THE ROUGH GUIDE TO
EUROPE
ON A BUDGET

written and researched by

Jonathan Bousfield, Tim Burford, Kiki Deere, Marc Di Duca,
Darragh Geraghty, E_____ _____hew Hancock,
Eva Hibbs, _____ton,
Phil Lee, Norm _____ Terry
Richardson _____te,
Steve Vickers, _____ _nd Matt Willis

ROUGH GUIDES

Contents

INTRODUCTION   4

Where to go	8	Ideas	14
When to go	12	Itineraries	22
Author picks	13		

BASICS   28

Getting there	29	Festivals and annual events	37
Getting around	31	Work and study	38
Accommodation	36	Travel essentials	40

THE GUIDE   47

1	Albania	47	19 Lithuania	697
2	Austria	61	20 Macedonia	715
3	Belgium & Luxembourg	87	21 Montenegro	727
4	Bosnia-Herzegovina	113	22 Morocco	741
5	Bulgaria	127	23 The Netherlands	773
6	Croatia	153	24 Norway	801
7	Czech Republic	183	25 Poland	831
8	Denmark	207	26 Portugal	859
9	Estonia	237	27 Romania	895
10	Finland	255	28 Russia	915
11	France	275	29 Serbia	939
12	Germany	351	30 Slovakia	957
13	Great Britain	415	31 Slovenia	977
14	Greece	495	32 Spain	997
15	Hungary	545	33 Sweden	1083
16	Ireland	569	34 Switzerland	1113
17	Italy	603	35 Turkey	1139
18	Latvia	681	36 Ukraine	1177

SMALL PRINT & INDEX   1193

Introduction to
Europe

There's no denying that Europe can be tough on the budget traveller – a potent mix of culture, landscape and history on the one hand and a cash-gobbling monster on the other, sticking to your daily allowance can prove tricky. But learn to zone out the "Spend! Spend! Spend!" siren song of its myriad restaurants, bars and shops and you'll find that this compact little continent is simply the world's greatest labyrinth. From London's Royal Parks and Amsterdam's canals to Istanbul's Grand Bazaar and Germany's Berlin Wall, just getting tangled up in its sights is a huge draw – you can do the Algarve, the Alps and the Arctic, all in one trip. There's time travel here too: with Stonehenge and Ephesus, cathedrals and castles, châteaux and palaces (not to mention statement-making modern architecture), Europe's man-made structures zoom you through millennia of civilization, a tumultuous history that scars and bejewels the continent by turns.

With its cultural kaleidoscope shifting not just from one country to the next but between towns and villages, relatively short distances can mean profound changes – bang for your backpacking buck, in other words, especially with the average gap-year trip getting shorter. And you needn't miss out even in some of the world's most **sophisticated cities**, with many iconic European experiences mercifully light on the pocket: think of *aperitivo* time in Rome, *blini* in Moscow, the freebie wonders at London's British Museum and bargain lunchtime concerts in Paris or Dublin. You will have to spend a few bob, of course. **Accommodation** and travel are bound to devour a fair chunk of your funds; the glass-half-full response is, "What do I spend the rest on?". Start by giving your **taste buds** the ride of their lives, be it in a Lyon *bouchon*, a smoky Turkish *ocakbaşi*, at a market or on the hoof (see Ideas, p.19). Don't be tempted to skip breakfast, either – an oven-fresh croissant or calorie-jammed "full English" are not to be missed, and all the more important in a morning-after-the-night-before context, especially since Europe lives for the wee hours. Whether it's Berlin and

ABOVE TAORMINA, SICILY **RIGHT** PORTOBELLO ROAD MARKET, LONDON

London's hipster dives, flamenco in Seville, Budapest's ruin bars or craft beer and organic wines in Bologna, there are countless reasons to stay up till sunrise. For fun en masse, check out the continent's **festivals** (see Ideas, p.16) – both traditional and modern – and the outdoor activities that animate its wide-open spaces (see Ideas, p.21), from horseriding in Bulgaria's Rila Mountains to surfing on Portugal's gnarled Alentejo coast. One advantage of **budget travel** is that it makes splurging all the sweeter – for a little flashpacking guidance, keep an eye out for our Treat Yourself tips throughout the Guide.

With just a few exceptions (see p.41), red tape won't be an issue thanks to Europe's unique "open borders" policy – you can travel **hassle-free** between countries that were once fierce enemies. To bolster your funds, consider working (see p.39), which can be a great way to meet people, immerse yourself in a country's day-to-day life and improve your language skills. But a word of caution – while you'll come across sleepy corners where things seem unchanged since some distant "Once upon a time" era, there's an atmosphere of unrest in others. The Eurozone financial crisis is rippling across the continent, having already destabilized governments from Ireland and Greece to Portugal and Slovenia, while 2016 saw Britain opt out of EU membership in the groundbreaking Brexit referendum. Recent terrorist attacks in France and Germany may make you wary, but remember that they're infrequent occurrences. When planning your trip and before you set off, keep an eye on the news and scour Twitter, which is also invaluable for up-to-the-minute reviews of new openings and off-the-beaten-track recommendations. The disaffected mood does have one upside: with its citizens so **politically engaged**, this is one of the most interesting times to travel in Europe for decades, and you're bound to have conversations and encounters that define your memories, whichever road you take.

Where to go

Europe has it all: sprawling cities and quaint villages; boulevards, promenades and railways; mountains, beaches and lakes. Some places will be exactly how you imagined: **Venice** is everything it's cracked up to be; springtime in **Paris** has even hardened cynics melting with the romance of it all; and **Oxford**'s colleges really are like Harry Potter film sets. But others will surprise, whether for their under-the-radar nature (see Author picks, p.13) or because they're stuck with an old-established, out-of-date reputation – but then, isn't tweaking your mental map all part of the fun?

Budget travellers are best off combining practicality with stick-a-pin-in-the-map impulsiveness. If you're flying out, look for where the cheap fares will take you and start from there – try our Itineraries section (see pp.22–27) for inspiration. Those getting around by train – still the best option – should note which countries are accessible with an InterRail Global pass and the equivalent Eurail pass (see p.34). Depending on your time and budget, choose one corner of the continent then consider a budget flight for that unmissable experience elsewhere, be it a foodie pilgrimage to **San Sebastián**, a cultural splurge at the **Edinburgh Festival**, or **St Petersburg**'s White Nights.

Great Britain maintains a certain psychological distance from its neighbours (as the Brexit referendum dramatically evidenced), and yet for many it's a European must-do, with iconic sights ranging from Big Ben and the Tower of London to Bath's Royal Crescent. North of the border, Scotland may opt for another independence referendum, given the population's dissatisfaction with Britain's decision to leave the EU. **London** has been feeling rather pleased with itself ever since the 2012 Olympics, and their legacy endures in the shape of the Queen Elizabeth Olympic Park. A reuse of the Games site, it's close to the hip, budget-friendly buzz of the city's East End. A quick flight away, **Ireland**'s west coast is an altogether more dramatic slice of the great outdoors, while a wander through **Galway**'s cobbled streets is the perfect way to explore 2020's European Capital of Culture. With steep fares in Great Britain especially, this is one region to really milk an InterRail card. Those without one should book tickets far in advance, or get ready for some very cosy long-distance bus rides.

The English-Scottish rivalry runs deep, but it's not a patch on the Catalan-Spanish equivalent, and Catalan capital **Barcelona** fairly pulsates with dynamism. From there, Spanish capital **Madrid** is within easy reach while, to the south, **Granada** and Andalucía's great city of **Seville** provide an undiluted shot of Spanishness. To the north and east, **France** and **Italy** could exhaust your rail pass in one fell swoop, with some of the world's finest cuisine, architecture, landscapes and museums. **Marseille** in the south of France recently had a spectacular shake-up, and the Vieux-Port is now studded with gleaming modern architecture. Out west, **Portugal** is relatively easy on the purse strings; its beautiful Douro Rail Route will make a veritable golden ticket of your rail pass, and even the **Algarve** has a thriving hostel scene these days. Further south again, voyage to **Morocco** the romantic way – by boat – and splash out on a stay at a traditional riad, where "Europe" can feel very far away indeed.

RIGHT FROM TOP SANTORÍNI, GREECE; ICEHOTEL, SWEDEN

Europe's best beaches

Mogren (Montenegro) Part of the so-called "Budva Riviera" that stretches either side of Montenegro's party town *par excellence* (p.735).

Olympos-Çıralı (Turkey) The 3km-long beach between the contrasting resorts of Olympos and Çıralı is among the most chilled in the Med (p.1168).

Ilha de Tavira (Portugal) Off the southern coast near the pretty town of Tavira (p.894) and backed by tufted dunes, this is one of the Algarve's finest, peaceful stretches.

Plage de la Rondinara (France) Shaped like a scallop shell, this vies with the turquoise waters of Santa Giulia and Palombaggia for title of "best Corsican beach" (p.350).

Chia (Italy) A sequence of shapely little bays lying just southwest of a quiet Sardinian village (p.679) – nearby lagoons are specked with flamingos, which come here to breed.

Hvar (Croatia) Hvar enjoys a growing reputation as the party capital of the Adriatic and there's a wealth of do-nothing-at-all beaches just a short bus or boat ride away (p.173).

Ksamil (Albania) This is still (just about) one of the Mediterranean's unspoiled corners – and with wonderful Butrint nearby, the beaches at the village of Ksamil (p.60) are an irresistible detour.

In spite of its famous Europe-Asia split, **Turkey** was supposedly closer to EU accession than Morocco. However, the terrorist attacks in Istanbul and Ankara in 2015 and 2016, the failed coup of July 2016 and the government's subsequent crackdowns have set back that schedule indefinitely, while nearby **Athens** experienced unrest in 2015 over Grexit fears. Still, both Athens and **Istanbul** remain excellent budget options. And with these countries' unforgettable ancient sites – not to mention **Greek island**-hopping or ballooning above the "fairy chimneys" of Turkey's **Cappadocia** – it's quite possible to feel blissfully removed from current affairs (should you so wish).

The "melting pot" cliché is often applied to Istanbul, but it's a fit for the **Balkans** too. Their rich diversity extends beyond the ethnic and cultural to landscape and urban make-up: the gorgeous coastlines of **Montenegro** and **Albania**; **Croatia**'s islands; **Romania**'s Saxon villages; the monasteries of **Serbia** and bridges of **Bosnia**; the architectural strangeness of Tirana and Skopje, capitals of **Albania** and **Macedonia**. Indeed, with evocative old quarters and (in some cases) relatively recent political turmoil, the Balkans' towns and cities are some of Europe's most fascinating – and affordable.

Into central Europe and the similarities between **Slovenia** and **Slovakia** don't begin and end with phonetics, these near-neighbours rivalling each other for mountain scenery and outdoorsy pursuits. Slovenian capital **Ljubljana** is an elegant charmer, while landlocked Slovakia boasts pretty **Bratislava** and **Košice**. Industrial **Plzeň** in the **Czech Republic** is regenerating around its own Capital of Culture 2015 award, while **Prague** is a treat just the way it is. Given their vast size, you'll be glad that **Poland** and **Ukraine** are enjoying improved infrastructure, a legacy of their stint as co-hosts of the 2012 UEFA European Football Championship – come for big city thrills with the likes of **Warsaw** and **Kyiv**, and a sense of discovery in less-touristed **Wrocław** and **L'viv**.

Once you hit **Germany** and its neighbours, you'll be glad of any money saved further east. That said, as nightlife hubs go, **Berlin** is pretty affordable; visit **Munich** for Oktoberfest if you like partying of a more traditional sort. Exploring the compact **Netherlands** by bike is both budget-friendly and oh-so-Dutch, while **Amsterdam** has some exciting new neighbourhoods to explore, especially around the former NDSM shipyard. Like the Netherlands, cultural heavyweight **Austria** does a whole lot with its modest size; yet with patches of mountainous terrain, this is one for the skis and snowboard rather than two wheels.

Finally, don't write off **Scandinavia** as unaffordable. Tourist cards, wild camping and university cafeterias – there are ways and means. And even if you can't quite stretch to the latest hot purveyor of "New Danish Cuisine", plenty of **Copenhagen**'s other famous pleasures can be enjoyed on the cheap – bakeries, *bodega* bars and cycling for starters. And the Northern Lights, visible from **Sweden**, **Norway** and **Finland**, might just be the greatest free show on earth. Finland serves up everything from the traditional culture of the reindeer-herding Sámi people to 2012 World Design Capital **Helsinki**. From there it's easy to reach the **Baltic** states of Latvia, Estonia and Lithuania. **Tallinn** and **Rīga** are two recent beneficiaries of the European Capital of Culture award, and a little more vibrant for it – or head boldly into **Russia**, where Moscow and St Petersburg have some truly blockbuster sights. From Marrakesh to Moscow – only in Europe.

When to go

Europe is, for the most part, a year-round destination. In terms of budget, it makes sense to travel in the off season (October through to May) – cheaper menus appear on restaurant tables, hotels drop their rates, and haggling over prices becomes a realistic option. This is especially true of tourist hotspots like Paris, Barcelona and Rome, which attract far bigger crowds in July and August.

If you do decide to travel during the peak **summer** season, try heading east – the Balkan coastline, the Slovenian mountains and Baltic cities are all fantastic places for making the most of your money. When tourist traffic dies down as **autumn** approaches, head to the Med. The famous coastlines and islands of southern Europe are quieter at this time of year, and the cities of Spain and Italy begin to look their best. **Wintertime** brings world-class skiing and snowboarding to European mountainsides (though not guaranteed), and countless festive markets pop up in the towns and cities below. There are epic New Year parties everywhere from Moscow to Lisbon and, despite the cold weather elsewhere at this time of year, there's still the possibility of sunshine in Turkey and Morocco. Come **spring** it's worth heading north to the Netherlands, Scandinavia, France and the British Isles, where you'll find beautifully long days and relatively affordable prices before the summer season kicks in around July.

While **weather** extremes are not the issue they are in, say, Asia or Africa, you should still bear them in mind when planning your trip. The Arctic winter in Scandinavia and Russia can bring temperatures as low as -35°C, with the sun barely rising above the horizon for months at a time. Conversely, summer days in central, southern and eastern parts of continental Europe can be sweltering – temperatures of around 40°C are not unheard of.

Author picks

From lungfuls of mountain air to gulps of super-strong beer, via floating taxis and hostels, cycle rides and kayaking, our authors share their top European tips.

Freewheeling Explore the Loire Valley's Renaissance châteaux, sampling delectable local wines (p.301); check out the street art in Málaga's SOHO district (p.1033); or glide around wonderful Copenhagen's famous cycle network (p.219).

Delicious dishes Relish the world's favourite cuisine at an Italian trattoria such as Florence's *Sostanza* (p.649); graze at the new gastromarkets in Córdoba (p.1036); and discover Britain's network of gastropubs and food markets (p.419).

Watery cities Spend the night in a floating hostel in Stockholm (p.1094); go wild swimming in Zürich (p.1130); board a boat to one of Helsinki's nearby islands (p.263); cruise along the canals of St Petersburg for a unique perspective on its historic sights (p.930); and absorb Venice's perennially stunning beauty from the seat of an affordable *traghetto* (p.638).

Under-the-radar towns Olomouc, Czech Republic (p.205), is a pint-sized Prague with fewer people and more charm (and cobblestones), while Berat (p.57) is a gorgeous Albanian town where row after row of Ottoman buildings loom down at you from the sides of a steep valley.

Drinking dens Order a knee-buckling Duvel beer at Brussels' historic *La Fleur en Papier Doré* (p.99) – a time-worn café once the favourite haunt of Surrealist painter Magritte and Tintin creator Hergé – or down a hefty home-brewed Columbus ale at Amsterdam's Brouwerij 't IJ (p.787), housed in an old public baths.

Saddle up Head for Bulgaria's Rila Mountains (p.131) on horseback (or by foot) to enjoy the spectacular scenery spread out beneath Mount Musala (2925m), the Balkan Peninsula's highest peak, or go galloping among the wild ponies on Great Britain's rugged Dartmoor (p.447).

Our author recommendations don't end here. We've flagged up our favourite places – a perfectly sited hotel, an atmospheric café, a special restaurant – throughout the guide, highlighted with the ★ symbol.

LEFT ISLE OF SKYE, SCOTLAND **FROM TOP** VENICE, ITALY; OLOMOUC, CZECH REPUBLIC; COPENHAGEN, DENMARK

Arts and culture

1 BERLIN WALL MEMORIAL, GERMANY
Page 364
An open-air exhibition of the Wall's most impressive remaining sections.

2 AYA SOFYA, TURKEY
Page 1146
Christianity and Islam meet in one magnificent Istanbul building.

3 BALLET, RUSSIA
Pages 929 & 937
Watch world-class performances at the Bolshoi or Mariinskiy theatres.

4 SISTINE CHAPEL, ITALY
Page 615
Michelangelo's jaw-dropping High Renaissance ceiling still inspires awe.

5 THE PARTHENON, GREECE
Page 503
The iconic image of Western civilization and template for buildings the world over.

6 SAGRADA FAMÍLIA, SPAIN
Page 1059
Gaudí's masterpieces are inseparable from the Barcelona experience.

7 TATE LIVERPOOL, UK
Page 462
Contemporary art displayed inside a beautifully converted warehouse.

Festivals

1 ST PATRICK'S DAY, IRELAND
Page 575
Dublin is the epicentre of March 17 shamrock-strewn, Guinness-fuelled fun.

2 SZIGET FESTIVAL, HUNGARY
Page 557
A week-long music and culture fest on Óbudai island, Budapest, which draws half a million revellers.

3 ROSKILDE, DENMARK
Page 226
Glastonbury's Scandinavian rival, with a mass naked run thrown in for good measure.

4 GENTSE FEESTEN, GHENT
Page 105
A two-week canal party so bacchanalian the entire city takes two weeks off work afterwards to recover.

5 FIESTAS DE SAN FERMÍN, SPAIN
Page 1071
Witness the hair-raising running of the bulls in Pamplona.

6 GLASTONBURY, GREAT BRITAIN
Page 447
You might end up caked in mud, but this legendary music festival is worth it.

7 EXIT FESTIVAL, SERBIA
Page 952
A beautiful fortress setting and top-name acts – what's not to like?

Eat like a local

1 FOOD MARKETS, GREAT BRITAIN
Page 429
Local, seasonal produce and a fantastic range of global influences.

2 CURRYWURST, GERMANY
Page 367
After a few steins, nothing else quite hits the spot like this curried street snack, a Berlin speciality.

3 SIMIT, TURKEY
Page 1143
Try one of these fresh bread rings with a little glass of sweet Turkish tea.

4 SMØRREBRØD, DENMARK
Page 211
Open sandwich as art form – and surprisingly filling.

5 PIZZA, ITALY
Page 607
Forget stuffed crust, the Neapolitan pizza is a thing of simple, unadorned beauty.

6 SNAILS, MOROCCO
Page 770
Tease out the flavoursome flesh with a toothpick, then slurp up the broth.

7 TAPAS, SPAIN
Page 1000
Small portions, big flavours – Spain's greatest gift to the world's taste buds.

The great outdoors

1 WINTER WONDERLAND
Pages 344 & 805

From Chamonix snowboarding to cross-country skiing in Norway.

2 THE NORTHERN LIGHTS
Pages 827 & 1110

Watch Mother Nature's greatest show in Tromsø or Swedish Lapland.

3 GET YOUR BOOTS ON
Pages 349 & 57

Tackle the GR20 in Corsica or go trekking in Valbona, Albania.

4 TAKE TO THE WATER
Pages 864 & 993

Try your hand at surfing in Portugal or rafting on the Soča, Slovenia.

5 GIDDY UP
Pages 109 & 573

Belgium's Ardennes region and Ireland's Connemara coast are perfect horseriding territory.

6 UNDER CANVAS
Page 37

Camping can help make Europe affordable – and even more beautiful.

7 TWO WHEELS
Pages 219, 1070 & 249

From freewheeling in Copenhagen and exploring Pamplona's medieval street maze, to wheeled marathons in Estonia's national parks.

Itineraries

You can't expect to fit everything Europe h
don't suggest you try. On the following p
that guide you through the different regi
from the misty Scottish Highlands to th
itineraries could be done in two to thre
don't push it too hard – with so much to s
waylaid somewhere you love or stray off th

GREAT BRITAIN AND IRELAND

Home to four proud nations, these two small
islands pack in a huge amount – from stately
homes and weather-beaten moors to theatre,
Premier League football and Europe's best music
festivals. Don't forget your brolly, drinking hat
and sense of humour.

❶ **London** As the saying goes, when a man is
tired of London, he is tired of life. One of the

world's
expensiv
your walle

❷ **Oxford** Th
chance to pur
college architec
medieval pub. **S**

❸ **Snowdonia** De
unpredictable weat
provide excellent hik
best hostels. **See p.47**

❹ **York** From a Viking m
streets to the soaring Go
to soak up some British h
to do it. **See p.467**

❺ **Edinburgh** With its stu
bars and – if you time it rig
festival, the Scottish capital
everyone. **See p.479**

❻ **The Highlands** Find you
knock back some whisky and
surrounded by Britain's most
See p.491

❼ **Belfast** A fascinating if tro
friendly locals and access poi
Europe's natural wonders, the
See p.596

**GREAT BRITAIN
AND IRELAND**

0   200
kilometres

ATLANTIC
OCEAN

SCOTLAND

N.
IRELAND

NORTH
SEA

REPUBLIC OF
IRELAND

ENGLAND

WALES

FRANCE

ABOV

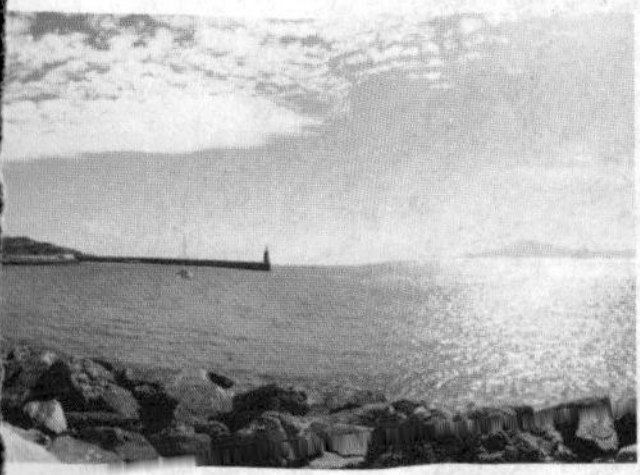

has to offer into one trip and we
ages is a selection of itineraries
ons of the continent, taking you
e souks of Morocco. Each of these
e weeks if followed to the letter, but
ee and do you're bound to get
e suggested route.

greatest cities is also one of the most
e, but follow our tips to emerge with
t intact. **See p.421**

e famous university town offers the
t along the river, admire the
ture or down a few pints in a
ee p.450

spite the notoriously
her, the Welsh mountains
ng and some of Britain's
7

useum and medieval
thic Minster, if you want
istory, York is the place

nning cityscape, lively
ht – international
has something for

inner Braveheart,
hike, climb or ski
stunning scenery.

ubled history,
nt to one of
Giant's Causeway.

E COSTA DE LA LUZ, SPAIN

❽ Dublin Yep, Guinness really does taste better here, though there's a lot more to see and do in Ireland's sophisticated capital. **See p.575**

❾ Wild Atlantic Way Explore the rugged cliffs, ancient monuments, windswept beaches, hidden villages and lively towns along Ireland's west coast. **See p.588**

FRANCE AND SWITZERLAND

Still the world's number one tourist destination, France can smugly claim to have it all, from mountains and sun-kissed beaches to unrivalled food and fashion. Pricey it may be, but nearby Switzerland is worth the expense for its attractive, appealingly relaxed cities and the jaw-dropping mountain views.

❶ Paris Laze over a coffee in a Left Bank café, arrange a romantic rendezvous or tick off the many museums in Europe's most elegant capital. **See p.281**

❷ The Loire Valley Some of the most impressive châteaux you'll see in the country grace this bucolic valley, which is also prime vineyard territory. **See p.299**

❸ Bordeaux An elegant, bustling city and world-famous wine-growing region, with some of Europe's top surf beaches just a short drive away. **See p.309**

❹ The Pyrenees Clear your head after all that wine with the fresh air and fine walks of this mountain range bordering Spain. **See p.316**

❺ The Côte d'Azur Nice, Cannes, Monaco – the names alone ooze glamour. Time to dress up and hit one of this chichi region's famed casinos. **See p.323**

❻ Corsica France's adventure playground, Corsica is home to one of Europe's toughest and most rewarding treks, the GR20. **See p.345**

❼ Lyon The country's gastronomic capital – eat at *Daniel et Denise*, a classic *bouchon*, to see how good traditional French cooking can be. **See p.339**

❽ The Alps Try your luck scaling Europe's highest mountains, or spend a season as a ski instructor or chalet monkey. **See p.343 & p.344**

❾ Zürich Laidback Zürich is still one of Europe's clubbing hotspots and has a wonderful riverside setting. **See p.1128**

BENELUX, GERMANY AND AUSTRIA

From fine chocolates and champion beers to fairytale castles, forests and clinking cowbells, this region has something for just about everyone. The cities can pass in a blur of late nights, but make time for the scenery too.

❶ Amsterdam Whatever you're looking for – cannabis, clubs, high culture or cuisine – the Netherlands' capital can provide it. **See p.779**

❷ Bruges It may be brazenly touristy but this gem of Flemish architecture is still worth a visit for its atmospheric canals and beautiful buildings. **See p.106**

❸ Cologne Linked to Brussels and beyond by super-fast trains, Cologne makes a perfect first stop in Germany with its spectacular cathedral and lively festivals. **See p.386**

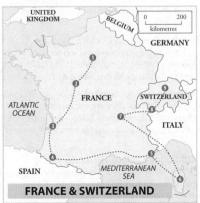

❹ Hamburg Germany's northern gateway boasts a vast port, magnificent red-brick warehouses and a riotous bar and live music scene. **See p.379**

❺ Berlin Some thirty years since the fall of the Wall, Berlin still has a raw, youthful energy that belies its history of division and destruction. **See p.358**

❻ Dresden Bombed to bits in World War II, Dresden is the classic phoenix-from-the-ashes story and now one of Europe's favourite backpacker hangouts. **See p.370**

❼ Munich From beer-fuelled thigh-slapping to modern art and mountain scenery, you'll find it all in Bavaria's capital. **See p.405**

❽ Salzburg Hit the Mozart trail, pose Julie Andrews-style in homage to *The Sound of Music* or pull on some skis and head for the mountains. **See p.77**

❾ Vienna Austria's capital is chock-full of palaces, museums and boulevards – with coffee and cake in a grand café never too far away. **See p.65**

SPAIN, PORTUGAL AND MOROCCO

Penélope Cruz, Cristiano Ronaldo, tapas, port and Rioja – it's hard not to warm to the Iberian peninsula. To the south, Morocco is just a short hop across the sea but seems a different planet in many respects.

❶ Bilbao Capital of the Basque country, Bilbao is Spain's friendliest city and home to one of Europe's most spectacular buildings: the Guggenheim. **See p.1074**

SPAIN, PORTUGAL & MOROCCO

❷ Barcelona Innovative architecture, city beaches, late-night bars and an enchanting old town – you'll find it hard to leave the Catalan capital. **See p.1053**

❸ Ibiza *Amnesia, Pacha, Ushuaia* – its nightclubs are famous the world over, but even on Europe's party island there are pockets of idyllic peace and quiet. **See p.1048**

❹ Madrid Take your cue from the locals in the Spanish capital – if you're dining before 10pm, dancing before midnight and asleep before dawn, you haven't experienced a truly Madrileño night out. **See p.1003**

❺ Porto Wander the winding cobbled streets of Portugal's second city – and sample a drop at one (or more) of the countless port lodges. **See p.881**

❻ Lisbon Portugal's immediately likeable capital has a great setting, delicious food and a huge amount of historic interest. **See p.865**

❼ Andalucía Spain in a nutshell – flamenco, fine wines, bullfighting and heat. If you're pushed for time, stick to the unmissable cities of Seville and Granada. **See p.1023**

❽ Fez Once across the Strait of Gibraltar from Tarifa or Algeciras, dive head first into Morocco with a stay in this medieval labyrinth of alleys, souks and mosques. **See p.755**

❾ Marrakesh Stunning, atmospheric city with the Atlas Mountains as a backdrop and the live circus that is the Jemaa el Fna square at its heart. **See p.768**

ITALY

If there's one country that deserves its own itinerary, it's Italy. Almost everyone who visits falls in love, whether with the designer-clad locals, the incomparable cuisine or the world's finest collection of art.

❶ Milan Prada, Gucci, Dolce & Gabbana… Milan is prime window-shopping territory, while the city's cathedral and da Vinci's *The Last Supper* are priceless experiences. **See p.622**

❷ Venice Despite seemingly sinking under the weight of its tourists, the most beautiful city in the world is frankly unmissable – and with some careful planning still possible to do on a budget. **See p.633**

❸ Bologna Capital of the foodie nirvana Emilia-Romagna (think Parma ham, Parmesan, balsamic vinegar), Bologna is a must-do for anyone with a digestive system. **See p.640**

ITALY

❹ Tuscany Birthplace of the Renaissance, Florence rightly pulls in the masses; nearby Siena is just as beautiful, full of fun-loving students and an excellent base to explore the region's hill towns. **See p.644 & p.651**

❺ Rome You can hardly "do" Europe and not "do" Rome. Whether you're stuck queuing for St Peter's, the Sistine Chapel or the Colosseum, you can at least rest assured that you're about to be wowed. **See p.610**

❻ Naples The home of pizza – and the best place to eat it – Naples is also a frenetic, crumblingly attractive city with an intriguing dark side. **See p.659**

❼ Pompeii From the ancient graffiti to plaster body casts, seeing a Roman town frozen in time is an experience you won't forget. **See p.664**

❽ Matera Try sleeping in a cave in this hand-carved stone city – the perfect introduction to Italy's captivating far south. **See p.668**

❾ Sicily Beaches, volcanoes and, in Palermo, one of Italy's most in-your-face cities – Sicilians simply do it better. **See p.670**

CENTRAL AND EASTERN EUROPE

Having long shrugged off the Iron Curtain, the region we used to regard as bleak and distant is now firmly at the beating heart of the continent. With elegant cities and vast tracts of unspoiled countryside, these countries provide a remarkable set of riches.

❶ Prague The Czech capital would probably win a pan-European beauty contest for its architecture. As for the beer…well, let's just say you won't be disappointed. **See p.188**

❷ Warsaw Beyond the Polish capital's immaculately reconstructed Old Town there are beautiful palaces and parks, not to mention restaurant, club and vodka-soaked bar scenes to explore. **See p.837**

❸ Kraków Arty and atmospheric, picture-postcard-pretty Kraków should not be missed, though neither should a sobering trip to nearby Auschwitz. **See p.848**

❹ L'viv This Central European gem has good backpacker hostels and a café-jammed, charming Old Town. **See p.1189**

❺ Tatra Mountains Stretching between Poland and Slovakia, the Tatras are that rare thing – majestic wilderness without hordes of Gore-Tex-clad tourists. **See p.854 & p.970**

❻ Budapest Two cities for the price of one: stately, museum-packed Buda and, across the not-so-blue Danube, nightlife and restaurant hotspot Pest. **See p.551**

❼ Ljubljana Repeat after me: "Lyoo-bly-AH-nah". The Slovenian capital is a small, perfectly formed pit stop between central Europe and the Adriatic. **See p.982**

CENTRAL AND EASTERN EUROPE

SCANDINAVIA

While it can hit your finances, Scandinavia is worth stretching the budget for. Apart from resembling Europe's answer to Middle Earth, it's also full of stylish cities, ingenious design and friendly locals.

❶ Copenhagen Picturesque and user-friendly, the Danish capital is a lively, welcoming introduction to the region. **See p.213**

❷ Gothenburg Sweden's second city boasts elegant architecture, fantastic nightlife and a fully functioning rainforest among its standout attractions. **See p.1098**

❸ Oslo Paying €8 for a beer can put people off the Norwegian capital, but if you can get over the prices, you'll understand why it frequently tops "best places to live" lists. **See p.807**

❹ The fjords No trip to Norway would be complete without a visit to the country's magnificent fjords. **See p.816**

❺ Lofoten Islands A mild climate, wild scenery and cute, laidback fishing villages pull in the crowds to this remote archipelago in Norway's far north. **See p.825**

❻ Lapland Synonymous with Santa, Lapland (whether Swedish or Finnish) fits the winter fantasy perfectly with reindeer, yapping huskies and the staggering Northern Lights. **See p.272 & p.1110**

❼ Stockholm Scandinavia's best-looking capital offers up an unspoilt medieval core, über-hip nightlife and, incongruously enough, some fine beaches. **See p.1089**

❽ Gotland Sweden's party island buzzes in summer when DJs hit the decks in Visby and the beaches fill with bronzed bodies. **See p.1106**

RUSSIA AND THE BALTIC COAST

Big scary bear it may be, but ever-changing Russia should not be missed, even if it's just to dip into its most "European" city, St Petersburg. Russia's compact Baltic neighbours, meanwhile, provide some of the most beautiful – and most fun – cityscapes in Eastern Europe.

❶ Moscow Big, brash, expensive, surreal and exciting, twenty-first-century Moscow is almost a nation in itself and well worth the effort to get to. **See p.922**

❷ St Petersburg With jaw-dropping architecture and priceless art collections, Russia's second city is at its best during the midsummer White Nights festival. **See p.930**

❸ Helsinki The love child of the Russian and Swedish empires, yet brought up to be proudly Finnish, Helsinki is a fascinatingly schizophrenic capital. **See p.261**

❹ Tallinn Having survived its tenure as a cheap stag- and hen-party hub, the beautifully preserved Estonian capital still retains a huge amount of charm. **See p.241**

❺ Rīga Larger and more cosmopolitan than its neighbours, Latvia's atmospheric capital is full of architectural treasures and is the gateway to some wonderful coastal scenery. **See p.686**

❻ Curonian Spit This narrow strip of lofty sand dunes and dense pine forest is perfect cycling and hiking territory. **See p.713**

❼ Vilnius The friendliest and perhaps prettiest of the Baltic capitals, Vilnius's largely undiscovered status means you can enjoy a break from the crowds. **See p.702**

SCANDINAVIA

RUSSIA AND THE BALTIC COAST

THE BALKANS

A fascinating cultural meeting point, the Balkans today are exciting, safe and mercifully cheap. While Croatia and Bulgaria have been on the scene for a while, a trip to Bosnia-Herzegovina, Macedonia or Albania still scores high in the intrepid stakes.

❶ Dalmatian coast Croatia's dramatic Dalmatian coast and islands are the perfect place to drop out for the summer, with unlimited watersports, cheap wine and vitamin D on offer. **See p.167**

❷ Sarajevo War-scarred it may be, but this mini-Istanbul might just be Europe's most welcoming capital – you're unlikely to leave without making a friend or two. **See p.118**

❸ Dubrovnik Rivalling Venice in its day, the "pearl of the Adriatic" has survived centuries of conquest and intrigue, not to mention being on an easyJet flight route. **See p.178**

❹ Budva Montenegro's star resort boasts the requisite pretty Old Town, but it's the unspoilt beaches and throbbing open-air bars that pull in the party set. **See p.734**

❺ Berat Whitewashed Ottoman houses huddle against the hillside in this gorgeous Albanian town, a UNESCO World Heritage Site. **See p.57**

❻ Ohrid Impossibly picturesque, set on the shimmering shores of the eponymous mountain-backed lake, Ohrid is the jewel in Macedonia's crown. **See p.725**

❼ Plovdiv Pay a visit to Bulgaria's buzzing second city to understand why the locals look down on Sofia, the country's capital. **See p.142**

❽ Belgrade Hectic and hedonistic, the Serbian capital is fast attracting the hip crowd thanks to its adrenaline-charged nightlife. **See p.944**

❾ Transylvania No, you probably won't see any vampires, but this history-steeped region holds myriad other attractions, from fairytale villages and colourful festivals to wolf tracking in the spectacular Carpathians. **See p.907**

GREECE AND TURKEY

Whether you're interested in classical antiquity and the founding of Western civilization or just sparkling blue seas and sandy beaches, Greece and Turkey are essential destinations.

❶ Kefalloniá Beautiful Kefalloniá is the best place to hop on a moped and discover that perfect beach. **See p.539**

❷ Athens Crowded, noisy and polluted the Greek capital may be, but once you've seen the sun set over the Parthenon you'll be hooked. **See p.502**

❸ Íos A favourite among hard-partying backpackers, Íos retains a bohemian, hippie-era charm and is the best stop on the Cyclades island-hopping trail. **See p.530**

❹ Crete Home to the Minotaur and a fair few trashy resorts, Crete also boasts the dramatic Samarian Gorge, Europe's answer to the Grand Canyon. **See p.540**

❺ Ephesus Turkey's best-preserved archeological site is a treasure-trove of ruined temples, mosaics, baths and some spectacular public conveniences. **See p.1162**

❻ Kaş Fill your days mountain biking, paragliding or diving, then relive it all in some of the Med's liveliest bars. **See p.1167**

❼ Cappadocia It's a long trip east but Cappadocia's unique volcanic landscape has an irresistible allure – stay in a cave hotel and visit a subterranean city. **See p.1173**

❽ Istanbul Squeeze every kuruş out of your Turkish lira shopping in the bazaars, having a rub down in a hammam and enjoying the surprisingly hectic nightlife. **See p.1146**

BERLIN

Basics

29 Getting there

31 Getting around

36 Accommodation

37 Festivals and annual events

38 Work and study

40 Travel essentials

Getting there

Europe can be easily reached by air from just about anywhere in the world, with flights to all major European cities. It's also possible to arrive by ferry from across the Mediterranean or Black Sea, or on the Trans-Siberian railway from East Asia.

Air fares will always depend on the **season**; they're usually highest in the summer and over the Christmas period, as well as over public holidays. Note also that flying at weekends or requiring a nonstop journey sometimes adds quite a bit to the round-trip fare. Barring special offers, the cheapest published **fares** usually require advance purchase of two to three weeks, and impose certain restrictions, such as heavy penalties if you change your schedule. Most cheap fares will only give a partial refund, if any, should you cancel or alter your journey, so check the restrictions carefully before buying. You can often cut costs by going through a youth or student travel specialist (see "Agents"; p.31), which may offer low-cost or special youth or student fares, as well as travel-related services such as travel insurance, rail passes and tours.

If Europe is only one stop on a longer journey, and especially if you are based in Australia or New Zealand, you might consider a **Round-the-World** (RTW) air ticket. Prices increase with the number of stops – figure on around £1550–2500/US$2000–3300/Aus$2660–3850/NZ$2820–4660 for a RTW ticket including one or two European stopovers.

From Britain and Ireland

Heading from Britain and Ireland to destinations in northwestern Europe, it's not just greener to go by train, long-distance bus or ferry – it can be quicker and cheaper too. However, it's normally cheaper to fly than take the train to most parts of southern Europe.

By plane

London is predictably **Britain**'s main hub for air travel, offering the highest frequency of flights and widest choice of destinations from its five airports (Heathrow, Gatwick, Stansted, Luton and City). Manchester also has flights to most parts of Europe, and there are regular services to the Continent from Birmingham, Southampton, Bournemouth, East Midlands, Bristol, Cardiff, Glasgow, Edinburgh, Leeds/Bradford, Liverpool and Newcastle. From the **Republic of Ireland**, you can fly direct to most major cities in mainland Europe from Dublin, Shannon and Cork. From **Belfast**, there are direct flights with easyJet to a handful of destinations; otherwise, you'll need to change in London or Manchester.

Budget airlines such as easyJet and Ryanair offer low-cost tickets to destinations around Europe (though not always the most convenient airports), though post-Brexit, prices may well go up as no-frills airlines have to negotiate their services in and out of the UK. There are also agents specializing in offers to a specific country or country group on both charters and regular scheduled departures.

EUROPEAN BUDGET AIRLINES

At the time of writing there were 39 budget airlines serving countries in or near Europe. We've listed the more established operators below, but for full details of routes visit ⓦflycheapo.com, while ⓦskyscanner.net is an invaluable price comparison resource.

Air Berlin ⓦ airberlin.com
Blue Air ⓦ blueairweb.com
Darwin ⓦ etihadregional.com
easyJet ⓦ easyjet.com
Flybe ⓦ flybe.com
Fly Niki ⓦ flyniki.com
Eurowings ⓦ eurowings.com
Jet2 ⓦ jet2.com
Norwegian Air Shuttle ⓦ norwegian.no
Ryanair ⓦ ryanair.com
Smart Wings ⓦ smartwings.com
Transavia ⓦ transavia.com
TUIfly ⓦ tuifly.com
Vueling ⓦ vueling.com
Wizz Air ⓦ wizzair.com

A BETTER KIND OF TRAVEL

At Rough Guides we are passionately committed to travel. We believe it helps us understand the world we live in and the people we share it with – and of course tourism is vital to many developing economies. But the scale of modern tourism has also damaged some places irreparably, and climate change is accelerated by most forms of transport, especially flying. All Rough Guides' flights are carbon-offset, and every year we donate money to a variety of environmental charities.

By train

Direct trains through the **Channel Tunnel** from London to Paris (17 daily; 2hr 30min) and Brussels (10 daily; 2hr) are run by Eurostar. Tickets to Paris for under-26s start at £27 one-way, £55 return. For over-26s, the cheapest and least flexible tickets cost £29 one-way or £58 return; the further in advance you book, the cheaper the deals. Through-ticket combinations with onward connections from Lille, Brussels and Paris can be booked through International Rail and Rail Europe (see p.35).

Other rail journeys from Britain involve a sea crossing by ferry or, sometimes, catamaran. **Tickets** can be bought from International Rail, and from most major rail stations or from Dutchflyer (W stena line.co.uk/ferry/rail-and-sail/holland) if routed via the Hook of Holland. For some destinations, there are cheaper SuperApex fares requiring advance booking and subject to greater restrictions. Otherwise, international tickets are valid for two months and allow for stopovers on the way, providing you stick to the prescribed route (there may be a choice, with different fares applicable). One-way fares are generally around two-thirds the price of a return fare. If you're under 26 you're entitled to special deals.

From **Ireland**, direct rail tickets to Europe via Britain generally include both boat connections, and are available from Irish Railways offices in the Republic (☎ 1850 366 222, W irishrail.ie), or Northern Ireland Railways in the North (☎ 028 9066 6630, W translink.co.uk).

For rail passes, contacts and other types of discounted rail travel, see p.34.

By bus

A **long-distance bus** is often the cheapest option, although much less comfortable than the train. The main operator is Eurolines (W eurolines.co.uk, W eurolines.ie), with a network of routes spanning the Continent. Prices can be up to a third cheaper than by train, and there are marginally lower fares on most services for those under 26. There's usually a discount if you buy your ticket in advance, and bigger discounts for journeys booked a week in advance. Connecting services from elsewhere in Great Britain add £15 each way to the price of the ticket from London. Eurolines sell fifteen- and thirty-day passes; alternatively, consider one of the various passes offered by Busabout for their services around Europe (see p.35).

By ferry

There are numerous **ferry services** between Britain and Ireland, and between the British Isles and the European mainland. Ferries from the southeast of Ireland and the south coast of England connect with northern France and Spain; those from Kent in southeast England reach northern France and Belgium; those from Scotland and the east coast and northeast of England cross the North Sea to Belgium, the Netherlands, Germany and Scandinavia.

FERRY OPERATORS

Brittany Ferries UK ☎ 0330 159 7000, W brittany-ferries.co.uk; Ireland ☎ 021 427 7801, W brittanyferries.ie. Cork to Roscoff (April–Nov); Portsmouth to Caen, Cherbourg, Le Havre, St Malo, Bilbao and Santander; Poole to Cherbourg; Plymouth to Roscoff, St Malo and Santander.

Condor Ferries UK ☎ 01202 207216, W condorferries.co.uk. Portsmouth to Cherbourg; Portsmouth, Poole and Weymouth to St Malo via Jersey and Guernsey.

DFDS Seaways UK ☎ 0871 522 9955, W dfdsseaways.co.uk. Newcastle to Amsterdam; Dover to Calais and Dunkerque; Newhaven to Dieppe.

Irish Ferries UK ☎ 0871 730 0400, Ireland ☎ 0818 300 400; W irishferries.com. Dublin to Holyhead and Cherbourg; Rosslare to Pembroke, Cherbourg (March–Dec) and Roscoff (May–Sept).

P&O Ferries UK ☎ 0800 130 0030, Ireland ☎ 01 868 9467; W poferries.com. Hull to Zeebrugge and Rotterdam; Dover to Calais; Larne to Cairnryan; Dublin to Liverpool.

Stena Line UK ☎ 0844 770 7070, W stenaline.co.uk; Ireland ☎ 01 907 5555, W stenaline.ie. Harwich to Hook of Holland; Rosslare to Fishguard; Dublin to Holyhead; Belfast to Cairnryan and Liverpool.

From the US

From the US the best deals are generally from the main hubs such as **New York, Washington DC** and **Chicago** to London. Fixed-date, nonstop advance-purchase tickets for midweek travel to London cost around US$420 in low season (roughly speaking, winter), US$710 in high season (summer, Christmas and Easter) from New York and Washington DC, US$775/890 from Chicago. For more flexible tickets, add at least a third to the price. Fixed-date advance-purchase alternatives include New York to Paris for US$645/815, US$650/800 to Frankfurt, US$730/830 to Madrid, or US$915/1115 to Rome; flying from Chicago, discounted tickets can be had for US$915/1380 to Paris and US$975/1140 to Frankfurt. There are promotional offers from time to time, especially off-peak, so check with individual airlines, or compare all available flights on W sky scanner.net and look at the whole month option to see which days are cheapest; allowing at least one stop can significantly reduce the price of a ticket.

From the **west coast** the major airlines fly at least three times a week and up to twice daily from Los Angeles, San Francisco and Seattle to the main

European cities. With fixed-price tickets, you can get from Los Angeles to London for US$770/815 (low/high season), to Paris for US$940/1245 and to Frankfurt for US$1000/1140.

From Canada

Most of the big airlines fly to the major European hubs from **Montreal** and **Toronto** at least once daily. From Toronto, London is your cheapest option, with the lowest direct round-trip fare around Can$470/700. Fares from Montreal to Paris start at Can$475/1000. **Vancouver** and **Calgary** have daily flights to several European cities, with round-trip fares to London from around Can$630/1280, depending on the season.

From Australia and New Zealand

There are flights from **Melbourne**, **Sydney**, **Adelaide**, **Brisbane** and **Perth** to most European capitals, with not a great deal of difference in the fares to the busiest destinations: a return from Sydney to London, Paris, Rome, Madrid, Athens or Frankfurt should be available through travel agents for around Aus$980 in low season (Australia's summer, Europe's winter) and slightly higher in high season (though you can sometimes get great deals). A one-way ticket costs slightly more than half that, while a return flight from **Auckland** to Europe is approximately NZ$1175 in low season and from around NZ$1735 in high season. Asian airlines often work out cheapest, and may throw in a stopover.

Some agents offer **"open jaw" tickets**, flying you into one city and out from another, which needn't even be in the same country. For **round-the-world** deals and other low-price tickets, the most reliable operator is STA Travel (see below), which also supplies packages with companies such as Contiki and Busabout, can issue rail passes, and advise on visa regulations – they'll also do all the paperwork for a fee.

From South Africa

Many major airlines fly from **Johannesburg** and **Cape Town** to a number of European hubs. Flights from Johannesburg cost about ZAR11,000/10,700 to London, ZAR9150/11,720 to Frankfurt in low season/high season, around ZAR11,620/10,370 to Paris, and slightly more from Cape Town. Many of the cheapest deals involve flying via the Middle East with companies such as Turkish Airlines or Emirates.

AGENTS

North South Travel UK ☎ 01245 608 291, ⓦ northsouthtravel .co.uk. Friendly, competitive travel agency, offering discounted fares worldwide. Profits are used to support projects in the developing world, especially the promotion of sustainable tourism.

STA Travel UK ☎ 0333 321 0099, ⓦ statravel.co.uk; US ☎ 1 800 781 4040, ⓦ statravel.com; Australia ☎ 134 782, ⓦ statravel.com .au; New Zealand ☎ 0800 474400, ⓦ statravel.co.nz; South Africa ☎ 0861 781 781, ⓦ statravel.co.za. Independent and student travel, air tickets, student IDs, travel insurance, car rental and rail passes.

Trailfinders England & Wales ☎ 020 7368 1200, ⓦ trailfinders .com; Scotland ☎ 0131 243 2800, ⓦ trailfinders.scot; Ireland ☎ 01 677 7888, ⓦ trailfinders.ie. One of the best-informed and most efficient agents for independent travellers.

Travel CUTS ☎ 1 800 667 2887, ⓦ travelcuts.com. Canadian youth and student travel firm.

USIT Ireland (Republic) ☎ 01 602 1906, USA ☎ 1 866 647 3697, Australia ☎ 1800 092 499; ⓦ usit.ie. Ireland's main student and youth travel specialists.

Getting around

It's easy to travel in Europe, and a number of special deals and passes can make it fairly economical too, especially for students and those under 26. Air links are extensive and, thanks to the growing number of budget airlines, flying is often cheaper than taking the train, but you'll appreciate the diversity of Europe best at ground level, by way of its enormous and generally efficient web of rail, road and ferry connections.

By train

Trains are generally the best way to tour Europe. The **rail network** in most countries is comprehensive and the region boasts some of the world's most scenic rail journeys. Costs are relatively low, too – apart from Britain, where prices can be absurdly steep – as trains are heavily subsidized, and prices are brought down further by passes and discount cards. We've covered the various passes here, as well as the most important international routes and most useful addresses; frequencies and journey times are given throughout the Guide.

During the summer, especially if you're travelling at night or a long distance, it's best to make **reservations** whenever you can; on some trains (TGV services, for example) it's compulsory. See our "Extra rail charges" box for more on supplements.

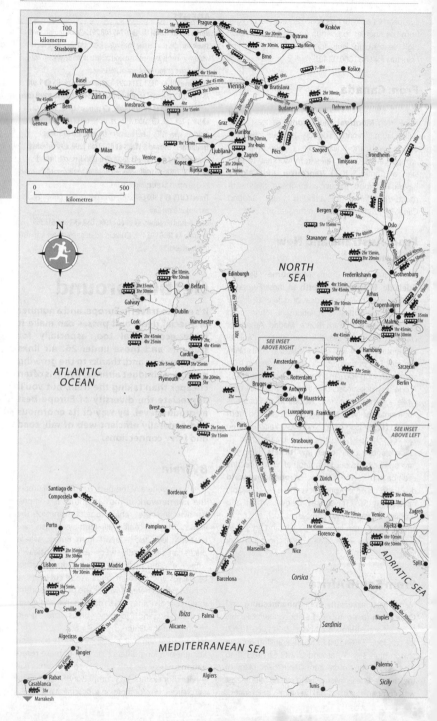

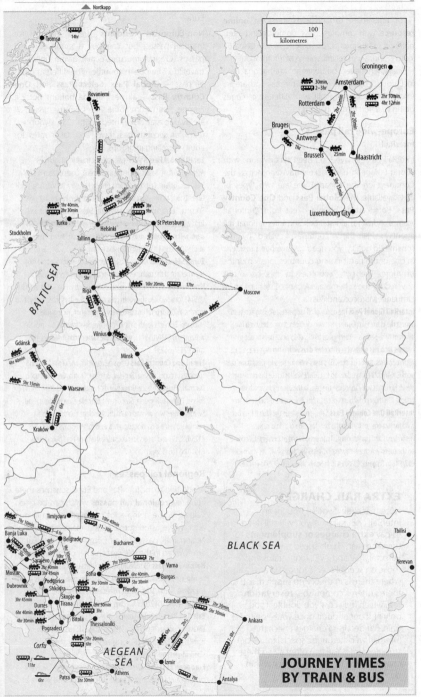

**JOURNEY TIMES
BY TRAIN & BUS**

For timetables, ⓦbahn.de is the best **online resource**, with comprehensive domestic and international rail listings across Europe, while ⓦseat61 .com is another excellent source of information.

Finally, whenever you board an international train in Europe, check the route of the car you are in, since trains frequently split, with different carriages going to different destinations.

Europe-wide rail passes
InterRail

InterRail passes have long been synonymous with young European backpackers travelling across the Continent on the cheap. There are two types of pass available: the **Global Pass** and **One Country Pass**. Both can be bought direct from ⓦinterrail .com and from main stations and international rail agents in all thirty countries covered by the scheme. To qualify, you need to have been resident in one of the participating countries for six months or more. The only countries in this book not covered by the scheme are Albania, Estonia, Latvia, Lithuania, Morocco and Russia.

InterRail Global Pass The daddy of all rail passes, offering access to almost the entire European rail network. You can choose between five different time periods – continuous blocks of 15 or 22 days or one month – or set amounts of travel – either five days within ten days or ten days within 22 days. Youth (under-26) passes valid for second-class travel start from €264/£221 for five days up to €626/£525 for a month's continuous travel. Note that you cannot use the pass in the country in which you bought it, although discounts of up to fifty percent are usually available.

InterRail One Country Pass Same principle as the Global Pass but valid for just one country (or the Benelux zone of Belgium, the Netherlands and Luxembourg). Time periods and prices vary depending on the country. A three-day second-class youth pass will set you back €57/£48 in Bulgaria, €131/£110 in Spain and €154/£129 in France.

EXTRA RAIL CHARGES

Note that even if you've bought an InterRail or Eurail pass, you will still need to pay **extra charges or supplements** to travel on many high-speed trains (such as Eurostar, TGV and AVE), night trains and those on special scenic routes. Even where there is in theory no supplement, there's often a compulsory **reservation fee**, which may cost you double if you only find out about it once you're on the train. For details of charges check the InterRail website under "special trains" or "supplements". You can often avoid these charges if you plan your journey within domestic networks.

Eurail

Non-European residents aren't eligible for InterRail passes, but can buy a range of Eurail passes (ⓦeurailgroup.org/eurail) giving unlimited travel in 27 European countries. The different types of pass – **Global Pass**, **Select Pass** and **One Country Pass** – all need to be bought outside Europe. Apart from some One Country passes, all are available at discounted youth (25 or younger) rates for second-class travel and saver rates for adults travelling in groups.

Eurail Global Pass A single pass valid for travel in 28 countries: Austria, Belgium, Bosnia-Herzegovina, Bulgaria, Croatia, Czech Republic, Denmark, Finland, France, Germany, Greece, Hungary, Ireland, Italy, Luxembourg, Montenegro, the Netherlands, Norway, Poland, Portugal, Romania, Serbia, Slovakia, Slovenia, Spain, Sweden, Switzerland and Turkey. There are seven different time periods available, from five days' travel within a month, up to three months' continuous travel. Prices start at €358/US$394 for a youth pass valid for five days.

Eurail Select Pass Allows you to select two, three or four bordering countries out of the countries above; the Benelux zone of Belgium, the Netherlands and Luxembourg counts as one country. Prices start at €130/US$143 for a two-country youth pass valid for five days' travel within two months. Prices depend on the country combination; for example, a Hungary–Romania youth pass valid for five days' travel in two months will cost you €130/US$143, whereas the same period for France–Italy costs €218/US$239.

Eurail One Country Pass Offers travel within one of the following countries or zones: Austria, Benelux, Bulgaria, Croatia, Czech Republic, Denmark, Finland, Greece, Greek Islands, Hungary, Ireland, Italy, Norway, Poland, Portugal, Romania, Scandinavia, Slovakia, Slovenia, Spain and Sweden. Prices vary depending on the size of the country/zone: for example, a youth pass in Scandinavia valid for three days' travel costs €175/US$192 and covers four countries; the same time period costs €151/US$166 in Spain.

Regional rail passes

In addition to the InterRail and Eurail schemes there are a few **regional rail passes** which can be good value if you're doing a lot of travelling within one area; we've listed some of the main ones below. National rail passes (apart from InterRail and Eurail) are covered in the relevant chapter of the Guide.

Balkan Flexipass ⓦraileurope.com. Offers unlimited first- and second-class travel through Bulgaria, Bosnia-Herzegovina, Greece, Macedonia, Serbia, Montenegro, Romania and Turkey. Prices start at US$163 (youth US$97) for five days' travel in one month.

Brit Rail Pass ⓦbritrail.com. A variety of passes available for travel in Britain, including country passes for England and Scotland. Prices start from US$325 (youth US$260) for a flexipass covering three days' standard-class travel within one month.

European East Pass ⓦraileurope.com. Gives five days' travel in a month in Austria, the Czech Republic, Hungary, Poland and Slovakia for US$276, plus up to five additional days at US$30 each.

RAIL CONTACTS

UK

eTrains4u ☎ 020 7619 1083, ⊛ etrains4u.com. Independent specialists for Continental rail travel.

Eurostar ☎ 03432 186186, outside the UK ☎ +44 1233 617 575, ⊛ eurostar.com. UK to Europe via the Channel Tunnel.

International Rail ☎ 0871 231 0790, ⊛ internationalrail.com. Global rail specialist.

InterRail ⊛ interrail.eu. Main website for buying InterRail passes.

The Man in Seat 61 ⊛ seat61.com. Comprehensive informational site set up by a rail enthusiast.

Voyages-sncf.com ☎ 0844 848 5848, ⊛ uk.voyages-sncf.com. British representative of SNCF French railways, sells rail tickets Europe-wide.

STA Travel ☎ 0333 321 0099, ⊛ statravel.co.uk.

US AND CANADA

ACP Rail International ☎ 1 866 938 7245, ⊛ acprail.com. Eurail agent.

BritRail Travel ☎ 1 866 938 7245, ⊛ britrail.com. British passes.

Eurail ⊛ eurail.com.

Rail Europe US ☎ 1 800 622 8600, Canada ☎ 1 800 361 7245; ⊛ raileurope.com. Official Eurail agent, with wide range of regional and one-country passes.

STA Travel US ☎ 1 800 781 4040, ⊛ statravel.com.

AUSTRALIA AND NEW ZEALAND

CIT Holidays Australia ☎ 1300 380 992, ⊛ cit.com.au. Eurail and Italian rail passes.

Rail Europe Australia ⊛ raileurope-world.com.au, New Zealand ⊛ raileurope.co.nz.

Rail Plus Australia ☎ 1300 555 003, ⊛ railplus.com.au; NZ ☎ 09 377 5415, ⊛ railplus.co.nz. Eurail and BritRail passes.

STA Travel Australia ☎ 134 782, ⊛ statravel.com.au; New Zealand ☎ 0800 474400, ⊛ statravel.co.nz.

SOUTH AFRICA

Rail Europe ☎ 011 628 2319, ⊛ raileurope.co.za. Official distributor for European rail in South Africa.

STA Travel South Africa ☎ 0861 781 781, ⊛ statravel.co.za.

By bus

Long-distance journeys by bus between major European cities are generally slower and less comfortable than by train and – if you have a rail pass – not necessarily cheaper. If you're only travelling to a few places, however, a **bus pass** or **circular bus ticket** can undercut a rail pass, especially for over-26s. There's also the option of a **bus tour** if you're on a tight schedule or simply want everything planned for you.

Eurolines ⊛ eurolines-pass.com. Offers the Eurolines pass, valid for travel between 51 cities in twenty countries. It costs £227/€270 (£269/€320 for over-26s) for fifteen days in high season (late June to

mid-Sept as well as Christmas/New Year) and £294/€350 (£357/€425) for 30 days. Prices are around a third lower in low season.

Busabout ⊛ busabout.com. Runs a hop-on, hop-off service throughout Western Europe operating May–Oct. There are four "loops" as well as a Flexitrip Pass where you design your own route. Prices start from £655/€758 for a one-loop pass or £417/€496 for a two-week Flexitrip Pass. You can also buy one-way passes for example, starting in Rome and heading to Paris via Spain.

Contiki ⊛ contiki.com. Long-established operator running bus tours throughout Europe for 18- to 35-year-olds from three to 46 days. A thirteen-day "European Discovery" tour taking in the Netherlands, Germany, Austria, Italy, Switzerland and France starts at £1284/€1528 including hotel accommodation and meals.

By car

Driving can be an inexpensive way of getting around Europe, particularly if you're travelling with several other people and splitting the costs. Even **renting a car** can work out as cheap as either bussing or taking the train, since car rental in many European countries starts from around €25 a day for a compact vehicle. A number of European countries have **car-sharing** schemes that allow travellers to get a cheap ride by linking up with drivers heading to their desired destination and sharing petrol costs. These include BlaBla Car (⊛ blablacar.co.uk) in the UK, GoMore (⊛ gomore .com) in Denmark and Drivy (⊛ drivy.de) in Germany.

By ferry

Travelling by **ferry** is sometimes the most practical way to get around, the obvious routes being from the mainland to the Mediterranean islands, and between the countries bordering the Baltic and Adriatic seas. There are countless routes serving a huge range of destinations, too numerous to outline here; we've given the details of the most useful routes within each chapter.

By plane

Most European countries now have at least one **budget airline** selling low-cost flights online, and invariably undercutting train and bus fares on longer international routes. Apart from its environmental impact, travelling by air means you miss the scenery and "feel" for a country that ground-level transport can provide; there's also the inconvenience of getting between airports and the cities they serve, often quite a haul in itself. But, if you're pressed for time, and especially if you want to get from one end of Europe to another, flying can be the cheapest option. See p.29 for a selective list of budget airlines.

Accommodation

Although accommodation is one of the key costs to consider when planning your trip, it needn't be a stumbling block to a budget-conscious tour of Europe. Indeed, even in Europe's pricier destinations the hostel system means there is always an affordable place to stay. If you're prepared to camp, you can get by on very little while staying at some excellently equipped sites. Come summer, university accommodation (see ⓦ university.com) can be a cheap option in some countries.

The one rule of thumb is that in the most popular cities and resorts – Venice, Amsterdam, Paris, Barcelona, the Algarve and so on – things can get very busy during the peak summer months. Be sure to book in advance.

Hostels

The cheapest places to stay around Europe are the innumerable **hostels** that cover the Continent. There are plenty of good-quality independent hostels in most major cities, including an increasing number of stylish designer hostels that can easily compete with lower-priced hotels on comfort, style and facilities. Many establishments are members of Hostelling International (HI), which incorporates the national youth hostel associations of every country in the world. Most are clean, well-run places, always offering dormitory accommodation, and often a range of private single and double rooms, or rooms with four to six beds. Many hostels also either have self-catering facilities or provide low-cost meals, and the larger ones have a range of other facilities – a swimming pool and a games room, for example. There is usually no age limit, but where there is limited space priority is sometimes given to those under 26. The best rates are usually available on the hostel website or through booking engines such as Hostelworld

(ⓦ hostelworld.com) or Hostelbookers (ⓦ hostel bookers.com). Strictly speaking, to use a HI hostel you have to have membership, although if there's room you can stay at most hostels by simply paying a bit extra. If you do plan to stay in hostels, however, it's certainly worth joining, which you can do through your home country's hostelling association. HI hostels can usually be booked through their country's hostelling association website, almost always over the counter at other hostels in the same country, and often through the international HI website ⓦ hihostels.com.

Some countries also offer their own **discount cards** or schemes. In the Netherlands, for example, 27 hostels belong to the StayOkay scheme (ⓦ stayokay.com) and purchasing a €17.50 card entitles travellers to a €2.50 discount a night. Students with ID get discounts in hostels across Germany, while in the Balkans many hostels belong to the Balkan Backpacker scheme (ⓦ thebalkanbackpacker.com), which offers discounts to travellers who stay in more than one of their network of hostels.

YOUTH HOSTEL ASSOCIATIONS

USA ☎ 1 301 495 1240, ⓦ hiusa.org.
Canada ☎ 613 237 7884, ⓦ hihostels.ca.
England and Wales ☎ 0800 019 1700 or ☎ 01629 592 700, ⓦ yha.org.uk.
Scotland ☎ 0845 293 7373, ⓦ syha.org.uk.
Ireland (Republic) ☎ 01 830 4555, ⓦ anoige.ie.
Northern Ireland ☎ 028 9032 4733, ⓦ hini.org.uk.
Australia ☎ 02 9218 9090, ⓦ yha.com.au.
New Zealand ☎ 0800 278 299, ⓦ yha.co.nz.
South Africa ⓦ hihostels.com.

Hotels and pensions

Most **hotels** in Europe are graded on some kind of star system. One- and two-star hotels are plain and simple on the whole, usually family-run, and rooms often lack private facilities; sometimes breakfast won't be included. In three-star hotels rooms will nearly always be en suite and prices will normally include breakfast. In the really top-level places breakfast isn't always included.

Obviously prices vary greatly, but you'll rarely pay less than €30 for a basic double room even in southern Europe, while between the Netherlands, Scandinavia and the British Isles the average price is around €85. In some countries a *pension* or **B&B** (also variously known as a guesthouse, *pensão*, *Gasthaus* or numerous other names) is a cheaper alternative, offering just a few rooms of simple

> ## ACCOMMODATION PRICES
>
> All **accommodation prices** listed are for high season. The prices we list for hotels, guesthouses, B&Bs, *pensions* and private rooms are for the cheapest double room. For hostels, it is the price of the cheapest dorm bed, and for campsites the cost of a night's stay per person, except where otherwise stated.

COUCHSURFING, AIRBNB AND WIMDU

Couchsurfing (Ⓦcouchsurfing.com) gives travellers the chance to stay with local people **free of charge**, with hosts verified through references and a vouching system. **Airbnb** (Ⓦairbnb.com) and **Wimdu** (Ⓦwimdu.com) are other good options for budget short-term stays with rooms, apartments and other (sometimes unusual) lodgings listed by private individuals.

Festivals and annual events

There's always some event or other happening in Europe, and the bigger shindigs can be reason enough for visiting a place. Be warned, though, that if you're intending to visit a place during its annual festival you need to plan well in advance; accommodation can be booked up months beforehand, especially for the most famous events.

accommodation. In some countries these advertise with a sign in the window; in others they can be booked through the tourist office for a small fee. There are various other kinds of accommodation – apartments, farmhouses, cottages, *gîtes* in France, and more – but most are geared to longer-term stays and we have detailed them only where relevant.

Camping

The cheapest form of accommodation is a **campsite**. Most sites charge per person, with additional charges per tent and/or per vehicle. Facilities can be excellent, especially in countries such as France where camping is very popular. If you don't have a vehicle you should add in the cost and inconvenience of getting to the site, since most are on the outskirts of towns. Some sites also have cabins, which you can stay in for a little extra, although these are usually fairly basic affairs, only really worth considering in regions like Scandinavia where budget options are thin on the ground. Tourist offices can often recommend well-equipped and conveniently located sites.

As for **camping rough**, it's a fine idea if you can get away with it. In some countries it's easy – in parts of Scandinavia it's a legal right, and in Greece and other southern European countries you can usually find a bit of beach to pitch down on – but in others it can get you into trouble with the law.

Camping Card International

If you're planning to do a lot of camping, a **Camping Card International** (CCI or "carnet"; Ⓦcampingcardinternational.com), gives discounts on member sites. Check the website for details of all the relevant organizations in various countries that issue the card.

Festival calendar

Many of the festivals and annual events you'll come across in Europe have their origin in – and in many cases still represent – religious celebrations, commemorating a local miracle or saint's day. Others are decidedly more secular – from film and music festivals to street carnivals.

JANUARY

Twelfth Night (Jan 6) Rather than Christmas Day, in Spain this is the time for present-giving, while in Orthodox Eastern Europe, Jan 6 is Christmas Day.
La Tamborrada, San Sebastián, Spain (Jan 20) Probably the loudest festival you will encounter as scores of drummers take to the streets of San Sebastián.

FEBRUARY

Berlin Film Festival, Germany (early to mid-Feb) Home of the Golden Bear award, this film bash is geared towards the general public.
Carnival/Mardi Gras (mid-Feb) Celebrated most famously in Venice, but there are smaller events across Europe, notably in Viareggio (Italy), Luzern and Basel (Switzerland), Cologne (Germany), Maastricht (Netherlands) and tiny Binche (Belgium).

MARCH

Las Fallas, Valencia, Spain (March 15–19) The passing of winter is celebrated in explosive fashion with enormous bonfires, burning effigies and plenty of all-night partying.
St Patrick's Day (March 17) Celebrated wherever there's an Irish community, in Dublin it's a five-day festival with music, parades and a lot of drinking.

APRIL

Easter Celebrated with most verve and ceremony in Catholic and Orthodox Europe, where Easter Sunday or Monday is usually marked with some sort of procession; note that the Orthodox Church's Easter can fall a week or two either side of the Western festival.
Feria de Abril, Seville, Spain (mid-April) A week of flamenco music and dancing, parades and bullfights, in a frenzied and enthusiastic atmosphere.

King's Day, Amsterdam, Netherlands (April 27) King Willem-Alexander's birthday is the excuse for this anarchic 24-hour drinking and dressing-up binge – remember your orange attire.

MAY

Cannes Film Festival, France (mid-late May) The world's most famous cinema festival is really more of an industry affair than anything else.

PinkPop Festival, Landgraaf, Netherlands (late May/early June) The Netherlands' biggest pop music festival.

JUNE

Festa do São João, Porto, Portugal (June 23–24) Portugal's second city puts on the mother of all street parties, culminating in revellers hitting each other with plastic hammers.

Glastonbury Festival, England (mid-late June) Despite being one of Europe's largest (and most expensive) music festivals, Glastonbury is a surprisingly intimate affair, thanks to its beautiful setting and hippie vibe.

Roskilde Festival, Denmark (late June/early July) An eclectic range of music (rock, dance, folk) and performance arts, with profits going to worthy causes.

JULY

The Palio, Siena, Italy (July 2 & Aug 16) Italy's most spectacular summer event: a bareback horse race between representatives of the different quarters of the city around the main square.

Montreux Jazz Festival, Switzerland (early July) These days only loosely committed to jazz, this festival takes in everything from folk to breakbeats.

Fiesta de San Fermín, Pamplona, Spain (July 6–14) Anarchic fun, centred on the running of the bulls through the streets of the city, plus music, dancing and of course a lot of drinking.

Exit Festival, Novi Sad, Serbia (early/mid-July) Europe's hippest music festival, held in a beautiful fortress and attracting top DJs and artists from around the world.

Avignon Festival, France (early/mid-July) Slanted towards drama but hosts plenty of other events too.

Dubrovnik Summer Festival, Croatia (July & Aug) A host of musical events and theatre performances against the backdrop of the town's beautiful Renaissance centre.

Gentse Feesten, Belgium (mid-July) A ten-day canalside party of music and theatre so bacchanalian that the whole city takes two weeks off work afterwards to recover.

The Proms, London (July–Sept) World-famous concert series that maintains high standards of classical music at egalitarian prices.

Ramadan (May–June in 2017, 2018 & 2019) Commemorating the revelation of the Koran to the Prophet Mohammed, the month of fasting from sunrise until sunset ends with a huge celebration called Eid el-Fitr. Morocco, Turkey, Kosovo, Bosnia-Herzegovina, plus Muslim areas of Bulgaria and Greece.

AUGUST

Locarno Film Festival, Switzerland (early/mid-Aug) Movies from around the world compete on the banks of Lake Maggiore.

Sziget Festival, Hungary (mid-Aug) Week-long music and culture fest on Obuda island, Budapest, drawing almost half a million revellers.

La Tomatina, Buñol, Spain The last Wednesday in August sees the streets of Buñol packed for a one-hour food fight disposing of 130,000 kilos of tomatoes.

Edinburgh Festival, Scotland (last three weeks of Aug) A mass of top-notch and fringe events in every performing medium, from rock to cabaret to modern experimental music, dance and drama.

Notting Hill Carnival, London (last weekend of Aug) Predominantly Black British and Caribbean celebration that's become the world's second-biggest street carnival after Rio.

Venice Film Festival, Italy (late Aug/early Sept) First held in 1932, this is the world's oldest film festival.

SEPTEMBER

Ibiza closing parties, Spain (mostly in Sept) The summer dance music Mecca goes out with a bang in September, with all the main clubs holding closing parties.

Regata Storica, Venice, Italy (early Sept) A trial of skill for the city's gondoliers.

Oktoberfest, Munich, Germany (late Sept/early Oct) A huge beer festival and fair, attracting vast numbers of people to consume gluttonous quantities of beer and food.

Galway International Oyster Festival, Ireland (last weekend in Sept) The arrival of the oyster season is celebrated with a three-day seafood, Guinness and dancing shindig.

OCTOBER

Combat des Reines, Switzerland (early Oct) Quirky cow-fighting contest held to decide the queen of the herd in the Valais region of Switzerland. The main event is the copious drinking and betting on the sidelines (and no, the cows don't get hurt).

NOVEMBER

Bonfire Night, Lewes, England (Nov 5) Huge processions and tremendous fireworks light up this sleepy town every year.

Madonna della Salute Festival, Venice, Italy (Nov 21) Annual candlelit procession across the Grand Canal to the church of Santa Maria della Salute.

DECEMBER

Christmas Festive markets sprout up across the Continent in the run-up to Christmas. One of the best is found in Cologne, Germany.

New Year's Eve Celebrated with parties across Europe, it's best experienced in Edinburgh where over a hundred thousand people cram the streets for Hogmanay, or in Moscow, with incredible fireworks over Red Square.

Work and study

The best way of getting to know a country properly is to work there and learn the language. Study opportunities are also a good way of absorbing yourself

in the local culture, though they invariably need to be organized in advance; look online and check newspapers for ads or contact one of the organizations listed below.

Working in Europe

There are any number of jobs you can pick up on the road to supplement your spending money. It's normally not hard to find bar or restaurant work, especially in large resort areas during the summer, and your chances will be greater if you speak the local language – although being able to speak English may be your greatest asset in more touristy areas. **Cleaning jobs**, **nannying** and **au pair** work are also common, if not spectacularly well paid, often just providing room and board plus pocket money. Some of them can be organized on the spot, while others need to be arranged before you leave home.

The other big casual earner is farm work, particularly **grape-picking**, an option from August to October when the vines are being harvested. The best country for this is France, but there's sometimes work in Germany too, and you're unlikely to be asked for documentation. Also in France, along the Côte d'Azur, and in other yacht-havens such as Greece and parts of southern Spain, there is sometimes crewing work available, though you'll need the appropriate experience.

Rather better paid, and equally widespread, if only from September to June, is **teaching** English as a foreign language (TEFL), though it's sometimes hard to find English-teaching jobs without a TEFL qualification. You'll normally be paid a liveable local salary, sometimes with somewhere to live included, and you can often supplement your income with more lucrative private lessons. The TEFL teaching season is reversed in Britain and to a lesser extent Ireland, with plenty of work available during the summer in London and on the English south coast (though again, some kind of TEFL qualification is usually required).

For further **information** on working abroad, check out the books published in the UK by Vacation Work; visit ⓦcrimsonpublishing.co.uk for their catalogue. Also try ⓦstudyabroad.com, a useful website with listings and links to study and work programmes worldwide.

Studying in Europe

Studying abroad invariably means **learning a language**, in an intensive course that lasts between two weeks and three months, and staying with a local family. There are plenty of places you can do this and you should reckon on paying around £230/US$300 a week, including room and board. If you know a language well, you could also apply to do a short course in another subject at a local university; check websites such as ⓦeurolingua.com, ⓦlanguagesabroad.com and ⓦeuropa-pages.com, and keep an eye out when you're on the spot. The EU **Erasmus** programme provides grants for university students from Britain and Ireland to study in one of 32 European countries for between three months and a full academic year if their university participates in the programme. Post-Brexit, British students may no longer be eligible for this scheme: check with your university's international relations office, or see ⓦbritishcouncil.org/erasmus.

WORK AND STUDY CONTACTS

AFS Intercultural Programs US ⓣ 1 800 AFS INFO, Canada ⓣ 1 800 361 7248, Australia ⓣ 1300131736, NZ ⓣ 0800 600 300, SA ⓣ 27114310113; ⓦ afs.org. Intercultural exchange organization.

American Institute for Foreign Study US ⓣ 1 866 906 2437, UK ⓣ 020 7581 7300, Australia ⓣ 02 8235 7000; ⓦ aifs.com. Language study and cultural immersion for the summer or school year.

ASSE US ⓣ 1 800 333 3802, Canada ⓣ 1 855 886 8381; ⓦ asse .com. International student exchanges and summer language programmes in various European countries.

British Council UK ⓣ 0161 957 7775, ⓦ britishcouncil.org. The Council's Recruitment Group recruits TEFL teachers with degrees and TEFL qualifications for posts, while its Education and Training Group runs teacher exchange programmes for those who already work as educators to find out about teacher development programmes abroad.

Council on International Educational Exchange (CIEE) US ⓣ 1 207 553 4000, ⓦ ciee.org. Leading NGO offering study programmes and volunteer projects.

Cultural Vistas US ⓣ 1 212 497 3500, ⓦ culturalvistas.org. Summer internships in various European countries for students who have completed at least two years of college in science, agriculture, engineering or architecture.

International House UK ⓣ 020 7611 2400, ⓦ ihlondon.com. Reputable English-teaching organization that offers TEFL training leading to a Certificate in English Language Teaching to Adults (CELTA), and recruits for teaching positions in Britain and abroad.

World Learning US ⓣ 1 800 257 7751 or ⓣ 1 802 257 7751, ⓦ worldlearning.org. The Experiment in International Living (ⓦ experiment.org) has summer programmes for high-school students, while the School for International Training (ⓦ sit.edu/studyabroad) offers accredited college semesters abroad, with language and cultural studies, homestay and other academic work.

WWOOF Europe ⓦ wwoofeurope.net. Volunteering on organic farms and with sustainable projects in various European countries.

Travel essentials

Costs

It's hard to generalize about what you're likely to spend travelling around Europe, but it's by and large **not cheap**. Some countries – Norway, Switzerland, the UK – are among the most expensive in the world, while in others (Turkey, for example) you can live quite well on a fairly modest budget. Remember, however, that all of Europe is modern and well touristed, which means higher prices than in the developing world. In general, countries in the north and west of Europe are more expensive than those in the south and east, though keep an eye on exchange rates.

Accommodation will be your largest single expense, and can really determine where you decide to travel. **Food and drink** costs also vary wildly, although again in most parts of Europe you can assume that a cheap restaurant meal will cost €12–20 a head, with prices nearer the top end of the scale in Scandinavia, at the bottom end in eastern Europe, and below that in Turkey and Morocco. **Transport** costs are something you can pin down more exactly if you have a rail pass. Nowhere, though, are transport costs a major burden, except perhaps in Britain where public transport is less heavily subsidized than elsewhere.

The bottom line for an average **daily budget** touring the Continent – camping, self-catering, hitching, etc – might be around €37 a day per person. Adding on a rail pass, staying in hostels and eating out occasionally would bring this up to

PRICES

At the beginning of each chapter you'll find a **guide to rough costs** including food, accommodation and travel. Prices are quoted in euros for ease of comparison. Within the chapter itself prices are quoted in local currency.

perhaps €60 a day, while staying in private rooms or hotels and eating out once a day would mean a personal daily budget of at least €110. See box below, for tips on keeping your costs down.

Crime and personal safety

Travelling around Europe should be relatively trouble-free, but, as in any part of the world, there is always the chance of **petty theft**. Conditions vary greatly depending on the country: in Scandinavia, for example, you're unlikely to encounter much trouble of any kind, whereas in certain areas of large cities such as London, Paris or Barcelona, the **crime** rate is significantly higher. Also take care in poorer regions such as Morocco, Turkey and southern Italy. France, Belgium, Germany and Turkey have been rocked by a number of terrorist attacks recently, and potential **terrorist activity** remains a concern throughout Europe. Be vigilant when you're in crowded public spaces.

Safety tips

In order to minimize the risks, you should take some basic precautions. First and perhaps most

---

GETTING BY ON A BUDGET

Buy a rail pass Whether you're planning to take in all of Europe or just a few countries, a rail pass will save you money (see p.34).

Find a roommate Accommodation in hotels, *pensions* and private rooms is cheaper if you share, so buddy up.

Student/youth discounts If you're a student or under 26, make sure you bring your student or youth card (see p.44), and always ask about discounts.

Head for the countryside Don't spend more time than you need to in cities – prices are always higher there.

Shun tourist traps Eat and drink with the locals and try regional food as it'll usually be cheaper – and frequently tastier.

Self-cater Markets are full of fresh, seasonal picnic fare, which makes self-catering a treat.

Drink at home Have a few drinks before you go out – you can usually pick up booze from local shops at a fraction of the bar price.

Be flexible Transport is often cheaper in off-peak hours.

Sleep on the train Make your longest journeys overnight – you'll forego accommodation costs for the night.

Bargain, bargain, bargain Don't be afraid to haggle (especially in places like Morocco where it's expected), but know when to stop.

important, try not to look too much like a tourist. Appearing lost, even if you are, should be avoided, and it's not a good idea – especially in southern Europe – to walk around flashing an obviously expensive camera or smartphone: the professional bag-snatchers who tour train stations can have your valuables off you in seconds.

If you're waiting for a train, keep your eyes (and hands if necessary) on your bags at all times; if you want to sleep, put everything valuable under whatever you use as a pillow. Exercise caution when choosing a train compartment and avoid any situation that makes you feel uncomfortable. **Padlocking** your bags to the luggage rack if you're on an overnight train increases the likelihood that they'll still be there in the morning. It's also a good idea to wear a **money belt**.

If you're staying in a hostel, take your valuables out with you unless there's a very secure store for them on the premises. It's a good idea to **photocopy your passport** and send it to your email account, and leave a copy of your address book with friends or family.

If the worst happens and you do have something stolen, inform the **police** immediately (we've included details of the main city police stations or tourist police throughout); the priority is to get a statement from them detailing exactly what has been lost, which you'll need for your insurance claim back home.

Customs

Customs and **duty-free restrictions** vary throughout Europe. Non-EU citizens arriving in the EU can bring in one litre of spirits, four litres of table wine, plus 200 cigarettes (or 250g tobacco, or fifty cigars). There is no duty-free allowance for travel within the EU: in principle you can carry as much in the way of duty-paid goods as you want, so long as it is for personal use. Note that Andorra, Gibraltar, the Canary Islands, Ceuta and the Channel Islands are outside the EU for customs purposes, and the UK may join them, depending on post-Brexit negotia-tions. If you are carrying prescribed drugs of any kind, it's a good idea to have a copy of the prescrip-tion to show to suspicious customs officers. Note also that all EU members restrict the importation from outside Europe of meat, fish, eggs and honey.

Drugs

Drugs such as amphetamines, cocaine, heroin, LSD and ecstasy are **illegal** all over Europe, and although use of cannabis is widespread in most countries, and legally tolerated in some (famously in the Netherlands, for example), you are never allowed to possess more than a tiny amount for personal use, and unlicensed sale remains illegal. Penalties can be severe (in certain countries, such as Turkey, even possession of cannabis can result in a hefty prison sentence) and your consulate is unlikely to be sympathetic.

Electricity

The supply in Europe is 220v (240v in the British Isles), which means that anything on North American voltage (110v) normally needs a trans-former – or at least a plug adapter if the power cord has a built-in transformer. Some countries (notably Spain and Morocco) still have a few places on 110v or 120v, so check before plugging in or you could fry your electronics. British and Irish sockets take three rectangular pins; elsewhere they take two round pins. A travel plug which adapts to these systems is useful to carry.

Entry requirements

Citizens of the UK (but not other British passport holders), Ireland, Australia, New Zealand, Canada and the US do not need a **visa** to enter most European countries, and can usually stay for between one and three months, depending on nationality. EU countries never require visas from Irish citizens, and currently British citizens don't need them either, though the situation may change post-Brexit. Always check visa requirements before travelling with the embassy of the country you are visiting, as they can and do change; this especially applies to Canadian, Australian, New Zealand and South African citizens intending to visit Eastern European countries.

VISA ALERT!

Everyone needs a **visa to visit Russia**, which must be obtained in advance, and if you're passing through Belarus to get there, you'll need a transit visa for that country as well. Citizens of most countries also need a visa for **Turkey**, which is available at the border (see p.1141). South Africans need a visa for most European countries, so be sure to check with the appropriate embassy before travelling.

Twenty-six countries (Austria, Belgium, Czech Republic, Denmark, Estonia, Finland, France, Germany, Greece, Hungary, Iceland, Italy, Latvia, Liechtenstein, Lithuania, Luxembourg, Malta, the Netherlands, Norway, Poland, Portugal, Slovakia, Slovenia, Spain, Sweden and Switzerland), known as the **Schengen group**, have joint visas which are valid for travel in all of them; in theory there are no immigration controls between these countries, though there may be spot-checks of ID within their borders.

Gay and lesbian travellers

Gay men and lesbians will find most of Europe a **tolerant** place in which to travel, the west rather more so than the east, where there can still be considerable hostility. Gay sex is no longer a criminal offence in any country covered by this book except Morocco, but some still have measures that discriminate against gay men (a higher age of consent, for example), and Russia has recently introduced a law against "gay propaganda", amid a new wave of **homophobia**. Lesbianism sometimes escapes such laws on the basis that its existence is not officially recognized, although that is not the case in Russia. For further information, check the International Lesbian and Gay Association's European region website at ⓦ ilga-europe.org.

Health

You don't need **inoculations** for any of the countries covered in this book, although for Morocco and Turkey typhoid jabs are advised, and in southeastern Turkey malaria pills are a good idea for much of the year – check ⓦ cdc.gov/travel for full details. Remember to keep your polio and tetanus boosters up to date.

EU citizens are covered by reciprocal health agreements for free or reduced-cost emergency treatment in many of the countries in this book (the main exceptions are Albania, Morocco, Russia, Turkey and Ukraine). To claim this, you will be asked for your proof of residence or **European Health Insurance Card** (EHIC). British citizens are currently eligible for an EHIC, and can apply for one at ⓦ ehic .org.uk, though post-Brexit this may change: check ⓦ gov.uk/european-health-insurance-card for the latest situation. Irish citizens can apply for a card at ⓦ ehic.ie. Without an EHIC, you won't be turned away from hospitals but you will almost certainly have to pay for any treatment or medicines. Also, in practice, some doctors and hospitals charge

anyway and it's up to you to claim reimbursement when you return home. Make sure you are insured for potential medical expenses, and keep copies of receipts and prescriptions.

Doctors, hospitals and pharmacies

For minor health problems it's easiest to go to a **pharmacy**, found pretty much everywhere. In major cities there should be at least one pharmacy open 24 hours – check any pharmacy window for a rota indicating the branch currently open all night. In cases of serious injury or illness contact your nearest consulate, which will have a list of English-speaking **doctors**, as will the local tourist office. In the accounts of larger cities we've listed the most convenient **hospital** casualty units/ emergency rooms.

Contraceptives

Condoms are available everywhere, and are normally reliable international brands such as Durex, at least in western Europe; the condoms in eastern European countries, Morocco and Turkey are of uncertain quality, however, so it's best to bring your own. **AIDS** is as much of a problem in Europe as in the rest of the world, and members of both sexes should carry condoms. The **pill** is available everywhere, too, though often only on prescription; again, bring a sufficient supply with you. In case of emergency, the **morning-after pill** is available from pharmacies without a prescription in Austria, Belgium, Bulgaria, Denmark, Estonia, Finland, France, Greece, Ireland, Lithuania, Morocco, the Netherlands, Norway, Portugal, Sweden, Switzerland, Turkey and the UK.

Drinking water

Tap water in most countries is **drinkable**, and only needs to be avoided in Morocco and parts of Turkey. Unfamiliar food may well give you a small case of the runs, normally over in a day or two.

Insurance

Wherever you're travelling from, it's a very good idea to have some kind of **travel insurance**. Before buying a policy, however, check whether you're already covered: students will often find that their student health coverage extends into the vacations and for one term beyond the date of last enrolment; and some credit cards include travel insurance.

Otherwise you should contact a specialist travel insurance company. A **typical policy** usually provides cover for the loss of baggage, tickets and –

ROUGH GUIDES TRAVEL INSURANCE

Rough Guides has teamed up with WorldNomads.com to offer great travel insurance deals. Policies are available to residents of over 150 countries, with cover for a wide range of adventure sports, 24hr emergency assistance, high levels of medical and evacuation cover and a stream of travel safety information. Roughguides.com users can take advantage of their policies online 24/7, from anywhere in the world – even if you're already travelling. And since plans often change when you're on the road, you can extend your policy and even claim online. Roughguides.com users who buy travel insurance with WorldNomads.com can also leave a positive footprint and donate to a community development project. For more information, go to ⓦroughguides.com/travel-insurance.

up to a certain limit – cash, as well as cancellation or curtailment of your journey. Make sure that the per-article limit covers your most valuable possession. Most policies exclude so-called **dangerous sports** unless an extra premium is paid: in Europe this can mean anything from scuba diving to mountaineering, skiing and even bungee-jumping. With **medical cover**, you should ascertain whether benefits will be paid as treatment proceeds or only after you return home, and whether there is a 24-hour medical emergency number.

Internet and email

In most European countries internet cafés are rare, since public **wi-fi** – often free – has taken over and data roaming has become significantly cheaper. Most hotels and many cafés and restaurants also offer free wi-fi.

Left luggage (baggage deposit)

Almost every train station of any size has facilities for depositing luggage – either lockers or a desk that's open long hours every day. We've given details in the accounts of the major cities.

Mail

We've listed the central **post offices** in major cities and given an idea of opening hours. Bear in mind, though, that in most countries you can avoid long waits in post offices by buying stamps from newsagents, tobacconists and street kiosks.

Maps

Though you can often buy **maps** on the spot, you may want to get them in advance to plan your trip: firms such as Stanfords in the UK (ⓦstanfords.co.uk) and Rand McNally in the US (ⓦrandmcnally.com) sell maps online or by mail order. For extensive

motoring, it's better to get a large-page road **atlas** such as Michelin's *Tourist and Motoring Atlas*. If you have a smartphone, the **Citymapper app** (ⓦcitymapper.com) is invaluable when navigating public transport in big cities; it currently covers London, Rome, Paris, Hamburg, Brussels, Berlin, Lyon, Lisbon, Milan, Madrid and Barcelona.

Money

The easiest way to carry your money is in the form of plastic. Hotels, shops and restaurants across the Continent accept major **credit and debit cards**, although cheaper places may not. More importantly, you can use them to get cash out of **ATMs** throughout the region, including Morocco and Turkey, as long as they are affiliated to an international network (such as Visa, MasterCard or Cirrus). Using a **cash card** pre-loaded with multiple currencies, such as Travelex (ⓦtravelex.com), is a good way to avoid paying bank withdrawal fees. In some countries **banks** are the only places where you can legally change money, and they often offer the best exchange rates and lowest commission. Local banking hours are given throughout this book. Outside normal hours you can use **bureaux**

THE EURO (€)

The **euro** is the currency of 19 EU countries (and a couple of others use the euro unilaterally). **Coins** come as 1c, 2c, 5c, 10c, 20c, 50c, €1 and €2, with one side of the coin stating the denomination while the other side has a design unique to the issuing country. Euro **notes** come as €5, €10, €20, €50, €100, €200 and €500. At the time of writing, £1 was worth €1.19, US$1 got you €0.90, Can$1 was €0.69, Aus$1 was €0.68, NZ$1 was €0.64 and ZAR10 was €0.63. Check ⓦxe.com for the latest exchange rates.

de change, often located at train stations and airports, though their rates and/or commissions may well be less favourable.

Phones

Since most people have mobile phones, **public call boxes** have become practically obsolete across Europe. It's easiest to call home via Skype or similar, though in some places it's still possible to go to a post office, or a special phone bureau, where you can call from a private booth and pay afterwards. Phoning from hotels tends to be very expensive.

To call **any country** in this book from Britain, Ireland, South Africa or New Zealand, dial ☎00, then the country code, then the city/area code (if there is one) without the initial zero – except for the following: Russia and Lithuania (where there is no initial zero); Italy, where the initial zero (or 3 for a cellphone) must be dialled; and Denmark, the Czech Republic, Latvia, Portugal, Spain, Andorra and Gibraltar, where there are no area codes, and the whole number must be dialled. From the US and most of Canada, the international access code is ☎011, from Australia it's ☎0011; otherwise the procedure is the same.

To **call home** from almost all European countries, including Morocco and Turkey, dial ☎00, then the country code, then the city/area code (without the initial zero if there is one), then the local number. The exception is Russia, where you dial ☎8, wait for a continuous dialling tone and then dial ☎10, followed by the country code, area code and number.

For **collect calls**, use the "Home Country Direct" service. In the UK and some other countries, international calling cards available from newsagents enable you to call North America, Australia and New Zealand very cheaply. Most North American, British, Irish and Australasian phone companies either allow you to call home on a credit card, or billed to your home number, though with mobile phone access becoming cheaper and easier worldwide, this would be a last resort.

Mobile/cellphones

Some North American **cellphones** may not work in Europe, though if your smartphone is unlocked, you can use it with a local SIM card in most European countries; in Australia and New Zealand, you can pre-order a SIM card from various countries from ⓦtravelgear.com.au. Mobiles from the UK, Ireland, Australia, New Zealand and South Africa can be used in most parts of Europe, and a lot of countries – certainly in Western Europe – have nearly universal coverage. There's a cap on **mobile phone charges** within Europe, so EU residents can use their own phones within all EU countries for the same price as at home – post-Brexit, this may or may not apply to British citizens: check with your mobile company first. Many service providers, including those in the United States, offer call and data packages that can be used abroad at little or no extra charge.

Student and youth discounts

It's worth flashing whichever discount card you've got at every opportunity. For students, an **International Student Identity Card** (ISIC for short) is well worth the investment. It offers reduced (usually half-price, sometimes free) entry to museums and other sights, as well as qualifying you for other discounts in certain cities. It can also save you money on some transport costs, notably ferries. The card costs £12 in the UK, €15 in Ireland, US$25 in the US, Can$20 in Canada, Aus$25 in Australia, NZ$25 in New Zealand and ZAR100 in South Africa. If you're not a student but under 26, get an **International Youth Travel Card**, which costs the same and can in some countries give much the same sort of reductions. Both cards are available direct from ⓦisic.org or from youth travel specialists such as STA. You can download the ISIC app that allows you to search for discounts in the country you're travelling in.

As well as the above options, the **European Youth Card** (ⓦeyca.org) entitles anyone under 26 (or under 30 in some countries) to a wide range of discounts on transport services, tourist attractions, activities and accommodation for up to a year. It is available online for people living outside Europe and at designated outlets in 38 European countries. Although the card is valid across the region, prices vary across individual countries (from around €5 to €19), as do the relevant discounts.

NEWSPAPERS

British and American newspapers and magazines are widely available in Europe, sometimes on the day of publication, more often the day after. They do, however, cost around three times as much as they do at home. Look too for locally produced English-language papers and websites.

CLOTHING AND SHOE SIZES

WOMEN'S DRESSES AND SKIRTS

American	4	6	8	10	12	14	16	18	
British	8	10	12	14	16	18	20	22	
Continental	38	40	42	44	46	48	50	52	

WOMEN'S BLOUSES AND SWEATERS

American	6	8	10	12	14	16	18		
British	30	32	34	36	38	40	42		
Continental	40	42	44	46	48	50	52		

WOMEN'S SHOES

American	5	6	7	8	9	10	11		
British	3	4	5	6	7	8	9		
Continental	36	37	38	39	40	41	42		

MEN'S SUITS

American	34	36	38	40	42	44	46	48	
British	34	36	38	40	42	44	46	48	
Continental	44	46	48	50	52	54	56	58	

MEN'S SHIRTS

American	14	15	15.5	16	16.5	17	17.5	18	
British	14	15	15.5	16	16.5	17	17.5	18	
Continental	36	38	39	41	42	43	44	45	

MEN'S SHOES

American	7	7.5	8	8.5	9.5	10	10.5	11	11.5
British	6	7	7.5	8	9	9.5	10	11	12
Continental	39	40	41	42	43	44	44	45	46

Time

This book covers four **time zones** (see map, p.46). GMT (Greenwich Mean Time), aka UTC, or Universal Time, is five hours ahead of Eastern Standard Time, eight hours ahead of Pacific Standard Time, eight hours behind Western Australia, ten hours behind eastern Australia, twelve hours behind New Zealand and two hours behind South Africa. Note that all countries in this book (except Morocco and Russia) have daylight saving time from March to October. This change, along with daylight saving in North America, Australia and New Zealand, can affect the time difference by an hour either way.

Tourist information

Before you leave, it's worth checking the websites of the **tourist offices** of the countries you're intending to visit. For parts of central and eastern Europe, where up-to-date maps can be hard to find within the country, it may be worth contacting the tourist office in advance and asking them to send you any free maps and brochures they may have:

note that a few countries do not have any official tourist offices abroad, and you may have to contact their embassy instead.

Once in Europe, most countries have a network of tourist offices that answer queries, dole out a range of (mostly free) maps and brochures, and can often book accommodation, or at least advise you on it. They're better organized in the UK, Scandinavia, the Netherlands, France, Switzerland and Spain – with branches in all but the smallest village, and mounds of information; in Greece, Turkey and eastern Europe you'll find fewer tourist offices and they'll be less helpful on the whole, sometimes offering no more than a couple of dog-eared brochures and a photocopied map. We've given further details, including a broad idea of opening hours, in the introduction for each country.

Travellers with disabilities

Prosperous northern Europe is easier for **disabled travellers** than the south and east, but the gradual enforcement of EU accessibility regulations is making life easier throughout the European Union

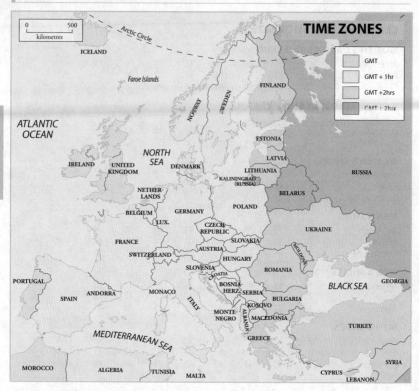

TIME ZONES

	GMT
	GMT + 1hr
	GMT +2hrs
	GMT + 3hrs

at least. Wheelchair access to public buildings nonetheless remains far from common in many countries, as is wheelchair accessibility to public transport. Most buses are still inaccessible to wheelchair users, but airport facilities are improving, as are those on cross-Channel ferries. As for rail services, these vary greatly: France, for example, provides well for disabled passengers, as do Belgium, Denmark, Switzerland and Austria, but many other countries make little if any provision. For comprehensive info on disabled travel, check out ⓦ disabledtravelers.com.

Women travellers

One of the major irritants for women travelling through Europe is sexual harassment, which, in Italy, Greece, Turkey, Spain and Morocco especially, can be almost constant for women travelling alone. By far the most common kind of harassment you'll come across simply consists of street whistles and catcalls; occasionally it's more sinister, and very occasionally it can be dangerous. Indifference is often the best policy, avoiding eye contact with men and at the same time appearing as confident and purposeful as possible. If this doesn't make you feel any more comfortable, shouting a few choice phrases in the local language is a good idea; don't, however, shout in English, which often seems to encourage them. You may also come across gropers on crowded buses and trains, in which case you should complain as loudly as possible in any language – the ensuing scene should be enough to deter your assailant.

VALBONA VALLEY NATIONAL PARK

Albania

HIGHLIGHTS

❶ **Tirana** Delve into Albania's past in a giant, underground Communist bunker. **See p.52**

❷ **Valbona** Rural life surrounded by stunning alpine mountains. **See p.57**

❸ **Berat** Explore a hilltop maze of Ottoman houses. **See p.57**

❹ **Gjirokastra** Beautiful valley views and a charming old town. **See p.58**

❺ **Ksamil's beaches** Relax on some of the Med's least-developed beaches. **See p.60**

HIGHLIGHTS ARE MARKED ON THE MAP ON P.49

ROUGH COSTS

Daily budget Basic €25, occasional treat €40

Drink Bottle of red wine €6

Food *Qoftë* (minced meat rissoles) €2

Hostel/budget hotel €10/€30

Travel Bus: Tirana–Saranda €8 Train: Tirana–Shkodra €1.50

FACT FILE

Population 3 million

Language Albanian (*Shqip*)

Currency Lekë (L)

Capital Tirana

International phone code ☎ 355

Time zone GMT +1hr

1

Introduction

Beyond vague recollections of its Communist past, few travellers know much about Albania. Its rippling mountains and pristine beaches, lands littered with historical Roman ruins and pretty Ottoman towns remain largely undiscovered. Most never see the alluring azure lakes or the picturesque valleys occupied by immensely hospitable locals, and instead bypass the country for its far more popular neighbours.

Following decades of isolationist rule, this rugged land still doesn't seem to fit into the grand continental jigsaw, with distinctly exotic notes emanating from its language, customs and cuisine. But it's those idiosyncrasies that make it such an intriguing and rewarding corner of Europe, begging to be explored.

Most travellers make a beeline for the capital, **Tirana**, a buzzing city with a mishmash of garishly painted buildings, traditional restaurants and trendy bars. However, those seeking to take Albania's true pulse should head to the mountainous hinterlands, particularly the sleepy hillside towns of **Berat** and **Gjirokastra** – both essentially open-air museums of life in Ottoman times. Keen hikers will want to explore the valley of Valbona, where karst limestone mountains harbour astonishing biodiversity, and as the snowcapped peaks of the interior drop down to the ocean, the immaculate beaches along the **Ionian coastline** are among the Mediterranean's least developed sands.

CHRONOLOGY

168 BC The Romans defeat the Illyrian tribe and establish rule over present-day Albania.

395 AD Division of Roman Empire; Albania falls under the rule of Constantinople.

300s–500s Invasions by Visigoths, Ostrogoths and Huns.

1343 Serbian invasions.

1443–79 Resistance against Ottoman rule, most of it led by national hero Skanderbeg.

1614 Founding of Tirana.

1912 Albania gains independence.

1922 Ahmet Zogu becomes prime minister and president before finally crowning himself King Zog in 1928.

1939 Mussolini annexes Albania; King Zog retreats to the *Ritz* in London.

1946 Proclamation of People's Republic of Albania, led by Enver Hoxha.

1967 "Cultural Revolution" sees agriculture collectivized, religious buildings destroyed and cadres purged.

1979 Mother Teresa, an ethnic Albanian, wins the Nobel Peace Prize.

1990 Thousands scramble into Tirana's Western embassies in an attempt to flee Albania.

1992 The Democratic Party wins elections, ending Communist rule.

1997 Collapse of financial pyramid schemes results in mass bankruptcies.

2000 Artist Edi Rama elected mayor of Tirana.

2009 Albania joins NATO and applies for EU membership.

2013 Edi Rama elected prime minister.

2015 Erion Veliaj elected mayor of Tirana.

ARRIVAL AND DEPARTURE

It's getting ever easier to **fly** into Albania, with a growing number of international connections. Low-cost carriers provide connections from all over Europe and direct British Airways flights from London can be quite reasonable. You can also fly cheaply to Corfu then get a ferry to Saranda (see p.59). Visas are not required for citizens of most nations; South Africa is a notable exception.

Greece offers by far the simplest international **bus** connections – there are daily services to Tirana from Athens and Thessaloniki (from €25), and it's also possible to get direct buses to a number of other Albanian cities. From Macedonia there are direct services from Skopje to Tirana, via Struga and Elbasan. It is still not straightforward to get here from

Montenegro – there are no services from the capital Podgorica, though there is a twice-weekly bus from Budva to Tirana and some unofficial minivans linking Shkodra and Ulcinj.

The most interesting form of arrival is by **ferry**. Several operators make overnight sailings to Durrës from Bari in Italy, including Ventouris Ferries (from €40; ⓦventouris.gr); there are hourly bus connections between Durrës and the capital. It's also possible to get to Saranda by ferry from Corfu (from €19; ⓦfinikas-lines.com), with at least two ferries per day making the forty-minute hop.

GETTING AROUND

Getting from A to B can be a little tricky in Albania – it's best to be flexible, exercise patience, and to treat travel information as a guideline rather than gospel.

Most travel is conducted by **bus**; the vehicles are usually Italian dinosaurs but fares are cheap, and the roads are being improved. However, the authorities have so far steadfastly refused to build any official bus stations – fine in smaller towns, but a nightmare in a city as large as Tirana where matters are utterly confusing. Buses are sometimes supplemented by minibuses known as **furgons**, which are technically illegal, especially in the big cities, though still run undeterred; they tend not to depart until full and will often roam around town until they have enough passengers.

There are no international **train** connections to Albania, but the country has a small rail network. As part of ongoing construction projects in the north of the city, Tirana's main train station has been demolished and relocated to the small town of Kashar near the airport. From here a limited service runs to a few destinations across the country.

ACCOMMODATION

Accommodation is surprisingly plentiful for a country with such low tourist numbers, and while state-owned

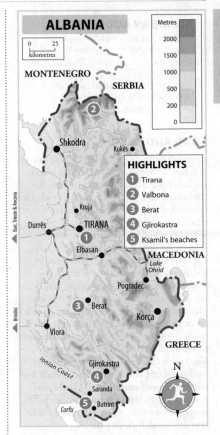

monstrosities were once the norm, there's now a decent selection of clean, good-value **hotels**. You should be able to find a double room for under €35 (prices are almost always quoted in euros), and breakfast is usually included. There don't tend to be any set rates for single rooms, but you can expect a small discount. During summer, it's advised to book ahead for private rooms on the coast. There are now **hostels** in Tirana, Saranda, Berat and Gjirokastra, charging €10–14 for dorm beds; all have free wi-fi. There are very few dedicated **campsites**, though the secluded beaches of the Ionian coast are great for those who can manage without facilities. Wild camping is fine in theory, but leaves you at the mercy of the (occasionally corrupt) local police.

1

FOOD AND DRINK

Albania's largely meat-based cuisine brings together elements of Slavic, Turkish and Italian cuisines. Spit-roasted lamb is the traditional dish of choice, though today it's *qebab* (kebabs) and *qoftë* (grilled lamb rissoles) that dominate menus, often served with a bowl of *kos* (yogurt). Another interesting dish is *fergesë*, a mix of cheese, egg, onions and tomatoes (and meat in some regions) cooked in a clay pot. **Vegetarians** will find that filling, generous salads are ubiquitous, and seafood is also plentiful around the coast. But for all this choice the modern Albanian youth – and many a tourist – subsists almost entirely on snack food, particularly *burek* (a pastry filled with cheese, meat or spinach) and *sufllaqë* (sliced kebab meat and French fries stuffed in a roll of flatbread). There are some excellent **desserts** on offer, including spongy *shendetlije*, cream-saturated *trilece*, and the usual Turkish pastries.

DRINK

Coffee is king in Albania. Consumed throughout the day, espresso now trumps the old traditional Turkish style, with grounds at the bottom (*kafe turke*). There are cafés on every corner, and it's worth noting that cafés and bars generally melt into the same grey area – what's one by day will usually morph into the other by night. The alcoholic drink of choice is **rakia** – like coffee, this spirit is something of a way of life in Albania, and usually consumed with meals. The country also produces some **wine**, mostly red, though most locals will admit to a preference for Macedonian varieties; Rilindja is a good, widely sold label. **Beer** is easy to find, and it's also worth sampling Skënderbeg **cognac**, which is cheap, available in shops everywhere and not too bad at all.

CULTURE AND ETIQUETTE

Albanians tend to go out of their way to welcome foreign guests – partly because of the low number of visitors – and generally do a fine job of eroding popular misconceptions.

Religious practice was largely stamped out following the 1967 Cultural Revolution, meaning that although seventy percent of the population is Muslim, the majority are non-practising; the same can be said of the Christian remainder.

One cultural nicety is that the **body language** used to imply "yes" and "no" is the diametric opposite of what you may be used to – a shake of the head (actually more of a wobble) means "yes", and a nod (actually more of a tilt) means "no". Younger folk and those used to foreigners may well follow international norms, which adds to the confusion.

Tipping at restaurants is generally an exercise in rounding up to the nearest lekë note, but with bigger bills ten percent is the norm. **Smoking** has been officially prohibited in public places since 2007, though the police are too busy smoking to fine anybody, and you'll still see ashtrays on every restaurant table.

SPORTS AND ACTIVITIES

In a mountainous country with a long coastline, the main attractions are pretty obvious – there are some delightful places to **swim** along the Ionian coast, while the most accessible **hiking** is in the national park area of Mount Dajti. More adventurous activities are thin on the ground, with a monopoly of sorts held by Outdoor Albania (❶04 222 7121, ❿outdooralbania.com), an adventurous young team that can organize treks and **ski-shoeing** trips, or more high-octane fun such as **rafting** and **paragliding**.

COMMUNICATIONS

Post offices are generally open Monday to Friday from 9am to 5pm. While their quality of distribution is improving – from a pretty low base – it's still prudent to hang onto any valuable parcels until you're out of the country. Public **phones**

ALBANIAN

Note that the dual nature of Albanian nouns – all have definite and indefinite forms – can cause some confusion with place names. Tirana is alternately referred to as Tiranë, Durrës as Durrësi, Berat as Berati, Saranda as Sarandë and Gjirokastra as Gjirokaster.

	ALBANIAN	PRONUNCIATION
Yes	Po	Paw
No	Jo	Yaw
Please	Ju lutem	Yoo lootem
Thank you	Faleminderit	Falemin-derit
Hello/Good day	Tungjatjeta	Toongya-tyeta
Goodbye	Mirupafshim	Meeropafshim
Excuse me	Më falni	Muh falni
Where?	Ku?	Koo?
Good	Mirë	Mir
Bad	Keq	Kek
Near	Afër	Afur
Far	Larg	Larg
Cheap	I lirë	Ee lir
Expensive	I shtrenjtë	Ee shtrenyt
Open	I hapur	Ee hapoor
Closed	Mbyllur	Mbeeloor
Today	Sot	Sawt
Yesterday	Dje	Dye
Tomorrow	Nesër	Nesur
How much is…?	Sa kushton…?	Sa kushton…?
What time is it?	Sa është ora?	Sa ushtu awra?
I don't understand	Unë nuk kuptoj	Oonuh nook koop-toy
Do you speak English?	A flisni anglisht?	Ah fleesnee anglisht?
One	Një	Nyuh
Two	Dy	Deeh
Three	Tre	Treh
Four	Katër	Katur
Five	Pesë	Pes
Six	Gjashtë	Gyasht
Seven	Shtatë	Shtat
Eight	Tetë	Tet
Nine	Nëntë	Nuhnt
Ten	Dhjetë	Dyet

are hard to track down, and almost all use cards; you may be offered these on the street but it's safer – and cheaper – to buy from a post office. Alternatively, a **SIM card** with unlimited data, messaging and up to an hour of international calls can cost as little as €10 for a month. **Wi-fi** is widespread, with most hostels, hotels, bars and cafés offering it for free.

EMERGENCIES

Despite its bad rap, the **crime rate** in Albania is actually very low by European standards, and you're extremely unlikely to find yourself stumbling into one of the famed blood feuds, some of which still bubble away up north. It is, however, worth being aware of a high **road accident** rate made vividly clear by the alarming number of memorial stones by the roadside.

Albania's **hospitals** are in very poor shape – most locals go abroad for

EMERGENCY NUMBERS
Police ☎ 129; Ambulance ☎ 127; Fire ☎ 128.

ALBANIA ONLINE

ⓦ **albania.al** Official site of the tourist board.

ⓦ **albania-hotel.com** Good for booking rooms online.

ⓦ **albanianhistory.net** Collection of historical articles.

ⓦ **journeytovalbona.com**
Comprehensive information on reaching the northern mountains.

treatment if they can afford it, and you should do likewise if possible. There are very few ambulances, so should you or a friend come across an accident it's usually best to hunt down a cab. **Pharmacies** exist in all urban areas, and are usually open 9am to 7pm.

INFORMATION

There are a few **tourist information offices** dotted around, though hours can be irregular to say the least – they can supply maps and book accommodation, but you're better off asking for information at your hotel or hostel.

MONEY AND BANKS

Albania uses the **lekë** (L), which is also often used in its singular form, lek. Coins of 5, 10, 20, 50 and 100 lekë are in circulation, as are notes of 200, 500, 1000, 2000 and 5000 lekë. Exchange **rates** are currently around €1 = 138L, £1 = 175L, and US$ = 122L. Accommodation prices are quoted in euros at all but the cheapest places, and some of the more upmarket restaurants do likewise; in these you can pay with either currency, although it often works out more expensive to pay in lekë. **Exchanges** are the best places to change money, and can be found in most cities. **ATMs** are everywhere in Tirana and all towns, while **credit cards** are increasingly accepted in hotels.

OPENING HOURS AND HOLIDAYS

Few **shops** and restaurants in Albania have set **working hours**, though you can expect restaurants to be open from breakfast to supper, and shops daily from 9am to 5pm. **Museums** are usually closed on Mondays.

Most shops and all banks and post offices are closed on **public holidays**: January 1 and 2, January 6, March 14, March 22, May 1, October 19, November 28 and 29, and December 25, as well as at Easter, both Catholic and Orthodox.

Tirana

Its buildings are painted in lurid colours, a gigantic, useless pyramid rises smack in the centre, the main square is a mess, the roads are potholed, and still there's no official bus station for this city of almost one million people, and yet for all these idiosyncrasies **TIRANA** is undeniably a charmer. The clash of architectural styles (from Italian to Communist to post-modern) is most evident in the central Blloku area, which was off-limits to all but Party members during Communist times. A generation or so down the line, espresso-sipping, fun-loving locals and trendy bar openings are vivid proof that the city is well on its way to becoming a "regular" European capital.

Tirana's Ottoman legacy was largely eroded by former dictator Enver Hoxha's failed regime, an era still evidenced by enormous boulevards and Brutalist architecture. In 2000, the Edi Rama period began with the city's charismatic mayor attempting to paint Tirana into the modern day; the resulting streetscape kaleidoscope performs a continuous palette shift from lemon to lime, saffron to cinnamon and burgundy to baby blue. Some locals grumble that their city looks to have fallen victim to a made-for-TV makeover.

WHAT TO SEE AND DO

Tirana is better for strolling than sightseeing, but there's plenty to keep you occupied in the southbound stretch from **Skanderbeg Square** to the **Grand Park**, which narrowly bypasses the trendy **Blloku** district on the way.

Skanderbeg Square

All roads in Tirana lead to **Skanderbeg Square**, centrepoint of the city and, therefore, the nation as a whole, marked at its southern end by an equestrian statue of national hero Skanderbeg, who led the ultimately unsuccessful resistance to fifteenth-century Ottoman invasions. The imposing **National History Museum** (Tues–Sat 10am–5pm, Sun 10am–2pm; 200L) sits at the north side of the square and is worth a quick visit, particularly for its coverage of Hoxha's concentration camps.

Heading clockwise around the square you'll find the **Palace of Culture**, which houses the National Theatre of Opera and Ballet. Then comes the pretty **Et'hem Bey Mosque** (daily 8am–11pm except during prayer times), which was closed off during Communist rule; one sunny day in 1991, thousands flocked here to make use of their new-found religious freedom.

Bulevard Dëshmorët e Kombit and Blloku

Heading south from Skanderbeg Square is the "Boulevard of National Martyrs". The first major sight is the **National Art Gallery** (Wed–Sun 10am–6pm; 100L), which is well worth visiting for its renowned icons by Onufri, and a collection of Socialist Realist paintings. On the parallel road, Ibrahim Rugova, there's the space-age **Resurrection of**

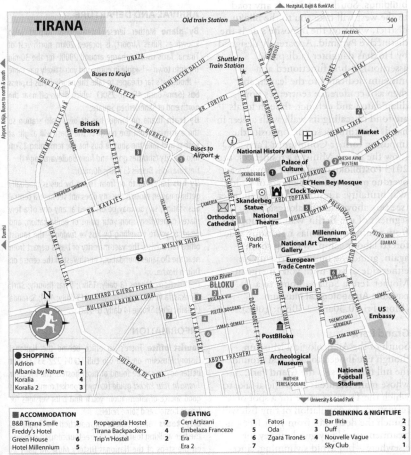

TIRANA

0 ——————— 500
metres

Hostpital, Dajti & Bunk'Art

Old train Station

UNAZA

Shuttle to Train Station

Buses to Kruja

MINE PEZA

HAXHI HYSEN DALLIU

BULEVARDI ZOGU I

RR. BARRIKADAVE

BARDHOK BIBA

RR. DEBRES

RR. TAFAJ

MAHMUT FORTUZI

ZOGU I 21

Airport, Kruja, Buses to north & south

MUHAMET GJOLLESHA

HUMERASHES

SKENDERBEG

RR. DURRESIT

RR. FORTUZI

QEMAL STAFA

HOXHA TAHSIM

Market

British Embassy

Buses to Airport ★

National History Museum

SHESHI AVNI RUSTEMI

FREDERIK SHIROKA

SKENDERBEG SQUARE

Palace of Culture

LUIGJ GURAKUQI

Et'hem Bey Mosque

RR. KAVAJES

RR. KAVAJES

ISKAM ALLAH

DESHMORET E K.

Clock Tower

ABDI TOPTANI

Skanderbeg Statue

PRESIDENTI GEORGE W BUSH

PETRO NINI LUARASI

CAMERIA

Orthodox Cathedral

National Theatre

MURAT TOPTANI

SKENDRIT

MYSLYM SHYRI

Youth Park

National Art Gallery

Millennium Cinema

Durrësi

MUHAMET GJOLLESHA

European Trade Centre

BULEVARD I GJERGJ FISHTA

BULEVARD I BAJRAM CURRI

SAMI FRASHERI

Lana River
BLLOKU

BRIGADA VIII

Pyramid

DESHMORET E KOMBIT

GJIK PART II

JUL VARIBOVA

RR. ELBASANIT

QEMAL GURANJAKU

N

PIETER BOGDANI

ISMAIL QEMALI

US Embassy

THEMISTOKLI GERMENJI

ABDYL FRASHERI

PostBlloku

SULEJMAN DE LVINA

Archeological Museum

MOTHER TERESA SQUARE

SHIH HAMIT

ASIM ZENELI

National Football Stadium

University & Grand Park

● SHOPPING	
Adrion	1
Albania by Nature	2
Koralia	4
Koralia 2	3

■ ACCOMMODATION				● EATING				■ DRINKING & NIGHTLIFE	
B&B Tirana Smile	3	Propaganda Hostel	7	Cen Artizani	1	Fatosi	2	Bar Iliria	2
Freddy's Hotel	1	Tirana Backpackers	4	Embelaza Franceze	5	Oda	3	Duff	3
Green House	6	Trip'n'Hostel	2	Era	6	Zgara Tironës	4	Nouvelle Vague	4
Hotel Millennium	5			Era 2	7			Sky Club	1

1

ALBANIA'S BUNKERS

Cross into Albania by land or sea, and you'll soon notice clutches of grey, dome-like structures dotting the countryside. Under Hoxha's rule, these **bunkers** were scattered around the country in tremendous numbers – estimates run as high as 750,000. These were no family shelters, but strategic positions to which every able-bodied man was expected to head, weapon in hand, at the onset of war. Though Western spies did indeed make attempts to infiltrate the country, the bunkers were never really put to the test. Huge underground government bunkers can also be found, most notably in Tirana where one 106-room shelter known as **Bunk'Art** (Tues–Sun: summer 9am–5pm; winter 9am–3.30pm; 300L; audioguide 600L; w bunkart.al) has been converted into an historical museum and art space, located near the Mount Dajti cable car station (see p.56).

Christ Orthodox Cathedral, which is particularly striking at night. South of here, the pleasant green verges of the **Lana** are a good place to get a handle on some of Tirana's famed **colourful buildings**. South of the river, any road to the west will take you to the **Blloku** district, while on the opposite side is the distinctive **Pyramid**. Apparently designed by Hoxha's daughter (a disputed assertion), it first functioned as a museum dedicated to the leader, and then as a conference centre; it's now dilapidated and defunct, though locals are fond of scaling its walls with a beer in hand. Continuing south, opposite the imposing former Communist Party HQ (now the Prime Minister's residence), the 2013 **PostBlloku monument** provides an overdue memorial to the years of Cold War brutality: a restored concrete bunker (see box above) stands alongside a segment of the Berlin Wall and supports from a mine at Albania's notorious Spaç forced labour camp. Walking south again, grandiose buildings rise up on either side of you until you emerge in Mother Teresa Square, home to a passable **Archeological Museum** (Mon–Fri 10.30am–2.30pm; 100L).

Grand Park

South of the Archeological Museum, though you'll need to curl west around the hill for access, is the **Grand Park**, whose main feature is an artificial lake to which the Tiranese come for a spot of relaxation. Its population of tiny fish will munch the dead skin from your feet – a treatment you'd pay good money for elsewhere – but avoid swimming, since villages on the far side of the lake empty their sewage into the waters. Note, too, that although the surrounding forest is full of beautiful fireflies come dusk, it also has snakes.

ARRIVAL AND DEPARTURE

By plane Mother Teresa International Airport (also known as Rinas Airport) is located 20km northwest of Tirana. Taxis usually charge around 2000L for the 30min trip into town – haggle in euros and you'll likely pay more – though it's far cheaper to take the hourly Rinas Express bus (6am–6pm; 45min; 250L), which drops off near the north end of Skanderbeg Square.

By train Tirana no longer has its own train station so those arriving from the north or the coast will alight at Kashar and take the shuttle bus for the remaining 15km into the city (shuttles go to and from Boulevard Zogu I).
Destinations Durrës (3 daily; 40min).

By bus Travelling to or from Tirana by bus is gradually getting easier, though the city does not yet have a central bus station, so you may be dropped at any one of a few places depending upon your point of embarkation, and whether you're travelling by bus or *furgon* – the tourist office can advise. The vast majority of buses depart from near the Doganës roundabout northwest of the centre on Dritan Hoxha.
Destinations Athens (8 daily; 15hr); Berat (hourly; 3hr); Gjirokastra (6 hourly; 4hr); Koman (3 daily; 4hr); Saranda (5 daily; 6hr); Skopje (4 daily; 6–7hr).

INFORMATION

Tourist office There's an office behind the National History Museum on Ded Gjo Luli (T 04 222 3313), but better advice can be found at most hostels. The irregular *Tirana In Your Pocket* guide (w inyourpocket.com) is also a good source of information; you'll find print versions for free in hostels and some hotels.

City tours An excellent introduction to Tirana is the free walking tour (w tiranafreetour.com) that meets on the steps of the National History Museum daily at

10am. Lasting around two hours, it takes in all the main sights and offers the chance to talk to a local who remembers the tail end of Communist rule. Tips are gladly received.

Activities Outdoor Albania (ⓦ outdooralbania.com) and Balkan Secrets (ⓦ balkansecrets.com) both organize fascinating out-of-Tirana excursions, such as mountain snowshoeing in the winter, kayaking in the summer, and jeep safaris.

GETTING AROUND

By bus Buses run every 5–10min (6am–10pm) on a few main routes and cost 30L for a one-way ticket.

By taxi Taxis should cost 400–500L for a trip within the city centre, though central Tirana is just about small enough to cover on foot. Speed Taxi and City Taxi have the best rates; not all have meters.

ACCOMMODATION

HOSTELS

Propaganda Hostel 75 Pjeter Bogdani ☎ 068 203 5261, ⓦ propagandahostel.com. This place is in a prime location for stumbling into bed after a night out in Blloku's best bars. There's a rooftop space where you can bring your own beers for a sundowner, and a variety of mixed and single-sex dorms. Dorms €9, doubles €27

Tirana Backpackers 3 Bogdanëve ☎ 068 468 2353, ⓦ tiranahostel.com. This centrally located hostel, with its retro and sometimes downright bizarre decor – see the preserved fish in jars from the old science museum – has good basic rooms and breakfast is included. The outdoor bar is beautiful on a summer afternoon. Dorms €10, doubles €30

★**Trip'n'Hostel** 1 Musa Maci ☎ 068 304 8905, ⓦ tripnhostel.com. A welcoming hostel with stylish communal areas, and dorm beds each with a curtain for privacy, a power socket and a handmade lamp. The breakfast is cooked fresh to order and the bar brews its own beer. Dorms €10, doubles €30

HOTELS

★**B&B Tirana Smile** Bogdanëve ☎ 04 224 3460, ⓦ bbtiranasmile.com. Spotless and charming, this place has huge, colourful rooms and a very friendly welcome. There's a comfortable communal room and breakfast is a mighty feast. Doubles €40

Freddy's Hotel 75 Bardhok Biba ☎ 068 203 5261, ⓦ freddyshostel.com. Formerly *Freddy's Hostel*, this family-run hotel has recently been renovated. Rooms are fresh and modern, and Freddy himself will often go out of his way to make you comfortable. Doubles €40

Hotel Millennium 25 Murat Toptani ☎ 04 225 1935. This colourful hotel is in a prime location, just 300m from the main square and on a quiet, leafy pedestrianized

street. Rooms are spacious and some have balconies. Doubles €40

EATING

Cen Artizani Mihal Duri. An incredibly cheap Italian restaurant where nine different types of pasta are freshly made in the adjoining glass-fronted kitchen. A huge plate with ham, calamari or shrimp costs just 300L. Daily 11am–11pm.

Embelaza Franceze 1 Dëshmorët e 4 Shkurtit. Come to enjoy cake and coffee served up in a lavish interior. Savoury dishes are available but most are overpriced (sandwiches from 350L, mains 1000L and up). Daily 7am–10pm.

Era 33 Ismail Qemali. A hugely popular restaurant with locals and visitors alike. There's Albanian grill and pasta, but the main event is the thin and crispy pizza (from 360L). They have a sister restaurant on Papa Gjon Pali II. Meal with wine under 1000L. Daily 11am–midnight.

Fatosi Luigj Gurakuqi. This is one of a handful of *qoftë* snack-shacks bunched together near the roundabout. All are extremely popular with locals and well priced. A decent-sized meal will set you back just 300L. Daily 8am–midnight.

★**Oda** Luigj Gurakuqi. Small place offering Ottoman-style meals on Ottoman-style sofas. The roasted peppers with cottage cheese (360L) are fresh and tangy, and the offal dishes (460L) far nicer than they sound; all is best washed down – if you're brave – with a shot of flavoured *rakia*. Daily 11am–11pm.

★**Zgara Tironës** Kavajës. An always-bustling restaurant split over two floors, this grill serves enormous meat platters and a variety of fresh, tasty salads. Meal with wine from 700L. Daily 8am–midnight.

DRINKING AND NIGHTLIFE

Tirana's nightlife scene gets better with each passing year. Almost everything of note is concentrated in the fashionable Blloku area, where most venues function as cafés by day and as bars come evening.

1

Bar Iliria Rruga Brigada VIII. A Tirana institution, this big but simple bar is run by just one man. Service can be slow but beers are cheap from 150L. Daily though hours vary; usually busy 8pm–midnight.

Duff Rruga Brigada VIII. A trendy bar/restaurant with comfy sofas outside and bar stools inside. There's a good selection of beer on tap and locals say the burgers are the best in the city. Daily 7am–late.

Nouvelle Vague Pjetër Bogdani. A retro, music-themed bar with cosy indoor and outdoor seating. Cocktails cost around 300L and there's a selection of Albanian and Italian beers from 200L. Daily 10am–late.

Sky Club 5 Dëshmorët e 4 Shkurtit. This surprisingly cheap top-floor revolving bar is somewhat outdated but has superb city views. Cocktails go for just 400L and shots of Skenderbeg cognac for 150L. It can get busy around sunset, so come a little earlier to ensure you get the best seats. Daily 8am–midnight.

ENTERTAINMENT

Academy of Film and Multimedia 78 Alexsandër Moisiu ☎ 04 236 5188, ⓦ afmm.edu.al. Occasional free screenings of foreign movies, all subtitled in English.

Millennium Cinema Murat Toptani. New Hollywood releases shown in a wonderful old theatre whose outdoor café is a delight on sunny days. Tickets from 400L.

SHOPPING

Tirana has a fascinating daily market (6am–10pm), which sprawls north of the Sheshi Avni Rustemi roundabout. Shops are generally open daily 9am–6pm.

Adrion Skanderbeg Square. Has English-language books, newspapers and magazines.

Albania by Nature Luigj Gurakuqi. The place to buy artisanal products, from olive-wood chopping boards to fruit juice, all handmade in Albania.

Koralia Abdyl Frashëri. Jewellery shop selling semi-precious stones and silver jewellery at reasonable prices. Sister shop on Myslym Shyri.

DIRECTORY

Embassies and consulates UK, Skanderbeg ☎ 04 223 4973; US, Elbasanit ☎ 04 224 7285.

Exchange Tirana is full of ATMs, and there's an exchange on almost every road in the centre, which tend to give better rates than the banks.

Hospital Civilian Hospital, Dibrës, northeast of the city centre.

Post office The office on Çameria is open Mon–Fri 8am–4pm.

Day-trips from Tirana

Local landmarks from which you can peer down on Tirana include the slopes of **Mount Dajti** and the hilltop town of **Kruja**, both of which can be visited on a day-trip from the capital.

MOUNT DAJTI

The dark, looming shape of **Mount Dajti** is easily visible from Tirana, a temptation that can prove too much for city dwellers, who head to the forested slopes in droves on sunny weekends. The mountain's network of paths feels surprisingly remote even though you're only 25km from the capital. There's no public transport to the mountain, but by taxi it should be no more than 700L to the base of the cable-car system (Mon & Wed–Sun: summer 10am–10pm; winter 10am–7pm; 800L return; ⓦ dajtiekspres .com) that whisks passengers to within a slog of the summit. There are a number of restaurants in the area, useful if you fancy refuelling before heading back down. It's worth combining this with an afternoon visit to Bunk'Art (see box, p.54), which is located near the cable-car station in Tirana.

KRUJA

Lofty **KRUJA**, 35km from Tirana, was the focal point of national hero Skanderbeg's resistance to the Ottoman invasions of the fifteenth century, and you'll see his likeness all over town. Most people make a beeline for the **castle**, which houses a number of restaurants and an excellent **History Museum** (Tues–Sun 9am–2pm & 4–7pm; 200L), whose diverting collection of weaponry, icons and the like is augmented by an impressive modern interior. Also within the castle walls is the **Ethnographic Museum** (Tues–Sun 9am–4pm; 300L), housed in a gorgeous building with a serene outdoor courtyard. Souvenir sellers have taken over the town, and the best place to buy your

Albania-flag T-shirt, Skanderbeg statuette or Mother Teresa lighter is the restored **Ottoman bazaar**, just below the castle access road. *Furgons* from Tirana (1hr; 200L) leave regularly from the Zogu i Zi roundabout northwest of the city centre.

The northern mountains

These remote mountains make up the southernmost part of the Dinaric Alps that stretch from Albania, through Serbia and as far north as Slovenia. The range is best explored by trekking around the valley of **Valbona**; it's a long but enjoyable journey from the capital, taking in a ferry crossing on the emerald waters of **Lake Koman**, but entirely worth it for this magnificent mountain scenery.

VALBONA

The picture-perfect valley of **VALBONA**, which follows a river of the same name, is nestled among a collection of towering karst limestone peaks that reach heights of up to 2690m. Home to some of the country's most picturesque homesteads, it offers a true taste of Albanian country living. There are well-marked trails to suit all abilities – maps are available from *Rilindja* restaurant, which doubles as an unofficial information and trekking hub.

ARRIVAL AND DEPARTURE

By bus The best way to reach Valbona is on the 5am bus to Koman from Tirana (1000L), which arrives in time for the 9am departure across Lake Koman (3hr; 800–1000L/person). On the other side of the lake, the ferry will be met by a bus connecting the arrival point (Fierze) and Valbona (700L). Ask the ferry staff to help you with connections to Valbona when you board. More detailed information at ⦿ journeytovalbona.com.

ACCOMMODATION AND EATING

There are a number of good budget options along the valley's main road offering dorms from €10, all of which can organize guides and picnics for day hikes and have adjoining restaurants.

Rilindja ⦿ 067 301 4637. Run by Alfred and his American wife, Catherine, this guesthouse has five basic but comfortable rooms, and is the best place to get information and maps on the local area. It also has the valley's finest restaurant serving ultra-fresh trout from the river (600L) and huge salads (350L). Doubles **€35**

Stani I Arif Kadris ⦿ 067 301 4643. One of the highlights of a visit to Valbona is a traditional lunch in a shepherd's stone house. This one can be reached by foot or 4WD from the main road near the Çeremi trailhead (maps available from *Rilindja*).

Southern Albania

With its jumble of rugged mountains fringed by pristine curls of beach, Albania's south is the most appealing part of the country. The interior route boasts the rewarding towns of **Berat** and **Gjirokastra**, each home to whole swathes of Ottoman buildings. Heading on down the **Ionian Coast** instead, you'll find one of Europe's few unspoilt sections of Mediterranean shore, a near-permanently sunny spot where the twin blues of sea and sky are ripped asunder by a ribbon of grey mountains – on a clear day you'll be able to see Italy from the 1027m-high **Llogaraja Pass**. Both routes converge at the beach town of **Saranda**, while further south are the fantastic ruins of **Butrint**.

BERAT

There are few better places to be in Albania than standing on the footbridge in the charming, easy-going town of **BERAT**. From this vantage point, you'll be surrounded by huddles of **Ottoman houses**, their dark, rectangular windows staring from whitewashed walls like a thousand eyes. On the south bank is the sleepy **Gorica** district, kept in shadow for much of the day by a muscular backdrop of rock; to the north is the relatively sun-drenched **Mangalemi** district, from which steep, cobblestoned paths lead up to the hill-top **Kalasa**, an old citadel whose wonderful interior is up there with the best old towns in the Balkans.

1

WHAT TO SEE AND DO

You'll have great views of Berat from the fourteenth-century **Kalasa**, a splendidly restored citadel (daily: April–Sept 8am–8pm; Oct–March 8am–5pm; 100L or free out of hours) towering above town, which is accessed via a steep, cobbled road. This is still a functioning part of town and home to hundreds, yet almost nothing dilutes its centuries-old vibe; visit at night and you're in for a wonderfully eerie treat. There were once over thirty **churches** here, but just a handful remain; oldest and most beautiful is the thirteenth-century **Church of the Holy Trinity**, sitting on the slope below the inner fortifications. Churches remain locked for most of the year, but the key-keepers are usually hanging around nearby. Also within the grounds is the **Onufri Museum** (Tues–Sun 9am–4pm; 200L), dedicated to the country's foremost icon painter, famed for his use of a particularly vivid red. Heading back down the access road, you'll come across the diverting **Ethnographic Museum** (daily: May–Sept 9am–1pm & 4–7pm, Sun 9am–2pm; Oct–April 9am–4pm, Sun 9am–2pm; 200L) and the first of the centre's three main **mosques**.

ARRIVAL AND ACTIVITIES

By bus The bus terminal is around 3km north of the town on Rruga Antipatrea. From there, it's a 30L bus ride on a local service to the centre of town.

Destinations Gjirokastra (2 daily; 4hr); Saranda (2 daily; 6hr); Tirana (every 30min; 3hr).

Tours Rafting excursions (around €50/person) and trips around nearby Mount Tomorri can be organized through Outdoor Albania (ⓦ outdooralbania.com). *Berat Backpackers* also lay on occasional tours.

ACCOMMODATION

Berat Backpackers ⓞ 069 306 4429, ⓦ beratbackpackers .com. Located over the river in Gorica and run by Scotty, an affable Geordie, this hostel remains the number one budget choice – the building is a bona fide Ottoman antique, the dorms are cosy, and the garden patio is a delightful place for evening drinks. Dorms €12, doubles €30

Klea ⓞ 032 234 970. Family-run guesthouse located just inside the citadel entrance. The tough climb to the top means it's not for all, but to stroll around the eerily quiet

old town by night is an utterly bewitching experience. Doubles €30

★**Mangalemi** ⓞ 068 232 3238, ⓦ mangalemihotel .com. Near the centre of town, on the road to the citadel, this traditional guesthouse has splendidly decorated rooms that offer excellent value; all are en suite with comfy beds and powerful showers. There's a superb on site restaurant, and the friendly staff are excellent sources of local information. Doubles €40

EATING AND DRINKING

Ajka On the Gorica side of the footbridge, this smart place is one of the few local bars that receives female customers. It's also good for coffee; head on up to the roof terrace to enjoy the evening sun with a drink. Daily 9am–11pm.

Mangalemi Inside the guesthouse of the same name. Professional service, large portions and reasonable prices – 500L can get you nicely full – and the salads are great. Head up to the terrace if the weather's nice. Reservations advised. Daily 10am–10pm.

Onufri Simple place inside the citadel walls, serving strong coffee and Albanian staples such as *pilaf* and stuffed peppers. Usually open 8am–6pm.

Spëtimi 2 ⓞ 032 238 707. Studenty snack-style joint on the river road, selling good pizzas (300L) and mouthwatering crêpes (150L). Daily 7am–11pm.

White House ⓞ 032 234 570. Riverside restaurant serving the best pizzas in town (from 300L; delivery service available), as well as seafood dishes and traditional Albanian grub. Daily 9am–11pm.

GJIROKASTRA

Sitting proudly above the sparsely inhabited Drinos valley, **GJIROKASTRA** is one of Albania's most attractive towns, and home to some of its friendliest people. It was once an important Ottoman trading hub and today a sprinkling of nineteenth-century **Ottoman-style houses** lines the maze of steep, cobbled streets. Gjiro is also etched into the nation's conscience as the birthplace of former dictator **Enver Hoxha**, and more recently the world-renowned author **Ismail Kadare**.

WHAT TO SEE AND DO

The Old Town's centrepiece is its imposing **citadel** (daily 9am–7pm; 200L), which is clearly visible from any point in town. Built in the sixth century and enlarged in 1811 by Ali Pasha Tepelna, it was used as a **prison** by King Zog, the

1

Nazis and Hoxha's cadres; the interior remains suitably spooky. There are tanks and weaponry to peruse, but most curious is the shell of an **American jet** that was (apparently) forced down in 1957 after being suspected of espionage by the Communist regime. Other than the castle, Gjiro's most appealing sight is its collection of Ottoman-style houses; a prime example is the eighteenth-century **Skenduli House** (daily 9am–7pm; 200L), where the owner's daughter gives English-language tours of its wonderfully preserved rooms throughout the day.

ARRIVAL AND DEPARTURE

By bus Buses and *furgons* stop on the highway intersection below the New Town. From here there's a local bus (30L) to take you up the steep climb to the Old Town main square; alternatively, it's a half-hour walk or a 300L taxi ride.
Destinations Berat (2 daily; 4hr); Korça (1 daily; 5hr); Saranda (hourly; 1hr 30min); Tirana (hourly; 4hr 30min).

ACCOMMODATION

None of these establishments has an address, but they're easy to find.
Gjirokastra Above the mosque on the road running under the castle wall ☎084 265 982. Modern guesthouse with an excellent location and pleasant patio for beers in the sun. Rooms are light and beautifully furnished. The traditional breakfast is superb. Doubles €30
Kotoni Signed from the road under the castle ☎084 263 526, ✉eda.goldemi@gmail.com. Cosy nineteenth-century building decorated in true Albanian style. Home-from-home touches include excellent breakfasts and handmade trimmings in the bedrooms. The adjoining restaurant is a welcoming family affair. Doubles €25
★**Stone City Hostel** Rruga Alqi Kondi (ask locals for directions to "Walter's hostel") ☎069 348 4271, ⊛stonecityhostel.com. Dutch-owned, modern hostel with original exposed brick walls and stylish communal area. Organizes fun day-trips in the surrounding hills. Dorms €12, doubles €30

EATING AND DRINKING

Kujtimi Qafa e Pazarit. Fantastic Albanian meals dished out under the dappled shade of a maple tree. A salad and small main will set you back 500L. The house speciality is juicy fried frogs' legs. Daily 9am–midnight.
Kuka Astrit Karagjozi. Run by two brothers, this modern restaurant serves excellent traditional Albanian and contemporary dishes. The leafy garden is huge and the inside very sophisticated. Traditional dishes from 200L; pasta 300L. Mon–Sat 8am–10pm.

SARANDA

Staring straight at Corfu, and even within day-trip territory of the Greek island, sunny **SARANDA** is perhaps Albania's most appealing entry point. A recent building boom has eroded some of the town's original genteel atmosphere, but it's still a great place to kick back, stroll along the promenade and watch the sun set over cocktails. There are beaches in town, but better are those in nearby **Ksamil**, some 20km to the south.

ARRIVAL AND DEPARTURE

By bus There's no station as such, but buses pick up and drop off just north of the centre on Vangjel Pandi, with the harbour a 5min walk away downhill.
Destinations Athens (1 daily; 10hr); Berat (2 daily; 6hr); Gjirokastra (hourly; 1hr 20min); Tirana (5 daily; 6hr).
By boat The small terminal on the west side of town has services to Corfu which run at least twice daily year-round, increasing to three per day June–Aug. Tickets (from €19) can be bought from the Finikas Lines (⊛finikas-lines .com) office on the access road.

ACCOMMODATION

As elsewhere around the Med, prices are at their highest in July and August and many hotels get fully booked far in advance. Discounts are negotiable at other times – even the hostels cut their dorm prices by €2 outside the summer months.

HOSTELS

★**Hairy Lemon** Koder 8f ☎069 355 9317, ⊛hairylemonhostel.com. Irish-owned hostel a 10min walk west of the centre, past the ferries. Clean and friendly, with very comfy beds and a great chill-out area for meeting new travel buddies. Dorms €12
Saranda (SR) Backpackers Mitat Hoxha 10 ☎069 434 5426, ⊛backpackerssr.hostel.com. This simple hostel is

---

THE BLUE EYE

On the way between Gjirokastra and Saranda is the wonderful **Blue Eye**, an underwater spring forming a pool of deepest blue (50L). Its setting in a cool, remote grove is quite spectacular, but the water is bracing to say the least. Hop on any bus or minivan plying the Saranda–Gjirokastra route, and ask to be let off at the Syri i Kaltër; the pool is 20min from the road on a clear path. There's a decent restaurant and hotel on site, with doubles from €30.

inconspicuously located in an apartment building next to an internet café near the ferry ticket office. Its dorms boast sea views and owner Tomi is always eager to help. Dorms €12

HOTELS

Hotel Real Off Ismail Tatzati ☎ 085 226 361. This is a simple place with spotless rooms – most of which have balconies. It's just a short walk from the seafront, the bus and ferry terminals, and dozens of bars and restaurants. Doubles €50
Kaonia Jonianet 2 ☎ 085 222 600. The best value of the hotels around the harbour, perhaps because of the unfinished building it's attached to. All rooms have balconies, but not all offer sea views so look before you pay. Doubles €50
Titania Jonianet 15 ☎ 085 222 869. Another excellent-value hotel considering its location right in the centre of the promenade. Sparklingly clean sea-view rooms with good low-season discounts. Doubles €60

EATING AND DRINKING

The town centre is filled with cheap joints selling *sufflaqe*, *burek* and the like, while there's also the well-stocked Alfa supermarket near the *Saranda (SR) Backpackers* hostel.
Bequa Telat Noga. Off the east side of Friendship Park. A small joint serving hearty Albanian food. Meat dishes from 200L; real penny-pinchers will appreciate the 70L *pilaf*. Daily 9am–11pm.
★**Limani** Jonianet. Jutting out into the harbour, this sprawling restaurant is by far the most popular in town. Staff are attentive, pizzas are cooked in a proper fired oven and the seafood (from 500L) is excellent: the raw marinated prawns are worth the 1500L splurge. Daily 7am–midnight.
Plazhi i Ri Jonianet. A low-key affair behind a row of palms on the promenade, which serves quality traditional dishes at pleasing prices. The seafood soup (500L) is a favourite. Pasta from 300L. Daily 7am–midnight.

NIGHTLIFE

Delight Bar Mitat Hoxha. Big, contemporary bar near the ferry terminal serving milkshakes (250L) by day and cocktails (500L) by night. Plays loud, cheesy chart music; open all day but is most fun 8pm–midnight.
Orange Bar Butrinti. Perhaps the most stylish bar in all of Saranda, this outdoor establishment is open 24 hours a day in summer. Come for cocktails in the evening and nurse your headache with a coffee the morning after.
Paparazzi Bar Mitat Hoxha. Near the top of the hill past the ferry terminal, this fun bar has a great atmosphere in the evenings. There are brilliant views of sparkling Saranda from the balcony. Daily 7am–late.

AROUND SARANDA

The main activity around Saranda is a visit to **Butrint** and the fantastic beaches of **Ksamil**, which can both be visited in a single day-trip from the town.

Ksamil beaches

The small coastal village of **KSAMIL** within **Butrint National Park** has a smattering of lovely public beaches lapped by spectacularly clear waters. Each cove is overlooked by a restaurant serving reasonably priced seafood (*Guvat* is the best of the bunch). The beaches are beautiful but busy in summer, and there are a few small islands close enough to swim to if you want a little extra space.

Butrint

Splendidly sited on an exposed nub of land, the isolated ruins of **BUTRINT** (daily 7am–7pm; 700L) offer a peek into over 2500 years of history, and are a delight to explore on its eucalyptus-lined trails. The area was first developed by the Greeks in the fourth century BC, and the expansive **theatre** and nearby **public baths** were built soon after. Butrint then reached its zenith during Roman times – Julius Caesar stopped by in 44 BC – though most of the statues unearthed from this period are now in the museums of Tirana. You can see most of Butrint's sights on a looped footpath, though do head up to the **Acropolis** for wonderful views and an excellent museum full of unearthed artefacts.

ARRIVAL AND DEPARTURE

You can pick up *furgons* to Butrint and Ksamil (hourly, on the same route; 30min; 100L) opposite the synagogue on Skënderbeu in Saranda (the road above the prom), but if you're a group you could opt for a taxi (around €30 including a few hours' waiting time at one or the other).

ACCOMMODATION

Livia ☎ 067 3477 077, ⓦ hotel-livia.com. Just 100m from the entrance to Butrint, this isolated hotel is fantastic value, with immaculate rooms and an excellent on-site restaurant. Doubles €55

HALLSTATT

Austria

HIGHLIGHTS

❶ **Viennese art** Feast your eyes on stunning paintings by Gustav Klimt and Egon Schiele. **See p.65**

❷ **Coffee and cake, Vienna** Indulge In mouthwatering treats in one of Vienna's ornate coffeehouses. **See p.71**

❸ **Salzburg** A fine Baroque city, home to Mozart and, of course, the sound of music. **See p.77**

❹ **Hallstatt** Visit this picture-postcard village in the lovely Salzkammergut region. **See p.82**

❺ **Adventure sports, Innsbruck** Hiking, mountain-biking and skiing in the stunning Austrian Alps. **See p.86**

HIGHLIGHTS ARE MARKED ON THE MAP ON P.63

ROUGH COSTS

Daily budget Basic €60, occasional treat €80

Drink Beer (0.5l) €4, wine or coffee €3

Food Schnitzel €10

Hostel/budget hotel €22/€65

Travel Train: Graz–Vienna €37.30; Vienna–Salzburg €25.50

FACT FILE

Population 8.7 million

Language German

Currency Euro (€)

Capital Vienna

International phone code ☎43

Time zone GMT +1hr

Introduction

Glorious Alpine scenery, monumental Habsburg architecture and the world's favourite musical – Austria's tourist industry certainly plays up to the clichés. However, it's not all bewigged Mozart ensembles and schnitzel; modern Austria boasts some of Europe's most varied museums and contemporary architecture, not to mention attractive and sophisticated cities whose bars, cafés and clubs combine contemporary cool with elegant tradition.

Long the powerhouse of the Habsburg Empire, **Austria** underwent decades of change and uncertainty in the early twentieth century. Shorn of her empire and racked by economic difficulties, the state fell prey to the promises of Nazi Germany. Only with the end of the Cold War did Austria return to the heart of Europe, joining the EU in 1995.

Politics aside, Austria is primarily known for two contrasting attractions – the fading imperial glories of the capital, and the stunning beauty of its Alpine hinterland. **Vienna** is the gateway to much of central Europe and a good place to soak up the culture of *Mitteleuropa*. Less renowned provincial capitals such as **Graz** and **Linz** are surprising pockets of culture, innovation and vitality. **Salzburg**, between **Innsbruck** and Vienna, represents urban Austria at its most picturesque, an intoxicating Baroque city within easy striking distance of the mountains and lakes of the **Salzkammergut**, while the most dramatic of Austria's Alpine scenery is west of here, in and around **Tyrol**, whose capital, **Innsbruck**, provides the best base for exploration.

CHRONOLOGY

1st century BC Romans take over Celtic settlements in present-day Austria.

788 AD Charlemagne conquers Austrian land.

1156 The "Privilegium Minus" gives Austria the status of Duchy.

1278 The Habsburgs seize control of much of modern Austria (except Salzburg), and retain it until World War I.

1683 The Siege of Vienna – the Habsburgs under Leopold I defeat the Ottoman Turks outside Vienna.

1773 Wolfgang Amadeus Mozart becomes Court Musician in Salzburg.

1797 Napoleon defeats Austrian forces, taking Austrian land.

1814 An Austrian coalition force defeats Napoleon. In the Congress of Vienna the Salzburg lands are given to Austria, ending centuries of independence under prince-archbishops.

1866 Austrian territory is lost as a result of the Austro-Prussian war.

1899 Sigmund Freud publishes *The Interpretation of Dreams*, introducing the concept of the ego.

1914 The assassination of the Austrian Archduke, Franz Ferdinand, begins the events that lead to World War I.

1920 A new constitution creates the Republic of Austria.

1938 Hitler incorporates Austria into Germany through "Anschluss".

1945 Austria is occupied by Allied forces as World War II ends.

1965 *The Sound of Music* draws attention to Austria on the big screen.

1980s Protests at election of President Kurt Waldheim, due to rumours implicating him in Nazi war crimes.

1995 Austria joins the EU.

2008 The world is shocked by the case of Josef Fritzl – who imprisoned his daughter in a cellar for 24 years, fathering seven children with her.

2016 In a photo-finish presidential election, left/liberal candidate Alexander van der Bellen triumphs over the far-right Norbert Hofer, though the results are later disputed, leading to a re-run of the election.

ARRIVAL AND DEPARTURE

Austria lies at the heart of Europe, bordered by seven countries. Excellent transport connections make it an easy stop-off on either a north–south or east–west route through Europe. Vienna has a major international airport, and you can also fly to Salzburg, Innsbruck, Graz and Linz or to the Slovak capital Bratislava, only a 75-minute bus journey

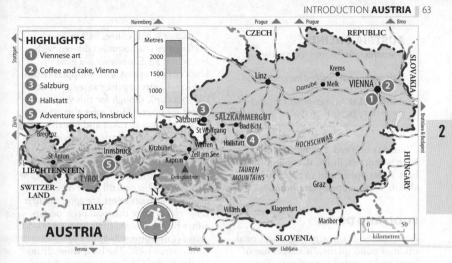

from Vienna. Vienna is also one of central Europe's major rail hubs, with **connections** including Budapest, Bratislava and Prague. Trains from Croatia and Slovenia stop in Graz, before also terminating here. Arriving in Vienna from northern Italy, it's likely you'll route via Venice and Klagenfurt. Innsbruck has good rail connections with both Italy and Munich, as does Salzburg.

GETTING AROUND

Austria's **public transport** is fast, efficient and comprehensive. ÖBB (⬝oebb.at) runs a punctual **train** network, which includes most towns of any size. All stations in cities and larger towns have left-luggage lockers. An Austria one-country pass with Eurail starts at €130 (3 days' validity in 1 month; under-25s), though individual train prices may be cheaper. From Vienna to Linz or Salzburg, it can be cheaper to travel on the privately operated Westbahn (⬝westbahn.at) out of the Westbahnhof rather than on ÖBB trains from the Hauptbahnhof.

Even cheaper connections between major cities are offered by German budget **bus** company Flixbus (⬝flixbus.at), with Vienna–Graz from €9 and Vienna–Munich from €19.90. Remoter areas including the Alpine valleys are served by the ÖBB-owned **Postbus** (⬝postbus.at). Daily and weekly regional travelcards

(*Netzkarte*), covering both trains and buses, are available in many regions.

Austria is bike-friendly, with **cycle lanes** in all major towns, and sometimes between towns. Many train stations rent **bikes** for around €12 per day; Vienna and Innsbruck also have public bike rental networks.

ACCOMMODATION

Outside popular tourist spots such as Vienna and Salzburg, **accommodation** need not be too expensive. Good-value **B&B** is usually available in the many small family-run hotels known as *Gasthöfe* and *Gasthäuser*, with prices from €60 per double. In the larger towns and cities a *pension* or *Frühstuckspension* will offer similar prices. Most places also have a stock of **private rooms** or *Privatzimmer*, although in well-travelled rural areas, roadside signs offering *Zimmer Frei* (vacancies) are common (double rooms from around €50). Local tourist offices have lists of these and will often ring around and book for you.

There are around a hundred **HI hostels** (*Jugendherberge* or *Jugendgästehaus*), run by or affiliated to ÖJHV (⬝oejhv.at) or ÖJHW (⬝oejhw.or.at). Rates are €20–27, normally including breakfast; non-members pay around €3.50 a night extra. There are also some excellent **independent hostels** in Salzburg and Vienna, plus affiliated youth hotel chains.

2

Austria's numerous **campsites** often have laundry facilities, shops and snack bars. Most open April to September, although some open year-round.

FOOD AND DRINK

Austrian food is hearty and traditional; often of good quality, it makes use of local and seasonal ingredients. For ready-made snacks, try a bakery (*Bäckerei*), confectioner's (*Konditorei*) or local market. **Fast food** centres on the *Würstelstand*, which sells hot dogs, *Bratwurst* (grilled sausage), *Käsekrainer* (spicy sausage with cheese), *Bosna* (spicy, thin Balkan sausage) and *Currywurst*. In *Kaffeehäuser* or cafés and bars you can get light meals and **snacks** starting at about €7; daily specials (under €10) and lunchtime set menus (*Tages-* or *Mittagsmenü*) are usually good value. Pizza and burgers are cheaper than main dishes (*Hauptspeisen*; €10–18) such as **schnitzel** (tenderized veal or pork): *Wienerschnitzel* is fried in breadcrumbs, *Jägerschnitzel* is served with a sauce (usually mushroom or tomato). There is usually something available for vegetarians – often *Käsespätzle*, similar to macaroni cheese. Two seasonal ingredients worth trying in spring and early summer are *Bärlauch* (wild garlic), delicious in soups and pasta sauces, and *Spargel* (asparagus), typically the white variety and served with hollandaise.

DRINK

For Austrians, daytime drinking traditionally centres on the **Kaffeehaus**, a relaxed place serving alcoholic and soft drinks, snacks and cakes, plus a wide range of coffees: a *Schwarzer* is small and black; a *Brauner* comes with a little milk;

a *Melange* is half coffee, half milk; a *Verlängerter* is an espresso diluted with hot water; an *Einspänner* is a glass of black coffee topped with whipped cream (*schlag*). Coffee is pricey in a *kaffeehaus* (€3–5 a cup), though for this you can linger for hours. Most cafés also offer a tempting array of cakes and pastries, as do *Café-Konditorei* (café-patisseries), where the cakes take centre stage.

Night-time drinking centres on **bars** and **cafés**, although traditional *Bierstuben* and *Weinstuben* are still thick on the ground. Austrian **beers** are good quality: most places serve the local brew on tap, either by the *Krügerl* (half-litre, €3.50–5), *Seidel* (third-litre, €2–4) or *Pfiff* (fifth-litre, €1–3). The local **wine**, drunk by the *Viertel* (25cl mug) or the *Achterl* (12.5cl glass), is often excellent. The *Weinkeller* is the place to go for this, or, in the wine-producing areas, a *Heuriger* or *Buschenschank* – a traditional tavern, usually serving cold food as well.

CULTURE AND ETIQUETTE

Austrian etiquette is much like the rest of Western Europe, with the leisurely café culture a central fixture. In restaurants, bars and cafés modest **tipping** – around ten percent or rounding up to the nearest euro – is expected (pay the waiter or waitress directly).

SPORTS AND ACTIVITIES

With stunning mountain scenery and beautiful lakes, Austria is an ideal destination for all sorts of outdoor sports. **Skiing** and snowboarding are major national pastimes (see box, p.86), and **hiking** and biking trails are clearly marked and graded. Tourist offices usually have a surfeit of details on local routes and activities.

2

LANGUAGE

A high proportion of Austrians speak English, though any attempt at **German** (see box, p.357) will be appreciated. Austrian accents and dialects can be tricky, however – the standard greeting throughout Austria is *Grüss Gott*.

COMMUNICATIONS

Most **post offices** are open Monday to Friday 8am to noon and 2 to 6pm; in larger cities they stay open through lunch and also open Saturday morning. **Stamps** can also be bought at tobacconists (*Tabak-Trafik*). Telekom Austria (A1) is the main **mobile phone** network and also operates call boxes; other mobile networks are T-Mobile and 3. You can search the phone book free online (⊕herold.at). Most hostels and hotels have **wi-fi**, and some cities, including Vienna, Salzburg and Linz, have free public wi-fi hotspots.

EMERGENCIES

Austria is law-abiding and reasonably safe. Dial ☉059133 for the nearest police station (*Polizei*). **Pharmacies** (*Apotheke*) follow shopping hours; a rota covers night-time and weekend opening, with details posted in pharmacy windows.

INFORMATION

Tourist offices (usually *Information*, *Tourismusverband*, *Verkehrsamt* or *Fremdenverkehrsverein*) are plentiful, often hand out free maps and almost always book accommodation.

MONEY AND BANKS

Austria's currency is the **euro** (€). Banking hours tend to be Monday to Friday 8am to 12.30pm and 1.30 to 3pm; Thursday until 5.30pm. Banks charge less commission than exchange bureaux.

EMERGENCY NUMBERS

Police ☉133; Ambulance ☉144; Fire ☉122.

OPENING HOURS AND PUBLIC HOLIDAYS

Most shops are open all day Monday to Saturday, though in the provinces they can close at lunch and on Saturday afternoons. Many **cafés**, **restaurants** and bars also have a weekly *Ruhetag* (closing day). Shops and **banks** close, and most museums have reduced hours, on **public holidays**: January 1, January 6, Easter Monday, May 1, Ascension Day, Whit Monday, Corpus Christi, August 15, October 26, November 1, December 8, December 24–26.

Vienna

Most people visit **VIENNA** (Wien) with a vivid image in their minds: a romantic place, full of imperial nostalgia, opera houses and exquisite cakes. Even so, the city can overwhelm with its eclectic feast of architectural styles, from High Baroque through the monumental imperial projects of the late nineteenth century, to the decorative Jugendstil (Art Nouveau) style of the early twentieth, used to great effect on several of the city's splendid U-Bahn stations.

Vienna became an important centre in the tenth century, then in 1278 the city fell to **Rudolf of Habsburg**, but didn't become the imperial residence until 1683. The great aristocratic families flooded in to build palaces in a frenzy of construction that gave Vienna its **Baroque character**. By the end of the Habsburg era the city had become a breeding ground for the ideological passions of the age, and the ghosts of Freud, Klimt and Schiele are now some of the city's biggest tourist draws.

WHAT TO SEE AND DO

Central Vienna is surprisingly compact, with the historical centre, or **Innere Stadt**, just 1km wide. The most important sights are concentrated here and along the Ringstrasse – the series of traffic- and tram-clogged boulevards that form a ring road around the centre. Efficient public transport allows you to

2

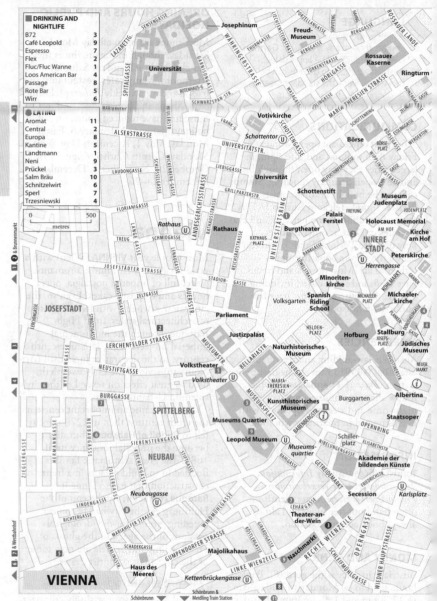

DRINKING AND NIGHTLIFE

B72	3
Café Leopold	9
Espresso	7
Flex	2
Fluc/Fluc Wanne	1
Loos American Bar	4
Passage	8
Rote Bar	5
Wirr	6

EATING

Aromat	11
Central	2
Europa	8
Kantine	1
Landtmann	5
Neni	9
Prückel	3
Salm Bräu	10
Schnitzelwirt	6
Sperl	7
Trzesniewski	4

0 — 500 metres

VIENNA

cross the city in less than thirty minutes, making even peripheral sights, such as the monumental imperial palace at **Schönbrunn**, easily accessible. However, for all the grand palaces and museums, a trip to Vienna would not be complete without spending a leisurely afternoon over a creamy coffee and a piece of cake in one of the grand, shabby-glamorous coffeehouses for which the city is famous.

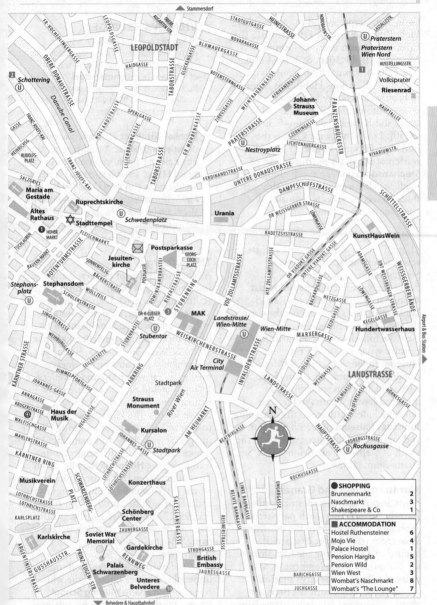

Stephansdom

The obvious place to begin exploration is **Stephansplatz**, the pedestrianized central square dominated by the hoary Gothic **Stephansdom** (Mon–Sat 6am–10pm, Sun 7am–10pm, except during services; free, but entry fees to most sections, combined ticket €17.90). It's worth paying to explore the interior more fully, with the highlights of the main section (English tours Mon–Sat 10.30am; €5.50) the Wiener Neustädter Altar, a late

2

Gothic masterpiece, and the tomb of the Holy Roman Emperor Friedrich III. The **catacombs** (tours every 15–30min, Mon–Sat 10–11.30am & 1.30–4.30pm, Sun 1.30–4.30pm; €5.50) contain the entrails of illustrious Habsburgs housed in bronze caskets. Stellar views reward those climbing the 137m-high (343 steps) south spire (daily 9am–5.30pm; €4.50). Lower, but with a lift, is the north tower (same hours; €5.50). The warren of alleyways north and east of **Stephansdom** preserves something of the medieval character of the city, although the architecture reflects centuries of continuous rebuilding.

Judenplatz

Though one of Vienna's prettiest little squares, **Judenplatz**, northwest of Stephansdom, is dominated by a deliberately bleak concrete **Holocaust Memorial** by British sculptor Rachel Whiteread. The square marks the site of the medieval Jewish ghetto and you can view the foundations of a fourteenth-century synagogue at the excellent **Museum Judenplatz** at no. 8 (Mon–Thurs & Sun 10am–6pm, Fri 10am–5pm; €10), which brings something of medieval Jewish Vienna to life. The ticket includes entrance to the intriguing **Jüdisches Museum** of Jewish tradition and culture, at Dorotheergasse 11 to the south of Stephansplatz (Mon–Fri & Sun 10am–6pm; ⓦjmw.at).

Kärntnerstrasse and Graben

From Stephansplatz, pedestrianized Kärntnerstrasse runs south past street entertainers and shops to the illustrious **Staatsoper** (ⓦwiener-staatsoper.at), opened in 1869 during the first phase of the Ringstrasse's development. A more unusual tribute to the city's musical genius is the state-of-the-art **Haus der Musik**, Seilerstätte 30 (daily 10am–10pm; €13; ⓦhausdermusik.com), a hugely enjoyable museum of sound.

Running west of Stephansplatz is the more upscale Graben, featuring an extremely ornate plague column (*Pestsäule*), built to commemorate the 1679 plague.

> ## VIENNA'S HEURIGEN
>
> To sample Austrian wines on a scenic excursion, visit one of the wine-producing villages on Vienna's outskirts. To the north of the Danube, **Stammersdorf** (tram #31 from Schottenring; 36min) is surrounded by vineyards and filled with traditional, family-run *Heurigen* (wine taverns).
>
> **Wienhof Wieninger** 21 Stammersdorferstr. 78 ⓦheuriger-wieninger.at. A great place to start, with a pleasant garden, good-value meals (from around €8) and an excellent selection of whites available by the glass (from €1.55). Mid-March to April Fri 3pm–midnight, Sat & Sun noon–midnight, May to mid-Dec Thurs & Fri 3pm–midnight, Sat & Sun noon–midnight.

The Hofburg

A block southeast of Graben is the immense, highly ornate **Hofburg** palace (ⓦhofburg-wien.at), housing many of Vienna's key imperial sights. Skip the rather dull **Kaiserappartements** in favour of the more impressive **Schatzkammer** (Mon & Wed–Sun 9am–5.30pm; €12), where you'll see some of the finest medieval craftsmanship and jewellery in Europe, including relics of the Holy Roman Empire and the Habsburg crown jewels. The Hofburg is also home to two of Vienna's most enduring tourist images: singing boys and prancing horses. Steps beside the Schatzkammer lead up to the **Hofmusik Kapelle** (Mon & Tues 10am–2pm, Fri 11am–1pm; free), where the **Vienna Boys' Choir** sings Mass (mid-Sept to June Sun 9.15am; ☎01 533 99 27, ⓦhofmusikkapelle.gv.at): you can obtain free, standing tickets from 8.30am (otherwise €10–36; book in advance).

On the north side of the Hofburg, the imperial stables are home to the white horses of the **Spanish Riding School**, known for their extraordinary, intricate performances. There are three main ways to see them: book a performance well in advance (mid-Feb to mid-June & mid-Aug to Dec, usually Sat & Sun at 11am, occasionally Fri & eves; standing from €25, seats from €50; ⓦsrs.at); attend a morning exercise session

(10am–noon: April–June, Sept & Oct Tues–Fri; Nov–March & Aug Tues–Sat; tickets for exercise session and tours from Michaelerplatz visitor centre Tues–Sun 9am–4pm; €15); or join a guided tour of the school and stables (March to mid-June & Aug to mid-Dec daily, otherwise 5–6 days per week; tours 2pm, 3pm & 4pm; tour €18; combined tour and training session €31). Alternatively, if you just want to take a peek at the horses, look into the stables (*Stallburg*) from the glass windows on Reitschulgasse.

Finally, at the Hofburg's southeastern tip, the **Albertina** (daily 10am–6pm, Wed till 9pm; €12.90; ⓦalbertina.at) houses one of the world's largest graphic art collections, with works by Raphael, Rembrandt, Dürer and Michelangelo.

The Ring and Rathausplatz

The Ring, the large boulevard that encircles the Innere Stadt, along with its attendant monumental civic buildings, was created to replace the town's fortifications, demolished in 1857; many of these buildings now house museums. On the western section is the showpiece **Rathausplatz**, a square framed by four monumental public buildings: the Rathaus (City Hall), the Burgtheater, Parliament and the Universität – all completed in the 1880s.

The Kunsthistorisches Museum

Of all Vienna's museums, the **Kunsthistorisches Museum** on Burgring still outshines them all (June–Aug daily 10am–6pm, Thurs till 9pm; Sept–May Tues–Sun 10am–6pm, Thurs till 9pm; €15; ⓦkhm.at). It's one of the world's greatest collections of Old Masters – comparable with the Hermitage or Louvre. Highlight is an unrivalled collection of sixteenth-century paintings by Brueghel the Elder, while the Peter Paul Rubens collection is also very strong and works by Vermeer and Caravaggio are worth seeking out. A number of Greek and Roman antiquities add breadth and variety. Set aside several hours at least: there is also an excellent café.

The MuseumsQuartier

Southwest of the Ring is Vienna's **MuseumsQuartier** (MQ; ⓦmqw.at), a collection of museums and galleries in the old imperial stables, where the original buildings are enhanced by a couple of striking contemporary additions. Stylish outdoor seating, plenty of good cafés and an interesting calendar of events make the area a focus for Vienna's cultural life. The best museum here is the **Leopold Museum** (Mon, Wed & Fri–Sun 10am–6pm, Thurs 10am–9pm; €13), with fine work by Klimt and the largest collection in the world of works by Egon Schiele.

The Secession

The eccentric, eye-catching building crowned with a "golden cabbage" by Karlsplatz is the **Secession building** (Tues–Sun 10am–6pm; €9.50; ⓦsecession.at), built in 1898 as the headquarters of the Secessionist movement, whose aim was to break with the Viennese establishment and champion new ideas of art and aesthetics. Designed by Joseph Maria Olbrech, the gallery was decorated by several luminaries of the group, including their first president Gustav Klimt. It still puts on contemporary exhibits today, with Klimt's *Beethoven Frieze* downstairs the only permanent artwork.

MAK

On the Ring's eastern section, beyond Stubenring, is the enjoyable **MAK** (Tues 10am–10pm, Wed–Sun 10am–6pm; €9.90, free Tues 6–10pm; ⓦmak.at), an applied arts museum whose eclectic collection spans the Romanesque period to the twentieth century and includes an unrivalled Wiener Werkstätte collection.

The Belvedere

South of the Ringstrasse, the **Belvedere** (daily 10am–6pm; Oberes €14, combined ticket €20; ⓦbelvedere.at; tram #D from the opera house) is one of Vienna's finest palace complexes. Two magnificent Baroque mansions face each other across a sloping formal garden. The loftier of the two, the **Oberes Belvedere**, has the best concentration of paintings by

2

Klimt in the city, including *The Kiss*, while the Unteres Belvedere and Orangerie show temporary exhibitions.

Schönbrunn

The biggest attraction in the city suburbs is the imperial summer palace of **Schönbrunn** (ⓜ schoenbrunn or; ⓜ4 to Schönbrunn), designed by Fischer von Erlach on the model of residences like Versailles. To visit the palace rooms or **Prunkräume** (daily: April–June, Sept & Oct 8.30am–5pm; July & Aug 8.30am–6pm; Nov–March 8.30am–4.30pm) there's a choice of two tours: the "Imperial Tour" (€13.30), which takes in 22 state rooms, and the "Grand Tour" (€16.40 with audioguide, €19.40 with tour guide), which includes forty rooms. The shorter tour misses out the best rooms – such as the Millions Room, a rosewood-panelled chamber covered from floor to ceiling with wildly irregular Rococo cartouches, each holding a Persian miniature watercolour. The palace gets unbearably overcrowded at the height of summer, with lengthy queues, so buy tickets in advance online. The splendid **Schlosspark** (daily 6.30am–dusk; free) is dotted with attractions, including the Gloriette – a hilltop colonnaded monument, now a café and terrace with splendid views (terrace daily: mid-March to June, Sept & Oct 9am–6pm; July & Aug 9am–7pm; late Oct to early Nov 9am–4pm; €3.60), fountains, a maze and labyrinth (same hours as Gloriette; €5.20) and Vienna's excellent **Tiergarten** or zoo (daily: Jan, Nov & Dec 9am–4.30pm; Feb 9am–5pm; March & Oct 9am–5.30pm; April–Sept 9am–6.30pm; €18.50; ⓦ zoovienna.at).

ARRIVAL AND DEPARTURE

By plane Vienna Airport (ⓦ viennaairport.com) is around 16km southeast of the city. The cheapest way to Wien-Mitte station in the centre is to take S-Bahn line ⓢ7 (every 30min; 25min; €3.90 one-way), though the City Airport Train (CAT; every 30min; 16min; €11 one-way) is faster. Buses (every 30min; €8 one-way) run to ⓤ Schwedenplatz (20min) in the centre and Westbahnhof (45min).

By train South of the centre, Vienna's ultra-modern Hauptbahnhof is Austria's most important international rail hub; all ÖBB's principal long-distance routes stop here, including trains from Prague, Budapest, Bratislava, Graz, Innsbruck and Munich, as well as those from Italy, Poland and Slovenia. Trains from Salzburg and Linz terminate either at the Hauptbahnhof or at the Westbahnhof (ⓤ3, five stops from the centre). Many long-distance services also stop at Vienna-Meidling station (ⓤ6, four stops south of Westbahnhof)

Destinations Bratislava (every 30min; 1hr); Budapest (every 1–2hr; 2hr 40min); Graz (hourly; 2hr 35min); Innsbruck (hourly; 4hr 25min); Linz (up to 5 hourly; 1hr 15min–1hr 35min); Melk (hourly; 1hr); Prague (every 2hr; 4hr); Salzburg (3 hourly; 2hr 20min–2hr 50min).

By bus Vienna international bus terminal is at Erdbergstr. (ⓤ Erdberg, southeast of the centre, six stops from Stephansplatz on line ⓤ3).

INFORMATION

Tourist information The main tourist office is on Albertinaplatz, behind the opera house (daily 9am–7pm; ⓣ01 245 55, ⓦ wien.info).

GETTING AROUND

So many attractions are in or around the Innere Stadt and can be visited on foot.

By public transport The network (ⓦ wienerlinien.at) consists of trams (Strassenbahn or Bim), buses, the U-Bahn (metro) and the S-Bahn (fast commuter trains). U-Bahns run from around 5am to 12.30am or so, with a reduced frequency of roughly four per hour between midnight & 5am on Fridays and Saturdays; trams run till around midnight. A network of nightbuses centres on Schottentor and Kärntner Ring/Oper.

Tickets Buy your ticket from booths or machines at stations, tobacconists or on board trams and buses (more expensive), then validate it at the start of your journey. One-way tickets are €2.20 (€2.30 on board buses and trams) and allow unlimited changes in one direction; day passes are better value (24hr/48hr/72hr for €7.60/€13.30/€16.50). The Vienna Card (48hr/72hr for €21.90/€24.90) provides unlimited travel plus discounts at attractions, though if you have an ISIC card, a simple travel pass will probably work out cheaper.

By boat DDSG (ⓦ www.ddsg-blue-danube.at) sightseeing boats dock at the Handelskai on the Danube northeast of the centre (ⓤ Vorgartenstrasse, four stops from Stephansplatz); Twin City Liners catamarans (ⓦ twincityliner.com) from Bratislava (April–Oct: up to 5 daily; 1hr 15min) dock at Schwedenplatz.

By bike Vienna has a very cheap city-wide bike scheme, CityBikes (ⓦ citybikewien.at), with 120 stations all over the city, including behind Stephansdom on Stephansplatz. The first hour is free, second is €1, third is €2. Bikes can be rented with a credit card or with a Citybike "tourist card"

VIENNESE ADDRESSES

Vienna is divided into **numbered districts** (*Bezirke*). District 1 is the Innere Stadt; districts 2–9 are arranged clockwise around it; districts 10–23 are a fair way out. Addresses begin with the number of the district, followed by the street name, then the house number and apartment number.

(€2 from the Radstation at the Hauptbahnhof; Mon–Fri 5.30am–8.30pm, Sat & Sun 6am–8pm).

ACCOMMODATION

For cheaper accommodation booking ahead is essential in summer. Several hostels are near the Westbahnhof, which is an easy few stops into the centre.

HOSTELS

★**Hostel Ruthensteiner** 15, Robert Hamerlinggasse 24 ☎01 893 42 02, ⓦhostelruthensteiner.com; ⓤWestbahnhof. Excellent, friendly and relaxed hostel an easy walk from the Westbahnhof. There's a spacious leafy courtyard, plus bar, musical instruments, kitchen, iPads, barbecue, laundry and free wi-fi. Dorms €20, doubles €66

Mojo Vie 7, Kaiserstr. 77/8 ☎0676 551 11 55, ⓦmymojovie.at; ⓤBurggasse-Stadthalle or tram #5 to Burggasse from Westbahnhof. Charming, stylish alternative to the standard hostel, with a network of local apartments housing dorms and private rooms. Excellent communal areas and personal, welcoming vibe. Reception 8am–1pm. Minimum two nights. Dorms €24, doubles €60

Palace Hostel 16, Savoyenstrasse 2 ☎01 481 00 30, ⓦhostel.at/en/palace-hostel-vienna; ⓤOttakring then bus #46a or #46b. Located amid leafy grounds up in the Vienna hills, with a view of the city. All rooms come with showers and some have direct access to the garden with its volleyball net and minigolf. Free sheets, parking and wi-fi. Dorms have a maximum of 4 beds. Dorms €22, doubles €60

Wombat's Naschmarkt 4, Rechte Wienzeile 35 ☎01 897 23 36, ⓦwombats-hostels.com; ⓤKettenbrückengasse. It's all about location at this branch of *Wombat's*, right by the Naschmarkt and within walking distance of the Innere Stadt. It's slick and well equipped, with en-suite dorms, a good bar, laundry and free wi-fi. Dorms €20, doubles €78

Wombat's "The Lounge" 15, Mariahilferstr. 137 ☎01 897 23 36, ⓦwombats-hostels.com. Smaller of Vienna's two party-oriented *Wombat's* hostels, close to the Westbahnhof. With kitchen, laundry, 24hr reception and free wi-fi. Dorms €21, doubles €68

HOTELS AND PENSIONS

Pension Hargita 7, Andreasgasse 1/8 ☎01 526 19 28, ⓦhargita.at; ⓤZieglergasse. Homely, Hungarian-owned

pension in a great location just off Mariahilferstr. The interior is decorated with blue country pottery, while the cabin-like common areas are lined with wood. All rooms contain washbasins, though en-suite costs extra. Breakfast €5. Doubles €54

Pension Wild 8, Lange Gasse 10 ☎01 406 51 74, ⓦpension-wild.com; ⓤVolkstheater. Friendly, laidback *pension*, a short walk from the Ring in a student district behind the university. En-suite costs extra. Especially popular with gay travellers; booking essential. Doubles €59

CAMPSITE

Wien West 14, Hüttelbergstr. 80 ☎01 914 23 14, ⓦwiencamping.at; bus #52 A or B from ⓤHütteldorf. In the plush far-western suburbs of Vienna, with two- and four-bed bungalows to rent. Closed Feb. Camping/person €7.50, plus per tent €7.50/8.50, bungalows/person €40

EATING

CAFÉS, CHEAP EATS AND SNACKS

With stalls selling giant savoury borek pastries from €2.50 or falafel sandwiches from €3.80, the Naschmarkt is the best place for cheap street food.

Central 1, Herrengasse 14; ⓤHerrengasse. Traditional meeting place of Vienna's intelligentsia, and Trotsky's favourite *Kaffeehaus* – of all Vienna's cafés, perhaps the most ornate. Breakfast (from €6.30) served until 11.30am weekdays, 1pm at weekends; main courses from €14.50 and a tempting cake display. Mon–Sat 7.30am–10pm, Sun 10am–10pm.

Europa 7, Zollergasse 8; ⓤNeubaugasse. Lively, modern café hosting a young, trendy crowd. The short menu includes breakfast from €5.90 and soups or salads from €3.20. Food is served into the small hours, but it's more bar than café by night; cocktails €7.80. Daily 9am–5am.

Kantine 7, Museumsplatz 1; ⓤMuseumsQuartier. One of the MuseumsQuartier's nicer cafés, serving breakfast until 3pm (€2.90), veggie-friendly stuffed pittas (from €6.90) and organic Schladminger beer. The vibe is relaxed and there's free wi-fi. Daily 9am–2am.

Landtmann 1, Universitätsring 4; ⓤSchottentor. One of Freud's haunts, this elegant Art Deco favourite feels fit for royals and has always attracted big-name celebrities and politicians, though also welcomes people from all walks of life. Breakfasts from €8.50, two-course Mittagsmenü €12.50. Daily 7.30am–midnight.

★**Neni** 6, Naschmarkt 510; ⓤKarlsplatz. Trendy Israeli café in the thick of the Naschmarkt's foodie scene, with delicious Mediterranean breakfasts served until noon (from €6.50), inexpensive mezze (from €3.50) and a two-course lunch menu for €11.50. Mon–Sat 8am–11pm.

★**Prückel** 1 Stubenring 24; ⓤStubentor. You could lose hours of your life to coffee, cake and the newspapers in this, one of the best and most relaxed of the classic

2

Viennese coffeehouses, with stylish 1950s decor and hot food from around €7. Live piano music Mon, Wed & Fri 7–10pm. Daily 8.30am–10pm.

★**Sperl** 6, Gumpendorferstr. 11; ⓌMuseumsquartier. With a slightly faded, *fin-de-siècle* interior this is among the finest of the city's coffeehouses, with reasonably priced daily specials (€9.80) and schnitzel (€11.40). Mon–Sat 7am–11pm. Sun 11am–8pm. July & Aug closed Sun.

Trzesniewski 1, Dorotheergasse 1. Just off Graben, this is a great place for a pit stop – grab a couple of small open sandwiches, with pâté toppings such as herring, egg or spicy pepper for €1.20 each, washed down with a *pfiff* (0.2l; €1.20) of beer. Mon–Fri 8.30am–7.30pm, Sat 9am–6pm, Sun 10am–5pm.

RESTAURANTS

Aromat 4, Margaretenstr. 52 ☎01 913 24 53; ⓌKettenbrückengasse. Tiny 1950s canteen-style place, with a short, daily changing evening menu of Mediterranean-influenced dishes (antipasti or Lebanese platters €7.90), plus sweet and savoury crêpes (from €5.90). Daily 5–10pm.

Salm Bräu 3, Rennweg 8; tram #71. With long outdoor tables in summer, this brew pub dishes up Viennese staples and huge salads (lunch menu €6.90, daily specials €15) as well as a fine selection of brewed-on-the-premises beers and spirits. Daily 11am–midnight.

Schnitzelwirt 7, Neubaugasse 52; tram #49. A convivial local favourite set in a wood-panelled space, perfect for getting cosy on cold nights. Great place for *wienerschnitzel* – a bargain at €7. Mon–Sat 11am–9.30pm.

DRINKING AND NIGHTLIFE

For a bar crawl or live music the string of clubs under the railway arches around ⓌThaliastr, Josefstädterstr. and Alserstr. are a good bet, while in summer beach bars line the Donaukanal.

BARS

Café Leopold 7, Museumsplatz 1 Ⓦca fe-leopold.at; ⓌMuseumsQuartier. Coolest of the MuseumsQuartier's cafés, in a stylish glass-walled space attached to the museum, with a roof terrace. Chic café during the day; DJs and cocktails (€8.80) at night. Mon–Wed & Sun 10am–midnight, Thurs 10am–4am, Fri & Sat 10am–6am.

★**Espresso** 7, Burggasse 57; ⓌVolkstheater. Stylish, friendly café/bar with street terrace and 1950s furniture; wines by the glass from €2.80. Mon–Fri 7.30pm–1am, Sat & Sun 10am–1am.

Rote Bar 7, Neustiftgasse 1; ⓌVolkstheater. Inside the Volkstheater, this sumptuous spot is decked out in red velvet and feels a bit like going back in time. Welcomes all ages, but be sure to wear your best threads. Admission price varies for DJ and tango nights. Mon–Fri 10pm–2am, Sat 10pm–4am, Sun 10pm–1am.

Wirr 7, Burggasse 70 Ⓦwirr.at; ❶Volkstheater. Hip, arty day-into-evening café-bar and basement club, with a terrace in summer and an eclectic weekend breakfast menu until 4pm (from €4.80). Mon–Wed & Sun 8am–2am, Fri & Sat 8am–4am.

CLUBS AND LIVE MUSIC

B72 8, Hernalser Gürtel 72, under the arches Ⓦb72.at; ❶Alserstr. or Josefstädterstr. Dark designer club featuring a mixture of DJs and often good live indie bands. Sun–Thurs 8pm–4am, Fri & Sat 8pm–6am.

Flex 1, Am Donaukanal Ⓦflex.at; ❶Schottenring. A stalwart in Vienna's club scene, this serious dance-music club by the canal attracts some of the city's best DJs. Entry price varies, but expect to pay around €8. Live gigs 7pm; club Thurs–Sat 11pm–6am.

Fluc/Fluc Wanne 2, Praterstern 5 Ⓦfluc.at; ❶Praterstern. This upstairs bar (*Fluc*) and underground club (*Fluc Wanne*) inside a former pedestrian tunnel could be mistaken for industrial containers. Come evening they transform into one of the best venues in the city, with interesting electro, house and hip-hop club nights. Entry €5–10. Mon–Sat 8pm–3am or later.

Passage 1, Babenberger Passage, Burgring 3 Ⓦclub -passage.at; ❶MuseumsQuartier/Volkstheater. Dressy, futuristic club in a converted pedestrian underpass, attracting a mixed crowd. Entry price varies depending on night. Tues–Thurs 10pm–5am, Fri & Sat 11pm–6am.

SHOPPING

Mariahilferstr. is best for high-street clothes shops and the big chains, though Neubaugasse, nearby, is more eclectic.

Brunnenmarkt Brunnengasse; ❶Josefstädter Strasse. With a distinctively local feel, Brunnenmarkt sells everything from homewares to Turkish breads and pastries. At Yppenplatz, its northern end, there's a farmers' market on Sat mornings, where you can pick up local produce or stop for brunch at one of the many cafés. Mon–Fri 6am–7.30pm, Sat 6am–5pm.

Naschmarkt ❶Karlsplatz. Large famous market with Turkish deli stalls, hip cafés and a plethora of stalls and snack joints, serving everything from falafel to sushi. On Sat mornings a flea market extends south from here near

⑩Kettenbrückengasse. Mon–Fri 6am–7pm, Sat 6am–6pm.
Shakespeare & Co 1, Sterngasse 2 ⓦshakespeare.co.at; ⑩Schwedenplatz. Friendly English-language bookshop; also sells translations of Austrian authors. Mon–Sat 9am–9pm.

ENTERTAINMENT

The local listings magazine *Falter* (ⓦfalter.at) has comprehensive details of the week's cultural programme. The tourist office also publishes the free monthly *Programm*.
Konzerthaus 3, Lothringerstr. 20 ☎01 24 20 02, ⓦkonzerthaus.at. A major classical venue which also hosts occasional jazz and world music performances.
Musikverein 1, Musikvereinsplatz 1 ☎01 505 81 90, ⓦmusikverein.at. Ornate concert hall, bastion of classical music, acclaimed for its acoustics and home to the Vienna Philharmonic.
Staatsoper 1, Opernring 2 ☎01 513 15 13, ⓦwiener-staatsoper.at. One of Europe's most prestigious opera houses. The season runs Sept–June and tickets range from €6 to well over €250. They often sell out, but the office also sells hundreds of standing-place tickets (*Stehplätze*) each night 1hr 20min before a performance (from €2–4).

DIRECTORY

Embassies Australia, 4, Mattiellistr. 2 ☎01 50 67 40; Canada, 1, Laurenzerberg 2 ☎01 531 38 30 00; Ireland, 1, Rotenturmstr. 16–18 ☎01 715 42 46; UK, 3, Jauresgasse 12 ☎01 71 61 30; US, 9, Boltzmanngasse 16 ☎01 31 33 90.
Hospital Allgemeines Krankenhaus, 9, Währinger Gürtel 18–20; ⑩Michelbeuern-AKH.
Post office Westbahnhof (Mon–Fri 8am–7pm, Sat 9am–6pm), Hauptbahnhof (Mon–Fri 8am–7pm, Sat 9am–3pm).

Central Austria

West of Vienna, the Danube snakes through the Wachau, one of its most scenic stretches, where castles and vineyards cling to steep slopes above quaint villages. The western end of this 40km stretch is marked by a stunning Baroque monastery in **Melk**. Further west the river steadily loses charm, though it's still a focus for several towns and cities, including **Linz**, whose high-tech Ars Electronica museum is particularly enjoyable. South of the Danube region, the land slowly climbs and rolls into the

hills of Styria, with its attractive and bustling capital **Graz**. Northwest of here, the land rises again up to the Salzkammergut, a region of fine Alpine scenery and pretty lakes within easy reach of **Salzburg**. Southwest of the Salzkammergut the peaks really start to soar, and resorts like **Zell am See** take full advantage of the landscape to offer great skiing and first-rate outdoor activities.

MELK

For real High Baroque excess, head for the early eighteenth-century **Benedictine monastery** at MELK – a pilgrimage centre associated with the Irish missionary St Koloman. The monumental coffee-cake monastery, perched on a bluff over the river, dominates the town. Highlights of the interior (daily: April–Oct 9am–5pm; tours in English 10.55am & 2.55pm; Nov–March guided tours only 11am & 2pm; €11, €13 with guided tour; ⓦstiftmelk.at) are the exquisite library, with a cherub-flecked ceiling by Troger, and the rather lavish monastery church, with similarly impressive work by Rottmayr.

ARRIVAL AND INFORMATION

By train The station is at the head of Bahnhofstrasse, which leads directly into the old quarter.
Tourist information Kremser Strasse 5 (March Mon, Wed, Fri 9.30am–3.30pm; April & Oct Mon–Sat 9.30am–5pm, Sun 10am–2pm; May–Sept Mon–Sat 9.30am–6pm, Sun 9.30am–4pm; ☎02 75 25 11 60, ⓦmelk.gv.at). Has a stock of private rooms; not all are central, but since Melk is small it's not a major Issue.

ACCOMMODATION

Junges Hotel Melk Abt Karl-Str. 42 ☎02 75 25 26 81, ⓦmelk.noejhw.at. HI hostel a 10min walk from the station, with wi-fi, bike parking and table tennis; reception 4–9pm. Breakfast included. Dorms <u>€22.50</u>, doubles <u>€57</u>

LINZ

Away from its industrial suburbs, **LINZ** is a pleasant Baroque city straddling the Danube, and steadily reinventing itself as a city of technology and innovation, most evident in a couple of show-stopping new museums.

WHAT TO SEE AND DO

Linz's two most striking contemporary attractions, Lentos Museum and Ars Electronica Center, face each other on either side of the Danube River – both are illuminated at night, their neon facades glowing dramatically opposite each other. To the south of the river is the city's compact Old Town, the hub of which is **Hauptplatz**, with its pastel-coloured facades and central Trinity Column, crowned by a gilded sunburst. Many of the city's liveliest bars are clustered just west of here, around the triangle formed by Hoffgasse, Altstadt and Hahnengasse. Heading south from the Hauptplatz, the busy shopping street Landstrasse leads south towards the train station.

Lentos

A modern addition to the city's cultural scene nestles beside the Danube: the shimmering, hangar-like steel-and-glass **Lentos** (Tues–Sun 10am–6pm, Thurs till 9pm; €8; ⒲lentos.at), which houses contemporary and modern art, including Klimt and Schiele.

Ars Electronica Center

An unusual, tardis-like temple to science and technology, **Ars Electronica Center**, Ars Electronica Strasse 1 (Tues, Wed & Fri 9am–5pm, Thurs 9am–7pm, Sat & Sun 10am–6pm; €9.50; ⒲aec.at) makes a trip to Linz worthwhile alone. Inside the glowing box of an exterior is an impressive series of interactive high-tech exhibits. One highlight is the Deep Space virtual-reality room with 3D projections on the walls and floor. Basement areas explore future developments in biology, materials, the brain and robots – set aside several hours and get stuck into the hands-on experiments.

ARRIVAL AND INFORMATION

By train 2km south of the centre, at the end of Landstr; all trams (lines #1, #2, #3 and #4) from the underground platform at the station (direction "Zentrum") run up Landstr. to Hauptplatz.

Destinations Salzburg (every 30min; 1hr 5min–1hr 15min); Vienna (3 hourly; 1hr 15min–1hr 35min).

Tourist information Altes Rathaus, Hauptplatz 1 (May–Sept Mon–Sat 9am–7pm, Sun 10am–7pm; Oct–April Mon–Sat 9am–5pm, Sun 10am–5pm; ⒯07 32 70 70 20 09, ⒲linz.at); sells the Linz Card (1-day €18, students €15; 3-day €30, students €25), which includes entry to museums and travel.

GETTING AROUND

By public transport Useful network of trams and buses: "mini" 4-stop ticket €1.10; single journey ("midi", transferable) €2.20; 24hr "maxi" ticket €4.40, under-21s €2.20. The Pöstlingbergbahn from Hauptplatz is a tourist tram (every 30min; 20min one-way; €6.10 return), up to the Pöstlingberg on the north side, a hill with good views over the city and a beer garden.

ACCOMMODATION

Campingplatz Linz-Pichlingersee Wienerstr. 937 ⒯07 32 30 53 14, ⒲camping-linz.at. Well-equipped campsite on a lake on the outskirts of Linz, with a restaurant, bar and laundry facilities. Tram #2 to Bahnhof Ebelsberg, then bus #11 or #19, direction Pichlinger See. Open mid-March to mid-Oct. Per person **€5.50**, plus per tent **€6**

Jugendherberge Stanglhofweg 3 ⒯07 32 66 44 34, ⒲jugendherbergsverband.at; bus #17, #19, #27 to "Ziegeleistr". Friendly youth hostel 2km from Hauptbahnhof. All bedrooms are en suite and breakfast is included. Reception Mon–Fri 7.30am–8.30pm, Sat & Sun 4–8.30pm. Dorms **€24.50**, doubles **€55**

Wilder Mann Goethestr. 14 ⒯07 32 65 60 78, ⒲wildermann.cc; tram one stop from the station to Goethestr. Simple, friendly and convenient hotel, between the train station and the centre; rooms with shared facilities or with en-suite showers. Doubles **€62**

EATING, DRINKING AND NIGHTLIFE

Alte Welt Hauptplatz 4. Unpretentious bar and wine cellar with tables on a cosy courtyard just off the Hauptplatz and on the main square itself. Hearty, Austrian/Italian-influenced mains €8–15. Occasional live music and cabaret. Mon–Fri 11.30am–2.30pm & 6–11pm, Sat noon–2.30pm & 6–11pm, Sun 6–10pm.

p'aa Altstadt 28. Contemporary vegetarian restaurant, with an imaginative, global menu including curries, Greek, Turkish and Italian-inspired dishes, salads and tasty juices. Lunch mains €9.50–15.50; evening €12.50–18.50. Opening hours vary, but usually Mon & Tues 11.30am–2.30pm, Wed–Fri 11.30am–2.30pm & 6–10pm.

★ Traxlmayr Promenade 16. The traditional coffeehouse in Linz serves excellent coffees and hot main courses (from €8) – treat yourself to a slice of Linzer Torte, the town's ubiquitous almond-and-jam cake (€3.80). Mon–Sat 7.30am–10pm, Sun 9am–7pm.

GRAZ

Austria's second-largest city, **GRAZ**, owes its importance to the defence of central Europe against the Turks. From the fifteenth century, it was constantly under arms, rendering it more secure than Vienna and leading to a modest seventeenth-century flowering of the arts. Today Graz celebrates its reputation as a city of design, thanks to a clutch of modern architectural adventures and a large student population, and it's a fun place to spend a few days without the tourists of Innsbruck or Salzburg.

WHAT TO SEE AND DO

Graz is compact and easy to explore, with most sights within easy walking distance of its central **Hauptplatz**, with its fantastically decorated Baroque facades.

The Altstadt

From Hauptplatz, it's a few steps to the River Mur and two examples of Graz's architectural renaissance: the **Murinsel** is an ultramodern floating bridge-cum-meeting-place with a café linking the two banks, inspired by an open mussel, while the giant bulbous **Kunsthaus Graz** (Tues–Sun 10am–5pm; €9, or Joanneum

2

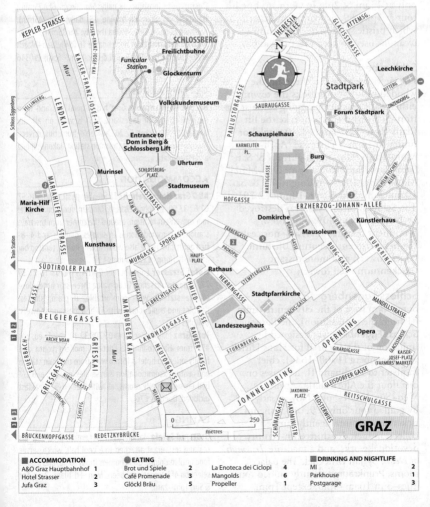

■ ACCOMMODATION		● EATING				■ DRINKING AND NIGHTLIFE	
A&O Graz Hauptbahnhof	1	Brot und Spiele	2	La Enoteca dei Ciclopi	4	MI	2
Hotel Strasser	2	Café Promenade	3	Mangolds	6	Parkhouse	1
Jufa Graz	3	Glöckl Bräu	5	Propeller	1	Postgarage	3

2

LANDESMUSEUM JOANNEUM TICKET

A combined ticket giving entrance to all **Landesmuseum Joanneum** museums comes in two versions: €13 for 24hr, €19 for 48hr.

ticket; ⊕ kunsthausgraz.at) is a museum of contemporary art, video installation and photography. Pick of the rest of the Joanneum museums is the **Landeszeughaus** city armoury on Herrengasse (Tues–Sun: April–Oct 10am–5pm; Nov–March guided tours only at 11am & 2pm in German; English tour at 1pm; €9, or Joanneum ticket), which bristles with sixteenth-century weapons used to keep the Turks at bay.

Schlossberg

For views over the city, head up the wooded hill that overlooks the town: either walk up the zigzagging stone stairs from Schlossbergplatz or take the lift (daily 8am–12.30am; €1.30 single) or funicular from Sackstrasse (April–Sept Mon–Thurs 9am–midnight, Fri & Sat 9am–2am, Sun 9am–11pm; Oct–March Mon–Thurs 10am–midnight, Fri & Sat 10am–2am, Sun 10am–10pm; €2.20). The **Schloss**, or fortress, was destroyed by Napoleon in 1809; only a few prominent features survive – noticeably the huge sixteenth-century **Uhrturm** (clock tower), and more distant **Glockenturm** (bell tower).

Schloss Eggenberg

Some 4km west of the city centre (tram #1 from the train station), the Baroque **Schloss Eggenberg** was designed in imitation of the Escorial for Hans Ulrich von Eggenberg (1568–1634), chief minister to Ferdinand II. It houses on one floor the **Alte Galerie** (April–Oct Wed–Sun 10am–5pm; Nov to early Jan by guided tour only; €9, or Joanneum ticket), whose intelligently curated collection includes thirteenth-century devotional works, and a macabre *Triumph of Death* by Jan Brueghel. The palace rooms, **Prunkräume** (hourly guided tours Tues–Sun 10am–4pm, except 1pm;

€11.50, or Joanneum ticket), were designed as an allegory of the universe (24 rooms, 365 windows on the outside, four towers and so on); the highlight is the "Room of the Planets", a great hall with an elaborate ceiling and wall paintings depicting the zodiac, and also the three Asian rooms, in particular the one decorated with rare Japanese panels from Osaka.

ARRIVAL AND INFORMATION

By train Graz's train station is on the western edge of town, a 15min walk or short tram ride (#1, #3, #6 or #7) from Hauptplatz.

Destinations Innsbruck (3 daily; 5hr 50min–6hr 25min); Hallstatt via Stainach-Irdning (5 daily; 2hr 45min); Salzburg (5 daily; 4hr); Vienna (hourly; 2hr 35min).

Tourist information Herrengasse 16 (daily: Jan–March & Nov 10am–5pm; April–Oct & Dec 10am–6pm; ☎ 0316 807 50, ⊕ graztourismus.at).

GETTING AROUND

By public transport Graz has a good bus and tram network; the 24hr Tageskarte (€5) is valid on all city transport; 1hr ticket €2.20, available from bus drivers, machines on trams and at the main station, Jakominiplatz and Hauptplatz.

ACCOMMODATION

A&O Graz Hauptbahnhof Eggenbergerstr. 7 ☎ 03 16 57 01 62 37 00, ⊕ aohostels.com; Modern, functional hostel in a convenient location, around the corner from the train station. Accommodation is in singles, doubles and 4–8-bed dorms; there are also women-only dorms, rooftop bar and wi-fi. Dorms €15, doubles €57

Hotel Strasser Eggenburger Gürtel 11 ☎ 03 16 71 39 77, ⊕ hotelstrasser.at. Good-value three-star hotel close to the station, with comfortable, if plain, singles, doubles and triple rooms with TV and massage showers. Doubles €63

Jufa Graz Idlhofgasse 74 ☎ 05 708 32 10, ⊕ jufa.eu; bus #50 from Hauptbahnhof. Friendly, modern youth and family-oriented hotel a 15min walk from the train station and centre. Accommodation is in singles, doubles and 3/4 bed en-suite family rooms, all with free wi-fi. Breakfast included. Doubles €76

EATING

Brot und Spiele Mariahilferstr 17. Central, unpretentious bar and restaurant attached to a pool hall, which serves food until midnight. Good burgers (from €6.30) and a good selection of international beers. Mon–Fri 10am–2am, Sat & Sun 1pm–2am.

GRAZ FARMERS' MARKET

Known for its wine-growing and farming, the region of Styria (Steiermarkt) produces local specialities, in particular **Kürbiskernöl** (pumpkin seed oil), which has a delicious, nutty flavour and is used in salad dressings and other dishes on many Graz menus. The excellent Graz's **farmers' market**, Kaiser-Josef-Platz (Mon–Sat 6am–1pm), is a good place to buy bottles of Kürbiskernöl, local cheeses, breads, meat and other produce. There are also snack stands, coffee joints and fresh juice bars.

★ **Café Promenade** Erzherzog-Johann-Allee 1. Attractive, Neoclassical pavilion, with stylish modern decor and a terrace beneath chestnut trees on the edge of the Stadtpark. Serves snacks (from €3), tapas (from €2.40), tortillas, sandwiches plus more substantial fare (€7–15). Mon–Thurs 9am–1am, Fri & Sat 9am–2am, Sun 9am–midnight.

Glöckl Bräu Glockenspielplatz 2–3. Traditional place, with busy beer terrace serving hearty Austrian dishes like *schnitzel* or *backhendl* for under €11; lunch specials €7. Daily 10.30am–midnight.

La enoteca dei Ciclopi Sackstr. 14 (in courtyard). This delightful Sicilian wine shop and restaurant, with a small cosy interior and a few courtyard tables, serves a short menu of delicious pasta dishes and antipasti. Lunchtime soup and pasta menu €6. Mon 5–10pm, Tues–Fri noon–11pm, Sat 11am–11pm.

Mangolds Griesgasse 11. Popular self-service place and excellent veggie option, with fresh juices and a large salad bar (pay by weight: €1.43/100g). Mon–Fri 11am–7pm, Sat 11am–4pm.

Propeller Zinzendorfgasse 17. Convivial student pub with a beer garden and a good menu that ranges from hearty Austrian classics to burgers. The generous portions cost €8.50–10 and there's also an all-you-can-eat student lunch buffet (Mon–Fri 11am–2pm; €7.90). Mon–Fri 10am–1am, Sat & Sun noon–1am.

DRINKING AND NIGHTLIFE

MI Färberplatz 1. Stylish, split-level third-floor café-bar (take the glass lift up), with a designer interior and an attractive roof terrace. Cocktails around €6.50. Mon–Fri 4pm–2am, Sat 9am–2am, Sun 4–11pm.

Parkhouse Stadtpark 2. Buzzing bar in a pavilion, tucked away in the park, with regular DJ nights and a young crowd spilling out onto the grass. Beers from €3.60; free entry. March–Oct daily 10am–late; Nov–Feb Fri & Sat from 9pm.

Postgarage Dreihackengasse 42 ⓦpostgarage.at. An interesting and varied programme of gigs and club nights in the four spaces here – free gigs, gay nights, techno and more. Generally open Wed–Sat: club nights 11pm–late, gigs start 7–8pm.

SALZBURG

For many visitors, **SALZBURG** represents the quintessential Austria, offering ornate architecture, mountain air and the musical heritage of the city's most famous son, Wolfgang Amadeus **Mozart**. The city and surrounding area were for centuries ruled by a series of independent prince-archbishops, and it is the pomp and wealth of their court that is evident everywhere in the fine Baroque Altstadt.

WHAT TO SEE AND DO

Salzburg's compact centre straddles the River Salzach, squeezed between two dramatic mountains – Mönchsberg on the west and Kapuzinerberg on the east. The **west bank** forms a tight-knit network of alleys and squares – Alter Markt, Residenzplatz, Mozartplatz (with obligatory statue of the composer) and Domplatz – overlooked by the medieval **Hohensalzburg fortress** high above.

Residenzplatz

The complex of Baroque buildings at the centre of Salzburg exudes the ecclesiastical and temporal power of Salzburg's archbishops, whose erstwhile living quarters, the **Residenz** (Mon & Wed–Sun 10am–4pm; €12, including access to the cathedral museums and organ gallery), dominates the west side of Residenzplatz. Take a self-guided audio-tour of the lavish **state rooms**, then head one floor up to the **Residenzgalerie**, whose collection includes a few interesting paintings, most notably Rembrandt's small, almost sketch-like *Old Woman Praying*.

On the east side of Residenzplatz, accessed from Mozartplatz, is the Neue Residenz, built by Archbishop Wolf Dietrich von Raitenau, and topped by the **Glockenspiel**, a seventeenth-century musical clock which chimes at 7am, 11am and 6pm. It now houses the

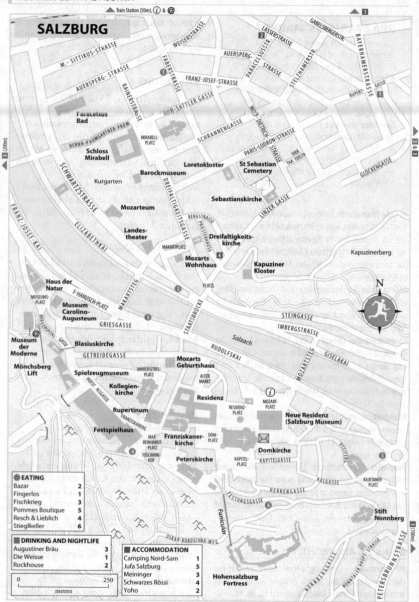

excellent **Salzburg Museum** (Tues–Sun 9am–5pm; €8.50; ⊛salzburgmuseum.at), which, as well as showing some of the archbishop's lavish rooms, explores Salzburg's history, its rediscovery by Romantic painters and the city's tourist industry.

Domplatz and Franziskanerkirche

The pale marble facade of the **Dom** dominates **Domplatz**, while inside, the impressively cavernous Renaissance structure dazzles with its ceiling frescoes. Across Domplatz, an archway leads through to the Gothic **Franziskanerkirche**, which houses a fine Baroque altar around an earlier *Madonna and Child*. The altar is enclosed by an arc of nine chapels and a frenzy of stucco. Look out for the twelfth-century marble lion that guards the stairway to the pulpit.

Mozarts Geburtshaus and Mozarts Wohnhaus

Getreidegasse, the main street in Salzburg's Old Town, is lined with opulent boutiques, painted facades and wrought-iron shop signs. At no. 9 is the canary-yellow **Mozarts Geburtshaus** (daily: July & Aug 8.30am–6.30pm; Sept–June 9am–5pm; €10, joint ticket with Wohnhaus €17; ⊚mozarteum.at), where the musical prodigy was born in 1756 and lived until the age of 17. Between the waves of tour parties it can be an evocative place, housing some fascinating period instruments, including one of his baby-sized violins. Over the Salzach River on Makartplatz, **Mozarts Wohnhaus** was the family home from 1773 till 1787 (same hours; €10), and now contains an engrossing multimedia history of the composer.

Hohensalzburg

Overlooking the city from the rocky mountain, the fortified **Hohensalzburg** (daily: May–Sept 9am–6.30pm; Oct–April 9.30am–4.30pm; €12, or €15.20 including funicular; ⊚salzburg -burgen.at) is Salzburg's key landmark. You can get up here on Austria's oldest funicular (daily every 10min: April–June, Sept, Oct & Dec 9am–8pm; July & Aug 9am–10pm; Nov & Jan–March 9am–5pm; €8.40 return) from Festungsgasse behind the Dom, although the walk up isn't as hard as it looks. Begun around 1070, the fortress gradually became a more salubrious courtly seat. Included in the price is an audioguide tour of the observation tower – with spectacular views – and battlements, access to the impressive state rooms and various exhibitions.

Mönchsberg

For some of the best views across to the Hohensalzburg, take the Mönchsberg

lift up to the **Mönchsberg** from Anton-Neumayr-Platz (July & Aug daily 8am–11pm; Sept–June Mon 8am–7pm, Tues–Sun 8am–9pm; €2.30 single, €3.60 return). At the summit, the sleekly concrete-and-glass **Museum der Moderne** (Tues–Sun 10am–6pm, Wed till 8pm; €8) is a stylish contrast to all the Baroque that puts on big-name art exhibitions.

Schloss Mirabell

Across the river from the Altstadt, **Schloss Mirabell** on Mirabellplatz stands on the site of a palace built by Archbishop Wolf Dietrich for his mistress Salome, with whom the energetic prelate was rumoured to have sired a dozen children. Familiar from *The Sound of Music*, the palace's ornate gardens offer a popular view back across the city.

Schloss Hellbrunn and the Untersberg

The Italianate palace **Schloss Hellbrunn** (daily: April & Oct 9am–4.30pm; May, June & Sept 9am–5.30pm; July & Aug 9am–9pm, Wasserspiele only after 6pm; €12.50; ⊚schlosshellbrunn.at) on Salzburg's southern fringe – 5km from the city centre – was built in the early seventeenth century by Salzburg's decadent archbishop Marcus Sitticus as a place for entertaining. The main attraction is the gardens' impressive array of fountains and watery gimmicks, or *wasserspiele*; guided tours take forty minutes, with the tour guide showing off all the tricks and hidden fountains, including an elaborate, water-powered mechanical theatre (prepare to be

---

THE SOUND OF MUSIC

Salzburg wastes no time cashing in on its connection with the legendary singing Von Trapp family, immortalized in the movie *The Sound of Music*. From its kiosk on Mirabellplatz, Panorama Tours (☎06 628 83 21 10, ⊚panoramatours.com) runs **The Original Sound of Music Tour** (daily 9.15am & 2pm; 4hr; €42) to the key film locations, such as Hellsbrun Palace and Mondsee Cathedral – they play the soundtrack and you're encouraged to sing along.

2

splashed). The palace itself features paintings of Sitticus's unusual animal collection, and a lavishly frescoed festival hall and music room.

To get to Schloss Hellbrunn take bus #25 from the train station or Mirabellplatz (every 20–30min). This bus continues to the village of St Leonhard, 7km further south, where a cable car (March–June & Oct–Nov 8.30am–4.30pm; July–Sept 8.30am–5pm; Dec–Feb 9am–3.30pm; return €23) climbs the 1853m **Untersberg** for impressive views of Salzburg to the north and the Alps to the south.

ARRIVAL AND DEPARTURE

By train The station is 2km north of Mozartplatz; numerous buses run to Mirabellplatz and Altstadt.

Destinations Graz (5 daily; 4hr); Hallstatt via Attnang-Puchheim (hourly 2hr 10min–2hr 35min); Innsbruck (hourly; 1hr 50min); Linz (up to 4 hourly; 1hr 15min); Munich (1–2 hourly; 1hr 30min); Werfen (1–2 hourly; 40–55min), Zell am See (every 2hr; 1hr 35min).

By bus If you're travelling on to Germany, note that Berchtesgaden, in Bavaria, is most easily accessed by bus from Salzburg.

Destinations Berchtesgaden, Bavaria (hourly; 45min); Strobl (for St Wolfgang; hourly; 1hr 10min).

INFORMATION

Tourist information Mozartplatz 5 (April–June & mid-Sept to mid-Oct daily 9am–6pm; July & first half Sept daily 9am–6.30pm, Aug daily 9am–7pm; mid-Oct to March Mon–Sat 9am–6pm; ☎06 62 88 98 73 30, ⓦsalzburg.info); also at the train station (daily: May & Sept 9am–7pm; June 8.30am–7pm; July & Aug 8.30am–7.30pm; Oct–April 9am–6pm).

Salzburg Card Both tourist offices sell this card (Nov–April €24/24hr, €32/48hr, €37/72hr; May–Oct €27/24hr, €36/48hr, €42/72hr), which includes public transport and admission to all the city's sights – if you go on the Unterbergs cable car it almost pays for itself.

GETTING AROUND

By public transport The bus network centres on the train station and Mirabellplatz. Single tickets available in blocks of five from tobacconists and transport offices at €1.80 per ticket (€2.60 on board).

ACCOMMODATION

Camping Nord-Sam Samstr. 22a ☎06 62 66 04 94, ⓦcamping-nord-sam.com; bus #23 from the train station to stop Mauermannstr. The most central campsite, well

equipped with a heated outdoor pool. Per person €12, plus per tent €6.50

Jufa Salzburg Josef Preis Allee 18 ☎05 708 36 13, ⓦjufa .eu; bus #25 from the train station. Large, very central, well-equipped hostel with accommodation in singles, doubles, 3-, 4- and 5-bed family rooms and 6–8-bed dorms. Breakfast included. Dorms €27.55, doubles €97

Meininger Fürbergstr. 18–20 ☎07 20 88 34 14, ⓦmeininger-hotels.com; Obus #2 from Hauptbahnhof to Sterneckstr. Large modern, well-equipped hostel/hotel located on a busy junction out of the centre. Some rooms and the fifth-floor terrace have views over Kapuzinerberg. Dorms €16, doubles €64

Schwarzes Rössl Priesterhausgasse 6 ☎06 62 87 44 26, ⓦacademiahotels.at. Wonderful, creaky old place – in term time a hall of residence – that's central and great value. Rooms have shared or private facilities. Open July–Sept. Doubles €88

Yoho Paracelsusstr. 9 ☎06 62 87 96 49, ⓦwww.yoho.at. Very popular and often fully booked hostel near the train station, with sociable bar, internet café, free wi-fi and laundry facilities. Dorms €22, doubles €132

EATING

★**Bazar** Schwarzstr. 3. Elegant coffeehouse with a pleasant river-view terrace, a fantastic place to unwind and nibble with a view. Snacks and soups from around €5, mains €14–16. Mon–Sat 7.30am–7.30pm, Sun 9am–6pm.

Fingerlos Franz-Josef-Str. 9. Stylish and relaxed Café-Konditorei, serving cakes as fine as you'll find in Salzburg, and excellent breakfasts. Breakfasts from €4.70, cakes from €2.60. Tues–Sun 7.30am–7.30pm.

Fischkrieg Hanuschplatz 4. Unpretentious riverside place serving fish and seafood in every form. Try the fishburgers (€2.50), paella (€8.70) or calamari (€7.70). Mon–Fri 8.30am–6.30pm, Sat 8.30am–1pm.

★**Pommes Boutique** Rudolfsplatz 1a. Some of the best burgers in Salzburg – including a decent veggie option – served from a tiny pavilion near the river. Portions are generous. From €4. Mon–Fri 11am–8pm, Sun noon–8pm.

Resch & Lieblich Toscaninihof 1a. Tucked away near the Festspielhaus, offering good-value Austrian cuisine in dining rooms carved out of the Hohensalzburg cliffs. Daily specials from €8.20. Mon–Sat noon–11pm; kitchen closes earlier.

Stieglkeller Festungsgasse 10. Enormous brewery-owned restaurant and beer garden with excellent views over the old town. Solid traditional food from €12. Daily 11am–10pm, closed Feb plus Mon in Jan & March.

DRINKING, NIGHTLIFE AND ENTERTAINMENT

The city hosts dozens of concerts of all musical persuasions year-round; check with Salzburg Ticket Service (ⓦsalzburg ticket.com), in the tourist office on Mozartplatz. The

Salzburg Festival (late July to late Aug; ☎06 628 04 50, ⓦsalzburgerfestspiele.at) is one of Europe's premier festivals of classical music, opera and theatre, with some outdoor concerts.

★ **Augustiner Bräu** Lindhofstr.7 (pedestrian entrance in Augustinergasse). A 15min stroll from the Old Town, this vast beer hall has a beautiful tree-shaded garden and own-brew beer, served in earthenware steins – €6.20 for 1l, €3.10 for 0.5l. It's good for inexpensive snacks and meals too. Mon–Fri 3–11pm, Sat & Sun 2.30–11pm.

Die Weisse 10 Rupertgasse. Lively microbrewery, well off the tourist track, with pleasant beer garden and great pub food. Goulash and dumplings €12. Mon–Sat 10am–midnight.

Rockhouse Schallmooser Hauptstr 46. Vibrant blend of bar, live rock venue and club, set in historic vaults in the flanks of the Kapuzinerberg. Gigs generally start at 8pm. Mon–Thurs 6pm–1am, Fri & Sat 6pm–2am.

DIRECTORY

Consulate UK, Alter Markt 4 ☎06 62 84 81 33.

Post office Residenzplatz 9, Mon–Fri 8am–6pm.

WERFEN

With its impressive fortification and spectacular ice caves, **WERFEN**, 40km south of Salzburg, offers a great day of sightseeing, but arrive early to comfortably see both. The moody castle **Festung Hohenwerfen** (April Tues–Sun 9.30am–4pm; May–Sept daily 9am–5pm; mid-July to mid-Aug daily 9am–6pm; Oct daily 9.30am–4pm; €12, €15.50 with lift), on an outcrop above town, lies a thirty-minute signed walk from Werfen's train station. Though much modified over the years, it has eleventh-century origins, with all the usual components – ornate chapel and torture chamber included – neatly gathered around a courtyard. There are daily falconry displays (April to mid-July & mid-Aug to Oct 11.15am & 3.15pm, mid-July to mid-Aug 11.15am, 2.15pm & 4.30pm) too.

Up the road from Werfen's castle, you can explore the first kilometre of a 40km underground network at the **Eisriesenwelt ice caves**. The caves are more than two hours' walk from the entrance building, so most visitors take a cable car. Tours run every 30min (daily: May–June, Sept & Oct 8am–3.45pm; July & Aug 8am–4.45pm; ticket office closes 45min before last tour; €12, €24 with cable car) and last around 75 minutes. It's cold, so take a jumper.

Trains from Salzburg frequently arrive at Werfen's station, from where **buses** (€7 return) to the caves depart daily at 8.18am, 10.18am, 12.18pm & 2.18pm; more buses leave (around every 20min) from the official Gries car park departure point across the river – it's signposted from the station and not far.

THE SALZKAMMERGUT

The **Salzkammergut**, Austria's lake district, features a spectacular series of lakes and mountains. You can get a feel for the area on a day-trip from Salzburg to St Wolfgang, or on a "Sound of Music tour", but if you want to hike, mountain bike or just chill out, head to a lakeside campsite or B&B for a few days' relaxation – picture-perfect Hallstatt is a good choice.

St Wolfgang

The pretty little village of **ST WOLFGANG**, on the north shore of Wolfgangsee, is undeniably picturesque, though it can get crowded in summer, and provides a good taster of the region, particularly if you take the vintage train to the top of the **Schafberg** peak (May–Oct 9.20am–3.30pm; last descent 5.05pm; €34 return; to avoid queuing, reserve a seat on ☎06 13 82 23 20,

---

GETTING AROUND THE SALZKAMMERGUT

A single **train** line runs north–south from Attnang-Puchheim via **Bad Ischl** (one of the region's main towns) and **Hallstatt** to Stainach Irdning (every two hours; 2hr 5min), with connections **from Salzburg** and Linz at Attnang-Puchheim and **from Graz** at Stainach Irdning. But **buses** are generally quicker, with Bad Ischl a useful hub for connections. Hourly bus #150 between Salzburg and Bad Ischl (1hr 35min) runs east along the southern shore of the Wolfgangsee; for St Wolfgang change at **Strobl** for connecting bus #546 (approx hourly; 15min).

2

ⓦschafbergbahn.at) from a station on the western edge of town.

In town, the **Pfarrkirche**, above the lakeshore, houses a high altar, an extravagantly pinnacled structure 12m in height, completed between 1471 and 1481. It features brightly gilded scenes of the *Coronation of the Virgin* flanked by scenes from the life of St Wolfgang.

ARRIVAL AND INFORMATION

By bus Buses from Strobl (see box, p.81) drop off at both ends of town, before and after the road tunnel that bypasses the centre.

By boat From April to October, Wolfgangsee Schifffahrt lake steamers run from St Gilgen (bus #150 from Salzburg) to the Schafberg station's jetty in St Wolfgang (April to mid-June, Sept & Oct 10.20am–6pm; mid-June to Aug 9am–6.50pm; €7.40; 40min; ⓦschafbergbahn.at).

Tourist office The tourist office (mid-May to June & first half Sept Mon–Fri 9am–6pm, Sat 9am–3pm, Sun 9am–noon/1pm; July & Aug Mon–Fri 9am–7pm, Sat 9am–6pm, Sun 10am–5pm; mid-Sept to mid-May Mon–Fri 9am–5pm, Sat 9am–noon; ☎06 138 80 03, ⓦwolfgangsee.at) is at the eastern entrance to the road tunnel.

Hallstatt

The jewel of the Salzkammergut is **HALLSTATT**, which clings to the base of precipitous cliffs on the shores of the Hallstättersee, 20km south of Bad Ischl. With towering peaks and a pristine lake, this is a stunning setting in which to hike, swim or rent a boat. Arriving **by train** is an atmospheric and evocative experience; the station is on the opposite side of the lake from the village, and the ferry, which meets all incoming trains, gives truly dramatic views.

WHAT TO SEE AND DO

Hallstatt gave its name to a distinct period of Iron Age culture after Celtic remains were discovered in the salt mines above the town. Many of the finds date back to the ninth century BC, and can be seen in the **Museum Hallstatt** (April & Oct daily 10am–4pm; May–Sept daily 10am–6pm; Nov–March Wed–Sun 11am–3pm; €8; ⓦmuseum-hallstatt.at).

The **Pfarrkirche** has a south portal adorned with sixteenth-century Calvary scenes. In the graveyard outside is a small stone structure known as the **Beinhaus**

OUTDOOR ACTIVITIES IN HALLSTATT

Boats can be rented on the lakeshore between the tourist office and the village centre (1hr; €15). The tourist office can advise on **hiking routes** and sells local hiking guides. At the southern end of town in the suburb of Lahn is a "Badinsel", an artificial island for sunbathing and swimming (changing facilities nearby).

(May–Oct daily 10am–6pm, €1.50), traditionally the repository for the skulls of villagers. The skulls, some quite recent, are inscribed with the names of the deceased and dates of their death, and are often decorated.

Steep paths zigzag up from the village centre and behind the graveyard to the **Salzachtal** (at least 1hr of hard hiking), the highland valley where **salt mines** (guided tours daily: April–Sept 9.30am–4.30pm; Oct 9.30am–3pm; Nov 9.30am–2.30pm; €22) once ensured the area's prosperity. Alternatively, take the **funicular** (daily: April to late Sept 9am–6pm; Oct 9am–4.30pm; Nov 9am–4pm; €16 return, combined ticket with tour €30) up from the suburb of Lahn.

ARRIVAL AND INFORMATION

By train The station is across the lake; ferries (€2.50) are timed to coincide with trains. Return ferry times are posted up at the ferry station and around town; the last train to Hallstatt arrives around 6.50pm.

By bus Buses stop in the suburb of Lahn, a 10min lakeside walk south of the centre.

Tourist information Tourist office at Seestr. 99 (Jan–April Mon–Fri 8.30am–5pm, Sat 9am–1pm; May–June Mon–Fri 8.30am–5pm, Sat & Sun 9am–2.30pm; July–Oct Mon–Fri 8.30am–6pm, Sat & Sun 9am–4pm; Nov & Dec Mon–Fri 8.30am–5pm; ☎06 134 82 08, ⓦhallstatt.net).

ACCOMMODATION AND EATING

Camping Klaussner-Höll Lahn 201 ☎06 134 83 22, ⓦcamping.hallstatt.net. A short way south from the tourist office at Lahn, on the outskirts of the village. Quiet and cyclist-friendly, with shop, bar, laundry service and wi-fi. Open mid-April to mid-Oct. Per person **€9.50**, plus per tent **€5.70**

Gasthaus zur Mühle Kirchenweg 36 ☎06 134 83 18, ⓦhallstatturlaub.at. Small, welcoming bar, restaurant and hostel uphill from the landing stage, with a good line

in pizzas (from €7.10). Upstairs are some basic dorm rooms. Dorms first night €27, subsequent nights €23
★ **Gasthof Simony** Wolfengasse 105 ☎ 06 13 42 06 37, ⓦ gasthof-simony.at. On the lakefront just off the main square, this relaxed guesthouse has a good range of rooms, some en-suite, with traditional wooden furniture and some with balconies overlooking the lake. The garden restaurant serves fresh lake fish from around €15. Good breakfast included. Doubles €80

ZELL AM SEE-KAPRUN

Some 80km south of Salzburg, **ZELL AM SEE** is a pretty old town wedged between a perfect alpine lake and an impressive mountainous hinterland. The quintessential Austrian resort, it's busy with skiers in winter and hikers in summer. Zell's twin village of **Kaprun** lures visitors for all-year glacier skiing on the 3203m Kitzsteinhorn.

WHAT TO SEE AND DO

The narrow streets of Zell's **Old Town** have charm, but they're mainly of interest for their bars, cafés and restaurants. The real attraction here is the scenery, whether enjoyed for its own sake or as a backdrop for summer hiking and cycling or winter sport. Zell's closest **skiing** fans out across the slopes of the 2000m **Schmittenhöhe** (ⓦ schmitten.at), with plenty of pistes for every standard. The most convenient ascent is via the CityXpress **cable car** (daily: summer 9am–5pm; winter 8.30am–4.30pm; ascent €19.50, descent €17; Schmittenhöhe day-passes include the CityXpress, €45) from the centre of Zell. In summer, the cable cars serve a web of **hiking trails**, stretching as far as the 2074m Maurerkogel, with a 360-degree panorama of 3000m-high peaks.

Towering above nearby **Kaprun**, the mighty **Kitzsteinhorn** is capped with snow and ice year-round. Just below the summit, the 3029m-high **Gipfelwelt** is the highest viewing platform in the region; in July and August there's a snow beach and ice bar on the glacier just below it. Making the ascent involves four cable cars from the base of the mountain near Kaprun (daily 8.15am–4.30pm; summer €40; winter ski pass €50;

ⓦ kitzsteinhorn.at); bus #660 runs from Zell to the base of the cable car.

ARRIVAL AND INFORMATION

By train Zell am See's station is on the lakeside, a few minutes' walk from the tourist office.
Tourist information Brucker Bundesstr. 1a (Mon–Fri 8am–6pm, Sat 9am–6pm, Sun 9am–1pm; ☎ 06 54 27 70, ⓦ zellamsee-kaprun.com). Has a list of private rooms in Zell and Kaprun (from €22 per person).
Zell am See Kaprun Summer Card Free from your hotel or hostel, it offers free entry or discounts on some transport, services and many attractions. Valid mid-May to mid-Oct.

ACCOMMODATION AND EATING

Junges Hotel Zell am See Seespitzstrasse Seespitzstr. 13 ☎ 06 54 25 71 85, ⓦ seespitz.hostel-zellamsee.at. HI-affiliated hostel on the lakeside 1200m south of Zell's centre, with bathing and sports facilities and accommodation in singles, doubles and 4–6-bed dorms. All rooms en-suite; breakfast included. Dorms €27, doubles €64
★ **Pinzgauer Diele** Anton Wallner Str. 6. Lively bar in Zell's Old Town with a fun, après-ski atmosphere and a wide choice of filling international fare from pizza (€7.50) and pasta (€8.90) to chilli and tortillas. Daily 4pm–4am.
Seecamp Thumersbacherstr. 33–34 ☎ 06 54 27 21 15, ⓦ seecamp.at. Modest-sized campsite on the lakeside 1.6km north of Zell's old town, with restaurant, wi-fi, laundry and shop. Open year-round. Bus #70 from Zell. Per person €9.70, plus per tent €6.20

Western Austria

West towards the mountain province of **Tyrol**, Austria's grandiose Alpine scenery begins to emerge. Most trains from Salzburg travel through a corner of Bavaria in Germany before joining the Inn valley and climbing back into Austria towards **Innsbruck**, Tyrol's main town. A less direct but more scenic route (more likely if you're coming from Graz or Zell) cuts by the majestic **Hoher Tauern** – site of Austria's highest peak, the Grossglockner.

INNSBRUCK

Nestled in the Alps and encircled by ski resorts, **INNSBRUCK** is a compact city cradled by towering mountains. It has a rich history: Maximilian I based his imperial court here in the 1490s, placing

2

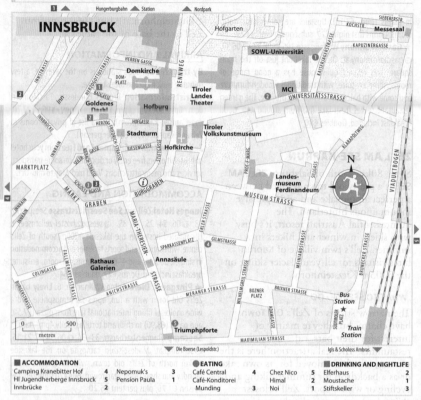

INNSBRUCK

■ ACCOMMODATION		● EATING				■ DRINKING AND NIGHTLIFE	
Camping Kranebitter Hof	4	Nepomuk's	3	Café Central	4	Chez Nico	5	Elferhaus	2
HI Jugendherberge Innsbruck	5	Pension Paula	1	Café-Konditorei		Himal	2	Moustache	1
Innbrücke	2			Munding	3	Noi	1	Stiftskeller	3

the city at the heart of European politics for a century and a half. This combination of historical pedigree and proximity to the mountains has put Innsbruck firmly on the tourist trail.

WHAT TO SEE AND DO

Most attractions are confined to the central **Altstadt**, bounded by the river and the Graben (Marktgraben and Burggraben), a road that follows the course of the medieval town's moat.

Maria-Theresien-Strasse

Innsbruck's main artery is **Maria-Theresien-Strasse**, famed for the view north towards the great Nordkette, the mountain range that dominates the city. At its southern end the triumphal arch, **Triumphpforte**, was built for the marriage of Maria Theresa's son Leopold in 1756. Halfway along, the **Annasäule**, a column supporting a statue of the Virgin,

commemorates the retreat of the Bavarians, who had been menacing Tyrol in 1703. Herzog-Friedrich-Strasse leads on into the centre, opening out into a plaza lined with arcaded medieval buildings. At the plaza's southern end is the **Goldenes Dachl**, or "Golden Roof" (though the tiles are really copper), built in the 1490s to cover an oriel window from which the court of Emperor Maximilian could observe the square below. The **Goldenes Dachl Museum** (May–Sept daily 10am–5pm; Oct & Dec–April Tues–Sun 10am–5pm; €4.80) has engrossing displays on the city's history, though it offers only a brief glimpse of the balcony.

Domplatz and the Hofburg

Standing on Domplatz, the ostentatious **Domkirche St Jakob** (Mon–Sat 10.15am–6.30/7.30pm, Sun 12.30–6.30/7.30pm) is home to a valuable *Madonna and Child* by German master

Lucas Cranach the Elder, although it's buried in the fussy Baroque detail of the altar.

The adjacent **Hofburg**, entered around the corner, has late medieval roots but was remodelled in the eighteenth century. Its Rococo state apartments are crammed with opulent furniture (daily 9am–5pm; €9).

The Hofkirche and Volkskunstmuseum

At the head of Rennweg is the **Hofkirche** (Mon–Sat 9am–5pm, Sun 12.30–5pm; €7), which contains the imposing (but empty) **mausoleum of Emperor Maximilian**. This extraordinary project was originally envisaged as a series of 40 larger-than-life statues, 100 statuettes and 32 busts of Roman emperors, but in the end only 28 of the statues were completed.

Housed in the same complex, the **Tiroler Volkskunstmuseum** (daily 9am–5pm; €11 including entry to Hofkirche and Landesmuseum), features a huge collection of folk art and objects including re-creations of traditional wood-panelled Tyrolean interiors.

Landesmuseum Ferdinandeum

A short walk south, the **Landesmuseum Ferdinandeum**, Museumstr. 15 (Tues–Sun 9am–5pm; €11, including Hofkirche and Volkskunstmuseum), contains one of the best collections of Gothic paintings in Austria; most originate from the churches of the South Tyrol (now in Italy).

Schloss Ambras

Set in attractive grounds 2km southeast of the centre, **Schloss Ambras** (daily 10am–5pm, closed Nov; €10; tram #6 or bus #C from the train station) was the home of Archduke Ferdinand of Tyrol. It features the impressive Spanish Hall, built from 1569–71, and exhibitions of armour and curios amassed from around the globe. Don't miss the inner courtyard covered in sixteenth-century frescoes, including depictions of the triumph of Bacchus.

Hungerburg plateau

A good starting point for hikes is the **Nordpark**, on the slopes of the Nordkette range, accessible from the swish Hungerburgbahn cable railway. Looking like a funky spaceship, the Zaha Hadid-designed Congress station is opposite the Hofgarten; take it to Hungerburg, then continue on a two-stage sequence of cable cars to just below the summit (daily 8.30am–5pm, Fri also 6–11.30pm; €27.20 return; ⓦnordkette.com). The rewards are stupendous views of the high Alps and access to all sorts of hikes.

ARRIVAL AND INFORMATION

By train Innsbruck station is on Südtirolerplatz, east of the Old Town, an easy walk from the centre.

Destinations Munich (every 2hr; 1hr 50min); Salzburg (18 daily; 1hr 45min–2hr); Venice (1 daily; 4hr 45min); Vienna (approx hourly; 4hr 15min); Zürich (9 daily; 3hr 40min).

By bus The bus station is immediately south of the train station; local buses stop in front of the train station.

Tourist information The tourist office at Burggraben 3 (daily 9am–6pm; ☎0512 598 50, ⓦinnsbruck.info) sells the Innsbruck Card (24hr/48hr/72hr for €39/€48/€55), which includes public transport, cable cars (some only in summer) and admission to all the sights.

GETTING AROUND

By public transport Buses and trams; single tickets €2.30 (€2.70 if bought on board), 24hr ticket €5.10. There's also a public bike rental scheme, Stadtrad (ⓦstadtrad.ivb .at; first 30min €2, second 30min €2, each extra hour €3; register with credit card).

ACCOMMODATION

Camping Kranebitter Hof Kranebittner Allee 216 ☎0512 28 19 58, ⓦkranebitterhof.at; bus #LK from Boznerplatz, a block west of the station, to Klammstr. Well-equipped campsite in the west of the city, close to the airport. Open year-round. Cash only, no cards. Per tent **€36**

HI Jugendherberge Innsbruck Reichenauerstr. 147 ☎05 12 34 61 79, ⓦjugendherberge-innsbruck.at; bus #O from Landesmuseum. Large, functional HI hostel on the outskirts of the city. Dorms **€21**, doubles **€58**

Innbrücke Innstr. 1 ☎05 12 28 19 34, ⓦgasthof-innbruecke.at. Plain but comfortable *Gasthof* on the west bank of the Inn, just over the bridge from the Altstadt. More expensive rooms have en-suite facilities, although most are without. Doubles **€74**

Nepomuk's Kiebachgasse 16 ☎05 12 58 41 18, ⓦnepomuks.at. Slightly ramshackle one-dorm hostel above *Café Munding*, whose owners also run the hostel and serve its good breakfasts. Also has a couple of doubles, though one is windowless and noisy. Dorm **€24**, doubles **€58**

2

SKIING AND OTHER ACTIVITIES

Innsbruck is great for outdoor activities; the tourist office has a wide range of brochures. Of Innsbruck's **ski areas** the closest to the city is **Nordpark** (see p.85), accessible via the Hungerburgbahn, with its fabulous panoramas, snow park for skiers and snowboarders and taxing expert-level runs. The other ski areas – including the Patscherkofel, Axamer Lizum, Glungezer, Muttereralm, Schlick 2000, Kühtai and Rangger Köpfl. – are all on the opposite, southern, side of the valley and offer mellower terrain ideal for relaxed, wide-turn skiing. At **Stubai Gletscher** (⊕ stubaier-gletscher.com) glacier skiing is possible from October to June.

In winter, **lift passes** cover all these ski regions: the Stubaier Gletscher, for example, has day-passes for €46 (less for part of the day), while the Olympia SkiWorld pass covers the whole Innsbruck area, including ski buses from the town centre, and costs €132 for three days. Passes are available from all lift stations or the Innsbruck tourist office.

Many **cycling** and **mountain-bike** routes are accessible from central Innsbruck, though some of the trails are for experts only: for bike rental try Die Böerse, Leopoldstr 4 (Mon–Sat 9am–6/6.30pm; ⊕ dieboerse.at). Innsbruck's tourist office runs an extensive programme of free **guided walks** – including sunrise and night-time hikes – from late May to late October.

Pension Paula Weiherburggasse 15 ☎ 0512 29 22 62, ⊕ pensionpaula.at; bus #W from the Marktplatz. Friendly, good-value *pension* in a chalet on a hillside north of the river – some rooms have balconies and mountain views. Doubles €62

EATING AND DRINKING

★ **Café Central** Gilmstr. 5. Venerable coffeehouse serving up excellent cakes and decent breakfasts (from €4). Good spot to linger over a coffee and slice of cake (from €2.80). Daily 6.30am–9pm.

★ **Café-Konditorei Munding** Kiebachgasse 16. Superb cakes (€3.80) and pastries, in a bustling traditional café in a quiet corner of the Altstadt, with a terrace primed for people-watching. Good breakfasts (from €3.90) too. Daily 8am–8pm.

Chez Nico Maria Theresienstr 49. While this vegetarian and vegan spot is fancier than some other recommendations, the portions are substantial and the modern-European creative twist is superb. Dinner is pricey (€34 for 4 courses), so go for the fabulous €14.50 two-course lunch special. Mon & Sat 6.30–10pm, Tues–Fri noon–2pm & 6.30–10pm.

Himal Universitätsstr. 13. Stylish Nepalese place serving fresh tasty curries; meat dishes from €11.50, with good veggie options plus lunch menus from €7.10. Mon–Sat 11.30am–2.30pm & 6–10.30pm, Sun 6–10pm.

Noi Kaserjägerstr. 1. Excellent, cheap Thai restaurant around the corner from the Hofkirche with tasty lunch menus from €7.90; main courses from €9.60. Mon–Fri 11.30am–2.30pm & 6–11pm, Sat 6–11pm.

DRINKING AND NIGHTLIFE

Elferhaus Herzog-Friedrich-Str. 11. Popular Old Town beer bar, with a lively atmosphere and a big selection of bottled and draught beers. Also serves good basic Austrian food. Hot mains from €8.40. Daily 10am–2am.

Moustache Herzog-Otto-Str. 8. A relaxed, studenty bar playing a good soundtrack of mainly British and American alternative tunes. Bottled beers €3.10, shots €2.50. On Sundays there's an all-you-can-eat brunch buffet from 11am (€12). Tues–Sun 11am–2am.

★ **Stiftskeller** Stiftsgasse 1–7. Cavernous traditional beer hall and restaurant close to the Hofkirche, and Hofburg, with Augustiner beers (from €2.70), Tyrolean snacks from around €5, baked potatoes from €6.30 and hearty meaty mains from around €10. Daily 10am–midnight.

DIRECTORY

Consulate UK, Kaiserjägerstr. 1/Top B9 ☎ 05 12 58 83 20.
Hospital Universitätklinik, Anichstr. 35 (☎ 05 050 40).
Laundry Bubble Point, Andreas-Hoferstr. 37 & Brixnerstr. 1 (Mon–Fri 8am–10/9pm, Sat & Sun 8am–8pm).
Post office Südtiroler Platz 10–12 (Mon–Fri 8am–6pm).

MARKT SQUARE, BRUGES

Belgium & Luxembourg

HIGHLIGHTS

❶ Brussels See the gold-fringed Grand-Place, Europe's prettiest square. **See p.96**

❷ Antwerp Discover the up-and-coming docks of Belgium's hip northern port. **See p.100**

❸ Ghent Sip local beers in lively bars and join the Gentse Feesten carnival. **See p.103**

❹ Bruges Explore this perfectly preserved medieval town's cobbled streets. **See p.106**

❺ The Ardennes Cycle, kayak or hike through gently rolling woods. **See p.109**

❻ Luxembourg City Discover the UNESCO-listed old town of this cliff-top capital. **See p.110**

HIGHLIGHTS ARE MARKED ON THE MAP ON P.89

ROUGH COSTS

Daily budget Basic €45, occasional treat €65

Drink Jupiler beer €1.60

Food Mussels with chips €15–20

Hostel/budget hotel €20/€60–90

Travel Train: Brussels–Antwerp €7.40

FACT FILE

Population Belgium: 11.4 million; Lux: 570,252

Language Flemish (Belgium), Letzebuergesch (Lux), French, German

Currency Euro (€)

Capital Brussels; Luxembourg City

International phone code Belgium: ☏32; Lux: ☏352

Time zone GMT +1hr

Introduction

A federal country with three official languages and an ongoing rivalry between its two main groups – Dutch-speaking Flemish and French-speaking Walloons – Belgium's dull reputation is definitely misleading. Lively, cultured cities in the predominantly urban north give way to beautiful forests and rugged hills in the south, while regular, affordable trains and an impressive range of good-value accommodation mean the country is a pleasure to explore. Factor in the Belgians' enthusiasm for beer and fine cuisine, and all the ingredients for a truly memorable trip are in place. With Europe's finest cliff-top city, little Luxembourg certainly does its bit too.

3

Roughly in the middle of Belgium lies the capital, **Brussels**, the heart of the EU and a genuinely vibrant and multicultural city. North of here stretch the flat landscapes of Flemish Belgium, whose main city, **Antwerp**, is a bustling old port with doses of fine art, cutting-edge fashion, and twice as many bars as Amsterdam. Further west, also in the Flemish zone, are the charismatic cities of **Bruges** and **Ghent**, each with a stunning concentration of medieval architecture. To the south of Brussels, Belgium's most scenic region, the Ardennes in Wallonia, has deep, wooded valleys, high elevations and dark caverns, with the town of **Namur** the obvious gateway.

The Ardennes reach across the border into the northern part of the Grand Duchy of Luxembourg, a dramatic landscape of rushing rivers and high hills topped with crumbling castles. The best base for rural expeditions is **Luxembourg City**, an exceptionally picturesque place straddling a steep valley.

CHRONOLOGY

BELGIUM

54 BC Julius Caesar defeats the Belgae tribes.

496 AD The King of the Franks, Clovis, founds a kingdom which includes Belgium.

1400–1500 The Belgian cities of Bruges, Brussels and Antwerp become the European centres of commerce and industry.

1477 Following the marriage of Austrian King Maximilian I and Mary of Burgundy, Belgium becomes part of Austria.

1713 Treaty of Utrecht transfers Belgian territory from French to Austrian rule.

1790 The Belgians form an independent state from Austria, though it does not last long. They are subsequently invaded by Austria, France and the Netherlands in quick succession.

1830 Belgium gains independence from the Netherlands.

1885 King Leopold II establishes a personal colony in the African Congo.

1908 The Belgian government takes over the Congo Free State after reports of Leopold's brutal regime are circulated.

1914–18 Belgium is invaded by Germany and sees heavy fighting before it is liberated.

1940–44 Nazi invasion, and ultimately liberation by Allied forces.

1957 Belgium is a founder member of the European Economic Community (EEC).

1960 Independence granted to the Congo.

1992 Belgium ratifies the Maastricht Treaty on the European Union.

2007 Following the resignation of Prime Minister Guy Verhofstadt, Belgium is without a government.

2011 In December, French-speaking Socialist leader Elio di Rupo is appointed prime minister of a six-party coalition, ending 541 days without a government. This is the longest period a country has ever been without an official government, exceeding Iraq's record of 289 days.

2012 Belgium holds municipal elections. Results show widespread gains for the New Flemish Alliance party seeking autonomy for Dutch-speaking Flanders.

2013 Crown Prince Philippe crowned new Belgian king after the abdication of his father Albert II.

2016 On March 22 Zaventem Airport and Maelbeek metro station suffer the worst terrorist attack in Belgian history – an IS atrocity that leaves 32 dead and 300 casualties.

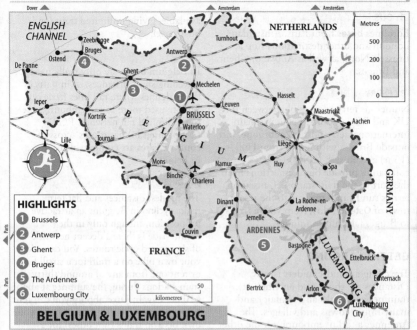

3

HIGHLIGHTS
1 Brussels
2 Antwerp
3 Ghent
4 Bruges
5 The Ardennes
6 Luxembourg City

BELGIUM & LUXEMBOURG

Map labels: Dover, Amsterdam, Amsterdam, ENGLISH CHANNEL, NETHERLANDS, Zeebrugge, Bruges, Turnhout, Ostend, Antwerp, De Panne, Ghent, Mechelen, Hasselt, Leuven, Maastricht, Ieper, Kortrijk, BRUSSELS, Aachen, Waterloo, Lille, Tournai, GERMANY, Liège, Mons, Namur, Huy, Spa, Binche, Charleroi, Dinant, La Roche-en-Ardenne, Jemelle, ARDENNES, Couvin, Bastogne, LUXEMBOURG, Ettelbruck, FRANCE, Echternach, Bertrix, Arlon, Luxembourg City, BELGIUM

Scale: 0 — 50 kilometres
Metres: 500, 200, 100, 0

LUXEMBOURG

963 AD Count Siegfried of Ardenne founds the capital of Luxembourg.

1354 Luxembourg's status is raised from fief to duchy by Emperor Charles IV.

1477 The Habsburgs take control of Luxembourg.

1715 Luxembourg is integrated into the Austrian Netherlands.

1867 Second Treaty of London ensures Luxembourg's independence and neutrality.

1890 Luxembourg announces its own ruling monarchy, relinquishing its ties to the Netherlands.

1914–1918 German occupation.

1920 Joins the League of Nations.

1939–1945 German occupation.

1957 Luxembourg is a founder member of the EEC.

2000 Grand Duke Jean abdicates, handing responsibility over to his son Henri.

2008 Constitutional crisis is provoked by Grand Duke Henri threatening to block a bill legalizing euthanasia. As a result, Parliament approves a reform which restricts the monarch to a purely ceremonial role.

2009 Luxembourg is commended for improving the transparency of its banking systems after being added to a "grey list" of countries with questionable banking arrangements by the G20.

2012 Crown Prince Guillaume weds Belgian Countess Stéphanie de Lannoy at the Notre-Dame Cathedral.

2014 Luxembourg's parliament votes to legalize same-sex marriage.

2015 A referendum proposal to allow foreigners to vote in national elections is rejected by a large margin.

ARRIVAL AND DEPARTURE

BY PLANE

The majority of airborne travel is into Brussels, which has two **airports**: the most conveniently located is Zaventem (also known as Brussels National), while Charleroi (which serves most budget airlines including Ryanair) lies about 55km from the centre.

BY TRAIN

There are frequent **rail** connections from London, Paris, Amsterdam and Luxembourg, with almost all international trains arriving at Bruxelles-Midi (Brussel-Zuid), and frequently also stopping in Ghent or Antwerp. Eurostar "Any Belgian Station" tickets are valid to all onward Belgian stations.

3

BY BUS

Eurolines **buses** from Paris, Amsterdam, London and other destinations stop at Brussels-Nord, as well as Antwerp, Ghent and Bruges.

BY FERRY

Numerous **ferry** services ply between the UK and Belgian ports. Belgium's main international ferry port is **Zeebrugge**, just outside Bruges, with ferries from Hull (15hr) and Rosyth (20hr). Ferry companies provide bus connections from the port to the train station. Transeuropa ferries run from Ramsgate to the resort town of **Ostend** (4hr), from where trains to Bruges take fifteen minutes.

GETTING AROUND

Travelling around Flanders is easy. Distances are short, and an efficient train network links all the major and many minor towns and villages. The Ardennes and Luxembourg, on the other hand, can be more problematic: the train network is not extensive and bus timetables can demand careful study for longer journeys.

BY TRAIN

Belgium's railway system (ⓦbelgianrail .be) – SNCB in French, NMBS in Flemish – is comprehensive and efficient, and fares are comparatively low. If you are under 26, don't have an InterRail or Eurail pass, and are spending some time in Belgium, ask for the **Go-Pass 10**, which buys you ten journeys between any Belgian stations for €51. (If you are planning on travelling from Belgium to Luxembourg and have a Go-Pass 10, use the pass to get to the Belgian border town of Arlon and buy an extension from there.) SNCB/NMBS also publishes information on offers and services in their comprehensive timetable book, which has an English-language section and is available at major train stations.

Luxembourg's railways (ⓦwww.cfl.lu) comprise one main north–south route down the middle of the country, with a handful of branch lines fanning out from the capital. There are a number of passes

available, giving unlimited train (and bus) travel.

BY BUS

In Belgium **buses** are only really used for travelling short distances, or in parts of the Ardennes where rail lines fizzle out. They're used more in Luxembourg, due to the limited rail network. RGTR (ⓦmobiliteit.lu) has routes across the country. Fares are comparable to those in Belgium.

BY BIKE

The modest distances and flat terrain make **cycling** in Belgium an attractive proposition, though only in the countryside is there a decent network of signposted cycle routes. You can take your own bike on a train for a small fee, or rent one from any of around thirty train stations during the summer at about €10 per day. In Luxembourg you can rent bikes for around €10 a day, and take your own bike on trains (not buses) for a minimal fee per journey. The Luxembourg Tourist Office has leaflets showing cycle routes and also sells cycling guides.

ACCOMMODATION

Accommodation is one of the major expenses on a trip to Belgium or Luxembourg but there are some **budget alternatives**, principally no-frills hotels, private rooms (effectively B&Bs) and plenty of good hostels. Whichever accommodation you choose, it's best to book ahead, especially in peak season.

In both countries, prices begin at around €60 for a double room in the cheapest one-star **hotel**; breakfast is normally included. Reservations can be made online or (for free) through most tourist offices on the day itself; the deposit they require is subtracted from your final hotel bill. **Private rooms** can be booked through local tourist offices too. Expect to pay €60–90 a night for a double, but note that they're often inconveniently situated on the outskirts of cities and towns. An exception is in Bruges, where private rooms – many of them in the centre – can be booked direct.

Belgium has around thirty **HI hostels**, run by two separate organizations: *Vlaamse Jeugdherbergcentrale* in Flanders (☎032 32 72 18, ⊛jeugdherbergen.be), and *Jeunesse de Wallonie* in Wallonia (☎022 19 56 76, ⊛lesaubergesdejeunesse.be). Most charge a flat rate per person of €19–25 for a bed in a dormitory or €60 for a double room, most with breakfast included. Some also offer lunch and dinner for €7–12. If you buy a yearly HI e-membership card (€11.52) you get a ten percent discount on your accommodation. Some of the more touristy cities such as Bruges, Antwerp and Brussels also have **privately run hostels**, which normally charge about €22 for a dorm bed. There are ten HI hostels in Luxembourg, all of which are members of the *Centrale des Auberges de Jeunesse Luxembourgeoises* (☎026 27 66 200, ⊛youthhostels.lu). Dorm bed rates for HI members are around €20, with non-members paying an extra €3. Breakfast is always included; lunch or dinner is €6–10.

In Belgium, there are hundreds of **campsites**, anything from a field with a few tent pitches through to extensive complexes. The vast majority are simpler one- and two-star establishments, for which two adults with a tent can expect to pay €20–30 per night; surprisingly, most four-star sites don't cost much more – add about €5. All Luxembourg's campsites are detailed in the Duchy's free tourist office booklet. Prices vary considerably, but are usually €5–7 per person, plus €5–7 for a pitch. In both countries, campsite phone numbers are listed in free camping booklets, and in Luxembourg the national tourist board (☎042 82 82 10, ⊛visitluxembourg.com) will make a reservation on your behalf.

STUDENT AND YOUTH DISCOUNTS

Most museums and galleries offer substantial discounts to those under 26, even if you don't have an ISIC card. Train travel is also cheaper for travellers aged under 26 if you buy a **Go-Pass 10** (see opposite).

FOOD AND DRINK

One of the great pleasures of a trip to **Belgium** is the cuisine, and if you stay away from tourist spots, it's hard to go wrong. Southern Belgian (or Wallonian) cuisine is similar to traditional French, with a fondness for rich sauces and ingredients. The Ardennes region is renowned for its smoked ham and pâté. **Luxembourg's food** is less varied and more Germanic, but you can still eat out extremely well.

In Flanders the food is more akin to that of the Netherlands, with steak and French fries the most common dish. Throughout Belgium, pork, beef, game, fish and seafood (mussels) are staple items, often cooked with butter, cream and herbs, or sometimes in beer; hearty soups are also common. *Hesprolletjes* (chicory and ham baked in a cheese sauce) and *stoemp* (puréed meat and vegetables) are two traditional dishes worth seeking out. Traditional Flemish dishes such as *waterzooi*, or "watery mess" (fish or chicken stew), and *carbonnade* (beef casserole) are also widely available. There are plenty of good **vegetarian** options too, such as quiche and salad, and you can find vegetarian restaurants in all of the larger cities.

In both countries, **bars** and **cafés** are a good source of inexpensive meals, especially at lunchtime when simple dishes – omelettes, steak, mussels – are offered as a dish of the day (*plat du jour/dagschotel*) for around €12. **Restaurants** are usually pricier, but the food is generally excellent. **Frituurs** (stands serving chips) are ubiquitous, cheap, and usually offer a variety of hot sauces, such as *stoofvlees* (beer-soaked beef).

Belgium is also renowned for its **chocolate**. The big *chocolatiers*, Godiva and Leonidas, have shops in all the main towns and cities, but high-quality chocolate is also available in supermarkets at a much lower price – try the Jacques or Côte d'Or brands.

Beer in Belgium is a real treat. Beyond the common lager brands – Stella Artois, Jupiler and Maes – there are about seven hundred speciality beers, from dark stouts to fruit beers, wheat beers and brown ales. The most famous are the strong ales brewed by the country's six **Trappist**

3

LANGUAGE

There are three official languages in **Belgium**: Dutch, French and German. Speaking French in the Flemish north is not appreciated, and vice versa. Most Belgians speak English. Natives of **Luxembourg** speak *Letzebuergesch*, a dialect of German, but most people also speak French and German and many speak English too. See p.280, p.357 and p.778 for some basic French, German and Dutch language tips.

monasteries; Chimay is the most widely available. Luxembourg doesn't really compete, but its three most popular brews – Diekirch, Mousel and Bofferding – complement the food wonderfully.

French **wines** are universally sold, but Luxembourg's wines, especially the *crémant* (sparkling wine), produced along the north bank of the Moselle, are light and refreshing. You'll also find Dutch-style **jenever** (similar to gin) in most bars in the north of Belgium, and in Luxembourg home-produced **eau-de-vie**, distilled from various fruits.

CULTURE AND ETIQUETTE

It's nearly impossible to make a faux pas among the Belgians – they're a relaxed bunch who take life at a leisurely pace (so don't be offended if a barman finishes polishing the glasses before serving you). Leave a ten percent tip in restaurants, and greet acquaintances with three kisses, not two.

SPORTS AND ACTIVITIES

The Ardennes is ideal for hiking, kayaking, cycling and horseriding (see p.110 for operators); cross-country skiing is also an option. La Roche-en-Ardenne and Bouillon make excellent bases in Belgium, while in Luxembourg the towns of Vianden and Echternach – each about an hour from Luxembourg City – are popular destinations for hikers and cyclists.

COMMUNICATIONS

Post offices are usually open Monday to Friday 9am–noon and 2–5pm. Some

BELGIUM'S PROVINCIAL & LINGUISTIC BORDERS

urban post offices also open on Saturday
mornings. Many **public phones** take only
phonecards, which are available from
newsagents and post offices. **Internet**
access is widespread, with more and
more hostels, hotels and cafés offering
free **wi-fi**.

EMERGENCIES

Both countries are safe. However, if
you're unlucky enough to have something
stolen, report it immediately to the
nearest police station and get a report
number – or better still a copy of the
statement itself – for your insurance
claim when you get home. With regard
to **medical emergencies**, if you're reliant
on free treatment within the EU health
scheme, try to remember to make this
clear to the ambulance staff and any
medics you subsequently encounter.
Outside working hours, all **pharmacies**
should display a list of open alternatives
in their window. Weekend rotas are also
listed in local newspapers.

INFORMATION

In both Belgium and Luxembourg, there
are **tourist offices** even in the smallest of
villages. They usually provide free local
maps, and the larger towns offer a free
accommodation booking service too.

MONEY AND BANKS

Belgium and Luxembourg both use the
euro (€). **Banks** are the best places to
change money and are generally open
Monday to Friday 9am–4/4.30pm in
both countries, though some have a
one-hour lunch break between noon and
2pm, and some close after lunch on
Friday. **ATMs** are commonplace.

OPENING HOURS AND HOLIDAYS

In both countries, most shops close on
Sunday (except in tourist towns), with
some only reopening on Monday
afternoon, even in major cities.
Nonetheless, normal **shopping hours** are
Monday to Saturday 9 or 10am to 6 or
7pm, with many urban supermarkets
staying open until 8 or 9pm on Fridays.
In the big cities, a smattering of
convenience stores (*magasins de nuit/
nachtwinkels*) stay open either all night or
until around 1 or 2am daily, and some
souvenir shops open late and on Sundays
too. Most **museums** are closed on
Mondays, though look out for occasional
late-night openings, especially in Brussels.
Restaurants also often close on Mondays.
Many **bars** have relaxed closing times,
claiming to stay open until the last
customer leaves. Less usefully, many
restaurants and bars close for at least a
couple of weeks in July or August.

Shops, banks and many museums are
closed on the following **public holidays**:
New Year's Day, Easter Sunday, Easter
Monday, May 1, Ascension Day (forty
days after Easter), Whit Sunday, Whit
Monday, June 23 (Luxembourg only),
July 21 (Belgium only), Assumption
(mid-Aug), November 1, November 11
(Belgium only), Christmas Day.

Brussels

Belgium's capital **BRUSSELS** (Bruxelles,
Brussel) boasts an exciting mish-mash
of modern museums, a well-preserved
medieval centre and an energetic
nightlife. Since World War II, the city's
appointment as headquarters of both

3

BRUSSELS

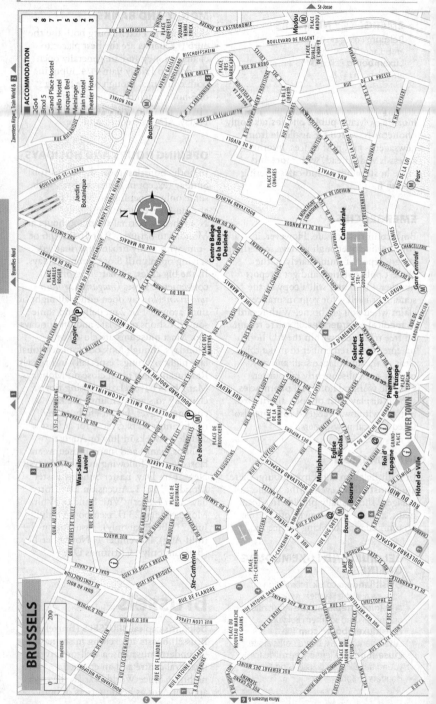

ACCOMMODATION
2Go4	4
Brxxl 5	8
Grand Place Hostel	7
Jello Hostel	1
Jacques Brel	5
Meininger	6
Train Hostel	2
Theater Hotel	3

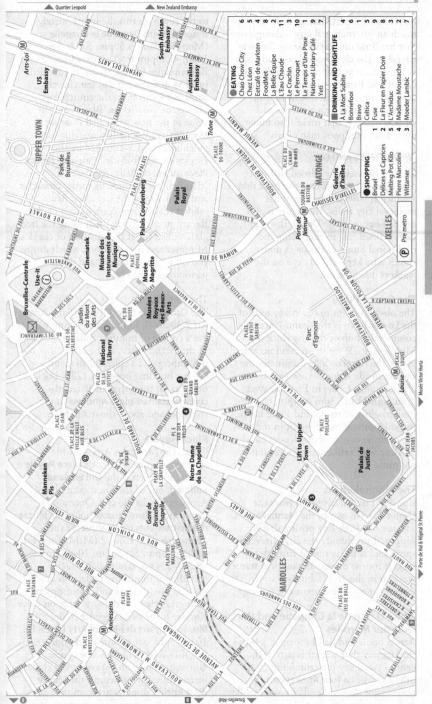

● EATING

Chao Chow City	6
Chez Léon	5
Eetcafé de Markten	4
FoodMet	8
La Belle Equipe	2
L'Eau Chaude	11
Le Crachin	3
Le Perroquet	10
Le Temps d'Une Pose	1
National Library Café	9
Yeti	7

● DRINKING AND NIGHTLIFE

À La Mort Subite	4
Bonnefooi	6
Bravo	1
Celtica	5
Fuse	9
La Fleur en Papier Doré	8
L'Archiduc	3
Madame Moustache	2
Moeder Lambic	7

● SHOPPING

Brüsel	1
Délices et Caprices	2
Melting Pot Kilo	5
Pierre Marcolini	4
Wittamer	3

3

NATO and the EU has made it very much an international city – though one that has little interest in being "branché" (trendy). The city's appeal certainly isn't as immediate as that of its neighbours Ghent and Bruges – and yet a day or two of wandering around reveals rooftop gardens, summer beach parties and vintage markets that make it so much more than the "poor man's Paris".

WHAT TO SEE AND DO

Central Brussels is enclosed within a pentagon of boulevards – the **petit ring** – which follows the course of the medieval city walls. The centre is also divided between the Upper Town and Lower Town, the former being the traditional home of the city's upper classes who kept a beady eye on the workers down below.

The Grand-Place

The obvious point to begin any tour of the **Lower Town** is the **Grand-Place**, the commercial hub of the city since the Middle Ages. With its stupendous spired tower, the **Hôtel de Ville** dominates the square; inside you can view various official rooms (tours in English: Wed 2pm, Sun 11am, 3pm & 4pm; €5). But the real glory of the Grand-Place lies in its **guildhouses**, mostly built in the early eighteenth century, their slender facades swirling with exuberant carving and sculpture.

The Manneken Pis

Rue de l'Etuve leads south from the Grand-Place down to the **Manneken Pis**, a statue of a little boy pissing that's supposed to embody the city's irreverent spirit, and is today one of Brussels' biggest tourist draws. The original statue was cast in the 1600s, but was stolen several times – the current one is a copy.

Notre Dame de la Chapelle and the Quartier Marolles

Across boulevard de l'Empereur, a busy carriageway that scars this part of the centre, you'll spy the crumbling brickwork of **La Tour Anneessens**, a remnant of the medieval city wall, while to the south gleams the immaculately restored **Notre Dame de la Chapelle** (Mon–Fri 9am–6.30pm, Sat & Sun 10am–6.30pm; free), a sprawling Romanesque-Gothic structure founded in 1134 and the city's oldest church. Running south from the church, rue Haute and parallel rue Blaes form the spine of the now gentrified **Quartier Marolles**, traditionally a working-class neighbourhood overlooked by the enormous, scaffold-clad **Palais de Justice**. **Place du Jeu de Balle**, the heart of Marolles, has retained its earthy character and is the site of the city's best **flea market** (daily 7am–2pm; busiest on Sun). Return to the Upper Town using the free glass-walled lift at the junction of rue des Minimes and rue de l'Epee, which drops you off in place Poelaert and offers a panorama of the city.

The Cathédrale

The **Cathédrale** (Mon–Fri 7.30am–6pm, Sat 7.30am–3.30pm, Sun 2–6pm; €1) lies a couple of minutes' walk to the east of the Grand-Place, at the east end of rue d'Arenberg. It's a splendid Brabantine-Gothic building begun in 1220. Look out also for the gorgeous sixteenth-century **stained-glass windows** in the transepts and above the main doors.

Place Royale

Climb the Mont des Arts – a wide stairway ascending towards **place Royale** – and on the left is the **Old England Building**, one of the finest examples of Art Nouveau in the city. Once a department store, it now holds the **Musée des Instruments de Musique**, at rue Montagne de la Cour 2 (MIM; Tues–Fri 9.30am–5pm, Sat & Sun 10am–5pm; €8, 19–25s €6; ⓦmim.be), which contains an impressive collection of musical instruments and a rooftop café with great views of the city. Back on place Royale, at rue de la Régence 3, the **Musées Royaux des Beaux-Arts** (Tues–Fri 10am–5pm, Sat & Sun 11am–6pm; €13, free first Wed of month from 1pm; ⓦfine-arts-museum.be) comprises three interconnecting museums: the **Musée d'Art Ancien** displays art from the

Renaissance to the early nineteenth century, including works by Brueghel and Rubens; the **Musée Fin-de-Siècle** covers art from the mid-nineteenth to the early twentieth century; while the **Musée Magritte** is devoted solely to the work of the Belgian Surrealist.

Northeast of the place Royale, on place des Palais, the haunting remains of the twelfth-century **Palais Coudenberg** (July & Aug Tues–Sun 10am–6pm; Sept–June Tues–Fri 9.30am–5pm, Sat & Sun & 10am–6pm; €6; ⓦcoudenburg.com), once home to Emperor Charles V, can be found beneath the BELvue museum.

Outside the petit ring

Brussels by no means ends with the petit ring. To the east of the ring road are the glass high-rises of the **EU**, notably the winged **Berlaymont** building beside métro Schuman and, nearby, on rue Wiertz 60, the lavish **European Union Parliament** building, which houses the **Parlamentarium** (Mon 1–6pm, Tues–Fri 9am–6pm, Sat & Sun 10am–6pm; free), an interactive multimedia visitors' centre explaining the complex workings of parliament.

Just south of the petit ring is the fashionable Ixelles district, filled with excellent examples of Art Nouveau and Art Deco architecture, as well as chic bars and restaurants. Its northern boundary is home to a large African community known as **Matongé**, named after a district

of Kinshasa in the Congo. Here you can explore the shops of **Galerie d'Ixelles** and sample fried plantain from one of the cafés on rue Longue Vie. To the southwest is the Saint-Gilles suburb where, at 25 rue Américaine, the **Musée Victor Horta** (Tues–Sun 2–5.30pm; €10, students €5; ⓦhortamuseum.be) occupies the innovative Art Nouveau architect's former home.

In the northern municipality of Schaerbeek, the new **Train World** museum, at place Princesse Elisabeth 5 (Tues–Sun 10am–5pm; €10, student €7.50; ⓦtrainworld.be) is a must for train geeks: it's far from dull, however, with unique film footage, props galore and a chance to sleep in a train (see p.98).

To the west of the city centre, at 39–41 Quai du Hainaut, is the new **Mima** (Wed–Sun 10am–6pm; €9.50 ⓦmimamuseum.eu), Brussels' version of the Tate Modern, showcasing thought-provoking contemporary art inside a former brewery.

ARRIVAL AND DEPARTURE

By plane The main airport is in Zaventem (ⓦbrusselsairport.be), 13km northeast of the centre. Trains to the city centre depart every 15min from Level -1 (20min; €8.50). No-frills airlines – principally Ryanair – fly into Charleroi (ⓦcharleroi-airport.com), 55km south of Brussels; shuttle buses leave every 30min for Bruxelles-Midi (1hr; €14 one-way).

By train Brussels has three main train stations – Bruxelles-Nord, Bruxelles-Central and Bruxelles-Midi, each a few minutes apart. Most international trains, including expresses from London, Amsterdam, Paris and Cologne, stop only at Bruxelles-Midi (Brussel-Zuid), roughly 2km southwest of the city centre. Bruxelles-Central is a 5min walk from Grand-Place; Bruxelles-Nord lies in the business area just north of the main ring-road. To transfer from one of the three main stations to another, simply jump on the next available main-line train. Travellers with Eurostar "Any Belgian Station" tickets can do so for free, otherwise you'll have to buy a new ticket.

Destinations Amsterdam CS (hourly; 2hr 30min); Antwerp (every 20–30min; 40min); Bruges (every 30min; 1hr); Ghent (every 30min; 30min); London (every 2hr; 1hr 50min); Luxembourg City (hourly; 3hr); Namur (hourly; 1hr); Ostend (every 30min; 1hr 10min); Paris (hourly; 1hr 30min).

By bus Eurolines (ⓦeurolines.co.uk) buses from London-Victoria arrive and depart at the Bruxelles-Nord station complex.

COMICS IN BRUSSELS

Brussels is a city made for comic book fans. The **Centre Belge de la Bande Dessinée** at 20 rue des Sables (Comic Strip Museum; daily 10am–6pm; €10, ISIC and IYHF card holders €7; ⓦcbbd.be) focuses on Belgian comics such as Tintin, Smurfs and so on. For shopping, head to **boulevard Lemonnier** which boasts ten comic book shops, or Multi BD at boulevard Anspach 122 (Mon–Sat 10.30am–7pm, Sun 12.30–6.30pm). Various walls around the city have been decorated with building-sized scenes from comic strips, and tourist information can supply you with a trail following the major ones.

3

3

BRUSSELS ONLINE

ⓦ **spottedbylocals.com/brussels**
Recommendations for places to eat and
visit from local residents.

ⓦ **bruxelleslabelle.com** Brussels local
shares her favourite haunts from clothes
shops to the best burger bars.

ⓦ **mysecretbrussels.com** Insider's guide
to the city by longtime Brussels resident
and journalist Derek Blyth.

INFORMATION

Tourist office VisitBrussels provides information and runs a
free same-night hotel booking service. It has offices at rue
Royale 2 (daily 9am–6pm; ☎ 02 513 89 40, ⓦ visit.brussels),
in the Hôtel de Ville on the Grand-Place (daily 9am–6pm)
and in the European Parliament (Mon 2–6pm, Tues–Thurs
9am–2pm), with smaller offices on the main concourse of
the Bruxelles-Midi train station (daily 10am–6pm) and in
the arrivals hall at Zaventem airport (daily 6am–9pm).
There's also a Visit Flanders information centre near the
Grand-Place at rue du Marché aux Herbes 61 (daily: April–
Sept 10am–6pm; Oct–March 10am–5pm; Sat & Sun closes
1–2pm). Pick up an Art Nouveau or comic strip trail map for
free at any of these offices. Use-It has an info desk at Galerie
Ravenstein 25 (Mon–Sat 10am–6.30pm; ⓦ brussels.use-it
.travel) with free wi-fi and maps tailored for younger
travellers (best bars, etc).

Discount cards All the tourist offices and some
museums sell the Brussels Card, which grants free entry
to over 30 museums, free use of public transport, and
discounts in selected bars and shops. It costs €22/30/38
for 1/2/3 days.

Listings Bruzz, published weekly in English and stocked
in tourist offices, has concert, film and exhibition listings.
Agenda is a useful English-language listings magazine,
available free in many hotels, hotels and shops. *Use-It*
annotated maps, free in hostels and tourist information
offices, are also extremely helpful.

GETTING AROUND

Central Brussels is easily walkable, but to reach some of
the outlying attractions you'll need public transport. The
system, called STIB (ⓦ stib-mivb.be), includes bus, tram,
métro and prémétro (underground trams) lines. Services
run from 6am until midnight, after which night buses take
over. A single flat-rate ticket costs €2.10 if bought before
you travel from kiosks or ticket machines, or €2.50 from
the driver (bus, prémétro or tram only). Alternatively, buy
a MOBIB card (€5), and add a JUMP ticket to it, available for
24/48/72hr and costing €7.50/14/18.

By taxi Hire a taxi from ranks around the city – notably
outside the train stations, on Bourse and place de

Brouckère; to book, phone Taxis Verts (☎ 02 349 49 49).
After 10pm, you pay an initial €4.40 and then €1.66/km.

By bike Villo! the city bike rental scheme, allows you to
pick up a bike at 180 locations around the city centre and
drop it off elsewhere at a very cheap rate. Full details are
on ⓦ villo.be and in the *Train & Vélo* leaflet (available at
stations).

ACCOMMODATION

HOSTELS

2Go4 bd Emile Jacmainlaan 99 ☎ 02 219 30 19, ⓦ 2go4
.be; ⓜ Rogier/De Brouckère. Excellent hostel with helpful
staff. TV snug and kitchen are bright and trendily decorated
with vintage finds, though the communal rooms and
reception are closed 1–4pm. Breakfast not included, but
you can help yourself to free hot drinks. Large groups (of
over six) not admitted. Dorms €18

Brxxl 5 Woeringenstraat 5 ☎ 025 02 37 100, ⓦ brxxl5
.com. New hotel/hostel ten minutes' walk from Midi-Zuid
station. All en-suite rooms have a/c, free wi-fi and
flatscreen TVs. No breakfast, vending machines. Dorms
€18, doubles €55

★ **Grand Place Hostel** Haringstraat 6–8 ☎ 02 219 30 19,
ⓦ 2go4.be; ⓜ Bourse/Gare Centrale. Situated on a side
street just off the Grand-Place, this is the best-located
hostel in the city. Dorms are finished to a high standard and
the en-suite bathrooms are positively luxurious. Kitchen
available. Bedding is included, but no breakfast. Dorms €18

Hello Hostel rue de l'Armistice 1 ☎ 0471 93 59 27,
ⓦ hello-hostel.eu; ⓜ Simonis. Snug, homely option in the
northwest of town, just outside the petit ring. Breakfast
area doubles as a common room and there are games,
books and a huge DVD collection. No laundry and doesn't
accept groups of more than six, but bedding and breakfast
are included. Dorms €21, doubles €55

Jacques Brel rue de la Sablonnière 30 ☎ 02 218 01 87,
ⓦ lesaubergesdejeunesse.be; ⓜ Botanique. Comfortable
HI hostel with a mix of en-suite dorm rooms. The free
organic breakfast is served in a fresh, bright communal
area. Laundry, games and *Babel Bar* (daily 7am–1am)
serving snacks and good beers. Bedding included. Rates
cheaper for under-26s. Dorms €24, doubles €56

★ **Meininger** quai du Hainaut 33 ☎ 025 88 14 74,
ⓦ meininger-hotels.com. Brilliant new hotel/hostel inside
a former red-brick brewery. Carbon neutral and with loft-
style rooms, there's lots of art, exposed brick walls and a
trendy bar. Family rooms too. Pets allowed. Dorms €16,
doubles €134

Train Hostel ave Georges Rodenbach 6 ☎ 02 808 61 76,
ⓦ trainhostel.be; tram #92 to Gare de Schaerbeek. A
hostel inside a train! Attached to the new Train World
museum (see p.97) at Schaerbeek, 30min north of the
centre, this quirky hostel has dorms kitted out with
authentic railway fittings including old dial-up telephones.

It's worth upgrading to a cabin or suite to sleep in an authentic railway carriage. Dorms €25, doubles €99

HOTELS

Theater Hotel rue van Gaver 23 ☎02 350 90 00, ⓦtheaterhotelbrussels.com; ⓜYser. It might be in the red-light district, but the excellent rooms at this hip boutique hotel mean you soon forget the seedy setting. Doubles €60

EATING

Brussels has an international reputation for its food, and even at the dowdiest snack bar you'll find well-prepared *Bruxellois* dishes featuring fusions of Walloon and Flemish cuisine. FoodMet at rue Ropsy Chaudron 24, to the left of Anderlecht Abbatoir (Fri–Sun 7am–2pm; ⓦfoodmet.brussels), is a new food market, ideal for picnic supplies.

CAFÉS

Eetcafé de Markten place du Vieux Marché aux Grains 5; ⓜSte-Catherine. Vibrant café offering good-quality hearty salads, sandwiches and soups at very reasonable prices. Mon–Sat 8.30am–midnight, Sun 10am–6pm.

L'Eau Chaude rue de Renards 25 ⓦleauchaude.be. Fill up at this cooperative vegetarian canteen where a plat du jour costs €9 during the week and €11 on Sundays. Breakfast available too. Thurs–Sun 10am–6pm.

National Library Café bvld de l'Empereur 2 ☎02 51 95 311. A secret spot that's calm not chic. The food is simple and cheap, but the views of the Hotel de Ville and an organic rooftop garden selling its produce (Mon, Wed & Fri 1–2pm) make it a real gem. Mon–Fri 9am–4pm.

Yeti rue de Bon Secours 4–6 ⓦiloveyeti.be; ⓜBourse. Eco-conscious café which uses only organic, local and/or Fairtrade products. Good breakfasts, sandwiches (€6), teas and popular for Sunday brunch. Thurs–Sat 9am–10pm, Sun 10am–5pm.

RESTAURANTS

Chao Chow City bd Anspach 89; ⓜBourse. Chinese food never came so cheap! Offers two dishes for either €4 at lunchtime or €6 in the evening. Options are typed up and posted on a piece of paper in the window. Daily noon–midnight.

Chez Léon rue des Bouchers 18 ⓦnl.chezleon.be; ⓜBruxelles-Central. Touristy, but worth a visit for their reliably tasty mussels. Ask for the Formule Leon which includes 500g of mussels, chips and a beer for a bargain €16. Daily 11.30am–11pm.

La Belle Équipe rue Antoine Dansaert 202 ☎02 502 11 02; ⓜPorte de Flandre. Authentic pizzeria which specializes in gourmet toppings (pizzas around €12). Everyone dines on one long bar top. Delivery service available. Daily 9am–10pm.

★**Le Crachin** rue de Flandre 12 ⓦlecrachin.net; ⓜSte-Catherine. Breton crêperie serving home-made sweet and savoury buckwheat pancakes and mugs of cider. Mains €12. Mon–Fri noon–2.30pm & 6.30–10.30pm, Sat & Sun noon–10.30pm.

Le Perroquet rue Watteeu 31; ⓜLouise. Come to this lively Art Nouveau café where they serve up good-value pittas and salads (€7–14). Tues–Sat noon–11.30pm, Mon & Sun noon–10.30pm.

Le Temps d'Une Pose rue de Laeken 116 ⓦletempsdunepose.be. Cracking local restaurant run by Sandrine who dishes up Belgian classics such as *stoemp* for €9, or the dish of the day for €8. Mon–Fri 7am–6pm.

DRINKING AND NIGHTLIFE

Brussels' bars are a joy. St-Géry, just to the west of Bourse, is the place to drink, especially during summer when bars spill out into the square. Rue du Marché au Charbon is the hub of gay nightlife.

BARS

À La Mort Subite rue Montagne aux Herbes Potagères 7 ⓦalamortsubite.com; ⓜGare Centrale. Atmospheric 1920s bar, famous for its Gueuze and Kriek beers. Mon–Sat 11am–1am, Sun noon–midnight.

Bonnefooi rue des Pierres 8 ⓦbonnefooi.be; Prémétro Bourse. Live music every night at this hip bar and a great atmosphere in summer when the crowds mingle on the street. Mon–Thurs & Sun 4pm–4am, Fri & Sat 4pm–8am.

★**Bravo** rue d'Alost 7 ⓦbravobxl.com. Industrial-style café that hides a banging basement jazz club where concerts are held almost daily: it also serves tapas (€4–9). Mon–Fri 9am–late, Sat & Sun 10.30am–late.

Celtica rue du Marché aux Poulets 55 ⓦcelticpubs.com; Prémétro Bourse. Football on big screens, DJs playing nightly from 11pm and the cheapest happy-hour prices in town – Trappist monastery beers just €3, beer on tap €1 1pm–midnight. Daily 1pm–late.

★**La Fleur en Papier Doré** rue des Alexiens 55 ⓦlafleurenpapierdore.be; ⓜGare Centrale. Traditional Belgian "brown" bar that was a favourite haunt of Hergé and Magritte. Serves Lambic beer the traditional way, in ceramic mugs. Tues–Sat 11am–midnight, Sun 11am–7pm.

L'Archiduc rue Antoine Dansaert 6 ⓦarchiduc.net; Prémétro Bourse. A pioneer of jazz in Belgium, this legendary Art Deco bar really gets going around midnight, earlier at weekends (5–7pm) – ring the doorbell to get in. Check out the beautiful purple Cointreau Teese cocktail created by burlesque artist Dita Von Teese. Daily 4pm–5am.

Moeder Lambic place Fontainas 8 ⓦmoederlambic.com; Prémétro Anneessens. Excellent place to try Belgium's many brews, with 46 beers on tap, including Brussels-brewed Cantillon – all served to you in snug wooden booths. Mon–Thurs & Sun 11am–1am, Fri & Sat 11am–2am.

3

CLUBS

Fuse rue Blaes 208 Ⓦ fuse.be; Ⓜ Gare du Midi. Get out your glow sticks at Belgium's finest techno club, which hosts some of the word's top DJs. Entry €58 before midnight, €12 after. Sat 11pm–7am.

Madame Moustache quai aux Bruler 5–7, Ⓦ madamemoustache.be. Hosts live bands from indie to garage and is very fond of a themed dance evening. Entry €5, €7 after midnight. Tues–Sat 8pm–4am.

SHOPPING

Aside from the Marolles flea market (see p.96), rue Blaes and rue Haute are lined with a mix of affordable and expensive antiques shops. High-street labels can be found on and around rue Neuve.

Brüsel blvd Anspach 100 Ⓦ brusel.com. Comic shop that stocks more than 8,000 new comic issues and specializes in French underground editions. Mon–Sat 10.30am–6.30pm, Sun noon–6.30pm.

Délices et Caprices rue des Bouchers 68, Ⓦ the -belgian-beer-tasting-shop.be. Central shop selling speciality beers. The owner, Pierre, can help you navigate through the hundreds of different brews on offer. Thurs– Mon 2–8pm.

Melting Pot Kilo rue Haute 154. Ladies roll up your sleeves – here you can rummage through piles of vintage clothes and pay just €15 per kilo. Daily 10am–6pm.

Pierre Marcolini rue des Minimes 1 (pl du Grand Sablon). Multi award-winning *chocolatier* renowned for his very posh, pretty and pricey "haute" creations and inventive flavour combinations. Mon–Thurs & Sun 10am–7pm, Fri & Sat 10am–8pm.

Wittamer pl du Grand Sablon 12. Esteemed *pâtissier* and *chocolatier* that's been around since 1910 and boasts the royal stamp of approval. Mon 9am–6pm, Tues–Sat 7am–7pm, Sun 7am–6.30pm.

DIRECTORY

Embassies Australia, av des Arts 56 ☎ 02 286 05 00 Ⓜ Trone; Canada, av de Tervuren 2 ☎ 02 741 06 11 Ⓜ Merode; Ireland, chaussée d'Etterbeek 180 ☎ 02 282 34 00 Ⓜ Schuman; New Zealand, 7th Floor, av des Nerviens 9–31 ☎ 02 512 10 40 Ⓜ Schuman; South Africa, rue Montoyer 17–19 ☎ 02 285 44 00 Ⓜ Trone; UK, av d'Auderghem 10 ☎ 02 287 62 11 Ⓜ Schuman; USA, bd du Régent 27 ☎ 02 811 40 00 Ⓜ Arts-Loi/Kunst-Wet.

Left luggage Self-service lockers at all three main train stations.

Pharmacy Multipharma, rue du Marché aux Poulets 37 (☎ 02 511 35 90; Mon–Fri 9.30am–6.30pm, Sat 10am–6pm).

Post office Gare du Midi, exit rue Fonsy (Mon–Fri 8am–7.30pm, Sat 10.30am–4.30pm).

Northern Belgium

Almost entirely **Flemish-speaking**, the region to the north of Brussels has a distinctive and vibrant cultural identity, its pancake-flat landscapes punctuated by a string of fine historic cities. These begin with **Antwerp**, a large old port that flourished during the sixteenth century and is now Flanders' most forward-thinking city, followed by **Ghent** and **Bruges**, which became prosperous during the Middle Ages on the back of the cloth trade. All three cities have great restaurants and a lively bar scene.

ANTWERP

ANTWERP, Belgium's second city, and the de facto capital of Flemish Belgium, fans out from the east bank of the Scheldt River about 50km north of Brussels. Many people prefer it to the capital; it is an immediately attractive place, famous for Rubens, fashion, diamonds and the best nightlife in Belgium.

WHAT TO SEE AND DO

At the centre of Antwerp is the spacious **Grote Markt**, where the conspicuous **Brabo fountain** features a bronze of Silvius Brabo, the city's first hero, depicted flinging the hand of the giant Antigonus – who terrorized passing ships – into the Scheldt. The north side of Grote Markt is lined with daintily restored sixteenth-century **guildhouses**, while the west is hogged by the handsome **Stadhuis (Town Hall)**.

Onze Lieve Vrouwe Kathedraal

Southeast of Grote Markt, the **Onze Lieve Vrouwe Kathedraal** (Mon–Fri 10am–5pm, Sat 10am–3pm, Sun 1–4pm; €6; Ⓦ dekathedraal.be) is one of the finest Gothic churches in Europe, dating from the middle of the fifteenth century. Four paintings by Rubens, including his masterpieces *Elevation of the Cross* and *Descent from the Cross*, are displayed here.

DRINKING AND NIGHTLIFE

Ampere	5
Café d'Anvers	1
De Duifkens	6
Hopper	7
Jazzcafé De Muze	4
Kathedraalcafé	3
Quinten Matsijs	2

EATING

Caravan	1
Comme Soupe	3
De Taloorkes	2
Fabiola	6
Fritkot Max	4
Kapitein Zeppos	7
Native	5

ACCOMMODATION

Abhostel	2
Alias	4
Pulcinella	3
Wake Up Sandwich	1
Zero Star Pension	5

ANTWERP

Koninklijk Museum voor Schone Kunsten (closed until 2018) & 7

Plantin-Moretus Museum

The newly refurbished UNESCO-listed **Plantin-Moretus Museum** at Vrijdagmarkt 22–23 (Tues–Sun 10am–5pm; €8; ⓦmuseumplantinmoretus.be) occupies the grand old mansion of Rubens' father-in-law, the printer Christopher Plantin. It provides a beautiful, richly decorated setting for two of the oldest printing presses in the world.

MoMu and Museum voor Schone Kunsten

In the heart of the city's fashion quarter along Nationalestraat, **MoMu** (Tues–Sun 10am–6pm; €8; ⓦmomu.be) showcases some of the avant-garde fashion for which the city is famous, with displays ranging from sixteenth-century lace dresses to pieces by Dries van Noten.

About fifteen minutes' walk further south at Leopold de Waelplaats, the **Koninklijk Museum voor Schone Kunsten** (Royal Museum of Fine Arts; ⓦkmska.be) has one of the country's best fine-art collections: it's currently closed for renovation (check website for the latest reopening date).

North of the Grote Markt

The impressively gabled **Vleeshuis** (Tues–Sun 10am–5pm; €5) is a short walk north of the Grote Markt. Built for the guild of butchers in 1503 and distinguished by its striped brickwork, it now holds a permanent exhibition covering 600 years of music and dance. Just north of here, along Vleeshouwersstraat, the elegant nave at the sixteenth-century **St Pauluskerk** (April–Oct Mon–Sat 2–5pm, Nov–Mar Sat–Sun 2–5pm; free) is decorated by a series of paintings depicting the Fifteen Mysteries of the Rosary, including Rubens' exquisite *Scourging at the Pillar* of 1617.

Rubenshuis and St Jacobskerk

Ten minutes' walk east of the Grote Markt is the **Rubenshuis**, at Wapper 9 (Tues–Sun 10am–5pm; €8; ⓦrubenshuis .be); the former home and studio of Rubens, it's now restored as a very popular museum. On his death in 1640, Rubens was buried in the chapel behind the high altar at **St Jacobskerk**, just to the north at Lange Nieuwstraat 73

3

(April–Oct daily 2–5pm; €3). The church features one of his last works, *Our Lady Surrounded by Saints*, featuring himself as St George, his two wives as Martha and Mary, and his father as St Jerome.

Het Eilandje

The docks north of the city centre are home to **MAS** (Museum aan de Stroom; Tues–Fri 10am–5pm, Sat & Sun 10am–6pm, last entry 1hr before closing time; permanent collection €5, temporary exhibitions €10, free entry last Wed of every month; ⓦmas.be), which brings together the collections of the former Ethnographic, National Shipping and Folklore museums in a dynamic display spread over floors four to eight. The top floor offers superb panoramic views of the city. Nearby at Montevideostraat 3, the **Red Star Line Museum** (Tues–Sun 10am–5pm; €8; ⓦredstarline.org) explores the lives and journeys taken by families sailing on the Red Star Line ocean liners which departed from Antwerp's docks for the USA between 1873 and 1934.

ARRIVAL AND DEPARTURE

By train Antwerp has two main-line train stations: Berchem and Centraal. The latter, located about 2km east of the Grote Markt, is the one you want for the city centre.

Destinations Bruges (hourly; 1hr 30min); Brussels (every 20min; 45min); Ghent (every 30min; 1hr).

INFORMATION

Tourist information Grote Markt 13 (Mon–Sat 9am–5.45pm, Sun 9am–4.45pm; ⓣ03 232 01 03, ⓦvisitantwerpen.be). Centraal Station also has a kiosk.

Discount cards Tourist offices sell the Antwerp City Card: it costs €27/35/40 for 24/48/72hr, and grants free access to all city museums and churches, free public transport use and discounts on attractions and bike rental.

GETTING AROUND

A flat-rate one-way ticket on any part of the city's transport system costs €3; a 24hr pass (*dagpas*) is €6 (€8 on board).

By tram/metro Antwerp is easily traversed on foot, but there are very good metro and tram services covering the city. Trams #9 and #15 (direction Linkeroever) run from the tram station beside Centraal Station to the centre; get off at Groenplaats.

ACCOMMODATION

Many mid-priced and budget establishments are around Centraal Station, where you should exercise caution at night.

★**Abhostel** Kattenberg 110 ⓣ0473 57 01 66, ⓦabhostel.com. Chic, family-run hostel a 15min walk from the centre. Each room has cool artwork on the walls. Rooftop terrace, kitchen and lounge with DVDs. Breakfast (with eggs) included. Dorms €20, doubles €50

Alias Provinciestraat 256 ⓣ03 230 05 22, ⓦaliasyouthhostel.com. Modernized hostel 2km from the centre. There's a homely TV room with adjoining breakfast room. Breakfast and bedding are included. Cash only. Dorms €21.50, doubles €50

Pulcinella Bogaardeplein 1 ⓣ03 234 03 14, ⓦjeugdherbergen.be. Sleek black-and-white minimalist hostel. Four- and six-bed en-suite dorms have individual reading lights and lockers. Stylish bar downstairs but no kitchen. Breakfast and sheets included; towels €6. Dorms €28, doubles €61

Zero Star Pension Minkelersstraat ⓣ078 05 40 50, ⓦhostelworld.com. Only open mid-June to Aug, this converted gas factory, 3km from the centre, offers the cheapest beds in town and includes an organic breakfast too: sheets €4 extra. Dorms €20

EATING

Antwerp is full of informal café-restaurants. Several of the best are clustered on Suikerrui and Grote Pieter Potstraat near the Grote Markt, and there's another concentration around Hendrik Conscienceplein. For fast food, try the kebab and falafel places on Oude Koornmarkt, or, of course, any of the *frituurs*.

CAFÉS AND SNACK BARS

★**Caravan** Damplein 17. The new owners here have spruced up the decor and revamped the menu to offer home-made breakfasts and lunch plus dinners with ingredients from New York to Japan. Mains €5–12. Wed–Fri 11am–11pm, Sat & Sun 10am–11pm.

Comme Soupe Hendrik Conscienceplein 11. Recommended by locals, this cute-as-a-button rustic bar serves sandwiches plus 3 different soups daily (€5), all cooked by the patron, Charlotte. Mon–Fri 11.30am–5pm, Sat 11.30am–6pm.

★**TREAT YOURSELF**

Wake-Up Sandwich Hoogstraat 68 ⓣ03 225 16 06, ⓦwakeupsandwich.be. Bright, well-located hotel, with breakfast in the lovely café downstairs included. The rooms sleeping four are a good deal. Book in advance in summer. Singles €53, doubles €87, quads €120

Fabiola Sint-Antoniusstraat 4. A rustic café with a fantastic range of croque monsieurs (€4–7). Sweet and savoury, traditional and gourmet – they're all here. Mon–Fri 10am–5pm, Sat 10am–7.30pm.

Fritkot Max Groenplaats 12. It doesn't look like much but this place might just serve the best chips in town (cornets cost €3) – ideal for a quick refuel between sightseeing. Daily noon–midnight.

RESTAURANTS

De Taloorkes Lange Koepoortstraat 61. Five minutes' walk from Grote Markt but a world away from its touristy offerings, this locals' restaurant serves mouth-watering stews and mussels for €15. Sun–Wed 11am–10pm, Thurs–Sat 11am–11pm.

Kapitein Zeppos Vleminckveld 78. Named after a famous 1960s cartoon hero, this restaurant has exposed brick walls, chunky wooden tables and excellent food – the €12 *dagschotel* is great value for money. Cash only. Mon–Fri 10am–10pm, Sat–Sun 11am–11pm.

★ **Native** Munstraat 8. Fancy a treat? Currently *the* place to go, this rustic café/restaurant serves inventive organic, seasonal food for around €16 a main. Great ambience. Tues & Wed 11am–6pm, Thurs–Sat 11am–9pm.

DRINKING AND NIGHTLIFE

BARS

De Duifkens Graanmarkt 5. A great place to try local beer Bolleke Koninck. Rumour has it the former owner's ashes are stored in the urn that sits on top of the fireplace! Daily 11am–midnight.

Hopper Leopold de Waelstraat 2 ⓦcafehopper.be. Best jazz bar in town, with live sessions on Mon at 9pm, Sun at 4pm and Oct–April Tues 9pm. Mon–Wed & Sun 10am–2am, Thurs–Sat 10am–3am.

Kathedraalcafé Torfbrug 10. Hard by the cathedral, this old bar is touristy but still worth visiting for the kitsch, nineteenth-century statues of the Virgin Mary that cram the interior. Daily 10am–late.

Quinten Matsijs Moriaanstraat 17. Established in 1545, this is Antwerp's oldest bar. The regal dark-wood interior is ideal for a quiet, relaxed drink of the local brew Triple d'Anvers, while the *hapjes* (appetizers) are hearty and delicious too. Wed–Sun noon–11pm.

CLUBS

Ampere Simonsstraat 21 ⓦampere-antwerp.com. Creative space beneath the railway tracks, just south of Centraal Station, that transforms into a club at weekends. They aim to mimic Berlin's underground music scene – and even have a piece of the wall to prove it. Good international DJs. Fri–Sat 11pm–7am.

Café d'Anvers Verversrui 15 ⓦwww.cafe-d-anvers.com. Club housed in a sixteenth-century church in the red-light

district. Mainly house music. Tickets can be bought online and range from €7–15. Thurs 11pm–6am, Fri & Sat 11pm–7.30am.

Jazzcafé De Muze Melkmarkt 15 ⓦjazzcafedemuze.be. Renowned jazz bar that puts on free live performances. Mon–Sat at 10pm and Sun at 3pm. Mon–Fri 11am–1am, Sat & Sun 11am–3am.

SHOPPING

Antwerp offers superb fashion shopping. High-street labels can be found along Meir and Huidevettersstraat, while Kammenstraat is good for vintage clothes shops. The haute-couture boutiques congregate around Nationaalstraat, Kammenstraat and Steenhouwersvese. Pricey antiques and cavernous junk shops can be found along Kloosterstraat.

DIRECTORY

Left luggage Self-service lockers in the Centraal train station under the stairs.

Post office Groenplaats 43 (Mon–Fri 9am–6pm, Sat 9am–3pm).

GHENT

The largest town in Western Europe during the thirteenth and fourteenth centuries, **GHENT** (Gent) was once at the heart of the medieval Flemish cloth trade. It's now the third-largest city in Belgium, and rivals Bruges thanks to its beautiful canals and well-preserved medieval architecture – without the stifling tourism.

WHAT TO SEE AND DO

A captivating university town with a spirited nightlife and its own **castle**, Ghent's main appeal lies in wandering the cobbled streets which line the canalside and sampling the city's bars.

Sint-Baafsplein

Ghent is famous for its three towers in a row. The first of these – and the best place to start exploring – is the mainly Gothic **Sint-Baafskathedraal**, squeezed into the corner of St Baafsplein (April–Oct Mon–Sat 8.30am–6pm, Sun 1–6pm; Nov–March Mon–Sat 8.30am–5pm, Sun 1–5pm; ⓦsintbaafskathedraal .be). Inside, a small chapel holds Ghent's greatest treasure, the altarpiece of the **Adoration of the Mystic Lamb** (April–Oct Mon–Sat 9.30am–5pm, Sun 1–5pm;

3

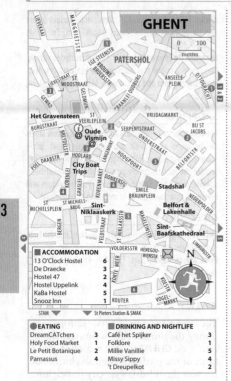

GHENT

ACCOMMODATION	
13 O'Clock Hostel	6
De Draecke	3
Hostel 47	2
Hostel Uppelink	4
KaBa Hostel	5
Snooz Inn	1

● EATING			■ DRINKING AND NIGHTLIFE	
DreamCATchers	3		Café het Spijker	3
Holy Food Market	1		Folklore	1
Le Petit Botanique	2		Millie Vanillie	5
Parnassus	4		Missy Sippy	4
			't Dreupelkot	2

Nov–March Mon–Sat 10.30am–4pm, Sun 1–4pm; €4 includes audioguide), a wonderful, early fifteenth-century painting by brothers Hubert and Jan van Eyck. It's undergoing a five-year restoration, so a panel may be missing.

On the west side of St Baafsplein lurks the medieval **Lakenhalle** (Cloth Hall), a gloomy hunk of a building. One of its entrances leads to the adjoining **Belfort** (Belfry; daily 10am–6pm; €8; ⓦbelfortgent.be), a much-amended edifice dating from the fourteenth century. A lift climbs up to the roof for excellent views over the city centre. St Niklaaskerk, at the western end of Emile Braunplein, completes the trio.

The Graslei and Patershol

The **Graslei** forms the eastern side of the old city harbour and is home to a splendid series of medieval guildhouses. On warm days it's packed with students sunning themselves, and is the departure point for

fifty-minute boat tours (€7 in cash) along the canals. Nearby just to the north are the narrow cobbled lanes and alleys of the **Patershol**, a pocket-sized district that was formerly home to the city's weavers, but is now Ghent's main restaurant quarter. To the west, on Sint-Veerleplein, stands **Het Gravensteen** (Castle of the Counts; April–Oct daily 10am–6pm; Nov–March 9am–5pm; €10 includes movieguide), a spectacular twelfth-century castle, now a chilling torture museum.

SMAK and STAM

Strolling south from the centre along Ghent's main shopping street, Veldstraat, it takes about twenty minutes to reach the former casino, now home to **SMAK**, Jan Hoetplein 1 (Mon–Fri 9.30am–5.30pm, Sat & Sun 10am–6pm; €8; ⓦsmak.be), a contemporary art museum known for its adventurous exhibitions.

Just north, across the canal at Godshuizenlaan 2, **STAM** (Mon–Fri 9am–5pm, Sat & Sun 10am–6pm; €8; ⓦstamgent.be) details the city's history via an array of artefacts, weapons, costumes and coins.

ARRIVAL AND DEPARTURE

By train Of Ghent's two train stations, Gent-Sint-Pieters, about 2km south of the city centre, is the handiest for town.
Destinations Antwerp (every 30min; 50min); Bruges (every 20min; 20min); Brussels (every 30min; 40min); Ostend (every 30min; 40min).
By bus The Flibco (ⓦflibco.com) shuttle bus from Charleroi airport takes 1hr 20min; tickets €5–15.

INFORMATION

Tourist information Oude Vismijn, Sint-Veerleplein 5 (daily: mid-March to mid-Oct 9.30am–6.30pm; mid-Oct to mid-March 9.30am–4.30pm; ☏09 266 56 60, ⓦvisitgent.be).
Discount cards The CityCard Gent grants free entry to all of the city's main museums and monuments, free use of public transport and a complimentary canal cruise. It costs €30 for 48 hours, or €35 for 72 hours, and can be bought from the tourist office, hotels, participating museums and offices of the public transport company De Lijn.

GETTING AROUND

By tram Trams depart from outside the train station. Tram #1 (direction Evergem or Wondelgem) runs up to the Korenmarkt, in the centre of town, every few minutes. The single journey flat-rate fare is €3; validate the ticket at the machine once you get on.

ACCOMMODATION

The tourist office publishes a comprehensive brochure detailing local accommodation, and operates a free hotel booking service. You can also ask them about camping options out to the west of town.

★ **13 O'Clock Hostel** Universiteitstraat 13 ☎ 047 13 313 13, ⓦ 13oclock.be. Converted university building that offers slick rooms with kitchenettes (no breakfast) right in the centre of town. Towel and linen included. Dorms **€29**, doubles **€60**

De Draecke St Widostraat 11 ☎ 09 233 70 50, ⓦ jeugdherbergen.be. Bang in the historic centre, this newly renovated hostel sports lots of beachy wood panelling, a bar and lounge. There's no kitchen, but bedding (not towels) and breakfast included. Three-course dinner €12. Dorms **€26**, doubles **€60**

Hostel 47 Blekerijstraat 47 ☎ 0478 71 28 27, ⓦ hostel47 .com. Trendy hostel in the north of town. Dorm rooms are finished to a high standard, and their communal showers and sinks are very swanky. No laundry, but breakfast and sheets are included. Cash only. Dorms **€30**, doubles **€69**

Hostel Uppelink Sint-Michielsplein 21 ☎ 09 279 44 77, ⓦ hosteluppelink.com. Excellent eleven-room hostel overlooking the central Korenlei canal. Some dorms (sleeping 2–4) have exposed brick, and one is for women only. Homely lounge and bar too. Fairtrade breakfast and sheets included. Dorms **€22**

KaBa Hostel Filips van Arteveld 35 ☎ 09 233 53 33, ⓦ kabahostel.be; bus #70/72 from train station to Gent Zuid then walk 400m. Fresh, bright and homely nine-room hostel run by couple Bart and Katrijn. Sunny garden and shared kitchen, with work by local artists adorning every wall. Towels €1. Dorms **€24**, doubles **€70**

EATING

Fancier restaurants are concentrated in Patershol, while less expensive options cluster around the Korenmarkt. Check out the new Holy Food Market, at Ottogracht 2 (ⓦ holyfood market.be), a permanent food market inside a sixteenth-century abbey. Thursday is vegetarian day citywide.

★ **TREAT YOURSELF**

Snooz Inn Ham 89 ☎ 0496 24 14 26, ⓦ snoozinn.be. Ultra-modern boutique B&B inside a converted printing house on the edge of the historic centre. Its three stylish rooms have posh showers or steam baths, projection TVs and polished concrete or parquet floors. Breakfast €12.20 extra. Doubles **€118**

DreamCATchers Schepenhuisstraat 17 ⓦ wearedream catchers.be. The Japanese craze for felines and food has reached Ghent. Run by young cat lovers Lana and Evelyne, this café offers coffee with a slice of cake and a cat to cuddle. Check website for opening times.

★ **Le Petit Botanique** Kammerstraat 19 ☎ 09 391 92 09. Part of an urban farming project that grows all its own organic vegetables. There is just one dish of the day, but it's wholesome, delicious and only €11. Reservations recommended. Mon–Fri 11am–9pm, Sat 10am–6pm.

Parnassus Oude Houtlei 122. Unique chance to dine inside a former Franciscan church and rub shoulders with locals at this lunchtime buffet frequented by students, professors and travellers on a budget. Fill up for around €8. Mon–Fri noon–2pm.

DRINKING AND NIGHTLIFE

Ghent boasts an energetic drinking scene thanks to its student population.

BARS

Café het Spijker Pensmarkt 3. Cosy candelit bar housed in a former thirteenth-century leprosy shelter. The terrace at the back has lovely views of the canal. Daily 10am–late.

Folklore Lange Steenstraat. One of Ghent's last true brown cafés. Hard-boiled eggs are served free with the drinks, chamber pots hang from the ceiling, and the clock is turned back one minute every year, so at "last call" at 1am it's actually only 12.30am! Thurs 8am–8pm, Fri 8am–1am, Sat 11am–1am, Sun 10.30am–8pm.

't Dreupelkot Groentenmarkt 12. Cigar-smoking owner Pol has been in charge for more than 40 years at the city's last traditional *jenever* bar. It stocks over 215 flavours, including home-made vanilla, all kept at icy temperatures. Mon–Sat 4pm–late.

CLUBS AND LIVE MUSIC

★ **Millie Vanillie** Sint-Niklaasstraat 2 ⓦ millievanillie .be. Oh-so-hip basement bar/club the owners wanted to

---

GHENT FESTIVAL

For ten days during the second half of July, Ghent transforms into a 24-hour party city as it pulsates with the **Gentse Feesten** (ⓦ gentsefeesten.stad.gent). Stages are set up in all the main squares and blast out every kind of music. Accommodation gets booked up months before the festival, so reserve in advance, and try to avoid visiting immediately afterwards – everything is shut for the next week or so as the city recovers.

name "Matt Damon", but their lawyers wouldn't let them. Dress up and get down to pop and dance music. Fri & Sat 10pm–5am.

Missy Sippy Klein Turkije ⓦ missy-sippy.be. New bar that's quickly gained a huge fan base thanks to its blues jams, poetry evenings and boogie nights. Tickets for some events €12. Tues–Sun 5pm–5am.

DIRECTORY

Pharmacy Apotheek Kouter, Kortedagsteeg 1 (ⓣ 09 225 18 49; Mon–Fri 8.30am–7pm, Sat 9.30am–6.30pm).

Post office Lange Kruisstraat 55 (Mon–Fri 9am–6pm, Sat 9am–3pm).

BRUGES

The reputation of **BRUGES** (Brugge) as one of the most perfectly preserved medieval cities in Europe has made it Belgium's tourist honeypot. Inevitably, the crowds tend to overwhelm the city's charms, but you would be mad to come to Belgium and skip it. Bruges boomed throughout the Middle Ages, its weavers turning English wool into clothing that was exported worldwide. By the end of the fifteenth century, however, the city fell into decline and its unique beauty went unnoticed until it was rediscovered some 400 years later, thanks to the popularity of Georges Rodenbach's novel *Bruges-la-Morte*.

WHAT TO SEE AND DO

The older sections of Bruges fan out from two central squares, Markt and Burg.

Markt

Markt, edged on three sides by nineteenth-century gabled buildings, is the larger of the two squares, an impressive open space flanked to the south by the mighty **Belfort** (Belfry; daily 9.30am–6pm; €10), built in the thirteenth century when the town was at its richest. Its tapering staircase leads up to the roof from where there are spectacular views over the city. Also on the square is the **Historium** (daily 10am–6pm, last tickets 5pm; €13.50, combination ticket with Groeningemuseum €17.50; ⓦ historium .be), which shows what life was like in Bruges during the fifteenth century

through its seven interactive rooms and a new "smart-glasses" tour.

The Burg and the Heilig Bloedbasiliek

From the Markt, Breidelstraat leads through to the **Burg**, whose finest building is the **Heilig Bloedbasiliek** (Basilica of the Holy Blood; April to mid-Nov daily 9.30am–noon & 2–5pm; mid-Nov to Dec Mon, Tues & Thurs–Sun 9.30am–noon & 2–5pm, Wed 9.30am–noon, Sun 9.30–11am & 2–5pm; €2.50; ⓦ holyblood.com). Its Upper Chapel holds a phial of the blood of Christ brought back from Jerusalem by the Crusaders. Stored in a grandiose silver tabernacle, the Holy Blood is still venerated on Ascension Day, when it is carried through the town in a colourful but solemn procession.

The Stadhuis

The **Stadhuis** has a beautiful, turreted sandstone facade, behind which is a magnificent **Gothic Hall** (daily 9.30am–5pm; €4). Nearby, at Burg 11, the former Court of Justice houses an impressive Renaissance ceremonial meeting room **'t Brugse Vrije** (daily 9.30am–12.30pm & 1.30–5pm; €4). Dating from the sixteenth century, it features an enormous oak chimneypiece carved in honour of the ruling Habsburgs.

The Groeningemuseum

The **Groeningemuseum**, at Dijver 12 (Tues–Sun 9.30am–5pm; €8, combination ticket with Historium €17.50), houses a superb collection of Flemish paintings, including several canvases by Jan van Eyck. From 2017, some rooms may be closed, so reduced entrance fees are on offer.

Onze Lieve Vrouwekerk

The **Onze Lieve Vrouwekerk** (Mon–Sat 9.30am–5pm, Sun 1.30–5pm; €6), on Mariastraat, features a delicate marble statue of *Madonna and Child* by Michelangelo and, in the chancel, the exquisite Renaissance mausoleums of Charles the Bold and his daughter Mary of Burgundy.

Sint-Janshospitaal and Begijnhof

Sint-Janshospitaal (Tues–Sun 9.30am–5pm; €8) has been turned into a lavish museum celebrating the city's history in general and the hospital in particular. In addition, the old chapel displays a small but distinguished collection of paintings by **Hans Memling**.

From Sint-Janshospitaal, it's a quick stroll down to the **Begijnhof** (Mon–Sat 10am–6.30pm, Sun 2.30–6.30pm; free), a circle of whitewashed houses around a tidy green that was established in the thirteenth century for pious women who had been widowed by the Crusades. Inside is the **Begijnhuisje** (€2), a small museum detailing daily seventeenth-century life. Nearby is the romantic **Minnewater**, often known as the "Lake of Love".

ARRIVAL AND DEPARTURE

By train Bruges's train station is situated 2km southwest of the centre.

Destinations Antwerp (hourly; 1hr 20min); Brussels (every 30min; 1hr); Ghent (every 20min; 20min); Ostend (every 30min; 15min); Zeebrugge (hourly; 15min).

INFORMATION

Tourist information The main office is in the city concert hall at 't Zand 34 (Mon–Sat 10am–5pm, Sun 10am–2pm; ☎ 05 044 86 86, ⚲ bezoekers.brugge.be), with smaller branches (both daily 10am–5pm) inside the Historium and inside the train station.

Discount card The Brugge City Card (⚲ bruggecitycard .be) grants free access to the main museums and attractions, includes a free canal boat ride and 25 percent discount on bicycle rental and public transport. It costs €47/53 for 48/72hr, and is cheaper for under-26s.

GETTING AROUND

By bus Local buses leave from outside the train station for the main square, the Markt; tickets cost €2 from the driver.

ACCOMMODATION

★ **Lybeer** Korte Vuldersstraat 31 ☎ 050 33 43 55, ⚲ hostellybeer.com. Modern, recently renovated hostel a 10min walk from the train station. Rooms are clean, and the common room cosy. Offers free walking tours themed on the film *In Bruges*, beer tastings and quiz nights. Dorms €30, doubles €110

Passage Dweersstraat 26 ☎ 05 034 02 32, ⚲ passagebruges.com. This hostel has very comfortable,

tasteful rooms sleeping two, three or four people. Breakfast is served in its excellent Art Deco restaurant. Dorms €32, doubles €64

Snuffel Ezelstraat 42 ☎ 050 33 31 33, ⚲ www.snuffel .be. Life at this hostel revolves around its laidback, late-opening bar. Perks include free walking tours, beer tastings every Wed at 7pm, and free concerts in summer. Bedding and breakfast included. Dorms €23, doubles €60

BRUGES

● EATING		■ DRINKING AND NIGHTLIFE	
#FOOD	5	Café Vlissinghe	2
Friterie 1900	3	De Coulissen	4
Oyya	4	Groot Vlaenderen	1
Pas Partout	1	Le Trappiste	3
Vino Vino	2		

● SHOPPING	
The Chocolate Line	3
t'Apostolientje	1
Think Twice	2

■ ACCOMMODATION	
St Christopher's Bauhaus	2
Lybeer	4
Passage	3
Snuffel	1

St Christopher's Bauhaus Langestraat 133–137; reception located at no. 145 ☎05 034 10 93, ⓦst-christophers.co.uk/bruges-hostels. Cheerful hostel with its own nightclub and excellent bar-restaurant. Ask for a "pod" bunk with curtains around it for privacy, power points and locker drawers. Free walking tours. Bedding and breakfast included. Dorms **€20**, doubles **€68**

EATING

★#FOOD Oude Burg 30 ⓦhashtagfood.be. Everything about this place is hip: from the hashtag in the name to the insect burger (€19.50) and healthy juices it serves up. Reservations recommended. Mon, Thurs–Sat noon–3pm & 5–8pm.

Friterie 1900 Markt 35. This simple shop-front counter has been serving up cornets of traditional Belgian *frites* for just €2 to the après-dancing crowd for donkey's years. Daily 10.30am–midnight.

Oyya Noordzandstraat 1. Need a sugar fix? This place serves the best ice cream, waffles (€2) and frozen yogurt with toppings galore. The salted caramel is a must. Daily 10am–11pm.

Pas Partout Jeruzalemstraat 1 ⓦsobo.be. A cash- and lunchtime-only place, 350m from the centre, that serves the cheapest *steak frites* (€10) in town. Dishes are prepared by once-unemployed individuals who are now learning a new trade. Mon–Sat 11.45am–2pm.

Vino Vino Grauwerkersstraat 15. Tattooed owner Achim serves delicious wines accompanied by superb tapas, such as *patatas bravas* and squid cooked in wine (€6–9). Great blues music in the background. Mon–Tues & Thurs–Sun 6pm–midnight.

DRINKING AND NIGHTLIFE

Café Vlissinghe Blekersstraat 2 ⓦcafevlissinghe.be. Open since 1515, this peaceful, tucked-away café is packed with historic relics. Has board games and a large terrace out the back. Cash only. Wed–Sat 11am–10pm, Sun 11am–7pm.

De Coulissen Jakob Van Oostraat 4. Bruges' largest nightclub (it's still small) has guest DJs on Thursdays, party tunes on Fridays and dance and R&B on Saturdays. Thurs–Sat 10pm–6am.

Groot Vlaenderen Vlamingstraat 94. Drag out your smartest pair of travelling trousers/dress for a gin cocktail at this "pre- & after-dinner" bar, which serves more than 70 different type of cocktails. Wed–Sat 5pm–2am, Sun 5pm–midnight.

Le Trappiste Kuipersstraat 33 ⓦletrappistebrugge.be. Choose from more than 100 specialist beers beneath the vaulted exposed-brick arches of this thirteenth-century cellar. It also hosts tasting evenings: check website for upcoming dates. Tues–Sun 5pm–midnight.

SHOPPING

Lace and chocolate are the best gifts to buy in Bruges.

't Apostolientje Balstraat 11. A trusted source for antique lace. Tues 1–5pm, Wed–Sat 9.30am–12.25pm & 1.15–5pm, Sun 9.30am–1pm.

The Chocolate Line Simon Stevinplein 19. Unusual option selling tobacco- and wasabi-flavoured chocolate. Tues–Sat 9.30am–6.30pm, Sun–Mon 10.30am–6.30pm.

Think Twice Sint Jakobsstraat 21. Quaint secondhand vintage shop that has a good turnover of stock. Mon–Sat 10am–6pm, Sun 1–5pm.

DIRECTORY

Internet The city has free wi-fi zones ("ZapFi") in the 't Zand, Markt and Burg squares.

Left luggage Self-service lockers located just inside the train station's main entrance.

Post office Markt 5 (Mon–Fri 9am–6pm, Sat 9am–3pm).

Southern Belgium

South of Brussels lies **Wallonia**, French-speaking Belgium, where a belt of heavy industry interrupts the rolling farmland that precedes the high wooded hills of the **Ardennes**. The latter spreads over three provinces – **Namur** in the west, **Luxembourg** in the south and Liège in the east – and is a great place for hiking and canoeing.

NAMUR

Capital of Namur province, the city of **NAMUR** is a charming place, with an antique centre that boasts a number of first-rate restaurants and bars full of university students. It is also the ideal base from which to explore the Ardennes forest.

WHAT TO SEE AND DO

Straddling the confluence of the rivers Sambre and Meuse, Namur's important strategic location is evidenced by the massive, rambling **citadel** that overlooks the town. One of the largest in Europe, explore it on foot or take the La Citad'n **tourist train** (April–June & mid-Sept to mid-Nov Sat & Sun; July to mid-Sept daily; €2), which departs every twenty minutes from place de l'Ange and rue du Grognon.

At rue de Fer 24 is the **Musée Provincial des Art Anciens**, also known as Trem.A (Tues–Sun 10am–6pm; €3, free first Sun of month), which now houses the Trésor du Prieuré d'Oignies, a spellbinding collection of reliquaries.

In the heart of the old town, at rue Fumal 12, is the **Musée Provincial Félicien Rops** (Tues–Sun 10am–6pm, open Mon July & Aug only; €3, audioguide €2; ⓦwww.museerops.be). Sexually liberated for his generation, Rops pushed the boundaries in his sketches and paintings – look for his saucy *Les Sataniques* series on the second floor.

A general **market** is held every Saturday on rue de Fer and a flea market every Sunday on quai de la Meuse (both 7am–1pm).

ARRIVAL AND DEPARTURE

By train Namur's train station is 500m north of the centre on place de la Station.

Destinations Brussels (every 30min; 1hr); Luxembourg City (hourly; 1hr 40min); Marloie for La Roche-en-Ardenne (hourly; 35min); Melreux for La Roche-en-Ardenne (hourly; 1hr).

INFORMATION

Tourist information Place de la Station (daily 9.30am–6pm; ☏081 24 64 49, ⓦnamurtourisme.be). There's also an info centre inside the Citadelle (daily: April–Sept 10am–6pm; Oct–March 10am–5pm) and inside the Halle Al'Chair at rue du Pont 21 (Jan–March & Oct–Dec Tues–Sun 10am–5pm; April–Sept daily 9.30am–6pm.

GETTING AROUND

By bike Li Bia Velo (ⓦwww.libiavelo.be) has blue bike rental areas around the city. A one-day ticket costs €1; the first 30min is free.
By boat Les Namourettes (July & Aug daily; June & Sept Sat & Sun; €1 one-way; ☏081 24 65 96) are river taxis that ferry passengers across the Meuse and Sambre rivers to the town of Jambes.

ACCOMMODATION

Auberge de Jeunesse av Félicien Rops 8 ☏081 22 36 88, ⓦlesaubergedejeunesse.be. On the southern edge of town, this hostel has doubles and dorms (sleeping 3–5), a bar with a terrace overlooking the river, a communal kitchen, TV room and laundry: it also serves breakfast and

evening meals (mains €5). It's 3km from the train station: walk along the river or take bus #3 or #4 from the centre (€1.75). Sheets and breakfast included. Dorms €25, doubles €62
Gîtes du Vieux Namur rue du Président 32 ☏475 45 76 00, ⓦlesgitesduvieuxnamur.be. Stylish self-catering apartments for stays of two nights or more, located in the centre of old Namur. €85 per night

EATING AND DRINKING

Local specialities include caramels called *biétrumé*, Wépion strawberries, and a sausage roll-like snack called *avisance*.
★**A Table!** rue des Brasseurs 21. Lively café serving organic light bites and veggie options (mains around €13). Tables at the back have views of the Sambre and the citadel. Tues–Wed 11.30am–2.30pm, Thurs–Sat 11.30am–2.30pm & 6.30–9pm.
La Mère Gourmandin rue du Président 13. Try the savoury crêpes (from €12) accompanied by tumblers of home-made cider at this romantic candelit restaurant. Mon–Sat noon–5pm, Sun noon–4pm.
Piano Bar place Marché-aux-Légumes 10. One of Namur's most popular bars, with live jazz on Fri and Sat from 10pm. Mon–Thurs & Sun noon–2am, Fri & Sat noon–4am.
Ursule & Pétula rue de Bruxelles 50. Reassuringly popular with locals, this café specializes in gourmet filled baguettes (€6), tasty soups such as carrot and coconut, and salads. Mon–Fri 11am–2pm.

LA ROCHE-EN-ARDENNE

If you've had enough of Belgian cities or flat landscape, head to the **Ardennes** for a change of scene. While its principal town, **La Roche-en-Ardenne**, is packed in the summer (mostly with young families), it remains one of the area's best bases for outdoor activities, and it's easy to escape into the gorgeous surrounding woods. The only downside is that, aside from the town's fairly impressive **castle ruins** (July & Aug daily 10am–6pm; April–June, Sept & Oct daily 11am–5pm; Nov–March Mon–Thurs 1–4pm; €5.50), there's not a whole lot to distract you if the weather's bad.

ARRIVAL AND DEPARTURE

By train The nearest stations to La Roche are Marloie and Melreux, both around 30min away by bus.
By bus Catch bus #13 from Melreux or #15 from Marloie (both: every 2hr; 35min). Passengers are dropped off in the centre of town.

3

INFORMATION AND TOURS

Tourist information place du Marché 15 (daily 9.30am–5pm, until 6pm July & Aug; ☎ 084 36 77 36, ⓦ la-roche-tourisme.com).

Ardenne Aventures rue de l'Eglise 35 ☎ 084 41 19 00, ⓦ ardenne-aventures.be. Long (€21; 5hr) and short (€16; 1hr 30min) kayak trips year-round, leaving hourly in high season; mountain biking (€25; 1hr); horseriding (€45, 2hr); rafting (Nov–April; €19; 1hr 30min). You can get good rates if you combine two activities on one day.

Brandsport Auberge La Laiterie, Mierchamps 15 ☎ 084 41 10 84, ⓦ brandsport.be. Orienteering (€12.50/half-day); kayaking (€20/half-day); caving (€55/half-day); archery (€25/half-day). Horseriding, abseiling and rock climbing can also be organized.

ACCOMMODATION AND EATING

Camping Le Vieux Moulin Petite Strument 62, about 800m to the south of the town centre along the Val du Bronze ☎ 084 41 13 80, ⓦ strument.com. Huge campsite with a picturesque setting beside a stream. Open March–Oct 31. Per person **€3.50**, plus per tent **€10**

La Stradella place du Marché 2. Garish decor, but the wood-fired Italian pizza is worth it. Very central. Daily 11.30am–2.15pm & 5.45–9.45pm.

Villa Le Monde rue du Nulay 9 ☎ 0496 67 62 19, ⓦ www.villalemonde.com. This family-run B&B in a villa is a short walk from the village centre, with four en-suite rooms, a homely lounge and leafy terrace. Doubles **€88**

Luxembourg

Famous as a tax haven, financial centre and headquarters for various European institutions, the **Grand Duchy of Luxembourg**, one of Europe's smallest sovereign states, unsurprisingly gets written off by many travellers. However, this is a mistake: **Luxembourg City** is incredibly charming and well worth visiting for a night or two.

LUXEMBOURG CITY

LUXEMBOURG CITY is one of the most spectacularly situated capitals in Europe. The valleys of the rivers Alzette and Pétrusse, which meet here, cut a green swathe through the city, their deep canyons formerly key to the city's defences.

WHAT TO SEE AND DO

Luxembourg City divides into four distinct sections: the old town (northern side of the Pétrusse valley), which holds most of the city's sights and is the most appealing quarter; the modern city, where the train station is located; the atmospheric valleys of the **Grund** area (east); and the **Kirchberg** section (northeast), home to sleek European Union buildings.

The old town

The UNESCO-listed old town focuses on two squares: the **place d'Armes**, fringed with cafés and restaurants, and the larger **place Guillaume II**, the venue for Luxembourg's main general market (Wed & Sat from 7am). Nearby, on rue du St-Esprit, the **Musée d'Histoire de la Ville de Luxembourg** (Tues, Wed & Fri–Sun 10am–6pm, Thurs 10am–8pm; €5; ⓦ mhvl.lu) houses a permanent exhibition explaining Luxembourg's history. Further history is on offer at the **Musée National d'Histoire et d'Art** (MNHA), on Marché-aux-Poissons (Tues, Wed & Fri–Sun 10am–6pm, Thurs 10am–8pm; €7; ⓦ mnha.lu), which displays a mish-mash of archeological finds, paintings and sculptures.

A few minutes' walk east of the museum on the montée de Clausen lies the entrance to 17km of underground tunnels known as the **Casemates du Bock** (daily: March & Oct to early Nov 10am–5.30pm; April–Sept 10am–8.30pm; €4), the earliest of which were excavated in 1644 under Spanish control.

The Grund

The dramatic **chemin de la Corniche** runs along the top of the cliff with great views of the slate-roofed houses of the quaint and leafy **Grund** down below. It leads to the gigantic **Citadelle du St-Esprit**, whose top has been levelled off and partly turned into a verdant park. The Grund is especially worth visiting on Wednesday (when students have a half-day) and Friday nights when its bars kick into action.

Kirchberg

Spread over a large area, the east of the city is largely dominated by European Union buildings; among them, at Park Dräi Eechelen 3, is the **Musée d'Art Moderne Grand-Duc Jean** (MUDAM; Wed–Fri 11am–8pm, Sat–Mon 11am–6pm; €7; ⊚mudam.lu). Down the hill from Mudam, at Park Dräi Eechelen 5, is the **Musée Dräi Eechelen** (Mon & Thurs–Sun 10am–6pm, Wed 10am–8pm; €5; ⊚m3e.public.lu), a restored fort detailing the Duchy's history.

A good way to see the city is to take the hour-long tours offered by the hop-on, hop-off **sightseeing bus** which leaves from place de la Constitution (April–Oct daily 9.40am–5.20pm; every 20min; €14, valid for 24hr).

ARRIVAL AND DEPARTURE

By train The train station, a 15min walk south of the old town, is the hub of all the city's bus lines. Buses departing from the depot on rue Aldringen will take you back to the train station.

Destinations Brussels (hourly; 3hr); Cologne (hourly; 5hr); Namur (hourly; 2hr); Nancy (hourly; 2hr); Strasbourg (hourly; 2hr).

INFORMATION

Tourist office place Guillaume II 30 (April–Sept Mon–Sat 9am–7pm, Sun 10am–6pm; Oct–March Mon–Sat 9am–6pm, Sun 10am–6pm; ⊙022 28 09, ⊚lcto.lu).

Discount card The Luxembourg Card grants free entry to 70 museums and tourist attractions nationwide and includes free cross-country travel. It is available for 1/2/3 days and costs €13/20/28.

GETTING AROUND

By bike Vél'oh! ⊚veloh.lu. City rental scheme with 72 stations dotted across town. There's a long-term card or a 7-day ticket. Book the latter and you only pay for what you use. Payment with bank card. First 30min free, then €5/24hr.

ACCOMMODATION

There are plenty of cheap hotels around the train station; you'll pay a little more to stay in the appealing Old Town – see the tourist information website for listings.

Campsite Kockelscheuer route de Bettembourg 22 ⊙047 18 15, ⊚ccclv.lu; bus #5. A well-equipped campsite 4km/20min bus ride from the city centre, with wi-fi, tennis courts, bowling, golf and two restaurants. Open March–Oct. Two nights minimum. Per person €4.50, plus per tent €6

Ibis Styles Centre Gare rue Jospeh Junck 30 ⊙04 92 496, ⊚ibis.com. It may be a chain, but you can't fault its good access to the city centre, and fresh modern interior. Doubles €80

Luxembourg City-Hostel rue du Fort Olisy 2 ⊙026 27 66 650, ⊚youthhostels.lu; bus #9, stop "Plateau Altmunster". Beneath imposing viaduct arches in the Pfaffenthal district, this big, bright HI hostel has four- and six-bed dorms (half en suite), a bar-restaurant with

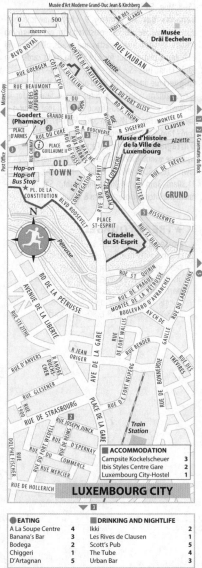

Musée d'Art Moderne Grand-Duc Jean & Kirchberg

LUXEMBOURG CITY

■ ACCOMMODATION	
Campsite Kockelscheuer	3
Ibis Styles Centre Gare	2
Luxembourg City-Hostel	1

●EATING		■ DRINKING AND NIGHTLIFE	
A La Soupe Centre	4	Ikki	2
Banana's Bar	3	Les Rives de Clausen	1
Bodega	2	Scott's Pub	5
Chiggeri	1	The Tube	4
D'Artagnan	5	Urban Bar	3

terrace, plus a pool table, book exchange and laundry. Dorms **€25**, doubles **€60**

EATING

French cuisine is popular here, but traditional Luxembourgish dishes, such as neck of pork with broad beans (*judd mat gaardebounen*), are found on many menus too.

A La Soupe Centre rue Chimay 9. Trendy soup bar just off place Guillaume II. A bowl of tasty soup plus bread costs €5–8. Mon–Fri 10am–7pm, Sat 10am–6pm.

Banana's Bar av Monterey 9. Lively American bar-restaurant whose walls are plastered with old advertising posters. Serves burgers, pastas and salads, all for around €12, and a plat du jour for €10.50. No credit cards. Mon 9am–11pm, Tues–Sat 9am–1am, Sun noon–7pm.

Chiggeri rue du Nord 15. Head upstairs to this bohemian bar-restaurant with funky decor that is famous for its *tartiflette* (€19) and 2200-strong wine list that features in the *Guinness Book of World Records*. Mon–Fri noon–3pm & 7pm–1am, Sat & Sun noon–3am.

D'Artagnan bd du Général Patton 92. Simple restaurant with one winning card: it serves the best horse steak in town (€20.50). Mon 6.30pm–midnight, Tues–Fri 11.30am–3pm & 6.30pm–midnight, Sat 6.30pm–midnight: kitchen closes at 2pm & 10pm.

★ TREAT YOURSELF

Bodega rue du Curé 5a. Adored by locals, this homely Iberian restaurant has personable service and excellent tapas and steaks. The huge helpings of paella are particularly good, as are the fish and lamb chops. Mains around €9.50–22. Mon–Sat 11.30am–2.30pm & 6.30–10.30pm.

DRINKING AND NIGHTLIFE

There's a lively bar scene in the old town and Grund, as well as Les Rives de Clausen, rue Emile Mousel 2 (10min walk from the HI hostel), a cluster of pubs and clubs that gets especially busy on Fri evenings.

Ikki Les Rives de Clausen ⊛ ikki.lu. Locals love this sleek and lively bar in the basement below a smart sushi restaurant. Mon–Thurs 5pm–1am, Fri & Sat 5pm–3am, Sun 3.30pm–1am.

★ Scott's Pub rue Bisserweg 4. Located in the Grund, this Irish bar is the most backpacker-friendly hangout in Luxembourg, with a lovely terrace that attracts a young, expat crowd. Mon–Sat 11am–1am, Sun 11am–midnight.

The Tube rue Sigfroi 8, Old Town. Youthful bar/club named after the London Underground. Most nights live DJs play everything from soul to techno. Mon–Fri 5pm–1am, Sat & Sun 5pm–3am.

Urban Bar rue de la Boucherie 2. One of the coolest bars in town, albeit in an understated way. There are good burgers and a filling dish of the day, and DJs play Wed–Sat. Mon–Thurs 11am–1am, Fri & Sat 11am–2am, Sun 11am–midnight.

DIRECTORY

Embassies UK, bd Joseph II 5 ☎ 02 298 64; US, bd Emmanuel Servais 22 ☎ 04 601 23.

Internet The entire city has a free wi-fi network called "CityLuxFree".

Luggage storage Located on platform 3CD of the train station.

Pharmacies Goedert, place d'Armes 5 (Mon–Sat 9am–5.30pm).

Post office rue Aldringen 25 (Mon–Fri 7am–7pm, Sat 7am–5pm).

Bosnia-Herzegovina

HIGHLIGHTS

❶ Sarajevo One of the friendliest capitals in Europe. **See p.118**

❷ Jajce Adorable Bosnian town with a resident waterfall. **See p.122**

❸ Bihać Rafting centre focused on the River Una. **See p.123**

❹ Mostar Much more than just a bridge. **See p.123**

❺ Trebinje Herzegovina's most appealing town, and another superb bridge. **See p.126**

HIGHLIGHTS ARE MARKED ON THE MAP ON P.115

ROUGH COSTS

Daily budget Basic €25, occasional treat €40

Drink Bosnian coffee €0.50–1

Food *Čevapčići* (meat rissoles) €2–4

Hostel/budget hotel €12/€25

Travel Bus: Sarajevo–Bihać €25; train: Sarajevo–Mostar €5

FACT FILE

Population 3.9 million

Languages Bosnian, Croatian, Serbian

Currency Convertible Mark (BAM or KM)

Capital Sarajevo

International phone code ☎ 387

Time zone GMT +1hr

Introduction

A land where turquoise rivers run swift and sheep huddle on steep hillsides, Bosnia-Herzegovina is one of Europe's most visually stunning corners. With muezzins calling the faithful to prayer under a backdrop of church bells, it also provides a delightful fusion of East and West in the heart of the Balkans. Appropriately, the country is now marketing itself as the "heart-shaped land", unintentionally revealing more perhaps than just the shape of its borders: this remains a country cleaved into two distinct entities, the result of a bloody war in the mid-1990s. However, while Bosnia-Herzegovina was not too long ago making headlines for all the wrong reasons, it's now busily, and deservedly, re-etching itself on the world travel map as a bona fide backpacker magnet of some repute.

Most travellers spend their time in the country's two major draws: Sarajevo and Mostar. **Sarajevo** has shrugged off its years under siege to become one of Europe's most likeable capitals, while the delightful city of **Mostar** is focused on an Old Bridge that, meticulously rebuilt after destruction during the war, must be the most photographed object in the Balkans. There are also some beguiling smaller towns to choose from, such as Bosnia's **Jajce**, or Herzegovina's **Blagaj**, while outdoor enthusiasts will be in their element in **Bihać**, one of Europe's foremost rafting destinations. **Trebinje** is easily the pick of the towns in the Republika Srpska.

CHRONOLOGY

9 AD Annexed by Rome.
395 Division of Roman Empire; the area that comprises today's Bosnia-Herzegovina stays under the rule of Rome.
553 Emperor Justinian I conquers the area for the Byzantine Empire.
1463 Bosnia falls to the Ottoman Empire.
1482 Herzegovina falls to the Ottoman Empire.
1878 Russian defeat of Turkey sees Bosnia-Herzegovina transferred to Austria-Hungary.
1914 Franz Ferdinand shot in Sarajevo by a Bosnian Serb, eventually leading to World War I.
1918 Bosnia-Herzegovina becomes part of the Kingdom of Serbs, Croats and Slovenes.
1961 Ivo Andrić, born near Travnik, wins the Nobel Prize for Literature.
1984 Sarajevo hosts the Winter Olympics.

1985 Emir Kusturica's film, *When Father Was Away on Business*, set in Bosnia, wins the Palme d'Or at Cannes.
1991 Following the fall of Yugoslavia, Croat-Muslim alliance declares independence and makes Sarajevo its capital; Serbs set up their own government just to the east.
1992 Led by Radovan Karadžić, Bosnian Serbs start campaign of "ethnic cleansing".
1993 Fighting breaks out between Croats and Muslims.
1995 NATO shelling ends siege of Sarajevo; peace terms set out by Dayton Agreement.
2001 *No Man's Land* becomes the first Bosnian movie to win an Academy Award.
2008 Radovan Karadžić arrested on charges of war crimes.
2011 Bosnia's Croat, Serb and Muslim political leaders agree to form new central government.
2011 Ratko Mladić arrested and transferred to the War Crimes Tribunal in The Hague.
2016 Radovan Karadžić found guilty of genocide and war crimes in The Hague.

ARRIVAL AND DEPARTURE

As close to landlocked as it's possible to get, Bosnia-Herzegovina is fairly easy to enter from all sides. There is one daily **train** service from Zagreb, in Croatia to Sarajevo. There are currently no trains from Belgrade or Budapest into Bosnia. **Bus** connections are more numerous and points of origin include Belgrade and Novi Sad in Serbia, and Split, Dubrovnik and Zagreb in Croatia. There are currently no direct **flights** from the UK to Bosnia, but a number of budget carriers fly to Zagreb (see p.159), Zadar

HIGHLIGHTS
1. Sarajevo
2. Jajce
3. Bihać
4. Mostar
5. Trebinje

4

(see p.167) and Dubrovnik (see p.178), from where you can get an onward bus.

GETTING AROUND

Bosnia-Herzegovina isn't the easiest country to get around, since much of its transport infrastructure – particularly the rail network – was damaged during the war. Things are improving, however, and decent **bus** services will almost always be able to get you where you want; it'll just take a little longer than you might expect. Connections between the Federation and the Republika Srpska aren't regular.

There are also a few **railway** lines across the country, though severe underfunding means that most trains are too slow or irregular to be worth considering; the one exception is the twice-daily route linking

Sarajevo and Mostar, which is fabulously scenic.

ACCOMMODATION

There are plenty of **hostels** in Sarajevo and Mostar (dorm beds cost around €12), as well as **private rooms** in these cities, though they're pretty rare elsewhere. Otherwise, **hotel** accommodation is pretty cheap – you should always be able to find a room in the €25–35 range. **Guesthouses** (*pansiona*) are available in some towns, though are nowhere near as numerous as in neighbouring countries. Free **wi-fi** is now almost standard in accommodation. There are a few **campsites** dotted around, most with reasonable facilities (ⓦen .camping.info/bosnia-herzegovina /campsites). The possible presence of

A TALE OF TWO ENTITIES

Travellers should be aware that, in many ways, Bosnia-Herzegovina functions as two separate countries. These are not Bosnia and Herzegovina, as one might infer from the name, since these are geographical regions (Bosnia makes up around 80 percent of the country, with Herzegovina a small triangle south of Sarajevo). Rather, the country is split along ethnic lines. To the west, and including Sarajevo, is the **Federation of Bosnia and Herzegovina**, a Muslim-Croat alliance; while to the east and north is the **Republika Srpska**, an ethnic-Serb territory of almost equal size, centred on its capital Banja Luka. To add to the confusion, there are three official languages – all essentially the same – and three presidents. "Most countries just have one idiot in charge", says a local, "but we've got three."

unexploded mines from the war means that wild camping is not a good idea.

FOOD AND DRINK

Centuries of Ottoman rule have left Turkish fingerprints on the nation's **cuisine**. You'll find *čevapčići* joints everywhere, selling grilled meat rissoles that are usually served up with *somun* (spongy bread) and chopped onion. Similarly hard to avoid are stands selling *burek*, greasy pastries filled with meat, spinach, cheese and sometimes pumpkin or potato; Sarajevo is often rated as the best *burek* city in the Balkans. Soups (*čorba*) and vegetables pop up all over the place on the country's menus, though more often than not the latter are stuffed with mincemeat; **vegetarians** will often have to satisfy themselves with salads, or something from the ubiquitous pizzerias. Sweets also have a Turkish ring to them, with syrupy *baklava* pastries available everywhere; added to this is an artery-clogging range of creamy **desserts**, most notable of which is *tufahije*, a marinaded apple topped with walnut and cream.

DRINK

The consumption of **coffee** (*kafa*) has been elevated to something approaching an art form (see box below). For alcohol, there are a few good domestic **beers** (*pivo*), and Herzegovina produces a lot of **wine** – try Blatina, a local variety of red. There's also *rakia*, a potent spirit as popular by night as coffee is by day. Locals are also fond of telling guests that Bosnian tap water is safe to drink – evidently a major source of pride.

CULTURE AND ETIQUETTE

It's imperative to note that there are three distinct **ethnicities** in Bosnia-Herzegovina – **Bosnian Serb**, mostly Orthodox; **Bosnian Croat**, mostly Catholic; and Muslims known as **Bosniaks**. Of course, all were constituent parts of the bloody war of the mid-1990s, and reverberations can still be felt today – it's never too far away from people's minds. Some locals are more than willing to talk about their experiences, particularly in Sarajevo, but of course it's best to let them make the first move.

Also worth noting is the **geographical split** evident in the country's name –

BOSNIAN COFFEE

Don't dare use the dreaded T-word – although Bosnian coffee is served **Turkish-style**, with hot water poured over unfiltered grounds, locals insist that their variety is unique. It's markedly weaker than Turkish coffee, mainly because of its function as a social lubricant – it's consumed fervidly throughout the day, with different coffee sittings ascribed different terms: *razgalica* in the morning, *razgovoruša* a little later on, and *sikteruša* following a meal. Coffee is **served** on a metal tray from a *džezva*, a cute metal pot, and poured into little tumblers (*fildžan*). Also on the tray will be a *šećerluk*, containing a few cubes of sugar – it's traditional to dip the corner of a sugar cube into your coffee for a flash, nibble it, then let the coffee wash it down. And, most importantly, do as the locals do and take your time.

you'll find yourself using "Bosnian" as an adjective most of the time, and this is accepted, though in Herzegovina it's a *tiny* bit of a faux pas to tell locals how much you're "enjoying Bosnia".

As for the more regular facets of travel etiquette, you should **dress** conservatively around religious buildings, leave small change or a little more as **tips** in a restaurant, and be aware that for all the ethnic rivalry, **smoking** is perhaps the country's dominant religion. Note, too, that some hostels will require you to remove your shoes before entering.

SPORTS AND OUTDOOR ACTIVITIES

Bosnia-Herzegovina is pretty good for outdoor pursuits. Beefy mountains mean that **hiking** is popular, though the continued presence of **landmines** means that you should seek local confirmation that an area is safe before setting off. During winter, a few **ski** slopes around Sarajevo come to life, while there's year-round **rafting** on several of the country's rivers – the best is the Una, near Bihać.

COMMUNICATIONS

Most **post offices** (*pošta*) are open weekdays from 9am to 5pm, and often on Saturday mornings too. Public **phones** use cards, which can be bought at post offices and kiosks. Better still, buy a **SIM card** from one of the main Bosnian mobile operators, which are BH Telecom, m:tel and Eronet; these typically cost around 5KM, including some starting credit. **Wi-fi** is common in Sarajevo and Mostar; where you do find an internet café, expect to pay 1–2KM/hr.

BOSNIA-HERZEGOVINA ONLINE

🌐 **bhtourism.ba** Official tourist board site.
🌐 **www.bhmac.org** Contains some useful information about landmine dangers.
🌐 **sonar.ba** Excellent site on all things to see and do in Sarajevo.

EMERGENCY NUMBERS
Police ☎ 122; Ambulance ☎ 124; Fire ☎ 123.

EMERGENCIES

With the war still fresh in many minds, travellers often arrive expecting Bosnia-Herzegovina to be a dangerous place; it will quickly become clear that this is not the case, and that the **crime rate** is very low by European standards. The country's two **police** forces are usually easy to deal with, but keep your passport or a copy handy in case of a spot check. One very important danger to note is the presence of **landmines**. Strewn liberally during the war, the vast majority have now been cleared, and there's no danger in any urban area. In the countryside, however, it's advisable to stick to clear paths.

Pharmacies usually follow shop hours, though in larger cities you'll find that some stay open until late, and are sometimes open 24 hours.

INFORMATION

Larger cities have **tourist information offices** with plenty of good English materials; some can make accommodation bookings. Free city **maps** are handed out at most hotels and all tourist offices.

MONEY AND BANKS

The currency of Bosnia-Herzegovina is the **convertible mark**, usually abbreviated to KM, though internationally it is BAM. Notes of 5, 10, 20, 50, 100 and 200KM are in circulation, as are coins of 10, 20 and 50 feninga (100 feninga = 1KM), and 1, 2 and 5KM. Exchange **rates** are currently around €1=1.95KM, £1=2.50KM and US€1=1.75KM. Accommodation prices are sometimes quoted in euros, as are meals at some upmarket restaurants. In urban areas you won't have to look too far for an **ATM**, and **exchange offices** (*menjačnica*) are plentiful in places used to tourists. **Banks** are usually open weekdays from 9am to 4pm, and often on Saturday mornings too. Credit/debit cards are accepted in most hotels, restaurants and shops.

4

BOSNIAN

The Bosnian language is essentially the same as Serbian, which in turn is essentially the same as Croatian (see p.158), and all three are listed as official languages in Bosnia-Herzegovina. Note that the Republika Srpska uses the **Cyrillic alphabet**, which may cause some problems with street signs, menus and timetables.

OPENING HOURS AND HOLIDAYS

Times are less rigid here than in most countries – **shops** usually open when they want to open, which in most cases is from 10am to 7pm, and in larger cities there's little difference at weekends. All banks and post offices will be closed on **public holidays**: January 1, March 1, May 1 and November 25 – though these dates are far from the end of the story as the Catholic and Orthodox churches celebrate Easter and Christmas at different times, and Muslims celebrate a biannual holiday known as *Bajram*.

Sarajevo

With their imaginations and travel memories fired by spiky minarets, grilled kebabs and the all-pervasive aroma of ground coffee, many travellers see in **SARAJEVO** a Slavic mini-Istanbul. The Ottoman notes are most prominent in Baščaršija, the city's delightful Old Town, which is home to umpteen mosques, bazaars, kebab restaurants and cafés. Further afield, burnt-out buildings evoke the catastrophic war of the mid-1990s, though the fun-loving, easy-going Sarajevans do a great job of painting over the scars of those tumultuous years – it's hard to walk around without being offered coffee, and it's hard to be invited for coffee without making friends.

Sarajevo gained importance during **Roman** times, and after a short slumber was reinvigorated as a trading hub during the **Ottoman** period, but sadly its recent history is far more pertinent. The international spotlight fell on the city as the host of the **1984 Winter Olympics**, but less than a decade later the world's eyes were retrained on it during a **siege** that lasted for almost four years – by some estimates, the longest in military history. Bosnian Serb forces made a near-unbroken ring around the city, shelling major buildings and shooting civilians dead on their way to work, while years of litter lay rotting in the streets. By the time the ceasefire was announced in 1996, around ten thousand people had been killed; on the ground you may notice some of the many **Sarajevo Roses** – flower-like scars of mortar shell explosions, poignantly filled in with red resin, though now badly fading.

WHAT TO SEE AND DO

The central district of **Baščaršija** is Sarajevo's prettiest and contains most of its sights. Heading west from here, the city's history unravels like a tapestry – Ottoman-era mosques slowly give way to the churches and elaborate buildings of the Austro-Hungarian period, before communist behemoths herald your arrival into "Sniper Alley" and its shells of war.

Baščaršija

The powerful waft of grilled *ćevapi* is a sure sign that you're about to enter **Baščaršija**, whose pedestrianized streets are a delight to wander around. It's most logical to approach here from the east, where you'll find the stunning **National Library**. In 1992, a single day's shelling destroyed over three million books, but reconstruction of this pink-and-yellow cream cake of faded beauty is now complete. A little way along is the central square, home to **Sebilj**, a small kiosk-like fountain, and **Baščaršija Mosque**. Far more beautiful is the **Gazi Husrev Beg Mosque** just down the way, which is worth a peep inside. Further west, you'll come across the **Bezistan**, an Ottoman-era bazaar now sadly filled with all manner of fake goods unsuited to such an elegant structure.

Baščaršija is also home to the six buildings that make up the **Museum of Sarajevo** – the largest is located inside the old Brusa Bezistan bazaar (Mon–Fri 10am–6pm, Sat 10am–3pm; 3KM; ⓦmuzejsarajeva.ba), just off the main

SARAJEVO: BAŠČARŠIJA

■ ACCOMMODATION
Balkan Han Hostel	2
Haris Youth Hostel	1
Hostel City Center Sarajevo	4
Hostel Franz Ferdinand	3
Residence Hostel	5
Traveller's Home	6

■ DRINKING & NIGHTLIFE
Baghdad	3
Barhana	2
Pivnica HS (Sarajevo Brewery)	4
Zlatna Ribica	1

■ SHOPPING
Butik Badem	2
Sprečo	1

■ EATING
Buregdžinica Bosna	8
Caffe Tito	3
Čajdžinica Džirlo	2
Cakum Pakum	4
Carigrad	6
Ćevabdžinica Petnica	9
Ćevabdžinica Željo	10
Dveri	5
Karuzo	1
Male Daire	7

0 ——— 100
metres

Bosnian Cultural Centre & National Theatre

4

square, which features a whole host of historical relics, all beautifully presented.

The Latin Bridge and 1878–1918 Museum

Modest in appearance, the **Latin Bridge** has some weighty history – this was the scene of the assassination of Archduke Franz Ferdinand and, by extension, the start of World War I; a plaque on the wall indicates the exact spot where Ferdinand met his fate. Off its northern end, the small, one-room **1878–1918 Museum** (Mon–Fri 10am–6pm, Sat 10am–3pm; 3KM) commemorates the incident, its most significant exhibits being the pistol used by the assassin, Gavrilo Princip, and the subsequent indictment against the perpetrators. Across the Miljacka River you'll see the fascinating **Papagajka**, a decaying yellow-and-green residential block apparently designed with hovercars in mind – this is how the Jetsons may have lived under Communism.

Ferhadija and around

Along and just off **Ferhadija**, the main pedestrianized thoroughfare, are several points of interest. Dominating the skyline just west of the Bezistan bazaar is the twin-turreted Catholic **cathedral** dating from the 1880s, while, just behind here, along Mula Mustafa Baseskije, stands the **central market place**. It was here, on February 5, 1994, that 68 people were killed following a mortar attack in what became the war's single most infamous incident; a blood red wall is inscribed with the names of all those who died. Adjacent to the cathedral, the superb **Galerija 11/7/95** (daily 10am–6pm; 10KM) is dedicated to the memory of the victims of the 1995 Srebrenica massacre.

"Sniper Alley" museums

Well worth the fifteen-minute walk west of Baščaršija is the **History Museum of Bosnia and Herzegovina** (Mon–Fri 9am–4pm, Sat & Sun 10am–2pm; 5KM). Don't be put off by the somewhat brutal exterior and shabby entrance, as the permanent exhibition detailing how Sarajevo functioned during the siege is sobering and superbly presented. The exhibits and photos are frequently harrowing, though the most striking aspect is the remarkable resourcefulness Sarajevans displayed, manifest in some ingeniously improvised implements for cooking, lighting, heating and the like.

On the other side of the main road stands the **Holiday Inn**, a distinctive yellow building that was the city's only functioning hotel during the siege, and as home to foreign journalists it was also one of its safest places.

Of even greater importance was the tunnel under the airport, part of which is now open as the **Tunnel Museum** (daily 9am–5pm; 10KM). During the siege, Sarajevo's UN-held airport was the only break in the city's surrounding ring of Serb forces – an 800m-long tunnel dug underneath the runways provided, for most locals, the only way into or out of the city. At the museum, you'll be played a home-movie-style DVD that describes the tunnel's creation before being led through a small section of the now-collapsed route.

ARRIVAL AND DEPARTURE

By plane Sarajevo's Butmir International Airport (☎ 033 289100, ⓦ sarajevo-airport.ba) is 12km from the city centre, a trip that will cost around 20KM by taxi, or take tram #3 to the final stop, then hire a cab.

By train The station is some 1.5km west of Baščaršija. It's a 30min walk into the centre, a short trip on tram #1, or a 7KM cab ride.

Destinations Mostar (2 daily; 2hr 45min); Zagreb (2 daily; 9hr).

By bus The main bus station is adjacent to the train station. Note that most buses to and from Belgrade (and to other towns in Republika Srpska) use Istočno bus station in the suburb of Dobrinja, in the Serbian part of the city; from here, exit right and walk for some 200m where you catch trolleybus #107 into the centre.

Destinations Belgrade (7 daily; 7hr); Bihać (3 daily; 7hr); Dubrovnik (2 daily; 6hr); Jajce (5 daily; 3hr 30min); Mostar (every 1hr–1hr 30min; 2hr 30min); Novi Sad (3 daily; 8hr); Split (5 daily; 7hr); Travnik (5 daily; 2hr); Trebinje (3 daily; 3hr); Zagreb (4 daily; 8hr).

INFORMATION AND TOURS

Tourist information Sarači 58 (July & Aug daily 9am–8pm; Sept–June Mon–Sat 9am–5pm; ☎ 033 580999, ⓦ sarajevo-tourism.com). You may stumble across a copy of *Sarajevo In Your Pocket*, but failing that, pick up *Sarajevo Navigator*, a useful monthly listings booklet.

Tours Insider Tours (☎ 033 534353, ⓦ sarajevoinsider .com) offers half a dozen excellent themed tours within the city, including the popular "Tunnel Tour" (see above) for €15, plus excursions further afield.

GETTING AROUND

Public transport An efficient system of buses, trams and trolleybuses operates throughout the city from 5am to 1am. Tickets can be bought from a kiosk for 1.60KM, or for 1.80KM from the driver; validate your ticket on board – fines are steep and ticket inspectors strict.

Taxis Journeys start at 1.5KM, and thereafter it's around 1KM/km, a ride in the centre should cost no more than 5KM.

ACCOMMODATION

The city has stacks of hostels, though many are unofficial, so best stick to the ones listed. If you get stuck, dozens of agencies around Baščaršija will be able to set you up with a private room.

HOSTELS

Balkan Han Dalmatinska 6 ☎ 061 538331, ⓦ balkanhan.com. Cracking and fairly central hostel with a mixture of boldly coloured dorms and doubles, as well as a common room-cum-bar (with Macs for use), and a lush garden featuring a very cool hammock. Dorms €14

Haris Youth Hostel Vratnik Mejdan 29 ☎ 061 518825, ⓦ hyh.ba. Super-relaxed hostel a 15min walk uphill from the centre. Check in at their office (Mon–Sat 8am–4pm), near the Baščaršija tram stop, and they'll give you a free ride up. Evenings can see anything from barbecues to impromptu guitar sessions. Dorms €14

Hostel City Center Sarajevo Muvekita 2/3 ☎ 062 280858, ⓦ hcc-sarajevo.com. Extremely clean hostel in a very central location, with four- to eight-bed dorms plus doubles, a cool lounge with PlayStation and musical instruments. Breakfast included. Dorms €13, doubles €30

★ **Hostel Franz Ferdinand** Jelića 4 ☎ 033 834625, ⓦ franzferdinandhostel.com. In honour of the assassinated archduke, and with rooms named and themed accordingly, this superbly conceived hostel also has a movie room and games lounge, bike rental and laundry. Breakfast included. Dorms €12, doubles €40

Residence Hostel Muvekita 1 ☎ 061 275188, ⓦ residencerooms.com.ba. This large, rambling hostel is more restful than *City Center* across the street, with spacious, high-ceilinged dorms, plus doubles with private bathrooms. Two kitchens for guest use. Breakfast included. Dorms €15, doubles €40

Traveller's Home Ćumurija 4 ☎ 070 242400, ⓦ myhostel.ba. A warm welcome awaits at this perky hostel near the river, with a good mix of dorms and private rooms, plus kitchen and laundry facilities. Breakfast included. Dorms €15, doubles €40

EATING

You can't walk more than 10m in Baščaršija without coming across a *ćevabdžinica* – note that many do not serve alcohol. *Burek* is similarly easy to hunt down, and many travellers rate it the best in the Balkans.

CAFÉS

Caffe Tito Bihaćka 19. Military-themed café-bar tucked under a wing of the Historical Museum. With socialist realist pictures on the inside and a gunship sitting outside, it's an interesting place to drink and chat. Daily 8am–midnight.

Čajdžinica Džirlo Kovaci 6. If the strong Bosnian coffee all gets a bit much, make tracks for this delightful Ottoman-styled teahouse – all low tables and stools, and thick patterned rugs – where you can partake in any number of flavours from around the globe. Daily 8am–10pm.

Carigrad Saraći 111. Mouthwatering selection of rich cakes, syrupy *baklava* and other sweet sins from just 1.50KM. Note that said desserts actually look bigger on your plate than they do behind the counter. Daily 9am–10pm.

Male Daire Luleđina bb. Peace-out café just behind the Baščaršija Mosque, where you can throw down good Bosnian coffee for 1.50KM, and suck on a *nargileh* for just 5KM. Daily 8am–11pm.

RESTAURANTS

Buregdžinica Bosna Bravadžiluk 9. With something as simple as *burek*, there should be very little to choose between purveyors, but the ones on offer here are simply a cut above the rest. Try the pumpkin (*tykva*) variety, with lashings of sour yoghurt (8KM). Daily 8am–11pm.

Cakum Pakum Kaptol 10. Sweet and savoury pancakes – as well as pasta – are the order of the day in this boxy but cosy little restaurant decked out in antique travel paraphernalia. Mon–Fri 10am–midnight, Sat noon–midnight.

★Ćevabdžinica Petica Bravadžiluk 21. If you must plump for just one *ćevabdžinica*, make it this one: unlike some places, meats (7KM) are grilled to order, while the accompanying *kajmak* and *somun* (spongy pitta bread) are similarly superb; snappy service too. Daily 8am–11pm.

Ćevabdžinica Željo Kundurdžiluk 12. Other Baščaršija kebab joints may be a little more polished, but this pair – there's another outlet a few paces away – are always packed with locals, who know that they provide the most bang for their buck. 7KM for ten *kebapči* and *somun*. Daily 9am–11pm.

Dveri Prote Bakovića 12. Nicely secreted away, this traditional Bosnian restaurant has a beautifully decorated interior, and the food is heavenly – try the house goulash, comprising hunks of beef with home-made gnocchi, porcini mushrooms and dried plums (18KM). Daily 8am–11pm.

Karuzo Dženetića Čikma bb. Here, in this rather delightful, maritime-themed restaurant, head chef Saša brings together meat-free dishes (quite a feat in Sarajevo) whose variety defies explanation, as well as sushi (20KM) – somehow, it all seems to work. Mon–Fri noon–3pm & 6–11pm, Sat 6–11pm.

DRINKING AND NIGHTLIFE

Sarajevo has a fair few quirky underground bars, which come and go with alarming regularity, so ask around. Locals go out late – most bars only start filling up after midnight, and all these places kick on until 1 or 2am at least.

Baghdad Bazerdžani 6. The white drapes, soft red lighting and mosaic lanterns ensure that, if nothing else, this is probably the best-looking bar in Sarajevo: a relaxing spot for a beer or cocktail, plus DJ sets at weekends.

Barhana Đjugalina 8. Set in a tucked-away courtyard, this groovy little bar is the place to come, above all, for a decent *rakija*. Try to bag one of the candlelit outdoor tables.

Pivnica HS (Sarajevo Brewery) Franjevačka 15. If you like Sarajevsko Pivo, why not head straight for the source? Their city-centre factory has a large, ornate bar out back, where it costs 5KM for a large glass of the good stuff. It's also more or less the only place in which you can try their delicious dark and unfiltered varieties.

Zlatna Ribica Kaptol 5. Currently the hottest spot in town, this place oozes character, from the eccentric decor and neatly attired staff to the great selection of drinks and groovy tunes. Even if you don't need to go, check out the loos.

ENTERTAINMENT

Bosnian Cultural Centre Branilaca Sarajeva 24 ⓦ bkc .ba. Large concert venue.

Chamber Theatre 55 Maršala Tita 56 ⓦ kamerni teatar55.ba. Cosy place used for experimental theatre productions, though rarely in English.

Kinoteka BiH Alipašina 19 ⓦ kinotekabih.ba. Interesting mix of subtitled movies shown weekdays at 7pm, and for just 3KM.

National Theatre Obala Kulina bana 9 ⓦ nps.ba. The largest theatre in the country, and home to Sarajevo's principal opera, drama and ballet companies.

> ## FESTIVALS IN SARAJEVO
>
> **Baščaršija Nights** ⓦ bascarsijskenoci.ba. Ballet, theatre, music and art exhibitions throughout July.
>
> **Jazz Fest** ⓦ jazzfest.ba. Excellent jazz festival, with some stellar names, usually held at the beginning of November.
>
> **MESS** ⓦ mess.ba. International, English-centred festival of theatre in October.
>
> **Sarajevo Film Festival** ⓦ sff.ba. In mid-August, this is one of the most prestigious film festivals in Europe, and largely focused on the region's output.
>
> **Saravejo Winter** ⓦ sarajevskazima.ba. Artistic festival (music, film, visual and performing arts) throughout February and March.

4

Sarajevo War Theatre Gabelina 16 ⓦsartr.ba. Established in 1992 in response to the closure of the city's theatres, this superb venue hosts a fascinating clutch of performances from home and abroad.

SHOPPING

Most useful to travellers is a small area around Mula Mustafa Bašeskije, where you'll find a couple of appealing markets – indoor and outdoor – and a few secondhand clothing stores.

Butik Badem Abadžiluk 12. Doles out superb Turkish sweets, dried mulberries, and a lot more besides. Daily 8am–11pm.

Srečo Kovači 15. One recommended souvenir purchase is a Bosnian coffee set: while whole teams of Baščaršija stands sell cheap ones, here you can get beautiful hand-made copper-and-tin sets for €30. Mon–Sat 9am–6pm.

DIRECTORY

Embassies and consulates; UK, Hamdije Čemerlića 39a ⓣ 033 282200; US, Robert C. Frasure 1 ⓣ 033 704000.

Hospital Kranjčevićeva 12 ⓣ 033 208100.

Pharmacy 24hr pharmacy at Obala Kulina bana 40 (ⓣ 033 272300).

Post office Zmaja od Bosne 88 (Mon–Sat 7am–8pm).

Bosnia

Occupying roughly four-fifths of the country, mountainous Bosnia contains some of the country's most appealing towns, and helpfully all can be visited on a fairly straight route linking Sarajevo and Zagreb. First up, get a sense of medieval history in **Travnik**, Bosnia's former capital, then head to **Jajce**, a tiny town with a waterfall crashing through its centre. Lastly there's laidback **Bihać**, one of Europe's best rafting spots.

TRAVNIK

Just a couple of hours out of Sarajevo, **TRAVNIK** is a good day-trip target, though its position on a main transport route detracts slightly from a delightful setting. This was the **Bosnian capital** during the latter part of Ottoman rule, and the residence of high-ranking officials known as viziers – you'll see their tombs (*turbe*) dotted around town. Travnik also gained fame as the birthplace of Ivo Andrić, a

Nobel Prize-winning novelist whose *Bosnian Chronicle* was set in his hometown.

The best place to soak up Travnik's history is at its majestic fifteenth-century **castle** (daily 10am–6pm; 2KM), built to hold off Ottoman forces but completed a few years too late. It's now great for a clamber around, and provides spectacular views of the surrounding mountains. Just under the castle is **Plavna Voda**, a quiet huddle of streamside **restaurants** where you can eat trout caught further upstream.

JAJCE

Whereas Travnik has grown a little too busy for its size, little **JAJCE** is simply adorable – even its name is cute, a diminutive form of the word "egg", and therefore translating as something like "egglet". The name is said to derive from the shape of a hill jutting up in the Old Town, ringed with walls and topped with an impressive **citadel**. In the Middle Ages, Bosnian kings were crowned just down the hill in the **Church of St Mary** (open to the public); the last coronation, of Stjepan Tomašević, took place here in 1461, but two years later the king had his head lopped off during the Ottoman invasion. Opposite the church are the **catacombs** (no set opening hours; 2KM), essentially an underground church, complete with a narthex, nave, presbytery and baptistry; if you're lucky, you'll find the keyholder in the restaurant opposite. Further downhill, the 21m-high **waterfalls** are a splendid sight, despite the pounding they took during the Bosnian conflict.

ACCOMMODATION AND EATING

Stari Grad Svetog Luke 3 ⓣ 030 654006, ⓦ jajcetours .com. One of very few places to stay in Jajce, this lovely hotel, slap-bang in the Old Town, offers tastefully furnished singles, doubles and suites (three of each), all with a/c. Breakfast included. Doubles **€45**

Vodopad Old Town. There are very few places to eat and drink, but this fun place just inside the gates doles out colossal double-scoop ice creams for just 1.5KM; if the weather's hot don't expect to get through the whole thing before it melts.

RAFTING AND KAYAKING IN NORTHWEST BOSNIA

Rafting in the Bihać area is possible year-round – the continuous flow of tourist traffic means that you'll usually be able to join a group (6–10 per boat) in any month, though the main season runs from March to October. Six kilometres from town, **Una Kiro** (☎037 361110, ⍟una-kiro-rafting .com) is the best established company for foreigners, and has a camping ground next to their base (€5 per tent plus €5 per adult). If you fancy something a little gentler, they also do a **kayaking** trip, which follows a 9km course over 2hrs (€50). There are three main **rafting routes** to choose from; listed per-person prices include equipment and transport, but not meals.
Kostela-Bosanska Krupa An easy 24km, 5hr stretch that's best for novices; €37.
Kostela-Grmuša Short, but packs in some meaty rapids on a 13km, 4hr course; €27.
Štrbački Buk-Lohovo An absolutely terrifying 15km, 4hr route featuring a 25m rapid ride; €43.

BIHAĆ

Herzegovina has no shortage of great **rafting** locales, but Bosnia's **BIHAĆ** beats them all. The crystal-clear **River Una** rushes through town, though it's a little further upstream that you'll find the best rafting; the river is highest in the spring and autumn. Adventure sports aside, Bihać is a pleasant, compact town with a cheerful pedestrianized zone in the centre. Here you'll find the **Church of Zvonik** and **Fathija Mosque**, both visitable, but most interesting is the **Captain's Tower**, once a prison, now a museum (Mon–Fri 9am–4pm, Sat 9am–2pm; 1KM).

ACCOMMODATION

Villa Una ☎037 311393, ⍟villa-una.com. Great location down by the river, and owned by the same outfit who run local rafting tours, this super value place has a combination of standard and superior rooms, though all are spotlessly clean. Breakfast included. Doubles €44

Herzegovina

Wedged into the far south of the country, little Herzegovina is less known than its big brother, Bosnia, but this land of muscular peaks and rushing rivers arguably has more to see. Pride of place goes to **Mostar** and its famed Old Bridge, but it's worth venturing outside the city to see little **Blagaj**, or to absorb the religious curiosities of **Međugorije**. Those on their way to Dubrovnik or Montenegro should also call in at **Trebinje**, by far the most pleasant town in the Republika Srpska.

MOSTAR

On arrival at the train or bus station, you may be forgiven for thinking that the beauty of **MOSTAR** has been somewhat exaggerated. There then begins a slow descent to the Old Town, during which it becomes more and more apparent that it really is a very special place indeed. Attentive ears will pick out rushing streams, salesmen crying their wares, as well as church bells and *muezzins* competing for attention, while steep, cobblestoned streets slowly wind their way down to the fast-flowing, turquoise-blue Neretva River and its Old Bridge, incredibly photogenic even when the Speedo-clad *mostari* – the brave gents who dive from the apex – aren't tumbling into the waters below. The city is hugely popular with tourists, though the dearth of high-end accommodation means that most visit on a day-trip – bad news for anyone on the Old Bridge around lunchtime, though great news for anyone staying the night; the best time to come is first thing in the morning or early evening.

Mostar's history is irrevocably entwined with that of its bridge. Like hundreds of locals, this was to fall victim in 1993 when the Croats and Muslims of the town, previously united against the Serbs, turned on each other: the **conflict** rumbled on for two long years, each side sniping at the other from opposing hills. Locals claim that, prior to the war, more than half of the city's marriages were mixed, but the figure has since dwindled to nothing; while relations are now much improved, the truce remains uneasy.

4

THE OLD BRIDGE

Transit point, dungeon, tourist attraction, war victim and macho launchpad, Mostar's small, hump-backed **Stari Most** has led an interesting life. With tradesmen terrified by the rickety nature of its wooden predecessor and the fast-flowing Neretva below, it was built in the 1560s at the instigation of Suleyman the Magnificent. Those employed to guard the bridge were called the **mostari**, a term later borrowed when naming the city, and then used to describe the men who dive from the apex, 21m down into the Neretva. After 427 years in service, the bridge was strategically destroyed by Croat forces in November 1993, symbolizing the ethnic division of the city. There then began the arduous process of rebuilding it piece by piece, using new materials but following the same techniques used in its initial construction, before it reopened in 2004. The mostari are still there, day after day; they'll try to work the crowd into shelling out an acceptable fee – typically around €25 – before taking the plunge. Join them if you dare, especially in July, when the annual **diving festival** marks the highlight of Mostar's year.

WHAT TO SEE AND DO

The **Old Town**, spanning both sides of the Neretva, contains most things of interest in Mostar, and in its centre is the **Old Bridge**, focal point of the city and the obvious place to kick off your sightseeing. On the eastern bank is the more interesting Muslim part of town, while the west is mainly home to Catholic Croats.

The east bank

Lined with trinket stores, cobblestoned Kujundžiluk climbs uphill, soon leading to the **Koski Mehmed Paša Mosque** (sunrise–sunset). For all its beauty, the panoply of souvenir sellers shows that tourism, rather than religious endeavour, is the current priority; eschew the 8KM it costs to climb the minaret and instead head down to the terrace where you can get superb head-on views of the bridge. Passing another mosque, the road segues quickly into modern Mostar, though pay attention to signs pointing out the **Turkish House** (irregular hours; 2KM) on your left, a fascinating peek into the Ottoman traditions of yesteryear. Above Kujundžiluk you'll see the **Cejvan Cehaj Mosque**, Mostar's oldest, on the way to the **Museum of Herzegovina** (Mon–Fri 9am–2pm, Sat 10am–noon; 2KM). Between the two lies a Muslim **graveyard**, and it's hard not to be moved when you notice that almost everybody laid to rest here died the same year, 1993.

Old Bridge Museum

Off the eastern end of the bridge is **Helebija**, a tower that now accommodates the enlightening **Old Bridge Museum** (April–Oct daily 10am–6pm; 5KM), spread over four levels, and topped with a viewing point. Of most interest is the archeological section, where you can see some of the few remaining chunks of the bridge that weren't swept away, alongside footage of its painstaking rebirth. There's sobering archive footage of the bridge's downfall in the neighbouring **Old Bridge Gallery**, which also stocks a superb range of books on the war and the history of Bosnia in English.

The west bank

Tara, the bridge's western tower, was once a dungeon into which prisoners were thrown to die, either from injury, starvation or – in rainy season – drowning. It's now the base of the diving club, and the **War Photo Exhibition** (daily: April, May, Oct & Nov 11am–6pm; June–Sept 9am–10pm; 6KM), an array of startling shots taken during the troubles by Kiwi photographer Wade Goddard. Just 22 at the time, Goddard spent this period with a family inside the Old Town, wandering the streets to document the hardships.

A little zigzagging will bring you to the **Crooked Bridge** – apparently built as a warm-up for the big boy, and almost as pleasing; although it (just about) remained standing during the war, it did finally collapse in 1999 due to flooding. Further along is the **Tabhana**, a former bathhouse now filled with bars and restaurants. Continue to the end of the street and you'll eventually reach Bulevar, the main road that, during the war, served as the front line – still today, the road is lined with a succession of battered buildings.

ARRIVAL AND DEPARTURE

By train The station is in an ugly area to the east of town, a 20min walk from the Old Bridge.
Destinations Sarajevo (2 daily; 2hr 45min).
By bus The station is next to the train station.
Destinations Dubrovnik (2 daily; 4hr); Sarajevo (hourly; 2hr 30min); Trebinje (2 daily; 3hr 30min).

INFORMATION AND TOURS

Tourist office Rade Bitange 5, behind the Tabhana, just west of the Old Bridge (daily: June–Aug 9am–9pm; May & Sept 9am–5pm; ☎033 580833, ⓦturizam.mostar.ba). Limited information available but they can help organize private accommodation.
Tours You'll find that most hostel owners offer tours (both of the city and further afield, typically costing €25–35), though the best ones are currently run by Bata, from *Hostel Majdas*, and Zika at *Hostel Nina* (see below).

ACCOMMODATION

The tourist office can help to organize private rooms, which cost €10–25/person depending upon the season, room size and proximity to the Old Town. All hostels listed offer a free pick-up from the train and bus stations.
Guesthouse Taso Maršala Tita 187 ☎061 523149. Some 400m south of the bridge, on the east bank, this sparkling little hostel offers fabulously clean and neat four- and six-bed dorms plus twins; a real home away from home. Dorms €12, twins €25
★**Hostel Majdas** Pere Lazetića 9 ☎061 382940. Friendly, cosy and within easy reach of the stations and the Old Town, this is Mostar's best hostel. There are four fresh and colourful rooms, a comfortable lounge and pretty courtyard where guests gather to chat and drink. Moreover, their day-long tours (see above) are the best in town. Breakfast included. Dorms €12, doubles €25
Hostel Nina Celebića 18 ☎061 382743, ⓦhostelnina.ba. Around 400m from the bridge, on the east bank, this modern, almost apartment-like building has spotless a/c dorms and double rooms. The genial host, Zika, also offers a couple of terrific tours. Dorms €10, doubles €20
Pansion Oscar Onešćukova 33 ☎036 580237. Nicely positioned on the edge of the Old Town (west bank), the double, triple and quad rooms (all a/c) at this sweet little guesthouse are perfectly adequate for the price; some with bathroom, some without. Breakfast included. Doubles €40

EATING AND DRINKING

Try to avoid eating noon–2pm, which is when the tour groups are led to their pre-booked tables.

Muslibegović House Osman Dikića 41 ☎036 551379, ⓦmuslibegovichouse.com. A rare and surprisingly affordable chance to stay in a national monument – this home has been in the hands of the noble Muslibegović family for over 300 years. Twelve rooms renovated with tasteful, individual designs, though a strong Ottoman theme prevails throughout; doubles €90, suites €100

Ali Baba East bank. The word "cavernous" is often misused, but this quirky place – café, bar and club all at once – is housed, literally, in a cave. It's the liveliest place in town of an evening, and summer months see DJs come in to spin some vinyl. The "Ali Baba" sign is on the little-used road entrance (the tunnel leading to it is worth a peek); the one at the lower entrance says "Open Sesame!".
Ćevabdžinica Tima-Irma Onešcukova bb. You can't come to Mostar and not feast on the likes of *čevapčiči* and *pljeskavica* (large hamburger), which this convivial establishment does better than anywhere else in town. Fun, hospitable, and dead cheap. Daily 9am–11pm.
★**Hindin Han** Jusovina bb. Just off Onešcukova and set picturesquely high above the water with a flower-bedecked terrace, the fine menu here comprises traditional Balkan grilled meats alongside trout, stuffed squid (13KM) and the like. Daily 11am–11pm.
Palma Burek Alekse Šantića 13. The best *burek* in town, no question, with meat, cheese or spinach fillings and a dollop of yoghurt (3KM); the café to the rear doles out coffee, big slices of cake and ice cream. Mon–Sat 7am–11pm, Sun 5–11pm.
Šadrvan Jusovina 11. It's all a bit hammed up for the tourist hordes, but you can't fault the setting – overlooking the bridge – or the menu, which offers a whole slew of meaty treats, such as *dolma* (grape leaves stuffed with minced meat, onion and rice, and slathered in sour cream), all at very affordable prices. Daily 10am–11pm.

EXCURSIONS FROM MOSTAR

Using Mostar as a base, you have a whole slew of destinations to choose from. Unfortunately, the paucity of public transport means that it's tough to see more than one in a day, and some places aren't accessible at all: often your best option is to visit on a **tour** from Mostar (see above).

4

Blagaj

Closest to Mostar is the village of **BLAGAJ**, just 12km to the east and accessible by local buses #10, #11 and #12 (7 services a day; 40min; 5KM return). Once you disembark, carry straight ahead through the town to the **Tekija** (daily 10am–6pm). Huddled into a niche in the cliff face, this wonky wooden building was once the residence of dervishes, and the interior – prayer rooms, washroom and kitchen – are all suitably spartan. The hammam, meanwhile, remains as it was. Right next to it, a never-ending torrent of water gushes out of the cliff, apparently reaching levels of 43,000 litres per second; some of this is skimmed off to make tea and coffee, which you can order at the adjacent terrace for just 1.5KM, including a chunk of *lokum* (Turkish delight).

Međugorje

Twenty-six kilometres south of Mostar is the curious village of **MEĐUGORJE**, a mere non-entity until June 1981, when a group of teenagers claimed to have been spoken to by the **Virgin Mary** here. Unlike Lourdes and Fatima, this has not been officially recognized by the Vatican, but that doesn't stop pilgrims arriving in such numbers that there are now thousands of rooms available to accommodate them. The main sights here are the **Church of St James** and the nearby "Weeping Knee" statue, so named as it apparently flouts the laws of thermodynamics by dribbling out a constant flow of fluid. You can reach here on local bus #48 from Mostar, though – get this – they don't run on Sundays.

Počitelj and the Kravice Waterfalls

A few kilometres south of Međugorje is the hillside village of **POČITELJ**, one of the most traditional in Herzegovina. The place is quite stunning, and dotted with remnants from the fifteenth century, most notably a citadel and a terrific mosque. Unfortunately there are no direct buses here, so it's best to join a tour. Groups will likely swing through to see the nearby **Kravice Waterfalls**, which are not accessible on public transport. High, wide and handsome, the pool below is a great place for a dip.

TREBINJE

The Republika Srpska's most appealing town by a country mile, **TREBINJE** is tucked into Herzegovina's southern extremity, and its proximity to Dubrovnik and the Montenegrin border makes it the ideal start or finish line to a race through the country. It's most famed for the sixteenth-century **Arslanagić Bridge** – a longer version of the one in Mostar – which sits a ten-minute walk from the town centre; in what must have been quite a feat, it was moved here, stone by stone, from the village of Arslanagić some 5km away, in 1972.

Back in the centre is the **Old Town**, a pretty warren of streets now largely filled with cafés; better yet for coffee-slurping is elegant **Jovan Dučić Trg**, home to a daily market and almost totally cloaked with maple leaves (*platani*).

There are also a couple of still-functioning **hilltop monasteries**, notably fourteenth-century Tvrdoš 6km west of Trebinje, which are a delight to roam around and well worth the climb.

INFORMATION

Tourist office Jovan Dučić bb (June–Sept Mon–Fri 8am–8pm, Sat & Sun 9am–3pm & 6–8pm; Oct–May Mon–Fri 8am–4pm, Sat 9am–3pm; ☎059 273410, ⊕trebinjeturizam.com).

ACCOMMODATION, EATING AND DRINKING

Azzaro Stari Grad 14. Cosy, convivial bar that's pretty much the most popular meeting place in town; occasional blues- and jazz-orientated evenings to boot. Daily 8am–11pm.
Hotel Polako Svetozara Ćorovica 8 ☎066 380722, ⊕hostelpolakotrebinje.com. With a super position on the Old Town margins, this sparky little hostel has two brightly decorated six-bed dorms and two doubles, plus a common area and self-catering kitchen – and there's a terrific pancake breakfast to set you on your way. Dorms €12, doubles €30

RILA MONASTERY

Bulgaria

HIGHLIGHTS

❶ Aleksandar Nevski Cathedral, Sofia The capital's most striking building. **See p.135**

❷ Rila Monastery Fabulous frescoes deep in the mountains. **See p.140**

❸ Bansko Skiing and snowboarding on the cheap, plus cosy traditional pubs. **See p.140**

❹ Plovdiv's Old Quarter Ornate Ottoman houses and Roman remains. **See p.142**

❺ The Black Sea Coast White sand, watersports and beach bars. **See p.148**

HIGHLIGHTS ARE MARKED ON THE MAP ON P.129

ROUGH COSTS

Daily budget Basic €25, occasional treat €40

Drink Beer (0.5l) €1

Food *Shopska* salad €3

Hostel/budget hotel €10/€20

Travel Train: Sofia–Plovdiv €4; bus: €7

FACT FILE

Population 7.2 million

Language Bulgarian

Currency Lev (Lv)

Capital Sofia

International phone code ☎ 359

Time zone GMT +2hr

5

Introduction

With dramatic mountain ranges, superb beaches, numerous historic towns and a web of working villages with traditions straight out of the nineteenth century, Bulgaria has a wealth of attractions crammed into a relatively compact country. More than anything else, this is a land of adventures: once you step off the beaten track, road signs and bus timetables often disappear (or are only in Cyrillic), and few people speak a foreign language, but almost everyone you meet will be determined to help you on your way.

Bulgaria's image has altered dramatically in recent years, thanks largely to the modernization of the country's tourist infrastructure coupled with soaring foreign interest in inexpensive rural and coastal properties. Independent travel is common: costs are relatively low, and for the committed there is much to take in. Romantic National Revival-era architecture, featuring timber frames and floral motifs, is a particular draw, with **Koprivshtitsa**, **Bansko** and **Plovdiv** foremost among examples of the genre. The monasteries are stunning, too – the finest, **Rila**, should be on every itinerary – while for city life aim for **Sofia**, **Plovdiv**, and the cosmopolitan coastal resorts of **Varna** and **Burgas**.

CHRONOLOGY

4000s BC Thracian tribes settle in the area of present-day Bulgaria.
600s BC Greeks settle in the area of present-day Bulgaria.
100s AD Romans invade the Balkan Peninsula.
200 A popular Roman amphitheatre draws people to Serdica (Sofia).
681 The First Bulgarian Kingdom is formed.
864 Bulgaria accepts the Orthodox Church.
1018 The country falls under Byzantine control.
1185 The Byzantines are repelled and the Second Bulgarian Kingdom is proclaimed.
1396 The Ottomans conquer Bulgaria, ushering in almost five hundred years of Turkish rule.
1876 Revolutionaries based at Koprivshtitsa carry out the ill-fated April Rising, which provokes savage Ottoman reprisals.
1877 War of Liberation sees Russia declare war on Turkey to win freedom for Bulgaria.
1886 The Treaty of Bucharest ends the Serbo-Bulgarian war begun the previous year, and Bulgaria gains territory.

1908 Bulgaria declares itself an independent kingdom.
1912 First Balkan War; Bulgaria sustains heavy losses in victory over the Ottomans.
1913 Second Balkan War; previous allies Serbia and Greece defeat Bulgaria.
1914–18 Bulgaria sides with the Central Powers during World War I.
1945 Soviet army invades German-occupied areas of Bulgaria.
1954 Todor Zhivkov becomes head of the Bulgarian Communist Party in power.
1989 Zhivkov ousted among calls for democratization.
1991 New constitution proclaims Bulgaria a Parliamentary Republic.
2001 Former king Simeon II is elected Prime Minister.
2004 Bulgaria joins NATO.
2007 Bulgaria joins the EU.
2009 Zhivkov's former bodyguard, Boiko Borisov, is elected Prime Minister.
2013 Borisov resigns following nationwide protests against poor living standards, rising energy costs, and corruption.
2014 Borisov is re-elected Prime Minister.

ARRIVAL AND DEPARTURE

Most tourists arrive at either of Sofia's two airport terminals, although in summer many fly directly to the coastal cities of Varna and Burgas on charter flights. Frequent **low-cost flights** from London and other European cities to Sofia are provided by easyJet and Wizz Air, which also has summer services to Varna and Burgas. The national carrier Bulgaria Air (Ⓦair.bg) serves most of Europe, but there are no direct flights to or from North America or Australasia.

Bulgaria has land borders with five countries and reliable international **rail**

HIGHLIGHTS

1. Alexsandar Nevski Cathedral, Sofia
2. Rila Monastery
3. Bansko
4. Plovdiv's Old Quarter
5. The Black Sea Coast

links. Popular routes include from Bucharest to Veliko Tarnovo (5–6hr) or to Sofia (11hr), and from Thessaloniki to Sofia (10hr), while trains from Istanbul traverse the country, stopping at Plovdiv (11hr) and Sofia (14hr) before continuing to Belgrade. Eurolines (ⓦeurolines.bg) runs frequent **bus** services to Sofia from many major European cities and has booking offices in Sofia, Plovdiv, Varna and Burgas.

GETTING AROUND

Public transport in Bulgaria is inexpensive but often slow and not always clean or comfortable. Travelling by **bus** (*avtobus*) is usually the quickest way of getting between major towns and cities. Generally, you can buy tickets (*bileti*) at the bus station (*avtogara*) at least an hour in advance when travelling between towns, but on some routes they're only sold when the bus arrives. On rural routes, tickets are often sold by the driver.

Bulgarian State Railways (BDZh; ⓦbdz .bg) can get you to most towns; trains are punctual and fares low. Express services (*ekspresen*) are restricted to main routes, but on all except the humblest branch lines you'll find so-called Rapid (*burz vlak*) trains. Where possible, use these rather than the snail-like *patnicheski* services. Long-distance or overnight trains have reasonably priced couchettes (*kushet*) and/or sleepers (*spalen vagon*). For these, on all expresses and many rapids, you need **seat reservations** (*zapazeni mesta*) as well as tickets (*bileti*). To ensure a seat in a non-smoking carriage (*myasto za nepushachi*), you will have to specify this when booking. **International tickets** must be bought in advance from the BDZh-Rila office located within stations. Most stations have **left luggage** offices (*garderob*). InterRail and Balkan Flexipass are valid, although it often works out cheaper to buy rail tickets as you go.

Cycling in Bulgaria's cities is becoming increasingly popular as cycle lane

5

networks expand, while the country's quiet minor roads linking towns and villages are a delight. Of the few bike rental outfits in Bulgaria, Zig-Zag Holidays in Sofia (Ⓦzigzagbg.com) is one of the most reliable and also runs organized tours.

ACCOMMODATION

Decent **hostels** charging around 20Lv for a dorm bed and 40–60Lv for double rooms can be found in Sofia, Plovdiv, Veliko Turnovo, Burgas and Varna. Budget **hotels** rent doubles from around 40Lv, a little more in Sofia and Plovdiv, while cosier family-run hotels with similar prices are common on the coast and in touristy towns such as Koprivshtitsa and Bansko.

The best **campsites** (*kamping*; summer only) are dotted along the coast. Campers are charged individually (around 9Lv per person) and two-person chalets (30–40Lv per night) are usually available. Camping rough is technically illegal and punishable with a fine, though authorities usually turn a blind eye. A number of hostels also offer camping space.

FOOD AND DRINK

Sit-down meals are eaten in either a **restorant** (restaurant) or a **mehana** (tavern). There's little difference between the two, save that a *mehana* is likely to offer folksy decor and a wider range of traditional Bulgarian dishes. Wherever you go, you're unlikely to spend more than 25Lv for a main course, salad and drink. The best-known traditional dish is *gyuvech* (which literally means "earthenware dish"), a rich stew comprising peppers, aubergines and beans, to which is added either meat or meat stock. *Kavarma*, a spicy meat stew (either pork or chicken), is prepared in a similar fashion. **Vegetarian meals** (*yastia bez meso*) are hard to obtain, although there is always a plentiful range of salads. *Gyuveche* (a variety of *gyuvech* featuring baked vegetables), *kachkaval pane* (cheese fried in breadcrumbs) and *chuskhi byurek* (baked peppers stuffed with egg and rice) are worth trying.

Foremost among **snacks** are *kebapcheta* (grilled sausages), or variations such as *shishche* (shish kebab) or *kyofteta* (meatballs). Another favourite is the *banitsa*, a flaky-pastry envelope with a filling – usually cheese – sold by bakeries and street vendors in the morning and evening. Elsewhere, *sandvichi* (sandwiches) and *pitsi* (pizzas) dominate the fast-food repertoire. Bulgarians consider their **yogurt** (*kiselo mlyako*) the world's finest, and hardly miss a day without consuming it.

DRINK

The quality of Bulgarian **wines** is constantly improving. Among the best reds are the heavy, mellow Melnik, and rich, dark Mavrud, while Dimyat is a good dry white. If you prefer the sweeter variety, try Karlovski Misket (Muscatel) or Traminer. Cheap native **spirits** are highly potent: *mastika* (like Greek *oúzo*) is drunk diluted with water; *rakiya* – brandy made from either plums (*slivova*) or grapes (*grozdova*) – is generally sipped, accompanied by salad. Bulgarian **beer** is as good as any, but local brands such as Kamenitza, Zagorka and Shumensko must now compete with the likes of Staropramen, Stella Artois and Heineken, which are brewed locally under licence.

Coffee (*kafe*) usually comes *espresso* style. **Tea** (*chai*) is nearly always herbal – ask for *cheren chai* (literally "black tea") if you want the real stuff, normally served with lemon.

CULTURE AND ETIQUETTE

Bulgarians are predominantly Orthodox Christian; Muslims of Turkish descent make up around nine percent of the population. Social etiquette in Bulgaria is still rather formal: shaking someone's hand is the most common form of **greeting** and you should address someone with their title and surname unless you know them well. It is appropriate to wait for the Bulgarian person to decide when to become less formal with you. When invited to someone's home it is polite to bring a small gift, and something from

5

BODY LANGUAGE

Bulgarians shake their heads when they mean "yes" and nod when they mean "no" – and sometimes reverse these gestures if they know they're speaking to foreigners, thereby complicating the issue further. Emphatic use of the words *da* (yes) and *ne* (no) should help to avoid misunderstandings.

your own country will be particularly appreciated.

As for **tipping**, leaving a ten percent tip will definitely be well received, although it is not obligatory.

SPORTS AND ACTIVITIES

Bulgaria's mountainous terrain offers plenty of adventurous options. The **ski season** lasts from December to March, and the country has several well-known resorts. Bansko (⊛banskoski.com), in the spectacular Pirin mountain range in the southwest, is the best known, with alpine peaks and challenging runs perfect for experienced skiers and snowboarders. Other large resorts include Pamporovo (⊛pamporovo.me) in the Rhodope Mountains, which is the best for beginners, and Borovets (⊛borovets-bg .com) in the Rila range; there are also ski facilities on Vitosha Mountain (⊛vitoshaski.com), just twenty minutes from the centre of Sofia. For more information see ⊛bulgariaski.com.

Of all Bulgaria's ranges, the Rila Mountains (⊛rilanationalpark.bg) provide some of the country's most attractive **hiking** destinations, including the highest peak – Mount Musala (2925m) – from where a two- to three-day trail leads to Rila Monastery. For the best maps, advice and organized hikes visit Zig-Zag Holidays (⊛zigzagbg .com) in Sofia. **Horseriding** is growing in popularity, and a small number of travel agencies can arrange trips of varying length (see box, p.141).

Despite the popularity of team sports such as basketball, handball and volleyball, none generates as much passion as **football**. Teams in the premier division ("A" Grupa) play on Saturday or Sunday afternoons. **Tickets** are generally cheap (around 5–10Lv) and sold at booths outside the grounds on the day of the match.

COMMUNICATIONS

You'll find that hotels, cafés, bars and restaurants generally offer free wi-fi. **Post offices** (*poshta*) are usually open Monday to Saturday 8.30am to 5.30pm, longer in big towns. **Phonecards** (*fonokarta*) for both Bulfon's orange phones and Betcom's blue phones are available from post offices and many street kiosks and shops. Cheap **SIM cards** from Bulgaria's three main network providers (Mtel, Globul and Vivacom) are widely available. The operator number for domestic calls is ☏121, for international calls ☏123.

EMERGENCIES

Petty theft is a danger on the coast, and the Bulgarian **police** can be slow in filling out insurance reports unless you're insistent. Foreign tourists are no longer a novelty in much of the country, but **women** travelling alone can expect to encounter stares, comments and sometimes harassment, while clubs on the coast are pretty much seen as meat markets. A firm rebuff should be enough to cope with most situations. Note that everyone is required to carry some form of **ID** at all times.

If you need a **doctor** (*doktor*) or dentist (*zabolekar*), go to the nearest hospital (*bolnitsa*), whose staff might speak English or German. Emergency treatment is free of charge, although you must pay for **medicines**. Larger towns will have at least one 24-hour pharmacy.

INFORMATION

Bulgaria's National Tourist Information Centre, located in Sofia at ploshtad Sveta

EMERGENCY NUMBERS

For any emergency dial ☏112

5

BULGARIAN

Hotel and travel agency staff in Sofia and the larger towns and coastal resorts generally speak some **English**, but knowledge of foreign languages elsewhere in the country is patchy; younger people are more likely to know a few words of English. Most street signs, menus and so on are written in the **Cyrillic** alphabet, but an increasing number have English transliterations.

	BULGARIAN	PRONUNCIATION
Yes	Да	Da
No	Не	Ne
Please	Моля	Molya
Thank you	Благодаря	Blagodarya
Hello/Good day	Добър ден	Dobur den
Goodbye	Довиждане	Dovizhdane
Excuse me	Извинявайте	Izvinyavite
Where?	Къде?	Kude?
Good	Добро	Dobro
Bad	Лошо	Losho
Near	Близо	Blizo
Far	Далече	Daleche
Cheap	Евтино	Eftino
Expensive	Скъпо	Skupo
Open	Отворено	Otvoreno
Closed	Затворено	Zatvoreno
Today	Днес	Dnes
Yesterday	Вчера	Vchera
Tomorrow	Утре	Utre
How much is...?	Колко струва...?	Kolko stroova...?
What time is it?	Колко е часът?	Kolko ai chasut?
I don't understand	Не разбирам	Ne razbiram
Do you speak English?	Говорите ли английски?	Govorite li Angleeski?
Do you have any vegetarian dishes?	Имате ли вегетерианска храна?	Imate li vegitarianska hrana?
Cheers	Наздраве	Nazdrave
The bill, please	Може ли сметката	Mozhe li smetkata
Is this the bus for...?	Това ли е автобусът за...?	Tova li avtobusat za...?
Is this the train to...?	Това ли е влакът за...?	Tova li e vlakut za...?
Have you got a single/double?	Имате ли единична двойна стая?	Imate li edinichna/dvoyna staya?
How much for the night?	Колко струва нощувката?	Kolko struva noshtuvkata?
One	Един/Една	Edin/edna
Two	Две	Dve
Three	Три	Tree
Four	Четири	Chetiri
Five	Пет	Pyet
Six	Шест	Shest
Seven	Седем	Sedem
Eight	Осем	Osem
Nine	Девет	Devet
Ten	Десет	Deset

Nedelya 1 (Mon–Fri 9am–5pm; ☎02 987 9778, ⍟bulgariatravel.org), is a smart, modern affair offering free maps and travel advice. Most major towns and cities have local **tourist information centres** where staff speak several languages and can provide maps, brochures and leaflets, although they aren't usually

authorized to make hotel reservations. The best general **maps** of Bulgaria and Sofia are published by Kartografiya and Domino; both are available in Latin alphabet versions and are sold at street stalls, petrol stations and bookshops.

MONEY AND BANKS

Until Bulgaria joins the Eurozone (estimated date: Jan 1, 2018) the currency remains the **lev** (Lv), which is divided into 100 stotinki (st). There are notes of 2Lv, 5Lv, 10Lv, 20Lv, 50Lv and 100Lv and coins of 1st, 2st, 5st, 10st, 20st and 50st, and 1Lv. Pegged to the euro, the lev is stable, and although hotels and travel agencies frequently quote prices in euros, you will be expected to pay in the local currency. At the time of writing, €1 = 1.95Lv, $1 = 1.75Lv, and £1 = 2.55Lv. Producing a **student ID card** at museums and galleries will often get you a discount of between a third and a half.

Banks are open Monday to Friday 9am to 4pm, and there are ATMs in every town. Private exchange bureaus, offering variable rates, are widespread – but beware of hidden commission charges. Also watch out for black market moneychangers who approach unwary foreigners with offers of better rates; if they sound too good to be true, they are. Credit and debit cards are acceptable at most shops, hotels and restaurants.

OPENING HOURS AND HOLIDAYS

Big-city **shops** and **supermarkets** are generally open Monday to Friday 8.30am to 6pm or later; on Saturday they close at 2pm. The massive malls that have sprung up in recent years are usually open daily from 10am to 10pm. In rural areas and small towns, an unofficial siesta may prevail between noon and 3pm. Many shops, offices, banks and museums are closed on the following **public holidays**: January 1, March 3, Easter Sunday and Monday, May 1, May 24, September 6, September 22, December 25 and December 31. Additional public holidays may occasionally be called by the government.

> **BULGARIA ONLINE**
> ⓦ **bulgariatravel.org** Comprehensive travel information.
> ⓦ **discover-bulgaria.com** Travel information and hotel booking.
> ⓦ **novinite.com** English-language news and features.
> ⓦ **questbg.com** News and features for foreigners living in Bulgaria.
> ⓦ **programata.bg** Up-to-date English-language cultural listings.

Sofia

With its drab suburbs and distinct lack of charming old buildings **SOFIA** (София) can seem an uninspiring place to first-time visitors. Yet once you've settled in and begun to explore, you'll find it a surprisingly vibrant city, especially on fine days, when its lush public gardens and pavement cafés buzz with life. Just 8km to the south looms verdant **Mount Vitosha**, promising fantastic hiking, biking and skiing.

Sofia was founded by a Thracian tribe some three thousand years ago, and various **Roman ruins** attest to its zenith as Serdika, a regional imperial capital in the fourth century AD. The Bulgars didn't arrive on the scene until the ninth century and, with the notable exception of the thirteenth-century Boyana Church, their cultural monuments largely disappeared during Ottoman rule (1396–1878). The architectural legacy of the Ottomans was mostly eradicated following liberation in 1878 and is now visible solely in a couple of stately **mosques**. The finest architecture postdates Bulgaria's liberation: handsome Neoclassical buildings, imposing Soviet-era government offices, vast parks, and the magnificent **Aleksandar Nevski Cathedral**.

WHAT TO SEE AND DO

Most of Sofia's sights are centrally located and within easy walking distance of each other. The pedestrianized Bulevard Vitosha forms the heart of the shopping district and leads north to the Church of Sveta Nedelya, from where Bulevard Tsar Osvoboditel passes the major public buildings, culminating with the grand Aleksandar Nevski Cathedral.

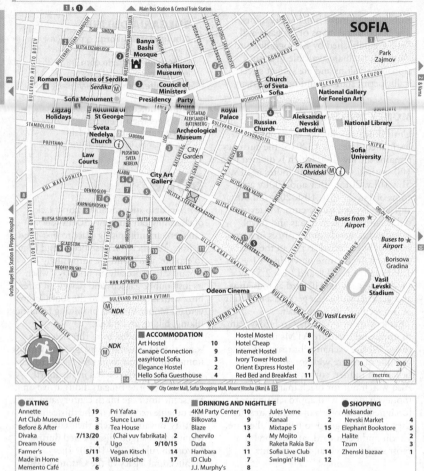

SOFIA

■ ACCOMMODATION			
Art Hostel	10	Hostel Mostel	8
Canape Connection	9	Hotel Cheap	1
easyHotel Sofia	3	Internet Hostel	6
Elegance Hostel	2	Ivory Tower Hostel	5
Hello Sofia Guesthouse	4	Orient Express Hostel	7
		Red Bed and Breakfast	11

● EATING				■ DRINKING AND NIGHTLIFE				● SHOPPING	
Annette	19	Pri Yafata	1	4KM Party Center	10	Jules Verne	5	Aleksandar	
Art Club Museum Café	3	Slunce Luna	12/16	Bilkovata	9	Kanaal	2	Nevski Market	4
Before & After	8	Tea House		Blaze	13	Mixtape 5	15	Elephant Bookstore	5
Divaka	7/13/20	(Chai vuv fabrikata)	2	Chervilo	4	My Mojito	6	Halite	2
Dream House	4	Ugo	9/10/15	Dada	3	Raketa Rakia Bar	1	Tzum	3
Farmer's	5/11	Vegan Kitsch	14	Hambara	11	Sofia Live Club	14	Zhenski bazaar	1
Made in Home	18	Vila Rosiche	17	ID Club	7	Swingin' Hall	12		
Memento Café	6			J.J. Murphy's	8				

Sveta Nedelya Church

At the heart of Sofia is **ploshtad Sveta Nedelya**, a pedestrianized square dominated by the distinctive **Sveta Nedelya Church** (daily 7am–7pm). Dating from 1863, its broad dome dominates the vast interior chamber, and colourful modern frescoes adorn every square centimetre of its walls.

The Largo

Laid out in the 1950s to demonstrate the power of Communist rule, the **Largo** is an elongated plaza flanked on three sides by severe monumental edifices built in Soviet Classicist style. They include the towering monolith of the former **Party House**, originally the home of the Communist hierarchy, and now serving as government offices. The plaza extends westwards to the **Sofia Monument**, the city's symbol, which represents the eponymous Goddess of Wisdom. On the northern side of the Largo is the **Council of Ministers**, Bulgaria's cabinet offices.

The Banya Bashi Mosque and the Sofia History Museum

The **Banya Bashi Mosque** was built in 1576 by Mimar Sinan, who also designed the great mosque at Edirne in Turkey. The mosque is not officially open to tourists, but modestly dressed visitors may visit outside of prayer times. Behind stands the **Sofia History Museum** (Tues–Sun 11am–7pm; 6Lv; ⑩ sofiahistorymuseum .bg), housed in a splendid yellow-and-red-striped *fin-de-siècle* building once home to the city's mineral baths. Highlights of its absorbing collection include a gleaming 1905 Mercedes owned by Prince Ferdinand I and an ornamental clock he received as a gift from Queen Victoria in the late nineteenth century. Locals gather daily to bottle the hot, sulphurous water that gushes from public taps into stone troughs outside the museum, opposite ulitsa Exzarh Iosif.

The Rotunda of St George and the Presidency
Sofia's oldest church, the **Rotunda of St George**, bul. Dondukov 2, dates back to the fourth century and contains frescoes from the eighth century onwards. It was built upon the Roman foundations of Serdika, which are open to the public and can also be seen in front of the nearby TSUM department store. Surrounding the church is the **Presidency**, guarded by soldiers in colourful nineteenth-century garb (Changing of the Guard hourly).

The Archeological Museum
A fifteenth-century mosque now holds the **Archeological Museum**, ul. Saborna 2 (May–Oct daily 10am–6pm; Nov–April Tues–Sun 10am–5pm; 10Lv; ⑩ naim.bg), whose prize exhibit is the magnificent Valchitran Treasure, a Thracian gold cauldron plus cups. Also on show is a collection of Thracian armour, medieval church wall paintings and numerous Roman tombstones.

The City Art Gallery
The **City Art Gallery** (Tues–Sat 10am–7pm, Sun 11am–6pm; free; ⑩ sghg.bg) in the City Garden, immediately to the south of ploshtad Aleksandar Batenberg, stages regular exhibitions of contemporary Bulgarian art. Displays feature the country's best-known artists, including bold expressive pieces by Vladimir Dimitrov (known as "The Master"),

and striking abstract works by Georgi Bozhilov-Slona.

The Russian Church and Aleksandar Nevski Cathedral
Built on the site of a mosque in the early twentieth century, the **Russian Church** (daily 8am–7pm) is a stunning golden-domed building with an emerald spire and an exuberant mosaic-tiled exterior, which conceals a dark, candle-scented interior. The nearby **Aleksandar Nevski Cathedral** (daily 7am–7pm, liturgy on Sun at 1pm; free) is one of the finest pieces of architecture in the Balkans. Financed by public subscription and built between 1882 and 1924 to honour the 200,000 Russian casualties of the 1877–78 War of Liberation, it's a magnificent structure, bulging with domes and semi-domes and glittering with gold leaf. Within the gloomy interior, a beardless Christ sits enthroned above the altar, and numerous scenes from his life, painted in a humanistic style, adorn the walls. The crypt, entered from outside (Tues–Sun 10am–6pm; 6Lv), contains a superb collection of icons from all over the country.

The National Gallery for Foreign Art
An imposing nineteenth-century building houses the **National Gallery for Foreign Art** (Mon & Wed–Sun 11am–6.30pm; 6Lv), which devotes a lot of space to Indian woodcarvings and second-division French and Russian artists, though there are a few minor works by the likes of Rodin, Chagall and Kandinsky. If you head back west past Aleksandar Nevski Cathedral, you'll pass two recumbent lions flanking the Tomb of the Unknown Soldier, set beside the wall of the plain, brown-brick **Church of Sveta Sofia** which gave the city its name in the fourteenth century.

Borisova Gradina
Southeast along bulevard Tsar Osvoboditel, past Sofia University, is **Borisova Gradina**, named after Bulgaria's interwar monarch, Boris III. The park – the largest in Sofia – has a rich variety of flowers and trees, outdoor bars, a couple

5

of football stadiums and two huge Communist monuments.

Mount Vitosha

A wooded granite mass 20km long and 16km wide, **Mount Vitosha**, 8km south of the city, is where Sofians go for picnics, hiking, biking and skiing. The ascent of its highest peak, the 2290m **Cherni Vrah**, has become a traditional test of stamina. Getting here on public transport is straightforward, although there are fewer buses on weekdays than at weekends. Take tram #5 from behind the Law Courts to Ovcha Kupel bus station, then change to bus #61, which climbs through the forests towards **Zlatni Mostove**, a beauty spot on the western shoulder of Mount Vitosha beside the so-called **Stone River**. Beneath the large boulders running down the mountainside is a rivulet which once attracted gold-panners. Trails lead up beside the stream towards the mountain's upper reaches: Cherni Vrah is about two to three hours' walk from here. Alternatively, use the Simeonovo **cable car** (daily in winter 8am–4pm; rest of the year Sat & Sun only 9am–5pm; 8/10Lv one-way/return) to reach the handful of ski pistes at Aleko (ⓦskivitosha.com). From here it's a two-hour hike up to the Cherni Vrah summit. To reach the Simeonovo cable car station take tram #10 from the centre to Hladilnik and change to bus #122.

ARRIVAL AND DEPARTURE

By plane Sofia airport (ⓦsofia-airport.bg) has two terminals: budget carriers arrive at Terminal 1; Bulgaria Air and other major airlines are handled by the newer and smarter Terminal 2. The terminals are connected by a free shuttle bus (every 30min) and the best way to get into the city centre is to catch the metro from Terminal 2 (5.30am–midnight). Bus #84 to the centre picks up from both terminals; tickets (1.60Lv) can be bought from the airport newspaper kiosk – you'll need additional tickets for any oversized bags. There's also *marshrutka* (private minibus) #30, which runs until around 10pm (every 15–30min; 1.50Lv). Taxis waiting outside Terminal 2 with fake OK Taxi signage will charge you an exorbitant 40Lv or more, so it's essential to book an official OK Taxi (ⓦoktaxi.net) at the booth in the arrivals hall (14–18Lv).

By train Trains arrive and depart from Central Station (Tsentralna Gara), a concrete hangar 2km from the centre

harbouring a number of exchange bureaus and snack bars, but little else to welcome the visitor. The metro station (5am–midnight) just outside is the quickest and easiest way to reach the centre.

Destinations Bansko (4 daily; 7hr via Septemvri); Belgrade (2 daily; 7hr 30min); Blagoevgrad (6 daily; 2hr 30min); Bucharest (1 daily; 9hr 30min); Burgas (5 daily; 8hr); Istanbul (1 daily; 11hr); Koprivshtitsa (8 daily; 2hr); Plovdiv (14 daily; 3hr); Septemvri (15 daily; 2hr); Thessaloniki (1 daily; 7hr); Varna (11 daily; 8hr); Veliko Turnovo (8 daily; 5hr via Gorna Oryahovitsa).

By bus Most buses arrive at the terminal, next to the train station, although some Bansko services and Blagoevgrad buses (for connections to Rila Monastery) use the Ovcha Kupel terminal, 5km southwest of the centre along bul. Tsar Boris III. Buses #11 and #60 head to the centre from here.

Destinations Bansko (6 daily; 3hr); Burgas (11 daily; 6hr); Koprivshtitsa (3 daily; 2hr); Plovdiv (hourly; 2hr); Varna (hourly; 7hr); Veliko Tarnovo (every 30min; 3hr 30min).

INFORMATION

Tourist office Both the National Tourist Information Centre at pl. Sveta Nedelya 1 (see p.131) and the Sofia Tourist Information Centre (July–Sept Mon–Fri 8am–8pm, Sat & Sun 10am–6pm; Oct–June Mon–Fri 9.30am–6pm; ☎02 491 8344, ⓦinfo-sofia.bg), in the underpass at the Kliment Ochridski metro station, provide city maps and local travel advice. An excellent alternative is the friendly travel agency Zig-Zag Holidays at bul. Stamboliiski 20 (entrance on ul. Lavele; Mon–Fri 9.30am–6.30pm, daily in summer; ☎02 980 5102, ⓦzigzagbg.com), which charges a 5Lv consultation fee, although not for accommodation booking.

GETTING AROUND

Public transport There's a flat fare of 1.60Lv on all urban routes, whether by bus (*avtobus*), trolleybus (*troleibus*), the two-line metro system, or tram (*tramvai*). Tickets (*bileti*) are sold from street kiosks and can be bought from machines on board trams or from the driver on buses and must be punched once you have entered the vehicle (inspections are frequent and there are 40Lv spot fines for fare dodgers). Kiosks at the main tram stops sell one-day tickets (*karta za edin den*; 6Lv) and a strip (*talon*) of ten tickets (12Lv) – the tickets can only be used by the purchaser and must be used in sequence. Metro tickets can only be bought from metro stations.

Taxis and minibuses The most reliable taxi company is OK Taxis (☎02 973 2121, ⓦoktaxi.net), charging 79st/km until nightfall, 90st afterwards, and 70st initial fare; make sure the driver has his meter running. Additionally, there's a fleet of private minibuses (*marshrutka*), acting like shared taxis and covering around forty different routes across the city for a flat fare of 1.50Lv. Destinations and routes are displayed on the front of the vehicles – in the Cyrillic alphabet – and passengers flag them down like normal taxis, calling out when they want them to stop.

ACCOMMODATION

Sofia has a number of good hostels, and some small, reasonably priced hotels in central locations. All hostels have free wi-fi and breakfast unless otherwise stated.

HOSTELS

Art Hostel ul. Angel Kanchev 21a ☎ 02 987 0545, ⓦ art-hostel.com. Sofia's trendiest hostel, hosting art exhibitions, live music, resident DJs and occasional drama performances. Guests have access to a kitchen and popular tea room-cum-bar with lovely garden, and free computer access. Dorms <u>20Lv</u>, doubles <u>60Lv</u>

Elegance Hostel ul. Bratya Miladinovi 33 ☎ 0888 450 107. Modern hostel located a 10min walk from the centre. Choice of spacious single-sex dorms or smartly furnished doubles. Shared kitchen and free tea and coffee. Dorms <u>16Lv</u>, doubles <u>40Lv</u>

★ **Hostel Mostel** bul. Makedoniya 2A ☎ 0889 223 296, ⓦ hostelmostel.com. Superb hostel located in a historic building a short walk from the centre. Besides the free all-you-can-eat breakfast, they offer a bowl of pasta and a bottle of beer for every night of your stay. The ground floor has a cavernous, comfortable lounge space with flat-screen TV, DVDs and travel library. Just up the road is the hostel's lively bar. Dorms <u>20Lv</u>, doubles <u>60Lv</u>

Internet Hostel ul. Alabin 50a ☎ 0889 138 298, ⓦ internethostelsofia.hostel.com. Friendly hostel with kitchen offering spacious but dated doubles, triples and quads, as well as studio apartments. Located on the second floor of a shopping arcade, above the *Dream House* restaurant. Dorms <u>18Lv</u>, doubles <u>48Lv</u>, studio apartment for two <u>70Lv</u>

Ivory Tower Hostel ul. Tsar Samuil 60 ☎ 0876 668 467. Welcoming hostel in a characterful part of downtown Sofia that's 5min from the centre. Neat single-sex dorms, a double/triple room with shared kitchen and living area. Dorms <u>24Lv</u>, doubles <u>65Lv</u>

Orient Express Hostel ul. Hristo Belchev 8A ☎ 0888 384 828, ⓦ orientexpresshostel.com. Small and cosy hostel, with high ceilings, modern fittings combined with antique and salvaged furniture, and TVs in every room. Its fifth-floor position makes for great views from the rooms, but some arduous stair climbing as there's no lift. Friendly and helpful staff. Dorms <u>22Lv</u>, doubles <u>48Lv</u>, apartment <u>70Lv</u>

HOTELS

Canape Connection ul. Gladston 12a ☎ 02 441 6373, ⓦ canapeconnection.com. Cosy, central guesthouse with rustic furniture and comfortable, extra-wide beds. Helpful staff are on hand to provide local information, and the breakfast is excellent. Doubles <u>62Lv</u>

easyHotel Sofia ul. Aldomirovska 108 ☎ 02 920 1654, ⓦ easyhotel.com. Despite being inconveniently located several blocks west of the centre, this is a great deal for anyone in search of a spotless, cheap en-suite room. Prices vary according to availability. Doubles <u>40Lv</u>

★ **Hello Sofia Guesthouse** bul. Stefan Stambolov 12 ☎ 0889 138 298, ⓦ hellosofia.hostel.com. Situated just a short distance from Sofia's thriving Women's Market (Zhenski Bazaar), this delightful guesthouse has been thoughtfully designed and features imaginative styling and home comforts that include widescreen TVs, spacious en-suite bathrooms, and a smart shared kitchen and lounge area. Doubles <u>50Lv</u>

Hotel Cheap ul. Knyaz Boris 203 ☎ 02 831 2123, ⓦ hotel-cheap.bg. Bland but decent place with spotless rooms. Conveniently located close to Lvov Most metro station and within walking distance of the bus and train stations. Doubles <u>60Lv</u>

Red Bed and Breakfast ul. Lyuben Karavelov 15 ☎ 0889 226 822, ⓦ redbandb.com. Occupying a charming historic building, this appealing guesthouse has huge rooms with high ceilings and parquet floors. Guests have the use of a washing machine and well-equipped kitchen. Doubles <u>40Lv</u>

EATING

The cheapest places to grab snacks, a beer or a coffee are the many cafés and kiosks on bul. Vitosha and pl. Slaveikov or in the city's public gardens. In recent years soup-focused places such as *Farmer's* (see p.138) have proliferated, serving up generous portions of wholesome, inexpensive fare that's proven immensely popular.

CAFÉS

Art Club Museum Café Corner of ul. Saborna and ul. Lege ⓦ artclubmuseum.bg. Chic café with a pleasant patio, set amid Thracian tombstones next to the Archeological Museum. Live DJs in the basement Thursday to Saturday nights. Serves a variety of light meals, desserts and inventive drinks, such as cappuccino with coconut and banana (3.80Lv). Open 24hr.

Memento Café bul. Vitosha 32. One of the countless cafés that have mushroomed along the city's main commercial strip in recent years, this tiny yet popular spot has a Mediterranean feel and serves top-notch coffee, cakes and sandwiches. Daily 8am–2am.

★ **Tea House (Chai vuv fabrikata)** ul. Georgi Benkovski 11 ⓦ teahousesofia.com. Atmospheric traditional teahouse with a formidable array of teas including Kashmiri *chai* and rose, priced from 2.50Lv. Check their Facebook page for upcoming live music performances. Daily 10am–11pm.

Vegan Kitsch ul. Parchevich 48 ⓦ vegankitsch.com. Tiny vegan café with just a couple of chairs that serves a

5

fabulous selection of sweet and savoury dishes to eat in or takeaway. Daily 9am–7pm.

Vila Rosiche ul. Neofit Rilski 26 ⓦvilarosiche.com. Enormously popular café within an elegant historic building. Treat yourself to sublime home-made cakes (6.90Lv), croissants and juices served inside or on the summer terrace. Daily 8.30am–10pm.

RESTAURANTS

Annette ul. Angel Kunchev 27 ⓦannette.bg. An excellent Moroccan restaurant with tree-shaded outdoor seating and a mouth-watering range of exotic dishes that include chicken baked with pear in wine sauce (13.90Lv). Daily 10am–10pm.

Before & After ul. Hristo Belchev 12 ⓦba.club-cabaret.net. Elegant and popular restaurant near the *Orient Express Hostel*, with a range of Bulgarian, Turkish and international dishes including some fantastic traditional desserts. Also great for vegetarian options, including grilled vegetables in yoghurt and dill (6Lv). Hosts tango dances on Sundays. Daily 8.30am–10pm.

Divaka ul. Gladston 54, with other branches at ul. Hristo Belchev 16 & ul. 6th Septemvri 41a. Small chain of bright and busy restaurants serving excellent, meat-heavy Bulgarian dishes. Chicken steak 6Lv, grilled vegetables 5.30Lv. Daily 10am–1am.

Dream House ul. Alabin 50a ☎02 980 8163, ⓦdreamhouse-bg.com. Intimate, friendly and well-established vegetarian restaurant above a shopping arcade. Has a good choice of meals and snacks using seasonal produce, including aubergine couscous (6.80Lv) and Asian bamboo soup (2.90Lv). They also deliver within the city centre area. Daily 11am–10pm.

Farmer's ul. Shishman 24, with another branch at pl. Garibaldi. Smart places serving a great range of soups (3Lv) as well as salads, chunky burgers and aubergine sandwiches. Eat-in or takeaway. Daily 9am–10pm.

Made in Home ul. Angel Kunchev 30A. Hugely popular place featuring distressed furniture, bare brick walls and retro ornaments. Serves a broad choice of well-prepared Bulgarian and international dishes. Daily 11am–11pm.

Pri Yafata bul. Dondukov 29. Brash but fun take on a traditional *mehana*, complete with live music, costumed staff and a great Bulgarian menu that includes tripe soup (*shkembe churba*; 3.90Lv) and a wide range of grilled meat dishes. Daily 11am–midnight.

★ **Slunce Luna** ul. Gladston 18b & ul. 6th Septemvri 39 ⓦsunmoon.bg. Popular vegetarian restaurants with rustic furniture and a bakery that supplies great wholemeal bread. Daily 9am–11pm.

Ugo bul. Vitosha 45, ul. Neofit Rilski 68 & ul. Han Krum 2 ⓦugo.bg. One of the better pizza and pasta restaurant chains in the centre, *Ugo* offers a broad range of dishes 24 hours a day.

DRINKING AND NIGHTLIFE

For evening entertainment, there's an ever-growing number of clubs, most playing a mix of pop, retro, rock or the ubiquitous local "folk pop" (*chalga*). Jazz and Latino music are also popular. Information on the city's small but thriving gay scene can be found at ⓦgay.bg.

BARS

Bilkovata ul. Tsar Shishman 22. A buzzing, smoky cellar with decent music and a young crowd, *Bilkovata* is something of a local legend: fondly remembered by successive generations of students, arty types and young professionals, it's still going strong. Packed beer garden in summer. Daily 10am–2am.

Dada ul. Benkovski 10 ⓦdadaculturalbar.eu. *Dada*'s regular cultural evenings – including film screenings and poetry readings – attract a mixed crowd of Bulgarians and expats. Daily noon–2am.

Hambara ul. 6-ti Septemvri 22. Hidden behind an unmarked doorway just off the street, this dark, candlelit, stone-floored bar is one of the most atmospheric places in the centre for a long night of drink-fuelled conversation. Live jazz several nights a week. Daily 7pm–2am.

J.J. Murphy's ul. Karnigradska 6 ⓦjjmurphys.bg. Sofia's top Irish bar, offering filling pub grub, big-screen sports and live music at the weekends. Daily noon–1am.

Jules Verne ul. Rakovski 127 (first floor). Simply furnished bar frequented by a lively crowd of arty young professionals. Daily 2pm–6am.

Kanaal bul. Madrid 2 ⓦkanaal.bg. Renowned for its vast choice of international beers, this stylish bar attracts a hip crowd. Ten minutes by taxi from the centre. Daily 5.30pm–2am.

Raketa Rakia Bar bul. Yanko Sakazov 15–17. One of the best places in the city to sample Bulgarian *rakia*, it's also gained a reputation for excellent local dishes. Daily 11am–midnight.

CLUBS

Entrance fees range from nothing to 20Lv depending on the venue; expect to pay more if a major DJ is manning the decks. A valid ID is compulsory.

4KM Party Center bul. Tsarigradsko shose 111 ⓦ4-km.com. Cavernous hall with giant sound system that holds regular concerts and all-night DJ parties – check their Facebook page for the latest events. Located 4km from the centre, it's best reached by taxi.

Blaze pl. Bulgaria 1. Lively bar and club beside NDK, with a good sound system pumping out mainstream pop for the trendy clientele. Daily 9pm–3am.

Chervilo bul. Tsar Osvoboditel 9. Stylish city-centre club offering the latest in house, techno and Latin over two floors. The action spreads out onto the terrace in summer,

5

when it's more like an elite, pay-to-enter pavement café than a club. Café daily 10am–10pm; club Thurs–Sat 10pm–7am.

ID Club ul. Karnigradska 19B ⓦidclub.bg. A popular gay club with plenty of dancing space that plays retro, *chalga* and pop until the early hours. So-called "face control" (only letting in those who look the part) is strict on busy nights. Daily 9pm–3am.

My Mojito ul. Ivan Vazov 12. This well-established club is one of Sofia's trendiest, with a laidback crowd and DJs playing a mix of mainstream dance and pop. Daily 9pm–5am.

LIVE MUSIC

Mixtape 5 NDK underpass beneath Lover's Bridge. Big club with central stage hosting hip local and international bands and DJs. Daily 9pm–late.

Sofia Live Club National Palace of Culture (NDK) ⓦsofialiveclub.com. Lying deep beneath NDK, a monolithic Communist-era building that dominates central Sofia, this plush club has hosted an impressive number of international world music and jazz groups. Daily 8pm–2am.

Swingin' Hall ul. Dragan Tsankov 8 ⓦswinginghall.bg. Cheerful, crowded bar that's been around for years and has live music (usually pop, rock or jazz) on two stages. Tues–Sat 9pm–4am.

ENTERTAINMENT

CINEMAS

Cinema City bul. Stamboliski 101 ☎02 929 2929, ⓦcinemacity.bg. Multi-screen cinema in the Mall of Sofia with lots of snack stands in the vicinity.

Odeon bul. Patriarh Evtimiy 1 ☎02 969 2469. Shows oldies and prize-winning art films past and present. Check ⓦprogramata.bg for listings. Small bar in the lobby.

SHOPPING

Until recently, the city's pedestrianized central street, bul. Vitosha, was the place where you were most likely to come across familiar high-street shops and brands; some remain but many were replaced by outdoor cafés when the retailers moved into the characterless yet immensely popular malls located south of the centre. Ul. Graf Ignatiev and ul. Tsar Ivan Shishman are now Sofia's busiest central shopping streets, home to a wide range of small independents selling everything from books to clothes, souvenirs and vegetables.

Aleksandar Nevski Located at the apex of the three central churches on pl. Aleksandar Nevski, this cluster of stalls offers an odd mix of religious paintings, Turkish-influenced silver jewellery, traditional Bulgarian peasant textiles, plus antique and replica Communist items. Be warned that there's Nazi memorabilia on sale too.

Elephant Bookstore ul. Tsar Ivan Shishman 31 ⓦelephantbookstore.com. A delightfully cosy shop crammed with new and used English books and a mesmerizing array of quirky gifts. Daily 10am–10pm.

Halite bul. Knyaginy Mariya Luiza, opposite the Banya Bashi Mosque. This elegant building houses Sofia's central food hall with two floors of shops and food stalls. Daily 7am–midnight.

Tzum Located just outside Serdika metro, this was once the preserve of the party elite and, although it's now been eclipsed by the much larger suburban malls, it remains the centre's premier shopping mall stocked with upmarket and luxury goods. Daily 10am–8pm.

Zhenski bazaar bul. Stefan Stambolov. One of the city's best outdoor markets, where trinkets, fresh fruit, vegetables and other foodstuffs are on sale. Daily 6am–5pm.

DIRECTORY

Embassies and consulates Canada, Pozitano 7 ☎02 969 9717; Ireland, Bacho Kiro 26–30 ☎02 985 3425; South Africa, Shipka 7 ☎02 983 3505; UK, Moskovska 9 ☎02 933 9222; US, Kozyak 16 ☎02 937 5100.

Hospital Pirogov hospital (bul. General Totleben 21 ☎02 915 4411, ⓦpirogov.eu).

Pharmacy Aronia 2001 at bul. Pencho Slaveikov 6, opposite Pirogov hospital, is open 24hr.

Post office ul. General Gurko 6 (daily 7am–8.30pm).

Southern Bulgaria

The route south from Sofia skirts the Rila and Pirin mountain ranges, swathed in forests and dotted with alpine lakes, and home to Bulgaria's highest peaks. Even those on a tight schedule should find time for a visit to the most revered of Bulgarian monasteries, **Rila**, around 30km east of the main southbound route. **Bansko**, meanwhile, on the eastern side of the Pirin range, boasts a wealth of traditional architecture, as well as being a major ski resort and a good base for hiking. Another much-travelled route heads southeast from Sofia towards Istanbul. The main road and rail lines now linking Istanbul and Sofia essentially follow the course of the Roman Serdica–Constantinople road, running past towns ruled by the Ottomans for so

5

long that foreigners used to call this part of Bulgaria "European Turkey". Of these, the most important is **Plovdiv**, Bulgaria's second city, whose old quarter is a wonderful mixture of National Revival mansions and classical remains. Some 30km south of Plovdiv is **Bachkovo Monastery**, containing Bulgaria's most vivid frescoes.

RILA MONASTERY

As the most celebrated of Bulgaria's religious sites, famed for its fine architecture and mountainous setting – and declared a World Heritage site by UNESCO – **Rila Monastery** receives a steady stream of visitors, many of them day-trippers from Sofia.

WHAT TO SEE AND DO

Ringed by mighty walls, the **monastery** (daily dawn–dusk; free; ⓦrilamonastery .pmg-blg.com) has the outward appearance of a fortress, but this impression is immediately dispelled when you see the beauty of the interior, which even the crowds can't mar. Graceful arches above the flagstoned courtyard support tiers of monastic cells, and stairways ascend to wooden balconies. Bold red stripes and black-and-white check patterns enliven the facade, contrasting with the sombre mountains behind and creating a harmony between the cloisters and the **church**. Richly coloured frescoes shelter beneath the church porch and cover much of its interior. The iconostasis is splendid, almost 10m wide and covered by a mass of intricate carvings and gold leaf. Beside the church is **Hrelyo's Tower**, the sole remaining building from the fourteenth century. Cauldrons, which were once used to prepare food for pilgrims, occupy the soot-encrusted kitchen on the ground floor of the north wing, while on the floors above you can inspect the spartan refectory and panelled guest rooms. Beneath the east wing is the **treasury** (daily 8.30am–5pm; 8Lv), where, among other things, you can view a wooden cross carved with more than 1500 miniature human figures, dating from the 1790s.

ARRIVAL AND DEPARTURE

Joining a day tour from the capital, booked through the Sofia Tourist Information Centre (see p.136), is by far the most sensible way of getting here, with group trips costing around 50Lv per person.

ACCOMMODATION

Pchelina ⓤ0888 393058, ⓦpchelina.com. Delightful hotel ensconced within the forest 3km away from the monastery. Pleasant en-suite rooms and a great restaurant that serves trout from the local river. Doubles 55Lv

Rila monastery ⓣ0705 42208. It's possible to stay on site in reasonably comfortable rooms. Gates close at 11pm. Doubles 65Lv

Zodiac 4km beyond the monastery ⓣ0887 362 186, ⓦcampingzodiacbg.com. Pleasant campsite occupying an attractive riverside spot, with smart double bungalows and a good restaurant. Camping/person 8Lv, double bungalows/person 15Lv

EATING

For cheap snacks, delicious bread and doughnuts, head for the bakery opposite the East Gate.

Drushliavitsa Built over a stream on the hillside just beyond the East Gate, this traditional-style Bulgarian restaurant offers polite service and shaded outdoor seating. The menu features Bulgarian standards and fresh local trout (7Lv). Daily 10am–10pm.

Rila Situated behind the bakery. Identical in style to the *Drushliavitsa* with a similar menu and prices. Daily 10am–10pm.

BANSKO

Lying some 40km east of the main Struma Valley route, **BANSKO** (Банско) is the primary centre for walking and skiing on the eastern slopes of the Pirin mountains. Originally an agricultural centre, ski tourism has prompted massive investment in recent years, resulting in the unappealing sight of apartment blocks and hotels squeezed into the backyards of stone-built nineteenth-century farmhouses. Despite this overdevelopment, the central old town, with its numerous traditional pubs hidden away down labyrinthine cobbled streets, is as attractive as ever and the perfect place to wind down after a hard day on the slopes.

Though connected to Sofia and other towns by bus, Bansko can also be reached by a **narrow-gauge railway**, which leaves the main Sofia–Plovdiv line at Septemvri and forges its way across the highlands. It's one of the most scenic trips in the Balkans, but also one of the slowest, taking five hours to cover just over 100km.

WHAT TO SEE AND DO

Bansko centres on the modern pedestrianized ploshtad Nikola Vaptsarov, where the **Nikola Vaptsarov Museum** (daily 8am–noon & 2–5.30pm; 3Lv) relates the life of the local-born poet and Socialist martyr. Immediately north of here, ploshtad Vazrazhdane is watched over by the solid stone tower of the **Church of Sveta Troitsa**, whose interior contains exquisite nineteenth-century frescoes and icons. On the opposite side of the square, the **Rilski Convent** houses an icon museum (Mon–Fri 9am–noon & 2–5.30pm; 3Lv) devoted to the achievements of Bansko's nineteenth-century icon painters.

From the main square, ulitsa Pirin leads north towards the **cable car** (Dec–April daily 8.30am–5pm; 28Lv), where there is a buzzing collection of ski-rental shops, bars and restaurants. Ski passes cost 58Lv per day (38Lv for children), and ski and snowboard equipment can be rented for around 30Lv per day. The cable car doesn't operate outside the ski season so the only option for reaching the summit in the summer months is to head west – on foot or by taxi – via a steep 14km uphill climb to the Vihren hut, where cheap dorm **accommodation** (12Lv per person) is available. This is the main trailhead for hikes towards the 2914m summit of **Mount Vihren**, Bulgaria's second-highest peak, or gentler rambles around the meadows and lakes nearby.

ARRIVAL AND DEPARTURE

By train The train station is on the northern edge of town, a 10min walk from pl. Vaptsarov.
Destinations Septemvri (4 daily; 5hr); Sofia (change at Septemvri, for the slow narrow-gauge railway; 4 daily; 7hr).
By bus The bus station is close to the train station.
Destinations Blagoevgrad (hourly; 1hr); Plovdiv (7 daily; 4hr); Sofia (hourly; 2hr 30min).

INFORMATION

Tourist information The tourist office is on pl. Nikola Vapzarov 4 (Mon–Fri 9am–6pm, Sat & Sun 10am–6pm; ☎0749 88580, ⓦbansko.bg).

ACCOMMODATION

Basecamp 5 Hostel ul. Ortze Popyordanov 1 ☎0888 110320. Excellent budget option with pristine four-bed dorms and shared kitchen and living area, 1km from the lift station. Dorms 20Lv
Bisser Family Hotel ul. El Tepe 16 ☎0749 88078, ⓦbisser-bansko.com. Pleasant hotel situated on a quiet street near the centre of town. En-suite rooms, wi-fi and breakfast included. Free daily bus to the lift station. Doubles 58Lv
Dedo Pene ul. Aleksandar Buynov 1 ☎0749 88348, ⓦdedopene.com. Located just south of pl. Vazrazhdane, there's an array of wonderfully atmospheric rooms in this restored nineteenth-century building. Doubles 60Lv
Zlatev Guest House ul. Nikola Popfilipov 1 ☎0899 969370. Family-run place in the heart of the old town, offering smart en-suite rooms and a secluded courtyard garden. Doubles 60Lv

EATING AND DRINKING

★**Dedo Pene** ul. Aleksandar Buynov 1 ⓦdedopene .com. Atmospheric restaurant serving reasonably priced traditional Bulgarian food and Bansko specialities such as *kapama*, a delicious stew of chicken, pork and cabbage. Sit inside among folksy decorations or opt for the vine-shaded courtyard in summer. Daily 11am–1am.
Irish Harp ul. Banderitsa 51 ⓦirishharpbansko.com. Popular pub in the town centre with good food and Guinness on tap. Daily 4pm–late.
Molerite ul. Glazne 41 ⓦmolerite.com. Two floors of wooden benches and ethnic textiles just north of pl. Nikola

---

HORSERIDING IN THE RILA MOUNTAINS

A unique way to experience the spectacular terrain of the **Rila Mountains** is on horseback. Some of the trails pass through virtually untouched forest areas and alongside staggering glacial lakes; there are also some seriously rocky options for experienced or adventurous riders. The Sofia-based tour operator Horseriding Bulgaria (ul. Orfey 9 ☎02 403 0107, ⓦhorseriding bulgaria.com) offers a number of tours setting out from their Iskar Ranch at the foot of the Rila Mountains, and costing from €600–900 for eight days.

5

Vaptsarov – try the superb local specialities such as roast lamb (18Lv) and sword-grilled shish kebabs (15Lv). Turns into a folk-pop disco after about 11pm. Daily 11am–2am.

PLOVDIV

Slated to be European Capital of Culture in 2019 and Bulgaria's second-largest city, **PLOVDIV** (Пловдив) has more obvious charms than Sofia, which the locals here tend to look down on. The old town embodies Plovdiv's long history – Thracian fortifications subsumed by Macedonian masonry, overlaid with Roman and Byzantine walls. Great timber-framed mansions, erected during the Bulgarian renaissance, loom over the derelict Ottoman mosques and artisans' dwellings of the lower town. But this isn't just another museum town: the city's arts festivals and trade fairs are the biggest in the country, and its restaurants and bars are equal to those of the capital.

WHAT TO SEE AND DO

Plovdiv centres on the large **ploshtad Tsentralen**, dominated by the monolithic *Hotel Trimontium Princess*.

Ploshtad Dzhumaya

Thronged with promenading Plovdivians and lined with shops, cafés and bars, the pedestrianized ulitsa Knyaz Aleksandar I leads onto the attractive **ploshtad Dzhumaya** where the substantial ruins of a **Roman stadium** that could hold thirty thousand spectators are on display beneath the square. Among the variously styled buildings here, the renovated **Dzhumaya Mosque**, with its diamond-patterned minaret and lead-sheathed domes, steals the show; it's believed that the mosque dates back to the reign of Sultan Murad II (1359–85).

The Old Quarter

Covering one of Plovdiv's three hills with its cobbled streets and colourful mansions, the **Old Quarter** is a painter's dream and a cartographer's nightmare. As good a route as any is to start from ploshtad Dzhumaya and head east up ulitsa Saborna. Blackened fortress walls dating from Byzantine times can be seen around Saborna and other streets, sometimes incorporated into the dozens of timber-framed National Revival houses that are Plovdiv's speciality. Outside and within, the walls are frequently decorated with niches, floral motifs or false columns, painted in a style known as *alafranga*. Turn right, up the steps beside the Church of Sveta Bogoroditsa, and continue, along twisting cobbled lanes, to the **Roman Theatre** (daily 9am–6pm; 6Lv), the best preserved in the country, and still an impressive venue for regular concerts and plays (advertised around the town and in the local press).

The City Gallery of Fine Arts and around

The **City Gallery of Fine Arts** on ulitsa Saborna (daily 9.30am–6pm; 3Lv; ⓦgalleryplovdiv.com) holds an extensive collection of nineteenth- and twentieth-century Bulgarian paintings, including some fine portraits by renowned National Revival realist painter Stanislav Dospevski. A short distance northeast, the **Church of SS Constantine and Elena** contains a fine gilt iconostasis, decorated by the prolific nineteenth-century artist Zahari Zograf, whose work also appears in the adjacent **Museum of Icons** (daily 9.30am–6pm; 3Lv). A little further uphill is the richly decorated Kuyumdzhioglu House, now home to the **Ethnographic Museum** (Tues–Sun 9am–6pm; 5Lv). Folk costumes and crafts are on display

---

THE NIGHT TRAIN TO ISTANBUL

There's a nightly **train** to Istanbul, which leaves Plovdiv at 10.12pm and arrives at 8am; tickets cost 54Lv and must be bought in advance from the BDZh-Rila office in Plovdiv's Central Station (Tsentralna Gara; daily 8am–noon & 1–4.45pm; ☎032 643120). Australian, US, UK and most EU citizens require Turkish **visas** (see p.1141) that can only be bought online at ⓦevisa.gov.tr.

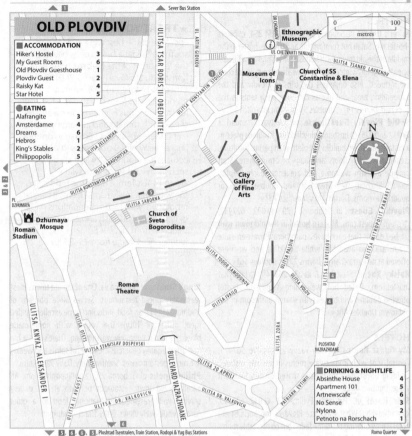

OLD PLOVDIV

ACCOMMODATION	
Hiker's Hostel	3
My Guest Rooms	6
Old Plovdiv Guesthouse	1
Plovdiv Guest	2
Raisky Kat	4
Star Hotel	5

EATING	
Alafrangite	3
Amsterdamer	4
Dreams	6
Hebros	1
King's Stables	2
Philippopolis	5

DRINKING & NIGHTLIFE	
Absinthe House	4
Apartment 101	5
Artnewscafe	6
No Sense	3
Nylona	2
Petnoto na Rorschach	1

on the ground floor; upstairs, the elegantly furnished rooms reflect the former owner's taste for Viennese and French Baroque.

ARRIVAL AND DEPARTURE

By train Plovdiv's train station is on bul. Hristo Botev, a 10min bus ride (#20 or #26) south of the centre.

Destinations Burgas (7 daily; 5hr); Istanbul (1 daily; 9hr); Koprivshtitsa (4 daily; 3hr 30min via Karlovo); Sofia (15 daily; 3hr); Varna (8 daily; 6hr).

By bus Two of Plovdiv's three bus stations are near the train station: Rodopi, serving the mountain resorts to the south, is just on the other side of the tracks; Yug, serving Sofia and the rest of the country, is one block east. The third, Sever, is north of the river (bus #3 or #99; 20min) and serves destinations such as Koprivshtitsa and Veliko Tarnovo. Several agencies at Yug station sell tickets for international buses. Hebros Bus (daily 8am–7pm; ☎ 032 657811, ⓦ hebrosbus.com), a Eurolines agent, can book

seats on buses to Greece, Turkey and Western Europe.

Destinations Avtogara Rodopi: Smolyan (hourly; 2hr 30min via Bachkovo monastery). Avtogara Sever: Koprivshtitsa (1 daily; 2hr 30min); Veliko Tarnovo (2 daily; 4hr). Avtogara Yug: Burgas (5 daily; 4hr); Sofia (hourly; 2hr); Varna (2 daily; 7hr).

INFORMATION

Tourist information In the old town at ul. Dr Stoyan Chomakov 1 (Mon–Fri 9am–5.30pm, Sat & Sun 10am–5pm; ☎ 032 620453), and in the new town behind the post office at pl. Tsentralen 1 (Mon–Fri 9am–6pm, Sat & Sun 10am–5pm; ☎ 032 656794, ⓦ visitplovdiv.com). Both offices provide maps and can reserve hotel rooms and arrange excursions.

ACCOMMODATION

Plovdiv's hotel prices are relatively high, but there are several excellent hostels and a few decent-value hotel options.

5

HOSTELS

Hiker's Hostel ul. Saborna 53 ☎0896 764 854, ⓦhikers
-hostel.org. Small but comfortable and friendly hostel in the
middle of the old town, with fantastic views and a traditional
open fire during winter. Breakfast, wi-fi and computer access
are included. Also organizes day-trips in Plovdiv and the
surrounding area, and guests can even pitch tents in the
backyard. Dorms 11Lv, doubles 50Lv, camping/pitch 10Lv

★**Old Plovdiv Guesthouse** ul. Chetvarti Yanuari 3
☎032 260 925, ⓦhosteloldplovdiv.com. Fabulous place in
a historic old-town building, replete with period furniture,
creaking wooden floors and bags of atmosphere. Staff
provide a warm welcome and are enormously helpful.
Shared kitchen, free breakfast and double, triple or
quadruple rooms. Dorms 26Lv, doubles 75Lv

Plovdiv Guest ul. Saborna 20 ☎032 622432,
ⓦplovdivguest.com. Modern hostel in the old town with
six-bed dorms that each have a bathroom. Private en-suite
rooms are also available, while breakfast and wi-fi are
offered at no extra charge. Dorms 22Lv, doubles 66Lv

Raisky Kat ul. Slaveikov 6 ☎032 268849, ⓦraiskykat
.hostel.com. Dated but welcoming family-run hostel
offering doubles and triples with shared bathroom in the
old town. Doubles 48Lv

HOTELS

My Guest Rooms ul. Ivan Vazov 29 ☎0896 567475.
Central spot with immaculate rooms in smartly restored
building. Guests have the use of a shared kitchen. Excellent
value. Doubles 40Lv

Star Hotel ul. Patriarch Evtiimi 13 ☎032 633599,
ⓦstarhotel.bg. What was once Plovdiv's top Socialist-era
hotel is now offering the same faded but comfortable rooms
(with a/c and wi-fi) at a fraction of their original price.
Central location, but breakfast not included. Doubles 40Lv

EATING

The most atmospheric restaurants are in the old town, many
occupying elegant old houses and serving good, traditional
Bulgarian food. In the new town, ul. Knyaz Aleksandar I is
awash with cheaper fast-food outlets, though better quality
can be found away from the main drag.

Alafrangite ul. Kiril Nektariev 17 ⓦalafrangite.eu.
Lovely National Revival-style restaurant housed in an old
town mansion serving traditional Bulgarian cuisine. Mid-
range prices, plus nightly live music in the fig-tree-shaded
courtyard. Daily noon–11pm.

Amsterdamer ul. Konstantin Stoilov 10 ⓦplovdiv
.amsterdambg.com. Stylish reproduction of a Dutch
restaurant serving Bulgarian and international cuisine such
as duck breast with fig sauce (11Lv). Daily 11am–midnight.

Dreams ul. Knyaz Aleksandar I 42 ⓦdreams-plovdiv.com.
A popular central spot for coffee, cocktails and cakes. Daily
8am–midnight.

King's Stables ul. Saborna 9a. One of the old town's most
reasonably priced restaurants. Serves large portions of
traditional Bulgarian food, including some excellent grilled
meat dishes (4–10Lv). The yogurt with home-made
blueberry jam is definitely worth trying. There's also a bar
that offers equally generous measures of spirits and weekly
live music performances. Summer only. Daily 9am–2am.

Philippopolis ul. Saborna 29, ⓦphilippopolis.com. An
excellent old town restaurant beneath an art gallery
serving well-presented international food in a quiet
garden with lovely views. Daily 10am–midnight.

DRINKING AND NIGHTLIFE

The best places to drink are the pavement cafés of ul.
Knyaz Aleksandar I. The Kapana area just north of the
Dzhumaya mosque is the place to head for late-night
tipples and dancing.

Absinthe House ul. Petko R. Slaveykov 8. Laidback bar
with an astounding and potentially mindbending choice
of absinthes. Daily 4pm–1am.

Apartment 101 ul. Gladston 8. Just off pl. Tsentralen,
this tiny, incredibly popular café-bar is crammed into the
first floor of a rickety old building. Daily 8am–midnight, Fri
& Sat until 2am.

Artnewscafe ul. Otets Paisii 38 ⓦartnewscafe.com. Tiny
café-bar with quirky interior that's frequented by hip, arty
Plovdivians. Daily 8am–11pm.

No Sense ul. Evlogi Georgiev 5. Popular place over two
floors that's been pumping out retro and rock every night
for years. Daily 10am–4am.

Nylona ul. Benkovski 8. With no sign outside, this dimly lit
rock bar in the Kapana area attracts an alternative crowd and
hosts irregular live music performances. Daily noon–4am.

Petnoto na Rorschach ul. Yoakim Gruev 36. Popular with the local alternative crowd, this vibrant club has regular live bands and even hosts the occasional literary event. Daily 9am–2am.

DIRECTORY

Hospital For 24hr emergency treatment try Medicus Alpha at ul. Veliko Tarnovo 21 (📞 032 634463, 🌐 medicusalpha .com), alongside the park next to pl. Tsentralen.
Pharmacy Kamea, ul. Hristo Danov 4, close to pl. Dzhumaya, is open 24hr.
Post office pl. Tsentralen 1 (Mon–Sat 7am–7pm, Sun 7am–11am).

BACHKOVO MONASTERY

Just 30km away and an easy day-trip from the city, the most attractive destination around Plovdiv is **Bachkovo Monastery** (daily 6.30am–9pm; free). Founded in 1038 by two Georgians in the service of the Byzantine Empire, this is Bulgaria's second-largest monastery. Through a great iron-studded door visitors reach the cobbled courtyard, surrounded by wooden galleries and adorned with colourful frescoes. Beneath the vaulted porch of Bachkovo's principal church, **Sveta Bogoroditsa**, are frescoes depicting the horrors in store for sinners; the entrance itself, overseen by the Holy Trinity, is rather more uplifting.

ARRIVAL AND DEPARTURE

Take one of the hourly buses from Rodopi station towards Smolyan; the stop for Bachkovo is 45min from Plovdiv.

ACCOMMODATION AND EATING

It's possible to stay in refurbished rooms in the monastery (📞 03327 2277; 40Lv/person with hot water and en suite), and there are three restaurants just outside; *Vodopada*, with its mini-waterfall, is the best.

Central Bulgaria

For over a thousand years, Stara Planina – known to foreigners as the **Balkan range** – has been the cradle of the Bulgarian nation. It was here that the Khans established the First Kingdom, and here, too, after a period of Byzantine control, that the Boyars proclaimed the Second

Kingdom and created a magnificent capital at **Veliko Tarnovo**. The nearby Sredna Gora (Central Mountains) were inhabited as early as the fifth millennium BC, but for Bulgarians this forested region is best known as the Land of the April Rising, the nineteenth-century rebellion for which the picturesque town of **Koprivshtitsa** will always be remembered.

Although they lie a little way off the main rail lines from Sofia, neither Veliko Tarnovo nor Koprivshtitsa is difficult to reach. The former lies just south of Gorna Oryahovitsa, a major rail junction midway between Varna and Sofia, from where you can pick up a local bus; the latter is served by the Koprivshtitsa stop, where nine daily trains from Sofia are met by local buses to ferry you the 12km to the village itself.

KOPRIVSHTITSA

Seen from a distance, **KOPRIVSHTITSA** (Копривщица) looks almost too lovely to be real, its half-timbered houses lying in a valley amid wooded hills. It would be an oasis of rural calm if not for the tourists drawn by the superb architecture and Bulgarians paying homage to a landmark in their nation's history.

WHAT TO SEE AND DO

All of the town's museums are open 9.30am–5.30pm, with half of them closing on Mondays, and the other half on Tuesdays. You can buy a combined ticket for five of the six museums for 5Lv at the tourist office and at any of the museums; otherwise they are priced at 3Lv each; tickets for Oslekov House can only be purchased on site (2Lv). It's also possible to hire an English-speaking guide for a two-hour tour (10Lv).

A street running off to the west of the main square leads to the **Oslekov House** (closed Mon). Its summer guest room is particularly impressive, with a vast wooden ceiling carved with geometric motifs. Cross the Freedom Bridge opposite the information centre to reach **Karavelov House** (closed Tues), the childhood home of Lyuben Karavelov, a

5

fervent advocate of Bulgaria's liberation who spent much of his adult life in exile where he edited revolutionary publications. Near the Surlya Bridge is the birthplace of the poet **Dimcho Debelyanov** (closed Mon), who is buried in the grounds of the hilltop Church of the Holy Virgin. A gate at the rear of the churchyard leads to the home of **Todor Kableshkov** (closed Mon), leader of the local rebels. Kableshkov's house now displays weapons used in the Rising and features a wonderful circular vestibule. Continuing south, cross the **Bridge of the First Shot**, which spans the Byala Reka stream, head up ulitsa Nikola Belodezhdov, and you'll come to the **Lyutov House** (closed Tues), once home to a wealthy yogurt merchant and today housing some of Koprivshtitsa's most sumptuous interiors. On the opposite side of the River Topolnitsa, steps lead up to the birthplace of another major figure in the Rising, **Georgi Benkovski** (closed Tues). A tailor by profession, he made the famous silk banner embroidered with the Bulgarian lion and "Liberty or Death!".

ARRIVAL AND INFORMATION

By train Buses to Koprivshtitsa usually meet trains arriving at the station 12km south of town.
Destinations Burgas (1 daily; 5hr 30min); Plovdiv (6 daily; 5hr); Sofia (9 daily; 2hr); Veliko Tarnovo (3 daily; 5–9hr).
By bus The small bus station is 200m south of the main square.
Destinations Plovdiv (1 daily; 2hr 30min); Sofia (5 daily; 2hr).
Tourist office The tourist office on the main square, pl. 20th April 6 (daily 9.30am–5pm; ☎07184 2191, ⓦ koprivshtitza.com), sells tickets for five of Koprivshtitsa's six house museums.

ACCOMMODATION

The tourist office can book private rooms (around 40Lv) in charming village houses. Advance reservations are recommended in summer.
Bolyarka ul. Petar Zhilkov 7 ☎07184 2043. Four-room B&B just uphill from the centre, offering bright, pine-furnished rooms and a lovely garden. Doubles 46Lv
Panorama ul. Georgi Benkovski 40 ☎07184 2035, ⓦ panoramata.com. A well-run complex south of the centre with smart modern rooms on the ground floor and traditional-style rooms above; most have sweeping views of the town. Doubles 70Lv
Trayanova Kashta ul. Gerenilo 5 ☎07184 3057. Just up the street from the Oslekov House, with delightful rooms in the National Revival style. Doubles 50Lv

EATING AND DRINKING

Dyado Liben Inn This fine nineteenth-century mansion opposite the main square serves traditional dishes such as *gyuvech* (meat stew) for around 6–15Lv. Daily 11am–midnight.
Lomeva Kashta A folk-style restaurant just north of the square, serving grills and salads from 6Lv. Daily 10am–midnight.

VELIKO TARNOVO

With its dramatic medieval fortifications and huddles of antique houses teetering over the lovely River Yantra, **VELIKO TARNOVO** (Велико Търново) holds a uniquely important place in the minds of Bulgarians. When the National Assembly met here to draft Bulgaria's first constitution in 1879, it did so in the former capital of the Second Kingdom (1185–1396), whose civilization was snuffed out by the Turks. It was here, too, that the Communists chose to proclaim the People's Republic in 1944.

KOPRIVSHTITSA AND THE APRIL RISING

From the "Bridge of the First Shot" to the "Place of the Scimitar Charge", there's hardly a part of Koprivshtitsa that isn't named after an episode or participant in the **April Rising of 1876**, a meticulously planned grassroots revolution against Ottoman control that failed within days because the organizers had vastly overestimated their support. Neighbouring towns were burned by the *Bashibazouks* – the irregular troops recruited by the Turks to put the rebels in their place – and refugees flooded into Koprivshtitsa, spreading panic. The rebels eventually took to the hills while local traders bribed the *Bashibazouks* to spare the village – and so Koprivshtitsa survived unscathed, to be admired by subsequent generations as a symbol of heroism. Although the home-grown Bulgarian revolution failed, the barbarity of the Turkish reprisals outraged the international community and led to the 1877–78 War of Liberation which won freedom for Bulgaria from over five hundred years of Ottoman rule.

WHAT TO SEE AND DO

Modern Veliko Tarnovo centres on **ploshtad Mayka Balgariya**: from here bulevard Nezavisimost (which becomes ulitsa Stefan Stambolov after a few hundred metres) heads northeast into a network of narrow streets that curve above the River Yantra and mark out the old town and its photogenic houses. From ulitsa Stambolov, the narrow cobbled ulitsa Rakovski slopes up into the **Varosh Quarter**, a pretty ensemble of nineteenth-century buildings once home to bustling artisans' workshops and now occupied by clothing and souvenir shops.

Sarafkina House

Clinging to the steep hillside at ulitsa General Gurko 88 is the **Sarafkina House** (Mon–Fri 9am–5.30pm; 6Lv), whose elegant restored interior is notable for its splendid octagonal vestibule and a panelled rosette ceiling.

Museum of the Bulgarian Renaissance and Constituent Assembly

Designed by the legendary local architect Kolyo Ficheto (1800–81), the blue-and-white building where the first Bulgarian parliament assembled in 1879 is now home to the **Museum of the Bulgarian Renaissance and Constituent Assembly** (summer daily 9am–6pm; winter Mon & Wed–Sun 9am–5.30pm; 6Lv), where you can see a reconstruction of the original assembly hall, and a collection of icons.

Tsarevets

Ulitsa Ivan Vazov leads directly from the museum to the medieval fortress, **Tsarevets** (daily: April–Oct 8am–7pm; Nov–March 9am–5pm; 6Lv). A successful rebellion against Byzantium was mounted from this citadel in 1185, and Tsarevets remained the centre of Bulgarian power until 1393, when, after a three-month siege, it fell to the Turks. The partially restored fortress is entered via the **Asenova Gate** halfway along the western ramparts. To the right, paths lead round to **Baldwin's Tower**, where Baldwin of Flanders, the so-called Latin Emperor of Byzantium, was incarcerated by Tsar

Kaloyan. Visitors can climb up to the parapet of the fully renovated tower for sweeping views of the town.

Don't miss the dramatic twenty-minute Tsarevets Sound and Light show held most evenings during the summer – it's free on public holidays, but on other days you'll have to wait for a large group to fork out for it, otherwise it doesn't go ahead. Call ☏062 636952 for show times.

ARRIVAL AND INFORMATION

By train All trains to Veliko Tarnovo actually stop at Gorna Oryahovitsa station from where bus #10 covers the 13km to the centre (30min). International trains must be booked in advance through the Rila-BDZh office beside the *Yantra Hotel* at ul. Stefan Stamolov 19 (Mon–Fri 8am–noon & 1–4.30pm; ☏062 622042).
Destinations Bucharest (2 daily; 6hr); Burgas (4 daily; 7hr); Istanbul (1 daily; 14hr); Sofia (8 daily; 5hr); Varna (5 daily; 4hr).

By bus Buses to and from Sofia and Varna use the small central bus terminal (*tsentralna avtogara*) just behind the Tourist Information Centre outside *Hotel Etar*. Buses to Plovdiv, Burgas and Ruse use the western terminal (*avtogara zapad*), 4km southwest of town accessed by bus #10 from the centre. From Ruse there are six daily buses to Bucharest (1hr 30min). Buses to Athens and Istanbul use the southern bus terminal (*avtogara yug*) which is a 10min walk south of the centre along bul. Hristo Botev.
Destinations Athens (1 daily; 16hr); Burgas (2 daily; 4hr); Istanbul (1 daily; 10hr); Plovdiv (2 daily; 4hr); Ruse (4 daily; 2hr 30min); Sofia (hourly; 3hr); Varna (hourly; 3hr 30min).

Tourist office bul. Hristo Botev 5 (summer Mon–Fri 9am–6pm, Sat & Sun 9am–5pm; winter Mon–Fri 9am–5pm; ☏062 622148, ⊛velikoturnovo.info).

ACCOMMODATION

Comfort ul. Paneyot Tipografov 5 ☏062 628 728, ⊛hotelcomfortbg.com. A spotless, family-run place, with wi-fi, a/c and splendid views of the Tsarevets fortress. Located just above the Varosh Quarter's bazaar. Doubles __60Lv__

Hikers Hostel ul. Rezervoarska 91 ☏062 604 019 or ☏0889 691 661, ⊛hikers-hostel.org. A friendly hostel with quirky wooden furniture tucked away in a narrow street high above the Varosh Quarter, looking out over Tsarevets. There's excellent dorm accommodation, tent space, kitchen and free wi-fi, computer access and pick-up service. Dorms __20Lv__, doubles __52Lv__, camping/person __10Lv__

★ **Hostel Mostel** ul. Iordan Indjeto 10 ☏0897 859 359, ⊛hostelmostel.com. Located in a beautifully restored

5

nineteenth-century Ottoman building south of the road leading to Tsarevets, with comfortable dorms and private en-suite rooms. Included in the price are a pick-up service, wi-fi, computer access, an all-you-can-eat breakfast, evening meal and a beer for every night of your stay. There's also a barbecue and tent space in the garden. Dorms 20Lv, doubles 60Lv, camping/person 18Lv

Stambolov ul. Stefan Stambolov 25 ☎0878 835 048, ⓦhotel-stambolov.com. Smart central option with single, double and triple rooms. Rooms at the back come with stunning views. Doubles 50Lv

EATING AND DRINKING

Club na Architecta ul. Velcho Dzhamdhziyata 14. Tucked away down a quiet alley and partially hewn into a rock face, this pleasant restaurant serves authentic Bulgarian cuisine and has a garden with lovely views. Daily 11am–midnight.

Melodie Bar pl. Slaveykov 1 ⓦbarmelodie.eu. Small, dimly lit jazz bar frequented by locals and expats. Daily 11.30am–2am.

Shastlivetsa ul. Stambolov 79. Perennially popular restaurant with fantastic views that offers local dishes, as well as a large range of pizzas and pastas. Main courses 6–30Lv. Daily 9am–midnight.

Stratilat ul. Rakovski 11. Located at the beginning of the Varosh Quarter, this relaxed café and cake shop occupies a restored old building with plenty of outdoor seating. Daily 10am–10pm.

The Black Sea coast

Bulgaria's **Black Sea** resorts have been popular holiday haunts for more than a century, though it wasn't until the 1960s that the coastline was developed for mass tourism, with Communist party officials from across the former Eastern Bloc descending on the beaches each year for a spot of socialist fun in the sun. Since then, the **resorts** have mushroomed and grown increasingly sophisticated, with the prototype mega-complexes followed by holiday villages. Fine weather is practically guaranteed, and the selling of the coast has been successful in economic terms, but with the exception of ancient **Sozopol** and touristy **Nesebar**, there's little to please the eye. The coast's two main cities – **Varna** and **Burgas** – can

both be used as a base for getting to less developed spots, such as the cliffs of **Kamen Bryag** and **Sinemorets'** superb beaches.

VARNA

VARNA (Варна) is a cosmopolitan place, and nice to stroll through: Baroque, nineteenth-century and contemporary architecture are pleasantly blended with shady promenades and a handsome seaside park. As a settlement it dates back almost five millennia, but it wasn't until seafaring Greeks founded a colony here in 585 BC that the town became a port. The modern city is used by both commercial freighters and the navy, as well as being a popular tourist resort in its own right.

WHAT TO SEE AND DO

Social life revolves around **ploshtad Nezavisimost**, where the opera house and theatre provide a backdrop for restaurants and cafés. The square is the starting point of Varna's evening promenade, which flows eastward from here along bulevard Knyaz Boris I and towards bulevard Slivnitsa and the seaside gardens. Beyond the opera house, Varna's main lateral boulevard cuts through ploshtad Mitropolit Simeon to the domed **Cathedral of the Assumption**. Constructed in 1886, it contains a splendid iconostasis and bishop's throne. The **Archeology Museum** on the corner of Mariya Luiza and Slivnitsa (daily 10am–5pm; 10Lv; ⓦarchaeo.museum varna.com) houses one of Bulgaria's finest collections of antiquities. Most impressive are the skeletons adorned with Thracian gold jewellery that were unearthed in Varna in 1972 and date back almost six thousand years.

South of the centre on ulitsa Han Krum are the extensive remains of the third-century **Roman baths** (Tues–Sun 10am–5pm; 4Lv). It's still possible to discern the various bathing areas and the once huge exercise hall. At the southern edge of the Sea Gardens, the **Navy Museum** (summer Tues–Sun 10am–6pm; winter Tues–Sat 9.30am–5.30pm; 5Lv; ⓦmuseummaritime-bg.com) is worth a trip to see the boat responsible for the Bulgarian Navy's only victory; it sank the Turkish cruiser *Hamidie* off Cape Kaliakra in 1912.

Beaches

Varna's municipal beach offers a perfunctory stretch of sand but little tranquillity as it's dominated by open-air bars and clubs. The beaches at the busy resorts of **Golden Sands** and **Albena** to the north are hardly any quieter, but are certainly wider and much more attractive. Beyond Albena the coastline turns rocky until the villages at **Krapets** and **Durankulak**, just short of the Romanian border, which boast some wonderful undeveloped sandy beaches.

ARRIVAL AND DEPARTURE

By plane Varna's international airport (ⓦvarna-airport .bg) lies 10km northwest of the city. Bus #409 (every 15min 6am–11pm; 1–3Lv) takes 20min to reach the centre where it stops opposite the Tourist Information Centre. Official OK Taxis (ⓦoktaxivarna.com) can be booked in the terminal (15–20Lv).

By train The train station is a 10min walk south of the centre along ul. Tsar Simeon.

Destinations Plovdiv (10 daily; 6–10hr); Sofia (11 daily; 7hr 30min–10hr).

By bus The bus terminal is a 10min journey (bus #1, #22 or #41) northwest of the centre on bul. Vladislav Varnenchik.

Destinations Albena (5 daily; 30min); Burgas (hourly; 2hr 30min); Durankulak (1 daily; 2hr 45min); Golden Sands (every 30min; 20min); Kamen Bryag (3 daily; 2hr 30min); Krapets (1 daily; 2hr 20min); Sofia (every 30min; 6–8hr); Sunny Beach (hourly; 2hr 10min); Veliko Tarnovo (hourly; 3hr 30min).

INFORMATION

Tourist office pl. Sv. Kiril i Metodi opposite the Cathedral of the Assumption (summer daily 9am–7pm; winter Mon–Fri 8.30am–5.30pm; ☎052 820690, ⓦvarnainfo .bg). The staff sell city maps, reserve hotel rooms and organize excursions.

ACCOMMODATION

Avocado Hostel bul. Maria Luisa 31 ☎0889 130 691. Superb new hostel with spacious air-conditioned dorms that each come with separate bathrooms. Excellent central location and lovely garden. Dorms 14Lv

Hostel Casablanca City ul. Krastio Mirski 1 ☎0887 821 901. Decent central option with reasonably comfortable mixed dorms and doubles. Dorms 14Lv, doubles 50Lv

Interhotel Cherno More bul. Slivnitsa 33 ☎052 612 235, ⓦchernomorebg.com. Once the city's flagship Socialist-era hotel, this central, sixteen-floor concrete monolith now offers its modernized rooms at reasonable prices. Fabulous views and a top-floor cocktail bar and restaurant. Doubles 80Lv

X Hostel ul. 16–19, Evksinograd ☎0885 049 084, ⓦxhostel.com. While it's a fair distance from the city (8km outside Varna on the road to Golden Sands) this sociable hostel is renowned for its wild parties – definitely not an option for those in search of a peaceful night's sleep. Dorms 18Lv

★**Yo Ho Hostel** ul. Ruse 23 ☎0887 933 340, ⓦyohohostel.com. Centrally located just off pl. Nezavisimost, this fun hostel sprawls over several colourful floors and hosts regular live bands and art exhibitions. Breakfast, wi-fi, computer access and pick-up service are all thrown in. Helpful staff can arrange day-trips and bike rental. Dorms 20Lv, doubles 48Lv

EATING AND DRINKING

There are plenty of bars to choose from along bul. Knyaz Boris I, while in summer the beach, reached by steps from the Sea Gardens, is lined with open-air bars, fish restaurants and a seemingly unending strip of nightclubs. Outside high season, though, it's pretty dismal.

Dom na Arkitekta ul. Musala 10. A traditionally furnished wooden townhouse west of the centre serving authentic Bulgarian dishes and plenty of grilled meat (from 7Lv), with a pleasant courtyard garden. Daily 11am–11pm.

Happy Bar and Grill pl. Nezavisimost. Reliable American-style restaurant with a picture menu offering a mixture of Bulgarian and international food. The *kashkaval pane* (battered cheese) is particularly good (5Lv). Daily 11am–11pm.

Interhotel Cherno More bul. Slivnitsa 33. Head to the sixteenth-floor cocktail bar for unrivalled views of the city; cocktails will set you back 8–15Lv. Daily 11am–1am.

★**Morske Vulk** ul. Odrin. Just south of pl. Exarch Yosef, this is one of the friendliest and cheapest restaurants in town, with a vibrant, alternative crowd and brilliant Bulgarian dishes, including vegetarian options such as pizza for around 8Lv. Daily 11am–2am.

Pench's Bar ul. Dragoman 25 ⓦpenchis.com. This stylish central bar has a mindboggling choice of cocktails (2014 and counting) that earned it the Guinness World Record for the number available in a single bar. Exemplary service and sophisticated atmosphere. Daily noon–2am.

Three Lions Pub pl. Slaveikov 1. Thriving English-themed pub located 100m east of the train station with regular live rock bands, big-screen TVs and good food. Daily 11am–1am.

5

BURGAS

The south coast's prime urban centre and transport hub, **BURGAS** (Бургас) provides easy access to the picture-postcard town of Nesebar to the north and Sozopol to the south. Often overlooked by tourists, Burgas' pedestrianized city centre, lined with smart boutiques, bars and cafés, is well worth a visit, though its best features are the delightful **Sea Gardens** overlooking the beach, and the pier at the eastern end of town.

ARRIVAL AND INFORMATION

By plane Burgas International Airport (ⓦ burgas -airport.com) is 15km north of the centre. Take bus #15 from the central bus station (every 30min, 6am–10pm); official Eko Taxis can be booked from within the airport (15–25Lv; ⓦ ekotaxiburgas.com).

By train The train station is at the southern edge of town, near the port.
Destinations Plovdiv (7 daily; 5hr); Sofia (6 daily; 8hr).

By bus The bus station is next to the train station.
Destinations Istanbul (3 daily; 7hr); Nesebar (every 30min; 50min); Plovdiv (6 daily; 4hr); Sinemorets (1 daily; 1hr 30min); Sofia (hourly; 6hr); Sozopol (every 30min; 50min); Varna (hourly; 2hr).

Tourist office Beneath bul. Hristo Botev in the underpass opposite the opera house (Mon–Fri 9.30am–5.30pm; ☎ 056 841542, ⓦ gotoburgas.com). Provides maps and can make hotel reservations.

ACCOMMODATION

Burgas has a reasonable choice of mid-range hotels but has long suffered from a shortage of budget accommodation.

Chi Hostel ul. Dr Nider 6A 14 ☎ 0899 908 422. One of only two decent budget options in town, this family-run hostel has a good central location and offers mixed dorms, shared kitchen and small garden. Dorms 16Lv

Fors ul. K. Fotinov 17 ☎ 056 828 852, ⓦ hotelfors-bg.com. Smart central hotel with good service, and spotless en-suite rooms with wi-fi and a/c. Doubles 80Lv

Fotinov ul. K. Fotinov 22 ☎ 056 993 031, ⓦ hotel fotinov.com. Pleasant family-run hotel near the *Fors*. Facilities include fitness equipment, wi-fi, sauna and a/c. Doubles 75Lv

Old House Hostel ul. Sofroniy 2 ☎ 0879 841 559. Cheap and cheerful place with choice of doubles or four-bed dorms within walking distance of the centre, the beach and the sea gardens. Doubles 40Lv, dorms 16Lv

EATING AND DRINKING

Burgas' pedestrianized central boulevards are crammed with bars, cafés and restaurants that spill out onto the streets in summer. There are several pleasant places to eat in the Sea Gardens and plenty more bars along the beach.

★**Neptun** Tsentalni plazh ⓦ neptunburgas.com. Fantastic bar and restaurant right on the beach with plush interior and shaded outdoor seating. Smart waiters provide a good level of service and the menu has a broad choice of local and international dishes – the Black Sea mussels in white wine (7.30Lv) are excellent. To reach it, follow ul. Tsar Simeon to the Sea Gardens then continue straight on to the beach. Daily 9am–midnight.

Rosé ul. Bogoridi 19. Stylish central restaurant serving excellent Mediterranean cuisine that includes chicken fillet with quinoa salad (14Lv). Daily 10am–midnight.

Zheleznyat Svetilnik ul. K. Fotinov 28. Great traditional-style restaurant with shaded outdoor seating serving typical Bulgarian dishes such as moussaka (5Lv) with an emphasis on grilled meat. Excellent wine list. Daily 11am–11.30pm.

NESEBAR

Famed for its delightful medieval churches, nineteenth-century wooden architecture and labyrinthine cobbled streets, **NESEBAR**'s (Несебър) old town, 35km northeast of Burgas, lies on a narrow, man-made isthmus connected by road to the mainland. It was founded by Greek colonists and grew into a thriving port during the Byzantine era; ownership alternated between Bulgaria and Byzantium until the Ottomans captured it in 1453. The town remained an important centre of Greek culture and the seat of a bishop under Turkish rule, which left Nesebar's **Byzantine churches** reasonably intact. Nowadays the town depends on them for its tourist appeal, which means there's often an over-whelming stream of summer visitors. Outside the hectic summer season, the place seems eerily deserted, with little open other than a few sleepy cafés.

WHAT TO SEE AND DO

Standing just inside the city gates, the **Archeological Museum** (summer daily 9am–7pm; winter Mon–Fri 9am–5pm, Sat & Sun 10am–5pm; 6Lv; ⓦ ancient -nessebar.com) has an array of Greek tombstones and medieval icons on display. Immediately beyond the museum is **Christ Pantokrator**, the first of Nesebar's churches, currently in use as an upmarket art gallery (summer only Mon–Fri 9am–8pm, Sat & Sun 9.30am–7pm; 3Lv). It features an unusual frieze of swastikas – an ancient symbol of fertility and continual change. Downhill on ulitsa Mitropolitska is the eleventh-century church of **St John the Baptist** (now also an art gallery; same hours; 3Lv), only one of whose frescoes still survives. Overhung by half-timbered houses, ulitsa Aheloi branches off from ulitsa Mitropolitska towards the **Church of Sveti Spas** (summer only daily 10.30am–7pm; 3Lv), outwardly unremarkable but filled with seventeenth-century frescoes.

A few steps to the east lies the ruined **Old Metropolitan Church**, dominating a plaza filled with pavement cafés and street traders. The church itself dates back to the sixth century, and it was here that bishops officiated during the city's heyday. Standing in splendid isolation beside the shore, the ruined **Church of St John Aliturgetos** represents the zenith of Byzantine architecture in Bulgaria. Its exterior employs limestone, red bricks, crosses, mussel shells and ceramic plaques for decoration.

Beaches

Visitors can either head for Nesebar's handful of small beaches or hop on a shuttle bus to the unattractive neighbouring resort of **Sunny Beach** where a great expanse of golden sand studded with thousands of umbrellas stretches for several kilometres along the overdeveloped coastline.

ARRIVAL AND INFORMATION

By bus Buses arrive at either the harbour at the western end of town, or further up Han Krum before turning around to head for the nearby Sunny Beach resort. Bus #1 connects the new and old towns.

Destinations Burgas (every 30min; 50min); Sofia (3 daily; 7hr); Varna (10 daily; 1hr 30min).

Tourist office Located in the centre of the old town at ul. Messemvria 10 (summer daily 10am–6pm; ☎0554 42611, ⊕ visitnessebar.org).

ACCOMMODATION

Ianis Paradise ul. Emona 20 ☎0554 45041. Old-town guesthouse offering simply furnished en-suite rooms with glorious sea views. Doubles 90Lv

Lebed ul. Avrora 8a ☎0899 841 872. Located on quiet backstreets at the eastern end of the old town, this popular place offers clean, simple rooms with modern furnishings. Doubles 100Lv

Preslav ul. Preslav 3 ☎0898 420 720. Simple family-run guesthouse in the new town with spotless en-suite rooms at bargain prices. Doubles 40Lv

Sandor ul. Georgi Rakovski 18 ☎0554 43309. Modern concrete hotel in the new town with pleasant rooms and good service. Doubles 65Lv

EATING AND DRINKING

There are plenty of places to eat, although most restaurants are aimed at the passing tourist crowd, serving predictably mediocre food. Snacks are available from summertime kiosks along the waterfront.

Kapitanska Sreshta ul. Mena 22. Atmospheric fish restaurant housed in a nineteenth-century building with a lovely shaded terrace overlooking the old town's harbour. Daily 10am–midnight.

Neptun ul. Neptun 1. Pleasant outdoor spot on the southeastern tip of the old town with great sea views. Serves a reasonably priced selection of Bulgarian standards. Daily 10am–midnight.

Plakamoto ul. Ivan Aleksander 8. Old-town favourite with outdoor seating beneath fig trees and sublime sea views. Daily 10am–midnight.

SOZOPOL

SOZOPOL (Созопол) is a busy fishing port and holiday resort, especially popular with Eastern European tourists. Its charm owes much to the **architecture** of the old town, where wooden houses jostle for space on a narrow peninsula, their upper storeys almost meeting across cobbled streets. The oldest settlement in Bulgaria, Sozopol was founded in the seventh century BC by Greek colonists.

WHAT TO SEE AND DO

The **Archeological Museum** (summer daily 9am–7pm; winter Mon–Fri 9am–5.30pm; 4Lv) behind the library holds a worthwhile collection of ancient ceramics, as well as a number of artefacts uncovered in the local area. Further into the town, follow the signs to the **Southern Fortress Wall and Tower Complex** (summer 9am–9pm; open by appointment only in winter; 4Lv; ⊕ sozopol-foundation.com), which gives access to a beautifully restored

5

tower and exhibits dating from the fourth century BC.

Sozopol's two small **beaches** are predictably overcrowded in high season, so it's worth making the short trip north to the emptier beaches around the *Zlatna Ribka* campsite (see below).

ARRIVAL AND INFORMATION

By bus Buses from Burgas arrive at pl. Han Krum on the southern edge of the old town. Those from other Bulgarian cities usually arrive at and depart from pl. Cherno More in the the new town.

Destinations Burgas (every 30min; 50min); Plovdiv (6 daily; 5hr); Sofia (6 daily; 7hr).

Tourist information In the absence of a municipal tourist office, the best source of information is the Aiatour travel agency, located high in the new town at ul. Musala 7 (summer daily 9am–9pm; irregular office hours out of season; ☏ 0550 23925, ⊚ aiatour.com).

ACCOMMODATION

Accommodation in Sozopol can be even harder to find during summer than in Nesebar, and most places shut down for the rest of the year. The Aiatour travel agency (see above) can arrange private rooms of varying standards (20–35Lv per person).

Art ul. Kiril I Metodii 72 ☏ 0550 24081, ⊚ arthotel-sbh .com. Smart modern hotel and restaurant perched on a rocky cliff at the northern end of the peninsula. Doubles 80Lv

Rusalka ul. Milet 36 ☏ 0550 23047. On the south of the peninsula, this is the best-value old town hotel with comfortable a/c rooms overlooking the sea. Breakfast not included. Doubles 80Lv

★**Tulen** ul. Tulen 7 ☏ 0888 808772. Fabulous old-town guesthouse with immaculate spacious rooms, cheerful decor and hospitable hosts. Excellent value. Doubles 70Lv

Zlatna Ribka 3km north of town on the Burgas bus route ☏ 0550 22534, ⊚ zlatna-ribka.com. Popular seaside campsite with great beach: the closer you are to the shore, the pricier the pitch. Camping/tent 35Lv, camper van 50Lv

EATING AND DRINKING

Art ul. Kiril I Metodii 72. Great old-town restaurant with outdoor tables on the cliff's edge at the northeastern end of the old town. Serves a mid-priced range of Bulgarian and international meals. Daily 10am–midnight.

Art Club Mishel ul. Apollonia 39. Central bar and café in a lovely old town building with plenty of comfy outdoor seating. Live jazz most nights. Daily 11am–1am.

Chuchura ul. Ribarska 10. Situated on the western side of the old town, this is a popular traditional-style restaurant with a particularly good selection of fish dishes (20–30Lv). Daily 11am–midnight.

Vyatarna Melnitsa ul. Morski Skali 27. Similar in style and price to the *Chuchura*, the "Windmill" has excellent service and perches on the northern tip of the peninsula. Daily 10am–midnight.

VIS ISLAND

Croatia

HIGHLIGHTS

❶ **Amphiteatre, Pula** Visit the sixth-largest amphitheatre in the world. **See p.165**

❷ **Zadar** Visit this buzzing town and discover its unique Sea Organ. **See p.167**

❸ **Diocletian's Palace, Split** Be amazed by this extraordinary 1700-year-old palace. **See p.169**

❹ **Vis Island** Relax on the Dalmatian Coast's most laidback island. **See p.175**

❺ **Dubrovnik** The ancient walled city is hardly undiscovered but can still work its unique magic. See p.178

HIGHLIGHTS ARE MARKED ON THE MAP ON P.155

ROUGH COSTS

Daily budget Basic €55, occasional treat €75

Drink Litre of local wine €6

Food *pohane lignje* (breaded squid) €5.50

Private room/hostel €42/€25

Travel Ferry: within Dalmatian islands €5–12; bus: Zagreb–Split €25

FACT FILE

Population 4.3 million

Language Croatian (Hrvatski)

Currency Kuna (kn)

Capital Zagreb

International phone code ☎ 385

Time zone GMT +1hr

Introduction

The serpentine coastline and sheer natural beauty of Croatia (Hrvatska) make it an irresistible European destination. Its tourist industry is now fully fledged, but the accompanying development has been fairly unobtrusive and there are still plenty of secluded rocky beaches and pristine old towns to explore. As well as a rich cultural heritage, the country offers a wealth of outdoor activities and a rapidly expanding festival scene. Already a hit destination among those in the know, Croatia looks set to grow even further in popularity.

The capital, **Zagreb**, is a lively central European metropolis, combining elegant nineteenth-century architecture with a vibrant bar and club scene. The peninsula of **Istria** contains many of the country's most developed resorts, with old Venetian towns like **Rovinj** rubbing shoulders with the raffish port of **Pula**. Further south lies **Dalmatia**, a dramatic, mountain-fringed stretch of coastline studded with islands. Dalmatia's main towns are Italianate **Zadar** and vibrant **Split**, an ancient Roman settlement and modern port that provides a jumping-off point to offshore destinations like high-society **Hvar**, untamed **Vis** and enchanting **Korčula**.

South of Split lies the medieval walled city of **Dubrovnik**, stuffed full of tourists but still a magical place to be.

CHRONOLOGY

600s Croatian Slavs settle in the region.

925 Tomislav is crowned the first King of Croatia.

1102 Inland Croatia accepts the authority of Hungarian kings.

1400s Coastal Croatia (independent city-state Dubrovnik excepted) falls under Venetian rule.

1526 Habsburg dynasty takes control of inland Croatia after the fall of Hungary to the Ottomans.

1918 After the defeat of the Habsburgs in World War I, Croatia joins the Kingdom of the Serbs, Croats and Slovenes.

1929 The kingdom becomes known as Yugoslavia.

1941 Croatian-Slovene communist Josip Broz Tito leads resistance to the Nazis and local quislings.

1945 Croatia becomes part of the communist Yugoslav federation.

1980 Tito dies without a clear successor, and political paralysis grips the country.

1990 Multi-party elections in Croatia produce a pro-independence majority.

1991 Croatia declares its independence. The Yugoslav army, backed by Serb irregulars, responds with force.

1995 Croatian forces retake areas occupied by Serbs, bringing the war to an end.

1999 Conservative president Franjo Tuđman dies, ushering in a more liberal era in Croatian politics.

2009 Croatia joins the NATO alliance.

2012 Croatian General Ante Gotovina is cleared of all charges on appeal at the International War Crimes Tribunal in the Hague.

2013 Croatia joins the EU on July 1.

2015 Conservative Kolinda Grabar-Kitarović becomes Croatia's first female president.

ARRIVAL AND DEPARTURE

The principal international **airports** are Dubrovnik, Pula, Rijeka, Split, Zadar and Zagreb. Ryanair runs services to Pula, Rijeka and Zadar, while easyJet flies to Pula, Split and Dubrovnik. Wizz Air flies to Split; Jet2 flies to Pula, Split and Dubrovnik; and BA flies to Dubrovnik, Split and Zagreb. The national carrier, Croatia Airlines (ⓦcroatiaairlines.com), operates routes throughout Europe, while European Coastal Airlines (ⓦec-air.eu) runs 20-seater flying boats from Ancona in Italy to Mali Lošinj, Zadar and Split.

Ferry routes to Croatia run frequently from Italy, with services to Split, Hvar and Zadar from Ancona, and Dubrovnik from Bari; passenger-only catamarans serve Poreč Pula and Rovinj from Venice: see ⓦjadrolinija.hr, ⓦvenezialines.com and ⓦsnav.it.

Croatia is served by many international **buses**, including services from Vienna,

CROATIA

HIGHLIGHTS

1 Amphitheatre, Pula
2 Zadar
3 Diocletian's Palace, Split
4 Vis Island
5 Dubrovnik

0 ___ 50
kilometres

Metres
1000
500
200
0

6

Belgrade and Sarajevo, most of them run by Eurolines (Ⓦeurolines.com), who are partnered with AutoTrans (Ⓦautotrans .hr). Several German cities are connected with Croatia too; see Ⓦeurolines.de. For services from Trieste check Ⓦautostazionetrieste.it.

Croatia is also linked with the rest of Europe by **rail**; see Ⓦbahn.de for timetables.

GETTING AROUND

Croatia's **train** service is pretty limited; you're much more likely to use the excellent **bus** network.

BY BUS

Croatia has an array of local bus companies. Leading ones include

AutoTrans (Ⓦautotrans.hr); services are well integrated and punctual, and bus stations tend to be well organized. If you're at a big city bus station, tickets (*karta*) must be bought from ticket windows before boarding. Elsewhere, buy them from the driver. You'll be charged around 7kn for items of baggage to be stored in the hold.

BY TRAIN

Croatian Railways (*Hrvatske željeznice*; Ⓦhzpp.hr) runs a smooth and efficient service, but it isn't very extensive. The most useful route is the Zagreb–Split line, which is served by high-speed, tilting trains. Trains (*vlak*, plural *vlakovi*) are divided into *putnički* (slow ones, which stop at every station) and IC (intercity trains that are faster and more

6

expensive). Timetables (*vozni red*) are usually displayed on boards in stations – *odlazak* means departure, *dolazak* arrival. **InterRail** passes are valid, and you must pay a small reservation fee for longer journeys.

Jadrolinija (ⓦjadrolinija.hr) operates numerous **ferry** services linking the main ports (Rijeka, Zadar, Split and Dubrovnik) to nearby islands. Split is the busiest, with both ferries and faster catamarans running to Brač, Hvar, Vis, Korčula and Dubrovnik. **Fares** are reasonable for short trips: Split to Hvar costs 47kn. Booking in advance is only possible on certain catamaran routes, and note that ferry timetables change around the end of May and end of September.

ACCOMMODATION

Private rooms (*privatne sobe*) and apartments (apartmani) have long been the mainstay of Croatian tourism. Many of these are advertised on international travel sites such as booking.com and airbnb.com. Otherwise bookings can be made through local travel agencies (usually open daily 8am–8/9pm in summer). High-season prices are around €40/310kn for a simple double sharing a toilet and bathroom and €60/450kn upwards for an en-suite double or a studio apartment; rates do not include breakfast unless otherwise stated. Places fill up quickly in July and August and stays of fewer than three nights are usually subject to a surcharge: arrive early or book ahead. Single travellers will find it difficult to get a private room unless they're prepared to pay the price of a double – although outside peak season you can negotiate.

It's likely you'll be offered a place to stay by elderly ladies waiting outside train, bus and ferry stations, particularly in southern Dalmatia. Don't be afraid to take a room offered in this manner, but be sure to establish the location and agree a price before setting off: expect to pay around twenty percent less than you

would with an agency. However you find a room, you can examine it before committing to paying for it. Official establishments with rooms should have a blue plaque saying "*sobe*" or "*apartmani*" outside – if they don't, they're not legal.

Independent **hostels** are cropping up more and more in Croatia – especially in the larger towns. The average price for a dorm bed is €24–29/180–220kn, and many also offer doubles and triples as well as dorms. Few of them are HI-affiliated; the Croatian Youth Hostel website (ⓦhfhs.hr) has details of those that are. Campsites usually open just for the summer season; see ⓦcamping.hr for a list.

FOOD AND DRINK

Croatia has a varied and distinctive range of **cuisine**, largely because it straddles two culinary cultures: the fish- and seafood-dominated cuisine of the Mediterranean and the hearty meat-oriented fare of Central Europe.

For **breakfasts** and **fast food**, look out for bakeries or snack-food outlets selling *burek* (about 15kn), a flaky pastry filled with cheese; or grilled meats such as *ćevapčići* (rissoles of minced beef, pork or lamb sold in a bun with relish; 37kn for a dozen from street stalls). Bread (*kruh*) is bought from a *pekarna* (bakery) or a supermarket.

A **restaurant** menu (*jelovnik*) will usually include starters such as *pršut* (home-cured ham) and *paški sir* (piquant hard cheese). Typical mains include some kind of *odrezak* (fillet of meat, often pan-fried), usually either *svinjski* (pork) or *teleški* (veal); and fresh fish, invariably grilled in one piece with head and bones intact. Other coastal staples are breaded or grilled squid (*lignje*), black squid risotto (*crni rižot*), and mixed fish stew (*brudet*). Real delicacies to be tried at least once are *škampi* (unpeeled prawns eaten with your fingers), *ostrige* (oysters), and *jastog* (lobster). No town is without at least one **pizzeria**, serving good stone-baked pizzas (around 40kn). A **konoba** is a no-frills, often family-run restaurant, usually serving local dishes at low prices.

Typical **desserts** include *palačinke* (pancakes) and *sladoled* (ice cream).

DRINK

Croatia is laden with relaxing **cafés** (*kavana*) for daytime drinking. Coffee (*kava*) is usually served black unless specified otherwise – ask for *mlijeko* (milk) or *šlag* (cream). Tea (*čaj*) is less available and drunk without milk.

Mainstream Croatian **beer** (*pivo*) is of the light lager variety; the superbly crafted pale ales and porters produced by Medvedgrad, Zmajska pivovara, San Servolo, Garden Brewery and Lab Pivo are definitely preferable if you can find them. The local **wine** (*vino*) is consistently good and reasonably cheap: in Dalmatia there are some pleasant, crisp whites such as Pošip and Bogdanjuša, as well as reds derived from the ubiquitous local Plavac grape. Ruling the roost in Istria are Malvazija, a palatable white, and Teran, a light fresh red. Local spirits (*rakija*) include *medica*, a honey-based, slow-burning nectar; *travarica*, a grape brandy infused with herbs; and *Pelinkovac*, a bitter spirit similar to Jägermeister.

CULTURE AND ETIQUETTE

With an almost ninety percent Roman Catholic population, religious holidays in Croatia are celebrated with gusto. A fun-loving people generally, especially among the younger generation, Croatians are welcoming and will happily engage you in conversations about food, wine and politics over a beer or two.

A service charge is not usually added to restaurant bills and it is the norm to leave a **tip** at your discretion (ten percent is quite acceptable).

SPORTS AND OUTDOOR ACTIVITIES

The Dalmatian coast is great for **watersports**, including sea kayaking, windsurfing, kite-surfing, wake-boarding and some less hardcore pursuits, such as banana-boating and renting a motorboat.

CROATIA ONLINE

ⓦ **croatia.hr** Official tourist board site.
ⓦ **istra.hr** One of the better official regional sites.
ⓦ **timeout.com/Croatia**. Good for events and festival information.
ⓦ **straysatellite.com**, ⓦ **travelhonestly.com**, ⓦ **chasingthedonkey.com** and ⓦ **zablogreb.blogspot.com** are the most engaging of the blogs.

6

Brač, Hvar and Vis have plenty of well-marked **cycling** and **hiking** trails.

Football remains the nation's favourite diversion. Croatia's national team has consistently proved to be one of the most successful in the whole of Central-Eastern Europe, regularly qualifying for major tournaments – an awesome achievement given Croatia's population of 4.3 million.

COMMUNICATIONS

Discernible by their bright yellow signs, **post offices** (*pošta* or HPT) are open Monday to Friday 7am to 7pm, Saturday 8am to 2pm. In big towns and resorts, some open daily and until 10pm. Stamps (*marke*) can also be bought at newsstands, and letterboxes are painted the same yellow as post office signs.

EU citizens can use their own mobile phones in Croatia free of any roaming costs as of June 2017. Most towns have **internet cafés** (expect to pay around 25kn/hr), and most apartments, hostels and cafés offer free wi-fi now too.

CRIME AND SAFETY

The crime rate is low by European standards and **police** (*policija*) are generally helpful when dealing with tourists. They often make routine checks on identity cards and other documents, so always carry your passport. In an **emergency**, call ☎112.

HEALTH

EU citizens in possession of a **European Health Insurance Card** (EHIC) are

6

CROATIAN

	CROATIAN	PRONUNCIATION
Yes	Da	Dah
No	Ne	Neh
Please	Molim	Mo-leem
Thank you	Hvala	Hvahlah
Hello/Good day	Bog/Dobar dan	Dobahr dan
Goodbye	Bog/Doviđenja	Doh veedehnyah
Excuse me	Izvinite	Izvineet
Sorry	Oprostite	Auprausteete
Today	Danas	Danass
Good	Dobro	Dobroh
Bad	Loše	Losheh
How much is…?	Koliko stoji…?	Koleekoh sto-yee…?
What time is it?	Koliko je sati?	Koleekoh yeh satee?
I don't understand	Ne razumijem	Neh rahzoomeeyehm
Do you speak English?	Govorite li engleski?	Govoreeteh lee ehngleskee?
Where is…?	Gdje je…?	Gdyeh ye…?
Where are…?	Gdje su…?	Gdyeh soo…?
Entrance	Ulaz	Oolaz
Exit	Izlaz	Eezlaz
Tourist office	Turistički Ured	Tooristichkee oored
Toilet	Zahod	Zah-haud
Private rooms	Sobe	Saubey
I'd like to book…	Ja bih revervirala…	Ya bee reserveerahla…
Cheap	Jeftino	Yeftinoh
Expensive	Skupo	Skoopoh
Open	Otvoreno	Otvoreenoh
Closed	Zatvoreno	Zatvoreenoh
One	Jedan	Yehdan
Two	Dva	Dvah
Three	Tri	Tree
Four	Četiri	Cheteeree
Five	Pet	Pet
Six	Šest	Shest
Seven	Sedam	Sedam
Eight	Osam	Osam
Nine	Devet	Devet
Ten	Deset	Deset

entitled to free emergency care in Croatia but are still required to pay a fee to cover the cost of materials and medicines. Travel insurance is therefore highly recommended. **Pharmacies** (*ljekarna*) tend to follow normal shopping hours (see opposite) and a rota system covers nights and weekends; details are posted in the window of each pharmacy.

INFORMATION

Most towns of any size have a **tourist office** (*turistička informacija*), which will give out brochures and local maps. Few offices book private rooms, but they will direct you to an agency that does.

MONEY AND BANKS

The local currency is the **kuna** (kn), which is divided into 100 lipa. There are coins of 1, 2, 5, 10, 20 and 50 lipa, and 1kn, 2kn and 5kn; and notes of 5kn, 10kn, 20kn, 50kn, 100kn, 200kn, 500kn and 1000kn. Accommodation and ferry prices are often quoted in euros, but you still pay in kuna. **Banks** (*banka*) are open

Monday to Friday 9am to 5pm (sometimes longer in summer), Saturday 8am to 1pm. Money can also be changed in post offices, travel agencies and **exchange bureaux** (*mjenjačnica*). Credit cards are accepted in a large number of hotels and restaurants. At the time of writing £1 = 9.5kn, €1 = 7.5kn and US$1 = 6.6kn. It's relatively hard to get rid of kuna once you've left Croatia (though exchange offices in neighbouring countries often accept it); spend up or exchange before leaving.

OPENING HOURS AND HOLIDAYS

Most **shops** open Monday to Friday 8am to 8pm and Saturday 8am to 3pm, although many supermarkets, outdoor markets and the like are open daily 7am to 7pm. Many newsagents, supermarkets and shopping malls open on Sundays. Most **museums and galleries** are closed on Mondays. Shops, banks and museums are closed on the following **public holidays**: January 1, January 6, Easter Monday, May 1, Corpus Christi, June 22, June 25, August 5, August 15, October 8, November 1 and December 25 & 26.

Zagreb

Croatian capital **ZAGREB** is very much Central Europe's surprise package, a city that challenges preconceptions and combines the gritty urban culture of northern Europe with the laidback vibe of the Mediterranean south. It has long been a quirky and creative place with a thriving alternative music scene, edgy fashions, creative clubbing and addictively eccentric bars, though Adriatic-bound travellers paid it little attention until recently. Zagreb is currently enjoying something of a moment, with a rapid increase in the number of things that make a city really purr – more good places to eat, more good places to drink, and a festival-driven sense that things are happening in the arts.

Central Zagreb falls neatly into three parts. **Donji Grad**, or Lower Town, which extends north from the train station to the main square, Trg bana Jelačića, is the bustling centre of the modern city. Uphill from here, to the northeast and the northwest, are the older quarters of **Kaptol** (the Cathedral Quarter) and **Gradec** (the Upper Town), both peaceful districts of ancient mansions and quiet squares.

Trg bana Jelačića and Ilica

Flanked by cafés, hotels and department stores, **Trg bana Jelačića** is Zagreb's main square, hectic with trams and hurrying pedestrians; the statue in the centre is of the nineteenth-century governor of Croatia, Josip Jelačić.

Running west from the square, below Gradec hill, is **Ilica**, the city's main shopping street. A little way along it and off to the right, you can take a **funicular** (daily every 10min, 6.30am–10pm; 4kn one-way) up to the Kula Lotrščak (see p.161).

Zagreb 360°

Take the lift to the top floor of this 1950s-era skyscraper, on the southwestern corner of Trg bana Jelačića, to reach **Zagreb 360°** (also known as Zagreb Eye; daily 10am–11.45pm; 20kn; ⓦzagreb360 .hr), a combined café and viewing deck that provides sweeping views of the city. It's from here that Zagreb reveals itself as a pretty, red-roofed Central-European city – something you don't always appreciate when mooching along at pavement level.

Preradovićev Trg and Trg maršala Tita

Head south of Ilica via **Preradovićev Trg**, a small, café-filled square where there's a flower market, and you will reach **Trg maršala Tita**. This grandiose open space is centred on the late nineteenth-century **National Theatre**, in front of which stands *The Well of Life*, a fountain by Croatia's greatest twentieth-century sculptor, Ivan Meštrović.

The Museum of Arts and Crafts

The beautiful **Museum of Arts and Crafts**, just west of the National Theatre

6

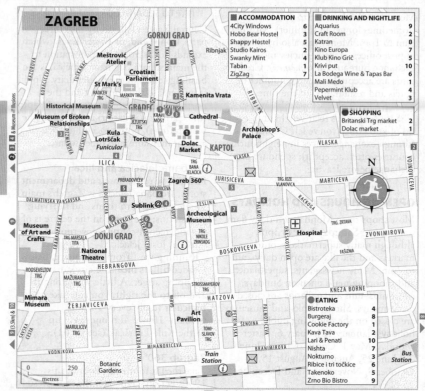

ZAGREB

ACCOMMODATION
4City Windows	6
Hobo Bear Hostel	3
Shappy Hostel	5
Studio Kairos	2
Swanky Mint	4
Taban	1
ZigZag	7

DRINKING AND NIGHTLIFE
Aquarius	9
Craft Room	2
Katran	8
Kino Europa	7
Klub Kino Grič	5
Krivi put	10
La Bodega Wine & Tapas Bar	6
Mali Medo	1
Pepermint Klub	4
Velvet	3

SHOPPING
Britanski Trg market	2
Dolac market	1

EATING
Bistroteka	4
Burgeraj	8
Cookie Factory	1
Kava Tava	2
Lari & Penati	10
Nishta	7
Nokturno	3
Ribice i tri točkice	6
Takenoko	5
Zrno Bio Bistro	9

Novi Zagreb, Museum of Contemporary Art & Airport

(Tues–Sat 11am–8pm, Sun 10am–2pm; 30kn), holds an impressive collection of furniture and textiles dating from the Renaissance to the present day.

Mimara Museum

The **Mimara Museum** at Rooseveltov Trg 5 (Tues–Fri 10am–7pm, Sat 10am–5pm, Sun 10am–2pm; 40kn) houses one of Zagreb's most prized art collections, a treasure-trove belonging to Zagreb-born Ante Topić Mimara. Highlights include Chinese art from the Shang through to the Song dynasty, as well as a fine collection of European paintings, although some of the attributions (can Zagreb really boast a Rembrandt or a Rubens?) have been questioned by experts.

The Art Pavilion and Archeological Museum

Tomislavov Trg, opposite the train station, is the first in a series of three shaded, green squares that form the backbone of the lower town. Its main attraction is the **Art Pavilion** (Tues–Thurs, Sat & Sun 11am–8pm, Fri 11am–9pm; 40kn), built in 1898 and now hosting art exhibitions in its gilded stucco and mock-marble interior. On the western edge of the most northerly square – tree-lined **Trg Nikole Zrinskog** (or Zrinjevac) – stands the **Archeological Museum** (Tues, Wed, Fri & Sat 10am–5pm, Thurs 10am–8pm, Sun 10am–1pm; 20kn), which houses a compelling collection of artefacts from prehistoric times to the Middle Ages.

Kaptol and the cathedral

The filigree spires of Zagreb's **cathedral** (Mon–Sat 10am–5pm, Sun 1–5pm) tower over the small district known as **Kaptol**, ringed by the ivy-cloaked turrets of the eighteenth-century **Archbishop's Palace**. Destroyed by an earthquake in

1880, the cathedral was rebuilt in neo-Gothic style, with a high, bare interior. Behind the altar lies a shrine to Archbishop Stepinac, head of the Croat church in the 1940s, imprisoned by the Communists after World War II, and beatified by the pope in 1998.

Tkalčićeva

On the western side of the Dolac market (see p.164), **Tkalčićeva** spears north along the path of the dried-up river that used to divide Kaptol and Gradec. Nowadays this is the city's prime people-watching spot – grab a seat at one of the many alfresco bars and cafés for the evening *korzo* (promenade) when well-heeled locals and their pooches strut their stuff.

Tortureum

Narrow alleys lead from Tkalčićeva to cobbled Radićeva, where the **Tortureum** or Museum of Torture at no. 14 (daily noon–8pm; 40kn; ⓦ tortureum.com) presents replicas of medieval torture instruments in an atmospherically lit, almost claustrophobically dark space that is more art installation than museum.

Gradec

The most ancient and atmospheric part of Zagreb, **Gradec** is a leafy, tranquil quarter of tiny streets, small squares and Baroque palaces. Gradec's main focus is **Markov Trg**, site of the Croatian Sabor or parliament. At its centre is the squat **Church of St Mark**, whose striking tiled roof displays the colourful coats of arms of the constituent parts of Croatia.

Gradec is entered from the upper end of Radićeva, via Kamenita Vrata, a tunnel-like gate with a small shrine holding a much-revered statue of Virgin and Child. Close by, the **Kula Lotršćak** (Burglars' Tower; Mon–Sat 9am–9pm, Sun 10am–9pm; 20kn) marks the top station of the funicular (see p.159) and provides fantastic views over the rest of the city and the plains beyond; a small cannon has been fired from the tower every day at noon since 1877.

Museum of Illusions

West of the lower station of the Gradec funicular at Ilica 72, the **Museum of Illusions** (daily 9am–10pm; 40kn; ⓦ muzejiluzija.com) fills two floors of a former residential building with visual tricks and mind games. Escheresque pictures, sloping floors and wonky walls ensure that this is good fun for adults and kids alike.

Museum of Contemporary Art

Arguably Zagreb's most stylish attraction, the **Museum of Contemporary Art** at Avenija Dubrovnik 17 (Tues–Fri & Sun 11am–6pm, Sat 11am–8pm; 30kn; ⓦ www.msu.hr; tram #14 to Siget stop) occupies a swish modern building in high-rise suburbs south of the river. The museum showcases both Croatian and international art: works by local iconoclasts Goran Trbuljak, Sanja Iveković and Mladen Stilinović reinforce Croatia's reputation for art that's witty, ironic and understated. You can also take a ride on Carsten Holler's toboggan tubes.

ARRIVAL AND DEPARTURE

By plane Zagreb airport is 10km southeast of the city; buses run to the main bus station (every 30min–1hr, 7am–8pm; 30kn).

By train Zagreb's central train station (*glavni kolodor*) is on Tomislavov Trg, on the southern edge of the city centre, a 10min walk from Trg bana Jelačića.

HEARTBREAK HOUSE: ZAGREB'S MUSEUM OF BROKEN RELATIONSHIPS

For a voyage into the more tumescent recesses of the human psyche there are few better starting points than Zagreb's **Museum of Broken Relationships** at Ćirilometodska 2 (daily 9am–9pm; 25kn; ⓦ brokenships.com), which began life as a travelling art installation. Based on mementoes donated by the public, it's a compelling and unique museum of wistful memory and raw emotion, with exhibits ranging from garden gnomes to prosthetic limbs. Each is accompanied by a text explaining its significance to the donor – some are touching, others quite kinky; and quite a few belong to the obsessive world of a David Lynch movie.

6

PLITVICE LAKES

Midway between Zagreb and the Dalmatian coast, the **Plitvice Lakes National Park** (daily: April, May, Sept & Oct 8am–6pm; June–Aug 7am–8pm; Nov–March 9am–4pm; July & Aug 180kn, April–June, Sept & Oct 110kn, rest of year 55kn; ⓦ np-plitvicka-jezera.hr) is the country's biggest single natural attraction. The 8km string of sixteen lakes, hemmed in by densely forested hills, presents some of the most eye-catching scenery in mainland Croatia, with water rushing from lake to lake via a sequence of falls and rapids. Wooden walkways traverse the foaming waters, allowing a close up view of the scenery. Most backpacker hostels in Zagreb, Zadar and Split offer day-trips to the lakes (around 200kn, not including entrance to the park itself), or try Wanderer Travel, Trpimirova 25 (ⓣ 091 222 2299, ⓦ wanderertravel.eu), a reputable agent. Independent travellers can get to the lakes by public bus – at least three daily Zagreb–Zadar and three Zagreb–Split services pass the park entrance.

Destinations Belgrade (2 daily; 6hr 40min); Budapest (2 daily; 6hr 30min); Ljubljana (6 daily; 2hr 20min); Munich (2 daily; 8hr 45min); Salzburg (2 daily; 7hr); Sarajevo (1 daily; 9hr); Split (2 daily, one of which is overnight; 5hr 30min–8hr); Vienna (1 daily; 6hr 30min).

By bus The main bus station (*autobusni kolodvor*) is a 10min walk east of the train station, at the junction of Branimirova and Držićeva – trams #2 and #6 run between the two stations, with #6 continuing to the main square.

Destinations Belgrade (5 daily; 6hr); Dubrovnik (8 daily; 9–11hr); Ljubljana (6 daily; 3hr); Munich (2 daily; 9hr 30min–11hr); Pula (hourly; 4hr–6hr 30min); Rijeka (hourly; 2hr 30min–3hr); Rovinj (6 daily; 4hr 30min–6hr); Sarajevo (4 daily; 7–8hr); Split (every 30min; 4hr 45min–8hr 30min); Trieste (5 daily; 4hr); Vienna (2 daily; 6hr); Zadar (hourly; 3–5hr).

INFORMATION

Tourist information Trg bana Jelačića 11 (June–Sept Mon–Fri 8.30am–9pm, Sat & Sun 9am–6pm; Oct–May Mon–Fri 8.30am–8pm, Sat 10am–5pm, Sun 10am–2pm; ⓣ 01 48 14 051, ⓦ zagreb-touristinfo.hr). Also at the main railway station (Mon–Fri 9am–9pm, Sat & Sun 10am–5pm); main bus station (Mon–Fri 9am–9pm, Sat & Sun 10am–5pm); and airport (Mon–Fri 9am–9pm, Sat & Sun 10am–5pm).

Discount cards The tourist office sells the Zagreb Card (72hr/90kn), which offers unlimited city transport and good discounts in museums and restaurants – perfect if you plan to do lots.

GETTING AROUND

By tram The easiest way to get about, with sixteen routes. Lines #2 and #6 run between the bus and train stations, #6 taking you into Jelačića, the main crossing point in the city. There's also a four-line network of night services.

By bus The bus network serves the capital's peripheries, setting off from the suburban side of the train station.

Tickets Tram and bus tickets (*karte*), valid for 1hr 30min if travelling in one direction, are sold at kiosks (10kn) or from the driver (12kn); day-tickets (*dnevne karte*) cost 30kn. Validate your ticket by punching it in the machines on board.

By taxi There are ranks at the station and the northeast corner of Trg bana Jelačića. The standard rate is 19kn plus 7kn/km, which goes up by twenty percent early in the morning and late at night, on Sun and holidays. Luggage costs 5kn/item. To book, call Cammeo (ⓣ 060 7100) or Ekotaxi (ⓣ 1414).

ACCOMMODATION

★4City Windows Palmotićeva 13 ⓣ 01 889 7999, ⓦ 4citywindows.com. A cute B&B in a beautifully converted downtown flat with small and imaginatively themed rooms. There's a bright, mood-enhancing kitchen packed with Pop Art, and breakfast is included. Doubles **580kn**

★Hobo Bear Hostel Medulićeva 4 ⓣ 01 48 46 636, ⓦ hobobearhostel.com; tram #6 from the bus or train station to Frankopanska. Stylish hostel in a great location near Ilica. There's a funky wine-cellar-like common room and a well-appointed kitchen. Dorms **112kn**, doubles **350kn**

Shappy Hostel Varšavska 8 ⓣ 01 48 30 483, ⓦ hostel-shappy.com. Bright, homely dorms and en-suite doubles, tucked in beside the Cvijetni shopping centre and with a lively downstairs café. An ideal base from which to explore the city. Dorms **130kn**, doubles **360kn**

Studio Kairos Vlaška 92 ⓣ 01 46 40 680, ⓦ studio-kairos.com; trams #4, #7, #11 and #12 to the Petrova stop. Located a 15min walk east of the main square, this cute and welcoming B&B consists of four small but neat rooms with smart en-suite bathrooms, flat-screen TVs and a/c. Most of the rooms are officially twins, but the slide-out, expandable beds will sleep three at a pinch. Doubles **530kn**

★Swanky Mint Ilica 50 ⓣ 01 400 4248, ⓦ swanky-hostel.com. Beautifully restored textile factory right behind Zagreb's main shopping street, offering quirky post-industrial decor, a large kitchen and a good social buzz. Breakfast can be bought at the hostel café, which boasts a retro interior and a wonderful back-yard terrace. Dorms 120kn, doubles 490kn

Taban Tkalčićeva 82 ☎ 01 55 33 527, ⓦ buzzbackpackers .com. At the top of the Tkalčićeva café-bar strip and with a well-stocked ground-floor bar of its own, *Taban* offers smartly furnished dorms with cubicle-like bunk beds, plus neat private doubles with TV. Dorms 150kn, doubles 500kn

ZigZag Petrinjska 9 ☎ 01 889 5433, ⓦ zigzag.hr. ZigZag have a selection of apartments around the city centre with the main reception area at the Petrinjska address. Apartments are all neat affairs with kitchenettes and cable TV. As something of a ZigZag trademark, each apartment features a blackboard with the staff's latest going-out tips written on it. Two-person apartments 850kn

EATING

Zagreb has plenty of cafés and bars with outdoor seating in the pedestrian area around Gajeva and Bogovićeva, and along trendy Tkalčićeva. For picnic food, head to Dolac market (see p.164).

CAFÉS
★**Cookie Factory** Tkalčićeva 21. "Life is uncertain: eat dessert first" is the motto of the *Cookie Factory* café, purveyor of some of the most addictive chocolate brownies in Central Europe. You can also fill up on cakes, ice cream and, of course, the eponymous cookies. Mon–Thurs & Sun 9am–10pm, Fri & Sat 9am–11pm.

Kava Tava Tkalčićeva 12. Filled with old radios and an odd jumble of furniture, Kava Tava is one of Zagreb's prime breakfasting spots, thanks to its fried-egg feasts, pancakes, good coffee and fresh juices. Daily 7am–midnight.

RESTAURANTS
Bistroteka Teslina 14. One of the leading lights of Zagreb's burgeoning bistro scene, *Bistroteka* chalks up a

---

★ TREAT YOURSELF

Takenoko Masarykova 22 ☎ 01 646 3385, ⓦ takenoko.hr. For quality Asian food in design-conscious interiors, moodily minimalist *Takenoko* does the trick. Most people come for the excellent sushi, although the menu also sweeps in steaks, teriyaki chicken, a broad range of wok-fried dishes and – fusion fans take note – wasabi-garnished lamb chops and Adriatic fish dressed with Asian spices. Mains around 150kn. Mon–Sat noon–11.30pm, Sun noon–5pm.

---

daily menu of sandwiches, pasta dishes, salads and main meals based on what seasonal products are currently stirring the chef's creative juices. Mains 65–120kn. Daily 8.30am–midnight.

Burgeraj Preradovićeva 13. "Burger Heaven" is a rough translation of the play-on-words title of this retro-styled diner celebrating the cult of the minced beef pattie. The menu is limited to about 4 or 5 burgers (35–49kn) but they are all well thought-out, with *Burgeraj's* own-recipe sauces and relishes proving the key ingredient. Daily 11am–11pm.

★**Lari & Penati** Petrinjska 42a. A small but perfectly formed deli-cum-restaurant with amazingly cheap and classy Mediterranean-meets-oriental dishes in the 40–60kn bracket. All served to a soundtrack of smooth jazz. Mon–Fri 8am–8pm, Sat 11am–5pm.

Nishta Masarykova 11. Vegetarian and vegan restaurant with an inventive, regularly changing menu which proves that meat-free cuisine can still spring a few surprises. Good-value soup of the day and a salad bar ensure that there are plenty of options here for light lunchers. Mains 60–70kn. Tues–Sun noon–11pm.

Nokturno Skalinska 4. On a cobbled street off Tkalčićeva, *Nokturno* has pleasant outdoor seating and tasty pizzas (50kn), meat and fish dishes (40–75n), and salads (25kn). Daily 9am–midnight.

Ribice i tri točkice Preradovićeva 7/1. A great place to sample Adriatic cuisine without having your wallet emptied afterwards, with traditional Dalmatian dishes (grilled squid, fried anchovies, fillets of hake) served at village-tavern prices (50–60kn for a main). Daily 9am–midnight.

Zrno Bio Bistro Medulićeva 20. Hidden away in a residential courtyard, *Zrno* is one of the key addresses in town for quality vegetarian and vegan food, with a broad-based menu of pasta and wok dishes and a popular daily set macrobiotic lunch. Mains 60–70kn. Mon–Sat noon–9.30pm.

DRINKING AND NIGHTLIFE

Pick up the free monthly *Events and Performances* pamphlet from the tourist office.

BARS
Craft Room Opatovina 35. Something of a temple to Croatia's emerging craft beer scene, this arty but cosy café-pub serves pretty much every decent ale in the country, with gourmet burgers providing the belly-lining accompaniment. Daily 10am–2am.

Kino Europa Varšavska 3. A lovely old interwar cinema that screens art movies, the Europa's café serves as a key meeting point for the city's art-and-culture tribes. There's a good choice of *rakijas* (12kn), and retro discos in the foyer at weekends. Mon–Thurs 8am–11pm, Fri & Sat 8am–2am, Sun noon–10pm.

ZAGREB FESTIVALS

Zagreb has an impressive array of annual **festivals** and events including INmusic (late June; ⓦinmusicfestival.com), a three-day rock-and-pop festival on the shores of Lake Jarun. The 2016 line-up included Florence & the Machine, PJ Harvey and Wilco. Check with tourist information for details of other events.

Klub Kino Gric Jurišićeva 6. Boasts both a private arthouse cinema and a small chilled-out bar with stripy walls. Enjoy a White Russian (30kn) in one of its stylish red director's chairs. Daily 7.30am–11.30pm.

Krivi put Savska 25. Near the Zagreb university students' union, this unassuming hut sucks in a huge cross section of young, boisterous and edgily alternative types, with a smoke-saturated inner sanctum and a vast wooden-bench yard with space for hundreds. Bottled Velebitsko beer (15kn) is the standard order. Daily 8am–1am.

La Bodega Wine & Tapas Bar Bogovićeva 5. One of the busiest outdoor terraces on the pedestrianized Bogovićeva strip belongs to *La Bodega*, a buzzing little place that serves good-quality but not too pricey wine and cocktails to draw in a predominantly young and stylish crowd. Wed–Sat 8am–2am, Sun–Tues 8am–midnight.

★**Mali Medo** Tkalčićeva 36 ⓦpivnica-medvedgrad.hr. Down a pint or two of the ruby-red lager Griška Vještica ("Witch of Grič") at this pub-restaurant run by the local Medvedgrad brewery. The pub itself is pretty small but the wooden-bench outdoor terrace spreads over a significant stretch of the Tkalčićeva drinking strip. Mon–Wed 10am–midnight, Thurs–Sat 10am–1am, Sun noon–midnight.

Velvet Dežmanova 9 ⓦvelvet.hr. Subdued lighting, antique furnishings, plush armchairs and sofas contribute a palpable sense of theatre at this one-off café-bar on the increasingly hip Dežmanova street. With good coffee, hot chocolate and decent pots of tea, this makes an ideal place for a lengthy break. Mon–Sat 8am–10pm, Sun 9am–2pm.

CLUBS

Aquarius Aleja Mira bb ⓦaquarius.hr; tram #17 from Trg bana Jelačića to Horvati. At the eastern end of Lake Jarun, 6km southwest of the centre, this club specializes in techno and drum'n'bass. International headline acts play here too (tickets from 190kn). Cover charge for club nights 30–40kn. Thurs–Sun 10pm–6am.

Katran Radnička 27. This post-industrial factory space is home to several ad-hoc clubs. Shock Show Industry (ⓦfacebook.com/ShockShowIndustry) and Super Super are two club nights currently occupying the former factory halls at weekends, but you should check with a local before setting out. Fri & Sat 11pm–6am.

Pepermint Klub Ilica 24. Look for the long queue of fashionistas on Ilica to find this fresh and trendy club, which plays a mix of music from funk to soul. Daily 10am–4am.

SHOPPING AND MARKETS

The principal area for shopping is along Ilica, off Trg bana Jelačića, which has several independent stores as well as familiar high-street names, punctuated by handsome coffee shops and a few tempting bakeries.

Britanski Trg market Britanski Trg. This bric-a-brac market is a magpie's dream – jewellery, traditional Croatian embroidery, farming implements, binoculars – you name it, it's there. Sun till 2pm.

Dolac market Dolac. Occupying a large terrace overlooking Trg bana Jelačića, Dolac is the city's principal market selling a feast of fruit and vegetables. It's at its liveliest on Thursdays and Fridays, when fresh Adriatic fish brings extra colour to the seafood pavilion. Daily 6.30am–3pm.

DIRECTORY

Embassies Australia, Nova Ves 11 ☎01 48 91 200; Canada, Prilaz Gjure Deželića 4 ☎01 48 81 200; UK, Ivana Lučića 4 ☎01 60 09 100; US, Thomasa Jeffersona 2 ☎01 66 12 200.

Exchange In the post office on Branimirova or at any bank. Privredna bank at Ilica 5 changes travellers' cheques.

Hospital For emergencies visit KBC Rebro, Kišpatićeva 6 ☎01 238 8888.

Internet Wi-fi is widespread. Best of the central internet cafés is *Sublink*, Teslina 12 (Mon–Sat 9am–10pm, Sun 3–10pm, 20kn/hr; ☎01 48 19 993, ⓦsublink.hr).

Left luggage At the train (24hr; 15kn/hr) and bus stations (daily 6am–10pm; 5kn/hr).

Pharmacies 24hr pharmacy at Radićeva 3.

Post offices Branimirova 4 (24hr); Jurišićeva 13 (Mon–Fri 7am–9pm, Sat 7.30am–2pm).

SUMMER IN THE CITY

A lot of Zagreb's clubs and live music venues close down for the summer, when most of the city's hip young things relocate to the Adriatic coast. Keeping life ticking over is the **Strossmartre (Ljeto na Strosu)** season of **open-air concerts and events** in Zagreb's Upper Town, with nightly happenings all summer long. It runs from May to early Sept: full schedule on ⓦljetonastrosu.com.

Istria

A large peninsula jutting into the northern Adriatic, **Istria** is Croatian tourism at its most developed. Many of the towns here were resorts in the nineteenth century and still attract an annual influx of sun-seekers. Yet the growth of tourism has done little to detract from the essential charm and beauty of the region. Istria's largest centre is the port city of **Pula**, which, with its Roman amphitheatre and other relics of Roman occupation, is a rewarding place to spend a couple of days. On the western side of the peninsula, the town of **Rovinj**, with its cobbled piazzas and shuttered houses, is the very image of Mediterranean chic.

ARRIVAL AND DEPARTURE

By bus and train The port city of Rijeka is the main travel hub for Istria, with regular buses to Zagreb, Pula, Rovinj, Zadar, Split and Dubrovnik. Rijeka's train station is 500m west of the centre at Krešimirova 5. The bus station is on the western fringe of the centre on Trg Žabica.

PULA

Once the chief port of the Austro-Hungarian Empire, **PULA** is an engaging combination of working port, naval base and vibrant riviera town. The Romans put the city squarely on the map when they arrived in 177 BC, transforming it into an important commercial centre.

WHAT TO SEE AND DO

The chief reminder of Pula's Roman heritage is its impressive amphitheatre; south of here, the town centre circles a pyramidal hill, scaled by secluded streets, dotted with Roman relics and topped with a star-shaped Venetian fortress.

The amphitheatre

The first-century BC **Roman amphitheatre** (daily: April 8am–8pm; May, June & Sept 8am–9pm; July & Aug 8am–midnight; Oct–March 9am–5pm; 40kn) is the sixth largest in the world, and once had space for over 23,000 spectators. The outer shell is fairly complete, as is one of the towers,

up which a slightly hair-raising climb gives a good sense of the enormity of the structure and a view of Pula's industrious harbour. The amphitheatre hosts the annual **Pula Film Festival** (ⓦ pulafilm festival.hr) at the end of July, as well as concerts throughout the summer.

The Archeological Museum

A short way south of the amphitheatre is Pula's **Archeological Museum** (Jan–April & Oct–Dec Mon–Fri 9am–2pm; May–Sept Mon–Sat 9am–8pm, Sun 10am–3pm; 20kn), where pillars and toga-clad statues mingle with ceramics, jewellery and trinkets from all over Istria, some of them prehistoric.

Zerostrasse

With its entrance beside the Archeological Museum, **Zerostrasse**, or "Zero Street", (mid-June to mid-Sept daily 10am–10pm; 15kn) was one of several pre-World War I tunnels built by the Austrian military to enable safe transport of men and armaments in the event of enemy bombardment. Featuring a central subterranean hall that could accommodate 6000 men, Zerostrasse is an atmospheric place that anyone with an interest in history – or indeed tunnels – will enjoy.

The Triumphal Arch and the Temple of Augustus

Central Pula's main street, Giardini, runs south to the first-century BC **Triumphal Arch of the Sergians**, through which the pedestrianized Via Sergia leads to the town's ancient Roman **Forum**, now the square at the centre of Pula's old quarter. On the far side of here, the slim but impressive **Temple of Augustus** was built between 2 BC and 14 AD to celebrate the cult of the emperor; its imposing Corinthian columns, still intact, make it one of the best examples of a Roman temple outside Italy.

ARRIVAL AND DEPARTURE

By plane Pula's airport is 6km northeast of the city. The bus ride to the centre costs 35kn; taxis are around 180kn.
By bus The bus station is 10min northeast of the centre, along Istarska Divizije.

6

Destinations Dubrovnik (1 daily; 15hr); Rijeka (roughly hourly; 1hr 30min–2hr 30min); Rovinj (roughly hourly; 45min); Split (2 daily; 12hr); Trieste (2 daily; 2hr 45min–3hr 45min); Venice (Mon–Sat 1 daily; 5hr); Zadar (3 daily; 7hr); Zagreb (hourly; 3hr 30min–5hr).

By ferry Pula's small passenger port is just east of the amphitheatre. Tickets can be booked through Libertas at Riva 14 (☎052 211 631).

Destinations Zadar (mid-July to Aug 4 weekly; 4hr 30min).

INFORMATION

Tourist information In the Forum (June–Sept daily 8am–10pm; Oct–May Mon–Sat 9am–7pm, Sun 10am–4pm; ☎052 212 987, ⊛pulainfo.hr).

ACCOMMODATION

Private rooms Book through Brioni Tours in the bus station (Mon–Fri 8am–4pm, Sat 8am–1pm; ☎052 544 219, ⊛brioni.hr). Doubles from 250kn

Hostel Pipištrelo Flaciusova 6 ☎052 393 568. An imaginatively designed hostel decked out in bold greens, yellows and salmon-pinks, with Pop Art adorning the walls of several rooms. There's a small kitchen on the ground floor and a social area next to the reception. Dorms 135kn, doubles 420kn

Pula Art Hostel Marulićeva 41 ☎098 874 078, ⊛pulaarthostel.com; bus #2a or #3 to Verudela from the bus station. Sociable hostel near central Pula (look out for the distinctive green building) with lots of creative touches, including a mosaic staircase. Free wi-fi and internet. Dorms 150kn

Stoja 3km southeast of town ☎052 387 144, ⊛arenacamps.com; bus #1 from Giardini. Simple campsite on a wooded peninsula with beautiful rocky beaches. Minimum two nights in summer. Per person 55kn, plus per tent 60kn

EATING AND DRINKING

Bistro Dva Ferala Kandlerova 32. *Dva Ferala* attracts a lively local crowd to its street-side seating for cheap Croatian cuisine, including *čevapčići*, and pork and chips (both 45kn). Mon–Sat 8am–11pm.

Jupiter Castropola 42. Perched on a hill near the fortress, this is a popular pizzeria with pretty Art Deco glass panels and a terrace. Sizeable pizzas from 40kn. Mon–Fri 10am–midnight, Sat noon–midnight, Sun 1pm–midnight.

Market Narodni Trg. Offers plenty of fresh fruit and veg and has a wealth of local deli products in the cast-iron Art Nouveau pavilion at its centre. Daily 7am–2pm.

Pietas Julia Riva 20. Grab a sofa and an apple martini (30kn) at this fun lounge bar in a pavilion west of the amphitheatre. Free wi-fi. Daily 10am–4am.

Rock Cafe Scalierova 8 ⊛myspace.com/rockcaffepula. A spacious place with a stage for live music, alcoves decorated with rock-star murals and a lot of fancy wood carving adorning the main bar and the wall panelling. Daily 8am–2am.

Uljanik Dobrilina 2. Counter-cultural club of many years' standing with a huge beer garden, DJ nights at weekends and live music in the summer. Cover charge varies – often free entry during the summer. Thurs–Sat 9pm–late.

ROVINJ

Once an island, charming **ROVINJ** lies 40km north of Pula. Refreshingly free of traffic, its hotchpotch of cobbled streets, terracotta roofs and shuttered windows teeters over the clear sea, and the harbour is an attractive mix of fishing boats and swanky yachts.

WHAT TO SEE AND DO

From the main square, **Trg maršala Tita**, the Baroque **Vrata svetog Križa** leads up to Grisia Ulica, lined with galleries selling local art. It climbs steeply through the heart of the Old Town to **St Euphemia's Church** (daily: April–June 10am–1pm; July–Sept 10am–6pm), dominating Rovinj from the top of its peninsula. This eighteenth-century Baroque church has the sixth-century sarcophagus of the saint inside, and you can climb its 58m-high tower (same hours; 10kn). Paths on the south side of Rovinj's busy harbour lead south towards **Zlatnirt**, a densely forested

---

PULA: EUROPEAN BASS-CULTURE CAPITAL

For those into reggae, dub, jungle, dubstep or any bass-heavy offshoots, Pula is one of the best places in the Mediterranean to spend the summer. Punta Christo, an abandoned seaside fortress just north of town, is the perfect venue for three highly recommended festivals – **Seasplash**, which concentrates on traditional reggae and dub (late July; ⊛seasplash-festival.com); **Outlook**, which focuses on reggae, dubstep and everything beyond (late Aug/early Sept; ⊛outlookfestival.com); and the more eclectic **Dimensions**, which ventures towards the outer frontiers of dance culture (late Aug; ⊛dimensionsfestival.com).

cape, crisscrossed by tracks. The best of the **beaches** – all rocky – are here, but you can also try the two islands just offshore: **Sveta Katarina**, the nearer of the two, and **Crveni otok**, just outside Rovinj's bay (linked by boats from the harbour; every hour; 30kn return).

ARRIVAL AND INFORMATION

By bus Rovinj's bus station is a 5min walk southeast of its centre, just off Trg na lokvi, at the junction of Carrera and Carducci.

Destinations Dubrovnik (1 daily; 16hr); Pula (roughly hourly; 45min); Rijeka (6 daily; 3hr); Split (1 daily; 11hr); Trieste (1 daily; 2–3hr); Venice (1 daily; 5hr 15min); Zadar (1 daily; 8hr); Zagreb (7 daily; 4–7hr).

By ferry Rovinj's small passenger port lies just north of the peninsula.

Destinations Trieste (mid-June to mid-Sept 1 daily; 1hr 30min–2hr 15min); Venice (summer only, Mon–Sat 1 daily; 5hr).

Tourist information On the waterfront promenade at Obala Pina Budicina 12 (June–Sept daily 8am–9pm; Oct–May Mon–Sat 8am–3pm; ☏052 811 566, ⓦtzgrovinj.hr).

ACCOMMODATION

Private rooms Try Natale, opposite the bus station at Via Carducci 4 (Mon–Sat 7.30am–9.30pm, Sun 8am–5pm; ☏052 813 365, ⓦrovinj.com). Rooms from 145kn

Porton Biondi Aleja Porton Biondi 1 ☏052 813 557, ⓦportonbiondi.hr. A pine-shaded campsite with its own beach, 700m north of town. Mid-March to Nov. Per person 55kn, plus per tent 85kn

EATING AND DRINKING

Trg Valdibora is home to a small produce market.

Art Public Bar Carera 88. Head through the passageway and into the back yard to locate this dark and welcoming drinking den, catering for a mixed bag of locals and tourists. There's a small outdoor terrace, and live music on Thurs. Daily 11am–midnight.

Da Sergio Grisia 11. Great pizzas – baby and normal-sized – from 50kn. Much better value than the places on the harbourfront. Daily 11am–11pm.

Maestral Obala V. Nazora. Located on the seafront towards Zlatni rt, with plenty of pine-shaded outdoor seating, and fresh seafood (from 50kn) grilled alfresco. Daily 8am–11pm.

Monte Carlo Svetoga Križa 23. This bar has a gorgeous terrace where you can intersperse drinks with refreshing dips in the sea. Bottled beer 20kn. Daily 8am–1am.

The Dalmatian Coast

Stretching from Zadar in the north to the Montenegrin border in the south, the **Dalmatian Coast** is one of Europe's most dramatic shorelines. All along, well-preserved medieval towns sit beneath a grizzled karst landscape that drops precipitously into some of the cleanest water in the Mediterranean. For centuries, the region was ruled by Venice, spawning architecture that wouldn't look out of place on the other side of the water. The busy northern port city of **Zadar** provides a vivacious introduction to the region. Otherwise, the main attractions are in the south: the lively provincial capital **Split**, built around a Roman palace and jumping-off point for the islands of Brač, Hvar, Vis and Korčula; and the walled city of **Dubrovnik**.

ARRIVAL AND DEPARTURE

Split is the main transport hub of the Dalmation Coast, with trains from Zagreb and onward bus connections to Dubrovnik. Ferry and catamaran services to the islands of Brač, Hvar, Vis and Korčula also run from Split.

ZADAR

A bustling town of nearly 100,000 people, **ZADAR** is one of the success stories of the Croatian Adriatic, combining ancient and medieval heritage with a vibrant bar scene and the kind of go-ahead architectural projects (such as the *Sea Organ* and the *Greeting to the Sun*) that give the seafront the appearance of an art installation.

WHAT TO SEE AND DO

Zadar displays a pleasant muddle of architectural styles, with Romanesque churches competing for space with modern cafés. The main sights are concentrated in the Old Town, which is hemmed in by the sea; the central Roman Forum is the best place to begin exploring.

6

6

THE SEA ORGAN AND GREETING TO THE SUN

Zadar's quirkiest feature, the **Sea Organ**, consists of wide marble steps leading into the sea, with a set of tubes and cavities carved underneath, which enable the sea and wind to orchestrate a constant harmony. Emitting a strange sound, a bit like panpipes crossed with whale song, the *Organ* is surprisingly melodic and relaxing. Next to it is another public artwork, **Greeting to the Sun**: a huge disc that accumulates solar power during the day and radiates a multicoloured hypnotic glow by night.

The Forum

Zadar's main square – or Forum – is dominated by the ninth-century **St Donat's Church** (daily: April, May & Oct 9am–5pm; June–Sept 9am–10pm; 10kn), a hulking cylinder of stone with a vast bare interior, built – according to tradition – by St Donat himself, an Irishman who was bishop here for a time. Opposite, the **Archeological Museum** (June–Sept Mon–Sat 9am–9pm; Oct–Nov Mon–Fri 9am–2pm, Sat 9am–1pm; 15kn) has an absorbing collection of Roman and medieval artefacts.

Behind St Donat's, the twelfth- and thirteenth-century **Cathedral of St Anastasia** has an arcaded west front reminiscent of Tuscan churches. Around the door frame stretches a frieze of twisting acanthus leaves, from which various beasts emerge – look out for the rodent and bird fighting over a bunch of grapes. You can climb the 56m campanile for great views over the city (Mon–Sat 10am–5pm; 10kn).

South of the Forum

Southeast of the Forum lies **Narodni Trg**, an attractive Renaissance square. A little further southeast, on Trg Petra Zoranića, the Baroque St Simeon's Church houses the exuberantly decorated reliquary of St Simeon, commissioned by Queen Elizabeth of Hungary in 1377 and fashioned from 250kg of silver by local artisans.

Overlooking the harbour at Poljana Zemaljskog odbora 1 is the state-of-the-art **Museum of Ancient Glass** (June–Sept daily 9am–9pm; Oct–May Mon–Sat 9am–4pm; 30kn), which contains a fine collection of Roman glassware and affords wonderful views over the harbour.

ARRIVAL AND DEPARTURE

By plane Zadar's airport is 12km east of town. Buses (7–9 daily depending on flight schedule; 25kn) run into town.

By train and bus The train and bus stations are about 1km east of the town centre, a 20min walk or a hop on bus #5 – tickets cost 10kn from the driver or 16kn (valid for two journeys) from kiosks.

Destinations (train) Split (2 daily; 5hr; change at Knin).
Destinations (bus) Dubrovnik (7 daily; 8hr 30min); Pula (3 daily; 6hr 30min); Rijeka (9 daily; 4hr 30min); Rovinj (1 daily; 8hr); Split (approx every 30min; 3hr–3hr 30min); Zagreb (hourly; 3–5hr).

By ferry Ferries arrive on Liburnska obala, just outside the walls of the Old Town.

Destinations Ancona (3–6 weekly; 6–9hr); Pula (mid-July to Aug 4 weekly; 4hr 30min).

INFORMATION

Tourist information Narodni Trg (June & Sept daily 8am–8pm; July & Aug daily 8am–midnight; Oct–May Mon–Fri 8am–3pm; ☎ 023 316 166, ⊛ tzzadar.hr).

ACCOMMODATION

Private rooms Jaderatours on Elizabete Kotromanić in the Old Town (☎ 023 250 350, ⊛ jaderatours.hr) has rooms from 150kn

Borik Majstora Radovana 7 ☎ 023 206 559, ⊛ campingborik.com; bus #5 or #8 from the bus and train stations. Well-equipped campsite in a large tourist complex with its own beach. Summer only. Per person 55kn, plus per tent 75kn

Boutique Hostel Forum Široka 20 ☎ 023 250 705, ⊛ hostelforumzadar.com. Designer hostel decked out by the team responsible for *Goli & Bosi* in Split (see p.171), offering a mixture of dorm rooms and hotel-standard private doubles (with breakfast included). Free wi-fi and a fully equipped kitchen are yours to use. Dorms 180kn, doubles 800kn

Drunken Monkey Hostel Skenderbega 21 ☎ 023 314 406, ⊛ drunkenmonkeyhostel.com. Out in the suburb of Arbanasi but still very handy for bus station and town centre, the *Monkey* offers clean dorms, a garden with a small pool, cosy communal areas and on-site bar. Free wi-fi and internet access. Dorms 165kn, doubles 440kn

EATING

For snacks and picnics, the daily market just inside the Old Town walls off Jurja Barakovića is the place to get fruit, vegetables, local cheeses and home-cured hams.

Konoba Na Po Ure Špire Brusine 8. Popular with locals and visitors alike, this homely restaurant is best known for its fish dishes, including heaps of juicy mussels (50kn) and fresh anchovies (30kn). Daily 10am–11pm.

★**Konoba Skoblar** Trg Petra Zoranića. Serving up the broad gamut of Dalmatian food at prices that won't lead to tears, *Skoblar* continues to draw in locals eager for *marende* (elevenses) or a more expansive mid-afternoon lunch. Daily specials (50kn) are chalked up on a board outside the door. Daily 9am–midnight.

★**Pašta & Svašta** Poljana Šime Budinića 1. Pasta is the name of the game at this rustic-but-chic street-corner restaurant, with several freshly made varieties and an imaginative choice of sauces to go with them. Mains 65–110Kn. Daily 9am–11pm.

★**Pet Bunara** Trg pet Bunara ☏023 224 010. Turning out refined Adriatic-Mediterranean cuisine, the "Five Wells" treats traditional ingredients with flair and imagination. The menu is seasonal, but local seafood predominates, and there is always something for vegetarians. Mains 80–120Kn. Daily 8am–1am.

DRINKING AND NIGHTLIFE

Hitch Kolovare. With a partially covered terrace jutting out into the Adriatic with views across the straits to the island of Ugljan, this is one of Zadar's best bets for sunset cocktail-sipping and after-sundown clubbing. Daily 8am–5am.

Kult Stomorica 6. One of a number of café-bars tucked down winding Stomorica, this fashionable spot has a large wooden terrace area on which to enjoy the pumping music. Daily 8am–1am.

★**The Garden** Bedemi zadarskih pobuna ⓦwatchthegardengrow.eu. This lounge-bar sits high up in the city walls: there are big beds to relax on, cocktail in hand, as well as a dancefloor that regularly boasts big-name DJs (cover charge for popular events). April–Oct daily 11am–2am.

SPLIT

6

The largest city in the region, and its major transit hub, **SPLIT** is a hectic place, but one of the most enticing spots on the Dalmatian Coast. At its heart lies a crumbling Old Town built within the walls of Diocletian's Palace, and including some of the most outstanding classical remains in Europe.

WHAT TO SEE AND DO

Diocletian's Palace is still the epicentre of the city – lived in almost continuously since Roman times, it has gradually become a warren of houses, tenements and churches. Almost everything worth seeing is concentrated here, behind the waterfront Riva, while to its west is the lush **Marjan peninsula**.

Diocletian's Palace

Built as a retirement home by Dalmatian-born Roman Emperor Diocletian in 305 AD, **Diocletian's Palace** is a jumble of original features and subsequent additions. The best place to start a tour is on its seaward side through the **Bronze Gate**, which once gave direct access to the

TISNO FESTIVALS

Tisno, a sprawling seaside village midway between Zadar and Split, shot into the limelight in 2012 when it became the new summer home of the Garden organization, the Zadar-based crew responsible for launching the legendary **Garden Festival** in 2007. Although the last Garden Festival was held in 2015, the team behind it hosts a growing roster of other festivals and events throughout the summer – July and August is just one huge party if you have the stamina to stick around. Getting there from Zadar or Split is easy – catch an inter-city bus to Šibenik and then change to a local bus to Murter, which calls at Tisno on the way. There's plenty of accommodation too, with apartments and camping on the site itself, or private rooms in Tisno village. **Tickets** for Tisno events and festivals cost around £120, not including transport and accommodation, and must be bought in advance.

Love International Early July; ⓦloveinternationalfestival.com.
Electric Elephant Mid-July; ⓦelectricelephant.co.uk.
Soundwave Festival Late July; ⓦsoundwavecroatia.com.
SuncéBeat Late July to early Aug; ⓦsuncebeat.com.
Stop making Sense Early Aug; ⓦstopmakingsense.eu.

6

water. Through the gate, you find yourself in a shady vaulted hall full of souvenir stalls. To your left is the atmospheric **palace basement** (daily: May–Sept 8am–8pm; Oct–April 8am–noon & 4–7pm; 10kn) that once sat beneath Diocletian's apartments, and where you can get some idea of the size and layout of his erstwhile home.

Carry on through the vaulted hallways and up the steps to the **Peristyle**, which these days serves as the main town square. At the southern end, more steps lead up to the **vestibule**, an impressive cone-shaped building that's the only part of the imperial apartments to be left anything like intact, despite losing its dome.

The cathedral

On the eastern side of the Peristyle stands one of two black granite Egyptian sphinxes, dating from around 15 BC, which originally flanked the entrance to Diocletian's mausoleum; the octagonal building, surrounded by an arcade of Corinthian columns, has since been converted into Split's **cathedral** (Mon–Sat 7am–noon & 5–7pm; 10kn; 5kn extra to visit the crypt). The cathedral's striking walnut and oak **doorway** was carved in 1214 and shows scenes from the life of Christ. Inside, the dome is ringed by two series of decorative Corinthian columns and a frieze that contains portraits of Diocletian and his wife. The church's finest feature is a cruelly realistic *Flagellation of Christ* depicted on the Altar of St Anastasius, completed by local artist Juraj Dalmatinac in 1448. To the right of the entrance is the **campanile** (same hours; 5kn), a restored Romanesque structure – from the top, the views across the city are magnificent.

Follow the alleyway directly opposite the cathedral to reach the intriguing **baptistry**, or Temple of Jupiter (Mon–Sat 7am–noon & 5–7pm; 10kn), originally built by a cult in Diocletian's time and later adapted by Christians.

The Golden Gate and Archeological Museum

North of the cathedral, along Dioklecijanova, is the grandest and best preserved of the palace entrances: the **Golden Gate**. Just outside there's a piece by Meštrović, a gigantic statue of the fourth-century Bishop **Grgur Ninski** – rubbing its big toe is said to bring good luck. Fifteen minutes' walk northwest of here, the **Archeological Museum**, at Zrinsko Frankopanska 25 (June–Sept Mon–Sat 9am–2pm & 4–8pm; Oct–May Mon–Fri 9am–2pm & 4–8pm, Sat 9am–2pm; 30kn), contains displays of Illyrian, Greek, medieval and Roman artefacts. Outside, the arcaded courtyard is crammed with gravestones, sarcophagi and decorative sculpture.

The Marjan peninsula

For peace and quiet, plus stunning views over the city, head for the woods of the **Marjan peninsula** west of the Old Town. It's accessible via Sperun and then Senjska, which cut up through the slopes of the **Varoš** district. There are tiny rocky **beaches** all round the peninsula.

ARRIVAL AND DEPARTURE

By plane Split airport is 16km west of town; Croatia Airlines buses connect with scheduled flights and run to the waterfront Riva (30kn); their office at Riva 9 has timetables. Alternatively, the #37 Split–Trogir bus runs from the main road outside the airport to the suburban bus station on Domovinskog rata, just north of the Old Town (every 20min; 20kn). A taxi costs 200kn.

By train and bus Split's main bus and train stations are next to each other on Obala Kneza Domagoja, a 5min walk round the harbour from the centre.

Destinations (train) Zadar (change at Knin; 2 daily; 5hr); Zagreb (2 daily, one of which is overnight; 6hr 20min–8hr 30min).

Destinations (bus) Belgrade (1 daily, overnight; 11hr 30min); Dubrovnik (make sure you take your passport, as you pass through a short stretch of Bosnia-Herzegovina on the way; 17 daily; 4hr–4hr 30min); Pula (3 daily; 13hr); Rijeka (6 daily; 8hr); Sarajevo (4 daily; 6hr 30min–8hr); Trieste (1 daily; 10hr 30min); Zadar (hourly; 3hr–3hr 30min); Zagreb (every 30min; 5hr–8hr 30min).

By boat The ferry terminal and Jadrolinija booking office (ⓦjadrolinija.hr) are both at the harbour, with the latter also selling Krilo Jet and SNAV tickets. Note that services are reduced outside the summer months.

Destinations Ancona (3 ferries daily; 10hr); Brač (Bol: 1 catamaran daily; 55min; Supetar: 1 ferry hourly; 50min); Dubrovnik (2 Krilo Jet catamarans daily; 3–4hr); Hvar (Hvar Town: 2 catamarans daily; 55min; Stari Grad:

7 ferries daily; 2hr); Korčula (Vela Luka: 2 ferries daily; 2hr 45min; 1 catamaran daily; 1hr 45min; Korčula Town: 2 catamarans daily; 2hr 25min); Vis (2–3 ferries daily; 2hr 20min; 1 catamaran daily; 1hr 15min).

INFORMATION

Tourist information There are offices at Riva 9 and in the Chapel of St Rock on the Peristyle (both June–Sept Mon–Fri 8am–8pm, Sat 8am–7pm, Sun 9am–1pm; Oct–May Mon–Fri 9am–5pm; ☎021 360 066, ⍟visitsplit .com).

Discount card The Splitcard, available from the tourist office (70kn/72hr; free on weekends between March and October), gets you free or discounted entrance to several of the sights, plus reductions on hostels and restaurants.

ACCOMMODATION

Private rooms Book through Turist Biro, Obala narodnog preporoda 12, on the waterfront (☎021 347 100, ⍟turistbiro-split.hr). Rooms from 345kn

★**Goli & Bosi** Morpurgova Poljana 2 ☎021 510 999, ⍟gollybossy.com. Sleek hostel decked out in eye-popping black and yellow, with tongue-in-cheek captions along the floors. Also includes the De Belly Café, a stylish restaurant and bar in the pretty courtyard outside (mains from 25kn). The smart dorms are the most affordable option, with each bunk built into its own cubbyhole. Dorms 240kn, doubles 750kn

Hostel Apinelo Petrova 42 ☎091 393 1287, ⍟apinelo .com. A restored stone house just outside the Old Town offering neat new dorms and a collection of 2-person apartments, plus a small communal kitchen. Dorms 130kn, apartments 600kn

Silver Central Kralja Tomislava 1 ☎021 490 805, ⍟silvercentralhostel.com. A modern, central hostel with a buzzy common area, bright and breezy dorms and doubles at various locations around the centre. Dorms 180kn, doubles 575kn

Split hostel booze & snooze Narodni trg 8 ☎021 342 787, ⍟splithostel.com. In the middle of the old city, this hostel is run by friendly Croatian-Australians who like partying with their guests. Also has a nearby sister hostel – Split Hostel Fiesta Siesta – with on-site bar at Kruževičeva 5. Dorms 200kn

Villa Varoš Miljenka Smoje 1 ☎021 483 469, ⍟villavaros .hr. Charming and cosy guesthouse in a lovingly restored house in the atmospheric Varoš quarter. Rooms are kitted out with homely, semi-rustic furnishings together with a/c and TV. Doubles 600kn

EATING

The daily market at the eastern edge of the Old Town is the place to shop for fruit, veg and local cheeses.

Buffet Fife Trumbićeva obala 11. Near the seafront this is a no-frills local favourite, serving dishes such as stuffed sweet peppers (35kn) and pašticada (beef stew with prunes; 45kn) in huge portions. Daily 6am–midnight.

★**Konoba Trattoria Bajamont** Bajamontićeva 3. Grab a seat at an old sewing machine table and watch the chef cook tasty Dalmatian dishes such as asparagus risotto (55kn) and calamari (50kn). Daily 8am–11pm.

Makrovega Leština 2. Hidden away in alleys just west of the Old Town, this chic café is a wonderful source of quality vegetarian food, with tofu and soya put to imaginative uses in a wide-ranging menu. The daily specials (soup, main and salad) are superb value at 60–70kn. Mon–Fri 9am–8pm, Sat 9am–4pm.

Villa Spiza Kružićeva 3. Only a handful of years old and already a Split institution, Villa Spiza ("spiza" is Split dialect for good nosh) serves traditional home cooking in a tiny Old Town space – the kitchen takes up most of the room, with small tables squeezed into what's left. Pan-fried fish dishes and old-school seafood stews rarely top the 70kn mark. Daily 11am–11pm.

DRINKING AND NIGHTLIFE

The beach at Bačvice, a few minutes' walk south past the train station, is a popular party place in summer.

Academia Club Ghetto Dosud. Despite periodic closures and reopenings this has remained a Split legend – a bar-come-art gallery with an extravagantly decorated interior and a lovely courtyard squeezed between ancient stone tenements. Frequent live DJ events, and a bohemian-friendly, gay-friendly, anything-friendly reputation. Daily 9am–1am.

Fabrique Trg Franje Tuđmana 3. Spacious pub just west of the Old Town with a lot of bare stone and brickwork adding character to the interior. Serves up a vast array of beer on draught and in bottles, including excellent local craft brews. Daily 8am–1am.

Figa Buvinina 1. This legendary Split bar (formerly known as Puls) offers a flashy-looking menu of sandwiches and light bites, a great list of cocktails and shots, and a to-die-for location on one of the Old Town's most atmospheric stepped alleys. Daily 8am–1pm.

DIRECTORY

Exchange At the bus station or any bank.

Hospital Firule, Spinčićeva 1 (☎021 556 111).

Launderette Modrulj, Šperun (daily: April–Oct 8am–8pm; Nov–March 9am–5pm).

Left luggage At the bus station (daily 7am–9pm; 5kn for first hour, then 1.5kn/hr) and train station (daily 6.30am–10pm; 15kn/hr).

Pharmacy Ljekarna Lučac, Pupačićeva 4, just east of the Old Town, is open 24hr.

Post office Kralja Tomislava 9 and Obala kneza Domagoja 2 (both Mon–Fri 7.30am–7pm, Sat 7.30am–2.30pm).

BRAČ

BRAČ is a bewitchingly bare, scrub-covered island fringed by fishing ports, coves and beaches. The easiest way to reach Brač is by **ferry** from Split to **Supetar**, an engaging, laidback fishing port on the north side of the island, from where it's an hour's bus journey to **Bol**, a major windsurfing centre on the island's south coast and site of one of the Adriatic's most beautiful beaches, **Zlatni Rat** (Golden Horn).

Supetar

Though the largest town on the island, **SUPETAR** is a rather sleepy village onto which package tourism has been painlessly grafted. There's a pretty old quarter set beside a parish church and a long curve of **beach** west of the harbour. Behind the beach is the **Petrinović Mausoleum**, a neo-Byzantine construction 1km west of town, built by sculptor Toma Rosandić to honour a local-born shipping magnate.

ARRIVAL AND INFORMATION

By ferry There are regular ferries between Supetar and Split (9–14 daily; 50min).

Tourist information Beside the ferry dock at Porat 1 (June–Sept daily 8–11am, 11.30am–6pm & 6.30–10pm; Oct–May Mon–Fri 8am–3pm; ☎021 630 900, ⓦ supetar.hr).

ACCOMMODATION

Private rooms Available from Atlas, on the harbourfront at Porat 10 (☎021 631 105, ⓦ atlas-supetar.com), and

> ## BRAČ ACTIVITIES
>
> **Scuba diving** Fun Dive Club in the *Supetrus* hotel complex at Put Vele Luke 4 (closed Oct–April; ☎098 130 7384, ⓦ fundiveclub.com) rents snorkelling and scuba gear and arranges crash courses (from 225kn).
>
> **Mountain biking** Rent a Roberts on Put Vele Luke (☎091 534 7575, ⓦ rentaroberts .com) rents out mountain bikes for 90kn/day.

Brač Travel, Put Vele Luke 9, opposite the ferry dock (☎021 630 236, ⓦ travel-brac.com). Rooms from **300kn**

Hostel D&D Put Vele Luke ☎098 344 790, ⓦ hostelbrac .com. Named after brother-and-sister management team Duje and Dora, *D&D* occupies a neatly decorated house near the beach. Space is limited, with accommodation consisting of two doubles, two triples and a quad. Doubles **350kn**

EATING AND DRINKING

Benny's Bar Put Vele Luke bb. West of town towards the *Supetrus* hotel complex, *Benny's Bar* has a large outdoor terrace with a pool where you can take in the sea air and enjoy live DJs and cocktails. June–Sept daily 8am–2am.

Bistro Palute Porat 4. The best of the places to eat on the harbourfront: serves good grilled fish from an open wood fire and meat dishes such as mixed skewers with fries (52kn) and goulash (55kn). Daily 8am–midnight.

Konoba Lukin Porat 32. Harbourside seating, a cosy, family atmosphere and well-prepared local dishes make this the best option for a meal. Cuttlefish salad (60kn) and pizzas (30–40kn). Daily noon–midnight.

Bol

Stranded on the far side of the Vidova Gora Mountains, the town of **BOL** has a beautiful setting and charming old stone houses. Its main attraction is **Zlatni Rat** beach, a long pebbly spit some 1.5km west of the centre, that gets very crowded during summer.

ARRIVAL AND INFORMATION

By bus From Supetar, 14 daily buses make the hour-long trip to Bol's harbour. Some buses take a slower route – check before you leave.

By ferry Catamarans dock at the western end of the town harbour.

Destinations Hvar (Jelsa: 1 daily; 20min); Split (1 daily; 55min).

Tourist information In the harbour (June & Sept daily 8.30am–3pm & 5–9pm; July & Aug daily 8.30am–10pm; Oct–May Mon–Fri 8.30am–3pm; ☎021 635 638, ⓦ bol.hr).

ACCOMMODATION

Private rooms Boltours, at Vladimira Nazora 18 (☎021 635 693, ⓦ boltours.com), can arrange private rooms and 2-person apartments. Alternatively, try More at Vladimira Nazora 28 (☎021 642 050, ⓦ more-bol.com). Rooms from **330kn**, apartments from **430kn**

Kito Camping Bračke ceste bb ☎021 635 551, ⓦ camping-brac.com. Large, friendly campsite close to the centre of Bol, with kitchens and a nearby supermarket. Per person **75kn**, plus per tent **25kn**

BOL ACTIVITIES

Hiking The 778m peak of Vidova Gora is within easy reach of Bol: a trail (2hr each way) heads uphill just beyond *Kito Camping* (see opposite). Check with the tourist office for details of the route.

Mountain biking The tourist office has free cycling maps. Next door, *Big Blue Café* rents bicycles (90kn/day).

Watersports Big Blue's watersports outlet, on the path leading to Zlatni Rat (April–Nov; ☎091 449 7087, ⓦbigblue sport.com), rents windsurfing boards (490kn/half-day) and sea kayaks (190kn/day).

EATING AND DRINKING

Arguola Vladimira Nazora 6. A sandwich bar that's a cut above the average, baking its own bread buns and stuffing them with local ingredients. The anchovy sandwich with capers is a tangy bargain at 22kn. Daily 10am–2am.

Konoba Mlin Ante Starčevića 11. A lovely restaurant in a pretty old stone mill, with live music and an outdoor wood-fired grill where freshly caught fish are cooked. Mains from 90kn. June–Oct daily 5pm–midnight.

Pizzeria Topolino Frane Radića 1. Located just metres from the sea, *Topolino* offers gorgeous views and a wide range of breakfast dishes, wood-oven-cooked pizzas (60–70kn), fresh salads (from 50kn) and home-made lemonade (18kn). May–Oct daily 8am–11pm.

Varadero Frane Radića. A prime position in the main square with DJs, a twelve-page cocktail menu (from 40kn) and a beach cabin feel – this is the place to be after dark. May–Oct daily 9am–2am.

HVAR

One of the most hyped of all the Croatian islands, **HVAR** is undeniably beautiful – a slim, green slice of land punctuated by jagged inlets and cloaked with hills of lavender. Despite Hvar's growing reputation as a high-society party island, tourist development hasn't been too overbearing. The island's Venetian-flavoured centre, **Hvar Town**, offers charm and affordability alongside plentiful opportunities for a cocktail-driven splash-out.

WHAT TO SEE AND DO

Hvar's central main square is flanked by the arcaded bulk of the **Venetian arsenal**, the upper storey of which was added in 1612 to house a **theatre** (summer 9am–1pm & 5–11pm; winter 11am–noon; 20kn), the oldest in Croatia. At the eastern end of the square is the **cathedral** (open mornings before services), a sixteenth-century construction with an eighteenth-century facade – a characteristic mixture of Gothic and Renaissance styles. Inside, the **Bishop's Treasury** (daily: June–Aug 9am–noon & 5–7pm; Sept–May 10am–noon; 20kn) holds a small but fine selection of chalices and reliquaries. The rest of the Old Town stretches back from the piazza in an elegant confusion of twisting lanes and alleys.

Up above, the **fortress** (daily: April & May 9am–4pm; June–Sept 8am–11pm; 25kn) was built by the Venetians in the 1550s and offers gorgeous sweeping views. From here, you can pick out the attractive fifteenth-century **Franciscan Monastery** (May–Oct Tues–Sat 9am–3pm & 5–7pm; 25kn) to the left of the harbour, and the pleasingly simple monastic church next door.

Beaches and islands

The **beaches** nearest to town are rocky and crowded, so it's best to make your way towards the **Pakleni otoci**. Easily reached by water taxi from the harbour (50–70kn return), the Pakleni are a chain of eleven wooded islands, three of which cater for tourists with simple bars and restaurants: Jerolim, a naturist island, is the nearest; next is Marinkovac; then Sv Klement, the largest of the islands.

ARRIVAL AND DEPARTURE

By boat Two daily Krilo Jet catamarans from Split arrive at Hvar Town itself; seven other ferries head for Stari Grad, 20km east. There's also one daily catamaran from Bol on Brač to Jelsa in the centre of the island. Tickets for Krilo Jet catamarans are available from Pelegrini Tours, by the ferry dock at Riva bb (☎021 742 743, ⓦpelegrini-hvar.hr), although be warned that these services can sell out days in advance.

Destinations from Hvar Town Korčula Town (2 Krilo Jet catamarans daily; 1hr 15min); Split (2 Krilo Jet catamarans daily; 55min); Vela Luka (1 catamaran daily; 45min); Vis (1 catamaran weekly; 1hr 30min).

6

Destinations from Stari Grad Ancona (June–Aug 2–5 weekly; 8–13hr; overnight), Split (7 ferries daily; 2hr). Destinations from Bol Jelsa (1 catamaran daily; 30min).
By bus Buses run from Stari Grad to Hvar Town (6–10 daily; 30min) and from Jelsa to both Hvar Town (3–4 daily; 45min) and Stari Grad (5–11 daily; 15min).

INFORMATION

Tourist information Branches at the bus station and on the main square at Trg sv. Stjepana bb (both June & Sept Mon–Sat 8am–1pm & 4–9pm, Sun 10am–noon & 6–8pm; July & Aug Mon–Sat 8am–2pm & 3–9pm, Sun 8am–1pm & 4–8pm; Oct–May Mon–Sat 8am–1pm; ☎021 741 059, ⦿tzhvar.hr).

ACCOMMODATION

Private rooms Contact Pelegrini Tours (see p.173). Rooms from <u>375kn</u>
Camping Mala Milna Milna ☎021 745 013. Terraced site right by the sea, 3km east of Hvar in the village of Milna. With a bit of luck, small-tent travellers might find a pitch beside the shore. Open May–Sept. Per person <u>50kn</u>, plus per tent <u>50kn</u>
★**Green Lizard Hostel** Domovinskog rata 13 ☎021 742 560, ⦿greenlizard.hr. A clean and comfy hostel uphill from the ferry port, with great sea views, fun cocktail evenings and hammocks to chill out in. Shared kitchen, free wi-fi. Open Easter–Oct. Dorms <u>150kn</u>, doubles <u>350kn</u>
Marinero Put svetog Marka 9 ☎091 410 2751, ⦿facebook.com/MarineroHostelHvar. Neat and tidy bunk-bed accommodation in historic stone house just steps away from the main square. It lacks kitchen and common room facilities but there's a solid restaurant downstairs. Breakfast 50kn extra. Dorms <u>150kn</u>
Orange Hostel Vandele Bozitkovića 16 (near *Green Lizard*) ☎091 515 7330, ⦿orange.hostel.com. More a

HVAR ACTIVITIES

Island tours Secret Hvar, Dolac bb (☎021 717 615, ⦿secrethvar.com) runs 4WD trips on the rough roads of inland Hvar, exploring abandoned villages and lavender plantations. Also does kayaking (350kn) and hiking trips (300kn).
Watersports Hvar Adventure, Obala bb, in the alleyway behind the Arsenal (☎021 717 813 or ☎091 154 3072, ⦿hvar-adventure .com), organizes a host of activities and day-trips, including wine tasting (420kn), sea kayaking around the Pakleni islands (350kn), guided hiking (300kn), sailing (420kn) and rock climbing (400kn).

★TREAT YOURSELF

Carpe Diem On the main seafront ⦿carpe-diem-hvar.com. Said to be Croatia's best cocktail bar, glamorous *Carpe Diem* is the epitome of jet-set. DJs spin crowd-pleasing tunes on the colonnaded terrace overlooking the harbour till the early hours, while skilled bartenders mix a long list of decadent cocktails (from 50kn). There is no cover charge but they do operate a "face control" admissions policy when busy, so it's worth dressing up. Taxi boats outside *Carpe Diem* transport revellers to its sister venue, *Carpe Diem Beach*, on the island of Marinkovac, which hosts DJ parties every night in peak season (cover charge for major events 100kn; check website for listings). *Carpe Diem* mid-June to late Aug daily 9am–2am; *Carpe Diem Beach* mid-June to late Aug daily 10am–5am.

peaceful private house than a hostel – there's no common room – with a leafy terrace and a mixture of rooms within its tangerine exterior. Doubles <u>400kn</u>

EATING

Bistro For Brace Bibića 17. The last of a dying breed, perhaps, *For* (local dialect for "Hvar") serves up the kind of authentic Dalmatian cooking that makes locals and tourists happy, and keeps its prices down too. The daily three-course lunch specials are a steal at 60kn, plus risottos and pastas for under 60kn, or steaks for under 100kn. Daily noon–3pm & 6–11pm.
Macondo Groda ☎021 742 850. This place has got style and quality, yet remains informal, and for a slap-up seafood feast there are few better places. The *škampi buzara* (unpeeled prawns in wine sauce; 120kn) is excellent. You'll need to book in summer. April–Oct Mon–Sat noon–2pm & 6.30pm–midnight, Sun 6.30pm–midnight.
Pizza Kogo Trg sv. Stjepana 34. A popular spot with pew-like seating inside and plenty of tables on the main square too. Reasonably priced mains include salads (45–55kn) and pizzas (70–80kn). Daily: June–Sept 10am–4am; Oct–May 10am–11pm.

DRINKING AND NIGHTLIFE

Hula Hula Majerovica. Hvar's premier après-beach bar, located on the shoreline path just beyond the *Amfora* hotel. Cold beers and cocktails served up on a big seaside terrace scattered with stools and beds, although it's standing room only on summer nights. May–Sept 9am–midnight.

Kiva Fabrika. Raucously enjoyable black hole of a place in an alleyway just off the portside path. Can be a tight squeeze on summer weekends. Daily 9pm–2am.

Pink Champagne Ive Miličića 4. Indoor clubbing venue that comes into its own when the last-orders bells have sounded elsewhere. Top DJ entertainment, theatrically clad staff and burlesque shows combine to provide an appealing mix of edgy decadence and mainstream fun. Midnight–6am: May–Sept daily; Oct–April Thurs–Sat only.

Red Baron Riva bb. Occupying a harbourside terrace with a pine tree growing out of the middle, this is an ideal vantage point from which to view the people looking at yachts. Classy list of cocktails (including the rum, strawberry and champagne Red Baron daiquiri, 65kn). May–Sept daily 8am–2am.

VIS

Wild and hilly, **VIS** is situated further offshore than any of Croatia's inhabited Adriatic islands. Closed to foreigners for military reasons until 1989, the island boasts two good-looking towns, **Vis Town** and **Komiža**, and great beaches and bars. Depending much more heavily on independent travellers and yachters than on the package crowd, it has a laidback atmosphere unique in the Adriatic.

Vis Town

VIS TOWN is a sedate arc of grey-brown houses on a deeply indented bay, above which loom the remains of abandoned agricultural terraces. A five-minute walk east from the harbour is the town's **history museum** (May–Oct Mon–Fri 9am–1pm & 5–9pm, Sat 9am–1pm; 20kn), and not far on from here is the suburb of **Kut**, an atmospheric, largely sixteenth-century tangle of narrow cobbled streets. Heading west around the bay soon brings you to the ruins of an ancient Greek cemetery and a Roman bath complex complete with preserved mosaics.

ARRIVAL, INFORMATION AND TOURS

By boat Ferries and catamarans arrive in the centre of Vis Town's harbour from where buses (5 daily; 15min) depart for Komiža on the western side of the island.

Destinations Hvar (1 catamaran weekly; 45min); Split (2–3 ferries daily; 2hr 20min; 1 catamaran daily; 1hr 30min).

Tourist information Just to the right as you leave the ferry dock (May–Sept Mon–Sat 8am–2pm & 5–8pm; Oct–April Mon–Fri 9am–1pm; ☎021 717 017, ⓦtz-vis.hr).

Tours Navigator (☎021 717 786, ⓦnavigator.hr), directly in front of the ferry dock, offers island tours, trips to the Blue Cave (see p.176; 250kn) and scooter rental (200kn/day).

ACCOMMODATION

Private rooms Enquire at Navigator (see above), or Ionios agency, 1km south of the ferry dock in Kut (☎021 711 532, ⊜ionios@st.t-com.hr), which offers a range of rooms and apartments from __330kn__

EATING, DRINKING AND NIGHTLIFE

There is a small supermarket near the harbour. Note that eating out on Vis is reasonably expensive and the island is extremely seasonal.

Bejbi Šetalište stare Isse. Pronounced "baby", this is a laid-back daytime coffee-drinking spot that bursts into life at night, with a funkily decorated café indoors, and bamboo-shaded bar in the yard. Daily: summer 6am–2am; winter 6am–midnight.

Fort George King George III Fortress ⓦfortgeorgecroatia .com. In the incomparable setting of a nineteenth-century fortress built by British occupiers just outside Vis Town, this open-air restaurant and bar runs club nights throughout the week, and live gigs by Croatian rock and jazz acts. June to mid-Sept daily 10am–4am (Wed & Sun may be closed for private parties).

Karijola Šetalište viškog boja 4. Perched on a terrace midway between the town centre and Kut, this is the best place for a quality thin-crust pizza (75–85kn). Settle your stomach with *Karijola*'s range of irresistible *rakijas* – the *rakija od mirte* (grappa flavoured with mistletoe) has proven aphrodisiac qualities. May–Sept 11am–midnight.

Konoba Vatrica Kralja Krešimira 15. Friendly, family-run restaurant in Kut, specializing in fresh fish cooked over a wood fire. More affordable options are the black squid risotto and macaroni in lobster sauce (both 60kn). May–Sept daily 9am–midnight; Oct–April Fri & Sat 5–11pm.

Paradajz Lost Pod Kulom 5. Just off the Riva behind a squat medieval tower, *Paradajz Lost* (a play on words based on the fact that *paradajz* is dialect for "tomato") serves an extensive range of excellent local wines in a courtyard strewn with a jumble of junk-shop furniture. June–Sept daily 6pm–2am.

Komiža

KOMIŽA, 10km from Vis Town, is the island's main fishing port – a picturesque town surrounded by lofty mountains. Dominating the southern end of the

6

harbour is the Kaštel, a stubby sixteenth-century fortress, which now houses the charming **Fishing Museum** (June–Sept Mon–Sat 10am–noon & 8–11pm; 15kn). Komiža's nicest beaches are ten minutes south of here, where you'll find a series of pebbly coves. Small boats leave the harbour for the **Blue Cave** on the nearby island of Biševo, a grotto filled with eerie shimmering light; expect to pay 150kn–250kn for a half-day trip, depending on the size and speed of the boat (see p.173).

ARRIVAL, INFORMATION AND TOURS

By bus Buses from Vis Town terminate about 100m behind the harbour.

Tourist information On the Riva just beyond the Kaštel (June–Aug Mon–Fri 8am–1pm & 6.30–8pm, Sat & Sun 6.30–8pm; Sept–May Mon–Sat 8am–1pm; ☎021 713 455, ⓦtz-komiza.hr).

Tours Alternatura, Hrvatskih mučenika 2 (☎021 717 239, ⓦalternatura.hr), organizes guided tours of the island's former military facilities (250kn), as well as scuba diving, free climbing, sailing in a traditional *falkuša* fishing boat and hang-gliding.

ACCOMMODATION

Private rooms Book through Alternatura (see above), or Srebrna, Ribarska 4 (daily 8am–1pm & 6–10pm; ☎021 713 668, ⓦsrebrnatours.hr). Rooms from 320kn

EATING, DRINKING AND NIGHTLIFE

Fabrika Riva svetog Mikule 12. *Fabrika* mixes thrift-store furnishing and post-industrial warehouse chic to create an arty-but-comfy lounge-bistro vibe. A snacking menu of burgers and wok-fried dishes in the 60–80kn range is backed up by a cracking choice of local wines and *rakijas*. May–Sept daily 9am–2am.

Kolđeraj Trg kralja Tomislava 1. This local bakery serves up fresh anchovy pasties (*komiška pogača*; 15kn), as well as other sweet and savoury pastries. Daily 6.30am–2am.

Konoba Bako Gundelićeva 1. Romantic beachside tavern complete with an indoor lobster pond. The fresh fish by the kilo is pricey, but there are also shrimp skewers (60kn) and *frutti di mare* (86kn) on offer. Daily: June–Aug 4pm–2am; Sept–May 5–11pm.

KORČULA

Like so many islands along this coast, **KORČULA** was first settled by the Greeks, who gave it the name Korkyra Melaina or "Black Corfu" for its dark and densely

MOREŠKA

Performances of Korčula's famous **folk dance**, the **Moreška**, take place outside the main gate to the Old Town every Monday and Thursday evening throughout the summer: tickets (100kn) are available from several agencies including Kaleta, Katun Tours and Atlas, all on Plokata 19, Travnja. This archaic, repetitive, sword-based dance is the story of a conflict between the Christians (in red) and the Moors (in black): the heroine, Bula, is kidnapped by the evil foreign king and his army, and her betrothed tries to win her back in a ritualized sword fight which takes place within a shifting circle of dancers.

wooded appearance. Even now, it's one of the greenest of the Adriatic islands, and one of the most popular. Medieval **Korčula Town** is the island's main settlement.

WHAT TO SEE AND DO

KORČULA TOWN sits on a beetle-shaped hump of land, a beautiful walled city ribbed with narrow alleys. The Venetians first arrived here in the eleventh century, and stayed, on and off, for nearly eight centuries, and their influence is particularly evident in the Old Town.

The Cathedral and Bishop's Treasury

The Old Town huddles around the **Cathedral of St Mark** (Mon–Sat: May & June 9am–2pm; July–Sept 9am–2pm & 5–7pm; Oct–April enquire at the tourist office to visit; 5kn), with a facade decorated with a gorgeous fluted rose window and a bizarre cornice frilled with gargoyles. The interior is one of the loveliest in the region – a curious mixture of styles, ranging from the Gothic forms of the nave to the Renaissance northern aisle, tacked on in the sixteenth century.

The best of the cathedral's treasures have been moved to the **Bishop's Treasury** (same hours as cathedral; 20kn, includes entrance to the cathedral), a couple of doors down. This small collection of fine and sacral art is one of the best in the country; look out for the Leonardo da Vinci sketch of a soldier wearing a costume bearing a striking resemblance to that of the Moreška dancers (see box opposite).

The Town Museum and the House of Marco Polo

On the main square, a former Venetian palace holds the **Town Museum** (daily: April–June 10am–2pm; July–Sept 9am–9pm; Oct–March 10am–1pm; 15kn), which displays everything from Greek amphorae to nineteenth-century furnishings. It is possible that Marco Polo was born in Korčula, though the seventeenth-century **House of Marco Polo** (daily: April–June, Sept & Oct 9am–3pm; July & Aug 9am–9pm; 20kn) has no link whatsoever with the explorer – there are, however, good views of town from its upper storeys.

Beaches

Your best bet for **beaches** is to head off by water taxi from the old harbour to one of the **Skoji islands** just offshore. The largest and nearest of these is **Badija** (40kn return), where there are some secluded rocky beaches, a couple of snack bars and a naturist section. There's also a sandy **beach** just beyond the village of **Lumbarda**, 8km south of Korčula (hourly buses in summer; 15min).

ARRIVAL AND DEPARTURE

By bus Korčula's bus station is 400m southeast of the Old Town. The bus service from Dubrovnik crosses the narrow stretch of water dividing the island from the mainland, by ferry from Orebić. Korkyra Info (ⓦ korkyra.info) also runs a door-to-door minibus service to Dubrovnik airport (May–Oct daily with frequency depending on demand; 2hr 45min; 250kn).
Destinations Dubrovnik (2 daily; 3hr 30min); Zagreb (1 daily, overnight; 11hr 30min).
By boat Ferry and catamaran services from Dubrovnik, Hvar and Split dock in Korčula Town harbour. In addition, there are also ferry and catamaran services from Hvar and Split to Vela Luka at the western end of the island, from where there's a connecting bus service to Korčula Town (3–6 daily; 1hr 10min). The Jadrolinja ticket office in Korčula Town is at Plokata 19 Travnja. Note that ferry departures may switch between the west and east harbours in bad weather, so check before you leave. G&V Line catamaran tickets are available from Korkyra Info (see above), Krilo Jet catamaran tickets from the kiosk at the west harbour.

Destinations from Korčula Town Dubrovnik (July & Aug 4 G&V Line catamarans weekly; 2hr 35min); Hvar (1 Krilo Jet catamaran daily; 1hr 15min); Split (1 Krilo Jet catamaran daily; 2hr 25min).
Destinations from Vela Luka Hvar (1 catamaran daily; 45min); Split (2 ferries daily; 2hr 45min; 1 catamaran daily; 2hr).

INFORMATION

Tourist information By the western harbour at Obala dr. Franje Tudmana 4 (June–Sept Mon–Sat 8am–8pm, Sun 8am–3pm; Oct–May Mon–Sat 8am–noon & 5–8pm, Sun 8am–noon; ☎ 020 715 701, ⓦ visitkorcula.eu).

ACCOMMODATION

Private rooms Kaleta (☎ 020 711 282, ⓦ kaleta.hr) and Kantun Tours (also left luggage and bike rental; ☎ 020 715 622, ⓦ ikorcula.net), both at Plokata 19 Travnja, offer rooms from **300kn**
Apartments Depolo ul. Hrvatske bratske zajednice 62 ☎ 020 721 172 or ☎ 098 357 582. Modern apartments on the top two floors of a historic stone house midway between the bus station and the Old Town. They can be rented out as four- to six-person apartments or as smaller two-person units. Two-person apartments **600kn**
Campsite Kalac ☎ 020 726 693, ⓦ korcula-hotels.com. Korčula's largest campsite, just 3km from town and with 600 pleasant pine-shaded pitches and a small sandy beach. Per person **60kn**, plus per tent **60kn**
Villa Depolo ul. Svetog Nikole bb ☎ 020 711 621, ⓔ tereza.depolo@du.t-com.hr. Four enormous, tastefully decorated rooms on the seafront, 150m west of the Old Town; some have brilliant sea views. **300kn**

EATING, DRINKING AND NIGHTLIFE

There's a daily fruit and veg market beside the entrance to the Old Town.
Adio Mare Svetog Roka 2. A long-standing tourist favourite, offering top-quality local food in a high-ceilinged room and on an upstairs terrace. It's an atmospheric place to eat in spring and autumn, but staff and kitchen are frequently rushed off their feet in high summer. April–Nov Mon–Sat noon–11pm, Sun 6–11pm.
Boogie Jungle Put Lokve ⓦ boogie-jungle.com. Located 3km out on the Žrnovo road, on a hill overlooking the town, this alfresco disco grouped around a series of curtain-draped pavilions is the place to enjoy wine and cocktails until sunrise. Cover charge 30–70kn. June–Sept daily 10pm–5am.
Dos Locos Šetalište Frana Kršinića. Live DJs and an alfresco bamboo bar draw the crowds to this spot behind the bus station. Cocktails for only 40kn during happy hour (8–10pm). Daily 9am–late.

6

Konoba Komin Šetalište Petra Kanavelića 26. Positioned on the restaurant-lined promenade that runs round the eastern side of the Old Town, *Konoba Komin* serves up consistently good fresh fish, grilled or baked over an open hearth. Mains 80–140kn. Daily noon–midnight.

DUBROVNIK

The walled city of **DUBROVNIK**, at Croatia's southern tip, is the country's irresistibly beautiful star attraction. Lapped by the glittering Adriatic Sea, sturdy walls encircle the city's white marble streets, which are lined with imposing Baroque buildings.

First settled by Roman refugees in the early seventh century and given the name Ragusa, the town soon exploited its favourable position on the Adriatic with maritime and commercial genius. By the mid-fourteenth century it had become a successful and self-contained city-state, its merchants trading far and wide. Dubrovnik continued to prosper until 1667, when an earthquake devastated the city. Though the city-state survived, it fell into decline, and in 1808 its political independence was ended by Napoleon.

An eight-month siege by Yugoslav forces in the early 1990s caused much destruction, but the city swiftly recovered. More recently, the city was used as a location for both *Game of Thrones* and *Star Wars*, earning it the attention of a whole new public.

WHAT TO SEE AND DO

Within its fabulous **city walls**, Dubrovnik is a sea of terracotta roofs punctured now and then by a sculpted dome or tower. The best way to get your bearings is by making a tour of the walls (daily: June–Aug 8am–7.30pm; May & Sept 8am–6.30pm; April & Oct 8am–5.30pm; Nov–March 9am–4pm; 100kn), which are 25m high with all five towers still intact. From here, you get spectacular views of the **Old Town**, bisected by the main street, Stradun. The main attractions, all within the walls, can easily be covered in a day and a half.

The Pile Gate

The **Pile Gate**, main entrance to the Old Town, is a fifteenth-century construction complete with a statue of St Blaise, the city's protector, set in a niche above the arch. Just through the gate sits **Onofrio's Large Fountain**, built in 1444, a domed affair at which visitors to this

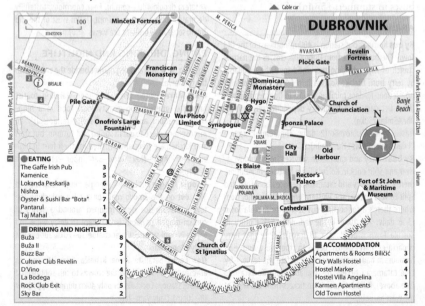

DUBROVNIK

EATING
The Gaffe Irish Pub	3
Kamenice	5
Lokanda Peskarija	2
Nishta	4
Oyster & Sushi Bar "Bota"	7
Pantarul	1
Taj Mahal	4

DRINKING AND NIGHTLIFE
Buža	8
Buža II	7
Buzz Bar	3
Culture Club Revelin	1
D'Vino	9
La Bodega	4
Rock Club Exit	5
Sky Bar	2

ACCOMMODATION
Apartments & Rooms Bilićić	3
City Walls Hostel	6
Hostel Marker	4
Hostel Villa Angelina	1
Karmen Apartments	5
Old Town Hostel	2

hygiene-conscious city used to have to wash themselves before they were allowed any further.

The Franciscan monastery and Stradun

Opposite Onofrio's Large Fountain, the museum of the peaceful fourteenth-century **Franciscan monastery** complex (daily: April–Oct 9am–6pm; Nov–March 9am–5pm; 30kn) holds some fine Gothic reliquaries and manuscripts tracing the development of musical scoring, together with objects from the apothecary's shop, dating from 1317; there is still a working on-site pharmacy. From here, **Stradun** (also known as Placa), the city's main street, runs dead straight across the Old Town, its limestone surface polished to a shine by thousands of feet. **War Photo Limited**, at Antuninska 6 (May–Oct daily 10am–10pm; 40kn), is a three-storey photo gallery housing changing exhibitions from some of the world's leading photographers – conflict, and its frequently innocent victims, is the main focus.

The far end of Stradun broadens into airy **Luža Square**, the centre of the medieval town and still a hub of activity. On the left, the **Sponza Palace** was once the customs house and mint, with a façade showing off an elegant weld of florid Venetian Gothic and more sedate Renaissance forms. Nowadays it houses free contemporary art exhibitions and a memorial to those who lost their lives during the Dubrovnik siege (daily: May–Oct 10am–10pm; Nov–April 10am–3pm; free).

The Dominican monastery

North behind the Sponza Palace lies the **Dominican monastery**, its arcaded courtyard filled with palms and orange trees. It also houses a small **museum** (daily: May–Oct 9am–6pm; Nov–April 9am–5pm; 30kn), with outstanding examples of local sixteenth-century religious art.

The Church of St Blaise and Rector's Palace

On the south side of Luža Square lies the Baroque-style **Church of St Blaise**. Built in 1714, it serves as a graceful counterpoint to the palace. Outside the church stands the carved figure of an armoured knight – known as **Orlando's Column**, it was once the focal point of the city-state. Adjacent sits the fifteenth-century **Rector's Palace**, the seat of the Ragusan government, in which the incumbent Rector sat out his month's term of office. Today it's given over to the rather uninspiring **City Museum** (daily: April–Oct 9am–6pm; Nov–March 9am–4pm; combined ticket with Maritime Museum and a couple of other sights not covered here – the Ethnographic Museum and Revelin Fortress – 100kn).

The cathedral

The seventeenth-century **cathedral**, south from the Rector's Palace, is a rather plain building, although there's an impressive Titian polyptych of *The Assumption* inside. The **Treasury** (mid-April to Oct Mon–Sat 9am–5pm, Sun noon–5pm; Nov to mid-April Mon–Sat 10am–noon & 3–5pm, Sun 3–5pm; 15kn) boasts a twelfth-century reliquary containing the skull of St Blaise; shaped like a Byzantine crown, it is covered with portraits of saints and frosted with delicate gold and enamel filigree work.

The Fort of St John and Church of St Ignatius

The city's small harbour is dominated by the monolithic hulk of the **Fort of St John**; upstairs it houses a **maritime museum** (daily: April–Oct 9am–6pm; Nov–March 9am–4pm; combined ticket with City Museum 100kn), which traces the history of Ragusan sea power through a display of naval artefacts and model boats. Skirting round the city's southern walls, you enter one of its oldest quarters, **Pustijerna**, much of which predates the seventeenth-century earthquake. Uphill sits the **Church of St Ignatius**, Dubrovnik's largest, a Jesuit confection modelled on Rome's enormous Gesù church. Steps sweep down from here to **Gundulićeva Poljana**, the square behind the cathedral, which is the site of the city's morning produce market.

6

The Dubrovnik Cable Car and Mount Srđ

For the best views in town take a ride on the **Dubrovnik Cable Car**, Petra Krešimira (daily: Feb, March & Oct 9am–5pm; April, May & Sept 9am–8pm; June–Aug 9am–midnight; Dec & Jan 9am–4pm; one-way 60kn, return 110kn), whose orange pods soar up to the top of Mount Srđ, offering a fantastic panorama of the city. You can also walk up or down the mountain via the winding footpath known as the Serpentina (90min up; 35min down). Note that the Serpentina is stony and unshaded – strong footwear and water are essential. The fort at Srđ's summit houses the **Museum of the Homeland War** (daily 8am–8pm; 20kn), featuring guns, shell cartridges and a rousing collection of photos.

Beaches

The noisy and crowded main city **beach** is a short walk east of the Old Town; less crowded and somewhat cleaner is the beach on the Lapad peninsula, 5km to the west (bus #6 from the Pile Gate). Or you can catch a boat from the old city jetty (April–Oct daily 8am–6pm; every 30min; 10min; 50kn return) to the wooded island of **Lokrum**. Covered in pine trees, Lokrum is home to an eleventh-century Benedictine monastery (which currently houses a *Game of Thrones* museum room detailing all the local shooting locations) and has extensive rocky beaches running along the eastern end of the island – with a naturist section (known as FKK) at the far eastern tip.

ARRIVAL AND DEPARTURE

By plane Atlas buses (30min; 35kn) run to the bus terminal at Gruž (enquire at the tourist office for times), dropping off at Pile Gate just outside the Old Town. Note that buses to the airport commence at the bus station and pick up passengers at the cable-car station on Zagrebačka; they do not call at Pile Gate.

By bus The bus terminal is located in the port suburb of Gruž, 4km west of town. If travelling to Split, take your passport, as you pass through Bosnia-Herzegovina en route.

Destinations Korčula (2 daily; 3hr 30min); Montenegro (various towns; 2–4 daily); Pula (1 daily; 15hr); Rijeka (4 daily; 11hr 30min–13hr); Rovinj (1 daily; 16hr);

Sarajevo (5 daily; 5–6hr); Split (17 daily; 4hr–4hr 30min); Trieste (1 daily; 15hr); Zadar (6–7 daily; 7hr–8hr 30min); Zagreb (8 daily; 11hr).

By boat The ferry terminal is located in the port suburb of Gruž, 4km west of town.

Destinations Bari, Italy (4–6 ferries weekly; 9hr); Korčula (July & Aug 4 G&V Line catamarans weekly; 2hr 35min); Split (2 Krilo Jet catamarans daily; 3–4hr).

INFORMATION AND TOURS

Tourist information The main branch is on the plaza outside the Pile Gate at Brsalje 5 (daily: July & Aug 8am–8pm; May, June & Sept 9am–8pm; Oct–April 9am–5pm; ☎020 321 011, ⊛tzdubrovnik.hr). There's also one opposite the ferry terminal in Gruž (same hours). The Dubrovnik Card (24hr/72hr/week for 150kn/200kn/250kn; ⊛dubrovnikcard.com) offers free entry to eight city attractions plus free public transport, and is available from the tourist office.

Tours Adriatic Kayak Tours, Zrinsko Frankopanska 6 (☎020 312 770, ⊛adriatickayaktours.com), and Adventure Dalmatia, Svetog Križa 3 (☎091 566 5942, ⊛adventuredalmatia.com), organize kayaking tours from 300kn for a half-day to Lokrum island.

GETTING AROUND

By bus City buses #1a or #1b (tickets 15kn from driver or 12kn from kiosk) run from the bus terminal to the main western entrance to the Old Town, the Pile Gate.

ACCOMMODATION

Dubrovnik is full in summer so always book accommodation well in advance.

Private rooms Locals offering private rooms meet bus and ferry arrivals. Alternatively, try Partner Travel/Direct Booker at Ante Starčevića 20 (☎020 638 194, ⊛direct-booker.com). Central rooms from 450kn, rooms in Gruž and Lapad from 400kn

Apartments & Rooms Biličić Privežna 2 ☎020 417 152 & ☎098 802 111, ⊛dubrovnik-online.com/apartments _bilicic. Well-equipped rooms and four-person

---

THE DUBROVNIK SUMMER FESTIVAL

Dubrovnik's prestigious **Summer Festival** (☎020 326 100, ⊛dubrovnik-festival.hr) from July 10 to August 25 is an enjoyable time to visit, with high-quality classical concerts and contemporary theatre performances in many of the city's courtyards, squares and bastions. Book well in advance or you may end up without a proper seat.

apartments a 10min walk uphill from town. There's a gorgeous garden – complete with tortoises – and genial owner Marija offers free picks-ups, internet access and laundry service. Doubles 450kn, apartments 900kn

City Walls Hostel Sv Šimuna 15 ☎091 799 2086, ⓦcitywallshostel.com. A fun, stylish hostel in a great Old Town location with superb views, free wi-fi and internet, and a communal kitchen. Breakfast included. Dorms 200kn, doubles 550kn

Hostel Marker Svetog Đurđa 6 ☎091 739 7545, ⓦhostelmarkerdubrovnik.hostel.com. A range of comfortable rooms and four-bed apartments spread between five old houses beneath the Lovrjenac Fort. Doubles 440kn, apartments 1500kn

Hostel Villa Angelina Old Town Plovani Skalini 17a ☎091 893 9089, ⓦhostelangelinaoldtowndubrovnik .com. Views of Dubrovnik's famous red-roofed skyline don't come much better than from the top floors of this tall house in the Old Town's northwest corner. Neat dorm rooms on site and some private doubles at a separate address just down the steps. Socializing areas are small, but staff are really helpful. Dorms 460kn, doubles 920kn

Karmen Apartments Bandureva 1 ☎020 323 433, ⓦkarmendu.com. Make like a real Ragusan and splash out on a stay at the exquisitely and artfully decorated *Karmen Apartments*. These four homely apartments (sleeping 2–3) are full of personal touches and offer amazing views of the harbour and city walls. Marc, the owner, is a wealth of local information. Apartments 650kn

Old Town Hostel Od Sigurate 7 ☎099 444 4111, ⓦfacebook.com/DubrovnikOldTownHostel. Functional twins and triples squeezed into a lovely Old Town house with plenty of exposed stonework. The communal kitchen/common room is snug and sociable and the staff are full of local knowledge. Breakfast included. Doubles 700kn

EATING

There's a morning market (Mon–Sat) at Gundulićeva Poljana in the Old Town, and a supermarket in the same square.

The Gaffe Irish Pub Miha Pracata 4. Ignore the sports pub exterior – *The Gaffe* offers excellent hearty home cooking at reasonable prices. Low-season lunch specials such as beef stew and dumplings are only 30kn. Food served at lunchtime only. Daily 9am–1am.

Kamenice Gundulićeva Poljana 8. A simple fish restaurant where waitresses in white clogs serve cheap portions of whitebait (56kn) and locals sometimes break into song over the delicious *kamenice* (oysters; 10kn each). Daily: summer 8am–midnight; winter 8am–9pm.

Lokanda Peskarija Na Ponti. Right on the old harbour with a huge terrace and great views, this seafood-only restaurant serves up a small but fantastic menu including mussels (60kn) and a fish platter (180kn for two people). Daily 8am–1am.

★ **Nishta** Prijeko bb. A meal at this stylish vegetarian café makes a welcome change from Croatia's meat and fish staples. A healthy portion of vegetable curry will set you back 85kn, and there's a fresh salad bar too (30–59kn). March–Dec Mon–Sat noon–11pm.

Oyster & Sushi Bar "Bota" Od Pustijerne bb. Worth splashing out on, *"Bota"* offers fresh-as-you-like sushi and sashimi for 7kn/piece, and tempura oysters (12kn/piece) straight from the restaurant's renowned oyster farm in Mali Ston. April–Oct daily 10am–1am.

Pantarul Kralja Tomislava 1 30 ☎020 333 486. A leading force in the trend for modern Adriatic cooking, *Pantarul* (or "fork" in local dialect) takes inspiration from both old-school recipes and modern fusion. Signature dishes like gnocchi with octopus (95kn) or monkfish *brodet* (110kn) use local ingredients; there are also some superbly crafted desserts and a serious list of wines and cocktails. Book ahead in summer. Daily noon–4pm & 6pm–midnight.

Taj Mahal Nikole Gučetića 2. Don't be fooled by the name – *Taj Mahal*, tucked away off the Stradun, offers traditional Bosnian dishes such as stuffed aubergines (40kn), veal in pastry (80kn) and *baklava* (25kn) in an exotic interior. Daily 10am–11pm.

DRINKING AND NIGHTLIFE

★ **Buža** Accessed from Ilije Sarake. Reached via a hole in the city walls, this is a stunning spot for a dip in the sea and a drink, with a cluster of tables perched on rocky terraces. Its more expensive (34kn/beer) sister bar, *Buža II*, is at Crijeviceva 9. Both daily 10am–late, depending on the weather.

Buzz Bar Prijeko 21. Convivial café-bar where a healthy mix of young locals and foreign interlopers makes up the crowd. A good choice of wines by the glass, the odd craft beer, inexpensive cocktails and milkshakes. Cover bands sometimes squeeze into the corner. Mon–Sat 7am–2am, Sun 9am–midnight.

Culture Club Revelin Sv. Dominika 3 ⓦclubrevelin .com. The stocky Revelin Fort makes an amazing venue for club nights and gigs, attracting international DJs – check their website and posters for listings and cover charge. Wed–Sat 10pm–late.

★ **D'Vino** Palmotićeva 4a. There are quite a few wine bars lurking in the Old Town's alleys, but *D'Vino* is one of the oldest and best. The alley invariably fills with enthusiastic drinkers on warm summer evenings. Daily noon–2am.

La Bodega Stradun bb. A wine bar on three floors that soon fills up despite its relatively large size. The recipe is simple: a serious but not over-expensive wine list; platters of Croatian *pršut*, cheese and olives to keep the stomach rumbles at bay; and a crowd-pleasing pop-disco soundtrack. Daily 8am–2am.

Rock Club Exit Boškovićeva 2. A year-round favourite with locals, although it loses out in the summer months due to its first-floor location. Setting the tone are album covers and rock-star photos on the walls, and more or less permanently hard-riffing background music. Daily 6pm–2am.

Sky Bar Brsalje 11, Pile. Formerly known as *Latino Club Fuego*, this popular disco just outside Pile Gate has been something of a nightlife landmark for successive generations of locals and tourists. Featuring mainstream

dance music and the odd themed party night, it's an enjoyable after-midnight option. Daily 11pm–6am.

DIRECTORY

Hospital Roka Mišetića 2 ☎ 020 431 777.

Left luggage Bus station (daily 4.30am–10.30pm; first hour 5kn, thereafter 1.5kn/hr).

Pharmacy Kod Zvonika, Stradun (Mon–Sat 7am–8pm).

Post office Široka (Mon–Fri 7.30am–9pm, Sat 10am–5pm).

TÝN CHURCH AT DUSK, PRAGUE

Czech Republic

HIGHLIGHTS

❶ **Prague** Row through the golden city at dusk. See p.188

❷ **Sedlec ossuary** See human bones in the subterranean ossuary at Sedlec. **See p.197**

❸ **Český Krumlov** Forget the Renaissance ever ended at this fairytale town. **See p.199**

❹ **Plzeň** Visit the home of Pilsner Urquell, the original lager. **See p.200**

❺ **Karlovy Vary** Indulge in some spa treatments at this lovely town in the mountains. **See p.201**

❻ **Olomouc** Discover the capital of an ancient empire. **See p.205**

HIGHLIGHTS ARE MARKED ON THE MAP ON P.185

ROUGH COSTS

Daily budget Basic €40, occasional treat €50

Drink Pilsner Urquell €1.50

Food Pork and dumplings €5

Hostel/budget hotel €15/€40

Travel Train: Prague–Karlovy Vary €12; bus: €6

FACT FILE

Population 10.5 million

Language Czech

Currency Czech koruna (Kč)

Capital Prague

International phone code ☎420

Time zone GMT +1hr

Introduction

"Prague never lets you go," said Franz Kafka, "this dear little mother has claws". Prague gets her golden claws into tourists too, and few ever make it outside the capital. But those who tear themselves away won't be sorry; the colonnade- and park-filled spa towns, Bohemia's Renaissance breweries and hilltop ruins, and the tumbling vineyards and rolling hills of Moravia are worth a week of anyone's time.

Sitting in the middle of Europe, with Germany to the west, Poland to the north, Slovakia to the east and Austria to the south, the Czech Republic is firmly entrenched in Central Europe. Although the country is relatively small, the variety in landscape and architecture is enormous, encompassing the forests and rolling countryside of **Bohemia**, peaceful spa towns like Karlovy Vary, **Moravia**'s spectacular karst region and historic towns like **Olomouc** and Český Krumlov.

CHRONOLOGY

Fourth century BC The Celtic "Boii" tribe inhabit the area now known as Bohemia.

500s AD Slavic tribes arrive.

830 AD The Great Moravian Empire is established on the Morava River.

907 Hungarians conquer the Great Moravian Empire.

1355 Charles IV, "the father of the Czech nation", is crowned Holy Roman Emperor.

1415 Protestant reformer Jan Hus is burned at the stake, sparking decades of religious conflict.

1458 George of Poděbrady is crowned.

1526 King Ferdinand I, a Habsburg, takes the Czech throne, and begins a project of re-Catholicization.

1620 The Protestant nobility is defeated by Catholic forces at the Battle of White Mountain.

1800s Rapid growth in nationalism and industrialization.

1918 The independent republic of Czechoslovakia is founded at the end of World War I.

1938 German troops annex the Sudetenlands along Bohemia's borders.

1945 German occupation ends as the Allies move in.

1948 The Communist Party seizes control of Czechoslovakia.

1968 The "Prague Spring" sees a brief period of political liberalization; the USSR responds by invading.

1989 The Velvet Revolution. Czechoslovakia becomes a democracy with playwright Václav Havel as president.

1993 The Czech Republic and Slovakia peacefully separate into two states.

2004 The Czech Republic joins the EU.

2007 The Czech Republic joins the EU's Schengen Treaty free movement zone.

2013 First direct presidential election is held, and Miloš Zeman becomes the new president.

2016 The government approves the use of Czechia as a catchier version of the country's name, though this fails to catch on with the public.

ARRIVAL AND DEPARTURE

There are direct **flights** from more than a dozen UK airports to Václav Havel Airport (☎ 220 111 888, ⓦ prg.aero), 10km northwest of Prague. Several international airlines (including Ryanair from London Stansted, and Wizz Air from London Luton) serve Brno (ⓦ brno-airport.cz). Prague is served by direct **train** services from numerous major European cities, including Bratislava, Berlin, Vienna and Budapest.

Student Agency (see opposite) is the principal **coach** operator between the UK and the Czech Republic: it also runs services between Prague and other Czech cities. Alternatively, Eurolines (ⓦ eurolines.com) also runs international bus services to the Czech Republic.

GETTING AROUND

Czech public transport is affordable and reliable. For train and bus times go to ⓦ idos.cz.

BY TRAIN

The Czech Republic has one of the most comprehensive **rail** networks in Europe.

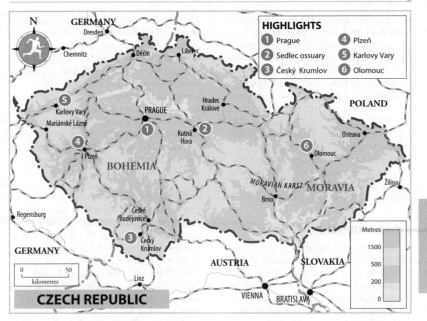

HIGHLIGHTS

1. Prague
2. Sedlec ossuary
3. Český Krumlov
4. Plzeň
5. Karlovy Vary
6. Olomouc

CZECH REPUBLIC

Czech Railways (České dráhy (ČD); ⓦcd.cz) runs several types of train: *rychlík* (R) or *spešný* (Sp) trains are faster, only stopping at major towns, while *osobní* trains stop at every small station, averaging 30km per hour. Fast trains are further divided into SuperCity (SC), which require reservations, EuroCity (EC) or InterCity (IC), which charge a supplement, and Expres (Ex), which don't. **Tickets** (*jízdenky*) for domestic journeys can be bought at the station (*nádraží*) before or on the day of departure. ČD runs reasonably priced **sleepers** to a number of neighbouring countries, which you should book in advance. **InterRail** and Eurail passes are valid in the Czech Republic.

BY BUS

Regional and national **buses** are mostly run by small private operators. **Bus stations** are often alongside train stations; some have ticket offices but you can usually buy tickets from the driver. For long-distance journeys, book your ticket at least a day in advance to guarantee a seat.

Student Agency (ⓞ841 101 101, ⓦstudentagency.cz) runs an excellent,

reasonably priced bus service, with direct routes between popular destinations.

BY BICYCLE

Cycling is popular in the Czech Republic, and the varied countryside provides good terrain whatever your level. Regional cycling maps (ⓦshocart.cz) are sold in bookshops. There's bike rental in all major cities and some smaller towns. See ⓦcyklistevitani.cz for more information.

ACCOMMODATION

Accommodation will be the largest chunk of your daily expenditure. The Czech Youth Hostel Association is affiliated with Hostelling International (ⓦczechhostels.com) and offers accommodation across the country. In addition to official hostels there are now independent backpacker digs, especially in hotspots such as Prague and Karlovy Vary. Making reservations through popular booking websites can get you some real bargains, especially in the capital which is always more expensive than the rest of the country.

Private rooms are available in all the towns on the tourist trail, and are often

7

the cheapest option. Look out for signs with the Czech word *Pokoje* (rooms) or the German *Zimmer Frei* (free rooms), or book through a local tourist office. Prices start at around 300Kč per person.

Campsites (*kemp*) are plentiful but facilities are often more basic than you might be used to. Pitch prices are about 50–100Kč. Most sites have simple **chalets** (*chaty* or *bungalovy*) for around 200Kč per person. The Shocart map *Kempy a chatové osady ČR* lists Czech campsites and is sold in many bookshops. See the Czech Camping Association website (ⓦcamp.cz) for more.

FOOD AND DRINK

Czech menus specialize in hearty, filling fare, traditionally a combination of meat, dumplings and sauerkraut. Staples such as roast duck (*pečená kachna*), sirloin in cream sauce (*svíčková na smetaně*) or roast pork (*vepřová pečeně*) are omnipresent, and can be delicious or boring, depending on the chef. Desserts include strudel (*závin*), fruit dumplings (*ovocné knedlíky*) and pancakes (*palačinky*).

Prague and bigger towns offer a fairly wide choice of non-Czech restaurants, and even small towns have a pizzeria and a Vietnamese/Chinese restaurant. **Vegetarian** food is easier to come by in cities, but in rural areas the choice is usually between fried cheese (*smažený sýr*) and fried cauliflower (*smažený květák*).

A **jídelna** or **bufet** is a self-service canteen selling cheap meals, sandwiches and snacks. A **bageterie** is a sandwich shop, and a **pekařství** is a bakery, which often sells open sandwiches as well as bread, rolls, buns and cakes – not to be confused with a **cukrárna**, or cake shop. A **pivnice** is a pub without food, while a **hospoda** or **hostinec** is a pub that serves meals. A **čajovna** is a teahouse, which might serve snacks, while **kavárna** means both coffeehouse and café, and will serve cakes and sometimes meals. A **vinárna** is a wine bar and a **restaurace** is a restaurant.

Restaurants and pubs usually open at about 11am and close between 11pm and 2am, but rarely serve food in the last few hours of the day. Lunchtime is early –

11.30am–1.30pm; if you arrive late, popular dishes will be gone. Waiters sometimes bring pretzels or a basket of bread to the table, which may seem free but will appear on the bill if eaten. Most restaurants and pubs do not charge service and **tipping** is not common – instead, round up the bill to the nearest 10Kč or 50Kč. In pubs it's customary to sit with strangers when seats are scarce: just ask if the space is free (*Máte tady volno?*), and wish fellow diners a good meal (*Dobrou chut'*).

DRINK

The Czechs drink more **beer** (*pivo*) per capita than anyone else in the world – hardly surprising given the high quality and low price of Czech beer. The most famous brands are Pilsner Urquell, from Plzeň, and Budvar, from České Budějovice. Even small canteens and cafés have beer on tap. Southern Moravia is a wine-growing region, and produces some good whites. Other specialities include Moravian *slivovice*, devilishly strong plum brandy, and Becherovka, a herb liquor from Karlovy Vary.

CULTURE AND ETIQUETTE

It can be easy to mistake the Czechs' shyness for surliness, and people who speak good English may well tell you that they don't speak it at all – it's often from lack of confidence rather than unfriendliness, and if you can get past some initial resistance, people are usually helpful and kind. Obviously, it helps if you learn some basic words – *Dobrý den* (hello), *Na shledanou* (goodbye), *Prosím* (please) and *Děkuji* (thank you) will take you far.

SPORTS AND ACTIVITIES

Football is the country's national sport. In Prague, you can see two of the top teams, Sparta (ⓦsparta.cz) and Slavia (ⓦslavia.cz). Matches are usually on Saturdays from August to November and March to May.

Almost as popular as football is **ice hockey**: bars in most towns show matches on the TV, or you can watch games in stadiums during the season: check

ⓦhokej.cz for details of fixtures and tickets. There are plenty of **outdoor activities** such as cycling, hiking and rock climbing to be enjoyed in Bohemia, as well as **caving** in the Moravian karst.

COMMUNICATIONS

Most **post offices** (*pošta*) are open Monday to Friday 9am to 5pm, Saturday 9am to noon. Signs over the counters show where to queue: *známky* (stamps), *dopisy* (letters) or *balíky* (parcels). Stamps are also sold at newsagents and kiosks. Some **public phones** take phonecards (*telefonní karty*), available from post offices, kiosks and some shops, though others still accept coins. Local **SIM** cards are cheap (200Kč) and call charges low, so non-EU citizens may want to buy a local SIM card. There are no roaming charges for EU citizens.

EMERGENCIES

Like any major city Prague has a **pickpocket** problem. Danger-spots are

CZECH

	CZECH	PRONUNCIATION
Yes	Ano	Ah-no
No	Ne	Neh
Please/You're welcome	Prosím	Pro-seem
Thank you	Děkuji	Dye-koo-yi
Good day/Hello	Dobrý den	Dob-ree den
Goodbye	Na shledanou	Nash-leh-dan-oh
Excuse me	Promiňte	Prom-in-teh
Sorry	Pardon	Pardon
Where?	Kde?	Kde?
Good	Dobrý	Dobree
Bad	Špatný	Shpatnee
Near	Blízko	Bleez-ko
Far	Daleko	Dah-lek-o
Cheap	Levný	Levnee
Expensive	Drahý	Dranee
Open	Otevřeno	Ot-evsh-en-o
Closed	Zavřeno	Zavsh-en-o
Today	Dnes	Dnes
Yesterday	Včera	Vch-er-a
Tomorrow	Zítra	Zeet-ra
How much is it?	Kolik to stojí?	Kol-ik toh sto-yee?
What time is it?	Kolik je hodin?	Kol-ik ye hod-in?
I don't understand	Nerozumím	Ne-rozoo-meem
Do you speak English?	Mluvíte Anglicky?	Mluv-ee-te ang-lit-skee?
I don't understand Czech	Nerozumím Český	Ne-rozoo-meem Chess-kee
Toilet	Toaleta	Toh-aleta
Square	Náměstí	Nam–yest-yee
Station	Nádraží	Nah-dra-shee
Platform	Nástupiště	Nah-stoopish-tyeh
One	Jeden	Yed-en
Two	Dva	Dva
Three	Tři	Trshi
Four	Čtyři	Shtiri
Five	Pět	Pyet
Six	Šest	Shest
Seven	Sedm	Sed-um
Eight	Osm	Oss-um
Nine	Devět	Dev-yet
Ten	Deset	Dess-et

7

7

Old Town Square, Charles Bridge, Wenceslas Square, the #22 tram and in the metro. The area around Hlavní nádraží (main station) and the park at Karlovo náměstí (Charles Square) are used by drug addicts and prostitutes at night. By law you should carry your **passport** with you.

Pharmacies (*lékárna*) are easy to find but not always English-speaking. If you need a repeat prescription take the empty bottle or remaining pills.

INFORMATION

Most towns have a **tourist office** (*informační centrum*) with English-speaking staff. You can find **maps** (*mapa*) in tourist offices, bookshops and petrol stations.

MONEY AND BANKS

The local **currency** is the Czech crown, or koruna česká (Kč), though some tourist-oriented services list prices in euros. At the time of writing £1 = 35Kč, €1 = 27Kč and $1 = 24Kč. **Banks** are usually open Monday to Friday 9am to 5pm and there are plenty of ATMs.

CZECH REPUBLIC ONLINE

ⓦ **czech.cz** Basic information on the Czech Republic.
ⓦ **czechtourism.com** Official tourist board website.
ⓦ **expats.cz** Website for Prague's expat community with useful practical information and events listings.
ⓦ **radio.cz/english** News and cultural events.
ⓦ **ticketpro.cz**, ⓦ **ticketstream.cz** Two good sites for finding out what's on around the country and booking tickets online.
ⓦ **slovnik.cz** Online dictionary.

OPENING HOURS AND HOLIDAYS

Most shops are open Monday to Friday 9am to 5 or 6pm, though in larger towns some shops open at weekends: corner shops (*večerka*) tend to stay open daily till 10 or 11pm. Museums and galleries generally close on Mondays but churches usually open daily; synagogues are closed on Saturdays and Jewish holidays.

Public holidays include January 1, Easter Monday, May 1, May 8, July 5 and 6, September 28, October 28, November 17, December 24–26.

Prague

Historical, whimsical, hedonistic and cynical, **PRAGUE** bewilders, bedazzles and befuddles its visitors in equal measure. Since the fall of the Iron Curtain in 1989, tourism and investment have poured in, turning the previously soot-streaked Communist capital into a buzzing metropolis.

Prince Bořivoj, an early Christian, founded the first Czech dynasty in 870, and his grandson, Prince Václav (the Good King Wenceslas of the Christmas carol), became the Czech patron saint after being murdered by his younger brother Boleslav I. Prague experienced a golden age under the urbane emperor, **Charles IV**, a polylingual patron of the arts whose court was the heart of fourteenth-century Europe. Charles founded the university as well as an entire new quarter, Nové Město, and built Charles Bridge, St Vitus' Cathedral and many other churches. A long period of Austro-Hungarian rule gave Prague its Italianate Baroque facades and high-minded coffeehouses, while the National Revival reasserted the Slavic identity of the city and added buildings such as the National Theatre and the Rudolfinum. The short-lived First Republic, modelled on American democracy, crashed when Nazi troops marched into Czechoslovakia, and President Beneš's decision to accept German "protection" was a dark moment in the nation's history, but probably saved the city from decimation. In 1948 Communism arrived in a wave of stained concrete, bringing a few architectural pearls along with the swine. The period since 1989 has seen rapid construction, but with a few exceptions, such as Jean Nouvel's Golden Angel in Smíchov and Karlín's Danube building, it's been unremarkable in character. Not so the restaurants, hotels, bars and clubs, which have, to some extent, re-awoken Prague's slumbering decadence.

WHAT TO SEE AND DO

Flowing from the east towards Germany, the Vltava divides Prague down the middle. Hradčany and Malá Strana, once home to the Austro-Hungarian elite, sit primly on the left bank, faced by the busier commercial quarters, Staré Město, Josefov and Nové Město.

Hradčany, home to the castle and St Vitus' Cathedral, tumbles into **Malá Strana** (Little Quarter), a maze of cobbles, distinctive house signs and red roofs, where you'll find the Czech senate's Baroque gardens **Valdštejnská zahrada** (Mon–Fri 7.30am–6pm, Sat & Sun 10am–6pm), which back onto Malostranská metro.

Over the river is **Staré Město** (Old Town), a delicate web of alleys and crooked streets that generally meet up at Staroměstské náměstí, the Old Town Square. Within Staré Město is the old Jewish quarter, **Josefov**, some of which is now a luxury shopping area.

Nové Město (New Town), the most central part of the modern city, spans the largest area of old Prague, with blocks stretching south and east of the old town in long strides.

Prague Castle

Once the heart of the Holy Roman Empire, **Prague Castle** (daily: buildings 9am–5pm; grounds 6am–10pm; Ⓦhrad .cz) is home to the Czech president and

crown jewels. Wandering the grounds is free, but to enter the buildings, including St Vitus Cathedral, the Old Royal Palace and the Basilica of St George, you need to buy a **ticket** from the Castle Information Centre, opposite the cathedral entrance (long-visit or short-visit options 250–350Kč; valid for two days).

St Vitus' Cathedral

Medieval **St Vitus' Cathedral**, which broods over the Prague skyline, is scarcely visible close up; the Third Courtyard surrounds it too tightly. The **Chapel of sv Václav**, by the south door, was built in the fourteenth century to commemorate the Czech prince Saint Wenceslas (Václav), murdered by his brother Boleslav I. A door in the south wall leads to the coronation chamber, which houses the **crown jewels**.

Old Royal Palace

The **Old Royal Palace** (Starý královský palác), across the courtyard from the south door of the cathedral, was home to Bohemian royalty from the eleventh to the seventeenth centuries. The massive Gothic **Vladislav Hall** (Vladislavský sál), where the early Bohemian kings were elected, is still used as the venue for the presidential swearing-in ceremony.

Basilica of St George

The **Basilica of St George** (Bazilika sv Jiří), with its beautifully austere Romanesque interior, was originally built in 1173. Classical music concerts are often held here.

Golden Lane

Golden Lane (Zlatá ulička), round the corner from the basilica, is a street of toy-sized tradesmen's cottages, as bright and compact as a watercolour box. Franz Kafka briefly lived at no. 22, his sister's house, during World War I.

The Royal Gardens

North of the castle walls, cross the **Powder Bridge** (Prašný most) to reach the **Royal Gardens** (Královská zahrada; April–Oct daily 10am–6pm; free), and enjoy the view over Little Quarter

7

7

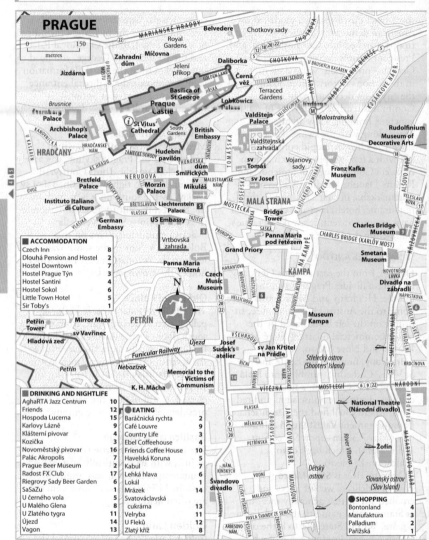

PRAGUE

0 — 150
metres

Mariánské Hradby · Belvedere · Chotkovy sady · Royal Gardens
Zahradní dům · Míčovna
Jízdárna
Jelení příkop · Daliborka · Chotkova · U Brusských kasáren
Golden Lane · Černá věž · Stare Zam. Schody
Basilica of St George · Jiřská · Terraced Gardens
Brusnice · Prague Castle · Lobkowicz Palace
Sternberg Palace · St Vitus' Cathedral · South Gardens · British Embassy · Valdštejn Palace · Malostranská · Rudolfinium Museum of Decorative Arts
Archbishop's Palace · HRADČANSKÉ NÁM. · Hradčanské · Valdštejnská zahrada
HRADČANY · Ke Hradu · Zámecké Schody · Hudební pavilón · Nunovská dům · sv Tomáš · Vojanovy sady · Franz Kafka Museum
Bretfeld Palace · NERUDOVA · Smiřických dům · sv MALOSTRANSKÉ NÁM. · sv Josef
Morzin Palace · Mikuláš · MALÁ STRANA
Instituto Italiano di Cultura · VLAŠSKÁ · BRETISLAVOVA · Liechtenstein Palace · TRŽIŠTĚ · Bridge Tower · Charles Bridge Museum
German Embassy · US Embassy · Vrtbovská zahrada · Panna Maria pod řetězem · Grand Priory · Charles Bridge (Karlův most) · Smetana Museum
Panna Maria Vítězná · Czech Music Museum · KAMPA · Divadlo na zábradlí
PETŘÍN · HELLICHOVA · Museum Kampa
Petřín Tower · Mirror Maze · sv Vavřinec · Hladová zeď' · VŠEHRDOVA · Josef Sudek's atelier · sv Jan Křtitel na Prádle · Střelecký ostrov (Shooters' Island)
Petřín · Nebozízek · Funicular Railway · Újezd · ŘÍČNÍ · Svandovo divadlo · VÍTĚZNÁ · MOST LEGII
Memorial to the Victims of Communism · K. H. Mácha
National Theatre (Národní divadlo) · Žofín
PLASKÁ · MĚLNICKÁ · PETŘÍNSKÁ · NÁM. KINSKÝCH · Slovanský ostrov (Slav Island)
Dětský ostrov

■ ACCOMMODATION	
Czech Inn	8
Dlouhá Pension and Hostel	2
Hostel Downtown	7
Hostel Prague Týn	3
Hostel Santini	4
Hostel Sokol	6
Little Town Hotel	5
Sir Toby's	1

■ DRINKING AND NIGHTLIFE	
AghaRTA Jazz Centrum	10
Friends	12
Hospoda Lucerna	15
Karlovy Lázně	9
Klášterní pivovar	4
Kozička	3
Novoměstský pivovar	16
Palác Akropolis	7
Prague Beer Museum	2
Radost FX Club	17
Riegrovy Sady Beer Garden	6
SaSaZu	1
U černého vola	5
U Malého Glena	8
U Zlatého tygra	11
Újezd	14
Vagon	13

● EATING	
Barácnická rychta	2
Café Louvre	9
Country Life	3
Ebel Coffeehouse	4
Friends Coffee House	10
Havelská Koruna	5
Kabul	7
Lehká hlava	6
Lokál	1
Mrázek	14
Svatováclavská cukrárna	13
Velryba	11
U Flekú	12
Zlatý kříž	8

● SHOPPING	
Bontonland	4
Manufaktura	3
Palladium	2
Pařížská	1

surrounded by fountains, sloping lawns and almond trees.

Hradčanské náměstí
Aristocratic palaces lie across Hradčanské náměstí like a pod of beached whales. A passage down the side of the Archbishop's Palace leads to **Šternberg Palace** (Tues–Sun 10am–6pm; 150Kč; ⊛ngprague.cz), home to the National Gallery's European **art collection** that contains pieces by Rubens, Cranch and El Greco. At Jiřská 3 is **Lobkowicz Palace** (daily 10am–6pm; 275Kč; ⊛lobkowicz.cz), full of aristocratic bric-a-brac. A passage at Pohořelec 8 leads to **Strahov Monastery** (Strahovský klášter) with its exquisite Baroque library (daily 9am–noon & 1–5pm; 100Kč; ⊛strahovskyklaster.cz), which displays peculiar and sublime artefacts from illuminated manuscripts to dried whale penises.

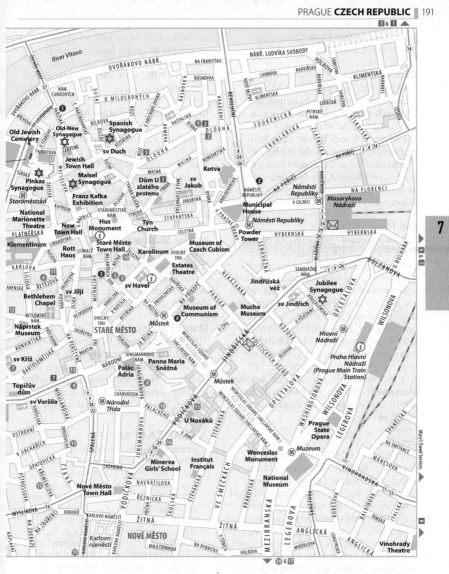

Sv Mikuláš

Malostranské náměstí, the main square in Malá Strana, forms a ring around the flamboyant church of **Sv Mikuláš** (daily: March–Oct 9am–5pm; Nov–Feb 9am–4pm; 70Kč), a triumph of Baroque opulence created by the Jesuits who were kicked out of Prague not long after it was completed.

Petřín

Head south down Karmelitská and you will see **Petřín hill** rising above, a bucolic spot ideal for a picnic. Above the **funicular railway** (daily 9am–11.30pm; every 10–15min; Prague transport tickets valid, available from the attendant in the station) is a nineteenth-century miniature copy of the Eiffel Tower, **Petřín Tower**, which you can climb or ascend by lift (daily: March & Oct 10am–8pm;

April–Sept 10am–10pm; Nov–Feb 10am–6pm; 120Kč).

Charles Bridge

Linking Malá Strana to Staré Město is Prague's most celebrated landmark, **Charles Bridge** (Karlův most), begun in 1357. Among the many statues that line the bridge is Czech patron saint John of Nepomuk, thrown off the bridge by Wenceslas IV for refusing to divulge the queen's confessions. It's best seen at dawn, or late at night, when the crowds have dispersed.

Old Town Square

Old Town Square (Staroměstské náměstí) was the city's main marketplace from the eleventh century until the nineteenth century. On the west side is the medieval **astronomical clock** (Pražský orloj), which gives a mechanical show featuring saints, deadly sins and Jesus (9am–9pm hourly on the hour). Across the square are the dour Gothic steeples of **Týn Church**; if you look closely, one steeple is slightly bigger – they represent Adam and Eve. In the centre of the square is the **Jan Hus Monument**, built in 1915 to mark the 500th anniversary of the Protestant reformer's execution.

Josefov

Northwest of Old Town Square is **Josefov**, a mixture of narrow cobbled streets – the remains of the old Jewish ghetto, and wide Art Nouveau boulevards – the legacy of 1890s slum clearance. The **Old Jewish Cemetery** is a poignant reminder of the ghetto, its inhabitants overcrowded even in death. To the south is the **Pinkas Synagogue**, inscribed with the names of 80,000 Czechoslovak Jews killed by the Nazis. The **Old–New Synagogue**, Europe's oldest, is the heart of Prague's Jewish community. Opposite is the **Jewish Town Hall** (Židovská radnice), with its distinctive anticlockwise clock. East of Pařížská is the gorgeous neo-Byzantine **Spanish Synagogue** (Španělská synagoga), which hosts classical concerts.

The Jewish Quarter sights can be accessed with one ticket, available from the office at ul Maiselova 38 (daily except Sat & Jewish holidays winter 9am–4.30pm, summer 9am–6pm; 480Kč, 320Kč for students under 26; ⓦjewishmuseum.cz).

Museum of Decorative Arts

In a neo-Renaissance palace opposite the Rudolfinum, the **Museum of Decorative Arts**, 17 Listopadu 2 (Tues 10am–7pm, Wed–Sun 10am–6pm; 120Kč; ⓦupm .cz) has a splendid collection of glass, clothes, pottery, clocks and dresses spanning a thousand years: it's currently closed for renovation.

Mucha Museum

A turning halfway along Na příkopě leads to the **Mucha Museum** at Panská 7 (daily 10am–6pm; 240Kč; ⓦmucha.cz), dedicated to the Czech Art Nouveau designer and painter Alfons Mucha.

Municipal House

The most impressive façade on náměstí Republiky is the **Municipal House** (Obecní dům), a delightful example of Czech Art Nouveau containing a concert hall, restaurants, café, and frescoes by Mucha. You can get in by taking the

FRANZ KAFKA

Franz Kafka was born in 1883 to middle-class Czech Jewish parents who ran a haberdashery in Old Town. His ambivalent relationship with Prague is reflected in his trademark tone of anxious claustrophobia – "A cage went in search of a bird", he once wrote. You can see the building where he worked as a clerk at **na poříčí 7**, and his homes on **Golden Lane** (no. 22) and **Old Town Square** (Oppelt building). Kafka went to fortnightly meetings at **Café Louvre** (see p.194) and also frequented **Café Savoy** in Malá Strana, where he first met the actor Isaac Lowy, who re-awakened his interest in Jewish culture. The **Kafka Museum** at Cihelna 2b (daily 10am–6pm; 200Kč; ⓦkafkamuseum.cz) displays first editions and manuscripts, personal letters, diaries and drawings – and gives an insight into one of the most intriguing minds of the twentieth century.

overpriced guided **tour** (two or three daily; 290Kč), or drink tea in the gilded café and enjoy a decent Czech meal in the basement restaurant for rather less.

Museum of Communism

Situated, with delicious irony, above *McDonald's*, the privately run **Museum of Communism** on Na Příkopě 10 (daily 9am–9pm; 190Kč; ⓦmuzeumkomunismu.cz) draws a sensational picture of life behind the Iron Curtain in all its grim monotony, from propaganda and labour camps to shopping and TV.

Wenceslas Square

The well-oiled axle of modern Prague is **Wenceslas Square** (Václavské náměstí), a mass of glitzy high-street shops, greasy sausage stands and the odd sleazy establishment dating back to the 1990s. It was here that protesters gathered to topple Communism in the Velvet Revolution. At the top end is a statue of St Wenceslas on his horse. Below is a small **memorial** to 21-year-old student **Jan Palach**, who burnt himself to death in protest against the Russian invasion of 1968, becoming a symbol of Czech resistance.

Museum of Modern Art

Take tram #12, #17 or #24 to the **Museum of Modern Art** (Veletržní palác; Tues–Sun 10am–6pm; 220Kč), in the Trade Fair Palace. This stately piece of 1920s functionalism houses works by Klimt, Picasso and the French Impressionists as well as Mucha's cycle of huge paintings called *The Slav Epic*.

DOX Centre for Contemporary Art

DOX (Wed & Fri 11am–7pm; Thurs 11am–9pm; Sat–Mon 10am–6pm; 180Kč, students 90Kč; ⓦdox.cz) showcases modern painting, sculpture, architecture, design and photography. One of the most intriguing venues in town, it's hosted the likes of Andy Warhol and Damien Hirst, as well as Czech artists such as sculptor David Černý and émigré architect Jan Kaplický.

ARRIVAL AND DEPARTURE

By plane Prague's Václav Havel airport (*letiště*) is 10km from the city centre (ⓦprg.aero). To get into town, catch a bus then a metro: bus #119 (4am–midnight; every 7–15min; 20min) goes to ⓜDejvická on line A, and bus #100 to ⓜZličín on line B. "Fixed-price" taxis are expensive, about 400Kč to the centre.

By train Coming by train, you'll arrive at one of Prague's four stations: Praha hlavní nádraží (Prague Main Station), where most international trains arrive/depart; Praha Holešovice station; Praha Masarykovo; or Praha Smíchov. All four are adjacent to metro stations.

Destinations Berlin (every 2hr; 4hr 30min); Bratislava (5 daily; 4hr); České Budějovice (up to 10 daily; 2hr 20min); Dresden (5 daily; 2hr 15min); Karlovy Vary (4 daily; 3hr 15min); Olomouc (1–2 hourly; 2–3hr); Plzeň (hourly; 1hr 40min); Vienna (3 daily; 4hr).

By bus The main bus station is Praha-Florenc on the eastern edge of Staré Město, right next to ⓜFlorenc (line B). At night this can be shady, so don't loiter. Most buses depart from Praha-Florenc. For Student Agency buses, book ahead (see p.185) at their main office in the Florenc bus station.

Destinations Berlin (hourly; 4hr 45min–5hr 30min); Bratislava (up to 10 daily; 5hr); Brno (every 30min–1hr; 2hr 20min–3hr); České Budějovice (up to 10 daily; 2hr 30min–3hr 30min); Český Krumlov (hourly; 3hr; typically leaves from Na Knížecí bus station near metro Anděl); Karlovy Vary (hourly; 2hr 10min–2hr 40min); Kutná Hora (Mon–Fri hourly; 1hr 40min; leaves from Háje metro station); Plzeň (hourly; 1hr); Vienna (hourly; 4–5hr).

INFORMATION

Tourist information Prague City Tourism can provide maps and brochures, and help with accommodation and tickets. There are several branches around town (Mon–Fri 9am–6/7pm, Sat 9am–3/5pm; April–Oct also Sun 9am–5pm; ⓦpraguewelcome.com), including the main office in the Old Town Hall at Staroměstské náměstí 5, and branches at Rytířská 31 at the bottom of Wenceslas Square (near ⓜMůstek) and at Prague Airport.

GETTING AROUND

By metro The metro (daily 5am–midnight) is fast, reliable and – with only three lines (for the time being) – easy to navigate.

By tram Running every 3–20min, Prague's trams cross the city's hills and cobbles with great dexterity. Tram #22, which runs through Vinohrady and Hradčany, is a good option for sightseeing. Night trams (numbers #51–#59; midnight–4.30am; every 30min) all pass through Lazarská in Nové Město.

By taxi Prague cabbies are notoriously wily, so it is best to call a taxi – AAA has English-speaking operators (☎14 0 14), as does ProfiTaxi (☎14 0 15). If you have to hail a cab,

7

RIVER CRUISE

Prague is most beautiful from the water. Boat trips down the Vltava last between an hour and a day; there are lunch and dinner cruises and jazz and club boats with live music. Buy tickets on the riverbank at Čechův Bridge or Embankment *nábřeži*, or pre-book with Prague Boats (☎ 724 202 505, ⓦ prague-boats.cz; prices start at 300Kč) or Jazzboat (☎ 731 183 180, ⓦ jazzboat.cz; 690Kč with option for dinner).

look for the Fair Place taxi sign, get a quote beforehand, and ask for a receipt (*účtenka*).

Travel passes If you're planning to use public transport regularly, buy a travel pass (110Kč/24hr, 310Kč/72hr); remember to validate it on your first journey. Alternatively, the Praguecard (ⓦ praguecard.com) gives you four days' unlimited transport and entry to fifty attractions (1780Kč, students 1300Kč): two-day (1300Kč) and three-day (1570Kč) versions are also available.

Tickets Buy tickets at tobacconists, kiosks or the ticket machines inside metro stations and by some tram stops, then validate them in the yellow machines on trams or at the metro entrance. There are two main tickets: the 32Kč ticket is valid for 90min; the 24Kč is valid for 30min. Plain-clothes inspectors check tickets and there is a fine of 800Kč on the spot (1500Kč to pay later) if you don't have a valid ticket.

Bike rental Praha Bike (Dlouhá 24; daily 9am–8pm; ⓦ prahabike.cz) rents bikes and organizes tours around Prague for 490Kč for a tour (2hr 30min) or 500Kč for an 8hr rental. City Bike (Královdvorská 5; daily 9am–7pm, ⓦ citybike-prague.com) offers bike rental with an optional MP3 audio tour (750Kč for 24hr).

ACCOMMODATION

Prague's most central hotels are in Staré Město, Nové Město and Malá strana, or you can pay less further out. Vinohrady is picturesque, with great wine bars and restaurants, Žižkov is down at heel but lively at night, Vyšehrad is pretty and sedate. You can find apartments and rooms on ⓦ prague-city-apartments.cz and ⓦ praguecentralapartments.com. The city's Charles University rents out student rooms over the summer; booking office at Voršilská 1, Nové Město (Mon–Fri only; ☎ 224 930 010; beds July to mid-Sept; from 350Kč).

★ **Czech Inn** Francouzská 76, Vinohrady ☎ 267 267 612, ⓦ czech-inn.com. With oak floors, brushed aluminium and discarded backpacks, *Czech Inn* has a part youth hostel, part luxury hotel vibe. In Vinohrady, it has a café-bar with live music, great staff and a 24-hour reception, plus dorms, private rooms (en-suite and shared bath) and apartments.

Metro to Náměstí Míru, then tram #4 or #22 to Krymská. Dorms **300Kč**, doubles **1520Kč**

Dlouhá Pension and Hostel (Travellers' Hostel) Dlouhá 33, Staré Město ☎ 224 826 662, ⓦ travellers.cz; ⓜ Náměstí Republiky. Large party hostel a 5min walk from Old Town Square and next door to *Roxy* music club. There's a kitchen and a 24hr reception. Breakfast included. Dorms **405Kč**, doubles **850Kč**

Hostel Downtown Národní 19, Nové Město ☎ 224 240 570, ⓦ hosteldowntown.cz. Clean, garishly decorated HI-affiliated hostel that offers dorms as well as private rooms with either shared or private baths. Dorms **720Kč**, doubles **2100Kč**

Hostel Prague Týn Týnská 19, Staré Město ☎ 224 808 301, ⓦ hostelpraguetyn.com; ⓜ Náměstí Republiky. Just 200m from Old Town Square, this funkily designed hostel is clean and colourful, if a bit small: price includes breakfast. Dorms **375Kč**

Hostel Santini Nerudova 14, Malá Strana ☎ 257 316 191, ⓦ hostelsantiniprague.com. In a prime position on the tourist trail up to the castle, this well-run hostel in a typical Malá Strana townhouse has antique touches and its own café bar. Dorms **630Kč**

Hostel Sokol Nosticova 2, Malá Strana ☎ 257 007 397, ⓦ hostelsokol.cz. Overlooking the river, this hostel has immaculate, spartan dorms (originally used by Communist athletes) full of brass and white linen. Dorms **350Kč**

Little Town Hotel Malostranské náměstí 11/260, Malá strana ☎ 242 406 965, ⓦ littletownhotel.cz; ⓜ Malostranská. In the shadow of St Nicholas Cathedral, this hostel/hotel is fresh, if a little barren. Choose from dorms or private rooms with en suite or shared bath. Dorms **400Kč**, doubles **1620Kč**

Sir Toby's Dělnická 24 ☎ 246 032 611, ⓦ sirtobys.com; ⓜ Nádraží Holešovice or tram stop Dělnická. Upmarket suburban hostel with a garden, cellar bar, lounge, large kitchen and dorms that look like pricey hotel rooms stretched. Dorms **530Kč**, doubles **1900Kč**

EATING

Prague food is not just meat and dumplings – now you can find anything from French and Korean to Mexican and Vietnamese. Restaurants are affordable, especially at lunchtime (11.30am–1.30pm) when pubs and bistros run cheap daily offers. Prague has a thriving café culture, and watching the streetlife from an old-fashioned coffeehouse, with a slice of strudel or honey cake, is one of the city's great pleasures.

CAFÉS

★ **Café Louvre** Národní 22, Nové Město ⓦ cafelouvre.cz; ⓜ Národní třída. Lovely Art Nouveau coffeehouse as rich and delectable as the classic sacher torte. There's a billiard hall, good-value lunch menu and a shady terrace. Mon–Fri 8am–11.30pm, Sat & Sun 9am–11.30pm.

Ebel Coffeehouse Řetězová 9, Staré Město; ⓂStaroměstská. Excellent place to escape the crowded streets and indulge in a good cup of coffee, breakfast or light snack. Mon–Fri 8am–8pm, Sat & Sun 8.30am–8pm.

Friends Coffee House Palackého 7, Nové Město Ⓦmilujikavu.cz; ⓂMůstek. Try their freshly roasted coffee and home-made sandwiches or sip a glass of wine. Hosts music performances, readings and photograph exhibitions. Mon–Fri 9am–9pm, Sat & Sun noon–8pm.

Svatováclavská cukrárna Václavská pasáž, Karlovo náměstí 6, Nové Město; ⓂKarlovo náměstí. Join the local pensioners for a glass of cheap Turkish coffee and a slice of strudel at this busy *cukrárna* within the glass-roofed Václavská pasáž. Mon–Fri 8am–7pm, Sat & Sun 8am– 9am.

Velryba Opatovická 24, Nové Město Ⓦkavarnavelryba.cz; ⓂNárodní třída. Long-established, grungy but authentic hippy-student hangout opposite the Church of sv Michala serving Žatec beer, cheap pasta and lots of meat. Mon–Fri 11am–midnight, Sat 5pm–midnight.

Zlatý kříž Jungmannovo nám. 19, Nové Město Ⓦlahudkyzlatykriz-praha.cz; ⓂMůstek. A meaty slice of Czech culture, this popular stand-up lunch-bar serves Prague's best *chlebíčky* (ornate open sandwiches) for only 16Kč, plus cold cuts, rolls and beer on tap. Mon–Fri 6.30am–7pm, Sat 9am–3pm.

RESTAURANTS

Baráčnická rychta Tržiště 23, Malá Strana Ⓦbaracnickarychta.cz; ⓂMalostranská. Popular local stashed in a back alley in the tourist district. Good food, outdoor seating in the quiet courtyard, and Svijany, a superb beer, on tap. Mains 150–295Kč. Mon–Sat 11am–11pm, Sun 11am–9pm.

Country Life Melantrichova 15, Staré Město Ⓦcountrylife.cz; ⓂMůstek. Around the corner from Old Town Square, this packed vegetarian lunch spot serves hot and cold cafeteria-style food by weight (a plateful for 100–120Kč). Mon–Thurs 10.30am–7.30pm, Fri 10.30am–5pm, Sun noon–6pm.

Havelská Koruna Havelská 21, Staré Město Ⓦhavelska-koruna.cz; ⓂMůstek. Just a 2min walk from Old Town Square, this is not for the health-conscious, with all grandma's favourite dishes plopped on a plate by grumpy dinner ladies. Mains 42–89Kč. Daily 10am–8pm.

Kabul Krocínova 5, Staré Město Ⓦkabulrestaurant.cz; ⓂNárodní třída. Prague's only Afghan restaurant offers a cheap and tasty lunch menu, hookah pipes and occasional evenings of traditional music. Mains 80–290Kč. Daily 11am–11pm.

Lehká hlava Boršov 2, Staré Město Ⓦlehkahlava.cz; ⓂNárodní třída. Cure for Czech pub fatigue – bright, chic, non-smoking and vegetarian. Daily lunch menu for 125Kč. Mains 150–200Kč. Mon–Fri 11.30am–11.30pm, Sat & Sun noon–11.30pm.

Lokál Dlouhá 33, Staré Město Ⓦambi.cz; ⓂNáměstí Republiky. A restaurant chain that re-creates the casual atmosphere of a Czech pub but cleaned up. It's very popular and the best bet for some authentically tasty Czech food. Mains 99–195Kč. Mon–Sat 11am–1am, Sun 11am–midnight.

Mrázek Bělehradská 82, Nové Město; ⓂNáměstí Míru. Join impoverished locals for a meat-sauce-dumpling combo at this traditional *jídelna* (stand-up self-service canteen). No English. Mains 20–85Kč. Mon–Fri 7am–6pm, Sat 7–11am.

U Fleků Křemencova 11, Nové Město Ⓦufleku.cz; ⓂNárodní třída. The look is there, and the beer is worth the trip, but this place can be a bit touristy. Food is pure Czech. Mains 199–349Kč. Daily 10am–11pm.

DRINKING AND NIGHTLIFE

7

Pubs close between 11pm and 2am – for late-night drinking head to the city centre's bars and clubs. Pub crawls are a good way to cover a lot of ground: one popular company is Prague Pub Crawl (Ⓦpubcrawl.cz; 500Kč), or for something perhaps more sedate, join the Sandemans beer tour (Ⓦnewpraguetours.com; 350Kč), which meets daily at 6pm on Old Town Square.

BARS AND PUBS

Hospoda Lucerna Vodičkova 36, Nové Město Ⓦhospodalucerna.cz; ⓂMůstek. Long, loud bar popular with everyone. Decent meals and a bit of history – the pub dates back to 1908. Mon–Thurs 11am–2am, Fri 11am–3am, Sat noon–3am, Sun noon–1am.

Klášterní pivovar Strahovské nádvoří 301, Hradčany Ⓦklasterni-pivovar.cz; ⓂMalostranská. Reward yourself for the steep walk up Petřín with a delicious beer – dark and light – brewed by the monks at Strahov Monastery. Daily 10am–10pm.

Kozička Kozí 1, Staré Město Ⓦkozicka.cz; ⓂStaroměstská. Popular place to start and round off an evening; the underground place stays open later than most and also serves proper meals. Mon–Thurs 4pm–4am, Fri 5pm–5.30am, Sat 6pm–5.30am, Sun 7pm–3am.

Novoměstský pivovar Vodičkova 20 Ⓦnpivovar.cz; ⓂMůstek. Outstanding microbrewery serving its own well-tapped misty eleven percent home brew, plus monster portions of Czech sustenance, in a series of twelve sprawling beer halls and rooms, some Gothic affairs deep underground. Mon–Fri 10am–11.30pm, Sat 11.30am–11.30pm, Sun noon–10pm.

★Prague Beer Museum Dlouhá 46, Staré Město Ⓦpraguebeermuseum.com; ⓂNáměstí Republiky. This smoky, no-nonsense temple to the lager gods serves up oddities rarely seen in the capital Bakalář from Rakovník, Konrad from Vratislavice and Prácheňská Perla from Protivín provide some intriguing variety. Daily 11.30am–3am.

Riegrovy Sady Beer Garden Riegrovy Sady, Vinohrady; ⓦ Jiřího z Poděbrad. Pints are sold from one hut, sausages from another. There's a big screen for sport, table-football and table-hockey. Daily noon–2am (dependent on weather).

U černého vola Loretánské náměstí 1, Hradčany; ⓦ Malostranská. Great traditional Prague pub doing a brisk business providing the popular light beer Velkopopovický kozel in huge quantities to thirsty local workers, plus a few basic pub snacks. Daily 10am–10pm.

U Zlatého tygra Husova 17, Staré Město ⓦ uzlatehotygra .cz; ⓦ Staroměstská. If you like authenticity, this tobacco-fugged local full of noisy old men is the place for you. Pilsner on tap and no food. Daily 3–11pm.

CLUBS

Friends Náprstkova 1, Staré Město ⓦ friendsclub.cz; ⓦ Národní třída. Low-key gay bar that transforms into a raucous club on Fri and Sat nights. Daily 7pm–6am.

Karlovy Lázně Novotného lávka 1, Staré Město ⓦ karlovylazne.cz; ⓦ Národní třída. Hyper-kitsch super-club on five floors, next to the Charles Bridge; techno on the top floor, progressively more retro as you descend towards the lobby. Daily 9pm–5am.

Palác Akropolis Kubelíkova 27, Žižkov ⓦ palacakropolis .cz; ⓦ Jiřího z Poděbrad. Art Deco mammoth *Akropolis* is a maze of live music, theatre, dancing and eating, with rock, house, pop, hip-hop, reggae and the rest. Mon–Thurs 11am–12.30am, Fri–Sun 11am–1.30am.

Radost FX Club Bělehradská 120, Vinohrady ⓦ radostfx .cz; ⓦ I. P. Pavlova. Popular central club decorated like a faux-oriental brothel and famous for its nightly parties. Visit during the day for a decent vegetarian meal. Daily 10pm–5am.

SaSaZu Bubenské nábřeží 306, Holešovice ⓦ sasazu.com; ⓦ Vltavská. Shiny goliath of Prague nightlife modelled on the slick clubs of New York's meatpacking district, with an oriental fusion restaurant. Fri & Sat 10pm–5am.

Újezd Újezd 18, Malá Strana ⓦ klubujezd.cz; ⓦ Národní třída. Three-floor club popular with the young, hedonist set. Mix of live music and DJs; the bottom floor is a pub and the corridors serve as an art gallery. Daily 2pm–4am.

ENTERTAINMENT

You can find entertainment listings on the sometimes difficult to navigate Prague Events Calendar (ⓦ pragueeventscalendar.cz), expat websites Expats.cz (ⓦ expats.cz) and Prague.tv (ⓦ prague.tv)

LIVE MUSIC

AghaRTA Jazz Centrum Železná 16, Staré Město ⓦ agharta.cz; ⓦ Staroměstská. Prague's best jazz club, with a good mix of top international names and local acts. Daily from 9pm.

U Malého Glena Karmelitská 23, Malá Strana ⓦ malyglen.cz; ⓦ Malostranská. Tiny, popular jazz venue in a Little Quarter cellar with a restaurant upstairs. Daily from 9pm.

Vagon Národní třída 25, Nové Město ⓦ www.vagon.cz; ⓦ Národní třída. Smoky music club playing a mix of rock and reggae, bursting at the seams with long-haired students and ageing rockers. Daily from 9pm.

CLASSICAL MUSIC, OPERA AND BALLET

Národní Divadlo (National Theatre) Národní 2, Nové Město ⓦ narodni-divadlo.cz; ⓦ Národní třída. Grand monument to nineteenth-century nationalism, built with a brick from every village in the country. Ballet and opera performed by national and touring companies. You can also get information on ballet and opera being shown at both the State Opera (Wilsonova 4, Nové Město) and Stavovské divadlo (Ovocný trh 1, Staré Město).

Obecní dům Nám. Republiky 5, Staré Město ⓦ obecnidum.cz; ⓦ Náměstí Republiky. Grand Art Nouveau building hosting a range of classical concerts and festivals.

Rudolfinum Alšovo nábřeží 12, Staré Město ⓦ ceskafilharmonie.cz; ⓦ Staroměstská. This neo-Renaissance concert hall next to the river houses the Czech Philharmonic Orchestra, creators of a thousand film soundtracks.

THEATRE

Lanterna Magika Národní 4, Nové Město ⓦ narodni -divadlo.cz; ⓦ Národní třída. A blend of circus, puppetry and dance. Czech theatre minus the language barrier.

National Marionette Theatre Žatecká 1, Staré Město ⓦ mozart.cz; ⓦ Staroměstská. Giant marionettes miming to a CD of Mozart's *Don Giovanni*. Silly but good fun.

Švandovo divadlo Štefánikova 57, Malá Strana ⓦ svandovodivadlo.cz; ⓦ Anděl. Czech theatre with English subtitles. Sit in the balcony for the best view.

CINEMA

Kino Lucerna Štěpánská 61, Nové Město ⓦ kinolucerna .cz; ⓦ Můstek. Nestling inside a 1930s shopping arcade off Wenceslas Square, Lucerna is a flamboyant, pint-sized Art Nouveau cinema. Czech, international, old and new films, and a quiet vintage bar.

Kino Světozor Vodičkova 41, Nové Město ⓦ kinosvetozor .cz; ⓦ Můstek. New releases, classics, art-house and documentaries.

ACTIVITIES

Boating Žofín or Střelecký island; ⓦ Národní třída. Pedalo and rowing boat rental from little firms on the river islands opposite the National Theatre. April–Oct; passport kept as deposit, approx 100Kč/hr.

HC Slavia 02 Arena, Libeň, ⓦhc-slavia.cz; ⓂČeskomoravská. Little can top an ice hockey match, beer in one hand and sausage in the other, surrounded by a thousand bellowing Czechs.

Podoli Swimming Complex Podolska 74, Kavčí hory ⓦpspodoli.cz; ⓂPražského povstání. Olympic-sized indoor and outdoor pools, waterslides, saunas and lawn for sunbathing. Take tram #3 or #17 to Kublov.

SHOPPING

Bontonland Václavské náměstí 1; ⓂMůstek. Music and film emporium buried bunker-like under the lower end of Wenceslas Square.

Manufaktura Melantrichova 17, Staré Město ⓦmanufaktura.cz; ⓂMůstek. Czech folk-inspired shop with a fantastic array of wooden toys, painted Easter eggs, straw decorations, honeycomb candles and sundry kitchen utensils. Daily 10am–8pm.

Palladium Náměstí Republiky 1, Nové Město ⓦpalladiumpraha.cz; ⓂNáměstí Republiky. Central mall with major European brands, supermarkets and a food court.

Pařížská Staré Město; ⓂStaroměstská. This street named "Paris" resembles the broad leafy boulevards of France's capital, and is home to Cartier, Hermes, Louis Vuitton et al. There's more shopping on nearby Celetná and Karlova.

DIRECTORY

Embassies and consulates Australia (honorary), Klimentská 10, Nové Město ☎296 578 350; Canada, Ve Struhach 2, Bubeneč ☎272 101 800; New Zealand, Václavské náměstí 11, Nové Město ☎234 784 777; Ireland, Tržiště 13, Malá Strana ☎257 530 061; UK, Thunovská 14, Malá Strana ☎257 402 111; US, Tržiště 15, Malá Strana ☎257 022 000.

Hospital Na Františku Hospital, Na Františku 8, Staré Město ☎222 801 211 (24hr number, English spoken), ⓦnnfp.cz.

Internet Most hostels and hotels have wi-fi (free, or for a small fee). There's unlimited free wi-fi at Prague Airport.

Left luggage There are lockers or left-luggage offices at all train stations.

Pharmacies Palackého 5, Nové Město (24hr; ☎224 946 982); Belgická 37, Vinohrady (24hr; ☎222 513 396).

Post office Jindřišská 14, Nové Město (daily 2am–midnight, but service is slow outside office hours).

Bohemia

Prague is encircled by the region of **Bohemia**, which covers the western two-thirds of the Czech Republic. To the west of Prague, **Karlovy Vary** is a picturesque spa town in the moody wooded mountains that mark the border with Germany. Southeast of here, the town of **Plzeň** brims with industrial vigour and Pilsner Urquell beer. Travelling east towards Slovakia you'll reach **Kutná Hora**, with its sinister bone church. South of Prague, close to the Austrian border, is another beer-brewing giant, **České Budějovice**, home of the original Budweiser, and **Český Krumlov**, with its rose-coloured churches and frescoed palaces.

KUTNÁ HORA

A short bus ride from Prague, **KUTNÁ HORA** has a handful of tourist attractions and a sleepy, provincial atmosphere. Beneath the town are kilometres of exhausted silver and gold mines. From 1308, Bohemia's royal mint at Kutná Hora converted its silver into coins that were used all over Central Europe, but when the mines ran dry the town dwindled.

WHAT TO SEE AND DO

Kutná Hora's old town is so small it can be explored in a couple of hours. Most of its sights sit between main square Palackého náměstí and the Cathedral of sv Barbora ten minutes to the southeast.

Sedlec ossuary

The town's most popular attraction is the ghoulish **ossuary** (*kostnice*), which houses 40,000 human skeletons (daily: April–Sept 8am–6pm; Oct & March 9am–5pm; Nov–Feb 9am–4pm; 90Kč, students 60Kč; ⓦossuary.eu) arranged in intricate patterns by local oddball František Rint, a carpenter, in 1870. Take bus #1 or #4 from Kutná Hora to Sedlec.

Cathedral of sv Barbora

A Gothic masterpiece dedicated to the patron saint of miners, the **Cathedral of sv Barbora** (Tues–Sun: Nov–March 10am–4pm; April–Oct 9am–6pm; 60Kč, students 40Kč) is approached by a street lined with Baroque saints and angels. To the right is the former Jesuit College, now the Kutná Hora Arts Centre.

7

7

Italian Court

From Palackého náměstí head down 28 října to the **Italian Court** (Vlašský dvůr) where coins were once minted. Exhibits re-create working conditions, and there's an exhaustive collection of Kutná Hora coins. Entrance is by guided tour only (daily; April–Sept 9am–6pm; March & Oct 10am–5pm; Nov–Feb 10am–4pm; 105Kč).

Czech Silver Museum

In a medieval fort at the junction of Barborská and Ruthardská is the **Czech Silver Museum** (Tues–Sun: April & Oct 9am–5pm; May, June & Sept 9am–6pm; July & Aug 10am–6pm; ⓦcms-kh.cz, 160Kč), where tourists can stroll the ancient mines in white coats and goggles.

ARRIVAL AND INFORMATION

By train Trains leave from Prague Main Station (10 daily; 50min). Kutná Hora's station is out of town, near Sedlec (useful for visiting the ossuary). Take bus #1 or #4 into the town centre.

By bus Buses leave from Prague's Háje metro station (hourly; 1hr).

Tourist office Palackého náměstí 377 (April–Sept daily 9am–6pm; Oct–March Mon–Fri 9am–5pm, Sat & Sun 10am–4pm; ☏327 512 378, ⓦkutnahora.cz). Can book private rooms and has internet access.

EATING AND DRINKING

Barborská Barborská 35. This miniature cocktail bar has a friendly vibe and really gets going at the weekends, when it's one of the last bars in town to close. Mon–Thurs 4pm–1am, Fri & Sat 4pm–3am.

Dačický Rakova 8. For hearty Czech meat-and-dumpling comfort food and local dark beer, head to this arched, dimly lit beerhall for the best Kutná Hora has to offer. Mains 149–790Kč. Daily 11am–11pm.

Kavárna na Kozím Plácku Dačického náměstí 10 ⓦkoziplacek.cz. This busy café near the Church of St James has a comfy interior, and is very popular with lovers of serious coffee. Daily 10am–10pm.

ČESKÉ BUDĚJOVICE

ČESKÉ BUDĚJOVICE is a sweet kernel of medieval town inside a tough shell of industrial sprawl. Settled in 1265, it has been associated with the brewing industry since the beginning, when citizens brewed lager for the Holy Roman Emperor. In the seventeenth century war and fire devastated the town, but it was lavishly rebuilt by the Habsburgs. Today its elegant arcades and winding backstreets are the perfect place to enjoy a Budvar beer (the original Budweiser) – which is, after all, the reason most people come here.

WHAT TO SEE AND DO

The compact medieval town centre forms a grid around magnificent **Přemysla Otakara II Square**, one of Europe's largest marketplaces. Just off the square is Black Tower (Černá věž; July & Aug daily 10am–6pm; Sept–June Tues–Sat 10am–6pm; 30Kč, students 20Kč), which you can climb for good views.

Budvar brewery

The **Budvar brewery** is 2.5km up the road to Prague, on Karolíny Světlé (bus #2). You'll need to book ahead for a one-hour English tour (March–Dec daily 9am–5pm; Jan & Feb Tues–Sat 9am–5pm; 120Kč; ☏387 705 347, ⓦvisitbudvar.cz).

ARRIVAL AND DEPARTURE

By train The train station is a 10min walk from the old town: head west along Lannova třída. It's possible to visit from Prague on a day-trip, but if you want to tour the brewery consider staying overnight: there's left-luggage storage at the station.

Destinations Brno (4 daily; 4hr 24min); Český Krumlov (10 daily; 45min); Plzeň (every 2hr; 1hr 52min); Prague (up to 10 daily; 2hr 20min).

By bus The bus station is by the train station, and has left-luggage facilities.

Destinations Brno (7 daily; 3hr 30min); Český Krumlov (approx every 30min; 35–45min); Prague (up to 10 daily; 2hr 30min–3hr 30min).

INFORMATION

Tourist office Náměstí Přemysla Otakara II. 1 (June–Sept Mon–Fri 8.30am–6pm, Sat 8.30am–5pm, Sun 10am–4pm; Oct–May Mon–Fri 9am–4pm, Sat 9am–1pm; ☏386 801 413, ⓦc-budejovice.cz).

ACCOMMODATION

Café Hostel Panská 13 ☏608 909 220, ⓦcafehostel.cz. This basic but well-maintained hostel lurks above a funky café in Kutná Hora's historical centre. There are only ten beds, so booking ahead is advisable. Dorms 380Kč

Penzion Centrum Biskupská 3 ☎387 311 801, ⓦpenzioncentrum.cz. Centrally located in a typical, renovated Kutná Hora townhouse, this guesthouse has bright, comfortably furnished rooms with en-suite facilities. The price includes a buffet breakfast. Doubles 1400Kč
Ubytovna u nádraží Dvořákova 14 ☎734 200 826, ⓦubytovna.vors.cz. České Budějovice isn't the cheapest city to stay in, so this is a decent choice, located in a dour housing block a 10min walk from the centre. The rooms are private but have shared facilities. Doubles 720Kč

EATING AND DRINKING

Hladový vokno Hroznová 34 ⓦhladovyvokno.cz. When your budget's tight and your belt's loose, head to *Hladový vokno* (Hungry Window) for a hefty kebab or burger (45–99Kč). Mon–Thurs 10.30am–11pm, Fri 10.30am–12.30am, Sat 6pm–12.30am.
Indická Resaurace Chelčického 10 ⓦindickarestaurace .cz. Climb a poky private staircase to find this well-loved, award-winning Indian restaurant, known for warm service and lovingly cooked food. Lunch specials 75–125Kč, mains 120–190Kč. Mon–Sat 11am–11pm.
Masné Krámy Krajinská 13 ⓦmasne-kramy.cz. Locals call it "the beer church" – an arched lofty Renaissance meat-market devoted to local beer. Don't miss the excellent unfiltered yeast beer (*kroužkovaný ležák*). Mains 149–369Kč. Mon–Thurs 10.30am–11pm, Fri & Sat 10.30am–midnight, Sun 10.30am–9pm.
Minipivovar Krajinská 27 Krajinská 27. Award-winning microbrewery producing five lagers that can give Budvar a good run for its money. Mains 120–190Kč. Mon–Thurs 11am–11pm, Fri & Sat 11am–11.45pm.
Pavlač Hroznova 9. Popular place just off the main square with a wide-ranging menu including vegetarian options. Mains 120–270Kč. Mon–Thurs 10am–10pm, Fri & Sat 10am–midnight, Sun 11am–10pm.

ČESKÝ KRUMLOV

Quaint, picturesque, red-roofed **ČESKÝ KRUMLOV** nestles amid the meanders of the sluggish River Vltava, just setting out on its journey to Prague. A UNESCO World Heritage Site since 1992, the town is deservedly popular, with tour buses unloading crowds of visitors at the city gates at noon for a five-hour stampede through the narrow streets – for a more enjoyable experience, stay overnight and avoid the crowds.

WHAT TO SEE AND DO

The twisting River Vltava divides the town into two: circular Staré Město on the right bank and the Latrán quarter on the left.

Krumlov Chateau

Krumlov Chateau (guided tours Tues–Sun: April, May, Sept & Oct 9am–4pm; June–Aug 9am–5pm; 130–240Kč; ⓦzamek-ceskykrumlov.eu) rises above the Latrán quarter. You can stroll through the castle's grounds and main courtyards for free day or night, or take a guided tour of the chateau itself. Climb the tower for beautiful views and explore the chateau's geometrical gardens and two theatres, the exquisite Rococo Chateau Theatre, and the cunning Communist Revolving Theatre, which spins on a mechanical axis.

The Eggenberg Brewery

A world away from the stainless-steel and fizz of the breweries at Plzeň and České Budějovice is the **Eggenberg**, which opened in 1630. Tours cost from 100Kč (daily at 11am; ☎380 711 225, ⓦeggenberg.cz). The restaurant serves good traditional food.

Egon Schiele Art Centrum

Just off the main square, on Široká, is the superb **Egon Schiele Art Centrum** (daily 10am–6pm; 160Kč; ☎380 704 011; ⓦschieleartcentrum.cz), devoted to the eponymous Austrian painter, who moved here in 1911 and caused outrage by painting nude teenagers and putting his feet on café tables. There are also temporary exhibitions of contemporary art and design.

ARRIVAL AND DEPARTURE

By train The train station is 1km south of the centre.
Destinations České Budějovice (10 daily; 45min); Prague (9 daily, 3hr 20min–4hr; change at České Budějovice).
By bus The bus station is a 5min walk northeast of the inner town.
Destinations České Budějovice (approx every 30min; 35–45min); Prague (hourly; 3hr).

INFORMATION AND TOURS

Tourist office Náměstí Svornosti 2 (April, May, Sept & Oct Mon–Fri 9am–6pm, Sat & Sun 9am–6pm, closed noon–1pm; June–Aug Mon–Fri 9am–7pm, Sat & Sun 9am–7pm, closed 1–2pm; Nov–March Mon–Fri

9am–5pm, Sat & Sun 9am–5pm, closed noon–1pm; ☎ 380 704 622, ⓦ www.ckrumlov.info).

Tours and rental Expedicion (Soukenická 33 ⓦ expedicion.cz) offers fishing (790Kč/5hr), horseriding (300Kč/hr), rafting/kayaking (from 550Kč/person) bike riding and climbing expeditions. Vltava Sport Service (Hradební 60 ⓦ ckvltava.cz) rents bikes, scooters, canoes and rafts. Bikes 330Kč/day, boat rental from 450Kč/4hr trip.

ACCOMMODATION

Hostel 99 Věžní 99 ☎ 775 276 253, ⓦ hostel99.cz. A kitchen, table tennis, movies, informative staff, a bar and (overpriced) restaurant. Come summer the dorms resemble high-school pyjama parties. The rafting pub crawl is famous. Dorms 300Kč, doubles 800Kč

Hostel Merlin Kájovská 59 ☎ 606 256 145, ⓦ hostelmerlin.com. Clean, cheap rooms overlooking the river with shared bathrooms and a kitchen. Dorms 250Kč, doubles 500Kč

★ **Krumlov House Hostel** Rooseveltova 68 ☎ 380 711 935, ⓦ krumlovhostel.com. A renovated Renaissance bakery as warm and cheering as fresh bread. There are private rooms and dorms, a common room, large kitchen and films. Dorms 385Kč, doubles 935Kč

U Čerta a Káči Dlouhá 100 ☎ 777 615 903, ⓦ certakaca .cz. This central *pension* looks like a dolls' house, with low wooden beams, heart-print curtains and a tiny kitchen. Doubles 1300Kč

Vodácký kemp Nové Spolí ☎ 777 640 946, ⓦ kempkrumlov.cz. Basic campsite in a picturesque spot by the river, 2km from the town, reachable by the #3 bus from the train or bus station. May–Sept. Per person 55Kč, plus per tent 50Kč

EATING AND DRINKING

Antre Horní 2 ⓦ www.klubantre.cz. This dapper 1930s café and music club in České's municipal theatre serves everything from breakfast, mid-morning snacks and cakes through to cocktails, wine and beer accompanied by live jazz. Daily 10am–midnight.

Cikánská Jizba Dlouh 31 ⓦ cikanskajizba.cz. Tightly packed into a medieval vaulted space, the *Cikánská Jizba* (Gypsy Cottage) is a standard Czech pub every night except

---

ČESKÝ KRUMLOV FESTIVALS

Five Petalled Rose Festival June at the summer solstice; ⓦ www.slavnostipeti-listeruze.eu. Medieval fair with jousting, fencing and theatre in the park.

International Music Festival July–Aug; ⓦ www.festivalkrumlov.cz. Large multi-genre music festival which usually attracts a few big names.

---

on Fridays, when talented local Roma musicians play. Daily 1pm–midnight.

Depo Pub Latrán 74. One of the new breed of clean-cut Czech pubs serving Plzeň beer and a higher class of Czech food in an industrial setting. Mains 70–280Kč. Daily 11am–11pm.

Egon Schiele Café Široká 71. A snug sitting room of a gallery café which locals say serves the best coffee in Krumlov. There's chess, board games, books and wi-fi. Tues–Sun 10am–6pm.

Na Louži Kájovská 66. This long-established hotel restaurant serves up the best Czech cooking in town. Local carp, roast duck and fruit dumplings (*ovocné knedlíky*), served with melted butter and sprinkled with hard sweet cheese, are the dishes to go for. Mains 114–239Kč. Daily 10am–11pm.

U dwau Maryí Parkán 104. Ye olde Bohemian food as it never was, but who's complaining? Gruel, rabbit, mead and millet all served up on a riverside terrace. Mains 70–185Kč. Daily 11am–11pm.

PLZEŇ

Rough and ready, industrial **PLZEŇ** (Pilsen) was built on beer and bombs. Bohemia's second city was founded in 1292 then swelled in the nineteenth century when the Industrial Revolution brought an ironworks and an armaments factory, and diversified to cars and trams under Communism. Most tourists come to pay their respects to Plzeň's greatest gift to the beverage world, Pilsner Urquell. The town's diverse architecture and unpretentious vigour come a distant second. Somewhat surprisingly, Pilzeň was European Capital of Culture in 2015, though the event has left little legacy in this gritty, working city.

WHAT TO SEE AND DO

The main square, náměstí Republiky, is dominated by the Gothic **Cathedral of sv Bartoloměj**, with the tallest spire in the country (103m). Opposite is the Italianate town hall, built in the Renaissance but sgraffitoed last century. Nearby, at Sady Pětatřicátníků 11, the **Velká synagoga** (April–Oct Sun–Fri, except Jewish holidays 10am–6pm; 70Kč adults, 40Kč students), the third largest in the world, was once the heart of the town's large Jewish community, but was decimated by the Holocaust. It now houses Jewish-themed exhibitions.

Pilsner Urquell and Brewery Museums

Plzeň's star attraction is the Plzeňský Prazdroj Brewery, better known by its German name, **Pilsner Urquell**, U Prazdroje 7 (English guided tours Mon–Fri 1pm plus 2.45pm or 4.15pm, Sat & Sun 10.45am, 1pm, 2.45pm & 4.30pm; 200Kč; ☎377 062 888, Ⓦprazdrojvisit.cz/en). In the original brewery, at Veleslavínova 6, the **Pivovarské Brewery Museum** provides some history and a film on brewing (daily: April–Sept 10am–6pm; Oct–March 10am–5pm; adult 90Kč).

Plzeň's Historical Underground

Tours leave from the Brewery Museum (see above) to explore **Plzeň's Historical Underground** (Plzeňské historické podzemí; daily: April–Nov 10am–6pm; Dec–March 10am–5pm; English tour daily at 2.20pm plus Sat & Sun 11.20am; 120Kč, students 90Kč; ☎377 235 574, Ⓦplzenskepodzemi.cz), 500m of tunnels under the town. The tunnels were once part of an underground network of passages that rivalled the streets above.

ARRIVAL AND INFORMATION

By bus You can get to Plzeň from Prague in around 1hr by bus from Zličín with Student Agency. The bus terminal (Pilzeň CAN on timetables) is on the west side of town, a 10min walk from the centre.
Destinations Karlovy Vary (7 daily; 1hr 40min); Prague (at least hourly; 1hr–1hr 30min).
By train The main train station (Hlavní nádraží) is just east of the city centre, a 10min walk away.
Destinations České Budějovice (every 2hr; 1hr 52min); Prague (hourly; 1hr 30min).
Tourist office Náměsti Republiky 41 (daily: April–Sept 9am–7pm; Oct–March 9am–6pm; ☎378 035 330, Ⓦpilsen.eu).

ACCOMMODATION

Euro Hostel Na Roudné 13 ☎377 259 926, Ⓦeurohostel.cz. This hostel offers basic, no-frills dorms and doubles just a 10min walk from the centre. Opt out of breakfast, which is overpriced. Dorms 400Kč, doubles 1000Kč
Pension City Sady 5 května 52 ☎377 326 069, Ⓦpensioncityplzen.cz. The rooms at this conveniently located guesthouse by the river are acceptable if slightly dated. A buffet breakfast is included in the price. Doubles 1490Kč

Pension Stará Plzeň Na Roudné 12 ☎377 259 901, Ⓦpension-sp.cz. The owners of this guesthouse have converted an old rustic house and stables into a handsome old-fashioned pension. Breakfast is an extra 130Kč. Doubles 900Kč
Pension V Solní Solní 8 ☎377 236 652, Ⓦvolny.cz /pensolni. Just off the main square, this cosy *pension* has just three rooms so should definitely be booked in advance. Breakfast is a very reasonable 85Kč extra. Doubles 1020Kč

EATING AND DRINKING

Anděl Bistro Bezručova 7 Ⓦandelcafe.cz. A city-centre restaurant serving extraordinarily fresh and healthy lunch specials (75–120Kč) to a hungry office-worker clientele. Mon–Thurs 7.30am–midnight, Fri 7.30am–1am, Sat 9am–1am, Sun 11am–10pm.
Francis Náměstí Republiky 3. 1950s rock-playing student bar-café with a wood-burning stove for winter, a courtyard for summer, sausages for the hungry and books for the antisocial. Mon–Fri 2–10pm, Sat & Sun 4–10pm.
Měšťanská Beseda Kavárna Kopeckého sady 13. Opulent Art Nouveau interior, beer on tap, old men playing chess and delectable honey chocolates (*medový koule*) make this the place for a rainy afternoon. Mon–Fri 9am–11pm, Sat 11am–11pm, Sun 11am–9pm.
Na Parkánu Veleslavínova 4 Ⓦnaparkanu.com. It may be the Brewery Museum pub, but lusty portions, unfiltered beer and decent prices make it popular with locals. Cheap lunch menu 110Kč (Mon–Fri 11am–2pm); mains 75–300Kč. Mon–Wed 11am–11pm, Thurs 11am–midnight, Fri–Sat 11am–1am, Sun 11am–10pm.
Rango Pražská 10 Ⓦrango.cz. Near the main square, this is one of Plzeň's best non-Czech restaurants serving up well-crafted Mediterranean fare in an atmospherically lit stone cellar. The wine list features some Czech vintages. Mains 150–400Kč. Daily noon–11pm.

KARLOVY VARY

You might be forgiven for thinking you took a wrong turn and left the Czech Republic when you reach the heart of **Karlovy Vary**. This over-renovated spa town, awash with fur hats and poodles in D&G handbags, feels decidedly un-Czech, largely due to its (now slightly waning) popularity with Russia's wealthy and partly because tourists outnumber locals. Peter the Great, Goethe and Beethoven all visited the town, and the old-style pleasures of central European spa life – hiking in the forest, bathing in hot spring water, and eating sweet nut

7

wafers (*oplatky*) to chase away the taste of the water – are still the best.

The town is orientated to Russian tourists, and finding English-speakers is harder than elsewhere – so bring your phrasebook. Euros are readily accepted.

WHAT TO SEE AND DO

Walking into town with the Communist eyesore *Thermal Hotel* on your right, you'll pass a series of colonnades built over the hot springs. The grandest is the **Mill Colonnade** (Mlýnská kolonáda), containing five springs. Further up Lázeňská street are **Market Colonnade** (Tržní kolonáda), a delicate timber construction, and the Communist-era **Hot Spring Colonnade** (Vřídelní kolonáda), a spring so hot and powerful (actually a geyser) that spa guests breathe the vapours instead of drinking the water.

Spa treatments

Sampling the bitter spring waters is free, though you'll need to buy a drinking cup from a kiosk, or bring a plastic bottle. For swimming, the cheapest option is the *Thermal Hotel*'s springwater hilltop pool (daily 10am–8pm, last entrance 7pm; 200Kč for 120min, 140Kč with ISIC; ⓦthermal.cz): follow the signs for "Bazén" (pool).

Hiking

The cool pine forests surrounding Karlovy Vary are perfect for **hiking**, and there are dozens of well-marked trails. One popular route climbs from *Grand Hotel Pupp* to a viewing tower and hilltop restaurant *Diana*, 1.5km away. Alternatively, you can take a **funicular** up to the viewing tower (daily: Feb–March & Nov–Dec 9am–5pm; April, May & Oct 9am–6pm; June–Sept 9am–7pm; 80Kč return).

Moser glassworks and museum

Luxury glass manufacturer **Moser** lies in the town's suburbs, at Kpt Jaroše 46. You can tour the glassworks and glass museum (tours every 30min; daily 9am–2.30pm; 180Kč, students 100Kč; ☎353 416 132, ⓦmoser-glass.com). Take bus #22 or #1 from Tržnice to the Moser stop.

ARRIVAL AND INFORMATION

By train Trains from Prague arrive at the newly renovated Horní station, to the north of town. Trains from Mariánské Lázně arrive at Dolní station, close to the main bus station and town centre.

Destinations Plzeň (7 daily; 3hr, with a change in Mariánské Lázně; 1 daily; 2hr 48min, direct); Prague (4 daily; 3hr 15min).

By bus Buses run to the spa from both train stations. From Prague, alight one stop early at Tržnice, right in the centre. The Student Agency bus from Prague Florenc is your best option (at least hourly; ☎800 100 300, ⓦstudentagency.cz).

Destinations Plzeň (7 daily; 1hr 40min); Prague (at least hourly; 2hr 15min).

Tourist office T.G. Masaryka 53 (Mon–Fri 8am–6pm, Sat & Sun 10am–1pm & 1.30–5pm; ☎355 321 171, ⓦkarlovyvary.cz). There's also tourist information at the Hot Spring Colonnade (see above).

ACCOMMODATION

Avoid the hotels that cluster around the spas: they're designed and priced for Russian oligarchs. Guesthouses and B&Bs are located around the bus and train stations. Private rooms are good value and can be booked through the tourist office. Karlovy Vary is generally not budget orientated – be prepared to stay outside the city for something affordable.

Březový Háj Campsite ☎777 944 252. Located on a riverbank, this small campsite 3km from the centre has tennis courts, a pool and bungalows. Catch the Březová bus from Tržiště bus station. April–Oct. Bungalows **400Kč**

Chebský Dvůr/Egerlander Hof Tržiště 39 ☎353 229 332, ⓦegerlanderhof.eu. Clean, basic rooms above a pub in the heart of the spa district. Doubles **1250Kč**

Kavalerie T.G. Masaryka 43 ☎353 229 613, ⓦkavalerie .cz. On the main street connecting the bus station and the centre, *Kavalerie* is a B&B over a café with homely rooms of three types: tourist, economy and standard (the difference is mostly in size), plus apartments. Price includes breakfast. Tourist doubles **920Kč**, economy doubles **1170Kč**

INTERNATIONAL FILM FESTIVAL

The **Karlovy Vary Film Festival** (ⓦkarlovyvary.cz) comes to town every July, bringing a smattering of A-listers and a carnival atmosphere. Anyone can buy tickets (80Kč) or day passes (250Kč/day) to the films, which range from Hollywood blockbusters to low-budget European indies. The town gets crowded so book accommodation and travel in advance.

Pension Fan U Trati 5 ☎ 353 997 085, ⓦ penzionfan.cz. On the north side of the River Ohře, near the main railway station, this much-lauded place has spick-and-span rooms and a tiny gym. Breakfast is a cheeky 190Kč extra. Doubles __1240Kč__

EATING AND DRINKING

Kavárna Čas T.G. Masaryka 3. Quiet little cinema coffee shop filled with the scent of popcorn and sweets, free of tour groups and serving excellent Italian espresso. Daily 10am–8pm.

KusKus Bělehradská 8 ⓦ kus-kus.cz. If you need a break from the usual Czech meat-and-dumpling combos, try this charming, simple café, which serves organic, vegetarian and vegan sandwiches, salads, cakes and snacks, eat-in or takeaway. Mon–Fri 7.30am–3pm.

Rad's Baguettes Zeyerova 2 ⓦ radsbaguettes.cz. The only inexpensive sandwich shop in the town centre serves up filling sandwiches, panini and baguettes – all for under 45Kč. Mon–Fri 7am–6pm, Sat 8am–noon.

Tandoor I.P. Pavlova 25. It's hard to find, hidden down a private driveway, but this rare Indian restaurant is worth searching out for the pleasant service and high price-to-portion-size ratio. Mains around 130Kč. Mon–Sat noon–9pm.

U Švejka Stará Louka 10 ⓦ svejk-kv.cz. The least overpriced of the central restaurants. High prices are balanced by the large portions of hearty Czech fare. Mains 139–360Kč. Daily 11am–11pm.

Moravia

The eastern third of the country, **Moravia** (Morava), moves at a slower pace than Bohemia, but is warmer, more welcoming and a touch more relaxed. It shares borders with Poland to the north, and Slovakia and Austria to the south. In the southeast of Moravia is bustling, industrial **Brno**, with red-brick houses and wide boulevards, while in the north is the ancient city of **Olomouc**, bursting with youthful energy.

BRNO

BRNO evolved into today's handsome, central European city during the nineteenth century, when it was a major textile producer and known as "rakouský Manchestr" (Austrian Manchester). The Czech Republic's

BURČÁK

From September, there are boisterous **vinobraní** festivals all over the country, marking the grape harvest – with the best in wine country, Moravia. Revellers dance, drink and feast in an event that dates back to the Middle Ages, and the star of the show is **burčák**, wine fresh from the press. Sweet and bubbly, it's only part fermented so it tastes as innocent as peach juice, but it's up to 8 percent alcohol. It's only available from late August to late November at festivals, wine bars and markets. For more information, check ⓦ wineofczechrepublic.cz.

7

second city and the capital of Moravia, Brno's energy has produced eleven universities, a powerful economy and a number of famous Czechs, including inventor of genetics Gregor Mendel, composer Leoš Janáček and novelist Milan Kundera.

WHAT TO SEE AND DO

Triangular **Svobody Square** (náměstí Svobody) sits funnel-like on the high street, Masarykova. To the right of the high street is **Zelný trh**, the old medieval Vegetable Market, still bustling with traders hawking onions and daffodils. **Špilberk Castle**, which houses historical exhibitions, dominates the skyline to the west, in a standoff with the hilltop **Cathedral of St Peter and St Paul** to the south.

Capuchin crypt

Below Zelný trh is the Capuchin monastery, with its popular **crypt** (April–Oct Mon–Sat 9am–6pm, Sun 11am–5pm; Nov–March Mon–Sat 10am–4pm, Sun 11am–4.30pm), which houses a charming collection of mummified monks.

The Old Town Hall

On Stará Radnice is the **Old Town Hall**, packed with strange artefacts clothed in fantastical legends. Its tower (April–Sept daily 8.30am–6pm; 60Kč) offers panoramic views of Brno.

7

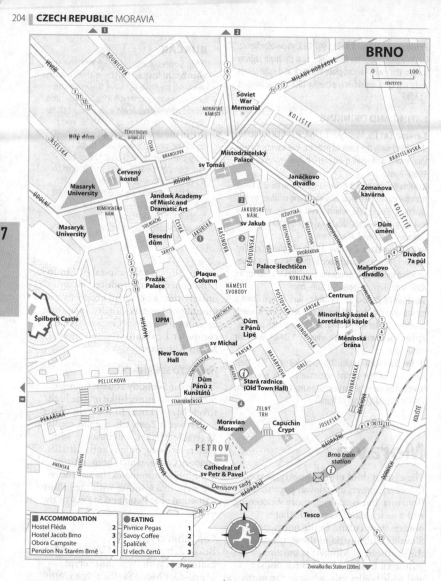

BRNO

0 _____ 100
metres

ACCOMMODATION
Hostel Fléda	2
Hostel Jacob Brno	3
Obora Campsite	1
Penzion Na Starém Brně	4

EATING
Pivnice Pegas	1
Savoy Coffee	2
Špalíček	4
U všech čertů	3

Brno Underground

It's possible to explore **Brno Underground**, some renovated cellars beneath the Zelný trh, including a labyrinth with an ossuary filled with 50,000 skeletons (Tues–Sun 9am–6pm; 160Kč).

ARRIVAL AND INFORMATION

By plane Brno's Tuřany airport (⊕ brno-airport.cz) is 8km from the centre. From the airport, take bus #76 to the main bus station. Both Ryanair and Wizz Air fly to Brno.

By train Brno's main train station is on the southern edge of the historical city centre. This is a large station with a full range of services.

Destinations Bratislava (every 2hr; 1hr 26min); České Budějovice (every 2hr; 4hr 30min); Olomouc (hourly; 1hr 33min–2hr 15min); Prague (at least hourly; 2hr 30min–3hr 30min).

By bus The old-fashioned Zvonařka bus station is a short walk from the train station. Some buses leave from a stop outside the *Grand Hotel* on Benešova třída.

Destinations Olomouc (at least hourly; 1hr–1hr 50min); Prague (3 hourly; 2hr 30min).

Tourist office Old Town Hall at Radnická 8 (Mon–Fri 8.30am–6pm, Sat & Sun 9am–6pm; ☎ 542 427 150, ☲ ticbrno.cz).

ACCOMMODATION

Brno hosts trade fairs from August to October, February and April, as well as a Moto GP in August, so book in advance during those months.

Hostel Fléda Štefánikova 24 ☎ 731 651 005, ☲ hostelfleda.com. Bare-bones, 48-bed hostel above a nightclub, *Club Fléda*. It's a bit of a party hostel so not for those in search of sleep at weekends. Catch tram #1 or #6 to Hrnčířská. Doubles have shared baths. Dorms 200Kč, doubles 800Kč

Hostel Jacob Brno Jakubské náměstí 7 ☎ 542 210 466, ☲ hosteljacob.cz. Clean and bright, the 37-bed *Jacob* is centrally located and has a well-equipped kitchen. Dorms 380Kč, doubles 1040Kč

Obora Campsite Rakovecká 72 ☎ 723 666 443, ☲ autocampobora.cz. Lakeside campsite 15min from the train station (tram #1 to the zoo, then bus #103). May–Sept. Camping/person 100Kč, plus per tent 80Kč, bungalows 500Kč

Penzion Na Starém Brně Mendlovo náměstí 1a ☎ 543 247 872, ☲ pension-brno.com. Genteel B&B in a former monastery. Go through Vankovka shopping centre from the train and bus stations and take tram #1 to Mendlovo náměstí. Breakfast 80Kč extra. Doubles 1200Kč

EATING AND DRINKING

As Brno gets classier, so do its restaurants and prices. It's still a university town though, so join the queues at one of the food stands on either Kobližná or Benešova for a cheap and filling *gyro* or pizza.

Pivnice Pegas Jakubská 4. Gregarious microbrewery rambling through numerous oak-panelled rooms. Dumplings with everything, wheat beer and a table shortage. Mains 80–370Kč. Mon–Sat 9am–midnight, Sun 11am–11pm.

Savoy Coffee Jakubské náměsti 1 ☲ savoy-brno.cz. Regal coffeehouse returned to its functionalist glory after decades as a Communist button shop. Mon–Fri 9am–midnight, Sat & Sun 11am–midnight.

Špalíček Zelný trh 12. Meat-and-potatoes Moravian cuisine, Starobrno beer, outdoor seating above the vegetable market and a 149Kč 3-course lunch menu. Mains 89–300Kč. Daily 11am–11pm.

U všech čertů Dvořákova 6/8 ☲ ucertu.cz. Popular pub with a good beer list and huge portions of food. Lunch specials 100Kč, mains 98–219Kč. Mon–Thurs 11am–midnight, Fri 11am–late, Sat noon–late, Sun noon–midnight.

OLOMOUC

One of the Czech Republic's most attractive towns, **Oloumouc** is often overlooked and remains one of the country's (virtually) undiscovered gems. In the Middle Ages the city was the capital of the Great Moravian Empire, and its wealth crystallized into magnificent palaces and churches before trickling away to Brno carrying a wave of industrial sprawl. The unspoilt city centre is home to 25,000 students, who ensure a rich supply of lively bars, cafés and clubs.

WHAT TO SEE AND DO

7

The old town clusters around two adjacent squares, **Horní** (upper) and **Dolní** (lower). The town hall on Horní has an astronomical clock, an object of exuberant Communist kitsch covered with gesticulating blonde peasants. Nearby is the polygonal Holy Trinity Column, protected by UNESCO, the largest plague column in the country.

Cathedral of sv Václav and the Archdiocesan Museum

Dwarfing tiny Václavské Square is the **Cathedral of sv Václav**, originally a Romanesque basilica, which contains a

> ## FESTIVAL FRENZY
>
> With its reputation as a cultural and artistic centre, Olomouc is a natural home for festivals. April brings **Academia Film** (☲ afo.cz), screening international science documentaries, and flower festival **Flora Olomouc** (☲ flora-ol.cz). In May, the **Dvořák Festival** (☲ mfo.cz) celebrates all the major Czech composers. The **Olomouc City Festival** (☲ olomouc.eu) is held at the beginning of June, while the **Summer of Culture in Olomouc** (☲ olomouckekulturniprazdniny.cz) runs through July and August with theatre, music and exhibitions throughout the city. In September, there's the **Organ Music Festival** and **Fall Festival of Sacred Music**, culminating, at the end of the month, in **Beerfest** (☲ beerfest.cz), an enjoyable combination of beer, rock music and gastronomy.

crypt (May–Oct Mon–Wed 10am–5pm, Thurs 9am–4pm, Fri & Sat 9am–5pm, Sun 11am–5pm) packed with reliquaries. Next door is the **Archdiocesan Museum** (Tues–Sun 10am–6pm; 70Kč), showcasing more than a thousand years of local history and a mind-blowing collection of church bling. The highlight is a gold-plated carriage covered with romping cherubs.

Olomouc Museum of Art

With interesting permanent exhibitions and great temporary ones, the **Olomouc Museum of Art** on Denisova (Tues–Sun 10am–6pm; 70Kč; ⓦwww.olmuart.cz) provides an enjoyable stroll through twentieth-century Czech art.

ARRIVAL AND INFORMATION

By train The train station is 1.5km east of the centre; catch tram #2, #4 or #6 to get into town.
Destinations Brno (hourly; 1hr 33min–2hr 15min); Prague (at least hourly; approx 2hr 20min).
By bus The bus station is 3km east of the city centre; catch tram #4.
Destinations Brno (at least hourly; 1hr–1hr 50min).
Tourist office Town Hall, Horní náměsti (daily 9am–7pm; ☎585 513 385, ⓦtourism.olomouc.eu).

ACCOMMODATION

Cosy Corner Hostel Sokolská 1 ☎777 570 730, ⓦcosycornerhostel.com. This Czech/Aussie-owned hostel occupies two brightly painted 1930s flats. The place has a now rare, old-school backpacker vibe, and there's a kitchen for self-caterers. Dorms 420Kč
Pension Moravia Dvořákova 37 ☎603 784 188, ⓦpension-moravia.com. Just a 10min walk from the city centre, this large suburban house has been converted into a welcoming B&B. Its owners are well clued up about what to see and do in the city. Doubles 900Kč
Pension U Jakuba 8. května 9 ☎585 209 995, ⓦpensionujakuba.cz. If you are looking for an affordable, central guesthouse with well-maintained, comfortable rooms, this is the place to head. Advance booking is recommended. Doubles 1190Kč, 4-bed apartments 2460Kč

EATING, DRINKING AND ENTERTAINMENT

CAFÉS AND RESTAURANTS

Café 87 Denisova 47. A great café near the museum that is celebrated for its fresh sandwiches, good coffee, excellent street-gazing opportunities and famous chocolate pie. It's naturally popular with students. Mon–Fri 7am–9pm, Sat & Sun 8am–9pm.
Caffè Dolce Vita Tř. 1. máje 38. This smart non-smoking café serves up well-priced Czech and international dishes and delicious coffee, accompanied by polite, competent service. Mon–Fri 8am–7pm, Sat 9am–7pm.
Green Bar Ztracená 3 ⓦgreenbar.cz. A self-service vegetarian canteen, where you pay by the weight – 21Kč per 100g – for fresh hot and cold meat-free dishes, salads and desserts. In summer there's a street-side alfresco seating area. Mon–Fri 10am–5pm.
Kathmandu Dolní náměstí 25 ⓦnepalirestaurant.cz. The 110Kč lunch menu is a great deal at this Nepalese restaurant – or go for the vegetarian version for 100Kč. Tandoori meals and other curries come in around 120Kč a dish. Mon–Sat 11am–10pm.
★**Moritz** Nešverova 2 ⓦhostinec-moritz.cz. Olomouc's finest microbrewery serves light, delicate lager and hearty Moravian cuisine. Try the open sandwiches with bitter *tvarůžky* cheese marinated in beer, or roast duck with cabbage and dumplings. There's a beer garden in summer with live music. Mains 95–290Kč. Sun–Thurs 11am–11pm, Fri & Sat 11am–midnight.

BARS AND CLUBS

15Minut Komenského 31. A few steps away from the university dorms and filled with wildly enthusiastic students every weekend. Their riotous two-day Erasmus Party in September is infamous. Daily 6pm–4am.
The Black Stuff Irish Pub 1. máje 19 ⓦblackstuff.cz. Railway tunnel meets hobbit drinking hole, popular with students. Lots of ethanol-based beverages on offer. Mon–Thurs 4pm–2am, Fri 4pm–3am, Sat 5pm–3am, Sun 5–11pm.
Koktejly & sny Uhelná 8 ⓦkoktejlyasny.cz. "Cocktails and Dreams" is a 1950s throwback, with retro kitsch decor and excellent cocktails. Mon–Wed 8am–midnight, Thurs–Fri 8am–1am, Sat 10.30am–1am, Sun 10.30am–9pm.
Vertigo Klub Univerzitní 6 ⓦklubvertigo.cz. Named after Hitchcock's masterpiece, this atmospheric underground student bar is filled with loquacious philosophy students and a smell that isn't quite tobacco. Mon–Thurs 1pm–2am, Fri & Sun 4pm–2am.

OLD SKAGEN, JUTLAND

Denmark

HIGHLIGHTS

① Copenhagen by bike Explore one of the world's best cycle networks. **See p.210**

② Kødbyen Dance all night in the capital's hipster hotbed. **See p.222**

③ Viking Ship Museum, Roskilde Gawk at the art of Viking shipbuilding at one of Denmark's best museums. **See p.226**

④ H.C. Andersens Hus Legendary author's fairytale museum. **See p.227**

⑤ Aalborg Parade the city's stunning new waterfront, then head out to Scandinavia's largest Viking burial site. **See p.233**

⑥ Skagen Breathtaking, heather-topped, sand-dune beaches. **See p.235**

HIGHLIGHTS ARE MARKED ON THE MAP ON P.209

ROUGH COSTS

Daily budget Basic €55, occasional treat €85

Drink Carlsberg (pint) €5

Food *Pølser* (Danish hot dog) €3.50

Hostel/budget hotel €25/€65

Travel Train: Copenhagen–Århus, €55; bus: €42

FACT FILE

Population 5.6 million

Language Danish

Currency Danish krone (kr)

Capital Copenhagen

International phone code ☎45

Time zone GMT +1hr

Introduction

From being a little-known, little-understood country wedged between mainland Europe and the rest of Scandinavia, Denmark has morphed into an international cultural powerhouse with multiple Michelin-starred restaurants and raved-about hit TV shows. But this international renown doesn't make the country any less thrilling to navigate on the ground and on a budget. Food-wise, you'd be hard pressed to find better butter, bacon and beer anywhere around, with some mean cheeses and pastries to boot. But don't expect this health-conscious people to sit around feasting all day: a bunch will have jogged past your table before you can say smørrebrød, and cycling is ubiquitous. With agriculture its primary industry, technological innovation and a focus on green energy is a big part of the economy of daily life. Culturally, too, it hits the high notes. Expect impeccable design and great musical offerings (especially jazz) at every turn. What's more, an ultra-efficient transport infrastructure makes Denmark one of Europe's most enjoyable countries to explore.

8

The nation has preserved its own distinct identity, exemplified by the universally cherished royal family and the reluctance to fully integrate with the EU (the Danish rejection of the euro was more about sovereignty than economics). There's also a sense of a small country that has long punched above its weight: it once controlled much of northern Europe and still maintains close ties with Greenland, its former colony.

Geographically, three main landmasses make up the country – the islands of Zealand and Funen and the peninsula of Jutland, which extends northwards from Germany. Most visitors make for **Zealand** (Sjælland) and, more specifically, **Copenhagen**, an exciting city with a beautiful old centre, an amazing array of museums and a boisterous nightlife. **Funen** (Fyn) has only one real urban draw, **Odense**, once home to Hans Christian Andersen; otherwise, it's renowned for cute villages and sandy beaches. **Jutland** (Jylland) has two of the sprightliest Danish cities in **Århus** and **Aalborg**, as well as scenery alternating between lonely beaches, gentle hills and heathland.

CHRONOLOGY

400 BC "Tollund Man" lives; his preserved body is discovered in a bog in 1950, and provides evidence of habitation during the Iron Age.

500 AD First mention of the "Dani" tribe is made by foreign sources.

695 First Christian mission to Denmark.

825 First Danish coinage introduced.

1397 The Union of Kalmar unites Denmark, Sweden and Norway (as well as Iceland, the Faroe Islands and the UK's Orkney and Shetland Islands) under a single Danish monarch.

1536 Reformation leads to the establishment of the Danish Lutheran Church.

1629 Sweden heavily defeats Charles IV's Denmark in the Thirty Years' War, resulting in Danish territorial losses.

1814 Denmark cedes Norway to Sweden.

1836 Hans Christian Andersen writes "The Little Mermaid".

1849 Constitutional monarchy established.

1864 Defeat by Prussia results in the loss of much territory.

1914 Neutrality is adopted during World War I.

1918 The vote is granted to all adult Danes.

1934 Children's playtime is transformed by the invention of Lego by Ole Kirk Christiansen.

1940 Nazi invasion meets minimal resistance.

1945 Denmark is liberated by Allied forces.

1979 Greenland is given greater autonomy by the Danish.

1989 First European country to legalize same-sex marriages.

1991 Danish police fire on protestors demonstrating against the country's acceptance of the Maastricht Treaty.

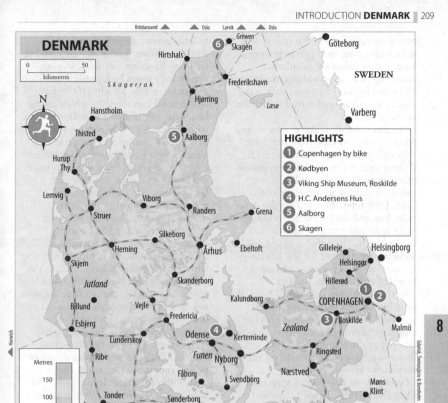

DENMARK

0 ————— 50
kilometres

N

S k a g e r r a k

Grèwen
Skagen
Hirtshals
Göteborg

SWEDEN

Frederikshavn

Hjørring

Hanstholm

Thisted

Læsø

Varberg

Hurup
Thy

Aalborg

Lemvig

Viborg

Struer

Randers

Grena

Skjern

Silkeborg

Herning

Jutland

Århus

Ebeltoft

Skanderborg

Billund

Vejle

Fredericia

Kalundborg

COPENHAGEN

Esbjerg

Lunderskov

Odense

Kerteminde

Zealand

Roskilde

Malmö

Ribe

Funen Nyborg

Ringsted

Gilleleje

Helsingborg

Helsingør

Hillerød

Tønder

Fåborg

Svendborg

Næstved

Møns
Klint

Sønderborg

Flensburg

Bagenkop

Rødby

Nykøbing

GERMANY

HIGHLIGHTS

1 Copenhagen by bike
2 Kødbyen
3 Viking Ship Museum, Roskilde
4 H.C. Andersens Hus
5 Aalborg
6 Skagen

Metres
150
100
0
below
sea level

Harwich

Gdańsk, Świnoujście & Bornholm

8

1992 Denmark wins European Football Championships.
2004 Crown Prince Frederick marries Tasmanian Mary Donaldson in a lavish ceremony.
2006 Cartoon depictions of the Prophet Mohammed in Danish newspapers spark mass protests in the Muslim world.
2009 UN climate change summit takes place in Denmark; the hoped-for global treaty does not materialize.
2011 Denmark criticized for reimposing border controls to stop flow of illegal immigration.
2014 Copenhagen restaurant *Noma* voted world's best restaurant by *Restaurant* magazine for third time.

ARRIVAL AND DEPARTURE

Visitors usually arrive in Copenhagen, either flying in to gleaming **Kastrup Airport** or pulling in to the city's **Central Station**, connected with the European rail network via Germany and, across the spectacular Øresund bridge, to Sweden.

Most international buses also arrive at Central Station. In addition, the **regional airports** at Aalborg, Århus and Billund handle a growing number of budget flights, mostly operated by Ryanair. There are regular **ferry services** to Sweden/Norway (via Frederikshavn or Hirtshals) and a rather lengthier connection to the Faroe Islands/Iceland (via Hirtshals).

GETTING AROUND

Denmark has a swift, easy-to-use public transport system. Danish State Railways (Danske Statsbaner or DSB; ⓦdsb.dk) runs an exhaustive, reliable **rail** network supplemented by a few privately owned rail lines. Services range from the large inter-city expresses (*lyntog*) to smaller local trains (*regionaltog*). InterRail/Eurail passes are valid on all DSB trains, with reduced rates on most privately owned lines. Ticket prices are calculated according to a countrywide zonal system, and travel by local transport within the zone of departure and arrival is included in the price.

The **bus** network is also extensive, and often supplements the train timetable, although prices don't work out much cheaper than trains. Some are operated privately and some by DSB itself; InterRail and Eurail passes are not valid. DSB **timetables** or *køreplan* detail train, bus and ferry services, including the S-train and metro systems in Copenhagen. The only buses not included are those of the few private companies; details of these can be found at train and bus stations.

Ferries or bridges link all of Denmark's principal islands. Where applicable, train and bus fares include the cost of crossings (although with ferries you can also pay at the terminal and walk on). Routes and prices are covered on the very useful HI map.

Cycling is the best way to appreciate Denmark's flat landscape (maps and information at ⓦcyklistforbundet.dk). Cycle paths proliferate, country roads have sparse traffic and all large towns have cycle tracks. Bikes can be rented at hostels, tourist offices and some train stations, as well as from bike rental shops (about 100kr/day, 400kr/week; 200–500kr deposit). All trains and most long-distance buses accept bikes, but you'll have to pay according to the zonal system used to calculate passenger tickets (12–60kr); 48kr to take your bike from Copenhagen to Århus by train. Reservations (30kr extra) are recommended (and obligatory on many trains May–Aug). In stations pick up a copy of *Bikes and Trains*, available in English, which goes into further detail.

ACCOMMODATION

Accommodation is a major expense, although there is a wide network of good-quality **hostels**. Most have a choice of private rooms, often with en-suite toilets/showers, as well as dorm accommodation; nearly all have cooking facilities. Rates are around 150kr per person for a dorm bed; non-HI members pay an extra 25kr a night (160kr for one-year HI membership, which can be bought at any affiliated hostel); travellers without bed linen will also need to pay to rent this. Danhostel Danmarks Vandrerhjem (ⓦdanhostel.dk) produces a free hostel guide. For a similar price, **sleep-ins** (smaller hostels aimed at backpackers) can be found chiefly in major towns, though some are open only in summer. There can be an age restriction (typically 35 or under). Local tourist offices have details.

Rooms at **hotels** can compare pricewise with private rooms in hostels. Expect to pay at least 550kr for a double room (and 450kr for a single), though note that this nearly always includes an all-you-can-eat breakfast. It's a good idea to book in advance, especially during peak season (this can also give you big discounts). Tourist offices can also supply details of **private rooms**, which usually cost 350–450kr for a double, plus a 50–70k booking fee. **Farmstays** (*Bondegårdsferie*; ⓦbondegaardsferie.dk) have become increasingly popular in recent years – digs can be either in rooms or camping (bring your own tent).

CAMPING

If you plan to **camp**, you'll need an international camping carnet, or a Camping Key Scandinavia (110kr), which is available at official campsites. A Transit Card (35kr) can be used for a single overnight stay. Most campsites are open from April to September, while a few stay open all year. There's a rigid **grading system**: one-star sites have toilets and showers; two-stars also have basic cooking facilities and a food shop within 2km; three-stars include a laundry and a TV room; four-stars also have a shop, while five-stars include a cafeteria. Prices are 75–100kr per person. Many campsites also have **cabins** to rent, usually with cooking facilities, for 2500kr–6000kr per week for a six-berth place, although they are often fully booked in summer months in advance (though occasionally you'll be able to rent a cabin for just a few days for around 300kr per night). Tourist offices offer a free leaflet listing all sites. **Camping rough** without permission is illegal, and an on-the-spot fine may be imposed. Good English-language information is available at ⓦdk-camp.dk; Danish Campsites (ⓦdanishcampsites.com) is a useful planning resource.

FOOD AND DRINK

Traditional **Danish food** is often characterized by rather stodgy meat or fish and veg combos, although the quality of ingredients is invariably excellent, especially with many chefs espousing the farm-to-plate or organic cooking ethos. Specialities worth seeking out include *stegt flæsk med persille sovs* (thinly sliced fried pork with boiled potatoes and parsley sauce) and the classic *røget sild* (smoked herring). **Breakfast** (*morgenmad*) is a treat, with almost all hotels and hostels offering a spread of cereals, freshly made bread, cheese, ham, fruit juice, milk, coffee and tea, for around 60kr (if not included in room prices). **Brunch**, served in most cafés from 11am until mid-afternoon, is a popular, filling option for late starters and costs 80–100kr. The traditional **lunch** (*frokost*) is *smørrebrød* – slices of rye bread heaped with meat, fish or cheese, and assorted trimmings – sold for 40–80kr a piece and very filling. An excellent-value set lunch can usually be found at restaurants and *bodegas* (bars selling no-frills food). *Tilbud* is the "special", *dagens ret* the "dish of the day"; expect to pay around 80kr for one of these, or 120–180kr for a three-course set lunch. The latest craze is *smushi*, the Danish take on sushi (about 50kr per piece).

For daytime **snacks**, there are hot-dog stands (*pølsevogn*) on all main streets and at train stations, serving hot dogs (*pølser*), toasted ham-and-cheese sandwiches (*parisertoast*) and chips (*pommes frites*) for around 25kr. Bakeries and cafés sell Danish pastries (*wienerbrød*), tastier and much less sweet than the imitations sold

abroad, and *rundstykker* (literally "round pieces"), a type of crispy bread roll. Restaurants are pretty expensive for dinner (reckon on 130–200kr), but you can usually find a Middle Eastern or Thai place offering **buffets** for around 80–100kr. Kebab shops are also very common and often serve pizza slices from around 30kr. If you plan on **self-catering**, head for the good-value Netto or Fakta supermarkets.

DRINK

The most sociable places to **drink** are pubs (variously known as a *værtshus*, *bar* or *bodega*) and cafés, where the emphasis is on **beer**. The cheapest is bottled lager – the so-called gold beer (Guldøl or Elefantøl; 25–35kr/bottle) is strongest. Draught lager (Fadøl) is more expensive and a touch weaker, but tastes fresher. The most common brands are Carlsberg and Tuborg, although microbreweries are now thankfully much more common, with many pubs making their own beer on the premises. Most international **wines** (from 40kr) and **spirits** (20–40kr) are widely available. There are many varieties of **schnapps**, including the potent Aalborg-made Aquavit.

CULTURE AND ETIQUETTE

Denmark is a liberal, tolerant country. The defining aspect of culture here is *hygge*: spending quality time with friends or loved ones over good food and drink. Remember that the Danish language

---

DENMARK ONLINE

ⓦ**visitdenmark.com** The excellent website of the Danish Tourist Board.

ⓦ**cphpost.dk** News and reviews from the *Copenhagen Post*, the capital's English-language weekly.

ⓦ**aok.dk** Listings for most of Zealand; some pages in English.

ⓦ**rejseplanen.dk** Public transport journey planner (with English-language option).

ⓦ**international.kk.dk** Practical information on studying, working and living in Denmark.

8

doesn't have a specific word for "please", so don't be upset if Danes leave it out when talking to you in English (which most Danes speak amazingly well). When wandering about, don't stray into the cycle lanes alongside most roads, and be aware that locals will always wait for the green "walk" light at pedestrian crossings – even when there isn't a car in sight.

Tipping is not expected, as service charges are included in hotel, restaurant and bar bills; however, if you think you've had particularly good service it's not unheard of to leave a few kroner. **Smoking** is banned in most restaurants, cafés and bars.

SPORTS AND OUTDOOR ACTIVITIES

Football (soccer) is by far the most popular **sport** in Denmark. The biggest team is FC Copenhagen who play in the twelve-team Superliga (⍵dbu.dk). As for **outdoor activities**, there's a series of cycle routes and hiking paths (⍵dvl.dk). Watersports are also popular. Over 200 beaches have Blue Flag status, and the extensive fjords of Zealand and Jutland provide further variety for the recreationally minded; ask at tourist offices where the best swimming is. Klitmøller on Jutland is the surfing capital.

COMMUNICATIONS

Post offices are open Monday to Friday from 9.30/10am to 5/6pm and Saturday from 9.30/10am to noon/2pm, with reduced hours in smaller communities. You can buy stamps from most newsagents. If you're in Denmark long-term, consider buying a **Danish SIM** for your mobile – prepaid cards from operators such as Telmore and CBB are available from petrol stations and post offices from 99kr. **Internet access** is free at libraries and some tourist offices; omnipresent coffee chain *Baresso* offers free wi-fi, as do many cafés and restaurants. Many towns and cities also have free wi-fi zones.

EMERGENCY NUMBERS
All emergencies ❶112.

EMERGENCIES

Danish **police** are generally courteous and most speak English. For **prescriptions**, doctors' consultations and dental work – but not hospital visits – you have to pay on the spot.

INFORMATION

Most places have a **tourist office** that can help with accommodation. They're open daily in the most popular spots, but have reduced hours from October to March. All airports and many train stations also offer a hotel booking service.

MONEY AND BANKS

Currency is the **krone** (plural kroner), made up of 100 øre. It comes in notes of 50kr, 100kr, 200kr, 500kr and 1000kr, and coins of 50øre, 1kr, 2kr, 5kr, 10kr and 20kr. **Banking hours** are Monday to Friday from 9.30/10am to 4pm, Thursday until 5.30/6pm. Banks are plentiful and are the easiest place to **exchange cash**, although they usually charge around 50kr per transaction: the rate charged by a bank for withdrawing from an ATM is just as competitive. Most airports and ferry terminals have late-opening exchange facilities, and ATMs are widespread. At the time of writing, €1 = 7.5kr, US$1 = 6.6kr and £1 = 9.4kr.

STUDENT AND YOUTH DISCOUNTS

Your **ISIC card** will get you thirty to fifty percent off most museum and gallery admission prices, although free entry is often available on Wednesdays and Sundays. If you're staying long-term a **DSB Wildcard** (185kr), which offers fifty percent off train fares for a year (⍵dsb.dk), can be worthwhile.

DANISH

	DANISH	PRONUNCIATION
Yes	*Ja*	Ya
No	*Nej*	Nye
Please	*Vær så venlig*	Verso venly
Thank you	*Tak*	Tagg
Hello/Good day	*Goddag*	Go-day
Goodbye	*Farvel*	Fah-vell
Excuse me	*Undskyld*	Unsgul
Good	*God*	Got
Bad	*Dårlig*	Dohli
Near	*Nær*	Neh-a
Far	*Fjern*	Fee-ann
Cheap	*Billig*	Billie
Expensive	*Dyr*	Duy-a
Open	*Åben*	Oh-ben
Closed	*Lukket*	Lohgget
Ticket	*Billet*	Bill-le
Today	*Idag*	Ee-day
Yesterday	*Igår*	Ee-goh
Tomorrow	*Imorgen*	Ee-mon
How much is...?	*Hvad koster...?*	Val kosta...?
I'd like...	*Jeg vil gerne ha...*	Yai vay gerna ha...
What time is it?	*Hvad er klokken?*	Val eayr cloggen?
Where is...?	*Hvor er...?*	Voa eayr...?
A table for...	*Et bord till...*	Et boa te...
I don't understand	*Jeg forstår ikke*	Yai fusto igge
Do you speak English?	*Taler de engelsk?*	Tayla dee engellsgg?
One	*En*	Ehn
Two	*To*	Toh
Three	*Tre*	Tray
Four	*Fire*	Fee-a
Five	*Fem*	Fem
Six	*Sex*	Sex
Seven	*Syv*	Syu
Eight	*Otte*	Oddeh
Nine	*Ni*	Nee
Ten	*Ti*	Tee

8

OPENING HOURS AND HOLIDAYS

Standard **shop hours** are Monday to Thursday from 9/10am to 5.30/6pm, Friday from 9/10am to 7/8pm, Saturday from 9am to 1/2pm (though in larger cities, several will stay open until 5pm on Saturday). Many larger shops and department stores are also open on Sundays for limited hours. All shops and banks are closed, and public transport and many museums run to Sunday schedules on **public holidays**: January 1; Maundy Thursday to Easter Monday; Prayer Day (4th Fri after Easter); Ascension (fortieth day after Easter);

Whit Sunday and Monday; Constitution Day (June 5); December 24 (pm only); December 25 and 26. On **International Workers' Day**, May 1, many offices and shops close at noon.

Copenhagen

Split by lakes and surrounded by sea, an energetic and hip waterside vibe permeates **COPENHAGEN** (København), one of Europe's most user-friendly (and trendy) capitals. It's a welcoming, compact city with a centre largely given over to pedestrians (and cyclists). There's an emphasis on café culture and top-notch museums by day, and a thumping live music, bar and club scene by night. Festivals like **Distortion** (June) and the **Jazz Festival** (July)

show the city off at its coolest and most inventive.

Until the twelfth century, when **Bishop Absalon** built a castle on Christiansborg's present site, there was little more than a tiny fishing settlement to be found here. Trade and prosperity flourished with the

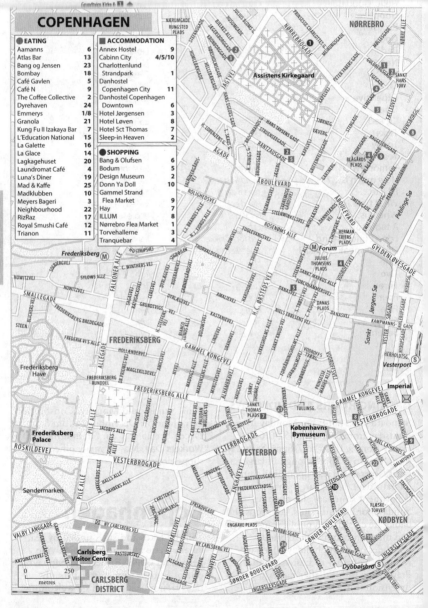

COPENHAGEN

● EATING	
Aamanns	6
Atlas Bar	13
Bang og Jensen	23
Bombay	18
Café Gavlen	5
Café N	9
The Coffee Collective	2
Dyrehaven	24
Emmerys	1/8
Granola	21
Kung Fu II Izakaya Bar	7
L'Education National	15
La Galette	16
La Glace	14
Lagkagehuset	20
Laundromat Café	4
Luna's Diner	19
Mad & Kaffe	25
Madklubben	10
Meyers Bageri	3
Neighbourhood	22
RizRaz	17
Royal Smushi Café	12
Trianon	11

■ ACCOMMODATION	
Annex Hostel	9
Cabinn City	4/5/10
Charlottenlund Strandpark	1
Danhostel Copenhagen City	11
Danhostel Copenhagen Downtown	6
Hotel Jørgensen	3
Hotel Løven	8
Hotel Sct Thomas	7
Sleep-in Heaven	2

● SHOPPING	
Bang & Olufsen	6
Bodum	5
Design Museum	2
Donn Ya Doll	10
Gammel Strand Flea Market	9
Hay	7
ILLUM	8
Nørrebro Flea Market	1
Torvehallerne	3
Tranquebar	4

introduction of the Sound Toll on vessels in the Øresund, and the city became the Baltic's principal harbour, earning the name **København** ("merchants' harbour"). By 1443, it had become the Danish capital. A century later, Christian IV created Rosenborg Castle, Rundetårn and the districts of Nyboder and Christianshavn, and in 1669 Frederik III graced the city with its first royal palace, Amalienborg. Since then, various kings and merchants have built up the city to be the amalgam of architectural styles and landscapes that you see today.

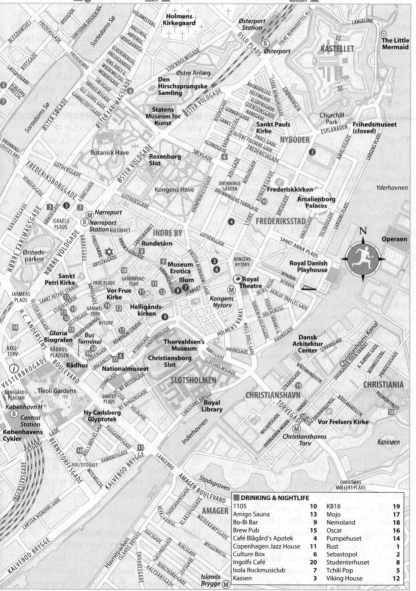

8

■ DRINKING & NIGHTLIFE			
1105	10	KB18	19
Amigo Sauna	13	Mojo	17
Bo-Bi Bar	9	Nemoland	18
Brew Pub	15	Oscar	16
Café Blågård's Apotek	4	Pumpehuset	14
Copenhagen Jazz House	11	Rust	1
Culture Box	6	Sebastopol	2
Ingolfs Café	20	Studenterhuset	8
Isola Rockmusicklub	7	Tchili Pop	5
Kassen	3	Viking House	12

WHAT TO SEE AND DO

The historic core of the city is **Slotsholmen**, originally the site of the twelfth-century castle and now home to the huge **Christiansborg** complex. Just across the Slotsholmen Kanal to the north is the medieval maze of **Indre By** ("inner city"), while to the south the island of **Christianshavn** is adorned with cutting-edge architecture in addition to the alternative enclave of **Christiania**. Northeast of Indre By are the royal quarters of Kongens Have and **Frederiksstaden**, while to the west the expansive Rådhuspladsen leads via Tivoli Gardens to Central Station and the hotspots of **Vesterbro** and **Nørrebro**.

Tivoli

Just off hectic Vesterbrogade outside the station is Copenhagen's most famous attraction, **Tivoli** (mid-April to mid-Sept Mon–Thurs & Sun 11am–10/11pm, Fri 11am–12.30am, Sat 11am–midnight; mid-Nov to end Dec closes one hour earlier; Mon–Thurs 100kr, Fri–Sun 110kr; ⊚tivoli.dk), an entertaining mixture of landscaped gardens, outdoor concerts (every Fri) and fairground rides. You'll probably hear it before you see it, thanks to its high perimeter walls and the constant screams from the roller coasters (multi-ride tickets 220kr). On a summer evening when the park is illuminated by thousands of lights and lamps reflected in the lake, it's one of Scandinavia's most magical experiences.

Ny Carlsberg Glyptotek

Founded by Carlsberg tycoon Carl Jacobsen, the **Ny Carlsberg Glyptotek** (Tues–Wed & Fri–Sun 11am–6pm, Thurs 11am–10pm; 95kr, Tues free; ⊚glyptoteket.com) is Copenhagen's finest classical and modern art gallery. There's a knockout selection of Greek and Roman sculpture on the first floor as well as some excellent examples of modern European art, including Degas casts, Monet's *The Lemon Grove* and works by Gauguin, Van Gogh and Danish Golden Age artists like Eckersberg, upstairs. Conclude your visit with a slice of delicious cake in the café beside the delightfully domed winter garden.

Thorvaldsens and the National museums

On the north side of Slotsholmen, the **Thorvaldsens Museum** (Tues–Sun 10am–5pm; 30kr, Wed free; ⊚thorvaldsensmuseum.dk) is home to an enormous collection of work of Denmark's most famous sculptor, Bertel Thorvaldsen. A short walk away over the Slotsholmen Kanal is the **Nationalmuseet** (National Museum; same hours, with guided tours Sun at 2pm; free; ⊚natmus.dk), which has excellent displays on Denmark's history from the Ice Age to the present day. The prehistory section in particular is fascinating, and includes amber animals, gold Viking horns, numerous corpses preserved in bogs and Denmark's oldest coin, struck around 995 AD.

Indre By and the Rundetaarn

West of Kongens Nytorv, the city's largest square and home to some of the best hotdog stalls in town, pedestrianized **Strøget** leads into the heart of **Indre By**. This is Denmark's premier shopping area. The quirky 35m-high **Rundetaarn** (Round Tower; mid-March to mid-May daily 10am–6pm; mid-May to mid-Sept daily 10am–8pm; mid-Sept to mid-Oct daily 10am–6pm; mid-Oct to mid-March Thurs–Mon 10am–6pm, Tues & Wed 10am–9pm; 25kr; ⊚rundetaarn.dk) dominates the skyline north of Strøget. Built as an observatory and finished in 1642, the main attraction is the view from the top, reached via a spiral walkway. A glass floor 25m up allows you to look down into the core of the tower. It's a still-functioning observatory, and you can view the night sky through its astronomical telescope (May–Sept 10am–8pm; Sept–May 10am–6pm).

Nyhavn and Frederiksstaden

Running east from Kongens Nytorv, a slender canal divides the two sides of **Nyhavn** ("new harbour"), picturesquely lined with colourful eighteenth-century

COPENHAGEN ON A BUDGET

Europe's fifth most expensive city, Copenhagen can be a tricky place to get by on a budget, but with a bit of planning you can make the most of your wallet. Museums with **free admission** include the Nationalmuseet (National Museum) and the Statens Museum for Kunst (National Gallery), see below, while many others offer free entry one day per week. Another great free activity in summer is swimming in Copenhagen harbour's outdoor pool on Islands Brygge, southwest across the canal from Indre By. You should also consider buying a CPHCARD (see p.219). As for getting around, you can walk to most places, use the free city bikes or take the harbour bus-boats. The city has plenty of free music on offer, including concerts at Tivoli almost weekly during summer. As for accommodation, having your own bed linen and HI card can save you upwards of 100kr nightly.

houses – now bars and cafés – and thronged with tourists year-round. Just north of Nyhavn, the royal district of **Frederiksstaden** centres on cobbled Amalienborg Slotsplads, home to the four **Amalienborg** royal palaces. Two remain as royal residences, and there's a changing of the guard at noon if the monarch is home. In the opposite direction is the great marble dome of **Frederikskirken**, also known as Marmorkirken or marble church (Mon–Thurs 10am–5pm, Fri–Sun noon–5pm; admission to dome Sat & Sun 1pm & 3pm, plus Mon–Fri June–Aug; free), modelled on St Peter's in Rome.

Kongens Have and Rosenborg Slot

West of Frederikskirken, **Kongens Have** is the city's oldest public park and a popular spot for picnics. Within the park is the fairytale **Rosenborg Slot** (daily: Jan–April & Nov to mid-Dec 10am–2pm; May, Sept & Oct 10am–4pm; June–Aug 9am–5pm; 80kr; ⓦkongernessamling.dk), the castle that served as the principal residence of Christian IV. The highlight is the downstairs treasury, where a gilded throne and the **crown jewels** and rich accessories worn by Christian IV are on display.

The Botanisk Have and art galleries

The **Botanisk Have** (Botanical Garden; May–Sept daily 8.30am–6pm, Oct–April Tues–Sun 8.30am–4pm; free; ⓦbotanik .snm.ku.dk), on the west side of Kongens Have, is dotted with greenhouses and rare plants. The neighbouring **Statens Museum for Kunst** (National Gallery; Tues–Sun 10am–5pm, Wed till 8pm; free, entry fee for some special exhibitions; ⓦsmk.dk) has bright and spacious galleries holding a vast

collection of art, from minor Picassos to major works by Matisse and Titian. Across the park on Stockholmsgade, **Den Hirschsprungske Samling** (The Hirschsprung Collection; Tues–Sun 11am–4pm; 75kr, free on Wed; ⓦhirschsprung.dk) holds a collection of twentieth-century Danish art, including work by the Skagen artists (see box, p.235), renowned for their use of light.

Little Mermaid

Just north of the **Kastellet**, a star-shaped fortress with five bastions on a corner overlooking the harbour, sits the diminutive (and, in all honesty, anticlimactic) **Little Mermaid**, a magnet for tourists since her unveiling in 1913. A bronze statue of the Hans Christian Andersen character, it was sculpted by Edvard Eriksen and paid for by the founder of the Carlsberg brewery. Over the years she's been the victim of several attacks, having her head and arms chopped off and even being blown up by a bomb in 2003 – and also spent much of 2010 at Shanghai's Expo – but she remains the most enduring symbol of the city.

Christianshavn

From Christiansborg, a bridge crosses to **Christianshavn**, built by Christian IV in the early sixteenth century and nicknamed "Little Amsterdam" thanks to its small canals, cute bridges and Dutch-style houses. Reaching skywards on the far side of Torvegade is one of the city's most recognizable features, the copper and golden spire of **Vor Frelsers Kirke** (daily 11am–3.30pm; tower May–Sept Mon–Sat 9.30am–7pm,

8

Sun 10.30am–7pm; free, tower 35kr;
ⓦwww.vorfrelserskirke.dk/english). Also
worth a look is the canalside **Dansk
Arkitektur Center** (daily 10am–5pm,
Wed till 9pm; 40kr, students 25kr or free
for architecture students; ⓦdac.dk), at
Strandgade 27B, with regular exhibitions
on design and architecture plus an
excellent café and bookshop.

Christiania

Christiania is a former barracks area
colonized by hippies after declaring itself
a "free city" in 1971. It has evolved into a
self-governing entity based on collective
ownership, with quirky buildings housing
alternative small businesses such as a
bicycle workshop and women's smithy,
as well as art galleries, cafés, restaurants,
Copenhagen's best falafel stand, music
venues and Pusherstreet, once an open
hash market. There are guided tours of
the area (late June to Aug daily 3pm;
rest of the year Sat & Sun only; 40kr;
ⓦrundvisergruppen.dk), starting at the
main gate by Prinsessegade, but it's just
as fun to wander around on your own.
No photos are allowed, unless by special
permission. The neighbourhood has been
racked by controversy since the off,
sitting as it does on prime real estate
while its population remain exempt from
the taxes most Danes pay. Although the
area's future is threatened by moves from
the Danish conservative government, as
its residents may tell you, the places earns
its keep: it's one of Copenhagen's most
visited attractions, and justifiably so.

Vesterbro

Directly behind the train station begins
Vesterbro, home to Copenhagen's
red-light district and one of the most
cosmopolitan areas in the city. It has a
great selection of shops, bars and
restaurants. While the area is perfectly
safe to walk around, male travellers may
want to give Istedgade (one of the main
thoroughfares) a wide berth at night to
avoid being propositioned.

Carlsberg Visitors Centre

"Probably the best beer in the world"
claims the advert. Well, you can decide

for yourself at the **Carlsberg Visitors
Centre** (Tues–Sun 10am–8pm; 95kr;
ⓦvisitcarlsberg.com) along Gamle
Carlsberg Vej (buses #18 and #26). As
well as learning how to create the perfect
pint at the Jacobsen Brewhouse, you also
get to sample two beers from a choice of
Carlsberg, Tuborg and Jacobsen brews.

Nørrebro

Nørrebro, an edgy area northwest across
the canal from Indre By (accessible from
the centre via buses #3A, #4A or #5A or a
25min walk), is crammed with some of
Copenhagen's best cafés, bars and clubs,
centred on Sankt Hans Torv. Caution is
advised, particularly at night: but it's
home to most of Denmark's most
happening hangouts and the resplendent
Assistens Kirkegård, a tranquil cemetery
which locals use as a park in summer, and
that has Hans Christian Andersen among
its permanent residents.

ARRIVAL AND DEPARTURE

By plane Kastrup airport is 11km southeast of the centre,
and is served by a main-line train to Central Station (5am–
midnight every 10min; midnight–5am hourly; 12min;
36kr).

By train Trains pull into Central Station (Københavns
Hovedbanegård or Københavns H on tickets) near
Vesterbrogade.

Destinations Aalborg (every 30min; 4hr 45min–5hr);
Århus (every 30min; 34hr); Hamburg (hourly; 4hr–6hr);
Helsingør (every 20min; 50min); Malmö (several hourly;
35min); Odense (3 hourly; 1hr 15min–1hr 30min);
Roskilde (every 20min; 30min).

By bus Long-distance buses from elsewhere in Denmark
stop at or near the Central Station.

Destinations Aalborg (3–5 daily; 4hr 45min); Århus (6–7
daily; 3hr); Malmö (hourly; 55min).

By boat Ferries dock an S-train ride away north of the
centre at Nordhavn (two stops from Nørreport station).

INFORMATION

Tourist information Vesterbrogade 4a, across from
Central Station (May, June & Sept Mon–Sat 9am–6pm,
Sun 9am–4pm; July & Aug daily 9am–7pm; Oct–April
Mon–Fri 9am–4pm, Sat 9am–2pm; ☏70 22 24 42,
ⓦvisitcopenhagen.com). Accommodation (including
private rooms) can be booked for free via their website.
Note that pickpockets operate in the tourist office and
thefts are common: be vigilant with your possessions (the
same applies in the train station).

Discount cards If you're sightseeing on a tight schedule, the CPHCARD (379/629kr for 24/72hr; ⓦ copenhagencard .com) is valid for the entire public transport network (including all Zealand) and gives entry to most attractions in the area. It's available at tourist offices, hotels, travel agents and the train station.

GETTING AROUND

By metro, S-tog and bus An integrated network of buses, electric S-trains (S-tog) and an expanding metro covers the city (5am–1am); night buses (*natbus*) take over after 1am, along with metro services on Thursday to Saturday nights, though the latter are less frequent. Night fares are double daytime fares, and if you're taking your bike, you'll need to buy a special ticket. Free route maps are available from stations.

Tickets The best deal is the 24hr, all-zone pass (130kr; valid on all trains /metro/buses) Other options include the CPHCARD (see above) and the city pass (for the four main city transport zones; 80/200kr for 24/72hr). There is also a range of tickets, from the single *billet* – a two-zone ticket valid for an hour (24kr) up to seven-day flexicards (250–675kr). Single *billets* can be bought on buses; all other tickets should be bought at train stations/newsagents. Make sure you validate your ticket before boarding at the yellow ticket-punching machines on the platform. Plain-clothes ticket inspectors operate on almost all train routes: there are instant 750kr fines for travelling without a ticket; don't even bother trying to play ignorant – your defence won't be bought, as all transport signs are printed in Danish and English.

By bike The city's Gobike scheme (ⓦ gobike.com) allows you to borrow any of 1260 hi-tech bikes from racks across the city. Integrated with onboard GPS and a tablet computer, the bikes feature navigation with route planning and map display, as well as real-time information on available bikes and docking stations all over the city. Payment is made by credit card (25kr/hr or 70kr/month if you subscribe on their website). Lower-tech cycle rental is available from CPH Bike Rental, Turesensgade 10 (daily 10am–6pm; from 50kr/6hr; profits go to helping cycling in Africa; ⓦ cph-bike-rental.dk), and Københavns Cykelbørs, Gothersgade 157 (Mon–Fri 9am–5.30pm, Sat 10am–1.30pm; plus June–Aug Sun 10am–1.30pm; from 50kr/day; ⓦ cykelborsen.dk); the latter also rents out hi-tech bicycles with GPS computers that have built-in guides of the city.

ACCOMMODATION

Copenhagen has a very good selection of hostels, mainly concentrated in the city centre and Nørrebro. Booking ahead is recommended on weekends and during summer months; otherwise turn up as early as possible during the day to ensure a bed. Hotel prices can verge on the

COPENHAGEN TOURS

When the weather's good, it's well worth forking out on a **city tour** to familiarize yourself with Copenhagen. There are hop-on/hop-off open-top **bus tours** around the key city sights (195kr; ⓦ stromma.dk) and also Netto Boats (daily late March–Oct 9.40am–8pm; 40kr; ⓦ havnerundfart.dk) operating hour-long canal and harbour **boat tours** past the old stock exchange (not open to the public), the island of Holmen and the Little Mermaid, leaving regularly from Nyhavn.

For bike enthusiasts, the best option is Bike Mike (daily 10.30am, plus April–Oct Wed & Sat 2.30pm; 299kr for 3hr including bike rental; ☏ 26 39 56 88, ⓦ bike copenhagenwithmike.dk), with themed **cycle tours** departing from Sankt Peders Stræde 47 in the Latin Quarter.

astronomical, but there are often online deals available and a few cheaper options in the centre. Private rooms (around 400kr) booked through the tourist office are usually an S-train ride away from the centre. Breakfast is not included, unless otherwise stated.

HOSTELS

Annex Hostel Helgolandsgade 15 ☏ 33 24 22 11, ⓦ annexcopenhagen.dk. Brightly coloured, recently refurbished hostel/hotel (with only private rooms). Rooms get LED TVs and wi-fi; the cheapest have wash basins but no private bathrooms. Singles **450kr**, doubles **495kr**

Danhostel Copenhagen City H.C. Andersens Boulevard 50 ☏ 33 11 85 85, ⓦ danhostelcopenhagencity.dk. Priding itself as Europe's largest "designer" youth hostel, this thousand-bed monster is friendly, efficient and centrally located in a multistorey building overlooking the harbour. There's a guest kitchen, a convivial café-bar and free wi-fi. Bikes for 100kr/day. All rooms en suite. Dorms **240kr**, doubles **775kr**

Danhostel Copenhagen Downtown Vandkunsten 5 ☏ 70 23 21 10, ⓦ copenhagendowntown.com. Affable hostel with mostly small four-person dorms and thirty private rooms, along with a cool café-bar, free wi-fi, pool table, chill-out cushions and a bang-in-the-centre location. Dorms **245kr**, doubles **410kr**

Hotel Jørgensen Rømersgade 11 ☏ 33 13 81 86, ⓦ hoteljoergensen.dk. Hostel offering six- to ten-bed dorms and basic rooms (with cable TV; some have their own bathroom), with a buffet breakfast included. Common room with TV, pool and table football. A stone's throw from Nørreport station on Israels Plads. Dorms **150kr**, doubles **575kr**

8

Sleep-in Heaven Struenseegade 7, Nørrebro ☎ 35 35 46 48, ⓦ sleepinheaven.com. Welcoming, irreverent hostel in a quiet spot next to Assistens Kirkegård. Six- or twelve-bed mixed dorms, plus double rooms (shared bathroom). Age limit 35; breakfast 40kr. Open 24hr; pool table; bar; free internet. Bus #12/#69, nightbus #92N from the centre (10min). Dorms __175kr__, doubles __375kr__

HOTELS

Cabinn City Mitchellsgade 14 ☎ 33 46 16 16, ⓦ cabinn .com. Clean cabin-style rooms close to Tivoli and the station. All are en suite and have TV; breakfast is 70kr extra. Two other branches in Frederiksberg. Singles __495kr__, doubles __625kr__

Hotel Løven Vesterbrogade 30 ☎ 33 79 67 20, ⓦ loevenhotel.dk. A real bargain for such a central location, in a historic nineteenth-century building (ring the bell marked "1st floor Løven" for admittance), with 46 airy and spacious rooms spread over five floors; most have a fridge, and some have a/c and bathroom. No breakfast, but has kitchen for self-catering. Occasional deals for longer stays. Reservations essential in summer. Doubles __699kr__

Hotel Sct Thomas Frederiksberg Allé 7 ☎ 33 21 64 64, ⓦ hotelsctthomas.dk. This gem of a three-star spot offers boutique-ish rooms close to hip Værnedamsvej and a short walk from glorious Frederiksberg Gardens. It's a bit of a trek from the city centre, but the friendly owners and very reasonable rates more than compensate. (Prices vary greatly; the best deals are online, quoted here). Singles __595kr__, doubles __850kr__

CAMPSITE

Charlottenlund Strandpark Strandvejen 144, Charlottenlund ☎ 44 22 00 65, ⓦ campingcopenhagen .dk. Beautifully situated 6km from Copenhagen at Charlottenlund Beach and with good, clean facilities. Very busy in summer. S-train line A, B or C to Svanemøllen then bus #14. Closed mid-Oct to early March. Per person __100kr__, plus per tent __35kr__

EATING

Mixing Michelin stars with budget bars, Copenhagen delights with its tremendously varied eating scene – which has helped to plant it on the map as Scandinavia's most sophisticated city. Head out of the centre as locals do towards Nørrebro and Vesterbro for the best deals. For self-caterers, bakeries are a good option, while for takeaway *smørrebrød* try the outlets at Centrum Smørrebrød, Vesterbrogade 6C; or Klemmen at Central Station. There are Netto supermarkets at Nørre Voldgade 94, Nørrebrogade 43 and Landemærket 11. If you fancy really getting to know the locals while filling up on home-made Danish food, you could always book a Dine With the Danes

evening, a long-running initiative which gets travellers into contact with locals who cook, serve and share a meal with you (from 480kr; ⓦ meetthedanes.com).

CAFÉS

Bang og Jensen Istedgade 130 ⓦ bangogjensen.dk. With high stucco ceilings, a mahogany counter left over from its former incarnation as a pharmacy, and plenty of swagger, this hip Vesterbro café-bar will never go out of fashion. Their casual bistro menu includes nachos with jerk chicken (80kr) and *croque chèvre* sandwiches (73kr). Tends to pack out before concerts in nearby Vega. Mon–Fri 7.30am–2am, Sat 10am–2am, Sun 10am–midnight.

Café Gavlen Ryesgade 1 ⓦ cafegavlen.dk. With breakfasts (from 40kr), delicious cakes (40kr) baked daily on the premises and good *smørrebrød* (44kr), this café is chic enough to grace Montparnasse: at night, speciality beers and cocktails replace coffee as the drink of choice. Mon–Thurs 8am–midnight, Fri & Sat 9am–2am, Sun 9am–11pm.

★ **The Coffee Collective** Jaegersborggade 10 ⓦ coffeecollective.dk. The best café in town, bar none. The joint is run by a former world champion barista. Ethically sourced coffee (espresso 20kr; long white 30kr), ultra-knowledgeable staff and coffee roasted right in front of you during the day. They have another branch at Godthåbsvej 34B. Mon–Fri 7am–7pm, Sat 8am–6pm, Sun 8am–7pm.

Dyrehaven Sønder Blvd 72 ⓦ dyrehavenkbh.dk. Cool café-bar-restaurant popular with in-the-know locals and expats. It serves real down-home Danish dishes such as *kartoffelmed* black bread with potatoes and grilled mackerel with lemon and dill. Breakfasts and lunches 18–88kr. Mon–Thurs & Sun 9am–9pm, Fri 9am–10pm, Sat 10am–10pm.

Granola Vernedamsvej 5 ⓦ www.granola.dk. Feel-good retro coffee bar serving delicious ice cream on one of the city's trendiest streets. Breakfasts/lunches 30–160kr. Mon–Fri 7am–10pm, Sat 9am–10pm, Sun 9am–3.30pm.

La Galette Larsbjørnsstræde 9 🌐 lagalette.dk. Authentic Breton pancakes made with organic buckwheat and an array of fillings – from ham and eggs to smoked salmon and caviar. Pancakes 30–60kr. Mon–Sat noon–4pm & 5.30–10pm, Sun 1–10pm.

Laundromat Café Elmegade 15 🌐 thelaundromatcafe .com. You can tell a good-value, popular café by the crowds, right? They certainly flock to this place, where breakfast goodies start at 45kr and big brunches at 88kr. Great cakes and coffees. Other branches in Frederiksberg (Gammel Kongevej 96) and Østerbro (Århusgade 38). Mon–Fri 8am–10pm, Sat & Sun 9am–midnight.

Luna's Diner Sankte Anne Gade 5 🌐 lunasdiner.dk. Bright little café in Christianshavn with street-front seating, the best milkshakes in town, burgers (from 134kr) and a massive weekend veggie brunch until 3pm (209kr). Mon–Thurs 9.30am–midnight, Fri & Sat 9.30am–1am, Sun 9.30am–11pm.

Mad & Kaffe Sønder Bvd 68 🌐 madogkaffe.dk. This is a recent winner of Copenhagen's best café amid mighty stiff competition. Famous for its breakfasts where you tick off exactly what you want. Nice lunches too (65–135kr). Daily 8.30am–8pm.

RESTAURANTS

Aamanns Øster Farimagsgade 10–12 🌐 aamanns.dk. Good place for cheap *smørrebrød* and other Danish dishes (from 60kr). Eat in or take away. Take away Mon–Sat 11.30am–5.30pm, Sun noon–4.30pm; restaurant Mon–Wed noon–4pm, Thurs & Fri noon–4pm & 6–11pm, Sat 11.30am–4pm & 6–11pm, Sun 11.30am–4pm.

Atlas Bar Larsbjørnsstræde 18 🌐 atlasbar.dk. Busy basement bar-restaurant with an imaginative range of world food from ostrich and Japanese beef to Mexican vegetarian burritos. Mains 135–165kr. Mon–Sat noon–10pm.

Bombay Lavendelstræde 13 🌐 eatatbombay.dk. The city's best Indian, with curries to eat in or take away for 120kr. Tues–Sun 4–11pm.

Café N Blågårdsgade 17 🌐 cafe-n-2200.dk. Bargain veggie burgers (49kr) and a "special" dish of the week (from 89kr) make this fabulous veggie/vegan café-restaurant a handy pit stop for budget-conscious travellers. Home-made bread, great coffee and pavement seating. Mon–Fri 8am–9pm, Sat & Sun 8am–10pm.

★**Kung Fu II Izakaya Bar** Ravnsborggade 16B 🌐 kungfubar.dk. Is it a bar? Is it a restaurant? The answer: both. An Izakaya bar is a Japanese informal bar where you drop in for a beer and a bite to eat. Exceptional value with cheap bites from 30kr and a tasting platter with a little bit of everything on the menu for 195kr. Food is served until 10pm. Mon–Fri 5.30pm–2am, Sat & Sun noon–2am.

L'Education National Larsbjornstrade 12 🌐 leducation .dk. Cute brasserie with friendly staff: the tasty French food is cheap (mains from 95–225kr), but the service and intimate atmosphere (candles and checked tablecloths) make the experience memorable. 11.30am–midnight.

Madklubben Store Kongensgade 66 🌐 madklubben.dk. Down-at-heel affordable chain restaurant that does simple Danish dishes (as little as 200kr for four courses). Efficient staff. Multiple branches, including at Vesterbro (Vesterbrogade 62). 5.30pm–midnight.

Neighbourhood Istedgade 27. All-organic Vesterbro pizza and cocktail joint. Pizzas are 145kr, the delicious salads 115kr. Mon–Wed 5–11pm, Thurs 5pm–1am, Fri 5pm–2am, Sat 10am–2am, Sun 10am–11pm.

COPENHAGEN'S BEST BAKERIES

The Danes take their bakeries seriously and you'll see them all around Copenhagen. The range of loaves and pastries on offer is almost intimidating, but staff will happily advise. As well as *rundstykker* and flaky pastries, most bakeries offer affordable sandwiches. The following five are among the city's best:

Emmerys Frederiksholms Kanal 1, Nørrebrogade 8, and Østerbrogade 51, among others 🌐 emmerys.dk. Trendy bakery chain with organic bread and filling sandwiches (from 49kr). Mon–Fri 7am–6pm, Sat & Sun 7am–4/5pm.

La Glace Skoubougade 3 🌐 laglace.dk. Set just east of Gammel Torv, Copenhagen's oldest confectioner (dating to 1870) is an essential stop for cakes and freshly made hot chocolate. Mon–Fri 8.30am–6pm, Sat 9am–6pm, Sun 10am–6pm.

Lagkagehuset Torvegade 45 🌐 lagkagehuset.dk. Opposite the Christianshavn metro station, this justifiably popular bakery offers a bewildering range of breads baked in stone ovens, as well as great pastries (from 15kr) and fruit-covered cakes. Mon–Thurs 6am–7pm, Fri 6am–7.30pm, Sat & Sun 6am–7pm.

Meyers Bageri Jaegersborggade 9 🌐 clausmeyer.dk. The focus is on bread here: it comes out of the oven the moment before the store opens, and the variety of loaves is incredible. Also at Store Kongensgade 46. Mon–Fri 7am–6pm, Sat & Sun 7am–4pm.

Trianon Hyskenstræde 8, east of Nytorv 🌐 trianon.dk. Purveyors to the queen – so the standard of breads and pastries here is top-notch. Mon–Fri 7.30am–5.30pm, Sat 8.30am–5pm.

8

RizRaz Kompagnistræde 20 ⓦrizraz.dk. Stylish, time-tested Mediterranean chain with excellent breakfast/evening buffets (lasagne/pizza/salad and the like) for 89/99kr. Daily 11.30am–midnight.

DRINKING AND NIGHTLIFE

Nørrebro vies for *the* place to be with hip Kødbyen, the city's still-functioning meatpacking district just southeast of Tivoli, where arty bars and clubs have taken over old warehouses. Bars across the city are generally open until midnight or 1am Mon–Wed & Sun, and until at least 2am Thurs–Sat.

BARS

1105 Kristen Bernikows Gade 4 ⓦ 1105.dk. It ain't cheap, but then the bartender here is inventor of the "Copenhagen", the city's signature cocktail. Phenomenal drinks and plenty of beautiful people. Wed, Thurs & Sat 8pm–2am, Fri 4pm–2am.

Bo-Bi Bar Klareboderne 4 ☎33 12 55 43. Simple, red hole-in-the-wall home to Copenhagen's oldest bar counter (from 1917), great cheap bottles of Danish and Czech beers, and a refreshingly diverse clientele of students, artists and writers. Daily noon–2am.

Brew Pub Vestergade 29 ⓦbrewpub.dk. Popular microbrewery bang in the centre of town, with a range of ales (40/58kr for small/large) and a great beer garden. Mon–Thurs noon–midnight, Fri & Sat noon–2am.

Café Blågård's Apotek Blågårds Plads 20 ⓦkroteket.dk. Unpretentious bar with a mixed crowd: students like the cheap beer, and an older crowd come for regular live blues/jazz. Two dozen of the beers on offer are home brews, which change regularly. Give the Vesterweisse, the summer wheat ale, a try. Mon–Sat noon–2am, Sun noon–midnight.

Ingolfs Café Ingolfs Alle 3 ⓦingolfskaffebar.dk. South of the centre in Amager via bus #5a, this is a mellow, Bohemian café-bar serving daytime organic brunches and often erupting into a live music venue at sundown. Come here for recuperation the morning after, then get the party started all over again. Mon & Tues 10am–10pm, Wed–Sat 10am–midnight, Sun 10am–9pm.

Kassen Nørrebrogade 18 ⓦkassen.dk. Known as one of Copenhagen's best-value cocktail bars. Friday two-for-one happy hour until 10pm. Thurs & Sat 8pm–4am, Fri 4pm–4am.

Nemoland Fabriksområde 52, Christiania ⓦnemoland.dk. Famous bar run by Christiania residents, and one of the city's most popular open-air hangouts, with picnic tables and decent café food. In winter, the crowd moves indoors to the pool tables and backgammon boards. Mon–Thurs 10am–1am, Fri–Sat 10am–3am, Sun 10am–1am.

Oscar Rådhuspladsen 77 ⓦoscarbarcafe.dk. Bright and lively café-bar popular with a gay clientele. DJs spin till late at weekends. Happy hour is 5pm to 9pm daily and there

are good sandwiches and burgers (from 79kr). Mon–Thurs & Sun 11am–11pm, Fri & Sat 11am–2am.

Sebastopol Sankt Hans Torv 2 ⓦsebastopol.dk. Trendy café-bar with a retro feel on the Sankt Hans Torv square. Small/large beer 34/50kr. Good brunches too (from 80kr). Mon–Thurs 8am–midnight, Fri 8am–1am, Sat 9am–1am, Sun 9am–10pm.

Studenterhuset Købmagergade 52 ⓦstudenterhuset.com. Friendly student hangout by the Rundetaarn, with table football and pinball machines. Live music (Thurs–Sat) and an international party every Wednesday for Erasmus students. Cakes from 15kr; large beer 25kr (a student card gets you a third off all prices). Happy hour (daily 7–10pm, plus Fri noon–10pm) gets you two draught beers for 35kr. Mon–Fri 8am–midnight, Sat & Sun 10am–midnight (sometimes later).

★**Tchili Pop** Rantzausgade 28 ⓦtjili.dk. *Tchili Pop's* oh-so-cool clientele keep coming back here for the laidback vibe and great live music sessions from up-and-coming Danish bands. It's one of Nørrebro's best bars. Mon & Tues 10am–midnight, Wed 10am–1am, Thurs 10am–2am, Fri & Sat 10am–3am, Sun 10am–midnight.

Viking House Vimmelskaftet 49 ⓦthevikinghouse.dk. Touristy but boisterous joint pumping out rock/heavy metal classics and with live music at weekends. In something of a drinkers' wasteland, and always lively. Mon–Thurs & Sun 3pm–3am, Fri & Sat 10am–7am.

CLUBS

Culture Box Kronprinsessegade 54A ⓦculture-box.dk. Stylish basement club and easily the best electronica venue in town. Cover charge 50–120kr. Fri & Sat 11pm–late.

Isola Rockmusiclub Linnésgade 16A ⓦisolabar.dk. Intimate club/bar playing mostly soul, rock and r'n'b. Free entry. Thurs–Sat 8pm–5am.

KB18 Kødboderne 18 ⓦkb18.net. Club/live music venue in the heart of Kødbyen hosting everything from electronica to blues/rock, and a renowned Saturday club night. Cover charge 60kr. Thurs 9pm–3am, Fri & Sat 9pm–7/8am.

Rust Guldbergsgade 8 ⓦrust.dk. Popular, long-running club and concert venue playing indie, rock and hip-hop. Cover charge 40–60kr. Wed–Sat 8.30pm–5am.

ENTERTAINMENT

LIVE MUSIC

Also check out the programmes at *Vega* at Enghavevej 40 in Vesterbro, and *Rust* (see above).

Copenhagen Jazz House Niels Hemmingsensgade 10 ⓦjazzhouse.dk. The city's premier jazz venue. Daily 7pm–late.

Mojo Løngangsstræde 21C ⓦmojo.dk. Atmospheric, divey blues venue with live acts every night. Entrance free or 70–120kr. Happy hour 8–10pm. Daily 8pm–5am.

LGBT COPENHAGEN

The Danish capital has a small but lively **gay scene** and hosts regular festivals and events including an annual Gay Pride march and one of the world's oldest LGBT film festivals, MIX, held each October (Ⓦ mixcopenhagen.dk). There are several gay **clubs** and numerous **bars** across the city; the big **sauna** is *Amigo Sauna* (Studiestrade 21a; Ⓦ amigo-sauna.dk). Check out Ⓦ visitcopenhagen.com/gay and Ⓦ rainbowbusinessdenmark.dk for more information.

Pumpehuset Studiestræde 52 Ⓦ pumpehuset.dk. Two concert venues in one, set into a former salt warehouse, with a total capacity of 1000. Hosts Danish bands and also attracts international names such as Kaiser Chiefs and Röyksopp. Entrance 50–250kr.

CINEMA

Grand Mikkel BryggersGade 8 ☎ 33 15 16 11, Ⓦ grandteatret.dk. Stylish arthouse cinema with a great café and lively events programme (films around 90kr).

Imperial Ved Vesterport 4 ☎ 70 13 12 11, Ⓦ imperialbio .dk. Copenhagen's largest cinema, with only one theatre, which can fit over 1100 people. Seats from 75–105kr.

OPERA AND THEATRE

If you're under 25 (or if you're buying after 4pm on performance day) then you may be able to get tickets at half price for the venues below: ask at the Royal Theatre box office for details.

Operaen Christianshavns Torv Ⓦ kgl-teater.dk. The city's spectacular opera house is as much an architectural as a musical attraction. Cheap tickets on the day of the performance can cost as little as 100kr. Guided tours July to late Aug (advance booking essential, 100kr).

Royal Theatre Kongens Nytorv Ⓦ kgl-teater.dk. Denmark's oldest and grandest theatre hosts ballet, opera, drama and concerts.

Skuespilhuset Sankt Annæ Plads 36 Ⓦ kgl-teater.dk. Strikingly modern waterside building with three stages, one of which can be opened for alfresco performances; plays are in Danish. The café has a great harbourside view. Guided tours early July to early Aug (100kr; daily 4pm).

SHOPPING

BOOKS

Tranquebar Borgegade 14. Huge bookshop-café specializing in travel literature (and great coffee). Mon–Fri 10am–6pm, Sat 10am–4pm.

CLOTHES

Istegade and the parallel Vesterbrogade have the best selection of boutiques including vintage and little-known designer wear.

Donn Ya Doll Istedgade 55 Ⓦ donnyadoll.dk. Has a great range of gadgets and Scandinavian designer labels. Mon–Fri 11am–6pm, Sat 10am–4pm.

DANISH DESIGN

Bang & Olufsen Østergade 18 Ⓦ bang-olufsen.dk. This flagship store sells audiophile stereo gear, top-end TVs and mobile-related sound products. Mon–Thurs 10am–6pm, Fri 10am–7pm, Sat 10am–4pm.

Bodum Østergade 10 Ⓦ bodum.com/dk. Offer a range of imaginative kitchenware including their classic cafetière. Mon–Thurs 10am–6pm, Fri 10am–7pm, Sat 10am–4pm.

Design Museum Bredgade 68 Ⓦ designmuseum.dk. It's worth checking the exhibition (100kr) and then the shop here for some fascinating examples of Danish design. Tues & Thurs–Sun 11am–5pm, Wed 11am–7pm.

Hay Østergade 61 Ⓦ hay.dk. Sells colourful, funky and affordable household accessories and *objets d'art*. Mon–Fri 10am–6pm, Sat 10am–5pm.

ILLUM Østergade 52 Ⓦ illum.dk. Hard to miss, halfway down Strøget, this is Copenhagen's premier department store: worth visiting just to marvel at the interior. Mon–Sat 10am–8pm, Sun 11am–6pm.

MARKETS

Gammel Strand flea market Gammel Strand 26. The most central market, celebrated but pricey, focusing on antiques. Fri & Sat 8am–5pm.

Nørrebro Flea Market Just outside Assistens Cemetery along Nørrebrogade. Head out here for cheaper deals on everything from porcelain to clothes. May to mid-Oct Sat 7am–2pm.

Torvehallerne Israels Plads Ⓦ torvehallernekbh.dk. Copenhagen's food market, near Norreport station, is an evocative covered market with stalls selling fairly upscale foodstuffs. Mon–Thurs 10am–7pm, Fri 10am–8pm, Sat 10am–6pm, Sun 11am–5pm.

DIRECTORY

Embassies Australia, Dampfærgevej 26 ☎ 70 26 36 76; Canada, Kristen Bernikowsgade 1 ☎ 33 48 32 00; Ireland, Østbanegade 21 ☎ 35 47 32 00; UK, Kastelsvej 36–40 ☎ 35 44 52 00; US, Dag Hammarskjölds Allé 24 ☎ 33 41 71 00.

Exchange Den Danske Bank at the airport (daily 6am–8.30pm); Forex and X-Change at Central Station (daily 8am–9pm).

8

Hospital Rigshospitalet, Blegdamsvej 9 ☎ 35 45 35 45; ⓦ rigshospitalet.dk.

Left luggage Lockers (Mon–Sat 5.30am–1am, Sun 6am–1am) are at Central Station by the entrance on Reventlowsgade, from 50kr for 24hr.

Pharmacies Steno Apotek, Vesterbrogade 6C; Sønderbro Apotek, Amagerbrogade 158. Both 24hr.

Police In Central Station and at Slotsherrensvej 113, near Islev train station.

Post office Købmagergade 33 and at Central Station.

DAY-TRIPS FROM COPENHAGEN

When the weather's good, you can top up your tan at the **Amager Strandpark beach**, just 5km from the centre (bus #12 or take the metro to Øresund, Amager Strand or Femøren then a 5min walk). If Tivoli hasn't exhausted your appetite, then make for the world's oldest amusement park at **Bakken** (mid-March till Sept daily noon/2pm–10pm/11pm/midnight; April, rides closed some weekdays; multi-ride ticket 219kr/249kr; ⓦ bakken.dk), close to the Klampenborg stop at the end of lines C and F+ on the S-train about 10km north of downtown. Besides slightly sinister clowns and vintage roller coasters it offers pleasant woods and nearby beaches to wander around.

There are two more excellent attractions on Zealand's northeastern coast. In the affluent town of **HILLERØD** at the end of S-train line C is the spectacular multi-turreted **Frederiksborg Slot** (daily April–Oct 10am–5pm; Nov–March 11am–4pm; 75kr; ⓦ frederiksborgslot.dk), a seventeenth-century castle built by Christian IV, surrounded by an ornamental lake and housing Denmark's national portrait gallery. Further north in **HUMLEBÆK**, and a short walk from its train station, is **Louisiana**, an outstanding modern art gallery, at Gammel Strandvej 13 (Tues–Fri 11am–10pm, Sat & Sun 11am–6pm; 115kr; ⓦ louisiana.dk). The gallery's setting is worth the journey alone – a harmonious blend of art, architecture and the natural landscape.

The rest of Zealand

As home to Copenhagen, **Zealand** is Denmark's most visited region, and, with a swift metropolitan transport network covering almost half of the island, you can always make it back to the capital in time for an evening drink. North of Copenhagen, **Helsingør** (Elsinore) is the departure point for ferries to Sweden and the site of legendary Kronborg Castle. To the west, and on the main train route to Funen, is **Roskilde**, with an extravagant cathedral that served as the resting place for Danish monarchs, and a superb location on the Roskilde fjord, from where five Viking boats were salvaged and are now displayed in a spectacular, specially built museum.

The northern coast of Zealand is scattered with quaint little fishing villages: consider a trip to **Gilleleje**, where you can buy fresh fish directly from the fishermen (connected by train to Helsingør).

HELSINGØR

Despite its status as a busy ferry port, **HELSINGØR** is a likeable town with some major historical attractions. Its position on the narrow strip of water linking the North Sea and the Baltic brought the town prosperity when, in 1429, the Sound Toll was imposed on passing vessels. Today it remains an important waterway, with ferries to and from Helsingborg in Sweden accounting for most of Helsingør's through-traffic and innumerable cheap booze shops.

WHAT TO SEE AND DO

Kronborg Castle

The town's single great tourist draw is **Kronborg Castle** (daily: June–Aug 10am–5.30pm; Sept–May 11am–4pm; Nov–March closed Mon; 90kr winter, 140kr summer; ⓦ kronborg.dk), principally because of its literary associations as Elsinore Castle, the setting for Shakespeare's *Hamlet*. There's no evidence Shakespeare ever visited Helsingør, and the tenth-century character Amleth on whom his hero was based long predates the castle. Nevertheless, the cottage industry of Hamlet souvenirs thrives here. The present castle dates from the sixteenth century when it jutted into the sound as a formidable warning to passing ships not to consider dodging the toll, and it remains a grand affair, enhanced immeasurably by its setting; the interior, particularly the royal chapel, is memorably ornate. Beneath the castle are the casemates, gloomy cavernous rooms that served as soldiers' quarters during times of war.

The historic shipyards

The big attraction just south of the castle is the revamped former shipyard area where the **Maritime Museum of Denmark** (Ny Kronborgvej 1; July & Aug daily 10am–5pm; Sept–June daily 11am–4pm; 110kr; ⓦmfs.dk) is one of the country's premiere places to learn about Denmark's seafaring past and present. Set underground in the old dry docks next to the Castle, the building comprises a continuous ramp that loops around the dock walls, allowing for unobstructed views from the Castle. Inside, the technologically advanced, well-curated collections span Viking, medieval and modern seafaring, exploration and merchant shipping. There are other unique finds, including a colossal Maersk freight container, relics from Denmark's conquests in Greenland, India, the West Indies and West Africa and – yes, really – the world's oldest surviving ship's biscuit (1852). The area is also the site of the **Culture Yard** (Mon–Fri 10am–9pm, Sat & Sun 10am–4pm; free; ⓦkulturvaerftet.dk), a theatre, concert venue, library and café-restaurant housed in an innovatively designed glass-steel structure created from old wharf buildings.

The medieval quarter

Helsingør's well-preserved **medieval quarter** is dominated by **Stengade**, the

> **FERRIES TO SWEDEN**
>
> The main ferry operator between Helsingør and **Helsingborg** in Sweden is Scandlines (ⓦscandlines.dk), making the twenty-minute crossing every fifteen to thirty minutes (78–108kr). All services leave from the main terminal by the train station. Eurail is valid on Scandlines, while InterRail and the Copenhagen Card give a 25 percent discount.

main shopping street, which is linked by a number of narrow alleyways to Axeltorv, the town's small market square – a nice place to enjoy a beer. Near the corner of Stengade and Skt Annagade is Helsingør's cathedral, **Skt Olai Kirke** (Mon–Sat: May–Aug 10am–4pm; Sept–April 10am–2pm; free; ⓦhelsingoerdomkirke.dk), while beyond is **Skt Mariæ Kirke** (mid-May to mid-Sept Tues–Sun 10am–3pm, mid-Sept to mid-May Tues–Sun 10am–2pm; free; guided tours at 2pm Mon–Fri; 20kr), whose Karmeliterklostret, built circa 1400, is now the best-preserved medieval monastery in Scandinavia (guided tours only; arrange via the church office). Its former hospital now contains the **Town Museum** (Tues–Sun noon–4pm, Sat till 2pm; 20kr), which displays surgical tools used in early brain operations.

ARRIVAL AND INFORMATION

By train The train station is on Jernbanevej, a 2min walk south of the centre.

Destinations Copenhagen (every 20min; 45min); Gilleleje (every 30min; 45min); Hillerød (hourly; 30min).

Tourist office Havnepladsen 3, just opposite the train station (Jan–June & Sept–Dec Mon–Fri 10am–4pm; July & Aug Mon–Fri 10am–5pm, Sat & Sun 10am–2pm; Aug closed Sun; ☏49 21 13 33, ⓦvisitnorthsealand.com).

ACCOMMODATION

Danhostel Helsingør Nordre Strandvej 24 ☏49 28 49 49, ⓦhelsingorhostel.dk. Beautifully located hostel in a restored villa bang on the beach (suitable for swimming) 2km north of town; bus #340 from the station (8min; get off at Højstrup Trinbraet stop). Rents bikes for 75kr/day. The cheapest rooms share baths off the corridor. Dorms 225kr, doubles 550kr

Helsingor Camping Strandalleen 2 ☏49 28 49 50, ⓦhelsingorcamping.dk. Near *Danhostel* on the same bus route, this magnificent site has great coastal views across to Kronborg Slot. Camping/person **75kr**, plus per tent **50kr**, cabins **420kr**

EATING AND DRINKING

Café Andre Kampergade 7 ⓦ cafeandre.dk. Tremendous-value stalwart of the town eating scene, which is popular with students. Sandwiches and salads from 59kr. Tues–Sat 10am–5pm.

Café Brostraede Brostraede 1. Unpretentious café with limited seating but the best sandwiches around (44kr), plus ice cream, frozen yoghurt and organic beers; down a tiny alley linking the port with the old town. Mon–Fri 10.30am–5.30pm, Sat 10.30am–3pm.

ROSKILDE

Once the capital of Denmark, **ROSKILDE** is worth a visit even if you can't make it to its famous annual rock festival (see box below). Its **Viking Ship Museum** is a world-class attraction, while the cathedral and old centre are lovely to wander around.

WHAT TO SEE AND DO

The fabulous **Roskilde Domkirke** (April–Sept Mon–Sat 10am–6pm, Sun 1–6pm; Oct–March Mon–Sat 10am–4pm, Sun 1–4pm; 60kr; ⓦ visit .roskildedomkirke.dk) was founded by Bishop Absalon in 1170 and largely completed by the fourteenth century. It's stuffed full of dead Danish monarchs, including twenty kings and seventeen queens. The most impressive chapel is that of Christian IV, full of bronze statues, frescoes and vast paintings of scenes from his reign. The current queen, the charismatic Margrethe II, has also expressed a desire to be buried here.

Next door is Roskilde Palace, housing the diverting **Museum of Contemporary Art** (Tues, Thurs & Fri noon–5pm, Wed noon–8pm, Sat & Sun 11am–4pm; 50kr, Wed free; ⓦ samtidskunst.dk).

Viking Ship Museum

Fifteen minutes' walk north of the centre on the banks of the fjord is the modern **Viking Ship Museum** (late June to Aug daily 10am–5pm; Sept to mid-June daily 10am–4pm; 115kr May–Sept, otherwise 80kr; ⓦ vikingshipmuseum.dk). Inside, five superb specimens of Viking

shipbuilding are displayed: a deep-sea trader, a merchant ship, a warship, a fishing vessel and a longship preserved incredibly from 1042, each retrieved from the fjord where they were sunk to block invading forces. You can board two life-size models of ships next door, and try on traditional Viking clothes. Outside, boat-building and sail-making demonstrations use only tools and materials available during the Viking era; when the weather allows, you can also experience a replica ship's seaworthiness on the fjord – you'll be handed an oar when you board and be expected to pull your weight as a crew member (50min; 80kr on top of the museum ticket; minimum twelve people). It's a humbling experience when you consider that similar ships made it all the way to Greenland.

ARRIVAL AND INFORMATION

By train The train station is at the southern edge of town.
Destinations Copenhagen (every 20min; 30min); Odense (hourly; 1hr 20min).

By bus The bus station is within the same complex as the train station.
Destinations Copenhagen (several hourly; 40min).

Tourist office On the main square, Stændertorvet 1 (Mon–Fri 10am–4/5pm, Sat 10am–1pm; ☎ 46 31 65 65, ⓦ visitroskilde.com).

Cycle rental Jupiter Cykler Roskilde at Gullandsstræde 3 offer cycle rental (75kr/day; 500kr deposit; Mon–Thurs 9am–5.30pm, Fri 9am–6pm, Sat 9am–2pm).

ACCOMMODATION

Roskilde Camping Baunehøjvej 7 ☎ 46 75 79 96, ⓦ roskildecamping.dk. 4km north of town via Frederiksborgvej on bus route #603, the campsite here has a gorgeous grassy, woodsy setting on the edge of the fjord.

ROSKILDE FESTIVAL

Book well in advance if you wish to stay during the **Roskilde Festival** (ⓦ roskilde -festival.dk), one of the largest open-air music festivals in Europe, attracting almost 100,000 people annually. Tickets go on sale in December and tend to sell out quickly. The festival usually takes place in early July, and there's a special free campsite beside the festival site, to which shuttle buses run from the train station every few minutes.

It's quite windy round here. Camping/person 80kr, plus tent 40kr, cabins 550kr

Roskilde Vandrerhjem Vindeboder 7 ☎46 35 21 84, ⓦ danhostel.dk/roskilde. Beautifully situated modern hostel of 40 rooms in the harbour area near the Viking Museum. Dorms 225kr, doubles 550kr

EATING AND DRINKING

★**Gimle** Helligkorvej 2 ⓦ gimle.dk. Set just 10min east of the tourist office, this café/live music venue serves burgers (99kr) and sandwiches (459kr); also turns into a club Friday and Saturday nights. Tues & Wed noon–midnight, Thurs noon–2am, Fri & Sat noon–5am, Sun 10am–5pm.

Konditor Bager Algade 6 ⓦ konditor-bager.dk. This is Roskilde's best bakery; breads and cakes 8–15kr. Mon–Thurs 7.30am–4pm, Fri 7am–4pm, Sat 7.30am–3pm.

Primo Piano Køgevej 1 ⓦ primo-piano.dk. Ridiculously good-value Italian with a wonderful range of pizzas, pastas and salads from 79kr. Wed–Sat 4–10pm.

Funen

Funen is the smaller of the two main Danish islands. Its pastoral outlook and laidback fishing villages along the coast draw many visitors, but the key attraction is **Odense**, Denmark's third city and the birthplace of writer Hans Christian Andersen and composer Carl Nielsen.

ODENSE

Named after Odin, chief of the pagan gods, **ODENSE** (pronounced Own-suh) is well over a thousand years old. An attractive little place, with a lush location on the River Odense Å, it has an engaging cultural scene and a surprisingly energetic nightlife with a focus on live music: it's one of Denmark's most enchanting places to spend a few days.

WHAT TO SEE AND DO

Odense's inner core is a network of cobbled streets flanked by photogenic medieval houses.

H.C. Andersens Hus and H.C. Andersens Barndomshjem

The city's (perhaps the country's) best attraction is the **H.C. Andersens Hus** at Bangs Boder 29 (June–Aug daily 10am–5pm; Sept–May Tues–Sun 10am–4pm; 95kr; ⓦ museum.odense.dk), where the writer was born in 1805. The museum includes a library of Andersen's

8

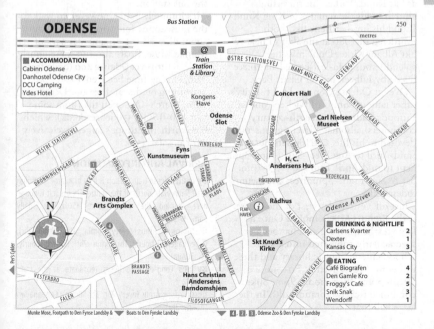

works and audio recordings of some of his best-known fairytales read by the likes of Sir Laurence Olivier. There's also intriguing paraphernalia including school reports, manuscripts, paper cuttings and drawings from his travels. The most striking feature, aside from the diminutive house itself, is the series of murals by Niels Larsen Stevns (1930) depicting different stages of Andersen's life. Check out the telling quotes on Andersen's unconventional looks and talent: "He is the most hideous man you could find but has a poetic childish mind", commented one contemporary.

Down the road, at Munkemøllestræde 3–5, is the tiny **H. C. Andersens Barndomshjem** (Childhood Home; June–Aug daily 10am–5pm; Sept–May Tues–Sun 11am–4pm; 30kr; ⓦmuseum .odense.dk), where the writer lived between the ages of 2 and 14.

The city centre

On Skt Knuds Plads just southwest of the Rådhus (town hall) is the crypt of Gothic **Odense Cathedral** (daily: April–Oct 10am–5pm; Nov–March 10am–4pm; free; ⓦodense-domkirke.dk). Also known as Skt Knuds Kirke, this travertine church holds the remains of King Knud II and his brother Benedikt, both murdered in 1086 at the altar of nearby Skt Albani Kirke. Don't miss the splendiferous gold-leaf-coated altarpiece inside by Lübeck master Claus Berg.

Over at Odense Concert Hall the city's other famous son, Carl Nielsen (one of Europe's leading nineteenth-century composers), also has a riveting museum devoted to his life, **Carl Nielsen Museet** (mid-April to Aug Wed–Sun 11am–3pm, Sept to mid-April Thurs & Fri 3–7pm, Sat & Sun 11am–3pm; free; ⓦmuseum .odense.dk).

Just off Vestergade, west of the centre, is the **Brandts Arts Complex**. Once a large textile mill, the area has been spectacularly converted into an art school, cinema, music library and three museums (Tues, Wed & Fri–Sun 10am–5pm, Thurs noon–9pm; 80kr combined ticket; ⓦbrandts.dk). In the large hall that

once housed the huge machinery is the **Kunsthallen**, which displays works by the cream of new talent in art and design, and the **Museet for Fotokunst**, featuring changing photography exhibitions. On the third floor the **Danmarks Mediemuseum** chronicles the development of printing, bookbinding and illustrating from the Middle Ages to the present day. There is another branch of Brandts at Jernbanegade 13 (Brandts 13; same opening hours) focusing on late nineteenth-century Danish art including stirring works by Vilhelm Hammershøi and Skagen artist P.S. Krøyer.

Den Fynske Landsby and Odense Zoo

South of the centre at Sejerskovvej 20 is **Den Fynske Landsby** (Funen Village; March–June & mid-Aug to late Oct Tues–Sun 10am–5pm; July to mid-Aug daily 10am–6pm; 60kr, June–Aug 85kr; ⓦmuseum.odense.dk), a living, breathing nineteenth-century village made up of buildings brought here from all over Funen, including a windmill and a school. In summer, free shows are staged at the open-air theatre. Buses #110 and #111 run to the village from the bus station.

It's infinitely better, however, to walk to the museum by following the river south about 4km via the ornamental park of Munke Mose. Boats also run there hourly (80kr return) via **Odense Zoo** (daily from 9am, closing time between 4 and 7pm, depending on day and season; Dec closes 2pm; March–Oct open till 10pm some Sat; 150–190kr; ⓦodensezoo.dk), which has Northern Europe's largest exclusively African safari park.

ARRIVAL AND INFORMATION

By train Odense train station is part of a large shopping mall 5min walk north of the centre. There's left luggage here, behind the ticket office (50kr/24hr; daily 5am–1.15am).

Destinations Århus (every 30min; 1hr 30min–2hr); Copenhagen (3 hourly; 1hr 30min–2hr); Esbjerg (hourly; 1hr 30min).

By bus Long-distance buses terminate at the train station.

Destinations Århus (every 2hr; 1hr 50min); Copenhagen (hourly; 2hr).

Tourist office At Vestergade 2 near the Rådhus (July & Aug 9.30am–6pm, Sat 10am–3pm, Sun 11am–2pm; Sept–June Mon–Fri 9.30am–4.30pm, Sat 10am–1pm; ☎ 63 75 75 20, ⓦ visitodense.com).

Bike rental CSV Cykeludlejning, at Nedergade 36 (100kr/day, plus 500kr deposit).

ACCOMMODATION

Cabinn Odense Østre Stationsvej 7–9 ☎ 63 14 57 00, ⓦ cabinn.com. Budget chain hotel close to the train station. All rooms are short on space but are en suite and have TV. Free internet access; buffet breakfast 70kr. Doubles 625kr

Danhostel Odense City Østre Stationsvej 31 ☎ 63 11 04 25, ⓦ cityhostel.dk. Conveniently located in a former hotel next to the train station, this five-star hostel has clean rooms (doubles are still bunks, though) and 24hr automated check-in. Doubles 570kr

DCU Camping Odensevej 102 ☎ 66 11 47 02, ⓦ odenseuk .dcu.dk/. Located near Den Fynske Landsby on the outskirts of Odense, this campsite has mini-golf and a heated pool. Take bus #22 from the train station towards Højby. Camping/person 78kr, plus per tent 25kr, cabins 550kr

Ydes Hotel Hans Tausens Gade 11 ☎ 66 12 11 31, ⓦ ydes .dk. One of the city's oldest hotels, but with a modern refurbishment and surprisingly competitive prices. Doubles 550kr

EATING

★ **Café Biografen** Brandts Passage 39–41 ⓦ cafebio .dk. Trendy bar attached to an artsy cinema, adorned with classic film posters. The bar gets going with thirty-somethings later on. Club sandwich 79kr; coffee 22kr. Brunch buffet (Fri–Sat till 2pm) 109kr. Mon–Thurs 10am–11pm, Fri & Sat 10am–midnight, Sun 10am–10.30pm.

Den Gamle Kro Overgade 23 ⓦ dengamlekro.eu. Set within a seventeenth-century courtyard, this traditional restaurant offers one of the best gastronomic experiences in Denmark. There's a basement wine cellar and a host of delicious *smørrebrød* (mostly 80–140kr) so you *can* have the experience for down-to-earth prices. Mon–Sat 11am–10pm, Sun 11am–9pm.

Froggy's Café Vestergade 68 ⓦ froggyscafe.dk. Bang-in-the-centre café-bar serving delicious salads (from 109kr) and the legendary *Froggy's* burger (124kr). Brunches from 109kr and divine fresh salmon (150kr) among the evening specials. DJs at weekends. Mon–Wed 9am–midnight, Thurs 9am–2am, Fri & Sat 9.30am–5am, Sun 9.30am–midnight.

Snik Snak Jernbanegade 14. Classy tapas place with knowledgeable staff who readily explain the only-in-Danish menu. Tapas 40–70kr – or the delicious charcuterie board for 79kr. Mon–Wed 10am–11pm, Thurs 10am–1am, Fri & Sat 10am–2am.

Wendorff Asylgade 16 ⓦ wendorff.dk. Wonderful bakery with two counters teeming with bread and cakes (9–15kr). Mon–Fri 7am–6pm, Sat & Sun 7am–4pm.

DRINKING AND NIGHTLIFE

★ **Carlsens Kvarter** Hunderupvej 19 ⓦ carlsens.dk. Cosy bar in the style of a country pub, with a relaxed atmosphere and Odense's best selection of beers (around 30kr for bottles), including all the Belgian Trappist ales. Mon–Sat noon–1am, Sun 1–7pm.

Dexter Vindegade 65 ⓦ dexter.dk. Jazz, blues and folk venue with live music a few times a week (entry 80–180kr, depending on the group playing) and a free jam night on Monday evenings. Good range of international beers too.

★ **Kansas City** Munkebjergvej 140 ⓦ kansascity.dk. This old clothes factory is now an experimental music venue epitomizing everything that's great about the local music scene: watch this space for tomorrow's big Danish names. It's 2km south of the centre via bus #29 or #63. Fri & Sat 7pm–late.

Jutland

8

Long ago, the Jutes, the people of **Jutland**, were a separate tribe from the more warlike Danes who occupied the eastern islands. By the Viking era, however, the battling Danes had spread west, absorbing the Jutes, and real power gradually shifted towards Zealand, where it has largely stayed ever since. Now, **Århus**, Denmark's second city halfway up the eastern coast, and **Aalborg**, capital of northern Jutland, are vibrant, cosmopolitan urban centres that draw those who dare to venture on from the other, more frequently visited, centres. To the west, the landscape becomes ever-more dramatic, with heather-clad moors and forests inland and both fjord and sea coastlines to explore – and the foreign tourists dry out completely. North of Aalborg the landscape becomes increasingly wind-battered and stark until it reaches **Skagen**, on the peninsula's tip.

ARRIVAL AND INFORMATION

By train You can reach the Jutland ferry terminals by train from other parts of the country. The train station in Esbjerg is at the end of Skolegade, with trains to and from Copenhagen (3hr 10min). All buses and most trains in Frederikshavn terminate at the central train station, a

WEST COAST WONDERS

Heading out to Denmark's west coast makes a tranquil diversion from the big urban centres further east. West from Århus you hit Esbjerg, from where ferries (hourly; 45kr; Ⓦ faergen.com) run to the artsy, folksy sandy island of **Fanø** (Ⓦ visitfanoe.dk). Just south of Esbjerg by train (hourly, 30min) is the oldest town in Denmark, **Ribe** (Ⓦ visitribe.com), with a beguiling medieval centre and several riveting museums.

short walk from the town centre; some trains continue to the ferry terminal itself.

By boat Jutland's main international ferry port is Frederikshavn, in the far north of the region (2hr 45min by train from Århus). It has express ferries to Götaborg in Sweden and Oslo, Norway (Ⓦ stenaline.nl). Its ferry terminal is near Havnepladsen, not far from the centre.

Tourist offices The tourist office in Esbjerg is at 33 Skolegade (self service; Mon–Wed & Sun 10am–8pm; Thurs–Sat 10am–6pm; ☎ 75 12 55 99, Ⓦ visitesbjerg.dk). In Frederikshavn, the tourist office is close to the ferry terminal at Skandiatorv 1 (mid-Aug to late June Mon–Fri 9.30am–4pm, Sat 10am–1pm; late June to mid-Aug Mon–Sat 9.30am–6pm, Sun 10am–1pm; ☎ 98 42 32 66, Ⓦ visitfrederikshavn.dk).

ÅRHUS

Denmark's second-largest city, **ÅRHUS**, is an attractive assortment of intimate cobbled streets, sleek modern architecture, brightly painted houses and student hangouts. It's small enough to get to grips with in a few hours, but lively enough to make you linger for days – an excellent music scene (especially for jazzophiles), interesting art, pavement cafés and energetic nightlife all earn it the unofficial title of Denmark's capital of culture. And Århus keeps ratcheting up its reputation – as European Capital of Culture in 2017 (Ⓦ aarhus2017.dk) it has been adding new events and attractions.

WHAT TO SEE AND DO

Århus's main street, pedestrianized Ryesgade/Søndergade, leads down from the train station, across the river and into the main town square, Bispetorvet. Running parallel one block west of

Ryesgade is Park Alle with the functionalist 1941 **Rådhus** (city hall), designed by Arne Jacobsen and Eric Moller; guided tours including the bell tower can be arranged through the tourist office (see p.232). Bispetorvet is dominated by the fifteenth-century **Domkirke** (May–Sept Mon & Wed–Sat 9.30am–4pm, Tues 10.30am–4pm; Oct–April Mon & Wed–Sat 10am–3pm, Tues 10.30am–3pm; Ⓦ aarhus-domkirke .dk), a massive Gothic church with exquisite frescoes as well as a miniature Danish warship hanging from the ceiling. The area to the north, known as the Latin Quarter, is crammed with shops, galleries and modern cafés.

ARoS

ARoS (Tues & Thurs–Sun 10am–5pm, Wed 10am–10pm; 120kr; Ⓦ aros.dk) is one of Europe's most beautiful contemporary buildings and a fantastic modern art museum. It contains seven floors of works from the late eighteenth century to the present day, accessed from a centrepiece spiral walkway reminiscent of New York's Guggenheim. The Skagen artists head the fine collection of home-grown art, though the likes of Warhol are also represented along with the eerie 5m-high *Boy*, by Australian sculptor Ron Mueck. Its standout permanent exhibit is artist Olafur Eliasson's fantastical addition to the roof, known as *Your Rainbow Panorama*. Suspended between city and sky, and loosely inspired by Dante's *Divine Comedy*, this 150m circular pathway spans the colour spectrum and gives panoramic views over the city.

Den Gamle By

A short walk northwest of the centre is one of the city's best-known attractions, **Den Gamle By**, on Viborgvej (The Old Town; daily: Jan 11am–3pm; early Feb to late March 10am–4pm; late March to June & mid-Aug to Dec 10am–5pm; July to mid-Aug 10am–6pm; 135kr; Ⓦ dengamleby.dk), an open-air museum of traditional Danish life, with half-timbered townhouses and actors in contemporary dress. Many buildings

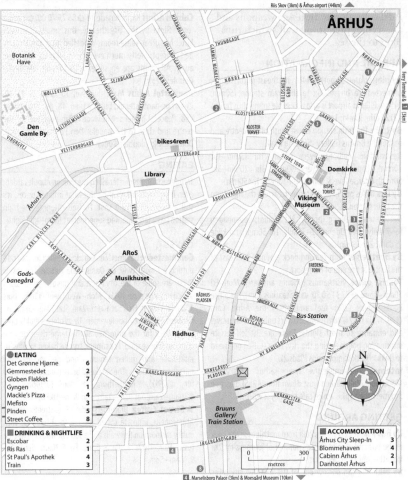

Riis Skov (3km) & Århus airport (44km)

ÅRHUS

Botanisk Have

Den Gamle By

bikes4rent

Library

ARoS

Musikhuset

Rådhus

Gods-banegård

Domkirke

Viking Museum

Bispe-torvet

Bus Station

Bruuns Gallery/ Train Station

N

8

●EATING

Det Grønne Hjørne	6
Gemmestedet	2
Globen Flakket	7
Gyngen	1
Mackie's Pizza	4
Mefisto	3
Pinden	5
Street Coffee	8

■ DRINKING & NIGHTLIFE

Escobar	2
Ris Ras	1
St Paul's Apothek	4
Train	3

■ ACCOMMODATION

Århus City Sleep-In	3
Blommehaven	4
Cabinn Århus	2
Danhostel Århus	1

0   300
metres

Marselisborg Palace (3km) & Moesgård Museum (10km)

date from the 1800s, but a new town expansion features shops and homes from the 1920s and 1970s. You can enter places such as a pastry shop, a haberdashery and a gynaecologist clinic, and there are also pony rides, a bookshop and a working central telephone switchboard. Close by are the pleasant **botanical gardens** (Mon–Sat 1–3pm, Sun 11am–3pm; free).

Marselisborg Palace and Moesgård Museum

Marselisborg Skov, 3km south of the centre, is the city's largest park, and home to the summer residence of the Danish

royals: its landscaped grounds can be visited when the monarch isn't staying (usually at all times outside Easter, Christmas and late June to early Aug; bus #19).

Ten kilometres south of Århus, the striking, just-refurbished **Moesgård Museum** (Tues & Fri–Sun 10am–5pm, Wed & Thurs 10am–9pm; 130kr; ⓦmoesmus.dk; bus #6) details Danish civilizations from the Stone Age onwards. Its most notable exhibit is the "Grauballe Man", a startlingly well-preserved sacrificial victim dating from around 100 BC discovered in a peat bog west of town in 1952. Also remarkable is the Illerup

Ådal collection of Iron Age weapons and the scenic "prehistoric trail" which runs 3km to the sea.

ARRIVAL AND INFORMATION

By plane Århus airport is 44km northeast of the centre, connected via bus #925x to the train station (50min; 115kr). Billund airport is also accessible from Århus by bus #912X (1hr 30min; 140kr).

By train The train station is just south of the centre and part of the Bruuns Gallery shopping mall.

Destinations Aalborg (every 30min; 1hr 15min–1hr 30min); Copenhagen (every 30min; 3hr 20min–3hr 50min); Odense (every 30min; 1hr 30min–1hr 50min).

By bus Buses pull in at the terminus across the road from the train station.

Destinations Aalborg (hourly; 2hr 30min); Copenhagen (6–7 daily; 3hr); Odense (2–3 daily, 1hr 50min); Roskilde (5 daily; 2hr 55min).

By boat Ferries from Zealand dock around 500m east of the centre at the end of Nørreport.

Tourist office VisitAarhus (phones answered Mon–Fri 10am–3pm; ☎ 87 31 50 10, ⓦ visitaarhus.com). The office books rooms (70kr fee) and offers the Århus Card (129/179kr for 24/48hr), which covers unlimited bus travel and entrance to most sights. There are 30 self-service information points around the city; for a staffed one head to Dokk1 (Hack Kampmanns Plads 2).

Internet The impressive new Aarhus Library on Møllegade, Mølleparken (just down from ARoS), has free internet access (plus a nice café to enjoy it with).

GETTING AROUND

By bus A basic ticket costs 20kr from machines in the back of the bus and is valid for any number of journeys for 2hr from the time stamped on it.

By bike You can borrow one of the 450 free city bikes (April–Oct; ⓦ aarhus.dk) dotted around the city centre (20kr coin deposit). Otherwise, bikes4rent at Skanderborgvej 107 (ⓦ bikes4rent.dk) rents out bikes from 95kr/day, with a 300kr deposit.

ACCOMMODATION

Århus City Sleep-In Havnegade 20 ☎ 86 19 20 55, ⓦ citysleep-in.dk. The most central hostel, with facilities including a guest kitchen, pool and TV rooms and a courtyard for summer barbecues. Organic breakfast is 70kr; also has free internet access. Dorms 190kr, doubles with shared bathroom 460kr, with private bathroom 520kr

Blommehaven Ørneredevej 35 ☎ 86 27 02 07, ⓦ camping-blommehaven.dk; bus #6 or #19. Overlooking a bay 5km south of the city centre, this campsite has access to a beautiful beach. Closed mid-Oct to mid-March. Camping/person 78kr, plus per tent 20kr, cabins 350kr

Cabinn Århus Kannikegade 14 ☎ 86 75 70 00, ⓦ cabinn .com. Right by the city theatre, this small, functional hotel has great-value rooms modelled after the Murphy bed concept: pretty much everything folds up and packs away. All rooms are en suite, with TV and telephone. Doubles 625kr

Danhostel Århus Marienlundsvej 10 ☎ 86 21 21 20, ⓦ aarhus-danhostel.dk; buses #1, #6, #8, #9, #16, #56 or #58. Peaceful hostel set in woods 3km northeast of the centre and close to the popular Den Permanente beach. Dorms 250kr, doubles 500kr

EATING

Trendy restaurants cluster along the river on Åboulevarden: even if you can't afford the somewhat inflated prices, it's still a lovely picnicking spot. For self-catering, the train station has a late-opening supermarket (8am–midnight).

CAFÉS

Gemmestedet Gammel Munkegade 1. Chilled, vibrant café putting a Turkish twist on Danish café culture. The salads (89kr) are some of the city's best and there's a novel tapas selection (large plate 105kr). Mon–Wed 10am–11pm, Thurs 10am–midnight, Fri & Sat 10am–2am, Sun 10am–9pm.

Globen Flakket Åboulevarden 18 ⓦ globen-flakket.dk. Locals flock for the brunches at this large riverside café with outdoor seating. For supper, try the baked trout with ratatouille and grilled lemon alongside one of their microbrewery beers. The weekend brunch buffets are a big hit (129kr). Mon–Thurs 8.30am–10.30pm, Fri 8.30am–2am, Sat 9am–2am, Sun 9am–10.30pm.

★ **Street Coffee** Brammersgade 15 ⓦ streetcoffee.dk. Atmospheric, intimate coffee shop: a local hangout with quirky cartoons on the walls and a sublime array of caffeine fixes. Mon–Thurs 7.30am–6pm, Fri 8.30am–5pm, Sat 9.30am–5pm.

RESTAURANTS

Det Grønne Hjørne Frederiksgade 60 ⓦ dgh-aarhus.dk. Great choice for a big feed on the cheap with an all-you-can-eat buffet (noon–4pm, 79kr; 4.30–10pm, 119kr). Mon–Sat noon–11pm.

Gyngen Mejlgade 53 ⓦ gyngen.dk. Impressive veggie burgers (120kr) and a mean chilli con carne with crème fraîche (78kr). Live music Tues–Sat (entrance 100–150kr). Tues 11am–4pm & 7pm–2am, Wed–Fri 11am–2am, Sat 6pm–2am.

★ **Mackie's Pizza** Sankt Clemens Torv 9 ⓦ mackiespizza.dk. Zany pizza joint with diner-style interior full of sports and music memorabilia. Delectable pizzas (from 65kr), with the rule that you have to eat them cutlery-free. Steaks, burgers and the like too. Mon–Sat 11.30am–10.30pm, Sun noon–10pm.

Mefisto Volden 28 ⓦ mefisto.dk. Less pricey than the beautiful building and mellow atmosphere might suggest.

In one of the city's prettiest townhouses, you can get good *smørrebrød* and light lunches (90–130kr) and even some dinnertime bargains (great fish dishes for 150kr). Mon–Fri 11.30am–10pm, Sat & Sun 10am–10pm.

Pinden Skolegade 29 ⓦpinden.dk. The best place in town for traditional Danish food, particularly for typical fish dishes (69–119kr). Mon–Wed noon–11pm, Thurs–Sat noon–1am.

DRINKING AND NIGHTLIFE

Escobar Skolegade 32. Popular student hangout with cheap beer (draught 40kr), loud music (frequently metal) and friendly bar staff. Mon–Thurs & Sun 7pm–3am, Fri 2pm–5am, Sat 7pm–5am.

Ris Ras Mejlgade 24 ⓦcaferisras.dk. Chilled student hangout with a vast range of beers. No food served, but you're welcome to bring your own. Mon–Thurs noon–2am, Fri–Sat noon–3am, Sun 2–7pm.

St Paul's Apothek Jægergårdsgade 76 ⓦ stpaulsapothek .dk. It's all about the cocktails, this place, and the trendy former apothecary shop certainly knows how to mix. Tues–Thurs 5.30pm–midnight, Fri & Sat 5.30pm–2am.

Train Toldbodgade 6 ⓦtrain.dk. Århus's most popular nightclub is also a concert venue pulling in big-name DJs and international acts. Entry fees for club nights 20–100kr, or up to 225kr for concerts.

NORTHWEST OF ÅRHUS

Mainland Denmark's loveliest scenery lies northwest of Århus, with the big draw being the country's first national park, **Thy** (ⓦnationalparker.naturstyrelsen.dk), created in 2008. It's a lonely tract of wild beach and inland heath containing the Danish surfing centre of **Klitmøller**, and backing onto vast fjords such as **Limfjorden**, producing some of the world's finest oysters.

ARRIVAL AND INFORMATION

By train and bus Trains run from Århus to Struer (hourly; 2hr 10min) where you change trains to continue by train into the park. Stenbjerg Landing is on bus route #313 from Thisted train station. Bus #322 runs from Thisted to Klitmøller.

Tourist information There's an information centre (and museum/café) at Stenbjerg Landing (April–Oct 1–5pm).

AALBORG

North Jutland's main city, **AALBORG** has undergone a renaissance in recent years. Long renowned for its raucous nightlife and nearby Viking burial ground, this city with nigh-on 200,000 within its metropolitan area has redeveloped its waterfront with hugely impressive results to showcase its industrial heritage, while not detracting from its substantial medieval core. It's also the main transport terminus for the region, and makes an exciting stopover on the way north to Skagen.

WHAT TO SEE AND DO

Huge investment on the stretch of Aalborg facing Limfjorden has transformed the once industrial **waterfront** district into a centre for design and entertainment, while there's plenty of historical charm in the sights and cobbled streets of the **old town**.

Kunsten Museum of Modern Art and Aalborg Tower

The stunning modern gallery that is **Kunsten Museum of Modern Art** (Tues–Fri 9am–5pm, Sat & Sun 10am–5pm; 95kr, free in Dec; ⓦkunsten.dk) is close to a sculpture park (take bus #15 or walk ten minutes west of the train station). Just west of here, up a staircase through woods, is the **Aalborg Tower** (late March to Oct 10/11am–5pm; 40kr), with spectacular city views and a restaurant.

The old town

Aalborg's well-preserved **old town** centres on the Gothic cathedral, the **Budolfi Kirke** (June–Aug Mon–Fri 9am–4pm, Sat 9am–2pm; Sept–May Mon–Fri 9am–3pm, Sat 9am–noon; ⓦaalborgdomkirke.dk). On the other side of Østerågade, sixteenth-century **Aalborghus Castle** is notable for its dungeon (May–Oct Mon–Fri 8am–3pm; free) and underground passages (open till 9pm).

Leading down to the waterfront is bar-lined **Jomfru Ane Gade**, Aalborg's booziest street.

Waterfront

The waterfront is undergoing substantial development, and has recently added a cruise-ship terminal and landscaped park, with more restaurants, bars and shops on the cards. The showpiece attraction is

8

8

Nordkraft (Kjellerups torv 5; ⓦnordkraft
.dk), housed in a former power station
five minutes' walk east of the centre, near
the big new shopping centre Friis, and
containing a cinema, theatre/concert
venue, several restaurants and the tourist
office. Just north, towards the water,
stands the **House of Music** (ⓦmusik
kenshus.dk), a cultural and performance
space, and home to the Royal Academy
of Music. A short walk west is the **Utzon
Center** (Tues–Sun 10am–5pm; 60kr;
ⓦutzoncenter.dk), designed by the man
who gave the world the Sydney Opera
House, Jørn Utzon. Utzon was born in
Aalborg and left the city this fitting
architectural masterpiece, inspired by the
old shipyards hereabouts, shortly before
his death. It's a showcase for contemporary design and has a wonderful café.
A ten-minute walk further west is the
distinctive **V&S Distillery** at Olesens Gade
1, home of the potent Scandinavian spirit
Aquavit, though unfortunately they only
offer tours for large groups.

Lindholm Høje

A few kilometres north of Aalborg via
bus #2 (15min), atmospheric **Lindholm
Høje** (Lindholm Hills; free; ⓦnordmus
.dk/lindholm-gb) is Scandinavia's largest
Viking burial site with more than seven
hundred graves. Visit early or late in the
day and you'll see the slanting sunlight
glint off the burial stones, many of
which are set in the outline of a Viking
ship. It's worth stopping by the site's
impressive **museum** (April–Oct daily
10am–5pm; Nov–March Tues–Sun
10am–4pm; 60kr).

ARRIVAL AND INFORMATION

By plane Aalborg airport (served by budget airline
Norwegian from London Gatwick 3–4 times weekly) is
7km northwest of the centre and connected by buses #2H,
#2J, #70 and #71 (20min; 22kr).
By train The train station is on J.F. Kennedys Plads, 10min
walk southwest of the centre. Left-luggage lockers are
available (50kr/24hr).
Destinations Århus (every 30min; 1hr 15min–1hr 30min);
Copenhagen (every 30min; 4hr 45min–5hr); Frederikshavn
(every 30min; 1hr15min); Odense (about hourly; 3hr).
By bus The bus terminal is on J.F. Kennedys Plads, next to
the train station.

Destinations Århus (hourly; 2hr 30min); Copenhagen
(every 2hr; 5hr 30min).
Tourist office In the Nordkraft building, Kjellerups torv 5
(Mon–Fri 10am–5.30pm, Sat 10am–2pm; ☎99 31 75 00,
ⓦvisitaalborg.com). Helpful service and touch-screen
information; they sell the Aalborg Card here (225kr/48hr),
which gives you free public transport, free admission to
many attractions and discounts in cafés/shops.

ACCOMMODATION

BBBB ☎98 11 60 44, ⓦhostel-aalborg.com. Large, well-
equipped hostel with 35 rooms and some cabins 3km west
of the town on the Limfjord bank beside the marina – take
bus #13 to the Egholm ferry junction and continue on foot
for 5min following the signs. Singles 460kr, doubles
575kr
Cabinn Aalborg Fjordgade 20 ☎96 20 30 00, ⓦcabinn
.com. Modern hotel with small, clean, en-suite rooms next
to the Riis shopping centre. Free wi-fi. Breakfast 70kr.
Doubles 625kr
Strandparken Skydebanevej 20 ☎98 12 76 29,
ⓦstrandparken.dk. Pleasant campsite 2km west of the
centre with access to an open-air swimming pool and
beach. Closed mid-Sept to late March. Per person 85kr,
plus per tent 30kr

EATING AND DRINKING

Jomfru Ane Gade is packed with late-opening bars, clubs
and restaurants offering bargain food/drink deals. Consider
buying the Aalborg Beerwalk card (ⓦvisitaalborg.com),
which gives you free drinks at loads of the bars here.
Flammen Østerågade 27 ⓦrestaurant-flammen.dk.
Hugely popular buffet restaurant with a dozen odd meats
and salads (all-you-can-eat buffet 199kr). It's a chain, but
a small, family-owned one. Mon–Wed & Sun 11am–8pm,
Thurs & Fri 11am–9pm, Sat 10am–9pm.
Irish House Østerågade 25 ⓦtheirishhouse.dk. Popular
pub serving traditional Irish food (until 9pm) and ales,
with regular drinks deals. Live music Thurs–Sat, jam
sessions on Mondays and sport on TV most evenings.
Mon–Wed 1pm–1am, Thurs 1pm–2am, Fri & Sat noon–
4am, Sun 2pm–midnight.
Penny Lane Boulevarden 1 ⓦpennylanecafe.dk.
Buzzing café serving filling sandwiches (85kr), lunches
(from 95kr) and brunches from 105kr. Mon–Fri 8am–6pm,
Sat 8am–5pm, Sun 9am–4pm.
★**Søgaards Bryghus** CW Obels Plads 1A
ⓦsoegaardsbryghus.dk. One of Denmark's best brewpubs,
with any of some 85 beers concocted here. The food is first-
rate too (they do a serious steak). Sunday all-you-can-eat
brunch buffet 198kr, dinner mains 188–258kr. Mon–Thurs
11am–11pm, Fri & Sat 11am–late, Sun 10.30am–9pm.
Studenterhuset Gammeltorv 11, opposite Budolfi
Domkirke ⓦstudenterhuset.dk. Student-run music

venue/café: the place to catch local Danish bands. International student night on Wednesdays. Also has a book exchange library and free internet. Coffee 14kr; large beer 29kr. Mon, Tues & Thurs 11.30am–midnight, Wed 11.30am–1am, Fri 11.30am–2am, Sat 3pm–2am.

SKAGEN

About 100km north of Aalborg, **SKAGEN** lies at the very top of Denmark amid breathtaking heather-topped sand dunes. A popular resort, it attracts thousands of visitors annually thanks to its artistic links to the past and spectacular seafood restaurants.

WHAT TO SEE AND DO

Much of Skagen's appeal lies in aimlessly wandering its marina or cycling out to its fabulous beaches. There is one star sight, however – the **Skagen Museum** (signposted from train station; May–Aug Mon, Tues & Thurs–Sun 10am–5pm, Wed 10am–9pm; Sept & Oct Tues–Sun 10am–5pm; 90kr; ⓦskagenskunstmuseer.dk), displaying much of the work of the influential Skagen artists (see box above). Nearby, at Markvej 2–4, is the former home of two of the group's leading lights: the **Michael and Anna Anchers Hus** (April & Oct Tues–Sun 11am–3pm; May–Aug daily 10am–5pm; 80kr; ⓦskagenskunstmuseer.dk). Around 2.5km southwest of the station is the **Buried Church**, which was engulfed by sand drift in 1795 and subsequently abandoned. Today the white spire is all that remains amid the dunes. **Old Skagen**, 4km west of the centre, is where Denmark's jet set have their villas: head to the **Solnedgangspladsen** here to watch the spectacular sunsets.

Grenen

Denmark's northernmost tip is at **Grenen**, 3km from Skagen along Strandvej and the beach, where two seas – the Kattegat and Skagerrak – meet, often with a powerful clashing of waves. You can get here by tractor-drawn bus (April to mid-Oct; 30kr return) – although it's an enjoyable walk through beautiful seaside scenery. At the tip you'll find some fascinating World War II heritage, an ambient restaurant and kilometres of blissful quiescence.

THE SKAGEN ARTISTS

Skagen has long been popular with artists, thanks to the warm, golden sunlight that illuminates its coastal scenery. During the 1870s, a group of painters inspired by naturalism settled here and began to paint the local fishermen working on the beaches, as well as each other. The **Skagen artists**, among them Michael and Anna Ancher and P.S. Krøyer, stayed until the turn of the century and achieved international recognition for their work, now on display at the Skagen Museum.

ARRIVAL AND INFORMATION

By train Skagen train station is on Sct Laurentii Vej, the town's main thoroughfare. It's served by privately operated trains from Frederikshavn (50 percent discount with Eurail/InterRail; 35min) roughly once an hour.
Tourist office Vestre Strandvej 10, close to the marina (Jan to mid-late June & mid-Aug to late Dec Mon–Fri 9.30am–4pm & Sat 10am–1/2pm; late June to mid-Aug Mon–Sat 9am–4pm & Sun 10am–2pm; ☏98 44 13 77, ⓦskagen-tourist.dk). Can arrange private rooms (around 400kr for 75kr fee).
Bike rental Skagen Cykeludlejning, by the train station (80kr/day, plus 200kr deposit; ⓦcykeludlejning-skagen.dk).

ACCOMMODATION

Danhostel Skagen Rolighedsvej 2 ☏98 44 22 00, ⓦdanhostelskagen.dk. A little way out of the centre, but the rooms are clean and good value. Breakfast 50kr. The nearest train station is actually Frederikshavnsvej. Reservations essential in summer. Closed Dec to mid-Feb. Dorms **190kr**, doubles **635kr**
Grenen Camping Fyrvej ☏63 60 63 61, ⓦcampone.dk. By the beach 1.5km along the road to Grenen. Closed mid-Sept to late March. Per person **76kr**, plus per tent **55kr**

EATING AND DRINKING

Skagen has fantastic "fresh-off-the-boat" seafood: treat yourself to a blowout meal at a marina restaurant like *Pakhuset* at Rødspættevej 6.
★**Brøndums Hotel** Anchersvej 3 ⓦbroendums-hotel .dk. Near the Skagen Museum and historically more important, as it was here that the Skagen Artists ate and socialized. You can do the same in the wonderfully atmospheric hotel restaurant; *smørrebrød* is a somewhat affordable 100–130kr, although otherwise it's pricey. Daily 11.30am–5pm & 6–10pm.
Buddy Holly Havnevej 16 ⓦfacebook.com/Buddy HollySkagen. Skagen's liveliest club, with plenty of drinks deals. Courtyard out the back. Daily 10pm–5am.

8

Jacobs Café & Bar Havnevej 4 @ jakobscafe.dk. Lively café-bar with outside seating and free wi-fi. Sandwiches 90–125kr. Café daily 9am–9.30pm; bar Mon–Thurs & Sun 9am–1am, Fri & Sat 9am–3am.

THE FAROE ISLANDS

Accessible only via plane or ferry, the remote and otherworldly Faroe Islands comprise an archipelago of eighteen wild, green and steeply pitching isles buffeted by North Atlantic winds, making for days of unforgettable adventure and some fascinating insight into Denmark's former colonial territories (though islanders prefer the term "autonomous region"). The islands are characterized by Denmark's most dramatic scenery and an abundance of sheep – which, incidentally, outnumber humans and have fuelled the trade in Faroese woollen products since being worn by the cast in the iconic Danish TV series *The Killing*. Krone is the currency, and Danish and English are understood.

WHAT TO SEE AND DO

The world's smallest capital city, **Torshavn**, a tranquil port of colourful turf-roofed houses, is the obvious starting point for explorations. The historic **Tingenes** area by the harbour is where most of the interest lies in town, along with the islands' now-famous woollen handicrafts showcased at Gudrun & Gudrun (Niels Finsensgøta 12; Mon–Fri 10am–5.30pm, Sat 10am–2pm; @ gudrungudrun.com). Northwest, on the island of Eysturoy, and connected by bus #400 from Torshavn, is **Leirvik**, a fishing village with an engaging **Boat Museum** (harbourfront; May–Sept Mon–Sat 10am–5pm; contact Torshavn tourist office before visiting). Further northwest from Torshavn is **Viðoy**, a wild island boasting some of Europe's highest sea

cliffs and a haven for birdlife. To reach the cliffs at **Cape Enniberg**, head to the village of Viðareiði (bus #400 from Torshavn to Klaksvik then bus #500; eight daily; 140kr) from where it's a tough, mountainous walk. The remotest of the Faroe Islands is spectacular **Mykines**, to the extreme west of the archipelago. Truly lost in time, it has some of the Faroes' best hiking. Get to Mykines via helicopter from Vágar Airport (Wed, Fri & Sun; 145kr; @ atlantic.fo) or boat from nearby Sørvágur (summer only; 60kr; @ ssl.fo).

ARRIVAL AND INFORMATION

By plane Vágar Airport, 45km west of Torshavn, has recently been refurbished and is connected to the capital by bus (10 daily; 1hr; 90kr). Atlantic Airways (@ atlantic .fo) is the sole carrier operating flights to the Faroe Islands. Destinations Copenhagen (2 daily; 1hr 20min).
By boat Ferries dock in central Torshavn; passages are operated by Smyril Lines (@ smyrilline.com).
Destinations Hirtshals (1–2 weekly; 28–31hr).
Tourist office Gongin 9. Can advise on accommodation, activities and transport on all the islands (@ 298 66 65 55; @ visitfaroeislands.com). Due to extreme conditions, a guide for any hike on the Faroes is strongly recommended.

ACCOMMODATION, EATING AND DRINKING

★**Áarstova** Gongin 1 @ aarstova.fo. Brilliant, snug restaurant in one of Torshavn's oldest houses, specializing in Faroese cuisine. Get your salted fish and wind-dried lamb here. 3/5-course dinners 500/700kr. Daily 6pm–midnight.
Barbora Fish House Gongin 4–6. Reasonably affordable and atmospheric locale specializing in local seafood. Daily 5.30–10pm.
Café Natur Aarvegur 7. The liveliest joint in town. Renovated harbourside café-bar sporting the Faroes' best beer selection, with live music at weekends. Mon–Thurs 11.30am–11.45pm, Fri 11.30am–3.45am, Sat 12.30pm–3.45am, Sun 1.30–11.45pm.
Kerjalon Hostel Oyggjarvegur 45 @ 298 31 75 00, @ hotelforoyar.com. The best budget accommodation in Torshavn, located next to the *Hotel Føroyar*. Dorms __250kr__

8

OLD TOWN, TALLINN

Estonia

HIGHLIGHTS

❶ **Tallinn's Old Town** Wander this beautifully preserved corner of the city. **See p.242**

❷ **Lahemaa National Park** Pristine wilderness on Estonia's north coast. **See p.249**

❸ **Saaremaa** A perfect island getaway with a beautiful castle and relaxing spa hotels. See p.250

❹ **Pärnu Beach** Enjoy a bracing dip in the Baltic or a mud bath in a local spa. **See p.251**

❺ **Tartu** Party the night away with the student population of Tartu. **See p.252**

HIGHLIGHTS ARE MARKED ON THE MAP ON P.239

ROUGH COSTS

Daily budget Basic €50, occasional treat €70

Drink Le Coq beer €2.50

Food Blood sausage and sauerkraut €5

Hostel/budget hotel €22/€45

Travel Bus: Tallinn–Saaremaa €15; Tartu–Tallinn €11

FACT FILE

Population 1.3 million

Language Estonian

Currency Euro (€)

Capital Tallinn

International phone code ☎372

Time zone GMT +2hr

9

Introduction

Visitors to Estonia encounter a mix of urbanity and wilderness, of the medieval and the contemporary, with crumbling castles and colourful design permeating urban landscapes. An efficient transport system makes it easy to get around, and the tech-savvy, dynamic residents welcome visitors with open arms. Friction between older generations of Russians and Estonians is a throwback to the Soviet era, while younger people mix freely, and those who get past the Estonians' natural reserve find them to be gregarious, uninhibited hosts.

Estonia's capital, **Tallinn**, has a magnificent medieval centre and lively nightlife, rivalled only by that of **Tartu**, an exuberant university town. **Pärnu**, a popular seaside resort, boasts fantastic sandy beaches. For inexpensive spa treatments, a fine castle and unspoilt countryside head for the island of **Saaremaa**, while **Lahemaa National Park**, outside Tallinn, offers a taste of pristine wilderness.

CHRONOLOGY

100s AD Tacitus refers to the Aestii people – the forebears of the Estonians.

1154 Estonia depicted on a map of the world for the first time.

1219 Danish conquer North Estonia, ushering in over a century of Danish rule.

1227 German crusaders invade the rest of Estonia.

1346 Danish territories in Estonia sold to the German Livonian Order.

1525 First book printed in the Estonian language.

1561 Livonian Order surrender their Estonian territory to Sweden.

1625 Sweden takes control over all Estonia.

1632 Estonia's first university opens in Tartu.

1721 Russia defeats Sweden in the Northern War and takes over Estonia.

1816 Serfdom is abolished in Estonia.

Late 1800s The spread of the Estonian language in schools is instrumental in increasing Estonian nationalism.

1918 Estonia states its claim to independence but is invaded by the Red Army.

1920 The Bolsheviks are defeated, giving Estonia full independence.

1934 Authoritarian rule is established by Prime Minister Konstantin Päts.

1940 Soviets invade Estonia, ushering in Communist rule.

1944 After four years of Nazi German occupation, the Soviet occupation returns.

1988 The "Singing Revolution" begins with huge crowds gathering to sing patriotic songs.

1991 Estonian independence is restored following the collapse of the Soviet Union.

2004 Estonia joins NATO and the EU.

2007 Estonia is the first country to introduce internet voting for national elections.

2009 Estonia rides the global economic crisis better than her Baltic neighbours.

2011 The euro becomes Estonia's official currency.

2015 Russian aggression against Ukraine leads to renewed edginess in Estonian-Russian relations.

ARRIVAL AND DEPARTURE

The compact and ultramodern **Tallinn Airport** (ⓦtallinn-airport.ee) is served by several European cities, including London, Dublin, Frankfurt, Barcelona and Stockholm. Ryanair, easyJet and airBaltic are among the main airlines. The national carrier Nordica (ⓦnordica.ee) currently has a limited fleet of aircraft and flies under the flag of Slovenian carrier Adria (ⓦadria.si). International **bus lines**, such as Ecolines (ⓦecolines .net) and Lux Express (ⓦluxexpress.eu), connect Tallinn via Tartu or Pärnu to Russia (Moscow, St Petersburg), Latvia (Rīga), Lithuania (Vilnius, Kaunas) and Germany (Berlin), among others. The only international **rail services** from Estonia are the daily train from Tallinn to St Petersburg and Moscow – book seats in advance on ⓦgorail.ee. Tallinn can also be reached by **ferry** from Helsinki, Finland, and from Stockholm, Sweden.

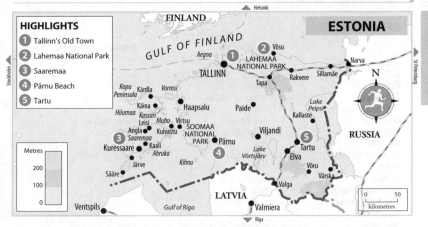

HIGHLIGHTS

1. Tallinn's Old Town
2. Lahemaa National Park
3. Saaremaa
4. Pärnu Beach
5. Tartu

ESTONIA

GETTING AROUND

Bus tickets can be bought either from the bus station ticket office or directly from the driver. Online schedules are available at ⓦtpilet.ee; buy tickets in advance if you're travelling in the height of summer or at weekends.

Although the **rail network** is limited, trains are as fast as buses and slightly cheaper (check ⓦedel.ee for times and prices); purchase your ticket from the conductor.

The bigger cities have efficient **public transport** systems, and the whole country is very bicycle-friendly. Due to the scarcity of public transport on the islands, many locals hitchhike; the usual precautions apply.

ACCOMMODATION

Though cheaper than in Western Europe, accommodation in Estonia will still take a large chunk out of most budgets. Tallinn has a vibrant **hostel** scene,

though outside the capital, some **hostels** are just student dorms converted for the summer. Beds cost €15–20 per person. Youth hostels aside, booking a **private room** is often the cheapest option (€18–25 per person). This can be arranged through tourist offices or private agencies. There are also plain guesthouse or *pension* rooms for €30–40 per person including breakfast, though the cheapest of these are not always centrally located.

FOOD AND DRINK

Mainstays of **Estonian cuisine** include soup (*supp*), dark bread (*leib*) and herring (*heeringas*), culinary legacies of the country's largely peasant past. Typical national dishes are *verevorst* (blood sausage) and *karbonaad* (pork chop), both traditionally served with *mulgikapsad* (sauerkraut). Various kinds of smoked fish, particularly eel (*angerjas*), perch (*ahven*) and pike (*haug*), are popular too, as are **Russian dishes** such as *pelmeenid* (ravioli with meat or mushrooms). Both Tallinn and Tartu also boast an impressive choice of ethnic **restaurants**. Outside these two cities, **vegetarians** will find their choice to be more limited.

When eating out, it's cheaper to head for bars and cafés, many of which serve **snacks** like pancakes (*pannkoogid*) and salads (*salatid*). A modest meal in a café

ESTONIA ONLINE

ⓦ**visitestonia.com** Extensive tourist board site covering all things Estonian.
ⓦ**baltictimes.com** English-language weekly newspaper.
ⓦ**inyourpocket.com** Excellent guide covering Tallinn, Tartu and Pärnu.
ⓦ**upnorth.eu** Culture and comment from Estonia and the Nordic region.

9

ESTONIAN

	ESTONIAN	PRONUNCIATION
Yes	*Jah*	Yah
No	*Ei*	Ey
Please	*Palun*	Palun
Thank you	*Aitäh/tänan*	Ayteh, tanan
Hello/Good day	*Tere*	Tere
Goodbye	*Head aega*	Heyad ayga
Excuse me	*Vabandage*	Vabandage
Where?	*Kus?*	Kus?
Student ticket	*Õpilase pilet*	Ypilahse pilet
Toilet	*Tualett*	Tualet
I'd like	*Ma sooviksin*	Mah sawviksin
I don't eat meat	*Ma ei söö*	Mah ay serr
The bill, please	*Palun arve*	Pahlun ahrrve
Good/Bad	*Hea/Halb*	Heya/Holb
Near/Far	*Lähedal/Kaugel*	Lahedal/Cowgal
Cheap/Expensive	*Odav/Kallis*	Odav/Kallis
Open/Closed	*Avatud/Suletud*	Avatud/Suletud
Today	*Täna*	Tana
Yesterday	*Eile*	Eyle
Tomorrow	*Homme*	Homme
How much is…?	*Kui palju maksab…?*	Kuy palyo maksab…?
What time is it?	*Mis kell praegu on?*	Mis kell prego on?
I don't understand	*Ma ei saa aru*	May saaru
Do you speak English?	*Kas te räägite inglise keelt?*	Kas te raagite inglise kelt?
One	*Üks*	Uks
Two	*Kaks*	Koks
Three	*Kolm*	Kolm
Four	*Neli*	Neli
Five	*Viis*	Vees
Six	*Kuus*	Koos
Seven	*Seitse*	Seytse
Eight	*Kaheksa*	Koheksa
Nine	*Üheksa*	Ooheksa
Ten	*Kümme*	Koome

costs €7–9, while in a typical restaurant two courses and a drink comes to around €27. **Self-catering** poses no major problems, as supermarkets and fresh produce markets are plentiful.

Restaurant opening hours tend to be between noon and midnight; cafés are open from 9am to 10pm or later.

DRINK

Estonians are enthusiastic drinkers, with **beer** (*õlu*) being the most popular tipple. The principal local brands are Saku and A. Le Coq, both of which are lager-style brews, although both companies also produce stronger, dark beers. Some great local craft beers have emerged in the last few years – Lehe, Põhjala, Õllenaut and Pühaste are among the names to look out for. In bars a lot of people favour **vodka** (*viin*) with mixers while local alcoholic specialities include **hõõgvein** (mulled wine) and **Vana Tallinn**, a pungent dark liqueur which some suicidal souls mix with vodka. **Pubs and bars** – most of which imitate global models – are taking over, especially in Tallinn. If you're not boozing, head for a *kohvik* (café); **coffee** (*kohvi*) is usually of the filter variety, and **tea** (*teed*) is served without milk (*piima*) or sugar (*suhkur*) – ask for both if necessary. Bars are usually open from noon until 2 or 4am at weekends.

CULTURE AND ETIQUETTE

Estonians tend to be reserved when you first meet them, though if you are lucky enough to be invited to a local home, you will see their warm and generous side. Unused to loud displays of emotion, they are scandalized by the loutish behaviour of foreign stag parties, although they do enjoy sociable drinking. A ten percent **tip** is sufficient in restaurants to reward good service; otherwise just round up the bill.

SPORTS AND OUTDOOR ACTIVITIES

Football and **basketball** are the national sports; for the former, go to the A. Le Coq Arena (Asula 4c; ☎627 9960), whereas Tallinn's Saku Suurhall (Paldiski mnt 104b; ☎665 9534) is the best place to see a basketball game. In the summertime, Estonia becomes a haven for **watersports**: windsurfing, kayaking, canoeing or simply hitting the beach. **Hiking**, **biking** and **horseriding** are popular both on the Estonian mainland and on the islands off its coast, such as Saaremaa and Hiiumaa. Almost twenty percent of Estonia is protected land, divided between four **national parks** and numerous **nature reserves**, which are home to many species of wild animals and birds. National parks are best visited between May and September; RMK (ⓦrmk.ee) manages the protected areas and campsites.

COMMUNICATIONS

Post offices (*postkontor*) are open Monday to Friday 8am to 6pm and Saturday 9am to 3pm. Users of **mobile phones** from EU counties should find call and data charges no more expensive than at home. Those with non-EU phones should consult their provider about roaming charges, and consider buying a local SIM card plus top-up talk time. There are few internet cafés due to the proliferation of **free wi-fi** hotspots: free wi-fi is available in most cafés and restaurants, and in all accommodation options in this chapter.

EMERGENCIES

Theft and street crime are at relatively low levels. The **police** (*politsei*) are mostly young and some speak English. **Emergency health care** is free and, in Tallinn at least, emergency operators speak English.

INFORMATION

Tourist offices (ⓦvisitestonia.com) can be useful for booking B&Bs and hotel rooms, as well as good-quality free **maps**; most bookshops also have good map sections. The *In Your Pocket* guides (ⓦinyourpocket.com) are excellent listings guides, available from tourist offices and kiosks for €2.50, or they can be downloaded free from their website.

MONEY AND BANKS

The Estonian **currency** is the euro (€). **Bank** (*pank*) opening hours are Monday to Friday 9am to 4pm, with most also open on Saturday from 9am to 2pm. **ATMs** are widely available. **Credit and debit cards** can be used in most hotels, restaurants and stores, but outside urban areas cash is preferred.

OPENING HOURS AND HOLIDAYS

Most **shops** open Monday to Friday 10am to 6pm and Saturday 10am to 3pm, but many larger ones stay open later and are also open on Sundays. **Public holidays**, when most shops and all banks are closed, are: January 1, February 24, Good Friday, Easter Sunday, May 1, Pentecost (50 days after Easter), June 23 and 24, August 20, December 24, 25 and 26.

Tallinn

TALLINN, Estonia's compact, buzzing capital, with its enchanting heart surrounded by medieval walls, has been

9

shaped by nearly a millennium of outside influence. While the fairytale Old Town has become the ideal weekend getaway for city-break tourists, the Estonian capital's growing importance as a regional centre for business, arts and technology has provided it with a go-ahead contemporary feel coupled with bags of hedonistic energy.

WHAT TO SEE AND DO

The heart of Tallinn is the **Old Town**, still largely enclosed by the city's medieval walls. At its centre is the **Raekoja plats**, the historic marketplace, above which looms **Toompea**, the hilltop stronghold of the German knights who controlled the city during the Middle Ages. East of the city centre there are several places worth a visit, such as **Kadriorg Park**, a peaceful wooded area with a cluster of historic buildings, and the forested island of **Aegna**.

Raekoja plats

Raekoja plats, the cobbled market square at the heart of the Old Town, is as old as the city itself. On its southern side stands the fifteenth-century **Town Hall** (Raekoda), boasting elegant Gothic arches at ground level, and a delicate steeple at its northern end. Near the summit of the steeple, **Vana Toomas**, a sixteenth-century weather vane depicting a medieval town guard, is Tallinn's city emblem. The well-labelled and informative **museum** inside the cellar hall (late June to Aug Mon–Sat 10am–4pm; rest of the year closed; €5) depicts Tallinn town life through the ages. For an expansive view of the town square, climb the spiral staircase of the **Town Hall Tower** (Raekoja Torn; May to mid-Sept daily 11am–6pm; €3).

THE TALLINN CARD

To do a lot of sightseeing in a short time, it can be worth buying a **Tallinn Card** (ⓦtallinncard.ee; €32/42/52 for 24/48/72hr), which gives you unlimited free rides on public transport as well as free entry to a plethora of attractions and discounts in shops and restaurants. Check website for details.

Church of the Holy Ghost and St Nicholas's Church

The fourteenth-century **Church of the Holy Ghost** (Pühä Vaimu kirik; Mon–Sat: May–Sept 9am–6pm; Oct–April 10am–3pm; €1) on Pühavaimu is the city's oldest church, a small Gothic building with stuccoed limestone walls, stepped gables, carved wooden interior, a tall, verdigris-coated spire and an ornate clock from 1680 – the oldest in Tallinn.

Contrasting sharply is the late Gothic **St Nicholas's Church** (Niguliste kirik; Tues–Sun 10am–5pm; museum €5), southwest of Raekoja plats. Dating back to the 1820s and rebuilt after being mostly destroyed in a 1944 Soviet air raid, it now serves as a museum of church art, including medieval winged altars and the haunting *Danse Macabre* ("Dance With Death") by Bernt Notke. It also hosts free organ recitals (Sat & Sun 4pm).

Toompea and the Aleksander Nevsky Cathedral

Toompea is the hill where the Danes built their fortress after conquering what is now Tallinn in 1219. According to legend, it is also the grave of **Kalev**, the mythical ancestor of the Estonians. Approach through the sturdy gate tower – built by the Teutonic Knights to contain the Old Town's inhabitants in times of unrest – at the foot of Pikk jalg. This is the cobbled continuation of Pikk, the Old Town's main street, that climbs up to Lossi plats, dominated by the impressively cake-like **Aleksander Nevsky Cathedral** (daily 8am–7pm; free). Bristling with domes, this structure was built at the end of the nineteenth century for the city's Orthodox population – an enduring reminder of the two centuries Tallinn spent under tsarist rule.

At the head of Lossi plats, the pink **Toompea Castle** stands on the site of the original Danish fortification. Rebuilt many times, the building is now home to the **Riigikogu**, Estonia's parliament.

Kiek-in-de-Kök and Bastion Tunnels

The imposing **Kiek-in-de-Kök tower** (Tues–Sun: March–Oct 10.30am–6pm; Nov–Feb 10.30am–4.30pm; €6; joint

9

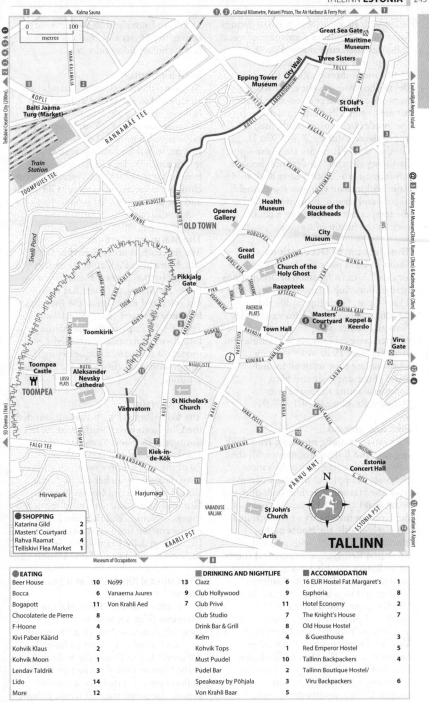

TALLINN

● SHOPPING	
Katarina Gild	2
Masters' Courtyard	3
Rahva Raamat	4
Telliskivi Flea Market	1

● EATING	
Beer House	10
Bocca	6
Bogapott	11
Chocolaterie de Pierre	8
F-Hoone	4
Kivi Paber Käärid	5
Kohvik Klaus	2
Kohvik Moon	1
Lendav Taldrik	3
Lido	14
More	12
No99	13
Vanaema Juures	9
Von Krahli Aed	7

■ DRINKING AND NIGHTLIFE	
Clazz	6
Club Hollywood	9
Club Privé	11
Club Studio	7
Drink Bar & Grill	8
Kelm	4
Kohvik Tops	1
Must Puudel	10
Pudel Bar	2
Speakeasy by Põhjala	3
Von Krahli Baar	5

■ ACCOMMODATION	
16 EUR Hostel Fat Margaret's	1
Euphoria	8
Hotel Economy	2
The Knight's House	7
Old House Hostel	
& Guesthouse	3
Red Emperor Hostel	5
Tallinn Backpackers	4
Tallinn Boutique Hostel/	
Viru Backpackers	6

9

ticket with Bastion Tunnels €10), dating from 1475, stands on Komandandi tee. It houses interactive displays on the development of the town and its fortifications throughout its history. Below the tower lies the entrance to a network of seventeenth-century **bastion tunnels**, originally built for defence by the Swedes but most recently used as bomb shelters during World War II. Guided tours (Tues–Sat 10.30am–6pm; frequency depends on demand; book in advance on ☎644 6686 or at Kiek-in-de-Kök; €6;) initiate you into the tunnels' history and legend; bring warm clothes as the temperature tends to be a cool 6–8°C even in the height of summer.

The Museum of Occupations

South of Lossi plats, on Toompea 8, the airy and modern **Museum of Occupations** (daily: June–Aug 10am–6pm; Sept–May 11am–6pm; €6) brings to life the personal experience of Estonians under Nazi and Soviet occupation through use of interactive exhibitions, and displays of artefacts from 1940 to 1991. It's well worth taking time to sit and watch some of the documentary films commemorating the anti-Soviet "Singing Revolution" of 1987–91.

Pikk and around

Pikk tänav, running northeast from Pikk jalg gate and linking Toompea with the port area, has some of the city's most elaborate examples of **merchants' houses** from the Hanseatic period, including the **Great Guild** at Pikk 17, headquarters of the German merchants who controlled the city's wealth; the **House of the Blackheads**, Pikk 26, with a lavishly decorated Renaissance facade; and the **Three Sisters**, a gabled group at Pikk 71. Supremely functional with loading hatches and winch-arms set into their facades, these would have served as combined dwelling places, warehouses and offices. Take the parallel street of Vene to the outstanding **Tallinn City Museum** at no. 17 (Mon & Wed–Sun: March–Oct 10.30am–6pm; Nov–Feb 10.30am–5.30pm; €4), which imaginatively recounts the history

of Tallinn from the thirteenth century through to Soviet and Nazi occupations and Estonian independence.

St Olaf's Church

At the northern end of Pikk stands the enormous Gothic **St Olaf's Church** (Oleviste kirik; daily 10am–6pm; free), first mentioned in 1267 and named in honour of King Olaf II of Norway, who was canonized for battling against pagans in Scandinavia. The church is chiefly famous for its 124m spire, which you can climb for a spectacular view of Old Town and the port (daily 10am–6pm, July & Aug until 8pm; €3).

The Maritime Museum

The sixteenth-century **Great Sea Gate**, which straddles Pikk at its far end, is flanked by two towers. The larger of these, Fat Margaret Tower, has walls 4m thick and now houses the **Estonian Maritime Museum** (Tues–Sun 10am–7pm; €4), a surprisingly entertaining four floors of nautical instruments, scale models of ships and antique diving equipment: some displays have English captions.

The city walls

The 4km-worth of walls that surrounded the Old Town were mostly constructed during the fourteenth century. Today, 1.85km of them still stand, along with 20 of the original 46 towers. One of the most dramatic stretches can be found along Laboratoriumi (subsequently Gümnaasiumi), where three of the oldest towers – Nunne, Kuldjala and Sauna – can be entered from Gümnaasiumi 3 (June–Aug: daily 11am–7pm; Sept–May daily except Thursday 11am–4/5pm; €2).

The Cultural Kilometre and Patarei Prison

Just north of the Old Town, the **Cultural Kilometre** (Kultuurikilomeeter) is a footpath that runs through an intriguing stretch of post-Soviet, post-industrial Tallinn. It begins beside the Kultuurikattel ("The Culture Boiler"), a former power station now converted into a concert venue. The power station's iconic chimney is where Russian film director Andrei Tarkovsky shot key scenes of his existential classic, *Stalker*. From here the path heads west past a small fishing harbour, and the Estonian Design House at Kalasadama 8 (ⓦestoniandesignhouse .ee), where young designers display and sell their wares. The path continues past the atmospheric old houses of the Kalamaja district before arriving at **Patarei Prison Museum** (May–Sept daily noon–7pm; €3; ⓦpatarei.org), a nineteenth-century fortress that was turned into a jail in 1920. Abandoned in 2004, it remains in pretty much the same state it was left in, providing an eerie, unsettling experience for visitors.

The Air Harbour
The Cultural Kilometre terminates outside Estonia's most astounding museum attraction, the **Air Harbour** (May–Sept daily 10am–7pm; Oct–April Tues–Sun 11am–7pm; €14; ⓦlennusadam.eu), a huge hangar built by the Russians in World War I to house a fleet of sea planes. A masterpiece of modern construction, this cavernous concrete space was reopened in 2012 as an extension of the Maritime Museum (see opposite). A system of raised walkways takes you past the exhibits – including fishing boats, mines, a replica World War I biplane and naval guns. The *pièce de résistance* is the Lembit submarine, built for the Estonian navy in Barrow-in-Furness in the 1930s. Outside, ice-breaker *Suur Toll* and several other ships are moored.

Telliskivi Creative City
Ten minutes' walk north of the Old Town, a former engineering works on the far side of the Balti Jaam station now houses the **Telliskivi Creative City** (ⓦtelliskivi.eu), a cluster of creative companies and artists' studios. It is also home to an assortment of cafés, restaurants and art-and-design shops, plus a popular Saturday flea market (see p.249).

Kadriorg Park
Kadriorg Park, a heavily wooded area 2km east of the Old Town along Narva maantee, was laid out according to the instructions of Russian tsar Peter the Great. The main entrance to the park is at the junction of Weizenbergi tänav and J. Poska (tram #1 or #3 from Viru väljak). Weizenbergi cuts through the park, running straight past **Kadriorg Palace**, a Baroque residence designed by the Italian architect Niccolò Michetti, which Peter had built for his wife Catherine. The palace houses the **Kadriorg Art Museum** (May–Sept Tues & Thurs–Sun 10am–5pm, Wed 10am–8pm; Oct–April closed Tues; €5.50), with a fine collection of Dutch and Russian paintings.

KUMU
Marking the eastern end of Kadriorg Park is the immense, futuristic-looking **KUMU** (April–Sept Tues & Thurs–Sun 11am–6pm, Wed 11am–8pm; Oct–April closed Tues; €6; ⓦkumu.ekm.ee), a must-see for anyone interested in twentieth-century Estonian art. It's certainly a wide-ranging collection: surrealism, pop art and abstraction flourished during the Soviet period, despite official hostility to such modernist excesses.

Aegna Island
An hour's boat ride (May–Sept Mon & Wed–Fri 2 daily, Sat & Sun 3 daily; double-check timetable with tourist office; €6 return) from **Pirita harbour** (bus #1, #34 or #38 from the underground stop at the Viru Centre), tiny peaceful

---

ESTONIA'S SONG FESTIVAL

The **Lauluväljak** at Narva maantee 95 (ⓦlauluvaljak.ee), just to the northeast of Kadriorg Park, is a vast amphitheatre which is the venue for Estonia's **Song Festivals**. These gatherings, featuring a 25,000-strong choir, are held every five years, and have been an important form of national expression since the first all-Estonia Song Festival held in Tartu in 1869. The grounds were filled to their 45,000-person capacity in summer 1988 when people assembled here spontaneously to sing patriotic songs in protest against Soviet rule, in what became known as the "**Singing Revolution**". The next Song Festival is in July 2019.

9

Aegna is an excellent day-trip destination. Its forest-covered interior and clean beaches attract locals who camp here in the summer.

ARRIVAL AND DEPARTURE

By plane The Lennart Meri Tallinn Airport (*lennu jaam*) is 3km southeast of the city centre and linked to the Viru shopping mall by bus #2 (every 20–40min, 6am–midnight; €2), a 5min walk from the Old Town's Viru Gate.

By train Tallinn's train station (*balti jaam*) is at Toompuiestee 35, just northwest of the Old Town, a 10min walk to the Town Square. There are ATMs by the front doors.

Destinations Moscow (1 daily at 5.10pm; 14hr); Pärnu (2 daily; 2hr 20min); St Petersburg (1 daily at 5.10pm; 6hr 40min); Tartu (8 daily; 2hr 10min).

By bus The city's bus terminal (*autobussi jaam*) is at Lastekodu 46, 2km southeast of the centre; there is an ATM and luggage storage. Trams #2 and #4 run from nearby Tartu mnt. to Viru väljak at the eastern entrance to the Old Town; alternatively, take any bus heading west along Juhkentali.

Destinations Kuressaare (up to 16 daily; 4hr–4hr 30min); Pärnu (every 30min, 6.20am–9pm; 2hr); Rīga (12 daily; 4hr 30min); St Petersburg (6–8 daily; 7–9hr); Tartu (every 30min, 5.45am–11pm; 2hr 30min); Vilnius (5 daily; 9–10hr).

By boat Arriving by sea, the passenger port (*reisisadam*) is just northeast of the centre at Sadama 25. For updated schedules see ⊚ www.portoftallinn.com.

Destinations Helsinki (10–15 daily; 2hr–3hr 30min); Stockholm (1 daily at 6pm; 16hr).

INFORMATION

Tourist information Tourist office at Niguliste 2 (April, May & Sept Mon–Sat 9am–6pm, Sun 9am–4pm; June–Aug Mon–Sat 9am–7pm, Sun 9am–6pm; Oct–March Mon–Sat 9am–5pm, Sun 10am–3pm; ☎645 7777, ⊚ tourism.tallinn.ee). You can also buy the Tallinn Card here (see box, p.242).

GETTING AROUND

By public transport Tallinn has an extensive tram, bus and trolleybus network. Locals travel for free; non-Tallinners must buy tickets (*talongid*) from the driver (€2); or buy a Smartcard (*Ühiskaart*) from a post office or news kiosk (€2 deposit necessary), topping it up according to what you think you will need – single journeys cost €1.10 (24/72hr €3/€5).

ACCOMMODATION

Demand for budget accommodation outstrips supply in summer, so book in advance.

10 Euro Hostel Fat Margaret's Põhja pst 27 ☎510 0916, ⊚ 16eur.ee. Just outside the Old Town walls, this tastefully decorated cheapie haven offers free use of its sauna (9–11am) to complement your stay in one of its en-suite rooms or dorms. The large kitchen/social area is a major boon. Dorms **€13**, doubles **€32**

Euphoria Roosikrantsi 4 ☎5837 3602, ⊚ euphoria.ee. A four-storey hostel with a great communal atmosphere, impromptu jam sessions, clean dorms and a couple of rooms, all with shared facilities. You can smoke a hookah and even paint your own mural in the large common room. Dorms **€13**, doubles **€70**

Hotel Economy Kopli 2c ☎667 8300, ⊚ economyhotel .ee. Refurbished 1920s hotel offering modern, comfortable rooms overlooking the train station area on the outskirts of the Old Town. Breakfast is included, as is wi-fi in the lobby. Doubles **€70**

★**The Knight's House** Rüütli 16 ☎631 1444, ⊚ knight -house.eu. Soothing hostel with floral murals in a characterful old house just steps from the main square. There's a mixture of dorms, quads and private doubles; a simple breakfast is included in the price. Dorms **€18**, doubles **€42**

Old House Hostel & Guesthouse Uus 26 ☎641 1281, ⊚ oldhouse.ee. Renovated, quiet Old Town house with attractive dorms and a handful of cosy twin rooms with shared bath, guest lounge and kitchen. Dorms **€15**, doubles **€60**

★**Red Emperor Hostel** Aia 10 ☎615 0035, ⊚ redemperorhostel.com. Ideally located on the eastern fringes of the Old Town, *Red Emperor* offers a choice of brightly decorated rooms ranging from quads to 10-bed dorms. Additional facilities include kitchen and a next-door bar with pool tables. Dorms **€10**

Tallinn Backpackers Olevimägi 11 ☎644 0298, ⊚ tallinnbackpackers.com. This party spot encourages

---

TALLINN TOURS

Tallinn can be explored in many different ways. Here are some of the more innovative tours:

City Bike Tours Vene 33 ☎511 1819, ⊚ citybike.ee. Tours of the Old Town and beyond (from €19) run by young, energetic guides. Self-guided tours of Estonian beauty spots also available.

EstAdventures ☎5308 8373, ⊚ estadventures.ee. Small-group tours of Tallinn, as well as day-trips to

Lahemaa National Park.

Tallinn Traveller Viru 6 ☎5837 4800, ⊚ traveller .ee. Excellent and inexpensive walking tours of Tallinn plus day-trips to Lahemaa National Park and coastal resort Haapsalu, led by young, knowledgeable guides.

bonding between fellow international travellers, be it through video screenings, communal dinners or bar crawls. Don't count on getting much sleep! Dorms €16
Tallinn Boutique Hostel/Viru Backpackers Viru 5 ☏ 644 6050, �ⓦ virubackpackers.com. The calmer sister hostel to *Tallinn Backpackers* with quiet singles, doubles and triples, as well as access to all *Tallinn Backpackers'* facilities and an invitation to join their raucous parties, but with the option of actually sleeping afterwards. Doubles €32

EATING

Self-caterers can try the Rimi supermarket at Aia 7 or else buy some cheap fresh produce at the Balti Jaama Turg (train station market) behind the train station.

CAFÉS, CHEAP EATS AND SNACKS

Bogapott Pikk jalg 9. This tiny family-run Tallinn institution, surrounded by part of the medieval wall, serves delicious sandwiches, coffee and pastries while you look around the art shop and ceramics studio. Coffee €1.80. Daily 10am–7pm.

Chocolaterie de Pierre Vene 6. Quaint café with vintage furnishings and a cobbled-alley terrace. Pierre's handmade chocolates are the stars of the show, although all manner of other sweets are on offer too. Carrot cake €3.50. Daily 9am–11pm.

Kohvik Klaus Kalasadama 8. In the same building as the Estonian Design House and perfectly situated for an assault on the Cultural Kilometre (see p.244), *Klaus* is a chic and cheery place in which to indulge in salads, pastas and main meals, as well as kick-start espressos and a full range of alcohol. Mon 9am–10pm, Tues–Sat 10am–11pm, Sun 10am–10pm.

Lido Solaris shopping centre, Estonia pst 9. It's a fast-food chain, captain, but not as we know it: traditional dishes from Estonia and all over the Baltic, some of which (potato pancakes, grilled meats) are cooked in front of you as you pass along the endless canteen counter. Scale models of Estonian buildings fill the dining space, staff in national costume man the tills. Fill your plate for under €4. Daily 10am–10pm.

More Viru Keskus shopping centre. Located on the top floor of the Rahvu Raamat bookshop in the Viru Centre, *More* represents the aristocratic end of the order-at-the-counter market, with Tallinn's beautiful things queuing up to grab an equally beautiful range of soups, pastries and cakes. The coffees and leaf teas are also top-notch. Quiche €4.30. Daily 9am–9pm.

RESTAURANTS

Beer House Dunkri 5. Vast, popular beer cellar which brews its own ales and serves up generous portions of imaginative meat dishes, such as elk and wild boar, as well as good, solid sausage-and-mash combos. Mains €8–12. Live music nightly. Daily 11am–midnight.

★**Bocca** Olevimägi 9. A chic cocktail spot in the evenings, this slick Italian restaurant serves superbly executed dishes that won't blow a hole in your budget if you stick to the soups and pastas. Try the linguine with grilled prawns and scallops (€12). Mon–Thurs noon–11pm, Sat noon–midnight, Sun 1–10pm.

F-Hoone Telliskivi 60A. Roomy restaurant in a post-industrial setting, with a broad and inexpensive range of Estonian-European fare served up in bare-brick, bare-floorboard surrounds. Breakfasts are served until 11.30am; two-course set lunches weigh in at around €6. Mon–Sat 9am–midnight, Sun 9am–10pm.

Kivi Paber Käärid Telliskivi 60A C4. In the C block of the Telliskivi factory complex, chef Kivi Paber cooks up delicious Nordic-meets-Mediterranean fare in a redesigned former factory hall. Try duck fillet with roasted veg (€10.90) or opt for one of the three-course daily specials (€8). All dishes gluten-free. Mon–Thurs & Sun 11am–11pm, Fri & Sat 11am–2am.

Kohvik Moon Vorgu 3. Just outside the Old Town near the start of the Cultural Kilometre, *Moon* ("Poppy") serves up Baltic-Mediterranean cuisine in contemporary surroundings. Borscht €3, duck breast €10. The dish of the day is a steal at €5. Mon–Sat noon–11pm, Sun 1–9pm.

Lendav Taldrik Telliskivi 60A. Indian cuisine in a former factory space, this time given a bright and colourful café makeover. Classics like Kahmiri lamb curry weigh in at around €10.50, and there's plenty of scope for vegetarians (Tarka dal €4.80). Mon–Thurs & Sun noon–10pm, Fri & Sat noon–1am.

No99 Sakala 3. Café-restaurant-bar in the foyer of the No99 Theatre, with outdoor seating under the colonnaded facade. Most punters come for the daily-special lunches (ranging in style from Italian pasta dishes to tofu cutlets; €5.20); there is also a full menu of drinks and the chance of catching live jazz on weekend evenings. Mon–Thurs noon–11pm, Fri & Sat noon–midnight.

Vanaema Juures Rataskaevu 10/12. A Tallinn favourite for many years, "Grandma's Place" serves no-nonsense Estonian home food in a cosy cellar setting. Menus change seasonally, although locally sourced trout, lamb, duck and elk are sure to feature. Mains €10–15. Mon–Sat noon–10pm, Sun noon–6pm.

★**Von Krahli Aed** Rataskaevu 8. The self-styled "Embassy of Pure Food" delivers delicious and imaginative fusion dishes, with locally sourced meat, fish and vegetables given a modern European makeover. There are plenty of vegetarian options; mains hover around the €8–11 mark. Mon–Sat noon–midnight, Sun noon–6pm.

DRINKING, NIGHTLIFE AND ENTERTAINMENT

Most of Tallinn's popular clubs cater for a mainstream crowd. More underground, cutting-edge dance music

9

SAUNAS

The first thing to do when you go to an Estonian **sauna** is get completely naked, though in mixed saunas wrapping a towel around you is at your own discretion. Once you get used to the heat, scoop some water onto the hot stones; it evaporates instantaneously, raising the temperature. Once everyone is sweating profusely, some might gently swat themselves or their friends with birch branches; this increases circulation and rids the body of toxins. Don't overdo it – ten minutes should be long enough, but get out immediately if you start to feel dizzy. Locals normally follow up with a plunge into a cold lake, although a cold shower will suffice. A good place to start is **Kalma** at Vana-Kalamaja 9a (Mon–Fri 11am–10pm, Sat & Sun 10am–11pm; public sauna for men only €9–10; private sauna for both sexes €14–20/hr); ☎627 1811, ⓦ kalmasaun.ee) – Tallinn's oldest public bath (built in 1928), containing private saunas for rent as well as men's and women's general baths (complete with swimming pool).

events change location frequently and are advertised by flyers, or try asking around in the city's hipper bars; expect to pay €4–10 admission.

BARS

Drink Bar & Grill Väike-Karja 8. The patrons at this lively bar are a mixed bunch: locals, backpackers and expats – but all are united in their love of unusual beers, organic ciders and the bar's own house brew. Daily noon–midnight.

Kelm Vene 33. This artsy-student-local bar hidden round a corner from the well-trodden thoroughfares of touristy Tallinn offers a nice mixture of grungy minimalism and domestic comfort, with distressed walls and dim lighting in one room; sofas, standard lamps and bookshelves in another. Occasional gigs and DJ evenings add to the fun. Daily 4pm–4am.

Kohvik Tops Soo 15. Housed in a ramshackle wooden house that's typical of the Kalamaja district just north of the Old Town, *Tops* proves the perfect hipster retreat with its jumble of retro furnishings, soundtracked by a mixture of indie, jazz and retro pop. Tues–Thurs 4–11pm, Fri 4pm–2am, Sat noon–2am.

Must Puudel Müürivähe 2. Cute and cosy café-bar decked out in a medieval-meets-1970s retro style, the "Black Poodle" serves daily specials (€4.50) at lunchtime, before filling up with a hedonistic local drinking crowd at night. Estonian craft beers on the menu and vinyl DJ nights

at weekends. Mon–Wed & Sun 9am–11pm, Thurs–Sat 9am–2am.

★ **Pudel Bar** Telliskivi 60A. Whitewashed brick and bare lightbulbs provide the requisite air of minimalist hip to this cool but welcoming bar dedicated to the art of a good brew. The list of craft beers from home and abroad (Brewdog Punk IPA €4) runs into the hundreds; platters of quality cheese and sausage will keep hunger pangs at bay. DJs, quiz nights and unplugged concerts add to the fun. Mon–Thurs 4pm–midnight, Fri 4pm–2am, Sat noon–2am, Sun 2pm–midnight.

Speakeasy by Põhjala Kopli 4. This outwardly nondescript, functionally furnished bar serves everything produced by the excellent Põhjala microbrewery, on tap as well as bottled. Local favourites include their Virmalised IPA and Rukkirääk rye ale; although they brew a lot of one-off seasonal specials too. Daily 6pm–2am.

Von Krahli Bar Rataskaevu 10/12. "Krahl" to regulars, this large hip hangout is always packed with a mix of local students and bohemian types. Frequent live music – from alternative to reggae to hip-hop. Good, cheap food: huge daily specials €4. Mon–Thurs & Sun noon–1am, Fri & Sat noon–3am.

CLUBS AND LIVE MUSIC

Clazz Vana Turg 2 ⓦ clazz.ee. One of the most popular venues in the Old Town for nightly live music – from blues to jazz to Latin. Shorter hours in winter. Sun–Thurs 11am–2am; Fri & Sat 11am–4am.

Club Hollywood Vana-Posti 8 ⓦ clubhollywood.ee. Large Old Town dance club playing techno, R'n'B and hip-hop. Very popular with a younger crowd as well as tourists. Cover €3–10; free entry for women on Wed. Wed–Sat 11pm–5am.

Club Privé Harju 6 ⓦ clubprive.ee. Style-conscious temple to cutting-edge dance culture, often attracting big-name DJs; check the schedule. Over 20s only. Entry €7–15. Thurs 11pm–5am, Fri & Sat midnight–6am.

Club Studio Sauna 1 ⓦ clubstudio.ee. A regular menu of house and cutting-edge dance music styles, plus frequent appearances from big-name visiting DJs, make *Studio* the place to be for the knowledgeable, party-hungry clubber. Entry €7–12. Wed–Sat 11pm–5am.

CINEMAS

Artis Estonia pst. 9 ⓦ kino.ee. Shows a full range of independent films. Entry €5–7.

Coca Cola Plaza Hobujaama 5 ⓦ forumcinemas.ee. Central multiplex showing the latest Hollywood productions. Entry €6–7.50.

SHOPPING

Katarina Gild Katarina käik. Alleyway just off Vene crammed with high-quality, highly original craft shops selling ceramics, stained glass, linen and more. Mon–Sat 11am–6pm.

Masters' Courtyard Vene 6 ⓦhoov.ee. Courtyard housing some of Tallinn's most original art and craft shops and galleries, where you can find ceramics, glassware, woodworks and candles for a very reasonable price. Mon–Fri 10am–6pm, Sat & Sun 10am–4pm.

Rahva Raamat 3rd floor, Viru Centre, Viru väljak. Large bookshop selling numerous English-language books and travel guides. Daily 9am–9pm.

Telliskivi Flea Market Telliskivi 60A. Furniture, books, clothes, crockery and wholefood snacks in the courtyard of the Telliskivi former factory complex. June–Sept Sat 10am–3pm.

DIRECTORY

Embassies Canada, Toomkooli 13, 2nd floor ⓣ627 3311; Ireland, Rahukohtu 4 ⓣ681 1870; UK, Wismari 6 ⓣ667 4700; US, Kentmanni 20 ⓣ668 8100.

Exchange Outside banking hours, try Tavid at Aia 5, though their overnight rates are not as favourable as their day rates.

Hospital Tallinn Central Hospital, Ravi 18 ⓣ666 1900. English-speaking doctors available.

Left luggage At the bus station (Mon–Sat 6.30am–10pm, Sun 7.45am–8pm; €4/24hr).

Pharmacies Aia Apteek, Aia 7 (8.30am–10.30pm); Tõnismäe Apteek, Tõnismägi 5 (24hr).

Police Pärnu mnt. 11 ⓣ612 3000.

Post office Narva mnt. 1, opposite the *Viru Hotel* (Mon–Fri 7.30am–8pm, Sat 8am–6pm).

The rest of Estonia

There are several attractions outside Tallinn that are well worth visiting, such as the vast, beautiful expanse of **Lahemaa National Park** and the pretty island of **Saaremaa**, home to the Bishop's Castle. The seaside resort of **Pärnu** is a slightly livelier affair, but outshone in vibrancy by the buzzy university town of **Tartu**.

LAHEMAA NATIONAL PARK

The largest of Estonia's national parks, 725-square-kilometre **Lahemaa** lies an hour's drive or bus ride from Tallinn. It stretches along the north coast, comprising lush forests, pristine lakes, and ruggedly beautiful coves and wetlands. The land is dotted with erratic boulders (giant rocks left over from the last Ice Age) and tiny villages throughout, while the forest is home to brown bears, wild boar, moose and lynx. The park is best explored by bicycle, as the villages are all connected by good paved roads. Parts of the park are doable as a day-trip, but you may well be charmed into staying longer.

EXPLORING THE PARK

If you go with Tallinn's Tallinn Traveller (see box, p.246), this is the day route that offers an excellent introduction to the park: start in the village of **Palmse**, where you can take in the grand German manor (May–Sept 10am–7pm; Oct–April shorter hours; €7), then cycle 8.5km northeast to **Sagadi Manor**, a well-preserved eighteenth-century aristocratic home (May–Sept daily 10am–6pm; €4), before heading north for 3km to **Oandu** – the start of several nature trails. Just before the fishing village of **Altja**, 2km to the north, you'll find the 1km **Beaver Trail**, where you can see dams built by beavers and stop for lunch at *Altja Korts* – an attractive tavern serving tasty fresh dishes, such as grilled salmon with grated potato pancakes (mains €8). From Altja you can cycle around the coast of the **Vergi peninsula**, taking in the picturesque villages (17km) surrounded by pine forest, before ending up on the wide, clean, windswept beach in **Võsu**. A seaside trail heads north from Võsu for 6km before arriving at the attractive village of **Käsmu**, which has a superb nautically themed **museum** (daily 9am–6pm; donations welcome) started by a local collector many years ago; look out for the giant sea mines in the front yard.

If you have any energy left, you can then tackle the rugged cycle trails along the western half of the Käsmu peninsula before getting picked up. Travelling independently, you can take the bus to Käsmu (see p.249), do the trail in reverse and then cycle up from Palmse to Võsu (6km) for an overnight stay before catching a bus back to Tallinn the following day.

9

ARRIVAL AND INFORMATION

By bus There are buses from Tallinn to Võsu (3 daily; 1hr 25min), Käsmu and Altja (both 1–2 daily; 1hr 10min–1hr 45min). For Palmse, take a morning bus from Tallinn to Rakvere (hourly; 1hr 30min) then catch a bus to Palmse (1 daily at 1.10pm; 25min).

Tourist information Located in tiny Palmse, the Lahemaa National Park Visitor Centre (daily. May–Aug 9am–7pm; Sept 9am–5pm; ☎ 329 5530, ⊚ lahemaa.ee) has helpful staff who can advise on accommodation, biking and hiking trails, plus nature tours, and provide a detailed map of the area.

GETTING AROUND

By bike Cycling is the best way to get around (locals do hitchhike, but the usual precautions apply). You can rent a bicycle at the *Palmse Hotel* (€4/hr or €15/day) and Sagadi Manor (see p.249), though bikes are sturdier and better maintained at Tallinn's Tallinn Traveller (see box, p.246), which also arranges transfers and day-trips to Lahemaa.

ACCOMMODATION

There are guesthouses and places to eat in Palmse, Sagadi, Altja, Võsu and Käsmu, as well as campsites, huts and forest houses throughout the park, maintained by RMK (⊚ rmk.ee).

Metsa Puhkemaja Võsu ☎ 323 8431, ✉ marika.innos @mail.ee. Simply furnished doubles and triples with shared bathrooms, kitchen facilities and a sauna. Free wi-fi throughout. Doubles €30

Toomarahva Turismitalu Altja ☎ 505 0850, ⊚ toomarahva.ee. A lovely traditional farmstead complete with thatched roof, log-panelled rooms, and a sauna hut at the bottom of a blissful garden. In summer, travellers can sleep in a barn on a bale of hay. Hay bales €5, doubles €45

SAAREMAA

The island of **SAAREMAA**, off the west coast of Estonia, is claimed by many to be one of the most authentically Estonian parts of the country. Buses from Tallinn, Tartu and Pärnu come here via a ferry running from the mainland village of Virtsu to Muhu Island, which is linked to Saaremaa by a causeway. The principal attraction is Kuressaare's thirteenth-century castle, one of the finest in the Baltic region, but the rest of the island also deserves exploration; **cycling** is the best way to get around.

Kuressaare

In **Kuressaare**'s Kesk väljak (main square) you'll find the yellow-painted **Town Hall**, dating from 1670, its door guarded by stone lions. From the square, Lossi runs south to the magnificent **Bishop's Castle** (Piiskopilinnus), set in the middle of an attractive park and surrounded by a deep moat. The formidable structure dates largely from the fourteenth century and is protected by huge seventeenth-century ramparts. The labyrinthine keep houses the **Saaremaa Regional Museum** (May–Aug daily 10am–7pm; Sept–April Wed–Sun 11am–7pm; €5; students €2.50), a riveting collection of displays charting the culture, nature and history of the island (including an excellent section on Soviet occupation). You can also climb the watchtowers, one of which houses stunning contemporary art and photography exhibitions.

Around the island

Cycling is a wonderful way of seeing Saaremaa, with its alternating landscapes of pine forest, tiny villages and vast fields. Highlights include the 37km route north from Kuressaare to **ANGLA**, its five much-photographed wooden windmills by the roadside. Halfway along, **KAALI** village, home to a giant meteorite crater thought to be at least 4000 years old, makes a worthy detour.

Ten kilometres southwest of Kuressaare, you can stop at **JARVE**, the local beach hangout, or do the 47km down to the tip of the Torgu peninsula, which ends in an amazing view from the jagged cliffs.

ARRIVAL AND INFORMATION

By bus From the bus station on Pihtla in Kuressaare, turn left onto Tallinna to reach the main square.

Destinations Leisi (5–6 daily; 55min); Pärnu (4 daily; 3hr); Tallinn (up to 16 daily; 4hr–4hr 30min); Tartu (2 direct daily; 6hr).

Tourist information The tourist office is in the Town Hall at Tallinna 2 (June–Aug Mon–Fri 9am–6pm, Sat & Sun 10am–4pm; Sept–May Mon–Fri 9am–5pm; ☎ 453 3120, ⊚ kuressaare.ee & ⊚ saaremaa.ee).

GETTING AROUND

By bike Bike rental from Bivarix Rattapood, Tallinna 26 (Mon–Fri 10am–6pm, Sat 10am–2pm; €8/4hr, €15/day).

Rüütli, cutting east–west through the centre, is the Old Town's main pedestrianized thoroughfare, lined with shops and a mix of seventeenth- to twentieth-century buildings, while parallel Kuninga boasts the largest concentration of restaurants. The entertaining **Pärnu Museum** is at Rüütli 53 (Tues–Sun 10am–6pm; €4, students €3), tracing local history from 9000 BC to World War II; ask for the information sheet in English. The oldest building in town is the **Red Tower** (Punane Torn; Tues–Sun 10am–5pm; free), a fifteenth-century remnant of the medieval city walls at Hommiku 11, a block north from Rüütli.

Follow Nikolai south from the centre and you'll reach the **Kunsti Museum** (daily: June–Aug 9am–9pm; Sept–May 9am–7pm; €3; ⓦchaplin.ee), set in the former Communist Party HQ at Esplanaadi 10. It holds excellent temporary exhibitions of contemporary art. South of here Nikolai joins Supeluse, which leads to the beach, passing beneath the trees of the shady Rannapark. Just beyond the sand dunes lies Pärnu's main attraction: the wide, clean sandy **beach**, lined with see-saws, changing booths and volleyball nets.

★ TREAT YOURSELF

Spa Hotel Rüütli, Pargi 12, Kuressaare ☏452 2133, ⓦsaaremaaspahotels.eu. Non-guests are welcome to sample a variety of inexpensive "medical" and "wellness" spa treatments at this hotel, including "Charcot's Shower" – strip naked and be pummelled with strong jets of water (€10). Treatments take place 8am–3pm; book in advance.

ACCOMMODATION

Kraavi Holiday Cottage 500m southeast of the castle at Kraavi 1, Kuressaare ☏5335 8784, ⓦkraavi.ee. Family-run guesthouse offering cosy, spacious doubles and triples with a hearty breakfast included. Use of sauna and bikes is extra. Little English spoken but the hostess is very welcoming. Doubles €25

Ovelia Majutus Suve 8, Kuressaare ☏518 5932, ⓦovelia.ee. Friendly and clean guesthouse with basic rooms, some with TVs. Some are also en suite, and have a shared kitchen. A 10min walk from the bus station. Doubles €25

Piibelehe Holiday Home Piibelehe 4, Kuressaare ☏453 6206, ⓦpiibelehe.ee. On the outskirts of town, this place has a number of airy guest rooms, some en suite and with use of a kitchen; camping also available. Discounts for multi-day stays; breakfast €6 extra. Camping/person €3, plus per tent €6, doubles €38

EATING AND DRINKING

Classic Café Lossi 9, Kuressaare. A great little spot to sample some of the best coffee and food in town while sitting in a cosy nook, surrounded by black-and-white photos of Kuressaare. Coffee €1.50. Daily 8.30am–10pm.

Kodulinna Lokaal Tallinna mnt. 11, Kuressaare. Popular café-pub on the main square dishing up inexpensive soups, light meals, and some filling daily specials (€3.50). Mon–Thurs & Sun noon–2am, Fri & Sat noon–5am.

Kohvik Retro Lossi 5, Kuressaare. An odd mix of furnishings and vinyl records pinned to the wall lend a vaguely hipsterish edge to this bar-restaurant serving a fine selection of Estonian-Mediterranean meals and a good choice of Estonian craft beers. Mains €9–11. Mon–Thurs & Sun noon–10pm, Fri & Sat noon–midnight.

PÄRNU

PÄRNU, Estonia's main seaside resort, comes into its own in summer, when it fills up with locals and tourists, and hosts daily cultural and musical events.

ARRIVAL AND INFORMATION

By train The train station is about 5km east of the centre at Riia mnt. 116.
Destinations Tallinn (2 daily; 2hr 20min).

By bus The bus station is on Pikk in the Old Town (information & ticket office round the corner at Ringi 3; daily 6.30am–7.30pm). Luggage storage by platform 8 (Mon–Fri 8am–7.30pm, Sat & Sun 9am–5pm; €3/day). Destinations Kuressaare (4–5 daily; 3hr); Rīga (3 daily; 2hr 30min); Tallinn (every 30min, 6am–9pm; 2hr); Tartu (up to 16 daily; 2hr 30min).

Tourist information The tourist office at Uus 4 (mid-May to mid-Sept daily 9am–6pm, mid-Sept to mid-May Mon–Fri 9am–5pm, Sat & Sun 10am–2pm; ☏447 3000, ⓦvisitparnu.com) stocks extensive information on Pärnu and the surrounding area.

ACCOMMODATION

Hommiku Hostel & Guesthouse Hommiku 17 ☏445 1122, ⓦhommikuhostel.ee. Both hostel and guesthouse-style accommodation are on offer at this attractive central budget option: all doubles and triples are en suite and

9

have their own kitchenettes; singles share a bathroom. Optional breakfast (€6) is served in a nearby café. Dorms €20, doubles €64

Hostel Lõuna Lõuna 2 ☎ 443 0943, ⓦ hostellouna.eu. Centrally located, with spartan, spacious dorms and basic rooms with shared facilities, popular with local students. Functional en suites on the ground floor. Dorms €15, doubles €55

Karjamaa Camping Asume Karjamaa 20a ☎ 564 8717, ⓦ karjamaacamping.ee. Just off the southeastern end of Pärnu's beach (and a 35-minute walk from the centre), Karjamaa offers tent space in a suburban garden setting, or dorm beds in 4-person chalets. Camping/person €5, plus per tent €6, dorms €25

EATING AND DRINKING

Postipoiss Vee 12. Wooden tavern, invoking nostalgia for tsarist Russia with its decor, and specializing in delicious Russian cuisine. You can't go wrong with home-made *pelmeni* (meat dumplings) in chanterelle sauce. Get in early to beat the groups. Mains €5–8. Mon–Thurs & Sun noon–11pm, Fri & Sat noon–2am.

Puhvet A.P.T.E.K Rüütli 40. Housed in a former pharmacy complete with tiled floor and wooden counter fittings, this buzzing bar offers an enticing list of shots and cocktails and DJ-driven dance action at weekends. The outdoor terrace is the place to hang out in summer. Wed & Thurs 6pm–2am, Fri & Sat 6pm–5am.

Sõõrikubaar Pühavaimu 15. An essential stop for caffeine addicts, this popular little café also does tasty pastries and *sõõrikud* (Estonian doughnuts). Mon–Fri 9am–9pm, Sat & Sun 9am–8pm.

Steffani Nikolai 24. Extremely popular restaurant serving a wide choice of tasty pizza and pasta dishes (huge calzone €7). There's a popular second branch between Ranna pst. and the beach in the summer, serving similar fare. Mon–Thurs & Sun 11am–11.30pm, Fri & Sat 11am–1.30am.

★ **Supelsaksad** Nikolai 32. Relaxing café on the ground floor of a former family house, with bare floorboards, lots of pinks and blues and the odd ravishing roll of retro wallpaper. Expect strong coffee, proper leaf teas, super salads and the cakes and pastries of your dreams. There's a small but exquisite menu of main meals (mushroom risotto €12). Garden seating in summer. Daily 9am–10pm.

Veerev Õlu Uus 3A. The "Rolling Beer" is an enjoyably unpretentious wooden-bench bar attracting an agreeable mixture of holidaymakers and garrulous locals. Mon–Sat 11am–midnight, Sun 1pm–midnight.

KIHNU

A short boat ride from Pärnu lies an island stuck in a delightful time warp. The four hundred or so inhabitants of **Kihnu** sustain

a traditional way of life that you won't find on the Estonian mainland. Young women still wear traditional striped woollen skirts here, just like their great-grandmothers, while little old ladies ride old-fashioned Soviet motorcycles with sidecars (there are no cars on the island).

ARRIVAL AND DEPARTURE

By boat To get to Kihnu, take a ferry from the quay at Munalaid, 45km west of Pärnu (June–Sept 2–4 daily; 1hr). There are connecting buses between Pärnu bus station and Munlaid (50min).

ACCOMMODATION

Rock City Guesthouse Sääre village ☎ 5626 2181, ⓦ rockcity.ee. One of the few places to stay, this is a simply furnished building set among trees near the shore. Open June–Aug only. Doubles €45

TARTU

Just over two hours southeast of Tallinn, **TARTU** is in many ways the undiscovered gem of the Baltic States, a small-scale university town that is full of youthful energy but happily free from the city-break tourism that tends to swamp the Estonian capital. With plenty of diversions, and events all year round, it's worth a stay of a couple of days.

WHAT TO SEE AND DO

The city's centre is its cobbled Raekoja plats, fronted by the Neoclassical Town Hall, a pink-and-white edifice with the "Kissing Students" statue in the fountain in front of it. The northeast corner features the **Leaning House** (a wonky-looking structure that is still essentially sound), home of the **Tartu Art Museum** (Wed & Fri–Sun 11am–6pm, Thurs 11am–9pm; €3), with edgy temporary exhibitions downstairs and works by Estonian masters upstairs. The Neoclassical theme continues in the cool white facade of the main **Tartu University** building at Ülikooli 18, just north of the square. Upstairs you can see the **Student Lock-up**, where students were incarcerated in the nineteenth century for such offences as the late return of library books and duelling (Mon–Sat 10am–6pm; €1). About 100m beyond the university is the red-brick Gothic **St John's Church** (Mon–Sat 10am–7pm; church free; tower €2), founded in 1330, and most famous for over one thousand pint-sized terracotta sculptures set in niches around the main entrance, although only about two hundred still survive.

Cathedral Hill and around

Behind the Town Hall, Lossi climbs **Cathedral Hill**, a pleasant park with the remains of the red-brick Cathedral at the top, housing the **University History Museum** (May–Sept Tues–Sun 10am–6pm; Oct–April Wed–Sun 11am–5pm; €4). Inside are some weird and wonderful scientific instruments, and a viewing terrace on one of the former cathedral towers. Nearby is the **Sacrifice Stone**, left over from Estonia's pagan

past; students now burn their lecture notes on it after the exams. Behind the stone you'll find **Kissing Hill**, where newlywed grooms carry their brides. South of Cathedral Hill, the infamous "Grey House" at Riia 15b – a place which filled the inhabitants of Tartu with dread in the 1940s and 50s – is now the **KGB Cells Museum** (Tues–Sat 11am–5pm; €4) with exhibits on deportations, Estonian resistance and life in the Soviet gulags, summarized in English.

ARRIVAL AND INFORMATION

By train The train station is about 900m southwest of the centre at Vaksali 6. There are no facilities at the station.
Destinations Tallinn (8 daily; 2hr 10min).

By bus The bus station is just east of the centre at Soola 2, and there is an ATM on the premises as well as a café and toilets. There's luggage storage at *Hotel Dorpat* next to the station (€1.50/bag).

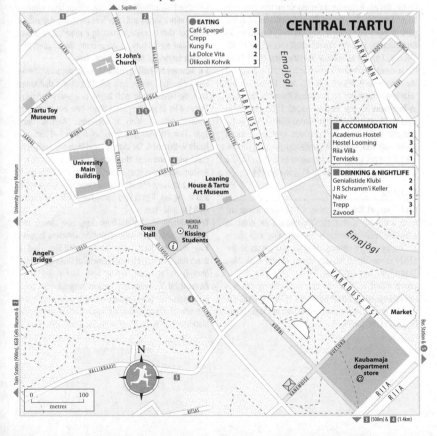

CENTRAL TARTU

EATING
Café Spargel	5
Crepp	1
Kung Fu	4
La Dolce Vita	2
Ülikooli Kohvik	3

ACCOMMODATION
Academus Hostel	2
Hostel Looming	3
Riia Villa	4
Terviseks	1

DRINKING & NIGHTLIFE
Genialistide Klubi	2
J R Schramm'i Keller	4
Naiiv	5
Trepp	3
Zavood	1

9

Destinations Kuressaare (2 direct daily; 6hr); Pärnu (up to 15 daily; 2hr 30min); Rīga (2 daily; 5hr); Tallinn (every 30min, 5.30am–11pm; 2hr 30min).

Tourist information The Tartu Visitors' Centre inside the old Town Hall (May to mid-Sept Mon–Fri 9am–6pm Sat & Sun 10am–5pm; mid-Sept to April Mon 9am–6pm, Tues–Fri 9am–5pm, Sat 10am–2pm; ☎744 2111, ⓦvisittartu .com) can book accommodation, store luggage and provide a wealth of info on Tartu and southern Estonia. You can pick up a copy of *Tartu in Your Pocket* here and surf the internet (free for 20min).

ACCOMMODATION

Academus Hostel Pepleri 14 ☎5306 6620, ⓦtartuhostel.eu. Cheap and fairly central accommodation in a well-appointed student dorm. Choose between self-contained doubles with TV and kitchenette, or a family room featuring two single beds and a pull-out sofa-bed (€50). Book well in advance. Doubles **€40**

Hostel Looming Kastani 38 ☎5699 4398, ⓦloominghostel.ee. Inside the Young Estonian Creativity Centre, this eco-hostel has an emphasis on recycling, with bright decor, friendly young staff, comfy beds and a spacious guest lounge. Bike rental from €10. Dorms **€14**, doubles **€56**

Riia Villa Riia 117a ☎738 1300, ⓦriiavilla.ee; bus #1, #8, #18 or #22 up Riia to Soinaste bus stop. West of Old Town, this tranquil guesthouse is well worth seeking out. Each of the six en-suite rooms has its own theme; choose "Glamorous Simplicity" or "Kleopatra's Room". Doubles **€42**

★Terviseks Raekoja Plats 10 ☎565 5382, ⓦterviseks bbb.com. Backpacker-favourite-turned-B&B run by friendly, energetic young staff, with spacious, brightly decorated doubles and dorms, modern lounge and gleaming kitchen. Special touches include reading lights by each bed and a guitar for guests to strum. Dorms **€15**, doubles **€44**

EATING

Café Spargel Kalevi 13. In an Art Nouveau house just west of the bus station, the "Asparagus Café" excels in affordable, well-presented European cuisine with plenty of healthy veggie options. Risottos and pastas in the €7–10 range. There's a shady terrace out the back. Mon 11am–9pm, Tues–Sat 11am–11pm.

Crepp Rüütli 16. Chic and busy café serving delicious salads, baguettes and filling crêpes (€3). The service is sometimes quite leisurely. Mon–Thurs & Sun 11am–11pm, Fri & Sat 11am–midnight.

Kung Fu Ülikooli 5. Small, unpretentious but satisfying Chinese restaurant that runs through the classics in dependable and eminently affordable style. Mains €7–9. Daily noon–11pm.

★La Dolce Vita Kompanii 10 (entrance from Gildi) ☎740 7545. Life seems pretty sweet when one of the thin-and-crispy, wood-fired pizzas is placed on your chequered tablecloth at this Italian-run restaurant. Mains €6–7. Mon–Thurs & Sun 11.30am–11pm, Fri & Sat 11.30am–midnight.

Ülikooli Kohvik (University Café) Ülikooli 20. Split-level establishment with an elegant café upstairs serving the likes of smoked duck with roast beetroot, and a bargain buffet on the ground floor, dishing up a selection of salads and hot meals to hungry students; pay by weight at €0.70/100g. Mon 11.30am–9pm, Tues 11.30am–10pm, Wed 11.30am–11pm, Thurs & Fri 11.30am–midnight, Sat noon–midnight.

DRINKING AND NIGHTLIFE

★Genialistide Klubi Magasini 5 ⓦgenklubi.ee. Tartu's self-styled "subcultural centre", this eclectic boho venue is a café (with a varied and tasty food menu) by day and an indie bar-club by night, attracting a mixed, arty crowd. Music and events vary, as do opening times; check the website for details. Mon–Sat noon–3am.

J R Schramm'i Keller Rüütli 11. Cellar bar under a low, vaulted ceiling, serving up a selection of ales that range from the latest Nordic craft brews to Newcastle Brown. There's a lot of standing room down here but it still gets rammed with students at weekends. Wed & Thurs 3pm–1am, Fri & Sat 3pm–2am, Sun & Mon 3–11pm.

Naiiv Vallikraavi 6. Set slightly apart from the main pub-crawl routes and much the better for it, *Naiiv* is a chic but welcoming bar that does a great line in local craft beers. It can be a tight squeeze at weekends when live gigs and DJs add to the fun. Tues & Wed 6pm–1am, Thurs 6pm–2am, Fri & Sat 6pm–3am.

Trepp Rüütli 16. Upstairs from *Crepp* (see above), this typically Tartu-esque slice of student bohemia features bare wooden floors, matt black furnishings, and a dangerously long and tempting menu of shots and spirits. Mon–Thurs 7pm–2am, Fri & Sat 8pm–4am.

Zavood Lai 30. Legendary student hangout with post-industrial decor, table football, eccentric indie sounds and a menu of cheap and tasty food chalked up on the blackboard. Mon–Fri 11am–4am, Sat & Sun 6pm–4am.

Finland

HIGHLIGHTS

❶ **Saunas** Don't be shy – strip off and join the locals. **See p.263, p.272 & p.274**

❷ **Design District, Helsinki** Sample the shops, cafés, galleries and nightlife of this vibrant, trendy area of the capital. **See p.264**

❸ **Tampere's museums** Industrial powerhouse Tampere has been revamped with impressive museums, including the new Moomin Museum at Tampere Hall **See p.269**

❹ **Olavinlinna Castle, Savonlinna** One of the best-preserved medieval castles in northern Europe – and with great watersports nearby. **See p.271**

❺ **Sámi Culture, Inari** One of Europe's last frontiers, where nomadic reindeer herders live in harmony with snowmobiles. **See p.274**

HIGHLIGHTS ARE MARKED ON THE MAP ON P.257

ROUGH COSTS

Daily budget Basic €40, occasional treat €65

Drink Salmiakki €4–6 shot

Food Reindeer stew with potatoes €10

Hostel/budget hotel €25/€60

Travel Train: Helsinki–Rovaniemi €80; bus: Helsinki–Tampere €27

FACT FILE

Population 5.4 million

Language Finnish and Swedish

Currency Euro (€)

Capital Helsinki

International phone code ☎ 358

Time zone GMT +2hr

Introduction

Drawing strong cultural influences both from its easterly neighbour, Russia, and from its western one, Sweden, Finland remains one of Europe's most enigmatic countries. It's a land best known for its laconic, pithy people with a penchant for kicking back in a sauna au naturel, for its bizarre annual festivals and for creating those quirky, hippo-like fairytale characters, the Moomins – its strangeness is a good part of the country's charm. And while it's far from a budgeteer's paradise, there are definitely ways to save – especially if you know where to drink.

10

The Finnish landscape is flat and punctuated by huge forests and lakes, with the drama heightening as you head north. The south is still peppered with stunning bodies of water, however. The capital, **Helsinki**, straddles several islands, brightened by brilliant fin-de-siècle architecture and superb collections of late modern and contemporary artworks. Former capital **Turku** is a cultural beacon too. Stretching from the thrumming industrial city of **Tampere** to the Russian border in the east, the vast waters of the **Lake Region** provide a natural means of transport for the timber industry – indeed, water here is a more common sight than land, with many towns lying on narrow ridges between lakes. North of here, the gradually rising fells and forests of **Lapland** are Finland's most alluring terrain and are home to the Sámi, semi-nomadic reindeer herders. For a few months on either side of midsummer, the midnight sun is visible from much of the region; in the dead of winter the north of the country is shrouded in polar darkness.

CHRONOLOGY

1800 BC Tribes from Russia settle in Lapland.

98 AD Roman historian Tacitus writes first recorded reference of the "Fenni".

1293 Sweden invades and defeats Finland, establishing dividing lines between the Catholic West and Orthodox East.

1642 First complete Finnish translation of the Bible produced.

1721 In the Treaty of Uusikaupunki, Sweden cedes Finnish land to Russia.

1809 Russians take Finland after military victory over Sweden.

1812 Helsinki is declared capital of Finland.

1837 The Kalevala, a collection of folklore-inspired poetry and Finland's most famous literary work, is first published.

1858 Confusion caused as Russia forces Finns to drive on the right-hand side of the road.

1860 Finland acquires its own currency, the markka.

1906 Finland gains its own national parliament. Finnish women are the first in the world to receive full political rights.

1917 Finland declares independence from Russia.

1939–40 Soviet troops invade Finland but meet fierce resistance during the "Winter War".

1941 Under the Moscow Peace Treaty, the southeast territory of Karelia is ceded to the Russians.

1945 Tove Jansson publishes the first of her Moomin books for children.

1952 Helsinki holds the Olympic Games.

1995 Finland joins the EU.

2000 Tarja Halonen becomes the first female president.

2002 Finland adopts the euro.

2006 Finnish death metal group Lordi win Eurovision song contest.

2008 Ex-president Martti Ahtisaari awarded the Nobel Peace Prize.

2009 Finnish government sells its share in Santa Park, signalling that the global economic crisis has reached the North Pole.

2011 Turku is joint European Capital of Culture.

2014 Finnish company Nokia sells its mobile phone business to Microsoft.

2017 Finland celebrates the centenary of its independence.

ARRIVAL AND DEPARTURE

There are over twenty airports dotted around the country (information at ⓦfinavia.fi/en), but you're most likely to arrive at Helsinki Vantaa Airport, which is the main hub for **international flights**. British Airways (ⓦba.com), Finnair

FINLAND

HIGHLIGHTS

1. Saunas
2. Design District, Helsinki
3. Tampere's Museums
4. Olavinlinna Castle, Savonlinna
5. Sámi Culture, Inari

10

(wfinnair.com), Norwegian (wnorwegian .no) and Scandinavian Airlines (wflysas .com) fly into Helsinki, with routes offered from most major European cities. **Ferries** arrive from Tallinn (Estonia) and Stockholm (Sweden) at Helsinki and Turku; contact either Tallink Line (wtallink.com) or Viking Line (wvikingline.fi) for tickets and timetables. Another popular route into the country is overland by **train** from St Petersburg to Helsinki, which thanks to a high-speed rail link takes under three and a half hours.

GETTING AROUND

Generally, trains and buses integrate well (in remoter areas they even connect with flights). Plan with care when travelling

through the far north and east where transport connections are more scant.

BY TRAIN

Trains are operated by Finnish State Railways (VR; wvr.fi). Comfortable Express and InterCity trains, plus faster, tilting Pendolino trains, serve the principal cities several times a day. If you're travelling by night train, it's better to go for the more expensive sleeper cars if you want to get any rest, as no provision is made for sleeping in the ordinary seated carriages. Elsewhere, especially on east–west hauls through sparsely populated regions, trains are often tiny or replaced by buses on which rail passes are still valid. InterRail (and Eurail) passes are valid on all trains. The best timetable is the *Rail Pocket Guide*, published by VR and available from all train stations and tourist offices.

BY BUS

Buses cover the whole country, but are most useful in the north. Tickets can be purchased at bus stations and most travel agents; only ordinary one-way tickets can be bought on board. Check ⓦmatka huolto.fi, which lists all bus routes and sells discounted tickets, or ask for the timetable (*Pikavuoroaikataulut*), available at all main bus stations. The private company Express Bus (ⓦexpressbus.fi) sells some particularly cheap fares – often as low as €2 – though you must book at least five days in advance for the most rock-bottom fares.

BY PLANE

Domestic flights can be comparatively cheap as well as time-saving, especially if you're planning to visit Lapland and the far north. Finnair (ⓦfinnair.com) operates the most flights, although Norwegian (ⓦnorwegian.com) also runs a few domestic routes. The cheaper tickets are generally only available if booked well in advance.

BY BIKE

Cycling can be an enjoyable way to see the country at close quarters, and the only appreciable hills are in the far north. You can take your bike along with you on an InterCity train for a €10 fee (reservations rarely necessary), and most youth hostels, campsites and some hotels and tourist offices offer bike rental from €15 per day; there may also be a deposit of around €30.

ACCOMMODATION

There's a good network of 65 official **HI hostels** (ⓦhostellit.fi) as well as a few independents. Most charge €5–6 for breakfast, and bed linen is often extra (€4–7), so if you're on a tight budget it's worth bringing your own sheets. Dorms are almost always single-sex in HI hostels; some independents have mixed dorms. The free *Finland: Budget Accommodation* booklet, available from any tourist office, contains a comprehensive list of hostels and campsites.

Hotels are expensive. Special offers in summer mean that you'll be able to sleep well on a budget in high season, but may have difficulty finding anything affordable out of season – the reverse of the norm. In many towns you'll also find **tourist hotels** (*matkustajakoti*) offering fewer frills for €45–60 per person, and **summer hotels** (*kesähotelli*; June–Aug only), which offer decent accommodation in student blocks for €25–45 per person.

Official **campsites** (*leirintäalue*) are plentiful. The cost to camp is roughly €15 per pitch, plus €5 per person, depending on the site's star rating. Most open from May or June until August or September, although some stay open longer and a few year-round. Many three-star sites also have cottages, often with TV, sauna and kitchen. To camp in Finland, you'll need a Camping Key Scandinavia, available at every site (and online: ⓦcamping.fi) for €16 and valid for a year. Camping rough is illegal without the landowner's permission – though in practice, provided you're out of sight of local communities, there shouldn't be any problems.

FOOD AND DRINK

Finnish food is a mix of Western and Eastern influences, with Scandinavian-style fish specialities and exotic meats such as reindeer and elk alongside dishes that bear a Russian stamp – pastries, and casseroles strong on cabbage and pork. Also keep an eye out for *karjalan piirakka* – oval-shaped pastries containing rice and mashed potato, served hot with a mixture of finely chopped hard-boiled egg and butter. *Kalakukko* is another inexpensive delicacy, if an acquired one: a chunk of bread with pork and whitefish baked inside it; it's legendary around Kuopio but available almost everywhere. Slightly cheaper but just as filling, *lihapiirakka* are envelopes of sweet pastry filled with rice and meat – ask for them with mustard (*sinappi*) and/or ketchup (*ketsuppi*). Don't pass over a chance to try a hearty bowl of *lohikeitto* (creamy salmon and potato soup) either.

Breakfasts (*aamiainen*) in hotels usually consist of a buffet of herring, eggs, cereals, cheese, salami and bread, while you can

FINLAND ONLINE

ⓦ **visitfinland.com** The official Finnish Tourist Board site.

ⓦ **finland.fi** A well-run, informative government site on Finnish culture and society.

ⓦ **sauna.fi** Everything you ever wanted to know about saunas but were afraid to ask, from the Finnish Sauna Society.

ⓦ **festivals.fi** A comprehensive listing of festivals throughout Finland.

ⓦ **nationalparks.fi** A handy starter for planning your visit to the Finnish outdoors.

lunch on the economical **snacks** sold in market halls (*kauppahalli*) or adjoining cafés. Most train stations and some bus stations and supermarkets also have cafeterias offering a selection of snacks, greasy nibbles and light meals, and street stands (*grillis*) turn out burgers and hot dogs for around €3. Otherwise, campus **mensas** are the cheapest places to grab a hot meal (€5 or less); theoretically, you have to be a student, but you're only asked for ID occasionally. In regular restaurants or *ravintola*, **lunch** (*lounas*) deals are good value, with many places offering a lunchtime buffet table (*voileipäpöytä* or *seisovapöytä*) stacked with a choice of traditional goodies for a set price of around €12. Pizzerias are another good bet, serving lunch specials for €7–10. For **evening meals**, cheap eats come in the form of pizzerias, along with, in bigger cities, Chinese, Thai or Nepalese. Authentic Finnish cuisine is invariably pricier.

DRINK

Finns are the world's biggest coffee consumers, knocking back an average 12kg per person annually: cafés fuel the trend and generally open 8am to 6pm. Most restaurants are fully licensed, and are often frequented more for drinking than eating. **Bars** are usually open till midnight or 1am (and clubs until 2am or 3am) and service stops half an hour before closing. You have to be 18 to buy beer and wine, 20 to buy spirits, and some places have a lower age limit of 24. The main – and cheapest – outlets for takeaway alcohol are the ubiquitous

government-run **ALKO** shops (Mon–Fri 9am–8pm, Sat 9am–6pm).

Beer (*olut*) falls into three categories: "light beer" (I-Olut), like a soft drink; "medium strength beer" (*keskiolut*; III-Olut), perceptibly alcoholic, sold in supermarkets and cafés; and "strong beer" (A-Olut or IV-Olut), on a par with the stronger European beers, and only available at licensed restaurants, clubs and ALKO shops. Strong beers, such as Lapin Kulta and Koff, cost about €1.30 per 300ml bottle at a shop or kiosk. Imported beers go for about €3 per can. Finlandia **vodka** is €20 for a 700ml bottle; Koskenkorva, a rougher vodka, is €15. You'll also find Finns knocking back **salmiakki**, a premixed vodka/liquorice cocktail which looks, smells and tastes like cough medicine, and *fisu*, another inexplicably popular drink that blends Fisherman's Friend lozenges with Koskenkorva.

CULTURE AND ETIQUETTE

Finnish people are normally an outsider's favourite thing about Finland: percipient, laconically humorous, self-deprecating and genuinely interested in those who care to find out more about their country. Yes, their brevity can make them come across as withdrawn, introspective, even downright odd: little value is put on exuberance, and you can have an entire conversation with a Finn without their making any discernible facial expression. But underneath this reserve, Finnish people are as full of enthusiasm and affection as any other nation. This is a people whose aversion to small talk and affinity for the awkward moment is rivalled only by their remarkable ability to drink several times their body weight in alcohol in an evening's sitting. Their underlying bonhomie does reveal itself when there's drink around, but alcohol abuse really has long been a problem here, and it's wise to avoid trying to keep up with the Finnish capacity for drinking.

Tipping is rare in Finland, and buying rounds is unheard of. Service is usually included in restaurant bills, although it's common to round the bill up to the nearest convenient figure when paying in cash (the same applies for taxi fares).

10

10

FINNISH

Stress on all Finnish words always falls on the first syllable.

	FINNISH	PRONUNCIATION
Yes	*Kyllä*	Koo-leh
No	*Ei*	Ay
Thank you	*Kiitos*	Keetos
Hello/Good day	*Hyvää päivää*	Hoo-veh pai-veh
Goodbye	*Näkemiin*	Nek-er-meen
Excuse me	*Anteeksi*	Anteksi
Where?	*Missä?*	Miss-eh?
Good	*Hyvä*	Hoo-veh
Bad	*Paha*	Paha
Near	*Lähellä*	Le-hell-eh
Far	*Kaukana*	Kau-kanna
Cheap	*Halpa*	Halpa
Expensive	*Kallis*	Kallis
Open	*Avoinna*	Avoyn-na
Closed	*Suljettu*	Sul-yet-oo
Today	*Tänään*	Ten-ern
Yesterday	*Eilen*	Aylen
Tomorrow	*Huomenna*	Hoo-oh-menna
How much is...?	*Kuinka paljon maksaa...?*	Koo-inka pal-yon maksaa...?
What time is it?	*Paljonko kello on?*	Palyonko kello on?
I don't understand	*En ymmärrä*	Enn oomerreh
Do you speak English?	*Puhutteko englantia?*	Poohut-tuko englantia?
One	*Yksi*	Uksi
Two	*Kaksi*	Kaksi
Three	*Kolme*	Col-meh
Four	*Nelja*	Nel-yeh
Five	*Viisi*	Veesi
Six	*Kuusi*	Coosi
Seven	*Seitsemän*	Sayt-se-men
Eight	*Kahdeksan*	Cah-deksan
Nine	*Yhdeksän*	Oo-deksan
Ten	*Kymmenen*	Kummenen

SPORTS AND OUTDOOR ACTIVITIES

The winter landscape lends itself to **cross-country skiing**, the season lasting from December until January in the south and April or May in northern and central Finland. There are ski slopes, too – Levi, Ylläs and Ruka are the main ones – see ⓦ ski.fi for more information. Several operators offer off-piste skiing. The hiking season is short (May to September) because of snow coverage, but trails like the 80km-long Karhunkierros (bear's ring; ⓦ nationalparks.fi/en/karhunkierros) remain popular. Watery pursuits like **kayaking** (or kitesurfing on the frozen lakes in the winter) are a worthwhile option in the lake regions, especially around Lake Inari. Popular national **sports** include the distinctively Finnish *pesäpallo*, similar to baseball, and ice hockey.

COMMUNICATIONS

Communications are dependable and quick. Free **internet access** is readily available, often at the local library. Major towns and cities usually have free, comprehensive wi-fi, with even remoter areas getting 3G coverage. **Post offices** are generally open 9am to 6pm Monday to Friday, with later hours in Helsinki. Public **phones** have been swiftly phased out in favour of mobile service; if you plan to make a lot of calls in Finland, invest in a Finnish SIM card; €20 will get you a Finnish number with about sixty minutes of domestic calling time or several hundred domestic text messages. Directory enquiries are ☎118 (domestic) and ☎020208 (international).

EMERGENCIES

You hopefully won't have cause to come into contact with the Finnish **police**, though if you do they are likely to speak English. As for **health problems**, if you're insured you'll save time by seeing a doctor at a private health centre (*lääkäriasema*) rather than waiting at a national health centre (*terveyskeskus*), though you're going to pay for the privilege. Medicines must be paid for at a **pharmacy** (*apteekki*), generally open daily 9am to 6pm; outside these times, a phone number for emergency help is displayed on every pharmacy's front door.

INFORMATION

Most towns have a **tourist office**, some of which will book accommodation for you, though in winter their hours are much reduced and some don't open at all. You can pick up a decent map of Finland free from tourist offices.

MONEY AND BANKS

Finland's currency is the **euro** (€). Banks are generally open Monday to Friday 9am to 4pm. Some **banks** have exchange desks at transport terminals, and **ATMs** are widely available. You can also change money at hotels, but the rates are generally poor. **Credit cards** are widely accepted right across the country.

OPENING HOURS AND HOLIDAYS

Most **shops** generally open Monday to Friday 9am to 6pm, Saturday 9am to 4pm. Along with banks, they close on **public holidays**, when most public

EMERGENCY NUMBERS

☎112 for all emergency services.

transport and museums run to a Sunday schedule. These are: January 1, January 6 (Epiphany), Good Friday and Easter Monday, May 1, Ascension (mid-May), Whitsun (late May), Midsummer (late June), All Saints' Day (early Nov), December 6 and 24 to 26.

10

Helsinki

Sitting across a series of islands in Finland's far south, **HELSINKI** has a maritime feel and a mood as much akin to Baltic Eastern Europe and Russian cities as to anywhere else in Scandinavia. For a century an outpost of the Russian Empire, Helsinki's very shape and form derives from its more powerful neighbour. Yet during the twentieth century it became a showcase for independent Finland, many of its impressive buildings reflecting the dawning of Finnish nationalism and the rise of the republic. This ushered in the so-called golden age of Finnish design in the 1950s, and the city is justifiably proud of its cutting-edge architecture. Today, visitors will find a youthful buzz on the streets, where the boulevards, outdoor cafés and restaurants are crowded with Finns who take full advantage of their short summer. At night the pace picks up in Helsinki's solid selection of bars and clubs.

WHAT TO SEE AND DO

Following a devastating fire in 1808, and the city's designation as Finland's capital in 1812, Helsinki was totally rebuilt in a style befitting its new status: a grid of wide streets and Neoclassical brick buildings modelled on the then Russian capital, St Petersburg.

Esplanadi and Senate Square

Esplanadi, a wide, tree-lined boulevard across a mishmash of tramlines from the harbour, is Helsinki at its most charming. A couple of blocks north of its eastern end, the suavely refurbished **City Museum** at Aleksanterinkatu 16 (Mon–Fri 11am–7pm, Sat & Sun 11am–5pm; free; ⓦhelsinginkaupunginmuseo.fi) offers a

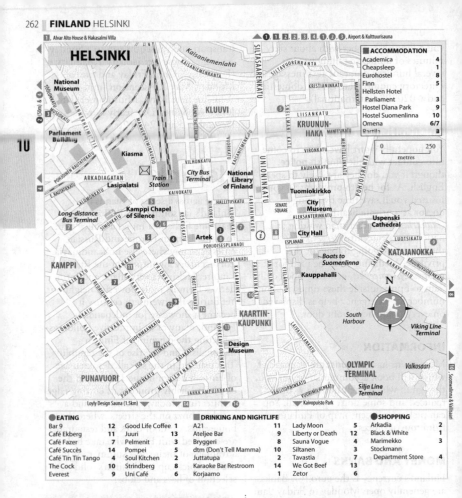

HELSINKI

Kaisaniemenlahti
KAISANIEMENRANTA
SILTASAARENKATU
SILTAVUORENRANTA

National
Museum
KRISTIANINKATU
MAURINKATU

KLUUVI
KRUUNUN-
HAKA
LIISANKATU
MANEESIKATU

Parliament
Building
TRÄ
Kiasma
VIRONKATU
RAUHANKATU
UNIONINKATU
KIRKKOKATU

ARKADIAGATAN
Lasipalatsi
Train
Station
City Bus
Terminal
National
Library
of Finland
Tuomiokirkko

KAIVOKATU
HALLITUSKATU
City
Museum

Long-distance
Bus Terminal
Kamppi Chapel
of Silence
SENATE
SQUARE
ALEKSANTERINKATU
Uspenski
Cathedral

Artek
City Hall
LUOTSIKATU
POHJOISESPLANADI
ESPLANADI
KATAJANOKKA
KRUUNUVUORENKATU

KAMPPI
ETELÄESPLANADI
Boats to
Suomenlinna

KALEVANKATU
Kauppahalli

N

EERIKINKATU
FREDRIKINKATU

KAARTIN-
KAUPUNKI
South
Harbour

Viking Line
Terminal

LÖNNROTINKATU
ALBERTINKATU
BULEVARDI

Design
Museum

OLYMPIC
TERMINAL
Valkosaari

PUNAVUORI
Silja Line
Terminal

Loyly Design Sauna (1.5km)
Kaivopuisto Park

ACCOMMODATION

Academica	4
Cheapsleep	1
Eurohostel	8
Finn	5
Hellsten Hotel Parliament	3
Hostel Diana Park	9
Hostel Suomenlinna	10
Omena	6/7
Rastila	2

0 ————— 250
metres

EATING

Bar 9	12	Good Life Coffee	1	
Café Ekberg	11	Juuri	13	
Café Fazer	7	Pelmenit	3	
Café Succès	14	Pompei	5	
Café Tin Tin Tango	4	Soul Kitchen	2	
The Cock	10	Strindberg	8	
Everest	9	Uni Café	6	

DRINKING AND NIGHTLIFE

A21	1	Lady Moon	5	
Ateljee Bar	9	Liberty or Death	12	
Bryggeri	8	Sauna Vogue	4	
dtm (Don't Tell Mamma)	10	Siltanen	3	
Juttatupa	2	Tavastia	7	
Karaoke Bar Restroom	14	We Got Beef	13	
Korjaamo	1	Zetor	6	

SHOPPING

Arkadia	2
Black & White	1
Marimekko	3
Stockmann Department Store	4

microcosm of 450 years of Helsinki life through wonderful interactive exhibitions.

Just west of City Museum is Senate Square (Senattintori), dominated by the exquisite form of the **Tuomiokirkko** (Cathedral; June–Aug daily 9am–midnight; Sept–May Mon–Sat 9am–6pm, Sun noon–6pm; ⓦhelsinginseurakunnat .fi). After the elegance of the exterior, the spartan Lutheran interior comes as a disappointment; more impressive is the gloomily atmospheric **crypt** (entrance on Kirkkokatu; June–Aug daily 9am–midnight; Sept–May Mon–Sat 9am–6pm, Sun noon–6pm), now often used for exhibitions. West across Unioninkatu, the city's most spectacular interior decoration awaits in the soaring ceilings and

mesmerizing decorative painting of the **National Library of Finland** (Mon–Fri 9am–6pm, plus some Sat; free; ⓦkansalliskirjasto.fi).

Uspenski Cathedral

The square towards the eastern end of Aleksanterinkatu is overlooked by the onion domes of the Russian Orthodox **Uspenski Cathedral** (May–Sept Mon–Fri 9.30am–4pm, Sat 9.30am–2pm, Sun noon–3pm, Oct–April closed Mon). Inside, there's a glitzy display of icons. Beyond is **Katajanokka**, a wedge of land extending between the harbours; with some beautiful Art Nouveau architecture, it's one of the city's most atmospheric places to walk around.

Kamppi Chapel of Silence
This tranquil, award-winning space
(Mon–Fri 8am–8pm, Sat & Sun
10am–6pm; ⓦevl.fi) west of the train
station on busy Narinkka Square (locally
referred to as Kamppi Square) is a
non-ecumenical structure designed to instil
a sense of calm in anyone needing respite
from the hustle and bustle of downtown.

Kiasma
Kiasma is Helsinki's museum of
contemporary art (Tues 10am–5pm,
Wed–Fri 10am–8.30pm, Sat 10am–6pm,
Sun 10am–5pm; €12; ⓦkiasma.fi), its
gleaming steel-clad exterior and hi-tech
interior making it well worth visiting.
Temporary exhibitions feature everything
from paintings to video installations.

The National Museum
North of Kiasma is the **National
Museum** (Tues–Sun 11am–6pm; €8;
ⓦkansallismuseo.fi), its design drawing
on the country's medieval churches
and granite castles. The exhibits, from
prehistory to the present, are exhaustive;
concentrate on a few specific sections,
such as the fascinating medieval church
art and the ethnographic displays. The
highlight could just be by the ticket desk
anyway: glance up for fabulous vivid
murals based on Finland's fabled national
epic poem, the *Kalevala* (which inspired
Tolkien's *Lord of the Rings*).

Hakasalmi Villa
There are four museums affiliated with the
City Museum scattered around town, of
which the lovely **Hakasalmi Villa** (Tues, Wed
& Fri–Sun 11am–5pm, Thurs 11am–7pm;
free), a rose-pink mansion in English-style
grounds that are good for a stroll, is most
eye-catching. It's northwest of the city
centre near the **Finlandia Hall**, a striking
conference centre designed by Alvar Aalto.

Suomenlinna
Built on five interconnected islands
by the Swedes in 1748 to protect Helsinki
from seaborne attack, the fortress of
Suomenlinna, fifteen minutes away by
boat, is the biggest sea fortress in the world.
Reachable by ferry (hourly; €5 return)
from the harbour, it's also a great place
to stroll around on a summer afternoon,
with superb views back across the water
towards the capital: you can either visit
independently or take one of the hour-long
summer **guided walking tours**, beginning
close to the ferry stage and conducted in
English (June–Aug daily 11am, 12.30pm
& 2.30pm; Sept–May Sat & Sun 1.30pm;
€11 high season, €4 low season).
Suomenlinna has a few museums, none
particularly riveting, but the best is
Suomenlinna Museum (daily: May–Sept
10am–6pm; Oct–April 10.30am–4.30pm;
€6.50), with a permanent exhibition on
the island. There are several atmospheric
places to eat and drink.

Vallisaari
The islands lying off the Finnish coast run
into the thousands, of which **Vallisaari** –
until 2016 private military property – is
the latest to become easily accessible. It's
an island for wildlife lovers, as the flora
here is superb, and marked trails criss-cross
it. Bring a picnic. The ferry (May–Aug
daily hourly; Sept Sat & Sun hourly;
€7.50 return) stops at Suomenlinna on
the return, so you can explore both.

ARRIVAL AND DEPARTURE

By plane Vantaa airport (ⓦhelsinki-airport.com) is 20km
to the north, connected by Finnair buses to the central
train station (every 20min; €6.30).
Destinations Ivalo (for Inari; 1–2 daily; 1hr 30min); Oulu
(13–15 daily; 1hr); Rovaniemi (5 daily; 1hr 15min).

10

10

DARING DESIGN

The Golden Age of Finnish Design started in the 1950s, driven by the innovation of architects like the celebrated **Alvar Aalto** who designed many of Helsinki's most striking modern buildings, cementing Helsinki's place as a European design capital. Design was there are plenty of attractions to check out and even a **Design District** (⊚ designdistrict.fi), an area fanning out from the Dianapuisto park at the northeastern end of Uudenmaankatu and full of fashion stores, galleries and showrooms.

DESIGN DESTINATIONS

Artek Keskuskatu 1B (Mon–Sat 9am–6pm; ⊚ artek.fi). Opposite Stockmann's Department Store, this is part museum paying homage to Alvar Aalto's visionary designs and part flashy furnishings store.
Design Museum Korkeavuorenkatu 23 (June–Aug daily 11am–6pm; Sept–May Tues 11am–8pm, Wed–Sun 11am–6pm; €10; ⊚ designmuseum.fi). A romp through Finnish design history.
Alvar Aalto Museum (July & Aug Tues–Fri 10am–6pm, Sat & Sun 11am–6pm; Sept–May Tues–Sun 10am 6pm; €6; ⊚ alvaraalto.fi). The architect's former home in the Töölönlahden puisto park shows the foresight of his early 1930s style when he acquired the property, with signs of the functionalist design he would become renowned for evident throughout. Tram #4.

By train The train station is in the heart of the city on Kaivokatu.
Destinations Oulu (11 daily; 6–9hr); Rovaniemi (4 daily; 10–13hr); St Petersburg (2 daily; 3hr 30min); Tampere (hourly; 1hr 30min); Turku (hourly; 2hr).
By bus The long-distance bus station is under the Kamppi shopping centre on Simonkatu.
Destinations Porvoo (15 daily; 1hr); Turku (hourly; 2hr 30min–2hr 50min).
By ferry Terminals are less than 1km from the centre; take tram #3T or #3B.
Destinations Stockholm (3 daily; 16hr); Tallinn (hourly; 2hr–4hr).

INFORMATION

Tourist office The excellent City Tourist Office at Pohjoisesplanadi 19 (mid-May to mid-Sept Mon–Sat

9am–6pm, Sun 9am–4pm; mid-Sept to mid-May Mon–Fri 9am–6pm, Sat & Sun 10am–4pm; ☎ 09 3101 3300, ⊚ visithelsinki.fi) hands out the useful, free listings magazines *Helsinki This Week* and *City*.
Discount card If you're staying a while, consider purchasing a Helsinki Card (€41/51/61 for 24/48/72hr; ⊚ helsinkicard .com), giving unlimited travel on public transport and free entry to more than fifty museums among other savings.

GETTING AROUND

The city's transport system (trams, buses and a limited metro) is very efficient.
Tickets One-way tickets can be bought on board (€3.20) or from the bus station, tourist office or kiosks around the centre (€2.50), while a tourist ticket (€12/24/36/48 for one/three/five/seven days) permits unlimited use of the whole network for the period covered. Tram #3T/#3B follows a useful figure-of-eight route around the centre.

ACCOMMODATION

Hostel beds are in short supply, especially during summer, so booking ahead is sensible. The Strömma tickets and tours desk at the tourist office can help with this in person, by phone, email or online (Mon–Fri 10am–4/4.30pm, Sat 10am–4pm; June–Aug also Sun 10am–4pm; ☎ 09 2288 1600, ⊚ stromma.fi).

HOSTELS

Academica Hietaniemenkatu 14 ☎ 09 1311 4334, ⊚ hostelacademica.fi. On the fringes of the city centre with single-sex dorms and double rooms. Breakfast and bed linen included in the price. June–Aug only. Tram #3T (stop "Kauppakorkeakoulu"). Dorms €29, doubles €70
Cheapsleep Sturenkatu 27B ☎ 04 5845 6188, ⊚ cheapsleep.fi. Does what it says on the tin, in a clean and amenable way, with 24hr reception and a supermarket downstairs. Dorms €29, doubles €59
Eurohostel Linnankatu 9 ☎ 09 622 0470, ⊚ eurohostel .fi. The biggest hostel in Finland, close to the ferry terminals and with a free sauna. Dorms €29, doubles €58.80
★ **Hostel Diana Park** Uudenmaankatu 9 ☎ 09 642 169, ⊚ dianapark.fi. Sociable, hip and atmospheric hostel (think shabby couches) in a grand old building on Helsinki's best street for bar-hopping. Dorms €28, doubles €68
Hostel Suomenlinna ☎ 09 684 7471, ⊚ hostelhelsinki .fi. Easily the most idyllic place to stay, and located on the fortress island of Suomenlinna (see p.263). Dorms €25, doubles €64

HOTELS

Finn Kalevankatu 3b ☎ 09 684 4360, ⊚ hotellifinn.fi. Peaceful modern rooms on the top floor of an office block, virtually in the city centre. Doubles €79

★ **TREAT YOURSELF**

In **Nuuksio National Park** thirty minutes' drive from Helsinki you can camp in the world's greenest campsite, where state-of-the-art tents are suspended from trees so barely a blade of grass gets trampled. Book through the outdoor adventure company **Honkalintu** (ⓦ honkalintu.fi) who arrange overnight camping adventures for €150 per two people.

Hellsten Hotel Parliament Museokatu 18 ☎ 09 251 1050, ⓦ hellstenhotels.fi. Sleek, large and well-appointed apartment-style rooms that are perfect for groups of friends. Operates another similar hotel in Katajanokka. Doubles €105

Omena Yrjönkatu 30 & Lönnrotinkatu 13 ⓦ omenahotels .com. Helsinki's best deals can often be found at either of these two centrally located, self-service, internet-reserved hotels (rates are very variable). Rooms are very sleek. Doubles €55

CAMPSITE

Rastila Karavaanikatu 4 ☎ 09 107 8517, ⓦ hel.fi /rastilaen. Great camping spot with cabins and dorms in an attached hostel. It's 13km east of the city centre, near the end of the metro line (Vuosaari) and served by night buses #90N till 1.30am during the week and 4.15am Fri & Sat. Camping/person €5, plus per pitch €15, cabins €85

EATING

Many places offer good-value lunchtime deals, and there are plenty of affordable ethnic restaurants and fast-food *grillis* for the evenings. At the end of Eteläesplanadi the *kauppahalli* (Mon–Fri 8am–7pm, Sat 8am–4pm) is good for snacks and sandwiches. Another bargain are the numerous university student cafeterias around the city. Kallio district, across the Kaisaniemenlahti 2km north of the city centre, has some great cheap Bohemian hangouts.

CAFÉS

Café Ekberg Bulevardi 9 ⓦ cafeekberg.fi. Nineteenth-century fixtures and a fin-de-siècle atmosphere, with waitresses bringing expensive sandwiches and pastries to marble tables. Lunch €9.30. Mon–Fri 7.30am–7pm, Sat 8.30am–5pm, Sun 9am–5pm.

Café Fazer Kluuvikatu 3 ⓦ fazer.fi. Owned by Finland's biggest chocolate company, with celebrated cakes and pastries. Lunch about €10. Mon–Fri 7.30am–10pm, Sat 9am–10pm, Sun 10am–6pm.

★ **Café Succès** Korkeavuorenkatu 2. Going strong over fifty years, *Succès* exudes classy tradition and has a huge local following. Great *korvapuusti* (cinnamon buns) and divine salmon soup. Snacks €3–10. Mon–Sat 8am–6pm.

Café Tin Tin Tango Töölöntorinkatu 7 ⓦ tintintango .info. Quirky café-bar with a laundry machine and sauna (book a day in advance) in the Töölö district northwest of the centre via tram #4. Breakfasts and light lunches around €10. Beer available. Mon–Fri 7am–midnight, Sat 9am–midnight, Sun 10am–9pm.

Good Life Coffee Kolmas Linja 17, ⓦ goodlifecoffee.fi. Exquisite coffee, pure and simple, at this hip Kallio joint: and there are a dozen more cool cafés within a five-block radius. Mon–Fri 8.30am–6pm, Sat 10am–6pm.

Strindberg Pohjoisesplanadi 33 ⓦ strindberg.fi. A classic Finnish café: the upstairs restaurant serves contemporary Scandinavian cuisine, while the street-level café is one of the places in town to see and be seen. Mains around €20. Mon–Tues 9am–10pm, Wed–Sat 9am–midnight, Sun 10am–10pm.

Uni Café Mannerheimintie 3 ⓦ hyyravintolat.fi. Cheap, filling dishes at this university cafeteria right in the city centre, with meals from as little as €5. Mon–Fri 11am–7pm, Sat 11am–6pm.

RESTAURANTS

Bar 9 Uudenmaakatu 9 ⓦ bar9.net. Though known as a great, unpretentious neighbourhood bar, they also serve excellent food all day. Massive grilled ham and cheese sandwiches, spicy pastas and salads from €10. Mon–Fri 11am–2am, Sat & Sun noon–2am.

★ **The Cock** Fabianinkatu 17 ⓦ thecock.fi. A refreshing find serving Helsinki's most creative and best-value lunch (€12 for a scrumptious soup and salad buffet) by a country mile. A more intimate lower level opens for dinner. Animated, atmospheric, and run by people who know about good food. Mon–Wed 7.30am–midnight, Thurs & Fri 7.30am–2am, Sat noon–2am.

Everest Luotsikatu 12 ⓦ everestyeti.fi. The best of several good Nepalese restaurants in Helsinki, on the Katajanokka peninsula. Main dishes start at €12. Mon–Fri 10.30am–10pm, Sat & Sun noon–10pm.

Juuri Korkeavuorenkatu 27 ⓦ juuri.fi. This cosy joint has popularized the concept of *sapas* (Finnish tapas) and you can come here to sample classic Finnish dishes prepared well and for cheap prices. A main – or four *sapas* – will set you back €16. Mon–Fri 11.30am–11pm, Sat & Sun noon–11pm.

Pelmenit Kustaankatu 7. This affordable hole-in-the-wall East European restaurant does amazing home-style comfort food such as blini, borscht and *pelmeni* (dumplings) for under €10. Mon–Thurs 11am–5pm, Fri–Sun 10am–10pm.

Pompei Snellmaninkatu 16 ⓦ facebook.com/ravintola pompei. Excellent, down-to-earth neighbourhood Italian restaurant run by a friendly Neapolitan. Good salads and pastas, and especially great pizzas from €10. Grappa and limoncello to boot. Mon–Fri 10.30am–11pm, Sat noon–11pm, Sun 10am–10pm.

Soul Kitchen Fleminginkatu 26–28 ⓦ soulkitchen.fi. American-style restaurant serving southern specialities such as macaroni cheese and succulent barbecue ribs from €10. Aretha and Ray play the tubes. Mon–Fri 11am–midnight, Sat 2pm–midnight, Sun 2–10pm.

DRINKING AND NIGHTLIFE

Wednesday is a popular night for going out, while on Friday and Saturday it's best to arrive as early as possible to get a seat. There are occasional free gigs on summer Sundays in Kaivopuisto Park, south of the centre. There's also a wide range of clubs and discos, which charge a small admission fee (€5–10). For details of what's on, read the back page of the culture section of *Helsingin Sanomat*, or the free fortnightly English-language paper *City*, found in record shops, bookshops and tourist offices.

10

BARS

A21 Annankatu 21 ⓦ a21.fi. This award-winning bar offers excellent if pricey cocktails, designer seating and cliques of there-to-be-seen clientele. Wed & Thurs 6pm–1am, Fri & Sat 6pm–3am.

Ateljee Bar *Hotel Torni*, Yrjönkatu 26. The best views of Helsinki from this stylish (but expensive) rooftop bar. Mon–Thurs 2pm–2am, Fri & Sat noon–2am, Sun 2pm–1am.

Bryggeri Sofiankatu 2 ⓦ bryggeri.fi. Just what the beer-lover needed: a sleek brewery restaurant just back from the harbourfront. Mon–Sat 11.30am–midnight, Sun noon–9pm.

Karaoke Bar Restroom Tehtaankatu 23A ⓦ karaokebar .net/restroom. One-time public lavatory rebuilt as a karaoke bar, with large gold-framed paintings on the walls. Popular with stag dos, so consider yourself forewarned. Mon–Fri 3pm–2am, Sat & Sun 2pm–2am.

Liberty or Death Erottajankatu 5 ⓦ libertyordeath.fi. Small exposed-brick cocktail bar that feels something like a Nordic speakeasy, with candles, jazz and regular changing menus of drinks bearing names such as Jabberwocky and Mutineer. As hip as you'll find in Helsinki. Mon–Thurs 4pm–2am, Fri & Sat 4pm–2am.

Siltanen Hämeentie 13B ⓦ siltanen.org. This great little red-brick spot is a Kallio favourite for local artists and musicians. They often play Finnish music from the 1960s. Great spot for its hulking large breakfasts and brunches (€16) too. Mon–Fri 11am–2am, Sat 11am–3am.

We Got Beef Iso Roobertinkatu 21. Helsinki's hippest-of-the-hipster bars has long been the place to come to hear DJs spin reggae, ska and funk, with a small dancefloor out the back. Wed–Sat 6pm–4am.

Zetor Kaivopiha, Mannerheimintie 3 ⓦ zetor.net. This classic Finnish bar-restaurant is filled with old rusty tractors and serves drinks and eats all day and night until 3.30am. A great place to try *sahti*, Finnish home-brewed ale. Mon & Sun noon–midnight, Tues noon–3am, Wed–Sat noon–4am.

CLUBS

Juttatupa Säästopankinranta 6. The city's best jazz club has live gigs Wednesdays and Saturdays. Mon–Wed 10.30am–midnight, Thurs–Sat 10.30am–1am, Sun 10.30am–11pm.

Korjaamo Töölönkatu 51B ⓦ korjaamo.fi. This well-managed cultural centre puts on superb indie rock, electronica and avant-garde concerts, and has a great bar. Opening hours depend on gigs but are at least Mon–Sat 11am–10pm.

Lady Moon Kalvokatu 12 ⓦ ladymoon.fi. Open nightly, this club claims you never need to drink the same drink there twice. The die-hard partiers love it. Opposite the train station. Daily 9pm–4am.

Tavastia Urho Kekossen Katu 4 ⓦ tavastiaklubi.fi. Finland's (perhaps Europe's) most legendary rock club and synonymous with the development of Finnish rock. Fri & Sat 8pm–4am, Sun 8pm–1am.

LGBT HELSINKI

The gay scene in Helsinki is small but spirited. For the latest details, pick up a copy of the widely available monthly *Z* magazine – in Finnish only but with a useful listings section – or drop into the state-supported gay organization SETA, Pasilanraitio 5 (ⓦ seta.fi).

dtm (Don't Tell Mamma) Mannerheimintie 6 B ⓦ dtm .fi. The capital's legendary gay nightclub still has all the charm: drag shows, gay karaoke and regular house music parties. Mon–Sat 9pm–4am.

Sauna Vogue Sturenkatu 27A ⓦ saunavogue.net. Finland's only gay sauna, with a bar, steamroom, terrace and masseur. €18 entry. Tues–Sat 3–10pm, Sun 3–11pm.

SHOPPING

Arkadia Nervanderinkatu 11 ⓦ arkadiabookshop.fi. Good international bookshop with hundreds of English titles. Tues–Fri noon–7pm, Sat 10am–6pm.

Black & White Toinen Linja 1 ⓦ blackandwhite.fi. Wonderful Kallio record store going strong over 30 years with lots of Finnish music (particularly strong on rock) besides an eclectic international mix. Mon–Fri 10am–6pm, Sat 10am–3pm.

Marimekko Mikonkatu 1 ⓦ marimekko.com. Signature snazzy Finnish clothing brand with many stores nation-wide. Mon–Sat 10am–8pm.

Stockmann Department Store Corner of Aleksanterinkatu and Mannerheimintie ⓦ stockmann .com. Sprawling Constructivist edifice selling everything from bubble gum to Persian rugs. Mon–Fri 9am–9pm, Sat 9am–6pm, Sun noon–6pm.

DIRECTORY

Embassies Australia (honorary consulate), Museokatu 25b; Canada, Pohjoisesplanadi 25b ⓣ 09 228 530; Ireland, Erottajankatu 7A ⓣ 09 682 4240; South Africa, Pohjoinen

Makasiinikatu 4 ☎ 09 6860 3100; UK, Itäinen Puistotie 17 ☎ 09 2286 5100; US, Itäinen Puistotie 14a ☎ 09 616 250.
Exchange Apart from the banks, try Change Group at the airport (6am–8/9pm) or Forex at the train station (Mon–Fri 8am–10pm, Sat & Sun 9am–7pm).
Hospital HUS Hospitals (ⓦ hus.fi/en/medical-care /hospitals) has 26 hospitals.
Left luggage Lockers (€4–8) in the train station (daily 5.20am–11pm).
Pharmacy Yliopiston Apteekki (☎ 0300 20 200, toll call, ⓦ yliopistonapteekki.fi) at Mannerheimintie 96 is open 24hr.
Post office Elielinaukio 2F (Mon–Fri 8am–8pm, Sat 10am–4pm, Sun noon–4pm).

PORVOO

About 50km east of Helsinki, **PORVOO** is one of the oldest towns on the south coast and among Finland's most charming places. Its narrow cobbled streets, flanked by brightly hued wooden buildings, give a sense of Finnish life before Helsinki's bold Neoclassical geometry came along. The **Porvoo Museum** (May–Aug Mon–Sat 10am–4pm, Sun 11am–4pm; Sept–April Wed–Sun noon–4pm; €8) includes the **Johan Ludwig Runeberg House** at Aleksanterinkatu 3 near the station where the famed Finnish poet lived from 1852; one of his poems provided the lyrics for the Finnish national anthem.

The old town is built around the hill on the other side of Mannerheimkatu, crowned by the fifteenth-century **Tuomiokirkko** (May–Sept Mon–Fri 10am–6pm, Sat 10am–2pm, Sun 2–5pm; Oct–April Tues–Sat 10am–2pm, Sun 2–4pm), where Alexander I proclaimed Finland a Russian Grand Duchy. The cathedral survived a serious arson attack in 2006 and reopened two years later.

ARRIVAL AND INFORMATION

By bus Buses run daily from Helsinki to Porvoo (from €9 one-way; 1hr).
Tourist office Aleksanterinkatu 1 (Mon–Fri 9am–7pm, Sat & Sun 10am–5pm; ☎ 040 489 9801, ⓦ visitporvoo.fi).

ACCOMMODATION

Porvoo Hostel Linnankoskenkatu 1–3 ☎ 019 523 0012, ⓦ porvoohostel.fi. Cosy 29-bed hostel, with ten rooms. There's an indoor pool and sports facilities nearby. Dorms €23, doubles €54

EATING

Hanna Maria Välikatu 6 ⓦ hanna-maria.fi. The cheapest place to eat in the Old Town, with lunches that range from €7 to €14. Stays open an extra hour later in the summer. Mon–Sat 8am–4pm, Sun 10am–4pm.

The southwest 10

The region immediately west of Helsinki comprises swathes of interminable forests interrupted only by modest-sized patches of water and wooden villa towns. The extreme southwestern corner is more interesting, with islands and inlets abutting a jagged shoreline, a spectacular archipelago stretching halfway to Sweden (so renowned it's known as *the* archipelago) and some distinctive Finnish–Swedish coastal communities.

TURKU

Co-host of the European Capital of Culture during 2011 (along with Tallinn), **TURKU** was once the national capital, but lost its status in 1812 and most of its buildings in a ferocious fire in 1827. These days it's a small and sociable city, bristling with history, culture and a sparkling nightlife, thanks to the students from its two universities. If you base yourself here for a few days, you'll be able to explore the fascinating coastal inlets and islands in the surrounding area.

WHAT TO SEE AND DO

To get to grips with Turku and its pivotal place in Finnish history, cut through the centre to the Aura River that splits the city. This tree-framed space is, as it was before the great fire of 1827, the community's bustling heart.

Tuomiokirkko

Overlooking the river, the **Tuomiokirkko** (daily 9am–6pm except during services) was erected in the thirteenth century and is still the centre of the Finnish Lutheran Church. Despite repeated fires, a number of features survive. A cathedral museum (€2) is located at the main entrance.

10

Turku Art Museum

The **Turku Art Museum** (Tues–Fri 11am–7pm, Sat & Sun 11am–5pm; €9; ⓦturuntaidemuseo.fi) is at the top of Aurakatu, housed in a lovely building constructed in 1904. It contains one of the better collections of Finnish art, with works by all the great names of the country's nineteenth-century Golden Age plus a commendable stock of modern pieces.

Aboa Vetus and Ars Nova

Turku's combined museum of **Aboa Vetus and Ars Nova** (daily 11am–7pm; €9; guided tours July & Aug daily 11.30am) sits on the riverbank. Digging the foundations of the modern art gallery revealed a warren of medieval lanes, now on show. The gallery comprises 350 striking works plus temporary exhibits, and there's a great café.

Turku Castle and harbour

Crossing back over Aurajoki and down Linnankatu and then heading towards the mouth of the river will bring you to harbour-hugging **Turku Castle** (Tues–Sun 10am–6pm; €9). If you don't fancy the walk, hop on bus #1 from the market square. The somewhat featureless whitewashed exterior conceals a maze of cobbled courtyards, corridors and staircases, with a bewildering array of finds and displays – a 37-room historical museum. The castle probably went up around 1280; its gradual expansion accounts for the patchwork architecture.

At the harbour several historic ships are moored, including the 1902-built 100m-long *Suomen Joutsen*, evoking something of the city's erstwhile maritime clout. To get the nitty-gritty on all things nautical, visit the diverting harbour-side **Forum Marinum** (June–Aug daily 11am–7pm; Sept–May Tues–Sun 11am–7pm; €8) where the new permanent exhibition colourfully runs the gamut of several centuries of maritime history.

Naantali

15km west of Turku, the small town of **Naantali** is one of the biggest and best-preserved examples of Finnish wooden architecture, and the gateway to a chunk of the archipelago lying off the southwest coast (much accessible by road). There are several good-quality restaurants here, though the big attraction is **Moominland** (daily mid-June to Aug; day ticket €28; moominworld.fi) theme park, devoted to the famous Finnish children's book characters. Needless to say, kids enjoy this most. Buses #6/7 from Turku's *kauppatori* (market square) run here.

ARRIVAL AND INFORMATION

By train The train station is just north of the city centre. It takes roughly 15min to walk into town.
Destinations Helsinki (hourly; 2hr); Tampere (9 daily; 1hr 40min).
By bus The bus station is next to the train station.
Destinations Helsinki (hourly; 2hr 5min–2hr 40min); Tampere (every 30min; 2–3hr).
By ferry From the Stockholm ferry, take the train to the terminal, 2km west, or catch bus #1 to Linnankatu.
Destinations Stockholm (4 daily; 10–11hr).
Tourist office Aurakatu 2 (April–Sept Mon–Fri 8.30am–6pm, Sat & Sun 9am–4pm; Oct–March Mon–Fri 8.30am–6pm, Sat & Sun 10am–3pm; ☎02 262 7444, ⓦvisitturku.fi).

ACCOMMODATION

It's worth contacting Kotimaailma (ⓦkotimaailma.com) for online offers on fully serviced apartments close to Turku city centre: these work out as little as €80 for two people. For staying out on the archipelago, contact Archipelago Booking of Finland (☎02 410 6600, ⓦarchipelagobooking.fi).
Campsite Ruissalo ☎02 262 5100; bus #8. On the island of Ruissalo, which has two sandy beaches and overlooks Turku harbour. There is also a villa in the grounds with rooms. June–Aug. Camping/person **€5**, plus per tent **€17**, doubles **€40**
Omena Hotelli Humalistonkatu 7 ⓦomenahotels.com. Alvar Aalto fans might fancy a stay in this building designed by Finland's most famous architect. The hotel is modern and self-service, with an automated reception area. Doubles **€55**
★ **River Hostel Turku** Linnankatu 72 ☎040 689 2541, ⓦwww.msborea.fi. Permanently docked on the river, the SS Borea is the most exciting place to stay in Turku on a budget. Staying on an ex-cruise ship is a novel quirk, and the en-suite cabin rooms are tidy and neat. Dorms **€23**, doubles **€42**
Tuure Bed and Breakfast Tuureporinkatu 17 C ☎02 233 0230, ⓦwww.netti.fi/~tuure2/en/. Clean, pleasant little guesthouse with friendly proprietors in Turku centre, where fifteen rooms are located in something of a drab office building. Doubles **€58**

EATING

Fresh produce is sold in the *kauppatori* (market square), near the tourist office, every day; in summer it's full of open-air cafés; nearby, the effervescent market hall or *kauppahalli* (Mon–Fri 8am–5pm, Sat 8am–2pm) offers a slightly more upmarket choice of delis and other places to eat.

Assarin Ullakko Rehtorinpellonkatu 4a. This rock-bottom-priced student cafeteria offers a lively atmosphere great for meeting local students. Lunch costs €5.60 (50 percent discount for students). Mon–Fri 10.30am–3pm.

Blanko Aurakatu 1 ⓦ blanko.net. Ever-popular bar-restaurant just opposite the tourist office. Good lunches and drum 'n' bass and house DJs till 3am at weekends. Mains from €10 to €17. Mon & Tues 11am–11pm, Wed & Thurs 11am–midnight, Fri 11am–3am, Sat noon–3am, Sun noon–6pm.

Café Art Läntinen Rantakatu 5 ⓦ cafeart.fi. Popular river-fronting café that don't scrimp on the strength of its espressos. Mon–Fri 10am–7pm, Sat 10am–5pm, Sun 11am–5pm.

Viikinkiravintola Harald Aurakatu 3 ⓦ ravintolaharald .fi. A fun Viking-style restaurant, this joint does hearty meals. Lunches around €10 served until 3pm. Mon noon–11pm, Tues–Thurs noon–midnight, Fri & Sat noon–1am, Sun 3pm–10pm.

DRINKING AND NIGHTLIFE

A drink at one of the many floating bar-restaurants moored along Itäinen Rantakatu is a popular summer tradition.

★**Brewery Restaurant** Koulu Eerikinkatu 18 ⓦ panimoravintolakoulu.fi. This former schoolhouse has been converted into a labyrinthine bar serving beer brewed on the premises and a fantastic range of whiskies. Mon–Sat 11am–2am.

Klubi Humalistonkatu 8 ⓦ klubi.net. Cavernous, studenty venue featuring live bands and DJ nights. Wed 10pm–4am, Thurs–Sat 9pm–4am.

Monk Humalistonkatu 3 ⓦ monk.fi. Cool spot with lots of live jazz. Mon 9pm–1am, Fri–Sat 9pm–4am.

The Lake Region

About a third of Finland is covered by the **Lake Region**, a massive area of bays, inlets and isles interspersed with dense pine forests. Despite holding much of Finland's industry, it's a remote, peaceful, verdant area, and even **Tampere**, a major industrial city, enjoys a laidback lakeside setting. The eastern part of the region is the most atmospheric: slender ridges furred with conifers link the few sizeable landmasses. The regional centre, **Savonlinna**, stretches gorgeously across several islands and boasts a fine medieval castle, inside which a famous opera festival is held every summer, while bustling **Kuopio** has superb museums and another enviable lakeshore location for water-based fun.

TAMPERE

10

Scandinavia's largest inland city, **TAMPERE** is a leafy place of cobbled avenues, sculpture-filled parks and two sizeable, placid lakes. It was long a manufacturing centre, but thanks to an impressive arts patronage, it has metamorphosed into one of Finland's most enjoyable cities, with free outdoor concerts, a healthy nightlife and cracking modern art. Even its old industry is now part of its edgy appeal: check the bars and the boutiques in the former factories and the hipsters hanging out alongside the weirs and canals.

WHAT TO SEE AND DO

The main streets run off either side of **Hämeenkatu**. At its western edge, **Hämeenpuisto** runs north–south. Further west, in undulations of parkland interspersed with churches and grand residential addresses, the isthmus that divides the two lakes of Näsijarvi and Pyhäjärvi stretches away.

Lenin Museum

The **Lenin Museum** at Hämeenpuisto 28 (June–Aug daily 11am–6pm; Sept–May Tues–Sun 11am–5pm; €6) was newly refurbished for 2016 and commemorates the revolutionary's ties with Finland.

Särkänniemi

At the northern end of Hämeenpuisto, **Särkänniemi** (one-day pass €38; ⓦ sarkanniemi.fi/en) is far more than the lake-fronting amusement park you see from afar. Aside from all the rides and a planetarium (which the day-pass gets you entry to, along with the tower), it's here that you will find **Näsinneula observation tower** (daily 11am–11pm; included in Särkänniemi ticket price, €5 by itself), topping out at 130m with a great view of the city and a restaurant. There's a lift if you don't fancy the climb.

With a separate admission charge, tremendous **Sara Hildén Art Museum** (May–Sept daily 10am–6pm; Oct–April Tues–Sun 10am–6pm; €10; ⓦtampere.fi /english/sarahilden.html) behind the observation tower is a quirky collection of Finnish and foreign modern works perched above the lakeshore.

Tampere Cathedral

Three blocks north of Hämeenkatu, stone-built **Tampere Cathedral** (daily May–Sept 10am–5pm; Oct–April 11am–3pm; free) is attractive from the outside. Inside, however, it is stunning, with some quite controversial decorative murals by Hugo Simberg and Magnus Enckell.

Tampere Hall

On the east side of the rail tracks, Scandinavia's largest conference centre is flash, but of note to sightseers as the new home of the adorable **Moomin Museum** (Tues–Fri 9am–5pm, Sat & Sun 10am–6pm; €6), a respectful and exhaustive overview of Tove Jansson's creations with touching models and sketches.

Rauhaniemi

About 3km north of Tampere Hall in Lappi neighbourhood, a woodsy park culminates in **Rauhaniemi** beach, complete with a **sauna** (Mon–Thurs 3–8pm, Fri 3–8.30pm, Sat & Sun 1–8pm; €4; ⓦrauhaniemi.net) where you cool off in the lake afterwards. Take bus #2 from outside the tourist office.

ARRIVAL AND INFORMATION

By plane Tampere-Pirkkala Airport is located 17km southwest of the city. Bus #1a operates between the airport and the train station, taking 40min (€6).

By train The train station is at Rautatienkatu 25, at the end of Hämeenkatu.

Destinations Helsinki (hourly; 2hr); Kuopio (4 daily; 3–4hr); Oulu (14 daily; 4hr 25min–8hr 30min); Savonlinna (5 daily; 5hr 30min–6hr 30min); Turku (9 daily; 1hr 40min).

By bus The long-distance bus station is in the town centre, off Hämeenkatu, two blocks west of the river.

Tourist office Hämeenkatu 14 (Sept–May Mon–Fri 10am–5pm, Sat 10am–3pm; June–Aug Mon–Fri 10am–6pm, Sat & Sun 10am–3pm; ☎03 5656 6800, ⓦvisittampere.fi).

ACCOMMODATION

★**Dream Hostel** Åkerlundinkatu 2 ☎045 236 0517, ⓦdreamhostel.fi. Wonderfully furnished, nigh-on hotel standard modern hostel with pretty much every amenity you could imagine, including a sauna and gym. Dorms **€19.80**, doubles **€59**

Härmälä Campsite ☎020 719 9777, ⓦsuomicamping fi: bus #1. 4km south of the city centre in gorgeous wooded environs with cabins. Early May to late Sept. Camping/person **€5**, plus per pitch **€15**, cabins **€47**

Omena Hotelli Hämeenkatu 7 & Hämeenkatu 28 ⓦomenahotels.com. Two excellent self-service hotels. No reception, so you must book online, but great deals are offered. Doubles **€55**

EATING

★**2H+K** Aleksanterinkatu 33 ⓦ2hk.fi. Time-tested but hip as ever, this vibrant restaurant, with exposed brick walls, serves fresh Italian-Finnish food. Mains are about €15. Mon–Thurs noon–midnight, Fri & Sat noon–1am, Sun 1–11pm.

Gopal Ilmarinkatu 16. Friendly vegetarian Indian lunch spot where you pay by weight (€1.85/100g). Mon–Fri 11am–5pm, Sat noon–4pm.

Kahvila Runo Ojakatu 3 ⓦkahvilaruno.fi. With some great Finnish rustic furniture, this bookish, high-ceilinged space is the best place in town for a coffee and cake. Mon–Fri 9am–8pm, Sun 10am–8pm.

Pizzeria Napoli Aleksanterinkatu 31 ⓦpizzerianapoli.fi. Tampere's best and longest-standing pizza place. Mon–Fri 10.45am–11pm, Sat noon–midnight, Sun noon–11pm.

Tivoli Smørrebrød & Øl Itäinenkatu 9–13. Good selection of Nordic sandwiches and beers in this resto-pub set in the Finlayson factory area. Mon & Tues 11am–9pm, Wed & Thurs 11am–10pm, Fri 11am–11pm, Sat noon–11pm, Sun noon–8pm.

DRINKING

Jack the Rooster Satakunnankatu 13 ⓦjacktherooster .fi. By the Satakunnankatu bridge, this legendary rock venue puts on great live gigs. Good food too. Mon, Thurs & Fri 4pm–4am, Tues & Wed 4pm–2am, Sat & Sun 1pm–4am.

Klubi Tullikamarinaukio 2 ⓦklubi.net. Busy nightclub and concert venue in an old customs house behind the train station. Wed 10pm–4am, Thurs–Sat 9pm–4am.

Telakka Tullikamarin aukio 3 ⓦtelakka.eu. The most popular watering hole among Tampere university students, serving good meals (from €13.50). Mon & Tues 11am–midnight, Wed & Thurs 11am–2am, Fri 11am–3am, Sat noon–3am, Sun noon–midnight.

SAVONLINNA AND AROUND

SAVONLINNA is one of Finland's most relaxed towns, renowned for its **opera**

festival (☎015 476 750, ⓦoperafestival.fi) in July. Book well ahead if you're visiting in summertime. Out of peak season, its streets and beaches are uncluttered, and the town's easy-going mood and lovely setting – amid a confluence of forests and lakes – make it a pleasant place to linger.

WHAT TO SEE AND DO

The best locations for absorbing the atmosphere are the **harbour** and **market square** at the end of Olavinkatu. At the square, try the Savonlinna speciality of *lörtsy*, a delicious meat-and-rice-filled pastry.

Follow the harbour around picturesque Linnankatu, or around the sandy edge of Pihlajavesi, which brings you to atmospheric and surprisingly well-preserved **Olavinlinna Castle** (hourly guided tours Jan–May Mon–Fri 10am–4pm, Sat & Sun 11am–4pm; June to mid-Aug daily 10am–6pm; mid-Aug to mid-Dec Mon–Fri 10am–4pm, Sat & Sun 11am–4pm; €8), perched on a small island. Founded in 1475, the castle witnessed a series of bloody conflicts until the Russians claimed possession of it in 1743 and relegated it to the status of town jail.

Nearby is the **Savonlinna Provincial Museum** in Riihisaari (Tues–Sun 11am–5pm, plus Mon same times June–Aug; €5), which occupies an old granary and displays an intriguing account of the evolution of local life, with rock paintings and ancient amber carved with human figures.

Punkaharju

Punkaharju, a densely forested ridge set amid the lakes 35km southeast of Savonlinna, and accessible by train, is your best opportunity to get out into the region's stunning countryside. A must-see near the train station is the **Finnish Forest Museum** (June–Aug daily 10am–7pm; May & Sept daily 10am–5pm; Oct–April Tues–Sun 10am–5pm; €10; ⓦwww.lusto.fi), which has riveting exhibits that bring the forests and their place in Finnish culture alive. There's a restaurant, and trails nearby.

ARRIVAL AND INFORMATION

By train There are two train stations: get off at Savonlinna-Kauppatori, across the main bridge from the tourist office.

Destinations Parikkala (for Helsinki; 6 daily; 50min); Punkaharju (4 daily; 30min); Tampere (5 daily; 5hr 30min–6hr 30min).

By bus The bus station is off the main island at the western end of Olavinkatu, but within easy walking distance of the town centre.

Destinations Kuopio (3–5 daily; 3hr).

Tourist office Puistokatu 1 (July to early Aug Mon–Sat 10am–6pm, Sun 10am–2pm; rest of year Mon–Fri 9am–5pm; ☎0600 30 007, ⓦsavonlinna.travel).

ACCOMMODATION

Kesähotelli Vuorilinna Kylpylaitoksentie ☎015 739 50. Nice, fairly central hostel on Vääräsaari island (road and boat connections) open June–Aug. Dorms **€30**

Perhehotelli Hospitz Linnankatu 20 ☎015 515 661, ⓦwww.hospitz.com. Attractive, central hotel. Prices go up by some 50 percent during the opera festival. Doubles **€98**

Wanha Pappila Opistokatu 13 ☎015 572 910, ⓦwww.sko.fi. 6km southwest of the centre in Poukkisilta, a beguiling former vicarage offering bed and breakfast. On-call reception June–Aug only. Doubles **€80**

EATING AND DRINKING

Good, cheap food is available at the pizza joints along Olavinkatu and Tulliportinkatu.

Café Alegria Puistokatu 3. Prettily painted café in the west of town with wickedly strong coffee and tasty snacks. Mon–Fri 9am–7pm, Sat 10am–3pm.

Majakka Satamakatu 11. Tasty Finnish nosh, and a definite maritime theme going on, with some good deals at lunchtime (around €10). Mon–Sat 11am–1am, Sun noon–midnight.

KUOPIO

The pleasant lakeside town of **KUOPIO** is best known for its enormous smoke sauna, the biggest in the world, and makes for a worthwhile pit stop on your way north to Lapland. One of the best times to visit is during **Kuopio Dance Festival** (ⓦkuopiodancefestival.fi) in mid-June.

WHAT TO SEE AND DO

Built on a grid system, the centre is easy to navigate. Just south of the train station is the main square, the *kauppatori*.

Museums

From the main square Kauppakatu leads east to the **Kuopio Museum** (Tues–Sat 10am–5pm; €8; ⓦkuopionmuseo.fi) at no. 23 with two floors of natural and cultural history. Further up the road, at

10

10

no. 35, the **Kuopio Art Museum** (Tues–Sat 10am–5pm; €6; ⓦtaidemuseo.kuopio.fi) has mainly modern Finnish art, housed in a converted bank. Two blocks down on Kuninkaankatu, the **Victor Barsokevitsch Photographic Centre** (Mon–Fri 11am–6pm, Sat & Sun 11am–4pm; €8; ⓦvb-valokuvakeskus.fi) is a real find – one of the best photography galleries in the country.

Puijo Tower

Every self-respecting Finnish city has a tower to look out over the flat lands below, and **Puijo Tower**, Puijontie 135, 2km north of the train station (Mon–Sat 10am–9pm, Sun 10am–7pm; €6; bus #10), is Kuopio's. The tower is modern but the woods nearby are ancient and undisturbed, plus there's a rare example of a sixteenth-century tenant farm to explore.

Woodsmoke sauna

Kuopio's **woodsmoke sauna** (Tues year-round, plus Thurs June–Aug; €12; ⓦrauhalahti.fi) is the main draw in town, and about as quintessentially Finnish an experience as you'll find: there are traditional Finnish evenings each night the sauna is open, which include a Lumberjack Show and great dinner buffet from mid-May to mid-August (€21). The sauna is located 4km south of the centre within the *Rauhalahti* spa hotel complex (see below).

ARRIVAL AND INFORMATION

By train Kuopio's train station is located just north of the *kauppatori*.

Destinations Helsinki (8–10 daily; 4hr 15min–4hr 50min); Oulu (5 daily; 4hr–4hr 40min); Rovaniemi (3 daily; 7hr); Tampere (6 daily; 3hr–3hr 30min).

By bus The bus station is connected to the train station by subway.

Destinations Savonlinna (3–5 daily; 3hr; some buses change at Varkaus).

Tourist office Kauppakatu 45, within Apaja shopping centre in the underground marketplace (Mon–Fri 8am–3pm; ☎017 182 584, ⓦkuopio.fi); ask here about boat trips on the lake.

ACCOMMODATION

Rauhalahti Spa Hotel & Resort Katiskaniementie 8, 5km from the city centre ☎017 473 000, ⓦrauhalahti.fi;

bus #7. It's a spa, it's a hotel, it's a hostel, it's the region's best campsite, with tent space and a wide range of cabins – in short, it's every type of accommodation you could possibly want, all set in attractive verdant lakeside grounds. Camping/person €6, plus per tent €13, camping cottage doubles €33, hostel double €70, hotel doubles €104

EATING AND DRINKING

The harbour area has several eateries that open up in summer and are good for a drink. Kuopio is famous for its fish- and pork-filled breads known as *kalakukko*.

★**Café Kaneli** Kauppakatu 22 ⓦkahvilakaneli.net. Charming little café cluttered with knick-knacks, serving superb coffee and cake. Mon, Tues, Thurs & Fri 9.30am–6pm, Wed 9.30am–7.30pm, Sat 11am–4pm, Sun 11am–3pm.

Intro Kauppakatu 20 ⓦravintolaintro.fi. The best restaurant in town, it's spacious, sophisticated but far from the most expensive. Especially good salads, and quite a few mains for €16. Mon–Thurs 11am–10pm. Fri & Sat 11am–midnight.

Sampo Kauppakatu 13. Proudly traditional fish restaurant that has been serving Finnish dishes loved by locals since 1931. Mains around €14. Mon–Thurs 11am–10pm, Fri & Sat 11am–midnight, Sun noon–10pm.

The north

The northern regions make up a vast portion of Finland: a full one third of the country lies north of the Arctic Circle. It's sparsely populated, with small communities often separated by long distances and little of anything in between besides tundra-like plains or dense forests. The coast of Ostrobothnia is affluent thanks to the flat and fertile farmland around; bustling **Oulu** is the major city, though it maintains a pleasing small-town atmosphere. Further north is the little-traipsed territory of **Lapland**, its wide-open spaces home to several thousand Sámi, who have lived more or less in harmony with this harsh environment for millennia. Up here are two good bases: the university town of **Rovaniemi** and, further north, the quiet spread-out village of **Inari**, a great jumping-off point for trips to more remote bits of the region; there is an extensive bus service and regular flights from Helsinki. Make sure you try Lappish **cuisine**, too – fresh cloudberries, smoked reindeer and wild salmon are highlights.

OULU

OULU, with its renowned university, is a great place to pause on your way up north, with a good collection of restaurants and cafés and a pulsing nightlife, mostly gathered around a nicely designed harbour. On Kirkkokatu, the copper-domed and stuccoed **Tuomiokirkko** (June–Aug daily 11am–8pm; Sept–May Mon–Fri noon–1pm) seems anachronistic amid the bulky blocks of modern Oulu. The few museums are nothing to write home about, but Oulu has won plaudits for its fabulous network of **cycling trails**, connecting the surrounding islands and woods, including Hietasaari Island with its lovely beach. Pick up a map of them at the tourist office.

ARRIVAL AND INFORMATION

By train The train station is located a few blocks east of the *kauppatori* and *kauppahalli*.
Destinations Helsinki (11 daily; 6–9hr); Rovaniemi (7 daily; 2hr 15min–2hr 45min); Tampere (14 daily; 4hr 25min–8hr 30min).
By bus The bus station is located next to the train station.
Destinations Helsinki (11 daily; 8hr–11hr 55min); Rovaniemi (6 daily; 3–4hr).
Bike rental Lappis Kiikelsilta (☎414 338 602, ⓦlappis .fi) on Kiikei island, accessed from the southern end of Oulu's Kauppatori. The office isn't always open, but give them a call and they can normally be there within 15min or so. €15/3hr or €25/day.
Tourist office Torikatu 10 (Mon–Thurs 9am–5pm, Fri 9am–4pm; mid-June to Aug until 5pm, plus Sat 10am–4pm; ☎08 5584 1330, ⓦvisitoulu.fi).

ACCOMMODATION

Nallikari Holiday Village ☎044 703 1353, ⓦcampingfinland.fi. Campsite with cabins (including some luxury ones) by the beach on Hietasaari island, 4km from town; take bus #17 from Isokatu in the town centre. Camping/person **€5**, plus per tent **€13**, cabins **€45**

EATING AND DRINKING

Rooster Café Torikatu 23 ⓦcaferooster.fi. This stylish, youthful café-cum-restaurant-cum-bar serves delicious and exciting brunches and dinners, although the large burger menu is what most diners tuck into (around €15). Mon–Thurs 10.30am–10pm, Fri 10.30am–11pm.
Sokeri Jussin Pikisaarentie 2 ⓦsokerijussinkievari.fi. A prettily painted wooden house on Pikisaari island where you can try delicious, creative Finnish cooking, such as roasted reindeer, or baked Arctic char in morel sauce. Mains from €18. Mon–Sat 11am–11pm, Sun noon–10pm.

ROVANIEMI

ROVANIEMI is touted as the capital of Lapland, and while its fairly bland shopping streets can't compare to the surrounding rural hinterland, the town's Arctic sensibility makes it worth spending a day here while gearing up for an exploration of truly wild northern Finland. The **midnight sun** is also visible from Rovaniemi for several weeks each side of midsummer.

Prepare yourself for what lies further north by visiting the 172m-long glass tunnel of **Arktikum** at Pohjoisranta 4 (mid-Jan to May & Sept–Nov Tues–Sun 10am–6pm; June–Aug daily 9am–6pm; Dec to mid-Jan daily 10am–6pm; €12; ⓦarktikum.fi). Subterranean galleries house fascinating insights into Sámi culture, the log-floating industry and all things circumpolar.

At Koskikatu 1, **Lapland Safaris** (branches also all over Lapland, including Inari; ☎016 331 1200, ⓦlaplandsafaris .com), and are the go-to adventure outfit for organizing excursions in Lapland proper, including their wonderful husky rides (€126 per person).

The biggest attractions are outside town. The **Arctic Circle**, 8km north, is connected by hourly bus #8 from the train station (€6.80 return). A few paces north is the **Santa Claus Village** (daily: early Jan to May 10am–5pm; June–Aug 9am–6pm; Sept–Nov 10am–5pm; Dec to early Jan 9am–7pm; free), a large, very commercialized log cabin where you can meet Father Christmas all year round.

ARRIVAL AND INFORMATION

By plane The airport is located 10km north of town, and connected by bus (€7).
Destinations Helsinki (5 daily; 1hr 15min).
By train The train station is 1km southwest of the town centre, at Ratukatu 3.
Destinations Helsinki (4 daily; 10–13hr); Kuopio (3 daily; 7hr); Oulu (7 daily; 2hr 15min–2hr 45min).
By bus The bus station is just west of the centre, off Postikatu, a few minutes' walk east from the train station.
Destinations Inari (3 daily; 4hr 40min–5hr 40min); Nordkapp, Norway (June to late Aug 1 daily; 10hr 35min).
Tourist office Maakuntakatu 29–31 (mid-June to mid-Aug Mon–Fri 9am–6pm, Sat & Sun 9am–3pm; rest of the year Mon–Fri 9am–5pm; ☎016 346 270, ⓦvisitrovaniemi.fi).

10

10

ACCOMMODATION

Guesthouse Borealis Asemieskatu 1 ☎044 313 1771, ⓦ guesthouseborealis.com. Family-run spot with colourful rooms and great service. Doubles €68

Hostel Rudolf Koskikatu 41, book via ☎016 321 321, ⓦ rudolf.fi. Modern hostel with colourful no-frills rooms a 10min walk from the centre. There are no staff on site; check in and reservations are handled by *Hotel Santa Claus*, Korkalonkatu 29. April–Nov. Doubles €49

Ounaskoksi Camping ☎016 345 304, ⓦ ounaskoski -camping-rovaniemi.com. Campsite on the far bank of Ounaskoski, facing town – a 20min walk from the station. Mid-May to late Sept. Per person €8.50, plus per tent €15

EATING AND DRINKING

★ **Café and Bar 21** Rovakatu 21 ⓦ cafebar21.fi. Lively little spot, serving salads, waffles, smoothies and coffee. Mon & Tues 11am–9pm, Wed & Thurs 11am–midnight, Fri 11am–2am, Sat noon–2am, Sun noon–9pm.

Kauppayhtiö Valtakatu 24. Unexpectedly fantastic café-bar with a mishmash of retro furniture. DJs at the weekend and a gallery at the back. "Best burgers in town" they claim: you may well agree. Mains €10–15. Tues–Thurs 11am–9pm, Fri 11am–3am, Sat 1pm–3am.

Monte Rosa Pekankatu 9 ⓦ monterosa.fi. Rovaniemi's best Italian restaurant, with excellent pan pizzas and pasta dishes, from €9.50. Mon–Fri 5–11pm, Sat 3–11pm, Sun 5–10pm.

Ravintola Roka Ainonkatu 3 ⓦ ravintolaroka.fi. Rovaniemi might not be the first place that comes to mind for sampling streetfood when the air temperature outside is invariably freezing, but in here it's warm and friendly, with massive hot sandwiches starting at €9. Mon–Thurs 10.30am–9pm, Fri 10.30am–11pm, Sat noon–11pm, Sun noon–9pm.

INARI

A half-day bus ride north of Rovaniemi, **INARI** lies along the fringes of Inarijärvi, one of Finland's largest lakes, and makes an attractive base from which to explore Lapland further. In the town, the excellent **SIIDA** (Sámi Museum; June–Sept daily 9am–7pm; Sept–May Tues–Sun 10am–5pm; €10; ⓦ siida.fi) has an outstanding outdoor section illustrating how the Sámi survived in Arctic conditions in their tepees, or *kota*, while the indoor section has a well-laid-out exhibition on life in the Arctic. Huge photographs depict how drastically the weather fluctuates here throughout the year. Towards the northern end of the village, summer **boat tours** (€20) depart from under the bridge to the ancient

Sámi holy site on the island of **Ukonkivi**. If walking's your thing, then check out the pretty **Pielpajärvi Wilderness Church**, a well-signposted 7km (2hr) hike from the village. Hotel Inari (☎016 671 016, ⓦ hotelliinari.fi) has an adjoining outdoor adventure company that organizes fun excursions in the surrounding wilderness.

ARRIVAL AND INFORMATION

By plane Ivalo airport in Törmänen is roughly 50km southeast of Inari. Buses meet flights and run via Ivalo to Inari (€8.50).

Destinations Helsinki (1–2 daily; 1hr 30min).

By bus Buses stop outside the tourist office, in the town centre, before continuing to Karasjok in Norway and – from June to Aug only – Nordkapp, about the most northerly point in mainland Europe.

Destination Ivalo (3–5 daily; 35min); Rovaniemi (3–4 daily; 4hr 40min–5hr 40min).

Tourist office The tourist office (June–Sept daily 9am–7pm; Sept–May Tues–Sun 10am–5pm; ☎040 168 9668, ⓦ inarisaariselka.fi) is in the SIIDA museum. Staff can advise on guided snow-scooter trips in winter and fishing trips in summer – as well as trips across the Russian border to Murmansk.

ACCOMMODATION

Hotel Kultahovi Saarikoskentie 2 ☎016 511 7100, ⓦ hotelkultahovi.fi. Not much to look at from afar but right by the river, and with the best restaurant, *Aanaar*, for a very long way (reindeer carpaccio, skewered tiger prawns). Doubles €104

Uruniemi Campsite ☎016 671 331, ⓦ uruniemi.fi. 2km south of the village In a gorgeous location right by the lake, with cabins and rooms arranged around manicured grounds. June–Sept. Camping/person €5, plus per tent €5, cottages €28

SAARISELKÄ

Saariselkä is a ski resort about the same distance (50km) from Ivalo airport as Inari, only heading south. It's not Finland's best ski centre but it is the easiest to access, as Rovaniemi–Inari buses stop by. South of town, try a stay at **Kiilopää** (☎016 668 741, ⓦ kiilopaa.fi), a delightful complex with a hotel, hostel, cabins and a legendary woodsmoke sauna. Here you can go fell-walking, snow-shoeing or partake of just about any outdoor activity you like. Dorms €30, doubles €82, four-person cabin €137

THE SEINE, VIEWED FROM NOTRE-DAME, PARIS

France

HIGHLIGHTS

❶ **Paris** Explore some of Europe's best museums, restaurants and nightlife. **See p.281**

❷ **Reims** Treat yourself to champagne tasting and a cellar tour. **See p.296**

❸ **Strasbourg** A city of striking architecture and hearty Alsatian food. **See p.305**

❹ **Marseille** Cycle along the dazzling Corniche for free. **See p.329**

❺ **Lyon** France's gastronomic capital also boasts some of the country's best nightlife. **See p.339**

❻ **Corsica** Marvel at the fiery red Calanques on L'Île de Beauté. **See p.345**

HIGHLIGHTS ARE MARKED ON THE MAP ON P.277

ROUGH COSTS

Daily budget Basic €55, occasional treat €80

Drink Glass of wine €3, beer €3.50

Food Baguette/sandwich €3.50–5

Hostel/budget hotel €19–35/€40–70

Travel Train: Paris–Nice €24 (if booked in advance)

FACT FILE

Population 66 million

Language French

Currency Euro (€)

Capital Paris

International phone code ☎ 33

Time zone GMT +1hr

Introduction

France is one of Europe's most stylish and dynamic countries. The largest country in Western Europe, it offers a variety of cultural and geographical experiences unmatched across the continent. Yet, despite its size, it's surprisingly easy to explore, with a fantastic high-speed train network which means that within hours of indulging in the café culture of the capital, you could be swimming in the clear waters of the Côte d'Azur.

Paris continues to captivate visitors with its world-class museums, distinctive neighbourhoods and exuberant nightlife. To the west, **Normandy** boasts some of the country's greatest Romanesque architecture, while the lush countryside and rocky coastline of neighbouring **Brittany** provide great surroundings for getting away from it all. To the east, you'll find the rolling vineyards and elegant towns of Champagne and **Burgundy**, while south lie the châteaux of the **Loire Valley** and the gorgeous hills and valleys of the **Dordogne** beyond. The Atlantic coast has a misty charm, including low-key **La Rochelle** and the surfing capital of **Biarritz**. Though most people push on south to the country's most obvious attractions, there's a lot to be said for exploring the Germanic towns of **Alsace** in the east and the high and rugged heartland of the **Massif Central**.

France's gastronomic capital, **Lyon**, acts as a gateway to the heady southern region of **Provence**, characterized by beautiful countryside, charming towns and sublime food. The **Côte d'Azur** retains something of its old glamour, while **Marseille** is more worthy of exploration than its reputation would have you believe. The very south of the country, marked by the canyons of the **Pyrenees**, hides the dream-like fortress of Carcassonne, and provides some of the country's best walking territory, alongside the **Alps**. The student cities of **Montpellier** and **Toulouse** should be stops on any budget traveller's itinerary, boasting cheap restaurants, excellent nightlife and a relaxed ambience.

CHRONOLOGY

51 BC Julius Caesar conquers Gaul.

486 AD Clovis I, leader of the Franks, establishes his rule over Gaul.

800 Charlemagne rules as King of the Franks.

1066 William, the Duke of Normandy, invades England and is crowned King of England.

1337 The Hundred Years' War with England begins.

1431 After leading the French army to victory, Joan of Arc is burnt at the stake for heresy, at the age of 19.

1589 Henry IV is the first of the Bourbon dynasty to become King of France; he enforces Catholicism in the country.

1789 The French Revolution ends the rule of the monarchy and establishes the First Republic.

1804 Napoleon I declares himself Emperor of the French Empire.

1815 Napoleon I is defeated at the battle of Waterloo; the monarchy is restored.

1871 Defeat in the Franco-Prussian War leads to the creation of the Third Republic.

1872 Monet ushers in the Impressionist Movement.

1889 Eiffel Tower is built, making it the tallest building in the world.

1905 Church and State are legally separated.

1914–18 World War I – over 1.5 million Frenchmen killed.

1939–44 Nazi Germany invades France, leading to four years of fascist rule. France is liberated by Allied forces in August 1944.

1968 Student revolts and national strike cripple the country.

2002 The euro replaces the franc.

2005 Civil unrest and riots across the country after the death of two teenagers who were running from police in one of Paris' impoverished housing estates.

2007 Nicolas Sarkozy is elected President.

2011 Full-face veils are banned from public places.

2012 Socialist François Hollande is elected President.

2015 Paris is attacked by Islamist terrorists in January and November, killing 30 and 130 people respectively, and injuring hundreds more.

11

HIGHLIGHTS
1. Paris
2. Reims
3. Strasbourg
4. Marseille
5. Lyon
6. Corsica

2016 In another act of terror, at least 85 people are killed when a man drives a lorry into the crowds celebrating Bastille Day on Nice's seafront.

ARRIVAL AND DEPARTURE

The main hub for arrivals by **plane** is Paris Charles de Gaulle, which is served by both major and budget airlines. In addition, there are around forty other airports, including Lyon, Nice, La Rochelle and Marseille. France has excellent **train** connections to the rest of Europe. The main access point is Paris: Gare du Nord links to Belgium, Germany and the UK; and Gare de Lyon to Italy, Spain and Switzerland. There are also excellent connections from the south of France to Italy and Spain.

The Eurolines **coach service** (ⓦ eurolines .com) connects most European countries to France; the main arrival point in Paris is the *gare routière* in the suburb of Bagnolet.

GETTING AROUND

France has one of the most extensive **rail** networks in Western Europe, run by the government-owned SNCF (ⓦ sncf.com). Bus services tend to be uncoordinated and are best used only as a last resort.

Train fares are reasonably high, but you can make savings by booking well in advance; Paris to Lyon, for example, can cost €25, but will be at least double that if booked on the day of travel.

InterRail and Eurail passes are valid on normal trains at all times. The high-speed TGVs (*Trains à Grande Vitesse*) require reservations (from €9), and there is a supplement to travel on certain other trains (from €1). Tickets (not passes) must be stamped in the orange machines in front of the platform on penalty of a steep fine. All but the smallest stations have an information desk but only a handful have left-luggage facilities. The word *autocar* on a timetable indicates that it's an **SNCF bus service**, on which rail tickets and passes are valid.

Bikes that can be dismantled and carried in a bike bag go free on all trains – if you can't collapse your bike then it can still travel free as long as the train doesn't require reservations and there's room. If you're catching a train that requires a reservation, your bike will also need a booking, and you'll have to pay a flat fee of €10. Bike rental shops (charging around €15 per day) are plentiful and many towns also have bike-sharing schemes.

ACCOMMODATION

Outside the summer season and school holidays, it's generally possible to turn up in any town and find accommodation. However, many hostels get booked up with school groups, so where possible it's worth reserving in advance.

All **hotels** are officially graded and are required to post their tariffs inside the entrance. Most **hostels** in France are operated by FUAJ, the French youth hostel association (part of the worldwide Hostelling International; ⓦhihostels.com). Many of the hostels are situated some distance from the centre of town, and the quality varies widely – from old-fashioned institutional accommodation to bright, modern, well-situated buildings. Many FUAJ hostels close in the middle of the day so you are unable even to leave your bags, and all require that you vacate the rooms by around 10am, even if you're not checking out. Almost all hostels provide bed linen, and most offer a free breakfast. **Gîtes d'étape** provide bunk beds and simple kitchen facilities in rural areas for climbers, hikers, cyclists, etc – they are listed, along with mountain refuges, on ⓦwww.gites-refuges.com. Local **campsites** provide a good budget alternative as they are generally clean, well equipped and often enjoy prime locations. Ask tourist offices for lists of sites or consult ⓦcampingfrance.com.

FOOD AND DRINK

Eating out in France isn't particularly cheap, but the quality of the food is often excellent and, even in the big cities, it's usually easy to find somewhere you can enjoy a *plat* and a glass of wine for under €20.

Generally the best place to eat **breakfast** (*petit déjeuner*) is in a bar or café. Most serve *tartines* (baguette with butter and/or jam) and croissants until around 11am. Coffee is invariably served black and strong – *un café* is an espresso, while *un café crème* is made with hot milk. Tea (*thé*) and hot chocolate (*chocolat chaud*) are also available – though the former is served without milk unless you request it on the side.

Cafés are often the best option for a light **lunch**, usually serving omelettes, sandwiches (generally half-baguettes filled with cheese or meat) and *croque-monsieur* (toasted ham and cheese sandwich; €5–8), as well as more substantial meals. Crêperies are ubiquitous throughout France and are usually very reasonably priced (from €5). Most cafés and restaurants have a midday *formule* (a set menu starting at around €12) of two or three courses, which will often allow you to enjoy high-quality restaurant food that you wouldn't otherwise be able to afford. Most restaurants serve food from noon to 2pm and 7 to 11pm.

Vegetarian restaurants are becoming more common, especially in large cities, and if you make it clear that you're *un végétarien(ne)*, something can normally be arranged in all but the most basic of places.

DRINK

Drinking is an important part of French life, with the local bar playing a central social role. **Wine** (*vin*) is the national drink, and drunk at just about every meal or social occasion. Even the most basic of cafés usually offer a wide range of French wines by the glass, and ordering a *pichet* or a carafe (usually ranging from a quarter bottle to a half bottle) is often great value.

11

FRANCE ONLINE

ⓦ**discoverfrance.net** Useful tourist information, with links to other sites.
ⓦ**france.fr** French tourist board.
ⓦ**tourisme.fr** Links to many tourist offices.
ⓦ**viafrance.com** Information on festivals, expos, events and concerts.

Beer can be very expensive, especially if ordered by the pint. Beer on tap (*à la pression*) is the best value – ask for *une pression* or *un demi* (0.33 litre). Spirits such as **cognac** and **armagnac**, and of course the notorious **absinthe**, are widely drunk but not cheap. A pleasant, inexpensive pre-dinner drink is *un kir*, a mix of white wine and crème de cassis, and if you're in the south of France it's definitely worth sampling the local **pastis**, drunk over ice and diluted with water – very refreshing on a hot day.

CULTURE AND ETIQUETTE

Making an effort to speak French, however dreadful your accent, is always highly appreciated; a few basic words will get you a lot further than any amount of grimacing and pointing.

It's customary to **tip** porters, tour guides, taxi drivers and hairdressers, around ten percent. Restaurant prices almost always include a service charge, so only leave an additional cash tip if you feel you've received service out of the ordinary.

SPORTS AND OUTDOOR ACTIVITIES

The main sport in France is undoubtedly **football**. The French football league (ⓦlfp.fr) is divided into Ligue 1 (the highest), Ligue 2 and National. Match tickets are available from specific club websites, or in the town they are playing – ask at the local tourist office.

Rugby is another major pursuit, especially in the southwest, and the country often puts up a good showing in the Six Nations tournament. Further details of rugby fixtures can be found at ⓦwww.ffr.fr. The annual Tour de France,

an epic 3000km **cycle race** across the country every July (ⓦletour.fr), is one of the country's most popular sporting events. The best **skiing** is in the Alps, and it's usually possible to ski from November to April. Prices can be high, however, so it's worth checking package prices in resort towns such as Chamonix (see p.344). France is also traced with lots of long-distance footpaths, known as *sentiers de grande randonnée* or GRs, and facilities for **hikers** are generally very good, including mountain refuges and excellent information centres in major hiking regions. The most popular areas for hiking are the Pyrenees and the Alps, though the Massif Central has some impressive, off-the-beaten-track routes.

COMMUNICATIONS

Post offices (*la poste*) are widespread and generally open from 8.30am to 6.30pm Monday to Friday, and 8.30am to noon on Saturday. **Stamps** (*timbres*) are also sold in *tabacs* (newsagents). For all calls within France you must dial the entire ten-digit number, including area code. The number for directory enquiries is ☎12. Almost all hotels and hostels, as well as an increasing number of campsites, offer **wi-fi**; you can also usually get online at the local tourist office.

EMERGENCIES

There are two main types of **police**, the Police Nationale and the Gendarmerie Nationale, and you can report a theft, or any other incident, to either.

To find a **doctor**, ask for an address at any *pharmacie* (chemist) or tourist information office. Consultation fees for a visit will be around €25 and you'll be given a *Feuille de Soins* (Statement of Treatment) for any insurance claims. EU citizens are, with an EHIC, exempt from charges (see p.42).

EMERGENCY NUMBERS

Police ☎17; Ambulance ☎15; Fire ☎18; or ☎112 for all three.

11

FRENCH

	FRENCH	PRONUNCIATION
Yes	*Oui*	Whee
No	*Non*	No(n)
Please	*S'il vous plait*	See voo play
Thank you	*Merci*	Mersee
Hello/Good day	*Bonjour*	Bo(n)joor
Goodbye	*Au revoir/à bientôt*	Orvoir/abyantoe
Excuse me	*Pardon*	pardo(n)
Today	*Aujourd'hui*	Ojoordwee
Yesterday	*Hier*	Eeyair
Tomorrow	*Demain*	Duhma(n)
What time is it?	*Quelle heure est-il?*	Kel ur et eel?
I don't understand	*Je ne comprends pas*	Je nuh compron pah
How much?	*Combien?*	Combyen?
Do you speak English?	*Parlez-vous anglais?*	Parlay voo onglay?
Where's the…?	*Où est…?*	Oo ay…?
Entrance	*Entrée*	Ontray
Exit	*Sortie*	Sortee
Tourist office	*Office de tourism*	Ofees der toureesmer
Toilet	*Toilettes*	Twalet
Hotel	*Hôtel*	Otel
Youth hostel	*Auberge de jeunesse*	Obairjh der jherness
Church	*Église*	Ay-gleez
Museum	*Musée*	Mewzay
What time does the… leave?	*À quelle heure part…?*	A kel er par…?
Boat	*Le bateau*	Ler bato
Bus	*Le bus*	Ler bews
Plane	*L'avion*	Lavyon
Train	*Le train*	Ler trun
Ticket	*Billet*	Beelay
Do you have a… room?	*Avez-vous une chambre…?*	Avay voo ewn shombrer…?
Double	*Avec un grand lit*	Avek un grand lee
Single	*À un lit*	A un lee
Cheap	*Bon marché*	Bo(n) marchay
Expensive	*Cher*	Share
Open	*Ouvert*	Oovair
Closed	*Fermé*	Fermay
One	*Un*	Uh(n)
Two	*Deux*	Duh
Three	*Trois*	Trwah
Four	*Quatre*	Kattre
Five	*Cinq*	Sank
Six	*Six*	Seess
Seven	*Sept*	Set
Eight	*Huit*	Wheat
Nine	*Neuf*	Nurf
Ten	*Dix*	Deess

INFORMATION

Most towns and villages have an *Office de Tourisme*, giving out local **information** and free maps. The larger ones can book accommodation anywhere in France, and most can find you a local room for the night, albeit with an added service charge.

STUDENT AND YOUTH DISCOUNTS

Most museums and attractions offer a student or under-26 discount, which can be anything up to a third off. To make the most of these, buy an **ISIC** (International Student) or **IYTC** (International Youth) card. For more information see ⓦisiccard .com. It's also worth noting that many museums have free entry on the first Sunday of every month.

MONEY AND BANKS

The currency of France is the **euro** (€). Standard **banking hours** are Monday to Friday 9am to noon and 2 to 4.30pm; in cities, some also open on Saturday morning. **ATMs** are found all over France and most accept foreign cards. Credit cards are generally accepted by most shops, restaurants and hotels.

OPENING HOURS AND HOLIDAYS

Basic **working hours** are 9am to noon/1pm and 2/3 to 6.30pm. The traditional closing **days** for shops (and some restaurants) are Sunday and Monday. **Museums** often have one closing day, frequently Mondays or sometimes Tuesdays, with reduced opening hours outside of summer. All shops, museums and offices are closed on the following **national holidays**: January 1, Easter Sunday and Monday, Ascension Day, Whit Monday, May 1, May 8, July 14, August 15, November 1, November 11, December 25.

Paris

All the clichés about **PARIS** are true – stylish, romantic, glamorous and utterly compelling – yet it retains surprises that continue to delight even the most seasoned visitors. The landscape of the city changes as you cross from *quartier* to *quartier*, and each area has a distinct style and atmosphere – from historic **St-Germain** and the genteel Luxembourg Gardens to the vibrant Marais, abuzz

with bars and cafés, and the steep cobbled streets of **Montmartre**. Paris is small for a capital city, and the best way to explore it is on foot – or do as the locals do and rent a bike (see p.289). Of course, it goes without saying that the café, bar and restaurant scene here is among the best in Europe, even for travellers on a budget.

WHAT TO SEE AND DO

Paris is split into two halves by the Seine. On the north of the river, the **Right Bank** (*Rive droite*) is home to the *grands boulevards* and its most monumental buildings, many dating from the civic planner Baron Haussmann's nineteenth-century redevelopment. Most of the major museums are here, as well as the city's widest range of shops around rue de Rivoli and Les Halles.

The **Left Bank** (*Rive gauche*) has a noticeably different feel. A legendary bohemian hangout since the nineteenth century, some of the city's most evocative streets can be found here. These days much of the area has given in to commerce, though it's not hard to discover some of its old spirit if you wander off the main roads around boulevard St-Germain and St-Michel.

Parts of Paris, of course, don't sit so easily within such definitions. **Montmartre**, rising up to the north and dominated by the great white dome of Sacré-Cœur, has managed to retain a village-like feel despite its tourist popularity, and the islands of the Seine (de la Cité and St-Louis), though touristy themselves, retain a charming, old-fashioned atmosphere within their side streets. In recent years, Paris's once run-down **eastern districts** have also been

PARISIAN ARRONDISSEMENTS

Paris is divided into twenty postal districts, known as *arrondissements*, which are used to denote addresses. The first, or *premier* (abbreviated as 1er), is centred on the Louvre and the Tuileries, with the rest (abbreviated as 2e, 3e, 4e etc) spiralling outwards in a clockwise direction.

11

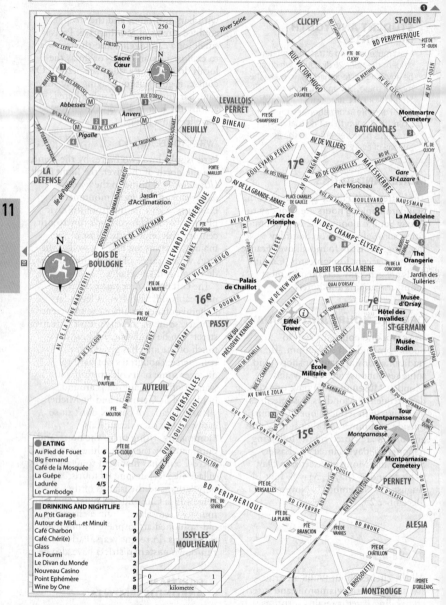

EATING

Au Pied de Fouet	6
Big Fernand	2
Café de la Mosquée	7
La Guêpe	1
Ladurée	4/5
Le Cambodge	3

DRINKING AND NIGHTLIFE

Au P'tit Garage	7
Autour de Midi…et Minuit	1
Café Charbon	9
Café Chéri(e)	6
Glass	4
La Fourmi	3
Le Divan du Monde	2
Nouveau Casino	9
Point Ephémère	5
Wine by One	8

revitalized and are now home to some of the city's best nightlife.

The Arc de Triomphe, Champs-Élysées and around

The **Arc de Triomphe** (daily: April–Sept 10am–11pm; Oct–March 10am–10.30pm; €9.50; ⓦarcde triompheparis.com; ⓜCharles-de -Gaulle-Etoile), at the head of the Champs-Élysées, is an imposing Parisian landmark, matched only by the Eiffel Tower, and offers panoramic views from the top. The celebrated **avenue des**

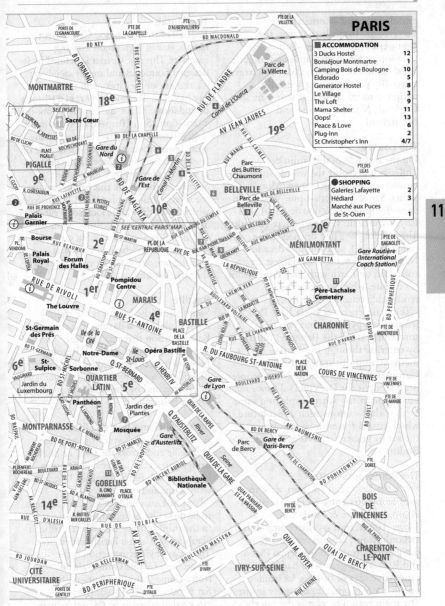

PARIS

■ **ACCOMMODATION**

3 Ducks Hostel	12
Bonséjour Montmartre	1
Camping Bois de Boulogne	10
Eldorado	5
Generator Hostel	8
Le Village	3
The Loft	9
Mama Shelter	11
Oops!	13
Peace & Love	6
Plug-Inn	2
St Christopher's Inn	4/7

● **SHOPPING**

Galeries Lafayette	2
Hédiard	3
Marché aux Puces de St-Ouen	1

11

Champs-Élysées is now, unfortunately, home to little more than a constant stream of tourists and too many chain shops. It leads to the vast, usually traffic-clogged **place de la Concorde**, whose centrepiece, a gold-tipped obelisk from the temple of Ramses at Luxor,

was given to King Louis-Philippe by the viceroy of Egypt in 1831. Beyond lies the formal **Jardin des Tuileries** (daily: April, May & Sept 7am–9pm; June–Aug 7am–11pm; Oct–March 7.30am–7.30pm; free; ⓜConcorde), the perfect place for a stroll with its grand vistas and symmetrical flowerbeds. Towards the river, the **Orangerie** (Mon & Wed–Sun 9am–6pm; €9; ⓦwww.musee-orangerie .fr; ⓜConcorde) displays Monet's largest water-lily paintings in a specially designed room, as well as works by Cézanne, Matisse, Urrillo and Modigliani.

The Louvre

On the east side of the Jardin des Tuileries is arguably the world's most famous museum, the **Louvre** (Mon, Thurs, Sat & Sun 9am–6pm; Wed & Fri 9am–9.45pm; €15; ⓦlouvre.fr; ⓜPalais Royal-Musée du Louvre/Louvre-Rivoli). The building was first opened to the public in 1793, and within a decade Napoleon had made it the largest art collection on Earth with the takings from his empire, which explains the remarkably eclectic collection.

The main entrance is via I.M. Pei's iconic glass pyramid, but you can sometimes avoid the (lengthy) queues by entering through the Louvre Rivoli métro station or through the Louvre Carousel shopping arcade. Most people head straight for Da Vinci's *Mona Lisa*, but it's definitely worth exploring some of the other sections such as **Sculpture**, which covers the entire development of the art in France from Romanesque to Rodin.

The Pompidou Centre

From the Louvre, it's a short walk to the **Pompidou Centre** on place Georges-Pompidou (Mon & Wed–Sun 11am–10pm; free; ⓦcentrepompidou.fr; ⓜRambuteau), famous for its striking design masterminded by Renzo Piano and Richard Rogers, who had the innovative idea of turning its insides out to allow for maximum space inside. The main reason to visit is the hugely popular **Musée National d'Art Moderne** (Mon & Wed–Sun 11am–9pm; €14), one of the world's great collections of modern art, spanning the period from 1905 to the present day, and taking in Cubism, Surrealism and much more along the way.

The Marais

Just east of the Pompidou Centre lies the **Marais**, one of Paris's more striking *quartiers*. This chic district is defined by its designer boutiques and trendy café-bars; it's also one of the city's main centres for gay nightlife. The **Musée d'Art et d'Histoire du Judaïsme**, 71 rue du Temple (Mon–Fri 11am–6pm, Sun 10am–6pm; €8; ⓦmahj .org; ⓜRambuteau), pays homage to the area's Jewish roots, with a major display of Jewish artefacts and historical documents as well as paintings by Chagall and Soutine. A short walk east brings you to the seventeenth-century Hôtel Juigné Salé, which holds the **Musée Picasso**, 5 rue de Thorigny (Tues–Fri 11.30am–6pm, Sat & Sun 9.30am–6pm; €12.50; ⓦmusee -picasso.fr; ⓜSt-Sébastien Froissart), housing one of the largest collections of the artist's work.

Bastille

Southeast of the Marais is the traffic-choked **place de la Bastille**, the site of the Bastille prison that was famously stormed in 1789, starting the French Revolution. Now the place is marked by the Colonne de Juillet, topped by a green bronze figure of Liberty, and by the strikingly modern Opéra Bastille.

Île St-Louis and Île de la Cité

A short walk southwest from place de la Bastille and across the pont de Sully brings you to the peaceful **Île St-Louis**, its main road, rue St-Louis en l'Île, lined with shops and restaurants.

Pont St-Louis bridges the short distance to **Île de la Cité**, where the city originated in the third century BC, when a tribe of Gauls known as the Parisii settled here. The most obvious attraction is the astounding Gothic **Cathédrale de Notre-Dame** (Mon–Fri 8am–6.45pm, Sat & Sun 8am–7.15pm; free; ⓦnotredamedeparis.fr; ⓜCité), which dates from the mid-fourteenth century and was extensively renovated in the nineteenth. It's worth climbing the towers (daily: April–Sept 10am–6.30pm, July & Aug Fri & Sat until 11pm; Oct–March 10am–5.30pm; €10) for an up-close view of the gargoyles and tower architecture.

At the western end of the island lies **Sainte-Chapelle**, 4 bd du Palais (daily: March–Oct 9.30am–6pm; Nov–Feb 9am–5pm; €10; Ⓦsainte-chapelle.fr; ⓂCité). One of the finest achievements of French Gothic style, it is lent fragility by its height and huge expanses of glorious stained glass.

The Eiffel Tower

Gustave Eiffel's iconic tower is, rightly or wrongly, the defining image of Paris for most tourists. Hugely controversial on its 1889 debut, it has come to be recognized as one of the city's leading sights. If you wish to ascend the tower (daily: mid-June to Aug 9am–midnight; Sept to mid-June 9am–11pm; €11 to second floor via lift, €7 to second floor via stairs, €17 to top; Ⓦtour-eiffel.fr; ⓂBir Hakeim/RER Champ de Mars-Tour Eiffel), be prepared for frustratingly long queues. It's at its most impressive at night, when fully illuminated – especially from the opposite side of the river.

Les Invalides and the Musée Rodin

A short walk from the Eiffel Tower is the Hôtel des Invalides, easily spotted by its gold dome. Built as a home for invalid soldiers on the orders of Louis XIV, it now houses the giant **Musée de l'Armée**, 129 rue de Grenelle (daily: April–Oct 10am–6pm; Nov–March 10am–5pm; €11; Ⓦmusee-armee.fr; ⓂVarenne). Military buffs will be fascinated by the vast collection of armour, uniforms, weapons and Napoleonic relics, and the section devoted to World War II.

Immediately east, at 77 rue de Varenne, the **Musée Rodin** (Tues–Sun 10am–5.45pm; €10; Ⓦmusee-rodin.fr; ⓂVarenne) contains many of Rodin's greatest and most famous works, including *The Kiss* and a bronze version of *The Thinker*. The collection is housed in an elegant eighteenth-century mansion, the Hôtel Biron, surrounded by a serene sculpture garden.

Musée d'Orsay

In a beautifully converted train station by the river, the celebrated **Musée d'Orsay**, 62 rue de Lille (Tues–Sun 9.30am–6pm, Thurs until 9.45pm; €12; Ⓦmusee-orsay.fr; RER Musée d'Orsay/ ⓂSolférino), is much more compact and manageable than the Louvre. Covering the periods between the 1840s and 1914, the collection features legendary artists such as Renoir, Van Gogh and Monet, and famous works including Manet's *Le Déjeuner Sur L'Herbe* and Courbet's striking *L'Origine du Monde*. The queues are always long, but booking tickets the day before at the advance ticket office on site will allow you priority entrance.

The Latin Quarter

The neighbourhood around the boulevards St-Michel and St-Germain has been known as the **Quartier Latin** since medieval times, when it was the home of the Latin-speaking universities. It is still a student-dominated area – its pivotal point being **place St-Michel** – now sadly dominated by tacky tourist traps. There are, however, some excellent bars and restaurants nearby.

Immediately south of here stand the prestigious Sorbonne and Collège de France universities, the jewels in the crown of French education and renowned worldwide. Nearby, the elegant surroundings of the **Jardin du Luxembourg** (daily dawn to dusk; RER Luxembourg) are perfect for a leisurely picnic.

St-Germain

The northern half of the *6e arrondissement* is an upmarket and expensive part of the city, but fun to wander through. The area is steeped in history: Picasso painted *Guernica* in rue des Grands-Augustins; in rue Visconti, Delacroix painted and Balzac's printing business went bust; and in the parallel rue des Beaux-Arts, Oscar Wilde died quipping "Either the wallpaper goes or I do." **Boulevard St-Germain** is home to the famous *Flore* and *Deux Magots* cafés, both with rich political and literary histories; however, the astronomical prices mean that gawping rather than sipping is the best option.

11

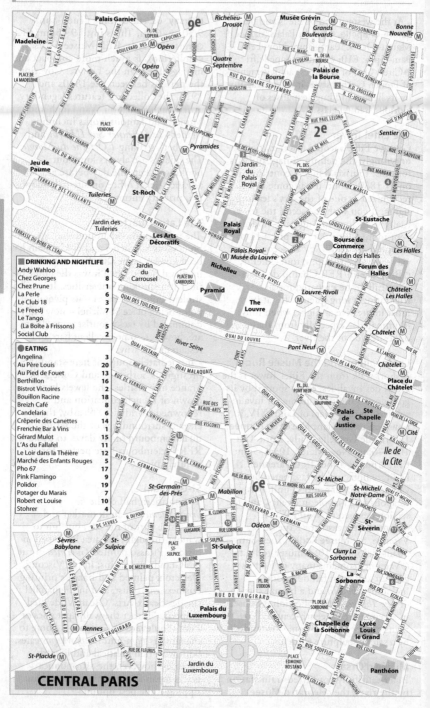

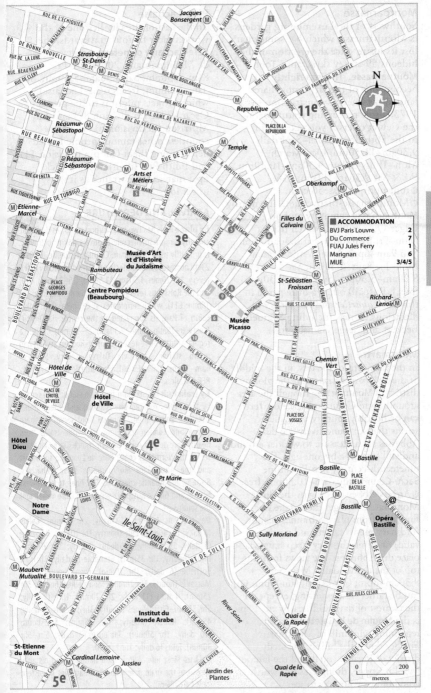

11

RUE DE L'ECHIQUIER
Jacques
Bonsergent M
BD. DE BONNE NOUVELLE
RUE DE LA LUNE
RUE BEAUREGARD
Strasbourg-
St-Denis M
BD.ST.
DENIS
RUE DE CLÉRY
RUE DU FAUBOURG ST-MARTIN
CITÉ RIVERIN
RUE TAYLOR
RUE CHÂTEAU D'EAU
R. ALBERT THOMAS
R. DELANCEY
R. BEAUREPAIRE
RUE BICHAT
RUE DU FAUBOURG DU TEMPLE
RUE ALEXANDRIE
RUE DU CAIRE
Réaumur-
Sébastopol M
RUE ST-DENIS
RUE RENÉ BOULANGER
BD. ST. MARTIN
RUE MESLAY
Republique
RUE LÉON JOUHAUX
RUE YVES TOUDIC
RUE DU FAUBOURG DU TEMPLE
RUE JULES FERRY
11e
PLACE DE LA
RÉPUBLIQUE
AV DE LA RÉPUBLIQUE

ACCOMMODATION

BVJ Paris Louvre	2
Du Commerce	7
FUAJ Jules Ferry	1
Marignan	6
MIJE	3/4/5

Montparnasse

Southwest of the Luxembourg gardens is Montparnasse, which has somewhat lost its lustre since the erection of the hideous 59-storey skyscraper, **Tour Montparnasse**. This has rightly become one of the city's most hated landmarks since its construction in 1973, a sole redeeming feature being the view it offers if you take the lift to the 56th floor (April–Sept daily 9.30am–11.30pm; Oct–March Mon–Thurs & Sun 9.30am–10.30pm, Fri & Sat 9.30am–11pm; €15; Ⓦtourmontparnasse56.com; ⓂMontparnasse-Bienvenüe). The nearby **Montparnasse cemetery** on boulevard Edgar-Quinet (mid-March to Oct Mon–Fri 8am–6pm, Sat 8.30am–6pm, Sun 9am–6pm; Nov to mid-March Mon–Fri 8am–5.30pm, Sat 8.30am–5.30pm, Sun 9am–5.30pm; free; ⓂRaspail) offers a little peace in this busy *quartier* and has plenty of illustrious names, including Samuel Beckett and Serge Gainsbourg.

Montmartre

In the far north of the city, in the middle of the *18ᵉ arrondissement*, is the glorious district of **Montmartre**. Though the area around Sacré-Cœur and place du Tertre can be horribly touristy, the quieter streets that surround lively rue des Abbesses are a pleasure to wander around, and still suggest a bygone age. The nineteenth-century neo-Byzantine **Sacré-Cœur** (daily 6am–10.30pm; free; ⓂAnvers/Abbesses) crowns the Butte Montmartre – to get there, take the funicular from place Suzanne Valadon (ordinary métro tickets and passes are valid) or climb the very steep stairs via place des Abbesses. The views from the top of the dome (daily: May–Sept 8.30am–8pm; Oct–April 9am–5pm; €6) can be rather disappointing, except on the clearest of days. Off nearby rue Lepic is the **Moulin de la Galette**, the last remaining windmill in Montmartre. Further down the hill, in the seedy district of Pigalle, you'll find the famous Moulin Rouge, though it's not worth going out of your way to see.

Père-Lachaise

To the east of the city lies one of the world's most famous graveyards, the **Père-Lachaise cemetery**, boulevard de Ménilmontant, 20ᵉ (Mon–Fri 8am–5.30pm, Sat 8.30am–5.30pm, Sun 9am–5.30pm; free; ⓂPère-Lachaise), which attracts pilgrims to the graves of Oscar Wilde (in division 89) and Jim Morrison (in division 6). There are countless other famous people buried here, among them Chopin (division 11) and Edith Piaf (division 97) – pick up a map at the entrance as it's easy to get lost.

ARRIVAL AND DEPARTURE

By plane Paris has two main airports: Charles de Gaulle and Orly. A much smaller one, Beauvais, 65km northwest, is primarily used by Ryanair. Charles de Gaulle (CDG) is 23km northeast and connected to Gare du Nord by RER B (every 10–20min 4.50am–11.50pm; 25–30min; €10) and the Roissybus (every 15–20min 6am–12.30am; 1hr 15min; €11), which terminates at ⓂOpéra. Orly, 14km south of Paris, is connected to the centre via Orlybus (every 8–15min 6am–12.30am; 25–35min; €7.70), a regular shuttle bus direct to Denfert-Rochereau RER and métro station, and via Orlyval (every 5–7min, 6am–11pm; 30min; €9.30), a fast shuttle train to Antony RER B station.

By train Paris has six main-line train stations, all served by the métro. You can buy national and international tickets at any of them. Gare du Nord serves northern France and London (on Eurostar), while trains from nearby Gare de l'Est go to eastern France. Gare St-Lazare serves the Normandy coast; Gare de Lyon the southeast and the Alps; Gare Montparnasse serves Chartres, Brittany, the Atlantic coast and TGV lines to southwest France; and Gare d'Austerlitz serves the Loire valley and the southwest.

Destinations Avignon (12 daily; 2hr 40min); Calais (6 daily; 1hr 40min); Lille (hourly; 1hr 10min); Bayonne (5 daily; 5hr 10min); Bordeaux (hourly; 3hr 20min); Dijon (hourly; 1hr 35min); Grenoble (5 daily; 3hr); La Rochelle (6 daily; 3hr 10min); Lyon (hourly; 2hr); Marseille (hourly; 3hr 20min); Montpellier (hourly; 3hr 25min); Nantes (11 daily; 2hr 20min); Nice (7 daily; 5hr 35min–6hr); Nîmes (hourly; 3hr); Reims (6 daily; 45min); Rouen (hourly; 1hr 15min); Strasbourg (10 daily; 1hr 50min); Toulouse (7 daily; 5hr–6hr 30min); Tours (6 daily; 1hr 15min).

By bus Most international and national long-distance buses use the main *gare routière* at Bagnolet in eastern Paris (ⓂGallieni).

INFORMATION

Tourist information There are tourist office branches all over the city. The most useful one is at 25 rue des Pyramides 1ᵉʳ (daily: May–Oct 9am–7pm; Nov–April 10am–7pm; ☎08 92 68 30 00, ⓦparisinfo.com; ⓜPyramides/RER Auber) and can help with last-minute accommodation, as can the booths at Gare de Lyon (Mon–Sat 8am–6pm) and Gare du Nord (daily 8am–6pm). You can also book tickets to museums at the tourist offices – handy for skipping the long queues.

Discount passes Many museums offer discounted entry to under-26s with ID (see box, p.281). They're also often free on the first Sunday of every month, but do get very busy because of it. The tourist office sells the Paris Museum Pass (€48/€62/€74 for 2/4/6 days; ⓦparismuseumpass .fr), valid for more than 35 museums and monuments in Paris, and which also allows you to skip the queues.

GETTING AROUND

Tickets Single tickets (€1.80) are valid on buses, the métro and, within the city limits (zones 1–2), the RER rail lines. If you're going to be using a fair bit of public transport, it makes more sense to buy a *carnet* of ten tickets (€14.10).

By métro The métro (Mon–Thurs & Sun 5.30am–12.30am, Fri & Sat 5.30am–2am) is an easy way of travelling around the city. The various lines are colour-coded and numbered, and the name of the train's final destination is visible.

By train Longer journeys across the city, or out to the suburbs, are best made on the underground RER express rail network (daily 5.30am–midnight).

By bus The bus network runs Mon–Sat 7am–8.30pm or 12.30am depending on the route, with a greatly reduced service on Sun. Night buses (ⓦnoctilien.fr) run 12.30–5.30am (every 30min–1hr) on 4 routes.

By bike There are over 1500 locations in the city from where you can rent a bike as part of the city's Vélib' scheme (€1.70/day, €8/week; first 30min free, €1/30min thereafter; ⓦvelib.paris). You'll need a credit card for a deposit in case the bike is damaged. When you've finished with them, bikes can be deposited at any of the Velib' stands in the city.

By taxi Taxis are plentiful after dark and can be hailed on the street. Rates start at €2.60, with a minimum charge of €7.

ACCOMMODATION

Accommodation is a lot more expensive in Paris than elsewhere in the country, and it's best to book in advance. The city has a good selection of independent hostels, some of which are more like boutique hotels than the usual standard of French hostel. All properties listed below have wi-fi and most hostels provide a rudimentary breakfast.

HOSTELS

★**3 Ducks Hostel** 6 place Etienne Pernet, 15ᵉ ☎01 48 42 04 05, ⓦ3ducks.fr; map pp.282–283. Lively, long-established and popular hostel in a historic building, offering colourful mixed and female-only dorms, plus a number of private rooms. Interior decor is stylish, and the terrace and lively streetside bar are nice places to hang out. Rates include breakfast and there's a kitchen for guests' use. Dorms €37, doubles €125

BVJ Paris Louvre 20 rue Jean-Jacques Rousseau, 1ᵉʳ ☎01 53 00 90 90, ⓦbvjhotel.com; ⓜLouvre Rivoli; map pp.286–287. The most central hostel in Paris, close to the Louvre and Les Halles, is rather institutional but excellently located. Dorms €30, doubles €70

FUAJ Jules Ferry 8 bd Jules-Ferry, 11ᵉ ☎01 43 57 55 60, ⓦfuaj.org; map pp.286–287. With a great position in the lively area by the Canal St Martin, this is a popular hostel despite being a little careworn. Dorms are on the small side. Dorms €27.70, doubles €62

★**Generator Hostel** 9–11 place du Coloniel Fabien, 10ᵉ ☎01 70 98 84 00, ⓦgeneratorhostels.com; ⓜColoniel-Fabien; map pp.282–283. New, well-run and friendly hostel right by the métro in a safe neighbourhood, with spotless dorms (four- to ten-beds) and private bathrooms. Facilities are excellent, with lots of storage space, a friendly bar and handy café. There's also some private doubles and quads. Dorms €27.90, doubles €88

Le Village 20 rue d'Orsel, 18ᵉ ☎01 42 64 22 02, ⓦvillagehostel.fr; ⓜAnvers; map pp.282–283. A friendly, independent hostel with good facilities, smarter than average dorms and an on-site bar. It might be located in the least picturesque area of Montmartre, but has a lovely terrace with views of the Sacré-Cœur. Dorms €30, doubles €85

The Loft 70 rue Julien Lacroix, 20ᵉ ☎01 42 02 42 02, ⓦtheloft-paris.com; ⓜBelleville; map pp.282–283. This boldly decorated hostel in up-and-coming Belleville is smart and stylish, but the paper-thin walls and pop rock endlessly pumped into the corridors mean it doesn't quite live up to its boutique hotel aspirations. Dorms €36, doubles €115

MIJE ☎01 42 74 23 45, ⓦmije.com; ⓜSt-Paul or Pont-Marie; map pp.286–287. A group of three hostels – *Le Fauconnier* (11 rue du Fauconnier), *Le Fourcy* (6 rue de Fourcy) and *Maubuisson* (12 rue des Barres) – situated just a few hundred metres apart in a set of magnificent mansions. Rooms are simple, but all guests can eat at *Le Fourcy*'s decent restaurant. There's a 1am curfew and additional obligatory purchase of MIJE membership (€2.50; valid for a year). Dorms €33.50, doubles €82

Oops! 50 av des Gobelins, 13ᵉ ☎01 47 07 47 00, ⓦoops -paris.com; ⓜPlace d'Italie; map pp.282–283. The city's first and much imitated "design hostel", situated south of the Latin Quarter near Place d'Italie. All rooms are en suite

11

and kept very clean, though doubles can be seriously overpriced in high season. Dorms €43, doubles €115

Peace & Love 245 rue La Fayette, 19ᵉ ☎01 46 07 65 11, ⓦparis-hostels.com; ⓜJaurès or Stalingrad; map pp.282–283. Right opposite the Canal St Martin, this small, welcoming hostel is a good choice if sleep isn't high on your priorities, with a cheap, popular bar that's open till 2am. Prices vary considerably with demand. Dorms €26, doubles €70

Plug-Inn 7 rue Aristide Bruant, 18ᵉ ☎01 42 58 42 58, ⓦplug-inn.fr; ⓜAbbesses; map pp.282–283. Small and swish hostel with designer decor and a great location on the slopes of Montmartre. The only downside is that some rooms are a little cramped. Dorms €32, doubles €99

★**St Christopher's Inn** 5 rue de Dunkerque, 10ᵉ ☎01 40 34 34 40, ⓦstchristophers.co.uk; ⓜGare du Nord; map pp.282–283. This whopper of a hostel (it has over six hundred beds) is a very slick operation: dorm beds all have lockable storage cages and USB points in the headboard, plus there are two on-site restaurants and a bar. Other perks include phones for free international calls, a female-only floor and a slew of nightly activities. There's a particular focus on private rooms here (four-bed apartments from €178), whereas their purpose-built "canal" branch (159 rue de Crimée, 19ᵉ) has a higher proportion of dorm beds. Dorms €40, doubles €128

HOTELS

Bonséjour Montmartre 11 rue Burq, 18ᵉ ☎01 42 54 22 53, ⓦhotel-bonsejour-montmartre.fr; ⓜAbbesses; map pp.282–283. In a great position just off lively rue des Abbesses, this charming family-run hotel offers great-value doubles and singles. The rooms are peaceful but not polished; some share a toilet and shower on the landing, and the best have small balconies. Book direct for the best rates. Doubles €69

Du Commerce 14 rue de la Montagne-Ste-Geneviève, 5ᵉ ☎01 43 54 89 69, ⓦcommerceparishotel.com; ⓜMaubert-Mutualité; map pp.286–287. Welcoming budget hotel on

---

★**TREAT YOURSELF**

Mama Shelter 109 rue de Bagnolet, 20ᵉ ☎01 43 48 48 48, ⓦmamashelter.com; ⓜPorte de Bagnolet; map pp.282–283. Doodle-covered blackboard ceilings and a graffiti theme distinguish this cool, Philippe Starck-designed hotel. Rooms come with an iMac, mini-bar and free movies, and facilities include a restaurant, pizzeria, bar and rooftop terrace. Book early for their ludicrously cheap starting rate. Doubles €99

---

a quiet street in the heart of the Latin Quarter. The rooms are decorated in bright, cheery colours, and there's a communal kitchen. Doubles €58

Eldorado 18 rue des Dames, 17ᵉ ☎01 45 22 35 21, ⓦeldoradohotel.fr; ⓜPlace de Clichy; map pp.282–283. Eclectic budget hotel near busy Place de Clichy and a 5min walk from Montmartre, with a bohemian atmosphere, quirkily decorated rooms and a good attached wine bar. Book well in advance. Doubles €65

Marignan 13 rue du Sommerard, 5ᵉ ☎01 43 54 63 81, ⓦhotel-marignan.com; ⓜMaubert-Mutualité; map pp.286–287. Excellent backpacker-oriented hotel, with laundry facilities, a kitchen and a good choice of triples and singles. The ebullient proprietor is a mine of information on Paris. Breakfast included. Doubles €85

CAMPSITE

Camping Bois de Boulogne allée du Bord de l'Eau ☎01 45 24 30 00, ⓦcampingparis.fr; shuttle bus to and from ⓜPorte Maillot; map pp.282–283. The city's major campsite is situated in the beautiful Bois de Boulogne and offers a range of facilities including showers, a canteen and bike rental. Per person and tent €11

EATING

Eating out in Paris need not be an extravagant affair, and even at dinner, it's possible to have a meal for around €15. Make a reservation Thursday to Saturday evening if you can.

CAFÉS, CHEAP EATS AND SNACKS

Angelina 226 rue de Rivoli, 1ᵉ; ⓜTuileries; map pp.286–287. Drinking a cup of the decadent *chocolat chaud à l'ancienne* (€8.20) at this historic tearoom is a Paris institution. Mon–Fri 7.30am–7pm, Sat & Sun 8.30am–7.30pm.

Berthillon 31 rue St-Louis-en-l'Île, 4ᵉ; ⓜPont Marie; map pp.286–287. Expect long queues for some of the best ice creams and sorbets in the city; the divine flavours include salted caramel and Earl Grey. Single scoop €2.50. Wed–Sun 10am–8pm.

Bouillon Racine 3 rue Racine, 6ᵉ; ⓜCluny-La Sorbonne; map pp.286–287. One of a few surviving *bouillons* (soup kitchens) that opened in the early 1900s, featuring gloriously extravagant Art Nouveau decor. The lunch *formule* is good value at €16.95 for two courses. Daily noon–11pm.

Café de la Mosquée 39 rue Geoffroy-St-Hilaire, 5ᵉ; ⓜPlace Monge; map pp.282–283. Attached to La Grande Mosquée, this Moorish café is an oasis of calm. Mint tea (€2.50) and baklava (€7 for three) are on offer in the intricately tiled *salon de thé*, or you can smoke shisha in the courtyard. Daily 9am–midnight.

★**L'As du Fallafel** 34 rue des Rosiers, 4ᵉ; ⓜSaint-Paul; map pp.286–287. Arguably the best falafel shop in the Jewish quarter. Their signature combination – pitta bread

TOP THREE PARISIAN PATISSERIES

You can't walk far in Paris without stumbling over a **patisserie**, many of which have been serving cakes for hundreds of years. Here are three of the best that are worth braving the queues for:

Gérard Mulot 76 rue de Seine, 6e; Ⓜ Odéon; map pp.286–287. This justifiably famous patisserie is usually crammed with locals. The many delights include lemon meringue tart (€4.70) and red fruit *millefeuille* (€5.20). Mon, Tues & Thurs–Sun 6.45am–8pm.

Ladurée 75 av des Champs-Élysées 8e; Ⓜ George V; map pp.282–283. Famous for its delectable *macarons* (€1.85/piece), which come in flavours such as salted

caramel and orange blossom. Indulge in one of their many treats over a cup of their delicate tea in this ornate tearoom, or head to the more intimate branch at 16 rue Royale. Daily 7.30am–11.30pm.

Stohrer 51 rue Montorgueil, 2e; Ⓜ Étienne-Marcel; map pp.286–287. The city's oldest patisserie serves arguably its most divine selection of cakes – try a *baba au rhum* (variations from €4.50), which was actually invented here. Daily 7.30am–8.30pm.

11

stuffed full of falafel, cabbage, aubergine, hummus and yoghurt – costs just €5 to take away. Mon–Thurs & Sun noon–midnight, Fri noon–3pm.

Le Loir dans la Théière 3 rue des Rosiers, 4e; Ⓜ St-Paul; map pp.286–287. The Sunday brunch (€19.50) at this laidback, cosy café is especially popular, as are their excellent cakes (€11 with tea). Get there early to bag a comfy leather armchair. Daily 9am–7.30pm.

★**Marché des Enfants Rouges** 39 rue de Bretagne, 3e; Ⓜ Filles du Calvaire; map pp.286–287. Not a café, but the oldest market in Paris. Take your pick from the freshly cooked food available at the stalls (including French, Moroccan and Italian) then grab a spot at the shared picnic tables. Tues–Sat 9am–2pm & 4–8pm, Sun 9am–2pm.

RESTAURANTS

Au Père Louis 38 rue Monsieur le Prince, 6e; ☎ 01 43 26 54 14; Ⓜ Odéon; map pp.286–287. This cosy, labyrinthine restaurant is a great choice for a long, relaxed meal. The menu is packed with classic dishes including onion soup (€9) and *crème caramel* (€7.50). Daily noon–3pm & 6pm–midnight.

★**Au Pied de Fouet** 45 rue de Babylone, 7e; ☎ 01 47 05 12 27; Ⓜ Saint-François-Xavier; map pp.282–283 & map pp.286–287. Tiny and charmingly old-fashioned restaurant with red-check tablecloths, picture-cluttered walls and wonky floors. Try the *pâté de campagne* (€3.50) and *confit de canard* (€12.50) with wine from €2.90 a glass. There's another branch at 3 rue Saint-Benoît, 6e. Mon–Sat noon–2.30pm & 7–11pm.

Big Fernand 55 rue du Faubourg Poissonnière, 9e; Ⓜ Poissonnière or Cadet; map pp.282–283. Run by a young and jolly team, this is *the* place to satisfy a burger craving in Paris (though there are now a number of branches in the city). Try one of their creations like *Le Bartholomé* (beef patty with raclette and caramelized onions; €12) or build your own. Mon–Sat noon–2.30pm & 7.30–10.30pm.

Bistrot Victoires 6 rue de la Vrillière, 2e; ☎ 01 42 61 43 78; Ⓜ Bourse; map pp.286–287. A convivial local bistro, tucked away near the Palais Royale. The fantastic old bar and big mirrors lend it a timeless appeal, and the food is surprisingly cheap for this part of the city (*poulet roti* €10). Daily 9am–11pm.

Breizh Café 109 rue Vieille du Temple, 3e; ☎ 01 42 72 13 77; Ⓜ Saint-Sébastien-Froissart; map pp.286–287. Authentic Breton *galettes* and crêpes (from €7) served in a refreshingly modern interior. The *galette complète* (ham, cheese and egg) is particularly good, as is the salted caramel crêpe. Wed–Sat 11.30am–11pm, Sun 11.30am–10pm.

★**Candelaria** 52 rue de Saintonge, 3e; Ⓜ Saint-François-Xavier; map pp.286–287. The queue usually snakes out the door for the excellent Mexican food here. There's no menu, but tortilla chips and home-made guacamole (€7) are a must, as are their potent cocktails (from €12). There are just six stools and scruffy sharing tables for diners (no reservations), with a crowded, dark cocktail bar behind. Restaurant Mon–Wed & Sun 12.30–11pm, Thurs–Sat 12.30pm–midnight; bar daily 6pm–2am.

Crêperie des Canettes 10 rue des Canettes, 6e; ☎ 01 42 65 20 27; Ⓜ St-Sulpice; map pp.286–287. A cosy little crêperie with a great range of *galettes* such as the *savoyarde* (raclette, potatoes, bacon and cream; €10) and *pichets* of Breton cider (from €4). Mon–Sat noon–2.30pm & 7–11pm.

La Guêpe 14 rue des Trois Frères, 18e; Ⓜ Abbesses or Anvers; map pp.282–283. This cheerfully decorated tapas bar, with a striking tile-topped counter, offers a refreshing change from the raft of so-so, tourist-oriented *bistrots* in the neighbourhood. For just €3–6 per dish, choose from a beautifully presented and creative selection of Spanish, Italian and Asian-inspired plates such as Comté spring rolls and cuttlefish croquettes. Tues–Sun 6pm–2am; closed Aug.

Le Cambodge 10 av Richerand, 10e; Ⓜ Goncourt; map pp.282–283. A laidback Cambodian restaurant with a unique ordering system where you write (or draw) your choice on a notepad. Try the *bo bun*, a fragrant noodle dish with beansprouts, carrots and peanuts (from €10). Mon–Sat noon–2.30pm & 7–11pm.

Pho 67 59 rue Galande, 5ᵉ ☎ 01 45 25 56 69; Ⓜ Maubert-Mutualité; map pp.286–287. A beacon of Southeast Asian authenticity in this desperately touristy area. The open kitchen produces a good range of Vietnamese dishes; go for the filling *pho* special (€14), made with French steak, or the three-course *menu* (€17). No credit cards. Mon 6.30–11pm, Tues–Sun noon–3pm & 6.30–11pm.

Pink Flamingo 105 rue Vieille du Temple, 3ᵉ ☎ 01 42 71 28 20; Ⓜ Saint-Sébastien-Froissart; map pp.286–287. The inventively named pizzas (from €13) at the Marais branch of this eclectic pizzeria include the Gandhi (sag paneer, baba ganoush and mozzarella) and the Bjork (smoked salmon, lumpfish caviar and crème fraîche). Tues–Fri noon–3pm & 7–11.30pm, Sat & Sun noon–11.30pm.

Polidor 41 rue Monsieur-le-Prince, 6ᵉ ☎ 01 43 26 95 34; Ⓜ Odéon; map pp.286–287. Historic bistro that was a favourite of James Joyce and Hemingway; service can be short-tempered but the food is good and reasonably priced. Try the *boeuf bourguignon* (€12). Mon–Sat noon–2.30pm & 7pm–12.30am, Sun noon–2.30pm & 7pm–midnight.

Potager du Marais 22 rue Rambuteau, 3ᵉ ☎ 01 57 40 98 57; Ⓜ Rambuteau; map pp.286–287. A tiny vegetarian restaurant serving interesting dishes like a "crusty" quinoa burger and goat's cheese with honey. Two-course menu €20. Wed–Sun noon–4pm & 7–10.30pm.

★ **Robert et Louise** 64 rue Vieille du Temple, 3ᵉ ☎ 01 42 78 55 89; Ⓜ Rambuteau or Saint Paul; map pp.286–287. The unassuming facade of this Marais institution doesn't betray anything of the restaurant's rustic, down-to-earth interior. The ground-floor dining room is permeated by the heady smell of the wood fire, over which the signature

---

★ **TREAT YOURSELF**

Frenchie Bar à Vins 6 rue du Nil, 2ᵉ ☎ 01 40 39 96 19; Ⓜ Sentier; map pp.286–287. Across the road from their very chic (and very popular) restaurant, this modern, bare-brick wine bar offers a more accessible taste of Gregory Marchand's cooking. He's worked in London (under Jamie Oliver) and New York, the influences of which can be seen in both his food and cosmopolitan clientele. All dishes are designed to share; expect savoury options like papardelle with lamb ragu, feta and olives (€15) followed by a divine chocolate pot with caramel butter and passion fruit (€8). Wines (from €6 a glass) are exceptionally well chosen. Daily 7–11pm.

---

dish, *côte de boeuf pour deux* (€42), is beautifully cooked. The weekday lunch *menu* (€12) is excellent value. Tues & Wed 7–11pm, Thurs–Sun noon–2.30pm & 7–11pm.

DRINKING AND NIGHTLIFE

Drinks are charged according to where you sit, with supplements for drinking on the terrace. The old working-class districts east of the Canal St Martin continue to hold some of the city's liveliest nightlife, while the Marais is the place to head for chic café-bars and trendy gay spots. The university quarter near St-Germain-des-Prés is also worth exploring. Most places are open all day until around 2am, and many offer an early-evening "happy hour". For listings, pick up the weekly guide *Pariscope*, which has a small section in English.

BARS

Au P'tit Garage 63 rue Jean-Pierre Timbaud, 11ᵉ; Ⓜ Parmentier; map pp.282–283. A young and rowdy crowd pack out this scruffy bar; expect to see plenty of double denim and check shirts. Cheap and sugary caipirinhas (€6.50) fuel the rock'n'roll atmosphere. Daily 5pm–2am.

Café Charbon 109 rue Oberkampf, 11ᵉ; Ⓜ Parmentier or rue Saint-Maur; map pp.282–283. Long a stalwart of the rue Oberkampf scene, the popularity of *Café Charbon* hasn't waned. The classic brasserie decor – oxblood booths, chandeliers and high ceilings – dates from the early twentieth century, and the long happy hour (daily 5–8pm) is particularly appealing. Wine starts at €4, with cocktails from €7. Mon–Wed & Sun 9am–2am, Thurs–Sat 9am–4am.

★ **Café Chéri(e)** 44 bd de la Villette, 19ᵉ; Ⓜ Belleville; map pp.282–283. This friendly neighbourhood bar is a great place to get a feel for Belleville's laidback "bobo" (bourgeois bohemian) vibe. Old school desks have been resurrected to provide the seats on the street, while the interior hosts exhibitions and DJs (Thurs–Sat). Drinks from €2.80. Daily 11am–2am.

Chez Georges 11 rue des Canettes, 6ᵉ; Ⓜ Mabillon or Saint-Sulpice; map pp.286–287. Fantastic, old-fashioned cellar wine bar (wine by the glass from €3.50), popular with students and older locals alike. Mon–Fri 5pm–2am, Sat noon–2am, Sun 6pm–1am.

Chez Prune 36 rue Beaurepaire, 10ᵉ; Ⓜ Jacques Bonsergent; map pp.286–287. As you might guess from the shabby-chic decor, mosaic floors and yellow walls, this relaxed café-bar is the quintessential canal-side hipster hangout. You'll need to get here early for a table outside. Wine from €3.50 a glass. Daily 10am–2am.

Glass 7 rue Frochot, 9ᵉ; Ⓜ Pigalle; map pp.282–283. Located in the seedy but slowly gentrifying area south of Pigalle (dubbed "SoPi"), *Glass* is a little slice of Americana in Paris. Ignore the menacing bouncer; there's a great

★TREAT YOURSELF

Andy Wahloo 69 rue des Gravilliers, 3e; Ⓜ Arts-et-Métiers; map pp.286–287. This very popular bar decked out in original Pop Art-inspired Arabic decor is fairly quiet during the week but gets packed to the gills at weekends. The bar serves mojitos and a few original cocktails, including the Wahloo julep (mint, rum, tobacco liquor, lime and cherry; €15). From Wednesday to Saturday DJs play a wide range of dance music, hip-hop, Moroccan rock and Algerian raï. Happy hour 6–8pm. Tues–Sun 7pm–1.45am.

atmosphere inside this small, packed bar. Try one of their whisky-based cocktails (€12) or craft beers (from €4). Tues–Thurs & Sun 7pm–4am, Fri & Sat 7pm–5am.

La Fourmi 74 rue des Martyrs, 18e; Ⓜ Pigalle; map pp.282–283. Refreshingly casual Montmartre café-bar with comfy red velvet benches, high ceilings and an enormous chandelier made from old wine bottles. Affordable beers (from €2.80) and cocktails keep things lively well into the night. Mon–Thurs 8am–2am, Fri & Sat 8am–3am, Sun 10am–1am.

La Perle 78 rue Vieille du Temple, 3e; Ⓜ Rambuteau or Saint-Sébastien-Froissart; map pp.286–287. This gay-friendly Marais bar might appear unremarkable, but it becomes enormously popular on weekend evenings. Prices aren't bad for this part of town either, with 50cl beers from €6.70 and wine from €3.50 a glass. Mon–Fri 6am–2am, Sat & Sun 8am–2am.

Wine by One 27 rue de Marignan, 8e; Ⓜ Franklin D. Roosevelt; map pp.282–283. An unpretentious concept wine bar with over a hundred wines to sample from snazzy self-service machines. Load a €2 card with as much money as you wish, then choose a wine to taste; prices start at €1.40 for a small sip. Tues–Fri noon–10pm, Sat 3–8pm.

CLUBS AND LIVE MUSIC

Autour de Midi...et Minuit 11 rue Lepic, 18e Ⓦ autourdemidi.fr; Ⓜ Blanche; map pp.282–283. A cosy subterranean jazz club with free jam sessions on Tuesdays and Wednesdays. Tues–Sat, hours vary.

Le Divan du Monde 75 rue des Martyrs, 18e Ⓦ divandumonde.com; Ⓜ Pigalle; map pp.282–283. Small venue with an eclectic selection of live music, from techno to Congolese rumba. See website for gig times.

Nouveau Casino 109 rue Oberkampf, 11e Ⓦ nouveaucasino.net; Ⓜ Parmentier or rue Saint-Maur; map pp.282–283. An interesting, experimental line-up of live gigs makes way for a relaxed, dancey crowd later on, with music ranging from electro-pop or house to rock.

Entry €5–12, depending on whether you reserve online and the time you arrive. Tues–Sun, hours vary.

Point Ephémère 200 quai de Valmy, 10e Ⓦ pointephemere.org; Ⓜ Jaurès; map pp.282–283. Grungy, concrete-floored bar, restaurant, club and gallery, which spills out onto the bank of the canal. Expect a mix of exhibitions, DJs and live acts. Tickets generally €11–18. Mon–Sat noon–2am, Sun noon–9pm.

Social Club 142 rue Montmartre, 2e Ⓦ parissocialclub .com; Ⓜ Bourse; map pp.286–287. Head to this unpretentious yet cool club to see big-name techno and electro DJs. Free–€20. Wed 11.30pm–3am, Thurs–Sat 11pm–6am.

LGBT PARIS

Paris has a well-established gay scene concentrated mainly in the Halles, Marais and Bastille areas. For information, check out *Têtu* (Ⓦ tetu.com), France's biggest gay monthly magazine, or visit the main information centre, Centre Gai et Lesbien de Paris, 63 rue Beaubourg, 3e (Ⓣ 01 43 57 21 47, Ⓦ centrelgbtparis.org; Ⓜ Ledru-Rollin/Bastille).

Le Club 18 18 rue du Beaujolais, 1er Ⓦ club18.fr; Ⓜ Palais Royal; map pp.286–287. The oldest gay club in Paris, but still fashionable, especially among a friendly, fresh-faced crowd. Tiny, too, which is part of the fun. Entry €10, which includes a drink. Fri & Sat midnight–6am.

Le Freedj 35 rue Ste-Croix-de-la-Bretonnerie, 4e; Ⓜ Hôtel-de-Ville; map pp.286–287. A stylish club in the heart of the Marais, attracting a young, trendy crowd. Daily 6pm–4am.

Le Tango (La Boîte à Frissons) 13 rue au Maire, 3e; Ⓦ boite-a-frissons.fr; Ⓜ Arts-et-Métiers; map pp.286–287. This old dancehall welcomes a mixed gay, lesbian and straight crowd for ballroom dancing before the music gives way to disco around 1am. Entry up to €15. Thurs 8pm–2am, Fri & Sat 10.30pm–5am, Sun 6–11pm.

ENTERTAINMENT

CINEMA

Tickets cost around €9 and discounts are offered across the city on Wednesdays. Films are identified as either *v.o.*, which means they're shown in their original language, or *v.f.*, which means they're dubbed into French.

Cinémathèque Française 51 rue de Bercy, 12e Ⓦ cinematheque.fr; Ⓜ Bercy. Housed in a striking Frank Gehry-designed building, Cinémathèque Française screens a range of films from avant-garde pieces to homages to Hollywood stars. Tickets €6.50.

Le Champo 51 rue des Ecoles, 5e Ⓦ lechampo.com; Ⓜ Cluny-La Sorbonne. This Latin Quarter cinema has been screening films since 1938. They now show an interesting selection of art-house classics and run *les nuits du Champo*: a night of three films followed by breakfast for €15.

11

THEATRE, OPERA AND CLASSICAL MUSIC

Concert venues and theatres sometimes offer standby tickets at a reduced rate. These are generally only released around 20min before the performance, and many offer discounted tickets to students.

Cité de la Musique 221 av Jean-Jaurès, 19e Ⓦ cite-musique.fr; Ⓜ Porte-de-Pantin. Modern venue in Parc de la Villette with an eclectic music programme that covers Baroque, contemporary works and world music. Tickets around €20.

Comédie-Française Ⓦ comedie-francaise.fr. For classical theatre by the likes of Molière or Racine, head to a production by this venerable company, staged in several theatres across Paris. Tickets from €13.

Palais Garnier place de l'Opéra, 9e Ⓦ operaderis.fr; Ⓜ Opéra. The city's original opera house stages both operas and ballets within its lavish interior. Tickets from €5.

SHOPPING

Galeries Lafayette 40 bd Haussmann, 9e Ⓦ galerieslafayette.com; Ⓜ Chaussée d'Antin-La Fayette; map pp.282–283. This massive department store sells everything from lingerie and designer fashion to books and DVDs. Worth a visit just to gawp at the astonishing architecture. Mon–Wed & Sat 9.30am–8pm, Thurs 9.30am–9pm.

Hédiard 21 place de la Madeleine, 8e Ⓦ hediard.fr; Ⓜ Madeleine; map pp.282–283. Gastronomes will be in seventh heaven in this shop, where the finest foods have been sold since 1854. Mon–Sat 9am–8.30pm.

Marché aux Puces de St-Ouen rue des Rosiers, 18e Ⓦ les-puces.com; Ⓜ Porte de Clignancourt; map pp.282–283. Bargain hunters congregate on this massive flea market (Europe's largest), with over 2500 stalls – be prepared to haggle. Mon, Sat & Sun 7.30am–6pm.

DIRECTORY

Embassies and consulates Australia, 4 rue Jean Rey, 15e ☏ 01 40 59 33 00; Canada, 35 av Montaigne, 8e ☏ 01 44 43 29 00; Ireland, 4 rue Rude, 16e ☏ 01 44 17 67 00; New Zealand, 7 rue Léonard de Vinci, 16e ☏ 01 45 01 43 43; South Africa, 59 quai d'Orsay, 7e ☏ 01 53 59 23 23; UK, 35 rue du Faubourg-St-Honoré, 8e ☏ 01 44 51 31 00; US, 2 av Gabriel, 8e ☏ 01 43 12 22 22.

Banks and exchange ATMs are located at all airports and mainline train stations, and at most of the banks in town. Beware that money-exchange bureaux and automatic exchange machines may advertise the selling rather than the buying rate and add on hefty commission fees.

Hospital Contact SOS-Médecins (☏ 36 24) for 24hr medical help, or dial ☏ 15 for emergencies.

Left luggage Lockers (€5.50–9.50) are available at all train stations.

Pharmacy Dérhy (☏ 01 45 62 02 41), 84 av des Champs-Élysées, is open 24hr.

Post office 52 rue du Louvre, 1er (Mon–Sat 7.30am–6am, Sun 10am–midnight).

DAY-TRIPS FROM PARIS

Within easy day-trip distance from Paris are two of the country's most popular sights – stately **Versailles** and Monet's beautiful garden at **Giverny**.

Versailles

The **Palace of Versailles** (Tues–Sun: April–Oct 9am–6.30pm; Nov–March 9am–5.30pm; €18 palace and gardens, €15 palace only; Ⓦ en.chateauversailles.fr) is the epitome of decadence and luxury, with its staggeringly lavish architectural splendour that is a homage to its founder, the "Sun King" Louis XIV. The **ornamental gardens** (daily: April–Oct 8am–8.30pm; Nov–March 8am–6pm) are particularly splendid and ostentatious, complete with canals, boating lakes and fountains. The easiest way to get to Versailles is on the half-hourly RER line C to Versailles-Rive Gauche (35min).

Giverny

Less than an hour northwest of Paris, **GIVERNY** is famous for **Monet's house and gardens**, complete with water-lily pond (April–Oct daily 9.30am–6pm; €9.50; Ⓦ fondation-monet.com). Monet lived here from 1883 until his death in 1926 and the gardens that he laid out were considered by many – including Monet himself – to be his "greatest masterpiece"; the best months to visit are May and June, when the rhododendrons flower around the lily pond and the wisteria hangs over the Japanese bridge, but it's overwhelmingly beautiful at any time of year. To get here, take a train to nearby **Vernon** from Paris-St-Lazare (around 5 daily; 45min; €29.40 return), then either rent a bike from the café opposite the station (€14 for the day) or take the shuttle bus (€8 return; timed to meet trains to/from Paris).

Northern France

Northern France includes some of the most industrial and densely populated parts of the country. However, there are some curiosities hidden away in the far northeastern corner. **Lille** with its *vieux ville* is lovely to amble around, while **Boulogne** is the most interesting port town. Further south, the *maisons* and vineyards of **Champagne** are the main draw, for which the best base is **Reims**, with its fine cathedral.

BOULOGNE-SUR-MER

BOULOGNE-SUR-MER is a pleasant Channel port with a long, sandy stretch of beach. Its **ville basse** (Lower Town), where the main port is located, is somewhat run-down, but within the medieval ramparts of the **ville haute** (Upper Town) rising above, there's a twelfth-century castle, a cathedral and a range of cafés and restaurants. It takes about 45 minutes to walk around the walls, from which you can enjoy panoramic views of the city.

ARRIVAL AND INFORMATION

By train The train station is on bd Voltaire, from where it's a 10min walk to the centre.
Destinations Calais (hourly; 30min); Lille (10 daily; 1hr); Paris (10 daily; 2hr 25min).
By bus Buses to Calais (4 daily; 40min) depart from the bus station on place de France, a few minutes' walk from the centre.
Destinations Calais (4 daily; 40min); Dunkerque (4 daily; 1hr 20min).
Tourist information The main tourist office is in Nausicaá aquarium, bd St-Beauve (Mon–Sat 10.30am–12.30pm & 2–5pm, with longer hours in summer; ☎03 21 10 88 10, ⓦtourisme-boulognesurmer.com).

ACCOMMODATION AND EATING

Faidherbe 12 rue Faidherbe ☎03 21 31 60 93, ⓦhotelfaidherbe.com. Don't be put off by the rather grim exterior; this is a great-value two-star near the sea and shops, with pretty rooms, a small bar-cum-breakfast room and friendly proprietors. Doubles **€69**
FUAJ Bologne-sur-Mer 56 place Rouget de Lisle ☎03 21 99 15 30, ⓦfuaj.org. The cheapest beds in town are at this friendly hostel opposite the station. It has a small bar with a pool table and *babyfoot* (table football). Dorms **€22.70**
La Grillardine 30 rue de Lille ☎03 21 80 32 94. Bright, small and cheerful restaurant in the *ville haute*, this has a growing and glowing reputation for its bistro dishes, using locally sourced meat. The €21 *menu* is particularly good value. Tues–Sat noon–2pm & 7–10pm, Sun noon–2pm.

CALAIS

CALAIS is one of the main ports for ferries to and from the UK. Unless you have an early-morning departure there's little reason to make a special stop here.

ARRIVAL AND DEPARTURE

By train Calais Ville (served by SNCF) is in the town centre; Calais Frethun (served by Eurostar) is on the outskirts.
Destinations Boulogne-Ville (hourly; 35min); Lille (2 hourly; 30min); Paris (5 daily; 1hr 30min).
By bus Buses for Boulogne (5 daily; 40min) depart from in front of Calais-Ville station.
By ferry For last-minute ferry bookings contact P&O Ferries (☎0825 120 156).

ACCOMMODATION AND EATING

Centre Européen de Séjour av du Maréchal de Lattre de Tassigny ☎03 21 34 70 20, ⓦauberge-jeunesse-calais .com; bus #3 from Calais Ville station. Decent hostel just a block from the beach, with small dorms and an on-site restaurant. Dorms **€24.50**
Histoire Ancienne 20 rue Royale ☎03 21 34 11 20. Family-run restaurant with a good-value *menu gourmand* (three courses €20.90) featuring dishes like salmon in a béarnaise sauce. Mon noon–2.30pm, Tues–Sat noon–2.30pm & 6–11pm.
Hotel Particulier Richelieu 17 rue Richelieu ☎03 21 34 61 60, ⓦhotel-richelieu-calais.co.uk. Delightful small hotel with individually decorated rooms (some with clawfoot tubs); don't be put off by the unpromising modern exterior. Doubles **€55**

LILLE

LILLE is a lively, modern city which is well worth visiting for a day or two. The winding, cobbled streets of the old town are lined with traditional patisseries, brasseries and a range of upmarket shops. The **Grand-Place**, also known as place du Général de Gaulle, is a busy square dominated by **Vieille Bourse**, the old exchange building, which now houses an afternoon book market (Tues–Sun

11

1–7pm). South of the old quarter lies the modern place Rihour, beyond which is the **Palais des Beaux-Arts**, place de la République (Mon 2–6pm, Wed–Sun 10am–6pm; €7; ☎03 20 06 78 00, ⓦpba-lille.fr), a notable fine arts museum with an excellent collection of Renaissance art and varying exhibitions.

ARRIVAL AND INFORMATION

By train Gare Lille-Flandres is on place de la Gare; Gare Lille-Europe is a 2min walk further east and has faster services.

Destinations from Gare Lille-Europe Boulogne (8 daily; 1hr); Brussels (7 daily; 40min); Calais (hourly; 30min); London (11 daily; 1hr 25min); Lyon (2 hourly; 3hr); Paris (23 daily; 1hr).

Destinations from Gare Lille-Flandres Brussels (16 daily; 35min); Paris (23 daily; 1hr).

Tourist information place Rihour (Mon–Sat 9.30am–6pm, Sun 10am–4.30pm; ⓦlilletourism.com).

ACCOMMODATION

Faidherbe 42 place de la Gare ☎03 20 06 27 93, ⓦhotel -faidherbe-lille.fr. Just opposite the station, this simple hotel is clean and welcoming. The cheapest rooms (with bathrooms down the hall) are great value. Doubles **€70**

FUAJ Lille 12 rue Malpart ☎03 20 57 08 94, ⓦfuaj.org. Centrally located but basic FUAJ hostel. Breakfast is included and there are simple cooking facilities. Note that reception is closed 11am–3pm. Dorms **€24.50**

Hotel Kanaï 10 rue de Bethune ☎03 20 57 14 78, ⓦhotelkanai.com. This stylish boutique hotel has a great location on a pedestrianized road in the heart of the city. As Lille is geared to business travellers, you can grab a real bargain at weekends. Doubles **€60**

EATING AND DRINKING

Estaminet T'Rijsel 25 rue de Gand ☎03 20 15 01 59. If you want the true Flemish *estaminet* (café) experience, this is the place. Decorated with hops, old photos and candles on the tables, this crowded bistro serves the whole gamut of regional dishes, and over forty beers. *Plats* from €12. Mon 7–10.30pm, Tues–Sun noon–2.30pm & 7–10.30pm.

L'Illustration 18 rue Royale. The pick of the bars on this lively stretch, thanks to the friendly bartenders and retro-pop soundtrack. They serve a good range of beers (from €4.50 for 50cl) and wine (from €3 a glass). Mon–Fri 12.30pm–2am, Sat 2pm–3am, Sun 3pm–2am.

MEERT 27 rue Esquermoise. A grand *patisserie* and *confiserie* selling all manner of pastries and chocolates, which you can eat in their *salon de thé* or take away. The éclairs (€3.10) are divine. Tues–Fri 9.30am–7.30pm, Sat 9am–7.30pm, Sun 9am–1pm & 3–7pm.

REIMS

REIMS is located at the heart of the Champagne region, so if you fancy a tipple or two it's worth stopping by. The town is also home to the spectacular Gothic **Cathédrale Notre Dame** (daily 7.30am–7.30pm), one of the most beautiful in France. The interior is renowned for the stained-glass designs by Marc Chagall in the east chapel and glorifications of the champagne-making process in the south transept.

If you're in town for the **champagne**, head to the tourist office for details of which *maisons* are currently offering tours; all have English-speaking guides. Cellar tours involve a small fee which includes a tasting at the end. The atmospheric *caves* of **Taittinger**, 9 place St-Nicaise (April to mid-Nov daily 9.30am–5.30pm; mid-Nov to March Mon–Fri 9.30am–1pm & 1.45–5.30pm; €16.50; ⓦtaittinger.fr), and the in-depth tours of **Lanson**, 66 rue de Courlancy (Mon–Fri 9.30am–noon & 1.30– 5.30pm; tours at 10am & 2.30pm; €15), which take you into the factory, are the only cellars you can visit without an appointment.

ARRIVAL AND INFORMATION

By train The train station is on bd Joffre, a short walk northwest of the centre.

Destinations Paris (7 daily; 45min).

Tourist information 4 rue Rockefeller (April–Sept Mon–Sat 9am–7pm, Sun 10am–6pm; Oct–March Mon–Sat 10am–6pm, Sun 10am–4pm).

ACCOMMODATION

CIS de Champagne Parc Léo Lagrange ☎03 26 40 52 60, ⓦcis-reims.com; tram A or B to "Comédie". The only dorm accommodation in Reims is predominantly group-oriented and a 15min walk from the train station. Dorms **€23.80**, doubles **€49.70**

Hotel Monopole 28 place Drouet d'Erlon ☎03 26 47 10 33, ⓦhotellemonopole.com. Like all of Reims' budget hotels, the *Monopole* is a little careworn, though it's cheap, friendly and well located on bustling place Drouet d'Erlon. Doubles **€45**

EATING

L'Apostrophe 59 place Drouet d'Erlon ☎03 26 79 19 89, ⓦrestaurant-lapostrophe.fr. Smart, modern café, bar, brasserie and terrace in an old building with a menu that goes from burgers (€14.60) to salmon with a creole sauce

11

and wild rice (€15.80). Lunch *menus* €13.50–18. Daily noon–1.45pm & 7–9.30pm.

Waïda 3–5 place Drouet d'Erlon ☎ 03 26 47 44 49. An old-fashioned bakery offering a mix of savoury and sweet pastries to eat in or take away; it's a good spot for a simple breakfast of baguette with butter and jam (€3.50). Tues–Sun 7.30am–7.30pm.

Normandy and Brittany

To the French, the essence of **Normandy** is in its food and drink: this is the land of butter and cream, cheese and seafood, cider and calvados. Many of the towns also have great historic importance: **Rouen** is where Joan of Arc was burned at the stake; **Bayeux** is rightly celebrated for its eponymous tapestry; the 80km stretch of northern coastline was the site of the **D-Day landings**; and the granite spectacle of **Mont St-Michel** dates back to the thirteenth century. The striking coastline, sandy beaches and lush countryside of **Brittany** feel like a world apart; it seems almost unbelievable that these verdant pastures are within easy reach of Paris. People here are both fiercely proud and defiantly isolationist.

ROUEN

ROUEN is a city of impressive churches, half-timbered houses and small cobbled streets. The town's focal point is place du Vieux-Marché, where Joan of Arc was burned at the stake in 1431. The old market square leads onto rue du Gros-Horloge, which has a colourful one-handed clock arching over the street. Walking along here brings you to the impressive **Cathédrale de Notre-Dame** (April–Oct Mon 2–6pm, Tues–Sat 9am–7pm, Sun 8am–6pm; Nov–March Mon 2–6pm, Tues–Sat 9am–noon & 2–6pm, Sun 8am–6pm), a Gothic masterpiece built in the twelfth and thirteenth centuries. The cathedral is best known as the subject of a series of paintings by Monet which explore the interaction between light and shadow on its facade.

★ **TREAT YOURSELF**

Gill Côté Bistro 14 place du Vieux Marché, Rouen ☎ 02 35 89 88 72. While the local two Michelin star restaurant, *Gill*, might be out of reach, its smart bistro offshoot is great value. Expect beautifully executed classics like beef tartare and chocolate fondant, with excellent-value lunch *formules* starting from €22.50 for two courses. Daily noon–2.30pm & 5.30–10.30pm.

ARRIVAL AND INFORMATION

By train The station is a 10min walk from the centre; there are hourly trains to Paris (1hr 10min).

Tourist information 25 place de la Cathédrale (May–Sept Mon–Sat 9am–7pm, Sun 9.30am–12.30pm & 2–6pm; Oct–April Mon–Sat 9.30am–12.30pm & 1.30–6pm; ⊛ rouentourisme.com).

ACCOMMODATION

FUAJ Rouen 3 rue du Tour, route de Darnétal ☎ 02 35 08 18 50, ⊛ fuaj.org; bus #2 or #3 to "Auberge de Jeunesse". Housed in a former dyeworks, this modern hostel has good communal areas. Dorms **€24.20**

★ **Le Sisley** 51 rue Jean Lecanuet ☎ 02 35 71 10 07. Take your pick from Monet, Manet, Degas or Renoir – each room here is decorated in the style of one of the great Impressionist painters. Some of the colours are pretty loud, but it has bags of personality. Doubles **€62**

EATING AND DRINKING

Brasserie Paul 1 place de la Cathédrale ☎ 02 35 71 86 07. An archetypal French brasserie, serving tasty traditional dishes and a great-value lunch *formule* at €17. Mon–Thurs & Sun 10am–11pm, Fri & Sat 10am–midnight.

Crêperie la Regalière 12 rue Massacre ☎ 02 35 15 33 33. This inexpensive but good-quality crêperie, with some outdoor seating just off the place du Vieux-Marché, is one of central Rouen's best bargains, with *menus* at €10 and €15. Tues–Sat 11.45am–11pm.

Delirium Café 30 rue des Vergetiers. In a splendid half-timbered house, this student-oriented pub, part of a Belgian chain, focuses entirely on beer, with a couple of dozen on draught – largely Belgian – and plenty more in bottles. Mon–Sat 1pm–2am.

BAYEUX

BAYEUX's world-famous **tapestry** depicting the 1066 invasion of England by William the Conqueror is one of the highlights of a visit to Normandy. The

11

70m strip of linen, embroidered over nine centuries ago, is housed in the **Centre Guillaume le Conquérant**, rue de Nesmond (daily: mid-March to mid-Nov 9am–6.30pm; mid-Nov to mid-March 9.30am–12.30pm & 2–6pm; €9; ⓦchateau-guillaume-leconquerant.fr). The **cathedral**, place de la Liberté (daily: Jan–March 9am–5pm; April–June & Oct–Dec 9am–6pm; July–Sept 9am–7pm), is a spectacular thirteenth-century edifice, with some parts dating back to the eleventh century.

ARRIVAL AND INFORMATION

By train The train station is a 15min walk southeast of the centre, just outside the ring road.

Destinations Caen (hourly; 20min); Paris (6 daily; 2hr 15min).

Tourist information pont St-Jean (Mon–Sat 9.30am–12.30pm & 2–5.30pm, Sun 10am–1pm & 2–5.30pm, with later opening July & Aug; ☎02 31 51 28 28, ⓦbayeux-bessin-tourisme.com).

ACCOMMODATION AND EATING

De la Gare 26 place de la Gare ☎02 31 92 10 70, ⓦhotel-delagare-bayeux.fr. Home to Normandy Tours (see box below), this conveniently situated hotel has fourteen rooms and a simple brasserie. Doubles **€44**

L'Insolite 16 rue des Cuisiniers ☎502 31 51 71 16. Cheap but chic crêperie serving an imaginative range of savoury *galettes* (around €8) and sweet crêpes. Set menus from €16. Tues–Sun noon–2pm & 7–9.30pm.

Mogador 20 rue A. Chartier ☎02 31 92 24 58, ⓦhotel-mogador-bayeux.fr. A small hotel in the centre of town offering cosy doubles as well as quads and triples. Doubles **€62**

ST-MALO

ST-MALO is a beautiful Breton coastal town with cobbled streets surrounded by medieval ramparts. You can easily spend a lazy day or so ambling through the lanes and strolling along the beaches. The **town museum**, in the castle to the right as you enter the main city gate, Porte St-Vincent (April–Sept daily 10am–12.30pm & 2–6pm; Oct–March Tues–Sun 10am–noon & 2–6pm; €6), covers the city's eventful history, which has encompassed colonialism, slave-trading and privateers.

There are plenty of windsurfing, sailing and wakeboarding opportunities at **Surf School St-Malo**, just off chaussée du Sillon along the bay, at 2 av de la Hoguette (☎02 99 40 07 47, ⓦsurfschool.org).

ARRIVAL AND INFORMATION

By train The station is a 20min walk east from the walled town. For Paris, you'll need to travel via Rennes.

Destinations Dol de Bretagne (hourly; 15min); Rennes (14 daily; 50min).

Tourist information Esplanade St-Vincent (Mon–Sat 9am–1pm & 2–6pm, with longer hours in summer; ⓦsaint-malo-tourisme.com).

ACCOMMODATION

Centre Patrick Varangot 37 av du Révérend Père Umbricht ☎02 99 40 29 80, ⓦcentrevarangot.com; bus #3 to "Auberge de Jeunesse". Spotlessly clean hostel located 1.5km from the train station and 150m from the beach. Book well in advance. Rates reduce after the first night. Dorms **€24.50**

Cité d'Alet Allée Gaston ☎02 99 81 60 91, ⓦville-saint-malo.fr. Perfectly positioned campsite on a peninsula by

---

D-DAY BEACHES

On June 6, 1944, 135,000 Allied troops stormed the beaches of Normandy in **Operation Overlord**. After heavy fighting, which saw thousands of casualties on both sides, the Allied forces took command of all the beaches, which was a major turning point of World War II. The 80km stretch of coastline north of Bayeux that saw the D-Day landings includes: **Omaha**, now home to the Musée Mémorial d'Omaha Beach (daily: mid-Feb to March & Oct to mid-Nov 10am–6pm; April–Sept 9.30am–6.30pm; €6.70; ⓦmusee-memorial-omaha.com), where exhibits include uniforms and a tank; and **Arromanches**, 10km northwest of Bayeux, which was the main unloading point for cargo (some four million tonnes of it). The interesting museum at Arromanches, **Musée du Débarquement**, place du 6 Juin (daily: Feb, Nov & Dec 10am–12.30pm & 1.30–5pm; March, April & Oct 9.30am–12.30pm & 1.30–5.30pm; May–Sept 9am–6pm; €7.90; ⓦmusee-arromanches.fr), has further information on France's liberation.

One of the best ways to see the beaches is on a **tour**: contact Normandy Sightseeing Tours (from €50; ☎02 31 51 70 52, ⓦnormandy-sightseeing-tours.com), or Normandy Tours (from €55; ☎02 31 92 10 70, ⓦnormandy-landing-tours.com).

the beach. Amenities include a café, shop and showers. Two people with a tent **€16**

Port Malo Hotel 15 rue Ste-Barbe ☎02 99 20 52 99, ⓦhotel-port-malo.com. Inside the town walls, this quaint hotel has surprisingly modern rooms, plus there's a bar right downstairs. Doubles **€72**

EATING AND DRINKING

Bouche en Folie 14 rue du Boyer ☎06 72 49 08 89. This little place offers classic, seasonal French dishes, with a good lunch *menu* for €15. Some outdoor seating. Mon & Thurs–Sun noon–2pm & 7–10pm.

La Brigantine 13 rue de Dinan ☎02 99 56 82 82. You won't find an English menu at this contemporary crêperie, but there is one British concession: the "queen mum", a marmalade and chocolate crêpe flambéed in whisky (€7.10). Daily noon–10pm, closed Mon & Thurs in winter.

La Java 3 rue Ste-Barbe. Fantastically cluttered and quirky cider bar with swings rather than stools at the bar and a toilet hidden in an old confessional. This is a great place to sample a *kir Breton* (cassis and cider; €4). Daily 8.30am–9pm, sometimes later.

MONT ST-MICHEL

Although part of Normandy, the island of **MONT ST-MICHEL** is easily reached from Brittany and can be visited on a day-trip from St-Malo. It's the site of the striking Gothic **Abbaye du Mont-Saint-Michel** (daily: May–Aug 9am–7pm; Sept–April 9.30am–6pm; €9; ⓦabbaye-saint-michel.fr), known as La Merveille, which is visible from all around the bay. The granite structure was sculpted to match the contours of the hill, and the overall impression is stunning. Until recently, the island was attached to the mainland by a long causeway, topped by a road. Now, thanks to a vast hydraulic and reconstruction project, it has become an island once again, connected to the island by a futuristic curved bridge.

ARRIVAL AND INFORMATION

By coach The easiest way of getting here is to take a Keolis coach (ⓦdestination-montsaintmichel.com) from Dol de Bretagne (€8 one-way) or Rennes (€15 one-way). You can reach Dol by train from St-Malo (hourly; 15min) and regular trains run from Paris to Rennes (hourly; 2hr 10min).

By train Very infrequent trains (2–4 daily; 20min) run from Dol de Bretagne to Mont St-Michel's nearest station,

Pontorson, where shuttle buses connect to the island (8–10 daily; 20min).

Tourist information In the lowest gateway (April–June & Sept Mon–Sat 9am–12.30pm & 2–6.30pm, Sun 9am–noon & 2–6pm; July & Aug daily 9am–7pm; Oct–March Mon–Sat 9am–noon & 2–6pm, Sun 10am–noon & 2–5pm; ☎02 14 13 20 15, ⓦbienvenueaumontsaintmichel.com).

The Loire Valley

With countless **châteaux** overlooking the stunning river and panoramic views over some of France's best vineyards, the Loire Valley is deservedly one of the country's most celebrated regions. Alongside the magnificent châteaux there are numerous lovely towns, including laidback **Saumur**, historic **Orléans** and the fairytale towns of **Amboise** and **Chinon**. The cathedral city of **Tours** is the best base for exploring the castles, while the modern metropolis of **Nantes** holds some unusual attractions.

NANTES

Part of Brittany until the 1960s, **NANTES** has transformed itself in the last decade. The star attraction is the **Machines de l'Île** (mid-April to June, Sept & Oct Tues–Fri 10am–5pm, Sat & Sun 10am–6pm; July & Aug daily 10am–7pm; Nov & Dec Tues–Fri 2–5pm, Sat & Sun 2–6pm; €8.50 for elephant ride or a spin on the carousel; ⓦlesmachines-nantes.fr), home to a disarmingly realistic mechanical **elephant** which takes regular walks along the riverside, and an intricate, multi-level merry-go-round.

Back in the centre of town, the **Château des Ducs** (courtyard, ramparts and garden daily: July & Aug 9am–8pm; Sept–June 10am–7pm; free; ⓦchateaunantes.fr), built by two of the last rulers of independent Brittany, François II and his daughter Duchess Anne, is now home to the high-tech **Musée d'Histoire de Nantes** (July & Aug daily 10am–7pm; Sept–June Tues–Sun 10am–6pm; €5). In 1800 the castle's arsenal exploded, shattering the stained glass of the **Cathédrale de St-Pierre et**

11

St-Paul (Mon–Fri 10am–noon & 2–5pm; Ⓦcathedrale-nantes.cef.fr), 200m away, just one of many disasters that have befallen the church.

ARRIVAL AND INFORMATION

By train The train station, on rue de Richebourg, is a 10min walk from the centre or a short tram ride to "Commerce".

Destinations Bordeaux (2 daily; 4hr 20min); Le Mans (for connections to Tours; hourly; 1hr 30min); Paris (hourly; 2hr 30min).

Tourist information 9 rue des Etats, opposite the Château des Ducs (mid-June to mid-Aug daily 9am–7pm; mid-Aug to mid-June daily 10am–6pm; ☎ 02 72 64 04 79, Ⓦnantes-tourisme.com).

ACCOMMODATION

FUAJ La Manu 2 place de la Manu ☎ 02 40 29 29 20, Ⓦfuaj.org; tram #1 to "Manufacture". Nantes' basic HI hostel is housed in an old tobacco factory a little east of the centre. Breakfast included. Reception daily 8am–noon & 3.30–10.30pm. Dorms €21.90

Saint Daniel 4 rue du Bouffay ☎ 02 40 47 41 25, Ⓦhotel -saintdaniel.com. You couldn't ask for a more central location, although the surrounding streets can be a little noisy at night. Rooms are plain but clean, and the staff are welcoming. Doubles €45

EATING AND DRINKING

Café Cult 2 rue des Carmes ☎ 02 40 47 18 49. Splashes of magenta and orange paint liven up this historic building. Grab one of the coveted tables outside on place du Change for classic bistro dishes (€22 for two courses) and wonderfully cheap wine (from €2.70 a glass). Mon–Wed noon–2pm & 7.30–10pm, Thurs–Sat noon–2pm & 7.30pm–2am.

La Ribouldingue 33 rue de Verdun. Table football, pinball and DJ sets are among the draws at this industrial-themed bar. Drinks are cheap, too, with cocktails from €6, shooters from €3 and half-litre beers for just €4. Mon 4pm–2am, Tues–Sat 11am–2am, Sun 2–8pm.

Le Melting Pot 26 bd de la Prairie au Duc ☎ 02 40 35 18 10. Cool, youthful burger joint with a big range of well-priced burgers (from €8.50, with chips), including vegetarian and gluten-free options. There are regular theme nights, too, such as a salsa evening and live comedy. Mon–Fri noon–2pm & 7.30–10.30pm, Sat 7.30–10.30pm.

TOURS

The elegant and compact regional capital **TOURS** makes a good base. The city has two main areas, situated on either side of the central rue Nationale. To the east loom the extravagant towers and stained-glass windows of the **Cathédrale St-Gatien**, with some handsome old streets behind. Adjacent, the **Musée des Beaux-Arts** (Mon & Wed–Sun 9am–12.45pm & 2–6pm; €5; Ⓦwww.mba.tours.fr), on place François Sicard, has some beautiful paintings in its collection, notably Mantegna's *Agony in the Garden*. The **old town** crowds around medieval place Plumereau, on the west side of the city, its half-timbered houses now packed with innumerable bars and restaurants.

ARRIVAL AND INFORMATION

By train The station is located to the south of the city on rue Édouard Vaillant.

Destinations Amboise (frequent; 20min); Chenonceaux (8 daily; 30min); Chinon (8 daily; 45min); Orléans (6–8 daily; 1hr 15min); Paris (hourly; 1–2hr); Saumur (frequent; 45min).

Tourist information The tourist office at 78–82 rue Bernard-Palissy, in front of the train station (April–Sept Mon–Sat 8.30am–7pm, Sun 10am–12.30pm & 2.30–5pm; Oct–March Mon–Sat 9am–12.30pm & 1.30–6pm, Sun 10am–1pm; ☎ 02 47 70 37 37, Ⓦtours-tourisme.fr), can arrange tours of the châteaux.

ACCOMMODATION

Colbert 78 rue Colbert ☎ 02 47 66 61 56, Ⓦtours-hotel -colbert.fr. If you want a hotel at the heart of the action, this is the place, with a huge selection of bars and restaurants right on the doorstep. The friendly hosts (and equally friendly dogs) and sunny garden terrace are an added bonus. Doubles €61

Des Arts 40 rue de la Préfecture ☎ 02 47 05 05 00, Ⓦhoteldesartstours.com. Located 5min from the station, this friendly hotel is no-frills but excellent value. Rooms are a little cramped, but nonetheless light and cheerful, some with little balconies. Doubles €54

EATING AND DRINKING

Comme Autre Fouée 11 rue de la Monnaie ☎ 02 47 05 94 78. An old-fashioned restaurant specializing in miniature sweet and savoury dough-based snacks, *fouée*, with local fillings such as *andouillette* and mustard (lunch *menu* from €10). Tues & Wed 7–10pm, Thurs–Sat noon–2.30pm & 7–10pm.

L'Atelier Gourmand 37 rue Etienne Marcel ☎ 02 47 38 59 87. A trendy, ultra-modern restaurant with superb fresh cuisine, not far from rue Colbert. Head here for lunch,

CYCLING THE LOIRE VALLEY

The **Loire à Vélo** scheme provides over 800km of safe cycling routes, with cycle paths meandering along the river all the way from Cuffy to St-Nazaire (Ⓦ loire-a -velo.fr has all the details). You can rent bikes in Tours from **Detours de Loire**, 35 rue Charles Gille (April–Oct Mon–Sat 9am–1pm & 2–7pm, Sun 9.30am–12.30pm & 6–7pm; Ⓣ 02 47 61 22 23, Ⓦ location develos.com), who allow you to drop the bike off at another town in their network for a small fee, depending on how far you've travelled.

when the *formule* is just €13. Daily noon–2pm & 7.30–10.30pm.

La Souris Gourmande 100 rue Colbert Ⓣ 02 47 47 04 80. Cheery local joint, where you'll be welcomed with a smile. The menu offers cheese dishes from all over France, including fondue (from €14), *raclette* and crêpes (from €8), and the cheese theme even extends to the decor. Tues–Sat noon–2pm & 7–10pm.

VILLANDRY

One of the Loire's most popular châteaux, **Villandry** (daily 9am–5pm, with later opening in summer; €10.50, €6.50 gardens only; Ⓦ chateauvillandry.fr) lies around 17km west of Tours. It boasts extraordinary ornamental Renaissance gardens that have marvellous views over the River Cher. The château itself dates from 1536 and has an interesting collection of Spanish paintings dating back to the seventeenth century.

ARRIVAL AND DEPARTURE

By bike There's no public transport, but Villandry is easy to reach by bike from Tours: cycle direct or take your bike on the train (3 daily; 12min) to Savonnières, 4km away.

By bus Shuttle buses operate July & Aug between Tours and the château (2–3 daily; 35min; timetables at Ⓦ filbleu.fr).

CHENONCEAU

Perhaps the finest Loire château is **Chenonceau** (daily 9.30am–5pm, with later opening in summer; €13; Ⓦ chenonceau.com), straddling the river 30km east of Tours. As with Villandry, the stunning formal gardens and

beautiful river views are the highlight. The château's charming interior is preserved in pristine condition and houses an excellent collection of paintings and tapestries.

ARRIVAL AND DEPARTURE

By train Regular trains run from Tours to the adjacent village of Chenonceaux (hourly; 30min) – note the additional "x" that differentiates it from the château.

CHINON

The ancient town of **Chinon** is an attractive and tranquil place to stop, with opportunities for kayaking on the River Vienne. The ruined **fortress** overlooking the town (daily 9.30am– 5pm, later hours in summer; €8.50; Ⓦ forteressechinon.fr) offers glorious views and is a fascinating relic of France's historic past: parts of it date from the twelfth and thirteenth centuries. It's been sensitively renovated, with interactive guidebooks and video projections that bring the ruins to life.

ARRIVAL, INFORMATION AND TOURS

By train The station, a 15min walk east of town, has good connections to Tours (8 daily; 45min–1hr).

Tourist information place Hofheim (May–Sept daily 10am–1.30pm & 2–7pm; Oct–April Mon–Sat 10am–12.30pm & 2.30–6pm; Ⓣ 02 47 93 17 85, Ⓦ chinon-valdeloire.com).

Kayak tours CLAN (daily April to mid-Oct; Ⓣ 06 23 82 96 33, Ⓦ loisirs-nature.fr), on quai Danton next to the campsite, offer combined kayak and bike excursions and also rent sit-on kayaks (€7.50/hr).

ACCOMMODATION AND EATING

Agnès Sorel 4 quai Pasteur Ⓣ 02 47 93 04 37, Ⓦ hotel -agnes-sorel.com. Delightful, family-run hotel well worth the schlep to the other side of town. The best of the modern, crisply decorated rooms have river views. Doubles **€68**

Café des Arts 4 rue Jean-Jacques-Rosseau Ⓣ 02 47 93 09 84. Offering reliable and reasonably priced brasserie grub at around €15 and specializing in local products, this café is especially popular with locals and visitors alike. Daily except Wed noon–2pm & 7.30–9.30pm.

Camping de l'Île-Auger quai Danton Ⓣ 02 47 93 08 35, Ⓦ camping-chinon.com. A 5min walk from the town, this campsite enjoys a lovely location by the river. Open April–Oct. Per person and tent **€7**

11

11

SAUMUR AND AROUND

SAUMUR is a peaceful, pretty riverside town, famous for its sparking wine and as a centre of spirit distillation. Above town, the **château** (Tues–Sun 10am–1pm & 2–5.30pm, with longer hours in summer; €6; ⓦ www.chateau-saumur.com) boasts great views, but only one wing is open to the public.

ARRIVAL AND INFORMATION

By train The station is on the north bank of the river; head over two bridges to the town.

Destinations Nantes (frequent; 1hr–1hr 30min); Tours (frequent; 40min).

Tourist information Quai Carnot (mid-May to Sept Mon–Sat 9.15am–7pm, Sun 10.30am–5.30pm; late Sept to mid-May Mon–Sat 9.15am–12.30pm & 2–6pm, Sun 10am–noon; ☎ 02 41 40 20 60, ⓦ ot-saumur.fr).

ACCOMMODATION AND EATING

Camping l'Île d'Offard Rue de Verden, l'Île d'Offard ☎ 02 41 40 30 00, ⓦ saumur-camping.com. This combined campsite and *centre de séjour* has a swimming pool, small bar and restaurant. In addition to waterfront tent pitches, there's clean and cheerful hostel accommodation. Camping/two people **€31**, dorms **€20**, doubles **€60**

Le Pot de Lapin 35 rue Rabelais ☎ 02 41 67 12 86. A relaxed vibe and exceedingly friendly staff make this contemporary bistro-restaurant a hit with both locals and out-of-towners. The large and varied menu might include delights like *boudin blanc* (€13) and rabbit tartin (€15), as well as tapas. Tues–Sat noon–1.45pm & 7–9.30pm.

Le Volney 1 rue Volney ☎ 02 41 51 25 41, ⓦ www .levolney.com. Simple, no-frills budget hotel that's great value, with clean rooms and comfy beds. Some rooms have shared showers. Doubles **€48**

ABBAYE DE FONTEVRAUD

The immense **Abbaye de Fontevraud** (daily: May–Oct 9.30am–6.30pm; Oct–April 10am–5pm; €11; ⓦ abbayedefontevraud.com), 15km southeast of Saumur, was founded in 1099 as both a nunnery and a monastery with an abbess in charge. Its chief significance is as the burial ground of the Plantagenet kings and queens, notably Henry II, Eleanor of Aquitaine and Richard the Lionheart; some of the tombs are extraordinarily elaborate.

ARRIVAL AND DEPARTURE

By bus The only way to get here by public transport is on the irregular bus #1 from Saumur (4–6 daily; 25min).

AMBOISE

Situated on the banks of the Loire, **AMBOISE** is a beautiful if heavily visited town. The main sight is the **Château Royal d'Amboise** (daily 9.30am–12.30pm & 2–4.45pm, with longer hours in summer; €11.20; ⓦ chateau-amboise.com), holding a majestic spot overlooking the river. It was built in the eleventh century and saw further additions by successive royals. Leonardo da Vinci's final residence, **Clos-Lucé**, is also located here (daily 10am–5pm, with longer hours in summer; €15; ⓦ vinci-closluce.com), housing a collection of some of his inventions with models dotted around the surrounding gardens.

ARRIVAL AND INFORMATION

By train The station is a 15min walk north of town on the opposite bank of the river.

Destinations Orléans (10 daily; 1hr); Tours (at least 4 hourly; 20min).

Tourist information By the river on quai du Général de Gaulle (Mon–Sat 10am–6pm, Sun 10am–12.30pm; ☎ 02 47 57 09 28, ⓦ amboise-valdeloire.co.uk).

ACCOMMODATION

Café des Arts 32 rue Victor Hugo ☎ 02 47 57 25 04, ⓦ www.cafedesarts.net. This pleasant café has a collection of two- to four-bed rooms hidden upstairs, all kitted out with sturdy pine bunks. It's not a hostel, so you don't share with people you don't know, but the prices are just as reasonable. Doubles **€45**

Camping de L'Île d'Or 100 rue de l'Île d'Or ☎ 02 47 57 23 37, ⓦ camping-amboise.com. A peaceful campsite located at the eastern end of L'Île d'Or. Camping/person **€3.20**, plus per tent **€3.90**

Le Blason 11 place Richelieu ☎ 02 47 23 22 41, ⓦ leblason.fr. Built as a school in 1490, this charming hotel has exposed beams in all of the rooms. It's slightly old-fashioned, but full of character. Doubles **€68**

EATING AND DRINKING

Anne de Bretagne 1 place du Chateau ☎ 02 47 57 05 46. This simple crêperie is a good choice for an affordable meal; the €13.80 *menu* will get you a savoury *galette*, sweet crêpe and a *bole* of cider. Daily noon–10pm.

Le Shaker 3 quai Francois Tissard, l'Île d'Or. With views across the water to the château, this riverside cocktail bar and *glacier* serves gigantic, fruity creations from €9 and non-alcoholic shakes for €5. Tues–Sun 6pm–3am.

ORLÉANS

Due south of Paris, **ORLÉANS** became legendary when Joan of Arc delivered the city from the English in 1429. Stained-glass windows in the nave of the enormous, Gothic **Cathédrale Sainte-Croix** (daily 9.15am–6pm) tell the story of her life, from her childhood through to her heroic military career and her eventual martyrdom. Immediately opposite, the **Musée des Beaux-Arts** (Tues–Sat 10am–6pm, Sun 1–6pm; €4) has an excellent collection of French paintings.

ARRIVAL AND INFORMATION

By train The station is a 15min walk north of the centre.
Destinations Amboise (10 daily; 1hr); Paris (hourly; 1hr); Tours (8 daily; 1hr –30min).
Tourist information 2 place de l'Etape (Tues–Sat 10am–1pm & 2–5pm, with longer hours in summer; ☎02 38 24 05 05, ⓦtourisme-orleans.com).

ACCOMMODATION

★**Archange** 1 bd de Vedun ☎02 38 54 42 42, ⓦhotelarchange.com. It's impossible not to smile on entering *Archange*, which is crammed with quirky artefacts, bold artworks and bohemian keepsakes. Each room has a distinct personality: from medieval in the Joan of Arc to monochrome in the yin-yang room. Doubles €49
Auberge de Jeunesse 7 av de Beaumarchais, 10km south of the city ☎02 38 53 60 06, ⓦaubergede jeunesseorleans.fr; tram A to "Université l'Indien". Pleasant modern hostel with helpful staff, although it's a bit of a trek from the centre of town. Dorms €17

★TREAT YOURSELF

De L'Abeille 64 rue Alsace-Lorraine ☎02 38 53 54 87, ⓦhoteldelabeille .com. A luxurious, family-run boutique hotel, decorated with beautiful wallpaper and antique furniture. In summer you can enjoy views over to the cathedral from their roof terrace. Three- and four-bed rooms available (from €146). Doubles €79

EATING AND DRINKING

La Pause 14 place du Châtelet ☎06 22 11 09 78. Simple but tasty dishes are the order of the day here, with quality burgers (€13.50), bagels and light bites, plus good vegetarian options. Wed–Fri 11.30am–3pm & 6.30–10.30pm, Sat & Sun 11am–10.30pm.
Le P'tit Barcelone 218 rue de Bourgogne. A laidback student haunt, this budget bar has cheapish drinks (€3–4 for a beer or glass of wine) and a range of tapas (from €5) to accompany them. Mon–Sat 11.30am–2am, Sun 5pm–1am.

Burgundy

Burgundy has some charming towns and villages, as well as some of the country's finest food and drink. **Dijon**, the capital, is an affluent place with great shops and lovely architecture. Heading south, the small town of **Beaune** is a good destination to sample the best of the region's famous wine, and to try local specialities such as *escargots à la bourguignonne* and *bœuf bourguignon*.

DIJON

Most famous for its mustard, **DIJON** is an elegant, historic town, based around a range of classical squares and narrow, winding streets. The Palais des Ducs, in the heart of the city, is notable both for the fifteenth-century **Tour Philippe le Bon** (guided tours only: April–Nov daily; Dec–March Wed, Sat & Sun; €3) and the fourteenth-century **Tour de Bar**, which houses the magnificent **Musée des Beaux-Arts** (Mon & Wed–Sun: May–Oct 9.30am–6pm; Nov–April 10am–5pm; free), the highlight of which are the Flemish paintings. Just to the north lies the stunning thirteenth-century Gothic **church of Notre-Dame** (Mon–Sat 9am–6.30pm), the exterior north wall of which holds a well-worn sculpted owl (*chouette*), which people touch for luck.

ARRIVAL AND INFORMATION

By train Dijon's train station is a 15min walk west from the centre.

BURGUNDY VINEYARDS

The Burgundy vineyards are justly famous for their complex wines, made predominantly from Pinot Noir and Chardonnay grapes. The best way to explore them is on the **Route des Grand Crus** (wroute-des-grands-crus-de-bourgogne.com), which takes in such places as **Vougeot** and **Puligny Montrachet**, famous for their high-calibre reds and whites respectively. The wine is cheaper if bought from source – expect to pay around €10 for a good bottle and €20 and upwards for an excellent one. If you fancy learning more about the wines, the **École des Vins de Bourgogne** in Beaune, 6 rue du 16ᵉ Chasseurs (℡03 80 26 35 10, wbourgogne -wines.com), offers crash courses in wine appreciation, some in English.

11

Destinations Beaune (1–3 hourly; 25min); Lyon (hourly; 2hr 10min); Paris (hourly; 1hr 30min); Reims (every 30min–1hr; 3hr 20min).

Tourist information 11 rue des Forges (April–Sept Mon–Sat 9.30am–6.30pm, Sun 10am–6pm; Oct–March Mon–Sat 9.30am–1pm & 2–6pm, Sun 10am–4pm; ℡08 92 70 05 58, wvisitdijon.com); there's another branch near the train station at 15 Cour de la Gare (same hours).

ACCOMMODATION

CRIS Dijon 1 av Champollion ℡03 80 72 95 20, wcri -dijon.com; bus #3 to "CRI-Dallas". The local hostel is comfortable, cheap and has good self-catering facilities. The only drawback is that it's 2.5km from the centre. Dorms **€23.10**

Le Jacquemart 32 rue Verrerie ℡03 80 60 09 60, wwww.hotel-lejacquemart.fr. A traditional hotel with warmly furnished rooms, the best with faux-marble bathrooms. The cheaper rooms aren't en suite. Doubles **€40**

Le Sauvage 64 rue Monge ℡03 80 41 31 21, whotellesauvage.com. Beautifully restored fifteenth-century hotel in a central location with a good restaurant. Doubles **€55**

EATING AND DRINKING

Au Vieux Léon 52 rue Jeannin. Decorated like an old-fashioned French café on acid, this alternative – and strictly antifascist, as it proudly proclaims – café-bar is a student favourite, with a lively, friendly atmosphere. Bottles of wine from €10. Mon–Sat 6pm–1.30am.

Chez Copains 10 Rue Quentin ℡03 80 40 20 10. The friendly, young proprietors and ingredients sourced in the adjacent market make this restaurant a hit. Try a Burgundian classic like *œufs en meurette* (poached eggs in red wine; £7). Tues–Sat noon–2pm & 7–10.30pm.

Le Shanti 69 rue Berbisey. Great little hookah joint, decked out with divans and South Asian decor, serving delicious teas, non-alcoholic cocktails, lassis and flavoured shisha. The food is all vegetarian – try the delicious Bombay burger. Dishes around €6–8. Mon–Sat noon–midnight.

BEAUNE

At the heart of the Côte d'Or region, **BEAUNE** is home to some of Burgundy's most prestigious wine cellars, many of which can be visited on guided tours (ask at the tourist office).

Its other major attraction is the fifteenth-century hospital, the **Hôtel-Dieu** on place de la Halle (daily: April to mid-Nov 9am–6.30pm; mid-Nov to March 9am–11.30am & 2–5.30pm; €7.50), now a museum with re-creations of the original wards and an exhibition of paintings and tapestries. On nearby rue d'Enfer is the old-fashioned **Musée du Vin** (April–Nov daily 9.30am–6pm; Dec–March Mon & Wed–Sun 11am–6pm; €5.80), which explains the history of the region's wine industry. The **Marché aux Vins**, 7 rue de l'Hôtel Dieu (daily: April–Oct 10am–7pm; Nov–March 10am–noon & 2–7pm; €11 for 6 wines), is a rather more taster-friendly experience, offering a self-guided tour of their modern cellars with some delectable wines to taste along the way.

ARRIVAL AND INFORMATION

By train Beaune station is a 10min walk east of the centre. **Destinations** Dijon (1–3 hourly; 25min); Lyon (hourly; 1hr 10min).

Tourist information 6 bd Perpreuil (Mon–Sat 9am–noon & 1–6pm, Sun 10am–12.30pm & 1.30–5pm, longer hours in summer; ℡03 80 26 21 30, wot-beaune.fr).

ACCOMMODATION AND EATING

Foch 24 bd Foch ℡03 80 24 05 65, whotelbeaune -lefoch.fr. Eleven pleasant rooms above a little café, run by a helpful family; some rooms sleep up to four. Doubles **€40**

Le Bistrot Bourguignon 8 rue Monge ℡03 80 22 23 24. Beaune's first wine bar has a good-value lunch *menu* (€14.90) featuring classics like *confit canard*, with wine from €3 a glass. Tues–Sat 11am–3pm & 6–11pm.

Les Cent Vignes 10 rue Auguste Dubois ☏03 80 22 03 91, ✉ campinglescentvignes@mairie-beaune.fr. Located just 1km out of Beaune, this good-value, pretty campsite has showers and a shop. Camping/person **€4.80**, plus per tent **€5.20**

Alsace and Lorraine

Dominated by the remarkable city of **Strasbourg**, Alsace often bears more similarity to Germany or Switzerland than to the rest of the country. The *mélange* of cultures is at its most vivid in the string of little wine towns that punctuate the **Route des Vins** along the eastern margin of the wet and woody Vosges mountains. The province of **Lorraine** is home to elegant eighteenth-century **Nancy**. Food and drink is excellent in the region, particularly the delicious white Rieslings and Gewürztraminers, served at the *winstubs* (or wine rooms) that predominate and offer inexpensive, unpretentious food based around pork, veal and beef, often in stews or casseroles.

NANCY

NANCY, capital of Lorraine, is a refined and beautiful town of opulent squares and splendid boulevards. At the centre is **place Stanislas**, a supremely graceful square dominated by the **Hôtel de Ville**. The roofline of this UNESCO World Heritage Site is topped by florid urns and lozenge-shaped lanterns dangling from the beaks of gilded cockerels. On the west side of the square, the **Musée des Beaux-Arts** (Mon & Wed–Sun 10am–6pm; €6; ⓦ mban.nancy.fr) boasts work by Caravaggio, Delacroix, Matisse and Picasso as well as contemporary installations. A little to the north the **Musée Lorrain**, 64 Grande-Rue (Tues–Sun 10am–12.30pm & 2–6pm; €4), devoted to Lorraine's history, is housed in the splendid Palais Ducal.

ARRIVAL AND INFORMATION

By train Nancy's station is a 10min walk from place Stanislas.
Destinations Lyon (3 daily; 4hr); Paris (hourly; 1hr 30min); Strasbourg (hourly; 1hr 25min).
Tourist information 1 place Stanislas (May–Sept Mon–Sat 9am–7pm, Sun 10am–5pm; Oct–April Mon–Sat 9am–6pm, Sun 10am–1pm; ☏ 03 83 35 22 41, ⓦ nancy-tourisme.fr).

ACCOMMODATION

Château de Rémicourt 149 rue de Vandoeuvre ☏ 03 83 27 73 67, ⓦ fuaj.org; bus #134 or #135 from outside the station to "Lycée Stanislas". The local hostel is a 20min bus ride from town, but it's spacious and friendly. Dorms **€15.30**
Revotel 43 rue Raymond Poincaré ☏ 03 83 28 02 13, ⓦ revotel-hotel.com. Just a 5min walk from the train station, this is a smartly decorated two-star with budget prices. The rooms are small, but they all come with flat-screen TV and free wi-fi. Doubles **€50**

EATING AND DRINKING

Bouche à L'Oreille 42 rue des Carmes ☏ 03 83 35 17 17. This bric-a-brac cluttered restaurant is the place to indulge a cheese craving; they have a huge range of *tartiflettes* and fondues, with good-value menus starting from €10.95 at lunchtime. Mon 7–10pm, Tues–Sat noon–1.30pm & 7–10pm.
Le Shortbus 2 ter rue de la Citadelle. Gay bar embraced by the mainstream student population. Packed to the rafters, loud and youthful, with a DJ spinning the decks after 10pm. Beers from €3. Wed–Sun 6pm–2am.

STRASBOURG

STRASBOURG is a major city with the feel of a charming provincial town. It has one of the loveliest cathedrals in France, an ancient but active university and is the current seat of the Council of Europe and the European Court of Human Rights, as well as part-time base of the European Parliament.

WHAT TO SEE AND DO

The **Grand Île** section of the city is the most striking, centred on two main squares, the busy **place Kléber** and, to the south, **place Gutenberg**, named after the fifteenth-century pioneer of printing type.

Cathédrale de Notre-Dame

The major landmark is the **Cathédrale de Notre-Dame** (daily 7–11.20am &

11

11

12.40–7pm; free), which beautifully combines ostentatious grandeur with chocolate-box fragility. Climb to the top platform for stunning views to the Black Forest (€5), and don't miss the tremendously complicated **astrological clock** (€2), built in 1842. Visitors arrive in droves to witness its crowning performance – striking the hour of noon with unerring accuracy at 12.30pm.

Musée de l'Oeuvre Notre-Dame

The **Musée de l'Oeuvre Notre-Dame**, 3 place du Château (Tues–Sun 10am–6pm; €6.50), houses the original sculptures from the cathedral exterior, as well as some of Europe's finest collected stained glass. A particular highlight is *Les Amants Trépassés* in room 23, which shows two lovers being punished, and makes the average Hollywood horror film look mild in comparison.

Petite France

Divided into three small islands by picturesque canals, the beautiful **Petite France** is made up of winding streets bordered by sixteenth- and seventeenth-century houses. The name Petite France was given to the area by the Alsatians in the seventeenth century, having been a quarantine area for patients of a devastating sixteenth-century venereal disease attributed to the French.

Musée d'Art Moderne et Contemporain

The **Musée d'Art Moderne et Contemporain**, 1 place Hans Jean Arp (Tues–Sun 10am–6pm; €7), stands on the west bank of the river and houses an impressive collection featuring Monet, Kandinsky, Klee and Picasso.

ARRIVAL AND INFORMATION

By train The station is a 15min walk west from place Kléber.

Destinations Lille (daily; 3hr 20min); Nancy (9–13 daily; 1hr 20min); Paris (1–2 hourly; 2hr 20min).

Tourist information 17 place de la Cathédrale (daily 9am–7pm; ☎03 88 52 28 28, ⓦotstrasbourg.fr).

ACCOMMODATION

Hotels get booked up early when the parliament is in session (one week a month); check ⓦ europarl.europa.eu.

Camping Indigo rue de l'Auberge de Jeunesse ⓣ 04 37 64 22 34, ⓦ camping-indigo.com; bus #2 from the train station to "Camping". This smart campsite offers simple pitches for tents, plus there's a pool on site, and free wi-fi. Per pitch with up to six people **€26.50**

Ciarus 7 rue de Finkmatt ⓣ 03 88 15 27 88, ⓦ ciarus.com. Pleasant and central hostel, set around a pretty internal courtyard and with a very cheap on-site restaurant. Dorms **€27**, twins **€72**

EtC... 7 rue de la Chaîne ⓣ 03 88 32 66 60, ⓦ etc-hotel .com. Surprisingly smart two-star just a short walk from the cathedral, offering cosy but nicely decorated rooms, some of which sleep up to four. Doubles **€60**

EATING

L'Epicerie 6 rue Vieux Seigle. A lovely café with vintage decor, situated in a reconstructed grocer's. Try one of their delicious *tartines* (open sandwiches) from €6.20. Daily 11.30am–1.30am.

★ **La Corde à Linge** 2 place Benjamin Zix ⓣ 03 88 22 15 17. Popular brasserie with a prime location in La Petite France and a contemporary interior. The canal-side terrace is perfect for people-watching and the simple, tasty food includes large salads (from €12), *spaetzle* pasta dishes (€11.50) and meaty Alsatian classics. Daily 11.45am–11pm.

DRINKING

Jeanette et les Cycleaux 30 rue des Tonneliers. Trendy, chilled-out bar serving wine (from €3.50), cocktails (from €7), milkshakes and light snacks. Daily 11.30am–1am.

L'Académie de la Bière 17 rue Adolphe-Seyboth. Head here for an enormous range of French and German beers: there are fifteen on tap with half-litres from €5.50. Daily 11am–4am.

The southwest

The varied landscapes of southwest France stretch from the vast horizons of Poitou-Charente to the ordered rows of Bordeaux's vineyards and the lush, heady green of the Dordogne. The Atlantic coast, lacking the busy glitz of the Côte d'Azur, has a slow, understated charm, best seen in **La Rochelle**. Further south, **Bordeaux**, justifiably famous for its wines, is a cosmopolitan and lively city that's worth a few days' exploration – from here, it's easy to strike east to **Périgueux**, a

good base for exploring the nearby prehistoric caves, or south to the Basque coast, home to **Biarritz**, the country's surf capital, and **Bayonne**, with its fine old timber-framed buildings and excellent chocolatiers.

The Pyrenees, marking the very south of France, are home to some of the country's best walking and one of its most vibrant cities, the rose-brick university town of **Toulouse**, whose youthful energy is matched only by **Montpellier**. Medieval **Carcassonne**, between the two, is undoubtedly the biggest tourist trap of the region, but it's hard not to be wowed when you first see its fairytale spires rising above the surrounding buildings.

LA ROCHELLE

The lively port town of **LA ROCHELLE** has an exceptionally beautiful seventeenth- and eighteenth-century centre and is a very pleasant place to linger for a few days. Granted a charter by Eleanor of Aquitaine in 1199, it rapidly became a port of major importance, trading in salt and wine. Following a makeover in the 1990s, which established a university, pedestrianized the centre and moved out the fishing operation, La Rochelle has become the largest Atlantic yachting port in Europe, without the exclusivity of some of its Mediterranean counterparts.

WHAT TO SEE AND DO

The heavy Gothic gateway of the Porte de la Grosse Horloge straddles the entrance to the old town, dominating the pleasure-boat-filled inner harbour, which is guarded by two of La Rochelle's three sturdy towers, **Tour de la Chaîne** and **Tour St-Nicolas** (daily: April–Sept 10am–6.30pm; Oct–March 10am–1pm & 2.15–5.30pm; €8.50 for all three towers). Behind the Grosse Horloge, the main shopping street, rue du Palais, is lined with eighteenth-century houses and arcaded shop fronts. The excellent **Musée du Nouveau Monde**, 10 rue Fleuriau (July–Sept Mon & Wed–Fri 10am–1pm & 1.45–6pm, Sat & Sun 2–6pm; Oct–June Mon & Wed–Fri

11

9.30am–12.30pm & 1.30–5pm, Sat & Sun 2–6pm; €6), commemorates the town's dubious fortunes from slavery, sugar, spices and coffee.

For beaches – and bicycle paths – you're best off crossing over to the **Île de Ré**, a narrow, sand-rimmed island immediately west of La Rochelle (take one of the Rébus buses from place de Verdun). Out of season it has a slow, misty charm, centred on the cultivation of oysters and mussels; in summer it's packed to the gills.

ARRIVAL AND DEPARTURE

By plane La Rochelle airport is located 2.5km northwest of the city. For the centre, take the #7 bus (Mon–Sat 7am–8.30pm; 20min) and get off at stop "Place de Verdun". On Sundays, take bus #47 to "Place de Verdun" (7am–8.30pm; 20min). Tickets cost €1.30 and can be bought on board.

By train From the train station, it's a 7min walk down av du Général de Gaulle to the town centre.

Destinations Bordeaux (7–14 daily; 2hr 20min); Cognac (6 daily; 1hr 20min–2hr); Nantes (5 daily; 1hr 50min); Paris (15–20 daily; 3hr 10min–4hr).

INFORMATION

Tourist information 2 quai Georges Simenon (April & May Mon–Sat 9am–6pm, Sun 9am–5pm; June & Sept Mon–Sat 9am–7pm, Sun 9am–5pm; July & Aug Mon–Sat 9am–8pm, Sun 9am–7pm; Oct–March Mon–Sat 9am–6pm, Sun 10am–1pm; ☎05 46 41 14 68, ⓦlarochelle-tourisme.fr).

GETTING AROUND

By bike There are two municipal bike stations, run by Yélo (ⓦyelo.agglo-larochelle.fr): one in place Verdun (all year) and the other on quai Verlin near the tourist office (May–Sept). On handing over ID you get 1hr of free bike rental; after this it's €2 for the second hour and €3 per 30min afterwards.

ACCOMMODATION

FUAJ La Rochelle av des Minimes ☎05 46 44 43 11, ⓦaj-larochelle.fr. Modern hostel, well positioned by Port des Minimes, a 30min walk from the station. The bright, nicely decorated rooms are all en suite; dinner is available and outdoor activities are often organized. From the station, follow signs to Porte des Minimes. Reception 8am–noon & 2–8pm. Dorms **€17.50**, doubles **€47.60**

Hotel de l'Océan 36 cours des Dames ☎05 46 41 31 97, ⓦhotel-ocean-larochelle.com. This small, friendly hotel is decked out in blues and yellows. Rooms are en suite, and

those at the front have excellent views of the port. Doubles **€75**

Hotel les Rosiers 56 bd André Sautel ☎05 46 67 42 27, ⓦhotel-lesrosiers.com. Located a short walk from the old town, what this basic hotel lacks in style it compensates for in price. More expensive en suites also available. Doubles **€75**

Le Soleil av Michel Crépeau ☎05 46 44 42 53. This municipal campsite has ping-pong, pétanque and hot showers, and allows barbecues. Fabulously located right by the sea, and just 800m from the town centre. Open late June to late Sept. Per person and tent **€10.38**

EATING, DRINKING AND NIGHTLIFE

Corrigans 20 rue des Cloutiers. A low-key but convivial little place down a quiet street near the market. Serves reasonably priced beer, with Irish music sessions every Sunday. Tues–Sat 6pm–2am, Sun 7pm–1am.

★ **Ernest le Glacier** 48 cours des Dames. The only place to head if you're looking for ice cream, making use of the best ingredients in an array of imaginative flavours, from lemon meringue to rice pudding. From €3.20. There's another branch at 16 rue du Port (closed Mon). Mon–Sat 11.30am–11pm, Sun 11.30am–7pm.

L'Amaranthe 14 rue Bletterie ☎05 17 83 07 21. Seating only fifteen, it's all rather cosy but the changing menu here offers fresh, inventive dishes and the €16 lunch *menu* is excellent value. Tues–Sat noon–10pm.

La Guignette 8 rue Saint Nicolas ☎05 46 41 05 75. Formerly a sailor's haunt, this is a wine bar beloved of students, who come at *l'heure de l'apéro* for a glass of its eponymous aperitif – white wine flavoured with fruit. Mon–Sat 10.30am–1.30pm & 4.30–9pm, Sun 4.30–9pm.

Le Soleil Brille Pour Tour le Monde 13 rue des Cloutiers ☎05 46 41 11 42. Decked out with luminous yellow furniture and cutesy sun motifs, this family-run restaurant is as vibrant and cheery as its name suggests. The good vibes infuse the food too, with fresh market ingredients whipped into delicious *tartes*, varied salads (from €10.50) and great vegetarian options. Tues–Sat noon–2pm & 7.30–10pm.

COGNAC

COGNAC is shrouded in the heady scent of its famous brandy. Of the various cognac *chais* (distilleries) huddled around the end of the Grande-Rue, **Baron Otard** is one of the best choices for a guided tour (€10; ⓦbaronotard.com), which recounts a history of the site, the principles of making cognac and, most importantly, a tasting.

ARRIVAL AND INFORMATION

By train The train station is southeast of the town centre, about a 15min walk.

Destinations Bordeaux (frequent, via Angoulême; 1hr 50min–2hr 50min).

Tourist information 16 rue du 14 Juillet (May, June & Sept Mon–Sat 9.30am–5.30pm; July & Aug Mon–Sat 9am–7pm, Sun 10am–5pm; Oct–April Mon–Sat 10am–5pm; ☎ 05 45 82 10 71, ⓦ tourism-cognac.com).

ACCOMMODATION AND EATING

L'Oliveraie 6 place de la Gare ☎ 05 45 82 04 15, ⓦ oliveraie-cognac.com. Though not exactly in the centre of town, this pleasant cheapie is right by the station and has simple rooms and a swimming pool. Doubles **€62**

Le St Jacques 8 rue Minotiers ☎ 05 45 32 43 07. Jolly worker's bistro with tables so close you can almost taste your neighbour's soup. Piquant, robust cooking and friendly service. Daily *menus* from €11 and the bar is open all day. Mon–Fri noon–2pm.

BORDEAUX

Though crammed with grand old buildings, **BORDEAUX** still has a surprisingly youthful feel. Café culture is in full swing here – indeed, one of the most pleasurable things about a visit to the city is sitting out on a sun-drenched terrace enjoying a glass or two of the region's fabulous wines. If you have time, and want to find out more about the justifiably world-famous wines of the region, it's definitely worth doing a wine tour (see box below).

WHAT TO SEE AND DO

The centre of Bordeaux bends around the west bank of the **Garonne** River in a crescent moon shape – and is colloquially known as *Porte de la Lune.*

Le Triangle d'Or and Quinconces

The "golden triangle", full of chic Parisian boutiques, runs between **place Gambetta**, with its eighteenth-century Porte Dijeaux, place de la Comédie with the classical 1780 **Grand Théâtre**, and place Tourny at the peak. In a breathtaking nineteenth-century colonial warehouse to the north of the vast Esplanade des Quinconces is the unmissable **CAPC musée**, 7 rue Ferrère (Tues–Sun 11am–6pm, Wed till 8pm; €4; ⓦ capc-bordeaux.fr). This is the finest contemporary art exhibition space in France, displaying pioneering national and international works with admirable use of space and lighting. The permanent collection includes Richard Long and Sol LeWitt, but the temporary installations are often the most exciting.

Sainte-Catherine, Saint Pierre and Place de la Victoire

The central pedestrian artery, **rue Ste-Catherine**, leads down from place de la Comédie to the **Musée d'Aquitaine**, 20 cours Pasteur (Tues–Sun 11am–6pm; €4; ⓦ musee-aquitaine-bordeaux.fr), which illustrates the history of the region from prehistoric times through to the 1800s. A few streets north stands the **Cathédrale St-André** (Mon 3–7.30pm, Tues–Sat 10am–noon & 2–6pm, Sun 9.30am–noon & 2–6pm, longer hours in summer), with its exquisite stained-glass windows and slender twin spires. Around the corner at 20 cours d'Albret, the **Musée des Beaux-Arts** (Mon & Wed–Sun

11

WINE TASTING IN THE BORDEAUX REGION

Along with Burgundy and Champagne, the wines of Bordeaux form the Holy Trinity of French **viticulture**. Bordeaux is mostly a red-wine region, growing high-class (and more expensive) **Cabernet Sauvignon** on the Left Bank (the countryside to the west of the Garonne River and Gironde estuary), while smaller growers make predominantly Merlot and Cabernet-Franc-based wines on the Right Bank. There are also some very good white wines, mainly from the Pessac and Graves regions to the south and southeast – largely based on **Sauvignon Blanc** and **Semillon**, that come in both dry and sweet forms. The easiest way to taste the wines is to visit the village of **St Emilion**, to the east of Bordeaux, where there are many wine shops that hold wine tastings. L'Envers du Décor, 11 rue du Clocher (☎ 05 57 74 48 31), is a good choice and has reasonable prices. The Bordeaux tourist office (see p.311) has information on château visits and wine tastings, and organizes a good variety of half- and full-day wine tours of the area.

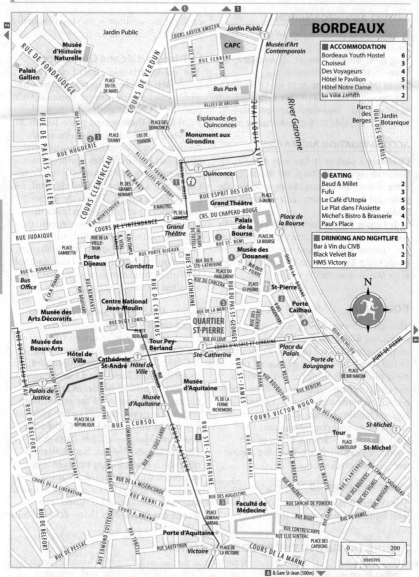

BORDEAUX

ACCOMMODATION

Bordeaux Youth Hostel	6
Choiseul	3
Des Voyageurs	4
Hôtel le Pavilion	5
Hôtel Notre Dame	1
La Villa Zénith	2

EATING

Baud & Millet	2
Fufu	3
Le Café d'Utopia	5
Le Plat dans l'Assiette	6
Michel's Bistro & Brasserie	4
Paul's Place	1

DRINKING AND NIGHTLIFE

Bar à Vin du CIVB	1
Black Velvet Bar	2
HMS Victory	3

11am–6pm; €4; ⓦmusba-bordeaux.fr) displays works by Rubens, Matisse and Renoir, as well as Lacour's evocative 1804 Bordeaux dockside scene, *Quai des Chartrons*. To the east of the centre lies the striking **place de la Bourse**, best viewed from the river's edge, reflecting in the glassy Font du Miroir, while farther south you'll find the student-friendly **place de la Victoire**, surrounded by cafés, restaurants and late-night bars.

Lacanau

Bordeaux's nearest beach, **Lacanau-Océan**, is well known for its beautiful lake and famous for its world-class **surfing**. If you fancy catching some waves, take bus #702 from opposite gare St Jean (6 daily;

1hr 50min; €2.60 one-way). You can rent boards and learn to surf at Lacanau Surf Club (☎05 56 26 38 84, ⱳsurflacanau .com), located on the corner of boulevard Plage and boulevard Liberty.

ARRIVAL AND DEPARTURE

By plane Bordeaux Mérignac airport, 12km west, is connected by regular shuttle bus (every 30min; €7.20) to Gare St Jean.

By train The station, Gare St-Jean, lies 2km southeast of central Bordeaux; bus #16 and tramline C run into town. Destinations Bayonne (3–10 daily; 1hr 40min–2hr 10min); Biarritz (6–12 daily; 2hr–2hr 45min); La Rochelle (4–6 daily; 2hr–2hr 20min); Lourdes (3–10 daily; 2hr 20min–3hr); Marseille (5 daily; 4hr); Nice (3–8 daily; 9–10hr); Paris (14–18 daily; 4hr); Périgueux (1–9 daily; 1hr–1hr 30min); Toulouse (10–17 daily; 2hr–2hr 40min).

INFORMATION

Tourist information 12 cours du 30-Juillet (May, June, Sept & Oct Mon–Sat 9am–7pm, Sun 9.30am–6.30pm; July & Aug Mon–Sat 9am–7.30pm, Sun 9.30am–6.30pm; Nov–April Mon–Sat 9am–6.30pm, Sun 9.45am–4.30pm; ☎05 56 00 66 00, ⱳbordeaux-tourisme.com). Organizes a plethora of wine and city tours. There are also branches at the train station and at the airport.

GETTING AROUND

By tram/bus The hubs of the comprehensive transport networks are place Gambetta for buses and Esplanade des Quinconces for trams. Buy tickets (€1.50) at the machines on the platforms before boarding and validate them on board.

By bike Bike rental from Liberty Cycles, 104 cours d'Yser (€10/day; book in advance; ☎05 56 92 77 18). There's also VCub, a city bicycle scheme with 31 stations across the city (first 30min free, €2/hr thereafter).

ACCOMMODATION

Bordeaux Youth Hostel 22 cours Barbey ☎05 56 33 00 70, ⱳauberge-jeunesse-bordeaux.com. A decent private hostel with a warm, relaxed vibe. A 15min walk from the centre by foot and a stone's throw from the station. Kitchen and laundry facilities available, and breakfast is included. Dorms €24

Choiseul 13 rue Huguerie ☎05 56 52 71 24, ⱳhotelchoiseul.com. Conveniently close to place Gambatta, this friendly hotel is great value. Check your room first as some are slightly cell-like. Every room has a private shower, but some share toilets. Doubles €58

Des Voyageurs 3bis av Thiers ☎05 56 86 18 00, ⱳhoteldesvoyageurs.net. This small two-star hotel is a short, picturesque walk from the centre across the Pont de

Pierre, and offers some of the nicest rooms in this price range. It has helpful staff and clean, well-furnished rooms. Doubles €75

★ **Hôtel le Pavillon** 6 rue Honoré Tessier ☎05 56 91 75 35, ⱳhotelpavillon.com. An absolute gem tucked away in the heart of town. Three tastefully furnished rooms with original art (the owner is a collector) and antiques. No en-suite bathrooms, but rooms have sinks. Doubles €40

Hôtel Notre Dame 36–38 rue Notre Dame ☎05 56 52 88 24, ⱳhotelnotredame33.fr. Just 10min from the Esplanade des Quinconces in Bordeaux's elegant antiques quarter, with small but pleasant rooms, all en suite. Doubles €59

La Villa Zénith 16 av Adjudant Guittard, Lacanau ☎06 84 60 88 08, ⱳlacanau-zenith.com. Out in Lacanau, but just 200m from the beach, with comfy dorms and rooms, a garden, cooking facilities and equipment lockers. Dorms €26, doubles €70

EATING

Baud & Millet 19 rue Huguerie. Enjoy a leisurely glass of wine (from €4) and a huge bowl of fondue to share (€18) at this fantastic wine shop where the friendly Monsieur Baud speaks excellent English. Mon–Sat 11am–11pm.

Fufu 37 rue St-Remi. A well-loved Japanese noodle bar in the heart of town; eat at the long bar, watching the chefs fry your noodles, or take away a hot box of ramen (from €8) and perch on a bench next to the Garonne, a few minutes' walk away. Tues–Sat noon–3pm & 7–11pm.

Le Café d'Utopia 5 place Camille Jullian. A lively, casual place in a beautiful old building that houses the Utopia arthouse cinema. Try one of their huge sandwiches (from €5.50) or delicious gourmet salads (from €8). May–Sept daily noon–10.30pm; Oct–April Mon–Fri noon–3pm & 7–10.30pm, Sat & Sun noon–10.30pm.

Le Plat dans l'Assiette 8 rue Ausone ☎05 56 01 05 01. One whole menu on a plate – that's the hook here – but it's no haute cuisine gimmick; the cheapest of the *assiettes* – the *Impression fromage levant* at €16.50 – still crams in roast camembert, gouda with cumin and speck, among relatively healthy stuff. Tues–Sat 7.30–10pm.

Michel's Bistro & Brasserie 15 rue du Pas-Saint Georges. A charming corner bistro with a sunny terrace, *Michel's* makes a great stop, with excellent mains from just €11, such as *boudin noir* with apples, and a number of beautifully presented (and delicious) desserts. Mon–Sat 8am–midnight, Sun 4–10pm.

Paul's Place 76 rue Notre Dame. Paul graciously welcomes you into his place, a delightful treasure-trove of old books, paintings and curios, while his son Jack prepares the good-value menu (€12.50). Host to regular film nights, poetry readings and gigs; glass of wine €2.80, beer €3.20. Tues noon–2.30pm, Wed–Fri noon–2.30pm & 6pm–midnight, Sat noon–2.30pm & 4.30pm–midnight.

11

DRINKING AND NIGHTLIFE

Bar à Vin du CIVB 1 cours du 30 Juillet. As promoters for Bordeaux wine growers and home to a wine-tasting school, the bar here is a good place to sample the region's excellent wines (from €2.50). Mon–Sat 11am–10pm.

Black Velvet Bar 9 rue du Chai des Farines ☎ 09 51 34 28 73. The atmospheric arches host regular concerts and open mic nights every Sunday — doubly intoxicating when combined with the happy hour (6–8pm). Mon–Sat 6pm–2am, Sun 6pm–midnight.

HMS Victory 3 Place Général Sarrail ☎ 05 56 92 78 47. Expect a packed dancefloor and merrymaking spilling onto the terrace at this lively student pub where you're welcome to bring your own food. Beer from €3. Happy hours: Mon–Fri 3–8pm, Sat & Sun 5–7pm. Live music Fri & Sat. Mon–Fri 3pm–2am, Sat 1.30pm–2am, Sun 2pm–midnight.

DIRECTORY

Consulates UK, 353 bd du Président-Wilson ☎ 05 57 22 21 10; USA, 10 place de la Bourse ☎ 05 56 48 63 80.

Health Centre Hospitalier Pellegrin-Tripode, place Amélie-Raba-Léon (☎ 05 56 79 56 79), to the west of central Bordeaux.

Police Commissariat Central, 23 rue François-de-Sourdis (☎ 05 57 85 77 77 or ☎ 17 in emergencies).

PÉRIGUEUX

The bustling market town of **PÉRIGUEUX**, with its beautiful Renaissance and medieval centre, makes a fine base for visiting the **Dordogne**'s prehistoric caves.

WHAT TO SEE AND DO

Place de la Clautre sits at the heart of the medieval old town, presided over by the striking **Cathédrale St-Front** (daily: April–June, Sept & Oct 8.30am–7pm; July & Aug 9am–8pm; Nov–March 8.30am–6pm) – its square, pineapple-capped belfry surging above the roofs of the surrounding medieval houses. During a nineteenth-century restoration, the architect Paul Abadie added five Byzantine domes to the roof, which served as a prototype for his more famous Sacré Cœur in Paris (see p.288). If you head north along rue St-Front, you'll reach the **Musée d'Art et d'Archéologie du Périgord**, at 22 cours Tourny (April–Sept Mon & Wed–Fri 10.30am–5.30pm, Sat & Sun 1–6pm; Oct–March Mon & Wed–Fri 10am–5pm, Sat & Sun 1–6pm;

€5.50; ⊛ perigueux-maap.fr), which boasts some beautiful Gallo-Roman mosaics found locally.

ARRIVAL AND INFORMATION

By train The station is a 15min walk from the cathedral. Destinations Bordeaux (9–15 daily; 1hr 15min–1hr 30min); Les Eyzies (4–8 daily; 35min).

Tourist information 6 place Francheville (mid-June to mid-Sept Mon–Sat 9am–7pm, Sun 10am–6pm; mid-Sept to mid-June daily 9am–12.30pm & 2–6pm; ☎ 05 53 53 10 63, ⊛ tourisme-perigueux.fr). It has a factsheet detailing how to get to the caves and back in a day (see opposite).

ACCOMMODATION

Camping Barnabé 80 rue des Bains ☎ 05 53 53 41 45, ⊛ barnabe-perigord.com. This peaceful campsite enjoys an excellent position on the banks of the River Isle. Plots are shady, and there's a bar, ping-pong and mini-golf on site. To get there cross pont des Barris and follow the south riverbank for 20min. April–Oct. Per person €4.80, plus per tent €4

★ **Des Barris** 2 rue Pierre Magne ☎ 05 53 53 04 05, ⊛ hoteldesbarris.com. A lovely little eighteenth-century hotel with twelve simple but attractive wood-furnished rooms. All are en suite and the best have views across the river to the cathedral. Doubles €55

Ibis 8 bd Georges Saumande ☎ 05 53 53 64 68, ⊛ ibis .com. The only hotel in the city where all the rooms boast either a river or – even better – a cathedral view, which makes up for their otherwise bare functionality. The lobby is deceptively grand, but staff are helpful. Book online for the best rates. Doubles €59

EATING AND DRINKING

Café Louise 10 place de l'Ancien Hôtel de Ville ☎ 05 53 08 93 85. This intimate *maison gourmande* is very popular for its blend of Italian and French flavours. *Menus* start from €14.50 and might include dishes like ravioli of foie gras. In fine weather you can sit out on the lovely *place*. Wed–Sun noon–midnight.

Le Saint Louis 26bis rue Eguillerie ☎ 05 53 53 53 90. An unpretentious bar-brasserie on one of the city's loveliest squares. Sit out under the umbrellas on the cobblestones, or inside the surprisingly smart interior. *Menus* start from €20 in the evenings, including dishes like scallops in a creamy pepper sauce. Mon–Sat 10am–11pm.

Les Toqués 38 rue Pierre Semard. An Irish pub/gig venue with over 160 bottled beers and seven on tap. The place accelerates from quiet evening drinks to no-holds-barred rowdiness at the drop of a hat. Mon–Wed 10am–2pm, Thurs 10am–2pm & 6–10pm, Fri 10am–2pm & 6pm–2am.

11

VÉZÈRE VALLEY CAVES

This lavish cliff-cut region, riddled with **caves** and subterranean streams, is half an hour or so by train from Périgueux. Cro-Magnon skeletons were unearthed here in 1868, and since then an incredible wealth of archeological evidence about the life of late Stone Age people has been found. The paintings that adorn the caves are remarkable not only for their age, but also for their exquisite colouring and the skill with which they were drawn.

WHAT TO SEE AND DO

The centre of the region is **LES EYZIES**, a rambling, somewhat unattractive village dominated by tourism. Worth a glance before or after visiting the caves is the **Musée National de la Préhistoire** (July & Aug daily 9.30am–6.30pm; June & Sept Mon & Wed–Sun 9.30am–6pm; Oct–May Mon & Wed–Sun 9.30am–12.30pm & 2–5.30pm; €6; ⓦmusee-prehistoire-eyzies.fr).

Font de Gaume caves

Just outside Les Eyzies, off the road to Sarlat, the **Grotte de Font-de-Gaume** (Mon–Fri & Sun: mid-May to mid-Sept 9.30am–5.30pm; mid-Sept to mid-May 9.30am–12.30pm & 2–5.30pm; €7.50; ⓣ05 53 06 86 00, ⓦsites-les-eyzies.fr) contains dozens of polychrome paintings, the colour remarkably preserved by a protective layer of calcite. The tours last 45 minutes, but only 80 people are admitted each day with a maximum of twelve people per group, so to be sure of a place you should reserve in advance by phone or arrive before 9.30am.

The Cap Blanc frieze

The **Abri du Cap Blanc** (Mon–Fri & Sun: mid-May to mid-Sept 10am–6pm; mid-Sept to mid-May 10am–12.30pm & 2–5.30pm; €7.50; ⓣ05 53 06 86 00, ⓦsites-les-eyzies.fr) is a steep 7km bike ride from Les Eyzies. This is not a cave but a rock shelter, containing a 15,000-year-old frieze of horses and bison; of only ten surviving prehistoric sculptures in France, this is undoubtedly the best.

Grotte des Combarelles

Three kilometres from Les Eyzies is the **Grotte des Combarelles** (Mon–Fri & Sun: mid-May to mid-Sept 9.30am–5.30pm; mid-Sept to mid-May 9.30am–12.30pm & 2–5.30pm; €7.50; ⓦsites-les-eyzies.fr), whose engravings of humans, reindeer and mammoths from the Magdalanian period (about 12,000 years ago) are the oldest in the region.

Lascaux

Up the valley of the Vézère River to the northeast, **Montignac** is more attractive than Les Eyzies. Its prime interest is the cave paintings at nearby **Lascaux** – or, rather, the tantalizing replica at Lascaux IV (due to open late 2016; for up-to-date information, visit ⓦprojet-lascaux .com, or speak to the tourist office in Montignac). Produced 17,000 years ago, the paintings are considered the finest prehistoric works in existence; the original has been closed since 1963 due to deterioration caused by the breath and body heat of visitors. The new replica experience aims to create the feeling of being inside the original cave, at a safe distance from Lascaux itself.

ARRIVAL

Les Eyzies The train station is a short walk northwest of town, and is served by trains from Périgueux (5–7 daily; 30–40min).

Montignac Buses run from place Tourny to Périgueux, but you'll need to reserve in advance (ⓣ05 53 59 01 48).

INFORMATION

Les Eyzies On the main street (Jan–March, Nov & Dec Mon–Fri 10am–12.30pm & 2–5pm; April & Oct Mon–Sat 9.30am–12.30pm & 2–6pm; May, June & Sept Mon–Sat 9.30am–12.30pm & 2–6pm, Sun 9.30am–12.30pm; July & Aug daily 9am–6.30pm; ⓣ05 53 06 97 05, ⓦlascaux -dordogne.com).

Montignac place Bertran-de-Born (July & Aug daily 9am–6.30pm; Sept–June Mon–Fri/Sat 9.30/10–12.30pm & 2–5/6pm; ⓣ05 53 51 82 60, ⓦlascaux-dordogne.com).

ACCOMMODATION

Des Falaises av de la Préhistoire, Les Eyzies ⓣ05 53 06 97 35, ⓔhotel-d-falaises@wanadoo.fr. At the quieter end of the main drag, this is the cheapest option in Les Eyzies. Rooms are fairly plain, but enlivened with colourful bed covers, and all are en suite. Doubles **€45**

11

Le Moulin du Bleufond av Aristide Briand, Montignac ☎ 05 53 51 83 95, ⓦ bleufond.com. On the riverbank 500m downstream from the centre of Montignac, this is a well-tended and very popular three-star campsite, with a great pool. Two people and a tent €25.30

BIARRITZ

A former Viking whaling settlement, **BIARRITZ** became famous in the nineteenth century when Empress Eugénie came here with the last French Emperor, Napoleon III. He built her a seaside palace in 1855, and an impressive list of kings, queens and tsars followed, bringing *belle époque* and Art Deco grandeur to the resort. Today Biarritz is the undisputed surf capital of Europe, hosting the prestigious week-long Surf Festival in July, which includes a longboard competition and nightly parties on the Côte des Basques beach. Despite its surf cachet, the town feels as though its glory days are well past, and it's actually a rather traditional (and tacky) seaside resort that can't compete with the Côte d'Azur.

WHAT TO SEE AND DO

The town's beaches are the main attraction. The best surfing is on the long competition beach, **plage de la Côte des Basques**, to the south – those less interested in surfing should try the intimate **Port-Vieux** beach for a calmer swim. A free beach shuttle, the Océane bus (Ligne 10), connects all the major beaches from Anglet to Ilbarritz in high season, departing from Biarritz Gare or outside the municipal casino on 1 boulevard du Général de Gaulle (July & Aug daily every 12min; ⓦ anglet -tourisme.com).

The **Biarritz Aquarium**, plateau Atalaye (April–June, Sept & Oct daily 9.30am– 8pm; July & Aug daily 9.30am–midnight; Nov–March Tues–Sun 9.30am–7pm; €14.50; ⓦ museedelamer.com), has one of Europe's best aquarium collections, including hammerhead sharks, turtles and seals. **Asiatica**, at 1 rue Guy Petit (Mon–Fri 2–6.30pm, Sat & Sun 2–7pm; €10; ⓦ museeasiatica.com), uphill and left off avenue Foch, houses an impressive collection of oriental art, including medieval jades and religious icons.

ARRIVAL AND DEPARTURE

By plane Biarritz airport is 4km inland from the town centre. Bus #14 (€1) heads into Biarritz.
By train The station is 4km southeast of the centre in La Négresse. Bus #A1 and #10 run between the station and the town centre.
Destinations Bayonne (14 daily; 15–30min); Bordeaux (hourly; 2hr 15min).
By bus Buses to Bayonne (#A1 & #A2) can be picked up from avenues Edouard VII and Louis Barthou respectively, beside the tourist office.

INFORMATION

Tourist information Square d'Ixelles (April–June & Sept to mid-Oct Mon–Fri 9am–6pm, Sat & Sun 10am–5pm; July & Aug daily 9am–7pm; mid-Oct to March Mon–Fri 10am–noon & 2–5pm, Sat & Sun 10am–1pm; ☎ 05 59 22 37 00, ⓦ tourisme.biarritz.fr).

GETTING AROUND

By bus Local operator Chronoplus have an information kiosk (☎ 05 59 24 26 53, ⓦ www.chronoplus.eu) near the main bus hub. Two free shuttle services operate from Square d'Ixelle (Mon–Sat 7.30am–7.30pm) – one for the town centre (every 10min) and another for the suburb of Saint-Charles (every 20min).
By bike and scooter Solibo, 24 rue Peyroloubilh (☎ 05 59 24 94 47), rents bikes and scooters; ID and credit card required (€20/day).

ACCOMMODATION

Biarritz Camping 28 rue Harcet ☎ 05 59 23 00 12, ⓦ biarritz-camping.fr. This reasonably basic campsite 3km south of town is the nearest to Biarritz, with a small pool and shop; the beach is a 10min walk. Early April to Sept. Two people plus tent €36
FUAJ Biarritz 8 rue Chiquito de Cambo ☎ 05 59 41 76 00, ⓦ fuaj.org; bus #9, #A1, or route B bus on Sun to "Bois de Boulogne". Just 1.5km from the beach and close to the station and the lake, this fantastic hostel has two- to four-bed dorms, rents out bicycles and has some good deals on surf lessons. Dorms €28.70
La Marine 1 rue des Goélands ☎ 05 59 24 34 09, ⓦ hotel -lamarine-biarritz.com. The best-value budget option in town offers a warm reception and has an ideal location near the old port. All rooms are en suite but can get a bit noisy thanks to the brasserie downstairs. Doubles €60
★ **Surf Hostel Biarritz** 27 av de Migron ☎ 06 63 34 27 45, ⓦ surfhostelbiarritz.com. The hippest hostel on the west coast, with bikes, boards and a hearty breakfast all included in the price. It is a bit out of the way; however, hostel shuttle buses run to and from the surf as well as the train station and airport. Booking essential. April–Oct. Dorms €40

11

EATING AND DRINKING

★**Bar Jean** 5 rue des Halles ☎ 05 59 24 80 38. Noisy and intimate, and with a lengthy list of fine Riojas, this local tapas favourite is the perfect place to pass any evening. Tapas around €3.50, paella €20. Very popular so worth booking ahead. Daily 9am–3pm & 6.30pm–1.30am; Oct–May closed Tues & Wed; closed Jan.

Crampotte 30 Port des Pêcheurs ☎ 05 35 46 91 22. An ideal place for an aperitif in the early evening, overlooking the pretty Petit Port. Try the plates of Basque ham and cheese (to share €8.90) with a glass of Basque *cidre* (€3.50). Wed–Sun 11am–11pm.

Le Surfing plage de Côte des Basques, 9 bd Prince de Galles. A sea-view shrine to the sport positioned near the water's edge, serving an interesting array of fish, meat and veggie dishes, from fish and chips to *mee goring* and risotto, with mains starting from €11. Wed–Sun 9am–2.30pm & 7.30–10.30pm.

Les Halles place Sobradiel. This recently restored *halles* is a fantastic spot to savour fresh, inexpensive seafood and local delicacies. Try fresh oysters and a glass of wine at *L'Ecaillerie*, a simple seafood stand that supplies most restaurants in town, yet whose €5-or-less dishes don't reflect restaurant prices. Daily 7am–1.30pm.

Miremont Patissier place Clémenceau. Established in 1872, this opulent boutique-cum-tearoom-cum-restaurant serves up devastatingly pretty cakes (from €2.50); the restaurant at the back has nice sea views. Daily 9am–8pm.

BAYONNE

Capital of the French Basque country and home of the bayonet, **BAYONNE** lies 6km inland at the junction of the Nive and Adour rivers. Having escaped the worst effects of mass tourism, it remains a cheerful and pretty town, with the shutters on the older half-timbered houses painted in the distinctive Basque tones of green and rust-red.

WHAT TO SEE AND DO

The town's two medieval quarters line the banks of the Nive, whose quays are home to many bars and restaurants. Grand Bayonne on the west bank is the administrative and commercial centre, while Petit Bayonne, to the east, has a more bohemian feel and is full of places to eat and drink. Chocolate-making techniques were brought to Bayonne by Jewish chocolatiers fleeing the Spanish Inquisition. It was here that a devilish brew, hot chocolate, was introduced to the country, much to the distaste of the Catholic Church due to its aphrodisiac qualities – the best place in town to try it is *Cazenave* (see p.316).

Petit Bayonne

On quai des Corsaires, along the Nive's east bank, stands the **Musée Basque** (April–June & Sept Tues–Sun 10am–6.30pm; July & Aug daily 10am–6.30pm, Thurs till 8.30pm; Oct–March Tues–Sun 10.30am–6pm; €6.50; ⓦmusee-basque.com), which provides a comprehensive overview of modern Basque culture.

Grand Bayonne

The **Cathédrale Ste-Marie** (daily 9am–12.30pm & 2–5pm), across the Nive, looks best from a distance, its twin spires rising with airy grace above the houses; the **cloister** rewards a visit with a good view of the stained glass and buttresses.

ARRIVAL AND DEPARTURE

By train and bus The train station is just off place de la République on the north bank of the Adour. Buses from Biarritz also arrive here.

Destinations Biarritz (every 30min; 10min); Bordeaux (hourly; 2hr); Hendaye (for the Spanish border; every 30min; 40min); Lourdes (4–6 daily; 1hr 40min; Paris (14–16 daily, some indirect; 4hr 45min–6hr); St Sébastien (from Hendaye; every 30min; 45min); Toulouse (3 daily; 3hr 30min).

INFORMATION

Tourist information 25 place des Basques (July & Aug Mon–Sat 9am–7pm, Sun 10am–1pm; Sept–June Mon–Fri 9am–6.30pm, Sat 10am–6pm; ☎ 08 20 42 64 64, ⓦbayonne-tourisme.com). It has an excellent scheme that lends bikes for free.

ACCOMMODATION

Hôtel des Arceaux 26 rue Port-Neuf ☎ 05 59 59 15 53. Many rooms don't have exterior windows, which can prove stuffy on hot days, but the hotel nevertheless has a pleasantly quirky character, with an agreeable mishmash of antique and faux-antique furniture. Doubles **€70**

Hôtel le Port Neuf 44 rue Port-Neuf ☎ 05 59 25 65 83. Excellently located within the picturesque old town and a 10min walk from the station. The rooms are stylishly furnished with en-suite bathrooms. Doubles **€60**

11

Monte Carlo 1 rue Sainte Ursule ☎ 05 59 55 02 68. Basic and charmless rooms, albeit with a handy location opposite the station. The restaurant and bar below may prove noisy at night. Doubles **€40**

EATING AND DRINKING

★ **Auberge du Petit Bayonne** 23 rue des Cordeliers ☎ 05 59 59 83 44. The welcome is warm and the food hearty at this husband-and-wife-run place. Be sure to try the roasted suckling lamb (*agneau de lait*) if it's available. *Menus* €11–19.50. Mon & Thurs–Sat noon–2.30pm & 7.30–10pm, Tues & Sun noon–2pm.

Chocolat Cazenave 19 Arceaux du Pont-Neuf. The pick of Bayonne's chocolatiers; try the famous *chocolat mousseux* – delicious, hand-whipped hot chocolate served with chantilly cream (€5.50) – with a serving of their hot, buttered toast (€3). Tues–Sat 9.15am–noon & 2–7pm.

La Karafe 25 quai Jaureguiberry. This cheap and lively wine bar is the place to go for *pintxos* (tapas), which might include local sheep cheese, *magret de canard* or chorizo (from €3), with glasses of wine starting from €2.50. Mon–Thurs 6pm–late, Fri & Sat noon–2.30pm & 6pm–late.

LOURDES

In 1858 Bernadette Soubirous, the 14-year-old daughter of a poor local miller in **LOURDES**, had eighteen visions of the Virgin Mary in a spot called the Grotte de Massabielle. Miraculous cures at the grotto soon followed and Lourdes grew exponentially; it now sees six million Catholic pilgrims a year and whole streets are devoted to the sale of religious kitsch. At the **grotto** itself – a moisture-blackened overhang by the riverside with a statue of the Virgin inside – long queues of the faithful process

HIKING IN THE PYRENEES

From either Gavarnie or Barèges, a few hours on the Pyrenees-spanning **hiking trail**, GR10, or the harder HRP (Haute Randonnée Pyrénéenne), brings you to staffed alpine refuges (rough camping is not generally allowed in the park). In summer, serious and properly equipped hikers may wish to continue on the trails, which are well served with refuges, though the weather and terrain make them highly dangerous in winter. The Lourdes and Bayonne tourist offices have information, or check ⓦ lespyrenees.net.

through. Above looms the first, neo-Gothic church built here, in 1871; nearby the massive subterranean **basilica** has a capacity of twenty thousand.

ARRIVAL AND INFORMATION

By train Lourdes train station is on the northeastern edge of town.

Destinations Bayonne (6 daily; 1hr 40min); Biarritz (frequent; 2hr 20min–4hr 10min); Toulouse (frequent; 2–3hr).

By bus The *gare routière* is located in the central place Capdevieille. There are two public transport networks, Ma Ligne and TER Midi-Pyrenees.

Destinations Barèges (7 daily; 1hr 17min); Gavarnie (June–Sept 1 daily; 1hr 40min).

Tourist information place Peyramale (Jan to mid-March, Nov & Dec Mon–Sat 9am–noon & 2–5.30pm; mid-March to May & Oct Mon–Sat 9am–12.30pm & 1.30–6.30pm, Sun 10am–12.30pm; June & Sept Mon–Sat 9am–6.30pm, Sun 10am–12.30pm; July & Aug Mon–Sat 9am–7pm, Sun 10am–6pm; ☎ 05 62 42 77 40, ⓦ lourdes -infotourisme.com).

ACCOMMODATION

Hotel Croix des Nordistes 29 bd de la Grotte ☎ 05 62 94 28 57, ⓦ hotelcroixdesnordistes-lourdes.com. There's an abundance of inexpensive hotels in Lourdes, including this simple place. Doubles **€42**

Plein Soleil 11 av du Monge ☎ 05 62 94 40 93, ⓦ camping -pleinsoleil.com. A well-equipped campsite with swimming pool, on-site bar and spotless facilities within close proximity of Lourdes. Camping for two people and tent **€24**

GAVARNIE AND BARÈGES

From Lourdes train station, several SNCF buses run daily to **Gavarnie** and **Barèges**, two resorts near the heart of the Parc National des Pyrénées Occidentales. Gavarnie is smaller and pricier than Barèges, but has an incomparable natural amphitheatre towering above, forming the border with Spain. From these two bases, you can embark on hikes in the park (see box above).

ACCOMMODATION

Camping La Bergerie Chemin du Cirque, Gavarnie ☎ 05 62 92 48 41, ⓦ camping-gavarnie-labergerie.com. A lovely campsite with basic facilities and a small on-site bar. The pitches are discreetly located in terraces to preserve the beauty of the surrounding landscape. June–Sept. Per person **€3.90**, plus per tent **€3.40**

Gîte L'Oasis 2 Pass Toys, Barèges ☎05 62 92 69 47, ⓦgite-oasis.com. A comfortable family-run gîte. Rooms are en suite, cosily furnished, and some have mountain views with balconies. Breakfast included with dorms; doubles are half-board. Dorms €25, doubles €92

La Ribère Route de Labatsus, Barèges ☎05 62 92 69 01, ⓦlaribere.com. One of the highest campsites in the French Pyrenees, offering stunning mountain views. Over 50 terrace-based pitches, with good, clean facilities. Camping for two people and tent €16

TOULOUSE

TOULOUSE is one of the most vibrant provincial cities in France, thanks to its sizeable student population – second only to that of Paris. The city has long been a centre for aviation – St-Exupéry and Mermoz flew out from here on their pioneering flights over Africa in the 1920s – and has more recently been developed as the country's centre of high-tech industry.

WHAT TO SEE AND DO

The centre of Toulouse is a rough hexagon clamped around a bend in the wide, brown Garonne River.

Place du Capitole and the old city

The **place du Capitole** is the site of Toulouse's town hall and a prime meeting place, with numerous cafés and a mammoth Wednesday market. South of the square, and east of rue Alsace-Lorraine, lies the **old town**. The predominant building material is the flat Toulousain brick, whose cheerful rosy colour gives the city its nickname of *ville rose*. Best known of these buildings is the Hôtel d'Assézat, west towards the river end of rue de Metz, which houses the marvellous private art collection of **Fondation Bemberg** (Tues–Sun 10am–12.30pm & 1.30–6pm, Thurs till 9pm; €8; ⓦfondation-bemberg.fr), including excellent works by Bonnard.

St-Sernin

Rue du Taur leads northwards from place du Capitole to place St-Sernin and the largest Romanesque church in France, **Basilique de St-Sernin** (daily 8.30am–6pm). Dating back to 1080, it was built to accommodate passing hordes of Santiago pilgrims and is one of the loveliest examples of its kind.

Les Jacobins

West of place du Capitole, on rue Lakanal, the church of **Les Jacobins** (Tues–Sun 9am–7pm) is another impressive ecclesiastical building. This is a huge fortress-like rectangle of unadorned brick, with an interior divided by a central row of slender pillars from whose capitals springs a colourful splay of vaulting ribs.

Across the Garonne

Across the Pont-Neuf on the west bank of the Garonne stands the brick tower of the inspirational **Chateaux d'Eau** (Tues–Sun 1–7pm; €3.50; ⓦgalerie chateaudeau.org), the first public gallery dedicated to photography in France and holding over four thousand pieces, along with antique equipment. Continue west from the river, then north up Allées de Fitte to the vaulted nineteenth-century slaughterhouse, **Les Abattoirs** (Wed–Sun noon–6pm; €7), whose comprehensive modern and contemporary art collections include a striking 8m-high Picasso theatre screen.

Aeroscopia

The city's major new aerospace museum, **Aeroscopia** (daily 9.30am–6pm; €11.50), is located right next to the airport (see below) and celebrates the city's close links with air travel. There are all sorts of sleek flying machines on display, from huge commercial Airbuses to supersonic military planes, alongside fascinating behind-the-scenes information about how these remarkable craft are made and then handled in mid-air.

ARRIVAL AND DEPARTURE

By plane Aéroport Toulouse-Blagnac (ⓦtoulouse.aeroport .fr) is 5km northwest of the town centre; shuttle buses connect to Gare Matabiau (every 20min, 5.30am–12.15am; 20min; €8). Alternatively, take the T2 tram (every 15min; €1.60) from the airport to Palais du Justice.

By bus and train Trains arrive into Gare Matabiau, buses into the *gare routière*, just to the right of the former on bd Pierre Semard, a 15min walk from the city centre down

11

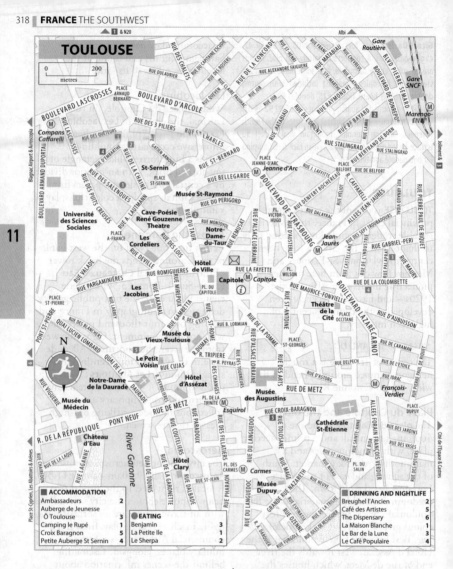

TOULOUSE

0   200
metres

■ **ACCOMMODATION**
Ambassadeurs	2
Auberge de Jeunesse	
Ô Toulouse	3
Camping le Rupé	1
Croix Baragnon	5
Petite Auberge St Sernin	4

● **EATING**
Benjamin	3
La Petite Ile	1
Le Sherpa	2

■ **DRINKING AND NIGHTLIFE**
Breughel l'Ancien	2
Café des Artistes	5
The Dispensary	6
La Maison Blanche	1
Le Bar de la Lune	3
Le Café Populaire	4

allées Jean-Jaurès. For details on buses to Andorra, see
ⓦ andorrabybus.com.

Destinations (train) Barcelona (3 daily, via Narbonne; 4hr
50min–5hr 45min); Bayonne (18–22 daily; 2hr 30min–3hr
45min); Bordeaux (18–22 daily; 2hr 30min); Carcassonne
(18 daily; 45min–1hr 15min); Lourdes (8–16 daily; 1hr
40min); Lyon (14–18 daily; 4–6hr); Marseille (22 daily; 3hr
30min–6hr); Paris (13 daily; 5hr 20min–6hr 45min).
Destinations (bus) Andorra (2 daily; 3hr 30min);
Carcassonne (1 daily; 2hr 20min).

INFORMATION AND GETTING AROUND

Tourist information Square Charles de Gaulle, by
Capitole *métro* station (June–Sept Mon–Sat 9am–7pm,
Sun 10.30am–5.15pm; Oct–May Mon–Fri 9am–6pm,
Sat 9am–12.30pm & 2–6pm, Sun 10am–12.30pm &
2–5pm; ☏08 92 18 01 80, ⓦ www.toulouse-tourisme
.com).

By bike VéloToulouse bike stands can be found
throughout the city – credit card guarantee required (first
30min free, around €2/hr thereafter).

ACCOMMODATION

Ambassadeurs 68 rue Bayard ☎ 05 61 62 65 84, ⓦ hotel-des-ambassadeurs.com. This friendly, family-run hotel offers spacious, good-value rooms, all en suite. Its location can't be beaten, a mere 5min walk from the station and 15min from the centre. Doubles **€54**

Auberge de Jeunesse Ô Toulouse 2 av Yves Brunaud ☎ 05 34 30 42 80, ⓦ otoulouse.org. Though not very central, this hostel is only 1km from the station and offers simple but clean dorm rooms. Dorms **€19**

Camping le Rupé 21 chemin du Pont de Rupé ☎ 05 61 70 07 35, ⓦ camping-toulouse.com; bus #59 to Rupé. The closest campsite, just north of the city in a leafy park, with waterskiing and fishing spots nearby. Two people and tent **€21.20**

Croix Baragnon 17 rue Croix-Baragnon ☎ 05 61 52 60 10, ⓦ hotelcroixbaragnon.com. Surprisingly airy rooms in this rarest of things, a central budget hotel. Be prepared to climb some stairs as there's no lift available. Doubles **€68**

Petite Auberge St Sernin 17 rue d'Embarthe ☎ 07 60 88 17 17, ⓦ lapetiteaubergedesaintsernin.com. A fantastic and friendly hostel in a buzzing part of town. Four-, six- and eight-bed dorms, some of which overlook a public park, with kitchenette and en-suite bathrooms. No arrival after 10.30pm. Dorms **€22**

EATING

Benjamin 7 rue des Gestes ☎ 05 61 22 92 66. A long-standing favourite for economical *terroir* food; service is pleasant and professional, although the atmosphere is somewhat anonymous. There's a wide selection of duck-based lunch and dinner *menus* from €17–23. Daily noon–2.30pm & 7.30–11pm.

La Petite Ile 30 rue des Salenques ☎ 05 61 21 54 31. A restaurant *reunaionnais* popular for its excellent-value Creole-inspired cuisine. The *plat du jour* consists of three changing dishes – a *rougail* (typical Creole dish using spices and tomatoes), a curry and a masala – and, at €7.50, is a bargain given the huge portions. Mon–Wed & Fri noon–3pm, Thurs noon–3pm & 6.30–10.30pm.

Le Sherpa 46 rue du Taur ☎ 05 61 23 89 29. The extensive menu of this busy crêperie and tea place is not only cheap (from €3) but encompasses every possible combination of filling. Daily 11am–midnight.

DRINKING AND NIGHTLIFE

Breughel l'Ancien 30 rue de la Chaine. A popular student-dominated bar with over thirty different, mainly Belgian, beers (from €4) and an infectiously lively atmosphere. Crowds regularly spill onto the neighbouring Place des Tiercerettes as impromptu live music fills the air. Mon–Fri 5pm–2am, Sat 5pm–3am.

Café des Artistes 13 place de la Daurade. A table on the sun-drenched terrace overlooking the Garonne is a deservedly popular spot. Come evening, it's perfect with a

beer (€3) from their wide-ranging selection. Mon–Wed 11am–1am, Thurs–Sat 11am–2am, Sun noon–10pm.

The Dispensary 1 rue Marthe Varsi. With its rock'n'roll aesthetic, impressive cocktail menu and delicious burgers (€13), this is an excellent option. Tues & Wed 6pm–12.30am, Thurs & Fri 6pm–2am, Sat noon–3am, Sun 6pm–12.30am.

La Maison Blanche 10 rue Arnaud Bernard ⓦ www .cafe-maison-blanche.fr. Sizzling, and not just because of the crowds that flock to this happening little venue. An Association Bar (you must register to gain free admittance) committed to staging fantastic live music. By day the café serves coffee (€1) and tapas (€2); come night, the wine flows (€1.50) and the party truly begins. Mon–Fri 2.30pm–midnight, Sat 6.30pm–1am.

Le Bar de la Lune 22 rue Palaprat. Relax with one of 120 types of beer (bottles such as Duvel from €5, a *demi* of well-kept beer €2) in this friendly little bar where the volume allows for conversation. Mon–Fri 7pm–2am, Sat 8pm–3am, Sun 6pm–2am.

Le Café Populaire 9 rue de la Colombette. This long-standing drinking den boasts some of the city's best happy hour bargains – on Wednesday, for example, you can buy ten beers for just €13 – which goes some way to explaining its buzzy atmosphere. Happy hour 7.30–8.30pm. Mon–Fri 1.30pm–2am, Sat 1.30am–3am, Sun 4pm–2am.

DIRECTORY

Consulates Canada, 10 rue Jules de Resseguier (☎ 05 61 52 19 06, ✉ consulat.canada-toulouse@amb-canada.fr); USA, 25 allées Jean-Jaurès (☎ 05 34 41 36 50, ⓦ france .usembassy.gov).

Health For medical emergencies contact SAMU (☎ 115). The network of university hospitals has facilities all over the city. For non-emergencies check their website for the appropriate centre (ⓦ chu-toulouse.fr).

CARCASSONNE

The fairytale aspect of **CARCASSONNE**'s old town (la Cité) was the inspiration for the castle in Walt Disney's *Sleeping Beauty*. Viollet-le-Duc rescued it from ruin in 1844, and his rather romantic restoration has been furiously debated ever since. Unsurprisingly, it's become a real tourist trap, its narrow lanes lined with innumerable souvenir shops and regularly crammed with hordes of day-trippers.

WHAT TO SEE AND DO

The **Cité** is a 25-minute walk from the station (20min from the new town) – well worth it to get a full view of the fortress from below. There's no charge for

11

11

CYCLING THE CANAL DU MIDI

The 240km-long **Canal du Midi**, which begins in Toulouse and ends at Sète, opening on to the Mediterranean, is a UNESCO World Heritage Site and renowned for its beauty. The towpath that runs along the canal beneath the dappled light of the plane trees is a picturesque cycle route, and you can explore this stretch of the canal by cycling between Carcassonne and Trèbes or Castelnaudary. Bikes can be **rented** from Génération VTT, Canal du Midi port opposite the station in Carcassonne (April–Oct daily 9.30am–1.30pm & 2.30–6.30pm; from €10/2hr; ☎06 09 59 30 85, ⓦgeneration-vtt.com).

admission to the main part of the Cité, or the grassy *lices* (moat) between the walls. However, to see the inner fortress of the **Château Comtal** (daily: April–Sept 10am–6.30pm; Oct–March 9.30am–5pm; €8.50), with its small museum of medieval sculpture, and to walk along the walls, you have to join a guided tour. In addition to wandering the town's narrow streets (though they can be a bit of a squeeze in summer), don't miss the beautiful, thirteenth-century church of **St-Nazaire** (daily: July & Aug 9am–7pm; Sept–June 9am–6pm) at the end of rue St-Louis.

ARRIVAL AND INFORMATION

By train The station is on the northern edge of the new town, at the end of av du Maréchal Joffre, from where it's a 35min walk to the Cité (very steep for the last 5min) or catch #4 from the bus stop on bd Omer Sarraut (Mon–Sat hourly, 7am–7pm; €1).

Destinations Arles (4–8 daily; 2hr 40min–3hr 30min); Barcelona (6 daily, via Narbonne; 4hr–5hr 10min); Bordeaux (18–22 daily; 3hr 20min–4hr 30min); Marseille (12–18 daily; 3hr 20min–5hr 30min); Montpellier (18 daily; 1hr 15min–1hr 45min); Nice (6 daily, via Marseille; 4–5hr); Nîmes (26 daily; 2hr 5min–3hr 10min); Paris (11–16 daily; 3–6hr); Perpignan (13 daily; 1hr 30min–2hr 15min); Toulouse (22 daily; 45min–1hr).

Tourist information 28 rue Verdun (April–June, Sept & Oct Mon–Sat 9.30am–6pm, Sun 10am–1pm; July & Aug daily 9.30am–7pm; Nov–March Mon–Sat 9.30am–12.30pm & 1.30–6pm; ☎ 04 68 10 24 30, ⓦtourisme-carcassonne .fr). There's also an annexe (April–June & Sept daily 9am–6pm; July & Aug 9am–7pm; Oct 9.30am–5.30pm; Nov–March Tues–Sun 9.30am–1pm & 1.30–5.30pm) just inside Porte Narbonnaise, the main gate to the Cité.

ACCOMMODATION

Camping la Cité rte St-Hilaire ☎04 68 10 01 00, ⓦcampingcitecarcassonne.com. A lovely riverside location (less than 10min from the Cité) and good sporting facilities. Two people and tent **€28**

★ **FUAJ Carcassone** rue du Vicomte Trencavel ☎04 68 25 23 16, ⓦfuaj.org. A fantastic hostel in an unsurpassable position in the heart of la Cité. Dorms are comfortable, facilities are modern and clean, and breakfast is substantial. There's also table tennis, themed nights in the bar, bike rental and organized trips to the surrounding countryside. Dorms **€24.90**, doubles **€52.60**

Hotel du Pont Vieux 32 rue Trivalle ☎04 68 25 24 99, ⓦhoteldupontvieux.com. Some rooms have tired decor but the building is atmospheric nevertheless, with a lovely garden behind ivy-covered walls, and the more expensive rooms offer views of the Cité. There's a roof terrace, too, with spectacular views. Doubles **€82**

Notre Dame de l'Abbaye 103 rue Trivalle ☎04 68 25 16 65, ⓦabbaye-carcassonne.com. A tranquil option, this former abbey has spick-and-span dorms (groups only) and doubles and a beautiful garden. The cheapest rooms share bathroom facilities. Breakfast included except for campers. Doubles **€51**

EATING AND DRINKING

Auberge de Dame Carcas 3 place du Chateau ☎04 68 71 23 23. A traditional bistro offering cassoulet and other regional dishes. Menus from €16.50. Daily: July & Aug noon–2pm & 7–10pm; Sept–June noon–2pm & 7–9pm.

L'Auberge des Lices 3 rue Raymond-Roger Trencavel. Set nicely apart from the main tourist traffic in the Cité. With mains starting at €21, the cheapest menu offers great value at €19.50 and features cassoulet. Mon & Thurs–Sun noon–2pm & 6.30–9.30pm; daily in summer.

Le Ponte Vecchio 22 rue Trivalle ☎04 68 71 33 17. Combining the romance of Italy with the fine dining of France, this intimate restaurant on the way up to the Cité oozes plenty of charm. The generous €20 menu offers cassoulet and an unmissable dessert list. Mon & Thurs–Sun noon–2pm & 6.30–9.30pm, Wed 6.30–9.30pm.

Le Trivalou 69 rue Trivalle ☎04 68 71 23 11. Options may be limited but the cooking is excellent: with *menus* starting at €16 and including delights like black bream on a vegetable risotto, it's well worth heading to this restaurant just a few minutes from the Cité. Tues–Sat noon–2pm & 6.30–10pm.

MONTPELLIER

MONTPELLIER is a vibrant city, renowned for its ancient university, once attended by such luminaries as Petrarch and Rabelais. Most of the central area is pedestrianized, which lends itself to unhurried exploration and many enjoyable evenings at terrace cafés.

WHAT TO SEE AND DO

At the city's hub is place de la Comédie, a grand oval square paved with cream-coloured marble and surrounded by cafés. The Opéra, an ornate nineteenth-century theatre, presides over one end, while the other end leads onto the pleasant Champs de Mars park. Nearby, at 39 bd Bonne Nouvelle, the much-vaunted **Musée Fabre** (Tues–Sun 10am–6pm; €8; ⓦ museefabre.montpellier3m.fr) has a wide art collection stretching from the Renaissance to the modern day, housed in a number of exceptionally beautiful buildings. The tangled, hilly lanes of Montpellier's old quarter lie behind the museum, and are full of seventeenth- and eighteenth-century mansions and small museums. The **Jardin des Plantes** (Tues–Sun: June–Sept noon–8pm; Oct–May noon–6pm; free), just north of the old town, with its alleys of exotic trees, is France's oldest botanical garden, founded in 1593. Opposite the gardens lies the **university quarter**, with its beautiful old buildings and lively café life.

ARRIVAL AND DEPARTURE

By plane The airport is 8km to the southeast of Montpellier, by the beaches, connected to the city by *navettes* (shuttle buses; timed for flights; 15min; €1.60, or €2.60 including one tram connection in town).

By bus and train The train station, Gare St Roch, is next to the *gare routière*, on the southern edge of town, a short walk down rue de Maguelone from the centre.

Destinations (train) Arles (hourly; 1hr 20min); Avignon (every 20–30min; 1hr 5min–2hr); Barcelona (4 daily, 2 via Port-Bou; 4hr 20min–7hr); Carcassonne (every 20–30min; 1hr 15min); Lyon (every 20–30min; 1hr 40min–3hr 30min); Marseille (every 20–30min; 2hr 20min); Nîmes (frequent; 30min); Paris (every 20–30min; 3hr 15min–6hr); Perpignan (hourly; 2hr 15min); Toulouse (every 20–30min; 2hr 15min–2hr 55min).

INFORMATION

Tourist information At the eastern end of place de la Comédie, opposite the Polygone shopping centre (July–Sept Mon–Fri 9am–7.30pm, Sat & Sun 9.30am–6pm; Oct–June Mon–Fri 10am–6pm, Sat & Sun 10am–5pm; ☎ 04 67 60 60 60, ⓦ ot-montpellier.fr).

ACCOMMODATION

FUAJ Montpellier Rue des Écoles-Laïques ☎ 04 67 60 32 22, ⓦ fuaj.org; tram stop "Louis Blanc". While the central location lends a real party atmosphere (noise can be a problem), the interior of this handsome building is tired and awaiting refurbishment. Closed noon–3pm. Dorms **€22.50**

Le Mistral 25 rue Boussairolles ☎ 04 67 58 45 25, ⓦ hotel-le-mistral.com. Simple, pleasant rooms; the location on a quiet street within a 5min walk of Place de la Comédie makes this a solid option. Doubles **€69**

Les Étuves 24 rue des Étuves ☎ 04 67 60 78 19, ⓦ hoteldesetuves.fr. A small family-run hotel, full of *belle époque* character. The spotless, plain rooms have en-suite showers or baths. Doubles **€49**

Nova 8 rue Richelieu ☎ 04 67 60 79 85, ⓦ hotelnova.fr. Ideally situated within close proximity to the station and old town, this hotel offers clean, spacious rooms at a bargain price, but it's the friendly welcome that's hard to beat. Doubles **€43**

EATING AND DRINKING

Barberousse 6 rue Boussairolles. Wooden from top to toe, with barrels for tables, this place feels a little like a ship's hold. Given that it's a *rhumerie* with nearly eighty different kinds available, you might find the floor starts listing too. Happy hour 6–8pm. Tues–Sat 6pm–1am.

Charlie's Beer 22 rue Aristide Ollivier ☎ 04 67 58 89 86. There are more than sixty beers on tap at this venerable, grungy old Montpellier institution. Live music at weekends. Mon–Sat 5pm–1/2am.

MONTPELLIER MARKETS

"Allez-allez-allez!" is the call of Montpellier's stallholders in the many **markets** around town. Here are three of the best.

Halles Jacques-Coeur Opposite the tram on bd Antigone. Stalls sell fresh local produce and home-cooked food. Mon–Sat 7am–8.30pm, Sun 7am–1.30pm.

Halles Castellane Rue de la Loge This graceful, iron-framed market hall is the city's main market.

Mon–Sat 7am–8pm, Sun 7am–1.30pm.

Marché Paysan Across the *place* from Les Halles Jacques-Coeur. A farmers' market specializing in local produce, seafood and artisanal products. Sun 8am–1.30pm.

La Fabrik 12 rue Boussairolles. Live music (think rock, blues, jazz and Irish), Belgian beers, whiskies from around the world and the occasional indoor boules tournament at this hipster hotspot. Daily 6pm–1am.

La Tomate 6 rue Four des Flammes ☎ 04 67 60 49 38. Truly a city institution, not least because of the prices – a midday menu is just €10, while the €13.90 evening menu offers fish soup and cassoulet among its options. Tues–Sat noon–2pm & 7.30–10.30pm.

Tripti Kulai 20 rue Jacques-Coeur ☎ 04 67 66 30 51. Quirky, friendly vegetarian/vegan restaurant. Dishes, including a good choice of salads, have an oriental flair, and the lassis and home-made chai are superb. Weekday *menus* from €12. Mon–Sat noon–3pm & 6–9.30pm.

11

PERPIGNAN

This far south, climate and geography alone ensure a palpable Spanish influence, but **PERPIGNAN** is actually Spanish in origin and home to the descendants of refugees from the Spanish Civil War. It's a cheerful city, with Roussillon's red-and-yellow-striped flag atop many a building, and makes an ideal stop-off en route to Spain or Andorra.

WHAT TO SEE AND DO

The centre of Perpignan is marked by the palm trees and smart cafés of **place Arago**. From here rue d'Alsace-Lorraine and rue de la Loge lead past the massive iron gates of the classical **Hôtel de Ville** to the tiny **place de la Loge**, the focus of the old heart of the city. Just north up rue Louis-Blanc is one of the city's few remaining fortifications, the crenellated fourteenth-century gate of **Le Castillet**, now home to the **Musée de l'Histoire de la Catalogne Nord**, a fascinating museum of Roussillon's Catalan folk culture (Tues–Sun 11am–5.40pm; €2).

ARRIVAL AND INFORMATION

By train The station is at the end of av General-de-Gaulle, a 15min walk from the city centre.

Destinations Barcelona (3 daily; 2hr 30min); Carcassonne (via Narbonne; 13–16 daily; 1hr 30min–2hr); Collioure (8–12 daily; 25min); Montpellier (16–20 daily; 1hr 30min–2hr); Paris (10–16 daily; 5hr–9hr 20min); Toulouse (16 daily; 1hr 30min–2hr).

By bus The bus station is on bd Saint Assiscle, to the west of the city centre. All regional bus journeys cost €1.

Tourist information place François Arago (June–Sept Mon–Sat 9am–7pm, Sun 10am–5pm; Oct–May Mon–Sat 9am–6pm, Sun 10am–1pm; ☎ 04 68 66 30 30, ⓦ perpignantourisme.com).

ACCOMMODATION

Camping Catalan Route de Bompas ☎ 04 68 63 16 92, ⓦ camping-catalan.com. A lively campsite 5km from the centre, with a swimming pool and frequent pétanque competitions. Ask for shade as not all pitches have it. Per person and tent €17.98

FUAJ Perpignan Parc de la Pépinière ☎ 04 68 34 63 32, ⓦ fuaj.org/perpignan. Backing onto a busy road isn't ideal but noise is limited and location is convenient for the station (5min). Dorms are basic, but staff are friendly and helpful, and the breakfast is excellent. Closed 10am–5pm. Dorms €20.40, doubles €42.60

Hotel de la Loge 1 rue des Fabriques d'en Nabot ☎ 04 68 34 41 02, ⓦ hoteldelaloge.fr. A beautiful hotel dating from 1650. Rooms have original beams, traditional Catalan furniture and some look out onto the lovely inner courtyard – all in all, a bargain. Doubles €79

Hotel du Berry 6 av du Général de Gaulle ☎ 04 68 34 59 02, ⓦ hotelduberry.com. Close to the station, the rooms (all en suite) really are basic but a night's sleep doesn't come much cheaper. Doubles €40

EATING AND DRINKING

Boulangerie Chez Ben Nouzid Place Cassanyes. Savour the scent of a true boulangerie as you enter this gourmet tribute to France's colonial past. Serves a selection of French and North African breads, plus irresistibly sticky pastries for little more than €1. Daily 8am–5pm.

Crêperie Bretonne 8 rue du Maréchal Foch. You may find yourself eating on the back of an old Renault Prairie at this charming crêperie, replete as it is with a dazzling array of vintage paraphernalia. Galettes €3.30–9.30. Mon & Tues noon–2pm, Wed–Sat noon–2pm & 7–11pm, Sun 7–11pm.

La Caféitère Catalane 17 rue de l'Ange. Located in a quiet courtyard, this distinguished café is a specialist in the

---

THE CÔTE VERMEILLE

The **Vermilion Coast** (ⓦ collioure.com) is named for its richly coloured rocks, which attracted artists such as Picasso, Dalí and Matisse. The latter's 1905–06 paintings of Collioure saw the birth of Fauvism, the forerunner to Cubism. Aside from these colourful rocks, the coast is also home to some lovely beaches and charming fishing towns. Frequent daily trains run between Perpignan and Collioure (see above).

brewing of aromatic teas and coffees. Select one of their slow-roasted coffee beans from the bean-filled drawers, perfectly accompanied by a home-made pastry (drinks from €2). Mon 1.30–7pm, Tues–Sat 8am–7pm.

New Bodega 3bis rue Voltaire 🕿 04 68 35 21 87. A tapas restaurant, with severely limited seating – booking is advisable at weekends. Straightforward classic tapas: *patatas bravas, gambas plaxa calamari* and the like, with prices mostly hovering around the €5 mark, and all prepared behind the large glass screen next to the tables. Daily noon–2pm & 7–11pm.

Provence and the Côte d'Azur

Provence is held by many to be the most irresistible region in France, with attractions that range from the high mountains of the southern Alps to the wild plains of the **Camargue**. Though technically part of the neighbouring region of Languedoc, the old Roman town of **Nîmes** is a good place to start exploring, as is nearby **Arles**, most famous for Van Gogh's paintings, and a great place to indulge in the area's café culture. **Avignon**, home of a wonderful summer festival, is so crammed full of history that it can sometimes feel like a living museum. Most of the region's towns are full of cobbled streets lined with brightly coloured, shuttered buildings, which are a delight to explore, and none more so than **Aix-en-Provence**.

By contrast, **Marseille**, France's second city, still hasn't shaken off its gritty image. Yet it rewards a little exploration and is home to some of the area's finest food. It also makes a good base for exploring the stunning **Calanques**. The Côte d'Azur certainly lives up to its name – taking a train along the coast reveals sparkling turquoise sea, packed in many places with the glitzy yachts of the rich and famous. **Nice** has all the trappings of a jet-set lifestyle, yet it feels a little more down-to-earth than nearby **Cannes**, and makes a great base for exploring small villages in the hills and other seaside towns.

NÎMES

NÎMES is intrinsically linked to two things: ancient Rome – whose influence is manifest in some of the most extensive **Roman remains** in Europe – and denim, a word corrupted from *de Nîmes*. First manufactured as *serge* in the city's textile mills, denim was exported to America to clothe workers, where a certain Mr Levi Strauss made it world-famous. These days, the town has a relaxed charm, and, with an excellent hostel as well, makes for a good place to relax for a few days.

11

WHAT TO SEE AND DO

The old centre of Nîmes spreads northwards from place des Arènes, site of the magnificent first-century **Les Arènes** (daily: April, May & Sept 9am–6.30pm; June 9am–7pm; July & Aug 9am–8pm; Nov–Feb 9.30am–5pm; €10; 🖳 arenes-nimes.com), one of the best-preserved Roman arenas in the world. Turned into a fortress by the Visigoths while the Roman Empire crumbled, the arena went on to become a huge medieval slum before it was fully restored. Now, with a retractable roof, it hosts opera, an international summer jazz festival and bullfights during the high-spirited Ferías on Pentecost and the third weekend of September. Another Roman survivor can be found northeast along boulevard Victor Hugo – the **Maison Carrée** (daily: March & Oct 10am–6pm; April, May &

PONT DU GARD

This stunning vestige of a 50km **aqueduct** built in the first century AD to carry spring water from Uzès to Nîmes is a poignant memorial to the hubris of Roman civilization. It sits peacefully in the valley of the Gardon River, and is a great place to cool off on hot summer days. Tours are run from the informative museum on the left side of the valley; *navettes* run from both Nîmes (1–2 daily; 35min) and Uzès (3 daily; 7min); bring a swimsuit, walking shoes and a picnic (🖳 ot-pontdugard.com).

Sept 10am–6.30pm; June 10am–7pm; July & Aug 9.30am–8pm; Nov–Feb 10am–1pm & 2–4.30pm; €6; ⓦarenes -nimes.com), a compact temple built in 5 AD and celebrated for its harmony of proportion – the entrance price includes a 3-D film about Roman Nîmes.

ARRIVAL AND DEPARTURE

By plane The Camargue airport, shared by Nîmes and Arles, is 15km southeast of the city. A shuttle service links it to the town centre (2–4 daily; timed with flights; "Gambetta" or "Imperator" stop; €6).

By bus and train Nîmes' adjacent bus and train stations are at the end of av Feuchères, a short walk southeast from the amphitheatre. Regional buses leave from bays situated at the rear.

Destinations (train) Arles (every 20–30min; 30–40min); Avignon (every 20–30min; 30min); Carcassonne (every 20–30min; 2hr 5min–3hr 10min); Clermont-Ferrand (every 20–30min; 5–6hr); Lyon (9 daily; 1hr 20min); Marseille (every 20–30min; 40min–1hr 15min); Montpellier (every 20–30min; 30min); Nice (6 daily, via Marseille; 4–5hr); Paris 20–30 daily; 3hr–9hr 30min); Perpignan (hourly; 2hr 45min).

INFORMATION

Tourist information 6 rue Auguste, by the Maison Carrée (April–June & Sept Mon–Sat 9am–7pm, Sun 10am–6pm; July & Aug Mon–Fri 9am–7.30pm, Sat 9am–7pm, Sun 10am–6pm; Oct–March Mon–Fri 9am–6.30pm, Sat 10am–6pm, Sun 10am–5pm; ⓞ04 66 58 38 00, ⓦot-nimes.fr); buy the monument and museum pass (€11) here, which gives access to the town's attractions for three days.

ACCOMMODATION

Acanthe du Temple 1 rue Charles Babut ⓞ04 66 67 54 61, ⓦhotel-temple.com. The rooms are basic but it's the service provided by owner Eric (who speaks English) that makes this place the pleasure that it is. Doubles **€63**

Cesar 17 av Feuchéres ⓞ04 66 29 29 90, ⓦhotel-nimes .net. A fine choice, 2min from the station, and with some rooms overlooking the elegant av Feuchéres. Check your room first, as some look onto a fire escape. Doubles **€55**

★**FUAJ Nîmes** 257 chemin de l'Auberge de Jeunesse, Cigale ⓞ04 66 68 03 20, ⓦfuaj.org; bus #i (Alès or Villeverte direction) from the station to Stade; last bus at 8pm. In a beautiful hillside arboretum, 2km west of Nîmes, this friendly, well-equipped hostel offers modern two-, four- or six-bed dorms and camping within their picturesque grounds. Camping/person and tent **€7.50**, dorms **€16.90**, doubles **€39**

EATING AND DRINKING

★**À la Tchatche chez Bertrand** 4 rue Saint-Antoine. A wonderful *bistrot à vins* with a young, convivial owner fiercely proud of the local provenance of all his produce, not least his mother's cured duck (€6.50). The *champignons à la brandade* (€4.80) are superb, as is the *pélardon* cheese with herbed honey (€6.50). Wed–Sat 10am–3pm & 6pm–1am; daily in summer.

Halles Auberge Central Halles, 5 rue des Halles. A popular counter bar in the bustling halles. Watch as the chefs prepare bold regional dishes such as *coeur de canard au balsamique*; *menus* from €13. Tues–Sun 10.30am–2.30pm.

Le Petit Mas Corner of rue Fresque and rue de la Madeleine ⓞ04 66 36 84 25. Generous salads (from €13) are the thing at this buzzing little spot, which is also popular for its tapas (from €6). Mon–Sat noon–3pm & 6pm–1am.

Maison Villaret 13 rue de la Madelaine. Since its foundation in 1775, this beautiful family bakery has become renowned for its trademark *croquant Villaret*, a small, almond-flavoured biscuit, now a city speciality. Mon–Sat 7am–7.30pm & Sun 8am–7.30pm.

Wine Bar "Le Cheval Blanc" 1 place des Arènes. With a terrace overlooking the arena, this Parisian-brasserie-style place is perfect for a tipple. The €14 lunch menu is excellent value. Mon–Sat noon–2pm & 7–11pm/ midnight.

ARLES

ARLES is a lovely, relaxed little Provençal town, steeped in Roman history. In 1888, Vincent Van Gogh was drawn in by the picturesque town, where he painted *Starry Night* and *Night Café*, but also got into a drunken argument with Gauguin and cut off the lower part of his own left ear. Today Arles, as home to the École Nationale de Photographie and host to the summer photographic **festival**, Les Rencontres (July–Sept; ⓦrencontres -arles.com), is the centre of French photography.

WHAT TO SEE AND DO

The focal point for tourists in Arles is the striking **amphitheatre** (Arènes), at the end of rue Voltaire (daily: April–Oct 9am–6pm; May–June & Sept 9am–7pm; July & Aug 9am–8pm; Nov–March 9am–5pm; €8), built at the end of the first century. The surrounding Rond-Point des Arènes is crammed full of

THE CARRIÈRES DE LUMIÈRES

Just outside of Les Baux-de-Provence, a fortified village15km northeast of Arles, lie some bauxite quarries that have been turned into a unique audiovisual experience called the **Carrières de Lumières** (daily: April–Oct 9.30am–7pm; Nov–March 10am–6pm; €12; ☎ 04 90 54 47 37, ⊛ carrieres-lumieres.com). Vast images are projected onto the floors, ceilings and walls of this cavernous quarry to the accompaniment of music, giving a unique resonance within the space. Wandering through these vast spaces and enveloped within a spectacular shifting projection of colours and shapes is a mind-blowing experience. Ligne #59 bus (late May to Sept 6 daily, 7.45am–6.15pm; 35min; €4.30) departs from Arles' train station to Les Baux-de-Provence village from where it is a short walk to the quarries.

touristy shops, cafés and restaurants, and can get very crowded on summer days. On place de la République you'll find the Église **St-Trophime** (mid-April to June Mon–Sat 8am–noon & 2–6pm, Sun 9am–1pm & 3–7pm; July–Sept Mon–Sat 8am–noon & 3–7pm, Sun 9am–1pm & 3–7pm; Oct to mid-April daily 8am–noon & 2–6pm; free), whose doorway is one of the most famous examples of twelfth-century Provençal carving, depicting a Last Judgement trumpeted by rather enthusiastic angels. No original Van Gogh paintings remain in Arles, but the **Fondation Vincent Van Gogh**, 33 rue du Dr-Fanton (daily 11am–7pm; €9; ⊛ fondation-vincent vangogh-arles.org), exhibits works based on his masterpieces by well-known contemporary artists such as Hockney and Bacon.

Around place Constantin

Housed in a splendid medieval building once used by the Knights of the Order of Malta, the **Musée Réattu** (10 rue du Grand Prieuré; Tues–Sun: March–Oct 10am–6pm; Nov–Feb 10am–5pm; €8; ⊛ museereattu.arles.fr) hosts a fine collection of modern art, including sketches and sculptures by Picasso. Opposite are the remains of the fourth-century **Roman baths** (daily: April & Oct 9am–6pm; May–Sept 9am–7pm; Nov–March 10am–5pm; €3).

Musée Départemental Arles Antique

The best insight into Roman Arles is at the **Musée Départemental Arles Antique** (Mon & Wed–Sun 10am–6pm; €8; ⊛ www.arles-antique.cg13.fr), west of the town centre, by the river. The fabulous

mosaics, sarcophagi and sculpture illuminate Arles' early history.

ARRIVAL AND INFORMATION

By train The train station is 5min walk from the amphitheatre on av Paulin.

Destinations Avignon (17–25 daily; 20min–1hr); Lyon (7–9 daily; 2hr 30min); Marseille (hourly; 45min–1hr); Montpellier (15–20 daily; 55min); Nîmes (7 daily; 30min); Paris (2 daily; 4hr).

By bus Buses to Saintes-Maries-de-la-Mer (for the Camargue; 9 daily; 50min) depart from bd Georges Clemenceau, east of rue Gambetta.

Tourist information bd des Lices (Easter–Sept Mon–Sat 9am–6.45pm, Sun 10am–1pm; Oct Mon–Sat 9am–5.45pm, Sun 10am–1pm; Nov–Easter Mon–Sat 9am–4.45pm, Sun 10–1pm; ☎ 04 90 18 41 20, ⊛ arlestourisme.com).

ACCOMMODATION

Acacias 2 rue de la Cavalerie ☎ 04 90 96 37 88, ⊛ hotel-acacias.com. Modern, simple but cheerfully decorated – and soundproofed – rooms in a friendly hotel, not far from the train station, with free parking nearby. Closed late Oct to March. Doubles **€80**

FUAJ Arles 20 av du Maréchal-Foch ☎ 04 90 96 18 25, ⊛ fuaj.org. The somewhat old-fashioned dorms are clean and airy, and there's a bar on site. Often gets overrun with noisy school kids, but the location is good – just 5min from town and a 15min walk from the station. Closed 10am–5pm. Dorms **€20.90**

VAN GOGH'S ARLES

The tourist office (see above) issues a good booklet of themed **walking tours** in Arles (€1). The best of these is the Van Gogh trail, which, by following various markers on the pavements, takes you to the sites of his most famous paintings – it's fascinating to see how the town has changed since he was here.

11

Le Régence 5 rue Marius Jouveau ☎04 90 96 39 85, ⓦhotel-regence.com. In the heart of the old district and within a 5min walk of the station. Rooms are clean and bright with some overlooking the tranquil Rhône River. Bike rental is available. Doubles **€75**

EATING AND DRINKING

Café la Nuit 11 place du Forum. The café immortalized in Van Gogh's *Café Terrace at Night*, this remains *the* spot to enjoy this pretty Roman *place*. Fine for a drink, but avoid the poor, overpriced food. Daily 8am–11pm.

Cuisine de Comptoir 10 rue Liberté. A simple, stylish place serving up excellent *tartines* on fine *poilâne* bread (from €10.90). It's no sandwich bar, though – served with soup (often gazpacho) and salad, they're worth savouring with a glass of wine. Mon–Sat 8.30am–2pm & 7–9pm.

L'Escaldadou 23 rue Porte-de-Laure ☎04 90 96 70 43. Behind its old-fashioned facade, this local favourite holds three substantial and usually very busy dining rooms. Service is friendly, and seafood lovers are in for a real treat. The one set *menu* is great value at €25 for three courses. Mon, Tues & Thurs–Sun noon–2pm & 7–10pm.

Le 16 16 rue du Dr-Fanton ☎04 90 93 77 36. A traditional little bistro serving a good-value lunch *formule* at €16 and dinner *menus* from €22. Mon–Fri noon–1.45pm & 7–9.30pm, Sat noon–1.45pm.

THE CAMARGUE

The flat, marshy delta immediately south of Arles – **the Camargue** – is a beautiful area, used as a breeding ground for the bulls that participate in local *corridas* (bullfights), and the white horses ridden by their herdsmen. The wildlife of the area also includes flamingos, marsh birds and sea birds, and a rich flora of reeds, wild flowers and juniper trees. The only town is **SAINTES-MARIES-DE-LA-MER**, best known for the annual Gypsy Festival held each May. It's a pleasant if touristy place, with some fine sandy beaches. If you're interested in birdwatching or touring the lagoons, your first port of call should be the tourist office (see below).

ARRIVAL AND INFORMATION

By bus Buses from Arles (9 daily; 50min) arrive and depart at the north end of place Mireille in Saintes-Maries-de-la-Mer.

Tourist information 5 av Van Gogh, Saintes-Maries-de-la-Mer (daily: Jan, Feb, Nov & Dec 9am–5pm; March & Oct 9am–6pm; April–June & Sept 9am–7pm; July & Aug 9am–8pm; ☎04 90 97 82 55, ⓦsaintesmaries.com). They can tell you where to rent bicycles, horses or 4WDs.

AVIGNON

AVIGNON, great city of the popes and for centuries one of the major artistic centres of France, is today one of the country's biggest tourist attractions and is always crowded in summer. It's worth putting up with the inevitable queues and camera-wielding hordes to enjoy the unique stock of monuments, churches and museums of this immaculately preserved medieval town. During the **Avignon festival** in July (see box, p.328), it's the only place to be – around 200,000 spectators come here for the show, though, so doing any normal sightseeing becomes virtually impossible.

WHAT TO SEE AND DO

Central Avignon is enclosed by thick **medieval walls**, built by one of the nine popes who based themselves here in the fourteenth century, away from the anarchic feuding and rival popes of Rome. Place de l'Horloge is lined with cafés and market stalls on summer evenings, beyond which towers the enormous **Palais des Papes** (daily: March 9am–6.30pm; April–June, Sept & Oct 9am–7pm; July 9am–8pm; Aug 9am–8.30pm; Nov–Feb 9.30am–5.45pm; €11, joint ticket with Pont St-Bénézet €13.50). Save your money, though: the denuded interior gives little indication of the richness of the papal court, although the building is impressive for sheer size. The nearby **Musée du Petit Palais** (Mon & Wed–Sun 10am–1pm & 2–6pm; €6) houses a collection of religious art from the thirteenth to sixteenth centuries. Jutting out halfway across the river is the famous **Pont St-Bénézet** (also known as Pont d'Avignon; same hours as Palais des Papes; €5). The struggle to keep the bridge in good repair against the ravages of the Rhône was finally abandoned in 1660, three and a half centuries after it was built, and today just four of the original 22 arches survive.

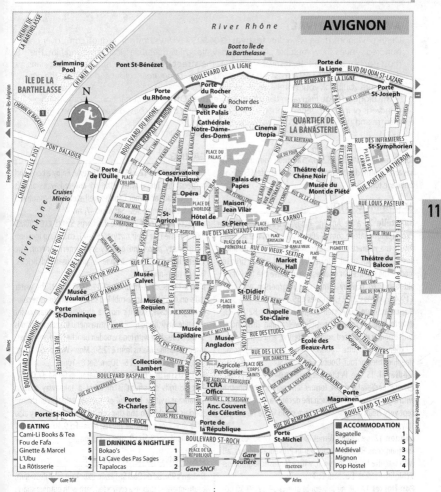

AVIGNON

● EATING			■ DRINKING & NIGHTLIFE			■ ACCOMMODATION	
Cami-Li Books & Tea	1		Bokao's	1		Bagatelle	1
Fou de Fafa	3		La Cave des Pas Sages	3		Boquier	5
Ginette & Marcel	5		Tapalocas	2		Médiéval	3
L'Ubu	4					Mignon	2
La Rôtisserie	2					Pop Hostel	4

On the south side of the city, the wonderful private collection of Jacques Doucet is on display at the **Musée Angladon**, 5 rue Laboureur (April–Sept Tues–Sun 1–6pm; Oct–March Tues–Sat 1–6pm; €8). The former home of museum founders Jean-Angladon Dubrujeaud and his wife Paulette Martin Avignon, it now houses some important pieces by Degas, Cézanne, Picasso, Modigliani and the only painting by Van Gogh displayed in Provence.

ARRIVAL AND DEPARTURE

By train Avignon's main train station is opposite the porte de la République on bd St-Roch, just 5min from the central place de l'Horloge. A regular shuttle bus (2–4 hourly; 13min; €3; from just inside porte de la République; ⓦ tcra .fr) and frequent trains (5min; €1.80) run to the separate TGV station, 3km to the southeast.

Destinations from Gare SNCF Arles (hourly; 20–40min); Lyon (12 daily; 2hr 30min); Marseille (14 daily; 1hr 5min– 1hr 55min); Nîmes (15 daily; 20–40min); Toulouse (11 daily, 8 via Nîmes or Montpellier; 3hr 10min–4hr 30min).

Destinations from Gare TGV Aix-en-Provence TGV (22 daily; 29min); Lille (5 daily; 4hr 30min); Lyon (14 daily; 1hr 10min); Nice (12 daily; 3hr–4hr 10min); Paris (17 daily; 2hr 40min).

INFORMATION

Tourist information The tourist office at 1 cours Jean-Jaurès (April–Oct Mon–Sat 9am–6pm, Sun 10am–5pm; Nov–March Mon–Fri 9am–6pm, Sat 9am–5pm, Sun

AVIGNON FESTIVAL

During Avignon's three-week July **festival** (❶04 90 27 66 50, ⓦfestival-avignon.com), over one hundred venues show multiple plays every day, alongside opera, classical music and film. The most popular aspect of the festival is probably the **street performers** – musicians, magicians, dancers, jugglers, clowns, artists and mime acts – who bring great colour and noise to the city. Make sure you book your hotel early.

The biggest fringe festival in the world, **Le Festival Off**, runs simultaneously, comprising hundreds of independent companies and representing the very best of cutting-edge fringe theatre and performance (ⓦwww.avignonleoff.com).

10am–noon; ❶04 32 74 32 74, ⓦavignon-tourisme.com) has an accommodation booking service and offers English-language tours.

ACCOMMODATION

Bagatelle 25 allée Antoine-Pinay ❶04 90 86 30 39, ⓦcampingbagatelle.com. A 20min walk from the station, this is the nearest campsite to town, with an adjoining hostel offering small, clean dorms and some private rooms. The on-site bar and restaurant have the feel of an old-fashioned holiday camp. Camping/person and tent **€19.47**, dorms **€21.21**, doubles **€59**

Boquier 6 rue du Portail Boquier ❶04 90 82 34 43, ⓦhotel-boquier.com. Extremely welcoming little hotel with brightly decorated, widely differing, and consistently inexpensive en-suite rooms, some very small, some sleeping three or four. Doubles **€65**

Médiéval 15 rue Petite-Saunerie ❶04 90 86 11 06, ⓦhotelmedieval.com. A former aristocratic townhouse with a grand staircase. Though the decor is a little tired, it's kept very clean and the studios are good value for longer stays. Doubles **€75**

Mignon 12 rue Joseph Vernet ❶04 90 82 17 30, ⓦhotel-mignon.com. Rooms decked out in Provençal colours, all with satellite TV, a/c and wi-fi, with a fantastic location on a chic little street. Doubles **€63**

Pop Hostel 17 rue de la République ❶04 32 40 50 60, ⓦpophostel.fr. Behind the nineteenth-century facade of this high-quality hostel lie stylish, inviting rooms and a smart bar/lounge. Dorms are four-, six- or eight-bed with shared bathrooms, and doubles are also available. Dorms **€21**, doubles **€83**

★TREAT YOURSELF

Fou de Fafa 17 rue des Trois Faucons ❶04 32 76 35 13. Book ahead, as this wonderfully intimate place is unmissable. Antonia's charming service and her partner Russell's spectacular dishes are a truly winning combination. *Menus* from €26. Tues–Sun 6.30–11pm (last reservations 9.30pm).

EATING

Camili Books & Tea 155 rue Carreterie. Enjoy a book and a special tea blend within the ivy-covered walls of this pretty terrace at owner Camili's well-stocked secondhand English bookshop. Tues–Sat noon–7pm.

Ginette & Marcel 25 place des Corps Saints ❶04 90 85 58 70. Famed for their *tartines* (€5–7), charming location on a pretty *place* and grocery-style interior decor. The three-cheese-and-pear *tartine* is particularly delicious. Daily 11am–midnight.

L'Ubu 13 rue des Teinturiers ❶04 90 80 01 01. The water mills on this picturesque cobbled street testify to its textile-dyeing heritage, but it's now a thriving destination for nightlife. Stylish and minimal with a menu to match, *L'Ubu* is an intimate affair with long wooden benches and an Italian-inspired cuisine. Mains from €12.50. Mon–Wed noon–2pm, Thurs–Fri noon–2pm & 8–10pm, Sat 8–10pm.

La Rôtisserie 2 rue Portail Matheron ❶09 84 37 04 62. This no-frills shopfront is more of a takeaway than a restaurant, with a handful of outdoor tables. Lunchtime specials like chicken and chips cost just €5, while they also offer sausages and other meats. Mon–Fri 9.30am–2pm & 5–7.30pm, Sat & Sun 9.30am–1.30pm.

DRINKING AND NIGHTLIFE

Bokao's 9bis bd du Quai St-Lazare ⓦbokaos.fr. Mainstream, youth-oriented club, in a converted barn with outdoor space, just outside the walls and across from the river, playing an eclectic mix of music. Tues–Sat midnight–7am.

La Cave des Pas Sages 41 rue des Teinturiers. A happening little bar where you can hang out beneath the dappled shade of the plane trees, with live gigs every Sat from 8.30pm. Mon, Tues & Thurs–Sat 12.30pm–midnight, Wed 4pm–1am.

Tapalocas 15 rue Galante. Spanish music, sometimes live, in a large, lively and very hectic three-storey bar, with outdoor seating. €3 tapas plates, plus a few larger dishes. Mon–Fri & Sun 11.45am–4pm & 6pm–1am, Sat 11.45am–1am.

AIX-EN-PROVENCE

For many visitors, **AIX-EN-PROVENCE** is the ideal Provençal city, the cobbled streets of its old town still retaining the romance of days past, especially when lit by the sun. The city has a (not entirely unfair) reputation for snobbishness, but it is still a relaxed and enjoyable place, where the greatest pleasure is in winding through the streets and relaxing in a shady place over a *pastis*.

WHAT TO SEE AND DO

Aix's old town stretches back from the leafy expanse of cours Mirabeau, and it's easy to spend a few hours just exploring the atmospheric streets, which are dotted with interesting shops and cafés. The only museum worth heading to is the **Musée Granet**, place St-Jean-de-Malte (Tues–Sun: June–Sept 10am–7pm; Oct–May noon–6pm; €5; ☎04 42 52 88 32), whose permanent collection includes some minor works by the town's most famous painter, Paul Cézanne, and a number of archeological finds from the region; it's the interesting and often inventive temporary exhibitions, however, that stand out. To find out more about Cézanne, you can visit his studio, the **Atelier Cézanne** at 9 av Paul-Cézanne (April–June & Sept Mon–Sat 10am–12.30pm & 2–6pm; July & Aug daily 10am–6pm; Oct–March Mon–Sat 10am–12.30pm & 2–5pm; €5.50; ☎atelier-cezanne.com), a ten-minute walk from the north end of the Vieille Ville; it looks exactly the same as it did at the time of his death.

ARRIVAL AND DEPARTURE

By train The SNCF station is located on rue Gustave-Desplaces, just 5min southwest of the old town. It's more likely that you'll arrive at the TGV station, 16km southwest of Aix and linked by regular *navette* (daily 4am–11.30pm every 30min; €5) to the *gare routière* on av de l'Europe.

Destinations from Gare SNCF Marseille (every 20min–30min; 30–45min).
Destinations from Gare TGV Avignon (22 daily; 20min); Lyon (20 daily; 1hr 30min); Marseille (frequent; 15min); Paris (4 daily; 3hr 30min).

INFORMATION

Tourist information 300 av Giuseppe Verdi, just west of Place du General du Gaulle (June–Sept Mon–Sat 8.30am–8pm, Sun 10am–1pm & 2–6pm; Oct–May Mon–Sat 8.30am–7pm, Sun 10am–1pm & 2–6pm; ☎04 42 16 11 61, ☎aixenprovencetourism.com).

ACCOMMODATION

Cheap accommodation is unfortunately hard to come by in Aix, especially in high season.
Auberge de Jeunesse 3 av Marcel Pagnol ☎04 42 20 15 99, ☎auberge-jeunesse-aix.fr; bus #4 from the *gare routière* to Vasarely. Situated 2km out of the city, offering modern dorms, a bar with cheap beers and inclusive breakfast. No communal kitchen facilities. Closed 2–4.30pm. Dorms **€23.10**
Cardinal 24 rue Cardinale ☎04 42 38 32 30, ☎hotel-cardinal-aix.com. Welcoming, rather old-fashioned establishment in a quiet though very central neighbourhood, with 29 sizeable, great-value antique-furnished a/c rooms. Doubles **€78**
Hôtel Paul 10 av Pasteur ☎04 42 23 23 89, ☎aix-en-provence.com/hotelpaul. A good budget option a 10min walk from the centre, with basic clean rooms, albeit rather tired. No credit cards accepted and expensive wi-fi charges. Doubles **€55**

EATING AND DRINKING

Bar Brigand place Richelme (place des Sangliers). A satisfyingly grungy little pub so beloved of the town's hipsters they spill out onto the street. *Pression* from €2.80, glass of wine from €2. Daily 10am–2pm.
Le Bouddoir 28 place des Tanneurs. A lovely place for a coffee on this little terrace beside a tinkling fountain, and their *plat du jour* is good value at €11.50. Come evening it livens up and makes a perfect spot to enjoy one of their cocktails. Mon–Sat 7am–2am, Sun 10am–8pm.

MARSEILLE

France's second most populous city, **MARSEILLE** has been a major centre of international maritime trade ever since it was founded by Greek colonists 2600 years ago. Like the capital, the city has suffered plagues, religious bigotry, republican and royalist terror, and had its own Commune and Bastille-storming

---

AIX STREET MARKETS

You cannot visit Aix and miss the colourful, vibrant **street markets** with which the town is synonymous. Held all year round, on Tuesdays, Thursdays and Saturdays (the main day), the flower market opposite the town hall, the antiques market on place de Verdun and the farmers' market on place Richelme are particularly impressive.

11

– it was the presence of so many revolutionaries from this city marching to Paris in 1792 that gave the name *Marseillaise* to the national anthem. A working city with little of the glamour of its ritzy Riviera neighbours, it is nevertheless a vibrant, exciting place, with a cosmopolitan population including many Italians and North Africans.

WHAT TO SEE AND DO

The old harbour, or **Vieux Port**, is the hub of the town and a good place to indulge in the sedentary pleasure of observing the city's street life over a *pastis*. Two fortresses guard the entrance to the harbour and the town extends outwards alongside the harbour from its three quais.

Musée des Civilisations d'Europe et de la Méditerranée (MuCEM)

One of two fortresses guarding the harbour entrance, medieval Fort St-Jean has been converted (with the addition of a modernist annexe) by Algerian-born architect Rudy Ricciotti into the **Musée des Civilisations d'Europe et de la Méditerranée**, or **MuCEM** for short (Mon & Wed–Sun: May, June, Sept & Oct 11am–7pm; July & Aug 10am–8pm, Fri till 10pm; Nov–April 11am–6pm; €9.50 exhibition; wmucem.org). With an enormous collection totalling a million works, and encompassing a broad range of disciplines including archeology, art history, sociology, religion and more, the museum transcends national boundaries to trace the important phases of Mediterranean civilization and culture through a series of permanent and temporary exhibitions.

There is a 115m-long bridge joining the fort to the new annexe, and a second bridge connecting the port and the church of St Laurent in the Panier district, linking the oldest parts of the city with the newly rejuvenated docklands.

Villa Méditerranée

Next to the MuCEM the spectacular **Villa Méditerranée** (Tues–Fri noon–6pm, Fri noon–10pm, Sat & Sun 10am–7pm; wvilla-mediterranee.org), designed by the

LE CORBUSIER

If you're interested in architecture, it's definitely worth taking the short bus journey out to Le Corbusier's **La Cité Radieuse**. Completed in 1952, this seventeen-storey block of flats is surprisingly striking even today, and you can take the lift up to the rooftop to enjoy fantastic views of the city and the surrounding area. You can even enjoy a drink while you're here. Take bus #21 from Centre Bourse to the Le Corbusier stop.

Italian architect Stegano Boeri, hosts exhibitions and events dedicated to the opening of dialogue between Mediterranean nations. There is an exciting programme of screenings, concerts, exhibitions and conferences; see website for details.

Euroméditerranée

The focus of the city's long-term regeneration plans is concentrated around the formerly industrial dockland area north of the Vieux Port, rechristened **Euroméditerranée**. These ambitious plans are currently transforming the hitherto neglected area surrounding the **Cathédrale de la Major** (Tues–Sun: summer 10am–7pm; winter 10am–6pm), an imposing nineteenth-century structure overlooking the modern docks. South from the cathedral on avenue Vaudoyer sits a low modernist structure built in 1948, formerly a sanitary station used to screen newly arrived immigrants, and now the home of the **Musée Regards de Provence** (daily 10am–6pm; €3.50; wmuseeregardsdeprovence.com). The museum houses the Fondation Regards de Provence's 850-strong collection of art from, and about, Provence, as well as frequent temporary exhibitions and a permanent exhibition telling the compelling story of the building and its role in the lives of immigrants entering the city.

Le Panier

On the northern side of the harbour is the original site and former old town of

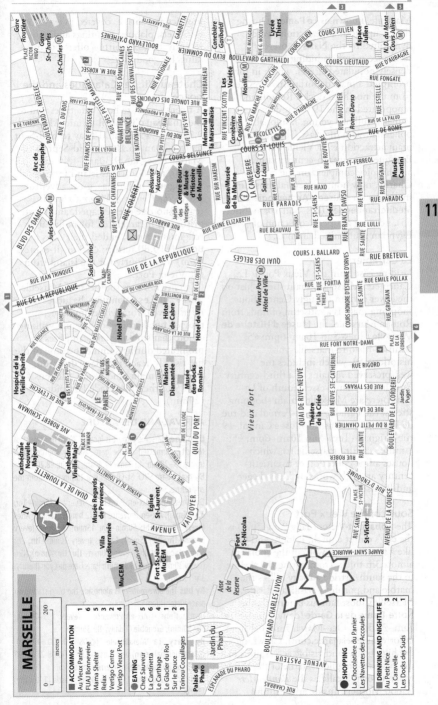

MARSEILLE

0 metres 200

11

■ ACCOMMODATION
Au Vieux Panier	1
FUAJ Bonneveine	6
Mama Shelter	5
Relax	3
Vertigo Centre	2
Vertigo Vieux Port	4

● EATING
Chez Sauveur	5
La Cantinetta	6
Le Carthage	4
Le Glacier du Roi	1
Sur le Pouce	2
Toinou Coquillages	3

● SHOPPING
La Chocolatière du Panier	1
Les Navettes des Accoules	2

■ DRINKING AND NIGHTLIFE
Au Petit Nice	3
La Caravelle	2
Les Docks des Suds	1

Marseille, known as **Le Panier**. During the occupation, large sections were dynamited by the Nazis to prevent resistance members hiding in the small, densely populated streets, which in turn prompted a mass deportation of residents from the northern docks. Rebuilt and repopulated in the 1950s, today's Le Panier is full of a young, fashionable and bohemian working class. The quarter's main attraction is La Vieille Charité, a Baroque seventeenth-century church and hospice complex, on rue de la Charité, now home to several museums, including the **Musée d'Archéologie Méditerranéenne** (Tues–Sun 10am–6pm; €5), housing a superb collection of Egyptian mummified animals.

La Canebière

Leading east from the Vieux Port is La Canebière, Marseille's main street. Just off the lower end, in the ugly Centre Bouse shopping mall, is a museum of finds from Roman Marseille, the **Musée d'Histoire de Marseille** (Tues–Sun 10am–6pm; €5; ꟷmusee-histoire-marseille-voie-historique.fr), which includes the well-preserved remains of a third-century Roman merchant vessel. South of La Canebière are Marseille's main shopping streets, rue Paradis, rue St-Ferréol and rue de Rome, as well as the **Musée Cantini**, 19 rue Grignan (Tues–Sun 10am–6pm; €5; ꟷmusee-cantini.marseille.fr), which houses a fine collection of twentieth-century art with works by Dufy, Léger and Picasso.

South of the Vieux Port

The **Abbaye St-Victor** (daily 9am–7pm) is the city's oldest church. It looks and feels like a fortress – the walls of the choir are almost 3m thick. Dominating the skyline to the south, astride a rocky hill, is the marble and porphyry basilica of Marseille's most famous landmark, the **Notre-Dame de la Garde** (daily: April–Sept 7am–7.15pm; Oct–March 7am–6.15pm; ꟷnotredamedelagarde.com). Crowning the high belfry, and visible across most of the city, is a 9m gilded statue of the Virgin Mary, known locally as the *Bonne Mère* (Good Mother). Inside are beautiful mosaics and shrines covered in ex-votos – trinkets, plaques, paintings and, more recently, football shirts – offered to the saints for good luck.

Chateau d'If, Les Calanques and the beach

A twenty-minute boat ride takes you to the **Château d'If** (April to mid-May daily 9.30am–4.45pm; mid-May to mid-Sept daily 9.30am–6.10pm; mid-Sept to March Tues–Sun 9.30am–4.45pm; €5.50), the notorious island fortress that figured in Dumas' great adventure story, *The Count of Monte Cristo*. In reality, no one ever escaped, and most prisoners, incarcerated for political or religious reasons, ended their days here. **Boats** (€10.80 return; ꟷfrioul-if-express .com) leave hourly for the island from the Vieux Port.

Twenty minutes southeast of Marseille (bus #20), **Les Calanques**, beautiful rocky inlets carved from white limestone, provide fine bathing, diving and walking – note that smoking and campfires are prohibited during summer because of the fire risk. To reach the **plage du Prado**, Marseille's main sand beach, take bus #47 or #19 to the Promenade Pompidou (20min).

ARRIVAL AND DEPARTURE

By plane Marseille airport is located 20km northwest of the city, connected to the gare SNCF by shuttle buses (every 15–20min, 4.50am–12.10am; 25min; €8.20).

By train Gare SNCF St-Charles is a 15min walk from the city centre.

Destinations Aix-en-Provence (every 15min–1hr; 35–45min); Aix-en-Provence TGV (2 hourly; 12min); Arles (every 30min–1hr; 50min–1hr 15min); Avignon (every 30min–1hr; 30–35min); Cannes (every 30min–1hr; 2hr 5min); Lyon Part Dieu (every 30min–1hr; 1hr 40min); Nice (every 30min–1hr; 2hr 35min); Paris Gare de Lyon (hourly; 3hr 15min).

By bus The *gare routière* is alongside the train station on place Victor Hugo.

Destinations Aix-en-Provence (every 5–20min; 30–50min); Grenoble (1 daily; 4hr 35min).

By ferry La Méridionale (☎08 10 20 13 20, ꟷlameridionale.com) and Corsica Linea (☎08 25 88 80 88, ꟷcorsicalinea.com) run ferries to Corsica.

Destinations Ajaccio (1–2 daily; 13hr); Bastia (1–2 daily; 13hr).

INFORMATION

Tourist information 11 La Canebière (Mon–Sat 9am–7pm, Sun 10am–5pm; ☎08 26 50 05 00, ⓦwww .marseille-tourisme.com).

GETTING AROUND

By public transport Marseille has an efficient public transport network (ⓦrtm.fr). The métro and trams run from 5am until just after midnight; buses run from 5/6am until 9pm, after which night-bus services take over until around 12.45am. *Solos* (single tickets; €1.60) can be used on journeys combining all three modes of transport if used within an hour; a good value day-pass, *Pass XL s4hr* (€5.20), can be bought from métro stations, RTM kiosks, and shops displaying the RTM sign.

By bike Blue bicycles belonging to Le Vélo scheme (ⓦlevelo-mpm.fr) can be rented from 130 self-service rental points throughout the city using a bank card (€1 for 7-day membership; usage first 30min free, €1 for each additional 30min).

By ferry RTM runs a ferry between the Vieux Port and Pointe Rouge in the south of the city for easier access to the beaches and Les Calanques (daily: late April to late June & Sept 8am–7pm; July & Aug 8am–10pm; hourly; €5).

ACCOMMODATION

FUAJ Bonneveine Impasse Dr Bonfils, off av Joseph Vidal ☎04 91 17 63 30, ⓦfuaj.org; bus #44 to the Bonnefon stop. At 5km from the city, yet in a fantastic location near Les Calanques and just 200m from the beach, this is a brilliant hostel, with friendly staff and clean dorms (2–6 beds). Tours, sea kayaking and horseriding can be arranged, and there's a bar on site. Dorms €21, doubles €55.20

★**TREAT YOURSELF**

Au Vieux Panier 13 rue du Panier ☎06 32 19 90 05, ⓦauvieuxpanier.com. In the heart of the trendy Le Panier district and 500m from the Vieux Port, the rooms of this seventeenth-century, former Corsican grocery store have been transformed into ephemeral works of art. Each year a different artist is commissioned to design a room within the house, creating unique spaces each with a distinctive atmosphere, equipped with en-suite bathrooms and design touches. There is a lounge area and exhibition space, communal kitchen and a beautiful roof terrace offering spectacular views of the ocean and the landmarks of Marseille. A truly spellbinding experience. Two-night minimum stay. Doubles €85

★**TREAT YOURSELF**

La Cantinetta 24 cours Julien ☎04 91 48 10 48. Savour classic Italian dishes (€12–19) in the sun-dappled garden or the convivial dining room of this gregarious restaurant that's evocative of a huge Italian family reunion. Reservation essential. Mon–Sat noon–2pm & 7.30–10.30pm.

Mama Shelter 63 rue de la Loubière ☎04 84 35 20 00, ⓦmamashelter.com; ⓜBaille or Notre Dame du Mont. Combining luxury and practicality, rooms at *Mama's* include a Mac TV, free movies and a kitchenette. The lively terrace bar is so happening there's no need to leave – unless you wish to visit the private beach. Doubles €79
Relax 4 rue Corneille ☎04 91 33 15 87, ⓦhotelrelax.fr. Homey and very friendly budget hotel, right next to the Opéra and near all the action. Public areas are a little overstuffed in style; rooms are simpler, with a/c and soundproofing. Prices are keen for the central location. Doubles €60
★**Vertigo Centre** 42 rue Petits Mariés ☎04 91 91 07 11, ⓦhotelvertigo.fr. Mere steps from the train station, this excellent hostel has bright, spacious dorms, all en suite, as well as a number of private rooms – the "deluxe" have private balconies. Staff are friendly and helpful, and there's a good kitchen, garden and a cheap bar. Dorms €22, doubles €70
★**Vertigo Vieux Port** 38 rue Fort Notre Dame ☎04 91 54 42 95, ⓦhotelvertigo.fr. A marvellous hostel spread across two former warehouses, each with quality modern art (all local commissions) on display. The communal spaces are very well conceived, the dorms are airy and breakfast is included. Dorms €25, doubles €70

EATING

Chez Sauveur 10 rue d'Aubagne ☎04 91 54 33 96. Established in 1943, this modest Sicilian restaurant close to the marché des Capucins is renowned locally for its excellent wood-fired pizzas (from €9), including a few made with *brousse*, a type of goat's cheese. Tues–Sat 11.30am–2pm & 7.30–10pm.
Le Carthage 8 rue d'Aubagne ☎04 91 54 72 85. This traditional *salon de thé* close to the marché des Capucins sells Tunisian sandwiches from €4.50, but it's the tempting piles of sticky North African pastries (from €1) that draw the eye. Daily 7am–8pm, closed Fri 12.30–2pm.
Le Glacier du Roi 4 place de Lenche. An artisan *glacier* with over 24 seasonal flavours. The *navetissimo* flavour is delicious – a blend of biscuit crumbs and orange flower water inspired by the traditional *navette* biscuits of Marseille. Two scoops €3.50. Daily except Tues 8.30am–7pm.

★**Sur le Pouce** 2 rue des Convalescents ☎ 04 91 56 13 28. Lively and inexpensive Tunisian restaurant in the *quartier* Belsunce, with a huge range of couscous from €5.50–10, plus grills, merguez sausages and *brochettes* from around €6. One of the city's best budget options. Daily noon–3pm & 6–11pm.

Toinou Coquillages 3 cours Saint-Louis ☎ 04 91 33 14 94. Popular with locals and visitors alike for the choice of more than forty types of shellfish, served in the restaurant and sold fresh from the counter at the front. *Moules* with chorizo €8.90, oyster *formules* from €9.20; they also do fish and chips. Daily 7am–10.30pm.

DRINKING AND NIGHTLIFE

Au Petit Nice 28 place Jean Jaurès. An institution among the locals for its cheap beer (from €2 *pression*) and constantly bustling terrace. It remains the spot to soak up the ambience of the city's most bohemian quarter. Tues & Thurs 10am–1.30am, Wed & Fri 9am–1.30pm, Sat 8.30am–1.30pm.

La Caravelle *Hotel Belle-Vue*, 34 quai du Port. The balcony of this intimate tapas bar overlooking the Vieux Port is a majestic spot come evening. Aperitifs and free tapas are served 6–9pm with live jazz (€3) every Wed & Fri evening. Daily 7am–1am.

Les Dock des Suds 12 rue Urbain V ☎ 04 91 99 00 00, ⓦ dock-des-suds.org; tram #2, stop "Arenc le Silo". Vast warehouse that hosts Marseille's annual Fiesta des Suds world music festival (Oct) and is a regular live venue for hip-hop, electro and world music. Entry €5–25. Hours vary.

SHOPPING

La Chocolatière du Panier 47 rue du Petit Puit. A beautiful old shop spanning three generations. With over three hundred varieties on offer, these seasonal creations are artisanal, inventive and delicious. Tues–Sat 9am–8pm.

Les Navettes des Accoules 68 rue Caisserie. Renowned for their croquants, macaroons, canistrelli and of course the orange-flavoured *navette* biscuits, which any self-respecting gourmet must sample. Mon–Sat 9.30am–7pm, Sun 10am–6pm.

DIRECTORY

Consulates UK, 24 av du Prado, 6e (☎ 04 91 15 72 10); USA, place Varian Fry, 6e (☎ 01 43 12 48 85).

Health Ambulance ☎ 15; doctor ☎ 3624; 24hr casualty department at Hôpital de la Conception, 147 bd Baille, 5e (☎ 04 91 38 00 00); medical emergencies for travellers at SOS Voyageurs, Gare St-Charles, 3e (☎ 04 91 62 12 80).

Police Commissariat Central, 2 rue Antoine-Becker, 2e (24hr; ☎ 04 91 39 80 00).

CANNES

Fishing village turned millionaires' playground, **CANNES** is best known for the International Film Festival, held in May, during which time it is overrun by the denizens of Movieland, their hangers-on and a small army of paparazzi. The seafront promenade, **La Croisette**, and the Vieux Port form the focus of Cannes' eye-candy life, while the old town, **Le Suquet**, on the steep hill overlooking the bay from the west, with its quaint winding streets and eleventh-century castle, is a pleasant place to wander.

ARRIVAL AND INFORMATION

By train The station is on rue Jean-Jaurès, a short walk north of the centre.

Destinations Marseille (frequent; 2hr); Monaco (frequent; 1hr–1hr 10min); Nice (frequent; 25–35min).

Tourist information The main tourist office is in the Palais des Festivals on the waterfront (daily 9/10am–7/8pm; ☎ 04 92 99 84 22, ⓦ cannes-destination .com). There is also a booth at the station (Mon–Sat 9am–1pm & 2–6pm).

ACCOMMODATION

Alnea 20 rue Jean de Riouffe ☎ 04 93 68 77 77, ⓦ hotel -alnea.com. Centrally located two-star with pleasant service and simple but colourful and well-equipped rooms with a/c, flatscreen TV and double-glazing. Doubles **€70**

Parc Bellevue 67 av Maurice Chevalier ☎ 04 93 47 28 97, ⓦ parcbellevue.com; bus #2 from the train station. The nearest campsite is in the suburb of La Bocca, 3km to the west of Cannes; most plots are shaded and there is a 40m pool. Per person **€4**, plus per tent **€29.50**

PLM 3 rue Hoche ☎ 04 93 38 31 19, ⓦ hotel-cannes-plm .com. A comfortable little hotel close to the station and a short walk from the beachfront. Rooms are decorated in soothing, neutral colours and there's free wi-fi. Doubles **€75**

EATING AND DRINKING

Chez Vincent & Nicolas 90 rue Meynadier ☎ 04 93 68 35 39. An original choice, with flamboyant staff, inventive food and a lovely setting. Try the scallops wrapped in bacon; meat or fish mains start at around €18. Daily 6.30–11.30pm.

La Crème de la Crêpe 9 rue Buttura. Cool, contemporary crêperie just a short walk from the train station. Galettes start at just €6 and crêpes from €3. Daily 10am–11pm.

Pint House 19 rue des Frères Pradignacs. Irish-style pub with live rugby on TV; the beers are mostly French or

Belgian (*pression* from €3.80). A bit of relief from the trying-too-hard excess of much of Cannes' nightlife. Daily 6pm–5am.

ANTIBES

The charming medieval town of **ANTIBES** has stupendous sea views shared by the Alps soaring majestically in the distance. Only 11km east of Cannes and easily visited as a day-trip, it has largely escaped the glitzy exclusivity and overdevelopment blighting so many neighbouring resorts, although the sea is still awash with millionaires' yachts.

WHAT TO SEE AND DO

The town's bustling streets are animated by many bars and restaurants, and there's a fine market selling fresh produce and local crafts (food June–Aug daily 6am–1pm; Sept–May Tues–Sun 6am–1pm; crafts mid-June to Sept Tues–Sun 3pm–midnight; Oct to mid-June Fri–Sun 3pm–midnight). Antibes also has the excellent **Musée Picasso** on Place Mariejol (mid-June to mid-July Tues–Sun 10am–6pm; mid-July to Aug Tues, Thurs, Sat & Sun 10am–6pm, Wed & Fri 10am–8pm; mid-Sept to mid-June Tues–Sun 10am–noon & 2–6pm; €6; ☎04 92 90 54 20, ⓦantibes -juanlespins.com), where you can see some of his lesser-known works in the beautiful surroundings of the sixteenth-century Chateau Grimaldi.

Antibes boasts some of the Riviera's most irresistible beaches – the long, sandy **Plage de la Salis** and the smaller **Plage de la Garoupe** are both free and unspoilt by big hotels.

ARRIVAL AND DEPARTURE

By train There are connections with Cannes (frequent; 7–10min) and Nice (frequent; 20–30min).

NICE AND AROUND

NICE, capital of the French Riviera and France's fifth-largest city, grew into a major tourist resort in the nineteenth century, when large numbers of foreign visitors – many of them British – were drawn here by the mild Mediterranean climate. The most obvious legacy of these early holidaymakers is the famous **promenade des Anglais** stretching along the pebble beach, which was laid out by nineteenth-century English residents to facilitate their afternoon stroll by the sea. These days, Nice is a busy, bustling city, but it's still a lovely place, with a beautiful location and attractive historical centre.

WHAT TO SEE AND DO

The old town, a rambling collection of narrow alleys lined with tall, rust-and-ochre houses, centres on place Rossetti and the Baroque **Cathédrale Ste-Réparate**. It's worth making nearby Le Château one of your first stops to take in the view, which stretches across the town and west over the bay. It's a steep walk up, or there's a lift, tucked just under the stairs (free) on the western side. A short walk north through the old town takes you to the promenade des Arts, where the **Musée d'Art Moderne et d'Art Contemporain** (Tues–Sun 10am–6pm; €10; ⓦmamac -nice.or) has a collection of Pop Art and neo-Realist work, including pieces by Andy Warhol and Roy Lichtenstein.

Cimiez

Up above the city centre is Cimiez, a posh suburb that was the social centre of the town's elite some seventeen centuries ago, when the city was capital of the Roman province of Alpes-Maritimae. To get here, take bus #15 from in front of the train station. The **Musée d'Archéologie**, 160 av des Arènes (Mon & Wed–Sun 10am–6pm; free), houses excavations of the Roman baths, along with accompanying archeological finds. Overlooking the museum on av des Arènes de Cimiez is the wonderful **Musée Matisse** (Mon & Wed–Sun 10am–6pm; €10;

11

> ### MUNICIPAL MUSEUMS IN NICE
> Many of Nice's museums and galleries are covered by the **French Riviera Pass** (€10/24hr; €20/7 days), including both the Chagall and Matisse museums. Considering that entry to the latter alone is €10, it provides excellent value.

11

■ ACCOMMODATION		●EATING		■ DRINKING AND NIGHTLIFE	
Backpackers Chez Patrick	2	Attimi	3	Akathor	4
Belle Meunière	4	Fenocchio	3	High Club	1
FUAJ Les Camélias	5	Le Bistro du Fromager	5	Juke House Café	1
Hôtel Baccarat	3	Lou Pilha Leva	2	Les Distilleries Idéales	3
Villa St-Éxupéry Gardens	1	Mets and Café	1	Wayne's	2
Wilson	6	Pasta Basta	6		

ⓦmusee-matisse-nice.org): Nice was the
artist's home for much of his life and the
collection covers every period. Nearby, the
beautiful **Musée Chagall**, 16 av du
Docteur Ménard (Mon & Wed–Sun:
May–Oct 10am–6pm; Nov–April
10am–5pm; €9), exhibits dazzlingly
colourful biblical paintings, stained glass
and book illustrations by Marc Chagall.

Day-trips from Nice

Nice is an excellent base from which to
explore the surrounding beaches and
picturesque resorts of the Riveria. The
medieval **Èze Village** is a labyrinthine
maze of vaulted passages and stairways,
its streets winding around a cone of rock
below the corniche. Towering 470m
above sea level, it offers spectacular
panoramic views of the coast. Take bus

#112 or #82 to Èze Vllage from tram
stop Garibaldi (hourly; 30min).

ARRIVAL AND DEPARTURE

By plane Nice airport is 6km southwest of the city,
connected to the main train station, Nice-Ville, by two fast
buses: #98 (every 20min, 5.40am–11.45pm) or #99 (every
30min, 7.53am–8.53pm); the single fare of €6 allows
unlimited travel on the Lignes d'Azur network for one day.
The slower regular bus #52 (every 30min, daily
6am–9.25pm; €1.50) also serves the main train station.
By train The main train station, Nice-Ville, is a 10min
walk northwest from the centre, on av Thiers.
Destinations Antibes (2–7 hourly; 15–28min); Avignon
TGV (10 daily; 2hr 50min–3hr 35min); Cannes (2–6
hourly; 25–41min); Genoa (7 daily via Ventimiglia;
3hr–4hr 30min); Marseille (every 30min–1hr; 2hr 35min–
3hr); Milan (7 daily via Ventimiglia; 4hr 50min–6hr
10min); Monaco (4 hourly; 15–25min); Paris (14 daily; 5hr
45min–6hr 25min).

By bus There is no actual *gare routière*. Instead, buses depart from the main thoroughfares in central Nice – av St Jean Baptiste, promenade des Anglais, and place Massèna. Check ⓦ lignesdazur.com for details.

Destinations Antibes (up to 4 hourly; 1hr); Cannes (up to 4 hourly; 1hr 30min); Èze-sur-Mer (up to 5 hourly; 32min); Èze Village (6 daily; 30min); Monaco (every 15min; 37min).

By ferry Corsica Ferries (ⓣ08 25 09 50 95, ⓦcorsica -ferries.fr) operate a year-round service to Corsica from the Gare Maritime.

Destinations Ajaccio (5–6 weekly; 6hr 30min); Bastia (8–9 weekly; 5hr 15min); Calvi (daily; 5hr 45min).

INFORMATION

Tourist information 5 promenade des Anglais (June–Sept daily 9am–7pm; Oct–May Mon–Sat 9am–7pm; ⓣ08 92 70 74 07, ⓦnicetourisme.com), with outlets at the airport and next to the station.

GETTING AROUND

By bus and tram Buses and trams in Nice and surrounding towns are run by Lignes d'Azur (ⓦlignesdazur .com). Single tickets for both buses and trams cost €1.50, and day pass tickets (€5) are also available.

By bike Nice's on-street bicycle rental scheme, Vélo Bleu (ⓦwww.velobleu.org), has 175 rental stations scattered throughout the city. You have to sign up online or call toll-free from a bike station (€1/day, €5/week), after which the first 30min is free; thereafter it costs €1 for the subsequent 30min and then €2/hr. Payment by credit card only.

ACCOMMODATION

Backpackers Chez Patrick First floor, 32 rue Pertinax ⓣ04 93 80 30 72, ⓦbackpackerschezpatrick.com. A friendly hostel with dorms of three to six beds and some private rooms, close to the station, with no curfew. Lacks a kitchen or communal space. Closed 11am–2pm. Dorms €35, doubles €80

Belle Meunière 21 av Durante ⓣ04 93 88 66 15. In a beautiful old building close to the station and a short walk from town, this friendly backpacker place offers simple but pleasant rooms and small dorms. Breakfast included. Dorms €35, doubles €86

FUAJ Les Camélias 3 rue Spitalieri ⓣ04 93 62 15 54, ⓦfuaj.org. In an excellent, central location, not far from the old town, this is a great, friendly hostel with clean, modern dorms and a good bar on site. Dorms €28.60

Hôtel Baccarat 39 rue d'Angleterre ⓣ04 93 16 14 25. This large hostel has mixed dorms (four to twelve beds), kitchen and a communal space. They have a flexible, helpful attitude, too, in spite of the 3–6am curfew. Private doubles are also good value. Dorms €23, doubles €85

★**TREAT YOURSELF**

Le Bistro du Fromager 29 rue Benoît Bunico ⓣ04 93 13 07 83. The cheesiest restaurant in Nice, their every offering built around France's fantastic *fromage*, coupled with wine from the cellar. The cooking is excellent, the produce local and the atmosphere buzzy, though expect to pay around €25 per person. Booking recommended. Mon–Sat 7–11pm.

★**Villa St-Éxupéry Beach** 6 rue Sacha Guitry ⓣ04 93 16 13 45, ⓦwww.villahostels.com. Well-equipped, a/c hostel close to place Masséna and Vieux Nice with a bar, 24hr gym, movie lounge, secure lockers and free wi-fi. There is a good range of smart private rooms, and the dorms (sleeping three to fourteen) are great too. Dorms €39.95, doubles €120

Wilson 39 rue de l'Hotel des Postes ⓣ04 93 85 47 79, ⓦhotel-wilson-nice.com. A stylish and gay-friendly budget guesthouse on the third floor in a great location, with individually themed rooms, the cheapest of which have washbasins only. Free wi-fi, but no lift. €50

EATING

Attimi 10 place Masséna ⓣ04 93 62 00 22. This bright terrace restaurant specializes in regional Italian dishes using organic, seasonal produce. Their specialities include colourful salads (from €7.50) and enormous pizzas (from €10.50). Daily noon–midnight.

★**Fenocchio** 2 place Rossetti. The master ice-cream maker of Nice, with a huge variety of flavours, like salted caramel and violet, alongside more traditional offerings. One scoop €2. Daily 9am–midnight.

Lou Pilha Leva 10 rue Collet. A self-proclaimed institution, this is nevertheless one of the best places in town to try classic Nice fast food like *socca* chickpea flatbreads (€2.80) and *pan bagnat* (tuna, olive and salad sandwich; €4). Daily 11am–8pm (later in summer).

Mets and Café 28 rue Assalit ⓣ04 93 80 03 57. Busy budget brasserie close to many of the backpacker hostels, serving traditional French food, with a €10.50 *formule* at lunchtime. Mon–Sat 11.30am–3pm & 8–9pm.

Pasta Basta 18 rue de la Prefecture ⓣ04 93 80 03 57. No-frills pasta place with fresh and dried pasta varieties, and a choice of sauces. Pasta from €4.60, sauce from €4, and rough wine by the *pichet* from €4. Daily noon–11pm.

DRINKING AND NIGHTLIFE

Akathor 32 cours Saleya. The fifty different European beers on offer attract both locals and tourists in their droves. Live music daily; beer from €4. Happy hour 5.30–9pm. Daily 5.30pm–2am.

High Club 45 promenade des Anglais. Large seafront club that attracts big-name international DJs and live PAs. There's also an eighties-themed club, *Studio 47*, and an LGBT-friendly club, *Sk'high*. Expect to pay €10, except for the occasional free nights. Fri–Sun 11.45pm–6am.

Juke House Café 8 rue Defly Tiny, American style cocktail and tapas bar that draws a young crowd. Happy hour is 6–8pm, when cocktails cost €5–6 and draught beers start at €2. As the name suggests, there's a jukebox. Tues–Sat 5pm–midnight.

Les Distilleries Idéales 40 rue de la Préfecture. This pleasant terrace bar in the heart of the old town has eight different draught beers (from €3.60), snacks (charcuterie and cheese platter €6) and a happy hour (6–8pm). Daily 9am–12.30am.

Wayne's 15 rue de la Préfecture. Live music and DJ sets every night at this boisterous Irish bar, which heaves with backpackers and Anglophone expats. Happy hour 5–8pm. Daily 10am–2am.

MONACO

The tiny independent principality of **MONACO** rears up over the rocky Riviera coast like a Mediterranean Hong Kong. The 3km-long state consists of the old town of Monaco-Ville; Fontvieille; La Condamine by the harbour; Larvotto, with its artificial beaches of imported sand; and, in the middle, **MONTE CARLO**. There are relatively few conventional sights – indeed, Monaco seems composed of little other than roads, fast cars and apartment blocks – but one worth heading to is the superb (though expensive) **Musée Océanographique** on avenue St-Martin (daily: Jan–March & Oct–Dec 10am–6pm; April–June & Sept 10am–7pm; July & Aug 9.30am–8pm; €14; ⍵oceano.mc), which displays a living coral reef, transplanted from the Red Sea into a 40,000-litre tank. If you want to try your luck at the famous **casino** (over-18s only; daily 2pm–very late; €10 after 2pm), you'll have to dress smartly – no shorts or T-shirts – and show your passport.

ARRIVAL AND INFORMATION

By train Monaco train station is wedged between bd Rainier III and bd Princess Charlotte and has several exits, signposted clearly.

Destinations Nice (up to 4 hourly; 15–20min).

By bus Buses following the lower corniche or autoroute stop at place d'Armes by the *gare* SNCF and in Monte Carlo.

Tourist information 2a bd des Moulins (Mon–Sat 9am–7pm, Sun 11am–1pm; ☎07 92 16 61 16, ⍵visitmonaco.com).

ACCOMMODATION, EATING AND DRINKING

Le Pinocchio 30 rue Comte-Félix-Gastaldi. A reliable, good-value Italian in a narrow street in Monaco-Ville, dishing up hearty portions from a long menu of antipasti and pasta, including the likes of *saltimbocca* and veal Milanese from €20, and pizzas from €9. Mon–Sat noon–2.30pm & 7–10.30pm.

RIJ Villa Thalassa ☎04 93 78 18 58, ⍵clajsud.fr. This clean and welcoming hostel is just 2km away from Monte Carlo along the coast near a good beach at Cap d'Ail. You can walk here in 30min from the city, or get the train to Cap d'Ail. Dorms **€20**

Stars 'n' Bars 6 quai Antoine 1er. This feisty, well-known bar on the quai serves up good-value food (for Monaco; prices from €11). Happy hour 5.30–7.30pm. Daily 11am–midnight.

Villa Boeri 29 bd du Général-Leclerc, Beausoleil ☎04 93 78 38 10, ⍵hotelboeri.com. A short walk uphill into France from Monte Carlo, this cheerful and welcoming two star has a nice terrace out the front. The a/c rooms are soundproofed, with satellite TV and bath or shower and WC. Doubles **€105**

The southeast

The southeast of France encompasses a geographically varied area, from the thick forests of the Massif Central to the dramatic peaks of the Alps. The Massif Central, not the most accessible part of the country, is worth going out of your way for, especially to see the dramatic landscape that surrounds **Le Puy-en-Velay**, which makes an excellent base for exploration. Most travel in the region will require passing through **Lyon**, a beautiful city that's worth lingering over, especially to try some of its exquisite restaurants. From here, a few hours on a train will take you to **Grenoble**, hemmed in by snowcapped mountains, and to **Chamonix**, which really comes alive during the ski season, and is a great place for extreme sports throughout the year.

LE PUY-EN-VELAY

LE PUY sprawls across a broad basin in the mountains, a muddle of red roofs and poles of volcanic rock; both landscape and architecture are completely theatrical. The town is a good base for explorations of the Massif Central – the tourist office (see below) is well stocked with information to help you plan your visit.

The **cathedral**, at the top of Mont Corneille, with its small, almost Byzantine cupolas and Romanesque facade, dominates the old town. The nearby **church of St-Michel** (daily: mid-Feb to mid-March 2–5pm; mid-March to April & Oct to mid-Nov 9.30am–noon & 2–5.30pm; May to mid-July & Sept 9am–6.30pm; mid-July to Aug 9am–7pm; €3.50), at the top of Rocher d'Aiguilhe, is an eleventh-century construction that appears to have grown out of the rock.

ARRIVAL AND INFORMATION

By train The train station is on place du Maréchal Leclerc, a 15min walk from central place du Clauzel.
Destinations Lyon (7 daily; 2hr 30min); Paris (8 daily via St Etienne and/or Lyon; 4hr 25min–5hr 30min).
Tourist information 2 place du Clauzel (Easter–June & Sept Mon–Sat 9am–noon & 1.30–6pm, Sun 10am–noon & 2–5.30pm; July & Aug Mon–Sat 8.30am–7pm; Sun 10am–noon & 2–5.30pm; Oct–Easter Mon–Sat 8.30am–noon & 1.30–5.30pm, Sun 10am–noon; ☎04 71 09 38 41, ⓦ ot-lepuyenvelay.fr).

ACCOMMODATION

Dyke 37 bd Maréchal Fayolle ☎04 71 09 05 30, ⓦ dykehotel.fr. This basic two star is 5min walk from the train station and 10min from the town's historic area, and so is always popular – make sure you book ahead. Doubles €51
FUAJ Centre Pierre Cardinal 9 rue Jules Vallès ☎04 71 05 52 40, ⓦ fuaj.org. This hostel has old but clean dorms, plus basic breakfasts (€3) and cooking facilities; reservations are compulsory for weekend stays. Check-in Mon–Sat 2–11.30pm only, Sun 6–9pm. Dorms €15
Le Régional 36 bd du Maréchal Fayolle ☎04 71 09 37 74, ⓦ hotelleregional.fr. A basic hotel attached to a friendly bar, offering cheap and comfortable doubles with shared bathroom. Doubles €30

EATING

Âme des Poètes 16 rue Séguret. In a lovely spot by the cathedral, this restaurant serves inexpensive regional food such as green lentil lasagne with salad (mains €11–20). Closed March & Oct. Daily 11am–11pm.
Marco Polo 46 rue Raphaël. The freshly cooked pasta is the thing at this Italian restaurant with a beautiful vaulted cellar, just moments from the cathedral. *Menus* from €17. Tues–Sat 11.30am–3pm & 7–11pm.

LYON

LYON is France's gastronomic capital, with more restaurants per square metre than anywhere else on Earth. The city also has a vibrant nightlife and cultural scene, the highlight of which is the summer-long festival Les Nuits de Fourvière, celebrating theatre, music and dance.

11

WHAT TO SEE AND DO

The city is split into three by its two rivers – the Saône and the Rhône. The elegant city centre, **Le Presqu'Île**, is made up of grand boulevards and public squares, while across the Saône lies the beautifully preserved and atmospheric old Renaissance quarter of Vieux Lyon.

Le Presqu'Île

North from Gare de Perrache, the pedestrian rue Victor-Hugo opens out onto the vast place Bellecour, which dwarfs even its statue of Louis XIV on horseback. On rue de la Charité, the **Musée des Tissus et des Arts Decoratifs** (Tues–Sun 10am–5.30pm; €10; ⓦ www.mtmad.fr) has an interesting collection of fabrics, clothes and tapestries dating from ancient Egypt to the present, alongside a collection of period furnishings. Northwest of place Bellecour, on the east bank of the Saône, the quai St-Antoine is lined every morning with a colourful food market; a book market takes place just upriver on Sundays.

North and inland from the river, Place des Terreaux is home to the **Musée des Beaux-Arts** (daily except Tues 10/10.30am–6pm; €7; ⓦ mba-lyon.fr). This absorbing collection includes ancient Egyptian, Greek and Roman artefacts as well as works by Rubens, Renoir and Picasso.

La Croix-Rousse

North of place des Terreaux, the old silk weavers' district of **La Croix-Rousse** has an

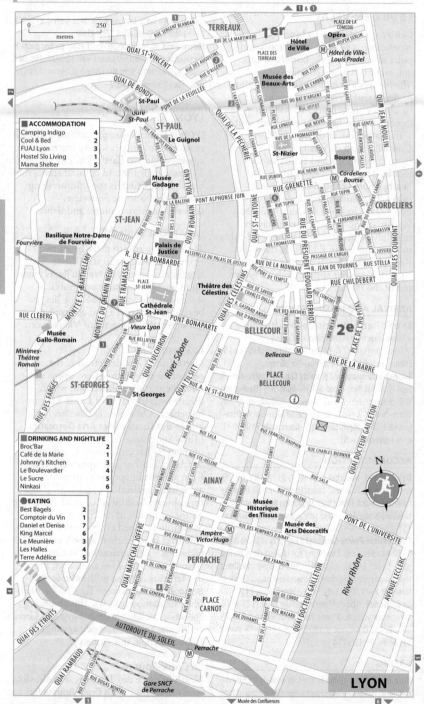

11

■ ACCOMMODATION

Camping Indigo	4
Cool & Bed	2
FUAJ Lyon	3
Hostel Slo Living	1
Mama Shelter	5

■ DRINKING AND NIGHTLIFE

Broc'Bar	2
Café de la Marie	1
Johnny's Kitchen	3
Le Boulevardier	4
Le Sucre	5
Ninkasi	6

● EATING

Best Bagels	2
Comptoir du Vin	1
Daniel et Denise	7
King Marcel	6
Le Meunière	3
Les Halles	4
Terre Adélice	5

LYON

authentic, creative feel to it. It is still a working-class area, but today only twenty or so people work on the computerized looms that are kept in business by the restoration and maintenance of tapestries within France's palaces and châteaux. The famous *traboules*, or covered alleyways, that run between streets were originally used to transport silk safely through town, later serving as wartime escape routes and hideouts for la Résistance. Look out for the small signs dotted about on walls in this area – follow the arrows to do a self-guided walking tour.

Vieux Lyon

The streets on the left bank of the Saône form an attractive muddle of cobbled lanes and Renaissance facades. The **Musée des Marionnettes du Monde & Musée d'Histoire de Lyon**, in the **Musée Gadagne** (Wed–Sun 11am–6.30pm; €6; ⓦgadagne .musees.lyon.fr), place du Petit Collège, is well worth an hour or two of your time, containing not just Lyon's famous puppets but also a collection of puppets from around the world. At the southern end of the rue St-Jean lies the **Cathédrale St-Jean**; though damaged during World War II, its thirteenth-century stained glass is in perfect condition.

Lyon Romain

Just beyond the cathedral, on avenue Adolphe-Max, is a funicular station, from which you can ascend (€1.80 one-way) to the two **Roman theatres** on rue de l'Antiquaille (daily: mid-April to mid-Sept 7am–9pm; mid-Sept to mid-April 7am–7pm; free), and the excellent **Musée de la Civilisation Gallo-Romaine**, 17 rue Cléberg (Tues–Sun 10am–6pm; €6), containing mosaics and other artefacts from Roman Lyon. Crowning the hill, the **Basilique de Notre-Dame** (daily 9am–7pm) is a gaudy showcase of multicoloured marble and mosaic, and there are fantastic views over the city from the gardens at the back of the church.

Elsewhere in the city

Reminders of the war are never far away in France, and the **Centre d'Histoire de**

la Résistance et de la Déportation, 14 av Berthelot (Wed–Sun 10am–6pm; €6), tells of the courage and ingenuity of the French Resistance. It also serves as a poignant memorial to the city's deported Jews. To the southeast of town, the **Musée Lumière**, 25 rue du Premier-Film (Tues–Sun 10am–6.30pm; €6.50; ⓦinstitut -lumiere.org), houses the Lumière brothers' cinematograph, which in 1895 projected the world's first film.

11

ARRIVAL AND DEPARTURE

By plane Lyon-St-Exupéry airport is 25km southeast of the city, connected by the Rhône Express tram (every 15min–30min; 4.25am–midnight; €15.80).

By train The main TGV train station, Gare de la Part-Dieu, is on bd Marius-Vivier-Merle, in the heart of the commercial district on the east bank of the Rhône, and connected to the centre by métro. Other trains arrive at the Gare de Perrache, by the southern edge of the centre on the Presqu'île.

Destinations Arles (7 daily; 2hr 40min); Avignon TGV (hourly; 1hr 10min); Dijon (hourly; 2hr); Geneva (13–15 daily; 1hr 45min–2hr 50min); Grenoble (every 30min; 1hr 15min–1hr 50min); Marseille (frequent; 1hr 45min–3hr 45min); Paris (every 30min; 2hr); Turin (via Chambery; 4 daily; 4–5hr).

INFORMATION

Tourist information place Bellecour (daily 9am–6pm; ☎04 72 77 69 69, ⓦen.lyon-france.com).

GETTING AROUND

By public transport Tickets for all city transport cost a flat €1.80, or buy the tourist office's *liberté* ticket for a day's unlimited travel on trams, buses and métro (€5.50).

By bike Vélo'v is a citywide cycling scheme where you take and leave a bike from one of about a hundred sites around town (€1.50/day ticket; first 30min free; ⓦvelov .grandlyon.com; credit card authorization required).

ACCOMMODATION

Camping Indigo Porte de Lyon ☎04 78 35 64 55, ⓦ camping-lyon.com; bus #89 from the bus station in Gare de Vaise, north of the city. The closest campsite to town, with a bar, restaurant, internet and a summer swimming pool. Per person and tent **€22.20**

Cool & Bed 32 Quai Arloing ☎04 26 18 05 28, ⓜ coolandbed.com. Located in a quiet courtyard next to the Saône River and a 20min walk from the old town (10min walk from metro stop Valmy), this is an excellent new hostel with stylish facilities and friendly staff. Dorms **€20**

★**FUAJ Lyon** 41–45 montée du Chemin Neuf ☎04 78 15 05 50, ⓦ fuaj.org. An excellent hostel, well worth the hike up from the métro station (Vieux Lyon; alternatively, take funicular to Minimes and walk down) for the fantastic views of the city from its terrace. Dorms are comfortable and clean, staff friendly and helpful, and there's a good bar. Dorms **€25.60**

★**Hostel Slo Living** 5 rue Bonnefoi ☎04 78 59 06 90, ⓦ slo-hostel.com. There are currently few better hostels in France than *Slo*, an easy-going place whose attractively designed, all-white rooms (four-, six- and eight-bedded dorms and private doubles) are located either side of a lovely wood-decked patio where you can play a game of *boules* or just kick back with a beer. Buffet breakfast €5. Dorms **€28**, doubles **€78**

Mama Shelter 13 rue Domer ☎04 78 02 58 00, ⓦ mamashelter.com. Another ultra-cool offering from the *Mama* family. Minimal, contemporary, with quality touches and luxuriously comfortable beds. Location is excellent (only three metro stops from the Gare de la Part-Dieu). Doubles **€69**

EATING

Best Bagels 1 place Tobie Robatel. With four addresses throughout the city, this bagel-bar is no longer a secret but its success is all in the name. Bagel, drink and accompaniment from €7.15. Mon & Tues 11.30am–10pm, Wed–Sat 11.30am–11pm, Sun 11am–2.30pm.

Comptoir du Vin 2 rue de Belfort ☎04 78 39 89 95. A fantastic local *bouchon* in the heart of the trendy Croix-Rousse district. Dishes are generous and delicious – the *andouillette* with mustard sauce (€3.80) is excellent. *Menus* from €13. Mon–Fri noon–2pm & 7–11pm, Sat noon–2pm.

King Marcel 31 rue Marcière ☎04 78 42 28 50. Choose from six juicy burgers (from €11), plus a veggie option, throw in some thick-cut fries and a green salad, then take a seat at one of the dinky tables (spread over two floors) and wait for it to be brought to you. Takeaway available too. Daily 11am–11pm.

Le Meunière 11 rue Neuve ☎04 78 28 62 91. Dyed-in-the-wool *bouchon* whose happily careworn demeanour is manifest in age-old furnishings and faded wall prints. Seating is arranged around a central "guest" table laden with various cuts of meat, cheeses and pâtés, while the menu states the likes of veal kidneys with port wine and mustard sauce. Good fun and good value. Mains €15. Tues–Sat noon–2pm & 7.30–9.30pm.

★**Les Halles** 102 cours Lafayette. Lyon's covered market has enough gorgeous produce to keep a gourmand happy for weeks – a great stop on sunny days when you can pick up everything you need for a picnic. There's also a good choice of bars and bistros for more leisurely lunches (mains from €11.50). Tues–Thurs 7am–12.30pm & 3–7pm, Fri & Sat 7am–7pm, Sun 7am–2pm.

Terre Adélice 1 place de la Baleine. Sparkling ice-cream parlour on a pretty old town square, though it's the sorbets that the locals really come here for. Choose, if you can, from over one hundred flavours, from the sublime (Armagnac, brandy and prune) to the ridiculous (cucumber). One scoop €4.60. April–Oct daily 12.30pm–midnight, Nov–March Wed–Sun noon–7pm.

DRINKING AND NIGHTLIFE

Broc'Bar 20 rue Lanterne. There's nothing obviously exciting about this street-corner café-cum-bar, with its battered-looking red and yellow tables and chairs, but the terrace is invariably packed with punters idly chatting over a daytime coffee or an evening beer. Sun & Mon 7am–1pm, Tues–Fri 7am–1am, Sat 8am–1am.

Café de la Mairie 4 place Sathonay. One of a number of low-key places on this pleasant *place* and a lovely spot for an early evening sundowner. Daily 7am–2am.

Johnny's Kitchen 48 rue St Georges. This Irish bar is where it's at, with a lively atmosphere, jovial bar staff and a great location in the old town. And sure, you're in gastronomic Lyon, but don't be embarrassed to order one of the burgers (€11 with fries and salad). *Pression* from €2.70. Mon–Thurs & Sun noon–1am, Fri & Sat noon–3am.

★ TREAT YOURSELF

Daniel et Denise 156 rue Créqui ☎04 78 60 66 53. If you've only got time to try one *bouchon* (a traditional Lyonnaise eating establishment), make it this one. This little corner restaurant will charm your socks off from the moment you step inside its old-fashioned interior, with its red-and-white-check-clothed table, tiled flooring and copper pots. On the menu are delicious dishes like sirloin of Angus beef with black pepper and Cognac, and poached pears with red wine and orange peel. Starters €14, mains €18. Closed Aug. Mon–Fri noon–2pm & 7–10pm.

Le Boulevardier 5 rue de la Fromagerie. A great little bar with a charming, relaxed feel that matches the jazz played here (both live and recorded). A good place to start or finish your night off (wine from €2.50, demi €2.70). Mon–Sat 7/8am–8pm, Sun 9am–3pm; till 3am Fri & Sat if there's a gig.
Le Sucre 50 quai Rambaud ⓦle-sucre.eu. Disused sugar factory on the banks of the Rhône that has been brilliantly converted into a cultural hub, the focal point of which is a rooftop bar playing host to an array of events, including techno club nights. Entry varies from free to €18. Thurs & Fri 10pm–5am, Sat 4pm–5am, Sun noon–midnight.
Ninkasi 267 rue Marcel Mérieux ⓦninkasi.fr. A high-spirited crowd is drawn here nightly to down a few refreshing house brews and soak up some cracking music, from live bands to world-renowned DJs. Entry free to €18 depending on event. Mon–Wed 10am–1am, Thurs 10am–2am, Fri & Sat 10am–4am, Sun 10am–midnight.

DIRECTORY

Health SAMU, emergency medical attention on ☎15; SOS Médecins ☎04 78 83 51 51. Hospitals: Croix-Rousse, 93 Grand rue de la Croix Rousse (☎04 72 07 10 46); Hôpital Edouard-Herriot, 5 place d'Arsonval, 3e (☎04 72 11 76 45).
Police The main commissariat is at 47 rue de la Charité, 2e (☎04 78 42 26 56).

GRENOBLE

The economic and intellectual capital of the French Alps, **GRENOBLE** is a thriving city, beautifully situated on the Drac and Isère rivers and surrounded by mountains. The old centre, south of the Isère, focuses on place Grenette and place Notre-Dame, both popular with local students, who lounge around in the many outdoor cafés. The central **Musée de Grenoble**, 5 place Lavalette (Mon & Wed–Sun 10am–6.30pm; €8; ⓦmuseedegrenoble.fr), is considered, by dint of its twentieth-century masterpieces, to be one of the best in Europe and includes works by Matisse, Chagall and Gauguin. Grenoble's highlight, however, especially in good weather, is the trip by **téléphérique** (May–Sept daily; Oct–April Tues–Sun; first ascent between 9.15am and 11am; last descent between 6.30pm and 12.15am according to the season; €5.50/8 one-way/return) from the riverside quai Stéphane Jay up to Fort de la Bastille on the steep slopes above the north bank of the Isère. It's a hair-raising ride to an otherwise uninteresting fort, but the views over the mountains and down onto the town are stunning, and the walk down is lovely and tranquil.

ARRIVAL AND INFORMATION

By bus and train The train and bus stations are on the northwestern edge of the city, at the end of av Félix Viallet, a 10min walk to the centre.
Destinations (train) Chamonix (5–9 daily with connections; 4hr 15min); Lyon (frequent; 1hr 15min–1hr 45min); Paris (several daily; 3hr); Turin (2–3 daily, via Chambéry; 3hr 30min–3hr 50min).
Tourist information 14 rue de la République, near place Grenette (May–Sept Mon–Sat 9am–7pm, Sun 9am–noon; Oct–April Mon 1–6pm, Tues–Sat 9am–6pm, Sun 9am–1pm; ☎04 76 42 41 41, ⓦgrenoble-tourisme.com).
Hiking information Maison de la Montagne, behind the tourist office at 3 rue Raoul Blanchard (Mon–Fri 9.30am–12.30pm & 1–6pm, Sat 10am–1pm & 2–5pm; ⓦgrenoble-montagne.com), is the place to go for information on mountain activities in the region.

GETTING AROUND

By bus and tram There are five tramlines in the city, of which lines A and B are the most useful, passing outside the train station and running through the city centre, plus a host of bus lines (ⓦtag.fr). A single ticket (€1.50; day pass €5) is valid for one hour on the TAG network, including changing vehicles.

HIKING IN THE ALPS

There are six **national and regional parks** in the Alps – Vanoise, Écrins, Bauges, Chartreuse, Queyras (the least busy) and Vercors (the gentlest) – each of which covers ideal walking country, as does the **Route des Grandes Alpes**, which crosses all the major massifs from Lake Geneva to Menton and should only be attempted by seasoned hikers. All walking routes are clearly marked and equipped with refuge huts, known as **gîtes d'étape** (ⓦwww.gites-refuges .com). The Maisons de la Montagne in Grenoble (see above) and Chamonix (see p.344) provide detailed information on GR paths (an abbreviation of Grande Randonnée, meaning "long ramble"), and local tourist offices often have maps of walks in their areas. Bear in mind that anywhere above 2000m will only be free of snow from early July until mid-September.

By bike Bike rental at Métrovélo, place de la Garem, lower level of the station (Mon–Fri 7am–8pm, Sat & Sun 9am–noon & 2–7pm; ⓦ metrovelo.fr; €3/24hr).

ACCOMMODATION

Alizé 1 place de la Gare ⓣ 04 76 43 12 91, ⓦ hotelalize .com. Just across the road from the station, Grenoble's cheapest hotel offers a friendly welcome and basic but surprisingly spacious and airy rooms. Doubles €43

De l'Europe 22 place Grenette ⓣ 04 76 46 16 94, ⓦ hoteleurope.fr. Faded grandeur in a seventeenth-century building with a central location overlooking the square. Rooms are generally small, and the cheapest have shared bathrooms. Doubles €59

★ **FUAJ Grenoble** 10 av du Grésivaudan ⓣ 04 76 09 33 52, ⓦ fuaj.org; bus #1 to la Quinzaine (the best option) or tram A to la Rampe. This smart, modern, eco-friendly hostel has ultra-clean dorms and a good atmosphere. There's excellent information about hiking in the area and skiing in winter; unfortunately it's 5km from the centre of town. Dorms €20.20

Les Trois Pucelles ⓣ 04 76 96 45 73, ⓦ camping3 pucelles-grenoble.fr; tram C in the direction of Le Prisme and get off at Mas des Îles. Located 4km from Grenoble, in Seyssins, this campsite has 65 pitches, two swimming pools and a restaurant in an arboretum by the Drac River (400m south of Mas des Îles). May–Sept. Per person and tent €10.50

Victoria 17 rue Thiers ⓣ 04 76 46 06 36, ⓦ hotelvictoria grenoble.com. A charming hotel in a quiet street close to town. Some rooms are spacious with traditional decor but some look onto grey rooftops; most are en suite. Doubles €53

EATING AND DRINKING

K Fée des Jeux 1 quai Stéphane Jay. A unique place specializing in board games, Sun brunch and, strangely,

---

★ **TREAT YOURSELF**

One of the most exhilarating experiences you can have in the Alps is not on the ground, but in the air. A number of companies operate **tandem paragliding flights**, which allow you to take in the fantastic scenery from a different perspective. Fly Chamonix (ⓣ 610 28 20 77, ⓦ fly-chamonix.com) offers tandem flights from €100 – for more information, or to book a flight, head to Chamonix Freeride Centre, 280 rue Paccard, Chamonix (daily 9am–noon & 3–7pm).

---

mead. The food is good value too, particularly the €12.80 lunch *formule*. Tues–Sat 11am–1am.

L'As de Pique 14 rue Lieutenant ⓣ 04 76 87 32 91. Enjoy a glass of wine (€2) in this pleasantly atmospheric and retro bar. The adjoining restaurant serves the regional speciality *Ravioles de Royans* (dishes €14–22). Mon–Fri 11am–midnight, Sat noon–2pm & 6pm–midnight.

La Gazzetta 30 av Félix Viallet ⓣ 04 76 50 22 22. A cut above your average Italian, *La Gazzetta* offers sublimely crafted dishes like mushroom and foie gras ravioli, and pappardelle with crayfish and asparagus tips (from €13), as well as pizza (from €9). The big bay windows and mezzanine-level seating lend this place a lounge-like feel. Mon–Fri noon–2pm & 7–10pm, Sat 7–10pm.

Le Café des Arts 36 rue St-Laurent ⓦ lecafedesarts38.fr. This intimate venue with stone walls and low lighting is suitably atmospheric for its varied programme, which ranges from African blues and Balkan jazz to classical and chanson. Check website for details. Mon–Sat 8pm–midnight.

Le Ferme à Dédé 1 place aux Herbes ⓣ 04 76 54 00 33. You could be forgiven for thinking you were halfway up a mountain in this fun restaurant, with its red-and-white-checked tablecloths and randomly scattered alpine junk. The big menu features hearty sausage casseroles, gooey Savoyard fondues and local favourites, *raclette* and *tartiflette*. Packed to the gills most nights. Mains from €14. Mon–Sat noon–2pm & 7–10pm.

Mark XIII 8 rue Lakanal. A two-floor bar and venue that draws in an exciting depth and variety of underground electronic DJ talent (progressive house, drum'n'bass, techno, ambient). Tues & Wed 2pm–1am, Thurs–Sat 2pm–2am.

CHAMONIX AND MONT BLANC

At 4810m, **Mont Blanc** is both Western Europe's highest mountain and the Alps' biggest draw. Nestled at its base, the town of **CHAMONIX** is lively year-round; in summer it's popular for rock climbing and hiking, while in winter its draw is the area's vast skiing possibilities. The pricey **téléphérique** (daily every 15min: May, June & Sept 8.10am–4pm; July & Aug 6.30am–5pm; Oct–April 8.10am–3.30pm; €58.50 return; ⓣ 04 50 53 22 75) soars to the Aiguille du Midi (3842m), a terrifying granite pinnacle on which the cable-car station and a restaurant are precariously balanced. Here, the view of Mont Blanc, coupled with the altitude, will literally leave you breathless. Book the téléphérique ahead to avoid the queues and get there early, before the clouds and the crowds close up.

ARRIVAL AND DEPARTURE

By train Chamonix train station is 3min walk from the centre, down av Michel Croz.

Destinations Grenoble (2 daily, via St Gervais; 6hr 10min); Lyon (8 daily, via St Gervais; 4–5hr).

By bus Buses leave from in front of the train station.

Destinations Courmayeur, Italy (2–6 daily; 45min); Geneva (2 daily; 2hr).

INFORMATION

Tourist information The tourist office at 85 place du Triangle-de-l'Amitié (daily: mid-April to mid-Dec 9am–12.30pm & 2–6pm; mid-Dec to mid-April 8.30am–7pm; ☏ 04 50 53 00 24, ⓦ chamonix.com) is able to book accommodation, provide good information on local activities and advise on weather and snow conditions.

Hiking information The Maison de la Montagne on place de L'Église is the place for organizing climbing, trekking, mountain biking and parapenting. On the top floor, l'Office de Haute Montagne (Mon–Sat 9am–noon & 3–6pm; July & Aug also Sun; ☏ 04 50 53 22 08, ⓦ ohm -chamonix.com) offer general advice on mountain conditions and activities. They also have good information about the Gîtes de Montagne that are situated along the major hiking trails.

ACCOMMODATION

Camping Les Marmottes 140 chemin des Doux ☏ 04 50 53 61 24, ⓦ camping-lesmarmottes.com. Situated off the main road south of Chamonix, this campsite is linked to the town via a free bus service. Facilities include a games room, use of barbecues and a laundry, and it enjoys great views of Mont Blanc. Per person **€6.80**, plus per tent **€3**

FUAJ Chamonix-Mont Blanc 127 Montée J. Balmat, les Pélerins d'en Haut ☏ 04 50 53 14 52, ⓦ fuaj.org; bus #3 from the town centre or the train to Les Pélerins. Situated in a traditional chalet 2km out of the centre, this hostel has good dorms and a friendly atmosphere, but no on-site kitchen. Closed noon–5pm & 7.30–8.30pm. Dorms **€29.80**

★ **Gîte Vagabond** 365 av Ravanel-le-Rouge ☏ 04 50 53 15 43, ⓦ gitevagabond.com. This lively and friendly hostel is a good choice year-round and invaluably cheap for the ski season (book ahead), when half-board packages are available. Dorms **€21**

Vert Hotel 964 rte des Gaillands ☏ 04 50 53 13 58, ⓦ verthotel.com; bus #1 stops outside. Around 1km west of the town centre, close to the Lac du Gaillands, this is a

welcoming place, offering a mix of double, triple and quad rooms. There's an atmospheric lounge bar-cum-restaurant that does fabulous cocktails and delicious food. Free pick-ups on request. **€70**

EATING AND DRINKING

L'Atelier Café quai D'Arve. This easy-going and colourful café serves up the best coffee (and pastries) in town, alongside light lunches (bagels and croques), breakfasts and brunches. Daily 8.30am–10pm.

Le Bartavel 26 cour du Bartavel ☏ 04 50 53 97 19. With its sprawling terrace edging out towards place Balmat, this is a good budget bet. Pizza (€10) and pasta (€12) form the mainstay of a long menu, which also includes soups, salads, crêpes and grillades. Daily 11.30am–11.30pm.

MBC 350 route du Bouchet. This microbrewery is perfect for those who find bière blonde doesn't quite hit the spot in the mountain air. Burger lovers will be satisfied, too (from €10). Food served 4–10.30pm. Daily 3pm–2am.

Moö Bar Cuisine 239 av Michel-Croz. A laidback Swedish-run bar-restaurant serving good-value dishes such as the plat du jour (€10.90) or pulled-pork burger €12.50 – all dishes served with salad. The bar has regular live bands. Daily 11.30am–1am.

Poco Loco 47 rue Paccard. It doesn't look like much, but this sliver of a snack bar does what it does – toasted sandwiches and other sur le pouce (on the go) goodies (from €4.40) – very well and very generously. Daily 11.30am–9.30pm.

Corsica

Known to the French as the "île de beauté", Corsica has an amazing diversity of natural landscape. One-third national park, its magnificent rocky coastline is interspersed with outstanding beaches, while the interior mountains soar as high as 2706m. Two French *départements* divide Corsica, each with its own capital: Napoleon's birthplace, **Ajaccio** on the southwest coast; and **Bastia**, which faces Italy in the north. The old capital of **Corte** dominates the interior, backed by a formidable wall of mountains. Of the coastal resorts, **Calvi** draws tourists with its massive citadel and long sandy beach; **Bonifacio**'s Genoan houses perch atop limestone cliffs, overseeing the clearest water in the Mediterranean, on the island's southernmost point. Still more dramatic landscapes lie around the

Golfe de Porto in the far northwest, where the famous red cliffs of the **Calanches de Piana** rise over 400m.

ARRIVAL AND DEPARTURE

By plane Air France (ⓦairfrance.fr) and its partner company Air Corsica (CCM; ⓦaircorsica.com) have regular flights to Corsica's four airports at Ajaccio, Bastia, Calvi and Figari (near Bonifacio) year-round. It's often possible to get discounts if you are under 25. In addition, easyJet (ⓦeasyjet .com) fly daily to Bastia and Ajaccio; Ryanair (ⓦryanair.com) fly daily to Figaro from Paris; Transavia (ⓦtransavia.com) fly from Nantes to Ajaccio three times weekly; and XL Airways (ⓦxlairways.com) fly to Figari from Paris during the summer. Bastia's airport, Poretta, is 20km south of town. Shuttle buses (35–40min; €9) meet all flights and stop outside the train station in the centre of town.

By ferry The island is served by a number of ferry companies which run services from both France (Marseille, Nice and Toulon) and Italy: Corsica Ferries (ⓦcorsica -ferries.com), La Méridionale (ⓦlameridionale.fr), Moby (ⓦmobylines.fr) and Corsica Linea (ⓦcorsicalinea.com). Prices range between €20 and €75 for foot passengers, plus between €100 and €250 for a vehicle, depending on the date. Routes are scaled back in winter (Oct–March) to several journeys a week; check websites for details. Bastia's port is in the north of town, a 5min walk from the centre.

Destinations from Nice Ajaccio (5–6 weekly; 6hr 15min–7hr); Bastia (7–8 weekly; 5hr 20min–7hr 30min); Calvi (daily; 5hr 45min).

Destinations from Marseille Ajaccio (1–2 daily; 13hr); Bastia (1–2 daily; 13hr).

Destinations from Livorno, Italy Bastia (1–2 daily; 4hr).

Destinations from Genoa, Italy Bastia (1 daily; 4hr 45min).

Destinations from Savona, Italy Bastia (4–14 weekly; 6hr).

Destinations from Santa Teresa di Gallura, Italy Bonifacio (late March to Sept 4–14 weekly; 50min).

GETTING AROUND

Corsica is somewhat difficult to navigate if relying on public transport, with services slow and infrequent. The unofficial website ⓦcorsicabus.org is helpful for train and bus timetables. Bastia is the island's main transport hub – while there's little of particular interest here, there's a good chance that you'll pass through the town at least once during your visit.

By train Corsica's narrow-gauge railway crosses the mountains to connect the island's main towns along the most scenic of lines. Lines run from Calvi to Ponte Leccia in the interior and from Ajaccio to Bastia via Corte. A single journey between Ajaccio and Bastia costs €21.60; InterRail tickets reduce fares to half for all services, while students can get a discount of 25 percent. Bastia's station is located west of place St-Nicolas.

Destinations from Bastia Ajaccio (3–5 daily; 3hr 45min); Calvi (change at Ponte Leccia; 3 daily; 3hr 15min); Corte (3–5 daily; 1hr 45min).

By bus Bus services are fairly frequent out of Bastia and Ajaccio, and along the east coast to Porto-Vecchio and Bonifacio. Elsewhere in the island, services are relatively infrequent. Fares are reasonable: tickets for the two-hour trip between Bastia and Calvi cost €16. Services are scaled back drastically Nov–May. Buses arrive in, and depart from, Bastia via either Rond Point de la Prefacture, near the train station, or rue du Nouveau Port.

Destinations Calvi (2 daily; 2hr); Porto-Vecchio (2 daily; 3hr).

By scooter With little public transport and many secluded beaches to visit, the roads that undulate and meander around Corsica mean it's a great place to rent a scooter. Try Scootloc at place du Marché in Ajaccio (€39–46/day; ☏ 06 26 17 31 07); Scoot Rent at 3 quai Banda del Ferro in Bonifacio (€50/day; ☏ 06 25 44 22 82); or Garage d'Angeli at 4 Quartier Neuf in Calvi (€35–50/day; ☏ 04 95 65 02 13).

By car Driving is by far the most convenient way to get around Corsica. Hertz (ⓦhertz.fr), Europcar (ⓦeuropcar .com) and Avis (ⓦavis.fr) all have offices in the big towns and airports; for the best prices, book via an online car rental portal.

AJACCIO

Set in a magnificent bay, **AJACCIO** has all the ingredients of a Riviera-style town with its palm trees, spacious squares, glamorous marina and street cafés. **Napoleon** was born here in 1769, but did little for the place except to make it the island's capital for the brief period of his empire. It is, however, a lovely place to spend time, particularly around the harbour and narrow streets inland from the fifteenth-century **Genoese** citadel. The **Palais Fesch: Musée des Beaux Arts**, rue Cardinal-Fesch (May–Sept Mon, Wed & Sat 10.30am–6pm, Thurs, Fri & Sun noon–6pm; Oct–April Mon, Wed & Sat 10am–5pm, Thurs, Fri & Sun noon–5pm; €8), is home to the country's most important collection of Renaissance paintings outside Paris, including works by Botticelli, Titian and Poussin. The best beach to head to is **plage Trottel**, ten minutes southwest from the centre along the promenade.

ARRIVAL AND DEPARTURE

By plane The airport, Napoléon Bonaparte, is 8km east and connected to the town by *navette* (shuttle bus; 3 hourly; €4.50).

By train The train station is a 10min walk north along the seafront.
Destinations Bastia (4 daily; 3hr 30min); Calvi (change at Ponte Leccia; 2 daily; 4hr); Corte (2–4 daily; 2hr).
By bus and ferry The ferry port and bus station occupy the same building off quai L'Herminier.
Destinations (bus) Bastia (2 daily; 3hr); Bonifacio (1–2 daily; 3hr 15min); Corte (3–5 daily; 2hr).

INFORMATION

Tourist information place du Marché (April–June & Sept Mon–Sat 8am–7pm, Sun 9am–1pm; July & Aug Mon–Sat 8am–8.30pm, Sun 9am–1pm & 4–7pm; Oct–March Mon–Fri 8.30am–6pm, Sat 8.30am–noon; ☏ 04 95 51 53 03, ⓦ ajaccio-tourisme.com).

ACCOMMODATION

Budget accommodation in Ajaccio is hard to find and hotels get booked up quite quickly. The tourist office can provide a list of those available as well as private apartments to rent.
Camping de Barbicaja Route des îles Sanguinaires ☏ 04 95 52 01 17; bus #5 from place Général-du-Gaulle. The most convenient campsite is 3km out of town, near the beach, a short bus ride away. Closed Nov–March. Two people and tent **€14.60**
Du Palais 8 bd Bévérini-Vico ☏ 04 95 22 73 68, ⓦ hoteldupalaisajaccio.com. A well-run place just a 10min walk north of the centre, within easy reach of the train station. The rooms are on the small side, but they're impeccably clean. Ask for one at the rear of the building if you want peace and quiet. Doubles **€80**
Marengo 2 rue Marengo ☏ 04 95 21 43 66, ⓦ hotel-marengo.com. A sweet little hotel with spacious, clean rooms. The cheapest have shared toilets, while some lead onto a floral courtyard. Doubles **€77.80**

EATING AND DRINKING

Da Mamma 3 passage Guingette ☏ 04 95 21 39 44. The set €17 *menu* (entrée, *plat* and dessert) doesn't compromise on quality in this traditional restaurant, pleasantly situated in the shade of a magnificent rubber tree; expect dishes like roast kid and seafood. Mon 6.30–11pm, Tues–Sat noon–2.30pm & 6.30–11pm.
Le Grand Café Napoleon 10 cours Napoléon ☏ 04 95 21 42 54. One of the oldest, grandest establishments in Ajaccio where you can eat in style – though not necessarily pay the price. Drop by for a pastry, or enjoy the good-value €20 *menu*. Mon–Sat 7am–11pm.
Le Temps des Oliviers 1 rue des Halles ☏ 04 95 28 36 72. Run by a pair of young sisters, this upbeat backstreet bistro occupies a secluded spot on a traffic-free alley. It serves quality Italian dishes: the pizzas (€12–15) are sublime, and so are the risotto and *grillades*. DJs play most

Thursday evenings. Mon–Sat noon–2.30pm & 6.30–11pm. Closed lunchtimes in July & Aug.
Vino de Diablo Port de l'Amirauté. A party place with live music and a lovely expansive terrace on the port. Three tapas and a drink for €13; good lunch *menu* at around the same price. Tues–Sat 5.30pm–2am.

LE GOLFE DE PORTO

Corsica's most startling landscapes surround the **Golfe de Porto**, on the west coast. A deep blue bay enfolded by outlandish red cliffs, among them the famous **Calanches de Piana** rock formations, the gulf is framed by snow-topped mountains and a vast pine forest. The entire area holds endless possibilities for outdoor enthusiasts, with a superb network of marked trails (free maps available from the Ajaccio tourist office) and **canyoning** routes, perfect bays for **kayaking** and some of the finest **diving** sites in the Mediterranean.

Porto

Less adventurous visitors can explore the coast on one of the excursion boats from the village of **PORTO**, the gulf's main tourist hub.

ARRIVAL AND INFORMATION

By bus Buses arrive and depart from the junction at the end of the route de la Marine, opposite the Banco supermarket, en route to the marina. The local bus operator is Autocars SAIB (ⓦ autocarsiledebeaute .com).
Destinations Ajaccio (1–2 daily; 2hr 10min); Calvi (May to mid-Oct 1 daily; 2hr 30min).
Tourist information Quartier la Marine (May, June & Sept daily 9am–6pm; July & Aug daily 9am–7pm; Oct–April Mon–Fri 9am–5pm; ☏ 04 95 26 10 55, ⓦ porto-tourisme.com).

ACCOMMODATION AND EATING

The village has a huge range of accommodation. For an inexpensive meal, try one of the pizzerias lining the roadside above the marina.
Camping Les Oliviers Along from the supermarket on the main road east from the village ☏ 04 95 26 14 49, ⓦ camping-oliviers-porto.com. Lovely campsite, with pitches under the shade of olive trees. Amenities include a bar, swimming pool, gym, hot tub, a hammam and massages. Per person **€10.80**, plus per tent **€4**

Le Golfe At the base of the rock in the marina ☎ 04 95 26 12 31, ⓦ hotel-le-golfe-porto.com. Small, cosy and unpretentious; every room has a balcony with a sea view. Among the cheapest at this end of the village. Closed Nov–Aug. Doubles €58

Le Romulus cours Napoléon. A good-value Italian, offering pizza (from €8.50), pasta dishes (€9.50) and lasagne. The terrace is a particularly lovely spot come evening. Mon–Sat noon–2pm & 7–10.30pm.

CALVI

Seen from the water, the great citadel of **CALVI** resembles a floating island, defined by a hazy backdrop of snow-capped mountains. The island's third port, it draws thousands of tourists for its 6km of sandy beach. The **ville haute**, a labyrinth of cobbled lanes and stairways encased by a citadel, rises from **place Christophe Colomb**, which links it to the town and marina of the *ville basse*. The square's name derives from the local belief that the discoverer of the New World was born here, in a now ruined house on the edge of the citadel. To reach the public **beach**, keep walking south, past the boats in the marina, and – unless you want to pay for a lounger and waited service – past the private beach bars.

ARRIVAL AND DEPARTURE

By plane Calvi's Ste-Catherine airport is 7km southeast of town, connected only by taxis (€25–30).

By train The train station, on av de la République, is just off the marina to the south of the town centre.

Destinations Ajaccio (2 daily; 4hr 10min); Bastia (2 daily; 3hr 20min); Corte (2 daily; 2hr 25min).

By bus Buses to and from Bastia and Calenzana stop in place Porteuse d'Eau, next to the station. Porto buses operate from the roadside behind the marina.

Destinations Bastia (1 daily; 1hr 45min–2hr 15min); Porto (1 daily; 2hr 30min).

By ferry The ferry port is on the opposite side of the marina, below the citadel.

INFORMATION

Tourist information quai Landry (mid-June to Sept daily 9am–7pm; Oct to mid-June Mon–Fri 9am–noon & 2–5.30pm, Sat 9am–noon; ☎ 04 95 65 16 67, ⓦ balagne -corsica.com).

ACCOMMODATION

Camping Bella Vista rte de Pietra-Maggiore, 1km southeast of the centre ☎ 04 95 65 11 76, ⓦ camping -calvi-bellavista.com. Much closer to the centre of town than the competition – though you pay a couple of euros extra a night for the privilege. Plenty of shade, nice soft ground and clean toilet blocks. Closed Nov–March. Two people and tent €17

Du Centre 14 rue Alsace-Lorraine ☎ 04 95 65 02 01. The most convenient budget accommodation, hidden away in the *ville basse*, with modest and well-kept rooms. Double €60

U Carabellu rte de Pietra-Maggiore ☎ 04 95 65 14 16, ⓦ clajsud.fr. Book ahead for this hostel, with tidy spacious dorms and a great out-of-town location overlooking the bay. From the station, turn left down av de la République, then right at the Total garage after 500m and keep walking for 3.5km. Also offers full- and half-board options. Dorms €20

EATING AND DRINKING

Bar de la Tour quai Landry. A lovely spot overlooking the water, and a great place for an early-evening beer. Daily noon–1am.

Best Of 1 rue Clemenceau, Port de Plaisance Area. The wood-fired bread topped with local specialities, panini and sandwiches made here are perfect for a snack on the move. Daily 11.30am–10pm.

La Tire Bouchon 15 rue Clemenceau ☎ 04 95 38 21 87. Serving traditional Corsican cuisine such as veal stew or tagliatelle with *brocciu* (fresh ewe's or goat's cheese). Mains €12–22, *menu* €25. April–Oct daily noon–2pm & 7–11pm.

Pizzeria Cappuccino Quai Landry ☎ 04 95 65 11 19. This restaurant has a great atmosphere and serves up good-value *calzones* (from €12) and pasta. Daily noon–3pm & 6–11pm.

CORTE

Perching on the rocky crags of the island's spine, **CORTE**, the island's only interior town, is regarded as the spiritual capital of Corsica, as this is where **Pasquale Paoli** had his seat of government during the brief period of independence in the eighteenth century. Paoli founded a university here and its student population adds some much-needed life. For outdoor enthusiasts, this is also an ideal base for **trekking** into the island's steep valleys, with two superb gorges stretching west into the heart of the mountains.

WHAT TO SEE AND DO

The main street, **cours Paoli**, runs the length of town, culminating in **place Paoli**, a pleasant market square lined with cafés. A cobbled ramp leads up to the **ville haute**, where you can still see the bullet marks made by Genoese soldiers during the War of Independence in tiny **place Gaffori**. Continuing north, you'll soon come to the gates of the **citadelle**, whose well-preserved ramparts enclose the ethnographic **Museu di a Corsica** (April to mid-June & mid-Sept to Oct Tues–Sun 10am–6pm; mid-June to mid-Sept daily 10am–8pm; Nov–March Tues–Sat 10am–5pm; €5.30). The best views of the citadel, the town and its valley are from the **Belvédère**, a man-made lookout post on the southern end of the ramparts.

ARRIVAL AND INFORMATION

By train Corte's train station is 1km southeast of town at the foot of the hill near the university.

Destinations Ajaccio (4 daily; 1hr 50min); Bastia (4 daily; 1hr 35min); Calvi (2 daily via Ponte Leccia; 2hr 30min).

By bus Buses to and from Porto (1 daily; 2hr 30min) work from outside the train station. Since the upgrade of the train line there are no longer any bus services from Ajaccio or Bastia.

Tourist information In the *citadelle* (July & Aug Mon, Wed & Sat 10am–5pm, Tues, Thurs & Fri 9am–7pm; Sept–June Mon–Fri 9am–noon & 2–6pm; ☎ 04 95 46 26 70, ⓦ corte-tourisme.com).

ACCOMMODATION

Ferme Équestre l'Albadu Ancienne route d'Ajaccio ☎ 04 95 46 24 55, ⓦ hebergement-albadu.fr. The nicest of the local campsites, located a 15min walk from town

– follow the main road south down the hill from place Paoli and take the second right after the second bridge. Per person **€6**, plus per tent **€3**

Gîte d'Étape U Tavignanu Behind the citadelle ☎ 04 95 46 16 85. Run-of-the-mill hikers' hostel with small dorms and a relaxing garden terrace that looks over the valley. Follow the signs for the Tavignano trail (marked with orange spots of paint) around the back of the citadelle. Breakfast included. Easter to mid-Oct. Dorms **€20**

HR Allée du 9 Septembre ☎ 04 95 45 11 11, ⓦ hotel-hr .com. Cheap and cheerful rooms in an old converted police station southwest of the station and just 10min from the centre. No credit cards. Doubles **€50**

EATING AND DRINKING

Café du Cours 22 rue Paoli. Student nights and well-priced drinks at this busy bar which also has internet access, some live Corsican bands and daytime left-luggage facilities; *demi* €3. Daily 7am–2am.

Les Délices du Palais cours Paoli. Frilly little crêperie-cum-*salon de thé* whose bakery sells a selection of delicious Corsican patisserie: try their *colzone* (spinach pasties) or *brocciu* baked in flaky chestnut-flour pastry. Mon–Sat 9am–2pm & 4–6pm.

U Valentinu 1 place Paoli ☎ 04 95 61 19 65. This great little Italian restaurant on the main street serves Corte's best pizzas, baked to perfection in a wood oven. The dining hall is spacious, staff are friendly, portions copious and prices reasonable. Go for one of their Corsican speciality options, featuring mountain charcuterie and ewe's cheese. Mains from €8. Daily noon–2.30pm & 6–10.30pm.

BONIFACIO

The port of **BONIFACIO** has a superb, isolated position on a narrow peninsula of dazzling white limestone at Corsica's southernmost point, only an hour away by

11

THE GR20

The **GR20 hiking trail** stretches across Corsica's dramatic granite spine from Calenzana in the north to Conza in the south. Covering a breathtaking landscape, the route takes you through some lush countryside and over the snowcapped peaks of the heart of the island. It is manageable for anyone in reasonable shape with basic trekking common sense, but proper hiking equipment is essential, as are nerves of steel for the ropes and vertical staircases built into the mountainside. Covering a distance of 180km, it takes around two weeks to complete, walking 2–6hr per day; red and white waymarks show the route, which is well serviced with bunked **mountain refuges**. Although the refuges cook and sell food, several days' supplies and a good stock of water are recommended. Do not attempt the route outside of the summer months; even then there is some residual snow in parts.

Buses go from Calvi to Calenzana (1–2 daily; 30min; €8), where the walk begins. Accommodation details and more information about the route itself can be found at ⓦ corsica.forhikers.com/gr20. Detailed maps can be obtained from the Calvi tourist office.

boat from Sardinia. For hundreds of years the town held the most powerful **fortress** in the Mediterranean and was a virtually independent republic. Nowadays, people are met with sights of precariously balanced houses edging their way into the sea. Bonifacio has become a chic holiday spot, sailing centre and deluxe day trip.

WHAT TO SEE AND DO

The **ville haute** is connected to the marina by a steep flight of steps at the west end of the quay, at the top of which you can enjoy glorious views across the straits to Sardinia. Within the massive fortifications of the citadel is an alluring maze of cobbled streets which bring you back down to the marina, where a **boat excursion** (from €17.50; try Rocca Croisières, ⓦ rocca-croisieres.com) round the base of the cliffs gives a fantastic view of the town and the **sea caves**. Some outstanding beaches lie near Bonifacio, most notably the shell-shaped **plage de la Rondinara**, 10km north; further north still, off the main Porto Vecchio road, the **plages de Santa Giulia** and **Palombaggia** wouldn't look out of place in the Maldives. Buses (1–4 daily; 30–40min) make the journey from Bonifacio to Porto Vecchio, passing the turn-off for la Rondinara. From Porto Vecchio a beach bus runs in July and August to Palombaggia (3 daily at 9.45am, 1.45pm, 4.20pm; 45min) and another to Santa Giulia (Mon–Sat 4 daily at 9.50am, 12.10pm, 3.05pm & 6.30pm; 20min).

ARRIVAL AND DEPARTURE

By plane Figari Sud-Corse Airport is located 20km from Bonifacio. A seasonal bus service is run by Transports Rossi (ⓣ 04 95 71 00 11) that should in theory meet incoming flights, stopping at Bonifacio en route to Porto Vecchio; otherwise your only option is to take a taxi into town – around €50.

By bus Buses drop passengers in the marina, next to the tourist office.

Destinations Ajaccio (2 daily; 3hr 30min); Bastia (2–4 daily; 3hr 25min); Porto Vecchio 1–4 daily; 30–40min).
By ferry Boats from Santa-Teresa-di-Gallura on Sardinia dock at the far end of the quay at the bottom of the hill.
Destinations Santa-Teresa-di-Gallura (late March to Sept 2–8 daily; 50min).

INFORMATION

Tourist information The tourist office is based in the *ville haute*, at the bottom of rue Fred Scamaroni (July–Sept daily 9am–7pm; Oct–June Mon–Fri 9am–noon & 2–5pm; ⓣ 04 95 73 11 88, ⓦ bonifacio.fr).

ACCOMMODATION

L'Araguina 33 av de Bonifaccio ⓣ 04 95 73 02 96, ⓦ camping-araguina-bonifacio.com. The only campsite close to the town has lumpy and sandy pitches but loans out tents and sleeping bags for those unprepared. It's north from the marina, 1km out of town with an unfortunate roadside location. Per person **€8**, plus per tent **€3.20**
Des Étrangers av Sylvère Bohn ⓣ 04 95 73 01 09. An absolute bargain just north of the harbour, offering spick-and-span rooms with tiled floor, plus more expensive rooms with a/c. Closed Nov–March. Doubles **€60**
Royal 8 rue Fred Scamaroni ⓣ 04 95 73 00 51, ⓦ hotel-leroyal.com. A good option in the centre of town, only minutes away from the tourist office. Don't let the slightly faded blue carpet and curtain-less showers put you off – the beds are comfy and it offers a decent night's sleep. Doubles **€75**

EATING AND DRINKING

B'52 Quai Camparetti. A laidback and tasteful late-night waterfront bar with tapas bites to accompany the house cocktails. Mid-June to mid-Sept daily 8pm–2am.
Cantina Doria 27 rue Doria ⓣ 04 95 73 50 49. A charming little place with odds and ends strung from the rafters, and serving traditional, hearty, Corsican specialities – try the fish soup or charcuterie. Three-course menu for €18. June to mid-Sept daily noon–3pm & 6–11pm; March–May & mid-Sept to Oct closed Sat.
Kissing Pigs 15 quai Banda del Ferro ⓣ 04 95 73 56 09. In spite of the prevailing pig theme (excellent *charcuterie*), the *aubergine à la bonifacienne* is one of the highlights and the €19 *châtaignes* ("chestnuts") *menu* is a steal. Worth reserving a table on the terrace for a dreamy view of the port. Daily 11am–late.

BEER PAVILION, OKTOBERFEST, MUNICH

Germany

HIGHLIGHTS

❶ **Berlin** Dramatic history and gritty modernity combine in this most untamed of European capitals. **See p.358**

❷ **Dresden** Glorious Baroque architecture by day; decadent bar-crawling by night. **See p.370**

❸ **Dom, Cologne** Cologne's cathedral is Gothic grandeur on a massive scale. **See p.387**

❹ **Heidelberg** Great romantic setting, buzzing student life and the best castle ruins in Germany. **See p.398**

❺ **Oktoberfest, Munich** The world's most famous beer festival. **See p.409**

HIGHLIGHTS ARE MARKED ON THE MAP ON P.353

ROUGH COSTS

Daily budget Basic €55, occasional treat €70

Drink Beer (half-litre) €2.90

Food Schnitzel €8

Hostel/budget hotel €25/€35

Travel Munich–Berlin: train €55–142, bus €22

FACT FILE

Population 81.2 million

Language German

Currency Euro (€)

Capital Berlin

International phone code ☏49

Time zone GMT +1hr

Introduction

Berlin and Munich deservedly draw the crowds, but the rest of Germany is often underrated as a destination, despite its picture-postcard medieval villages, dynamic modern cities and swathes of idyllic countryside. But those who do explore more widely will find a rich regional diversity, which harks back to a time when the country was made up of a patchwork of independent states, and a robust respect for the past. There are plenty of unique customs, festivals, castles, historic town centres, food, beers and wines to discover. Juxtaposed with all this tradition is – in Germany's cities, at least – a wholehearted embracing of modernity. Here inventiveness is celebrated in dynamic modern architecture, slick engineering, cutting-edge contemporary art museums and luxurious spas.

No German city celebrates innovation and creativity quite like **Berlin**, which bursts with youth, art and energy. Counter-culture also thrives in the other great eastern German city of **Dresden**, which is also known for its Baroque finery. This, too, is a key draw in the many palaces of **Potsdam**, while small but cultured **Weimar** is another significant town that rewards travel in this region.

In northern Germany the large, bustling harbour city of **Hamburg** with its rambunctious nightlife is a key draw. Further south, straddling the banks of the River Rhine, **Cologne** is another dynamic city, famed for a skyline dominated by a spectacular cathedral begun in 1248, and its huge and decidedly impious Carnival celebrations.

Munich is the key city in southern Germany, with its fine museums and bustling beer halls, but in general the region is best appreciated in smaller towns which preserve the country's pastoral and romantic side. Among them are the beautiful university town of **Heidelberg**; **Trier** with its many Roman remains; the spa town of **Baden-Baden**; and the attractive and youthful town of **Freiburg**. Many of Germany's scenic highlights can be found in the south too, including the **Bavarian Alps** along the Austrian border; the **Bodensee** (Lake Constance) near the Swiss border; the **Black Forest** and the **Rhine Valley**, whose majestic sweep has spawned a rich legacy of legends and folklore.

CHRONOLOGY

57 BC Julius Caesar invades and conquers "Germania Inferior".

800 AD Charlemagne, the Frankish ruler over territory including Germany, is crowned Holy Roman Emperor.

1438 Habsburg dynasty rules over Germany with election of Albert I.

1517 Martin Luther writes his *95 Theses* against corruption in the Catholic Church, a protest that culminates in the Protestant Reformation.

1648 End of the Thirty Years' War between European Catholic and Protestant powers leads to the division of Germany into princely states.

1806 Napoleon dissolves the Holy Roman Empire.

1871 Unification of Germany under Chancellor Otto von Bismarck, after German success in the Franco-Prussian War.

1880s Bismarck establishes German colonies in Africa.

1918 Germany is defeated in World War I; the Treaty of Versailles enforces heavy reparation payments upon Germany.

1919 The Weimar Republic is established.

1923 Hyperinflation causes economic meltdown.

1933 Hitler becomes Chancellor of Germany.

1939 World War II begins as Germany invades Poland.

1939–45 Millions die in Nazi concentration camps during the Holocaust.

1945 Germany is defeated, the Allies occupy the country.

1949 Germany is divided between Communist East and Democratic West.

1961 The Berlin Wall is constructed.

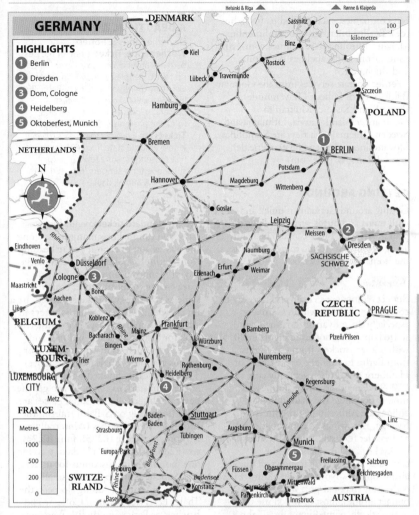

1989 Following mass protests, the Berlin Wall is torn down.

1990 The two Germanys are reunited.

2002 Germany reluctantly abandons the Deutschmark and adopts the euro.

2005 Angela Merkel becomes the first female – and first east German – Chancellor.

2009–2013 Euro crisis; Germany emerges as the dominant power in the euro bloc and starts moves towards a banking union.

2015–2016 Refugee crisis: over a million Syrian war refugees and other migrants arrive, due to Germany's unique open-door policy, while populist parties gain power.

ARRIVAL AND DEPARTURE

Flying is the cheapest and most convenient way to get to Germany from outside Europe and from many other European countries too, thanks to the proliferation of budget airlines. The largest airport is Frankfurt Airport (FRA), and there are over forty others to choose from.

Germany is well connected by train and bus with destinations throughout continental Europe. Check Deutsche Bahn's website (ⓦbahn.de) for international routes; several private

bus companies, such as Flixbus (⊛flixbus
.de), BerlinLinienBus (⊛berlinlinienbus
.de) and Eurolines (⊛eurolines.com), run
routes from as far afield as Barcelona
and Bucharest.

Ferries operate services from the German
Baltic ports of Lübeck (Travemünde),
Rostock and Sassnitz-Mukran to
Denmark, Finland, Latvia, Lithuania and
Sweden. The major carriers are Scandlines
(⊛scandlines.de), Stena (⊛stenaline.de)
and TT-Line (⊛ttline.com).

GETTING AROUND

Getting around Germany is quick and easy,
with **trains** and **buses** very affordable if you
plan in advance. Buses can also be handy
along designated "scenic routes", such as
the Romantic Road (see box, p.405).

BY PLANE

Budget **airlines** are a cheap and fast way to
cover long distances within Germany –
especially since Ryanair (⊛ryanair.com)
started operating domestic flights in 2015,
with one-way tickets from €5. Flights
from Berlin to Cologne or Stuttgart, or
Hamburg to Munich, generally cost
€20–90 depending on the airline and
time of booking. The main **domestic
airlines** are Airberlin (⊛airberlin.com),
Ryanair, Eurowings (⊛eurowings.com)
and easyJet (⊛easyjet.com). Skycheck
(⊛skycheck.de) is a handy flight
comparison website that shows all budget
airline options. Note that Frankfurt (FRA)
is the only major airport not served by
budget airlines, most of which use the
optimistically named Frankfurt-Hahn
(HHN), 120km west of the city.

BY TRAIN

Trains are mainly run by Deutsche Bahn
(DB; ⊛bahn.de). Main train stations
have good information desks, and
left-luggage lockers (€3–6/day depending
on size). The fastest service is the
InterCityExpress (ICE). InterCity (IC)
and EuroCity (EC) trains are next in line.
Slower Regional trains (RE/RB) run on
less used routes and are often significantly
cheaper. Major cities often have an
S-Bahn commuter rail network.

> ## A BEAUTIFUL WEEKEND
> Deutsche Bahn's **Schönes-
> Wochenende-Ticket** is one of the best
> bargains around: on Saturday or Sunday,
> up to five people can travel anywhere in
> Germany on regional trains (S-Bahn, RB,
> IRE, RE) for €40 a day for the first
> passenger, plus €4 for every second,
> third, etc passenger. Similar **Länder-
> Tickets** are available for a day's travel
> within a single state from €23 for the
> first passenger plus a few euros for
> subsequent passengers (Mon–Fri from
> 9am, Sat & Sun all day).

With **standard tickets**, valid for two
days, you can make as many stops along
the way as you like. So if you're heading
from Berlin to Cologne, you can take a
day in Hannover on your way for no
extra charge. A return ticket costs the
same as two one-way tickets. Tickets are a
lot cheaper if booked for set journeys in
advance (from 3–90 days before the trip;
look for Sparpreis tickets online), and
there are numerous discount passes for
groups and individuals (see box above).
Tickets are easily booked online, but staff
at the train stations can help you get the
best rate. InterRail and Eurail passes are
valid (including on S-Bahn trains). The
InterRail Germany Pass (⊛interrailnet
.eu) provides three (€203), four (€223),
six (€283) or eight (€313) days' travel in
one month – with discounts for under
26s. **Supplements** apply on a small
number of trains including sleepers, the
Thalys (a service between Cologne and
Brussels or Paris), the Berlin–Warszawa
Express, and ICE Sprinters – fast trains
between key cities.

BY BUS

Although not as fast as trains, **Buses** are
excellent value for cheap intercity travel
and connect all major cities and airports.
They have toilets, (limited) free wi-fi on
board, and are generally punctual. **Prices**
are very low, even if you book just before
travelling: Berlin to Munich (8hr) costs
€20–30; Dresden to Leipzig (under 2hr)
€5; Cologne to Frankfurt (2hr) around
€8. The main **bus companies** are Flixbus

(ⓦflixbus.de), Berlinlinienbus (ⓦberlinlinienbus.de) and Eurolines (ⓦeurolines.com).

BY LOCAL BUS AND TRAM

All cities have reliable local **buses**, though in more rural areas they can be infrequent. You can usually buy tickets from the driver; stops are marked "H" for *Haltestelle*. Major cities also have a **U-Bahn** and/or a tram system, where you'll normally need to buy and validate your ticket before boarding or, sometimes, as you're boarding. U-Bahns are patrolled, albeit infrequently, by plain-clothes ticket inspectors who levy on-the-spot fines on passengers without valid tickets.

BY BICYCLE

Cyclists are well catered for: many smaller roads have cycle paths, and bike-only lanes are ubiquitous in cities, where it's often a great way to get around. There are also some excellent long-distance cycle routes. Many train stations have bicycle rental outlets (around €15/day).

Two national **bike rental schemes** allow travellers to use bicycles in cities and pay by credit card for the time used. Deutsche Bahn's Call A Bike service (ⓦcallabike.de, €3 registration fee, usually €1 per 30min, up to €15 for 24hr) is in over 40 cities, while Nextbike (ⓦnextbike.de, free online registration, usually €1 per 30min, up to €9 for 24hr) covers 45 cities. Register or log in at one of the bike station terminals, or call the number written on the bike, and you obtain a code to open the lock. Bikes can be returned at any other bike station, or in some cities at any central street corner. Bikes need their own ticket (*Fahrradkarte*) on a train: €5/day on regional trains and €9/day on IC/EC trains; they are not allowed on ICE services.

ACCOMMODATION

It's often best to reserve **accommodation** in advance, especially in the cities, where trade fairs and seasonal tourism create high demand. Nearly all tourist offices will reserve accommodation for a fee.

You're never far from a large, functional **HI hostel** (*Jugendherberge*) run by DJH (ⓦjugendherberge.de) – though they are often block-booked by school groups, so book in advance, and they aren't particularly cheap (around €23, including breakfast and sheets). There are usually no curfews or lockouts, but reception hours may be limited. **Independent hostels** are a much better choice in cities – friendly, relaxed and often an excellent source of local advice. The larger ones may book their beds budget-airline-style: the greater the demand and closer to the arrival day you book, the more you pay. Expect to pay €15–30; breakfast (around €6–9) and sheets (around €2–4) are not always included.

Hotels are graded, clean and comfortable. In rural areas, prices start at about €30 for a double room; in cities, at about €50. *Pensions* and **B&Bs** are plentiful; local tourist offices will have a list (or look for signs saying *Fremdenzimmer* or *Zimmer frei*). Online **apartment rental** services, such as Airbnb, are very popular, despite resistance from cities and locals fighting rising rents and gentrification.

Even the most basic **campsites** have toilets, washing facilities and a shop. For a full list of campsites see ⓦbvcd.de.

FOOD AND DRINK

German **food** is both good value and high quality, and though traditionally solid and meat-heavy, there's often a wide range of international choices in cities at least: Italian restaurants are the most reliable, but Greek, Turkish and Chinese places are also common. Some hotels and guesthouses include **breakfast** in the price of the room – typically cold meats and cheeses, bread and jams.

Traditionally **lunch** tends to be the main meal, with good-value daily menus on offer. Pubs and inns – a **Gaststätte**, **Gasthaus** or **Gasthof** – are usually cosy and serve hearty home cooking, particularly pork and sausages along with distinct regional variations.

The distinction between café, restaurant and bar is often blurred, with many offering good simple breakfasts, salads

12

and some mains. *Gaststätten* – along with
the brewery-affiliated *Brauhäuser* – also
offer their own beer alongside filling
soups, salads and snack dishes. The easiest
option for snacks, however, is to head for
the ubiquitous **Imbiss** street stalls and
shops, which range from traditional *Wurst*
sellers to popular *Döner kebap* places.

Traditional German cuisine generally
offers little for **vegetarians**, but nowadays
you should be able to find vegetarian
food in all but the most diehard of
country inns.

DRINK

For **beer** drinkers, Germany is paradise.
Munich's beer gardens and beer halls are
the most famous drinking dens in the
country, offering a wide variety of
premier products, from dark lagers
through tart *Weizens* to powerful *Bocks*.
Cologne holds the world record for the
number of city breweries, which all
produce the beer called *Kölsch*, but
wherever you go you can be fairly sure of
getting a locally brewed variety. There are
also many high-quality German **wines**,
especially those made from the Riesling
grape. Finally, **Apfelwein** is a sour variant
of cider beloved in and around Frankfurt.

CULTURE AND ETIQUETTE

Most Germans are friendly, hospitable
and helpful, and if you stand at a corner
long enough with map in hand,
someone's bound to help. **Jaywalking** is
illegal in Germany, so only cross on the
green man – you could be fined if you
don't, though are most likely to get off
with disapproving looks from passers-by.

When paying at a German café, if
you're in a group, you'll be asked if you
want to pay individually (*getrennt*) or all
together (*zusammen*). To **tip** in a café,

round your bill up to the next €0.50 or
€1 and give the total directly to the
waiter; at restaurants you should leave
around ten percent of the bill.

SPORTS AND OUTDOOR ACTIVITIES

Football (ⓦbundesliga.de/en) is the major
spectator sport in Germany, with
world-class clubs playing in top-notch
stadiums. Tickets can be purchased from
the clubs' websites or via ⓦeventim.de;
important matches sell out well in advance.

Germany's great outdoors has a lot to
offer, particularly to **hikers** and **cyclists**.
The most popular regions for hiking are in
the Black Forest and the Bavarian Alps,
but there are well-maintained, colour-
coded hiking routes all over Germany. The
country is crisscrossed with long-distance
cycling routes. The cycling page on
Germany's tourism website (ⓦgermany
.travel) is excellent for planning.

COMMUNICATIONS

Post offices are open Monday to
Friday 8am to 6pm and Saturday 8am to
1pm. Call shops are the cheapest way to
phone abroad and often offer internet
access as well; expect to pay €1–2 per
hour. EU citizens pay no **mobile phone**
roaming charges: non-EU citizens may
want to buy a local SIM card with a
German number that lets you call and
surf at local rates – Aldi and Lidl sell
good-value prepaid SIM cards. German
businesses have been slow to offer **wi-fi**,
but now many cafés, hotels and hostels
provide free access – though you may
need to ask for the password.

EMERGENCIES

The **police** (*Polizei*) treat foreigners with
courtesy. Reporting thefts at local police
stations is straightforward, but there'll be
a great deal of bureaucracy to wade

EMERGENCY NUMBERS
Police ☎110; Fire & Ambulance ☎112.

12

GERMAN

Pronunciation Consonants: "w" is pronounced like the English "v" and the "v" like "f"; "sch" is pronounced "sh"; "z" is "ts". The German letter "ß" is a double "s". Vowels: a is like in "car", e is "eh", "ie" and "i" are "ee", "ei" is "eye", "eu" is "oy"; u is "oo", o is "awe", ä is like in "ma'am", ü is like the French "plus" and ö like the French "oeuf".

	GERMAN	PRONUNCIATION
Yes	Ja	Yah
No	Nein	Nine
Please	Bitte	Bitteh
Thank you	Danke	Duhnkeh
Hello/Good day	Guten Tag	Gooten tahg
Goodbye	Tschüss, ciao, or auf Wiedersehen	Chuss, chow, or owf veederzain
Excuse me	Entschuldigen Sie, bitte	Enshooldigen zee, bitteh
Today	Heute	Hoyteh
Yesterday	Gestern	Gestern
Tomorrow	Morgen	Morgen
I don't understand	Ich verstehe nicht	Ich vershtayeh nicht
How much is…?	Wieviel kostet…?	Vee feel costet…?
Do you speak English?	Sprechen Sie Englisch?	Shprechen zee aing-lish?
I'd like a beer	Ich hätte gern ein Bier	Ich hetteh gairn ein beer
Entrance /exit	der Eingang/der Ausgang	dare eingahng/dare owsgahng
Toilet	das WC/die Toilette	dahs vay-tsay/dee toyletteh
HI hostel	die Jugendherberge	dee yougendhairbairgeh
Main train station	der Hauptbahnhof	howptbahnhof
Bus	der Bus	dare boos
Plane	das Flugzeug	das floog-tsoyg
Train	der Zug	dare tsoog
Cheap/expensive	Billig/teuer	Billig/toy-er
Open/closed	Offen/auf geschlossen/zu	Uhffen/owf gehshlossen/tsoo
One	Eins	Einz
Two	Zwei	Tsveye
Three	Drei	Dry
Four	Vier	Fear
Five	Fünf	Foonf
Six	Sechs	Zex
Seven	Sieben	Zeeben
Eight	Acht	Ahkt
Nine	Neun	Noyn
Ten	Zehn	Tsehn

12

through. Doctors generally speak English. **Pharmacies** (*Apotheken*) can deal with many minor complaints; all display a rota of local pharmacies open 24 hours.

INFORMATION

You'll find a good **tourist office** in every town, with a large amount of literature and maps; town and regional tourist websites are usually bilingual and excellent. City tourist offices often offer discount cards, covering public transport and free or discounted entry to major sights. These can be worthwhile if you visit several sights, but check first what discounts are offered – sometimes they're no cheaper than the student price. Most museums and attractions offer significant reductions for students and young people.

MONEY AND BANKS

German currency is the **euro** (€). **Exchange facilities** are available in most banks, post offices and commercial exchange shops called *Wechselstuben*.

The Reisebank has branches in the train stations of most main cities (generally open daily, often till 10/11pm). Basic **banking hours** are Monday to Friday 8.30am to noon and 1.30 to 3.30/4pm, Thursdays till 5/6pm. **Credit and debit cards** are generally accepted – but certainly not universally – with budget restaurants, cafés and many shops requesting cash. **ATMs** are widespread.

OPENING HOURS AND HOLIDAYS

Shops open at 8 or 9am and close around 6 to 8pm weekdays and 2 to 4pm on Saturdays; they are generally closed all day Sunday, though regulations vary by state. Pharmacies, petrol stations and shops in and around train stations tend to stay open late and at weekends. **Museums** and **historic monuments** are, with few exceptions (mainly in Bavaria), closed on Monday. **Public holidays** are: January 1, January 6 (regional), Good Friday, Easter Monday, May 1, Ascension Day, Whit Monday, Corpus Christi (regional), August 15 (regional), October 3, November 1 (regional) and December 25 and 26.

Berlin

Energetic and irreverent, **BERLIN** is a welcoming, exciting city where the speed of change over the past few decades has been astounding. With a long history of decadence and cultural dynamism, the revived national capital has become a magnet for artists and musicians. Culturally, it has some of the most important archeological collections in Europe, as well as an impressive range of galleries and museums, and an exuberant, cutting-edge nightlife.

The city resonates with modern European history, having played a dominant role in Imperial Germany, both during the Weimar Republic after 1914 and in the Nazis' Third Reich. After 1945 the city was partitioned by the victorious Allies and, as a result, was the front line of the Cold War. In 1961, its division into two hostile sectors was given a very visible expression by the construction of the notorious Berlin Wall. After the Wall fell in 1989, Berlin became the national capital once again in 1990. These days, parliament (**Bundestag**) sits in the renovated Reichstag building, and the city's excellent museum collections have been reassembled. The physical revival of Berlin has put it at the forefront of contemporary architecture, and there is a plethora of dramatic new buildings around the city.

WHAT TO SEE AND DO

Most of Berlin's main sights are in the central **Mitte** district, which extends from the leafy boulevard of Unter den Linden to the bustling area of restaurants, shops and bars around Hackescher Markt a short walk northeast. To the south lies Potsdamer Platz and the museums of the Kulturforum. This overlooks the Tiergarten park, while further west lies the adjacent area City West, a neighbourhood known for its shopping, particularly along the Ku'damm. The residential city districts beyond Mitte – particularly **Kreuzberg**, **Prenzlauer Berg**, **Friedrichshain** and **Neukölln** – are wonderful to stroll through and have many of the city's liveliest hangouts.

The Brandenburg Gate and the Reichstag

The most atmospheric place to start a tour of Berlin is the **Brandenburg Gate**, the city-gate-cum-triumphal-arch built in 1791. To its north stands the **Reichstag**, the nineteenth-century home of the German parliament, which was remodelled by Norman Foster for the resumption of its historic role in 1999, when the much-photographed glass cupola was added. You can climb a spiral walkway to the top of the **dome** (daily 8am–midnight; free; ⓦbundestag.de; ID required) for fine views over the surrounding government quarter and Tiergarten park, and an excellent free audiotour, though you'll have to register online weeks in advance. If you haven't booked in advance, you may get a last-minute slot by asking at the nearby Service Centre, across Scheidemannstrasse (daily: April–Oct 8am–8pm; Nov–March 8am–6pm). Alternatively, those with a fat

WALKING TOURS

Walking tours of Berlin are a popular way for budget travellers to get a handle on the city and meet other travellers. All companies offer four-hour city tours for around €14, plus more specialized ones such as Third Reich sites; Cold War Berlin; Jewish life; Potsdam; and Sachsenhausen. Operators include **Original Berlin Walks** (☎030 301 91 94, ⓦberlinwalks .com), **Insider Tours** (☎030 692 31 49, ⓦinsidertour.com) and **New Berlin Tours** (☎030 510 50 030, ⓦnewberlintours.com), whose city-centre tour is free, though tips are expected. **Alternative Berlin** (☎0162 819 82 64, ⓦalternativeberlin.com) runs tours of Berlin's graffiti art and squats, while **Christopher Isherwood's Neighbourhood Tour** (usually Sat at 11.30; ⓦcabaret-berlin.com) provides fascinating insights into the gay, arts and revue theatre scene of the 1920–30s, as depicted in *Cabaret*.

wallet can book a table at the gourmet rooftop restaurant *Käfer* (daily 9am–4.30pm & 6.30pm–midnight; ☎030 22 62 990).

The Holocaust Memorials

The bold **Holocaust Memorial** (officially the "Memorial to the Murdered Jews of Europe") lies south of the Brandenburg Gate, where 2711 upright concrete slabs have been arranged in a dizzying grid. The exhibition in its underground information centre (Ort der Information; Tues–Sun: April–Sept 10am–8pm; Oct–March 10am–7pm; free) is carefully presented and moving. Over the road, on the fringes of the Tiergarten park, another concrete oblong forms the **Gay Holocaust Memorial**, which remembers those convicted of homosexual acts under the regime. Leaning to one side, the memorial is defiantly not straight, and has a small window behind which a film of two men kissing permanently plays.

Just west of the Brandenburg Gate, a pond surrounded by fragmented stones is the **Memorial to the Sinti and Roma Victims of National Socialism**: a fresh flower is placed daily on a central stone in the pond. At the southern edge of Tiergarten park, the **T4 Memorial for the Victims of the Nazi Euthanasia Programme** commemorates some 300,000 people who were murdered under the Nazis' euthanasia programme that was coordinated from the building that once stood here.

Unter den Linden

East of the Brandenburg Gate stretches broad and stately **Unter den Linden**, once Berlin's most important thoroughfare.

Post-unification renewal, including oversized embassies and museums flanking the boulevard, only hints at its former grandeur.

Bebelplatz, at Unter den Linden's eastern end, was the site of the infamous Nazi book-burning of May 10, 1933; an unusual memorial – an underground room housing empty bookshelves, visible through a glass panel set in the centre of the square – marks the event.

More than anyone, it was architect Karl Friedrich Schinkel who shaped nineteenth-century Berlin, and one of his most famous creations stands opposite the **Staatsoper** further along Unter den Linden: the **Neue Wache**, a former royal guardhouse resembling a Roman temple and now a memorial to victims of war and tyranny. Next door the Baroque old Prussian Arsenal now houses the excellent **Deutsches Historisches Museum** (daily 10am–6pm; €8, students €4). It covers two thousand years of German history in imaginative displays that often focus on social history, making good use of the vast selection of artefacts in the collection: from a seventeenth-century Turkish tent taken during the siege of Vienna to parallel displays of life in 1950s East and West Berlin.

The Gendarmenmarkt

Following Charlottenstrasse south from Unter den Linden, you come to the elegant **Gendarmenmarkt**, where the Französischer Dom and lookalike Deutscher Dom dominate on either side of the square. The former was built as a church for Berlin's influential Huguenot community at the beginning of the

12

▲ Tegel Airport (4km)

DRINKING AND NIGHTLIFE
Golgatha — 3
Ritter Butzke — 2
Schleusenkrug — 1

EATING
Curry 36 — 1
Knofi — 2/3

12

eighteenth century. Between them stands the Neoclassical Konzerthaus by Schinkel. A block west of here lies **Friedrichstrasse**, a high-class shopping street.

Schlossplatz and Museuminsel

At the eastern end of Unter den Linden is the Schlossplatz, former site of the original imperial palace, then of the GDR's Palast der Republik parliament building, which was dismantled in 2008 to make way for a re-creation of the **Stadtschloss**, due for

completion in 2019. The Platz stands at the midpoint of the Spree island whose northern half, Museuminsel, is the location of **Berliner Dom**, the city's grandest church, and five of Berlin's top museums. The largest is the **Pergamonmuseum** (Mon–Wed & Fri–Sun 10am–6pm, Thurs 10am–8pm; €12, students €6), whose treasure-trove of the ancient world includes the huge Ishtar Gate from sixth-century BC Babylon; the hall housing the spectacular Pergamon Altar from 160 BC

CENTRAL BERLIN

is closed for renovations until 2019. The **Alte Nationalgalerie** (Tues, Wed & Fri–Sun 10am–6pm, Thurs 10am–8pm; €12, students €6) houses a collection of nineteenth-century European art, while at the island's northern tip the beautifully restored **Bode-Museum** (Tues, Wed & Fri–Sun 10am–6pm, Thurs 10am–8pm; €12, students €6) displays Byzantine art and medieval to eighteenth-century sculpture. Meanwhile, the **Altes Museum** (Tues, Wed & Fri–Sun 10am–6pm, Thurs 10am–8pm; €10, students €5) focuses on Greek and Roman antiquities, while the **Neues Museum** (Mon–Wed & Fri–Sun 10am–6pm, Thurs 10am–8pm; €12, students €6) houses the city's impressive Egyptian collection with Berlin's single most famous exhibit – a 3,300-year-old bust of Nefertiti.

Alexanderplatz

To reach Alexanderplatz, the stark commercial square that was the hub of

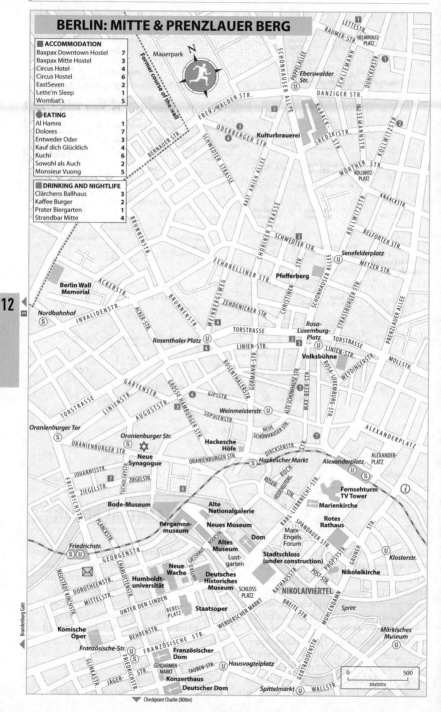

BERLIN: MITTE & PRENZLAUER BERG

■ ACCOMMODATION
Baxpax Downtown Hostel	7
Baxpax Mitte Hostel	3
Circus Hotel	4
Circus Hostel	6
EastSeven	2
Lette'm Sleep	1
Wombat's	5

● EATING
Al Hamra	1
Dolores	7
Entweder Oder	3
Kauf dich Glücklich	4
Kuchi	6
Sowohl als Auch	2
Monsieur Vuong	5

■ DRINKING AND NIGHTLIFE
Clärchens Ballhaus	3
Kaffee Burger	2
Prater Biergarten	1
Strandbar Mitte	4

12

0   500
metres

communist East Berlin, head along Karl-Liebknecht-Strasse (the continuation of Unter den Linden), past the Neptunbrunnen fountain beside the thirteenth-century Marienkirche. Like every other building in the vicinity, the church is overshadowed by the gigantic **Fernsehturm** (TV tower; daily: March–Oct 9am–midnight; Nov–Feb 10am–midnight; €13), whose 203m-high observation platform and revolving café offer unbeatable views. Southwest of here lies the **Nikolaiviertel**, a quarter of reconstructed medieval buildings and winding streets, which was razed overnight in June 1944.

Hackescher Markt and around

The area north of the River Spree around ⑤ Hackescher Markt emerged as one of the most intriguing parts of the city when Berlin was reunified. Artists' squats, workshops and galleries sprang up here in the early 1990s, and some still survive. But today the district's appeal is based on its history as Berlin's affluent pre-war **Jewish quarter** and its current status as a booming, if fairly touristy, shopping, restaurant and nightlife quarter, with fashionable boutiques, ethnic restaurants and stylish bars. One highlight is the quarter's distinctive Höfe, or courtyards; particularly the elegant **Hackesche Höfe** whose network of eight courtyards features cafés, galleries and designer shops.

The district's Jewish legacy is evident in the rebuilt Moorish-style **Neue Synagoge** on Oranienburger Strasse (April–Sept, Mon–Fri 10am–6pm, Sun 10am–7pm; €5, students €4). Little remains of the building beyond the facade, but there are exhibitions on the history of the synagogue and on Jewish culture.

Potsdamer Platz

The heart of prewar Berlin lay to the south of the Brandenburg Gate, around **Potsdamer Platz**, which for decades lay dormant and bisected by the Berlin Wall. Post-reunification, huge commercial development has produced a business district that gathers around the impressive Sony Center, with its cinema, shops and massive atrium.

MUSEUM ENTRY

Berlin's superb **state museums and galleries** (including all Museuminsel and Kulturforum museums; ⓦ smb.museum) offer a day-ticket for each cluster of museums called a **Bereichskarte** (area ticket; €10–18, students €6–9). Meanwhile, a **three-day ticket** for all Berlin's state-owned museums, plus dozens of others including the Jüdischen Museum, is a steal at €24/12. With a **student ID card** almost all sights and museums give up to fifty percent discount, while under-18s often have free access.

The Kulturforum

Just west of Potsdamer Platz lies the **Kulturforum**, a gathering of museums centred on the unmissable **Gemäldegalerie** (Tues, Wed & Fri 10am–6pm, Thurs 10am–8pm, Sat & Sun 11am–6pm; €10, students €5; ⑤/ⓤ Potsdamer Platz), with its world-class collection of old masters. The interconnected building to the north houses the **Kunstgewerbemuseum** (Tues–Fri 10am–6pm, Sat & Sun 11am–6pm; €8, students €4), a sparkling collection of European arts and crafts. A couple of minutes' walk south, Mies van der Rohe's impressive **Neue Nationalgalerie** is closed for renovations until 2019; its permanent collection of twentieth-century German paintings includes Berlin portraits and cityscapes by George Grosz and Otto Dix.

The course of the Wall

It's nearly three decades since the **Berlin Wall** came down, and much of its course is marked by a double row of cobblestones, with information panels at key points. There are also several stretches preserved as memorials to those who died trying to cross it. Immediately east of Potsdamer Platz, a sizeable, crumbling section of Wall runs along Niederkirchnerstrasse, beside the captivating **Topography of Terror** (daily 10am–8pm; free), an exhibition on the former site of the Gestapo and SS headquarters which documents their chilling histories. To the east, Niederkirchnerstrasse meets

12

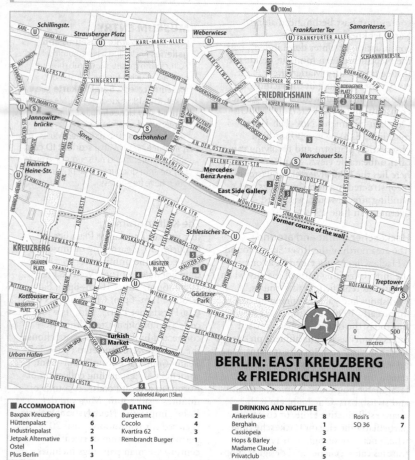

BERLIN: EAST KREUZBERG & FRIEDRICHSHAIN

■ ACCOMMODATION		● EATING		■ DRINKING AND NIGHTLIFE			
Baxpax Kreuzberg	4	Burgeramt	2	Ankerklause	8	Rosi's	4
Hüttenpalast	6	Cocolo	4	Berghain	1	SO 36	7
Industriepalast	2	Kvartira 62	3	Cassiopeia	3		
Jetpak Alternative	5	Rembrandt Burger	1	Hops & Barley	2		
Ostel	1			Madame Claude	6		
Plus Berlin	3			Privatclub	5		

Friedrichstrasse at the site of the Wall's most infamous crossing, **Checkpoint Charlie**. Here, along with a reconstruction of the US checkpoint booth, is a fascinating open-air display on the Wall's history.

The most rewarding section of Wall can be seen at Bernauer Strasse, just north of Mitte, where a short stretch has been preserved as the **Berlin Wall Memorial**. This is the only section where the two parallel walls plus "death strip" between remain, viewable from a lookout at the visitor centre over the road. Extending from the no-man's land for several blocks is a stretch of memorials with plaques and images that tell you stories of tunnels

and escape attempts and life in a city with the wall (visitor centre Tues–Sun 10am–6pm; open-air exhibition and memorial ground daily 8am–10pm; free; ⑤ Nordbahnhof/⑩ Bernauer Str.).

Stretching along the River Spree, near Friedrichshain, a 1300m-long section of the Wall known as the **East Side Gallery** (⑤ Ostbahnhof) is covered with paintings by international artists, originally done in the months after the fall of the Iron Curtain, but since touched up and partially fenced off.

Jüdisches Museum

Daniel Libeskind's striking zinc-skinned **Jüdisches Museum**, Lindenstr. 9–14 in west Kreuzberg (Jewish Museum; Mon 10am–10pm, Tues–Sun 10am–8pm; €8, students €3; ⓌHallesches Tor/Kochstr.), is part museum, part memorial. Its lower ground level is Libeskind's reflection on three strands of the Jewish experience in Berlin – exile, Holocaust and continuity – and is a disorientating but compelling experience. On the upper two floors, a more conventional exhibition documents the culture, achievements and history of Berlin's Jewish community.

Ku'damm and around

The focus of the city's western side, a short walk south of Bahnhof Zoo station, is the start of the **Kurfürstendamm**, or Ku'damm, a 3.5km strip of ritzy shops, cinemas, bars and cafés. Western Berlin's most famous landmark here is the **Kaiser-Wilhelm-Gedächtniskirche**, mostly destroyed by British bombing in 1943, the broken spire left as a reminder of the horrors of war, with a modern church built alongside. Opposite, the new **Bikini Berlin** mall, inside a listed 1950s building, is worth visiting for its quirky fashion and pop-up shops, plus a rooftop garden (free) with views over the monkey enclosures of the zoo.

Tiergarten

Berlin Zoo, beside Zoologischer Garten station, forms the beginning of the giant **Tiergarten**, a restful expanse of woodland and a good place to wander along the banks of the Landwehrkanal. Strasse des 17 Juni heads all the way through the Tiergarten to the Brandenburg Gate, with the **Siegessäule**, the iconic victory monument, at the central point.

Schloss Charlottenburg

The sumptuous **Schloss Charlottenburg** with its splendid gardens is on Spandauer Damm 10–22 (Old Palace; Tues–Sun: April–Oct 10am–6pm; Nov–March 10am–5pm; €10, students €7; 10min walk from ⓈWestend or bus #M45 from the zoo). Commissioned by the future Queen Sophie Charlotte in 1695, it was added to throughout the eighteenth and early nineteenth centuries. Admission to the Old Palace includes a tour of the

main state apartments and self-guided visits to the private chambers, while the New Wing includes an array of paintings by Watteau and other eighteenth-century French artists.

The Olympiastadion

Located in the far west of the city is the site of the 1936 Olympics, and of the 2006 Football World Cup final, the **Olympiastadion**, one of the very few impressive Nazi-era buildings that survived. If you can't make it to a Hertha BSC (Ⓦherthabsc.de) match, you can visit the stadium at other times (daily: April–July, Sept & Oct 9am–7pm; Aug 9am–8pm, Nov–March 10am–6pm; €7, students €5.50; various tours available €11–13; Ⓦolympiastadion-berlin.de; Ⓢ/ⓊOlympiastadion).

ARRIVAL AND DEPARTURE

By plane Berlin's two international airports (Ⓦberlin -airport.de) lie within easy reach of the city centre. The closer of the two is Tegel airport (TXL), from which the frequent #TXL express bus runs to the Hauptbahnhof and Alexanderplatz, while #X9 express or local #109 buses run to Bahnhof Zoo (all covered by a public transport zone AB ticket; €2.70). Schönefeld (SXF) is southeast of the centre and reachable on S-Bahn line S9 via Ostkreuz, or by regional train RE7 or RB14 to Alexanderplatz, the Hauptbahnhof and Bahnhof Zoo (every 10min; 30min); bus #X7 runs to nearby Ⓤ Rudow (all require a public transport zone ABC ticket; €3.30). The new Berlin Brandenburg International (BBI) airport – which will incorporate Schönefeld – is years behind schedule with no opening date in sight; when it finally opens, Tegel will close.

By train The huge Hauptbahnhof (main station) northeast of the Brandenburg Gate is well connected to the rest of the city by S-Bahn, regional trains and trams.

Destinations Cologne (hourly; 4hr 20min); Dresden (every 2hr; 2hr); Frankfurt (hourly; 4hr); Hamburg (hourly; 1hr 40min); Hannover (hourly; 2hr); Leipzig (hourly; 1hr 15min); Munich (hourly; 6hr); Paris (4 daily, including overnight; 8–10hr); Prague (every 2hr; 4hr 30min); Warsaw (4 daily; 5hr 15min); Weimar (every 2hr; 2hr 20min).

By bus Most international and intercity buses stop at the central bus station (ZOB), Masurenallee 4-6, which is linked to the Ku'damm area by many local buses, including the #M49 service, and U-Bahn line #2 from Kaiserdamm station.

Destinations Cologne (hourly; 7hr 30min); Frankfurt (hourly; 6hr 30min); Hamburg (hourly; 3hr); Hannover (hourly; 3hr); Leipzig (hourly; 2hr 10min); Munich (hourly; 7hr).

12

INFORMATION

Tourist information Main tourist office at the Hauptbahnhof (daily 8am–10pm; ☎030 25 00 25, ⓦvisitberlin.de), with branches at Brandenburg Gate (daily 10am–7pm; Kurfürstendamm 21 (daily: April–Oct 9.30am–7pm; Nov–March 9.30am–6pm); and in the TV Tower at Alexanderplatz (daily: April–Oct 10am–6pm; Nov–March 10am–4pm).

Discount passes The WelcomeCard (Berlin zones AB 48hr/72hr/5-day for €19.50/€27.50/€35.50; Berlin and Potsdam zones ABC 48hr/72hr/5-day for €21.50/€29.50/€40.50; ⓦberlin-welcomecard.de) provides free travel and up to fifty percent off many of the major tourist sights, though not those on the Museuminsel: note that many of the discounts are the same as student prices.

GETTING AROUND

Berlin has an efficient, integrated system of U- and S-Bahn train lines, buses and trams (ⓦbvg.de), though cycling in Berlin is also very easy.

By U- and S-Bahn Trains run daily 4.30am–12.30am (Fri & Sat all night).

By bus and tram The city bus network – and the tram system in eastern Berlin – covers the gaps left by the U-Bahn; several useful tram routes centre on Hackescher Markt, including the #M1 to Prenzlauer Berg. Night buses and trams operate, with buses (around every 30min) generally following U-Bahn line routes; free maps are available at most stations.

Tickets Available from machines at U/S-Bahn stations, on trams or from bus drivers: zone AB single ticket €2.70; zone ABC (includes Schönefeld airport) single €3.30; short-trip ticket (*Kurzstrecke*) for 3 train or 6 bus/tram stops €1.70; zone AB day ticket €7; for 2/3/5 days the WelcomeCard (see above) can be good value. Validate all tickets in the yellow or red machines on platforms or inside trams and buses before travelling.

By bike Rental bikes from the Call a Bike and Nextbike schemes (see p.355) can be found across the city, while many hostels also rent out bikes for €12–15 per day. Fat Tire beneath the TV tower at Alexanderplatz (daily: Oct–April 9.30am–6pm; May–Sept 9.30am–8pm; ☎030 240 479 91, ⓦfattirebiketours.com/berlin) rents bikes and runs bike tours (€28 for 4hr 30min).

ACCOMMODATION

Berlin has plenty of great hostels, primarily in Mitte, Prenzlauer Berg, Kreuzberg and Friedrichshain; several new options are more like budget hotels and are often the best choice for private rooms: book at least a couple of weeks in advance in high season. All hostels listed have wi-fi.

HOSTELS

Baxpax Downtown Hostel Ziegelstr. 28 ☎030 27 87 48 80, ⓦbaxpax.de; ⓢ/ⓤFriedrichstr; map p.362. This hostel is a little more hotel-like than its sister branches. Most rooms en suite; linen €2.50. Dorms €22, doubles €100

Baxpax Kreuzberg Hostel Skalitzer Str. 104 ☎030 69 51 83 22, ⓦbaxpax.de; ⓤGörlitzer Bahnhof; map p.364. One of a trio of backpacker outfits with clean, bright rooms, cooking facilities and bike rental. Dorms €17, doubles €70

Baxpax Mitte Hostel Chausseestr. 102 ☎030 28 39 09 65, ⓦbaxpax.de; ⓤZinnowitzer Str.; map p.362. Same vibe as all the Baxpax hostels but in a fantastic location amid oodles of bars and restaurants. Dorms €13, doubles €78

Circus Hostel Weinbergsweg 1a, Mitte ☎030 20 00 39 39, ⓦcircus-berlin.de; ⓤRosenthaler Platz; map p.362. Clean, welcoming, fun and deservedly popular base in a great location between Mitte and Prenzlauer Berg, with helpful staff and its own bar. Dorms €19, doubles €58

EastSeven Schwedter Str. 7, Prenzlauer Berg ☎030 93 62 22 40, ⓦeastseven.de; ⓤSenefelderplatz; map p.362. Cosy, small, independent hostel with kitchen and pretty garden, including a barbecue. Some nice touches, such as communal meals on Mon and discounts in local shops. Dorms €26, doubles €74

Industriepalast Warschauer Str. 43, Friedrichshain ☎030 74 07 82 90, ⓦip-hostel.com; ⓢ/ⓤWarschauer Str; map. p.364. Central for Berlin's main party zone, this former factory has functional but spacious dorms and great-quality private rooms with en-suite facilities. Dorms €17, doubles €80

Jetpak Alternative Görlitzerstr. 38 ☎030 62 90 86 41, ⓦjetpak.de; ⓤSchlesisches Tor; map p.364. Attractive high-end hostel in a lively neighbourhood close to all the action in Kreuzberg and Friedrichshain. Perks include a buffet breakfast and under-floor heating, along with bicycle rental, laundry facilities and cheap beer. Dorms €28, doubles €64

Lette'm Sleep Lettestr. 7, Prenzlauer Berg ☎030 44 73 36 23, ⓦbackpackers.de; ⓤEberswalder Str.; map p.362. Chilled-out hostel with free internet, a kitchen and a good location, on a particularly attractive square in Prenzlauer Berg. Dorms €18, doubles €72

Plus Berlin Warschauer Platz 6, Friedrichshain ☎030 311 69 88 20, ⓦplushostels.com; ⓢ/ⓤWarschauer Str; map p.364. Lively large hostel just behind the U-Bahn station with its own pool and sauna. Dorms €22, doubles €68

Wombat's Alte Schönhauser Str. 2 ☎030 84 71 08 20, ⓦwombats-hostels.com/berlin; ⓤRosa-Luxemburg-Platz; map p.362. Bright, friendly and well-equipped new hostel in a great location near some good bars. All dorms are en suite, the spacious, 2-person apartments with kitchens are stylish and the roof bar has superb views over the city. Breakfast €4. Dorms €26, doubles €78, apartments €90

HOTELS

Circus Hotel Rosenthalerstr. 1 ☎030 20 00 39 39, ⓦcircus-berlin.de; ⓤRosenthaler Platz; map p.362. Fantastic, stylish budget hotel run by the *Circus Hostel* over the road. Helpful staff provide local advice and some nice extras like free laptop loans. All rooms are en suite, though those overlooking the street are a little noisy. Doubles **€85**

Hüttenpalast Hobrechtstr. 65 ☎030 37 30 58 06, ⓦhuettenpalast.de; ⓤHermannplatz; map p.364. Funky and quirky place with a garden on the border of trendy Kreuzberg and Neukölln, offering standard hotel rooms, wooden cabins and vintage caravans. Breakfast €6.50 (cabins and caravans include morning coffee and croissant). Doubles **€74**, caravans/cabins **€69**

Ostel Wriezener Karree 5 ☎030 25 76 86 60, ⓦostel.eu; Ⓢ Ostbahnhof; map p.364. *Ostalgie*-themed hotel, decked out in 1970s GDR-style, though with modern facilities. Breakfast €8. Singles **€30**, doubles **€39**, 4–5 person apartments **€80**

EATING

Many cafés, bars and restaurants serve food, with plenty offering a good weekend brunch. The bustling Kreuzberg/ Neukölln Turkish market (Tues & Fri 11am–6.30pm), on Maybachufer (USchönleinstr.), is great for cheap meals, breads, vegetables, meat and Turkish sweets.

CAFÉS, CHEAP EATS AND SNACKS

Al Hamra Raumerstr. 16, Prenzlauer Berg; ⓤEberswalder Str. or Ⓢ Prenzlauer Allee; map p.362. Relaxed, extremely popular Arabian-style café-bar. Good food and cheap drinks every day – Sun brunch until 5pm is especially tasty (€12). Daily 11am–11pm.

Burgeramt Krossener Str. 22, on Boxhagener Platz; ⓤFrankfurter Tor or Ⓢ Warschauer Str.; map p.364. *Imbiss* place with an eccentric line in burger toppings – pineapple, teriyaki and gouda appear together – but there are plenty of classic and veggie versions, making it a perfect bar-hopping pit stop in Friedrichshain. Burgers €4–8. Mon–Thurs noon–midnight, Fri–Sun noon–3am.

Curry 36 Mehringdamm 36, west Kreuzberg; ⓤMehringdamm; map pp.360–361. One of the best places to try Berlin *Currywurst* (€1.50) – a traditional fast-food combo of grilled sausage, hot tomato sauce and curry powder. Daily 9am–5am.

Dolores Rosa-Luxemburg-Str. 7, Mitte; Ⓢ /ⓤAlexanderplatz; map p.362. Mouthwatering California-style Mexican fast food, complete with San Francisco decor and a high concentration of expats. Burritos from €4. Daily 11am–10pm, Sun 1–10pm.

Entweder Oder Oderberger Str. 15, Prenzlauer Berg; ⓤEberwelder Str.; map p.362. Friendly café-bar, with a tasty menu of German dishes that's perfect for a hangover-beating breakfast: a big platter for two costs €16. Mon,

Wed–Sat 10am–midnight, Tues 3pm–midnight, Sun 10am–10pm.

Kauf dich Glücklich Oderberger Str. 44, Prenzlauer Berg; ⓤEberwelder Str.; map p.362. Super-cute, café-bar-waffle shop and ice-cream parlour, all done out in 1950s retro furniture (that's for sale). Mon–Fri 10.30am–1am, Sat & Sun 10am–1am.

Knofi Bergmannstr. 11 & 98, Kreuzberg; ⓤMehringdamm; map pp.360–361. The *Gözleme* – filled Turkish crêpes – are cheap (€4.50), huge and delicious at this lively local Mediterranean bistro (no. 11) and deli (opposite, no. 98); there's the same menu of soups, salads and some hot dishes at both. Daily: bistro 8am–midnight; deli 9am–midnight.

Kvartira 62 Lübbener Str. 18; ⓤSchlesisches Tor; map p.364. Atmospheric Russian café with 1920s-era dark red and gold decor serving Russian classics such as *borscht* soup (€4), delicious *pelmeni* (dumplings; €5) and tea flavoured with jam – as well as some great chocolate cake. Sun–Thurs 6pm–2am, Fri & Sat 6pm–4am.

Rembrandt Burger Richard-Sorge-Str. 21, Friedrichshain; ⓤFrankfurter Tor; map p.364. Away from the crowds, this relaxed joint serves excellent beef and veggie burgers (from €8) served with Dutch-style or sweet potato fries. Dutch snacks like deep-fried cheese and spicy sausages (from €2) too. Daily noon–10pm.

Sowohl als Auch Kollwitzstr. 88, Prenzlauer Berg; ⓤEberswalder or Senefelderplatz; map p.362. This café has an excellent selection of cakes, with an extensive coffee and tea menu to boot; it's also popular for breakfast. Daily 8am–midnight.

RESTAURANTS

Cocolo Ramen Paul-Lincke-Ufer 39, Kreuzberg ☎030 98 33 90 73; ⓤSchönleinstr.; map p.364. Authentic and delicious Japanese ramen plus good-value lunch menus from €6. Mon–Sat noon–11pm, Sun 6–11pm.

Kuchi Gipsstr. 3, Mitte; ⓤWeinmeister Str.; map p.362. Deliciously fresh, imaginative sushi, prepared in front of you, is the speciality at this stylish Mitte restaurant. Well worth

12

the slightly higher prices: sushi selection from around €11. Mon–Sat noon–midnight, Sun 6pm–midnight.

Monsieur Vuong Alte Schönhauser Str. 46, Mitte; ⓊWeinmeisterstr.; map p.362. Small, hip and popular Vietnamese place with a high-quality, low-price menu that changes daily. Meals €9. Mon–Thurs noon–11pm, Fri–Sun noon–midnight.

DRINKING AND NIGHTLIFE

Among the best in the world, Berlin's nightlife is centred on several different neighbourhoods. As Hackescher Markt and Oranienburger Str. become more upmarket and touristy, the best bars tend to be in the inner-city residential areas: in Prenzlauer Berg, try the area around Kastanienallee for places with a relaxed, neighbourhood feel; in Friedrichshain, the Simon-Dach-Strasse is a premier twenty-something late-night hangout, while many of the city's best clubs and alternative hangouts are in or around the adjoining ramshackle districts of Kreuzberg and Neukölln.

BARS

Ankerklause Kottbusser Damm 43, Neukölln; ⓊSchönleinstr.; map p.364. Everything-goes bar with a nautical theme, a deck overlooking the canal, a cosy interior with comfy booths, a jukebox and a laidback vibe. They also dish up basic food like nachos and sandwiches (€4–12) until about 9pm. Mon 4pm–2am, Tues–Sun 10am till at least 2am.

Golgatha Viktoriapark, Kreuzberg; ⓊPlatz der Luftbrücke; map pp.360–361. Lively, legendary Biergarten at the foot of Kreuzberg hill serving Löwenbräu (€2.90), Kreuzberger Klosterbier and excellent fresh food and grilled meat dishes for a couple of euros. Daily: April–Aug 9am–late; Sept–March hours depend on weather.

Hops & Barley Wühlischstr. 22–23; Ⓢ/ⓊWarschauer Str.; map p.364. One of Berlin's better spots to drink beer

---

GAY BERLIN

Berlin's diverse **gay scene** is spread across the city, but there's a discernible gay village just south of ⓊNollendorfplatz in Schöneberg. Check out the gay listings magazine *Siegessäule* (Ⓦsiegessaeule.de), which is available in many local cafés and shops. Look out for the Café Fatal and Rollerdisko nights at *SO36* (see opposite), club nights by *GMF* (Ⓦgmf-berlin.de) at various venues, or check out *Berghain* (see below), a club with a strong gay presence. The annual Christopher Street Day Gay Pride **festival** is in June or July (Ⓦcsd-berlin.de).

---

brewed on-site, offering seasonal beers and signature brews like the malty Dunkles (dark), a refreshing pilsner and tart cider. Sun–Fri 5pm–2am, Sat 3pm–4am.

Madame Claude Lübbener Str. 19, Kreuzberg; Ⓢ/ⓊWarschauer Str.; map p.364. Quirky, grungy subterranean space with furniture on the ceiling (is that an upside-down chair?), making you think you've leapt into a rabbit hole. Gets packed later, with DJs spinning a mix of techno, house, funk, rock and a mish-mash of whatever they like. Daily 7pm till at least 3am.

Prater Biergarten Kastanienallee 7–9; ⓊEberswalder Str.; map p.362. Large and relaxed Prenzlauer Berg beer garden. The attached *Gaststätte* serves German classics year-round. Winter Mon–Sat 6pm–late, Sun noon–late; summer daily noon–late (weather permitting).

Schleusenkrug Müller-Breslau-Str.; ⓈTiergarten; map pp.360–361. Outstanding, relaxed beer garden overlooking the canal lock at the western end of Tiergarten park. Besides beer (€4) there's everything from breakfast (€5–9) to Flammkuchen pizza (€9), organic grilled sausages, schnitzel and healthy salads. Daily 10am–midnight.

Strandbar Mitte Monbijoustr. 3, Mitte; ⓈHackescher Markt; map p.362. Popular, seasonal city beach bar with deckchairs and a dancefloor overlooking the River Spree opposite the Bodemuseum. Great spot to lounge in the afternoon with a beer, attracting a mixed, 20–40-something crowd. April–Oct daily 10am–late.

CLUBS

Don't bother arriving before midnight at Berlin's clubs. To find out what's on, go with the flow from Warschauer Strasse or pick up one of the listings magazines, *Zitty* (Ⓦzitty.de), *Tip* (Ⓦtip-berlin.de) or the English-language *Exberliner* (Ⓦexberliner.com).

Berghain Am Wriezener Bahnhof, Friedrichshain Ⓦberghain.de; ⓈOstbahnhof; map p.364. Legendary techno club in a huge former power station, attracting a mixed gay-straight crowd; entrance policy is strict and generally turns away anyone who looks like a foreign backpacker. Try arriving Sunday at noon. Upstairs *Panorama Bar* Fri & Sat 8pm–late; *Berghain* usually Fri 11pm non-stop till Mon morning.

Cassiopeia Revaler Str. 99 Ⓦcassiopeia-berlin.de; Ⓢ/ⓊWarschauer Str.; map p.364. A popular club in a former rail maintenance yard with four dancefloors and a mad combination of skate-park, climbing wall, cinema and beer garden. Always worth a look. Club nights Wed–Sun 11pm–late.

Clärchens Ballhaus Auguststr. 24 Ⓦballhaus.de; ⓈHackescher Markt; map p.362. Classic 1913 dancehall, hosting dance nights from 9pm, often with instruction: Mon salsa, Tues tango, Wed swing, Thurs & Sun ballroom, Fri & Sat *Schwoof* disco parties (€7). Also serves great pizzas. Daily 11am till at least midnight.

Kaffee Burger Torstr. 60, Mitte ⓦ kaffeeburger.de; ⓤ Rosenthaler Platz/Rosa-Luxemburg-Platz; map p.362. Small, former GDR bar decorated in deep red, with an eclectic range of live music, spoken word events and club nights, including the infamously funky Russian disco twice monthly. Sun–Thurs 9pm–4am, Fri & Sat 9pm–6am.

Privatclub Skalitzer Strasse 85, Kreuzberg ⓦ privatclub-berlin.de; ⓤ Görlitzer Bhf; map p.364. Intimate club inside a former post office building, with an eclectic range of live bands from around the world and parties. Thurs–Sat from 7pm.

Ritter Butzke Ritterstr. 26, Kreuzberg ⓦ ritterbutzke.com ⓤ Moritzplatz; map pp.360–361. Exciting club in a former factory building in an up-and-coming part of Kreuzberg, with three dancefloors, an outdoor area and music with a more local focus than other clubs.

Rosi's Revalerstr. 29, Friedrichshain ⓦ rosis-berlin.de; ⓢ Warschauer Str.; map p.364. Quirky and hugely fun with Berlin's hallmark improvised feel. There's a sense of crashing a house party here, with a small kitchen and living room to hang out in between bouts on dancefloors where indie or techno pounds. Outdoor table tennis too. Thurs–Sat 6pm–late, Sun 2pm till late.

SO 36 Oranienstr. 190, Kreuzberg ⓦ so36.de; ⓤ Görlitzer Bhf; map p.364. Cult punk club with a large gay and lesbian following. Sunday's *Café Fatal* – ballroom dance class at 7pm, dancing from 8pm – is a fantastic, friendly gay and mixed free-for-all. Also frequent live music. See website for exact hours.

ENTERTAINMENT

For last-minute tickets to just about any kind of show or event, try Hekticket (☎ 030 230 99 30, ⓦ hekticket.de), which sells half-price tickets from 2pm and has two locations: Hardenbergstr. 29d, Charlottenburg, opposite the main entrance to ⓢ/ⓤ Zoologischer Garten, and Alexanderstr. 1, Mitte, northeast of Alexanderplatz, ⓢ/ⓤ Alexanderplatz.

CineStar Potsdamerstr. 4 ⓦ cinestar.de/en; ⓢ/ⓤ Potsdamer Platz; map pp.360–361. Sony Center Cinema that screens films in English; €8.50, students €7.

Philharmonie Herbert-von-Karajan-Str. 1 ☎ 030 25 48 80, ⓦ berliner-philharmoniker.de; ⓢ/ⓤ Potsdamer Platz; map pp.360–361. Custom-built home of the world's most celebrated orchestra, the Berlin Philharmonic, with free Tuesday lunchtime concerts at 1pm (Sept to mid-June).

Staatsoper Bismarckstr. 110 ☎ 030 20 35 44 38, ⓦ staatsoper-berlin.org; ⓤ Ernst-Reuter-Platz; map p.362. Excellent operatic productions, temporarily based in the Schiller Theatre while their beautiful building on Unter den Linden is being renovated.

DIRECTORY

Banks and exchange ATMs and exchange at the airports, and major stations. The Reisebank has offices at

BARGAINS AND BOUTIQUES

Boutiques and local designers are in good supply in Berlin, though bargains are rare. The area just northeast of ⓢ Hackescher Markt is the best place for a cluster of fashion boutiques. Head to Prenzlauer Berg (from Kastanienallee to Helmholzplatz) for high-quality, high-priced **local designers**, and to the Boxhagener Platz area of Friedrichshain for the latest hipster apparel. **Flea markets** (*Flohmärkte*) abound in Berlin; head to the busy Mauerpark market in Prenzlauer Berg (Sun 9am–6pm; tram #M10 to Friedrich-Ludwig-Jahn-Sportpark) for the best bargains.

Hauptbahnhof, Friedrichstrasse and Ostbahnhof stations (daily 8am–10pm).

Embassies and consulates Australia, Wallstr. 76–79 ☎ 030 880 08 80, ⓦ germany.embassy.gov.au/beln/home .html; Canada, Leipziger Platz 17 ☎ 030 20 31 20, ⓦ canadainternational.gc.ca/germany-allemagne; Ireland, Jägerstr. 51 ☎ 030 22 07 20, ⓦ embassyofireland.de; New Zealand, Friedrichstr. 60 ☎ 030 20 62 10, ⓦ mfat.govt.nz /en/countries-and-regions/europe/germany/berlin; South Africa, Tiergartenstr. 18 ☎ 030 22 07 30, ⓦ suedafrika.org; UK, Wilhelmstr. 70–71 ☎ 030 20 45 70, ⓦ www.gov.uk /government/world/organisations/british-embassy-berlin; US, Clayallee 170 ☎ 030 830 50, ⓦ de.usembassy.gov.

Hospital There's an emergency room at Campus Charité Mitte, entrance Luisenstr. 65, Mitte (☎ 030 450 531 000)

Pharmacy Apotheke Haupbahnhof, at the main station (24hr).

Post office The post office (Postamt) with the longest hours is at Bahnhof Friedrichstr., at Georgenstr. 12 (Mon–Fri 6am–10pm, Sat & Sun 8am–10pm).

DAY-TRIPS FROM BERLIN

Easy and engaging day-trips by train include the town of **Potsdam**, just southwest of Berlin, famous for the lavish summer palaces and gardens of the Prussian royalty at Sanssouci. Just beyond Berlin's northern edge lies the sombre site of the **Sachsenhausen** concentration camp.

Potsdam: Park Sanssouci

Stretching west from **POTSDAM**'s charming town centre is **Park Sanssouci** (park entry free, but €2 donation gets

12

12

you a useful map; day ticket for all sights €19, students €14), a dazzling collection of eighteenth- and nineteenth-century Baroque and Rococo palaces and ornamental gardens that were once the fabled retreat of the Prussian kings. Dotted with follies, fountains and themed gardens, it's a place you could easily spend a day exploring. **Schloss Sanssouci** (Tues–Sun: April–Oct 10am–6pm; Nov–March 10am–5pm; €12, students €8), the star attraction, was a pleasure palace completed in 1747, where Frederick the Great could escape the stresses of Berlin and his wife. Head here first, as tickets are timed and sell out fast. East of the palace is the **Bildergalerie** (May–Oct Tues–Sun 10am–6pm; €6, students €5), a restrained Baroque creation with paintings by Rubens, Van Dyck and Caravaggio. On the opposite side of the Schloss, the **Neue Kammern** (April–Oct Tues–Sun 10am–6pm; €6, students €5) was originally used as an orangery and later converted into a guest palace in similar lavish Rococo style.

West of here, the **Orangery** (April Sat & Sun 10am–6pm; May–Oct Tues–Sun 10am–6pm; €4, students €3), a later, Neoclassical palace built by Frederick William IV in 1826, features the astonishing Raphael Hall, covered with quality copies of many of Raphael's most famous works. At the west end of the 1.5km-long stylized gardens stands the massive Rococo **Neues Palais** (Mon & Wed–Sun: April–Oct 10am–6pm; Nov–March by guided tour only 10am–5pm), €8, students €6, including audioguide or guided tour), which has an exquisitely opulent interior.

ARRIVAL AND INFORMATION

By train and bus Take ⑤1 or 7 (every 10min; 35min; zone C) or a regional train to Potsdam. From Potsdam train station, take bus #614, #695 or #X5 to Schloss Sanssouci (every 5–10min; 2km); #695 also stops at the Neues Palais, Orangery and the Dachhaus.

Tourist information Potsdam tourist offices are in the train station (Mon–Sat 9.30am–8pm), at the Luisenplatz (April–Oct Mon–Sat 9.30am–6pm, Sun 10am–4pm; Nov–March Mon–Sat 9.30am–6pm) and at the Alter Markt (Mon–Sat 9.30am–7pm & Sun 10am–4pm).

Gedenkstätte Sachsenhausen

More than 200,000 people were imprisoned at **Sachsenhausen concentration camp** between 1936 and 1945, of which many tens of thousands died at the hands of the Nazis. Several of the original buildings across the site house exhibitions about the camp's history (daily: mid-March to mid-Oct 8.30am–6pm; mid-Oct to mid-March 8.30am–4.30pm, exhibitions closed on Mondays in winter; guided tour €3, students €2; Ⓦstiftung-bg.de/gums/en /index.htm).

ARRIVAL AND DEPARTURE

By train and bus Take ⑤1 or a regional train to Oranienburg (every 10min; 25–45 min; zone C), and then bus #804 or #821, or walk for 20min, following the signs to Sachsenhausen.

Eastern Germany

Berlin stands apart from the rest of the East, but its dynamism finds an echo in the two other main cities in the region: particularly **Dresden**, the beautiful Saxon capital so ruthlessly destroyed in 1945, now rebuilt and thriving, and **Leipzig**, which provided the vanguard of the 1989 revolution. Both combine some interesting sights and excellent museums and galleries, with a fun, irreverent bar and club scene. Equally enticing are some of the smaller places, notably the beautiful, diminutive **Weimar**, the fountainhead of much of European art and culture, while small-town **Meissen** retains the appearance and atmosphere of prewar Germany.

DRESDEN

Once regarded as Germany's most beautiful city, **DRESDEN** survived World War II largely unscathed until the night of February 13, 1945. Then, in a matter of hours, it was reduced to ruins in saturation bombing, with around 18,000 to 25,000 people killed. Post-reunification, the city has slotted easily into the economic framework of

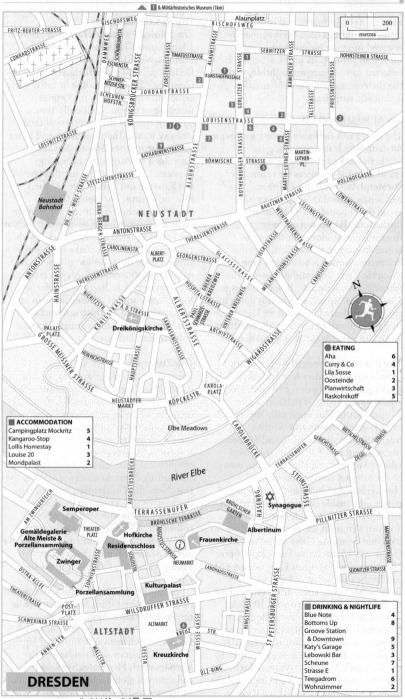

DRESDEN

ACCOMMODATION
Campingplatz Mockritz	5
Kangaroo-Stop	4
Lollis Homestay	1
Louise 20	3
Mondpalast	2

EATING
Aha	6
Curry & Co	4
Lila Sosse	1
Oosteinde	2
Planwirtschaft	3
Raskolnikoff	5

DRINKING & NIGHTLIFE
Blue Note	4
Bottoms Up	8
Groove Station	
& Downtown	9
Katy's Garage	5
Lebowski Bar	3
Scheune	7
Strasse E	1
Teegadrom	6
Wohnzimmer	2

12

12

the reunited Germany, and most of the historic buildings have been brilliantly restored in an ambitious and hugely successful project. Its physical revival is reflected in its resurgent nightlife, with the thriving scene around Neustadt a hedonistic surprise.

WHAT TO SEE AND DO

The city's main sights are in the picturesque **Altstadt**, which stretches along the southern bank of the River Elbe. The grand Baroque set pieces are centred on **Theaterplatz** – with the Zwinger, Residenzschloss and Semperoper (the grand opera house) – and **Neumarkt** further east. Between the two is Augustusstrasse, along which runs a porcelain-tiled mural, while the formal **Brühlsche Terrasse** is an elegant promenade along the river. The southern part of the Altstadt is more prosaic, though the large 1960s Prager Strasse, which runs down to the Hauptbahnhof, is useful for high-street shopping. North of the river, the **Neustadt** is the best place to eat, drink and sleep.

The Frauenkirche and Albertinum

Dominating Dresden Altstadt's skyline is the elegant, soaring dome of the Baroque **Frauenkirche** (Mon–Fri 10am–noon & 1–6pm, Sat & Sun open only for special events) on the **Neumarkt**. Only a fragment of wall was left standing after the war, and in 1991 the decision was taken to rebuild the church, using many of the original stones, creating a chequerboard of light and dark stones in places. The inside is gloriously light, with an impressive 37m-high interior dome. You can climb up the dome for a close-up look and stunning views across town (Mon–Sat 10am–6pm, Sun 12.30–6pm; Nov–Feb closes at 4pm; €8, students €6). Just to the east, overlooking the Brühlischer Garten, the **Albertinum** (daily 10am–6pm; €10, students €7.50; ⓦskd .museum) houses the outstanding New Masters Gallery: it displays art from the nineteenth-century onwards, much of it by German artists – look out for works by the Romantic Caspar David Friedrich, the Expressionist Otto Dix, Van Gogh and the more modern work of Gerhard Richter.

The Residenzschloss

The colossal **Residenzschloss** (Wed–Mon 10am–6pm; €12; timed ticket for the Historisches Grünes Gewölbe €12; Residenzschloss plus Historisches Grünes Gewölbe €21; book online or arrive early; ⓦskd.museum) houses the **Grünes Gewölbe** or Green Vault collection, a dazzling array of the Saxon royal family's treasury items. The three thousand items of the **Historisches Grünes Gewölbe**, assembled by Augustus the Strong between 1723 and 1730, are displayed in the Baroque mirrored rooms of their historic setting. The **Neues Grünes Gewölbe** exhibition features some of the collection's most impressive items, such as the famous carved cherry stones – with 185 carved faces squeezed onto a single stone. Inside the 60m-long Riesensaal hall, the **Rüstkammer** displays a collection of weaponry including a magnificent Renaissance suit of armour for man and horse, while the **Türckische Cammer** exhibits Augustus the Strong's Ottoman fashions and armour.

The Zwinger

Baroque Dresden's great glory was the palace known as the **Zwinger** (Tues–Sun 10am–6pm; €10, students €7.50, includes all Zwinger museums plus audioguide; ⓦskd.museum), which faces the Residenzschloss and contains several museums. It's free to enter the palace's magnificent courtyard and view the enchanting Nymphenbad fountain at the rear. Near the Theaterplatz entrance, in the nineteenth-century extension, is the **Gemäldegalerie Alte Meister**, whose collection of Old Masters ranks among the best in the world, including Raphael's *Sistine Madonna*, plus masterpieces by Titian, Veronese, Dürer, Holbein and Cranach.

Beautifully displayed in the southeastern pavilion, entered from Sophienstrasse, is the **Porzellansammlung**, featuring porcelain items from the famous Meissen factory, as well as from China and Japan. The southwestern pavilion houses the **Mathematisch-Physikalischer Salon**'s collection of globes, clocks and scientific instruments. These two museums can also be visited separately (each museum €6, students €4.50).

The Altmarkt and Kreuzkirche
At the north end of Prager Strasse is the **Altmarkt**; the only building of note here is the **Kreuzkirche**, a church that mixes a Baroque body with a Neoclassical tower. On Saturdays at 6pm, and at 9.30am Sunday services, it usually features the Kreuzchor, one of the world's leading boys' choirs.

The Neustadt
Across the River Elbe, the **Neustadt** was a planned Baroque town. The north bank of the Elbe features the green open space of the Elbe Meadows, with a couple of beer gardens and the best views of the Altstadt skyline. The area around Louisenstrasse is the focus of the city's alternative culture, with a burgeoning art scene; wander through the bohemian **Kunsthofpassage** with its courtyards, houses and arty shops.

On a hill north of Neustadt, a grand old arsenal building, on Olbrichtplatz 2, houses the excellent **Militärhistorisches Museum** (Military museum; daily 10am–6pm, Mon until 9pm; €5, Mon after 6pm free, ⓦmhmbw.de). Designed by US architect Daniel Libeskind, the building is dramatically split into two by a giant wedge, dividing the exhibitions inside into the permanent and fascinating temporary exhibitions. The top of the wedge has a viewing platform overlooking the city.

ARRIVAL AND DEPARTURE

By plane Dresden Airport (ⓦdresden-airport.de) is connected to the Hauptbahnhof and the Neustadt Bahnhof by Ⓢ 2 (every 30min; 13–23min; €2.20).
By train Dresden has two main train stations – the Hauptbahnhof, south of the Altstadt, and Neustadt Bahnhof, at the northwestern corner of the Neustadt.
Destinations Berlin (every 2hr; 2hr 15min); Frankfurt (hourly; 4hr 45min); Leipzig (every 30min; 1hr 15min–1hr 40min); Meissen (every 30min; 35min); Prague (every 2hr; 2hr 10min); Weimar (hourly; 2hr 10min); Wrocław (3 daily; 4hr).

INFORMATION

Tourist information Tourist office at Neumarkt 2, inside the QF Passage next to the Frauenkirche (Mon–Fri 10am–7pm, Sat 10am–6pm, Sun 10am–3pm; ☎0351 50 15 01, ⓦdresden.de/tourism). Pick up the excellent, free USE-IT Dresden map at hostels and train station information desks, or download it from the website (ⓦuse-it.travel).
Discount passes The Dresden-City-Card (€35/48hr) includes public transport, entrance to all Dresden state museums, except the Historisches Grünes Gewölbe, and sundry discounts.

GETTING AROUND

By public transport The network of trams, buses and S-Bahn is frequent and reliable, though the main sights are easily walkable. Trams #8 (to Theaterplatz) and #7 (to the Synagoge by Brühlischer Garten) are useful for getting between the Neustadt and Altstadt. One-way €2.30; day ticket €6.

ACCOMMODATION

Campingplatz Mockritz Boderitzer Str. 30 ☎035 14 71 52 50, ⓦcamping-dresden.de; bus #76 from the Hauptbahnhof. Basic campsite with some nice shady spots. Open year-round. Reception 8–11am & 4–9pm. Per person **€6**, plus per tent **€4.50**
Kangaroo-Stop Erna-Berger-Str. 8–10, Neustadt ☎035 13 14 34 55, ⓦkangaroo-stop.de. Cheap, spacious hostel with a kitchen on a quiet street 3min from Neustadt station, 10min from the bar district. Dorms **€17**, doubles **€46**, apartments **€90**
★ **Lollis Homestay** Görlitzer Str. 34, Neustadt ☎035 18 10 84 58, ⓦlollishome.de. This wonderfully cosy hostel is in lively Neustadt, with friendly staff, quirky rooms, a kitchen (plus free communal dinners weekly) and bikes for rent – though the central location means it can be loud at night. Tram to Alaunplatz or 20min from Neustadt Bahnhof. Sheets €2 extra. Dorms **€17**, doubles **€47**
Louise 20 Louisenstr. 20, Neustadt ☎035 18 89 48 94, ⓦlouise20.de. Bright, quiet, if slightly bland, hotel-quality hostel in a courtyard in the midst of the bar district. Dorms **€18**, doubles **€44**
Mondpalast Louisenstr. 77, Neustadt ☎035 15 63 40 50, ⓦmondpalast.de. A great backpackers' place with artistically decorated rooms on one of Neustadt's liveliest streets. Bike rentals €8/day. Sheets €2. Dorms **€14**, doubles **€48**

EATING

Aha Kreuzstr. 7, Altstadt. Slightly hippy-ish fair-trade café and shop, with a good-value menu of soups such as potato and leek, plus healthy main courses like goats' cheese with figs (€13). Daily 10am–midnight.
Curry & Co Louisenstr. 62, Neustadt. This ultra-hip, minimalist *Currywurst* joint serves up cheap, quick and satisfying snacks on the go. *Currywurst* and fries €4.30. Sun–Thurs 11am–10pm, Fri & Sat 11am–2am.

12

Lila Sosse Kunsthof passage, Alaunstr. 70, Neustadt Ⓦ lilasosse.de. A great spot for relaxing and unwinding, this cool bistro in an arty courtyard prepares modern German dishes – try the home-made cheese *Spätzle* (€6.90). Mon–Fri 4–11pm, Sat & Sun noon–11pm.

Oosteinde Preissnitzstr. 18, Neustadt. Delicious, good-value food served beneath a low-vaulted roof or outside in a peaceful beer garden. Burgers start at €7.80, mains from €9. Mon–Sat 4pm–midnight, Sun 11am–midnight.

Planwirtschaft Louisenstr. 20, Neustadt; Ⓦ planwirtschaft -dresden.de. Popular café-bar-restaurant and *Biergarten* with a great breakfast buffet (Mon–Fri €9.80, Sat & Sun €14.50). Convivial tables set under trees offer the chance to chat with new friends. Daily 7.30am–1am.

Raskolnikoff Böhmische Str. 34, Neustadt; Ⓦ raskolnikoff.de. A large, rambling, bohemian Russian bar-café and restaurant. Great food and an atmospheric beer garden that gets very crowded at weekends. Mon–Fri 10am–2am, Sat & Sun 9am–2am.

DRINKING AND NIGHTLIFE

The Neustadt is home to more than 130 bars and clubs clustered around a handful of narrow streets, where crowds drink peacefully outside on warm nights. For nightlife listings, pick up a copy of *Sax* or *Dresdner* (German only) from the tourist office or hostels.

BARS

Blue Note Görlitzer Str. 2b, Neustadt Ⓦ jazzdepartment .com. Dark and boozy jazz bar, packed to the gills nightly for its live music starting at 9pm. To get a seat, arrive when it opens. Daily 7pm till at least midnight.

Bottoms Up Martin-Luther-Str. 31, Neustadt. Down a quiet backstreet away from the main action, this easy-going café-bar and beer garden is an unpretentious favourite that serves good weekend breakfasts. Mon–Fri 5pm–5am, Sat & Sun 10am–5am.

Lebowski Bar Gorlitzer Str. 53, Neustadt. Kick back with a cocktail (a white Russian, of course, just like the Dude) while the Big Lebowski plays in the background. Daily 6pm till at least 1am.

Scheune Alaunstr. 36, Neustadt Ⓦ scheune.org. A bastion of the alternative scene with a studenty bar and beer garden, tasty Indian food, a cinema and occasional gigs. Mon–Fri 4pm–midnight, Sat & Sun 10am–midnight.

Teegadrom Louisenstr. 48, Neustadt; Ⓦ teegadrom.de. A more tranquil alternative to the Neustadt hipster scene: it's calm and candlelit, with board games, and attracts a mixed crowd of 20- and 30-somethings. Daily 4pm–2am.

Wohnzimmer Alaunstr. 27/Jordanstr. 19, Neustadt; Ⓦ wohnzimmer-dresden.de. On two levels, this living-room-themed bar has comfy couches and serves up a good selection of cocktails including mojitos and martinis. Daily 1pm till at least 1am.

CLUBS

Groove Station & Downtown Katherinenstr. 11–13, Neustadt Ⓦ groovestation.de, Ⓦ downtown-dresden.de. Set around a courtyard, this rough-and-ready rock, hip-hop and dance bar/live music complex has been a Neustadt cornerstone for years. Fri & Sat 8pm–2am.

Katy's Garage Alaunstr. 48, Neustadt Ⓦ katysgarage.de. Neustadt institution – and one of the few clubs to open daily – with a chilled beer garden at the front, and club behind (from 8pm); Mon is student night. Daily 5pm till at least 1am.

Strasse E Werner-Hartmann-Str. 2 Ⓦ strasse-e.de; tram #7 or S-Bahn to Industriegelände, along Hermann-Mende-Str. then right onto Werner-Hartman-Str. Industrial area turned venue/music mini-city north of the Neustadt, where there's always something interesting going on. Fri & Sat 6pm till at least 2am.

DAY-TRIPS FROM DRESDEN

Around Dresden there is stunning scenery in **Saxon Switzerland** and the quaint unspoilt town of **Meissen**, making the city a good base for exploring the region. Both are within Dresden's regional transport network.

Sächsische Schweiz

The **Sächsische Schweiz** (Saxon Switzerland) region southeast of Dresden is a natural wonderland of majestic sandstone mountains, stunning views of the River Elbe and ample opportunities for hiking, cycling and climbing. One classic hiking route is the 115km **Malerweg** (Painter Route), overnighting in tourist-friendly villages along the way. There are also countless day hikes, easily reached by train from Dresden, such as Königstein to Rathen via Lilienstein (7km), through woods and open vistas.

ARRIVAL AND INFORMATION

By S-Bahn and bus It's easy to visit this region from Dresden; just take Ⓢ 1 (every 30min; single €6.20) to Kurort Rathen, Königstein or Bad Schandau and follow trailheads from there; ferries across the Elbe connect to the trains.

Tourist information The tourist office in Dresden (see p.373) has general information; the friendly office inside Bad Schandau train station sells good maps and can recommend day hikes suited to your abilities (April & Oct Mon–Fri 8am–5pm, Sat & Sun 9am–noon; May–Sept Mon–Sat 8am–5pm, Sat & Sun 9am–4pm; Nov–March Mon–Fri 8am–5pm, Sat 9am–noon, Jan & Feb closed Wed; Ⓦ saechsische-schweiz.de).

Meissen

The cobbled square and photogenic rooftop vistas are reason enough to visit the porcelain-producing town of **MEISSEN**, which, unlike its neighbour Dresden, survived World War II almost unscathed. Walking towards the centre from the **train station** (a 20min walk over the railroad bridge or the Altstadtbrücke; both are signposted), on the opposite side of the River Elbe, you see Meissen's commandingly sited castle almost immediately, rising just back from the Elbe's edge. The **Albrechtsburg** (daily: March–Oct 10am–6pm; Nov–Feb 10am–5pm; €8, students €4; ⓦ albrechtsburg-meissen .de) is a late fifteenth-century combination of military fortress and residential palace, which housed a porcelain factory in the eighteenth and nineteenth centuries. Much of its current interior is nineteenth century, with murals celebrating Saxon history. Cocooned within the castle precinct is the Gothic **Dom** (daily: April–Oct 9am–6pm; Nov– March 10am–4pm; €4, students €2.50); inside, look out for the brass tomb-plates of the Saxon dukes.

The **Staatliche Porzellan-Manufaktur** is at Talstr. 9 (daily: May–Oct 9am–6pm; Nov–April 9am–5pm; €9, students €6; ⓦ meissen.de), about 1.5km south of the central Markt. It's the most famous factory to manufacture Dresden china, which was invented when Augustus the Strong imprisoned the alchemist Johann Friedrich Böttger, ordering him to produce gold. Instead, he accidentally invented the first true European porcelain. You can view many of the factory's finest creations in the attached **museum** (same hours) and shop.

ARRIVAL AND INFORMATION

By S-Bahn S-Bahn line 1 from Dresden to Meissen station (35–40min, every 30min; single €6.20).

Tourist information Meissen's tourist office is located on Markt 3 (April–Oct Mon–Fri 10am–6pm, Sat & Sun 10am–3pm; Nov–March Mon–Fri 10am–5pm, Sat 10am–3pm, Jan closed Sat & Sun; ⓣ 03521 419 40, ⓦ touristinfo-meissen.de).

LEIPZIG

LEIPZIG has always been among the most dynamic of German cities. With its influential and respected university, and a tradition of trade fairs dating back to the Middle Ages, it never experienced the same degree of isolation as other cities behind the Iron Curtain. Leipzigers have embraced the challenges of reunification, and the city's imposing monuments, cobbled backstreets and wide-ranging nightlife make for an inviting visit.

WHAT TO SEE AND DO

Most points of interest lie within the old centre, a compact mix of traditional and often strikingly modern, with several Passagen, or covered shopping arcades, often with stylish Art Nouveau touches, running between the main streets.

Nikolaikirche and Markt

Following Nikolaistrasse due south from the train station brings you to the **Nikolaikirche**, a rallying point during the collapse of the GDR, when its weekly peace prayers, which had been going on for several years, escalated into large protests. Although a sombre medieval structure outside, inside the church is a real eye-grabber thanks to rich decoration, works of art and pink columns with palm-tree-style capitals. A couple of blocks west is the **Markt**, whose eastern side is entirely occupied by the **Altes Rathaus**, built in the grandest German Renaissance style with elaborate gables and an asymmetrical tower. To the rear of the Altes Rathaus is the Baroque **Alte Handelsbörse**, formerly the trade exchange headquarters. South of the Markt, **Mädler Passage** is an elegant arcade famous for the restaurant *Auerbach's Keller*, which features in Goethe's *Faust*.

Museum der bildenden Künste

Immense and striking, the modern perspex-skinned cube of the **Museum der bildenden Künste**, at Katharinenstr. 10 (Tues & Thurs–Sun 10am–6pm, Wed noon–8pm; €10, students €7), houses a distinguished collection, from Old Masters through to twentieth-century artists, and is particularly strong on

12

12

Leipzig-born Max Beckmann. Traditional galleries are interspersed with airy, two-storey spaces featuring imaginative and playful contemporary pieces, many by local artists. To further explore the thriving local art scene, check out the excellent **Galerie für Zeitgenössische Kunst**, Karl-Tauchnitz-Str. 11, just outside the Ring southwest of the centre (Gallery for Contemporary Art; Tues–Fri 2–7pm, Sat & Sun noon–6pm; €5, students €3, Wed free), while more contemporary art can seen in the galleries of the wonderful **Spinnerei**, at Spinnereistrasse 7, an old cotton mill complex west of the centre (Tues–Sat 11am–6pm; free ⓦspinnerei.de; ⓢPlagwitz).

The Thomaskirche and Bach-Museum

Just southwest of the Markt, on Thomaskirchhof, stands the predominantly Gothic **Thomaskirche**, where Johann Sebastian Bach served as cantor for the last 27 years of his life. The most remarkable feature is its musical tradition: the Thomanerchor choir, which Bach once directed, can usually be heard on Fridays (6pm), Saturdays (3pm) and during the Sunday service (9am). Directly across from the church is the **Bach-Museum** (Tues–Sun 10am–6pm; €8, students €6), which showcases Bach relics such as his manuscripts and evokes his period and music through modern displays.

Runde Ecke and Zeitgeschichtliches Forum

In the autumn of 1989 Leipzig was at the forefront of protests against the GDR, and one focus for this was the **Runde Ecke**, at Dittrichring 24, the city's headquarters for the Stasi, East Germany's secret police (daily 10am–6pm; €4, students €3; English audioguide €3). Much of it has been preserved as it was, complete with a Stasi official's office, making it a fascinating trawl through the methods and machinery of the Stasi. Less atmospheric but slicker is the **Zeitgeschichtliches Forum** (Mon–Fri 9am–6pm, Sat & Sun 10am–6pm; free), just south of the Markt at Grimmaische Str. 6, a multimedia museum on the history of the GDR.

The Völkerschlachtdenkmal

East of the centre on Strasse des 18 Oktober stands the colossal **Völkerschlachtdenkmal** (daily: April–Oct 10am–6pm; Nov–March 10am–4pm; €6; ⓢ Völkerschlachtdenkmal or tram #15), a 91m-high concrete-and-granite war memorial. It commemorates the 54,000 allied soldiers who died in the 1813 Battle of Nations, which pitted the combined might of the Prussian, Austrian and Russian forces against Napoleon's army. A lookout platform offers great views, and at its base the **Forum 1813** exhibition provides context to the battle.

ARRIVAL AND INFORMATION

By plane Leipzig-Halle Airport (ⓦleipzig-halle-airport.de) is connected with the main train station by the Airport Express train (every 20min; 15min).

By train Leipzig's enormous Hauptbahnhof is at the northeastern corner of the city centre.

Destinations Berlin (hourly; 1hr 20min); Dresden (every 30min; 1hr 15min–1hr 40min); Frankfurt (hourly; 3hr 30min); Meissen (hourly; 1hr 20min); Weimar (hourly; 1hr).

Tourist information Beside the Museum der bildenden Künste at Katharinenstr. 8 (Mon–Fri 9.30am–6pm, Sat 9.30am–4pm, Sun 9.30am–3pm; ☎0341 71 04 260, ⓦleipzig.de). The Leipzig Card (1/3-days for €11.50/25.50), which includes public transport and various discounts, is unlikely to be good value – particularly if you get student discounts, which are often the same.

GETTING AROUND

By train, tram and bus S-Bahn trains connect the Hauptbahnhof to the city centre, the Völkerschlachtdenkmal and Plagwitz; trams #9 and #11 from the Hauptbahnhof are useful for Karl-Liebknecht-Str. One-way ticket €2.50, day ticket €6.90.

ACCOMMODATION

Auensee Gustav-Esche-Str. 5 ☎034 14 65 16 00, ⓦcamping-auensee.de; tram #10 or #11 to Wahren Rathaus, then walk or bus #80 to Auensee. Open May–Dec, with bungalow doubles also available. Reception daily: May–Oct 8am–1pm & 2–8.30pm; Nov & Dec 8am–1pm & 2–5.30pm. Camping/person €6,50, plus per tent €4, bungalows €35

Central Globetrotter Kurt-Schumacher-Str. 41 ☎034 11 49 89 60, ⓦglobetrotter-leipzig.de. Popular backpacker spot just north of the Hauptbahnhof. Rooms facing the street can be noisy. Sheets €3. Breakfast €4. Dorms €15, doubles €24

Sleepy Lion Jacobstr. 1 ☎034 19 93 94 80, ⓦhostel-leipzig.de. This is a spacious, well-run hostel west of the centre, 15min walk from the station. Bed linen free, sleeping bags not allowed. Dorms €11, doubles €38

EATING, DRINKING AND NIGHTLIFE

Gottschedstrasse, just west of the Thomaskirche, is lined with attractive cafés and bars, while Karl-Liebknecht-Strasse, a couple of tram stops south of the centre (#10 or #11), is lively and studenty.

Die Versorger Spinnereistr. 7, Plagwitz ⓦ die-versorger .com. Cosy villa inside the Spinnerei complex with cheap pub food (schnitzel and fries €6.50; soup from €3), occasional concerts and a lovely summer garden with scattered seating and table tennis. Mon–Fri 8.30am–7pm, Sat 10am–7pm, Sun 11am–7pm.

Ilses Erika Bernhard-Göring-Str. 152, Südvorstadt ⓦ ilseserika.de; tram to Connewitz Kreuz. Indie bar, club and music venue Thurs–Sat; beer garden all summer. Attracts a nice mix of ages and people from students to families with kids in the beer garden. Wed–Sun times vary.

Luise Bosestr. 4, corner of Gottschedstr ⓦ luise-leipzig .de. Chic café-bar with an attractive, vaguely Pop Art decor, serving excellent breakfasts (from €6) and small pasta dishes. Sun–Thurs 9am–1am, Fri & Sat 9am–3am.

KH70 Karl-Heine-Str. 70, Plagwitz ⓦ kh70.de. One of several studenty options en route to the Spinnerei complex. The soul food served up includes tasty burgers (around €7), chilli con carne and "groove salad". Sun–Thurs 6pm–1am, Fri & Sat 6pm–3am.

Moritzbastei Universitätsstr. 9 ⓦ moritzbastei.de. A cavernous student cellar bar and club in a former bastion, with lots of events, including live music. There are also beer gardens and a cheap student canteen. Mon–Fri 10am–1am, Sat noon–1am.

naTo Karl-Liebknecht-Str. 46, Südvorstadt ⓦ nato-leipzig .de; tram #10 or #11 to Südplatz. Focus of the city's alternative scene with a popular bar, gigs of indie, alt-folk and jazz music, theatre, cabaret and an art-house cinema. Daily 5 or 6pm til at least midnight.

WEIMAR

Despite its modest size, **WEIMAR** has played an unmatched role in the development of German culture: Goethe, Schiller and Nietzsche all made it their home, as did the architects and designers of the Bauhaus school. The town was also chosen as the drafting place for the constitution of the democratic republic established after World War I, a regime whose failure ended with the Nazi accession. Add to this the town's cobbled streets and laidback, quietly highbrow atmosphere, and Weimar makes an attractive stop for a day or two.

WHAT TO SEE AND DO

Weimar's main sights are concentrated in the city's walkable centre, south of the main train station and on the west side of the River Ilm. The lovely **Park an der Ilm** stretches 2km southwards from the **Schloss** on both sides of the river. The **Buchenwald** concentration camp memorial is a bus ride to the northwest.

The Schloss and Markt

Weimar's former seat of power was the **Schloss**, set by the River Ilm at the eastern edge of the town centre, a Neoclassical complex of a size more appropriate for ruling a mighty empire. It's now a **museum** (Tues–Sun: Jan–Easter, Nov & Dec 9.30am–4pm; Easter–Oct 9.30am–6pm; €7.50, students €6), with a collection of Old Masters on the ground floor, including pieces by both Cranachs and Dürer, while the first-floor rooms are grand Neoclassical chambers, with lavish memorial rooms to great poets – most notably Goethe and Schiller. South of nearby Herderplatz is the spacious **Markt**, lined with a disparate jumble of buildings, the most eye-catching of which is the green and white gabled Stadthaus on the eastern side, opposite the neo-Gothic Rathaus.

The Goethewohnhaus und Nationalmuseum

On Frauenplan, south of the Markt, the **Goethewohnhaus und Nationalmuseum** (Tues–Sun: Jan–March, Nov & Dec 9.30am–4pm; April–Oct 9.30am–6pm; €12, students €8.50) is where Goethe lived for some fifty years until his death in 1832. The house and garden have been atmospherically preserved as they were in his lifetime, complete with the chair in which he died, while the museum showcases his extensive collections of art and natural specimens.

Theaterplatz and around

Weimar's most photographed symbol is the large double statue of Goethe and Schiller on **Theaterplatz**, a spacious square west of the Markt. The Nationaltheater on the west side of

12

12

the square was founded and directed by Goethe, though the present building is a modern copy. Directly opposite is the small but interesting **Bauhaus museum**, with a collection of artefacts and photos relating to the influential architecture and design movement (Wed–Mon: April–Oct 10am–6pm; Nov–March 10am–4pm, €4, students €3) – a large new museum is planned just north of the town centre for 2019 to commemorate the hundredth anniversary of the Bauhaus movement. Schillerstrasse snakes away from the southeast corner of Theaterplatz, with the **Schillerhaus** at no. 12 (Tues–Sun: April–Oct 9.30am–6pm; Nov–March 9.30am–4pm; €7.50, students €6), the home of the poet and dramatist for the last three years of his life.

Konzentrationslager Buchenwald

The **Konzentrationslager Buchenwald** (Tues–Sun: April–Oct 10am–6pm; Nov–March 10am–4pm; free; ⓦbuchenwald.de) is situated north of Weimar on the Ettersberg heights, and can be reached by bus #6 (hourly from Goetheplatz and the train station; 20min). Over 240,000 prisoners were incarcerated in this concentration camp, with 65,000 dying here. Very few original buildings remain, but an audioguide (€3) and the historical exhibition paint a vivid picture of life and death in the camp.

ARRIVAL AND INFORMATION

By train Weimar's train station, on the Leipzig line, is a 20min walk north of the main sights.
Destinations Dresden (hourly; 2hr 30min); Eisenach (every 30min; 50min); Frankfurt (hourly; 2hr 30min); Leipzig (hourly; 1hr).
Tourist information Tourist office at Markt 10 (April–Oct Mon–Sat 9.30am–7pm, Sun 9.30am–3pm; Nov–March Mon–Fri 9.30am–6pm, Sat & Sun 9.30am–2pm; ⓣ03643 7450, ⓦweimar.de).

ACCOMMODATION

A&O Hostel Buttelstedter Str. 27c ⓣ030 809 47 51 10, ⓦaohostels.com. Large new hostel with spacious rooms, just five minutes' walk north of the Hauptbahnhof. Dorms €18, doubles €51
Labyrinth Hostel Goetheplatz 6 ⓣ036 43 81 18 22, ⓦweimar-hostel.com. Fantastic, central and friendly hostel, with attractive spotless rooms individually

designed by local artists. There's a good kitchen, a relaxed communal area and a courtyard. Dorms €14, doubles €50
Pension Savina Meyerstr. 60 ⓣ036 438 66 90, ⓦpension-savina.de. Convenient *pension* where the cosy, spotless and simply furnished rooms come with en-suite bathrooms and kitchenettes. A fine choice. Doubles €62

EATING, DRINKING AND NIGHTLIFE

ACC Burgplatz 1. A relaxed bar and restaurant with an upstairs gallery and quiet candlelit tables lining a cobbled side street. Mains from €6.50. Mon–Fri noon–1am, Sat & Sun 10am–1am.
Estragon Herderplatz 3. Small soup bar that's part of an organic supermarket, with a daily-changing menu of tasty, filling soups (€3–6) and salads (pay by weight). Mon–Fri 10am–7pm, Sat noon–7pm.
Giancarlo Schillerstr. 11. Gloriously old-fashioned Italian ice-cream parlour, with over sixty home-made flavours – try the bitter chocolate – plus extravagant sundaes and waffles. The €1.20 coffee-and-croissant breakfast (9–11am) is unbeatable value. Daily 9am–8pm, often later in summer.
Kasseturm Goetheplatz 10. Student club in an atmospheric brick tower – it puts on some good live music nights, which are always sweaty and occasionally rowdy. Mon–Sat 8pm till at least 1am.
San Eisfeld 4. Cosy Korean restaurant with authentic classics such as veg or meat *bibimbap* (fried rice, from €7), a fireplace in winter and lovely home-made ceramics for sale. Tues–Sat noon–4pm & 5–10pm.

EISENACH: THE WARTBURG

A small town on the edge of the Thuringian Forest, **EISENACH** is home to Germany's best-loved medieval castle, the **Wartburg**. The castle complex (guided tours only, every 15min; daily: April–Oct 8.30am–5pm; Nov–March 9am–3.30pm; €9, students €5; English translation available), first mentioned in 1080, includes one of the best-preserved Romanesque palaces this side of the Alps, with several newer additions, including the Festsaal, a nineteenth-century interpretation of medieval grandeur so splendid that Ludwig II of Bavaria had it copied for his fairytale palace, Neuschwanstein. The tour takes you through its ornately decorated rooms. Also on view is a small exhibition of paintings – including some elegant portraits by Cranach the Elder – and the **Lutherstube**, the room in which Martin Luther translated the New Testament into the German vernacular while in hiding in 1521–22.

ARRIVAL AND INFORMATION

By train Eisenach is 45min–1hr 10min from Weimar by train (every 30min) – an easy day-trip. The Wartburg is a good hour's walk from the train station (get a map from DB information at the train station or tourist office). From the station head southwest along Wartburgallee; after 20–30min, at the Reuter-Wagner-Museum, there's a signposted footpath up to the Wartburg, a steep 30min climb from here. Alternatively, bus #10 runs hourly (April–Oct) from the train station to the Eselstation (donkey station), from where it's a 15min steep climb to the castle. Electric bikes can be rented from Cycle Service, Markt 18.

Tourist information Tourist office inside the Stadtschloss palace at Markt 24 (Mon–Fri 10am–6pm, Sat & Sun 10am–5pm; ☎ 03691 792 30, ⌨ eisenach.info).

ACCOMMODATION AND EATING

There's a traditional restaurant at the Wartburg, plus cheap and tasty Thuringian *Rostbratwurst* stalls near the donkey station and a dozen or so cafés and restaurants around the Markt in the town centre.

Jugendherberge Eisenach Mariental 24 ☎ 03691 74 32 59, ⌨ eisenach.jugendherberge.de; bus #3 or #10 to "Unterhalb der Herberge". Spacious hostel at the foot of the Wartburg hill, 1km from the main square. Dorms €23, doubles €46

Northern Germany

Hamburg, Germany's second city, is infamous for the sleaze and hectic nightlife of the Reeperbahn strip – but it is far more than this, with a sophisticated cultural scene, handsome warehouse quarter and big-city allure. Another maritime city, **Lübeck**, has a strong pull, with a similar appeal to the mercantile towns of the Low Countries. To the south lies **Hannover**, worth a visit for its museums and gardens.

HAMBURG

Stylish media centre and second-largest port in Europe, **HAMBURG** is undeniably cool – more laidback than Berlin or

Frankfurt, more sophisticated than Munich, and with nightlife to rival the lot. Its skyline is dominated by the pale green of its copper spires and domes, but a few houses and churches are all that's left from older times. Though much of the subsequent rebuilding isn't especially beautiful, the result is an intriguing mix of old and new, coupled with an appealing sense of open space – two-thirds of Hamburg is occupied by parks, lakes or canals.

WHAT TO SEE AND DO

Much of the fun of Hamburg is in exploring different quarters, each with a distinct feel and purpose. The centre, defined by the Binnenalster and Aussenalster lakes to its northeast, and the docks and port to the south, is focused on the oversized **Rathaus**. The streets that span north, particularly **Jungfernstieg** and around, are classy and commercial. But the focus of Hamburg is the **docks and warehouses** along the Elbe River. North from the port are the best neighbourhoods after dark: **St Pauli** and its infamous Reeperbahn, the studenty **Schanzenviertel** further north, and chic **Altona** off to the west.

The Rathaus

The commercial and shopping district centres on **Binnenalster** lake and the neo-Renaissance **Rathaus** (guided tours Mon–Fri 11am–4pm, Sat 10am–5pm, Sun 10am–4pm; €4, tours in English on request; ☎ 040 428 312 064), a magnificently pompous demonstration of the city's power and wealth in the nineteenth century.

Nikolaikirche and St Michaelis

Hamburg's skyline is punctuated by a series of church spires – it's worth climbing one to appreciate the surrounding watery expanses. The most dramatic ascent is the glass lift up through the skeletal spire of **Nikolaikirche** on Willy-Brandt-Strasse, which is pretty much all that remains of the church, the rest having been destroyed in 1943. A small, poignant exhibition is displayed in

12

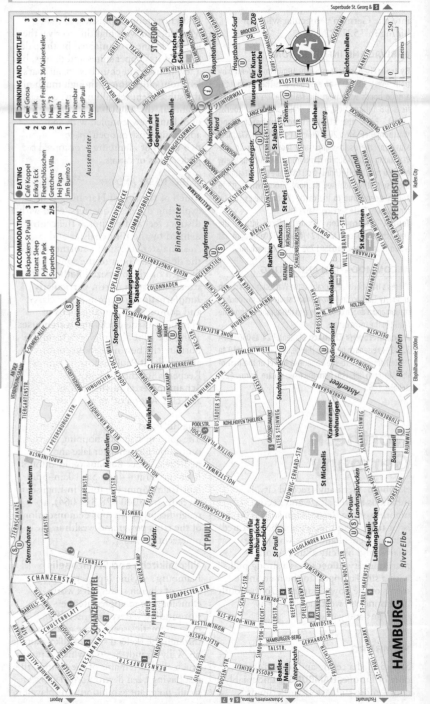

Superbude St. Georg & 5

■ ACCOMMODATION
Backpackers-St Pauli	3
Instant Sleep	1
Pyjama Park	4
Superbude	2/5

● EATING
Café Koppel	4
Erika's Eck	1
Fleetschlösschen	6
Gretchens Villa	2
Hej Papa	3
Jim Burrito's	5

● DRINKING AND NIGHTLIFE
Caxé Gnosa	3
Fabrik	6
Grosse Freiheit 36/Kaiserkeller	4
Haus 73	7
Knuth	1
MuTter	8
Prinzenbar	9
StrandPauli	9
Waxd	5

HAMBURG

the crypt (daily: May–Sept 10am–6pm; Oct–April 10am–5pm; €5 for spire and crypt). Hamburg's city church is the elegant Baroque **St Michaelis**, on Englische Planke. You can go up the tower (daily: May–Oct 9am–7.30pm; Nov–April 10am–5.30pm; €5, students €4) for a panorama over the docks.

The waterfront

From the red-brick **Speicherstadt** immediately south of the Markt, via eye-catching new developments of the **HafenCity** area to the impressive utilitarian **port** to the west, Hamburg's waterfront is its most distinctive area. With its tall, ornate warehouses, the nineteenth-century **Speicherstadt** quarter is the most attractive part to wander and crisscross the bridges at will – Hamburg has more of them than Venice or Amsterdam. Its modern counterpart behind is **HafenCity**, a docklands development project with futuristic architecture, such as the **Elbphilharmonie** concert hall with its stunning interior (opens in 2017; check Welbphilharmonie.de for details of guided tours).

Further west, the harbour area is dominated by the solid wharf building of **St Pauli Landungsbrücken**, while west again along Hafenstrasse is the location for the legendary **Fischmarkt**. Come early on Sunday to witness an amazing trading – and drinking, as it's a post-club institution – frenzy; it's in full swing by 6am then all over by 10am. Around the harbour you can pick up a **boat tour** (from €14; 1hr), giving an intriguing look at the port and its industrial containers.

St Pauli and the Schanzenviertel

The former dockers' quarter, **St Pauli**, is now the red-light district and nightlife centre. Its main artery is the **Reeperbahn** – ugly and unassuming by day, blazing with neon at night. Running off here is **Grosse Freiheit**, the street that famously hosted The Beatles' first gigs – the junction of the two is now Beatles-Platz, with a sculpture of the Fab Four. The neighbourhood north of here, centred on Schulterblatt, is the **Schanzenviertel** (or Schanze), home to a riotously good fun,

scruffy and studenty bar scene and cool urban ateliers.

The Kunsthalle

Just northeast of the Hauptbahnhof, on Glockengiesserwall, is the **Kunsthalle**, Hamburg's unmissable art collection (Tues, Wed & Fri–Sun 10am–6pm, Thurs 10am–9pm; Mon–Fri €12, students €6; Sat & Sun €14, students €7; Thurs after 6pm €8, students €4). The main building features an outstanding collection, ranging from Old Masters to the twentieth century, and includes works by Rembrandt and Munch. An attached glass cube, reached via an underground passageway, houses the **Galerie der Gegenwart** (Contemporary Art; same ticket), with late twentieth-century works plus big temporary exhibitions and installations.

ARRIVAL AND DEPARTURE

By plane Hamburg Airport, roughly 11km north of the city, is connected with the main train station via S-Bahn line S1 (every 10min; 25min; €3.20).

By train The Hauptbahnhof is at the eastern end of the city centre.

Destinations Århus (2 daily; 4hr 30min); Berlin (hourly; 1hr 40min); Copenhagen (5 daily; 5hr); Frankfurt (hourly; 3hr 30min); Hannover (every 30min; 1hr 20min); Lübeck (every 30min; 40min); Munich (hourly; 5hr 40min).

INFORMATION

Tourist information In the Hauptbahnhof (Mon–Sat 9am–7pm, Sun 10am–6pm; ☏040 30 05 17 01, ⓦhamburg-travel.com); at the airport (daily 6am–11pm) and at Landungsbrücken 4/5, St Pauli (Sun–Wed 9am–6pm, Thurs–Sat 9am–7pm).

Discount pass The Hamburg Card (€9.90/25.50/40.90 for 1/3/5 days) gives free use of public transport and reduced admission to some of the city's museums.

GETTING AROUND

By public transport Hamburg is big, with an extensive public transport network, made up of U-Bahn, S-Bahn and buses. A short trip costs €2.20, a one-way trip €3.20, a day ticket €6.20 (after 9am, €7.60 before); a day ticket for up to five people is €11.60.

By bike Bike rental from the Nextbike and StadtRad (Call a Bike) schemes and from Fahrradladen St Georg, Schmilinskystr. 6, 10min from Hauptbahnhof (Mon–Fri 10am–7pm, Sat 10am–1pm; €10/day), and Fahrradstation, Schlüterstr. 11 (ⓢDammtor; Mon–Fri 10am–6pm; €12/day).

12

12

ACCOMMODATION

Backpackers-St Pauli Bernstorffstr. 98 ☏ 040 23 51 70 43, ⓦ backpackers-stpauli.de; ⓣ Feldstr. Small backpacker hostel run by St Pauli locals, well located for both St Pauli and the Schanze, with a good communal area and bar next door. Sheets €2.50 (own sleeping bags not permitted). Dorms €17, doubles €30

Instant Sleep May-Brauer-Alee 277 ☏ 010 13 100 100, ⓦ instantsleep.de; S/ⓣ Sternschanze. Centrally located in the lively Schanze area, this laidback, independent hostel has basic rooms and a kitchen, though it's on a noisy corner above a bar. Dorms €19,50, doubles €49

Pyjama Park Reeperbahn 36 ☏ 040 31 48 38, ⓦ pyjama -park.de. Comfortable hotel and hostel with nicely designed and individually styled rooms, a bar with DJs and a rooftop terrace in summer. Dorms €21, doubles €63

Superbude St Pauli Juliusstr 1–7 ☏ 040 807 91 58 20, ⓦ superbude.de; S/ⓣ Sternschanze. Trendy and hip hotel-hostel hybrid with stylish communal areas and lots of yellow – smack in the middle of St Pauli. Dorms €16, doubles €60

EATING

Café Koppel In Koppel 66 arts centre, Lange Reihe 75, northeast of the train station in St Georg district; S/ⓣ Hauptbahnhof. Relaxed, classy vegetarian café-restaurant that's part of an arts centre, with a small menu of home-made breakfasts and daily specials (around €7), delicious cakes and a pretty summer garden. Daily 10am–11pm, garden until 7pm.

Erika's Eck Sternstr. 98; S/ⓣ Sternschanze. A firm student favourite, serving huge portions of traditional German dishes almost round the clock with breakfast served from midnight, making it popular post-clubbing. Mon–Fri 5pm till 2pm the next day, Sat & Sun 5pm–9am.

Fleetschlösschen Brooktorkai 17; ⓣ Messberg. Atmospheric little café in a small building in the Speicherstadt – worth stopping in to browse through its collection of books on Hamburg and the harbour. Good coffee and a short menu of rolls and soups. Daily 8am–10pm.

Gretchens Villa Marktstr. 142; ⓣ Messehallen. Cute, bright little café with a short daytime menu and heavenly cakes – a good spot for people-watching on this street of stylish shops. Tues–Sun 10am–7pm.

Hej Papa Poolstr. 32 ⓦ hej-papa.de. The "kitchen and coffee" concept here with healthy snacks, great drinks and fabulous breakfasts at weekends draws in a relaxed mix of locals. Mon–Fri 9am–5pm, Sat & Sun 10am–5pm.

Jim Burrito's Schulterblatt 12, Schanzenviertel; S/ⓣ Sternschanze. Laidback, with a nicely shabby charm to the place: tasty, cheap and filling Mexican dishes, if not particularly spicy (a range of chilli sauces is at hand). Burritos €5–9. Daily noon–midnight.

DRINKING AND NIGHTLIFE

Hamburg's nightlife is outstanding: the Schanzenviertel for studenty bar-crawling; St Pauli for clubs and live music venues; while Altona attracts an older, more relaxed crowd. For information on the gay scene check *Hinnerk magazine* (German only, ⓦ blu.fm/hinnerk), available from the tourist office, cafés and bars.

BARS

Café Gnosa Lange Reihe 93; St Pauli. Well-known gay bar-café northeast of the train station that also attracts a mixed crowd. Packed at weekends. Marvellous cakes at €4, and good breakfasts. Sun–Thurs 10am–midnight, Fri & Sat 10am–1am.

Knuth Grosse Rainstr. 21; S Altona. Relaxed, stylish neighbourhood café-bar with comfy chairs and a convivial atmosphere where you can lounge and read or just grab a bite. Mon–Sat 9am till late, Sun 10am–8pm.

Mutter Stresemannstr. 11; S/ⓣ Sternschanze. Small, atmospheric retro-styled bar that's often the last to shut. Attracts a good mix of ages and manages to be hip without any attitude. Daily 9pm–6am.

StrandPauli Hafenstr. 89; S/ⓣ Landungsbrücken. Cool urban beach-bar on the old wharf, with cocktails, Caribbean vibes and an unrivalled view of the port. Summer Mon–Thurs 11am–11pm, Fri & Sat 11am–midnight, Sun 10am–11pm; winter Fri & Sat 11am–midnight, Sun 10am–11pm, Mon–Thurs only when weather permits.

CLUBS AND LIVE MUSIC

Fabrik Barnerstr. 36 ⓦ fabrik.de; S Altona. Major live music and club venue in Altona, with a huge range of music and occasional mixed gay nights. See website for times.

Grosse Freiheit 36 & Kaiserkeller Grosse Freiheit 36 ⓦ grossefreiheit36.de; ⓣ St Pauli or S Reeperbahn. A tourist attraction in itself, *Grosse Freiheit 36* books major acts most weekends, with an emphasis on goth and rock. The massive *Kaiserkeller* below plays mostly alternative music, and is famous for hosting The Beatles in the early 1960s. *Grosse Freiheit 36* (venue) Thurs from 9pm, Fri & Sat from 10pm; *Kaiserkeller* Wed, Fri & Sat from 10pm.

Haus 73 Schulterblatt 73 ⓦ dreiundsiebzig.de; S/ⓣ Sternschanze. Something is always on in this ramshackle building, somewhere between a community centre and a club, from dance classes to film and reggae club nights. Daily 7pm till at least midnight, usually later at weekends.

Prinzenbar Kastanienallee 20 ⓦ prinzenbar.net; ⓣ St Pauli or S Reeperbahn. This wonderfully atmospheric venue, all crumbling Baroque cherubs, chandeliers and dark corners, hosts small club nights and live gigs; mainly indie. Tues–Sat 7pm till at least midnight.

Wald Großneumarkt 45. Relaxed beer bar in the Neustadt district with fresh, smooth unpasteurised Pilsner Urquell and a wide range of liquor. Light meals and snacks served too. DJs play at weekends. Tues–Sat 4pm–3am.

DIRECTORY

Bank and exchange Reisebank, at Hauptbahnhof, Dammtor and Altona stations.

Consulates New Zealand, Domstr. 19 ☎ 040 442 55 50; UK, Neuer Jungfernstieg 20 ☎ 040 448 032 36; US, Alsterufer 27/28 ☎ 040 411 711 00.

Pharmacy At the Hauptbahnhof, Steindamm 2 (Mon–Fri 8am–8pm, Sat 9am–6pm).

Post office In the Altstadt at Mönckebergstr. 7 (Mon–Fri 9am–7pm, Sat 9am–3pm).

LÜBECK

Just an hour from Hamburg, **LÜBECK** makes a great day-trip. Set on an egg-shaped island surrounded by the water defences of the River Trave and the city moat, the pretty Altstadt is a compact place to wander, with many small lanes and courtyards to explore.

WHAT TO SEE AND DO

The city's emblem – and your first view of the Altstadt as you approach from the station – is the twin-towered, leaning **Holstentor** (Jan–March Tues–Sun 11am–5pm; April–Dec daily 10am–6pm; €7, students €3.50), with a small city museum inside. Straight ahead, over the bridge and up Holstenstrasse, the first church on the right is the Gothic **Petrikirche**; an elevator goes to the top of its spire (daily: Oct–March 10am–7pm; April–Sept 9am–8pm, €3, students €2) for great views over the town. Back across Holstenstrasse is the Markt and the elaborate **Rathaus.** Just behind, you'll find **Café Niederegger**, a renowned shop crammed with marzipan products and a free museum dedicated to the sugary substance.

Behind the north wing of the town hall stands the **Marienkirche**, Germany's oldest brick-built Gothic church. The interior makes a light and lofty backdrop for treasures like a 1518 high altar. The church's huge bells remain embedded in the floor where they fell when the church was bombed in 1942. **Katharinenkirche**, on the corner of Königstrasse and Glockengiesserstrasse, has three sculptures on its facade by Ernst Barlach; only three of the nine commissioned in the early 1930s had been completed when his work was banned by the Nazis. To the north at Königstrasse 9–11 are the **Behnhaus** and the **Drägerhaus**, two patricians' houses now converted into a museum (Tues–Sun: Jan–March 11am–5pm; April–Dec 10am–5pm; €7, students €3.50) housing modern and nineteenth-century paintings. More art – excellent medieval plus modern exhibitions – can be found in the **St Annen Museum** (Tues–Sun: Jan–March 11am–5pm; April–Dec 10am–5pm; €7, students €3.50) in a former convent at St Annen-Strasse, which also has good displays on merchant life in Lübeck.

ARRIVAL AND DEPARTURE

By train The train station is 5min west of the Altstadt: walk down Konrad-Adenauer-Str. to the Holstentor.

Destinations Copenhagen (4 daily; 4hr 20min); Hamburg (every 30min; 40min).

By ferry Lübeck's port, Travemünde, is 20min by train from Lübeck. Lisco Baltic Service (☎ 045 02 88 66 90, Ⓦ dfdslisco.com) runs to Rīga; Finnlines (☎ 045 028 05 43, Ⓦ www.ferrycenter.fi) to Helsinki and Malmö; and TT-Line (☎ 045 028 01 81, Ⓦ ttline.com) to Trelleborg.

Destinations Helsinki (6 weekly; 28hr); Malmö (3 daily; 8–9hr); Trelleborg (6 daily; 7hr).

INFORMATION

Tourist information The tourist office at Holstentorplatz 1 (Jan–March, Oct & Nov Mon–Fri 9am–6pm Sat 10am–3pm; April & Sept Mon–Fri 9am–6pm, Sat 10am–4pm, Sun 10am–3pm; May–Aug & Dec Mon–Fri 9am–7pm, Sat 10am–4pm, Sun 10am–3pm, ☎ 018 058 89 97 00, Ⓦ luebeck.de) has a café, arranges walking tours and has information on boat tours.

Discount passes The Happy Day Card (€12/14/17 for 24/48/72hr) gives free public transport and up to fifty percent discount at museums.

EATING

Hüxstrasse, which runs east from the Markt, has several good cafés and bars.

Colestreet Beckergrube 18, west of the Markt, off Breite Str. Named after a south London street where the owner once lived, this shabby-chic café and bar is good for snacks, cake or cocktails. Tues–Sun 11am–3am.

12

HANNOVER

A major transport hub and trade-fair city, **HANNOVER** looks fairly dull. The city's showpiece – refreshingly – is not a great cathedral, palace or town hall, but a series of **gardens** and first-class **museums**. Hannover's location at the intersection of major cross-country rail lines makes it a good place to stop over on your way to somewhere else.

WHAT TO SEE AND DO

Hannover's commercial centre is a short walk southwest of the train station. The best **museums** are further south, on the other side of Friedrichswall, while the splendid **royal gardens** are northwest of the centre. The centre is pretty bland, but there are some attractive corners and interesting neighbourhoods if you explore a bit further out.

12

The Altes Rathaus and Marktkirche

A short distance southwest of the train station, a few streets of rebuilt half-timbered buildings convey some impression of the medieval town. The elaborate brickwork of the high-gabled fifteenth-century **Altes Rathaus** is impressive, despite the modern interior. Alongside is the fourteenth-century red-brick Gothic **Marktkirche**, with some miraculously preserved stained glass and a shockingly frank depiction of twentieth-century German history depicted on the modern church doors, complete with a Nazi dictator, tanks, executions and corpses.

Niedersächsisches Landesmuseum and Sprengel Museum

Southeast of the Marktkirche, across Friedrichswall on Willy-Brandt-Allee, the **Niedersächsisches Landesmuseum** (Tues–Fri 10am–5pm, Sat & Sun 10am–6pm; €4, students €3, Fri 2–5pm free; Ⓤ Aegidientorplatz) houses a fine collection of paintings from the Middle Ages to the early twentieth century, plus archeology and ethnology collections. Further down the road lies the **Sprengel Museum** (Tues 10am–8pm, Wed–Sun 10am–6pm; €7, students €4, Fri free; Ⓦ sprengel-museum.de), with a first-rate

collection of twentieth- and twenty-first-century painting and sculpture.

The Neues Rathaus

West of the Landesmuseum on Friedrichswall is the vast, green-domed **Neues Rathaus**, built at the start of the twentieth century. In the foyer are four models of Hannover in 1689, 1939, 1945 and today, illuminating the extent of wartime loss, something that is all too clear as you look over the city from the top of the town hall's **dome** (March to mid-Nov Mon–Fri 9am–6.30pm, Sat & Sun 10am–6.30pm; €3, students €2), reached via a curved lift.

The gardens

The royal gardens of **Herrenhausen**, featuring Europe's highest garden fountain, stretch out northwest of the centre. Proceeding north from town along Nienburger Strasse, the **Georgengarten**, an English-style landscaped garden, is to the left, a foil to the city's pride and joy, the magnificent formal **Grosser Garten** beyond (daily 9am till dusk; €5; trams #4 and #5 to Herrenhäuser Gärten, main entrance just by the stop on Herrenhäuser Str.). If possible, time your visit to coincide with the fountain displays (late March to late Oct daily 11am–noon & 2/3–5pm). Directly opposite, on Herrenhäuser Strasse, is the entrance to **Berggarten**, the botanic garden (same hours and ticket).

ARRIVAL AND DEPARTURE

By plane Hannover Airport and the train station are connected with S-Bahn line #5 (every 30min; 20min; €3.40).
By train The train station is in the centre of town, just northeast of main shopping district Kröpke.
Destinations Amsterdam (every 2hr; 4hr 20min); Berlin (hourly; 1hr 40min); Cologne (hourly; 2hr 40min); Frankfurt (hourly; 2hr 20min); Hamburg (every 30min; 1hr 35min); Munich (hourly; 4hr 20min–4hr 40min).

INFORMATION

Tourist information Tourist office opposite the train station, Ernst-August-Platz 8 (Mon–Fri 9am–6pm, Sat 10am–3pm; April–Oct Sat 10am–5pm, Sun 10am–3pm; Ⓣ 0511 123 451 11, Ⓦ hannover-tourism.de).
Discount pass The HannoverCard (individual €9.50/18 for 1/2 days, up to 5 people €20/27 for 1/2 days) covers

public transport and provides discounts to the main museums and sights.

GETTING AROUND

By public transport The best of Hannover is outside the centre, so its excellent transport network of tram/U-Bahn, S-Bahn and buses – centred on the Hauptbahnhof, Kröpke and Aegidientorplatz – is useful. The tram/U-Bahn network has some overground tram lines (such as #17 and #10) and some hybrid tram/U-Bahn lines where central stops are underground, with lines emerging above ground to become street-level trams further out (such as #4 and #5). One-way tickets €2.60, day tickets €5.

ACCOMMODATION

There are very few budget options in Hannover, and prices double or more during trade fairs.

Bed 'n Budget City Hostel Osterstr. 37 ☎0511 360 61 07, ⓦbednbudget.de. Central hostel and budget hotel with modern appearance and sturdy bunks. Most rooms have a private bathroom, TV, desk and fridge. Dorms €18, doubles €72

Flora Heinrichstr. 36 ☎051 138 39 10, ⓦhotel-flora -hannover.de. Spotless hotel with slightly old-fashioned furniture, located behind the train station. The welcome is always very warm and the front-desk staff very helpful. Breakfast included. Doubles €68

Hostel Hannover Lenaustr. 12 ☎051 11 31 99 19, ⓦhostelhannover.de; trams #10 & #17 to Goetheplatz. Basic but friendly, this slightly old-fashioned hostel has decent communal areas but packed dorms. Though it's located outside the centre, it's good for the Linden-Limmer nightlife. Check-in from 11am. Sheets €4. Prices €5 extra at weekends and during trade fairs. Dorms €20

EATING AND DRINKING

In the centre, slightly twee, touristy Kramerstr. and Knochenhauerstr. near the Markt are your best options. More fun for nightlife is the sprawling Linden-Limmer district west of the centre, particularly around Goetheplatz or midway along Kötnerholzweg. Lister Meile, behind the station, is also a good bet.

Café Glocksee Glockseestr. 35 ⓦcafe-glocksee.de; tram #10 to Goetheplatz. Great, scruffy little club and venue; head along Lenaustr. and it's the graffitied building at the end (entrance round the back). Mon–Sat 8am–midnight.

Café Safran Königsworther Str. 39, corner of Braunstr; tram #10 to Glocksee. This laidback café-bar has some sort of cheap deal every day, such as beer and a pizza for €7. Daily 9am–2pm, Fri & Sat till 3pm.

Lulu In der Steinriede 12 ⓦcafe-lulu.com; ⓤSedanstrasse. Handsome café with seating on a pretty cobbled square a block east of the Lister Meile. It serves Alsatian Flammküchen

and burgers for around €7 plus an excellent weekday lunch for €6. Mon–Sat 9am–1am, Sun 10am–1am.

Markthalle Karmaschstr. 49, near the Markt, ⓦmarkthalle -in-hannover.de. The indoor market is packed full of dozens of food stalls – German, Italian, Spanish, Turkish and Japanese, and even a cocktail bar – selling good-value meals. It's also very popular for a quick after-work drink. Mon–Wed 7am–8pm, Thurs & Fri 7am–10pm, Sat 7am–4pm.

Spandau Projekt Engelbosteler Damm 30 ⓦspandauprojekt.de; ⓤChristuskirche. Cool, retro-styled café-bar on a street of restaurants north of the centre. There are Italian dishes and Thai veggie curries at fair prices, plus organic breakfast buffets at weekends. Mon–Fri noon–1am, Sat & Sun 10am–1am.

BREMEN

Famous for a fairytale of four animal musicians, **BREMEN** is an attractive small city located about an hour from Hannover and Hamburg. Maritime trade via the Weser River led to it becoming a wealthy medieval merchant city with a liberal mindset, something for which Bremen remains famous today. Their legacy is such attractive architecture as one of the finest town squares in North Germany, listed as a UNESCO World Heritage Site, and a small but enjoyable nightlife district.

WHAT TO SEE AND DO

The town's geographic and cultural heart is the **Markt**, with a **Rathaus** fronted by a fabulous Renaissance facade of ornate allegorical carving. Rooms within (Mon–Sat tours at 11am, noon, 3pm and 4pm, Sun 11am and noon; €5.50) live up to the looks, especially the Güldenkammer with gilded Jugendstil leather wall-hangings. Outside, a statue of Roland, a chivalric knight and protector of civic rights, brandishes a sword at the **Dom** opposite, to champion the citizens' independence from the archbishops; a church lackey burned down its wooden predecessor. Running south off the Markt, **Böttcherstrasse** was remodelled in the 1920s from a decaying alley into an Art Deco and Expressionist fantasy by a team of avant-garde artists, notably sculptor Bernhard Hoetger. Here, the **Paula-Modersohn-Becker Museum** (Tues–Sun 11am–6pm; €8, students €6) is the world's first museum dedicated to a female artist, who worked in the nearby art colony at Worpswede, while revamped Gothic merchant's house **Roselius-Haus** (same ticket) displays late medieval art and furniture.

South of the Dom is the **Schnoorviertel**, the traditional quarter of fishermen, sailors and craftsmen on the Weser's banks at the edge of the old town. Today the cottages contain upmarket boutiques, galleries and restaurants – touristy, but cute nonetheless. East of the Schnoor, the **Kunsthalle** (Tues 10am–9pm, Wed–Sun 10am–5pm; €9, students €5) has an excellent gallery of German and international art, including works by Rubens and Delacroix, alongside works by Worpswede artists.

ARRIVAL AND INFORMATION

By train Head straight out of the train station; it's a 10min walk into the centre.

Destinations Hamburg (every 30min; 1hr); Hannover (every 30min; 1hr 5min).

Tourist information Just off Markt on the corner of Obernstr. and Liebfrauenkirchhof (Mon–Fri 9.30am–6.30pm, Sat 9.30am–5pm, Sun 10am–4pm; ☎0421 308 00 10, ⓦbremen-tourism.de), plus smaller branch in the train station (Mon–Fri 9am–6.30pm, Sat & Sun 9.30am–5pm).

ACCOMMODATION, EATING AND DRINKING

In the centre, Schlachte is a line of bars on the riverbank, while the main student bar and nightlife district is the Ostertorviertel east of the old town.

Lila Eule Bernhardstr. 10. Cheap, grungy and fun little basement club – one of the oldest in Germany – with wild alternative, disco-punk, electrorock, hip-hop and other parties. Free admission on Thursday's student night. Thurs–Sat 11pm–late.

Piano Fehrfeld 64. Lazy-paced café-bar at the heart of the Ostertorviertel whose menu of pizzas, pastas and steaks, most priced under €15, is popular with everyone from families to friends. Daily 9am–1am.

Ratskeller Am Markt 21. Touristy and not cheap at around €16 a main, but the cellar restaurant beneath the Rathaus is one of the most famous in Germany for historic atmosphere as much as traditional cooking. Daily 11am–midnight.

Townside Am Dobben 62 ☎042 17 80 15, ⓦtownside .de; tram #6 from the train station. Friendly modern hostel in Bremen's nightlife district, with eco ethics such as Fairtrade products plus a kitchen and women's dorm. Dorms €15, doubles €52

Central Germany

Central Germany is the country's most populous region and home to its industrial heartland – the Ruhrgebiet. **Cologne** stands out here, with its reminders of long centuries as a free state, cheek-by-jowl bars and a populace that's legendary for its friendliness. Neighbouring **Bonn**, Beethoven's birthplace, makes for a good day-trip, while nearby **Aachen** is of interest as the first capital of the Holy Roman Empire. To the south, the Rhineland-Palatinate (*Pfalz*) is famed for the romantic vineyard-lined stretch of the Rhine from Cologne to Mainz, which passes through a gorge of impressive rock outcrops, studded with the sort of castles that have given rise to many a fairytale. Nowadays pleasure cruisers – and a railway line – make the attractive journey through the gorge, and beyond to the state capital of **Mainz**, where the printing press was invented, as celebrated in the excellent Gutenberg Museum. The Mosel, which joins the Rhine at the city of Koblenz, has a similar parade of vineyards and ruined castles leading south to the ancient town of **Trier**, with its extraordinarily well-preserved Roman remains – possibly the best outside Italy. To the northeast, in the state of Hesse, dynamic **Frankfurt** dominates, with its financial sector providing the region's economic powerbase.

COLOGNE (KÖLN)

COLOGNE (Köln) has a population of one million, and its huge Gothic Dom is Germany's most visited monument. Despite its long history, much of the city is modern – the legacy of World War II – but though it's not the most beautiful city in Germany, it's certainly one of the liveliest and friendliest. Try to catch the annual pre-Lent **Carnival** – when huge parties fill the streets – or the summer Christopher Street Day (Gay Pride) celebrations, which can attract up to a million visitors. Cologne has a long and glorious history – as a Roman colony

(Colonia), a pilgrimage centre, trading city, marketer of eau de Cologne and recently as Germany's media capital.

WHAT TO SEE AND DO

Cologne's major sights are all within walking distance of the train station, in a dense centre on the west bank of the Rhine.

The Dom

Begun in 1248, and only finished in 1880, Cologne's gigantic **Dom**, next to the train station (May–Oct Mon–Sat 6am–9pm; Nov–April Mon–Sat 6am–7.30pm, Sun 1–4.30pm, ⓦkoelner-dom.de), is one of the largest Gothic buildings ever built and its archbishop was one of the seven Electors of the Holy Roman Empire. Its treasures are many and it's worth paying €1 for the explanatory English booklet inside. Climb the 509 steps to the top of the **south tower** (daily: March, April & Oct 9am–5pm; May–Sept 9am–6pm; Nov–Feb 9am–4pm; €4, students €2) for a breathtaking panorama over the city and the Rhine. The **Domschatzkammer** (daily 10am–6pm; €6, students €3) in the vaults on the north side of the building contains a stunning array of treasury items.

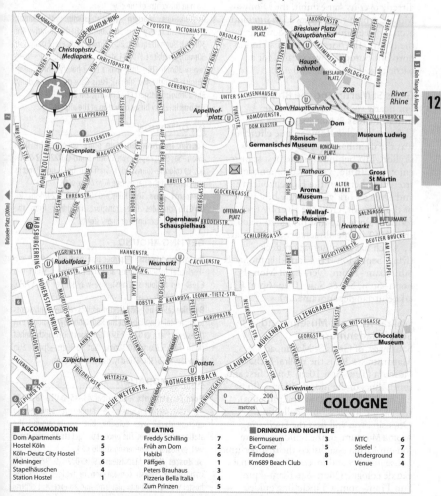

COLOGNE

■ ACCOMMODATION		● EATING		■ DRINKING AND NIGHTLIFE			
Dom Apartments	2	Freddy Schilling	7	Biermuseum	3	MTC	6
Hostel Köln	5	Früh am Dom	2	Ex-Corner	5	Stiefel	7
Köln-Deutz City Hostel	3	Habibi	6	Filmdose	8	Underground	2
Meininger	6	Päffgen	1	Km689 Beach Club	1	Venue	4
Stapelhäuschen	4	Peters Brauhaus	3				
Station Hostel	1	Pizzeria Bella Italia	4				
		Zum Prinzen	5				

Museum Ludwig and the Römisch-Germanisches Museum

In a modern building next to the Dom, the spacious **Museum Ludwig** (Tues–Sun 10am–6pm, first Thurs in month 10am–10pm; €13, students €8.50, first Thurs in month €7; ⊛museumludwig.de) is one of Germany's premier collections of modern art, particularly strong on American Pop Art and German Expressionism. The neighbouring **Römisch-Germanisches Museum** (Tues–Sun 10am–5pm, first Thurs in month 10am–10pm; €9, students €5; ⊛roemisch -germanisches-museum.de) was built directly over its star exhibit, the Dionysus Mosaic, which can be viewed *in situ* (and even for free through the windows facing the Dom). The finest work of its kind in northern Europe, it was created for a patrician villa in about 200 AD.

Gross St Martin and the Rhine

For nearly six hundred years, the tower of **Gross St Martin**, one of Cologne's twelve Romanesque churches, was the dominant feature of the city's skyline. Just behind it is the best spot to enjoy the Rhine, a grassy promenade stretching between the Hohenzollern and Deutzer bridges. For the best view of the Altstadt, cross the river by the footway along the first bridge to reach the **Köln Triangle** skyscraper at Ottoplatz 1, which has an observation deck (May–Sept Mon–Fri 11am–11pm, Sat & Sun 10am–11pm; Oct–April Mon–Fri noon–6pm, Sat & Sun 10am–6pm; €3; ⊛koelntrianglepanorama.de).

Wallraf-Richartz-Museum and Schokoladenmuseum

Southwest of Gross St Martin, at Martinstrasse 39, is the **Wallraf-Richartz-Museum** (Tues–Sun 10am–6pm, first and third Thurs of the month 10am–10pm; €8, students €4.50; ⊛wallraf.museum), with a fine Impressionist collection. Opposite, you will find the fascinating **Aroma Museum**, in the building where Johann Farina established the first perfume house in 1709 and invented the original eau de cologne (Mon–Sat 10am–7pm, Sun 11am–5pm; €5 including guided tour; ☎0221 399 8994, ⊛farina-haus.de). Further south, on the banks of the Rhine, the thoroughly enjoyable **Chocolate Museum** (Tues–Fri 10am–6pm, Sat & Sun 11am–7pm; July & Aug also Mon 10am–6pm; €9, students €6.50; ☎022 19 31 88 80, ⊛chocolatemuseum -cologne.com) focuses on the history and production of chocolate.

ARRIVAL AND DEPARTURE

By plane Cologne/Bonn Airport is connected to the train station with line Ⓢ13 and Ⓢ19 (every 30min; 15min; €2.70).

By train The Hauptbahnhof is immediately north of the Dom in the centre of the city.

Destinations Aachen (every 30min; 35–55min); Amsterdam (every 2hr; 3hr 20min); Berlin (hourly; 4hr 30min); Bonn (frequent; 20–30min); Brussels (7 daily; 1hr 50min); Frankfurt (10–11 daily; 1hr 20min); Heidelberg (every 30min–1hr; 2hr); Mainz (1–2 hourly; 1hr 45min); Munich (hourly; 4hr 30min); Paris Gare du Nord (4 daily; 3hr 20min); Stuttgart (1–2 hourly; 2hr 20min).

By bus Intercity buses only stop at the airport.

INFORMATION

Tourist information Main office opposite the Dom (Mon–Sat 9am–8pm, Sun 10am–5pm; ☎022 122 13 04 00, ⊛cologne-tourism.de). Staff can book hotel rooms and hand out the handy free *Köln Miniguide*.

Discount pass The KölnCard (valid for 24/48hr for €9/€18) provides free transport, including from the airport, plus discounts for many sights.

GETTING AROUND

By bus and tram The public transport network (⊛kvb -koeln.de) includes buses and trams/U-Bahn. Short trip €1.90 (up to four stations), one-way longer trip €2.80, day-pass €8.50.

By bike Call-a-bike and Nextbike bikes can be found across town; rental is available at the Radstation by the north exit (Breslauer Platz, ☎022 11 39 71 90) from the Hauptbahnhof (Mon–Fri 5.30am–10.30pm, Sat 6.30am–8pm, Sun 8am–8pm; €5/3hr, €10/day, deposit €50 cash).

ACCOMMODATION

Dom Apartments Johanniststr 43–45 ☎022 19 77 11 44, ⊛domapartment.de. A range of self-catering apartments all over Cologne, but mostly around the station and the Dom. The price of budget studios compares well to hostels. Two-person studio **€69**

★**Hostel Köln** Marsilstein 29 ☎022 19 98 77 60, ⊛hostel.ag. Stylish combination of budget hotel and hostel with a children's play area and an excellent central

12

location. No dorms as such; rooms are only rented whole. Breakfast included. Doubles €79, six-bed room €174

Köln-Deutz City Hostel Siegesstr. 5 ☎022 181 47 11, ⓦkoeln-deutz.jugendherberge.de. Large and functional DJH hostel close to Deutz station, directly across the Rhine from the Altstadt. Facilities include a disco room. Normally booked by large groups. Good weekend deals online. Dorms €25, doubles €77

Meininger Engelbertstr. 33–35 ☎022 199 76 09 65, ⓦmeininger-hotels.com. This branch of the hostel chain has a great location and a wide range of services: kitchen, bar, laundry facilities, a female dorm and bike rental €12. Dorms €19, doubles €59

Stapelhäuschen Fischmarkt 1–3 ☎022 12 72 77 77, ⓦkleines-stapelhaeuschen.de. Charming Altstadt hotel-restaurant rebuilt to resemble its seventeenth-century appearance, and located by Gross St Martin. Rooms overlooking the river are the nicest. Doubles €70

Station Hostel Marzellenstr. 44–56 ☎022 19 12 53 01, ⓦhostel-cologne.de. Large, independent hostel just north of the station, with 24hr reception and kitchen. A good buffet breakfast (€6) is served in the restaurant next door. Dorms €17, doubles €48

EATING

The Altmarkt area is the main focus of nightlife for visitors, though locals tend to prefer the western part of the city along the Ring, while students gather around Zülpicher Platz and Brüsseler Platz.

Freddy Schilling Kyffhäuserstr. 34. Delicious organic burgers (from €6) and fries served with home-made sauce by friendly staff. Also has some vegan options. Sun–Thurs noon–10pm, Fri & Sat noon–11pm.

Früh am Dom Am Hof 12–18. Near the Dom and fronted by a marvellous fountain with dwarves, this huge, heavily touristed *Brauhaus* has excellent food. Main courses from around €10, snacks €5. Daily 8am–midnight.

★**Habibi** Zülpicher Str. 28. Plastered with posters, this lively Lebanese restaurant in the student neighbourhood is perfect for fantastic falafel and other late-night munchies. Falafel in pita €1.90. Sun–Thurs 11am–1am, Fri & Sat 11am–3am.

Päffgen Friesenstr. 64–66. Less touristy than the places near the Dom, with a younger clientele, and *Kölsch* brewed on the premises. Local dishes from €10. Sun–Thurs 10am–midnight, Fri & Sat 10am–12.30am.

★**Peters Brauhaus** Mühlengasse 1 ☎022 12 57 39 50. Reservations only to eat in this popular beer tavern, but it's worth visiting if only to admire the grand Art Deco room. The beans with smoked bacon and potato fill you up for €11. Daily 11am–12.30am.

Pizzeria Bella Italia 1 Friesenwall 52. Super-cheap Italian with pasta dishes and pizzas from €4; needless to say, its benches are packed shoulder to shoulder.

Mon–Thurs 11.30am–midnight, Fri & Sat 11.30am–1am, Sun 1pm–midnight.

Zum Prinzen Alter Markt 20–22. Typical, old-style restaurant that is much cosier than most. It serves house beer and huge portions of food, with Cologne specialities from around €10 and Flammekuchen pizza €8.80. Daily 11am–1am.

DRINKING AND NIGHTLIFE

Cologne's unique beer, *Kölsch*, is a light, aromatically bitter brew served in small, thin glasses.

Biermuseum Buttermarkt 39. Loud, busy Altstadt bar tucked away near the river, serving 18 beers on tap as well as countless more in bottles, all costing less than €3.50. Daily 2pm–3am.

Filmdose Zülpicher Str. 39 ⓦfilmdose-koeln.de. Quiet wine bar that's packed with students; it has a cabaret stage for live theatre during term time. Snacks from €2. Mon–Fri 9am–1am, Fri & Sat 9am–3am.

Km689 Beach Club Rheinparkweg 1 ⓦkm689.de. A relaxed beach club with sand and palm trees overlooking the Rhine near the Köln Triangle skyscraper. Admission is free if you spend €6 on cocktails (from €6) or snacks like *currywurst* (€4). Mid-May to Sept Fri–Sun 4pm–late.

MTC Zülpicher Str. 10 ⓦmtcclub.de. Studenty basement venue on Cologne's best street for nightlife, featuring live rock and metal bands. Go early to avoid the long queues. Fri & Sat punk parties 11pm–late.

Stiefel Zülpicher Str.18. Dilapidated and relaxed punk-rock bar in the student quarter. A great place to down a beer or shoot pool. Sun–Thurs 6pm–2am, Fri & Sat 6pm–5am.

Underground Vogelsanger Str. 200 ⓦunderground -cologne.de; ⓣVenloer Str. Great for live gigs, especially rock and punk, the *Underground* has a lovely beer garden, table football and a big indie/alternative following. Daily 6.30pm–late.

GAY NIGHTLIFE

Cologne's gay scene is second only to Berlin's: see ⓦheart -of-cologne.de.

> ## COLOGNE'S CARNIVAL
>
> Though Cologne's **carnival** actually begins as early as November 11, the real fun starts with Weiberfastnacht on the Thursday before Lent. The city goes wild for the next five days until Ash Wednesday; prepare yourself for drunken dancing in the streets and wild costumes. The best of the numerous parades are the alternative **Geisterzug Saturday night**, complete with fire-juggling and drumming, and the spectacular **Rose Monday Parade**, with music, floats and political caricatures.

12

Ex-Corner Schaafenstr. 57–59. This corner bar is one of a triangular cluster of gay bars just south of Rudolfplatz and is busy every night of the week. Daily 7pm–5am.

Venue Hohe Str. 14 ⓦvenue-cologne.de. The biggest, loudest, brashest gay club in Cologne, with different music nights attracting a variety of clubbers every weekend. Fri & Sat 11pm–late.

DIRECTORY

Internet Gigabyte, Hohenzollernring 7–11 (24hr; €1–1.50/hr, ⓦgiga-byte.info). Giant internet café with 130 terminals.

Hospital Out-of-hours medical service (ⓣ01805 04 41 00; calls 14 cents/min).

Left luggage At the train station (€3/2hr, €6/24hr).

Pharmacy At the north exit from the train station (Mon–Fri 6am–9.30pm, Sat 8am–9.30pm, Sun 10am–6pm); there's also a digital notice board giving details of out-of-hours service.

Post office Breite Str. 6 (Mon–Fri 9am–7pm, Sat 9am–2pm).

12 BONN

A great day-trip from Cologne, lovely, riverside **BONN** was West Germany's unlikely capital from 1949 until unification in 1990. But even with its role diminished, the city is still worth a visit to see the birthplace of Ludwig van Beethoven, a string of top-rated museums and an attractive Old Town.

WHAT TO SEE AND DO

The small pedestrianized **Old Town** (Altstadt) centres on two spacious squares. The square to the south is named after the **Münster**, whose central octagonal tower and spire are the city's most prominent landmarks. The **Market square** (Marktplatz) is dominated by the pink Rococo **Rathaus** and hosts a market every day except Sunday.

The Beethoven-Haus and the Schloss

A couple of minutes' walk north of Marktplatz, at Bonngasse 20, is the **Beethoven-Haus** (April–Oct daily 10am–6pm; Nov–March Mon–Sat 10am–5pm, Sun 11am–5pm; €6, students €4.50; ⓣ228 98 17 525, ⓦbeethoven -haus-bonn.de), where the composer was born in an attic room in 1770. Beethoven left Bonn for good aged 22, but the city

nevertheless has the best collection of memorabilia of its favourite son. To the east is the Baroque **Schloss**, once the seat of the Archbishop-Electors of Cologne and now part of the university.

The Museumsmeile

The **Museumsmeile** (ⓤHeussallee) is home to the **Kunstmuseum** at Friedrich-Ebert-Allee 2 (Tues & Thurs–Sun 11am–6pm, Wed 11am–9pm; €7, students €3.50; ⓦkunstmuseum-bonn .de), with its fine Expressionist collection. Next door is the **Kunst- und Ausstellungshalle** (Tues & Wed 10am–9pm, Thurs–Sun 10am–7pm; price depends on exhibition; ⓦbundeskunsthalle.de), an arts centre hosting major temporary exhibitions. The Kunstmuseum's other neighbour is the **Haus der Geschichte** at Willy-Brandt-Allee 14 (Tues–Fri 9am–7pm, Sat & Sun 10am–6pm; free; ⓦhdg.de), a fascinating museum exploring German history from the end of World War II to the present.

ARRIVAL AND INFORMATION

By train and bus Bonn's train station lies in the middle of the city; just to the east is the bus station, whose local services, along with the trams, form part of a system integrated with Cologne's.

Tourist information Windeckstr. 1, am Münsterplatz (Mon–Fri 10am–6pm, Sat 10am–4pm, Sun 10am–2pm; ⓣ0228 77 50 00, ⓦbonn-region.de).

Discount pass The Bonn Regio Welcome-Card (valid 24hr; from €10) is a great deal, including travel and free admission to almost all museums and sights.

EATING AND DRINKING

Biergarten Alter Zoll Brassertufer 1. Lovely Biergarten shaded by huge trees, right by the Rhine near the Schloss. It serves up pizza (from €5), good German and Asian dishes, and hosts occasional concerts. Daily 11am–midnight.

Cassius Garten Maximilianstr. 28d, opposite the station. Offers daily-changing hot vegetarian and vegan specials, buffet-style meals (pay by weight €1.85/100g, cheaper after 7pm), and great soups from €2.50. Mon–Sat 11am–8pm.

Pawlow Heerstr. 64. Fashionable café-bar in the bohemian Nordstadt district, with benches outside, great coffees and small measures of wine for tight budgets from €2. At weekends after 10pm it becomes a club. Mon–Thurs 11am–1am, Fri & Sat 11am–late, Sun 10am–1am.

AACHEN

AACHEN has a laidback atmosphere that reflects its large student population, making it a good day-trip from Cologne. Bordering Belgium and the Netherlands, it was the hub of Charlemagne's Europe-wide eighth-century empire. The choice was partly strategic but also because of the presence of hot springs. Relaxing in these waters was one of the emperor's favourite pastimes, and they remain a major draw at the luxurious **Carolus Thermen** spa, overlooking Kurgarten park, just northeast of the centre (daily 9am–11pm, last entry 9.30pm; from €12 for 2hr 30min; ⓦcarolus-thermen.de) – alternatively, you can taste the smelly, 53°C hot thermal water for free in the pavilion beside the tourist information office (see below).

WHAT TO SEE AND DO

Little of Charlemagne's architectural legacy survives, but its crowning jewel, the former **Palace chapel**, has pride of place at the heart of the **Dom** (Mon–Sat 11am–7pm, Sun 1–7pm; ⓦaachendom.de), a UNESCO World Heritage Site. At the rear of the chapel, the gilded shrine of Charlemagne, finished in 1215 after fifty years' work, contains the emperor's remains, while the gallery has the imperial throne, viewable only on a tour (English tour daily at 2pm; €4, students €3; tickets from the Dominformation office opposite the Schatzkammer). Next to the Dom is the dazzling treasury or **Schatzkammer** (Jan–March Mon 10am–1pm, Tues–Sun 10am–5pm; April–Dec Mon 10am–1pm, Tues–Sun 10am–6pm; €5, students €4; entrance on Johannes-Paul-II-Strasse). Its highlights are the tenth-century Lothar Cross and a Roman sarcophagus once used as Charlemagne's coffin. The emperor's palace once extended as far as the expansive **Markt**. Here two of the palace towers remain, incorporated into the **Rathaus**, whose fourteenth-century facade is lined with the figures of fifty Holy Roman Emperors, 31 of whom were crowned in Aachen. The glory of the interior (daily 10am–6pm; €5, students €3) is the massive twelfth-century Coronation Hall, repository of the reproduction crown

jewels. Behind the Rathaus at Katschhof 1, an excellent interactive exhibition in the new **Centre Charlemagne** (Tues–Sun 10am–6pm, €5, students €3; ⓦwww .centre-charlemagne.eu) provides the low-down on the city's rich history.

ARRIVAL AND INFORMATION

By plane Aachen-Maastricht airport is 41km from Aachen and is best reached via Maastricht train station; Cologne's airport can be reached by train in about 1hr 15min.

By train The centre is 10min walk from the train station – down Bahnhofstrasse, then left into Theaterstrasse.

Destinations Brussels (hourly; 1–2hr); Cologne (every 30min; 35–55mins); Liège (hourly; 25–50mins); Paris Gare du Nord (4 daily; 2hr 40min).

Tourist information In the Elisenbrunnen pavilion on Friedrich-Wilhelm-Platz (Jan–March Mon–Fri 10am–6pm, Sat 10am–2pm; April–Dec Mon–Fri 10am–6pm, Sat & Sun 10am–3pm; ☎0241 180 29 50, ⓦaachen-tourist.de); hands out the free *Aachen at a glance* guide and map.

EATING, DRINKING AND ACCOMMODATION

Leading northeast out of the Markt, Pontstrasse is the student quarter and lined with bars, cheap cafés and restaurants.

A&O Hostel Hackländerstr. 5 ☎024 1463 07 33 00, ⓦaohostels.com. Large new chain hostel by the station with comfy modern rooms, a roomy communal area and a bar. Breakfast €7. Dorms €22, doubles €69

Alt-Aachener Kaffeestuben Büchel 18. Historic wood-clad café with great cakes and particularly good *Printen*, a spiced gingerbread that's the main local speciality. Breakfasts from €7. Mon–Fri 9am–6.30pm, Sat 9am–6pm, Sun 10am–6pm.

Kittel Pontstr. 39. Relaxed bohemian café serving great inexpensive food, such as pasta from €6, plus cheap daily breakfast specials. DJs man the decks from 8pm on Sat. Daily 10am–2am.

Sowiso & Ocean Pontstr. 164–166. One of a cluster of lively sports and cocktail bars, with student-friendly prices, plenty of outdoor seating and a cheerful atmosphere. Guinness on tap, Jägermeister €2. Daily 10am–late.

MAINZ

At the confluence of the Rhine and Main rivers, **MAINZ** is an agreeable mixture of old and new, with an attractively restored centre and a jovial populace who are responsible for Germany's second-biggest carnival bash after Cologne. Its long-standing ecclesiastical power aside – the archbishop of Mainz was the head of German bishops – the city is also famous for Johannes Gutenberg, who invented printing here around 1450.

WHAT TO SEE AND DO

Rearing high above central Mainz, the **Dom** (March–Oct Mon–Fri 9am–6.30pm, Sat 9am–4pm, Sun 12.45–3pm & 4–6.30pm; Nov–Feb Mon–Fri 9am–5pm, Sat 9am–4pm, Sun 12.45–3pm & 4–5pm) is unusual for sharing its outer walls with rows of eighteenth-century houses. Inside, the choirs at both ends indicate it as an imperial cathedral, with one for the emperor and the other for the clergy; seven coronations have taken place here. The bustling **market square** outside (markets Tues, Fri & Sat 7am–2pm) adjoins Liebfrauenplatz and the fascinating **Gutenberg Museum** (Tues–Sat 9am–5pm, Sun 11am–5pm; €5, students €3; ⓦgutenberg-museum.de), which pays tribute to the Gutenberg Press. One of the greatest inventions of all time, it enabled the mass production of books – don't miss the original Gutenberg Bibles on the third floor. Next door in the **Druckladen** (Printing shop; Mon–Fri 9am–5pm, Sat 10am–3pm; free), visitors can learn how to hand-set type, and buy posters and souvenirs.

ARRIVAL AND DEPARTURE

By plane From Frankfurt airport take ⑤8 to Mainz Hauptbahnhof (2 hourly; 25min).

By train The station is a 15min walk northwest of the city centre; head down Bahnhofstrasse or take a tram or bus (single ticket €2.75).

Destinations Cologne (1–3 hourly; 1hr 20min–1hr 55min); Frankfurt (very frequent; 35min); Heidelberg (several hourly; 55min); Stuttgart (2–3 hourly; 1hr 50min).

By boat KD Lines sail along the Rhine between Mainz and Cologne via Bacharach and Koblenz (late March to late Oct 1–2 daily; 5hr 45min/2hr 45min to Bacharach; ☏0221 208 83 18; ⓦk-d.com).

INFORMATION

Tourist information Brückenturm am Rathaus Rheinstrasse 55 (Mon–Fri 9am–5pm, Sat 10am–4pm; ☏061 31 24 28 88, ⓦwww.touristik-mainz.de) – it's tricky to find, in an isolated location above the street beside a pedestrian bridge. There's also an office in the Landesmuseum, Grosse Bleiche 49–51 (Tues 10am–8pm, Wed–Sun 10am–5pm).

Discount pass The MainzPlus card, sold at the tourist office and in the local transport office in front of the central station at Bahnhofplatz 6a, costs €11.95 and includes access to all museums, a city tour and transport in the Mainz/Wiesbaden conurbation for 48hr.

GETTING AROUND

By bike Bike rental from Mainzer Rad Verleih Bingerstr 19 (on the viaduct south of the station; from €8.90/day, deposit €50 with ID; ☏06131 33 61 225, ⓦcjd-mainz.de).

ACCOMMODATION

DJH Otto-Brunfels-Schneise 4 ☏06131 853 32, ⓦjugendherberge.de; buses #62 & #63 from the Hauptbahnhof to stop "Am Viktorstift/Jugendherberge". Modern HI hostel, with single, twin and four-bed rooms and dorms, in the wooded heights of Weisenau with great views over the Rhine. Breakfast included. Dorms €23, doubles €57

Mainzer Hof Kaiserstr. 98 ☏06131 9 72 40, ⓦhotel -mainzerhof.de. Along the Rheinpromenade a 15min walk from the station, this is the cheapest of the city-centre hotels, with decent rooms (some with river views) and a sauna. Doubles €69

EATING, DRINKING AND NIGHTLIFE

Mainz boasts more vineyards on its outskirts than any other German city; its many lovely wine bars are the best places to sample their produce.

Altdeutsche Weinstube Liebfrauenplatz 7. The oldest wine bar in town (established in 1462) is still going strong – it offers daily dishes for around €12, served up with local wine for €3–4. Mon–Sat 4pm–midnight.

Annabatterie Gartenfeldpl. 2 ⓦannabatterie.de. In the student district near the train station, this small and cosy café serves breakfast until 3pm, plus sandwiches and salads (from €5). Daily 10am–8pm.

Heiliggeist Mailandsgasse 11. Attractive bistro in the Gothic vaults of a fifteenth-century hospital; main courses are around €15 and include *Croustarte*, a kind of local pizza-cum-pancake. Mon–Fri 4pm–1am, Sat & Sun 9am–2am.

THE RHINE GORGE

North of Mainz, the Rhine snakes west to **BINGEN**, where the spectacular 80km-long Rhine Gorge begins. Its most famous sight is the Lorelei, a rocky projection between Oberwesel and St Goar, where legend has it that a blonde maiden lured passing mariners to their doom with her song. The region is best visited by boat or by bike, spending a night in Bacharach, but if you're pressed for time, the train will do.

ARRIVAL AND DEPARTURE

By train The railway between Mainz and Koblenz runs along the riverbank, offering wonderful gorge views from the windows – sit on the right.

By boat Some river cruises depart from Mainz, but KD begin at Bingen (summer 2–3 daily; ⓦ kd-rhein-main .de). The one-way fare from Bingen downstream to Koblenz is €38.40 (4hr; 6hr upstream).

Bacharach

Pretty, half-timbered **BACHARACH**, 15km from Bingen, huddles behind a fourteenth-century wall, which you can walk along for a brilliant view. The town is chock-full of alleyways and quirky buildings, such as the celebrated **Altes Haus** at Oberstrasse 61, so wonky it seems to lean in all directions at once. Many of the buildings house *Weinstuben* (wine bars), where you can try local favourite *Hahnenhof* Riesling.

ACCOMMODATION

Im Malerwinkel Blücherstrasse 41–45 ☎ 067 43 12 39, ⓦ im-malerwinkel.de. Bacharach's best budget hotel is this lovely half-timbered place built into the old town wall; the path into town next to the brook nearby is a delight. Doubles €69

Jugendherberge Bacharach Burg Stahleck ☎ 067 43 12 66, ⓦ djh.de. The twelfth-century castle of Burg Stahleck above town houses Germany's most atmospheric hostel. It's a steep uphill climb to get there, but the views of the Rhine Valley are worth it; book well in advance in high season. Dorms €22, doubles €55

TRIER

Birthplace of Karl Marx, and the oldest city in Germany, **TRIER** was once the capital of the Western Roman Empire. Today, it's merely a regional centre for the upper Mosel valley, giving it a relaxed air. Despite a turbulent history, the city's past is well preserved, particularly in the most impressive group of Roman remains north of the Alps.

WHAT TO SEE AND DO

The centre corresponds roughly to the Roman city and can easily be covered on

foot. From the train station, it's a few minutes' walk down Theodor-Heuss-Allee to the impressive **Porta Nigra**, Roman Trier's northern gateway (daily: March & Oct 9am–5pm; April–Sept 9am–6pm; Nov–Feb 9am–4pm; €4). From here, Simeonstrasse runs down to the **Hauptmarkt**, a busy pedestrian area, where market stalls sell groceries and flowers. At the southern end of the Hauptmarkt, a half-hidden Baroque portal leads to the exquisite Gothic church **St Gangolf**, built by the burghers of Trier to aggravate the archbishops, whose political power they resented.

The Dom and Konstantinbasilika

Up Sternstrasse from the Hauptmarkt, the magnificent Romanesque **Dom** (daily: April–Oct 6.30am–6pm; Nov–March 6.30am–5.30pm; ⓦ dominformation.de) lies on the site of the one built in the fourth century by Emperor Constantine. The present church dates from 1030, and the original facade has not changed significantly since then. From here, take Liebfrauenstrasse and turn left on An der Meerkatz, to the **Konstantinbasilika** (April–Oct Mon–Sat 10am–6pm, Sun 3–6pm; Nov–March Tues–Sat 10am–noon & 2–4pm, Sun 1–3pm; Dec also open Mon 10am–noon & 2–4pm). Built as Emperor Constantine's throne hall, its dimensions are awe-inspiring: 36m high and 71m long, it is completely self-supporting. It became a church for the local Protestant community in the nineteenth century.

The Rheinisches Landesmuseum and the Kaiserthermen

Just beyond the formal gardens southwest of the Konstantinbasilika, the **Rheinisches Landesmuseum** (Tues–Sun 10am–5pm; €8, students €6; ⓦ landesmuseum-trier .de) is easily the best of Trier's museums, with a permanent display that conveys the sophistication and complexity of Roman civilization; the prize exhibits are the richly sculpted tombstones from Neumagen and the collection of Roman mosaics, the largest north of the Alps. A few minutes' walk further south, the **Imperial Baths** (daily: March & Oct

12

BOAT TRIPS ON THE MOSEL

The stretch of the Mosel connecting Trier with the city of Koblenz cuts a sinuous and attractive gorge that gives Germany some of its steepest vineyards and best full-bodied wines. **Boats** offer an ideal way to explore the valley: Gebrüder Kolb (ⓦ moselfahrplan.de) runs regular sailings from Trier to Bernkastel-Kues, while the Princesse Marie-Astrid (ⓦ visitmoselle.lu/en /what-to-do/au-bord-de-l-eau) sails along the Luxembourg border on the upper Moselle; Mosel-Schiffs-Touristik (ⓦ moselpersonenschifffahrt.de) concentrates on the middle leg around Traben-Trarbach and Bernkastel-Kues, while Köln-Düsseldorfer (ⓦ k-d.com) covers the northern stretch between Cochem and Koblenz. Pick up the latest timetables from the tourist information office in Trier.

9am–5pm; April–Sept 9am–6pm; Nov–Feb 9am–4pm; €4) was one of the largest bath complexes in the Roman world. Its extensive underground heating system has survived, and you can walk through its passages.

The Karl-Marx-Haus

Southwest of the Hauptmarkt, the **Karl-Marx-Haus**, Brückenstrasse 10 (late March to Oct daily 10am–6pm; Nov to late March Mon 2–5pm, Tues–Sun 11am–5pm; €4, students €2.50 including free audioguide; ⓦ fes.de/karl-marx-haus), is where Karl Marx was born. It now houses a modern three-storey museum on his life and work, as well the influence of his ideas in history up to the present.

ARRIVAL AND INFORMATION

By train The train station is slightly east of the centre; walk 500m straight up the Christophstrasse to reach the Porta Nigra.

Destinations Cologne (hourly; 2hr 45min–3hr 30min); Luxembourg (1–2 hourly; 50min).

Tourist office At the Porta Nigra (Jan & Feb Mon–Sat 10am–5pm, Sun 10am–1pm; March, April, Nov & Dec Mon–Sat 9am–6pm, Sun 10am–3pm; May–Oct Mon–Sat 9am–6pm, Sun 10am–5pm; ☎0651 97 80 80, ⓦ trier -info.de).

Discount cards The Antiquity Card (€12–18) includes free admission to the Landesmuseum and two Roman structures plus reductions for other sights. The Trier-Card (€9.90/3 days) includes transport plus discounts to the museums.

GETTING AROUND

By bike Bike rental (€12/day) is in the underground bicycle garage next to the Porta Nigra (mid-April to Oct Mon–Sat 9am–6pm, Sun 10am–5pm), and inside the train station by platform 11 (May–Sept daily 9am–6pm; Oct to mid-April Mon–Sat 10am–6pm, Sun 10am–2pm).

ACCOMMODATION

Camping Treviris Luxemburgerstr. 81 ☎065 18 20 09 11, ⓦ camping-treviris.de. Campsite on the western bank of the Mosel, over the Konrad-Adenauer bridge, with a beer garden and barbecue. Open April–Oct. Per person €5.90, plus per tent €5.10

DJH An der Jugendherberge 4 ☎065 114 66 20, ⓦ djh.de; buses #5, #7, #8 and #12. Spotless modern HI hostel, with games rooms and sports facilities. Some single-bed rooms. Dorms €23, doubles €57

Hille's Gartenfeldstr. 7 ☎065 17 10 27 85, ⓦ hilles -hostel-trier.de. Homely, clean and sociable independent hostel, just 10min walk south of the station. Breakfast €6 extra, sheets €3. Dorms €74, doubles €52

EATING, DRINKING AND NIGHTLIFE

Alt Zalawen Zurlaubener Ufer 79. This traditional tavern, complete with outdoor seating overlooking the Mosel, makes an excellent place to try out the local cider, Viez. Meat platter €6. April–Oct daily 3–11pm; Nov–March Mon–Sat 3–11pm.

Astarix Karl-Marx-Str. 11. This relaxed student bar is your best bet for good and inexpensive food, such as oriental snacks for €7.50 or pizza from €3.50, and there's often live music at night. It's tricky to find, behind the *Miss Marples* pub, down a side alley. Mon–Thurs 11.30am–11pm, Fri Sat 11.30am–11.30pm, Sun 1–11.30pm.

Irish Club Trier Jakobstr. 10. Central, reliably popular and fun bar offering quiz nights, karaoke, live bands and DJs at weekends. Pint of Guinness €5.50. Mon–Thurs 4pm–1am, Fri 4pm–3am, Sat noon–3am, Sun 2pm–1am.

FRANKFURT (AM MAIN)

Straddling the River Main just before it meets the Rhine, **FRANKFURT** is known as Germany's financial capital and the home of the European Central Bank. But it also has some of Germany's best museums – no other German city spends as much on culture – and some excellent, if expensive, nightlife. Over half of the city, including almost all of the centre, was destroyed during World War II, and the rebuilders often opted for innovation over restoration, resulting in an architecturally mixed skyline – part quaint, Germanic red sandstone, part skyscraper, giving rise to the name Mainhattan.

WHAT TO SEE AND DO

Frankfurt's centre is defined by its old city walls, now a semicircular stretch of public gardens. Presided over by the gabled **Römer** or town hall, the broad, irregular piazza of **Römerberg** is the historical and geographical heart of the Altstadt, where Charlemagne built his fort to protect the original *frankonovurd* (ford of the Franks). The whole quarter was flattened by bombs in 1944, but significant landmarks were rebuilt or restored afterwards – recently the horrendous 1970s town hall was demolished to make way for fifteen reconstructions of the original pre-war buildings, plus twenty other houses. Each December, Römerberg is the focus for Frankfurt's delightful Christmas Market.

Kaiserdom

The Altstadt's most significant survivor is the thirteenth-century church of St Bartholomäus, known as the **Kaiserdom** (Sat–Thurs 9am–8pm, Fri noon–8pm; free), where for two centuries Holy Roman Emperors were crowned. To the right of the choir is the restored **Wahlkapelle** (electoral chapel), where the seven Electors would choose the Holy Roman Emperor. You can climb up the tower for a great view of the city (April–Oct daily 10am–6pm; Nov–March 10am–5pm; €3). Alternatively, take the lift up 200m to the 56th floor of the **Main Tower** at Neue Mainzer Strasse 52–58 (April–Oct Sun–Thurs 10am–9pm, Fri & Sat 10am–11pm; Nov–March Sun–Thurs 10am–7pm, Fri & Sat 10am–9pm; €6.50, students €4.50).

Goethehaus

A must-visit, the **Goethehaus**, Grosser Hirschgraben 23–25 (Mon–Sat 10am–6pm, Sun 10am–5.30pm; €7, students €3), was where Johann Wolfgang Goethe was born in 1749

and lived on and off until his move to Weimar in 1775. After being destroyed in a 1944 bombing raid, the mansion was painstakingly reconstructed and filled with paintings and furniture that had been evacuated in time. The museum gives you an excellent overall description of Germany's literary giant.

Museum für Moderne Kunst

Dividing Braubachstrasse from Berliner Strasse at the eastern end of the Altstadt, the **Museum für Moderne Kunst** at Domstrasse 10 (MMK; Tues & Thurs–Sun 10am–6pm, Wed 10am–8pm; €12, students €6; ⊚mmk-frankfurt.de) is a three-storey affair featuring major modern artists such as Lichtenstein and Beuys, alongside innovative temporary exhibitions.

Sachsenhausen and Museumsufer

For a laidback evening out, head for **Sachsenhausen**, the city-within-a-city on the south bank of the Main. The network of streets around Affentorplatz is home to the apple-wine (*Ebbelwei*) houses, while the Schaumainkai – also known as **Museumsufer** – is lined with excellent museums. Pick of the bunch is the recently extended **Städel**, at no. 63 (Tues, Wed, Sat & Sun 10am–6pm, Thurs & Fri 10am–9pm; €14, students €12; ⊚staedelmuseum.de). All the big names in German art are represented, including Dürer, Holbein and Cranach the Elder – as well as other European masters from Rembrandt to Picasso. The **Deutsches Filmmuseum** at no. 41 (Tues & Thurs–Sun 10am–6pm, Wed 10am–8pm; €6, students €3; ⊚deutschesfilmmuseum.de) has its own cinema and is popular for foreign films and arthouse screenings. Another engaging choice is the lively **Museum für Kommunikation** at no. 53 (Tues–Fri 9am–6pm, Sat & Sun 11am–7pm; €3; ⊚www.mfk-frankfurt .de), installed in a bright, glassy modern building, whose exhibits include a Salvador Dalí lobster telephone.

ARRIVAL AND DEPARTURE

By plane Frankfurt Airport (⊚frankfurt-airport.com) is Germany's busiest, though it's not used by budget airlines.

12

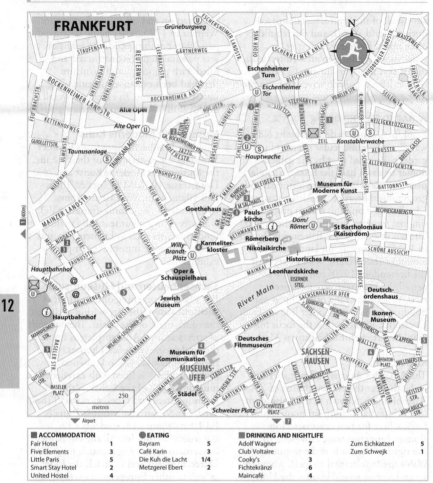

■ ACCOMMODATION		● EATING		■ DRINKING AND NIGHTLIFE			
Fair Hotel	1	Bayram	5	Adolf Wagner	7	Zum Eichkatzerl	5
Five Elements	3	Café Karin	3	Club Voltaire	2	Zum Schwejk	1
Little Paris	5	Die Kuh die Lacht	1/4	Cooky's	3		
Smart Stay Hotel	2	Metzgerei Ebert	2	Fichtekränzi	6		
United Hostel	4			Maincafé	4		

It has rail links to many German cities and Frankfurt's Hauptbahnhof (Ⓢ8 and Ⓢ9; 10min; €4.65). The deceptively named Frankfurt Hahn Airport (ⓦhahn -airport.de) is a distant 125km west, midway between Trier and Koblenz. It is connected to Frankfurt by bus that stops just south of the Hauptbahnhof (12 daily; 1hr 45min; €15; ⓦbohr.de).

By train From the Hauptbahnhof it's a 15min walk to the centre; take Ⓤ4 or Ⓤ5, or tram #11 or #12.

Destinations Berlin (hourly; 4hr 10min); Cologne (1–3 hourly; 1hr–1hr 20min); Hamburg (hourly; 3hr 40min); Hannover (1–2 hourly; 2hr 30min); Heidelberg (hourly; 50min); Mainz (frequent; 35min); Munich (hourly; 3hr 10min); Nuremberg (1–2 hourly; 2hr 5min).

By bus The bus station is just south of the Hauptbahnhof.

INFORMATION

Tourist information In the train station (Mon–Fri 8am–9pm, Sat & Sun 9am–6pm; ☏069 21 23 88 00, ⓦfrankfurt-tourismus.de), and at Römerberg 27 (Mon–Fri 9.30am–5.30pm, Sat & Sun 9.30am–4pm). They can book accommodation.

Discount passes The Frankfurt Card (€10.50/15.50 for 1/2 days) can be bought from tourist offices and allows travel throughout the city, plus fifty percent off entry charges to most museums. The two-day Museumsufer Ticket (€18, students €10) provides free entrance to 34 museums.

GETTING AROUND

By public transport Frankfurt has an integrated public transport system (ⓦrmv.de) made up of S-Bahn, U-Bahn and trams. Tickets €2.80, short trip €1.80 (permitted destinations shown at every stop), day ticket €7 (€9.10 includes airport).

ACCOMMODATION

Accommodation is pricey, thanks to the business clientele; rates can triple during or just before trade fairs. The flipside is that they tumble at weekends (when you are strongly advised to come).

Fair Hotel Europaallee Mainzer Landstr. 120 ☏ 069 74 26 28, ⓦ fairhotelfrankfurt.de. Pleasant budget hotel just north of the train station, away from the sleazier streets. Good weekend rates. Doubles €62

Five Elements Moselstr. 40 ☏ 069 24 00 58 85, ⓦ frankfurt.5elementshostel.de. Lively hostel a short walk from the main station, with 24hr reception, all-you-can-eat breakfast until noon (€4.50) and laundry. The bar is a great place to socialize and there's live music every Sat. Dorms €19, doubles €59

Little Paris Karlruherstr. 8 ☏ 069 273 99 63, ⓦ little-paris-hotel.de. Delightful little hotel in a side street south of the station, where each room is designed around a French movie star. Breakfast included. An excellent choice. Doubles €79

Smart Stay Hotel Niddastr. 45–47, ☏ 069 25 78 10 60, ⓦ hotel-frankfurt.smart-stay.de. Large new hostel near the station with neat private rooms and spacious dorms, each with en-suite bathrooms and TVs. Dorms €16, doubles €59

United Hostel Kaiserstr. 52 ☏ 069 256 67 80 00, ⓦ united-hostel-frankfurt.com. A lot of money has been spent on this bright, hip hostel, with double-glazed windows, hotel-quality bathrooms, a huge kitchen and cinema-size TV screen. Breakfast €4.50. Dorms €19

EATING AND DRINKING

Bayram Münchnerstr. 29. Turkish restaurant and kebab house going since 1991, popular and highly recommended by the locals. All food is fresh and cooked on a wooden grill. Massive portions from €9. Mon–Thurs & Sun 8am–2am, Sat 8am–6am.

Café Karin Grosser Hirschgraben 28. Frankfurt institution that's friendly, unpretentious and well worth a visit. Breakfast till 6pm (from €3.20) and a bistro-bar later on; pasta €9.80. Mon–Sat 9am–7pm, Sun 10am–7pm.

Die Kuh die Lacht Schillerstr. 28 & Friedensstr. 2. Excellent burgers at the "Laughing Cow" – including meat-free falafel and nut options – with side dishes ranging from fries to salad or veggie tempura. Classic burger €7.25. Both branches Mon–Sat 11am–11pm, Sun noon–10pm.

Metzgerei Ebert Grosse Eschenheimer Str. 5. A family butchery which also sells cooked food in Frankfurt's pedestrian area. A plateful of Frankfurters and potato salad costs €6.50 – try the famous *Zeppelinwurst*, cooked since 1909 from a patented recipe. Mon–Fri 8am–7pm, Sat 8am–6pm.

NIGHTLIFE

Apfelwein (acidic cider) is Frankfurt's speciality, and Sachsenhausen's taverns are the most atmospheric places to try it.

Adolf Wagner Schweizer Str. 71. One of the most popular of the *Apfelwein* taverns, with a lively clientele of all ages and a cosy terrace. Meals from €9, *Apfelwein* €1.90. Daily 11am–midnight.

Club Voltaire Kleine Hochstr. 5. Politically committed, alternative bar and club that hosts various events from art exhibitions to live music (entry €5–10). Beer €3. Mon–Sat 6pm–1am, Sun 6pm–midnight.

Cooky's Am Salzhaus 4 ⓦ cookys.de. Stylish hip-hop, house and soul club north of Berliner Strasse, hosting popular DJ nights plus occasional live acts. Beer €3.50, entry €5–10. Tues–Sun 11pm–late.

Fichtekränzi Wallstr. 5. Lovely *Apfelwein* tavern with a tree-shaded courtyard, wood-panelled interior and a more extensive menu than many. *Apfelwein* €1.80; "Frankfurt butcher's platter" €7.80. Daily from 5pm, garden closes at 11pm.

Maincafé Schaumainkai 50. Situated on the river quay, this is the perfect place to sit on the grass, drink beer and chill, while watching the sun set behind the skyscrapers opposite. Daily 10am–midnight.

Zum Eichkatzerl Dreieichstr. 29, Sachsenhausen. An excellent, traditional *Apfelwein* tavern with a large courtyard; meaty main courses, such as Frankfurt Schnitzel with green sauce from €9. Mon–Fri 5pm–midnight, Sat & Sun 4pm–midnight.

Zum Schwejk Schäfergasse 20, ⓦ schwejk-frankfurt .de. A lively, straight-friendly gay bar in the middle of Frankfurt's gay triangle, with seasonally changing over-the-top decoration and outside seating. Tues–Thurs 4pm–1am, Fri 4pm–3am, Sat noon–3am, Sun 6pm–1am.

DIRECTORY

Consulates Australia, Main Tower, Neue Mainzer Str. 52–58 ☏ 069 90 55 80; UK, Barclays Capital, Bockenheimlandstr. 38–40 ☏ 069 71 67 53 45; US, Giessenerstr. 30 ☏ 069 753 50.

Hospital Bürgerhospital, Nibelungenallee 37–41 ☏ 069 15 00 0.

Pharmacy At the train station, lower concourse (Mon–Fri 6.30am–9pm, Sat 8am–9pm, Sun 9am–8pm).

Post office Branches at the train station, next to platform 23 (Mon–Fri 7am–7pm, Sat 9am–4pm), and in the Karstadt department store at Zeil 90 (Mon–Sat 10am–8pm).

12

Baden-Württemberg

The southwestern state of **Baden-Württemberg** is Germany's most prosperous. The motorcar was invented here in the late nineteenth century, and the region has stayed at the forefront of technology ever since, with **Stuttgart** still the home of Daimler (Mercedes) and Porsche. The state is also home to the famous university city of **Heidelberg**. Baden-Württemberg's scenery is wonderful: its western and southern boundaries are defined by the Rhine and its bulge into Germany's largest lake, the **Bodensee** (Lake Constance). Within the curve of the river lies the **Black Forest**, source of another of the continent's principal waterways, the Danube.

HEIDELBERG

Quintessentially German and home to Germany's oldest university, **HEIDELBERG** lies majestically on the banks of the swift-flowing Neckar, 85km south of Frankfurt. For two centuries, it has seduced travellers, most notably Mark Twain, like no other German city and it still draws them to its bosom. The centrepiece is the **Schloss**, a compendium of magnificent buildings, made more atmospheric by their ruined condition; this is one castle where you won't end up traipsing through over-decorated bedchambers. The rest of the city has some good museums, but the main appeal lies in its picturesque cobbled streets, crammed with traditional restaurants and student pubs. In spring and early summer the streets hum with activity and late-night parties – by July and August, most students have left, to be replaced by swarms of visitors.

WHAT TO SEE AND DO

Actually a group of Renaissance palaces, the dominating **Heidelberg Schloss** (daily 8am–6pm; €7, students €4 including funicular, audioguide €5; ⍟schloss -heidelberg.de) can be reached from the Kornmarkt by the Bergbahn funicular (daily 9am–8pm, every 10min), which continues to the **Königstuhl** viewpoint (€7, students €5.50 return); you can also walk up to the castle in ten minutes via the steep Burgweg. At the southeastern corner is the most romantic of the ruins, the **Gesprengter Turm**; a collapsed section lies intact in the moat, leaving a clear view into the interior. The Schloss is also home to the **Grosses Fass**, an eighteenth-century wine barrel capable of holding 220,000 litres, plus the diverting **Pharmacy Museum** with exhibits in English (daily: April–Oct 10am–6pm; Nov–March 10am–5.30pm; €6, students €4).

The Altstadt

The Altstadt's finest surviving buildings are grouped around the sandstone **Heiliggeistkirche** on Marktplatz. Note the tiny shopping booths between its buttresses, a feature ever since the church was built. The striking Baroque **Alte Brücke** is reached from the Marktplatz down Steingasse; dating from the 1780s, the bridge was painstakingly rebuilt after being blown up by the German army during World War II. The **Palais Rischer** on Untere Strasse (now a private dwelling) was the most famous venue for the university's *Mensur*, or fencing match; wounds were frequent and prized as badges of courage – for optimum prestige, salt was rubbed into them, leaving scars that remained for life.

Universitätsplatz, the heart of the Old Town, is flanked by the eighteenth-century **Alte Universität** (April–Oct Tues–Sun 10am–6pm; Nov–March Tues–Sat 10am–4pm; €3, students €2.50) with its impressive conference room **Alte Aula** (1886) and the **Neue Universität**, built with US donations in 1931. Heidelberg's students didn't come under civil jurisdiction: offenders were dealt with by the university authorities, and could serve their punishment at leisure. The **Studentenkarzer** (Students' Prison) around the corner at Augustinergasse 2 (same hours and ticket as Alte Universität) was used from 1778 to 1914; its spartan cells are covered with some fantastic graffiti.

Finally, check out the wonderful, quirky **Packaging Museum** at

12

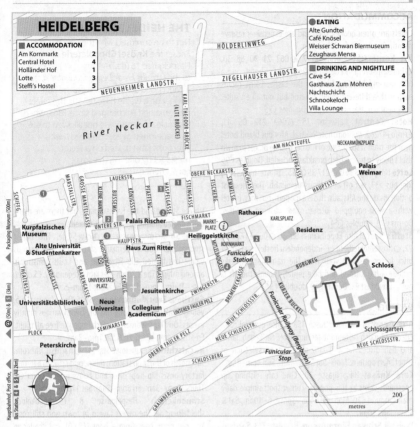

HEIDELBERG

■ ACCOMMODATION
Am Kornmarkt	2
Central Hotel	4
Holländer Hof	1
Lotte	3
Steffi's Hostel	5

● EATING
Alte Gundtei	4
Café Knösel	2
Weisser Schwan Biermuseum	3
Zeughaus Mensa	1

■ DRINKING AND NIGHTLIFE
Cave 54	4
Gasthaus Zum Mohren	2
Nachtschicht	5
Schnookeloch	1
Villa Lounge	3

12

Hauptstrasse 22 (Wed–Fri 1–6pm, Sat & Sun 11am–6pm; €5, students €3; ⓦverpackungsmuseum.de), displaying consumer products like 1890s carbolic toilet paper, 1900s Knorr cubes and Persil washing powder from 1907.

ARRIVAL AND DEPARTURE

By plane Ryanair, Wizz Air and other budget flights fly into Karlsruhe/Baden-Baden airport, 90km to the south (ⓦbadenairpark.de), which is connected to Heidelberg's train station by bus #140 (1–2 daily; 1hr 30min; €20; ⓦhahn-express.de).

By train and bus Heidelberg's train and bus stations are next to each other in an anonymous quarter 20min walk west of the Altstadt. All trams except the #24 run to the old centre; bus #33 stops at the Bergbahn below the Schloss.
Destinations Frankfurt (1–2 hourly; 54min); Mainz (1–2 hourly; 51min); Munich (hourly; 2hr 20min); Stuttgart (1–2 hourly; 45min).

INFORMATION

Tourist information In the Rathaus on Marktplatz (April–Oct Mon–Fri 8am–5pm, Sat 9am–3pm. Nov–March Mon–Fri 8am–5pm; ☏062 215 84 02 24, ⓦheidelberg-marketing.de) and on the square outside the station (April–Oct Mon–Sat 9am–7pm, Sun 10am–6pm; Nov–March Mon–Sat 9am–6pm).

Discount pass The Heidelberg Card (1/2/4 days for €15/17/19) includes transport in the city, entry to the Schloss and reductions in museums, attractions and restaurants.

GETTING AROUND

By bus and tram Although Heidelberg is small, the bus and tram system is useful for journeys from the train or bus stations. A bus from the station to the old town is €1.30 one-way; longer trip €2.34; day ticket for one person €6.50, extra people €2.70 each.

By bike Heidelberg is covered by the Nextbike and Call-a-Bike rental schemes.

ACCOMMODATION

Hotels are often booked solid and are expensive; reserve months in advance for July & Aug.

Am Kornmarkt Kornmarkt 7 ☎062 21 90 58 30, ⓦhotelamkornmarkt.de. Excellent-value hotel in a 600-year-old building beneath the castle. Large rooms each with a different colour scheme but not all en suite. Continental buffet breakfast €9. Doubles **€75**

Hotel Central Kaiserstr. 75 ☎062 212 06 41, ⓦinfo147262.wix.com/hotelcentral. Airy but bland hotel near the train station. One of the best-value places in town that's likely to have a bed: breakfast included. Doubles **€95**

Lotte Burgweg 3 ☎062 217 35 07 25, ⓦlotte-heidelberg .de; bus #33, get off at Rathaus-Bergbahn. The cheapest option inside the Altstadt, this is a modern, but cosy, hostel with a well-equipped kitchen and washing facilities. Dorms **€23**, doubles **€64**

Steffi's Hostel Alte Eppelheimer Str. 50 ☎062 217 78 27 72, ⓦhostelheidelberg.de. Independent hostel in a former brick factory a short walk from the train station. Perks include a big kitchen and bike rental, though the lift is noisy. Breakfast €3. Dorms **€18**, doubles **€56**

EATING

Alte Gundtei Zwingerstrasse 15a ⓦalte-gundtei.com. Friendly Turkish restaurant serving excellent kebab, lamb and fish dishes for €11–16, plus a good selection of vegetarian options. Mon–Sat 5pm–1am, Sun 4pm–1am.

Café Knösel Haspelgasse 20. Chic café dishing up enormous cakes at this popular corner spot; simple daily mains around €10. Mon–Fri noon–3pm & 6–10pm, Sat & Sun noon–10pm.

Weisser Schwan Biermuseum Hauptstr. 143. Spacious establishment offering thirty types of beer and much loved by the locals for its good-value lunch menu. Try the *Fleischkäse* (meatloaf) for €7. Daily 11am–11.45pm.

Zeughaus Mensa Im Marstallhof. Inside the old barracks is a student refectory that's open to everyone. Fill up from a basic warm buffet and pay by weight. Around €6 for a plateful. Daily 11am–10pm.

DRINKING AND NIGHTLIFE

Because of its large student community Heidelberg punches well above its weight in nightlife. The focus is

TREAT YOURSELF

Holländer Hof Neckarstaden 66 ☎062 216 05 00, ⓦhollaender-hof.de. Possibly the most comfortable hotel in this romantic town, with dreamily furnished, cosy rooms facing the Alte Brücke. Breakfast and half a bottle of sparkling wine included. Doubles **€129**

THE HEIDELBERG KISS

Not to be confused with the nearby *Café Knösel*, the **Knösel Chocolaterie** at Haspelgasse 16 (daily 11am–7pm) is home to the famous *Heidelberger Studentenkuss*, a dark chocolate filled with praline and nougat on a waffle base (€2.50). The sweet has remained unchanged since 1863, when the male students were not allowed to talk to chaperoned girls, so showed their affections (and passed on a secret message) by offering this small confectionery.

Untere Strasse and the Rathausplatz, but there are many clubs dotted around the new city as well.

Cave 54 Krämmergasse 2 ⓦcave54.de. The oldest student jazz club in Germany, since 1954, this famous venue has hosted Ella Fitzgerald and Louis Armstrong, among others. The 8.30pm Tues jam is legendary. €5 cover. Tues–Thurs 10pm–3am, Fri & Sat 10pm–5am.

Gasthaus Zum Mohren Untere Str. 5. One of several hip, young drinking spots along this alley, with various nightly events. On Thurs women drink champagne free all night. Fri–Thurs 4pm–3am, Fri & Sat 1pm–3am.

Nachtschicht Bergheimer Str. 147 ⓦnachtschicht.com. Just north of the train station, this popular club in a former factory hosts hip-hop, disco and house nights. Cover €6. Thurs 10pm–3am, Fri 8pm–3am, Sat 11pm–4am.

Schnookeloch Haspelgasse 8 ⓦschnookeloch -heidelberg.de. The oldest tavern in town and still cosy. You can drink beer from a boot (€7.60) and challenge yourself to finish the enormous schnitzels for €13.50. Daily 7.30am–3am.

Villa Lounge Hauptstr. 187. Popular to the point of bursting with under 25s who flock here for cheap drink specials – if you're lucky, you'll get cocktails for €4, or an all-night Happy Hour. Mon–Thurs & Sun 9am–2am, Fri & Sat 9am–3am.

FREIBURG (IM BREISGAU)

FREIBURG basks in the laidback atmosphere you'd expect from Germany's sunniest city. It's been a university town since 1457 and its youthful presence is maintained year-round with a varied programme of festivals. It's a thoroughly enjoyable place to visit, and makes the perfect urban base for exploring the surrounding **Black Forest**. Home of the cuckoo clock and source of the Danube, the Black Forest, stretching 170km north to south, and up to 60km east to west, is

Germany's largest and most beautiful forest. Its name reflects the mountainous landscape darkened by endless pine trees and, as late as the 1920s, much of this area was eerie wilderness, a refuge for boars and bandits. Today, many of its villages are geared toward tourism, brimming with souvenir shops, while old forest trails provide easy and enjoyable hiking.

WHAT TO SEE AND DO

The city's most impressive sight is the dark-red sandstone **Münster** (Mon–Sat 10am–5pm, Sun 1–7.30pm), with its intricate openwork spire. Begun in about 1200, the church has a masterly Gothic nave, with flying buttresses, gargoyles and statues – the stained-glass windows are all original, having survived World War II. From the **tower** (April–Oct Mon–Sat 9.30am–5pm, Sun 1–5pm; €2, students €1.50) there's a fine panorama of the city and the surrounding forested hills. Walking south from here on Kaiser-Josef-Strasse, Freiburg's central axis, you come to the **Martinstor**, one of two surviving towers of the medieval fortifications. Just southeast of here is the main channel of the *Bächle* (medieval rain canals that supplied water in case of fire); follow it along Gerberau, to the **Schwabentor**, the other thirteenth-century tower. Nearby, at Oberlinden 12, you can find Germany's oldest surviving inn, **Zum Roten Bären** (established 1120). Opposite here, the Schwabentor footpaths lead up the **Schlossberg**, with a ruined French fortress and great views over the city.

Schauinsland

The hills of the Black Forest almost rise out of Freiburg's Altstadt, giving the town a convenient outdoor playground for hikers and mountain bikers: the tourist information office has good maps, and details of numerous trailheads accessible by public transport. The largest of these forested peaks, **Schauinsland**, lies 7km south of the city and is easily ascended on the **Schauinslandbahn cable car** (daily: July–Sept 9am–6pm; Oct–June 9am–5pm; one-way €9, students €8.50, return €12.50, students €11.50;

⊙0761 4511 777, ⊙schauinslandbahn .de; tram #2 to Günterstal then bus #21). From its summit a five-minute walk leads to a lookout tower and the top of several well-marked trails. These offer first-class hiking and mountain biking – with almost the entire 14km journey back to Freiburg downhill – plus great views along the way.

ARRIVAL AND DEPARTURE

By plane The EuroAirport Basel-Mulhouse-Freiburg (just across the border in France) is 70km south of Freiburg; Flixbus runs to Freiburg train station (hourly; €20 single; 55min; ⊙ flixbus.de).
By train The train station is on Bismarckallee about a 10min walk west of the city centre.
Destinations Basel (2 hourly; 45min–1hr); Frankfurt (hourly; 2hr 20min); Stuttgart (hourly; 2hr); Zürich (hourly; 2hr).
By bus The bus station is on Bismarckallee just below the train station. Ticket for city buses and trams cost €2.20, a 24hr ticket is €5.60 or €11.20 for up to 5 people. The Freiburg WelcomeKarte (€25, 3 days) includes all local transport plus the Schauinslandbahn cable car.

INFORMATION AND TOURS

Tourist information Rathausplatz 2–4 (June–Sept Mon–Fri 8am–8pm, Sat 9.30am–5pm, Sun 10.30am–3pm; Oct–May Mon–Fri 8am–6pm, Sat 9.30am–2.30pm, Sun 10am–noon; ⊙076 13 88 18 80, ⊙freiburg.de). For €3, they'll also find you a room.
Tours Tours in English (1hr 30min) are run by Freiburger Leben (May–Oct Wed–Fri 10am & 2pm, Sat 10.30am, noon & 3.30pm; €9; ⊙076 11 37 69 18, ⊙freiburgerleben.com).

ACCOMMODATION

★ **Black Forest Hostel** Kartäuserstr. 33 ⊙076 18 81 78 70, ⊙blackforest-hostel.de; tram #1 from the station to Schwabentorbrücke. Buzzing backpackers' hostel in an old factory near the centre, and by far the best place to stay in town. Well-equipped kitchen, and bikes for €8/day. Sheets €4. No wi-fi, but there are several PCs with internet access. Dorms **€17**, doubles **€60**
Camping Hirzberg Kartäuserstr. 99 ⊙076 13 50 54, ⊙freiburg-camping.de; tram #1 to Musikhochschule, then turn left through the subway, cross the river and follow the signs. The most accessible (on foot) of Freiburg's three campsites. Open all year. Per person **€8.80**, plus per tent **€4.70**
Helene Staufenerstr. 46 ⊙076 14 52 10 29, ⊙hotel -helene-freiburg.de. Just over 1km south of the train station (take tram #5), just beyond the Dreisam River, this is the best-value central hotel in Freiburg. Breakfast buffet included. Doubles **€75**

12

KL Freiburg Kartäuserstr. 41 ☎076 12 11 16 30, ⓦkl -freiburg.de. Very modern, clean hotel-cum-hostel, near the centre, with a cafeteria. Though it's almost always full, it's worth trying. Students get thirteen percent discount. Breakfast included. Doubles **€69**

EATING, DRINKING AND NIGHTLIFE

Freiburg has great nightlife; pick up a free *Tipps* magazine to see what's on, or just head into the bar area around Löwenstrasse and make some new friends.

Brennessel Eschholzstr. 17 ⓦbrennessel-freiburg.de. Local students pack out this slightly shabby restaurant behind the station for the unbeatable €1.80 spaghetti bolognese (from 6–7.30pm and 10.30–11.30pm only). Also has roast pork for €9.80 and vegetarian dishes from €8. Mon–Sat 6pm–1am, Sun 5pm–1am.

Jazzhaus Schnewlinstr. 1 ⓦjazzhaus.de. Club in an old wine cellar attracting a range of ages and hosting musical events, from world music concerts to blues, jazz, rock and hip-hop. Club night cover €7. Fri & Sat club nights 11pm–4am, gigs from 8pm.

Karma Bertoldstr. 51–53 ⓦkarma-freiburg.de. The *Karma* complex has it all: a café-bar, a good Indian restaurant with a weekday all-you-can-eat buffet (€8), and a club in the cellar (cover €6). Café-bar Mon–Thurs 9.30am–2am, Fri & Sat 9.30am–3am, Sun 9am–1am; restaurant Mon–Thurs 11.30am–2.30pm & 6–11pm, Fri & Sat 11am–1am, Sun 11am–11pm; club Fri & Sat 11pm–5am.

Kastaniengarten Schlossbergring 3 ⓦkastaniengarten -freiburg.de. A beautiful *biergarten* shaded by chestnut trees on the Schlossberg, accessed by elevator from opposite the Schwabentor. A litre of beer is €7.50, *Weisswurst* with a pretzel is €6. April–Oct daily 11am–midnight.

Markthalle Grünewalderstr. 4 ⓦmarkthalle-freiburg.de. This food court bustles with locals visiting different kiosks.

EUROPA PARK

Some 40km north of Freiburg, Germany's largest **theme park** (daily: mid-March– Oct 9am–6pm or later; late Nov & Dec 11am–7pm; €44.50; ☎078 22 77 66 88, ⓦeuropapark.de) is great fun. Fairytale figures like Rapunzel and Hansel & Gretel plus eleven roller coasters entertain you during the day, while variety shows, cinemas, pop concerts and restaurants in the fourteen country-themed areas amuse you at night. Flixbus has a daily bus service from Freiburg at 9.30am (30min; €8; ⓦflixbus.de), or take the train to Ringsheim, then a connecting bus. You can stay overnight at the Europa-park campsite (per person **€10.50**).

---

that dish up quality regional Swabian and international dishes. Mon–Thurs 8am–8pm, Fri & Sat 8am–midnight.

Martin's Bräu Kaiser-Joseph-Str. 237 (down the Martinsgässle alley). Typical *bierstube* brewing its own beer and offering cheap local specialities such as cheese noodles for €8.90 and standard international dishes. Mon–Thurs & Sun 11am–midnight, Fri & Sat 11am–2am.

★ **Schlappen** Löwenstr. 2 ⓦschlappen.com. Cool café-bar attracting mainly students – it starts as a restaurant and pub and ends as a club with late-night music. Try the delicious local *Maultaschen* dumplings (€7), washed down with one of the many beers (€3). Mon–Wed 11am–1am, Thurs 11am–2am, Fri & Sat 11am–3am, Sun 3pm–1am.

STUTTGART

In the centre of Baden-Württemberg, 85km southeast of Heidelberg, **STUTTGART** is home to the German success stories of Bosch, Porsche and Mercedes. Founded in 950 as a stud farm (*Stuotgarten*) by Duke Liudolf of Swabia, it became a town only in the fourteenth century. Set amid rolling hills, it has some unique museums and sparkling nightlife.

WHAT TO SEE AND DO

From the train station, Königstrasse passes the brutalist modern Dom and enters Schlossplatz, on the south of which is the **Altes Schloss**, built to defend Duke Liudolf's stud farm and now home to the **Württemberg State Museum** (Tues–Sun 10am–6pm; €5.50, students €4.50; ⓦlandesmuseum-stuttgart.de). This large and varied museum explores the history of the region from the Stone Age to the present through archeological exhibitions as well as arts and crafts. On the western side of Schlossplatz, the shiny glass box of the **Kunstmuseum** (Tues, Wed & Fri–Sun 10am–6pm, Thurs 10am–8pm; €7, students €5, Wed free; ⓦkunstmuseum -stuttgart.de) boasts a rich permanent collection including some harsh Weimar-era paintings by Otto Dix, plus excellent temporary exhibitions.

Northeast of Schlossplatz at Konrad-Adenauer-Strasse 30–32, the **State Gallery** is one of Germany's most visited art museums (Tues & Thurs 10am–8pm, Wed & Fri–Sun 10am–6pm; €5.50; Wed & Sat free; ⓦstaatsgalerie.de). There's an Old Masters section as well as a New

Gallery focusing on various schools within twentieth-century art movements.

The Weissenhofmuseum

Over five months in 1927, pioneering modern architects including Le Corbusier and Mies van der Rohe built Stuttgart's residential **Weissenhofsiedlung** area, 3km north of the centre, to demonstrate radical new ideas and materials. Eleven buildings have survived here and Le Corbusier's semi-detached house at Rathenaustr. 1 – recently granted UNESCO World Heritage status – now houses the **Weissenhofmuseum** (Tues–Fri 11am–6pm, Sat & Sun 10am–6pm; €5, students €2; ⓦweissenhofmuseum.de; ⓤKillesberg). Inside is a fascinating exhibition about the district and Le Corbusier's revolutionary ideas on architecture, plus various original interiors.

The Mercedes and Porsche museums

As much as they are collections of vintage cars, the Mercedes and Porsche museums are also temples to fine engineering, human ingenuity and thousands of hours of careful hard work. So slick are the museums – their modern architecture airy and futuristic, the displays self-confident, seamless and high-tech – that they can't fail to inspire. The **Mercedes-Benz-Museum**, Mercedesstr. 100 (Tues–Sun 9am–6pm; €8, students €4; ⓦmercedes -benz.com; ⓢNeckarpark), is strong on the early parts of motoring history, since its founders invented both the motorbike and the motorcar. The **Porsche Museum**, Porscheplatz 1 (Tues–Sun 9am–6pm; €8, students €4; ⓦporsche.com/museum; ⓢ6 to Neuwirtshaus) is no less flashy – and allows you to pose inside a Carrera GTS. Dozens of priceless, highly polished examples of fine engineering are explained by an intelligent audioguide and touch-screen monitors. The success of the brand is underlined by a display of some of Porsche's 28,000 trophies.

ARRIVAL AND DEPARTURE

By plane Stuttgart Airport is linked to the train station by ⓢ2 and ⓢ3 (frequent; 30min).
By train Stuttgart's train station is located in the centre of town.

Destinations Berlin (4–5 daily; 5hr–5hr 45min); Cologne (8 daily; 2hr 14min); Frankfurt (hourly; 1hr 17min); Hamburg (6–7 daily; 5hr 30min); Konstanz (10 daily; 2hr 20min); Munich (1–2 hourly; 2hr 15min); Zürich (every 2hr; 3hr).
By bus There's no bus station in the city centre. Some buses use the station at Hafenbahnstr. 15 in Obertürkheim, while others use Burgunderstr. 39 in Zuffenhausen. Both are 15–20min by S-Bahn from the central train station.

INFORMATION

Tourist information Opposite the train station at Königstr. 1a (Mon–Fri 9am–8pm, Sat 9am–6pm, Sun 10am–6pm; tours & tickets ☎071 12 22 81 11, hotel bookings ☎071 12 22 81 00, ⓦstuttgart-tourist.de), and in Terminal 3 at the airport (Mon–Fri 8am–7pm, Sat 9am–1pm & 1.45–4.30pm, Sun 10am–1pm & 1.45–5.30pm). Stuttgart has free wi-fi in the city centre; log in to the Unitymedia network.
Discount passes The StuttCard (€15/20/25 for 1/2/3 days) gives free admission to various attractions and numerous discounts; the Combination StuttCard (€25/35/45 respectively) includes use of local public transport.

GETTING AROUND

By public transport A day ticket for the extensive integrated public transport network costs €6.80, a one-way ticket €0.80.

ACCOMMODATION

Alex 30 Alexanderstr. 30 ☎0711 838 89 50, ⓦalex30 -hostel.de; ⓤOlgaeck. Established independent hostel near the Bohnenviertel that has a bar, café, kitchen and terrace. Breakfast buffet €8. Dorms €25, doubles €64
A&O Stuttgart City Rosensteinstr. 14 ☎0711 25 27 74 00, ⓦaohostels.com; ⓤMilchhof. Large and functional new chain hostel, 2km north of the station, with a kitchen and bar. Good breakfast buffet €7. Dorms €15, doubles €60
International Studenthotel Neckarstr. 172 ☎0711 41 43 00, ⓦsw-stuttgart.de; ⓤStöckach. Excellent-value modern student hotel just east of the centre. Breakfast is included and there's a communal lounge for socializing. Non-students pay €10 extra. Singles with shared facilities €28, en-suite doubles €58
Jugendherberge Stuttgart International Haussmannstr. 27 ☎0711 664 74 70, ⓦjugendherberge -stuttgart.de; ⓤEugensplatz. Large, well-organized but run-of-the-mill DJH hostel, on a hillside, with great views over town from the terrace. Dorms €32, doubles €64

EATING, DRINKING AND NIGHTLIFE

Stuttgart is surrounded by vineyards, and its numerous *Weinstuben* are excellent places to try good-quality local

12

12

wines at low cost. It is also great for nightlife with the focus below Schlossplatz, around the Hans-im-Glück fountain on Geisstrasse and west of Rotebühlplatz, while to the southwest, hip Marienplatz has casual cafés and ice-cream parlours.

Brauhaus Schönbuch Bolzstr. 10. Independent brewery, beer hall and garden in the middle of the pedestrian district serving filling lunch dishes for €8 or schnitzel and fries for €12. Try a half-litre of its Ur-Edel lager for €3.80. Sun–Wed 11am–midnight, Thurs–Sat 11am–1am.

Café Galao Tübinger Str. 90. Small, quirky café off Marienplatz with healthy breakfasts, home-made cake and lethal cocktails, plus concerts ranging from jazz to African to Middle Eastern psych rock. Mon–Fri noon–10pm, Sat & Sun 3–10pm.

Kiste Hauptstätterstr. 35 ⓦkiste-stuttgart.de. Live venue that hosts interesting jazz sessions as well as performances by local indie rock bands. Entrance €5. Mon–Thurs 6pm–2am, Fri & Sat 7pm–3am.

Lehmann Seidenstr. 20 ⓦlehmannclub.de. One of techno's cathedrals with a reputation inside Germany second only to legends like Berlin's *Berghain* – check out the We Are Techno nights. Cover €10–15. Fri & Sat 11pm–late.

★**Mata Hari** Geissstr. 3. Standing room only in this bar/café, very popular with the under 25s, and always packed to the rafters, often spilling out to the street. Daily dish €8. Mon–Thurs & Sun 3pm–2am, Fri & Sat 2pm–3am.

Palast der Republik Friedrichstr. 27. Offbeat cult place: a former public loo that's now a beer kiosk. On sunny days drinkers line the pavement outside and (amazingly for Germany) DJs play loud music on the pavement at night. Sun–Wed 11am–2am, Thurs–Sat 11am–3am.

Udo's Snack Calverstrasse 23. Hole-in-the-wall snack bar offering quality burgers for €4.50 and loud techno for free: an irresistible combination that's been going strong for over 30 years. Mon–Wed 11am–10pm, Thurs 11am–11pm, Fri & Sat 11am–1am.

KONSTANZ AND THE BODENSEE

In the far south, hard on the Swiss border, **KONSTANZ** lies at the tip of a tongue of land sticking out into the huge **Bodensee** (Lake Constance). The town itself is split by the lake, giving Konstanz the air of a sea town. Its convivial atmosphere is best experienced in the summer, when street cafés tempt prolonged stays and the water is a bustle of sails.

WHAT TO SEE AND DO

Konstanz's most prominent building is the Romanesque **Münster** church, in the heart of the Altstadt (Mon–Sat 10am–5pm, Sun 12.30–5pm; €2), while its regional highlights are two small Bodensee islands, both connected to the mainland by a bridge. The nearby **Mainau** island (daily dawn to dusk; March–Oct €19, Nov–Feb €9.50, half-price after 5pm; ⓦmainau.de; bus #4 from Konstanz) has a royal park featuring magnificent floral displays, formal gardens, greenhouses, forests, a butterfly house and a handful of well-placed restaurants. The larger, but still tranquil, island of **Reichenau**, 8km west of Konstanz, is home to the Romanesque Benedictine **St Georg Abbey**, a UNESCO World Heritage Site (daily 9am–5pm; ⓦreichenau -tourismus.de).

ARRIVAL AND INFORMATION

By train The train station is at the southern edge of the city on the border with Switzerland. For Reichenau take the train to Reichenau station (frequent; 9min), then change to bus #7372 to "Mittelzell" (frequent; 15min).

Destinations Munich (2 hourly; 4hr 15min–5hr); Zürich (hourly; 1hr 20min).

Tourist information Beside the train station at Bahnhofplatz 43 (April–Oct Mon–Fri 9am–6.30pm, Sat 9am–4pm, Sun 10am–1pm; Nov–March Mon–Fri 9.30am–6pm; ☎075 31 13 30 30, ⓦkonstanz-tourismus .de); staff can book private rooms.

GETTING AROUND

By bike Bike rental from Kultur-Rädle, Bahnhofplatz 29 (Easter–Oct Mon–Fri 9am–12.30pm & 2.30–6pm, Sat 10am–4pm, Sun 10am–12.30pm; €13/day; ☎07531 273 10; ⓦkultur-raedle.de).

By boat Bodensee-Schiffsbetriebe (BSB), Hafenstr. 6 (☎075 313 64 00, ⓦbsb-online.com). Ferries and cruises run regularly around the lake and to the Bodensee islands and they also offer scenic trips to Switzerland.

ACCOMMODATION

Campingplatz Bruderhofer Fohrenbühlweg 45 ☎075 313 13 92, ⓦcampingplatz-konstanz.de; bus #1 to Tannenhof then a 10min walk. One of two pleasant neighbouring campsites on the lakeshore 4km northeast of the centre and around 1km from the car-ferry dock. Per person **€7**, plus per tent **€5.50**

DJH Konstanz Zur Allmannshöhe 16 ☎075 313 22 60, ⓦjugendherberge-konstanz.de; bus #4 to Jugendherberge. Excellent hostel uniquely located in and around an old water tower, 5km out of town. Dorms **€23.20**, over 26s **€29.20**

Bavaria

Bavaria (Bayern), Germany's largest federal state, fills the southeast of the country. It's the home of almost all German clichés: beer-swilling men in *Lederhosen*, piles of *Sauerkraut* and sausages galore. But that's only a small part of the picture, and one that's almost entirely restricted to the Bavarian Alps that lie south of the magnificent state capital, **Munich**. Eastern Bavaria – whose capital is **Regensburg** – is dominated by rolling forests where life revolves around logging and minor industries like glass production. To the north, **Nuremberg** is the hub of Protestant **Franconia** (Franken), a region known for its vineyards and natural parks as well as beautifully preserved and atmospheric medieval towns – notably **Rothenburg ob der Tauber**, which is but a highlight among the glut of attractive places that dot Bavaria's **Romantic Road**.

MUNICH

Founded in 1158, **MUNICH** (München) has been the capital of Bavaria since 1504, and as far as the locals are concerned it's the centre of the universe. Impossibly energetic, it bursts with a good-humoured self-importance that is difficult to dislike. After Berlin, Munich is Germany's most popular city – and with its compact, attractive old centre it's far easier to digest. It has a great setting, with the mountains and Alpine lakes just an hour's drive away. The best time to come is from June to early October, when the beer gardens, cafés and bars are in full swing – not least for the world-famous **Oktoberfest** beer festival.

> ## THE ROMANTIC ROAD
>
> The charming, picturesque **Romantic Road** (ⓦromantischestrasse.de) is Germany's best-loved tourist route, running from the vineyards of Würzburg in northern Bavaria over 385km of pastoral scenery and quaint medieval villages to the fairytale castle of Füssen in the south. Touring buses (April–Oct 1 daily; ☎069 719 12 61 00, ⓦtouring -travel.eu) run in each direction between Frankfurt and Füssen via Munich, with short stops in many of the towns and free audioguides included (12hr 20min).

WHAT TO SEE AND DO

Just ten minutes' walk east of the train station, the twin onion-domed towers of the red-brick Gothic **Frauenkirche** (Dom; daily 7.30am–8.30pm) form the focus of the city's skyline. The pedestrian shopping street, **Kaufingerstrasse**, just below, heads east to the centre and the main square, the Marienplatz.

Marienplatz

The **Marienplatz** is the bustling heart of Munich, thronged with crowds being entertained by street musicians and artists. At 11am and noon (March–Oct also 5pm), the square fills with tourists as the glockenspiel in the **Neues Rathaus**, Marienplatz 8 (Tower daily: May–Sept 10am–7pm; Oct–April 10am–5pm; €2.50), jingles into action. To the right is the plain Gothic **Altes Rathaus**, whose tower now houses the **Spielzeugmuseum** (daily 10am–5.30pm; €4), with its vast toy collection.

Alter Peter and the Viktualienmarkt

On the south side of Marienplatz, the **Peterskirche** tower (summer Mon–Fri 9am–7pm, Sat & Sun 10am–7pm; winter Mon–Fri 9am–5.30pm, Sat & Sun 10am–5.30pm; €2, students €1) offers the best views of the Altstadt. Directly below, you'll find the **Viktualienmarkt**, an open-air food market selling everything

12

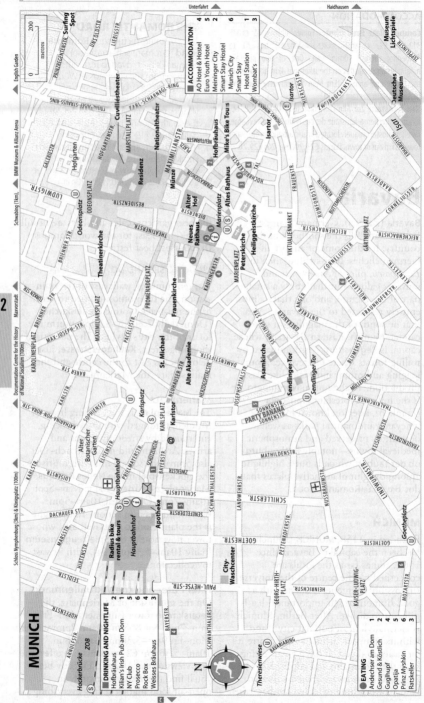

MUNICH

Schloss Nymphenburg (3km) & Königsplatz (100m) ◀
Documentation Centre for the History of National Socialism (100m) ◀
Maxvorstadt ◀
Schwabing (1km) ◀
BMW Museum & Allianz Arena ◀
English Garden ◀

Unterfahrt ▲   Haidhausen ▲

ACCOMMODATION
AO Hotel & Hostel	4
Euro Youth Hotel	5
Meininger City	2
Smart Stay Hostel Munich City	6
Smart Stay Hotel Station	1
Wombat's	3

DRINKING AND NIGHTLIFE
Hofbräuhaus	2
Kilian's Irish Pub am Dom	1
NY Club	5
Prosecco	6
Rock Box	4
Weisses Bräuhaus	3

EATING
Andechser am Dom	1
Gesund & Köstlich	2
Gughupf	4
Opatija	5
Prinz Myshkin	6
Ratskeller	3

N

from *Weisswurst* and beer to fruit and veg. West of here, at Sendlinger Str. 62, stands the pint-sized **Asamkirche** (Mon–Fri 7.30am–6pm; Sat 8am–7pm, Sun 8am–3pm; free), one of the most splendid Rococo churches in Bavaria.

The Hofbräuhaus, the Residenz and Königsplatz

Northeast of Marienplatz is the **Hofbräuhaus**, Munich's largest and most famous drinking hall (see p.408). North of here, on Residenzstrasse, is the entrance to the palace of the Wittelsbachs, the immense **Residenz** (daily: April to mid-Oct 9am–6pm; mid-Oct to March 10am–5pm; €7, students €6; ⓦ residenz -muenchen.de). One of Europe's finest Renaissance buildings, it was so badly damaged in the last war that it had to be almost totally rebuilt. The splendid 66m-long Antiquarium, the oldest part of the palace, is the highlight of the visit. A separate ticket is necessary to see the fabulous treasures of the **Schatzkammer** (same hours as Residenz; €7, students €6, or €11, students €9 combined with Residenz); the star piece is the dazzling stone-encrusted statuette of St George, made around 1590. Across Odeonsplatz from the Residenz is one of the city's most regal churches, the **Theatinerkirche**, whose golden-yellow towers and green copper dome add a splash of colour to the roofscape.

Northwest of the Residenz, the grand neo-classicist district around **Königsplatz** was the centre of Nazi power from the early 1930s and regularly used for mass rallies. Standing on the location of the former Nazi party headquarters, the new **Documentation Centre for the History of National Socialism**, Brienner Strasse 34 (Tues–Sun 10am–7pm, €5, students €2.50), has an excellent exhibition about Munich's role in the rise and fall of the Nazi movement.

The Deutsches Museum

Munich's most impressive museum – the **Deutsches Museum** at Museumsinsel 1 (daily 9am–5pm; €11, students €4; ⓦ deutsches-museum.de) – occupies a midstream island in the Isar, southeast of

the centre. Covering every conceivable aspect of scientific and technical endeavour, from historical scientific instruments to the latest medical research, this is the most compendious collection of its type in Germany.

The English Garden

Munich's open central park is a delight to walk around in, especially in the summer. Check out the **surfers** in the fast-flowing river at the bottom of the garden on Prinzregentenstrasse, walk up for a Hofbräu beer and a sausage in the **Chinesischen Turm** (daily 10am–11pm), lie naked if you dare in the nudist section in the middle of the garden (west of the stream), or rent a pedalo on the large lake at the top.

North Munich

There are two main attractions a short trip north of the centre: right by U-Bahn Olympiapark, **BMW World** (Mon–Sat 7.30am–midnight, Sun 9am–midnight; free) is in reality a big showroom for the car giant's latest models but impressive nevertheless, while the **BMW museum** opposite (Tues–Sun 10am–6pm; €10, students €7) has vintage cars and motorcycles on display as well as electric cars and hydrogen engine models. Further north is the futuristic **Allianz Arena**, home of **Bayern Munich** and the site of its interesting museum (daily except match days 10am–6pm; €12, students €10; combi ticket including arena tour €19, students €17) where the club's silverware (and goldware) is on display along with photos, mementoes, videos and biographies of their greats.

West Munich

Schloss Nymphenburg (daily: April to mid-Oct 9am–6pm; mid-Oct to March 10am–4pm; €6, students €5, combined ticket for all Nymphenburg sights €11.50, students €9; ⓦ schloss-nymphenburg.de), the summer residence of the Wittelsbachs, is reached by tram #17 from the train station. Its kernel is a small Italianate palace begun in 1664 for the Electress Adelaide, who dedicated it to the goddess Flora and her nymphs – hence the name.

ARRIVAL AND DEPARTURE

By plane Munich's airport, Franz Josef Strauss Flughafen (ⓦmunich-airport.de), 35km north of the city, is connected to the Hauptbahnhof and Marienplatz by ⓢ1 and ⓢ8 – buy the €12.40 Airport-City-Day-Ticket.

By train The Hauptbahnhof is at the western end of the city centre.

Destinations Berlin (hourly; 6hr 30min); Cologne (1–2 hourly; 5hr); Nuremberg (2 hourly; 1hr); Regensburg (hourly; 1hr 30min); Salzburg (2 hourly; 1hr 45min); Stuttgart (2 hourly; 2hr 15min); Vienna (1–2 hourly; 4hr).

By bus The bus station (ZOB) is on Arnulfstrasse, behind the train station.

INFORMATION AND TOURS

Tourist information At Bahnhofplatz 2 (Mon–Sat 9am–8pm, Sun 10am–6pm; ⓦmuenchen.de) and in the Neues Rathaus on Marienplatz (Mon–Fri 9.30am–7.30pm, Sat 9am–4pm, Sun 10am–2pm): both can help book rooms. There is also a telephone accommodation line ☎089 23 39 65 55.

Tours Radius, Arnulfstr. 3 (☎089 54 34 87 7740, ⓦradiustours.com; 3hr bike tour €25), and Mike's Bike Tours, Bräuhausstr. 10 (☎089 25 54 39 87, ⓦmikesbiketours.com; 4hrs €31), both do fun bike tours around Munich and beyond as well as bike rentals for around €15–20 per day. Both also arrange Neuschwanstein bus tours.

GETTING AROUND

By public transport Regular one-zone tickets cost €2.70 and are valid for 3 hours; a *Kurzstrecke* short trip ticket valid for up to two S- or U-Bahn stops or four bus or tram stops costs €1.40 (ⓦmvv-muenchen.de). Day tickets (€6.40); 3-day tickets (€16); group tickets for up to five people (€12.20/28.20 for 1/3 days).

ACCOMMODATION

The cheap hotel area is south of the station below the length of Bayerstrasse. Accommodation can be hard to find during the Oktoberfest, when prices rocket.

AO Hotel Hostel Bayerstr. 75 ☎089 45 23 57, ⓦaohostels.com. Modern hotel-cum-hostel with clean, warm rooms on the large side. Discounts for early bookers. Breakfast €6, sheets €3. Dorms €16, doubles €67

★**Euro Youth Hotel** Senefelderstr. 5 ☎089 59 90 88 11, ⓦeuro-youth-hotel.de. Good atmosphere and location in an 1880s building with a late-closing bar and friendly staff. Breakfast €4.90. Dorms €17.50, doubles €60

Meininger City Landsbergerstr. 20 ☎089 55 05 30. Functional, well-managed hostel about 15min from the station. Every room/dorm has shower and WC, while the singles and doubles have a TV. The beer garden is good in the summer. Buffet breakfast included. Dorms €16, doubles €45

Smart Stay Hostel Munich City Mozartstr. 4 ☎089 558 79 70, ⓦsmart-stay.de; U-Bahn to Goetheplatz. Welcoming hostel within spitting distance of the Oktoberfest grounds, a 15min walk south from the train station. Breakfast buffet and sheets included. Dorms €15, doubles €89

Smart Stay Hotel Station Schützenstr. 7 ☎089 552 52 10, ⓦsmart-stay.de. Good location between the station and the centre, overlooking a pedestrianized street with a terrace in summer. What this clean, basic hotel lacks in charm it makes up for in convenience. Buffet breakfast €6.90. Dorms €20, doubles €79

Wombat's Senefelderstr. 1 ☎089 59 98 91 80, ⓦwombats-hostels.com. Modern, lively and central, with a bright and warm winter garden and friendly staff. There's a great bar, too, with daily happy hours. Breakfast €4.50. Dorms €25, doubles €80

EATING

A good place to fuel up is the bustling Viktualienmarkt, which has an array of outdoor or stand-up eating options.

★**Andechser am Dom** Weinstr. 7a ⓦandechser-am-dom.de. Traditional place serving solid Bavarian food and beer from the Andechs monastic brewery. Mains €14.50 and a half-litre of Helles Bier €3.80. Daily 10am–1am.

Gesund & Köstlich Marienplatz 1 ⓦgesund-und-koestlich.de. The self-service canteen inside the courtyard of the Neues Rathaus has great-value, freshly cooked lunch deals (from €8) and a pay-by-weight buffet (from €1.50/100g). Mon–Fri 11am–6.30pm, Sat noon–4pm.

★**Guglhupf** Kaufingerstr. 5 ⓦcafe-guglhupf.de. This cosy café hidden in a courtyard off Kaufingstrasse is a good budget option. Great selection of salads for €8; schnitzel and chips €10.50 and *Apfelstrudel* with ice cream for €6.50. Mon–Sat 8am–7pm, Sun 10am–7pm.

Opatija Hochbrückenstr. 3 ⓦopatija-restaurant.com. This cosy Croatian and international restaurant serves grilled meat, schnitzel, pasta and pizza at low prices. Simple mains start at €7.50. Daily noon–10pm.

Prinz Myshkin Hackenstr. 2 ⓦprinzmyshkin.com. Excellent vegetarian and vegan restaurant serving filling international dishes, such as vegetable curry or chilli con tofu, beneath a high vaulted ceiling. Lunch special €7.50. Daily 11am–12.30am.

DRINKING AND NIGHTLIFE

The main focus for clubbers is the "Party Banana" semicircle on the inner ring road between Maximilianplatz and Sendlinger Tor. For listings check out the free magazine *In München* (in German).

Hofbräuhaus Platzl 9 ⓦhofbraeuhaus.de. The most famous and touristy of the beer halls, but beer and food prices are reasonable. *Mass* (1l beer) €8.40, fried sausage €7.90. Daily 9am–11.30pm.

Ratskeller Marienplatz 8 ☎089 219 98 90, ⓦ ratskeller.com. The labyrinthine cellar of the Neues Rathaus is always full. The food is hearty and good, everything from *Weisswurst* with bread (€6) to elegant seasonal dishes including game. Two-course lunch menu with drink €15. Daily 10am–1am.

Kilian's Irish Pub am Dom Frauenplatz 11 ⓦ kiliansirishpub.com. A popular expat watering hole, with Murphy's Guinness and Kilkenny on tap, massive hamburgers (€11–13) and live music nightly at 8pm. Mon–Thurs 4pm–1am, Fri & Sat 11am–2am, Sun noon–1am.

★**Rock Box** Hochbrückenstr. ⓦ rockboxbar.de. Lounge-club in a tiny, tried-and-tested venue full of young locals, all eager to practise their English on you. Cocktails from €6.50. DJs on Fri & Sat. Mon–Sat 3pm–late, Sun 7pm–late.

Weisses Bräuhaus Tal 7 ⓦ schneider-brauhaus.de. Famous for its Schneider *Weissbier* (€4.10) and cosier than the *Hofbräuhaus*. Try the traditional two-sausage breakfast for €2.70, or a roast pork dinner for €9.90. Daily 8am–12.30am.

GAY AND LESBIAN NIGHTLIFE

Munich has a lively and visible gay scene mostly south of the Sendlinger Tor.

NY Club Sonnenstr. 25 ⓦ nyclub.de. Munich's top gay club, with lush decor and a great sound system; international DJs play on Sat. Fri 10pm–late, Sat 11pm–late.

Prosecco Theklastr. 1 ⓦ prosecco-munich.de. Tiny bar that blends Alpine kitsch with every other variety of decorative excess. The music is a mix of *Schlager* (schmaltzy German pop) and Eurodisco hits. Thurs–Sat 10pm–late.

DIRECTORY

Consulates Canada, Tal 29 ☎089 219 95 70; South Africa, Sendlinger-Tor-Platz 5 ☎089 231 16 30; UK, Möhlstr. 5 ☎089 21 10 90; US, Königinstr. 5 ☎089 288 80.

OKTOBERFEST

The huge **Oktoberfest** (ⓦ oktoberfest .de), held on the Theresienwiese fairground for sixteen days following the penultimate Saturday in September, is an orgy of beer drinking spiced up by hairy fairground rides. The event began with a fair held to celebrate a Bavarian royal wedding in October 1810, and it proved so popular that it's been repeated ever since.

Hospital 24hr A&E at Rotkreuz Krankenhaus, Nymphenburger Str. 163 (☎089 13 030).

Pharmacy Bahnhofplatz 2, Mon–Fri 7am–8pm, Sat 8am–8pm. For 24hr pharmacies call ☎089 59 44 75.

Post office Bahnhofplatz 1 (Mon–Fri 8am–8pm, Sat 9am–4pm).

KZ-GEDENKSTÄTTE DACHAU

On the northern edge of Munich, the town of **Dachau** was the site of Germany's first **concentration camp** (daily 9am–5pm; free; English audioguide €3.50, students €2.50; maps free; ⓦ kz-gedenkstaette-dachau.de). Many original buildings still stand, including the crematorium and gas chamber; a replica hut gives an idea of the conditions prisoners endured. In the former maintenance building there's a sobering exhibition in English detailing the history of the camp, including graphic colour film shot at liberation. There's also a 22-minute documentary film in English shown five times daily (10am–3pm). Dachau's S-Bahn station is on line ⑤2 from the central station (20min); from the S-Bahn take bus #726 to the KZ-Gedenkstätte stop (Mon–Fri & peak time Sat every 20min, Sun every 40min).

THE BAVARIAN ALPS

It's amid picture-book mountain scenery that you'll find the classic Bavarian folklore and customs, and the **Bavarian Alps** encompass some of the most famous places in the province, such as the fantasy castle of **Neuschwanstein** and Hitler's **Eagle's Nest** near Berchtesgaden. Visit these hotspots outside the July and August peak season and you'll find the crowds less oppressive. Note that the popular resort of Berchtesgaden is more easily accessible from Salzburg (see p.77).

Neuschwanstein and Schloss Hohenschwangau

Lying between the Forggensee reservoir and the Ammer mountains, **FÜSSEN** and the adjacent town of **SCHWANGAU** are the bases for visiting Bavaria's two most popular castles. **Schloss Hohenschwangau** (obligatory guided tours daily: April–Sept

12

12

NEUSCHWANSTEIN AND HOHENSCHWANGAU TICKETS

Tickets for both castles must be bought at the **ticket centre** at Alpseestrasse 12, Hohenschwangau village. If you are visiting both castles, you can buy a **combination ticket** for €23.

5am–5pm; Oct–March 9am–4.30pm; €12; ⓦhohenschwangau.de), originally built in the twelfth century but heavily restored in the nineteenth, was where "Mad" King Ludwig II spent his youth. Ludwig's stamp is firmly imprinted on **Schloss Neuschwanstein** (guided tours daily: April–Sept 9am–6pm; Oct–March 10am–4pm; €12; ⓦneuschwanstein.de), the storybook castle which he had built on a crag overlooking Hohenschwangau. The inspiration for Disneyland's castle, it's an architectural hotchpotch with a stunning Byzantine throne hall. Still incomplete at Ludwig's death, it's a monument to a sad and lonely character.

ARRIVAL, INFORMATION AND TOURS

By train Take the train to Füssen (hourly from Munich; 2hr) and then bus #73 or #78 to Hohenschwangau.

Tourist information Füssen's tourist office, Kaiser-Maximilian-Platz 1 (Mon–Fri 9am–6pm, Sat 9.30am–1.30pm, Sun 9.30am–12.30pm; ☏083 629 38 50, ⓦfuessen.de), can book accommodation.

Tours Füssen is also the end of the Romantic Road from Würzburg via Augsburg (see box, p.405), served by tour buses in season. You can visit both of the area's castles in a day; get a Bayern-Ticket for €23, which allows unlimited transport in Bavaria until 3am next day, including city transport in Munich.

ACCOMMODATION

Old King's Hostel Franziskanergasse 2 ☏083 628 83 73 85, ⓦoldkingshostel.com. An intimate design hostel in a medieval building in the old town of Füssen, with individually styled rooms, tours, activities and bike rental. A 7min walk from the train station. Dorms €27, doubles €64

BERCHTESGADEN

Almost entirely surrounded by mountains at Bavaria's southeastern extremity, the area around **BERCHTESGADEN** has a magical atmosphere, especially in the mornings, when mists rise from the lakes and swirl around lush valleys and rocky mountainsides.

Unsurprisingly, Berchtesgaden has some great **mountain walks** to take you away from the summer crowds (the tourist office has maps). Its star attraction, however, is the stunning emerald **Königssee**, Germany's highest lake, which bends around the foot of the towering **Watzmann** mountain (2713m), 5km south of town – regular buses run out here – and there are lake **cruises** (April–Oct daily 9am–4.15pm; €16 return). The town is also home to an unexpected diversion, the **Salzbergwerk**, a historic salt mine that's been refurbished with an hour-long amusement-park-like ride/tour through its underground caverns (tours daily: May–Oct every 10min, 9am–5pm; Nov–April every 25min, 11am–3pm; €16.50; ⓦsalzbergwerk.de).

ARRIVAL AND INFORMATION

By bus and/or train From Munich you must change trains at Freilassing (1 hourly; 2hr 55min), so it's quicker and no more costly to take a direct Munich–Salzburg train (1–2 hourly; 1hr 30min), then take a direct bus from Salzburg to Berchtesgaden (hourly; 45min).

Tourist information The tourist office is in the town centre, Maximilianstr. 9 (Mon–Sat 9am–6pm, Sun 10am–1pm & 2–6pm; ☏086 52 94 45 300, ⓦberchtesgaden.de).

ACCOMMODATION

DJH Berchtesgaden Struberberg 6 ☏086 529 43 70, ⓦberchtesgaden.jugendherberge.de. Berchtesgaden's youth hostel is in the Strub district west of the town centre and has views of the Watzmann massif. Breakfast included. Dorms €22.40, doubles €50.80

HITLER'S HIDEOUT

Berchtesgaden is indelibly associated with **Adolf Hitler**, who rented a house in the nearby village of Obersalzberg, which he later enlarged into the **Berghof**, a stately retreat where he could meet foreign dignitaries. High above the village, Hitler's Kehlsteinhaus, or "**Eagle's Nest**", survives as a restaurant, and can be reached by bus and lift from Obersalzberg (mid-May to late-Oct daily 8.30am–4pm; €16.10 bus and lift return ticket; ⓦkehlsteinhaus.de).

Haus Achental Ramsauer Strasse 4 ☎086 52 45 49, ⓦgaestehaus-achental.de. A friendly alternative to the youth hostel, located close to the station, this is a large, typically Bavarian family hotel complete with hanging geraniums on balconies. Breakfast included. Doubles €60

REGENSBURG

The undisturbed medieval ensemble of central **REGENSBURG**, stunningly located on the banks of the Danube midway between Nuremberg and Munich, can easily be visited as a day-trip, but it makes a tempting overnight stop too. Getting lost in the web of cobbled medieval lanes with patrician palaces and towers, nursing a drink in one of the sunny squares or cycling along the Danube are the main draws here. It's also a university city, with a lively nightlife scene for its size.

WHAT TO SEE AND DO

A good place to start is the 336m-long, twelfth-century **Steinerne Brücke**, the only secured crossing along the entire length of the Danube at the time it was built. At the southern end of the bridge, a medieval salt barn houses the **World Heritage Exhibition** (daily 10am–7pm; free), which relates the history of the town via modern media installations. It's here that you purchase tickets to climb the adjoining **Brückturm** (same times; €2.50), the last survivor of the bridge's watchtowers, for excellent views of the old town and river. Just south, the Gothic Dom, **St Peter's** (daily: April, May & Oct 6.30am–6pm; June–Sept 6.30am–7pm; Nov–March 6.30am–5pm), begun in 1273, has some beautiful fourteenth-century stained-glass windows. Regensburg's medieval **Alte Rathaus** contains the magnificent fourteenth-century Gothic Reichssaal, which was, from 1663 to 1806, the fixed venue for the imperial Diet or Reichstag of the Holy Roman Empire. It can now be visited as part of the **Reichstagsmuseum** (guided tours in English daily: April–Oct 3pm; Nov, Dec & March 2pm; €7.50, students €4). There's also a prison and torture chamber in the basement. In the southern part of the Altstadt is **Schloss Thurn und Taxis** (guided tours in English July to mid-Sept daily 1.30pm; €13.50;

ⓦthurnundtaxis.de), one of the largest inhabited palaces in Europe, occupying the converted monastic buildings of the abbey of St Emmeram.

ARRIVAL AND INFORMATION

By train Maximilianstrasse leads straight from the train station north to the centre.
Destinations Munich (hourly; 1hr 33min); Nuremberg (hourly; 1hr); Vienna (every 2hr; 4hr).
Tourist information Tourist office at Rathausplatz 4 (April–Oct Mon–Fri 9am–6pm, Sat 9am–4pm, Sun 9.30am–4pm; Nov–March Mon–Fri 9am–6pm, Sat 9am–4pm, Sun 9.30am–2.30pm; ☎0941 507 44 10, ⓦregensburg.de) hands out free city maps.

GETTING AROUND

By bike Bike rental from Bikehaus, Bahnhofstr. 18 (Mon–Sat 10am–7pm, ☎0941 599 88 08; €13/24hr), on the left as you leave the Hauptbahnhof on the northern (Altstadt) side.

ACCOMMODATION

Brook Lane Hostel Obere Bachgasse 21 ☎094 16 90 09 66, ⓦhostel-regensburg.de. Independently run hostel in the Altstadt, with accommodation in snug dorms or spartan singles and doubles. Open 24hr. Dorms €16, doubles €50
Jugendherberge Regensburg Wöhrdstr. 60 ☎094 14 66 28 30, ⓦregensburg.jugendherberge.de. DJH youth hostel on an island in the Danube, within easy walking distance of the Altstadt. Breakfast included. Dorms €28

EATING AND DRINKING

Brauhaus am Schloss Waffnergasse 6 ⓦbrauhaus-am-schloss.com. The Thurn und Taxis' *Brauhaus*, with a copper microbrewery behind the bar, a shady beer garden and own-brew Helles, Marstall Dunkell and Braumeister Weisse beers. Light meals from €6, main courses from €10. Mon–Fri 11am–midnight, Sat & Sun 10am–midnight.
Dicker Mann Krebsgasse 6 ⓦdicker-mann.de. Vine-covered and candlelit café-restaurant on an alley off Haidplatz serving delicious, good-value meals, with breakfast from €4 and dinner specials from around €8. Daily 9.30am–1am.
★**Spitalgarten** St. Katharinenplatz 1 ⓦgarten.spital .de. Traditional brewhouse and *Biergarten* with 10 different beers and great city views from the northern end of the bridge. Schweinebraten €9, lighter meals around €6. Daily 10am–11pm.
Wurstkuchl Thundorfer Str. 3. Next to the Steinerne Brücke and looking like somewhere a hobbit might cook, this 500-year-old institution was originally the stonemasons' and dock workers' kitchen and has a menu dominated by delicious Regensburg sausages (plate of 6 €9). Daily 9am–7pm.

12

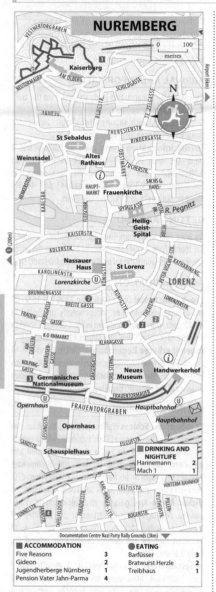

NUREMBERG

ACCOMMODATION		● EATING	
Five Reasons	3	Barfüsser	3
Gideon	2	Bratwurst Herzle	2
Jugendherberge Nürnberg	1	Treibhaus	1
Pension Vater Jahn-Parma	4		

■ DRINKING AND NIGHTLIFE	
Hannemann	2
Mach 1	1

Documentation Centre Nazi Party Rally Grounds (3km) ▼

NUREMBERG

In many minds, the medieval town of
NUREMBERG (Nürnberg) conjures up
images of the Nazi rallies, the 1935
"Nuremberg Laws" which deprived Jews
of their citizenship and forbade them
relations with Gentiles, and then the
war-crime trials. Yet all this infamy is a
world away from the friendly, bustling
city of today. Nuremberg's relaxed air
makes a day spent exploring its half-
timbered houses, fine museums and beer
halls hard to beat.

WHAT TO SEE AND DO

Meticulous postwar rebuilding means
you'd never guess that World War II
bombs reduced ninety percent of
Nuremberg's centre to rubble. The
reconstructed medieval core is
surrounded by ancient city walls and
neatly bisected by the River Pegnitz.
The most charming original streets lie
at the western end of the city centre.

The Kaiserburg

The **Kaiserburg** (imperial castle; guided
tours daily: April–Sept 9am–6pm;
Oct–March 10am–4pm; €7, students €6;
Palas and museum only €5.50, students
€4.50; tower and well only €3.50,
students €2.50), which forms the
northwest corner of the medieval
fortifications, was where Holy Roman
Emperors held their "Reichstag" or
imperial diet. Inside are the impressive
thirteenth-century **Palas** castle halls and
chapel, and the castle museum, while in
the courtyard are the **Tiefer Brunnen** –
the castle's 47m-deep well – and the
Sinwellturm tower for views of the city.

The Germanisches Nationalmuseum

The sprawling **Germanisches
Nationalmuseum**, Kartäusergasse 1
(Tues & Thurs–Sun 10am–6pm, Wed
10am–9pm; €8, students €5; ✆gnm.de),
presents the country's cultural history
through its large, important collection of
artefacts and art from German central
Europe, from the Bronze Age to the
present. Look out for the first globe,
made by Martin Behaim in 1492 – just
before Columbus "discovered" America.

The Fascination and Terror exhibition

The Nazi Party rallies were held on the
Zeppelin and March fields in the suburb
of Luitpoldhain. Here, the gargantuan
but never-completed Congress Hall
houses the **Documentation Centre Nazi**

Party Rally Grounds (Mon–Fri 9am–6pm, Sat & Sun 10am–6pm; €5, students €3; ⓦmuseen.nuernberg.de; tram #9 to Doku-Zentrum), an unmissable multimedia exhibition documenting the history and significance of the rally grounds, and the Nazis' ruthless misuse of propaganda and power.

ARRIVAL AND DEPARTURE

By plane The driverless U2 metro connects Nürnberg airport with the train station (every 10–12min; 13min).
By train The Hauptbahnhof is just outside the southern edge of the city walls; follow Königstrasse into the centre.
Destinations Berlin (every 30min–1hr 30min; 5hr); Frankfurt (every 30min–1hr; 2hr 10min); Munich (every 30min; 1hr 10min); Regensburg (hourly; 55min); Vienna (every 2hr; 4hr 40min).

INFORMATION

Tourist information At Königstrasse 93 opposite the Hauptbahnhof (Mon–Sat 9am–7pm, Sun 10am–4pm; ☏091 12 33 60, ⓦtourismus-nuernberg.de), plus smaller office at Hauptmarkt 18 (Mon–Sat 9am–6pm, Sun 10am–4pm).
Discount pass The Nürnberg Card (€25/2 days) includes public transport plus entrance to museums.

GETTING AROUND

By public transport There are S- and U-Bahn trains, trams and buses; a one-way trip costs €3, a 1-day (Mon–Fri) or 2-day weekend ticket costs €7.70.
By bike Nuremberg's NorisBike rental network (ⓦnorisbike.de) is linked to the Nextbike scheme, with dozens of rental points across the city.

ACCOMMODATION

Five Reasons Frauentormauer 42 ☏0911 99 28 66 25, ⓦfive-reasons.de. Neat and spacious new hostel and hotel with nicely designed communal spaces at the southern edge of the Altstadt. Dorms €18, doubles €69
Jugendherberge Nürnberg Burg 2 ☏091 12 30 93 60, ⓦkaiserstallung-nuernberg.de; ⓤ2 to Rathenauplatz, then bus #36 to Burgstrasse. The DJH hostel has a

---

wonderful location in the massive fifteenth-century imperial stables next to the Kaiserburg, overlooking the Altstadt, a 25min walk from the Hauptbahnhof. Dorms €31, doubles €87
Pension Vater Jahn-Parma Jahnstr. 13 ☏091 144 45 07, ⓦhotel-vaterjahn-parma.de. Immaculate and friendly guesthouse just south of the Opernhaus on the other side of the railway tracks, close to the Hauptbahnhof and Altstadt. Doubles €50

EATING AND DRINKING

There are plenty of snack stops in the pedestrian shopping zone and at the Hauptbahnhof; bars and cafés are scattered throughout the Altstadt.
Barfüsser Hallplatz 2. This popular beer hall in the cavernous cellars of the huge Mauthalle warehouse brews its own beer (€2.60) and serves good food. Daily specials from €8; six *Rostbratwurst* €7. Daily 11am–1am.
Bratwurst Herzle Brunnengasse 11. A bit less obviously tourist-oriented than other options, *Herzle* is a great place for sampling Nuremberg's mini-sausages. Six *Bratwürste* plus a dollop of potato salad will set you back just €7.70. Mon–Sat 11am–10pm.
Hannemann Johannesgasse 22. A cosy bar with retro decor and good vibes, just off Königstrasse. It serves craft beers, wine and long drinks from €7. Tues–Thurs 7pm–1am, Fri & Sat 7pm–2am.
Mach 1 Kaiserstr. 1–9 ⓦmacheins.club.de. Stylish club with a main floor that pumps out house and electro sounds, plus a futuristic tunnel and a more intimate lounge area. Fri & Sat 11pm–4am.
★ **Treibhaus** Karl-Grillenberger-Str. 28 ⓦcafetreibhaus.de. Refreshingly out of the way yet still in the Altstadt, (close to ⓤWeisser Turm) this hip café-bar serves from morning to night, with breakfasts from €5, pancakes and light meals from €6, and cocktails from €5. Mon–Wed 9am–1am, Thurs–Sat 9am–2am, Sun 9.30am–1am.

ROTHENBURG OB DER TAUBER

The Romantic Road (see box, p.405) winds its way along the length of western Bavaria, running through the most visited – and most beautiful – medieval town in Germany, **ROTHENBURG OB DER TAUBER**. In a fairytale location, it's besieged by tour groups during the day, so spend the night – or at least an evening – to appreciate it in relative peace.

WHAT TO SEE AND DO

The views of the surrounding countryside from the fourteenth-century town walls

---

12

★ **TREAT YOURSELF**

Gideon Königstrasse 45 ☏0911 660 09 70, ⓦgideonhotels.de. Modern and comfortable budget, boutique-style hotel with a rooftop terrace in the Altstadt, close to the train station. There's an excellent buffet breakfast (€10), too. Doubles €99

12

are magnificent, but Rothenburg's true charms lie among its medieval houses and cobbled streets.

Marktplatz and St Jakobs-Kirche

The focus of the Altstadt is the sloping **Marktplatz**, dominated by the arcaded front of the Renaissance Rathaus; the narrow, 60m tower of the **Altes Rathaus** (April–Oct daily 9.30am–12.30pm & 1–5pm; Nov & Jan–March Sat & Sun noon–3pm; Dec Mon–Thurs & Sun 10.30am–2pm & 2.30–6pm, Fri & Sat 10.30am–2pm & 2.30–8pm; €2) provides the best views. The other main attractions on the Marktplatz are the mechanical figures on the facade of the **Ratsherrntrinkstube**. Eight times a day these figures re-enact an episode in which former mayor Nusch allegedly saved Protestant Rothenburg from the wrath of Catholic General Tilly during the Thirty Years' War, by downing three litres of wine in one go. Northwest of the Marktplatz is the impressive Gothic **St Jakobs-Kirche** (daily: April–Oct 9am–5pm; Nov & Jan–March 10am–noon & 2–4pm; Dec 10am–4.45pm; €2), with the exquisite Heilig-Blut-Altar, a masterpiece of woodcarving by Tilman Riemenschneider, tucked away on an upper level.

The Mittelalterliches Kriminalmuseum

Of the local museums, the most interesting is the **Mittelalterliches**

Kriminalmuseum at Burggasse 3–5 (daily: Nov–March 1–4pm; April–Oct 10am–6pm; €7, students €4; ⓦ kriminalmuseum .eu), which contains collections of medieval torture instruments and related objects, such as the beer barrels that drunks were forced to walk around in.

ARRIVAL AND INFORMATION

By train From the station, a 10min walk east of the centre, head left on Bahnhofstr., then right on Ansbacherstr., which takes you straight through Röder city gate.
Destinations Würzburg (hourly; 1hr 10min).
Tourist information Tourist office in the Ratsherrntrinkstube on Marktplatz (May–Oct Mon–Fri 9am–6pm, Sat & Sun 10am–4pm; Nov–April Mon–Fri 9am–5pm, Sat 10am–1pm; ☏ 09861 404 800, ⓦ rothenburg.de).

ACCOMMODATION AND EATING

DJH Mühlacker 1 ☏ 098 619 41 60, ⓦ rothenburg .jugendherberge.de. A short walk from the train station and the town centre, this hostel is housed in two beautifully restored buildings and a modern annexe off the bottom of Spitalgasse. Dorms €23
Gästehaus Raidel Wenggasse 3 ☏ 098 61 31 15, ⓦ gaestehaus-raidel.de. Located in a wonderfully creaky 600-year-old building, this guesthouse oozes character, with lots of antiques and a feeling of yesteryear. Doubles €69
Roter Hahn Obere Schmiedgasse 21 ☏ 098 61 97 40 ⓦ roterhahn.com. Franconian regional specialities are served up in the historic setting of a fourteenth-century inn, with main courses from €12. Daily 11am–11pm. Doubles €89

QUIRAING, ISLE OF SKYE

Great Britain

HIGHLIGHTS

❶ **The British Museum** Arguably the world's finest museum. **See p.424**

❷ **Bath** Regency and Roman splendour in England's most beautiful city. **See p.443**

❸ **York** Medieval city bursting with bars and bistros. **See p.467**

❹ **Hiking Wales** Dream-like hikes from the Brecon Beacons to Snowdonia. **See p.476 & p.478**

❺ **Edinburgh Festival** The world's biggest arts festival. **See p.481**

❻ **Scotland's islands** Otherworldly landscapes and wonderful hospitality. **See p.493**

HIGHLIGHTS ARE MARKED ON THE MAP ON P.417

ROUGH COSTS

Daily budget Basic €60, occasional treat €85

Drink Lager €5

Food Fish and chips €11

Hostel/budget hotel €27/€80–100

Travel Train: London–Brighton €25–35; bus: London–Manchester €10–40

FACT FILE

Population 64 million (includes Northern Ireland)

Language English

Currency Pound sterling (£)

Capital London

International phone code ☎44

Time zone GMT

13

Introduction

A famous British newspaper headline in the 1950s declared: "Fog in Channel, Continent Cut Off". Britain's outlook on the world has always been unique, born of its status as an island nation on the western edge of Europe. And yet within this compact territory there's not just one country but three – England, Wales and Scotland – and a multitude of cultural identities: God forbid you should call a Scot or a Welshman English.

London, the capital, is the one place that features on everyone's itinerary. **Brighton** and **Canterbury** offer contrasting diversions – the former a lively seaside resort, the latter one of Britain's finest medieval cities. The southwest of England holds the rugged moorlands of **Devon**, the rocky coastline of **Cornwall**, and the historic spa city of **Bath**, while the chief attractions of central England are the university cities of **Oxford** and **Cambridge**, and Shakespeare's home town **Stratford-upon-Avon**. Further north, the former industrial cities of **Manchester**, **Liverpool** and **Newcastle** are lively, rejuvenated places, and **York** has splendid historical treasures, but the landscape, especially the uplands of the Lake District, is the biggest magnet. For true wilderness, head to the **Welsh mountains** or **Scottish Highlands**. The finest of Scotland's lochs, glens and peaks, and the magnificent scenery of the West Coast islands, can be reached easily from **Glasgow** and **Edinburgh** – the latter perhaps Britain's most attractive urban landscape.

CHRONOLOGY

54 BC The Romans attack Britannia but are forced back until a successful invasion in 43 AD.

1066 AD Duke William II of Normandy defeats the last Anglo-Saxon ruler, King Harold II, at the Battle of Hastings.

1215 The Magna Carta forms the basis upon which English law is built.

1301 Edward I conquers Wales, giving his heir the title Prince of Wales.

1534 Henry VIII breaks with the Catholic Church. The Head of State becomes Head of the Church of England.

1603 King James VI of Scotland also becomes James I of England in the Union of the Crowns.

1653–58 A brief period of republicanism under Oliver Cromwell, following the English Civil War.

1707 The Act of Union unites the parliaments of Scotland and England, with the addition of Ireland in 1800.

1800s The Industrial Revolution helps Britain to expand her empire and become a dominant world force.

1914–18 Britain fights in World War I.

1928 Women attain full suffrage after a hard-fought campaign.

1939–45 Britain fights in World War II. London and other major centres are heavily bombed during the Blitz.

1947 Indian independence from British rule heralds the gradual demise of the British Empire.

1960s The Beatles sing their way through the swinging sixties.

1979 Margaret Thatcher becomes Britain's first female prime minister.

1998 Devolution in Scotland and Wales.

2005 On July 7 London is rocked by terrorist bombings, leaving 52 dead.

2012 London hosts the Olympics.

2016 The UK holds a referendum and narrowly votes to leave the European Union.

"**Great Britain**", or just "Britain", is a geographical term encompassing England, Scotland and Wales, including their islands. However, it can also be used politically, in the context of central government, "British" nationals, or for national teams at sporting events such as the Olympics, in which case it includes Northern Ireland. "**United Kingdom**" is a political term, referring to the sovereign state of England, Scotland, Wales and Northern Ireland. In this guide Northern Ireland is covered with the rest of the island in the Ireland chapter.

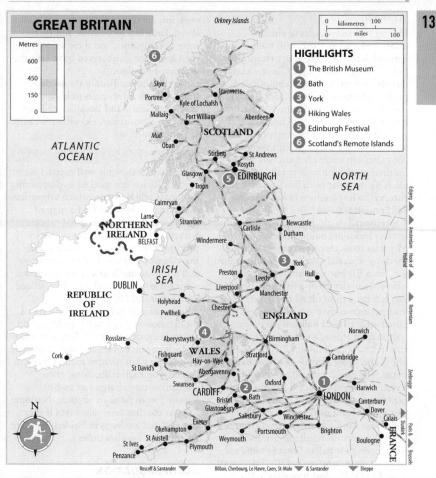

GREAT BRITAIN

Metres
600
450
150
0

Orkney Islands

0 — kilometres — 100
0 — miles — 100

HIGHLIGHTS

1. The British Museum
2. Bath
3. York
4. Hiking Wales
5. Edinburgh Festival
6. Scotland's Remote Islands

Skye
Portree
Mallaig
Mull
Oban
Kyle of Lochalsh
Fort William
Inverness
Aberdeen
SCOTLAND

ATLANTIC
OCEAN

Stirling
Glasgow
Troon
Rosyth
St Andrews
EDINBURGH

NORTH
SEA

Cairnryan
Larne
**NORTHERN
IRELAND**
BELFAST
Stranraer
Carlisle
Newcastle
Durham
Windermere

*IRISH
SEA*

DUBLIN
Holyhead
Pwllheli
Chester
Preston
Leeds
Liverpool
Manchester
York
Hull

**REPUBLIC
OF
IRELAND**

Rosslare
Cork
Fishguard
St David's
Aberystwyth
WALES
Hay-on-Wye
Abergavenny
Swansea
CARDIFF
Bristol
Glastonbury
Okehampton
St Austell
St Ives
Penzance
Plymouth
Exeter
Weymouth
Bath
Salisbury
Winchester
Portsmouth
Stratford
Oxford
ENGLAND
Birmingham
Cambridge
LONDON
Harwich
Canterbury
Dover
Calais
Brighton
Boulogne
Norwich
Weymouth

FRANCE

N

Esbjerg ▶
Amsterdam ▶
Hook of Holland ▶
Rotterdam ▶
Zeebrugge ▶
Dunkirk ▶
Paris & Brussels ▶

Roscoff & Santander ▼   Bilbao, Cherbourg, Le Havre, Caen, St-Malo ▼   & Santander ▼   Dieppe ▼

ARRIVAL AND DEPARTURE

If you're travelling from outside mainland Europe or Ireland, you're most likely to arrive by **plane**. Long-haul flights land at a range of destinations throughout the UK, including Manchester, Edinburgh and Glasgow, though most air passengers still find themselves passing through London's main airports – Gatwick, Heathrow, Stansted and Luton – the latter two the principal hubs of no-frills carriers like Ryanair and easyJet, which also operate out of smaller regional airports around the country and provide many internal flights.

Greener alternatives for getting to Britain from mainland Europe include the high-speed **Eurostar** train (ⓦeurostar.com) from Paris or Brussels to St Pancras International in London, Eurolines **buses** (ⓦeurolines.co.uk), and **ferries**, with boats from Ireland, France, Belgium, the Netherlands, Denmark and Spain docking at ports across the UK.

GETTING AROUND

Most places are accessible by train and/ or coach, though costs are among the highest in Europe: check **Traveline** (ⓣ0871 200 2233, ⓦtraveline.org.uk) for advice on trains, coaches, ferries and, most usefully, local buses.

13

BY TRAIN

Having suffered decades of chronic under-investment, the British **train** network is slowly beginning to improve, though **fares** remain high. Cheap tickets do exist, but the bafflingly complicated pricing system makes them hard to find, and they can only be obtained (sometimes far) in advance. Avoid rush hours, and if you're booking online be prepared to make several attempts – trying again even an hour later can make cheap tickets appear (or disappear) seemingly at random, while often it's the same price (and occasionally cheaper) to buy a return ticket. **National Rail Enquiries** (☎0845 748 4950, ⓦnationalrail.co.uk) has details of all train services including online booking. Megabus (ⓦuk.megabus.com) is worth checking separately as they run Megatrains too, from £1, but with limited routes.

If you're under 26 or a full-time student, you can get a third off all rail tickets (except some early-morning services) by purchasing a **16–25 Railcard** from any train station (though not at Heathrow airport), or apply online. You'll need a photo and proof of your age or student status. The card costs £30 and is valid for a year. Adding the railcard to your Oyster card (see box, p.430) in London also gets you a 34 percent discount on off-peak daily price caps. European travellers (excluding British residents) are also eligible for an **InterRail Great Britain Pass** (ⓦinterrailnet.com; see p.430). Prices start from £118/£157 for three days' train travel in one month for under/over-25s.

BY BUS

Long-distance buses are referred to as **coaches** in Britain. Services between cities are frequent and cheaper than trains, though long journeys take considerably longer: **National Express** (☎08717 818178, ⓦnationalexpress.com) serve the most routes. If you are student or under 26 you can buy a National Express Coachcard (£10), which gives up to thirty percent off standard fares, or their BritXplorer Pass offering unlimited travel for £79 for seven days, £139 for two weeks and £219 for 28 days for all ages. **Megabus** (ⓦuk.megabus .com) is generally the cheapest coach

operator; the cheap seats go fast, so book ahead. **Local bus services** are run by an array of companies, and there are very few rural areas that aren't served by at least the occasional minibus.

You can also see Britain via **guided tours**; Haggis Adventures (ⓦhaggis adventures.com) and Backpacker Tours (ⓦbackpackertours.co.uk) offer a wealth of budget options.

BY BIKE

Cyclists are reasonably well catered for in Britain. Routes are marked as part of the **National Cycle Network**, which crisscrosses the country – you can find a map of them all at ⓦcyclestreets.net. Ordnance Survey Landranger maps, available in tourist offices and outdoor shops, also mark some routes, as well as footpaths and minor roads. Many cities now have some **cycle lanes**, which are often shared with buses and taxis.

Bikes can generally be taken on **trains**, though not on all London underground trains (see ⓦtfl.gov.uk for details of when and where you can take a bike), and there is usually a limit on how many bikes can be taken on each train. Some train companies may charge you and/or require you to book in advance. National Express **coaches** only take bikes if they can fold and are bagged. Folded bikes are accepted on London buses.

ACCOMMODATION

Accommodation in Britain is expensive and it's a good idea to reserve in advance. Britain has an extensive network of **HI hostels** operated by the Youth Hostel Association (ⓦyha.org.uk for England and Wales; ⓦsyha.org.uk for Scotland). A bed for the night with YHA can cost as little as £13, but in cities expect to pay up to £29. YHA membership (£15/year) will save you £3 per night. Most places of interest also have at least one **independent hostel**, which will generally be of a comparable standard and price but often more centrally located.

In tourist cities it's hard to find a double room in a **hotel** for less than £70 a night, though there are a few cheaper chain hotels, which offer special deals: Premier Inn (ⓦpremierinn.com) sometimes offer identikit rooms from £29, while Travelodge (ⓦtravelodge.co.uk) can be as low as £25 per room. EasyHotel (ⓦeasyhotel.com) have small rooms decked out in their signature orange; London rooms start at £31, Edinburgh rooms from £28. A nicer option for budget accommodation, and often cheaper outside London (particularly if you're on your own), are **guesthouses** and **B&Bs** – usually a comfortable room in a family home, plus a substantial breakfast – starting at around £30 a head: tourist offices often have a list of nearby accredited B&Bs. Airbnb (ⓦairbnb.com), too, is an excellent way of staying with locals – it tends to be cheaper than a regular B&B and is widespread across the country.

There are more than 750 official **campsites** in Britain, charging from around £6 per person. Camping wild in England and Wales requires the landowner's permission, while in Scotland it is mostly legal as long as you're unobtrusive and leave the site as you found it.

FOOD AND DRINK

Long lampooned as a culinary wasteland, Britain has seen a transformation in both the quality and variety of its restaurants over the past two decades. **Modern British cuisine** – in effect anything inventive – has been at the core of this change, though wherever you go you'll find places serving Indian, Italian and Chinese food, and often plenty of other international cuisines. If you're on a tight budget, the temptation is still to head for the nearest fast-food joint or one of the ubiquitous sandwich chains, but with a little effort, alternatives can easily be found, with even higher-end establishments often offering reasonably priced lunchtime or early-evening deals.

Wherever you stay you'll almost certainly be offered an "**English breakfast**" – basically eggs, bacon, sausage, and any combination of fried or grilled sides such as tomatoes, mushrooms, black pudding, bread and baked beans; you'll also be given the option of cereal, toast and fruit. Every major town will have upmarket restaurants and so-called **gastropubs** serving daintily

presented cuisine, but traditional British cooking – the mainstay of pub food – is hearty and filling. Typical dishes include the quintessential fish and chips, steak and kidney pie, shepherd's pie (minced lamb topped with mashed potato), and – mainly on Sundays – roast dinners, served with roast potatoes, veg and (particularly with beef) Yorkshire pudding, made from savoury batter. Britain is one of Europe's better countries for **vegetarians**, and wherever you eat there'll always be at least one veggie choice.

DRINK

Drinking traditionally takes place in the **pub**, where you can buy draught beer (sold by the pint or half-pint), wine, bottled beer and spirits. Despite the popularity of cold, fizzy lager, traditional British beer, known as real ale or bitter, is undergoing something of a renaissance; richer and often darker than lager, and served at cellar temperature rather than chilled, it comes in thousands of varieties. In England pubs are generally open Monday to Saturday from 11am to 11pm, and on Sunday from noon to 10.30pm (though many places may open longer at weekends); hours are often longer in Scotland, while Sunday closing is common in Wales.

In Scotland, the national drink is **whisky**. The best – and most expensive – are single malts, best drunk neat or with a splash of water to release the flavour.

CULTURE AND ETIQUETTE

Famed for their stiff upper lip and polite reticence, the British tend to be more reserved than many of their continental counterparts. Possibly the most cosmopolitan place in Europe – in the larger cities anyway – Britain has developed a reputation for liberal tolerance and benefits from a diverse range of faiths, creeds and colours.

Tipping is expected (if not mandatory) in restaurants; around ten percent of the total is the norm. Technically this is optional, though you will be frowned at if you ask for it to be removed. It is not necessary to tip bar staff at bars and pubs.

13

SPORTS AND OUTDOOR ACTIVITIES

Football (soccer) is a British obsession. "The beautiful game" was codified here in 1863, and seeing a match is a must for any sports fan, though it can be extremely difficult and costly to acquire tickets for Premier League games. you'll have more luck with lower-league clubs, such as Fulham, in London (wfulhamfc.com). **Rugby** and **cricket**, though popular, do not generally inspire the same fervent tribalism as football, and consequently can offer a more relaxed spectator experience. You can turn up and buy tickets on the day for domestic matches at Lord's cricket ground in London (wlords.org) during the season (April–Sept). Tennis fans make a beeline for the world-famous championships at **Wimbledon** (wwimbledon.com): it's not cheap and tickets are very difficult to come by, but if you are prepared to queue, you can see some great matches on the outside courts for around £25.

Britain's diverse geography and geology, with access to large bodies of fresh and salt water, mean that venues for **outdoor pursuits** are easily accessible. **Walking** is one of the finest ways to see the country, and an excellent infrastructure of long-distance footpaths crisscrosses Britain (wwalkingbritain.co.uk). The uplands of Wales (wvisitwales.co.uk /active), Scotland (wactive.visitscotland .com) and the English Lake District (wgolakes.co.uk) are particularly good for hiking, climbing and watersports, while Devon and Cornwall (wvisitsouthwest .co.uk) have the best **surfing** in the UK.

COMMUNICATIONS

Wi-fi is ubiquitous, and free access is offered at most accommodation, including hostels. **Post offices** open Monday to Friday 9am to 5.30pm, and some open on Saturday 9am to noon. Of the few remaining **public phones**, most take phonecards, which can be bought from post offices and newsagents, or credit cards. For the **operator**, call ☎100 (domestic) or 155 (international). Increasingly, European mobile phones can be used in the UK at no extra charge (including data packages).

EMERGENCIES

Tourists aren't a particular target for criminals except in crowds in big cities, where you should be on your guard against **pickpockets**. Britain's bigger conurbations all contain areas where you may feel uneasy after dark, but these are usually away from tourist sights.

For health complaints that require immediate attention, go to the **emergency** department of the local hospital (known as A&E). These are run by the **National Health Service** (NHS; wnhs.uk to find your nearest) and will be free at the time of treatment, though depending on your country (some have mutual agreements with Britain) you may get billed later. For minor injuries you can also use NHS **walk-in clinics**. **Pharmacies** dispense only a limited range of drugs without a doctor's prescription. Most are open standard shop hours, though in large towns there may be ones that stay open late or even 24hr.

INFORMATION

Tourist offices exist in virtually every British town, offering information and a basic range of maps. **National parks** (wnationalparks.gov.uk) also have their own information centres, which are better for guidance on outdoor pursuits. The most comprehensive series of **maps** is produced by the **Ordnance Survey** (wordnancesurvey.co.uk) – essential if you're planning serious hiking.

BRITAIN ONLINE

w**visitbritain.com** Official tourist board site with links to regional sites.
w**streetmap.co.uk** Detailed UK street maps.

EMERGENCY NUMBERS

Police, fire and ambulance ☎999 or 112.

MONEY AND BANKS

The **pound sterling** (£), divided into 100 pence, remains the national currency. There are coins of 1p, 2p, 5p, 10p, 20p, 50p, £1 and £2; and notes of £5, £10, £20 and £50; notes issued by Scottish banks are legal tender but sometimes not accepted south of the border. At the time of writing, £1 was worth €1.20 and $1.47. Normal **banking hours** are Monday to Friday 9.30am to 5pm, though some branches also open on Saturday mornings. **ATMs** accept a wide range of debit and credit cards: freestanding ATMs usually charge around £2 to take money out on top of your bank charges, so use one attached to a bank. Shops, hotels, restaurants and most other places readily accept **credit cards** for payment.

OPENING HOURS AND HOLIDAYS

General **shop hours** are Monday to Saturday 9am to 5.30/6pm, although many places in big towns are also open Sunday (usually 11am–5pm in England and Wales, longer in Scotland) and until 7/8pm – or later – at least once a week, often on a Thursday. **Public holidays** are: January 1, January 2 (Scotland only), Good Friday, Easter Monday (not Scotland), first Monday and last Monday in May, last Monday in August, St Andrew's Day (Nov 30, or nearest Mon if weekend; Scotland only), Christmas Day and Boxing Day (Dec 25 & 26) – though in practice it's only on January 1, January 2 (Scotland only) and Christmas Day that everything shuts down; on other holidays, many shops in larger towns and cities – as well as nearly all sights – remain open.

London

With a population of around 8.5 million, **LONDON** sprawls over an area of more than 600 square miles either side of the River Thames. The city exudes an undeniable buzz of success; it is where the country's news, art and money are made, the pace of life is fast and there's always something new and exciting happening.

Living costs are high here – accommodation and transport are among the most expensive in the world – but Londoners put up with this precisely because there is just so much to see and do here, much of it free.

Skip exorbitantly priced palaces in favour of London's (mostly free) world-class museums and galleries, and be sure to visit at least a couple of the outdoor spaces; London is one of the world's greenest cities, with many parks, cemeteries and canals to explore. London's famous department stores and offbeat weekend **markets** offer limitless **shopping**, while its cultural scene caters for all tastes and budgets, churning out everything from epic theatre productions to experimental live music. London's multicultural society means that there is an unparalleled variety of cuisine, too, often very affordable.

WHAT TO SEE AND DO

The majority of sights are north of the **River Thames**, and a good place to start is the political and regal centre; the area around Whitehall, with **Trafalgar Square** at one end, **Parliament Square** at the other and **Buckingham Palace** off to the side.

Trafalgar Square and the National Gallery

Trafalgar Square's focal point is **Nelson's Column**, featuring the one-eyed admiral who died defeating the French at the 1805 Battle of Trafalgar. Extending across the north side of the square is the **National Gallery** (daily 10am–6pm, Fri till 9pm; free; ⊚nationalgallery.org.uk), one of the world's great art collections. Masterpieces include paintings by Raphael, Michelangelo, Da Vinci and Rembrandt, along with Van Gogh's *Sunflowers* and Seurat's *Bathers at Asnières*. Round the side of the National Gallery, in St Martin's Place, is the fascinating **National Portrait Gallery** (daily 10am–6pm, Thurs & Fri till 9pm; free; ⊚npg.org.uk), which houses images of the great and good, from Hans Holbein's larger-than-life drawing of Henry VIII to Sam Taylor-Wood's video portrait of David Beckham.

13

13

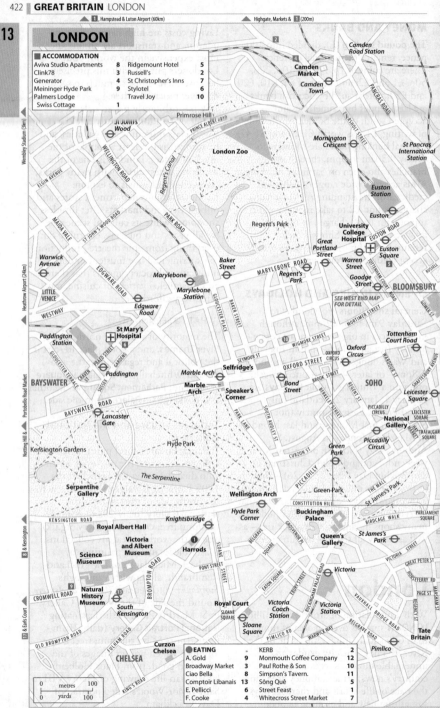

LONDON

■ ACCOMMODATION

Aviva Studio Apartments	8	Ridgemount Hotel	5
Clink78	3	Russell's	2
Generator	4	St Christopher's Inns	7
Meininger Hyde Park	9	Stylotel	6
Palmers Lodge		Travel Joy	10
Swiss Cottage	1		

Camden Road Station

Camden Market

Camden Town

St John's Wood

Primrose Hill

PRINCE ALBERT ROAD

London Zoo

Regent's Canal

Mornington Crescent

St Pancras International Station

Euston Station

Euston

Regent's Park

PARK ROAD

University College Hospital

Great Portland Street

Warren Street

Euston Square

Baker Street

MARYLEBONE ROAD

Regent's Park

Goodge Street

BLOOMSBURY

Marylebone

Marylebone Station

SEE WEST END MAP FOR DETAIL

Warwick Avenue

LITTLE VENICE

WESTWAY

Edgware Road

St Mary's Hospital

MORTIMER STREET

Tottenham Court Road

Paddington Station

Paddington

SEYMOUR ST

Marble Arch

Selfridge's

OXFORD STREET

Oxford Circus

Oxford Circus

SOHO

BAYSWATER

BAYSWATER ROAD

Marble Arch

Speaker's Corner

Bond Street

Leicester Square

Lancaster Gate

National Gallery

Kensington Gardens

Hyde Park

PARK LANE

PICCADILLY CIRCUS

Piccadilly Circus

TRAFALGAR SQUARE

The Serpentine

Green Park

Serpentine Gallery

Wellington Arch

CONSTITUTION HILL

Green Park

St James's Park

KENSINGTON ROAD

Hyde Park Corner

Buckingham Palace

PARLIAMENT SQUARE

Royal Albert Hall

Knightsbridge

Queen's Gallery

St James's Park

Victoria and Albert Museum

1 Harrods

Victoria

Science Museum

PONT STREET

Natural History Museum

South Kensington

Royal Court

Victoria Coach Station

Victoria Station

Tate Britain

CROMWELL ROAD

Sloane Square

OLD BROMPTON ROAD

Curzon Chelsea

Pimlico

CHELSEA

KING'S ROAD

●EATING

A. Gold	9	KERB	2
Broadway Market	3	Monmouth Coffee Company	12
Ciao Bella	8	Paul Rothe & Son	10
Comptoir Libanais	13	Simpson's Tavern.	11
E. Pellicci	6	Sông Quê	5
F. Cooke	4	Street Feast	1
		Whitecross Street Market	7

0	metres	100
0	yards	100

13

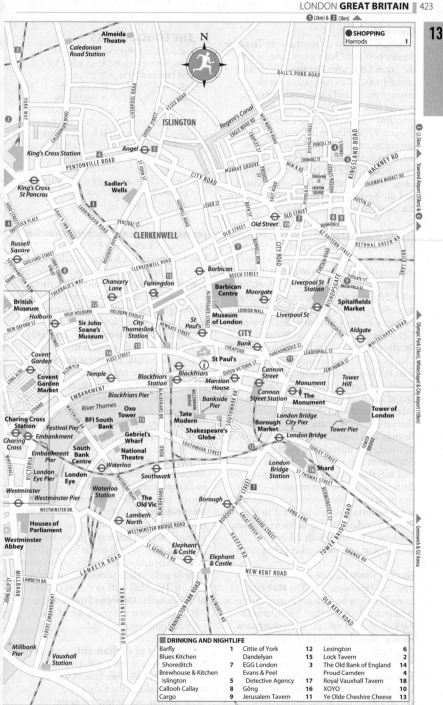

● **SHOPPING**

Harrods 1

❸ (2.5km) ►

Stansted Airport (55km) & ❻ ►

Olympic Park (3km), Whitechapel & City Airport (10km) ►

N

BALL'S POND ROAD

YORK WAY

Almeida Theatre

Caledonian Road Station

CALEDONIAN ROAD

❸

❷

LIVERPOOL ROAD

ESSEX ROAD

ISLINGTON

Regent's Canal

EAGLE WHARF RD

NEW NORTH ROAD

PACKLES ST

PURCELL ST

PITFIELD STREET

❹

PURCELL ST

LYMPUS

HACKNEY RD

KINGSLAND ROAD

UPPER STREET

King's Cross Station

Angel ⊖ ❺

ST JOHN ST

PENTONVILLE ROAD

MURRAY GROOVE

PREVOST ST

CRONDALL ST

❺

NEW N RD

FANSHAW ST

COLUMBIA MARKET RD

AUSTIN ST

Sadler's Wells

FARRINGDON ROAD

GOSWELL ROAD

CITY ROAD

HOXTON ST

HOXTON SQUARE

King's Cross St Pancras

❸

LEVER ST

BATH ST

OLD STREET

PITFIELD ST

ESSEX RD

JUDD STREET

GRAY'S INN ROAD

PERCIVAL ST

Old Street ⊖ ❿

OLD STREET

❼

❽ ❾

RIVINGTON ST

GT EASTERN STREET

BRICK LANE

TAVISTOCK PLACE

THEOBALD'S WAY

CLERKENWELL

CLERKENWELL ROAD

BUNHILL ROW

CITY ROAD

CURTAIN ROAD

BETHNAL GREEN RD

Russell Square

GUILFORD STREET

SOUTHAMPTON ROW

LAMB'S CONDUIT STREET

ROSEBERY AVENUE

Barbican ⊖

BEECH STREET

Liverpool St Station

BISHOPSGATE

TOLGATE ST

BRUSH FIELD ST

Chancery Lane ⊖

Farringdon ⊖

❶❶

Barbican Centre

Moorgate ⊖

Spitalfields Market

GRAY'S INN ROAD

HIGH HOLBORN

❶❷

HOLBORN VIADUCT

ALDERSGATE STREET

LONDON WALL

Liverpool St ⊖

HOUNDSDITCH

British Museum

Holborn ⊖

Sir John Soane's Museum

City Thameslink Station

St Paul's ⊖

Museum of London

CITY

Aldgate ⊖

WHITECHAPEL ROAD

NEW OXFORD ST

KINGSWAY

❶❸

NEWGATE STREET

CHEAPSIDE

Bank ⊖

THREADNEEDLE ST

LEADENHALL ST

FENCHURCH ST

Covent Garden ⊖

FLEET STREET

❶❹

St Paul's ⓘ

QUEEN VICTORIA ST

❶❶

Tower Hill ⊖

Covent Garden Market

Temple ⊖

Blackfriars ⊖

Cannon Street ⊖

Monument ⊖

ALDWYCH

LONG ACRE

STRAND

Blackfriars Station

Mansion House ⊖

Cannon Street Station

The Monument

Tower of London

EMBANKMENT

Blackfriars Pier

MILLENNIUM BRIDGE

BLACKFRIARS BR

Bankside Pier

SOUTHWARK BR

London Bridge City Pier

Tower Pier

TOWER BRIDGE

Charing Cross Station

WATERLOO BRIDGE

River Thames

Oxo Tower

Tate Modern

Borough Market

London Bridge

Festival Pier

BFI South Bank

Shakespeare's Globe

TOOLEY STREET

Charing Cross ⊖

Embankment ⊖

Gabriel's Wharf

SOUTHWARK ST

❶❷

London Bridge Station

ST THOMAS STREET

Shard ❶❻

WHITEHALL

Embankment Pier

South Bank Centre

National Theatre

SOUTHWARK STREET

VICTORIA EMB

Waterloo ⊖

Southwark ⊖

BERMONDSEY ST

London Eye Pier

London Eye

BLACKFRIARS ROAD

LONG LANE

TOWER BRIDGE ROAD

Westminster ⊖

Westminster Pier

Waterloo Station

The Old Vic

Borough ⊖

TABARD STREET

GREAT DOVER ST

GRANGE RD

WESTMINSTER BR.

WATERLOO ROAD

Lambeth North ⊖

Houses of Parliament

WESTMINSTER BRIDGE ROAD

BOROUGH HIGH STREET

HARPER RD

Greenwich & O2 Arena ►

Westminster Abbey

LAMBETH ROAD

ST GEORGE'S RD

Elephant & Castle ⊖

Elephant & Castle

NEW KENT ROAD

OLD KENT ROAD

MILLBANK

ALBERT EMBANKMENT

LAMBETH BR.

KENNINGTON ROAD

KENNINGTON PARK ROAD

WALWORTH RD

Millbank Pier

Vauxhall Station

VAUXHALL ST

■ **DRINKING AND NIGHTLIFE**

Barfly	1	Cittie of York	12
Blues Kitchen		Dandelyan	15
Shoreditch	7	EGG London	3
Brewhouse & Kitchen		Evans & Peel	
Islington	5	Detective Agency	17
Calloon Callay	8	Gŏng	16
Cargo	9	Jerusalem Tavern	11

Lexington	6
Lock Tavern	2
The Old Bank of England	14
Proud Camden	4
Royal Vauxhall Tavern	18
XOYO	10
Ye Olde Cheshire Cheese	13

▼ ❶❻ (100m)

13

Covent Garden

A minute or so's walk northeast of Trafalgar Square between Shaftesbury Avenue and the Strand is **Covent Garden**, a lively area centred around an early seventeenth-century piazza and nineteenth-century market hall, which housed the city's principal fruit and vegetable market until the late 1970s. The structure is now full of boutiques, stalls and quirky, arty shops, while buskers perform in front of Inigo Jones's classical **St Paul's Church**. Across Long Acre from the station is **Neal Street** and the **Seven Dials**, both lined with shops, bars and restaurants.

The British Museum

A short walk from the northern end of Neal Street near Holborn tube station is the magnificent **British Museum**, Great Russell Street (daily 10am–5.30pm, Fri till 8.30pm; free; ⓦbritishmuseum.org), one of the world's great museums. Inside, Norman Foster's glass-and-steel covered Great Court surrounds the **Round Reading Room**, where Karl Marx penned *Das Kapital*. The museum houses some four million exhibits from around the world, with gems such as the Easter Island moai, an exceptional, turquoise-inlaid Aztec skull, Chinese porcelain and Britain's own Neolithic remains. The Roman and Greek antiquities are second to none, and include the **Parthenon Sculptures** – taken by Lord Elgin in 1801 and still the cause of discord between the British and Greek governments – while the museum's other most famous exhibit is the **Rosetta Stone**, which led to the modern understanding of hieroglyphics. High-profile exhibitions take place throughout the year (ticket prices vary).

Buckingham Palace

The tree-lined sweep of **The Mall** runs from Trafalgar Square southwest through Admiralty Arch, flanked by **St James's Park** on the left and on to **Buckingham Palace** (State Rooms daily: late July to Aug 9.15am–7.45pm, last admission 5.15pm; Sept 9.15am–6.45pm, last admission 4.15pm; adult/student £21.50/19.60; ⓦroyalcollection.org.uk), which has served as the monarch's

THE LONDON PASS

Many of London's major attractions come with whopping entry costs, so **The London Pass** (1/2/3/6-day £59/79/95/129; ⓦlondonpass.com) may save you money. It provides free entrance to around 60 sights, including major attractions like London Zoo, the Tower of London and St Paul's Cathedral, as well as allowing you fast-track entrance and giving extras like audioguides at galleries, and a free bus tour and river cruise. It can also be used as an Oyster card (see box, p.430) by adding the public transport option.

permanent residence since the accession of Queen Victoria in 1837. The building's exterior, last remodelled in 1913, is pretty bland, but it's actually the rear of the Palace: the much finer front overlooks the monarch's garden. When Buckingham Palace is closed, many mill about outside the gates to catch the **Changing of the Guard** (April–July daily at 11.30am), while over on the other side of St James's Park, the **Horse Guards** stage a more elaborate equestrian ceremony (Mon–Sat at 11am, Sun 10am). From Buckingham Palace you can retrace your steps to go down Whitehall towards Westminster, or head west through Green Park to Hyde Park Corner.

Whitehall and Westminster

Whitehall, flanked by government buildings, leads off south from Trafalgar Square towards the area known as **Westminster**, the country's political seat of power for nearly 1000 years. The original White Hall was a palace built for King Henry VIII, but a fire in 1698 meant subsequent monarchs had to move to St James's Palace (closed to the public), just off The Mall. Off to the west side of Whitehall is **Downing Street**, where No. 10 has been the residence of the prime minister since 1732.

The Houses of Parliament

Clearly visible at the south end of Whitehall is London's finest Gothic Revival building, the Palace of Westminster, better known as the

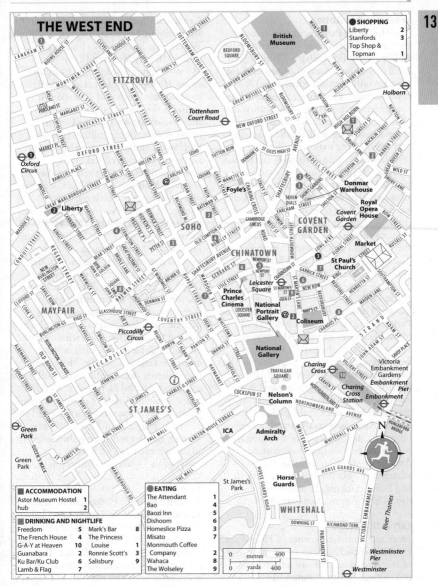

THE WEST END

● SHOPPING
Liberty 2
Stanfords 3
Top Shop &
Topman 1

FITZROVIA

British
Museum

BEDFORD
SQUARE

Tottenham
Court Road

Holborn

Oxford
Circus

Foyle's

Donmar
Warehouse

Liberty

SOHO

COVENT
GARDEN

Royal
Opera
House

Covent
Garden

Market

CHINATOWN

St Paul's
Church

Prince
Charles
Cinema

Leicester
Square

National
Portrait
Gallery

Coliseum

MAYFAIR

Piccadilly
Circus

National
Gallery

Charing
Cross

Victoria
Embankment
Gardens

Embankment
Pier

Charing
Cross
Station

Embankment

TRAFALGAR
SQUARE

Nelson's
Column

ST JAMES'S

Green
Park

ICA

Admiralty
Arch

Green
Park

St James's
Park

Horse
Guards

WHITEHALL

N

River Thames

■ ACCOMMODATION
Astor Museum Hostel 1
hub 2

■ DRINKING AND NIGHTLIFE
Freedom 5
The French House 4
G-A-Y at Heaven 10
Guanabara 2
Ku Bar/Ku Club 6
Lamb & Flag 7
Mark's Bar 8
The Princess
Louise
Ronnie Scott's 3
Salisbury 9

● EATING
The Attendant 1
Bao 4
Baozi Inn 5
Dishoom 6
Homeslice Pizza 3
Misato 7
Monmouth Coffee
Company 2
Wahaca 8
The Wolseley 9

0 metres 400
0 yards 400

Westminster
Pier

Westminster

Houses of Parliament. It is distinguished above all by the ornate, gilded clock tower popularly known as **Big Ben**, after the thirteen-ton bell that it houses. The original royal palace, built by Edward the Confessor in the eleventh century, burnt down in 1834. The only part to survive is the magnificent Westminster Hall, which can be glimpsed en route to the **public galleries** from which you can watch parliament's proceedings (check parliament is in session; queue 1–2hr before session starts outside the Cromwell Green visitor entrance; free; ⓦ parliament .uk); guided tours (£25.50) can also be booked on the website.

13

Westminster Abbey

The Houses of Parliament overshadow their much older neighbour, **Westminster Abbey** (Mon–Fri 9.30am–3.30pm, Wed until 6pm, Sat 9.30am–1.30pm, Sun for worship only; adult/student £20/17; ⍵westminster-abbey.org). Encompassing the grand sweep of England's history, the abbey has been the venue for all but two coronations since William the Conqueror, and many of the nation's monarchs, together with some of its most celebrated citizens, are interred here; of particular note is **Poets' Corner**, where the likes of Chaucer, Tennyson and Charles Dickens are buried. More recently, the abbey was the venue chosen for the 2011 wedding of Prince William and Kate Middleton, now the Duke and Duchess of Cambridge. The new Queen's Diamond Jubilee Galleries are due to open in 2018.

Hyde Park

Central London's largest green space, **Hyde Park** is made up of manicured gardens, forest-like glades and shaded nature zones. In the middle of the park is **The Serpentine**, a lake with a popular lido; the nearby **Serpentine Gallery** (daily 10am–6pm; free; ⍵serpentinegallery.org) hosts excellent contemporary art exhibitions. In the northeast corner of the park, towards Marble Arch, **Speakers' Corner** has long been associated with public free speech, as well as the famous British eccentricity. Anyone can turn up to discourse on whatever subject they choose, as Orwell and Lenin once did; Sunday is the best day to hear impassioned oratory.

Exhibition Road

From the southwest corner of Hyde Park, **Exhibition Road** leads to an excellent trio of free museums. The visually striking, interactive **Science Museum** (daily 10am–6pm, closes 7pm on summer weekends; ⍵sciencemuseum.org.uk) has exhibitions on space exploration, the industrial age and medicine through the ages, with inventions ranging from Crick and Watson's DNA model to *Puffing Billy*, the world's oldest surviving steam train, plus ways to convert waste matter into energy, and more. Further south on Cromwell Road, a distinctive German Romanesque building designed by Alfred Waterhouse in the 1880s houses the **Natural History Museum** (daily 10am–5.50pm, last Fri of the month closes 10.30pm; ⍵nhm.ac.uk), dedicated to mammals, birds and evolution. It contains the famous Dinosaur Gallery, the state-of-the-art Darwin Centre housing over twenty million biological specimens, and a section on volcanoes and earthquakes accessed by an atmospheric escalator: there are also special exhibitions on the likes of space photography (extra charge).

In terms of sheer variety and scale, the nearby **Victoria and Albert Museum** (Mon–Thurs, Sat & Sun 10am–5.45pm, Fri 10am–10pm; ⍵vam.ac.uk) is the greatest museum of applied arts in the world, with five floors of treasures. Highlights include the *Raphael Cartoons*, fashion from the eighteenth century through to modern *haute couture*, an immense jewellery collection, and the two striking Cast Courts, filled with casts of priceless marble works, such as the immense Trajan's Column. The ground-floor galleries dedicated to Asia display the enormous Ardabil carpet – the world's oldest – splendid suits of samurai armour, golden tonsure scissors from Thailand and an ornate beggar's bowl from Pakistan.

South Kensington tube is the closest to all three museums and has an underground walkway connecting them.

Tate Britain

A short walk from Parliament Square west along Millbank, **Tate Britain** (daily 10am–6pm; free; ⍵tate.org.uk) displays British art from 1500 onwards, including a whole wing devoted to Turner. The permanent galleries usually include a selection of works by the likes of Hogarth, Constable and Bacon, and the gallery hosts the controversial Turner Prize for contemporary British artists each year, along with other temporary exhibitions (entry charges apply). The **Tate to Tate Boat** carries passengers from Millbank to Tate Modern on Bankside (see opposite; every 40min during Tate opening hours; £7.50 one-way or £5 with a Travelcard).

13

South Bank

The **South Bank** forms the stretch by the Thames roughly from Westminster Bridge to London Bridge (a 50min walk). The riverside footpath buzzes with life, as people stroll and jog past street entertainers and art installations, or sit out at the many restaurants. The focal point is the **London Eye** (Mon–Fri 10am–8.30pm, Sat & Sun 10am–9.30pm; £21.20; ⓦ londoneye.com), a 135m-tall observation wheel that revolves above the river. Head north from here past the brutalist **South Bank Centre** (see p.436) – which encompasses the Royal Festival Hall and the Hayward Gallery – the adjacent **National Theatre** and **British Film Institute**. You'll pass craft shops and restaurants in Gabriel's Wharf and the OXO Tower before reaching Bankside (see below).

Bankside and Tate Modern

Contemporary **Bankside** is dominated by the colossal **Tate Modern** (daily 10am– 6pm, Fri & Sat till 10pm; free; ⓦ tate.org .uk), built in a minimalist postwar power station. There are temporary exhibitions (around £10; book ahead for major exhibitions), but as the permanent collection includes works by just about every famous modern artist including Monet, Bonnard, Matisse, Picasso, Dalí, Mondrian, Warhol and Rothko, you should get your fill of modern art for free.

Directly outside Tate Modern, Norman Foster's **Millennium Bridge**, with its spectacular views, will take you across the river to the City of London and St Paul's Cathedral.

Globe Theatre to London Bridge

Dwarfed by Tate Modern is **Shakespeare's Globe** (ⓦ shakespearesglobe .com), a reconstruction of the polygonal playhouse where most of the Bard's later works were first performed. If you're happy to stand in the pit, you can catch a show from as little as £5. A short stroll further east winds away from the river under Victorian railway arches to **London Bridge** and the popular **Borough Market** (see box, p.429), a fantastic place to refuel. Towering above Borough Market

is London's tallest skyscraper, the **Shard**. Head up to the observation deck on the 62nd floor (daily 9am–10pm; £26; ⓦ theviewfromtheshard.com) for unparalleled 360-degree views of the capital, or for the price of a cocktail (around £18) you can enjoy slightly less lofty views from the *Gong Bar* on the 52nd floor.

The City of London

Despite the newer development of Canary Wharf stealing many companies further east, the **City of London** remains London's financial hub and can feel hauntingly empty out of office hours. The oldest part of London, it was built on the original Roman Londinium, and its appeal lies in the contrast of tiny chapels on narrow, winding streets with towering, iconic skyscrapers, such as The Gherkin, The Cheesegrater and The Walkie Talkie, at 20 Fenchurch St, whose 155m-high **Sky Garden** (Mon–Fri 10am–6pm, Sat & Sun 11am–9pm, Fri & Sat till 10pm; book free visits online; ⓦ skygarden .london) is particularly worth visiting.

St Paul's Cathedral

On the western edge of the City is one of London's most famous landmarks, **St Paul's Cathedral** (Mon–Sat 8.30am– 4pm; adult/student £18/16; ⓦ stpauls .co.uk). The most distinctive feature of architect Christopher Wren's Baroque edifice is the vast dome, one of the largest in the world. Highlights include the **Whispering Gallery**, up in the dome, so-called because words whispered to the wall on one side are clearly audible on the other; the broad exterior Stone Gallery; and the uppermost Golden Gallery, which offers panoramas over London. The **crypt** is the resting place of Wren, Turner, Reynolds and other artists, but the most imposing sarcophagi are those occupied by the Duke of Wellington and Lord Nelson.

Museum of London

Just north of St Paul's, situated in the 1970s-designed **Barbican Centre**, is the **Museum of London** (daily 10am–6pm; free; ⓦ museumoflondon.org.uk). It tells

13

the story of the city from prehistoric times to the present day, with particularly interesting displays on Roman London and the Great Fire, plus the Lord Mayor's state coach dating to 1757. The Barbican Centre itself (Ⓦbarbican.org.uk) is one of London's cultural hotspots, housing cinemas, theatres and galleries.

Tower of London

Justifying all the hype, the **Tower of London** (March–Oct daily 9am–5.30pm; Nov–Feb Mon–Fri 9am–4.30pm, Sat & Sun 10am–4.30pm; adult/student £25/19.50; online discounts; Ⓦhrp.org.uk), on the river a mile southeast of St Paul's by the iconic Tower Bridge, remains one of London's most remarkable buildings. Begun by William the Conqueror, and pretty much completed by the end of the thirteenth century, the Tower is the most perfectly preserved (albeit heavily restored) medieval fortress in the country. The central **White Tower** holds part of the Royal Armouries collection, and, on the second floor, the Norman Chapel of St John, London's oldest church. Close by is Tower Green, where two of Henry VIII's wives were beheaded. Look out for the ravens; according to legend, the monarchy will fall if they ever leave, so their wings are clipped accordingly. The Waterloo Barracks house the **Crown Jewels**, among which are the three largest cut diamonds in the world.

The East End

A short walk from the Tower brings you to Aldgate and the start of the **East End**. The area has always drawn large immigrant populations due to its proximity to the river – it has been in turn Huguenot, Jewish and, most recently, Bangladeshi and Pakistani. Walk down Whitechapel Road from Aldgate and you'll pass one of Britain's largest mosques, as well as the excellent **Whitechapel Gallery** (Tues–Sun 11am–6pm, Thurs until 9pm; free; Ⓦwhitechapelgallery.org), which shows off a cutting-edge mix of contemporary art. **Brick Lane** meanders off to the left (take Osborn St), lined with curry houses, trendy street markets, retro shops and boutiques.

At the other end of Brick Lane are the funky, creative areas of **Shoreditch**, **Hoxton** and **Old Street**, full of restaurants, galleries, cafés and design stores. A two- to three-mile walk further east down Whitechapel Road brings you to what was once a desolate industrial area, transformed into the Olympic Park for the 2012 Games. The site reopened as the **Queen Elizabeth Olympic Park** in July 2013 (Ⓦqueenelizabetholympicpark .co.uk), with major sporting and events venues surrounded by parkland, plus Anish Kapoor's 115m-high **Orbit**, Britain's largest piece of public art: its sky-high platforms offer fantastic views across London and a hair-raising 40-second ride down the world's longest tunnel slide (daily: April–Oct 10am– 6pm; Nov–March 11am–5pm; tower only £10, slide and tower £15; Ⓦarcelormittalorbit.com).

Regent's Park and Camden

As with almost all London's royal parks, Londoners have Henry VIII to thank for **Regent's Park**: he confiscated it from the Church for yet more hunting grounds and it's now a popular picnicking spot. Flanked by some of the city's most elegant residential buildings, the park is home to **London Zoo** (daily: Easter–Aug 10am–6pm, Sept & Oct 10am–5pm; Nov–Easter 10am–4pm; £24.25; Ⓦzsl .org), one of the world's oldest and most varied collections of animals. Take the tube to Baker Street, Regent's Park or Great Portland Street to enter the park at its southernmost edge and walk north to the zoo, or get the tube to **Camden Town** with its famous **market** (see box opposite) and music scene, and walk west down **Regent's Canal**, which runs through the middle of the zoo.

Hampstead Heath and Highgate Cemetery

Camden gives way to the affluent suburb of Hampstead and the vast **Hampstead Heath**, which offers the perfect antidote to London's highly manicured parks. East of Hampstead is **Highgate Cemetery**, ranged on both sides of Swains Lane (ⓊHighgate/Archway). Karl Marx lies in the East Cemetery (Mon–Fri 10am–5pm,

MARKETS

At the weekend, visit one of London's high-quality markets: some are well established, some trendy pop-ups, but wherever you go, you're sure to find tasty food and a lively, relaxed atmosphere. Unless specified, markets tend to run 10am–5pm.

Borough ⓘ London Bridge; ⓦ boroughmarket.co.uk; map pp.422–423. Where serious foodies stock up on hard-to-source ingredients. Not cheap, but there are free tasters and excellent food stalls. Mon–Thurs 8am–5pm, Fri noon–6pm, Sat 8am–5pm; limited stalls on Mon & Tues.

Brick Lane and Spitalfields ⓘ Liverpool St; ⓦ bricklanemarket.com; map pp.422–423. Two separate markets, but punters wander between the two on Sundays, when Brick Lane is thick with food stalls. Spitalfields draws an eclectic mix of artists, jewellers and designers in a restored covered market. Brick Lane Sun 9am–5pm; Spitalfields Mon–Fri 10am–5pm, Sun 9am–5pm.

Camden ⓘ Camden Town; ⓦ camdenlock.net; map pp.422–423. A punk hangout in the 1970s, with plenty of Dr. Martens and studded jackets still on offer today, mixed with every other sub-culture going. Daily 10am–6pm.

Columbia Road Shoreditch High Street Overground; ⓦ columbiaroad.info; map pp.422–423. An easy walk from Brick Lane, this lovely plant and flower market is also full of boutique stores and hip coffee shops. Sun 8am–3pm.

Greenwich Cutty Sark DLR; ⓦ greenwichmarketlondon .com; map pp.422–423. Covered market with quirky handmade gifts and crafts (Tues, Wed & Fri–Sun) as well as vintage clothes stores and antiques (Tues, Thurs & Fri). Tues–Sun 10am–5.30pm.

Portobello Road ⓘ Notting Hill; ⓦ portobelloroad .co.uk/market; map pp.422–423. The most iconic London market thanks to the film *Notting Hill*, with stalls peddling antiques, rare books and vintage finds (Sat only), as well as fashion and crafts. Mon–Wed 9am–6pm, Thurs 9am–1pm, Fri & Sat 9am–7pm.

---

the East Cemetery (Mon–Fri 10am–5pm, Sat & Sun 11am–5pm; £8; ⓦ highgate -cemetery.org); more atmospheric is the overgrown West Cemetery (guided tours only: March–Nov Mon–Fri 2pm, Sat & Sun hourly 11am–4pm; Dec–Feb Sat & Sun hourly 11am–3pm; £12, includes entry to East Cemetery), with its eerie Egyptian Avenue and terraced catacombs.

Greenwich

One of London's most beguiling spots, and offering respite from the frenetic centre, **Greenwich** is worth the short trip. Transport links are good: there are regular riverboats (see p.431), trains from London Bridge, or the DLR scoots from Bank via the redeveloped Docklands south to the **Cutty Sark** (daily 10am–5pm, last admission 4pm; entry by timed ticket only, best to pre-book online; £13.50; ⓦ rmg.co.uk). This famous tea clipper has recently been dazzlingly restored after a devastating fire, and now you can walk beneath the 143-year-old hull, as well as stroll the decks and explore the hold. Hugging the riverfront to the east is Wren's beautifully symmetrical Baroque ensemble of the **Old Royal Naval College** (daily 10am–5pm; free; ⓦ ornc.org). Across the

road, the **National Maritime Museum** (daily 10am–5pm, closes 8pm Thurs; free; ⓦ rmg.co.uk) has model ships, charts and globes, and hosts sea-themed exhibitions. From here Greenwich Park stretches up the hill, crowned by the Wren-inspired **Royal Observatory** (daily 9am–5pm; £9.50), where you can straddle the Greenwich Mean Time meridian and catch a show at the excellent planetarium.

ARRIVAL AND DEPARTURE

BY PLANE

Flying into London, you'll arrive at one of the capital's five international airports: Heathrow (ⓦ heathrowairport .com), Gatwick (ⓦ gatwickairport.com), Stansted (ⓦ stanstedairport.com), Luton (ⓦ london-luton.co.uk) or City (ⓦ londoncityairport.com). EasyBus (ⓦ easybus .co.uk) has buses from Gatwick, Stansted and Luton to central London, while National Express operate from all airports. From Heathrow, Gatwick and Stansted, there are express trains every 15min that will get you there faster than other modes of transport, but cost around £20 one-way; fares are often discounted online.

Heathrow 15 miles west. Served by Piccadilly Line on the Tube (every few min, 6am–11.50pm; 1hr; £6 cash or £5.10/3.10 Oyster peak/off-peak). In addition to the express train services, Heathrow Connect trains offer a slower stopping service to Paddington Station (every 30min; 25min; £10.20). National Express coaches go to

13

Victoria Coach Station (every 10–15min; 50min; £6). After midnight, night bus #N9 runs to Trafalgar Square (every 20min; 1hr 10min; £2.50 cash/1.50 Oyster).

Gatwick 30 miles south. Connected by several train companies: Southern trains run on the same route as the Gatwick Express, but are cheaper (every 15min; 35min; £15.50), and First Capital Connect trains run to London Bridge, Blackfriars and St Pancras International (every 15min; 30–40min; around £12).

Stansted 34 miles northeast. Regular National Express services run to Victoria Coach Station via Baker Street and Marble Arch (every 15min; 1hr 45min; £10), or Liverpool Street (every 15min; 1hr–1hr 15min; £8 advance booking); Terravision buses also go to Victoria and Liverpool Street (every 20–40min; 40–55min; £10).

Luton 37 miles north. Served by shuttle buses to Luton Airport Parkway station, from which there are services to St Pancras (every 5–20min; 25–45min; £14) and other stations with First Capital Connect (see Gatwick). Green Line bus #757 also runs from the airport terminal into central London (every 20min–1hr; 1hr 30min; £17 or £25 return within 3 months).

London City 10 miles east. Served by the Docklands Light Railway (DLR), with regular services to Bank (every 8–15min; 22min; £4.90 cash or £3.30/2.80 Oyster peak/off-peak).

BY TRAIN

Eurostar services terminate at St Pancras International. Trains from the English Channel ports arrive at Victoria, Waterloo or Charing Cross stations, while those from elsewhere in Britain come into one of London's numerous main-line termini (namely Waterloo and Paddington from the southwest, Euston or King's Cross from the north, and Liverpool Street from the east), all of which have tube stations.

Destinations from Charing Cross Canterbury (every 30min; 1hr 45min); Dover (every 30min; 1hr 10min–2hr). Euston Glasgow (hourly; 4hr 30min–5hr 40min); Liverpool (every 20min; 2hr 10min–2hr 30min); Manchester (every 20min; 2hr 10min).

King's Cross Cambridge (every 15min; 50min–1hr 20min); Durham (every 30min; 2hr 45min–3hr); Edinburgh (every 30min; 4hr 20min–5hr 40min); Glasgow (hourly; 4hr 30min–5hr 40min); Newcastle every 30min; 2hr 50min–3hr 15min); York (every 30min; 1hr 50min–2hr 20min).

London Bridge Brighton (every 15min; 1hr 5min).

Marylebone Stratford-upon-Avon (hourly; 2–3hr).

Paddington Bath (every 30min; 1hr 30min); Bristol (every 15min; 1hr 20min–1hr 45min); Oxford (every 10–20min; 1hr–1hr 50min); Penzance (13 daily; 5hr 10min–8hr 10min); Cardiff (every 15min; 2hr 10min).

St Pancras International Brussels (10 daily; 2hr–2hr 15min); Lille (8 daily; 1hr 20min–1hr 40min); Paris (hourly; 2hr 15min–2hr 50min).

BY BUS

Long-distance buses from around Britain and continental Europe arrive at Victoria Coach Station, a 500-yard walk south of Victoria train station.

Destinations Amsterdam (4 daily; 10–12hr); Bath (every 1hr 30min; 2hr 50min–3hr 20min); Berlin (1–2 daily; 24hr); Brighton (hourly; 2hr 15min–3hr 15min); Bristol (hourly; 3hr); Cambridge (every 90min; 2hr 30min); Cardiff (hourly; 3hr 15min–3hr 45min); Dover (hourly; 2hr 30min–3hr); Dublin (1 daily; 12hr 30min); Durham (4 daily; 6–7hr); Edinburgh (2 daily; 9hr–9hr 45min); Glasgow (5 daily; 8hr 15min–9hr 45min); Inverness (1 daily; 13hr); Liverpool (every 2hr; 4hr 40min–5hr 45min); Manchester (hourly; 4hr 35min–5hr 20min); Newcastle (5 daily; 6hr 25min–7hr 25min); Oxford (every 20–30min; 1hr 50min–2hr); Paris (6 daily; 10hr); Penzance (6 daily; 8hr 45min–9hr 45min); Stratford-upon-Avon (3 daily; 3hr 15min–3hr 25min); York (4 daily; 4hr 50min–5hr 25min).

INFORMATION

Tourist information London's flagship tourist office is the City of London Information Office (Mon–Sat 9.30am–5.30pm, Sun 10am–4pm; ☏020 7332 1456,

---

OYSTER AND CONTACTLESS CARDS

The cheapest way to pay for public transport in London is to use a **contactless credit or debit card** or an **Oyster** touch card (✆tfl.gov.uk; £5 refundable deposit). They both work in exactly the same way – you touch in at the beginning and end of each journey – and are valid on the underground, buses, trams, the DLR, the London Overground rail network and most National Rail services in London, as well as giving money off some riverboats. You can store cash on the Oyster card ("pay as you go") as well as weekly travel cards (from £32.40); simply "top up" at stations or Oyster Ticket Stops, including newsagents and other shops with an Oyster logo outside. When using an Oyster or contactless card, one-way bus fares are almost half the cash price (£1.50 instead of £2.50) and tube fares in Zone 1 are £2.40 instead of £4.90 – also, your overall fee is capped, no matter how many journeys you make (currently £6.50 a day for Zones 1 and 2). If you don't have an Oyster or contactless card, a one-day paper **Travelcard** for Zones 1 to 4 (£12.10) is still cheaper than buying individual tickets.

ⓦ visitlondon.com), opposite St Paul's Cathedral. There are other branches all over the city – the website details them on a map.

GETTING AROUND

Transport for London (TfL) oversees the city's public transport, and their website (ⓦ tfl.gov.uk) is a vital tool for all Londoners and visitors to help navigate this enormous city by tube, bus, boat or bike. TfL's six tourist information centres are in the following stations: Piccadilly Circus tube station, Heathrow Terminals 1, 2 and 3, Euston, Liverpool Street, Victoria and King's Cross (all open daily). There's also a 24hr phone line for information on all services, including up-to-date closures or diversions (ⓣ 0843 222 1234). Central London is very walkable and Citymapper (ⓦ citymapper .com) is an excellent navigational app that gives you route options from A to B using both public transport, taxis, bikes or just walking, showing times, prices and even when the next bus/train is due.

BY UNDERGROUND

The quickest way to get around is via the London Underground network, known as "the tube" (daily 5.30/7.30am–12.30am approx, with trains running all night on Fri & Sat on several lines; check "first and last" tube on TfL website). Tickets must be bought in advance from the machines or booths in station entrance halls and need to be kept until the end of your journey so that you can leave the station. If you use Oyster, always touch the card reader on the way in and out of each station. If you cannot produce a valid ticket or Oyster card on demand, you'll be charged an on-the-spot penalty fine of £80. Avoid the packed tube during rush hour.

BY BUS

A great way to see the city, especially from the top of London's famous red double-deckers. Many run 24hr, though be aware that night buses prefixed with the letter "N" may not run the same route as their day counterpart. If you don't have an Oyster or a contactless debit/credit card, you will need to buy a single ticket (£2.50) from the machine at the bus stop before boarding (in central London), or, outside the centre, simply pay the driver (use small change). Hail buses by sticking your arm out. Most buses are modern, but classic London Routemaster buses, complete with conductor, still run on two routes: Charing Cross station to the Tower of London (#15) and Kensington High St to Aldwych (#9).

BY BOAT

Riverboat services on the Thames are a pleasant and quick way to get between east and west. Having an Oyster or contactless debit/credit card or a paper Travelcard will get

you a third off riverboat tickets (otherwise £3.50 single), while if you've got a pay-as-you-go Oyster you'll get ten percent off single fares. Westminster Pier, Embankment Pier and Waterloo Pier are the main central embarkation points and there are regular sailings to Bankside, London Bridge, Tower Bridge and Greenwich. Timings and services alter frequently, so pick up the *Thames River Services* booklet from a TfL travel information office, or see ⓦ tfl .gov.uk/river.

BY TAXI

If you're in a group, London's metered black cabs (just wave to hail one when their orange "taxi" light is illuminated) can be a viable way of travelling. Cost depends on time of day, distance travelled and travel time and there's a minimum £2.40 fare, plus a £2 phone call charge. A two-mile journey (10–20min) should cost around £15 (6am–8pm). To book in advance, call ⓣ 020 7272 0272, ⓦ www.londonblackcabs.co.uk or find your nearest black cab via the Hailo (ⓦ hailocab.com) app. Minicabs look just like regular cars and are considerably cheaper than black cabs (a black cab to Heathrow will cost up to £85, while a minicab will charge £40–60), but need to be booked by phone in advance. To get numbers for local registered minicab companies, check out ⓣ minicabit.com and ⓦ minicabsinlondon.com, download the Cabwise app or text CAB to ⓣ 60835. Cheaper still is Uber (ⓦ uber.com).

BY TRAIN AND TRAM

There is a variety of different train lines in London. The Overground and the Docklands Light Railway (DLR) are operated by TfL and form part of the tube map – most interchanges are as simple as on the tube. National Rail services from London out to Greater London suburbs and commuter towns are run by outside agents, but you can use Oyster cards for most journeys in and around the city (details on TfL website). Oyster can also be used on the trams in south London.

BY BIKE

London is becoming more bike friendly with new cycle superhighways and a public bike rental scheme (ⓦ tfl .org.uk; credit or debit card needed to rent at docking stations found all over central London). "Boris Bikes", named after Boris Johnson, the mayor who installed them, cost £2 to rent for the day or £10 for a week, then you pay an hourly incremental charge after that; as the first half an hour is free, so long as you keep docking the bikes and picking up new ones, it can be a great and cheap way to see London. Alternatively, you can find standard rental shops through the London Cycling Campaign (ⓦ lcc.org.uk). Pick out cycle-friendly routes using the free guides available from transport information offices, or check the TfL website.

13

ACCOMMODATION

West London offers easy access to the museums and central London, though it tends to be expensive for eating and nightlife. Northeast London is currently London's hippest area, with a vibrant atmosphere and some of the best nightlife in town, while anywhere near the South Bank is central enough to walk into the West End. Student rooms are available July–Sept; try Imperial College (☎020 7594 9507, ⍵imperial.ac.uk/summeraccommodation) or LSE (☎020 7955 7676, ⍵lsevacations.co.uk). For classy, modern budget B&Bs, try the Bed and Breakfast Club (⍵thebedandbreakfastclub.co.uk) or stay with locals via Airbnb (⍵airbnb.com).

HOSTELS

The YHA (see p.418) has seven HI-affiliated London hostels, most in unbeatable locations (Oxford Street, St Pancras, St Paul's, Central near Regent's Park, Earls Court and Thameside), and most with cheap twins and doubles as well as dorms. Prices shown are for the cheapest weeknight dorm in high season; in low season beds start from around £17. A continental breakfast is included at the hostels below unless specified.

Astor Museum Hostel 27 Montague St ☎020 7580 5360, ⍵astorhostels.com; ⍴Russell Square; map pp.422–423. Right next to the British Museum, this venerable mansion combines a stellar location with ample self-catering facilities and a large guest lounge. 18–35-year-olds only. Sociable without being a party hostel. Breakfast £1. Dorms £21, doubles £95

Clink78 78 King's Cross Rd ☎020 3475 3000, ⍵clinkhostels.com; ⍴King's Cross; map pp.422–423. Quirky hostel housed in a Victorian courthouse with dorms of various sizes (some female-only) painted in cheerful colours. Chill-out space is in the actual courtrooms, while the cheapest of the private rooms are the cramped former police cells. Dorms £20, doubles £90

Generator 37 Tavistock Place ☎020 7388 7666, ⍵generatorhostels.com; ⍴Russell Square; map pp.422–423. Part of a Europe-wide range of design-led hostels, this huge, raucous place combines clubby, neon-lit social spaces with luxurious digs, on-site bar, games room and free walking tours for its youthful clientele. Dorms £52, doubles £122

Meininger Hyde Park 67 Queen's Gate ☎020 3318 1407, ⍵meininger-hotels.com; ⍴Gloucester Road; map pp.422–423. Right near Hyde Park and the Victoria & Albert Museum, this spotless, minimalist German hostel/hotel has comfortable beds in dorms (for over-18s only) plus stylish en-suite rooms. Dorms £17, doubles £121

★**Palmers Lodge Swiss Cottage** 40 College Crescent ☎020 7483 8470, ⍵palmerslodges.co.uk; ⍴Swiss Cottage; map pp.422–423. One of a mini-chain of boutique hostels, this is a superb option within a converted Victorian mansion, with privacy curtains around bunks, comfy guest lounge and helpful staff around the clock. Free bed linen, too. Extensive breakfast £4.50. Dorms £19, doubles £77

St Christopher's Inns 121 Borough High St ☎020 7939 9710, ⍵st-christophers.co.uk; ⍴London Bridge; map pp.422–423. Self-styled "international party house" in three separate buildings near London Bridge: *The Village* has a nightclub and comedy bar; *The Inn* is above a pub and a little more tranquil; while *The Oasis* is women-only. No curfew. Dorms £19, doubles £78

Travel Joy 111 Grosvenor Rd ☎020 7834 9689, ⍵traveljoyhostels.com; ⍴Pimlico or bus #24 from central London; map pp.422–423. Right on the river in tranquil Pimlico, this friendly hostel is set above the *King William IV* pub, with a terrace hosting barbecues on sunny days and live music on Sat. Some dorms are en suite. Dorms £28

HOTELS, B&BS AND SELF-CATERING

Most budget hotels and B&Bs in central London are grotty or old-fashioned; with a short commute from the centre, you get much better value for money. See p.418 for budget chain hotels.

★**Aviva Studio Apartments** 42 Glenthorne Rd ☎07976 020304, ⍵avivastudio-apartments.co.uk; ⍴Hammersmith; map pp.422–423. On a residential street in West London but with plenty of local restaurants and just 5min from the tube, these well-equipped 1- and 2-person studio apartments are clean and comfortable, and the owners are friendly and knowledgeable. Doubles £70

★**hub** 110 St Martin's Lane ☎333 321 3104, ⍵hubhotels.co.uk; ⍴Covent Garden; map pp.422–423. Right in the heart of West End, this stylish hotel borders on capsule, with cleverly designed, high-tech, compact rooms, all with monsoon showers and a/c. Good deli downstairs. Doubles £65

Ridgemount Hotel 65–67 Gower St ☎020 7636 1141, ⍵ridgemounthotel.co.uk; ⍴Euston Square; map pp.422–423. This Georgian terraced house has a great location near the British Museum and a tranquil garden – you can choose cheaper rooms with wash basins or fancier en suites (£20 more). Doubles £90

Russell's 123 Chatsworth Rd, Hackney ☎0797 666 9906, ⍵russellsofclapton.com; Homerton Overground or #38 bus from central London; map pp.422–423. The out-of-the-way location in an ungentrified part of Hackney means you get a boutique B&B offering vintage-style luxury, not to mention a great breakfast, courtesy of the former music industry manager/owner. A good location for exploring trendy Shoreditch and Dalston. Doubles £80

Stylotel 160–162 Sussex Gardens ☎020 7723 1026, ⍵stylotel.com; ⍴Paddington; map pp.422–423. Ultra-modern budget hotel inside two Georgian townhouses, with aluminium wall coverings, floor-to-ceiling mirrors, excellent beds and a Stylolounge for hanging out. Buffet breakfast included. Doubles £79

EATING

Few cities can match London for the sheer diversity of eating experiences on offer. You'll find restaurants for every cuisine you can think of and competition keeps prices low. If you're after a quick bite to eat, *Pret a Manger* and *Eat* chains are ubiquitous and serve freshly made, imaginative sandwiches, wraps and soups.

CAFÉS, CHEAP EATS AND SNACKS

A. Gold 42 Brushfield St ⓦ agoldshop.com; ⓣ Liverpool Street; map pp.422–423. Right by Spitalfields Market (see box, p.429), this superb traditional food shop sells tasty, made-to-order sandwiches and salad boxes, crammed with gourmet ingredients such as smoked Cheddar with pear chutney or smoked duck breast (£5–5.50). Mon–Fri 10am–4pm, Sat noon–5pm.

★**The Attendant** 27a Foley St ⓦ the-attendant.com; ⓣ Goodge Street; map p.425. Salads, imaginative breakfasts, wraps, pastries, smoothies and juices, all made with fresh local produce, are all on offer at this Victorian public lavatory turned café. Speciality coffees are *de rigueur* here, and special diets are catered for. Mon–Sat noon–8.30pm, Sun noon–5.30pm.

★**E. Pellicci** 332 Bethnal Green Rd; ⓣ Bethnal Green; map pp.422–423. Run by the Pellicci family since the 1900s and a favourite haunt of gangster brothers the Krays, this is an East End institution, serving hearty cooked breakfasts (£5.50) and Italian specials. Mon–Sat 7am–4pm.

F. Cooke 150 Hoxton St; ⓣ Old Street; map pp.422–423. Get the very traditional London pie, mash & liquor (parsley gravy) with house chilli vinegar for under £4.50, or if you dare, jellied eels in this spit 'n' sawdust Cockney place. Mon–Thurs 10am–7pm, Fri & Sat 9.30am–8pm.

★**Homeslice Pizza** 13 Neal's Yard ⓦ homeslicepizza .co.uk; ⓣ Covent Garden; map p.425. Buzzy, friendly spot serving 20-inch wood-fired pizzas big enough for two (£20; several are available by the slice too (£4). Wonderful, unusual ingredients: try goat shoulder with sumac yogurt or oxtail with horseradish and sorrel cream. No reservations. Daily noon–11pm.

Monmouth Coffee Company 27 Monmouth St, Seven Dials ⓦ monmouthcoffee.co.uk; ⓣ Holborn; map p.425; also at Borough Market (see box, p.429); ⓣ London Bridge; map pp.422–423. *Monmouth* have made a name for themselves by making the best coffee in London – look out for other cafés selling their blends. Mon–Sat 8am–6.30pm; Borough branch Mon–Sat 7.30am–6pm.

Paul Rothe & Son 35 Marylebone Lane ⓦ paulrotheand sondelicatessen.co.uk; ⓣ Bond Street; map pp.422–423. Established in 1900 and still run by the Rothes, this deli puts together an exemplary array of hot and cold sandwiches (£3.50) and ladles toppings on jacket potatoes (£5). Mon–Fri 8am–6pm, Sat 11am–5pm.

RESTAURANTS

★**Bao** 53 Lexington St ⓦ baolondon.com; ⓣ Oxford Circus or Piccadilly Circus; map p.425. Taiwanese street stall gone upmarket, this tiny, trendy eatery specializes in *bao* (steamed, filled buns), as well as other small, tapas-style dishes – pig blood cake and century egg with eryngii mushroom are revelations: dishes from £3. No reservations, so be prepared to queue. Mon–Sat noon–3pm & 5–10pm.

Baozi Inn 26 Newport Court ⓣ 020 7287 6877; ⓣ Leicester Square; map p.425. Kitsch Communist decor is combined here with authentic northern Chinese dishes. The noodles, buns and dumplings are a treat, and the spicy beef noodle

---

LONDON STREET FOOD

London's latest trend is for **gourmet street food**, and food vans are popping up all over the capital selling everything from pulled-pork sandwiches to custard tarts. Locations change frequently, but the following, along with Borough Market and Portobello Market (see box, p.429), are good bets for a gourmet lunch on a budget.

Broadway Market From London Fields Park to the Regent's Canal ⓦ broadwaymarket.co.uk; London Fields rail or Haggerston Overground; map pp.422–423. There's been a produce market on this site in Hackney since the 1890s; these days more than a hundred stalls sell everything from Vietnamese coffee and meze to gourmet sausage rolls and cupcakes. Sat 9am–5pm.

KERB at Cubitt Square, Stable St ⓦ kerbfood.com; ⓣ Kings Cross; map pp.422–423. "Making cities taste better", gourmet street food vendors bring their lunchtime action to Kings Cross, with epic burgers, Scandi-style smoked fish, Indonesian *rendang*, burritos, *tonkatsu* and Filipino BBQ. Wed–Fri noon–2pm.

Street Feast Dalston Yard, Hartwell St ⓦ streetfeastlondon.com; ⓣ Dalston Junction Overground; map pp.422–423. Probably London's most exciting night market, with cuisines spanning Mexican, Vietnamese, Korean, Hawaiian-style sushi and much more, plus the Gin Store and Tequila Treehouse providing after-dinner tipples. Fri & Sat 5pm–midnight; £3 entry after 7pm.

Whitecross Street Market Whitecross St ⓣ Barbican; map pp.422–423. Mexican and Italian street food are both specialities at this bustling food market in the heart of the City. Mon–Fri 11.30am–3pm.

13

soup is topped with a layer of tongue-numbing chilli oil. Cheap, spicy and filling. Mains from £8. Mon–Thurs & Sun noon–10.30pm, Fri & Sat noon–midnight.

Ciao Bella 86–90 Lamb's Conduit St ⓦ ciaobellarestaurant .co.uk; ⓣ Russell Square/Holborn; map pp.422–423. Jolly, extremely popular old-style Italian, serving huge plates of classic pasta dishes, pizza, calzones plus hearty mains from £9. Mon–Sat noon–11.30pm, Sun noon 10.30pm.

Comptoir Libanais 1–5 Exhibition Rd ⓦ comptoir libanais.com; ⓣ South Kensington; map pp.422–423. Super-handy for three of London's best museums, this colourful Lebanese-style canteen, with tables on the street outside, serves tasty hot and cold meze, wraps, tagines and grilled meats: meze from £3.50, mains from £9. Several other branches. Mon–Sat 8.30am–midnight, Sun 8.30am–10pm.

Dishoom 12 Upper St Martin's Lane ⓦ dishoom.com; ⓣ Covent Garden or Leicester Square; map p.425. Bombay Café mini-chain that specializes in Indian street-food-style dishes, ideal for sharing. Gunpowder potatoes, spiced chickpeas and prawn koliwada stand out; dishes from £4.20. Another branch at 22 Kingley St, ⓣ Oxford Circus. Mon–Fri 8am–11pm, Sat & Sun 9am–11pm.

Misato 11 Wardour St; ⓣ Piccadilly Circus; map p.425. This Japanese café attracts a lot of students from the Far East with its enormous portions of *katsu* curry and other Japanese dishes: mains from £7.50. Daily noon–11pm.

Simpson's Tavern Ball Court, 38½ Cornhill ⓦ simpsonstavern.co.uk; ⓣ Bank; map pp.422–423. This historic chophouse, tucked away down a Dickensian alley in the City, dates from 1757 and the interior and menu seem to have changed little since. Settle into one of the wood-panelled booths and feast on doorstop sandwiches (from £4.50) or hearty mains such as sausage and mash (£7). Mon–Fri 8am–4pm.

Sông Quê 134 Kingsland Rd ⓦ songque.co.uk; Hoxton Overground; map pp.422–423. On a strip of road packed with Vietnamese restaurants, this unpretentious place is a

cut above the rest, with authentic flavours and efficient service: mains from £8.50. Mon–Fri noon–3pm & 5.30–11pm, Sat noon–3pm, Sun noon–10.30pm.

★**Wahaca** 66 Chandos Place ⓦ wahaca.co.uk; ⓣ Charing Cross or Covent Garden; map p.425. Part of a nationwide chain, this vast basement restaurant serving Mexican street food is always packed. It's noisy and fun, and the tapas-size servings of tacos, tostadas and quesadillas are delicious: tapas from £4, mains from £10. Mon–Sat noon–11pm, Sun noon–10.30pm.

DRINKING AND NIGHTLIFE

From Victorian pubs serving ale to old gents, to hip bars and clubs frequented by an eternally young, edgy clientele, London has it all. In the east, there's a thriving bar and club scene around Shoreditch, Hoxton and Old Street, while Soho and north London also get their share of the action. In recent years, craft beer has taken London by storm, with numerous brewpubs serving their own microbrews.

BARS AND PUBS

Brewhouse & Kitchen Islington Torrens St, Highbury ⓦ brewhouseandkitchen.com/islington; ⓣ Angel; map pp.422–423. One of a small chain of brewpubs, this congenial spot serves fifty of its very own microbrews, as well as guest beers and freshly cooked food to go with it. Beer tastings arranged. Mon–Thurs 11am–11pm, Fri & Sat 11am–midnight, Sun noon–11pm.

The French House 49 Dean St ⓦ frenchhousesoho.com ⓣ Leicester Square; map p.425. One of Soho's most iconic pubs, attracting a bohemian crowd. Charles de Gaulle was based here during WWII and the French connection is evident in its collection of wines, champagnes and beers. Mon–Sat noon–11pm, Sun noon–10.30pm.

★**Jerusalem Tavern** 55 Britton St ⓣ Farringdon; map pp.422–423. Cool Clerkenwell's the setting for this packed pub, serving some of the best ales in London from barrels in the wall amidst eighteenth-century decor. Mon–Fri 11am–11pm.

Lamb & Flag 33 Rose St ⓣ Covent Garden or Leicester Square; map p.425. A respite from hectic Covent Garden, this compact, atmospheric pub was once known as the *Bucket of Blood* – after the prize fights held here. Mon–Sat 11am–11pm, Sun noon–10.30pm.

Lexington 96 Pentonville Rd ⓣ Angel; map pp.422–423. This luxuriously decorated bourbon joint puts on events like a pop pub quiz, as well as cheap live music and club nights upstairs. Mon–Wed & Sun noon–2am, Thurs noon–3am, Fri & Sat noon–4am.

Lock Tavern 35 Chalk Farm Rd ⓦ lock-tavern.com ⓣ Chalk Farm; map pp.422–423. This laidback Camden pub is ever-popular, thanks to its free live music, tasty food and buzzing atmosphere. The roof terrace and garden are in high demand on summer weekends. Mon–Thurs noon–midnight, Fri & Sat noon–1am, Sun noon–11pm.

★**TREAT YOURSELF**

The Wolseley 160 Piccadilly ⓦ thewolseley.com; ⓣ Piccadilly Circus; map p.425. Traditional British afternoon tea doesn't come much more special than this, within the beautiful Art Deco surroundings of the opulent *Wolseley*. If you only do it once in your life, it's worth splashing out £27.50 for a full afternoon tea, with finger sandwiches, cakes and scones (cream teas from £11.50). Dressing up? Smart casual is fine. Afternoon tea served Mon–Fri 3–6.30pm, Sat 3.30–5.30pm, Sun 3.30–6.30pm.

DRINKING ON A BUDGET

For a break from London's sky-high drink prices check out the sensitively restored Victorian pubs owned by the **Sam Smith's** brewery. Prices are kept low as everything, including spirits and soft drinks, comes from the same brewery; a pint of lager starts at just £3. The *Cittie of York*, 22 High Holborn (❶Chancery Lane; map pp.422–423), *Ye Olde Cheshire Cheese* at 145 Fleet St (❶Blackfriars; map pp.422–423), and *The Princess Louise* at 208 High Holborn (❶Holborn; map p.425) all have historical interiors, but there are plenty of others.

The Old Bank of England 194 Fleet St; ❶Holborn/ Temple; map pp.422–423. You're unlikely to sip a pint in a grander setting than this nineteeneeth-century bank with ceiling frescoes, chandeliers, marble and dark wood. Great pies and a solid wine list, too. Mon–Fri 8am–11pm.

Salisbury 90 St Martin's Lane; ❶Leicester Square; map p.425. Beautiful old gin palace and pub packed with original features, dark wood, mirrors and glassware in the heart of Theatreland. Mon–Thurs 11am–11.30pm, Fri & Sat 11am–midnight, Sun noon–10.30pm.

CLUBS

Blues Kitchen Shoreditch 134–146 Curtain Rd ⓦtheblueskitchen.com/shoreditch; ❶Old Street; map pp.422–423. A converted Victorian warehouse with a New Orleans vibe, this place is a lively restaurant by day, serving BBQ, steak, ribs and bourbon cocktails, before morphing into a live blues/jazz/soul joint by night. Mon–Wed noon– midnight, Thurs noon–1am, Fri noon–2.30am, Sat 11am–3am, Sun 11am–10.30pm.

Cargo 83 Rivington St ⓦcargo-london.com; ❶Old Street; map pp.422–423. Live music bar/club playing global music, with decked gardens for socializing and DJs playing their sets into the wee hours. Mon–Thurs 6pm–1am, Fri & Sat 6pm–3am, Sun 6pm–midnight.

EGG London, 200 York Way, Kings Cross ☎0207 871 7111, ⓦegglondon.co.uk; map pp.422–423. Spread over five separate spaces that include one of London's biggest dance floors, EGG has a 24-hour licence and parties until morning most nights. Friday nights see up-and-coming DJs at the decks, while on Saturdays it's a mix on international DJ superstars and fresh talent. Daily approx 10pm–9am.

Guanabara Parker St ⓦguanabara.co.uk; ❶Holborn; map p.425. Nightly samba, bossa-nova and Latin beats keep the punters on the dancefloor at this fun Brazilian club. Free Wed, Thurs & Sun, Fri £10 after 9pm, Sat £10 after 8pm. Mon–Sat 5pm–2.30am, Sun 5pm–midnight.

Proud Camden The Stables Market, Chalk Farm Rd ⓦproudcamden.com; ❶Camden Market; map pp.422–423. This former horse hospital is a chilled-out bar by day that turns into a burlesque club at night. Groove to the live music and the DJs or head out to the Alice in Wonderland-esque rooftop bar for an alfresco drink. Entrance £3–8. Sun–Wed 11am–1.30am, Thurs–Sat 11am–2.30am.

XOYO 32–37 Cowper St, Shoreditch ⓦxoyo.co.uk; ❶Old Street; map pp.422–423. Spread over two floors, with an industrial, street-arty vibe, this club benefits from a superb sound system and plays host to London's biggest house event, Sneak, every Tuesday, and guest DJs on other nights. Tickets £4–10. Mon–Thurs 10pm–3am, Fri & Sat 9pm–4am, Sun 8pm–midnight.

LIVE MUSIC AND SPORTS VENUES

Barfly 49 Chalk Farm Rd ⓦthebarflylondon.com; ❶Camden Town/Chalk Farm; map pp.422–423. Where a large array of punk, rock and indie bands make their debut, with club nights too. Mon & Thurs 3pm–2am, Tues & Wed 3pm–1am, Fri & Sat 3pm–3am, Sun 3pm–midnight.

02 Arena Peninsula Square ⓦtheo2.co.uk; ❶North Greenwich. Excellent mid-sized concert and event venue on the south side of the Thames. Past performers have included Leonard Cohen, Rihanna, Prince, Alice Cooper and more. You can also sign up for guided walks along the top

★TREAT YOURSELF

If you fancy a change from pints of lager, head for one of the city's stylish **cocktail bars** for a barrel-aged daiquiri or smoky negroni. The drinks are pricey (£10–15), but they pack a punch, and the bars are open till the early hours. For speakeasy-style cool, try *Evans & Peel Detective Agency*, 310c Earls Court Rd ⓦevansandpeel.com (❶Earls Court; map pp.422–423), while the eclectic, Lewis-Carroll-themed *Callooh Callay*, 65 Rivington St ⓦcalloohcallaybar .com (❶Old Street; map pp.422–423), serves creative cocktails. *Dandelyan* inside the *Mondrian* hotel, 20 Upper Ground (❶London Bridge; map pp.422–423), offers some of the most unusual cocktails in London by award-winning mixologist Mr Lyan, *Gŏng* inside the *Shangri-La* hotel at the Shard, 32 London Bridge St ⓦgong-shangri-la.com (❶London Bridge; map pp.422–423), has the loftiest views in London from its 52nd-floor setting, while *Mark's Bar*, 66 Brewer St, Soho (❶Piccadilly Circus; map p.425), is a lavish subterranean haven with classic British cocktails and an extensive gin and Scotch list.

13

of the arena.

Ronnie Scott's 47 Frith St ⓦronniescotts.co.uk; ⓣTottenham Court Rd; map p.425. London's most famous jazz club; big-name acts play in the dimly lit, red-velvet downstairs club. Mon–Sat 6pm–3am, Sun 6.30pm–midnight.

South Bank Centre Belvedere Rd, by Waterloo Bridge ⓦsouthbankcentre.co.uk; ⓣWaterloo; map pp.422–423. Vast arts complex, showcasing high quality music of all genres, from classical to the likes of Mary Chapin Carpenter; it includes the Royal Festival Hall and the Purcell Room, both top classical music venues.

Wembley Stadium Wembley ⓦwembleystadium.com; ⓣWembley Park. With a capacity of 90,000, this immense stadium hosts major football games and the biggest names in rock and pop, from Bruce Springsteen and Beyoncé to Coldplay and Ed Sheeran.

GAY AND LESBIAN NIGHTLIFE

Freedom 66 Wardour St ⓦfreedombarsoho.com; ⓣTottenham Court Road; map p.425. Stylish, glamorous cocktail bar and nightclub that attracts those who work in fashion and entertainment. Cabaret, drag and comedy are on weeknights. Mon–Fri 4pm–3am, Sat & Sun 2pm–3am.

G-A-Y at Heaven Under The Arches, Villiers St ⓦheavennightclub-london.com; ⓣCharing Cross/ Embankment; map p.425. Britain's most popular gay club, this legendary, 2000-capacity club continues to reign supreme. Expect disco divas and big acts. Free entry vouchers on website. Regular club nights Mon & Thurs– Sat; for other events see website.

Ku Bar/Ku Club 30 Lisle St ⓦku-bar.co.uk; ⓣLeicester Square/Tottenham Court Rd; map p.425; smaller branch at 25 Frith St. Ever-popular bar over three floors with a huge variety of inventive club nights. Tues is lesbian night. Free entry; £5 after 11pm Fri & Sat. Mon–Sat noon–3am, Sun noon–2am.

Royal Vauxhall Tavern 372 Kennington Lane ⓦrvt.org .uk; ⓣVauxhall; map pp.422–423. From cabaret to comedy and from drag shows to discos, London's oldest gay venue has it all. An international gay institution. Entry around £8

ENTERTAINMENT

CINEMAS

Leicester Square is where film premieres take place and where you can catch blockbusters at the Odeon and Vue.

BFI Under Waterloo Bridge, South Bank ⓦbfi.org.uk; ⓣWaterloo; map pp.422–423. Serious arts cinema showing up to ten different films each day and screening the London Film Festival (Oct) and London Lesbian and Gay Film Festival (late March).

Prince Charles 2–7 Leicester Place ⓦprincecharlescinema .com; ⓣLeicester Square; map p.425. The bargain basement of London's cinemas, with a programme of newish movies, singalong events and cult favourites.

THEATRES AND OPERA

Almeida Theatre Almeida St, Islington ⓦalmeida .co.uk; ⓣHighbury & Islington; map pp.422–423. Theatre known for launching independent, original performances.

Coliseum St Martin's Lane ⓦeno.org; ⓣLeicester Square; map p.425. Home to the English National Opera, and more radical and democratic than the Royal Opera House, with opera (in English) and ballet. Expect the likes of Madam Butterfly and Tristan and Isolde.

Donmar Warehouse 41 Earlham St ⓦdonmar warehouse.com; ⓣCovent Garden; map p.425. Formerly the spiritual home of director Sam Mendes, and the best bet for a central off-West End show. Front-row tickets £10 on Mon when bought two weeks in advance (see website); standing tickets are £7.50.

National Theatre by Waterloo Bridge, South Bank ⓦnationaltheatre.org.uk; ⓣWaterloo; map pp.422–423. The NT has three separate theatres putting on consistently good productions. Tickets often go on sale at £10; ask about discounted day seats or standing tickets.

Old Vic The Cut, off Waterloo Rd ⓦoldvictheatre.com; ⓣWaterloo; map pp.422–423. A venerable theatre, which mostly showcases classic drama.

Royal Court 50–51 Sloane Square ⓦroyalcourttheatre .com; ⓣSloane Square; map pp.422–423. With an emphasis on new work by cutting-edge young writers, this intimate space is a great place to catch emerging talent.

Sadler's Wells Rosebery Ave ⓦsadlerswells.com; ⓣAngel; map pp.422–423. London's biggest dance venue puts on a truly varied mix of contemporary dance – from tap to hip-hop – as well as more traditional forms such as ballet and flamenco.

CULTURE ON THE CHEAP

Many **theatres** offer student discounts, and have standing, restricted view, or standby tickets available last minute. ⓦlastminute.com often have cheaper tickets for most of the big shows, such as *Phantom of the Opera*, *The Lion King* and *Mamma Mia!*, while the TKTS booth in Leicester Square sells half-price tickets (Mon–Sat 9am–7pm, Sun 10.30am–4.30pm; ⓦtkts.co.uk) for that day's performances, with tickets also available up to a week in advance. For classical music, between July and September, you can't beat the **Proms** (ⓦbbc.co.uk/proms), the annual classical music festival held at the Royal Albert Hall. Simply queue up a few hours before the performance to get standing tickets for around £5.

SHOPPING

London's up there with Paris and New York for the sheer variety of its shopping, and there are many stores and boutiques you simply won't find anywhere else. If you're on a budget, window-shopping is still a great way of spending time; better still, visit one of the capital's many markets (see box, p.429). Westfield, the mammoth mall with outlets in west London (Ⓣ Shepherd's Bush) and east London (Ⓣ Stratford and Stratford Overground), has all the big names, both high-end and high-street. For shopping by street, see box below.

Harrods Brompton Rd, Ⓦ harrods.com; Ⓣ Knightsbridge; map pp.422–423. London's grandest department store and a place where many tourists come just to browse; check out the incredible food hall and the art gallery. Daily 10am–8pm, Sun noon–6pm.

Liberty Great Marlborough St Ⓦ liberty.co.uk; Ⓣ Oxford Circus; map p.425. Famous for its iconic prints, with jewellery, scarves, bags and designer clothes in opulent surroundings. Mon–Sat 10am–8pm, Sun noon–6pm.

Topshop & Topman 214–216 Oxford St Ⓦ topshop .com; Ⓣ Oxford Circus; map p.425. "World's largest fashion store" attracts huge crowds in search of the latest fashions. Mon–Sat 9am–9pm, Sun 11.30am–6pm.

★**Stanford's** 12–14 Long Acre Ⓦ stanfords.co.uk; Ⓣ Covent Garden/Leicester Square; map p.425. The best travel shop in the UK, with several floors of maps, guidebooks, travel literature and related paraphernalia. Mon–Fri 9am–8pm, Sat 10am–8pm, Sun noon–6pm.

QUINTESSENTIAL LONDON SHOPPING STREETS

Charing Cross Road A great place to pick up reading material. Rummage in one of the many secondhand bookshops, or browse new titles in Foyles.

Covent Garden Plenty of high-street stores, plus independent fashion outlets around the Neal St area, Floral St, Seven Dials and Long Acre.

Knightsbridge to Sloane Square Every high-end designer has their flagship store near here.

Oxford Street London's most famous and frequented shopping strip, home to gargantuan branches of high-street shops including Primark and Nike Town.

Soho and Carnaby Street Seedy Soho is crammed with quirky fashion shops, independent record stores and erotica. At its western boundary, Carnaby Street (Ⓦ carnaby.co.uk) trades heavily on its association with the swinging Sixties, but is still a good bet for cool trainers and young fashion.

DIRECTORY

Banks and exchange Shopping areas such as Oxford St and Covent Garden are littered with private exchange offices, but their rates are usually worse than the banks. Any post office (see p.420) will exchange money commission-free and any large bank will offer competitive rates.

Embassies Australia, Australia House, Corner of Aldwych with the Strand ☎ 020 7379 4334, Ⓦ uk.embassy.gov.au (Ⓣ Holborn/Temple); Canada, Canada House, Trafalgar Square ☎ 020 7258 6600, Ⓦ UnitedKingdom.gc.ca (Ⓣ Charing Cross); Ireland, 17 Grosvenor Place ☎ 020 7235 2171, Ⓦ embassyofireland.co.uk (Ⓣ Hyde Park Corner); New Zealand, 80 Haymarket ☎ 020 7930 8422, Ⓦ nzembassy.com/uk (Ⓣ Piccadilly Circus); South Africa, South Africa House, Trafalgar Square ☎ 020 7451 7299, Ⓦ southafricahouseuk.com (Ⓣ Charing Cross); United States, currently at 24 Grosvenor Square (☎ 020 7499 9000, Ⓦ uk.usembassy.gov; Ⓣ Bond Street), but due to move south of the river to Nine Elms in 2017.

Hospitals St Mary's Hospital, Praed St (☎ 020 3312 6666; Ⓣ Paddington); University College Hospital, 235 Euston Rd (☎ 0845 1555 000; Ⓣ Euston Square or Warren Street).

Left luggage At all airport terminals and major train stations.

Pharmacy Boots at Piccadilly Circus is open until midnight (6pm on Sun), or Zafash at 233 Old Brompton Rd is 24hr (Ⓣ Earls Court).

Post office 24 William IV St (Mon & Wed–Fri 8.30am–6.30pm, Tues 9.15am–6.30pm, Sat 9am–5.30pm; Ⓣ Leicester Square/Charing Cross).

Southeast England

Leafy and prosperous, **southeast England** is well served by swift, frequent rail and coach services from London, making it ideal **day-trip** territory. The medieval ecclesiastical power base of **Canterbury** is full of history, while on the coast the upbeat, hedonistic resort of **Brighton** is London's summer playground by the sea.

DOVER

DOVER is the main port of entry along this stretch of coast, and the country's busiest: **ferries** sail to Calais and Dunkirk from the Eastern Docks. Besides the spectacular **white cliffs of Dover**, a symbol

13

of Britain's wartime defiance, and the impressive **Dover Castle**, with its war tunnels and Roman lighthouse remains, there's little to detain you here.

ARRIVAL AND INFORMATION

By train The main train station is Dover Priory, a 10min walk west of the centre and served by shuttle buses from the Eastern Docks.

Destinations Canterbury (2 hourly; 16–27min) and London (2 hourly; 2hr).

By bus Coaches to London pick up from both the docks and the town-centre bus station on Pencester Road.

Destinations London (hourly; 2hr 25min–3hr 20min).

Tourist information The tourist office is in Dover Museum, Market Square (daily 9.30/10am–3/5pm; Oct–March closed Sun; ☎ 01304 201066, ⓦ whitecliffscountry.org.uk).

CANTERBURY

CANTERBURY, still home to England's pre-eminent Archbishop, was one of medieval Europe's hottest pilgrimage destinations, as Chaucer's *Canterbury Tales* attest. Pilgrims flocked to the shrine of Archbishop Thomas à Becket, who was brutally murdered in the cathedral nave in 1170, victim of an unseemly spat between Church and State. Enclosed on three sides by medieval walls that you can stroll along, this World Heritage town hosts a sizeable student population, with the cathedral the main visitor draw.

WHAT TO SEE AND DO

Built in stages from 1070 onwards, **Canterbury Cathedral** (Mon–Sat 9am–5.30pm, Sun 12.30–2.30pm; ⓦ canterbury-cathedral.org; adult/student £10.50/9.50) is dominated by the central, sixteenth-century Bell Harry tower, with late Gothic towers giving the cathedral its distinct appearance. Its interior is austere, with a modern sculpture comprising ragged swords, suspended over the place in the northwest transept where Becket met his violent end. Its Romanesque crypt is one of the few remaining visible relics of the Norman cathedral with religious murals dating back to the eleventh century.

For more on local history, check out the **Beaney House of Art & Knowledge**, 18 High St (Mon–Wed, Fri & Sat

9am–5pm, Thurs 9am–7pm, Sun 10am–5pm; free; ⓦ canterburymuseums .co.uk/beaney), whose Explorers' Gallery also features such exotica as a nineteenth-century Chinese face-slapper, weaponry from the Indian Raj, an Egyptian cat mummy and ancient Greek pottery.

ARRIVAL AND DEPARTURE

By train Canterbury has two train stations: Canterbury East serves London Victoria and Dover Priory, while Canterbury West serves London Paddington, London Charing Cross and St Pancras – the stations are 10min east and southwest of the centre respectively.

Destinations Brighton (change at London or Ashford International; hourly; 2hr 45min); Dover (every 30min; 30min); London St Pancras (hourly; 1hr 15min); London Victoria (every 30min; 1hr 35min); London Charing Cross (every 30min; 1hr 45min).

By bus The bus station is at St George's Lane, below the High St.

Destinations Dover (hourly; 40min); London (hourly; 2hr).

INFORMATION

Tourist information The tourist office is located in the Beaney (see above; same hours; ☎ 01227 378100).

ACCOMMODATION

★ **Canterbury YHA** 54 New Dover Rd ☎ 0845 371 9010, ⓦ yha.org.uk. A 10min walk from the centre, this large, well-run hostel with excellent kitchen facilities and a good ratio of guests per bathroom is a friendly place despite its somewhat institutional decor. Dorms **£15**, doubles **£69**

Kipps Canterbury 40 Nunnery Fields ☎ 01227 786121, ⓦ kipps-hostel.com. Homely independent hostel near Canterbury East station and an easy walk to the centre. There's a communal kitchen, free wi-fi and a garden with pool table. Dorms **£19.50**, doubles **£65**

EATING AND DRINKING

Burgate Coffee House 43 Burgate. Steps away from the cathedral entrance, this snug independent café, decorated with photos of Burma, is an excellent stop for good coffee and imaginative sandwiches (£5.50–6.50), including veggie options. Mon–Sat 8.30am–5.30pm, Sun 10am–4.30pm.

★ **Goods Shed** Canterbury West station ⓦ thegoodsshed .co.uk. Top-notch local picnic ingredients and cheap lunch specials in this atmospheric restaurant and farmers' market that also stocks up to 300 different ale varieties. Head for *Whitstable Larder* for gourmet sausage rolls (80p), quiches, pies and tarts. Tues–Sat 9am–6pm, Sun till 4pm.

Kitch 4 St Peter's St. This tiny, whitewashed eatery specializes in generous cooked breakfasts (£8–9), superfood salads and home-made hummus and soup, with an emphasis on local, organic produce: vegetarians and vegans are well-catered for. Mon–Fri 8.30am–5pm, Sat & Sun 9am–5pm.

BRIGHTON

BRIGHTON has been a magnet for day-tripping Londoners since the Prince Regent (later George IV) started holidaying here in the 1770s with his mistress, launching a trend for the "dirty weekend". One of Britain's most entertaining seaside resorts, the city has emerged from seediness to embrace a new, fashionable hedonism, becoming one of the country's gay centres. This factor – along with a large student presence – has endowed Brighton with a buzzing nightlife scene, and there's a colourful music and arts festival (⊕brightonfestival.org), which runs for three weeks in May, coinciding with Brighton Fringe Festival (⊕brightonfringe .org), followed by Brighton Pride (⊕brighton-pride.org) in August.

WHAT TO SEE AND DO

Most people head straight for the beach, a four-mile-long stretch of pebbles bordered by a balustraded promenade. Brighton's cultural attractions and the shops and cafés of The Lanes are a short stroll from here.

The seafront

The wonderfully tacky half-mile-long **Brighton Pier** is an obligatory call; it's a huge amusement arcade, peppered with booths selling fish and chips, candyfloss and the famous Brighton rock. The **Brighton Wheel** provides sky-high views of the pier and coastline from its glass pods (Mon–Thurs & Sun 10am–9pm, Fri & Sat 10am–11pm; £8, ⊕brightonwheel.com), while a short stroll further east is the oldest electric railway in the world, **Volk's Electric Railway** (Easter–Sept daily every 15min, Mon–Fri 10.15am–5pm, Sat & Sun 11.15am–6pm; £3.80 return, ⊕volkselectricrailway.co.uk), whose antiquated locomotives run eastward towards the marina and the nudist beach. Brighton's newest attraction, a

controversial, 531ft observation tower with Sky Bar, the **British Airways i360** (Sun–Thurs 10am–10pm, Fri & Sat 10am–11pm; £15; ⊕britishairwaysi360 .com), opened in summer 2016 on the seafront by the old West Pier.

The Royal Pavilion and around

Inland, wedged between The Lanes and North Laine (see below) and flanked by the Theatre Royal, is the square known as Pavilion Gardens, home to the flamboyant **Royal Pavilion** (daily: April–Sept 9.30am–5.45pm; Oct–March 10am–5.15pm; £12.30; ⊕brighton museums.org.uk/royalpavilion). The closest you'll get to the Taj Mahal in Britain, the Royal Pavilion is a wedding-cake confection of pagodas, minarets and domes built in 1817 as a pleasure palace for the Prince Regent. Its interior is even more impressive than the exterior, decorated with ostentatious chandeliers and exotic chinoiserie.

Opposite the Pavilion is the **Brighton Museum and Art Gallery** (Tues–Sun & Mon bank hols 10am–5pm; free; ⊕brightonmuseums.org.uk), worth a visit for its excellent collection of twentieth-century art and design and a pair of the corpulent Prince Regent's enormous trousers.

The Lanes and North Laine

Between the seafront and Trafalgar Street lie Brighton's "lanes", offering some of the UK's best shopping. The narrow alleys of **The Lanes** preserve the layout of the fishing port that Brighton once was, while to the north the arty, bohemian quarter of **North Laine** is not in fact one road but many thin streets. Both are packed with stalls, independent second-hand clothes-, record- and bookshops, quirky boutiques and cosy coffee houses.

ARRIVAL AND DEPARTURE

By train From the train station on Queen's Road it's a 10min stroll straight down to the seafront.
Destinations Gatwick airport (every 15min; 25–40min); London (Victoria, King's Cross, St Pancras, Blackfriars and London Bridge; every 15min; 50min–1hr 5min).
By bus Coaches arrive at the Pool Valley bus station, very near the seafront.

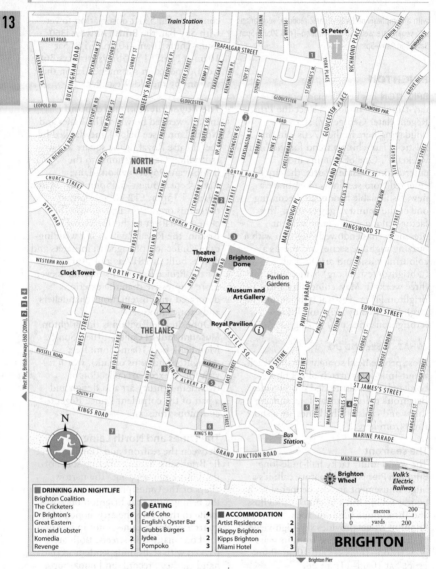

West Pier, British Airways i360 (200m), 2, 3 & 4

N

DRINKING AND NIGHTLIFE
Brighton Coalition	7
The Cricketers	3
Dr Brighton's	6
Great Eastern	1
Lion and Lobster	4
Komedia	2
Revenge	5

EATING
Café Coho	4
English's Oyster Bar	5
Grubbs Burgers	1
Iydea	2
Pompoko	3

ACCOMMODATION
Artist Residence	2
Happy Brighton	4
Kipps Brighton	1
Miami Hotel	3

| 0 | metres | 200 |
| 0 | yards | 200 |

BRIGHTON

Brighton Pier

Destinations Gatwick airport (hourly; 1hr); London Victoria (hourly; 1hr 50min–2hr 15min).

INFORMATION

Tourist information There's no tourist office, but contact ☎01273 290337, ⓦvisitbrighton.com for info.

ACCOMMODATION

Most accommodation options in Brighton require a two-night minimum stay at weekends, while prices in hostels go up at weekends, too: book well in advance for festivals and other events.

★**Happy Brighton** 23 Broad St ☎01273 676826, ⓦhappybrighton.com. Run by friendly, young, multilingual hosts, this great hostel is near the sea and the main attractions – you can choose between regular bunks or sleeping pods in a shared room. Dorms £21

Kipps Brighton 76 Grand Parade ☎01273 604182, ⓦkipps-brighton.com. Independent, friendly hostel run by the same people as *Kipps Canterbury* (see p.438), with a bar, terrace, and all other usual amenities for backpackers. Breakfast £2. Dorms **£20**, doubles **£90**

Miami Hotel 22 Bedford Square ☎01273 778701, ⓦ themiamihotel.co.uk. This is a handsome Grade II-listed Regency townhouse just a short stroll from the beach and town centre. The furniture went out of fashion in the 1970s, but some rooms come with sea views and balconies, and attached kitchenettes allow you to self-cater too. Doubles **£45**

EATING

Café Coho 53 Ship St ⓦ cafecoho.co.uk. This bijou independent café with a handful of outdoor tables is a great spot for people-watching in The Lanes. It does posh overstuffed sandwiches (bacon, brie and cranberry £4.25), as well as delicious cakes and coffee. Mon–Fri 8am–6.30pm, Sat & Sun 9am–7pm.

Grubbs Burgers 13 York Place & 89 St James' St. This Brighton micro-chain is legendary for its succulent burgers, with around 15 inventive combos: burger and fries/wedges £5.60. Sun–Thurs noon–midnight, Fri & Sat noon–3am.

★**Iydea** 17 Kensington Gardens ⓦ iydea.co.uk. Veggie café with an emphasis on freshness and eco-friendliness, with a Middle Eastern and Mediterranean bent; expect delicious globally influenced mains (£4.70–7.70 including two sides), tempting breakfasts, as well as cakes, salads, smoothies and organic beer and wine. Daily 9.30am–5.30pm.

Pompoko 110 Church St ⓦ pompoko.co.uk. Extremely popular no-frills Japanese with speedy service and tasty rice dishes such as teriyaki chicken don (£5.20) – everything on the menu is under £6. Daily 11.30am–11pm.

DRINKING AND NIGHTLIFE

Packed with bars, pubs and clubs, Brighton's frenetic nightlife can compete with that of many larger cities: for full listings, pick up a copy of *The Brighton Magazine* or check out ⓦ brighton.co.uk. It also has a lively gay scene; check out the free listings magazine *3Sixty*.

★**TREAT YOURSELF**

Rooms at the vibrant **Artist Residence boutique hotel** (33 Regency Square, ☎01273 324302, ⓦ arthotelbrighton .co.uk) have been decorated by artists, with each in a different style: some are emblazoned with graffiti, some feature pop art-style murals, while others are more soberly decorated while still retaining an arty feel. The smaller "micro sea view" rooms and standard doubles (without sea view) are a bargain, and breakfasts are a treat. Doubles **£120**

★**TREAT YOURSELF**

English's Oyster Bar 29–31 East St ☎01273 327980, ⓦ englishs.co.uk. Superior seafood in appealingly old-school surroundings. The two-course set menu is great value at £18, with dishes such as mussels steamed in cider followed by haddock in a pesto crust. Have your oysters raw or cooked three different ways. Daily noon–10pm.

PUBS

★**The Cricketers** 15 Black Lion St ⓦ cricketersbrighton .co.uk. This historic pub – Brighton's oldest – was immortalized by Graham Greene in the classic *Brighton Rock*, and its cosy, rich-red interior with plenty of hidden nooks has changed little since. A good selection of ales, and the food's decent too. Sun–Thurs noon–10pm, Fri–Sun noon–8pm.

Dr Brighton's 16 Kings Rd ⓦ doctorbrightons.co.uk. Friendly gay pub– Brighton's oldest – on the seafront, which is popular with all ages and has DJ sets at weekends. On Mon, Tues, Thurs & Sun the happy hour lasts all day. Mon–Thurs 1pm–midnight, Fri & Sat 1pm–2am, Sun 1–11pm.

Great Eastern 103 Trafalgar St. A tiny, 150-year-old traditional pub, serving over 60 American whiskeys and a great selection of real ales. Live music on Thurs and DJs every other Fri/Sat, as well as traditional roast lunches on Sun. Mon–Thurs & Sun noon–midnight, Fri & Sat noon–1am.

★**Lion and Lobster** 24 Silwood St ⓦ thelionandlobster .co.uk. A classic pub serving excellent food in rambling dining quarters (book at weekends), and a two-storey outdoor terrace. Mon–Thurs 11am–1am, Fri & Sat 11am–2am, Sun noon–midnight.

CLUBS AND LIVE MUSIC VENUES

Brighton Coalition 171–181 Kings Rd Arches ⓦ drinkinbrighton.co.uk/coalition. Right on the seafront, this club puts on a range of events, from club nights to karaoke. Thurs hosts *District*, dedicated to alternative rock and indie, with cheap drinks and popular with students. Daily 10pm–late.

Komedia 44 Gardner St ⓦ komedia.co.uk. Cool venue offering everything from cabaret and comedy to rock gigs, club nights and spoken word. Live music nights vary 7.30–11pm; club nights Fri & Sat 11pm–3am; comedy Thurs, Fri & Sun 8–10.30pm, Sat 7–9.30pm & 11pm–1.30am.

Revenge 32 Old Steine ⓦ revenge.co.uk. Brighton's biggest gay club is a three-floor affair, including a roof terrace, with a cheesy soundtrack. Bar Mon–Wed & Sun noon–1am, Thurs 9pm–1am, Fri & Sat noon–6am; club Tues–Sat 10.30pm–5am.

13

The West Country

As you approach England's **West Country**, the cosmopolitan feel of the southeast begins to fade into a slower, rural pace of life from **Salisbury** onwards, becoming more pronounced the further west you travel. In Neolithic times a rich and powerful culture evolved here, shown by monuments such as **Stonehenge** and **Avebury**. Urban attractions include vibrant **Bristol** and the elegant spa town of **Bath**, with its extensive Roman ruins, while those in search of bleakly picturesque rural landscapes should head for the ancient woods of **Dartmoor**. The southwestern extremities of Britain include some of the country's most beautiful stretches of coastline: with rugged, rocky shores, excellent white sandy beaches and surfable waves, **Cornwall** is one of Britain's busiest corners over the summer.

SALISBURY

Over a millennium ago, **SALISBURY** was founded after clergy living in the fort at **Old Sarum**, two miles north of the city, moved down the valley and created a walled sanctuary and the magnificent cathedral at the site where five rivers meet. Lined with half-timbered tudor houses, its central streets follow a grid pattern, so it is easy to find your way from the train station off Fisherton Street east over the River Avon to the bus station and Market Square (market on Tues & Sat), or to the cathedral south down the High Street through North Gate.

WHAT TO SEE AND DO

The city's dominant feature is the elegant spire of its thirteenth-century Gothic **cathedral** (Mon–Sat 9am–5pm, Sun noon–4pm; £7.50 for 45min tour, or £12.50 for 90min tour including spire; ⓦsalisburycathedral.org.uk), the tallest in the country at over 400ft. Don't miss the world's oldest working clock, dating from 1386, in the north aisle, or the lofty octagonal **chapterhouse**, approached via the cloisters (Mon–Fri 9.30–4.30pm, Sat 10am–4.30pm, Sun 12.45–3.45pm; free), which holds one of the four extant copies of the 1215 **Magna Carta**, England's most famous constitutional document, as well as one of Europe's finest medieval friezes.

Most of Salisbury's remaining sights are grouped in a sequence of graceful historic houses around **Cathedral Close**. The **Salisbury Museum** on West Walk (Mon–Sat 10am–5pm; June–Sept also Sun noon–5pm; £8; ⓦsalisburymuseum .org.uk) is a good place to bone up on the Neolithic history of the region – don't miss the Stonehenge Archer – before heading out to Stonehenge.

ARRIVAL AND DEPARTURE

By train The station is on the northwest edge of town, a 10min walk from the cathedral.
Destinations Bath (every 30min; 1hr); Bristol (every 30min; 1hr 10min); Exeter (for Dartmoor; hourly; 2hr); London (every 30min; 1hr 40min).
By bus Buses terminate behind Endless St, a short walk northeast of the cathedral.
Destinations Bath (1 daily; 1hr 15min); Bristol (1 daily; 2hr 15min); London via Heathrow Airport (3 daily; 3hr).

INFORMATION

Tourist information Tourist office on Fish Row, just off Market Square (Mon–Fri 9am–5pm, Sat 10am–4pm, Sun 10am–2pm; ☎01722 342860, ⓦvisitwiltshire.co.uk).

ACCOMMODATION

Alderbury Caravan & Camping Park Southampton Rd, Whaddon ☎01722 710125, ⓦalderburycaravanpark .co.uk; bus #X7. Three miles south of Salisbury, this pleasant campsite with launderette and wi-fi is easily reached from the city centre (15min). Per tent £13
Spire House 84 Exeter St ☎01722 339213, ⓦsalisbury -bedandbreakfast.com. A terrific base for exploring Salisbury, this welcoming B&B has four double rooms with funky wallpaper and comfortable furnishings, chosen with care. Excellent breakfasts, too. Doubles £75

EATING AND DRINKING

Gallery Café at Fisherton Mill 108 Fisherton St. Fantastic café-cum-art-and-craft gallery where you can get a great stone-baked bread sandwich (£6), soup or salad and watch sculptors or milliners at their craft. Tues–Fri 10am–5pm, Sat 9.30am–5.30pm.
★**Haunch of Venison** 1 Minster St ⓦhaunchpub.co.uk. Tiny, atmospheric old pub supposedly home to the ghost of the "Demented Whist Player", whose amputated mummified

hand resides in a nook in a side room as a warning to card game cheats everywhere. Also boasts an outstanding whisky selection. Mon–Sat 11am–11pm, Sun noon–6pm.

STONEHENGE

In deepest darkest Wiltshire, between Salisbury and Bath, the countryside was once home to a thriving Neolithic civilization, the greatest legacy of which is the mysterious stone circle of **Stonehenge** (daily: mid-March to April, May & Sept to mid-Oct 9.30am–6pm; June–Aug 9am–7pm; mid-Oct to mid-March 9.30am–5pm; £15.50; ⓦenglish-heritage .org.uk). Built in several distinct stages and adapted to the needs of successive cultures, the first stones were raised about 3000 BC, and during the next six hundred years the incomplete blue-stone circle was transformed into the familiar formation observed today. The way in which the sun's rays penetrate the enclosure at dawn on midsummer's day has led to speculation about Stonehenge's role as either an astronomical observatory or a place of sun worship.

A smart **visitor centre** at Airman's Corner features a wonderful 360-degree projection of Stonehenge, as well as reconstructed Neolithic huts: free shuttle buses run from here to the stones – or you can walk the 1.5 miles. The stones are cordoned off, but you can walk round the outside and view them from about 100 yards away. To walk among the stones, you have to pre-book a half-hourly time slot, though there's free access once a year on the evening of the summer solstice, when tens of thousands of revellers party at the stones until sunrise (see website for details).

ARRIVAL AND DEPARTURE

By bus The Stonehenge Tour bus (mid-March to early June & Sept to mid-Oct 10am–4pm hourly; early June to Aug 9.30am–5pm every 30min; ⓦwww.stonehengetour.info; £14) connects Salisbury's train station to Stonehenge.

BATH

BATH is surely the prettiest small city in Britain. It became important under the Romans, who worshipped at the hot springs, creating the eponymous **baths**,

one of Britain's top sights. Revived and reconstructed in the eighteenth century as a retreat for the wealthy and fashionable, the city has a harmonious and elegant look, constructed from the local honey-coloured sandstone and still retaining the genteel air of refinement Jane Austen satirized in her novels *Persuasion* and *Northanger Abbey*. However, the large student population makes it a vibrant place and there are numerous festivals throughout the year, such as the eclectic two-week International Music Festival in May and, naturally, the Jane Austen Festival in September, when a Regency dress parade takes place: see ⓦvisitbath .co.uk for all festivals.

WHAT TO SEE AND DO

Bounded on three sides by the River Avon, Bath's core is relatively compact. From Bath Spa train station, head north along Manvers Street which becomes Pierrepoint Street in the direction of Pulteney Bridge, then turn off left up York Street to reach the Abbey, Roman Baths and tourist office. Carry on winding northwest from the Abbey until you reach Queen Square and walk through Royal Victoria Park to reach the most famous streets in Bath, the Royal Crescent and the Circus.

The Roman Baths and Bath Abbey

The Romans considered natural hot springs a gift from the gods, and Bath's, being the only ones in Britain, received very special treatment when they conquered in 43 AD. Hidden underground for years, the springs were rediscovered by the Victorians: today, they house the wonderfully interactive **Roman Baths museum** (daily: March–June, Sept & Oct 9am–5pm; July & Aug 9am–9pm; Nov–Feb 9.30am–5pm; £15, combined ticket with Fashion Museum £21; ⓦromanbaths.co.uk). Highlights include the almost perfectly preserved bronze head of Minerva, Roman goddess of the sacred spring, a large portion of the decorative front of the Temple that would have stood as part of the bath complex, as well as an extensive warren of spa rooms. The **Pump Room**, built in the eighteenth century, is

13

---

now a restaurant and tearoom; the Roman Baths entrance ticket entitles you to a free glass of the tepid ferrous spa water inside.

The Royal Crescent and Assembly Rooms

The best of Bath's eighteenth-century architecture is on the high ground to the north of the town centre, where the well-proportioned Georgian urban planning is showcased by the elegant **Circus** and adjacent **Royal Crescent**, former home to the likes of David Livingstone and Clive of India. The first house to be built here, no. 1 (Mon noon–5pm, Tues–Sun 10.30am–5.30pm; £8.50; ⍈ no1royalcrescent.org.uk), has been sumptuously restored to its former glory; you can wander the elegant Georgian rooms above stairs, as well as the original servants' quarters.

Just east of the Circus, the elegant **Assembly Rooms** (daily 10.30am–6pm; £2.50, or included in entry to the Fashion Museum) were the hub of fashionable Georgian society. The building also houses the **Fashion Museum** (daily: Jan, Feb, Nov & Dec 10.30am–4pm; March–Oct 10.30am–5pm; £8.75 or joint ticket with Roman Baths £21; ⍈ fashionmuseum.co.uk), with displays showcasing the changing dress code from the sixteenth to the twentieth centuries.

The Holburne Museum

A ten-minute walk from the centre along Great Pulteney St, the **Holburne Museum** (Mon–Sat 10am–5pm, Sun 11am–5pm; free; ⍈ holburne.org) is an excellent fine-arts collection housed in a stately villa with a bold glass extension. On display are paintings by Gainsborough, who was born in Bath, and his contemporaries

Stubbs and Zoffany, as well as some fine Dutch paintings and exquisite small-scale sculptures, ceramics and porcelain.

ARRIVAL AND DEPARTURE

By train Bath Spa train station is on Dorchester St at the end of Manvers St, 5min south of the Abbey.
Destinations Bristol (every 20min; 15min); London Paddington (every 30min; 1hr 30min); Oxford (change at Didcot Parkway; 1–2 hourly; 1hr 10min–1hr 30min); Salisbury (1–2 hourly; 1hr).

By bus The bus station is along from the train station on Dorchester St.
Destinations Bristol (every 20min; 1hr); Bristol Airport (hourly; 1hr 15min); Glastonbury (1 direct daily from Bath Spa; 1hr); London (hourly; 2hr 45min–4hr).

INFORMATION

Tourist information The tourist office is just off the Abbey churchyard (Mon–Sat 9.30am–5pm, Sun 10am–4pm; ☎ 0906 711 2000, ⍈ visitbath.co.uk). Free walking tours leave from the Pump Room (Sun–Fri 10.30am & 2pm; Sat 10.30am; 2hr; ⍈ bathguides.org.uk), or you can download a self-guided walking tours app from the Visit Bath website.

ACCOMMODATION

Bath YHA Bathwick Hill ☎ 0845 371 9303, ⍈ yha.org.uk; bus #18 or #U18. Stunning hillside villa a couple of miles uphill east of town with an unloved interior that's due to be refurbished. Dorms £20, doubles £48

Bath YMCA Broad St Place ☎ 01255 325900, ⍈ bathymca .co.uk. Large, no-frills hostel in a great location in the centre of town. The staff are friendly and breakfast is good, but cleanliness is an issue. Dorms £23, doubles £60

University of Bath Claverton Down ☎ 01225 386079, ⍈ bath.ac.uk/accommodation. Simply furnished, great-value en-suite rooms at the university, east of the centre, with hotel-style extras such as free toiletries, tea and coffee; most rooms are available July–Sept, but some can be booked all year. Doubles £60

White Hart Inn Widcombe Hill ☎ 01225 313985, ⍈ whitehartbath.co.uk. A 10min walk from the station: although it is a bit further out of the centre, this old inn offers simple but excellent-value dorms, singles and doubles, with a good restaurant and bar downstairs, plus a little sun-trap garden. Dorms £15, doubles £40

EATING, DRINKING AND NIGHTLIFE

★ The Bell Inn 103 Walcot St ⍈ thebellinnbath.co.uk. Everything you want from a neighbourhood pub: a range of beers, a mixed and lively crowd, a garden, live music most days and vinyl DJs at weekends, plus good roasts at weekends and barbecues in summer. Mon–Sat 11.30am–11pm, Sun noon–10.30pm.

Made by Ben 100 Walcot St ⓦmadebyben.com. Delicious gourmet sandwiches, pies, quiches and cakes. There's a handful of tables out back, or you can take away (quiche with salad £6.50). Mon–Fri 8am–5pm, Sat 9am–6pm, Sun 10am–5pm.

Moles 14 George St ⓦmoles.co.uk. This popular live-music venue attracts a good mix of bands, while club nights (Tues–Sat) range from indie and alternative to The Big Cheese. Tues–Sat 10pm–3 or 4am.

The Raven of Bath 6–7 Queen St ⓦtheravenofbath .co.uk. As well as micro-brewed ales and a relaxed atmosphere, this pub serves up fantastic pies with mash and gravy (£9.80). Mon–Thurs & Sun 11.30am–11pm, Fri & Sat 11.30am–midnight.

★ **Wild Café** 10a Queen St ⓦwildcafe.co.uk. A trendy local favourite for brunch (served all day) and mains such as lamb and falafel burgers. Great organic and fairtrade food, and the café is powered by renewable energy. English breakfast £7. Mon–Fri 8am–5pm, Sat 9am–6pm, Sun 10am–5pm.

Yak Yeti Yak l2 Pierrepont St ☎01225 443473, ⓦyakyetiyak.co.uk. Not the cheapest, but you may not get another Nepalese meal this good in Britain; for £10.50, the 3-course set meal is a great deal (noon–2pm & before 7pm). Booking essential at weekends. Mon–Thurs noon–2pm & 6–10.30pm, Fri & Sat noon–2pm & 5–10.30pm, Sun 6–10.30pm.

BRISTOL

Situated on a succession of chunky hills twelve miles west of Bath and just inland from the mouth of the River Avon, **BRISTOL** grew rich on transatlantic trade – the slave trade, in particular – in the eighteenth century. It remains a wealthy, commercial centre, and is home to a population of around 450,000, a major university, a thriving music scene that produced some of the most significant artists of the 1990s (Portishead, Tricky, Massive Attack), and Banksy – guerrilla artist and *agent provocateur* whose subversive stencils adorn neglected city walls throughout the world. More ethnically diverse than other cities in the southwest, Bristol manages to combine clued-up arty urban culture with enticing green spaces and striking industrial architecture. In August, the city hosts Europe's largest hot-air balloon fiesta (ⓦbristolballoon fiesta.co.uk) – a spectacular sight.

The city centre is an elongated traffic interchange, known as the **Centre Promenade**. Walking from the station, detour via the church of **St Mary Redcliffe** (Mon–Sat 8.30am–5pm, Sun 8am–8pm; donation expected), a glorious Gothic confection begun in the thirteenth century, before continuing across the river, through elegant Queen's Square.

The Floating Harbour

The southern end of the centre gives way to the city's **Floating Harbour**, an area of waterways that formed the hub of the old port. It is now the location of numerous bars and restaurants as well as **M Shed** (Tues–Fri 10am–5pm, Sat & Sun 10am–6pm; free; ⓦmshed.org), a museum whose engaging, interactive exhibits provide an excellent overview of all things Bristolian, from the city's role in the transatlantic slave trade to its contemporary music scene. Nearby are two of Bristol's contemporary arts venues: the **Arnolfini** (Tues–Sun 10am–6pm ⓦarnolfini.org.uk; free), a cool, white gallery and performing arts space that stages modern art and photography exhibitions, and the **Watershed** cinema complex (ⓦwatershed.co.uk), with an excellent café. Just north of here, **College Green** is overlooked by the city's Gothic Revival **cathedral** and the curvaceous red-brick Council House. A short walk west along the southern side of the harbour, or a brief ride on the ferry (£1.60 return; 10min), brings you to Isambard Kingdom Brunel's majestic **SS Great Britain** (Mon–Fri 10am–4.30pm, Sat & Sun 10am–5.30pm; adult £14, student £11; ⓦssgreatbritain.org), the world's first propeller-driven iron ship, which first launched from here in 1843, and has been sensitively restored to its original glory. One of the most technologically advanced ships of its time, the passenger liner zipped between Bristol and New York in just two weeks.

Stokes Croft

The main road leading north from the centre, **Stokes Croft**, has become the city's cultural pulse as artists and creative types

13

have turned what was until recently a grotty road littered with derelict buildings into a buzzing and fashionable part of the city with an array of vintage shops, cool cafés and street art.

Clifton

Reached by bus #8 from the Centre Promenade, genteel **Clifton Village** is a great place to wander, its streets lined with Georgian mansions, airy terraces, enticing pubs and antiques shops. Overhanging the limestone abyss of the Avon Gorge is the **Clifton Suspension Bridge**, another creation of the indefatigable engineer Brunel. From the Clifton side of the Suspension Bridge, **the Downs**, the city's largest green space, stretches north for a couple of miles. On the way back down to the centre, the **Bristol Museum and Art Gallery** (Mon–Fri 10am–5pm, Sat & Sun 10am–6pm; free; ⓦ bristol.gov.uk /museums) is home to Banksy's controversial *Paint Pot Angel* sculpture, as well as an excellent Eastern Art collection, exhibits on prehistory and more.

ARRIVAL AND DEPARTURE

By plane Bristol Airport (ⓦ bristolairport.co.uk), eight miles south of town, is served by easyJet and Ryanair flights from Edinburgh, Glasgow and Newcastle as well as European destinations. Regular Bristol International Flyer buses (ⓦ flyer.bristolairport.co.uk) run to the stations and the city centre (£7 one-way; 30min).

By train The main station, Bristol Temple Meads, is a 5min bus ride southeast of the centre (bus #8 or #9), or a 15min walk.

Destinations Bath (every 10–30min; 15min); Cardiff (every 20min; 40min–1hr); Exeter for Dartmoor (every 30min; 1hr); London (hourly; 1hr 45min); Penzance (hourly; 5hr 15min); Oxford via Reading or Didcot Parkway (every 30min; 1hr–1hr 30min); Salisbury (every 30min–1hr; 1hr 10min); York (hourly; 4hr).

By bus The bus station is near the Broadmead shopping centre on Marlborough St.

Destinations Bath (every 20min; 1hr); Cardiff (every 2hr; 1hr 15min); Glastonbury (some via Wells; every 30min; 1hr 20min); Oxford (1 daily; 3hr); Penzance (5 daily; 5hr 45min–8hr 15min); Salisbury (1 daily; 2hr 10min).

INFORMATION

Tourist information The tourist office is at E Shed, Canons Rd, just off Centre Promenade on the water (Mon–Fri & Sun 11am–4pm, Sat 10am–4pm; ⓣ 0906 7112191,

ⓦ visitbristol.co.uk): Bristol Highlights Walk (ⓦ bristol walks.co.uk; £6) tours of the old town depart from outside here at 11am every Saturday (March–Nov).

ACCOMMODATION

Bristol YHA 14 Narrow Quay ⓣ 0845 3719726, ⓦ yha .org.uk. This splendidly situated hostel is in an old wharfside building – a former grain house – next to the Arnolfini. Staff are helpful and the rooms are clean, though fairly institutional and with cheap beds. Dorms **£20**, doubles **£48**

Clifton House 4 Tyndall's Park Rd ⓣ 0117 9735407, ⓦ cliftonhousebristol.com. Boutique B&B in a Victorian villa in Clifton, behind the museum, offering en-suite triple and quad rooms with a luxurious feel. Full English breakfast included. Doubles **£85**

Rock and Bowl Motel 22 Nelson St ⓣ 0117 3251980, ⓦ rocknbowlmotel.com. For energetic night owls rather than for light sleepers, this loud, convivial, mural-covered place in the city centre has basic but clean dorms and rooms above a retro bowling alley; there's on-site bowling, live music and a large lounge for socializing. Dorms **£18**, doubles **£45**

EATING

Boston Tea Party 75 Park St, 156 Cheltenham Rd, 97 Whiteladies Rd & 1 Princess Victoria St, Clifton. Chain of cafés dotted around the southwest, each with its own personality and an emphasis on locally sourced produce. Cooked breakfast £7. Mon–Sat 7.30am–8pm, Sun 9am–7pm.

★ **Canteen** 80 Stokes Croft ⓦ canteenbristol.co.uk. In a refurbished 1960s office block, this cooperative-run bar with restaurant serves slow, locally produced food such as Cornish fish stew for just £8. Live alternative music for all tastes starts from around 9.30pm. Mon–Thurs & Sun 10am–midnight, Fri & Sat 10am–1am.

Eat a Pitta 67a Gloucester Rd ⓦ eatapitta.co.uk. The short but sweet menu has just three items and they all involve Bristol's best falafel (£6), with home-made sauces. Daily Mon–Sat 10.30am–8.30pm, Sun 10.30am–6pm.

Mud Dock Café 40 The Grove. Bike shed café-restaurant on the quayside, with great views over the water from their balcony, and dishes such as spinach and feta omelette on the £6 weekday lunch menu. Mon 10am–5pm, Tues–Fri & Sun 10am–10pm, Sat 9am–10pm.

Simply Thai 67 Gloucester Rd ⓦ simplythaibristol.com. One of several inexpensive, good restaurants along Gloucester Rd, north of the centre, this is an authentic take on Thai food, with favourites such as spicy papaya salad and masaman chicken curry (£7). Daily noon–3pm & 5–11pm.

St Nicolas' Market Corn St. For a budget meal on the go, this great market has a huge array of local and ethnic food stalls. Mon–Sat 9.30am–5pm.

★ **Thali Cafe** 12 York Rd, Montpelier, 1 Regents St, Clifton, & 1 William St, across the river from Temple Meads ⓦ thethalicafe.co.uk. Colourful mini-chain of Bristol Indian

GLASTONBURY FESTIVAL

The world-famous five-day **Glastonbury Festival** (ⓦglastonburyfestivals.co.uk), held annually over the last weekend in June, is one of the West Country's biggest draws. When it was first held in 1970, this small-scale event cost £1; today it draws 175,000-plus people to a binge of music and hedonism and the tickets (£228) sell out in hours. Anyone who is anyone has played here – and there's still nothing else quite like it.

restaurants serving up a fantastic range of street food and thalis (£9). Clifton daily noon–10pm; Montpelier Mon–Fri 6–11pm, Sat & Sun 10am–11pm; William St daily 6–11pm.

DRINKING, NIGHTLIFE AND ENTERTAINMENT

The Apple Cider Boat Welsh Back, at the end of King St ⓦapplecider.co.uk. A fantastic array of West Country ciders, cider cocktails and snacks such as sausage rolls, all served on a floating canal boat on the harbour. Mon–Sat noon–midnight, Sun noon–10.30pm.

Copper Jack's Crafthouse 30 Clare St. Mural-decorated cocktail bar that hosts live music on Tues, Thurs & Sat – nurse a craft beer on a Chesterfield sofa, or order one of the edgy cocktails that the staff dream up. Tues–Sat 5pm–2am.

Milk Thistle Quay Head House, Colston Ave ⓦmilkthistlebristol.com. Inside this four-storey speakeasy in a plush townhouse, the beautiful oak-panelled bar serves equally attractive cocktails with a supporting cast of craft beers, wine and cider. Mon–Wed 5pm–1.30am, Thurs–Sat 5pm–3am.

Old Vic King St ☎0117 9877877, ⓦbristololdvic.org.uk. Britain's longest continuously running theatre has undergone a state-of-the-art refurbishment and now has several diverse performance spaces.

★ **Start The Bus** 7–9 Baldwin St ⓦstartthebusbristol .co.uk. A buzzing live music bar with local art on the walls, delicious American diner-style food (2 for 1 burgers on Tues) and a happy crowd. Mon–Wed & Sun noon–1am, Thurs noon–2am, Fri & Sat noon–3am.

★ **Thekla** The Grove, East Mud Dock ⓦtheklabristol .co.uk. Legendary riverboat venue staging eclectic events, gigs and Bristol's best club nights, ranging from disco to indie. Thurs–Sat 9.30pm–4am.

DARTMOOR

DARTMOOR, an expanse of uplands some 75 miles southwest of Bristol, is one of England's most beautiful wilderness areas. It's home to an indigenous breed of **wild pony** and dotted with **tors**, natural outcrops of granite. The area is renowned for outdoor pursuits, from cycling and horseriding to canoeing and climbing, and was the setting for the Sherlock Holmes

adventure, *The Hound of the Baskervilles*. Don't go unprepared, especially if you plan to camp, as the moor has an unforgiving weather system and explorers regularly get lost in its thick fogs. The northern part of the moor is more easily accessible from Exeter while the southern moor is best approached from Plymouth.

Okehampton and Lydford

The wildest parts of the moor, around its highest points of **High Willhays** and **Yes Tor** (which at over 2000ft are classified as southern England's only mountains), lie a few miles south of the market town of **OKEHAMPTON**. Four miles east of here, the **Finch Foundry** (mid-March to Oct daily 11am–5pm; £5; ⓦnationaltrust .org.uk/finch-foundry) is England's last water-powered forge, while the village of **LYDFORD** lies nine miles southwest of Okehampton, in a lovely gorge setting: there's a great 1.5-mile ramble from the village to the 30m-high **White Lady waterfall**, via the churning whirlpools of Lydford Gorge.

ARRIVAL AND INFORMATION

By train and bus There are train stations at Exeter, Newton Abbot, Totnes, Ivybridge and Plymouth; buses run from these towns onto the moor. The Haytor Hoppa bus runs on Sat (June–mid-Sept 4 daily) from Newton Abbot or Bovey Tracey (both serviced by frequent buses from Exeter) up to the northeast corner of the moor. Okehampton is served by regular buses from Plymouth and Exeter.

Tourist information Tourist office located off Fore Street, Okehampton (summer Mon–Sat 10am–5pm; winter Mon, Fri & Sat 10am–4.30pm; ☎01837 53020, ⓦokehamptondevon.co.uk), or check ⓦdartmoor.gov.uk for free downloadable walks.

ACCOMMODATION

Dartmoor YHA Postbridge ☎0845 371 9622, ⓦyha.org .uk. This remote and cosy YHA hostel, a mile south of Postbridge, makes a great base for local circular walks. There are basic bunks in the dorms upstairs and a social

13

CAMPING ON DARTMOOR

Camping wild on certain common land in Dartmoor is permitted for one or two nights, though you shouldn't pitch on farmland, within 100 yards of a road, house or on an archeological site; check out ⓦdartmoor.gov.uk/visiting /vi-enjoyingdartmoor/camping /camping-map for a helpful map. Always obtain consent from the landowner if pitching on private land.

---

area with books and games downstairs. Small discount for arrival on foot/bike. Dorms **£20**, doubles **£44**

Okehampton YHA Klondyke Rd ⓣ01837 53916, ⓦyha .org.uk. YHA hostel and activity centre in a converted goods shed at Okehampton station, with an on-site restaurant and cycle workshop; it's a popular base for cyclists and there's excellent abseiling and rock climbing in the area, too. Dorms **£29**, doubles **£74**

★**Sparrowhawk Backpackers** 45 Ford St, Moretonhampstead ⓣ01647 440318, ⓦsparrowhawk backpackers.co.uk. A converted barn with a dorm in the old hayloft, plus comfortable if basic private rooms. There's a relaxing communal area including a large kitchen and a sunny courtyard. Dorms **£17**, doubles **£38**

PENZANCE AND AROUND

The busy market and port town of **PENZANCE** with its colourful, pirate-rich history forms the natural gateway to the westernmost extremity of Cornwall, the Penwith Peninsula, and has the best transport links – all the major sights in the region can be reached on day-trips from here.

WHAT TO SEE AND DO

Penzance itself makes a pleasant base – to explore the town's historic buildings, pick up a self-guided walking tour booklet (£1) from the tourist office. The bigger attractions, however, are a bus ride away along the coast.

St Michael's Mount

The view east across the bay is dominated by **St Michael's Mount** (ⓦstmichaelsmount .co.uk), site of a fortified medieval monastery perched on an offshore pinnacle of rock. At low tide, the Mount is joined by a cobbled causeway to the mainland

village of Marazion (bus #2 runs here from Penzance every 30 minutes); at high tide, a boat or amphibious vehicle can ferry you over (£2 each way). You can amble partway along the Mount's shoreline, but most of the rock lies within the grounds of the **castle**, now a stately home (mid-March to Nov Mon–Fri & Sun 10.30am–5pm; castle £9; gardens £6) that has been inhabited by the St Aubyn family since the seventeenth century.

The Minack Theatre

Clinging to a craggy cove near Porthcurno beach, seven miles west of Penzance, the **Minack Theatre** (daily: April–Sept 9.30am–5.30pm; Oct–March 10am–4pm; £4 entrance to site, prices for evening performances vary; ⓦminack .com) is a splendid sight, a craggy amphitheatre with seats carved into the rocks that overlook the waves below.

ARRIVAL AND DEPARTURE

By train Penzance train station is at the northeastern end of town, a step away from Market Jew St.
Destinations Bristol (5 daily; 4hr); London (7 daily; 5hr 40min); Par (for Newquay; hourly; 1hr); St Ives (change at St Erth; hourly; 20–50min).

By bus The bus station is next to the train station.
Destinations Bristol (4 daily; 6hr 10min–8hr); Marazion (every 30min; 10min); Land's End (hourly; 55min); London (4 daily; 8hr 35min); Newquay (3 daily; 1hr 35min–2hr); St Ives (every 30min; 30min).

INFORMATION

Tourist information There's a National Trust visitor centre just outside the train and bus stations (Mon–Wed, Fri & Sat 10am–4pm; ⓣ01736 335530, ⓦpurelypenzance.co.uk).

GETTING AROUND

By bus From Penzance, bus #1 or #1A takes you to Land's End (8 daily; 55min) – some stop at Porthcurno (35min) from where it is a 400m steep climb to the Minack Theatre; bus #2 runs to Marazion; #17 runs to St Ives. A £10 day travel card gives you unlimited travel on all buses in Cornwall.

ACCOMMODATION

★**Con Amore Guesthouse** 38 Morrab Rd ⓣ01736 363423, ⓦcon-amore.co.uk. A 5min walk from the centre of town, this spotless, homey guesthouse offers a handful of snug en-suite rooms with nice extra touches such as bath robes and kettles. The owners couldn't be more helpful and breakfast costs £5 extra. Singles **£35**, doubles **£65**

THE EDEN PROJECT

One of Cornwall's major draws, occupying a 160ft-deep disused clay pit, the **Eden Project** (daily: April–Oct 9am–6pm; Nov–March 10am–4pm; school holidays 10am–6pm; £25; ticket valid for one year, discounts if arriving by public transport or booking online; ⓦedenproject.com) showcases the diversity of the planet's plant life in a stunningly landscaped site. The centrepiece is two vast geodesic "biomes", or conservatories, one holding plants from the Mediterranean, and the larger housing the **world's largest indoor rainforest**; a new canopy walkway allows you to take in the view from the treetops. For an extra £20 you can glide above the biomes on England's longest zip wire or take a 65ft freefall: see ⓦhanglooseadventure.com for details. The Eden Project lies four miles northeast of St Austell in Bodelva (bus #101 from St Austell train station).

★ **Easy PZ Backpackers** 29 Lannoweth Rd ☏01736 368136, ⓦeasypz.info. A lot of thought has gone into this welcoming hostel: from reading lights by each bunk in the individually decorated dorms to a fully equipped kitchen, lounge and room for drying wet gear. It's a 5min stroll from the bus/railway station; summer season only. Dorms **£20**, doubles **£50**

Penzance Backpackers Alexandra Rd (no number; about halfway up) ☏01736 363836, ⓦpzbackpack.com. Good independent hostel on a quiet tree-lined road 10min walk from central Penzance. With kitchen, cosy lounge and wi-fi. Dorms **£16**, doubles **£36**

EATING AND DRINKING

Archie Browns Bread St. Welcoming veggie café above a health-food shop using locally sourced ingredients. Specialities include mango and sweet potato curry, black bean stew and homity pie. Breakfasts from £3. Mon–Sat 9am–5pm.

★ **Mackerel Sky** 45 New St ⓦmackerelskycafe.co.uk. Excellent café-restaurant specializing in locally caught fish and seafood. It's hard to go wrong with the crab rarebit (£9) or smoked mackerel fishcakes (£11). Mon, Wed & Sun 10am–2.30pm, Thurs–Sat 10am–2.30pm & 6–9pm.

The Turk's Head Chapel St ⓦturksheadpenzance.co.uk. Knock back a pint of local Turk's Head ale at this cosy thirteenth-century pub with a pirate heritage and a smugglers' tunnel that runs all the way to the harbour. Excellent food accompanies the local ales and ciders on tap. Mon–Sat 11.30am–11pm, Sun noon–10.30pm.

ST IVES

13

Across the peninsula from Penzance, the fishing village of **ST IVES** is the quintessential Cornish resort, featuring a tangle of narrow streets lined with whitewashed cottages, fringed by three wide sandy beaches. The village's erstwhile tranquillity attracted several major artists throughout the twentieth century, including Ben Nicholson and Barbara Hepworth, and every other shop in town is a gallery making the most of its arty heritage. There is even a diminutive outpost of the **Tate gallery** here overlooking Porthmeor Beach (closed for renovation until Spring 2017, but likely to be same hours and price as Hepworth Museum; ⓦtate.org.uk/stives), that focuses on St Ives' School artists such as Patrick Heron and Barbara Hepworth, and features changing exhibitions of contemporary artists. The **Barbara Hepworth Museum and Garden** on Barnoon Hill (March to late July, Sept & Oct daily 10am–5.20pm; late July & Aug daily 10am–6.20pm; Nov–Feb Tues–Sun 10am–4.20pm; £6.60, or £10 combined with Tate St Ives) preserves the sculptor's studio and you can view some of her more striking abstract works in the beautiful garden.

Of the town's three beaches, the largest, north-facing **Porthmeor**, usually has good surf; rent a surfboard (£10/2hr) or paddle-board (£18/2hr), or take a lesson at the St Ives Surf School (£35/2hr; ☏01736 793938, ⓦstivessurfschool .co.uk). Alternatively, ramble along the

LAND'S END

Mainland Britain's westernmost point is a bleakly beautiful promontory, its steep cliff sides buffeted by relentless waves. Unfortunately, it's also topped by a tacky 1980s monument, shopping arcade and overpriced hotel. However, it's a good starting point for some fantastic day walks along the dramatic coast: you can walk south to Porthcurno (3–4 hours), taking in the Minack Theatre en route and then catching the #1A bus back to Penzance; or walk north to the gorgeous, pristine Sennen Cove (45min), then catch bus #1 back to Penzance.

13

coastal path south towards **Zennor** for beautiful views of craggy coves and wild flowers.

ARRIVAL AND INFORMATION

By train The train station is at Porthminster Beach.
Destinations London (via St Erth; 7 daily; 5hr 35min–6hr 20min); Penzance (hourly; 30–50min).
By bus The bus station is at The Malakoff, next to the train station. Buses #17 and #18 run to Penzance (1–2 hourly; 45min).
Tourist information The St Ives Visitor and Information Centre (Mon–Fri 9am–5pm, Sat & Sun 11am–4pm; ☎ 0905 2522250, ⓦ stivestic.co.uk) is in the Guildhall.

ACCOMMODATION AND EATING

Blas Burgerworks The Warren ☎ 01736 797272. Tuck into the best burgers in the southwest, with a great choice for vegetarians, too: specialities include halloumi stack with caper aioli and black bean burger with guacamole. Daily noon–9.30pm.
Cohort Hostel The Stennack, Town Centre ☎ 01736 791664, ⓦ stayatcohort.co.uk. The refurbished *St Ives Backpackers* hostel occupies an enormous old Wesleyan chapel and comes with seriously comfortable beds, a chill-out room and surfer-friendly facilities. It's built around a central courtyard where barbecues are organized in summer. Dorms **£19**, doubles **£40**

NEWQUAY

Buffeted by Atlantic currents, Cornwall's north coast is the area of the West Country most favoured by the **surfing** set. King of the surf resorts is tacky **NEWQUAY**, whose seven miles of golden sands, including Fistral Beach, host surfing championships. Equipment can be rented on most beaches or from one of the surf shops around town.

ARRIVAL AND INFORMATION

By plane Newquay's airport (ⓦ newquaycornwallairport .com) is three miles north of town; destinations include London Gatwick, Glasgow, Liverpool and Manchester: bus #56 runs to the centre (hourly; 20min).
By train The train station (change in Par or Plymouth) is just east of the centre.
Destinations London (5 daily; 5hr); Penzance (6 daily; 2hr).
By bus The bus station is on Manor Rd.
Destinations Eden Project (hourly; 1hr); St Ives (every 30min; 1hr).
Tourist information The tourist office at Marcus Hill (Mon–Fri 9.15am–5.30pm, Sat & Sun 10am–4pm;

reduced hours in winter; ☎ 01637 854020, ⓦ visitnewquay .org) has a left luggage facility and books surfing lessons.

ACCOMMODATION

Base Surf Lodge 20 Tower Rd ☎ 07766 132124, ⓦ basesurflodge.co.uk. Overlooking Fistral Beach, just thirty seconds from the UK's best waves, this lively lodge welcomes surfers with dorm-style digs of two to six beds per room. Surf lessons arranged and stag and hen parties welcome. Three-night minimum July to August. Dorms **£25**, doubles **£50**
Smarties Surf Lodge 84 Crantock St ☎ 01637 872391, ⓦ smartiessurflodge.co.uk. Hospitable Jackie plies her guests with cake and cold beer on arrival, the downstairs common area is a sociable chill-out spot and the place is just a short walk from both the beaches and the nightlife. Dorms **£20**

Central England

Encompassing both the old industrial towns and cities of the Midlands and some postcard-pretty countryside, alongside some of England's major cultural landmarks, **CENTRAL ENGLAND** defies easy categorization. With close on a million residents, Birmingham is the Midlands' largest city, but despite boasting one of the best concert halls in the country, is still unlikely to feature on a whistle-stop national tour. More appealing for a quick fix of history and culture are **Stratford-upon-Avon**, birthplace of William Shakespeare, and the rival university cities of **Oxford** and **Cambridge**.

OXFORD

Thoughts of **OXFORD** inevitably conjure up the university, revered as one of the world's great academic institutions. The city's skyline is dominated by its "dreaming spires", while the streets and narrow lanes of its compact medieval heart form a dense maze lined with historic honey-stone buildings containing the university's 38 grand colleges. Its combination of workaday vitality with hallowed academia, hidden centuries-old taverns and thousands of students strolling its lanes makes Oxford one of Britain's most appealing cities.

If you're looking to visit the colleges, plan your visit in advance (check ⓦox.ac.uk) since access may be restricted at exam time – especially in May and June – as well as during conferences and functions.

Christ Church College and the cathedral

The largest and most ostentatious of Oxford's colleges, **Christ Church** (Mon–Sat 10am–4.30pm, Sun 2–4.30pm; £8; ⓦchch.ox.ac.uk) was founded by Cardinal Wolsey in 1524; today, a great number of visitors come to view its grand **dining hall** (open from 2.30pm) and Great Staircase, which featured in the *Harry Potter* films. The college chapel is in fact the city of Oxford's beautiful **cathedral**.

Christ Church Meadow, Merton and Magdalen

South of Christ Church, **Christ Church Meadow** offers scenic views and gentle walks – either east along Broad Walk to the River Cherwell or south along New Walk to the River Isis. From the Broad Walk, paths lead to **Merton College**

(Mon–Fri 2–5pm, Sat & Sun 10am–5pm; £3; ⓦmerton.ox.ac.uk), founded in 1264 and home to Oxford's first quad, the Mob Quad, as well as the oldest medieval library in use, where Tolkien wrote much of *Lord of the Rings*. Nearby Rose Lane emerges at the eastern end of the High Street opposite **Magdalen College** (pronounced "maudlin"; daily noon–6/7pm; £6; ⓦmagd.ox.ac.uk), with a beautiful medieval chapel and cloisters – the wealth of gargoyles and grotesques perching on its buttresses is said to have inspired C.S. Lewis' stone statues in *The Chronicles of Narnia*.

The Bodleian Library and around

Just north of the High Street stands the **Bodleian Library** (term time: Mon–Fri 9am–10pm, Sat 9am–4pm, Sun 11am–5pm; holidays: Mon–Fri 9am–7pm, Sat 10am–4pm; 1hr tour £8; ⓦwww.bodleian.ox.ac.uk/bodley), the country's second-largest copyright library, with a staggering 4000 books added every week. Tours take in the fifteenth-century Divinity School (Hogwarts' infirmary in the *Harry Potter* films) and Duke Humphrey's medieval library, while

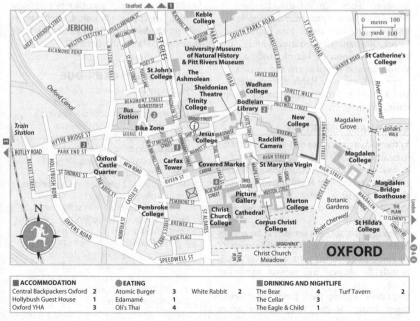

■ ACCOMMODATION		● EATING			■ DRINKING AND NIGHTLIFE		
Central Backpackers Oxford	2	Atomic Burger	3	White Rabbit 2	The Bear	4	Turf Tavern 2
Hollybush Guest House	1	Edamamé	1		The Cellar	3	
Oxford YHA	3	Oli's Thai	4		The Eagle & Child	1	

13

extended tours (Wed, Sat & Sun; 90min; £14; booking essential, ☎01865 287400) include the circular **Radcliffe Camera**, a spectacular reading room with Britain's third-largest dome.

South of the Radcliffe Camera, you can scale the spire of the University Church, **St Mary the Virgin**, on the High Street (Mon–Fri 9.30am–4.30pm, Sat 9.30am–5pm, Sun 11.45am–4.30pm; £4), for fantastic panoramic views of central Oxford.

University museums

A few minutes' walk north along Parks Road, and accessed through the Natural History Museum, the **Pitt Rivers Museum** (Mon noon–4.30pm, Tues–Sun 10am–4.30pm; free; ⓦprm.ox.ac.uk) is a treasure trove of anthropological miscellanea gathered from around the world by Victorian adventurers. Its fascinating collection includes displays of ceremonial masks, weaponry, tattooing implements, shrunken heads, body adornments and more.

Five minutes' walk west along Museum Road and south along St Giles is the mammoth Neoclassical **Ashmolean Museum** (Tues–Sun & Bank Holiday Mondays 10am–5pm; free; ⓦashmolean .org). Its extensive collections include Greek, Roman, Mesopotamian and Egyptian antiquities, Islamic, Indian, European and Chinese art, the world's largest collection of Raphael drawings and a priceless Stradivari "Messiah" violin dating from 1716.

ARRIVAL AND DEPARTURE

By train Oxford's train station is a 5min walk west of the centre along Park End St.

Destinations Bath (change at Didcot Parkway or Reading; 1–2 hourly; 1hr 20min–1hr 40min); London (2–3 hourly; 1hr–2hr); Manchester (every 30min; 2hr 50min); Stratford-upon-Avon (change at Leamington Spa; every 2hr; 1hr 30min).

By bus Long-distance buses terminate at the centrally located Gloucester Green bus station, off George St. Of the various London–Oxford coach services, the #X90 is currently the cheapest (£15 one-way; ⓦoxfordbus .co.uk).

Destinations Cambridge (every 30min; 3–4hr); Gatwick Airport (hourly; 2hr–2hr 30min); Heathrow Airport

(every 30min; 1hr 20min); London (every 10–15min; 1hr 40min); Stratford-upon-Avon (1 daily at 11.05am; 1hr 10min).

INFORMATION AND TOURS

Tourist information At the tourist office, 15 Broad St (Mon–Sat 9.30am–5pm, Sun 10am–3.30pm; ☎01865 686430, ⓦvisitoxfordandoxfordshire.com), you can book themed walking tours (£12–24), rent bikes or buy a visitors' guide (£1).

GETTING AROUND

By bike Bainton Bikes at 78 Walton St (☎01865 311610, ⓦbaintonbikes.com; £10–15/day) rents out hybrids, standard bikes and mountain bikes and organizes guided bike tours; advance booking necessary.

ACCOMMODATION

Out of term time, some colleges rent student rooms to tourists (single/double from £50/90; ⓦoxfordrooms .co.uk); singles tend to have shared facilities. It's advisable to book in advance and to check whether you're in picturesque medieval grounds or in less characterful modern accommodation. There are also a few Airbnb (ⓦairbnb.com) rooms on offer, particularly in the Jericho area, a short walk north of the centre.

★**Central Backpackers Oxford** 13 Park End St ☎01865 242288, ⓦcentralbackpackers.co.uk. A central location, helpful staff, spacious but spartan dorms and a friendly vibe make this a good place to meet fellow travellers: there's free wi-fi throughout, a rooftop terrace and light breakfast, plus earplugs provided due to the location on top of a nightclub. Dorms __£22__

PUNTING IN OXBRIDGE

Renting a punt – essentially a flat-bottomed Venetian-style gondola powered by a brave soul brandishing a pole – is one of the finest ways to experience Oxford and Cambridge. In **Oxford**, Magdalen Bridge Boathouse (ⓦoxfordpunting.co.uk), on the High Street, rents punts, rowboats and pedaloes for £22 per hour. In **Cambridge**, Trinity College Punts (ⓦtrin.cam.ac.uk /visiting/punting), down a side street behind Trinity College, offers the cheapest punt rental in town at £16 per hour – perfect for a cruise downstream past the architectural splendours of the college Backs or a trip upstream to rural Grantchester. Punting tours are available in both Oxford and Cambridge – just ask the ubiquitous touts.

Hollybush Guest House 530 Banbury Rd ☎01865 554886, ⓦhollybushguesthouse.com. This appealing, family-run guesthouse offers a handful of singles and doubles, as well as a family room; continental breakfast included. It's 2.5 miles north of the centre; buses #2 and #7 pass by. Doubles **£75**

Oxford YHA 2a Botley Rd ☎0845 371 9131, ⓦyha.org .uk. Next to the train station, this large, modern HI hostel is somewhat impersonal but spotlessly clean, efficiently run and offers inexpensive meals, a kitchen, bar, wi-fi and laundry. Dorms **£19**, doubles **£49**

EATING

The Covered Market is a good bet for independent, daytime cafés, while the Jericho district (north of the centre) or Cowley Rd out east have plenty of independent cafés and restaurants.

Atomic Burger 96 Cowley Rd. With comic books for wallpaper, this Oxford institution is an ode to Americana. Burger-wise, choose from the likes of Chuck Norries (BBQ pulled pork, cheese and fried onions), Molly Ringwald (bacon, camembert & BBQ sauce), or supersize it with a double-stacked Dolly Parton (double burger, bacon and cheese). Burgers available in beef, chicken or veggie (£8.25–17.50). Daily 11.30am–10.30pm.

Edamamé 15 Holywell St ⓦedamame.co.uk. Terrific Japanese food at fair prices (mains £6–9.50) – it's no wonder the queue for this tiny restaurant snakes down the street. Lunch consists of Japanese curries, ramen and tonkatsu dishes, while Thursday night is sushi night. Wed 11.30am–2.30pm, Thurs–Sat 11.30am–2.30pm & 5–8.30pm, Sun noon–3.30pm.

★**Oli's Thai** 38 Magdalen Rd ☎01865 790223 ⓦolisthai .co.uk. With a succinct menu of beautifully executed, authentic Thai dishes (£9–14) and just a handful of tables, this tiny place, 15min walk from the centre, is wildly popular. While it's often reserved weeks in advance, there are a few unreserved seats at the bar for walk-ins – their confit duck panang alone is worth it. Tues noon–3pm, Wed–Sat noon–2pm & 5–9pm.

★**White Rabbit** Friar's Entry ⓦwhiterabbitoxford .co.uk. This cosy pub serves up a good selection of local craft beers and a range of award-winning stonebaked pizzas (£7.50–10). There are numerous veggie options, but we're big fans of the Zola (Gorgonzola, pear and pancetta pizza). Daily noon–midnight.

DRINKING AND NIGHTLIFE

For listings of gigs and other events, consult *Daily Info*, a poster put up in colleges and all around town on Tues and Fri (ⓦdailyinfo.co.uk).

The Bear 6 Alfred St. Oldest pub in Oxford (1242) with very low ceilings, real ales and snippets from neckties – proffered by their owners in exchange for a pint. Decent pub grub, too. Mon–Thurs & Sun 11am–11pm, Fri & Sat 11pm–midnight.

The Cellar Frewin Court, off Cornmarket St ☎01865 244761, ⓦcellaroxford.co.uk. Nightly, mostly live music, from rock and pop acts to Afrobeat, Goth and electronica. Popular with students. Tickets from £4. Daily 7.30pm–2 or 3am.

The Eagle & Child 49 St Giles. This pub, a.k.a. "Bird & Baby", was once the haunt of J.R.R. Tolkien, C.S. Lewis and friends, and serves a good selection of local ales, though the ordering system is odd and the food can be hit-and-miss. Mon–Thurs 11am–11pm, Fri & Sat 11am–1am, Sun noon–10.30pm.

★**Turf Tavern** 4 Bath Place One of Oxford's oldest drinking establishments (c. 1280), this tavern is hidden away down narrow twisting passages (look for the Bridge of Sighs). With its heavy wooden beams, low ceilings and crooked floors, it's suitably characterful and serves local beers, as well as generous portions of tasty pub food. Mon–Sat 11am–11.15pm, Sun 11am–10.30pm.

STRATFORD-UPON-AVON

The pretty town of **STRATFORD-UPON-AVON** is synonymous with its most famous citizen, William Shakespeare, who was born here in 1564. The town revels in its links to the Bard and successfully plays up the "merrie olde England" image. Most people come to see the five attractively restored Shakespeare-related properties, but you could simply soak up the atmosphere by meandering along the river, lined with Tudor buildings.

WHAT TO SEE AND DO

Top of the Bardic itinerary is **Shakespeare's Birthplace** on Henley Street (daily: April–June, Sept & Oct 9am–5pm; July & Aug 9am–6pm; Nov–March 10am–4pm; £17.50 including Nash's House/New Place & Hall's Croft, or pass including all five houses £26.25; ⓦshakespeare.org.uk). The heavily restored Tudor building where the great man was born features interesting displays on his life plus plentiful graffiti from devotees through the ages.

A short walk away on Chapel Street are **Nash's House/New Place** (daily: April–Oct 10am–5pm; Nov–March 11am–4pm; for ticket price see above). The former was once the property of Thomas Nash, first husband of Shakespeare's granddaughter,

13

Elizabeth Hall, and is kitted out with period furnishing, temporary exhibitions and archeological findings excavated from beneath the New Place plot next door. New Place is the site of Shakespeare's last home, where he died in 1616, though the house itself is long gone. A five-minute walk away, Old Town Street is home to the medieval **Hall's Croft** (daily 10am–5pm; for ticket price see above), former home of Shakespeare's eldest daughter, Susanna, and her husband, John Hall. Inside, you can learn about medicine in the sixteenth and seventeenth centuries.

About half a mile west of the town centre in Shottery is the thatched, wood-beamed **Anne Hathaway's Cottage** (same hours as Shakespeare's Birthplace, but closes 5pm July & Aug; £10.25), surrounded by beautiful gardens said to be where Shakespeare courted Anne. Two and a half miles from here (clearly signposted) is Shakespeare's mother's family home, now called **Mary Arden's Farm** (mid-March to early Nov daily 10am–5pm; £13.25): a classily re-created Tudor working farm complete with rare-breed animals, as well as weavers, falconers and farmers in period costume.

Back in town, a short walk from Hall's Croft towards the river, is the handsome **Holy Trinity Church** (April–Sept Mon–Sat 8.30am–6pm, Sun 12.30–5pm; Oct–March Mon–Sat 9am–3.45pm, Sun 12.30–4.45pm). William and Anne Shakespeare are buried here in the chancel (£2, or free with ticket to one of Shakespeare's houses).

THE ROYAL SHAKESPEARE COMPANY

Seeing a play at the Royal Shakespeare Theatre (box office Mon–Sat 10am–6pm; ☎01789 403493, ⓦrsc.org.uk), home to the fantastically talented **Royal Shakespeare Company**, is a Stratford highlight. The Company works on a repertory system, which means you could see three or four different plays in a visit of a few days (though not all by the Bard himself). Ticket prices vary and the most popular shows get booked up months in advance.

ARRIVAL AND INFORMATION

By train Stratford's train station is on the northwestern edge of town, a 10min walk from the centre.

Destinations London Marylebone (change at Birmingham, Dorridge or Leamington Spa; hourly; 2hr); Oxford (change at Banbury or Leamington Spa; every 2 hours; 1hr 30min).

By bus Long-distance buses pull into the Riverside Station on the east side of the town centre, off Bridgeway.

Destinations London Victoria (3 daily; 3hr 5min–3hr 50min); Oxford (1 daily at 4pm; 1hr 10min).

Tourist information Tourist office at Bridgefoot, opposite Bancroft Gardens (March–Oct daily 9am–5.30pm; Nov–Feb Mon–Sat 9am–5.30pm, Sun 10am–4pm; ☎01789 264 293, ⓦdiscover-stratford.com).

ACCOMMODATION

★**Hamlet House** 52 Grove Rd ☎07968 702434, ⓦhamlethouse.com. Friendly B&B a 5min walk from the centre, with quirky themed rooms. Free internet, bikes and jumbo breakfasts, with specialities such as omelette cooked with herbs from the garden. **£60**

Stratford YHA Hemmingford House, Alveston ☎0845 371 9661, ⓦyha.org.uk; buses #X15, #18A and #X18 from Bridge St or bus station. Rambling Georgian mansion with its own café-bar on the edge of the pretty village of Alveston, two miles east of town. Dorms **£17**, doubles **£39**

EATING AND DRINKING

El Greco 27 Rother St ⓦel-greco.co.uk. Conveniently located right near Shakespeare's birthplace, this Greek restaurant serves up Mediterranean tapas (dolmades, keftedes, grilled halloumi) plus more substantial lunch and pre-theatre menus (£14.50 for two courses). Daily 10am–10pm.

★**HR Coffee Bar** 12 Windsor St ⓦhrcatering.co.uk. This fresh and funky café makes the most of locally sourced, seasonal ingredients. Come here for hearty breakfasts, toasties, imaginative salads and the Reuben sandwich for lunch, or wonderful cakes plus coffee from an award-winning local micro-roastery. Mon–Sat 8am–5pm.

Old Thatch Tavern Market Place ⓦoldthatch tavernstratford.co.uk. The only thatched building in the centre of Stratford, and one of the few historic inns that hasn't lost its character, this fifteenth-century pub serves good British food and ales. Mon–Sat 11.30am–11pm, Sun noon–6pm.

CAMBRIDGE

Tradition has it that the University of **CAMBRIDGE** was founded by refugees from Oxford, who fled that town after one of their number was lynched by hostile townsfolk in the 1220s; there's been rivalry between the two institutions ever since, though nowadays it's manifested in the annual boat race. More walkable and tranquil than its rival, Cambridge features "**the Backs**", a green swathe of land straddling the River Cam, which overlooks the backs of the old colleges and provides the town's most enduring image of grand academic architecture. Access to the colleges is restricted during examinations, conferences and functions. For four days in late July, the town hosts the popular **Cambridge Folk Festival** (ⓦcambridgefolkfestival.co.uk).

WHAT TO SEE AND DO

Cambridge city centre is bound to the west by the Cam and is dominated by historic university buildings. A logical place to start a tour is King's Parade, originally the medieval High Street.

King's College

Flanking King's Parade, Cambridge's grandest college is **King's College**, with a much-celebrated, beautiful **chapel** (term time Mon–Sat 9.30am–3.15pm, Sun 1.15–2.30pm; hols daily 9.30am–4.30pm; £9; ⓦkings.cam.ac.uk) and an equally vaunted choir (term time Evensong Mon–Sat 5.30pm, Sun 10.30am & 3.30pm) – its Christmas services are renowned worldwide. At the northern end of King's Parade, the **Senate House** is the scene of graduation ceremonies.

Trinity College

Just north of King's, **Trinity College** (daily 10am–5pm; £3; ⓦtrin.cam.ac.uk) is the largest of the Cambridge colleges. Beyond the Great Gate lies the vast asymmetrical expanse of Great Court, which displays a fine range of Tudor buildings, the oldest of which is the fifteenth-century clock tower – the annual race against its midnight chimes is now common currency thanks to the film *Chariots of Fire*. The west end of Nevile's Court is enclosed by the beautiful **Wren Library** (term time Mon–Fri noon–2pm, Sat 10.30am–12.30pm; hols Mon–Fri only; free). Back outside Trinity, it's a short hop to the River Cam, where you can go **punting** – the quintessential Cambridge pursuit (see box, p.452).

St John's College and the Round Church

Founded by Henry VII's mother, Lady Margaret Beaufort, **St John's College** (daily 10am–5pm, closes 3.30pm Jan, Feb, Nov & Dec; £8; ⓦwww.joh.cam .ac.uk) is worth a peek for its chapel ceiling depicting saints and scholars standing shoulder to shoulder, as well as its mishmash of architectural styles. The lovely **Bridge of Sighs**, modelled on its famous counterpart in Venice and built in 1813, links the college's New Court with Third Court. On Bridge Street, the strange and distinctive twelfth-century **Round Church** (Mon–Sat 10am–5pm, Sun 1–5pm; £2) is not only the second-oldest building in the city, but also directly influenced by the Church of the Holy Sepulchre in Jerusalem.

Queens' College and the Fitzwilliam Museum

Queens' College (Jan to mid-March, Nov & Dec daily 2–4pm; mid-March to mid-May & mid-June to Sept daily 10am–4.30pm; Oct Mon–Fri 2–4pm, Sat & Sun 10am–4.30pm; £3; ⓦqueens .cam.ac.uk), with its twin Tudor courtyards, is accessed through the gate on Queen's Lane. Equally eye-catching is the wooden Mathematical Bridge over the Cam, a copy of the mid-eighteenth-century original which, it was claimed, would stay in place even if the nuts and bolts were removed. From Queens', it's a short stroll in the opposite direction from the colleges down Trumpington Street to the excellent **Fitzwilliam Museum** (Tues–Sat 10am–5pm, Sun noon–5pm; free; ⓦfitzmuseum.cam.ac.uk). The ground floor is a treasure trove of antiquities, from Egyptian sarcophagi and funereal offerings to Roman statuary, while the first floor displays applied arts and European painting, including masterpieces by Rubens, Hogarth, Renoir and Picasso.

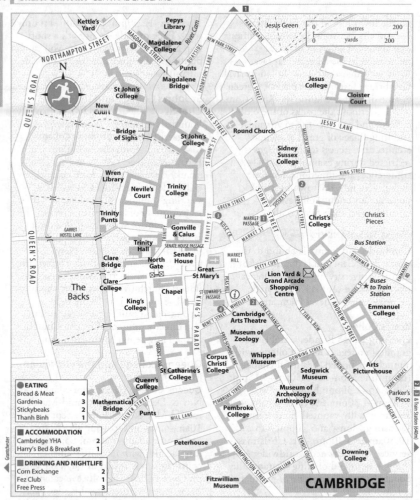

CAMBRIDGE

EATING
Bread & Meat	4
Gardenia	3
Stickybeaks	2
Thanh Binh	1

ACCOMMODATION
Cambridge YHA	2
Harry's Bed & Breakfast	1

DRINKING AND NIGHTLIFE
Corn Exchange	2
Fez Club	1
Free Press	3

ARRIVAL AND DEPARTURE

By train Cambridge train station is a mile or so southeast of the city centre, off Hills Rd. It's a 20min walk into the centre, or else cross the street and take Citi buses #1, #2, #3, #7 or #8 (£1.60) from the bays to the left of the station exit.

Destinations Birmingham (12 daily; 2hr 30min); London (every 15min; 50min–1hr 30min); Stansted Airport (every 30min; 30min).

By bus Coaches stop at the Drummer St bus station or along Parkside Piece.

Destinations Heathrow Airport (hourly; 2hr 30min); Gatwick Airport (7 daily; 4hr); London (13 daily; 2hr 30min); Oxford (every 30min; 3hr 30min–4hr 20min); Stansted Airport (9 daily; 45min).

INFORMATION

Tourist information In the Guildhall, Peas Hill, near Market Square (Mon–Sat 10am–5pm; May–Oct also Sun 11am–3pm; ☎ 01223 457581, ⊚ visitcambridge.org).

ACCOMMODATION

Staying in one of the university college rooms is an excellent bet for centrally located, cheap accommodation out of term time; see ⊚ cambridgerooms.co.uk for details.

Cambridge YHA 97 Tenison Rd ☎ 0845 371 9728, ⊚ yha .org.uk. Fully refurbished, large hostel near the train station comprises a clutch of private en-suites, basic doubles and a dorm, with good facilities for self-caterers, social areas, and a canteen/bar serving local ales.

Somewhat lacking in atmosphere, though, and occasionally overrun with school groups. Dorms £25, doubles £65

Harry's Bed & Breakfast 39 Milton Rd ☎01223 503866, ⓦwelcometoharrys.co.uk. This welcoming B&B with four cosy en-suite rooms is an easy 10min walk from the centre across Jesus Green. The Full English breakfast is top-notch. Doubles £65

EATING

★**Bread & Meat** 4 Bene't St ⓦbreadandmeat.co.uk. The budget place does just four types of meaty sandwiches on sourdough (with a roast vegetable version for vegetarians) – our favourite is the porchetta. Generous sides include poutine and slaw. Mon–Sat 11.30am–8pm, Sun 11.30am–5pm.

Gardenia 2 Rose Crescent ⓦgardis.co.uk. A beloved Cambridge student institution, "Gardis" provides late-night nourishment in the form of lamb souvlakia, falafel and superior kebabs: mains from £4.70. Daily 11am–5am.

Stickybeaks 42 Hobson St. This independent café is always justifiably busy; come here for breakfast, lunch (chunky sandwiches and home-made soup), or just linger over coffee and cake: mains from £5. Mon–Fri 8am–5.30pm, Sat 9am–5.30pm Sun 10am–5pm.

Thanh Binh 17 Magdalene St. The only non-chain Vietnamese place in town, with an excellent 2-course lunch menu (£11.50) and the best *nem nuong* (pork meatballs) this side of Hanoi. Mon–Sat noon–2pm & 6–10pm.

DRINKING AND NIGHTLIFE

To find out about current club nights, theatre productions and comedy nights, browse the flyers hanging from the railings down King's Parade.

Corn Exchange Corn Exchange St ☎01223 357851, ⓦcornex.co.uk. Entertainment venue in the heart of town where you can catch anything from the Shaolin monks on tour to Mary Chapin Carpenter and various comedy shows.

Fez Club 15 Market Passage ⓦcambridgefez.com. A much-loved Cambridge student haunt, the *Fez*'s eclectic music policy and pseudo-Arabian decor keep it ahead of the competition. Tuesday *Fresh* is student night, with r'n'b, hip-hop and dancehall on the menu. Entry £4–6. Daily 10pm–3am.

★**Free Press** 7 Prospect Row ⓦfreepresspub.com. In the backstreets behind Emmanuel College this tiny pub is off the tourist trail: it serves local brews, real ales and guest beers and has a beer garden and great food. Mon–Thurs noon–2pm & 6–11pm, Fri & Sat noon–11pm, Sun noon–2.30pm & 7–10.30pm.

Northern England

13

The great outdoors grabs the headlines in lake-laden, mountain ravine-scored **Northern England**. The best-known area is the **Lake District**, encompassing picturesque stone-built villages, sixteen huge lakes and England's highest mountains. Less explored but equally beautiful is **Northumberland** in the northeast and the southern **Peak District**. Northern England is also home to some of the country's major cities, including **Manchester** and **Liverpool** in the west and **Newcastle** in the northeast – they each combine the ostentatious civic architecture of nineteenth-century capitalism with vigorous twenty-first-century renewal. In the ecclesiastical hotbeds of **Durham** and **York**, their famous cathedrals provide a focus for fascinating, medieval-themed meanderings.

MANCHESTER

Sprawling northern metropolis **MANCHESTER** has one of the country's most vibrant social and cultural scenes, enlivened by the student population of its two major universities, its stylish Gay Village, the glitzy Curry Mile and its buzzing, bohemian Northern Quarter. In many ways it is the flagship for multifaceted Britishness: it shot to prominence courtesy of its Industrial Revolution riches, later becoming a powerhouse of music and football.

WHAT TO SEE AND DO

From the main Piccadilly train station, it's a few minutes' walk northwest to **Piccadilly Gardens**, an obvious starting point for an exploration of the city.

Manchester Art Gallery

The **Manchester Art Gallery** (daily 10am–5pm, till 9pm Thurs; free; ⓦmanchestergalleries.org) has a fine collection of Pre-Raphaelite paintings, Impressionist pictures of Manchester by Adolphe Valette, twentieth-century

13

British art by the likes of Lucien Freud and Stanley Spencer, and an excellent interactive gallery. It is located a quarter of a mile from the gardens, on Mosley Street. Just to the west, the **Town Hall** (Mon–Fri 9am–5pm, free; guided tours Tues and occasional Sun at 11am; £5) is the country's pinnacle of Victorian civic aspiration: check out the Ford Madox Brown murals inside.

Royal Exchange Theatre and National Football Museum

St Ann's Square is home to the wonderful **Royal Exchange Theatre** (w royalexchange .co.uk). If you don't have time to see a show, pop in and have a look at the building – formerly the Cotton Exchange – whose florid, pink marble columns and lofty cupolas surround the spherical performance space, an egg-like module squatting in the centre. A short walk north in Cathedral Gardens you'll find the **National Football Museum** (daily 10am–5pm; free; w nationalfootball museum.com), a spectacular, wedge-shaped glass building housing artefacts that tell the story of football, from its earliest beginnings around the world to the birth of the women's game. You can also try Football Plus, an interactive simulator that tests your footballing skills and commentating prowess.

Museum of Science and Industry

South down Deansgate and right onto Liverpool Road, the superbly informative **Museum of Science and Industry** (daily 10am–5pm; free; w msimanchester.org .uk) spreads over several old factory buildings to celebrate the triumphs of industrialization. Exhibits include working steam engines, textile machinery, a hands-on science centre and atmospheric re-creations of period rooms. There's also a chance to walk through a rebuilt Victorian sewer, complete with its unique aroma.

Salford Quays and Old Trafford

Metrolink trams from Piccadilly and Deansgate-Castlefield run to Harbour City, jumping-off point for the revamped **Salford Quays**, scene of a massive urban renewal scheme in the old dock area. Here,

the spectacular waterfront arts hub, **The Lowry** (Mon–Fri 9.30am–8pm, Sat & Sun 10am–8pm; free; w thelowry.com), houses performance spaces and galleries, where you can view the work of the artist L.S. Lowry, best known for his "matchstick men" scenes. You can also get here by walking down the docks from the Salford Quays tram stop. A footbridge runs across the docks to the **Imperial War Museum North** (daily 10am–5pm; free; w north .iwm.org.uk), a striking aluminium-clad building imaginatively exploring the effects of war in the twentieth century, with the main conflicts covered through a series of thoughtful displays and films. Looming nearby is **Old Trafford**, home of Manchester United Football Club, whose museum, a must-see for any football fan, is situated in the Sir Alex Ferguson Stand (northern side of stadium; daily 9.30am–5pm; museum & tour £25, museum only £18; advance booking essential for tours ☏ 0161 868 8000, w manutd.com; Metrolink towards Altrincham to Old Trafford, or towards Eccles to Exchange Quay).

ARRIVAL AND DEPARTURE

By plane Manchester Airport (w manchesterairport.co.uk) is ten miles south of the city centre, with a fast, frequent train service to Manchester Piccadilly (every 5–10min; 15–20min).

By train Most trains arrive at Piccadilly station, on the city's east side.

Destinations Chester (every 30min; 1hr–1hr 30min); Edinburgh (every 2hr; 3hr 20min); Glasgow (hourly; 3hr 10min); London Euston (3 hourly; 2hr 15min); Liverpool (frequent; 45min–1hr 10min); Newcastle (hourly; 2hr 40min); York (3 hourly; 1hr 25min).

By bus Long-distance coaches stop at Chorlton St coach station, just west of Piccadilly station.

Destinations Chester (3 daily; 1hr 15min–1hr 40min); Glasgow (4 daily; 4–5hr); Liverpool (hourly; 1hr 15min); London (hourly; 3hr 45min); York (via Leeds; 18 daily; 2hr 20min–2hr 40min).

INFORMATION

Tourist information Manchester Visitor Centre is in Piccadilly Plaza, on Portland St (Mon–Sat 10am–5.15pm, Sun 10.30am–4.30pm; ☏ 0871 222 8223, w visitmanchester.com).

GETTING AROUND

By bike Bike rental from Bicycle Boutique, Hillcourt St (Mon–Fri 8.30am–6.30pm, Sat & Sun 10am–4pm;

Mon–Fri £15/day, Sat & Sun £12/day; ☎0161 273 7801 ⓦhillcourtstreetcycles.co.uk).

By Metrolink The handy Metrolink (ⓦwww.metrolink .co.uk) tram system runs around central Manchester. Buy tickets from machines on the platform.

ACCOMMODATION

Hatters Hilton Chambers 15 Hilton St ☎0161 236 4414, ⓦhattersgroup.com. This clean Northern Quarter hostel has a roof terrace, complimentary all-day breakfast and feels fresher than its sister property on

Newton St. Weekend rates are higher. Dorms £19, doubles £56

Hatters Hostel 50 Newton St ☎0161 236 9500, ⓦhattersgroup.com. Inside a refurbished factory, this hostel is a good option if you want to party and just need somewhere cheap to lay your head. Dorms £18, doubles £49

★**Manchester YHA** Potato Wharf, Castlefield ☎0871 371 9647, ⓦyha.org.uk. Close to the Museum of Science and Industry, this swanky HI hostel (all dorm rooms have en-suite bathrooms) has a great canalside location. Dorms £19, doubles £55

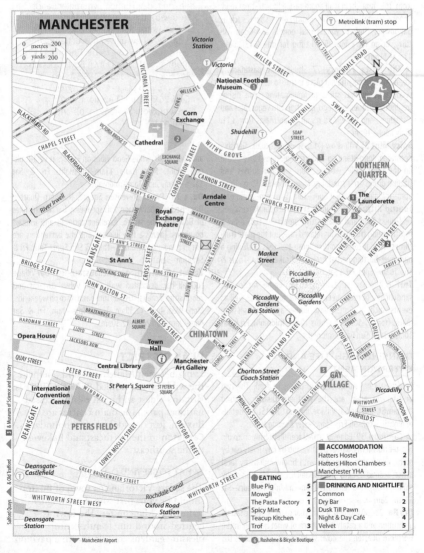

MANCHESTER

● **EATING**

Blue Pig	5
Mowgli	2
The Pasta Factory	1
Spicy Mint	6
Teacup Kitchen	4
Trof	3

■ **ACCOMMODATION**

Hatters Hostel	2
Hatters Hilton Chambers	1
Manchester YHA	3

■ **DRINKING AND NIGHTLIFE**

Common	1
Dry Bar	2
Dusk Till Pawn	3
Night & Day Café	4
Velvet	5

13

EATING

For good, cheap eats, try the decent mini-chains around Exchange Square, or head for the "Curry Mile", Wilmslow Rd in Rusholme (bus #18 from the city centre; 25min) for some of Britain's best budget Asian cooking.

Blue Pig 69 High St ⓦthebluepigmcr.co.uk. Brasserie-style bar-restaurant serving small plates for sharing (3 for £13), such as harissa lamb meatballs and masala fish fingers, plus hearty burgers, ribs and steaks. Daily 10am–midnight or 1am.

Mowgli 16 Corn Exchange House ⓦmowglistreetfood .com. This mini-chain is all about casual Indian street food. Choose several small dishes (from £4) to share, such as gunpowder chicken, yogurt chat bombs and Goan fish curry, or go for a four-tiered tiffin for one (£12). Daily 11am–11pm.

★**The Pasta Factory** 77 Shudehill ⓦpastafactory .co.uk. This friendly Italian place is true to its name with a succinct menu that sticks to imaginative pasta dishes (reginette with venison ragu, bucatini with vegetables and pistachios) and wine. And it's all great. Mains from £11. Daily noon–10pm.

Spicy Mint 35 Wilmslow Rd ⓦspicymint.co.uk. Garishly decorated, long-standing and unpretentious curry house on the Curry Mile, whose award-winning curries and sizzling dishes are a speciality. Mains from £9. Mon–Thurs 5pm–midnight, Fri & Sat 6pm–1am, Sun 3pm–midnight.

Teacup Kitchen 55 Thomas St ⓦteacupandcakes.com. Feel-good food and imaginative breakfasts (£8) draw a mostly young crowd to this relaxed café, but the place truly shines when it comes to their loose-leaf teas (including a hangover-busting herbal brew) and cakes. Mon–Thurs & Sun 10am–6pm, Fri & Sat 10am–8pm.

Trof 8 Thomas St ⓦtrofnq.co.uk. Come for coffee, sandwiches, burgers, beer or eclectic cocktails, as well as events such as Sun's roast dinner-and-vinyl session: mains from £7.50. Mon–Thurs 10am–midnight, Fri & Sat 10am–3am, Sun 9am–midnight.

DRINKING, NIGHTLIFE AND ENTERTAINMENT

Manchester has no shortage of places to drink. The two best-known areas are the Northern Quarter, around Oldham St, and the Gay Village, around Canal St. For details of nightlife, consult Fri's *Manchester Evening News*.

★**Common** 39 Edge St ⓦaplacecalledcommon.co.uk. Hipster Northern Quarter creative hub by day, lively bar by night, *Common* is decorated with bright murals by local artists – amid its extensive cocktail list, the Martinis really shine. Mon–Wed & Sun 11am–midnight, Thurs–Sat 11am–2am.

Dry Bar 28–30 Oldham St ⓦdrybar.co.uk. A "Madchester" institution and a catalyst for much of what goes on in the Northern Quarter. The downstairs music venue hosts DJs

MANCHESTER MUSIC

In 1978, local TV personality Tony Wilson founded **Factory Records** and gave voice to a movement that came to define both Manchester and Britain's post-punk musical soundscape. Bands like Joy Division and New Order emerged and embraced the new electronic music that was played at Factory's club, **The Hacienda**, the prototype for the industrial warehouse spaces ubiquitous in club design today. Homegrown guitar bands followed – the Stone Roses, Happy Mondays, the Smiths – succeeded in the 1990s by a new generation of bands, from Oasis and The Verve to The Chemical Brothers and Badly Drawn Boy. Although *The Hacienda* closed in 1997, its legacy lives on, with places like the *Night & Day Café*, 26 Oldham St (ⓦnightnday .org), providing a stage for up-and-coming talent.

and live bands, while Good Vibes on Fridays is soul/funk/pop night. Mon–Thurs 11am–midnight, Fri & Sat 11am–4am, Sun 11am–midnight.

Dusk Till Pawn Stevenson Square, Northern Quarter. Disguised as a pawnshop, this speakeasy bar has the likes of Bowie on the stereo, excellent cocktails and infused bourbons. There's a free jukebox and the bartenders are fun to hang out with. Tues–Thurs & Sun 5pm–1am, Fri & Sat 5pm–3am.

Velvet 2 Canal St. Elegant, Renaissance-style Gay Village cocktail bar, decorated with plush velvet curtains and zebra-striped chairs. DJs play funks and disco on weekends. Mon–Wed 4pm–12.30am, Thurs 4pm–1am, Fri & Sat 4pm–2am, Sun 2pm–12.30am.

PEAK DISTRICT

Lying between Manchester and Sheffield, the wild, cavern-riddled **PEAK DISTRICT** is Britain's oldest and most easily accessed national park. The main centres are **Buxton**, just outside the park boundaries, **Castleton** to the northeast and **Bakewell** in the southeast.

WHAT TO SEE AND DO

The sedate Victorian spa town of **Buxton** should be your first stop if coming by train from Manchester. The town is centred around nineteenth-century pleasure gardens complete with a pavilion theatre and the legendary **St Ann's Well**, where the famous mineral water is sourced. There are spectacular caverns just outside town at **Poole's Cavern** (daily: March–Oct 9.30am–5pm; Nov–Feb Sat & Sun 10am–4pm; ⓦpoolescavern.co.uk; £9.75), while in **Castleton**, a beautiful stone village 10 miles northwest, there are three showcaves and dozens more challenging subterranean passageways to explore: details at the National Park Centre (see below). A five-mile hike or one stop on the Hope Valley line further brings you to **Edale**, where the area's best hike begins and climbs up to **Kinder Scout** (8 miles) on the bleak Kinder Plateau. From **Bakewell**, famed for its jam-filled pudding, it's a ten-minute ride on bus #215 or #218 to **Chatsworth House** (get off at Baslow; house daily 11am–5.30pm; garden daily 11am–6pm; £23; ⓦchatsworth.org), one of Britain's grandest country houses: set in a 35,000-acre estate, its garden features the stately home's iconic cascades, as well as woods, valleys, fountains and tumbling rivers.

ARRIVAL AND INFORMATION

By train Trains from Manchester Piccadilly run to Buxton (hourly; 1hr) and Hope (hourly; 50min), two miles east of Castleton.

By bus Several direct buses a day run from Manchester to Bakewell (2hr) and Buxton (1hr 20min). TransPeak buses run three times daily between Bakewell and Buxton (30min): other routes include the #173 (Castleton–Bakewell) and the #68 (Buxton–Castleton).

Tourist information The main offices are at Pavilion Gardens in Buxton (daily: 9am–5pm; ☎01298 25106) and Castleton's National Park Centre, Buxton Rd (daily: Jan–March 10.30am–4.30pm; April–Dec 10am–5.30pm; ☎01629 816572, ⓦpeakdistrict.gov.uk).

ACCOMMODATION AND EATING

Castleton YHA Castleton ☎08453 719628, ⓦyha.org .uk. This YHA hostel in a fabulous Gothic mansion just outside Castleton is a fantastic base for hiking, and there's also a planetarium and a Celtic roundhouse for campfires. Dorms **£20**, doubles **£65**

Ye Olde Cheshire Cheese Inn How Lane, Castleton ⓦwww.cheshirecheeseinn.co.uk. Pretty half-timbered coaching inn selling sandwiches (£6 with Cheshire cheese and apple chutney), plus home-made pies. Food daily noon–8.30 or 9pm.

Youlgreave YHA Fountain Square, Youlgreave ☎0845 3719151, ⓦyha.org.uk; bus #170/#171. A 42-bed hostel in a converted Victorian shop, 3 miles outside Bakewell. It has cycle storage and self-catering facilities. Dorms **£18**, doubles **£39**

LIVERPOOL

Thanks to an astounding twenty-first-century revival, **LIVERPOOL** leads the way as the region's most liveable, loveable big city: a major turnaround from its infamous post-war poverty. The rediscovered sense of cultural pride is almost as palpable as in the days when it was Britain's main transatlantic port and the empire's second city. The Albert Dock has been the focus of regeneration, where converted warehouses and glitzy, glassy architecture showcase Liverpool's cultural spoils. Acerbic wit and loyalty to one of the city's two football teams are the linchpins of Liverpool's identity, along with an underlying pride in the local musical heritage – which is fair enough from the city that produced The Beatles.

WHAT TO SEE AND DO

From Lime Street train station it's a short walk to William Brown Street and the impressive **Walker Art Gallery** (daily 10am–5pm; free; ⓦliverpoolmuseums .org.uk/walker), which takes you on a jaunt through British art history: Hogarth, Gainsborough, Hockney and local boy Stubbs are all well represented, while modern British art is a highlight – don't miss Ben Johnson's vivid 2008 Liverpool cityscape.

The Waterfront

From the **Pier Head** and Liverpool's waterfront, it's worth taking a "Ferry 'cross the Mersey" (as sung by Gerry and the Pacemakers) to Birkenhead for the views back towards the city; ferries serve commuters during morning and afternoon rush hours (£2.60 single, £3.20 return), but in between there are hourly cruises with commentary (£10). Just behind the ferry terminal, but best seen from the river itself, stands the grandiose **Royal Liver Building**, with its enormous clock faces and local mascots – a Liver

13

(pronounced lie-ver) bird perched on each tower.

A short stroll south at **Albert Dock**, you'll find **Tate Liverpool** (daily 10am–5.50pm; free; ⊛ tate.org.uk /liverpool), northern home of the national collection of modern art, which also showcases touring exhibitions from Tate Modern.

On the other side of the dock, the **Merseyside Maritime Museum** (daily 10am–5pm; free; ⊛ liverpoolmuseums .org.uk/maritime) presents a thorough history of Liverpool's docks, complete with models of notable ships built there, and an exhibition on the city's role in the Battle of the Atlantic. Particularly compelling are the displays on emigration from the city to North America and Australia, and another on Liverpool's *Titanic* connections. Inside the same building, the superb **International Slavery Museum** (daily 10am–5pm; free; ⊛ liverpoolmuseums.org.uk/ism) focuses on Liverpool's role in the transatlantic slave trade, with exhibits on the conditions aboard slaving ships and some original shackles. The museum also explores modern-day slavery in India, with powerful displays on racism, including moving first-hand video testimonies.

The cathedrals

To the east of the city, at either end of Hope Street, stand two very different twentieth-century cathedrals. The Roman Catholic **Metropolitan Cathedral** (Mon–Fri 7.30am–5pm, Sat & Sun 7.30am–6pm; donation requested), a ten-minute walk up Mount Pleasant, is a vast inverted funnel of a building, while the pale red Anglican **Liverpool Cathedral** (daily 8am–6pm; free) is the largest in the country: a neo-Gothic creation, designed by Sir Giles Gilbert Scott in 1903 but not completed until 1978. Climb the colossal tower (£5.50) to get fabulous 360-degree views of the city. On clear days, you can see Blackpool Tower, 28 miles to the north.

ARRIVAL AND DEPARTURE

By plane Liverpool John Lennon Airport (⊛ liverpoolairport.com) is nine miles southeast of the city and connected to the Liverpool One bus station in the city centre by Arriva's #500 buses (every 30min).

By train Regional destinations such as York, Manchester and London Euston arrive and depart from Liverpool Lime Street station, on the eastern edge of the city centre.

Destinations Cardiff (via Crewe/Chester/Birmingham; 3–4 hourly; 4hr); London Euston (hourly; 2hr 15min); Manchester (every 15min; 45min); York (hourly; 2hr 15min).

By bus Regional coaches stop on Norton St, northeast of Liverpool Lime Street.

Destinations Cardiff (1–2 daily; 6hr 45min); Chester (4 daily; 50min); London (6 daily; 6hr); Manchester (every 30min; 1hr); Newcastle (4 daily; 5–6hr); Oxford (2 daily; 5hr 15min–6hr).

THE FAB FOUR

Liverpool's most famous sons, The Beatles, account for a large number of the city's tourist attractions, with plenty of pubs and shops providing a high dose of Fab Four nostalgia. Spread over two venues on Albert Dock and Pier Head, **The Beatles Story** (daily: April–Oct 9am–7pm; Nov–March 10am–6pm; £15; ⊛ beatlesstory.com) is a multimedia attempt to capture the essence of the band's rise. The audioguide tour covers everything, from the Beatles' upbringing and early years to Beatlemania in the 1960s and the Fab Four's final split and solo careers. There may be few revelations for true fans, but the painstakingly put-together collection of photos, memorabilia and videos, as well as re-creations of the *Casbah* and *The Cavern Club*, where they used to play, is a labour of love.

Buses depart twice daily from Albert Dock's tourist information centre for a two-hour **Magical Mystery Tour** (book on ☎ 0151 703 9100 or at tourist offices; £17.95) of sites associated with the band, such as Penny Lane and Strawberry Fields. Hardcore fans will also want to visit **20 Forthlin Rd**, once home of the McCartney family, and the **Mendips**, the house where John Lennon lived between 1945 and 1963 (both are accessible on a pre-booked minibus tour Feb–Nov Sat & Sun; £23; ☎ 0151 427 7231, ⊛ nationaltrust.org.uk). Finish your Fab tour with a night at **The Cavern Club** (see p.463).

13

By boat P&O ferries (@poferries.com) from Dublin (3 daily; 8hr) dock at Liverpool Freeport, 5 miles north of the centre; Stena Line ferries (@stenaline.co.uk) from Belfast 1–2 daily; 8hr) dock at the Seacombe 12 Quays Ferry Terminal, across the river from Albert Dock.

INFORMATION

Tourist information Albert Dock (daily: April–Sept 10am–5.30pm; Oct–March 10am–5pm; @0151 233 2008, @visitliverpool.com), plus branches at St Georges Place (daily 10am–5pm) and Liverpool John Lennon Airport (daily 8am–6pm).

ACCOMMODATION

Embassie Hostel 1 Falkner Square @0151 707 1089, @embassie.com. This nineteenth-century, former Venezuelan consulate exudes character, with a games room, two kitchens and a garden. Breakfast included, plus free entry to *The Cavern Club*. Dorms £18

International Inn 4 South Hunter St, off Hardman St @0151 709 8135, @internationalinn.co.uk. Converted Victorian warehouse with four- to ten-person, en-suite dorms, plus cheap doubles and apartments. The staff are helpful and there's a 24-hour reception. Dorms £24, doubles £50, apartments £70

Liverpool YHA 25 Tabley Street, off Wapping @0845 371 9527, @yha.org.uk. Reliable HI hostel, a 5min walk from Albert Dock, with smart three- to six-bed rooms, all with private bathrooms. Dorms £14, doubles £49

The Old Dairy 39a Kempton Rd @theolddairyliverpool .co.uk; bus #14/#79c/#79d from Queen Square. Popular guesthouse a couple of miles from the centre, with clean double rooms (most en-suite). Doubles £49

EATING

As well as the places below, Liverpool's Chinatown, around Berry and Nelson Streets, is a good spot to look for cheap food.

Cuthbert's Bakehouse 103 Mount Pleasant @cuthbertsbakehouse.co.uk. Relaxed coffee shop with a little garden, serving stuffed bagels, soups, jacket potatoes, panini and excellent cream teas with scones. Mon–Fri 9am–6pm, Sat 10am–5pm, Sun 11am–5pm.

The Egg Café 16–18 Newington, 2nd floor @eggcafe .co.uk. Gem of a veggie/vegan café doing mammoth quiches, salads and vegan-friendly cakes: mains from £5. Bring your own wine. Mon–Fri 9am–10.30pm, Sat & Sun 10am–10.30pm.

★Etsu Japanese Restaurant Beetham Plaza, 25 the Strand @etsu-restaurant.co.uk. Beautiful, authentic Japanese food in light, bright surroundings. Get your fill of gyoza, tempura, Japanese curry (£10), donburi (£13), udon noodles and varied sushi sets (from £4). Tues, Thurs & Fri noon–2.30pm & 5–9pm, Wed & Sat 5–9pm, Sun 4–9pm.

HoSt 31 Hope St @ho-st.co.uk. This pan-Asian brasserie conjures up fresh, imaginative dishes – some may be a little ambitious, but the duck coconut curry, slow-cooked Korean meatballs and the smoked baby-back ribs are spot-on: mains from £10. Daily 9.30am–11pm.

Lucha Libre 96 Wood St @lucha-libre.co.uk. Lively Mexican restaurant serving street food (think tacos, quesadillas and burritos): the Baja fish tacos (£5) and pork pibil burritos (£7) stand out, while the home-made salsas are ace. Daily noon–10 or 11pm.

DRINKING AND NIGHTLIFE

Serious clubbers and live-music fans gravitate towards the streets around Wolstenholme Square, while the Cavern Quarter around Mathew St is home to myriad cheesy late-night bars, often Beatles-themed. The evening paper, the *Liverpool Echo*, has what's-on listings. Keep an eye out, too, for the free local music fanzine Bido Lito.

Alma Da Cuba St Peters' Church, Seel Street. Catholic church spectacularly converted into a bar/restaurant, which turns into a pumping party venue later on in the night. Mon–Wed & Sun 11am–midnight, Thurs–Sat 11am–2am.

★Berry and Rye 48 Berry St. Hidden behind an all-black shop front (no sign), this speakeasy-style cocktail bar specializes as the name suggests, in whisky and gin. Knowledgeable staff and candlelit snugs make it a good pre-club bar. Tues–Sat 5pm–2am, Sun 7pm–1am.

Kazimier Garden 32 Seel St @thekazimier.co.uk. This rickety outdoor offshoot of the defunct Kazimier club has a refreshing boho vibe, interesting drinks and a fine roster of gigs (there's also a train carriage to sit in). Mon–Fri 4pm till late, Sat & Sun noon till late.

The Cavern Club 8–10 Mathew St @cavernclub.org. Rebuilt version of The Beatles' original venue (not quite in the same place), hosting nightly live bands, such as the Kinks and Small Faces tributes (Thurs–Sun nightly admission charge of up to £5). Daily 10am–midnight/2am.

Leaf on Bold St 65–67 Bold St @thisisleaf.co.uk. An unusual combination of teashop, bar and venue for self-expression, with regular yoga classes, clothing fairs and Scrabble sessions. Mon–Thurs 9am–midnight, Fri 9am–2am, Sat 10am–2am, Sun 10am–midnight.

The Philharmonic 36 Hope St. Remarkable, ornate pub with mosaic floors and gilded wrought-iron gates, designed by the shipwrights of the *Lusitania*. Skip the food in favour of the guest ales. Daily 11am–midnight.

ENTERTAINMENT

FACT 88 Wood St @fact.co.uk. The Foundation for Art and Creative Technology shelters two galleries showing film/video/new media projects, an arthouse cinema and café-bar. Mon–Sat 10am–9pm, Sun 11am–9pm.

13

O2 Academy 11–13 Hotham St ⓦo2academyliverpool .co.uk. The best medium-sized live music venue in town, with good club nights.

CHESTER

The heart of genteel **CHESTER** is surrounded by Britain's most intact city walls and its narrow streets are lined with Victorian and Tudor Rows (covered walkways high above street level lined with shops and cafés). Timber-framed houses sit sedately beside the River Dee, which in Roman times made it a port and one of the most important strongholds in the empire. Today, Chester makes a good base for visiting Liverpool or North Wales.

WHAT TO SEE AND DO

Walking the 2.5 miles round the Roman **city walls** is the best introduction to the city. Outside the walls to the east on Vicar's Lane is Britain's largest **Roman Amphitheatre** (daily; free), hinting at Chester's former importance within the empire. For more on the Romans, visit the red-brick **Grosvenor Museum** (Mon–Sat 10.30am–5pm, Sun 1–4pm; free; ⓦgrosvenormuseum.co.uk) on Grosvenor Street, or stroll along a reconstructed Roman street at the **Dewa Roman Experience** (Mon–Sat 9am–5pm, Sun 10am–5pm; £5.50; ⓦdewaromanexperience.co.uk) on Pierpoint Lane. The northeastern section of the walls skirts the 1000-year-old **Cathedral** (Mon–Sat 9am–5pm, Sun 1–4pm; £3), a grand monastic complex with wonderfully preserved cloisters. Another fun way to explore is via a river or canal boat: **Chester Boat** (ⓦchesterboat.co.uk; £14; 1hr 30min) tours leave from the dock on Souters Lane, along the Dee to Eaton Estate, home to the duke and duchess of Westminster.

ARRIVAL AND INFORMATION

By train Trains arrive and depart from the station on the eastern edge of the city, a 10min walk from the centre.
Destinations Conwy (hourly; 1hr); Liverpool (every 15min; 45min); London (hourly; 2hr); Manchester (2–3 hourly; 1hr 15min).

By bus Coaches stop just north of Princess St, in the city centre.
Destinations Liverpool (4 daily; 1hr); Manchester (4 daily; 1hr 15min).
Tourist information The main tourist office, inside the town hall on Northgate St (daily 9am–5.30pm; ☎08456 477 868), arranges themed walking tours of the city.

ACCOMMODATION AND EATING

The Brewery Tap 52–54 Lower Bridge St ⓦthe-tap .co.uk). Seventeenth-century hall with a fantastic selection of cask ales and meals – like grilled ox heart – for £9.95. Mon–Thurs noon–11pm, Fri & Sat noon–midnight, Sun noon–10.30pm.

Chester Backpackers 67 Broughton St ⓦchesterback packers.co.uk. The best budget option in town: a quirky former pub with en-suite singles, twins and doubles, a large guest lounge and a 24-hour kitchen. Doubles £38

★ **Urbano 32** 32 Bridge St ⓦwww.urbano32chester .co.uk. An ideal place for brunch (from £6), lunch (sourdough pizzas from £8) or cocktails, this trendy, independent joint with exposed brick walls sits right in Chester's medieval heart. Daily 9am–11pm.

THE LAKE DISTRICT

The site of England's highest peaks and its biggest concentration of lakes, the glacier-carved **Lake District National Park** is the nation's most popular walking area. Weather here in Cumbria changes quickly, but the sudden shifts of light on the bracken-bedaubed moorland, and on the slate of the local buildings, are part of the area's appeal. The region is informally divided into the South Lakes, including **Windermere** and **Ambleside**, and the North Lakes, which include **Keswick**.

ARRIVAL AND DEPARTURE

By train From London, use the main-line service from Euston to Glasgow, disembarking at Lancaster or Oxenholme: from Oxenholme a branch line runs to Windermere and Kendal.
Destinations from Windermere Lancaster (5 daily; 40min); Oxenholme (hourly; 20min).
Destinations from Kendal Lancaster (5 daily; 25min); Oxenholme (hourly; 5min).
By bus National Express coaches run daily from London Victoria and Manchester to the Lake District.
Destinations from Windermere London (1 daily; 8hr 40min); Manchester (via Preston; 1 daily; 5hr 35min).
Destinations from Kendal London (1 daily; 8hr); Manchester (via Preston; 1 daily; 5hr 30min).

GETTING AROUND

By bus Stagecoach buses go everywhere in the region: Explorer Tickets provide unlimited bus travel across all of Cumbria and Lancashire (1-day £10.50, 3-days £25). The main routes are #555 from Lancaster to Kendal, Windermere, Ambleside, Grasmere and Keswick, and the open-top #599 from Bowness to Ambleside and Grasmere via Windermere and Brockhole: tourist offices can provide a complete list of other services.

Windermere and Bowness

Windermere is the largest of the lakes, with its main town of **WINDERMERE** set a mile or so back from the water. Other than the short climb up to the viewpoint of **Orrest Head** (30min), it has a motor museum and an aquarium, and it is the region's main service centre.

There are also buses (#555 and #599 from outside the train station) to the **Lake District National Park Visitor Centre** at Brockhole, which has an excellent information centre as well as exhibitions on the Lake District past, present and future (daily: mid-March to Oct 10am–5pm; Nov to mid-March 10am–4pm; free; ☎01539 446601). Boats (£8) run from Ambleside (see below) to the Visitor Centre.

For trips onto Lake Windermere itself, catch bus #508 or #599 from outside Windermere train station to the photogenic, but often more crowded, lakeshore town of **BOWNESS**. Lake **ferries** (☎01539 443360, ⓦwindermere-lakecruises.co.uk) run to Lakeside at the southern tip (£10 return) or to Waterhead (for Ambleside) at the northern end (£8 return).

INFORMATION

Tourist information The Windermere tourist office is located outside the train station (Mon–Fri 9am–4.30pm, Sat & Sun 9.30am–5pm; ☎01539 446499).

GETTING AROUND

By bike Bikes can be rented from Country Lanes at Windermere train station (from £23/day; ☎01539 444544, ⓦcountrylaneslakedistrict.co.uk).

ACCOMMODATION, EATING AND DRINKING

Lake District Backpackers' Lodge High St, Windermere ☎01539 446374, ⓦlakedistrictbackpackers.co.uk. This little hostel just downhill from the station has simple, cosy dorms.

Booking ahead is recommended; cash only if paying on arrival. Breakfast included. Dorms £17, doubles £39

The Hole in't Wall Low Side, behind the church in Bowness ☎01539 443488. Don't miss the chance to enjoy a pint of cask ale (£3.50) at the oldest hostelry in Bowness, once supposedly frequented by Dickens. Mon–Sat 11am–11.30pm, Sun 11am–10.30pm.

Lazy Daisy's Lakeside Kitchen Crescent Rd, Windermere. Welcoming coffee shop serving sandwiches and snacks (from £6) throughout the day and a more sophisticated evening menu that includes fish dishes and salads. Daily 9am–9pm.

Ambleside

Pretty but touristy, **Ambleside** is good for stocking up on outdoor gear, and makes a reasonable base between the north and south lakes. The **Armitt Museum** (Mon–Sat 10am–5pm; £3.50; ⓦarmitt.com) exhibits items of local geological, archeological and literary interest.

INFORMATION

Tourist information Limited info is available at The Hub of Ambleside (look for the post office sign) by the Market Cross (daily 9am–5pm; ☎01539 432582).

ACCOMMODATION AND EATING

Ambleside Backpackers Old Lake Rd ☎01539 432340, ⓦenglishlakesbackpackers.co.uk. Independent family-run

SOUTH LAKES

13

hostel located in a quiet part of town, with immaculate dorms. Breakfast included. Dorms £20, doubles £50

Ambleside Youth Hostel Waterhead ☎ 0845 3719620, ⍟ yha.org.uk. Huge YHA hostel in a prime lakeside location. It's a great base for outdoor adventures, from kayaking to scrambling, and there are excellent facilities, including a licensed restaurant. Dorms £23

Zeffirelli's Compston Rd ⍟ zeffirellis.com. A cinema with its own daytime café and a pizza restaurant (margheritas £8.45). Daily 10am–10pm.

Elterwater and Langdale

The #516 Stagecoach bus from Ambleside runs four miles west to the charming hamlet of **ELTERWATER**. The valley here offers dramatic scenery and plenty of good walking, such as routes up to Stickle Tarn and the peaks of **Langdale** (including England's highest point, Scafell Pike). The *Sticklebarn Tavern*, two miles beyond Elterwater on the same bus route, is a good place to start from, though you should make sure you have good shoes, waterproofs and a map.

ACCOMMODATION AND EATING

★ **Baysbrown Farm Campsite** A few minutes' walk west of the village of Chapel Stile ☎ 01539 437150, ⍟ baysbrownfarmcampsite.co.uk. Canny campers shun expensive hotels in favour of this spectacular site, which has views down the valley. Per person £6

Brambles Café In the centre of Chapel Stile. Attractive little café serving coffee and light meals (from £6) to a mix of tourists and locals. Daily 9am–5pm.

Keswick and Derwent Water

Principal hiking and tourist centre for the northern lakes, **KESWICK** (pronounced "kez-ick") lies on the shores of **Derwentwater**. The **Keswick Launch** (mid-March to Nov & school hols daily; Dec to mid-March Sat & Sun; £10.25 return trip, ☎ 01768 772263, ⍟ keswick-launch.co.uk) runs right around the lake: you can get off at Hawes End to climb **Cat Bells** (1481ft), for the best lakeside vantage point. From Keswick you can hike up to Latrigg (1203ft; 3hr) for breathtaking views or the more challenging **Skiddaw** (3050ft; 5hr), among the more straight-forward of the area's many true mountain hikes. Walks round the lake via **Borrowdale**, perhaps the most beautiful valley in England, take three to five hours, depending on whether you stick to the lakeside or climb above it. A mile and a half's stroll eastwards is **Castlerigg Stone Circle** (free), a Neolithic monument commanding spectacular views.

ARRIVAL AND INFORMATION

By bus The terminal is behind Booths Foodstore, off Keswick's Main St.

Destinations Ambleside (hourly; 45min); Grasmere (hourly; 30min); Kendal (hourly; 1hr 30min); Windermere (hourly; 1hr 10min).

Tourist information Moot Hall, Market Square (Mon–Fri 9.30am–4.30pm, Sat & Sun 9.30am–5.30pm; ☎ 01768 772645).

LAKE DISTRICT LUMINARIES

The lakeland landscape has been an inspiration to some of England's most revered literary figures. **William Wordsworth** lived at both **Rydal Mount** (March–Oct daily 9.30am–5pm; Nov–Feb Wed–Sun 11am–4pm; £7.50, gardens only £5), three miles northwest of Ambleside on the #555 bus, and the more interesting **Dove Cottage**, Grasmere (Mon–Fri 9.30am–4.30pm, Sat & Sun 9.30am–5pm; closed Jan; £7.50), which still holds many of Wordsworth's possessions. Both he and his sister Dorothy lie in simple graves in the village churchyard of St Oswald's.

Beatrix Potter, author, illustrator and botanist, lived at **Hill Top** (Mon–Thurs, Sat & Sun: mid-Feb to mid-March 10.30am–3.30pm; mid-March to mid-May 10.30am–4.30pm; mid-May to Aug 10.30am–5.30pm; Sept & Oct 10.30am–4.30pm; £11; ticket numbers limited; ⍟ nationaltrust.org.uk), a lovely seventeenth-century house in the hamlet of Near Sawrey. You can take a ferry from Bowness (see p.465) and cover the steep two miles to the house on foot or by minibus. Get there early to beat the crowds.

From the village of Coniston, reached by bus #505 from Windermere or Ambleside, you can take the wooden *Coniston Launch* (£11 return; ☎ 01768 775753, ⍟ conistonlaunch.co.uk) to the elegant lakeside villa, **Brantwood** (Mon–Fri 9.30am–4pm, Sat & Sun 9.30am–5pm; £8, gardens only £5.50), former home of artist and critic **John Ruskin**. The house is full of Ruskin's drawings and sketches, as well as items relating to the Pre-Raphaelite painters he inspired.

13

GETTING AROUND

By bike Bike rental available from Keswick Mountain Bikes, Southey Hill (daily 9am–5.30pm; ☏ 01768 775202, ⓦ keswickbikes.co.uk; £25/day).

ACCOMMODATION, EATING AND DRINKING

Denton House Penrith Rd ☏ 01768 775351, ⓦ dentonhouse-keswick.co.uk. Sprawling, laidback hostel that focuses on the Lake District's outdoor attractions, and can organize activities in the area. Dorms £19

The George 3 St John's St. Old coaching inn with Jennings ales on tap, serving a much-in-demand Cow Pie (£11.95 for a half portion). Daily 11am–11pm or midnight.

Keswick YHA Station Rd ☏ 08453 719746, ⓦ yha.org.uk. Well-maintained YHA hostel in a serene riverside spot with impressive mountain scenery: its licensed restaurant serves cheap evening meals. Dorms £30, doubles £59

Lakeland Pedlar Henderson's Yard, off Main St. Keswick's most agreeable café: vegetarian-friendly, with excellent home-made cakes and scones, as well as soups and sandwiches. Try the "boneshaker" salad with organic bread (£5.50). Mon–Fri 9am–4pm, Sat & Sun 9am–5pm.

YORK

Affluent **YORK** is a layer cake of history: the Romans used the city as their capital in northern Britain, as did Edwin of Northumbria, whose conversion to Christianity in 627 granted it huge spiritual importance. Then the Vikings swept through in 866, and ruled until 954, when Eric Bloodaxe lost Jorvik – as it was then known – to King Edred, who brought it into his unified England. Today its sinuous centuries-old cobbled streets are filled with cafés and craft shops, surrounded by picturesque medieval ramparts and centred on the spectacular Gothic Minster cathedral.

WHAT TO SEE AND DO

Start your sightseeing with a stroll along the **city walls** (daily till dusk), a three-mile circuit that takes in the various medieval "bars", or gates, with fine views of the Minster. Guided walks (daily 10.15am; April–Sept also 2.15pm; July & Aug also 2.15pm & 6.45pm; free; 2hr) depart from outside the art gallery in Exhibition Square; just turn up.

York Minster

Ever since Edwin built a wooden chapel on the site, **York Minster** (Mon–Sat 9am–5pm, Sun 12.45–5pm; adult £15, student £14; ⓦ yorkminster.org) has been the centre of religious authority for the north of England. Most of what's visible now was built in stages between the 1220s and the 1470s, and today it ranks as the country's largest Gothic building. Inside, the scenes of the East Window, completed in 1405, and the abstract thirteenth-century Five Sisters window, represent Britain's finest collection of stained glass. You can also climb up the central tower, which gives views over the medieval pattern of narrow streets to the south known as **The Shambles**.

Yorkshire Museum

Southwest of the Minster, just outside the city walls, Museum Gardens leads to the ruins of the Benedictine abbey of St Mary and the **Yorkshire Museum** (daily 10am–5pm; £7.50; ⓦ yorkshiremuseum .org.uk), which contains much of the abbey's medieval sculpture, and a selection of Roman, Saxon and Viking finds. The displays give a good insight into life in Roman-era Eboracum (York), with exhibits on Viking and medieval York too.

Jorvik, Dig and Castle Museum

From the Minster, shopping streets spread south and east, focusing eventually on Coppergate, former site of the city's Viking settlement. The blockbuster experience that is **Jorvik Viking Centre** (daily: April–Oct 10am–5pm; Nov–March 10am–4pm; ⓦ jorvik-viking-centre.co.uk; £10.25) provides an entertaining taste of the period through a re-creation of Viking streets, complete with appropriate sounds and smells: book online to skip the queues. Just north of here, within St Saviour's Church, is the hands-on museum **Dig** (daily 10am–5pm; £6.50 or £14.45 including Jorvik; ⓦ digyork .com), where visitors carry out their own excavations, discovering artefacts and learning about the science and processes of archeology. Further south, the superb **Castle Museum** (daily

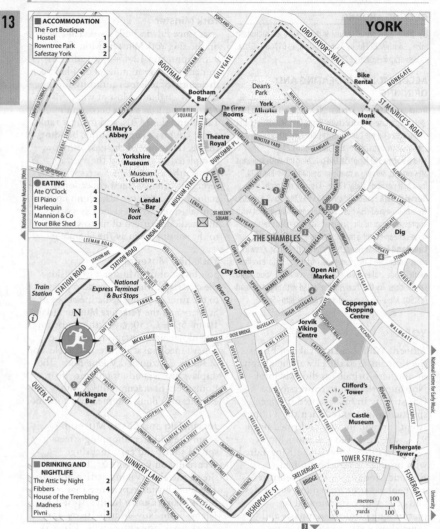

YORK

■ **ACCOMMODATION**
The Fort Boutique
  Hostel 1
Rowntree Park 3
Safestay York 2

● **EATING**
Ate O'Clock 4
El Piano 2
Harlequin 3
Mannion & Co 1
Your Bike Shed 5

■ **DRINKING AND
NIGHTLIFE**
The Attic by Night 2
Fibbers 4
House of the Trembling
  Madness 1
Pivni 3

9.30am–5pm; £10; ⓦyorkcastle
museum.org.uk) has full-scale
re-creations of life in bygone times,
with evocative street scenes of the
Victorian and Edwardian periods.

ARRIVAL AND DEPARTURE

By train York's train station lies outside the city walls on
Station Rd.
Destinations Edinburgh (every 30min; 2hr 30min);
London King's Cross (every 30min; 2hr); Manchester (every
15–30min; 1hr 30min); Newcastle (every 30min; 1hr).

By bus Long-distance coaches stop outside the train
station, as well as on Rougier St, 200 yards northeast, just
before Lendal Bridge.
Destinations Edinburgh (1 daily; 6hr 30min); London (3
daily; 5hr 30min); Manchester (hourly via Leeds; 2hr
45min); Newcastle (2 daily; 2hr 45min).

INFORMATION

Tourist information 1 Museum St (Mon–Sat
9am–5pm, Sun 10am–4pm; ⓣ01904 550099,
ⓦvisityork.org), sells the York Pass (£38 for one day),
which includes access to nearly all the city's sights.

ACCOMMODATION

Outside term time, the University of York (☎01904 328431, ⓦ york.ac.uk) rents out good-value double rooms on its campus.

★**The Fort Boutique Hostel** 1 Little Stonegate ☎01904 639573, ⓦ thefortyork.co.uk. Bang in the centre, this upmarket hostel has spacious, characterful rooms with flat-screen TVs and local artwork. Rooms (but not all dorms) are en suite; there's a bar-café downstairs, which makes the place a little noisy. Dorms £16, doubles £96

Rowntree Park Terry Ave ☎01904 658997, ⓦ caravanclub.co.uk. Conveniently placed campsite on the banks of the River Ouse, just south of town, within easy walking distance. Per person £9.60, plus per tent £12.30

★**Safestay York** 88–90 Micklegate ☎02033 268471, ⓦ safestay.com. Wonderful boutique hostel in a Grade I-listed Georgian terrace house. Expect wood-panelled rooms, luxurious private rooms, privacy curtains for bunk beds, a basement games room, plus a bar and other comfy spaces to socialize in. Dorms £29, doubles £93

EATING

El Piano 15–17 Grape Lane ⓦ el-piano.com. Bright, family-run vegan restaurant serving plenty of nut-free and raw dishes (mains £9.95), with flavours from South America, Spain and East Africa. Mon–Sat 11am–11pm, Sun noon–9pm.

Harlequin 2 King's Sq ⓦ harlequinyork.com. This first-floor tearoom serves generous lunches (jacket potatoes, salads, baguettes), excellent cream teas with freshly baked scones and ethically sourced coffee (espresso £1.90). Mon–Sat 10am–4pm, Sun 11am–3pm.

★**Mannion & Co** 1 Blake St ⓦ mannionandco.co.uk. Deli, bistro, bakery, patisserie – this sweet place wears a lot of hats and wears them well. Queue for Yorkshire rarebit for breakfast, charcuterie platters and more substantial mains (£6–10) for lunch and artisan coffee anytime. Mon–Fri 9am–5.30pm, Sat 9am–6pm, Sun 10am–5pm.

Your Bike Shed 148–150 Micklegate ⓦ yourbikeshed .co.uk. A bike repair workshop, coffee shop and café serving hearty meals to hungry cyclists – expect toasties, imaginative sandwiches, superfood salads and overflowing jacket potatoes. Mains from £5. Mon–Sat 9am–5pm, Sun 10am–5pm.

DRINKING AND NIGHTLIFE

The Attic by Night 2 King's Sq, on the second floor, above *Harlequin*. A youthful, art-filled coffee shop run by the same team as *Harlequin*, with occasional cabaret nights, gin tastings and bottled craft beer. Thurs noon–6pm, Fri & Sat noon–8pm.

Fibbers Stonebow House, Stonebow ⓦ fibbers.co.uk. Long-established, this is still York's best live music venue, with bands and musicians from around the

world playing most nights of the week. Gigs nightly from 7.30pm.

House of the Trembling Madness 48 Stonegate. Hidden away above a bottle shop, this taxidermy-filled pub serves a great range of Belgian beers in a shadowy, candlelit hall. Daily 11am–midnight.

Pivni 6 Patrick Pool ⓦ pivni.co.uk. A proper beer drinkers' pub in a timber-framed building dating back to 1190. While some of its many bottled beers from around the world go for up to £20, the ales on tap are much cheaper. Mon–Sat 11.30am–11.30pm, Sun noon–11.30pm.

ENTERTAINMENT

City Screen Picturehouse 13–17 Coney St ⓦ picturehouses.co.uk. Arthouse cinema with a riverside café-bar and live music. Also screens Hollywood films.

National Centre for Early Music St Margaret's Church, Walmgate ⓦ ncem.co.uk. Hosts a prestigious early music festival in July, plus world, jazz and folk gigs throughout the year.

DURHAM

A "perfect little city" according to travel writer Bill Bryson, **DURHAM** is known for its spectacular cathedral and castle perched high on a bluff enclosed by a loop of the River Wear (pronounced "weer"). Once one of northern England's power bases, today it's a quiet city with cobbled streets and a young vibe, being home to one of Britain's most prestigious universities. Visit as a day-trip from Newcastle or stay over to soak up the medieval vibe.

WHAT TO SEE AND DO

Durham hit the limelight after the remains of St Cuthbert, the patron saint of Northumbria, were moved here in the ninth century because of Viking raids. His shrine at the eastern end of the beautiful eleventh-century **cathedral**

13

(Mon–Sat 9.30am–6pm, Sun 12.30–5.30pm; till 8pm daily mid-July to early Sept; ⓦdurhamcathedral.co.uk; donation requested) soon became a pilgrimage site. The cathedral is England's finest example of Norman architecture, and also contains the tomb of the Venerable Bede, the country's first historian. Its tower gives breathtaking views (Mon–Fri 10am–3pm, Sat 10am–4pm; £5). On the opposite side of Palace Green, **Durham Castle** (tours daily at 1.15pm, 2.15pm, 3.15pm & 4.15pm; during university hols, also at 10.15am, 11.15am & 12.15pm; £5; ⓦdur.ac.uk/durham.castle) is a much refurbished Norman edifice that started out as a motte-and-bailey fort in 1072 and is now a university hall of residence: the Black Staircase is one of its most impressive features.

ARRIVAL AND INFORMATION

By train Durham train station is a 10min walk from the centre, via either of the two main river bridges.
Destinations Edinburgh (hourly, 2hr); London (hourly; 3hr); Newcastle (every 20min; 15min); York (4 hourly; 50min).
By bus The bus station is just south of the train station on North Rd.
Destinations London (3 daily; 7hr); Newcastle (every 30min; 1hr).
Tourist information The World Heritage Site Visitor Centre (☎01913 343 805, ⓦthisisdurham.com; Mon–Fri 9.30am–4.30pm, Sat & Sun 9.30am–5pm), near the castle at 7 Owengate, has information on the city's attractions.

ACCOMMODATION

Durham University has rooms available – including within the castle – at Easter and from July to Sept (☎0800 289 970, ⓦdur.ac.uk/conferences).
Castle View Crossgate ☎0191 386 8852, ⓦcastle-view.co.uk. The city's best-value guesthouse with homely rooms, internet access and great views of Durham Castle. Doubles £100
Durham City YHA St Chad's College, near the cathedral ☎0191 334 3358, ⓦyha.org.uk. Open only during the summer holidays and at Easter, this well-located college block has great-value single, double and twin rooms, some en suite. Doubles £28

EATING, DRINKING AND ENTERTAINMENT

★**Flat White** 21a Elvet Bridge. Home-made cakes are served on floral plates at this café/wine bar just off Saddler St. Its stone walls and wooden beams are

decorated with colourful sprigs of dried flowers. Cheap breakfasts (from £3.50) and excellent coffee. Tues–Sat 9am–5.30pm, Sun 10am–4pm.
Gala Theatre & Cinema Millennium Place ⓦgaladurham.co.uk. Durham's large theatre and cinema complex hosts drama, concerts, comedy shows and film nights. Daily 10am–late.
Shakespeare Tavern 63 Saddler St. Splendidly British, this allegedly haunted twelfth-century watering hole has nooks to snuggle up in and an extensive range of beers and spirits. Daily 11am–11.30pm.
Vennel's Café Saddler's Yard, off Saddler St. Café everything from cakes to pies and quiches (£5) in a lovely little hidden courtyard. Mon–Sat 9.30am–5pm, Sun 10.30am–5pm.

NEWCASTLE-UPON-TYNE

NEWCASTLE-UPON-TYNE has shaken off its image as being all bare-chested football fans and raucous nightlife. While still possessing both in abundance, this formerly industrial city is now as trendy as it is tough, and more about culture than clubbing. It boasts a slew of fine galleries and arts venues, as well as a handsome Neoclassical downtown area fanning out from the lofty Grecian column of **Grey's Monument**, the city's central landmark. Facing Newcastle across the Tyne is rejuvenated Gateshead, a former industrial area and now the hub of the city's art scene.

WHAT TO SEE AND DO

Arriving by train from the south, your first view is of the **River Tyne**, flanked by redeveloped quaysides and crossed by a series of bridges linking Newcastle to the **Gateshead** side of the river. Most famous is the single steel-arched **Tyne Bridge**, built in 1928 and complemented by the hi-tech "winking" **Millennium Bridge**, a wonderful sweeping arc of sparkling steel channelling pedestrians cross-river. North of the centre is student- and bar-filled Jesmond, while east is the trendy, regenerated area of Ouseburn.

Laing Gallery, Baltic and The Sage

The northeast's main art collection is housed in the **Laing Gallery** on New Bridge Street (Tues–Sat 10am–5pm, Sun 2–5pm; free; ⓦlaingartgallery.org.uk), though it's overshadowed by the excellent **BALTIC Centre for Contemporary Art** (daily 10.30am–6pm; free; ⓦbalticmill.com) next to the Millennium Bridge in Gateshead. One of the biggest contemporary galleries outside London, this converted former flour mill hosts visiting shows by some of the biggest names in contemporary art. On a similarly ambitious scale, the **Sage Gateshead** (daily roughly 9am–11pm; free; ⓦthesagegateshead.org) is a billowing steel, aluminium and glass structure by Norman Foster, that hosts a programme of concerts (classical and contemporary), events and activities.

Discovery Museum and Great North Museum

The **Discovery Museum** at Blandford Square (Mon–Fri 10am–4pm, Sat & Sun 11am–4pm; free; ⓦdiscoverymuseum .org.uk) zips through Tyneside's exciting history, from the city's technological and scientific achievements to Newcastle's most famous sons and daughters. The showpiece is the **Turbinia**, a 100ft-long ship that was the world's fastest back in 1897. Further north, near the Haymarket bus station, the university-run **Great North Museum**, Barras Bridge (Mon–Sat 10am–4pm, Sun 11am–4pm; free; ⓦgreatnorthmuseum .org.uk), has exhibitions on prehistory (dinosaurs) and ancient Egypt plus an interactive model of Hadrian's Wall.

ARRIVAL AND INFORMATION

By plane Newcastle International Airport (ⓦnewcastleairport.com) is five miles north of the city centre, and served by the local Metro system (daily 5.45am–midnight): a DaySaver ticket for unlimited travel in all three zones costs £4.80.

By train Newcastle's Central Station is a 2min walk from the centre.

Destinations Durham (around 3 hourly; 10–15min); Edinburgh (every 30min; 1hr 30min); Glasgow (every 30min, most via Edinburgh; 2hr 30min–3hr); London (every 30min; 3hr); York (up to 5 hourly; 1hr); Manchester (via York; every 15min; 2hr 35min–3hr 20min).

By bus The coach station, on St James's Boulevard, is a few mins' walk west of the station.

Destinations Durham (every 30min; 50min); Edinburgh (3 daily; 3hr 15min); Glasgow (2 daily; 4hr 30min–5hr); Liverpool (7 daily; 5hr 15min–6hr 50min); London (4

daily; 7hr–8hr 15min); Manchester (8 daily; 3hr 40min–4hr 50min); York (5 daily; 2hr 20min–4hr 50min).

Tourist information The main tourist office is at Central Arcade (Mon–Sat 9.30am–5.30pm, Sun 10am–4pm; ☎0191 277 8000, ⓦvisitnewcastlegateshead.com).

ACCOMMODATION

The University of Northumbria (☎0191 227 4209, ⓦnorthumbria.ac.uk) and Newcastle University (☎0191 222 6318, ⓦncl.ac.uk) offer good-value, summertime B&B (mostly single rooms) in their halls of residence.

Albatross Backpackers Inn 51 Grainger St ☎0191 233 1330, ⓦalbatrossnewcastle.co.uk. The most convenient place to stay in Newcastle, this large, friendly hostel is both central and full of nice touches, such as the games room with Xbox, large guest kitchen and bike storage. Dorms **£17**, doubles **£46**

Euro Hostel 17 Carliol Square ☎0845 490 0371, ⓦeurohostels.co.uk/newcastle. Clean, smart, en-suite rooms at this refurbished, 256-bed converted warehouse hostel on top of one of the city's best bars. Staff are friendly but a bit disorganized. Dorms **£20**, doubles **£70**

EATING

Many restaurants are grouped around Bigg Market, a block west of Grey St.

★**Fat Hippo Underground** 2 Shakespeare St ⓦfathippo.co.uk. Enormous, juicy burgers (from £8) in brioche buns in a cavernous subterranean setting. We love PB&J (with peanut butter and bacon jam) and the signature Fat Hippo with chorizo and cheese. Veggie options on offer, too. Daily noon–10pm.

Kafeneon 8 Bigg Market ⓦkafeneon.co.uk. Central, Greek bar/restaurant with a bargain happy-hour menu (5–8pm) of two courses for £10 – the pulled pork gyros gets our vote. Mon–Sat 11am–10pm.

★**TREAT YOURSELF**

Blackfriars Restaurant Friars Street ☎0191 261 5945, ⓦblackfriarsrestaurant .co.uk. Located in a thirteenth-century monastery, and claiming to be Britain's oldest continually used dining room, this characterful place specializes in "modern medieval" cuisine. Dishes include pan haggerty (a northeastern speciality of potatoes, onions and cheese) and roast pork belly followed by sticky toffee pudding with salted caramel sauce. Go for the set menu (2 courses for £15) or an early evening weekday meal to get the best deals. Mon–Sat noon–2.30pm & 5.30–9.45pm, Sun noon–2.45pm.

13

Nudo Noodles 54–56 Low Friar St ⓦ nudonoodles .co.uk. Plush, popular noodle house with sushi sets from £7.50 and noodle dishes from £8: authentic dishes include Japanese-style grilled eel. Daily noon–10pm.

Pink Lane Coffee Pink Lane ⓦ pinklanecoffee.co.uk. Independent specialist coffee shop just up from the station with staff who really know their beans. Good sandwiches, too (£4). Mon–Fri 7am–7pm, Sat 9am–5pm, Sun 10am–4pm.

DRINKING AND NIGHTLIFE

Free monthly entertainment listings magazine, *The Crack*, available in pubs and record shops, is the best way to find out what's on.

Centurion Bar Central Station ⓦ centurion-newcastle .com. This wonderfully grand Victorian bar used to be the First Class waiting room at the Central Station. Today, it's a great place to kick off a night out, with beers and wines from around the globe. Sun–Thurs 10am–11pm, Fri & Sat 10am–1am.

The Cluny Lime St, Ouseburn. Intimate live music venue hosting rising stars of the music scene: also serves decent burgers (£7.95) and a good international beer selection. Mon–Sat 8–11pm or midnight, Sun 8–10.30pm.

Digital Times Square ⓦ yourfutureisdigital.com. Proud owner of the best sound system in the city. Plenty of world-class DJs have headlined here, with music running the full gamut from 1980s cheese through to rave, with rock'n'roll on Rebel Thursdays. See website for opening and closing times.

HADRIAN'S WALL

A phenomenal construction that was erected between 122 and 128 AD and spanned 73 miles, **Hadrian's Wall** once separated Roman England from barbarian Scotland. It can be a wonderfully atmospheric place, especially on a rainy day, when it's not difficult to imagine Roman soldiers gloomily contemplating their bleak northern posting from atop the wall. Today the **Hadrian's Wall Path**, an 84-mile way-marked trail (5–7 days) runs coast to coast across Northumberland and Cumbria. It starts four miles east of Newcastle at **Segedunum**, the last outpost of Hadrian's great border defence, where you can look round the remains of the Roman fort (daily: April–Oct 10am– 5pm; Nov–March 10am–3pm; £5.25; ⓦ Wallsend). Otherwise, the best jumping-off point and base for longer

exploration is the abbey town of **HEXHAM**, 45 minutes west of Newcastle by train or bus. Some of the finest preserved sections of wall include **Housesteads** (Mon–Fri 10am–4pm, Sat & Sun 10am–6pm; £7), the most complete Roman fort in Britain, set in spectacular countryside, and the partly re-created fort and lively museum at **Vindolanda Roman Fort** (ⓦ vindolanda .com; Mon–Fri 10am–5pm, Sat & Sun 10am–6pm; £6.50). The circular route, which can be started from either Housesteads or Vindolanda, provides a decent walk, covering around 7.5 miles and taking in both Housesteads and Vindolanda, as well as some dramatic scenery.

ARRIVAL AND INFORMATION

By bus The Hadrian's Wall #AD122 bus (daily Easter–Oct up to 5, though not all services cover the whole route; 1-day ticket £12) runs between Hexham and Carlisle via all the main sites.

Tourist information Hexham has a tourist office in the main car park (April–Oct Mon–Sat 9.30am–5pm, Sun 11am–4pm; Nov–March Mon–Sat 10am–4.30pm; ☎ 01434 652220), or check out ⓦ visithadrianswall.co.uk.

ACCOMMODATION AND EATING

Hadrian's Wall Camping Melkridge, Haltwhistle ☎ 01434 320495, ⓦ hadrianswallcampsite.co.uk. Small, level site near the Wall with a centrally heated bunk barn. Camping/person **£10**, bunk barn **£15**

Twice Brewed Inn ☎ 01434 344534, ⓦ twicebrewedinn .co.uk. Just 1.5 miles from the Vindolanda Roman Fort, this friendly pub offers cosy rooms, pub grub throughout the day plus more refined meals in the evening, such as haggis-stuffed chicken, washed down with local beers. Doubles **£65**

Wales

Picturesque **WALES** has long appealed to British holidaymakers, drawn by unspoilt countryside and some of the UK's most dramatic mountains. The relationship between Wales and England, however, has never been entirely easy. Fed up with demarcation disputes, the eighth-century Mercian king Offa constructed a dyke to separate the two countries: the 177-mile **Offa's**

Dyke Path still (roughly) marks the border to this day, though Wales came under English rule in the late thirteenth century. Nevertheless, Wales retains a strong national identity, most clearly manifested in the Welsh language (see box below), and the arrival, in 1999, of the National Assembly for Wales, the first all-Wales tier of government for nearly six hundred years, is a sign that power is starting slowly to shift back.

Much of the country, particularly the **Brecon Beacons** in the south and **Snowdonia** in the north, is relentlessly mountainous and offers wonderful hiking terrain, while **Pembrokeshire** to the west boats a striking coastline. The biggest towns, including the capital **Cardiff** in the south, **Aberystwyth** in the west, and **Caernarfon** in the north, all cling to the coastal lowlands, but even then the mountains are only a short bus-ride away. **Holyhead**, on the island of **Anglesey**, is the main British port for ferry sailings to Dublin.

CARDIFF

Though once shackled to the fortunes of the coal-mining industry, Wales' capital city, **CARDIFF** (Caerdydd), has been revitalized over the past decade, not least due to the arrival of the Welsh Assembly. The city's narrow Victorian arcades are interspersed with new shopping centres and wide pedestrian precincts.

WHAT TO SEE AND DO

Cardiff's city centre extends north of Cardiff Central train station. To the west of the centre, overlooking the River Taff, is the gleaming **Millennium Stadium** (ⓦmillenniumstadium.com), where the country's top rugby is played. Cardiff's main historical landmark, the castle, is a short stroll northeast of here, while the revitalized Cardiff Bay, with its cutting-edge architecture, lies south of the centre.

Cardiff Castle and the National Museum

Cardiff Castle (Mon–Fri 10am–5pm, Sat & Sun 9am–6pm; £12; ⓦcardiffcastle .com) is the historical heart of the city. Standing on a Roman site developed by the Normans (with a twelfth-century Norman keep in the centre), the castle was embellished by the English architect William Burges in the 1860s, and each room in the sumptuous apartments is now a wonderful example of Victorian "medieval" decoration: the Banqueting Hall and the ceiling in the Arab Room steal the show. Look out, too, for the splendid Clock Tower and the Animal Wall, with its menagerie in stone, leading up to the castle.

Five minutes' walk northeast, the ground floor of the **National Museum Cardiff** in Cathays Park (Tues–Sun 10am–5pm; free; ⓦmuseumwales.ac.uk) is devoted to natural history and archeology. Upstairs is a fine collection of Impressionist paintings, landscapes and

---

WELSH CULTURE AND LANGUAGE

Indigenous **Welsh culture** survives largely through language and song. Music, poetry and dance are celebrated at Eisteddfod festivals throughout the country; most famous is the annual Royal National Eisteddfod (ⓦeisteddfod.org.uk) in different locations across the country in early August.

The **Welsh language** has undergone a revival and you'll see it on road signs all over the country, although you're most likely to hear it spoken in the north, west and mid-Wales, where, for many, it's their first language. Some Welsh place names have never been anglicized, but where alternative names do exist, we've given them in the text.

SOME BASICS

Hello	*Helo*	Hello
Goodbye	*Hwyl*	Huh-will
Please	*Os gwelwch chi'n da*	Oss gway-look un tha
Thank you	*Diolch*	Dee-ol'ch

13

portraits by Welsh artists, abstract art and ceramics – look out for the incredible glass art pioneered by Maurice Marinot.

Cardiff Bay

A half-hour walk south of the centre is the **Cardiff Bay** area, most easily reached by bus #7 from Cardiff Central. Once known as Tiger Bay, the long-derelict area has seen massive redevelopment since the Welsh Assembly opened. The architectural masterpiece that is the **Wales Millennium Centre** dominates, with its gleaming copper roof and huge theatre (see opposite). The **Doctor Who Experience** (Wed–Mon 10am–5pm; £14; ⓦ doctorwhoexperience.com) explains Cardiff's links to the programme – much of it was filmed here – and you can play Dr Who's sidekick before exploring a warehouse full of props and sets. Nearby is the Cardiff Bay **Visitor Centre** (see below), known as "The Tube" for its unique, award-winning design. There are also waterfront walks, glittering millennium architecture and an old Norwegian seamen's chapel, converted into a cosy café.

ARRIVAL AND DEPARTURE

By plane Cardiff Airport (ⓦ cardiff-airport.com) is around 35min west of the centre; the Cardiff Airport Express Bus (every 20min; £5) runs to Cardiff Central train station.

By train Long-distance services (including all those listed below) arrive and depart from Cardiff Central. Some local trains also depart here, while others use Queen St station, east of the centre.

Destinations Abergavenny (every 30min; 40min); Birmingham (hourly; 2hr); Bristol (Temple Meads; every 30min; 50min); Conwy (3 daily; 4hr 20min); London (every 30min; 2hr 10min); Manchester (hourly; 3hr 25min); Pembroke (2 daily; 3hr).

By bus Long-distance coaches and buses from the airport arrive at the bus terminal, right beside Cardiff Central train station, south of the city centre off Penarth Rd.

Destinations Abergavenny (hourly; 1hr 45min–2hr 30min); Aberystwyth (3 daily; 4hr); Brecon (8 daily; 1hr 30min); Bristol (hourly; 1hr 30min); London (hourly; 3hr 20min–4hr).

INFORMATION

Tourist information The Old Library on The Hayes (Mon–Sat 9.30am–5.30pm, Sun 10am–4pm; ☎ 029 2087 3573,

ⓦ visitcardiff.com), and Cardiff Bay Visitor Centre (daily 10am–6pm; ☎ 029 2087 7927). The former is also home to The Cardiff Story (Mon–Sat 10am–5pm, Sun 11am–4pm; free; ⓦ cardiffstory.com), an interactive museum that uses videos, sound effects and smells to show how the city went from "coal to cool".

ACCOMMODATION

Austins Guest House 11 Coldstream Terrace ☎ 029 2037 7148, ⓦ hotelcardiff.com. Friendly guesthouse by the river, with compact, spotless singles and doubles with flat-screen TVs. Most share bathrooms. Doubles **£45**

NosDa Studio Hostel 53–59 Despenser St ☎ 029 2037 8866, ⓦ nosda.co.uk. Just across the river from the Millennium Stadium, this lively, well-run hostel has bright, modern dorms and rooms, as well as a bar and computers. Beware, though, if you get a stag party in the room next to yours, as the walls are pretty thin. Breakfast included. Dorms **£11**, doubles **£40**

★**River House Backpackers** 59 Fitzhamon Embankment, along the riverbank ☎ 029 2039 9810, ⓦ riverhousebackpackers.com. Spotlessly clean, this intimate riverside hostel feels more like a B&B than a budget crash pad and attracts a sedate clientele. The dorms (4- and 6-bed) and double rooms share a well-equipped kitchen, dining area, lounge and decked outside seating area. The free breakfast is extensive. Dorms **£17**, doubles **£42**

EATING, DRINKING AND NIGHTLIFE

Clwb Ifor Bach (The Welsh Club) 11 Womanby St ⓦ clwb.net. Little club playing an eclectic range of music, though rock and indie by up-and-coming local bands dominates. Entry £4–10. Tues–Sat 10pm–2/3am.

Coffee Barker 13 Castle Arcade. Arguably Cardiff's best coffee shop, with a great choice of beans and squishy sofas you can sink into for a spot of breakfast or brunch: coffee from £2.50. Mon–Sat 8.30am–5pm, Sun 11am–4.30pm.

Gwdihŵ 6 Gilford Crescent ⓦ gwdihw.co.uk. Fun little bar (pronounced goody-hoo) with a beer garden that turns into a live music venue by night. Rock, indie and soul dominate. Mon–Thurs & Sun 3pm–midnight, Fri & Sat noon–2am.

Madame Fromage 18 Castle Arcade ⓦ madamefromage .co.uk. One of the best cheese specialists in the country, serving up delicious soups (£5), cold platters and home-cooked "slow food" in a pretty Victorian arcade opposite the castle. Mon–Fri 10am–5.30pm, Sat 9.30am–6pm & occasional Sun 11am–4pm.

★**Purple Poppadom** 185a Cowbridge Rd East ⓦ purplepoppadom.com. A 10min walk from the castle, this restaurant dazzles your tastebuds with a contemporary take on Indian cuisine, such as wonderfully tender, intensely tasty chicken tikka and tangy prawn curry with mango. The 2-course weekday lunch is a steal at £11. Tues–Sat noon–2pm & 5.30–11pm, Sun 1–9pm.

Zerodegrees 27 Westgate St ⓦzerodegrees.co.uk /cardiff. This sleek, industrial-themed bar-restaurant and microbrewery close to the Millennium Stadium serves up stone-fired pizzas with imaginative toppings from £8.50. Mon–Sat noon–midnight, Sun noon–11pm.

ENTERTAINMENT

Wales Millennium Centre ⓣ 029 2063 6464, ⓦwmc .org.uk. Cardiff Bay's arts hub has a wide-ranging, year-round programme that includes opera, ballet, contemporary dance, music and comedy.

CHEPSTOW AND TINTERN ABBEY

The sleepy market town of **CHEPSTOW** (Cas-Gwent) is bunched around Britain's first stone **castle** (March–Oct daily 9am–5pm; Nov–Feb Mon–Sat 10am–4pm, Sun 11am–4pm; adult £6, student £4.20; ⓦcadw.wales.gov.uk), built by the Normans in 1067 and much of which is still impressively intact. Nothing in town, however, can match the six-mile stroll north along the Wye to South Wales' main historical treasure, the eerie ruins of **Tintern Abbey**, built in 1131 and now in a state of majestic disrepair (same hours and price as castle).

ARRIVAL AND DEPARTURE

By bus Bus #69 (Mon–Fri 8 daily, Sat 6 daily, Sun 4 daily) runs from Chepstow to Tintern then on to Monmouth, eight miles north.

Tourist information For information on Chepstow and the Offa's Dyke Path contact the tourist office on Bridge Street (daily: April–Oct 9.30am–5pm; Nov–March 9.30am–3.30pm; ⓣ01291 623772, ⓦchepstow.co.uk).

ACCOMMODATION

St Briavels Castle YHA hostel ⓣ08453 719 042, ⓦyha.org.uk; bus #69. Allegedly "Britain's most haunted", this hostel occupies a moated Norman castle seven miles northeast of Chepstow. Dorms £15

THE BRECON BEACONS

The **Brecon Beacons National Park** (ⓦbreconbeacons.org) is a vast area of bare, rocky uplands and wooded valleys that makes perfect walking country. The terrain is tough, though – the SAS train here – and you should always be prepared

for inclement weather. The Beacons themselves, accessed from Brecon town, share the limelight with the **Black Mountains** in the park's eastern portion, which rise north of pretty Crickhowell. Climbing the area's tallest peak, **Pen-y-Fan** (886m), is a popular three- to- four hour round hike along a well-marked trail which leaves from the car park just south of the *Storey Arms*, 11 miles south of Brecon. An alternative route – less busy and wonderfully scenic – up the peak starts from Cwm Gwdi near Brecon town, and takes around five or six hours round trip.

Crickhowell and around

Friendly **CRICKHOWELL** (Crughywel) lies five miles west of Abergavenny and makes a picturesque base. A great six-mile hike into the **Black Mountains** from here takes you through remote countryside to tiny **Partrishow Church**; inside, you'll find a rare carved fifteenth-century rood screen complete with a dragon, and an ancient mural of the grim reaper. For more dramatic scenery, the six-and-a-half-mile round trip to Table Mountain (1481ft) or the still-longer hike up to **Sugar Loaf** (1955ft), offer great views of the Black Mountains.

Brecon

The largest of the central Brecon Beacons rise just south of **BRECON** (Aberhonddu), a lively little town eight miles west of Crickhowell known for its mid-August international jazz festival (ⓦbreconjazz .com). Accommodation is scarce during the festival and prices high, so book ahead.

ARRIVAL AND INFORMATION

By bus Stagecoach's (ⓦstagecoachbus.com) #T4 bus service runs from Cardiff to Brecon (every 2hr; 1hr 30min), where you can transfer to their #X43 service to Crickhowell (hourly; 25–45min): buses from Brecon stop on the square in Crickhowell, near the tourist office. Buses from Hereford in England (accessible by rail) also run to Brecon.

TOURIST INFORMATION

Crickhowell The tourist office (Mon–Sat 10am–5pm, Sun 10am–1pm; ⓣ01873 811970, ⓦvisitcrickhowell .co.uk) is on Beaufort Street.

13

THE BEACON WAY

The 100-mile **Beacon Way** traverses the entire Brecon Beacons National Park from Abergavenny to Llangadog (allow 8 days). Check the weather before setting out as conditions change rapidly on the hills. Regular trains run from Cardiff to Abergavenny.

Brecon For details of the area's numerous hiking routes call at the tourist office in Brecon's Cattle Market car park (Mon–Sat 9.30am–5pm, Sun 10am–4pm; ☎01874 622485).

ACCOMMODATION

CRICKHOWELL
Gwyn Deri B&B Mill St ☎01873 812494 ☎gwynderibedandbreakfast.co.uk. Welcoming owners run this homey B&B with three modern, immaculate double rooms. An excellent breakfast is included. Doubles **£70**

BRECON
YHA Brecon Beacons Seven miles south of Brecon along the A470 ☎0845 371 9506, ☎yha.org.uk. Particularly handy for hiking Pen-y-Fan, this converted farmhouse comprises snug dorms, rooms and camping pods, with a large guest kitchen and on-site bar. Dorms **£18**, doubles **£55**

PEMBROKESHIRE AND ST DAVID'S

The sleepy town of **Pembroke** (Penfro), accessible by train from Cardiff, is a handy jumping-off point from which to explore the southern part of the **Pembrokeshire Coast National Park** (☎pcnpa.org.uk), which covers 240 square miles of wooded estuaries, rocky cliffs and isolated beaches. Walkers can hail buses that run along the coast.

St David's
Around thirty miles north of Pembroke, the city of **ST DAVID'S** (Tyddewi), Britain's smallest, is one of the most enchanting spots in Britain (☎stdavids.co.uk). Its beautiful **cathedral** (daily 9am–5.30pm; £3 donation requested; ☎stdavids cathedral.org.uk), delicately tinted purple, green and yellow by a combination of lichens and geology, hosts a prestigious classical music festival in late May or early June. Nearby, the remains of

the magnificent fourteenth-century **Bishop's Palace** (March–Oct daily 9.30am–5/6pm; Nov–Feb Mon–Sat 10am–4pm, Sun 11am–4pm; £3.50) add to the wonderful setting.

ARRIVAL AND INFORMATION

By bus Travel first to Haverfordwest, served by frequent trains from Cardiff (every 2hr; 2hr 30min) and National Express buses from Pembroke (2 daily; 35min). From here take hourly bus #411 sixteen miles west to St David's.
By car St David's is around 2hr 30min drive west of Cardiff along the M4 and A40.
Tourist information The national park visitor centre in town at the Oriel y Parc Landscape Gallery (daily: March–Oct 9.30am–5.30pm; Nov–Feb 10am–4.30pm; ☎01437 720392, ☎pembrokeshirecoast.org.uk) has maps of scenic walks around St David's.

ACCOMMODATION AND EATING

Bishops 22–23 Cross Sq ☎thebish.co.uk. Friendly pub on the main square serving delicious British standards, such as fish and chips and bangers and mash. Mains from £10. Daily 11am–midnight.
St David's YHA Llaethdy, close to Whitesands Beach ☎0845 371 9141, ☎yha.org.uk. Converted farmhouse two miles northwest of town that appeals to surfers and climbers, who get a kick out of exploring the surrounding coastline. Dorms **£22**, doubles **£55**

ABERYSTWYTH

ABERYSTWYTH, a lively, thoroughly Welsh seaside resort of neat Victorian terraces, has a thriving student culture. The flavour of the town is best appreciated from the seafront, where one of Edward I's castles bestrides a windy

FERRIES TO IRELAND

Two ferries daily to Rosslare in Ireland (4hr; ☎irishferries.com) leave from **Pembroke Dock**, two miles north of Pembroke. About 17 miles further north, at the end of the main London to Cardiff train line, is **Fishguard** (Abergwaun), from where Stena Line ferries depart twice daily to Rosslare (4hr; ☎stenaline.co.uk). **Holyhead** (Caergybi), on Anglesey, is the busiest Welsh ferry port, with six ferries and catamarans (run by Stena Line and Irish Ferries) leaving for Dublin each day (2hr 20min–3hr 15min).

13

headland to the south. The picturesque bluff to the north of town can be reached via a clanking **cliff railway** (April–Oct daily 10am–5pm; Nov–March limited timetable in operation; £4.50 return). For a more extended rail trip, you can take the **Vale of Rheidol** narrow-gauge steam train to **Devil's Bridge**, a picturesque canyon where three bridges span a dramatic waterfall (late March to Oct; £20 return; ⍵rheidolrailway.co.uk).

ARRIVAL AND INFORMATION

By train The train station is 10min south of the seafront, reached by walking up Terrace Rd.

Tourist information The tourist office is also on Terrace Rd, near the junction with Bath St (Mon–Sat 10am–5pm; July & Aug also Sun 10am–5pm; ☎01970 612125).

ACCOMMODATION AND EATING

Baravin Llys y Brenin, Terrace Rd ⍵baravin.co.uk. Near the waterfront, this bistro/bar combines Italian dishes with Welsh ingredients – try the pizza with pulled Penlan pork and Perl Wen cheese: mains from £8.50. The horseshoe-shaped bar is the place to make merry, fuelled by imaginative cocktails. Mon–Sat 10am–late.

Maes y Mor 25 Bath St ☎01970 639270, ⍵maesymor .co.uk. While the town seafront is lined with genteel guesthouses, this smart place, located a block back, offers snug singles, doubles and family rooms, with a self-catering kitchen available. Doubles **£55**

SNOWDONIA NATIONAL PARK

With its jagged peaks, towering waterfalls and glacial lakes, **Snowdonia National Park** (⍵visitsnowdonia.info) attracts walkers in large numbers, with a steady stream even in the bleakest months. The park covers an enormous area stretching from Aberdyfi in the south to Conwy on the north coast. Its highlight, though, is the glory of North Wales – **Mount Snowdon**, at 3560ft the highest mountain in England and Wales.

GETTING AROUND

By bus and train There are two main access routes. From Porthmadog, a few miles north of Harlech (both on the local rail network), buses skirt the base of Snowdon north to Caernarfon and Llanberis; main-line trains from Crewe and Chester hug the north coast through Bangor to Holyhead, passing through Llandudno Junction and Conwy (the latter is a request stop).

Llanberis

LLANBERIS is a popular lakeside village in the shadow of **Snowdon** and a convenient base for exploring the area. The slate quarries that seared Llanberis's surroundings now lie idle, but the excellent **Welsh Slate Museum** (Easter–Oct daily 10am–5pm; Nov–Easter Mon–Fri & Sun 10am–4pm; free; ⍵museumwales.ac.uk) takes an in-depth look at the town's former lifeblood, with slate-cutting demonstrations and immense machinery.

ARRIVAL AND INFORMATION

By bus Regular buses run the seven miles southeast from Caernarfon (see p.478), stopping on the high street. Sherpa Bus services encircle Snowdon itself; most routes cost £2 in each direction.

Tourist information The tourist office is a few minutes' walk away from the high street on the A4086, inside the Electric Mountain building (Mon, Tues & Fri–Sun 10am–4pm; ☎01286 870765, ⍵visitsnowdonia.info).

ACCOMMODATION

There's a good choice of accommodation for walkers, particularly in Llanberis. The Sherpa Bus provides access to several well-equipped HI hostels (⍵yha.org.uk), each at the base of a footpath up the mountain.

Bryn Gwynant YHA Nantgwynant, 10 miles south of Llanberis along the A498 ☎0845 371 9108, ⍵yha.org.uk /hostel/bryn-gwynant. This converted Victorian mansion has views across Llyn Gwynant lake and is conveniently located near the Watkin Path up Snowdon. Meals available on request. Dorms **£20**, doubles **£60**

Idan House 12 High St, Llanberis ☎01286 670 873, ⍵idanhouse.vpweb.co.uk. Centrally located, family-run guesthouse, where most of the rooms share bathrooms. A generous cooked Welsh breakfast is included in the price. Doubles **£55**

Pen-y-Pass YHA Five miles south of Llanberis along the A4086 ☎0845 371 9534, ⍵yha.org.uk/hostel/pen-y -pass. Popular hostel along the Pen-y-Pass mountain pass, at the start of the Miners' Track and Pyg Track, with dorms and private rooms, some en suite. Dorms **£18**, doubles **£55**

EATING

Pete's Eats 40 High St, Llanberis ⍵petes-eats.co.uk. Busy, bright café that acts as hiker central, serving huge portions of soup, pasta and daily specials to a Goretex-clad crowd. Mains from £4. Daily 8am–8 or 9pm.

13

CLIMBING SNOWDON

There are six main tracks up Snowdon, varying in length and difficulty.

Llanberis Path (5 miles; 3hr) The longest but easiest ascent of the mountain from Llanberis.

Snowdon Ranger Path (4 miles; 3hr) Runs from *Snowdon Ranger YHA* and has two steep sections.

Miners' Track (4 miles; 2hr 30min) Largely flat trail that runs from the Pen-y-Pass car park, past Llyn Llydaw, and then climbs steeply up to meet the Pyg Track and Llanberis Path.

Pyg Track (3.5 miles; 2hr 30min) Also starts from the Pen-y-Pass car park, but climbs quite steeply straight away.

Rhyd Ddu Path (4 miles; 3hr) An uncrowded, gentle ascent past the rim of Cwn Clogwyn from the Caernarfon–Beddgelert road (A4085).

Watkin Path (4 miles; 3hr) Steep and challenging route from Nantgwynant that involves a scramble up Bwlch Ciliau then a further climb up Snowdon.

Snowdon Horseshoe (8-mile-loop) Combines the Pyg Track with a scramble up the knife-edge Crib Goch ridge (for experienced hikers only), and a loop around Llyn Llydaw lake from Snowdon that eventually descends to join the Miners' Track.

Alternatively, you can take the steam-hauled **Snowdon Mountain Railway** (mid-March to early Nov daily; £25 single, £37 return; discounts for 9am departure; ⓦ snowdonrailway.co.uk), which operates from Llanberis (see p.477) to the summit, weather permitting. Whichever way you come, make sure you're equipped with suitable shoes, warm clothing, and food and drink to see you through any unexpected hitches.

CAERNARFON

CAERNARFON is a handy springboard for trips into Snowdonia. **Caernarfon Castle** (March–Oct Mon–Fri 9.30am–5pm, Sat & Sun 9.30am–6pm; Nov–Feb Mon–Sat 10am–4pm, Sun 11am–4pm, adult £7.95, student £5.60; ⓦ caernarfon-castle .co.uk), built in 1283, is arguably one of the most splendid castles in Britain, with atmospheric towers and rambling stone passageways. It's here that heirs to the throne, the princes of Wales, are ceremonially invested.

ARRIVAL AND INFORMATION

By bus Buses stop at the station on Penllyn, just across Castle Square from the tourist office.

Tourist information Castle St (April–Oct daily 9.30am–4.30pm; Nov–March Mon–Sat 10am–3.30pm; ☎ 01286 672232, ⓦ visitsnowdonia.info).

ACCOMMODATION AND EATING

Black Boy Inn Northgate St ☎ 01286 673604, ⓦ black -boy-inn.com. Smart (but pricey) en-suite doubles. Also serves great pub food (mains from £8.50) and Welsh cream teas. **£90**

Totters 2 High St ☎ 01286 672963, ⓦ totters.co.uk. An excellent independent hostel with lockers in spick-and-span dorms, cosy rooms and an atmospheric fourteenth-century basement. Dorms **£18.50**, doubles **£44**

NORTH WALES COAST

From Caernarfon, buses run northeast to Bangor which is connected to the pretty little island of **Anglesey** (Ynys Môn) by the Menai Bridge, built by Thomas Telford in 1826. Eighteen miles east of Bangor is the medieval walled town of **CONWY** and its impressive UNESCO-listed **Conwy Castle** (March–Oct Mon–Fri 9.30am–5pm, Sat & Sun 9.30am–6pm; Nov–Feb Mon–Sat 10am–4pm, Sun 11am–4pm; adult £8, student £5.60). Built in 1307 by Edward I as one of his "Iron Ring" of fortresses to pacify the rebellious Welsh, the castle has eight towers enclosing a cavernous Great Hall, and is rumoured to have a resident ghost.

ACCOMMODATION AND EATING

Conwy YHA Larkhill, Sychnant Pass Rd ☎ 0845 371 9732, ⓦ yha.org.uk. Just west of the centre, Conwy's modern HI has a full range of facilities and its private rooms are mostly en suite. Dorms **£19**, doubles **£45**

Press Room 3 Rose Hill St, Conwy. With an outdoor courtyard facing the castle, this café-cum-arty-shop serves quiches, full breakfasts and daily specials, such as gourmet takes on Welsh rarebit: mains from £6. Daily 10.30am–3.30pm.

Scotland

With its kilted bagpipers, brooding castles on craggy highland hilltops, mystery-steeped lochs and whisky, **SCOTLAND** has a unique character, which is apparent as soon as you cross the border from England. This is partly due to the Scots, unlike the Welsh, successfully repulsing the expansionist designs of England down the centuries. Although the "old enemies" formed a union in 1707, Scotland retained many of its own institutions, notably distinctive legal and educational systems. However, Scottish **political nationalism** has been on the rise since 1997's referendum, when the Scottish people voted in favour of devolution. The Scottish Parliament held its first meeting in 1999, and the 2011 elections saw the Scottish National Party (SNP) gain a historic majority. Buoyed by its success, the SNP-led government held a **referendum** on complete independence in late 2014, in which the Scots voted narrowly in favour of remaining part of the UK. Scotland voted strongly to stay in the EU in the 2016 referendum when the UK voted to leave, leading SNP supporters to call for a second independence referendum – whatever happens, the issue of Scottish sovereignty is far from settled.

Most of Scotland's population clusters around the two principal cities: stately **Edinburgh**, the national capital, with its magnificent architecture and imperious natural setting, and revitalized **Glasgow**, a former Industrial Revolution powerhouse now renowned for its culture, nightlife and cuisine. Outside this Central Belt, Scotland is overwhelmingly rural, and just beyond Glasgow the wild, mountainous, loch-strewn bulk of the **Highlands** rears up and doesn't stop until it hits the north coast. Off the west coast lie the majority of Scotland's beach-fringed islands, surviving largely on fishing and agriculture. All this makes for terrific outdoor fun, with many of the most scenic spots – such as the famous **Loch Lomond** and **Loch Ness** – easily accessible.

EDINBURGH

EDINBURGH, so said former resident Robert Louis Stevenson, "is what Paris ought to be". For many centuries Scotland's capital rivalled Europe's greatest cities in terms of learning, cultural clout and setting. It straddles two extinct volcanoes: Castle Rock – topped with an imposing castle – and Arthur's Seat, which shelters the official residence of the Royal Family in Scotland. In between is a beautiful city, made up of steeply twisting alleyways (wynds) and stone-built houses. The population usually hovers around the half-million mark, but swells massively in high season, peaking in August during the **Edinburgh Festival**.

WHAT TO SEE AND DO

The centre has two distinct parts. The castle rock is the core of the medieval city – the **Old Town** – where nobles and servants lived side by side for centuries within tight defensive walls: Edinburgh earned its nickname "Auld Reekie" from the smog and smell generated by the cramped inhabitants. To the north, the **New Town**, designed by eminent architects of the day, was begun in the late 1700s: still largely intact, it's an outstanding example of Georgian town planning.

The Old Town and castle

The cobbled **Royal Mile** – composed of Castlehill, Lawnmarket, High Street and Canongate – is the central thoroughfare of the **Old Town**, running down to the Palace of Holyroodhouse from the **castle** (Mon–Fri 9.30am–5pm, Sat & Sun 9.30am–6pm; £16.50; ⓦedinburghcastle .gov.uk), a formidable edifice perched on sheer volcanic rock, with fantastic views of the city from its battlements. Within its precincts are St Margaret's Chapel, Edinburgh's oldest surviving building dating from 1110, and the venerable fifteenth-century siege cannon, Mons Meg, complete with enormous cannonballs. Other castle highlights include the richly decorated Great Hall, an exhibition displaying the Honours of Scotland (the Scottish Crown Jewels) and the Stone of Destiny – the coronation stone that was returned to Scotland in

EDINBURGH

DRINKING AND NIGHTLIFE

Bramble	3
Cabaret Voltaire	2
Café Royal	5
Dirty Dick's	6
Jekyll & Hyde	4
Liquid Room	7
Sandy Bell's	8
Sheep Heid Inn	9
Whistle Binkie's	1

■ **ACCOMMODATION**

Ardenlee Guest House	4
Castle Rock	8
CODE Hostel Edinburgh	7
Haggis Hostel	6
Hermitage Guest House	5
High Street Hostel	2
Pub by Premier Inn	1
Malone's Old Town Hostel	9
Smart City Hostel	3

● **EATING**

Brew Lab	7	Mother India's Café	9
The Dogs	10	Mums	5
Elephant House	6	Oink	8
Fishers	4	Papii	1
Hanedan	2	Tapa	12
Mosque Kitchen	3	Valvona and Crolla	11

13

1997 after spending 700 years in Westminster Abbey. The castle esplanade provides a dramatic setting for the Military Tattoo, a lavish display of martial pomp staged during the Festival. Year-round, at 1pm (Mon–Sat), the One O'Clock Gun is fired from the Mills Mount Battery.

National Museum of Scotland

At the eastern end of Lawnmarket, George IV Bridge leads south from the Royal Mile to Chambers Street, where the **National Museum of Scotland** (daily 10am–5pm; free; ⓦnms.ac.uk) is home to many of the nation's historical treasures, ranging from Celtic pieces to twentieth-century icons.

High Kirk of St Giles and Parliament House

On the Royal Mile, High Street starts at Parliament Square, dominated by the **High Kirk of St Giles** (May–Sept Mon–Fri 9am–7pm, Sat 9am–5pm, Sun 1–5pm; Oct–April Mon–Sat 9am–5pm, Sun 1–5pm; £3 donation; ⓦstgilescathedral.org .uk) with its crown-shaped spire and Thistle Chapel sporting some impressive mock-Gothic woodcarving. On the south side of Parliament Square are the Neoclassical law courts, incorporating the seventeenth-century **Parliament House**, under whose spectacular hammerbeam roof the Scottish parliament met until the 1707 Union.

John Knox's House and Scottish Parliament

The westernmost section of the Royal Mile, Canongate, starts just beyond **John Knox's House** (Mon–Sat 10am–6pm; July & Aug also Sun noon–6pm; £5; ⓦscottishstorytellingcentre.co.uk), atmospheric home of the city's fierce Calvinist cleric (look out for the Devil on the ceiling), and the Scottish Storytelling Centre. The road leads to the new **Scottish Parliament** (Mon–Sat 9am–5pm except during February recess; free), a costly, controversial but undoubtedly striking piece of contemporary architecture.

The Palace of Holyroodhouse and Arthur's Seat

The Royal Family's official Scottish residence is the imposing **Palace of Holyroodhouse** (daily: April–Oct 9.30am–6pm; Nov–March 9.30am–4.30pm; £12), which has been entwined with its fair share of historical figures including Oliver Cromwell and Mary, Queen of Scots. The public are admitted to the sumptuous state rooms unless the royals are in residence. The **Queen's Gallery** (same hours; £6.70) displays works of art from the royal collection. The palace looks out over Holyrood Park, from where fine walks lead along the **Salisbury Crags** and up **Arthur's Seat** beyond; a fairly stiff climb is rewarded by magnificent views over the city and the Firth of Forth.

The New Town

The wide grassy valley of Princes Street Gardens marks a clear divide between the Old and New Towns. Along the north side runs **Princes Street**, the main shopping area. Splitting the gardens halfway along is the **Scottish National**

THE EDINBURGH FESTIVAL

By far the biggest arts event in Europe, August's **Edinburgh Festival** is really a multitude of festivals, mostly theatre-based, attracting artists, performers, comedians and tourists in their thousands. **The Edinburgh Festival Fringe** (ⓦedfringe.com), begun as a sideline to the International Theatre Festival to showcase alternative performances, is now the largest draw, mainly for its up-and-coming and big-name comedians. But with a ticket even on the Fringe often hitting £10 or more, and accommodation prices soaring, the only way to experience the Festival cheaply is often to work at it. Pretty much everywhere in Edinburgh becomes a venue during the festival, and every venue needs box office, front of house, technical and bar staff. You won't make much money, but you'll often end up with accommodation and free passes for your venue's shows, and sometimes others. The main Fringe venues to approach are the Assembly Rooms (ⓦassemblyfestival.com), Gilded Balloon (ⓦgildedballoon.co.uk), Underbelly (ⓦunderbelly.co.uk) and Pleasance (ⓦpleasance.co.uk/edinburgh).

13

Gallery (daily 10am–5pm, Thurs till 7pm; free; ⓦnationalgalleries.org), an Athenian-style sandstone building. One of the best small collections of pre-twentieth-century art in Europe, it displays works by major European artists including Botticelli, Titian, Rembrandt, Gauguin and Van Gogh. Look out for Sir Henry Raeburn's charming *Skating Minister* – a postcard favourite. The gallery is linked, via a Neoclassical underground chamber, to the **Royal Scottish Academy** (Mon–Sat 10am–5pm, Sun noon–5pm; free), an exhibition space originally designed in 1826 that hosts changing exhibitions of contemporary art.

The Scott Monument and Calton Hill

Northeast of the National Gallery you can climb the peculiar Gothic spire of the **Scott Monument** (daily: April–Sept 10am–7pm; Oct–March Mon–Fri 10am–4pm, Sat & Sun 10am–6pm; £5), a tribute to Scottish author Sir Walter Scott. Further on down Princes Street **Calton Hill** rises up above the New Town and is worth climbing, both for the citywide views and for the surreal collection of Neoclassical follies, including the unfinished **National Monument**, perched on the very top.

Scottish National Portrait Gallery

At the eastern end of Queen Street stands the **Scottish National Portrait Gallery** (daily 10am–5pm, Thurs till 7pm; free), a remarkable red-sandstone building modelled on the Doge's Palace in Venice. Inside, the collection of portraits offers an engaging procession through Scottish history from Robert Burns to Sean Connery.

Scottish Modern Art Galleries

In the northwest corner of the New Town lies **Stockbridge**, a smart residential suburb with vintage shops, cool cafés and a bohemian vibe. From here Belford Road leads up to the **Scottish National Gallery of Modern Art** (daily 10am–5pm; free), whose two buildings (named Modern One and Modern Two) offer an accessible introduction to all the notable movements of twentieth-century art, with a sculpted garden area designed by Charles Jencks.

Leith

Once rough-round-the-edges Leith, Edinburgh's historic port two miles northwest of the city centre, has been revitalized in recent years and now has a cool collection of lively waterside bars and restaurants. It's also home to the Royal Yacht *Britannia* (daily: April–June & Oct 9.30am–4pm; July–Sept 9.30am–4.30pm; Nov–March 10am–3.30pm; adult £15, student £13.50; ⓦroyalyachtbritannia.co.uk), the Queen's former luxury yacht, now berthed at Ocean Terminal. The vessel has hosted some of the world's most important figures in its 44 years of service, from Gandhi and Nelson Mandela to Bill Clinton: check out the surprisingly modest royal quarters (the Queen's are separate from Prince Philip's).

Rosslyn Chapel

Located on the eastern edge of the village of Roslin, seven miles south of Edinburgh, is the remarkable, mystery-steeped **Rosslyn Chapel** (Mon–Sat 9.30am–5pm, Sun noon–4.45pm; £9; ⓦrosslynchapel.com), reachable on

Lothian bus #15. Its intricate fifteenth-century design and imagery associated with Freemasonry and the Knights Templar contributed to its starring role in Dan Brown's bestseller *The Da Vinci Code* and the subsequent Hollywood film.

ARRIVAL AND DEPARTURE

By plane Edinburgh Airport (ⓦedinburghairport.co.uk) is eight miles west of the centre. From the airport to the city centre, you can take Airlink bus #100 (4am–midnight every 10–15min; 40min; £4.50 single; ⓦflybybus.com) or Edinburgh Trams (6am–midnight every 10–15min; 30min; £5 single; ⓦedinburghtrams.com).

By train Edinburgh's Waverley Station is bang in the centre, just south of Princes St.

Destinations Aberdeen (hourly; 2hr 30min); Durham (every 30min; 1hr 45min); Glasgow (every 15min; 50min); Inverness (10 daily; 3hr 30min); Leuchars (for St Andrews; every 30min; 1hr); London (1–2 hourly; 4hr–7hr 30min); Newcastle (3 hourly; 1hr 30min); Stirling (every 30min; 50min); York (2 hourly; 2hr 30min).

By bus Edinburgh Bus Station is on Elder Street, just south of York Place, and is served by a mixture of long-distance and local buses.

Destinations Aberdeen (hourly; 3hr); Glasgow (every 15min; 1hr 20min); Inverness (every 1–2hr; 3hr 45min–4hr 45min); Manchester (3 daily; 5hr 40min–6hr 25min); Newcastle (5 daily; 2hr 45min–3hr 30min); St Andrews (hourly; 2hr); Stirling (at least hourly; 1hr 30min).

INFORMATION

Tourist information 3 Princes St, above the station on the top level of Princes Mall (July & Aug Mon–Sat 9am–8pm, Sun 10am–8pm; Sept–June Mon–Sat 9am–5pm, Sun 10am–5pm; ☏0131 473 3868, ⓦvisitscotland.com). There's also a branch at the airport. Both tourist offices sell the Edinburgh Pass: it includes a free airport transfer and access to more than thirty of the city's attractions (1-day pass £29; 2-day £39; 3-day £49), though not Edinburgh Castle or Holyroodhouse Palace, so you have to do a lot of sightseeing to make it worthwhile.

GETTING AROUND

By bus The city is covered by an extensive network of Lothian (ⓦlothianbuses.com) and First (ⓦfirstgroup .com) buses. Lothian buses #10, #12, #16 & #22 run from Princes St to Leith via Leith Walk: day passes are available on board for £3.60 (exact change required). First buses charge £3.50 for a day pass and give change.

By bike Edinburgh Cycle Hire, 29 Blackfriars St (☏0131 556 5560, ⓦcyclescotland.co.uk), rents bikes (from £20/ day) and offers customized cycling tours of Scotland.

By tram Edinburgh Trams (ⓦedinburghtrams.com) run from the airport to the city centre via Haymarket (£5). A single within the city costs £1.60; an unlimited day rider ticket costs £4 (£9 including the airport).

ACCOMMODATION

If you want to stay during the Festival (early Aug to early Sept), you'll need to book months in advance and, in many cases, be prepared to pay more than the high season prices listed here. Minto St, which starts about a mile and a half south of the train station, and Pilrig St, just west of Leith Walk, hold a myriad B&Bs.

HOSTELS

★**Castle Rock** 15 Johnston Terrace ☏0131 225 9666, ⓦscotlandstophostels.com. Friendly 200-bed hostel tucked below the castle ramparts. It comes with a comfortable lounge, period features and, allegedly, its own ghost. Dorms £17, doubles £45

★**CODE Hostel Edinburgh** 50 Rose St N Lane ☏0131 659 9883, ⓦcodehostel.com. This boutique hostel has comfy sleeping pods providing privacy plus electric sockets for your rechargeables. Thoughtfully designed communal spaces and a roof terrace encourage socializing, and the staff are helpful. There's a great 2-person apartment, too. Dorms £25, apartment £99

Haggis Hostel 5/3 West Register St ☏0131 557 0036, ⓦhaggishostels.co.uk. Small, clean, fresh-feeling dorms high up in a building near Princes St. TV room, laundry facilities, clean showers and breakfast provided: single-sex dorms available, too. Dorms £22

High Street Hostel 8 Blackfriars St ☏0131 557 3984, ⓦscotlandstophostels.com. Large hostel in a sixteenth-century building just off the Royal Mile, with basic rooms, a mural-filled lounge area and a huge kitchen. The cleanliness could be better, but staff are friendly and the location is excellent. Dorms £20, doubles £70

Malone's Old Town Hostel 14 Forrest Rd ☏0131 226 5954, ⓦmaloneshostel.com. Dorms at this hostel above an Irish bar are a little stark, but the location is excellent and guests get discounts on food at the pub below. Dorms £13

Smart City Hostel 50 Blackfriars St ☏0131 524 1989, ⓦsmartcityhostels.com. This modern hostel has spotless, hotel-standard en-suite rooms and dorms, with a stylish bar, terrace and restaurant. Dorms £12, doubles £69

GUESTHOUSES AND HOTELS

Ardenlee Guest House 9 Eyre Place ☏0131 556 2838, ⓦwww.ardenlee.co.uk. Welcoming guesthouse near the Royal Botanic Garden with comfortable rooms; unusually, solo travellers pay exactly half the price of a double. Doubles £80

Hermitage Guest House 16E Hermitage Place ☏0131 555 4868. Friendly spot a short walk from Leith. The singles and doubles may be of the can't-swing-a-cat variety, but

13

they're warm, clean, and breakfast is included. Lothian bus #25 takes you almost to the doorstep. Doubles **£60**

★ **hub by Premier Inn** 37E Market St ☎ 0871 527 9580, ⓦ hubhotels.co.uk. All creams and lime greens, these ultra-compact, ultra-modern rooms are designed with comfort in mind: excellent beds, monsoon showers, fast wi-fi and control panels for the light and temperature. And it's right on the Royal Mile. Doubles **£59**

EATING

CAFÉS, CHEAP EATS AND SNACKS

Brew Lab 6–8 South College St ⓦ brewlabcoffee.co.uk. Artisan coffee bar favoured by design-conscious students, who come for the locally made cakes and pastries (from £2), exposed brick interiors and free wi-fi. Daily 9am–6pm.

Elephant House 21 George IV Bridge ⓦ elephanthouse .biz. Popular café with a cavernous back room, best known as the place where J.K. Rowling wrote the first *Harry Potter* book. Simple dishes like chilli con carne cost £5.50. Mon–Fri 8am–10pm, Sat & Sun 9am–11pm.

★ **Oink** 34 Victoria St ⓦ oinkhogroast.co.uk. Busy little takeaway shop specializing in hog roast rolls (look for the pig in the window). Choose your bread, stuffing and sauce, then tuck in (from £4). Daily 11am–5pm, but may close earlier if pork runs out.

Papii 101 Hanover St. Smart, pastel-coloured interiors make this bright café a popular place to stop for a coffee made from locally roasted beans, accompanied by toasted bagels, waffles or a granola breakfast. Mon–Fri 7.30am–4pm, Sat 8am–5pm, Sun 9am–4pm.

Valvona and Crolla 19 Elm Row ⓦ valvonacrolla.co.uk. Stylish deli (Scotland's oldest) selling picnic treats with a Mediterranean slant (great Italian wines and cheeses). Mon–Thurs 8.30am–6pm, Fri & Sat 8am–6.30pm, Sun 10.30am–4pm.

RESTAURANTS

The Dogs 110 Hanover St ⓦ thedogsonline.co.uk. No-nonsense Scottish restaurant with a good-value lunch menu (mains £5–6) and a pricier evening one (mains £10–14) – dishes range from seafood barley risotto to devilled ox liver. Daily noon–10pm.

Fishers 1 The Shore, Leith ⓦ fishersrestaurants.co.uk. Among several seafood restaurants on this upmarket stretch beside Leith docks, *Fishers* is famous for its high-quality fish sourced from around Scotland's coast, and the weekday set menu (two courses for £15) is a good deal. Mains from £16. Daily noon–10.30pm.

Hanedan 41 W Preston St ⓦ hanedan.co.uk. Justifiably popular, this tiny authentic Turkish place serves fantastic hot and cold meze, meaty and veggie moussaka and chargrilled meats. Meze from £3.50, mains from £9. Tues–Sun noon–3pm & 5.30pm–late.

Mosque Kitchen 31 Nicholson Square ⓦ mosquekitchen .com. "Curry in a hurry": this simple, canteen-style establishment is super-popular with students and visitors and serves large portions of curry, koftas and biriyani for £6. Daily 10am–9.30pm.

Mother India's Café 3 Infirmary St ⓦ motherindia .co.uk. This buzzy, popular spot specializes in Indian tapas, with a couple of dishes (from £4.25) enough for one person. Feast on the likes of lamb saag, fish masala and aubergine fritters. Mon–Thurs noon–2pm & 5–10.30pm, Fri–Sun noon–10.30pm.

★ **Mums** 4a Forrest Rd. Gravy-drizzled comfort food in a laidback, retro-style diner. *Mums* serves up more than a dozen types of mashed potato with its gourmet, gluten-free sausages (from £7.50), and has a good selection of bottled Scottish ales and ciders to wash the food down with. Daily 10am–10pm.

★ **Tapa** 19 Shore Place ⓦ tapaedinburgh.co.uk. Atmospheric tapas bar in Leith, serving authentic Spanish specialities that include aubergine with honey, goat's cheese and beetroot towers and plenty of cold cuts. Spanish wines and sherries abound and the El Classico lunch for two (£15) is good value for 6 tapas. Sun–Thurs 1–9pm, Fri & Sat 1–10pm.

DRINKING AND NIGHTLIFE

Pick up a copy of *The List* or *The Skinny* to find out what's going on with Edinburgh's lively nightlife. If you're just out for a drink, try the New Town's traditional pubs, or the bar-restaurants along the waterfront in Leith. The top of Leith Walk is the place for gay nightlife.

PUBS AND BARS

★ **Bramble** 16A Queen St ⓦ bramblebar.co.uk. Unmarked, refined subterranean bar that has earned its place in the World's Top 20 Bars with its remarkable cocktails. Nary a beer drinker in sight. Daily 4pm–1am.

Café Royal 19 West Register St ⓦ caferoyaledinburgh .co.uk. Make a point of visiting this Grade A listed pub, arguably Edinburgh's most beautiful watering hole, which serves a wide selection of wines and beers. There's a pricier restaurant below serving classic dishes (mains from £13; 2-course early bird menu £20). Mon–Sat 11am–midnight, Sun 12.30–11pm.

Dirty Dick's 159 Rose St. Cluttered with old curios, this pub boasts cask-conditioned ales, an animated atmosphere and legendary steak-and-ale pies (£9.50). Mon–Fri 11am–1am, Sat & Sun noon–1am.

Jekyll & Hyde 112 Hanover St ⓦ eerie-pubs.co.uk/jekyll -hyde. Ghoulish, Gothic, gimmicky and fun, this themed pub serves creepily named concoctions from the bar. Daily 11am–10pm.

Sheep Heid Inn 43–45 The Causeway, Duddingston ⓦ thesheepheidedinburgh.co.uk. Edinburgh's oldest pub has great ales, an extensive wine list, tasty food and the world's oldest-known skittle alley. It's a 20min walk around the southern edge of Holyrood Park, near Arthur's Seat. Mon–Thurs 11am–11pm, Fri & Sat 11am–midnight, Sun 12.30–11pm.

CLUBS AND LIVE MUSIC

Cabaret Voltaire 36–38 Blair St ⓦthecabaretvoltaire .com. Eclectic beats, live acts, comedy, theatre and the occasional live band. Most nights 11pm–3am.

Liquid Room 9c Victoria St ⓦliquidroom.com. Hosts house nights and cheap, midweek indie parties. It's also a popular live venue; Kasabian, Feeder and the Dead Kennedys have all played here. Most nights keep going until 3am.

Sandy Bell's 25 Forrest Rd ⓦsandybellsedinburgh.co.uk. Music fans and whisky drinkers prop up the long, mirror-backed bar at this corner pub, which has live folk music nightly from 9.30pm. The highland, island and lowland malts are joined by a respectable beer list. Daily noon–1am.

Whistle Binkie's 4–6 South Bridge ⓦwhistlebinkies .com. Terrific live music bar in a cellar near the Royal Mile that features several bands nightly, the genres veering from jazz to rock and blues. Sun–Wed 11am–midnight, Thurs–Sat 11am–1am.

DIRECTORY

Banks and exchange Several big bank branches on and around St Andrew's Square, Hanover St and along George St.

Embassies and consulates Australia (Honorary Consulate), 5 Mitchell St ☏0131 538 0582; Canada: Mr John Rafferty ☏07702 359 916; US, 3 Regent Terrace ☏0131 556 8315.

Hospital Royal Infirmary, Old Dalkieth Rd ☏0131 536 1000, has a 24-hour emergency department.

Left luggage At Waverley Station (£8 per item/day).

Post office St James' Shopping Centre, near the eastern end of Princes St (Mon–Sat 9.30am–5.30pm).

GLASGOW

Having shrugged off its post-industrial malaise, rejuvenated **Glasgow**, Scotland's largest city, has undergone a revamp these last two decades and now basks in the light of its outstanding achievement, which was epitomized by its successful hosting of the 2014 Commonwealth Games. The River Clyde on which it sits now bustles again with prosperity, and the city is also home to one of the world's best art schools and a fantastic live music scene. It's rightly favoured for its down-to-earth ambience, die-hard "Glesga" party spirit and innovative architecture ranging from lavish

> ### SCOTLAND'S MUSIC FESTIVALS
>
> The summer festival season is a great time to visit Scotland. For mainstream acts, check out **T in the Park**, near Kinross (July; ⓦtinthepark.com). For something more alternative, try the **Wickerman Festival** (July; ⓦthewickermanfestival .co.uk), near Dundrennan in Dumfries and Galloway, which culminates in the burning of a huge wicker effigy.

eighteenth-century mansions through to cutting-edge twenty-first-century design.

WHAT TO SEE AND DO

Glasgow's centre lies on the north bank of the River Clyde, around the grandiose **George Square**, a little way east of Central Station. Here, in the West End and on the South Side, lies the legacy of grand civic buildings, such as the impressive **City Chambers**, on the east side of the square, that led the Victorians to label Glasgow the "second city of the Empire".

The Gallery of Modern Art

Just south of George Square, down Queen Street, is the lavish eighteenth-century **Gallery of Modern Art (GoMA)** (Mon–Wed & Fri 10am–5pm, Thurs 10am–8pm, Sat & Sun 11am–5pm; free; ⓦglasgowlife.org .uk), which houses changing exhibitions by contemporary Scots, such as photography by Wolfgang Tillman, music, performance and textiles by Cosima von Bonin and sculpture by Tessa Lynch.

The National Piping Centre

Just across from Glasgow's Theatre Royal at 30–34 McPhater Street, the **National Piping Centre** (Mon–Fri 9am–5pm, Sat 9am–1pm; free; ⓦthepipingcentre.co.uk) tells the story of the Scottish bagpipe, from its role in clan conflicts to the seemingly impossible task of putting pipe music to paper. Attached is the independently run hotel, *The Pipers' Tryst* (see p.488).

Cathedral and Necropolis

Northeast of George Square is the **cathedral** on Castle Street (Mon–Sat 9.30am–5.30pm, Sun 1–4pm;

13

GLASGOW

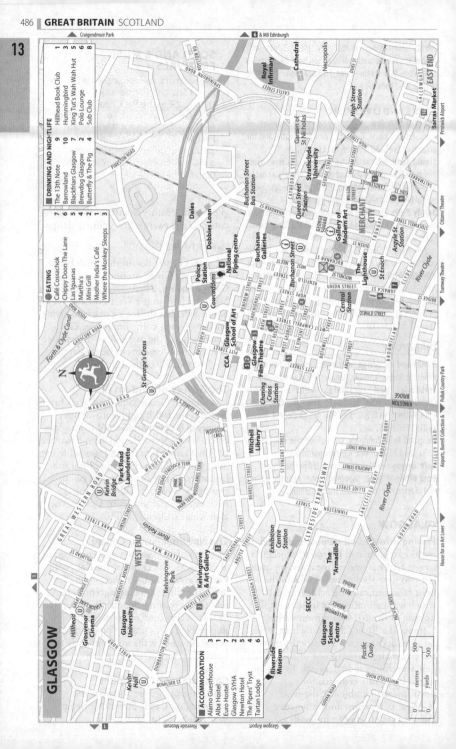

ACCOMMODATION
Alamo Guesthouse	3
Alba Hostel	1
Euro Hostel	7
Glasgow SYHA	2
Newton Hotel	5
The Pipers' Tryst	4
Tartan Lodge	6

EATING
Café Cossachok	7
Chippy Doon The Lane	6
Las Iguanas	5
Martha's	4
Mini Grill	2
Mother India's Café	1
Where the Monkey Sleeps	3

DRINKING AND NIGHTLIFE
The 13th Note	9	Hillhead Book Club	1
Barrowland	10	Hummingbird	3
Blackfriars Glasgow	5	King Tut's Wah Wah Hut	5
Brewdog Glasgow	7	Polo Lounge	6
Butterfly & The Pig	4	Sub Club	8

Ⓦglasgowcathedral.org.uk), which was built in 1136, and is the only Scottish mainland cathedral to have escaped the country's sixteenth-century religious reformers. The adjacent **Necropolis**, a hilltop cemetery for the magnates who made Glasgow rich, has great views across the city.

Kelvingrove Art Gallery and the West End

The boundaries of the leafy **West End** are marked by the magnificent Baroque crenellations of **Kelvingrove Art Gallery**, Argyle Street (Mon–Fri 10am–5pm, Sat & Sun 11am–5pm; free; Ⓦglasgowlife.org.uk), which houses pieces by Rembrandt, Degas, Millet, Van Gogh and Monet, as well as an impressive body of Scottish painting. Don't miss Dalí's *Christ of St John of the Cross* – an arresting vision of the Crucifixion.

River Clyde

The **Riverside Museum** along Glasgow's redeveloped waterfront at 100 Pointhouse Place (Mon–Fri 10am–5pm, Sat & Sun 11am–5pm; free; Ⓦglasgowlife.org.uk) showcases the city's shipbuilding heritage. In summer you can take a cruise from the quay outside here on the world's last ocean-going paddle steamer (☎0845 130 4647, Ⓦwaverleyexcursions.co.uk) to Dunoon (£27) and Rothesay (£33), as well as other destinations around the Clyde Estuary.

The Burrell Collection

About four miles south of the centre, in **Pollok Country Park** (buses #3, #45, #48 & #57 from Union Street, or train to Pollokshaws West), is the astonishing **Burrell Collection**, amassed by William Burrell and housed in a custom-built gallery (Mon–Fri 10am–5pm, Sat & Sun 11am–5pm; free; Ⓦglasgowlife.org.uk). Works by Memling, Cézanne, Degas, Bellini and Géricault feature among the paintings, while adjoining galleries display antiquities from ancient Rome, Greece, China and medieval Europe, as well as Islamic art and Persian rugs.

ARRIVAL AND DEPARTURE

By plane Glasgow International Airport lies eight miles west of the city, with regular bus #500 shuttling to Buchanan St bus station (15min; £7 single). Glasgow Prestwick Airport, thirty miles south, is connected to the city centre by trains (3 hourly; 30min) and buses.

By train Glasgow has two main train stations, around 10min walk apart: Central serves all points south and west, as well as Edinburgh; Queen St serves Edinburgh and the north.

Destinations from Queen Street Balloch (every 30min; 45min); Edinburgh (every 15min; 50min); Inverness (some change at Perth; every 2hr; 3hr 25min); Mallaig (for Skye; 2–3 daily; 5hr 20min); Oban (for Mull; 2 daily; 3hr); Newcastle (most change in Edinburgh; hourly; 2hr 30min–3hr); Stirling (every 30min; 45min–1hr).

Destinations from Glasgow Central Edinburgh (up to 4 hourly; 1hr–1hr 30min); Liverpool (via Wigan/Preston; every 30min; 3hr 30min); London (hourly; 4hr 30min–5hr 30min); Manchester (3 direct, around 23 daily via Preston/Carlisle; 3hr 15min–3hr 45min).

By bus Buchanan St bus station sits at the northern end of Buchanan St.

Destinations Edinburgh (every 15min; 1hr 20min); Inverness (every 1hr 30min; 3hr 45min–4hr 30min); Liverpool (1 daily; 6hr 30min); London (6 daily; 8hr–9hr 45min); Manchester (7 daily; 5hr–5hr 30min); Newcastle (4 daily; 4hr–4hr 30min); Oban (for Mull; 3 daily; 3hr); St Andrews (hourly; 2hr 30min); Skye (3 daily; Kyle of Lochalsh 5–6hr, Portree 6–7hr, Uig 7–8hr); Stirling (up to 3 per hour; 50min–1hr 45min).

INFORMATION

Tourist information The tourist office is at 170 Buchanan St, just west of Glasgow Queen St (Mon–Sat

---

CHARLES RENNIE MACKINTOSH

There aren't many architects who have made a bigger impression on a city than **Charles Rennie Mackintosh** (1868–1928). Little-appreciated in his lifetime, his fascinating, pioneering building designs around the city are among the best examples of early modernist architecture, and are now finally getting the recognition they deserve. See his work for yourself at his first commission, the **Lighthouse** on Mitchell Lane (Mon–Sat 10.30am–5pm, Sun noon–5pm; free; Ⓦthelighthouse.co.uk), and climb the tower from the third floor for expansive views of Glasgow's rooftops: check Ⓦglasgowmackintosh.com for details of the city's other examples of the great man's work.

13

9am–6pm, Sun noon–4pm; ☎0141 204 4400, ⓦpeoplemakeglasgow.com); there's a smaller office at Glasgow International Airport.

GETTING AROUND

By bus Most city bus services are run by First (ⓦfirstglasgow.com); single tickets cost £1.40 (carry exact change) and an unlimited Day-rider costs £4.50.

By subway The subway is cheap and easy: it has a circular chain of fifteen stations with a flat fare of £1.40 (Discovery Ticket £4 for a day's unlimited travel). If you buy a rechargeable Subway Smartcard (£3), unlimited day travel costs £2.75.

By train The Roundabout ticket (£6.60) gives one day unlimited travel by suburban rail and subway.

By bike Dales at 150 Dobbies Loan has mountain bikes to rent (Mon–Fri 9am–6pm, Thurs 9am–7pm, Sat 9am–6pm, Sun 11am–4pm; £22/day; ☎0141 332 2705, ⓦwww.dalescycles.co.uk).

ACCOMMODATION

Alamo Guesthouse 46 Gray St ☎0141 339 2395, ⓦalamoguesthouse.com. Quiet and attractive Victorian tenement near Kelvingrove Park, whose twelve immaculate rooms come with antique furnishings; the more affordable rooms are downstairs and share facilities. Doubles **£59**

Alba Hostel 6 Fifth Ave ☎0141 334 2952, ⓦalbahostelglasgow.co.uk. This good-value West End hostel is a fair way out of town (10min train ride to Anniesland railway station or 30min bus ride) and the furnishings are rather unloved, but the staff try hard to keep guests happy. Dorms **£15**, doubles **£48**

Euro Hostel 318 Clyde St ☎08455 399 956, ⓦeurohostels .co.uk/glasgow. Its handy central location near the subway and nightlife areas makes up for the rather impersonal feel at this huge hostel. The bar at street level sells cheap cocktails Mon–Thurs & Sun. Dorms **£15**, doubles **£36**

Glasgow SYHA 8 Park Terrace ☎0141 332 3004, ⓦsyha .org.uk. Friendly hostel in a listed building beside Kelvingrove Park, with helpful staff, en-suite rooms and dorms. Reachable via an uphill slog, it's handy for the West End, less so for central Glasgow. Dorms **£18**, doubles **£50**

Newton Hotel 248–252 Bath St ☎0141 332 1666, ⓦnewtonhotel.co.uk. Centrally located, family-run hotel encompassing a clutch of cosy, carpeted singles, doubles and family rooms with power showers and flat-screen TVs. Full Scottish breakfast included. Doubles **£60**

The Pipers' Tryst 30–34 McPhater St, at the National Piping Centre ☎ 0141 353 5551, ⓦthepipingcentre.co.uk /hotel-restaurant. Its profits supporting the adjacent bagpipe centre, this venerable hotel has decor that pays homage to Scotland: all the beds are tartan-wrapped and just a short stagger upstairs from the bar selling a good selection of single malts. Doubles **£89**

Tartan Lodge 235 Alexandra Parade ☎0141 554 5970, ⓦtartanlodge.co.uk. A 10min walk east of Glasgow Cathedral, this hostel nestles inside a former church. Dorms (including a women-only dorm) are snug, en-suite and come with plenty of secure storage. The staff are very helpful, though noise from the main road might disturb lighter sleepers. Dorms **£18**, doubles **£50**

EATING

Café Cossachok 10 King St ⓦcafecossachok.com. Russian restaurant, gallery and occasional live music venue, serving an excellent-value lunchtime menu (two courses for £10) and Slavic mains such as pork shashlik, pelmeni (Russian dumplings) and borscht. Daily noon–11pm.

Chippy Doon The Lane McCormick Lane, off Buchanan St ⓦthechippyglasgow.com. Down a tiny alleyway, this chippy specializes in sustainably sourced fish; the golden battered chunks are light and crispy and the portions are huge. Mains from £8. Daily noon–9.30pm.

Las Iguanas 10–14 W Nile St ⓦiguanas.co.uk. Yes, it's a chain, but a good one at that – come for Latin American-style tapas, such as ceviche, glazed pork ribs and fiery prawns, or opt for a supporting cast of burritos and Brazilian moqueca: three tapas £14.70. Daily 10am–11pm.

Martha's 142a St. Vincent St ⓦmymarthas.co.uk. With a mission to bring fast, healthy food to the people of Glasgow, this slick café dishes up subtly spiced veggie and meat dishes, serving them either as a main course with rice, or as a takeaway wrap (from £4.50). Mon–Fri 7.30am–4pm, Sat 11am–4pm.

★ Mini Grill 224A Bath Rd ⓦminibarglasgow.co.uk. Trendy modern Scottish restaurant doing wondrous things with local produce. Go for a gourmet burger at lunchtime (£8) or choose the two-course pre-theatre menu (£14) featuring the likes of haggis trio, scallops with pancetta or seared duck. Daily noon–11.30pm.

Mother India's Café 1355 Argyle St ⓦmotherindia .co.uk. An innovative, tapas-style approach to Indian street food makes this bustling place near the Kelvingrove Art Gallery a winner. Dishes from £4. Daily noon–11pm.

Where the Monkey Sleeps 182 West Regent St ⓦmonkeysleeps.com. This basement coffee shop attracts a student crowd with good tunes and vast selection of filled bagels (from £4), panini, toasties and American pancakes. Mon–Fri 7am–4pm.

DRINKING AND NIGHTLIFE

Pubs and clubs cluster around the city centre, the suave Merchant City to the east of Queen St, and the West End around Ashton Lane.

PUBS AND BARS

Blackfriars Glasgow 36 Bell St ⓦblackfriarsglasgow .com. The somewhat dated decor belies the excellent beer selection at this brewpub. It sources beers from various Scottish microbreweries, as well as craft beers from the US, Norway and elsewhere. A real beer-lover's pub. Sun–Thurs 11am–midnight, Fri & Sat 11am–3am.

Brewdog Glasgow 1397 Argyle St ⓦ brewdog.com. The place to come for top-quality craft beers by the Scottish brewery Brewdog. There's usually at least half a dozen IPAs on tap, plus occasional guest ciders. Feeling brave? Try the 9.2% Hardcore IPA (£3.50 for half a pint). Mon–Sat noon–midnight, Sun 12.30pm–midnight.

Butterfly & The Pig 153 Bath St ⓦ thebutterflyand thepig.com. Eclectic, shabby-chic basement pub with live music, a decent food menu and a good selection of beers and ales. The tearoom upstairs serves cracking Scottish breakfasts, too. Daily noon–10pm; tearooms open from 8.30am.

★**Hillhead Book Club** 17 Vinicombe St ⓦ hillheadbookclub.co.uk. Attractive bar-restaurant in an old cinema, with a high, sculpted ceiling lit by huge lanterns. There are two menus (one for veggies), and the well-presented mains all cost less than £10. It also has ping-pong and retro computer games for pre-club fun. Mon–Fri 11am–10pm, Sat & Sun 10am–10pm.

Hummingbird 186 Bath St. One of several cheap bars along Bath St, *Hummingbird* is cool and dingy, with candles hanging from the ceiling in birdcages. Does a good line in gourmet burgers (from £8) and has cocktails named after subjects like travel, politics and food. Mon–Thurs noon–1am, Fri & Sat noon–3am.

CLUBS AND LIVE MUSIC

The 13th Note 50–60 King St ⓦ 13thnote.co.uk. A Glasgow institution hosting up-and-coming bands from metal to indie via acoustic rock. Also serves great veggie food. Daily noon–midnight.

Barrowland 244 Gallowgate ⓦ glasgow-barrowland .com. Glasgow's most famous live venue, with a medium-size capacity for soon-to-be-big bands and more established acts. Gig nights 7–11pm.

★**King Tut's Wah Wah Hut** 272a St Vincent St ⓦ kingtuts.co.uk. Famous as the place where the likes of Oasis, Pulp, Radiohead and Manic Street Preachers played at the start of their careers, this intimate venue hosts excellent indie gigs. Daily from 8pm.

Polo Lounge 84 Wilson St ⓦ pologlasgow.co.uk. Popular gay club that mixes refined drinking upstairs with a packed, cruisey dancefloor in the basement. Tues, Thurs & Sun 11pm–3am, Wed & Fri 10pm–3am, Sat 9pm–3am.

Sub Club 22 Jamaica St ⓦ subclub.co.uk. Underground club and purveyor of the finest techno and electro, regularly hosting DJs from Glasgow, London and beyond. Fri & Sat 11pm–3am, plus some midweek parties (see website).

ENTERTAINMENT

Centre for Contemporary Arts (CCA) 350 Sauchiehall St ⓦ cca-glasgow.com. Cultural centre that has a reputation for a programme of controversial performances and exhibitions.

Citizens' Theatre 119 Gorbals St ⓦ citz.co.uk. South Side theatre famous for sourcing top Scottish talent; a great place to catch a performance.

Glasgow Film Theatre 12 Rose St ⓦ glasgowfilm.org /theatre. This wonderful cinema shows art films and old favourites, as well as documentaries by British filmmakers.

DIRECTORY

Hospital Royal Infirmary, 84 Castle St (☎ 0141 211 4000). **Police** Pitt St (☎ 0141 532 2000).
Post office 59 Glassford St (Mon–Sat 8.30am–5.30pm).

STIRLING

STIRLING's strategic position between the Lowlands and Highlands at the easiest crossing of the River Forth has shaped its major role in Scottish history. Its steep cobbled streets and stupendous castle atop a crag are its loveliest features, though the area beyond Old Town is less appealing.

WHAT TO SEE AND DO

Set on a rocky volcanic outcrop, the atmospheric **castle** (Mon–Fri 9.30am–5pm, Sat & Sun 9.30am–6pm; £14.50) was the seat of the Stuart monarchs and is, arguably, Scotland's most important castle. Highlights within the complex are the late Renaissance **Royal Palace**, with its sumptuous Queen's bedchamber, and the earlier **Great Hall**, with a restored hammerbeam roof. Look out, too, for the tapestry exhibition and the all-encompassing views from the ramparts.

Stirling's oldest part huddles around the narrow, winding streets leading up to the castle. Look out for the Gothic, timber-roofed **Church of the Holy Rude** (daily 10am–5pm), where the infant James VI – later James I of England – was crowned King of Scotland in 1567. From here, Broad Street slopes down to the lower town, passing the **Tolbooth**, the city's arts and cultural centre.

Stirling is famous as the scene of Sir William Wallace's victory over the English in 1297, a crucial episode in the Wars of Independence. The Scottish hero

13

was commemorated in the Victorian era with the **Wallace Monument** (daily: April–May, Sept & Oct 10am–5pm; June–Aug 9.30am–5pm; Nov–March 10.30am–4pm; £10; bus #62A or #63A from the Stirling Bus Station), a bizarre Tolkienesque tower providing stupendous views.

ARRIVAL AND INFORMATION

By train The train station is just east of the lower part of Old Town, off Burgh Muir Rd.

Destinations Aberdeen (hourly; 2hr–2hr 30min); Edinburgh (every 30min; 1hr); Glasgow (3 hourly; 1hr); Inverness (6 daily; 3hr).

By bus Long-distance buses depart from Goosecroft Rd, beside the train station.

Destinations Edinburgh (up to 3 hourly; 2hr 20min); Glasgow (1–2 hourly; 50min); St Andrews (every 2hr; 2hr).

Tourist information Old Town Jail, St John St (daily 10am–5pm; ☎01786 475 019, ⊛visitscotland.com); maps of town and helpful info provided.

ACCOMMODATION

Stirling SYHA St John St ☎01786 473442, ⊛syha.org .uk. Inside a former church just a few minutes' walk from the castle, this compact hostel offers snug en-suite dorms and rooms and the staff are friendly and helpful. There are full self-catering facilities on-site and inexpensive meals available during high season. Dorms **£22**, doubles **£44**

Willy Wallace Hostel 77 Murray Place ☎01786 446773, ⊛willywallacehostel.com. Lively backpacker hostel with large, colourful yet spartan dorms, double rooms with iPod docks and a welcoming common area where you can play the piano or pick up a guitar. Dorms **£15**, doubles **£52**

EATING AND DRINKING

Breá 5 Baker St ⊛brea-stirling.co.uk. Contemporary bistro that makes the most of fresh, locally sourced ingredients and brings you the likes of Shetland Isles mussels, chunky sandwiches, gourmet burgers (from £9.75), stone-baked pizzas and an excellent selection of local brews, gins and whiskies. Sun–Thurs noon–9pm, Fri & Sat noon–10am.

The Portcullis Castle Wynd ☎01786 472 290 ⊛theportcullishotel.com. Right by the castle, this eighteenth-century hotel has one of the city's best pubs, complete with beer garden and fire. It also serves reasonable pub food (mains from £10) too. Daily 11.30am–midnight.

ST ANDREWS

Scotland's oldest university town and an important medieval pilgrimage centre, **ST ANDREWS** lies on a gorgeous stretch of

the Fife coast 56 miles northeast of Edinburgh. With Prince William and Kate as former alumni of its university, the town is a young-feeling, well-to-do place with a clutch of atmospheric ruins, and seven swanky golf courses that are some of the oldest and most revered in the world.

WHAT TO SEE AND DO

A wonderful crescent of sandy beach sweeps north from St Andrews' famous Old Course, while immediately south of it runs North Street, one of the town's two main arteries, largely taken up with grand university buildings.

The castle and cathedral

St Andrews' two main roads converge on the ruins of the magnificent Gothic **cathedral** (daily: April–Oct 9.30am–5.30pm; Nov–March 10am–4pm; free), the largest and grandest ever built in Scotland and an important medieval pilgrimage centre. The bones of St Andrew allegedly lie beneath the altar. You can scale the nearby **St Rule's Tower** (Mon–Fri 9.30am–4pm; Sat & Sun 10am–5.30pm; £4.50, combined ticket with castle £8) for some great views. Nearby, off the seafront The Scores, the small thirteenth-century ruined **castle** (Mon–Fri 9.30am–4pm; Sat & Sun 10am–5.30pm; £5.50, combined ticket with Tower £8) was the former fortified home of the bishop of St Andrews and site of the grisly murder of Cardinal David Beaton in 1546.

The Old Course

Located on the northwestern fringes of town, the **Old Course** is St Andrews' most famous golf course and – according to Jack Nicklaus – the world's best. If you want to step onto its famous fairways and try your hand at the sport, head to the **Himalayas putting green** at The Links (April–Sept Mon–Sat 9.30am–6pm, Sun noon–6.30pm; £3 per round).

Arrival and information

By train There are direct trains from nearby Leuchars (five miles away) to Edinburgh (twice hourly; 1hr). Frequent buses (10min) connect with the train station.

By bus The bus station is west of town on City Rd.

13

Destinations Edinburgh (hourly; 2hr); Glasgow (hourly; 2hr 30min).

Tourist information 70 Market St (Mon–Fri 9.15am–5pm, Sat 9.30am–7pm; April to mid-Oct also Sun 11am–5pm; ☎ 01334 472021, ⊛ visitstandrews.com).

ACCOMMODATION AND EATING

If you want to stay in summer or during one of the big golf tournaments, book well ahead.

Doll's House 3 Church Square ⊛ dollshousestandrews .co.uk. Tucked away off the main street, this quirky bistro does wonderful things with seasonal local produce and the market menu is your best bet. Expect the likes of haggis balls with mustard sauce, hearty soups and smoked haddock with new potatoes and wilted spinach: two-course lunch £11. Daily 10am–midnight.

St Andrews Tourist Hostel St Mary's Place ☎ 01334 479911. The only hostel in town, in a very central location. While the staff are friendly and helpful, the facilities are basic, the furnishings rather tired and a spring clean wouldn't go amiss. £14

University of St Andrews ☎ 01334 463000, ⊛ bnb .st-andrews.ac.uk Between June and September you can lodge in plush doubles in one of three historic university halls or some self-catering apartments belonging to the university. Doubles £59

THE HIGHLANDS

The beguiling **Highlands** are a stunning mix of bare hills, green glens and silvery lochs, which extend up to the country's northern coast. The distances involved, along with scarce public transport, mean that you'll need several days to explore any one part properly. **FORT WILLIAM** is the Highlands' key outdoor base, served by train from Glasgow and bus from Inverness. On the outskirts of town is the **Nevis Range**, with skiing in winter and superb hiking and mountain biking in summer, and, sixteen miles south, **Glen Coe**, where soaring scenery and poignant history combine like nowhere else in the country. Fort William also marks one end of the West Highland Way, which runs all the way to Glasgow, and it's a good base from which to climb **Ben Nevis**, Britain's highest peak.

AVIEMORE, at the foot of the looming **Cairngorm** range, another national park, is also a good base for challenging hiking, ancient pine forests and winter sports. With **outdoor activities** the big draw across the region, most tourist information centres and hostels carry information on local hiking routes and adventure sports.

ARRIVAL AND DEPARTURE

By train Some scenic spots are served by ScotRail's train network (⊛ scotrail.co.uk), which has good-value travel passes available.

By minibus tour A couple of rival companies offer lively minibus tours of the Highlands designed specifically for backpackers: Haggis (☎ 08452 578345, ⊛ haggisadventures .com) and award-winning Macbackpackers (☎ 0131 558 9900, ⊛ macbackpackers.com) depart from Edinburgh on trips lasting between one and ten days, covering the likes of Loch Ness, Skye and the Highlands. Three-day tours to Skye cost around £129.

ACCOMMODATION AND EATING

FORT WILLIAM

Glen Nevis Hostel ☎ 01397 702336, ⊛ syha.org.uk. If you're looking to climb Ben Nevis, it's better to stay in Glen Nevis than Fort William itself. This fully equipped SYHA hostel is at the foot of Ben Nevis, a 2.5-mile walk out of town, and private rooms are available for solo travellers. Dorms £22, doubles £70

AVIEMORE

Glenmore Lodge ☎ 01479 861256, ⊛ glenmorelodge .org.uk. As well as running excellent, if expensive, outdoor courses in rock climbing, mountaineering, kayaking and mountain biking, this famous lodge also offers en-suite B&B rooms. Doubles £80

CLIMBING BEN NEVIS

There are two main routes up Ben Nevis, Scotland's highest mountain. The shorter, steeper and more well-trodden **Mountain Track** (7hr return) starts from the Glen Nevis car park, 2.5 miles east of Fort William, and involves many stone steps. The longer, gentler and more rewarding **North Face Route** (9 hours return) starts from the North Face car park, around 10 miles north of Fort William, off the road towards Inverness, and gives you full views of the mountain during your riverside approach. For the best of both worlds, ascend via the North Face approach then descend to Glen Nevis, and get a taxi back to your starting point. Never underestimate the mountain and make sure you wear suitable clothing, and take food, water, map and compass, as capricious weather conditions and poor visibility can descend rapidly.

13

Aviemore SYHA Grampian Rd ☎01479 810345, ⊛syha .org.uk. Just south of the train station, this hostel is well equipped for hikers. Dorms are simple, but there's a handy drying room and a sociable dining space. Dorms £18, doubles £50

INVERNESS

Lying 160 miles north of Edinburgh, **INVERNESS** is the capital of the Highlands, a grey but affable town at the mouth of the River Ness, with a vibrant dining scene. The chief historical attraction nearby is the ever-popular **Culloden Visitor Centre** (daily: April–Oct 9am–5.30pm; Nov–March 10am–4pm; £11), six miles east on bus line #2B from the city centre. In 1746, Culloden Moor was the scene of the last pitched battle on British soil, when Bonnie Prince Charlie's Jacobite army was crushed in just forty minutes, ending Stuart ambitions of regaining the monarchy forever. Infinitely more dramatic is the fairytale fourteenth-century **Cawdor Castle** (May–Oct daily 10am–5.30pm; £10.70; ⊛cawdorcastle .com), the legendary home of Shakespeare's Macbeth, twelve miles northeast. Take bus #10 to Nairn and transfer there to #252, walking the last ten minutes or so to the castle.

ARRIVAL AND DEPARTURE

By plane Inverness Airport (⊛hial.co.uk/inverness -airport) is seven miles northeast of the town and served by regular bus (roughly every 30min; 25min).

By train The train station is just northeast of the centre on Station Square.

Destinations Aviemore (every 1–2hr; 45min); Edinburgh (8 daily; 3hr 30min); Glasgow (4 direct daily, or change at Perth; 3hr 30min); Kyle of Lochalsh (for Skye; Mon–Sat 4 daily; Sun 2 daily; 2hr 30min); Stirling (some change at Perth; 11 daily; 2hr 30min–3hr).

By bus The bus station is just northwest of the train station.

Destinations Edinburgh (hourly; 3hr 30min–4hr 40min); Fort William (via Loch Ness, 5 daily; 2hr 30min); Glasgow (hourly; 3hr 30min–4hr 30min); Stirling (2 daily; 3hr 20min).

INFORMATION

Tourist information Castle Wynd (April–Oct Mon–Fri 9am–5pm, Sat 9am–6pm, Sun 10am–5pm; Nov–March Mon–Sat limited hours; ☎01463 234353, ⊛inverness -scotland.com) rents out bikes.

ACCOMMODATION AND EATING

★**Bazpackers** 4 Culduthel Rd ☎01463 717663, ⊛bazpackershostel.co.uk. The smallest hostel in town, and the best, with an open fire, good mattresses and individual reading lights in dorms, plus friendly staff and an excellent ratio of showers per guest. Dorms £19, doubles £50

Café 1 75 Castle St ⊛cafe1.net. Snug Scottish restaurant serving Scottish and European dishes created from fresh, locally sourced ingredients – expect super-fresh fish and seafood. Lunch and early-bird menus are a steal at £10 for two courses. Mon–Sat noon–2.30pm & 6–9.30pm.

Hootananny 67 Church St. Lively pub that specializes in traditional music and weekly ceilidhs and serves solid Scottish food like haggis in puff pastry. Mon–Thurs noon–1am, Fri & Sat noon–3am, Sun 6.30pm–midnight.

Inverness Student Hotel 8 Culduthel Rd ☎01463 236556, ⊛invernessstudenthotel.com. This welcoming hostel has dorms sleeping between 5 and 10 people, a quiet location by the castle and excellent self-catering facilities. Dorms £19

LOCH NESS

Loch Ness forms part of the thickly forested natural fault line of the Great Glen, which slices across the southern edge of the Highlands between Inverness and Fort William. Most visitors are eager to catch a glimpse of the elusive **Loch Ness Monster**: to find out the whole story, take a bus to **DRUMNADROCHIT**, fourteen miles southwest of Inverness, where the **Loch Ness Exhibition Centre** (daily: Easter–Oct Mon–Fri 9am–5pm; Sat & Sun 9.30am– 6pm; Nov–Easter 10am–3.30pm; £7.95; ⊛lochness.com) attempts to breathe life into the old myth. A couple of miles

---

THE LOCH NESS MONSTER

Tales of **Nessie** date back at least as far as the seventh century, when the monster came off second best in an altercation with St Columba. However, the possibility that a mysterious prehistoric creature might be living in the loch only attracted worldwide attention in the 1930s, when sightings were reported during the construction of the road along its western shore. Numerous appearances have been reported since, but even the most high-tech surveys of the loch have failed to come up with conclusive evidence.

south, the ruined **Castle Urquhart** (daily: April–Sept 9.30am–6pm; Oct 9.30am–5pm; Nov–March 9.30am–4.30pm; £8.50) is one of Scotland's most beautifully sited fortresses.

THE ISLE OF MULL AND AROUND

The **Isle of Mull** is the most accessible of the Inner Hebrides off Scotland's west coast: just 45 minutes by ferry from **Oban**, which is linked by train to Glasgow. Its three hundred miles of rugged coastline are the main draw, peppered with castles, beautiful beaches, idyllic chocolate-box villages like Tobermory, and Iona, the birthplace of Christianity in Britain.

Craignure and Tobermory

CRAIGNURE is the ferry terminal for boats from Oban. Two miles' walk along the bay is dramatic thirteenth-century **Duart Castle** (April Mon–Thurs & Sun 11am–4pm; May to mid-Oct daily 10.30am–5pm; £6; ⍵duartcastle.com), where you can peek into the dungeons and ascend to the rooftops. Mull's "capital" **TOBERMORY**, 22 miles northwest of Craignure, is easily the most attractive fishing port in the west of Scotland, with brightly coloured houses and boats sheltering in a bay backed by a steep bluff.

Fionnphort and Staffa

Some 35 miles west of Craignure, tiny **Fionnphort** is nevertheless one of Mull's

---

MIDGE ALERT

During the summer months, particularly in wetter areas, the Highlands and Islands are blighted by **midges** – tiny biting insects that appear in swarms. If you're camping or hiking, make sure you have insect repellent – locals swear by Avon's Skin So Soft moisturizer – as well as a midge hood, a net fitting over a wide-brimmed hat which, while making no concessions to fashion, should protect the face. Even a light breeze will blow the midges away, though, so try and pick somewhere that isn't completely still to camp.

---

metropolises. A few miles south at Knockvologan is the gorgeous sandy beach of **Erraid**, inspiration for Robert Louis Stevenson's thriller *Kidnapped*. The *Iolaire* (☎01681 700358; ⍵staffatrips .co.uk; £30; also stops on Iona) runs from Fionnphort to **Staffa**, a moody, uninhabited basaltic island marking the northern end of the Giant's Causeway (see p.600) with the cathedral-like **Fingal's Cave**, whose haunting noises inspired Mendelssohn's *Hebrides Overture*.

Isle of Iona

Serene little **Iona** has been a place of pilgrimage for several centuries: it was here that St Columba fled from Ireland in 563 AD and established a monastery subsequently responsible for the conversion of more or less all of pagan Scotland. The present **abbey** (Mon–Fri 9.30am–4.30pm, Sat & Sun 9.30am–5.30pm; £7.10; ⍵iona.org.uk) dates from 1200, while Iona's oldest building, **St Oran's Chapel**, lies just south. It stands at the centre of the burial ground, Reilig Odhrain, which is said to contain the graves of sixty kings.

ARRIVAL AND INFORMATION

By ferry Regular ferries (up to 7 daily; 45min; £3.45 per passenger single, £13 per car) run from Oban to Craignure. Iona is served by Calmac ferries (at least 9 daily; 10min; £1.65 single) from Fionnphort.

Tourist information The island's main tourist office is at The Pier, Craignure (April to mid-Oct Mon–Sat 8.30am–5pm, Sun 10am–5pm; mid-Oct to March Mon–Sat 9am–5pm, Sun 10.30am–noon & 3.30–5pm; ☎01680 812377, ⍵visitscottishheartlands.com), while the Explore Mull Visitor Centre, on the edge of Main Street's car park, Tobermory (daily 9am–5pm; ☎01688 302875, ⍵exploremull.com), can arrange trips and rent bikes.

ACCOMMODATION

Iona Hostel A mile from the ferry, Iona ☎01681 700781, ⍵ionahostel.co.uk. This excellent hostel – a working croft – has comfortable beds in the mixed-sex dorms, a well-equipped kitchen/lounge and a beautiful beach nearby. Dorms **£21**

Tobermory Youth Hostel Main Street, Tobermory, Mull ☎01688 302481. Dorms here are a little stark, but the setting – among multicoloured harbour-front houses – is undeniably pretty. Open March–Oct only. Dorms **£20**

13

ISLAND-HOPPING

The sea off Scotland's west coast is dotted with islands, from tiny rocks to substantial landmasses. The main ferry company, **Caledonian MacBrayne** (CalMac; ⓦ calmac.co.uk), connects most of them, and offers a range of island-hopping trips. Arran, Islay and the Small Isles (Rum, Muck and Eigg) are all worth visiting, too.

THE ISLE OF SKYE

The deeply indented coastline, azure water and spectacular summits of the **Isle of Skye** make it one of the most captivating spots in Britain. The island's stunning topography once shielded Bonnie Prince Charlie from capture by government forces; now the high, jagged peaks of the **Cuillin** ridge are some of Britain's best (and most demanding) walking and climbing terrain. Equally dramatic are the rock formations of the **Trotternish peninsula** in the north.

Elgol and the Cuillins

The best approach to the **Cuillins** is by #55 bus from Broadford on the dramatic road to **ELGOL**, from where there are boat trips on the *Bella Jane* (late March to Oct daily; one-way £14, return £26; ☎0800 731 3089, ⓦbellajane.co.uk) to stunning Loch Coruisk, where there's a seal colony. With adequate planning, you can hike from the loch up into the Cuillins or back to Elgol. Serious hikers also head for **GLENBRITTLE**, west of the Cuillins.

Portree, Dunvegan, Old Man of Storr and Uig

Skye's capital is **PORTREE**, an attractive fishing port in the north of the island. Some nine miles from Portree on the **Trotternish peninsula** are Skye's geological highlights: a 165ft sea stack called the **Old Man of Storr** and, soaring above Staffin Bay ten miles north, the **Quiraing** – a spectacular forest of rock formations. The tranquil village of **UIG**, on the west coast,

has ferries to the islands of the Outer Hebrides. Twenty-one miles northwest of Portree is Dunvegan, and the fourteenth-century **Dunvegan Castle** (April–Oct daily 10am–5.30pm; £12.10; ⓦwww .dunvegancastle.com), seat of the chief of the Clan MacLeod – check out the dungeons and the ragged Fairy Flag, subject of many myths.

ARRIVAL AND INFORMATION

By train Skye is connected to the mainland via a bridge to Kyle of Lochalsh, from where several trains daily serve Inverness (2hr 35min). Trains also run from Mallaig to Glasgow (3 daily; 5hr 20min).

By ferry Ferries run between Armadale in southeastern Skye and Mallaig on the mainland (April–Oct 6–8 daily; 30min).

By bus Regular buses link Skye with Glasgow (3 daily; 7hr).

By car Having your own transport makes exploration of the island considerably easier.

Tourist information Portree has the island's main tourist office just off Bridge Rd (Mon–Fri 9am–5pm, Sat 9am–6pm; April–Oct also Sun 10am–4pm; ☎01478 614906).

ACCOMMODATION AND EATING

GLEN BRITTLE

Glenbrittle Hostel Glen Brittle ☎01478 640278, ⓦsyha.org.uk. No-frills youth hostel with a self-catering kitchen and a small shop selling snacks and supplies. Closed Oct–Feb. Dorms £20, doubles £60

PORTREE

Portree Independent Hostel ☎01478 613737, ⓦhostelskye.co.uk. Cheery, paint-daubed hostel in the middle of Skye's attractive capital with single-sex dorms. Cosy living room and free tea and coffee. Dorms £20

L'Incontro The Green. "Italy with a Skye flavour" serves pizza with classic Scottish ingredients (from £11) – our favourite comes with haggis and Stornoway black pudding. May–Sept Tues–Sun 4–11pm.

UIG

★**The Cowshed Boutique Bunkhouse** Just off the A87 ☎07917 536 820, ⓦskyecowshed.co.uk. A couple of minutes from the Outer Hebrides ferry, this gorgeous bunkhouse has snug dorms (all beds with privacy curtains), and shingled sleeping pods for up to three people. Great sea views and well-designed kitchen and common spaces make this a real treat to stay in. Dorms £17, pods £70

FRESCO AT THE PALACE OF KNOSSOS, CRETE

Greece

HIGHLIGHTS

❶ **Athens** Wander at the ancient, awe-inspiring Acropolis and hit the capital's clubs. **See p.502**

❷ **Meteora** Magical Byzantine monasteries perched on dramatic rock stacks. **See p.518**

❸ **Thessaloníki** A multicultural hub, springboard to northern Greece and Vergína. See p.520

❹ **Olympia** Explore historic Olympia, birthplace of the famous Games. **See p.526**

❺ **Santoríni** Take in the sunset from Ía on this spectacular island. **See p.531**

❻ **Knossos** Visit the impressive site of Knossos, legendary home of the Minotaur. **See p.541**

HIGHLIGHTS ARE MARKED ON THE MAP ON P.497

ROUGH COSTS

Daily budget Basic €30, occasional treat €40

Drink Ouzo €3

Food *Souvláki* (shish kebab) €3

Hostel/budget hotel €20/€30

Travel Bus: Athens–Delphi €16; ferry: Athens–Crete €40

FACT FILE

Population 11 million

Language Greek

Currency Euro (€)

Capital Athens

International phone code ☎ 30

Time zone GMT +2hr

Introduction

With 227 inhabited islands and a landscape ranging from Mediterranean to Balkan, Greece has enough appeal to fill months of travel. The beaches are distributed along a convoluted coastline, with cosmopolitan resorts lying surprisingly close to remote islands where boats may call only twice a week. The initial glimpse of sapphire water or the discovery of millennia-old ruins bordered by ancient olive groves is intoxicating, and it's the mingling of history and hedonism that ensures Greece's enduring appeal. Island-hopping is still popular, but if you're on a tight budget, consider exploring the mainland or the Peloponnese by bus, or save on multiple, pricey ferry trips by focusing on a few highlights.

The country is the sum of an extraordinary diversity of influences. Romans, Arabs, Frankish Crusaders, Venetians, Slavs, Albanians, Turks, Italians, as well as the thousand-year Byzantine Empire, have all been and gone since the time of Alexander the Great. Each has left its mark: the **Byzantines** through countless churches and monasteries; the **Venetians** in impregnable fortifications such as Monemvasiá in the Peloponnese; the **Franks** with crag-top castles, again in the Peloponnese but also in the Dodecanese and east Aegean. Most obvious, perhaps, is the heritage of four hundred years of **Ottoman Turkish** rule, which exercised an inestimable influence on music, cuisine, language and way of life.

Even before the fall of Byzantium in the fifteenth century, Greek peasants, fishermen and shepherds had created one of the most vigorous and truly **popular cultures** in Europe, which found expression in song and dance, costumes, embroidery, furniture and the distinctive whitewashed houses. Though having suffered a decline under Western influence, Hellenic culture – architectural and musical heritage in particular – is undergoing a renaissance.

CHRONOLOGY

c. 800 BC Homer writes *The Iliad* and *The Odyssey*.
776 BC First Olympic Games are held in Olympia.
438 BC The building of the Parthenon is completed.

399 BC The trial and execution of Socrates, the founding father of philosophy, takes place.
387 BC Plato establishes the Athens Academy.
323 BC Alexander the Great dies heralding the beginning of the Hellenistic period.
146 BC Greece becomes a province of the Roman Empire.
330 AD The Roman capital moves to Constantinople and the Byzantine Empire is established. Christianity becomes the dominant religion.
1453 Ottoman Turks invade Constantinople. End of the Byzantine Empire.
1821 Greek National Revolution against Ottoman rule.
1832 The Treaty of London recognizes Greek Independence. Greece becomes a monarchy under King Otto I.
1833 Athens becomes the capital of modern Greece.
1864 King Otto ousted, King George I introduces parliamentary democracy.
1896 The first modern Olympic Games are held in Athens.
1912–13 During the Balkan wars Greece doubles its size, gaining Thessaloníki and parts of Macedonia and Thrace.
1923 War with Turkey ends in defeat, an exchange of populations and an end to the Greek presence in Asia Minor.
1940–41 Greece is invaded and occupied by German, Italian and Bulgarian armies. Liberation comes in October 1944 with the help of heavy resistance fighting.
1945–49 Greek Civil War between Communists and pro-Western forces.
1952 A new constitution is passed which retains the monarchy as head of state.
1967 Military coup led by Colonel George Papadopoulos.
1974 Turkish invasion of Cyprus. The colonels' junta

14

HIGHLIGHTS

1. Athens
2. Meteora
3. Thessaloníki
4. Olympia
5. Santoríni
6. Knossos

GREECE

---

collapses. New constitution established and the monarchy abolished with a referendum.

1981 Greece joins the EU.

2002 Greece adopts the euro.

2004 "The year of Greece" – the country wins the UEFA Euros and stages a successful Olympic Games.

2010 The economic crisis forces the Greek government to seek help from the European Union and the IMF, leading to five years of recession.

2015 Alexis Tsipras' far-left government tries to renegotiate an end to austerity. Faced with the possibility of a euro exit, it accepts a new bailout with more stringent economic conditions.

ARRIVAL AND DEPARTURE

There are international **airports** on the mainland at Athens and Thessaloníki, while budget flights serve numerous other mainland and island destinations including Crete, Corfu, Mýkonos, Santorini and Rhodes.

By **boat**, there are regular ferries from Ancona, Bari, Brindisi, Trieste and Venice in Italy, arriving at Corfu, Igoumenítsa and Pátra. Eurail and InterRail pass holders travel free from the above ports with Superfast Ferries (ⓦsuperfast.com) or Minoan Lines (ⓦminoan.gr) to Igoumenítsa or Pátra on the mainland. From there, regular onward bus services leave for Athens and Thessaloníki. You can also travel by boat from Turkey to the Dodecanese, the northern Aegean islands and from Albania to Corfu.

By **bus**, land crossings into Greece are possible from Albania, Macedonia, Bulgaria, Romania and Turkey, all arriving in Thessaloníki, from where onward travel to the rest of the country is easy and straightforward. Finally, Thessaloniki is served by **train** from Belgrade and Sofia.

GETTING AROUND

BY TRAIN AND BUS

While Greece's **rail** network is limited, there are reliable lines operating from Athens to Thessaloníki and onwards to Alexandhroúpoli on the Turkish border, from Athens to Kláto, Athens to Kalambáka (for Metéora) and Pireás to Halkída, as well as local tourist lines (see box, p.510). **Eurail** and **InterRail** are valid, though pass holders must reserve like everyone else, and there's a small supplement on the intercity services. You can book train tickets in advance on ⓦtrainose.gr.

Buses form the bulk of public land transport, and service on the major routes is efficient, with companies organized nationally into a syndicate called **KTEL**. If starting a journey from a bus station, you'll be issued a ticket with a seat number. Return tickets are open-ended and must be validated at the ticket office before you board the bus.

BY BOAT

Greek island **ferries** are all in private ownership so frequencies, destinations and sailing times are likely to change in line with demand. As this can't be forecast reliably in the current crisis, planning months ahead is likely to prove futile. Your best bet is to book your ferry tickets a few days in advance from one of the many port agencies, who receive new timetable info first. While daily boats between the most popular islands in July and August are certain to continue running, this may not be the case outside of these months. All ferry schedules shown here are for summer; ferries are much less frequent off-season. Leave plenty of time for your journey as ferries are often late or take longer to reach their destinations than scheduled.

Hydrofoils and high-speed **catamarans** are roughly twice as fast but twice as expensive as ordinary ferries. In season, *kaïkia* (caïques) sail to more obscure islets. For more information on ferry and hydrofoil schedules, see ⓦgtp.gr.

BY BIKE AND SCOOTER

Once on the islands, almost everybody rents a **scooter** or a bicycle. Scooters cost from €12 a day, bikes less. To rent a scooter you must produce a motorcycle licence from your country of origin.

ACCOMMODATION

Most of the year you can turn up pretty much anywhere and find a **room**. Only around Orthodox Easter and in July and August are you likely to experience problems; at these times, it's worth booking well in advance.

Hotels are categorized from "Luxury" down to "E-class", but these ratings have more to do with amenities and number of rooms than pricing – a budget hotel will typically cost €60–80 for a double. There are few **hostels** in Greece, but plenty of privately let **rooms** (*dhomátia*), which are divided into three classes (A–C), and are usually cheaper than hotels. As often as not, rooms find you: owners descend on ferry and bus arrivals to tout any space they have. On the islands, minibuses from campsites and hotels meet new arrivals for free transfers. Increasingly, rooms are being eclipsed by **self-catering facilities**, which are excellent value. If signs or touts are not apparent, ask for studios at travel agencies, which usually cluster around arrival points.

GREECE IN THE MOVIES

It's no surprise that Greece's photogenic sea, sands and dazzling light have provided the backdrop to numerous films. Worth watching before your trip is the Bond film **For Your Eyes Only** (1981), set amid the spectacular cliff-top monasteries of the Metéora (see p.518); **Shirley Valentine** (1989), the story of a downtrodden housewife's discovery of Mýkonos (see p.526) and alfresco love; the romantic musical comedy **Mamma Mia!** (2008), filmed on Skópelos (see p.536); the tender **Before Midnight** (2013), shot around Kardhamýli (see p.515); and the youth comedy **The Inbetweeners** (2011) that satirizes the 18–30 drinking culture in Mália, Crete (see p.542).

BUDGET EATING

Snacks are one of the pleasures of Greek eating – head to a supermarket and stock up on Greek yogurt and honey for breakfast and buy *tyrópites* and *spanakópites* (cheese and spinach pies respectively) from a bakery for lunch (€2). Good budget food chains include *Woodys* and *Everest*.

Bringing a tent increases your options for cheap accommodation. Official **campsites** range from basic island compounds to highly organized complexes, most of which close in winter (Nov–April). Many sites rent tents or have more permanent accommodation in the form of cabins and bungalows. Rough camping is forbidden.

FOOD AND DRINK

Eating out in Greece is popular and reasonably priced: €10–15 per person for a meal with beer or cheap wine. Typical **taverna** dishes to try include *moussaka* (aubergine and meat pie), *yígandes* (giant haricot beans in tomato sauce), *tzatzíki* (yogurt, garlic and cucumber dip), *melitzanosaláta* (aubergine dip), *khtapódhi* (octopus) and *kalamarákia* (fried baby squid). Quintessentially Greek establishments **ouzerí** and **mezedhopolía** serve filling *mezédhes* (the Greek version of tapas) with drinks, adding up to a substantial meal. Note that people eat late: 1.30–3pm for lunch & 9–11.30pm for dinner, although most places serve food all day.

As for **drinks**, the traditional coffee shop or **kafenío** is the pivot of rural life; like tavernas, these range from the sophisticated to the old-fashioned. Their main business is sweet Greek coffee, but they also serve spirits such as aniseed-flavoured *ouzo* and brandy, as well as beer and soft drinks. Islanders take pre-dinner *ouzo* an hour or two before sunset: you'll be served a glass of water alongside, to be tipped into your *ouzo* until it turns milky white. **Bars** are ubiquitous in the largest towns and resorts. Drinks, at €5–8, are invariably more expensive than at a *kafenío*.

GREECE ONLINE

ⓦ **visitgreece.gr** Greek National Tourist Organization.
ⓦ **trainose.gr** Greek Railways (OSE).
ⓦ **gtp.gr** Greek ferries, hotels, restaurants.
ⓦ **aferry.co.uk** Greek ferry bookings.
ⓦ **www.greececamping.gr** Greek campsites.
ⓦ **odysseus.culture.gr** Greek Ministry of Culture site; the most up-to-date source for opening hours of museum and archeological sites.

CULTURE AND ETIQUETTE

It is important to be respectful when visiting one of Greece's many **churches** or **monasteries**, and appropriate clothing should be worn – covered arms and legs for both sexes. The more popular sites often provide such clothing, should you be without it. Photography is also banned in sacred places. Another important part of Greek life is the afternoon **siesta**, when peace and quiet are valued. In restaurants, **tipping** is normally expected and usually customers leave a little more for service. **Topless bathing** is usually fine on virtually all Greek beaches, but, especially in smaller places or town beaches, check first before stripping off. Full nudity is tolerated only at designated or isolated beaches.

SPORTS AND OUTDOOR ACTIVITIES

The larger islands and resorts on the mainland have countless opportunities for **watersports** – including waterskiing, windsurfing, diving and snorkelling.

PERÍPTERA PAVEMENT KIOSKS

There are more than 11,000 **períptero**, or pavement kiosks, across the country with a good 1300 in central Athens alone, including the first one that opened in 1911 on Panepistimíou St. Selling everything from bus tickets to condoms, razors and stationery, they're often the first port of call for directions, too. Many open 24 hours.

14

14

GREEK

	GREEK	PRONUNCIATION
Yes	Ναί	Né
No	Όχι	Óhi
Please	Παρακαλώ	Parakaló
Thank you	Ευχαριστώ	Efharistó
Hello/Good day	Γειά σας/Χαίρετε	Yiá sas/Hérete
Goodbye	Αντίο	Adío
Excuse me	Συγνώμη	Signómi
Sorry	Λυπάμαι	Lipáme
When?	Πότε;	Póte?
Where?	Πού;	Poú?
Good	Καλό	Kaló
Bad	Κακό	Kakó
Near	Κοντά	Kondá
Far	Μακριά	Makriá
Cheap	Φτηνό	Ftinó
Expensive	Ακριβό	Akrivó
Open	Ανοιχτό	Anikhtó
Closed	Κλειστό	Klistó
Today	Σήμερα	Símera
Yesterday	Χθές	Khthés
Tomorrow	Αύριο	Ávrio
How much is…?	Πόσο κάνει…;	Póso káni…?
What time is it?	Τί ώρα είναι;	Tí óra íne?
I don't understand	Δέν καταλαβαίνω	Thén katalavéno
Do you speak English?	Ξαίρετε Αγγλικά;	Ksé'rete angliká?
Do you have a room?	Έχετε ένα ελεύθερο δωμάτιο;	Éhete éna eléfthero domátio?
Where does this bus go to?	Πού πηγαίνει αυτό τό λεωφορείο;	Poú piyéni aftó tó leoforío?
What time does it leave?	Τί ώρα φεύγει;	Tí óra févyi?
A ticket to…	Ένα εισιτήριο γιά…	Éna isitírio yiá…
I'm going to…	Πάω στό…	Páo stó…
Can I have the bill please?	Τό λογαριασμό παρακαλώ;	Tó loghariazmó, parakaló?
One	Ένα /Μία	Éna/mía (for 1am/pm)
Two	Δύο	Dhýo
Three	Τρία/Τρείς	tría/trís(for 3am/pm)
Four	Τέσσερα/Τέσσερεις	Téssera/tésseris (for 4am/pm)
Five	Πέντε	Pénde
Six	Έξι	Éxi
Seven	Εφτά	Eftá
Eight	Οκτώ	Októ
Nine	Εννέα	Enéa
Ten	Δέκα	Théka

There are usually information kiosks at the main beaches. The country's mountainous landscape provides plenty of **walking** and **climbing** options, particularly in the spring or autumn. The most rewarding areas are in northern Greece and the Peloponnese, but there are now some good, signposted treks on the islands too. Always wear sturdy walking boots and carry plenty of water.

For serious hiking, it's worth buying a specialist map.

COMMUNICATIONS

Post offices operate Monday to Friday 8am to 2pm. **Stamps** can also be bought at minimarkets, newsstands or stationers. **Public phones** are mainly card-operated; buy phonecards from newsagents and kiosks. It's possible to make collect (reverse-charge) or charge-card calls from these phones (☎139 for international operator), but you need €2.50 credit on a Greek phonecard to begin. Mobile phones from EU countries have free roaming charges: those from non-EU countries may find it cheaper to buy a local pay-as-you-go **SIM card** for about €5 from kiosks, minimarkets or mobile-phone chains like Germanos. There are few remaining internet cafés, since almost every café, bar and restaurant has a strong **wi-fi** signal.

EMERGENCIES

The most common causes of a run-in with the **police** are drunken loutishness and camping outside an authorized site. For minor medical complaints go to a local **pharmacy** (open Mon & Wed 8am–2pm, Tues, Thurs & Fri 8am–1.30pm & 5–8pm): details of out-of-hours places are posted in all pharmacy windows or call ☎1434. For serious medical attention you'll find English-speaking doctors in all bigger towns and resorts; ask the tourist police for names or dial ☎1016. Emergency treatment is free in state hospitals, though you'll only get the most basic level of nursing care.

INFORMATION

National Tourist Organization (EOT) offices have been scaled down considerably during the economic crisis. You will only find them in the largest of towns and resorts; in other places, try private local agencies near the ports or bus stations.

MONEY AND BANKS

Greece's currency is the **euro** (€). **Banks** are normally open Monday to Thursday 8am to 2.30pm, Friday 8am to 1.30pm.

EMERGENCY NUMBERS

Any emergency ☎112; Police ☎100; Ambulance ☎166; Fire ☎199; Tourist police ☎1571.

STUDENTS AND YOUTH DISCOUNTS

Many state-owned **museums and sites** are free or heavily discounted for students from EU countries – a valid student card is required. Non-EU students generally pay half-price.

14

A few branches stay open longer, the most central of which in Athens is Pireaus Bank at the junction of Stadhíou and Amerkís St near Sýndagma Square (Mon–Fri 8am–8pm, Sat 10.30am–3pm). **ATMs** accept foreign cards, and **credit and debit cards** are generally accepted in most hotels, restaurants and shops, though in isolated areas cash will prove useful.

OPENING HOURS AND HOLIDAYS

Shops generally open Monday to Saturday from 8.30/9am to 2/2.30pm, with afternoon shopping on Tuesdays, Thursdays and Fridays from 5.30/6pm to 8/8.30pm. In Athens and tourist areas shops and offices often stay open right through the day. On Sunday shops are generally closed, while in rural areas **public transport** reduces dramatically or ceases completely, so be careful not to get stranded. Opening hours for **museums**

FAR FROM AN OPEN AND SHUT CASE

One of the results of Greece's current economic crisis is the **erratic opening times** of state museums, tourist offices and archeological sites. Many museums employ extra staff for the summer season with its longer opening hours. However, due to new anti-corruption laws, in order to take on new staff they have to go through a lengthy public tendering process – even when employing guards for just a few months in the summer. As a result, summer opening hours are fairly fluid – they can start as early as April or as late as July and end in early September or continue until October. Hence, in some of our opening times, we just state summer and winter, rather than giving exact months.

14

and **ancient sites** change with exasperating frequency (see box, p.501), though most state museums are closed on Mondays: smaller sites and monasteries may close for a siesta, even when they're not supposed to. There's a vast range of **national holidays** and **festivals**. The most important, when almost everything will be closed, are: January 1 and 6, first Monday of Orthodox Lent (February 23 2017; February 19 2018), March 25, May 1, Orthodox Good Friday & Easter Monday April 14 & 17 2017; April 6 & 9 2018), Whit Monday (June 5 2017, May 28 2015), August 15, October 28, December 25 and 26.

Athens

Exasperating and exhilarating, **ATHENS** has been inhabited continuously for over seven thousand years. Vastly improved by a vigorous scrub for the 2004 Olympics, it now has an efficient, ever-expanding, user-friendly metro and its mix of contemporary culture, nightlife and heritage rivals that of any European city. Part of Athens' charm is the mix of retro and contemporary: cutting-edge clothes shops and designer bars stand by the remnants of the Ottoman bazaar, while modernist 1960s apartment blocks stand shoulder to shoulder with Neoclassical mansions.

Athens' Acropolis, protected by a ring of mountains and commanding views of all seagoing approaches, was a natural choice for prehistoric settlement. Its development as a city-state reached its zenith in the fifth century BC with a flourish of art, architecture, literature and philosophy that has pervaded Western culture ever since. The **ancient sites** are the most obvious of Athens' attractions, but the pleasant cafés, markets and landscaped stair-streets, the startling views from the hills of **Lykavitós** and **Filopáppou**, and, around the foot of the Acropolis, the scattered monuments of the Byzantine and nineteenth-century town, all have their appeal.

WHAT TO SEE AND DO

Pláka is the best place to begin exploring the city. One of the few parts of Athens with unified architecture, its narrow streets and stepped lanes are flanked by nineteenth-century Neoclassical houses. The interlocking streets provide countless opportunities for watching the world – or at least the tourists – go by. While the Acropolis complex is an essential sight, it can be rewarding to stumble across smaller and more modest relics, such as the fourth-century BC Monument of Lysikrátis, or the first-century Tower of the Winds. Or take a walk through the pleasant National Gardens, away from the chaos of Athens' traffic-choked streets. Save some energy for the balmy evenings, however – with fantastic restaurants and funky bars, Athens knows how to juxtapose the ancient with the modern.

The Acropolis

A rugged limestone outcrop, watered by springs and rising abruptly from the plain of Attica, the **Acropolis** (daily: summer 8am–7pm; winter 8.30am–4pm; €20, including entrance to the Theatre of Dionysos) was one of the earliest settlements in Greece, supporting a Neolithic community around 5000 BC. During the ninth century BC, it became the heart of the first Greek city-state, and in the fifth century BC, Pericles had the complex reconstructed under the direction of architect and sculptor Pheidias, producing most of the monuments visible today, including the Parthenon. Having survived more or less intact for over two millennia, the Acropolis was blown up by a shell in

---

ACROPOLIS COMBINED TICKET

If you are visiting several of Athens' ancient sites, the **combined ticket** for €30 (valid for 5 days) is excellent value. It includes the Acropolis, the Theatre of Dionysus, the Ancient Agora and the Roman Forum, as well as other minor sites such as the Lykeion, Hadrian's Library, Kerameikos and Olympieion.

1687 during the Ottoman-Venetian war. In 1811 Lord Elgin controversially sawed off parts of the frieze (the "Elgin Marbles"), which he later sold to the British Government. While the original religious significance of the Acropolis is now nonexistent, it is still imbued with a sense of majesty. The vistas alone are worth the climb, as the Acropolis's height affords a rare bird's-eye view over the capital. Go early or late to beat the crowds and savour a moment alone with this icon of Western civilization.

The Parthenon

With the construction of the **Parthenon**, fifth-century BC Athens reached an artistic and cultural peak. No other monument in the ancient Greek world had achieved such fame, and it stood proud as a symbol of the greatness and the power of Athens. The first and largest building constructed by Pericles' men, the temple is stunning, achieving an unequalled harmony in temple architecture. Built on the site of earlier temples, it was intended as a new sanctuary for Athena and a house for her cult image, a colossal statue decked in ivory and gold plate that was designed by Pheidias and considered one of the Seven Wonders of the Ancient World; unfortunately the sculpture was lost after the fifth century AD.

The Erechtheion

To the north of the Parthenon stands the **Erechtheion**, the last of the great works of Pericles. The building is intentionally unlike anything else found among the remnants of ancient sites. The most bizarre and memorable feature is the Porch of the Caryatids, as the columns are replaced by six maidens from the town of Caryae (Caryatids) holding the entablature gracefully on their heads. The significance of this design continues to puzzle both historians and visitors.

The Acropolis Museum

In a striking, purpose-built building at the foot of the rock, the **Acropolis Museum** (April–Oct Mon 8am–4pm,

Tues–Thurs, Sat & Sun 8am–8pm, Fri 8am–10pm; Nov–March Mon–Thurs 9am–5pm, Fri 9am–10pm, Sat & Sun 9am-–8pm; €5; ⊛theacropolismuseum .gr) stands above a set of excavations visible through a see-through floor. It contains nearly all the portable objects removed from the Acropolis since 1834. Prize exhibits include the *Moschophoros*, a painted marble statue of a young man carrying a sacrificial calf; the graceful sculpture of Athena Nike adjusting her sandal, known as *Nike Sandalizoussa*; and four Caryatids from the Erechtheion. Athens now has a suitable facility for the storage and display of the Elgin Marbles – but whether the British Museum will return them remains to be seen.

Herodes Atticus Theatre and Theatre of Dionysus

Dominating the southern slope of the Acropolis hill is the second-century Roman **Herodes Atticus Theatre**, restored for performances of music and classical drama during the summer festival (the only time it's open). The main interest hereabouts lies in earlier Greek sites to the east, pre-eminent among them the **Theatre of Dionysus** (same hours as the Acroplis; entrance included in the €20 Acropolis ticket). Masterpieces of Aeschylus, Sophocles, Euripides and Aristophanes were first performed here, at one of the most evocative locations in the city. The ruins are impressive; the theatre, rebuilt in the fourth century BC, could hold some seventeen thousand spectators.

The Ancient Agora

Northwest of the Acropolis, the **Ancient Agora** (daily: summer 8am–7pm; winter 8.30am–4pm; €8) was the nexus of ancient Athenian city life, where acts of administration, commerce and public assembly competed for space. The site is a confused jumble of ruins, dating from various stages between the sixth century BC and the fifth century AD. For some idea of what you are surveying, head for the **museum** in the rebuilt Stoa of Attalos. At the far corner of the precinct sits the nearly intact but distinctly clunky

ATHENS

● SHOPPING

Monastiráki	2
flea market	
Travel Bookstore	1

■ EATING

Amvrosia	7
Dhióskouri	6
Greco's Project	3
Oinopoleion	2
Savvas	4
Thanassis	5
To Athinaïkon	1

■ DRINKING AND NIGHTLIFE

Baba Au Rum	6
Bios/Tesla	9
Booze Cooperativa	3
Brettos	8
Couleur Locale	10
Dora Stratou Theatre	1
Gagarin 205	4
Handlebar	2
Mike's Irish Bar	7
Six D.O.G.S.	5

■ ACCOMMODATION

Athens Backpackers	8
Athens Studios	9
Athens Style	3
City Circus	1
Dióskouros	5
Guest House	2
Fivos	1
Marble House	10
Phaedra	6
Student and Travellers' Inn	4
Youth Hostel	
Pagration	7

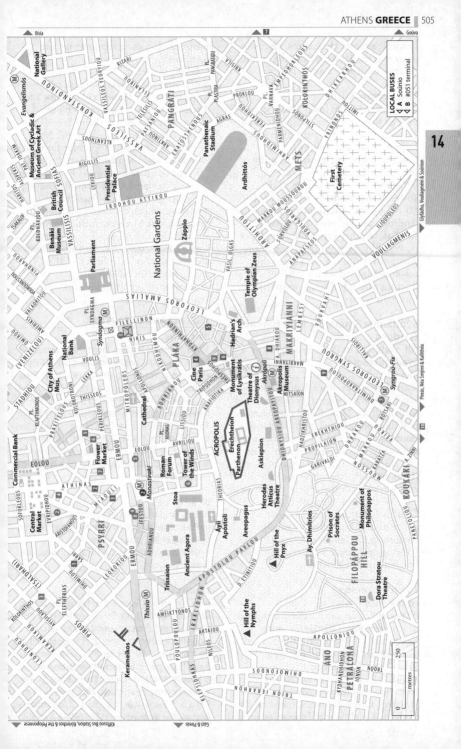

14

LOCAL BUSES
▽ A Soúnio
▽ B #051 terminal

National Gallery

Museum of Cycladic & Ancient Greek Art

Evangelismós Ⓜ

National Gallery

KONSTANDINOU

VASSILEOS YEORYIOU

RIZARI

ELLANIKOU

PANGRÁTI

PL. PANGAIOU

PL. PLASTIRA

KRISSA

PROKLOU

PL. VARNAVA

KOLOKINTHOS

ERATOSTHENOUS

EMPEDOKLEOUS

ARRIANOU

AGRAS

ANTINOROS

PARMENIDHOU

DHIKEARHOU

TELESILIS

PLATONOS

ARNINDHOUS

STILPONOS

ROLLINI

EFRONOS

Panathenaic Stadium

Ardhittós

METS

First Cemetery

Museum of Cycladic & Ancient Greek Art

VASSILEOS SOFIAS

KLEANTHOUS

ARNINTHIDHOU

MARKOU MOUSSOUROU

HERONDHOU

YOUFIGAITOS

ILIOUPOLEOS

SOTIRIHOU

ARDHITTOU

AMARASSIS

TSOSEMBASLON

VOULIAGMENIS

Benáki Museum

RIGILIS

PL. KOLONAKIOU

LYKIOU

Presidential Palace

British Council

 PINDHAROU

VALAORITOU

PLOUTARHOU

AKADIMIAS

KOUMBARI

SEKERI

IRODHOU ATTIKOU

VASSILISIS

National Gardens

Záppio Ⓜ

Temple of Olympian Zeus

MARKOU MOUSSOUROU

MAKRIYIÁNNI

VOURVAHI

LEMBESI

AMERIKIS

OMIROU

(VENIZELOU)

PINDHAROU

Parliament

PL. SYNDAGMA Ⓜ

Syndagma Ⓜ

FILELLINON

NIKIS

NIKODIMOU

KIDHATHINEON

Hadrian's Arch

VASIL. OLGAS

AMALIAS

LEOFOROS

VASIL. OLGAS

National Bank

City of Athens Mus.

STADHIOU

VOULIS

LEKKA

PERIKLEOUS

MITROPOLEOS

APOLLONOS

FILELLINON

NIKIS

PLÁKA

Cine Paris

TRIPODHON

Monument of Lysikrátis

AREOPAYITOU

A. DHIAKOU

Akrópoli Ⓜ

Acropolis Museum

MAKRIYIANNI

MITSAÍON

PROPLEON

SYNGROU

LEOFOROS

DHIMITRAKOPOULOU

Syngroú-Fix Ⓜ

BOTSARI

VEIKOU

Commercial Bank

PL. KLEFTHMONOS

PRAXITELOUS

KOLOKOTRONI

THISSEOS

Cathedral

PL. AGORAS

LISSIOU

ADHRIANOU

ANAFIOTIKA

ACROPOLIS

Erechtheion

Parthenon

Theatre of Dionysus

Asklepion

DHIONYSIOU

EREKHTHIOU

HADZIKHRISTOU

MAKRI

KARIATA

MOUSSON

PROPILEON

GARIVALDI

KOUKÁKI

A. ZINNI

EOLOU

Flower Market

ERMOU

EOLOU

Roman Forum

Tower of the Winds

THEORIAS

Herodes Atticus Theatre

DHIONYSIOU

AREOPAYITOU

PANEOLLIOU

Monument of Philopappos

TRIARIOU

PANEOLLIOU

TROON

ATHINAS

MONASTIRAKI

Monastiráki Ⓜ

IFESTOU

MIAOULI

Stoa

Ancient Agora

Ayii Apóstoli

Areopagus

Hill of the Pnyx

Ay. Dhimítrios

Prison of Socrates

FILOPÁPPOU HILL

Dora Stratou Theatre

DHIMITRAKOPOULOU

KARTZA

Central Market

ARISTOFANOUS

EVRIPIDHOU

SARRI

PSYRRÍ

ADHRIANOU

ERMOU

LEOKORIOU

Trissáion

APOSTOLOU PAVLOU

IRAKLIDHON

POULOPOULOU

AMFIKTYONOS

AKTAIOU

Hill of the Nymphs

APOLLONIOU

ANO PETRÁLONA

TRION IERARHON

KYDHANDIDHON

SOFOKLEOUS

(TSALDHARI)

DHIMOFONDOS

DHIMOFONDOS

SOFRONIOU

KOLOKYNTHOS

AVTISSIOU

PL. ELEFTHERIAS

PIREOS

LEONIDHOU

DHIODHOU

KERAMIKOU

Kerameikós

PL. AVISSINIAS

Thissío Ⓜ

KLEPSIDHRAS

NILEOS

0   250
metres

Doric Temple of Hephaistos, otherwise known as the **Thissíon** from the exploits of Theseus depicted on its friezes.

The Roman Forum

The **Roman Forum** (daily 8am–3pm; €6), or Roman Agora, was built as an extension of the Hellenistic Agora by Julius Caesar and Augustus. The best-preserved and most intriguing of the ruins, though, is the graceful, octagonal structure known as the **Tower of the Winds**. It was designed in 50 BC by the Macedonian astronomer Andronicus, and served as a compass, sundial, weather vane and water clock powered by a stream from one of the Acropolis springs. Each face of the tower is adorned with a relief of a figure floating through the air, personifying the eight winds.

Sýndagma Square and the National Gardens

All roads lead to Platía Syndágmatos – **Sýndagma Square** – with its pivotal metro station. It is geared to tourism, with a main post office, banks, luxury hotels and travel agents grouped around it. Behind the Neoclassical parliament buildings off the square, the **National Gardens** provide the most refreshing spot in the city, a shady oasis of trees, shrubs and creepers. South of the gardens stands **Hadrian's Arch**, erected by the Roman emperor to mark the edge of the classical city and the beginning of his own. Directly behind are sixteen surviving columns of the 104 that originally comprised the **Temple of Olympian Zeus** – the largest temple in Greece, dedicated by Hadrian in 132 AD.

Town museums

At the northeastern corner of the National Gardens is the fascinating and much-overlooked **Benáki Museum**, Koumbári 1 (Wed & Fri 9am–5pm, Thurs & Sat 9am–midnight, Sun 9am–3pm; €7, students €5; ⓦwww .benaki.gr), with a well-organized collection that features Mycenaean jewellery, Greek costumes, memorabilia from the Greek War of Independence and

historical documents, engravings and paintings.

Taking the second left off Vassilísis Sofías after the Benáki Museum will bring you to the **Museum of Cycladic and Ancient Greek Art**, Neofýtou Dhouká 4 (Mon, Wed, Fri & Sat 10am–5pm, Thurs 10am–8pm, Sun 11am–5pm; €7, Mon €3.50; ⓦcycladic.gr), impressive for both its subject and the quality of its displays.

To the northwest, beyond Omónia, the fabulous **National Archeological Museum**, Patissíon 44 (daily 8am–8pm; €10; ⓦnamuseum.gr), contains gold from the grave circle at Mycenae, including the so-called Mask of Agamemnon, along with an impressive classical art collection and findings from the island of Thíra, dating from around 1600 BC, contemporary with the Minoan civilization on Crete.

ARRIVAL AND DEPARTURE

BY PLANE

Athens' Eleftheríos Venizélos airport, 33km southeast of Athens, is on metro Line #3 (every 30min, 6am–11.30pm; €10), which runs into the city centre in about 40min. There are four buses from the airport: bus #X93 runs to Kifissoú bus station at 100 Kifissoú St (every 30min; 1hr 10min); the #X95 goes direct to Sýndagma Square (every 10min; 1hr 15min); the #X96 runs to Pireás port (every 30min; 1hr 40min); and the #X97 to Dafni Metro station (every 30–40min; 1hr 10min). All bus tickets cost €6 one-way. A fixed-fare taxi to the centre will cost you €38 or, from midnight to 5am, €54.

BY TRAIN

Thessaloníki trains arrive at the Laríssis train station to the northwest of the city centre, with its own metro station on Line #2 and on the Proasteiakos Line.

Destinations Kórinthos (hourly; 1hr 20min); Thessaloníki (6 daily; 5hr 30min).

BY BUS

Buses from northern Greece and the Peloponnese arrive at Kifissoú bus station, 10min from the centre by bus #051 (5am–midnight). Buses from central Greece arrive closer to the centre at Liossíon bus station, 260 Liossíon St, north of the train station. From here bus #024 goes to Sýndagma Square (5am–midnight). Most international buses drop off at Laríssis train station or Kifissoú; a few will drop you right in the city centre upon request. Attica buses to Lávrio, Rafína and Soúnio leave from the KTEL/Mavromatéon terminal at the southwest corner of the Pédhion Áreos park.

14

Destinations from Kifissoú Corfu (3 daily; 10hr); Igoumenítsa (4 daily; 7hr); Ioánnina (6–8 daily; 8hr); Kalamáta (2 daily; 3hr 30min); Kefalloniá (5 daily; 8hr); Kórinthos (1–2 hourly; 1hr 20min); Mycenae-Fíkhti (hourly; 2hr); Monemvasiá (3–4 daily; 4hr); Náfplio (hourly; 2hr 30min); Pátra (1–2 hourly; 3–4hr); Pýrgos (10 daily; 5hr); Spárti (11 daily; 4hr); Thessaloníki (11–12 daily; 7hr).

Destinations from Liossíon Delphi (4–5 daily; 3hr); Kými, for Skýros ferries (5 daily; 3hr 30min); Tríkala (9 daily; 4hr 30min); Vólos (10–12 daily; 5hr).

Destinations from KTEL/Mavromatéon Rafína (every 30min; 1hr 30min); Soúnio (hourly; 2hr); Lávrio (1–2 hourly; 1hr 30min).

BY BOAT

Effectively an extension of Athens, the port of Pireás lies at the end of metro Line #1 and is the main terminus for international and inter-island ferries. Blue-and-white buses shuttle passengers around the port for free. The other ports on the east coast of the Attic peninsula, Rafína and Lávrio, are alternative departure points for some Cycladic and northeastern Aegean islands. Frequent buses connect them with Platia Eghýptou in central Athens.

Destinations from Pireás Haniá (1–2 daily; 9–10hr); Íos (4–5 daily; 3hr 30min–5hr 30min); Iráklion (1–2 daily; 7hr); Mýkonos (3–4 daily; 2hr 30min–4hr 30min); Náxos (3–6 daily; 4–6hr); Páros (3–6 daily; 3–5hr); Pátmos (1–3 weekly; 9hr); Rhodes (1–2 daily; 16–18hr); Santoríni (4–6 daily; 5–7hr); Sífnos (4–5 daily; 2hr 50min); Sýros (2–3 daily; 4hr).

INFORMATION

Tourist office GNTO information desks at Dhionysíou Areopayítou 18–20 (Mon–Fri 9am–8pm, Sat 10am–4pm; ☎ 210 3310 392, ✉ info@gnto.gr; Ⓜ Akropolis) and at the airport (Mon–Fri 9am–5pm, Sat 10am–4pm).

Tours Alternative Athens (ⓦ alternativeathens.com) runs a range of tours off the beaten track, such as the Street Art Tour (€30pp), or the Hip Athens Orientation Tour, which takes in the hotspots and trendy neighbourhoods of the city (€40pp).

GETTING AROUND

All public transport operates daily 5.30am–midnight, while on Fri & Sat the metro and trams run until 2am.

Tickets Single-journey tickets are valid on all forms of transport for 90min (€1.40). Travelcards are also available (€4.50 for 24hr, €9 for 5 days), while a 3-day bus and metro ticket for greater Athens that includes one trip to or from the airport costs €22. If you travel without a valid ticket you are liable for a fine up to sixty times the value of your ticket.

CRIME

Though safer than many European cities, Athens has seen a **crime rise** in the last few years as the result of tensions between new immigrant communities and the police, an increase in drug use and unemployment, and the city's history of anti-establishment protest. Though not quite no-go areas as such, it's best to avoid walking in parks after dark (especially Pedhíon Áreos), in unlit areas around Omónia Square and in the backstreets behind the Athens Polytechnic. Petty theft is also increasing, especially in the centre and around Ⓜ Victoria.

By bus and trolley Athens' bus and trolley network is extensive but very crowded at peak times.

By tram A tram line runs from Sýndagma through Athens to the seaside resorts of Glyfádha and Voúla.

By metro Line #1 runs from Pireás to Kifissiá, with central stops at Thissío, Monastiráki and Omónia; Line #2 runs from Anthoúpolis to Ellinikó via Sýndagma and a station at the foot of the Acropolis; Line #3 heads east from Ayía Marína all the way to the airport. Tickets (€1.40) are available at all stations from automatic coin-op dispensers or staffed windows. They must be validated before boarding. You are unlikely to use the Suburban railway (Proastiakós) unless you want to travel to Corinth or Kiato and onwards to Pátra.

By taxi Taxis can be fairly expensive. Drivers may pick up several passengers along the way, each paying the full fare for their journey – so if you're picked up by an already occupied taxi, memorize the meter reading. There's a minimum fare of €3.20.

ACCOMMODATION

The city can be deserted in August when a lot of establishments close for holidays and the nightlife moves to the islands and to the seaside.

HOSTELS

Athens Backpackers Makri 12, Makriyiánni ☎ 210 9224 044, ⓦ backpackers.gr. Relaxed hostel in a prime location with clean, simple dorms, internet access, rooftop bar with Acropolis views and a buzzing atmosphere. The €6 walking tour makes it a great place to meet fellow travellers. Very popular, so best to book ahead. Dorms **€22.50**

★**Athens Style** Ayías Theklas 10, Monastiráki ☎ 210 3225 010, ⓦ athenstyle.com. Superb hostel, a few minutes' walk from Monastiráki metro. The roof terrace bar has lounge music DJs in the summer until 1am when the

14

action moves to the club next door, called appropriately *Next Door*, until 4am. Breakfast €4; locker luggage storage (€2/day). Dorms €24, doubles €76, apartment for four €100

City Circus Sarrí 16 ☎213 0237 244, ⓦcitycircus.gr. Surrounded by some of the best street art in Athens, bright by day, less so by night, this is one of the best-equipped hostels in Athens with effusive, obliging staff. The deal with the restaurant below is good: breakfast for €5, two-course meal €11.50, 3 courses €14.50. Offers free city tours. Dorms €25, doubles €55

Dióskouros Guest House Pittakoú 6 ☎210 3248 165, ⓦhoteldioskouros.com. Basic, cheap hostel in the Pláka, with female-only dorms, good at organizing further trips to the islands. Price includes continental breakfast in a beautiful garden. No private bathrooms. Dorms €20, doubles €50, triple €70

Fívos Athinás 23 ☎210 3226 657, ⓦhotelfivos.gr. Gloomy hostel in an old five-floor building that shows its age, but central, cheap, clean and secure with 24hr reception and a healthy, fruit-and-muesli-based breakfast included. Dorms sleep a maximum of four people and all except those on the top floor have an en-suite bathrooms. Dorms €15, doubles €50

Student and Travellers' Inn Kydhathinéon 16, Pláka ☎210 3244 808, ⓦstudenttravellersinn.com. Popular, clean and well-run official hotel-cum-hostel in a prime location close to nightlife. Cheerful rooms, many with private bathrooms, as well as luggage storage, good wi-fi access and a garden bar in season. Dorms €16, doubles €50

Youth Hostel Pagration Dhamáreos 75, Pangráti ☎210 7519 530, ⓦathensyhostel.com; trolley bus #2 or #11. Old-style youth hostel in a congenial (if remote) neighbourhood away from the centre with cooking and laundry facilities. Students only, and they insist on seeing an ISIC. Dorms €12

HOTELS AND APARTMENTS

★**Athens Studios** Veikou 3a, Makriyiánni ☎210 9235 811, ⓦathensstudios.gr. Well-priced dorms and serviced apartments (sleeping 2–4) run by the team at *Athens Backpackers*. Simple, spacious and clean with kitchen, TV, laundromat and a sports bar on site (beer €3). Extra sleepers can be accommodated on fold-out beds. Luggage storage €3/day. Breakfast included. Dorms €25, apartments €140

★**Marble House** Cul-de-sac at Anastasíou Zínni 35, Metro Syngroú-Fix ☎210 9228 294, ⓦmarblehouse.gr. Beautifully renovated in 2015, this peaceful, welcoming *pension* lies south of the Acropolis. Most rooms are en suite and with balcony, and all have ceiling fans and a fridge: a/c is €5/day extra. Breakfast €5. Doubles €45

Phaedra Adhriánou & Herefóndos 16, Pláka ☎210 3238 461, ⓦhotelphaedra.com. Cheerful and clean rooms with

a/c, just over half of which are en suite. Excellent location on a pedestrianized street overlooking the Byzantine church of Ayía Ekateríni. Doubles €70

EATING

If you can stand the touts and tourist hype, Pláka still provides a pleasant setting for an evening meal, though for good-value, good-quality cuisine, outlying neighbourhoods such as Psyrrí, Monastiráki, Gázi and Exárhia are much better bets. To really leave other tourists behind, take metro Line #1 and try the cafés and restaurants around Metro Maroússi, Neo Iráklio and Kifissiá up north.

Amvrosia Dhrákou 3–5. Right by Syngroú-Fix metro station, this is the best grill on this pedestrian street and always packed. Enjoy a whole roast chicken, choose from a large selection of veggie dishes or munch through a huge kebab platter (€6–9) at the outdoor tables. Take away *souvlaki* (€2.20). Daily noon–12.30am.

Dhióskouri Dhioskoúron 13, Pláka. Popular, atmospheric café with an unbeatable view of the Agora, where cold drinks and coffees take precedence over slightly pricey snacks. *Mezédhes* €5–9. Daily noon–late.

Greco's Project Mitropoleos 5 & Nikis, Sýndagma. This Greek food joint took Athens by storm when it opened in 2015, offering both takeaway and waiter service at knockdown prices without compromising quality. Kebabs from €2.50. Daily 7am–1am.

Oinopoleion Aischýlou 12, Psyrrí. Straightforward taverna, the best in a cluster, that excels in grilled/fried seafood, vegetable starters and wine from basement barrels. Arrive early (remember Greeks eat late) or wait for a table (no reservations). Mains €8–9. Sun–Thurs 7am–midnight, Fri & Sat noon–1am.

★**Savvas** Ermou 91, Monastiráki ☎210 3211 167, ⓦsavvas-restaurant.gr. Slightly upmarket though still good-value, sleek kebab restaurant, serving Armenian and

THE ATHENS FESTIVAL

The **Athens Festival** (☎210 327 2000, ⓦgreekfestival.gr), from June to late August, encompasses classical Greek theatre, contemporary dance, classical music, big-name jazz, traditional Greek music plus rock concerts. Most performances take place at the Herodes Atticus Theatre – an atmospheric venue on a warm summer's evening. There are also some performances at the ancient theatre of Epidaurus (see p.512). The main festival box office is at Panepistimíou 39 (Mon–Fri 9am–5pm, Sat 9am–3pm); tickets from €15.

Pontian dishes (€9). Its great selling point is the roof garden, but you must reserve in advance. If unlucky, stop by for a takeaway *souvláki* (€2.20) anyway. Daily 9.30am–2am.

Thanássis Mitropóleos 69, Monastiráki. Reckoned to serve the best *souvláki* (€2.50) and Middle Eastern kebabs in Monastiráki. Always packed with locals at lunchtime, but worth the wait. Take away or eat in the garden at the back. Kebab platter €8.90. Daily 9am–2am.

To Athinaïkón Themistokléous 2, corner with Panepistimíou. In business since 1932, this is a sophisticated *ouzerí* with marble tables and old posters, popular with local workers at lunch; strong on fresh seafood. Great prices, too, with main courses for €8–9. Mon–Sat 11.30am–12.30am.

DRINKING, NIGHTLIFE AND ENTERTAINMENT

Clubs and bars do not start filling up until after midnight and stay open until dawn. If you have no idea where to go, just get off at Metro Monastiráki around midnight and walk around.

BARS

★**Baba Au Rum** Kleitíou 6, Sýndagma. Very trendy bar with colourful decor that sparked a Greek mixology revolution – sample the great selection of enormous rum-based cocktails (€9) from the 160-plus types of rum on offer. Sun–Fri 7pm–3am, Sat 1pm–4am.

Booze Cooperativa Kolokotróni 57–59. Dark, cavernous space with a cool daytime crowd draped at long tables supping draught beer (€3) and playing board games. Stick around at night for DJs, exhibitions and the latest from the Athens avant-garde. Daily 11am–late.

Brettos Kydathinéon 41, Pláka. With multicoloured bottles and wooden barrels lining the walls, this must-go bar is a sophisticated spot which exudes Greekness, full of reminders of its hundred-year-plus history. *Ouzo* €3.50; cocktails €8. Daily 10am–3am.

★**Couleur Locale** Normanoú 3, Monastiráki. Difficult to find even though it's signposted, but persist and climb up the three floors that separate the young and fit on the roof terrace from the young and not so fit on the ground floor – the view over the Acropolis is breathtaking. Cocktails €7.50. Sun–Fri 10am–2am, Sat 10am–3am.

Handlebar Melanthíou 8, Psyrri. Run by Welsh Gareth in conjunction with the bike shop next door, this cosy little bar has become the hub of the Athens' budding cycling community since 2014. Simple snacks till 6pm, 500ml draught beer for €2.50 and live DJs at weekends. Sun–Thurs 11am–midnight, Fri & Sat 11am–1.30am.

CLUBS AND LIVE MUSIC

Bios/Tesla Pireós 84 ⓦbios.gr. *Bíos* comprises the small, cosy *Tesla Bar* upstairs, and a raw, minimalist club

STARLIT CINEMAS
Outdoor cinema is a charming Greek tradition with hundreds of alfresco screens throughout the country. A balmy evening watching a classic in a bougainvillea-draped courtyard with a few beers is hard to beat. Try the centrally located Cine Paris at Kydhathinaíon 22 in Athens, ⓦcineparis.gr (€8), or the Cinema Kamari just outside Kamari on Santoríni ⓦcinekamari.gr (see p.532). Both open mid-May to mid-Sept.

14

downstairs with an adjoining terrace. From the Stereo MCs to Performance Art – you'll find it here. Fri & Sat 11am–late.

Dora Stratou Theatre Filopáppou Hill ⓦgrdance.org. Dancers, singers and folk musicians unite to give spectators an insight into local Greek traditions. Tickets from €15. Late May to mid-Sept Wed–Fri 9.30pm, Sat & Sun 8.15pm.

Gagarin 205 Liossíon 205 ⓦgagarin205.gr. Located near Attikí metro station, this is the place to watch the best international up-and-coming bands and more established acts. Gigs start around 9.30pm: check website for details.

Mike's Irish Bar Sinópis 6, Pyrgos Athinón, Ambelókipi ⓦmikesirishbar.com. A lively watering hole which has something to suit everyone, including karaoke, live blues music and big screens for sport. Guinness in cans and Murphy's on draught. Mostly free, some live nights €6. Daily 10pm–late.

★**Six D.O.G.S.** Avramiotou 6-8, Monastiraki ⓦsixdogs .gr. A garden bar with an indoor live venue that has taken Athens by storm; there's hardly a local under 30 who hasn't passed through its doors. Its eclectic choice of international bands and a large, shady garden have played as important a role in its popularity as its reasonable prices (beer €5; cocktails €7). Sun–Thurs 10am–3am, Fri & Sat 10am–7am.

SHOPPING

For high-street shopping, head to the boutique stores around Sýndagma square. Souvenir shops abound in Pláka, where leather goods, foodstuffs and jewellery are good value; most remain open all day.

Monastiráki flea market An interesting selection of weird and wonderful goods for sale. Sunday is the best time for a visit, when the market expands into the surrounding streets. The nearby Central Market sells local foods. Daily; hours vary according to stall.

Travel Bookstore Sólonos 71. The largest stock of foreign-language travel books in town, plus walking maps. Mon, Wed, Sat 8.30am–4.30pm, Tues, Thurs & Fri 8.30am–8.30pm.

DIRECTORY

Embassies and consulates Australia, Kifissías & Alexándhras Level 6 Thon Bldg ☎210 8704 000; Canada, Ethnikís Andistáseos 48 Halándri ☎210 7273 400; Ireland, Vassiléos Konstandínou 7 ☎210 7232 771/2; New Zealand, Kifissiás 76 ☎210 6924 136; UK, Ploutárhou 1, Kolonáki ☎210 7272 600; US, Vassilísis Sofías 91 ☎210 721 2951/9.

Hospitals Evangelismós (☎213 2041 000) is the most central, but KAT (☎213 2086 000), way out in Maroússi, is the designated Greater Athens emergency hospital. Both have their own metro stops. The pharmacy at Larissis station is open Mon–Sat 7.30am–11.30pm.

Internet Although there are no internet cafés as such, it's hard to find a café or a taverna that doesn't offer free wi-fi.

Post office The branch at Sýndagma Square has the longest hours (Mon–Fri 7.30am–8.30pm, Sat 7.30am–2.30pm, Sun 9am–1.30pm).

CAPE SOÚNIO AND TEMPLE OF POSEIDON

The 70km of shoreline south of Athens has good but highly developed beaches. At weekends the sands fill fast, as do innumerable bars, restaurants and clubs. But for most visitors, this coast's attraction is at the end of the road. **Cape Soúnio** is among the most imposing spots in Greece, and on it stands the fifth-century BC **Temple of Poseidon** (daily 9.30am–sunset; €8), built in the time of Pericles as part of a sanctuary to the sea god. In summer you've faint hope of solitude unless you arrive before the tours do, but the temple is as evocative a ruin as Greece can offer. Doric in style, it preserves sixteen of its thirty-four columns, and the view is stunning. Below the promontory lie several coves, the most sheltered of which is a five-minute walk east from the car park and site entrance.

The main Soúnio **beach** is more crowded, but has a group of tavernas at the far end, which – considering the location – are reasonably priced. Buses to Soúnio leave every hour from Athens' KTEL/Mavromatéon terminal: some take the coastal route, which is more scenic than the inland route and takes around two hours (€6.90).

The Peloponnese

The appeal of the **Peloponnese** is hard to overstate. The **beaches** of this southern peninsula are among the finest and least developed in the country, while its ancient sites include the Homeric palace of Agamemnon at **Mycenae**, the Greek theatre at **Epidaurus** and the sanctuary of **Olympia**, host to the Olympic Games for a millennium. Medieval remains run from the fabulous castle at **Acrocorinth** and the strange tower-houses and frescoed churches of the **Máni**, to the extraordinary Byzantine towns of **Mystra** and **Monemvasiá**. The Peloponnese also boasts Greece's most spectacular train route, an hour-long journey on the **rack-and-pinion rail line** from Dhiakoftó to Kalávryta (see box below).

ARRIVAL AND DEPARTURE

By bus and train The usual approach from Athens is on the frequent buses and trains that run via modern Kórinthos (Corinth).

By boat From Italy and the Adriatic, Pátra (see p.516) is the main port of the Peloponnese, although some ferries from the Ionian Islands arrive at Kyllíni.

KÓRINTHOS

Whoever possessed **Kórinthos** – the ancient city that displaced Athens as capital of the Greek province in Roman times – controlled both the trade between northern Greece and the Peloponnese, and the short cut between the Ionian and Aegean seas. It's

---

DHIAKOFTÓ TO KALÁVRYTA RAILWAY

A contender for one of Europe's quirkiest railway journeys, this **rack-and-pinion rail line** (Odondotós; ⊚odontotos.com) from Dhiakoftó to Kalávryta celebrated its 120th anniversary in 2016, and is a must for any visitor to the region (3–5 daily; €19 return). Trains grind their way up vertiginous slopes, rattle through tunnels and clank over crazily narrow bridges on their way through the dramatic Vouraïkós Gorge.

unsurprising, therefore, that the city's history is a catalogue of invasions and power struggles, until it was razed by the Romans in 146 BC. The site lay in ruins for a century before being rebuilt, on a majestic scale, by Julius Caesar in 44 BC. St Paul stayed for 18 months and preached there in 51/52 AD.

WHAT TO SEE AND DO

Nowadays, the remains of the city occupy a rambling site below the acropolis hill of Acrocorinth, itself littered with medieval ruins. To explore both you need a full day, or better still, to stay close by. The modern village of **ARHÉA KÓRINTHOS** spreads around the main archeological zone, where you'll find plenty of places to eat and sleep, including a scattering of **rooms** to rent in the backstreets.

Ancient Corinth

The main excavated site of **Ancient Corinth** (daily: Nov to mid-April 8am–3pm; mid-April to Sept 8am–8pm; first two weeks of Oct 8am–7pm; second two weeks of Oct 8am–6pm; €8) is dominated by the remains of the Roman city. You enter from the south side, which leads straight into the **Roman agora**. The real focus, however, is a survival from the classical Greek era: the fifth-century BC **Temple of Apollo**, whose seven austere Doric columns stand slightly above the level of the forum.

Acrocorinth

Towering 575m above the lower town, **Acrocorinth** (Tues–Sun 8am–3pm; €2) is an amazing mass of rock still largely encircled by 2km of wall. During the Middle Ages this ancient acropolis of Kórinthos became one of Greece's most powerful fortresses. It's a 4km climb (about 1hr), but well worth it. Amid the sixty-acre site, you wander through a jumble of semi-ruined chapels, mosques, houses and battlements, erected in turn by Greeks, Romans, Byzantines, Franks, Venetians and Ottomans.

ARRIVAL AND DEPARTURE

By train Kórinthos is connected to Athens via the suburban rail line to Elefthérios Venizélos airport. The train station is 3km from town with shuttles running between the two.
Destinations Athens (1–2 hourly; 1hr 20min).
By bus The KTEL bus station is at Dimokratías 4, some 200m east of the centre of Kórinthos, with frequent local buses to Isthmós for connections to the rest of the Peloponnese.
Destinations from Kórinthos Ancient Kórinthos (hourly; 20min).
Destinations from Isthmós Athens (hourly; 1hr); Fíchti for Mycenae (8–10 daily; 1hr); Kalávryta (2 daily; 45min–1hr 30min); Kalamáta (7–8 daily; 3hr 15min–4hr); Pátra (1–2 hourly; 1hr 50min–2hr 30min); Náfplio (10–12 daily; 1hr 20min); Spárti (8 daily; 4hr).

ACCOMMODATION

Hotel Korinthos Damaskinoú 26 ☎ 27410 26710. One block from the port and three blocks from the bus station, this small and simple hotel is conveniently located: its owners are keen to show you their city. Breakfast €5. Doubles €50

Marinos Rooms Arhéa Kórinthos, Sysyphus St ☎ 27410 31994, ⊛ marinos-rooms.gr. Very popular, family-run hotel right by Ancient Corinth with comfortable rooms. There's a decent restaurant downstairs: breakfast €8. Book in advance. Doubles €50

MYKÍNES (MYCENAE)

Southwest of Kórinthos, the ancient site of **MYCENAE** is tucked into a fold of the hills just 2km northeast of the modern village of **Mykínes**. Agamemnon's citadel, "well-built Mycenae, rich in gold", as Homer wrote, was uncovered in 1874–76 by the German archeologist Heinrich Schliemann, who was convinced that Homer's epics had a factual basis. Brilliantly crafted gold and sophisticated architecture bore out the accuracy of Homer's words. The buildings unearthed by Schliemann show signs of having been occupied from around 1950 BC until 1100 BC, when the town, though still prosperous, was abandoned. No coherent explanation has been found for this event, but war between rival kingdoms was probably a major factor.

WHAT TO SEE AND DO

You enter the **Citadel of Mycenae** (daily: April 8am–7pm; May–Oct 8am–8pm; Nov–March 8am–6pm; €12) through

14

14

the mighty **Lion Gate**. Inside the walls to the right is **Grave Circle A**, the cemetery which Schliemann believed contained the bodies of Agamemnon and his followers, murdered on their triumphant return from Troy. In fact the burials date from about three centuries before the Trojan war, but they were certainly royal, and the finds are among the richest yet unearthed. Schliemann took the extensive **South House**, beyond the grave circle, to be the Palace of Agamemnon. But a much grander building was later discovered on the summit of the acropolis. Rebuilt in the thirteenth century BC, it is, like all Mycenaean palaces, centred on a **Great Court**. The small rooms to the north are believed to have been royal apartments, and in one of them the remains of a red stuccoed bath have led to its fanciful identification as the place of Agamemnon's murder.

Outside the walls of the citadel lay the main part of the town, and extensive remains of **merchants' houses** have been uncovered near to the road. A few minutes' walk down the road is the astonishing **Treasury of Atreus**, a royal burial vault entered through a majestic 15m-long corridor.

ARRIVAL AND DEPARTURE

By bus Three daily buses from Náfplio (see below) stop at the gate.

ACCOMMODATION

The modern village of Mykínes has one main street, where all accommodation and places to eat are located.

Oraia Eleni (Belle Hélène) ☎ 27510 76225, ✉ bellhel @otenet.gr. Former home of archeologist Heinrich Schliemann, this second-oldest hotel in Greece looks rather run-down, but it's full of history. What's more, its rooms are spacious and the shared bathrooms spotless. Breakfast included. Doubles **€40**

NÁFPLIO

NÁFPLIO, 44km south of Kórinthos, a lively, beautifully sited town with a faded elegance, inherited from when it was briefly modern Greece's first capital, makes an attractive base for exploring the area or for resting up by the sea.

WHAT TO SEE AND DO

The main fort, **Palamídhi** (daily: April–Oct 8am–8pm; Nov–March 8am–5pm; €8), is most directly approached by 890 stone-hewn steps up from Polyzoïdhou Street. Within its walls are three self-contained castles, all built by the Venetians in the 1710s. To the west, the **Acronafplía** fortress (free to enter) occupies the ancient citadel, whose walls were adapted by successive medieval occupants. The third fort, the photogenic **Boúrtzi** (free to enter), occupies the islet offshore from the harbour and allowed the Venetians to close the shallow shipping channel with a chain. In the town itself, **Platía Syndágmatos**, the main square, is a great place to relax over a coffee. There's also a thriving nightlife, with a string of bars along the waterfront at Bouboulínas Street and at Staïkopoúlou Street in the centre.

ARRIVAL AND DEPARTURE

By bus Buses arrive on Syngroú, just south of the interlocking squares Platía Trión Navárhon and Platía Kapodhístria.

Destinations Athens (hourly; 3hr); Epidaurus (4–6 daily; 45min); Mycenae (3–4 daily; 1hr).

ACCOMMODATION AND EATING

Byzantio Vassiléos Alexándhrou 15. Sit beneath a cloud of pink and purple bougainvillea and feast on specialities such as home-made sausages, organic wine and an enormous coal-grilled platter of meat. Expect to pay about €10/person. Daily noon–1pm.

★**Latini** Óthonos 47 ☎ 27520 96470, ⊕ latinihotel.gr. Old but refurbished hotel in a quiet street in the centre of the Old Town with spacious rooms. Pay extra for the top-floor rooms for great views of Bourtzi. Breakfast included. Doubles **€50**

EPIDAURUS

From the sixth century BC to Roman times, **EPIDAURUS**, 30km east of Náfplio, was a major spa and religious centre; its **Sanctuary of Asclepius** (daily: Jan–March 8am–5pm; April 8am–7pm; March–Oct 8am–8pm; Nov & Dec 8am–3pm; €12) was the most famous of all shrines dedicated to the god of healing. The magnificently preserved 14,000-seat theatre is the venue for some **classical-theatre performances** during the Athens Festival (June–Aug; ⓦgreekfestival.gr).

ACCOMMODATION AND EATING

Camping Nicholas I & II Paleá Epídavros ☎27530 41297/41445, ⓦnicolasgikas.gr. Two campsites, 2.5km apart, which have wonderful pitches on grass among orange and mulberry groves, right on the beach. An on-site taverna, *Mouria*, serves *Nicholas I* and has played host to many a celebrity appearing at the Epidaurus Festival – from Pavarotti to Dame Helen Mirren. Open May–Sept. Book well ahead. Per person **€6.50**, plus per tent **€5.50**

SPÁRTI (ANCIENT SPARTA)

Today, **SPÁRTI**, 112km southwest of Náfplio, is just a large provincial town. As the ancient Spartans left no tangible cultural legacy like the Athenians, don't expect any ruins of note. Because of its good road connections, however, and decent hotels and restaurants, it's best suited for an overnight stay and a day-trip to **Mystra** (see below).

ARRIVAL AND DEPARTURE

By bus The KTEL bus station is at the far eastern end of Lykoúrgou, a 10min walk from the centre.
Destinations Areópoli (5 daily; 2hr); Athens (10 daily; 4hr); Monemvasiá (3 daily; 2hr 30min); Mystra (6–7 daily; 30min); Yíthio (5 daily; 1hr).

ACCOMMODATION

Hotel Cecil Paleológou 125 ☎27310 24980, ⓦhotelcecil .gr. A warm welcome awaits at this centrally located, if rather noisy, 1930s hotel, with clean en-suite rooms furnished in wood, silk and lace. No breakfast. Doubles **€55**
Lakonía Paleológou 89 ☎27310 28951. Surprisingly cheery hotel on a noisy road, this is your best bet if you are to stay overnight in Sparta. Large clean rooms, fluffy beds, modern bathrooms, the lot. Breakfast in room. Doubles **€45**

EATING

Diethnés Paleológou 105. The garden here is an oasis of calm, and especially atmospheric in the evenings. Hearty Greek favourites are dished up to the sound of birdsong. Meals around €12–12. Daily noon–midnight.
Zeus Paleológou 72. Modern Greek cuisine and a wide selection of local wines served in minimalist surroundings. A bit pricey but worth it; specialities include roast goat and artichoke bake (€12–18). Daily noon–midnight.

MYSTRA (MYSTRÁS)

A glorious, airy place, hugging a steep flank of the Taïyetos mountains, **MYSTRA** is an astonishingly complete Byzantine city that once sheltered a population of some twenty thousand. The castle on its summit was built in 1249 by Guillaume II de Villehardouin, fourth Frankish Prince of the Morea (as the Peloponnese was then known), and together with the fortresses of Monemvasiá and the Máni it guarded his territory. In 1262 the Byzantines drove out the Franks and established the Despotate of Mystra.

To explore the site of the **Byzantine city** (daily: April–Aug 8am–8pm; Sept 8am–6.30pm; Oct 8am–5.30pm; Nov–March 8am–3pm; €12), take the bus from Spárti which stops at the village of Néos Mystrás and then continues up the hill. Make for the top entrance, then explore a leisurely downhill route. Following this course, the first identifiable building you come to is the fourteenth-century church of **Ayía Sofía**. The **Kástro**, reached by a path that climbs directly from the upper gate, maintains the Frankish design of its thirteenth-century construction, though modified by successive occupants. Heading down from Ayía Sofía, there are two possible routes. The right fork winds past the ruins of a Byzantine mansion, while the left fork passes the massively fortified **Náfplio Gate** and the vast, multistorey complex of the **Despots' Palace**. At the **Monemvasiá Gate**, linking the upper and lower towns, turn right for the **Pandánassa convent**, which is perhaps the finest that survives in the town. Further down on this side of the lower town make sure you see the diminutive **Perívleptos monastery**, whose single-domed church, partly carved out of the rock, contains Mystra's most complete cycle of frescoes. The **Mitrópolis**, or cathedral, immediately beyond the gateway, ranks as the oldest of Mystra's churches, built from 1270 onward.

ACCOMMODATION

Castleview Néos Mystrás ☎27310 83303, ⓦcastleview .gr. Shady and quiet, this campsite is 500m from the village. A small pool and a good traditional taverna are just two of its attractions. Open April–Oct. Camping per person €6.50, plus per tent €4, bungalows €40

Paleologio Mystras 2.5km from Spárti, 4km from Néos Mystrás ☎ 27310 22724, ⓦ campingpaleologio.com; buses to Néos Mystrás stop at the entrance (tell the driver in advance). Well-run campsite with good facilities (wi-fi, pool, laundry, minimarket). Open all year. Per person €7, plus per tent €5

MONEMVASIÁ

Set impregnably on a great eruption of rock connected to the mainland by a causeway, the Byzantine seaport of **MONEMVASIÁ** is a place of grand, haunted atmosphere. At the start of the thirteenth century it was the Byzantines' sole possession in the Morea, eventually being taken by the Franks in 1249 after three years of siege. Regained by the Byzantines as part of the ransom for the captured Guillaume II de Villehardouin, it served as the chief commercial port of the Despotate of the Morea. At its peak in the Byzantine era, Monemvasiá had a population of almost sixty thousand.

WHAT TO SEE AND DO

A causeway connects the mainland village of **Yéfira** to Monemvasiá. The twenty-minute walk provides some wonderful views, but there is also a free shuttle bus. The **Lower Town** once sheltered forty churches and over 800 homes, though today a single main street harbours most of the restored houses, plus cafés, tavernas and a scattering of shops. The foremost monument is the **Mitrópolis**, the cathedral built by Emperor Andronikos II Komnenos in 1293, and the largest medieval church in southern Greece. Across the square, the tenth-century domed church of **Áyios Pétros** was transformed by the Ottomans into a mosque and is now a small **museum** of local finds (Tues–Sun 8am–3pm; €2). Towards the sea is a third church, the **Khrysafítissa**, with its bell hanging from an old acacia tree in the courtyard. The climb to the **Upper Town** is highly worthwhile, not least for the solitude.

ARRIVAL AND INFORMATION

By bus Intercity buses arrive in the village of Yéfira on the mainland, from where a free daily shuttle leaves for Monemvasiá every 10–15min. For all onward destinations change in Spárti.

Destinations Athens (3–4 daily; 4hr).

Tourist information Malvasia Travel (by the bus stop) runs all tourist information services, and sells bus tickets.

ACCOMMODATION

All the budget accommodation is in Yéfira, with room prices in Monemvasiá going through the roof in summer.

Filoxenía Yéfira ☎ 27320 61716, ⓦ filoxenia -monemvasia.gr. A stylish hotel by the causeway with good views of the rock from the more expensive rooms. There is a beach in front but it's rather uninviting. Breakfast, a/c, satellite TV all included. Doubles €65

★**Malvasia** Kastro, Monemvasiá ☎ 27320 61160, ⓦ malvasiahotel-traditional.gr. A peaceful hotel on the rock, full of charm and retaining many traditional features. The views from the more expensive rooms are breathtaking, though to bag one of the two budget rooms in high season, you'll need to book months in advance. Breakfast, a/c, satellite TV, all included. Doubles €65

EATING

Matoula Kastro, Monemvasiá. This long-running family restaurant has plenty of fresh fish on offer, and a shady terrace on which to enjoy the food and the views. Main courses €12. Daily noon–11pm.

To Kanoni Kastro, Monemvasiá. A small and friendly place inside the castle with split-level seating, offering a variety of vistas from its balcony. Mains €7–10. April–Oct daily noon–midnight.

YÍTHIO

YÍTHIO, Sparta's ancient port, is the gateway to the dramatic Máni peninsula and one of the south's most attractive seaside towns. Its low-key harbour, with occasional ferries, has a graceful nineteenth-century waterside, while out to sea, tethered by a long narrow causeway, is the islet of **Marathoníssi** (ancient Kranae), where Paris and Helen of Troy spent their first night after her abduction from Sparta.

ARRIVAL AND DEPARTURE

By bus Buses from Athens and Spárti drop you close to the centre of town, at the bus station located on Vassiléos Pávlou.

Destinations Areópolis (4 daily; 30min); Athens (4–6 daily; 5hr); Kalamáta (2 daily; 2hr); Kórinthos (6 daily; 2hr 45min); Spárti (6 daily; 50min); Trípoli (3 daily; 2hr 30min).

ACCOMMODATION

★ **Meltemi** On the Yíthio–Areópoli road ☎ 27330 23260, ⓦ campingmeltemi.gr. Excellent campsite served by four buses from Yíthio (ask the driver to stop at the site), where facilities include pool with a bar, restaurant and free wi-fi. Also 2-person bungalows. Disabled access. Open April–Oct. Camping per person €6, plus per tent €5, bungalows €30

Saga Pension Tzanetáki ☎ 27330 23220, ⓦ sagapension .gr. Looks like a Greek apartment block, but it contains spacious and comfortable rooms, most with balconies overlooking the bay. There's also a popular restaurant downstairs. Breakfast €5. Doubles €50

EATING

Barba Sideris Ermoú & Xantháki. Now run by its third generation, this family taverna is right by the sea and specializes in skewered and grilled meat in *ladhókolla* (wrapping paper). Dishes from €10. Daily noon–midnight.

To Korali Platía Yíthiou. This is the place to do as the locals do – order some *ouzo* and watch the world go by from the corner of the square. Mains from €8. Daily noon–midnight.

THE MÁNI PENINSULA

The southernmost peninsula of Greece, the **Máni peninsula**, stretches from Yíthio in the east and Kalamáta in the west down to Cape Ténaro, mythical entrance to the underworld. It's a wild and arid landscape with an idiosyncratic culture and history: nowhere else in Greece seems so close to its medieval past. There are numerous opportunities for outdoor activities too.

Areópolis

The quickest way into the Máni is to take a bus from Yíthio to **AREÓPOLIS**, gateway to the so-called Inner Máni. For onward travel to the Outer Máni, a change at Ítylo is involved. Should you get stuck overnight, there are a few decent hotels.

ARRIVAL AND DEPARTURE

By bus The bus station is in the main square, Platía Athánatos.

Destinations Ítylo (3 daily; 20min); Yíthio (2–4 daily; 45min).

ACCOMMODATION

Hotel Kouris Main Square ☎ 27330 51340. Not the best-looking hotel facade in the Peloponnese but inside it's surprisingly pleasant and modern with soundproofed rooms all with balconies and galloping wi-fi. Doubles €50

Kardhamýli and Outer Máni

Various attractions lie to the north of Areópolis, along the 80km road to Kalamáta, which has views as dramatic and beautiful as any in Greece. There are numerous cobbled paths for hiking and a series of **small beaches**, beginning at **NÉO OÍTILO** with its fine sandy beach, and extending more or less through to Kardhamýli. The fishing village of **ÁYIOS NIKÓLAOS** has the best fish tavernas and rooms. **STOÚPA**, with possibly the best beach, is geared towards British tourism, with several small hotels, two **campsites**, supermarkets and tavernas.

KARDHAMÝLI, 8km north of Stoúpa, is a beautiful place, where orange groves descend to a long pebbly beach from the restored tower-house quarter of **ANO KARDHAMÝLI**. The former stomping ground of Bruce Chatwin (who wrote *The Songlines* here) and English author Patrick Leigh Fermor, who lived in neighbouring Kalamítsi, the village also formed the scenic backdrop to the film *Before Midnight* (2013), starring Ethan Hawke and Julie Delpy.

ARRIVAL AND INFORMATION

By bus Buses stop in Kardhamýli next to the main square.

Destinations Kalamáta (1–4 daily; 1hr); Ítylo (Mon–Fri 1 daily; 1hr).

ACCOMMODATION AND EATING

Iphigenia Rooms Kardhamýli ☎ 27210 73648. Just 100m from the seafront, this makes a wonderful base for exploring the area, with apartments featuring small kitchenettes and bougainvillea-draped balconies – some have great views over the Messenian Gulf. No breakfast. Doubles €50

★ **Lela's** Kardhamýli. Run by Patrick Leigh Fermor's former cook, *Lela's* is ideal for a delicious, home-cooked meal with a menu that changes regularly. Go early to grab a table with the best views. Mains €8. Daily noon–11pm.

14

14

OLYMPIA

The historic resonance of **OLYMPIA**, which for over a millennium hosted the Panhellenic Games, is rivalled only by Delphi or Mycenae. Its site, too, ranks with this company, for although the ruins are confusing, the setting is as perfect as could be imagined: a luxuriant valley of wild olive and plane trees beside the twin rivers of Alfiós and Kladheós, overlooked by the pine-covered Mount Kronion. The modern village of **ARHÉA OLYMBÍA** is adjacent to the site.

WHAT TO SEE AND DO

The entrance to the **ancient site** (summer: daily 8am–8pm; winter daily 8am–3pm; €12 including museum; ☏ 26240 22517) leads along the west side of the sacred precinct wall, past a group of public and official buildings. Here the fifth-century BC sculptor Pheidias was responsible for creating the great gold-and-ivory cult statue in the focus of the precinct, the great Doric **Temple of Zeus**. The smaller **Temple of Hera**, behind, was the first built here; prior to its completion in the seventh century BC, the sanctuary had only open-air altars. Rebuilt in the Doric style in the sixth century BC, it's the most complete structure on the site. However, it's the 177m track of the **Stadium** itself that makes sense of Olympia: the start and finish lines are still there, as are the judges' thrones in the middle and seating banked to each side, which once accommodated up to thirty thousand spectators. Finally, in the **archeological museum**, the centrepiece is the statuary from the Temple of Zeus, displayed in the vast main hall. Most famous of the individual sculptures is the **Hermes of Praxiteles**, dating from the fourth century BC: one of the best preserved of all classical sculptures, it retains traces of its original paint.

ARRIVAL AND INFORMATION

By bus Most people arrive via Pýrgos, which has frequent buses to Olympia. The bus stop is at the end of Praxitéles Kondhýli in Arhéa Olymbía.

Destinations Pýrgos (hourly; 45min); Trípoli (3 daily; 3hr).

Guided Tour You can download a free Olympia self-guided tour mp3 (48min) from ⓦ elladaguides.com.

ACCOMMODATION

Camping Diana ☏ 26240 22314, ⓦ campingdiana.gr. The closest campsite, 1km uphill from the site, has some good facilities (pool, internet though mostly at reception, café bar, currency exchange), but there's not much to do except visit Olympia. Open all year. Per person €7, plus per tent €5

Neda Karamanlí 1 ☏ 27210 22563, ⓦ hotelneda.gr. Central and quiet hotel that offers a lot for its price: bathtubs, large pool, roof garden (though the view is nothing to write home about) and private parking, which is difficult in Olympia. Doubles €60

EATING

★**Aegeon** Yeoryíou Doúma 4. Unassuming taverna with a welcoming atmosphere, offering everything from baked lamb to pizza – its vegetarian stews can tempt the most committed carnivores. It's a bit pricier than other local restaurants, with mains around €9, but worth it. April–Nov daily 8am–midnight.

PÁTRA

The city of **PÁTRA** is the third largest in the country, and connects the mainland to Italy and the Ionian Islands. Unlike many other destinations in the Peloponnese, Pátra is a thriving working city and has a life of its own which extends far beyond tourism, despite the number of travellers passing through. There are enough sites to fill a day's sightseeing, in particular the **twin churches of Áyios Andhréas** and **the tomb of St Andrew** who was martyred in Pátra, though most people pass through quickly. The city is best enjoyed in the evening, when thousands of party-going university students transform the streets. At the heart of the drinking scene are the streets of Ayíou Nikoláou, Ríga Feréou and Pandanássis, all pedestrianized and crammed with bars. Pátra's **carnival** (ⓦ carnivalpatras.gr) is the best-known in Greece.

ARRIVAL AND DEPARTURE

By bus Buses arrive at the KTEL Achaïa bus station next to the Pátra Infocenter at Agorá Argýri.

Destinations Athens (every 30min; 2hr 30min–3hr); Dhiakoftó for Odondotós train (4 daily; 1hr 30min); Ioánnina (2 daily; 5hr); Kalamáta (2 daily; 4hr); Pýrgos (6–10 daily; 2hr); Thessaloníki (3 daily; 7hr).

By ferry Ferries arrive at Néo Limáni, south of the city. Bus #18 (€1.20) takes you from the port to the centre, while a taxi costs €5.

Destinations Ancona (7–8 weekly; 17–24hr); Bari (2–3 weekly; 17hr); Brindisi (1 daily; 16hr); Corfu (1 daily; 6–7hr); Igoumenítsa (1 daily; 8–10hr); Itháki (1 daily; 6hr); Kefaloniá (1 daily; 2hr 10min); Trieste (1 weekly; 29hr 30min); Venice (1–2 weekly; 32hr).

INFORMATION

Tourist information Infocenter Agorá Argýri, Ayíou Andréou 12 (daily 7.30am–9pm; ☎ 2610 461740, ⓦ patrasinfo.com), is one of the best, most helpful and well-manned tourist offices in Greece.
Tourist Police Goúnari 52, by the Italian ferry terminal (☎ 2610 455 833).

ACCOMMODATION

Adonis Kapsáli 9 ☎ 2610 224 213, ⓦ adoniscityhotel.gr. High-rise hotel straight out of a J.G. Ballard novel, that is showing its age, but is conveniently situated by the bus station. It's also the cheapest option in town. Doubles €45
Delfíni Iróon Polytechníou 102 ☎ 2610 421 001, ⓦ delfini-hotel.gr. North of the centre, but with frequent buses into town, this is a generic, functional budget hotel that is amenable to bargaining over its room prices off-season. Doubles €50

The centre and north

Central and northern Greece has a multifaceted character, encompassing both ancient and modern, from the mythical home of the gods on **Mount Olympus** to the urban splendour of **Thessaloníki**, and a plethora of landscapes. The highlights lie at the fringes: site of the ancient oracle **Delphi**, and further northwest at the otherworldly rock-monasteries of **Metéora**. Access to these monasteries is through **Kalambáka**, beyond which the **Katára pass** over the Píndhos mountains provides a stunning backdrop. En route lies **Métsovo**, perhaps the easiest location for a taste of mountain life, though blatantly commercialized. Nearby **Ioánnina**, once the stronghold of the notorious Ali Pasha, still retains a lot of character. To the south, closer to Athens, is the monastery of **Ósios Loukás**, one of Greece's finest Byzantine buildings and worth a detour en route to Delphi.

DELPHI

With its position on a high terrace overlooking a great gorge, in turn dwarfed by the ominous crags of Parnassós, it's easy to see why the ancients believed the extraordinary site of **DELPHI**, 150km northwest of Athens, to be the centre of the Earth. But what confirmed this status was the discovery of a chasm that exuded strange vapours and reduced all comers to frenzied, incoherent and obviously prophetic mutterings. For over a thousand years a steady stream of pilgrims toiled their way up the dangerous mountain paths to seek divine direction, until the oracle eventually expired with the demise of paganism in the fourth century AD. Today it makes for a pleasant day-trip from the capital.

14

WHAT TO SEE AND DO

You enter the **Sacred Precinct of Apollo** (daily: summer 8am–8pm; winter 8am–3pm; €12, including museum) by way of a small agora, enclosed by ruins of Roman porticoes and shops selling votive offerings. The paved **Sacred Way** begins after a few stairs, zigzagging uphill between the foundations of memorials and treasuries to the **Temple of Apollo**. The theatre and stadium used for the main events of the Pythian games are on terraces above the temple. The **theatre**, built in the fourth century BC, was closely connected with Dionysus, god of drama and wine. A steep path leads up through pine groves to the stadium, which was banked with stone seats in Roman times.

The **museum** (summer Mon & Tues 10am–5pm, Wed–Sun 8am–8pm; winter Tues–Sun 8am–3pm) contains a collection of ancient sculpture matched only by finds on the Acropolis in Athens; the most famous exhibit is *The Charioteer*, one of the few surviving bronzes of the fifth century BC. Following the road east of the sanctuary towards Aráhova, you reach a sharp bend. To the left, the celebrated **Castalian spring** still flows from a cleft in the cliffs, where visitors to Delphi were obliged to purify themselves. Across and below the

14

road from the spring is the **Marmaria** or Sanctuary of Athena Pronoia (same hours as main site; free), the "Guardian of the Temple". The precinct's most conspicuous building is the **Tholos**, a fourth-century BC rotunda whose purpose remains a mystery. Above the Marmaria, a **gymnasium** also dates from the fourth century BC, though it was later enlarged by the Romans.

ARRIVAL AND DEPARTURE

By bus The small bus station is on Pávlou & Fridheríkis, at the opposite end of the modern town of Delphi to the archeological site.
Destinations Athens (4 daily; 3hr); Pátra (1–2 daily; 3hr); Thessaloníki (1 daily; 5hr).

ACCOMMODATION

Apollon Camping 1.5km west towards Ámfissa ⊕ 22650 82750, ⦿ apolloncamping.gr. The closest campsite to Delphi with a bus stop outside. Facilities include bungalows (sleeping 2), a swimming pool, minimarket and a restaurant with views towards the Corinthian Gulf. Open all year. Dorms **€11.50**, camping/person **€7.50**, plus per tent **€3.50**, bungalows **€23**
Dimákos Rooms Pávlou & Fridheríkis 55, Delphi ⊕ 22650 82080/82323. Most rooms at this guesthouse have spectacular views towards the valley, and all have a/c and access to wi-fi, but no breakfast. Open April–Oct. Doubles **€25**
Sibylla Pávlou & Fredheríkis 9, Delphi ⊕ 22650 82335, ⦿ sibylla-hotel.gr. Located close to the archeological site, this hotel has spotless and comfortable rooms, and the staff are helpful. There's also a basic self-service breakfast available for €1.50. Doubles **€35**

EATING

Taverna Vakhos Apóllonos 31. This taverna has a wonderful setting and serves filling, home-made dishes including a choice of vegan and vegetarian options and wine from Parnassos. Main courses €6–8. Daily noon–11pm.

KALAMBÁKA AND METÉORA

Few places are more exciting to arrive at than **KALAMBÁKA** and the neighbouring village of **Kastráki**, about twenty minutes' walk away. Your eye is immediately drawn to the weird grey cylinders of rock overhead – these are the outlying monoliths of the extraordinary valley of **Metéora**, familiar to many through films

such as the James Bond classic *For Your Eyes Only*. The earliest religious communities in the valley emerged during the late tenth century, when hermits made their homes in the caves that score many of the rocks. In 1336 they were joined by two monks from Mount Áthos, one of whom established the first monastery here.

WHAT TO SEE AND DO

Today, the four most visited monasteries are essentially museums. Only two others, Ayías Triádhos and Ayíou Stefánou, continue to function with a primarily religious purpose. Each monastery levies an **admission charge** of €3 and operates a strict **dress code**: skirts for women (supplied at the monasteries), long trousers for men and covered arms for both sexes.

Beyond the monastery of **Ayíou Stefánou**, firmly planted on a massive pedestal, stretches a chaos of spikes, cones and stubbier, rounded cliffs. Visiting the monasteries demands a full day, which means staying two nights nearby. Opening times vary because of particular saints' days, masses, fast days etc, so check before you leave.

Ayíou Nikoláou Anápavsa and Varlaám

From Kastráki, the fourteenth-century **Ayíou Nikoláou Anápavsa** (Sat–Thurs: April–Oct 9am–3.30pm; Nov–March 9am–2pm; ⊕ 2432 022375) is reached first. Some 250m past the car park and stairs to Ayíou Nikoláou, a clear path leads up a ravine between assorted monoliths; soon, at a fork, you've the option of bearing left (for Megálou Meteórou; see below) or right to **Varlaám** (April–Oct Sat–Thurs 9am–4pm; Nov–March Sat–Wed 9am–3pm; ⊕ 2432 022277), which is one of the oldest and most beautiful monasteries in the valley.

Megálou Meteórou and Roussánou

From the fork below Varlaám the path also takes you northwest to **Megálou Meteórou** (April–Oct Wed–Mon 9am–5pm; Nov–March Thurs–Mon

9am–3pm; ☎2432 022278), the grandest of the monasteries and also the highest. Next you follow trails until you reach the signed access path for the tiny, compact convent of **Roussánou** (Thurs–Tues: April–Oct 9am–5pm; Nov–March 9am–2pm; ☎2432 022649).

Ayías Triádhos and Ayíou Stefánou

It's less than a half-hour from Roussánou to the vividly frescoed **Ayías Triádhos** (April–Oct Fri–Wed 9am–5pm; Nov–March Fri–Tues 10am–4pm; ☎2432 022220), approached up 130 steps carved through a tunnel in the rock. The convent of **Ayíou Stefánou** (Tues–Sun: April–Oct 9.30am–1.30pm & 3.30–5.30pm; Nov–March 9am–1pm & 3–5pm; ☎2432 022279), the last of the monasteries, lies a further fifteen minutes' walk east of Ayías Triádhos; bombed in World War II, it's the one to omit if you've run out of time.

ARRIVAL AND DEPARTURE

By train Kalambáka train station is located 100m south of the bus station.
Destinations Athens (1 daily; 5hr); Thessaloníki (1 daily; 3hr).
By bus Buses arrive at the bus station in Kalambáka on Ikonómou. All long-distance buses involve a change at Tríkala.
Destinations Athens to Tríkala (6 daily; 4hr 30min); Thessaloníki to Tríkala (4–5 daily; 2hr 45min); Tríkala (hourly; 30min).

ACCOMMODATION

Hotel Metéora Ploutárhou 14 ☎24320 22367, ⊚hotel -meteora.gr. The pick of the Kalambáka hotels. Great value for the location and high standard of service: the en-suite rooms come with wi-fi, a/c and delicious breakfasts. Doubles €40
★ **Hotel Tsikeli** Kastráki ☎24320 22438, ⊚tsikelihotel .gr. A wonderful, relaxing guesthouse, with traditionally furnished rooms, free wi-fi and stunning views. Breakfast is served in the lush garden. Doubles €45
Plakias Kastráki ☎24320 22504, ⊚meteora-plakias.gr. A homely feel accompanies these clean and crisp en-suite rooms, not far from the main square – ask for an upper-floor room for views of Metéora. Breakfast included. Doubles €35
Vrachos Camping At the entrance to Kastráki ☎24320 22293, ⊚campingkastraki.com. A well-equipped shady campsite with a large swimming pool (with view of the rocks) and good restaurant. Per person €8

EATING

Parádhissos Kastráki. This traditional taverna offers a spacious terrace with beautiful views and a variety of barbecued specialities that are very popular with locals. Service can get rather overwhelmed when busy. Mains €6–8. Daily noon–11pm.
Stéfanos Kastráki. A traditional coal-grill taverna, with a forecourt shaded by a large awning and surrounded by flower beds. It prides itself on the freshness of the ingredients – the lamb kebab is particularly recommended. Mains €5–7. Daily noon–midnight.

IOÁNNINA

The fortifications of **IOÁNNINA**'s old town, former capital of the Albanian Muslim chieftain Ali Pasha, are punctuated by towers and minarets. From this base Ali, "the Lion of Ioánnina", prised from the Ottoman Empire a fiefdom encompassing much of western Greece. Disappointingly, most of the city is modern and undistinguished; however, the fortifications of Ali's citadel, the **Kástro**, survive more or less intact. Apart from this, the most enjoyable quarter is the old **bazaar** area, outside the citadel's main gate.

On the far side of the lake from Ioánnina, the island of **Nissí** is served by water-buses (every 30min; €2) from the quay northwest of the Froúrio. Its village, founded during the sixteenth century, is flanked by several beautiful, diminutive monasteries, with the best thirteenth-century frescoes in the **Monastery of Filanthropinón**.

ARRIVAL AND INFORMATION

By bus The local and Intercity KTEL station is at Yeoryíou Papandhreou.
Destinations Athens (5–6 daily; 8hr); Igoumenítsa (6–8 daily; 2hr 30min); Pátra (2 daily; 3hr 30min); Thessaloníki (5–6 daily; 9hr 30min).
Tourist office Dhodhónis 39 (Mon–Fri 7am–3pm; ☎26510 41868) can provide information on the whole Epirus region.

ACCOMMODATION

Filyra Andhroníkou Paleológou 18 ☎26510 83560, ⊚hotelfilyra.gr. Five bright, modern two-person studios with small kitchenettes, ideal for self-catering, located in the historic Kástro – with its own car park, a big plus in the Old City. Studios €65

14

14

Kendrikon Kolétti 5 ☎ 26510 71771. Centrally located stone mansion with rooms sporting traditional hardwood floors and furniture scoring high on atmosphere without compromising on modern facilities, such as flat-screen TV, wi-fi and a/c. Offers a two-course lunch for €10. Doubles €50

EATING

Fysa Roufa Avéroff 55. This long-standing traditional restaurant specializes in tripe soup (*patsa*) and serves large portions of oven-baked dishes, which you can inspect yourself in the kitchen. Very popular with locals. Mains €8–10. 24hr.

★**To Souvlaki tou Vounou** Amfithea. A 10min drive from the town centre by car or taxi, this grill taverna is in a fantastic location by the lake and is a top recommendation by locals. Athens prices, but worth it for the food and location. Free wi-fi. Mains €10–12. Daily 7pm–2am.

THESSALONÍKI

THESSALONÍKI, Greece's second-largest city, feels more Central European and modern than Athens. During the Byzantine era, it was also the second city after Constantinople, enjoying a cultural "Golden Age" until the Ottoman conquest in 1430. As recently as the 1920s, the city's population was as mixed as any in the Balkans: besides the Greeks there were Turks, who had been in occupation for close on five centuries, Slavs, Albanians, and the largest European **Jewish** community in the Mediterranean – 80,000 at its peak. Finally, with a student population of 120,000, the city's **nightlife** is buzzing, with many bars and clubs concentrated either in the regenerated warehouse area of **Ladhádhika** by the port or further up in **Valaorítou Street**.

WHAT TO SEE AND DO

Thessaloníki boasts many excellent sights – including a superb archeological museum and some lovely frescoed Byzantine churches – but the most obvious pleasures of Greece's second city are in its street life: its myriad bars, first-rate yet affordable restaurants and pumping clubs.

The Archeological Museum

The renovated **Archeological Museum** (daily: April–Oct 8am–8pm; Nov–March 9am–4pm; €8) is on Andhronikou 6, a few paces from the White Tower. The museum's highlights are the "Macedonian gold" rooms on the ground floor, containing precious finds from various tombs in the area. There are startling amounts of gold and silver – masks, crowns, necklaces, earrings, bracelets – all of extraordinary craftsmanship.

The Museum of Byzantine Culture and White Tower

The well-curated **Museum of Byzantine Culture** at 2 Stratou Ave (same hours as the Archeological Museum; €8) is also worth a look for its finely preserved tombs, splendid mosaics, icons and jewellery. Close by, on the waterfront, Thessaloníki's enduring landmark, the **White Tower** (daily April–Oct 8am–8pm, Nov–March 9am–4pm; €4), the last surviving bastion of the city's medieval walls, tells the story of the city through a high-tech multimedia exhibit. Go to the top for an unforgettable view of the city.

Churches

Among the city's many **churches**, the unmissable ones are the **Rotónda**, in the east of the city, originally a Roman rotunda built in 306 AD, decorated with golden mosaics (winter daily 8am–5pm; summer Mon–Sat 10am–4pm, Tues & Fri also 6–9pm; €2); **Áyios Dhimítrios** (built originally in 413 AD, though the current building dates from 1948), with several seventh-century mosaics and the relics of the saint; the eighth-century **Ayía Sofía**, a few blocks west of "Rotónda", with superb mosaics of the Ascension and the Virgin Enthroned, and nearby **Panayía Ahiropíitos** (fifth century AD), the largest Paleochristian church in the Balkans (all churches open 8am–7pm; free).

COMBINED MUSEUM TICKET

You can pay to enter each site individually or buy a **combined ticket** for €15 (valid for three days), which gives entry to the Archeological Museum, the Museum of Byzantine Culture, the White Tower and the Roman Forum: it can be bought at any of the sites.

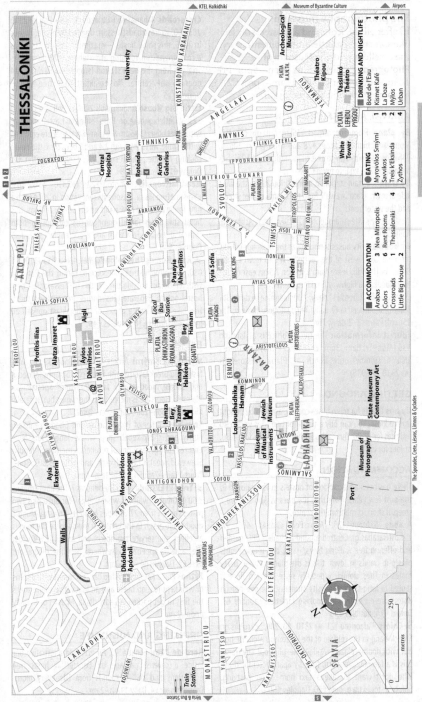

▲ KTEL Halkidhíki   ▲ Museum of Byzantine Culture   ▲ Airport

THESSALONÍKI

14

■ DRINKING AND NIGHTLIFE
Bord de l'Eau	1	Mylos	2
Kismet Kafé	4	Urban	4
La Doze	5		

● EATING
Myrovólos Smýrni	5	Treis k'Eksínda	4
Savvíkos	3	Zýthos	2
Nea Mitrópolis	1		

■ ACCOMMODATION
Arabas	3	Rent Rooms	6
Colors	6	Thessaloníki	2
Crossroads	1		
Little Big House	2		

▲ The Sporades, Crete, Lésvos, Límnos & Cyclades

▼ Véria & Bus Station

0 ___ 250 metres

The photography museum

If, after all the icons and alabaster, you feel like something a little more contemporary, the excellent portside **Museum of Photography** (Tues–Thurs 10am–5pm, Fri 10am–10pm, Sat & Sun 11am–7pm; €2) is worth a few hours' exploration.

ARRIVAL AND INFORMATION

By plane From the airport, 16km out on the Néa Moudhaniá highway, buses #78 and #78N (every 30min, 24hr/day; 45min) run to the train station and KTEL bus terminal (€2). Taxi into town €20.

By train The train station at Monastiriou 28, on the west side of town, is a short walk from the central grid of streets and the waterfront.

Destinations Alexandroupolis (2 daily; 6hr); Athens (6 daily; 5–6hr).

By bus Most city buses terminate at the Makedonia KTEL terminal, 5km west of the centre (taxi into town €5–6). Buses for Halkidikí leave from a station 7.5km east on the Néa Moudhaniá highway (taxi into town €12).

Destinations Athens (11 daily; 7hr); Ioánnina (6 daily; 3hr 30min); Igoumenítsa (2 daily; 4hr); Litóhoro (hourly; 1hr 15min); Pátra (2–3 daily; 7hr).

Tourist information The tourist office is at Tsimiskí 136 (Mon–Fri 8am–3pm; ☎ 2310 221 100) and there's also a summer-only booth at Platía Aristotelous (☎ 2310 222 935).

GETTING AROUND

By bus Tickets for town buses cost €1, and can be bought from a kiosk. You can buy a ticket for two trips within 70 minutes for €1.20; three trips within 90 minutes for €1.30; or four for €2.

ACCOMMODATION

There has been an explosion of hostels in Thessaloníki in the past few years. Note that the ones in Ano Poli are a steep, if short, climb from the centre.

Arabas Sahtouri 28, Ano Poli ☎ 6944 466 97, ⊚ hostelarabas.gr. Centred around a shaded BBQ garden and offering free walking tours, game and movie nights plus pub crawls in town, this is the place to meet party mates in Thessaloníki, especially since the top floor is rented to long-term university students. The five-person dorms are en suite with cooking facilities. Laundry €3. Dorms €14, doubles €38

★**Colors** Valaoritou 21 ☎ 2310 502280, ⊚ colors.gr. Smack-bang in the middle of the Valaoritou nightlife hub but with double-glazed windows keeping out any noise, this is a fabulous, modern, friendly apart-hotel for those who don't want to take a taxi home after partying. Sofabeds for extra people €20. Doubles €50

Crossroads Athanassíou Dhiákou 1, Ano Poli ☎ 2310 203 700, ⊚ crossroadsthess.gr. Opened by owner Yorgos in 2015, this small hostel – maximum ten guests – has a cosy, friendship-forming atmosphere. #23 bus comes straight from the train station (stop Ayios Pavlos), #24 goes to the centre. No breakfast, but free coffee. Dorms €15

Little Big House Andokídhou 24, Ano Poli ☎ 2313 014 323, ⊚ littlebighouse.gr. Busy, efficient hostel and café with quiet hours (3–5pm & 11pm–7am) that are enforced with a smile. All rooms with 2,4 and 6 beds have their own cooking facilities, shower and WC. Breakfast buffet €2. Dorms €17, doubles €48

Nea Mitrópolis Syngroú 22 ☎ 2310 530 363, ⊚ neametropolis.gr. Despite its renovation in 2014 with a new lobby area and new paint on the stucco ceilings, this hotel still oozes faded grandeur. Its location is both central and quiet. Free wi-fi and a/c. Breakfast included. Doubles €40

★**Rent Rooms Thessaloniki** Melenikou 9 ☎ 2310 204 080, ⊚ rentrooms-thessaloniki.com. Facing the Rotonda with a fabulous outside terrace, this is Thessaloníki's best hostel option. Separate girls' dorms, free walking tours, free bike rental and a choice of six breakfast options all included. Dorms €18, doubles €49

EATING

Myrovólos Smýrni Arcade off Komninón 32. An old-fashioned Greek taverna with faded photographs for decor, and simple, good-quality food (Smyrniot specialities). Mains €8. Hours are as mercurial as the owner, but generally Mon–Sat noon–2am, Sun noon–4pm.

Savvíkos Corner of Polytechníou and Dhodhekaníssou. Classy and shiny kebab shop whose long hours have ensured that generations of revellers remember it fondly. Skewered meat €1.80, chicken and pitta €3.80. Mon–Thurs 11am–7am Fri & Sat 11am–9am.

★**Treis ki Eksinda** Ayías Theodhoras 7. The name means 3.60 in Greek – which is what you pay for ouzo plus two plates chosen from 27 varieties of meze. An astonishingly good-value *ouzeri* in the centre of town where the food is excellent, the service top-notch, and mains (€5–6) cost the same as appetizers elsewhere. Half litre of draught beer €2. Daily noon–12.30am.

Zýthos Platía Katoúni 5. A hip bar-restaurant with dozens of well-kept foreign beers and an innovative menu that's the first to get packed in Ladhádhika. Mains €6–8. Daily noon–2am.

DRINKING AND NIGHTLIFE

Bord de l'Eau Egnatía 45. An arty and alternative bar inside a covered passage on Egnatía. It hosts free exhibitions and chilled sounds from DJs every night. Draught beer €4. Daily 11am–2am.

Kismet Kafé Katoúni 11. Intimate and cosy, with hard DJ sounds inside, while the candlelit tables outside make a perfect spot for a relaxed drink. Daily 9pm–late.
La Doze Vilara 1. Dead in the middle of the hip Valaoritou area and flanked by many more bars, this is the one that packs them to the rafters, offering the best cocktails in the area (€8.50). Tues–Sun 8pm–late.
Mýlos Andhréou Yeoryíou 56 ⓦ mylos.gr. The main town music venue is the *Mýlos* complex, in an old flour mill by the port, where you'll find bars, exhibition galleries and a club occasionally plying *rembétika*. Daily 10am–late.
Urban Zefksidhos 7. This was the first café/bar in what has become a pedestrian, sit-down-with-your-mates-and-a-beer zone below Ayía Sofía. Quirky decor that reminds you of Budapest's ruin pubs and a delicious €6 mojito. Daily 10am–4am.

DIRECTORY

Consulates Australia, Frágon 13 ☎ 2310 553 355; Canada, Koundouriótou 19 ☎ 2310 256 350; UK, Aristotélous 21 ☎ 2310 278 006; US, Tsimiskí 43 ☎ 2310 242 905. If you need a visa for onward Balkan travel, it's best to get it in Athens.
Hospital Yenikó Kendrikó, Ethnikís Amýnis 41 ☎ 2310 211 221/2.
Post office Vasiléos Irakliou 38 (Mon–Fri 7.30am–8.30pm, Sat 7.30am–2pm, Sun 9am–1.30pm).

HALKIDHIKÍ

When entering **HALKIDHIKÍ** you leave behind rocky outcrops, stunted shrubs and salt cedars by the seashore and say hello to a French Mediterranean landscape – all chestnuts, oaks, beeches and poplars. Many travellers insist that no other place in Greece can boast beaches like Halkidhikí's, and with 550km of coastline over its three peninsulas of **Kassándhra**, **Sithonía** and **Mount Áthos**, they may well be right. Kassándhra, being closer to Thessaloníki, is the more developed, while Sithonía, further out, is the quieter location.

WHAT TO SEE AND DO

Although for quite some time Halkidhikí has been the exclusive domain of package tourists, recent initiatives by local tour operators have developed a range of backpacker-oriented activities including mountain biking, watersports, hiking and horseriding (ⓦ gohalkidiki.com).

If clubbing is your scene, then the town of **Kallithéa** in **KASSÁNDHRA** makes a good destination. Just 1km outside the town no fewer than four hangar-like superclubs line up to compete nightly for your euros – at weekends, when the Thessaloníki crowd descends en masse, partying carries on nonstop from Saturday afternoon to Sunday evening. Kallithéa also hosts an unmissable summer cultural event, the **Sáni Festival** (July & Aug; ⓦ sanifestival.gr), bringing together world-class rock and jazz acts, as well as Greek superstars.

For a more tranquil, romantic stay, sandy, scenic **SITHONÍA** has hidden coves and secret beachheads that provide privacy even in high season. The towns of **Nikíti** and **Neos Marmarás** are easily accessible, though you'll need your own car to explore further.

Although **MOUNT ATHOS** itself is out of bounds to women – a ban that extends to all female animals including chickens and cows – both genders can visit **Ouranoúpolis**, the last Greek town before the monastic border. Known as the "City of Heaven", it's surprisingly loud and expensive, but is a great place from which to take a trip on one of the two daily boats that circumnavigate the peninsula. If you want to stay overnight, however, you're better off heading to nearby **Ierissós** with its enormous Blue Flag beach and cheap municipal campsite.

The region's most interesting archeological site is the partly and sensitively restored **STÁYIRA** on Halkidhiki's east coast, the birthplace of Aristotle (Tues–Sun 8am–3pm; free), conveniently situated next to the green, unspoilt village of **OLYMBIÁDA**.

ARRIVAL AND DEPARTURE

By bus KTEL buses for Halkidhikí leave from a station 7.5km east of Thessaloníki on the Néa Moudhaniá highway. To get there, take bus #45/#45A which starts at the Makedonia bus station, 5km west of Thessaloníki city centre, stopping along Egnatias street en route. Buses for Olymbiáda also leave from the Makedonia station; almost all city buses going west stop there.
Destinations Kallithéa (1–12 daily; 1hr 30min); Nikíti/Néos Marmarás (3–5 daily; 1hr 45min); Olymbiáda (2 daily; 2hr); Ouranoúpolis (6 daily; 2hr 30min).

14

14

Car rental Local operator Drive Hellas rents cars from €18/day and has offices in Thessaloníki, the airport and the Halkidhikí KTEL station (☎ 23104 72600, ⓦ drive-hellas .com).

ACCOMMODATION

★ **Armenistís Camping Armenistís** Sithonía ☎ 23750 91497, ⓦ armenistis.gr. Set on its own sheltered beach opposite the jagged-tooth peak of Mount Athos, this is more of a village than a campsite, with an open-air cinema, ATM, basket-ball court, spa and watersports. It also offers dorms in large safari canvas tents. Bus from Thessaloníki stops outside the campsite. Open late April to Sept. Per person €7.80, plus per tent €7.80

Blue Dream Sáni ☎ 23750 31249, ⓦ campingbluedream .gr. High-quality campsite right on the beach with restaurant and lively beach bar; conveniently situated for the Sáni Festival. Open May–Sept. Per person €8.50, plus per tent €7.50

Ierissós Camping Ierissós ☎ 23770 21125. Cheap, municipal campsite that won't win first prize for facilities or services, but its location, on a massive, sandy beach, makes up for any shortcomings. Per person €4.50, plus per tent €4

★ **Liotopi** Olymbiáda ☎ 23760 51257/51255, ⓦ hotel -liotopi.gr. A family-run hotel at the entrance to the village with lovely rooms and idiosyncratic owners. Free cooking demonstrations show you what you can eat at the excellent nearby *Akroyáli* taverna that belongs to the hotel. The half-board option (€94 for two) is highly recommended and includes a cooked breakfast and à la carte dinner at the *Akroyáli*. April–Oct. Doubles €58

★ **M.E.L.I** Kallithéa ☎ 23740 24220, ⓦ hotelmeli.gr. One of the best-located hotels in Kallithéa: set in a quiet backstreet two blocks from the highway, and also near the nightlife epicentre. Huge rooms with kitchenette and ultra-fast wi-fi and a large common pool with jacuzzi. The young owners are helpful and friendly. May–Sept. Doubles €65

White Rabbit Guest House Psakoúdhia, at the crossroads to Ormyliá ☎ 23710 52682, ⓦ whiterabbit.gr.

Run by students, Halkidhikí's only hostel is in a charming, modern villa 800m from the wonderful beach and village of Psakoúdhia. With a drum set in the common room, this is more of a retreat than a rowdy backpackers' joint – songbirds twitter in the large garden and psychedelic paintings adorn the walls. Bikes and scooters for rent. Breakfast €3. Dorms €15, doubles €40

EATING

★ **Anthoúlas** Kriopiyí, Kassándhra. A real find and definitely worth the schlep to the tiny village of Kriopiyí, 5km south of Kallithéa. With a Balkan ambience, good fresh seafood and the best moussaka west of Istanbul, this small family restaurant keeps winning Greek food awards, with good reason: the local suppliers are listed in the menu. Mains €12–15. May–Oct Mon–Fri 5pm–midnight, Sat & Sun 1pm–1am.

VERGÍNA (ANCIENT AEGAE)

In 1977, archeologists discovered the burial sanctuary of the ancient Macedonian dynasty, including Alexander the Great's father and son, at the village of **VERGÍNA**. The four **Royal Tombs** (Mon noon–8pm, Tues–Sun 8am–8pm; €8) constitute the focus of an unmissable underground museum. It features delicate gold and silver funerary artefacts, the facades of the tombs, the kings' armours, frescoes (uniquely, with perspective) and the ashes of the deceased royals in ornate ossuaries.

ARRIVAL AND DEPARTURE

By bus It's easy to make this a day-trip from Thessaloníki: hourly buses run to Véria (1hr; €9.80 return), from where onward buses (10–12 daily; €3.20 return) cover the final 20min to modern Vergína village. A taxi from Véria to Vergína costs €15 one-way.

CLIMBING MOUNT OLYMPUS

Four to five hours' walking along the well-marked, scenic E4 long-distance path up the Mavrólongos canyon brings you to **Priónia**, from where there's a sharper three-hour trail-climb to the *Spilios Agapitos* refuge. It's best to stay overnight here, as you need to make an early start for the three-hour ascent to **Mýtikas**, the highest peak (2917m) – the summit frequently clouds over towards midday. The path continues behind the refuge, reaching a signposted fork above the tree line in about an hour; straight on, then right, takes you to Mýtikas via the ridge known as Kakí Skála, while the other fork, an abrupt right, continues for an hour to the *Yiosos Apostolidhis* hut. From the hut there's an enjoyable loop down to the **Gortsiá** trailhead and from there back down into the Mavrólongos canyon, via the medieval monastery of Ayíou Dhionysíou. If you are short of time, you can hike the short 30-minute trail along Enipéas Gorge to the village's water reservoir.

MOUNT OLYMPUS AND LITÓHORO

Highest, most magical and most dramatic of all Greek mountains, **Mount Olympus** – the mythical seat of the gods – rears straight up nearly 3000m from the shores of the Thermaïkós Gulf. Dense forests cover its lower slopes and its wild flowers are gorgeous. If you're well equipped, no special expertise is necessary to reach the top between mid-June and October, though it's a long hard pull, and its weather is notoriously fickle. The usual approach to Mount Olympus is via **LITÓHORO** on the eastern slopes, a pleasant village in a magnificent mountain setting. You can buy a proper **map** of the range in Athens, Thessaloníki or Litóhoro.

ARRIVAL AND DEPARTURE

By bus Litóhoro's KTEL terminal is just south of the main square.
Destinations Thessaloníki (hourly; 1hr 15min).

ACCOMMODATION

Enipéas Litóhoro ☎ 23530 84328, ⌨ hotel-enipeas.gr. This hotel, with a central location and balconied rooms with views over a gorge, is the best-value accommodation in the village. Free wi-fi. Breakfast €5. Doubles **€50**
Olympios Zeus Pláka Litohórou 10km from Litóhoro ☎ 23520 22115. Shady upmarket beach campsite at the foot of Mt Olympus with bungalows to rent (sleeping 2), a pizzeria, grill restaurant and beach bar. Camping/person **€7**, plus per tent **€4**, bungalows **€60**
Summit Zero Gritsa, 5km from Litóhoro ☎ 23520 61406, ⌨ summitzero.gr. You can combine a stay by the sea and a climb up Mount Olympus by staying at this funky hostel. The whole place is highly congenial plus they organize hikes and mountain-bike rides on Mount Olympus. Dorms **€15**

★ TREAT YOURSELF

Gastrodrómio en Olympo Ayíou Nikoláou 36, Litóhoro ☎ 23520 21300, ⌨ gastrodromio.gr. Who would have thought that Litóhoro would sport one of the most acclaimed restaurants in Greece? If you make it there, splash out on the casseroles made with locally sourced meats and mountain herbs, fresh fish or a platter with thirty different types of Greek cheeses. For those on a budget, the three-course menu starts from €10. Booking recommended July & Aug. Daily noon–late.

The Cyclades

The **Cyclades** (pronounced with a hard C throughout) is the most satisfying Greek archipelago for island-hopping, with its vibrant capital on **Sýros**. The majority of the islands are arid and rocky, with brilliant-white, cuboid architecture, making them enormously popular with tourists. **Íos**, the original hippie island, is still a backpacker's paradise, while **Mýkonos** – with its teeming old town, nudist beaches and highly sophisticated clubs and bars (many of them gay) – is by far the most visited (and most expensive) of the group. Arriving by ferry at the partially submerged volcanic caldera of **Santoríni**, meanwhile, is one of the world's great travel adventures. **Páros**, **Náxos** and **Sífnos** are nearly as popular, while the one major ancient site worth making time for is **Délos**, the commercial and religious centre of the classical Greek world. Note that accommodation prices quoted below can be thirty to forty percent cheaper outside July and August.

ARRIVAL AND DEPARTURE

By boat Almost all the Cyclades are served by boats from Pireás, but there are also ferries from Rafína, one hour by bus north of Athens.

SÝROS

Sýros is the most populous island in the archipelago, and **ERMOÚPOLIS** is its capital and port (and capital of the Cyclades as a whole). It's a lively spot, bustling with a commercial life that extends far beyond tourism. Crowned by two imposing churches, the Catholic Capuchin **Monastery of St Jean** in the medieval quarter of Ano Sýros, and the Orthodox **Anástasis**, the city is one of the most religiously and culturally diverse places in the whole of Greece.

ARRIVAL AND INFORMATION

By ferry The ferry port is in the centre of Ermoúpolis.
Destinations Íos (1–2 weekly; 5–7hr); Mýkonos (2 daily 1hr 15min); Náxos (1–2 daily; 1hr 30min–2hr); Páros (1–3 weekly; 3hr); Pireás (2–3 daily; 4hr); Santoríni (1–2 weekly; 8hr 30min); Sífnos (1–2 weekly; 3hr–4hr 30min).

14

14

Tourist information Teamwork, Akti Papagou 18 (📞 22810 83400, 🌐 teamwork.gr), is the best place to ask for directions, accommodation and tours.

ACCOMMODATION

Palladion Proïou 3 📞 22810 86400, 🌐 palladion-hotel .com. Quiet, clean, old-school 1970s hotel that has been renovated and modernized with rooms overlooking a garden – excellent value if you're not overly fussy about the decor. Breakfast included. Doubles €55
Zannikos Rooms Proïou 103 📞 22810 82735. Simple, basic rooms with thin walls, but very well located for both the port and the nightlife. You may have to exercise your mime skills – or speak Greek – to communicate, though. Doubles €40

EATING

Stin Ithaki tou Aí Klonos & Stefanou. Tucked down a side street, this welcoming taverna serves up all the Greek classics, with a vibrant bougainvillea growing overhead. Mains €10. Daily noon–midnight.
Yiannena Platía Kanári. Popular, friendly spot, seemingly unchanged since the 1950s, serving great kebabs and other Greek standard fare with views of the seafront promenade. Mains €7. Daily 11am–1am.

SÍFNOS

Although **Sífnos** – notable for its classic Cycladic architecture and pottery – often gets crowded, its modest size makes exploring the picturesque island a pleasure, whether by the excellent in-season bus service or on foot over a network of old stone pathways.

KAMÁRES, the port, is tucked in at the base of high, bare cliffs in the west. A steep twenty-minute bus ride takes you up to APOLLONÍA, a rambling collage of flagstones, belfries and flowered courtyards. The island bank, post office and tourist police are all located here. As an alternative base, head for KÁSTRO, a short bus ride below Apollonía on the east coast; built on a rocky outcrop with an almost sheer drop to the sea on three sides, this medieval capital of the island retains much of its character. The island's finest beach is, however, VATHÝ, a fishing village regularly connected by bus to and from Apollonía.

ARRIVAL AND INFORMATION

By boat The ferries dock at the port of Kamáres.

Destinations Íos (1–2 daily; 2hr 45min–3hr 15min); Mýkonos (1 weekly; 5hr 30min); Náxos (1 weekly; 4hr 30min); Páros (1 weekly, 2hr 50min); Pireás (4–5 daily; 2hr 50min); Santoríni (1–2 daily; 3hr 30min); Sýros (1–2 weekly; 8hr 30min).
Tourist information There is an information booth opposite the dock (summer only Mon–Fri 8am–3pm).

ACCOMMODATION

★ **Hotel Stavros** Kamáres 📞 22840 33383, 🌐 sifnos travel.com. Harbourfront hotel whose huge, traditional Greek island rooms have kitchenettes, plus balconies with panoramic beach views. No breakfast. Doubles €60
Makis Camping Kamáres 📞 22840 32366, 🌐 makiscamping.gr. One of the best in the Cyclades, this beach campsite has excellent facilities with a laundry open to non-guests, as well as studios sleeping 1–2 people. Open May–Sept. Camping/person €8, plus per tent €4, studios €50

MÝKONOS

Mýkonos has become the most popular and expensive of the Cyclades, visited by several million tourists a year. If you don't mind the crowds, the upmarket capital, **MÝKONOS TOWN** (also known as **HÓRA**), is still the most beautiful and vibrant of all island capitals. Dazzlingly white, it's the archetypal Greek island town with sugar-cube buildings stacked around a cluster of seafront fishermen's dwellings.

The closest **beach** is **Áyios Stéfanos**, 4km north and connected by a very regular bus service, though **Platýs Yialós**, 4km south, is marginally less crowded. A bus service from Mýkonos town and a *kaïki* service from **Órnos**, 2km south, connect almost all the beaches east of

---

DAY-TRIP TO DÉLOS

Boats from the west end of Mýkonos harbour leave for ancient **Délos** (€38 return), the sacred isle, where Leto gave birth to Artemis and Apollo. It's worth a half-day trip for the magnificent views across to the nearby Cyclades from Mount Kýnthos (a 15min walk to the top), and for the archeological site (Tues–Sun 8.30am–3pm; €5), with remains of ancient temples, mosaics and its monumental lion avenue.

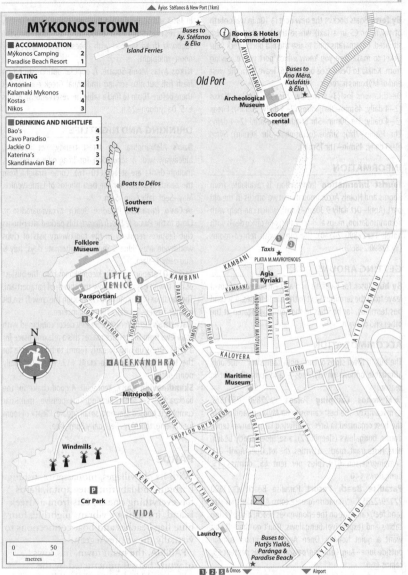

MÝKONOS TOWN

■ ACCOMMODATION
Mýkonos Camping   2
Paradise Beach Resort 1

● EATING
Antonini   2
Kalamaki Mykonos 1
Kostas   4
Nikos   3

■ DRINKING AND NIGHTLIFE
Bao's   4
Cavo Paradiso   5
Jackie O   1
Katerina's   3
Skandinavian Bar 2

Áyios Stéfanos & New Port (1km)

Buses to
Ay. Stéfanos
& Élia

Island Ferries

Rooms & Hotels
Accommodation

Old Port

Buses to
Áno Méra,
Kalafátis
& Élia

Archeological
Museum

Scooter
rental

14

Boats to Délos

Southern
Jetty

Taxis
PLATIA M.MAVROYENOUS

Folklore
Museum

LITTLE
VENICE

KAMBANI

KAMBANI

Agia
Kyriaki

KAMBANI

Paraportianí

ÁYION ANARYÍRON

K. YIÓRGOULI

DRAKOPOÚLOU

DHÍLOU

AY. YERÁSIMOU

ANDRHONÍKOU MATOYÁNNI

ZOUGANÉLI

MAVROYÉNI

AYIOU STÉFANOU

AYÍOU IOÁNNOU

N

ALEFKÁNDHRA

KALOYERA

LITOU

Maritime
Museum

Mitrópolis

MITRÓPOLIS

ENÓPLON DHYNÁMEON

IPÍROU

TOURLIANÍS

 R O H A R I

Windmills

XENÍAS

AY. EFTHÍMIOU

VIDA

Car Park

Laundry

Buses to
Platýs Yialós,
Paránga &
Paradise Beach

AYÍOU IOÁNNOU

0   50
metres

■1■, ■2■, & Órnos ▼   ▼ Airport

Platýs Yialós: gorgeous, pale-sand **Paránga** beach, popular with campers; **Paradise**, well sheltered by its headland dominated by the eponymous campsite and club; and **Super Paradise**, partly nudist and gay. Probably the island's best beach is **Eliá** – mainly gay – on the south-central coast: a broad, sandy stretch with a verdant backdrop. Less busy, but harder

to get to, are **Kaló Livádhi**, **Kalafátis** and **Liá** further east, as well as the northern, more windswept beaches of **Fteliá** and **Áyios Sóstis**.

ARRIVAL AND DEPARTURE

By plane The airport is about 3km out of town, a short taxi ride away (€8–10). Frequent buses run in high season (10min; €2).

14

By ferry Boats dock at the new port (a 10min walk north of town, or €5 in a taxi) where the bus station is also situated. Catamarans tend to use the old port: check your ticket to make sure you know which port you're leaving from. Kaïkia to Délos (see box, p.526) leave from the west end of Mýkonos harbour.

Destinations Íos (3–4 weekly; 2hr–5hr 30min); Náxos (2–4 daily; 45min–3hr); Páros (2–3 daily; 50min); Pireás (3–4 daily; 3hr 30min–5hr 30min); Santoríni (2–4 daily; 2hr 15min–7hr); Sífnos (occasional; 3hr 30min); Sýros (1–3 daily; 45min–1hr 15min).

INFORMATION

Tourist information Information is available from Rooms and Hotels Accommodation, two offices in the old port (April–Oct daily 9.30am–5pm), which can help with accommodation, maps and activities; one office deals with hotels (☎ 22890 24540), the other with rented rooms (☎ 22890 24860).

GETTING AROUND

By bus Buses for Kalafátis and all beaches east of town leave from the terminus next to the island ferries. A second bus terminus, for beaches to the south, is located at the other end of town.

ACCOMMODATION

The bus to town stops outside both campsites – the only affordable options on Mýkonos – and runs all night in season.

★**Mykonos Camping** Paraga ☎ 22890 25915/6, ⓦ mycamp.gr. The best campsite on Mýkonos and one of the best organized in Greece, offering large canvas tents, dorms, bungalows (sleeping 2), a secluded sandy beach, bars, restaurant, maps, activities, the lot. Open April–Oct. Camping/person €10, plus per tent €5, dorms €15, bungalows €40

Paradise Beach Resort Paradise Beach ☎ 22890 22129/22852, ⓦ paradise-greece.com. An industrial-size (and feel) campsite on the eponymous beach, also offering cabins and (expensive) bungalows. Don't go there If you want a quiet holiday. Open April–Oct; prices tumble outside June–Aug. Camping/person €10, plus per tent €5, cabins €66

EATING

Antonini Platía Mantó. A reliable choice on the main square, serving Greek family cooking since 1955. Go to the kitchen to choose your dish. Mains €12. Daily noon–late.

Kalamaki Mykonos Platía Mantó. Central and open all hours, it's the only grill left in town to quench the clubbers' munchies. An essential pit stop. Chicken skewers €2.20, salads €5, kebab plate €11. April–Oct 24hr.

Kostas Mitropóleos 5. Small, family restaurant, founded

in 1963 and buried deep in the town's labyrinthine centre. It serves everything from seafood to grills – don't miss the saganaki (fried seafood with cheese). Mains €12. Daily noon–midnight.

Nikos Ayias Monís Square. A popular option, strong on fresh fish but also serving traditional Greek cuisine. Get there before 10pm to find a table (no reservations). Mains €15. Daily noon–2am.

DRINKING AND NIGHTLIFE

Bao's Alefkándhra. The latest trendy, yet informal, hideaway, with a reputation for imaginative cocktails, though drinks are steep (€10–16). Come straight from the beach at sunset for the best photos of Little Venice. May–Sept daily 6pm–5am.

★**Cavo Paradiso** Paradise Beach ⓦ cavoparadiso.gr. Close to the Paradise Beach Resort, this packed after-hours club features regularly in the top-twenty lists of clubs worldwide. May, June & Sept open alternate days; July & Aug daily 1–9am.

Jackie O Paraportianí ⓦ jackieomykonos.com. The busiest of the town's gay clubs, below the church of Paraportianí. The top floor (if you can reach it through the crowd) is a bit quieter. Easter–Oct daily 10pm–6am. Free.

Katerina's Little Venice. Low-key decor combined with sea views from the terrace makes this a relaxing place for a drink. Dress up and go early (6pm) to find a table for the legendary sunsets. Cocktails €12. April–Oct daily noon–late.

Skandinavian Bar K. Yeorgouli. A good choice for the backpacker set, this buzzing, inexpensive multi-bar complex is housed around a small square. Plenty of room for dancing, too. May–Sept daily 8pm–late.

PÁROS

With its old villages, monasteries, fishing harbour and labyrinthine capital, **Páros** has everything one expects from a Greek island, including a vibrant nightlife, four blue flag beaches and boat connections to virtually the entire Aegean.

PARIKIÁ, the main town, has rows of white houses punctuated by the occasional Venetian-style building and church domes. Just outside the centre, the town also has one of the most interesting churches in the Aegean – the fourth-century **Ekatondapylianí** (daily 7am–9pm; free). The place culminates in a seaward Venetian **kastro**, whose surviving east wall incorporates a fifth-century BC round tower. The second-largest village of Páros, **NÁOUSSA**, a twenty-minute bus ride from Parikiá, retains much of its original character as a fishing village with winding, narrow alleys and simple Cycladic houses.

ARRIVAL AND INFORMATION

By ferry All ferries dock at Parikiá, the main town.
Destinations Íos (4 daily; 1hr); Mýkonos (4–5 daily; 50min–2hr); Náxos (6–8 daily; 30–55min); Pireás (3–6 daily; 3–5hr); Santoríni (5–7 daily; 2hr 30min); Sífnos (1 weekly; 2hr 50min); Sýros (2–4 daily; 2hr 40min).
Tourist information Located in the windmill in the centre of the roundabout opposite the quay (summer only, during ferry arrivals). Any of the agencies by the ferry docks can help with maps and information.

GETTING AROUND

By bus The bus stop is centrally located in Parikiá next to the quay. There are buses to Náoussa every 30min in July & Aug, less frequently at other times.

ACCOMMODATION

★ **Captain Manólis** Market St, Parikiá ☎ 22840 21244, ⓦ paroswelcome.com. Central but unbelievably quiet and freshly renovated; all rooms have inner garden views and free wi-fi, though the bathrooms are on the small side. Breakfast €5. Doubles €55
Dina Market St, Parikiá ☎ 22840 21325, ⓦ hoteldina .com. Small family *pension*, showcasing the Cycladic colours of white and blue; it's spotlessly clean and right in the middle of the action, so a bit pricey. Doubles €80
Jimmy's Hostel Livadhia ☎ 698 252 4025, ⓦ jimmyshostel.com. Whitewashed hostel with a café, facing the closest beach to Parikiá and run by an extrovert Zorba-like character, this is a place to let rip. Dorms €25, doubles €60
★ **Kriós Beach Camping** 2km north from Parikiá ☎ 22840 21705, ⓦ krios-camping.gr. Excellent facilities in a shady site, hosting occasional parties with plate smashing. There are cabins (sleeping 2) and a pool, but why go there when the beach is so much better? Open June–Sept. Camping/person €8, plus per tent €3, cabins €28

EATING, DRINKING AND NIGHTLIFE

Dubliner/Paros Rock By the bridge, Parikiá. Young, lively and OTT, this complex of bars and clubs is where you will probably end up dancing after a night drinking in town. Cocktails €8–10. Entrance with drink €5. June–Sept daily 11pm–7am.
Happy Cows Just behind the National Bank in Parikiá. This place serves excellent, inventive vegetarian food in kitsch, colourful surroundings: it also makes some concessions for carnivores, such as chicken or seafood. Mains €12. April–Oct daily noon–2am.

Tráta Parikiá. Down a side street off the road heading east out of town. This popular taverna specializes in seafood served beneath a vine-covered patio. Mains €10–12. April–Oct daily noon–midnight.

NÁXOS

Náxos is the largest and most fertile of the Cyclades, with high mountains, intriguing central valleys, a spectacular north coast, sandy beaches in the southwest, and Venetian towers and fortified mansions scattered throughout.

WHAT TO SEE AND DO

A long causeway protecting the harbour connects **NÁXOS TOWN** with the islet of Palátia, where the huge stone portal of an unfinished sixth-century BC **Temple of Apollo** still stands. Most of the town's life goes on down by the port or in the streets just behind it; the quaint Old Market Street has narrow stone paths leading to small shops and a handful of restaurants and cafés. From here, stepped lanes lead up past crumbling balconies and through low arches of the **Bourgo** to the fortified medieval **kastro**, near the **Archeological Museum** (Tues–Sun 8.30am–3pm; €3), with its important Early Cycladic collection. The town has a laidback feel, with unashamedly long happy hours which last for most of the day. There's a thriving nightlife, with plenty of bars scattered along the waterfront.

Beaches

The island's best **beaches** are regularly served by buses in season. Within Náxos Town itself is **Áyios Yeóryios**, a long sandy bay, part of the hotel and restaurant quarter. A short bus ride south, however, you'll find the more inviting **Áyios Prokópios** and **Ayía Ánna** beaches, with plenty of rooms to let and many good tavernas. Beyond the headland stretches **Pláka** beach, a 5km-long vegetation-fringed expanse of white sand, which comfortably holds the summer crowds of nudists and campers from the two campsites nearby.

ARRIVAL AND INFORMATION

By plane The airport is a 10min taxi ride south of Náxos Town (€10).

14

14

By ferry Boats dock at the quay at the northern end of Náxos Town.

Destinations Íos (2–3 daily; 1hr 45min–2hr 30min); Mýkonos (3–4 daily; 30min–1hr 30min); Páros (4–5 daily; 50min–2hr); Pireás (3–4 daily; 2hr 30min–4hr 30min); Santoríni (1–4 daily; 2hr 15min–2hr 30min); Sífnos (1 weekly; 5hr 30min); Sýros (2 daily–1hr 15min).

Tourist information You can obtain information at Zas Travel (☎ 22850 23330) or Auto Tour car rental (☎ 22850 25480) opposite the quay, where you can pick up leaflets or leave your luggage (both daily 9.30am–9.30pm).

GETTING AROUND

By bus The bus stop in Náxos Town is opposite the quay.

ACCOMMODATION

Camping Marágas ☎ 22850 24552, ⓦ maragascamping .gr. A shaded campsite right on Maragas beach and the closest to town. Also offers doubles in a hotel behind the campsite. Open April–Oct. Camping/person €9, plus per tent €5, doubles €45

Camping Pláka Ayía Anna ☎ 22850 42700/42031, ⓦ plakacamping.gr. Flanked by *Pláka I* and *Pláka II* hotels (where the double rooms include breakfast), this large modern site with its own sandy beach (50m away), surf school and restaurant feels more like a resort than a campsite. Camping/person €8, plus per tent €2, doubles €60

Despina's Rooms Náxos Town ☎ 22850 22356. Hidden (but well signposted) beneath the castle in the Bourgo. Rooms are small but clean and airy, with shared kitchen and bathroom and balconies with sea views. No breakfast. Doubles €45

★**Soula** Áyios Yeóryios ☎ 22850 23196, ⓦ soulahotel .com. Clean, whitewashed, bright and beautiful, this is one of the best hostels in the Cyclades. It has everything you need, from secure lockers to free ferry transfers. Breakfast €6. Dorms €18, doubles €45

EATING AND DRINKING

Manólis Garden Old Market St, Bourgo. A peaceful spot for an evening meal, with overhanging vines and an overwhelming scent of jasmine, offering stews and grills and a fantastic vegetarian moussaka. Mains €8–10. May–Oct daily 6pm–1am.

Meze Meze On the seafront. In the centre of the seafront and serving fresh seafood, this is the pick of a row of tavernas. Service is excellent so don't be put off if it's busy, which it always is. Mains €8. April–Oct daily 11am–midnight.

★**Scirocco** Platía Evripéous. In the centre of town, this restaurant is something of an institution with a high reputation among locals who flock here for its Naxiot specialities, many based on the local hard cheese. Mains €7–9. Daily noon–midnight.

Íos

Once a hippie hangout, Íos remains popular with a younger crowd seeking fun and sun, and as party capital of the Aegean, the island provides this in abundance. However, although no other island attracts more under-25s, Íos has miraculously maintained much of its traditional Cycladic charm, with picture-perfect whitewashed houses and churches. Lively nights lead to lazy days, perfect for exploring the island beaches.

WHAT TO SEE AND DO

Don't expect a quiet stay in the town of **HÓRA**, as every evening the streets throb to music, with the larger **clubs** clustered near the bus stop. To get the most out of the nightlife, start around 11pm with the bars and clubs around the central square, which tend to close at 3am. Around this time the larger clubs just outside town begin to liven up, and the party continues (even if you don't) until 9am.

Mylopótas and Manganári

The most popular stop on the island's bus routes is **MYLOPÓTAS**, site of a magnificent beach where there's a mini-resort (run by Far Out Camping; see below) offering plenty of activities including quad biking, watersports and diving, as well as parties. It gets very crowded, so for a bit more space, head away from the Mylopótas bus stop, where there are dunes behind the beach. From Yialós, boats depart daily at around 10am to **MANGANÁRI** on the south coast, where there's a superb blue flag beach.

ARRIVAL AND DEPARTURE

By ferry Boats dock at the quay in Yialós. Regular buses connect the port to Hóra and Mylopótas (every 15min, 8am–12.30am), but many hotels and hostels offer free transfers.

Destinations Mýkonos (4–5 daily; 2hr); Náxos (2–3 daily; 1hr 45min–2hr 30min); Páros (4 daily; 1hr); Pireás (4–5 daily; 3hr 30min–5hr 30min); Santoríni (6–9 daily; 45min–1hr 30min); Sífnos (1–2 daily; 2hr 45min–3hr 15min); Sýros (1–2 weekly; 5–7hr).

ACCOMMODATION

Far Out Camping Mylopótas ☎ 22850 91468, ⓦ faroutclub.com. By far the most popular campsite, thanks to its facilities, fun factor and the on-site club. Two-person bungalows also available. Open April–Sept. Camping/person €10, bungalows €50

★ **Francesco's** Old Town ☎ 22860 91223, ⓦ francescos .net. A favourite option with backpackers, who come for the vibe and not just the cheap dorm beds or private rooms. Lively bar and terrace with sea views, late breakfast till 2pm and a pool with a view. Dorms €14, doubles €52

Lófos Hóra ☎ 22860 91481. Right up from the archeological site, this family-owned complex with basic but well-furnished rooms is very conveniently located for both the bus stop and the Hóra nightlife opposite. It's peaceful and quiet– a rarity on Íos. Open May–Oct. Doubles €40

EATING

Lord Byron Old Town. An intimate restaurant with funky decor, serving generous meze plates to share (€12). A restaurant for those with an appetite and a thirst for a good mojito. May–Oct daily 6pm–1am.

The Nest Old Town. Here's where you'll find the locals enjoying veal in a clay pot (*youvétsi*) for €8. Chatty waiters who love to explain every dish, quick service and reasonable prices. April–Oct daily noon–midnight.

DRINKING AND NIGHTLIFE

Red Bull Bar Main square. Small bar specializing in dance music – and the well-known energy drink, mixed with large doses of spirits. Cocktails €8. May–Oct daily 10pm–3am.

Slammer Bar Main square. Legendary bar, where you should avoid saying the word "slammer" too loudly. Plays popular music ranging from the 1980s to current tunes. Entry €5 including a free drink. May–Oct daily 10pm–3am.

Sweet Irish Dreams Main street, in front of the church. Satisfy your cravings for a pint of the black velvet drink and dance till dawn – on the tables. Entry €7 including a free drink. June–Sept 6pm–late.

SANTORÍNI (THÍRA)

Santoríni is the epitome of relaxation, with its sun-drenched beaches and ambling, whitewashed stone paths. The island (a partially submerged volcanic

> ### COMBINED TICKET
>
> If you're in Santoríni for a while, consider buying a €14 **combined ticket** covering the four main museums and archeological sites: it can be bought from any of the main museums.

caldera poking above the ocean's surface in five places) is a welcome destination for those who have spent too many nights partying on Íos or Mýkonos. As the ferry manoeuvres into the great bay, gaunt, sheer cliffs loom hundreds of metres above. Nothing grows to soften the view, and the only colours are the reddish-brown, black and grey pumice strata layering the cliff face of **Thíra**, the ancient name of Santoríni. Despite a past every bit as turbulent as the geological conditions that formed it, the island is now best known for its spectacular views, dark-sand beaches and light, dry white wines.

WHAT TO SEE AND DO

Regular buses meeting the ferries at **Órmos Athiniós** make their way to the island's capital **FIRÁ**, half rebuilt after a devastating earthquake in 1956 and lurching dementedly at the cliff's edge. Besieged by day-trippers from cruise ships, it's somewhat tacky and commercialized, though watching the sunset from the cliff-hugging terrace of any of the overpriced restaurants, you'll understand why it's so popular. With a post office, travel agencies and a few hostels, it makes a good base from which to explore the island. The town boasts a couple of museums: the **Archeological Museum** (Tues–Sun 8am–3pm; €2) and the astonishing **Museum of Prehistoric Thíra** (Mon & Wed–Sun 8.30am–3pm; €6), between the cathedral and the bus station, where you will find a range of stunning artefacts documenting an advanced civilization that perished forty centuries ago.

Around the island

Near the northwestern tip of the island is one of the most dramatic towns of the Cyclades, **ÍA**. Jaw-droppingly beautiful and magical, the town is still worth visiting despite the back-to-back chain of luxury hotels clinging to the cliff face. Try to avoid coming from 6–8pm when buses ferry throngs of tourists to admire its legendary sunset views and the narrow winding main street becomes choc-a-bloc with bodies bearing cameras.

14

14

BOAT TRIPS TO THE VOLCANO

Take a **boat trip** from Firá or Ía to explore the magma-encrusted islets of the caldera and to swim in the sulphurous hot springs. You can book trips of varying lengths costing €18–38 from Dakoutros travel in Firá (daily 9am–9pm; ⓦ santorini excursions.com).

Santoríni's **beaches** are bizarre: long black stretches of volcanic sand that get blisteringly hot in the afternoon sun. There's little to choose between **KAMÁRI** and **PERÍSSA**, the two main resorts – both have long beaches and a mass of restaurants, rooms and apartments. Períssa gets more backpackers, but Kamari is also the gateway to the classical-era **Ancient Thíra** (Tues–Sun 8am–3pm; €4).

At the southwestern tip of the island, a prehistoric Minoan-era village was unearthed at **Akrotíri** from beneath banks of volcanic ash (April–Oct daily 8.30am–8pm; €12; bus from Firá or Períssa). Signposted nearby is the spectacular **Red Beach**, now sadly roped off, as falling rocks have made swimming dangerous – take a picture from afar only.

ARRIVAL AND DEPARTURE

By plane The airport is on the east side of the island, and served by infrequent buses to Firá and Monólithos beach (€2.20; 20min). As there are fewer than forty taxis on the island (fare to Firá €40), try to negotiate a free transfer with your hotel.

By ferry Most boats arrive at the functional port of Órmos Athiniós from where buses depart for the island's capital.
Destinations Íos (6–9 daily; 45min–1hr 30min); Iráklion (1–2 daily; 1hr 30min–6hr); Mýkonos (1–4 daily; 2hr 15min–2hr 30min); Náxos (4–6 daily; 2hr 15min); Páros (5–7 daily; 2hr 30min); Pireás (4–6 daily; 5–7hr); Sífnos (1–2 daily; 3hr 30min); Sýros (1–2 weekly; 8hr 30min).

GETTING AROUND

By bus In contrast to the airport, bus services are plentiful enough between Firá and other destinations around the island, but timetables vary widely from month to month.

ACCOMMODATION

★**Fira Backpackers Place** Firá ⓣ 22860 31626, ⓦ firabackpackers.com. Ultra-modern, well-organized hostel with 24hr reception, late check-out, cooking facilities, free laundry and female-only dorms. Its bright,

yellow-and-green common lounge with comfortable sofas and digital jukebox makes a great place to chill out. No breakfast. Dorms €30, doubles €67

Kykladonisia Firá ⓣ 22860 22458, ⓦ santorinihostel .com. Sleek, upmarket hostel with a swimming pool, single-sex dorms and free wi-fi. Try to get one of the rooms with a sunset view. Dorms €28, doubles €70

Perissa Camping Períssa ⓣ 22860 81343, ⓦ perissa camping.com. The happening beach campsite on Santorini with an open shaded area where you can kip with your sleeping bag, plus bungalows (sleeping 2). There's a taverna, beach bar and ferry transfers, too. Camping/person €7, plus per tent €3, bungalows €35

San Giorgio Firá ⓣ 22860 23516, ⓦ sangiorgiovilla.gr. Tucked away to the left of the car park next to the main square, this hotel has clean, excellent-value rooms with a/c, some with balconies. No breakfast. Doubles €80

Santorini Camping Firá ⓣ 22860 22944, ⓦ santorinicamping.gr. A shady campsite with a pool and restaurant, 350m from the centre of Firá. Prices vary wildly according to season. Camping/person €10, dorms €15

The Dodecanese

The **Dodecanese** islands lie so close to the Turkish coast that some are almost within hailing distance of the shore. They were only included in the modern Greek state in 1948 after centuries of occupation by Crusaders, Ottomans and Italians. Medieval **Rhodes** is the most famous, but almost every one has its classical remains, its Crusader castles, its traditional villages and grandiose, Italian-built Art Deco public buildings. The main islands of Rhodes and **Pátmos** are well connected with each other, and neither is hard to reach.

ARRIVAL AND DEPARTURE

By ferry Rhodes is the principal transport hub, with ferry services to Turkey, as well as connections with Crete, the northeastern Aegean islands, selected Cyclades and the mainland.

RHODES

It's no surprise that **Rhodes** is among the most visited of Greek islands. Not only is its east coast lined with sandy beaches, but the core of the capital is a beautiful and remarkably preserved medieval city.

WHAT TO SEE AND DO

RHODES TOWN divides into two unequal parts: the compact old walled city and the new town sprawling around it. There's plenty to explore in the rest of the island too, not least the charming and lively resort of **Haráki** and **Líndhos**.

Rhodes Town

First thing to meet the eye, and dominating the northeast sector of the city's fortifications, is the **Palace of the Grand Masters** (summer daily 8am–8pm, winter Tues–Sun 8am–3pm; €6, fortifications €2). Two excellent **museums** occupy the ground floor: one devoted to medieval Rhodes, the other to ancient Rhodes. The heavily restored **Street of the Knights** (Odhós Ippotón) leads due east from the front of the palace. The "Inns" lining it housed the Knights of St John for two centuries, and at the bottom of the slope the Knights' Hospital now houses the **Archeological Museum** (same hours; €8), where the star exhibits are the two famous statues of *Bathing Aphrodite* and the *Marine Venus*, the last of which inspired *Reflections on a Marine Venus* by Lawrence Durrell. Heading south, it's hard to miss the most conspicuous Ottoman monument in Rhodes, the candy-striped **Süleymaniye Mosque**, now only open for major events and weddings. The only Muslim sight you can visit is the **Hafiz Ahmed Aga Library**, which was built in 1793 and still contains 1256 manuscripts out of the original 1995 (Mon–Sat 9.30am–3pm; €1).

14

ARRIVAL AND INFORMATION

By plane Rhodes' Diaghoras airport lies 15km east of Rhodes Town, and is served by frequent buses to the centre (€2.30). A taxi to town costs €20–24. Rhodes is connected directly with many European capitals via charter flights.
Destinations Athens (4–5 daily; 1hr); Iráklion (1 daily; 55min); Thessaloníki (1 daily; 1hr 15min).

By ferry Ferries dock at the port of Akandia east of the Old Town; cruise ships anchor at Kolóna; pleasure boats and local traffic use Mandráki. There's a ticket office at Kolóna (7.30am–9pm).

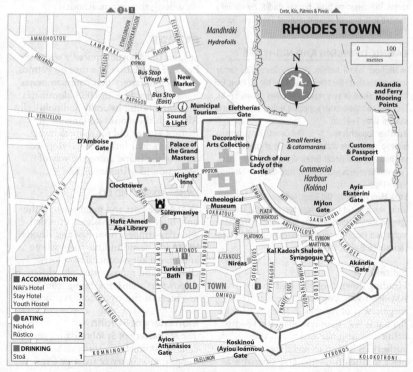

RHODES TOWN

Crete, Kós, Pátmos & Pireás

Mandhráki
Hydrofoils

N

0   100
metres

Bus Stop (West)
New Market
Bus Stop (East)
PL. KYPROU
Municipal Tourism
Sound & Light
Eleftherías Gate

AMMOHOSTOU
ETHELONDON
DHODHEKANISON
LAMBRAKI
ELEFTHERIAS
PLASTIRA
S. VENIZELOU
DHIAKOU
A. PAPAGOU

EL. VENIZELOU

D'Amboise Gate
Palace of the Grand Masters
Decorative Arts Collection
Small ferries & catamarans
Customs & Passport Control

Akandia and Ferry Mooring Points

Knights' Inns
IPPOTON
Church of our Lady of the Castle

Clocktower
ORFEOS
Archeological Museum
Commercial Harbour (Kolóna)

NAVARINOU

Süleymaniye
SOKRATOUS
PLATIA IPPOKRATOUS
ERMOU
AKTI
Mýlon Gate
Ayía Ekateríni Gate

Hafiz Ahmed Aga Library
APELLOU
ARISTOTELOUS
SAKHTOURI
PINDHAROU

PLATONOS
PL. EVREON MARTYRON
ELHADEF

PL. ARIONOS
IPPODHAMOU
AYIOU FANOURIOU
AZFANOUS
Niréas
SOFOKLEOUS
Kal Kadosh Shalom Synagogue
PYTHAGORA
PERIKLEOUS
DHIMOSTHENOUS
Akándia Gate

Turkish Bath
OLD TOWN
OMIROU
PRAVIE LOUS

RIGA FEREOU

ACCOMMODATION
Niki's Hotel   3
Stay Hotel   1
Youth Hostel   2

EATING
Niohóri   1
Rústico   2

DRINKING
Stoá   1

KOMNINON
Áyios Athanásios Gate
FILELLINON
Koskinoú (Ayíou Ioánnou) Gate
VYRONOS
KOLOKOTRONI

14

Destinations Iráklion (1–2 weekly; 14–17hr); Kós (2–3 daily; 2hr 30min–3hr); Pátmos (1–2 daily; 5hr); Pireás (1 daily; 16–18hr); Sýros (3 weekly; 9hr).

By bus Buses for the rest of the island leave from two departure points on Averoff St.

Destinations Faliraki (3 hourly; 35min); Líndhos (1–2 hourly; 1hr).

Tourist information The municipal tourist office at Averoff 3 (Mon–Fri 7am–3pm; ☎ 22410 35945, ⊛ rhodes .gr) can provide maps and bus timetables.

ACCOMMODATION

★ **Niki's Hotel** Sofokléous 39, Old Town ☎ 22410 25115, ⊛ nikishotel.gr. Wonderful views over the old town from the roof garden, and breakfast (€5) served outside on a lovely patio. Very quiet, despite being close to all-night bars. Doubles €70

Stay Lohagoú Fanouráki 19–21 New Town ☎ 22410 24024, ⊛ stay-rhodes.com. Opened in 2015, this well-managed, smart new hostel has up-to-date facilities, including a cinema, restaurant, roof terrace and female-only dorms. Dorms €14, doubles €28

Youth Hostel Ergíou 12, Old Town ☎ 22410 30491 or ☎ 6939 663 054, ✉ hostel-gr19@gmail.com. Old-fashioned youth hostel with four-bed dorms and double rooms. The dorms are basic, but the studios are carefully restored with original features retained. Free wi-fi. Dorms €10, doubles €40

EATING, DRINKING AND NIGHTLIFE

★ **Niohóri** Ioánni Kazoúli 29, New Town. This family restaurant is worth the 10min walk out of the old town, for its Greek cuisine at very reasonable prices (mains €7–8). They also own the butcher's opposite, where all the meat is sourced. Daily 1–11pm.

Rústico Ippodhámou 3–5, Old Town. Busy taverna under a shady vine with a wide range of choices, from seafood and traditional Greek dishes to Italian pasta. Two-course menus including aperitif for €10–12. Daily 9am–11pm.

Stoá Menekléous 32, Old Town. Opposite the old Turkish Baths, this is one of the few busy bars in the Old Town not catering solely to tourists. Come to one of its Friday tango nights and make friends with everyone on the island. Cocktails €6. Daily 10am–late.

Faliráki

Heading down the east coast from Rhodes Town, you reach the island's mega-resort of **Faliráki**. A few years back, the name was synonymous with 18–30s drink-and-disgrace antics, but the authorities have clamped down and the place is much friendlier and amenable as

a result, while the nearby Water-Park also attracts many families. That's not to say that its notorious nightlife has abated: its two main streets are called Bar Street and Club Street, after all.

Líndhos and around

LÍNDHOS, Rhodes' number two tourist attraction, lies 35km south of Faliráki, its charm undiminished by commercialism and crowds. On the steep hill above the town, the Doric **Temple of Athena** and Hellenistic stoa (porch-like building used for meetings and commerce), as well as the Knights' castle, stand inside the town's famed Acropolis (daily 8am–7.40pm; winter closed Mon; €12). Líndhos's two beaches on either side of the Akropolis are crowded in summer; you'll find better ones heading south past Lárdhos, the start of 15km of intermittent coarse-sand beach up to and beyond the growing resort of **Yennádhi**. Inland near here, the late Byzantine frescoes in the village church of **Asklipió** are among the best on Rhodes.

PÁTMOS

St John the Apostle reputedly wrote the Book of Revelation in a cave on **Pátmos**, and the monastery that commemorates him, founded here in 1088, dominates the island both physically and politically. Although the monks no longer run Pátmos as they did for more than six centuries, their influence has stopped most of the island going the way of Mammon like Rhodes or Kós.

WHAT TO SEE AND DO

SKÁLA, the port and main town, is the only busy part of the island, crowded with day-trippers from Kós and Rhodes. **HÓRA** is a beautiful little town whose antiquated alleys conceal over forty churches and monasteries, plus dozens of shipowners' mansions dating from the seventeenth and eighteenth centuries.

Monastery of St John

The **Monastery of St John** (daily 8am–1.30pm; Tues, Thurs & Sun also 4–6pm; monastery & treasury €4) shelters behind massive defences in the hilltop capital of Hóra. Buses go up (€1), but the thirty-minute walk along a beautiful old cobbled path is much more worthwhile.

Monastery of the Apocalypse

Just over halfway up the hill to Hóra is the **Monastery of the Apocalypse** (same hours; €2), built around the cave where St John heard the voice of God issuing from a cleft in the rock. This is merely a foretaste, however, of the main monastery, whose fortifications guard a dazzling array of religious treasures dating back to medieval times.

Beaches

The bay north of the main harbour in Skála shelters **Méloï beach**, with a well-run campsite. For swimming, the second beach north, **Agriolivádhi**, is usually less crowded. From Hóra a good road runs above the package resort of Gríkou to the isthmus of **Stavrós**, from where a thirty-minute trail leads to the excellent beach, with one seasonal taverna (summer *kaïki* from Skála).

ARRIVAL AND INFORMATION

By ferry Boats arrive at the harbour, in the middle of Skála.

Destinations Pireás (1–3 weekly; 9hr); Rhodes (1–2 daily; 5hr).

By bus The bus stop is next to the harbour; most journeys take about 10min.

Destinations Hóra (7–11 daily); Gríkou (6 daily); Kámbos (4 daily).

Tourist information The tourist office is located close to the police station opposite the harbour (summer Mon 9am–5pm, Tues–Sat 9am–9pm; ⓣ 22470 31666) and can assist with accommodation.

ACCOMMODATION

Siroco Cochlakas, Skála ⓣ 22470 33262, ⓦ siroco.patmos.eu. Situated 5min from the port, these fully equipped self-contained, two-person apartments with kitchenette have large private balconies and beautiful sunset views. April–Oct. Doubles €70

Studios Irene Skála ⓣ 694 655 8123. Four modern apartments in a wonderful secluded complex with tiled floors, solid wooden furniture and a large shaded garden smelling of basil plants. Free ferry transfers and gourmet meals offered. Doubles €50

EATING

Art Café Skála, behind the post office. A great café-bar to relax in – there are flickering candles, draught beer (€4) and a breezy roof garden with views to the harbour and the monastery. Daily 7pm–4am.

Hiliomodhi Skála. As its nautical decor suggests, this is the place to come for fish and seafood dishes that won't disappoint, with a tasty grilled octopus (€8) the main speciality. Daily 5pm–1am.

14

The Sporades

The **Sporades**, scattered across the northwestern Aegean, are an easy group to island-hop. The two most popular islands, **Skiáthos** and **Skópelos**, have good beaches, transparent waters and thick pine forests, while less-visited Alónissos is woodier with fewer beaches. **Skýros**, the fourth of the Sporades, is isolated from the others and less scenic, but with perhaps the most character; for a relatively uncommercialized island within a day's travel of Athens it's unbeatable.

SKIÁTHOS

Despite the throngs of holidaymakers, **Skiáthos** remains pretty and alluring, combining a cosmopolitan side with extensive pine forests that descend onto broad sandy beaches. All these elements come together in **KOUKOUNARIÉS**, 12km southwest from the capital, regularly voted among the best beaches in Greece, with the naturist-friendly **Banana beach** just beyond it. In **SKIÁTHOS TOWN**, you can explore the typical two-storey stone houses and visit the church of **Áyios Nikólaos** built on a large rock beside the old port for some great sweeping views. Near the main town, other beautiful beaches include **Kanapitsa**, **Megáli Ammos** and **Ahladhiés**, or, for something more secluded, you can venture north to the cave seascape of **Lalária** and the unfussy village of **Asélinos**.

ARRIVAL AND DEPARTURE

By plane Charter flights from all over Europe (May–Sept) arrive at the Aléxandhros Papadhiamántis airport, 3km north of Skiáthos Town, which is served by a regular bus to Koukounariés Beach, via Skiáthos Town.

Destinations Athens (1–5 daily; 35min).
By ferry Boats arrive in the new port at the centre of Skiáthos Town.
Destinations Skópelos (3–5 daily; 1hr); Vólos (3–5 daily; 1hr 45min–2hr 30min).
By bus The bus stop is by the ferry disembarkation point.
Destinations Koukounariés (1–3 hourly; 20min).

ACCOMMODATION

Camping Koukounariés Koukounariés ☎ 24270 49250, Ⓦ campingkoukounariesskiathos.gr. Camping is the best way to experience this glorious beach – and this campsite won't let you down. Shady and serene with good facilities but no pets, no open fires and no noise at night. June–Aug. Per person **€11**, plus per tent **€4**
Matoúla Paraliakós ☎ 24270 23252. Simply the best budget option on Skiáthos, these self-catering studios are bright, balconied and breezy, and easy to get to from the port. Free airport and ferry shuttle. Cash only. Doubles **€55**

EATING

★**Lo&La** Moraïtídhou Skiáthos Town ☎ 694 888 8352. This beautiful Italian restaurant serving home-made pasta (€8) and fresh fish makes a change from the usual Greek island grilled-meat diet and it's deservedly popular. Book in advance. May–Oct daily 5pm–midnight.
Lyhnári End of Papadhiamánti, Skiáthos Town. Run by a Greek-Norwegian couple, this tucked-away taverna has thrived by word of mouth due to its tasty Greek and international dishes and the excellent service. May–Oct daily 7pm–midnight.

SKÓPELOS

More rugged yet better cultivated than neighbouring Skiáthos, **Skópelos** is also very much more attractive. **SKÓPELOS TOWN** slopes down one corner of a huge crescent of a bay. Within the town, spread below the oddly whitewashed ruins of a Venetian *kastro*, stand many churches – 123 reputedly, though some are small enough to be mistaken for houses.

Beaches

Buses run along the island's main road to Loutráki, stopping at the turn-offs to all the main beaches and villages. **Stáfylos** beach, 4km out of town, is the closest, but it gets quite crowded; the overflow flees to **Velanió**, just east and officially nudist. Much more promising, if you're after relative isolation, is sandy

Limnonári, a fifteen-minute walk or short *kaïki* ride from **Agnóndas** (which has tavernas and rooms). The large resort of **Pánormos** has become overdeveloped, but slightly further on, **Miliá** offers a tremendous 1500m sweep of tiny pebbles beneath a bank of pines, while nearby **Kastáni's** fine grey sands are the location where scenes from the film *Mamma Mia!* were shot – don't be surprised to see groups of tourists trying to re-create the dance for *Does Your Mother Know* on the sands.

ARRIVAL AND DEPARTURE

By ferry Boats arrive at the quay in the middle of Skópelos Town. The island also has another small port at Loutráki.
Destinations Áyios Konstandínos (4 daily; 2hr 10min–4hr); Skiáthos (3–5 daily; 1hr); Vólos (3–5 daily; 1hr 30min–3hr).
By bus The bus stop is next to the quay, near the taxi rank.
Destinations Loutráki and all beaches (4–7 daily; 45min–1hr).

ACCOMMODATION

Eleni Harbourfront Skópelos Town ☎ 24240 22393. Simple, clean hotel with nautical decor and a homely atmosphere, situated dead on the harbourfront. All rooms have large balconies and a/c. No breakfast. Doubles **€50**
Regina Panormos ☎ 24240 22280. Surrounded by a lush pine forest, these traditional studios with cooking facilities have large comfortable beds, and balconies with superb views of Panormos Bay. No breakfast. Doubles **€40**

EATING

Wherever you eat, ask first if serve they the local delicacy, Skópelos cheese pie.
Alexander's Garden Skópelos Town. A delightful garden restaurant, serving traditional Greek food alongside more unusual local specials, such as pork with plums (€14). Mains from €9. Daily 7pm–late.
★**O Molos** Old Harbour, Skópelos Town. The pick of the tavernas on the waterfront, serving typical Greek cuisine with an excellent salad selection. Speciality is fried cheese with honey (€6). Mains from €8. Daily noon–midnight.

SKÝROS

Skýros remains a very traditional and idiosyncratic island. Some older men still wear the vaguely Cretan-looking costume of cap, vest, baggy trousers, leggings and clogs, while the women favour yellow scarves and long embroidered skirts.

Unlike the other Sporades which are accessed via Vólos on the mainland, Skýros is reached from Kými on the island of Évia.

WHAT TO SEE AND DO

A **bus** connects Linariá – a functional little port with a few tourist facilities – to **SKÝROS TOWN**, spread below a high rock rising precipitously from the coast. Traces of classical walls can still be made out among the ruins of the Venetian *kastro*; within the walls is the crumbling, tenth-century monastery of **Áyios Yeóryios**. Despite the town's peaceful afternoons, the narrow streets come alive in the evening, as the sun sets behind the hills, bathing the white buildings in a soft light.

ARRIVAL AND DEPARTURE

By plane There is a small domestic airport on the northern tip of the island, 10km from the town. There are no buses; a taxi to town costs about €15.
Destinations Athens (3 weekly; 40min); Thessaloníki (3 weekly; 40min).
By ferry Boats arrive at the functional port of Linariá. Buses wait for the boats and connect the port to Skýros Town (€1); taxis are a steep €15.
Destinations Kými (1–2 daily; 1hr 40min).

ACCOMMODATION

Hotel Elena Skýros Town ☎ 22220 91738. Centrally located, with tiled floors, white walls and wooden furniture. The rooms are clean and comfortable with a/c and free wi-fi, but no breakfast. Doubles **€45**

EATING

Adráchti Skýros Town. Tasty local dishes including wild green salads are served on a rooftop terrace with a panoramic view over the town. Mains around €8. No credit cards. Daily noon–midnight.
O Pappous k'Ego Skýros Town. Popular spot with tables spilling out onto the cobbled pavement – it serves up tasty Skyriot specialities such as goat in lemon sauce and pork & onion stew. Mains €8–10. Daily 6pm–late.

Ionian islands

The six **Ionian islands** are geographically and culturally a mixture of Greece and Italy. Floating on the haze of the Adriatic, their green silhouettes come as a surprise to those more used to the stark outlines of the Aegean. The islands were the Homeric realm of Odysseus, and here alone of all modern Greek territory the Ottomans never held sway. After the fall of Byzantium, possession passed to the Venetians, and the islands became a keystone in that city-state's maritime empire from 1386 until its collapse in 1797 when they passed to the French, the British and finally the Greeks in 1864. Tourism has hit **Corfu** in a big way but none of the other islands has endured anything like the same scale of development. For a less sullied experience, head for **Kefalloniá**.

CORFU (KÉRKYRA)

A visit to **Corfu** is an intense experience, if sometimes a beleaguered one, for it has more package hotels and holiday villas than any other Greek island. The commercialism is apparent the moment you step ashore at the ferry dock, or cover the 2km from the airport. That said, **CORFU TOWN**, the capital, has a buzzy appeal: cafés on the Esplanade and in the arcaded Listón have a civilized air, and become lively bars when the sun sets. The rest of the island is dotted with some lovely beaches and charming villages.

WHAT TO SEE AND DO

Corfu Town and around
In Corfu Town, the Palace of Sts Michael and George at the north end of the Spianádha is worth visiting for its private **Asiatic Museum** (daily: summer 8am–8pm; winter 9am–4pm; €6), **Archeological Museum** (currently closed for renovations) and **Byzantine Museum** (Tues–Sun 8am–3pm; €4). A combined ticket for both museums plus the **Old Fort** (daily: summer 8am–sunset; winter 8am–3pm; €6) costs €14. The island's patron saint, Spyrídhon, is entombed in a silver-covered coffin in his own church on Vouthrótou, and four times a year, to the accompaniment of much celebration and feasting, the relics are paraded through the streets. Some 5km south of town lies the picturesque convent of **Vlahérna**,

14

14

which is joined to the plush mainland suburb of Kanóni by a short causeway; the tiny islet of **Pondikoníssi** in the bay is visited by frequent *kaïkia* (€5 return).

Vátos and Pélekas

Much of the island's coastline has been remorselessly developed; the tiny village of **VÁTOS**, just inland from west-coast Érmones, is the one place within easy reach of Kérkyra Town that has an easy, relaxed feel to it and reasonable rooms and tavernas. It's the best option for independent travellers, and there's a free bus service to the beach of Glyfadha. Thanks to the village's hilltop location, there are some fine views over the surrounding countryside towards the coast. Nearby **PÉLEKAS** is rather busy and also inland but it's a good alternative base.

Áyios Górdhis and around

Further south, **ÁYIOS GÓRDHIS** beach is more remote, but that hasn't spared it from the crowds who come to admire the cliff-girt setting. **Áyios Yeóryios**, on the southwest coast, consists of a developed area just before its beautiful beach, which extends north alongside the peaceful Korissíon lagoon. **Kávos**, near the cape itself, with its many clubs and discos, is the nightlife capital of the island; for daytime solitude and swimming, you can walk to beaches beyond the nearby hamlets of Sparterá and Dhragotiná.

ARRIVAL AND INFORMATION

By plane In summer charter flights from all over Europe arrive at the airport, 2km south of Corfu Town. Local blue buses #5 and #6 run into town from a stop near the airport (hourly; 10min). A taxi costs €15.
Destinations Athens (2–3 daily; 1hr).
By ferry Boats arrive at the new port, 1km west of Corfu Town.
Destinations Brindisi (3–5 weekly; 4–9hr); Igoumenítsa (5–8 daily; 1hr 30min); Sarande, Albania (3 daily; 30min–1hr 15min).
By bus The long-distance "green" bus terminal is at Lefkímis 7, in Corfu Town (@ greenbuses.gr). The suburban "blue" buses start from Saroko Square.
Destinations Áyios Górdhis (2–8 daily; 45min); Athens (3 daily; 10hr); Kávos (10 daily; 1hr 30min); Paleokstrítsa (6–11 daily; 1hr); Thessaloníki (2 daily; 6hr).

Tourist information There's an Info Point at the entrance to the Old Fortress (Mon–Fri 9am–5pm; @ 26610 20355).

ACCOMMODATION

CORFU TOWN
Atlantis Ksenophóndos Stratigoú 48 @ 26610 35560, @ atlantis-hotel-corfu.com. Conveniently located near the New Port. It may be rather colourless and functional, but it has large rooms with a/c and a good breakfast is included. Doubles **€75**
Dionysus Camping Village Dhassiá, 8km north of Corfu Town @ 26610 91417, @ dionysuscamping.gr; bus #7 (ask the bus driver to stop here). Campsite with excellent facilities, pitches under olive trees, bungalows (sleeping 2) and sporting activities on offer. Open April–Oct. Camping/person **€6.50**, plus per tent **€4.50**, bungalows **€24**

AROUND THE ISLAND
Corfu Traveler's Inn Áyios Górdhis @ 26610 53935, @ corfubackpackers.com. Beachside accommodation with plenty of activities on offer, including kayak rental and organized club crawls. The prices include a free pickup, breakfast and dinner. Dorms **€23**, doubles **€45**
Pension Martini Pélekas @ 26610 94326, @ pensionmartini.com. The friendly owners here offer simple rooms with small balconies that boast great views over Albania. There's a lush garden too, where they put on the occasional barbecue party. Doubles **€35**
The Pink Palace Áyios Górdhis @ 26610 53103/4, @ thepinkpalace.com. Raucous but fun holiday complex, with jacuzzis, excursions, sports facilities, on-site club, 24hr bar and more. Prices include breakfast and dinner. Dorms **€24**, doubles **€56**

EATING AND DRINKING

CORFU TOWN
Pane e Souvlaki Town Hall Square. Freshly grilled meats at astonishingly good prices? Yes, and the result is a daily scrum outside this incredibly popular kebab shop. Salads €5, souvlaki €6.50. Daily noon–midnight.
To Paradosiakon Solomoú 20. This colourful restaurant with pavement seating serves traditional dishes such as beef and onion stew, and chicken or veal in tomato sauce. Mains €8–9. April–Oct daily 10.30am–midnight.

PÉLEKAS
Jimmy's At the crossroads of the road to the beach and Kaiser's Throne lookout. A friendly brick-and-stone taverna that serves excellent breakfast and dinner with a great choice of vegetarian dishes – the house wine is good, if a little on the pricey side. Mains €8–10. Daily 8am–11am & 5–11.30pm.
Zanzibar Below the central square on the road to Corfu Town. Very popular bar with an extensive cocktail

menu and DJs in the evenings. Beers €5, cocktails €7. Easter–Oct 24hr.

KEFALLONIÁ

Kefalloniá is the largest, and, at first glance, least glamorous, of the Ionian islands; the 1953 earthquake that rocked the archipelago was especially devastating here, with almost every town and village levelled and rebuilt. The 2001 film adaptation of Louis de Bernières' novel, *Captain Corelli's Mandolin*, was filmed here, attracting a steady stream of tourists.

WHAT TO SEE AND DO

There's plenty of interest: beaches to compare with the best on Corfu, good local wine and the partly forested mass of Mount Énos (1628m). The island's size, skeletal bus service and shortage of summer accommodation make renting a motorbike or car a must for extensive exploration.

Argostóli and the north

ARGOSTÓLI is the bustling, concrete island capital. North of here, the beach of **Mýrtos** is considered the best on the island, although it lacks facilities – the closest places to **stay** are nearby Dhivaráta and almost bus-less **Ássos**, a beautiful fishing port perched on a narrow isthmus linking it to a castellated headland. At the end of the line, pretty **Fiskárdho**, with its eighteenth-century houses, is the most stylish place on the island, Greece's own St-Tropez where you can often play "spot-the-celeb".

The east coast

Busy **SÁMI**, set against a natural backdrop of verdant, undulating hills, nestles itself into a sweeping bay. The town is the second port on the island, with boats to Itháki and Pátra. However, **AYÍA EFIMÍA**, 10km north, makes a far more attractive base. Between the two towns, 3km from Sámi, the **Melissáni cave** (summer daily 8.30am–6.30pm; winter Sat & Sun 10am–4pm; €6), a partly submerged, Capri-type "blue grotto", is well worth a stop. Southeast

from Sámi are the resorts of **PÓROS**, with regular ferries to Kyllíni.

ARRIVAL AND INFORMATION

By plane Summer flights from many European destinations arrive at Kefalloniá international airport, 7km south of Argostóli. There's no airport bus; taxis to town cost €15.
Destinations Athens (2 daily; 1hr).
By ferry Ferries from Kyllíni in the Peloponnese dock at Póros (5–8 daily; 1hr 15min); ferries from Pátra dock at Sámi (1 daily; 2hr 10min); while ferries from Zákynthos dock at Pessádha (2 daily; 1hr 30min).
By bus The bus station in Argostóli is just past the causeway, on I. Metaxa.
Destinations Fiskárdho (1–2 daily; 1hr 30min); Póros (2 daily; 30min); Sámi (3–4 daily; 40min).
Tourist information Customs Office Pier (Mon–Fri 7am–2.30pm; ☏ 26710 22248).

ACCOMMODATION

Camping Argostóli Fanári, 2km north of town ☏ 26710 23487, ⓦ camping-argostoli.gr. Good facilities including a taverna, minimarket and newly renovated toilets. This is your best bet if you want to be close to town. June–Sept. Per person **€6.50**, plus per tent **€5**
Karavomilos Beach 1km outside Sámi ☏ 26740 22480, ⓦ camping-karavomilos.gr. A shady campsite near the beach, 1km from town with a pool, minimarket and a decent restaurant. Open May–Sept. Per person **€8.50**, plus per tent **€5**
Regina Studios Fiskárdo ☏ 26740 41125, ⓦ regina-studios.gr. Centrally located doubles in a detached house on the road to Magano idiosyncratically furnished with floral fabrics in bright colours: rooms come with cooking facilities, a/c and balconies overlooking a large garden. Breakfast €5. Doubles **€65**

EATING AND DRINKING

Captain's Table Rizospáston 2, Argostóli. A waterfront restaurant with a nautical theme serving everything from home-made pizza to fresh fish in large portions. Always busy, so service can be slow at times. Mains €8–10. Daily noon–midnight.
Mermaid Restaurant Sámi. In a wonderful location on the seafront, this friendly restaurant uses local produce to create hearty dishes including a signature meat pie. Mains €7–9. May–Oct daily noon–midnight.
Tzívras Vandhóroui 1, Argostóli. Small traditional restaurant near the market with all Greek fare cooked to a high standard. There's a good selection for vegetarians, such as courgette-and-aubergine bake for €7. Daily 11am–5pm.

14

14

Crete

CRETE is distinguished as the home of the **Minoan** civilization, Europe's earliest, which made the island the centre of a maritime trading empire as early as 2000 BC and produced artworks unsurpassed in the ancient world. The capital, **Iráklion**, is not the prettiest town on the island, although visits to its superb Archeological Museum and the Minoan palace at nearby **Knossos** are all but compulsory. There are other great Minoan sites at **Mália** on the north coast and at **Phaestos** in the south. Near the latter are the remains of the Roman capital at **Gortys**.

Historical heritage apart, the main attractions are that inland this is still a place where traditional rural life continues, and that the island is big enough to ensure that, with a little effort, you can still get away from it all. There's also a surprisingly sophisticated club scene in the north-coast cities, and plenty of manic, beer-soaked tourist fun in some resorts in between.

IRÁKLION

The best way to approach bustling **IRÁKLION** is by sea; that way you see the city as it should be seen, with Mount Ioúktas rising behind and the Psilorítis range to the west. As you get closer, it's the fifteenth-century city walls that first stand out, still dominating and fully encircling the oldest part of town, and finally you sail in past the great Venetian fort defending the harbour entrance. The excellent **Archeological Museum**, at Xanthoudhidhou 2 (April–Oct daily 8am–8pm; Nov–March Mon 11am–5pm, Tues–Sun 8am–3pm; €10, €16 including Knossos), hosts a collection that includes almost every important prehistoric and Minoan find on Crete.

ARRIVAL AND DEPARTURE

By plane Nikos Kazantzakis airport is 4km east of the city with regular buses to the centre (every 10min; €1.10). A taxi costs €14.

Destinations Athens (4–6 daily; 50min); Thessaloníki (1 daily; 1hr 15 min).

By bus For all points along the north-coast highway and Knossos, use the Liménos bus station close to the ferry dock; services on inland routes to the south and west (for Phaestos, for example) leave from the Hanióportas terminal outside the city walls at Haniá Gate.

Destinations from Liménos Haniá (hourly; 1hr 20min); Hersónissos (every 30min; 40min); Knossos (every 10min; 20min); Mália (every 30min; 1hr); Réthymnon (hourly; 1hr 30min); Sitía (5–6 daily; 3hr 15min).

Destinations from Hanióportas Phaestos (8 daily; 1hr).

By ferry Boats dock at the quay at the eastern end of town. As you arrive, turn right to reach the centre.

Destinations Pireás (1–2 daily; 7hr); Rhodes (1–2 weekly; 14–17hrs); Santoríni (1–2 daily; 6hr); Sitía (2 weekly; 3hr).

INFORMATION

Tourist information Platía Nikifórou Foká (daily; 8.30am–2.30pm; ☎ 28134 09777/80). For what's on (and

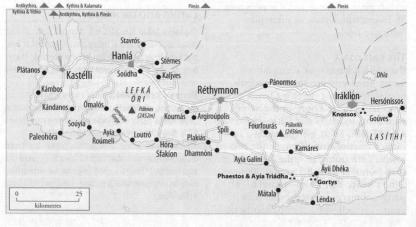

much more) in Crete's vibrant capital ⓦ nowhereaklion.com is an excellent website, run by a British expat.

ACCOMMODATION

★**Kronos** Sof. Venizelou 2 and M. Agarathou ☎ 2810 282 240, ⓦ kronoshotel.gr. Iráklion's best budget hotel, recently renovated with double-glazed windows and sea views. Its common areas are leather-clad while the spacious rooms have a/c and wi-fi; the buffet breakfast (included) is pretty good, too. Doubles **€60**

Lena Lahaná 10 ☎ 2810 223280, ⓦ lena-hotel.gr. Two-star hotel, in a residential street 500m from the harbour. Quiet, functional, clean and cheerful with a/c in every room plus free wi-fi: en-suite rooms cost €55. Breakfast €8. Doubles **€38**

Rea Kalimeráki 1 ☎ 2810 223 638, ⓦ hotelrea.gr. A clean, comfortable *pension* in a quiet and convenient central location behind the museum, with super-friendly staff: en-suite rooms cost €45. Breakfast €3. Open March–Nov. Doubles **€35**

EATING

50-50 Bar & Grill Odhós 1866 20 ☎ 2810 286 220. Possibly the best place to try Cretan cuisines and wines, with a great atmosphere on the occasional *rebétika* music night – reserve in advance for these. Mains from €7. Daily 10am–midnight.

Dipolo Cafe-Taverna Monis Odiyítrias. Not just a taverna but also a grocery shop, this place serves delicious authentic Cretan *mezédhes*, such as six different types of local cheese and traditionally smoked pork. Mains from €6. Mon–Sat 9am–midnight.

Johnny Burger Minótavrou 4 (El Greco Park). Yummy, innovative burgers that use home-made buns, local *graviéra* cheese, truffles and seventeen different sauces. Vegetarians are well catered for, too. Mains from €7. Daily 10am–midnight.

THESEUS AND THE MINOTAUR

Legend has it that King Minos built the labyrinth at Knossos to contain the **minotaur**. This terrifying creature with a man's body and a bull's head fed on fresh maidens and young men – until Theseus arrived to slay the monster, and, helped by Minos's daughter Ariadne, escaped the maze. Theseus subsequently ditched Ariadne on Náxos; yet she fared well, marrying the god Dionysus. On the way back, Theseus forgot to change the ship's sails from black to white – a signal to his father, Aegeus, that he'd survived and slayed the Minotaur – and caused his father's suicide from grief. Aegeus jumped from Cape Soúnio (p.510) into the sea that was subsequently named after him.

KNOSSOS AND PHAESTOS

The largest of the Minoan palaces, **KNOSSOS** (daily: April–Oct 8am–8pm; Nov–March 8am–3pm; €15) reached its cultural peak over 3500 years ago. Evidence of a luxurious lifestyle is plainest in the **Queen's Suite**, off the grand **Hall of the Colonnades** at the bottom of the stunningly impressive **Grand Staircase**. The site was excavated by Sir Arthur Evans from 1900 onwards. At the same time, the Italian Federico Halbherr was excavating the Minoan Palace at **PHAESTOS**, 35km west of Gortys (see below). Unlike the reconstruction work at Knossos, however, Phaestos remains totally pristine, which, to many, adds to its value and magnificence (daily: summer 8am–8pm; winter 8am–3pm; €8).

GORTYS

About 1km west of the village of Áyii Dhéka, where the bus drops you off, **GORTYS** (summer daily 8am–8pm; winter Tues–Sun 8am–3pm; €6) is the ruined capital of the Roman province of Cyrenaica, which included not only Crete but also much of North Africa. If you walk here from Áyii Dhéka you'll get an idea of the huge scale of the place at its height in the third century AD.

14

At the main entrance to the fenced site, north of the road, is the ruined but still impressive basilica of **Áyios Títos**, the island's first Christian church and burial place of the saint (Titus) who converted Crete and was also its first bishop. Beyond this is the **Odeon**, which houses the most important discovery on the site, the **Law Code** – ancient laws inscribed on stones measuring about 10m by 3m.

HERSÓNISSOS AND MÁLIA

The coast east of Iráklion was the first to be developed, and is still the domain of the package tourist. There are some good beaches, but all of them fully occupied. The heart of the development lies around **HERSÓNISSOS** and **MÁLIA**, which these days form virtually a single resort. If it's the party-holiday spirit you're after, this is the place to come – its reputation became even more notorious after scenes from *The Inbetweeners* movie were shot here – and wherever you go, you'll have no problem finding bars, clubs and British (or Irish) pubs.

SITÍA

Sleepy **SITÍA**, the port and main town of the relatively recently "discovered" eastern edge of Crete offers a plethora of waterside restaurants, a blue flag beach and a less hectic lifestyle than nearby **ÁYIOS NIKÓLAOS**. At the far eastern end of the island, **VAÏ BEACH** is the most famous on Crete, thanks to its ancient grove of palm trees. In season, though, its undoubted charms are diluted by crowds of day-trippers. Other beaches at nearby **Ítanos** or **Palékastro** – Crete's main windsurfing centre – are less exotic but emptier.

ARRIVAL AND DEPARTURE

By bus The bus station is on the southern edge of town, a short walk from the centre.
Destinations Iráklion (4–5 daily; 3hr 15min); Vaï (3–4 daily; 1hr).
By ferry The harbour is located 500m north of town.
Destinations Iráklion (2 weekly; 3hr); Pireás (2 weekly; 18hr); Rhodes (2 weekly; 10hr).

ACCOMMODATION

El Greco Arkadhíou 13 ☎ 28430 23133, ⊛ elgreco-sitia .gr. Central, friendly and old-fashioned – in attitude rather than in furnishings – this is an old-school hotel where a daily chat with the receptionist is *de rigueur*. Breakfast €4. Doubles €45

RÉTHYMNON

West of Iráklion, the old town of **RÉTHYMNON** is a labyrinthine tangle of Venetian and Turkish houses set around an enclosed sixteenth-century harbour and wide sandy beach. Medieval minarets lend an exotic air to the skyline, while dominating everything from the west is the superbly preserved outline of the **Venetian fortress** (summer 8am–7pm; winter 10am–5.30pm; €4). Much of the pleasure is in wandering the streets of the old town once the sun has set; there's an unbroken line of tavernas, cafés and cocktail bars right around the waterside and into the area around the old port. Better-value places are found around the seventeenth-century Venetian **Rimóndi Fountain**, an easily located landmark. The heart of Réthymnon's sparkling nightlife centres on the old port from around midnight.

ARRIVAL AND INFORMATION

By bus The bus station is to the west of the city; head around the inland side of the fortress to reach the centre.
Destinations Haniá (hourly; 1hr); Iráklion (hourly; 1hr 30min).
Tourist information Mégaro Delfíni at Sofokli Venizelou (Mon–Fri 9am–3pm; ☎ 28310 29148).

ACCOMMODATION

Camping Elizabeth Missiria, 4km east of Réthymnon ☎ 28310 28694, ⊛ camping-elizabeth.net. This campsite is in the hotel strip along the beach, served by frequent buses. Also rents bungalows (sleeping 2). Open May–Oct. Camping/person €8.50, plus per tent €5, bungalows €42
Olga's Pension Soulíou 57 ☎ 697 622 3018. These small but attractive rooms are individually decorated and have free wi-fi and a/c. The flower-filled roof garden is a gem; ask to feed the venus flytrap. Breakfast included. Doubles €50
Youth Hostel Tombázi 41 ☎ 28310 22848, ⊛ yhrethymno.com. This friendly and relaxed hostel at the edge of the Old Town has clean facilities, cheap breakfasts, women-only dorms and 24hr CCTV for security. Dorms €10

EATING, DRINKING AND NIGHTLIFE

Ice Club Salamínos 12. The town's biggest nightclub, hosting occasional live gigs from bands and Greek acts (normally starting at 8.30pm, prices vary). Their "Hell" club nights are notorious. June–Sept daily 11.30pm–late.

Metropolis Neárchou 15. A funky bar with DJs from a local, eponymous radio station that attracts a lively, hipster/studenty crowd. It also puts on a scattering of themed events, karaoke and live music. Cocktails €8. March–Nov 11pm–6am.

To Pigádhi Xanthoúdhidhou 31. This unpretentious restaurant is great value and recommended by locals. There's an atmospheric garden where you can eat excellent food, and the service is attentive. Mains €7–12. May–Oct noon–midnight.

PLAKIÁS

Réthymnon lies at one of the narrower parts of Crete, so it's relatively quick to cut across from here to the south coast. The obvious place to head is **PLAKIÁS**, a growing resort that's managed to retain a small-town atmosphere. There are numerous **rooms**, though it becomes very busy in August.

ACCOMMODATION

Youth Hostel ☎ 28320 32118, ⓦ yhplakias.com. Proud to be the most southerly hostel in Europe, it is set in an olive grove and, with its relaxed atmosphere, it feels more like a taverna or a beach bar. Book well ahead. Open Easter–Oct. Dorms €̶1̶1̶

HANIÁ

HANIÁ is the spiritual capital of Crete; for many, it is also the island's most attractive city – especially in spring, when the snowcapped peaks of the Lefká Óri (White Mountains) seem to hover above the roofs.

WHAT TO SEE AND DO

The **port area** is the oldest and the most interesting part of town. The little hill that rises behind the landmark domes of the quayside Mosque of the Janissaries is called **Kastélli**, site of the earliest Minoan habitation and core of the Venetian and Turkish towns. Beneath the hill, on the inner harbour, the arches of sixteenth-century Venetian arsenals survive

---

HIKING THE SAMARIAN GORGE

The **Samarian Gorge** – one of Europe's longest – makes an easy day-trip, with regular buses from Haniá (May–Oct only). Be warned, however, that you won't be alone – dozens of coaches set off before dawn for the dramatic climb into the White Mountains and the long (at least 4hr) walk down. At the bottom of the gorge is the village of Ayía Roúmeli from where boats will take you east to Hóra Sfakíon and your bus home, or west towards the pleasant resorts of Soúyia and Paleohóra. The mountains offer endless other **hiking challenges**: Soúyia and Paleohóra are both good starting points, as is Loutró, a tiny place halfway to Hóra Sfakíon, accessible only by boat.

---

alongside remains of the outer walls. Behind the harbour lie the less picturesque but livelier sections of the old city. Around the cathedral on Halídhon are some of the more animated shopping areas, particularly leather-dominated **Odhós Skrydhlóf**.

Beaches

Haniá's **beaches** all lie to the west: the packed city beach is a ten-minute walk beyond the Maritime Museum, but for good sand you're better off taking the bus from the east side of Platía 1866 along the coast road to Kalamáki. In between you'll find emptier stretches if you're prepared to walk some of the way.

ARRIVAL AND INFORMATION

By plane The airport is located in Acrotiri, 15km from Haniá. Buses run regularly into town (5.30am–23.45pm; €2.50). Taxis cost €30.
Destinations Athens (3–4 daily; 50min).

By bus The bus station is on Odhós Kydhonías, within easy walking distance of the centre.
Destinations Iráklion (hourly; 3hr); Omalós (for the Samarian Gorge; 4 daily when the gorge is open; 1hr); Réthymnon (hourly; 1hr).

By ferry Ferries dock about 10km away at the port of Soúdha: frequent city buses run from here to the market on the fringes of Haniá old town.
Destinations Pireás (1–2 daily; 9–10hr).

14

Tourist information Municipal Tourist Office, inside the Town Hall at Milonoyánni 53 (Mon–Fri 8.30am–2.30pm; ☏ 28213 41666).

ACCOMMODATION

Camping Chania 5km west of town ☏ 28210 31138, ⓦ camping-chania.gr. Close to no fewer than four beaches, this small but lively site has Cretan music and karaoke nights, a pool and a restaurant. Any west-heading bus from Platía 1866 will take you there. March–Oct. Per person €7, plus per tent €4

Earini Rooms Halídhon 27 ☏ 28210 57666, ⓦ earini.gr. You'll be sure of a hospitable welcome and clean, decent en-suite air-conditioned rooms at this well-situated guesthouse run by a lovely old lady. No breakfast. Doubles €32

Mme Bassia Betólo 45–51 ☏ 28215 02750, ⓦ mmebassia.gr. A charming *pension* with a homely atmosphere tucked away in the harbour backstreets. The traditionally decorated rooms are a good size, and there's a tiny roof garden too. Breakfast €5.50. Doubles €60

Pension Nora Theotokopoúlou 60 ☏ 28210 72265, ⓦ pension-nora.com. The charming air-conditioned rooms here have use of a shared kitchen. The size and facilities of the rooms vary, as do the prices accordingly. No breakfast. Doubles €40

EATING AND DRINKING

Ellotia Pórtou 6. It can be tricky to find this cosy garden taverna, but it's worth it, as it serves delicious traditional fare in a leafy setting. Grills €8–10. Daily noon–midnight.

Fáka Arholéontos 15. Not facing the port and thus considerably cheaper, this is nevertheless one of the best budget restaurants in Haniá, whose quality hasn't diminished through the years. Cretan lyra-based folk music at the weekends. Daily 11am–midnight.

Tamam Zambelíou 49. A converted Turkish bathhouse that serves up an adventurous menu, including vegetarian food, plus dishes ranging from stuffed goat roll to veal with aubergine purée. Especially popular with veggies and wine-lovers. Mains €8–10. Daily noon–midnight.

SZECHENYI BATHS, BUDAPEST

Hungary

HIGHLIGHTS

❶ Castle hill, Budapest The heart of historic Buda. **See p.551**

❷ Thermal Baths, Budapest Wallow in the city's historic baths. **See p.555**

❸ Siófok A must if you're a party animal. See p.559

❹ Badacsony Enjoy the walks in this gorgeous region. **See p.560**

❺ Pécs Explore this compact town's UNESCO treasures. **See p.562**

❻ Valley of the Beautiful Woman, Eger Taste local wines in the main square's cellars. See p.564

HIGHLIGHTS ARE MARKED ON THE MAP ON P.547

ROUGH COSTS

Daily budget Basic €60, occasional treat €80

Drink Beer (large) €2–2.50

Food Goulash €3–4

Hostel/pension €15–30

Travel Train: Budapest–Eger €8.50

FACT FILE

Population 10 million

Language Hungarian

Currency Forint (Ft)

Capital Budapest

International phone code ☎36

Time zone GMT +1hr

Introduction

Bordered by countries as diverse as Austria, Serbia and Ukraine, Hungary is a crossroads at the centre of the continent – what was once known as Mitteleuropa – and it fuses old Europe and new in its mix of Habsburg grandeur and Communist-era grittiness. There is a Central European solidity to its food, buildings and culture, but the more exotic, and undeniably romantic, founding myth of the nomadic, warrior Magyars from the Central Asian steppe is also key to Hungarians' fiery national pride.

15

Budapest, the capital, is a city of imposing scale and wide Danube vistas, split by the river into historic Buda and buzzy Pest, and offering both the old (imperial-era boulevards, Art Nouveau coffeehouses, bubbling Turkish baths) and the new (quirky warehouse bars and summer riverboat clubs). A few hours' travel beyond Budapest is enough to access Hungary's other key charms, from Serb-influenced **Szentendre**, a short way north along the Danube bend, to the lush wine-growing **Badacsony** region on the shores of **Lake Balaton** to the southwest. Balaton, the "nation's playground", also plays host to crowded summer party resorts such as **Siófok**, or gentler **Keszthely**. Hungary's three most culture-rich towns beyond Budapest are scattered across the country but not to be missed: **Sopron**, close by the border with Austria; **Pécs**, on the far southern tip, ringed by alpine hills; and **Eger**, just northeast of Budapest, a mellow, historic city famous for its Bull's Blood wine. Across southeast Hungary stretches the enormous Great Plain, covering half the country and home to some beautiful national parks and the cities of **Szeged**, **Kecskemét** and **Debrecen**.

CHRONOLOGY

9 BC Area around the Danube is conquered by the Romans.

434–453 AD Attila the Hun's feared empire is centred in modern-day Hungary.

568 The Avars, nomads from Inner/Central Asia, arrive.

Around 896 The Magyars in Hungary begin the *honfoglalás* or land-taking (conquest of the region).

1000 Kingdom of Hungary established by King Stephen.

1242 The Mongols attack Hungary.

1526 The Hungarian army is defeated by the Ottomans in the Battle of Mohács and the country is split into three regions, under different forms of government.

1552 The Hungarians hold back the Turks at the Eger fortress – a major date in national consciousness.

1699 The Turks are defeated and expelled from Hungary by the Austrian Habsburgs.

1867 In order to quell separatist calls, Austria accepts greater Hungarian autonomy – in what is known as the Compromise – and the dual monarchy of Austria-Hungary is formed.

1896 Huge celebrations across Hungary for the millennial anniversary – 1000 years since the arrival of the Magyars.

1918 After World War I, Austria-Hungary is split into two countries.

1920 Treaty of Trianon in which Hungary loses two-thirds of its prewar territory.

1919–41 The right-wing dictatorship of Admiral Horthy.

1944 Germany occupies Hungary and installs the Arrow Cross party (Hungarian fascists) in government.

1944–45 Hungary's large prewar Jewish community is decimated as Jews are deported under Nazi occupation.

1945 Soviets invade Hungary.

1947 Soviets consolidate their postwar power in Hungary.

1956 National uprising against Soviet occupation is brutally repressed.

1989–91 Collapse of Communism in the Soviet Union and the eastern bloc.

1990 Hungary's first free elections held.

2004 Hungary joins the EU.

2010 Pécs becomes European City of Culture.

2011 A new constitution is approved by a right-wing Parliament; new election and media laws cause concern among Hungary's EU partners.

2015 Hungary builds a fence across the Serbian border after 200,000 migrants enter the country over the summer hoping to moving to Germany.

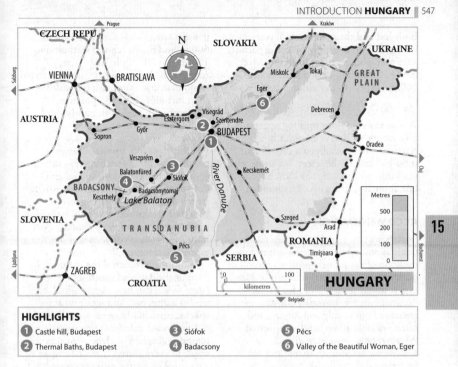

HIGHLIGHTS

① Castle hill, Budapest ③ Siófok ⑤ Pécs

② Thermal Baths, Budapest ④ Badacsony ⑥ Valley of the Beautiful Woman, Eger

ARRIVAL AND DEPARTURE

Flights to Budapest arrive at Ferenc Liszt airport, 20km from the centre; a bus and metro combination will take you into central Budapest, and there's also an airport bus that will drop you at your accommodation. Wizz Air also flies directly from London to Debrecen.

Most international **trains** arrive at Keleti station in Budapest, although Déli also handles a few arrivals from Belgrade. Global or One Country InterRail **passes** are valid on all trains. The international **bus** terminal is at Népliget (Metro Line 3) in Budapest, with international buses generally operated by Volánbusz. Mahart runs **hydrofoils** from Vienna which dock at the International Landing Stage on Belgrád rakpart in Budapest.

GETTING AROUND

Public transport in Hungary is cheap and fairly reliable, although the air-conditioning doesn't always work in trains or buses. The biggest problem can be getting information, as English is by no means uniformly spoken.

BY TRAIN

Intercity **trains** (marked "IC" on the timetable) are the fastest way of getting to the major towns. Seat reservations, a separate numbered piece of card available at any MÁV office (🌐mav-start.hu), are compulsory for services marked ⓞon timetables, and cost around 480Ft extra. You can buy **tickets** (*jegy*) for domestic services at the station (*pályaudvar* or *vasútállomás*) on the day of departure, but it's best to buy tickets for international trains (*nemzetközi gyorsvonat*) in advance. When buying your ticket, specify whether you want a one-way ticket (*egy útra*), or a return (*retur* or *oda-vissza*).

BY BUS

Volánbusz (🌐volanbusz.hu) runs the bulk of Hungary's **buses**, which are often the quickest way to travel between the smaller towns. Arrive early to confirm times and get a seat. For **long-distance services** from

Budapest and the major towns, you can book a seat up to 30min before departure; after that, you get them from the driver (and risk standing). For a journey of 100km, expect to pay around 2600Ft.

Private taxis are notorious for ripping off tourists, so always ask your hotel/restaurant/bar to call you a cab. If you must hail one in the street, use those with markings on the side that show a local taxi company, its logo and its number.

15 ACCOMMODATION

Hostels are common in the main tourist destinations, while across the country the tradition of the homely *pension* (*panzió*) or **guesthouse** (*vendégház*) still thrives. Here, expect to pay from 8000Ft for a double. Alternatively, try **university dorms** – rooms are rented out in July and August, and often available at weekends year-round. **Private rooms** (*vendégszoba*) and apartments are also affordable and can be arranged through the Ibusz agency (ⓦibusz.hu), or local tourist offices. Doubles range from 8000Ft in provincial towns to around 10,000Ft in Budapest. Outside Budapest and Lake Balaton (where prices in the summer can double), a three-star **hotel** (*szálló* or *szálloda*) will charge from around 12,000Ft for a double; solo travellers may have to pay this too, since singles are not always on offer.

Campsites range from deluxe to third class. In high season, expect to pay around 2000Ft for two people with a tent, and up to twice as much around Lake Balaton.

FOOD AND DRINK

You are unlikely to go hungry in Hungary. Cafés and restaurants (*étterem* or *vendéglő*) proliferate and portions are usually large. Eating out is generally affordable: choose well and you can stuff yourself, plus enjoy a few beers, for under 2000Ft.

Kebabs, falafel and small dishes – such as *hortobágyi palacsinta* (pancakes stuffed with mince and doused in creamy paprika sauce) – cost from as little as 600Ft, and mains tend to start around 1200Ft (or 2000Ft in higher-end restaurants).For foreigners, the archetypal **Hungarian dish** is goulash (*gulyásleves*) – a soup including beef and potatoes, brilliantly coloured with paprika and traditionally served in a cauldron (*bogrács*).

Hungarians like a protein-heavy **breakfast** (*reggeli*) featuring cheese, eggs and salami, plus bread and jam. **Coffeehouses** (*kávéház*) are increasingly trendy and you'll find many serving breakfast and coffee with milk (*tejeskávé*) or whipped cream (*tejszínhabbal*). For most Hungarians coffee means one thing: espresso (*eszpresszó*).

Traditionally, **lunch** is the main meal of the day, and lunch set menus (*napi menü*) can be a highly affordable way of eating out. You won't want for **snacks**, particularly sweet ones: the old-fashioned *cukrászda* or patisserie with tempting displays of elaborate cakes is a staple of every town centre. Marzipan is a national favourite, as is ice cream (*fagylalt*). **Pancakes** (*palacsinta*, from around 350Ft) are very popular, as are strudels (*rétes*; about 600Ft).

Hungary's mild climate and diversity of soils are ideal for **wine** (*bor*), which is cheap whether you drink it by the bottle (*üveg*) or the glass (*pohár*). The country's best-known wine-producing region is the Tokaj-Hegyalja, known predominantly for dessert wine. *Bikavér*, produced around Eger and meaning "Bull's Blood", is a robust red. Good whites can be found around the Badacsony in the Balaton region and near Sopron.

Wine bars (*borozó*) are common, but the best way to taste is at source at the wine cellars (*borpince*) around Pécs and Eger. Harder drinkers favour **brandy** (*pálinka*), with popular flavours being distilled from apricots (*barack*), plums (*szilva*) or pears (*körte*). Local **beers** (*sör*) to try are Soproni Ászok and Pécsi Szalon, while in Budapest a craft beer scene is well established in the city's famous "ruin bars" (see p.557).

CULTURE AND ETIQUETTE

Hungarians are generally very ready to help if you need directions or assistance. The biggest barrier is still the language – in Budapest you can survive on English but elsewhere you'll need to muster a little German, as well as the polite basics in Hungarian. Never say "thank you" when paying; this is understood in Hungary as "keep the change". If you want to leave a tip, ten percent will do, and, in restaurants, is expected.

Hungary's dominant **religion** is Catholicism but there are many Protestant churches. Respectful clothing is expected in places of worship. **Women travellers** should not expect any particular hassle in Hungary.

SPORTS AND OUTDOOR ACTIVITIES

Hungary is a predominantly rural country, one-fifth covered in forests. The Great Plain, especially the area around Kecskemét and the Kiskunság National Park, offers some of the best **horseriding** in Europe as well as fantastic horse shows during the summer. It's cheapest to select an independent horseriding operator.

Cycling is very well provided for: Tourinform (see box below) can provide cycling maps with recommended routes, and bikes can be rented in most towns for around 1500–2000Ft a day. Particularly scenic cycling routes can be found around Lake Balaton. There are limited **hiking** opportunities in Hungary; however, walks in the Badacsony region offer stunning views over Lake Balaton.

COMMUNICATIONS

Post offices (*posta*) are usually open Monday to Friday 8am to 4pm, Sat 8am to 1pm. The few **public phones** that are left use cards that can be bought from post offices and newsstands. To make national calls, dial ☎06, wait for the buzzing tone, then dial the area code and number. To make an international call, dial ☎00, wait for the buzzing tone, then dial the country code and number. All hotels and hostels (certainly those covered

in this Guide), as well as many cafés and bars, offer free wi-fi.

HUNGARY ONLINE

Ⓦ **tourinform.hu** National tourist office.
Ⓦ **ibusz.hu** Handy portal for viewing and booking cheap private rooms all across Hungary.
Ⓦ **budapestinfo.hu** Comprehensive site with up-to-the-minute listings.
Ⓦ **bkv.hu** Timetables and info for all public transport in Budapest.
Ⓦ **mavcsoport.hu/en** Hungarian train timetables in English.
Ⓦ **volanbusz.hu/en** Bus timetables.
Ⓦ **jegymester.hu** Buy tickets for events and exhibitions online.

EMERGENCIES

Tourists are treated with respect by the **police** (*rendőrség*) unless they're suspected of smuggling drugs or driving under the influence of alcohol. Always carry a photocopy of your passport. **Pharmacies** are identifiable by their green cross signs. Opening hours are generally Monday to Friday 9am to 6pm, Saturday 9am to noon; signs in the window give the location of all-night pharmacies (*ügyeletes gyógyszertár*). Tourist offices can direct you to local medical centres or doctors' surgeries (*orvosi rendelő*); these will probably be in private (*magán*) practice, so be sure to carry health insurance. EU citizens have reciprocal arrangements for emergency treatment, but only at state hospitals.

MONEY AND BANKS

Currency is the **forint** (Ft or HUF), which comes in notes of 500Ft, 1000Ft, 2000Ft, 5000Ft, 10,000Ft and 20,000Ft, and in coins of 5Ft, 10Ft, 20Ft, 50Ft, 100Ft and 200Ft. At the time of writing, €1=315Ft, US$1=280Ft, and £1=400Ft.

EMERGENCY NUMBERS

Police ☎107; Ambulance ☎104; Fire ☎105; General hotline ☎112.

15

15

HUNGARIAN

	HUNGARIAN	PRONUNCIATION
Yes	*Igen*	I-gen
No	*Nem*	Nem
Please	*Kérem*	Kay-rem
Thank you	*Köszönöm*	Kur-sur-nurm
Hello/Good day	*Jó napot*	Yo nopot
Goodbye	*Viszontlátásra*	Vee-sont-lah-tarsh-rah
Excuse me	*Bocsánat*	Botch-ah-not
Good	*Jó*	Yo
Bad	*Rossz*	Ross
Today	*Ma*	Ma
Yesterday	*Tegnap*	Teg-nop
Tomorrow	*Holnap*	Hall-nop
How much is…?	*Mennyibe kerül…?*	Men-yi-beh keh-rool…?
What time is it?	*Hány óra van?*	Hine-ora von?
I don't understand	*Nem értem*	Nem air-tem
Do you speak English?	*Beszél Angolul?*	Beh-sail ong-olool?
Where is/are?	*Hol van/vannak?*	Hawl-von/von-nok?
Entrance	*Bejárat*	Beyah-rot
Exit	*Kijárat*	Kiyah-rot
Women's toilet	*Női*	Nuy
Men's toilet	*Férfi mosdó*	Fayr-fi maws-daw
Toilet	*WC*	Vait-say
Hotel	*Szálloda*	Sahlaw-da
Railway station	*Vasútállomás*	Voh-sootal-law-mass
Bus/train stop	*Megalló*	Meh-gall-oh
Plane	*Repülőgép*	Repoo-lur-gepp
Near	*Közel*	Kur-zel
Far	*Távol*	Tav-oll
Single room	*Egyágyas szoba*	Eggy-ah-yas saw-ba
Double room	*Kétágyas szoba*	Kay-ta-yas soba
Cheap	*Olcsó*	Ol-cho
Expensive	*Drága*	Drah-ga
Open	*Nyitva*	Nyeet-va
Closed	*Zárva*	Zah-rva
One	*Egy*	Eggy
Two	*Kettő*	Ket-tur
Three	*Három*	Hah-rom
Four	*Négy*	Naidge
Five	*Öt*	Urt
Six	*Hat*	Hot
Seven	*Hét*	Hait
Eight	*Nyolc*	Nyolts
Nine	*Kilenc*	Kee-lents
Ten	*Tíz*	Teez

Accommodation and tour prices are often quoted in euros, but you still pay in forints. Standard **banking hours** are Monday to Thursday 8am to 4pm, Friday 8am to 1pm. Bureaux de change operate longer hours and can be found in the centre of most larger towns. **ATMs** are widespread, and you can use a **credit/** **debit card** to pay in most hotels, restaurants and shops.

OPENING HOURS AND HOLIDAYS

Shops are generally open Monday to Saturday 9am to 6pm. They close on Sundays and public holidays including

January 1, March 15, Easter Monday, May 1, Whit Monday, August 20, October 23, November 1, December 25 and 26. Shopping centres operate later hours and are generally open every day.

Budapest and around

Over two million people – one-fifth of Hungary's population – live in **BUDAPEST**, and it is the political, cultural and commercial heart of the country. After the 1867 Compromise, which gave the Hungarian monarchy equal status with Austria under the final half-century of the Habsburg Empire and ushered in a high age of Hungarian nationalism, the city was rapidly developed to become a standing celebration of Hungarian culture and power. The sheer scale of its vast iconic buildings, from the castle to the Parliament to the Gellért Baths, testifies to Hungary's central role in European history.

Pest is located on the eastern bank of the Danube and **Buda** on the hilly west bank. Since the unification of these two distinct cities in 1873, the **Danube** (Duna) is less a dividing line, more the heart of the capital itself, providing its most splendid vistas, from both banks. Each of Budapest's 23 districts (*kerületek*) is designated on maps and at the beginning of addresses by a Roman numeral; "V" is Belváros (inner city), on the Pest side; "I" is the Castle district in Buda.

WHAT TO SEE AND DO

Castle Hill (Várhegy) is the crowning feature of the **Buda** side; a plateau 1.6km long, it rises steeply from the Danube bank, bearing the imposing Buda Palace, a web of cobbled streets and the Mátyás Church, symbolic of Hungarian nationalism. **Pest** is thick with hip cafés and bars, as well as being home to the historic Belváros (central old town) and the intimate Jewish district.

Buda: Castle Hill

Castle Hill stands on the western bank of the **Chain Bridge** (Széchenyi lánchíd), opened in 1849, and – amazingly – the first permanent bridge between Buda and Pest. From Clark Ádám tér on the Buda side, you can reach Castle Hill on the dinky nineteenth-century funicular or **Sikló** (daily 7.30am–10pm; 1200Ft) or take bus #16/16A from Széll Kálmán tér metro station direction Disz tér.

Mátyás Church and Fishermen's Bastion

On **Szentháromság tér**, the busy square at the heart of Buda, stands the bright-roofed **Mátyás Church** (Mon–Sat 9am–5pm, Sun 1–5pm; 1500Ft). Inside, the church is fabulously exuberant, with the original thirteenth-century structure used as the base for a late nineteenth-century redesign in a Romantic Nationalist style. The splendid gold leaf and nationalist motifs clearly reclaimed the church as Hungarian – it had been a mosque for a time under Ottoman rule. A statue of **King Stephen** (Szent Istvan) on horseback stands outside – he is revered as the founder of the Hungarian state and the one responsible for converting Hungarians to Christianity.

Behind the church is the neo-Romanesque **Fishermen's Bastion** or Halászbástya, constructed in 1902 on the spot supposedly defended in the past by the guild of fishermen against would-be invaders. Today it's an excellent place for looking out across the river to the splendid Parliament building rising up on the east bank.

Buda Palace

Topping the crest of Castle Hill, close by the point where the funicular railway emerges, stands **Buda Palace**. The fortifications and interiors have been endlessly remodelled, with the palace's destruction in World War II only the latest in a long line of onslaughts since the thirteenth century. The **National Gallery** (Tues–Sun 10am–6pm, last ticket 5pm; 1800Ft; ☎01 201 9082, ✺mng .hu), which occupies the central wings B, C and D of the palace compound,

15

contains Hungarian art from the Middle Ages onwards, including heavily symbolic nineteenth-century representations of idealized national myths.

On the other side, facing the Palace's Lion Courtyard, the **Budapest History Museum** in Wing E (Tues–Sun: March–Oct 10am–6pm; Nov–Feb 10am–4pm; 2000Ft; ☎01 487 8800, ⓦbtm.hu) gives some further historical context with a gathering of artefacts from Budapest's dark ages and medieval past, but is rather old-fashioned, and arguably underwhelming for the price.

15

Gellért Hill

Close by the Szabadság híd (Freedom bridge) on the Buda side is **Gellért Hill** (Gellérthegy), home to the best known of the city's baths, Gellért Baths (see box, p.555), and topped by the **Liberation Monument**, constructed in 1947 to commemorate Hungary's liberation from Nazi rule. Known by locals as The Bottle Opener, it depicts a woman holding aloft the palm of victory and is one of the few Soviet monuments to survive the fall of the Iron Curtain *in situ* (most have been destroyed or moved out of town to the Statue Park). Below, the **Citadella**, a mock-medieval fortress built by the Habsburgs to cow the population after the 1848–49 revolution, hugs the west bank of the Danube.

Statue Park

The **Statue Park** (Szoborpark; daily 10am–sunset; 1500Ft; ☎01 424 7500, ⓦmementopark.hu), on the Buda side of the river 15km south of town, houses statues of Marx, Engels, Lenin and friends, as well as heroic scenes from Communist legends, and gives a lively glimpse into Hungary's Communist past for the uninitiated. Buses #101, #101B and #101E depart from Kelenföld metro station (Line 4) every 10 minutes; get off at the Memento park stop. The easiest option, though far from cheap, is to take the private tour bus from Deák tér (daily 11am; July & August also at 3pm; 4900Ft return, includes entrance fee).

Pest: around Vörösmarty tér

Central **Vörösmarty tér** is flooded with crowded café terraces, and dominated by the **Gerbeaud** patisserie, a *belle époque* high-society haunt, now sadly partly converted to a bistro and a cocktail bar. By *Gerbeaud*'s terrace is the entrance to Budapest's underground Line 1, continental Europe's first metro line, and the second in the world after London's, when it opened in 1896. It is now a UNESCO World Heritage Site.

Váci utca, a mix of chic shops and tourist tat stalls, runs south from **Vörösmarty tér** past the Pesti Theatre, where the twelve-year-old Franz (Ferenc) Liszt made his concert debut. It then continues south to the **Central Market Hall** (Mon 6am–5pm, Tues–Fri 6am–6pm, Sat 6am–3pm), a grand high-roofed hall whose stalls are laden with Hungarian products and pricey street food. Halfway along the central aisle stands the Kmetty & Kmetty stall with a picture of Margaret Thatcher who famously shopped there during her 1984 visit.

National Museum

At Muzeumkörút 14–16 (the road named after it), and easily accessed by ⓜKálvin tér, is the grandiose Neoclassical **National Museum** (Tues–Sun 10am–6pm; 1600Ft; ☎01 338 2122, ⓦhnm.hu), which gives a comprehensive overview of Hungarian history from the Magyar tribes' arrival to the collapse of Communism.

The Great Synagogue and Jewish museum

On the corner of Wesselényi and Dohány utca stands the **Great Synagogue** or Dohány Street synagogue (March Sun–Thurs 10am–6pm, Fri 10am–3.30pm; April–Oct Sun–Thurs 10am–6pm, Fri 10am–4.30pm; Nov–Feb Sun–Thurs 10am–4pm, Fri 10am–2pm; 3000Ft; ☎01 343 0420, ⓦdohanystreet synagogue.hu). It is the world's second-largest synagogue (the largest is in New York) and the central place of worship for what remains – despite the devastation of the Holocaust – of Central Europe's largest Jewish community. The Byzantine-Moorish interior is worth a

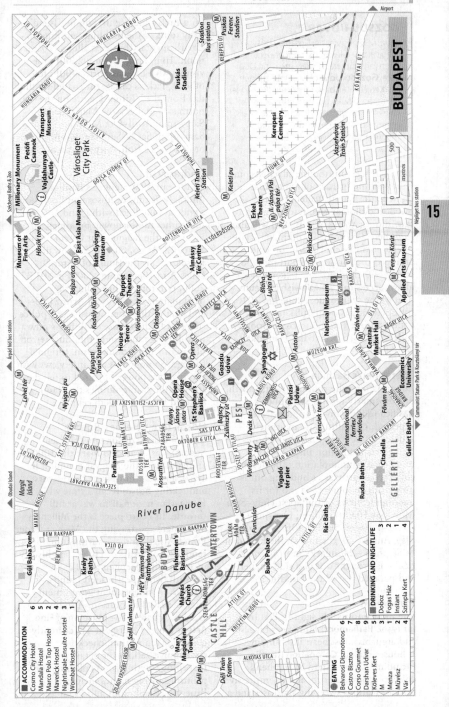

BUDAPEST

▲ Airport

15

ACCOMMODATION

Cosmo City Hotel	6
Mandala Hostel	5
Marco Polo Top Hostel	2
Maverick Hostel	4
Nightingale Ensuite Hostel	3
Wombat Hostel	1

DRINKING AND NIGHTLIFE

Doboz	3
Fogas Ház	2
Instant	1
Szimpla Kert	4

EATING

Belvarosi Disznotoros	6
Castro Bisztro	7
Corso Gourmet	8
Darshan Udvar	9
Köleves Kert	5
Menza	3
Művész	2
Vár	4

> ### GOZSDU UDVAR
>
> Extremely popular and insanely busy, a magical complex of six interconnecting courtyards between Kiraly utca and Dob utca, **Gozsdu Udvar** houses an antique market, cocktail bars, American diner-style restaurants, pull-your-own-pint pubs, cafés, handicraft stalls, Latin-themed bars, penny arcades, a gym – and, did we mention, bars?

15

look, but seek out too the silver weeping willow in the "garden of remembrance" named after Raoul Wallenberg, the Swedish diplomat who rescued many Jews during World War II. You will also find there a prominent commemorative plaque to Sir Nicholas Winton who arranged the Kindertransport in 1938, saving 669 children. The ticket also allows access to a new **Jewish Museum**, next to the synagogue: opened in 2016, it displays items from 1681 (a marriage contract from Verona) to contemporary Judaica (a 2015 octahedral Hannukah Minorah).

St Stephen's Basilica

Looming over the rooftops to the north of Vörösmarty tér lies **St Stephen's Basilica** (daily 9am–7pm; donation expected; ⓦbasilica.hu), an assertive nineteenth-century cathedral whose heavy ornamentation inspires awe more than contemplation. The dome collapsed shortly after building but is now sturdy enough to climb for its panoramic views of Budapest (July–Sept Mon–Sat 10am–6.30pm; Oct–June 10am–4.30pm; 500Ft). On St Stephen's Day, August 20, the mummified hand of St Stephen – Hungary's most revered relic – is brought out of a side-chapel and paraded round the building.

Parliament

The most unmissable sight in Pest by far is the **Parliament**, Hungary's biggest and arguably most beautiful building. It houses the old **Coronation Regalia**, including national hero St Stephen's crown, sceptre and orb, and its impressive interior features sweeping staircases and a

96m-high gilded central dome. There are daily **tours** of the building – in English – if parliamentary business allows (10am, noon, 1pm, 2pm & 3pm; 2200Ft for visitors with EU passport, 5400Ft for others). Tickets can be purchased on the day from the Visitors' Centre on the north side (daily; Nov–March daily 8am–4pm; April–Oct Mon–Fri 8am–6pm, Sat & Sun 8am–4pm) or in advance from ⓦjegymester.hu.

Andrássy út

To the east of St Stephen's Basilica, **Andrássy út** runs dead straight for 2.5km, a wide avenue lined with grand, if sometimes tumbledown, buildings, including the magnificent Opera House at no. 22. At no. 60, out east towards Hősök tere, is the **House of Terror** (Tues–Sun 10am–6pm; 2000Ft; ☎01 374 2600, ⓦterrorhaza.hu). Once the headquarters of the fascist Arrow Cross and later of the Communist secret police (the ÁVO), the House of Terror is now a hard-hitting museum to the "dual terror" of Fascism and Communism. Original footage, photographs and interviews with survivors are powerfully used to tell the story of the twin tyrannies that Hungary suffered in the twentieth century.

Hősök tere – Heroes' Square

The bombastic **Hősök tere** (Heroes' Square) was created to mark the 1000th anniversary of the Magyar conquest in 1896, and its triumphant conquerors and rearing horses recall a time when Hungarian nationalism was at full throttle. Its centrepiece is the **Millenary Monument**, portraying the Magyar leader Prince Árpád, and the surrounding semicircle of greats of Hungarian history includes King Stephen and Lajos Kossuth, who spearheaded Hungary's short-lived independent government after the 1848 revolution. Also on Heroes' Square is the **Museum of Fine Arts** at Dózsa György út 41 (currently closed for renovation; check ⓦszepmuveszeti.hu for details on its reopening), with a good collection of paintings by big names including Brueghel, Rembrandt and El Greco.

BATHING IN STYLE: BUDAPEST'S SPA SCENE

Budapest has some of Europe's grandest **baths**, and they are much more affordable than you might expect. Hungarians love to wallow in the thermal waters bubbling up from subterranean springs, and a Budapest spa visit is a must-do experience – it's fantastically restorative and sure to ease any aches and pains. A basic ticket covers three hours in the pools, sauna and steam rooms (*gözfürdo*), with services such as mud baths (*iszapfürdo*) or massages (*masszázs*) extra: for information on all Budapest's baths check ⓦ budapestgyogyfurdoi.hu.

Built in 1913 on the Buda side of Freedom Bridge, the magnificent **Gellért baths**, with original Art Nouveau furnishings, stunning mosaics, sculptures and stained glass, offer the most exclusive experience (daily 6am–8pm; from 5100Ft pool and locker). The atmospheric **Rudas baths** at Döbrentei tér 9 on the Buda side of Erszébet bridge, house a charming octagonal pool beneath a characteristic Turkish dome (men only Mon & Wed–Fri, women only Tues, mixed Sat & Sun; daily 6am–8pm; from 3200Ft). The popular, highly recommended **Széchenyi Baths**, by Heroes' Square in Pest, are the hottest in the capital, with large outdoor pools where old men play chess on floating boards, and fun features such as water rapids and underwater bubble jets (daily 6am–10pm; from 4700Ft). On Saturday nights they stage steamy, extravagant SPArties with drinks, DJs and dancing in and out of the water (10.30pm–3am; tickets from €35/10,900Ft at ⓦ spartybooking.com).

15

The Városliget and Vajdahunyad Castle

The **Városliget** (City Park), which starts just behind the Hősök tere, holds the **Vajdahunyad Castle**, a somewhat kitsch imitation Transylvanian castle which incorporates no fewer than 21 architectural styles from across Hungary's regions and was built in 1896 as a celebration of Hungarian art and design. In the courtyard is a statue of the monk Anonymus – a celebrated twelfth-century chronicler of Hungarian history. An artificial lake at the foot of the castle is filled with water for rowing and pedaloes in summer, and ice-skating in winter.

ARRIVAL AND DEPARTURE

BY PLANE

From Ferenc Liszt airport, take bus #200E (5.05am–11.45pm; every 7–15min) to Kobánya-Kispest metro station (20 min), from where it's ten metro stops to the centre (Deák tér station). As this involves a journey by bus and metro, buy a transfer ticket (530Ft) from the newsagents at the terminal. An airport shuttle (ⓣ 01 296 8555, ⓦ minibud.hu) will take you to any address you ask for (typically 3900Ft for one, 4900Ft for two to the city centre; tickets from their office in the terminal building) but you may have to wait for other passengers going your way. If you opt for a taxi, use only the official Fő airport company (around 6500Ft to the centre).

BY TRAIN

The three main train stations are all directly connected by metro with Deák tér metro station. Keleti (ⓣ 01 313 6835) handles all international trains; Nyugati (ⓣ 01 349 0115)

receives domestic trains from the Danube Bend and the Great Plain; and Déli (ⓣ 01 355 8657) handles services to Lake Balaton. For general train information see ⓣ 01 444 44999, ⓦ mavcsoport.hu/en.

Destinations from Keleti Bratislava (11 daily; 2hr 40min); Bucharest (4 daily; 16hr); Eger (8 daily; 2hr); Kraków (1 daily; 11hr 40min); Pécs (10 daily; 3–4hr); Prague (8 daily; 7–10hr); Sopron (12 daily; 3hr 20min); Vienna (12–13 daily; 3–4hr); Zagreb (3 daily; 6hr).

Destinations from Nyugati Debrecen (1–2 hourly; 2hr 26min–3hr); Kecskemét (hourly; 1hr 20min); Szeged (hourly; 2hr 20min).

Destinations from Déli Siófok (hourly; 1hr 20min); Badacsonytomaj (10 daily; 2hr 30min).

BY BUS

The international bus station is at Népliget (Line 3), which also serves most domestic destinations, while Puskás Ferenc Stadion bus station (Line 2) serves areas in east Hungary. Volánbusz operates all routes except Budapest–Vienna, which is run by Flixbus.

Destinations from Népliget Badacsony (10 daily; 3hr); Bratislava (2 daily; 2hr 50min); Kecskemét (1–2 hourly; 1hr 20min–1hr 45min); Keszthely (10 daily; 2hr 15min–3hr); Kraków (1 daily; 7hr); Pécs (6 daily; 3hr 30min–4hr 15min); Prague (2 daily; 7hr 15min); Szeged (6 daily; 3–4hr); Vienna (8 daily; 2hr 55min); Zagreb (1 daily; 5hr).

Destinations from Puskás Ferenc Stadion Eger (1–2 hourly; 1hr 50min–2hr 10min).

BY BOAT

Regular passenger cruises on the Danube are operated by Mahart (May–Sept; ⓣ 01 484 4013, ⓦ mahartpassnave .hu), leaving from Vigadó tér pier. International hydrofoils dock at Belgrád rakpart.

Destinations from Vigadó tér pier Szentendre (April Sat & Sun 10am; May–Sept daily 10am; 1hr 30min).
Destinations from Belgrád rakpart Vienna (Tues, Thurs, Sat; 9am; 6hr 30min).

INFORMATION AND TOURS

Tourist information The main Tourinform office in Budapest is at *Sütő* utca 2, just around the corner from Deák tér metro (daily 8am–8pm; ☎01 438 8080). Other branches are at Heroes Square (daily 9am–7pm) and Ferenc Liszt Airport Terminal 2A (daily 8am–10pm) and 2B (daily 10am–10pm).

Discount passes The Budapest Card (4900/7900/9900Ft for 24/48/72hr; ⓦbudapest-card.com), available at the airport and tourist offices, hotels and major metro stations, gives unlimited travel on public transport, free or discounted admissions to museums and attractions, and discounts on the airport minibus. All museums offer reduced entry to students.

Tours Budapest Tours offers various free excursions (☎70 428 9674, ⓦfreebudapesttours.hu), the most popular of which is the Orientation Tour (daily 10.30am from Deák tér; 2hr 30min). Budapest Underguide (☎30 908 1597, ⓦunderguide.com) runs many specialized tours in English, including the recommended "Tipsy" tour (a pub crawl at €49pp – four minimum – including two drinks).

GETTING AROUND

Tickets A basic 350Ft ticket is valid for a single journey on the metro, buses, trolleybuses and trams within city limits. If you travel by metro and bus in a single journey, buy a transfer ticket (530Ft). Tickets are available from metro stations and must be validated in the machines at the entrance before the journey starts, or on board buses, trolleybuses and trams. Travel cards are valid on all metro and bus lines within Budapest and are available in 24hr/72hr/weekly (1650/4150Ft/4950Ft) versions, as well as the 30/5 version (valid for any 5 days in 30; 4550Ft). If you don't have the correct ticket you can be fined up to 12,000Ft.

By metro The metro (daily 5.30am–11.15pm) has four lines (yellow, red, blue and green); services run every 2–15min.

By bus and tram Buses (*busz*) generally run every 10–15min. Express buses, with the red suffix "E", go nonstop between termini. Trams (*villamos*) and trolleybuses (*trolibusz*) run regularly throughout the day. Nightbuses have three-digit numbers beginning with 9 and run every 30–60min from midnight to 5am. Tram #6 also operates through the night.

By taxi Avoid hailing taxis on the street – you are likely to get ripped off. Instead, use reliable firms such as Főtaxi (☎01 222 2222, ⓦfotaxi.hu), Citytaxi (☎01 211 1111, ⓦcitytaxi.hu), Taxi4 (☎01 444 4444, ⓦtaxi4.hu) and

Taxi5 (☎01 555 5555, ⓦtaxi5.hu). Charges are 450Ft (flag drop) plus 280Ft/km.

ACCOMMODATION

If you want to be close to Budapest's nightlife, cafés and central sights, the best districts to stay in are V, VI and VII in Pest.

★**Cosmo City Hotel** V, Vaci utca 77 ☎01 799 0077, ⓦcosmohotel.hu. At the southern, quieter, tip of Vaci utca this designer hotel for budget-conscious travellers offers everything you need for little more than a hostel: lovely purple-and-black colour scheme, large rooms, comfortable beds, galloping wi-fi. Breakfast included. Doubles €70

Mandala Hostel VIII, Krúdy Gyula 12 ☎01 789 9515, ⓦmandalahostel.com. Beautifully decorated boutique hostel in a listed 1909 Art Nouveau building. Large six- to eight-bed dorms in open-plan/loft-style rooms, rather than the usual bunk beds. Tends to fill last, so definitely worth a try if stuck. Dorms €10, doubles €35

Marco Polo Top Hostel VII, Neár utca 6 ☎01 413 2555, ⓦmarcopolohostel.com. Very well-organized hostel with double rooms and twelve-bed dorms with bunks separated by curtains so they don't feel cramped (though they get hot in the summer). The bar downstairs is the starting point for pub crawls. Wi-fi on first floor only. Dorms €14.50, doubles €50

Maverick Hostel V, Ferénciek Tére 2 ☎01 267 3166, ⓦmavericklodges.com/eng. Cheery, clean hostel with no bunk beds (dorms have a split-floor open-plan area instead) and good service: rooms with private bathrooms cost a reasonable €48. *Maverick* also runs a more upmarket hostel in Kazincky utca which is pricier and not as quiet. Dorms €12, doubles €30

★**Nightingale Ensuite Hostel** VIII, József Körút 2 ☎70 947 9676, ⓔnightingale.minihotel.budapest @gmail.com. Fresh, chic decor in this friendly hostel offering double and triple rooms only. All but one have their own bathroom and that one has sole use with a private key. Although it overlooks Budapest's busiest road junction, you'll notice little noise. Doubles €33

Wombat Hostel V, Kiraly utca 20 ☎01 883 5005, ⓦwombats-hostels.com/budapest. With four massive floors, a pop-art common room straight out of a Lichtenstein painting, breakfast buffet for 1000Ft, CCTV for safety, and lighters, earplugs and condoms available at reception, this new kid on the block is setting high standards in Budapest. Dorms €17, doubles €50

EATING

It's easy to refuel cheaply in Budapest with a growing number of outlets serving falafels and kebabs. The two street food areas to explore are the junction of October 6 utca with Zrínyi utca in front of St Stephen's Basilica or the Central Market at Fövam tér.

CAFÉS, CHEAP EATS AND SNACKS

Belvarosi Disznotoros V, Kiraly utca 1d. Farm-to-kitchen self-service grill where you choose cuts of fresh meat and have them cooked in front of you. Great range of pickles and salads with home-made mayo: egg, cheese, potato salad – you name it, they have it. Mon–Thurs 10am–10pm, Fri–Sat 10am–midnight, Sun 10am–8pm.

★**Corso Gourmet** V, Vaci utca 54. Astonishingly good-value self-service restaurant on the second floor of a gourmet shop with mains less than 1000Ft (soups and salads at 300Ft are often included in the price of the main course). The entrance leads into the wine section of the gourmet shop – walk through it and take the lift to the second floor. Mon–Sat 8am–9pm, Sun 8am–7pm.

Müvész VI, Andrássy út 29. Classic old coffeehouse (est. 1898), across from the Opera House, decorated in a traditional style with crystal chandeliers and dark wood furnishings. Try a slice of the chocolate and caramel Dobos cake for 850Ft. Mon–Sat 9am–10pm, Sun 10am–10pm.

Vár I, Dísz tér 8. The only budget option on the Buda hill, this is a great self-service café serving filling dishes for under 1000Ft especially from the daily lunch menu (11.30am–2pm). Even if you're not hungry, have a seat and sample the best cappuccino in Buda. Daily 8am–8pm.

RESTAURANTS

Castro Bisztro V, Madách Imre tér 3. Shabby-chic bistro close to Deák tér, with a laidback feel and eclectic decor including chintzy floral tablecloths. There's a wide range of vegetarian and vegan options, but the goulash at 1150Ft is the winner. Mon–Thurs 11am–midnight, Fri 11am–1am, Sat noon–1am, Sun 2pm–midnight.

Darshan Udvar VIII, Krúdy Gyula utca 7. Part of a cluster of bar-restaurants in a cul-de-sac off a charming pedestrianized street, convenient if you're staying at *Mandala Hostel*. Yummy pizzas (1000Ft) sit alongside Hungarian specialities with mains around 1800Ft. Daily 11am–midnight.

Kőleves Kert VII, Kazinczy utca 41. Fun garden gastropub with Hungarian fusion dishes cooked by the same chef as the more upmarket restaurant next door (mains 1300–1400Ft). Go if only to lie in one of their hammocks. Mon–Fri 8am–1am, Sat & Sun 9am–1am.

M VII Kertesz utca 48 (off Liszt Ferenc tér). ☎ 01 322 3108. Cosy little restaurant that feels both low-key and very special with quirky interior design and delicious Hungarian-inspired food – the desserts are particularly generous. Mains around 2500Ft. Reservations recommended. Mon–Fri 6pm–midnight, Sat & Sun noon–4pm & 6pm–midnight.

★**Menza** VI, Liszt Ferenc tér 2. Stylish, if self-consciously so. Enjoy Hungarian dishes alfresco on the see-and-be-seen Liszt Ferenc tér, consistently one of the best eats in Budapest offering mains around 2000–3000Ft. Daily 10am–midnight.

DRINKING, NIGHTLIFE AND ENTERTAINMENT

For nightlife, head to District VII with its atmospheric "ruin pubs", namely bars inside run-down and disused buildings. The fortnightly *Budapest Funzine* (ⓦ funzine.hu) is a free listings and events magazine in English available from hotels, cafés and tourist information points. Tickets for most music events can be bought through Ticket Express (VI, Andrássy út 18; ☎ 30 303 0999, ⓦ eventim.hu).

Doboz VII, Klauzál utca 10 ⓦ doboz.pm. Ruin-style hotspot in Budapest set around an inner courtyard where a model of King Kong made out of planks is climbing a plane tree – anyone over 25 might feel out of place. Draught beer 500Ft. Fri & Sat cover 1500Ft. Mon–Thurs 5pm–3am, Fri & Sat 5pm–6am.

★**Fogas Ház** VII, Akácfa utca 51 ⓦ fogashaz.hu. This former dentist's practice became a "ruin pub" with a garden and has now expanded to a multi-level hangout with six bars, three dancefloors (disco, techno, house) and a live acoustic venue – yet it still manages to capture the anarchic spirit that started it off. Daily 6pm–4am.

Instant VI, Nagymező utca 38 ⓦ instant.co.hu. Labyrinthine venue set around an open courtyard with an offbeat energy and surreal, arty decor. It doesn't fill up until 1am. Mon–Thurs & Sun 4pm–6am, Fri & Sat 4pm–11am.

Szimpla Kert VII, Kazinczy utca 14 ⓦ szimpla.hu. The original "ruin pub" occupies a chaotic warehouse space with seven bars and a smokers' yard, but is far too often full of stag parties and hostel pub crawls. Daily noon–4am.

15

SZIGET FESTIVAL

Missed out on Glastonbury? Then head to Budapest in mid-August for one of Europe's "must-do" music festivals. Every year about 400,000 fans ("szitizens") from more than 80 countries descend on Óbudai island in the Danube, just north of Budapest, for the **Sziget Festival** (ⓦ szigetfestival .com). The week-long event attracts top international acts, such as Rihanna, Muse and David Guetta, but also offers a variety of cultural programmes, including theatre, circus, exhibitions, a Roma stage and a large LGBT tent. If you buy the discounted early-bird tickets (sold until the end of May), you'll pay €55–65 per person for a day pass, €219 for a five-day pass and €249 for a seven-day pass. The passes include free transport in the capital and, as the connections with Budapest are excellent, they provide a great opportunity to explore the city during the day.

15

DIRECTORY

Embassies and consulates Australia, XII, Királyhágó tér 8–9 ☎01 457 9777, ⊕hungary.embassy.gov.au; Canada, XII, Ganz utca 12–14 ☎01 392 3360; Ireland, V, Szabadság tér 7 ☎01 301 4960; New Zealand Consulate, VII, Nagymező utca 47 ☎01 302 2484; UK, V, Harmincad utca 6 ☎01 266 2888; US, V, Szabadság tér 12 ☎01 475 4400, ⊕hungary.usembassy.gov

Hospitals You can find 24hr medical help in the centre at Semmelweis utca 14/b (entrance on Gerlóczy utca) ☎01 311 6816, and at Dob utca 86 ☎01 321 0440.

Pharmacies The pharmacy at Teréz körút 41, near Oktogon, is open 24hr; pharmacies inside shopping centres also tend to be open longer hours.

Police 24hr tourist hotline ☎01 438 8080.

Post office The branch in Keleti station is open 24hr while the branch in Nyugati station is open daily 7am–midnight.

SZENTENDRE

SZENTENDRE on the west bank of the **Danube Bend** is a popular day-trip from Budapest, a picturesque if rather touristy "town of artists" with narrow cobbled streets and quaint houses.

WHAT TO SEE AND DO

Szentendre was originally populated by Serbs seeking refuge from the Ottomans in the late seventeenth century, and the Serbian cultural imprint remains, particularly in the rococo **Blagovestenska Church** (April–Oct Tues–Sun 10am–5pm; 400Ft; ☎26 312 399), on the north side of the main square, **Fő tér**. Just around the corner at Vastagh György utca 1 is the **Margit Kovács Museum** (daily 10am–6pm; 1200Ft; ☎26 310 244), displaying the lifetime work of Hungary's greatest ceramicist and sculptor, born in 1902.

There's a charming view over Szentendre's steeply banked rooftops and gardens from the hilltop **Templom tér**, above Fő tér, where the **Serbian Orthodox Cathedral** is visible inside its walled garden; tourists are generally not admitted, but you can see the cathedral iconostasis and treasury in the adjacent museum (May–Sept Tues–Sun 10am–6pm; Oct–April Tues–Sun 10am–4pm; 700Ft; ☎26 312 399).

Try and spend some time in Szentendre, as there are at least half a dozen more art collections, exhibitions and galleries worth a look – indeed, you won't want to miss the **Marzipan Museum** with its sculpted pastries at Dumtsa Jenő utca 12 (daily: April–Oct 9am–7pm; Nov–March 9am–6pm; 500Ft; ☎26 311 931). There are spring-welcoming folk dances on March and April weekends, music festivals over the summer and a rich programme leading to New Year's Eve. Ask Tourinform for details.

ARRIVAL AND INFORMATION

By train Suburban HÉV trains depart from Batthyány tér in Budapest. Szentendre's train station is located a 5min walk south of town. If you have a Budapest travel card you have to pay a small surcharge of around 600Ft return at the ticket office at Batthyány tér before boarding.

Destinations Budapest (2–7 hourly; 40min).

By boat Boats depart from Budapest's Vigadó tér pier (1 daily; 1hr 30min). Szentendre's docking station is 100m north of the town centre.

Tourist information Tourinform, Dumtsa Jenő utca 22 (May–Aug daily 10am–6pm; Sept–Oct daily 9am–5pm; Nov–April Tues–Sun 9am–5pm; ☎26 317 965, ⊕iranyszentendre.hu).

ACCOMMODATION

Centrum Panzió Bogdanyi utca 15 ☎26 302 500, ⊕hotelcentrum.hu. Homely, moderately plush rooms with modern bathrooms, right opposite the riverbank. Breakfast 1000Ft. Doubles 12,000Ft

Ilona Panzió Rákóczi F utca 11 ☎26 313 599. Simple rooms in a pleasant location in the heart of the old quarter. Breakfast included. Doubles 12,000Ft

Pap-Sziget Pap Island, 1.5km north of town ☎26 310 697, ⊕camping-budapest.com; Pap Sziget bus from Ujpest metro station north of Budapest. Well-organized campsite with two-person caravans, bungalows and motel rooms to rent. Convenient for the Hungaroring Formula 1 race and the Sziget festival. Open May to mid-Oct. Camping/tent 4000Ft, doubles 4800ft, bungalows 8600Ft

EATING AND DRINKING

Aranysárkány Alkotmány utca 1a. Cosy and popular, Hungary's first ever private restaurant, established in 1977, serves up traditionally filling Magyar cuisine – try the goulash soup served in bread casing for 1200Ft. Daily noon–10pm.

Görög Kancsó Duna Korzó 9. A Greek restaurant with a summer-holiday feel and sophisticated decor; offers glass-enclosed seating along the main Danube bank. Great moussaka for 1990Ft. Free wi-fi. Daily 10am–10pm.

Palapa Batthyani utca 2 just off Dumtsa Jenő utca. Brightly decorated, fun Mexican outfit with lively garden and tequila cocktails. Mains from 1700Ft. Mon–Thurs & Sun noon–10pm, Fri & Sat noon–midnight.

Western Hungary

The major tourist attraction to the west of the capital is **Lake Balaton**, dubbed the "Hungarian sea", and all that remains of the Pannonian Sea which once covered this part of Europe. Its built-up southern shore features loud resorts such as **Siófok**, which brands itself as the "Capital of Summer", while gentler **Keszthely** perches on the western tip. Worth a visit if you fancy a spot of swimming during the day while boozing and dancing at night, Siófok is Hungary's answer to the notorious nightlife of resorts such as Kavos, Malia and Magaluf – without the Mediterranean coyness. By contrast, the four villages that cluster around **Badacsony**, a hulk of volcanic rock on the northern shore of the lake, are very charming indeed and the perfect starting point for walks and wine-tasting tours in the Balaton region. Being flat, the lakeshore lends itself to cycling and there are plenty of places where you can rent bikes for around 1500Ft a day.

The wider region of **Transdanubia** – of which Lake Balaton and Badacsony are part – is the most ethnically diverse in the country. Its valleys and hills, forests and mud flats have been settled by Magyars, Serbs, Slovaks and Germans, and occupied by Romans, Ottomans and Habsburgs. Its towns have been through multiple evolutions and it shows: the delightful **Sopron** has a gorgeous medieval centre, Roman ruins and Baroque finery to its name, while **Pécs** boasts the country's best-preserved Ottoman mosque as well as some fascinating early Christian excavated finds.

SIÓFOK

The biggest, trashiest resort on Balaton, **SIÓFOK** throbs with summer crowds intent on sunbathing, boozing and clubbing. The two main resort areas are Aranypart (Gold Shore) to the east of the centre and Ezüstpart (Silver Shore) to the west. Though the central stretch of sand consists of a paying **beach** (daily mid-May to mid-Sept 7am–7pm; 600Ft), there are free beaches 1km either side. You can rent windsurfing equipment and wakeboards from 3000Ft per hour at most beaches.

ARRIVAL AND INFORMATION

By train The train station is on Fő utca at the centre of town.
Destinations Budapest (9 daily; 1hr 30min).
By bus The bus station is at Fő utca 71–81 (☎84 310 220). Bus #12 goes all along the south shore, aided by the #21 between July 10 and Aug 20. Bus #2 runs east of Siófok and #61 runs west.
Destinations Budapest (3 daily; 1hr 30min); Keszthely (3 daily; 1hr 30min); Pécs (4 daily; 3hr).
Tourist information The Tourinform office is inside the Víztorony (Water Tower), the town's landmark on the main square (May to mid-June & mid-Aug to mid-Sept Mon–Fri 8am–6pm, Sat 9am–1pm; mid-June to mid-Aug Mon–Sat 8am–8pm, Sun 9am–1pm; mid-Sept to April Mon–Fri 8am–4.30pm; ☎84 310 117, ⓦsiofokportal.com).

ACCOMMODATION

Hostels are geared towards Hungarian students, so campsites are a better bet. Tourinform can book private rooms, of which there are plenty during the summer.
Aranypart Camping Szent László utca 185 ☎84 353 899, ⓦbalatontourist.hu; bus #2, Szabadifürdő stop. Located 3km east of the centre, this large, well-equipped campsite also has bungalows (2–4 people) to rent. Open May to mid-Sept. Camping/person 1400Ft, plus per tent 1000Ft, bungalows 26,000Ft
Ifjúság Camping Siófok-Sóstó, Pusztatorony tér ☎84 352 851, ⓦbalatontourist.hu; bus #2, final stop. This smaller, quiet campsite lies 9km east of the centre, not on Balaton itself, but on the shore of a fishing lake. It also has 2-person bungalows. Open end of May to mid-Sept. Camping/person 1000Ft, plus per tent 750Ft, bungalows 4500Ft

EATING

★**Amigo** Fő utca 99. Good-value pizzeria offering much more than pizzas (around 1400Ft) with a roast pork platter, for example, at 1900Ft. Well worth walking the 200m east from the bus station. Mon–Thurs & Sun 11am–midnight, Fri & Sat 11am–1am.
Café Roxy Szabadság tér 1. Very pleasant and central wood-panelled café-restaurant; great for a relaxed glass of wine, mid-morning coffee or oven-baked pizza (around

15

1500Ft). Daily: June–Aug 8am–1am; Sept–May 8am–11.30pm.

DRINKING AND NIGHTLIFE

Flört Sió utca 4 ⓦflort.hu. High-energy techno club with special nights such as *XXLparty* and – no prizes for guessing the theme – *Bunga Bunga*. Still, Tiësto, Sasha, Paul van Dyk and many more top DJs have appeared here. Aug daily 10pm–5am, plus occasional nights throughout the year.

Palace Dance Club Siófok-Ezüstpart, Vécsey Károly utca 20 ⓦpalace.hu. Hosting 20-hour marathons, Siófok's most notorious club has been open since 1990 and is still going strong, with two floors of house, dance and techno. Party buses will take you there for free if you call ☏ 30 200 8888. Tickets 1000–3000Ft. June–Aug on party nights 10pm–late.

KESZTHELY

KESZTHELY is a gentler counterpart to brash Siófok, with a pleasant waterfront encompassing two bays (one for swimming, the other for ferries). There are stretches of grass and small paying **beaches** (June–Aug 8am–7pm; Városi Strand 1000Ft; Helikon Strand and Libás Strand 500Ft) that give peaceful views over the seemingly never-ending lake.

WHAT TO SEE AND DO

Walking up from the train station along Martírok útja, you'll pass the **Balaton Museum** on your left at Muzeum utca 2 (Jan–April & Oct–Dec Tues–Sat 9am–4pm; May & Sept Tues–Sat 9am–5pm; June–Aug daily 9am–6pm; ☏83 312 351, ⓦbalatonimuzeum.hu), hosting exhibits on the region's history and wildlife. Kossuth utca, swarming with cafés and shops, leads up towards the beige, Baroque **Festetics Palace**, which also houses hunting, coach and model railway museums (July–Aug daily 9am–6pm; May, June & Sept daily 10am–5pm; Oct–April Tues–Sun 10am–5pm; palace & coach museum 2500Ft, all museums 4200Ft; ☏83 314 194, ⓦhelikonkastely.hu). The third-largest palace in Hungary, it was built in 1745 by Count György Festetics, who attracted the leading lights of the eighteenth-century literary and high society scenes. Highlights include the mirrored ballroom, but, given the entry fee, those on a budget may prefer to admire the exterior and pretty surrounding gardens. The palace stages regular summer concerts, and in its cellars you can find the **Wines of Balaton museum** exhibiting 1500 wines (Tues–Sun 10am–5pm; entrance 600Ft or 1500Ft including three tastings, 2500Ft including five tastings).

ARRIVAL AND INFORMATION

By train The train station is located a 15min walk south of the centre at the junction of Kazinczy utca and Mártirok utja.

Destinations Budapest (7 daily; 3hr 30min); Siófok (7 daily; 1hr 30min).

By bus The bus station is next to the train station, at Kazinczy utca.

Destinations Badacsony (7 daily; 30min); Budapest (7 daily; 3hr 30min); Pécs (4 daily; 3hr); Siófok (2 daily; 1hr 30min); Sopron (2 daily; 3hr).

By ferry The quay is a 10min walk south of the centre, along Erzsébet királyné útca.

Destinations Badacsony (mid-July to Aug 1–2 daily; 2hr).

Tourist information Tourinform, Kossuth Lajos utca 30 (Sept–May Mon–Fri 9am–5pm, Sat 9am–1pm; June to mid-June Mon–Fri 9am–6pm, Sat 9am–2pm; mid-June to Aug Mon–Fri 9am–7pm, Sat & Sun 10am–4pm; ☏83 314 144, ⓦwest-balaton.hu). There is also an infopoint at the Lake Balaton promenade (June–Aug daily 9am–7pm).

ACCOMMODATION

Ambient Apartments Sopron utca 10 ☏30 460 3536, ⓦkeszthely-apartman.fw.hu. En-suite doubles and small apartments for two or more are offered in this handily located apartment house next to the Festetics Palace. Doubles 7000Ft, apartments 8400Ft

Castrum Camping Móra Ferenc utca 48 ☏83 312 120, ⓦcastrum.eu. Over 150 pitches in this large campsite 300m from the lakefront, with hedges and trees providing plenty of shade. Open May to Sept. Per person 1600Ft, plus per tent 2000Ft

EATING AND DRINKING

John's Pub Kossuth Lajos utca 46 ⓦjohnspubkeszthely.hu. Saloon-style bar with a long but affordable cocktail list and music late into the night. Daily lunch menu for 1150Ft. Club nights at weekends. Mon–Thurs noon–midnight, Fri noon–4am, Sat 6pm–4am.

BADACSONY

The **BADACSONY** – a hefty hunk of volcanic rock, forming a plateau visible from many kilometres around – is the iconic centre-point of the beautiful wine-growing region that is named after it. Four villages nestle at its feet, and it makes for a lovely base for walks, wine tasting and swimming in Lake Balaton. In particular, **Badacsonytomaj** has a small-scale charm enhanced by sampling a glass of local wine, never hard to come by, given the abundance of boutique wine cellars and roadside bars (*borozó*). You can rent bikes at various points along Park utca, the main road by the lake. There is also a clean, paying **beach** (Strandfürdő May & Sept 9am–5pm; June–Aug 8am–7pm; 700Ft).

WHAT TO SEE AND DO

The Baroque **Róza Szegedy House** (March–May Wed–Mon 10am–5pm; June–Aug daily 10am–7pm; Sept–Oct Wed–Mon 10am–6pm; Nov–Feb Fri–Sun 11am–5pm; 800Ft; ⓦszegedyrozahaz.hu) is on Kisfaludy utca, the only road going uphill from Római utca. The walk is a steep but picturesque 2.5km through the Badacsony vineyards. A little further up stands **Rose Rock** (Rózsa kő), where local legend has it that if a man and woman sit together with their backs facing Lake Balaton and think about each other, they will marry within a year. The Rose Rock is a good starting point for an invigorating hike to the Kisfaludy lookout tower (437m) and, twenty minutes further north, the Stone Gate (Kőkapu), formed by two great basalt towers. Both points offer splendid views of the lake and the patchwork of Badacsony's vineyards. Several wineries in the area offer **wine tasting**, including Laposa at Káptalantóti Bogyai L. utca 1 (ⓦbazaltbor.hu), Szási, at Szentgyörgy-hegy Hegymagas (ⓦszaszipince.hu), and Istvándy Winery at Káptalantóti, Rózsadomb 121 (ⓦistvandy-pinceszet.hu).

ARRIVAL AND INFORMATION

By train The train station is opposite the ferry pier on Park utca.
Destinations Budapest (3 daily; 3hr).
By bus Buses stop on Park utca by the ferry pier.
Destinations Keszthely (8 daily; 30min).
By ferry The ferry dock is in the middle of town (mid-July to Aug only).

Destinations Keszthely (1–2 daily; 2hr).
Tourist information Park utca 14 (Jan–April & Nov–Dec Mon–Fri 8am–4pm; May–June & Sept–Oct Mon–Fri 9am–5pm, Sat & Sun 10am–3pm; July & Aug Mon–Fri 9am–7pm, Sat & Sun 10am–7pm; Sept Mon–Fri 9am–5pm; ☎87 531 013, ⓦbadacsony.com). They can book accommodation and hiking tours in English.

ACCOMMODATION

Borbaratok Római utca 88, Badacsonytomaj ☎87 471 000, ⓦborbaratok.hu. Outstanding *panzió*, with large, beautifully comfortable rooms, and an excellent restaurant (mid-March to Dec daily 11.30am–9pm) serving superb Hungarian dishes. Breakfast included. Doubles 17,000Ft
Tomaj Camping Balaton utca 13, Badacsonytomaj ☎87 471 321, ⓦtomajcamping.hu. Pretty campsite by the lakeside, also known as the "Riviera", around a 10min walk east of the train station. Also rents wooden bungalows with kitchenette. Open May–Sept. Camping/person 1000Ft, plus per tent 1400Ft, bungalows 10,500Ft

15

SOPRON

A captivating town close to the Austrian border, **SOPRON** retains its original medieval layout with no fewer than 240 listed buildings. From its fourth-century Roman-era town walls to its Baroque central square, it is steeped in history, and its proximity to Vienna makes it a perfect day-trip from the Austrian capital (see p.65).

WHAT TO SEE AND DO

The horseshoe-shaped **Belváros** (inner town) is north of Széchenyi tér and the main train station. At its southern end, beautiful **Orsolya tér** (Bear Square) features Renaissance edifices and the yellow and cream Gothic church. Heading north towards the main square, **Új utca** (New Street – actually one of the town's oldest thoroughfares) is a gentle curve of perfectly preserved homes painted in red, yellow and pink. At no. 22 stands a **medieval synagogue** (April–Sept daily 10am–6pm; Oct Tues–Sun 10am–6pm; 800Ft; ☎99 311 327) that flourished when the street was Zsidó utca (Jewish Street).

Fő tér

Fő tér features an exquisite assembly of Gothic and Baroque architecture. Its

15

centrepiece is the **Goat Church** at Templom utca 1 (April–Oct Tues–Sun 10am–6pm; Nov–March 10am–4pm; 900Ft), so-called because, according to legend, its construction in the thirteenth century was financed by a goatherd whose flock unearthed a cache of gold coins. The attached **Chapter house** (same hours & ticket), which served as a prayer house and burial chapel, is considered one of Hungary's best examples of Gothic architecture. The Renaissance **Storno House**, at Fő tér 8, has a good exhibition on the colourful history of Sopron county (Tues–Sun 10am–6pm; 700Ft; ☎99 311 327, ⓦmuzeum.sopron.hu), but its highlight is the Storno family apartment on the second floor, a superb example of nineteenth-century bourgeois living quarters (1000Ft extra).

Firewatch Tower
North of Storno House rises Sopron's symbol, the **Firewatch Tower** (Jan–March Tues–Sun 10am–6pm; April–Sept daily 10am–8pm; Oct–Dec daily 10am–6pm; 1150Ft), founded upon the stones of a fortress originally laid out by the Romans. The **Gate of Loyalty** at the base of the tower commemorates the townsfolk's decision to remain part of Hungary when offered the choice of annexation to Austria in 1921.

ARRIVAL AND INFORMATION

By train The station is on Mátyás Király utca, 500m south of Széchenyi tér.
Destinations Budapest (6 daily; 2hr 40min); Vienna (2–4 hourly; 1hr 10min).
By bus The station is northwest of the old town, a 5min walk along Lackner Kristóf utca from Ógabona tér.
Destinations Keszthely (2 daily; 3hr); Pécs (1 daily; 6hr 30min).
Tourist information Tourinform is inside the Liszt Cultural Centre at Liszt Ferenc utca 1 (June–Sept daily 10am–8pm, Oct–May Mon–Fri 9am–5pm, Sat 9am–1pm; ☎99 517 560, ⓦturizmus.sopron.hu).

ACCOMMODATION AND EATING

Cézár Cellar Hátsókapu utca 2. A shabby exterior hides a cosy candlelit medieval wine cellar serving a tasting of four glasses of wine plus a meat-and-cheese board for 3000Ft. Mon–Sat noon–midnight, Sun 4–11pm.

Fehér Rózsa Pócsi utca 21 ☎99 335 270, ⓦfeherrozsa .hu. Pleasant, spotless air-conditioned rooms (a rarity in Sopron) in a 300-year-old inn, 200m east of the centre. It also has an excellent restaurant (daily 11am–11pm) serving mains around 1600–2500Ft. Breakfast included. Doubles **12,000Ft**

★ **Gambrinus** Fő tér 3. Inexpensive food, smiling waiters and great service in the middle of the main square? You'd better believe it, so go there before the tourists spoil this gem of a traditional restaurant that's housed in the old Town Hall. Try their Bramboráky (filled pancakes) for 1200–1800Ft. Daily 10am–midnight.

PÉCS

PÉCS is everyone's second-favourite town after Budapest, with a strong religious and scholarly heritage (Hungary's first university was founded here in 1367). Its remarkable history is summarized by its landmark mosque, synagogue and cathedral plus a clutch of fascinating Roman-era finds. The surrounding Mecsek hills help create a warm microclimate in the Pécs basin, where vineyards thrive.

WHAT TO SEE AND DO

Pécs is a small and navigable town, its cultural attractions concentrated in the **Belváros** (Old Town), radiating outwards from Széchenyi tér. Start with the synagogue by Kossuth tér, then head through charming Jokai tér towards the leafy western side, where you'll find the magnificent Peter and Paul cathedral.

Synagogue and Mosque of Gázi Kászim Pasha
Heading up Bajcsy-Zsilinszky utca from the bus terminal, you'll pass the imposing **synagogue**, which dominates Kossuth tér (April–Oct Mon–Fri & Sun 10am–4pm; 500Ft; ☎72 315 881). Its beautiful nineteenth-century interior is hauntingly impressive. Over 4000 Pécs Jews perished in the Holocaust and only a tenth of that number live in Pécs today. During the Ottoman occupation (1543–1686), Pécs' chief church, in a commanding position on Széchenyi tér 2, was converted into the **Mosque of Gázi Kászim Pasha** (Mon–Sat 9am–5pm, Sun 1–5pm; 1000Ft; ☎30 373 8900), which now stands as

the last remaining of seventeen mosques the Ottomans built in Pécs. The building has again been converted to serve as a church – and a cross is placed atop the crescent on its roof – but the underlying design is unmistakably Islamic.

Archeological World Heritage Sites and cathedral

From the centre of town, follow either Káptalan or Janus Pannonius utca towards the pristine Art Nouveau **Peter and Paul Basilica** (Mon–Sat 9am–5pm, Sun 1–5pm; 1200Ft includes Crypt; ☎72 513 080, ⓦpecsiegyhazmegye.hu): topped with all twelve Apostles, it is built on an epic scale. Next door, you can visit the **Episcopal Palace**, whose interior styles span four centuries providing a veritable history of European design (guided tours only daily 9am–4pm; 2000Ft). Nearby at Szent Istvan tér 17 (in the gardens just below the steps to the cathedral), the **Cella Septichora visitor centre** gives access to a wealth of Roman and early Christian archeological remains (April–Oct Tues–Sun 10am–6pm; Nov–March Tues–Sun 10am–5pm; 1700Ft; ☎72 224 755, ⓦpecsorokseg.hu). Pécs fell under Roman rule as the empire expanded into the Balkans in the second century, and became Christian with the conversion of the Emperor Constantine in 313 AD. The excavated rooms include the Peter and Paul burial chamber and a Christian cemetery site. Visitors can get a 360-degree view through glass panels placed above, below or on the side of the chambers.

Zsolnay Cultural Quarter

Pécs was the headquarters of the Zsolnay family, producers of unique Hungarian pottery and pyrogranite tiles. One of the highlights of the town is a stroll through the historic city, known as the **Zsolnay Cultural Quarter**, where fifteen historic buildings have been renovated, and whose parks and promenades feature 88 Zsolnay statues.

ARRIVAL AND INFORMATION

By train The train station is a 20min walk south of the centre on Indoház tér. Sadly, there are no more international trains south from Pécs.

Destinations Budapest (9 daily; 3hr).
By bus The bus station is northeast of the train station by the Arkád shopping centre.
Destinations Budapest (8 daily; 3–4hr); Siófok (4 daily; 2–3hr); Sopron (1 daily; 6hr 30min); Szeged (7 daily; 3hr 20min).
Tourist information Tourinform, at Széchenyi tér 7 (April–Oct Mon–Fri 9am–8pm, Sat & Sun 10am–6pm; Nov–March Mon–Fri 9am–8pm, Sat 9am–6pm; ☎72 213 315, ⓦiranypecs.hu), can book accommodation and English-language tours.

ACCOMMODATION

Arkadia Hunyádi utca 1 ☎72 512 550, ⓦhotelarkadiapecs.hu. Central but quiet three-star hotel with sophisticated grey-black decor: rooms spread over two buildings, so you can choose between modern cool or older traditional. Free parking and breakfast included. Doubles **€64**

Főnix Hotel Hunyádi utca 2 ☎72 311 680, ⓦfonixhotel .com. Just north of Széchenyi tér, the simple en-suite rooms in this hotel are good value. Breakfast included. A/c 1500Ft/day. Doubles **12,990Ft**

★ **Hungária Apartmanház** Hungária utca 17 ☎72 251 184, ⓦapartmanhotelpecs.hu. Superb self-catering modern studio apartments with cable TV, wooden floors, kitchenette and wi-fi. Washing facilities on site (€2). Free parking. Apartments **9500Ft**

NAP Hostel Kiraly utca 23–25 ☎72 950 684, ⓦnaphostel.com. Centrally located hostel with bright if rather crammed dorms and graffiti-style decor. Entrance through the *Nappali Bar* below. Dorms **€10**, doubles **€44**

EATING

The Arkád shopping centre (Mon–Sat 7am–9pm, Sun 8am–7pm) has many fast-food outlets offering Asian, Italian, Turkish, American and Hungarian dishes.
Az Elefánthoz Jokai tér 6 ⓦelefantos.hu. Excellent Italian serving delicious thin-crust pizzas on Pécs' best square for people-spotting. Beers 450Ft, pizzas from 1650Ft. Sun–Thurs 11.30am–11pm, Fri & Sat 11.30am–midnight.
★ **Flekken 1** Hungária utca 16. Popular budget tavern just off the centre serving a wide selection of dishes from pizzas (980Ft) to goulash (690Ft) and huge salads (Caesar 940Ft). Daily 11am–11pm.
Hungária Vendéglő Opposite *Flekken* at Hungária utca 13 ⓦhungariavendeglo.hu. As cheap and popular as *Flekken 1*, though not always open in the evenings. Two-course menu 590–850Ft. Sun–Thurs 11am–3pm, Fri & Sat 11am–9pm.

DRINKING AND NIGHTLIFE

Ti-Ti-Tá Líceum utca 4 ⓦtitita.club. The main club, bar and live music venue in Pécs, offering a variety of events.

15

Whether you like reggae, rock or techno, you'll find it here late into the night. Entrance fee varies depending on act. Beer 500Ft. Wed–Sat 7pm–late.

Eastern Hungary

The gorgeous town of **Eger**, set among the rolling Bükk hills, is a must on any trip to Hungary long enough to allow you to foray beyond Budapest, while oenophiles won't want to miss its celebrated "Valley of the Beautiful Woman".

EGER

Atmospheric **EGER** boasts a fabled fortress which famously repulsed Ottoman attack in 1552, expansive cobbled streets and a feeling of bonhomie which may well have something to do with its famous Bull's Blood cuvée wine (*Egri Bikavér*). A white version (*Egri Csillagok*) was launched in 2012 and is equally delicious. Eger's university, opposite the cathedral, ensures that, during term time, the town enjoys a nightlife out of proportion to its size.

WHAT TO SEE AND DO

Eger's Baroque centre is quite large and stretches either side of the main square, **Dobó István tér**, extending to the compact, cobbled streets around the castle.

Cathedral

The splendid Neoclassical **cathedral** or basilica on Pyrker tér (daily 9am–6pm; donation 300Ft; ☎36 470 970, ⓦeger -bazilika.plebania.hu) is the country's second-largest church after Estergom. Painted a Habsburg royal yellow, it is five minutes' walk southwest from the main square, approached by a grand set of steps. Inside, it is grandiosely decorated with toffee-coloured columns and pastel frescoes.

Archbishop's Palace

On pleasant, pedestrianized Széchenyi Istvan utca 3, the newly restored **Archbishop's Palace** (April–Sept Tues–Sun 10am–6pm; Oct–March Tues–Sat 10am–4pm; 1800Ft) is a u-shaped Baroque building, housing a

treasury, a history of the bishopric of Eger as well as the art collection of the town's prince-bishops. Although the bulk of the collection was moved to Budapest's Fine Arts Museum, some fine paintings are still on show here – among the oils on the second floor, *Boy Lighting a Pipe* by Hendrick ter Brugghen (1623) is said to be the earliest Western painting depicting smoking.

Minaret and the Turkish Tent

Walk down Sandor utca, cross the bridge and head to the left to climb Europe's most northerly **minaret**, an iconic memento of Eger's Ottoman occupation (daily: April & Oct 10am–5pm; May–Sept 10am–6pm; 300Ft). Legend has it that when the Habsburgs tried to pull down the minaret, even a hundred oxen couldn't topple it: in the end they just put a cross at the top. Returning to the castle via Dobó utca, you can pop into the authentically lavish **Nine-Sided Turkish Tent**, at no. 40, to admire its dazzling interior and sip a coffee brewed in hot sand (March–May & Sept–Dec Tues–Sun 10am–10pm; June–Aug daily 9am–11pm; free; ⓦegripasasatra.com).

Eger Castle

Uphill from Dobó István tér is Hungary's most famous **castle** (May–Sept daily 10am–6pm; Oct–April Tues–Sun 10am–4pm; 1600Ft including museums and casements; ☎36 312 744, ⓦegrivar .hu). Inside, you get a powerful sense of the sheer scale of the fortress, and can easily imagine the scene in 1552 when soldiers and local women (who volunteered to help) saw off a Turkish force six times their number – a cannon is fired every day at 15.52 to commemorate the event. There are three museums inside the fortress, but it's the hundreds of metres of underground **casements** – reopened in May 2016 – that are an absolute must, and give you an insight into the techniques employed by the besiegers and the besieged.

Valley of the Beautiful Woman

A twenty-minute walk southwest of the town centre in an area known as **Valley of**

15

the Beautiful Woman is a big square crammed with wine cellars, where you can enjoy back-to-back wine tastings – an integral part of a trip to Eger. A tourist train runs down here every thirty minutes from Egészségház utca (10am–10pm; 800Ft).

ARRIVAL AND INFORMATION

By train The station is on Állomás tér. The centre is a 10min walk to the right of Deák Ferenc utca, just up from the station.

Destinations Budapest (9 daily; 2hr).

By bus The bus station is at Barcóczy utca 2 behind the Basilica (☎ 36 517 777).

Destinations Budapest (2 hourly; 1hr 50min–2hr 10min); Debrecen (8 daily; 2hr 30min).

Tourist information The Tourinform office is at Bajcsy-Zsilinszky utca 9 (April–June & Sept–Oct Mon–Fri 8am–5pm, Sat 9am–1pm; July–Aug Mon–Fri 8am–6pm, Sat & Sun 9am–1pm; Nov–March Mon–Fri 8am–5pm; ☎ 36 517 715, ⊚ eger.hu). There's also a useful English-language expat site at ⊚ ieger.com.

GETTING AROUND

By bike You can rent bikes from Prana at Bajcsy-Zsilinszky utca 17 (Mon–Sat 9.30am–6pm; ☎ 36 419 221, ⊚ pranaeger.hu) from 1500Ft/6hr.

ACCOMMODATION

As in most of Hungary, colleges convert their dorms to hostels in July and Aug. Try St Hedvig at Dobó tér 6 (☎ 36 320 788, ⊚ kissne@szenthedvig.hu).

★ **Aphrodite Apartments** Dobó utca 22 ☎ 36 415 535, ⊚ aphroditeapartmentsandcafe.com. Great-value large self-catering apartments in the middle of the historic centre, sleeping 2–4 people. Price includes wi-fi, parking and a room service breakfast. Reception at *Görög Café* next door. 12,000Ft

Tulipán Szépasszonyvölgy 71 ☎ 70 385 1166, ⊚ tulipancamping.com. Basic campsite in the Valley of the Beautiful Woman – there's a dearth of shady spots, but with 40-odd wine cellars within walking distance, who cares? Open mid-March to mid-Oct. Per person 800Ft, plus per tent 900Ft

Várkapu Panzió Kossuth L. utca 21 ☎ 36 322 592, ⊚ varkapupanzio.hu. Large, high-ceilinged parquet-and-pine rooms in this listed Baroque building just outside the castle gate. A/c only on the first floor. Breakfast included. Doubles 15,000Ft

EATING AND DRINKING

Biboros Bajcsy-Zsilinszky utca 6. The main watering hole of the Eger youth, this popular bar with a great inner courtyard stays busy until the early hours every day. Beer 320Ft. Mon–Fri 11am–3am, Sat 1pm–3am, Sun 3pm–midnight.

★ **Macok** Tinódi Sebestyén tér 4. Bistro serving innovative Hungarian dishes at prices that would normally put it outside the scope of this Guide were it not for its tremendous lunch menu served on weekdays from noon until it runs out: two dishes 1500Ft, three dishes 1800Ft out of a choice of five. Mon–Thurs noon–10pm, Fri & Sat noon–11pm, Sun noon–6pm.

The Great Plain

Spanning half of Hungary, the **Great Plain** is its key horseriding region – horseriding being a core part of Magyar folklore: this warrior people's stunning success in conquering this part of Europe is often attributed to their skill and agility as archers on horseback. The prime destinations here are **Debrecen**, and the nearby **Hortobagy National Park**. Further south, between the Danube and the Tisza rivers, are **Kecskemét** and **Szeged**, both towns with some interesting turn-of-the-twentieth-century architecture and well worth a stop.

KECSKEMÉT

Possible as a day-trip from Budapest, **KECSKEMÉT** is a small town chiefly remarkable for several striking pieces of architecture from Hungary's "Romantic Nationalist" period at the turn of the twentieth century. Its name comes from the Hungarian for goat, *kecske*, as its thirteenth-century bishop apparently used to give the cloven-footed creatures to each new Christian convert.

WHAT TO SEE AND DO

Kecskemét's main attraction is the ornate **Cifra Palace** on Szabadság tér – a large building on a street corner that you might overlook, were it not for the daring Art Nouveau design. Designed by Markus Géza in 1902, it now houses the **Kecskemét Art Gallery** (Tues–Sun 10am–5pm; 700Ft; ☎ 76 480 776, ⊚ muzeum.kecskemet.hu). Szabadság tér runs into the other main square, Kossuth tér, where the **Town Hall** stands tall, a masterpiece of Romantic Nationalist architecture. You can visit its Ceremonial Hall (Mon–Fri 10–11.30am; 300Ft), but must reserve first at the Tourinform office (see below). Finally, the **Hungarian Photography Museum** at Katona József tér 12 (Tues–Sun noon–5pm; 500Ft; ☎76 403 221, ⊛fotomuzeum.hu) has excellent exhibitions of photography from the nineteenth century to the present day.

ARRIVAL AND INFORMATION

By train It's about a 15min walk down Nagykőrösi utca from the station at Kodaly Zoltan tér, to Szabadság tér.
Destinations Budapest (15 daily; 1hr 15min); Szeged (10–12 daily; 1hr).
By bus Located right next to the train station at Noszlopy Gaspár park 1.
Destinations Budapest (1–3 hourly; 1hr 10min–2hr); Szeged (1–2 hourly; 1hr 30min–2hr).
Tourist information The Tourinform office is in the corner of the Town Hall at Kossuth tér 1 (mid-May to Sept Mon–Fri 8.30am–5.30pm, Sat 9am–1pm; Oct to mid-May Mon–Fri 8am–4pm; ☎76 481 065, ⊛iranykecskemet .hu). They also rent out bikes (2500Ft/day).

ACCOMMODATION AND EATING

In July & Aug, hostel accommodation is available in the colleges at Piaristák tere 4 (☎76 506 912) and Nyíri utca 28 (☎76 486 322).
Fábián Panzió Kápolna utca 14 ☎76 477 677, ⊛panziofabian.hu. Very friendly *pension* with smart, spacious rooms around a beautifully tended garden. Note that beds are only 1.95m long. Breakfast included. Doubles __12,500Ft__
★**Lordok Kávezó** Kossuth tér 6–7. Central café bar that offers enormous gateaux time-stamped for freshness (450Ft) during the day, while it later packs a young crowd in to sample the cocktails (600–1000Ft). Mid-May to Sept Sun–Thurs 9am–midnight, Fri & Sat 9am–2am; Oct to mid-May Sun–Thurs 9am–10pm, Fri & Sat 9am–midnight.
Technika Kavezó Rácoczi utca 2 ⊛technikakavezo.hu. An atmospheric rock club inside the old Kecskemét Synagogue. The mainly student crowd is attracted by the frequent gigs on offer and the cheap beer (400Ft/half litre). Mon–Wed noon–4pm, Thurs & Fri noon–midnight, Sat 8pm–midnight.

SZEGED

The most sophisticated city in the Great Plain, **SZEGED** straddles the River Tisza as it flows south towards Serbia. The present layout of the city, and its beautiful Art Nouveau architecture, date from after the great flood of 1879, when Szeged was rebuilt with strapping new buildings and squares thanks to foreign funding. The student population gives the city a real energy, and it's more than pleasant for a day or two's stopover.

WHAT TO SEE AND DO

Szeged's biggest monument is **Dom tér**, ringed by scholarly cloisters and busts of celebrated Hungarians. It was created in 1920 to complement the enormous double-spired **Votive Church** (daily 9am–7pm; Tower 700Ft; ☎62 420 32, ⊛fogadalmitemplom.hu), which leading townspeople pledged to erect after the great flood. There's an interesting interactive exhibition on the town's history in the crypt (Tues–Sun 9am–5pm; 400Ft, combined ticket with Tower 1000Ft), while at 12.15pm and 5.45pm, the **Musical Clock** on the south side of the square comes alive, as figurines from inside pop out and trundle around to the chiming of bells.

Móra Ferenc Museum

The **Móra Ferenc Museum** at Roosevelt tér 1–3 (daily 10am–6pm; 1490Ft; ☎62 549 040, ⊛moramuzeum.hu) contains folk art, fine art and archeological remains that offer an insight into the Avars, the people who ruled much of the Central-Eastern European Pannonian plain from the sixth to ninth centuries. From the museum, it's a short walk to green, pretty Széchenyi tér, home to the neo-Baroque **town hall** with its decorative tiled roof. Look out for the "Bridge of Sighs", modelled on the Venetian original, which links the hall to a neighbouring house.

Great Synagogue

The **Great Synagogue** at Jósika utca 10 (April–Sept Mon–Fri 9am–noon & 1–4pm; Oct–March Mon–Fri 9am–2pm, 500Ft; ☎62 423 849, ⊛zsinagoga.szeged .hu) was built between 1900 and 1903 by architect Lipót Baumhorn. It is one of Hungary's most beautiful buildings, sporting a blue glass dome with stars picked out in gold, and a stunning Art Nouveau interior that is full of life: the

15

frescoes and stained glass replicate exactly the plants and flowers that the then chief rabbi, a keen botanist, thought might have grown in ancient Jerusalem.

ARRIVAL AND INFORMATION

By train The train station is on Indóház tér, south of the centre, a short tram ride on the #1 or #2 (400Ft).
Destinations Budapest (hourly; 2hr 20min); Kecskemét (hourly; 1hr).
By bus The station is on Mars tér, a 10min walk west from Roosevelt tér down Híd utca.
Destinations Budapest (6 daily; 3hr); Kecskemét (1–2 hourly; 1hr 45min); Novi Sad (2 daily; 3hr); Pécs (6 daily; 3hr 30min); Subotica (3 daily; 1hr–1hr 30min).
Tourist information Tourinform, Dugonics tér 2 (April & May Mon–Fri 9am–5pm, Sat 9am–1pm; June–Aug Mon–Fri 9am–6pm, Sat 9am–1pm; Sept–March Mon–Fri 9am–5pm; ☎ 62 488 690, ⊕ szegedtourism.hu). Very organized and helpful office that can help with accommodation – ask for their Art Nouveau walk guide. There is also a seasonal office in Széchenyi tér (June–Aug daily 8am–8pm).

ACCOMMODATION

Eötvös Loránd Youth Hostel Tisza Lajos krt 103 ☎ 62 544 388, ✉ szallas@eotvos.u-szeged.hu. In summer, Eötvös College rents beds in its dorms right in the centre of town. Email them to book in advance; if they're full they will suggest other colleges. July & Aug only. Dorms **3210Ft**
Hostel 66 Petőfi Sándor sgt 66 ☎ 702 159 990, ✉ booking@hostel66.com. Basic but modern and clean hostel with uncrowded dorms and largish twin rooms not too far from the centre. Free coffee. Dorms **€14**, doubles **€50**
★ **Lila Vendégház** József Attila sgt 9 ☎ 62 635 166, ⊕ lilahaz.hu. Friendly budget hotel with modern, well-furnished rooms, each with its own small hall – a nice touch. Free parking available, plus cooked breakfast for 1000Ft. Doubles **12,000Ft**
Partfürdő Camping Középkikötő sor 1–3 ☎ 62 430 843, ⊕ szegedkemping.hu. Located on the riverbank in Újszeged, a 10min walk from the centre across the Belvárosi bridge, this large campsite has a swimming pool and private river beach. Open May–Sept. Per person **1490Ft**, plus per tent **590Ft**

EATING AND DRINKING

Corso Café Kárász utca 16. Open-fronted café/restaurant in Szeged's pedestrianized heart, attracting a student crowd for its large portions. Mains from 1200Ft. Mon–Wed 9am–midnight, Thurs & Fri 9am–1am, Sat 10am–1am, Sun 10am–midnight.
Dugonics Teri Kisvendeglő Dugonics tér 2. A patisserie with a good restaurant at the back, where tall indoor yuccas rise above the cherry-wood tables. Three-course menus 1200Ft during the week, 1500Ft at weekends. Daily 7am–9pm.
★ **Halászcsárda** Roosevelt tér 12–14 ☎ 62 555 980, ⊕ szegedihalaszcsarda.hu. A Szeged riverside institution, where a cauldron of brilliant-red fish goulash goes down swimmingly with a glass of local Riesling. Mains from 1700Ft; half-portions available (and, frankly, recommended). Reservations recommended. Daily 11am–midnight.

DEBRECEN

DEBRECEN and its surrounding countryside is where you should go to experience the real Hungary of the *betyar* (cowboys) and the *czardas* (inns). Far from Budapest and its Germanic influences, this is a city where the nineteenth-century patriotism that awoke the Hungarian nation is still running strong, aided and abetted both by a Calvinist stubbornness and by the youthful idealism of its large student population. Although it's Hungary's second city, it is both easy to manage and – with a forest within city limits – as close to nature as a city can be. It is also the gateway to the stunning Hortobagy National Park, a piece of Asian steppe in Central Europe.

WHAT TO SEE AND DO

Debrecen's identity as the centre of Calvinism in Hungary is confirmed by the dominating presence of the **Great Reformed Church** on Kossuth tér (March–May Mon–Fri 9am–4pm, Sat 9am–1pm, Sun noon–4pm; June–Aug Mon–Fri 9am–6pm, Sat 9am–1pm, Sun noon–4pm; Sept & Oct Mon–Fri 9am–4pm, Sat 9am–1pm, Sun noon–4pm; Nov–Feb Mon–Fri 10am–3pm, Sat 9am–1pm, Sun noon–4pm; 600Ft; ☎ 52 412 695, ⊕ nagytemplom.hu), with its sparse and austere interior. Inside, you can browse the Hungarian Declaration of Independence (in English), which Lajos Kossuth proclaimed here on April 13, 1849, and see his chair and memorabilia, or simply take the lift up the Eastern tower to the panorama bridge for a bird's-eye view of the city.

Behind the church is the **Déri museum** (Tues–Sun 10am–6pm; 2000Ft; ☎ 52 322 207, ⊕ derimuzeum.hu), whose

15

permanent art collection includes Munkácsy's awe-inspiring paintings of Christ.

The other focus of the town is located at the end of the #1 tram line running north from the station via Kossuth tér: the area around the **University** and **The Great Forest** (*Nagyerdő*), which is really a fancy name for the admittedly large city park. There, you can find restaurants, bars, a botanical garden, a zoo and a large amusement park, as well as the august **Aquaticum** spa (ⓦaquaticum.hu).

ARRIVAL AND INFORMATION

By plane The airport (served by Wizz Air) is only about 10min by bus south of the main train station. An airport shuttle runs regularly between the airport and the train station (300Ft).
Destinations London Luton (10 weekly; 2hr 35min).
By train The train station is south of town on Petőfi tér and joined to the centre by tram #1.
Destinations Budapest (hourly; 2hr 30min); Hortobagy (10 daily; 45min).
By bus The bus station is about a 15min walk west of the centre on Külső-Vásártér, at the end of Széchenyi utca.
Destinations Eger (8 daily; 2hr 20min); Szeged (3 daily; 5hr).
Tourist information Tourinform is at 20 Piac utca (mid-June to Aug Mon–Fri 9am–5pm, Sat 9am–1pm; Sept to mid-June Mon–Fri 9am–5pm; ☎52 412 250). They have a free bicycle scheme (20,000Ft deposit) and sightseeing tours in English (2hr; 15,000Ft per group).

GETTING AROUND

By tram and bus Debrecen's public transport is very easy to negotiate, with tram line #1 running from the train station north to the university and looping back again, taking in all important sights. Line #2 heads toward the residential areas in the northwestern part of the city. A bus ticket costs 300Ft (buy from kiosks). A one-day card valid on trams and buses costs 1000Ft, while a three-day card costs 2400Ft. Public transport information is on ⓦdkv.hu.

ACCOMMODATION

Debrecen University (☎52 512 950 & ☎52 512 940) offers beds in various student residences around the town in July and Aug.
★**Regi Posta** Széchenyi utca 6 ☎52 325 325, ⓦregiposta.hu. Great location, great hosts and great inclusive breakfast in the oldest building in Debrecen, where Sweden's Charles XII stayed in 1714 (you can book his room). Free parking and an excellent Hungarian traditional restaurant in the basement. Doubles **€57**
Szív Panzió Szív utca 11 ⓦszivpanzio.hu. Spotlessly clean *pension* in a quiet residential street a 10min walk from the station. The red ochre inner courtyard has a covered wooden benchstand, great for sipping a coffee in the summer. Free parking. Breakfast 1000Ft. Doubles **7800Ft**

EATING, DRINKING AND NIGHTLIFE

Palma Simonyi út 44 ⓦpalmapub.hu. Feels like an English pub, albeit of the gastro persuasion, and the food is as good as the drinks. Pizzas 1600Ft, with a weekday three-course lunch menu for only 1100Ft. Daily 10am–midnight.
★**Roncsbar** Csapó utca 27 ⓦroncsbar.hu. When you walk into Debrecen's only "ruin pub" you think you've entered the scene of an Iron Maiden album cover – no wonder, as it belongs to the drummer of local metal band, *Tankcsapda*. Don't worry, they're friendly and the beer is cheap (360Ft). Mon, Tues & Sun 11am–midnight, Wed & Thurs 11am–2am, Fri & Sat 11am–4am.

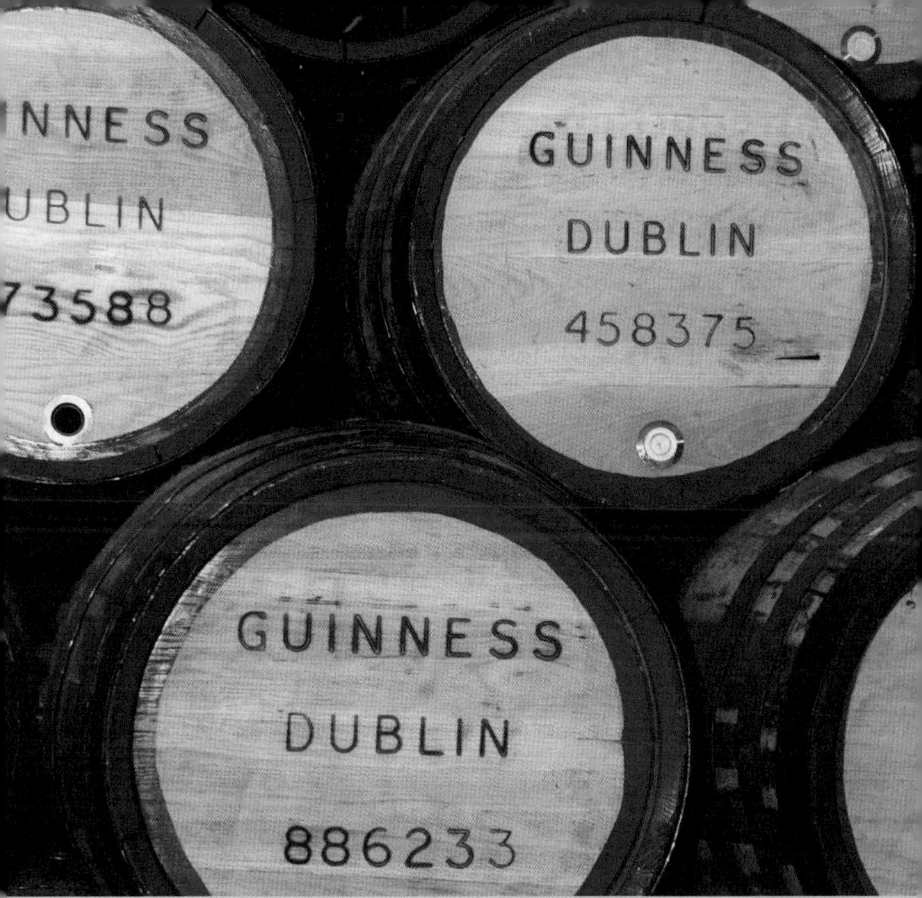

Ireland

HIGHLIGHTS

❶ **Dublin** Visit the home of world-famous Guinness. **See p.575**

❷ **Glendalough, Wicklow** Explore the ruins of a sixth-century monastery in the "Garden of Ireland". **See p.582**

❸ **Wild Atlantic Way** Experience Ireland's rugged west coast on a stunning 2500km touring route. **See p.588**

❹ **County Clare** The stunning landscapes of the Cliffs of Moher and the Burren alongside traditional Irish music. **See p.590**

❺ **Slieve League** Witness astounding views from Europe's highest sea cliffs. **See p.595**

❻ **Giant's Causeway** Marvel at the astonishing basalt columns. **See p.600**

HIGHLIGHTS ARE MARKED ON THE MAP ON P.571

ROUGH COSTS

Daily budget Basic €50, occasional treat €70

Drink Guinness €4.50/pint

Food Irish stew €10

Hostel/budget hotel €16/€35–45

Travel Train: Dublin–Belfast (2hr 10min) €20; bus: Kilkenny–Dublin (2hr 20min–3hr) €13

FACT FILE

Population 6.4 million

Language English; Gaelic

Currency Euro € (Republic); pound sterling £ (N. Ireland)

Capitals Dublin (Republic); Belfast (N. Ireland)

International phone code ☏353 (Republic); ☏44 (N. Ireland)

Time zone GMT

Introduction

In both Northern Ireland and the Republic, Ireland's lures are its landscape and people – the rain-hazed loughs and wild coastlines, the talent for conversation and wealth of traditional music. While economic growth has transformed Ireland's cities, the countryside remains relatively unchanged.

Ireland's west draws most visitors; its coastline and islands – especially **Aran** – combine vertiginous cliffs, boulder-strewn wastes and dramatic mountains. The interior is less spectacular, though the southern pastures and low wooded hills are classic landscapes. Northern Ireland's principal highlight is the bizarre basalt formation of the **Giant's Causeway**.

Dublin is an extraordinary mix of youthfulness and tradition, of revitalized Georgian squares and vibrant pubs. **Belfast** has undergone a massive rejuvenation, while the cities of **Cork** and **Galway** sparkle with energy.

No introduction can cope with the complexities of Ireland's **politics**, which still permeate most aspects of daily life in many areas in the North. However, regardless of partisan politics, Irish hospitality is as warm as the brochures say, on both sides of the border.

CHRONOLOGY

c. 3000 BC Neolithic tombs first constructed.

c. 500 BC Celts arrive, heralding the Iron Age.

c.100 BC Romans refer to Ireland as "Hibernia".

432 AD Saint Patrick arrives in Ireland, converting pagans to Christianity.

795 Viking raids on Ireland.

1167 Arrival of Anglo-Norman invaders, ushering in eight hundred years of English rule.

1558–1603 Policy of Plantation of Irish lands under Queen Elizabeth I.

1649–53 Cromwell re-conquers Ireland, after a bloody campaign against Irish Catholics and English Royalists.

1690 Battle of the Boyne marks decisive victory by the Protestant king William of Orange over Catholic James II of England.

1704 Penal Code introduced, barring Catholics from voting, education and the military.

1759 Arthur Guinness begins to brew his famous stout in Dublin.

1798 Rebellion of the United Irishmen led by Wolfe Tone and supported by French troops is suppressed.

1801 Act of Union makes Ireland officially part of Great Britain.

1803 Second United Irishmen Rebellion under Robert Emmet defeated.

1845–49 Potato famine causes widespread starvation and prompts mass migration to the United States.

1879–82 Land War increases support for the Home Rule movement led by Charles Stewart Parnell.

1916 Easter Rising by Irish nationalists is brutally repressed by the British.

1922 Irish War of Independence ends with secession of 26 Irish counties from the UK to form the Irish Free State. Six counties in the North remain part of the UK.

1922 James Joyce's *Ulysses* is published.

1949 The Republic of Ireland is declared.

1970s The Provisional IRA steps up violent campaigns in Northern Ireland and the UK.

1972 British troops kill thirteen civilians in Derry, Northern Ireland, in an event known as Bloody Sunday.

1973 Ireland joins the European Community.

1998 Good Friday Agreement signed by the British and Irish governments heralding a new era of peace in Northern Ireland.

2002 The euro is introduced in the Republic of Ireland.

2005 The Provisional IRA announces a full ceasefire.

2007 Agreement between rival party leaders, Ian Paisley and Gerry Adams, to share power in an elected assembly for Northern Ireland.

2008 Crisis in the Irish banking system combines with a worldwide recession, bringing an end to economic prosperity.

2010 Police and justice powers for Northern Ireland transferred from London to Belfast; the EU and International Monetary Fund approve an €85 billion loan to bail out the Irish economy.

2011 Queen Elizabeth makes historic first State visit to Ireland.

2015 Ireland becomes the first country to approve same-sex marriage by popular vote.

ARRIVAL AND DEPARTURE

Ireland has five international **airports**: Dublin, Cork, Shannon and Knock in

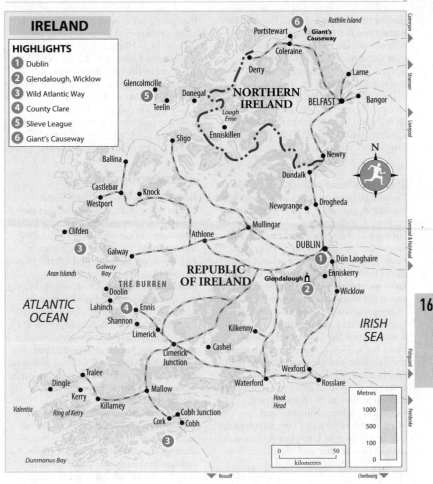

IRELAND

HIGHLIGHTS

1 Dublin
2 Glendalough, Wicklow
3 Wild Atlantic Way
4 County Clare
5 Slieve League
6 Giant's Causeway

Rathlin Island
Portstewart
6 **Giant's Causeway**
Coleraine
Derry
Larne
NORTHERN IRELAND
BELFAST
Bangor
Glencolmcille
5 Donegal
Teelin
Lough Erne
Newry
Sligo
Enniskillen
Ballina
Dundalk
Castlebar
Knock
Newgrange
Drogheda
Westport
Mullingar
Clifden
Athlone
DUBLIN
3 Galway
1 Dún Laoghaire
Aran Islands
Galway Bay
REPUBLIC OF IRELAND
Glendalough
Enniskerry
THE BURREN
2
Wicklow
ATLANTIC OCEAN
Doolin
Lahinch 4 Ennis
Shannon
Kilkenny
IRISH SEA
Limerick
Cashel
Limerick Junction
Tralee
Wexford
Dingle
Mallow
Waterford
Rosslare
Kerry
Killarney
Hook Head
Valentia
Ring of Kerry
Cobh Junction
Cork
Cobh
3
Dunmanus Bay

Metres
1000
500
100
0

0   50
kilometres

Cairnryan
Stranraer
Liverpool
Liverpool & Holyhead
16
Fishguard
Pembroke

Roscoff
Cherbourg

---

the Republic, and Belfast International in the North. Regional airports, which also serve Britain, are Belfast City, Derry, Donegal, Galway, Kerry and Sligo.

Ferry routes from the UK comprise Cairnryan–Larne, Fishguard–Rosslare, Fleetwood–Larne, Holyhead–Dublin, Holyhead–Dún Laoghaire, Isle of Man–Belfast, Isle of Man–Dublin, Liverpool–Belfast, Liverpool–Dublin, Pembroke–Rosslare, Stranraer–Belfast and Troon–Larne. Travelling by ferry without a vehicle is not expensive (about €80 return), but taking a car is pricey (€200–300 in high season).

GETTING AROUND

You can save money on rail and bus services by booking online and buying multi-journey tickets in advance; the **Freedom of Northern Ireland/Irish Rover** tickets give you unlimited bus/rail travel for three, five, eight or fifteen days. See ⓦtranslink.co.uk or ⓦbuseireann.ie.

BY TRAIN

In the Republic, Iarnród Éireann (ⓦirishrail.ie) operates **trains** to most major towns and cities; book online for substantial discounts. Few routes run north–south, so, although you can easily get to the west coast by train, you can't use the railways to explore. The **Dublin–Belfast line** is the only cross-border service, and the journey takes a little over two hours (€20). NI Railways (walink.co.uk) operates just a few routes in Northern Ireland.

The Global and One Country **InterRail** (see p.34) passes are valid in Ireland – though you need two separate One Country passes for the Republic and Northern Ireland.

BY BUS

The express **buses** of the Republic's Bus Éireann (wbuseireann.ie) cover most of the island, including several cross-border services. Citylink also runs a good service between Dublin, Galway, Limerick and Cork (wcitylink.ie) at slightly cheaper rates. Aircoach (waircoach.ie) run buses direct from Dublin airport to Cork. Bus **fares** are generally cheaper than trains, especially midweek. Remote villages may only have a couple of buses a week, so it's essential to find out the times – major bus stations stock free timetables. Private buses operate on major routes throughout the Republic and are often cheaper than Bus Éireann: J.J. Kavanagh & Sons, for instance, provide an efficient service from Dublin airport to Shannon airport, Limerick, Galway, Kilkenny and Waterford (☎056 883 1106, wjjkavanagh.ie). In the North, Ulsterbus (wtranslink.co.uk) runs regular and reliable services.

BY CAR

Driving is the best way to see the country, and **car rental**, if shared between a few people, can also work out cheaper than public transport. Budget (☎090 662 7711, wbudget.ie) and Thrifty (☎01 844 1944, wthrifty.ie) have the cheapest rates, around €15–60 per day depending on the season. Book online for the best deals. Note that the driver must be over 25 years of age.

BY BIKE

Cycling is an enjoyable and reasonably safe way of seeing Ireland. In the Republic, bikes can be rented in most towns and Raleigh is the main operator (€15/day, €70/week; from €100 deposit; ☎01 465 9659, wraleigh.ie); local dealers (including some hostels) are cheaper. It costs an extra €10 to carry a bike on a bus, and €3–10 on a train, though not all buses or trains carry bikes; check in advance. In the North, bike rental (around £15/day) is more limited; tourist offices have lists of local operators. Taking a bike on a bus costs half the adult one-way fare (up to a maximum of £5) and, on a train, a quarter of the adult one-way fare (with no upper limit).

ACCOMMODATION

Hostels run by **An Óige** (Irish Youth Hostel Association; wanoige.ie) and **HINI** (Hostelling International Northern Ireland; whini.org.uk) are affiliated to Hostelling International. Overnight prices start at €11–17 in the Republic and £9.50–13 in the North. Most Irish hostels are **independent hostels**, which usually belong to either Independent Holiday Hostels (☎01 836 4700, whostels-ireland.com) or the Independent Hostels network (☎074 973 0130, windependenthostelsireland.com). In the Republic, expect to pay €12–20 for a dorm bed, €17–32 (rising to €46 in some Dublin hostels) per person for private rooms where available; in the North, it's £9–14/£16–27.

B&Bs vary enormously, but most are welcoming, warm and clean. Expect to pay from around €30/£25 per person sharing; most **hotels** are a little pricier but you can find bargains online. Booking ahead is always advisable during high season and major festivals.

Camping costs around €8–12 a night in the Republic, £7–10 in the North. In out-of-the-way places it may be possible to camp in the wild, but ask the landowner's permission first: farmers in popular tourist areas may ask for a small fee. Some hostels also let you camp for around €8/£5 per person.

FOOD AND DRINK

Irish **food** is meat-orientated. B&Bs usually provide a "traditional" **Irish breakfast** of sausages, bacon and eggs (although many offer vegetarian alternatives). **Pub lunch** staples are usually meat or fish and two veg, with a few veggie options, while specifically vegetarian places are sparse outside major cities and popular tourist areas. All towns have fast-food outlets, but traditional fish and chips is a better bet, especially on the coast. For the occasional treat, there are some very good seafood restaurants, particularly along the southwest and west coasts. Most towns have daytime cafés serving a selection of affordable hot dishes, salads, soups, sandwiches and cakes.

DRINK

The stereotypical view of the "Irish national pastime" has a certain element of truth; especially in rural areas, the **pub** is the social heart of the community and the focus for the proverbial **craic** (pronounced "crack"), a particular blend of Irish fun involving good company, witty conversation and laughter, frequently against a backdrop of music. The classic Irish drink is **Guinness**, which is made in Dublin, while the Cork stouts, Beamish and Murphy's, have their devotees. For English-style keg **bitter**, try Smithwicks. Irish **whiskeys** are world-famous – try Paddy's, Jameson's or Bushmills.

CULTURE AND ETIQUETTE

With the huge influx of visitors to Ireland in recent years, the country has acquired an increasingly **cosmopolitan** feel, particularly in the big cities, but the sense of national identity and heritage remains strong. Traditional music sessions are still the primary form of evening entertainment in pubs, especially in rural areas.

Despite the decreasing influence of Catholicism in Ireland, family values still reign. It's hard to miss the hospitality and friendliness that most clearly define the Irish.

Smoking is banned in all indoor public places. In restaurants and cafés, a ten percent **tip** is generally expected.

SPORTS AND OUTDOOR ACTIVITIES

Walking and **cycling** in Ireland are great ways of enjoying the country's beautiful landscapes (see ⓦirishtrails.ie for suggested routes). There are great opportunities for **horseriding** (see ⓦdiscoverireland.ie); a lovely ride is along the white sands of Connemara. **Watersports** are popular: Ireland is increasingly praised for its surfing spots, such as Portrush in the north, Bundoran in Donegal, and Lahinch in Clare (see ⓦisasurf.ie).

The two great Gaelic sports, **hurling** (the oldest field game in Europe, and similar to hockey) and **Gaelic football** (a mixture of soccer and rugby, but predating both), are very popular spectator sports. Croke Park Stadium in Dublin is home to the big fixtures (see ⓦgaa.ie and ⓦcrokepark.ie).

Horse racing (ⓦgoracing.ie) looms large on the sporting agenda: you'll never be far from a race, whether it's a big racecourse like Galway or a soggy village affair.

COMMUNICATIONS

Main **post offices** are open Monday to Friday 9am to 5.30pm, Saturday 9am to 1pm. Stamps and phonecards are also often available in newsagents. **Public phones** are becoming increasingly rare. **International calls** are cheaper at weekends or after 6pm (Mon–Fri). To call the Republic from Northern Ireland dial ☏00353 followed by the area code (without the initial 0) and the local number (note cross-border calls are charged at the international rate). To call the North from the Republic use the code ☏048, followed by the eight-digit local number. **Wi-fi access** is widely available in hotels and hostels, and pubs and cafés; just ask the proprietor for the log-in details.

16

IRELAND ONLINE

ⓦ**discoverireland.ie** Fáilte Ireland website with comprehensive tourist information.
ⓦ**discovernorthernireland.com** Northern Ireland Tourist Board.
ⓦ**heritageireland.com** Information on Ireland's main heritage sites.
ⓦ**visitdublin.ie** Accommodation, eating and drinking listings for the capital.

EMERGENCIES

The Republic's police are known as the **Gardaí** (pronounced "gar-dee"), while the **PSNI** (Police Service of Northern Ireland) operates in the North. **Hospitals** and medical facilities are high quality; you'll rarely be far from a hospital, and both Northern Ireland and the Republic are within the European Health Insurance Card scheme. Most **pharmacies** open standard shop hours, though in large towns some may stay open until 10pm; they dispense only a limited range of drugs without a doctor's prescription.

INFORMATION

Tourist offices are abundant in Ireland, in the smaller as well as larger towns on the tourist trail. **Fáilte Ireland** provides tourist information in the Republic; the **Northern Ireland Tourist Board** in the North. They provide free maps of the city/town and immediate vicinity, and sell a selection of more extensive and specialized maps.

MONEY AND BANKS

Currency in the Republic is the **euro** (€); in Northern Ireland it is the **pound sterling** (£). Standard **bank hours** are Monday to Friday 9.30am to 4.30pm (Republic and Northern Ireland). There

STUDENT DISCOUNTS

A **student card** usually gives reduced entrance charges of up to fifty percent, and if you're visiting sites run by the Heritage Service in the Republic (ⓦ heritageireland.ie) it's worth buying a **Heritage Card** (€25, students €10), which provides a year's unlimited admission.

are **ATMs** throughout Ireland – though not in all villages – and most accept a variety of cards. The exchange rate at the time of writing was €1.25/£1.

OPENING HOURS AND HOLIDAYS

Business hours are roughly Monday to Saturday 9am to 6pm, with some late evenings (usually Thurs) and Sunday opening. **Museums** and attractions are usually open regular shop hours, though outside the cities, many only open during the summer. Some museums are closed on Mondays. **Cafés** usually open daily from 8am till 6pm, and most **restaurants** from noon till 10pm. **Pubs** operate strict trading hours, and those without a late-night licence must close at 11.30pm Sunday to Thursday and 12.30am on Friday & Saturday. **Nightclubs** close at 2.30am.

Public holidays in the Republic are: Jan 1, St Patrick's Day (March 17), Easter Monday, May Day (first Mon in May), June Bank Holiday (first Mon in June), August Bank Holiday (first Mon in Aug), October Bank Holiday (Halloween, last Mon in Oct), December 25 and 26. Note that some places may also close on Good

16

THE IRISH LANGUAGE

Though **Irish** is the first language of the Republic, you'll rarely hear it spoken outside the areas officially designated as *Gaeltacht* ("Irish-speaking"), namely West Cork, West Kerry, Connemara, some of Mayo and Donegal, and a tiny part of Meath. However, two important words you may encounter sometimes appear on the doors of pub toilets: *Fir* (for men) and *Mná* (for women). You'll also find the word *Fáilte* (welcome) popping up frequently as you enter towns and tourist spots. A few other words to get your tongue round:

Sláinte	cheers, good health
Gardaí	police
An lár	city centre
Dia dhuit	hello
Slán	goodbye

More information on the Gaeltacht areas is available at ⓦ gaelsaoire.ie.

Friday. In the North: January 1, St Patrick's Day (March 17), Good Friday, Easter Monday, May Day (first Mon in May), Spring Bank Holiday (last Mon in May), July 12, August Bank Holiday (last Mon in Aug), December 25 and 26.

Dublin and around

Set on the banks of the River Liffey, **DUBLIN** is a splendidly monumental city with a cosmopolitan feel and an internationally renowned nightlife. It was the centre of Ireland's booming economy during the "Celtic Tiger" years up to 2007, which brought rejuvenation and renewed energy, and which still remains despite high unemployment.

Dublin began as the Viking trading post **Dubh Linn** (Dark Pool), which soon amalgamated with the Celtic settlement of **Baile Átha Cliath** (Town of the Hurdle Ford) – still the Irish name for the city. The city's fabric is essentially **Georgian**, hailing from when the Anglo-Irish gentry invested their income in new townhouses. After the 1801 Act of Union, Dublin entered a long economic decline, but remained the focus of much of the agitation that eventually led to independence.

The city is an excellent base for excursions to the picturesque mountains, lakes, forested estates and rural villages of **County Wicklow**, or to the five-thousand-year-old passage tombs at **Newgrange** in the Boyne Valley, County Meath.

WHAT TO SEE AND DO

Dublin's fashionable **Southside** is home to the city's trendy bars, restaurants and shops – especially in the cobbled alleys of **Temple Bar** leading down to the **River Liffey** – and most of its historic monuments, centred on **Trinity College**, **Grafton Street** and **St Stephen's Green**. But the **Northside**, with its long-standing working-class neighbourhoods and inner-city communities, is the real heart of the city. Across the bridges from Temple Bar are the shopping districts around **O'Connell Street**, where you'll find a flavour of the old Dublin. Here, you'll also come across a fair amount of graceful – if slightly shabby – residential streets and squares, with plenty of interest in the museums and cultural centres around the elegant **Parnell Square**.

The Vikings sited their assembly and burial ground near what is now **College Green**, a three-sided square where Trinity College is the most famous landmark.

Trinity College

Founded in 1592, Trinity College played a major role in the development of a Protestant Anglo-Irish tradition: right up to 1966, Catholics had to obtain a special dispensation to study here, though now they make up the majority of the students. The stern grey and mellow red-brick buildings are ranged around cobbled quadrangles in a larger version of the quads at Oxford and Cambridge. **The Old Library** (June–Sept Mon–Sat 8.30am–5pm, Sun 9.30am–5pm; Oct–May Mon–Sat 9.30am–5pm, Sun noon–4.30pm; €11, students €9; ⓦbookofkells .ie) owns numerous Irish manuscripts; pride of place goes to the illustrated ninth-century **Book of Kells**, which contains the four Gospels written in Latin on vellum, the script adorned with patterns and fantastic animals intertwined with the text's capital letters. The first of the great Irish illuminated manuscripts, the **Book of Durrow**, which dates from between 650 and 680, is also on display.

Grafton Street and around

Just south of College Green, the streets around pedestrianized **Grafton Street** frame Dublin's quality shopping area – featuring boutiques, department stores and designer outlets, as well as some secondhand, more alternative, shops. At the southern end of Grafton Street lies **St Stephen's Green**, whose pleasant gardens and ponds are a nice picnic spot on a sunny day. At 15 St Stephen's Green you'll find the charming **Little Museum of Dublin** (daily 9.30am–5pm, Thurs until 8pm; €7). Housed in a magnificent eighteenth-century townhouse, it charts the history of Dublin since 1900. Running parallel to

16

16

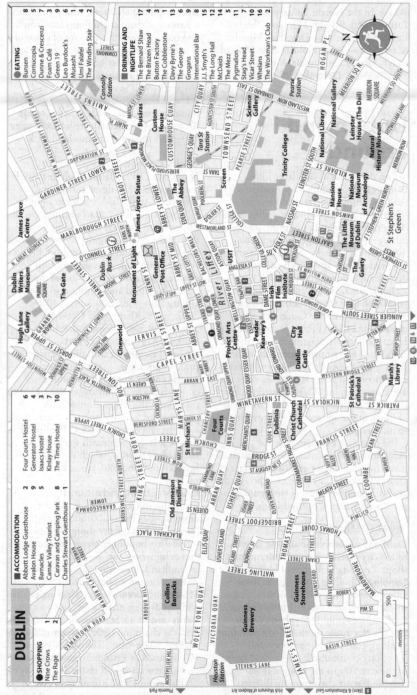

● EATING

Bunsen	8
Cornucopia	5
Dunne & Crescenzi	7
Foam Café	3
Green 19	6
Leo Burdock's	1
Musashi	4
Umi Falafel	4
The Winding Stair	2

● DRINKING AND
NIGHTLIFE

The Bernard Shaw	17
The Brazen Head	4
Button Factory	3
The Cobblestone	1
Davy Byrne's	13
The George	6
Grogans	9
International Bar	8
J.J. Smyth's	15
The Long Hall	12
McDaids	14
The Mezz	5
Pygmalion	11
Stag's Head	7
Vicar Street	10
Whelans	16
The Workman's Club	2

■ ACCOMMODATION

Abbott Lodge Guesthouse	2
Avalon House	9
Barnacles	3
Camac Valley Tourist Caravan and Camping Park	8
Charles Stewart Guesthouse	1
Four Courts Hostel	6
Generator Hostel	4
Isaacs Hostel	5
Kinlay House	7
The Times Hostel	10

● SHOPPING

Nine Crows	1
The Rage	2

Grafton Street, Kildare Street harbours the imposing **Leinster House**, built in 1745 as the Duke of Leinster's townhouse, and now the seat of the Irish parliament, the **Dáil** (pronounced "doyle").

National Museum of Archaeology and the Natural History Museum

Alongside the Dáil is the **National Museum of Archaeology** (Tues–Sat 10am–5pm, Sun 2–5pm; free; ⓦmuseum .ie), the repository of the treasures of ancient Ireland. Much of its prehistoric gold was found in peat bogs, along with the Lurgan Longboat and the collection of "Bog Bodies", preserved victims of Iron Age human sacrifice. The Treasury and the Viking exhibitions display such masterpieces as the Ardagh Chalice and Tara Brooch – perhaps the greatest piece of Irish metalwork – and St Patrick's Bell.

The **Natural History Museum** (Tues–Sat 10am–5pm, Sun 2–5pm; free) has more than 10,000 animals from Ireland and overseas on display, some dating from the eighteenth century when the museum was first opened.

Merrion Square and the National Gallery

The back of Leinster House overlooks **Merrion Square**, the finest Georgian plaza in Dublin. No. 1 was once the home of Oscar Wilde, and a flamboyant statue on the green opposite shows the writer draped insouciantly over a rock; on Sundays the square's railings are adorned with artwork for sale. On the west side of the square, the **National Gallery** (Mon–Sat 9.30am–5.30pm, Thurs until 8.30pm, Sun noon–5.30pm; free) features a collection of works by European Old Masters and French Impressionists, but the real draw is the trove of Irish paintings, best of which is the permanent exhibition devoted to Ireland's best-known painter, Jack B. Yeats.

Temple Bar

Dame Street, leading west from College Green, marks the southern edge of the **Temple Bar** quarter, where you'll find a hub of lively restaurants, pubs, boutiques and arts centres. At night the area plays host to tourists out looking for a good time, as well as to stag and hen parties – so expect a particularly raucous kind of fun.

Dublin Castle

Tucked away behind City Hall, **Dublin Castle** (Mon–Sat 10am–4.45pm, Sun noon–4.45pm; €6.50; ⓦdublincastle.ie) was founded by the Normans, and symbolized British power over Ireland for seven hundred years. Though parts date back to 1207, it was largely rebuilt in the eighteenth century following fire damage. Tours of the State Apartments reveal much about the extravagant tastes and foibles of the viceroys, and the real highlight is the excavations in the Undercroft, where elements of Norman and Viking Dublin are still visible. The Clock Tower building now houses the **Chester Beatty Library** (Mon–Fri 10am–5pm, Sat 11am–5pm, Sun 1–5pm; Oct–April closed Mon; free; ⓦcbl.ie), a sumptuous and massive collection of books, objects and paintings amassed by the twentieth-century American collector Sir Arthur Chester Beatty on his travels around Europe and Asia.

Christ Church Cathedral

Over the brow of Dublin Hill, **Christ Church Cathedral** (June–Sept Mon–Sat 9am–7pm, Sun 12.30–2.30pm & 4.30–6pm; Oct–May Mon–Sat 9am–5pm, Sun 12.30–2.30pm; €6; ⓦchristchurchdublin.ie) was built between 1172 and 1240 and heavily restored in the 1870s. The crypt museum now houses a small selection of the cathedral's treasures, the least serious of which include a mummified cat and rat, found trapped in an organ pipe in the 1860s.

Located in a part of the cathedral known as Synod Hall, **Dublinia** (daily 10am–6pm; €8.50; ⓦdublinia.ie) is home to some brilliantly interactive and hands-on exhibits focusing on Viking and medieval Dublin.

St Patrick's Cathedral

Five minutes' walk south from Christ Church is Dublin's other great Norman edifice, **St Patrick's Cathedral** (Mon–Fri 9.30am–5pm, Sat 9am–6pm, Sun

16

9–10.30am, 12.30–2.30pm, 4.30–6pm; €6; ⓦstpatrickscathedral.ie), founded in 1191, and replete with relics of Jonathan Swift, author of *Gulliver's Travels*, its dean from 1713 to 1747. Just round the corner on St Patrick's Close sits **Marsh's Library** (9.30am–5pm, Sat 10am–5pm, closed Tues & Sun; €3; ⓦmarshlibrary .ie), a magnificently preserved late Renaissance public library.

Guinness Brewery

West of Christ Church, the **Guinness Brewery** covers a large area on either side of James's Street. Guinness is the world's largest single beer-exporting company, dispatching some 300 million pints a year. Set in the centre of the brewery, the **Guinness Storehouse** (daily 9.30am– 7pm; July & Aug until 8pm; €20 including pint of Guinness, ten percent discount if you book online; ⓦguinness -storehouse.com) serves as a kind of theme park for Guinness-lovers – and even if you're not a fan, you can't fail to be entertained by the interactive displays and activities, which include learning how to pour the perfect pint and watching some of those great Guinness TV ads again. Visits to the Storehouse end with reputedly the best pint of Guinness in Dublin, in the panoramic *Gravity Bar* at the top of the building, with amazing views over the city.

Irish Museum of Modern Art

Regular buses (#26, #51, #79 and #90) run along The Quays to Heuston Station from where it's a five-minute walk to the **Royal Hospital Kilmainham**, Ireland's first Neoclassical building, dating from 1680, which now houses the **Irish Museum of Modern Art** (Tues–Sat 10am–5.30pm, Wed opens 10.30am, Sun noon–5.30pm; free; ⓦimma.ie). Its permanent collection of Irish and international art includes works by Gilbert and George, Damien Hirst, Sean Scully, Francesco Clemente and Peter Doig.

General Post Office and the Monument of Light

Halfway up O'Connell Street looms the **General Post Office** (Mon–Sat

8.30am–6pm; free), the insurgents' headquarters in the 1916 Easter Rising; only the frontage survived the fighting, and you can still see where bullets were embedded in the pillars. The building is still a functioning post office, and home to a state-of-the-art **museum** dedicated to the Rising (daily 9am–5.30pm, €10, ⓦgpowitnesshistory.ie). Across the road on the corner of Essex Street North is a **statue of James Joyce**. At the same junction, where the city's most famous landmark, Nelson's Pillar, once stood (it was blown up by the IRA on the fiftieth anniversary of the Easter Rising in 1966), stands a huge, illuminated stainless-steel spire – the **Monument of Light** – representing the city's hopes for the new millennium.

Parnell Square

At the northern end of O'Connell Street lies Parnell Square, one of the first of Dublin's Georgian squares. Its plain red-brick houses are broken by the grey-stone **Hugh Lane Gallery** (Tues–Thurs 9.45am–6pm, Fri 9.45am–5pm, Sat 10am–5pm, Sun 11am–5pm; free; ⓦhughlane.ie), once the Earl of Charlemont's townhouse and the focus of fashionable Dublin. The gallery exhibits work by Irish and international masters, and features a reconstruction of Francis Bacon's working studio. Almost next door, the **Dublin Writers Museum** (Mon–Sat 9.45am–4.45pm, Sun 11am–4.30pm; €7.50; ⓦwritersmuseum.com) whisks you through Irish literary history from early Christian writings up to Samuel Beckett. Two blocks east of Parnell Square, at 35 North Great George's St, the **James Joyce Centre** (Tues–Sat 10am–5pm, Sun noon–5pm; €5; ⓦjamesjoyce.ie) runs intriguing walking tours of the novelist's haunts (€10, combined tickets with the Dublin Writers Museum are available; ⓣ01 878 8547).

Old Jameson Distillery

Fifteen minutes west of O'Connell Street, on Bow Street, is the **Old Jameson Distillery** (Mon–Sat 9am–6pm, Sun 10am–6pm; €16; ⓦjamesonwhiskey.com). Tours cover the history and method of distilling what the Irish called *uisce beatha* (anglicized to whiskey and meaning "water of life") – which differs from Scotch whisky by being three times distilled and lacking a peaty undertone – and end with a tasting session. The Distillery also has two **bars**, which pride themselves on their Jameson cocktails, and a **restaurant** (9am–4.45pm; light lunch €12).

Phoenix Park

Phoenix Park is one of the world's largest urban parks, a great escape from the hustle and bustle of the centre (bus #10 from O'Connell Street or #25 from Wellington Quay); originally priory land, it's now home to the Presidential Lodge, **Áras an Uachtaráin** (free tours every Sat 10.30am–4.30pm; ⓦpresident.ie), and **Dublin Zoo** (daily: Feb 9.30am–5pm; March–Sept 9.30am–6pm; Oct 9.30am–5.30pm; Nov–Jan 9.30am–4pm; €17; ⓦdublinzoo.ie).

ARRIVAL AND DEPARTURE

By plane The airport (ⓦdublinairport.com) is 10km north of the city; Airlink buses #747 and #748 run to Busáras bus station (every 10–20min; 30min; €6 one-way, €10 return), or there are regular Dublin Bus services #16, #41, #41B (every 10–20min; €1.85). Aircoach (ⓦaircoach.ie) run services to the city centre and South Dublin (€6–14 one-way/€10–21 return depending on distance travelled), and a cheap, comfortable coach all the way to Cork (€16/24) and Belfast (€17/24). A taxi to Dublin centre should cost €25.

By train Trains terminate at either Connolly Station on the Northside, or Heuston Station on the Southside.

Destinations (Connolly) Belfast (8 daily Mon–Sat, 5 Sun; 2hr 10min); Drogheda (33 daily; 30min–1hr); Rosslare (3–6 daily; 3hr); Sligo (6–11 daily; 3hr 10min–3hr 30min).

Destinations (Heuston) Cork (12–15 daily; 2hr 50min); Ennis (4 daily, via Limerick; 2hr 55min–3hr 40min); Galway (9–11 daily; 2hr 20min–2hr 50min); Kilkenny (6 daily Mon–Sat, 4 on Sun; 1hr 40min–1hr 50min); Killarney (7 daily; 3hr 30min–3hr 50min); Westport (3 daily; 3hr 20min–3hr 40min).

By bus Bus Éireann coaches arrive at Busáras bus station, off Beresford Place, just behind The Custom House; private buses use a variety of central locations.

Destinations Belfast (20 daily; 2hr 55min); Cashel (6 daily; 2hr 50min); Cork (6 daily; 4hr 25min); Derry (11 daily; 4hr); Donegal town (11 daily; 3hr 45min–4hr 10min); Doolin (2 daily; 6hr 15min); Drogheda (35 daily; 1hr 20min); Ennis (13 daily; 4hr 20min–6hr 50min); Enniskillen (11 daily; 2hr 20min–3hr); Galway (15 daily; 3hr 30min); Kilkenny (7 daily; 2hr 10min–2hr 30min); Killarney (5 daily; 6hr 10min);

Newgrange (3 daily; 1hr 40min–1hr 55min); Portrush (1–2 daily; 5hr 40min); Rosslare Harbour (18 daily; 3hr 20min); Sligo (7 daily; 4hr); Westport (4 daily; 5hr–5hr 40min).

By boat Ferries dock at either Dún Laoghaire, 10km south of the city centre, from where DART railway connects to the city (every 15min; €3.25; 20min), or at the closer Dublin Port, where the #53 bus (€2.70; 35min) meets arriving ferries; through-coaches from Britain usually drop you at Busáras.

INFORMATION AND TOURS

Tourist office Suffolk St, off College Green (Mon–Sat 9am–5.30pm, Sun 10.30am–3pm; ⓦvisitdublin.com), with branches at 14 Upper O'Connell St, the Dún Laoghaire ferry terminal and the airport.

Travel agency USIT on Aston Quay, by O'Connell Bridge (Mon–Fri 10am–6.30pm, Thurs until 7pm, Sat 9.30am–5pm; ⓣ01 602 1904, ⓦusit.ie).

Bus tours City Sightseeing (ⓦcitysightseeingdublin .com) and Dublin Bus Tours (ⓦdublinsightseeing.ie) run similar hop-on, hop-off tours to all the major sights in the city (€19–22); both collect from the front of Trinity College.

Walking tours Tour Gratis (ⓦneweuropetours.eu) operate free walking tours, picking up from all of the listed hostels (see p.580) every morning. The fantastic 1916 Rebellion walking tours (March–Oct Mon–Sat 11.30am, Sun 1pm; meet at the *International Bar*, 23 Wicklow St; €13; ⓦ1916rising.com) visit sights of interest relating to the 1916 Rising.

Organized pub crawls Dublin Literary Pub Crawl (April–Oct daily 7.30pm; Nov–March Thurs–Sun 7.30pm; meet at *The Duke Pub*, 9 Duke St; €12; ⓦdublinpubcrawl .com); and the more raucous Backpacker Pubcrawl (daily 8pm; meet at *The Mercantile* on Dame St; €12; ⓦbackpackerpubcrawl.com).

GETTING AROUND

Pre-paid Leap Cards, available online (ⓦleapcard.ie; refundable deposit of €5) or from newsagents, are valid on Dublin Bus, LUAS trams, DART and commuter rail services, and work out cheaper than paying cash fares.

By bus Dublin has an extensive route network and all buses are exact fare only. Fares range from €0.75 for short city-centre journeys to €3.30, and a one-day bus pass is €7.60. Free bus timetables are available from Dublin Bus, 59 Upper O'Connell St. Nitelink night buses cost €6.50.

By tram The LUAS tram service operates along two routes: from Connolly Station to Tallaght via Abbey St to Heuston Station, and from St Stephen's Green to Sandyford. Tickets cost €1.90–3.10 one-way, €3.50–5.60 return.

By train The DART railway links Howth and Malahide to the north of the city with Bray and Greystones to the south via Pearse, Tara St and Connolly stations in the city centre (maximum fare €4.60). A trip on the DART is an activity in itself, affording stunning views of the Dublin suburbs and

16

coastline. Get off at Howth, Malahide, Sandymount, Dún Laoghaire, Killiney, Bray or Greystones for pleasant seaside walks.

Bike rental Cycle Ways, 185 Parnell St ☎ 01 873 4748.

ACCOMMODATION

Although Dublin has lots of accommodation, anywhere central fills up at weekends, around St Patrick's Day (March 17), at Easter and in high summer, so it's wise to book ahead. The cheaper places are generally north of the river, especially around the bus and train stations northeast of the centre. All hostels listed provide free breakfast.

HOSTELS

Avalon House 55 Aungier St ☎ 01 475 0001, ⓦ avalon -house.ie. Bustling and friendly hostel with slightly cramped dorms but plenty of twin or four-bedded rooms. Performers get a free night's accommodation for an evening recital in the café. Dorms €16, doubles €50

Barnacles 19 Temple Lane ☎ 01 671 6277, ⓦ barnacles .ie. Hugely popular hostel on a cobbled street in the heart of Temple Bar. Dorms €22, doubles €68

★ **Four Courts Hostel** 15–17 Merchants Quay ☎ 01 672 5839, ⓦ fourcourtshostel.com. In a very central location, this hostel is housed in Georgian buildings overlooking the River Liffey. Excellent facilities and helpful staff. Dorms €17, doubles €48

Generator Hostel Smithfield Square ☎ 01 901 0222, ⓦ generatorhostels.com. Chic and contemporary hostel in a great location, adjacent to the Jameson Distillery. There's always a good buzz thanks to the open social spaces and excellent café/bar. Dorms €25, doubles €90

Isaacs Hostel 2–5 Frenchman's Lane ☎ 01 855 6215, ⓦ isaacs.ie. Housed in an eighteenth-century wine warehouse with its own restaurant and a free sauna in the basement. Close to the bus station. Dorms €20

Kinlay House 2–12 Lord Edward St ⓦ kinlaydublin.ie. Large, friendly and popular hostel right beside Christ Church Cathedral. Dorms €12.50, doubles €60

★ **The Times Hostel** 8 Camden Place ☎ 01 475 8588, ⓦ timeshostels.com. Small and convivial hostel close to some of the city's best pubs and restaurants, with free pancake breakfasts and organized tours, pub crawls and game nights. Dorms €14, doubles €60

GUESTHOUSES

Abbott Lodge Guesthouse 87–88 Gardiner St Lower ☎ 01 836 5438, ⓦ abbott-lodge.com. Georgian townhouse with large, high-ceilinged rooms and floral bedspreads. Welcoming and family-run with plenty of kitsch decor involving fake flowers and ornaments. Singles €69, doubles €89

Charles Stewart Guesthouse 5/6 Parnell Square ☎ 01 878 0350, ⓦ charlesstewart.ie. Very reasonably priced

accommodation in elegant Georgian surroundings, opposite the Gate Theatre. Doubles €62

CAMPSITE

Camac Valley Tourist Caravan and Camping Park Naas Rd, Clondalkin ☎ 01 464 0644, ⓦ camacvalley.com. The most convenient campsite, with excellent facilities, located on the N7, a 35min drive from the centre. Bus #69 from the centre (Aston Quay, near O'Connell Bridge) stops right outside the campsite. The last bus is at 11.15pm, so if you're any later, a taxi (around €25) is your only option. Per person €10

EATING

★ **Bunsen** 3 South Anne St. With a menu so minimal it fits on a business card, *Bunsen* serves up the best burgers in the city (from €7). Mon–Wed noon–9.30pm, Thurs–Sat noon–10.30pm, Sun 1–9.30pm.

Cornucopia 21 Wicklow St. One of the city's few vegetarian cafés and very popular for its generous portions of home-made soups, salads, curries and gratins. Mains €9–14. Mon–Sat 8.30am–9pm, Sun noon–8.30pm.

Dunne & Crescenzi 14–16 South Frederick St. Authentic Italian restaurant serving delicious bruschetta (€6.50), antipasti, panini and simple pasta dishes (from €12), washed down with the cheapest (yet very palatable) house wine in Dublin. Daily 8am–late.

★ **Foam Café** 24 Strand St Great. Fabulously kitsch café in the heart of the Italian Quarter serving light meals and a moreish selection of cakes. Pizzas €11.50. Daily 11am–9pm.

Green 19 19 Camden St. Simple yet top-quality dishes like slow-braised pork belly with sautéed spinach and butternut squash (€12) or gnocchi with wild mushrooms (€14). Excellent cocktails and a funky vibe complete the picture. Mon–Sat 10am–11pm, Sun noon–10pm.

Leo Burdock's 2 Werburgh St. Dublin's best fish and chips – takeaway only. Fresh cod and chips (known as "Dubliners caviar") is €9.25. There's another branch on Liffey St Lower. Daily noon–midnight.

★ TREAT YOURSELF

For high-end organic Irish food, it is hard to beat **The Winding Stair** (40 Ormond Quay; ☎ 01 872 7320, ⓦ winding-stair.com). Dishes are thoughtfully prepared using ingredients from small, carefully selected producers. The menu changes daily, but expect dishes like steamed cockles and mussels with Clogherhead crab and Irish rib-eye steak with roasted garlic truffle butter. The dining room is bright and airy, with gorgeous views over the River Liffey. Mains €24. Daily noon–10.30pm.

Musashi 15 Capel St. Chow down on some of the city's finest (and cheapest) sushi, accompanied by a jazz soundtrack. BYOB. Daily noon–10pm.

Umi Falafel 13 Dame St. Cheap and cheerful Middle Eastern restaurant famous for their falafels (€6) made from a traditional family recipe. Dine in or take-out. Daily noon–10pm.

DRINKING AND NIGHTLIFE

Most of Dublin's eight hundred pubs serve food, and can be the best place to sample traditional Irish cuisine. The music scene – much of which is pub-based – is changeable, so it's always best to check the listings magazines like *Hot Press* (€3.50). See ⓦ dublineventguide.com for listings of free events, or *In Dublin* (ⓦ indublin.ie) and *Totally Dublin* (ⓦ totallydublin.ie). Camden Street is the best place to find live rock; hit Temple Bar for clubs playing pop and dance music, as well as touristy traditional sessions.

BARS

★**The Bernard Shaw** 11–12 South Richmond St ⓦ bodytonicmusic.com. The walls of this "bar, café and creative space" are covered in graffiti outside and the works of local artists inside. There's a colourful beer garden, nightly DJs playing everything from reggae to house, a pool table and a Big Blue Bus serving excellent pizzas (€9). Mon–Fri 8am–midnight/1am, Sat & Sun 4pm–midnight/1am.

Davy Byrne's 21 Duke St ⓦ davybyrnes.com. An object of pilgrimage for *Ulysses* fans, since Leopold Bloom stopped here for a snack. Attracts a sophisticated crowd and also serves good food (traditional Irish stew €12.50). Mon–Wed 11am–11.30pm, Thurs & Fri 11am–12.30am, Sat 10.30am–12.30am, Sun 12.30–11pm.

Grogans 15 South William St ⓦ groganspub.ie. Popular spot among Dublin's bohemian set, with paintings by local artists adorning the walls. On sunny evenings the crowd spills onto the pedestrian street outside. Mon–Thurs 10.30am–11.30pm, Fri & Sat 10.30am–12.30am, Sun 12.30–11pm.

The Long Hall 51 South Great George's St. Victorian pub encrusted with mirrors and antique clocks. Mon–Wed 4–11.30pm, Thurs 1–11.30pm, Fri & Sat 1pm–12.30am, Sun 1–11pm.

McDaids 3 Harry St. Intimate old-school pub serving the perfect Guinness. One of Republican writer Brendan Behan's favourite watering holes. Mon–Sat 10.30am–11.30pm/12.30am, Sun 12.30–11pm.

Stag's Head 1 Dame Court, Dame St, almost opposite the Central Bank. Wonderfully intimate pub, full of mahogany, stained glass and mirrors. Very popular with local Dubliners, and does good pub lunches. Mon–Sat 10.30am–1am, Sun 10.30am–midnight.

CLUBS

Button Factory Curved St ⓦ buttonfactory.ie. Housed in the refurbished Temple Bar Music Centre, this is the place to find top Irish and international DJs in the Thurs–Sat club. Opening hours are erratic but club nights are 11pm–2.30am.

The George South Great George's St ⓦ thegeorge.ie. Dublin's oldest and most popular gay bar and club. Mon 2–11.30pm, Tues–Fri 2pm–2.30am, Sat 12.30pm–2.30am, Sun 12.30pm–1.30am.

Pygmalion Powerscourt Townhouse ⓦ pyg.ie. Located in the vaults of Powerscourt Townhouse, this bar/restaurant transforms into one of the best clubs in the city every weekend. Daily until late.

The Workman's Club 10 Wellington Quay ⓦ theworkmansclub.com. A maze of interconnecting rooms in a red-brick building fronting the River Liffey houses dancefloors, venues for live music and poetry readings, themed bars and a rooftop terrace. Daily 5pm–3am.

LIVE MUSIC

★**The Brazen Head** 20 Lower Bridge St ⓦ brazenhead .com. The oldest pub in Dublin, with traditional music nightly from 9.30pm. Daily until late.

The Cobblestone 77 King St North ⓦ cobblestonepub.ie. Atmospheric pub on the edge of the Smithfield Plaza, famous for its nightly traditional sessions. Daily until late.

International Bar 23 Wicklow St ⓦ international-bar .com. Large saloon with rock bands, jazz and a comedy club upstairs or in the cellar. Daily until late.

J.J. Smyth's 12 Aungier St ⓦ jjsmyths.com. One of the few places to catch local jazz and blues talent. Opening hours depend on gigs and events.

The Mezz 23–24 Eustace St ⓦ mezz.ie. Café-bar with live rock, jazz, blues funk, soul and reggae every night. Brazilian food served noon–7.30pm. Mains from €5. Opening hours depend on gigs and events.

Vicar Street 58–59 Thomas St ⓦ vicarstreet.com. One of the city's finest music venues, offering a varied programme of major music and comedy acts. Opening hours depend on the events programme.

Whelans 25 Wexford St ⓦ whelanslive.com. Notorious music pub and club attracting a host of up-and-coming international stars as well as local talent. Daily until late.

ENTERTAINMENT

THEATRES

Dublin's theatres are among the finest in Europe, offering a good mix of classical and more avant-garde performances. Tickets start at around €20, with concessions offered on Monday to Thursday nights and for matinees. Visit ⓦ entertainment.ie for listings.

The Abbey Lower Abbey St ⓦ abbeytheatre.ie. Ireland's most historic theatre, founded in 1899 by W.B. Yeats to promote Irish culture and drama.

The Gaiety South King St ⓦ gaietytheatre.ie. Dublin's oldest and most ornate theatre, showing pantomimes and popular plays.

16

The Gate 1 Cavendish Row ⓦ gate-theatre.ie. Showcases contemporary Irish drama, alongside European classics.

CINEMAS
Cineworld Parnell St ☎ 1520 880 444, ⓦ cineworld.ie. Seventeen-screen multiplex.
Irish Film Institute 6 Eustace St, Temple Bar ☎ 01 679 5744, ⓦ irishfilm.ie. Shows classics and new independent films, and has a good bar and restaurant.

SHOPPING
Dundrum Town Centre, Dundrum; ⓦ dundrum.ie. Home to the biggest shopping centre in Europe; take LUAS from St Stephen's Green to Balally. Mon–Fri 9am–9pm, Sat 9am–7pm, Sun 10am–7pm.
Nine Crows 5 Ormond Quay Lower ⓦ shopninecrows .com. Hand-picked vintage clothing with a 90s revival feel. The beating heart of Dublin's fashion scene. Mon noon–6pm, Tues, Wed, Fri & Sat 11am–6.30pm, Thurs 11am–7pm, Sun 1–5pm.
The Rage 16B Fade St ⓦ therage.ie. A great little store selling secondhand vinyl and retro video games. Friendly staff will help you pick out a bargain. Mon–Sat 10.30am–7pm, Sun noon–6pm.

DIRECTORY
Embassies Australia, Fitzwilton House, Wilton Terrace ☎ 01 664 5300; Canada, 7–8 Wilton Terrace ☎ 01 234 4000; UK, 29 Merrion Rd ☎ 01 205 3700; US, 42 Elgin Rd, Ballsbridge ☎ 01 668 8777.
Exchange General Post Office, O'Connell St; most city centre banks.
Hospitals Southside: St James's, James St ☎ 01 410 3000; Northside: Mater Misericordiae, Eccles St ☎ 01 885 8888.
Internet There are free wi-fi spots around the city; look out for the DublinFree mosaics or see ⓦ dublincity.ie for locations.
Left luggage Busáras, Heuston and Connolly stations.
Pharmacy Dame Street Pharmacy, 16 Dame St; O'Connell's, 55 O'Connell St.
Post office GPO O'Connell St (Mon–Sat 8.30am–6pm); St Andrew's St (Mon–Fri 9am–6pm, Sat 9am–1pm).

COUNTY WICKLOW

Referred to as the "Garden of Ireland", the picturesque mountains, lakes, forested estates and rural villages of **County Wicklow** provide a stunning backdrop for a bracing country walk or scenic drive. Given its proximity to the capital, the region is easily visited on a day-trip from Dublin, but there are plenty of B&Bs and hostels in the area.

The wonderfully unspoilt 127km mountain trail, the **Wicklow Way**, bisects the Wicklow Mountains, looping through glacial valleys, farmland and forests. The trail passes through the villages of **Roundwood, Rathdrum** and **Enniskerry**, from where the eighteenth-century **Powerscourt Estate** gardens and waterfall (house and gardens daily 9.30am–5.30pm; €9.50, waterfall only €6; ⓦ powerscourt.ie) are easily accessible.

Some 30km south of Enniskerry, the beautifully tranquil monastic site of **Glendalough** ("valley of the two lakes") forms one of the most dramatic landscapes in the country. The monastery was founded in the sixth century by St Kevin, and the 30m-high tapering round tower on the bank of the Lower Lake has epitomized mystical Ireland in tourist brochures for decades.

ARRIVAL AND DEPARTURE
By bus You can get to the three villages of Roundwood, Rathdrum and Enniskerry (all on the Wicklow Way) on bus #44 from O'Connell St in Dublin city centre (hourly; €2.80). For Glendalough, take the St Kevin's bus (4 daily; €13 one-way/€20 return; ⓦ glendaloughbus.com) from outside the Mansion House on Dawson St.

INFORMATION AND TOURS
Tourist office The Glendalough visitor centre is at Lower Lake (daily 9.30am–6pm; March–Oct closes 5pm; €4), and the Wicklow Mountains National Park Information Centre (Upper Lake; March–Oct daily 9.30am–6pm; Oct–March daily 9.30am–5pm, ⓦ wicklowmountainsnationalpark.ie) can provide information on walking routes.
Tours The visitor centre at Lower Lake runs tours (daily 2pm) of Glendalough monastic site. Several companies run day-tours to Glendalough from Dublin (including Over the Top Tours, ⓦ overthetoptours.com, and Wild Wicklow Tours, ⓦ wildwicklow.ie; both €25–28).

ACCOMMODATION
Glendalough Hostel On the R757 near the Upper Lake ☎ 0404 45342, ⓦ anoige.ie. Ideally located in an old lodge near the monastic settlement. Dorms €16, twins €50

NEWGRANGE

One of the foremost visitor attractions in the country, **Brú na Bóinne** ("the palace of the Boyne") encompasses the 5000-year-old passage graves of **Newgrange**, Knowth

16

and Dowth. Three rotund mounds of earth rise above these Neolithic graves – now excavated and reconstructed – south of the River Boyne in County Meath.

The **exhibition** (€3, €6 with entrance to Newgrange and €11 for all three passage graves) in the visitor centre (see below) includes information on the sites, how they were built and the artwork of enigmatic spirals carved into the stone walls. There is also a full-scale replica of the chamber at Newgrange as well as a model of one of the smaller tombs at Knowth.

The **guided tour** of Newgrange is led by the visitor centre (see blow), and includes a simulation of the rising sun during the winter solstice, during which the rays of light enter through a strategically positioned slit above the entrance, casting first light on the burial chamber before spreading along the 19m length of the passage.

ARRIVAL AND INFORMATION

By bus To get to the visitor centre, take the Bus Éireann service #100 from the Busáras bus depot in Dublin city centre (see p.579) to Drogheda, from where shuttle bus #163 connects to the visitor centre.

Tourist information Access to the monuments is by guided tour from the visitor centre only (daily: May–Sept 9am–6.30pm; Oct–April 9.30am–5pm; ⓦnewgrange .com), located on the south side of the River Boyne, 5km east of the village of Slane.

The southeast

The southeast is Ireland's sunniest and driest corner. The region's medieval and Anglo-Norman history is richly concentrated in **Kilkenny**, a bustling, quaint inland town, while to the west, at the heart of County Tipperary, is the **Rock of Cashel**, a spectacular natural formation topped with Christian buildings from virtually every period. In the southwest, **Cork** is both relaxed and spirited, the perfect place to ease you into the exhilarations of the west coast.

KILKENNY

KILKENNY is Ireland's finest medieval city, its castle set above the broad sweep of the

River Nore and its narrow streets laced with carefully maintained buildings. In 1641, the city became the virtual capital of Ireland, with the founding of a parliament known as the Confederation of Kilkenny. The power of this short-lived attempt to unite resistance to English persecution of Catholics had greatly diminished by the time Cromwell's wreckers arrived in 1650. Kilkenny never recovered its prosperity, but enough remains to indicate its former importance.

WHAT TO SEE AND DO

Left at the top of Rose Inn Street is the broad **Parade**, which leads up to the castle. To the right, the High Street passes the eighteenth-century **Tholsel**, once the city's financial centre and now the town hall.

Rothe House

Beyond the Tholsel is **Parliament Street**, the main thoroughfare, where the **Rothe House** (Mon–Sat 10.30am–5pm, Sun noon–5pm; €5.50; ⓦrothehouse.com) provides a unique example of an Irish Tudor merchant's home, comprising three separate houses linked by cobbled courtyards.

St Canice's Cathedral

The thirteenth-century **St Canice's Cathedral** (June–Aug Mon–Sat 9am–6pm, Sun 2–6pm; Sept–March Mon–Sat 10am–1pm & 2–4/5pm, Sun 2–4/5pm; €4; ⓦstcanicescathedral.com) has a fine array of sixteenth-century monuments, many in black Kilkenny limestone. The **round tower** next to the cathedral (same hours; €3; combined ticket with cathedral €6) is the only remnant of a monastic settlement reputedly founded by St Canice in the sixth century; there are superb views from the top.

Castle

It's the imposing twelfth-century **Castle** that defines Kilkenny (tours daily: 9/9.30am–4.30/5.30pm; €7; ⓦkilkennycastle.ie). Its library, drawing room, bedrooms and Long Gallery of family portraits are open for viewing, as is the **Butler Gallery** (daily 10am–1pm & 2–4.30/5.30pm; free; ⓦbutlergallery .com), housing exhibitions of modern art.

16

ARRIVAL AND DEPARTURE

By train The train station is just north of the centre, off John St.
Destinations Dublin (7 daily; 1hr 40min–2hr).
By bus The bus station is next to the train station, off John Street. Some services stop on Patrick St.
Destinations Cork (3 daily; 2hr 50min); Dublin (6 daily; 2hr 15min–2hr 45min).

INFORMATION

Tourist office Rose Inn St, in the sixteenth-century Shee Alms House (May–Sept Mon–Sat 9.30am–5.30pm; Oct–April Tues–Sat 9.30am–1pm & 2–5pm; ☎ 056 775 1500, ⓦ visitkilkenny.ie).
Listings The weekly *Kilkenny People* (€1.80) has listings information. See also ⓦ kilkenny.ie.
Festivals The town is renowned for The Cat Laughs comedy festival in June (ⓦ thecatlaughs.com) and its Arts Festival in August (ⓦ kilkennyarts.ie).

ACCOMMODATION

★ **Kilkenny Tourist Hostel** 35 Parliament St ☎ 056 776 3541, ⓦ kilkennyhostel.ie. An excellent budget option in a rambling Georgian building. Dorms €17, doubles €42
MacGabhainn's Backpackers Hostel 24 Vicar St ☎ 056 777 0970, ⓦ macgabhainns-backpackers.hostel.com. Small and friendly hostel in the centre of town, with a barbecue area for sunny days. Dorms €16
Tree Grove camping Danville House, New Ross Rd ☎ 056 777 0302, ⓦ treegrovecamping.com. Campsite 1.5km south of the city on the R700, open March–Nov 15. Bike rental available. Per person €8

EATING

Billy Byrne's 39 John St ☎ 056 772 1783. Fine pub lunches for €9. Regular themed nights like Taco Tuesday and Movie Night Pizza are always good fun. Mon–Thurs 9.30am–11.30pm, Fri & Sat 9.30am–12.30am, Sun 12.30pm–11pm.
★ **Café Sol** William St ☎ 056 776 4987. Award-winning café-restaurant which is pricey in the evenings, but good for salads and light mains (from €9) at lunch. Mon & Tues 11.30am–5pm, Wed–Sun 11.30am–9.30pm.
Gourmet Store 56 High St. Hummus, panini, bagels and wraps made to order at this little deli. From €3. Mon–Sat 8am–6pm.
Kyteler's Inn St Kieran St ⓦ kytelersinn.com. Decent pub grub (from €10) in medieval surroundings, accompanied by regular traditional music sessions. Food served noon–9pm. Daily until late.

DRINKING AND NIGHTLIFE

Parliament and Ormonde streets are best for live traditional and rock music; John St has a more commercial feel with clubs and pop music.

Edward Langton's 69 John St. Swanky hotel with four bars and a popular club (Tues, Thurs & Sat 10pm–2.30am). There's a swing club (Thurs–Sat) in the *67 Bar* and regular comedy nights, live music and theatre in the Set Theatre. Also serves good pub grub (mains €12) daily noon–10pm.
★ **The Hole in the Wall** 17 High St ⓦ holeinthewall.ie. Housed in the oldest surviving townhouse in Ireland, this cosy tavern really comes alive in the evenings, with live music and an incredibly friendly atmosphere. Mon, Wed & Thurs 8pm–midnight, Fri 8pm–1am, Sat 2.30pm–1am, Sun 2–11pm.
The Pumphouse 26–28 Parliament St. Popular with young and old, locals and travellers alike. Music most nights, and there's also a pool table. Mon–Thurs & Sun 2–11.30pm, Fri & Sat 2pm–12.30am.
Tynan's 2 Horseleap Slip, St John's Bridge. Riverside bar with cosy Victorian interior and beer garden; there are still relics from its days as a pharmacy and grocery store. Late bar Mon, Wed & Thurs; live music Mon–Thurs from 9pm. Daily until late.

THE ROCK OF CASHEL

The extraordinary **ROCK OF CASHEL** (daily: mid-Sept to mid-Oct 9am–5.30pm; mid-Oct to mid-March 9am–4.30pm; mid-March to early June 9am–5.30pm; early June to mid-Sept 9am–7pm; €7) appears as a mirage of crenellations rising bolt upright from the vast encircling plain. This is where St Patrick reputedly used a shamrock to explain the doctrine of the Trinity. **Cormac's Chapel**, built in the 1130s, is the earliest and most beautiful of Ireland's Romanesque churches, and the limestone **Cathedral**, begun in the thirteenth century, is a fine example of Anglo-Norman architecture, with its Gothic arches and lancet windows. The tapering **round tower** is the earliest building on the Rock, dating from the early twelfth century. The **Cashel Heritage Centre** (daily 9.30am–5.30pm; closed Sat & Sun Nov–Feb; free; ⓦ cashel.ie) on Main Street has a small exhibition that covers the history of the town.

ARRIVAL AND DEPARTURE

By bus Cashel is most often visited as a day-trip from Cork or Kilkenny; buses from Cork drop off outside *The Bakehouse* bakery, those from Kilkenny and Dublin on the other side of the street.

ACCOMMODATION

★**Cashel Lodge** Dundrum Rd ☎ 062 61003, ⓦ cashel -lodge.com. A beautifully renovated coach house blessed with spectacular views and located close to the Rock. Doubles €̲8̲5̲, camping €̲1̲2̲

EATING AND DRINKING

The Bakehouse 7 Main St. Cosy café offering fresh baked scones, pastries, soups and sandwiches (€5–7). Daily 8am–5.30pm.
Mikey Ryan's Bar 76 Main St. Atmospheric traditional pub with occasional live music. Fresh soup and sandwiches served Mon–Sat noon–3pm.

CORK

Everywhere in **CORK** there's evidence of its history as a great mercantile centre, with grey-stone quaysides, old warehouses, and elegant, quirky bridges spanning the River Lee to each side of the city's island core – but the lively atmosphere and large student population, combined with a vibrant social and cultural scene, are equally powerful draws. Massive stone walls built by invading Normans in the twelfth century were destroyed by William III's forces during the **Siege of Cork** in 1690, after which waterborne trade brought increasing prosperity, as witnessed by the city's fine eighteenth-century bow-fronted houses and ostentatious nineteenth-century churches.

WHAT TO SEE AND DO

The graceful arc of **St Patrick's Street** – which with **Grand Parade** forms the commercial heart of the centre – is crammed with major chain stores. Just off here on Princes Street, the **English Market** (Mon–Sat 9am–5.30pm) offers the chance to sample local delicacies like *drisheen* (a peppered sausage made from a sheep's stomach lining and blood). On the far side of St Patrick's Street, chic Paul Street is a gateway to the bijou environs of French Church Street and Carey's Lane. The west of the city is predominantly residential, though Fitzgerald Park is home to the **Cork Public Museum** (Mon–Fri 11am–1pm & 2.15–5pm, Sat 11am–1pm & 2.15–4pm, plus April–Sept Sun 3–5pm; free), which focuses on Republican history.

Shandon area

North of the River Lee is the historic **Shandon area**, a reminder of Cork's eighteenth-century status as the most important port in Europe for dairy products. The striking **Cork Butter Exchange** survives, stout nineteenth-century Neoclassical buildings given over to craft workshops. At one corner of the old butter market on O'Connell Square is the **Cork Butter Museum** (March–June, Sept & Oct 10am–5pm; July & Aug 10am–6pm; Nov–Feb Sat & Sun 10am–3.30pm; €4; ⓦ corkbutter.museum), which exhibits, among other items, a keg of thousand-year-old butter. Behind the square is the pleasant Georgian church of **St Anne's Shandon** (March–May & Oct Mon–Sat 10am–4pm, Sun 11.30am–3.30pm; June–Sept Mon–Sat 10am–5pm, Sun 11.30am–4.30pm; Nov–Feb Mon–Sat 11am–3pm, closed Sun; €5), easily recognizable from all over the city by its weather vane – a 3.5m salmon. The church tower gives excellent views over the city and an opportunity to ring the famous bells. Around 2km west along North Mall, in the Sunday's Well area of the city, is the nineteenth-century **Cork City Gaol** (daily: March–Oct 10am–4pm; Nov–Feb 9.30am–5pm; €8; ⓦ corkcitygaol.com), with wax figures and an excellent audioguide focusing on social history.

ARRIVAL AND DEPARTURE

By train The train station is 1km east of the city centre on Lower Glanmire Road.
Destinations Dublin (15 daily Mon–Sat, 12 Sun; 2hr 35min–3hr 35min); Killarney (8 daily; 1hr 30min–2hr).
By bus The bus station is on Parnell Place by Merchant's Quay.
Destinations Cashel (6 daily; 1hr 35min–1hr 50min); Dublin (6 daily; 4hr 25min); Galway (13 daily; 4hr 20min); Kilkenny (3 daily; 3hr 10min–4hr 15min); Killarney (11 daily; 2hr).
By ferry Boats from Roscoff arrive at Ringaskiddy, 13km from town. A shuttle bus runs to the centre.

INFORMATION

Tourist office Grand Parade (Mon–Sat 9.30am–5pm, July & Aug also Sun 10am–5pm; ☎ 021 425 5100, ⓦ discoverireland.ie/southwest).
Festivals Cork's international jazz festival takes place in late October (ⓦ corkjazzfestival.com) and there's a film festival in November (ⓦ corkfilmfest.org).

16

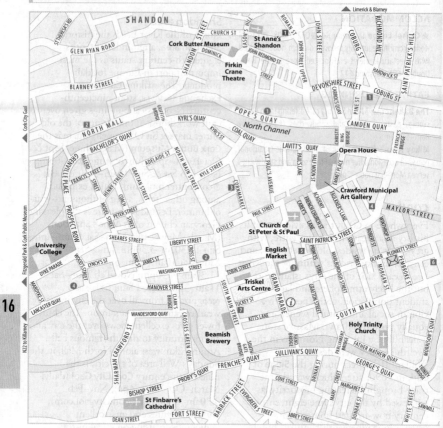

Limerick & Blarney

16

ACCOMMODATION

Aaran House Tourist Hostel Lower Glanmire Rd ☎021 455 1566, ✉tracy_flynn3@hotmail.com. Friendly and very convenient for train and bus stations. Dorms €14, doubles €38

Brú Hostel 57 McCurtain St ☎021 455 9667, ⓦbruhostel .com. Enjoy modern facilities at the affordable hostel with a bar attached, where guests can claim a free pint. Live music every night. Dorms €18, doubles €50

Gabriel House Summerhill North ☎021 450 0333, ⓦgabrielhousebb.com. This old Christian Brothers building has been beautifully renovated and offers quality accommodation with sweeping views of the city. Singles €55, doubles €85

Kinlay House Bob & Joan's Walk, off Upper John St, Shandon ☎021 450 8966, ⓦkinlayhousecork.ie. With great facilities (self-catering, kitchen, laundry, service, health club), this large but friendly hostel is in a lovely part of town near St Anne's Shandon. Dorms €15, doubles €50

★**Sheila's** 4 Belgrave Place, Wellington Rd ☎021 450 5562, ⓦsheilashostel.ie. Set back from the hustle and bustle of town, *Sheila's* is comfortable, clean and well run, with extras such as a small cinema room and a sauna (€2). Dorms €16, doubles €38

EATING

Cafe Paradiso 16 Lancaster Quay ⓦcafeparadiso.ie. A Cork institution for over 20 years, this vegetarian restaurant serves top-class food in a casual atmosphere. At €23 for two courses, the pre-theatre menu is good value. Mon–Sat 5.30–10pm.

★**Farmgate Café** English Market ⓦfarmgate.ie. Enjoy wholesome, fresh food sourced from the surrounding market in a bustling atmosphere. Mains €9–14, gourmet sandwiches €7. Mon–Fri 8.30am–5pm, Sat 8.30am–4.30pm.

Liberty Grill 32 Washington St ⓦlibertygrill.ie. Brunch (served till 5pm Mon–Sat) and burgers – try the lamb and feta one – are this restaurant's specialities. Mains from €10. Mon–Sat 8am–9pm.

THE SOUTHEAST IRELAND | 587

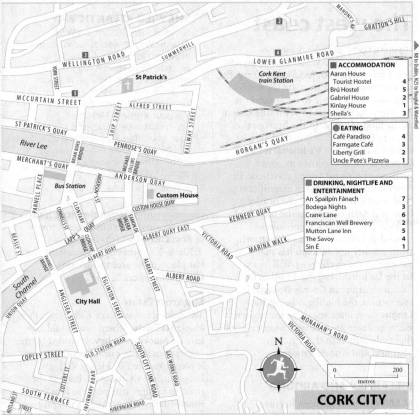

Aaran House	
Tourist Hostel	4
Brú Hostel	5
Gabriel House	2
Kinlay House	1
Sheila's	3

EATING
Café Paradiso	4
Farmgate Café	3
Liberty Grill	2
Uncle Pete's Pizzeria	1

DRINKING, NIGHTLIFE AND ENTERTAINMENT
An Spailpín Fánach	7
Bodega Nights	3
Crane Lane	6
Franciscan Well Brewery	2
Mutton Lane Inn	5
The Savoy	4
Sin É	1

CORK CITY

Airport, Passage West, Ringaskiddy & Kinsale

16

★**Uncle Pete's Pizzeria** 31 Pope's Quay Ⓦ unclepetes.ie. Grab a €2 slice of thin-crust pizza from this quality Italian takeaway. Toppings encompass anything from king prawns to black pudding. Daily noon–late.

DRINKING AND NIGHTLIFE

For listings, pick up the free *Whazon*? (Ⓦ whazon.com).

Bodega Nights Cornmarket St, Coal Quay Ⓦ bodegacork.ie. Popular club with regular DJs (Tues, Fri & Sat until 2.30am). The bar-restaurant serves good fusion food for lunch and dinner, with live jazz to accompany Sunday brunch.

Franciscan Well Brewery 14 North Mall. A microbrewery with a medieval heritage serving delicious craft beers and wood-fired pizzas. Mon–Thurs & Sun 1–11.30pm, Fri & Sat 1pm–12.30am.

★**Mutton Lane Inn** 3 Mutton Lane. Cosy candlelit pub open since 1787, down an alleyway painted with colourful murals. Plays funk and soul, with occasional trad sessions. Daily 10.30am–late.

The Savoy St Patrick St Ⓦ savoytheatre.ie. Cork's premier club housed in an old cinema building, with DJs and live music. Thurs–Sat 10pm–2.30am.

ENTERTAINMENT

LIVE MUSIC

An Spailpín Fánach South Main St. Traditional music every night, except Saturday, in this famous bar.

Crane Lane Phoenix St Ⓦ cranelanetheatre.ie. Billed as the "House of Jazz, Blues and Burlesque", this theatre has a late bar (open until 2am daily), and regular shows and gigs.

★**Sin É** 8 Coburg St. Intimate music bar, usually packed for its traditional sessions and other live music, Tuesday to Thursday from 9.30pm, and Fridays and Sundays at 6.30pm.

THEATRE AND CINEMA

Triskel Arts Centre Tobin St ☎021 427 2022, Ⓦ triskelart.com. A lively spot housed in the eighteenth-century Christchurch, with cinema, exhibitions, readings and concerts.

The west coast

If you've come to Ireland for mountainous scenery, sea and remoteness, you'll hit the jackpot in County Kerry. By far the most visited areas are the town of **Killarney** and a scenic route around the perimeter of the Iveragh Peninsula known as the **Ring of Kerry**. In the heart of the Burren, **Doolin** in County Clare is a marvellous spot for **traditional music**. **Galway** is a free-spirited city, and a gathering point for young travellers. To its west lies **Connemara**, a magnificently wild coastal terrain, with the nearby beautiful **Aran Islands**, in the mouth of Galway Bay. The landscape softens around the historic town of **Westport**, while further north, **Sligo** has many associations with the poet W.B.Yeats. In the far northwest, the 1134km of folded coastline in **County Donegal** is spectacular, the highlight being **Slieve League**'s awesome sea cliffs, the highest in Europe. There are plenty of international flights directly into the region (to Shannon and Knock airports).

KILLARNEY AND AROUND

KILLARNEY town has been heavily commercialized and has little of architectural interest, but the surrounding **Killarney National Park**, with some of the best lakes, mountains and woodland in Ireland, definitely compensates. **Cycling** is a great way of seeing the terrain, and makes good sense – local transport is sparse.

WHAT TO SEE AND DO

Around the town, three spectacular **lakes** – Lough Leane, Muckross Lake and the Upper Lake – form an appetizer for MacGillycuddy's Reeks, the highest mountains in Ireland.

Knockreer Estate

The entrance gates to the **Knockreer Estate**, part of the Killarney National Park, are just over the road from Killarney's cathedral. Tall wooded hills, the highest being **Carrantuohill** (1041m), form the backdrop to **Lough Leane**, and

---

THE WILD ATLANTIC WAY

Stretching over 2500km, the **Wild Atlantic Way** (⬤ wildatlanticway.com) is the world's longest coastal touring route, which traverses Ireland's rugged west coast. From Cork to Donegal, the route takes in hundreds of sites and towns including the Cliffs of Moher, Skellig Michael, Dingle and Malin Head. Bus Éireann (⬤ buseireann.ie) offer an "Open Road" ticket allowing you to hop on and off. Tickets start from €57 for three days of unlimited travel, with extra "stamps" costing €15 per day.

---

the main path through the estate leads to the restored fifteenth-century tower of **Ross Castle** (March–Nov daily 9.30am–5.45pm; €6, gardens free), the last place in the area to succumb to Cromwell's forces in 1652.

Muckross Estate

Two kilometres south of Killarney is the **Muckross Estate**, where you should aim first for **Muckross Abbey**. Founded by the Franciscans in the mid-fifteenth century, it was suppressed by Henry VIII, and later, finally, by Cromwell. Back at the main road, signposts point to **Muckross House** (daily: July & Aug 9am–7pm; Sept–June 9am–5.30pm; €9 or €15 joint ticket with farm; ⬤ muckross-house.ie), a nineteenth-century neo-Elizabethan mansion with wonderful gardens and a traditional working farm. The estate gives access to well-trodden paths along the shores of Muckross Lake where you can see one of Killarney's celebrated beauty spots, the **Meeting of the Waters**. Close by is the massive shoulder of Torc Mountain, shrugging off **Torc Waterfall**. The Upper Lake is beautiful, too, with the main road running along one side up to **Ladies' View**, from where the view is truly spectacular.

Gap of Dunloe and the Black Valley

West of Killarney lies the **Gap of Dunloe**, a natural defile formed by glacial overflow that cuts the mountains in two. *Kate Kearney's Cottage*, a pub located 10km from Killarney at the foot of the track leading up to the Gap, is the last fuelling stop before *Lord Brandon's Cottage*, a summer tearoom (June–Aug 10am–5pm), 11km away on the other side of the valley. The track winds its way up the desolate valley between high rock cliffs and waterfalls, past a chain of icy loughs and tarns to the top, to what feels like one of the most remote places in the world: the **Black Valley**, named after its entire population perished during the famine (1845–49). There's a wonderfully isolated An Óige hostel here (see below).

The quickest way to Killarney from here is to carry on down to *Lord Brandon's Cottage* and take the boat back across the Upper Lake.

ARRIVAL AND DEPARTURE

By train The train station is on Park Rd, a short walk east of the centre.

Destinations Cork (8 daily; 1hr 20min–1hr 40min); Dublin (7 daily; 3hr 15min–3hr 30min).

By bus The bus station is next to the train station on Park Rd.

Destinations Cork (13 daily; 1hr 35min–1hr 50min); Dingle (2–5 daily; 2hr–2hr 40min); Dublin (10 daily; 6hr 10min–7hr 30min); Waterville (1 daily; 1hr 55min).

INFORMATION

Tourist office Beech Rd off New St (daily 9am–6/8pm; ☎ 064 31633, ⍵ discoverireland.ie/southwest).

Listings *The Kerryman* (€2) ⍵ kerryman.ie.

ACCOMMODATION

Black Valley Hostel Beaufort ☎ 064 34712, ⍵ blackvalleyhostel.com. Ideally located for nature lovers, with the Kerry Way, Killarney National Park, the MacGillycuddy Reeks and Carrantuohill mountain close by. Sits 22km from Killarney; follow signs for Black Valley off the Killarney to Kenmare Rd. Dorms €19, twins €42

★ Dunloe View Hostel 8km west of Killarney town on the Ring of Kerry (N72) road ☎ 064 664 4187, ⍵ dunloeviewhostel.ie. Pleasant hostel on a working farm, overlooking the MacGillycuddy Reeks. Dorms €17, doubles €45

Flesk Caravan and Camping Muckross Rd ☎ 064 663 1704, ⍵ killarneyfleskcamping.com. 1.5km south of the centre on the N71 Kenmare road. Per pitch with two adults €25

Neptune's Town Hostel Bishop's Lane, off New St ☎ 064 663 5255, ⍵ neptuneshostel.com. Large, welcoming hostel with colourful rooms. Dorms €18, doubles €44

The Súgan Hostel Lewis Rd ☎ 064 663 3104, ⍵ suganhostelkillarney.com. Cosy, family-run hostel with colourful decor. There's also bike rental, cheaper if you're a guest. Dorms €15, doubles €40

EATING AND DRINKING

The Country Kitchen 17 New St. Cheap, hearty food, including full Irish breakfast (€9). Mon–Sat 9.30am–6pm.

★ Courtney's 24 Plunkett St ⍵ courtneysbar.com. Huge and informal bar, popular with young people for its midweek traditional sessions, live bands on Fri and DJ sets on Sat. Daily 2pm–late.

McSorley's 10 College St ⍵ mcsorleyskillarney.com. Traditional music in the main bar every night until around 10pm in summer, followed by a live band. The upstairs club is the biggest in Killarney. Daily until 2am.

O'Connor's Bar 7 High St. Old and intimate little pub with local Irish musicians on Thursdays and Fridays. You can book Gap of Dunloe tours here. Daily until late.

THE RING OF KERRY

Most tourists view the spectacular scenery of the 179km **Ring of Kerry**, west of Killarney, without ever leaving their tour coach or car – so anyone straying from the road, or waiting until the afternoon, will experience the slow twilights of the Atlantic seaboard in perfect seclusion.

GETTING AROUND

By bus Buses from Killarney circle the Ring in summer (May–Sept 2 daily; from €20 return). The public bus departs from the bus station and private tour operators (book through the tourist office in Killarney) from their respective offices in town. For the rest of the year, buses travel only the largely deserted mountain roads as far as Cahersiveen.

By bike Cycling the Ring (216km) takes at least three days. Most of the route is off the main road, but it is well signposted and passes through the main towns and villages. Several places in Killarney offer bike rental for around €15 per day, including O'Sullivan's Cycles (⍵ killarneyrentabike.com) on Lower New St, beside the entrance to Killarney National Park.

DINGLE

The fishing village of **DINGLE** is the best base for exploring the peninsula. Kerry's leading port in medieval times, then later a centre for smuggling, the town's main attractions nowadays are aquatic: the star of the show is undoubtedly **Fungi** the dolphin, who's been visiting the town's harbour since 1983 (boats offer trips out to see him from around €16).

16

ACCOMMODATION

Hideout Hostel Dykegate St ☎066 915 0559, ⓦthehideouthostel.com. The best budget option in town, combining a communal hostel feel with the comfort of a small hotel. Dorms €16, doubles €40

Rainbow Hostel 1km west of the centre in Miltown ☎066 915 1044, ⓦrainbowhosteldingle.com. Laidback family-run hostel on the edge of town. Dorms €16, doubles €40, camping €9

EATING AND DRINKING

Chowder Café Strand St. As you'd expect, the chowder here is the main attraction (and at €6.95 it's a steal), but there's plenty more on offer – the crab tart is a particular delight. Daily 10am–4pm, till 6pm in high season.

John Benny's Strand St ⓦjohnbennyspub.com. Popular pub renowned for its excellent fresh oysters, seared king scallops and seafood pies. There's live music Mon–Sat. Daily until late.

O'Flaherty's Bar Bridge St ⓦoflahertysbardingle.com. The proprietor Fergus leads local and visiting musicians in nightly trad sessions in a space packed with memorabilia documenting the history of Dingle. Mon–Thurs 11am–11.30pm, Fri & Sat 11am–12.30am, Sun noon–11pm.

DINGLE PENINSULA

The **Dingle Peninsula** is a place of intense, shifting beauty: spectacular mountains, long sandy beaches and splinter-slatted rocks. The highlight is the stunning promontory of **Slea Head**, which has fabulous views over to the **Blasket Islands**.

The Irish-speaking area west of Dingle is rich in relics of the ancient Gaelic and early Christian cultures. The spectacular fort of **Dún Beag** (daily Feb–Nov 10am–5pm; €3; ⓦdunbegfort.com) is about 6km west of Ventry village, and has four earthen rings as defences and an underground escape route by the main entrance. West of the fort, the hillside above the road is studded with stone beehive huts, cave dwellings, forts, churches, standing stones and crosses – over five hundred in all. The beehive huts were built and used for storage up until the late nineteenth century, but standing among ancient buildings – such as the **Fahan group** – you're looking over a landscape that's remained essentially unchanged for centuries.

GETTING AROUND

Public transport in the west of the peninsula amounts to a very irregular bus from Dingle to Dunquin, making cycling the best way to explore.

COUNTY CLARE

With its stunning natural landscape and unique culture, **County Clare** is one of the most popular stops along the Wild Atlantic Way (see box, p.588). Though home to the stunning Burren National Park and the Cliffs of Moher, it has more to offer than just scenery. The true spirit of the West Coast can be found in cosy pubs of the colourful villages that dot the countryside, and in historic towns such as Ennis.

Some 40km northwest of Ennis is the tiny seaside village of **DOOLIN**, famed for a steady, year-round supply of **traditional music**.

The village is the perfect base from which to explore the mystically barren expanse of **The Burren**, a vast landscape of cracked limestone terraces stretching to the wild Atlantic Ocean. The area is dotted with well-preserved megalithic remains such as the **Poulnabrone Dolmen** (on the R480, 20min drive from Doolin), an imposing tomb constructed from three massive limestone slabs dating from 2500 BC. **The Cliffs of Moher**, 4km south of Doolin, are the area's most famous tourist attraction, with their great bands of shale and sandstone rising 200m above the waves.

LAHINCH, a small village 20km south of Doolin, attracts hordes of surfers (see opposite) for its famous beach break.

ARRIVAL AND DEPARTURE

By bus Ennis Bus Station is a 10min walk from the town centre.
Destinations Galway (4 daily; 1hr 20min); Limerick (4 daily; 1hr, 1hr 35min).

By train Ennis train station is in the same location as the bus station.
Destinations Dublin (7–10 daily; 3–4hr); Galway (4 daily; 1hr 15min).

By ferry A ferry (April–Sept) runs from Doolin pier to the Aran Islands (see p.593).

GETTING AROUND

If you don't have your own vehicle, the best way to see the area is by bus. Bus Eireann daily route #350, for example, takes in Ennis, the Cliffs of Moher, Doolin and Galway. Tickets start from €12. Check ⒲buseireann.ie for further details.

INFORMATION

Tourist office The visitors' centre is beside the car park in Doolin (daily: March & Oct 9am–6pm; April 9am–6.30pm; May & Sept 9am–7pm; June 9am–7.30pm; July & Aug 9am–9pm; Nov–Feb 9am–5pm; €6; ⒲cliffsofmoher.ie) and can organize tours to O'Brien's Tower, built in 1835 as a viewing point for visitors.

Surfing You can rent boards from Lahinch Surf Shop (☏065 708 1543, ⒲lahinchsurfshop.com) or organize lessons at the Lahinch Surf School (☏087 960 9667, ⒲lahinchsurfschool.com).

ACCOMMODATION

★**Aille River Hostel** Doolin ☏065 707 4260, ⒲ailleriverhosteldoolin.ie. Renovated 300-year-old cottage with camping facilities (enquire for prices), beautifully located overlooking the Aille River in the centre of Doolin village. Dorms €17, doubles €45

★**Doolin Hostel** Sea Rd ☏087 282 0587, ⒲doolinhostel.com. Doolin's oldest hostel has been completely renovated and feels more like a modern hotel, with a coffee shop on site serving fresh cakes and scones. Dorms €18, doubles €48

Lahinch Hostel Church St, Lahinch ☏065 708 1040, ⒲lahinchhostel.ie. Basic dormitory accommodation popular with surfers. Dorms €17

Rainbow Hostel Roadford ☏065 707 4415, ⒲rainbowhostel.net. A welcoming, family-run place offering bike rental (€8–12/day) and free guided walks of the area around Doolin. Dorms €16, doubles €40

EATING AND DRINKING

Doolin Café Roadford ⒲thedoolincafe.com. The self-proclaimed philosophy here is "why buy it when you can make it", with all dishes on the seasonal menu made using local artisan produce. The veggie breakfast with home-made baked beans and grilled halloumi is a real treat. Daily 8.30am–4pm, plus Thurs–Mon 6.30–9.30pm.

O'Connor's Fisher St ⒲gusoconnorsdoolin.com. One of three pubs in Doolin famous for their nightly traditional music sessions, offering giant portions of steaming mussels (€12) and other fresh seafood dishes. If you can't find a seat here, try McGann's or McDermott's close by. Mon–Thurs 10am–11.30pm, Fri & Sat 10am–12.30am, Sun 10am–11pm.

GALWAY

County **GALWAY** is home to the country's largest Irish-speaking Gaeltacht region, and, as a lively university city, its

reputation as party capital of Ireland is well justified. University College Galway guarantees a high number of young people in term time, but the energy is most evident during Galway's **festivals**, especially the lively **Arts Festival** in the last two weeks of July (⒲galwayartsfestival .com), and the **Galway Races** in the last week of July (⒲galwayraces.com).

WHAT TO SEE AND DO

Granted city status in 1484, **Galway** developed in the Middle Ages into a flourishing centre of trade with the Continent, a period of prosperity that is evident in its impressive architecture. Merchant townhouses line pedestrianized Shop Street, where buskers perform at all hours of the day and night outside some of the city's liveliest bars and cafés. **Lynch's Castle** on Shop Street, which now houses the Allied Irish Bank, dates from the fifteenth century and is a fine example of a medieval townhouse, with its stone facade decorated with carved panels, gargoyles and a lion devouring its prey.

Down by the River Corrib stands the **Spanish Arch**, a sixteenth-century structure that was used to protect galleons unloading wine and rum. Across the river lies the **Claddagh** district, the old fishing village that once stood outside the city walls and gave the world the Claddagh ring as a symbol of love and fidelity. Past the Claddagh the river widens out into **Galway Bay**; for a pleasant sea walk follow the road until it reaches **Salthill**, the city's seaside resort. There are several beaches along the promenade, though the best are 5km from Salthill at **Silverstrand** on the Barna road.

ARRIVAL AND DEPARTURE

By train The train station is off Eyre Square, on the northeast edge of the city centre.

Destinations Dublin (9–11 daily; 2hr 30min–3hr).

By bus The bus station is located on Forster St, beside the train station.

Destinations Cork (12 daily; 4hr 25min); Doolin (4 daily; 1hr 40min–2hr 50min); Dublin (15 daily; 3hr 30min–3hr 45min); Killarney (7 daily; 4hr 40min); Westport (6 daily; 1hr 35min–3hr 45min).

INFORMATION

Tourist office Forster St (daily 9am–5.45pm; ☎ 091 537 700, ⦿ irelandwest.ie).

ACCOMMODATION

Barnacles 10 Quay St ☎ 091 568 644, ⦿ barnacles.ie. Buzzing hostel conveniently located for pubs and cafés on Quay St; the larger dorms are a little crowded, but smaller ones are bright and comfortable. Dorms €17, doubles €50

Kinlay House Merchant's Rd ☎ 091 565 244, ⦿ www .kinlaygalway.ie. Enormous, impersonal hostel just off Eyre Square. Day-trips to the Aran Islands, the Cliffs of Moher and Connemara depart right outside the door. Dorms €19, doubles €60

Salthill Caravan Park Ballyloughlane, Renmore ☎ 091 523 972, ⦿ salthillcaravanpark.com. Family-run park located right on the beach, less than 2km from the centre. April–Sept. Per person €12

GALWAY CITY

ACCOMMODATION
Barnacles	3
Kinlay House	2
Salthill Caravan Park	4
Sleepzone	1

EATING
Dough Bros	1
Fat Freddy's	5
Griffin's Bakery	3
Kai Café	6
McCambridges	2
McDonagh's	4

DRINKING AND NIGHTLIFE
Blue Note	5
Crane Bar	6
The Quays	3
Róisín Dubh	4
Taaffe's	1
Tigh Neachtain	2

★**Sleepzone** Bóthar na mBan, Wood Quay ☎ 091 566 999, ⦿ sleepzone.ie. Ultramodern hostel with a mini-hotel feel, bright en-suite rooms and a huge communal kitchen. Dorms €17, doubles €60

EATING

Dough Bros 24 Upper Abbeygate St. Starting out as a wildly popular food truck, the *Dough Bros* now have a permanent residence where they serve the best wood-fired pizzas in Galway. Their "Posh Pepperoni" (€9) is an instant classic. Daily noon–10pm.

Fat Freddy's The Halls, Quay St ⦿ galwayrestaurants.net. Good pizzas, salads and antipasti at this fun, colourful bistro. Mains €10–15. Daily noon–10pm.

★**Griffin's Bakery** 21 Shop St ☎ 091 563 683, ⦿ griffinsbakery.com. The café above this long-established bakery is the ideal spot to rest your weary legs, with plenty of hot sandwiches and cakes to choose from. Lunch €7. Mon–Sat 8am–6pm.

★**Kai Café** 20 Sea Rd ⦿ kaicaferestaurant.com. An absolute gem of a café serving soul-nourishing food. Menu changes often, but expect things like West Coast crab salad (€11) for lunch. Mon 9.30am–3pm, Tues–Fri 9.30am–3pm & 6.30–10.30pm, Sat noon–3pm & 6.30–10.30pm, Sun noon–3pm.

McCambridges 38–39 Shop St ⦿ mccambridges .com. The queues run out the door every lunchtime at this gourmet deli renowned for its sandwiches, wraps and rolls (€3–5). Mon–Sat 8am–7pm, Sun noon–6pm.

McDonagh's 22 Quay St ⦿ mcdonaghs.net. A must for the freshest seafood at any time of day. The takeaway next door has a few informal tables and is much cheaper than the restaurant. Mains €8–34. Mon–Sat 5–10pm; takeaway daily noon–midnight.

DRINKING AND NIGHTLIFE

The Quay St area leading down to the river is known as the "Left Bank" due to the proliferation of popular pubs, restaurants and cafés. See the weekly *Galway Advertiser* (free; ⦿ advertiser.ie/galway) or *Galway City Tribune* (€1.60) for listings.

Blue Note 3 West William St. Atmospheric pub with intimate booths and snugs, a heated smoking garden, and DJs most nights.

★**Crane Bar** 2 Sea Rd ⦿ thecranebar.com. Holds revered traditional music sessions nightly from 9pm.

The Quays Quay St. One of the city's best-loved pubs, whose atmospheric interior was taken from a medieval French church. Daily until late.

Róisín Dubh Dominick St ⦿ roisindubh.net. Popular music bar and venue which plays host to top-class Irish and international acts. Opening hours depend on gigs and events.

Taaffe's 19 Shop St. One of the best places to hear traditional music, where there are nightly sessions until late.

Tigh Neachtain 17 Cross St ⓦ tighneachtain.com. Old-fashioned pub that attracts an eccentric, arty crowd. Great live music, too. Daily until late.

THE ARAN ISLANDS

The **Aran Islands – Inishmore**, **Inishmaan** and **Inisheer**, 50km out across the mouth of Galway Bay – are spectacular settings for a wealth of early remains and some of the finest archeological sites in Europe. The isolation of the Irish-speaking islands prolonged the continuation of a unique, ancient culture into the early twentieth century.

Inishmore

Inishmore is a great tilted plateau of limestone with a scattering of villages along the sheltered northerly coast. The land slants up to the southern edge, where dramatic cliffs rip along the entire shoreline. As far as the eye can see is a tremendous patterning of stone, the bare pavements of grey rock split into bold diagonal grooves and latticed by dry-stone walls.

WHAT TO SEE AND DO

Most of Inishmore's sights are to the northwest of **KILRONAN**, the island's principal town, where minibuses and ponies and traps offering island tours (see below) wait by the pier. Past the *American Bar* and up the hill to the west of Kilronan is a small settlement called Mainistir, from where it's a short signposted walk to the twelfth-century **Teampall Chiaráin** (Church of St Kieran). Five kilometres west along the main road from here is Kilmurvey, a small cluster of houses with a sandy beach which is a fifteen-minute walk from the most spectacular of Aran's prehistoric sites, **Dún Aonghasa**, accessed via its **visitor centre** (April–Oct 9.45am–6pm; Nov–March 9.30am–4pm; closed Mon & Tues in Jan & Feb; €4). The spectacular fort, which is 2500 years old, is perched on the edge of a sheer cliff, beaten relentlessly by the Atlantic Ocean below. The **Seven Churches**, just east of the village of Eoghanacht, is a monastic site dating from the ninth century,

believed to be one of the most significant medieval pilgrimage destinations in the west of Ireland.

ARRIVAL AND DEPARTURE

By ferry Boats from Galway city, Rossaveal and Doolin (see box above) dock at Kilronan.

INFORMATION AND TOURS

Tourist office Just west of where the ferry docks at Kilronan (daily: March–Oct 10am–5pm; Nov–Feb 11am–5pm; ☎ 099 61263).

Tours Seasonal minibuses (€10) run tours up through the island's villages. Pony-and-trap tours depart from the pier (€40 for a group of up to 4 people).

Bike rental Mullin's and BNN's near the pier (€10/day).

ACCOMMODATION

Accommodation can be booked through the Kilronan tourist office, or when you buy your ferry ticket in Galway.

Kilronan Hostel Kilronan ☎ 099 61255, ⓦ kilronan hostel.com. Cheery hostel with great facilities. Very convenient for the ferry. Dorms **€22**, doubles **€60**

Mainistir House Hostel Mainistir ☎ 099 61318, ⓦ aranislandshostel.com. A 20min walk west from the pier, this peaceful hostel offers a renowned "all you can eat" buffet every night for €15. Dorms **€20**, doubles **€50**

EATING AND DRINKING

Seafood is the island's great speciality, with most of the popular restaurants located in Kilronan.

★**Joe Watty's Bar** A great pub with traditional music most nights; serves good soups and stews, from €6. Food served daily noon–9pm.

The Old Courthouse (The Ould Pier). Simple and cheap place serving fresh fish and chips and seafood chowder, with a few outdoor tables. Closed Nov–Feb. Daytime only.

Inishmaan

Compared to Inishmore, **Inishmaan** is lush, with stone walls forming a maze that chequers off tiny fields of grass and clover. The island's main sight is **Dún Chonchubhair**: built sometime between the first and seventh centuries, its massive oval wall is almost intact and commands great views. Ask at the *Teach Ósta* pub for information (☎099 73003) – it's a warm and friendly place that also serves snacks in summer.

ACCOMMODATION

An Dún ☎099 73047, ⓦinismeainaccommodation.ie. Comfortable B&B right on the sea, also near Dún Chonchubhair. March–Nov only. Doubles €90

Ard Álainn ☎099 73027, ⓦgalway.net/pages/ard -alainn. Perched on a hill near Dún Chonchubhair offering lovely views over the island and neighbouring Inishmore. April–Sept only. Doubles €55

Inisheer

Inisheer, less than 3km across, is the smallest of the Aran Islands. A great plug of rock dominates the island, its rough, pale-grey stone dripping with greenery, topped by the fifteenth-century **O'Brien's Castle**, standing inside an ancient ring fort. Set around it are low fields, a small community of pubs and houses, and windswept sand dunes.

INFORMATION

Tourist office The Inisheer Island Cooperative hut by the pier (Mon–Sat 10.30am–3.30pm, summer only; ☎099 75008, ⓦdiscoverinisoirr.com) will give you a map and a list of B&Bs.

ACCOMMODATION

Brú Radharc na Mara ☎099 75024, ⓦbruhostelaran .com. Comfortable and clean family-run hostel, offering tours of the island on request. March–Oct only. Dorms €15, doubles €40

Campsite This campsite has toilets and washing facilities, and is near the pier. May–Sept only. Free

Radharc an Chláir Castle Village ☎099 75019. Bright yellow bungalow by the castle offering views across the sea to the Cliffs of Moher. Doubles €70

EATING AND DRINKING

Óstán Inis Oírr ☎099 73020. Tasty meals are available daily at the island's only hotel.

Tigh Ned's The place to head for music, coffee and snacks.

SLIGO

SLIGO is, after Derry, the biggest town in the northwest of Ireland. The legacy of **W.B. Yeats** – perhaps Ireland's best-loved poet – is still strongly felt here: the **Yeats Memorial Building** on Hyde Bridge (Mon–Fri 10am–5pm; free; ⓦyeats-sligo .com) features a photographic exhibition and film on his life, while the poet's Nobel Prize for Literature and other memorabilia are on show in the **Sligo County Museum** in the library on Stephen Street (Tues–Sat 10am–noon & 2–4.30pm; free). The **Model Arts Centre** on The Mall (Tues–Sat 10am–5.30pm, Sun noon–5pm; free; ⓦthemodel.ie) has works by the poet's brother, **Jack B. Yeats**, along with a broad collection of modern Irish art.

ARRIVAL AND DEPARTURE

By train The station is in the town centre on Lord Edward St.

Destinations Dublin (6 daily; 3hr 40min).

By bus The bus station is next to the train station, on Knappagh Rd.

Destinations Dublin (4 daily; 3hr 50min); Galway (4 daily; 2hr 40min).

INFORMATION

Tourist office O'Connell St, in the Ground Floor Old Bank Building. (Mon–Fri 9am–5pm, Sat 10am–5pm; ☎071 916 1201, ⓦsligotourism.ie).

ACCOMMODATION

Arrowrock Lodge, 25km south of Sligo town ☎071 966 6073, ⓦarrowrocklodge.com. This farmhouse-turned-hostel is the perfect base to explore the surrounding historic sites and stunning scenery. Comfortable rooms and a fully equipped kitchen give it a nice cosy feel. Dorms €15, doubles €50

Railway Hostel 1 Union Place ☎071 914 4530, ⓦtherailway.ie. Small hostel with comfortable communal areas and a lovely kitchen. Dorms €16, doubles €40

Tree Tops B&B Cleveragh Rd, 1km southeast along Pearse Rd ☎071 916 0160, ⓦtreetopssligo.com. Bright and comfortable rooms with sparklingly white bedspreads, great breakfasts and friendly hosts. Singles €40, doubles €72

EATING AND DRINKING

Hargadon's 4–5 O'Connell St ⓦhargadons.com. Award-winning but reasonably priced pub grub, including an excellent seafood chowder, home-made pâté and fresh seafood. Mains from €11. There's also a wine shop attached. Mon–Sat noon–3.30pm & 4–9pm.

16

Shoot the Crows Gratton St. One of the best places in Sligo for live traditional music. There are also regular sessions in *Earley's* and *Furey's*, both on Bridge Street. Opening hours depend on gigs.

Sweet Beat Café 3 Bridge St ⓦ sweetbeat.ie. Bright and welcoming vegan café serving superfood salads and an ever-changing "daily warmer". If you're feeling brave, go for the ginger shot – guaranteed to put pep in your step. Mon–Fri 10am–5pm, Sat 11am–5pm.

DONEGAL TOWN

DONEGAL TOWN is focused around its old marketplace – The Diamond – and makes a fine base for exploring the stunning coastal countryside and inland hills and loughs. Just about the only sight in the town itself is the well-preserved shell of **O'Donnell's Castle** on Tírchonaill Street by The Diamond (April–Oct daily 10am–6pm; Nov–March daily 9.30am–4.30pm; €4), a fine example of Jacobean architecture. On the left bank of the River Eske stand the few ruined remains of **Donegal Friary**, while on the opposite bank a woodland path known as Bank Walk offers wonderful views of **Donegal Bay** and the **Blue Stack Mountains**.

ARRIVAL AND DEPARTURE

By bus The stop for Bus Éireann departures and arrivals is outside the *Abbey Hotel*.
Destinations Derry (3–7 daily; 1hr 30min); Dublin (9–11 daily; 3hr 30min–5hr 55min); Glencolmcille (2 daily; 1hr 25min); Sligo (8 daily; 1hr).

INFORMATION

Tourist office The Quay (June–Aug Mon–Sat 9am–5.30pm, Sun 11am–3pm; Sept–May Mon–Sat 9am–5pm; ☎074 972 1148, ⓦ discoverireland.ie /northwest).

ACCOMMODATION

There are dozens of B&Bs in Donegal – you can book at the tourist office.
Atlantic Guesthouse Main St ☎074972 1187, ⓦ atlanticguesthouse.ie. Family-run establishment in the centre of town with bright and cheery rooms. Doubles **€52**
★**Donegal Town Independent Hostel** ☎074972 2805, ⓦ donegaltownhostel.com. Just past the roundabout on the Killybegs Rd, a 5min walk from town, this peaceful and very friendly hostel also has camping. Dorms **€17**, doubles **€42**, camping/person **€9**

EATING AND DRINKING

The Blueberry Tea Room Castle St. Good-quality, reasonably priced food served in a very cosy atmosphere. It has an internet café upstairs. Mains up to €12. Mon–Sat 9am–7pm.

The Reel Inn Bridge St. A lively bar packed with local old-timers, even at midday. Traditional music every night.

Simple Simon The Diamond. Deli in an organic food store offering healthy takeaway lunches (€2–5). Mon–Sat 10am–6pm.

SLIEVE LEAGUE

To the west of Donegal town lies one of the most stupendous landscapes in Ireland. There are two routes up to the ridge of **Slieve League**: a back way following the signpost to Baile Mór just before Teelin, and the road route from Teelin to Bunglass, a sheer 300m above the sea. The former path has you looking up continually at the ridge known as One Man's Pass, on which walkers seem the size of pins, while the front approach swings you up to one of the most thrilling cliff scenes in the world, the **Amharc Mór**. On a good day you can see a third of Ireland from the summit.

GLENCOLMCILLE

Since the seventh century, following Columba's stay in the valley, **GLENCOLMCILLE** has been a place of pilgrimage: every June 9 at midnight the locals commence a three-hour barefoot itinerary of the cross-inscribed slabs that stud the valley basin, finishing up with Mass at 3am in the small church. If you want to attempt *Turas Cholmcille* ("Columba's Journey") yourself, get a map of the route from the Glencolmcille Hill Walkers Centre, which also has lovely modern budget accommodation (see p.596), or the **Folk Village Museum** (Easter–Sept Mon–Sat 10am–6pm, Sun noon–6pm; €4.50; ⓦ glenfolkvillage .com), a cluster of replica, period-furnished thatched cottages.

ACCOMMODATION

Dooey Hostel ☎074 973 0130. A path to the left of the Folk Village Museum leads to this very basic but wonderfully positioned hostel run by a chatty local lady called Mary and her son Leo. Dorms **€15**, doubles **€30**, camping **€10**

16

Ionad Siul Guesthouse ☎074 973 0302, ⌨ionadsuil
.ie. Very modern and comfortable rooms at the
Glencolmcille Hill Walkers Centre, with use of a cosy
communal area and self-catering facilities. Doubles €50

EATING AND DRINKING

An Cistin Part of the Foras Cultúir Uladh Irish language
and culture complex, and the best place for food and drink.
Biddy's Bar Main St. Small bar located in the centre of
town. In the summer there's live music most nights, from
traditional and folk to blues.
Roarty's Main St. Good for a drink and lively traditional
music sessions most nights.

Northern Ireland

In 1998, after thirty years of the
Troubles in Northern Ireland, its people
overwhelmingly voted in support of a
political settlement and, it was hoped, an
end to political and sectarian violence
between Catholic republicans and
Protestant unionists. For a time the
political process gradually inched
forwards, hampered by deep mistrust and
suspicion on both sides. In recent years,
however, considerable headway has been
made in the peace process, with the
resumption of devolved government in
Northern Ireland, and a greater sense of
hope evident on both sides of the
community. **Belfast** and **Derry** are lively
and attractive cities that have benefited
from considerable investment and
regeneration in recent years, and the
northern coastline – especially the bizarre
geometry of the **Giant's Causeway** – is as
spectacular as anything in Ireland.

BELFAST

A quarter of Northern Ireland's
population lives in the capital, **BELFAST**.
The legacy of **the Troubles** is still clearly
visible in areas like West Belfast, where
peace walls currently divide Catholic and
Protestant communities (although there
are plans to remove them by 2023) and
political murals adorn street corners.
Security measures have been considerably
eased, though there are certain flashpoints
such as the Short Strand and the Ardoyne.

The city is going from strength to
strength, with a flourishing arts scene and
many new restaurants and clubs. Despite its
turbulent history, the city is imbued with a
zest for life, and a palpable cross-
community desire for a peaceful future.

WHAT TO SEE AND DO

City Hall is the central landmark of Belfast,
and divides the city conveniently into
north and south. The area to the north
of it, known as the **Cathedral Quarter**,
contains most of Belfast's official buildings,
as well as the main shopping areas, cosy
pubs and cool warehouse restaurants. The
southern section of the city, the so-called
Queen's Quarter, hosts many of the city's
museums and student bars, while the
Titanic Quarter across the river is the city's
most recently developed area.

Donegall Square and around

Belfast City Hall, presiding over central
Donegall Square, is an austere
Presbyterian building (tours Mon–Fri
11am, 2pm & 3pm, Sat 2pm & 3pm;
free). At the northwest corner of the
square stands the **Linen Hall Library**
(Mon–Fri 9.30am–5.30pm, Sat
9.30am–4pm; free; ⌨linenhall.com),
entered on Fountain Street, where the
Political Collection houses over eighty
thousand publications covering Northern
Ireland's political life since 1966. The
streets heading north off Donegall Square
North lead to the main shopping area.

The Cathedral Quarter and river area

Towards the river, either side of Ann
Street, are the narrow alleyways known as
The Entries, with some great old saloon
bars and warehouse restaurants. The area
is becoming the focus of the city's arts
scene, especially with the opening of the
Metropolitan Arts Centre, 10 Exchange St
West (MAC; daily 10am–7pm, later on
performance nights; ⌨themaclive.com),
which hosts regular art and photography
exhibitions, and music, theatre and dance
performances.

At the end of High Street the clock
tower is a good position from which to
view the world's second- and third-largest
cranes, Goliath and Samson, across the

16

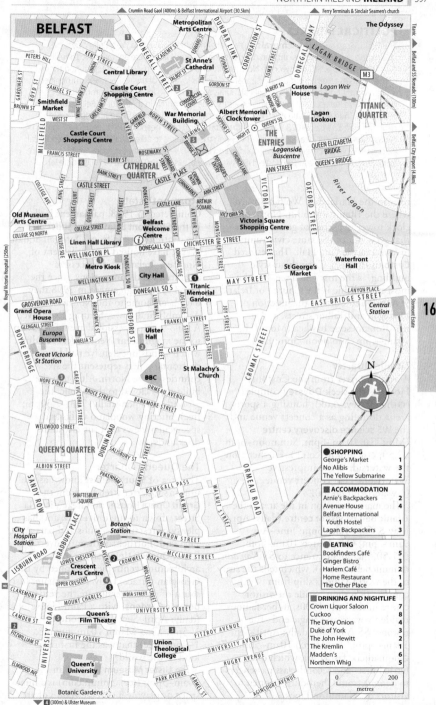

BELFAST

The Odyssey

Titanic

Metropolitan
Arts Centre

PETERS HILL

St Anne's
Cathedral

KENT STREET

Central Library

Customs
House

Lagan Weir

DONEGALL QUAY

LAGAN BRIDGE

M3

Belfast and SS Nomadic (100m)

Smithfield
Market

Castle Court
Shopping Centre

SAMUEL ST

War Memorial
Building

Albert Memorial
Clock tower

Lagan
Lookout

TITANIC
QUARTER

Belfast City Airport (4.8km)

Castle Court
Shopping Centre

FRANCIS STREET

CATHEDRAL
QUARTER

THE
ENTRIES

*Laganside
Buscentre*

QUEEN ELIZABETH
BRIDGE

QUEEN'S BRIDGE

River Lagan

Old Museum
Arts Centre

COLLEGE SQ NORTH

Belfast
Welcome
Centre

Linen Hall Library

CHICHESTER STREET

Waterfront
Hall

Sirmount Estate

16

Metro Kiosk

City Hall

Titanic
Memorial
Garden

MAY STREET

St George's
Market

LANYON PLACE

EAST BRIDGE STREET

Central
Station

Royal Victoria Hospital (250m)

Grand Opera
House

Europa
Buscentre

HOWARD STREET

Ulster
Hall

Great Victoria
St Station

BBC

St Malachy's
Church

ORMEAU AVENUE

BANKMORE STREET

N

QUEEN'S QUARTER

DUBLIN ROAD

DONEGALL PASS

ORMEAU ROAD

City
Hospital
Station

Botanic
Station

VERNON STREET

Crescent
Arts Centre

MCCLURE STREET

Queen's
Film Theatre

Union
Theological
College

Queen's
University

Botanic Gardens

(300m) & Ulster Museum

● **SHOPPING**

George's Market	1
No Alibis	3
The Yellow Submarine	2

■ **ACCOMMODATION**

Arnie's Backpackers	2
Avenue House	4
Belfast International Youth Hostel	1
Lagan Backpackers	3

● **EATING**

Bookfinders Café	5
Ginger Bistro	3
Harlem Café	2
Home Restaurant	1
The Other Place	4

■ **DRINKING AND NIGHTLIFE**

Crown Liquor Saloon	7
Cuckoo	8
The Dirty Onion	4
Duke of York	3
The John Hewitt	2
The Kremlin	1
Madden's	6
Northern Whig	5

0   200
metres

POLITICAL MURALS

The Republican and Loyalist **murals** on the Falls and Shankill roads in West Belfast provide a fascinating and moving insight into the city's complicated past. There are over two thousand examples of this political artwork in Northern Ireland altogether, mostly painted during the height of the Troubles to represent the political and religious loyalties of the respective communities. More recently, community-led, apolitical murals are becoming increasingly common. The open-topped Belfast City Sightseeing buses include the murals in their tour of Belfast, departing every 30–45min from Castle Place (£12.50, student £10.50). Taxi Trax (Castle Junction on King St, near City Hall; £30/car; ☎028 9031 5777, ⓦtaxitrax.com) offer bespoke taxi tours including West Belfast, but the most interesting way of viewing the murals is to take a walking tour with political ex-prisoners, who present both Republican and Loyalist viewpoints (tours Mon–Sat 11am & Sun 2pm; 2hr; £8; assemble at the bottom of Divis Towers, Falls Rd; ☎028 9020 0770, ⓦcoiste.ie).

river in the Harland & Wolff shipyard where the **Titanic** was built. North of the clock tower is a series of grand edifices that grew out of the same civic vanity as invested in the City Hall. The restored **Customs House**, a Corinthian-style building, is the first you'll see, but the most monolithic is the Church of Ireland **St Anne's Cathedral** at the junction of Donegall and Talbot streets, a neo-Romanesque basilica (Mon–Fri 10am–4pm, Sun noon–3pm; free).

Titanic Quarter

Across the river from the Customs House is the sleek **Odyssey** complex (ⓦtheodyssey.co.uk), housing a sports arena doubling as a concert venue and the **W5 science discovery centre** (Mon–Sat 10am–6pm, Sun noon–6pm; £8.50; ⓦw5online.co.uk). Further along the waterside is the impressive Waterfront Hall concert venue (ⓦwaterfront.co.uk).

The main attraction in the area is the **Titanic Belfast visitor centre** (daily: April, May & Sept 9am–6pm; June–Aug 9am–7pm; Oct–March 10am–5pm; £17.50, includes entrance to SS *Nomadic*; ⓦtitanicbelfast.com), which tells the story of the world-famous ship from construction right beside the visitor centre in the early 1900s, to her famous maiden voyage and tragic end. The restored SS *Nomadic* (daily: April–Sept 10am–6pm; Oct–March 10am–5pm; £7; ⓦnomadicbelfast.com), which once ferried first- and second-class passengers to *Titanic* from Cherbourg, is open to visitors on Hamilton Dock.

Stormont Estate

Completed in 1938, parliament buildings in the **Stormont Estate**, four miles east of the centre (bus #4a from Donegall Square West), have housed the parliament of Northern Ireland and successive assemblies and conventions; since the Good Friday Agreement in 1998 they have been home to the Northern Irish Assembly and Power Sharing Executive. A mile-long processional avenue leads up to the magnificent Neoclassical building, which stands in extensive parkland. The six frontal pillars represent the six counties of the North. Although the building is closed to the public, the grounds are open (daily: 7am–7.30pm; free), offering woodland walks and spectacular views over the city and docklands.

The Queen's Quarter

The area of **South Belfast** known as the Queen's Quarter stretches from the **Grand Opera House**, on Great Victoria Street, down to the university, and has plenty of restaurants, pubs and bars at each end. Further south on University Road, **Queen's University** is the architectural centrepiece, flanked by the Georgian terrace, University Square. Just south of the university are the verdant **Botanic Gardens**, with a Palm House (daily: April–Sept 10am–noon & 1–5pm; Oct–March 10am–noon & 1–4pm; free) that was the first of its kind in the world.

The **Ulster Museum** (Tues–Sun 10am–5pm; free; ⓦnmni.com) is a huge space displaying a rich collection of art and artefacts including prehistoric and Celtic objects such as the famous Malone Hoard, a collection of sixteen Neolithic stone axes; other exhibitions explore Belfast's shipbuilding and linen-producing industries.

ARRIVAL AND DEPARTURE

By plane Belfast International Airport is 30km west of town (buses every 10–30min to Europa bus station; £7 one-way, £10 return; ☎028 9448 4848, ⍵belfastairport .com); George Best Belfast City Airport is 4.8km northeast (bus #600 every 20min to city centre 5.30am–10pm; £2.50 return; ☎028 9093 9093, ⍵belfastcityairport.com).
By train Most trains call at the central Great Victoria St Station, though those from Dublin and Larne terminate at Central Station on East Bridge St.
Destinations Coleraine (9–10 daily; 1hr 20min–1hr 45min); Derry (5–9 daily; 2hr 30min); Dublin (8 daily; 2hr 10min); Larne Harbour (9–25 daily; 1hr 10min).
By bus Buses from Derry, the Republic, the airports and ferry terminals arrive at Europa Buscentre beside Great Victoria St train station; buses from the north coast use Laganside Bus Centre in Queen's Square. A regular Centrelink bus connects all bus and train stations.
Destinations Derry (11–32 daily; 1hr 50min); Dublin (20 daily; 3hr); Enniskillen (5–16 daily; 2hr–2hr 20min).
By boat Ferries from Stranraer dock at Corry Rd (taxi £9), and those from Liverpool further north on West Bank Rd (taxi £8), while ferries from Cairnryan dock 30km north at Larne (bus or train to centre).

INFORMATION

Tourist office The Belfast Welcome Centre, 10–12 Donegall Square North (Mon–Sat 9am–5.30/7pm, Sun 11am–4pm; ☎028 9024 6609, ⍵visit-belfast.com). Offers internet access.

GETTING AROUND

Information on all buses and trains is available at ☎028 9066 6630 or ⍵translink.co.uk.
By bus The city is served by Metro bus service. Day tickets for the whole network cost £3.70 (Mon–Sat). One-way tickets cost £1.20–1.80. The metro kiosk in Donegall Square West provides free bus maps. Ulsterbus serves outlying areas.
Discount passes The one-, two- or three-day Belfast Visitor Pass (£6.50/£11/£14.50) offers unlimited travel and discounts for visitor attractions around the city.
Bike rental Lifecycles, Unit 35, Smithfield Market (£10/ day, £16 for 2hr guided tour).

ACCOMMODATION

★**Arnie's Backpackers** 63 Fitzwilliam St ☎028 9024 2867, ⍵arniesbackpackers.co.uk. Cheerful and relaxed independent hostel with a homely atmosphere and colourful garden, near the university. Dorms £12, twins £44
Avenue House 23 Eglantine Ave ☎028 9066 5904, ⍵avenueguesthouse.com. A homely guesthouse in a red-brick Victorian townhouse, with a warm welcome, pretty garden and great breakfasts. Doubles £70, triple £85
Belfast International Youth Hostel 22–32 Donegall Rd ☎028 9031 5435. Large, well-equipped but characterless modern HINI hostel, just west of Shaftesbury Square. Dorms £15, doubles £50
Lagan Backpackers 121 Fitzroy Ave ☎028 9514 0049, ⍵laganbackpackers.com. Friendly, clean and comfortable place in an old red-brick house, with free English breakfast included and regular barbecue nights in summer. Dorms £15, doubles £40

EATING

Many of the best places to eat and the liveliest pubs are located in the Cathedral Quarter, with plenty of budget options and student bars around Great Victoria Street and in the university area.
Bookfinders Café 47 University Rd. Bohemian café at the back of a charmingly messy bookshop. Poetry nights on Fridays from 8pm. Lunch from £3. Mon–Sat 10am–5.30pm.
★**Ginger Bistro** 7–8 Hope St ⍵gingerbistro.com. Fresh seasonal ingredients are sourced locally from farmers and fishermen, and whipped into tasty and imaginative dishes with an international twist. Mains £13–20. Tues–Sat noon–3pm & 5–9.30pm.
Harlem Café 34 Bedford St ⍵harlembelfast.co.uk. A lunchtime institution with days-gone-by comfort and charm. Fantastic dinner at weekends. Home-made pie £8. Mon–Thurs 8am–4pm, Fri & Sat 8/9am–late, Sun 9am–5pm.
Home Restaurant 22 Wellington Place ⍵homebelfast .co.uk. Delicatessen serving home-made comfort food from locally sourced ingredients. £6–12. Mon–Thurs noon–4pm & 5–9.30pm, Fri & Sat noon–4pm.
The Other Place 78 Botanic Ave ⍵theotherplace.co.uk. Fine breakfasts, and plenty of pizzas, pastas and baked potatoes (£5–10). Daily 8am–10pm.

DRINKING AND NIGHTLIFE

Belfast's best entertainment is pub music, though there's also a vibrant club scene and plenty of DJ bars. For listings check *The Big List* (free; ⍵thebiglist.co.uk), available in pubs, record shops and hostels, and the *Belfast Telegraph* (70p; ⍵belfasttelegraph.co.uk).

PUBS

★**Crown Liquor Saloon** 46 Great Victoria St. The city's most famous pub, decked out like a spa bath, serves a good range of Ulster food, such as champ and colcannon (both potato dishes) and Strangford oysters in season.

16

Mon–Wed 11.30am–11pm, Thurs–Sat 11.30am–midnight, Sun 12.30–10pm.

Cuckoo 149 Lisburn Rd. Quirky bar popular with students, with a graffitied floor, cuckoo clocks on the walls, and jam jars of cocktails (£4.95). Daily until 1am.

The Dirty Onion 3 Hill St ⓦ thedirtyonion.com. Housed in one of the oldest buildings in Belfast, *The Dirty Onion* is one of the most buzzing pubs in the city. Expect live music nightly and queues at weekends. Daily noon–1am.

Duke of York 7–11 Commercial Court ⓦ dukeofyork belfast.com. Traditional bar on one of Belfast's oldest cobbled streets, with regular live trad sessions, an upstairs disco and a courtyard area which gets packed on sunny days. Daily until late.

The John Hewitt 53 Donegall St ⓦ thejohnhewitt.com. Owned by Belfast Unemployed Resource Centre, this popular bar has some of Belfast's best traditional music sessions on Tuesdays, Wednesdays and Saturday evenings, blues on Thurdays and jazz on Fridays.

Madden's 52–74 Berry St. Unpretentious and atmospheric pub, with regular traditional music sessions (Fri & Sat).

CLUBS

The Kremlin 90 Donegall St ⓦ kremlin-belfast.com. Northern Ireland's biggest gay venue, with a host of events throughout the week.

Northern Whig 2–10 Bridge St ⓦ thenorthernwhig .com. Massive upmarket bar in the premises of the old newspaper, featuring pre-club DJs most nights.

SHOPPING

The main shopping area is the long stretch of Donegall Place and Royal Ave, where you'll find big fashion and retail names. The big shopping centres are Victoria Square on Victoria St and Castle Court on Royal Ave. Unsurprisingly, things get more alternative in the university area.

George's Market May St, east of City Hall. Specializes in food on Friday and artisan produce at the weekends. Fri 6am–2pm, Sat 9am–3pm, Sun 10am–4pm.

No Alibis 83 Botanic Ave ⓦ noalibis.com. A great independent bookshop specializing in crime. It often holds music events and readings. Opening hours depend on events.

The Yellow Submarine 44 Botanic Ave. You don't get much cooler than this. Five floors filled with an eclectic mix of vintage clothing, vinyl, books and furniture at very reasonable prices. Mon–Sat 11am–6pm, Sun 1–5pm.

DIRECTORY

Exchange The Belfast Welcome Centre (see p.599), and all major bank branches.

Hospitals Belfast City Hospital, Lisburn Rd (☎ 028 9032 9241); Royal Victoria, Grosvenor Rd (☎ 028 9024 0503).

Left luggage Belfast Welcome Centre, 47 Donegall Place.

Police North Queen St ☎ 028 9065 0222.

Post office Castle Place.

THE GIANT'S CAUSEWAY

Since 1693, when the Royal Society publicized it as one of the great wonders of the natural world, the **Giant's Causeway** has been a major tourist attraction. Lying 65 miles northwest of Belfast, it consists of an estimated 37,000 polygonal basalt columns; it's the result of a massive subterranean explosion some sixty million years ago which spewed out a huge mass of molten basalt onto the surface which, as it cooled, solidified into massive polygonal crystals. Taking the 1km path down the cliffs from the **visitor centre** (daily: Feb, March & Oct 9am–6pm; April–June & Sept 9am–7pm; July & Aug 9am–9pm; Nov–Jan 9am–5pm; £9; ⓦ giantscausewayofficial guide.com), or the shuttle bus (every 15min; £2 return), brings you to the most spectacular of the blocks where many people linger, but if you push on, you'll be rewarded with relative solitude and views of some of the more impressive formations high in the cliffs. One of these, **Chimney Point**, has an appearance so bizarre that the ships of the Spanish Armada opened fire on it, believing that they were attacking Dunluce Castle, a few kilometres further west. An alternative 3.2km circuit follows the spectacular cliff-top path from the visitor centre, with views across to Scotland, to a flight of 162 steps leading down the

THE MOURNE MOUNTAINS

If you're based in Belfast but fancy a day-trip out of the metropolis, the beautiful **Mourne Mountains** provide the perfect escape. The mountain range comprises twelve peaks, of which Slieve Donard, at 850m, is the highest in Northern Ireland. From Belfast, buses #20, #720 and #237 run from the Europa Buscentre to Newcastle (up to 15 daily; 1hr); from Newcastle, the Mourne Rambler service (June–Aug) tracks a loop through the area (£5.50 day-ticket; ⓦ www.mourne-mountains.com).

GETTING TO THE GIANT'S CAUSEWAY

Trains from Belfast go to Coleraine, where there's a regular connection to Portrush; from either, you can catch the "open-top" **bus** (July & Aug 4 daily; £9 for day ticket) to the Causeway, or from Portrush there's bus #172, both running via Bushmills. A restored **narrow-gauge railway** runs between Bushmills and the Causeway (July & Aug 7 daily, plus some days in other months; 20min; one-way £5.25, return £6.75; ☎028 2073 2844).

Alternatively, take a direct **coach** (Goldline Express #221) from the Belfast Europa Buscentre to the Causeway (July & Aug 4 daily; 1hr 35min; one-way £11.50, return £17.50). The Antrim Coaster coach (Goldline Express #252) runs from Larne direct to the Causeway (April–Sept only; 2 daily; 2hr 30min; one-way £10, return £17.50) and on to Coleraine via Bushmills, Portrush and Portstewart, Antrim Glens and stunning seascapes en route.

If you prefer to travel **by foot**, you can walk the "Causeway Coast Way" (⟆causewaycoastway .com), a spectacular 33-mile trail starting from Ballycastle that will earn you a "green discount" admission to the visitor centre.

cliff to a set of basalt columns known as the **Organ Pipes**.

Carrick-a-Rede

Don't miss the **Carrick-a-Rede Rope Bridge**, which sits 13km east of the Causeway (daily: March–Oct 10am–6/7pm, June–Aug 10am–7pm, weather permitting; £5.90; ⟆national trust.org.uk). For the past two hundred years, fishermen had reputedly erected a bridge from the mainland cliffs to Carrick-a-Rede island over a vast chasm, so they could check their salmon nets. Now, the National Trust is in charge. Venturing across the swaying rope bridge high above the water is an exhilarating experience, but not for the faint-hearted. Ulsterbus #252 runs between Bushmills and the rope bridge via the Causeway in summer months.

PORTSTEWART

PORTSTEWART is a pleasant coastal resort ten miles west of the Giant's Causeway, with a long sandy beach and good surf. Barmouth Wildlife Reserve behind the strand has bird hides offering opportunities to view waterfowl, waders and nesting birds.

ACTIVITIES

Ocean Warriors 80 The Promenade ☎028 7083 6500. Surf shop offering boards and wetsuits for sale or rent.

ACCOMMODATION

Rick's Causeway Coast Hostel 4 Victoria Terrace ☎028 7083 3789, ⟆rickscausewaycoast.hostel.com. The bus stop for the Giant's Causeway is 100m from the hostel. Dorms £15, doubles £40

EATING AND DRINKING

Harbour Café 18 The Promenade. Huge, hearty portions of lasagne, roast dinners and fish and chips (from £7.50) served up by friendly staff daily. There's an ice-cream parlour too for a sweet treat. Open daily.

Shenanigans 78 The Promenade. The steaks, fresh fish and vegetables used for the seasonal menu in this gastropub are all sourced in Northern Ireland. The meal deal for two including wine is just £20. They serve a great strawberry daiquiri (£5.90) in the bar, and there's a popular student nightclub *Havana* upstairs. Daily noon–1.30am.

DERRY-LONDONDERRY

DERRY-LONDONDERRY (traditionally referred to as "Derry" by Nationalists, "Londonderry" by Unionists – and now often pinned together as "Derry-Londonderry") lies at the foot of Lough Foyle, less than three miles from the border with the Republic. The city presents a beguiling picture, its two hillsides terraced with pastel-shaded houses punctuated by stone spires, and, being seventy percent Catholic, has a very different atmosphere from Belfast. Despite the Catholic dominance, from Partition in 1921 until the late 1980s, the Protestant minority maintained control of all important local institutions. The situation came to a head after the Protestant Apprentice Boys' March in August 1969, when the police attempted to storm the Catholic estates of the Bogside. In the ensuing tension, British troops were widely deployed for the first

16

time in Northern Ireland. On January 31, 1972, the crisis deepened when British paratroopers opened fire on civilians, killing thirteen unarmed demonstrators in what became known as **Bloody Sunday**.

Derry-Londonderry is now greatly changed: tensions eased considerably here long before Belfast, although defiant murals remain and marching is still a contentious issue. The city centre has undergone much regeneration, and Derry-Londonderry's justifiable reputation for innovation in the arts resulted in it becoming the UK City of Culture in 2013 (ⓦcityofculture2013.com).

WHAT TO SEE AND DO

You can walk the entire mile-long circuit of Derry-Londonderry's seventeenth-century **city walls** – some of the best-preserved defences in Europe. Reinforced by bulwarks, bastions and an earth rampart with parapet, the walls encircle the original medieval street pattern with four gateways – Shipquay, Butcher, Bishop and Ferryquay.

The **Bogside murals** are in the streets that were once the undisputed preserve of the IRA, and **Free Derry Corner** marks the site of the original barricades erected against the British army at the height of the Troubles. Nearby are the Bloody Sunday and Hunger Strikers' memorials. Further along the city wall is the **Royal Bastion**, former site of the Revd George Walker statue, which was blown up in 1973. It is in Walker's and their predecessors' memory that the Protestant Apprentice Boys march around the walls every August 12. The new **Peace Bridge** crosses the River Foyle to the redeveloped Ebrington Square, a former World War I military base that has been transformed into an outdoor event space.

ARRIVAL AND DEPARTURE

By plane City of Derry airport (☎028 7181 0784, ⓦcityofderryairport.com) is 7 miles northeast, connected to the centre by the Airporter bus (£5).

By train Trains from Belfast arrive on the east bank of the Foyle with a free connecting bus to the bus station. Destinations Belfast (4–9 daily; 2hr 30min); Coleraine (5–9 daily; 1hr).

By bus The station is on Foyle St, beside Guildhall Square.

Destinations Donegal (3–7 daily; 1hr 25min–1hr 45min); Dublin (11 daily; 4hr); Enniskillen (5–15 daily; 2hr–4hr 20min); Sligo (3–5 daily; 2hr 30min).

INFORMATION

Tourist office 44 Foyle St (July–Sept Mon–Fri 9am–7pm, Sat 9am–6pm, Sun 10am–5pm; Oct–June Mon–Fri 9am–5pm, Sat 10am–5pm, Sun 10am–4pm; ☎028 7126 7284, ⓦvisitderry.com).

Tours City Tours offer walking tours of the walls (11 Carlisle Rd; daily 10am, noon & 2pm; £4; ☎0771 293 7997, ⓦderrycitytours.com) and taxi tours (£25/hr for 4 people), which explore fifteen hundred years of history and provide an introduction to the Bogside murals.

ACCOMMODATION

Derry City Independent Hostel 44 Great James St ☎028 7128 0524. A friendly, bohemian hostel with furniture from around the world. Hosts regular barbecues in the summer. Dorms __£18__, doubles __£50__

★ **The Saddler's House** 36 Great James St ☎028 7126 9691, ⓦthesaddlershouse.com. Beautifully decorated Georgian townhouse run by knowledgeable hosts and serving excellent breakfasts. This, together with its sister B&B *The Merchant House*, is a real treat. They also have self-catering cottages and two-bed apartments available to rent. Late-night revellers not welcome. Doubles __£60__

EATING

Badgers Bar & Restaurant 16–18 Orchard St. Located in the heart of the city, close to the walls, this hugely popular bar serves good pub grub using locally sourced ingredients. Daily noon–10pm.

★ **Primrose Café** 15 Carlisle Rd ☎028 7126 4622. This atmospheric café is the ideal spot to enjoy a bit of people-watching while indulging your sweet tooth. Alfresco dining in their gorgeous "secret garden" is a treat. Mains £5–8. Mon–Sat 8am–5pm, Sun 11am–4pm.

DRINKING AND NIGHTLIFE

Mason's Bar 10 Magazine St. Much-loved live music venue which also runs Derry's only comedy club (two Thursdays every month). Mon–Sat 11am–1am, Sun noon–12.15am.

Peadar O'Donnell's/The Gweedore Bar 59–63 Waterloo St ⓦpeadars.com. Traditional and contemporary music every night until late.

Sandino's Café Bar Water St ⓦsandinoscafebar.com. Intimate candlelit café-bar with a Che Guevara theme downstairs, and a live music venue upstairs, which opens late. Traditional music on Sun from 5pm.

DUOMO, FLORENCE

Italy

HIGHLIGHTS

❶ **Turin** Italy's first capital is home to spectacular royal palaces. **See p.620**

❷ **Venice** Visit St Mark's Square after midnight when it's almost tourist-free. **See p.633**

❸ **Florence** Marvel at Renaissance masterpieces. See p.644

❹ **Pompeii and Herculaneum** Explore the evocative remains of two cities buried by ash. See p.664

❺ **Matera** A cavernous city with dwellings entirely hewn out of rock. **See p.668**

❻ **Taormina** Breathtaking views of Mount Etna at this former bohemian retreat. **See p.673**

HIGHLIGHTS ARE MARKED ON THE MAP ON P.605

ROUGH COSTS

Daily budget Basic €35, occasional treat €50

Drink Wine €2.50/glass

Food Local pasta dish €5–8; pizza slice €2

Hostel/budget hotel €15–30/€45–60

Travel Train: Rome–Naples €20; bus: €12

FACT FILE

Population 60 million

Language Italian

Currency Euro (€)

Capital Rome

International phone code ☎39

Time zone GMT +1hr

17

Introduction

Of all the countries in Europe, Italy is perhaps the hardest to classify. A modern industrialized nation and a harbinger of global style, its designers lead the way with each season's fashions. But it is also a Mediterranean country, with all that that implies. If there is a single national characteristic, it is to embrace life to the full, manifest in its numerous local festivals and in the importance placed on good food. There is also, of course, the country's enormous cultural legacy: Tuscany alone has more classified historical monuments than any country in the world, and every region holds its own treasures.

Italy wasn't unified until 1861, a fact that's borne out by the regional nature of the place today. The well-to-do cities of **Turin** and **Milan** epitomize the wealthy, industrial north; to their south is **Genoa**, a bustling port with a long seafaring tradition. By far the biggest draw in the north is **Venice**, a unique and beautiful city – though you won't be alone in appreciating it. The centre of the country, specifically **Tuscany**, boasts classic, rolling countryside and the art-packed towns of Florence, Pisa and Siena, while neighbouring **Umbria** has a quieter appeal. **Rome**, the capital, harbours a dazzling array of ancient and Renaissance gems. South of here in Campania, **Naples**, a vibrant, unforgettable city, is the spiritual heart of the economically undeveloped Italian south, while close by are fine ancient sites and the spectacular **Amalfi Coast**. The region of Basilicata is home to spellbinding **Matera**, a unique troglodyte settlement where cave dwellings are carved into rock. Puglia, the "heel" of Italy, has underrated pleasures – most notably **Lecce**, a Baroque gem of a city. **Sicily** is a law unto itself, with attractions ranging from Hellenic remains to the drama of Mount Etna, and the beguiling city of Palermo. **Sardinia**, too, feels far removed from the mainland, especially in its relatively undiscovered interior.

CHRONOLOGY

753 BC Rome founded by Romulus and Remus.
509 BC The city becomes a Republic.
49 BC Julius Caesar wages war against the Senate and extends the Roman Empire across Europe.

80 AD Building of the Colosseum.
476 Last Roman Emperor Romulus Augustus overthrown by barbarians.
756 Papal States created after Frankish forces defeat the Lombards.
1173 Building of the Tower of Pisa begins.
1512 Michelangelo completes his frescoes in the Sistine Chapel, as the Italian Renaissance flourishes.
1804 Napoleon declares himself emperor of Italy.
1814 Following Napoleon's defeat, Italy is divided into various states.
1861 Unification of Italian states into a Kingdom by Giuseppe Garibaldi.
1898 First Italian football league established.
1915 Italy joins World War I on the side of the Allies.
1922 Fascist Benito Mussolini becomes prime minister.
1929 The Lateran Treaty declares Vatican City an independent state. It is the smallest state in the world.
1940 Italy enters World War II on the side of the Nazis.
1943 Allies capture Sicily and imprison Mussolini. Italy declares war on Germany.
1945 Mussolini is captured and executed by Italian Communists.
1946 Republic replaces the monarchy.
1957 The Treaty of Rome establishes the European Economic Community.
1970s The military left-wing organization Brigate Rosse terrorizes the country with murders, kidnappings and sabotage.
1992 Silvio Berlusconi becomes Prime Minister and the so-called Second Republic begins.
2013 Pope Benedict XVI unexpectedly resigns and is replaced by Francis I. The Governor of Sicily declares state of emergency when hundreds of African migrants die in shipwrecks off the coast.
2016 In August, over 240 people are killed when a powerful earthquake hits Amatrice and nearby towns in Central Italy.

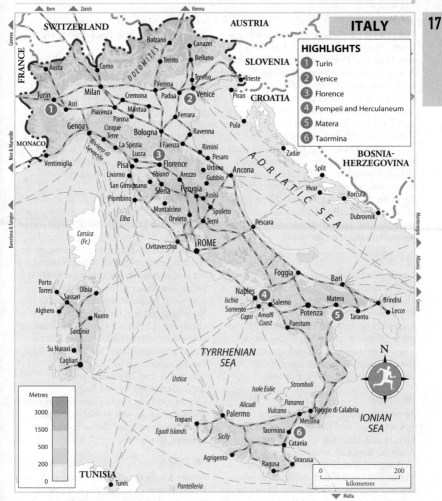

SWITZERLAND

AUSTRIA

FRANCE

Bern   Zürich   Vienna

Bolzano   Canazei

SLOVENIA

Aosta   Como   Trento   Belluno   Treviso   Trieste

Turin   Milan   Verona   Padua   Venice   Piran   CROATIA

Asti   Cremona   ②

Piacenza   Mantua   Ferrara

Genoa   Parma   Bologna   Ravenna   Pula

Cinque   Faenza   Rimini

MONACO   Terre   La Spezia   Lucca   Pesaro

Riviera di   Levante

Ventimiglia   Pisa   ③ Florence   Urbino   Ancona   Zadar   BOSNIA-
                                                              HERZEGOVINA

Livorno   Chianti   Arezzo   Gubbio   Split

San Gimignano   Siena   Perugia   Assisi   Hvar   Korčula

Piombino   Montalcino   Spoleto   Dubrovnik

Elba   Orvieto   Terni   Pescara

ROME   ④ Naples   Foggia   Bari

Civitavecchia   Salerno   Matera   Brindisi

Corsica
(Fr.)

ADRIATIC SEA

HIGHLIGHTS

① Turin
② Venice
③ Florence
④ Pompeii and Herculaneum
⑤ Matera
⑥ Taormina

Porto   Olbia
Torres   Sassari

Alghero   Nuoro

Sardinia

Su Nuraxi   Cagliari

TYRRHENIAN
SEA

Ustica

Ischia   Sorrento   Capri   Amalfi   Paestum   Potenza   ⑤ Taranto   Lecce
                    Coast

Isole Eolie   Stromboli

Alicudi   Panarea
         Vulcano   Reggio di Calabria
Trapani   Palermo   Messina

Egadi Islands   Sicily   Taormina   ⑥ Catania   IONIAN
                                                SEA

Agrigento   Ragusa   Siracusa

TUNISIA   Tunis   Pantelleria

Malta

Metres
3000
1500
500
200
0

0   200
kilometres

N

ARRIVAL AND DEPARTURE

BY PLANE

The majority of tourists arrive at the **airports** of Rome or Milan, although low-cost European airlines Ryanair and easyJet also offer services to Bari, Bologna, Brindisi, Genoa, Naples, Palermo, Parma, Perugia, Pisa, Rimini, Turin and Venice, plus destinations in Sardinia and Sicily. Budget Italian airline blu-express (wblu-express.com) flies from Greece and Albania and a number of destinations in Italy including Milan and Rome, as well as

between many Italian cities; Meridiana (wmeridiana.it) has routes between many European and Italian cities. From North America, national carrier Alitalia (walitalia.com) runs direct flights to Milan, Rome and Venice, with numerous connecting flights to other cities, although you may find cheaper deals with US airlines such as Delta and American Airlines. Meridiana operates direct flights from New York to Cagliari, Catania, Olbia, Naples and Palermo. The cheapest option, though, can be to fly to London and get a budget flight onward from there.

17

BY TRAIN

Train travel from the UK often works out more expensive than flying, but there is a vast choice of routes, mostly arriving in Milan. From elsewhere in Europe, look into Trenitalia's Smart Price fares; in theory you can travel from Paris for €35, Lugano and Zurich for €9, Geneva, Bern and Basil for €19, Munich for €33 and Vienna for €29, but in practice availability is extremely limited and seats must be booked at least a month ahead. If you're under 26, and planning to travel extensively by rail, consider Trenitalia's **Carta Verde**, which gives you 10 percent off domestic fares and 25 percent off international fares (€40; valid 1 year); see ⓦtrenitalia.com for details.

BY BUS

Getting to Italy **by bus** can take a soul-destroyingly long time and is rarely cheap enough to be worth it. Eurolines (ⓦeurolines.co.uk) runs services around Europe; London to Venice costs €95 and takes 30 hours. Busabout (ⓦbusabout .com) runs hop-on, hop-off services to Rome and cities further north from destinations throughout Europe.

BY FERRY

Ferries ply routes from Albania to Ancona, Bari and Brindisi; Corsica to Genoa and Livorno; Croatian ports to Ancona, Bari and Venice; ports in Greece to Ancona, Bari, Brindisi, Trieste and Venice; Bar and Kotor in Montenegro to Ancona and Bari; Tangiers in Morocco to Genoa and Livorno; and Barcelona to Genoa, Livorno and Civitavecchia. See ⓦdirectferries.it for details.

GETTING AROUND

BY TRAIN

The rail network is extensive, less so in the south, though delays are common. **Trains** are operated by Italian State Railways (Ferrovie dello Stato or FS; ⓦtrenitalia.com). For most journeys you'll have a choice between Eurostar – expensive but fast – the slower, mid-priced Intercity and the cheap, snail-paced Diretto, Interregionale and Regionale. Seat reservations are obligatory on Eurostar and Intercity lines, and should be made a week in advance on busy routes. **InterRail** and **Eurail** passes are valid on the whole FS network, though you'll pay supplements for the fast trains and most long-distance trains. **Tickets** must be validated in the yellow machines at the head of the platform. Call Trenitalia on ☏06 6847 5475 or consult the website for information and online tickets.

BY BUS

Some parts of the country – notably parts of the south and Sicily – are better served by **bus** than by train, though schedules can be sketchy. Buy tickets at *tabacchi* or the bus terminal rather than on board; for longer journeys you can normally buy them in advance direct from the bus company. Major companies running long-haul services include Marozzi (Rome to the Amalfi Coast and Brindisi; ⓦwww2.marozzivt.it), SAIS (connects major mainland cities with Sicily; ⓦsaistrasporti.it), SITA (Puglia, Campania and Basilicata; ⓦwww .sitasudtrasporti.it) and Sulga (destinations in Puglia, Emilia Romagna and Umbria, as well as Milan, Naples, Florence, Rome and Rome Fiumicino Airport; ⓦsulga.it).

BY FERRY

Ferries for Sicily and Sardinia depart from Genoa, Livorno, Naples, Salerno (near Naples; Sicily only) and Civitavecchia (near Rome). Smaller islands such as Capri, plus towns in the Bay of Naples and along the Amalfi Coast, are served by speedier **hydrofoils**. Book well in advance for the longer routes in high season to find the cheapest fares; for timetables, see ⓦdirectferries.it.

ACCOMMODATION

Book **hotels** in advance in the major cities and resorts, especially in summer. Rates vary greatly, but on average you can expect to pay €65 for a double without private bathroom (*senza bagno*) in a one-star hotel, and at least €90 for a double in a three-star. Very busy places might ask you to book a minimum of three nights.

B&Bs and **agriturismi** (farmstays) can make a good-value alternative. They are often in spectacular locations and provide excellent Italian home cooking, though you may need a car to get to them: ask for a list from the local tourist office.

There are **hostels** in every major Italian city, charging €15–30 per person for a dorm bed, though for two people travelling together, this isn't much cheaper than a budget hotel room. You can see the full list of Italy's HI hostels on ⓦaighostels.it. **Student accommodation** is a popular budget option in university towns (July & Aug only); alternatively, ask the tourist board about local **case reliogiose** or **pensioniati**, religious houses with rooms or beds to let. They can be better value than hostels but often have curfews. Short-term flat rentals can be cheaper than staying in hotels, in particular in cities like Rome and Florence. ⓦcross-pollinate.com lists rooms and apartments for rent in a number of Italian cities.

There are plenty of **campsites**, and in most cases you pay for location rather than facilities, which can vary enormously. Daily prices are around €8 per person, plus €10 for a two-person tent. See ⓦcamping.it for information.

FOOD AND DRINK

There are few places in the world where you can eat and drink as well as in Italy. If you eat only pizza and sandwiches, you'll be missing out on the distinctive **regional cuisines**; don't be afraid to ask what the *piatti tipici* (local dishes) are. Most Italians start their day in a bar, with a cappuccino and a *cornetto* (croissant), a **breakfast** that should cost around €2 if you stand at the counter – at least double that if you take a seat. At **lunchtime**, bars sell *tramezzini*, sandwiches on white bread, and *panini* (sandwiches). Another stopgap is arancini, fried meat- or cheese-filled rice balls, particularly prevalent in the south. Italian **ice cream**

(*gelato*) is justifiably famous and usually costs €1.50–2.50 a cup or cone. **Markets** sell fresh, tasty produce for next to nothing, and work out much cheaper than supermarket shopping.

The ultimate budget option for sit-down food is **pizza**. Although trattorias or restaurants often offer a fixed-price *menù turistico*, it's generally better to steer clear if you want an authentic experience. A **trattoria** is traditionally cheaper than a restaurant, offering *cucina casalinga* (home-style cooking). But in either, pasta dishes go for around €5–9; main fish or meat courses for €7–15. Order vegetables (*contorni*) separately. Afterwards there's fruit (*frutta*), desserts (*dolci*) and liquors such as *grappa* and *limoncello*.

DRINK

Bars are less social centres than functional places for a quick coffee or beer. You pay first at the cash desk (*la cassa*), present your receipt (*scontrino*) and give your order. Coffee comes small and black (*caffè*), with a dash of milk (*macchiato*), iced (*shakerato*) in summer, or there's the ever-popular *cappuccino*. Tea (*tè*) comes with lemon (*con limone*) unless you ask for milk (*con latte*); it's mainly served cold as ice-tea (*tè freddo*). A *spremuta* is a fresh orange juice; crushed-ice fruit *granite* are refreshing in summer.

Wine (vino) is invariably drunk with meals, and is very cheap. Go for the local stuff: ask for *un mezzo* (a half-litre) or *un quarto* (a quarter) *della casa* (house). Bottles are pricier but still good value; expect to pay at least €12 in a restaurant. The cheapest and most common brands of **beer** (*birra*) are the Italian Peroni and Moretti. Draught beer (*alla spina*) is

17

STUDENT AND YOUTH DISCOUNTS

Entrance to many of Italy's state-owned museums and archeological sites is free or reduced for EU citizens aged under 25. Students are often eligible for discounts too; carry a valid ISIC card or equivalent. A number of museums and archeological sites also offer free entry the last Sunday of the month.

served in measures of a pint (*una media*) and half-pint (*piccola*). A generous shot of spirits, limoncello, or grappa – made from grape pips and stalks – costs from €2. Amaro is a bitter after-dinner liqueur. Drinking in bars (*locali*) can be pricey – around €5 for a beer and €5–9 for a cocktail – while drinking in clubs can be ruinous, although the entrance fee of €10–15 usually includes one drink.

Some places will be happy to serve you **tap water** (*acqua del rubinetto*), most certainly in the mountains, although it's not common in cities as the quality of water is low. For bottled water, ask for *acqua naturale* (still) or *acqua frizzante* (sparkling).

CULTURE AND ETIQUETTE

Italy remains strongly **family-oriented**, with an emphasis on the traditions and rituals of the Catholic Church, and it's not unusual to find people living with their parents until their early thirties. While the north is cosmopolitan, the south can be rather provincial; women travelling on their own may attract unwanted attention in smaller areas. When entering churches, ensure that your knees and shoulders are covered. In towns and villages all over the country, life stops during the middle of the day for a long lunch.

Tipping is not a big deal in Italy; in restaurants – if a service charge is not included – it's acceptable to reward good service with a couple of euros. In bars, some Italians leave a coin on the counter after finishing their coffee, but it is by no means expected. Likewise, taxi drivers will not expect a tip. **Smoking** is outlawed in all enclosed public places.

SPORTS AND OUTDOOR ACTIVITIES

Spectator sports are popular, particularly **football** (*calcio*), though cycling, motorcycling, motor racing and women's volleyball are also high-profile sports. A football match in Italy can be exhilarating to watch. The season runs from the end of August to May; see ⊕legaseriea.it for details; tickets cost from €25.

Campania, Sardinia and Sicily, with their clear waters, provide excellent conditions for **scuba diving** and **snorkelling**, while Rome, Milan, Turin, Venice and, at the other end of the country, Mount Etna in Sicily, are within easy reach of **ski resorts**. The same mountainous terrain is perfectly suited to summertime **hiking**. For mountain biking try the rolling hills of Umbria and Tuscany, although serious bikers might consider the infamous Passo dello Stelvio near the Swiss border.

COMMUNICATIONS

Post office opening hours are usually Monday to Friday 8.30am to 6.30pm, with branches in larger towns also open Saturdays 8.30am–12.30pm. Stamps (*francobolli*) can also be bought at *tabacchi* – ask for *posta prioritaria* if you want letters to arrive home before you do. Public **phones** are card-operated; get a phonecard (*scheda telefonica*) from *tabacchi* and newsstands for €5/10. For land-line calls – local and long-distance – dial all digits, including the area code. Directory enquiries (☎1240) are pricey. Virtually all hostels and a number of cafés offer free **wi-fi**; there are internet cafés in most towns too; hourly rates are around €2–4.

EMERGENCIES

Most of the **crime** you're likely to come across is small-time. You can minimize the risk of this by being discreet, not flashing anything of value and keeping a

EMERGENCY NUMBERS

Police ☎112 for all emergencies.

ITALIAN

	ITALIAN	PRONUNCIATION
Yes/No	*Si/No*	See/Noh
Please	*Per favore*	Pear fah-vure-ay
You're welcome	*Prego*	Pray-goh
Thank you	*Grazie*	Grraat-see-ay
Hello/Good day/Hi	*Ciao/buongiorno/salve*	Chow/boo-on jawr-noh/salvay
Goodbye	*Ciao/arrivederci*	Chow/arrivi-derchee
Excuse me	*Mi scusi*	Mee scoo-see
Good	*Buono*	Bwo-noh
Bad	*Cattivo*	Cat-ee-voh
Near	*Vicino*	Vih-chee-noh
Far	*Lontano*	Lont-ah-noh
Today	*Oggi*	Ojj-ee
Yesterday	*Ieri*	Ee-air-ee
Tomorrow	*Domani*	Doh-mahn-ee
How much is...?	*Quanto è...?*	Cwan-toe ay...?
What time is it?	*Che ore sono?*	Keh orr-ay son-noh?
I don't understand	*Non capisco*	Non kapee-skoe
Do you speak English?	*Parla Inglese?*	Parr-la inglay-zay?
Ticket	*Biglietto*	Bil-yettoh
Where is...?	*Dov'è...?*	Doh-vay...?
Entrance	*L'ingresso*	Lingress-oh
Exit	*L'uscita*	Loo-shee-tah
Platform	*Il binario*	Il bin-ah-ree-oh
Toilet	*Il bagno*	Il ban-yo
Ferry	*Il traghetto*	Il trag-ettow
Bus	*L'autobus*	Lout-o-boos
Plane	*L'aereo*	Lah-air-ay-oh
Train	*Il treno*	Il tray-no
I would like a...	*Vorrei...*	Vorr-ay...
Bed	*Letto*	Lett-oh
Single/double room	*Camera singola/doppia*	Cam-errah singolah/doppiah
Cheap	*Economico*	Eck-oh-no-micoh
Expensive	*Caro*	Car-oh
Open	*Aperto*	Apairt-oh
Closed	*Chiuso*	Queue-zoh
Breakfast	*Colazione*	Coll-ats-ioh-nay
Hotel	*L'hotel*	Lott-ell
Hostel	*L'ostello*	Lost-ellow
One	*Uno*	Oo-noh
Two	*Due*	Doo-ay
Three	*Tre*	Tray
Four	*Quattro*	Cwattr-oh
Five	*Cinque*	Chink-way
Six	*Sei*	Say
Seven	*Sette*	Set-tay
Eight	*Otto*	Ot-toe
Nine	*Nove*	Noh-vay
Ten	*Dieci*	Dee-ay-chee

firm hand on your camera and bag, particularly on public transport. The police come in many forms: the *Vigili Urbani* deal with traffic offences and the *Carabinieri* with public order and drug control; report thefts to the *Polizia di Stato*. Italy treats soft and hard drugs offences with equal severity.

17

Pharmacies (*farmacie*) can give advice and dispense prescriptions; there's one open all night in towns and cities (find the address of the nearest on any pharmacy door). For serious ailments, go to the *Pronto Soccorso* (casualty) section of the nearest hospital (*ospedale*).

INFORMATION

Most towns, major train stations and airports have a **tourist office** (*ufficio turistico*), which will give out maps for free. Kompass has excellent hiking maps mainly covering the north of the country, as does Club Alpino Italiano, available throughout Italy.

MONEY AND BANKS

Italy's currency is the euro (€). You'll get the best rate of exchange at a **bank**; hours are Monday to Friday 8.30am to 1.30pm and 2.30 to 4pm. ATMs (*bancomat*) are widespread. The Italian way of life is cash-based, and many smaller restaurants and B&Bs will not accept credit cards.

OPENING HOURS AND HOLIDAYS

Most shops and businesses open Monday to Saturday 8/9am to 1pm and 4–7/8pm, though in the north, offices work a 9am to 5pm day. Just about everything, with the exception of bars and restaurants, closes on Sunday. Most churches keep shop hours. Museums traditionally open Tuesday to Sunday 9am to 7pm. Most archeological sites open daily from 9am until an hour before sunset.

Many of Italy's inland towns close down almost entirely for the month of August,

when Italians head for the coast. Everything closes for national holidays: January 1, January 6, Easter Monday, April 25, May 1, June 2, August 15, November 1, December 8, December 25 and 26.

Rome

Of all Italy's historic cities, **ROME** (Roma) exerts the most fascination. Its sheer weight of history is endlessly compelling. Classical features – the Colosseum, the Roman Forum, the spectacular Palatine Hill – stand alongside ancient basilicas containing relics from the early Christian period, while Baroque fountains and churches define the city centre. But it's not all history and brickwork: Rome has a vibrant, chaotic life of its own, its crowded streets thronged with traffic, locals, tourists and students.

WHAT TO SEE AND DO

Rome's city centre is divided into distinct areas. The **Centro Storico** (historic centre) occupies a hook of land on the east bank of the River Tiber, bordered to the east by Via del Corso and to the north and south by water. The old Campus Martius of Roman times, it became the heart of the Renaissance city and is now an unruly knot of narrow streets holding some of the best of Rome's classical and Baroque heritage, as well as much of its nightlife.

From here, Rome's central core spreads east, across Via del Corso to the major shopping streets around the **Spanish Steps** and the main artery of Via Nazionale, and south to the **Roman Forum**, **Colosseum** and **Palatine Hill**. The west bank of the river is home to the **Vatican** and **St Peter's** and, to the south of these, charming **Trastevere**. East of Termini Station is student-hub San Lorenzo, home to Rome's main university and some of its best nightlife.

The Roman Forum

The best place to start a tour of the city is the **Roman Forum** (daily 8.30am–1hr before sunset; 2-day joint ticket with

Colosseum and Palatine Hill €12, €7.50
for 18–25-year-olds), the bustling centre
of the ancient city. It's worth getting the
audioguide (€5, must be returned by
4.30pm) as there is next to no textual
information displayed on site.

Running through the heart of the
Forum, the **Via Sacra** was the best-known
street of ancient Rome, lined with its
most important buildings, such as the
Curia – begun in 45 BC, this was the
home of the Senate during the Republican
period. Next to the Curia is the **Arch of
Septimius Severus**, erected in the early
third century AD to commemorate the
Emperor's tenth anniversary in power. In
the centre of the Forum is the **House of
the Vestal Virgins**, where the six women
charged with keeping the sacred flame of
Vesta alight lived. On the far side of the
site, the towering **Basilica of Maxentius** is
probably the Forum's most impressive
relic. From the basilica, the Via Sacra
climbs to the **Arch of Titus** on a low arm
of the Palatine Hill, its reliefs showing the
spoils of Jerusalem being carried off by
eager Romans.

Palatine Hill

From the Forum, turn right at the Arch
of Titus to reach the **Palatine Hill** (same
hours and ticket as Roman Forum), now a
beautiful archeological garden. In the days
of the Republic, the Palatine was the most
desirable address in Rome. From the
Farnese Gardens, on the right, a terrace
looks back over the Forum, while the
terrace at the opposite end looks down
on the alleged centre of Rome's ancient
beginning – an Iron Age hut, known as
the **House of Romulus**, the best-preserved
part of a ninth-century BC village.

Close by, steps lead down to the
Cryptoporticus, a passage built by Nero
to link the Palatine with his palace on
the far side of the Colosseum. A left turn
leads to the **House of Augustus** (entrance
daily at 12.45pm only), which holds
beautiful frescoes dating back to 30 BC
and is considered to be among the most
magnificent examples of Roman wall
paintings anywhere; even the builders'
ancient graffiti has been meticulously
preserved.

The Capitoline Hill

Formerly the spiritual and political centre
of the Roman Empire, the Capitoline
Hill lies behind the Neoclassical
Vittoriano monument on Piazza Venezia.
Atop the Capitoline is **Piazza del
Campidoglio**, designed by Michelangelo
in the 1530s and flanked by the two
wings of one of the city's most important
museums of ancient art – and the oldest
public gallery in the world, dating back
to 1471 – the **Capitoline Museums** (daily
9.30am–7.30pm; €14; ⓦmuseicapitolini
.org). The Palazzo Nuovo, the museum's
left-hand wing, contains some of the best
of the city's Roman and Greek sculpture.
Highlights of the Palazzo dei
Conservatori opposite include various
parts of the colossal statue of the
Emperor Constantine which once stood
in the Forum, and sixteenth-century
frescoes.

Colosseum

Immediately outside the Forum, the
fourth-century **Arch of Constantine** marks
the end of the Via Sacra. Across from
here is Rome's most awe-inspiring ancient
monument, the **Colosseum** (same hours
and ticket as Roman Forum; bypass
queues by buying tickets at the Palatine
Hill). Begun by the Emperor Vespasian in
72 AD, construction was completed by
his son Titus about eight years later – an
event celebrated with one hundred days
of games. The arena was about 500m in
circumference and could seat fifty
thousand people; the Romans flocked
here for gladiatorial contests and cruel
spectacles. Mock sea battles were also
staged here – the arena could be flooded
in minutes. After the games were
outlawed in the fifth century, the
Colosseum was pillaged for building
material, but the magnificent shell
remains.

Campo de' Fiori and the Ghetto

From Piazza Venezia, Via del Plebiscito
forges west; take a left turn into the maze
of cobbled streets that wind down to
pretty **Campo de' Fiori**, one-time heart
of the medieval city, now home to a
colourful produce market (Mon–Sat

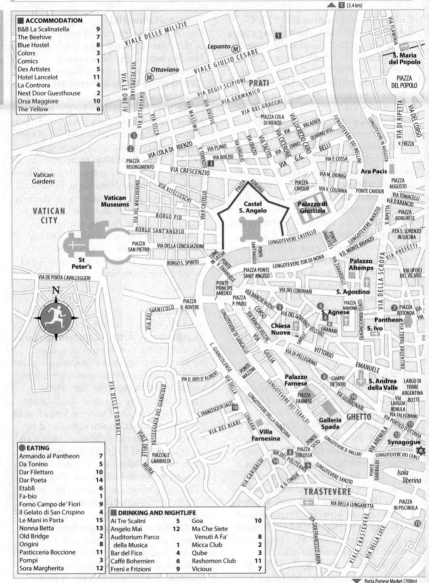

▲ **1** (3.4 km)

■ **ACCOMMODATION**

B&B La Scalinatella	9
The Beehive	7
Blue Hostel	8
Colors	3
Comics	1
Des Artistes	5
Hotel Lancelot	11
La Controra	4
Next Door Guesthouse	2
Orsa Maggiore	10
The Yellow	6

● **EATING**

Armando al Pantheon	7
Da Tonino	5
Dar Filettaro	10
Dar Poeta	14
Etablì	6
Fa-bío	1
Forno Campo de' Fiori	9
Il Gelato di San Crispino	4
Le Mani in Pasta	15
Nonna Betta	13
Old Bridge	2
Origini	8
Pasticceria Boccione	11
Pompi	3
Sora Margherita	12

■ **DRINKING AND NIGHTLIFE**

Ai Tre Scalini	5	Goa	10
Angelo Mai	12	Ma Che Siete	
Auditorium Parco		Venuti A Fa'	8
della Musica	1	Micca Club	2
Bar del Fico	4	Qube	3
Caffè Bohemien	6	Rashomon Club	11
Freni e Frizioni	9	Vicious	7

▼ Porta Portese Market (700m)

6.30am–2pm). Surrounded by bars, it's a great spot to watch the *passeggiata* (early-evening stroll).

A short walk from here, east of Via Arenula, a warren of narrow streets makes up the **Ghetto**. Having moved here from Trastevere in the thirteenth century, the city's Jews were walled off from the rest of the city in 1556, and subsequently suffered centuries of ill-treatment, culminating in the deportations of World War II, when a quarter of the Ghetto's population died in concentration camps. Today, the area has an intimate, backstreet feel, and is an atmospheric place for a wander and a delicious deep-fried artichoke.

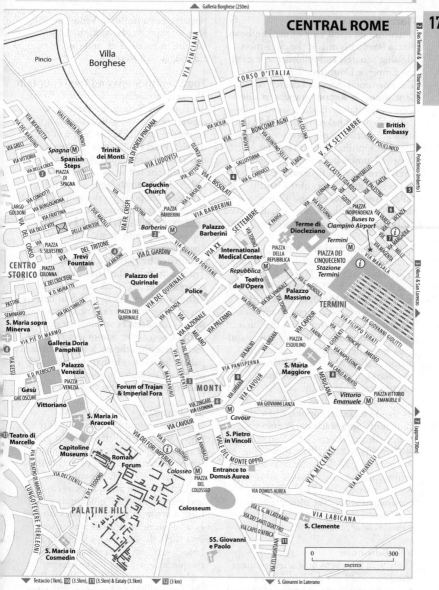

Pantheon

One of the Centro Storico's main draws is the **Pantheon** (Mon–Sat 9am–7.30pm, Sun 9am–6pm; free), the most complete ancient Roman structure in the city, finished around 125 AD. Inside, the diameter of the dome and height of the building are precisely equal, and the hole in the dome's centre is a full 9m across; there are no visible arches or vaults to hold the whole thing up – instead, they're sunk into the concrete of the walls of the building. The coffered ceiling was covered in solid bronze until the seventeenth century, and the niches were filled with statues of the gods.

17 ## Piazza Navona

A ten-minute stroll west of the Pantheon, **Piazza Navona** is one of the city's most pleasing squares, and follows the lines of the Emperor Domitian's chariot arena. The Borromini-designed church of **Sant'Agnese in Agone** on the west side supposedly stands on the spot where St Agnes, exposed naked to the public in the stadium, miraculously grew hair to cover herself. Opposite, the **Fontana dei Quattro Fiumi** is by Borromini's arch-rival, Bernini; each figure represents one of the four great rivers of the world – the Nile, Danube, Ganges and Plate – though only the horse was actually carved by Bernini.

The Ara Pacis and around

Walking north along the Lungotevere (riverside drive) from Piazza Navona, you'll arrive at the striking **Ara Pacis** (daily 9.30am–7pm; €10.50; ⓦarapacis.it). Built in 13 BC to celebrate Augustus's victory over Spain and Gaul, the "altar of peace" is housed in a slick travertine-and-glass container designed by American architect Richard Meier in 2006. Inside, the altar supports a frieze showing Augustus and his family.

Via di Ripetta arrows north from here to grand **Piazza del Popolo**, where the church of **Santa Maria del Popolo** (Mon–Thurs 7.15am–12.30pm & 4–7pm, Fri & Sat 7.30am–7pm, Sun 9–10am & 4.30–6.30pm; free) holds some of the best Renaissance art of any Roman church. Two pictures by Caravaggio attract the most attention – the *Conversion of St Paul* and the *Crucifixion of St Peter*.

Villa Borghese

Leafy **Villa Borghese**, just a few minutes' stroll east of Piazza del Popolo, is a tranquil haven from the noise of the city. It harbours several fine museums, not least the **Galleria Borghese** (Tues–Sun 8.30am–7.30pm; timed entry every 2hr; €11; ☏06 32 810; call to book at least a day in advance), a dazzling collection of mainly Italian art and sculpture. Highlights include Canova's sculpted marble *Pauline*, the sister of Napoleon

portrayed as a reclining Venus, in Room 1; spectacular sculptures by Bernini in rooms 2–4; and five Caravaggios in Room 8.

The Spanish Steps and Trevi Fountain

The area immediately southeast of Piazza del Popolo is historically the artistic quarter of the city, with a distinctly cosmopolitan air. At the centre of the district, **Piazza di Spagna** features the distinctive boat-shaped Barcaccia fountain, the last work of Bernini's father. The **Spanish Steps** – a venue for international posing – sweep up from the piazza to the sixteenth-century church of **Trinità dei Monti**. From the top of the Spanish Steps, narrow Via Sistina winds down to Piazza Barberini, dominated by Bernini's Fontana del Tritone, its muscular Triton held up by four dolphins. West down Via del Tritone, hidden among a web of narrow streets, is one of Rome's more surprising sights – the **Trevi Fountain**, a deafening gush of water over Baroque statues and rocks built onto the back of a Renaissance palace; legend has it that throwing a coin over your shoulder into the pool guarantees your return to Rome.

San Lorenzo

Packed in around Via Tiburtina is the edgy **San Lorenzo** district, a tight grid of streets named after ancient Italian tribes. The area badly suffered the Allied bombing of 1943, and it still has a slightly unkempt air to it. Street art and posters advertising upcoming gigs form a constantly evolving backdrop on every centimetre of spare wall space, interspersed with vintage shops and hole-in-the-wall pizza takeaways. It's the place to go for cheap eats and a night out; young people gather at Piazza dell'Immacolata and surrounding streets for drinks in the early evening, before heading to one of the many busy bars and live music venues.

Trastevere

Over on the Tiber's west bank, picturesque **Trastevere**, once the city's shabby bohemian quarter, is now somewhat gentrified, and home to vibrant nightlife and some of the city's best restaurants.

The area's hub is **Piazza di Santa Maria in Trastevere**, and the magnificent twelfth-century church of the same name on the western side of the square. Held to be the first official church in Rome, built on a site where a fountain of oil is said to have sprung on the day of Christ's birth, it is resplendent with thirteenth-century mosaics. The square is a good starting point for a mooch through the district's alleys, lined with enticing cafés, bars, markets, boutiques and *gelaterias*.

St Peter's Basilica

The **Vatican City**, a tiny territory north of Trastevere, is partly hemmed in by high walls, but opens its doors to the rest of the city in the form of Bernini's **Piazza San Pietro**. **St Peter's Basilica** (daily 7am–7pm; Oct–March till 6.30pm; free) was built to a plan initially conceived at the end of the fifteenth century by Bramante and finished off over a century later by Carlo Maderno, bridging the Renaissance and Baroque eras. The first thing you see, on the right, is Michelangelo's moving *Pietà*, completed when he was just 24. On the right-hand side of the nave, the bronze statue of St Peter was cast in the thirteenth century by Arnolfo di Cambio. Bronze was also used in Bernini's imposing 28m-high *baldacchino*, the centrepiece of the sculptor's embellishment of the interior. To the right of the main doors, you can ascend by stairs or lift to the **roof**, from where there's a steep walk up 320 steps to the **dome** (daily 8am–6pm; Oct–March till 5pm; €6, €8 with lift), well worth the effort for its glorious views over the city.

The Vatican Museums

A ten-minute walk from the northern side of Piazza San Pietro takes you to the **Vatican Museums** (Mon–Sat 9am–6pm; last admission 4pm; €16, students under 26 €8; last Sun of the month 9am–2pm, last admission 12.30pm, free; ⓦmv .vatican.va) – quite simply the largest, richest museum complex in the world, stuffed with treasures from every period of

the city's history. The queues to get in can be daunting so it's best to book ahead online. Highlights include the **Stanze di Raffaello**, a set of rooms decorated for Pope Julius II by Raphael among others, including the *School of Athens* fresco, which depicts his artistic contemporaries as classical figures: Leonardo is Plato and Michelangelo Heraclitus. Further on is the **Galleria Chiaramonte**, a superb collection of Roman statues, and the **Galleria delle Carte Geografiche**, a stunning corridor adorned with incredibly precise, richly pigmented maps of Italy.

The **Sistine Chapel**, of course, is the main draw. Built for Pope Sixtus IV in 1481, it serves as the pope's private chapel and hosts the conclaves of cardinals for the election of each new pope. The paintings down each side wall depict scenes from the lives of Moses and Christ by Perugino, Botticelli and Ghirlandaio, among others. But it's Michelangelo's ceiling frescoes of the *Creation* that everyone comes to see, executed almost single-handedly over a period of about four years for Pope Julius II. The *Last Judgement*, on the west wall of the chapel, was painted by Michelangelo over twenty years later. The nudity caused controversy from the start, and the pope's zealous successor, Pius IV, insisted that loincloths be added, although these were later removed.

ARRIVAL AND DEPARTURE

By plane Rome has two airports. Leonardo da Vinci, better known as Fiumicino (ⓦadr.it/fiumicino), and Ciampino (ⓦadr.it/ciampino), which is exclusively for low-cost flights. Two train services link Fiumicino to Rome: the Leonardo Express to Termini (every 30min until 11.23pm; 32min; €14), and the FL1 to Trastevere (27min), Ostiense (32min) and Tiburtina (47min) stations (every 15–30min until 11.27pm; €8). Terravision coach services (every 20min; 55min; €4; ⓦterravision.eu) and SIT buses (every 30–45min; 1hr; €6; ⓦsitbusshuttle.com) travel to Termini station and Via Crescenzio, east of Vatican City. From Ciampino, Terravision (every 20min; €4) and SIT buses (every 30–45min; €4) make the 40min trip to Termini station.

By train The main train station is Termini, meeting point of the metro lines and city bus routes. Some long-distance services use Stazione Tiburtina. The two stations are connected by metro and bus.

17

Destinations Bologna (every 15min; 2–4hr); Florence (every 15min; 1hr 20min–3hr 20min); Milan (every 15min; 3hr–6hr 30min); Naples (every 30min; 1hr 10min–2hr 40min); Paris (1 daily; 14hr 50min); Turin (hourly; 4–6hr); Vienna (1 daily; 13hr 20min); Zürich (via Milan; 5 daily; 6hr 50min–7hr 30min).

By bus Domestic bus services use the bus terminal outside Stazione Tiburtina (ⓜ Tiburtina).

Destinations Agrigento (1 daily; 12hr); Amalfi (1 daily; 4hr); Bologna (2 weekly; 4hr 30min); Florence (1–2 daily; 3hr 20min); Lecce (4 daily; 8hr 30min); Naples (1 daily; 2hr); Palermo (1 daily; 11hr); Perugia (5 daily; 2hr 20min); Sorrento (2 daily; 4hr).

INFORMATION AND TOURS

Tourist office The department of tourism Roma Capitale (ⓦ turismoroma.it) has a tourist information booth at Termini Station at platform 24 (daily 8am–6.45pm), and green tourist information kiosks (PIT) near every major sight (daily 9.30am–7pm), as well as at both of the city's airports at arrivals (Fiumicino daily 9am–5.45pm; Ciampino daily 8.30am–6pm). The tourist information line ⓣ 060608 is open daily 9am–9pm.

Discount passes The Roma Pass (€36 for three days; ⓦ romapass.it) gives you free access to all public transport within the city, as well as free entry to the first two sites you visit, plus many further discounts. Buy the pass from tourist information kiosks or from participating sites.

Tours The Yellow Guides (ⓦ theyellowguides.com) run fun walks around the historical centre, while Eating Italy Food Tours (ⓦ eatingitalyfoodtours.com) offer entertaining food and cultural tours.

GETTING AROUND

Tickets Public transport is cheap and reasonably reliable. A day-pass (BIG; €7), one-way ticket (BIT; valid for 100min on all public transport, including one trip on the metro; €1.50), three-day pass (€18) or one-week ticket (€24) for the metro and bus network can be bought from most newspaper stalls and *tabacchi*, and from ticket machines in metro stations. Stamp tickets to validate them at the entrance gates to metros and on board buses and trams.

By bus The bus network is extensive; useful routes include the #40 from Termini station, which passes through the centre en route to the Vatican, and #116 from the ⓜ Barberini, which serves both Villa Borghese and the Centro Storico. A network of night buses (*bus notturni*) serves most parts of the city, running until about 5.30am. #N1 follows metro line A; #N2 calls at all stops along metro line B; and #N8 runs from Trastevere to Termini station.

By metro The city's two metro lines, A and B, meet beneath Termini station, while the B1 line connects Bologna and Jonio stations. The metro is the quickest

way to get around, with trains every 3–5min (5.30am–11.30pm, Fri & Sat till 1.30am).

By taxi Meters start at €3 by day (€4.50 on Sun) and €6.50 after 10pm. Depending on luggage and the time of travel, it should cost around €10 to get from Termini to the centre. You can hail one in the street, or at the ranks at Termini or Argentina (opposite Feltrinelli), or call ⓣ 06 06069 free of charge for public taxis of the Municipality of Rome.

ACCOMMODATION

In high season (April–July, Sept & major religious holidays) Rome is very crowded, so book accommodation as far in advance as possible. Many of the city's hostels and cheaper hotels are located close to Termini station, but it's pretty insalubrious; pay a bit more to stay in the centre if you can.

HOSTELS

★**The Beehive** Via Marghera 8, Termini ⓣ 06 4470 4553, ⓦ the-beehive.com. This wonderful hostel has spacious rooms with artisan mirrors and designer furnishings, a vegetarian organic café, a massage room and a quiet leafy patio perfect to unwind with a book. Dorms €35, doubles with shared bathroom €80, doubles with bathroom €100

Comics Viale Giulio Cesare 38, Prati ⓣ 06 9437 9873, ⓦ comicsguesthouse.it. Unique quirky hostel with the world's favourite comics characters decorating every nook and cranny; all rooms are immaculate and each has a/c, TV, DVD player and private bath. There's also a chill-out area with beanbags, DVDs and a Playstation. Dorms €30, doubles €100

La Controra Via Umbria 7, Termini/Centro Storico ⓣ 06 9893 7366, ⓦ lacontrora.com. A laidback, quiet hostel where guests socialize at the breakfast table; all dorms have a/c, parquet floors and private bath. Dorms €35, doubles €110

Next Door Guesthouse Via Nomentana 316 ⓣ 06 4565 4938, ⓦ nextdoorguesthouse.com. This friendly hostel is decorated with lovingly restored, quirky twentieth-century furniture and accessories. Dorms are brightened up with splashes of colour, and there's a kitchen and terrace for guests' use. A 20min bus ride from the centre. Dorms €30, doubles €70

Orsa Maggiore Via San Francesco di Sales 1a, Trastevere ⓣ 06 6893 753, ⓦ foresteriaorsa.altervista.org. In an exceptional location in Trastevere, this municipal-run women's hostel is housed in a former convent. Rooms are ample, bright and functional and the atmosphere calm and laidback. Dorms €26, doubles with shared bath €72, doubles with bath €110

★**The Yellow** Via Palestro 44, Termini ⓣ 06 4938 2682, ⓦ the-yellow.com. The comfortable dorms here all have individual hanging bars for clothes and personal reading lamps, sockets and lockers. The bustling friendly bar at this

★TREAT YOURSELF

Just a stone's throw away from the Colosseum, the family-run **Hotel Lancelot** (Via Capo d'Africa 47 ☎ 06 7045 0615, ⊕ lancelothotel.com), in a leafy residential neighbourhood, has charmingly quaint rooms, some with private balconies; those on the upper floors boast incredible views over the nearby Colosseum. Staff are welcoming and encourage guests to mingle at the convivial breakfast tables. Excellent low- and mid-season rates (Nov–Feb, July & Aug) make the hotel more affordable. Doubles **€196**

party hostel attracts plenty of locals too and the fun continues until the wee hours in the soundproof basement. Dorms **€24**, doubles **€90**

B&B AND HOTELS

B&B La Scalinatella Via Urbana 48 ☎ 06 488 0547, ⊕ lascalinatellaroma.com. Located in a seventeenth-century palace a short walk to major sights, this lovely B&B has three tastefully furnished rooms with whitewashed wood beams, antique furniture and spacious bathrooms. Doubles **€150**

★**Blue Hostel** Via Carlo Alberto 13, Termini ☎ 340 925 8503, ⊕ bluehostel.it. This intimate little hotel with only six doubles has bright and airy rooms with original timber ceilings; windows give on to a peaceful interior courtyard, which echoes with birdsong and the bells of nearby Santa Maria Maggiore. There's also a private apartment, with kitchen, sleeping five. All rooms have Nespresso machines. Doubles **€150**, apartment **€170**

Colors Via Boezio 31, Prati ☎ 06 687 4030, ⊕ colorshotel .com. Located right by the Vatican, this colourful hotel has spick-and-span rooms with modern amenities. From mid-June to September there are a few dorms available. Dorms **€32**, doubles **€99**

Des Artistes Via Villafranca 20, Termini ☎ 06 4454 365, ⊕ hoteldesartistes.com. The a/c rooms here are spacious and pleasantly decorated with classical prints and wooden furniture; some rooms operate as two- to six-bed dorms. There's a large rooftop terrace, perfect to meet other travellers and kick back in the sun in the warmer months. Dorms **€26**, doubles **€95**

EATING

All of Rome's neighbourhoods have at least one food market (generally Mon–Sat 7am–2pm); Campo de' Fiori is the most famous, while Piazza Vittorio Emanuele near Termini sells African fruits and Asian food too. The large food temple Eataly (⊕ www.roma.eataly.it; Ⓜ Piramide) is home to plenty of superb restaurants, bars and cafés, perfect to sample Italian dishes.

CAFÉS, SNACKS AND ICE CREAM

Fa-bìo Via Germanico 43, Prati ⊕ fa-bio.com. Organic fresh juices made with fruit and/or vegetables from €3 and zingy salads with ingredients like tofu, lentils and lovely dressings for €5 are the perfect antidote to too much pizza and sun. Good vegetarian choices. Mon–Fri 11am–5.30pm, Sat 11am–4pm.

Forno Campo de' Fiori Piazza Campo de' Fiori 22, Centro Storico ⊕ fornocampodefiori.com. This little bakery is the perfect spot to grab some "pizza bianca" (white pizza, focaccia style) or "pizza rossa" (red pizza, with tomatoes) on the go for about €2 a slice. Mon–Sat 7.30am–2.30pm & 4.45–8pm; July & Aug closed Sat.

★**Il Gelato di San Crispino** Via della Panetteria 42, Centro Storico ⊕ ilgelatodisancrispino.it. Close to the Trevi fountain, this artisan *gelateria* rustles up exceptional ice-cream flavours, all made using natural in-season fruits. The signature *crespino al miele* (creamy vanilla with honey) is a must. Mon–Thurs & Sun 11am–12.30am, Fri & Sat 11am–1.30am.

Old Bridge Viale Bastioni di Michelangelo 5, Prati ⊕ gelateriaoldbridge.com. The perfect pit stop for a refreshing ice cream (around €2.50) after a long day of sightseeing at the nearby Vatican Museums. Daily 10am–2am.

Origini Via del Gesù, corner Piè di Marmo, Centro Storico. Friendly *gelateria* offering exquisite home-made ice cream (€3), *granite* and yogurt with a choice of toppings (both €4). Staff will happily let you sample the flavours on offer. Daily 10am–11.30pm.

Pasticceria Boccione Via del Portico d'Ottavia 1, Ghetto. Historic Jewish bakery with marvellous ricotta and dried fruit-filled cakes. Mon–Thurs & Sun 7am–7pm, Fri 7am–3pm.

Pompi Via della Croce 82, Centro Storico ⊕ barpompi.it. Savour Rome's best tiramisù (€4) at this long-standing favourite café. The five different flavours include piña colada and banana and chocolate, and come in a little box perfect to take away and enjoy on nearby Piazza di Spagna. Daily 10am–10.30pm.

RESTAURANTS AND PIZZERIAS

The Centro Storico, Trastevere, Testaccio and Monti are full of small, family-run restaurants.

Armando al Pantheon Salita de' Crescenzi 30, Centro Storico ☎ 06 6880 3034, ⊕ armandoalpantheon.it. Authentic and honestly priced food at this long-standing staple with old-fashioned interior, close to the Pantheon. *Primi* €10, *secondi* €15. Reservations required. Mon–Fri 12.30–3pm & 7–11pm, Sat 12.30–3pm.

17

WATER FOUNTAINS

All over Rome, there are small water fountains from which you can drink. The water is ice-cold, clean and free, so bring a water bottle and fill up.

Da Tonino Via del Governo Vecchio 18–19, Centro Storico. Basic but tasty dishes are served at this laidback restaurant. Pasta dishes start at €6, while *straccetti*, strips of beef with rocket, are €7. Mon–Sat noon–3pm & 7–11pm.

Dar Filettaro Largo dei Librari 88, Centro Storico. A true Rome experience: chaotic and delicious. The order of the day is fried fish (€5), along with whatever salad is in season. Mon–Sat 5.30–11pm.

Dar Poeta Vicolo del Bologna 45, Trastevere ⓦ darpoeta .com. The pizzas (€5–9) are made using a special dough recipe, with the final result being partially Roman (crunchy) and partially Neapolitan (sloppy). Daily noon–1am.

★ **Etablì** Vicolo delle Vacche 9, Centro Storico ⓦ etabli.it. This wonderful wine bar with high ceilings and a cosy fireplace for the winter months hosts live jazz and funky blues bands (Tues & Wed 8.30–11.30pm) and Thursday jam sessions (8pm–midnight). Wine, tapas (both €5) and cocktails (€8). Mon–Wed 7am–1am, Thurs–Sat 7am–2am, Sun 9am–1am.

★ **Le Mani in Pasta** Via dei Genovesi 37, Trastevere ⓦ lemaniinpasta.net. Wonderful home cooking with an emphasis on fish-based dishes and traditional Roman cuisine in the heart of Trastevere – you can peer at the flurry of activity in the kitchen from the welcoming little dining area. *Primi* €9–13. Tues–Sun 12.30–3pm & 7.30–11.30pm.

Nonna Betta Via del Portico d'Ottavia 16, Ghetto ⓦ nonnabetta.it. Authentic Jewish Roman home cooking, such as deep-fried artichokes (€5) when in season, with recipes all handed down by grandma Betta. *Primi* €9, *secondi* €10. Mon & Wed–Sun noon–6pm & 6.30–11pm.

Sora Margherita Piazza delle Cinque Scole 30, Ghetto. This intimate family-run place with a handwritten menu offers all manner of local dishes including handmade pasta (mains €11), served in a tiny dining area where customers inevitably socialize over their dishes. Daily 12.30–3pm, plus Mon, Wed, Fri & Sat 8–10.30pm.

DRINKING AND NIGHTLIFE

The two main areas to go for a drink are Trastevere and the Centro Storico, particularly around Campo de' Fiori. Bohemian Monti, near the Colosseum, and studenty San Lorenzo are full of bars frequented by locals. For clubs, the door charge can be anything from €5 to €25, and normally includes a complimentary drink.

BARS

★ **Ai Tre Scalini** Via Panisperna 251, Monti. Monti's laidback wine bar with old-school knick-knacks attracts a cool young crowd who are here for the exceptional wine (there are over 250; from €4.50 a glass), which can be enjoyed with top-notch regional dishes (€8). Daily 12.30pm–1am.

Bar del Fico Piazza del Fico 26, Centro Storico. This trendy spot attracts Rome's cool set, who gather here to mingle over an *aperitivo* (glass of wine €5, cocktails €8) on the leafy cobbled square. Daily 8am–2am.

Caffè Bohemien Via degli Zingari 36, Monti ⓦ caffebohemien.it. Intimate boho hangout with mismatched vintage furniture, dim lighting, and books lining the walls, perfect for an evening drink (wine €5, cocktails €6). There's an *aperitivo* buffet (7–9pm; €8). Mon, Wed & Thurs 5.30pm–1.30am, Fri & Sat 6pm–2am.

Freni e Frizioni Via del Politeama 4/6, Trastevere ⓦ freniefrizioni.it. This ex-garage (the name means "Brakes and Clutches"), cluttered with vintage machinery, is a popular early-evening hangout, thanks to its generous *aperitivo* buffet (7–10pm) – just buy a drink (from €6) and dig in. Daily 6.30pm–2am.

Ma Che Siete Venuti A Fa' Via di Benedetta 25, Trastevere ⓦ football-pub.com. Quench your thirst at this tiny drinking hole serving sixteen top-notch beers (€4) on tap, to be enjoyed with local and international footie matches on screen. Daily 11am–2am.

CLUBS AND LIVE MUSIC VENUES

For information in English, check the Entertainment section of *WHERE Rome* magazine ⓦ wheretraveler.com. Much of the club scene moves down to the beach at Ostia in the summer – look for posters around town.

Angelo Mai Viale delle Terme di Caracalla 55 ⓦ angelomai .org. This laidback arty venue is a centre for theatre, cinema, contemporary art and music, attracting DJs from Italy and beyond. Check the website for what's on.

Auditorium Parco della Musica Viale P. de Coubertin, Flaminio ⓦ auditorium.com. Bus #910 from Termini. See big international acts in this magnificent venue, one of the few modern constructions in the city. In the summer gigs are held in the outdoor amphitheatre, which seats 3000.

Goa Via di Libetta 13, Ostiense ⓦ goaclub.com. One of Rome's historic clubs, with ethno-industrial decor and big-name DJs spinning techno, jungle and house. Thurs–Sat 11pm–4.30am.

Micca Club Via degli Avignonesi 73, Piazza Barberini ⓦ miccaclub.com. This lively venue hosts popular burlesque and cabaret shows. Admission around €15, including a drink. Check the website to see what's on.

Qube Via di Portonaccio 212, Pigneto ⓦ qubedisco.com. Set on three floors, this large popular club hosts university nights on Mondays, gay nights on Fridays and an eclectic mix of DJs on Saturdays, spinning all sorts from '60s to electronica. Check the website for event details. Oct–May Mon, Fri, Sat 10.30pm–3am.

Rashomon Club Via degli Argonauti 16/20 Ⓦ rashomonclub.com. One of the city's most popular clubs, this place oozes an underground vibe and is always a step ahead in terms of music trends. Bar Mon–Thurs 10pm–4am; club Fri & Sat 11.30pm–5am.

Vicious Via Achille Grandi 7a, Esquilino Ⓦ viciousclub .com. Step into this underground joint with dark interiors where a hip crowd soaks in techno, electronica, rock and indie beats. Tues–Sat 10pm–4am.

ENTERTAINMENT

Cinemas Nuovo Olimpia (Via in Lucina 16, off Via del Corso) is the main English-language cinema. Check Ⓦ romereview.com for original-language cinemas and film listings.

Classical music The city's churches host a wide range of concerts, many of them free. The Auditorium Parco della Musica is home to the Accademia di Santa Cecilia, the city's prestigious classical academy.

Opera The opera scene is concentrated on the Teatro dell'Opera, Piazza B. Gigli, in winter (Ⓣ 06 481 7003, Ⓦ operaroma.it), and moves to the spectacular Terme di Caracalla in summer.

FESTIVALS

Festival delle Letterature
Ⓦ festivaldelleletterature.it. The floodlit Basilica of Maxentius provides a stunning backdrop to readings by international authors. May & June.

Lungo il Tevere Roma
Ⓦ lungoiltevereroma.it. Cultural events and food tasting along the banks of the Tevere River. June–Sept.

Festa de Noantri Piazza Santa Maria in Trastevere and around. Trastevere's traditional summer festival in honour of the Virgin, with street stalls selling snacks and trinkets, and a grand finale of fireworks. Last two weeks of July.

RomaEuropa Festival Ⓦ romaeuropa .net. A cutting-edge performing arts festival, generally with some big-name acts, in locations around town. Mid-Sept to Nov.

Rome Film Festival Ⓦ romacinemafest .it. A host of film stars descend on the city for its annual film festival, and there are English-language screenings all around town. Mid- to end Oct.

SHOPPING

With the exception of the Galleria Alberto Sordi on Via del Corso, malls and department stores are few and far between. The boutiques around Piazza di Spagna are for big-spenders only, but nearby Via del Corso is lined with shops selling cheap to mid-range clothing and books. Other mainstream outlets can be found along Via Cola di Rienzo near the Vatican, and Via Nazionale, off Piazza della Repubblica. Via del Governo Vecchio off Piazza Navona has a string of great vintage stores; the alleys off Campo de' Fiori and the streets of San Lorenzo harbour independent jewellery and clothing shops.

Markets Porta Portese flea market is the city's best known (Sun mornings; catch any bus from Termini to Piazza Torre Argentina, then change for tram #8 to Porta Portese). Via Sannio (Mon–Sat 9am–1.30pm; Ⓜ San Giovanni) is also a great place to find vintage bargains.

DIRECTORY

Embassies Australia, Via Antonio Bosio 5 Ⓣ 06 852 721; Canada, Via Salaria 243 Ⓣ 06 854 441; New Zealand, Via Clitunno 44 Ⓣ 06 853 7501; UK, Via XX Settembre 80a Ⓣ 06 4220 0001; US, Via V. Veneto 121 Ⓣ 06 46 741.

Exchange Offices at Termini station operate out of banking hours.

Hospitals Ambulance Ⓣ 118; central hospital: Policlinico Umberto I, Viale del Policlinico 155 Ⓣ 06 49 971, Ⓦ www .policlinicoumberto1.it; International Medical Center, Via Firenze 47 Ⓣ 06 488 2371, Ⓦ www.imc84.com. Call Ⓣ 060608 who can help find the nearest medical service open to foreign tourists.

Left luggage At Termini station (daily 6am–11pm; €6 for the first 5hr, then €0.90/hr).

Pharmacy Piram, Via Nazionale 228 (24hr), near Termini. The rota is posted on pharmacy doors.

Police Emergencies Ⓣ 112; main police station at Via S. Vitale 15 Ⓣ 06 46 861.

Post office Piazza San Silvestro 19 (Mon–Fri 8.30am–7pm, Sat 8.30am–12.30pm).

Northwest Italy

The northwest of Italy is many people's first experience of the country, and while it often represents its least stereotypical "Italian" aspect, there are some iconic towns here. The vibrant city of **Turin** was the first capital of Italy after the Unification in 1861, and still holds many reminders of its past. **Milan**, the upbeat capital of the heavily industrial region of **Lombardy**, continues to be taken

17

seriously for its business and fashion credentials, while the region of **Liguria** to the south is home to one of the country's most spectacular stretches of coastline. The chief town of the province is the sprawling port of **Genoa**, while southeast, towards Tuscany, the **Cinque Terre**'s rugged stretch of coastline continues to wow travellers with its cliff-top villages and clear blue waters.

TURIN

The seat of the House of Savoy, **TURIN** (Torino) is home to gracious avenues, opulent palaces, splendid galleries and genteel *belle époque* cafés. Fourteen of the city's Savoy palaces have been named UNESCO World Heritage Sites, and are well worth seeking out. Located at the foot of the mountains, in winter the city serves as the perfect base to ski in the nearby Alps.

WHAT TO SEE AND DO

The grid plan of the Baroque centre makes finding your way around easy. Grand Via Roma is the central spine, punctuated by Piazza San Carlo, a grand cloister-like space fronted by Baroque facades.

Museo Egizio

The superb **Museo Egizio** at Via Accademia delle Scienze 6 (Mon 9am–2pm, Tues–Sun 8.30am–7.30pm; €15; ⓦmuseoegizio.it) houses the world's second-largest collection of Egyptian antiquities. The collection began under Carlo Emanuele III in the mid-eighteenth century and was added to over the years. On the ground floor is an impressive space with massive granite

---

SKIING THE VIALATTEA

The snow-capped peaks surrounding Turin are home to some of the best ski slopes in the Alps. Known collectively as the **Vialattea** (ⓦvialattea.it), the eight Italian resorts hosted the 2006 Winter Olympics. Sestriere is the most sophisticated, while Sauze d'Oulx is great for its après-ski scene. All the towns are linked by ski lifts, and a daily ski pass costs €37. Getting to the slopes involves a train from Turin to Oulx (hourly; 1hr 15min), and then a bus to your chosen destination. Bardonecchia, the western-most town in Italy, has more than 100km ski runs reachable from Torino in less than one hour by train. See ⓦbardonecchiaski.it.

---

sphinxes, gods and pharaohs, while upstairs there are mummy cases, everyday objects and even food, along with two of the collection's highlights: a statue of Ramses II and the Tomb of Kha and Mirit.

Polo Reale

Beautiful Piazza Castello is home to the **Polo Reale** (royal museums complex; Tues–Sun 9am–7pm; €12; ⓦpoloreale .beniculturali.it), which includes the Palazzo Reale (Royal Palace) plus the Armeria Reale, Galleria Sabauda and Museo d'Antichità, whose collections span two thousand years of history. The palace was the residence of the kings of Sardinia until 1859 and then of Vittorio Emanuele II, King of Italy, until 1865. Its sumptuous interiors feature magnificent gilded rooms, while the Armeria Reale has a collection of over 1200 pieces of armour and weapons.

Museo del Cinema

East of Via Roma is the **Mole Antonelliana**, whose dome, topped by a pagoda-like spire, is a Turin landmark and boasts great views over the city (a lift takes you to the top). The building also contains the excellent **Museo del Cinema** (Mon, Wed–Fri & Sun 9am–8pm, Sat 9am–11pm; €10, €14 including lift, €7 for lift only; ⓦmuseocinema.it), which celebrates Turin's involvement with cinema since the early twentieth century.

BATTLE OF THE ORANGES

In the week leading up to Shrove Tuesday, locals in the town of **Ivrea**, some 55km north of Turin, stage an annual three-day battle armed only with the cheerful-looking but painful-feeling fruit. If you fancy getting juiced – and quite possibly bruised – you can visit by train from Turin (hourly; 1hr 10min). See ⓦstoricocarnevaleivrea.it.

ARRIVAL AND DEPARTURE

By plane Turin airport (⊚ aeroportoditorino.it) is 16km north of the city. It is connected by bus with Porta Susa and Porta Nuova train stations (every 20–30min; 50min; €6.50, or €7.50 on the bus) or by train to Dora-GTT Station (19min; €3, valid for 120min on Turin public transport).

By train Turin's main train station is Porta Susa on Corso Bolzano, west of the centre. Some trains also stop at Porta Nuova on Corso Vittorio Emanuele II at the southern end of Via Roma, which is more convenient for the city centre.

Destinations Genoa (every 1–2hr; 2hr); Milan (every 30min; 50min–1hr 30min); Nice (2 daily; change at Genoa; 5hr 30min); Rome (hourly; 4hr 30min); Venice (frequent; 4hr).

INFORMATION

Tourist office Piazza Castello/Via Garibaldi (daily 9am–6pm); Piazza Carlo Felice in front of Porta Nuova train station (daily 9am–6pm). There's a screen at the airport from where you can contact the tourist office in town (daily 9am–12.30pm & 2.30–6pm). Tourist information hotline daily 9am–12.30pm & 2.30–6pm; ⊕ 011 535 181; ⊚ turismotorino.org.

Discount pass Pick up a Torino Piemonte Card (€23/1 day, €35/2 days, €42/3 days), which covers entrance to museums and exhibitions, and discounts on many cultural sites and events, as well as reduced tickets on main tourist services.

ACCOMMODATION

★**Foresteria degli Artisti** Via degli Artisti 15 ⊕ 011 837 785, ⊚ foresteriadegliartisti.it. This cosy attic apartment with kitchenette has parquet floors with rugs that give the place a warm, lived-in feel. The friendly owner bakes cakes which she serves for breakfast. The family have a number of apartments around town. **€90**

Garibaldi 18 Via Garibaldi 18/56 ⊕ 011 521 2184, ⊚ garibaldi18torino.it. Tucked away on a small square just off Via Garibaldi, this B&B in an eighteenth-century building has three Turin-themed rooms: the automobile museum room features a Playstation with steering wheel; the Cinema museum room has a selection of Italian films on DVD; and the spacious Egyptian museum room sleeps up to five (€120). **€80**

★**Tomato** Via Silvio Pellico 11 ⊕ 011 020 9400, ⊚ tomato.to.it. Characterful hostel in the happening San Salvario district, with a cosy lounge area and a small courtyard. The rooms have recycled tomato-tin lampshades and wooden fruit-and-veg crate bedside tables. Free tea and coffee all day in the little bar area. Dorms **€25**, doubles **€65**

EATING

Slow Food (⊚ slowfood.com), the non-profit international organization promoting gastronomic traditions and locally sourced produce, was born in Bra, just a few kilometres from Turin. The city restaurants and food shops often support the movement, serving local dishes, wines and food.

★**Al Bicerin** Piazza della Consolata 5 ⊕ 011 436 9325, ⊚ bicerin.it. This tiny, beautiful café has been here since 1763 and age has not withered it – it's *the* place to try a *bicerin* (€5). Mon, Tues & Thurs–Sun 8.30am–7.30pm.

La Maison de Marie Via Giuseppe Garibaldi 18 ⊕ 011 521 4875. Tucked away on a small courtyard off Via Garibaldi, this welcoming place offers Piemontese and French dishes in a laidback setting; the menu changes daily according to the market produce. *Primi* at €8.50, *secondi* €12. Daily 7am–8pm.

★**Mara dei Boschi** Via Berthollet 30h ⊕ 011 076 9557, ⊚ maradeiboschi.it. The best *gelateria* in the city, serving exquisite ice cream made with fresh fruits. There are over twenty flavours, most scribbled on a blackboard – don't miss the chocolate fondant with orange. Two flavours €2.50. Mon 3–11pm, Tues–Sun 11.30am–11pm.

M**bun Corso Siccardi 8/A ⊕ 011 561 097, ⊚ mbun.it. A great alternative to *McDonald's, M**Bun* (*bun* means "good" in Torinese dialect) is a fast-food member of the Slow Food movement, which uses locally sourced meat, biodegradable utensils and organic produce. Although the speciality is the burgers (€6), you'll find plenty of gluten-free and vegetarian options. Daily noon–midnight.

Taverna dell'Oca Via dei Mille 24 ⊕ 011 837 547, ⊚ tavernadelloca.com. An excellent restaurant tucked away on a pleasant square that specializes in goose dishes (*Taverna dell'Oca* translates as "Goose Tavern"); there's a great-value lunch menu with *primi* at €5.50 and *secondi* at €7.50; otherwise *primi* €11, *secondi* €16. Tues–Fri 12.15–2.15pm, Sat & Sun 12.15–2.15pm & 7.45–10pm.

DRINKING AND NIGHTLIFE

The Beach Via Murazzi del Po 22 ⊕ 392 288 3024, ⊚ thebeachmurazzi.it. This happening club right by the river gets particularly crowded on Thursday and Friday evenings when top-class DJs spin techno and electronica. Thurs–Sun 8.30pm–3am.

Chalet Viale Virgilio 25 ⊕ 011 668 9777, ⊚ chaletdelvalentino.com. In the Parco del Valentino, this popular club has been going strong for decades; its outdoor areas are pleasant in summer. Wednesday night sees the place fill with university students, while on Friday and Saturday it tends to attract an even younger crowd. Wed, Fri & Sat 11am–4am.

★**Smile Tree** Piazza della Consolata 9C ⊕ 331 1848 136, ⊚ www.smiletree.it. Award-winning mixologists shake up inventive cocktails (€9) at this popular bar on Piazza della Consolata. There's seating on the square in the summer and a vegan *aperitivo* is served daily 7–10pm (€12). Tues & Wed 7pm–2am, Thurs–Sat 7pm–3am, Sun 7pm–2am.

17

MILAN

MILAN (Milano) is the capital of Italy's fashion and design industry, with the reputation as a fast-paced and somewhat unfriendly business city ruled by consumerism and the work ethic. But don't be put off: coupled with the swanky shops and excellent nightlife, Milan boasts a lovely canal area, friendly suburbs and unmissable historical sites – the Gothic cathedral has few peers in Italy, while Leonardo da Vinci's iconic fresco of *The Last Supper* is a must.

WHAT TO SEE AND DO

Piazza del Duomo

A good place to start a tour of Milan is **Piazza del Duomo**, the city's historic centre and home to the world's largest Gothic cathedral (daily 8am–7pm; free; ⍟duomomilano.it), begun in 1386 and not completed until almost five centuries later. One of the highlights of the building is the **cathedral roof** (daily 9am–7pm; €13 by elevator, €8 on foot), where you are surrounded by a forest of lacy Gothic carving and subjected to superb views of the city.

On the north side of the piazza, the opulent **Galleria Vittorio Emanuele II** is a cruciform glass-domed gallery designed in 1865 by Giuseppe Mengoni, who was killed when he fell from the roof a few days before the inaugural ceremony. The Galleria leads through to the world-famous eighteenth-century **La Scala** opera house.

Pinacoteca di Brera

At the far end of Via Brera is Milan's most prestigious gallery, the awe-inspiring **Pinacoteca di Brera** (Tues–Sun 8.30am–7.15pm; €10; ⍟pinacotecabrera .org), opened in 1809 by Napoleon who filled it with works looted from the churches and aristocratic collections of French-occupied Italy.

Castello Sforzesco

The **Castello Sforzesco** (castle grounds daily 7am–7.30pm, closes 6pm in winter; free; ⍟milanocastello.it) rises imperiously from the mayhem of **Foro Buonaparte**, laid out by Napoleon as part of a grand plan for the city. The castle houses a number of museums (Tues–Sun 9am–5.30pm; combined ticket €12) including the **Museo d'Arte Antica**, which houses Michelangelo's *Rondanini Pietà*, while the **Torre Falconiere** houses an art collection with paintings by Vincenzo Foppa, the leading Milanese artist before Leonardo da Vinci, as well as some Canalettos.

Santa Maria delle Grazie and the Last Supper

South of the Castello, the church of **Santa Maria delle Grazie** is Milan's main attraction. A Gothic pile, partially rebuilt by Bramante (who added the massive dome), it is famous for its fresco of *The Last Supper* by Leonardo da Vinci, which covers one wall of the refectory. Advance booking is essential (viewing Tues–Sun 8.15am–7pm; €6.50; ⍟www .cenacolovinciano.net).

ARRIVAL AND DEPARTURE

By plane Linate (⍟milanolinate-airport.com) is Milan's closest airport, 7km from the city centre and connected by the airport bus to Stazione Centrale (every 20min; 5.40am–9.30pm; 20min; €5; buy ticket on board). City buses (#73; every 10min; 5.30am–midnight; 30min; €1.50) run from Linate to Piazza San Babila. Malpensa airport (⍟milanomalpensa-airport.com) is 50km northwest of the city near Lago Maggiore and connected by the Malpensa Express train to Cadorna station (every 30min; €12; ⍟www.malpensaexpress.it) and by bus with Stazione Centrale (every 15–20min until 1.20am; 1hr; €10; ⍟malpensashuttle.com). Bergamo Orio al Serio is 50km away and connected to Stazione Centrale (Orioshuttle every 30min, 4.25am–10.20pm; 50min; from €5; ⍟orioshuttle.it).

By train Most international trains pull in at the Stazione Centrale, northeast of the centre on Piazza Duca d'Aosta (metro lines M2 or M3).

Destinations Bologna (frequent; 1–3hr); Geneva (4 daily; 4hr); Genoa (frequent; 1hr 30min); Paris (6 daily with 1 change; 7hr 40min–12hr 30min); Rome (frequent; 3hr–3hr 30min); Venice (every 30min; 2hr 30min); Verona (every 30min; 1hr 30min–2hr).

By bus Buses arrive at and depart from Lampugnano bus station (⍟Lampugnano) northwest of the city centre, seven stops from Cadorna station on the M1.

Destinations Bologna (3 daily; approx 3hr); Florence (4 daily; 4hr 35min); Naples (1 daily; 11hr); Palermo (2 daily; 20hr); Rome (4 daily; 8hr); Siena (4 daily; 4–5hr); Venice (2 daily; 5hr).

INFORMATION

Tourist office Piazza Castello 1 (Mon–Fri 9am–6pm, Sat 9am–1.30pm & 2–6pm, Sun & public hols 9am–1.30pm & 2–5pm; ☎02 7740 4343, ⓦvisitamilano.it). There is also a tourist booth at Stazione Centrale (Mon–Fri 9am–5pm, Sat & Sun 9am–12.30pm; ☎02 7740 4318).

GETTING AROUND

By bus, metro and tram An efficient network of trams, buses and the metro runs 6am–12.30am. There are interconnecting stations so you can change from the metro onto the overground and back. For detailed maps and route information head to the ATM office in Duomo metro station (ⓦatm.it).
By night bus These take over after the other options close, and run until 1am following the train routes, or until about 3am following alternative routes.
Tickets Tickets (normally valid 75min; €1.50) can be used for one journey only on the metro or as many bus and tram journeys as you can make in that time, or a 24hr ticket (€4.50), valid on metro, tram and buses, available from any metro station or *tabacchi*. A 48hr ticket costs €8.25.
Bike sharing Bikes can be picked up and deposited at various points around the city. You need a credit card to access the service. A daily subscription costs €4.50 (ⓦwww.bikemi.com).

ACCOMMODATION

When there is an "exposition" on (there are about 25 a year, lasting 2–3 days each) prices rocket.
Five Stars ☎338 182 0717, ⓦifivestars.it Tastefully furnished apartments sleeping from four to eight people in various locations around the city. All the apartments feature modern amenities and the friendly landlady will make you feel at home – guests will find complimentary food upon arrival as well as tea, coffee and toiletries. **€80**
Gogol'Ostello Via Chieti 1 ☎02 3675 5522, ⓦgogolostello.it; tram #1. This pleasant hostel and literary café to the north of Parco Sempione hosts cultural events including book presentations and theatre performances. Communal areas are warm and colourful with books scattered here and there, while the dorms are neat and tidy. Bike rental, too (€16/day). Dorms **€29**, doubles **€84**
★**LaFavia Four Rooms** Via Carlo Farini 4 ☎0347 784 2212, ⓦlafavia4rooms.com; ⓜPta Garibaldi. A charming B&B in a nineteenth-century building with warm and welcoming rooms, featuring retro armchairs and lamps, hand-woven carpets and designer wallpaper. Breakfast is served on the leafy roof terrace garden. **€100**
★**Ostello Bello** Via Medici 4 ☎02 3658 2720, ⓦwww .ostellobello.com; ⓜMissori. An award-winning hostel with mismatched coloured furniture, terraces with hammocks and a communal area dotted with curios. Welcoming dorms have reading lamps and lockers, and

there's a cosy kitchen for guests' use. Their sister-hostel *Ostello Bello Grande* is by Stazione Centrale. Dorms **€30**, doubles **€98**

EATING

★**Bello e Buono** Viale Sabotino 14 ☎02 9455 3407, ⓦbelloebuonogastronomia.it; ⓜPorta Romana. This tiny laidback place attracting students from nearby Bocconi University offers exceptional home cooking at incredible prices. Expect traditional family Mediterranean recipes – the *melanzane parmigiana* (€7.50) is to die for. The pasta and bread are home-made, too, and lunch is a bargain €6. Mon–Sat 10.30am–1am.
★**Chocolat** Via Boccaccio 9 ☎02 4810 0597, ⓦchocolatmilano.it; ⓜCadorna. A sleek, stylish café and *gelaterie* offering 26 delicious flavours, including seven chocolate options (€2.50), and some with unusual ingredients such as chilli, aniseed and vinegar. The café also offers delicious cakes that can be enjoyed at the tables on the ground floor or on the mezzanine. Mon–Fri 7.30am–1am, Sat 8am–1am & Sun 10am–1am.
Ex Mauri Via Federico Confalonieri 5 ☎02 6085 6028, ⓦexmauri.com; ⓜIsola. An atmospheric restaurant with barebrick walls, serving traditional Italian recipes with a twist. The menu includes some Venetian favourites, including *sarde in soar* (sardines marinated in caramelized onions; €10) and tasty home-made desserts. Mon–Fri noon–2pm & 8–11pm.
Luini Via S. Radegonda 16 ⓦwww.luini.it; ⓜDuomo. A city institution that's been serving *panzerotti* (deep-fried mini-*calzone*) round the corner from the Duomo for over 150 years; be prepared to queue. There are a couple of benches in nearby Piazza San Fedele if you want to eat sitting down. Mon 10am–3pm, Tues–Sat 10am–8pm.

DRINKING AND NIGHTLIFE

Nightlife centres on the streets around the Brera gallery, the club-filled Corso Como, and the Navigli and Ticinese quarters, clustered around Milan's thirteenth-century canals. Drinks go for around €5 a beer and €7 for cocktails.

> ### LA SCALA
>
> The season at **La Scala** (☎02 861 827, ⓦteatroallascala.org), one of the world's most prestigious opera houses, runs from December to July. Although seats are expensive and can sell out months in advance, there is often a chance of picking up a seat in the gods (from €25) an hour or so before a performance, by heading to the Theatre ticket office on Via Filodrammatici 2.

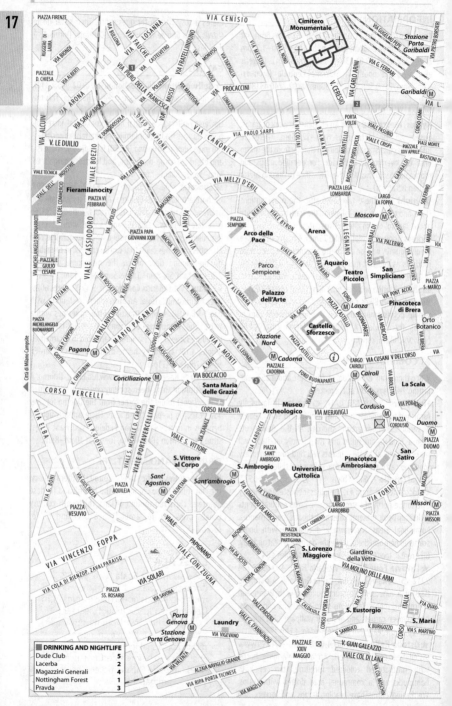

DRINKING AND NIGHTLIFE	
Dude Club	5
Lacerba	2
Magazzini Generali	4
Nottingham Forest	1
Pravda	3

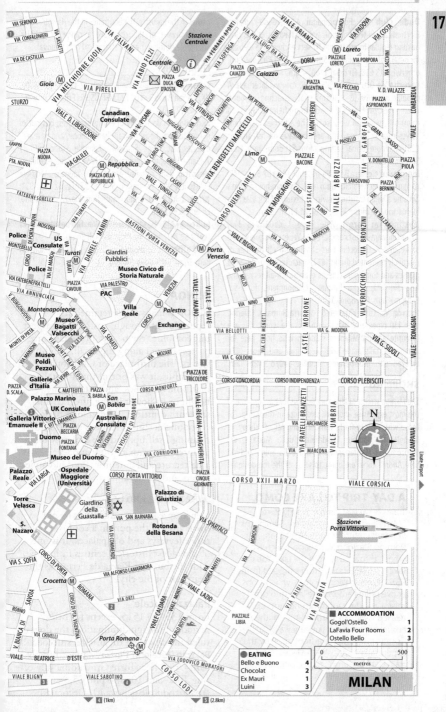

MILAN

N

17

Dude Club Via Boncompagni 44 ⊛dude-club.net. Electronica and techno music are the flavours at this club hosting regular international DJ sets – check the website for details of who's playing. Students pay €12 before 2am, otherwise it's €18. Fri & Sat 11pm–5am.

Lacerba Via Orti 4 ☎02 545 5475, ⊛www.lacerba.it. A popular *aperitivo* (8–9.30pm) spot attracting a young alternative crowd for its laidback atmosphere, seating is on colourful stools and worn sofas. The attached restaurant serves creative dishes with an emphasis on fish (mains €20) in a more formal setting. Mon–Sat 6pm–1am, Fri & Sat 6pm–2am.

Magazzini Generali Via Pietrasanta 14 ☎02 539 3948, ⊛magazzinigenerali.it; tram #24. Ex-warehouse that's become a Milan institution with a mixture of popular club nights and live music. Wed, Fri & Sat 11pm–5am.

Nottingham Forest Viale Piave 1 ☎02 798 311, ⊛nottingham-forest.com; ⊕Porta Venezia. Arguably one of Milan's best cocktail bars shaking up all manner of creatively presented drinks (€12), each served in different glasses and containers (there's even a cocktail served in a first aid kit) in an intimate environment. Tues–Sat 6.30pm–2am, Sun 6pm–1am.

Pravda Via Carlo Vittadini 6; ⊕Porta Romana. Offering over 150 types of vodka from across the world, this is a favourite among Milanese students who flock here for potent cocktails made with fresh fruit and juices (€7), enjoyed on the little pavement outside. Daily 6.30pm–1am.

SHOPPING

The fashion streets of Milan are famous for having some of the most expensive and exclusive shops in the world. For those with cash to flash, wander along Milan's shopping triangle, the famous Quadrilatero della Moda – Via Manzoni, Via Montenapoleone, Via della Spiga and Via Sant Andrea Corso are home to some of the top designer

names in the industry. The boutiques in the Navigli area in the southwest of the city have a range of quirkier, affordable clothing (nearest station ⊕Porto Genova).

DIRECTORY

Consulates Australia, Via Borgogna 2 ☎02 7767 4200; UK, Via San Paolo 7 ☎02 723 001; US, Via Principe Amedeo 2/10 ☎02 290 351.

Exchange Banks usually offer the best rates, but out of normal banking hours you can change money and travellers' cheques at the Stazione Centrale office (daily 7.45am–10.15pm). The airports all have exchange facilities.

Hospital 24hr casualty service at Ospedale Maggiore Policlinico, Via Francesco Sforza 35 (☎02 55 031, ⊛policlinico.mi.it), a short walk from Piazza del Duomo. Emergency ☎118.

Police ☎113. Headquarters at Via Fatebenefratelli 11 (☎02 62 261), near the Pinacoteca di Brera.

Post office Via Cordusio 4, off Piazza Cordusio (Mon–Fri 8am–7pm, Sat 8.30am–noon).

GENOA

GENOA (Genova) has retained its reputation as a tough, cosmopolitan port but combines the beauty of Renaissance palaces dotted along the small, winding streets. The birthplace of Christopher Columbus, it was one of the five Italian maritime republics, and reached the height of its power in the fifteenth and sixteenth centuries. After a long period of economic decline, Genoa is successfully cleaning itself up, and the city now offers an interesting mix of ultra-modern architecture and amenities, and old-style streets and restaurants.

WHAT TO SEE AND DO

Genoa spreads outwards from its old town around the port in a confusion of tiny alleyways and old palaces. It is one of the oldest historical centres in Europe, with the buzzing Piazza de Ferrari as the heartbeat of the city.

Palazzo Ducale

From 1384 to 1515, except for brief periods of foreign domination, the doges ruled the city from the ornate, stuccoed **Palazzo Ducale** in Piazza Matteotti (daily 9am–7pm; free; Torre Grimaldina July & Aug Tues–Sun 10am–7pm; €5; ⊛palazzoducale.genova.it). Decorated

---

A DAY-TRIP TO LAKE COMO

Trains leave for Como regularly from Milan's Cadorna station (every 30min; 1hr; last direct return train to Milan is around 9pm) to Stazione Nord Lago, which is a stone's throw away from the lake. You can take a cruise (hop-on, hop-off ticket from €8.90; ⊛navigazionelaghi.it), which stops at five points around the lake, and don't miss a wander round the enchanting, relaxed village of **Torno** in the southeast corner of the lake. If you fancy a picnic on Como's beautiful waterfront, drop by the supermarket opposite the North Como train station. Como's tourist office is at Piazza Cavour 17.

with elaborate frescoes, the rooms are a sight to behold. Walk up the Torre Grimaldina to the palace's cramped prison cells, which still contain the shackles and scrawled graffiti of prisoners past.

Cattedrale di San Lorenzo

The Gothic **Cattedrale di San Lorenzo** (daily 8am–noon & 3–7pm), complete with Baroque chancel, is home to the Renaissance chapel of St John the Baptist, whose remains once rested in the thirteenth-century sarcophagus. After a particularly bad storm, priests carried his casket through the city to placate the sea, and a commemorative procession takes place each June 24 to honour him. His reliquary is in the **treasury** (Mon–Sat 9am–noon & 3–6pm; €6, including entry to the Diocesan Museum, same hours), along with a polished quartz plate on which, legend says, Salome received his severed head.

The waterfront

After generations of neglect, Genoa's waterfront has undergone restoration and is gaining tourist appeal with a huge aquarium and lively markets and cafés near Piazza Caricamento.

Piazza Banchi and around

Behind Piazza Caricamento is a thriving commercial zone centred on **Piazza Banchi**, formerly the heart of the medieval city, off which the long **Via San Luca** leads north to the **Galleria Nazionale di Palazzo Spinola** (Tues–Sat 8.30am–7.30pm, Sun 1.30–7.30pm; €4, €6.50 joint ticket with the Palazzo Reale, €2/€3.25 18–25 years; ⓦpalazzospinola .beniculturali.it), displaying work by the Sicilian master Antonello da Messina. North of here is the wonderful **Via Garibaldi**, lined with frescoed and stuccoed Renaissance palaces; a walk down the street at night is a must. Two palaces are now museums housing Genoese paintings: the **Palazzi Bianco and Rosso** (late March to early Oct Tues–Fri 9am–7pm, Sat & Sun 10am–7.30pm; early Oct to late March Tues–Fri 9am–6.30pm, Sat & Sun 9.30am–6.30pm; joint ticket with

Palazzo Tursi €9), adorned with fantastic chandeliers, mirrors, gilding and frescoed ceilings. Palazzo Bianco provides access to the next-door **Palazzo Tursi**, the largest of Genoa's palaces.

Christopher Columbus House

The childhood home and museum (April, May, Sept & Oct Tues–Sun 11am–5pm; June–Aug Tues–Sun 11am–6pm; Nov–March Fri–Sun 11am–3pm; €5) dedicated to the man who discovered the New World is on Piazza Dante. It is small but gives a fascinating insight into Columbus's life. Highlights include a bell reputedly from his flagship the *Santa Maria*.

ARRIVAL AND DEPARTURE

By plane Genoa's airport (ⓦaereoportodigenova.com) is 6km west of the city centre and is connected by Volabus service to Stazione Principe, Piazza de Ferrari and Stazione Brignole (every 40min; 30min; €6 incl. 1hr of public transport in the city).

By train Most trains stop at Genoa's two stations, Stazione Principe on Piazza Acquaverde and Stazione Brignole on Piazza Verdi. Both stations are well connected by metro line and bus (#36, among others).

Destinations Milan (hourly; 1hr 30min); Pisa (frequent; 1hr 40min); Rome (every 1–2hr; 4hr 30min).

By bus Buses from the Riviera and inland arrive at Piazza della Vittoria, a few minutes' walk south of Brignole (for most destinations you're better off catching the train).

Destinations Nice (1 daily; 3hr).

By ferry Genoa is one of Italy's biggest passenger ports, for cruise ships and ferry routes. Check ⓦmoby.it, ⓦgnv .it, ⓦtirrenia.it for up-to-date schedules.

Destinations Barcelona (2 weekly; 19hr); Bastia (1–2 daily; 6hr 30min); Olbia (1–2 daily; 11hr); Palermo (daily; 20hr); Porto Torres (1–2 daily; 13hr).

INFORMATION

Tourist office Via Garibaldi 12r (daily 9am–6.20pm; ☏010 557 2903, ⓦvisitgenoa.it). There's also an information centre at the Stazione Marittima (daily 8.30–11.30am) and at the Porto Antico (Jan–daily: March & Oct–Dec 9am–5.50pm; April–June & Sept 9am–6.20pm; July & Aug 9am–7.50pm), as well as at the airport (daily 9am–5.20pm).

Discount passes The tourist office sells a Genoa pass, which covers use of all transport in the city, including lifts and funiculars (€4.50/24hr). The Museum Card gives access to most of the city's museums as well as bus travel (€15/1 day, €25/2 days).

17

ACCOMMODATION

The best areas to stay are the roads bordering the old town, Piazza Colombo and on Via XX Settembre, Genoa's main shopping street near Stazione Brignole.

Cairoli Via Cairoli 14/4 ☎010 246 1454, ⓦwww .hotelcairoligenova.com. A superior three-star, with a choice of doubles, triples and family rooms, all brightly furnished, modern, en suite and soundproof. The location, on the edge of the old town but handy for Principe station, is excellent, and there's also a roof terrace and two apartments for rent. €75

Genova Passo Costanzi 10 ☎010 242 2457, ⓦostellogenova.it. A simple HI hostel a 30min bus ride from the centre with great views over the port. Single-sex dorms. Take bus #40 or #640 (evening) from Stazione Brignole. From Stazione Principe take bus #35 to Via Napoli and change to bus #40 or #640. Dorms €15, doubles €38

Manena Vico alla Chiesa della Maddalena 9/1 ☎010 860 8890, ⓦmanenahostel.it. On the edge of the old town, down a lane just off Via Garibaldi, this place offers clean five-, eight- and twelve-bed dorms and free wi-fi. The friendly staff arrange free city tours and weekend pub crawls, and the (somewhat cramped) shared spaces make it a good place to meet fellow travellers. Dorms €22

Villa Doria Via al Campeggio Villa Doria 15/N, Pegli ☎010 696 9600, ⓦcampingvilladoria.it. Leafy campsite 8km from Genoa, with its own café, shop and solarium: take a train to Pegli and then bus #93. Per person €9, plus per tent €10

EATING AND DRINKING

Genoa is home to plenty of cheap trattorias, and you can readily find delicious *farinata* and focaccia at street outlets.

★ **Gran Ristoro** Via Sottoripa 29r ☎010 247 3127. The humble appearance of this hole-in-the-wall sandwich shop, tucked away along the old arcades of Via Sottoripa, belies its city-wide fame. Its sandwiches (from €4) are packed with excellent meats and fillings. If you're not sure what to choose, let them guide you towards building the sandwich of your dreams. Mon–Sat 7am–8pm.

Louisiana Jazz Club Via S. Sebastiano 36r ⓦlouisianajazzclub.com. A drum reveals the entrance to this established and excellent jazz venue. Cocktails and generous snacks are €7. Thurs only 9pm–midnight.

Sa Pesta Via Giustiniani 16r ☎010 246 8336, ⓦsapesta.it. Extremely popular with locals, this place is well known for its good local cooking. Dishes from €9. Booking essential. Mon–Sat noon–2pm, dinner Thurs–Sat 7–8.30pm.

Taggiou Via Superiore del Ferro 8 ☎010 275 9225, ⓦtaggiou.it. More of a wine bar and delicatessen than a restaurant, but very popular, drawing crowds at lunch and dinner for its good selection of Italian wine, plates of cold cuts and cheese, sandwiches (€5–7) and blackboard of hot dishes – typically pastas, *polpettone* (meatloaf) or *involtini*

(thin slices of meat rolled with filling). Good-value lunch specials (pasta plus a drink and a coffee for €7). Mon–Sat noon–3pm & 6pm–midnight.

Trattoria da Maria Vico Testadoro 14r ☎010 581 080. No-nonsense, endearingly chaotic place up a grubby side street, which serves up simple Ligurian cooking at rock-bottom prices; a two-course meal and drink will set you back just €10. Mon–Sat noon–3pm, Thurs & Fri 7–10pm.

THE RIVIERA DI LEVANTE

A superb stretch of lush green hills sheltering beautiful seaside resorts, the **RIVIERA DI LEVANTE** stretches eastwards from Genoa. The ports that once survived on navigation, fishing and coral diving are now well versed in the ways of tourism, and while the resorts are hectic during summer months, the towns are still charming enough to ensure they're worth visiting. The coastline is wild and beautiful in parts and a coastal path meanders over the clifftops to each of the resorts. All the towns can be reached by train and boat.

Santa Margherita Ligure

Pretty **SANTA MARGHERITA LIGURE** is a small, palm-tree-lined resort, with a little pebble beach and concrete jetties to swim from. Quieter than its more famous neighbours, the town has a charming and sleepy fishing village atmosphere.

INFORMATION

Tourist office On the waterfront at Piazza Vittorio Veneto (daily 9.30am–1pm & 3–7pm; ☎0185 287 485).

GETTING AROUND

By scooter and bike Scooters and bikes are a fun way of getting around: go to Via XXV Aprile 11 (☎0185 284 420, ⓦgmrent.it).

By boat Boats depart regularly in summer for Rapallo (€5.50 return) and the millionaires' playground that is the small village of Portofino (return Mon–Sat €9.50, Sun & public hols €10).

ACCOMMODATION

B&B L'Ora Blu Corso Rainusso 20 ☎329 614 5604. In an enviable location in the heart of Santa Margherita Ligure and a short stroll to the beach and train station, this welcoming B&B offers spick-and-span rooms painted in mellow hues. There's a communal kitchen and lounge area too. €100

Flory Via Luigi Bozzo 3 ☎0185 286 435, ⓦhotelflory.it. A friendly mid-priced hotel nicely located on a quiet side street, with good-sized rooms, some en suite. There's a panoramic roof terrace, small library and free bike loan for guests. **€120**

EATING

Il Faro Via Maragliano 24a ☎0185 286 867. Friendly family-run restaurant that has been going strong for over five decades with a focus on fresh fish and seafood dishes. *Primi* €8, *secondi* €10. Mon & Wed–Sun noon–2.30pm & 7–10.30pm.

Trattoria Baicin Via Algeria 5 ☎0185 286 763. A good-value family-run seafood restaurant in the centre of town, just back from the waterfront park, with outdoor seating in a tiny alley. It serves Ligurian specialities such as swordfish with tomato sauce and olives, a great *fritto misto* and home-made pasta with pesto. Starters around €8, mains €12–17. Tues–Sun noon–3pm & 7–10pm.

Rapallo

RAPALLO is a lovely Riviera town just a forty-minute train ride from Genoa. Brightly coloured beach huts line parts of the pebbled shore, backed by an intriguing tangle of narrow lanes that are well worth a wander.

INFORMATION

Tourist office Lungomare Vittorio Veneto 7 (Mon–Sat 9.30am–12.30pm & 3.30–6.30pm; ☎0185 230 346).

ACCOMMODATION

Bandoni Via Marsala 24 ☎0185 187 0900, ⓦalbergobandonirapallo.com. Housed in a fine old palazzo, this is one of the best bargains in town, with a mix of en-suite (from €80) and shared-bath rooms. It's old-fashioned and a bit tatty in places, but clean and simple, and has a great location on the waterfront. **€70**

Rapallo Via San Lazzaro 4 ☎0185 262 018, ⓦcampingrapallo.it. This well-equipped campsite is a haven of green and just 2km from the sea. Per person **€7**, plus per tent **€10**

EATING AND DRINKING

Enoteca Il Castello 10 Lungomare Castello 6 ☎0185 52426. This bar has lovely views of the castle and sea as well as great cocktails and nibbles. Mon, Tues & Fri–Sun 11.30am–1am, Wed 11.30am–3pm.

O Bansin Via Venezia 105 ☎0185 231 119, ⓦtrattoriabansin.it. An authentic trattoria in the heart of the old town with a bargain weekday lunch menu for €5, €7 or €10. Daily noon–2pm & 7–10pm; closed Mon eve.

CINQUE TERRE

The **CINQUE TERRE** (ⓦparconazionale5 terre.it) is a series of five beautiful villages – **Monterosso**, **Vernazza**, **Corniglia**, **Manarola** and **Riomaggiore** – perched on tiny cliff-bound inlets lapped by azure-blue sea and linked by a coastal pathway. It's possible to visit all the villages in one day via the pathway, although it can get busy at peak seasons. The liveliest of the villages is probably Monterosso, with its excellent large beach.

ARRIVAL AND INFORMATION

By train Slow trains run between Levanto and La Spezia (roughly every 30min), stopping at every village.

Tourist office Each village has a tourist office at its train station.

GETTING AROUND

Passes The Cinque Terre Parco Card, 1 day (€7.50) or 2 days (€14.50), sold at the tourist offices, gives access to the paths and village lifts (where available). Other cards include train and hiking combos (€12/1 day; €23/2 days).

By boat A boat stops at each of the villages every hour (Corniglia has no harbour; prices vary depending on where you start your journey; see ⓦnavigazionegolfodeipoeti.it).

ACCOMMODATION

Accommodation tends to be expensive in summer months, at about €120 for a double room, or there are rental apartments that have to be taken for a week at a time.

Ostello Cinque Terre Via Riccobaldi 21, Manarola ☎0187 920 215, ⓦwww.hostel5terre.com. A great hostel with separate male and female dorms – clean, friendly and well situated near the church of San Lorenzo at the upper end of Manarola. Very popular, so book in advance in summer. Reception daily 8am–1pm & 4–8pm. Dorms **€25**, doubles **€70**

EATING AND DRINKING

La Scogliera Via Birolli 103, Manarola ☎0187 920 747. Right on the main street down to the harbour, this serves a fine signature seafood spaghetti (€10) on its outside terrace, along with great lobster pasta and tuna carpaccio. Pizzas too (from €6.50). Mon–Thurs & Sat & Sun 11am–11pm.

Trattoria Billy Via Rollandi 122 ☎0187 920 628, ⓦtrattoriabilly.com. For great views over Manarola and good local food, this trattoria is worth the steep uphill walk and the €30–40 bill. Booking is recommended. Mon–Wed & Fri–Sun noon–2.30pm & 6–10pm.

17

Northeast Italy

Venice, the premier draw in northeast Italy, is one of Europe's most stunning – and unmissable – cities. The region around it, the **Veneto**, still bears the imprint of Venetian rule and continues to prosper. Gorgeous, vibrant **Verona** plays on its Shakespeare connections and centres on a fairly intact Roman amphitheatre, while nearby **Padua** hums with student activity and has some artistic and architectural masterpieces. South, between Lombardy and Tuscany, **Emilia-Romagna** is the heartland of northern Italy, a patchwork of ducal territories formerly ruled by a handful of families, whose castles and fortresses still stand proudly in well-preserved medieval towns. **Parma** is a wealthy provincial town worth visiting for its easy-going ambience and delicious food as well as masterful paintings by Parmigianino and Correggio. The coast is less interesting, but, just south of the Po delta, **Ravenna** boasts probably the finest set of Byzantine mosaics in the world.

VERONA

The romantic city of **VERONA**, with its Roman sites and cobbled streets of impressive medieval buildings, stands midway between Milan and Venice. It reached its zenith as an independent city-state in the thirteenth century under the Scaligeri family, who were energetic patrons of the arts; many of Verona's finest buildings date from their rule.

WHAT TO SEE AND DO

The city centre nestles in a deep bend of the River Adige, and the main sight of its southern reaches is the central hub of **Piazza Bra** and its mighty **Roman Arena** (Mon 1.30–7.30pm, Tues–Sun 8.30am–7.30pm; July & Aug closes 3.30pm on performance days; €10). Dating from the first century AD, this Roman amphitheatre originally held seating for twenty thousand, and offers a tremendous panorama from the topmost of the 44 marble tiers. It now houses the

largest outdoor opera stage in the world (see box above).

Historical centre

To the north of the Roman amphitheatre, Via Mazzini, a narrow traffic-free street lined with expensive clothes shops and pricey *gelaterias*, leads to a number of squares. The biggest and most appealing is Piazza Erbe, with a market in the middle and cafés lining either side. The adjacent Piazza dei Signori is flanked by the medieval **Palazzo degli Scaligeri**. At right angles to this is the fifteenth-century **Loggia del Consiglio**, the former assembly hall of the city council and Verona's outstanding early Renaissance building, while, close by, the twelfth-century **Torre dei Lamberti** (daily 10am–7pm; €8 including Galleria di Arte Moderna) gives dizzying views of the city; be prepared to block your ears for the hourly ringing of the tower's bells. **Juliet's house** is situated on the nearby Via Cappello 23 (Mon 1.30–7.30pm, Tues–Sun 8.30am–7.30pm; €6) – even if you don't go inside the house, you can see the famous balcony, rub the right breast of her statue (supposedly for luck) and read some of the thousands of love messages dotted around the place.

Arche Scaligere and the Duomo

In front of the Romanesque church of **Santa Maria Antica**, the **Arche Scaligere** are the elaborate Gothic funerary monuments of Verona's first family, set in a wrought-iron palisade decorated with ladder motifs, the emblem of the Scaligeri. Nearby, at Via Arche Scaligere 4, is **Romeo's House**, marked by a lopsided sign. Verona's **Duomo** (Mon–Sat 10am–5.30pm, Sun 1.30–5.30pm; Nov–Feb closes 5pm; €2.50, or Verona

Card), with its unfinished bell tower, lies just around the river's bend, a mixture of Romanesque and Gothic styles that houses an *Assumption* by Titian.

Roman theatre

The **Roman theatre** (Mon 1.30–7.30pm, Tues–Sun 8.30am–7.30pm; €4.50, including Museo Archeologico), on the north side of the river, is worth visiting for its gorgeous views. In the summer months, a Shakespeare festival (in Italian, but it's still great to soak up the atmosphere) and a jazz festival make use of this amazing venue (see below). Reached by a lift, the **Museo Archeologico** features a number of Greek, Roman and Etruscan finds. From here, head up to Castel San Pietro round the corner for the ultimate views of Verona.

Basilica di San Zeno Maggiore

The **Basilica di San Zeno Maggiore** (March–Oct Mon–Sat 8.30am–6pm, Sun noon–5pm; Nov–Feb Mon–Sat 10am–1pm & 1.30–5pm, Sun noon–5pm; €2.50) is one of the most significant Romanesque churches in northern Italy. Its rose window, representing the Wheel of Fortune, dates from the twelfth century, as do the magnificent portal and medieval frescoes.

ARRIVAL AND DEPARTURE

By train From the train station it's a 20min walk to Piazza Bra.

Destinations Milan (every 30min; 1hr 20min–2hr); Padua (every 30min; 45min–1hr 20min); Rome (8 direct daily; 3hr); Venice (every 30min; 1hr 10min–2hr 15min).

INFORMATION

Tourist office Via degli Alpini 6 (Mon–Sat 10am–6pm, Sun 10am–4pm; ☎045 806 8680, ⍟tourism.verona.it). As well as providing information, it organizes walking tours, runs a hotel-booking service and can book tickets for the Arena.

Discount passes The Verona Card (€22/1 day or €22/2 days) covers most of Verona's museums and churches and can be purchased at the tourist offices, *tabacchi* and most museums.

Festivals If you're interested in the Shakespeare and jazz festivals that take place in the Roman theatre in the summer, head to the box office on Via Pallone 16 (☎045 8011 154 or you can buy at the venue; ticket prices start at €10).

ACCOMMODATION

Arena Stradone Porta Palio 2 ☎045 803 2440, ⍟albergoarena.it. There are hardly any one-star hotels in central Verona – this one, next to Castelvecchio (not as close to the Arena as its name might suggest), has been refurnished quite recently, and is the best of the bunch. **€125**

Campeggio Castel San Pietro Via Castel S. Pietro 2 ☎045 592 037, ⍟campingcastelsanpietro.com; bus #41 or #95 from the station to Via Marsala and then a steep walk up the hill. This pleasant shady site out by the old city walls offers marvellous views over the city. Open April–Sept. Per person **€10**, plus per pitch **€10**

Ostello della Gioventù Salita Fontana del Ferro 15 ☎045 590 360, ⍟ostelloverona.it; bus #73, or #91 after 7.45pm and on Sun, from the station to Piazza Isolo. HI hostel in the lovely setting of sixteenth-century Villa Francescatti. Offering 241 beds, including family rooms (bunk beds only); some rooms have frescoed ceilings, others a private terrace; many have splendid views over the rooftops. Dinner is available for €8. Dorms **€18**, family rooms (per person) **€20**

EATING AND DRINKING

★**Antica Osteria al Duomo** Via Duomo 7/A ☎045 800 7333. There has been an *osteria* here for at least a century, and it still serves old Veronese favourites such as *pastissada* (horse stew) and *bigoli* with *sugo d'asino* (donkey sauce). Prices are low (most *secondi* around €10), the decor is quirky and the hosts are terrific. Mon–Sat 11.30am–3pm & 7pm–midnight.

★**Osteria La Mandorla** Via Alberto Mario 23 ☎045 597 053. This tiny, old-fashioned, authentic bar is just a minute's stroll from the Arena; the atmosphere is great, and the wines and snacks are very good. Mon 5pm–2am, Tues–Sun 11am–2.30pm & 5pm–2am.

Trattoria Dal Ropeton Via Fontana del Ferro 1 ☎045 803 0040, ⍟trattoriadaropeton.it. Friendly restaurant tucked away among a maze of streets serving delicious dishes. Try the handmade *penne del Ropeton* (€7), with a sauce of fresh peppers, sausage, cream and curry. Booking is recommended. Mon & Wed–Sun noon–2.30pm & 7.30–11pm.

PADUA

Hemmed in by industrial sprawl, **PADUA** (Padova) is not the most alluring city in northern Italy. However, it's a particularly ancient place with a relaxed air and a sense of the real Italia. Donatello and Mantegna both worked here, and in the seventeenth century Galileo researched at the university.

17

WHAT TO SEE AND DO

Cappella degli Scrovegni

Just outside the city centre, through a gap in the Renaissance walls off Corso Garibaldi, **Cappella degli Scrovegni**, affectionately referred to as the "scrawny chapel" for its diminutive size (daily 9am–7pm, slots for a 15 or 20min viewing should be booked 24hr in advance, but bookable on the day if there is space; €13; ☎049 201 0020, ⓦwww .cappelladegliscrovegni.it), features some stunning Giotto frescoes beneath a lapis-blue ceiling. These are the main reason for coming to Padua. Commissioned in 1303 by Enrico Scrovegni in atonement for his father's usury, the chapel's walls are covered with breathtakingly detailed and largely well-preserved illustrations of the life of Mary, Jesus and the story of the Passion. It's a bit of a rush to see forty masterpieces in fifteen minutes, but well worth it.

Piazza del Santo

In the southwest of the city, down Via Zabarella from the *cappella*, is the starkly impressive **Piazza del Santo**. The main sight here is Donatello's **Monument to Gattamelata** of 1453, the earliest large bronze sculpture of the Renaissance. On one side of the square, the basilica of San Antonio, or **Il Santo**, was built to house the body of St Anthony (a famous disciple of St Francis of Assisi); the **Cappella del Tesoro** at its far end (daily 7am–12.45pm & 2.30–7.30pm) houses the saint's tongue and chin in a head-shaped reliquary.

The university

From the basilica of San Antonio, Via Umberto leads back towards the university, which was established in 1221, and is older than any other in Italy except Bologna. The main block is the **Palazzo del Bo**, where Galileo taught physics from 1592 to 1610. The major sight is the sixteenth-century **anatomy theatre** in the Palazzo del Bo (45min tours in English & Italian; March–Oct Mon, Wed & Fri 2.30pm, 3.30pm, 4.30pm, Tues & Thurs 9.30am, 10.30am, 11.30am, plus Thurs 2.30pm, 3.30pm & 4.30pm, Sat 9.30am, 10.30am, 11.30am; Nov–Feb Mon, Wed & Fri 2.30pm & 3.30pm, Tues, Thurs & Sat 10.30am & 11.30am; €7; ☎049 827 3047, ⓦunipd.it). The university's botanical garden, the oldest in the world, is a green haven in the city (Via Orto Botanico 15; April & May daily 9am–7pm; June–Sept Tues–Sun 9am–7pm; Oct Tues–Sun 9am–6pm; Nov–March Tues–Sun 9am–5pm; €10; ☎049 827 3939, ⓦortobotanicopd.it).

ARRIVAL AND DEPARTURE

By plane Venice airport is most convenient for Padua. There are regular buses from Marco Polo (every 30min–1hr; €8.50).

By train Trains arrive in the north of the city centre, just a few minutes' walk up Corso del Popolo from the old city walls.
Destinations Bologna (frequent; 1hr–1hr 30min); Milan (every 30min; 2hr–2hr 50min); Venice (every 20min; 25–50min); Verona (every 30min; 40min–1hr 20min); Vicenza (every 20min; 15–30min).

INFORMATION

Tourist office There are tourist offices at the train station (Mon–Sat 9am–7pm, Sun 10am–4pm; ☎049 201 0080) and in the centre of the city at Galleria Pedrocchi 9 (Mon–Sat 9am–7pm; ☎049 201 0080, ⓦwww.turismopadova.it).

Discount passes The tourist office sells the Padova Card (€16/48hr; €21/72hr), which gives access to certain museums (including Scrovegni Chapel frescoes), free bus travel and a parking space.

ACCOMMODATION

Ostello Città di Padova Via Aleardo Aleardi 30 ☎049 875 2219, ⓦostellopadova.it. Padua's friendly HI hostel is in a quiet street in the south of the city; it's a 30min walk from the station, but the tram goes to nearby Prato della Valle. Beds are in six-bed dorms, with some four-bed rooms for families. Wi-fi and laundry facilities. Rates include breakfast. Dorms **€19**

Sporting Center Via Roma 123 ☎049 793 400, ⓦsportingcenter.it. Extremely well-equipped, spacious campsite 15km away in Montegrotto Terme, with a reasonable two-star hotel on site. Also a restaurant, large swimming pool and thermal spa. Served by frequent trains (15min). Per person **€9.40**, plus per tent **€13.50**

Verdi Via Dondi dell'Orologio 7 ☎049 836 4163, ⓦalbergoverdipadova.it. A friendly small three-star, very near to Piazza dei Signori. The fourteen rooms are all a good size and have modern furnishings, and the tariffs are low. **€110**

EATING AND DRINKING

For eating on the go, there's a daily fruit market on Piazza Erbe, which also has a few cheap restaurants and bars. There is a supermarket, Pam, at Piazzetta della Garzeria 3 (Mon–Sat 8am–9pm, Sun 9am–8pm).

★**La Folperia** Piazza della Frutta. Max and Barbara bring their seafood stall to the square every night. Mouthwatering and generous portions of *gamberi fritta*, calamari and other seafood served on paper plates. Portion around €5. Daily 5–9pm.

★**Osteria L'Anfora** Via del Soncino 13 ☎049 656 629. Fantastic *osteria* near Piazza Erbe serving hearty portions of delicious fresh pasta is served in a large ramshackle room. *Primi* around €10, *secondi* €16. Booking recommended. Mon–Sat 9am–11.30pm; kitchen 12.30–3.15pm & 8–11.30pm.

Piccola Trattoria Via Rolando da Piazzola 21 ☎049 656 163, ⓦpiccolatrattoria.it. Very popular trattoria, with a distinctive menu that mixes local recipes with Sardinian specialities such as suckling pig, all superbly presented. Its *secondi* are around €16, and it offers a bargain €15 set lunch. Mon 8–11pm, Tues–Sat noon–2pm & 8–11pm.

VENICE

The first-time visitor to **VENICE** (Venezia) arrives with a heavy load of expectations, most of which won't be disappointed. It is an extraordinarily beautiful city, and the major sights are all they are cracked up to be. The downside is that Venice is very expensive and deluged with tourists. Twenty-seven million come here each year, most seduced by the famous motifs – Carnival (see p.640), glass ornaments and singing gondoliers. To avoid the mêlée, stroll down one of the intriguing and peaceful side streets or take a boat across to the Lido and relax on its lovely beach.

WHAT TO SEE AND DO

The 118 islands of central Venice are divided into six districts known as *sestieri*, with that of **San Marco** (enclosed by the lower loop of the Canal Grande) home to most of the essential sights. To the east is **Castello**, to the north **Cannaregio**. On the other side of the Canal Grande is **Dorsoduro**, which stretches from the fashionable quarter at the southern tip of the canal to the docks in the west. **Santa Croce** roughly follows the curve of the Canal Grande from Piazzale Roma to a point just short of the Rialto, where it joins the smartest of the districts on this bank, **San Polo**.

Piazza San Marco

Flanked by the Grand Canal, **Piazza San Marco** is probably the busiest square in the whole of Italy. It's lined with some stunning architecture such as the dominating **Campanile** (daily: Easter–June & Oct 9am–7pm; July–Sept 9am–9pm; Nov–Easter 9.30am–3.45pm; €8; ⓦwww.basilicasanmarco.it), which began life as a lighthouse in the ninth century, but is in fact a reconstruction: the original tower collapsed on July 14, 1902. It is the tallest structure in the city, and the 98m-high tower provides magnificent views of the neighbouring islands and lagoons, as well as the red-clay rooftops of the city.

Basilica di San Marco

Across Piazza San Marco, the **Basilica di San Marco** (Mon–Sat 9.45am–5pm, Sun 2–5pm; Nov–Easter Sun closes 4pm; free) is the most exotic of Europe's cathedrals, modelled on Constantinople's Church of the Twelve Apostles, finished in 1094 and embellished over the succeeding centuries with trophies brought back from abroad. Inside, a steep staircase leads from the church's main door up to the **Museo di San Marco** and the **Loggia dei Cavalli** (daily 9.45am–4.45pm; €5), where you can enjoy fine views of the city and the Gothic carvings along the apex of the facade. However, it's the **Sanctuary**, off the south transept (Easter–Oct Mon–Sat 9.45am–5pm, Sun 2–5pm; Nov–Easter Mon–Sat 9.45am–4pm, Sun 2–4pm; €2), that holds the most precious of San Marco's treasures, the **Pala d'Oro**, or golden altar panel, commissioned in 976 in Constantinople. This mind-blowingly intricate explosion of gold, enamel, pearls and gemstones is generally considered to be one of the greatest accomplishments of Byzantine craftsmanship. The **Treasury** (same hours as Pala d'Oro; €3) is a similarly dazzling warehouse of chalices, reliquaries and candelabra, while the tenth-century **Icon of the Madonna of Nicopeia** (in the chapel on the east side

17

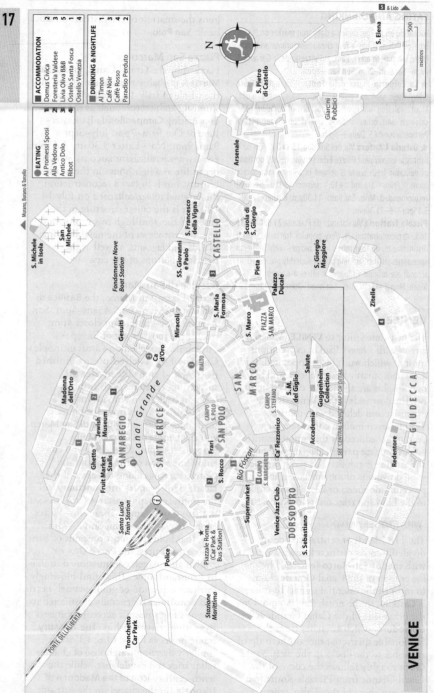

ACCOMMODATION
Domus Civica	2
Foresteria Valdese	3
Livia Oliva B&B	5
Ostello Santa Fosca	1
Ostello Venezia	4

DRINKING & NIGHTLIFE
Al Timon	1
Café Noir	3
Caffè Rosso	4
Paradiso Perduto	2

EATING
Ai Promessi Sposi	2
Alla Vedova	3
Antico Dolo	3
Ribot	4

Murano, Burano & Torcello

S. Michele in Isola

San Michele

S. Pietro di Castello

S. Elena

Giardini Pubblici

Arsenale

Scuola di S. Giorgio

S. Francesco della Vigna

Fondamente Nove Boat Station

Gesuiti

SS. Giovanni e Paolo

Miracoli

Pietà

S. Giorgio Maggiore

Ca' d'Oro

S. Maria Formosa

S. Marco

Palazzo Ducale

PIAZZA SAN MARCO

Zitelle

Madonna dell'Orto

Jewish Museum

Ghetto

Fruit Market Stalls

CANNAREGIO

Canal Grande

SANTA CROCE

RIALTO

SAN MARCO

Salute

S. M. del Giglio

Guggenheim Collection

Accademia

CAMPO S. POLO

SAN POLO

CAMPO S. STEFANO

Ca' Rezzonico

SEE CENTRAL VENICE MAP FOR DETAIL

Frari

S. Rocco

Rio Foscari

CAMPO S. MARGHERITA

DORSODURO

Supermarket

Venice Jazz Club

S. Sebastiano

Redentore

LA GIUDECCA

Santa Lucia Train Station

Police

Piazzale Roma (Car Park & Bus Station)

Stazione Marittima

Tronchetto Car Park

PONTE DELLA LIBERTÀ

VENICE

CASTELLO

N

5 & Lido

500 metres
0

of the north transept) is the most revered religious image in Venice. Considered by Venetians to be the protector of the city after being brought here from Constantinople by Doge Enrico Dandolo in 1204, she was carried at the head of the Imperial Army in battles.

Palazzo Ducale

The **Palazzo Ducale** (daily: April–Oct 8.30am–7pm; Nov–March 8.30am–5.30pm; ticket office closes 1hr earlier; €19; ⓦpalazzoducale.visitmuve.it) was principally the residence of the doge. Like San Marco, it has been rebuilt many times since its foundation in the first years of the ninth century, but the earliest parts of the current structure date from 1340. As well as fabulous paintings and impressive administrative chambers, the Palazzo contains a maze of prison cells, reached by crossing the world-famous **Ponte dei Sospiri** (Bridge of Sighs).

Dorsoduro

In the Dorsoduro area west of San Marco is the impressive European art collection of the **Galleria dell'Accademia** (Mon 8.15am–2pm, Tues–Sun 8.15am–7.15pm; €15; ⓦgallerie accademia.org). Five minutes' walk from here the unfinished Palazzo Venier dei Leoni is home to the **Guggenheim Collection** (daily except Tues 10am–6pm; €15; ⓦguggenheim-venice.it). Peggy Guggenheim lived here for thirty years until her death in 1979. Her private collection is an eclectic mix of pieces from her favourite Modernist artists, with works by Brancusi, De Chirico, Max Ernst and Malevich.

San Polo

On the northeastern edge of **San Polo** is the former trading district of **Rialto**. It still hosts the lively Rialto market, which is located on the far side of the Rialto bridge and has stalls heaving with fresh fruit and vegetables and a shiny array of fish.

Fifteen minutes' walk west of here is the mountainous brick church **Santa Maria Gloriosa dei Frari** (Mon–Sat 9am–6pm, Sun 1–6pm; €3; ⓦchorus venezia.org). The collection of artworks

here includes a couple of rare paintings by Titian – most notably his radical *Assumption*, painted in 1518. Titian is also buried in the church. At the rear of the Frari is the **Scuola Grande di San Rocco** (daily 9.30am–5.30pm; €10; ⓦscuolagrandesanrocco.it), home to a cycle of more than fifty major paintings by Tintoretto.

Cannaregio

In the northernmost section of Venice, **Cannaregio**, you can walk from the bustle of the train station to some of the quietest and prettiest parts of the city in a matter of minutes. The district boasts one of the most beautiful *palazzi* in Venice, the **Ca D'Oro**, or Golden House (Mon 8.15am–2pm, Tues–Sun 8.15am–7.15pm; €6; ⓦcadoro.org), whose facade once glowed with gold leaf, and what is arguably the finest Gothic church in Venice, the **Madonna dell'Orto** (Mon–Sat 10am–5pm, Sun noon–5pm; €2.50), which contains Tintoretto's tomb and two of his paintings. Cannaregio also has the dubious distinction of containing the world's first **ghetto**: in 1516, all the city's Jews were ordered to move to the island of the **Ghetto Nuovo**, an enclave that was sealed at night by Christian guards. Even now it looks quite different from the rest of Venice, its many high-rise buildings a result of restrictions on the growth of the area. The **Jewish Museum** (Mon–Fri & Sun: June–Sept 10am–7pm; Oct–May 10am–5.30pm; €4; ⓦwww.museoebraico.it) in Campo Ghetto Nuovo organizes hourly tours in English and Italian of the synagogues (€10, including museum admission).

Castello

Campo Santi Giovanni e Paolo is the most impressive open space in Venice after Piazza San Marco, dominated by the huge brick church of **Santi Giovanni e Paolo** (Mon–Sat 9am–6pm, Sun noon–6.30pm; €2.50), founded by the Dominicans in 1246 and best known for its funeral monuments to 25 doges. The other essential sight in **Castello** is the **Scuola di San Giorgio degli Schiavoni** (Mon 2.45–6pm, Tues–Sat 9.15am–1pm

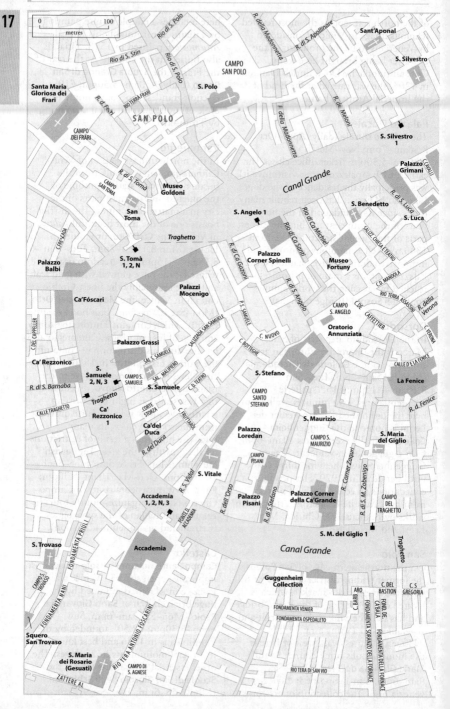

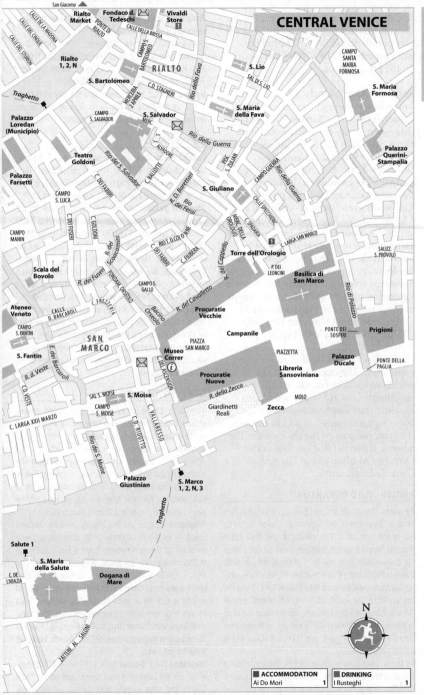

CENTRAL VENICE

San Giacomo

Rialto Market
Fondaco d. Tedeschi
Vivaldi Store
CALLE DELLA BRISSA
PONTE DI RIALTO
CALLE DELLA FAVA
Rio della Fava
S. Lio
SAL DI S. LIO
CAMPO SANTA MARIA FORMOSA
S. Maria Formosa

CALLE DE LA MADONA
CALLE DEL CINQUE
CALLE DE STURION

Rialto 1, 2, N
CAMPO S. BARTOLOMEO
RIALTO
S. Bartolòmeo
C.D. STAGNERI
S. Maria della Fava

Traghetto
MOCENIGO 2 APRILE
CAMPO S. SALVADOR
MERC
S. Salvador
Rio della Guerra
S. Maria della Fava

Palazzo Loredan (Municipio)
Rio del S. Salvador
S. SALVADORE
PISC
S. TULIAN
S. Giuliano
CAMPO GUERRA
Rio della Guerra

Teatro Goldoni
C. BALLOTTE
R. D. Baretani
CALLE SPECHIERI
Palazzo Querini-Stampalia

Palazzo Farsetti
C. DEI FABBRI
Rio dei Ferali
S. SPADARIA
MERC. DELLA OROLOGIO

CAMPO S. LUCA
C. DEI FUSERI
C. GOLDONI
R. del Scoacamini
C. RIO T. D.COLONNE
C. FIUBERA
C. LARGA SAN MARCO

CAMPO MANIN
FONDAM. ORSEOLO
R. dei Fuseri
C. DEI FABBRI
R. del Cappello
Torre dell'Orologio
SALIZZ. S. PRÒVOLO

Scala del Bovolo
CAMPO S. GALLO
R. del Cavalletto
P. DEI LEONCINI
Basilica di San Marco
Rio di Palazzo

Ateneo Veneto
CALLE D. BARCAROLI
C. FREZZERIA
Bacino Orseolo
Procuratie Vecchie
Campanile
PONTE DEI SOSPIRI
Prigioni

CAMPO S. FANTIN
PIAZZA SAN MARCO
PIAZZETTA

S. Fantin
E. dei Barcaroli
R. D. Veste
SAN MARCO
Museo Correr
Procuratie Nuove
Libreria Sansoviniana
Palazzo Ducale
PONTE DELLA PAGLIA

C.D. VESTE
SAL S. MOISE
CALLE D'ASCENSION
R. della Zecca
MOLO

C. LARGA XXII MARZO
S. Moise
CAMPO S. MOISE
C. VALLARESSO
Giardinetti Reali
Zecca
Zecca

Rio del S. Moise
C.D. RIDOTTO

Palazzo Giustinian
S. Marco 1, 2, N, 3

Traghetto

Salute 1
C. DE L'ABAZIA
S. Maria della Salute
Dogana di Mare

N

■ ACCOMMODATION		■ DRINKING	
Ai Do Mori	1	I Rusteghi	1

17 & 2.45–6pm, Sun 9.15am–1pm; €5), to the east of San Marco, set up by Venice's Slav population in 1451. The building has a superb cycle by Vittore Carpaccio on the ground floor.

Venice's other islands

Immediately south of the Palazzo Ducale, Palladio's church of **San Giorgio Maggiore** (May–Sept Mon–Sat 9.30am–6.30pm, Sun 8.30–11am & 2.30–6.30pm; Oct–April Mon–Sat 9.30am–dusk, Sun 8.30–11am & 2.30pm–dusk; free, campanile €6) stands on the island of the same name and has two pictures by Tintoretto in the chancel – *The Fall of Manna* and *The Last Supper*. On the left of the choir a corridor leads to the **Campanile**, one of the best vantage points in the city. The long island of **La Giudecca**, to the west, was where the wealthiest aristocrats of early Renaissance Venice built their villas. The main reason to come today is the Franciscan church of the **Redentore** (Mon–Sat 10am–5pm; €3), designed by Palladio in 1577 in thanks for Venice's deliverance from a plague that killed a third of the population. The **Lido**, home to the world's oldest film festival, is a ten-minute boat ride from San Marco Zaccaria (take *traghetto vaporetto* #1, #2 May–Sept only, or #5.1) and in summer is a great place to escape the crowds. The quietest stretch of free beach is at the Ospedale Al Mare end of Lungomare Gabriele D'Annunzio.

ARRIVAL AND DEPARTURE

By plane Marco Polo airport (ⓦ veniceairport.it) is 7km north of the centre on the edge of the lagoon, linked by bus to the terminal at Piazzale Roma: the ATVO coach (Azienda Trasporti Veneto Orientale; every 30min; 20min; €6; ⓦ www.atvo.it), or the ACTV (Azienda del Consorzio Trasporti Veneziano; €6; ⓦ actv.it) bus #5, which is equally frequent but usually takes a little longer. For €12 you can buy an ACTV bus-and-boat ticket, which gets you to Piazzale Roma then gives you one *vaporetto* journey of up to 90min. Alilaguna water-buses operate on three routes from the airport (hourly; just over 1hr to San Marco; €15 to central Venice).

By train Santa Lucia train station is on the north side of the canal, to the west of the city centre (ⓦ trenitalia.com). Waterbus services run to San Marco, and you can cross over

Ponte degli Scalzi to reach San Polo or follow the canal along to get to Cannaregio.

Destinations Bologna (frequent; 1hr 15min–2hr); Florence (hourly; 2hr); Milan (every 30min; 2hr 10min–3hr); Padua (every 10min; 25–50min); Trieste (frequent; 2–3hr); Verona (frequent; 1hr–1hr 30min).

By bus All road traffic comes into the city at Piazzale Roma, at the head of the Canal Grande, from where waterbus services run to all parts of Venice.

INFORMATION

Tourist office There are information points at the train station (daily 8am–8.50pm), at the airport (8.30am–7pm) and at Museo Correr in Piazza San Marco (9am–7pm). Call centre Hello Venezia (☎ 0412424, ⓦ veneziaunica.it).

Discount passes There are two museum cards for the city's civic museums (ⓦ visitmuve.it). The Musei di Piazza San Marco card costs €17 (€10 for students under 26), is valid for three months, and covers the Palazzo Ducale, Museo Correr, Museo Archeologico and the Libreria Sansoviniana. The Museum Pass, costing €24/€18, covers these four, plus other civic museums. It's valid for six months. Both passes allow one visit to each attraction and are available from any of the participating museums. The sights covered by the Musei di Piazza San Marco card can be visited only with a museum card; at the other places you have the option of paying an entry charge just for that attraction. Accompanied disabled people have free access to all civic museums.

GETTING AROUND

Despite its tangle of narrow, people-choked streets, walking is the fastest way of getting around Venice – you can cross the whole city in an hour.

Gondola Gondolas are expensive although an astonishingly graceful craft, perfectly designed for negotiating the tortuous and shallow waterways. To hire one costs €80/40min for up to six passengers, rising to €100 between 7pm and 8am; you pay an extra €40 for every additional 20min, or €50 from 7pm to 8am.

Traghetti There are just four bridges spanning the Canal Grande – the Ponte Calatrava (at Piazzale Roma), Ponte dei Scalzi (at the train station), Ponte di Rialto and Ponte dell'Accademia – so the *traghetti* (gondola ferries) that cross it can be useful time-savers. Costing €2 (€0.70 if you're a resident), they are also the only cheap way of getting a ride on a gondola, albeit a stripped-down version, with none of the trimmings and no padded seats: most locals stand rather than sit. There used to be almost thirty gondola *traghetti* across the Canal Grande, but today there are just seven.

Waterbus There are two basic types of boat: *vaporetti*, which are the lumbering workhorses used on the Canal Grande and other heavily used routes, and *motoscafi*, smaller vessels employed on routes where the volume of traffic isn't as great. The standard fare is an exorbitant €7 for a single journey, so it's better to get a multi-day travel tourist card that includes all *vaporetti* and bus transport (€20/1 day, €30/2 days, €40/3 days; ⓦ veneziaunica.it); a single ticket is valid for an hour, and for any number of changes of water-bus, as long as you're travelling from point A to point B – it cannot, in other words, be used as a return ticket. Should you have more than one piece of large luggage, you're supposed to pay €7/additional item. Note that all tickets and travel cards have to be swiped before each journey at the meter-like machines that are at every stop. If you're 14–29 years old, make sure you buy the Rolling Venice card for just €4, which gives large reductions on transport in the city.

ACCOMMODATION

Accommodation is the major expense in Venice and you should always book ahead – you might also consider staying in nearby Padua, 30min away by train (see p.631), Mestre or on the Lido. High season officially runs from March 15 to Nov 15 and then from Dec 21 to Jan 6, but many places don't recognize the existence of a low season any more. There is a booking office at the tourist office outside the train station.

★ **Ai Do Mori** Calle Larga S. Marco 658 ☎ 041 520 4817, ⓦ hotelaidomori.com; map pp.636–637. Very friendly, and situated a few paces off the Piazza, this is a top recommendation for budget travellers. The top-floor room has a private terrace looking over the roofs of the Basilica and the Torre dell'Orologio, and is one of the most attractive (and, of course, expensive) one-star rooms in the city. All rooms have their own bathroom. €150

Domus Civica Calle Campazzo, San Polo 3082 ☎ 041 721 103, ⓦ domuscivica.com; map p.634. This Catholic women's student hostel is open to tourists from mid-June to mid-Sept. Most rooms are double with running water; showers free; no breakfast; midnight curfew. Dorms €25

Foresteria Valdese Calle S. Maria Formosa, Castello 5170 ☎ 041 528 6797, ⓦ foresteriavenezia.it; map p.634. Run by Waldensians, this hostel is installed in a wonderful *palazzo*, with flaking frescoes in the rooms and a large communal salon. It has bedrooms for one to four people and small dormitories that can accommodate up to nine; most of the smaller rooms have a private bathroom. Registration 9am–1pm & 6–8pm. Dorms €32, doubles €105

★ **Livia Oliva B&B** Via Aldo Manuzio 5, Lido ☎ 041 526 2981; map p.634. An unbeatable choice on the Lido, close to the ferry station and near a lovely sandy beach. The rooms are spotless and there's a lovely terrace overlooking the quiet canal-lined street. Doubles €58

Ostello Santa Fosca S. Maria dei Servi, Cannaregio 2372 ☎ 041 715 775, ⓦ ostellosantafosca.it; map p.634.

Student-run hostel in an atmospheric former Servite convent in a quiet part of Cannaregio, with rudimentary bedrooms sleeping two to seven people (the larger rooms are female-only), nearly all of them with shared bathrooms. 12.30am curfew. Dorms €27

Ostello Venezia Fondamenta Zitelle 86, Giudecca ☎ 041 523 8211, ⓦ ostellovenezia.it; map p.634. The city's 240-bed, 29-room HI hostel occupies a superb location looking over the water to San Marco, and has been completely revamped, making it one of the best in Italy – bright, spacious, comfortable and even stylish. Rooms range from doubles to sixteen-bed dorms. Breakfast and sheets are included – but remember to add the expense of the boat from central Venice. No kitchen, but you can eat cheaply in the hostel canteen. No curfew. Dorms €25

EATING

Venice is full of great restaurants but it can be a minefield to find cheap places. Avoid the tourist hotspots like Piazza San Marco where prices rocket, and make sure you head to a *bàcaro*, a bar that offers a range of snacks called *cicheti* (or *ciccheti*). Some *bácari* also produce one or two more substantial dishes each day, such as risotto or seafood pasta.

Ai Promessi Sposi Calle dell'Oca, Cannaregio 4367 ☎ 041 241 2747; map p.634. This moderately priced (mains around €15) and cosy little *osteria* specializes in *baccalà* and other traditional fish recipes. Excellent range of *cicheti* at the bar. Tues & Thurs–Sun 11.30am–2.15pm & 6–11pm, Wed 6–11pm.

Alla Vedova Calle del Pistor 3912, Cannaregio ☎ 041 528 5324; map p.634. This long-established little restaurant is fronted by a bar offering a mouthwatering selection of *cicheti* and a good range of wines. One of the best-value places in town (antipasti and main courses from just €10), so book ahead. Mon–Wed, Fri & Sat 11.30am–2.30pm & 6.30–10.30pm, Sun 6.30–10.30pm.

Antico Dolo Ruga Rialto, San Polo 778 ☎ 041 522 6546, ⓦ anticodolo.it; map p.634. You can pop into this tiny and long-established *osteria* for a few *cicheti* and a glass of Merlot and come away just a few euros poorer; or you can take a table and eat an excellent meal for something in the region of €40. For lunch, the €18.50 plate of assorted *cicheti* is a tempting offer. Daily noon–10pm.

Ribot Fondamenta Minotto, Santa Croce 158 ☎ 041 524 2486, ⓦ ristoranteribot.com; map p.634. Named after a famous racehorse, *Ribot* is an old-fashioned, good-value, unfussy and relaxed restaurant, with a menu that draws on recipes from beyond the Veneto, and a lovely garden out back. Main courses are mostly under €20, and there are some very well-priced set menus. The wine list is excellent, and the location – near the Tolentini – is off the main tourist routes. Mon–Sat noon–2.30pm & 7–10.30pm.

17

DRINKING AND NIGHTLIFE

Venice is short on clubbing action, but there are plenty of bars, particularly around Campo Santa Margherita and Campo San Giacomo.

Al Timon Fondamenta degli Ormesini, Cannaregio 2754 ☎041 524 6066; map p.634. With its attractively spartan neo-traditional decor, this *osteria* is a big hit with Venice's students and 20-somethings — most nights, the crowd spills out onto the canalside. The meals are generally good, but this is really a place for a snack and a drink or two. Mon–Sat 11am–4pm & 7pm–1am.

Café Noir Crosera S. Pantalon, Dorsoduro 3805 ☎041 710 227. A favourite student bar, often with live music on Tues. Mon–Fri 11am–2am, Sat & Sun 7pm–2am.

Caffè Rosso Santa Margherita, Dorsoduro 2963 ⓦcafferosso.it; map p.634. This tiny bar draws a large crowd. Either stand outside or join the chilled-out throng who sit in the square. Mon–Sat 7am–1am.

I Rusteghi Corte del Tentor, San Marco 5513 ☎041 523 2205; map pp.636–637. A small *osteria*, secreted away in a tiny courtyard close to Campo San Bartolomeo, with great *cicheti*, nice wine and a congenial host – plus a few outside tables. The perfect place for a quiet snack in the San Marco area. Mon–Sat 10am–3pm & 6pm–midnight.

Paradiso Perduto Fondamenta della Misericordia, Cannaregio 2540 ☎041 720 581, ⓦilparadisoperduto .com; map p.634. A fixture on the Venice scene, *Paradiso Perduto* is packed to the rafters most nights with a young crowd. The restaurant section is like a boho refectory and the atmosphere is usually terrific, though there are better kitchens in the neighbourhood. Go for the drinks, the *cicheti* and the buzz. Mon & Thurs–Sun 9am–2am.

ENTERTAINMENT

To find out about concerts and events going on throughout the city, head to one of the tourist offices (see p.638). Alternatively, check out websites ⓦmusicinvenice.com or ⓦveniceconcerts.com.

La Fenice ☎041 786 511, ⓦteatrolafenice.it. The city's opera house was completely rebuilt after a calamitous fire in 1996 and puts on excellent performances. Tickets range €15–200.

Venice Jazz Club Ponte dei Pugni, Dorsoduro 3102 ☎041 523 2056, ⓦvenicejazzclub.com. Live jazz takes place throughout the year at this popular venue.

DIRECTORY

Hospital Ospedale Civile, Campo SS. Giovanni e Paolo (☎041 529 4111).

Police To notify police of a theft or lost passport, report to the *questura* at Rampa S. Chiara 500, on the north side of Piazzale Roma (☎041 271 5511).

Post office Calle delle Acque 5016, close to San Salvador (Mon–Fri 8.30am–7pm, Sat 8.30am–12.30pm).

BOLOGNA

BOLOGNA is the oldest university town in Europe (the institution dates back to the eleventh century) and teems with students and bookshops. Known for its left-wing politics, "Red Bologna" has long been the Italian Communist Party's spiritual home. The birthplace of Marconi boasts some of the richest food in Italy, a busy cultural life and a convivial café and bar scene.

WHAT TO SEE AND DO

The compact, colonnaded city centre is famous for its 38km of covered arcades, built to cover the horses brought to Bologna by the first university students, and is still startlingly medieval in plan.

Piazza Maggiore and around

Buzzing **Piazza Maggiore** is the heart of the city, dominated by the basilica of **San Petronio**, and was originally intended to have been larger than St Peter's in Rome. Just north of the square, in the centre of Piazza del Nettuno, is the marble and bronze **Fountain of Neptune**, a famous emblem of the city. Created by Giambologna in the late sixteenth century, it shows the sea god lording it over an array of cherubs, mermaids and dolphins. Northwest of the piazza, at Via Don Minzoni 14, is the **MAMbo**, the Modern Art Museum of Bologna (Tues, Wed & Fri noon–6pm, Thurs, Sat & Sun noon–8pm; €6; ⓦmambo-bologna.org). Housed in an ex-bakery, the museum contains works by Italian and international artists and hosts regular temporary exhibitions by contemporary artists. MAMbo currently houses the **Museo Morandi**, while its home in the Palazzo d'Accursio on Piazza Maggiore is restored. The museum is dedicated to the works of Giorgio Morandi, one of Italy's most important twentieth-century painters.

Archiginnasio

Bologna's university – the **Archiginnasio** – was founded at more or less the same time as the Piazza Maggiore, though it didn't get a special building until 1565. The most interesting portion is the **Teatro Anatomico** (Mon–Fri 10am–6pm, Sat 10am–7pm, Sun 10am–2pm; €3; ⓦwww .archiginnasio.it), the original medical faculty dissection theatre, whose tiers of seats surround a professor's chair, covered with a canopy supported by figures known as *gli spellati* – the skinned ones.

Piazza San Domenico

South down Via Garibaldi, **Piazza San Domenico** is the site of the church of **San Domenico**, built in 1251 to house the relics of St Dominic. The angel and figures of saints Proculus and Petronius were the work of a very young Michelangelo. It also holds a crucifix by Pizzano.

Due Torri

At Piazza di Porta Ravegnana, the **Torre degli Asinelli** (daily: March–Oct 9am–6pm; Nov–Feb 9am–5pm; €3) and perilously leaning **Torre Garisenda** are together known as the Due Torri, the only significant survivors of 180 towers that were scattered across the city during the Middle Ages, when possession of the towers determined the ranks of power within the city. Superstition holds that any student who enters these towers before graduation won't graduate at all. The climb up the 498 steps to the top of the Torre degli Asinelli is tough and takes about fifteen minutes but you'll be rewarded with spectacular views over Bologna's rooftops.

ARRIVAL AND DEPARTURE

By plane Bologna's airport (ⓦbologna-airport.it) is northwest of the centre, linked by Aerobus (every 15min; 25min; €6) to the train station and Via dell'Indipendenza in the centre of town.

By train The train station is on Piazza delle Medaglie d'Oro. Buses #A, #11, #25 and #27 run to Piazza Maggiore or Via Rizzoli, or it's a 20min walk.

Destinations Ferrara (every 30min; 25min–50min); Florence (frequent; 35min); Milan (every 30min; 1–2hr); Rimini (every 30min; 50min–1hr 30min); Rome (frequent; 2hr–2hr 20min); Turin (every 2hr; 2hr 10min–2hr 30min); Venice (frequent; 1hr 30min–2hr); Verona (every 1–2hr; 50min–1hr 30min).

By bus All long-distance buses terminate in Piazza XX Settembre 6, next to the train station. Sena (ⓦsena.it) runs services to Naples, Rome and Siena.

Destinations Naples (5 daily; 9hr); Rome (7 daily; 6hr 15min); Siena (7 daily; 2hr 40min–4hr).

INFORMATION

Tourist office Piazza Maggiore 1 (Mon–Sat 9am–7pm, Sun 10am–5pm; ☏051 239 660, ⓦbolognawelcome.it). Packed with information, including details of gourmet tours and cookery courses. There's a second office at the airport (Mon–Sat 9am–7pm, Sun 9am–4pm; ☏051 647 2201).

Discount passes The 48-hour Bologna Welcome Card costs €20 and includes admission to many of the major museums, plus either free public transport for 24 hours or a free shuttle bus to and from Bologna's airport.

GETTING AROUND

Walking is the best way to see Bologna, as the compact centre can be crossed in under 30min.

City Red Bus This bus (ⓦcityredbus.com) offers a day ticket for just €13 and is a great way to explore Bologna outside the city centre.

By bike Demetra Social Bike at Via Capo di Lucca 37, near the bus station, rents bikes for €15/day.

ACCOMMODATION

Trade fairs take place several times a year (March to early May & Sept–Dec are peak times), during which prices can double – so it's best to book ahead. The tourist office has a helpful and free booking service.

★**Garisenda** Galleria del Leone 1/Via Rizzoli 9 ☏051 224 369, ⓦalbergogarisenda.com. The seven rooms here are basic – only three have private bathrooms (€85) – but the location is great and the welcome genuine. It's surprisingly quiet for its location, above the Via Rizzoli shops right opposite the two towers. **€65**

Il Nosadillo Via Nosadella 15 ⓦilnosadillo.com. This small hostel in the old centre is more convenient, though pricier than Bologna's official HI hostel (6km out of town). As the staff aren't around all day, it feels more like a shared apartment than a hostel, with three mixed dorms sleeping five to seven. They share the bathrooms, kitchens and living room. Check-in 2–8pm. Dorms **€24**, doubles **€70**

17

Panorama Via Livraghi 1 ☎051 221 802, ⓦhotelpanoramabologna.it. Offering excellent value, this fourth-floor, one-star hotel has three- and four-bed rooms as well as large doubles and singles; it's a little old-fashioned but spotlessly clean. Only one room comes with private bath; the rest share pleasant facilities down the corridor. Helpful owners. €55

EATING

For a snack, head for the Mercato di Mezzo, the former market hall at Via Clavature 12 where you can buy salads, *calamari*, platters of ham and cheese plus wine and beer from different stalls and sit at convivial shared tables – or take away (daily 8.30am–midnight).

Al Sangiovese Vicolo del Falcone 2 ☎051 583 057, ⓦalsangiovese.com. Tucked away on an unprepossessing backstreet by the Porta San Mamolo, this traditional trattoria serves excellent pasta dishes such as *strozzapreti* with porcini mushrooms, peas and ham (€8), as well as meaty mains (€12–16), washed down with a fine Sangiovese red from the family vineyard. Mon–Sat noon–2.30pm & 7–10.30pm.

Clorofilla Strada Maggiore 64/C ☎051 235 343. This warmly inviting fish and vegetarian place is just the spot if the "fat of Bologna" has been weighing you down, offering enticing salads with predominantly organic products, all around €8, as well as tofu and seitan dishes and fish specialities from €12. Mon–Sat noon–3pm & 7.30–11pm.

Osteria dell'Orsa Via Mentana 1/F ☎051 231 576. Bustling, friendly and cheap, this is where both students and locals go for simple good food. Pastas (€6), salads (€8) and main dishes €10–12. Share one of the big tables and join in the pub-like conviviality. Daily 12.30pm–1am.

★**Tamburini** Via Caprarie 1 ☎051 234 726. A fabulous deli with hanging hams and counters bulging with giant cheeses. It's also got a popular wine bar selling roasted meats and plates of filled pasta for around €5–7. Mon–Sat 8.30am–8pm, Sun 10am–6.30pm; wine bar daily noon–11pm.

DRINKING AND NIGHTLIFE

One of the cheapest and liveliest areas is the pub-and bar-lined Via Zamboni, where the university students hang out. Piazza Verdi pulls in the crowds on summer evenings with its open-air bars and live music. West of the centre, there is a buzzing scene in the streets around the Mercato delle Erbe, while the nearby Via del Pratello is also lined with bars and restaurants. There's a free open-air cinema in Piazza Maggiore in the summer (late June to late July; 10pm) showing arty and black-and-white films – ask at the tourist office (see p.641).

Altotasso Piazza San Francesco 6/D ☎051 238 003. Small *enoteca* offering a great spread of *aperitivi*, with an emphasis on zero kilometre produce. Craft beers on tap and

the wines are mostly local and organic. Live jazz and rock in the large back room on Wednesdays. Daily 4.30pm–3am.

Cantina Bentivoglio Via Mascarella 4/B ☎051 265 416, ⓦcantinabentivoglio.it. This place has live jazz from around 10pm in the cellars of a sixteenth-century *palazzo*, and the food (snacks to full meals; mains €9–18) and wines are excellent. Daily 8pm–2am; closed Sun in summer.

Enoteca des Arts Via San Felice 9 ☎051 236 422. This tiny, dark bar is a proper *enoteca* – all warm wood and dusty bottles – serving cheap local wine and preparing simple snacks (panini, cold meat platters) on request. Mon–Sat 5pm–3am.

PARMA

PARMA is an extremely pleasant town, with dignified streets, large green spaces, a wide range of good restaurants and an appealing air of provincial affluence. The home of Parmesan and Parma ham also offers plenty to see, not least the works of two key late Renaissance artists – Correggio and Parmigianino.

WHAT TO SEE AND DO

Piazza Garibaldi is the fulcrum of Parma, and its cafés and surrounding alleyways are liveliest at night. The mustard-coloured **Palazzo del Governatore** flanks the square, behind which stands the Renaissance church of **Santa Maria della Steccata** (daily 7.30am–noon & 3–6.30pm; free). Inside there are frescoes by a number of sixteenth-century painters, notably Parmigianino. It's also worth visiting the **Duomo** (daily 9am–12.30pm & 3–7pm), on Piazza del Duomo in the northeast of the city centre, to see the octagonal **Baptistery** (€6), considered to be Benedetto Antelami's finest work, built in 1196. Frescoes by Correggio are in the **Camera di San Paolo** (Tues–Fri & Sun 8.30am–1.30pm, Sat 8.30am–5.30pm; €2), in the former Benedictine convent off Via Melloni, a few minutes' walk north.

East of the cathedral square, it's hard to miss Parma's biggest monument, the **Palazzo della Pilotta**, begun for Alessandro Farnese in the sixteenth century and rebuilt after World War II bombing. It now houses the city's main art gallery, the **Galleria Nazionale** (Tues–Sun 8.30am–1.30pm; €6; €3 after 2pm; ⓦwww.gallerianazionaleparma.it), whose extensive collection includes more works by Correggio and Parmigianino. The grassy area around the Palazzo is a popular place for a picnic. If you've had enough of all things cultural and fancy checking out some shopping streets, stroll down the wide and laidback **Strada della Repubblica**, or alternatively people-watch from a café on Via Farini, take a walk along the river or escape the heat of the day at the Parco Ducale.

ARRIVAL AND DEPARTURE

By plane Ryanair flies three times weekly from London Stansted to Parma's airport (☎0521 9515, ⓦparma -airport.it), 5km from the train station. Bus #6 (every 30min) runs to the station; a taxi will cost around €10.
By train Parma's train station is a 15min walk from the central Piazza Garibaldi, or take bus #1, #8, #9 or #13.
Destinations Bologna (every 30min–1hr; 1hr–1hr 10min); La Spezia (every 1–2hr; 2hr); Milan (frequent; 1hr 15min–1hr 40min).

INFORMATION

Tourist office Piazza Garibaldi 1 (Mon 1–7pm, Tues–Sat 9am–7pm, Sun 9am–1pm & 2–6pm; ☎0521 218 889, ⓦturismo.comune.parma.it). Ask here about connecting to free wi-fi.
Festivals and events Events include the annual Verdi festival in October, held at the Teatro Regio on Via Garibaldi (☎0521 203 999, ⓦteatroregioparma.org).

ACCOMMODATION

Al Battistero d'Oro Strada Sant'Anna 22 ☎338 490 4697, ⓦalbattisterodoro.it. Two delightful rooms in a B&B filled with local eighteenth-century furniture. The friendly owner, Patrizia, can help with information, and also rents out a well-equipped apartment round the corner. **€100**
D'Autore Strada Nino Bixio 89 ☎348 898 2304, ⓦbbdautore.it; bus #1, #6 or #20 from the station. A welcoming B&B in a quiet location on the western side of the river, impeccably run by Giacomo and Roberto, who provide free bikes. Breakfast €5. Cash only. **€75**
Ostello della Gioventù Via S. Leonardo 86 ☎0521 191 7547, ⓦostelloparma.it; a 10min bus ride north of the centre (#2 & #13 from the train station and the city centre). This hostel offers spick-and-span six-bed dorms, doubles and triple rooms with private bathrooms, and a host of extra facilities. Open 24hr. Breakfast €3 extra. Dorms **€20**, doubles **€44**
Palazzo dalla Rosa Prati Piazza Duomo 7 ☎0521 386 429, ⓦpalazzodallarosaprati.it. Luxurious conversion of an old *palazzo* in the heart of town with fabulous rooms and suites – suite 5 looks out over the Baptistery, and if the lights are on in the evening you can see the frescoes. It's a friendly place – owned and run by the same family since the 1600s. Breakfast is served in the café downstairs. **€110**

EATING AND DRINKING

★**Ciacco** Strada Garibaldi 11 ☎0521 234 063. Artisan ice-cream parlour, named after a Dante character, where the range of seasonal flavours includes some unusual combinations, such as the delicious *strudel* and the curious liquorice sorbet. Mon–Thurs noon–11pm, Fri–Sun noon–midnight.
★**Gallo d'Oro** Borgo della Salina 3 ☎0521 208 846. Atmospheric trattoria on a quiet side street off Strada Farini. Excellent filled pastas such as pumpkin ravioli (€8), while the *secondi* include a tasty rabbit with herbs (€9). Daily noon–2.30pm & 7.30–11pm.
★**Panino d'Artista** Strada Farini 19–21 ☎0521 236 512. This narrow bar bustles with customers and serves a superb array of *antipasti* (a glass of wine plus snacks €5). At their Verdi-themed restaurant next door, *La Cucina del Maestro*, the *risotto Verdi* is masterful – and great value (€9.50). Mon–Thurs & Sun 7am–1am, Fri & Sat 7am–2am.
★**Tabarro** Strada Farini 5/B ☎0521 200 223. Cosy little wine bar with geometric-tiled floor, copper-topped bar and beer barrels as tables – a convivial spot for an *aperitivo*. The meat and cheese plates (from €7) are locally sourced. Tues–Thurs & Sun 5pm–midnight, Fri & Sat 5pm–1am.

RAVENNA

RAVENNA'S colourful sixth-century mosaics are one of the crowning achievements of Byzantine art – and undoubtedly the main reason for visiting the town. The mosaics are the legacy of a quirk of fate 1500 years ago, when Ravenna briefly became capital of the Roman Empire, and can be seen in a day. The **Basilica of San Vitale**, ten minutes northwest of the centre, was completed in 548 AD. Its mosaics, showing scenes from the Old Testament and the life of Christ, are in the apse. Across from the basilica is the tiny **Mausoleo di Galla Placidia** (daily: April–Sept 9.30am–7pm; Nov–Feb 10am–5pm; March & Oct 9.30am–5.30pm; entry with Museum card), whose mosaics glow with a deep-blue lustre. Galla Placidia was the daughter, sister, wife and mother of various Roman emperors, and the interior of her fifth-century mausoleum, whose cupola is covered in tiny stars, is breathtaking. East of here, on the Via di Roma, is the

17

sixth-century basilica of **Sant'Apollinare Nuovo** (daily: April–Sept 9.30am–7pm; Nov–Feb 10am–5pm; March & Oct 9.30am–5.30pm; entry with Museum card). Mosaics run the length of the nave, depicting processions of martyrs bearing gifts. Five minutes' walk up Via di Roma, the **Arian Baptistery** has a fine mosaic ceiling (daily 8.30am–7.30pm; Nov– March closes at 4.30pm; free). Ravenna does have other strings to its bow, including some lovely sandy beaches (take bus #70 from the station).

ARRIVAL AND INFORMATION

By train Ravenna's train station is a 5min walk from the centre.
Destinations Bologna (hourly; 1hr 20min–2hr); Ferrara (hourly; 1hr 15min); Rimini (hourly; 1hr–1hr 10min).
Tourist office Piazza Caduti per la Libertà 2 (April–Sept Mon–Sat 8.30am–7pm, Sun 10am–6pm; Oct–March Mon–Sat 8.30am–6pm, Sun 10am–4pm; ☎0544 35 404, ⓦturismo.ravenna.it). The Classe tourist office is by the church at via Romea Sud 226 (Sat & Sun 9.30am–12.30pm; ☎0544 473 661).
Museum card A combined ticket (€9.50) is valid for seven days and covers all the church-controlled sights. It's available from any of the participating museums.

ACCOMMODATION

Hostel Dante Via Nicolodi 12 ☎0544 421 164, ⓦhostelravenna.com. HI hostel a 10min walk east of the station, handily opposite a large Co-op supermarket. An all-you-can-eat buffet breakfast is included in the price. Lock-out between noon and 2.30pm. Dorms **€21**, doubles **€27**

EATING AND DRINKING

Ca' De Ven Via C. Ricci 24 ☎0544 30 163, ⓦcadeven.it. Stunning wood-panelled *enoteca* with painted ceilings that has expanded into the airy glass-covered courtyard next door. It offers a simple menu of a few pizza and pasta dishes, as well as a selection of *piadine* for around €4.50. There's also a huge range of vintages to sample by the glass from €1.50 upwards. Tues–Sun 10am–2.30pm & 6–10.30pm.

Central Italy

The Italian heartland of **Tuscany** is one mass of picture-postcard landscapes made up of lovely, walled hill-top towns and rolling, vineyard-covered hills. **Florence** is the first port of call, home to a majestic Duomo, the extensive Uffizi gallery and the elegant Ponte Vecchio. **Siena**, one of the great medieval cities of Europe, is also the scene of Tuscany's one unmissable festival – the Palio – which sees bareback horseriders careering around the cobbled central square, while **Pisa's** leaning tower, a feat of engineering against gravity, and intricately decorated cathedral justifiably attract hordes of tourists. To the east lies **Umbria**, a beautiful region of thick woodland and undulating hills; the capital, **Perugia**, is an energetic student-dominated town, while **Assisi** is famed for its gorgeous setting and extraordinary frescoes by Giotto.

FLORENCE

FLORENCE (Firenze) is undoubtedly the highlight of Tuscany. Its chapels, galleries and museums are works of art in themselves, and every corner brings you face to face with architectural splendour. Some of the most famous pieces in Western art are on display here, including Michelangelo's *David* in the Accademia and Botticelli's *Birth of Venus* in the Uffizi.

WHAT TO SEE AND DO

Florence's major sights are contained within an area that can be crossed on foot in a little over half an hour. From Santa Maria Novella train station, most visitors gravitate towards **Piazza del Duomo**, beckoned by the pinnacle of the dome. **Via dei Calzaiuoli**, which runs south f rom the Duomo, is the main catwalk of the Florentine *passeggiata*, a broad pedestrianized avenue lined with shops. It ends at Florence's other main square, the **Piazza della Signoria**, fringed on one side by the graceful late fourteenth-century **Loggia della Signoria** and dotted with statues, most famously a copy of Michelangelo's *David*.

The Duomo

The **Duomo** (daily 10am–5pm; free; €15 il Grande Museo del Duomo ticket includes entry to the sights below; ⓦilgrandemuseodelduomo.it) was built between the late thirteenth and mid-fifteenth centuries. The third-largest church in the world, its ambience is more that of a great assembly hall than of a devotional building. The seven stained-glass roundels, designed by Uccello, Ghiberti, Castagno and Donatello, are best inspected from a gallery that forms part of the route to the top of the dome (daily 8.30am–6.20pm), from where the views are stupendous. Next door to the Duomo stands the **Campanile** (daily 8.15am–6.50pm), begun by Giotto in 1334. As well as offering an impressive bird's-eye view of Florence, this contains several enormous bells and more than fifty intricately carved marble reliefs. Opposite, the **Baptistery** (daily 8.15–10.15am & 11.15am–6.30pm), generally thought to date from the sixth or seventh century, is the oldest building in the city. Its gilded bronze doors were cast in the early fifteenth century by Lorenzo Ghiberti, and described by Michelangelo as "so beautiful they are worthy to be the gates of Paradise". Inside, it is equally stunning, with a thirteenth-century mosaic floor and ceiling and the tomb of Pope John XXIII, the work of Donatello and his pupil Michelozzo.

The Palazzo Vecchio

The tourist-thronged **Piazza della Signoria** is dominated by the colossal **Palazzo Vecchio**, Florence's fortress-like town hall (April–Sept Mon–Wed & Fri–Sun 9am–11pm, tower closes at 9pm, Thurs 9am–2pm; Oct–March Mon–Wed & Fri–Sun 9am–7pm, tower closes 5pm, Thurs 9am–2pm; palazzo €10, tower €10, combined ticket €14), begun in the last year of the thirteenth century as the home of the Signoria, the highest tier of the city's republican government. A staircase leads to its **tower**; the view at the top of the 223-step climb rivals that from the cathedral dome.

The Uffizi

Immediately south of the Palazzo Vecchio, the **Galleria degli Uffizi** (Tues–Sun 8.15am–6.50pm; booking advisable online; €8; ⓦwww.uffizi.firenze .it) is the greatest picture gallery in Italy. Highlights include Filippo Lippi's *Madonna and Child with Two Angels*

and some of Botticelli's most famous works, notably the *Birth of Venus*. While the Uffizi doesn't own a finished painting that's entirely by Leonardo da Vinci, there's a celebrated *Annunciation* that's mainly by him, and Michelangelo's *Doni Tondo*, found in Room 18, is his only completed easel painting.

Bargello

The **Bargello** museum (Tues–Sat 8.15am–1.50pm, plus 2nd & 4th Sun of month and 1st, 3rd & 5th Mon of month, same hours; €4, €7 during exhibitions) lies just northwest of the Uffizi in Via del Proconsolo. The collection contains numerous works by Michelangelo, Cellini and Giambologna. Upstairs is Donatello's sexually ambiguous bronze *David*, the first freestanding nude figure since classical times, cast in the early 1430s.

San Lorenzo

The church of **San Lorenzo** (Mon–Sat 10am–5pm, Sun 1.30–5pm; Nov–Feb closed Sun; €7 combined ticket with Biblioteca Medicea-Laurenziana), north of Piazza del Duomo, has a strong claim to be the oldest church in Florence. At the top of the left aisle and through the cloisters, the **Biblioteca Medicea-Laurenziana** (Mon–Sat 9.30am–1.30pm; same ticket) was designed by Michelangelo in 1524; its most startling feature is the vestibule, a room almost filled by a flight of steps resembling a solidified lava flow.

Accademia

Northeast of San Lorenzo, the **Accademia** (Tues–Sun 8.15am–6.50pm; €8), Europe's first school of drawing, is swamped by people wanting to see Michelangelo's *David*. Finished in 1504, when the artist was just 29, and carved from a gigantic block of marble, it's an incomparable show of technical bravura.

Santa Croce

Down by the river, to the southeast of the centre, the church of **Santa Croce** (Mon–Sat 9.30am–5.30pm, Sun 2–5.30pm; €6), begun in 1294, is

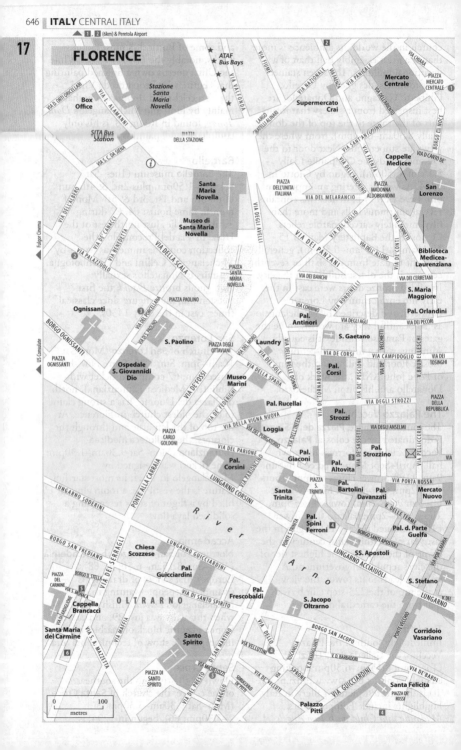

17

FLORENCE

★ ATAF
★ Bus Bays
★
★
★

Box
Office

Stazione
Santa
Maria
Novella

SITA Bus
Station

ℹ

Fulgor Cinema

US Consolate

2

VIA D. ORTI ORICELLARI

VIA L. ALAMANNI

VIA S. C. DA SIENA

VIA DELL'ALBERO

VIA DE CAMACCI

VIA DELLA SCALA

VIA DE PALAZZUOLO

VIA BENEDETTA

PIAZZA
SANTA
MARIA
NOVELLA

Santa
Maria
Novella

Museo di
Santa Maria
Novella

VIA FIUME

VIA VALFONDA

LARGO
FRATELLI ALINARI

DELLA STAZIONE

VIA DEGLI AVELLI

VIA SANT'ANTONINO

VIA PANICALE

VIA FAENZA

VIA NAZIONALE

VIA DEL MELARANCIO

PIAZZA
DELL'UNITA
ITALIANA

VIA DELL'AMORINO

PIAZZA
MADONNA
ALDOBRANDINI

Supermercato
Crai

Mercato
Centrale

PIAZZA
MERCATO
CENTRALE **1**

VIA DELL'ARIENTO

VIA CHIARA

BORGO LA NOCE

VIA D. CANTO DE NELLI

Cappelle
Medicee

San
Lorenzo

VIA FAENZA

PIAZZA
SAN
GIOVANNI

2

VIA DEI PANZANI

VIA DEI BANCHI

VIA DEL GIGLIO

VIA DE CONTI

VIA DELL'ALLORO

VIA ZANNETTI

Biblioteca
Medicea-
Laurenziana

S. Maria
Maggiore

Pal. Orlandini

VIA DEI CERRETANI

VIA DEI RONDINELLI

Ognissanti

BORGO OGNISSANTI

PIAZZA
OGNISSANTI

PIAZZA PAOLINO

VIA DEL PORCELLANA

VIA S. PAOLINO

S. Paolino

Ospedale
S. Giovanni di
Dio

VIA DE FOSSI

S. Maria
Maggiore

Pal.
Antinori

S. Gaetano

Laundry

Museo
Marini

Pal. Rucellai

VIA DEL MORO

VIA DELLE BELLE DONNE

VIA DEI CORNINO

VIA DEGLI AGLI

VIA DEI PECORI

VIA DE' CORSI

VIA CAMPIDOGLIO

VIA DE' PESCIONI

VIA DE'

VIA DE' TORNABUONI

Pal.
Corsi

Pal.
Strozzi

VIA DEGLI STROZZI

VIA DEGLI ANSELMI

PIAZZA
DELLA
REPUBBLICA

VIA BRUNELLESCHI

VIA DE' TOSINGHI

PIAZZA
DELLA
REPUBBLICA

VIA DELLA SPADA

VIA DEL SOLE

VIA DELLA VIGNA NUOVA

VIA DELL'INFERNO

Loggia

VIA DEL PURGATORIO

VIA DE' FEDERIGHI

PIAZZA
CARLO
GOLDONI

Pal.
Corsini

PONTE ALLA CARRAIA

LUNGARNO CORSINI

VIA DEL PARIONE

VIA DEL PARIONCINO

Pal.
Giaconi

Pal.
Altovita

Pal.
Strozzino

VIA DE SASSETTI

VIA PORTA ROSSA

VIA PELLICCERIA

Pal.
Bartolini

Pal.
Davanzati

Mercato
Nuovo

V. DELLE TERME

3

Santa
Trinita

PIAZZA
S.
TRINITA

PONTE S. TRINITA

Pal.
Spini
Ferroni

4

BORGO SANTI APOSTOLI

Pal. d. Parte
Guelfa

SS. Apostoli

VIA POR S. MARIA

LUNGARNO ACCIAIUOLI

R i v e r

A r n o

LUNGARNO SODERINI

BORGO SAN FREDIANO

PIAZZA
DEL
CARMINE

VIA S. MONACA

BORGO D. STELLA

VIA DE SERRAGLI

Chiesa
Scozzese

LUNGARNO GUICCIARDINI

Pal.
Guicciardini

5

Cappella
Brancacci

Santa Maria
del Carmine

6

VIA M. D'ANGIOLINO

VIA S. A. MAZETTA

VIA MAFFIA

O L T R A R N O

Pal.
Frescobaldi

VIA DI SANTO SPIRITO

Pal.
Frescobaldi

Santo
Spirito

PIAZZA DI
SANTO
SPIRITO

VIA DEL PRESTO

VIA MAGGIO

VIA MICHELOZZI

VIA DELLO SPRONE

VIA DI SAN MARTINO

VIA SANT'AGOSTINO

S. Jacopo
Oltrarno

VIA DELLO

VIA DE' VELLUTI

VIA TOSCANELLA

S. R. RANGIANTI

VELLUTINI

BORGO SAN JACOPO

V. D. BARBADORI

SPRONE

S. Stefano

LUNGARNO

V. DEI

Corridoio
Vasariano

PONTE VECCHIO

BORGO SAN JACOPO

VIA GUICCIARDINI

VIA DE' BARDI

Santa Felicita

PIAZZA DE'
ROSSI

4

Palazzo
Pitti

SDRUCCIOLO DE' PITTI

0   100
      metres

0   100

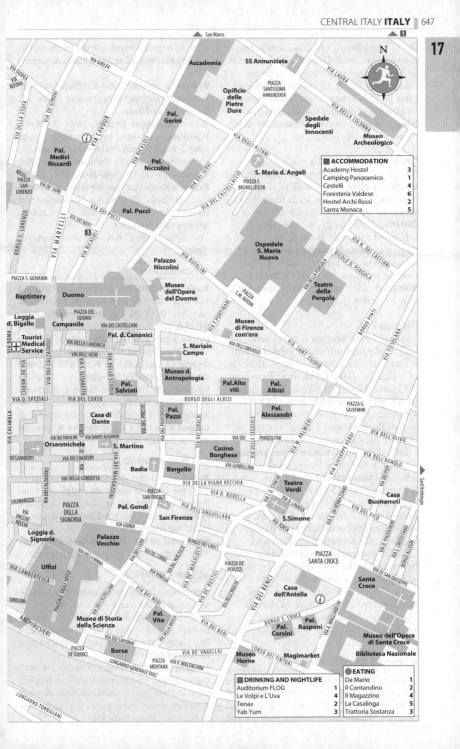

▲ San Marco

▲ ❶

N

VIA TADDEA
VIA ROSINA
VIA GUELFA
VIA DE' GINORI
VIA DELLA STUFA
VIA CAVOUR
VIA RICASOLI
VIA DEGLI ALFANI
VIA DELLA COLONNA
VIA LAURA

Accademia
SS Annunziata
Opificio delle Pietre Dure
PIAZZA SANTISSIMA ANNUNZIATA
Pal. Gerini
Spedale degli Innocenti
Museo Archeologico
Pal. Medici Riccardi
Pal. Niccolini
S. Maria d. Angeli
NELLI PIAZZA SAN LORENZO
VIA DE' GORI
VIA DEI SERVI
PIAZZA F. BRUNELLESCHI
VIA DEL CASTELLACCIO

BORGO S. LORENZO
VIA MARTELLI
VIA DEI BIFFI
VIA DEI PUCCI
Pal. Pucci
VIA RICASOLI

ACCOMMODATION
Academy Hostel	3
Camping Panoramico	1
Cestelli	4
Foresteria Valdese	6
Hostel Archi Rossi	2
Santa Monaca	5

❸

VIA BUFALINI
Palazzo Niccolini
Ospedale S. Maria Nuova
VIA N. DEI CACCINI
VICOLO D. PERGOLA
VIA DELLA PERGOLA

PIAZZA S. GIOVANNI
Museo dell'Opera del Duomo
PIAZZA S.M. NUOVA
Teatro della Pergola
BORGO PINTI

Baptistery
Duomo
PIAZZA DEL DUOMO
Campanile
VIA DEI CASTELLANI
Museo di Firenze com'era
VIA SANT'EGIDIO

Loggia d. Bigallo
VIA ROMA
Pal. d. Canonici
VIA DELL'ORIUOLO
VIA DE' PORTINARI
VIA FIESOLANA

Tourist Medical Service
VIA DELLA CANONICA
VIA DELLE OCHE
VIA DELLO STUDIO
S. Maria in Campo
VIA DE' MEDICI
VIA DEI CALZAIUOLI
VIA S. ELISABETTA
Pal. Salviati
Museo d. Antropologia
Pal. Alto viti
Pal. Albizi

VIA D. SPEZIALI
VIA DEL CORSO
BORGO DEGLI ALBIZI
PIAZZA G. SALVEMINI

VIA CALIMALA
Casa di Dante
Pal. Pazzi
Pal. Alessandri
VIA DELL'ULIVO

VIA DEI TAVOLINI
VIA DANTE ALIGHIERI
VIA DEL PRESTO
VIA DEL PROCONSOLO
VIA DEI GIRALDI
VIA DELLE SEGGIOLE
PANDOLFINI
VIA M. PALMIERI
VIA GIUSEPPE VERDI
VIA DELL'AGNOLO

DE' LAMBERTI
Orsanmichele
S. Martino
VIA DEI CIMATORI
Casino Borghese
VIA DEI
VIA DE PEPI

VIA DEI CALZAIUOLI
Badia
Bargello
VIA GHIBELLINA
Teatro Verdi
VIA GHIBELLINA
Casa Buonarroti
VIA DEL FICO

VIA DELLA CONDOTTA
VIA DELLA VIGNA VECCHIA
VIA D. PINOCHERE

CALIMARUZZA
PIAZZA SAN FIRENZE
VIA D. BURELLA
VIA D. STINCHE
VIA D. LAVATOI
VIA GHIBELLINA DE' MACCI
VIA S. CRISTOFANO
BORGO ALLEGRI

VIA VACCHE-RECCIA
PIAZZA DELLA SIGNORIA
Pal. Gondi
San Firenze
VIA DELL'ANGUILLARA
S.Simone
VIA TORTA
PIAZZA SANTA CROCE

Loggia d. Signoria
Palazzo Vecchio
VIA GONDI
BORGO DEI GRECI
Santa Croce

Uffizi
VIA DELLA NINNA
VIA DEI LEONI
VIA DEL CORNO
VINEGIA
VIA DE' MAGALOTTI
PIAZZA DE' PERUZZI
PIAZZA SANTA CROCE
VIA DI SAN GIUSEPPE
VIA S. GIUSEPPE

VIA LAMBERTESCA
PIAZZALE DEGLI UFFIZI
VIA DE' RUSTICI
VIA DELLE BRACHE
Casa dell'Antella
VIA A. MAGLIABECHI
Museo dell'Opera di Santa Croce

GIROLAMI
VIA DEI NERI
VIA DEI BENCI
Santa Croce

ARCHIBUSIERI
VIA DEI CASTELLANI
Pal. Vita
VIA DELLA MOSCA
VIA DEI NERI
BORGO S. CROCE
Pal. Rasponi
Pal. Corsini

Museo di Storia della Scienza
VIA DEI SAPONAI
Borsa
PIAZZA DE' GIUDICI
PIAZZA MENTANA
VIA DE' VAGELLAI
VIA V. MALENCHINI
CORSO DEI TINTORI
Museo Horne
Magimarket
Museo dell'Opera di Santa Croce
Biblioteca Nazionale

LUNGARNO GENERALE DIAZ
LUNGARNO TORRIGIANI

DRINKING AND NIGHTLIFE
Auditorium FLOG	1
Le Volpi e L'Uva	4
Tenax	2
Yab Yum	3

EATING
Da Mario	1
Il Contandino	2
Il Magazzino	4
La Casalinga	5
Trattoria Sostanza	3

17

full of tombstones and commemorative monuments, including Vasari's memorial to Michelangelo and, on the opposite side of the church, the tomb of Galileo, built in 1737 when it was finally agreed to give the scientist a Christian burial. Most visitors, however, come to see the dazzling frescoes by Giotto.

Oltrarno and beyond

The photogenic thirteenth-century **Ponte Vecchio**, loaded with jewellers' shops overhanging the water, leads from the city centre across the river to the district of **Oltrarno**. Head west, past the relaxed, café-lined square of **Santo Spirito**, to the church of **Santa Maria del Carmine** – an essential visit for the superbly restored frescoes by Masaccio in its **Cappella Brancacci** (Mon & Wed–Sat 10am–5pm, Sun 1–5pm; €6).

Palazzo Pitti

South of Ponte Vecchio is the massive bulk of the fifteenth-century **Palazzo Pitti**. It contains six separate museums, the best of which, the **Galleria Palatina** (Tues–Sun 8.15am–6.50pm; €8.50 combined ticket with Galleria d'Arte Moderna, €13 if a special exhibition is on), houses some superb Raphaels and Titians. The rest of the first floor is dominated by the state rooms of the **Appartamenti Monumentali**. The Pitti's enormous formal garden, the delightful **Giardino di Boboli** (Tues–Sun 8.15am–4.30pm; March till 5.30pm; April, May, Sept & Oct till 6.30pm; June–Aug till 7.30pm; €7, €10 during exhibitions; ticket includes the Bardini Gardens, the Argenti, Porcellane and Costume museums), is also worth a visit. Beyond here, the multicoloured facade of **San Miniato al Monte** (Mon–Sat 9.30am–1pm & 3–7pm, Sun 3–7pm; free) lures troops of visitors up the hill. The interior is like no other in the city, and its form has changed little since the mid-eleventh century.

ARRIVAL AND DEPARTURE

By plane Pisa's Galileo Galilei airport (see p.651) is the main airport for Tuscany. A small number of international air services use Peretola (or Amerigo Vespucci) airport (☎ 055 306 1300, ⓦ aeroporto.firenze.it), 5km northwest

of the city centre; the Volainbus service provides shuttles from here into Florence Santa Maria Novella station every 30min.

By train The main train station is at Piazza Santa Maria Novella, in the northwest of the city centre, a 10min walk from the Piazza del Duomo.

Destinations Bologna (frequent; 35min–1hr 20min); Milan (frequent; 1hr 40min); Naples (hourly; 3hr); Perugia (every 2–4hr; 2hr 10min); Pisa (every 20min; 50min–1hr 25min); Rome (frequent; 1hr 30min); Venice (hourly; 2hr); Verona (every 1–2hr; 1hr 35min–2hr 30min).

By bus The main bus station is close to the train station on Via Santa Caterina da Siena. Use bus company Sena (ⓦ sena.it) for longer journeys. ATAF (ⓦ www.ataf.net) runs the reliable local service.

Destinations Perugia (1 daily; 4hr); Siena (hourly; 1hr 30min).

INFORMATION

Tourist office The main tourist office is at Via Cavour 1r, a 5min walk north of the Duomo (Mon–Fri 9am–6pm, Sat 9am–2pm; ☎ 055 290 832, ⓦ www.firenzeturismo.it); this office provides information on the whole Florence province. Smaller offices are at the Loggia del Bigallo, by the Baptistery (Mon–Sat 9am–7pm, Sun 9am–2pm), and opposite the train station, at Piazza della Stazione 5 (Mon–Sat 9am–7pm, Sun 9am–2pm).

Discount card Pick up the Firenze card (ⓦ www .firenzecard.it) at the offices; it's pricey at €72/3 days but includes scores of the city's museums and all use of all transport in the city; it also enables you to bypass the queues at the major museums.

GETTING AROUND

By bus For cross-town journeys you might want to use ATAF buses. Tickets are valid for unlimited journeys within 90min (€1.20), 24hr (€5) or 72hr (€12). A Biglietto Multiplo gives four 90min tickets for €4.50; they can be bought from *tabacchi*.

Bike rental Rentway, Piazza San Benedetto 1r (daily 10am–7.30pm; €14/day; ⓦ segwayrentflorence.com).

ACCOMMODATION

Florence's most affordable hotels are close to the station, in particular along and around Via Faenza, Via Fiume, Via della Scala and Piazza di Santa Maria Novella. Advance booking is advisable, or head to the tourist office on Piazza Della Stazione where there is a hotel booking office inside the same building.

Academy Hostel Via Ricasoli 9 ☎ 055 239 8665, ⓦ academyhostel.it. Set in a seventeenth-century *palazzo* just a short walk from the Duomo, this hostel offers airy, high-ceilinged rooms and a common area with flatscreen TV, plus a sunny terrace. Dorms **€38**

17

Camping Panoramico Via Peramondo 1, Fiesole ☎055 559 069, ⓦflorencecamping.com. Located in Fiesole, a short bus ride from central Florence, this 120-pitch three-star site has a bar, restaurant, pool and small supermarket. Mid-March to Nov. Pitches per adult €7, plus per tent €6

Cestelli Borgo SS. Apostoli 25 ☎055 214 213, ⓦhotelcestelli.com. Spotlessly maintained by its young Florentine-Japanese owners and offering excellent value for money, this eight-roomed one-star occupies part of a house that once belonged to a minor Medici. The rooms are a good size, and most are en suite. €100

Foresteria Valdese Firenze–Istituto Gould Via dei Serragli 49 ☎055 212 576, ⓦfirenzeforesteria.it. Run by the Waldensian Church, this hostel-cum-evangelical college occupies part of a seventeenth-century *palazzo*. The 99 beds are extremely popular, so book in advance. Street-front rooms can be noisy but the old courtyard, terracotta floors and stone staircases provide atmosphere. Dorms €25

Hostel Archi Rossi Via Faenza 94r ☎055 290 804, ⓦhostelarchirossi.com. Lively, arty and ultra-efficient hostel right by the station with a superb private garden. Cheap evening meals are available. There are also free pizza and pasta nights and free daily walking tours. Dorms €30, doubles €100

Santa Monaca Via S. Monaca 6 ☎055 268 338, ⓦostello .it. This hostel in Oltrarno, close to the Carmine, has 115 beds in rooms sleeping up to 22, both mixed and female-only. Kitchen facilities (no utensils), washing machines and a useful noticeboard with information on lifts and onward travel. Check-in 6am–2am; bedrooms have to be vacated between 10am and 2pm. Curfew 2am. Dorms €20

EATING

The best place to find picnic food and snacks is the Mercato Centrale, just east of the train station, or Mercato di Sant'Ambrogio. Both markets close at 2pm. Supermarket Il Centro is at Borgo Degli Albizi 57.

Da Mario Via Rosina 2r ☎055 218 550, ⓦtrattoria-mario .com. Located close to the Mercato Centrale, *Da Mario* has probably been packed out every lunchtime since the Colsi family started running the place in 1953. For earthy Florentine cooking at very low prices, there's nowhere better. Mon–Sat noon–3.30pm.

Il Contadino Via Palazzuolo 69–71r ☎055 238 2673. This small place is an excellent choice for lunch, with set meals at €9 or €11. Set dinner starts at €13.50. Daily noon–10pm.

Il Magazzino Piazza della Passera 2–3 ☎055 215 969. This earthily authentic osteria-*tripperia* serves hearty dishes of pasta, tripe and beef at around €10–18. Daily noon–3pm & 7.30–11pm.

La Casalinga Via Michelozzi 9r ☎055 218 624, ⓦtrattorialacasalinga.it. People are willing to queue a long time for a table at this great-value trattoria that serves old-style family Italian cooking. *Primi* around €7. Mon–Sat noon–2.30pm & 7–10pm.

★**Trattoria Sostanza** 25 Via Porcellana ☎055 212 691. Affectionately known as "the trough", this is where the real Florentines have been going for the best *bistecca* in town (about €25 for two) since 1869. A simple, no-frills affair, with hearty portions of superlative food. Booking recommended. Mon–Fri 12.30–2pm & 7.30–9.45pm; April, May, Sept & Oct open Sat.

DRINKING AND NIGHTLIFE

Mercato Centrale, just east of the train station, has some of Florence's cheapest bars. For listings information, call in at the box office, Via Delle Vecchie Carceri 1 (☎055 210 804).

Auditorium FLOG Via Michele Mercati 24b ☎055 477 978, ⓦwww.flog.it; bus #4 or #28 from Santa Maria Novella. One of the city's best-known mid-sized venues, and a perennial student favourite for all forms of live music (and DJs), but particularly local indie-type bands. It's usually packed, despite being way out in the northern suburbs.

★**Le Volpi e L'Uva** Piazza dei Rossi 1r, off Piazza di Santa Felicità ☎055 239 8132. This friendly and successful little *enoteca* serves at least two dozen wines by the glass, most of them from small vineyards. A selection of tasty cold meats and snacks is on offer, and there are a few tables on the nice little terrace. Mon–Sat 11am–9pm.

Tenax Via Pratese 46 ⓦtenax.org. Bus #29 or #30. The city's biggest club and one of its leading venues for new and established bands, playing an eclectic mix of indie, trance, pop and old classics. Admission €20–25. Mid–Sept to Mid–May Thurs–Sat 10pm–3am.

Yab Yum Via de' Sassetti 5r ☎055 215 160, ⓦyab.it. Smart city-centre basement club near the Duomo, known throughout the country for Monday's Yabsmoove – Italy's longest-running hip-hop night. Oct–May Mon & Wed–Sat 7pm–4am.

FLORENCE'S FESTIVALS AND EVENTS

In summer there are often open-air screens at various places – check *Firenze Spettacolo* for the latest screenings. In May the **Maggio Musicale** (ⓦmaggiofiorentino .com) puts on concerts, gigs and other events throughout the city, while **St John's Day** (June 24) sees a massive fireworks display on Piazzale Michelangelo and the final of the Calcio Storico on Piazza Santa Croce, a violent hybrid of rugby, boxing and wrestling, played out between the city's four *quartieri*.

17

DIRECTORY

Consulates The UK consulate for northern Italy is in Milan; the US has a consulate in Florence, at Lungarno Amerigo Vespucci 38 (☎055 266 951).

Hospitals Santa Maria Nuova, Piazza Santa Maria Nuova 1 ☎055 69 381, ⓦwww.asf.toscana.it. English-speaking doctors are on 24hr call at the Tourist Medical Service, Via Roma 4 ☎055 475 111, ⓦmedicalservice .firenze.it.

Post office Via Pellicceria 3 (Mon–Fri 8.20am–7.05pm, Sat 8.20am–12.35pm).

PISA

The Leaning Tower in **PISA** is an iconic image, yet its stunning beauty is often underrated, with its intricate carvings appearing as though they are icing details on a very large wedding cake. It's set alongside the **Duomo** and **Baptistery** on the manicured grass of the lovely **Campo Piazza dei Miracoli**, whose buildings date from the eleventh and twelfth centuries, when Pisa was one of the great Mediterranean powers. Beyond this pretty square, the city synonymous with Galileo, Shelley and Byron may lack the polish of a Siena or a Florence but it is still definitely worth a meander along its charming narrow streets.

WHAT TO SEE AND DO

Leaning Tower

Perhaps the strangest thing about the **Leaning Tower** (daily: Jan & Dec 10am–5pm; Feb & Nov 9.40am–5.40pm; March 9am–6pm; April–Sept 9am–8pm; Oct 9am–7pm; €18; book ahead at ⓦwww.opapisa.it/ boxoffice), begun in 1173, is that it has always tilted; subsidence disrupted the foundations when it had reached just three of its eight storeys. For the next 180 years a succession of architects was brought in to try to correct the tilt, until 1350 when the angle was accepted and the tower completed. Eight centuries after its construction, it was thought to be nearing its limit, and the tower, supported by steel wires, was closed to the public in the 1990s – though it's open for visits once again now that the tilt (and 3.9m overhang) has been successfully halted.

PISA'S FESTIVALS

Pisa is known for its **Gioco del Ponte**, usually held on the last Sunday in June, when teams from the north and south banks of the city stage a series of "battles", including pushing a seven-tonne carriage over the Ponte di Mezzo. But the town's most magical event is the **Luminara** on June 16, when buildings along the river are festooned with candles to celebrate San Ranieri, the city's patron saint.

Duomo and Baptistery

The **Duomo** (daily: March 10am–6pm; April–Sept 10am–8pm; Oct 10am–7pm; Nov–Feb 10am–12.45pm & 2–5pm; no admittance to tourists before 1pm on Sun; free) was begun a century earlier than the Tower, its facade – a delicate balance of black and white marble, and tiers of arcades – setting the model for Pisa's highly distinctive brand of Romanesque. The third building of the Miracoli ensemble, the circular **Baptistery** (daily: March 9am–6pm; April–Sept 8am–8pm; Oct 9am–7pm; Nov–Feb 10am–5pm; €5), is a slightly bizarre mix of Romanesque and Gothic, embellished with statues (now largely copies) by Giovanni Pisano and his father Nicola. The originals are displayed in the Opera del Duomo **museum** (March 9am–6pm; April–Sept 8am–8pm; Oct 9am–7pm; Nov–Feb 10am–5pm; €5) to the east of Piazza del Duomo.

Camposanto

Along the north side of the Campo dei Miracoli is the **Camposanto** (daily: March 9am–6pm; April–Sept 8am–8pm; Oct 9am–7pm; Nov–Feb 10am–5pm; €5), a cloistered cemetery built towards the end of the thirteenth century. Most of its frescoes were destroyed by Allied bombing in World War II, but two masterpieces survived relatively unscathed in the Cappella Ammannati – a fourteenth-century *Triumph of Death*, and *The Last Judgement*, a ruthless catalogue of horrors painted around the time of the Black Death.

ARRIVAL AND DEPARTURE

By plane Pisa's airport (ⓦwww.pisa-airport.com) is about 1km south of the city centre. The PisaMover rail connects the airport to the city centre every 5–8min in less than 10min. Alternatively, the LAM Rossa city bus (€1.30) connects the airport to Pisa Centrale.

By train Pisa's picturesque train station is south of the centre on Piazza della Stazione, a 30min walk from Campo dei Miracoli. Take bus LAM Rossa for the 10min journey to the Leaning Tower.

Destinations Florence (every 15–30min; 50min–1hr 20min); Lucca (every 30min; 25min).

By bus A bus shuttles between Florence and Pisa airport (hourly; 1hr 10min).

INFORMATION

Tourist office Piazza Vittorio Emanuele 16, near the train station (daily 10am–1pm & 2–4pm; ☎050 42 291, ⓦwww.turismo.pisa.it and ⓦpisaunicaterra.it). There's usually also an information desk at Piazza del Duomo 7, by the Leaning Tower (daily 9.30am–5.30pm).

Discount card A tourist ticket (€9) gives admission to most of Piazza dei Miracoli's sights and museums, but not the Leaning Tower. Available from the ticket office on the north side of the Leaning Tower, and inside the Museo delle Sinopie (or book online ⓦwww.opapisa.it).

ACCOMMODATION

Campeggio Torre Pendente Viale delle Cascine 86 ☎050 561 704, ⓦcampingtorrependente.it. Large, well-maintained campsite 1km west of Campo Piazza dei Miracoli, with a restaurant, shop and large outdoor swimming pool. Open week before Easter–early Nov. Per person €11, plus tent €11

Hostel Pisa Via Corridoni 29 ☎050 520 1841, ⓦhostelpisa .it. An excellent hostel a 5min walk from the train station. Great courtyard and facilities including billiards and chess; rental bikes from €5/day. Dorms €15, doubles €40

Michele Guest House Via Vespucci 103 ☎333 601 1287, ⓦguest-house.it. Run by photographer Michele, this excellent B&B has luxurious rooms full of his work. Take advantage of the owner's extensive knowledge of the area. Doubles €65

EATING

Avoid eating around the Tower if you can, as prices here are sky-high for tourists. There are plenty of cheap eateries and studenty bars around Piazza Dante and Piazza delle Vettovaglie, and between Piazza Garibaldi and Piazza Cairoli.

Da Cucciolo Vicolo Rosselmini 9. The family-run *Cucciolo* has been in business for almost half a century, and is one of the city's most reliable trattorias, offering unfussy and delicious traditional meals, at around €10 for a main course. Mon–Sat noon–2.30pm & 7.30–10pm.

De' Coltelli Lungarno Pacinotti 23. The De' Coltelli family are credited with having devised the recipe for ice cream back in the seventeenth century, and the shop that bears their name is one of Italy's top-rank *gelaterie*, with a penchant for adventurous concoctions – anyone for seafood ice cream? Mon–Thurs & Sun noon–10.30pm, Fri & Sat noon–midnight.

Osteria dei Cavalieri Via San Frediano 16. Tucked away behind Piazza dei Cavalieri, this restaurant boasts a great menu (most *secondi* under €15) and wine list. Reservations recommended in high season. Mon–Fri 12.30–2pm & 7.45–10.30pm, Sat 7.45–10.30pm.

Vineria di Piazza Piazza delle Vettovaglie 13. Reliable and good-value dishes (mains about €8–10) are served at this friendly little place where the menu is scribbled on a blackboard. Tues–Sun 12.15–2.30pm.

SIENA

SIENA, 60km south of Florence, is the perfect antidote to its better-known neighbour. Self-contained behind excellently preserved medieval walls, its cityscape is a majestic Gothic attraction that you can roam around and enjoy without venturing into a single museum. During the Middle Ages, Siena was one of the major cities of Europe – the size of Paris, it controlled most of southern Tuscany and developed a highly sophisticated civic life, with its own written constitution and a quasi-democratic government.

WHAT TO SEE AND DO

The **Campo** is the centre of Siena in every sense: the main streets lead into it, the Palio (see box, p.653) takes place around its café-lined perimeter, and it's the natural place to gravitate towards. It deserves its reputation as one of Italy's most beautiful squares, and taking a picnic onto the red stones to watch the shadows move around the square is a good way to while away an afternoon.

The Palazzo Pubblico

The **Palazzo Pubblico** with its 107m-high bell tower, the **Torre del Mangia**, occupies virtually the entire south side of the square, and although it's still in use as Siena's town hall, its principal rooms have been converted into a museum (daily: mid-March to Oct 10am–7pm; Nov to

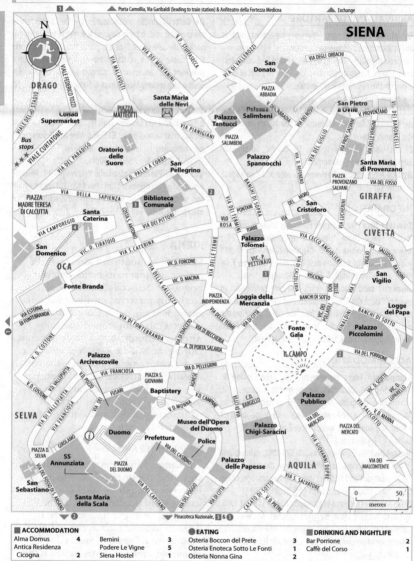

SIENA

■ ACCOMMODATION			● EATING		■ DRINKING AND NIGHTLIFE	
Alma Domus	4	Bernini	3	Osteria Boccon del Prete	3	Bar Porrione	2
Antica Residenza		Podere Le Vigne	5	Osteria Enoteca Sotto Le Fonti	1	Caffè del Corso	1
Cicogna	2	Siena Hostel	1	Osteria Nonna Gina	2		

mid-March 10am–6pm; €9), frescoed with themes integral to the secular life of the medieval city.

Around the Campo

Between buildings at the top end of the Campo, the fifteenth-century **Loggia di Mercanzia**, built as a dealing room for merchants, marks the intersection of the city centre's principal streets. From here **Via Banchi di Sotto** leads east to the **Palazzo Piccolomini** and on into the workaday quarter of **San Martino**. From the Campo, Via di Città cuts west across the oldest quarter of the city, fronted by some of Siena's finest private *palazzi*. At the end of the street, Via San Pietro leads to the **Pinacoteca Nazionale** (Mon & Sun

9am–1pm, Tues–Sat 10am–6pm; €4; ⓦpinacotecanazionale.siena.it), a fourteenth-century palace housing a roll call of Sienese Gothic painting.

The Duomo

Southwest of Il Campo, the **Duomo** (March–Oct Mon–Sat 10.30am–7pm, Sun 1.30–6pm; March only Sun 1.30–5.30pm; Nov–Feb Mon–Sat 10.30am–5.30pm, Sun 1.30–5.30pm; €4, or €7 during the summer uncovering of the marble pavement; early Nov & early Jan–Feb entrance free, but €2 for Libreria Piccolomini) was completed to virtually its present size around 1215; plans to enlarge it withered with Siena's medieval prosperity. The building is a delight, its style an amazing mix of Romanesque and Gothic, delineated by bands of black and white marble on its facade. Inside, a startling sequence of 56 panels, completed between 1349 and 1547, features virtually every artist who worked in the city. Midway along the nave, the **Libreria Piccolomini**, signalled by Pinturicchio's brilliantly coloured fresco of the *Coronation of Pius II*, has superbly vivid frescoes.

Museums

Opposite the Duomo is the complex of **Santa Maria della Scala** (May–Oct daily 10.30am–6.30pm; Nov–April Mon, Wed & Thurs 10.30am–4.30pm, Fri–Sun 10.30am–6.30pm; €9), the city's hospital for over eight hundred years and now a vast museum that includes the frescoed Sala del Pellegrinaio. The **Museo dell'Opera del Duomo** (March–Oct Mon–Sat 10.30am–7pm, Sun 1.30–6pm, March only Sun 1.30–5.30pm; Nov–Feb Mon–Sat 10.30am–5.30pm, Sun 1.30–5.30pm; €7), tucked into a corner of the Duomo extension, offers a fine perspective: follow the "Panorama dal Facciatone" signs to steep spiral stairs that climb up to the top of the building; the views are sensational but the topmost walkway is narrow and scarily exposed.

ARRIVAL AND DEPARTURE

By train Siena's train station is 2km northwest of town. Cross the road and take bus #3 or #9 to Tozzi; #7, #17 or #77 to Garibaldi/Sale; #8 or #10 to Gramsci (it's a good 20–25min uphill walk to the centre from the station, and not recommended).

Destinations Florence (hourly; 1hr 30min); Pisa (via Empoli; every 30min–1hr; 1hr 45min).

By bus Most intercity buses arrive on or near Viale Federico Tozzi, the road running alongside Piazza Gramsci–Piazza Matteotti, or at nearby La Lizza, but some terminate at the train station or at San Domenico. Buses are run by Tiemme (ⓣ0577 204 111, ⓦsienamobilita.it), which also runs services to and from Florence.

Destinations Bologna (2 daily; 3hr); Florence (30 daily; 1hr 15min–3hr); Pisa airport (1 daily; 1hr 50min); San Gimignano (10 daily; 1hr 5min–1hr 15min); Turin (4 weekly; 6hr 45min); Venice (2 daily; 5hr 20min).

THE SIENA PALIO

The **Siena Palio** is the most spectacular festival in Italy, a minute-and-a-half-long bareback horse race around the Campo contested twice a year (July 2 and August 16, each of which is preceded by all manner of trial races and processions) between the seventeen ancient wards – or *contrade* – of the city. Even now, a person's *contrada* frequently determines which churches they attend and where they socialize. There's a big build-up, with trials and processions for days before the big event, and traditionally all Sienese return to their *contrada* the night before the race; emotions run too high for rivals to be together, even if they're husband and wife. The Palio itself is a hectic spectacle whose rules haven't been rewritten since the race began – thus, supposedly, everything is allowed except to gouge your opponents' eyes out. On occasions it can take up to an hour to even start the race due to false starts. For the best view, you need to have found a position on the inner rail by 2pm and to keep it for the next seven hours. Beware that toilets, shade and refreshments are minimal, the swell of the crowd can be overwhelming, and you won't be able to leave the Campo for at least two hours after the race. If you haven't booked a hotel room, reckon on staying up all night (for more information see ⓦilpalio.org).

17

FESTIVALS

Open-air film festival **Cinema in Fortezza** runs from the end of June until the beginning of September. Screenings of the films, varying from slapstick American comedies and world arthouse to old Italian classics, begin at 9.45pm at the Anfiteatro della Fortezza Medicea (Ⓦ cinemanuovopendola.it). There are also a number of open-air jazz concerts (Ⓦ sienajazz.it) and wonderful operas held in different evocative settings all over Siena and the surrounding areas (Ⓦ www.chigiana.it).

INFORMATION

Tourist office Santa Maria della Scala, Palazzo Squarcialupi, Piazza Duomo 1 (Mon–Fri 10.30am–4.30pm, Sat & Sun 10.30am–6.30pm; Ⓣ 0577 280 551, Ⓦ www.terresiena.it).

ACCOMMODATION

In summer, Siena gets ridiculously booked up, especially during the Palio; book far in advance.

★ **Alma Domus** Via Camporegio 37 Ⓣ 0577 44 177, Ⓦ hotelalmadomus.it. Originally a pilgrim hostel, this fourteenth-century building, reached via a stairway close to San Domenico church, offers great-value and remarkably peaceful accommodation; its en-suite doubles, triples and quads enjoy wonderful views. **€82.50**

★ **Antica Residenza Cicogna** Via delle Terme 75 Ⓣ 0577 285 613, Ⓦ anticaresidenzacicogna.it. Charming B&B on the first floor of a medieval *palazzo* not far north of the Campo, with seven a/c, soundproof en-suite rooms, all beautifully decorated. The breakfast is delicious, there's free computer use and wi-fi, and free tea and biscuits add to the home-from-home feel. **€85**

Bernini Via della Sapienza 15 Ⓣ 0577 289 047, Ⓦ albergobernini.com. Charming one-star hotel run by a friendly family; the views from the huge windows and wonderful breakfast terrace are breathtaking. Midnight curfew. Doubles with shared bathroom **€80**, en suite **€100**

★ **Podere Le Vigne** Via Tufi 56 Ⓣ 0577 286 952, Ⓦ poderelevigne.it. Picturesque B&B in a typical Tuscan farmhouse a 20min walk from the centre. There is lots of outdoor space to enjoy and the charming Federica also offers cooking lessons. Take bus #54 from the centre. Doubles **€90**

Siena Hostel Via Fiorentina 89 Ⓣ 0577 169 8177, Ⓦ sienahostel.it. A friendly and comfortable hostel that is a bit of a walk (1.5km) from the centre; take bus #10 from the train station or Piazza Gramsci, or bus #35 and #36 from Piazza Gramsci. If you're coming from Florence, ask the bus driver to let you off at "Lo Stellino". Rates include breakfast. Dorms **€21**, doubles **€48**

EATING

You can buy pizza by weight from many central hole-in-the-wall places, or gourmet supplies at De Miccoli, Via di Città 95 (daily 8am–8pm), for cheeses and cold meats.

Osteria Boccon del Prete Via di S. Pietro 17. A cellar-like little restaurant, with a vaulted ceiling, close to the Pinacoteca. Starters include classic bruschetta and *crostini*, *primi* dishes such as gnocchi with sea bream (from €8), and mains from €10 such as pork fillet with roast potatoes. Mon–Sat 12.15–3pm & 7.15–10pm.

Osteria Enoteca Sotto le Fonti Via Esterna di Fontebranda 114. This friendly *osteria* with a rustic, homespun feel offers Tuscan specialities such as *ribollita* (vegetable soup), *pappardelle* with wild boar (€7.50) and an array of meaty mains from €10. It's also an *enoteca*, with over a hundred wines, many offered by the glass. Mon–Sat 12.30–2.30pm & 7.30–10pm.

Osteria Nonna Gina Piano del Mantellini Ⓣ 0577 287 247. No-nonsense, ultra-fresh, Italian home cooking in a friendly family atmosphere with some outdoor tables. Most dishes are under €10 (it's renowned for its gnocchi). Tues–Sun 12.30–2.30pm & 7.30–10.30pm..

DRINKING AND NIGHTLIFE

The main action of an evening is the *passeggiata* from Piazza Matteotti along Banchi di Sopra to the Campo – and there's not much in the way of nightlife after that, though there are a handful of bars scattered over town.

Bar Porrione Via del Porrione 14. Just an ordinary bar off the Campo, but it's popular with a studenty crowd at weekends thanks to its late opening hours. Tues–Sun 9am–3am.

Caffè del Corso Banchi di Sopra 25 Ⓣ 0577 226 656. This diminutive bar serves up a decent *aperitivo* with snacks from 7 to 9pm, and gets lively later on with students thanks to its loud music and cheap cocktails (€3.50). It has a few tables on the tiny alley outside too. Tues–Sun 8am–3am.

SAN GIMIGNANO

One of the best-known villages in Tuscany, **SAN GIMIGNANO**'s skyline of towers, framed against the classic rolling hills of the Tuscan countryside, has justifiably caught the tourist imagination, and in high season can get uncomfortably busy. The little hill town was a force to be reckoned with in the Middle Ages: it had a large population of fifteen thousand but was hit hard by the Black Death and never quite recovered – today there's half that number.

You can walk across the town in fifteen minutes and around the walls in an hour. The main entrance gate, facing the bus terminal on the south side of town, is **Porta San Giovanni**, from where **Via San Giovanni** leads to the town's interlocking main squares, **Piazza della Cisterna** and **Piazza del Duomo**. The more austere Piazza Duomo, off to the left, is flanked by the **Collegiata** (April–Oct Mon–Fri 10am–7.30pm, Sat 10am–5.30pm, Sun 12.30–7.30pm; Jan 1–14, Feb, March, Nov 1–14 & Dec Mon–Sat 10am–5pm, Sun 12.30–5pm; Jan 15–31, March 12 & Nov 15–30 closed except for services; €4), frescoed with Old and New Testament scenes. The **Palazzo Comunale** next door (daily: March 10am–5.30pm; April–Oct 9.30am–7pm; Nov–Feb 11am–5.30pm; €6) gives you the chance to climb the 218 steps of the **Torre Grossa**, the town's highest surviving tower. North from Piazza Duomo, **Via San Matteo** is one of the grandest and best preserved of the city streets, with quiet alleyways running down to the walls. The small **Wine Museum** (call ☎0577 941 267 for details), at the Parco della Rocca, is free to enter, and you can enjoy a glass of wine at the adjoining bar while admiring some of the most spectacular views the town has to offer.

ARRIVAL AND DEPARTURE

By bus From Siena catch one of the direct buses (#130) from Via F. Tozzi (10 daily; 1hr 5min–1hr 20min), or take a bus to Poggibonsi station (hourly; 45min) and change there for the bus to San Gimignano. Buses from Florence to Poggibonsi run at least hourly (50min).

By train From Siena take a train to Poggibonsi (40min) and change there for the 20min bus trip (every 15–30min) up to San Gimignano.

INFORMATION

Tourist office On the south side of Piazza del Duomo (daily: March–Oct 10am–1pm & 3–7pm; Nov–Feb 10am–1pm & 2–6pm; ☎0577 940 008, ⓦsangimignano.com).

ACCOMMODATION

Boschetto di Piemma Località Santa Lucia 38/c ☎0577 907 134, ⓦboschettodipiemma.it. The nearest campsite, with camping pitches and chalets as well as a bar, restaurant and pool. Closed Nov to mid-March. Per person €11, plus per pitch €9

Foresteria del Monastero S Girolamo Via Folgore 30 ☎0577 940 573, ⓦmonasterosangirolamo.it. Run by Benedictine monks, this basic but excellent budget choice

in a quiet monastery has comfortable rooms. Booking essential. €60

Le Vecchie Mura 15 Via Piandornella 15 ☎0577 940 270, ⓦvecchiemura.it. The most fabulous restaurant in San Gimignano also rents out private rooms with a/c, and dinner on your doorstep. Doubles €65

EATING AND DRINKING

Take a picnic up to the Parco Della Rocca or the Parco di Montestaffoli and enjoy the views of the village and surrounding countryside.

Di Vinorum Piazza Cisterna 30/Via degli Innocenti 5. Despite the inauspicious entrance on the piazza, this is a lovely spot for an early evening drink. The bar is built into the town wall and has a cool stone interior. The outdoor tables have fantastic views. Wine from €3. Bruschetta from €5. Daily 11am–9pm, reduced opening times in winter.

Il Trovatore Viale dei Fossi 17. A cheerful, no-frills place just outside the walls, serving forty types of deliciously crispy pizzas cooked in a wood-fired oven (€5.50–9.50). Daily except Wed 6.30pm–midnight.

Le Vecchie Mura Via Piandornella 15 ☎0577 940 270, ⓦvecchiemura.it. Romantic restaurant with wonderful views of the Tuscan hillside from its well-kept terrace. Booking essential. *Primi* €9, *secondi* €13. Mon & Wed–Sun 6–10pm.

PERUGIA

PERUGIA, the Umbrian capital perched on a hill, is an attractive medieval university town dominated by young people of every nationality, many at the Università per Stranieri (Foreigners' University). It's known for its nightlife, people-watching, and chocolate – some of Italy's most famous chocolate, Perugini, is made here.

WHAT TO SEE AND DO

Perugia hinges on a single street, **Corso Vannucci**, a broad pedestrian thoroughfare. At the far end, the austere **Piazza Quattro Novembre** is backed by the plain-faced **Duomo San Lorenzo** (Mon–Sat 7.30am–12.30pm & 3.30–6.45pm, Sun 8am–1pm & 4–7pm; free) and is interrupted by the thirteenth-century Fontana Maggiore. The lavishly decorated **Collegio di Cambio** (Mon–Sat 9am–12.30pm & 2.30–5.30pm, Sun 9am–1pm; Nov–March closed Mon pm; €4.50) sits at Corso Vannucci 25. This is the town's medieval money exchange, frescoed by the famous architect Perugino and said to be the most beautiful bank in

17

the world. The Palazzo dei Priori houses the **Galleria Nazionale dell'Umbria** (daily 8.30am–7.30pm; €6.50), one of central Italy's best galleries, whose collection includes statues by Cambio, frescoes by Bonfigli and works by Perugino. **Via dei Priori** is a lovely, winding, cobbled street that bends gently through the rambling white buildings. This leads down to Agostino di Duccio's colourful **Oratorio di San Bernardino**, whose richly embellished facade is by far the best piece of sculpture in the city. On the southern side of town, along Corso Cavour, the cloisters of the large church of **San Domenico** hold the **Museo Archeologico Nazionale dell'Umbria** (Tues–Sun 10am–7.30pm; €4), home of one of the most extensive Etruscan collections around.

ARRIVAL AND DEPARTURE

By air Arriving by air (Ryanair flies from the UK), you'll land at the Aeroporto "San Francesco d'Assisi" (☎075 592 141, ⓦairport.umbria.it), 12km east of the centre. ACAP-SULGA shuttles meet incoming flights and run to Piazza Italia (2–4 daily; 15min; €8), with intermediate stops, including Perugia's train station; these should be booked in advance by phone (☎075 500 9641).
By train Trains arrive well away from the centre of Perugia on Piazza Vittorio Veneto; buses go from outside the station to Piazza Italia or Piazza Matteotti (20min).
Destinations Assisi (every 30min–1hr; 20–30min); Florence (every 2hr; 2hr); Rome (hourly; 2–3hr).
By bus Buses arrive at Pian di Massiano; take the Minimetrò (see below) up to Piazza Italia.
Destinations Florence (1 daily; 2hr–2hr 30min); Rome (5 daily; 2hr 30min); Rome Fiumicino airport (2–4 daily; 3hr 45min); Siena (3–7 daily; 1hr 30min).
By minimetrò The light-rail system takes people up and down the hill of Perugia in 12min (daily; every 2–3min; Mon–Sat 7am–9.20pm, Sun 9am–8.45pm, €1.50).

THE UMBRIA JAZZ FESTIVAL

One of the most prestigious jazz events in Europe, the **Umbria Jazz Festival** (ⓦumbriajazz.com) has featured stars such as Dizzy Gillespie and Keith Jarrett. It takes place in July, and while the main events tend to be in Perugia, there are offshoots – performances and workshops that often make use of stunning churches, courts and open-air spaces – in towns across the region.

INFORMATION

Tourist office Piazza Matteotti 18 (daily 9am–7pm; ☎075 573 6458, ⓦturismo.comune.perugia.it).

ACCOMMODATION

Centro Internazionale di Accoglienza per la Gioventù Via Bontempi 13 ☎075 572 2880, ⓦostello .perugia.it. The town's original hostel is perfectly situated in a historic *palazzo* just 2min from the Duomo. It has frescoed common areas and a panoramic terrace that some of the rooms share. Dorms **€17**
★**Hotel Rosalba** Piazza del Circo 7 ☎075 572 8285, ⓦhotelrosalba.com. Standing alone and impossible to miss with its pink facade, this friendly place offers fresh rooms equipped with Sky TV, kettle and tea in a quiet but central location. Doubles **€75**
Little Italy Hostel Via della Nespola 1 ☎075 966 1997, ⓦlittleitalyhostel.it. A fine, modern "design" hostel housed in an ancient church, with a bright dorm room for twelve (in three-tier bunks), and a smaller room for eight (with four two-tier bunks) that costs an extra €2. Free, light breakfast. Check-in is 2–6pm. Dorms **€18**, doubles **€70**
Ostello AIG Mario Spagnoli Via Cortonese 4, Località Pian di Massiano ☎075 501 1366, ⓦhihostels.com. Down near the main station, this hostel has 186 beds in 33 four- and six-bed dorms. It has its own restaurant, and breakfast is included. Dorms **€14**, singles **€27**, doubles **€31**

EATING

Being a student city, there are plenty of cheap cafés and takeaways. Co-op supermarket is on Piazza Matteotti 19, while the market on Piazza Circo (daily 8am–1pm) sells plenty of fresh produce.
Al Mangiar Bene Via della Luna 21 ☎075 573 1047, ⓦalmangiarbene.it. This lovely, brick-vaulted space is a rare find: all organic, with produce sourced from local farms. Pasta dishes start from €6 (with pizzas in the evening only from just €5). Tues–Sat 12.30–2.45pm & 7.30–11.45pm, Mon & Sun 7.30–11.45pm.
Civico 25 Via della Viola 25 ☎075 571 6376, ⓦcivico25 .com. Wine bar with food close to the Università degli Stranieri, great for a glass of wine with a bruschetta of fava beans, chickpeas or chicken-liver pâté, or for a full meal. Expect to pay around €30 for a full meal. Mon–Sat 7pm–2am.
Dal Mi'Cocco Corso Garibaldi 12 ☎075 573 2511. They keep it beautifully simple at this local favourite. The four-course meal costs €13 and the portions are large and hearty. It's best to book. No credit cards. Tues–Sun 1–3pm & 8–10.30pm.
Mediterranea Piazza Piccinino 11 ☎075 572 4021. Simple and tasteful pizzeria with a small wood-fired oven and a couple of brick-vaulted rooms, a few steps beyond the entrance to the Pozzo Etrusco. It has over 25 varieties (€6). Daily 12.30–2.30pm & 7.30–11pm.

PERUGIA FESTIVALS

As well as its jazz festival, Perugia has a stream of eclectic events throughout the year. Around September there's a **chocolate festival** (ⓦeurochocolate .com) that lasts for ten days, while the **Christmas market** is splendid in its scale and opulence.

DRINKING AND NIGHTLIFE

La Terrazza Via Matteotti 18a. Outdoor bar with sweeping views over the Umbrian countryside. Cocktails around €6. Open late May–Sept. Daily 11am–2am.

Punto di Vista Viale dell'Indipendenza 2. Extremely popular bar with beautiful views of the rolling countryside and snowcapped peaks in the distance. Beer €4. Daily 5.30pm–2.30am; closed in winter.

Velvet Fashion Café Viale Roma 20 ☎075 572 1321. Perugia's most central club. Offers smart dining, drinking and occasional live music. Daily 9pm until late; closed Mon–Wed in winter and all summer.

ASSISI

ASSISI is Umbria's best-known town thanks to St Francis, Italy's premier saint and founder of the Franciscan order. It has a medieval hill-town charm and is easy to navigate around in just a few hours.

The **Basilica di San Francesco**, now restored to its former glory after a devastating earthquake in 1997, is at the end of Via San Francesco (Lower Church Mon–Sat 6am–7pm; Nov–March closes 5.45pm; Upper Church Mon–Sat 8.30am–7pm; Nov–March closes 6pm; free). It houses one of the most overwhelming collections of art outside a gallery anywhere in the world. St Francis lies under the floor of the Lower Church, in a crypt only brought to light in 1818. The walls have been lavishly frescoed by artists such as Cimabue and Giotto, and the stained-glass windows cast a dim light that enhances the magical atmosphere. The Upper Church, built to a light and airy Gothic plan, is richly decorated too, with dazzling frescoes about the life of St Francis. A short trek up the steep Via di San Rufino leads to the thirteenth-century **Duomo** (daily: April–July, Sept & Oct 7am–12.30pm & 2.30–7pm; Aug 7am–7pm; Nov–March 7am–1pm &

2.30–6pm), which holds the font used to baptize St Francis.

ARRIVAL AND INFORMATION

By train Bus #C connects the station, 5km southwest of the centre, with Piazza Matteotti every 30min.

Tourist office Piazza del Comune (April–Oct Mon–Fri 8am–2pm & 3–6/6.30pm, Sat 9am–7pm, Sun 9am–6pm; Nov–March Mon–Fri 8am–2pm & 3–6pm, Sat & Sun 9.30am–5pm; ☎075 81 381, ⓦvisit-assisi.it).

ACCOMMODATION

Ostello della Pace Via di Valecchie 4 ☎075 816 767, ⓦassisihostel.com. In a quiet setting a 10min walk downhill from Piazza dell'Unità d'Italia, this hostel occupies an old farmhouse, and has a garden, lots of facilities and welcoming staff. Ask to be dropped at "Villa Guardi" if you're arriving by bus from the station. Dorms €18, doubles €50

EATING

Buca di San Francesco Via Eugenio Brizzi 1 ☎075 812 204. The *Buca* has been around for ever, and is generally a reliable choice for a decent meal, with typical *primi* (from €9) that might include handmade spaghetti with roast mushroom, beef and herbs, and mains (from €12) such as lamb cooked with wild herbs. Tues–Sun 12.30–2.30pm & 8–10.30pm.

Pallotta Via Volta Piana 2 ☎075 812 649. An unpretentious and welcoming trattoria with a lovely wood-beamed dining room. *Primi* (€5–9) include *stringozzi alla Pallotta*, handmade pasta (without egg) served with mushroom, chilli flakes and a generous swirl of local olive oil. *Secondi* (€6–15) might include suckling pig, lamb chops or braised pigeon. Daily set three-course menu with wine €25 (vegetarian menu €24). Daily except Tues noon–3pm & 7–10.30pm.

SPOLETO

SPOLETO is a tiny hill-top town adorned with small and winding cobbled streets, beautiful Romanesque churches and the remains of an ancient amphitheatre.

Piazza della Libertà is where you will find the **Museo Archeologico** (daily 8.30am–7.30pm; €4), and where you can also glimpse the ancient arena. From here it's a short walk to the elegant **Duomo** (daily: April–Oct 8.30am–12.30pm & 3.30–7pm; Nov–March closes 5.30pm; free). The apse frescoes inside were painted by the fifteenth-century Florentine artist Fra Lippo Lippi – he died shortly after their completion amid rumours that he was poisoned for

17 seducing the daughter of a local noble family. The **Ponte delle Torri**, a photo-favourite, is an astonishing piece of medieval engineering, best seen as part of a circular walk (allow around 5hr 30min) around the base of the **Rocca**. **Piazza del Mercato** and its surrounding streets are a great place to head for a spot of lunch.

ARRIVAL AND DEPARTURE

By train The station is just northwest of the Lower Town; shuttle buses (€1.30 or €2 on board; buy tickets from the station bar) to the centre depart from outside the station. Destinations Florence (1 daily; 2hr 50min); Rome (14 daily; 1hr 20min–1hr 45min).

INFORMATION

Tourist office Piazza della Libertà 7 (April–Oct Mon–Sat 9am–1.30pm & 2–7pm, Sun 9am–1pm & 3–5.30pm; Nov–March Mon–Sat 9am–1.30pm & 2.30–6.15pm, Sun 9.30am–1pm & 3–5pm; ☎0743 218 620, ⓦwww .comunespoleto.gov.it).

ACCOMMODATION

Camping Monteluco ☎0743 220 358, ⓦcampeggiomonteluco.com. An attractively small pastoral site behind San Pietro, with several bungalows, 35 camping places and a bar/pizzeria, but quite an uphill trek to the Upper Town. April–Sept. Pitches **€12**
Gattapone Via del Ponte 6 ☎0743 223 447, ⓦhotelgattapone.it. A welcoming and beautifully styled family-run hotel with lovely views from most rooms, which are spectacularly situated above the gorge and almost alongside the Ponte delle Torri. **€110**

EATING

Canasta Piazza della Libertà 14 ⓦcanastaspoleto.it. Historic café on the main square, which keeps the townspeople happy with tasty savouries and tempting pastries. Set three-course menus at €18 and €25. A great place to start the day. Daily except Wed, all day.
La Lanterna Via della Trattoria 6. A convivial, central place and the best of the town's mid-price trattorias, on a side street left off the hill between Piazza della Libertà and Piazza Fontana. It serves huge helpings of delicious pasta from €7 and grilled meats and other mains from €8. Daily except Wed 12.30–3pm & 7.30–10.30pm.

URBINO

URBINO boasted one of the most prestigious courts in Europe in the fifteenth century, and today the highlight of a visit to this hill-top town is the grand

> ### FERRIES FROM ANCONA
> The main arrival and departure port on Italy's eastern coast is the transit town of **Ancona**, with ferries taking you to Croatia, Albania, Greece and Montenegro. Ferries leave from Ancona's Stazione Marittima, a couple of kilometres north of the train station (bus #1 or #4), close to the centre of town. For the best at-a-glance idea of timetables and routes, visit ⓦdoricaportservices.it. Each of the main ferry lines has a ticket office (closed 1–3pm) and you can also buy tickets from the agencies all around the port, but booking online gets you the cheapest deals. Always aim to arrive at the Stazione Marittima two hours before departure (3hr if you're taking a camper van).

Palazzo Ducale and its impressive collection of Renaissance paintings.

The Palazzo Ducale was built by the extravagant Federico da Montefeltro, the fifteenth-century Duke of Urbino. It is now home to the excellent **Galleria Nazionale delle Marche** (Mon 8.30am–2pm, Tues–Sun 8.30am–7.15pm; €6.50). Among the paintings in the Appartamento del Duca is Piero della Francesca's strange *Flagellation* and the portrait of *The Mute* by Raphael, who was born in Urbino. The most interesting of the Palazzo's rooms is Federico's Studiolo, a triumph of illusory perspective.

Buzzy **Piazza della Repubblica** is a great place for lunch or a drink.

ARRIVAL AND DEPARTURE

By bus Urbino has no train station, and its bus station is at Borgo Mercatale at the foot of the Palazzo Ducale. The easiest way to reach the city is by train to Fano or Pesaro and then by bus from there. Destinations Fano (at least hourly; 1hr 10min); Pesaro (every 30min; 45min–1hr).

INFORMATION

Tourist office Piazza Duca Federico 35 opposite the Palazzo Ducale (Mon–Sat 9am–1pm & 2.30–5.30pm, Sun 9am–1pm; ☎0722 2613, ⓦwww.turismo.pesarourbino .it). There's a small office at Borgo Mercatale by the entrance to the ramp and lift (daily 7am–9pm).

ACCOMMODATION

Il Cortegiano Via Veterani 1 ☎340 844 1181, ⓦilcortegiano.it. Urbino's best-situated B&B, just across from the Palazzo Ducale above a bar-restaurant, has six large basic rooms, some with shared bathrooms. Free wi-fi and a ten percent discount in the restaurant for guests. **€60**

Raffaello Via Santa Margherita 40 ☎0722 4896, ⓦalbergoraffaello.com. In a typical red-brick, shuttered old-town building, this hotel has fourteen simply furnished rooms with panoramic views over the pantiled roofs of Urbino. Changing art exhibitions in the communal areas and free wi-fi. **€65**

EATING AND DRINKING

Angolo Divino Via Sant'Andrea 14 ☎0722 327 559. Geranium-covered on the outside, and atmospheric within, this *osteria* is located in a pink *palazzo* near the Botanical Gardens. It's well known for regional delicacies, including home-made pasta (*primi* around €10), and there are some good vegetarian choices. Tues–Sun noon–3pm & 7pm–midnight.

Da Franco Via del Poggio 1 ☎0722 2492. Studenty lunchtime hangout (self-service) with *primi* such as home-made *strozzapreti* pasta – "strangled priests" – with vegetables, and *secondi* including rabbit cooked with fennel. A meal will set you back around €20 including wine. Mon–Sat noon–2.30pm.

Southern Italy

The Italian **south** (*mezzogiorno*) offers a decidedly different experience from that of the north; indeed, few countries are more tangibly divided into two distinct, often antagonistic, regions. **Naples** is the obvious focus of the south, an utterly compelling city just a couple of hours south of Rome. In the **Bay of Naples**, highlights are the resort of Sorrento and the island of **Capri**, crawling with tourists but beautiful enough to be worth your time, while the ancient sites of **Pompeii** and **Herculaneum** are Italy's best-preserved Roman remains. South of Naples, the **Amalfi Coast** is a contender for Europe's most dramatic stretch of coastline. In the far south, **Matera**, jewel of the Basilicata region, harbours ancient cave dwellings dug into a steep ravine. Puglia – the long strip of land that makes up the "heel" of Italy – boasts the Baroque wonders of **Lecce**, and is also useful for ferries to Greece and Croatia.

NAPLES

Wherever else you travel south of Rome, the chances are that you'll wind up in **NAPLES** (Napoli). It's the kind of city people visit with preconceptions, and it rarely disappoints: it is dirty and overbearing; it is crime-ridden; and it is most definitely like nowhere else in Italy – something the inhabitants will be keener than anyone to tell you. One thing, though, is certain: a couple of days here and you're likely to be as staunch a defender of the place as its most devoted inhabitants.

WHAT TO SEE AND DO

The area between the vast and busy Piazza Garibaldi, the city's transport hub, and Via Toledo, the main street a kilometre or so west, makes up the old part of the city – the **Centro Storico**, whose buildings rise high on either side of the narrow, crowded streets. South of here is the busy port, and, to the northwest, Naples' finest museums.

The Duomo

From Piazza Garibaldi, Via dei Tribunali cuts through to Via Duomo, where you'll find the tucked-away **Duomo** (Mon–Sat 8.30am–1.30pm & 2.30–8pm, Sun 8.30am–1.30pm & 4.30–7.30pm; free), a Gothic building from the early thirteenth century dedicated to San Gennaro, the patron saint of the city, martyred in 305 AD. Two phials of his blood miraculously liquefy three times a year – on the first Saturday in May, on September 19 and on December 16. If the blood refuses to liquefy, disaster is supposed to befall the city. The first chapel on the right as you walk into the cathedral holds the precious phials, as well as Gennaro's skull.

MADRE

A short walk up Via Duomo, Naples' superb modern art museum, **MADRE**, at Via Settembrini 79 (Mon, Wed–Fri 10am–7.30pm, Sun 10am–8pm; €7; ⓦmadrenapoli.it), shows off works by some big-name contemporary artists. The most prominent of these is by Francesco Clemente, a New York-based Neapolitan artist who created the huge, vibrant mural of Naples. The museum also holds

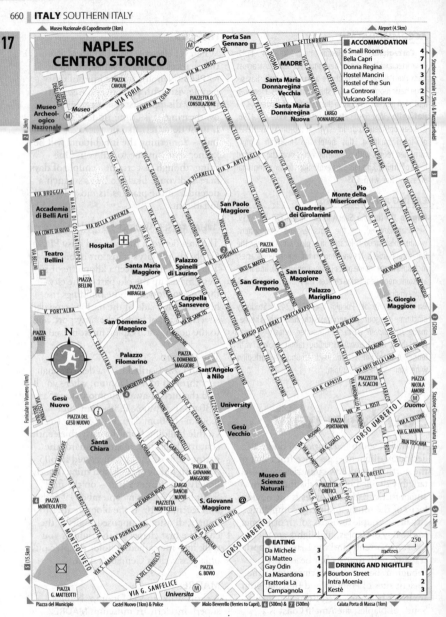

NAPLES CENTRO STORICO

■ ACCOMMODATION
6 Small Rooms	4
Bella Capri	7
Donna Regina	1
Hostel Mancini	3
Hostel of the Sun	6
La Controra	2
Vulcano Solfatara	5

● EATING
Da Michele	3
Di Matteo	1
Gay Odin	4
La Masardona	5
Trattoria La Campagnola	2

■ DRINKING AND NIGHTLIFE
Bourbon Street	1
Intra Moenia	2
Kestè	3

works by the likes of Jeff Koons and Anish Kapoor, as well as a massive anchor – symbolizing the city's maritime roots – by Jannis Kounellis.

Spaccanapoli and around

Busy Via dei Tribunali and its parallel, Via San Biagio dei Librai – commonly known as **Spaccanapoli** – make up the heart of the old city and Naples' busiest and architecturally richest quarter. A maelstrom of hurrying pedestrians, revving cars and buzzing scooters, this is the best place to get a sense of the city and its inhabitants. At 253 Via dei Tribunali is the **Cappella Pio Monte della**

Misericordia (Thurs–Tues 9am–2.30pm; €7; ⓦpiomontedellamisericordia.it), an unassuming jewel of a church thanks to its breathtaking altarpiece: Caravaggio's *Seven Works of Mercy*, which elegantly juxtaposes warm acts of charity with ribald picaresque street life, reflecting something of Naples's own appeal. The picture gallery is well worth a visit, containing works by Francesco de Mura, Luca Giordano and others.

Gesù Nuovo and Santa Chiara

West up Spaccanapoli is the **Gesù Nuovo** church, distinctive for its lava-stone facade, prickled with pyramids that give it an impregnable, prison-like air. Facing it, the church of **Santa Chiara** is quite different, a Provençal-Gothic structure built in 1328 (and rebuilt after World War II). The attached **cloister** (Mon–Sat 9.30am–5.30pm, Sun 10am–2.30pm; €6; ⓦmonasterodisantachiara.com), covered with colourful majolica tiles depicting bucolic scenes, is one of the gems of the city.

Castel Nuovo

A ten-minute walk south of Santa Chiara, **Piazza del Municipio** is a busy traffic junction that stretches down to the waterfront, dominated by the brooding hulk of the **Castel Nuovo** (Mon–Sat 9am–7pm; €6). It was built in 1282 by the Angevins and later the royal residence of the Aragon kings. It's the views over the port from the upper terrace that steal the show – along with the **Sala dei Baroni**, accessed from the courtyard, a huge room with magnificent umbrella-ribbed vaults that were once covered in frescoes by Giotto.

Palazzo Reale and around

Some 500m west of the castle, **Piazza del Plebiscito**, with its impressive sweep of columns, was modelled on Bernini's Piazza San Pietro in Rome. On one side of the square, the dignified **Palazzo Reale** (daily except Wed 9am–8pm; €4; ⓦpalazzorealenapoli.it) was built in 1602 to accommodate a visit by Philip III of Spain. Upstairs, the first-floor rooms are sumptuously decorated with gilded furniture, *trompe-l'oeil* ceilings, and seventeenth- and eighteenth-century paintings.

Just beyond the castle, the opulent **Teatro San Carlo** is the largest opera house in Italy, and one of the most distinguished in the world (guided tours Mon–Sat hourly 10.30am–12.30pm & 2.30–4.30pm; Sun 10.30am, 11.30am & 12.30pm; €6; ⓦteatrosancarlo.it).

Museo Archeologico Nazionale

Arrowing north from the Piazza del Plebiscito, Via Toledo leads to the **Museo Archeologico Nazionale** (Wed–Mon 9am–7.30pm; €8), home to the best of the finds from the nearby Roman sites of Pompeii (see p.664) and Herculaneum (see p.664). The ground floor concentrates on sculpture, the mezzanine houses the museum's collection of mosaics, while upstairs, wall paintings from the villas of Pompeii and Herculaneum are the museum's other major draw. Don't miss the "secret" room of erotic Roman pictures and sculptures, once thought to be a threat to public morality.

Museo Nazionale di Capodimonte

The city's second major museum, the **Museo Nazionale di Capodimonte** (Thurs–Tues 8.30am–7.30pm; €7.50; €6.50 after 2pm; ⓦmuseocapodimonte .beniculturali.it) is a bus ride away from town (#R4 from Via Toledo or #178 from the Museo Archeologico). The former residence of the Bourbon King Charles III, built in 1738, it has a huge and superb collection of Renaissance and Flemish paintings, including a couple of Brueghels, canvases by Perugino and Pinturicchio, an elegant *Madonna and Child with Angels* by Botticelli, and Lippi's soft, sensitive *Annunciation*.

Vomero

Vomero, the district topping the hill immediately above the old city, can be reached by funicular from Corso Vittorio Emanuele, west of the Gesù Nuovo, or Piazza Augusteo near the Teatro San Carlo. A five-minute stroll from the station, the star-shaped fortress of **Castel Sant'Elmo** (Wed–Mon 8.30am–7.30pm;

17

€5) was built in the fourteenth century and hosts occasional exhibitions. Occupying Naples' highest point, it has lovely views which are only topped by those from the terraced gardens of the **Certosa e Museo di San Martino** (Mon, Tues & Thurs–Sun 8.30am–7.30pm; €6), a former Carthusian monastery. Now a museum, it contains seventeenth- and eighteenth-century Neapolitan painting and sculpture.

ARRIVAL AND DEPARTURE

By plane Capodichino airport (ⓦ aeroportodinapoli.it) is about 7km north of the centre. The red-and-white official airport bus Alibus (every 20min; €3) connects the airport to Piazza Garibaldi (20min) and Piazza Municipio (30min).

By train Trains arrive at Piazza Garibaldi, the main hub of all transport services.

Destinations Lecce (5 daily; 5hr 30min); Palermo (3 daily; 9hr 30min–11hr); Pompeii (from Stazione Circumvesuviana; every 30min; 40min); Rome (hourly; 1hr 10min–2hr 40min); Siracusa (3 daily; 8hr 30min–10hr 30min); Sorrento (from Stazione Circumvesuviana; every 30min; 1hr 5min; reach Amalfi by bus or ferry from Sorrento).

By bus Most long-distance, inter-regional buses and local buses use Corso Meridionale behind the train station by Piazza Garibaldi.

Destinations Assisi (2 daily; 5hr); Lecce (3 daily; 5hr 30min); Matera (2 daily; 4hr); Perugia (2 daily; 4hr 30min).

By ferry Ferries arrive at Calata Porta di Massa, and are connected with Molo Beverello by free shuttle bus. Hydrofoils dock at Molo Beverello, a short bus ride or a 15min walk from the centre.

Ferry destinations Capri (10 daily; 1hr 20min); Palermo (2 daily; 8hr–10hr 30min).

Hydrofoil destinations Capri (every 30min–1hr; 40min); Sorrento (6 daily; 45min).

INFORMATION

Tourist office Information desk at Capodichino airport (daily 8am–11pm), and two offices in the centre of the city: Piazza del Gesù Nuovo (Mon–Sat 9am–5pm, Sun 9am–1pm; ☎081 551 2701); and Via S. Carlo 9, on the south side of Galleria Umberto I across from Teatro San Carlo (Mon–Sat 9am–5pm, Sun 9am–1pm; ☎081 402 394).

Discount cards If you are around for more than a day, invest in the Artecard (from €21; sold in the train station, museums and online at ⓦ www.campaniaartecard.it), which is valid on various combinations of city transport, along with free and discounted museum entrance.

GETTING AROUND

Tickets TIC tickets (issued by UnicoCampania; ⓦ unicocampania.it) are valid on all city buses, metro lines and funiculars as well as the Circumvesuviana and Cumana lines (within Naples), and can be bought in advance from *tabacchi*, newsstands or metro stations. Fares cost a flat €1.50 (valid 90min), or you can buy an all-day ticket (€4.50) or a weekly ticket (€15.80).

By bus and metro City buses will get you almost everywhere, although they are crowded and slow. The bus system is supplemented by the *metropolitana*, which is more useful for longer hops across the city. Two urban lines are handy for visitors, each snaking across the city centre from Piazza Garibaldi. The older Line 2 has three stops between Garibaldi and Mergellina before continuing on to Pozzuoli Solfatara. The newer Line 1 has useful stops at Municipio (for the harbour), Toledo, Museo, Dante and Vanvitelli (for Vomero).

By funicular Three funiculars scale the hill of the Vomero every 10–15min: the Funicolare di Chiaia (daily 6.30am–12.30am), from Piazza Amedeo; the Funicolare Centrale (daily 6.30am–12.30am), from the Augusteo station, just off the bottom end of Via Toledo; and the Funicolare di Montesanto (daily 7am–10pm), from the station on Piazza Montesanto. A fourth, the Funicolare di Mergellina, runs up the hill above Mergellina from Via Mergellina (daily 7am–10pm).

ACCOMMODATION

6 Small Rooms Via Diodato Lioy 18 ☎081 790 1378, ⓦ 6smallrooms.com. Located in a crumbling historical building, this small artsy hostel with quirky murals attracts a laidback boho crowd. Dorms €18, doubles €45

Bella Capri Via Melisurgo 4 ☎081 552 9494, ⓦ bellacapri.it. Right by the port, this hostel offers private

---

★ **TREAT YOURSELF**

If you're going to splurge on accommodation anywhere in Italy, Naples is the place: your money will go a lot further. Try, for example, **Donna Regina** (Via Settembrini 80; ☎081 446 799, ⓦ discovernaples.net; doubles €93), run by a family of artists. A warm and welcoming B&B in a beautifully restored ex-convent, it has spacious, individually furnished rooms with period antiques and wonderfully high ceilings. The walls are jam-packed with books and paintings, giving a cosy touch, while the lively breakfast table adds to the convivial feel. The B&B also offers fun 3hr pizza tours. Look at ⓦ discovernaples.net for more boutique B&Bs in the city.

rooms with TV and a/c, and dorms, most with lockers. There's also a little kitchen for guests' use. Ten percent discount with this book. Dorms €21, doubles with shared bath €60, with private bath €66

Hostel Mancini Via Mancini 33 ☏081 553 6731, ⊛hostelmancininaples.com. Family-run hostel right across from the station with large dorms (mixed & female only) with lockers and private bathrooms, and recently renovated private rooms. There's a fully equipped kitchen and free luggage storage. Rates include breakfast. Ten percent discount with this book. Dorms €20, doubles with shared bath €50, with private bath €70

★**Hostel of the Sun** Via Melisurgo 15 ☏081 420 6393, ⊛hostelnapoli.com. This fun hostel with lively staff has a chilled-out lounge area with board and computer games; dorms have lockers and a/c, while doubles are all equipped with TV and DVD player. There's a buzzing bar and staff organize tours in the area, including Vesuvius on horseback. Dorms €18, doubles with shared bath €60, with private bath €80

★**La Controra** Piazzetta Trinità alla Cesarea 231 ☏081 549 4014, ⊛lacontrora.com. Clean, cool hostel with a glass lift, modern kitchen and a leafy garden. Dorms all have lockers, individual reading lamps and sockets. Dorms €17, doubles €60

Vulcano Solfatara Via Solfatara 161, Pozzuoli ☏081 526 2341, ⊛campeggiovulcanosolfatara.it. Metro to Pozzuoli, then a 10min walk uphill. This well-equipped campsite, on the edge of a volcanic crater, has a swimming pool, minimarket and takeaway. Camping/person €11, plus per tent €7, two-person bungalows €54

EATING

Colourful produce markets are found all over the centre; one of the best (daily 8am–1pm) takes up the streets around Via Pignasecca, a few streets west of the Gesù Nuovo.

Da Michele Via Cesare Sersale 1–3 ⊛damichele.net. Historic pizzeria serving some of Naples' best pizzas: marinara, margherita or double margherita are the sole choices here, from €4. Arrive early as the queues can get epic (get a ticket from the cash desk), or order to take away if you can't wait. Mon–Sat 10.30am–11pm.

★**Di Matteo** Via Tribunali 94. A must for a truly exceptional pizza (€3–6). Order a *frittatina* (€1) as you wait, a heavenly bundle of pasta, mince, peas, cheese and black pepper, deep-fried. Mon–Sat 7pm–midnight.

Gay Odin Via Benedetto Croce 61 (plus other branches around the city) ⊛gay-odin.it. This well-established chocolate shop offers a selection of superb ice creams whose many flavours were inspired by the 300-plus inventive chocolate fillings. About €1.80 for a cup or cone. Mon–Thurs 9am–8.30pm, Fri & Sat 9am–11.30pm, Sun 10am–8.30pm.

La Masardona Via Giulio Cesare Capaccio 27. Truly local street-food joint a few minutes from the train station specializing in authentic fried pizzas stuffed with tomatoes, pork scratchings and provola and ricotta cheese (€2); watch owner Enzo at work as he expertly kneads while his wife Anna fries, and enjoy the exquisite result. Tues, Wed, Fri & Sun 7am–3pm, Sat 6.30am–10pm.

Trattoria La Campagnola Via dei Tribunali 47. Small, busy, and serving excellent, well-priced Neapolitan food, with great *spaghetti con polpette* (spaghetti with meatballs; €10) and hearty mains like *salsiccia* (sausage), *cotoletta* (breaded cutlet) and *scaloppina* (veal escalope). Mon & Sun 7.30–11pm, Wed–Sat noon–3pm & 7.30–11pm.

DRINKING AND NIGHTLIFE

Most clubs close in July and August and move to the beach; the Neapolitans who remain congregate for a beer in the studenty bars around Piazza Bellini and Piazza del Gesù Nuovo.

Bourbon Street Via Bellini 52/53 ☏338 825 3756, ⊛bourbonstreetjazzclub.com. A premier venue for Italian and international jazz acts, bringing a slice of New Orleans to the heart of Naples' *centro storico*. Tues–Sun 8pm–3am.

Intra Moenia Piazza Bellini 70 ⊛intramoenia.it. This café-cum-bar located in one of the city's most popular nightlife spots is dotted with knick-knacks, books and trinkets for sale, with Thurday jazz, fusion and bossanova sessions at 10pm. Cocktails (€7), beer and wine (both €4). Mon–Thurs & Sun 11am–2am, Fri & Sat until 3am.

Kestè Largo San Giovanni Maggiore Pignatelli 26–27 ⊛keste.it. Fun little bar with tables spilling onto the square attracting a laidback crowd. DJs liven the scene on Wednday and Fridays plus there are weekly jazz, reggae and rock sessions. *Aperitivo* at 6.30pm; cocktails €5. Tues–Sun 6.30pm–2.30am.

DIRECTORY

Consulates UK, Via dei Mille 40 ☏081 423 8911; US, Piazza della Repubblica ☏081 583 8111.

Hospital Ospedale Ascalesi, Via Egiziaca Forcella 31 (☏081 254 2117); Ospedale Cardarelli, Via Cardarelli 9 (☏081 747 1111).

Pharmacy At the train station (24hr).

Police ☏113. Main police station is at Via Medina 75 ☏081 794 1111.

Post office Piazza Matteotti 2 (Mon–Fri 8am–6.30pm, Sat 8am–12.30pm).

THE BAY OF NAPLES

Of the islands that dot the bay, **Capri** is the best place to visit if you're here for a short time. **Sorrento**, the brooding presence of **Vesuvius** and the incomparable Roman sites of **Herculaneum** and **Pompeii** are further draws.

17

Vesuvius

Its most infamous eruption, in 79 AD, buried the towns and inhabitants of Pompeii and Herculaneum, and **VESUVIUS** has long dominated the lives of those who live on the Bay of Naples. It's still an active volcano – the only one on mainland Europe – and there have been hundreds of (mostly minor) eruptions over the years, the last in 1944 when 28 people died. Considered to be one of the world's most dangerous volcanoes, a future eruption would lead to the evacuation of nearly one million inhabitants who populate the surrounding area.

The **walk** up to the crater from the bus stop takes about half an hour on marked-out paths. At the top (admission €10), the crater is a deep, wide, jagged ashtray of red rock emitting the odd plume of smoke. You can walk round halfway (700m) while soaking in breathtaking sea views. See ⓦwww.vesuviopark.it for information on trails.

ARRIVAL AND DEPARTURE

By train and bus Catch the Circumvesuviana train to either Pompeii or Ercolano Scavi. EAVBus buses leave from Pompeii's main station and Piazza Anfiteatro (roughly every 2hr; 8am–3.30pm; just over 1hr, last bus back 4.40pm; €10 return). Busvia del Vesuvio runs 4WD truck excursions from Pompeii-Villa dei Misteri station to within 600m of the summit (hourly, 9am–3pm; €22 including park admission; ☏ 340 935 2616, ⓦ busviadelvesuvio.com). From Ercolano train station, buses run by Vesuvio's Express head to the car park by the crater (every 40min; 9.45am–4pm; last bus back to Ercolano at 5.30pm; €10 return; ☏ 081 739 3666, ⓦ vesuvioexpress.it). There are two buses daily from Naples, starting at Piazza Piedigrotta in Mergellina (9am & 10am) and stopping in Piazza Garibaldi (*Hotel Terminus*; 9.25am & 10.25am), reaching the car park by the crater at about 10.30am and 11.30am, and returning at 12.30pm and 2pm; tickets cost €15 return.

Pompeii

Destroyed by Vesuvius, **POMPEII** (daily: April–Oct 8.30am–7.30pm, last entry 6pm; Nov–March 8.30am–5pm, last entry 3.30pm; €13; ⓦpompeiisites.org) was, in Roman times, one of Campania's most important commercial centres. Of a total population of twenty thousand, it's thought that two thousand perished in the great eruption of 79 AD, asphyxiated by the toxic fumes of the volcanic debris, their homes buried under several metres of ash and pumice. The full horror of their death is apparent in plaster casts made from the shapes their bodies left in the volcanic ash – gruesome, writhing figures, some with their hands covering their eyes.

Seeing the site will take you half a day at least. Entering from the Pompeii-Villa dei Misteri side, you come across the **Forum**, a slim open space surrounded by the ruins of some of the town's most important official buildings. North of here lies a small baths complex, and beyond, the **House of the Faun**, its "Ave" (Welcome) mosaic outside beckoning you in to view the atrium and the copy of a tiny bronze dancing faun. A few streets southwest, the **Lupanare** was Pompeii's only purpose-built brothel, worth a peek for its racy wall paintings. A short walk from the Porta Ercolano is the **Villa dei Misteri**, the best preserved of all Pompeii's palatial houses, which contains frescoes depicting the initiation rites of a young woman into the Dionysiac Mysteries, an orgiastic cult transplanted to Italy from Greece in the Republican era.

On the other side of the site, the **Grand Theatre** is still used for performances, as is the **Little Theatre** on its far left side. From here, it's a short walk to the **Amphitheatre**, one of Italy's most intact and also its oldest, dating from 80 BC.

ARRIVAL AND INFORMATION

By train The Circumvesuviana links Pompeii Scavi-Villa dei Misteri with Naples (35min) and Sorrento (30min). **Tourist office** Via Sacra 1, just off the modern town's main square (Mon–Fri 9am–3.30pm; ☏ 081 850 7255).

Herculaneum

The town of **Ercolano** is the modern offshoot of the ancient site of **HERCULANEUM** (daily: April–Oct 8.30am–7.30pm; Nov–March 8.30am–5pm; €11; ⓦpompeiisites.org), situated at the seaward end of Ercolano's main street. A residential town destroyed by the eruption of Vesuvius on August 2, 79 AD, it's much smaller than Pompeii, and as such is a more manageable site –

less architecturally impressive, but with better-preserved buildings. Highlights include the **House of the Mosaic Atrium**, with its mosaic-laid courtyard, the large baths complex and the **Casa del Bel Cortile**, which contains a group of skeletons, poignantly lying in the pose they died in.

ARRIVAL AND INFORMATION

By train Ercolano is a 15min hop on the train from Naples on the Circumvesuviana line (€2.50 one-way).
Tourist office Via IV Novembre 44 (Mon–Fri 8am–4pm, Tues & Thurs 8am–5pm; ☏081 788 1243, ⓦwww .comune.ercolano.na.it).

SORRENTO

Topping the rocky cliffs close to the end of its peninsula, **SORRENTO**'s inspired location and pleasant climate have drawn travellers from all over Europe for two hundred years. Nowadays it caters mostly to the package-tour industry, but this bright, lively place retains its southern Italian roots. Accommodation and food, though not exactly cheap, are much better value than most of the other resorts along the Amalfi Coast, making it a good base from which to explore the area. Sorrento's centre, **Piazza Tasso**, makes a lively focus for the evening *passeggiata*. The town isn't well provided with beaches: most people make do with the rocks and a tiny, crowded strip of sand at **Marina Grande** – fifteen minutes' walk or a short bus ride from Piazza Tasso.

ARRIVAL AND DEPARTURE

By train Sorrento's train station lies about 300m east of the main Piazza Tasso. Trains depart roughly every 30min to Naples (1hr 10min), with stops in Pompeii (35min) and Ercolano (15min).
By bus The bus station – for buses to the Amalfi Coast and the airport – is just in front of the train station. Tickets on SITA buses to the Amalfi Coast are available from *tabacchi* and can't be bought on board (Positano €1.80; Amalfi €2.70).
By hydrofoil There are connections to Naples (6 daily; 35min; €12.30) and Capri (every 30min–1hr; 25min; €18.30).

INFORMATION

Tourist office Via de Maio 35, just off Piazza Sant'Antonino (Mon–Fri 9am–7pm, Sat 9am–1pm; June–Sept also Sun 9am–6pm; ☏081 807 4033, ⓦsorrentotourism.com).

ACCOMMODATION

Camping Nube d'Argento Via del Capo 21 ☏081 878 1344, ⓦnubedargento.com. A 15min walk south from Piazza Tasso up the main road, this campsite has a pool, restaurant, minimart with basic food provisions and wonderful sea views. Closed mid-Jan to mid-March. Per person **€12**, plus per tent **€6**
Seven Via Iommella Grande 99, Sant'Agnello ☏081 878 6758, ⓦsevenhostel.com. A 20min walk north of town or one stop north on the Circumvesuviana train. Set in a former monastery, this large modern hostel has clean and functional dorms, all with a/c, lockers, individual reading lamps and sockets; the views from the rooftop terrace with deckchairs are, quite simply, breathtaking. Dorms **€23**, doubles **€80**
Ulisse Via del Mare 22 ☏081 877 4753, ⓦulissedeluxe .com. More of a four-star hotel than hostel, "deluxe" *Ulisse* has sparkling rooms, all with a/c, fridge, satellite TV and private bath; there are only two six-bed dorms (one male, one female), so book way ahead. Guests have access to the spa next door. Dorms **€25**, doubles **€100**

EATING

Da Emilia Via Marina Grande 62 ⓦdaemilia.it. This trattoria serves simple food in perhaps Sorrento's best location – on the waterfront at Marina Grande. Very good for pasta dishes, with half a dozen great seafood and tomato-based *primi* (seafood *paccheri* €13), and the same number of principally fish *secondi*. Daily noon–3pm & 6.30–10pm.
Da Gigino Via degli Archi 15. A good, no-nonsense restaurant and pizzeria, and one of the oldest spots in town, with a menu of standards, including decent pasta dishes from €8, main courses from around €10 (good *saltimbocca alla romana* €10) and excellent pizzas from €8. Daily noon–11.45pm.
★Inn Bufalito Vico Fuoro I 21 ⓦinnbufalito.it. Warm, friendly mozzarella bar and restaurant serving great pasta dishes and inventive mains, big baskets of country breads, cheese platters, delicious *antipasti misti*, and excellent daily chef recommendations such as *paccheri* with buffalo sauce (€13). Daily noon–midnight; closed Jan & Feb.

DRINKING AND NIGHTLIFE

Chaplin's Pub Corso Italia 18. True Irish pub serving pints of lager (€5), Guinness and Magners (both €6), with major sporting events shown on screen. Soak up the booze with some fish and chips (€9). Daily 11am–3am.
Fauno Piazza Tasso 13 ⓦfaunonotte.it. Sorrento's only club attracts tourists and locals alike with its themed nights and weekly live music shows. No entry fee, but obligatory €10 spend on drinks. Daily 11.30pm–3am; Oct–March Sat only.

17

CAPRI

Rising from the sea off the far end of the Sorrentine peninsula, the island of **Capri** is the most sought-after destination in the Bay of Naples. During Roman times the Emperor Tiberius retreated here to indulge in debauchery; more recently the Blue Grotto and the Island's remarkable landscape have drawn tourists in their droves. Capri is a busy and expensive place, but it's easy enough to visit as a day-trip (there's no budget accommodation on the island). In July and August, however, you may prefer to give it a miss rather than fight through the crowds.

WHAT TO SEE AND DO

CAPRI TOWN is a very pretty place, with winding alleyways converging on the tiny main square of Piazza Umberto. The Giardini di Augusto give tremendous views of the coast below and the towering jagged cliffs above. Opposite, take the hairpin path, Via Krupp, down to **MARINA PICCOLA**, a huddle of houses and restaurants around a few patches of pebble beach – pleasantly quiet out of season, though in summer it's heaving. You can also reach the ruins of Tiberius' villa, the **Villa Jovis**, from Capri Town (Mon & Wed–Sun: April–Oct 9am–6pm; Nov–March 10am–2pm; €2; free first Sun of the month), a steep 45-minute trek east. The site is among Capri's most exhilarating, with incredible views.

ANACAPRI, the island's other main settlement, though less picturesque, is the starting point for some worthwhile excursions: from here a chairlift (daily: March & April 9.30am–4pm; May–Oct 9.30am–5pm; Nov–Feb 9.30am–3.30pm; €7.50 one-way, €10 return) carries you up 596m **Monte Solaro**, the island's highest point, where there's a pricey but picturesquely sited café. The island's most famous attraction, the **Blue Grotto**, is an hour's trek down Via Lo Pozzo, but it's best to take a bus from the main square. At €13.50 it's a bit of a rip-off, with boatmen whisking visitors through the grotto in five minutes flat, but the intense, glowing blue of the cave is undeniably beautiful.

ARRIVAL AND DEPARTURE

By ferry Ferries and hydrofoils dock at Marina Grande, from where it's a steep walk up 300 steps (20–45min) or a short funicular ride (€1.80) to Capri Town, which perches on the hill above. Buses link the main centres – Marina Grande, Capri Town, Marina Piccola and Anacapri – every 10min (€1.80, or €8.60 for a day ticket).

INFORMATION

Tourist office There are offices in Marina Grande (April–Oct Mon–Sat 9am–1pm & 3–6pm, Sun 9.30am–1.30pm; Nov–March Mon–Sat 9am–3pm; ☎081 837 0634, ⓦ capritourism.com); in Capri Town in the Piazzetta (April–Oct Mon–Sat 9.30am–1.30pm & 4–6.45pm, Sun 9.30am–1.30pm; Oct–April closed Sun; ☎081 837 0686); and Anacapri, at Via G. Orlandi 59 (Mon–Sat 9am–3pm; ☎081 837 1524).

EATING

Picnics are a good way to avoid paying Capri's inflated restaurant prices.

Capri Pasta Via Canale 12, Capri Town. This local delicatessen offers a great selection of home-made dishes to go; try the *ravioli caprese* or the *melanzane parmigiana* (both €6). For dessert, head to Buonocore nearby for the island's best ice cream. Mon–Sat 9am–8pm, Sun 9am–2pm.

Il Solitario Via G. Orlandi 96 ⓦ trattoriailsolitario.it. A family-run restaurant where the food is excellent – they do a very generous *spaghetti alle vongole* with home-made pasta, and great pizzas too; the prices are moderate, and the service very friendly. Mon, Tues & Thurs–Sun noon–3pm & 7pm–midnight; closed two months in winter.

THE AMALFI COAST

Occupying the southern side of Sorrento's peninsula, the **Amalfi Coast** is one of Europe's most beautiful stretches of coast, its corniche road winding around the towering cliffs. There are no trains; buses from Sorrento and Naples take the coast road – a spectacular ride of hairpin bends with fantastic views of the undulating coastline.

Amalfi

In Byzantine times, **AMALFI** was an independent republic and a naval superpower, with a population of some seventy thousand. Vanquished by the Normans in 1131, it was then devastated by an earthquake in 1343. A few remnants of Amalfi's past glories

BARI AND BRINDISI TRANSPORT

Numerous ferries arrive at the busy ports of **Bari** and **Brindisi** daily, and the two cities are also served by budget airlines Ryanair and easyJet.

BARI

By plane Bari airport (☎080 580 0200, ⓦaeroportidipuglia.it) is 25km northwest of the city centre. Pugliairbus (ⓦpugliairbus.aeroportidipuglia .it) connects Bari airport with those of Brindisi and Foggia, and with Lecce, Taranto, Matera and the Gargano promontory.

By train Bari has excellent rail connections and three train stations.

Destinations Alberobello (FSE, every 30min–1hr; 1hr 30min); Brindisi (36 daily; 1hr 20min); Lecce (33 daily; 1hr 30min–2hr); Locorotondo (20 daily; 1hr 40min); Matera (FAL, 14 daily; 1hr 30min); Rome (5 daily; 4hr 40min); Taranto (20 daily; 1hr 20min).

By bus From the coastal towns north of Bari you'll arrive at Piazza Eroi del Mare; SITA buses from inland and southern towns, Miccolis buses from Rome and FAL buses from Basilicata pull up in Largo Sorrentino (behind the train station). FSE buses from Brindisi pull in at Largo Ciaia (Mon–Sat), and on Largo Sorrentino (Sun), when they substitute for the train service. Bus services to Naples (3hr) are quicker than the train.

By ferry Ferries all use the Stazione Marittima, next to the old city, which is connected with the main FS train station by bus #20.

Destinations Albania (Durrës: 2 daily; 8hr); Croatia (Dubrovnik: 6 weekly; 10hr); Montenegro (Bar: 5 weekly; 9hr); and Greece (Igoumenitsa: 2–3 daily; 8hr 30min; Corfu: 3 weekly; 8hr; Pátra: 6 weekly, 16hr 30min).

BRINDISI

By plane Brindisi's airport (☎080 580 0200, ⓦaeroportidipuglia.it) is 7km from the city centre. There are buses from the airport direct to Lecce (€7.50), Bari (€10) and Taranto (€6.50).

By train The train station is on Piazza Crispi, at the foot of Corso Umberto, a 10- to 15min walk from the port.

Destinations Lecce (36 daily; 30min); Ostuni (25 daily; 25min); Taranto (13 daily; 1hr).

By bus Services to Rome, Florence and Pisa (Marozzi buses) and Naples (Miccolis buses) arrive at, and depart from, Viale P. Togliatti, a continuation of Viale A. Moro in the new part of town.

Destinations Florence (1 daily; 13hr); Naples (3 daily; 5hr 30min); Pisa (1 daily; 14hr); Rome (4 daily; 7hr).

By ferry Arriving by ferry from Greece leaves you at Costa Morena, a couple of kilometres southeast of town; a shuttle bus run by the port authority links this with the town centre, dropping off and picking up at the intersection of Corso Garibaldi and Lungomare Regina Margherita, in front of the maritime station, before continuing to the airport.

Destinations Cephallonia (weekly in July & Aug; 16hr); Corfu (6 weekly; from 7hr); Igoumenitsa (6 weekly; 8hr); Patras (at least 1 daily in summer; 13hr).

---

survive, and its narrow alleyways and tucked-away piazzas make it fun to wander through. The **Duomo** dominates the main piazza, its toy-town facade topped by a glazed-tiled cupola. St Andrew is buried in its crypt, though the most appealing part of the building is the cloister (daily 9am–7pm, earlier in winter; €3) – Arabic in feel, with its whitewashed arches and palms. Opposite Piazza Gioia, the **Arsenale** (daily 11am–6pm; €2) displays the Tavole Amalfitane – the book of maritime laws that governed the Republic, and the rest of the Mediterranean, until 1570, as well as an exhibition about the evolution of the compass, which was said to have been invented by Amalfitan Flavio Gioia in 1302. Beyond these, the focus is the busy seafront, where there's a crowded **beach**.

ARRIVAL AND DEPARTURE

By bus Buses stop at Piazza Flavio Gioia, on the waterfront.

Destinations Ravello (every 30min; 30min); Rome (Marozzi bus; 3 daily; 5hr 30min); Sorrento (hourly; 1hr 40min); Salerno (hourly; 55min).

By ferry Ferries and hydrofoils use Amalfi's tiny harbour, a stone's throw away from the centre.

Destinations Capri (4 daily; 1hr 30min); Positano (hourly; 30min); Salerno (hourly; 25min); Sorrento (hourly; 50min).

By train The nearest major train station is at Salerno, from where there are SITA buses and ferries to Amalfi.

INFORMATION

Tourist office Via delle Repubbliche Marinare, on the seafront (Mon–Sat 9am–1pm & 2.30–5.30pm; ☎089 871 107, ⓦamalfituristoffice.it).

17

ACCOMMODATION

Almost all the hotels in Amalfi are expensive; it makes sense to base yourself in a hostel in one of the nearby towns, such as Atrani, a 10min bus ride from Amalfi.

A' Scalinatella Piazza Umberto I 5–6, Atrani ☎089 871 492, ⓦhostelscalinatella.com. SITA bus to Atrani or 1km walk from Amalfi. This budget hostel-cum-hotel has small rooms, some with private kitchen, in Atrani, as well as accommodation at a country farmhouse nearby. Dorms **€30**, doubles **€90**

Centrale Largo Piccolomini 1 ☎089 872 608, ⓦamalfihotelcentrale.it. An excellent location, with good-sized and pleasantly furnished rooms – some with a great view of Amalfi's Duomo – and breakfast served on the hotel's lovely roof terrace. **€120**

Sant'Andrea Salita Costanza d'Avalos 1 ☎089 871 145, ⓦalbergosantandrea.it. One of the cheaper options in town, this pleasant hotel on the central square has views of the Duomo from most rooms. Doubles **€90**

EATING

Stock up on food provisions at the grocery Melchiorre Alimentari, just off Piazza dei Dogi; you can order freshly made sandwiches to go for €2.50.

★**Cuoppo d'Amalfi** Via Supportico dei Ferrari 10, just off Piazza dei Dogi. This little joint offers a selection of dishes sizzled in front of your eyes: take your *cuoppo* – a paper cone filled with shrimps, squid and small local fish (€8) – to the beach with a glass of white wine (€3) and enjoy. Daily noon–midnight.

Taverna Buonvicino Largo S. Maria Maggiore 13, ⓦtavernabuonvicino.com. This restaurant and wine bar makes the most of its atmospheric little square – perhaps Amalfi's prettiest – offering a seasonal menu with local favourites such as squid stuffed with potatoes (€14). Book ahead. Daily noon–3pm & 6.15–10.15pm.

Ravello

The best views of the coast are inland from Amalfi, in **RAVELLO**. For a time an independent republic, nowadays it's little more than a large village. What makes it more than worth the thirty-minute bus ride up from Amalfi is its unrivalled location, spread across the top of one of the coast's mountains. The **Duomo** (daily 9am–noon & 5.30–8pm) is a bright eleventh-century church with a richly ornamented interior, but Ravello's real draws are its two villas: by the Duomo are the gardens of the **Villa Rufolo** (daily 9am–8pm, earlier in winter; €5), the spectacular venue for a renowned arts festival in the summer (tickets from €25,

some events free; ⓦwww.ravellofestival .com); a ten-minute walk south is the stunning **Villa Cimbrone** (daily 9am–sunset; €7), undoubtedly worth a visit for the spectacular views of the coast from the Terrace of Infinity, adorned with eighteenth-century marble busts.

INFORMATION

Tourist office Via Roma 18 (daily: March–Oct 9am–6pm; Nov–Feb 9am–4pm; ☎089 857 096, ⓦravellotime.it).

MATERA

Tucked into the instep of Italy in the Basilicata region, **MATERA** is one of the south's most fascinating cities. The main point of interest is its *sassi*, rock dwellings dug out of a ravine. During the 1950s and 1960s the residents were evicted, as the city had degenerated into a slum. New blocks were constructed outside the town to house the population and the *sassi* were left empty, but in 1993 the area was declared a World Heritage Site and has since been slowly repopulated with hotels, restaurants and workshops, as well as starring as the set of many a film, including *The Passion of The Christ*. In 2019, it will be one of Europe's Capitals of Culture.

The focus of the sassi district, a warren of rock streets, is the **chiese rupestri** or rock-hewn churches, of which you can visit two, the spectacular **Santa Maria de Idris** (daily: April–Oct 10am–7pm; Nov–March 10am–2pm; €3), with frescoes dating from the fourteenth century, and, adjacent, **Santa Lucia alle Malve** (daily: April–Nov 10am–7pm; Nov–March 10.30am–1.30pm; €3, or €5 for both churches). For an insight into what life was like for the *sassi*-dwellers, stop by the **Casa Grotta**, just below Madonna de Idris (daily: April–Oct 9.30am–7.30pm; Nov–March 9.30am–5.30pm; €2), or the **C'era una Volta** exhibition at Via Fiorentini 251 (daily 8.30am–8pm; €1.50), a *sassi* dwelling with its life-size inhabitants and their furniture sculpted out of the local tufa by generations of the same family. The **Palombaro Lungo Cistern** (daily 9am–1pm & 4–8pm; €3, includes 20min guided tour), entirely dug by hand and with a

If you're going to splash out on one of the atmospheric cave hotels, the **Antica Locanda San Martino** (Via Fiorentini 71; ☎0835 256 600, ⓦlocandadisanmartino.it; doubles €185) is a special choice: a cool, fragrant *sassi* conversion with individual terraces and an underground swimming pool and sauna. The **Hotel Sassi** (Via S. Giovanni Vecchio 89; ☎0835 331 009, ⓦhotelsassi.it; doubles €94) has gorgeous rooms with film-set-worthy views, some of which can sleep large groups on request to make it more affordable.

capacity of over five million litres of water, served as a vital water supply for inhabitants of the area. **Musma** at Via San Giacomo (Tues–Sun: April–Sept 10am–2pm & 4–8pm; Oct–March 10am–2pm; €5; ⓦmusma.it) is a museum of contemporary sculpture strikingly set in rooms gouged out of the rock.

ARRIVAL AND DEPARTURE

By plane Matera is 60km southwest of Bari airport. Buses operated by Pugliairbus (5 daily; 1hr 15min; €5) run to Piazza Matteotti.
By bus Coaches stop at the Matera Villa Longo station, a 20min walk out of town but connected by bus.
Destinations Naples (2 daily; 4hr); Rome (3 daily; 7hr).
By train The train station, on Piazza Matteotti, is served by the private FAL rail line (ⓦferrovieappulolucane.it) from Bari. If you're travelling from Naples, consider a train running to Ferrandina, 30km outside Matera, from where buses to Matera meet the trains.

INFORMATION

Tourist office Via Ridola (Mon–Sat 9.30am–1.30pm & 3–7pm, Sun 9.30am–7pm; ☎0835 311 655, ⓦaptbasilicata.it). Further information on Matera and the region of Basilicata at ⓦdiscoverbasilicata.com and ⓦbasilicataturistica.com.

Tours Bike Basilicata (ⓦbikebasilicata.it) rent mountain bikes (€25/day), while Walk Basilicata (ⓦwalkbasilicata.it) offer hiking tours of the surrounding area.

ACCOMMODATION

★ **La Dolce Vita** Rione Malve 51 ☎0835 310 324, ⓦladolcevitamatera.it. This small, intimate B&B with welcoming management has two beautiful cave-like doubles, as well as two mini apartments equipped with kitchen. Rates include breakfast. Doubles €80

Le Monacelle Via Riscatto 9/10 ☎0835 344 097. This ex-friary is now a smart hostel, with two large dorms sleeping 13 and 16, both nicely decorated with wooden furniture. The latter has partitioned areas for privacy, while the former preserves a wonderful original stone floor. There's a 1am curfew for the dorms. Dorms €19, doubles €90

EATING AND DRINKING

L'Arturo Piazza del Sedile 15. This welcoming wine and food shop prepares great sandwiches (€3) and offers excellent cheese and meat boards. Daily 10am–3.30pm & 7pm–midnight.
La Gatta Buia Via Margherita 90/92. Popular restaurant and wine bar with tables on a pretty square offering a selection of creatively prepared local dishes which change monthly. *Primi* €8–10, *secondi* €10–17. Tues–Sun noon–3pm, 7.30pm–midnight.
Oi Marì Via Fiorentini 66 ⓦoimari.it. Authentic Neapolitan pizzas (€4–9) and a selection of regional dishes made with local ingredients to be enjoyed in a cavernous setting. *Primi* and *secondi* from €8. Daily dinner only 8–11pm, plus Fri & Sat lunch 1–3pm.

LECCE

LECCE, 40km south of Brindisi port, is often called the "Florence of the south". These alleys may be well trodden, but a real sense of discovery still accompanies a visit to the city's vine-enveloped stonework. Carved from soft sandstone, these buildings were built for wealthy families, churchmen and merchants during the fifteenth to seventeenth centuries, and are among the most beautiful examples of the style. A short walk from the central Piazza Sant'Oronzo is **Santa Croce** (daily 9am–noon & 5–8pm, earlier in winter; free), the most famous of Lecce's churches, where delicate engravings soften the Baroque outline of the building. Inside, the excess continues with a riot of stars, flowers and foliage covering everything from the top of columns to chapel altarpieces. Lecce's other highlight is the **Piazza del Duomo**, an elegantly proportioned square surrounded by Baroque *palazzi*. The **Duomo** itself (daily 9am–noon & 4–6.30pm, earlier in winter; free) is an explosion of Baroque detail.

ARRIVAL AND DEPARTURE

By plane Lecce is 40km from Brindisi airport (ⓦbrindisiairport.net); Pugliairbus (9 daily; €7.50) connects the airport to the City Terminal on Piazza Carmelo Bene in the centre of town.

By train The train station is a 15min walk south of the centre on Viale Oronzo Quarta.

Destinations Bari (9 daily; 1hr 20min–1hr 50min); Bologna (9 daily; 7–9hr); Brindisi (every 30min–1hr; 25min); Naples via Caserta (5 daily; 6hr); Rome (3 daily; 5hr 30min); Turin (2 daily; 13hr); Milan (8 daily; 8 12hr).

By bus Buses arrive at the City Terminal, a 10min walk from the centre; some buses for southern destinations also use the train station.

Destinations Bologna (1 daily; 10hr 50min); Naples (3 daily; 5hr 20min); Palermo (1 daily; 11hr 30min); Rome (4 daily; 8hr).

INFORMATION

Tourist office Corso Vittorio Emanuele 24 (daily: June–Sept 9.30am–1.30pm & 3.30–7.30pm; Oct–May 10am–1pm & 4–6pm; ⓣ0832 682 985). Infopoints also at Piazza Sant'Oronzo (daily: June–Sept 9.30am–9pm; Oct–May 9.30am–1.30pm & 3.30–7.30pm; ⓣ0832 242 099) and in the castle, at Viale 25 July (June–Aug 9.30am–9pm, open until 11pm mid-July–end Aug; Oct–May 9am–8.30pm; closed Sept; ⓣ0832 246 517).

ACCOMMODATION

B&B Azzurretta Via Vignes 2b ⓣ0832 242 211, ⓦbblecce.it. Occupies the top floors of a sixteenth-century *palazzo* boasting a glorious terrace. Pleasantly furnished, with large wooden beds and airy rooms. Doubles €70

Centro Storico B&B ⓣ0832 242 727, ⓦbedandbreakfast.lecce.it. This attractive B&B occupies the same *palazzo* as *B&B Azzurretta*. Doubles without bath €60, with bath €80

Le Comari Salentine Via Duca degli Abruzzi 67 ⓣ347 426 9404, ⓦlecomarisalentine.it. This itty bitty B&B has three neatly presented rooms decked out in minimalist Ikea furniture; all are spotless, and two have a kitchenette, ideal for self-caterers. Doubles €50

EATING AND DRINKING

In the evenings, the bars that line Piazza Vittorio Emanuele II liven up, with DJs, live music, and tables spilling onto the leafy square.

Caffè Letterario Via G. Paladini 46 ⓦcaffeletterario.org. This arty café-bar with mismatched furniture and board games organizes a wealth of events, including theatre performances and live music. Check the website for the full programme. *Aperitivo* from €5. Tues–Sat 7pm–2.30am, Sun 5pm–2am; open Mon in summer.

La Vecchia Osteria Via Dasumno 3. You will see owner and chef Totò hard at work in the kitchen rustling up excellent home-made dishes; the vegetables are mostly home-grown, the olive oil is from Totò's own olive grove and he even makes the house wine. *Primi* €5–12, *secondi* €6–12. Tues–Sun 1–3pm & 8pm–midnight.

★**Le Zie** Via Costadura 19 ⓣ0832 245 178. A simple trattoria serving superb home-style cooking – try Puglia's famous *orecchiette* pasta (€8); more adventurous types can go for the local speciality, horsemeat in spicy sauce (€12). The home-made liqueurs are a must-try. Booking advisable. Tues–Sat 12.30–2.30pm & 8–10.30pm, Sun 12.30–2.30pm.

Sicily

Perhaps the most captivating of Italy's islands, **SICILY** (Sicilia) feels socially and culturally separate from the rest of Italy. Occupying a strategically vital position, the largest island in the Mediterranean has a history and outlook that have less in common with its modern parent than with its erstwhile rulers – from the Greeks who first settled the east coast, in the eighth century BC, through a bewildering array of Romans, Arabs, Normans, French and Spanish, to the Bourbons, seen off by Garibaldi in 1860. Substantial relics remain, and temples, theatres and churches are scattered across the island.

The capital, **Palermo**, is a bustling city with an unrivalled display of Norman art and architecture and Baroque churches. The most obvious other target is the chic eastern resort of **Taormina**. From here you can visit **Mount Etna**, or travel south to the ancient Greek centre of **Siracusa**. To the west, the greatest draw is the grouping of temples at **Agrigento**, the largest concentration of the island's Greek remains.

PALERMO

In its own wide bay beneath the limestone bulk of Monte Pellegrino, **PALERMO** is stupendously sited. Originally a Phoenician, then a Carthaginian, colony, this remarkable city was long considered a prize worth capturing, and under Saracen and Norman rule in the ninth to twelfth centuries it became the greatest city in Europe, famed for the wealth of its court and peerless as a centre of learning. Nowadays it's a brash, exciting city, whose uniquely varied architecture and museums are well worth exploring.

WHAT TO SEE AND DO

Around the Quattro Canti

The heart of the old city is the Baroque **Quattro Canti** crossroads, with **Piazza Pretoria** and its racy fountain just around the corner. In nearby Piazza Bellini, the church of **La Martorana** (Mon–Sat 8am–1pm & 3.30–5.30pm, 6.30pm in summer, Sun 8.30am–9.45 & noon–1pm; free) is one of the finest survivors of the medieval city. Its slim twelfth-century campanile and spectacular mosaics make a marked contrast to the adjacent squat chapel of **San Cataldo** (daily 9.30am–12.30pm & 3–6pm; €2.50) with its little Arab red golfball domes representing the Trinity.

Alberghiera

In the district of Alberghiera, a warren of narrow streets, you'll find the deconsecrated church of **San Giovanni degli Eremiti** (Via dei Benedettini; Tues–Sun 9am–6.30pm; €6), built in 1148. Established on the remains of a mosque, it's topped with five rosy domes and has late thirteenth-century cloisters. From here it's a few paces north to the **Palazzo dei Normanni** (generally Mon–Sat 8.15am–5.40pm, Sun 8.15am–1pm, but check ⓦfedericosecondo.org; Fri–Mon €8.50, Tues–Thurs €7 when the Royal Apartments are closed; entrance on Piazza Indipendenza), the seat of the Sicilian regional parliament. It was originally built by the Saracens and was enlarged by the Normans, under whom it housed the most magnificent of medieval European courts. The beautiful **Cappella Palatina** (closed to visitors Sun 9.45am–11.15am), the private royal chapel of Roger II, is almost entirely covered in glorious twelfth-century mosaics.

The impressive Norman **Cattedrale** (Mon–Sat 9am–5.30pm, Sun 4.30–6pm; free) boasts a fine portal and tombs containing the remains of some of Sicily's most famous monarchs (entry €1.50).

The Museo Archeologico Regionale, Vucciria and around

17

The beautiful Neoclassical Teatro Massimo, Italy's largest opera house, built in honour of King Victor Emmanuel II, is on Via Roma. Regular performances take place, and the interior of the theatre can be visited as part of a guided tour (every 20min; 30min; daily 9.30am–6pm, last tour at 5.30pm; €8). Although the **Museo Archeologico Regionale** (ⓦwww.regione.sicilia.it/beniculturali/salinas), to the northeast of the Teatro off Via Roma, has been closed for restoration for years, small sections open sporadically, while occasional **temporary exhibitions** offer a chance to see some of its magnificent collection of artefacts, which spans the island's Phoenician, Greek and Roman heritage.

Southeast of the Museo Archeologico is the **Vucciria market** area (daily from 8am), which offers glimpses of the Palermo of old. You can cut through to Sicily's **Galleria Regionale** (Tues–Sat 9am–6pm with sporadic Sunday openings; €8), on Via Alloro, in the rough-and-ready La Kalsa district. It's a stunning art collection, with works from the eleventh to the seventeenth centuries.

ARRIVAL AND DEPARTURE

By plane Palermo airport (☏ 091 702 0273, ⓦ gesap.it) is 35km west of town. Prestia e Comandè buses meet arrivals and have stops at various city-centre locations before reaching the terminal at the train station – tell the driver where you're going and he can advise where best to get off (55min; €6.10). Trinacria Express run trains to the central station (1hr; €6.30).

Destinations Milan (several daily; 1hr 30min); Naples (2 daily; 55min); Pisa (2 daily; 1hr 25min); Rome (several daily; 1hr).

By train Trains arrive at the Stazione Centrale, at the southern end of Via Roma – bus #101 runs to the centre. Buy tickets (€1.30; valid for 1hr 30min) at *tabacchi* shops.

Destinations Agrigento (10 daily; 2hr 10min); Siracusa (change at Messina; 4 daily; 6hr 30min–7hr 30min); Taormina (change at Messina; 8 daily; 4hr–5hr 20min).

By bus Buses (services run by SAIS and Interbus) are quicker than trains in Sicily, taking scenic cross-country routes rather than lumbering round the coast. The bus terminal is at Piazza Cairoli right by the train station.

17

■ ACCOMMODATION		● EATING		■ DRINKING AND NIGHTLIFE	
A Casa di Amici Hostel & Rooms	1	Franco "U Vastiddaru"	2	Ai Chiavettieri	2
Al Giardino dell'Alloro	2	Il Maestro del Brodo	3	Qvivi	3
Casa Orioles	3	Osteria lo Bianco	1	Taverna Azzurra	1
La Casa dei Limoni	4	Pasticceria Cappello	4		

Destinations Agrigento (every 1hr 30min; 2hr); Naples (1 daily; 12hr); Rome (2 daily; 13hr); Siracusa (3 daily; 3hr 15min); Taormina (change at Catania; hourly; 4hr).

By ferry Services dock just off Via Francesco Crispi, from where it's a 10min walk up Via E. Amari to Piazza Castelnuovo.

Destinations Genoa (1 daily; 19hr); Naples (1 daily; 11hr 15min).

INFORMATION

Tourist office Via Principe di Belmonte 92 (Mon–Fri 8.30am–7.30pm, Sat 8.30am–6pm; ☎ 091 585 172). Also council-run information kiosks (all Mon–Wed, Sat & Sun 9am–1pm & 3–7pm, Thurs & Fri 9am–1pm & 3–6pm, though hours may be reduced) scattered around the city centre, in places like Piazza Politeama, Piazza Bellini and at the Stazione Centrale.

GETTING AROUND

By bus Tickets for the *linea gialla, linea rossa* and *linea verde*, and the *circolare* (which all weave in and out and over the *centro storico*) minibus services, cost just €0.52 for a day's use.

ACCOMMODATION

A Casa di Amici Hostel & Rooms Via Dante 57 ☎ 091 584 884, ⓦ acasadiamici.com. This friendly hostel has a yoga studio and offers music workshops and bike rental. There's also a café-bar as well as a kitchen for self-caterers. Dorms €20, doubles without bath €50, with bath €60

Al Giardino dell'Alloro Vicolo S. Carlo 8 ☎ 338 224 3541, ⓦ giardinodellalloro.it. Lovely B&B in the heart of La Kalsa with books for guests to borrow, a courtyard where breakfast is served and a living room used as an exhibition space for contemporary Sicilian artists. The five rooms feature original works of art, and have kettles and mugs. There is a small kitchen for guests' use. **€85**

★**Casa Orioles** Via alla Piazza dei Tedeschi 4 ☎339 874 2001 or ☎091 652 6890, ⓦcasaorioles.it. This arty B&B in a sixteenth-century building has palatial, beautifully presented rooms with period furniture, all with kitchenette and private bath. There are also larger mini apartments sleeping four. Doubles **€60**, apartment **€100**

La Casa dei Limoni Piazza Giulio Cesare 9 ☎334 834 3888 or ☎338 967 8907, ⓦlacasadeilimoni.it. A friendly B&B right opposite the train station that's great value for money, and a good choice if you're catching an early train. **€60**

EATING

The city's markets are a great place to pick up a picnic; try Ballarò, between Piazza Carmine and Piazza Ballarò in the Alberghiera district. There's a GS supermarket in Piazza Marina.

Franco "U Vastiddaru" Corso Vittorio Emanuele 102, corner Piazza Marina. A local hangout with outdoor seating serving traditional *panelle* (fried chickpea flour; €2.50) and *arancini* (€2), as well as the much-loved *focaccia* with *milza* (veal spleen and lung; €2.50). Daily 8am–2am.

Il Maestro del Brodo Via Pannieri 7. Simple Sicilian home cooking with a focus on fish dishes; there's a wonderful buffet selection of *antipasti* (€8) to choose from. Tues–Sun 12.30–3.30pm, Fri & Sat also 8–11pm; July & Aug lunch only.

Osteria lo Bianco Via E. Amari 104 ☎091 251 4906. Decorated with Juventus souvenirs and religious brick-a-brac, this is one of the cheapest places to eat in town, serving traditional Palermitano food. *Primi* €5, *secondi* €7. Mon–Sat 12.30–2.30pm & 7.30–10.30pm, Sun 12.30–2.30pm.

Pasticceria Cappello Via Colonna Rotta 68 ⓦpasticceriacappello.it. A sweet lover's delight, offering all manner of cakes and tarts (from €2.50), as well as artisanal ice cream including lactose-free fruit options, to take away or to enjoy at one of the little tables outside. Mon, Tues & Thurs–Sun 7am–9.30pm.

DRINKING AND NIGHTLIFE

In summer, nightlife shifts to the beach resort of Mondello, which is full of lively bars, a half-hour bus ride from Palermo (#806 from Teatro Politeama). The Vucciria district, in particular Via dei Chiavettieri, Piazza Rivoluzione and nearby Piazza Maggiore, has scores of bars that are packed most nights of the week. Piazza Marina also attracts a crowd and a half.

★**Ai Chiavettieri** Via Chiavettieri 16/18. Welcoming bar with handcrafted wooden furniture, attracting a hip artsy crowd who flock here for the great cocktails (€6), selection of over sixty wines (€4), cheap *chiputos* (shots €2) and the friendly vibe. Main dishes (€6–13), too. Tues–Sun 7pm–3am.

Qvivi Piazza della Rivoluzione 5. A young studenty crowd spills in for the great *aperitivo* that kicks off as doors open at 6.30pm; drinks are knocked back on the lively square and are sometimes accompanied by live jazz, blues or rock. Tues–Sun 6.30pm–3am.

Taverna Azzurra Discesa Maccheronai 9. A rustic bar attracting a large crowd for the cheap beers (€1.50) and *sangue* (literally "blood", fortified wine €1) enjoyed on the street outside. Mon–Sat 9am–2pm & 5pm–4am.

DIRECTORY

Consulates UK, Via Cavour 117 ☎091 326 412; US, Via Vaccarini 11 ☎091 305 857.

Hospital Policlino, Via del Vespro 129 ☎091 655 1111.

Police Piazza della Vittoria 8 ☎091 210 111.

Post office Via Roma 320 (Mon–Fri 8.30am–7pm, Sat 8.30am–12.30pm).

TAORMINA

On Sicily's eastern coast, and dominating two grand sweeping bays, **TAORMINA** is the island's best-known resort. The outstanding remains of its classical theatre, with Mount Etna as an unparalleled backdrop, arrested passing travellers when Taormina was no more than a medieval hill village. Nowadays it's rather chichi, full of designer shops and pricey cafés, but still has plenty of charm. Its pedestrianized main street, Corso Umberto I, is lined with fifteenth- to nineteenth-century *palazzi* interspersed with intimate piazzas. The **Teatro Greco** (daily 9am–1hr before sunset; €8) was founded by the Greeks in the third century BC, though most of what's left is a Roman rebuilding from the first century AD, when a deep trench was dug in the orchestra to accommodate animals and gladiators. Don't miss the beautiful **Villa Comunale**, a charming public garden once part of a sumptuous private villa owned by Lady Florence Trevelyan. For breathtaking views of the bay and Mount Etna, climb the steps up the **Via Crucis** footpath to the church of the Madonna della Rocca. From here it's a steep but beautiful uphill walk to the wonderful hamlet of **Castelmola**, one of Italy's most beautiful villages, renowned for its almond wine (for an unusual experience sample a glass at *Bar Turrisi* (see p.674).

17

The closest beach to Taormina is at **MAZZARÓ**, with its much-photographed islet, **Isola Bella**: it's a scenic thirty-minute descent on foot, or use the cable car (every 15min; €3 each way) from Via Pirandello.

ARRIVAL AND DEPARTURE

By plane The closest airport is Catania (⍟catania -airport.com), 45km south; buses run between the airport and Taormina (11 daily; 1hr 25min; €7.90).

By bus The bus terminal is at Via Pirandello, a 5min walk from the centre.

Destinations Catania (every 30min; 1hr 10min); Palermo (via Catania; hourly; 3hr 40min).

By train The train station, Taormina-Giardini Naxos, is way below town – it's a steep 30min walk up or a short bus ride to the centre (€1.90).

Destinations Catania (15 daily; 40–50min); Palermo (via Messina; 12 daily; 4hr 30min–5hr 40min); Siracusa (6 daily; 2hr–2hr 50min).

INFORMATION

Tourist office Palazzo Corvaja, Piazza Santa Caterina (Mon–Fri 8.30am–2.30pm & 3.30–7pm; ☎0942 23 243).

ACCOMMODATION

★**Hostel Taormina** Via Circonvallazione 13 ☎0942 625 505, ⍟taorminahotel.net. Welcoming intimate hostel equipped with a kitchen for guests' use, dorms with lockers, and a wonderful terrace with lounge chairs and great views over the bay. The friendly staff are always ready to help. Dorms €22, doubles €66

Taormina's Odyssey Via Paternò di Biscari 13 ☎0942 24 533, ⍟taorminaodyssey.com. Comfortable, with four double rooms and two dorms. There is a kitchen for guest use, rooms have a/c and TV, and there's even a terrace. It is understandably popular, so book well ahead. Dorms €20, doubles €40

★**TREAT YOURSELF**

Smarten up and head to Taormina's luxurious and historic **Grand Hotel Timeo** (Via Teatro Greco 59 ☎0942 627 0200, ⍟grandhoteltimeo.com), whose guests have included all manner of illustrious figures, from D.H. Lawrence to Somerset Maugham. Sip a cocktail (€12) on the wonderful terrace – the panoramic views over Etna and the bay are, quite simply, breathtaking. Dinner will set you back about €70 per person.

EATING

★**Bam Bar** Via di Giovanni 45. This pleasant café with outdoor seating serves over twenty natural flavours of icy sweet *granita* (€3.50), including ricotta and pistachio, typically enjoyed with a freshly baked brioche. Heavenly. Tues–Sun 7am–9pm.

★**Da Cristina** Via Strabone 2. The town's best freshly baked *arancini* (€2.50) come in six exquisite flavours, including pistachio, aubergine and wild fennel; you can also get bargain take-away or eat-in pasta dishes for €5. Daily 7.30am–1am.

Tutti ccá Fratelli Ingegnere 12. The candle-lit tables of this welcoming restaurant line the steps of a quiet cobbled street with views over the Roman Theatre. *Primi* €8–16, *secondi* €10–22. Daily 11am–1am.

DRINKING AND NIGHTLIFE

In town, the action takes place in picturesque but posey Piazza Paladini, off the Corso. Alternatively, the summer beach-bars of nearby Spisone are reachable on foot from Taormina or by bus from Via Pirandello.

Bar Turrisi Piazza Duomo 19, Castelmola. This unique bar in the beautiful neighbouring village of Castelmola attracts crowds from all over keen to sample traditional almond wine (€3) in an unusual setting – how often have you visited a bar decked out entirely in phallic memorabilia? Daily 9.30am–3am.

Daiquiri Piazza Duomo. This trendy lounge bar knocks up exceptional cocktails – including over ten types of daiquiris and even Pimm's – to be enjoyed on the lantern-lit cushioned seats lining the outdoor steps. Cocktails €8. Daily 5pm–2am.

★**Morgana Bar** Scesa Morgana 4. Dress up for this snazzy bar and nightclub with open-air lounge area that attracts a well-heeled local crowd who sip cocktails (from €10) until the early hours. DJs spin a melange of musical flavours: contemporary commercial, vintage Italian and international hits. Daily 8pm–3am; Nov & Dec closed Tues.

MOUNT ETNA

Mount Etna's massive bulk looms over much of the coastal route south of Taormina. At 3340m, it is a substantial mountain and the **ascent** is a spectacular trip; the fact that it's also one of the world's biggest volcanoes – and still active – only adds to the draw. Getting up can be costly and is weather-dependent, so get as much advice as possible on the ground beforehand (see box, p.675).

CLIMBING MOUNT ETNA

The safest and easiest way to ascend Mount Etna is with a **tour** from Taormina. Etna People (ⓦetnapeople.com) offer a range of tours, including classic full day and sunset tours, from €58. If you do decide to go it alone, catch the bus (daily, leaves 8am; 1hr) from **Catania** train station (Catania is approx 50km south of Taormina) up to the huddle of souvenir shops and restaurants at the **Rifugio Sapienza** (see below), which marks the end of the drivable road up the south side of Etna. To get as high up as possible, you can either take a **cable car then a jeep** with guide (2hr 30min; €57.50 return), or take the cable car (daily 9am–5pm; €29.50 return) and walk up the remaining 400m. Alternatively, if you're an experienced walker, go **on foot**: the trip up will take four hours, the return a little less. Take warm clothes, good shoes and glasses to keep the flying grit out of your eyes. The return bus to Catania leaves at 4.30pm, so if you want to walk all the way you'll have to stay the night in the *rifugio*.

If you don't have the time or funds to reach the summit, the **Circumetnea rail service** (€7.25; no service on Sundays; InterRail passes not valid; ⓦcircumetnea.it) train offers a hop-on hop-off service stopping off at a number of towns. It trundles around the base from **Giarre-Riposto**, thirty minutes by train or bus from Taormina. The whole tour takes three and a half hours and ends in Catania.

ACCOMMODATION

Rifugio Sapienza North Nicolosi, Etna Sud ☎095 915 321, ⓦrifugiosapienza.com. A cosy, chalet-style *rifugio* hotel equipped with central heating for the colder months. Each of the 25 en-suite rooms has a TV, the restaurant's worth a look, and you can reach it on public transport. Breakfast included. Per person **€55**

SIRACUSA

SIRACUSA (ancient Syracuse), 115km south of Taormina, was first colonized by the Greeks in 733 BC and grew to become their main power base in Sicily. Today, the city boasts some of the best Greek archeological remains anywhere, and also has a strong Baroque character in its old town, squeezed onto the island of **Ortygia**, and connected to the new town by two bridges.

WHAT TO SEE AND DO

Ortygia

Near the bridge that connects Ortygia to the mainland, the **Temple of Apollo**, built in the sixth century BC, is probably Sicily's most ancient Doric temple. Over the years, it was transformed into a Byzantine church, then an Arab mosque, and into a church again under the Normans. At the centre of the island, the most obvious attraction is the **Duomo** (daily 8am–noon & 4–8pm; €3), set in a piazza studded with Baroque architecture, and itself incorporating twelve fluted columns from the fifth-century BC temple that originally stood here. At the other end of the square, the church of **Santa Lucia** (Tues–Sun 11am–2pm & 3–7pm; free) harbours a Caravaggio

painting, the *Burial of Santa Lucia*. Round the corner at Via Capodieci 16 is the severe thirteenth-century facade of the **Galleria Regionale di Palazzo Bellomo** (Tues–Sat 9am–7pm, Sun 9am–1pm; €8), an outstanding collection of medieval art, and paintings by Antonello da Messina.

The Archeological Museum

North of the train station the city is mainly new, though the best of Siracusa's archeological sights are also here. It's a twenty-minute walk to Viale Teocrito (or take bus #12 from Riva Nazario Sauro), from where you walk east for the **Museo Archeologico Regionale** (Tues–Sat 9am–6pm, Sun 9am–1pm; €8, €13.50 including entrance to Parco Archeologico, valid 3 days), housing a wealth of material from the early Greek colonies, including a wonderful coin and jewellery collection; the museum's highlight is a headless marble *Venus*, sculpted rising from the sea. Round the corner, the ruined **Basilica di San Giovanni** has interesting catacombs (daily 9.30am–12.30pm & 2.30–5pm; €8 ticket includes guided tour departing every 30min; 40min).

17

The Archeological Park

Siracusa's extensive **Parco Archeologico** (daily 9am–1hr before sunset; €10, €13.50 combined ticket with Museo Archeologico Regionale) is a ten-minute walk west of the archeological museum. Here, the **Ara di Ierone II**, an enormous third-century BC altar, is the first thing you see, though the highlight is the **Teatro Greco**. Cut out of the rock and looking down towards the sea, it hosts a summer season of Greek plays (windafondazione .org). Nearby, the **Latomia del Paradiso**, a leafy quarry, is best known for the **Orecchio di Dionisio**, an S-shaped cave, 65m long and 20m high, that Dionysius is supposed to have used as a prison.

ARRIVAL AND DEPARTURE

By plane Interbus run services from Catania airport (wcatania-airport.com) to Siracusa (hourly; 1hr 15min).
By train Siracusa's train station is on Via Crispi, a 20min walk from Ortygia.
Destinations Agrigento (via Catania and Caltanissetta; 1 daily; 5hr); Catania (8 daily; 1hr 10min); Palermo (via Messina; 4 daily; 7hr 20min); Taormina (10 daily; 2hr).
By bus Buses stop in Corso Umberto, near the train station.
Destinations Agrigento (via Catania; hourly; 4hr 30min); Palermo (3 daily; 3hr 15min); Taormina (hourly; 3hr 10min).

INFORMATION

Tourist office Via Roma 31 (Mon–Sat 8am–8pm, Sun 9.30am–6.30pm; t 800 055 500, toll-free).

ACCOMMODATION

Ares Via Mirabella 49 t 0931 461 145, waresbedand breakfast.it. Comfortable B&B on a quiet street, near the sea. Rooms are smart and spotless, there's a lovely roof terrace, and owner Enzo is a great source of information on Ortigia. €80
Casa Cristina Via Chindemi 8 t 0931 62 205, wcasa cristinasr.it. The airy a/c rooms at this little B&B all have wonderful views over the temple of Apollo; there's a kitchen for guests' use and all-day tea and coffee. Doubles €80
Casa Mia Corso Umberto 112 t 0931 463 349, wbbcasamia.it. More of a small hotel than a B&B, Casa Mia has pleasant rooms with a/c and private bath in a nineteenth-century palazzo; there's also a pleasant sunny breakfast terrace. Doubles €90
★ **Lol Hostel** Via F. Crispi 94 t 0931 465 088, wlolhostel .com. Siracusa's only hostel has a spacious lounge area, a modern kitchen and immaculate dorms with lockers and reading lamps. Private rooms all have flat-screen TVs and are en suite. Dorms €23, doubles €75

EATING

Fratelli Burgio Piazza Cesare Battisti 4 wfratelliburgio .com. Tickle your taste buds as you explore the food market in the morning, then head to this wonderful deli for a large plate of exceptional cold cuts for around €10. Mon–Sat 8am–3.30pm.
La Gazza Ladra Via Cavour 8 t 340 060 2428, wgazzaladrasiracusa.com. The owners of this cosy, itty-bitty restaurant head to the market every morning to stock up on fresh produce, which they lovingly prepare all afternoon. Try the sought-after pasta alla palermitana (€10). Book ahead. Tues–Sun 7.30–11.30pm.
Viola Bakery Café Via Roma 43 t 331 861 8415. A contemporary urban look, free, reliable wi-fi and friendly staff have made the Via Roma branch of Viola popular. At lunchtime there are salads, focaccia and scacce (a bread pie stuffed with combinations of vegetables, cheeses and ham) all priced at €5 and under. Daily 7.30am–9pm.

DRINKING AND NIGHTLIFE

Nightlife centres on the lively little square of the Corte dei Bottari and Piazzetta San Rocco in Ortygia.
Enoteca Solaria Via Roma 86 wwww.enotecasolaria .com. Laidback wine bar with a few tables dotting the pavement serving Sicilian wines (€3) and tasty nibbles (€5–15). Mon–Sat 11am–2.30pm & 6pm–midnight.
Sale Via Amalfitania 56/2. Happening bar with brick vaulted ceilings and tables spilling onto the lively square; there are live jazz and blues bands on Thursday (Sept–June). Cocktails €5. Daily 7.30pm–late.
Tinkitè Via della Giudecca 61/63, corner of Via Minniti. A happening little bar-cum-café, serving lovely cakes for breakfast and delicious snacks come aperitivo hour (cocktails €5). Sporadic live music bands. Daily 8.30am–1am & 5.30–11pm, Wed 5.30–11pm only.

AGRIGENTO

Halfway along Sicily's southern coast, **AGRIGENTO** is primarily of interest for its substantial Greek remains, strung out along a ridge facing the sea a few kilometres below town. The series of Doric temples here, mostly dating from the fifth century BC, are the most evocative of Sicily's remains. They are also the focus of a constant procession of tour buses, so budget accommodation should be booked in advance (though Agrigento could be a day-trip from Palermo). A road winds down from the modern city to the sites; buses (#1, #2 and #3 from outside the train station, tickets from the bar inside station) drop off at a car park between the two separate zones of archeological remains at the **Valle dei Templi** (daily 8.30am–7pm; €10, €13.50 combined ticket with archeological museum). The eastern zone is home to the scattered remains of the oldest of the temples: the **Tempio di Ercole**, probably begun in the last decades of the sixth century BC; the better-preserved **Tempio della Concordia**, dating to around 430 BC, with fine views of the city and sea; and the Doric Tempio di Giunone, probably completed in 440 BC.

The western zone, back along the path and beyond the car park, is less impressive but still worth wandering around. The mammoth construction that was the **Tempio di Giove**, the largest Doric temple ever known, was left in ruins by the Carthaginians and further damaged by earthquakes. Valle dei Templi leads back to the town from the car park via the excellent **Museo Archeologico Regionale** (Tues–Sat 9am–1pm & 2–7pm, Mon & Sun 9am–1pm; €8, €13.50 joint ticket with Valle dei Templi) – an extraordinarily rich collection devoted to local finds. From June/July to mid-September the Valle dei Templi usually opens at **night**: once the sun has set over the ruins, they're spectacularly illuminated by floodlights.

ARRIVAL AND DEPARTURE

By plane The closest airports are Catania and Palermo. Regular buses serve Catania airport (hourly; 2hr 40min) and Palermo airport (3 daily; 2hr 30min) from the terminal at Piazza Rosselli.

By bus The bus terminal is at Piazza Rosselli.
Destinations Catania (hourly; 2hr 50min); Naples (1 daily; 12hr); Palermo (every 1hr 30min; 2hr); Rome (2 daily; 14hr).

By train Trains arrive at Agrigento Centrale at the edge of the old town (don't get out at Agrigento Bassa).
Destinations Palermo (every 2hr; 2hr).

INFORMATION

Tourist office Via Atene 272 (Mon–Fri 9.30am–1.30pm plus Tues & Thurs 3.30–7.30pm; ☎0922 596 168).

ACCOMMODATION

★**Camere a Sud** Via Ficani 6 ☎349 638 4424, ⓦcamereasud.it. Welcoming B&B with five cute and cosy rooms, all with private bath, decked out in mellow colours. Staff are exceptionally friendly and there's a pleasant little roof terrace. Doubles **€70**

Piccolo Gellia Vicolo Gozza 2 ☎0922 27157, ⓦpiccologellia.com. An enchanting B&B set in a nineteenth-century building: artsy photos grace the walls, a convivial breakfast is laid out in the morning and the two roaming cats make you feel at home. Doubles with shared bath **€55**, with private bath **€69**

Villa Pirandello Via Francesco Crispi 34 ☎0922 22 275, ⓦvillapirandello.it. A Sicilian-Yorkshire family run this B&B in a nineteenth-century villa with five rooms, a shady garden and a sunny terrace. A more therapeutic post-temples spot is hard to imagine. Breakfasts, featuring fresh fruit and artisan pastries, are superb. **€75**

EATING AND DRINKING

In town, Piazza San Francesco off Via Atenea livens up substantially in the evenings. Along the beachfront, the area of San Leone has plenty of places offering cheap drinks.

Ambasciata di Sicilia Via Giambertoni 2 ⓦristorantel ambasciatadisicilia.it. Revel in the wonderful views over the bay as you dig into a hearty plate of *linguine all'ambasciata* (linguine with bacon, calamari and courgette; €9). Tues–Sun noon–3pm & 7–11pm; mid July & Aug only.

Le Cuspidi Piazza Cavour 19. The best ice creams in town (small cone €1.30), with unusual flavours such as fresh ricotta and almond, as well as the classics. Mon & Wed–Sun 7.30am–midnight.

Mojo Piazza San Francesco 11. Popular bar with thumping music attracting a young crowd who mingle on the square over €6 cocktails. Tues–Sun 7.30pm–3am.

Sardinia

Just under 200km from the Italian mainland, **SARDINIA** (Sardegna) is often regarded as the epitome of Mediterranean Europe. Its blue seas, white sands and rolling hills are beautiful and its way of life relaxed. Sardinia also holds fascinating vestiges of the various powers – Roman, Carthaginian, Genoese and Pisan – that have passed through, alongside striking remnants of Sardinia's only significant native culture, known as the Nuraghic civilization, in the seven thousand tower-like *nuraghi* that litter the landscape. The capital, **Cagliari**, is worth exploring for its excellent museums and some of the island's best nightlife. From here, it's only a short trip to the renowned ruined city at **Nora**, and the quieter beaches at **Chia**. The other main ferry port and airport is Olbia, in the north, little more than a transit

17

town for the exclusive resorts of the Costa Smeralda. There's a third airport at the relaxed resort of **Alghero** in the northwest.

CAGLIARI

Rising up from its port and crowned by an old citadel squeezed within a protective ring of fortifications, **CAGLIARI** has been Sardinia's capital since at least Roman times and is still the island's biggest town. Nonetheless, its centre is easily explored on foot, with almost all the wandering you will want to do encompassed by the citadel.

WHAT TO SEE AND DO

The citadel
The most evocative entry to the citadel is from the monumental **Bastione San Remy** on Piazza Costituzione. From here, you can potter in any direction to enter its intricate maze. The citadel has been altered little since the Middle Ages, though the tidy Romanesque facade on the mainly thirteenth-century **cathedral** (Mon–Sat 8am–8pm, Sun 8am–1pm & 4.30–8.30pm; free) in Piazza Palazzo is in fact a fake, added in the twentieth century in the old Pisan style.

Piazza dell'Arsenale
At the opposite end of Piazza Palazzo, a road leads into the smaller **Piazza dell'Arsenale**, site of several museums including the **Museo Archeologico Nazionale** (Tues–Sun 9am–8pm, last entry 7.15pm; €5). In the same complex, the **Pinacoteca Nazionale** (Tues–Sun 9am–7.15pm; €5) features some glowing fifteenth-century altarpieces, while the **Museo delle Cere** (Tues–Sun 9am–1pm & 4–7pm; €1.55) displays a series of thought-provoking anatomical waxworks executed by Clemente Susini for nineteenth-century medical students.

Towers
Off Piazza Palazzo stands the **Torre San Pancrazio**, the best preserved of Cagliari's fortified towers, from where it's a ten-minute walk to the **Torre dell'Elefante** (both towers daily: May–Sept 10am–7pm; Oct–April 9am–5pm; €3 each),

named after the small carving of an elephant on one side; climb to the top of either for stupendous views over the city and coast.

Beaches
To get to **Poetto Beach**, the long stretch connected to Cagliari, take bus #PF or #PQ from outside the train station for the fifteen-minute ride and get off wherever a patch takes your fancy.

ARRIVAL AND DEPARTURE

By plane Cagliari's airport (ⓦ www.sogaer.it) is linked to town by train (every 15–30min; 5–10min).

By ferry Cagliari's Stazione Marittima is a short walk from Via Roma and the train and bus stations. Tirrenia's ticket office is at Via Riva di Ponente (☎ 070 666 065 or ☎ 892 123, ⓦ tirrenia.it).

Destinations Civitavecchia (1 daily; 13–15hr); Naples (2 weekly; 13hr 30min); Palermo (1–2 weekly; 12hr).

By train The train station is on Piazza Matteotti.

Destinations Alghero (3 daily via Sassari; 4hr 30min); Olbia (1 direct daily; 4hr).

By bus The bus station is on Piazza Matteotti.

Destinations Chia (hourly; 1hr 15min); Olbia (1–2 daily; 4hr 15min–5hr); Pula (hourly; 50min); Sassari (1 daily; 3hr 40min).

INFORMATION

Tourist office In the Palazzo Civico on Piazza Matteotti (daily: April–Oct 9am–8pm; Nov–March 9am–5pm; ☎ 070 677 7397, ⓦ www.cagliariturismo.it). In summer, an information kiosk sometimes opens outside the Stazione Marittima when cruise ships dock at the port.

ACCOMMODATION

Hostel Marina Piazza Scalette San Sepolcro 2 ☎ 070 670 818, ⓦ hostelmarinacagliari.it. This excellent YHI-affiliated hostel is located in the heart of the old town, only a short walk from the train station. Enthusiastic staff, an outdoor café and a cinema room. Room 108 is the best. Dorms €20, doubles €54

La Ghirlanda Via Baylle 7 ☎ 070 204 0610 or ☎ 339 889 2648, ⓦ bnblaghirlanda.com. Central B&B in a late nineteenth-century building with painted ceilings and hospitable hosts. The five large rooms are equipped with TV, a/c, fridges and bathrooms; breakfast is at a bar on Via Roma. €80

La Terraza Sul Porto Largo Carlo Felice 36 ☎ 339 876 0155, ⓦ laterrazzasulporto.com. This fabulous B&B close to the centre has a huge kitchen, cheery decor and a stunning roof terrace. Doubles €50

Rosso e Nero Via Savoia 6 ☎070 656 673, ⓦrossoenerobeb.it. Ideally located for the restaurants of the Stampace area, this small B&B has clean, tastefully decorated rooms. Doubles **€66**

EATING AND DRINKING

★**Lillicu** Via Sardegna 78 ☎070 652 970. Locals cram into this excellent trattoria that serves traditional Cagliari food, often at shared long wooden tables. The large portions, excellent seafood and singing waiters make this an unforgettable experience. Pasta and a quart of wine €15. Mon–Sat 1–3pm & 8.30–11pm.

L'Isola del Gelato Piazza Yenne 35. This extremely popular *gelateria* serves many flavours of ice cream but also offers everything from breakfast cakes to aperitifs. Outdoor seating available. Daily 7am–3am (closes earlier out of season).

Vinvoglio Via Lamarmora 45–47 ☎070 204 2094. Squeezed into a tiny space in Castello, this "wine jazz bar" has a cool, late-night ambience and live jazz most nights. There's a great selection of wines and beers, and you can eat here too (booking recommended). Tues–Sat 7pm–3am.

PULA AND NORA

The charming little town of **Pula**, an hour south of Cagliari, is a great base to explore **Nora** and the stunning southern beaches at **Chia**.

Nora Archeological Centre

Nora is the site of an **ancient city** (daily: mid-Feb to March 10am–6pm; April–Sept 10am–8pm; Oct 10am–6.30pm; Nov to mid-Feb 10am–5.30pm; last entry 1hr before closing; €7.50), thought to date from the eighth century BC. An administrative, religious and commercial centre for over 1000 years, it was abandoned around the seventh century AD when the Arab invasion forced the inhabitants to retreat inland. The monuments – a theatre, thermal baths (which made use of natural springs here), a forum, a temple, an aqueduct and noble houses – suggest a sophisticated people, and many of the intricate mosaics decorating the town remain intact.

To get here from Pula, take an eight-minute ride on the Follesa bus (ⓦfollesa.com) from Piazza Giovanni XXIII, or follow the signs and walk (25min).

Laguna di Nora

Next to the Nora Archeological Centre is the **lagoon** (daily: June–Aug 10am–8pm; Sept 10am–7pm; €8; ☎070 920 9544, ⓦlagunadinora.it), originally a fish farm and now an environmental park where you can observe nesting birds and local wildlife, paddle around in a **canoe** (€25/3hr, including entry to the lagoon park), or take a **snorkelling** trip to see the Roman remains on the bed of the bay (€25/3hr). Nora beach itself, flanked by the **Torre del Coltellazzo** and the **Torre di Sant Efisio** (which you can climb up for a view over the mountains of Santa Margherita), is a lovely, family-orientated place for a swim.

Chia

For secluded beaches, take a bus from Pula's Via Lamarmora to **Chia** (hourly; 25min); Chia beach is a five-minute walk from where the bus terminates. From here, white sands lapped by turquoise-blue waters stretch along the west coast for about 4km.

ARRIVAL AND DEPARTURE

By bus ARST buses connect Pula with Cagliari roughly every hour, less frequently on Sun (50min). From Pula, a local minibus runs to Nora and the campsites at Santa Margherita di Pula (5–9 daily; Oct–May Mon–Sat only).

INFORMATION

Tourist office Piazza del Comune (Tues–Sun 10.15am–1pm & 2–4.30pm; ☎070 920 9033).

ACCOMMODATION

If you get stuck for accommodation in Pula, your best bet is to ask at the helpful tourist office.

Campeggio Torre Chia ☎070 923 0054, ⓦcampeggiotorrechia.it. A large campsite just a stone's throw from Chia beach, which has a small on-site shop and restaurant; take a left off the main road from the Chia junction and head towards the sea. Per person **€9.50**, plus per tent **€9**

Hotel Quattro Mori Via Cagliari 10, Pula ☎070 920 9124. Basic but clean hotel that's also the cheapest accommodation option in town. Doubles **€40**

EATING

Su Furriadroxu Via XXIV Maggio 11, Pula ☎070 924 6148. With an arcaded courtyard, this place specializes in

17

dishes from the Campidano area. Try the ravioli stuffed with ricotta and saffron, cooked in butter and orange, or a mixed meat grill. Pastas and soups are €7, mains €10–13. Mon, Tues & Thurs–Sun 8–10.45pm.

ALGHERO

In the northwest of Sardinia, **ALGHERO** is a lively resort with a Catalan flavour. From the **Giardino Pubblico**, the **Porta Terra** is the first of Alghero's seven defensive towers, erected by the prosperous Jewish community before their expulsion in 1492. **Via Roma** runs down from here through the old town's puzzle of lanes to the pedestrianized **Via Carlo Alberto**, home to most of the bars and shops. Turn right to reach **Piazza Civica**, the old town's main square, at one end of which rises Alghero's mainly sixteenth-century **cattedrale** (daily 7am–7.30pm; free).

Coastal trips

The best excursions are northwest along the coast, past the long bay of **Porto Conte** to the point of **Capo Caccia**, where the spectacular sheer cliffs are riddled by deep marine caves. The most impressive of these is the Grotta di Nettuno, or **Neptune's Grotto** (daily: April & Oct 10am–6pm; May–Sept 9am–8pm; Nov–March 10am–4pm; last tour 1hr before closing; €13), a long snaking passage that delves far into the rock and is full of stalagmites and stalactites. To get there, join a boat trip from the port (€16, excluding entrance to the caves; 20–40min), or take the bus from Alghero's Giardini Pubblici (1–3 daily; €4.50 return), leaving you at the top of a long and steep flight of steps that corkscrews down to the cave mouth. If you do have time for another excursion, head down the coast to the picturesque town of **Bosa** (4 daily buses; 1hr).

ARRIVAL AND DEPARTURE

By plane From Alghero airport (🖥 aeroportodialghero.it) there are hourly local buses into the centre of town (30min; €1 from machines in the terminal, €1.50 on board), or direct services to Sassari and, in summer, Cagliari.
By train Trains arrive 2km north of the centre and are connected to the port by regular local buses. Destinations Sassari (frequent; 35min).
By bus Buses from the airport and from out of town arrive at the Giardini Pubblici, by the port and old centre. Destinations Bosa (2–5 daily; 55min); Sassari (4–10 daily; 1hr).

INFORMATION

Tourist office Piazza Porta Terra (April–Sept Mon–Sat 8am–8pm, Sun 10am–1pm; Oct–March Mon–Sat 8am–8pm; ☎ 079 979 054, 🖥 alghero-turismo.it).

ACCOMMODATION

Hostal de l'Alguer Via Parenzo 79 ☎ 079 930 478, 🖥 algherohostel.com. This slightly shabby HI hostel is located in a fairly distant but tranquil spot 5km along the coast at Fertilia, reachable by local bus from Alghero. Dorms €15, doubles €35
La Mariposa Via Lido 22 ☎ 079 950 480, 🖥 lamariposa.it. Popular, friendly, well-equipped campsite 2km north of town, with direct access to the seaweed-covered beach. April to mid-Oct. Per person €13, plus per tent €12
★ **L'Ioc D'or B&B** Via Logudoro 26 ☎ 334 289 7130, 🖥 llocdor.com. Friendly B&B a short walk from the old town, with two large, airy rooms and a self-contained apartment. Breakfasts on the patio include fresh fruit and yoghurt. Doubles €80

EATING AND DRINKING

Al Vecchio Mulino Via Don Deroma 3. In the heart of the old town, this locals' favourite serves up tasty seafood and meat dishes (mostly €12–16) and pizzas in low-vaulted rooms. Daily 7pm–midnight; mid-Sept to mid-June closed Tues.
Casablanca Via Umberto 76. With vaulted rooms, this is a great venue for a straightforward pizza or pasta dish in a convivial atmosphere; mains are €10–15. Oct–May Mon, Tues & Thurs–Sun 12.30–2.30pm & 7.30–11.30pm; June–Sept closed all day Mon & Thurs lunchtime.
Poco Loco Via Gramsci 8 ☎ 079 983 604. Superb modern pizzeria and cocktail bar hosting live music gigs. The metre-long pizza serves four (€32), while cocktails start at €6. Daily 7.30pm–midnight.

HOUSE OF THE BLACKHEADS, RĪGA

Latvia

HIGHLIGHTS

❶ **Rīga** Admire the exquisite Art Nouveau architecture before exploring the expanding bar scene. **See p.686**

❷ **Jūrmala** Join the Latvian summer beach party at this string of seaside resorts. **See p.693**

❸ **Sigulda** Explore the castle ruins and hiking trails of the gorgeous Gauja Valley. **See p.694**

❹ **Ventspils** Vibrant port city with one of Latvia's best beaches. **See p.695**

❺ **Kolka** Explore seaside villages and windswept coast. **See p.696**

HIGHLIGHTS ARE MARKED ON THE MAP ON P.683

ROUGH COSTS

Daily budget Basic €60, occasional treat €70

Drink Aldaris beer €2.70

Food Pork with potatoes and sauerkraut €7

Hostel/budget hotel €15/€30–45

Travel Bus: Rīga–Ventspils €7.55; train: Rīga–Sigulda €1.90

FACT FILE

Population 2 million

Language Latvian; Russian also widely spoken

Currency Euro (€)

Capital Rīga

International phone code ☎371

Time zone GMT +2hr

Introduction

Since becoming a member of the European Union in 2004, Latvia has enjoyed a bumpy ride of boom and slump, although the decision to adopt the euro in January 2014 seems to point to a measure of stability in future. The Soviet occupation left the country with a large Russian minority population, and it remains a place divided by language and culture – Rīga in particular is a strikingly bilingual city, although all road signs and public notices are in Latvian. While it's the country's boisterous capital to which most visitors are attracted, to experience the true spirit of Latvia you'll need to head into the spectacularly unspoiled countryside, with its lakes, forests and sandy beaches.

18

The most obvious destination is the capital, **Rīga**. Its architectural treasures, lively nightlife and countless eating options make it a prime destination for budget travellers. Places within easy reach of the capital include the palace of **Rundāle**, while those wishing to hit the beach can head either to the nearby resort area of **Jūrmala** or to the port city of **Ventspils**. In the scenic **Gauja Valley**, the attractive small town of **Sigulda** makes a good base for hiking, biking, canoeing and other outdoor pursuits.

CHRONOLOGY

2500 BC The Balts (ancestors of today's Latvians and Lithuanians) occupy present-day Latvia.
1201 German crusaders found the city of Rīga.
1285 Rīga joins the Hanseatic League, bringing closer economic ties with the rest of Europe.
1500s Protestantism takes hold in much of Latvia except the south – which falls under Polish-Lithuanian rule and remains Catholic.
1629 Most of Latvia is conquered by Sweden.
1721 Sweden loses its Latvian possessions to Peter the Great of Russia.
Late 1800s Cultural and intellectual movements led by the "Young Latvians" increase Latvian national consciousness.
1905 A peasant revolt against the land-owning German nobility is followed by brutal repression.
1918–1920 Latvia gains independence, despite German and Soviet military intervention.
1940 Latvia is taken by the Soviets at the beginning of World War II, then occupied by the Germans a year later. Both occupations cause horrendous suffering for Latvians.
1945 By the end of the war, Soviet occupation is re-imposed.

1991 Collapse of the Soviet Union brings about the restoration of independence.
1999 Vaira Vike-Freiberga, the first female president of Latvia, takes office.
2004 Latvia joins the EU and NATO.
2008–11 A period of rapid economic growth is followed by recession.
2014 Latvia adopts the euro.
2015 Russian aggression in Ukraine places Latvia on the front line of defence against a newly militant Muscovite empire.

ARRIVAL AND DEPARTURE

Rīga International Airport (Lidosta Rīga) is served by numerous European airlines, including Ryanair, Lufthansa, Turkish Airlines and Wizz Air as well as Latvia's low-cost airBaltic (wairbaltic.com).

Options for cross-border **train** travel are fairly limited, with connections to Moscow and St Petersburg, but not to Lithuania or Estonia. Eurolines (weurolines-latvia.lv), LuxExpress (wluxexpress.eu) and Ecolines (wecolines.net) offer frequent **bus** services linking Rīga with Tallinn, Vilnius and St Petersburg, among other international destinations.

A daily overnight **ferry** service runs from the Rīga terminal to Stockholm, Sweden (wtallinksilja.com), as well as from Ventspils daily to Nynäshamn, Sweden (60km from Stockholm), and twice weekly to Travemünde in Germany.

GETTING AROUND

Rīga has plentiful cheap public transport. Buy **train** tickets in advance: stations have separate windows for long-distance (*starpilsetu*) and suburban (*pirpilsetu*) trains. Long-distance services are divided into "passenger" (*pasazieru vilciens*) and "fast" (*ātrs*) – both are quite slow but the latter, usually requiring a reservation, stops at fewer places. On timetable boards, look for *atiet* (departure) or *pienāk* (arrival). Check train timetables online at ⦿pv.lv.

Buses are slightly quicker than trains, though marginally more expensive. Buy long-distance tickets in advance from the ticket counter and opt for an express (*ekspresis*) bus if possible.

Cycling is a great way of getting around the resort areas and small towns – an increasing number of local agencies can organize bike rental.

ACCOMMODATION

Outside Rīga and Jūrmala, there are few backpacker hostels, though inexpensive guesthouses and campsites can be found in many Latvian towns. **Hostels** are particularly prolific in the centre of Rīga, while a number of small, good-value **hotels** and **guesthouses** are also available, though rooms are in short supply in peak season and advance reservations are required in summer. In Rīga and Jūrmala, agencies offer well-priced **private rooms** (*istabas*) of a reasonable standard. There's a handful of decently equipped **campsites** in Rīga, Jūrmala, Sigulda and Ventspils.

FOOD AND DRINK

While meat or fish and potatoes remain the bedrock of Latvian cuisine, Rīga has something to suit every palate, with a lot of good international cuisine and vegetarian options. **Eating out**, particularly in the capital's classier joints, is fairly expensive, but there are plenty of self-service fast-food places, offering filling meals for around €5–6. Numerous supermarkets and markets make **self-catering** a viable option too.

Restaurants tend to be open from noon to midnight, with bars keeping similar hours (although some stay open past 2am). Cafés typically open at 9 or 10am.

Popular national **starters** include cabbage soup (*kāpostu zupa*), sprats with onions (*sprotes ar sīpoliem*) and *pelēkie zirņi* (mushy peas in pork fat). Slabs of pork garnished with potatoes and sauerkraut constitute the typical **main course**, although freshwater fish (*zivs*) is common too. *Rasols* (cubes of potato, ham and gherkin drenched in cream) is the staple salad. *Pelmeni* (Russian ravioli) are ubiquitous – you'll find them on most menus.

DRINK

Rīga has excellent **bars**, though some are expensive. Imported **beer** (*alus*) is widely available, and local lager beers like Aldaris and Cēsu are perfectly palatable.

18

LATVIAN

In Latvian, the stress always falls on the first syllable of the word. The exception is the word for thank you (*paldies*), which has the stress on the second.

	LATVIAN	PRONUNCIATION
Yes	*Jā*	Jah
No	*Nē*	Neh
Please	*Lūdzu*	Loodzoo
Thank you	*Paldies*	Paldeeass
Hello/Good day	*Labdien*	Labdeean
Goodbye	*Uz redzēšanos*	Ooz redzehshanwas
Excuse me	*Atvainojiet*	Atvainoyet
Today	*Šodien*	Shwadien
Yesterday	*Vakar*	Vakar
Tomorrow	*Rīt*	Reet
What time is it?	*Cik ir pulkstenis?*	Tsik ir pulkstenis?
Open/Closed	*Atvērts/Slēgts*	Atvaerts/Slaegts
Good/Bad	*Labs/Slikts*	Labs/Slikts
Do you speak English?	*Vai jūs runājat angliski?*	Vai yoos roonahyat angliski?
I don't understand	*Es nesaprotu*	Es nesaprwatoo
How much is…?	*Cik tas maksā…?*	Tsik tas maksah…?
Cheap/Expensive	*Lēts/Dārgs*	Laets/Dahrgs
Student ticket	*Studentu biļeti*	Studentu bilyeti
Boat	*Kuģis*	Kugyis
Bus	*Auto*	Owto
Plane	*Lido*	Lidaw
Train	*Dzelzceļa*	Dzelzcelyuh
Where is the…?	*Kur atrodas…?*	Kur uhtrawduhs…?
Near/Far	*Tuvs/Tāls*	Tuvs/Taals
I'd like…	*Es vēlos…*	Es vaalaws…
I'm a vegetarian	*Es esmu veģetārietis/te (m/f)*	Es asmu vejyetahreatis/te
The bill, please	*Lūdzu rēķinu*	Loodzu rehkyinu
Toilet	*Tualete*	Tuuhlete
One	*Viens*	Viens
Two	*Divi*	Divi
Three	*Trīs*	Trees
Four	*Četri*	Chetri
Five	*Pieci*	Pietsi
Six	*Seši*	Seshi
Seven	*Septiņi*	Septinyi
Eight	*Astoņi*	Astonyi
Nine	*Deviņi*	Devinyi
Ten	*Desmit*	Desmit

Boutique-brewed ales are increasingly common in Rīga – check out the better-quality beers produced by small breweries like Valmiermuiža. Worth trying once is *Rīga Melnais Balzāms* (Rīga Black Balsam), a bitter liqueur (45 percent) made from a secret recipe of roots and herbs, and supposed to cure all ailments.

Coffee (*kafija*) and tea (*tēja*) are usually served black – ask for milk (*piens*) and/or sugar (*cukurs*).

CULTURE AND ETIQUETTE

Latvians are reserved and greet each other with handshakes rather than effusive hugs. The distinctive Russian and Latvian communities do not mix much and some resent being mistaken for the other. At work, **women** still fill more traditional roles, and the general attitude to women travelling alone can be mildly sexist, although there is little risk of harassment. Leave a ten percent **tip** for good service in a restaurant.

SPORTS AND ACTIVITIES

Ice hockey is the national sport, and the revered national team plays at the 12,500-seat Arena Rīga (Skanstes 21, ☎6738 8200, ⓦarenariga.com). You'll need to book in advance for important games.

Outside Rīga there is plenty of scope for **outdoor pursuits**. A number of beautiful **national parks**, best visited in the summer and home to dozens of protected species, offer extensive hiking and biking trails ripe for exploration. Canoeing, rafting and extreme sports such as mountain boarding, quad biking and bungee jumping are on offer around Cēsis and Sigulda in the Gauja Valley. Skiing and snowmobiling take over in winter, while the port of Ventspils attracts kitesurfers.

COMMUNICATIONS

Post offices (*pasts*) are generally open from 8am to 7pm during the week and from 8am to 3pm on Saturdays. Those with mobile phones from EU countries pay no roaming charges in Latvia; visitors from non-EU countries should check roaming charges with their phone company and consider buying a local SIM card. An increasing number of **wi-fi hotspots** in Rīga has led to few internet cafés remaining, and free internet and wi-fi is offered by almost all guesthouses, hotels and youth hostels.

EMERGENCIES

Theft is the biggest hazard. If you're staying in a cheap hotel, don't leave valuables in your room. Muggings and casual violence are not unknown in Rīga; avoid parks and backstreets after dark. **Police** (*policija*), who are unlikely to speak much English, will

EMERGENCY NUMBERS

Police ☎02; Ambulance ☎03; Fire ☎01; universal emergency number ☎112.

18

penalize you if you're caught drinking in public – expect a stiff fine. Some **strip clubs** and **pubs** are notorious for ripping off drunk foreign males.

Pharmacies (*aptieka*) are well stocked with over-the-counter painkillers, first aid items, sanitary products and the like. In larger cities, they tend to be open from 8am until 8pm. There are 24-hour pharmacies in the capital, where, with some luck, you'll find an English-speaker. **Emergency medical care** is free, but if you fall seriously ill, try and head for home, as many Latvian medical facilities still lag behind those in Western Europe.

INFORMATION

Tourist offices run by the Latvian tourist board (ⓦlatvia.travel) are located at the centre of most major cities and well-touristed towns. Jāņa Sēta, Elizabetes iela 83–85, Rīga, is well stocked with guides, and publishes its own maps. *Rīga in your Pocket* (ⓦinyourpocket.com; €3) is an excellent English-language **listings** guide. *The Baltic Times* (ⓦbaltictimes.com) provides weekly updates on current affairs and events.

MONEY AND BANKS

In January 2014 Latvia adopted the euro (€) as its official **currency**. Bank (*banka*) **hours** vary, but in Rīga many are open Monday to Friday from 9am to 5pm, and on Saturdays from 10am to 3pm. Outside the capital, many close at 1pm and most are closed at weekends. **Exchanging cash** is straightforward, even outside banking hours, as Rīga is full of currency exchange offices (*valutas maiņa*); shop around to get the best rate. **ATMs** are plentiful nationwide and accept most international cash cards. Credit cards are accepted in an increasing number of establishments.

OPENING HOURS AND HOLIDAYS

Shops are usually open weekdays from either 8 or 10am to 6 or 8pm, and on Saturdays from 10am to 7pm. Some food shops are open until 10pm and are also open on Sundays. In Rīga there are a few 24-hour shops, which sell food and alcohol. Most shops and all banks close on the following **public holidays**: January 1, Good Friday, Easter Sunday, Easter Monday, May 1, May 4, the second Sunday in May, June 23 and 24, November 18, December 24, 25, 26 and 31.

Rīga

RĪGA is the largest, liveliest and most cosmopolitan of the Baltic capitals, with a great selection of accommodation to suit any budget and a wide variety of world cuisine. A heady mixture of the medieval and the contemporary, the city has much to offer architecture and history enthusiasts in the narrow cobbled streets of Old Rīga and the wide boulevards of the New Town, where beautiful examples of Art Nouveau architecture line Strēlnieku iela and Alberta iela.

The city also has all the trappings of a modern capital, with excellent shopping, and a notoriously exuberant nightlife.

WHAT TO SEE AND DO

Old Rīga (Vecrīga), grouped loosely around Town Hall Square (**Rātslaukums**) and Cathedral Square (Doma laukums), forms the city's nucleus and is home to most of its historic buildings. With its cobbled streets, narrow lanes and hidden courtyards, it gives the impression of stepping back in time. To the east, Old

Rīga is bordered by Bastejkalns Park, beyond which lies the **New Town** (known locally as "Centrs"). Built during rapid urban expansion between 1857 and 1914, its wide boulevards are lined with four- and five-storey apartment buildings, many decorated with extravagant Art Nouveau motifs.

Town Hall Square

Rīga's **Rātslaukums**, or Town Hall Square, is dominated by the **House of the Blackheads** (Melngalvju nams), whose facade is an opulent masterpiece of Gothic architecture and which once served as the headquarters of Rīga's bachelor merchants, who adopted the North African, non-white St Maurice as their patron (hence the name "Blackheads"). Largely destroyed in 1941, the House was lovingly reconstructed for the 800th anniversary of Rīga's foundation in 2001.

The ugly oblong structure next door belongs to the old **Occupation Museum** (Latvijas okupācijas muzejs), which is currently closed for renovation – you can see its collection on temporary display in the former US embassy building at Raiņa bulvāris 7 (see p.689).

Museum of the Sun

One of Rīga's most intriguing sights is the quaint and curious **Museum of the**

LOFTY VIEWS

If you want to see the city unfold before you, with its melange of church domes, vast parks, ribbon of river and squat Soviet creations, follow the urban throng to Šķūņu iela to **St Peter's Church** (Pēter baznīca; Tues–Sun; May–Aug 10am–7pm; Sept–April 10am–5pm), a large red-brick structure with a graceful three-tiered spire; climb the tower (€9) for excellent panoramic views. Battling the church for the finest vistas of Rīga is "Stalin's Birthday Cake" – the **Academy of Sciences** (April–Sept daily 8am–8pm; €3.60), a 1950s Empire State Building lookalike at Akadēmijas laukums 1. The 65m skyscraper, adorned with hammers and sickles near the top, has a 360-degree viewing platform on the 17th floor.

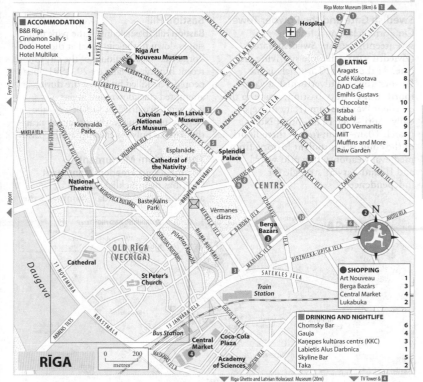

Riga Motor Museum (8km) &

■ ACCOMMODATION

B&B Rīga	2
Cinnamon Sally's	3
Dodo Hotel	4
Hotel Multilux	1

● EATING

Aragats	2
Café Kūkotava	8
DAD Café	1
Emihls Gustavs Chocolate	10
Istaba	7
Kabuki	6
LIDO Vērmanītis	9
MiiT	5
Muffins and More	3
Raw Garden	4

● SHOPPING

Art Nouveau	1
Berga Bazārs	3
Central Market	4
Lukabuka	2

■ DRINKING AND NIGHTLIFE

Chomsky Bar	6
Gauja	4
Kaņepes kultūras centrs (KKC)	3
Labietis Alus Darbnīca	1
Skyline Bar	5
Taka	2

RĪGA

18

Riga Ghetto and Latvian Holocaust Museum (20m) ▼   TV Tower & **4** ▼

Sun at Valnu iela 30 (Saules muzejs; Mon–Sat 9am–6pm; €4), a private collection of artworks, ornaments and cult objects connected with the fiery life-giving orb in the title. Visually attractive throughout, the display also has interesting things to say about the position of the sun in religion and folk belief, and the development of astronomy.

Cathedral Square

Cathedral Square is dominated by the towering red-brick **Rīga Cathedral** (daily 10am–5pm; €3), established in 1211 and featuring one of the biggest organs in Europe. On the other side of the cathedral, at Palasta 4, is the worthwhile **Museum of Rīga's History and Navigation**, featuring Bronze Age and medieval artefacts, such as a mummified criminal's hand, as well as temporary art exhibitions (Wed–Sun 11am–5pm; €4.50).

Rīga Bourse Art Museum

Opposite the cathedral, the former building of the Latvia stock exchange at Doma laukums 6 contains the **Rīga Bourse Art Museum** (Mākslas muzejs Rīgas birža; Tues–Thurs, Sat & Sun 10am–6pm, Fri 10am–8pm; €3; ⓦ rigasbirza.lv), the nation's collection of old masters and archeological treasures. A small Monet landscape and a Rodin sculpture are the main big-name draws, although the Flemish still lifes and classical antiquities are enough to keep the interest from flagging.

The Castle and the Three Brothers

From Cathedral Square, Pils iela runs down to Castle Square (Pils laukums) and **Rīga Castle** (Rīgas pils), built in 1515 and now home to the Latvian president. Follow Mazā Pils iela from Pils laukums to see the **Three Brothers** (Trīs brāli), three charming medieval houses, one of which, built in the fifteenth century, is thought to be the oldest in Latvia.

18

Swedish Gate and the Powder Tower

On Torņa iela, you'll find the seventeenth-century **Swedish Gate** (Zviedru vārti), the sole surviving city gate. At the end of Torņa iela is the Powder Tower (Pulvertornis), a vast, fourteenth-century bastion, home to the excellent **War Museum** (Kara muzejs, daily: April–Oct 10am–6pm; Nov–March 10am–5pm; free) – three floors of the country's turbulent history, from medieval weaponry to world wars I and II, and Latvia's struggle for independence.

Bastion Hill

Bastion Hill (Bastejkalns) – the park that slopes down to the city canal at the end of Torņa iela – is a reminder of the city's more recent history: on January 20, 1991, four people were killed by Soviet fire during an attempted crackdown on Latvia's independence drive. Stones bearing the victims' names mark where they fell near the Bastejas bulvāris entrance to the park.

The Freedom Monument

The modernist **Freedom Monument** (Brīvības piemineklis), known affectionately as "Milda", dominates the

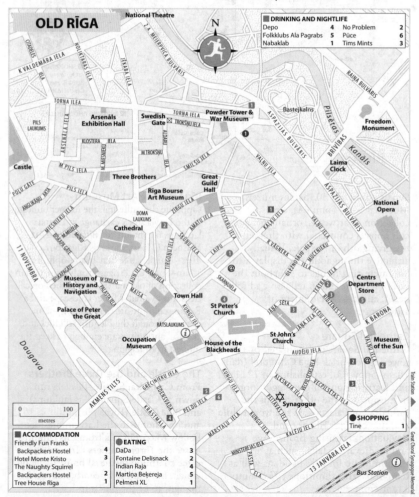

OLD RĪGA

National Theatre

N

DRINKING AND NIGHTLIFE
Depo	4	No Problem	2
Folkklubs Ala Pagrabs	5	Pūce	6
Nabaklab	1	Tims Mints	3

PILS LAUKUMS

Arsenāls Exhibition Hall

TORŅA IELA

Swedish Gate

TROKŠŅU IELA

Powder Tower & War Museum

Bastejkalns

Freedom Monument

KLOSTERA IELA

M.TROKŠŅU

Castle

M PILS IELA

Three Brothers

SMILŠU IELA

Laima Clock

Great Guild Hall

Riga Bourse Art Museum

DOMA LAUKUMS

ZIRGU IELA

National Opera

Cathedral

AMATU IELA

KALKU IELA

LAIPU

SKAŅU IELA

Museum of History and Navigation

M.SKOLAS

SKĀRŅU IELA

R.VAGNERA

Centrs Department Store

Palace of Peter the Great

MAISA

Town Hall

St Peter's Church

JAŅA SĒTA

K BARONA

RĀTSLAUKUMS

KUNGU IELA

House of the Blackheads

St John's Church

AUDĒJU IELA

Museum of the Sun

Daugava

Occupation Museum

GRĒCINIEKU IELA

Synagogue

0   100
metres

ACCOMMODATION
Friendly Fun Franks Backpackers Hostel	4
Hotel Monte Kristo	3
The Naughty Squirrel Backpackers Hostel	2
Tree House Rīga	1

EATING
DaDa	3
Fontaine Delisnack	2
Indian Raja	4
Martiņa Beķereja	5
Pelmeni XL	1

SHOPPING
Tine	1

AKMENS TILTS

PELDU IELA

13 JANVĀRA IELA

Bus Station

Train Station

Great Choral Synagogue Memorial

18

JEWS IN LATVIA

Jews living in Rīga and other parts of Latvia suffered the same fate as Jews in other parts of Eastern Europe when Latvia was overrun by Nazis. The **Rīga Ghetto and Latvian Holocaust Museum**, Maskavas 14a (entry from Krasta; Mon–Fri & Sun 10am–6pm; suggested donation €5; ⓦrgm.lv), built on the site of the Jewish ghetto behind the Central Market, consists of two outdoor exhibits: a seemingly endless wall of victims' names, and photographs and text illustrating the life of the Jewish community in different parts of Latvia before World War II. On Peitavas iela 6/8, you'll find the last surviving **synagogue** in Rīga; when all the synagogues in the city were burned down by the Nazis in 1941, this building and its treasures – the sacred scrolls – escaped destruction due to its close proximity to other buildings. There's a memorial on Gogoļa iela where the **Great Choral Synagogue** was burnt down in July 1941 with a large number of Lithuanian Jewish refugees trapped inside. At Skolas 6, you will find a small but gritty and informative **Jews In Latvia Museum** (Mon–Thurs & Sun 11am–5pm; donation; ⓦjewishmuseum.lv), telling the history of Jewish life in Latvia from the eighteenth century onwards, including persecution by both Nazis and Soviets, and the survival and rebirth of Judaism in independent Latvia.

view along Brīvības bulvāris as it enters the **New Town**, holding aloft three stars symbolizing the three regions of Latvia. Incredibly, the monument survived the Soviet era, and nowadays two soldiers stand guard here in symbolic protection of Latvia's independence.

Occupation Museum

Temporarily housed in the former building of the American Embassy at Raiņa bulvāris 7, the **Occupation Museum** (Latvijas okupācijas muzejs; May–Sept daily 11am–6pm; Oct–April Tues–Sun 11am–5pm; donation welcomed; ⓦokupacijasmuzejs.lv) documents the atrocities committed against Latvia's population by both Nazi and Soviet occupations. Harrowing and moving

exhibits include letters to loved ones thrown from trains by Latvians forcibly removed to Siberia, and the simple household items (children's toys, Christian crosses) they fashioned by hand to make life bearable once they got there.

National Art Museum

Esplanade Park runs north from Brīvības bulvāris. At the far end of the park, the **Latvian National Art Museum** (Valsts mākslas muzejs; Tues–Thurs 10am–6pm, Fri 10am–8pm, Sat & Sun 10am–5pm; €3.50; ⓦlnmm.lv) contains an impressive array of twentieth-century Latvian paintings, by artists from post-impressionist Vilhelms Purvitis to doyen of Soviet agit-prop Gustavs Klucis. In a separate building on Torņa iela 1, the **Arsenāls Exhibition Hall** (Tues, Wed & Fri noon–6pm, Thurs noon–8pm, Sat & Sun noon–5pm; €3.50) stages cutting-edge temporary exhibitions by contemporary artists.

Rīga Art Nouveau Museum

The **Rīga Art Nouveau Museum** at Alberta iela 12 (Tues–Sun 10am–6pm; May–Sept €6; Oct–April €3.50), housed in the former apartment of renowned artist and engineer Konstantīns Pēkšēns, is a must for anyone with an interest in Art Nouveau. You can view original period furniture and some of Pēkšēns' work, and the visit culminates in the viewing of a short video which will enable you to tell the difference between "romantic" and "vertical" Art Nouveau facades on the city's streets.

Rīga Motor Museum

It's worth travelling 8km out of town to one of Rīga's odder attractions – the **Motor Museum** (Rīgas motormuzejs; daily 10am–6pm; €10). Home to an impressive collection of vehicles through the ages, its pride and joy are those belonging to Soviet heads of state – see Stalin lounging in the back seat of his bulletproof ZIS. To get here, take bus #21 east along Brīvības to the Pansionāts stop (20min), cross the road and take the main road that runs to the right of the housing development (5min).

18

ARRIVAL AND DEPARTURE

By plane Rīga Airport (Lidosta Rīga; ⓦ riga-airport.com) is located about 13km west of the city centre. Bus #22 (every 20min; €1.15 if ticket is bought from vending machine or newspaper kiosk; €2 if bought from driver) drops passengers at Strēlnieku laukums, just west of Rātslaukums, and by the train station. A taxi from the airport should cost no more than €20.

By train Rīga's main train station (Centrālā stacija) is just southeast of Old Rīga on 13 Janvāra iela; it takes about 15min to walk to Rātslaukums from here. Facilities include ATMs, currency exchange and an information centre.

Destinations Majori, Jūrmala (every 30min; 40min); Moscow (1 daily at 5.30pm; 16–18hr); Salaspils (1–2 hourly; 15min); Sigulda (8–10 daily; 1hr); St Petersburg (1 daily at 5.30pm; 15hr).

By bus Rīga's bus station (Autoosta) is a 5min walk west of the train station along 13 Janvāra iela; luggage storage, ATM and tourist information available. To get to Old Rīga, turn left out of the front entrance and pass through the underpass.

Destinations Bauska (every 30min; 1hr 10min–1hr 30min); Kaunas (1–2 daily; 4hr 30min); Klaipēda (3 daily; 5hr); Moscow (1 daily; 17hr); Pärnu (9–11 daily; 3hr 30min); Sigulda (at least 8 daily; 1hr 15min); St Petersburg (4 daily; 12–14hr); Tallinn (9–11 daily; 5hr 30min); Tartu (3 daily; 5hr); Ventspils (hourly; 3hr); Vilnius (8 daily; 5hr–5hr 30min).

By ferry The ferry terminal (Jūras pasazieru stacija) is to the north of Old Rīga. Tram #5, #7 or #9 runs from the stop in front of the terminal on Ausekļa iela to Aspazijas bulvāris in the city centre (two stops).

Destinations Stockholm (1 daily; 16hr).

INFORMATION AND TOURS

Tourist information The main tourist office, at Rātslaukums 6 in the centre of the Old Town (daily 10am–6pm; ☏ 6703 7900, ⓦ liveriga.com), has plenty of information on Latvia's attractions and sells copies of Rīga In Your Pocket (€3) as well as the Rīga Card (€25/€30/€35 for 24/48/72hr; ⓦ rigacard.lv), which gives unlimited use of public transport plus museum discounts.

Tours EAT Rīga/Rīga Explorers Club (☏ 2246 9888, ⓦ rigaexplorersclub.com or ⓦ eatriga.lv) organizes a big range of themed walking tours, bike tours and food tours, all with an English-speaking guide. Prices (anything from €15 to €80 per person) depend on numbers.

GETTING AROUND

Both Old Rīga and the New Town are easily navigated on foot, and you can reach outlying attractions by frequent and efficient public transport.

By bus, tram and trolleybus Buses, trams and trolleybuses run 5.30am–midnight. You can buy flat-fare one-way tickets from the driver for €2, or purchase cheaper e-talons from public transport ticket machines or

from Narvesen newsstands for one (€1.15), two (€2.30), five (€5.75) or ten rides (€10.90); or for one, three or five days of travel (€5/€10/€15).

ACCOMMODATION

Rīga has extensive budget accommodation, mostly concentrated in the southern half of Old Rīga, with a few options in nearby New Town and by the Central Market. Reserve in advance in summer. All accommodation options listed offer wi-fi.

OLD TOWN

Friendly Fun Franks Backpackers Hostel Novembra krastmala 29 ☏ 2599 0612, ⓦ franks.lv; map p.688. Clean, laddish, Aussie-run hostel for those seeking crush-your-beer-can-against-your-forehead action. Perpetually full and not shying away from hosting stag parties, this firm favourite welcomes you on arrival with a free beer at its 24hr bar. Raucous fun. Dorms €15, doubles €50

Hotel Monte Kristo Kalēju 56 ☏ 6735 9100, ⓦ hotelmontekristo.lv; map p.688. Reliable three-star hotel that's enduringly popular due to its location; on the fringes of the Old Town but only a short hop away from the bus station. Small but comfortable rooms; buffet breakfast included. Doubles €65

The Naughty Squirrel Backpackers Hostel Kalēju iela 50 ☏ 6722 0073, ⓦ thenaughtysquirrel.com; map p.688. One of the most sociable places to stay in the Old Town, with daily tours and themed nights – from Movie Night to Latvian Food Night. Lockers are provided, and the location is hard to beat. Dorms €13, doubles €45

★**Tree House Riga** Kaļķu iela 11a ☏ 2571 3126, ⓦ facebook.com/TreeHouseRiga; map p.688. One of many hostels occupying the upper floors of historic central buildings, Tree House has smooth stylish dorms (including one female-only room), a cosy communal space that looks like a domestic living room, yoga classes twice a week, and a yoga practice room. They don't mind you partying providing you do it outside. Dorms €15.50

NEW TOWN

B&B Riga Ģertrūdes iela 43 ☏ 6727 8505, ⓦ bb-riga.lv; map p.687. A friendly family-run guesthouse in Central Rīga offering en-suite rooms equipped with cable TV, fridges and microwaves. Breakfast vouchers and airport transfers available. Doubles €70

★**Cinnamon Sally's** Merkela iela 1, 3rd floor ☏ 2204 2280, ⓦ cinnamonsally.com; map p.687. More like the luxury apartment of a good friend than a hostel, this place has spacious dorms (with extra touches like a make-up table in the girls' dorm); the combined lounge/kitchen is a great place to socialize and the incomparable Sally herself is always ready for a chat with her guests. Dorms €15, doubles €35

Dodo Hotel Jersikas iela 1 ☎ 6724 0220, ⓦ dodohotel .com; map p.687. Budget hotel offering tastefully decorated, spacious en-suite rooms with flat-screen TVs and free wi-fi, as well as a French pancake breakfast (€4), all just a 15min walk or short tram ride from Old Rīga. Doubles €50

Hotel Multilux Barona iela 37 (entrance from Ģertrūdes) ☎ 6731 1602, ⓦ multilux.lv; map p.687. This Art Nouveau building in Central Rīga boasts thoroughly modern en-suite rooms with cable TV, wi-fi and breakfast buffet included in the price. Doubles €35

EATING

Many bars and cafés offer cheap and filling food and there are also plenty of reasonably priced restaurants serving international cuisine.

CAFÉS, CHEAP EATS AND SNACKS

Café Kūkotava Tērbatas iela 10/12; map p.687. Cosy café that not only serves some of the city's best coffee but also tantalizes you with its delectable home-made cakes. Mon–Fri 8am–8pm, Sat & Sun 10am–6pm.

Emihls Gustavs Chocolate Blaumaņa iela 11a; map p.687. Try the exquisite chocolate truffles or sip the bliss-in-a-cup white and dark molten chocolate (with a glass of water on the side in case it proves too rich for you). Hot chocolate €2.50. Mon–Fri 9am–10pm, Sat 10am–10pm, Sun 10am–8pm.

Fontaine Delisnack Teatra iela 2; map p.688. Tucked in an alley behind the Centrs department store, this has quickly become *the* place in the Old Town for freshly flipped gourmet burgers (€5.50), all-day breakfasts and a handful of Asian- and Mexican-inspired snacks – although the chilli con carne tends to run out by teatime. There's a fully stocked bar if you want to make a night of it. 24hr.

LIDO Vērmanītis Elizabetes iela 65; map p.687. Pretty much everything in the Baltic culinary repertoire is available at this vast order-at-the-counter canteen restaurant, decked out in kitsch-folklore style and patrolled by staff in traditional costume. Mains €3–4. Daily 9am–10pm.

Martiņa Beķereja Valnu iela 28; map p.688. Locals queue at the counter of this café-patisserie to stock up on freshly baked *piragi* (from €0.40), doughy parcels filled with bacon bits, shredded cabbage or eggs and leeks. It's also a comfortable city-centre venue for a coffee-and-cake break. Mon–Fri 7.30am–9pm, Sat & Sun 8am–9pm.

★ **MiiT** Lāčpleša iela 10; map p.687. Vegetarian café-bar with sleek modern interior, excellent-value lunch menus (€4.80) and Valmiermuižas beer. *MiiT* also houses a bicycle design workshop and is a popular meeting spot for cyclists. Mon 7am–9pm, Tues–Thurs 7am–11pm, Fri 7am–2am, Sat 9am–2am, Sun 10am–6pm.

Muffins and More Ģertrūdes iela 9; map p.687. You'll smell the delicious muffins even before you set foot in this tiny, welcoming café. There are more than a dozen varieties and the blueberry ones just might be the best in

Eastern Europe. The "More" of the name consists of soup and baguettes. Muffins €1.10; soup €3.75. Mon–Fri 8am–8pm, Sat 10am–6pm, Sun 11am–6pm.

Pelmeni XL Kaļķu iela 7; map p.688. Popular canteen-style eatery offering six types of *pelmeni* (Russian ravioli) filled with meat or cheese, plus soups and drinks. Gourmet cuisine it ain't, but it *will* fill your belly. €1.65/200g. Mon–Sat 9am–4am, Sun 10am–4am.

RESTAURANTS

Aragats Miera iela 15; map p.687. The effusive hostess won't have to tell you off for not finishing your food, because you will: the Armenian-style grilled meats and stews, with the fresh herbs chopped up right at your table, are the best in the city. Mains €9–15. Tues–Sun 1–10pm.

DAD Cafe Miera iela 17; map p.687. Homely café with simple rustic furnishings and a largely vegetarian menu that's particularly strong on pastas and salads. With two-course set lunches weighing in at €4.50, it's a great place for a daytime feed. Mon–Sat noon–9pm.

DaDa Audēju iela 16 (Centrs department store); map p.688. Its decor reflects the anarchist art movement, but *DaDa* specializes in Mongolian barbecue. Fill up a bowl with fresh meat, seafood, vegetables and noodles, pick a sauce and have it cooked in front of you. Small/large bowl €7.25–10. Mon–Thurs & Sun 10am–10pm, Fri & Sat 10am–midnight.

Indian Raja Skarnu iela 7; map p.688. Authentic, flavourful Indian food in a cosy cellar setting – an expat favourite. The menu is varied and there's plenty for vegetarians. Huge mains €12–15. Daily noon–11pm.

Istaba Barona 31A; map p.687. Cosy, chic and quirky café tucked into the second floor of an enjoyably odd art gallery-cum-gift shop. Coffee, tea and cakes are tip-top, and there's a range of meals – the menu is not written down, and you'll be asked what kind of food you like by a waiter-cum-chef. Mon–Sat noon–midnight.

Kabuki Tērbatas 46 (entrance from Mārtas); map p.687. One of the most pleasant and reliable among the crop of sushi restaurants that has opened in Rīga in recent years, with a functional but chic interior, a big choice of sushi and noodle dishes, generous pots of tea and reasonable prices. Daily 11am–10.30pm.

Raw Garden Skolas iela 12; map p.687. A stylish, vegan non-dairy restaurant, where no dish is cooked above 45°C, and where you'll probably join the crowd of satisfied patrons clamouring for more. Two-course set lunches are a steal at €6.50. Mon–Fri 8am–9pm, Sat 11am–9pm.

DRINKING, NIGHTLIFE AND ENTERTAINMENT

The Old Town offers innumerable opportunities for bar-hopping, with a wide range of watering holes (many serve decent food too) filling up with fun-seeking locals. Many double as restaurants during the day but close at 1/2am.

18

18

BARS

Chomsky Bar Lačplēša iela 68; map p.687. Looking a bit like a roomy student flat, the gruff but welcoming *Chomsky Bar* is a refreshing alternative to the mass-tourist pubs of the Old Town. A mural of left-wing guru Noam Chomsky sets the tone. Affordable local beers and spirits, and a lively front yard in summer. Mon–Thurs 4pm–midnight, Fri & Sat 4pm–3am.

Gauja Terbatas 56, map p.687. Loving re-creation of a Latvian domestic interior circa 1973, complete with mismatching furniture, frumpy textiles, old-style board games and shelves of boring-looking books. Good draught beer. Daily noon–11pm.

Kaņepes kultūras centrs (KKC) Skolas iela 15 ⓦ facebook.com/Zoo.KKc; map p.687. Alternative cultural centre offering art exhibitions, occasional theatre and live music, and a supremely mellow bar. Daily 1pm–2am.

Labietis Alus Darbnīca Aristīda Briāna iela 9A; map p.687. Wooden tables and lights made out of beer glasses provide a suitably solid-but-stylish atmosphere in which to sample the outstanding ales produced by the Labietis brewery – which you can see through a glass window at the back. With a big choice of seasonal brews on tap (€2.50–5.50/0.5Lt) there's a lot to work your way through. Mon 4–10pm, Tues 3–11pm, Wed & Fri 3pm–3am, Thurs 3pm–1am, Sat & Sun 1pm–1am.

No Problem Tirgoņu 5/7; map p.688. The best of the capital's beer gardens, *No Problem* boasts a prime spot overlooking Doma laukums (Cathedral Square), more than 20 beers on tap, live music nightly and some of the best burgers in town, served by friendly, efficient staff. Daily 11am–3am.

Skyline Bar Elizabetes iela 55; map p.687. Behold Rīga's splendour from a window seat on the 26th floor of the *Reval Hotel Latvija*. There's a long list of quality cocktails (€9–12) Mon–Wed & Sun 11.30am–1am, Thurs 11.30am–2am, Fri & Sat 11.30am–3am.

Taka Miera iela 10; map p.687. Intimate bar with beat-up furniture and a hip young clientele drawn by an indie-rock soundtrack and an excellent range of craft beers. With set lunches at €4 it's also a good place to eat. Mon & Tues 2pm–midnight, Wed 3pm–midnight, Thurs & Sat 2pm–2am, Fri 3pm–3am, Sun 6–10pm.

Tims Mints Jaņa Sēta 5; map p.688. Located in an Old Town courtyard, this quirky living room-style bar serves improvised cocktails in jam jars and packs 'em in at weekends when eclectic DJs draw an arty-but-hedonistic crowd. Tues & Wed noon–2am, Thurs & Fri noon–4am, Sat 2pm–4am, Sun 2–10pm.

CLUBS AND LIVE MUSIC

Depo Vaļņu iela 32 ⓦ klubsdepo.lv; map p.688. Post-industrial cellar space with alternative DJ nights, live garage bands and an eclectic mix of experimental, reggae, punk, metal and other genres. Daily noon–5am.

Folkklubs Ala Pagrabs Peldu iela 19 ⓦ folkklubs.lv/en; map. p.688. Live folk music is just as popular as rock in Latvia, and this welcoming, barrel-vaulted cellar club is the ideal place to find out why. With a full menu of food (and a choice of over 25 beers on tap), it's a popular place to dine – so don't be surprised if all the tables are booked. Mon & Tues noon–1am, Wed noon–3am, Thurs noon–4am; Fri noon–6am, Sat 2pm–5am, Sun 2pm–1am.

Nabaklab Z. A. Mierovica bulvāris 12 ⓦ nabaklab.lv; map p.688. Part art gallery, part bohemian club with live bands, DJs and a summer terrace for enjoying their own *Nabaklab* brew. Mon–Wed & Sun noon–2am, Thurs, Fri & Sat noon–6am.

Pūce Peldu iela 26/28 ⓦ facebook.com/KlubsNaktiPuce; map. p.688. A dark roomy space centred on a splendid circular bar, this is an excellent place to drink the night away while listening to an eclectic menu of indie, house and 1980s pop. Wed 8pm–2am, Thurs 8pm–4am; Fri 6pm–6am, Sat noon–6am, Sun noon–midnight.

CINEMA

Forum Cinemas (Coca-Cola Plaza) 13 Janvāra iela 8 ⓦ forumcinemas.lv; map p.687. Second-largest cinema in northern Europe, with 14 screens. Tickets €6–9.

Splendid Palace Elizabetes iela 61 ⓦ splendidpalace.lv; map p.687. Rīga's oldest cinema, showing art films as well as blockbusters. Tickets €5.

SHOPPING

Art Nouveau Rīga Strēlnieku 9 ⓦ artnouveauriga .lv; map p.687. Dedicated entirely to Art Nouveau merchandise, such as small plaster faces copied from the decorations on Rīga's facades. Daily 10am–7pm.

Berga Bazārs Elizabetes iela 83/85; map p.687. Soviet kitsch, freshly baked bread, organically grown produce and gourmet food samples. Every Saturday 10am–4pm.

Central Market (Centrāltirgus) Next to the bus station; map p.687. This row of massive 1930s former Zeppelin hangars is worth visiting just to appreciate the sheer size of it. It sells everything from half a cow to bread, smoked meats and fake designer watches. Daily 8am–5pm.

Lukabuka Gertrudes 62; map p.687. Art and design bookshop with cards and stationery – they also sell cool comic books (including titles in English) by local independent publisher Kuš!. Mon–Sat 10am–7pm.

Tine Vaļņu 2; map p.688. Large store selling ceramics, amber trinkets, linen goods and plenty of woolly mittens and socks. Mon–Sat 9am–7pm, Sun 10am–5pm.

DIRECTORY

Embassies Canada, Baznīcas iela 20/22 ☎ 6781 3945; Ireland, Alberta iela 13 ☎ 6703 9370; UK, Alunāna iela 5 ☎ 6777 4700; US, Samnera Velsa 1 ☎ 6710 7000.

Exchange Marika: Brīvības bulvāris 30 and Dzirnavu iela 96 (both 24hr).

Hospital ARS, Skolas iela 5 ☏ 6720 1007. Some English-speaking doctors.

Left luggage At the bus station (daily 6.30am–11pm; from €0.35/hr, depending on weight). Also lockers at the left-luggage office (Rokas Bagāias) in the train station basement (4.30am–midnight; €3/day).

Pharmacy Saules aptieka, Brīvības iela 68 (Mon–Fri 8am–10pm, Sat & Sun 10am–10pm).

Post office Brīvibas bulvāris 32 (Mon–Fri 7.30am–7pm, Sat 9am–3pm).

The rest of Latvia

In summer, the whole of Latvia seems to head to the beach – be it **Jūrmala**, the lively string of seaside resorts near Rīga, or the picturesque port of **Ventspils**, with its unspoiled stretch of sand and its music festival. Nature lovers can head inland to the picturesque little town of **Sigulda**.

JŪRMALA

A 20km string of small seaside resorts lining the Baltic coast west of Rīga, **JŪRMALA** was originally favoured by the tsarist nobility and later drew tens of thousands of holiday-makers from all over the USSR. It continues to be a popular beach resort today, with its wide, clean, sandy **beach** backed by dunes and pine woods, and dotted with beer tents and climbing frames. It pulses with sun worshippers during the summer, especially during the week-long **music festival** in July. The central resort of the Jūrmala strip, **Majori**, is the best place to get off the train if you're just here for the day.

WHAT TO SEE AND DO

Jomas iela, the pedestrianized main street running east from the station square, teems with people and has a number of excellent restaurants and cafés, as well as craft stalls and art exhibitions. A few paths lead to the beach from Jūras iela, north of Jomas iela. The beach aside, Jūrmala's attractions include the wonderful new interactive **Jūrmala City Museum**, Tirgonu 29, Majori (Wed–Sun 10am–5pm; free), which charts the town's history as a popular beach resort. Upstairs is reserved

for excellent temporary art and photography exhibitions.

The next settlement east of Majori is Dzintari, home to the **Forest Park** (Dzintaru mežaparks), a dense rectangle of pinewoods criss-crossed by footpaths, with a children's playground and space for rollerskating and skateboarding. Skates can be hired from the Skritulslidu noma kiosk at the park's western end (Mon–Fri 5–9pm, Sat & Sun noon–8pm). A **viewing tower** in the middle of the park provides sweeping views of Jūrmala, the Lielupe River and the coast.

A further 3km east of Majori, beside the Lielupe River, **Livu Akvaparks** at Viestura iela 24 (Mon–Sat 11am–10pm, Sun 11am–9pm; €21 for 2hr, or day pass €29; ⓦ akvaparks.lv) is Latvia's biggest swimming complex, with a variety of wave pools, palm trees and plummet-down waterslides: it's a fifteen-minute walk from both Bulduri and Lielupe train stations.

ARRIVAL AND INFORMATION

By train Trains leave Rīga's station from platforms 3 and 4. Majori is the main stop for Jūrmala, eleven stops from Rīga. Destinations Riga (roughly every 30min until around 11pm; 30min).

By minibus Minibuses depart from Rīga's Central Minibus Station, opposite the train station (every 10min, 6am–midnight; 25min). Take either the Rīga–Sloka or the Rīga–Dubulti minibus and get off in front of the Majori train station.

Tourist information Lienes iela 5, Majori (Mon 9am–6pm, Tues–Fri 9am–5pm, Sat 10am–5pm, Sun 10am–3pm; ☏ 6714 7900, ⓦ tourism.jurmala.lv). Helpful staff have info on the town's attractions and accommodation.

ACCOMMODATION

Elina Lienes iela 43, Majori ☏ 6776 1665, ⓦ elinahotel.lv. This popular guesthouse has clean en-suite rooms with TV, in a quiet residential street a 10min walk from the beach. Doubles **€60**

Kempings Nemo Atbalss iela 1, Vaivari ☏ 2610 0500, ⓦ nemo.lv. Large campsite at the western end of Jūrmala (alight at Vaivari station) in a pleasant middle-of-the-forest location just behind the beach, with reasonably clean facilities and a small aquapark on site. There are also double rooms in cabins. Camping/person **€4.50**, plus per tent **€6**, cabins **€23**

EATING AND DRINKING

Kalnakrastu Raušu Fabrika Vienības prospekts 35, Lielupe. Located at the Livu Akvaparks end of the resort,

18

this popular bakery with a scattering of eat-in tables is very much a cult destination among locals. Stop by to gorge on delicious pastries, tarts and speķa pīrāgi (savoury buns filled with bacon bits). Daily 8am–8pm.

Sue's Asia Jomas iela 74, Majori. Busy restaurant serving large portions of excellent Indian, Thai and Chinese cuisine. The Tom yum kuung is spicy and flavoursome (€9). Daily noon–11pm.

Zangezur Jomas iela 80, Majori. Popular Armenian restaurant specializing in grilled meats and other tasty dishes, such as aubergines with garlic and walnuts. Try the hinkale – large meat dumplings (€6). Daily 11am–11pm.

SALASPILS

The concentration camp at **SALASPILS**, 14km southeast of Rīga, is where most of the city's Jewish population perished during World War II. One hundred thousand people died here, including prisoners of war and Jews from other countries. The site is marked by monumental sculptures, with the former locations of the barracks outlined by white stones. Look for the offering of toys by the children's barracks, and the bunker, inscribed with the words "Behind this gate the earth groans" – here there's a haunting exhibition (open access; free) about the camp.

ARRIVAL AND DEPARTURE

By train To get here take a suburban train from Rīga central station in the Ogre direction and alight at Dārziņi (at least one hourly; 30min), though be aware that the stop is not well signposted; it's the first one to be completely surrounded by pine forest. From here a clearly signposted path leads to the clearing, a 15min walk through the forest.

RUNDĀLE PALACE

One of the architectural wonders of Latvia, Baroque **Rundāle Palace** (Rundāles Pils; daily: May–Oct 10am–6pm; Nov–April 10am–5pm; combined ticket to the palace, exhibitions and gardens €6; ⓦrundale.net) lies 77km south of Rīga. Its 138 rooms were built in two phases during the 1730s and 1760s, and designed by **Bartolomeo Rastrelli**, the architect responsible for the Winter Palace in St Petersburg. It was privately owned until 1920 when it fell into disrepair, but has been meticulously restored pretty much to its former glory.

Each opulent room is decorated in a unique fashion and there are changing art exhibitions both inside the palace and in the vast landscaped gardens.

ARRIVAL AND DEPARTURE

By bus There are frequent buses from Rīga to Bauska (every 30min, 7am–8pm; 1hr 30min); then take a local service to Pilsrundāle (up to 9 daily; 30min). The palace is across the street from the bus stop.

SIGULDA

Dotted with parks and clustered above the southern bank of the River Gauja around 50km northeast of Rīga, **SIGULDA** is Gauja National Park's main centre and a good jumping-off point for exploring the rest of the **Gauja Valley**.

WHAT TO SEE AND DO

From the train station, Raiņa iela runs north into town, passing the bus station. After about 800m a right turn into Baznīcas iela brings you to the impressive seven-hundred-year-old **Sigulda Church** (Siguldas baznīca).

Turaida Castle

Sigulda is home to three castles: Krimulda Castle (Krimuldas pilsdrupas), Sigulda Castle (Siguldas pilsdrupas), a former stronghold of the German Knights of the Sword, and from which you can see **Turaida Castle** (Turaidas pilsdrupas), the most impressive of the three. Built on the site of an earlier stronghold by the bishop of Rīga in 1214, the castle was destroyed when lightning hit its gunpowder magazine in the eighteenth century. Today, its exhibitions chart the castle's history (daily: May–Sept 9am–7pm; €5; Oct–April 10am–5pm; €3) and it's possible to climb up the main tower for 360-degree views of the valley below.

You can reach the castle by bus #12 (for Turaida or Krimulda) from Sigulda bus station (several daily; €0.70). Alternatively, take the **cable car** from Poruka iela, 20 minutes' walk northwest of Sigulda bus station (daily 10am–6.30pm, every 30min; Mon–Fri €2, Sat & Sun €3), across the Gauja River to Krimulda Castle –

18

daredevils can bungee jump from the cable car (Thurs–Sun 6.30pm until the last customer; €60; ⓦbungee.lv). From Krimulda Castle, descend the wooden staircase signposted "Gūtmaņis Cave", then follow the path past the cave – the setting for a legend of "star-crossed lovers". The path turns to the right before rejoining the main road just short of Turaida itself.

The bobsleigh track

West of Sigulda train station along Ausekļa iela is a **bobsleigh track** where you can hurtle down a concrete half-tube at 80km an hour (June–Sept Sat & Sun 11am–6pm; €10/person/ride), or try the exhilarating professional winter bob (Oct–March daily noon–7pm; €50).

ARRIVAL AND INFORMATION

By train The train station is a 10min walk southwest of the bus station.
Destinations Rīga (up to 9 daily; 1hr 15min).
By bus Frequent buses from Rīga serve Sigulda's bus station, located a 2min walk south of the town centre.
Destinations Rīga (at least hourly; 1hr 15min).
Tourist information Raiņa iela 3, just to the left of the entrance to the bus station (Mon–Fri 8am–7pm, Sat 9am–2pm; ☎6797 1335, ⓦtourism.sigulda.lv). Helpful multilingual staff can book you into private rooms and provide information on exploring the Gauja Valley. They can also arrange hot-air ballooning (book in advance; ☎2928 8448, ⓦwww.altius.lv) and bungee jumping from the cable car.
Gauja National Park Administration Turaidas iela 2a (daily: May–Oct 9am–7pm; Nov–April 9am–6pm; ☎2665 7661, ⓦgnp.gov.lv). Located on the north side of the river, this helpful office provides information on hiking trails in the Gauja National Park, including the popular trail from Sigulda to the village of Ligatne. Hiking map €3.

ACCOMMODATION

Kaķis Pils iela 8 ☎2661 6997, ⓦcathouse.lv. Spotless, compact rooms with a bar and canteen-style restaurant next door. The disco may keep you awake on Fri and Sat. Doubles €̶3̶5̶
Livkalns Pēteralas iela 4b ☎2651 7416. This charming hotel's appeal lies in its secluded location, attractive rooms (the more luxurious doubles have their own jacuzzis), some with a/c and satellite TV, and a splendid cellar restaurant serving regional cuisine. Breakfast included. Doubles €̶6̶5̶
Siguldas Pludmale Peldu iela 2 ☎2924 4948, ⓦmakars .lv. Large campsite in a shady riverside spot northwest and downhill from the town centre; the only drawback is the

queue for the bathroom. Arranges canoeing and rafting trips. Open May–Sept. Camping/person €̶6̶, plus per tent €̶3̶

EATING AND DRINKING

Kaķu Māja Pils iela 8. The Black Cat café offers large helpings of inexpensive canteen-style food and a tempting range of cakes in the bakery next door. Main and a drink: €5.50. Daily 11am–midnight.
Zalumnieku Piestātne Kafejnica Pils iela 9. Another canteen-style place with a roomy, rustic interior serving large portions of Latvian food; pay by weight. Complete meal €4.50. There's also a separate pizza restaurant; medium pizza €5. Daily noon–10pm.

VENTSPILS

An attractive seaside city, **VENTSPILS**, 200km northwest of Rīga, is Latvia's biggest commercial port. The city's Old Town, with its cobbled streets, its beach – the best in Latvia – and handful of museums, makes Ventspils a great place to while away a couple of days.

WHAT TO SEE AND DO

One of the city's main draws is the long stretch of clean white-sand **beach** at the town's western end – a worthy recipient of the Blue Flag and popular with sun worshippers, volleyball players and kitesurfers in summer. Still, it's so big that you needn't jostle other beachgoers for elbow space even at the height of peak season. In Jūrmalas Park near the beach, you'll find the popular **Beach Aquapark**, with slides, wavepools and other watery attractions (Mon–Fri noon–10pm, Sat 10am–10pm, Sun 10am–7pm; €7/2hr,

> #### GAUJA NATIONAL PARK
> Encompassing a diverse range of flora and fauna, **Gauja National Park** (ⓦfacebook.com/GaujaNPF) covers more than 920 square kilometres of near-pristine forested wilderness, bisected by the 425km Gauja River. The valley is ideal for exploring by bike, as most of the hiking trails are accessible to cyclists. Numerous "wild" campsites are located along the river's banks, and major campsites in Sigulda, Cēsis and Valmiera, at the north end of the park, can arrange overnight canoeing and rafting trips.

18

18

plus €1 for each extra hour; ⓦudensparks
.lv), and also an **open-air museum** (daily
11am–6pm; €2), with ethnographic
displays featuring traditional fishermen's
dwellings and equipment.

At the northern end of the beach, a
long boardwalk, overlooked by a viewing
tower, stretches towards the lighthouse.
Here you can spot one of several
specimens from Ventspils' bizarre **Cow
Parade** – the Sailor Cow. Other cow
sculptures are found along the Ostas iela
promenade that leads east towards the
ferry port; don't miss the **Travelling Cow**,
shaped like a giant suitcase. South of the
promenade lies the Old Town, with its
Art Nouveau buildings and attractive
main square, overlooked by the jolly
yellow **Nicholas Evangelical Lutheran
Church** and featuring a giant quill
sculpture due to the town's popularity
with international writers. The Old
Town's most interesting feature is the
thirteenth-century **Castle of the Livonian
Order** at Jāņa iela 17 (Tues–Sun
10am–6pm; €2.20), home to an excellent
interactive museum featuring the history
of the city and port and a disturbing
exhibit on the Soviet prison in the
barracks.

ARRIVAL AND INFORMATION

By bus The bus station is in the centre at Kuldīga iela 5.
Destinations Liepāja (6 daily; 2hr 45min–3hr); Rīga
(hourly; 3hr); Talsi (4–5 daily; 1hr 40min).
By ferry Ferries from Travemünde in Germany, Nynashamn
in Sweden and Saaremaa in Estonia arrive at the ferry
terminal at Dārza iela 6: check ⓦstenaline.lt for schedules.
Destinations Nynashamn, Sweden (Tues–Thurs, Sat &
Sun 1 daily; 10hr); Saaremaa, Estonia (check schedule with
tourist office); Travemünde, Germany (Tues & Sat 1 daily;
27hr 30min).
Tourist information At the ferry terminal building at
Dārza iela 6 (May–Sept Mon–Fri 8am–7pm, Sat 9am–7pm,
Sun 10am–4pm; Oct–April Mon–Fri 8am–5pm, Sat & Sun
10am–3pm; ☎6362 2263, ⓦvisitventspils.com).

ACCOMMODATION

Kupfernams Kārļa iela 5 ☎6362 6999,
ⓦhotelkupfernams.lv. Delightful, centrally located
guesthouse with funky en-suite attic rooms with sloping

roofs. Wi-fi and breakfast included, and there's a good
restaurant downstairs. Doubles €59
Ventspils Piejūras Kempings Vasarnīcu iela 56 ☎6362
7925, ⓦcamping.ventspils.lv. To the southwest of the city
centre, right next to its white sandy beach, this large, popular
campsite offers tent spaces and fully equipped 4-person
holiday cottages, as well as a guest kitchen and sauna.
Camping/person €4.50, plus per tent €5, cottages €40

EATING AND DRINKING

Don Basil Annas iela 5. Cosy bistro-style place with a fair
selection of freshwater fish dishes, pastas and risottos.
Mains €10–12. Mon–Thurs 11am–8pm, Fri & Sat
11am–10pm, Sun noon–6pm.
Kupfernams Kārļa iela 5. Cosy café and restaurant
serving tasty local staples such as grilled fish with grated
potato pancakes and crêpes with a variety of fillings. Mains
€5–8. Mon–Sat 8am–10pm, Sun 8am–6pm.
Skroderkrogs Skroderu iela 6. A traditional-style pub-
restaurant bang in the centre serving up lashings of
traditional Latvian pork-and-potatoes fare. Also a great place
for a quick coffee and cake. Mains €5–8. Daily 11am–10pm.

CAPE KOLKA AND SLĪTERE NATIONAL PARK

To really get away from it all, take a trip
to the village of Kolka at the northernmost tip of **Cape Kolka**, where the Gulf
of Rīga meets the Baltic Sea, passing
through pine forest and numerous coastal
villages along the way. Kolka is part of
Slītere National Park, a former Soviet
military base turned protected nature
reserve, and there are a number of nature
trails to be hiked, not to mention the
seemingly endless expanse of virtually
deserted beach.

ARRIVAL AND DEPARTURE

By bus Direct bus from Rīga (3 daily; 3hr 45min). If
coming from Ventspils, change at Talsi: Ventspils–Talsi (4
daily; 1hr 40min); Talsi–Kolka (3 daily; 1hr 15min–2hr).

ACCOMMODATION AND EATING

Ūši 10min walk north of the bus stop ☎2947 5692,
ⓦkolka.info. You can stay at this friendly guesthouse (go
past the church on your left, then a field to your right), or
pitch a tent in the adjacent meadow. Meals are provided
on request, or you can buy local smoked fish. Camping/
person €4, doubles €46

HILL OF CROSSES (KRYŽIŲ KALNAS), ŠIAULIAI

Lithuania

HIGHLIGHTS

❶ Genocide Museum, Vilnius A haunting reminder of man's inhumanity. **See p.705**

❷ Trakai A fairytale medieval castle sitting on its own little island. **See p.707**

❸ Hill of Crosses A spiritual monument to Lithuanian identity. **See p.711**

❹ Palanga Lithuania's premier beach resort; the place to hear live music and party all night. See p.712

❺ Curonian Spit A wild, beautiful national park on the Baltic Coast. See p.713

HIGHLIGHTS ARE MARKED ON THE MAP ON P.699

ROUGH COSTS

Daily budget Basic €55, occasional treat €75

Drink Utenos beer €2

Food *Cepelinai* (potato and meat parcels) €4

Hostel/budget hotel €12/€40

Travel Bus: Kaunas–Klaipeda €15; train: Vilnius–Kaunas €5

FACT FILE

Population 2.9 million

Language Lithuanian

Currency Euro (€)

Capital Vilnius

International phone code ☎370

Time zone GMT +2hr

Introduction

Lithuania is a vibrant, quirky and largely unspoiled country, which has undergone rapid change since becoming independent from the Soviet Union in 1991. You'll find a lively nightlife, both in Vilnius and on the coast, ample grounds for outdoor pursuits in the national parks and a number of great beaches, as well as a stark contrast between city life and rural simplicity. Fiercely proud of their country, Lithuanians are more exuberant and welcoming than their Baltic neighbours and you are likely to encounter their hospitality everywhere.

19

Lithuania's small size makes getting around inexpensive; even in well-trodden destinations the volume of visitors is low, leaving you with the feeling that there's still much to discover here. **Vilnius**, with its Baroque Old Town and narrow alleys, also boasts a boisterous nightlife, while the second city, **Kaunas**, has an attractive centre and a couple of interesting museums, along with some excellent restaurants and bars. The port city of **Klaipėda** is a great place to break your journey en route to the resorts of **Neringa** (the Curonian Spit), a unique sliver of sand dunes and forest that shields Lithuania from the Baltic Sea, or to **Palanga**, Lithuania's party town, where everyone flocks in the summer for a good time.

CHRONOLOGY

2000 BC The ancestors of the Lithuanians settle in the Baltic region.

1009 AD First recorded mention of the name Lithuania in the Quedlinburg Annals.

1236 Grand Duke Mindaugas unites Lithuania to ward off German crusaders.

1386 After an arranged marriage between the King of Lithuania and the Queen of Poland, Lithuania converts to Christianity.

1410 The Polish–Lithuanian alliance defeats the Teutonic Knights, increasing their hold over the Baltic region.

1547 First Lithuanian book, *The Simple Words of Catechism*, is published.

1795 Russia takes control of Lithuania.

1865 Growth of the liberation movement leads to violent repression by the Russians.

1900 Mass emigration across the world to escape Russian repression and rural poverty.

1918 Lithuania gains independence.

1940 Lithuania is occupied by the Soviet Union.

1941 Lithuania is invaded by Nazi Germany. Thousands of Lithuanian Jews are killed.

1944–5 Soviet occupation returns. Thousands are deported.

1991 (Jan) Soviet crackdown on the independence movement leaves 14 dead.

1991 (Aug) The Soviet Union collapses and Lithuania regains independence.

2004 Lithuania joins the EU; thousands emigrate to work in Western Europe.

2009 Dalia Grybauskaitė becomes the country's first female president. She is re-elected in 2014.

2015 Lithuania adopts the euro.

ARRIVAL AND DEPARTURE

Most tourists arrive by **air**; Vilnius airport is served by several European airlines, including budget airlines Wizz Air (ⓦwizzair.com), Norwegian Air Shuttle (ⓦnorwegian.com) and Ryanair (ⓦryanair .com); the latter also flies to Kaunas. Lithuania has poor **rail** connections with its neighbours; international **buses** from neighbouring countries to Vilnius and Kaunas are far more numerous, with plenty of services from Latvia and Estonia. There are also frequent **ferries** from Kiel in Germany, and Karlshamn in Sweden, to Klaipėda on Lithuania's Baltic coast (ⓦdfdsseaways.co.uk).

GETTING AROUND

Buses are slightly quicker, more frequent and more expensive than trains. It's best to buy long-distance bus tickets in advance, and opt for an express (*ekspresas*),

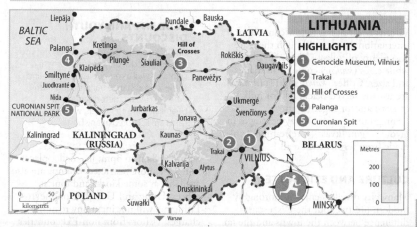

to avoid frequent stops. You can also pay for your ticket on board, although this doesn't guarantee you a seat.

You should also buy long-distance **train** tickets in advance – stations have separate windows for long-distance and suburban (*priemiestinis* or *vietinis*) trains. Long-distance services are divided into "passenger" (*keleivinis traukinys*) and "fast" (*greitas*); the latter usually require a reservation. On timetable boards, look for *isvyksta* (departure) or *atvyksta* (arrival).

In Vilnius and Kaunas public transport is frequent and efficient: buses, trolleybuses and route taxis cover most of the city. The Curonian Spit is best explored by **bicycle**; bike rentals are inexpensive and plentiful.

ACCOMMODATION

A good way to keep accommodation costs down is by staying in **private rooms**, which typically cost €35–40 with breakfast. The most reliable agency for these is Litinterp (wlitinterp.com), which has offices and guesthouses in Vilnius, Kaunas and Klaipėda; the latter can book rooms in Palanga and on the Curonian Spit. Spartan double rooms in **budget hotels** can cost as little as €30; smarter mid-range places charge €40–60.

There are an increasing number of **hostels**, especially in Vilnius and Kaunas, usually charging €10–15 per night for a dorm bed; it's best to reserve in advance. There are also plenty of **campsites** in rural areas; expect to pay €3–6 per person, plus the same per tent.

FOOD AND DRINK

Lithuanian **cuisine** is based on traditional rural fare. Typical starters include marinated mushrooms (*marinuoti grybai*), herring (*silkė*) and smoked sausage (*rukyta dešra*) along with cold beetroot soup (*saltibarščiai*). A popular **national dish** is *cepelinai*, or zeppelins – cylindrical potato parcels stuffed with meat, mushrooms or cheese. Others include potato pancakes (*bulviniai blynai*), and *koldūnai* – ravioli-like parcels filled with meat or mushroom. Popular **beer snacks** include deep-fried sticks of black bread with garlic (*kepta duona*) and smoked pigs' ears. Pancakes (*blynai, blyneliai* or *lietiniai*) come in a plethora of sweet and savoury varieties.

Most cafés and bars serve reasonably priced food. Well-stocked supermarkets, such as Iki and Maxima, are found in the main cities and towns. Many restaurants are open between 11am and midnight daily, with cafés open from 8/9am and bars closing at 2am at the earliest.

Beer (*alus*) is popular, with big local brands like Švyturus, Utenos and Kalnapilis competing with a healthy microbrewery scene. Also popular is **mead** (*midus*), Lithuania's former nobleman's drink. The leading local **firewaters** are Starka, Trejos devynerios and Medžiotojų – invigorating spirits

19

flavoured with herbs. Most bars in Vilnius and Kaunas follow contemporary international styles, although there are also plenty of folksy Lithuanian places, while cafés (*kavinė*) come in all shapes and sizes. Coffee (*kava*) and tea (*arbata*) are usually served black; ask for milk (*pienas*) and/or sugar (*cukrus*).

Forego international fizzy beverages in favour of *gira* (kvass), a refreshing drink made from fermented bread.

CULTURE AND ETIQUETTE

Many city dwellers enjoy a thoroughly modern lifestyle, but there is a stark difference between the towns and the far poorer rural Lithuania, where **traditional culture** remains firmly in place. If eating with locals, it is rude to refuse second helpings of food; when toasting someone, always look them in the eye. Always give an odd number of flowers when visiting Lithuanians, as even numbers are for the dead. Shaking hands across the threshold is bad luck. Family ties are strong, and extended family gatherings are common. Only tip in restaurants to reward good service; ten percent is fair.

SPORTS AND ACTIVITIES

Lithuania's top sport is **basketball**, and locals religiously follow the matches on TV. Try to catch a game at Vilnius's Siemens Arena (ⓦsiemensarena.lt). Lithuania's **national parks**, as well as the Curonian Spit, offer various opportunities for **outdoor activities** such as hiking, biking and canoeing.

COMMUNICATIONS

In major towns, **post offices** (*pastas*) are open Monday to Friday 8am to 6pm and

LITHUANIA ONLINE

ⓦ**vilnius-tourism.lt** Vilnius tourist information.
ⓦ**en.delfi.lt** Lithuanian news portal with news and views in English.
ⓦ**lietuva.lt** General information about the country.

STUDENT AND YOUTH DISCOUNTS

An ISIC or an IYTC card will usually get you fifty percent discount on museums and sights, as well as on public transport and some long-distance trains during term time. A YHA card gets discounts at HI-affiliated youth hostels, while ISIC/IYTC cards are accepted at any hostel.

Saturday 8am to 3pm; in smaller places hours are more restricted. **Stamps** are also available at some kiosks and tourist offices. Using an EU mobile phone in Lithuania will not incur any roaming charges; visitors from non-EU countries should contact their operator about charges, or consider buying a local prepaid SIM card with either Bitė, Omnitel or Tele 2 (€3). Most cafés and restaurants have free **wi-fi**.

EMERGENCIES

You're unlikely to meet trouble in Lithuania; pickpocketing, car theft and late-night mugging are the most common crimes. One common scam involves foreign men being accosted by beautiful women, who invite them for a drink in a nearby rip-off bar – the victims are then charged extortionate amounts for drinks. The **police** expect to be taken seriously, so be polite if you have dealings with them. **Emergency health care** is free, but if you get seriously ill, head home.

INFORMATION

Most major towns have **tourist offices**, often offering accommodation listings and event calendars in English. The **In Your Pocket** guides to Vilnius, Kaunas and Klaipėda (available from bookshops, newsstands, tourist offices and some hotels; ⓦinyourpocket.com; €2) are indispensable sources of practical

EMERGENCY NUMBERS

Fire ☏01; Police ☏02; Ambulance ☏03. For general emergencies call ☏112.

information. Regional **maps** and detailed street plans of Vilnius are available in bookshops and kiosks.

Curonian Spit; **credit** and **debit cards** are widely accepted.

MONEY AND BANKS

Lithuania adopted the euro (€) in January 2015. **Bank** (*bankas*) opening hours vary widely from one firm to another (Mon–Fri 8am–3/4pm is a fairly typical schedule). If you're looking to exchange money or get a cash advance outside banking hours, find an **exchange office** (*valiutos keitykla*). There are plentiful **ATMs** in all major towns as well as at the

OPENING HOURS AND PUBLIC HOLIDAYS

Opening hours for **shops** are 9/10am to 6/7pm. Outside Vilnius, some places take an hour off for lunch; most close on Sunday (though some food shops stay open). Most shops and all banks close on the following **public holidays**: January 1, February 16, March 11, Easter Sunday, Easter Monday, May 1, June 24, July 6, August 15, November 1, December 25 and 26.

19

LITHUANIAN

	LITHUANIAN	PRONUNCIATION
Yes	*Taip*	Tape
No	*Ne*	Ne
Please	*Prašau*	Prashau
Thank you	*Ačiu*	Achoo
Hello/Good day	*Labas*	Labass
Goodbye	*Viso gero*	Viso gero
Excuse me	*Atsiprašau*	Atsiprashau
Sorry	*Atleiskite*	Ahtlayskita
Where?	*Kur?*	Kur?
Can you show me?	*Galėtumėt man parodyti?*	Gahlehtumet mahn pahrawdeeteh?
Student ticket	*Studento billetas*	Studantoh bileahtahs
Toilet	*Tualetas*	Tuahlatas
I'd like to try…	*Aš norėčiau išbandyti*	Ahsh nawrehchow ishbahndeeteh
I don't eat meat	*Aš nevalgau mėsos*	Ahsh navahlgow mehrsaus
Bill	*Saskaita*	Sahskaitah
Good/Bad	*Geras/Blogas*	Gerass/Blogass
Near/Far	*Artimas/Tolimas*	Artimass/Tolimass
Cheap/Expensive	*Pigus/Brangus*	Piguss/Branguss
Open/Closed	*Atidarytas/Uždarytas*	Atidaritass/Uzhdaritass
Today	*Šiandien*	Shyandyen
Yesterday	*Vakar*	Vakar
Tomorrow	*Rytoj*	Ritoy
How much is…?	*Kiek kainuoja…?*	Kyek kainwoya…?
What time is it?	*Kiek valandų?*	Kyek valandoo?
I don't understand	*Nesuprantu*	Nessuprantoh
Do you speak English?	*Ar jus kalbate angliškai?*	Ar yoos kalbate anglishkay?
One	*Vienas*	Vyenass
Two	*Du/dvi*	Doh/Dvee
Three	*Trys*	Triss
Four	*Keturi*	Keturee
Five	*Penki*	Penkee
Six	*Šeši*	Sheshee
Seven	*Septyni*	Septinee
Eight	*Aštuoni*	Ashtuonee
Nine	*Devyni*	Devinee
Ten	*Dešimt*	Deshimt Lithuanian

Vilnius

A cosmopolitan city with an ancient, Baroque heart, **VILNIUS** is relatively compact and easy to get to know, with a variety of inexpensive attractions and a lively nightlife. Its numerous churches and palaces jostle for space in the Old Town's winding cobbled alleys, where glitzy restaurants stand incongruously beside dilapidated old buildings. The large student population lends the place a tangible air of energy and optimism. Beguiling, and sometimes downright odd, Vilnius has an addictive quality.

WHAT TO SEE AND DO

At the centre of Vilnius, poised between the medieval and nineteenth-century parts of the city, is **Cathedral Square** (Katedros aikštė). To the south of here along Pilies gatvė and Didžioji gatvė is the **Old Town**, containing perhaps the most impressive concentration of Baroque architecture in northern Europe. West of the square in the **New Town** is Gedimino prospektas, a nineteenth-century boulevard and the focus of the city's commercial and administrative life. The traditionally **Jewish areas** of Vilnius between the Old Town and Gedimino prospektas still retain some sights, and the community that once lived here is remembered in a brace of good museums.

Cathedral Square

Cathedral Square is dominated by the Neoclassical **cathedral** (daily 7am–7pm), which started out as a thirteenth-century wooden church built on the site of a pagan temple. The highlight of the airy, vaulted interior is the opulent **Chapel of St Casimir**, the patron saint of Lithuania. Next to the cathedral on the square is the white belfry, once part of the fortifications of the vanished Lower Castle. Between the cathedral and the belfry lies a small coloured tile with *stebuklas* (miracle) written on it, marking the spot from where, in 1989, two million people formed a human chain that stretched all the way to Tallinn, Estonia, to protest against Soviet occupation.

The Grand Dukes' Palace

Immediately behind the cathedral stands the **Grand Dukes' Palace** (Valdovu rumai; Tues, Wed, Fri & Sat 10am–6pm, Thurs 10am–8pm, Sun 10am–4pm; €3; ⓦvaldovurumai.lt), a twenty-first-century reconstruction of a Renaissance palace that fell into ruin at the end of the eighteenth century. Rebuilt more or less accurately by following old paintings and drawings, the courtyard-edged complex now holds a sumptuous collection of furnishings and artworks displayed in over thirty rooms, reflecting the opulent style in which Lithuania's Grand Dukes might once have lived.

Gediminas Castle and Museum

Rising behind Cathedral Square is the tree-clad Castle Hill, its summit crowned by the red-brick **Gediminas Castle** – one of the city's best-known landmarks – founded by Grand Duke Gediminas – the Lithuanian ruler who consolidated the country's independence. The tower houses a small **museum** (daily: April–Sept 10am–9pm; Oct–March 10am–6pm; €4), with models showing the former extent of Vilnius's fortifications. The view of the Old Town from the top is unparalleled. Take the **funicular** (same times as castle museum; €2 return) from the courtyard of the Applied Art Museum.

The Lithuanian National Museum

About 100m north of the cathedral, the **Lithuanian National Museum**, at Arsenalo 1 (Lietuvos Nacionalinis Muziejus; Tues–Sun 10am–6pm; €2; ⓦlnm.lt), traces the history of Lithuania from the Middle Ages to 1940: its fascinating collection of folk crafts, paintings and photographs includes a display of wooden crucifixes and ethnographic reconstructions of peasant life. A little further north on Arsenalo, the much snazzier **Prehistoric Lithuania Exhibition** (Tues–Sun 10am–6pm; €2) displays flint, iron, bronze and silver objects covering the history of Lithuanians up to the Middle Ages.

The National Art Gallery

On the north side of the River Neris, on Konstitucijos 22, the **National Art Gallery**

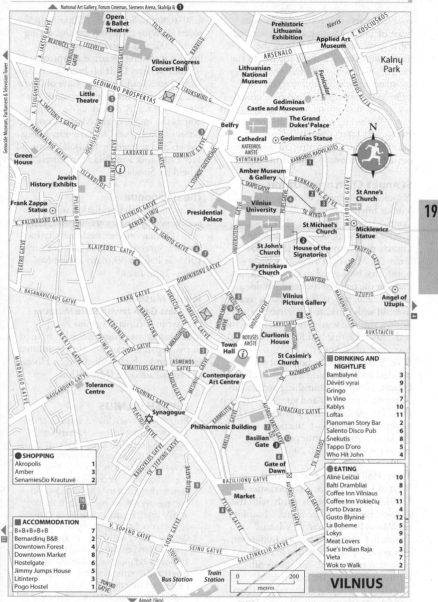

National Art Gallery, Forum Cinemas, Siemens Arena, Skalvija & ❶

Genocide Museum, Parliament & Television Tower

Opera & Ballet Theatre

A. JAKŠTO GATVE
BEATRIČES G.
J. LELEVELIO
A. VIENUOLIO GATVE
VILNIAUS GATVE
TILTO GATVE
RADVILŲ

Vilnius Congress Concert Hall

ARSENALO

Neris

T. KOSČIUŠKOS

Prehistoric Lithuania Exhibition

Applied Art Museum

Kalnų Park

A. STUGLINSKIO
A. SMETONOS GATVE
GEDIMINO PROSPEKTAS
LIAUKSMINO G.

Little Theatre

Lithuanian National Museum

Funicular

T. KSKIRDOS ALEJA

Gediminas Castle and Museum

PAMĖNKALNIO GATVE
JOGAILOS GATVE
LABDARIŲ G.
TOTORIŲ GATVE
ODMINIŲ GATVE
L. STUIKOS-GUCEVIČIAUS

Belfry

The Grand Dukes' Palace

Green House

Cathedral ◉ **Gediminas Statue**

KATEDROS AIKŠTĖ

ŠVENTARAGIO

N

Jewish History Exhibits

ISLANDIJOS
PYLIMO GATVE
ⓘ

BARBOROS RADVILAITĖS G.

Amber Museum & Gallery

S. SKAPO GATVE

BERNARDINŲ GATVE

MAIRONIO GATVE

St Anne's Church

Frank Zappa Statue ◉

K. KALINAUSKO GATVE
LIEJYKLOS GATVE
BENEDIKTINŲ
SV. IGNOTO GATVE
UNIVERSITETO GATVE
PILIES GATVE
SV. MYKOLO

Presidential Palace

Vilnius University

St Michael's Church

Mickiewicz Statue

PAUPIO GATVE

Vilnia

St John's Church

House of the Signatories

KLAIPĖDOS GATVE

Pyatnitskaya Church

DOMINIKONŲ GATVE

ĮSGANYTOJO

TEATRO GATVE

J. BASANAVIČIAUS GATVE
TRAKŲ GATVE
PRANCIŠKONŲ
VOKIEČIŲ GATVE
STIKLIŲ GATVE
DIDŽIOJI GATVE
SAVIČIAUS
BOKŠTO GATVE
MAIRONIO GATVE

Vilnius Picture Gallery

UŽUPIO

Angel of Užupis

AUKŠTAIČIŲ

YMGRI GATVE
KĖDAINIŲ G.
PYLIMO GATVE
LYDOS GATVE
SV. MIKALOJAUS
ŠVARCO GATVE
ANTOKOLSKIO
ROTUŠĖS AIKŠTĖ

Town Hall ⓘ

Čiurlionis House

AUGŠTINŲ

MINDAUGO GATVE
NAUGARDUKO GATVE
ŽEMAITIJOS GATVE
ASMENOS GATVE
MĖSINIŲ
ŠALTINIŲ GATVE

Tolerance Centre

Contemporary Art Centre

St Casimir's Church

KAZIMIERO GATVE

LIGONINES GATVE

Synagogue ✡

ARKLIŲ
KARMELITŲ G.
AUŠROS VARTŲ GATVE

Philharmonic Building

SUBAČIAUS GATVE

Basilian Gate

RAUGYKLOS GATVE
SV. STEPONO GATVE
SODŲ GATVE

Gate of Dawn

BAZILIJONŲ GATVE

Market

PYLIMO GATVE
AUŠROS VARTŲ GATVE
LAPŲ GATVE
DIKSNOS

V. SOPENO GATVE
SEINŲ GATVE
GELEŽINKELIO GATVE

Bus Station

Train Station

PUNSKO GATVE

0   200
metres

Airport (5km)

■ DRINKING AND NIGHTLIFE
Bambalynė	3
Dėvėti vyrai	9
Gringo	1
In Vino	7
Kablys	10
Loftas	11
Pianoman Story Bar	2
Salento Disco Pub	6
Šnekutis	8
Tappo D'oro	5
Who Hit John	4

● EATING
Alinė Leičiai	10
Balti Drambliai	8
Coffee Inn Vilniaus	1
Coffee Inn Vokiečių	11
Forto Dvaras	4
Gusto Blyninė	12
La Boheme	5
Lokys	9
Meat Lovers	6
Sue's Indian Raja	3
Vieta	7
Wok to Walk	2

● SHOPPING
Akropolis	1
Amber	3
Senamiesčio Krautuvė	2

■ ACCOMMODATION
B+B+B+B+B	7
Bernardinų B&B	2
Downtown Forest	4
Downtown Market	8
Hostelgate	6
Jimmy Jumps House	5
Litinterp	3
Pogo Hostel	1

VILNIUS

(Nacionalinė Dailės Galerija; Tues, Wed, Fri & Sat 11am–7pm, Thurs noon–8pm, Sun 11am–5pm; ⓦndg.lt; €2) houses a permanent display of eleven galleries of Lithuanian art since 1900, as well as temporary exhibitions. The works explore Lithuania's frequently dramatic historical context of war, independence and Soviet occupation; check out the photo documentaries of Antanas Sutkus in particular.

The Old Town

The **Old Town**, just south of Cathedral Square, is a network of narrow, often cobbled streets that forms the Baroque heart of Vilnius, with the pedestrianized Pilies gatvė cutting into it from the southeastern corner of the square. To the west of this street is **Vilnius University**, constructed between the sixteenth and eighteenth centuries around nine linked courtyards that extend west to Universiteto gatvė. Within its precincts is the beautiful Baroque **St John's Church** (Šv Jono baznyčia), founded during the fourteenth century, taken over by the Jesuits in 1561.

St Anne's Church and Užupis

Napoleon Bonaparte, who stayed in Vilnius briefly during his ill-fated campaign against Russia in 1812, is said to have been so impressed by **St Anne's Church**, on Maironio gatvė (Šv. Onos Bažnyčia; May–Sept Tues–Sun 10am–6pm), that he wanted to take it back to Paris on the palm of his hand. Studded with skeletal, finger-like towers, its facade overlaid with intricate brick traceries and fluting, this late sixteenth-century structure is the finest Gothic building in the capital. Just south of St Anne's, a bridge over the River Vilnia forms the border of the self-declared independent republic of **Užupis**, home to a flourishing population of artists, bohemians and yuppies. Stroll up from *Užupio Café* across the bridge to find a gaggle of bars and art galleries as well as the Užupis Angel, a trumpet-blowing statue unveiled in April 2001.

Town Hall Square and around

West of Užupis, Pilies gatvė becomes Didžioji gatvė as it heads south, with the restored Baroque palace at no. 4 housing the **Vilnius Picture Gallery** (Vilniaus Paveikslų Galerija; Tues–Sat 11am–6pm, Sun noon–5pm; €2), with a marvellous collection of sixteenth- to nineteenth-century paintings. The colonnaded Neoclassical building at the end of **Town Hall Square** (Rotušės aikštė) is the **Town Hall** itself. The **Contemporary Art Centre** (Suolaikinio meno centras or SMC; Tues–Sun noon–8pm; €2.50; ⓦcac.lt) lies behind it, hosting modern art exhibitions with interactive elements and a good café. East of the square is the striking **St Casimir's Church** (Šv. Kazimiero Bažnyčia; Mon–Fri

4.30–6.30pm, Sun 9am–1.30pm), the oldest Baroque church in the city, dating from 1604, and possessing a beautiful interior including a marble altarpiece.

South of here, Didžioji becomes Aušros Vartų gatvė, leading to the **Gate of Dawn** (Aušros Vartų), the sole survivor of the nine city gates. A chapel above the gate houses the image of the Madonna of the Gates of Dawn, said to have miraculous powers and revered by Catholics from all over Lithuania and Poland; open-air Mass is held on Sundays.

The synagogue

Today the Jewish population of Vilnius numbers only five thousand, and, out of over 100 that once existed, the city has just one surviving **synagogue**, built in 1903, at Pylimo 39 (daily except Sat 10am–2pm; free).

Jewish Museum

The **Vilna Gaon Jewish State Museum** (Valstybinis Vilniaus Gaono Žydų Muziejus; ⓦwww.jmuseum.lt) is housed in two separate branches. The **Holocaust Exhibition** in the so-called Green House at Pamėnkalnio 12 (Mon–Thurs

---

JEWISH VILNIUS

Before World War II, Vilnius was one of the most important centres of **Jewish** life in Eastern Europe. The Jews – first invited to settle in 1410 by Grand Duke Vytautas – made up around a third of the city's population, mainly concentrated in the western fringes of the Old Town around present-day Vokiečių gatvė, Zydų gatvė and Antokolskio gatvė. Massacres of the Jewish population began soon after the Germans occupied Vilnius on June 24, 1941, and those who survived the initial killings found themselves herded into two **ghettos**. The smaller of these ghettos centred on the streets of Zydų, Antokolskio, Stiklių and Gaono, and was liquidated in October 1941, while the larger occupied an area between Pylimo, Vokiečių, Lydos, Mikalojaus, Karmelitų and Arklių streets, and was liquidated in September 1943. Most of Vilnius's 80,000 Jewish residents perished in Paneriai forest, 10km southwest of the city.

9am–5pm, Fri 9am–4pm, Sun 10am–4pm; €3; combined ticket with Tolerance Centre €5) contains a harrowing display on the fate of Vilnius and Kaunas Jews during World War II, including eyewitness accounts, and many extremely disturbing photographs with some captions in English. The most recent addition to the Jewish State Museum is the **Tolerance Centre**, Naugarduko 10/2 (Mon–Thurs 10am–6pm, Fri & Sun 10am–4pm; €3; combined ticket with Holocaust Exhibition €5), housing some excellent twentieth-century Jewish artwork and an engrossing display charting the history of Jews in Lithuania from the fourteenth century until the present day.

Frank Zappa statue

On Kalinausko Street, the bronze head of rocker **Frank Zappa** is perched on a column against a backdrop of street art. Civil servant Saulis Paukstys founded the local Zappa fan club and, in 1992, commissioned the socialist-realist sculptor Konstantinas Bogdanas to create this unique memorial.

Gedimino prospektas and the Genocide Museum

Gedimino prospektas, running west from Cathedral Square, is the most important commercial street. On the southern side of **Lukiskių aikštė**, a square around 900m west of Cathedral Square, is Gedimino 40, Lithuania's former KGB headquarters. The building also served as Gestapo headquarters during the German occupation, and, more recently, the Soviets incarcerated political prisoners in the basement. It's now the **Genocide Museum**, entrance at Aukų 2a (Genocido aukų muziejus; Wed–Sat 10am–6pm, Sun 10am–5pm; €4; ⓦgenocid.lt /muziejus) with torture cells and an execution chamber that make a grim impression. Well-labelled, detailed exhibits on Soviet occupation, deportation and Lithuanian partisan resistance are upstairs; the optional English-language audio commentary (€3) is worthwhile if you want a detailed prison tour.

ARRIVAL AND DEPARTURE

By plane The airport is 5km south of the centre, with regular trains to the central station (every 30min, 6.30am–7.30pm; 7min; €1). Buses #1 and #2 (every 30min; 20min; €1) will also take you to the centre. A taxi costs around €15.

By train The main train station is at Geležinkelio 16, with 24hr luggage storage in the basement, a 24hr currency exchange, ATMs, detailed timetables, information office and a Maxima supermarket.

Destinations Kaunas (every 30min; 1hr 15min–1hr 45min); Klaipėda (4 daily; 3hr 50min–4hr 35min); Moscow (1–2 daily; 13–15hr); St Petersburg (2 weekly; 18hr 30min); Trakai (8 daily; 35min).

By bus The bus terminal, just across the road from the train station, has luggage storage and an ATM.

Destinations Kaunas (every 20–30min; 1hr 30min–2hr); Klaipėda (hourly; 4hr); Nida (via Klaipėda; 1 daily at 7am; 5hr 50min); Palanga (10 daily; 5hr); Rīga (8 daily; 5hr–5hr 30min); Tallinn (5 daily; 9–10hr); Trakai (every 30min; 30min); Warsaw (2 daily; 8hr 30min).

INFORMATION

Tourist information The two main tourist office branches at Vilniaus 22 (daily 9am–6pm; ☎ 5262 9660, ⓦvilnius -tourism.lt) and Didžioji 31, in the town hall (daily 9am–1pm and 2–6pm; ☎ 5262 6470), offer advice on accommodation, events listings and festivals (ⓦvilniusfestivals.lt).

GETTING AROUND

By bus Tickets cost €1 from newspaper kiosks or from the driver. Validate your ticket by punching it in the machine on board. An electronic ticket (vilniečio kortelė; €1.50 deposit) is more useful if you're travelling around, and can be topped up in increments of €3.50/€6.20/€12 for 1/3/10 days.

By taxi Prices are usually reasonable and fares should cost no more than €0.60/km. Phoning ahead guarantees you a better rate; try Ekipažas (☎ 1446).

ACCOMMODATION

B+B+B+B+B Kauno 5 ☎ 6264 5614, ⓦ 5bhostelvilnius .com. In the same building as *Kablys* club (see p.707), this won't appeal to early risers. There is however a good mix of dorms and private rooms, in an intelligently designed thrift-chic space. Late breakfast €3 extra in the *Kablys* café. Dorms €12, doubles €30

★**Bernardinų B&B House** Bernardinu 5 ☎ 6720 3277, ⓦ bernardinuhouse.com. Great-value B&B with spacious, tastefully decorated rooms, all with cable TV and some en suite. Offers excursions throughout Lithuania. Breakfast €4 extra. Doubles €45

Downtown Forest Paupio 31a ☎ 6868 4523, ⓦ downtownforest.lt. A large suburban mansion some fifteen minutes' walk east of the Old Town, with neat bright dorms and private rooms, and a large garden with

19

19

tent space. It also has an outdoor bar and bike rental: breakfast is included. Dorms €10, doubles €40

Downtown Market Pylimo 57 ☏6798 5476, ⓦdowntownmarket.lt. A quirky, friendly boutique hotel close to the Gate of Dawn. The six en-suite rooms are each decorated in market themes (flower market, flea market etc). Organic breakfast included. Doubles €40

Hostelgate Aušros Vartų 17-1 ☏6383 2818, ⓦhostelgate.lt. This bustling central hostel, run by outgoing, helpful staff, offers clean dorms, kitchen, table football and wi-fi. Organized excursions include sauna tours and trips to fire weaponry in the countryside. Private doubles are located a few streets away at Mikalojaus 3. Dorms €9, doubles €32

★**Jimmy Jumps House** Savičiaus 12 ☏5231 3847, ⓦjimmyjumpshouse.com. Difficult to find but worth it, this backpackers' hostel has a great party feel and offers free walking tours of Vilnius. Kitchen and breakfast included. Dorms €10, doubles €32

Litinterp Bernardinų 7 ☏5212 3850, ⓦlitinterp.com. Stay in this central guesthouse with airy, comfortable rooms and shared bathrooms and kitchenettes. Book in advance in summer. Breakfast delivered to your door for an extra €3. Doubles €46

Pogo Hostel Barboros Radvilaites 3-1 ☏6846 7060, ⓦfacebook.com/pogohostel. A bright, neatly renovated town house in the heart of the action, with modern design touches and pop art on the walls. Dorms €15, doubles €42

EATING

There's a fast-growing range of eating options in Vilnius plus a variety of cuisines. Bars and cafés serve both snacks and meals, and often represent better value for money than restaurants.

CAFÉS, CHEAP EATS AND SNACKS

Coffee Inn Vilniaus 17; also at Vokiečių 18. It may be a café chain, but it's local and has character, boasting homely mix-and-match furnishings and a young crowd. Excellent coffee, smoothies, muffins, sandwiches, wraps – and cheesecake to die for. Mon–Fri 7am–midnight, Sat & Sun 8am–midnight.

Forto Dvaras Pilies 16. An excellent place to try fairly authentic *cepelinai* (€4), which come with a variety of fillings as well as the usual minced meat version, or stuffed potato pancakes (€3.50). Cheap, tasty and filling. Daily 11am–11pm.

Gusto Blyninė Aušros Vartų 6. Substantial, tasty crêpes with every imaginable sweet or savoury filling (€2.50). A good place to enjoy Lithuania's legendary potato pancakes, served with lashings of sour cream and bacon bits. Daily 9am–10pm.

Wok To Walk Vilniaus 19. A great little spot where you choose from an array of noodles, rice, vegetables and sauce, all wok-fried in front of you. Quick and tasty. Mains €4. Mon–Thurs 11am–10pm, Fri 11am–3am, Sat noon–midnight, Sun noon–8pm.

RESTAURANTS

Alinė Leičiai Stiklių 4. Quality Lithuanian food in a part modern, part medieval building, offering filling inexpensive staples (*cepelinai*; €4.50) as well as hearty feasting fare (pork knuckle marinated in beer; €10). They brew their own ales too; try the hemp beer (€3/0.5lt). Daily 11am–midnight.

Balti Drambliai Vilniaus 41. Vegetarian restaurant with a loyal, mildly bohemian clientele, in a many-chambered, red-brick basement decorated with pictures of deities. Tasty, inexpensive tofu-based stews with couscous or rice form the backbone of the menu. Live bands and DJs on summer weekends lend a clubby feel. Mains €4. Mon–Thur & Sun 11am–10pm, Fri & Sat noon–midnight.

La Boheme Šv Ignoto 4/3 ☏5212 1087. Wine bar-cum-restaurant in a fine barrel-vaulted setting. Food is modern European with a Mediterranean slant, including excellent risottos, pastas and tapas-style nibbles. Lived-in wooden furnishings and candles add to the atmosphere. Mains €8–11. Mon–Wed 11am–midnight, Thurs 11am–1am, Fri 11am–2am, Sat noon–2am, Sun noon–midnight.

Lokys Stiklių 8 ☏5262 9046. Cosy Lithuanian cellar restaurant specializing in well-cooked game dishes that are worth the splurge. Beaver stew with mushrooms €12; quail with pear and blackberry sauce €16. Daily noon–midnight.

Meat Lovers Šv Ignoto 14. This small, smart and functional restaurant serves expertly grilled steaks (€15) and succulent pork roasts (€8), washed down with tasty small-brewery Lithuanian beers (€2.70/0.5lt). Mon–Fri 11.30am–midnight, Sat noon–midnight, Sun noon–8pm.

★**Sue's Indian Raja** Odminių 3 ☏5266 1888. One of the best restaurants in town, this place is popular with expats and locals alike. Gorge yourself on excellent curry (€9–12), though be warned that the dishes are authentically spicy. Mon & Sun 11am–10pm, Tues–Sat 11am–11pm.

Vieta Šv Ignoto 12. Vegetarian restaurant and wine bar with a regularly changing menu of soups, stews and pies, many with an East-West fusion approach to the spicing. Only problem is they tend to run out of mains come the evening. Mains €4–7. Daily noon–10pm.

DRINKING AND NIGHTLIFE

A rapidly developing bar strip along Vilniaus gatvi (and adjacent Islandijos) has given Vilnius a new-found every-night-of-the week buzz. Most bars are open late and many feature DJs at weekends, offering effective competition to the pay-to-enter disco clubs.

BARS

Bambalynė Stiklių 7. A vaulted brick cellar harbours this popular beer shop and bar selling over 100 Lithuanian beers – including a handful of its own tasty brews at €3/0.5lt. Furnished with chairs and tables that look like they belonged to impoverished nineteenth-century aristocrats, it's delightfully odd. Tues–Sat 11am–midnight, Sun & Mon 11am–10pm.

Dėvėti vyrai Sodų 3. Just outside the Old Town but still within bar-crawl distance, this dark but welcoming bar serves beers from the renowned Dundulis brewery and decent cocktails. Cheap set lunches bring in a discerning daytime crowd on weekdays. Mon–Fri 9am–1am, Sat & Sun 5pm–1am.

Gringo Vilniaus 31. Animated and cheerful café-bar with sofas and tables in the back corner and a constant crush around the bar. One of the key stations on the Vokiečių-Vilniaus crawl, it attracts a fair crowd come the weekend. Mon–Wed & Sun 11am–2am, Thurs 11am–3am, Fri & Sat 3pm–4am.

In Vino Aušros vartų 7. Wine bar and much more besides, with candlelight and wooden chairs and tables creating a nineteenth-century French-farmhouse-kitchen feel in the main room, and a more loungey area around the corner. Background jazz and chansons create a bit of extra class. Sun–Thurs 4pm–2am, Fri & Sat 4pm–4am.

Pianoman Story Bar Islandijos 1. One of a string of bars along Islandijos, *Pianoman* is in many ways the ideal pub – a good place to sit and talk, watch midweek sport on TV, or enjoy the raw party mood come the weekend. Mon–Thurs 5pm–2am.

Šnekutis Šv. Stepono 8. An excellent place to sample microbrews and ales from all over Lithuania (€2.50/0.5lt). The rustic decor and tasty bar snacks are a nice touch. Mon–Sat 11am–11pm.

Tappo D'oro Vokiečiu 8. Wine bar with a mildly bohemian edge – it's constantly full of everyone from students to established cultural figures, with the weekend fun usually extending out onto the pavement. Mon–Sat 5pm–4am.

Who Hit John Didžioji 19. This cupboard-sized bar with barely room to swing a cocktail umbrella has become something of a cult thanks in large part to its eclectic music policy and equally eclectic clientele. Very good for cocktails, a list of which is chalked up above the bar. Mon–Thurs & Sun 8pm–5am, Fri & Sat 8pm–6am.

CLUBS

Kablys Kauno 5 ⓦ facebook.com/kablysvilnius. Housed in an elegantly colonnaded Soviet-era cultural centre, "The Hook" has long been at the centre of indie activity in Vilnius, with regular alt-rock gigs, and DJ nights from hip-hop to dub reggae. Daily 11am–2am.

Loftas Švitrigailos 29 ⓦ menufabrikas.lt. A big post-industrial space that hosts hands-in-the-air DJ events as well as gigs by international jazz and rock acts. Thurs–Sat 10pm–4am.

Salento Disco Pub Didžioji 28. Various themed nights (most involving foam), cheesy pop tunes, large TV screens and a young and up-for-it crowd. Entry €3. Daily 10pm–6am.

ENTERTAINMENT

Forum Cinemas Akropolis Ozo 25 ⓦ forumcinemas.lt. Modern, multi-screen cinema in Vilnius's largest shopping mall, showing the latest blockbusters in original language, with subtitles. Entry €6.

Opera & Ballet Theatre Vienuolio 1 ☎ 5262 0727, ⓦ opera.lt. Stunning building featuring well-attended performances by local opera and ballet companies.

Skalvija Goštauto 2/15 ☎ 5261 0505, ⓦ skalvija.lt. International art films are shown in this central venue by the river. Entry €3–5.

Vilnius Congress Concert Hall Vilniaus 6/14 ☎ 5261 8828, ⓦ lvso.lt. Chamber music, orchestra performances and ballet.

SHOPPING

Akropolis Ozo 25. Huge shopping complex around 3km north of town with a variety of clothing and jewellery shops, plus an indoor ice rink and the Vichy Aqua Park with water slides (€20). Daily 8am–10pm.

Amber Aušros Vartų 9. An extensive array of amber jewellery and handicrafts. Mon–Fri 10am–7pm, Sat & Sun till 5pm.

Senamiesčio Krautuvė Literatų 5. Fresh Lithuanian fare including pickles, sausages and cakes, all laid out in baskets for you to sample. Mon–Sat 10am–8pm, Sun 11am–5pm.

DIRECTORY

Banks and exchange ATMs are plentiful. Citadele, outside the station at Geležinkelio 6 (24hr), changes money at decent rates.

Embassies and consulates Australia, Vilniaus 23 ☎ 5212 3369; Canada, Jogailos 4 ☎ 5249 0950; Ireland, Gedimino 1 ☎ 5262 9460; UK, Antakalnio 2 ☎ 5246 2900; US, Akmenų 6 ☎ 5266 5500.

Hospital Vilnius University Emergency Hospital, Šiltnamiu 29 ☎ 5216 9069.

Left luggage Train station has 24hr luggage storage in the basement. Bus station also has baggage room (5.30am–9.45pm).

Pharmacy Eurovaistinė, Gedimino 18 (Mon–Fri 7am–9pm, Sat 9am–9pm, Sun 9am–8pm); Gedimino Vaistinė, Gedimino 27 (Mon–Fri 7.30am–8pm, Sat & Sun 10am–5pm).

Police Saltoniškiu 19 ☎ 5271 9731.

Post office Gedimino prospektas 7 (Mon–Fri 7.30am–7pm, Sat 9am–4pm).

TRAKAI

Around 30km west of Vilnius lies the little town of **TRAKAI**, a mix of concrete Soviet-style buildings merging with the wooden cottages of the Karaite community, Lithuania's smallest ethnic

19

minority. Standing on a peninsula jutting out between two lakes, Trakai is the site of two impressive medieval castles and makes for a worthwhile day-trip from the capital.

Once you arrive, follow Vytauto gatvė and turn right down Kęstučio gatvė to reach the remains of the **Peninsula Castle**, now partially restored after having been destroyed by the Russians in 1655. Skirting the ruins along the lakeside path, you will see the spectacular **Island Castle** (Salos pilis), one of Lithuania's most famous monuments, accessible by two wooden drawbridges and preceded by souvenir and rowing-boat rental (€5) stalls. You can also rent yachts here (€25 for 40min cruise with skipper). Built around 1400 AD by Grand Duke Vytautas, under whom Lithuania reached the pinnacle of its power, the castle fell into ruin from the seventeenth century until a 1960s restoration returned it to its former glory (May–Sept daily 10am–7pm; March, April & Oct Tues–Sun 10am–6pm; Nov–Feb Tues–Sun 10am–5pm; €6, students €3, permission to take photos €2). The history museum inside displays artefacts discovered while excavating the site.

Trakai is home to three hundred Karaim – a Judaic sect of Turkish origin whose ancestors were brought here from the Crimea by Grand Duke Vytautas to serve as bodyguards. You can learn more about their cultural contribution to Trakai at the **Karaite Ethnographic Exhibition**, 22 Karaimų gatvė (Wed–Sun 10am–5pm; €1.50).

ARRIVAL AND DEPARTURE

By bus and train Take a bus from Vilnius's main bus station (at least one hourly; 35min; last bus from Trakai at 8.45pm) or a train (8 daily; 35min).

EATING

Kybynlar Karaimų 29. Several places in Trakai serve *kibinai*, traditional Karaite pasties stuffed with minced meat, mushrooms or other savoury fillings. This place, just off the main street, has the biggest choice (€2–3 per pasty), as well as grilled meats and salads. Wash it down with *gira*, a semi-alcoholic drink made from fermented bread. Mon–Thurs & Sun noon–9pm, Fri & Sat noon–10pm.

The rest of Lithuania

Lithuania is predominantly rural – a gently undulating, densely forested landscape scattered with lakes, and fields dotted with ambling storks in the summer. The major city of **Kaunas**, west of the capital, rivals Vilnius in terms of its historical importance. Further west, the main highlights of the coast are the **Curonian Spit**, whose dramatic dune-scapes can be reached by ferry and bus from **Klaipėda**, and **Palanga**, which fills up in summer with thousands of people looking for fun.

KAUNAS

KAUNAS, 98km west of Vilnius and easily reached by bus or rail, is Lithuania's second city, seen by many Lithuanians as the true heart of their country; it served as provisional **capital** during the interwar period of 1920–39. It is undergoing rapid modernization, with the mirror-like exteriors of new buildings reflecting parts of the medieval city wall. While much of Kaunas is a busy urban sprawl, visitors will invariably be drawn to the old heart of the city where the main attractions lie.

WHAT TO SEE AND DO

The most picturesque part of Kaunas is the **Old Town** (Senamiestis), centred on **Town Hall Square** (Rotušės aikštė), on a spur of land between the Neris and Nemunas rivers. The square is lined with fifteenth- and sixteenth-century merchants' houses in pastel stucco shades, but the overpowering feature is the magnificent Town Hall itself, its tiered Baroque facade rising to a graceful 53m tower.

The cathedral and castle

Occupying the northeastern shoulder of the square, the red-brick tower of Kaunas's austere **cathedral** stands at the western end of Vilniaus gatvė. Dating back to the reign of Vytautas the Great, the cathedral was much added to in subsequent centuries. After the plain exterior, the lavish gilt-and-marble interior comes as a

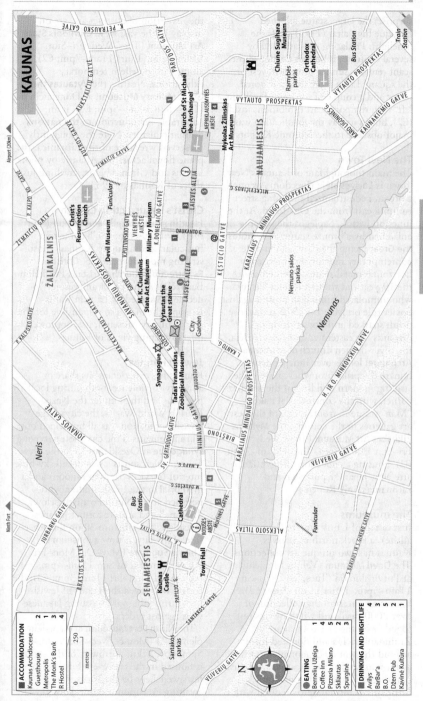

KAUNAS

K. PETRAUSKO GATVĖ

Chune Sugihara Museum

Orthodox Cathedral

Ramybės parkas

Bus Station

Train Station

VYTAUTO PROSPEKTAS

Church of St Michael the Archangel

NEPRIKLAUSOMYBĖS AIKŠTĖ

Mykolas Žilinskas Art Museum

VYTAUTO PROSPEKTAS

NAUJAMIESTIS

KAUNAKIEMIO GATVĖ

KARO LIGONINĖS G.

MICKEVIČIAUS G.

Christ's Resurrection Church

Funicular

Devil Museum

ŽEMAIČIŲ GATVĖ

VIENYBĖS AIKŠTĖ

VYDŪNO GATVĖ

Military Museum

LAISVĖS ALĖJA

DAUKANTO G.

MINDAUGO PROSPEKTAS

M. K. Čiurlionis State Art Museum

SAVANORIŲ PROSPEKTAS

KĘSTUČIO GATVĖ

KARALIAUS

Nemuno salos parkas

ŽALIAKALNIS

Vytautas the Great statue

City Garden

LAISVĖS ALĖJA

A. MACKEVIČIAUS GATVĖ

K. DONELAIČIO GATVĖ

Nemunas

Neris

P. KALPOKO GATVĖ

Synagogue

Tadas Ivanauskas Zoological Museum

E. OŽEŠKIENĖS

V. PUTVINSKIO GATVĖ

S. GERTRŪDOS GATVĖ

I. KANTO G.

H. IR O. MINKOVSKIŲ GATVĖ

JONAVOS GATVĖ

VILNIAUS GATVĖ

GRUODŽIO G.

KARALIAUS MINDAUGO PROSPEKTAS

BIRŠTONO

ŽEMAIČIŲ GATVĖ

A. MAPŲ G.

M. DAUKŠOS G.

VEIVERIŲ GATVĖ

Funicular

Bus Station

Cathedral

MUITINĖS GATVĖ

ALEKSOTO TILTAS

Kaunas Castle

Town Hall

ROTUŠĖS AIKŠTĖ

SENAMIESTIS

PAPILIO G.

L. A. JAKŠTO GATVĖ

SANTAKOS GATVĖ

ŠV. GERTRŪDOS GATVĖ

S. DARIAUS IR S. GIRĖNO GATVĖ

JURBARKO GATVĖ

BRASTOS GATVĖ

Santakos parkas

VEIVERIŲ GATVĖ

Airport (20km)

Ninth Fort

N

0 — 250 metres

ACCOMMODATION

Kaunas Archdiocese Guesthouse	2
Metropolis	1
The Monk's Bunk	3
R Hostel	4

EATING

Bernelių Užeiga	1
Coffee Inn	4
Pizzeria Milano	5
Skilautas	2
Spurginė	3

DRINKING AND NIGHTLIFE

Avilys	4
BarBar'a	3
B.O.	5
Džem Pub	2
Kavinė Kultūra	1

19

surprise; the large, statue-adorned Baroque high altar (1775) steals the limelight. Predating the cathedral by several centuries is **Kaunas Castle**, whose scant remains survive just northwest of the square. Little more than a restored tower and a couple of sections of wall are left, with temporary art exhibitions inside (€2), but in its day the fortification was a major obstacle to the Teutonic Knights.

The New Town

The main thoroughfare of Kaunas's New Town is **Laisvės alėja** (Freedom Avenue), a broad, pedestrianized shopping street running east from the Old Town. At the junction with L. Sapiegos the street is enlivened by a bronze statue of **Vytautas the Great** facing the City Garden. Here, a contemporary memorial composed of horizontal metal shards commemorates the 19-year-old student Romas Kalanta, who immolated himself in protest against Soviet rule on May 14, 1972 and whose death sparked anti-Soviet rioting. Towards the eastern end of Laisvės alėja, the silver-domed **Church of St Michael the Archangel** looms over Independence Square (Nepriklausomybės aikštė). The striking modern building in the northeast corner, with the controversial naked "Man" statue in front, is one of the best art galleries in the country, the **Mykolas Žilinskas Art Museum** (Tues, Wed, Fri–Sun 11am–5pm, Thurs 11am–7pm; €2), housing a collection of Egyptian artefacts, Japanese porcelain and Lithuania's only Rubens.

The museums

Just north of Unity Square (Vienybės aikštė), a block north of Laisvės, Kaunas has two unique art collections. The **Devil Museum** (Velnių Muziejus), at Putvinskio 64 (Tues, Wed, Fri–Sun 11am–5pm, Thurs 11am–7pm; €2), houses an entertaining collection of over 2000 devil and witch figures put together by the artist Antanas Žmuidzinavičius and donated from around the world. Diagonally opposite, at Putvinskio 55, the dreamy, symbolist paintings of Mikalojus Čiurlionis, Lithuania's cultural hero credited with

the invention of abstract art, are on display in the vast **M. K. Čiurlionis State Art Museum** (Tues, Wed, Fri–Sun 11am–5pm, Thurs 11am–7pm; €2), along with excellent temporary exhibitions. Nearby, the **Vytautas the Great Military Museum**, at Donelaičio 64 (Tues–Sun 10am–5pm; €2), is an admirable introduction to the nation's dramatic history. Note the poignantly preserved wreckage of the Lituanica, the plane flown across the Atlantic by pilots Darius and Girenas before crashing just short of Kaunas in 1933.

Christ's Resurrection Church

Heading east along V. Putvinskio from the Devil Museum, you'll come to a funicular, leading up to Kaunas's most striking modernist church, **Christ's Resurrection Church** (Kristaus Prisikėlimo Bažnyčia). A marvel or an eyesore? You decide. Designed by Latvian Kārlis Reisons, the man also responsible for the city's Military Museum, its 70m tower offers sweeping views of Kaunas (€2).

Jewish Kaunas

Kaunas has experienced its share of anti-Jewish violence, both during local pogroms and then under the Nazis. During World War II, the city's large Jewish population was all but wiped out; all that remains is the city's sole surviving **synagogue** at Ožeškienės 13 in the New Town, which sports a wonderful sky-blue interior (services Sat 10am–noon) and a **memorial** to the 1700 children who perished at the Ninth Fort (see below). The small and austere former Japanese consulate, at Vaižganto 30 on the other side of the city, is now a **museum to Chiune Sugihara** (May–Oct Mon–Fri 10am–5pm, Sat & Sun 11am–4pm; Nov–April Mon–Fri 11am–3pm; €3), the consul who saved thousands of Jewish lives during the war by issuing Japanese visas against orders.

The **Ninth Fort Museum**, at Žemaičių plentas 73 (Mon & Wed–Sun 10am–6pm; €3), 24km northwest of the centre, is housed in the tsarist-era fortress where Jews were kept by the Nazis while awaiting execution: exhibits cover extermination of Jews by the Nazis and the deportation of Lithuanians by the Soviets. A massive, jagged stone memorial crowns the site. Take bus #35 from Kaunas bus station (every 30min) and get off at the IX Fortas stop.

ARRIVAL AND DEPARTURE

By plane Kaunas's international airport is located around 20km north of Kaunas. Bus #29 (€1) passes through the Old Town and stops at the main bus and train stations.

By bus and train Kaunas's bus and train stations are both along Vytauto at the southeastern end of the centre, a 10min walk from Laisvės alėja; take any trolleybus passing in front of the stations to the Old Town (€0.80). There is luggage storage at both, and an ATM out on the main street.

Destinations (train) Vilnius (every 30min; 1hr 15min–1hr 45min).

Destinations (bus) Klaipėda (hourly; 3hr); Nida (1 daily at 7am; 4hr 10min); Palanga (7 daily; 3hr 30min); Rīga (9–14 daily; 4hr–4hr 30min); Tallinn (1 daily via Riga at 9pm; 9hr); Vilnius (every 20–30min; 1hr 30min–2hr); Warsaw (4 weekly; 7hr).

INFORMATION

Tourist information Laisvės 36 (June–Aug Mon–Fri 9am–7pm, Sat 10am–6pm, Sun 10am–3pm; Sept–May Mon–Thurs 9am–6pm, Fri 9am–5pm; ☏37 323 436, ⓦ visit.kaunas.lt). Provides useful maps and copies of *Kaunas in Your Pocket* (€1). There's another office at Rotušės aikštė 29 (same hours).

ACCOMMODATION

★ **Kaunas Archdiocese Guest House** Rotušės 21 ☏37 322 597, ⓦ kaunas.lcn.lt/guesthouse. With a hard-to-beat location between two churches, this charming place has clean doubles and free internet. Consumption of alcohol is forbidden. A real bargain. Doubles €25

Metropolis Daukanto 21 ☏37 205 992, ⓦ metropolishotel.lt. Much renovated nineteenth-century hotel in a great location with 75 inexpensive en-suite rooms. The wood-panelled lobby area still has bags of *belle époque* charm. Breakfast included. Doubles €43

R Hostel Vytauto 83 ☏690 45 329, ⓦ r-hostel.lt. A welcome addition to Kaunas's hostel scene, offering a good mix of bunks and private rooms, plus a lounge with table football, beer-tasting evenings and barbecues. Dorms €10, doubles €23

The Monk's Bunk Laisves 48-2 ☏620 99 695, ⓔ kaunashostel@gmail.com. Relaxed, traveller-friendly hostel with a great kitchen and homely lounge, complete with free-to-use djembe drums and guitar. Offers free walking tours of the city. Dorms €11, doubles €32

EATING

Bernelių Užeiga Valančiaus 9 ☏37 200 913. Dine on huge portions of meaty Lithuanian staples in an attractive rustic interior. Tuck in to traditional fare like rabbit stew with potato and red cabbage (€6.30), or a pile of potato pancakes with a choice of dips (€3.50). Mon–Wed & Sun 11am–11pm, Thurs 11am–midnight, Fri & Sat 11am–1am.

Coffee Inn Laisvės 72. Great coffee, smoothies and a good choice of wraps (€4), plus cosy sofas and free wi-fi. Mon–Fri 7am–10pm, Sat 10am–10pm, Sun 10am–9pm.

Pizzeria Milano Mickevičiaus 19. Tucked away in a functional 1930s block, this busy but informal restaurant serves up fairly authentic pizzas (€4–6) and pasta dishes (€3–5). Mon–Thurs & Sun 10am–1am, Fri & Sat 10am–2am.

Skliautas Rotušės 26. Set in a courtyard near the town hall, this small bar/restaurant has a brick-vaulted ceiling and evokes the atmosphere of the 1940s with old clocks, photos, candles and interwar music. Pork with cranberry sauce €4. Live gigs on the terrace in summer. Mon–Thurs 11am–midnight, Fri 11am–2am, Sat 11am–2am, Sun 11am–11pm.

★ **Spurginė** Laisvės 84. Traditional café that hasn't changed in decades, dishing out delicious springy Lithuanian doughnuts (*spurgos*), and also tasty small pies stuffed with cabbage, mushroom and other savoury fillings. Mon–Fri 8.30am–8pm, Sat & Sun 9am–7pm.

DRINKING AND NIGHTLIFE

Avilys Vilniaus 34. Excellent microbrewery in a cosy cellar offering two types of honey-flavoured beer (€4/0.5lt), beer soup and a range of standard meat dishes and bar snacks. Wash down a plate of fried plums and bacon with a

---

HILL OF CROSSES

Up on a hill, 12km north of the town of Šiauliai, 188km northwest of Vilnius and 170km east of Klaipėda, lies the **Hill of Crosses** (Kryžių Kalnas), an ever-growing, awe-inspiring collection of more than 200,000 crosses, statues and effigies. There are many myths surrounding the Hill's origin, some dating back to pagan times, although the most plausible is that it was to commemorate rebels killed in nineteenth-century uprisings against the Russian Empire. In the Soviet era, they were planted by grieving families to commemorate killed and deported loved ones, and kept multiplying despite repeated bulldozing by the authorities. Today, crosses are often planted to give thanks for a happy event in a person's life. To get here, take a train to Šiauliai from Vilnius (5–8 daily; 2hr 30min) or Klaipėda (5 daily; 2hr) and then take a taxi (15min; €10).

19

19

pint of grog (warmed honey beer with extra honey and lemon). Mon–Fri noon–midnight, Fri & Sat noon–2am.

BarBar'a Vilniaus 56. Dress smart, look beautiful and if you make it in, enjoy some cocktails along with Kaunas's pretty young things. Theme nights, happy hours and weekend DJs keep the crowd happy. Wed–Sat 11pm–5am.

B.O. Muitinès 9. This friendly, popular and unpretentious bar is one of the best places to hook up with a young, arty crowd. The choice of Lithuanian and international beers is among the best in the city. Mon–Thurs & Sun 5pm–2am, Fri & Sat 5pm–3am.

Džem Pub Laisvės 59. Take the lift up to this cosy bar with regular live bands, a good range of beers and a superb view of the city. Tues–Thurs 4pm–3am, Fri & Sat 6pm–4am.

Kavinė Kultūra Donelaičio 14–16. This laidback bohemian hangout with shabby-chic furnishings is a great place to snap up a set lunch (Mon–Fri only; €4) or enjoy a beer or few on the outdoor terrace. Mon–Thurs & Sun noon–10pm, Fri & Sat noon–2am.

KLAIPĖDA

KLAIPĖDA, Lithuania's third-largest city and most important port, lies on the Baltic coast, 275km northwest of Vilnius. Home to an evocative Old Town and a medieval castle, the city serves as an ideal staging post en route to the Curonian Spit, or to the party town of Palanga.

WHAT TO SEE AND DO

Just east of the Old Town, Klaipeda's Old Castle Port is a former industrial zone renovated to create an attractive area of seaside promenades backed by nineteenth-century warehouses. It is reached via the cast-iron **Swing Bridge**, which is opened (by a manually operated cog mechanism) to allow boats into the marina once every hour. The nearby **Castle Museum** (Pilies muziejus; Tues–Sat 10am–6pm; €1.80) tells the history of the city through a varied collection of exhibits – from medieval weapons to Renaissance ceramics.

ARRIVAL AND DEPARTURE

By bus and train Klaipėda's train and bus stations lie on opposite sides of Priestoties gatvė, a 10min walk north of the Old Town.
Destinations (train) Vilnius (4 daily; 3hr 50min–4hr 35min).
Destinations (bus) Kaunas (hourly; 3hr); Nida (direct: 1–2 Fri–Sun; from Smiltynė: 8 daily; 50min); Palanga (every 30min; 30min); Rīga (4 daily; 4–5hr); Vilnius (hourly; 4hr).
By ferry The old ferry terminal at Pilies 4 – which you'll

want instead of the new ferry terminal at Nemuno 8 if you don't have a car – has regular departures to Smiltynė, the gateway to the Curonian Spit.
Destinations Smiltynė (June–Aug every 30min; 5am–2am; Sept–May at least 1 hourly, 7am–9pm; 15min).

INFORMATION

Tourist Information The tourist office in the Old Town at Turgaus 7 (Mon–Fri 9am–7pm, Sat & Sun 10am–4pm; ☎ 46 412 186, ⓦ klaipedainfo.lt) stocks the excellent *Klaipėda in Your Pocket* (€1).

ACCOMMODATION

Klaipėda Hostel Butkų Juzės 7–4 ☎ 6559 4407, ⓦ klaipedahostel.com. Handy if you arrive late, this basic but friendly HI-affiliated hostel is located right next to the bus station. Dorms €11
Litinterp Guest House Puodžių 17 ☎ 46 410 644, ⓦ litinterp.lt. A 15min walk west along S. Daukanto gatvė from the bus and train stations, this is a better bet than *Klaipėda Hostel*, with clean, attractive rooms and a facility for booking private rooms in Klaipėda or Nida (see p.714). Reception open: Mon–Fri 8.30am–7pm, Sat 10am–3pm. Doubles €40

EATING AND DRINKING

Ararat Liepų 48a. An outstanding Armenian establishment serving tender, delicately spiced grilled meats (from €7), excellent red wine, and Armenian "Ararat" cognac. Mon–Sat noon–midnight, Sun 1–11pm.
Herkus Kantas Kepėjų 17. Welcoming Old Town cellar pub with a magnificent array of Lithuanian and international beers. The food menu features everything from Irish stew to quiche, with plenty of bar snacks in between. Tues–Sat 5pm–1am.

PALANGA

Around 25km north of Klaipėda, **PALANGA** is Lithuania's top seaside resort – and party central in the summer.

WHAT TO SEE AND DO

Palanga's biggest attraction is its white, 18km-long sandy **beach**; throughout the summer months it hosts a number of outdoor all-night music events. The wooden **pier**, jutting into the sea at the end of Basanavičiaus gatvė, is where families and couples gather to watch the sunset (around 10pm in July).

From the beach, head east along pedestrian **Basanavičiaus** with the rest of the human tide, past the street musicians and vendors, countless restaurants, arcade games, amusement park rides and amber stalls. You can dance until morning at one of the clubs on Vytauto gatvė, the main street, or on S. Darius ir S. Girėno gatvė, which leads off Vytauto gatvė to the beach.

The lush Botanical Garden (Botanikos Sodas) houses a fascinating **Amber Museum** (June–Aug Tues–Sat 10am– 8pm, Sun 10am–7pm; Sept–May Tues–Sat 11am–5pm, Sun 11am–4pm; €2.30; ⓦpgm.lt) displaying around 25,000 pieces of "Baltic Gold", many with insects and plants trapped inside.

ARRIVAL AND INFORMATION

By bus The bus station on Kretingos gatvė is a couple of blocks away from Basanavičiaus gatvė, the main tourist street.

Destinations Kaunas (7 daily; 3hr 30min); Klaipėda (every 30min; 30min); Rīga via Liepāja (1 daily at 11.15am; 4hr 30min); Vilnius (10 daily; 5hr).

Tourist information Vytauto 94 (June–Aug Mon–Fri 9am–7pm, Sat & Sun 10am–4pm; Sept–May Mon–Fri 9am–5pm, Sat 10am–2pm; ☎460 48811, ⓦpalangatic .lt). Helpful, multilingual staff can book private rooms, organize excursions and provide information on events in and around town.

ACCOMMODATION

Due to the town's immense summertime popularity, advance bookings are advised. Otherwise the cheapest option is to haggle with the locals holding up "Nuomojami kambariai" (rooms for rent) signs as the bus enters Palanga, although the quality may vary considerably. Outside high season prices can fall to around half of those quoted below.

Ema Jurates gatvė 32 ☎460 48608, ⓦema.lt. This brightly painted guesthouse has seven cute rooms with TV, most featuring cosy attic ceilings, plus a colourfully decorated café on site. Doubles **€44**

Vandenis Birutės 47 ☎460 53530, ⓦvandenis.lt. A comfortable hotel away from the bustle, home to a good café-restaurant with outdoor seating and a live music club. All rooms are en suite and have cable TV. Breakfast included. Doubles **€70**

Vila Ramybė Vytauto 54 ☎460 54124, ⓦvilaramybe.lt. A great boutique hotel with colourful themed rooms, all en suite and some with kitchen or balcony. The restaurant-bar downstairs is one of the best in town. Breakfast included. Doubles **€70**

EATING, DRINKING AND NIGHTLIFE

1925 Basanavičiaus 4. Bar-restaurant resembling a log cabin, with a rustic wooden interior and an open fire in winter. Also has a pleasant patio garden. Mains around €8. Daily 10am–midnight.

Čagino Basanavičiaus 14. With its glass-box architecture and patio seating, this bright Russian restaurant is good for people-watching and ample portions of hearty meat dishes (€9), soups and pancakes. Daily noon–midnight.

Exit Nēries 39. Two-tiered entertainment: lively disco with kitschy decor upstairs, and a packed nightclub downstairs. Upstairs Mon–Thurs & Sun 7pm–3am, Fri & Sat 9pm–6am; downstairs daily 10pm–6am.

Laukinių Vakarų Salūnas Basanavičiaus 16. Packed with a young crowd and offering nightly karaoke and wet T-shirt competitions plus the occasional live band. Cocktails around €5. Mon–Thurs & Sun 9pm–5am, Fri & Sat 9pm–6am.

★Žuvinė Basanavičiaus 37a. Fish restaurant with books on the shelves and a smart interior; the generous portions of well-prepared seafood dishes, such as monkfish in spinach sauce (€26) or mussels in white wine (€12), cannot be faulted. Daily 11am–midnight.

THE CURONIAN SPIT

Shared between Lithuania and Russia's Kaliningrad province, the **CURONIAN SPIT** is a 98km sliver of land characterized by vast sand dunes and pine forests. Much of the Lithuanian stretch is covered by the Curonian Spit National Park (ⓦnerija.lt). Some of the area can be seen as a day-trip from Klaipėda, though it really warrants a

> ### CYCLING THE SPIT
>
> The best way to explore the Curonian Spit is by **cycling** along well-marked biking trails that meander through pine forest and along the sand dunes. **Juodkrantė**, 30km away from Nida, is home to **Witches' Hill** (Raganų kalnas), an entertaining wooden sculpture trail in the woods with wonderfully macabre statues of devils, witches and folk heroes. *Vila Flora*, right on Juodkrantė's waterfront, serves simple but excellent fresh fish (€6–8) and pancakes (€3.70). Heading back towards Nida, stop off at the side of the road to catch a glimpse of the huge **heron and cormorant colony** in the trees. When passing through **Preila**, look for the *rūkyta žuvis* (smoked fish) signs and stop at a smokery for some delicious samples, cheaper here than in Nida. Numerous informal bike rental stalls pop up throughout central Nida in summer (€3/hr, €10/day).

19

stay of several days to soak up the unique atmosphere.

ARRIVAL AND DEPARTURE

By ferry and minibus Ferries depart from the quayside towards the end of Žvejų gatvė in Klaipėda (€0.80 return), sailing to Smiltynė on the northern tip of the spit. From the landing stage, frequent minibuses (€3.40) run south towards more scenic parts of the spit, stopping at the villages of Juodkrantė, Pervalka and Preila, and terminating at Nida, 35km south.

NIDA

NIDA is the most famous village on the spit – a small fishing community boasting several streets of attractive blue- and brown-painted wooden houses. Although there are plenty of visitors in the summertime, it never feels crowded. There are several good **restaurants** on Naglių gatvė and Lotmiškio gatvė, as well as along the waterfront. From the end of Naglių, a shore path runs to a flight of wooden steps leading up to the top of the **Parnidis dune** south of the village. From the summit you can gaze out across a Saharan sandscape stretching to Russia's Kaliningrad province. Retrace the trail along the waterfront to see elaborate **weather vanes** with unique designs – each village has its own. Stop by the **Neringa History Museum**, Pamario 53 (June–Aug daily 10am–6pm; Oct–May Tues–Sat 10am–5pm; €1), which traces the village's heritage through photos of crow-eating locals and fishing paraphernalia. Also along Pamario is the church cemetery, with **krikštai** – carved wooden grave monuments – placed upright at the foot of the resting body. Nida's long, luxuriant **beach** is on the opposite side of the spit, a thirty-minute walk through the forest from the village.

ARRIVAL AND INFORMATION

By bus Buses from the mainland and from Smiltynė stop on Naglių, Nida's main street. Everything in Nida is within walking distance.

Destinations Kaunas (via Klaipėda; 1 daily; 4hr 10min); Smiltynė (8 daily; 1hr 30min); Vilnius (via Klaipėda; 1 daily; 5hr 50min).

Tourist information The tourist office at Taikos 4 (June–Aug Mon–Sat 10am–7pm, Sat & Sun 10am–1pm & 2–7pm; Sept–May Mon–Sat 9am–1pm & 2–6pm; ☎ 469 52345, ⓦ visitneringa.com) has info on lodging and events.

ACCOMMODATION

Nida has a few budget guesthouses, but as they tend to fill up in the summer, advance reservations are recommended. Private rooms (€35–50) and local B&Bs (€50–70) can be booked via the tourist office.

Inkaro Kaimas Naglių 26 ☎ 469 52123, ⓦ inkarokaimas .lt. A beautifully decorated double, quad and a two-room apartment are on offer at this welcoming seaside guesthouse. All are en suite and have satellite TV and kitchenette. Doubles **€64**, apartment **€87**

Misko Namas Pamario 11 ☎ 469 52290, ⓦ miskonamas .com. Colourful house with a range of en-suite rooms and apartments, a communal kitchen and a lovely private garden. Breakfast €7.50; bike rental €8/day. Doubles **€65**, 4-person apartment **€90**

EATING AND DRINKING

Baras Bangomūša Naglių 5. Homely, informal place, and one of the best spots in Nida to try the local smoked fish. Koldūnai (ravioli-like meat parcels; €3.80) and other Lithuanian dishes also available. Daily 9am–midnight.

In Vino Taikos 32. Enjoy the best views in Nida from the terrace of this popular wine bar on the roof of the Urbo Kalnas hotel, uphill from the village centre. Extensive drinks menu, and good tapas. Daily 10am–midnight.

Kuršis Naglių 29. Popular and breezy café-restaurant with good views of the coast, serving a range of Lithuanian dishes, including smoked fish, roast pike-perch (€8.30) and excellent šaltibarščiai (cold beetroot soup; €2). Daily 9am–midnight.

SVETI JOVAN KANEO, OHRID

Macedonia

HIGHLIGHTS

❶ **Skopje** The capital boasts great food, quirky bars and some downright weird architecture. **See p.720**

❷ **Šutka** Europe's largest Roma community makes for a fascinating day-trip. **See p.722**

❸ **Sveti Jovan Bigorski** Remote monastery seemingly plucked straight from a fairytale. **See p.724**

❹ **Bitola** Go off the tourist radar in this charming southern town. **See p.724**

❺ **Ohrid** Sitting next to a mountain-fringed lake of the same name, this is Macedonia's prettiest and most likeable town. **See p.725**

HIGHLIGHTS ARE MARKED ON THE MAP ON P.717

ROUGH COSTS

Daily budget Basic €25, occasional treat €35

Drink Wine from €2.50 per bottle

Food *Tavče gravče* (bean casserole) €1.50

Hostel/budget hotel €10/€25

Travel Bus: Skopje–Ohrid €7; train: Skopje–Bitola €4

FACT FILE

Population 2.1 million

Language Macedonian

Currency Denar (MKD)

Capital Skopje

International phone code ☎389

Time zone GMT +1hr

Introduction

Macedonia is, quite simply, one of Europe's most relaxing travel destinations. Outside the capital it's almost all countryside, with vineyards, mountains, forests and rolling fields lending their hues to a pleasantly green patchwork. Look a little closer at the few urban areas, though, and you'll likely come to understand why the French refer to a mixed salad as a *macédoine*: this hotchpotch of Ottoman rule, Yugoslav domination, Orthodox faith and Albanian influence represents one of Europe's most varied societies.

The capital, **Skopje**, is something of a Yugoslav symphony in grey, though one whose brutal architecture is softened by an appealing Ottoman centre, as well as by friendly locals. Most travellers prefer to base themselves around **Lake Ohrid**, a delightful, mountain-fringed expanse straddling the Albanian border. Between Skopje and Ohrid, a glut of immaculately painted **monasteries** competes for your attention; **Sveti Jovan Bigorski** is the most enjoyable, and lies within **Mavrovo**, a national park that provides great hiking opportunities, as well as skiing in the winter.

CHRONOLOGY

168 BC The Macedonian area is absorbed by the Roman Empire.

395 AD The Roman Empire splits. Macedonia falls under Byzantine rule.

447 Attila the Hun rampages through the area.

1394 Five hundred years of Ottoman rule begin.

1878 Russian victory over the Ottoman Empire; Macedonia is ceded to Bulgaria, though soon returned at the instigation of Western powers.

1910 Gonxha Agnesë Bojaxhiu, an ethnic Albanian, known to the world as Mother Teresa, is born in Skopje.

1912 The Turks are ousted in the Balkan Wars; Macedonia is shared between Serbia and Greece.

1918 The Serb-ruled area that comprises today's Macedonia is given to the Kingdom of Serbs, Croats and Slovenes.

1945 Macedonia becomes part of socialist Yugoslavia.

1963 Over one thousand people killed by an earthquake in Skopje.

1991 Macedonia gains independence from Yugoslavia.

1993 Admitted to the UN as "Former Yugoslav Republic of Macedonia".

2001 Civil war between government and ethnic Albanian insurgents.

2005 Macedonia becomes an official candidate for EU membership.

2008 Greece blocks Macedonia's entry to NATO over name dispute (see box below).

2014 Completion of the "Skopje 2014" project, a gigantic facelift of Macedonia's capital city.

ARRIVAL AND DEPARTURE

Skopje's "Alexander the Great" **airport** (ⓦairports.com.mk) hosts a few Balkan flag carriers and European budget airlines; the one with most connections is Wizz Air (ⓦwizzair.com), whose destinations include London, Brussels and Stockholm. Ohrid also has an international airport but flights are few and far between; Thessaloniki and Sofia are also within striking distance. Most,

---

"THEN WHAT ARE WE? FYROMANIANS?"

As soon as Macedonia declared independence from Yugoslavia, a different kind of battle broke out along the Greek border, one regarding two matters integral to a new country: **name** and **flag**. Athens objected to the use of the name – the bulk of historical Macedonia now lies under Greek control – and also to a flag featuring the ancient kingdom's sixteen-pointed Vergina Sun. The new nation squeezed into the UN as the "Former Yugoslav Republic of Macedonia", or FYROM for short, and later changed its flag to end a Greek economic blockade. Many nations now recognize the "Republic of Macedonia", but this battle of nomenclature remains locked in stalemate, and is unlikely to end anytime soon.

20

MACEDONIA

SERBIA

KOSOVO

Kumanovo

BULGARIA

Tetovo

SKOPJE

Lake Matka

Gostivar

Veles

MAVROVO
NATIONAL
PARK   *Mavrovo*

Debar   Kicero

Negotino

Prilep

Vevčani
Struga
Lake   Ohrid   GALIČICA
Ohrid   NATIONAL PARK
Resen   Bitola

Gradište   Malovište

Brajčino

ALBANIA   GREECE

Belgrade

0 — 25
kilometres

HIGHLIGHTS

1 Skopje
2 Šutka
3 Sveti Jovan Bigorski
4 Bitola
5 Ohrid

Metres

2000

1000

500

200

0

N

Thessaloniki

20

however, make their way to Macedonia overland. There are a couple of daily **bus** services from Tirana in Albania (via Struga), but poor neighbourly relations mean that there are very few direct services from Greece. In summer you may be able to catch a minibus from Thessaloniki to Skopje; this was once easier by train but the Greek government, in its wisdom, cut off all international services in 2011. Mercifully, the daily service from Belgrade to Skopje is still running. Citizens of some countries (notably South Africa and India) still need **visas** to enter Macedonia; check ⓦmfa.gov.mk for more information.

GETTING AROUND

Almost all travel in Macedonia is by **bus**. Services are punctual and reasonably frequent, and the vehicles themselves could be worse. Note that buses take one of two routes between Skopje and Ohrid: one through Bitola, and a shorter, more picturesque trip through Kičevo. The

limited **train** network suffers from slow and irregular services and is rarely used by visitors. The best domestic line is the thrice-daily service between Skopje and Bitola, which passes through wonderful mountain scenery.

ACCOMMODATION

Accommodation is not terribly varied but it's generally quite affordable. Skopje's overpriced **hotels** are now supplemented by a number of cut-price alternatives (from around €25), while in the hinterlands – including Ohrid – you'll be able to make use of **private rooms**, known as *sobi*; you'll often be met at bus stations by homeowners with rooms to spare. Prices vary wildly depending upon location and facilities, but generally expect to pay from €10 to €30 for a double room. There are a few **hostels** in Skopje and Ohrid, each costing around €10 for a dorm bed, while **campsites** can be found around the lakes of Ohrid and Prespa; the cost of camping is usually less than €10 per tent.

FOOD AND DRINK

The Macedonian diet is dominated by barbecued **meat** (*skara*), of which the most popular variety are sausage-shaped kebabs (*kebapčinja*), usually served with chopped onion and spongy, freshly baked bread. Other items to look out for on a regular menu are soups (*čorba*) and *tavče gravče*, a bean casserole served on a hot clay plate. The ubiquitous *burek* – pastry filled with meat, cheese or spinach – is a good, cheap **breakfast**. **Vegetarians** can find solace in excellent salads and *ajvar* – a meze-like starter made from red peppers – while pizzerias are everywhere and always offer veggie choices. You'll find baklava – syrupy Turkish **sweets** – all over the country.

DRINK

The consumption of **coffee** (*kafe*) seems almost obligatory, and it's traditionally served Turkish-style (black, with grounds at the bottom), though espresso is gaining currency. More local in nature is **boza**, a refreshing millet-based drink available in cake shops come summer. There are some good domestic **beers** (*pivo*), with Skopsko the most popular brand, but Macedonia is more famed for uniformly good **wines**. Vranec (red) and Smederevka (white) are two local grape varieties worth trying; you may be lucky enough to find shops selling fresh, home-made concoctions for just €1.50 per litre, but otherwise Tikveš is a reliable, widely sold bottled brand. After 7pm, alcohol can only be bought in bars and licensed restaurants.

CULTURE AND ETIQUETTE

Macedonia is a real mishmash of cultures, and it's very important to take note of a few **political and ethnic issues** – taking Greece's side in the country's naming or flag disputes (see box, p.716) won't win you any friends, nor will promoting Albanian or Macedonian nationalism to the "wrong" side. Only two-thirds of the population are Macedonians of Slav ethnicity – the vast majority of whom belong to the **Orthodox Church** – while most of the remaining third are ethnic Albanian. Tensions still run high between the two groups – 2001 saw a civil war between the government and Albanian insurgents – though travellers are unlikely to be affected.

Smoking regulations have been tightened of late, while **tipping** at restaurants is generally a simple exercise in rounding up.

SPORTS AND ACTIVITIES

Activities in Macedonia centre on the mountains. The national parks of Mavrovo, Galičica and Pelister are excellent for **hiking** – Mavrovo and Pelister also offer good **skiing** opportunities – while the crystal waters of Lake Ohrid make it the country's most appealing place for **diving** and **swimming**. The country's empty roads are ideal for **cycling**, but since there are precious few places to rent bikes it makes sense to bring your own.

COMMUNICATIONS

Most **post offices** (*pošta*) are open Monday to Friday 7am to 5pm, and sometimes on Saturday mornings. These are the best places to make **phone calls** or purchase phonecards. International roaming charges have fallen in recent years, but apps such as Skype or Viber are the best deal for calling abroad. **Wi-fi** is widely available in hotels, hostels, bars, restaurants and cafés.

EMERGENCIES

The crime rate is pretty low by European standards, even in Skopje. However, it's prudent always to carry your passport, or

20

MACEDONIA ONLINE

Ⓦ **exploringmacedonia.com** National tourism portal.
Ⓦ **macedoniaexperience.com** Information about cultural events, tours and active holidays.
Ⓦ **balkaninsight.com** News from Macedonia and its neighbours.

EMERGENCY NUMBERS

For police, ambulance or the fire department call ☎ 112.

MACEDONIAN

Macedonia uses the **Cyrillic alphabet**, which poses problems with street signs, train and bus timetables. For most of these there's no transliteration into Latin script, but many restaurants have dual-language menus, and a decent level of English is spoken across the country.

	MACEDONIAN	PRONUNCIATION
Yes	Да	Da
No	не	Ne
Please	молам	Molam
Thank you	благодарам	Blago-daram
Hello/Good day	здраво	Zdravoh
Goodbye	до гледање	Dog-led-anyeah
Excuse me	извинете	Eezvee-neteh
Where?	каде?	Ka-deh?
Good	добар	Dobar
Bad	лош	Losh
Near	блиску	Bleeskoo
Far	далеку	Dalekoo
Cheap	евтин	Evteen
Expensive	скап	Skap
Open	отворен	Otvoren
Closed	затворен	Zatvoren
Today	денес	Denes
Yesterday	вчера	Vchera
Tomorrow	утре	Ootre
How much is…?	колку чини тоа…?	Kolkoo chinee toe-ah…?
What time is it?	колку е часот?	Kolkoo eh chasot?
I don't understand	не разбирам	Ne razbee-ram
Do you speak English?	зборувате ли англиски?	Zbo-roo-vateh lee Angliskee?
One	еден	Eh-den
Two	два	Dva
Three	три	Tree
Four	четири	Cheh-tee-ree
Five	пет	Pet
Six	шест	Shest
Seven	седум	Sedum
Eight	осум	Ossum
Nine	девет	Devet
Ten	десет	Deset

20

a photocopy of the picture page. You'll find **pharmacies** (*apteka*) in all major towns and cities, and a surprising number have English-speaking staff; opening hours vary but some are 24hr. If you need a **hospital**, outside Skopje taxis may be faster than ambulances.

INFORMATION

There are now a number of **tourist information offices** dotted around the country. They're slowly starting to learn what travellers require, though many keep irregular hours.

MONEY AND BANKS

The currency is the **denar** (usually abbreviated to MKD), comprising coins of 1, 2, 5, 10 and 50MKD, and notes of 10, 50, 100, 500, 1000 and 5000MKD. Exchange **rates** are currently around €1 = 61MKD, £1 = 78MKD and US$1 = 54MKD. Accommodation prices are usually quoted in euros, though you can also pay in denar. Money can be **exchanged** at an exchange office or bank; the latter are usually open Monday to Friday 8am to 5pm. **ATMs** are easy to find in urban areas, though stock up on cash if you're heading into the sticks.

OPENING HOURS AND HOLIDAYS

Most **shops** stay open until 8pm on weekdays, and mid-afternoon on Saturdays. Sundays are still special in Macedonia – don't expect too much to be open, even in central Skopje. Things also grind to a halt on **public holidays**: January 1, 2 and 7, Orthodox Easter (March or April), May 1 and 24, August 2, September 8 and October 11.

20

Skopje

Other than the mazy lanes of the delightful, Ottoman-era **Čaršija** district, **SKOPJE** (Скопje) is best described as "appealingly ugly"; the city was ravaged by an earthquake in 1963, and its stately buildings were replaced by brutal Yugoslav-era designs. These have, in turn, been superseded by the works of **Skopje 2014**, a government-sponsored renovation scheme. Almost universally unpopular with locals, its focal point is a chain of monumental **Neoclassical buildings** along the riverfront, joined by literally hundreds of new **statues**. For the traveller, all of this change is rather absorbing, and worth keeping tabs on while you're sampling the city's excellent food and nightlife.

WHAT TO SEE AND DO

The **Čaršija** district north of the river contains the bulk of Skopje's sights, and is the obvious place from which to kick off a trip around the city. Despite the recent completion of two pedestrian bridges (each sporting thirty statues), the area remains in a state of flux as new statues continue to be installed on a regular basis.

Čaršija and the Kale

Turkish times linger on in the shape of several mosques, of which **Mustapha Pasha** is the largest and most intricately decorated. Two splendid former bathhouses, the copper-domed **Daud Pasha** on ulitsa Kruševska and the nearby **Čifte Amam**, are long out of use as hammams and both now serve as homes of the **National Gallery** (Tues–Sun 10am–6pm; 100MKD; ⓦnationalgallery.mk). Those seeking history instead can head to the **National Museum of Macedonia** (Tues–Sat 9am–5pm, Sun 9am–1pm; 100MKD), which is well worth an hour or two. All are outdone, however, by wonderful little **Sveti Spas** (ul. Makarija Frchkovski; daily 9am–4pm; 120MKD), a secluded fourteenth-century monastery. Its church was built mostly underground – under Ottoman rule churches were not allowed to be higher than mosques – and its carved-walnut iconostasis is jaw-dropping. Northwest of Čaršija, and up from the eastern ramparts of the old castle (now closed to visitors), is the excellent **National Museum of Contemporary Art** (Tues–Sat 10am–5pm, Sun 9am–1pm; free; ⓦmsuskopje.org.mk), from where you can see the whole of Skopje. The collection, which comprises mainly local art, is not bad, either.

South of the Vardar

Cross the **Stone Bridge** (Kamen Most) and you'll find yourself in Skopje's main square, **Ploštad Makedonija**. You won't be able to miss the gigantic equestrian statue of the original Ali G, Alexander the Great (although, owing to political sensitivities with Greece, its official name is *Warrior on Horse*) – it's by far the largest of the truly bewildering number of statues in the area. Just west of the bridge's southern end are two of the most distinctively Yugoslav buildings in the city. The **Mepso building** is a fusion of Le Corbusier-style design and Communist-era factory, now used as office space; behind it is the **Central Post Office**, a bizarre concrete spaceship whose lavish interior will once more count as a Skopje must-see if repairs following a catastrophic fire in 2013 are ever completed.

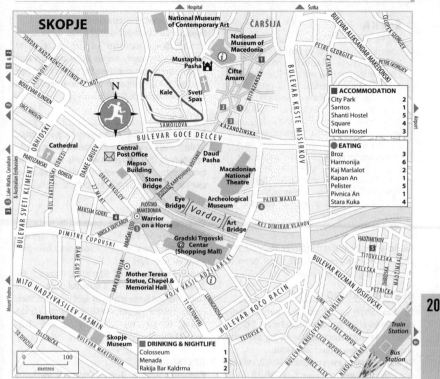

SKOPJE

▲ Hospital   ▲ Šutka

National Museum
of Contemporary Art   ČARŠIJA

National
Museum of
Macedonia

Mustapha
Pasha

Čifte
Amam

Kale   Sveti
Spas

SAMOILOVA

KAZANDŽINSKA

BULEVAR GOCE DELČEV

Cathedral

Central
Post Office

Daud
Pasha

Mepso
Building

Macedonian
National
Theatre

Stone
Bridge

Eye
Bridge

Archeological
Museum

PAJKO MAALO

Vardar

Warrior
on a Horse

Art
Bridge

KEJ DIMIRAR VLAHOV

Gradski Trgovski
@ Centar
(Shopping Mall)

Mother Teresa
Statue, Chapel &
Memorial Hall

Ramstore

Skopje
Museum

■ ACCOMMODATION	
City Park	2
Santos	1
Shanti Hostel	5
Square	4
Urban Hostel	3

● EATING	
Broz	3
Harmonija	6
Kaj Maršalot	2
Kapan An	1
Pelister	5
Pivnica An	1
Stara Kuka	4

■ DRINKING & NIGHTLIFE	
Colosseum	1
Menada	3
Rakija Bar Kaldrma	2

0   100
metres

Train
Station

Bus
Station

20

Marking the start of largely pedestrianized **Makedonija**, a crescent of elegant
buildings (survivors of the quake) provides
some much-needed respite from all the
new construction. **Mother Teresa** was born
further up the road, and a memorial hall,
chapel and statue have been placed here in
her honour. At the very end of the road,
you'll see the imposing **Skopje Museum**
(Mon–Sat 9.30am–5pm, Sun 9.30am–
1pm; 100MKD); fronted by a large clock
that stopped during the earthquake, it's
worth a quick look.

Mount Vodno

Look south from any vantage point in
Skopje and you'll see Mount Vodno,
within walking distance of the city and
topped with a huge cross. The mountain
is great for hiking – the 1066m peak is
only a couple of hours' walk from central
Skopje. A cable car from the base of the
mountain whisks visitors to the top in
just seven minutes (Tues–Sun: April–Sept

10am–8pm; Oct–March 10am–5pm;
100MKD return). To reach the cable car
costs 250MKD by taxi or 35MKD on
hourly buses from the bus station.

ARRIVAL AND INFORMATION

By plane Skopje's Alexander the Great airport is 21km
east of the city. Taxis are expensive at around €20
(1220MKD), though buses are an option: Vardar Ekspres
(⟨w⟩ vardarekspres.com.mk) runs shuttles (7–9 daily;
150MKD) to a schedule loosely connected to flight times.
You can board at several places; the most useful spots are
the bus station, and the central *Holiday Inn*.

By train The train station is located a 20min walk or
150MKD taxi ride southeast of the centre. It's not the kind
of place you'll want to hang around for too long.

Destinations Belgrade (2 daily; 9hr); Bitola (3 daily;
3hr–3hr 50min).

By bus The main bus station sits alongside the train
station, and is marginally more pleasant.

Destinations Belgrade (11 daily; 6hr); Bitola (12 daily; 2hr
40min); Debar (2 daily; 3hr); Istanbul (4 daily; 14hr);
Mavrovi Anovi (7 daily; 1hr 45min); Ohrid (12 daily;
3–4hr); Sofia (4 daily; 5hr); Tirana (1 daily; 7hr).

ŠUTKA

The Skopje district of Šuto Orizari, more commonly referred to as **Šutka**, is home to Europe's largest **Roma** community. The area is impoverished and dilapidated, but a visit can be quite fascinating – colourful buildings, litter-lined streets and a bustling daily market make it feel something like an Indian town transported to the Balkans. It's also one of Macedonia's foremost centres of song and dance (see w culturalcorner stones.org for images and audio samples), but events run to no schedule – sunny summer afternoons are your best bet. Buses #19 and #20 run here from the post office and train station respectively, or it's only 250MKD by taxi.

Tourist office The staff at the office on Vasil Agilarski bb (daily 8.30am–4.30pm; ☎02 322 3644) hand out pamphlets and give practical advice.

GETTING AROUND

By bus Skopje surely has the world's greatest concentration of London buses outside London. Tickets on these Chinese-built replicas and the old Yugoslav models that run in tandem with them cost 35MKD.
By taxi Fares start at a very reasonable 50MKD, and a city-centre trip will rarely cost more than 200MKD. It's the normal way of getting around, even for locals.

ACCOMMODATION

HOSTELS

★**Shanti Hostel** Rade Jovcevski Koragin 11 ☎02 609 0807, w shantihostel.com. A short walk from the bus and train stations, this is still the best hostel in town, despite its slightly cramped common areas. There's also a second hostel around the corner; staff at both are friendly and knowledgeable, and if you fancy a walk into town it's a simple stroll along the river. Dorms €8
Urban Hostel Mother Teresa 22 ☎02 614 2785, w urbanhostel.com.mk. Good, modern hostel a 20min walk west of the town centre, and accessible on a number of bus routes from the station. The common area is large and inviting, with a piano its focal point, while the dorm rooms are clean and spacious. Dorms €9

HOTELS

City Park Mihail Cokov 1 ☎02 329 0860, w hotelcitypark .com.mk. Friendly and modern boutique-style hotel located right next to a park – bring your jogging shoes. You'll almost always be able to knock a little off the rack rate. Doubles €80
Santos Bitpazarska 125 ☎02 322 6963. A great budget option with cute little rooms that's full of local character.

You'll see it signed off Bitpazarska. Doubles €30
Square Nikola Vapcarov 2 ☎02 322 5090, w hotelsquare .com.mk. Stylish mini-hotel set atop an apartment complex; its thoroughly modern rooms are a pleasant surprise after the Communist-era lifts used to access their floor, and you can gaze down at the Alexander statue as you eat breakfast (included). Doubles €40

EATING

The terms "café" and "bar" are somewhat fuzzy; what passes for the former during the day will generally morph into the latter by night. The Čaršija area has become one of the most buzzing parts of town, though it's rivalled by the row of café-bars along the waterfront east of Ploštad Makedonija.

CAFÉS

Broz Crvena Voda 4. A bizarre Communist-themed coffee-chain parody – Starbuckski? – whose walls are lined with subtle revolutionary pictures. Upstairs seats have good mountain views. Open 24hr.
Kapan An Kapan An, off Bitpazarska. Housed in the fifteenth-century Kapan An, a delightful former traders' hostel, this tiny venue is a lovely spot in the old town, serving coffee from just 40MKD and nargile (Turkish hookah) for the same ridiculously low price. Daily noon–11.30pm.

RESTAURANTS

Harmonija Skopjanka Shopping Centre 37. A world away from Macedonia's typically meaty fare, this tranquil spot serves superb macrobiotic and vegan dishes sold by weight (400MKD/kg). Mon–Sat 11am–midnight.
Kaj Maršalot Guro Gakovik 8. Take a trip back to Tito times at this Yugoslav-themed restaurant. The food is little different to what you'll find elsewhere in the city, but where else would you be served by students dressed as Young Pioneers? Daily 8am–10pm.
Pelister Makedonija 1. Hugely popular with both locals and tourists – you may well struggle to get a seat. Order a pizza (from 260MKD), something more interesting like breaded mozzarella with saffron, or go for the healthy salad bar option. Daily 8am–midnight.
Pivnica An Kapan An, off Bitpazarska. Don't let the name (which means beerhouse) deceive you – this is a classy restaurant in the charming ground level of Kapan An. Extensive and inventive local menu, with grills starting at around 200MKD – the sausages are particularly good. Daily 10am–midnight.
Stara Kuka Pajko Maalo 14. Highly regarded traditional restaurant within one of the city's oldest buildings serving hearty meals that are worth splurging on; the casseroles are excellent. Walking distance from the centre, and taxi drivers know the name. Mains 250–650MKD. Daily 10am–midnight.

SKOPJE'S FESTIVALS

Buskerfest ⓦbuskerfestmakedonija
.com. Over a week of eclectic street
performances, usually taking place in
May or June.

Pivo-Lend ⓦpivolend.com.mk. Beer
festival held each September within the
fortress walls.

Skopje Jazz Festival ⓦskopjejazzfest
.com.mk. Acclaimed event featuring
musicians from around the world, spread
over a week each October.

Skopje Film Festival
ⓦskopjefilmfestival.com.mk. Well worth
checking out. Screenings in the Kultura
cinema at Luj Paster 2. April.

Vino-Skop ⓦvinoskop.com. Wine festival
offering the opportunity to taste local
produce, usually held in October.

DRINKING AND NIGHTLIFE

Colosseum Železnička 66. A surprisingly polished house
venue that regularly ropes in DJs from overseas. In summer
they host outdoor events in Gradski Park. Admission
200MKD. Daily 10pm–4am.

Menada Podraje bb. Overlooking the old Daud Pasha
baths, this is a favourite with Skopje's artier set, largely due
to the regular live music sets. Also a great place to head for
coffee or a light lunch in the daytime. Daily 10am–late.

Rakija Bar Kaldrma Podgradje 14. The most
expensive *rakija* at this buzzing bar costs 240MKD a
glass and tastes quite good; the cheapest goes for
50MKD and may well make you heave. Either way, you
won't remember in the morning. Daily 8am–midnight,
Fri & Sat till 2am.

ENTERTAINMENT

Macedonian National Theatre Ilijo Vojvoda bb. A new
venue, built as part of the Skopje 2014 project, that plays
host to ballet and operatic performances. Tickets from
200MKD. Ticket office Mon–Fri 9am–8pm, Sat
noon–8pm.

Milenium Kej 13 Noemvri. Multiplex cinema in the
Trgovski Centar shopping mall; tickets 180MKD.

DIRECTORY

Embassies and consulates Australia, Londonska 11b
☏ 02 306 1834; Canada, Praska bb ☏02 322 5630; UK,
Salvador Aljende 73 ☏02 329 9299; US, Samoilova 21
☏02 310 2000.

Hospital Re-Medika, Makedonska Brigada 18
☏ 02 260 3100.

Money There are ATMs all around the city centre, and in
the bus station, which also has exchange booths.

Pharmacy Apteka Viola. Vostanichka 59 (24hr).

Post office Orce Nikolov (Mon–Sat 7am–5.30pm,
Sun 7am–2.30pm).

LAKE MATKA

A mere half-hour drive from Skopje,
pretty **LAKE MATKA** (Матка езеро)
provides an easy break from the grey
of the capital. The artificial lake is
surrounded by richly forested peaks, and
its edges are dotted with restaurants,
many of which can only be accessed by
boat. You'll be approached by boat
owners, who typically charge €10 for a
short ride around, and a trip to either a
restaurant or some nearby **caves**. Ask at
the Skopje tourist office about the
lake-side guesthouses here. Take bus #60
from the station (8 daily; 60MKD), or
hop in a taxi (600MKD).

Western Macedonia

Travellers heading from Skopje to Ohrid
have two bus routes to choose from. The
first heads south through the major – for
Macedonia – city of **Bitola**, a pleasant
place with some interesting nineteenth-
century architecture. Heading west
instead will bring you close to the
national park of **Mavrovo**, good for
hiking in summer and skiing in winter.
This latter route also takes an hour less.
Ohrid itself is Macedonia's prime
attraction, the name referring both to a
large, mountain-ringed lake, and the
beautiful old town that sits on its
northern shore. Just to the east, and
sitting next to another pristine lake, is
charming **Pelister National Park**.

MAVROVO NATIONAL PARK

Mavrovo National Park (Националниот
Парк Маврово; ⓦnpmavrovo.org.mk)
spreads its wings over one of Macedonia's
most beautiful corners, a rich and rugged
land where rushing streams tumble down
slopes cloaked with pine and birch. There

20

is a wealth of sights and activities to choose from – the wonderful monastery of **Sveti Jovan Bigorski** is a particular delight to visit. **Camping** and **hiking** are possible most of the year, while winter snows make for some of the most affordable **skiing** and **snowboarding** in Europe.

Mavrovo

Most travellers base themselves in the little town of **Mavrovo** (Маврово). Popular with locals, this resort sits next to a lake of the same name, but is sadly not accessible on public transport; to get here, head by bus to **Mavrovi Anovi**, 8km away on the other side of the lake, from where it'll be a 250MKD taxi ride. *Hotel Bistra* (☎042 489 027, ⊛bistra.com; doubles €100) is right next to the ski slopes; although rooms here are beyond the budget of most backpackers, staff can help to organize (cheaper) private accommodation.

Sveti Jovan Bigorski

Macedonia has no shortage of wonderful monasteries, but **Sveti Jovan Bigorski** (Свети Јован Бигорски; daily 8am–8pm; free) takes the biscuit. Tucked away in delightfully bucolic countryside near the Albanian border, its whitewashed buildings are edged with dark wood, and should the fireflies come out to play in the evening it will feel like you've stepped into a Hayao Miyazaki anime. Most of the older buildings were destroyed in a fire in 2009, though reconstruction was swift. Travellers can stay for a nominal fee; this is best arranged through the hostels or tourist offices of Skopje or Ohrid. To get here, jump on any bus heading between Debar and Gostivar (both accessible from Skopje and Ohrid), and ask to be let off at the monastery.

SKIING IN MAVROVO

Mavrovo (⊛skimavrovo.com) is the best place to head for wintertime fun. The season lasts from mid-Nov to mid-April, day-passes cost just 1100MKD (half-day 850MKD), and skis can be rented for a similar price.

BITOLA

Pretty little **BITOLA** (Битола) is one of Macedonia's few attractive urban centres; you'll doubtless wonder if it can really be the second-largest city in the country. Its laidback air also disguises some historical pedigree – in the Ottoman era, such was the importance of this trading hub that a string of consulates set up on the main thoroughfare. Amazingly, some remain: the Turkish one still functions because of Bitola's sizeable Turkish minority, while both the UK and France retain a small diplomatic presence here. All are housed in splendid nineteenth-century buildings, more of which line the city's pedestrianized main road, Maršal Tito.

ARRIVAL AND DEPARTURE

Bitola's train and bus stations sit side by side in contrasting states of disrepair, a 15min walk south of the centre.

Train destinations Skopje (5 daily; 3hr 30min).

Bus destinations Ohrid (hourly; 1hr 30min); Skopje (hourly; 2hr 40min).

ACCOMMODATION

There's no real reason to stay overnight, but it makes a convenient break on the Skopje–Ohrid route.

Domestika Hostel Ivo Lola Ribar bb ☎070 496 585. Cheap and cheerful hostel with dated interior but adequate facilities and a great €2 breakfast. Shared kitchen, double, triple and quadruple rooms. Dorms **€5**

PELISTER NATIONAL PARK

A pristine national park between Bitola and Ohrid, **Pelister** (Националниот парк пелистер) overlooks **Lake Prespa**, a shimmering expanse that, while nowhere near as deep as Ohrid, boasts surrounding mountain scenery every bit as beautiful. On the northern side of the park sits the small **Pelister ski resort**. From here a spine trail zigzags south to Malo Ezero, a picturesque lake at the park's centre. The lake can also be approached from the wonderfully unspoilt village of **Brajčino** (Брајчино), a great hiking base to the southwest. With its hand-stacked stone walls it shows almost no signs of the modern day. **Malovište** (Маловиште) is another gorgeous old village whose population has nose-dived to almost nothing. Now being thrown funds to polish up and lure people back, it's well worth a visit to walk the cobbled streets, breathe some fresh air and admire this relic of a bygone age.

ARRIVAL AND DEPARTURE

Pelister ski resort is accessible from Bitola: take a bus to Turnovo and then a taxi the rest of the way (€20 all in). Buses to Brajčino leave on the half-hour from Resen, a town on the main Ohrid–Bitola stretch. Malovište is off the Resen–Bitola road; ask to be dropped off the bus in Kažani, from where it's a 4km walk, hitch or taxi ride south.

ACCOMMODATION

It's quite easy to score a *sobi* (private room) in Brajčino; in summer you'll likely be met coming off the bus.
Vila Raskrsnica ☎ 075 501 830. The only official accommodation in the village is at this delightfully rustic hotel and restaurant where most rooms have stunning mountain views. Doubles **€40**

LAKE OHRID

Vast almost to the point of appearing sea-like, **Lake Ohrid** (Охридско Езеро) is Macedonia's major draw. A backdrop of **mountains** encircles it like a torn sky, looping through Albanian territory on the way back around. This is the only place in the country that can be described as touristy, but even in peak season the combination of Ohrid town's genteel streets and quietly lapping waves produces a relaxed air.

Not only is this one of the **deepest lakes** in Europe – over 300m in places – but it's also one of the oldest. Appropriately, it has played host to lakeside communities since the **Neolithic period**, but it was not until Roman times that **OHRID** (Охрид), on the lake's northeastern fringe, developed as a town. Large basilicas were constructed from the fifth century, and Slavic tribes started moving in shortly after that. Ohrid's importance as a religious centre was maintained under Ottoman rule, the town becoming a tourist destination during the Yugoslav period.

WHAT TO SEE AND DO

Many sights are located among the steep lanes of the walled **Old Town**. There are a couple of monasteries in the area, but most visitors are here for the timeless

majesty of **Lake Ohrid** itself – locals swear that the water remains clean enough to drink, and with visibility of up to 20m they may well be right. Motorized "water-taxis" are available for tours of varying lengths (from €10).

The Old Town

The best place to start a tour around the Old Town is the **Upper Gate**. In the area immediately to the south you'll find a fascinating **icon gallery** (Tues–Sun 10am–2pm & 6–9pm; free), home to some of the best examples found in the Ohrid area. Staff here should also be able to open up the adjacent **Sveta Bogorodica**, a thirteenth-century church with wonderful interior frescoes.

West of the gate you've a choice of uphill paths; one heads to the **Fortress of Tsar Samoil** (daily 9am–7pm; 30MKD), which has a disappointingly messy interior but some superlative views of the town and lake. The other path leads past an old **Roman amphitheatre** to **Sveti Kliment** (daily 8am–8pm; free), a large, modern church inside which you'll see the remains of twelfth-century graves; Saint Clement himself is interred in the far corner. The church is built next to the ruins of another that dates from the fifth century; its foundations (including tremendous mosaics) are on display under a rather ugly shelter.

From Sveti Kliment it's a hop and a skip down the slopes to **Sveti Jovan Kaneo** (daily 8am–6pm; 100MKD), whose lakeside setting makes it Ohrid's most appealing church. The walk east back into town is rather lovely, and passes the tranquil residential enclave of **Kaneo**. Back in the centre you'll find the **National Museum** (Tues–Sun 10am–2pm & 6–9pm; 100MKD), full of historical relics and an interesting place to while away an hour or two.

The monasteries

Some 30km south along the eastern shore of the lake is the wonderful monastery of **Sveti Naum**, which lies within walking distance of the Albanian border. Magical grounds surround the seventeenth-century building, whose interior (daily

20

7am–7pm; 100MKD) is filled with vivid frescoes. In the summer you can get here by boat from Ohrid town, and buses (600MKD return) run every couple of hours during the day; it'll cost the same in a shared taxi. The road heads between the lake and **Galičica National Park** (⊚galicica.org.mk), which is a great place for a hike. On the way to Sveti Naum from Ohrid town you'll pass the village of Gradište, which boasts remains of a Bronze Age village hauled from the bottom of the lake. You can also dive into the surrounding crystal waters from €40 per person (⊚amfora.com.mk).

Heading north then west instead from Ohrid will eventually bring you to the wonderful lakeside monastery of **Kalište**, where monks once lived in caves dug into the cliffs – these, and other mural-lined halls, are open to visitors (100MKD), though you'll probably have to ask around for the key.

ARRIVAL AND INFORMATION

By bus The station is inconveniently located 2km north of the Old Town; it'll cost 100MKD by cab, although it's certainly walkable if your bag isn't too big. To get to Debar, it's usually best to catch a bus from nearby Struga (5 daily; 1hr 30min); to get to Struga, you're usually best off grabbing a shared taxi (15min) for 100MKD per person from the main road just north of the tourist area.

Destinations Bitola (3 daily; 1hr 30min); Resen (6 daily; 50min); Skopje (9 daily; 3–4hr).

Tourist information The General Turist 2000 agency at Partizanska 6 (daily 9am–8pm; ☎046 260 423) is the best option for tours and local information.

ACCOMMODATION

There are some great places to stay in Ohrid, but *sobi* (private rooms) are also an option, especially when the hotels are booked up in summer months. You're likely to be met at the bus station by those with rooms to spare. Camping is possible at three sites along the lake between Ohrid and Sveti Naum (around 400MKD/tent).

Di Angollo Just off the main square ☎046 260 003, ⊚apartmanidiangolo.com.mk. So what if the reception is inside a pizza restaurant? The dorms at this simple, central hostel are clean and colourful, and there's a decent little communal area. Dorms **€10**

★**Sunny Lake** Klimentov Univerzitet 38 ☎075 629 571, ⊚sunnylakehostel.mk. Superb hostel that strikes the right balance between relaxation and partying. The common areas are great places to meet people, especially in the summer over barbecued meat and a few glasses of *rakija*. Dorms **€10**

Vila Lucija Kosta Abraš 29 ☎046 265 608. So close to the lake that you may wake to see your ceiling shimmering with reflected sunlight. The spick-and-span rooms are excellent value, and come with almost painfully powerful showers. Doubles **€35**

Vila Sofija Kosta Abraš 64 ☎046 254 370, ⊚vilasofija .com.mk. Well-equipped boutique rooms set in a beautiful, traditionally styled building – great value, especially for the €30 single rooms. Doubles **€65**

EATING AND DRINKING

Ohrid's culinary scene is terribly uninspired for a place with such tourist appeal. In summer, a curl of "beach" bars opens up along the lakeside east of the Old Town. More interesting, for some, will be the Skovin Winery (Dimche Malenko 12, just off the main pedestrian square), where a litre of freshly made wine – fired into plastic bottles from petrol-station-like pumps – costs just 70MKD. You can buy regular bottles too, but it's not half as much fun.

Liquid Kosta Abraš 52. This bar is busy most nights with a young and fun-loving clientele, so it's a good place to make new friends, get drunk with existing ones, or combine the two. Daily 6pm–late.

★**Plaza Potpeš** Kaneo. This marvellous Kaneo restaurant is so close to the lake you can bathe your feet in the water as you eat. Prices are generally reasonable, while some items on the menu are just plain cheap, such as the 100MKD hamburger (it puts many a fast-food version to shame). Come for drinks in the evening – the boardwalk stroll alone is quite magical. Daily 11am–11pm.

Sveta Sofija Tsar Samoil 88. Popular spot with a delightful patio overlooking the church. Mains start at around 200MKD and include Ohrid trout, fried squid and traditional local dishes baked in clay pots. Daily 8am–midnight.

THE REPUBLIC OF VEVČANI

Fancy a quirky half-day trip? Head to **Vevčani**, a village that declared tongue-in-cheek independence after the fall of Communism. The only real evidence of this is its weird banknotes, and even these are rarely available; ask at Domkinska Kuka, a terrific restaurant. Instead, it's best to come for the pleasant **springs** area, signed uphill from town – the water here may be the best in the Balkans, and the energetic can make use of a 5.2km-long mountain trail. To get here you'll need to take a bus from the town of Struga, located on Lake Ohrid.

WHITEWATER RAFTING ON THE TARA RIVER, DURMITOR

Montenegro

HIGHLIGHTS

❶ **Kotor** Head up to St Ivan's Castle for jaw-droppingly beautiful views over Montenegro's prettiest town. **See p.732**

❷ **Budva** The former Yugoslav beach-party place of choice has got its mojo back. **See p.734**

❸ **Cetinje** The one-time Montenegrin capital is a sleepy town dotted with stately old embassy buildings. **See p.738**

❹ **Podgorica** A unique opportunity to go off the tourist radar in a European capital. See p.738

❺ **Durmitor National Park** Great for skiing in winter or rafting in the summer. **See p.740**

HIGHLIGHTS ARE MARKED ON THE MAP ON P.729

ROUGH COSTS

Daily budget Basic €30, occasional treat €50

Drink Nikšičko Tamno beer €1 (bottle from shop)

Food Sarma €2.50–4

Hostel/budget hotel €20/€50

Travel Bus: Budva–Kotor €3; train: Podgorica–Virpazar €1

FACT FILE

Population 625,000

Language Montenegrin

Currency Euro (€)

Capital Podgorica

International phone code ☏ 382

Time zone GMT +1hr

21

Introduction

The tiny state of Crna Gora is better known under its Italian name, Montenegro. The English translation – "Black Mountain" – may sound a little bleak, but Montenegro is a land exploding with colour. Carpeted with flowers for much of the year, the country's muscular peaks are dappled with the dark greens of pine, beech and birch from which turquoise streams rush down to a tantalizingly azure blue sea. Fringing it, the coastline is dotted from border to border with beaches of yellow and volcanic grey, and huddles of picturesque, orange-roofed houses – a postcard come to life.

While the **coastline** is most appealing for the traveller, Montenegro's most precious jewel – phenomenally photogenic **Kotor** – sits just a little inland at the end of a fjord-like bay. The beach town of **Budva** is the other real highlight, but you should also try to make time for the ruins of **Stari Bar**. Away from the coast, the country's pleasures are mainly confined to the mountains, particularly the spectacular national park of **Durmitor**, while the old Montenegrin capital of **Cetinje** is also well worth a visit; the present-day capital, **Podgorica**, gets few visitors but certainly has its charms.

CHRONOLOGY

9 AD Roman annexation of the region incorporates most of present-day Montenegro into the province of Dalmatia.
395 The Roman Empire splits into eastern and western halves, with Montenegro lying on the line of division.
990 Slav state of Duklja established.
1190 Successor state of Zeta annexed by Serbia.
1499 Much of Montenegrin interior falls to the Ottoman Empire; the Venetian Empire controls the coast.
1697 Ottomans defeated in the Great Turkish War; Petrović clan assumes control.
1797 Venice falls to Napoleon, who transfers the Gulf of Kotor to Austrian rule.
1878 Montenegro granted independence following the Congress of Berlin.
1918 Kingdom of Serbs, Croats and Slovenes formed, incorporating Montenegro.
1929 Montenegro becomes part of the new Kingdom of Yugoslavia.
1945 Tito becomes prime minister (president from 1953) and ushers in the era of Communist rule; Podgorica renamed Titograd.

1979 The coast between Bar and Ulcinj is damaged by an earthquake.
1991 Break-up of Yugoslavia; Montenegro votes to stay with Serbia in a referendum.
2006 Montenegro gains independence following a second referendum.
2012 Montenegro opens negotiations for accession to the EU.
2015 NATO invites Montenegro to join, with a view to full membership in 2017.

ARRIVAL AND DEPARTURE

Flights to Montenegro are in surprisingly short supply. National flag carrier Montenegro Airlines (ⓦmontenegro airlines.com) has a monopoly of sorts, and the only budget carrier to have been able to enter the market is Ryanair (ⓦryanair.com), with cheap flights twice a week between Podgorica and Brussels. However, Montenegro is easily reached overland from Croatia – there are **buses** along the coast from Dubrovnik (served by budget flights) and Split, though some of these will require a bus change after a short walk across the border. From Serbia, there are several daily buses between Belgrade and the Montenegrin coast, via Podgorica; daily **trains** – including a night service – also run from Belgrade to Bar along the same route. From Bosnia-Herzegovina there are direct buses to Podgorica from Trebinje and Sarajevo. The only decent connection with Albania is a daily bus (ⓦkotortotirana.com) that departs at 8.30am from Tirana and Kotor with stops at Budva, Podgorica and Shkodra

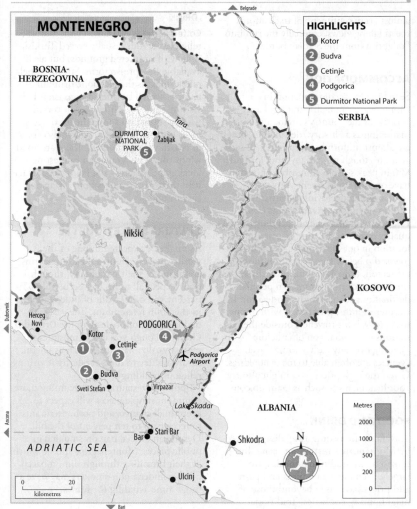

HIGHLIGHTS
1 Kotor
2 Budva
3 Cetinje
4 Podgorica
5 Durmitor National Park

along the way; alternatively, *Montenegro Hostel* (see p.734) can organize taxis direct to Tirana from Budva or Kotor for around €35 per person.

Perhaps the most romantic way to arrive in Montenegro is by **ferry** from Italy – Montenegro Lines (wmontenegrolines .net) runs between two and six weekly services to Bar from Bari (from €50).

Note that citizens of some countries, notably South Africa and India, still need **visas** to enter Montenegro; check online at wvisit-montenegro.com. You may have to apply at a Serbian embassy, since Montenegrin ones remain a little thin on the ground.

GETTING AROUND

For a country with such a small population, the frequency of intercity **buses** is quite remarkable. In addition, Montenegro has poured substantial funds into upgrading its main travel arteries, and travel times are accordingly short.

A **train** line heads to Bar from the Serbian border – a beautiful journey. While services are infrequent, prices are dirt-cheap and

21

almost every centimetre of track affords breathtaking views, especially the run into Podgorica from the Serbian border.

ACCOMMODATION

Searching for accommodation in Montenegro can be frustrating. Partly because of the country's premature marketing as a "luxury" destination, **hotels** are almost uniformly overpriced – in some areas, it's tough to find anything for under €50 in peak season. A number of **hostels** have opened up in recent years and standards are improving. Many travellers end up staying in **private rooms** (*sobe*). Prices vary dramatically depending on the quality of room, the time of year and the location in question – rates in less heralded towns dip below €10 per person in the off-season, though you may pay three times more during summer in popular destinations such as Budva and Kotor. In warmer months, proprietors with rooms to spare wait for travellers outside the bus stations – see what's on offer before handing over any cash – while travel agencies are often able to make bookings. Given the high prices, you might also try your luck on a site such as ⓦairbnb.com.

FOOD AND DRINK

Travellers often come away disappointed by Montenegro's **restaurant** scene. In tourist areas, traditional meals have largely been ousted by pizza and pasta, and prices have risen beyond those of neighbouring countries. Traditional restaurants are known as *konoba*, and can help those willing and able to escape said Italian staples. Menu items to look out for include grilled kebabs (*čevapčići*), cabbage leaves stuffed with mincemeat (*sarma*), bean soup with flecks of meat (*pasulj*), goulash (*gulaš*), and the artery-clogging *karađorđe vasnicla*, a breaded veal cutlet roll stuffed with cheese. **Vegetarians** can take refuge in the hearty salads available almost everywhere. Also ubiquitous are the Turkish snack staples of *burek*, pastry filled with meat, cheese, spinach and occasionally mushroom, and syrupy baklava sweets.

DRINK

Coffee (*kafa*) is consumed with almost religious fervour, usually served Turkish-style with unfiltered grounds, but also available in espresso form. Strong-as-hell **rakija** remains the alcoholic drink of choice – you'll be offered it constantly if visiting someone's home – but travellers usually subsist on some fine local beers, most notably Nikšićko, which also comes in a dark variety (*tamno*). There are good **wines** too, with Vranac an interesting local grape variety – the Plantaže label has it in their roster, and is both cheap and easy to find.

CULTURE AND ETIQUETTE

As might be expected in one of the world's newest countries, Montenegrins are proud of their **nationality**, though don't expect all to be anti-Serb: only 55 percent voted in favour of independence in the 2006 referendum. The vast majority of locals belong to the **Orthodox Church**, though you'll find mosques in majority-Albanian areas, such as Ulcinj. As always, try to dress modestly if visiting religious buildings.

Tipping at restaurants is becoming more common; simple places will expect to keep small change, and posh restaurants to receive up to ten percent of the bill. Despite an official ban on **smoking** in public places, Montenegrins still do much of their breathing through slim, tobacco-filled cylinders: non-smokers may have a tough time avoiding the fumes.

SPORTS AND ACTIVITIES

Outdoor activities come in two main flavours: mountain and coastal. **Hiking** is a joy around the peaks of Montenegro's

---

MONTENEGRIN

Montenegrin is the official language, though it's essentially the same as Serbian (except that it uses the Roman alphabet rather than Cyrillic). You should be able to get by using Croatian (see box, p.158), with which it has strong similarities, though English is widely spoken in tourist areas.

21

national parks, most notably Durmitor, which is also good for **kayaking**, and **skiing** in winter. On the beach, **watersports** including jet-skiing, parasailing and zorbing are all available at various points along the coast – Budva is the prime spot, though kayaking around Kotor Bay is a delight.

COMMUNICATIONS

Most **post offices** (*pošta*) are open Monday to Friday 8am to 7pm, Saturday 8am to noon. These are also your best bet for **phone calls** as public phones are in extremely short supply; local landlines are cheap to call, though calls to mobile phones are more expensive. International roaming charges have fallen in recent years, but apps such as Skype or Viber are the best deal for calling abroad. Hotels, hostels, restaurants, bars and cafés usually offer **wi-fi**.

EMERGENCIES

Montenegro has a pretty low crime rate as far as muggings and petty theft go, though of course it pays to be vigilant, especially around bus stations. The **police** (*policija*) are generally easy-going, and some speak basic English.

Pharmacies (*apoteka*) tend to follow shop hours, though you'll find emergency 24-hour telephone numbers posted in the windows. If they can't help, you'll be directed to a **hospital** (*bolnica*).

INFORMATION

Many towns and resorts now have a **tourist information office**, but hours can be infrequent and staff do not always speak English. Although they can advise on local accommodation, it's unlikely that they'll book rooms for you – head to a travel agent instead.

MONEY AND BANKS

Though not yet a member of the EU, Montenegro uses the **euro** (€). **Banks** are generally open Monday to Friday 9am to 6pm and Saturday 9am to noon, while **ATMs** are widespread.

OPENING HOURS AND HOLIDAYS

Most **shops** open Monday to Saturday 9am to 8pm, with many closed on Sundays. Very few museums are open on Mondays, and all shops and banks close on **public holidays:** January 1, 6 and 7, Orthodox Easter (April or May), May 1 and 21, and July 13.

The coast

Blessed with sunshine, pristine beaches lapped by clear Adriatic waters, and appealing, whitewashed old towns, the **Montenegrin coast** has become one of Europe's hottest properties. Heading north–south from Croatia to the Albanian border, you'll first hit charming **Herceg Novi**, before the coast ducks inland to meet magnificent **Kotor** – without doubt the most picturesque town in the land. South of here, the littoral swings back out to the beaches

21

of **Budva**, which is something of a party capital during the summer. It's then mountain-edged coast all the way to **Bar**, home to some terrific ruins.

HERCEG NOVI

Developed as a coastal resort during eighteenth-century Austro-Hungarian rule, little **HERCEG NOVI** is a thoroughly likeable town, and yet one that is usually bypassed by tourists. Its steep maze of lanes is lined with stately, crumbling villas, while plants and flowers from around the world abound, bequeathed by countless sailors down the years. Nearby **beaches**, meanwhile, make for excellent swimming.

Most sights are concentrated within Herceg Novi's appealing, walled **Old Town**. At its centre you'll find the **Church of Archangel Michael**, which is barely over a hundred years old, yet looks like it has been around rather longer. From here you can climb the steps to take in views from **Kanli Kula** tower (summer only daily 9am–10pm; €1). Down from the Old Town, the seafront **promenade** makes for a delightful walk. Head east for twenty minutes, then turn inland to find the elegant, seventeenth-century **Savina Monastery** (daily 6am–8pm; free).

ARRIVAL AND INFORMATION

By bus There's a small station on Jadranski put, a 5min walk from the Old Town. Heading south, most buses cross the Bay of Kotor by ferry (no extra charge). Travelling via Kotor increases the following journey times – except to Kotor – by around 45min.

Destinations Bar (6 daily; 2hr 30min); Budva (every 30min–1hr; 1hr 15min); Dubrovnik (3 daily; 1hr 15min); Kotor (hourly; 45min); Podgorica (every 30min; 3hr).

Information and tours The Tourist Information Centre is close to the bus station at Jova Đabovića 12 (Mon–Sat 8am–2pm; ⓦ hercegnovi.travel). The nearby Black Mountain agency, Pet Danica 21 (daily 8am–8pm; ☎ 067 640869, ⓦ montenegroholiday.com), can book tours and also arrange rafting trips to Durmitor (see box, p.740).

ACCOMMODATION

There's a dearth of hotel accommodation in the centre, though the Black Mountain agency (see above) can book private rooms from €10/person and apartments can be booked online through sites such as ⓦ booking.com; most hotels are on the outskirts of town.

Apartments Pavlovic Njegoševa 156 ☎ 068 623328. Spotless apartments with self-catering kitchens and wonderful sea views located within walking distance of the old town. €45

Autocamp Zelenika Sunčana obala ☎ 067 678631. Campsite 3km east of town; open April–Oct. Pitches €13

Garni Hotel Bokeška Noć Brace Grakalica 42A ☎ 069 341018, ⓦ garnihotelbokeskanoc.com. Lovely place in the vicinity of Savina Monastery with glorious sea views from most rooms. €80

Villa Živanović Zelenica bb ☎ 031 678148, ⓦ villazivanovic.com. Great budget option on the outskirts of town with comfortable a/c rooms and good breakfast. €30

EATING

Cafés, bars and restaurants cluster around the harbour.

Kafana Pod Lozom Trg Nikole Đurkovića. A 2min walk from the church (past the clock tower and turn right), this restaurant cooks up cheap local specialities – you'll be able to fill up for €5. Try the *gulaš*, or the *sarma*. Daily 10am–9pm.

Konoba Feral Šetalište Pet Danica 47. A great harbourside fish restaurant renowned for its generous portions and excellent service. Local seafood options include cuttlefish, mussels and octopus – the superb seafood platter is more than enough for two. Daily 9am–midnight.

KOTOR

Perched on the edge of a majestic bay, the medieval Old Town of **KOTOR** is the undisputed jewel in Montenegro's crown. Though no longer Europe's best-kept secret, Kotor's sudden elevation to the tour-bus league has failed to dim the timeless delights of its cobbled alleyways and secluded piazzas. Enclosing cafés and churches galore, the town **walls** are themselves glowered down upon by a series of hulking peaks. Down below, a harbour bustling with sleek yachts marks the end of the **Bay of Kotor**, made fjord-like by the 1000m cliffs that rise almost vertically from the serene waters.

First colonized by the Greeks, Kotor came to prominence in the twelfth century, then passed through Serb, Austro-Hungarian and Bosnian hands before fifteenth-century Ottoman conquests forced it under the protective wing of Venice. Venetian rule ended in 1797, the shape of today's Kotor having been laid out in the intervening years.

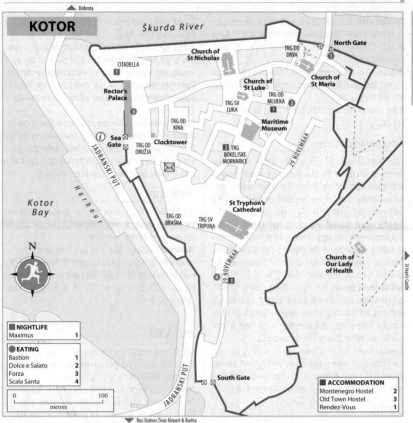

KOTOR

Škurda River

▲ Dobrota

North Gate

CITADELLA

Church of
St Nicholas

TRG OD
DRVA

Rector's
Palace

Church of
St Luke

TRG OD
MLIJEKA

Church of
St Maria

TRG SV
LUKA

Maritime
Museum

TRG OD
KINA

ⓘ Sea
Gate

Clocktower

TRG OD
ORUŽJA

TRG
BOKELJSKE
MORNARICE

29 NOVEMBAR

*Kotor
Bay*

Harbour

JADRANSKI PUT

St Tryphon's
Cathedral

TRG OD
BRAŠNA

TRG SV
TRIPUNA

N

Church of
Our Lady
of Health

St Ivan's Castle

NIGHTLIFE
Maximus   1

EATING
Bastion   1
Dolce e Salato   2
Forza   3
Scala Santa   4

0   100
    metres

29 NOVEMBAR

JADRANSKI PUT

South Gate

ACCOMMODATION
Montenegro Hostel   2
Old Town Hostel   3
Rendez-Vous   1

▼ Bus Station, Tivat Airport & Budva

WHAT TO SEE AND DO

Kotor's charms are best appreciated by heading to the **Old Town**, *sans* map, and getting lost in the labyrinthine streets. You'll likely enter through the Sea Gate, next to the harbour, and emerge onto the main square, Trg od Oružja. Cafés spill out from glorious buildings, the most notable of which are the old **Rector's Palace** and a leaning **clock tower**. Burrow through the streets and before long you'll end up at **St Tryphon's Cathedral** (daily 8am–7pm; €2.50), backed by a wall of mountains and perfect for photos; it's well worth the entry fee for a peek inside. Elsewhere there are several churches that merit a look, as well as a fascinating **Maritime Museum** (July–Sept Mon–Fri 8am–11pm, Sat & Sun 10am–4pm; Oct–June Mon–Fri 9am–5pm, Sat & Sun 9am–noon; €4), a repository of nautical maps and model ships.

The old **fortress walls** (daily 8am–8pm; €3) sit proudly above the town, and make for a rewarding climb that's best begun from the North Gate. Allow at least ninety minutes for the round-trip to **St Ivan's Castle**, from which you'll have tremendous views of the fjord. On hot summer days it's best to set off early or wait until evening, and note that the first building you come to, the **Church of Our Lady of Health**, is not even halfway up.

ARRIVAL AND INFORMATION

By bus The bus station is a 5min walk south of the Old Town.

Destinations Bar (5 daily; 1hr 45min); Budva (every 30min; 30min); Cetinje (hourly; 1hr); Podgorica (hourly; 1hr 30min).

21

Tourist office Located just outside the main entrance to the Old Town (daily 8am–5pm; July & Aug to 8pm; ☎ 032 322886, ⓦ tokotor.me), and able to book accommodation.

Tours Both hostels lay on good day-trips; the *Montenegro Hostel's* famous 12hr "Big Montenegro" tour (€40) covers much of the country.

Bike rental The *Old Town Hostel* rents bikes from €7 per day.

ACCOMMODATION

At all times of year, you're likely to be approached by *sobe* owners as you get off the bus. Rooms are mainly grouped in two areas: Škaljari, uphill from the industrial mess near the bus station, and the more pleasant area of Dobrota, on the bayside just north of the Old Town.

Montenegro Hostel Trg od Muzeja ☎ 069 039751, ⓦ montenegrohostel.com. There's a bit of noise from bars at night and churches in the morning, but the location is excellent – right in the heart of the Old Town – and the rooms in the back are quieter. Dorms €15

★ **Old Town Hostel** In from south gate ☎ 032 325317, ⓦ hostel-kotor.me. Fantastic hostel, located in a rambling, centuries-old building which once belonged to local nobility. Dorms are spick-and-span, and their private rooms even better. Dorms €20, doubles €54

Rendez-Vous Trg od Mlijeka ☎ 032 323931. The Old Town's cheapest hotel option sits on "Milk Square", a lovely place off the tour-group trail. Its comfortably furnished rooms are en suite with wi-fi and a/c. Doubles €60

EATING

Given the Old Town's status as a tourist magnet, its culinary scene is disappointing, especially for those on a budget – though you'll find places serving slices of pizza for €2.

Bastion Trg od Drva. Seafood restaurant offering a more authentic Old Kotor atmosphere than you'll find elsewhere; the interior is far from showy, and the outdoor terrace is located in a charming square. Tuna steak with shrimp sauce €15, fish salad €5. Daily 10am–midnight.

Dolce e Salato Trg od Mlijeka. Outdoor seats in this quiet square are a perfect place for breakfast – a slice of *burek*, a

Turkish coffee and a piece of strudel will come to just €3.50. Daily 7am–5pm.

Forza Trg od Oružja. Despite occasionally lethargic service, this is the best of a whole clutch of cafés on the main square, and a perfect place to watch Kotor strolling by. Don't dare step inside to peek at their cakes – you'll almost certainly emerge €4 lighter and a little heavier elsewhere. Daily 8am–10pm.

Scala Santa Just inside the south gate. This pricey but attractive restaurant is one of the few places in the Old Town specializing in Montenegrin food, rather than pizza and pasta – try the huge *njeguški* steak (€15), topped with *prosciutto*-like cured ham. Daily 10am–midnight.

NIGHTLIFE

The nightlife in Kotor can be surprisingly good, and there's usually live music at weekends, which see the cobbled streets thumping until midnight.

Maximus Citadella. Take your pick from several music-themed floors at the country's biggest nightclub which lies right in the heart of the Old Town and occasionally hosts big-name DJs. Entry can be €10–15 on weekends. Daily 9pm–late.

BUDVA

Of Montenegro's seemingly never-ending chain of picturesque coastal towns, **BUDVA** is by far the most popular. Filled to the brim with bars, restaurants and limestone houses, its Old Town is almost as pretty as the one in nearby Kotor, and there's plenty of fun to be had on the beaches, as well as at the seafront bars which pop up in the summer.

WHAT TO SEE AND DO

Budva's focal point is the **Old Town** – more of a place to stroll and sip coffee than to sightsee – though most travellers are here for the **beaches**, and there are plenty to choose from.

FESTIVALS IN AND AROUND KOTOR

Kotor's festival year kicks off on February 1, with folk dances and church music on the **day of St Tripun**; this is closely followed by the **Masked Ball**, a colourful event that sees processions through the Old Town. In April there's the wonderfully varied **Montenegrin Dance Festival**, before the **International Summer Carnival** (late July/early August) celebrates the sunny season with theatrical and musical performances. Around the same time is **Refresh** (ⓦ refreshfestival.me), a four-day music festival that ropes in some big-name DJs. All pale in comparison, however, to late August's **Boka Nights**, when boats fill the bay, fireworks electrify the night sky, and everyone goes just a little bit mad.

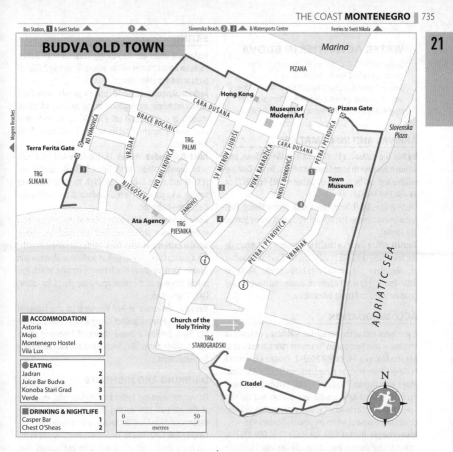

BUDVA OLD TOWN

Mogren Beaches

Marina

PIZANA

Hong Kong

CARA DUŠANA

Museum of Modern Art

Pizana Gate

Slovenska Plaza

KO IVANOVICA

BRAĆE BOCARIĆ

VRZDAK

Terra Ferita Gate

PETRA I PETROVICA

TRG PALMI

TRG SLIKARA

IVO MILKOVICA

SV MITROV LJUBIŠE

VUKA KARADŽIĆA

CARA DUŠANA

NIKOLE ĐUROVICA

Town Museum

NJEGOŠEVA

ZANOVICI

Ata Agency

TRG PJESNIKA

PETRA I PETROVICA

VRANJAK

ⓘ

ⓘ

ADRIATIC SEA

Church of the Holy Trinity

TRG STAROGRADSKI

Citadel

N

0   50
metres

ACCOMMODATION
Astoria	3
Mojo	2
Montenegro Hostel	4
Vila Lux	1

EATING
Jadran	2
Juice Bar Budva	4
Konoba Stari Grad	3
Verde	1

DRINKING & NIGHTLIFE
Casper Bar	1
Chest O'Sheas	2

The Old Town

The highlight of the Old Town is the area around the **Church of the Holy Trinity** (daily July–Sept 8am–noon & 5pm–midnight; Oct–June 8am–noon & 4–7pm), home to frescoes that, while far from ancient, are rather beautiful. Looming over this is the fifteenth-century **citadel** (May–Oct daily 8am–midnight; €2), which offers splendid views of the Adriatic waves pummelling in. Still, you're best advised to try instead to hunt down the entrances to the **Old City wall**, which boasts even better views. There are only two of these, and almost no tourists ever get up there – one is just to the left when you enter through the Terra Ferita gate, and the other is down an alley opposite *Hong Kong* restaurant at Vuka Karadžića 1. Also in the Old Town are

the **Town Museum** (Tues–Fri 9am–10pm, Sat & Sun 10am–5pm; €2), which houses Greek and Roman booty from the ruins being unearthed beneath the citadel, and a **Museum of Modern Art** (Mon–Sat 8am–2pm & 4–10pm; €2).

Beaches and islands

The main beach, **Slovenska Plaža**, curls a few pebbly kilometres east from the Old Town, but far nicer are the sandy **Mogren** beaches, west of the Old Town, which attract a more youthful crowd – just follow the path around the cliffs from the *Mogren Hotel*. Better still is the beach on uninhabited **Sveti Nikola Island**, which you'll see jutting up offshore. In summer, regular water taxis will shuttle you across; prices start at around €5 per person, though you'll have to haggle.

WATER ACTIVITIES IN BUDVA

Slovenska Plaža, the main beach, is the place to head for all kinds of watery fun. Jet-skis and parasailing are on offer for the adventurous (from €40), while kayaks and pedaloes are a calmer option (€4–8/hr).

ARRIVAL AND INFORMATION

By bus The station is a 15min walk from the Old Town, and a 10min walk north form Slovenska Plaza. Terrae Taxis are reliable and can be booked by phone or SMS (☎ 19717 or ☎ +382 69 444334).

Destinations Bar (hourly; 1hr); Cetinje (every 30min; 1hr); Kotor (every 30min–1hr; 30min); Podgorica (every 30min; 1hr 30min).

Tourist office There's a tourist information centre outside the town hall (☎ 033 453416) in the Old Town and another at Njegoševa 28 ☎ 033 452750 (both Mon–Sat 8am–8pm). They won't advise on accommodation, but are good for maps and travel information.

ACCOMMODATION

If you're not met at the bus station – almost a certainty in summer – your best option for private rooms is to head to Ata (Iva Mikovića 14; ☎ 069 240242, ⓦ atabooking.com) in the Old Town who can make bookings for €20–45/room.
Mojo Vojvodanska 3 ☎ 069 711986, ⓦ mojobudva.com. Perfectly located between the bus station and the Old Town, this offers a cheap yet relaxing stay in immaculately clean rooms, most of which are private. Doubles €55
Montenegro Hostel Vuka Karadzića 12 ☎ 069 039751, ⓦ montenegrohostel.com. Colourfully decorated hostel in the Old Town. The three dorms are effectively private rooms with more beds inside (each has its own kitchenette and bathroom), and there's a handy common area up top. Dorms €18
Vila Lux Jadranski put bb ☎ 033 455950, ⓦ vilalux.com. Delightful central hotel with high standards and free breakfasts that will fill you up until lunchtime. Good discounts for single travellers. Doubles €75

★ TREAT YOURSELF

Astoria Njegoševa 4 (☎ 033 451110, ⓦ astoriamontenegro.com). Friendly boutique hotel just inside the Old Town, offering artistically designed rooms and wonderful views from a rooftop terrace. Doubles from €200, though off-season you may get a suite for the same price. They also have a hugely popular restaurant that spills out from the town walls. €200

EATING

Restaurant prices are surprisingly reasonable in Budva; those on a tight budget will be able to fill up on €2 slices of pizza around the Old Town.
Jadran Slovenska Obala 10. Hugely popular waterfront restaurant whose international menu includes *schnitzels*, mussels or stuffed squid (all €10). In the summer, they even have a bunch of tables on the beach itself. Daily 9am–1am.
Juice Bar Budva Vranjak 13. Top rated Old Town café with superb salads, fresh juices (€3–5), sandwiches (€3–4) and other light dishes. With its shaded outdoor seating, it's a great spot to relax and watch the world go by. Daily 9am–midnight.
Konoba Stari Grad Njegoševa. One of the better venues in the Old Town, serving excellent seafood dishes – their squid is excellent whether fried, stuffed or grilled, as is the black risotto (all €10) – as well as traditional Montenegrin cuisine. There's a grand beach terrace outside, which also makes this one of the most appealing places for coffee. Daily 11am–1am.
Verde At the corner of Velji Vinogradi bb and Jadranski put. Highly regarded budget eatery a short walk from the Old Town serving a broad choice of takeaway salads (€2–3), pasta dishes (€3), fresh juices and pancakes. Daily 8am–midnight.

DRINKING AND NIGHTLIFE

On summer evenings Budva can be quite wild, especially at the open-air bars dotting the harbour road – pole-dancers, *rakija* and Russian tourists are a potent mix.
Casper Bar Cara Dušana 10. Still the trendiest bar in the Old Town, this is a tiny place with a fun but loungey vibe, and regular DJ sets. Daily 10am–2am.
Chest O'Sheas Mitrov Ljubiše. Small and appealing Irish pub right in the middle of the Old Town, with sports events on screen and Guinness (€7) on tap. Daily noon–1am.

BAR

The pleasant town of **BAR** is literally the first port of call for many visitors to Montenegro, thanks to regular ferry connections with Italy. While the beach is rocky and there are no real attractions in the centre, it's worth at least an afternoon thanks to the magnificent ruins of **Stari Bar** (daily: June–Aug 8am–10pm; Sept–May 8am–8pm; €2) – *stari* means old – which sit 5km up the hill. The beauty of its setting is quite staggering – sheer cliffs surround this old town on all sides, and tiny farming communities dot the valleys below.

Fragments of pottery found in the area date it as far back as 800 BC, though it wasn't until the **sixth century** that the Byzantine Empire created what you see today; the destruction also in evidence was caused during the Ottoman resistance battles of the 1870s. A trip to Stari Bar should set you back no more than €6 by taxi, or grab one of the marked buses from the main drag or the bus and train stations (every 15min; €1).

ARRIVAL AND INFORMATION

By train The station is located 2km south of town, a €4 taxi ride from the centre.
Destinations Belgrade (2 daily; 11hr); Podgorica (10 daily; 1hr); Virpazar (9 daily; 25min).
By bus 300m from the train station; you can often hop on or off buses far nearer the town centre.
Destinations Budva (hourly; 1hr); Kotor (9 daily; 1hr 45min); Podgorica (hourly; 1hr 45min).
By ferry The terminal is immediately west of the centre, serving daily ferries from Bari year-round (see box, p.667).
Tourist office Obala 13 Jula, on the opposite side of the main road from the ferry terminal (June–Sept daily 8am–9pm; Oct–May Mon–Sat 8am–4pm; ☎030 311633, ⊛ bar.travel).

ACCOMMODATION

There are few *sobe* rooms in central Bar, so it's best to head to Šušanj, a pleasant district hanging over the almost unpronounceable beach of Zukotrlica. It's a 20min walk north along the seafront, or a €2 taxi ride; once there, keep your eyes open for "*sobe*" signs.
Le Petit Chateau Obala Kralja Nikole ☎030 314400. Located on the seafront opposite the port, this characterful old building is one of the few central hotels. Rooms are smartly furnished and many have lovely sea views. Doubles **€65**
Villa Monegro Ilino bb ☎069 915415. Good-value hotel in the Šušanj district, a short walk from the beach, with a/c doubles and apartments with self-catering kitchens. Doubles **€35**

EATING AND DRINKING

Kaldrma Stari Bar. Adorable veggie restaurant – think cushions and rugs – near the entrance to the ruins. Summer daily 11am–10pm; often closed in the winter.
Karađuzović Stari Bar. Cosy family-run café near the ruins that's great for breakfast; €3 will buy you a slice of *burek*, a Turkish sweetie and an espresso. Daily 9am–8pm.
Pulena Vladimira Rolovića 11. Popular pizzeria-pub tucked into the fantastic Yugoslav-era Robna Kuka centre on the main drag. They have a nice range of local dishes as well as their Italian roster, and you can fill up for under €10. Daily 11am–11pm.

ULCINJ

ULCINJ sits near the Albanian border, and most travellers use the town as a simple conduit between the nations – the twice-daily bus connections to and from Shkodra (see p.728) are the only scheduled services of any kind linking Albania and Montenegro. You won't need to stay the night, and few foreign travellers choose to, but it's an attractive place for sure – from the bus station, a €4 taxi ride or 30min walk will bring you to the main beach, which sits under a delightful **Old Town**. The latter is a diametric opposite to those in Kotor and Budva – scruffy, unpolished, and quite fascinating as a result.

The interior

The mountains visible from the Montenegrin coast hint at the beauty of its interior, an area sadly bypassed by most travellers. The capital, **Podgorica**, is overlooked by backpackers but certainly merits a visit, while **Cetinje**, the former capital, makes a delightful stopover. Best of all is the mountainous north, particularly **Durmitor**, a spectacular

21

national park where you can hike through unspoilt pastureland, ski past 2000m-plus peaks, or raft through the colossal Tara Canyon.

CETINJE

Sleepy CETINJE sits just over the mountainous crest from Budva and Kotor, and is well placed for a visit if you're heading between coast and interior. Cetinje became Montenegro's **capital** on independence in 1878, and of the clutch of embassies that were established, many remain visible today as faded relics of the city's proud past. Though the status of capital has long been passed to Podgorica, many government offices – and, in fact, the presidential seat – remain in Cetinje.

WHAT TO SEE AND DO

Central Cetinje is small enough to walk around in an hour or two, and almost all sights are located on or near **Njegoševa**, a mostly pedestrianized central thorough-fare. The sights listed below are all open daily 9am–5pm, and can be visited on a €10 combined ticket (available from any of the museum ticket offices) or cost from €3 to €5 each.

Trg Dvorski and Trg Revolucije

The **Palace of King Nikola** sits at the southern end of Trg Dvorski. Prior to becoming king in 1910, Nikola was a military leader and poet (as well as a prince, of course), and his old palace is full of regal bric-a-brac. Opposite this is the **Ethnographic Museum**, which mainly features nineteenth-century costumes. Down the road in Trg Revolucije you'll find the **Biliarda**, once the residence of King Petar II, and named after a billiard

table – still visible today – that he once had hauled here from Kotor. Near the Biliarda you'll find the **National Museum**, worth visiting for its first-floor art gallery, and nestled into the hillside across the square is **Cetinje Monastery**.

ARRIVAL AND INFORMATION

By bus Buses pull into a tiny terminal that's a 10min walk into town; there's a small map at the station.
Destinations Budva (every 30min; 1hr); Kotor (hourly; 1hr 15min); Podgorica (every 30min; 45min).
Tourist office Njegoševa 39, in the large car park near the *Grand Hotel* (June–Sept daily 8am–7pm; Oct–May Mon–Fri 9am–2pm; ☎041 230250, ⍟cetinje.travel). It's good for local maps but little more.

ACCOMMODATION AND EATING

Grand Njegoševa st. 1 ☎041 231652, ⍟hotelgrand.me. Yugoslav-era beast at the end of Njegoševa that'll be of great interest to fans of well-worn retro interiors. Doubles **€65**
Kole Crnogorskih Junaka 12. Great-value local favourite that serves up generous portions of local dishes and seafood accompanied by delicious homebaked bread. Mains €5–10. Daily 7am–midnight.
La Vecchia Casa Vojvode Batrića 6 ☎067 629660. Rooms and apartments in a glorious old house with a wonderful garden right in the centre of town. Highly recommended. Doubles **€30**
Restoran Vinoteka Vasa Raičovića. Rich and varied menu of local specialities, including delicious *gulaš* and *sarma*. Dine with a view on the outdoor terrace, head up to the quiet upper level or down to the basement wine bar. Mains €5–10. Daily 10am–8pm.

PODGORICA

Though there may not be a great deal to see in **PODGORICA**, the Montenegrin capital has been attracting an increasing number of backpackers in recent years, and the hostel scene has expanded to accommodate them. It is the newest capital city in Europe, one of the

---

CETINJE'S EMBASSIES

Cetinje's former **embassies** are quite fascinating, and it's fun to track them down – basically, look for any oldish building sporting a crest. Nearest the bus station is the grey **French embassy**, covered with an assortment of lemon and blue tiles. Down on Trg Dvorski, the **Serbian embassy** contains the aforementioned ethnographic museum, and the **Bulgarian** one is now a great café. Further down the road, the crumbling **British embassy** is now a music academy; turn left for the **Turkish embassy**, now home to the University of Cetinje's Faculty of Drama, and the pick of the bunch – the gorgeous, peach-coloured **Russian embassy**.

smallest, and, until recently, one of the least visited. It also might be the only European capital in which the river water looks positively drinkable – the city centres on the **Morača**, a fast-flowing turquoise river edged by parkland and spanned by a couple of pedestrian bridges, one of which – the Gazela – dives down below street level. There are also some interesting fortress remains in this area, while **Gorica Forest Park** is worth a visit for its pleasant walking trails; it's to the north of town, behind the easy-to-find national stadium.

ARRIVAL AND INFORMATION

By plane The airport lies 11km south of the city. A minibus usually meets incoming Montenegro Airlines flights to transport passengers to Podgorica's central square (€3). The only other alternative is to take a taxi – those parked outside will expect €20 to the centre; taxis booked by phone (Alo Taxi ☎ 19700; City Taxi ☎ 19711; Taxi Gold ☎ 19805) charge €5–10 for the same journey.

By train The train station is a 15min walk from the centre.
Destinations Bar (11 daily; 1hr); Belgrade (2 daily; 10hr); Virpazar (9 daily; 35min).

By bus The terminal is adjacent to the train station.
Destinations Bar (8 daily; 1hr 45min); Budva (every 30min; 1hr 30min); Cetinje (every 30min; 30min); Herceg Novi (hourly; 2hr 30min); Kotor (hourly; 2hr); Žabljak for Durmitor National Park (5 daily; 2hr 30min).

Tourist office Slobode 47 (June–Oct Mon–Fri 8am–8pm, Sat 9am–1pm; Nov–May Mon–Fri 8am–4pm; ☎ 020 667535, ⓦ podgorica.travel). A good source of information, and can advise on accommodation.

ACCOMMODATION

Evropa Orahovačka 16 ☎ 020 623444, ⓦ hotelevropa .co.me. How convenient – Podgorica's cheapest hotel is located down a side street leading from the train and bus stations. Rooms are good and there's a restaurant downstairs. Doubles **€50**

Hostel Podgorica Bratstva Jedinstva 7-III, Apartment 1 ☎ 069 206909, ⓦ hostelpodgorica.com. Expect a warm welcome at this converted apartment that lies 5min east of the stations and offers comfortable four- and six-bed dorms. Dorms **€11**

Montenegro Hostel Radoja Jovanovića 52 (old street name)/Spasa Nikolića 52 (new street name) ☎ 069 255501, ⓦ montenegrohostel.com. A 15min walk east from the stations, with bright spacious dorms and private rooms in a detached house close to the river. Pleasant common area, shared kitchen, laundry and bike rental (€7/ day). Dorms **€11**

EATING AND DRINKING

Restaurants in Podgorica are better value than the hotels, and *burek*-serving snack bars are easy to find. For nightlife, the best streets are Njegoševa and Bokeška – take your pick from the various bars on offer.

Buda Bar Stanka Dragojevića 26. Though it's a poor copy of the hip *Buddha Bar* chain, this popular place attracts a lively young crowd that parties till the early hours. Daily 8am–3am.

Duhovny Centar Njegoševa 27. Scoff down cheap, tasty local fare – mostly veggie – in this church-run and church-like restaurant: try the salty pancakes with cream. You can eat for under €5. Daily 8am–midnight.

★**Karver** Obala Ribnice. Charming riverside café set inside an old Turkish bath, whose top was lopped off to make room for a bridge. Squashed it may be, but this is as cool as Podgorica gets – it's a great hangout for evening drinks, and also has a bookshop with a few English-language titles. Latte €1.50. Daily 9am–11.30pm.

Lanterna Imarka Miljanova 41. Traditional-style restaurant with rough stone walls and chunky wooden furniture that's renowned for its superb pizzas (extra large €7) and attentive service. Daily 10am–11pm.

★**Stara Kuca** Iva Andrića 5. The "Old House" occupies a charming stone building with roaring open fire in winter and shaded rustic terrace for the hot summer months. Serves hearty portions of fish dishes and meat-based local specialities. Daily 10am–midnight.

DIRECTORY

Embassies and consulates UK, Ulcinjska 8 ☎ 020 618010; US, Džona Džeksona 2 ☎ 020 410500.

Hospital Podgorica Hospital, Ljubljanska 1 ☎ 020 225125.

Post office Slobode 1 (Mon–Sat 7am–8pm). Has telephones for public use.

LAKE SKADAR

Oozing over the Albanian border, beautiful **Skadar** is the largest lake in the Balkans, and also one of its most untouched. However, since it lies on the train line, it's easily accessible and can make a good stopoff on your way to or from the coast. The main jump-off point is **Virpazar**, a cute little fishing village at the northern end of the lake, 1km back down the line to Podgorica from the station. From here it's a pleasant walk along the lake's western shore, and though there's nowhere to rent bikes, if you've brought one along you'll be in heaven – an hour's ride will bring into

ACTIVITIES IN DURMITOR

There's plenty to do in and around the park, though this area is most famed for its **rafting**, which is among the best in Europe. This can be arranged through agencies on the coast, *Montenegro Hostel* in Kotor or Budva, or in Žabljak itself – try Summit, Njegoševa bb (☎069 016502, ⓦ summit.co.me), which charges €45 per person for a half-day trip and also runs jeep, mountain biking, canyoning and hiking tours. **Hiking** is great from June to September, but do come prepared since this is a wild area, and be warned that the weather can change rapidly, even in summer. The aforementioned agencies can provide maps. Wintertime opens up **skiing** possibilities, and **snowboarding** is on the rise too; the main slopes are accessible from Žabljak, with day-passes costing around €15, and ski rental almost the same.

sight a clutch of **offshore monasteries**, though to get any nearer you'll have to search for a boat.

ACCOMMODATION AND EATING

Country House Djurisic Boljevci bb ☎69 406584. Perched on a picturesque hillside just outside Virpazar, this charming guesthouse has a lovely garden and clean, cosy rooms with wonderful views. Inexpensive home-cooked meals are available and the breakfasts are exceptional. Tours of the region can be arranged by the affable owners who also offer free bikes for guests to use. Doubles €40

Pelikan Virpazar ☎020 711107, ⓦ pelikan-zec.com. A one-stop shop for lodging, dining and motorboat tours; the simply furnished rooms are comfortable, though they're outdone by the excellent lakeside restaurant, which specializes in local fish. Doubles €55

★ **TREAT YOURSELF**

Boskovica Brvnare ☎069 541728. A little south of Žabljak (call to be picked up), this highly appealing clutch of self-catering pine-clad chalets makes for great value – the views are simply stupendous. Discounts for stays of over five days. Chalets €110

DURMITOR NATIONAL PARK

A land of jagged, pine-cloaked mountains and alpine pastureland, **Durmitor** is the most scenic place in inland Montenegro, and a hive of **outdoor activity** throughout the year, a prime spot for skiing, hiking, camping, rafting and far more.

Dozens of 2000m-plus peaks drop down to the spectacular **Tara Canyon**, a 1000m-deep rip in the Earth bisected by a crashing river. The park is centred on the mountain town of **Žabljak**, accessible by bus along a winding road that can turn even the stomachs of the locals; it's a two-and-a-half-hour bus ride from Podgorica (five daily).

ACCOMMODATION

There's plenty of accommodation in the area, though as elsewhere in the country the hotels are a little dear. Better for budget travellers are private rooms – from €10 per person – which you'll be offered on getting off the bus. Durmitor is also a great place for camping, and there are a number of sites around the park.

Ivan Do Autocamp Žabljak ☎069 041749, ⓦ autocamp -ivando.com. Well-established campsite in stunning location just outside town. Caravans (€5) and camper vans (€5) are also catered for. Per person €2, plus per tent €2

TILEWORK, MEDINA, TANGIER

Morocco

HIGHLIGHTS

❶ Tangier The former International Zone retains a delightfully seedy charm. **See p.748**

❷ Chefchaouen Charming little mountain town full of blue houses. **See p.752**

❸ Medina, Fez The world's best-preserved medieval city. **See p.755**

❹ Kasbah des Oudaïas, Rabat Ancient citadel with a splendid gateway. **See p.760**

❺ Jemaa el Fna, Marrakesh A spontaneous open-air circus every evening. **See p.768**

❻ Essaouira Laidback seaside resort that's become famous for its excellent windsurfing. See p.771

HIGHLIGHTS ARE MARKED ON THE MAP ON P.743

ROUGH COSTS

Daily budget Basic €35, occasional treat €50

Food *Tagine* €4–5

Drink Pot of mint tea €1

Hostel/budget hotel €8–15

Travel Marrakesh–Casablanca: train €8; bus €5.50–7.50

FACT FILE

Population 33.3 million

Languages Arabic, Berber languages, French, Spanish

Currency Dirham (dh)

Capital Rabat

International phone code ☎212

Time zone GMT

Introduction

It's just an hour's ferry ride from Spain, yet Morocco seems worlds away from Europe. Its culture is Islamic and, despite its 44 years of French and Spanish colonial rule, a more distant past constantly makes its presence felt. A visit here is a challenging, intense and rewarding experience.

22

Berbers, the indigenous people, make up over half of Morocco's population; only around ten percent of Moroccans claim to be "pure" Arabs. Until independence in 1956, the country was divided into Spanish and French zones, the latter building Villes Nouvelles (new towns) alongside the long-standing Medinas (old towns) in all the country's main cities.

Many people come to Morocco on cheap flights, mainly to Marrakesh, but coming by boat from Europe, your most likely introduction to the country is **Tangier** in the north, still shaped by its heyday as an "international zone" in the 1950s. To its south, in the Rif Mountains, the town of **Chefchaouen** is a small-scale and enjoyably laidback place, while inland lies the enthralling city of **Fez**, the greatest of the four imperial capitals (the others are Meknes, Rabat and Marrakesh). The sprawl of **Meknes**, with its ancient walls, makes an easy day-trip from Fez.

The power axis of the nation lies on the coast in **Rabat** and **Casablanca**. "Casa" looks a lot like Marseille, while the elegant, orderly capital, **Rabat**, has some gems of Moroccan architecture. Further south, **Marrakesh** is an enduring fantasy that won't disappoint. The country's loveliest resort, **Essaouira**, a charming walled seaside town, lies within easy reach of both Marrakesh and Casablanca.

CHRONOLOGY

42 AD Romans take control of the coastal regions of Morocco.
600s Arabs conquer Moroccan lands, introducing Islam.
1062 Marrakesh is built by the Berber dynasty of Almoravids.
1195 Almoravids are replaced by the Almohads, who conquer southern Spain.
1269 The capital is moved to Fez.
1415 The Portuguese capture the Moroccan port of Ceuta.

1492 Influx of Muslim and Jewish Andalusian refugees following the fall of Granada.
1524 Foundation of Saadian kingdom at Tagmadert.
1666 English occupy Tangier, introduce tea to Morocco.
1672 Alaouites under Moulay Rashid take power in Fez.
1860 Spanish wage war with Morocco, ultimately gaining land in Ceuta.
1904 France and Spain divide various areas of influence in Morocco.
1912 Treaty of Fez divides Morocco into protectorates controlled by France and Spain.
1943 Moroccan Independence Party, Istiqlal, is founded.
1956 Morocco declares independence from France.
1963 First general elections.
1975 Morocco occupies the Western Sahara.
1999 Accession of Mohammed VI to the throne.
2006 Introduction of cheap flights to Marrakesh.
2011 Bomb in Marrakesh kills fifteen people in April. Moderate Islamist PJD wins parliamentary elections in November.
2015 High turnout in local elections.

ARRIVAL AND DEPARTURE

To reach Morocco from Europe you can either fly or take a ferry. The main **airports** are in Casablanca, Fez and Marrakesh, the last of which is served regularly by budget airlines from UK and European airports. Ryanair (⊕ryanair .com) and easyJet (⊕easyjet.com) both sell cheap online tickets.

Ferries from Algeciras (Spain) take you to the new port of Tangier Med or the Spanish enclave of Ceuta. Ceuta is 3km from the Moroccan town of Fnideq, where you can take buses or shared taxis to Tangier or Tetouan. Tangier Med – also served by ferries from places like Sète, Genoa and Barcelona – is inconveniently situated but has shared *grands taxis* to Tangier. Only ferries from Tarifa (served by a free shuttle bus from Algeciras for ferry ticket holders) actually

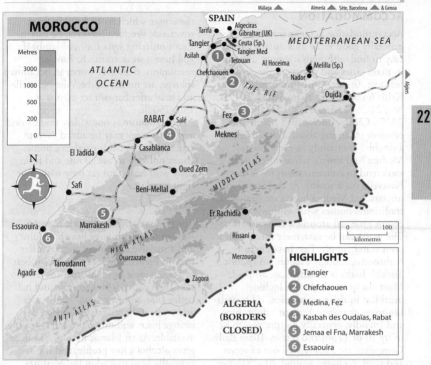

take you to Tangier, which has all the major transport links, and is itself worth a visit. Boat tickets can be booked online (ⓦtrasmediterranea.es, ⓦbalearia.com and ⓦfrs.es) or at the ports of departure.

GETTING AROUND

BY TRAIN

For travel between the major cities, **trains** are the best option. A table of direct and connecting services to any other station is available at any station ticket office or on the website of the national rail company, ONCF (ⓦwww.oncf.ma). Couchettes (154dh extra) are available on night trains from Tangier to Marrakesh (10hr 15min), and are worth the money for extra comfort and security. Only direct trains are listed in this chapter.

BY TAXI

Shared *grands taxis* are usually big Peugeots or Mercedes, plying set routes for a set fare, and are much quicker than buses, though the drivers can be reckless. Make clear you only want *une place* (one seat), otherwise drivers may assume you want to charter the whole car. Expect to wait until all six places in the taxi are taken, though you can pay for the extra places if you are in a hurry. Within towns **petits taxis** do short trips, carrying up to three people. They queue in central locations and at stations and can be hailed on streets when they're empty. Payment – usually no more than 20dh – depends on distance travelled.

BY BUS

Buses are marginally cheaper than shared *grands taxis*, and cover longer distances, but are slower. The national company, CTM (ⓦctm.ma), is the most reliable. Supratours (ⓦsupratours.ma) run express buses that connect to train services.

ACCOMMODATION

Accommodation is **inexpensive**, generally good value and usually pretty easy to find, although it's more difficult in main cities and resorts in the peak seasons: August, Christmas, and Aïd el Kebir (expected dates are Sept 1 2017; Aug 21 2018, Aug 11 2019, July 31 2020). Cheap, unclassified hotels and *pensions* (charging about 120–200dh for a double) are mainly in each town's Medina (old town), while hotels with stars tend to concentrate in the Ville Nouvelle (new town). At their best, unclassified Medina hotels are beautiful, traditional houses with whitewashed rooms grouped around a central patio. The worst can be extremely dirty, with a poor water supply. Few have en-suite bathrooms, though a hammam (public Turkish bath) is usually close at hand. Most cheap hotels do not include breakfast in their room price. HI hostels (*auberges de jeunesse*), often bright, breezy and friendly, generally require you to be in by 10 or 11pm and out by 10am daily. Campsites are usually well out of town and tend to charge around 20–25dh per person plus the same again for your tent.

FOOD AND DRINK

Moroccan cooking is wholesome and filling. The main dish is usually a **tajine** (casserole). Classic *tajines* include chicken with lemon and olives, and lamb with prunes and almonds. The most famous Moroccan dish is **couscous**, a huge bowl of steamed semolina piled with vegetables, mutton, chicken or fish. Restaurant starters include *salade marocaine*, a finely chopped salad of tomato and cucumber, most often the spicy, bean-based *harira*. Dessert will probably be fruit, yogurt or a pastry. **Breakfast** is cheapest if you buy *msimmen* or *melaoui* (which taste like pancakes), *harsha* (a heavy gritty griddle bread) or pastries from street-side shops and eat them at cafés.

The best **budget meals** are at local diners, where *tajines* or roast chicken with chips and salad are usually under 60dh. Even cheaper are sandwiches and *shwarmas*, which cost 15–20dh from street-side vendors; however, be careful about ordering *kefta* (minced lamb) if you have a weak stomach. Fancier restaurants, definitely worth an occasional splurge, are mostly in the Ville Nouvelle and may offer bargain set menus at 130–250dh.

Vegetarianism is not widely understood and meat stock may be added even to vegetable dishes. If invited to a home, you're unlikely to use a knife and fork; copy your hosts and eat only with your right hand.

DRINK

The national drink is **thé à la menthe** – green tea with a large bunch of mint and a massive amount of sugar. Coffee (*café* in French; *qahwa* in Arabic) is best in French-style cafés. Moroccans tend to take their coffee with half milk and half coffee (*nus-nus*) in a glass. Many cafés and street stalls sell freshly squeezed orange juice, and mineral water is readily available. As an Islamic nation, Morocco gives **alcohol** a low profile, and it's generally hard to find in the Medinas, although bars are always around in the Ville Nouvelle. Moroccan wines, usually red, can be very drinkable, while the best-value **beer** is Flag Speciale. Most local bars are male domains; hotel bars, on the other hand, are more mixed and not much more expensive. Supermarkets often sell alcohol; ask a *petit taxi* to take you to the nearest Acima or Marjane.

CULTURE AND ETIQUETTE

Morocco is a Muslim country, and in rural areas particularly, people can be quite **conservative** about dress and displays of affection. It's not the done thing to kiss and cuddle in public, nor even for couples to hold hands. Dress is more conservative in rural areas, though even in the cities you can feel uncomfortable in sleeveless tops, short shorts or skirts above the knee. The heat can also be oppressive, so long, light, loose clothing is best. A shawl allows women to cover up while wearing sleeveless tops.

SHOPPING

You can pick up bargains throughout Morocco, and you will kick yourself if you go home empty-handed. However, getting a price you can brag about in the hostel requires a willingness to enter into the spirit of **haggling**. The first price you will be given may be three to ten times more than the going rate; if you're a student, it's always worth pointing that out when bargaining. Though quality makes a difference, we've included rough prices for some popular goods you could reasonably fit into a backpack. Fixed-price shops in the Ville Nouvelle also give a good approximation of what you should be paying in the Medina.

- Small kilims (coarse rugs) 500–800dh
- Leather bags (cheaper in Fez than Marrakesh) 150–500dh
- Leather babouches (slippers) 50–250dh
- Cotton scarves 10–100dh
- Jelaba (traditional Moroccan dress) 200–2000dh

Be sensitive when taking **photographs**, and always ask permission. In certain places, particularly the Jemaa el Fna in Marrakesh, people may demand money from you just for happening to be in a shot you have taken. Also note that it is illegal to photograph anything considered strategic, such as an airport or a police station.

When invited into people's homes, remove footwear before entering the reception rooms. If invited for a meal, take a gift: a box of sweets from a posh patisserie usually goes down well.

It is acceptable (and a good idea) to try **bargaining** at every opportunity (see box above). If you do it with a smile, you can often get surprising reductions.

Morocco is inexpensive but poor, and **tips** can make a big difference; it's customary to tip café waiters a dirham or two.

SPORTS AND ACTIVITIES

Casablanca and Essaouira cater to **surfers**: the former has better waves while the latter is excellent for windsurfing. **Mohammedia**, a thirty-minute ride from both Rabat and Casablanca, is also a great destination for surfers. Tangier and Rabat have decent surf beaches but with less developed services.

The Moroccan mountain ranges offer great **hiking** opportunities. Good starting points include: Chefchaouen, in the Rif; Fez and Meknes near the Middle Atlas; and Marrakesh, two hours away from

Mount Toubkal – the second-highest mountain in Africa. Consult local tourist information offices or hotels for advice and details of the trails.

Horseriding is an increasingly popular tourist pursuit in Morocco. *La Roseraie Hotel*, located in the High Atlas, 60km from Marrakesh (☎0524 439128, ⓦlaroseraiehotel.com), is a great place from which to hire horses and venture into the mountainous countryside. Prices depend on your itinerary but it's not cheap.

Football is Morocco's most popular sport. You will see it being played in every conceivable open space. If you start up a game on a beach it won't be long before you are joined by some Moroccans; equally you'll usually be welcome in pick-up games. All the major cities have teams and money is being poured into new stadiums.

COMMUNICATIONS

Post offices (La Poste) are open Monday to Friday 8am to 4.15pm; larger ones stay open until 6pm, and open Saturday 8am to noon. You can also buy stamps at

MOROCCO ONLINE

ⓦ**muchmorocco.com** Moroccan tourist board's website.

ⓦ**babelfan.ma** Arts and culture, including information on festivals throughout Morocco, but in French only.

ⓦ**morocco.com** Huge collection of links to sites about every aspect of Morocco.

postcard shops and sometimes at tobacconists. International phone calls are best made with a phonecard (from post offices and some tobacconists). Alternatively, there are privately run *téléboutiques*, open late. You must dial all ten digits of Moroccan phone numbers. Internet access is available pretty much everywhere, and at low rates: 5–10dh per hour is typical. Tourist hotels (even cheap ones) often have wi-fi, as do some trendy cafés and all major rail stations; Casablanca even has a few public wi-fi hotspots.

22

EMERGENCIES

Street robbery is rare but not unknown, especially in Tangier and Casablanca. Hotels are generally secure for depositing money; campsites less so. There are two main types of **police** – grey-clad *gendarmes*, with authority outside city limits; and the navy-clad *sûreté* in towns. There's sometimes a brigade of "tourist police" too. Steer clear of marijuana (*kif*) and hashish – it's illegal, and buying it leaves you vulnerable to scams, as well as potentially large fines and prison sentences.

Moroccan **pharmacists** are well trained and dispense a wide range of drugs. In most cities there is a night pharmacy, often at the town hall, and a rota of *pharmacies de garde* that stay open till late and at weekends. You can get a list of English-speaking doctors in major cities from consulates.

Also be aware that there have been occasional bomb attacks on Western and tourist targets, the most recent occurring in 2011 at a café on Marrakesh's Jemaa el Fna, in which seventeen people were killed; you may wish to check the travel advice offered by organizations such as the US State Department (⑥ travel.state .gov) or UK Foreign Office (⑥ gov.uk /foreign-travel-advice) before visiting.

EMERGENCY NUMBERS

Police – *Sûreté* ❶ 19, *Gendarmes* ❶ 177; Fire and ambulance ❶ 15.

INFORMATION

There's a **tourist office** (Délégation du Tourisme) run by the Office National Marocain du Tourisme (ONMT) in every major city, and sometimes also a locally funded Syndicat d'Initiative. They stock a limited selection of leaflets and maps, and can put you in touch with official guides. Local bookshops and street-side kiosks sometimes sell local maps. There are scores of "unofficial guides", some of whom are students, while others are out-and-out hustlers (though these have been clamped down on). If they do find you, be polite but firm; note that it's illegal to harass tourists.

MONEY AND BANKS

The unit of currency is the **dirham** (dh), divided into 100 centimes; in markets, prices may be in centimes rather than dirhams. There are coins of 10c, 20c, 50c, 1dh, 5dh and 10dh, and notes of 20dh, 50dh, 100dh and 200dh. At the time of writing, £1 = 14dh, $1 = 9.80dh, €1 = 11.20dh. Note that different accommodation establishments quote their prices in different currencies. You can get dirhams in Algeciras (Spain) and Gibraltar, and can usually change foreign notes on arrival at major sea- and airports. For exchange purposes, the most useful and efficient chain of banks is the **BMCE** (Banque Marocaine du Commerce Extérieur). Post offices will also change cash, and there are **bureaux de change** in major cities and tourist resorts. Many banks give cash advances on credit cards, which can also be used in tourist hotels (but not cheap unclassified ones) and the ATMs of major banks. Banking hours are Monday to Friday 8.15am to 3.45pm (Mon–Fri 9.30am–2pm during the holy month of Ramadan).

OPENING HOURS AND HOLIDAYS

Shops and stalls in the souk (bazaar) areas open roughly 9am to 1pm and 3 to 6pm. Ville Nouvelle shops are also likely to close for lunch, and also once a week, usually Sunday. Islamic **religious holidays** are calculated on the lunar calendar and

MOROCCAN ARABIC

Moroccan Arabic is the country's official language, and there are three Berber languages, but much of the country is bilingual in French. For some useful French words and phrases see p.280.

	MOROCCAN ARABIC
Yes	Eyeh
No	La
Please	Afek/Minfadlik
Thank you	Shukran
Hello	Assalam aleikum
Goodbye	Bissalama
Excuse me	Issmahli
Where?	Fayn?
Good	Mezziyen
Bad	Mish Mezziyen
Near (here)	Krayb (min hina)
Far	Baeed
Cheap	Rkhis
Expensive	Ghalee
Open	Mahlul
Closed	Masdud
Today	El Yoom
Yesterday	Imbarih
Tomorrow	Ghedda
How much is...?	Shahal...?
What time is it?	Shahal fisa'a?
I (m) don't understand	Ana mish fahim
I (f) don't understand	Ana mish fahma
Do you (m) speak English?	Takellem ingleezi?
Do you (f) speak English?	Takelma ingleezi?
One	Wahad
Two	Jooj
Three	Tlata
Four	Arba'a
Five	Khamsa
Six	Sitta
Seven	Seba'a
Eight	Temeniya
Nine	Tisaoud
Ten	Ashra

22

change each year. In 2017–2020 they fall (approximately) as follows: Ramadan (when all Muslims fast from sunrise to sunset) is in May–June; the end of Ramadan is celebrated with Aïd es Seghir (aka Aïd el Fitr), a two-day holiday; Aïd el Kebir, in August or September, is when Abraham offered to sacrifice his son for God; the Muslim New Year is a couple of weeks after that, with Mouloud (the birthday of Mohammed) in November or December. Non-Muslims are not expected to observe Ramadan, but should be sensitive about not breaking the fast in public. **Secular holidays** are considered less important, with most public services (except banks and offices) operating normally even during the two biggest ones – the Feast of the Throne (July 30), and Independence Day (Nov 18).

Northern Morocco

The northern tip of Morocco alone justifies the short ferry ride from Spain: in three days or so you could check out

22

the delightfully seedy city of **Tangier** and the picturesque mountain town of **Chefchaouen** in the Rif Mountains.

TANGIER

For the first half of the twentieth century TANGIER (Tanja in Arabic; Tanger in French) was an "International City" with its own laws and administration, attracting notoriety through its flamboyant expat community. With independence in 1956, this special status was removed and the expat colony dwindled. Its mixed colonial history and proximity to Spain means that Spanish is a preferred second language. Today Tangier is a grimy but energetic port, mixing modern nightclubs and seedy Moroccan bars with some fine colonial architecture.

The **Grand Socco**, or Zoco Grande – once the main market square (and, since Independence, officially Place du 9 Avril 1947) – offers the most straightforward approach to the Medina. The arch at the northern end opens onto Rue d'Italie, which leads up to the **Kasbah**. To the right, Rue es Siaghin leads to the atmospheric but seedy **Petit Socco**, or Zoco Chico, the Medina's main square. Rue des Almohades (aka Rue des Chrétiens) and Rue Ben Raisouli lead to the lower gate.

Kasbah

The **Kasbah** (citadel), walled off from the Medina on the highest rise of the coast, has been the palace and administrative quarter since Roman times. The main point of interest is the former Sultanate Palace, or **Dar el Makhzen** (Mon & Wed–Sun 9–11.30am & 1.30–4pm; 10dh), now converted into a museum of crafts and antiquities, which gives you an excuse to look around, though the exhibits are rather sparse.

Beaches

Tangier's best **beaches** are a twenty-minute ride out of town. There are few vendors selling refreshments, so it's best to bring your own food and drink. **Plage Sidi Kacem** has a trendy beach restaurant,

L'Océan (daily noon–5pm; ☎0539 338137), which rents out deckchairs and serves hamburgers and European food, as well as being licensed. A *petit taxi* from town will cost around 150dh each way.

Caves of Hercules

Perhaps the area's most popular tourist spot is the **Caves of Hercules** (Grottes d'Hercule), 16km southwest of town, where the sea has eroded the cave entrance to form the shape of Africa. In summer there are very occasional buses (#2 from St Andrew's Church near the Grand Socco), but otherwise you'll have to charter a *grand taxi* to get here (around 100dh for the round trip including waiting time. The caves (9am–sunset; 5dh) have been occupied since prehistoric times, later serving as a quarry for millstones (you can see the erosion on the walls) and in the 1920s becoming a rather exotic brothel.

ARRIVAL AND DEPARTURE

By plane The airport is 15km southwest of the city centre. A *petit taxi* into town is 150dh.

By train All trains terminate at Tanger Ville station 2km east of town. A *petit taxi* into town is around 20dh on the meter, but drivers may demand more. The overnight train from Tangier to Marrakesh allows you to venture south without losing time.

Destinations Casablanca Voyageurs (8 daily; 4hr 40min); Fez (3 daily; 4hr 35min); Marrakesh (1 nightly; 10hr 15min); Meknes (3 daily; 4hr); Rabat (8 daily; 3hr 40min).

By bus The *gare routière* bus station, used by all intercity buses and shared *grands taxis*, is 1.5km southeast of the centre on Av Youssef Ben Tachfine.

Destinations Casablanca (14 daily; 6hr); Chefchaouen (11 daily; 3hr); Fez (8 daily; 7hr); Fnideq (for Ceuta; 10 daily; 2hr); Marrakesh (6 daily; 9hr 30min); Meknes (11 daily; 5hr); Rabat (14 daily; 5hr); Tetouan (24 daily; 1hr 30min).

By boat Ferries from Tarifa dock at the terminal immediately below the Medina, while ferries from Algeciras arrive at Tangier Med, 40km east of town.

Destinations from Tangier (city) Tarifa (12 daily; 1hr).

Destinations from Tangier Med Algeciras (16–22 daily; 1hr–2hr 30min); Genoa, Italy (2 weekly; 48hr); Gibraltar (1 weekly; 1hr 30min); Sète, France (3 weekly; 35–40hr).

INFORMATION

Tourist information The tourist office is at 29 Bd Pasteur, just down from Place de France (Mon–Fri 8.30am–4.30pm; ☎0539 948050).

ACCOMMODATION

There are dozens of hotels and *pensions*, but the city can get crowded in summer, when some places double their prices.

MEDINA

Al-Andalusi 64 Rue Ibn Battuta 0539 936052. Friendly hostel with dorm rooms sleeping 2–4, as well as a welcoming salon and a rooftop terrace with sweeping views of the city. Dorms 125dh

Mamora 19 Rue des Postes 0539 934105. A good-value option with pleasant rooms, some with en-suite showers; make sure you ask for a room facing the mosque, as the views are worth it. Doubles 120dh

Melting Pot 3 Rue de Tsouli 0539 331508, meltingpothostels.com. Clean and well-run hostel with a choice of double rooms or dorms sleeping 4–8. Bathrooms are shared but there's plenty of hot water. Dorms €11, doubles €35

VILLE NOUVELLE

Camping Miramonte Off Rue Shakespeare, 300m west of Stade Marshan 0672 207055, campingmiramonte .com. Often closed for no apparent reason, so call ahead before trekking out here. Per person 25dh, plus per tent 25dh

★ **El Muniria** 1 Rue Magellan 0539 935337. Pick of Tangier's hotels, decorated in a laidback modern Moroccan style. William Burroughs wrote his most famous book, *The Naked Lunch*, here. Doubles 250dh

Magellan 16 Rue Magellan 0539 372319. Great value for money: sparkling clean with tangerine-coloured public areas and tastefully painted rooms. Doubles 150dh

Pension Dar Omar Khayam 8 Rue el Antaki 0539 343036, daromarkhayam.com. Former convent with cell-like singles or a/c en-suite doubles. Rooms at the back are quieter. Doubles 150dh

Pension Miami 126 Rue de la Plage 0539 932900. Beautifully tiled old Spanish townhouse with pleasant rooms, and bathrooms on each corridor. Doubles 150dh

EATING

Tangier is best enjoyed from a café, and the Petit Socco is packed with them, each offering the opportunity to relax and observe the hustle on the street. The two main centres for food in general are the Grand Socco, where you can pick up cheap, filling Moroccan staples, and the more diverse (and licensed) strip on Av d'Espagne.

CAFÉS, CHEAP EATS AND SNACKS

Africa 83 Rue de la Plage. The 55dh (plus 7dh tax) four-course set menu here is one of the best bargains in town, or you can settle for the usual *tajine* and brochette dishes instead (45–65dh). Daily 11am–10pm.

Café de Paris Place de France. For a more upmarket choice, head to Tangier's most famous and reputedly oldest café. Daily 7am–11pm.

Café Hafa Off Rue Shakespeare by the Punic Tombs. Cut into the cliff face and looking across the Mediterranean to Spain, this place offers basic snacks (including *bissara*, a fava bean soup usually eaten for breakfast) and cakes or croissants to go with your tea. Daily 10am–7pm.

Dolcy's Eastern end of Bd Pasteur. A great spot for breakfast, offering eggs, toasted sandwiches and fresh juices. Daily 7am–11pm.

Eric's Hamburger Shop Arcade Mentoubi, between Bd pasteur and Rue el Moutanabi. Wooden stools lined up against a stainless-steel counter, and a menu consisting of hamburgers and hot dogs. Daily 24hr.

RESTAURANTS

Anna e Paolo 77 Rue Prince Heritier 0539 944617. The pastas are the speciality at this Italian family-run restaurant (mains 75–145dh). Licensed. Mon–Sat noon–3pm & 7.30–11pm.

El Dorado 23 Rue Allal ben Abdallah. There's a wide variety of marine denizens to be had at this Spanish fish restaurant, as well as couscous on Fridays and paella on Sundays (mains 60–140dh). Daily noon–3pm & 7.30–11pm.

Le Nabab 4 Rue al Kadiria 0661 442220. Former *fondouk* (or caravanserai, an old merchants' hostel) restored to a classy restaurant. The Moroccan menu includes both traditional dishes and some more inventive offerings. Mains 90–140dh, set menu 175dh. Mon–Sat noon–3pm & 7.30–11pm.

Rif Kabdani 14 Rue dar el Baroud 0539 371760. Small French-style bistro with a menu of Moroccan standards, complimentary tapas and mint tea. Mains 55–85dh. Daily noon–10pm.

San Remo 15 Rue Ahmed Chaouki 0539 938451. Good-value Mediterranean cooking, including seafood and meat grills (mains 70–240dh), and pizzas. They also have a cheaper pizzeria across the road. Daily noon–3pm & 7–11pm.

Valencia 6 Av Youssef Ben Tachfine 0539 945146. Very popular fish restaurant, whose straightforward menu includes a variety of fried and grilled dishes (mains 35–80dh). Mon & Wed–Sun 11am–10pm.

DRINKING AND NIGHTLIFE

Many of Tangier's nightlife venues attract a rather seedy crowd; the places listed here are the most dependable.

Atlas Bar 30 Rue Prince Héritier. Intimate, atmospheric dive-bar that's been serving beer and tapas (and barely changed) since 1928. Daily 8pm–1am.

Dean's Bar 2 Rue d'Amérique du Sud. Former haunt of Tennessee Williams, Francis Bacon and Ian Fleming, now a smoky but cheap and welcoming Moroccan drinking hole. Daily noon till late.

22

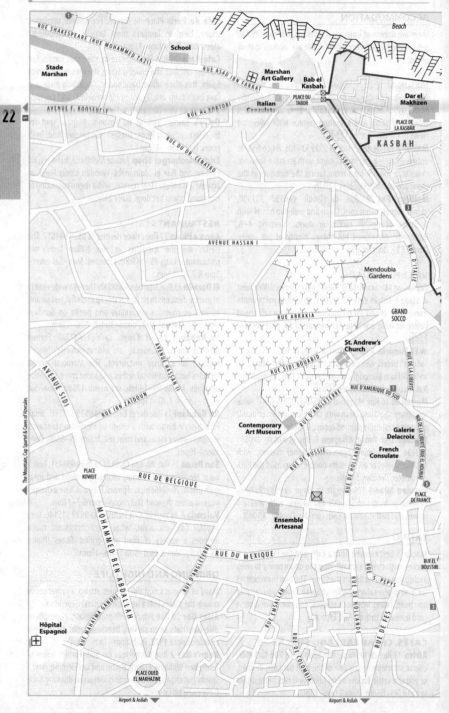

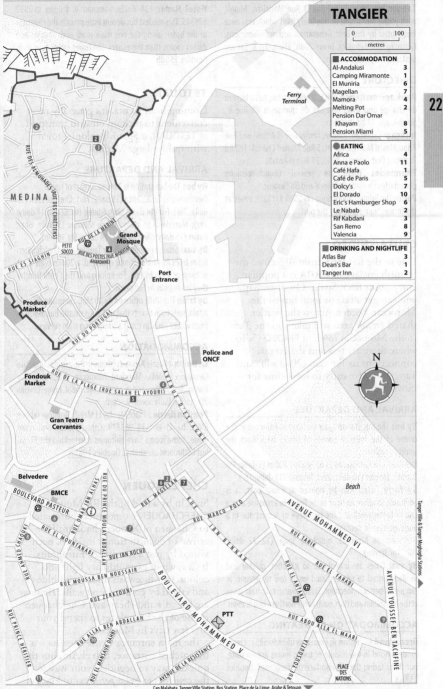

TANGIER

0 — 100 metres

ACCOMMODATION

Al-Andalusi	3
Camping Miramonte	1
El Muniria	6
Magellan	7
Mamora	4
Melting Pot	2
Pension Dar Omar Khayam	8
Pension Miami	5

EATING

Africa	4
Anna e Paolo	11
Café Hafa	1
Café de Paris	7
Dolcy's	7
El Dorado	10
Eric's Hamburger Shop	6
Le Nabab	2
Rif Kabdani	3
San Remo	8
Valencia	9

DRINKING AND NIGHTLIFE

Atlas Bar	3
Dean's Bar	1
Tanger Inn	2

Ferry Terminal

MEDINA

RUE DES ALMOHADES (RUE DES CHRETIENS)

RUE DE LA MARINE

Grand Mosque

PETIT SOCCO

RUE ES SIAGHIN

RUE DES POSTES (RUE MOKHTAR AHARDANE)

Port Entrance

Produce Market

RUE DU PORTUGAL

Police and ONCF

Fondouk Market

RUE DE LA PLAGE (RUE SALAH EL AYOURI)

AVENUE D'ESPAGNE

Gran Teatro Cervantes

N

Beach

Belvedere

BMCE

BOULEVARD PASTEUR

RUE DU PRINCE MOULAY ABDALLAH

RUE OMAR IBN ALKHYS

RUE EL MOUNTANABI

RUE AHMED CHAQUI

RUE IBN ROCHD

RUE MAGELLAN

RUE MARCO POLO

RUE IBN BENNAR

AVENUE MOHAMMED VI

RUE TARIK

RUE EL FARABI

RUE MOUSSA BEN NOUSSAIR

BOULEVARD MOHAMMED V

RUE ZERKTOUNI

RUE EL ANTAKI

RUE ABOU ALLA EL MAARI

AVENUE YOUSSEF BEN TACHFINE

RUE ALLAL BEN ABDALLAH

PTT

RUE PRINCE HERITIER

RUE EL MANSAUR DAHBI

AVENUE DE LA RESISTANCE

AVENUE MOHAMMED V

RUE YOUSSOUFIA

PLACE DES NATIONS

Tanger Ville & Tanger Moghogha Stations

Cap Malabata, Tanger Ville Station, Bus Station, Place de la Ligue, Arabe & Tetouan ▼

Tanger Inn Hotel El Muniria, 1 Rue Magellan. Mingle with young Moroccans at this lively joint which was once frequented by the Beat Generation authors (Burroughs, Ginsberg and Kerouac); beers 20dh. Thurs, Fri & Sat are best. Mon–Sat 10pm–2am.

DIRECTORY

Bank and exchange BMCE, 21 Bd Pasteur, has a bureau de change and ATM. Bureaux de change at 68 Rue es Siaghin and 47 Bd Pasteur.
Internet Cybercafé Juliana, corner Rue el Antaki and Rue Abou Alaa al Maari; Euronet, 5 Rue Ahmed Chaouki (off Bd Pasteur); Club Internet 3000, 27 Rue el Antaki.
Pharmacies There are several English-speaking pharmacies on Place de France and Bd Pasteur.
Police The Brigade Touristique (✆ 0539 931129), based at the former train station by the port.

CEUTA/FNIDEQ

Due to the fast ferry from Algeciras, the Spanish enclave of **CEUTA** is a popular entry point from Spain. On disembarking you can get a taxi or local bus to the Moroccan border. Across the border, shared *grands taxis* will take you the 3km to the Moroccan town of **FNIDEQ** (5dh) where there are bus and shared taxi connections to Tetouan (20–35dh) and Tangier. Arrive early to leave time for moving on.

ARRIVAL AND DEPARTURE

By bus The bus station (*gare routière*) in Fnideq is in the centre of the town, a couple of blocks back from the seafront highway.
Destinations Casablanca (3 daily; 6hr); Rabat (3 daily; 4hr 30min); Tangier (10 daily; 2hr); Tetouan (11 daily; 1hr).
By ferry Tickets can be booked at Ceuta port; it is advisable to arrive an hour early. Times to avoid are at the end of Easter week and the last week of August due to a huge increase in demand.
Destinations Algeciras, mainland Spain (12–22 daily; 1hr–1hr 30min).
By taxi Buses are infrequent, so it's often quicker and similarly priced to get a shared *grand taxi* to Tetouan or Tangier for better connections. Shared *grands taxis* have ranks at the bus station and (for Ceuta) at the northern end of town.

ACCOMMODATION AND EATING

Dreamland Av Hassan II, Fnideq ✆ 0539 976357. Clean, modern hotel in the middle of town; rooms are en suite, but those facing the sea also face the busy road. Doubles 258dh

Hotel Nador 134 Av Mohammad V, Fnideq ✆ 0539 675345. This modest but decent little place is the cheapest of the hotels along the one main road, with smaller and darker rooms than the others, but lower prices to match. Doubles 150dh

TETOUAN

Coming from Ceuta, it's generally most convenient to pick up onward transport at **TETOUAN**, a Spanish colonial town with quite a large Medina.

ARRIVAL AND DEPARTURE

By bus The bus station is 1km southeast of town.
Destinations Casablanca (15 daily; 7hr); Chefchaouen (15 daily; 2hr); Fez (14 daily; 6hr); Fnideq (for Ceuta; 11 daily; 1hr); Marrakesh (6 daily; 10hr); Meknes (5 daily; 6hr); Rabat (15 daily; 6hr); Tangier (24 daily; 1hr 30min).
By taxi Shared *grands taxis* for Tangier and Chefchaouen leave from Av Khaled Ibnou el Oualid, a 20min walk west of town or 15dh by taxi. For Fnideq and the Ceuta frontier they leave from Av Hassan II.
By train The ONCF office on Av 10 Mai, alongside Place Al Adala, sells train tickets that include a shuttle bus to Asilah from where you can catch a connecting train service.

ACCOMMODATION

La Unión 1 Pasaje Achaach (through the arcades opposite Cinema Español). Standard Moroccan fare, including *harira*, brochettes and a reasonable meat *tajine* (mains 25–40dh). Daily noon–9.30pm.
Pensión Iberia 5 Place Moulay el Mehdi, 3rd floor (above BMCE bank) ✆ 0533 963679. Central, clean and good value. Some rooms have balconies overlooking the Plaza, but bathrooms are shared. Doubles 108dh

CHEFCHAOUEN

Shut in by a fold of the Rif Mountains, **CHEFCHAOUEN** (sometimes abbreviated to Chaouen or Xaouen) had, until the arrival of Spanish troops in 1920, been visited by just a handful of Europeans. It's a town of extraordinary light and colour, its whitewash tinted with blue and edged by golden stone walls. *Pensions* are friendly and cheap and Chefchaouen is one of the best places to spend your first few days in Morocco.

The main entrance to the Medina is a tiny arched entrance, Bab el Ain, but the quickest way to negotiate your way to the centre is to get a *petit taxi* to **Place el**

Makhzen (ask for the Kasbah), where you will find *Hotel Parador*, an expensive hotel but a good place to pop into for a beer or a swim. From here it is only a two-minute walk to **Place Outa el Hammam**, where most of the town's evening life takes place. By day the town's focus is the **Kasbah** (Mon, Wed, Thurs & Sun 10am–2pm & 4–7.30pm, Tues 4–7.30pm, Fri 10am–1pm & 4–7.30pm; 10dh), a quiet ruin with shady gardens and a small museum, which occupies one side of the square.

Chefchaouen is best enjoyed pottering around the Medina or relaxing at coffee shops. For the more adventurous there are **hiking** trails that start from the town. Or you can charter a *grand taxi* from Place el Makhzen to go to the **Oued Laou beach**, about 60km away, or hike along rivers and waterfalls at **Akchour**, a thirty-minute *grand taxi* ride away.

ARRIVAL AND DEPARTURE

By bus Buses arrive at the station southwest of town; it's a 15min uphill walk into the centre, or a 10dh *petit taxi* ride. Buy tickets a day in advance for Fez and Meknes.
Destinations Casablanca (3 daily; 6hr); Fez (9 daily; 4hr 30min); Meknes (3 daily; 5hr 30min); Rabat (3 daily; 5hr); Tangier (11 daily; 3hr); Tetouan (15 daily; 2hr).
By shared taxi Tangier and Tetouan services operate from Av Jamal Dine el Afghani, off the west side of Pl Mohammed V.

ACCOMMODATION

Camping Azilan Rue Sidi Abdelhamid ☎0539 986979. Located up on the hill above town, by the modern *Hôtel Asma*. Chefchaouen's campsite is inexpensive but can be crowded in summer. Price is for two people and a tent. **95dh**
Hotel Andaluz 1 Rue Sidi Salem ☎0539 986034. Behind the jolly blue-and-white entrance, the rooms are a bit sombre, but staff are friendly and there's a very decent English-language book collection. Doubles **120dh**
Hotel Ouarzazat Rue de Alkharazine ☎0539 988990. Rooms are decked out in local furniture and bathrooms are pretty spick and span. Doubles **140dh**
Hotel Salam 39 Av Hassan II ☎0539 986239. Cheap, friendly and a favourite with backpackers who don't want to be in the Medina, with high-ceilinged rooms and shared bathrooms. Doubles **120dh**
Pension La Castellena 4 Sidi Ahmed El Bouhali ☎0539 986295. The rooms are a little bit small at this perennially popular *pension*, but they're all beautifully decorated,

individually furnished and painted by hand with colourful motifs. Doubles **150dh**

EATING AND DRINKING

Al Azhar At the bottom of the steps on Av Moulay Idriss. Popular local snack restaurant with good food and service. Fast and cheap (mains 20–50dh). Daily 10am–10pm.
Assada On a nameless lane just north of Bab el Aïn, opposite the *Hôtel Bab el Aïn*. Extending across the lane and above to an open rooftop terrace, a favourite of locals and travellers alike. Food served all day (breakfasts 18–25dh, mains 20–45dh). Daily 9am–9pm.
Casa Aladin Rue Targi 17, off the north end of Place Outa El Hammam. Two floors and a terrace, beautifully done out in *Arabian Nights* style, as its name suggests, serving great *tajines*, couscous (including vegetarian) and other staples (mains 45–85dh, set menus 75dh). Daily 11am–11pm.

22

Central Morocco

Between the mountain ranges of the Rif to the north and the Atlas to the south lie the cities that form Morocco's heart: the great imperial centres of **Meknes** and **Fez**, the modern capital, **Rabat**, and the country's largest city and commercial capital, **Casablanca**.

MEKNES

More than any other Moroccan town, **MEKNES** is associated with a single figure, the Sultan Moulay Ismail, during whose reign (1672–1727) the city went from provincial centre to spectacular capital showcasing over fifty palaces and 24m of exterior walls. Today Meknes is a more sedate and calm version of Marrakesh, and the palaces and monuments of its Medina reward a day's exploration. The town also serves as a perfect base to explore the nearby ancient site of **Volubilis** and holy town of **Moulay Idriss**.

WHAT TO SEE AND DO

The heart of the town, **Place El Hedim**, originally formed the western corner of the Medina, but Moulay Ismail had the houses here demolished to provide a grand approach to his palace quarter. There are a fair few sights to explore leading off the *place*.

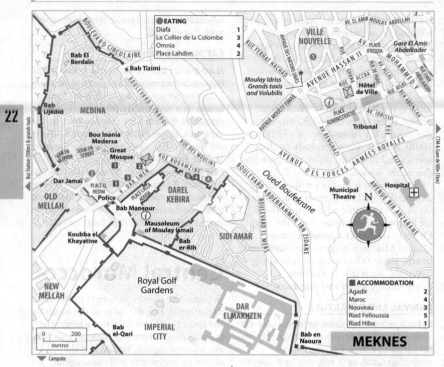

22

Bus Station (500m) & grands taxis

Dar Jamaï and the souks

The **Dar Jamaï** (Mon & Wed–Sun 9am–6pm; 10dh), at the back of Place El Hedim, is a superb example of a nineteenth-century Moroccan palace, and the museum inside is one of the best in Morocco, with a fantastic display of Middle Atlas carpets. The lane immediately to the left of the Dar Jamaï takes you to the Medina's major market street: on your left is **Souk en Nejjarin**, the carpet souk; on your right, leading to the Great Mosque and Bou Inania Medersa (a *medersa* is a Koranic school), are the fancier goods offered in the **Souk es Sebbat**. The **Bou Inania Medersa** (daily 9am–6pm; 10dh), constructed around 1340–50, has an unusual ribbed dome over the entrance hall, and from the roof you can look out to the tiled pyramids of the Great Mosque.

Koubba el Khayatine and Moulay Ismail's Mausoleum

Behind the magnificent Bab Mansour (open for occasional exhibitions) is Place

Lalla Aouda. Straight ahead from that gate, and bearing left, you come into another open square, on the right of which is the green-tiled dome of the **Koubba el Khayatine** (daily 10am–6pm; 10dh), once a reception hall for ambassadors to the imperial court. Below it a stairway descends into a vast series of subterranean vaults, known as the **Prison of Christian Slaves**, though it was probably a storehouse or granary. Nearby is the entrance to **Moulay Ismail's Mausoleum** (Mon–Thurs, Sat & Sun 9am–noon & 2.30–6pm; free), where you can approach the sanctuary.

Moulay Idriss and Volubilis

A short *grand taxi* ride from Meknes takes you to two of the most important sites in Morocco's history. **Moulay Idriss**, 25km north of Meknes (10dh by shared *grand taxi* from Avenue des Nations Unies) was established by the Prophet's great-grandson, who is credited with bringing Islam to Morocco. Today, it is a small but bustling town, which

Moroccans treat with great respect. It is worth a trip for the views from the top of the town and for an insight into the religious heart of Morocco (particularly true in the **festival**, or *moussem*, that takes place in the second week of August). Note that non-Muslims are barred from visiting the religious shrines of Moulay Idriss for which the town is famous.

Five kilometres northwest of Moulay Idriss, **Volubilis** (daily 8am–6.30pm; 10dh) was once the Roman capital of the province; it's still possible to follow the outline of the old city and walk among some well-preserved ruins. A small on-site museum houses Roman artefacts found here.

ARRIVAL AND INFORMATION

By train Meknes has two train stations, both in the Ville Nouvelle. All trains stop at Gare de Ville, but Gare el Amir Abdelkader (some services only) is more central.

Destinations Casablanca Voyageurs (19 daily; 3hr); Fez (23 daily; 40min); Marrakesh (8 daily; 6hr 55min); Rabat (19 daily; 2hr); Tangier (4 daily; 4hr).

By bus and taxi Private buses and most shared *grands taxis* arrive west of the Medina by Bab el Khemis. CTM buses arrive at their terminus on Av de Fès, near the Gare de Ville.

Destinations (private) Casablanca (10 daily; 4hr 30min); Chefchaouen (3 daily; 5hr 30min); Fez (12 daily; 1hr); Marrakesh (8 daily; 9hr); Rabat (10 daily; 2hr 30min); Tangier (9 daily; 5hr 30min); Tetouan (4 daily; 6hr).

Destinations (CTM) Casablanca (9 daily; 4hr); Fez (15 daily; 1hr); Marrakesh (3 daily; 7hr 15min); Rabat (10 daily; 2hr); Tangier (5 daily; 5hr); Tetouan (1 daily; 6hr).

Tourist information 27 Place Administrative, Ville Nouvelle (Mon–Fri 8.30am–4.30pm, Sat 8–11am; ☎0535 516022).

ACCOMMODATION

All places listed here are in the Medina, the most atmospheric place to stay, where everything is on your doorstep.

Agadir 9 Rue Dar Smen ☎0535 530141. Clean and friendly, with small basic rooms tucked away in odd crannies of an eccentric, rambling building. Hot showers are available (7dh), and there's a hammam nearby. Doubles 100dh

Maroc 7 Rue Rouamzine ☎0535 530075. The spartan rooms on the interior courtyard benefit from a welcome cross-breeze, while the hole-in-the-floor bathrooms could do with similar ventilation. In summer, those on restricted budgets can sleep on the roof terrace for 50dh. Doubles 200dh

★TREAT YOURSELF

Riad Felloussia 23 Derb Hammam Jdid ☎0535 530840, ⊕riadfelloussia.com. The quaint labyrinthine corridor leads to a beautiful indoor garden with tiled fountain and cedar beams, and the *Riad*'s four suites are beautifully decorated with local fabrics and materials. Breathtaking views from the rooftop terrace, too. Breakfast included. Doubles €90

Nouveau 65 Rue Dar Smen ☎0667 309317. This blue-tiled place claims to be the first hotel in the Medina (despite the name). It's cool and shady, but staff are rather surly, the facilities are basic and there are no external windows. Hot showers 5dh. Doubles 120dh

Riad Hiba 20 Rue Lalla Aicha Addouya ☎0535 460109, ⊕riadhiba.net. Heavy ornate furnishings and added bonuses like flatscreen cable TV, a/c and wi-fi. Breakfast included. Doubles €32

EATING

There are cheap eats on Rue Rouamzine near *Hôtel Maroc* and you can also pick up inexpensive bites from one of the many restaurants in Place Hedim.

Diafa 12 Rue Badr el Kobra ☎0535 528302. Looks like a private house, with extremely good and reasonably priced cooking, but only a choice of five mains on the menu (set menu 150dh). Daily noon–midnight.

Le Collier de la Colombe 67 Rue Driba ☎0535 555041. The speciality here is Atlas mountain trout, to be savoured on the rooftop terrace with sunset views over the golden Medina. Mains from 80dh. Daily 11am–3pm & 7pm–midnight.

Omnia 8 Derb Ain El Fouki. Friendly restaurant set in a family home courtyard brimming with local knick-knacks. Sit in one of the little cushioned salons as fresh aromas waft out of the kitchen. Mains around 85dh. Daily noon–3pm & 7–10pm.

Place Lahdim Derb Sidi Amar Bouaouada (just off the northern corner of Place El Hedim). Tuck into generous portions of tasty Moroccan food or unwind on the terrace with some mint tea as you watch the world go by in the square below. Daily 8.30am–11pm.

FEZ (FÈS)

The most ancient of the imperial capitals, **FEZ** (Fès in French) stimulates the senses with its colours, sounds and smells, and seems to exist somewhere between the Middle Ages and the modern world. Some two hundred thousand of the city's

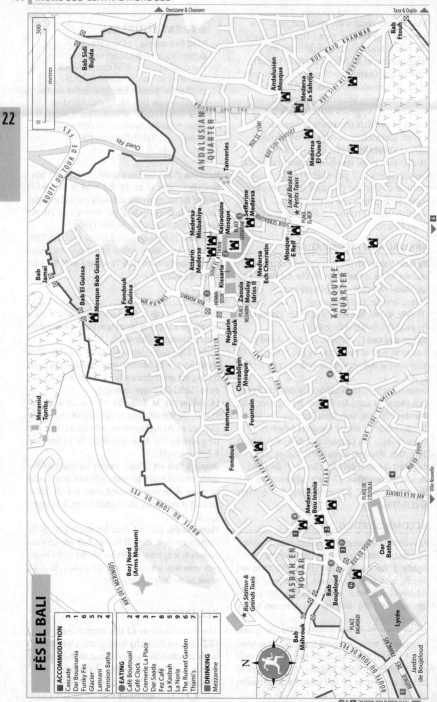

FÈS EL BALI

ACCOMMODATION

Cascade	3
Dar Bouanania	1
Funky Fès	6
Glacier	5
Lamrani	2
Pension Batha	4

EATING

Café Boutouail	2
Café Clock	4
Cremerie La Place	3
Dar Saada	8
Fez Café	5
La Kasbah	9
La Noria	6
Thami's	7

DRINKING

Mezzanine	1

Bab Sidi Bujida

Bab Frouh

RUE KAID KHAMMAR

Andalusian Mosque

Medersa Es Sahrija

RUE SIDI ALI BOUGHALEB

RUE SIDI BOUJIDA

ANDALUSIAN QUARTER

Tanneries

RUE ES TEM

RUE SIDI YOUSSEF

Medersa El Oued

Bab El Frouh

Oued Fès

ROUTE DU TOUR DE FÈS

Medersa Misbahiya

Kairaouine Mosque

Seffarine Medersa

Local Buses & Petits Taxis

PLACE SEFFARINE

SOUK SEBBAGHINE

PLACE EL NEJJARIN

Bab Jamai

Bab El Guissa

Mosque Bab Guissa

Fondouk Guissa

RUE HOMIS

Attarin Medersa

SOUK EL ATTARIN

Kissaria

Mosque E Reif

Medersa Ech Cherratin

HENNA SOUK

RUE HORMIS

Zaouia Moulay Idriss II

KAIROUINE QUARTER

Nejjarin Fondouk

PLACE NEJJARIN

RUE CHERABLIYIN

SAFI

RUE BEN

Merenid Tombs

Cherabliyin Mosque

Hammam

Fountain

RUE SIDI EL MIYAT

Fondouk

AVE DES MERINIDS

Borj Nord (Arms Museum)

TALAA SEGHIRA

TALAA KEBIRA

RUE ED DOUH

Medersa Bou Inania

PLACE DE L'ISTIQLAL

AVE DE LA LIBERTE

Bus Station & Grands Taxis

ROUTE DU TOUR DE FÈS

KASBAH EN NOUAR

Bab Boujeloud

Dar Batha

RUE ED DOUH

PLACE BAGHDADI

Lycée

Bab Mahrouk

Jardins de Boujeloud

AVENUE DES FRANÇAIS

ROUTE DU TOUR DE FÈS

N

300

0

metres

FEZ ORIENTATION

The Medina in Fez is uniquely vast and beautiful, with two distinct parts: the newer section, **Fès el Jedid**, established in the thirteenth century, is mostly taken up by the Royal Palace; the older part, **Fès el Bali**, founded in the eighth century on the River Fez, was populated by refugees from Tunisia on one bank – the **Kairaouine** quarter – and from Spain on the other bank – the **Andalusian** quarter. In practice, almost everything you will want to see is in the Kairaouine quarter.

There are several different gates through which you can enter Fès el Bali. The blue-tiled **Bab Boujeloud** gateway at its western end is the most popular and recognizable entry point and is a useful landmark. From here you can turn left at the *Restaurant La Kasbah* to get on to Talâa Kebira, the Medina's main thoroughfare. From the north, **Bab el Guissa** offers another port of entry. For views of the Medina, have a drink at the *Hotel Palais Jamaï* (next to Bab Jamaï) or *Hotel les Merinides*. There's also an impressive view from the **Arms Museum** in the fort above the bus station (Mon & Wed–Sun 8.30am–noon & 2.30–6pm; 30dh).

22

---

half-million inhabitants (though actual figures are probably much higher than official ones) live in the oldest part of the Medina, Fès el Bali.

WHAT TO SEE AND DO

Getting lost is one of the great joys of the Fez Medina. However, if you want a more informed approach, pick up a small green book called *Fès* from newsstands (100dh); it ties in with tourist trails in the Medina that are marked out by coloured stars. Tour guides can be found at Bab Boujeloud; the official ones wear medallions to identify themselves.

Talâa Kebira
Talâa Kebira, the Medina's main artery, is home to the most brilliant of Fez's monuments, the **Medersa Bou Inania** (daily 9am–5.30pm; closes 4pm during Ramadan, and sometimes closes briefly for prayers; 10dh), which comes close to perfection in every aspect of its construction, with beautiful carved wood, stucco and *zellij* tilework. Continuing down Talâa Kebira you reach the entrance to the **Souk el Attarin** (Souk of the Spice Vendors), the heart of the city. To the right, a street leads past the charming **Souk el Henna** – a tree-shaded square where traditional cosmetics are sold – to Place Nejjarin (Carpenters' Square). Here, next to the geometric tilework of the Nejjarin Fountain, is the imposing eighteenth-century **Nejjarin Fondouk**, now a woodwork museum (daily 10am–5pm; 20dh), though the building

is rather more interesting than its exhibits. Immediately to the right of the fountain, Talâa Seghira is an alternative route back to Bab Boujeloud, while the alley to the right of that is the aromatic **carpenters' souk**, ripe with the scent of sawn cedar, and top on the list of great Medina smells.

Zaouia Moulay Idriss II
The street opposite the Nejjarin Fountain leads to the **Zaouia Moulay Idriss II**, one of the holiest buildings in the city. A *zaouia* is a shrine dedicated to a local saint: buried here is the son and successor of Fez's founder, who continued his father's work. Only Muslims may enter to check out the *zellij* tilework, original wooden *minbar* (pulpit) and the tomb itself. Just to its east is the Kissaria, where fine fabrics are traded. Over to your left (on the other side of the Kissaria), Souk el Attarin comes to an end opposite the fourteenth-century **Attarin Medersa** (daily 9.30am–6pm; 10dh), the finest of the city's medieval colleges after the Bou Inania.

Kairaouine Mosque
To the right of the Medersa, a narrow street runs along the north side of the **Kairaouine Mosque**. Founded in 857 AD by a refugee from Kairouan in Tunisia, the Kairaouine is one of the oldest universities in the world, and the fountainhead of Moroccan religious life. Its present dimensions, with sixteen aisles and room for twenty thousand worshippers, are

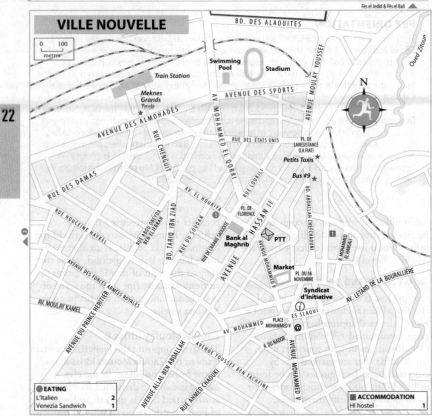

VILLE NOUVELLE

BD. DES ALAOUITES

0   100
metres

Train Station

Meknes
Grands
Taxis

Swimming
Pool

Stadium

AVENUE DES SPORTS

AVENUE MOULAY YOUSSEF

N

Oued Zitoun

AVENUE DES ALMOHADES

RUE CHENGUIT

AVENUE MOHAMMED EL QORRI

RUE DES ÉTATS UNIS

PL. DE
LARESISTANCE
(LA FIAT)

Petits Taxis

RUE DES DAMAS

Bus #9

RUE HOUCEINE HAYKEL

AV. EL HOURIYA

RUE LOUKILI

BD. TARIQ IBN ZIAD

RUE ABOU OBEYDA
BEN ELKERRAN

RUE DU SOUDAN

RUE DE LABBAYE SAOUTE

PL. DE
FLORENCE

Bank al
Maghrib

AVENUE   HASSAN II

PTT

AVENUE MOHAMMED V

BD. ABDALLAH CHEFCHAOUNI

R. MOHAMMED
EL HANSALI

AVENUE DES FORCES ARMEES ROYALES

AV. MOULAY KAMEL

AVENUE DU PRINCE HERITIER

Market

PL. DU 16
NOVEMBRE

Syndicat
d'Initiative

AV. LETARD DE LA BOURALLIÈRE

ES SLAOUI

AVENUE ALLAL BEN ABDALLAH

AVENUE YOUSSEF BEN TACHFINE

AV. MOHAMMED

PLACE
MOHAMMED V

@

R. DU NADOR

AVENUE MOHAMMED V

RUE AHMED CHAOUKI

EATING
L'Italien   2
Venezia Sandwich   1

ACCOMMODATION
HI hostel   1

Place de l'Atlas & CTM Terminal ▼

essentially the product of tenth- and twelfth-century reconstructions. Non-Muslims can look into the courtyard through the main door.

Place Seffarine

The street emerges in **Place Seffarine**, strikingly picturesque with its faïence fountain, gnarled fig trees and metalworkers hammering away. On the west side of the square, the thirteenth-century **Seffarine Medersa** is still in use as a hostel for students at the Kairaouine.

Souk Sabbighin

If you're beginning to find the medieval prettiness of the central souks and *medersas* slightly repetitive, then the area beyond the square should provide the antidote. The dyers' market – **Souk Sabbighin** – is directly south of the

Seffarine Medersa, and is draped with fantastically coloured yarn and cloth drying in the heat. Below, workers in grey toil over cauldrons of multicoloured dyes. **Place er Rsif**, nearby, has buses and taxis to the Ville Nouvelle, the French-built part of town, outside the city walls.

The tanneries

The street to the left (north) of the Seffarine Medersa leads to the rather smelly tanneries, constantly visited by tour groups with whom you could discreetly tag along if you get lost. Inside the tanneries, water deluges through holes that were once windows of houses. Hundreds of skins lie spread out on the rooftops, above vats of dye and others containing the pigeon dung that's used to treat the leather. Straight on, the road eventually leads back round to the Attarin Medersa.

ARRIVAL AND DEPARTURE

By train The train station is in the Ville Nouvelle, a 15min walk north of the hotels around Place Mohammed V. If you prefer to stay in the Medina, take a *petit taxi* (12dh), or bus #19 which will drop you off at R'cif in the Medina; alternatively, walk down to Place de la Résistance (aka La Fiat) and pick up bus #9 to Dar Batha/Place de l'Istiqlal, near the western gate to Fès el Bali, Bab Boujeloud.

Destinations Casablanca Voyageurs (19 daily; 3hr 30min); Marrakesh (8 daily; 7hr 30min); Meknes (23 daily; 35min); Rabat (19 daily; 2hr 30min); Tangier (4 daily; 5hr 20min).

By bus The bus station is just outside the walls near Bab Boujeloud. The terminal for CTM buses is off Rue de l'Atlas, which links the far end of Av Mohammed V with Place de l'Atlas.

Destinations (private) Casablanca (18 daily; 5hr); Chefchaouen (7 daily; 5hr); Marrakesh (8 daily; 10hr); Meknes (approximately every 30min; 1hr); Rabat (15 daily; 4hr); Tangier (5 daily; 8hr); Tetouan (12 daily; 6hr).

Destinations (CTM) Casablanca (16 daily; 4hr 30min); Chefchaouen (4 daily; 4hr); Marrakesh (6 daily; 9hr); Meknes (11 daily; 1hr); Rabat (17 daily; 3hr); Tangier (6 daily; 6hr); Tetouan (4 daily; 5–6hr).

By taxi Shared *grands taxis* mostly operate from the bus station; exceptions include some of those serving Meknes (from the train station).

INFORMATION

Tourist information Staff at the office on Place Mohammed V (Mon–Fri 8.30am–4.30pm; ☎0535 624769) can tell you about June's seven-day Festival of World Sacred Music (☎0535 740535, ⊕fesfestival.com) and the five-day cherry festival which usually follows immediately after it in nearby Sefrou.

ACCOMMODATION

There's a shortage of hotel space in all categories, so be prepared for higher-than-usual prices; booking ahead is advisable. For atmosphere and character, the Medina is the place to be.

Cascade Just inside Bab Boujeloud, Fès el Bali ☎0535 638442; map p.756. An old building with a useful public hammam just behind. Rooms are small and basic, but the management is friendly; the fantastic view from the terrace, where you can drink if you bring your own, is the real draw. Doubles 150dh

★**Dar Bouanania** 21 Derb ben Salem (signposted on Talâa Kebira), Fès el Bali ☎0535 637282, ⊕darbouanania@gmail.com; map p.756. Not quite a *riad*, but the budget equivalent, with spacious rooms and traditional decor for reasonable enough prices. Doubles 300dh

Funky Fes 60 Arset Lamdissi, Fès el Bali ☎0535 633196, ⊕funkyfes.com. Mellow hostel on the southern fringes of the Medina, a popular spot for backpackers, with a range of dorms and en-suite doubles. Breakfast included. Dorms 100dh, doubles 370dh

Glacier 9 Derb Jedid, Mellah (down an alleyway off Rue des Merenides) ☎0535 626261. The best budget choice in the old Jewish ghetto, a brightly painted hotel with basic but tidy rooms, some overlooking the Jewish cemetery. Doubles 100dh

HI hostel 18 Rue Abdeslam Seghrini, Ville Nouvelle ☎0535 624085; map p.758. One of Morocco's best hostels – well kept, friendly and spotlessly clean. Breakfast included. Dorms 75dh, doubles 170dh

Lamrani Talâa Seghira, Fès el Bali ☎0535 634411; map p.756. Friendly place in a very central location, with small but bright and clean rooms, most with double beds, some with shared bathrooms (hot showers 10dh). Doubles 150dh

Pension Batha 8 Sidi Lakhayat, Batha, Fès el Bali ☎0535 741150; map p.756. Airy pension, difficult to miss thanks to its pink shutters, with half a dozen pleasant, old-fashioned rooms, and a terrace overlooking Pl Batha. Doubles 250dh

EATING

Fès el Bali has two main areas for cheap local food: around Bab Boujeloud and along Rue Hormis (running from Souk el Attarin towards Bab Guissa), while the Ville Nouvelle is mainly home to pricier Western-style restaurants serving European cuisine.

CAFÉS, CHEAP EATS AND SNACKS

Café Boutouail Rue Boutouail, Fès el Bali; map p.756. Coffee and pastries in the heart of the old city, with extra seating hidden away upstairs. The speciality is *panaché*, a mixture of cow's milk, almond milk, raisins and ice cream (10dh). Daily 7.30am–9pm.

Café Clock 7 Derb El Magana, Fès el Bali ⊕fez.cafeclock .com; map p.756. A maze of comfy little salons leads off the three-tiered courtyard; forget *tajines* – you're here for the camel burger (95dh) or the falafel with hummus and tabbouleh (55dh). Daily 8.30am–10.30pm.

★**Cremerie La Place** On the northeast corner of Place Seffarine, Fès el Bali; map p.756. Tiny café perfect for enjoying a tea and delectable patisseries as you watch the coppersmiths hammering and shaping merchandise under the shade of the picturesque plane tree. Daily 7am–7pm.

Fez Café 13 Akbat Sbaa, Fès el Bali; map p.756. Walk through a beautiful oasis of greenery to reach the shady patio of this quiet café where you can relax with a tea or juice; the menu changes every day, so there's always something new to try (mains 190dh). Daily noon–3pm & 7.30–10pm.

La Kasbah Inside Bab Boujeloud, Fès el Bali; map p.756. The draw here is the roof terrace overlooking the blue gate

22

22

and the windy Medina alleyways below; the *tajines* (40dh) can be a little insipid, though. Menus 70dh. Daily 9am–midnight.

La Noria Off Av Moulay Hassan, Fès el Jedid; map p.756. Quiet spot by a water wheel, good for breakfast (until 11am) and a bargain cup of coffee, though you can also grab *harira* soup (25dh) or a Berber omelette (40dh), with set menus from 80dh. Daily 7am–11.30pm.

Venezia Sandwich 7 Av el Houria; map p.758. A superior fast-food joint in a row of similar places, with grilled sausages, fried fish and a range of cheap panini (20dh). Daily noon–1am.

RESTAURANTS

Dar Saada 21 Rue el Attarine, Fès el Bali; map p.756. Tasty Moroccan dishes (grilled meat from 80dh, *tajines* from 90dh) all in vast portions in an old palace. Licensed. Daily 10am–9pm.

★ **L'Italien** Av Omar Ibnou Khattab, Champs de Course; map p.758. Fun and fashionable restaurant that is by far the best Italian in town, with proper wood-fired pizzas (70–115dh) and exquisite pastas. Daily noon–4pm & 7pm–midnight.

Thami's 50 Serrajine, Bab Boujeloud, Fès el Bali; map p.756. People-watch to your heart's content over simple but satisfying food, great value at around 40dh for dishes such as egg-topped *kefta tajine*. Daily 9am–midnight.

DRINKING

★ **Mezzanine** 17 Ksbat Chams, Av des Français, Fès el Bali; map p.756. Sun yourself on the funky lounge terrace at lunchtime or soak in the trendy atmosphere over a chilled beer and a *tapa* (from 50dh) as you peer over the city ramparts at the spectacular gardens below. Mon–Sat 1pm–1am, Sun 1pm–midnight.

DIRECTORY

Banks and exchange ATMs at Place R'cif and Bab Boujeloud in the Medina; plenty of banks (all with ATMs) on Mohammed V in the Ville Nouvelle, including BMCE on Place Mohammed V; also on Place de l'Atlas and Place Florence.

Internet Cyber, above the *téléboutique* on Av Hassan II (daily 9am–10pm).

Pharmacy There are pharmacies opposite the SGMB bank by Bab Boujeloud, on Batha and on the Grande Rue des Merenides in the Mellah, plus numerous ones throughout the Ville Nouvelle. The Pharmacie du Municipalité, just up from Pl de la Résistance, on Av Moulay Youssef, is open overnight.

Police At the Préfecture de Medina around the corner from the Musée Batha, and by the post office on Bd Mohammed V.

Post office Corner of avenues Mohammed V and Hassan II, Ville Nouvelle; also in Place Batha and Place des Alaouites, Medina.

RABAT

Often undervalued by tourists, Morocco's capital city, **RABAT**, has a modern political centre (with elegant French architecture), several historical monuments, accessible bars and an ancient Kasbah overlooking a sandy beach. Though it should not take priority over Fez, Marrakesh or Chefchaouen, it is worth a visit if you have the time.

WHAT TO SEE AND DO

Rabat's compact Medina – the whole city until the French arrived in 1912 – is wedged on two sides by the sea and the river, on the others by the twelfth-century Almohad and fifteenth-century Andalusian walls. Laid out in a simple grid, its streets are very easy to navigate.

Kasbah des Oudaïas and around

North of the Medina lies the **Kasbah des Oudaïas**, a charming and evocative quarter whose principal gateway – **Bab el Kasbah** or Oudaïa Gate, built around 1195 – is one of the most ornate in the Moorish world. Its interior is now used for art exhibitions. Down the steps outside the gate, a lower, horseshoe arch leads directly to **Moulay Ismail's Palace** (Mon & Wed–Sun 9am–4pm; 20dh), which hosts quite an interesting jewellery museum.

The adjoining **Andalusian Garden** – one of the most delightful spots in the city – was actually constructed by the French in the last century, though true to Arab Andalusian tradition, with deep, sunken beds of shrubs and flowering annuals.

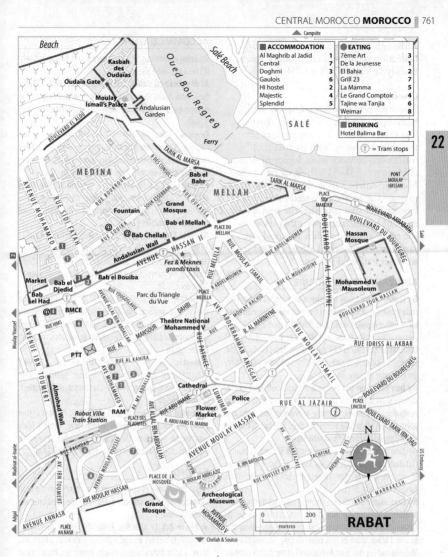

■ ACCOMMODATION	
Al Maghrib al Jadid	1
Central	7
Doghmi	3
Gaulois	6
HI hostel	2
Majestic	4
Splendid	5

● EATING	
7ème Art	3
De la Jeunesse	1
El Bahia	2
Grill 23	7
La Mamma	5
Le Grand Comptoir	4
Tajine wa Tanjia	6
Weimar	8

■ DRINKING	
Hotel Balima Bar	1

RABAT

Hassan Mosque

The most ambitious of all Almohad buildings, the **Hassan Mosque** (daily 24hr; free), with its vast minaret, dominates almost every view of the city. Designed by the Almohad ruler Yacoub el Mansour as the centrepiece of the new capital, the mosque seems to have been more or less abandoned at his death in 1199. The minaret, despite its apparent simplicity, is among the most complex of all Almohad structures: each facade is different, with a distinct combination of patterning, yet the whole intricacy of blind arcades and interlacing curves is based on just two formal designs. Facing the tower are the Mosque and Mausoleum of Mohammed V, begun on the sultan's death in 1961 and dedicated six years later.

Archeological Museum

On the opposite side of the Ville Nouvelle from the mausoleum is the **Archeological Museum** on Rue el Brihi (Mon & Wed–Sun 9am–4.30pm; 10dh), the most important in Morocco.

Although small, it has an exceptional collection of Roman-era bronzes, found mainly at Volubilis (see p.754).

Chellah

The royal burial ground, **Chellah** (daily 8am–6pm; 10dh), is a startling sight as you emerge from the long avenues of the Ville Nouvelle, with its circuit of fourteenth-century walls, legacy of Abou el Hassan (1331–51), the greatest of the Merenid rulers. Off to the left of the main gate are the partly excavated ruins of the Roman city that preceded the necropolis. A set of Islamic ruins is further down to the right, situated within a second inner sanctuary, approached along a broad path through half-wild gardens.

ARRIVAL AND DEPARTURE

By train The best way to arrive is by train, as Rabat Ville train station is at the heart of the Ville Nouvelle; don't get off at Rabat Agdal station, 2km from the centre.

Destinations Casablanca Port (every 30min; 1hr); Casablanca Voyageurs (27 daily; 1hr); Fez (19 daily; 2hr 30min); Marrakesh (9 daily; 4hr 25min); Meknes (19 daily; 2hr); Tangier (8 daily; 3hr 50min).

By bus The main bus terminal is 3km southwest of the centre, served by local buses #17, #30 and #41, and by *petits taxis*. It's easier, if you're arriving by bus from the north, to get off in Salé across the river, and take a tram or shared *grand taxi* from there into Rabat.

Destinations Casablanca (frequent; 1hr 30min); Essaouira (10 daily; 8hr 30min); Fez (at least hourly; 4hr 30min); Marrakesh (hourly; 5hr 30min); Meknes (hourly; 3hr); Tangier (14 daily; 5hr).

By taxi Shared *grands taxis* for most intercity destinations operate from outside the main bus station; those to Casablanca cost only a couple of dirhams more than the bus and leave more or less continuously. Shared taxis to Meknes and Fez run from Av Hassan II at the corner with Av Chellah.

INFORMATION

Tourist information Corner Rue Oued el Makhazine and Rue Zalaka, Agdal (Mon–Fri 8.30am–4.30pm; ⓣ 0537 278300).

GETTING AROUND

By bus Local buses to the intercity bus station leave opposite Bab el Had.

By tram There are two tram lines, both serving Salé and the Hassan Mosque, from which one runs to Rabat Ville train station, the other along Av Hassan II.

ACCOMMODATION

Accommodation can fill up in summer and during festivals; it's best to phone ahead.

Al Maghrib al Jadid 2 Rue Sebbahi ⓣ 0534 732207. Basic and clean, though the candy-pink and bright blue decor is garish. Hot showers 8am–9.30pm (10dh). Doubles **120dh**

Central 2 Rue al Basra ⓣ 0537 707356. One of the better cheapies, conveniently located, as its name suggests. Most rooms have patterned colonial floor tiles. Hot water mornings and evenings only. Doubles **200dh**

Doghmi 313 Av Mohammed V, just inside Bab Jedid ⓣ 0537 723898. Clean and simple rooms lead off a pleasant white and azure veranda, all with shared bathrooms. Doubles **130dh**

Gaulois 1 Rue Hims (corner of Av Mohammed V) ⓣ 0537 723022. Two-star with grand entrance and decent rooms, some en suite. Pricier than other options if the cheap rooms have gone, but can be good value for money. Doubles **220dh**

HI hostel 43 Rue Marrassa ⓣ 0537 725769. Just outside the Medina walls north of Av Hassan II, this centrally located hostel has plain and simple dorms with shared bathroom facilities. HI membership sometimes required. Dorms **60dh**

Majestic 121 Av Hassan II ⓣ 0537 722997, ⓦ hotelmajestic.ma. Excellent option with a 24hr reception and porter; rooms are bright and spotless. Doubles **366dh**

Splendid 8 Rue Ghazza ⓣ 0537 723283. A great option with clean rooms, some of which give onto a leafy courtyard – perfect for relaxing in after a day of exploration. Hot water evenings only. Doubles **226dh**

EATING

Rabat has a wide range of good restaurants serving both Moroccan and international dishes. The cheapest ones are in the Medina.

★**7ème Art** Av Allal Ben Abdallah. Trendy good-value café with tables set around a garden area with a fountain, serving light dishes such as salads, omelettes, burgers and panini, and more substantial *tajines*, pastas and grillés (20–75dh). Daily 7am–7pm.

De la Jeunesse 305 Av Mohammed V. One of the city's better budget restaurants, with generous portions of couscous, and decent *tajines* (10–25dh). Upstairs is quieter and has more seating. Daily noon–10pm.

El Bahia Av Hassan II, built into the Andalusian wall, near the junction with Av Mohammed V. Sit at one of the tables that line the Andalusian wall or retreat to the leafy inner patio for reasonably priced *tajines*, brochettes and salads (25–65dh), though service can be slow. Daily noon–10pm.

Grill 23 386 Av Mohammed V. Cheap but delicious *shwarma*, burgers (28–38dh) and big, crunchy salads

★TREAT YOURSELF

★**TREAT YOURSELF**

Le Grand Comptoir 279 Av Mohammed V ☎0537 201514, ⓦlegrandcomptoir.ma. Classy, Parisian-style brasserie with wonderful 1920s-style decor and live music that ranges from jazz to traditional Moroccan. Serves excellent meat and seafood dishes and a decent selection of wines. Main courses 85–280dh. Daily 9am–1am.

(15–35dh). Convenient for a takeaway to carry with you on a train journey (it's just up the street from the station). Daily 7am–1am.

La Mamma 6 Rue Tanta, behind the *Hôtel Balima*. Good pasta dishes and wood-oven pizzas in a rustic trattoria setting (mains 45–95dh). Daily noon–3pm & 7.30pm–midnight.

★**Tajine wa Tanjia** 9 Rue Baghdad. This lovely little place – all low cushioned seating and Moroccan paintings – serves a wide range of excellent *tajines* and *tanjia* (jugged beef or lamb). Mains 76–120dh. Mon–Sat 11am–3pm & 6pm–midnight.

Weimar 7 Rue Sana'a, inside the Goethe Institute. Studenty, expat hangout serving pastas, salads and meats, or a "half-half" (half pizza and half-size salad, 70dh), washed down with German beer. Daily 9am–10pm.

DRINKING AND NIGHTLIFE

Avenues Mohammed V and Allal Ben Abdallah have some good cafés, but the best bars are situated in Agdal, a bit of a trek from the centre. Those itching for a boogie should head to the Centre Commercial Prestige along the Route des Zaers, a 10min taxi ride out of town, home to a cluster of nightclubs.

Hotel Balima Bar Av Mohammed V. This bar is conveniently located in the centre of town and has a terrace overlooking the parliament. Daily noon–10pm.

DIRECTORY

Banks and exchange BMCE at the northern end of Av Mohammed V has a bureau de change (daily 8am–8pm). Others are on Av Moulay Youssef between hotels *Bélère* and *Caleche d'Or*, and on the corner of Av Mohammed V & Rue Ghaza.

Embassies Australia represented by Canada; Canada, 66 Av Mehdi Ben Barka, Souissi ☎0537 544949; New Zealand represented by the UK; UK, 28 Av S.A.R. Sidi Mohammed, Souissi ☎0537 633333; US, km 5.7, Av Mohammed VI, Souissi ☎0537 637200. Ireland has an honorary consul in Casablanca (☎0522 272721).

Internet Most open daily 9am–9pm, 5–8dh/hr; cheapest places are on or off Rue Souika in the Medina; in the Ville Nouvelle, try 113 Av Hassan II by Hôtel Majestic.

Police Av Tripoli, near the cathedral. Police posts at Bab Jedid and north end of Rue des Consuls.

Post office Halfway down Av Mohammed V.

CASABLANCA

Morocco's main city and economic capital, **CASABLANCA** (or "Casa") is also North Africa's largest port. Casa's Westernized image does not fit with most travellers' stereotype of Morocco but the city offers good food, beaches and fun nightlife.

WHAT TO SEE AND DO

Casablanca's Medina, above the port and recently gentrified, is largely the product of the late nineteenth century, when Casa began its modest growth as a commercial centre. Film buffs will be disappointed to learn that Bogart's *Casablanca* wasn't shot here (it was filmed entirely in Hollywood) – *Rick's Café* (expensive) commemorates it as a gimmick at 248 Boulevard Sour Jedid.

Mosquée Hassan II

The awe-inspiring **Mosquée Hassan II** (guided tours only Mon–Thurs, Sat & Sun 9am, 10am, 11am & 2pm, Fri 9am & 2pm; 120dh) is a must-see. After Mecca and Medina, it's the world's third-largest mosque, with a minaret soaring 200m, and space for a hundred and five thousand worshippers. Commissioned by the last king, who named it after himself, it cost an estimated US$800m. It's a short taxi ride northeast of the centre.

Musée du Judaïsme Marocain

Five kilometres south of town, in the suburb of Oasis, the **Musée du Judaïsme Marocain** at 81 Rue Chasseur Jules Gros (Mon–Fri winter 10am–5pm, summer 10am–6pm; 40dh; wheelchair accessible; ☎0522 994940, ⓦcasajewishmuseum .com) is the only Jewish museum in any Muslim country. Many Moroccan Muslims are proud of the fact that Jewish communities have, historically, been protected in Morocco. The museum gives an insight into the disproportionate role that Jews have played in Moroccan life.

22

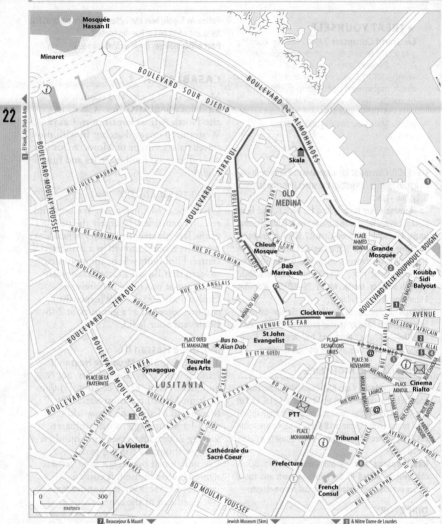

El Hank, Aïn Diab & Anfa

Mosquée
Hassan II

Minaret

BOULEVARD SOUR DJEDID

BOULEVARD DES ALMOHHADES

BOULEVARD MOULAY YOUSSEF

RUE JULES MAURAN

RUE DE GOULMINA

BOULEVARD DE

BOULEVARD ZIRAOUI

BOULEVARD ZIRAOUI

BOULEVARD TAH AR ET ELTTOUL

RUE DE GOULMINA

RUE DES ANGLAIS

RUE JEMAA ACH CHLEUH

OLD MEDINA

Skala

Chleuh
Mosque

Bab
Marrakesh

R MORA OU SAID

RUE CHAKIB ARSALANE

PLACE
AHMED
BIDAOUI

Grande
Mosquée

Koubba
Sidi
Balyout

BOULEVARD FELIX HOUPHOUET BOIGNY

AVENUE

RUE LEON L'AFRICAIN

RUE ALLAL

Clocktower

AVENUE DES FAR

BOULEVARD

BORDEAUX

D'ANFA

Synagogue

PLACE DE LA
FRATERNITÉ

La Violetta

BOULEVARD

AVE HASSAN SOUKTANI

RUE JEAN JAURES

BOULEVARD MOULAY YOUSSEF

PLACE OUED
EL MAKHAZINE

Tourelle
des Arts

LUSITANIA

D'ALGER

BOULEVARD

Bus to
★ Aïn Diab

St John
Evangelist

R F ET M GUEDJ

AVENUE MOULAY HASSAN I

RUE
RACHIDI

PLACE
DESNATIONS
UNIES

BD DE PARIS

PTT

PLACE
MOHAMMED
V

Cathédrale du
Sacré Coeur

BD MOULAY YOUSSEF

PLACE 16
NOVEMBRE

AVE HOUMAN

PLACE
AKNOUL

RUE IDRISS

LAHRIZI

MOULAY ABDALLAH

RUE PRINCE

Tribunal

Prefecture

French
Consul

RUE EL HARRAR

BOULEVARD DU 11 JANVIER

RUE MUST APHA

Cinema
Rialto

AVENUE LALA YAKOUT

0   300
metres

7, Beausejour & Maarif   Jewish Museum (5km)   3 & Nôtre Dame de Lourdes

The beaches

The **Ain Diab beach**, to the west of Mosque Hassan II, and at the end of the tram line, is one of Morocco's best and most easily accessible beaches. Surf lessons and equipment are readily available along the corniche, which runs alongside the beach. **Mohammedia**, 30km from Casa, is a less crowded option, with better surf. Take the train (16dh) from Casa Port station.

ARRIVAL AND DEPARTURE

By plane If you're arriving at Mohammed V airport, catch one of the regular trains (hourly 5.55am–9.55pm; 35min) to Casa Voyageurs and the more convenient Casa Port. *Grands taxis* are 250dh (300dh at night) for the 45min drive.

By train Intercity trains stop at Casa Voyageurs (2km southeast of the centre). From there, trams run into town (6dh); otherwise, it's a 20min walk or a *petit taxi* ride. Local services from Rabat (every 30min 6.30am–8pm; 1hr 10min) continue to Casa Port station (Gare du Port), between the town centre and the port.

CASABLANCA

■ DRINKING & NIGHTLIFE
Bao	1
La Cigale	3
Trica Bar	2

Ⓣ = Tram stops

■ ACCOMMODATION
Camping Oasis	
Dar Bouazza	7
Colbert	5
Du Centre	1
Galia	6
Miramar	3
Mon Rêve	3
Negociant	4
Touring	2

● EATING
Al Mounia	6
La Bodega	3
La Taverne du Dauphin	2
Le Petit Poucet	5
Ostrea	1
Rôtisserie Centrale	4

22

Ain Sebaa & Mohammedia by coast (S111) ▶

Casa Port Station

Centre Zoo

BOULEVARD *Mohammedia buses & taxis*
R ZAID OU HMAD
★ **Tour Atlas**
DES FORCES
CTM
PLACE ZELLAQA
ARMÉES ROYALES (F.A.R.)
MOULAY ABDERRAHMAN
PLACE MIRABEAU
AVENUE PASTEUR
AVENUE PASTEUR

BEN ABDALLAH
Grands Taxis to/from Rabat ★
Marché Central
PLACE EN PAQUET
RUE KARACHI
BOULEVARD DE LA RÉSISTANCE
Ⓣ BOULEVARD MOHAMMED V
PLACE ELYASSIR
BOULEVARD EMILE ZOLA

EL FETOUAKI
HASSAN I
RUE OULED ZAINE
PLACE DE BANDOENG
RUE MOHAMMED DIOURI
BOULEVARD EMIL EZOLA
PLACE DE LA GARE

PLACE DU 20 AOÛT
MAANI
RUE MOHAMMED SMIHA
BOULEVARD DE STRASBOURG
BOULEVARD ABDELLAH BEN YACINE
Ⓣ

PLACE DE LA VICTOIRE
RUE KHOURIBGA
BOULEVARD IBN TACHFINE
BOULEVARD D'OUJDA
B.D BA
Casa Voyageurs

◀ Gare Ouled Ziane   ◀ Mohammedia & Rabat by motorway

Destinations from Casa Voyageurs Fez (hourly; 4hr); Marrakesh (9 daily; 3hr 20min); Meknes (hourly; 3hr 15min); Rabat (27 daily; 1hr); Tangier (8 daily; 5hr).

By bus Arrive by CTM if possible, as it drops you downtown on Rue Léon l'Africain by the *Sheraton Hotel*. Private buses use the Gare Ouled Ziane bus station southeast of town on Route des Ouled Ziane.

Destinations (CTM) Essaouira (4 daily; 6hr 15min); Fez (15 daily; 5hr); Marrakesh (17 daily; 3hr 30min); Meknes (11 daily; 4hr); Rabat (31 daily; 1hr 20min); Tangier (7 daily; 5hr 30min); Tetouan (6 daily; 6hr 30min).

Destinations (private) Essaouira (10 daily; 8hr); Fez (10 daily; 5hr); Marrakesh (roughly every 30min; 4hr); Meknes (10 daily; 4hr); Rabat (frequent; 1hr 30min); Tangier (10 daily; 6hr 30min); Tetouan (10 daily; 7hr).

By taxi Most shared *grands taxis* arrive at Gare Ouled Ziane; some from Rabat arrive a block east of the CTM terminal; those from Essaouira come into a station south of the centre on Bd Brahim Roudani in Maarif, a longish walk (2km) or a cheap taxi ride away.

INFORMATION

Tourist information The Syndicat d'Initiative at 98 Bd Mohammed V (Mon–Fri 8.30am–4.30pm, Sat 8.30am–noon; ☏0522 221524) has free maps. The Délégation de Tourisme is south of the centre at 55 Rue Omar Slaoui

22

(Mon–Fri 8.30am–4.30pm; ☎0522 271177). The Conseil Régional du Tourisme have a kiosk just north of Pl Mohammed V, on Av Hassan II, and another next to the Hassan II Mosque (both Mon–Sat 8.30am–12.30pm & 2.30–6.30pm; ⊛visitcasablanca.ma).

Internet Most internet cafés are open daily from 9am–10pm and cost 10dh/hr. Club Internet, Bd Mohammed V, soukalina.net, 38 Rue Mouflakei Abdelkader.

Police Bd Brahim Roudani (☎0522 989865).

ACCOMMODATION

There are plenty of hotels, though they are often near capacity; cheaper rooms in the centre can be hard to find by late afternoon.

Camping Oasis Dar Bouazza Rte d'Azzour, 25km from town ☎0522 290767. Spacious, with modern, clean ablutions, but rather a long way from town. Price is for two people and a tent. __120dh__

Colbert 38 Rue Chaouia ☎0522 314421, ⊛hotelcolbert .ma. Huge (103 rooms) well-priced hotel with decent rooms (some with shower), and good-value singles (100dh). Doubles __210dh__

Du Centre Rue Sidi Balyout ☎0522 446180. A warm welcome at reception, along with clean and pleasant, honey-hued, en-suite rooms, makes this an excellent option in the centre. Doubles __200dh__

★**Galia** 19 Rue Ibnou Batouta ☎0522 481694, ✉galia_19 @hotmail.fr. The city's best budget option, with friendly English-speaking management and a handy location by the Marché Central tram station near the CTM. Doubles __270dh__

Miramar 22 Rue León l'Africain ☎0522 310308. One of the cheapest among the little hotels in the city centre, with some en-suite rooms (otherwise a shower is 10dh). Doubles __140dh__

Mon Rêve 5 Rue Chaouia ☎0522 311439. Long-standing budget travellers' favourite, also popular among locals. Book ahead. Doubles __220dh__

Negociant 116 Rue Allal Ben Abdallah ☎0522 314023. A popular choice with Moroccan families – clean, comfortable rooms, some en suite, and shared-bathroom singles (120dh). Doubles __220dh__

Touring 87 Rue Allal Ben Abdallah ☎0522 310216. Refurbished old French hotel that's friendly and excellent value; the best option in a street of cheap hotels. Doubles __200dh__

EATING

Al Mounia 95 Rue du Prince Moulay Abdallah. Excellent Moroccan cuisine in a palatial salon or shaded garden. Vegetarians will love the meze and salads, while the house specialities are chicken *tajine* and pigeon *pastilla* (mains 120–150dh). Licensed. Mon–Sat 7.30–11pm.

La Bodega 127 Rue Allal Ben Abdallah ⊛bodega.ma. Jam-packed with Latino and Spanish memorabilia as well as a large TV screen for sporting events, this lively place serves a decent selection of tapas (60dh); once the drinks (beers from 35dh) start flowing, the downstairs bar and little dancefloor liven up a fair amount. Mon–Sat noon–3pm & 7pm–2am, Sun 7pm–2am.

La Taverne du Dauphin 115 Bd Felix Houphouët Boigny ☎0522 221200. One of Casa's most famous and popular spots, with great seafood served in the restaurant and bonhomie dished up in the cramped bar. Mains 46–145dh, fixed-price menu 115dh. Mon–Sat noon–11pm.

Le Petit Poucet 86 Bd Mohammed V ☎0522 275420. A slice of old Casablanca, this restaurant is dressed up like a 1920s Parisian salon. The food (mains 45–125dh) is fine but nothing special, though the *soupe à l'oignon* is pretty good. Licensed. Daily 9am–10pm.

Ostrea Port de Pêche. Excellent, super-fresh seafood, although not cheap: Oualidia oysters, lobster or crayfish by weight, and for non-seafood eaters, there are grillés, pasta dishes and even frogs' legs *à la provençale* (mains 75–240dh). Licensed. Daily noon–11pm.

Rôtisserie Centrale 36 Rue Chaouia. Best of a bunch of cheap chicken-on-a-spit joints on this little stretch of road opposite the Marché Central. Chicken, chips and salad here won't set you back much more than 30dh. Daily 11am–11pm.

DRINKING AND NIGHTLIFE

There are scores of bars and clubs along the Corniche, 10min west of the centre, playing everything from hip-hop to house music.

Bao Bd de la Corniche, Aïn Diab. African beats and a laidback atmosphere make this a popular spot to get down to the sound of West African rhythms. Entry 100dh. Fri & Sat are the best days. Daily 11pm–4am.

La Cigale 10 Bd Brahim Roudani. The room at the back is where it all takes place – once the first tune is on the jukebox, the night has begun. Come for couscous Fri lunchtime. Daily 11am–midnight.

Trica 5 Rue al Moutanabi. You could nearly be in NYC at this stylish warehouse bar with brick walls and old-school tunes in the background. Mon–Sat 6.30pm–1am, Sun 6.30pm–midnight.

Southern Morocco

Few places on earth can better the abiding memory of the Sahara desert meeting the Atlantic, while **Marrakesh**, with its colourful Medina, is undoubtedly Morocco's best-known city; further south loom the scenic **Atlas Mountains** and west lies the coastal city of **Essaouira**, the country's best windsurfing spot.

MARRAKESH

MARRAKESH (Marrakech in French) is a city of immense beauty, sitting low and pink before a great range of mountains. It's an immediately exciting place, especially its ancient Medina. Marrakesh's population is growing and it has a thriving industrial area; the city remains the most important market and administrative centre in southern Morocco.

WHAT TO SEE AND DO

Marrakesh's **Medina** is big, taking up a fair part of the city. At its heart is the **Jemaa el Fna**, from which most things of interest radiate. There are lots of cheap *pensions* and hotels near here. To the north of the Jemaa are the famous **souks** of Marrakesh, where you can spend hours getting lost and picking up bargains. Just to the west is the great minaret of the **Koutoubia** mosque. This towers over the start of Avenue Mohammed V, which connects the Medina to **Gueliz**, where you can find the train station, CTM office and tourist information as well as some modern cafés, supermarkets and bars. It's a fairly long walk between Gueliz and the Medina, but there are plenty of taxis and the regular buses #1 and #16 between the two. Further west of the Koutoubia, just past Bab Jedid, there is a district of opulent hotels with fantastic, if pricey, bars.

Jemaa el Fna

There's nowhere in the world like the **Jemaa el Fna**: by day it's basically a market, with a few snake charmers and an occasional troupe of acrobats; in the late afternoon it becomes a whole carnival of musicians, storytellers and other entertainers; and in the evening dozens of stalls set up to dispense hot food to crowds of locals, while the musicians and performers continue. If you get tired of the spectacle, or if things slow down, you can move over to one of the numerous cafés' rooftop terraces.

Koutoubia

Nearly 70m high and visible for many kilometres, the minaret of the **Koutoubia** mosque was begun shortly after the Almohad conquest of the city, around 1150, and displays many features that were to become widespread in Moroccan architecture – the wide band of ceramic inlay, the pyramid-shaped merlons, and the alternation of patterning on the facades.

The northern Medina

Just before the red ochre arch at its end, **Souk Smarine** (an important Medina thoroughfare) narrows and you get a glimpse through passageways of the **Rahba Kedima**, a small and fairly ramshackle square whose most interesting features are its apothecary stalls. At the end of Rahba Kedima, a passageway to the left gives access to another, smaller, square – a bustling, carpet-draped area known as **La Criée Berbère**, which is where slave auctions used to be held.

Cutting back to the main thoroughfare, whose next section is named Souk el Kebir rather than Souk Smarine, you emerge at the **kissarias**, the covered markets at the heart of the souks. Kissarias traditionally sell more expensive products, which today means a predominance of Western designs and imports. Off to their right is **Souk des Bijoutiers**, a modest jewellers' lane, while at the north end is a convoluted web of alleys comprising the **Souk Cherratin**, essentially a leatherworkers' market.

Ben Youssef Medersa

If you bear left through the leather market and then turn right, you should arrive at the open space in front of the **Ben Youssef Mosque**. The originally fourteenth-century **Ben Youssef Medersa** (daily 9am–5pm; 10dh) – the annexe for students taking courses in the mosque – stands off a side street just to the east. It was almost completely rebuilt in the sixteenth century under the Saadians, with a strong Andalusian influence.

22

22

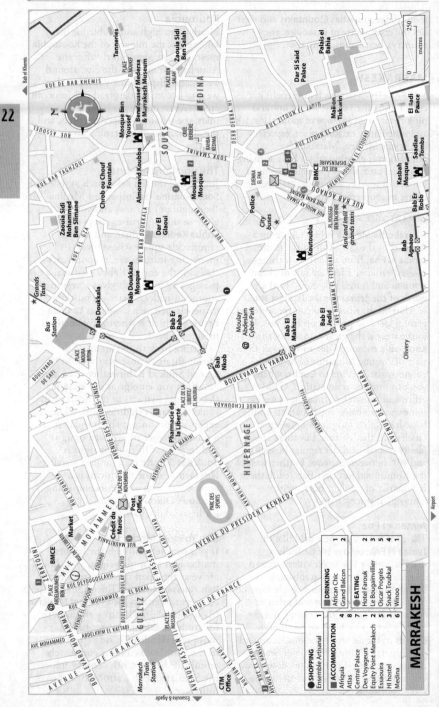

● SHOPPING
Ensemble Artisanal 1

■ ACCOMMODATION
Afriquia 4
Atlas 8
Central Palace 7
Des Voyageurs 1
Equity Point Marrakech 2
Essaoura 5
HI hostel 3
Medina 6

■ DRINKING
African Chic 1
Grand Balcon 2

● EATING
Hotel Farouk 1
Le Bougainvillier 3
Oscar Progrès 5
Snack Toubkal 4
Winoo 6

0   250
metres

Marrakesh Museum and Almoravid Koubba

Next door to the Medersa is the **Marrakesh Museum** (daily 9am–6pm; 50dh), which exhibits jewellery, art and sculpture, both old and new, in a beautifully restored nineteenth-century palace. Almost facing it, the small **Almoravid Koubba** (daily 9am–6pm; closed for restoration at time of writing but visible from the street) is easy to pass by, but it is the only building in the whole of Morocco from the eleventh-century Almoravid dynasty still intact. The motifs you've just seen in the Medersa – the pine cones, palms and acanthus leaves – were all carved here first.

The Saadian Tombs

Sealed up by Moulay Ismail after he had destroyed the adjoining El Badi Palace, the sixteenth-century **Saadian Tombs** (daily 9am–4.45pm; 10dh), accessed by a narrow alley near the Kasbah Mosque south of Jemaa el Fna, are home to two main mausoleums. The finer is on the left as you come in, a beautiful group of three rooms built to house El Mansour's own tomb and completed within his lifetime. The tombs of over a hundred more Saadian princes and royal household members are scattered around the garden and courtyard, their gravestones likewise brilliantly tiled and often elaborately inscribed.

El Badi Palace

Though largely in ruins, enough remains of Ahmed el Mansour's **El Badi Palace** (daily 9am–4.45pm; 10dh) to suggest that its name – "The Incomparable" – was not undeserved. It took a later ruler, Moulay Ismail, over ten years of systematic work to strip the palace of everything moveable or of value but, even so, there's a lingering sense of luxury. What you see today is essentially the ceremonial part of the palace complex, planned for the reception of ambassadors. To the rear extends the central court, over 130m long and nearly as wide, and built on a substructure of vaults in order to allow the circulation of water through the pools and gardens. In the southwest corner of the complex is the original (and, in its day, much celebrated) *minbar* (pulpit) from the Koutoubia mosque (admission is an extra 10dh, payable at the main gate).

Rue Zitoun el Jedid

Heading north from El Badi Palace, **Rue Zitoun el Jedid** leads back to the Jemaa, flanked by various nineteenth-century mansions. Many of these have been converted into carpet shops or tourist restaurants, but one of them has been kept as a museum, the **Palais el Bahia** (daily 9am–4.45pm; 10dh), former residence of a grand vizier. The name of the building means "The Brilliance"; indeed, it's a beautiful old palace with two lovely patio gardens and some classic painted wooden ceilings. Further north is the **Maison Tiskiwin** (8 Rue de la Bahia; daily 9.30am–12.30pm & 2.30–6pm; 20dh), which houses a superb collection of Moroccan and Saharan artefacts. If you're pressed for time, however, prioritize the lovely **Dar Si Said** palace nearby on Derb Si Said, as it also houses the **Museum of Moroccan Arts** (Mon & Wed–Sun 9am–4.45pm; 10dh), with a plethora of interesting historical arts and crafts.

CLIMBING MOUNT TOUBKAL

Imlil, the setting-off point for trekkers wanting to climb **the second-highest peak in Africa**, is within two to three hours' *grand taxi* drive of Marrakesh (30dh for a place, leaving from Place Youssef Tachfine, and usually changing taxis at Asni; 180dh to charter the taxi one-way). Most trekkers set out early to mid-morning from Imlil to stay the night at the Toubkal refuge (5–7hr), which gets crowded in summer. It's best to start from here at first light the next morning in order to get the clearest possible panorama from Toubkal's heights (afternoons can be cloudy). The ascent is not difficult if you are fit, but it can be very cold. Reckon on 2hr 30min–4hr going up by the southern route, 4hr 30min by the northern, and 2hr–2hr 30min to descend by either route.

22

ARRIVAL AND DEPARTURE

By plane From the airport, 4km southwest of town, bus #19 runs to Place Foucauld by the Jemaa and along Av Mohammed V (every 30min 7am–9.30pm; 30dh) – petits taxis (70dh by day, 120dh by night) are a more convenient option.

By train From the train station, west of Gueliz, cross Av Hassan II and take bus #8/#10/#14/#66 or a petit taxi (15dh) for Place Foucauld by the Jemaa.

Destinations Casablanca Voyageurs (11 daily; 3hr 20min); Fez (8 daily; 7hr 35min); Meknes (8 daily; 6hr 46min); Rabat (9 daily; 4hr 25min); Tangier (1 daily; 10hr 15min).

By bus The bus terminal is just outside the northwestern walls of the Medina by Bab Doukkala; from here it's a 20min walk to the Jemaa, or take bus #6/#8/#10/#14/#16 (opposite Bab Doukkala), or a petit taxi (10dh). CTM buses arrive and depart from their office south of the train station, though you can buy tickets and sometimes pick them up at the main terminal.

Destinations (private) Casablanca (every 30min, 4am–9pm; 3hr 30min); Essaouira (18 daily; 3hr); Fez (8 daily; 10hr); Meknes (8 daily; 9hr); Rabat (24 daily; 5hr 30min); Tangier (6 daily; 10hr).

Destinations (CTM) Casablanca (20 daily; 3hr 30min); Essaouira (2 daily; 2hr 30min); Fez (5 daily; 8hr); Meknes (3 daily; 7hr); Rabat (9 daily; 4hr 30min); Tangier (2 daily; 9hr 30min).

INFORMATION

Tourist information Place Abdelmoumen Ben Ali (Mon–Fri 8.30am–4.30pm; ☎ 0524 436239).

ACCOMMODATION

The Medina has the main concentration of cheap accommodation – most of the places quite pleasant – and, unusually, has a fair number of classified hotels too. Given the attractions of the Jemaa el Fna and the souks, this is the first choice. Booking in advance is advisable. Our recommendations are in the Medina unless stated otherwise.

Afriquia 45 Sidi Bouloukate ☎ 0524 442403. Basic but hospitable rooms with a Gaudíesque top-floor terrace. The shady orange trees twitter with swallows (be warned that this invariably means an early-morning wake-up call). En-suites cost 100dh extra. Doubles 150dh

★**Atlas** 50 Sidi Bouloukate ☎ 0524 391051, ⊛ hotel -atlas-marrakech.com. Calm and clean hotel set around two courtyards, with decorative iron and woodwork throughout; there's an appealing rooftop chill-out lounge for the weary tourist. Excellent rates for single travellers (90dh). Rooms with a/c are twice the price. Doubles 170dh

Central Palace 59 Sidi Bouloukate ☎ 0524 440235, ⊛ lecentralpalace.com. A peaceful haven set in a leafy

three-tiered courtyard with pleasantly decorated rooms, some en suite. There's also a couscous restaurant on the roof terrace. Doubles 155dh

Des Voyageurs 40 Av Zerktouni, Gueliz ☎ 0524 447218. Old-fashioned hotel with welcoming management, spacious rooms and a little patio-cum-garden. Doubles 144dh

Equity Point Marrakech 80 Derb el Hammam Mouassine ☎ 0524 440793, ⊛ equity-point.com. A hostel in a riad, with a fun crowd, four- to eight-bed dorms (each with its own bathroom), plus a pool, bar and restaurant. Dorms €13, doubles €65

Essaouira 3 Derb Sidi Bouloukate ☎ 0524 443805. The entrance opens onto a beautiful courtyard with intricately painted woodwork. Be prepared for the vibrantly tiled rooms – the patterns might just make you dizzy after a heavy night. Doubles 100dh

HI hostel Rue El Jahid, Gueliz ☎ 0524 447713, ✉ aubergemarrakech@hotmail.fr. Neat and tidy single-sex dorms, good for those with an early start as it's close to the train station and the CTM. Dorms 70dh

Medina 1 Derb Sidi Bouloukate ☎ 0524 442997. A perennial favourite among the cheapies, this place is clean, friendly and good value, and there's always hot water in the shared showers. Doubles 110dh

EATING

The most atmospheric place to eat is the Jemaa el Fna, where food stalls set up around sunset and serve up everything from harira soup and couscous to stewed snails and sheep's heads, all eaten at trestle tables. Cheap restaurants gather in the Medina, along with French-style cafés and virtually all the city's bars. You'll find more upmarket places uptown in Gueliz.

Hotel Farouk 66 Av Hassan II, Gueliz. Excellent-value set menu with soup or salad, then couscous, tajine or brochettes, and dessert, for 50dh. Wood-oven pizzas 30–40dh. Daily 6am–11pm.

Le Bougainvillier Rue El Mouassine 33. Old French crooners set the mood at this atmospheric café with a leafy sunny patio and little salons, serving teas and tajines (90dh). Daily 10am–10pm.

Oscar Progrès 20 Rue Bani Marine. One of the best budget restaurants in town, with large servings of couscous (veg 30dh, lamb 40dh), or be a real pig and go for the 100dh set menu. Daily noon–11pm.

Snack Toubkal In the southeast corner of Jemaa el Fna. Despite its touristy appearance, the food here is popular with locals and tourists alike. Set menus are 45–50dh. Daily 24hr.

★**Winoo** 77 Bd Moulay Rachid, Gueliz. Justifiably popular café-restaurant serving big salads (25–50dh) and tajines (20–25dh), all freshly made, well presented and very inexpensive. Daily 7am–3am.

SHOPPING IN THE SOUKS

Marrakesh is famous for its **souks**, where you can buy goods from all over Morocco. Prices are rarely fixed, so before you set out, head to the supposedly fixed-price **Ensemble Artisanal** (Mon–Sat 9am–7pm, Sun 9am–noon), on Avenue Mohammed V, midway between the Koutoubia and the ramparts at Bab Nkob, and get an idea of how much things are worth. It pays to bargain hard, as the first price you are told can easily be five or ten times the going rate, with the most obscene prices to be found around the edges of the souks.

DRINKING

African Chic 5 Rue Oum Errabia. One of Marrakesh's most congenial bars, with cocktails, wines and beers, tapas (five for 70dh, eight for 100dh), not to mention live Latin and Gnaoua music every night from 10pm. Daily 8pm–4am.

Grand Balcon On top of the *Café Glacier* on Jemaa el Fna. "Obligatory consumption" is required here – you won't be allowed in unless you pay for your drinks or passable *tajines* (50–55dh) at the door. The incredible view over the square attracts a large crowd, though. Daily 10am–10pm.

DIRECTORY

Banks and exchange BMCE has branches with adjoining bureaux de change and ATMs in the Medina (Rue Moulay Ismail, facing Place Foucauld) and Gueliz (114 Av Mohammed V).

Internet Moulay Abdeslam Cyber-Park on Av Mohammed V opposite the Ensemble Artisanal (daily 10am–1pm & 2–7pm; 5dh/hr); Jawal, behind 12 Bd Mohammed Zerktouni (daily 9am–9pm; 6dh/hr).

Pharmacies and doctor Pharmacie du Progrès, Place Jemaa el Fna at the top of Rue Bab Agnaou; Pharmacie de la Liberté, just off Place de la Liberté. If you're in need of a doctor, try Dr Abdelmajid Ben Tbib, 171 Av Mohammed V (☏0524 431030).

Police Tourist police on Jemaa el Fna (24/7; ☏0524 384601).

Post office Place du 16 Novembre, midway along Av Mohammed V, and on the Jemaa el Fna (Mon–Fri 8am–7.15pm, Sat 8.30am–5.30pm).

ESSAOUIRA

ESSAOUIRA, the nearest beach resort to Marrakesh, is a lovely eighteenth-century walled seaside town. A favourite with the likes of Frank Zappa and Jimi Hendrix back in the 1960s, its tradition of hippy tourism has created a much more laidback relationship between local residents and foreign visitors than you'll find in the rest of Morocco. Today Essaouira is a centre for arts and crafts in addition to being the country's top windsurfing spot.

WHAT TO SEE AND DO

22

Orientation in Essaouira is simple, and it's a great place for a wander; the **ramparts** are an obvious starting point. Heading north along the lane at the end of Place Prince Moulay el Hassan, you can access the **Skala de la Ville** (daily sunrise till sunset), a great sea bastion topped by a row of cannons, which runs along the northern cliffs. At the end is the circular **North Bastion**, with panoramic views. Along the Rue de la Skala, built into the ramparts, are woodcarving workshops, where artisans use **thuja**, a distinctive local hardwood. You can find another impressive bastion by the harbour, the **Skala du Port** (daily 9am–5pm; 10dh).

The souks

The town's **souks** spread around and to the south of two arcades, on either side of Rue Mohammed Zerktouni, and up towards the **Mellah** (former Jewish ghetto), in the northwest corner of the ramparts. Don't miss the **Marché d'Épices** (spice market) and **Souk des Bijoutiers** (jewellers' market). Art studios and hippie-style clothing shops cluster around **Place Chefchaouni** by the clock tower. For those wanting to spice up their **culinary skills**, Atelier Madada (7 Rue Youssef el Fassi ☏0524 475512, ⓦlateliermadada.com) offers cookery classes in local specialities.

The beaches

The southern **beach** (the northern one is less attractive) extends for many kilometres, past the Oued Ksob river bed and the ruins of an old fort known as the Borj el Berod. If you're after **watersports**, Club Mistral (☏0524 783934) on the south beach rents out surfboards, kayaks and wind/kitesurfing gear, and offers lessons too.

22

ARRIVAL AND INFORMATION

By bus The bus station is about 500m (10min walk) northeast of Bab Doukkala gate. It's worth taking a *petit taxi* (about 7dh), especially at night.

Destinations Casablanca (20 daily; 7hr); Marrakesh (18 daily; 3hr 30min); Rabat (15 daily; 8hr 30min).

By taxi Shared *grands taxis* to Marrakesh and Casablanca operate from just next to the bus station, though they may drop arrivals at the more central Bab Doukkala or Place Prince Moulay el Hassan.

Tourist information Tourist office at Av du Caire (Mon–Fri 9am–4pm; ☎ 0524 783532).

ACCOMMODATION

Accommodation can be tight over Easter and in summer, when advance booking is recommended.

Camping Sidi Magdoul 1km south of town behind the lighthouse ☎ 0524 472196, ✉ labo.flash@hotmail.com. Clean, friendly and well managed, with hot showers, campervan pitches and an area of soil and trees for pitching tents in. Per person 17dh, plus per tent 20dh

Cap Sim 11 Rue Ibn Rochd ☎ 0524 785834, ⓦ hotelcapsim.com. Rooms at this refurbished budget hotel with fourth-floor sun terrace are beautifully kept and decorated, in colours as warm as the welcome. Breakfast included. Doubles 220dh

Central 5 Rue Dar Eddhab, off Av Mohammed Ben Abdallah ☎ 0524 783623. Cheap and cheerful basic rooms and friendly staff in a nice old house around a patio with a fig tree. Shared hot showers (8dh). Doubles 120dh

Majestic 40 Rue Laâlouj ☎ 0524 474909. The lobby and stairs in this budget hotel (formerly the French colonial courthouse) aren't very inspiring, but the rooms are decent enough for the price – nothing fancy, but fresh and clean. Doubles 150dh

Souiri 37 Rue Attarine ☎ 0524 475339, ⓦ hotelsouiri .com. Very central and deservedly popular, this welcoming

little hotel offers a range of rooms, the cheaper ones having shared bathroom facilities. Rooms at the front are considered the best, though those at the back are quieter. Doubles 228dh

EATING AND DRINKING

For an informal meal, you can do no better than eat at the line of grills down at the port. Restaurants can be a bit expensive, but there are plenty of places to pick up cheap sandwiches.

Bab Laâchour By Pl Prince Moulay el Hassan. A café with a restaurant upstairs, overlooking the plaza, with fish dishes and *tajines* (mains 30–100dh), and an 85dh set menu. Licensed. Daily: café 8am–9pm, restaurant noon–3pm & 7–10pm.

Dar Tata In the grain souk. A budget restaurant right in the middle of the Medina. The 95dh fish menu starts with delicious fish soup, followed by whatever's good from the day's catch, all beautifully presented. Daily 9.30am–6.30pm.

Essalam 23 Place Prince Moulay el Hassan. A great-value no-frills restaurant which serves up some of the cheapest set menus in town (30–65dh). The walls are decorated with watercolours by Breton artist Charles Kérival. Daily 9am–4pm & 7–10pm.

La Petite Perle 2 Rue el Hajjalli. Sit on cushioned benches in this restaurant, styled like a Berber tent, and dig into a good-value *tajine* or couscous. Set menus 60–95dh. Daily noon–3pm & 7–10.30pm.

Laayoune 4 bis Rue Hajjali. A popular place for Moroccan staples in a warm, relaxed setting with low-lying, candlelit tables and friendly service. Set menus based on *tajines* or couscous go for 78–98dh. Daily noon–3pm & 7–10.30pm.

Taros Place Moulay Hassan. Along the theme of a boat deck on a Greek island tour, with palm parasols and patio furniture, this jolly rooftop bar is a perfect spot to enjoy an early-evening beer (35dh) or a cocktail (from 75dh). Daily 9am–1am.

HERENGRACHT, AMSTERDAM

The Netherlands

HIGHLIGHTS

❶ **Amsterdam** Canals, coffeeshops and world-famous art. **See p.779**

❷ **Delft** Enjoy wonderful apple cake in Vermeer's home town. **See p.793**

❸ **Rotterdam** Adventurous architecture and buzzing nightlife. **See p.794**

❹ **Utrecht** A relaxing antidote to Amsterdam, just 20min from the capital. **See p.797**

❺ **Hoge Veluwe National Park** Cycle through woods to the world's best collection of Van Goghs. **See p.799**

❻ **Maastricht** A cosmopolitan university town with a tranquil old quarter. **See p.799**

HIGHLIGHTS ARE MARKED ON THE MAP ON P.775

ROUGH COSTS

Daily budget Basic €55, occasional treat €75

Drink Beer €2.80

Food Pancake €8

Hostel/budget hotel €20–35/€70–95

Travel Train: Amsterdam–Rotterdam €14

FACT FILE

Population 16.9 million

Language Dutch

Currency Euro (€)

Capital Amsterdam

International phone code ☎ 31

Time zone GMT +1hr

Introduction

Despite the popular reputation of its most celebrated city, Amsterdam, the Netherlands is not all sex and drugs (and there's little rock'n'roll). Delve deeper and you will find a diminutive country with a heavyweight cultural heritage: its A-list of art superstars, Rembrandt, Vermeer and Van Gogh, rivals that of any country, and you could easily spend a solid week just scraping the surface of its museums. Dutch cities also provide plenty of architectural eye candy with pretty gabled houses and peaceful canals perfect for aimless wandering, while its flat fertile landscape means cycling can get you almost anywhere, from iconic tulip fields to sandy, dune-backed islands.

23

Though most people travel only to atmospheric **Amsterdam**, nearby is a group of worthwhile towns known collectively as the **Randstad** (literally "rim town"), including **Haarlem** and **Delft** with their old canal-girded centres, and **Den Haag** (The Hague), a stately city with fine museums and easy beach access. The dynamic port city of **Rotterdam** is a showcase for noteworthy architecture and alternative art. Outside the Randstad, life moves more slowly. To the south, the landscape undulates into heathy moorland, best experienced in the **Hoge Veluwe National Park**. Further south lies the compelling city of **Maastricht**, squeezed between the German and Belgian borders.

CHRONOLOGY

58 BC Julius Caesar conquers the area of the present-day Netherlands.

1275 Amsterdam is founded by Count Floris V of Holland.

1477 The Austrian Habsburgs take control.

1500s Protestant Reformation spreads through the Netherlands, leading to wars against the Catholic Habsburg rulers based in Spain.

1579 The Union of Utrecht is signed by seven provinces to form the United Provinces against Spain. The Netherlands are declared independent two years later, heralding a "Golden Age" of trade and colonial expansion.

1603 The Dutch East India Company establishes its first trading post in Indonesia, an area that it would gradually colonize.

1806 Napoleon annexes the Kingdom of Holland for France.

1813 The French are driven out and the Prince of Orange becomes sovereign of the United Netherlands.

1853 Vincent Van Gogh is born.

1914–18 The Netherlands remains neutral during World War I.

1940 Nazi Germany invades the Netherlands, forcing the deportation and murder of Dutch Jews, including Anne Frank's family.

1944 Operation Market Garden sees heavy fighting around Arnhem but fails to dislodge German troops.

1947 Anne Frank's diary is published.

1953 More than 1800 killed in severe flooding on Jan 31. The disaster forms the inspiration for the massive Delta land reclamation project.

1975 Cannabis is decriminalized – tourism booms.

1980 Coronation of Queen Beatrix.

1992 The Maastricht Treaty is signed, transforming the European Community into the European Union.

1997 Treaty of Amsterdam clears the way for the introduction of a single European currency.

2001 The Netherlands becomes the first country to legalize same-sex marriage.

2002 Anti-immigration politician Pim Fortuyn is killed shortly before elections.

2004 Film-maker Theo Van Gogh is murdered by a radical Islamist.

2010 Coalition government led by Geert Wilders collapses following dispute over troops in Afghanistan.

2012 Maastricht bans tourists from smoking cannabis in coffeeshops. Attempts to instil a nationwide ban fail.

2013 Queen Beatrix, aged 75, abdicates in favour of her son Prince Willem-Alexander – the first male monarch in over a century.

2016 Study published by eLife pronounces Dutch men officially world's tallest, with an average height of 6ft (1.8m).

ARRIVAL AND DEPARTURE

Regular high-speed **trains** (ⓦthalys.com) run to Amsterdam from Brussels (1hr

THE NETHERLANDS

HIGHLIGHTS

1. Amsterdam
2. Delft
3. Rotterdam
4. Utrecht
5. Hoge Veluwe National Park
6. Maastricht

23

50min) and Paris (3hr 15min), with
Eurostar (w eurostar.com) trains from
London connecting at Brussels Midi
(total journey time 4hr). German ICE
(w nsinternational.nl) trains also run
direct to Amsterdam from Cologne
(2hr 40min) and Frankfurt (3hr 45min).
Coming from the UK it is cheaper to use
the overnight **ferry** from Harwich to the
Hook of Holland (w stenaline.co.uk
/ferry-to-holland) or Hull to Rotterdam
(w poferries.com).

Low-cost **airlines** operate flights from
across Europe to five Dutch airports:
Amsterdam Schiphol, Eindhoven,

Groningen, Maastricht and Rotterdam.
Of these, Schipol offers by far the widest
choice of routes and is a mere fifteen
minutes by train to Amsterdam Central.

GETTING AROUND

Trains (w ns.nl) are fast and efficient,
fares relatively low, and the network
comprehensive. With any ticket, you're
free to stop off en route and continue
later that day. **Buses** are rarely used for
long-distance journeys except for the
more remote areas of the country not
covered in this guide. The website

23

ⓦ9292.nl is a useful journey planner for both trains and buses.

The Netherlands has a nationwide **public transport ticket** (ⓦov-chipkaart.nl) that is valid on all trains, metro, trams and buses, and comes in two formats – paper and plastic. Sold at NS automatic ticket machines and by most tram and bus drivers, the paper (disposable) **OV-chipkaart** is designed for occasional transport use – either for single journeys or one- or two-day bus or rail passes. For extended stays, a rechargeable, plastic OV-chipkaart – valid for five years – costs €7.50 and is sold only at train and bus stations, not by drivers. Before your journey, load up the card with credit – a minimum of €6 for urban transport and €20 for rail: unspent credit can be reclaimed at any public transport ticket office. Bear in mind that most ticket machines do not accept foreign debit or credit cards or cash – though ticket offices do.

The Netherlands has a nationwide system of **cycle** paths. You can rent bikes cheaply from main train stations and outlets in almost any town and village. Theft is rife: never leave your bike unlocked, and don't leave it on the street overnight – most stations have a storage area. For more on cycling see "sports and activities".

ACCOMMODATION

Accommodation can be pricey, especially in Amsterdam during peak season. Many of the smaller towns such as Haarlem have few budget options, so it may be cheaper to stay in Den Haag or Rotterdam and make day-trips to the Randstad towns. The cheapest one- or two-star **hotel** double rooms start at around €70; three-star hotel rooms begin around €95. Prices usually include a reasonable breakfast. The national hostel association **Stayokay** (ⓦstayokay.com) runs 27 clean, efficient (and bright orange) hostels nationwide, charging around €20–35 per person including a decent breakfast. If you use them extensively then it may be worth buying a **Stayokay Card**, which costs €17.50 and gives a discount of €2.50 a night. Larger cities have independent hostels with slightly lower prices but a tad more character. There are plenty of well-equipped **campsites**: expect to pay around €6 per person, plus €3–5 for a tent. Some sites also have **cabins** for up to four people, for around €40 a night.

FOOD AND DRINK

Dutch **food** largely revolves around bread, cheese and deep-fat fryers. Some specialities to look out for include: *kroketten*, bite-size chunks of meat and cheese sauce deep-fried in breadcrumbs; *fricandel*, a frankfurter-like sausage; and *poffertjes*, delicious airy little pancakes dusted in icing sugar. Seafood is often excellent, though the national craze for downing a whole salted herring (*maatjes*) may require some practice. As in Belgium, *frites* and mayo are served on almost any street corner.

In **restaurants**, the dish of the day (*dagschotel*) is the cheapest option. Usually the best-value restaurants are **Indonesian** (a legacy of Dutch colonial history), serving lots of lovely *nasi* or *bami goreng* (rice or noodles with meat), while another former colony, **Surinam**, has brought South American/Indian fusion cuisine (roti and curried plantain, anyone?) to the streets of major Dutch cities. Turkish-style kebabs (*shoarma*) and falafel are on offer almost everywhere.

DRINK

Sampling the Dutch and Belgian **beers** is a real pleasure, often done in a cosy brown café (*bruine kroeg*, named after the tobacco-stained walls); the big brands Heineken, Amstel, Oranjeboom and Grolsch are just the tip of the iceberg. A standard, small glass is *een fluitje*; a bigger glass is *een vaasje*. You may also come across *proeflokalen* or tasting houses, small, old-fashioned bars that close around 8pm, and specialize in **jenever**, Dutch gin, drunk straight; *oud* (old) is smooth, *jong* (young) packs more of a punch.

DRUGS

Purchases of up to 5g of cannabis, and possession of up to 30g (the legal limit) are tolerated; in practice, many "**coffeeshops**" offer discounted bulk purchases of 50g with impunity. When you walk in, ask to see the **menu**, which lists the different hashes and grasses on offer. Take care with spacecakes (cakes or biscuits baked with hash), mainly because you can't be sure what's in them, and don't ever buy from street dealers. All other narcotics are illegal, and don't even think about taking a "souvenir" home with you.

CULTURE AND ETIQUETTE

The Dutch are renowned for their liberal and laidback attitude, so there isn't much in the way of etiquette to observe. Don't be embarrassed about speaking to locals in **English** – unlike many of their fellow Europeans, the Dutch are happy to converse in English and are generally helpful. **Tipping** is not usually expected and service charges are often added to the bill in restaurants. Many bars and cafés continue to allow **smoking** (tobacco, that is), despite a national ban. **Prostitution** is legal, regulated and somewhat in your face in the form of window brothels in Amsterdam and other cities.

SPORTS AND ACTIVITIES

The Netherlands is a nation of **cyclists**. Renting bikes and cycling from city to city is very easy. For a more rural experience, the island of Texel and the Hoge Veluwe National Park near Arnhem are ideal, with the park even providing free bicycles for visitors. **Football** is also extremely popular, with the season

---

THE NETHERLANDS ONLINE

ⓦ**dutchnews.nl** English-language news and a useful "Dictionary of Dutchness".
ⓦ**holland.com** National tourist board.
ⓦ**iamsterdam.com** Exhaustive official site of Amsterdam's tourist board.
ⓦ**invadingholland.com** Entertaining blog by an Englishman in Amsterdam.

DISCOUNT CARDS

The **European Youth Card** (ⓦeyca.org; €14) offers discounts at most museums, galleries and tourist attractions throughout the country, as well as theatre, film and other leisure activities. Amsterdam and Rotterdam also offer **tourist cards** (see p.785 & p.796), with Rotterdam's being by far the best deal.

---

running from September to May and matches held on Sunday at around 2.30pm, with occasional games on Wednesday too. The major teams are PSV Eindhoven, Feyenoord in Rotterdam, and Amsterdam's Ajax.

COMMUNICATIONS

Free **wi-fi** is available in most cafés, hostels and hotels and many libraries and museums; just ask for the password. KPN, T-Mobile and Vodafone are the main **mobile** operators and offer a range of SIM-only deals. There are only a few **public phones** left near train stations, mainly for tourists – most take phonecards, which can be bought from TNT stores and tourist offices. The Dutch **postal service** is run by TNT and called PostNL, with counters within large stores and supermarkets. Stamps are sold at a wide range of outlets, mini-markets and hotels. Postboxes are legion – post international items in the "*Overige*" slot.

EMERGENCIES

The Netherlands is one of the safest countries in Europe, and most brushes with the law involve tourists who have overindulged in coffeeshops or bars or both (note that urinating in the street carries a €50 fine). **Pharmacies** (*apotheek*) are open Monday to Friday 8.30am to 5.30pm; if they are closed there'll be a note of the nearest open pharmacy on the door. When in need of a doctor, enquire at the reception of your accommodation; otherwise head for any hospital (*ziekenhuis*). If you need the emergency services, police, ambulance and fire are all on ☏112.

23

DUTCH

	DUTCH	PRONUNCIATION
Yes	*Ja*	Yah
No	*Nee*	Nay
Please	*Alstublieft*	Alstooblee-eft
Thank you	*Dank u/Bedankt*	Dank yoo/Bedankt
Hello/Good day	*Hallo*	Halloh
Goodbye	*Dag/Tot ziens*	Dahg/Tot Zeens
Excuse me	*Pardon*	Pardon
Where?	*Waar?*	Waah?
Good	*Goed*	Gud
Bad	*Slecht*	Slecht
Near	*Dichtbij*	Dichtbye
Far	*Ver*	Vare
Cheap	*Goedkoop*	Gudkoop
Expensive	*Duur*	Dooer
Open	*Open*	Open
Closed	*Gesloten*	Gesloten
Push	*Duwen*	Doowen
Pull	*Trekken*	Trekken
Today	*Vandaag*	Vandahg
Yesterday	*Gisteren*	Histehren
Tomorrow	*Morgen*	Morgen
How much is…?	*Wat kost…?*	Wat kost…?
I don't understand	*Ik begrijp het niet*	Ick bechripe het neet
Do you speak English?	*Spreekt u Engels?*	Spraicht oo Engels?
One	*Een*	Ayn
Two	*Twee*	Tway
Three	*Drie*	Dree
Four	*Vier*	Veer
Five	*Vijf*	Vife
Six	*Zes*	Zess
Seven	*Zeven*	Zayven
Eight	*Acht*	Acht
Nine	*Negen*	Nehen
Ten	*Tien*	Teen

INFORMATION

Official Dutch tourist offices known as VVVs are usually in town centres or by train stations and have information in English, including maps and accommodation lists; they will also book rooms for a small charge.

MONEY AND BANKS

The Dutch currency is the **euro** (€). **Banking hours** are Monday 1 to 5/6pm, Tuesday to Friday 9am to 5/6pm; in larger cities some banks also open Thursday 7 to 9pm and occasionally on Saturday mornings. **GWK exchange offices** at train stations open late daily.

You can also change money at most VVV tourist offices, though rates are worse. **ATMs** are widespread.

OPENING HOURS AND HOLIDAYS

Many **shops** close on Monday mornings, although markets open early. Otherwise, opening hours tend to be 9am to 5.30/6pm, with many shops staying open late on Thursdays or Fridays. Sunday opening is becoming increasingly common, with many shops open between noon and 5pm. In major cities, night shops (*avondwinkels*) open 4pm to 1/2am. **Museum** times are generally Tuesday to Saturday 10am to 5pm,

Sunday 1 to 5pm, although these vary widely. Shops and banks are closed, and museums adopt Sunday hours, on **public holidays**: January 1, Good Friday, Easter Sunday and Monday, April 27, May 5, Ascension Day, Whitsun and Monday, December 25 and December 26.

Amsterdam

A "bucket-list" city for many travellers, **AMSTERDAM** is a cosmopolitan capital packed with world-class attractions such as the **Rijksmuseum**, the **Van Gogh Museum** and the heart-rending **Anne Frank House**.

Gradually growing from a fishing village at the mouth of the River Amstel to a major European trading centre, Amsterdam accommodated its expansion with the cobweb of **canals** that gives the city its distinctive and elegant shape today.

In the 1960s Amsterdam emerged as a fashionable centre for the **alternative movement**, famously hosting John Lennon and Yoko Ono's "Bed-In for Peace". The city still takes a progressive approach to social issues, with its **cannabis café culture** and red-light district, though recent years have seen a more conservative shift. The tacky city centre souvenir and sex shops and the famous red-light windows are slowly being replaced by boutiques and artists' studios. And today, many of the city's trendsetters are heading out of the centre to the vibrant up-and-coming districts such as Amsterdam Noord and NDSM.

WHAT TO SEE AND DO

Amsterdam's compact **Old Centre** contains many of the city's attractions and takes about forty minutes to walk across. Centraal Station lies on its northern edge, and from here the city fans south in a web of concentric canals (*grachts*), surrounded by expanding suburbs. To the south is the city's main square and energetic party venue, **Leidseplein**, with the leafy **Vondelpark** and Museum quarter just over the Singelgracht to the south. The **Jordaan** to the northwest features mazy cobbled

streets and dreamy canals, and offers perfect strolling territory. North and east of Centraal Station are the expanding **docklands**, full of sleek modern architecture, bars and restaurants.

Centraal Station and the Damrak

The cathedral-esque **Centraal Station** is most people's first impression of Amsterdam. Exiting the station, you're greeted with chaotic **Stationsplein** which has for years resembled a building site crisscrossed with tram tracks, cyclists, buses and pedestrians, a legacy of the Metro works due to continue until 2020. From here, the busy thoroughfare **Damrak** marches into the heart of the city, lined with overpriced restaurants and bobbing canal boats, and flanked on the left first by the Modernist stock exchange, the **Beurs van Berlage** (now a concert hall), and then by the enormous De Bijenkorf department store.

The Red Light District

East of Damrak, the infamous **Red Light District**, stretching across two canals – Oudezijds Voorburgwal and Oudezijds Achterburgwal – is a curious mixture of unabashed sleaze (live sex shows and vibrator shops) and some quite lovely cafés, restaurants and bars. It's perhaps more fun to visit at night, when the neon-lit window brothels become strangely scenic. A few frivolous attractions worth seeking out here include the **Condomerie**, the world's first condom speciality shop (see p.788), and the **Hash Marihuana Hemp Museum** at Oudezijds Achterburgwal 148 (daily 10am–10pm; €9). Similarly frolicsome is the **Erotic Museum**, Oudezijds Achterburgwal 54 (Mon–Thurs & Sun 11am–1am, Fri & Sat 11am–2am; €7), which has some hilarious exhibits.

ROYAL REVELRY

The annual **King's Day** – on 27 April – is the city's biggest party, with up to half a million people dusting off their orange wigs and packing the streets and canals until it looks like a waterside disco: book accommodation well ahead for this date.

23

23

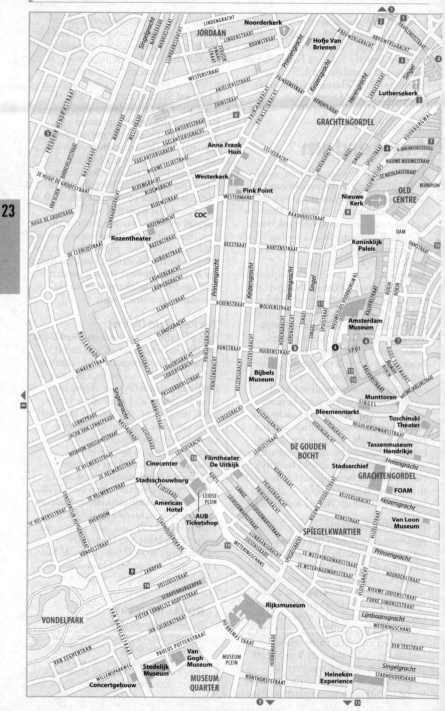

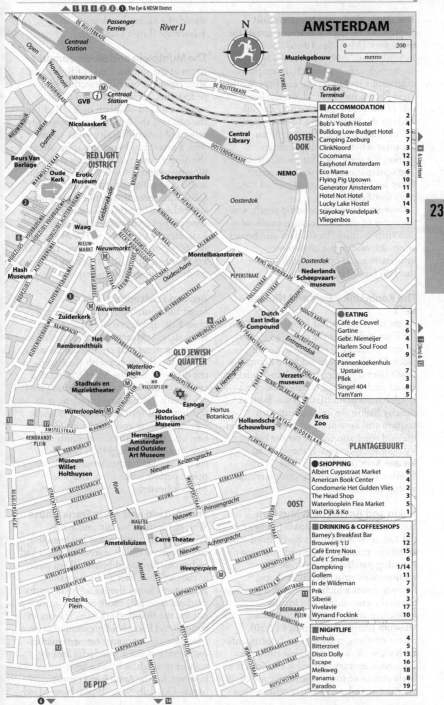

AMSTERDAM

N

River IJ

Passenger Ferries

Muziekgebouw

Cruise Terminal

Central Station

Centraal Station

GVB

St Nicolaaskerk

OOSTER-DOK

Central Library

NEMO

Oosterdok

Beurs Van Berlage

RED LIGHT DISTRICT

Oude Kerk

Erotic Museum

Scheepvaarthuis

Waag

Hash Museum

NIEUW-MARKT

Nieuwmarkt

Montelbaanstoren

Nederlands Scheepvaart-museum

Zuiderkerk

Nieuwmarkt

Dutch East India Compound

Het Rembrandthuis

OLD JEWISH QUARTER

Waterloo-plein

Verzets-museum

Stadhuis en Muziektheater

Waterlooplein

MR VISSERPLEIN

Esnoga

Joods Historisch Museum

Hortus Botanicus

Hollandsche Schouwburg

Artis Zoo

Museum Willet Holthuysen

Hermitage Amsterdam and Outsider Art Museum

REMBRANDT-PLEIN

PLANTAGEBUURT

OOST

Carré Theater

Amstelsluizen

Weesperplein

Frederiks Plein

DE PIJP

23

0   200
metres

■ ACCOMMODATION
Amstel Botel	2
Bob's Youth Hostel	4
Bulldog Low-Budget Hotel	5
Camping Zeeburg	7
ClinkNoord	3
Cocomama	12
Easyhotel Amsterdam	13
Eco Mama	6
Flying Pig Uptown	10
Generator Amsterdam	11
Hotel Not Hotel	8
Lucky Lake Hostel	14
Stayokay Vondelpark	9
Vliegenbos	1

● EATING
Café de Ceuvel	2
Gartine	6
Gebr. Niemeijer	4
Harlem Soul Food	1
Loetje	9
Pannenkoekenhuis Upstairs	7
Pllek	3
Singel 404	8
YamYam	5

● SHOPPING
Albert Cuypstraat Market	6
American Book Center	4
Condomerie Het Gulden Vlies	2
The Head Shop	3
Waterlooplein Flea Market	5
Van Dijk & Ko	1

■ DRINKING & COFFEESHOPS
Barney's Breakfast Bar	2
Brouwerij 't IJ	12
Café Entre Nous	15
Café t' Smalle	6
Dampkring	1/14
Gollem	11
In de Wildeman	7
Prik	9
Siberië	3
Vivelavie	17
Wynand Fockink	10

■ NIGHTLIFE
Bimhuis	4
Bitterzoet	5
Disco Dolly	13
Escape	16
Melkweg	18
Panama	8
Paradiso	19

The Oude Kerk and Nieuwmarkt

Behind the Beurs, off Warmoesstraat, the **Oude Kerk** (Mon–Sat 10am–6pm, Sun 1–5.30pm; €7.50), a bare, mostly fourteenth-century church, often puts on exhibitions including the excellent World Press Photo. Just beyond, on the other side of the Red Light District, Zeedijk leads to the **Nieuwmarkt square**, usually full of market stalls, particularly on Saturday when an organic farmers' market is a great spot for picnic treats. The square is centred on the turreted **Waag** building, an original part of the city's fortifications.

Kloveniersburgwal, heading south, was the outer of the three eastern canals of sixteenth-century Amsterdam and boasts, at no. 29, one of the city's most impressive canal houses, built for the Trip family in 1662.

The Koninklijk Paleis and Nieuwe Kerk

At the southern end of Damrak, the **Dam** (or Dam Square) is the centre of the city, its war memorial serving as a meeting place. On the western side, the **Koninklijk Paleis** (Royal Palace; daily 10am–5pm but closed during official ceremonies, check ⓦpaleisamsterdam.nl; €10) was built as the city hall in the mid-seventeenth century and now hosts state functions and the odd royal appearance on the balcony. Vying for importance is the adjacent **Nieuwe Kerk** (exhibitions daily 11am–5pm), a fifteenth-century church rebuilt several times.

Rokin and Amsterdam Museum

South of Dam Square, **Rokin** follows the old course of the Amstel River, lined with grandiose nineteenth-century mansions. Running parallel, **Kalverstraat** is a monotonous strip of clothes shops, halfway down which, at no. 92, a gateway forms the entrance to the former orphanage that's now the **Amsterdam Museum** (daily 10am–5pm; €12.50), where artefacts, paintings and documents survey the city's development from the thirteenth century. Close by, the **Spui** is a lively corner of town whose mixture of bookshops and packed bars centres on a statue of a young boy known as *'t Lieverdje* (Little Darling).

The Muntplein and Bloemenmarkt

Right at the southern end of Rokin, the **Muntplein** is a busy intersection where pedestrians, cyclists, cars and trams conduct a kind of urban ballet. Right in the centre is the Munttoren – originally a mint and part of the city walls, topped with a seventeenth-century spire. Across the Singel canal is the fragrant daily **Bloemenmarkt** (Flower Market). To the south is **Reguliersgracht**, an appealing canal with seven distinctive steep bridges stretching in line from Thorbeckeplein. One of the canals which crosses it, Keizersgracht, is home to **FOAM** at no. 609 (Sat–Wed 10am–6pm, Thurs & Fri 10am–9pm; €10; ⓦfoam.org), a hip, modern photography gallery.

Around Leidseplein

From the Spui, trams and pedestrians cross Koningsplein onto Amsterdam's main drag, **Leidsestraat** – a long, slender shopping street that cuts across the main canals. On the corner with Keizersgracht, the department store Metz & Co has a top-floor café with one of the best views of the city. Leidsestraat broadens at its southern end into **Leidseplein**, home to a vast Apple store and lined with identikit bars and clubs that form the hub of the city's mainstream nightlife. On the far corner, the **Stadsschouwburg** is the city's prime performance space after the Muziektheater.

The Jordaan and Anne Frank House

West of Centraal Station and across Prinsengracht, the **Jordaan** is a beguiling area of narrow canals, narrower streets and architecturally varied houses. With some of the city's best bars and restaurants, alternative clothes shops and good outdoor markets, especially those on the square outside the **Noorderkerk** (which hosts an antique and household goods market on Mondays and a popular farmers' market on Saturdays), it's a wonderful area to wander through. It is most famous, however, for the **Anne Frank House** (April–Oct daily 9am–10pm; Nov–March

AMSTERDAM CYCLING: A ROUGH GUIDE

Pretty much all Amsterdammers own a bike (*fiets*) and around two-thirds use them every day to get around. If you're thinking of joining them, it's worth bearing in mind some tips:

• start off with a bicycle tour (see p.785); you'll get your bearings and learn some useful road etiquette.

• to warn the locals that you're a beginner, rent a bright-red cycle from MacBike (Ⓦmacbike.nl). If you want to blend in, try a classic Dutch *burco* from Ajaxbike (Ⓦajaxbike.nl).

• beware tram tracks (these can buckle a wheel in seconds). You can't take a bike on a tram, but trains are okay providing you have the right ticket.

• always lock your bike to something solid. Bike thieves simply carry off cycles that only have a wheel lock.

• a lot of traditional Dutch bikes have pedal brakes rather than handlebar brakes – you may want to pay a little more for a regular bike.

Sun–Fri 9am–7pm, Sat 9am–9pm; before 3.30pm entrance is only with online tickets for a booked time slot; after 3.30pm tickets sold at the entrance; €9; Ⓦannefrank.org), where the young diarist lived, at Prinsengracht 267. It's deservedly one of the most popular tourist attractions in town. Anne, her family and friends went into hiding from the Nazis in 1942, staying in the house for two years until they were betrayed and taken away to labour camps. The plain, small rooms have been well preserved, and include moving details such as the film-star pin-ups on Anne's bedroom wall and video interviews with her former classmates.

On the Prinsengracht, south of Anne Frank House, stands the **Westerkerk** (April–Nov Mon–Fri 10am–3pm, Sat 11am–3pm; Dec–March Mon–Fri 10am–3pm; free), burial place of Rembrandt. You can climb its impressive 85m tower (June–Sept Mon–Sat 10am–3pm guided tours every 30min; €7.50).

The Vondelpark

The lush **Vondelpark** – immediately south of the buzzing Leidseplein – is the city's most enticing open space, packed in summer with young Amsterdammers lazing by the lake and listening to music; in June, July and August there are free concerts every Sunday at 2pm. Southeast of the park is a residential district, with designer shops and delis along chic **P.C. Hooftstraat** and **Van Baerlestraat**, and some of the city's major museums grouped around the grassy wedge of **Museumplein**.

The Rijksmuseum

One of the world's premier art museums, the **Rijksmuseum**, accessed from Museumstraat (daily 9am–5pm; €17.50; Ⓦrijksmuseum.nl), displays a chronologically organized collection, ranging from Dutch masters (pre-eminent among them Rembrandt, Frans Hals and Vermeer) to Van Gogh self-portraits and some wonderful Southeast Asian and Japanese art. Highlight is Rembrandt's huge *The Night Watch,* but don't miss the Dutch landscapes by Jan van Goyen, the intricate scale model of an East India Company merchant ship and the comically smug 1642 portrait of one Gerard Andriesz Bicker (son of the mayor of Amsterdam) by Bartholomeus van der Helst (all covered in the excellent multimedia tour; €5). Buy tickets online to avoid the queues.

The Van Gogh Museum and Stedelijk Museum

An Amsterdam institution, the **Van Gogh Museum** at Paulus Potterstraat 7 (Sat–Thurs 9am–6pm, Fri 9am–10pm; €17; Ⓦvangoghmuseum.nl) features paintings from the artist's early years in Holland including the dark *The Potato Eaters*, and continues through to the celebrated colourful works he produced after moving to Arles in the south of France, such as *The Yellow House* and the *Sunflowers* series (again, book online to avoid the queues). Along the street, the bold new-look **Stedelijk Museum of Modern Art** (daily 10am–6pm, Fri until 10pm; €15; Ⓦstedelijk.nl) has acres of

23

23

exhibition space dispaying major works by Van Gogh, Mondrian, Kandinsky and Matisse – look out for Picasso's *Seated Woman with Fish-Hat*.

The Heineken Experience and De Pijp

The vast **Heineken Experience** at Stadhouderskade 78, cast from the Rijksmuseum (July & Aug daily 10.30am–9pm; Sept–June Mon–Thurs 10.30am–7.30pm, Fri–Sun 10.30am–9pm; €16; ⓦheinekenexperience.com), provides a slick overview of one of the Netherlands' biggest brands, with a couple of free beers thrown in afterwards. South of here is the neighbourhood known as **De Pijp** (The Pipe) after its long canyon-like streets of brick tenements. It's a lively close-knit community with numerous inexpensive Surinamese and Turkish restaurants mixed in among the hip bars and organic delis. The main focus is lengthy **Albert Cuypstraat**, whose **market** (see p.788) is the largest in the city. Just south is the lovely landscaped **Sarphatipark**.

Waterlooplein and the Rembrandt House

East of Rembrandtplein across the Amstel, the large, squat **Muziektheater** and **Stadhuis** (commonly known as Stopera) flank **Waterlooplein**, home to the city's excellent **flea market** (see p.788). Behind, Jodenbreestraat was once the main street of the Jewish quarter (emptied by the Nazis in the 1940s); no. 6 is **Het Rembrandthuis** (Rembrandt House; daily 10am–6pm; €13; ⓦrembrandthuis.nl), which the painter bought in 1639 at the height of his fame. The main attraction here is the house itself, decorated in seventeenth-century style, rather than its relatively modest collection of Rembrandt etchings.

The Jewish Quarter and Hermitage Amsterdam

The award-winning **Joods Historisch Museum**, at Nieuwe Amstelstraat 1 (Jewish Historical Museum; daily 11am–5pm; closed Yom Kippur; €15; ⓦjhm.nl), is cleverly housed in a complex of Ashkenazi synagogues dating from the late seventeenth century and gives a vivid impression of Amsterdam's long-gone Jewish ghetto, while interactive pieces explain Jewish customs.

From here it's a short stroll towards the River Amstel and the **Hermitage Amsterdam** at Amstel 51 (daily 10am–5pm; €17.50; ⓦhermitage.nl), the first foreign branch of Russia's leading art museum in St Petersburg, possessing an extensive collection of paintings of Old Masters, as well as Oriental art and Post-Impressionist work. Inside, the new **Outsider Art Museum** promotes work by artists who did not study at art academies, such as Shinichi Sawada.

The Scheepvaartmuseum

One of the city's most popular attractions, the **Scheepvaartmuseum** (Maritime Museum) on Kattenburgerplein in the eastern docklands (daily 9am–5pm; €15; ⓦscheepvaartmuseum.nl) occupies the old arsenal of the Dutch navy built on its own mini-islet in the 1650s. Highlight is the full-scale replica of an East Indian merchant ship *De Amsterdam* – you can explore its decks and galleys, storerooms and gun bays.

ARRIVAL AND DEPARTURE

By plane Trains run from Schiphol airport, 15km southwest of Amsterdam, to Centraal Station (6am–midnight every 10min, midnight–6am hourly; 15min; €4.10 one-way;

HIT THE DOCKS

For a change of perspective head out to the wide-open spaces of the **eastern docklands**. A short tram trip (#26) or cycle ride east of Centraal Station, you'll find the futuristic Muziekgebouw concert venue (ⓦmuziekgebouw.nl) and the *Lloyd Hotel* (ⓦlloydhotel.com), a one- to five-star hotel and "cultural embassy", which hosts exhibitions and events in its huge light-filled public spaces.

A 10min (free) ferry ride north of Centraal Station takes you to the former shipyards of the Amsterdam Shipping Company. Now known as **NDSM**, this area is being rapidly redeveloped and boasts a couple of cool places to eat and drink, and rummage for antiques. Check ⓦndsm.nl for information.

ⓦns.nl). Alternatively, the Airport Express bus #197 (ⓦbus197.nl) leaves from platform B9 at Schiphol Plaza for the city centre (stopping at Museumplein, the Rijksmuseum and Leidseplein) every 15min; €4.75 one-way.

By train Centraal Station is the hub of all bus and tram routes and just 5min walk from central Dam Square.

Destinations Arnhem (for Hoge Veluwe National Park; every 15min; 1hr 5min); Brussels (every 1–2hr; 1hr 49min); Cologne (every 2hr; 2hr 40min); Den Haag HS (every 15min; 50min); Den Helder (every 30min; 1hr 15min); Frankfurt (every 2–3hr; 3hr 45min). Haarlem (every 10min; 15–20min); Leiden (every 15min; 35–45min); Maastricht (every 30min; 2hr 30min); Paris (hourly; 3hr 15min); Rotterdam (every 15min; 1hr 10min); Texel (via Den Helder; every 30min; 1hr 15min); Utrecht (every 5–15min; 30min).

By bus International buses arrive at Amstel Station, 10min southeast of Centraal Station by metro.

Destinations Brussels (hourly; 2hr 45min); Cologne (7 daily; 4hr 15min); Frankfurt (7 daily; 6hr 15min); London (7 daily; 10hr); Paris (6 daily; 7hr).

INFORMATION AND TOURS

Tourist office The main VVV is opposite Centraal Station, at Stationsplein 10 (daily 9am–6pm; ☎020 702 6000, ⓦiamsterdam.com); there's also an office in the airport in Arrivals hall 2 (daily 7am–10pm).

Discount card The Iamsterdam City Card (€55/65/75/85 for 24/48/72/96hr; ⓦiamsterdam.com) covers city transport and entry to many attractions. Given the price, though, it's only worth considering if you visit a lot of museums (note that it doesn't include the Rijksmuseum or Anne Frank House).

Bike tours Mike's Bike Tours (☎020 233 0216, ⓦmikesbiketoursamsterdam.com) does a good city tour leaving at noon from Prins Hendrikkade 176 (€25; 3hr 30min). Yellow Bike, at Nieuwezijds Kolk 29 (☎020 620 6940, ⓦyellowbike.nl), offers similar excursions departing at 1.30pm (€27.50), while Toms Travel Tours (☎06 1311 9892, ⓦtomstraveltours.com) runs bike trips plus photo and eco tours.

GETTING AROUND

By public transport There's an excellent network of trams, buses and metro (all daily 6/7am–midnight). The GVB public transport office in front of Centraal Station (Mon–Fri 7am–9pm, Sat & Sun 8am–9pm; ☎0900 8011, ⓦgvb.nl) has free route maps and sells OV-chipkaart (see p.776). After midnight, night buses take over, running roughly hourly from Centraal Station to most parts of the city (one-way ticket €4).

By bike Most hostels rent bikes for around €10 per day. Otherwise try MacBike (from €14.75 per day; ☎020 620 0985, ⓦmacbike.nl), which has convenient branches at

Centraal Station, Leidseplein, Marnixstraat and Waterlooplein, or the slightly cheaper Ajax Bike (from €8.50 per day; ☎0615 6 8 4831, ⓦajaxbike.nl) in De Pijp.

ACCOMMODATION

It's always worth booking ahead in high season, and at weekends throughout the year. Some hostels demand a two-night minimum stay.

HOSTELS

Bob's Youth Hostel Nieuwezijds Voorburgwal 92 ☎020 623 0063, ⓦwww.bobsyouthhostel.nl. This lively and legendary backpackers' favourite is just a 10min walk southwest of Centraal Station. Bar open til 3am. 30 max age limit. Dorms €22

Bulldog Low-Budget Hotel Oudezijds Voorburgwal 220 ☎020 620 3822, ⓦbulldog.nl. Super-smart "five-star" hostel with a bar, DVD lounge, roof terrace and laundry facilities. Accommodation ranges from dorms with TVs and showers to doubles and apartments. Dorms €33, doubles €123

ClinkNoord Badhuiskade 3, Amsterdam Noord ☎020 214 9730, ⓦclinkhostels.com. This brand-new hostel, housed in the 1920s former headquarters of Shell, offers four- to ten-bed dorms (including women-only dorms) and private en-suite rooms. Facilities include a free cinema, self-catering kitchen, café, library and bar with live music. Dorms €25

Cocomama Westeinde 18 ☎020 627 2454, ⓦcocomama.nl. Boutique hostel with upmarket two- to six-bed wooden bunk dorms, plus lovely en-suite private doubles and family rooms. It has a super communal kitchen, a lounge area showing movies and a lush garden (plus friendly house cat). Dorms €38, doubles €131

Eco Mama Valkenburgerstraat 124, Eastern Docklands ☎020 770 9529, ⓦecomamahotel.com. Superb light, bright eco-hostel with green roof, water-saving system and rooms that range from "El Cheapo" twelve-bed dorms to very stylish private en-suite doubles; there's a women-only dorm too. Dorms €42, doubles €142

Flying Pig Uptown Vossiusstraat 46–47, Museum Quarter ☎020 400 4187, ⓦflyingpig.nl. The better of the city's two Flying Pig hostels. It's immaculately clean with dorms sleeping four to fourteen, and a few have queen-size bunks that can be shared. There's a kitchen, no curfew, good tourist information and a strong party atmosphere – they serve the cheapest beer in town. Dorms €16, doubles €45

★ Generator Amsterdam Mauritskade 57 ☎020 708 5600, ⓦgeneratorhostels.com; tram #9 to Alexanderplein. Once the university's zoology department, this hotel-style hostel is the hippest new option in town. Light-filled modern rooms; cocktails served in the lecture-hall-turned-bar; pizza and espresso at an on-site café, plus free bikes. Dorms €15, doubles €85

23

★ TREAT YOURSELF

Lucky Lake Hostel ⓦluckylake.nl; metro to Holendrecht station then free shuttle bus. This rural idyll by the manmade Vinkeveen lakes, 15km southeast of central Amsterdam, offers a mixture of brightly decorated caravans, cabins sleeping two to three, and four-bed dorms. Rent a bike or kayak, cook in the outdoor kitchen or chill out in the lounge. Free breakfast. April to mid-Sept. Dorms €36, caravans €60, cabins €66

Stayokay Vondelpark Zandpad 5, Museum Quarter ⓣ020 589 8996, ⓦstayokay.com. One of the largest hostels in Europe, with bar, restaurant, secure lockers, and bike rental and shed; no curfew. Book two months ahead in high season. Dorms €40, doubles €115

HOTELS

Amstel Botel NDSM Pier 3 ⓣ020 626 4247, ⓦamstelbotel.nl. This three-star floating hotel in the NDSM district has "waterside" or "landside" rooms, plus five designer "Loftletter" rooms – one even has a half pipe for skateboarders! Rooms are fairly functional, but the bar has a pool table, juke box and pinball machine. Doubles €120

Easyhotel Amsterdam Van Ostadestraat 97 ⓣ020 3769 5901, ⓦeasyhotelamsterdam.com; tram #16 or #24 stop at Albert Cuypstraat. South of the centre, this clean, modern hotel charges for extras such as flatscreen TV, hairdryer and wi-fi. No breakfast, just vending machines. Doubles €58

Hotel Not Hotel Piri Reïsplein 34 ⓣ020 820 4538, ⓦhotelnothotel.com. Here each room is a work of art created by young designers. And the art is not just hanging on the walls – you can sleep in a tram cart, in a printed house or behind a secret bookcase. On-site bar serves Thai food and cocktails. Doubles €113

CAMPSITES

Camping Zeeburg Zuider IJdijk 20 ⓣ020 694 4430, ⓦcampingzeeburg.nl; tram #26 from Centraal Station to Zuiderzeeweg or night bus #359 to Flevoweg. Located on an island amid trees, this campsite also rents out eco-cabins. Min two-night stay. Free wi-fi. Open all year. Camping/person €14, plus per tent €10, cabins €100

Vliegenbos Meeuwenlaan 138 ⓣ020 636 8855, ⓦvliegenbos.com; bus #32, #33 or night bus #361 from Centraal Station. Located a 10min ferry ride away in Amsterdam North, this site is well equipped with a homely restaurant and lots of shade. April–Oct. Per tent €22

EATING

Amsterdam has many ethnic restaurants, especially Indonesian, Surinamese and Thai, as well as *eetcafés* that serve decent, well-priced food in an unpretentious setting.

CAFÉS

★ Café de Ceuvel Korte Papaverweg 4 ⓦcafedeceuvel.nl. Genial vegetarian café whose friendly owners have transformed a polluted shipyard into a sustainable green "business" park, of which the café – constructed from recycled materials – forms the hub. The quiches, salads and sandwiches (€8) include ingredients and herbs grown from their converted houseboat garden. Mon–Thurs & Sun noon–midnight, Fri & Sat noon–2am; closed Mon in winter.

Gartine Taksteeg 7 ⓦgartine.nl. Tucked down an alleyway just off the Kalverstraat, *Gartine* is an oasis of calm, and most of the ingredients in its delicious sandwiches (€7), salads (€11.50) and afternoon teas are grown in its own allotment. Wed–Sun 10am–6pm.

★ Gebr. Niemeijer Nieuwendijk 35 ⓦgebroeders niemeijer.nl. A great spot for a continental breakfast, *Gebr. Niemeijer* serves wonderful pastries and bread (also available to take away) with top-quality organic hams, cheeses, jams and more. The coffee is excellent too. Tues–Fri 8.15am–6.30pm, Sat 8.30am–5pm, Sun 9am–5pm.

Singel 404 Singel 404. A favourite among students for decades, *Singel 404* serves arguably the best sandwiches in Amsterdam – try the smoked chicken, avocado, sun-dried tomatoes and Brie. Get there early or you'll wait for a table. Daily 10am–6pm.

RESTAURANTS

Harlem Soul Food Haarlemmerstraat 77. Stylish New Orleans-style joint knocking out filling nachos (€8), jerk chicken (€5.40), plus more sophisticated evening dishes (crayfish salad €14). Daily 10am–1am, Fri & Sat until 3am.

Loetje Johannes Vermeerstraat 52 ⓦloetje.com. The original Amsterdam branch, this restaurant serves excellent steaks and salads on a pleasant outdoor terrace in summer: mains around €11.50. Other branches at Centraal Station (Stationsplein 10), Werfkade 14 and Ruyschstraat 15. Daily 10am–10.30pm.

Pannenkoekenhuis Upstairs Grimburgwal 2 ⓦupstairspannenkoeken.nl. Minuscule place in a tumbledown house, accessible via a steep staircase/ ladder, and with dozens of teapots hanging from the ceiling. It serves hearty sweet and savoury pancakes for under €10. Wed–Sun noon–6pm.

★ Pllek Tt. Neveritaweg 59 ⓦpllek.nl. One of several hip venues at the NDSM wharf, *Pllek* is housed in co-joined shipping containers. Dishes are international and affordable: mains like wild boar stew will set you back around €19. Mon–Thurs & Sun 9.30am–1am, Fri & Sat 9.30am–3am.

23

YamYam Frederik Hendrikstraat 88-90 ☎ 020 681 5097, ⓦ yamyam.nl. Top pizzeria with traditional dining room and open kitchen. Excellent pizza toppings include fresh rucola and truffle sauce. Pizzas €8–13. Booking strongly advised. Tues–Sat 6–10pm, Sun 5.30–10pm.

DRINKING AND NIGHTLIFE

There is a distinction between bars and coffeeshops, where smoking dope is the primary pastime (ask to see the menu). You must be 18 or over to enter these, and don't expect alcohol to be served. Drinks cost double those in a bar, but entry prices are low and there's rarely any kind of door policy. Check ⓦ djguide.nl to see who's hitting the decks.

BARS

★ **Brouwerij 't IJ** Funenkade 7 ⓦ brouwerijhetij.nl. Long-established brewery in the old public baths adjoining the Gooyer windmill. Serves up an excellent range of home-made beers and ales, from the thunderously strong Columbus amber ale to the easier-drinking Natte. Daily 2–8pm.

Café 't Smalle Egelantiersgracht 12 ⓦ t-smalle.nl. Candlelit café-bar with a pontoon on the canal out front for relaxed summer afternoons. In winter, be sure to try the gluhwein. Mon–Thurs & Sun 10am–1am, Fri & Sat 10am–2am.

Gollem Raamsteeg 4 ⓦ cafegollem.nl. Cosy split-level bar with rickety furniture, wood panelling and a comprehensive selection of Belgian beers, plus a few Dutch brews. Three other branches at Overtoom 160, Daniel Stalpertstraat 74 and Amstelstraat 34. Mon–Fri 4pm–1am, Sat & Sun noon–3am.

★ **In de Wildeman** Kolksteeg 3 ⓦ indewildeman.nl. A peaceful escape from the tacky shops of nearby Nieuwendijk, this lovely old-fashioned watering hole still boasts its original low bar and shelving. One of the centre's most appealing beer houses. Mon–Thurs & Sun noon–1am, Fri & Sat noon–2am.

★ **Wynand Fockink** Pijlsteeg 31 ⓦ wynand-fockink.nl. Just off Dam Square, this is one of the city's oldest *proeflokalen*, and it offers a vast range of its own flavoured jenevers. It's standing room only here. Daily 3–9pm.

COFFEESHOPS

Barney's Breakfast Bar Haarlemmerstraat 102 ⓦ barneys.biz. This popular café-cum-coffeeshop is one of the most civilized places in town to enjoy a big hit with a fine breakfast at any time of day. A few doors down, at no. 98, *Barney's Farm* affords a nice sunny spot in the morning and serves alcohol, while across the street the trendier *Barney's Uptown* serves cocktails. Daily 8am–1am.

Dampkring Handboogstraat 29 ⓦ dampkring-coffeeshop -amsterdam.nl. Colourful coffeeshop with loud music and a laidback atmosphere, known for its good-quality hash. There's a second branch on Haarlemmerstraat, just west of Centraal Station. Daily 10am–1am.

Siberië Brouwersgracht 11. Bright, modern coffeeshop that is less commercial than some of the larger chains. Very relaxed and friendly with a good selection of magazines and a chessboard – worth a visit whether you smoke or not. Mon–Thurs 9am–11pm, Fri & Sat 9am–midnight, Sun 10am–11pm.

CLUBS

Bitterzoet Spuistraat 2, Old Centre ⓦ bitterzoet.com. Spacious but cosy two-floor bar and theatre hosting a mixed bag of events: DJs playing punk and disco, film screenings and occasional urban poetry nights. Mon–Thurs & Sun 8pm–3am, Fri & Sat 8pm–4am.

Disco Dolly Handboogstraat 11, Old Centre ⓦ discodolly .nl. The reincarnation of the *Dansen bij Jansen* club, this two-floor club plays a soundtrack of soul, boogie-woogie, disco, deep house and occasional hip-hop. Very popular with students. Mon–Thurs 10pm–4am, Fri–Sun 10pm–5am.

Escape Rembrandtplein 11, Grachtengordel ⓦ escape .nl. A feature of Amsterdam's clubbing scene since the 1980s, this vast place can hold two thousand people. Recently updated, with an impressive sound system and visuals, its new café and lounge pull in the crowds. Thurs 11pm–4am, Fri & Sat 11pm–5am, Sun 11pm–4.30am.

Panama Oostelijke Handelskade 4, eastern docklands ⓦ panama.nl. Overlooking the River IJ and hosting top-name international DJs (Thurs–Sun), this club also has a restaurant, *Mercat*. Dress to impress. Mon–Wed noon–1am, Thurs & Sun noon–3am, Fri & Sat noon–4am.

LIVE MUSIC

Bimhuis Piet Heinkade 3, eastern docklands ☎ 020 788 2150, ⓦ bimhuis.nl. The city's premier jazz and improvised music venue is located right next to the Muziekgebouw. There are gigs from Dutch and international artists throughout the week, as well as jam sessions and workshops, plus a bar and restaurant for concertgoers, with pleasant views over the river. Mon–Thurs & Sun 6.30pm–1am, Fri & Sat 6.30pm–3am.

Melkweg Lijnbaansgracht 234a, Grachtengordel ☎ 020 531 8181, ⓦ melkweg.nl. A former dairy, the Melkweg ("Milky Way") is probably Amsterdam's most respected entertainment venue, with two halls for live music covering a broad range of genres, from reggae to rock. There's also a café-restaurant (Marnixstraat entrance; Wed–Sun noon–9pm).

Paradiso Weteringschans 6–8, Grachtengordel ☎ 020 626 4521, ⓦ paradiso.nl. This converted church just around the corner from the Leidseplein is popular with an alternative crowd. On Wed and Thurs eclectic dance night "Noodlanding" draws in the crowds, and DJ sets feature live performances on Sat. Hours vary.

23

23

ENTERTAINMENT

Amsterdam buzzes with places offering everything from English-language comedy to arthouse cinema. Grab a copy of *A-mag* from the tourist office or visit the "what's on" section of ⓦiamsterdam.com for the latest listings. Last-minute tickets are sold by ⓦlastminuteticketshop.nl.

★ **Boom Chicago** Rozengracht 117, Jordaan ☎020 217 0400, ⓦboomchicago.nl. This rapid fire improv comedy troupe hailing from the US performs nightly to crowds of both tourists and locals, and receives rave reviews. Inexpensive food, cocktails and beer served in pitchers.

Concertgebouw Concertgebouwplein 2–6, Museum Quarter ☎0900 671 8345, ⓦconcertgebouw.nl. One of the most impressive venues in the city, with a star-studded international programme, yet very reasonable prices (€15–50). Free 30min Wednesday lunchtime concerts are held from September to May (doors open 12.15pm; arrive early), and in July and August there's a heavily subsidized series of summer concerts.

EYE IJ promenade 1 ⓦeyefilm.nl; take the GVB Buiksloterwegveer passenger ferry service across the River IJ from the back of Centraal Station. This sleek riverside cinema screens a mixture of blockbusters and arthouse films (€9) and provides engaging views of the river and city centre.

GAY AMSTERDAM

Amsterdam has one of the biggest and best-established gay scenes in Europe. The nationwide organization COC (ⓦcocamsterdam.nl) can provide information and contacts. Otherwise check ⓦgayamsterdam.com.

Café Entre Nous Halvemaansteeg 14. Camp brown café that's packed at peak times, when everyone joins in the sing-alongs to cheesy 1980s music. Women welcome. Mon–Thurs & Sun 8pm–3am, Fri & Sat 8pm–4am.

Prik Spuistraat 109 ⓦprikamsterdam.nl. Voted the Netherlands' best gay bar of 2015 by Rainbow Awards, with tasty cocktails, smoothies and snacks, plus DJs at weekends. Mon–Thurs 4pm–1am, Fri & Sat 4pm–3am, Sun 3pm–1am.

Vivelavie Amstelstraat 7 ⓦvivelavie.net. Casual lesbian bar, where gay men are very welcome. Quiet during the week, but packed at the weekends. Mon–Thurs & Sun 4pm–3am, Fri & Sat 3pm–4am.

SHOPPING AND MARKETS

Albert Cuypstraat Market Albert Cuypstraat. Amsterdam's biggest market stretches for over 1km along De Pijp's longest street. As well as cheap clothes and homewares you'll find plenty of ethnic food stalls. Mon–Sat 9am–5pm.

American Book Center Spui 12, Old Centre ⓦabc.nl. This store has a vast stock of titles in English, as well as lots of imported US magazines and books. Mon noon–8pm, Tues, Wed & Fri 10am–8pm, Thurs 10am–9pm, Sun 11am–6.30pm.

Condomerie Het Gulden Vlies Warmoesstraat 141, Old Centre ⓦcondomerie.com. This shop sells condoms of every shape, size and flavour imaginable (and unimaginable) – all in the best possible taste. Mon–Wed & Fri 11am–6pm, Thurs & Sat 11am–9pm, Sun 1–6pm.

The Head Shop Kloveniersburgwal 39, Old Centre ⓦheadshop.nl. Every dope-smoking accessory you could possibly need, along with assorted marijuana ephemera. Mon–Fri 11am–6pm, Sat 11am–7pm, Sun noon–7pm.

★ **Van Dijk & Ko** Papaverweg 46, NDSM ⓦvandijkenko .nl. A treasure trove of reasonably priced vintage furniture, books, school supplies, glassware, etc. Can deliver internationally. Tues–Sat 10am–6pm, Sun noon–6pm.

Waterlooplein Flea Market Waterlooplein behind the Stadhuis ⓦwaterllooppleinmarkt.nl. An Amsterdam institution and the city's best central flea market is sprawling and chaotic, with wonderful antique/junk stalls to root through. Mon–Sat from 9am.

DIRECTORY

Embassies and consulates In Den Haag (p.793).

Exchange GWK Travelex Stationsplein 13f, Kalverstraat 150, and Leidsestraat 103.

Hospital VU Medisch Centrum De Boelelaan 1117 ☎020 444 4444, ⓦwww.vumc.nl.

Internet Wi-fi is available at all hostels and hotels, and pretty much all cafés and restaurants. If you need a terminal, try the Central Library at Oosterdokskade 143 (daily 10am–10pm; €1/30min; ⓦoba.nl).

Left luggage Bankcard-operated left-luggage lockers (daily 7am–11pm), at Centraal Station near platform 2b.

Post office Amsterdam's main post office is at Singel 250 (Mon–Fri 7.30am–6.30pm, Sat 9am–5pm; ⓦpostnl.nl). Otherwise postal transactions can be carried out at stores with the PostNL logo and branches of Albert Heijn supermarkets (including Jodenbreestraat 21).

Police Dial ☎0900 8844 and the operator will direct you to the nearest police station.

The Randstad

The string of towns known as the **Randstad**, or "rim town", situated amid a typically Dutch landscape of flat fields cut by canals, forms the country's most populated region and still recalls the landscapes painted in the seventeenth century. Much of the area can be visited as day-trips from Amsterdam. **Haarlem** is worth a look for the outstanding Frans Hals Museum, while to the south, the university centre of **Leiden** makes a pleasant detour before you reach the refined tranquillity of **Den Haag** (The Hague) and the modern urban landscape of **Rotterdam**. Nearby **Delft** and **Gouda** repay visits too, the former with one of the best-preserved centres in the region.

HAARLEM

Just over fifteen minutes from Amsterdam by train, **HAARLEM** is a handsome, mid-sized town that can be easily explored in a few hours. It also makes a good alternative base to Amsterdam at busy times. Those after a decent pint will also love the **Jopenkerk**, a church converted into a brewery.

WHAT TO SEE AND DO

The core of Haarlem is **Grote Markt** and the adjoining Riviervismarkt, flanked by the gabled, originally fourteenth-century **Stadhuis** and the impressive bulk of the **Grote Kerk** (Mon–Sat 10am–5pm; €2.50). Inside, the mighty Christian Müller organ of 1738 is said to have been played by Handel and Mozart. The town's main attraction is the wonderful **Frans Hals Museum**, at Groot Heiligland 62 (Tues–Sat 11am–5pm, Sun noon–5pm; €12.50; ⓦfranshalsmuseum.nl), that houses a number of his lifelike seventeenth-century portraits, including the *Civic Guard* series, which established his reputation.

ARRIVAL AND INFORMATION

By train The train station is north of the centre, about a 10min walk from the Grote Markt.
Destinations Alkmaar (every 30min; 30min); Amsterdam CS (every 10min; 15min); Delft (every 30min; 40min); Den Haag HS (every 30min; 30min); Leiden (every 10min; 20min).
Tourist office Stadhuis, Grote Markt 2 ⓣ023 531 7325, ⓦvvvhaarlem.nl (April–Sept Mon–Fri 9.30am–5.30pm, Sat 9.30am–5pm, Sun noon–4pm; Oct–March Mon 1–5.30pm, Tues–Fri 9.30am–5pm, Sat 10am–5pm).

ACCOMMODATION

★**Hello I'm local** Spiegelstraat 4 ⓣ023 844 6916, ⓦhelloimlocal.nl. Boutique twelve-room B&B/hostel with three dorms sleeping 8–14 and nine doubles/twins and quads, each beautifully decorated and many boasting lovely views. Dorms €19, doubles €75

Stayokay Haarlem Jan Gijzenpad 3 ⓣ023 537 3793, ⓦstayokay.com. Spick-and-span modern hostel near the sports stadium, about 3km north of the town centre. To get there, take bus #2 from the station – a 10min journey. Dorms €33, doubles €115

EATING AND DRINKING

De Roemer Botermarkt 17 ⓦcafederoemer.nl. Cosy bar with a covered outside terrace, tucked away on the edge of the old centre. It serves sandwiches and salads (€5–9) at lunch, and decent burgers and excellent steaks at dinner. Mon–Thurs 10am–1am, Fri & Sat 10am–2am, Sun noon–1am.
De Vlaminck Warmoesstraat 3. Takeaway serving classic crispy Dutch *frites* served with a dollop of fresh mayo. Mon–Wed & Fri–Sun 11am–7pm, Thurs 11am–9pm.
★**Jopenkerk** Gedempte Voldersgracht 2 ⓦjopenkerk .nl. A converted church that is home to the Jopen microbrewery, bar and restaurant, with long benches, comfy sofas and its own cloudy, unfiltered beer. The food is simple rather than splendid, but you should at least try one of the dozen or so Jopen brews at the bar. Daily 10am–1am; lunch noon–3pm; dinner 5.30–8pm.

LEIDEN

The charm of **LEIDEN** lies in the peace and prettiness of its gabled streets and canals, though the town's museums are varied and comprehensive enough to merit a visit. It also has a thriving student population thanks to a university consistently rated one of Europe's finest.

WHAT TO SEE AND DO

The most appealing quarter is **Rapenburg**, a peaceful area of narrow pedestrian streets and canals that is home to the country's best archeological museum, the **Rijksmuseum Van Oudheden** (National Museum of Antiquities; Tues–Sun 10am–5pm; €9.50; ⓦrmo.nl). Outside sits the first-century AD Temple of Teffeh, gifted by the Egyptian government, while inside are more Egyptian artefacts, along with classical Greek and Roman sculptures and exhibits from prehistoric, Roman and medieval times. Across Rapenburg, a network of narrow streets converges on the Gothic **Pieterskerk**. East of here, Breestraat marks the start of a vigorous **market** (Wed & Sat), which sprawls right over the sequence of bridges into Haarlemmerstraat, the town's major shopping street. Close by,

23

23

FLOWER POWER: THE KEUKENHOF

Along with Haarlem to the north, Leiden and Delft are the best bases for seeing the famous Dutch **bulbfields** that flourish in spring. The view from the train as you travel from Haarlem to Leiden can be sufficient in itself as the line cuts directly through the main growing areas, the fields divided into stark geometric blocks of pure colour. Otherwise, head for **Lisse**, home to the **Keukenhof** (mid-March to mid-May daily 8am–7.30pm; €16; ⓦ keukenhof.nl), the world's largest flower gardens. Some six million blooms are on show, complemented by five thousand square metres of greenhouses. Bus #54 (every 30min; 25min) runs to the Keukenhof from Leiden bus station. To skip the queues, it's worth getting Connexxion's combined bus and entry ticket (€20; available from Leiden Station as well as Schiphol and Amsterdam VVV).

the **Burcht** (daily 10am–10pm; free) is a shell of a fort, whose battlements you can clamber up for views of the town centre. The **Molenmuseum de Valk**, on Molenwerf at 2e Binnenvestgracht 1 (Tues–Sat 10am–5pm, Sun 1–5pm; €4; ⓦ molenmuseumdevalk.nl), is a museum housed in a classic Dutch windmill. Walk west along the 2e Binnenvestgracht and soon you'll hit the **Museum Volkenkunde** (Museum of Ethnology; Tues–Sun 10am–5pm; €14), with an impressive collection of artefacts from every continent.

ARRIVAL AND INFORMATION

By train Leiden's train station is on the northwest edge of town next to the bus station.

Destinations Amsterdam CS (every 10min; 35min); Amsterdam Schiphol (every 10min; 20min); Delft (every 10min; 20min); Den Haag HS (every 10min; 15min); Haarlem (every 10min; 20min); Rotterdam (every 15min; 35min).

Tourist office Right outside the train station at Stationsweg 41 (Mon–Fri 8am–6pm, Sat 10am–4pm, Sun 11am–3pm; ☏ 071 516 6000, ⓦ www.leiden.nl).

ACCOMMODATION

Rembrandt Nieuwe Beestenmarkt 10 ☏ 071 5144 233, ⓦ rembrandthotel.nl. City-centre three-star hotel with canal views and light, modern rooms. *Grand Café* on the

ground floor serves a buffet breakfast and finger food until late. Doubles €86

Vliet 39 Vliet 39 ☏ 071 513 40 48, ⓦ menscorpus.nl. In a seventeeth-century canalhouse, 1km from the centre, this first-floor en-suite suite comes with DVD player, free wi-fi and sitting room. Breakfast €12.50 per person. Cash only. Doubles €124

EATING AND DRINKING

Barrera Rapenburg 56 ⓦ cafebarrera.nl. A fashionable café-bar and student favourite with a traditional brown interior. Has a great canal-side location, a good, long beer menu and a pavement terrace. Also many wines by the glass and filling bar food – try the Rapenburger for €7.50. Mon–Sat 10am–1am, Sun 11am–1am.

★**De Bonte Koe** Hooglandsekerkkoorsteeg 13 ⓦ cafedebontekoe.net. One of the grooviest café-bars in Leiden, "The Colourful Cow" occupies vintage premises – apparently it was a butcher's shop (hence the tiles) that never managed to open. Serves a good range of beers on draught and a tasty home-made burger. Mon–Thurs 4pm–1am, Fri 4pm–3am, Sat 12.30pm–3am & Sun 1.30pm–1am.

La Bota Herensteeg 9 by the Pieterskerk ⓦ labota.nl. Hidden studenty spot which serves great-value food and beers. *Dagschotel* for €7 and steak or salmon for €10. Daily 5pm–1am; kitchen open 5–10pm.

DEN HAAG

Urbane **DEN HAAG (THE HAGUE)** is different from any other Dutch city. Since the sixteenth century it has been the Netherlands' political capital and from 1945 the home of the International Court of Justice. The main attraction for visitors is its wonderful **museums** packed with Dutch masters and its proximity to **Scheveningen**, the Netherlands' biggest beach resort.

WHAT TO SEE AND DO

The modern and historical centres of the city interweave about 1km north of Den Haag HS station, with the main sights clustered together. More attractions – including the seaside at **Scheveningen** – are further north, all of which are easily accessible on public transport.

The Binnenhof, Mauritshuis and around

The central **Binnenhof** is the home of the Dutch parliament and incorporates elements of the town's thirteenth-century

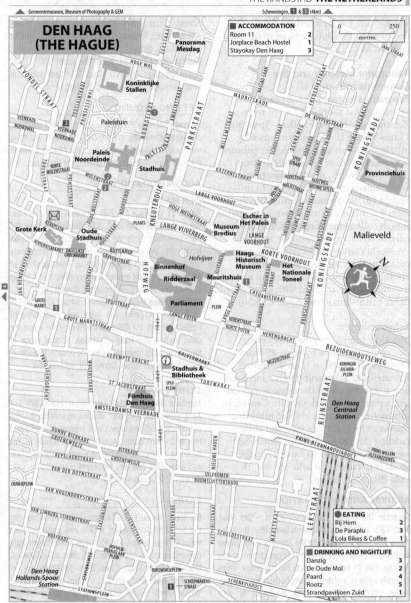

**DEN HAAG
(THE HAGUE)**

■ ACCOMMODATION	
Room 11	2
Jorplace Beach Hostel	1
Stayokay Den Haag	3

0	250
	metres

23

Malieveld

● EATING	
Bij Hem	2
De Paraplu	3
Lola Bikes & Coffee	1

■ DRINKING AND NIGHTLIFE	
Danzig	3
De Oude Mol	2
Paard	4
Rootz	5
Strandpaviljoen Zuid	1

castle set around a pretty, tree-lined lake. Immediately east of here, at Plein 29, is the **Mauritshuis** (Mon 1–6pm, Tues, Wed & Fri–Sun 10am–6pm, Thurs 10am–8pm; €14; ⓦmauritshuis.nl), a magnificent seventeenth-century mansion housing an extensive range of Flemish and Dutch

paintings including Vermeer's *Girl with a Pearl Earring* and *View of Delft*, plus one of Rembrandt's final self-portraits. Best to visit after 3pm or on Thursday evening to avoid the crowds. For an artistic contrast don't miss the nearby **Escher in Het Paleis**, at Lange Voorhout 74 (Tues–Sun

11am–5pm; €9; ⓦescherinhetpaleis.nl), dedicated to the Dutch master of optical illusion, M.C. Escher.

Panorama Mesdag and the Gemeentemuseum

Panorama Mesdag, just west of the pedestrianized shopping area of town at Zeestraat 65 (Mon–Sat 10am–5pm, Sun 11am–5pm; €10; ⓦpanorama-mesdag .nl), is an astonishing 360-degree painting of seaside scenes of Scheveningen from the 1880s. North, the **Gemeentemuseum,** Stadhouderslaan 41 (Tues–Sun 11am–5pm; €13.50; ⓦgemeentemuseum.nl; tram #17 from Centraal Station), contains superb collections of musical instruments, Islamic ceramics and modern art, with the world's largest collection of Mondrian paintings. The attached **Museum of Photography** and **GEM** contemporary art museum can be accessed with a combined ticket (Tues–Sun noon–6pm; €18.50).

Scheveningen

Just 4km from Den Haag city centre and easily accessible by tram #9 from Den Haag Central or tram #1 from Kneuterdijk, **Scheveningen** is a big brash beach resort with all the usual attractions like a pier, casino and Sea Life Centre. In summer it becomes a kind of mini Ibiza thanks to its beachside bars and surfers tackling the (bone-chilling) North Sea swells. Another way to experience the sands is to take a "fat bike" tour with Lola Bikes (see below).

ARRIVAL AND INFORMATION

By train The city has two train stations – Den Haag Central (CS) and Den Haag Hollands Spoor (HS), the latter about 1km southeast, close to the *Stayokay* hostel. There are frequent rail services between the two (5min), or you can take tram #1 from HS direct to the city centre. Trains generally arrive at, and depart from, both stations, so your choice will be down to which is closest to your accommodation. The exceptions are the slow intercity trains to Belgium which only stop at HS (connecting to the Thalys service at Rotterdam is much faster), and services to Schiphol which are slightly more frequent from CS.

Destinations Amsterdam CS (every 30min; 50min); Amsterdam Schiphol (every 15–20min; 28min); Antwerp (Den Haag HS only; every 2hr; 1hr 32min); Brussels (Den Haag HS only; every 2hr; 2hr 13min); Delft (every 15min;

12min); Gouda (every 20min; 20min); Leiden (every 30min; 20min); Rotterdam (every 15min; 25min); Utrecht (every 15min; 40min).

Tourist office Spui 68, inside the public library (Mon noon–8pm, Tues–Fri 10am–8pm, Sat 10am–5pm, Sun noon–5pm; ☎070 361 8860, ⓦdenhaag.com).

GETTING AROUND

By tram Trams are the best way to get around Den Haag and out to Scheveningen. A day card costs €6.50, less if you own an OV-chipkaart (see p.776). Line #1 runs between the train stations, then continues north to the beach.

ACCOMMODATION

DEN HAAG

Room 11 Veenkade 6 & 7–9; reception at *Café de Bieb*, Veenkade 7 ☎070 346 3657, ⓦhotelroom11.nl; tram #17 from Den Haag CS to the Noordwal tram stop. Bargain hotel with ten rooms spread over three three-storey terrace houses. Although they are far from luxurious, all are en suite, pleasant enough and very affordable. A handy location, too, plus organic breakfasts. Doubles **€70**

Stayokay Den Haag Scheepmakersstraat 27 ☎070 315 7888, ⓦstayokay.com. This large and comfortable HI hostel is located just 400m northeast of – and across the canal from – Den Haag HS station. A good range of facilities includes luggage and bicycle storage, bike rental, a café and a small library. Dorms **€19**, doubles **€60**

SCHEVENINGEN

Jorplace Beach Hostel Keizerstraat 296 ☎070 338 3270, ⓦjorplace.nl; tram #1. Within easy walking distance of the beach, Scheveningen's well-equipped hostel offers ten- to 24-bunk dorms. Also has several double rooms, including a campervan in the back garden. There's a café and a bar, plus bike and longboard rental. Dorms **€22**, doubles **€50**, campervan **€30**

EATING

Bij Hem Molenstraat 21a. Inventive sandwiches (try the Surinam spicy chicken, €9.75) and some excellent mains (Wagyu burger, €18.95) await at this bright little café-restaurant on one of the city's most chi-chi streets. Mon–Wed & Sun 10am–11pm, Thurs–Sat 11am–late.

De Paraplu Bagijnestraat 9 ⓦparaplu-eetcafe.nl. Simple *eetcafé* always jam-packed with people looking for good food at a reasonable price. Known for its Giant Plu-burger for around €16. Mon–Thurs & Sun 4–11pm, Fri–Sat 4pm–1am.

★**Lola Bikes & Coffee** Noordeinde 91, ⓦlolabike sandcoffee.nl. Bike shop/espresso bar with cool artwork and retro cycles hanging on the wall. Don't miss their Fatbike Experience cycle tour of the beach and dunes (every Sun 8.30am; €35). Daily 8am–6pm.

DRINKING AND NIGHTLIFE

Danzig Lange Houtstraat 9 ⓦ danzig.nl. Basement dance bar, hugely popular with students for its free entrance and cheap beer. Thurs–Sat 11pm–4am/5am.

De Oude Mol Oude Molstraat 61. Good old traditional bar and neighbourhood joint down a narrow side street. Oodles of atmosphere and an enjoyable range of beers. Upstairs is a tiny tapas bar. Daily from 5pm; kitchen Wed–Sat from 5.30pm.

Paard Prinsegracht 12 ⓦ paard.nl. Den Haag's main music venue, often featuring international acts (Florence and the Machine and Calvin Harris have appeared), and frequent DJ nights (many with free entry). Check online for the full schedule, show times and early bird discounts.

Rootz Grote Marktstraat 14 ⓦ rootz.nl. This large, heaving café-bar debunks Den Haag's staid reputation. Its saloon-style interior serves more than 200 Dutch and Belgian beers. Mon–Thurs & Sun 10am–12.30am, Fri & Sat 10am–1am.

Strandpaviljoen Zuid Wieringse Pad Stroke 11, Duindorp ⓦ gmdh.nl/zuid; tram #12 to Duindorp and follow the signs. Popular beach bar-restaurant south of the main Scheveningen strands. Also hosts live music and DJ sets. Summer daily 9am–11pm.

DIRECTORY

Embassies and consulates Australia, Carnegielaan 4, Den Haag ☎ 070 310 8200; Canada, Sophialaan 7, Den Haag ☎ 070 311 1600; Ireland, Scheveningseweg 12, Den Haag ☎ 070 363 0993; New Zealand, Eisenhowerlaan 77N, Den Haag ☎ 070 346 9324; UK, Lange Voorhout 10, Den Haag ☎ 070 427 0427; US, Lange Voorhout 102, Den Haag ☎ 070 310 2209.

DELFT

DELFT, 2km inland from Den Haag, is perhaps best known for **Delftware**, the delicate blue and white ceramics to which the town gave its name in the seventeenth century, and as the home of the painter **Johannes Vermeer**. With its gabled red-roofed houses standing beside tree-lined canals, the town has a faded tranquillity – though one that can suffer beneath the tourist onslaught in summer.

WHAT TO SEE AND DO

Delft's main square, the **Markt**, is framed by the impressive **Nieuwe Kerk** (Feb–March Mon–Sat 10am–5pm; April–Oct Mon–Sat 9am–6pm; Nov–Jan Mon–Fri 11am–4pm, Sat 10am–5pm; church €4 including entrance to Oude Kerke, tower

€4, churches & tower €7; ⓦ oudeen nieuwekerkdelft.nl) and the Renaissance **Stadhuis** opposite. William the Silent – leader of the struggle for Dutch independence in the sixteenth century – is buried in the Nieuwe Kerk, and you can climb the 370 steps of the **tower** for spectacular views. West of here, **Wynhaven**, an old canal, leads to Hippolytusbuurt and the Gothic **Oude Kerk** (same hours and fee as Nieuwe Kerk), with an unhealthily leaning tower. Vermeer fans should check out the **Vermeer Centrum** at Voldersgracht 21 (daily 10am–5pm; €8; ⓦ vermeerdelft.nl), which explains Vermeer's technique well with the aid of reproduction paintings.

A fifteen-minute walk south of the centre at Rotterdamseweg 196 is the **Royal Delft Experience** (daily 9am–5pm; Nov to mid-March as above but noon–5pm Sun; €12.50; ⓦ www.royaldelftexperience.nl) where you can see Delftware being painstakingly painted.

ARRIVAL AND INFORMATION

By train Delft's glassy new train station is a 10min walk from the Markt.

Destinations Amsterdam (every 15min; 1hr); Den Haag CS (every 10min; 10min); Rotterdam (every 5min; 10min).

Tourist office Delft's VVV, called TIP, is just off the Markt at Kerkstraat 3 (April–Sept Sun & Mon 10am–4pm, Tues–Sat 10am–5pm; Oct–March Tues–Sat 10am–4pm; Sun 11am–3pm; ☎ 05 215 40 51, ⓦ www.delft.nl).

ACCOMMODATION

Hostel Delft Voldersgracht 17a ☎ 061 649 6621, ⓦ hosteldelft.nl. Recently revamped, this bright and breezy city-centre hostel ambles round three old buildings, its six en-suite dorms sleeping between four and sixteen guests in tidy bunk beds. The six-bunk attic room is especially convivial. Has a communal kitchen, a TV lounge and four rooftop terraces. No breakfast. Dorms **€22**

Leeuwenbrug Koornmarkt 16 ☎ 015 214 7741, ⓦ leeuwenbrug.nl. Pleasant, medium-sized, three-star hotel occupying attractively renovated, canal-side premises – nothing fancy, just cosy and homely. Rooms are perhaps a little spartan, but those at the front have nice views and the breakfasts are very good. Doubles **€90**

EATING AND DRINKING

Café Zondag Voldersgracht 7 ⓦ zondag-delft.nl. "Every day is Sunday" at this relaxed café on pretty Voldersgracht. Good coffee and snacks (sandwiches €7.45), plus a decent

23

range of beers. Mon–Wed 10am–5.30pm, Thurs 10am–6pm, Fri & Sun 10am–10pm, Sat 9am–10pm.

★ **Kleijweg's Stadskoffyhuis** Oude Delft 133 ⓦ stads -koffyhuis.nl. Charming little café that regularly wins awards for its inventive range of sandwiches (€6–9) and also serves the best pancakes in town (€6–12). Mon–Fri 9am–8pm & Sat 9am–6pm.

Kobus Kuch Beestenmarkt 1 ⓦ kobuskuch.nl. Located on one of Delft's most atmospheric squares, this café is famous for its homebaked apple pie with whipped cream (€4) served in an old-fashioned woodpanelled setting; sandwiches around €7. Great terrace too. Mon–Thurs 9.30am–1am, Fri & Sat 9.30am–2am, Sun 10am–1am.

★ **Lunchcafé Vrij** Branantse Turfmarkt 61 ⓦ lunchcafevrij.nl. Buzzing little café serving some of the best coffee in the Netherlands, plus home-made pastries and Portuguese platters (€15.50) served with artisan bread: gluten-free options too. Tues–Fri 9.30am–5.30pm, Sat 9am–5pm, Sun 10.30am–5.30pm.

★ **Trappistenlokaal** 't Klooster Vlamingstraat 2 ⓦ www .trappistenlokaal.nl. Smashing little bar with traditional decor and an excellent range of international beers, both on tap and bottled. They often organize tastings. Mon–Thurs & Sun 4pm–1am, Fri 4pm–2am, Sat 2pm–2am.

ROTTERDAM

Looming skyscrapers, gritty docklands – **ROTTERDAM** is the Netherlands but not as we know it. The largest seaport in Europe, Rotterdam's urban landscape is largely a result of the hammering it received during World War II when bombing completely levelled the city. Today, with its elegant **Erasmus bridge**, playful Blaak **cube houses** and the vast Tetris-block "De Rotterdam", the city can boast some of the most adventurous architecture in the world. There's also plenty to keep you entertained, including a great **museum park**, the bohemian **Witte de Wittstraat** artistic quarter and, last but not least, the welcoming and independent-spirited Rotterdammers themselves.

WHAT TO SEE AND DO

You can get a feel for the city by walking from Centraal Station (or taking tram #7 from just outside) down to the Museumpark along Mauritsweg. More idiosyncratic attractions lie further east, while Delfshaven is a short, and rewarding, journey southwest.

The Museumpark and around

The impressive **Boijmans Van Beuningen Museum**, at Museumpark 18 (Tues–Sun 11am–5pm; €15; ⓦ boijmans.nl), has a superb collection of works by Monet, Van Gogh, Picasso, Gauguin and Cézanne, as well as several by Bosch (don't miss his *Tower of Babel*) Brueghel the Elder and Rembrandt. A stroll south through the Museumpark brings you to the **Kunsthal** at Westzeedijk 341 (Tues–Sat 10am–5pm, Sun 11am–5pm; €12; ⓦ kunsthal.nl), which hosts first-rate exhibitions of contemporary art, photography and design, and the **Natuur Museum** (Tues–Sun 11am–5pm; €7; ⓦ hetnatuurhistorisch.nl), displaying more than 400,000 objects related to natural history. For alternative art, you can't do better than a browse around the tiny, inexpensive galleries along **Witte de Withstraat**, northeast of the Museumpark.

The Maritiem Museum and the Kubuswoningen

The chief exhibit of the entertaining **Maritiem Museum** at Leuvehaven 1 (Maritime Museum; Tues–Sat 10am–5pm, Sun 11am–5pm; €10; ⓦ maritiemmuseum .nl), is the iron-clad *Buffel*, a nineteenth-century Dutch navy ship. A short walk east along Blaak is a remarkable series of 1980s cube-shaped houses, the *Kubuswoningen*: you can look round one, the **Kijk Kubus**, at Overblaak 70 (Show Cube; daily 11am–5pm; €2.50; ⓦ kubuswoning.nl).

Delfshaven

Little in Rotterdam city centre can be called postcard pretty, but **Delfshaven**, a short metro ride from Beurs, makes up for it. Its two canals are lined with lovely old warehouses and it was from here that the Pilgrim Fathers set sail for the New World in 1620, a connection marked by the elegant **Pelgrimvaderskerk** (Pilgrim's Church) and the excellent **De Pilgrim brewery** (see p.797).

The Erasmusbrug and Wilhelminakade

To experience Rotterdam's new architecture, cross the 800m **Erasmusbrug** to Wilhelminaplein (or take metro line

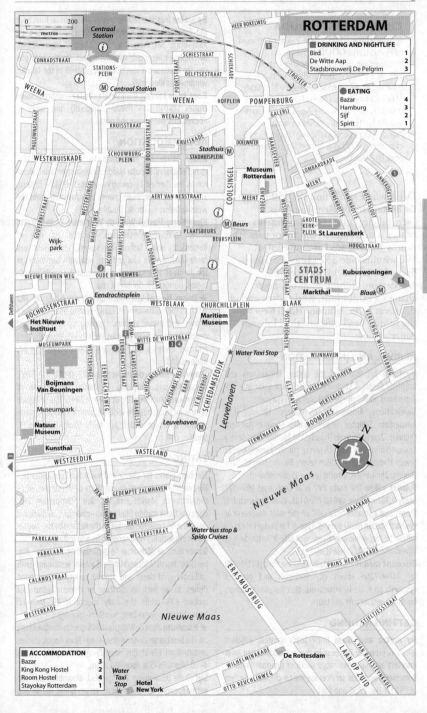

ROTTERDAM

0 200
metres

Centraal Station

DRINKING AND NIGHTLIFE
Bird	1
De Witte Aap	2
Stadsbrouwerij De Pelgrim	3

EATING
Bazar	4
Hamburg	3
Sijf	2
Spirit	1

ACCOMMODATION
Bazar	3
King Kong Hostel	2
Room Hostel	4
Stayokay Rotterdam	1

23

CONRADSTRAAT
STATIONS-PLEIN
Centraal Station
SCHIESTRAAT
POORTSTRAAT
DELFTSESTRAAT
SCHIEKADE
HEER BOKELWEG
STROVEER
WEENA
WEENA
HOFPLEIN
POMPENBURG
WEENAZUID
GALERIJ
KRUISSTRAAT
KRUISKADE
DOELWATER
HAAGSEVEER
LOMBARDKADE
PANNEKOEKSTRAAT
BOTERSLOOT
SCHOUWBURG-PLEIN
Stadhuis
STADHUISPLEIN
Museum Rotterdam
MEENT
BINNENROTTE
WESTKRUISKADE
PAULOWNASTRAAT
GOUVERNESTRAAT
WESTERSINGEL
MAURITSWEG
JACOBUSSTR.
MAURITSSTRAAT
KARL DOORMANSTRAAT
SCHOUWBURG
AERT VAN NESSTRAAT
MEENT
RODEZAND
WESTWAGENSTR.
Beurs
PLAATSBEURS
BEURSPLEIN
GROTE-KERK-PLEIN
St Laurenskerk
HOOGSTRAAT
Wijk-park
NIEUWE BINNEN WEG
OUDE BINNENWEG
Eendrachtsplein
KARL DOORMANSTRAAT
KEIZERSTRAAT
STADS-CENTRUM
Kubuswoningen
Markthal
Blaak
ROCHUSSENSTRAAT
WESTBLAAK
CHURCHILLPLEIN
BLAAK
Het Nieuwe Instituut
Maritiem Museum
POSTHOORNSTR.
MUSEUMPARK
WESTERSINGEL
WITTE DE WITHSTRAAT
BOOM-STRAAT
GAARDSSTRAAT
EENDRACHTSSTRAAT
EENDRACHTSWEG
SCHIEDAMSESINGEL
SCHIEDAMSE VEST
BAAN
JE BLEKERHOF
SCHIEDAMSEDIJK
Water Taxi Stop
WIJNHAVEN
SCHEEPMAKERSHAVEN
HERTEKADE
Boijmans Van Beuningen
Museumpark
BRAKELSTR.
Leuvehaven
Leuvehaven
GLASHAVEN
BOOMPJES
Natuur Museum
Kunsthal
WESTZEEDIJK
VASTELAND
TERWENAKKER
MAASKADE
VAN VOLLENHOVENSTRAAT
GEDEMPTE ZALMHAVEN
Nieuwe Maas
N
PARKLAAN
HOUTLAAN
WESTERSTRAAT
PARKLAAN
Water bus stop & Spido Cruises
PRINS HENDRIKKADE
CALANDSTRAAT
ERASMUSBRUG
WESTERKADE
Nieuwe Maas
STIELTJESSTRAAT
Water Taxi Stop
Hotel New York
WILHELMINAKADE
De Rottesdam
OTTO REUCHLINWEG
LAAN OP ZUID
S VAN RAVESTEYNKADE
Delfshaven

CHEESE FEAST: GOUDA

A pretty little town some 25km northeast of Rotterdam, **GOUDA** makes an enchanting day-trip. Its Markt – the largest in the Netherlands – hosts a touristy **cheese market** every Thursday (April to late Aug 10am–1pm), an event dates from the Middle Ages when farmers would barter their goods using a *handjeklap* (hand-clapping) ritual. Gouda can also easily be reached from Utrecht and The Hague.

23

D/E), where you'll find the 150m-high **De Rotterdam** by Rem Koolhaas, a "vertical city" of upscale apartments, offices, a hotel and a handful of bars. The nearby **Nederlands Fotomuseum**, at Wilhelminakade 332 (Tues–Fri 10am–5pm, Sat & Sun 11am–5pm; €9; ⓦnederlandsfotomuseum.nl), hosts changing exhibitions, while at the end of the street is the fabulous **Hotel New York**, the former head office of the Holland-America Line.

ARRIVAL AND INFORMATION

By train Just north of the centre, Rotterdam's vast futuristic Centraal Station is served by regular intercity departures plus high-speed Thalys and Frya trains.

Destinations Amsterdam CS (every 10min; 1hr); Amsterdam Schiphol (every 10min; 50min); Antwerp (hourly; 32min); Brussels (hourly; 1hr 10min); Delft (every 5min; 10min); Den Haag CS (every 10min; 25min); Gouda (every 10min; 20min); Leiden (every 10min; 30min); Paris (hourly; 2hr 40min); Utrecht (every 15min; 40min).

Tourist office The main VVV is at Coolsingel 195–197 (daily 9.30am–6pm; ☎010 790 0185, ⓦrotterdam.info); there's also a smaller "info café" on the main concourse at Centraal Station (daily 9am–5.30pm). For budget ideas on where to eat, drink and sleep, visit Use-It Rotterdam at Vijverhofstraat 47 (ⓦuse-it.nl).

Discount card The Rotterdam Welcome Card (€11/16/20 for 24/48/72hr) covers city transport and provides discounts on entry to attractions, plus discount vouchers for shops, restaurants and tours.

GETTING AROUND

By metro and tram Rotterdam's spotless, efficient metro is probably the best in the Netherlands (all lines intersect at Beurs, two stops south of Centraal Station). Both metro and tram services use the ov-chipkaart system (€3.50 for 2hr; €7.50 one day).

By water bus This fast ferry runs every 30min from near the Erasmusbrug to Dordrecht, 15km south (Mon–Fri 7am–8pm, Sat 8am–9m, Sun 11am–7.30pm; €2–6; ov-chipkaart accepted; ⓦwaterbus.nl). On the way you can see Rotterdam's vast docklands as well as the famous windmills at Kinderdijk.

Boat trips Leaving from beside the Erasmusbrug, Spido cruises (☎010 275 9988, ⓦspido.nl) runs tours of Rotterdam's waterways and port.

ACCOMMODATION

Bazar Witte de Withstraat 16 ☎010 206 5151, ⓦhotelbazar.nl. Popular Middle Eastern-style hotel whose rooms are themed by country – African, Middle Eastern, South American etc – so choose your favourite from the website before you book. Doubles **€80**

King Kong Hostel Witte de Withstraat 74 ☎010 818 8778, ⓦkingkonghostel.com. Located on one of Rotterdam's most fashionable streets, this bright and breezy hostel has a cool and arty vibe with hammocks in the dorms and (private) rain showers in the single/double rooms. Dorms **€26**, doubles **€100**

★ **Room Hostel** Van Vollenhovenstraat 62 ☎010 282 7277, ⓦroomrotterdam.nl. Funky central hostel in bright orange and purple colours, sleeping up to a hundred people in dorms with themes such as art, festivals, port and zoo. There's a busy bar downstairs. Dorms **€16.50**, doubles **€65**

Stayokay Rotterdam Overblaak 85 ☎010 436 5763, ⓦstayokay.com. Inspiring HI hostel inside one of Rotterdam's *kubuswoningen* (see p.794). Has a handy central location, but the facilities, which include luggage storage and bike rental, are fairly basic. Dorms **€21**, doubles **€60**

EATING

The best places for cheap and tasty food are Oude and Nieuwe Binnenweg, and groovy Witte de Withstraat, while the futuristic Market Hall, Ds. Jan Scharpstraat 298, opposite Blaak station (daily noon–midnight; ⓦmarkthal .nl) – the first covered market in the Netherlands – houses a host of speciality food shops, bars and restaurants.

Bazar Witte de Withstraat 16 ⓦbazarrotterdam.com. Big, bustling North African/Middle Eastern restaurant with strikingly vivid decor and a good variety of vegetarian dishes. Mains such as couscous or chicken kebab cost around €13, while the daily special is €9. Mon–Fri 8am–1am, Sat 9am–2am, Sun 9am–midnight.

★ **Hamburg** Witte de Withstraat 94B ⓦrestauranthamburg .nl. The best burgers in town (free-range Black Angus, chicken or tofu from €7) at this new US-style diner. Mon–Thurs 4–10.30pm, Fri–Sun noon–10.30pm.

Sijf Oude Binnenweg 115 ⓦsijf.nl. Downbeat café-bar with appealing Art Deco decor; serves filling snacks and light meals such as wild salmon or satay for around €14. There's an intimate little terrace too, great for people-watching. Sun & Mon 10am–midnight, Tues–Sat 10am–1am; kitchen till 10pm, 11pm on the weekend.

Spirit Mariniersweg 9 ⓦspiritrotterdam.nl. A New York loft-style one hundred percent organic vegetarian restaurant with a pay-by-weight buffet that will fill you up nicely for around €12.50. Mon–Sat 8am–11pm.

DRINKING AND NIGHTLIFE

Bird Raampoortstraat 26 ⓦbird-rotterdam.nl. You can hear anything from jazz to Latin to hip-hop at this club/restaurant under the arches of the Hofbogen viaduct. Tues–Thurs 5.30pm–1am, Fri & Sat 5.30pm–4am.

De Witte Aap Witte de Withstraat 78 ⓦdewitteaap.nl. Funky little café-bar with faded furniture, an arty clientele and displays of modern art on the walls. Occasional DJ sounds too – and a lively spill-out pavement terrace. Daily 1pm–4am.

★Stadsbrouwerij De Pelgrim Aelbrechtskolk 12 ⓦpelgrimbier.nl. Rotterdam's most popular brewery is located in the old Delfshaven council building, dating from 1580 with an attractive terrace overlooking the harbour. Its Mayflower Tripel beer with a hint of caramel is especially tasty. Wed–Sun noon–midnight.

UTRECHT

A short hop from Amsterdam, **UTRECHT**, with its world-class university, stunning medieval architecture and canals full of people lazily boating about in summer, has an almost Oxbridge feel. The city is perhaps best known for the 1713 **Peace of Utrecht**, a series of treaties which ended the War of the Spanish Succession.

WHAT TO SEE AND DO

Although it boasts few stellar sights, Utrecht's historic centre is perfect for aimless wandering. Its focal point is the fourteenth-century 110m-high **Dom Tower** – the highest church tower in the country. A one-hour guided tour (April–Sept Mon & Sun noon–4pm hourly; Tues–Sat 11am–4pm hourly; Oct–March Mon–Fri & Sun 3 daily; Sat noon–4pm hourly; €9; ⓦdomtoren.nl) takes you unnervingly close to the top, from where you can see Rotterdam and Amsterdam on a clear day.

Around 1km south of the centre at Nicolaaskerkhof 10, the **Central Museum** (Tues–Sun 11am–5pm; €12.50, includes

---

UTRECHT FROM THE WATER

The best way to experience the low-slung canals and architecture of Utrecht is from the water – the main Oudegracht and Nieuwegracht loop can be done in under an hour by kayak. Kanoverhuur at Oudegracht 275 (March to mid-Oct Mon 1–8pm, Tues–Sun 10am–8pm; €5/hour; ⓦkanoverhuurutrecht.nl) rents out kayaks and Canadian-style canoes.

---

entrance to Miffy Museum; ⓦcentraal museum.nl; bus #2) is worth a visit for its collection of Dutch art, mostly by local Utrecht artists. The nearby **Miffy Museum**, at Agnietenstraat 1 (Tues–Sun 10am–5pm; over 12s €3.50, 2–12s €8.50, under 2s free; ⓦnijntjemuseum .nl), is devoted to Dick Bruna, Utrecht artist and creator of children's favourite and global bestselling cartoon rabbit Miffy.

ARRIVAL AND INFORMATION

By train Utrecht's train station is located inside the large Hoog Catharijne shopping centre. Follow the signs and you will eventually be spat out at Vrdenburg which leads to the main canal, Oudegracht.

Destinations Amsterdam (every 15min; 30min); Arnhem (every 30min; 40min); Gouda (every 10min; 20min); Maastricht (every 30min; 2hr); Rotterdam (every 15min; 45min).

Tourist office Beside the Dom Tower at Domplein 9 (Sun & Mon noon–5pm, Tues–Sat 10am–5pm; ☏030 236 0000, ⓦvisit-utrecht.com). It offers the usual services and organizes tours of the Domtoren (see above). Pick up the Use-It Utrecht (ⓦuse-it.travel) map filled with budget eating suggestions and free sights.

ACCOMMODATION

Stayokay Utrecht-Bunnik Rhijnauwenselaan 14b ☏030 656 1277, ⓦstayokay.com; bus #40 or #41 from the train station direction Wijk bij Duurstede to Rhijnauwen. Peaceful, family-orientated HI hostel located a good 5km out of the centre in an old country manor house. Dorms __€25__, doubles __€59__

Strowis Budget Hostel Boothstraat 8 ☏030 238 0280, ⓦwww.strowis.nl. This central hostel, in a seventeenth-century townhouse on a tatty side street, has a good range of facilities including a small library, bike rental and a self-catering kitchen. Rooms, painted in cheerful colours, range from single to large dorms. Breakfast €6. Dorms __€20__, doubles __€65__

23

EATING, DRINKING AND NIGHTLIFE

Andersom Vismarkt 23. There aren't too many coffeeshops in the centre of Utrecht, but this well-established place fits the bill – and it's metres from the Domtoren. Mon–Sat 10am–11pm, Sun noon–11pm.

Beers & Barrels Oudegracht aan de Werf 125 ⓦ beersbarrels.nl. Pick of the old brick cellars along the Oude Gracht canal, this deep and dark, busy and atmospheric bar has a great range of local and foreign beers, some brewed on the premises, plus inexpensive barbecue food, from pulled pork (€7.50) through to burgers (€12). Daily 4pm–midnight; kitchen till 10pm, 11pm Thurs–Sat.

Broodje Mario Oudegracht 132. This market stall is a local institution, selling pizza slices and the famous Mario sandwich with cheese, salami and red pepper. Fill up for only €3.50. Mon–Sat 10.30am–6pm.

Kimmade Mariastraat ⓦ kimmade.nl. Arguably the best Vietnamese restaurant in town, this well-established place offers everything from honey pork through to fried tofu at excellent prices; mains are around €7. Mon–Sat noon–10pm, Sun 1–8pm.

★**The Village** Voorstraat 46, ⓦ thevillagecoffee.nl. Probably the hippest café in Utrecht – all exposed brickwork, bearded baristas and boasting a great location for people-watching. Mon–Fri 8am–6pm, Sat 9am–6pm, Sun 10am–6pm.

Beyond the Randstad

Outside the Randstad towns, the Netherlands is relatively unknown territory to visitors. To the north, there's superb cycling and hiking to be had through scenic **dune reserves** and delightful villages, with easy access to pristine beaches, while the island of **Texel** offers the country's most complete beach experience, and has plenty of birdlife. The **Hoge Veluwe National Park**, near Arnhem, boasts one of the Netherlands' best modern art museums and has some delightful cycle paths. Further south, a rougher landscape of farmland and forests leads to **Maastricht**, a city with a vibrant, pan-European feel.

TEXEL

The largest of the islands off the north coast – and the easiest to get to (2hr from Amsterdam) – **TEXEL** (pronounced "tessel") offers diverse and pretty landscapes, and is one of Europe's most important bird-breeding grounds.

WHAT TO SEE AND DO

Texel's main settlement, **DEN BURG**, makes a convenient base and has bike rental outlets. On the coast 3km southeast of Den Burg, **OUDESCHILD** is home to the new **Kaap Skil Museum van Jutters & Zeelui** at Heemskerckstraat 9 (April–Oct Mon–Sat 10am–5pm, Sun noon–5pm; €8.50; ⓦ kaapskil.nl), a fascinating collection of marine-related miscellanea. On the way into town, at Schilderweg 214, the **Texelse Bierbrouwerij** (tours Tues–Fri 2pm & 3pm, Sat 2pm, 3pm & 4pm; €11.50; ⓦ texels.nl) offers tours of the brewery and tastings. In the opposite direction is **DE KOOG**, with a good sandy beach and the **EcoMare nature centre**, at Ruijslaan 92 (daily 9.30am–5pm; €9.75; ⓦ ecomare.nl), a bird and seal sanctuary as well as natural history museum. **Fishing boat tours** from Oudeschild harbour (several daily year-round; ⓦ hetwadop.nl) stop at the **Wad**, banks of sand and mud to the east of the island, where seals and birds gather.

ARRIVAL AND INFORMATION

By boat Car ferries, run by Teso (Mon–Sat 6.30am–9.30pm, Sun 7.30am–9.30pm; ☎ 0222 369 600, ⓦ teso.nl), leave Den Helder for Texel hourly on the half-hour with extra departures in high season, and the journey takes about 20min. Return tickets cost €2.50 for foot passengers, plus €2.50 for a bike or moped; cars including passengers cost €37 at peak times. Once on Texel, various buses greet the ferry's arrival and depart for destinations across the island.

By bus Texelhopper bus #28 from Den Helder's train station uses the ferry to cross to Texel and then drives on to Den Burg and De Koog. It departs at twelve minutes past the hour and the tickets (€5.50 to anywhere on the island) include the ferry.

Tourist office Den Burg's VVV is at Emmalaan 66 (☎ 314 741, ⓦ texel.net; June–Oct Mon 9am–9pm, Tues–Fri 9am–5.30pm, Sat 9am–5pm, Sun 6–9pm; Nov–May Mon–Fri 9am–5.30pm, Sat 9am–5pm).

ACCOMMODATION

Camping is the most popular option here, with good campsites dotted around the island. The VVV website has a full list including some funky yurt options.

HOGE VELUWE NATIONAL PARK

Just north of **Arnhem** (80km from Amsterdam/55km from Utrecht) is the huge, privately owned **Hoge Veluwe National Park** (daily: Jan–March, Nov & Dec 9am–6pm, April & Sept 8am–8pm, May & Aug 8am–9pm, June & July 8am–10pm, Oct 9am–7pm; €9.15; ⓦ hogeveluwe.nl). Apart from being a wonderful place to hike and cycle (there are 1700 free "White Bikes" to use), it's also home to the superb **Kröller-Müller Museum** (Tues–Sun 10am–5pm; €18.30 including park admission; ⓦ krollermuller.nl), a collection of fine art that includes nearly three hundred paintings by Van Gogh, plus works by Picasso, Seurat, Léger and Mondrian, and is surrounded by an imaginative **sculpture garden**.

To get to the park, take the train from Amsterdam to Ede-Wageningen (every 30min; 1hr) and then bus #108 to Otterlo (every 30min; 20min), then cycle (30min), or catch bus #106 to Hoenderloo (every 30min; 15min), which stops near the entrance. If you fancy staying, there's an excellent **campsite** near the Hoenderloo entrance (open April–Oct; per person €8, plus per tent €7; ⓦ pampel.nl).

Kogerstrand Badweg 33 ☎0222 390 112, ⓦ texelcampings.nl. Campsite set among the beachside dunes in De Koog, the island's busiest resort. Part of a network of four sites across the island. Closed Oct–March. Per person **€17**

Stayokay Texel Haffelderweg 29 ☎0222 315 441, ⓦ stayokay.com. HI hostel on the outskirts of Den Burg that's well suited to families and groups, and it has a big bar and terrace. Dorms **€32**, doubles **€75**

EATING AND DRINKING

De Twaalf Balcken Weverstraat 20 ⓦ 12balcken.nl. The *Tavern of the Twelve Beams* is a Texel institution, an *eetcafé* serving well-priced salads, tortilla and ribs (mains from €16). Mon–Thurs 10am–1.30am, Fri & Sat 10am–3am, Sun 5pm–1.30am.

Pangkoekehuus Kikkertstraat 9 ⓦ pangkoekehuus.nl. They serve a great line in pancakes here – both sweet and savoury – and you can sit outside on the large terrace and watch the world go by. Prices start at around €4. Daily noon–8.30pm, July & Aug until 9pm.

Van der Star Heemskerckstraat 15, Oudeschild ⓦ vispaleistexel.nl. Well-priced seafood café located on Oudeschild harbour. It's pretty basic – wicker chairs and tables – but you won't care when you taste the delicious fresh and smoked fish. Mon–Sat 8am–6pm.

MAASTRICHT

Squashed between the Belgian and German borders, **MAASTRICHT** is one of the most delightful cities in the Netherlands. A university town popular with foreign students, it made a fitting location for the 1992 treaty that established the modern EU and the euro (you'll find € symbols decorating the pavement). It's worthy of a couple of nights to explore properly. If you can, try to time your visit to coincide with the excellent **pinkpop music festival** (mid-June; ⓦ pinkpop.nl) in nearby Landgraaf.

WHAT TO SEE AND DO

A short walk from the train station is the trendy **Wyck quarter**, home to a cluster of bars, restaurants and the city's most interesting shopping street, **Rechstraat**. From here the pretty Sint Servaasbrug leads west over the Maas River to the old town.

The old town and caves

The heart of the old town is busy **Markt square**, set around the impressive seventeenth-century **Stadhuis**. South of here are several notable churches, the most affecting being the **Onze Lieve Vrouw Basiliek** (daily 7.30am–5pm; free) which houses a beautiful Gothic chapel of Our Lady, full of flickering candles.

Continuing south brings you to the ancient **city walls** and the **university quarter**, with its pretty cobbled streets, shady squares and affordable cafés. You can explore a series of defensive tunnels beneath the city walls at **Casemates** (book guided tours in Dutch only €6.40; ⓦ maastrichtunderground.nl), though far more impressive are the labyrinthine **Zonneburg Caves**, a short boat ride away (gaslit tours in English at 2pm; €5.90 including boat trip from Maaspromenade 58; ⓦ maastrichtunderground.nl).

Bonnefantenmuseum

On the east side of the river, the newest part of Maastricht, Céramique, offers a complete contrast to the historic city, and is home to Maastricht's main art gallery, **Bonnefantenmuseum**, at Avenue Céramique 250 (Tues–Sun 11am–5pm; €10; ⓦbonnefanten.nl). Its collection ranges from Old Masters to contemporary artists, but the building itself, designed by Aldo Rossi, with its stunning cupola and monumental stairs, is just as impressive.

ARRIVAL, INFORMATION AND TOURS

By train The train station is on the east side of town, a 5min walk from the Sint Servaas Bridge. The nearest high-speed international services depart from Liège in Belgium. Destinations Amsterdam (every 30min; 2hr 25min); Eindhoven (for Rotterdam or Den Haag; every 30min; 1hr); Liège (hourly; 35min); Utrecht (every 30min; 2hr).

Tourist office The VVV is at Kleine Staat 1, at the end of the main shopping street (May–Oct Mon–Sat 10am–6pm, Sun 11am–5pm; Nov–April Mon–Fri 10am–6pm, Sat 10am–5pm; ⓣ043 325 2121, ⓦvvvmaastricht.nl).

★**Maastricht Running Tours** ⓦmaastrichtrunning tours.nl. Grab some exercise and discover hidden historical details on this excellent 6km running tour. €25 for one or two runners; cheaper for groups.

ACCOMMODATION

Camping Mooi Bemelen Gasthuis 3 ⓣ043 407 1321, ⓦmooibemelen.nl; bus #53. The most convenient campsite, just 10min east of town by bus. Open all year. Per person €4.20, plus per tent €4.20

De Hofnar Capucijnenstraat 35 & Keizer Karelplein 13 ⓣ043 351 0396, ⓦhofnarmaastricht.nl. Cosy B&B divided over two buildings with reasonable rooms, varying in size and shape: some have shared facilities. It has a homely atmosphere right in the heart of the city, though can be a bit noisy. €75

Stayokay Maastricht Maasboulevard 101 ⓣ043 750 1790, ⓦstayokay.com. Modern hostel sleeping around two hundred, right on the banks of the River Maas and within walking distance of the Onze Lieve Vrouweplein. There's a great terrace overlooking the water in summer. Dorms €35

EATING AND DRINKING

★**Café Sjiek** Sint Pieterstraat 13 ⓦcafesjiek.nl. Pleasant *eetcafé* serving a wide selection of regional dishes at affordable prices (mains around €15). Its cheese platter is a must for connoisseurs. It's also a great place to try local *zoervleis* (meat marinated in apple syrup and ginger). Mon–Thurs 5pm–2am, Fri–Sun noon–2am.

Coffeelovers Dominikanerkerkstraat 1. A stylish café within a bookshop in a beautiful converted church. The great coffee and sandwiches (€5.50) are a perfect accompaniment to browsing the books. Mon 10am–6pm, Tues, Wed & Fri–Sat 9am–6pm, Thurs 9am–9pm, Sun noon–5pm.

Take One Café Rechstraat 28 ⓦtakeonebiercafe.nl. Over 100 varieties of beer can be sampled in this Maastricht institution run by husband and wife Peet and Mery. Be prepared to be quizzed in depth on your taste preferences. Mon & Thurs–Sun 4pm–2am.

Tasty Thai Rechtstraat 29 ⓦtastythai.nl. Fast, flawless Thai food (mains €9) is served up in this canteen-style restaurant on the boutique-lined Rechtstraat. Mon 3–9pm, Tues–Sun noon–9pm.

★**Zondag** Wijckerbrugstraat 42 ⓦcafezondag.nl. Cool café-bar with huge windows serving snacks, soups (around €5) and salads (€10) until 10pm, after which DJs and stiff cocktails are the order of the day. Mon–Fri 10am–2am, Sat–Sun 10am–3am.

LOFOTEN ISLANDS

Norway

HIGHLIGHTS

❶ Oslo Opera House Gorgeous, sprawling arts space. **See p.809**

❷ Grünerløkka Buzzy, trendy Oslo neighbourhood with plenty of nightlife. See p.813

❸ Norwegian Canning Museum Engaging, history-rich exhibitions in Stavanger. **See p.814**

❹ Bryggen Atmospheric Bergen quarter with handsome wooden structures. **See p.816**

❺ Balestrand Quaint, fjordside village with glacier access. **See p.820**

❻ Lofoten Stunning Arctic archipelago with evocative land and seascapes. **See p.825**

❼ Northern Lights Fiery swathes of celestial illumination. **See p.827**

HIGHLIGHTS ARE MARKED ON THE MAP ON P.803

ROUGH COSTS

Daily budget Basic €80, occasional treat €115

Drink Beer €8

Food Meatballs with potatoes €20

Hostel/budget hotel €45–65/€100

Travel Train: Oslo–Bergen €95; bus: Oslo–Bergen €60

FACT FILE

Population 5.3 million

Language Norwegian

Currency Norwegian krone (kr)

Capital Oslo

International phone code ☎47

Time zone GMT +1hr

Introduction

Norway's extraordinary, postcard-perfect landscapes put the country at the top of any bucket list. Though its high prices will stretch your wallet, the payoff comes in the country's mix of likeable, easy-going cities and magnificent wilderness – during summer, you can hike up a glacier in the morning and thaw out in an urban bar in the evening, watching the sun dip below the horizon for all of half an hour, if at all. Deeper into the countryside, you'll find vast stretches of forests surrounded by distinctive glacier-formed landscapes. And because of Norway's small population, it really is possible to travel for hours in this natural grandeur without seeing a soul.

Beyond **Oslo** – a pretty and increasingly cosmopolitan capital surrounded by mountains and fjords – the major cities of interest are historic **Trondheim**, **Bergen**, on the edge of the fjords, and northern **Tromsø**. Anyone with even a passing fondness for the great outdoors should head to the **western fjords**: dip into the region from Bergen or **Ålesund**, or linger in one of the many quiet waterside towns and villages. Further north, deep in the Arctic Circle, the astounding **Lofoten Islands** have some of the most striking mountain scenery and clearest waters in Norway. To the north of here, the tourist trail focuses on the long journey to **Nordkapp**, the northernmost accessible point in Europe; the route leads through **Finnmark**, one of the last strongholds of the Sámi and their reindeer herds. Tourism reaches its height from late June to August when opening hours are long and activities plentiful; the rest of the year, you'll find many establishments closed unless you're in major towns.

CHRONOLOGY

10,000–2000 BC Seal- and reindeer-hunting tribes move into present-day Norway.
800–1050 AD Norwegian Vikings become a powerful force in Europe.
900 King Harald becomes the first ruler of a united Norway.
1030 The Norwegians adopt Christianity.
1262 Norway increases her empire, colonizing Greenland and Iceland.

1350 Almost two-thirds of the population die during the Black Death.
1396 The Kalmar Union unites Norway with Denmark and Sweden under a single ruler.
1536 Sweden leaves the Kalmar Union, leaving Norway under Danish control.
1814 Norwegian hopes of independence are dashed after Sweden invades and takes control.
1905 Parliament declares independence from Sweden. Haakon VII is crowned the first king of an independent Norway in 525 years.
1911 Explorer Roald Amundsen's expedition is the first to reach the South Pole ahead of the ill-fated Scott expedition.
1913 Norway becomes one of the first countries in the world to give women the vote.
1914 Norway remains neutral during World War I.
1940–45 German forces overrun Norway in sixty days, and it's five years before the country is liberated in May 1945.
1960s The discovery of oil and gas in the North Sea leads to greater economic prosperity.
1981 Gro Harlem Brundtland becomes Norway's first female prime minister.
1994 EU referendum: Norwegians decide not to join the EU.
2005 Prime Minister Kjell Bodevik is defeated in the general elections, and is replaced by Labour candidate Jens Stolenberg.
2011 Right-wing extremist Anders Breivik kills 77 people and wounds 319 in a combined shooting spree and the bombing of government buildings in Oslo.
2014 A major in the Norwegian army becomes the first woman to command a UN peacekeeping force.
2016 Decline in world oil prices leads to economic retrenchment.

NORWAY

Metres	
2000	
1000	
400	
0	

0   250
kilometres

NORWEGIAN
SEA

RUSSIA

Nordkapp
Honnigsvåg
Hammerfest
Lakselv
Kirkenes
Tromsø
Alta
Karasjok
Narvik
Kiruna
Lofoten
Islands
Svolvær
Å
Bodø
Fauske
Arctic Circle
Mo-i-Rana

HIGHLIGHTS

1 Oslo Opera House
2 Grünerløkka
3 Norwegian Canning Museum
4 Bryggen
5 Balestrand
6 Lofoten
7 Northern Lights

SWEDEN

FINLAND

Gulf of Bothnia

Trondheim
Ålesund
Åndalsnes
Geirangerfjord
Dombås
Nordfjord
Jostedalsbreen
Glacier
Stryn
Mundal
Østersund
Balestrand
Sognefjord
Bergen
Flåm
Lillehammer
Finse
HELSINKI
Haugesund
JOTUNHEIMEN
NATIONAL PARK
OSLO
Preikestolen
(Pulpit Rock)
Stavanger
Sandefjord
STOCKHOLM
Larvik
TALLINN
Kristiansand
BALTIC
SEA
ESTONIA

Newcastle

Hirtshals   Gothenburg & Denmark

24

ARRIVAL AND DEPARTURE

The four busiest **airports** for budget travellers are Oslo, Bergen, Trondheim and Stavanger. The main low-cost carrier is Norwegian (wnorwegian.no), an excellent budget airline serving a wide range of destinations, both direct and indirect. Its main rivals are Ryanair (wryanair.com), SAS (wflysas.com) and Widerøe (wwideroe.no).

Oslo and Norway's southern coastline can be reached by **car ferry** from Germany and Denmark by Color Line (wcolorline .com), DFDS Seaways (wdfdsseaways. com) and Fjordline (wfjordline.com). Fjordline boats also link Denmark with Bergen and Stavanger.

There are international **trains** to Oslo from Stockholm and Gothenburg in

Sweden and to Trondheim from Östersund. International **buses** run from various Swedish cities to Oslo (wswebus .se), and from northern Finland to northern Norway (weskelisen.fi).

GETTING AROUND

Public transport is very reliable, but in the winter (especially in the north), services can be cut back severely. Regional bus, ferry and train timetables are available at all tourist offices.

There are four main **train** routes, linking Oslo to Stockholm in the east, to Kristiansand and Stavanger in the southwest, to Bergen in the west and to Trondheim and on to Bodø in the north. The main discount scheme for train tickets is the advance-booking **Minipris**, which can save you upwards of 50 percent. InterRail and Eurail **rail passes** are valid in Norway. For train timetables, check ⓦnsb.no.

You'll need to use a combination of ferries and **buses** principally in the western fjords and mainly buses in the far north. Long-distance bus tickets can be expensive, though seats are always guaranteed and tickets are usually bought on board; in addition, the country's principal bus company, Nor-Way Bussekspress (ⓦnor-way.no), gives a ten percent discount for online purchases.

Travelling by **ferry** is one of the real pleasures of a trip to Norway. The **Hurtigruten** ferry (ⓦhurtigruten.co.uk) still retains its traditional role of connecting remote coastal towns, linking Bergen with Kirkenes, on the Russian border in the far north, with ferries running once a day in each direction. Shorter port-to-port trips can be surprisingly economical, especially if you are not obliged to book a cabin (as you are on longer voyages). There are also scores of **car ferries**, especially in the western fjords, as well as a plethora of **Hurtigbåt** (express passenger ferries).

If you book in advance and particularly if you are travelling long distances, **flying** is far quicker and often cheaper than taking a bus; check ⓦwideroe.no or ⓦnorwegian.no for offers.

Norway is a great place for **cycling**, but be prepared for narrow mountain roads, long distances and many tunnels that are closed to non-motorized traffic. Bike Norway (ⓦbike-norway.com) has all the information you need.

ACCOMMODATION

For budget travellers as well as hikers, climbers and skiers, **hostels** provide the accommodation mainstay; most are run by Norske Vandrerhjem (ⓦhihostels.no), but there are some excellent independent hostels too.

Expect to pay 300–400kr for a dorm bed, and 500–700kr for a double room. Sleeping bags are not allowed, but bringing a sleeping bag liner saves paying bed linen costs. The more expensive hostels nearly always include breakfast in the price of the room. HI members get a fifteen percent discount. Some HI hostels close between 11am and 4pm, there's often an 11pm/midnight curfew and most hostels tend to be inconveniently located. Many hostels close altogether during the winter months.

There are around four hundred official **campsites** around the country (ⓦcamping.no), plenty of them easily reached by public transport. Expect to pay 150–180kr per night for two people using a tent. Sites also often have **cabins** (*hytter*), usually four-bedded affairs with kitchen facilities, with prices ranging between 300 and 750kr. Many campsites come equipped with a guest kitchen, lounge, wi-fi access and sauna. A Camping Card Scandinavia (CCS), available from campsites or online (ⓦwww.camping.no), gives you numerous discounts. DNT (Norwegian Mountain Touring Club; ⓦdnt.no) maintains several hundred **mountain huts** along popular wilderness routes in Norway's national parks, which range from staffed lodges to unmanned huts

---

PLANNING YOUR TRIP

Travelling the length of Norway involves serious logistical planning, since each part of the country is covered by its own baffling array of buses and boats. Furthermore, some bus routes are only open in summer. Below are some useful websites to assist you with planning.

ⓦ**nsb.no** Norway train timetables and tickets.

ⓦ**rutebok.no** Compendious route-planner site covering boats, buses, trains and flights.

ⓦ**nor-way.no** National bus company connecting all major cities as far north as Trondheim.

ⓦ**177nordland.no** Buses and ferries in Nordland, from Trondheim northwards.

ⓦ**hurtigruten.no** Timetables and tickets for Norway's main coastal ferry.

ⓦ**skyss.no** Buses in the western fjords.

ⓦ**norled.no** Boats and buses in the western fjords.

ⓦ**torghatten-nord.no** Ferries to the Lofoten Islands from the mainland.

with kitchen facilities (pick up the key at the nearest DNT office). You can **camp rough** in any wild area in Norway as long as you are at least 150m from houses or water sources, and leave no trace.

Hotels are generally pricey, beginning at about 900kr, although rates are linked to demand and vary greatly. **Guesthouses** (*pensjonat* or *gjestehus*) cost around 750kr for a double, and B&Bs (ⓦbbnorway .com) can offer even better value. Finally, in the Lofoten Islands, **sjøhus** (literally "sea houses") and **rorbuer** (converted fishermen's cabins) can be rented from 500kr per cabin and sleep between two and eight people.

FOOD AND DRINK

Norwegian **food** is excellent: fish is plentiful, while reindeer steak and elk can be sampled in the north. However, eating well on a tight budget can be difficult. Breakfast (*frokost*) – bread, cheese, eggs, jam, cold meat and fish buffet, washed down with unlimited tea and coffee – is usually decent at hostels, and very good in hotels. If it isn't included in the room rate, reckon on an extra 75kr.

Picnic food is the best stand-by, and most supermarkets sell disposable barbecues for spontaneous fry-ups. **Fast-food** alternatives include kebab and burger joints, *pølse* (hot dogs) and pizza slices at any Narvesen or 7-Eleven, and sandwiches and cakes at Deli de Luca branches in Oslo, Bergen and Stavanger. Food markets sell *smørbrød*, huge open sandwiches heaped with a variety of garnishes. In the larger towns, traditional cafés (*kaffistovas*) serve good-quality Norwegian food at reasonable prices. At lunchtime (*lunsj*), most restaurants offer a separate lunch menu (mains 150–200kr) or cheaper daily specials (*dagens rett*), while dinner (*middag*) can be prohibitively expensive, with mains from 220kr. All large towns have authentic Thai, Chinese and Indian restaurants, which offer cheaper meals than their Norwegian equivalents. Restaurant business hours are usually 11am/noon to 3pm for lunch and 4/6 to 11pm for dinner.

The Norwegians have a complicated relationship with alcohol, with the result that booze is both heavily regulated and taxed; alcohol prices are the highest in Europe. Buying from the supermarkets and **Vinmonopolet** (state-run off-licences) is cheapest: in a bar, **beer** costs from around 70kr for 500ml. It comes in three strengths: class I is light, class II is what you get in supermarkets, while class III is the strongest and only available at Vinmonopolet. In the cities, bars stay open until at least 1am, if not later; in the smaller towns, they tend to close at 11pm. Look out for the national drink, *aquavit*, served ice-cold in little glasses; at forty percent ABV, it's real headache stuff. Outside bars and restaurants, **wines** and **spirits** can only be purchased from Vinmonopolet; opening hours are usually Monday–Friday 10am–5/6pm, Saturday 9am–1/3pm. You have to be 18 to buy wine and beer, 20 to buy spirits. No shop will sell you alcohol on a Sunday.

CULTURE AND ETIQUETTE

Norwegian people are generally scrupulously polite, helpful and self-deprecating. The famous **Nordic reserve** is apparent, but usually evaporates under the influence of direct friendliness.

In most restaurants it's common to round up the bill, whereas in upmarket places a ten percent **tip** is generally expected. Almost everyone speaks excellent English, even in the most isolated towns.

SPORTS AND OUTDOOR ACTIVITIES

Every type of snow-based sport is enjoyed in Norway, but **skiing** (both cross-country and downhill) is the national winter pastime and is taken very seriously indeed. In the north of the country, **dogsledding** and **snowmobile trips** can also help you make the most of the snow, though you pay dearly for the privilege, while **sailing** and **kayaking** are great ways to enjoy the western fjord region. The chill, clear waters around the Lofoten Islands are prime **snorkelling**, **diving** and **whale-watching**

24

NORWEGIAN

	NORWEGIAN	PRONUNCIATION
Yes	Ja	Ya
No	Nei	Ney
Please	Vær så snill	Veyr saw snil
Thank you	Takk	Takk
Hello/Good day	God morgen/God dag	God mor-gan/Go-daag
Goodbye	Adjø	Ad-yur
Excuse me	Unnskyld	Ewn-shewl
Where is?	Hvor er…?	Vor ayr…?
Good	God	God
Bad	Dårlig	Dawr-lig
Near	Nær	Neyr
Far	Langt	Laangt
Cheap	Billig	Billig
Expensive	Dyrt	Deert
Open	Åpen	Aww-pen
Closed	Stengt	Stengt
Today	I dag	Ee-daag
Yesterday	I går	Ee-gawr
Tomorrow	I morgen	Ee maw-ren
How much is it?	Hvor myer koster det?	Vor mew-e kaws-ter de?
What time is it?	Hva er klokka?	Vaa eyr klaw-ka?
I don't understand	Jeg forstår ikke	Yai fawr-stawr ik-ke
Do you speak English?	Snakker du engelsk?	Snack-er doo eyng-elsk?
Help!	Hjelp!	Yelp!
Cheers!	Skål!	Skol!
One	En	En
Two	To	Taw
Three	Tre	Trey
Four	Fire	Fee-reh
Five	Fem	Fem
Six	Seks	Seks
Seven	Sju	Shoo
Eight	Åtte	Aw-teh
Nine	Ni	Nee
Ten	Ti	Tee

territory, while Norway's vast national parks are a hiker's dream. There are plentiful hiking and climbing routes, as well as glacier walk excursions, with transport details and maps available from local tourist offices and DNT offices.

COMMUNICATIONS

Most accommodation options offer (usually) **free wi-fi** access, and most libraries have free internet access for at least 15 minutes at a time. **Post office** opening hours are Monday to Friday 9am to 5pm, Saturday 10am to 2/3pm. Mobile phone coverage is excellent almost everywhere, and EU citizens will pay minimal or no roaming charges.

EMERGENCIES

Violent crime is extremely rare. Hotels, pharmacies and tourist offices have lists of local **doctors** and dentists. Norway is not in the EU, but it is in the EEA and reciprocal health agreements mean EU/EEA citizens get free hospital treatment with the appropriate proof of identity.

EMERGENCY NUMBERS

Police ☏ 112; Ambulance ☏ 113; Fire ☏ 110.

INFORMATION

Every town has a helpful **tourist office** (ⓦvisitnorway.com). Many book accommodation, some rent out bikes and change money. During the high season – late June to August – they normally open daily for long hours; outside of these months, they mostly adopt shop hours, and many close down altogether in winter. Some cities, such as Oslo, Bergen and Stavanger, also have local DNT offices (Den Norske Turistforening; ⓦdnt.no) which stock hiking maps and information on Norway's national parks.

MONEY AND BANKS

Norway's currency is the **krone** (kr), divided into 100 øre. Coins come in 50 øre, 1kr, 5kr, 10kr and 20kr denominations; notes are in 50kr, 100kr, 200kr, 500kr and 1000kr denominations, though many retailers aren't keen on the latter. At the time of writing €1 = 9.20kr; £1 = 10.6kr; and US$1 = 8.20kr.

   Banking hours are Monday to Friday 8am to 3pm, Thursday till 5pm. Most airports and some train stations have exchange offices, open evenings and weekends. **ATMs** are commonplace even in the country's villages, and **credit and debit cards** are accepted pretty much everywhere.

OPENING HOURS AND HOLIDAYS

Supermarkets are open Monday to Friday 9am to 9pm and on Saturdays 9am to 6pm. Opening hours for **shops** are Monday to Wednesday and Friday 10am to 5pm, Thursday 10am to 7pm, Saturday 10am to 2pm. Almost all shops and supermarkets close on Sundays, the main exceptions being newspaper and snack-food kiosks (*Narvesen*). Most businesses are closed on **public holidays**: January 1, Maundy Thursday, Good Friday, Easter Sunday and Monday, May 1 (Labour Day), Ascension Day (mid-May), May 17 (Norway's National Day), Whit Monday, December 25 and 26.

Oslo

Downtown **OSLO** is largely the work of the late nineteenth and early twentieth centuries, an era reflected in the wide avenues, dignified parks and gardens, solid buildings and long, classical vistas. Oslo's residents enjoy the trappings of metropolitan life yet live but a stone's throw from dense forest and sandy beaches.

WHAT TO SEE AND DO

Oslo is graced by a clutch of first-rate museums and sights, a growing number of (admittedly expensive) cafés and restaurants, and a hip bar, clubbing and live music scene, all of which will keep you happily occupied for a few days.

Oslo Cathedral and Stortinget

The **cathedral** (Domkirke; Mon–Thurs, Sat & Sun 10am–4pm, Fri 4–6pm; free; ⓦoslodomkirke.no) is located just off Karl Johans gate. Its elegant interior and striking altarpiece are well worth a visit. From here, it's a brief stroll up Karl Johans gate to the **Stortinget**, the parliament building, an imposing chunk of neo-Romanesque architecture that was completed in 1866. In front of the parliament, a narrow park-piazza flanks

24

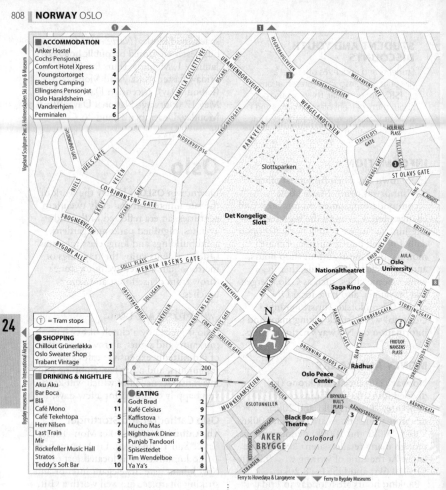

Karl Johans gate; in summer, it teems with promenading city folk, while in winter, people flock to its floodlit open-air skating rinks.

National Gallery

At Universitetsgata 13, the **National Gallery** (Nasjonalgalleriet; Tues, Wed & Fri 10am–6pm, Thurs 10am–7pm, Sat & Sun 11am–5pm; 100kr; ⓦnasjonalmuseet.no) is home to Norway's largest and best collection of fine art. A room devoted to Edvard Munch holds the original version of his famous *Scream*, and there are also wonderfully striking landscapes by Johan Christian Dahl and Thomas Fearnley.

City Hall

You can't miss the monolithic brickwork of the massive **City Hall** or **Rådhus** (daily 9am–4pm; free; ⓦrft.oslo.kommune.no), near the waterfront, which opened in 1950 to celebrate the city's 900th anniversary. Venture inside to admire an enormous hall decorated with murals by several prominent Norwegian artists – this is where the Nobel Peace Prize is awarded on December 10 each year.

Nobel Peace Center

No visitor to Oslo should miss the **Nobel Peace Center** (Mid-May to Aug daily 10am–6pm; Sept to mid-May Tues–Sun 10am–6pm; 100kr; ⓦnobelpeacecenter .org), a state-of-the-art interactive

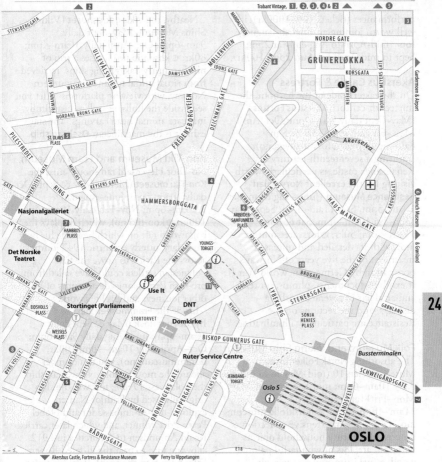

Akershus Castle, Fortress & Resistance Museum ▼   Ferry to Vippetangen ▼   Opera House ▼

OSLO

24

museum charting the history of the world's most prestigious prize and the lives and work of its winners. The excellent temporary exhibitions often include shows of modern photography.

Holmenkollen Ski Jump & Museum

At the **Ski Jump & Museum** (June–Aug daily 9am–8pm; May & Sept daily 10am–5pm; Oct–April daily 10am–4pm; 130kr; ⓦholmenkollen.com), the ski-jump tower gives you an exhilarating view of the city and of the ski jump itself, which attracts the world's best ski jumpers during the annual ski festival in March. The absorbing museum immerses you in the 4000-year history of skiing, while the entertaining **ski-jump** simulator

(separate entry fee: 75kr), complete with movement and sound effects, is not for the weak of stomach. Take T-bane line 1 towards Frognerseteren and alight at Holmenkollen.

Oslo Opera House

One of the most striking pieces of architecture in Oslo, the **Opera House** (foyer Mon–Fri 10am–7pm, Sat 11am–6pm, Sun noon–6pm; free; ⓦoperaen.no) is all white and blue angles, like the icebergs from which its shape takes its inspiration. Wander up onto its sloped roof, play the musical rods on the roof or by the entrance, or explore the beautiful, light-filled interior. Even if you don't attend one of the ballet or opera performances (tickets 100–1000kr), it's well worth joining an English-language **tour** (mid-April to Aug daily at 2pm; Sept to mid-April Fri–Sun 2pm; 100kr).

Akershus Castle & Fortress

On the eastern side of the harbour, the thirteenth-century **Akershus Fortress** (May–Sept daily 8am–9pm; Oct–April Mon–Fri 7am–6pm, Sat & Sun 8am–6pm; free; ⓦforsvarsbygg.no), featuring a seventeenth-century Renaissance castle, is particularly worth visiting for the excellent **Norwegian Resistance Museum** (June–Aug Mon–Sat 10am–5pm, Sun 11am–5pm; Sept–May Mon–Fri 10am–4pm, Sat & Sun 11am–4pm; 50kr; ⓦforsvaretsmuseer .no), with its detailed and unbiased treatment of the five years of Norway's occupation by Germany in World War II. It exhibits documents, photos, posters and artefacts in several absorbing displays, and the sections on the Resistance are particularly illuminating.

Folk Museum and Viking Ship Museum

The absorbing **Norsk Folkemuseum**, at Museumsveien 10 (mid-May to mid-Sept daily 10am–6pm; mid-Sept to mid-May Mon–Fri 11am–3pm, Sat & Sun 11am–4pm; 125kr; ⓦnorskfolkemuseum .no), combines an extensive collection of nineteenth-century household objects with folk art, lots of wonderful painted wooden furniture, and an open-air display of around 150 buildings from different periods of Norwegian history.

GETTING TO THE BYGDØY PENINSULA

The leafy **Bygdøy peninsula** is easily reached by passenger **ferry** from the Rådhusbrygge, behind the Rådhus (pier 3; April–Oct 8am–8.45pm, every 20min; shorter hours outside summer months; 60kr each way on board, 60kr return from the pierside ticket machine). Boats stop first at Dronningen pier (15min from Rådhusbrygge) for the Viking Ship and Folk museums, and then the Bygdøynes piers (20min) for the Kon-Tiki and Fram museums. Alternatively, take **bus** #30 (every 10–20min), which runs from Oslo S.

Nearby, the **Vikingskipshuset** (Viking Ships Museum; May–Sept daily 9am–6pm; Oct–April daily 10am–4pm; 80kr; ⓦkhm.uio.no) houses a trio of ninth-century oak Viking ships, retrieved from ritual burial mounds in southern Norway, with viewing platforms to let you see inside the hulls, as well as beautifully intricate animal head carvings. The star exhibit is the magnificent **Oseberg ship**.

Kon-Tiki Museum and Fram Museum

No Thor Heyerdahl fan should miss the **Kon-Tiki museet** (March–May & Sept–Oct daily 10am–5pm; June–Aug daily 9.30am–6pm; Nov–Feb daily 10am–4pm; 100kr; ⓦkon-tiki.no), which displays the balsawood raft on which he made his now legendary, utterly eccentric 1947 journey across the Pacific to prove the first Polynesian settlers could have sailed from pre-Inca Peru, alongside accounts of his other journeys and his life's work.

Inside the **Frammuseet**, next to the Bygdøynes dock (May & Sept daily 10am–5pm; June–Aug daily 9am–6pm; Oct–April daily 10am–4pm; 100kr; ⓦframmuseum.no), you can clamber aboard the most famous Norwegian ship, the polar vessel *Fram*; this was the ship originally used by Fridtjof Nansen, explorer-turned-ambassador and Nobel Peace Prize winner, and which later carried Roald Amundsen to Antarctica in 1912, allowing him to beat the ill-fated Robert Falcon Scott to the South Pole. Complete with most of its original fittings, the interior gives a superb insight into the life and times of these early polar explorers.

Munch Museum

The **Munchmuseet**, Tøyengata 53 (Mid-June to late Sept daily 10am–5pm; late Sept to mid-June daily 10am–4pm; 100kr; ⓦmunchmuseet.no), is reachable by T-bane – get off at the Tøyen station and it's a signed 5min-walk. Born in 1863, **Edvard Munch** is Norway's most famous painter. His lithographs and woodcuts are on display here, as well as his early paintings plus a handful of the great signature works of the 1890s. The museum owns one version of *The Scream* – there are four versions in total. The museum will be closed and moved to the harbourfront near the Opera House (see p.809) by 2020.

Vigeland Sculpture Park

Reachable by tram #12 from the centre (get off at the Vigelandsparken stop), Frogner Park's star feature is the wonderful open-air **Vigeland Sculpture Park** (daylight hours; free), the remarkable lifetime's achievement of another modern Norwegian artist, Gustav Vigeland. Vigeland started on the sculptures in 1924 and was still working on them when he died in 1943. A long sequence of life-size bronze and granite figures frowning, fighting and playing leads up to the central fountain, an enormous bowl representing the burden of life, supported by straining, sinewy bronze Goliaths, with an intricately carved obelisk towering behind it.

ARRIVAL AND DEPARTURE

By plane Oslo Gardermoen International Airport is located 45km north of the city centre. From the airport, FlyToget express trains go straight to Oslo S (daily every 10–20min 5am–11.30pm; 180kr one-way, 360kr return; w flytoget .no), as do the cheaper and slower NSB (Norwegian rail) intercity and local trains (hourly, fewer on Sat; 30min; 95kr each way). The Flybussen airport bus (Mon–Fri 5.20am–1am, Sat & Sun 5.30am–1am; every 20–30min; 180kr one-way, 275kr return; w flybussen.no) runs to the bus station, which is attached to Oslo S. Ryanair flights land at Torp airport, some 110km southwest of Oslo; Torp-Ekspressen buses connect arriving flights with Oslo bus terminal (2hr; 240kr one-way, 440kr return; w torpekspressen.no).

By train All trains arrive at Oslo Sentralstasjon (Oslo S), at the eastern end of the city centre.

Destinations Åndalsnes (4 daily, change at Dombås; 5hr 30min); Bergen (3–4 daily; 6hr 50min); Stavanger (4 daily; 8hr); Tønsberg (hourly; 1hr 20min); Trondheim (3 daily; 6hr 40min).

By bus Connected to Oslo S by a pedestrian bridge, the Oslo bus terminal handles long-distance and international buses. The website w rutebok.no has public transport timetables for all the different bus companies and routes.

Destinations Bergen (1–2 daily; 9hr 30min); Sogndal (2 daily; 7hr 30min); Stavanger (1–2 daily; 9hr); Trondheim (1–2 daily; 8hr 30min).

By boat DFDS Seaways (w dfdsseaways.co.uk) operates car ferries between Copenhagen and Oslo, while Stena Line (w stenaline.co.uk) runs car ferries from Fredrikshavn, in Denmark, to Oslo. Ferries dock at the Vippetangen quay, a 15min walk (1200m) from Oslo S – or catch bus #60

marked "Jernbanetorget" (every 20–30min; 8min). Color Line (w colorline.co.uk) car ferries from Kiel berth at the Hjortneskaia, some 3km west of the city centre. A connecting bus runs from the quay to Jernbanetorget and then Oslo bus station.

INFORMATION

CITY TOURIST OFFICE

Oslo Visitor Centre Jernbanetorget 1, in the Østbanehallen, a converted former railway station next to Oslo S train station (Sept–May daily 9am–6pm; June–Aug Mon–Sat 8am–8pm & Sun 9am–6pm; t 81 53 05 55, w visitoslo.com). The Oslo Visitor Centre has a full range of information about Oslo and its environs. They issue handy, free city maps marked with tram and principal bus routes and supply free copies of both the thorough *Oslo Guide* and the listings brochure *What's On in Oslo*. They also sell public transport tickets, concert tickets and the Oslo Pass (see p.807), as well currency exchange and accommodation reservations.

YOUTH INFORMATION CENTRE

Unginfo (Use-it) Møllergata 3, a brief walk from Oslo S (Mon–Fri 11am–5pm, Sat noon–5pm; t 24 14 98 20, w use-it.no). Oslo's Youth Information Centre provides help and support to young people (26 years and below). They also do a sideline in youth tourism, producing an annual *Free Map for Young Travellers*, which provides tips and hints and gives a roundup of their favourite bars and clubs, etc – and marks them on a map. They carry all manner of fliers for gigs and concerts as well, plus there's lots more information on their website.

HIKING INFORMATION OFFICE

Den Norske Turistforening (DNT) Storgata 3 (Mon–Fri 10am–5pm, Thurs 10am–6pm, Sat 10am–3pm; t 22 82 28 00, w dntoslo.no). The Norwegian hiking organization's city-centre office stocks a full range of Norwegian hiking maps, books and equipment. Also sells DNT membership (640kr per annum), which confers substantial discounts at DNT huts.

GETTING AROUND

By tram and bus Trams run on six lines, crossing the centre from east to west. Most bus routes, of which there are many, converge at Oslo S.

By metro The *Tunnelbanen* (T-bane or metro) has five lines and they share a common slice of track crossing the city centre from Majorstuen in the west to Tøyen in the east, with Jernbanetorget/Oslo S in between.

By passenger boat Numerous local ferries cross the Oslofjord to the south of the centre, connecting the city with its outlying districts and archipelagos; ferries leave from the jetties behind the Rådhus.

24

24

Tickets The Oslo conurbation is divided into zones, and the more zones you cross, the higher the fare. However, central Oslo and its immediate surroundings are all in Zone 1, where flat-fare tickets cost 32kr if purchased before the journey, 50kr if purchased from a bus or tram driver. A Zone 1 unlimited 24hr pass (*Dagskort*) costs 90kr and can be bought at the automatic ticket machines.

ACCOMMODATION

HOSTELS

Anker Hostel Storgata 55 ☎ 22 99 72 00, ⓦ ankerhostel .no. Enormous, clean and friendly hostel on the edge of the hip Grünerløkka district, attracting an international clientele. Amenities include guest kitchens and a bar. The attached hotel has somewhat better-turned-out rooms for 1000kr. Dorms 260kr, en-suite doubles 700kr

★ **Oslo Haraldsheim Vandrerhjem** Haraldsheimveien 4, Grefsen ☎ 22 22 29 65, ⓦ haraldsheim.no. Best of the HI hostels, 4km northeast of the centre, consisting mostly of four-bed dorms, many en-suite. To get there, take tram #17 from outside Oslo S train station, and get off at the Sinsenkrysset stop, from where it's a signed 5min walk. Open all year except Christmas week. Dorms 255kr, doubles 610kr

HOTELS AND GUESTHOUSES

Cochs Pensjonat Parkveien 25 ☎ 23 33 24 00, ⓦ cochspensjonat.no. Pleasant guesthouse just north of the royal palace, with spartan but well-kept rooms. The least expensive rooms are those with shared facilities – en-suites cost 850kr (single 650kr) and those with a kitchenette 900kr (single 690kr). Breakfasts (42kr extra) are served just along the street at *Espresso House*. Doubles 720kr

Comfort Hotel Xpress Youngstorget Møllergata 26 ☎ 22 03 11 00, ⓦ nordicchoicehotels.com. Opened in 2011, and aimed firmly at the youth/clubbing market, this chain hotel in a seven-storey block does its best to create a cool/relaxed vibe, beginning with the striking Pop Art decor in the foyer. There are few formalities at reception – you check in at the electronic kiosks – and the 175 guest rooms beyond (modernism-meets-spartan) are similarly hi-tech. Doubles 650kr

Ellingsens Pensjonat Holtegata 25 ☎ 22 60 03 59, ⓦ ellingsenspensjonat.no. Competitively priced accommodation in a large, well-equipped and attractively decorated late nineteenth-century house on the west side of the city centre, just beyond the Slottsparken. Rooms are spacious and those with en suite cost 990kr. Guests have access to a small garden. Doubles 800kr

Perminalen Øvre Slottsgate 2 ☎ 24 00 55 00, ⓦ perminalen.no. This hostel-like hotel has two things going for it – a central location and budget prices: a bed in a four- or six-berth room costs just 425kr, a single 685kr. At these rates, it's hardly surprising that the guest rooms are positively frugal, though at least all the doubles and singles are en suite. Popular with the Norwegian military. Doubles 960kr

CAMPSITE

Ekeberg Camping Ekebergveien 65 ☎ 22 19 85 68, ⓦ www.ekebergcamping.no. Sprawling campsite in a field just 3km southeast of the city centre – and on the east side of the Ekebergparken. Rudimentary but still popular. Take bus #34 from Oslo S – it's a 10min journey. June–Aug. Per tent (sleeping up to 4) 300kr

EATING

For those counting their kroner, Godt Brød, Thorvald Meyersgate 49, is best for freshly baked bread and doorstop sandwiches. You can also buy a bag of freshly cooked prawns from a fishing boat at the Rådhusbrygge pier, or head to the open-air market on Youngstorget (Mon–Sat 7am–2pm).

Kafé Celsius Rådhusgata 19 ⓦ kafecelsius.no. Great little café-bar in refurbished old premises off a cobbled square, with a fetching courtyard for sunny days and fresh, light dishes such as chicken salad (190kr). Mon–Fri 11am–11pm, Sat noon–11pm, Sun 11am–11pm.

Kaffistova Rosenkrantz gate 8 ⓦ kaffistova.com. Set in a hotel, this self-service café feels a bit like a canteen but serves open sandwiches and traditional Norwegian dishes such as meatballs and reindeer cakes – reckon on 160kr for a main course. Mon–Fri 11am–9pm, Sat & Sun 11am–7pm.

Mucho Mas Thorvalds Meyersgate 36 ⓦ muchomas.no. Cute, relaxed bar-restaurant that does a roaring trade in less-than-authentic (but still tasty) Mexican food. The portions are enormous. Mains from 120kr. Mon–Thurs & Sun noon–midnight, Fri & Sat noon–3am.

★ **Nighthawk Diner** Seilduksgata 15 ⓦ nighthawk diner.com. Immensely popular replica 1930s diner, complete with original jukebox. The burgers are not cheap (from 150kr) but are truly excellent; most dishes are organic, and the blueberry milkshakes are to die for. Mon 7am–11pm, Tues & Wed 7am–midnight, Thurs 7am–1am, Fri 7am–2.30am, Sat 10am–2.30am, Sun 10am–11pm; kitchen closes 9pm Mon & Sun, 11pm otherwise.

Punjab Tandoori Grønland 24 ⓦ punjabtandoori.no. Superb curries at bargain prices served up at this simple, canteen-style restaurant in Grønland; mains from 70kr. Mon–Sat 11am–11pm, Sun noon–10pm.

Spisestedet Hjelmsgate 3 ⓦ spisestedet.vpweb.co.uk. A centrally located vegetarian restaurant with a thirty-year reputation; there's an emphasis on organic produce, and dishes are mostly vegan. Meal 50–100kr. Mon–Thurs 2–8pm, Fri 2–7.30pm.

Tim Wendelboe Grünersgata 1 ⓦ timwendelboe.no. Run by an award-winning coffee grinder, this café serves high-quality coffee that's slightly above average in price. Mon–Fri 8.30am–6pm, Sat & Sun 11am–5pm.

★**Ya Ya's** Øvre Vollgate 13 ⓦyayas.no. The *som tum* (green papaya salad) at this superb Thai restaurant is spicy enough to satisfy the harshest of palates, the red curry is authentic down to the tiny pea aubergines, and the decor (complete with artificial thunderstorm during meal) manages to convince you that you're in a tropical Thai garden. Mains 179kr. Daily 4–10pm.

DRINKING AND NIGHTLIFE

Oslo's hippest cafés and bars can be found in the trendy Grünerløkka area. The capital also has a lively music scene, with everything from local bluegrass bands to metal to clubs featuring top DJs. For entertainment listings, consult Use-It's website (ⓦuse-it.no) or *What's On Oslo*, a free, monthly English-language brochure produced by Oslo tourist office.

BARS

Aku-Aku Thorvald Meyersgate 32 ⓦwww.akuaku.no. Tiki bar with a South Pacific vibe, great tropical cocktails and a boat strapped to the ceiling that belonged to Thor Heyerdahl, on loan from the Kon-Tiki Museum. Try their signature Chilli Punch. Mon–Thurs 6pm–1am, Fri & Sat 3pm–3am, Sun 3pm–1am.

Bar Boca Thorvald Meyers gate 30. Tiny, friendly 1950s retro bar in Grünerløkka, with great cocktails. Live jazz once or twice weekly. Get there early. Mon–Thurs 2pm–1am, Fri & Sat 2pm–3am, Sun noon–1am.

Café Tekehtopa St Olavs plass 2 ⓦtekehtopa.no. This busy little bar, set within a former pharmacy, draws in a student crowd on account of its quirky environs and wide range of draught and bottled beers. They also serve inexpensive pizzas, salads and omelettes. Mon–Fri 11am–midnight, Sat noon–midnight & Sun noon–10pm.

Mir Toftesgate 69 ⓦlufthavna.no. Popular with local rockers, this adorably oddball bar is tucked away in a courtyard, complete with old aeroplane seats, candlelight and even a book exchange. Live music and other events three or four nights a week. Daily 8pm–1am.

Stratos Youngstorget 2 ⓦstratos.as. Set atop a large Art Deco tower, this inviting summer rooftop bar has great panoramas and even better cocktails served in a cool brickwork setting. Accessible by lift. Late June to mid-Aug Tues–Sat 3pm–3am, Sun 8pm–3am.

Teddy's Soft Bar Brugata 3. A local stalwart, this genuine 1950s US dive bar is a good place to wind down with a beer or a milkshake. Mon–Sat 11am–3am.

CLUBS

Café Mono Pløensgate 4 ⓦcafemono.no. Popular rock 'n' roll bar-club just by Youngstorget. The decor and music are rock-themed; you can often catch local and international bands here. Mon–Sat 11am–3am, Sun 6pm–3am.

Herr Nilsen C.J. Hambros plass 5 ⓦherrnilsen.no. Small and intimate jazz club whose brick walls are decorated with jazz

memorabilia. Live jazz – sometimes traditional and bebop – most nights. In a handy, central location too. Daily 2pm–3am.

LIVE MUSIC

★**Blå** Brenneriveien 9c ⓦblaaoslo.no. Cultural nightspot that's rated in the world's top 100 jazz clubs, featuring primarily live jazz, but DJs, salsa and metal nights, public debates and poetry readings too. Open daily, hours dependent on acts; till 3.30am at weekends.

Last Train Karl Johans gate 45 ☎22 41 52 93, ⓦlasttrain .no. Premier hard rock club with gritty decor, that hosts great live bands. Mon–Fri 3pm–3.30am, Sat 6pm–3.30am.

Rockefeller Music Hall Torggata 16 ⓦrockefeller.no. One of Oslo's major concert venues, hosting well-known and up-and-coming bands – mostly rock or alternative.

ENTERTAINMENT

Black Box Theatre Stranden 3 ⓦblackbox.no. Cutting-edge alternative dance and theatre at this arty venue in Aker Brygge.

Saga Kino Stortingsgata 28 ⓦnfkino.no. Six-screen cinema showing the latest Hollywood blockbusters and other international films.

SHOPPING

Chillout Markveien 55, Grünerløkka ⓦchillout.no. Excellent travel shop stocking a wide range of guidebooks, maps and travel gear, with a little café serving perk-me-ups to assist with the browsing. Mon–Fri 10am–7pm, Sat 10am–6pm, Sun noon–6pm.

Oslo Sweater Shop Tullins gate 5 ⓦshopatnorway.com. Classic Norwegian sweaters are not known for being affordable, but this shop – the largest selection in the city – frequently has items on sale. Also sells trolls, shoes and *bunads* (national dress). Mon–Fri 10am–6pm, Sat 10am–3pm.

Trabant Vintage Markveien 56 ⓦtrabantclothing.com. Pick up vintage and vintage-inspired fashions at this impeccably cool Grünerløkka boutique. Its other branch at Youngstorvet 4 specializes in rock-related designs. Mon–Fri noon–6pm, Sat 11am–5pm.

DIRECTORY

Embassies and consulates Canada, Wergelandveien 7 (☎22 99 53 00); Ireland, Haakon VII's gate 1 (☎22 01 72 00); UK, Thomas Heftyes gate 8 (☎23 13 27 00); US, Henrik Ibsens gate 48 (☎ 21 30 89 96).

Hospital Oslo Kommunale Legevakten, Storgata 40 ☎23 48 72 00. 24hr emergency clinic.

Left luggage Oslo S (daily 4.30am–1am) has luggage lockers, as does Use-It (see p.811).

Pharmacy Jernbanetorgets Apotek (24hr), Jernbanetorget 4b ☎23 35 81 00, opposite Oslo S.

Post office Tollbugata 17 at Kirkegaten (Mon–Fri 8am–5pm, Sat 9am–11am; ⓦposten.no).

24

JOTUNHEIMEN NATIONAL PARK

North of Oslo, the 1151-square-kilometre **Jotunheimen** is the country's largest and most popular national park. Its valleys, lakes and mountains are a veritable playground for hikers and climbers. The park boasts northern Europe's highest peak, Galdhøpiggen (2469m), the Sognefjellet – possibly Norway's most scenic road (and a tough challenge for serious cyclists) – plus numerous trails with DNT staffed huts along many of them. Popular hikes include the precarious Besseggen ridge, which scythes its way between two glacial lakes; the Hurrungane massif, with fabulous views from the summit of Fanaråken (2069m); and Galdhøpiggen, a tough day-hike showcasing some dramatic glaciers. You'll need to equip yourself with Staten kartveerk's *Jotunheimen Aust* and *Jotunheimen Vest* maps, and Oslo's DNT office (see p.811) can help you with trip planning. Public transport to the park only runs between late June and mid-August, so check schedules in advance.

Southern Norway

Regular trains run from Oslo to the lively harbour town of **Stavanger** on the south coast. Near Stavanger, the spectacular **Lysefjord** accounts for some of the most dramatic landscape in this part of the country and features one of Norway's biggest hiking attractions, **Preikestolen (Pulpit Rock)** – a dramatic clifftop viewpoint overlooking the fjord far below. The region's forests provide ample opportunity for camping and walking, while watersports, sailing in particular, are popular on the many lakes and beaches; and Stavanger has a vibrant harbourside bar and restaurant scene.

STAVANGER

STAVANGER is a breezy and busy fjordside city that has prospered as the hub of Norway's oil industry. The presence of a thriving university gives the town a real buzz, and there's a number of excellent but unpretentious bars that wouldn't be out of place in any of the Scandinavian capitals.

WHAT TO SEE AND DO

The heart-shaped pond, **Breiavatnet**, in the middle of the compact town centre is a helpful reference point; the twelfth-century **Norman cathedral** (June–Aug daily 9am–6pm; Sept–May Mon–Thurs 9am–4pm, Fri 9am–6pm & Sat 11am–4pm; 30kr) is just north of here, and the tapering harbour is visible from the cathedral steps.

Stavanger's delightful **old town** is just northwest of the cathedral – stroll around the charming cobbled streets or drop into the entertaining **Norwegian Canning Museum** at Øvre Strandgate 88 (mid-May to mid-Sept daily 10am–4pm; mid-Sept to mid-May Tues–Fri 11am–3pm, Sat & Sun 11am–4pm; 90kr; ⓦmuseumstavanger.no), part of the multi-site **Stavanger Museum**, which takes you through the twelve-step process of canning fish – a traditional local industry – from the salting to the smoking and packing; freshly smoked sardines are available to taste. Further east along the harbour, the excellent must-see **Norwegian Petroleum Museum** (June–Aug daily 10am–7pm; Sept–May Mon–Sat 10am–4pm, Sun 10am–6pm; 120kr; ⓦnorskolje.museum.no) is a slick, well-designed space detailing the history of Norway's most important industry.

ARRIVAL AND DEPARTURE

By plane Stavanger airport, 15km south of the city, is connected to the bus station by regular *flybussen* (120kr one-way, 180kr return; ⓦflybussen.no).

By train The train station is on Jernbaneveien, facing Breiavatnet, the small and central lake.
Destinations Kristiansand (4–6 daily; 3hr); Oslo (2–4 daily; 8hr).

By bus The bus terminal is right next to the train station.
Destinations Bergen (every 1–2hr; 5hr to 5hr 30min); Kristiansand (5 daily; 4hr).

By boat Most domestic ferries from the islands and fjords around Stavanger, including both Hurtigbåt passenger express boats and car ferries, dock at the Fiskepiren terminal, a shortish walk northeast of lake Breiavatnet – and about 800m from the train and bus stations.

INFORMATION

Tourist office Opposite the cathedral at Domkirkeplassen 3 (June–Aug daily 9am–8pm; Sept–May Mon–Fri 9am–4pm, Sat 9am–2pm; ☎ 51 85 92 00, ⓦ regionstavanger.com).

ACCOMMODATION

Budget accommodation anywhere near the centre is hard to come by; book ahead.

Stavanger Bed and Breakfast Vikedalsgaten 1A ☎ 51 56 25 00, ⓦ stavangerbedandbreakfast.no. This friendly, hostel-like B&B has over 20 simple modern rooms, most with showers and sinks (but shared toilets). Every evening, guests gather in the dining room for the complimentary coffee and waffles – and a very sociable affair it is too. The B&B is in a residential area just 10min walk from the train station. A real snip, even if some of the inter-room walls are paper-thin. Doubles 890kr

Stavanger Camping Mosvangen Henrik Ibsensgate 21 ☎ 51 53 29 71, ⓦ stavangercamping.no. On the south side of lake Mosvatnet, just 3km from the centre – and not far from the nearest HI hostel (see below) – this large and well-equipped campsite has space for tents and caravans as well as a selection of cabins for up to six people. Open May to mid-Sept. Camping/tent (sleeping 2) 280kr, cabins 500kr

Stavanger Vandrerhjem St Svithun Gerd-Ragna Bloch, Thorsensgate 8 ☎ 51 51 26 00, ⓦ hihostels.no. In a modern block attached to the university hospital, this all-year HI hostel has self-catering facilities, a laundry and a café. Most of the rooms are en-suite singles or doubles, but there are 6-bunk dorms with shared facilities. The hostel is located about 2km south of the train/bus station – a 20min walk or take bus #4 or #11 and ask to be put off. Dorms 295kr, doubles 900kr

EATING

★**Bøker og** Børst Øvre Holmegate 32 ⓦ bokerogborst.no. Charming café-bar where the decor really does set the tone – from the vintage posters and Oriental bric-a-brac through to the jam-packed bookshelves. There's a pavement terrace at the front and a mini-courtyard at the back. The drinks – both soft and alcoholic – are the main event, but they also sell snacks and there are live gigs here too. Daily 9/10am–2am.

Nero Øvre Holmegate 8 ⓦ restaurant-nero.no. Well-turned-out Italian restaurant where they make good use of local ingredients – from rhubarb to cheese and seafood. The menu is creative and imaginative – and a three-course set meal costs 600kr. Tues–Sat 6pm–1am.

24

STAYING IN A LIGHTHOUSE

The rocks and reefs of the **southwest coast** between Kristiansand and Stavanger house a string of disused **lighthouses**, several of which offer simple, hostel-like **accommodation** for the intrepid traveller. Lighthouse lodging is inexpensive, though you'll have to bring your own food, water and bed linen – if you don't speak Norwegian, the local tourist office can help book the accommodation. Getting there by boat can be both difficult and pricey: most people arrive on their own boats, and scheduled ferries are rare – again, ask the local tourist office who will sail where and at what cost. The number of lighthouses offering accommodation varies from year to year – check ⓦ northsearoad.co.uk and the more detailed ⓦ lighthousesof norway.com for an up-to-date list.

LIGHTHOUSES OFFERING ACCOMMODATION

Hatholmen Fyr Hatholmen ☎ 95 94 75 82, ✉ mandalkystlag@gmail.com. Out in the Skaggerak, about 15min by boat from Mandal, the stumpy Hatholmen lighthouse perches on a rocky headland with a trio of white-painted houses in its lee. There are 20 beds here, with self-catering facilities, an outside toilet and a cold shower – and they do mean cold. The return boat trip from Mandal costs about 250kr; the tourist office will make the necessary arrangements, or call the boatman on ☎ 90 28 27 62. Late June to late Aug. Per person 200kr

Lindesnes Fyr Lindesnes ☎ 38 25 54 20, ⓦ lindesnesfyr .no. At Norway's most southerly point, on a knobbly, lichen-stained headland that's accessible by car, the old lighthouse keeper's cottage has been modernized to house an apartment sleeping six. There's a couch for two in the living room and a first-floor bedroom for a maximum of four, plus a shower, toilet and kitchen – and superb views out to sea. The most dramatic time to visit is during bad weather: the headland is exposed to ferocious storms, when the warm westerly currents of the Skagerrak meet cold easterly winds. Apartment 1200kr

Ryvingen Fyr Ryvingen ☎ 97 77 93 50, ⓦ www .ryvingensvenner.no. There's been a lighthouse way out in the Skagerrak on the rocky islet of Ryvingen since 1867. The present lighthouse, a sturdy red and white structure, is glued to a large shank of rock with the churning ocean down below. Nearby, the old lighthouse keeper's quarters have been pleasantly modernized with eight cheerful rooms (19 beds) and an outside toilet, but no showers. Late June to late Aug. Several boat owners will make the 45min journey from Mandal, near Kristiansand, for a round trip price of about 600kr: ring Knut Joseland (☎ 90 17 44 21) or ask the nearest tourist office to make the necessary arrangements. Per person 400kr

PREIKESTOLEN (PULPIT ROCK)

The region's biggest highlight, **Pulpit Rock** is responsible for one of Norway's most arresting images: people balancing precariously on the edge of the sheer cliff with a 604m drop into Lysefjord below. To get there from Stavanger, take the ferry east from the Fiskepiren terminal to Tau (every 40min–1hr; 40min; passengers 52kr; ⓦnorled.no), from where there are connecting buses (mid-March to mid-May 4 daily; mid-May to mid-Sept every 40min to 1hr; 35min; 175kr return) to the Preikestolen car park. From the car park, it's a **four-hour hike** there and back to Preikestolen along a clearly marked trail. The first half of the hike is steep in parts and paved with uneven stones, while the second half – over bedrock – is a good bit easier. The change in elevation is 350m and you should take food and water; the hike is not feasible in winter unless you really know what you are doing; sturdy footwear is essential.

Thai Cuisine Kirkegata 41 ⓦthaicuisine.no. Sociable and very popular restaurant in trim modern premises that serves the best Thai food in Stavanger. The menu, which covers all the classics and then some, has main courses from around 260kr. Mon–Fri 11am–11pm, Sat noon–11pm & Sun 2–11pm.

DRINKING AND NIGHTLIFE

★**Café Sting** Valberget 3 ⓦcafesting.no. Next to the Valbergtårnet watchtower, this laidback café-bar attracts a youthful, vaguely arty crew. The food is filling and inexpensive, there's a pleasant albeit small pavement terrace, and the place doubles as an art gallery and live music venue. Mon–Wed 11am–midnight, Thurs–Sat 11am–1am, Sun 1pm–midnight.

Cardinal Skagen 21 ⓦcardinal.no. One of the best pubs in town with a dark and antique interior, a long wooden bar and a first-rate range of ales, both in bottle and on draught. Rammed at the weekend – quite rightly so. Sun–Thurs 3pm–1.30am, Fri & Sat noon–1.30am.

Taket Nattklubb Nedre Strandgate 13 ☎51 84 37 01, ⓦherlige-stavanger.no. The best club in town, strong on house music with great cocktails too; don't be surprised if you have to queue. It's located a few metres west of Torget. Wed–Sun midnight–3.30am.

Bergen and the fjords

The **fjords** are the most familiar and alluring image of Norway – huge forested clefts in the landscape which dwarf the large ferries that travel along them. Bergen is a handy springboard for the fjords, notably the **Flåm valley** and its inspiring mountain railway, which trundles down to the Aurlandsfjord, a tiny arm of the mighty **Sognefjord** –

Norway's longest and deepest. North of the Sognefjord, **Nordfjord** is the smaller and less stimulating, though there's superb compensation in the **Jostedalsbreen** glacier (Europe's largest), which nudges the fjord from the east. The tiny S-shaped **Geirangerfjord**, further north again, is magnificent too – narrow, sheer and rugged.

BERGEN

Norway's first capital, **BERGEN** is now the second-biggest city in Norway, but somehow doesn't feel like it – its centre is relaxed and easygoing, its cobbled streets a pleasure to explore. It's one of the rainiest places in rainy Norway, but benefits from a lovely setting among seven hills, and is altogether one of the country's most enjoyable cities, with a lively student scene.

WHAT TO SEE AND DO

There's plenty to see in Bergen, from fine old buildings to a series of good museums. The city is also in the heart of **fjord country**, within easy reach of some of Norway's most stunning scenic attractions.

Torget and Bryggen

The obvious place to start a visit is **Torget**, an appealing harbourside plaza that's home to the best fish market in the country. From here, it's a short stroll round to **Bryggen**, where a string of distinctive, brightly painted wooden buildings (a UNESCO protected site) lines the waterfront. These once housed the city's merchants and now hold shops,

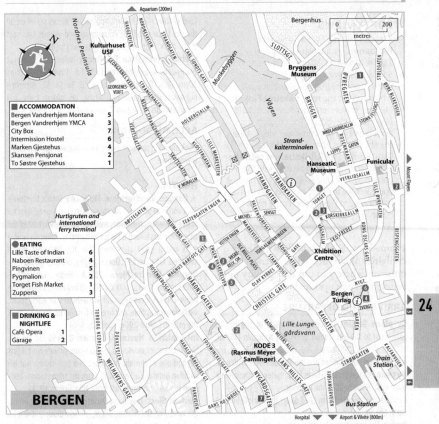

ACCOMMODATION
Bergen Vandrerhjem Montana	5
Bergen Vandrerhjem YMCA	3
City Box	7
Intermission Hostel	6
Marken Gjestehus	4
Skansen Pensjonat	2
To Søstre Gjestehus	1

EATING
Lille Taste of Indian	6
Naboen Restaurant	4
Pingvinen	5
Pygmalion	2
Torget Fish Market	1
Zupperia	3

DRINKING & NIGHTLIFE
Café Opera	1
Garage	2

BERGEN

Hospital ▼   ▼ Airport & Vilvite (800m)

24

restaurants and bars. Although most of the original structures were destroyed by fire in 1702, they carefully follow the original Hanseatic German design. Among them, the **Hanseatic Museum** (May–Sept daily 9am–5pm; Oct–April Tues–Sat 11am–2pm, Sun 11am–4pm; 100kr; ⓦmuseumvest.no), an early eighteenth-century merchant's dwelling kitted out in late Hansa style, is the most diverting.

Nearby, the **Bryggens Museum** (mid-May to Aug daily 10am–4pm; Sept to mid-May Mon–Fri 11am–5pm, Sat noon–3pm, Sun noon–4pm; 80kr; ⓦbymuseet.no) features a series of imaginative exhibitions that attempt to re-create local medieval life.

KODE 3

The pick of Bergen's art museums is the **KODE 3**, Rasmus Meyers Allé 7 (Rasmus Meyer Samlinger; daily 11am–5pm; mid-Sept to mid-May closed Mon; 100kr; ⓦkodebergen.no), which displays an extensive collection of Norwegian paintings spanning the eighteenth to early twentieth centuries and including several prime works by Edvard Munch and beautiful landscapes by Thomas Fearnley and J.C. Dahl.

Aquarium and VilVite

Bergen's other attractions include a large **Aquarium** at Nordnessbakken 4 (daily 9am–7pm May–Aug; Sept–April 10am–6pm; 250kr; ⓦakvariet.no), featuring a shark tunnel and fish and sea mammals from around the world. For hands-on fun, it's well worth heading to **VilVite** at Thormølensgate 51 (late June to mid-Aug daily 10am–5pm, mid-Aug to late June Tues–Fri 9am–3pm, Sat & Sun

LOFTY VIEWS

If it's not raining, take a ride on the **Fløibanen**, a funicular railway (every 15min: Mon–Fri 7.30am–11pm/midnight, Sat 8am–11pm/midnight, Sun 9am–11pm/midnight; 45kr each way), which runs to the top of **Mount Fløyen** (320m), from where there are incredible panoramic views over the city and the fjord beyond. For even wider views, take the shuttle bus from Torget (May–Sept 9am–6pm) to the **Ulriksbanen cable car** (100kr one-way, 160kr return), which takes you up Mount Ulriken (620m). From here, you can hike the well-marked trail to the top of Mount Fløyen and come back down on the funicular.

10am–5pm; 175kr. Children 135kr; ⓦvilvite.no), an interactive science museum where you can defy gravity by riding a bicycle upside down.

ARRIVAL AND DEPARTURE

By plane Bergen's airport, 20km south of the city, is connected to the bus station by regular *flybussen* (45min; 100kr each way; ⓦ flybussen.no), which stops at Torget, the main bus and train stations and the *Radisson SAS Royal Hotel*.
By train The train station faces Strømgaten, a 10min walk southeast of the head of the harbour.
Destinations Myrdal/Flåm (3–4 daily; 2hr/3hr); Oslo (3–4 daily; 6hr 30min).
By bus The bus station is adjacent to the train station.
Destinations Ålesund (1 daily; 9hr 30min); Oslo (express 3 weekly, 9hr; otherwise 1–3 daily, 11hr); Stavanger (every 1–2hr; 5hr); Trondheim (1 daily; 14hr 20min).
By boat International ferries and cruise ships arrive at Skoltegrunnskaien quay on the northeast tip of the harbour; domestic ferries and catamarans (ⓦ skyss.no) line up on the opposite side of the harbour at the Strandkaiterminalen. A bus (5pm daily; 50kr) runs to the Hurtigruten ferry terminal near Nøstebryggen, a 25min walk from the *Radisson SAS Royal Hotel*.
Destinations Norled (ⓦ norled.no) operates a Hurtigbåt high-speed ferry to Balestrand (May–Sept 1–2 daily; 4hr); and Flåm (May–Sept; 1 daily; 5hr 30min). The Hurtigruten coastal ferry heads north to Ålesund (12hr 45min).

INFORMATION

Tourist office Torget (May & Sept daily 9am–8pm; June–Aug daily 8.30am–10pm; Oct–April Mon–Sat 9am–4pm; ☏ 55 55 20 00, ⓦ visitbergen.com). Issues maps and the excellent *Bergen Guide* booklet; books Norway in a Nutshell tours and other trips; and sells the very worthwhile Bergen

Card (240kr/24hr, 310kr/48hr), which allows travel on all the city's buses and free entrance to (or discounts for) most of the city's sights, including sightseeing trips.
Hiking information The Bergen Turlag DNT office at Tverrgaten 4–6 (Mon–Wed & Fri 10am–4pm, Thurs 10am–6pm, Sat 10am–2pm; ☏ 55 33 58 10, ⓦ bergen oghordalandturlag.no) can advise on hiking trails and mountain huts in western Norway and also sells hiking maps.

ACCOMMODATION

Book ahead in summer, especially if you want to stay in the town centre.

HOSTELS

★**Bergen Vandrerhjem Montana** Johan Blyttsveie 30, Landås ☏ 55 20 80 70, ⓦ montana.no. A good spot for active travellers, this large, well-run hostel 4km east of the city centre has hiking trails on its doorstep, bikes for rent, a gym and a great view over the city. Breakfast buffet included. Take bus #31. Dorms **235kr**, doubles **660kr**
Bergen Vandrerhjem YMCA Nedre Korskirkeal-lmenningen 4 ☏ 55 60 60 55, ⓦ bergenhostel.no. The super-central location, mini kitchenettes in each room, sociable atmosphere and free wi-fi make up for the size of the rooms. Dorms **290kr**, doubles **580kr**
Intermission Hostel Kalfarveien 8 ☏ 55 30 04 00, ⓦ intermissionhostel.no. Christian-run, private hostel just beyond one of the old city gates in a two-storey, old-ish wooden building, a 5min walk from the train station. Mid-June to mid-Aug. Breakfast costs 40kr. Dorms **190kr**
Marken Gjestehus Kong Oscarsgate 45 ☏ 55 31 44 04, ⓦ marken-gjestehus.com. Bright, modern decor and helpful staff make this 21-room hostel one of Bergen's better accommodation options. Dorms **250kr**, doubles **710kr**

HOTELS AND GUESTHOUSES

City Box Nygårdsgaten 31 ☏ 55 31 25 00, ⓦ citybox.no. *City Box*'s slick, modern design extends to its reservation system; you book online and use your booking number to check yourself in and print your key card at the door. Rooms are frugal with minimalist decor (the cheaper ones share bathrooms); there's free wi-fi too. Doubles **1100kr**
Skansen Pensjonat Vestrelidsallmenningen 29 ☏ 55 31 90 80, ⓦ skansen-pensjonat.no. This attractive seven-room B&B inside a nineteenth-century stone house sits just above the funicular entrance. Excellent views, a Norwegian breakfast and the welcoming couple who run it make it a top place to stay. Doubles **900kr**
★**To Søstre Guesthouse** Nedre stølen 4c ☏ 93 06 60 46, ⓦ tosostre.no. This lovely, family-run guesthouse – "The Two Sisters" – is special. On a narrow cobbled lane, among a small pocket of wooden houses close to the Bryggen, it's a lovingly renovated old timber house with three tastefully decorated en-suite rooms in a modern

rendition of period style. The attic room is fantastically cosy. Doubles <u>**1000kr**</u>

EATING

Lille Taste of Indian Marken 12 ⓦlilletasteofindian .com. Authentic, inexpensive Indian food with a number of vegetarian dishes. Three dishes (including one vegetarian) are picked daily for the 79kr lunchtime special. Daily 1pm–midnight.

Naboen Restaurant Sigurds gate 4 ⓦgrannen.no. Excellent, innovative Swedish dishes at decent prices in this easy-going spot. Their marinated salmon with mustard sauce (250kr) and oven-baked wolf fish with barleycorn risotto (280kr) are especially tasty. Mains average 250kr. Mon–Thurs 4pm–1am, Fri & Sat 4pm–3am.

Pingvinen Vaskerelven 14 ⓦpingvinen.no. Informal resto-bar specializing in small-town Norwegian cooking. Lunch specials include hearty pea soup with bacon, while more substantial dinner dishes feature whale, reindeer and meatballs. Lunch mains from 100kr; dinner mains from 190kr. Daily 11am–3am.

★**Pygmalion** Nedre Korskirke allmenning 4 ⓦpygmalion.no. Cosy organic brick-and-candles café with modern art on the walls and a good choice of vegetarian dishes, including salads, pancakes and ciabattas. Salads 120–150kr, pancakes from 80kr. Daily 9am–11pm.

Torget Fish Market Torget. Feast your eyes on the colourful displays of fish and seafood, shop for local smoked salmon, venison salami and cloudberry jam, or grab one of the delicious open sandwiches (100kr). June–Aug daily 7am–9pm, Sept–May Mon–Sat 7am–4pm.

Zupperia Vaskerelven 12 ⓦzupperia.no. Choose from an almost endless menu of soups (from 60kr) including Thai chicken and reindeer with wild mushrooms. More solid dishes include salads, burgers and meat and fish mains. Two other branches at Nordahl Bruns gate 9 and Torget 13. Mon–Fri noon–11pm, Sat 1–11pm, Sun 2–11pm.

DRINKING AND NIGHTLIFE

Café Opera Engen 18 ⓦcafeopera.org. Arty café by day that serves some of the city's best coffee and transforms into a hot nightspot, playing soul, blues and funk on Wed & Thurs, hip-hop on Fri and reggae on Sat. Mon 10am–12.30am, Tues 10am–2am, Wed–Fri 10am–3.30am, Sat 11am–3.30am, Sun 11am–11.30pm.

Garage Christies gate 14 ⓦgarage.no. Near-darkness and sticky floors in the club downstairs, playing anything from rockabilly to soul, plus a friendly bar upstairs. Look out for the unusual door handles – they're trophies handed out in the Norwegian equivalent of the Grammies, donated by musicians.

BERGEN'S FESTIVALS

Bergen International Festival (ⓦfib.no) Twelve days of music, ballet, folklore and drama in May/June.

Borealis (ⓦborealisfestival.no) A big music festival in late March, celebrating all genres of music.

Octoberfestival Beer-related festivities at Bergen's version of Oktoberfest.

FLÅM VALLEY

One of the most spectacular attractions in the region is the **Flåmsbana**, a remarkable railway line that plummets 866m from the village of Myrdal down the verdant **Flåm valley** to the **Aurlandsfjord**. The track is one of the steepest anywhere in the world, making a wondrously dramatic journey.

Flåm

The village of **FLÅM**, the train's destination, lies alongside meadows and orchards on the Aurlandsfjord, a matchstick-thin branch of the Sognefjord. There are some excellent opportunities for both kayaking and hiking: hikers can get off the train at **Berekvam** station, the halfway point, and stroll down from there. Flåm itself is a tiny village that has been developed for tourism to within an inch of its life, but out of season – or on summer evenings, when the day-trippers have gone – it can be a pleasantly restful place.

ARRIVAL AND INFORMATION

By train To get to Flåm, take a train from Bergen to Myrdal, where you change for the Flåmsbana; the round trip takes the whole day and you can combine the Flåmsbana with a fjord cruise on the "Norway in a Nutshell" excursion (see box, p.820).

Information The tourist office (April–Oct daily 9am–6pm; Oct–March Thurs–Sat 9am–3pm; ☎95 43 04 14, ⓦsognefjord.no), by the train station, can book ferry tickets and provide information on local hikes.

EATING AND ACCOMMODATION

You can pick up groceries at the Coop behind the tourist office or grab a large helping of Norwegian staples at the dockside café (mains 150kr).

Flåmsbrygga ⓦflamsbrygga.no. Metres from the train station, this recent addition to the Flåm scene boasts a bar built in the style of a Viking long hall. The architecture may

24

NORWAY IN A NUTSHELL

If you're short of time, **Norway In a Nutshell** is the prime offering of Fjord Tours (Ⓦfjordtours.com), who specialize in coordinating tours of the fjord country, using either Bergen or Oslo as the starting/finishing point. These range from day-trips to the Flåm valley, Sognefjord and Hardangerfjord to multi-day excursions up and down the coast. Guides are not provided; Norway In a Nutshell simply saves you the trouble of trying to coordinate the complex local boat and bus timetables by booking the relevant transport for you. Pick up the tickets at the train station or the Bergen tourist office using the reference number provided.

be strange, but it serves excellent beer made in the on-site Ægir microbrewery. Daily 11am–5pm, later in summer.

Flåm Camping og Vandrerhjem ☏ 94 03 26 81, Ⓦ flaam-camping.no. This large, excellent campsite across the river from the train station also has sparkling hostel facilities. March to Oct. Camping/person 220kr, dorms 290kr, doubles 850kr

SOGNEFJORD AND JOSTEDALSBREEN

With the exception of Flåm, the southern shore of the **Sognefjord** remains sparsely populated and relatively inaccessible, whereas the north shore boasts a couple of very appealing villages. Pretty **Balestrand** makes an ideal base for excursions to the breathtaking **Jostedalsbreen glacier**.

Balestrand

A particularly pretty place to base yourself, scenic **BALESTRAND** has been a tourist destination since the mid-nineteenth century. The beauty of the fjord aside, there is little to see in town apart from the quaint little stave church of **St Olaf**, though Fjærland and Jostedalsbreen (see box below) are within easy striking distance; daily excursions from Balestrand will take you to the village, glacier museum and glacier itself for around 750kr.

ARRIVAL AND INFORMATION

By bus Buses from Bergen (via Vadheim) and Flåm (via Sogndal) arrive at Balestrand's minuscule harbourfront.
Destinations Bergen (3 daily; 4–6hr); Oslo (3 daily; 8hr 10min–8hr 50min).
By boat Boats from Bergen and Flåm arrive at the small dock just north of the *Kviknes* hotel.
Destinations Aurland (May–Sept 1–2 daily; 1hr 45min); Bergen (May–Sept 2 daily; 4hr); Flåm for passengers (May–Sept 1–2 daily; 2hr); Flåm via Dragsvik and Vangsnes for vehicles (every 40min–1hr; 30min).
Tourist office At the harbourfront (mid-June to mid-Aug Mon–Sat 7.30am–6pm; mid-Aug to mid-June Mon–Fri 10am–5.30pm; ☏ 57 69 12 55, Ⓦ sognefjord.no); it provides a map of hikes around the village.

ACCOMMODATION AND EATING

Cider House Sjøtunsvegen 32, Ⓦ ciderhuset.no. Summertime-only restaurant specializing in innovative local dishes with a Turkish influence made from organic produce and home-made cider. Give the white scallops with caviar appetizer (100kr), or *manti*, Turkish dumpling main (205kr), a try. Late June to late Aug daily 4–10pm.
Kafé Me Snakkast Holmen 13. A simply furnished café with an outdoor terrace, just behind the tourist office. They

24

VISITING THE JOSTEDALSBREEN GLACIER

The **Jostedalsbreen glacier** is a vast ice plateau that dominates the whole of the inner Nordfjord region. The glacier's many arms – or nodules – melt down into the nearby valleys, giving the local rivers and glacial lakes their distinctive blue-green colour. The glacier is protected within the **Jostedalsbreen Nasjonalpark**, and it's possible to organize **glacier walks** on Nigardsbreen, its longest arm, with Jostedalen Breførarlag, based in Jostedalen village (June–Sept; from 550kr; Ⓦ bfl.no). Walks range from two-hour excursions to all-day, fully equipped hikes. If you just want to see the glacier, it's possible to do so on a day-trip from Bergen (the ferry from Balestrand to Fjærland – Norway's book town – from where the bus takes you to the glacier, is timed to meet the boat from Bergen), though an overnight stay in Balestrand is highly recommended. Along the way, the bus makes a stop at the diverting **Glacier Museum** (April, May, Sept & Oct 10am–4pm; June–Aug 9am–7pm; 120kr; Ⓦ bre.museum.no), which features an interesting panoramic film on the glacier and climate change.

serve inexpensive local dishes, such as salads (from 80kr) and soups, plus cakes, ice cream and wine. June–Aug daily 10am–10pm, Sept–May Fri 10.30am–6pm, Sat 10.30am–4pm.

Sjøtun Camping Sjøtunsvegen 1 ☎ 95 06 72 61, ⓦ sjotun.com. This fully equipped campsite is a 10min walk along the shoreline road. June to mid-Sept only. Camping/person <u>40kr</u> plus per tent <u>130kr</u>, two-person cabins <u>300kr</u>

ÅLESUND

An overnight ferry ride from Bergen, the fishing and ferry port of **ÅLESUND**, which many Norwegians consider to be the best place to live in the country, is immediately – and quite obviously – different from any other Norwegian town. In 1904, a disastrous fire destroyed the town centre, which was then speedily rebuilt largely in the German Jugendstil (Art Nouveau) style, though with original Norwegian touches, such as the recurring dragon motif. The finest buildings are concentrated on the main street, **Kongensgate**, and around the slender, central harbour and the **Brosundet**. The excellent **Jugendstil Art Nouveau Centre** (June–Aug 10am–5pm; Sept–May Tues–Sun 11am–4pm; 80kr; ⓦ jugendstilsenteret.no) tells the story of Art Nouveau and the rebuilding of the city through the entertaining visual "From Ashes to Art Nouveau" exhibition.

Not to be missed is the vast **Atlantic Ocean Park** (June–Aug Mon–Fri & Sun 10am–7pm, Sat till 4pm; Sept–May Tues–Sun 11am–4pm; 180kr; ⓦ atlanterhavsparken.no), 3km from the town centre. As one of the best aquariums in Norway, it provides a comprehensive introduction to the North Atlantic undersea world.

ARRIVAL AND DEPARTURE

By plane Ålesund's airport is located on Vigra island just outside of town. *Flybussen* (100kr single, 150kr return; 25min) are timed to correspond with flight arrivals and departures.

Destinations Bergen (3 daily; 45min); Oslo (up to 10 daily; 55min); Trondheim (2 daily; 40min).

By bus The town's bus station is by the waterfront on Sjøgata, a few metres south of the town harbour, Brosundet.

Destinations Åndalsnes (2 daily; 2hr 20min); Bergen (at least 2 daily; 7hr); Trondheim (2–3 daily; 7hr 30min).

By boat The Hurtigruten ferry docks just north of the tourist office by the harbour.

Destinations Hurtigruten ferry once daily to: Bergen (13hr); Geiranger (mid-April to mid-Sept; 3hr 45min); Trondheim (mid-April to mid-Sept, 23hr; mid-Sept to mid-April, 15hr).

INFORMATION

Tourist office On the harbourside at Skateflukaia 1 (June–Aug daily 8.30am–6pm; Sept–May Mon–Fri 9am–4pm; ☎ 70 15 76 00, ⓦ visitalesund-geiranger .com), this tourist office hands out a free walking tour booklet covering Ålesund's architectural high points.

ACCOMMODATION

Ålesund Vandrerhjem Parkgata 14 ☎ 70 11 58 30, ⓦ hihostels.no. Central HI hostel in a creaky but clean old building, with self-catering facilities. Dorms <u>300kr</u>, doubles <u>750kr</u>

EATING AND DRINKING

Anno Apotekergata 9 ⓦ anno.no. Sleek bar, with atmospheric lighting, hardwood floors and leather banquettes, plus an outside terrace. Mon–Thurs 11am–11pm, Fri & Sat 11am–3am, Sun 1–8pm.

Lyspunktet Kipervikgata 1 ⓦ lyspunktet.as. Modern café with a massive chandelier and generous coffees. Big slouchy sofas, tacos (135kr), burgers (175kr) and imaginative meaty dishes at low prices. Mon noon–5pm, Tues–Fri 10am–10pm, Sat noon–5pm, Sun noon–6pm.

Maki Brosundet Hotel, Apotekergata 5 ⓦ brosundet .no. Immaculate, intimate restaurant, with harbour views and an always excellent, locally sourced menu. Mains average around 300kr. Mon–Sat 6–11pm.

GEIRANGERFJORD

Inland from Ålesund lies the S-shaped **Geirangerfjord**, one of the region's smallest and most breathtaking fjords. It cuts deeply inland, before terminating at the small village of **Geiranger**, which is invaded daily by cruise-ship passengers in summer. Many impressive waterfalls can be seen throughout the fjord, and the sheer cliffs rising on either side dwarf the cruise ships passing through.

It's best to approach the Geirangerfjord by bus from the north, if you can, as the views are

24

prettiest from this direction. From Åndalsnes (see below), the nerve-racking hairpin bends of the wonderfully scenic **Trollstigen Highway** climb through some of the country's highest mountains before sweeping down to the tiny Norddalsfjord. From here, it's a quick ferry ride and dramatic journey along the Ørnevegen, the Eagle's Highway, for a first view of the Geirangerfjord.

ARRIVAL AND DEPARTURE

By bus The twice-daily bus only runs between Geiranger and Åndalsnes from late June to August (timetables on ⓦ rutebok.no; 3hr).

By boat In the summer, an enjoyable alternative to taking the bus, with fantastic views, is to take the Hurtigruten ferry from Ålesund (June–Aug; 4hr each way); the same ferry heads back to Ålesund at 1.30pm.

ÅNDALSNES

Whether you're coming from the south via the dramatic Trollstigen, or from Oslo by train (via Dombås) on the incredible Rauma line, arriving in **ÅNDALSNES** is nothing short of spectacular. Its magnificent setting amid lofty peaks and looking-glass water makes for a good day hike up a mountain overlooking the town.

ARRIVAL AND INFORMATION

By train The train station is located at Jernbanegata 1.
Destinations Dombås (2 daily; 1hr 40min); Oslo (4 daily via Dombås; 5hr 30min–6hr).

By bus Buses arrive to the same complex as the train station.
Destinations Ålesund (2–3 daily; 2hr 10min); Geiranger (mid-June to Aug; daily at 8.20am, also Mon–Fri & Sun at 5.15pm, Sat at 3.45pm; 3hr 10min).

Tourist office Next to the train station (July–Aug Mon–Fri 8am–4pm, Sat & Sun 8am–2pm, Sept–June Mon–Fri 9am–3pm; ☏71 22 16 22, ⓦ visitandalsnes .com).

ACCOMMODATION

Åndalsnes Hostel Setnes ☏71 22 13 82, ⓦ hihostels.no. Located 1.5km outside of town, the HI-affiliated hostel is a great place to stay overnight. The bus to and from Geiranger stops right outside. Dorms <u>345kr</u>, doubles <u>860kr</u>

Central and Northern Norway

The long, thin counties of **Trøndelag** and **Nordland** mark the transition from pastoral southern to blustery northern Norway. Trondheim, Trøndelag's appealing main town, is easily accessible from Oslo by train. In **Nordland**, you reach the **Arctic Circle**, beyond which the land becomes ever more spectacular, not least on the exquisite, mountainous **Lofoten Islands**. Further north still, the provinces of **Tromsø** and **Finnmark** appeal to those who appreciate untamed, severe natural beauty, with the lively university town of **Tromsø** the obvious stopping (and jumping-off) point. As for Finnmark, many visitors head straight for **Nordkapp**, from where the midnight sun is visible between early May and the end of July, while those interested in Sámi culture go east towards Finland and the Sámi town of **Karasjok**.

TRONDHEIM

TRONDHEIM, a loveable and atmospheric city with much of its partly pedestrianized nineteenth-century centre still intact, has been an important Norwegian power base for centuries, its success guaranteed by the excellence of its harbour. The early Norse parliament, or **Ting**, met here, and the city was once a major pilgrimage centre.

WHAT TO SEE AND DO

Easy-going Trondheim possesses a marvellous cathedral and several low-key sights, as well as a clutch of good restaurants, cafés and popular student bars.

Nidaros Cathedral and Archbishop's Palace

The colossal **Nidaros Cathedral** – Scandinavia's largest medieval building, gloriously restored following the ravages of the Reformation and several fires – remains the focal point of the city centre (May Mon–Fri 9am–3pm, Sat

9am–2pm, Sun 1–4pm; June–Aug
Mon–Fri 9am–6pm, Sat 9am–2pm,
Sun 1–5pm; Sept–April Mon–Sat
9am–2pm, Sun 1–4pm; cathedral 90kr,
tower 40kr; ⊛nidarosdomen.no). Taking
Trondheim's former name (Nidaros
means "mouth of the River Nid"), the
cathedral is dedicated to King Olav,
Norway's first Christian ruler, who was
buried here. Now it is the traditional
burial place of Norwegian royalty and
the place of coronation for Norwegian
monarchs. Highlights of the interior
include the Gothic choir with its
pointed arches.

Behind the cathedral lies the heavily
restored twelfth-century Archbishop's
Palace, home to the **Norway Crown
Regalia** (May Mon–Sat 10am–3pm,
Sun noon–4pm; June–Aug Mon–Fri
10am–5pm, Sat 10am–3pm, Sun
noon–4pm; Sept–April Tues–Fri
10am–1pm, Sat 10am–2pm, Sun
noon–4pm; 90kr; combined ticket with
cathedral and palace museum 180kr) –
the crowns, sceptres and ermine
ceremonial robes are presented in an
atmospheric cellar. Another wing of the
palace houses the absorbing **Army and
Resistance Museum** (May–Sept Mon–Sat
10am–4pm & Sun noon–4pm; free). Its
most interesting section is on the top
floor and details the German occupation
of World War II.

Torvet

Torvet is the main city square, a spacious
open area anchored by a statue of the
Viking Olav Tryggvason, perched on a
stone pillar. The broad and pleasant
avenues of Trondheim's centre that
radiate out from here were laid out
in the late seventeenth century.

Rockheim

Down on the harbourfront, in a recycled
warehouse, **Rockheim** (Home of Rock;
Tues–Sun 10am–6pm 120kr; ⊛rockheim
.no) is a gallant attempt to make a
museum out of popular music. Some
exhibits are for listening, others for
playing, and there's a "wall of sound" too
– where you can stand on a dated circle
and see clips of Norway's most popular

bands of yesteryear. It's all really rather
enjoyable, and you can try to get to grips
with one of Norway's specialities too, **Black
Metal**, with a whole room devoted to this
genre of music – insert a tape (yes, a tape)
and hear those guitars shriek with the likes
of Mayhem, Darkthrone and Gorgoroth.

Munkholmen

If you have an extra day in Trondheim, and
the weather's fine, squeeze in a day-trip by
ferry (daily: late May 10am–4pm & late
Aug to early Sept 11am–4pm hourly on
the hour; June to mid-Aug 10am–6pm
every 30min; 90kr return) to the "Monk's
Island" from the harbour. This lovely island
with a great beach has a rich history: it was
originally the town's execution grounds,
but later housed a monastery, which then
became a prison and finally a customs
house before becoming the recreation spot
that it is today.

ARRIVAL AND DEPARTURE

24

By train The city's train terminal, Sentralstasjon, is on the
northern edge of the centre, a 10min walk from the main
square, Torvet.
Destinations Bodø (2 daily; 10hr); Oslo (4 daily via
Dombås, Lillehammer and Oslo Gardermoen airport; 6hr
30min–7hr 45min); Stockholm (2 daily; 12hr).
By bus The bus terminal, Rutebilstasjon, is next to the
train station.
Destinations Ålesund (1–2 daily; 7hr); Bergen (1 daily;
14hr); Oslo (1–3 daily; 8hr 30min).
By boat The all-year Kystekspressen (⊛kystekspressen
.no) passenger express boat from Kristiansund (1–3 daily;
3hr 15min) docks at the Pirterminalen, 5min walk north of
the train/bus stations. The quay for the Hurtigruten coastal
boat is near the Pirterminalen, another 300m or so to the
north.
Destinations Hurtigruten to Ålesund (daily at 10pm;
14hr); Bodø (daily at noon; 24hr 30min).

INFORMATION

Tourist office On the first floor of Nordre gate 11 (mid-
June to mid-Aug daily 9am–6pm; mid-Aug to mid-June
reduced hours; ☏73 80 76 60, ⊛visittrondheim.no).

ACCOMMODATION

City Living Schøller Hotel Dronningens gate 26 ☏73
87 08 00, ⊛cityliving.no. Independent, economy hotel in
the heart of the city. Fifty simple rooms spread over three
floors. Competitively priced, but no breakfast. Doubles
800kr

★**Pensjonat Jarlen** Kongens gate 40 ☎73 51 32 18, ⊕jarlen.no. Friendly central guesthouse, each of its rooms, bar the single, has a gleaming bathroom, a kitchenette, a comfortable armchair and free wi-fi. Doubles 690kr

Singsaker Sommerhotell Rogertsgata 1 ☎73 89 31 00, ⊕sommerhotell.singsaker.no. Charming summer-only hotel/hostel with a nice courtyard a short walk or bus ride on bus #63 from the centre. Mid-June to mid-Aug. Doubles 780kr

Trondheim Vandrerhjem Weidemannsveien 41 ☎73 87 44 50, ⊕trondheimvandrerhjem.no. Completely razed and rebuilt in 2013, this modern building calls to mind something of a designer hospital, but the dorms are spacious and only sleep 4–5. A 20min, 2km hike east from the centre, or to save your legs, take any bus up Innherredsveien and ask the driver to let you off as close as possible. Open all year. Dorms 330kr, doubles 625kr

EATING AND DRINKING

★**Baklandet Skydsstasion** Øvre Bakklandet 33 ⊕skydsstation.no. Serves up tasty traditional dishes and is particularly famous for its *bacalao* (dried salted cod); mains from 250kr. Daily: June–Aug 10am–1am; Sept–May 11am–1am.

Bar Passiar Dokkparken 4 ⊕dokkhuset.no. Managing to straddle that fine line between trendy and pretentious, this high-ceilinged spot is the pick of the bars along the Nedre Elvehavn dockside strip, not least for its roof terrace. Mon–Thurs 3–11.30pm, Fri 3pm–2.30am, Sat noon–2.30am.

Bare Blåbær Innherredsveien 16, Nedre Elvehavn ⊕barebb.no. Run by the same folks who operate the nearby *Bar Passiar* (see above), this fast-moving café-restaurant offers excellent-value stone-baked pizzas (from 100kr), which make it very popular with a youthful clientele. A separate area better known as *Bær & Bar* has house and electro DJs spinning till late. Mon–Thurs 11am–1.30am, Fri & Sat 11am–2.30am, Sun 11am–1.30am.

Café 3B Brattørgata 3B ⊕cafe3b.no. Rock'n'roll and indie club-cum-bar, where you can drink well into the wee hours. One of the grooviest places in town. Daily 6pm–2.30am.

Café Ni Muser Bispegata 9A ⊕nimuser.no. Fashionable café occupying an older building that might be glum but for the modern art on the walls (for sale) and the terrace out the back. Features a creative menu that emphasizes local, seasonal ingredients – try the simply wonderful creamy cauliflower soup (145kr) or the vegetarian lasagne (165kr). Daily 11am–11pm.

BODØ

North of Trondheim, it's a long, 730km haul beyond the Arctic Circle to **BODØ**, literally the end of the line: this is where all trains and some long-distance buses from the south terminate. The nine-hour train trip is a rattling good journey, with the scenery becoming wilder and bleaker the further north you go. Bodø is also a stop on the Hurtigruten coastal boat route and the main port of departure for the Lofoten Islands.

ARRIVAL AND INFORMATION

By train The train station is on Jernbaneveien at the northeast edge of the city centre, immediately next to the ferry terminal. Most days, it's possible to get off a night train from Trondheim and catch a ferry to the Lofoten Islands straight away (see opposite), or take a bus north to Narvik via Fauske (2 daily; 6hr 30min).

Destinations Fauske (2 daily; 40min); Oslo (2 daily, change at Trondheim; 17hr); Trondheim (2 daily; 9hr 40min).

By bus The station for long-distance Nor-Way Bussekspress buses is located at the Sentrumsterminalen, at the far end of Sjøgata.

Destinations Ålesund (3–4 daily; 7hr); Bergen (1 daily; 14hr).

Tourist office In the centre at Tollbugata 13 (mid-June to late Aug Mon–Fri 9am–8pm, Sat 10am–6pm & Sun 10am–6pm; late Aug to mid-June Mon–Fri 9am–3.30pm; ☎75 54 80 00, ⊕visitbodo.com). They give out information on connections to the Lofoten Islands, rent out bikes and also issue a detailed town and district guide.

ACCOMMODATION

Bodøsjøen Camping Båtstøveien 1 ☎75 56 36 80, ⊕bodocamp.no. This year-round fjordside campsite is roughly 3km southeast of the centre, not far from the Bodin kirke. Flanked by a ridge of evergreens and spread over a somewhat bleak-looking field is a set of cabins of various shapes and sizes, the smallest just a single small room with two beds. Camping/tent 260kr, cabins 250kr

Bodø Vandrerhjem Sjøgata 57 ☎75 50 80 48, ⊕hihostels.no. All-year, HI-hostel with 71 bunk beds in 23 rooms – from singles to an 8-bunk dorm. The rooms are neat and trim in a frugal sort of way, and there are self-catering facilities, a common room and a laundry. Handily located in a three-storey, red-brick block next to the train station. Dorms 325kr, doubles 840kr

EATING, DRINKING AND NIGHTLIFE

Bryggerikaia Sjøgata 1 ⊕bryggerikaia.no. Attractive and modern café/restaurant, where you can pop in for a coffee or a beer or sample some excellent seafood with mains from around 200kr. The verandah offers harbour views, and look out for their special buffet deals. Mon–Sat 11am–11pm, Sun noon–11pm.

Løvolds Kafé Tollbugata 9. A quayside spot with a traditional and inexpensive Norwegian menu of canteen-style dishes featuring local ingredients. Mains around 120kr. Mon–Fri 9am–6pm & Sat 9am–3pm.

LOFOTEN ISLANDS

A skeletal curve of mountainous rock stretched out across the Norwegian Sea, the **Lofoten Islands** rise dramatically out of the clear waters as you approach from the mainland. Snow-covered mountains loom behind trim little fishing villages with cod drying on traditional wooden racks. Life moves (much) more slowly up here, but there's plenty to keep an active traveller occupied: the islands are perfect for rambling, cycling, sea kayaking, sailing, diving, snorkelling and even whale watching – to say nothing of the cross-country ski opportunities come wintertime. The weather is exceptionally mild, and there's plentiful **accommodation** (⑩lofoten.info) in *rorbuer* (originally fishermen's huts), hostels and campsites.

ARRIVAL AND DEPARTURE

By plane Among several airports, you can fly to the Lofoten Islands from Bodø and Tromsø with Widerøe (⑩wideroe.no).

By bus Lofotenekspressen (☎177, ⑩177nordland.no) provides the main bus service from the mainland to the Lofoten, leaving Narvik twice daily for Svolvær via a series of bridges (2 daily; 4hr), then arriving at Å roughly four hours later.

By boat The Hurtigruten calls at two ports in the Lofoten Islands, Stamsund and Svolvær (daily from Bodø, 4/6hr; daily from Tromsø, 17/19hr). In addition, the southern Lofoten car ferry (⑩thn.no) leaves Bodø for Moskenes, Værøy and Røst (1–2 daily; 3hr 30min/5hr 15min/7hr 15min; 196kr per person), while the Nordlandexpressen Hurtigbåt passenger express boat (⑩thn.no) links Bodø with Svolvær (1 daily; 3hr 30min–3hr 45min).

Austvågøy

Austvågøy is the largest and northernmost island of the Lofoten group, with **SVOLVÆR** its main town and transport hub. Svolvær is home to the excellent **War Museum**, Fiskergata 12 (June–Sept Mon–Sat 10am–10pm, Sun noon–3pm; Oct–May by appointment; 80kr; ⑩lofotenkrigsmus.no), comprising a well-presented collection of rare World War II objects that chronicle the British commando raids on Lofoten.

ARRIVAL AND INFORMATION

By boat The Hurtigbåt passenger express boat from Bodø (see p.824) docks in the centre of Svolvær, as does the Hurtigruten (see p.804).

By bus The Svolvær bus station is located just in front of the Hurtigruten dock.

Destinations Å (4 daily; 3hr 30min); Narvik (2 daily; 3hr 30min); Sortland (1–4 daily; 2hr 30min).

Tourist office The busy tourist office is on Torget, the main square, near the harbour (March to mid-Oct Mon–Fri 9am–3.30pm; mid-Oct to Feb Mon–Fri 8.15–11.15am & 12.15–3.30pm; mid-May to early Sept also Sat 10am–2pm; early June to early Aug also Sun 10am–9pm; ☎76 07 05 75, ⑩lofoten.info); they have maps, accommodation lists and public transport details for all the Lofoten Islands.

ACCOMMODATION

Lofoten Rorbuer Jektveien 10, Svolvær ☎91 59 54 50, ⑩lofoten-rorbuer.no. There are eighteen modest rooms, some with bunk beds, at this long-established place on the Marinepollen lagoon. A few of the rooms share a kitchen and/or a bathroom, while others have self-contained kitchenettes. About 1km north of town along the E10. Doubles 800kr

Svinøya Rorbuer Gunnar Bergsvei 2, Svinøya ☎76 06 99 30, ⑩svinoya.no. At the northeast end of town, a causeway crosses over to the long and slender island of Svinøya, which is home to this well-appointed set of *rorbuer*. They range from the plain and simple to the deluxe. Doubles 1100kr

EATING

★**Børsen Spiseri** Svinøya Rorbuer, Gunnar Bergsvei 2, Svinøya ☎76 06 99 30, ⑩svinoya.no. Lofoten's most atmospheric restaurant, in a gorgeous old waterfront building, adorned with maritime paraphernalia. Its speciality is stockfish (*bacalao*), but whatever you order will be skilfully and delicately prepared. Reservations recommended. Daily 6–10pm; closed Mon–Wed in winter.

★**Du Verden** Torget 15, Svolvær ☎76 07 09 75, ⑩duverden.no. On the central square, this place aspires to cover a lot of bases – seafood, pizza, pasta, sushi – and just about succeeds. The food is always attractively presented and the place is generally heaving. Mains average 240kr. Kitchen: Mon–Sat 11am–10pm & Sun 1–10pm; bar till 11pm, 2.30am on Fri & Sat.

Vestvågøy: Stamsund

The next large island to the southwest, **Vestvågøy**, is the one that really

24

captivates many travellers, due in no small part to the atmospheric village of **STAMSUND**, whose older buildings are strung along a rocky, fretted seashore. The scenery on this island is truly spectacular, and hikers are rewarded with stunning views.

ARRIVAL AND DEPARTURE

By plane The island's airport is located 15km west of Stamsund, in the dull administrative centre of Leknes.
Destinations Bodø (8 daily; 25min).
By bus Regular buses run between Stamsund and Leknes, from where you can catch another bus to Å or Svolvær. Buses arrive at the lot alongside the Hurtigruten quay.
Destinations Leknes (6 daily; 30min).
By boat The Hurtigruten (see p.804) calls here on its way north from Bodø and south from Tromsø.
Destinations Honningsvåg (41hr); Svolvær (2hr); Tromsø (19hr).

ACCOMMODATION AND EATING

Skjærbrygga Hjellskjæret ☎ 76 05 46 00, ⓦ skjaerbrygga .no. This restaurant and bar is located right by Stamsund's harbour in an old and attractively renovated *sjøhus*. The menu is strong on seafood with mains going for around 250kr. June–Sept daily noon–midnight, kitchen till 10pm; check website for hours at other times of the year.
Stamsund Vandrerhjem Hartvågen 13 ☎ 76 08 93 34, ⓦ hihostels.no. This popular and relaxing hostel comprises several *rorbuer* and a bright yellow *sjøhus*, all perched on the edge of a bonny little bay. You can rent bikes here (100kr/day) and there are self-catering facilities. About 1.2km north of Stamsund's harbour. March to mid-Oct. Dorms 160kr, doubles 460kr

Flakstadøya and Moskenesøya

By any standard, two of the more southerly Lofoten Islands, **Flakstadøya** and **Moskenesøya**, are extraordinarily beautiful, their rearing peaks crimping a sea-shredded coastline and studded with a string of fishing villages. Remarkably, the E10 road travels along almost all of this dramatic shoreline, by way of tunnels and bridges, to **MOSKENES**, the **ferry port** midway between Bodø and the remote, southernmost islands of **Værøy** and **Røst**.

The delightful village of **Å**, a huddle of old houses on stilts wedged in tight between the grey-green mountains and the surging sea, is located at the end of the E10 road, 6km south of Moskenes. Highlights in town include the

Norwegian Fishing Village Museum (June to late Aug daily 9am–7pm; late Aug to May Mon–Fri 10am–5pm; 80kr; ⓦ museumnord.no), a collection of buildings devoted to traditional trades, such as the 1844 bakery which still bakes amazing cinnamon buns (see below). Å is also home to the excellent **Tørrfiskmuseum** (Stockfish Museum; June to late Aug daily 9am–7pm; late Aug to May Mon–Fri 10am–5pm; 50kr; ⓦ lofoten-info.no), a great museum on stockfish, the air-dried fish that served as the staple diet of most Norwegians well into the twentieth century. It's presided over by a gregarious curator who will tell you more than you ever wanted to know about the history of this very typical Norwegian foodstuff.

ARRIVAL AND DEPARTURE

By bus The Lofoten Ekspressen (ⓦ 177nordland.com) runs the length of the E10, stopping at most destinations between Narvik and Å.
Destinations Moskenes (6 daily; 10min); Narvik (1–2 daily; 8hr 15min); Svolvær (1–2 daily; 3hr 45min).
By boat Ferries sail between Bodø and Moskenes, 5km from Å. Buses don't always coincide with sailings to and from Moskenes though, so if you're heading from the ferry port to Å, you may have to walk the fairly easy 5km or take an expensive taxi.
Destinations Bodø (2–3 daily; 4hr).

ACCOMMODATION AND EATING

Å-Hamna Rorbuer & Vandrerhjem Å **i Lofoten** Å ☎ 76 09 12 11, ⓦ hihostels.no. In the centre of Å, by the waterside, this appealing HI hostel has an assortment of smart one- to eight-bedded *rorbuer*. Also offers equally smart, hotel-standard rooms in the adjacent *sjøhus*. Open year round. Dorms 260kr, doubles 540kr
Gammelgården Bakery Å in the Norwegian Fishing Village Museum. Built in the 1880s, this good-looking, late nineteenth-century building, with its gabled slate roof, started out as a lodging house for seasonal fishermen. Today, it's Lofoten's best bakery, cooking excellent cinnamon buns in a vintage oven (15kr). Mid-June to mid-Aug daily 9am–5pm.
Hotel Smaken av Lofoten Å ☎ 76 09 21 00, ⓦ smakenavlofoten.no. In the centre of Å, down by the harbour, this collection of buildings features *rorbuer* of various shapes and sizes. Some of the nicest are extremely comfortable and the pick have period furnishings; others have shared facilities. Doubles 1200kr

TROMSØ

Friendly **TROMSØ**, the "gateway to the arctic", is the de facto capital of northern Norway. Set on an island, connected to the mainland by bridge and tunnel, and surrounded by dramatic mountains and craggy shoreline, it offers easy access to a multitude of winter and summer activities.

WHAT TO SEE AND DO

TROMSØ has two cathedrals, a clutch of interesting museums and a lively nightlife, patronized by its significant student population.

Domkirke and the Polar Museum

In the centre of town, you can't miss the striking woodwork of the **Domkirke**. From the church, it's a short walk north along the harbourfront to one of the most diverting museums in the city, the **Polar Museum**, Søndre Tollbodgate 11 (daily: mid-June to mid-Aug 10am–7pm; mid-Aug to mid-June 11am–5pm; 60kr; ⓦpolarmuseum.no), whose varied displays include skeletons retrieved from the permafrost of Svalbard and accounts of expeditions by polar explorers Fridjof Nansen and Roald Amundsen.

Polaria

Also on the waterfront, **Polaria**, Hjalmar Johansens gate 12 (daily: mid-May to Aug 10am–7pm; Sept to mid-May noon–5pm; ⓦpolaria.no; 125kr), the city's star attraction, draws coach-loads of tourists to see the 3pm feeding of the bearded seals. This state-of-the-art aquarium combines its tanks of

ART IN TROMSØ

Tromsø has a couple of excellent free art museums. The **Art Museum of Northern Norway**, Sjøgata 1 (daily 10am–4pm), focuses on landscape paintings by northern Norwegian artists, as well as modern sculpture and photography exhibitions, while **Perspektivet**, Storgata 95 (Tues–Sun 11am–5pm), stages cutting-edge photography exhibitions, the most recent including "In Cod we Trust".

cold-water fish with a walk-through seal tunnel, displays about the region's fragile ecosystem and a stunning panoramic film on Svalbard.

Arctic Cathedral

Across the long Tromsø Bridge from the centre, the white, pointy, ultramodern **Ishavskatedralen** (mid-May to late May daily 3–6pm; June to mid-Aug Mon–Sat 9am–7pm, Sun 1–7pm; mid-Aug to May daily 3–6pm; 40kr; midnight sun concerts in summer 140kr; ⓦishavskatedralen.no) is outstanding, its shape inspired by the Hoja mountain near Tromsø. It's made up of eleven immense triangular concrete sections representing the eleven Apostles left after the betrayal, with a stunning stained-glass window.

Tromsø Museum

This excellent anthropological and geological **museum** (June–Aug daily 9am–6pm, Sept–May Mon–Fri 10am–4.30pm, Sat noon–3pm, Sun 11am–4pm; 60kr; ⓦvisittromso.no) should not be missed by anyone with

24

THE NORTHERN LIGHTS AND THE MIDNIGHT SUN

Tromsø's northerly location but relatively mild climate has made it one of the most popular spots in the world from which to view the **Northern Lights**, or Aurora Borealis, which are seen here regularly between November and April. Caused by solar winds as they hit the Earth's atmosphere, they light up the sky in shimmering waves of blue, yellow and green – a spectacle of celestial proportions.

In the summertime there's an entirely different Arctic phenomenon to behold: the **midnight sun**. In Tromsø you're so far north that the sun never actually dips beneath the horizon. Head for Fjellheisen, a cable car that runs to the top of **Mount Storsteinen** (take bus #26; mid–May to mid–Aug daily 10am–1am; mid–Aug to mid-May daily 10am–10pm; 170kr) between May 18 and July 25 around midnight, and you'll see the sun, hovering over the horizon in the west, setting the sky spectacularly aglow.

an interest in all things northern. Apart from the excellent displays on both traditional and modern Sámi culture, complete with ceremonial objects, traditional dress and household implements, downstairs you can learn about the Aurora Borealis phenomenon how it works – as well as create your own. Take bus #37 from the centre.

ARRIVAL AND INFORMATION

By bus Long-distance buses arrive at and depart from the Prostneset, metres from the tourist office.
Destinations Alta (1 daily; 6hr 30min); Honningsvåg (3 daily; 3hr 20min); Narvik (3–5 daily; 4hr 15min).
By boat The Hurtigruten coastal boat docks in the centre of town at the foot of Kirkegata.
Destinations Honningsvåg (daily at 6.30pm; 17hr); Svolvær (daily at 1.30am; 17hr 30min).
Tourist office Kirkegate 2, near the Domkirke (mid-May to Aug Mon–Fri 9am–7pm, Sat & Sun 10am–6pm; Sept to mid-May Mon–Fri 9am–4pm, Sat 10am–4pm; ☎ 77 61 00 00, ⓦ visittromso.no); produces a comprehensive Tromsø guide.

ACCOMMODATION

Ami Skolegata 24 ☎ 77 62 10 00, ⓦ amihotel.no. In an old wooden villa on the hillside behind the town centre, this few-frills guesthouse-cum-hotel has twenty-odd simple rooms, both en-suite and with shared facilities. One bonus is the wide views over the city centre. Doubles **1100kr**
Tromsø Camping Elvestrandvegen ☎ 77 63 80 37, ⓦ tromsocamping.no. Reasonably handy waterside site, about 2km east of the cathedral, on the mainland side of the main bridge, with 55 modern and "rustic" cabins. Open year-round. Take bus #20 or #24. Camping/tent (sleeping 2) **300kr**, cabins **700kr**
Viking Hotel Grønnegata 18 ☎ 77 64 77 30, ⓦ vikinghotell.no. The 24 bright and modern rooms at this breezy guesthouse are appealing. They also have several

contemporary apartment-style rooms with kitchenettes and large living spaces. Centrally located near the Mack Brewery. **1000kr**

EATING

You can buy freshly caught cooked prawns straight off the boats at the Stortorget pier, and at weekdays a Thai food stall on Stortorget sells succulent spicy chicken and pork skewers (25kr).
Kafé Globus Storgata 30 ⓦ globuskafe.no. Popular Eritrean café with a global menu that includes pitas, salads, Moroccan meat dishes and *injera* – a large, sponge-like pancake topped with mounds of spicy beef curry, lentils and wilted spinach (175kr). Mon–Fri 10am–7pm, Sat 11am–5pm.
Thai House Storgata 22 ⓦ thaihouse.no. Decent Thai cooking – if a little hit and miss – with the welcome inclusion of some excellent fish and vegetable dishes; mains from 220kr. Daily 3–11pm.
Verdensteatret Storgata 93b ⓦ verdensteatret.no. Popular café-bar housed in Norway's oldest movie theatre that attracts an arty young crowd with its cheap lunch food, drinks, independent film screenings and pumping DJ nights. Mon–Thurs 11am–2am, Fri & Sat 11am–3.30am, Sun 1pm–2am.

DRINKING AND NIGHTLIFE

Blå Rock Café Strandgata 14. Definitely the place to go for loud – that's very loud – rock music. Also features regular live acts, plus the best burgers in town – try the amazing blue-cheese Astroburger. They serve several dozen beers, most priced at around 70kr. Mon–Thurs 11.30am–2am, Fri & Sat 11.30am–3.30am, Sun 1pm–2am.
Ølhallen Pub Storgata 4 ⓦ olhallen.no. With its cosy cellar decor and winning location (attached to the Mack Brewery), the city's favourite pub serves a full range of microbrews (70kr/pint). Mon–Fri 10am–6pm, Sat 9am–6pm.
Studentsamfunnet Driv Storgata 6 ⓦ driv.no. This large, ambitious and artsy hangout never wants for its share of barflies. In part of the Mack Brewery, it holds four bars and three stages, which together cater for every musical taste, including DJ nights, live concerts and disco. Come early to get a seat. Mon–Thurs noon–1.30am, Fri & Sat noon–3am.

TREAT YOURSELF

Emma's Drømmekjokken Kirkegata 8 ⓦ emmasdrommekjokken.no. "Emma's Dream Kitchen" serves sublime locally sourced fare from Arctic char to reindeer at prices to match. At the downstairs café, *Emma's Under*, prices are slightly lower but the dishes, such as whale steak in peppercorn sauce or grilled fish, are just as delicious. Lunch mains from 190kr. Downstairs: Mon–Fri 11am–10pm, Sat noon–10pm; Upstairs: Mon–Sat 6–10pm.

FINNMARK, MAGERØYA AND NORDKAPP

Beyond Tromsø, the northern tip of Norway, **FINNMARK**, enjoys no less than two and a half months of permanent daylight either side of the summer solstice. Here, the bleak and treeless island of **Magerøya** is connected to the northern edge of the mainland by an ambitious combination of tunnels and bridges, and the prime target on the island is Nordkapp – the North Cape.

Alta

A modest north Norwegian town, **ALTA**'s primary claim to fame is the most extensive area of **prehistoric rock carvings** in northern Europe, which are impressive enough to have been designated a UNESCO World Heritage Site. The settlement is also the obvious place to overnight if you're heading from Tromsø to the far north, since there's a direct bus to Nordkapp (May–Sept 1–2 daily; 4hr 20min).

Alta's prehistoric rock carvings form part of the **Alta Museum**, Altaveien 19 (May to mid-June daily 8am–5pm; mid-June to Aug daily 8am–8pm; Sept–April Mon–Fri 8am–3pm, Sat & Sun 11am–4pm; May–Sept 105kr, Oct–April 70kr; ⊛alta.museum.no). The museum itself has displays of prehistoric rock art and exhibits on the social history behind these carvings, touching upon the role of religion and commerce in the region. A limited local bus service – *bybussen* – runs from the main Alta bus station south to the borough of Bossekop and the museum (Mon–Fri every 15–30min; Sat & Sun hourly; 7min).

Count on at least an hour to view the carvings, **Helleristningene i Hjemmeluft**, and appreciate the site, which is accessed along the E6. The carvings extend down the hill from the museum to the fjordside along a clear and easy-to-follow footpath and boardwalk that stretches for just under 3km. On the trail, there are a dozen or so vantage points offering close-up views of the carvings, recognizable though highly stylized representations of boats, animals and people picked out in red pigment.

ARRIVAL AND INFORMATION

By bus Long-distance buses arrive at the tourist office in the centre of Alta.

Destinations Honningsvåg (1–2 daily; 4hr); Karasjok (2 weekly; 3hr 30min); Nordkapp (May–Sept 1–2 daily; 4hr 20min); Tromsø (1 daily; 6hr 30min).

Tourist office The main branch is located at Bjorn Wirkolas vei 11, in the same building as the bus terminal

(June & Aug daily 9am–6pm; July daily 9am–8pm; Sept–May Mon–Fri 9am–3.30pm, Sat 10am–3pm; ☎99 10 00 22, ⊛visitalta.no). It issues free town maps, will advise on hiking the Finnmarksvidda and help with finding accommodation.

ACCOMMODATION AND EATING

Alta River Camping ☎78 43 43 53, ⊛alta-river -camping.no. This well-equipped site is set on a large green riverside plot, with tent spaces as well as hotel-style rooms and cabins, some of which have en-suite baths, plus a sauna right on the water. Located about 5km out of town along Highway 93. Open year-round. Camping/tent 190kr, doubles 600kr, cabins 500kr

Bårstua Gjestehus Kongleveien 2a ☎78 43 33 33, ⊛baarstua.no. The most appealing of Alta's several guesthouses, this is located just off the E6 on the north side of town. The eight large rooms are pleasant enough, all with kitchenettes. 800kr

Du Verden Matbar Markedsgata 21 ⊛duverden.no/alta. In the centre of Alta, this friendly restaurant has a menu covering all the Norwegian basics – the king crab (460kr) and the grilled stock fish (375kr) come especially recommended. Mon–Sat 10am–11.30pm & Sun 1–10.30pm.

Honningsvåg

The fishing village of **HONNINGSVÅG**, Magerøya's only significant settlement and a place that claims to be the most northerly "city" in the world, is your last port of call before Nordkapp – the North Cape – just 34km away.

ARRIVAL AND DEPARTURE

By plane Widerøe (⊛wideroe.no) operates flights from Tromsø to Honningsvåg airport.

Destinations Tromsø (1–3 daily; 1hr 30min).

By bus Buses from the mainland, including the long-distance Nordkappexpressen, pull into the bus station at the southern end of the village.

Destinations Alta (1–3 daily; 4hr); Nordkapp (mid-May to mid-Aug 3 daily; mid-Aug to mid-Sept 2 daily; 45min).

By boat Hurtigruten coastal boats dock at the jetty, adjacent to the bus station, with northbound boats arriving at 11.45am and departing 3.15pm; southbound, the boats don't overlay here, arriving at 6am and departing 15min later; the northbound service is met by special Nordkapp excursion buses – details on board.

Destinations Tromsø (1 daily; 18hr).

ACCOMMODATION AND EATING

Arctico Icebar Sjøgata 1 ⊛articoicebar.com. Opened a decade ago by two Spaniards, this large storage freezer

24

THE SÁMI IN NORWAY

Norway's original inhabitants, the **Sámi**, have survived as reindeer herders in the north of the country for thousands of years. Though their traditions and culture were long under threat by the Norwegian state, today's Sámi are very much alive and kicking; they have their own independence day, their own flag and even their own parliament in the town of **Karasjok**. A detour to Karasjok, linked by twice-daily buses from Alta, is particularly worthwhile, and you can take a guided tour of the **Sámi Parliament**, Kautokeinoveien 50 (late June to mid-Aug hourly from 8.30am–2.30pm; mid-Aug to late June Mon–Fri 1pm; free), visit the **Sámi National Museum**, Mari Boine geaidnu 17 (June–Aug daily 9am–3pm; Sept–May Tues–Fri 9am–3pm; 75kr), with its displays of traditional clothing, tools and art by contemporary Sámi artists, or take a more light-hearted look at Sámi culture at the **Sápmi Park**, Porsangerveien (daily: Jan–May 10am–2pm; June to mid-Aug 9am–7pm; mid-Aug to late Aug 9am–4pm; Sept Mon–Fri 9am–4pm; 150kr; ⓦ visitsapmi.no), an excellent high-tech theme park. A great place to stay is the *Engholm's Design Lodge* (ⓦ engholm.no), a collection of rustic cabins 6km south of Karasjok along the Rv92, which doubles as the town's HI hostel and arranges husky safaris in winter; hearty meals are available too.

offers a wintertime Arctic experience in the spring- and summertime ice bar. 140kr entrance, which includes two (non-alcoholic) drinks. April to mid-Oct daily 9am–9pm.

Corner Fiskeriveien 2 ⓦ corner.no. This modern bistro serves fresh seafood (as you would expect) – try the sautéed herb-baked king crab symphony (125kr) – but also does good burgers and stews, and even whale steak (229kr). Daily 10am–11pm (kitchen closes 9pm).

Nordkapp Camping Skipsfjorden ☎78 47 33 77, ⓦ nordkappcamping.no. Set outside Honningsvåg on the road to Nordkapp, this is a good bet for camping out in the middle of nowhere. Camping/tent (sleeping 2) **260kr**, doubles **700kr**, cabins **600kr**, bungalows **1200kr**

Scandic Nordkapp Skipsfjord ☎78 47 72 60, ⓦ scandichotels.com. In a solitary location just off the E69 about 9km from Honningsvåg, this is the largest hotel on Magerøya, with nearly 300 rooms. The rooms are fine, if a little frugal, and there is a canteen-style restaurant. It's popular with groups bound to and from Nordkapp. June–Sept. Doubles **1300kr**

Nordkapp

While the 307m-high cliff known as **Nordkapp** isn't actually the northernmost point of mainland Europe (that honour

belongs to Knivskjellodden, reached along an 18km signposted track from Highway E69), it is as far north as you can get by public transport. It's a hassle to reach, but there is something exhilarating about this bleak, wind-battered promontory, bespeckled with grazing reindeer. It is the only viewpoint in Norway that you have to pay to visit, though officially you're paying to enter the blight on the landscape that is **Nordkapphallen** (North Cape Hall; daily: early to mid-May & Sept to mid-Oct 11am–3pm; mid-May to Aug 11am–1am; mid-Oct to April 12.30–2pm; 260kr), a flashy tourist centre that contains Europe's northernmost (and possibly its most expensive) souvenir shop, café, restaurant, bar, panoramic movie theatre, chapel and post office.

ARRIVAL AND DEPARTURE

By bus Regular buses run between Honningsvåg and Nordkapp.

Destinations Alta (1–3 daily; 4hr); Honningsvåg (May–Sept 4–6 daily; 45min).

MARKET SQUARE, WROCŁAW

Poland

HIGHLIGHTS

❶ Night out in Warsaw Live it up in the bars of the country's dynamic capital. **See p.841**

❷ Sopot Relax on the vast stretch of white sand near this lively summertime resort. **See p.846**

❸ Kazimierz, Kraków Explore Poland's Jewish heritage in this hip neighbourhood. **See p.850**

❹ Tatra Mountains Hike among jagged alpine peaks and enjoy unique mountain culture. See p.854

❺ Wrocław Discover this elegant gem, unspoilt by tourist hordes. **See p.855**

HIGHLIGHTS ARE MARKED ON THE MAP ON P.833

ROUGH COSTS

Daily budget Basic €50, occasional treat €70

Drink Vodka (50ml shot) €1

Food *Żurek* soup €2–3

Hostel/budget hotel €12/€35

Travel Train: Warsaw–Kraków €33; bus: €15

FACT FILE

Population 38.5 million

Language Polish

Currency Złoty (zł/PLN)

Capital Warsaw

International phone code ☏48

Time zone GMT +1hr

25

Introduction

Poland has long been a nation steeped in tradition and history, although the past twenty-five years have witnessed such dizzying economic development that the country is starting to feel more and more like the rest of Europe. Still, beneath the gleaming surface lies a culture firmly rooted in hospitality, community values and national pride, while reminders of the country's turbulent past are everywhere. Poland is also a land of considerable natural beauty, whose idyllic lakes, beaches and mountains provide a nice contrast to the urban buzz of the cities.

The capital **Warsaw** is a fascinating hybrid, its historic centre rubbing up against neighbourhoods of communist-era grey, glittering modern office blocks and energetic pockets of vibrant nightlife. **Kraków**, the ancient royal capital in the south, is the real crowd-puller, rivalling the elegance of Prague and Vienna, while **Gdańsk** in the north offers an insight into Poland's turbulent history as well as its Baltic-riviera beach life. In the west, **Wrocław** charms visitors with its stately architecture and buzzy student life, while **Poznań** offers a mixture of historical attractions and urban diversions that is quintessentially Polish. The **Tatra Mountains** on the Slovak border offer exhilarating hiking and affordable skiing.

CHRONOLOGY

966 AD Mieszko I unites Slav tribes to create the Polish state.

1025 Bolesław I, Mieszko's son, is crowned the first King of Poland.

1300s Gdańsk and several other northern cities join the Hanseatic League, and trade prospers.

1386 Polish queen Jadwiga marries Lithuanian Grand Duke Jogaila, creating a dynastic union between the two countries.

1410 Polish-Lithuanian forces defeat the Teutonic Knights at the Battle of Grunwald.

1500s The Renaissance sweeps through Poland-Lithuania, giving it significant cultural importance in Europe.

1700s Russia, Prussia and Austria divide Poland-Lithuania between them in the Three Partitions.

1863 The January Uprising against Russian authority is brutally repressed.

1918 An independent Polish state is created following the collapse of German, Russian and Austro-Hungarian empires.

1939 Poland is invaded by Nazi Germany, beginning World War II.

1945 By the end of the war more than six million Poles are dead. Soviets drive out the Nazis and occupy large parts of Poland; the country's borders shift 200km west.

1947 Polish communists win fixed elections.

1978 Karol Wojtyła, Archbishop of Kraków, is elected Pope, taking the name John Paul II.

1980 A strike in Gdańsk, led by Lech Wałęsa, leads to the formation of Solidarity, a free trade union.

1981 Communist leaders attempt to stamp out Solidarity by declaring martial law.

1990 Wałęsa becomes the first popularly elected president of Poland.

2004 Poland accedes to the EU.

2010 A plane carrying conservative President Lech Kaczyński and over 90 dignitaries crashes near Smolensk, Russia, killing everyone on board.

2015 Elections give the nationalist and anti-liberal PiS ("Law and Justice") party a majority in the Polish parliament.

ARRIVAL AND DEPARTURE

Several budget **airlines** fly into Warsaw, Kraków, Gdańsk, Wrocław and Poznań.

Poland has **rail** connections with all its neighbouring countries. Several direct trains arrive daily in both Kraków and Warsaw from Prague, Budapest and Vienna, while Poznań, Wrocław and Warsaw all have regular connections to Germany.

Eurolines (wⓔeurolines.pl) provide **bus** services from all major European capitals to Warsaw, Kraków, Gdańsk and other Polish cities. In addition, Polski Bus (ⓦpolskibus.com) runs to Poland from Berlin, Vienna and Prague; while Tiger

HIGHLIGHTS

1. Night out in Warsaw
2. Sopot
3. Kazimierz, Kraków
4. Tatra Mountains
5. Wrocław

Metres

1000
500
200
100
0

POLAND

Express (🌐tigerexpress.eu) operates minibuses from Brno, Vienna and Prague to Kraków and Wrocław. On the southern border, there are daily buses to Zakopane from the Slovakian resort of Poprad.

GETTING AROUND

BY TRAIN

The Polish railway companies operate many different types of **train**. International passes such as Eurail and InterRail are valid for all of them, although supplements are charged on the fastest services. If you are buying individual-journey tickets, however, beware that tickets valid for one type of service are rarely valid for another.

Biggest of the rail companies is PKP Intercity, which runs Express InterCity Premium (EIC Premium) using extra-fast pendolino trains, Express InterCity (EIC), InterCity (IC) and TLK trains. EIC Premium, EIC and IC trains run on key routes (such as Warsaw–Kraków or Warsaw–Gdańsk, and Warsaw–Poznań) and only stop at major cities. They're the fastest, most comfortable but also most expensive means of getting around, and seat reservations (*miejscówka*; 10–12.50zł) are compulsory. TLK are slightly slower than express trains but are around fifty percent cheaper than travelling by EIC Premium or EIC.

The Przewozy Regionalne company is responsible for running Regio and InterRegio services; Regio are usually local

25

services that travel at snail-like speeds and stop at every wayside halt; InterRegio are faster, longer-distance trains that frequently link important cities. To complicate matters further, Koleje Mazowieckie operates local trains in Warsaw and central Poland, while the Warsaw Municipal Transport Company (ZKM) operates commuter trains in and around the capital.

The main city stations are generally termed *główny*; departures (*odjazdy*) are printed on yellow posters; arrivals (*przyjazdy*) on white; *peron* means platform. You can check times and ticket prices on the PKP timetable online (Ⓦ rozklad-pkp.pl).

BY BUS

It's in rural districts not served by the railway network that **buses** come into their own, although a growing number of bus companies are offering inter-city routes that provide a viable alternative to rail travel.

BY BIKE

Poland's predominantly flat landscape is a tempting place for **cyclists**. There are repair shops in many cities and you can transport bikes on most trains. Note, however, that due to poor roads and dangerous driving, Poland is one of Europe's leading nations for traffic fatalities.

ACCOMMODATION

Backpacker-friendly hostels proliferate in all major cities. They generally offer excellent service, with free wi-fi and laundry, for around 45zł per bed; many also offer private doubles too. There's a small but growing choice of **apartments** and **B&Bs** in the cities, and family-run **pensions** in rural resorts. Prices in these categories hover around 120–180zł for a double room.

Polish **campsites** are often a fair distance out of town and are not always much cheaper than a hostel dorm bed (20–40zł). Though some sites have excellent facilities, in others you'll find a toilet and little else. For a list of campsites in Poland, check Ⓦ eurocampings.co.uk/poland.

FOOD AND DRINK

Poles are passionate about their food, and their cuisine is an intriguing mix of Slavic and Central European influences. While often wonderfully flavoursome and nutritious, it does live up to its reputation for heaviness. **Meals** generally start with soups, the most popular of which are *barszcz* (beetroot broth) and *żurek* (a sour soup of fermented rye). The basis of most main courses is fried or grilled meat, such as *kotlet schabowy* (breaded pork chops). Two inexpensive specialities (10–15zł) you'll find everywhere are *bigos* (sauerkraut stewed with a variety of meats) and *pierogi*, dumplings stuffed with cottage cheese (*ruskie*), meat (*z mięsem*), or cabbage and mushrooms (*z kapustą i grzybami*). The national snack is the *zapiekanka*, a baguette topped with mushrooms, melted cheese and tomato sauce. There are a few veggie cafés for **vegetarians** sick of cabbage, including the *Green Way* chain.

Restaurants stay open until 9 or 10pm, later in city centres, and prices are lower than in Western Europe: in most places outside of Warsaw and Kraków you can have a two-course meal with a drink for 40zł. The cheapest option is the local **milk bar** (*bar mleczny*; usually open from breakfast until 6 or 7pm), which provides fast and filling meals for workers, students and anyone else looking for affordable Polish food.

DRINK

The Poles can't compete with their Czech neighbours when it comes to **beer** (*piwo*), but a growing range of microbreweries is beginning to challenge the bland national brands. Even in Warsaw, you won't pay more than 12zł for a half-litre. Tea (*herbata*) and coffee (*kawa*) are both popular; the former comes with lemon rather than milk. But it's **vodka** (*wódka*), ideally served neat and cold, which is the national drink (see box, p.842).

CULTURE AND ETIQUETTE

As a nation in which around 75 percent of people are practising Roman Catholics, Poland maintains fairly conservative religious and social customs, especially in the countryside. Poland's young, urban population tend to be both more relaxed and wilder than their parents. Yet Poles of all ages are also warm, passionate people, fond of handshakes and of lively, informal conversation over a vodka. Table manners follow the Western norm and it is common to reward good service with a **tip** (either by leaving ten percent or by rounding up the bill to the nearest convenient figure).

SPORTS AND OUTDOOR ACTIVITIES

The most popular **sport** is football, and the national and top league teams often attract sell-out crowds. Poles are enthusiastic **cyclists** and the pavements of Warsaw and Kraków are increasingly full of them. For most **hikers**, the highlight of Poland is the Tatra Mountains in the south, though the country's 23 national parks offer plenty of opportunities for beautiful walks and horseriding. **Watersports** are concentrated around Sopot in the north and Mazury in the northeast, while the **skiing** season (Nov–Feb) brings tourists flocking to southern mountain resorts like Zakopane.

COMMUNICATIONS

Free **wi-fi** is ubiquitous, and available in city-centre hotspots, bars, cafés, hostels, hotels and trains. A few **internet cafés** still exist here and there, charging 4–6zł per hour. Main post offices (*Poczta*) are usually open Monday to Saturday 8am to 8pm; branches close earlier. For public phones you'll need a card (*karta telefoniczna*), available at post offices and RUCH newsagent kiosks.

POLAND ONLINE

ⓦ **poland.travel/en** The official tourist website with general details on Poland's major sights and visa information.
ⓦ **thenews.pl** Polish radio's English-language service, focusing on national news and current events.
ⓦ **culture.pl** News and essays on Polish cultural events and history.
ⓦ **inyourpocket.com** Reliable source of restaurant and bar listings in the big cities.

EMERGENCIES

Poland is a very safe country to travel in, though inevitably thefts from dorms and pickpocketing do occur. Safely store your valuables whenever possible and, on night trains, lock your compartment when you sleep. Polish **police** (*policja*) are courteous but unlikely to speak English. **Medical care** can be basic and most foreigners rely on the expensive private medical centres run by Medicover (☎ 500 900 500, ⓦ medicover.pl). For non-prescription medication, local pharmacists are helpful and often speak English.

INFORMATION

Most cities have a **tourist office** (*informacja turystyczna*, or IT), usually run by the local municipality, though some are merely private agencies selling tours.

MONEY AND BANKS

Currency is the **złoty** (zł/PLN), divided into 100 groszy. Coins come in 1, 2, 5, 10, 20 and 50 groszy, and 1, 2 and 5 złoty denominations; notes as 10, 20, 50, 100 and 200 złoty. At the time of writing, €1 = 4.4zł, US$1 = 3.9zł and £1 = 5.50zł. **Banks** (usually Mon–Fri 7.30am–5pm, Sat 7.30am–2pm) and exchange offices (*kantors*) offer similar exchange rates. Major credit and debit cards are widely

25

POLISH

	POLISH	PRONUNCIATION
Yes	*Tak*	Tahk
No	*Nie*	Nyeh
Please	*Proszę*	Prosh-eh
Thank you	*Dziękuję*	Djen-ku-yeh
Hello/Good day	*Dzień dobry*	Djen doh brih
Goodbye	*Do widzenia*	Doh veed-zen-yah
Excuse me/Sorry	*Przepraszam*	Psheh-pra-shahm
Today	*Dzisiaj*	Djyish-eye
Yesterday	*Wczoraj*	Vchor-eye
Tomorrow	*Jutro*	Yoo-troh
What time is it?	*Która godzina?*	Ktoo-rah go-djee-nah?
I don't understand	*Nie rozumiem*	Nyeh roh-zoom-yem
How much is…?	*Ile kosztuje…?*	Ill-eh kosh-too-yeh…?
Do you speak English?	*Pan/i/mówi po angielsku?*	Pahn/ee/movee poh ahn-gyel-skoo?
Where is the…?	*Gdzie jest…?*	G-djeh yest…?
Entrance	*Wejście*	Vey-shche
Exit	*Wyjście*	Viy-shche
Toilet	*Toaleta*	To-a-le-ta
Hotel	*Hotel*	Ho-tel
Hostel	*Schronisko/hostel*	Sro-nees-ko
Church	*Kościoł*	Kosh-choow
What time does the…	*O ktorej odchodzi/*	O ktoo-rey ot-ho-djee/
Leave/arrive?	*Przychodzi…?*	Pshih-ho-djee…?
Boat	*Łódź*	Woodj
Bus	*Autobus*	Aw-tow-boos
Plane	*Samolot*	Sa-mo-lot
Train	*Pociąg*	Po-chonk
I would like a…	*Proproszę…*	Po-pro-she…
Bed	*Łóżko*	Woosh-ko
Single room	*Pokoj jednoosobowy*	Po-koi yed-no-o-so-bo-vi
Double room	*Pokoj lózkiem*	Po-koi woosh-kyem
Cheap	*Tani*	Tah-nee
Expensive	*Drogi*	Droh-gee
Open	*Otwarty*	Ot-var-tih
Closed	*Zamknięty*	Zahmk-nee-yen-tih
One	*Jeden*	Yed-en
Two	*Dwa*	Dvah
Three	*Trzy*	Trshih
Four	*Cztery*	Chter-ih
Five	*Pięć*	Pyench
Six	*Sześć*	Sheshch
Seven	*Siedem*	Shedem
Eight	*Osiem*	Oshem
Nine	*Dziewięć*	Djyev-yench
Ten	*Dziesięć*	Djyesh-ench

accepted, and **ATMs** are common in cities. Few places accept euros.

OPENING HOURS AND HOLIDAYS

Most shops open on weekdays from 10am to 6pm, and all but the largest close on Saturday at 2 or 3pm and all day Sunday. RUCH kiosks, selling public transport tickets (*bilety*), open at 6 or 7am. Most museums and historic monuments are closed once a week. Entrance tends to be inexpensive, and is often free one day of the week. **Public**

holidays are: January 1, January 6, Easter Monday, May 1, May 3, Whitsun (May/June), Corpus Christi (May/June), August 15, November 1, November 11, December 25 and 26.

Warsaw

Packed with a bizarre mix of gleaming office buildings and grey, Communist-era apartment blocks, **WARSAW** (Warszawa) often bewilders backpackers. Yet if any city rewards exploration, it is the Polish capital. North of the lively centre are stunning Baroque palaces and the meticulously reconstructed Old Town; to the south are two of Central Europe's finest urban parks; and in the east lie reminders of the rich Jewish heritage extinguished by the Nazis.

Warsaw became the capital in 1596 and flourished as one of Europe's most prosperous cities. Absorbed by the Russian Empire in 1815, it wasn't until 1918 that Warsaw again became the capital of an independent Poland. The Germans invaded in 1939 and herded the city's large Jewish population into a ghetto, prior to their transportation to the death camps. The Warsaw Uprising of 1944 so infuriated Hitler that he ordered the total destruction of the city, leaving 850,000 Varsovians dead and 85 percent of Warsaw in ruins. Rebuilt after the war, the historic core of the city now stands at the centre of a dynamic, fast-developing metropolis.

WHAT TO SEE AND DO

The main sights are on the western bank of the Wisła (Vistula) River where you'll find the central business and shopping district, **Śródmieście**, grouped around Centralna station and the nearby Palace of Culture. The more picturesque **Old Town** (Stare Miasto) is just to the north.

The Old Town

The title **Old Town** (Stare Miasto) is, in some respects, a misnomer for the historic nucleus of Warsaw. During World War II the beautifully arranged Baroque streets were destroyed, after which they were painstakingly reconstructed so accurately that the area has been named a UNESCO World Heritage Site. The Old Town comes alive in the summer, as tourists, street performers and festivals take over the cobblestone streets.

Royal Castle

Plac Zamkowy (Castle Square), on the south side of the Old Town, is dominated by the thirteenth-century **Royal Castle**, now home to the Castle Museum (May–Sept Mon–Wed, Fri & Sat 10am–6pm, Thurs 10am–8pm, Sun 11am–6pm; Oct–April Tues–Sat 10am–4pm, Sun 11am–4pm; 23zł, audioguide 17zł; ⊚zamek-krolewski.pl). Though the structure is a replica, many of its furnishings are originals. After passing the lavish Royal Apartments of King Stanisław August, you visit the **Ballroom** with its allegorical ceiling paintings symbolizing the *Apotheosis of the Genius of Poland*.

Old and New Town squares

On ul. Świętojańska, north of the castle, stands St John's Cathedral, the oldest church in Warsaw. A few metres away, the **Old Town Square** (Rynek Starego Miasta) is one of the most remarkable bits of postwar reconstruction anywhere in Europe. Flattened during the Uprising, its three-storey merchants' houses have been rebuilt in near-flawless imitation of the Baroque originals.

Crossing the ramparts heading north brings you to the **New Town Square** (Rynek Nowego Miasta) at the heart of the so-called New Town (Nowe Miasto), the town's commercial hub in the fifteenth century but now a quiet spot to escape the bustling Old Town.

Krakowskie Przedmieście and Nowy Świat

Running south from pl. Zamkowy is **Krakowskie Przedmieście** and its continuation **Nowy Świat**, lined with stately buildings and churches. One highlight is the **Church of the Nuns of the Visitation**, one of the few buildings in central Warsaw to have come through

25

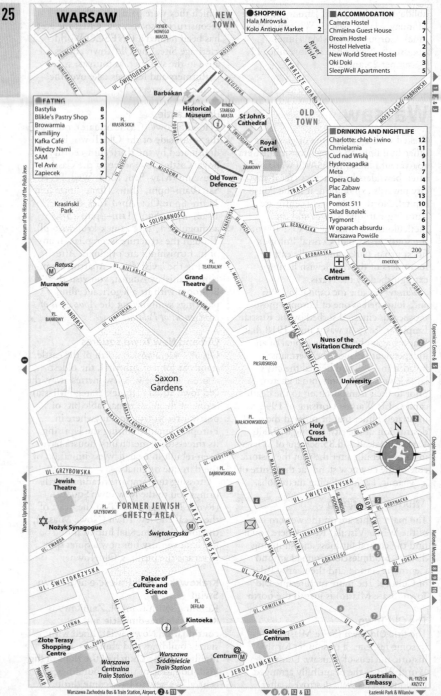

WARSAW

● SHOPPING
Hala Mirowska	1
Kolo Antique Market	2

■ ACCOMMODATION
Camera Hostel	4
Chmielna Guest House	7
Dream Hostel	1
Hostel Helvetia	2
New World Street Hostel	6
Oki Doki	3
SleepWell Apartments	5

■ EATING
Bastylia	8
Blikle's Pastry Shop	5
Browarmia	1
Familijny	4
Kafka Café	3
Między Nami	6
SAM	2
Tel Aviv	9
Zapiecek	7

■ DRINKING AND NIGHTLIFE
Charlotte: chleb i wino	12
Chmielarnia	11
Cud nad Wisłą	9
Hydrozagadka	1
Meta	7
Opera Club	4
Plac Zabaw	5
Plan B	13
Pomost 511	10
Skład Butelek	2
Tygmont	6
W oparach absurdu	3
Warszawa Powiśle	8

Barbakan

Historical Museum

St John's Cathedral

Royal Castle

OLD TOWN

Old Town Defences

Krasiński Park

Ratusz

Muranów

Grand Theatre

Nuns of the Visitation Church

University

Saxon Gardens

Holy Cross Church

Med-Centrum

0   200
metres

Jewish Theatre

FORMER JEWISH GHETTO AREA

Nożyk Synagogue

Świętokrzyska

Palace of Culture and Science

Kintoeka

Galeria Centrum

Złote Terasy Shopping Centre

Warszawa Centralna Train Station

Warszawa Śródmieście Train Station

Centrum

Australian Embassy

N

Museum of the History of the Polish Jews

Warsaw Uprising Museum

Copernicus Centre & 5

Chopin Museum

National Museum & 6 & 10

the war unscathed. Much of the rest of Krakowskie Przedmieście is occupied by university buildings, including several fine Baroque palaces and the **Holy Cross Church**. Sealed inside a column to the left of the nave is an urn containing Chopin's heart.

Chopin Museum

Warsaw's most lavish tribute to its favourite son is the achingly modern **Chopin Museum**, east of Krakowskie Przedmieście at ul. Okolnik 1 (Tues–Sun 11am–8pm; 22zł; ⓦchopin.museum). With interactive handsets to guide visitors through exhibits on the musician's life, it's a must for Chopin enthusiasts, though only a hundred people are allowed into the museum at a time so tickets must be reserved in advance.

The Copernicus Centre

Downhill from the Chopin Museum on the banks of the river, the **Copernicus Centre** at Wybrzeże Kościuszkowskie 20 (Tues–Fri 8am–6pm, Sat & Sun 10am–7pm; 27zł; ⓦkopernik.org.pl) is a hands-on science museum in a spectacularly contemporary building. Aimed mainly at entertaining children and game-playing adults, its wealth of touch-screen computers and mind-bending challenges can keep you occupied for hours.

National Museum

At the southern end of Nowy Świat and east along al. Jerozolimskie is the **National Museum** (Tues–Fri & Sun 10am–6pm, Thurs 10am–8pm; 15zł; free Tues; ⓦmnw.art.pl), housing an extensive collection of archeology and fine art, as well as Christian frescoes from medieval Sudan. The contemporary galleries upstairs contain an all-embracing introduction to Polish modern art.

Palace of Culture and Science

Towering over central Warsaw's main east–west thoroughfare, al. Jerozolimskie, the **Palace of Culture and Science** was a post-World War II gift from Stalin. Today, its vast interior contains theatres, bars and a swimming pool, while the platform on the thirtieth floor (Mon–Thurs & Sun 9am–8pm, Fri & Sat 9am–11pm, 20zł; ⓦpkin.pl) offers impressive views of the city.

Jewish Ghetto

West of the New and Old towns is the former **ghetto** area, in which an estimated 380,000 Jews – one-third of Warsaw's total population – were crammed from 1939 onwards. By the war's end, the ghetto had been razed to the ground, with only around three hundred Jews and just one synagogue, the **Nożyk Synagogue** at ul. Twarda 6, left. You can still get an idea of what Jewish Warsaw looked like on the miraculously untouched ul. Próżna.

Museum of the History of the Polish Jews

Located in the midst of the former ghetto area at Anielewicza 6, the **Museum of the History of the Polish Jews** (Mon, Thurs & Fri 10am–6pm, Wed, Sat & Sun 10am–8pm; 25zł; ⓦpolin.pl) is worth visiting for the building alone – a futuristic glassy slab filled with organic, curvy surfaces. The display pays tribute to the rich Jewish civilization that flourished on the soil of Poland, until all but snuffed out by the Holocaust. The painted wooden ceiling of the seventeenth-century Gwozdziec synagogue is one obvious highlight. Opposite the museum is the **Ghetto Heroes Monument**, commemorating the doomed Warsaw Ghetto Uprising of April 1943, when lightly armed ghetto inhabitants took on the might of the German SS.

Warsaw Uprising Museum

About 1.5km west of the centre is the **Warsaw Uprising Museum** at ul. Grzybowska 79 (Mon, Wed & Fri 8am–6pm, Thurs 8am–8pm, Sat & Sun 10am–6pm; 18zł, free Sun; ⓦ1944.pl; tram #22 from Centralna Station). Set in a century-old brick power station, this ultra-modern audio-visual museum retells the grim story of how the Varsovians fought and were eventually crushed by the Nazis in 1944 – a struggle that led to the deaths of nearly two hundred thousand

25

Poles and the destruction of most of the city. Special attention is given to the equivocal role played by Soviet troops, who watched passively from the other side of the Wisła as the Nazis defeated the Polish insurgents. Only after the city was a charred ruin did they move across to "liberate" its few remaining inhabitants.

Łazienki Park

About 2km south of the centre, on the eastern side of al. Ujazdowskie, is the much-loved **Łazienki Park** (bus #116, #180 or #195 from Nowy Świat). Once a hunting ground, the area was bought in the 1760s by King Stanisław August, who turned it into a park and built the Neoclassical **Łazienki Palace** (Mon 11am–6pm, Tues, Wed & Sun 9am–6pm, Thurs–Sat 9am–8pm; 25zł) across the lake. But the park itself is the real attraction, with its oak-lined paths alive with peacocks and red squirrels.

Wilanów Palace

The grandest of Warsaw's palaces, **Wilanów** (May–Sept Mon 9.30am–7pm, Tues, Thurs & Fri 9.30am–4pm, Wed, Sat & Sun 9.30am–6pm; Oct–April Mon & Wed–Sun 9.30am–4pm; 20zł, free Thur; ⓦwilanow-palac.pl) makes an easy excursion from the centre: take bus #180 south from Krakowskie Przedmieście or Nowy Świat to its terminus. Converted in the seventeenth century from a small manor house into the "Polish Versailles", the palace displays a vast range of decorative styles, a mixture mirrored in the delightful palace **gardens** (daily 9am–dusk; 5zł, free Thurs).

ARRIVAL AND DEPARTURE

By plane Okęcie airport is 8km southwest of the Old Town. Suburban trains run from the airport to Warszawa Śródmieście (near Centrum) every 30min and Warszawa Centralna every hour (both 6.30am–10.30pm; 25min). Outside these hours night bus #N32 runs into town.

By train The main train station, Warszawa Centralna, is in the modern centre just west of the Centrum crossroads.

Destinations Berlin (4 daily; 5hr 45min); Budapest (2 daily; 1 of which overnight; 9hr 30min–11hr 30min); Gdańsk (hourly; 2hr 50min); Kyiv (1 daily; overnight; 16hr); Kraków (hourly; 2hr 30min); Poznań (hourly; 2hr 45min–3hr); Prague (3 daily; 1 of which overnight; 8hr

30min–12hr); Sopot (hourly; 3hr 5min); Toruń (10 daily; 2hr 20min); Vienna (5 daily; of which 2 overnight; 8hr 30min–9hr 30min); Wrocław (5 daily; 3hr 40min).

By bus The main bus station, Dworzec PKS, is located right next to the Warszawa Zachodnia train station, 3km west of Centralna Station. Catch eastbound buses #127, #130, #158 or #517 into town.

Destinations L'viv (2 daily; 12hr); Rīga (1–2 daily; 13hr); Tallinn (1–2 daily; 17hr); Wrocław (1 daily; 6hr 30min); Vilnius (2 daily; 8–10hr).

INFORMATION

Tourist information In the Old Town Square at 19/21 (daily: May–Aug 9am–9pm; March & April, Sept & Oct 8am–7pm; Nov–Feb 8am–6pm; ☎22 194 31, ⓦwarsawtour.pl). There are also tourist offices at the Palace of Culture and the airport.

Travel agents STA Travel, ul. Krucza 41/43 (☎22 529 3800), can reserve international or domestic flights and train tickets, and sells ISIC Cards.

GETTING AROUND

Tickets Tickets for trams, buses and the metro (single trip 4.40zł; single trip of up to 20min duration 3.40zł) are available at green RUCH kiosks or automatic ticket machines. Always punch your tickets in the machines on board, as Warsaw's inspectors are extremely thorough. There are also good-value 1-day passes available (13zł), which should be punched the first time you use them. Tickets for students (ulgowy) are half-price, but you need to show ID.

By bus A well-developed if busy network of buses runs until around 11pm; after that, night buses leave every 30min from behind the main train station.

By tram A crowded but efficient means of transport, running till 11pm.

By metro Warsaw's subway system consists of a north–south line running through the centre of town and an east–west route that connects the centre with the suburb of Praga across the river. Świętokrzyska is where the two lines meet.

By taxi Generally with an initial charge of 8zł, then around 3zł/km, 4.50zł/km after 10pm and on Sun. English is spoken at Ele (☎22 811 1111) and Euro Taxi (☎2219668).

ACCOMMODATION

Warsaw has many good private hostels, mainly in Śródmieście; all the hostels listed below offer free internet, breakfast and free/cheap laundry services unless otherwise stated.

HOSTELS

Camera Hostel ul. Jasna 22 ☎22 828 8600, ⓦcamerahostel.pl. Functional dorms with film-themed decor, a good range of social areas and hard-to-beat, central location. Dorms 55zł, doubles 160zł

Dream Hostel Krakowskie Przedmieście 55 ☎ 22 419 4848, ⓦ facebook.com/dreamhostelwarsaw. Superbly located hostel occupying four floors of a renovated town house, *Dream* comes with modern furnishings, well-equipped social areas and never seems too crowded or frantic. The loft rooms are particularly cute. Breakfast and snacks available for a few extra złotys. Dorms 60zł, doubles 240zł

Hostel Helvetia ul. Sewerynów 7 30 ☎ 22 826 7108, ⓦ hostel-helvetia.pl. Dead central yet in a quiet street, this nicely furnished hostel has plenty of showers, a women's dorm and a separate apartment. They also offer swish doubles and apartments in *Helvetia Plus* a 3min walk away (reception at the *Helvetia*) – breakfast is included at both locations. Dorms 59zł, doubles 170zł

★**New World Street Hostel** ul. Nowy Świat 27 ☎ 22 828 1282, ⓦ nws-hostel.pl. Friendly staff and a cosy common room (complete with board games and books) make this the pick of Warsaw's hostels. While the in-hostel atmosphere is calming, neighbouring streets are packed with bars. Dorms 42zł, doubles 180zł

Oki Doki pl. Dąbrowskiego 3 ☎ 22 828 0122, ⓦ okidoki.pl. With its eccentric, individually designed rooms and bar (0.5lt beer 7zł), this hostel has the liveliest feel of any in town. Breakfast available for 15zł. Dorms 65zł, doubles 190zł

APARTMENTS

Pragapartments ☎ 792 217 313, ⓦ pragapartments .com.pl. A superb option if you're aiming to stay on the up-and-coming east bank of the Wisła River, offering a mixture of smartly furnished, 2-person studio, 1-room and 2-room apartments in different locations in the Praga district. Studio 240zł, 1-room apartment 300zł

★**SleepWell Apartments** ul. Nowy Świat 62 ☎ 600 300 749, ⓦ sleepwell-warsaw.pl. Just off Warsaw's main café strip, this restored apartment offers fairly small rooms (they're cute en-suite doubles rather than "apartments" in the real sense of the word), decked out in bold, kitschy colours. Doubles 227zł

B&B

Chmielna Guest House ul. Chmielna 13 ☎ 22 828 1282, ⓦ chmielnabb.pl. Surprisingly intimate place for such a central location, with seven rooms arranged around a spacious living room and adjoining kitchen. Some rooms are quite small and share a bathroom in the hallway, but all are stylishly decorated with soothing colours. Doubles 190zł

EATING

CAFÉS, CHEAP EATS AND SNACKS

Blikle's Pastry Shop ul. Nowy Świat 35. *Blikle's* is renowned throughout the nation for its soft springy doughnuts (*paczki*), but there's a lot more besides including a mouthwatering array of pastries, cakes and chocolates. Cake slices 3.80zł. Daily 9am–9pm.

Familijny ul. Nowy Świat 29. Conveniently located milk bar serving good soups, pancakes and traditional Polish dishes for just a couple of złoty. A Warsaw student favourite. Mains 5–10zł. Mon–Fri 7am–8pm, Sat & Sun 9am–5pm.

★**Kafka Café** ul. Obozna 3. Tasty sandwiches (14zł), pasta dishes (23zł) and strong coffee make this stylish café popular with a student crowd, who spill out onto the chairs outside on the lawn in summer. Mon–Fri 9am–10pm, Sat & Sun 10am–10pm.

SAM ul. Lipowa 7. Bakery with diner attached, serving soups, main dishes and delicious fresh bread. Opt for a roast beef sandwich (14zł) or settle down with the Thai rice and vegetables (25zł). Mon–Sat 8am–10pm, Sun 9am–10pm.

Tel Aviv Poznańska 11. Middle Eastern/vegan café celebrated city-wide for its huge selection of own-recipe hummus spreads. Order something classic like stuffed aubergine (40zł) from the à-la-carte menu, or opt for the two-course set lunch (Mon–Fri only; noon–4pm; 25zł). Mon–Sat 9am–midnight, Sun 10am–10pm.

RESTAURANTS

Bastylia ul. Mokotowska 17. Legendary pancake bar with a chic interior, serving up a large number of sweet and savoury pancakes. Pancake with prosciutto and gruyère 24zł. Daily 8am–11pm.

Browarmia ul. Królewska 1. Roomy beer hall and grill-restaurant with a hugely popular street-facing terrace, brewing its own pilsner and wheat beers (from 12zł/0.5 litre). Use them to wash down a hearty dish of pork knuckle (69zł) or a steak (from 40zł). Daily noon–11pm.

Między Nami ul. Bracka 20. Cultured, gay-friendly café-restaurant that's excellent for a light meal, with some innovative vegetarian choices and a pleasant summer patio. Mains 20–35zł. Mon–Thurs 10am–11pm, Fri & Sat 10am–midnight, Sun 2–11pm.

Zapiecek al. Jerozolimskie 28. A wide variety of *pierogis*, *golabki* (stuffed cabbage leaves), *nalesniki* (pancakes) and other traditional Polish specialities, served by waitresses decked out in folk costumes. *Pierogis* 22zł. Daily 11am–11pm.

DRINKING AND NIGHTLIFE

The bar scene in Warsaw has really taken off over the last decade, and the city now provides a great night out that rivals Prague and needn't blow your budget. Praga, across the river, boasts a lively, bohemian bar scene – an interesting alternative to the more glitzy hangouts you'll find downtown.

POLAND'S ELIXIR: VODKA STRIKES BACK

The tipple most associated with Poland, **vodka** is making a major comeback after decades of being overshadowed in the fashion stakes by imported Western drinks. Traditionally made from cereal grains, potatoes or beets, Polish vodka is usually served chilled and neat – although increasingly mixed with fruit juice. Żubrówka, infused with bison grass, is delicious on its own or mixed with apple juice. Other vodkas usually consumed as down-in-one shots include Żołądkowa Gorzka (an amber-coloured herbal vodka), Wiśniówka (from cherries) and the honey-flavoured Krupnik.

BARS

Charlotte: chleb i wino al. Wyzwolenia 18 (entrance on pl. Zbawiciela). Chic and spacious café-bar dishing out coffee and croissants during the daytime, wine and spirits at night. There's outdoor seating beneath plac Zbawiciela's colonnades. Mon–Thurs 7am–midnight, Fri 7am–1am, Sat 9am–1am, Sun 9am–10pm.

Chmielarnia Marszalkowska 10/16. Bustling multi-tap beer pub with one of the best choices of ale in the city, from Polish boutique brews to international craft favourites. Punters also flock here for the irresistible Nepalese food – daily specials (served 11am–4pm; 19–26zł) always include at least one vegetarian choice. Daily 11am–midnight.

Meta ul. Foksal 21. A time capsule stuffed with pop-cultural ephemera from the 1970s and 80s, *Meta* serves up vodka shots, excellent small-brewery beers (Kasztelan 7zł) and late-night snacks (including the most popular steak tartare in town). Daily 11am–6am.

Plan B al. Wyzwolenia 18. Leading hipster hangout on the popular pl. Zbawiciela, featuring red sofas, rickety wooden chairs and a standing-room-only terrace in the spring and summer. Mon–Sat 11am–3am, Sun 4pm–2am.

Skład Butelek ul. 11 Listopada 22, Praga. Wonderfully quirky gathering place for Warsaw's creative types, serving obscure Ukrainian beers in an old factory. 0.5lt beer 10zł. Wed–Sat 4pm–3am.

W Oparach Absurdu ul. Zabkowska 6, Praga. Chaotic, lively and decorated with all the haphazard charm of a flea market. 0.5lt beer 9zł. Daily noon–3am.

Warszawa Powiśle ul. Kruckowskiego 3b. Located in the UFO-shaped former ticket hall of the Warszawa-Powiśle station, this self-styled "kiosk for wódka and culture" serves drinks and snacks (burgers 12zł) until late. Summer evenings bring the best out in the place, when crowds spill across the pavement out front. Daily 9am–midnight.

CLUBS AND LIVE MUSIC

Hydrozagadka ul. 11 Listopada 22 ⓦ hydrozagadka .waw.pl. Courtyard bar-cum-nightclub featuring a bare-bones interior: expect to hear leftfield DJs, and the kind of visiting indie bands that attract an informed alternative audience. Cover 25–50zł. Fri, Sat and gig nights (check the website) 7pm–4am.

Opera Club pl. Teatralny 1. Dancefloors and semi-private rooms scattered throughout the cavernous chambers beneath the Grand Theatre, making for a novel night out. Cocktails 19–25zł. Fri & Sat 10pm–5am.

Tygmont ul. Mazowiecka 6/8 ⓦ tygmont.com.pl. The city's top jazz club, with a regular gig roster, retro discos and a stylish, upmarket clientele. Entrance 10zł and upwards depending on event. Tues–Thurs 9pm–2am, Fri & Sat 7pm–4am.

SUMMER-ONLY RIVERSIDE BARS

Between June and September Warsaw nightlife migrates to the banks of the Wisła, home to a variety of al-fresco bars and clubs.

Cud nad Wisłą bul. Flotylli Wiślanej. Sprawling open-air hangout north of the Pilsudski bridge offering drinks, bar snacks, live music, weekend food markets and DJ events. June–Sept daily noon–midnight.

Plac Zabaw bul. Grzymały-Siedlieckiego ⓦ facebook .com/placzabawnadwisla. Located on the west bank of the river just south of the Świętokrzyskie bridge, the "Playpark" spreads its deckchairs over a grassy part of the riverbank and organizes al-fresco gigs and open-air film screenings throughout the summer. An attached pontoon structure (named "Barka") hosts late-night DJ events. May–Sept daily 11am–11pm; Barka Thurs–Sat until 4am.

Pomost 511 ul. Flotylli Wiślanej ⓦ facebook.com /Pomost511. On the same riverside stretch as *Cud nad Wisłą* and with a similar mixture of culture, music and cold beers, *Pomost* offers open-air theatre as well as film shows and crowd-pulling DJs. May–Sept Mon–Wed & Sun noon–midnight, Thurs–Sat noon–3am.

MARKETS AND MALLS

For mainstream **fashion brands**, first explore the gleaming Złote Terasy shopping centre, behind Centralna train station, before passing through to the mainly pedestrianized streets of ul. Chimielna and ul. Nowy Świat. The daily Hala Mirowska market on al. Jana Pawła II is the place to go for **fresh fruits and vegetables**, while **antique** hunters should head for the Kolo Antique Market on ul. Obozowa (Sun 7am–2pm; trams #13 & #23 from the Old Town), where you'll find everything from war medals to old Christian icons.

ENTERTAINMENT

A wealth of cultural festivals brings the city to life in summer, especially the Warsaw "Summer Jazz Days" in June, and "Jazz in the Old Town" (a series of outdoor concerts) throughout July and Aug. Films are usually shown in their original language with Polish subtitles. Tickets 17–30zł.

Grand Theatre (Teatr Wielki) pl. Teatralny 1 ☎ 22 692 3288, ⓦ teatrwielki.pl. Worth visiting just for its Neoclassical facade, but it also hosts the best of Poland's National Opera. 28–320zł depending on seats.

Kinoteka pl. Defilad 1 ⓦ kinoteka.pl. Multiplex in the Palace of Culture and Science showing the latest blockbusters.

Muranów ul. Gen. Andersa 1 ⓦ muranow.gutekfilm.pl. Art-house cinema that screens a range of films from around the world.

DIRECTORY

Embassies and consulates Australia, ul. Nowogrodzka 11 ☎ 22 521 3444, ⓦ poland.embassy.gov.au; Canada, ul. Matejki 1/5 ☎ 22 584 3100, ⓦ canadainternational.gc.ca /poland-pologne; Ireland, ul. Mysia 5 ☎ 22 849 6633, ⓦ dfa.ie/irish-embassy/poland; New Zealand, al. Ujazdowskie 51 ☎ 22 521 0500, ⓦ nzembassy.com /poland; South Africa, ul. Koszykowa 54 ☎ 22 622 1031, ⓦ www.dirco.gov.za/warsaw; UK, ul. Kawalerii 12 1 ☎ 22 311 0000, ⓦ gov.uk/government/world/poland; USA, ul. Ujazdowskie 29/31 ☎ 22 504 2000, ⓦ pl.usembassy.gov.

Exchange The Old Town has a host of *kantor* stores that exchange foreign cash, though you will have to shop around for the best rates. Interchange Poland at ul. Chmielna 30 (Mon–Fri 8am–10pm, Sat & Sun 9am–10pm) is also a reliable option.

Hospitals The nearest public hospital to the centre is the Praski, al. Solidarności 67 (☎ 22 619 1979). The private Damian clinic at ul. Foksal 3/5 (☎ 22 566 2222, ⓦ damian .pl) has English-speaking staff and 24hr service.

Internet *Arena Cafe*, Centrum metro station (daily 7am–midnight; 6zł/hr).

Left luggage Centralna Station has a 24hr left-luggage room and lockers with storage for up to ten days.

Pharmacies There is a 24hr pharmacy on the top floor of Centralna train station.

Post office ul. Świętokryzska 31/33 (24hr).

Northern Poland

Even in a country accustomed to shifting borders, **northern Poland** presents an unusually tortuous historical puzzle. Successively the domain of the Teutonic Order, Hansa merchants and the Prussians, it's only in the last seventy years that the region has become definitively Polish. The conurbation of **Gdańsk**, **Sopot** and **Gdynia**, known as the Tri-City, lines the Baltic coast with its dramatic shipyards and sandy beaches, while highlights inland include the medieval centres of **Malbork** and **Toruń**.

GDAŃSK

Both the starting point of World War II and the birthplace of the anti-communist Solidarity movement, **GDAŃSK** has played more than a fleeting role on the world stage. Traces of its past are visible in the steel skeletons of shipyard cranes and the Hanseatic architecture of the old town. After all the social and political upheavals of the last century, the city is now busy reinventing itself as a tourist hub.

WHAT TO SEE AND DO

With its medieval brick churches and narrow eighteenth-century merchants' houses, Gdańsk certainly looks ancient. But its appearance is deceptive: by 1945, the core of the city lay in ruins, and the present buildings are almost complete reconstructions.

The Main Town (Główne Miasto)

Huge stone gateways guard both entrances to ul. Długa, the main thoroughfare. Start from the sixteenth-century gate at the top,

25

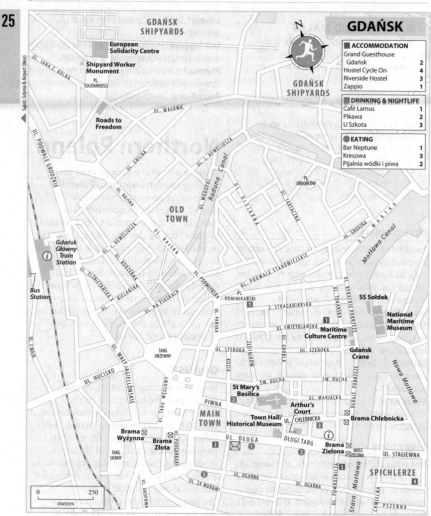

GDAŃSK

■ ACCOMMODATION

Grand Guesthouse	
Gdańsk	2
Hostel Cycle On	4
Riverside Hostel	3
Zappio	1

■ DRINKING & NIGHTLIFE

Café Lamus	1
Pikawa	2
U Szkota	3

● EATING

Bar Neptune	1
Kresowa	3
Pijalnia wódki i piwa	2

Brama Wyżynna, and carry on east through the nearby Brama Zlota. You'll soon come across the imposing Town Hall, which houses a **Historical Museum** (June–Sept Mon 9am–1pm, Tues–Thurs 9am–4pm, Fri & Sat 10am–6pm, Sun 10am–4pm; Oct–May Tues 10am–1pm, Wed, Fri & Sat 10am–4pm, Sun 11am–4pm; 12zł, free Mon) with shocking photos of the city's wartime destruction.

Further down, the street opens onto the wide expanse of ul. Długi Targ, where the ornate facade of **Arthur's Court** (same hours as Historical Museum; 10zł) stands out among the fine mansions. The surrounding streets are also worth exploring, especially ul. Mariacka, brimming with amber traders, at the end of which stands **St Mary's Basilica** (Mon–Sat 8.30am–6.30pm, Sun 11am–noon & 1–5pm; 4zł), the largest church in Poland.

The waterfront and the Maritime Museum

At the end of ul. Długi Targ the archways of **Brama Zielona** open directly onto the waterfront. Halfway down is the fifteenth-century **Gdańsk Crane**, the biggest in medieval Europe, part of the **National Maritime Museum** (July & Aug daily 10am–6pm; Jan–June & Sept–Nov Tues–Sun 10am–4pm; Dec Tues–Sun 10am–3pm; 8zł; ⓦnmm.pl). Highlights include an exhibition of primitive boats; for an extra 10zł you can also tour the cargo ship SS *Soldek* docked outside. The museum's annexe on the opposite banks of the river, the **Maritime Culture Centre** (same times; 14zł), has four fascinating floors of interactive displays covering storms and sea life as well as boats from around the world.

The shipyards and the European Solidarity Centre

Further north loom the cranes of the famous Gdańsk **shipyards**, crucible of the struggle to topple communism in Poland. Poignantly set outside the shipyard gates is the monument to the workers killed during peaceful anti-government demonstrations in 1970. Ten years later, the Solidarity union led by Lech Wałęsa turned a shipyard strike into a snowballing national movement. It's an inspiring story, told by the multimedia exhibition at the **European Solidarity Centre** (daily 10am–8pm; 17zł; ⓦecs.gda.pl), a modern building in front of the shipyards that commemorates freedom movements across Central Europe as well as in Poland.

ARRIVAL AND DEPARTURE

By plane Gdańsk Lech Wałęsa airport lies 8km from the city centre. Trains (every 20min; 35min; 3.50zł) run to Gdańsk Central Station (see below), although some services require a change at Gdańsk-Wreszcz. Taxis cost 50–80zł.

By train Make sure to get off at the Główny (Central) Station, a 10min walk northwest of ul. Długa, the heart of the Main Town.

Destinations Kraków (every 2hr; 5hr 30min); Malbork (every 30min; 30–50min); Poznań (5 daily; 3hr); Sopot (every 15min; 20min); Toruń (6 daily; 2hr 20min); Warsaw (hourly; 2hr 50min); Wrocław (4 daily; 5hr).

By bus The bus station is just behind the train station, reached via an underpass.

Destinations Riga (1 daily; 16hr); Tallinn (1 daily; 21hr); Vilnius (1 daily; 11hr).

INFORMATION

Tourist information Tourist office at Długi Targ 28/29 (daily: June–Aug 9am–7pm; Sept–May 9am–5pm; ☎0505 877 021, ⓦgdansk4u.pl). There are also offices at the airport (24hr) and the train station (Mon–Fri 9am–7pm, Sat till 5pm, Sun till 4pm).

ACCOMMODATION

Grand Guesthouse Gdansk ul. Dluga 4 ☎666 061 350, ⓦgrandguesthouse.pl. Bright, simple doubles (some en-suite) and a small kitchen/social area in a restored townhouse right in the centre. Breakfast included. **230zł**

Hostel Cycle On ul. Spichrzowa 15 ☎531 153 700, ⓦhostelcycleon.com. Small but colourful dorms and private rooms in an evocative red-brick street. There's a small common area and breakfast included. Also rents out bikes (25zł/day). Dorms **70zł**, doubles **230zł**

Riverside Hostel ul. Powroźnicza 18/24 ☎58 718 3854, ⓦfacebook.com/RiversideHostel. Situated among historic dockside warehouses, this hostel combines relaxing social areas and a fully equipped kitchen with neat, classy dorms and some cute doubles. Dorms **65zł**, doubles **180zł**

★ **Zappio** ul. Świętojańska 49 ☎58 322 0174, ⓦzappio.pl. Budget hotel and youth hostel in a beautiful prewar building, with big windows and period woodwork. Dorms **55zł**, doubles **170zł**

EATING

Bar Neptune ul. Długa 33/34. Legendary milk bar with the usual Polish *barszcz*, *pierogi* and pork-chop fare. Dishes tend to run out well before closing time. Mains from 5zł. Mon–Fri 7.30am–7pm, Sat & Sun 10am–5pm.

★ **Kresowa** ul. Ogarna 12. Cuisine from the Polish-Lithuanian-Ukrainian borderlands (*kresy*), served in a refined atmosphere for a reasonable price. Much of the food is based on historic recipes: don't miss the *Zrazy Radziwilowskie* (beef rolls stuffed with mushrooms; 29zl). Other mains 20–40zł. Daily 10am–10pm.

Pijalnia wódki i piwa ul. Dlugi targ 35/38. One of Poland's new breed of round-the-clock drinks-and-snack bars, serving vodka shots, beer (4zł), herring snacks and *gzik* (sour cream, onion and cottage cheese; 8zł) in a communist-era interior. Daily 9am–5am.

DRINKING AND NIGHTLIFE

Local clubbers prefer the nightlife in Sopot (see p.846), but there are several bars on Piwna and Chlebnicka to keep you entertained.

Café Lamus ul. Lawndowa 8 (entrance from ul. Straganiarska). An artful mixture of old furniture and retro wallpaper sets a suitably bohemian tone to this beer-drinkers' favourite, with a fridge full of craft ales from Poland and beyond. Daily noon–2am.

25

Pikawa ul. Piwna 14/15. Something of a shrine to hot chocolate, which comes in all guises (from 6.50zl) and with varying dollops of cream. Apple pie and ice cream provide further reasons to overindulge. Daily 10am–11pm.

U Szkota Pub ul. Chlebnicka 9/10. A friendly Scottish pub that comes complete with kilted waiters and Belhaven Scottish Ale on tap, alongside Irish beers such as Kilkenny and Guinness on tap (14zl for 0.4lt). Mon–Thurs & Sun 4pm–1am, Fri & Sat 4pm–2am.

SOPOT

Some 15km northwest of Gdańsk lies Poland's trendiest coastal resort, which boasts Europe's longest wooden pier (512m) and a broad stretch of golden sand. With its vibrant nightlife, **Sopot** is a magnet for young party animals. All roads lead to the beach, where aside from lounging you can meander up the pier (entry 7.50zl May–Sept), on which you'll find boat tours operating in summer.

ARRIVAL AND INFORMATION

By train The train station lies 400m west of the beach and a 5min walk from the main street, ul. Monte Cassino.

Tourist information The tourist office is on the way to the pier at plac Zdrojowy 2 (daily 10am–6pm; ☎ 790 280 884, ⓦsts.sopot.pl), and helps with accommodation, which fills up quickly in summer.

ACCOMMODATION

Cheap accommodation can be hard to find in Sopot. Your best bet is to look for "Wolny Pokoj" (free room) signs in private houses, where you can rent rooms for around 50zl/person.

Central Hostel ul. Monte Casino 15 ☎ 53 085 8717, ⓦhostelcentral.pl. Bang in the centre of town, this hostel is sparsely furnished but has a lively party atmosphere and sunny rooms. Dorms __60zl__, doubles __250zl__

OPEN'ER FESTIVAL

Taking place just north of Gdańsk and Sopot at Gdynia's Kosakovo airfield, the **Open'er Festival** (ⓦopener.pl) in early July is one of Europe's largest outdoor rock events. It's very much Central Europe's answer to Reading or Roskilde: 2016's line-up included Red Hot Chilli Peppers, Pharrell Williams, Tame Impala and the ubiquitous Florence & the Machine. Four-day tickets weigh in at around 600zl; add an extra 80zl for camping.

EATING

For best value, avoid ul. Monte Cassino and head for the restaurants around 1km south along the beach.

Bar Przystan al. Wojska Polskiego 11. A touristy but great-value restaurant with a big glass-enclosed dining room right above the beach. Fresh Baltic fish such as cod, halibut or flounder 8–11.50zl/100g. Daily 10am–11pm.

Mocno Nadziane ul. Haffnera 7/9. Contemporary-style *pierogi* bar serving several variations on the pastry-pocket theme, including some intriguing local fish-flavoured options. Also a good place to drink spirits and cocktails come the evening. Mains 10–20zl. Daily 11am–10pm.

DRINKING AND NIGHTLIFE

Atelier al. Mamuszki 2 ⓦklubatelier.pl. Seafront bar and weekend club attracting a hedonistically inclined, bohemian set. Music policy is broader here than elsewhere, with indie rock regularly colliding with retro disco and hip-hop. Mon–Thurs 3pm–midnight, Fri 3pm–5am, Sat 11am–5am, Sun 1am–midnight.

Zatoka Sztuki al. Mamuszki 14, ⓦzatokasztuki.pl. Multi-themed café, restaurant, art gallery and club situated on the beach just north of the pier. Follow up fusion food in the restaurant (salmon in teriyaki sauce 44zl) with a long night of cocktails and DJ-induced dancing. May–Sept 10am–2am.

MALBORK

The spectacular fortress of **MALBORK** (Tues–Sun: mid-April to mid-Sept 9am–7pm; rest of year 10am–3pm; high season 39.50zl, low season 29.50zl; ⓦzamek.malbork.pl) was built as the headquarters of the Teutonic Order in the fourteenth century and still casts a threatening shadow over an otherwise sleepy town. As the Teutonic Knights sank into deep financial crisis, they were eventually forced to sell the castle in the mid-fifteenth century. The place was then employed as a royal residence and a stopover for Polish monarchs en route between Warsaw and Gdańsk.

You enter over a moat and through the daunting main gate, before reaching an open courtyard. Brooding above is the **High Castle**, which harbours the vast **Castle Church** with its faded chivalric paintings. You'll be given an English audioguide for the three-hour self-guided tour, or, in July and August, you can opt for a live tour instead (both are included in the ticket price).

ARRIVAL AND DEPARTURE

By train The train station is about a 10min walk south of the castle; there are regular trains to and from Gdańsk (every 30min; 30–50min).

TORUŃ

Once one of the most beautiful medieval towns in Central Europe, **TORUŃ** was founded by the Teutonic Knights and is still rich with their architectural legacy. It's also famous for being the birthplace of Nicolaus Copernicus, whose house still stands. Now a friendly university city, with bars and cafés sprinkled throughout the compact streets, Toruń combines lively nightlife with its status as a UNESCO World Heritage Site.

WHAT TO SEE AND DO

The highlight of Toruń is the mansion-lined Market Square (Rynek) and its fourteenth-century Town Hall, now the **District Museum** (Tues–Sun: May–Sept 10am–6pm; Oct–April 10am–4pm; 11zł), with a fine collection of nineteenth-century paintings and intricate woodcarvings. South of the Rynek at ul. Kopernika 15/17, the **Copernicus Museum** (same hours as District Museum; 11zł), in the house where the great man was born, contains a fascinating model collection of his original instruments as well as facsimiles of the momentus *De Revolutionibus* and a selection of early portraits. The large, Gothic **St John's Cathedral** (Mon–Sat 8.30am–7.30pm, Sun 4.30–7.30pm; 5zł), at the eastern end of ul. Kopernika, has a tower offering panoramic views over the city (April–Oct only; 3zł extra). Further north stands the **Contemporary Art Centre** at Waly Gen. Sikorskiego 13 (Tues–Thurs & Sun 10am–6pm, Fri & Sat 10am–8pm; 10zł), a contemporary building hosting cutting-edge art exhibitions.

ARRIVAL AND DEPARTURE

By train Toruń Główny, the main train station, is 2km south of the river; buses #22, #25 and #27 (every 10min; 2.80zł) run from outside the station to pl. Rapackiego on the western edge of the Old Town, the first stop after crossing the bridge.

Destinations Gdańsk (6 daily; 2hr 20min); Poznań (9 daily; 1hr 30min); Warsaw (10 daily; 2hr 20min).

> **PIERNIKI**
>
> You can't leave Toruń without trying the local **pierniki**, or gingerbread, which has been made here since the town was founded. *Pierniczek* on Żeglarska 25 offers a mouthwatering range.

By bus The bus station is on ul. Dąbrowskiego, just north of the centre.

INFORMATION

Tourist information Tourist office at Rynek Staromiejski 25 (Mon–Fri 9am–6pm, Sat–Sun 10am–6pm; ⓣ 56 621 0930, ⓦ it.torun.pl).

ACCOMMODATION

Hostel Freedom Rynek Staromiejski 10 ⓣ 731 218 415, ⓦ freedomtorun.pl. Nicely decorated hostel in a creaky-floored main-square apartment, with small kitchen, free breakfast and neat bunk-bed dorms. Dorms **40zł**, doubles **100zł**

Orange Plus ul. Jeczmienna 11 ⓣ 56 651 8457, ⓦ hostelorange.pl. A bright, cosy hostel with friendly staff, comfortable dorms, relaxing social areas but not much of a kitchen. Dorms **35zł**, doubles **100zł**

EATING AND DRINKING

★ **Café Fajka** ul. Małe Garbary 1. Chilled-out place filled with cushions, offering a huge range of cocktails and shishas that bubble milk or gin instead of water. Cocktails from 12zł. Mon–Wed & Sun 3pm–2am, Thurs–Sat till 3am.

Manekin ul. Wysoka 5. The perfect place for pancake lovers, with a lengthy menu of innovative meat, veg and sweet fillings (try the salmon and camembert pancake for 17zł). It's not all batter, though – soups and salads also feature. Mon–Thurs & Sun 10am–10pm, Fri & Sat 10am–11pm.

Oberza ul. Rabiańska 9. Cosy restaurant near the Market Square offering quick, traditional buffet meals such as stuffed cabbage parcels or pork chop with plums, served up in a farmhouse interior. Mains 15–30zł. Daily 11am–10pm.

Pod Arkadami ul. Rozana 1. Clean, bright milk bar on the Market Square serving superb, filling soups and potato dishes. Potato pancakes 6zł. Mon–Fri 9am–7pm, Sat & Sun 9am–4pm.

Southern Poland

Southern Poland attracts more visitors than any other region in the country, and its appeal is clear from a glance at the map. The **Tatra Mountains** bordering

25

Slovakia are the most spectacular in the country, snowcapped for much of the year and markedly alpine in feel. The former royal capital of **Kraków** is an architectural gem. Pope John Paul II was archbishop here until his election in 1978, but equally important are the city's Jewish roots: before the Holocaust, this was one of Europe's most vibrant Jewish centres. This multicultural past echoes in the old district of Kazimierz, and its culmination is starkly enshrined at the death camps of **Auschwitz-Birkenau**, 50km west of the city.

KRAKÓW

KRAKÓW was the only major city in Poland to come through World War II essentially undamaged. The city's Old Town (Stare Miasto) swarms with visitors in summer, but retains an atmosphere of *fin-de-siècle* stateliness, its streets a cavalcade of churches and palaces. A university centre, Kraków has a tangible buzz of arty youthfulness and enjoys a dynamic nightlife.

WHAT TO SEE AND DO

Kraków is bisected by the River Wisła, with virtually everything of interest on the north bank. At the heart of the **Old Town** is the Main Square, with **Wawel Hill**, ancient seat of Poland's kings and Church, and the rejuvenated old Jewish suburb of **Kazimierz** lying to the south.

The Market Square

The largest square in medieval Europe, the Market Square (Rynek Główny) is now a broad expanse with the vast **Cloth Hall** (Sukiennice) at its centre, ringed by magnificent houses and towering spires. Originally a collection of outdoor market stalls, the Cloth Hall was first built in 1300 and reconstructed during the Renaissance, and still houses a bustling covered market.

The Rynek Underground

Central Kraków's newest and most entertaining tourist attraction is the **Rynek Underground** (April–Oct Mon 10am–8pm, Tues 10am–4pm, Wed–Sun 10am–10pm; Nov–March Mon & Wed–Sun 10am–8pm, Tues 10am–4pm; closed second Mon of every Month; 19zł), an extensive subterranean museum that stretches beneath the market square. Recent archeological excavations have been left *in situ* and covered by glass walkways, allowing you to explore the layout of the medieval marketplace. The display also features touch-screen computers and videos of role-playing actors dressed up as medieval traders.

St Mary's Church

On the east side of the Market Square is the Gothic **St Mary's Church** (Tues–Sat 11.30am–6pm, Sun 2–6pm; 10zł), the taller of its two towers, which you can climb in summer (May–Aug Tues–Sat 9–11.10am & 1.10–5.30pm, Sun 1–5pm; 10zł), topped by an amazing ensemble of spires. Inside is the stunningly realistic triptych high altar (1477–89), an intricate woodcarving depicting the Virgin Mary's Quietus among the apostles.

The university

West from the Rynek is the university area, whose first building was the fifteenth-century **Collegium Maius** at ul. Jagiellońska 15, today housing the **University Museum** (Mon, Wed, Fri & Sat 10am–2.20pm, Tues & Thurs 10am–5.20pm; 16zł). An optional guided tour is included in the price if you want it – the museum office will sign you up for the next English-language departure. Inside, the ground-floor rooms retain the mathematical and geographical murals once used for the teaching of

---

THE HEJNAŁ

Legend has it that during one of the thirteenth-century **Tatar raids** on Kraków, a guard watching from the tower of St Mary's Church saw the invaders approaching and blew his trumpet, only for his alarm to be cut short by an arrow through the throat. Every hour a local fireman now plays the sombre melody (*hejnał*) from the same tower, halting abruptly at the point when the guard is supposed to have been hit.

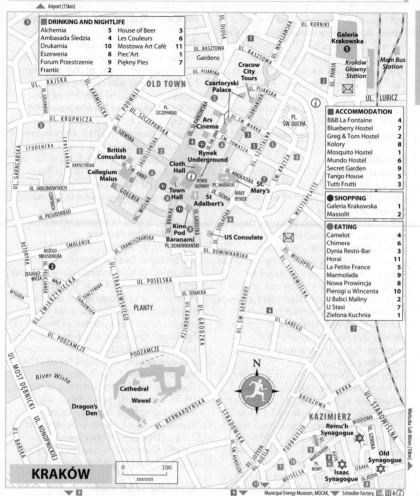

Airport (15km)

DRINKING AND NIGHTLIFE

Alchemia	5	House of Beer	3
Ambasada Śledzia	4	Les Couleurs	6
Drukarnia	10	Mostowa Art Café	11
Eszeweria	8	Piec' Art	1
Forum Przestrzenie	9	Piękny Pies	7
Frantic	2		

ACCOMMODATION

B&B La Fontaine	4
Blueberry Hostel	7
Greg & Tom Hostel	2
Kolory	8
Mosquito Hostel	1
Mundo Hostel	6
Secret Garden	9
Tango House	5
Tutti Frutti	3

SHOPPING

Galeria Krakowska	1
Massolit	2

EATING

Camelot	4
Chimera	6
Dynia Resto-Bar	3
Horai	11
La Petite France	5
Marmolada	9
Nowa Prowincja	8
Pierogi u Wincenta	10
U Babci Maliny	2
U Stasi	7
Zielona Kuchnia	1

Municipal Energy Museum, MOCAK, Schindler Factory, 10, 11 & (i)

figures like Copernicus, one of the university's earliest students.

Wawel Hill

For over five hundred years, Wawel Hill (wwawel.krakow.pl) was the seat of Poland's monarchy. The original **cathedral** (Mon–Sat 9am–5pm; Sun 12.30–5pm; 8zł) was built in 1020, but the present basilica is a fourteenth-century structure, with a crypt that contains the majority of Poland's 45 monarchs. Their tombs and side chapels are like a directory of European artistic movements, not least the Gothic Holy

Cross Chapel and the Renaissance Zygmuntowska chapel. The excellent **Cathedral Museum** (Mon–Sat 9am–4pm; 12zł) features religious and secular items dating from the thirteenth century, including all manner of coronation robes.

Visitor numbers are restricted, so arrive early or book ahead to visit the various sections of **Wawel Castle** (ticket office Mon–Fri 9am–5.45pm, Sat & Sun 10am–4.45pm), including the State Rooms (Tues–Sun: April–Oct 10am–5pm; Nov–March 10am–4pm; 18zł), furnished with Renaissance paintings

25

and tapestries, and the grand Royal Private Apartments (same times as State Rooms; 25zł). Much of the original contents of the Royal Treasury and Armoury (April–Oct: Mon 9.30am–1pm, Tues–Sun 10am–5pm; Nov–March: Tues–Sat 9.30am–4pm; 18zł) were sold to pay off royal debts, but still feature some fine works, including the Szczerbiec, the country's original coronation sword.

Kazimierz

A **Jewish centre** from the fourteenth century onwards, Kraków's Kazimierz district had grown by 1939 to accommodate some 65,000 Jews. After the Nazis took control, however, this population was forced into a cramped ghetto across the river. Waves of deportations to the death camps followed before the ghetto was liquidated in March 1943, ending seven centuries of Jewish life in Kraków. Kazimierz is now a fashionable and bohemian residential district, filled with **synagogues** – although present-day Kazimierz's Jewish population is a tiny fraction of what it was before 1939.

Just off pl. Nowy, a colourful square surrounded by chic cafés, is the **Isaac Synagogue** at ul. Kupa 18 (Mon–Thurs & Sun 9am–8pm, Fri 9am–2.30pm; 7zł) – now a working synagogue once again, it contains sizeable chunks of Hebrew inscriptions on its walls. At ul. Szeroka 24 is the **Old Synagogue** (Mon 10am–2pm, Tues–Sun 9am–5pm; 10zł), the oldest surviving example of Jewish religious architecture in Poland and home to the **Museum of Kraków Jewry**, with its traditional paintings by the area's former inhabitants. Nearby, the **Remu'h Synagogue**, also on ul. Szeroka (Mon–Fri: May–Sept 9am–6pm; Oct–April 9am–4pm; 8zł) contains lovely original furnishings; in the cemetery behind the synagogue you'll find restored eighteenth-century gravestones.

At the southern end of Kazimierz, the **Municipal Engineering Museum** at św Wawrzynca 15 (Tues–Sun: June–Sept 10am–6pm; Oct–May 10am–4pm; 10zł) contains a fantastic display of vehicles in a former tram depot.

MOCAK Museum of Contemporary Art

The former industrial district of Podgorze/Zabłocie just across the river from Kazimierz is one of contemporary Kraków's fastest-developing districts, thanks in part to the opening of the **MOCAK Museum of Contemporary Art** at ul. Lipova 4 (Tues–Sun 11am–7pm; 10zł; ⑩mocak.com.pl) in 2011. Occupying renovated buildings that once formed part of Oskar Schindler's Emalia Factory (see below), it contains a compelling collection of Polish contemporary art and hosts a regular programme of big-name exhibitions.

The Schindler Factory

Immediately next door to MOCAK, **The Schindler Factory** is where German industrialist Oskar Schindler manufactured enamel pots during World War II, employing over a thousand Kraków Jews specifically to save them from the death camps – a tale immortalized in Steven Spielberg's Oscar-winning film, *Schindler's List*. The factory is now home to a superbly arranged exhibition entitled **Kraków Under Nazi Occupation** (Mon 10am–4pm, Tues–Sun 9am–8pm; first Mon of month 10am–2pm; 21zł), which fills several rooms with photo displays, period newsreels and interviews with survivors. Telling the stories of both Jewish and Gentile Kraków with equal weight, it's an engrossing and rewarding experience.

Wieliczka salt mines

Ten kilometres from Kraków is the "underground salt cathedral" of **Wieliczka**, 300km of subterranean tunnels that have been used to mine salt since the thirteenth century (daily: April–Oct 7.30am–7.30pm; Nov–March 8am–5pm). The ticket price includes a tour (84zł English, 55zł Polish), which passes by an underground lake and a number of impressive statues and edifices – including chandeliers – carved out of rock salt. Trains to Wieliczka-Rynek run from Kraków Głowny roughly every hour.

ARRIVAL AND DEPARTURE

By plane Kraków airport is situated 15km west of the city centre. It's easiest to catch the free shuttle bus to the airport's train station, which has regular trains to Kraków Główny (every 30min, 4.14am–11.44pm; 18min; 22zł). The equivalent taxi ride costs 70–90zł.

By train Kraków Główny, the central train station, is located a 5min walk northeast of the city's historic centre. Destinations Bratislava (1 daily; 8hr); Budapest (1 daily; 10hr 30min); Gdańsk (every 2 hours; 5hr 30min); Oświęcim/Auschwitz (15 daily; 1hr 45min); Poznań (4 daily; 5–7hr); Prague (1 daily; 8hr 30min); Warsaw (hourly; 2hr 30min); Wrocław (every 2 hours; 3hr 10min); Zakopane (3 daily; 3hr 40min).

By bus The main bus station is located directly opposite the train station. Nearby, Eurolines (see p.00) runs services to all major European capitals.
Destinations Oświęcim/Auschwitz (2–3 hourly; 1hr 45min); Zakopane (every 20min; 2hr).

INFORMATION AND TOURS

Tourist information The municipal tourist office (Mon–Fri 8am–8pm, Sat & Sun 9am–5pm; ☎ 012 430 2646, ⊛ krakow.pl) operates information booths at four central locations: the circular pavilion in the Planty near the train station underpass; the Town Hall Tower on Rynek Główny; the Wyspiański 2000 Pavilion on plac Wszystkich Świętych; and ul. Jozefa 7 in Kazimierz.

Tours You'll be bombarded with tour offers for the city and surrounding sights, but these are often rushed and cost four times as much as public transport. If you do want a tour, Cracow City Tours at ul. Floriańska 44 (daily 9am–9pm; ☎ 12 421 1327, ⊛ cracowcitytours.pl) offers a wide range of itineraries and discounts for students.

ACCOMMODATION

The number of hostels has mushroomed in the last few years, but it is still worth booking ahead if you want to stay in the most central spots. All hostels have free wi-fi, breakfast and cheap laundry services.

HOSTELS

Blueberry Hostel ul. Wrzesińska 5/5 ☎ 12 426 4664, ⊛ blueberryhostel.com. Small, intimate hostel in a beautifully decorated, parquet-floored flat near Kazimierz. Free breakfast and a relaxing boutiquey feel. Dorms 65zł, doubles 165zł

★ **Greg & Tom Hostel** ul. Pawia 12/7 ☎ 12 422 4100, ⊛ gregtomhostel.com. The ideal hostel for those who want home comforts as well as a place to crash, this suave option opposite the train station offers single beds in snazzily designed dorms (no bunks), neat doubles and relaxing social/kitchen space. Dorms 57zł, doubles 150zł

Mosquito Hostel Rynek Kleparski 4/6 ☎ 12 430 1461, ⊛ mosquitohostel.com. Comfortable and sharply decorated hostel just round the corner from the Stary Kleparz market, offering a mixture of dorms and private

room; buffet breakfast and a cosy galley kitchen. Dorms 65zł, doubles 230zł

★ **Mundo Hostel** ul. Sarego 10 ☎ 12 422 6113, ⊛ mundohostel.eu. Probably the most beautiful hostel in Kraków, with each room decorated according to a different national theme. Relaxing kitchen-cum-lounge, and a decent-sized breakfast. Dorms 60zł, doubles 170zł

Secret Garden ul. Skawinska 7 ☎ 12 430 5445, ⊛ thesecretgarden.pl. Spacious, bright and cheerful hostel on a quiet street which provides hotel-like standards at hostel prices – there are no dorms, with all the rooms being doubles, triples or quads. There's a roomy kitchen, and a swish first-floor TV lounge. Doubles 150zł

Tutti Frutti ul. Floriańska 29 ☎ 12 428 0028, ⊛ tuttifruttihostel.com. This welcoming hostel does the basics (especially breakfast) very well and also provides guides for guests seeking the best places to go out. As well as dorms, it has 4-bed apartments. Dorms 50zł, apartments 260zł

B&BS

B&B La Fontaine ul. S ławkowska 1 ☎ 12 422 6564, ⊛ bblafontaine.com. Surprisingly affordable B&B in the Old Town, with cute homey rooms located on the attic floor of an apartment block. A good breakfast in the downstairs restaurant is included. Doubles 285zł

Kolory ul. Estery 10 ☎ 12 421 0465, ⊛ kolory.com.pl. Bright en-suite rooms above *Les Couleurs* (see p.852), all with TV and folk-style design details. Some rooms overlook the lively plac Nowy; marginally quieter rooms are at the back. Doubles 240zł

Tango House ul. Szpitalna 4 ☎ 12 429 3114, ⊛ tangohouse.pl. Hidden in a secluded courtyard just round the corner from the main square, *Tango* is a B&B of two halves: the old part has a spectacular nineteenth-century staircase and en-suite rooms in soothing citrus colours, while the new part houses smart studios with kitchenettes. All rooms come with electric kettle; breakfast is 20zł extra. Doubles 280zł

EATING

Kraków's centre is renowned for its restaurants and cafés, which offer much beyond the Polish culinary staples.

CAFÉS, CHEAP EATS AND SNACKS

Camelot ul. św. Tomasza 15. A chic, artsy café with wooden furnishings, peasant-art motifs on the walls, and occasional cabaret shows in the basement. Excellent desserts, including the best apple pie in town (12.50zł). Daily 9am–midnight.

Chimera ul. św. Anny 3. Expansive buffet selection in a soothing courtyard, with attractively priced main courses, a salad bar and plenty of vegetarian choices. Single portions 5zł, plateful 18zł. Daily 11am–10pm.

25

La Petite France ul. św. Tomasza 25. An attractive deli-bistro with five small tables and a row of stools pushed against the street-facing window ledge. This is a fantastic place to tuck into what is arguably the best quiche in Kraków (10zł) or a more filling baguette sandwich (13zł). Daily 9am–10pm.

★ **Nowa Prowincja** ul. Bracka 3–5. Homely, relaxed café owned by local musical legend Grzegorz Turnau, with a wonderful wooden loft, thick hot chocolate and Kraków's best lattes (10zł). Daily 9am–11pm.

U Babci Maliny ul. Sławkowska 17. Upmarket milk bar with a mountain hut interior, serving suitably wholesome Polish classics. Mains 9–18zł. Mon–Fri 9am–7pm, Sat & Sun 10am–5pm.

U Stasi ul. Mikołajska 16. Lunchtime classic favoured by locals, hidden behind a pizzeria, with unusually friendly service and delicious *knedle* (dumplings) stuffed with plums (7zł). Mon–Fri 12.30pm until the food runs out.

RESTAURANTS

Dynia Resto-Bar ul. Krupnicza 20. The city's most stylish student hangout, complete with blissful walled garden, has amazing breakfasts (15–30zł), healthy salad or pasta lunches and seductive desserts. Mon–Sat 8am–11pm, Sun 9am–10pm.

Horai Plac Wolnica 4. Long-established pan-Asian eatery that consistently rates highly for quality and price. The menu covers everything from dim sum to sushi sets, although it's the devilishly spicy Thai dishes that stand out. Mains in the 30–35zł bracket. Daily noon–10pm.

Pierogi u Wincenta ul. Bozego Ciala 12. Tiny six-table place with a huge selection of own-recipe *pierogi*, including plenty of vegetarian options (such as *pierogi* with broccoli and feta). Mon–Wed & Sun noon–10pm, Thurs noon–11pm, Fri & Sat noon–midnight.

Zielona Kuchnia ul. Grabowskiego 8/9. Hidden away just northwest of the Old Town and with a wonderful garden courtyard, "Green Kitchen" serves up Polish-Mediterranean fusion cuisine with a contemporary twist. The risotto with seasonal vegetables (29zł) makes for a perfect summertime lunch. Mon–Sat 1–10pm, Sun 1–8pm.

★**TREAT YOURSELF**

Marmolada ul. Grodzka 5. Traditional Polish cuisine with an Italian twist – the Saltimbocca veal (50zł) and roast goose with cherries (52zł) are both memorably rich and satisfying – and there's a lot more to choose from, too. With candles on the tables and floral decor, it's as relaxing as they come. Daily noon–11pm.

DRINKING AND NIGHTLIFE

For best value head to Kazimierz or the student quarter to the west of the Old Town.

BARS

★**Alchemia** ul. Estery 5. Murky, quirky and always packed, this candlelit rabbit warren has a stuffed crocodile over the bar and a full programme of live jazz, rock and cabaret in the adjoining basement club: 0.5lt beer 7.50zł. Mon 10am–3am, Tues–Thurs 9am–3am, Fri & Sat 9am–4am, Sun 9am–2am.

Ambasada Śledzia ul. Stolarska 8/10. The *Herring Embassy* doffs an ironic cap to the drinking culture of the communist era, with cheap drinks and retro bar snacks (like marinated herring and jellied meats) in a trendy minimalist matt-black interior. Note that sister bar *Śledź u Fryzera* across the road at Stolarska 5 is open until 5am. Daily 8am–midnight.

Drukarnia Nadwiślańska 1 ⓦ drukarniaclub.pl. Roomy bar just over the river from Kazimierz, with several rooms decked out in different styles, from arty Parisian café to brash party pub. There's also a basement-level club venue hosting regular DJs and live music. Mon–Thurs & Sun 9am–1am, Fri & Sat 9am–4am.

Eszeweria ul. Jozefa 9. Characteristically dimly lit Kazimierz café bar that is sometimes so dark inside that you can't even see the person behind the counter, never mind the range of drinks on offer. Once you've succeeded in choosing your tipple, sink into one of the salvage-chic armchairs indoors, or head for the lush garden courtyard at the back. Sun–Thurs 10am–2am, Fri & Sat 10am–5am.

Forum Przestrzenie ul. Marii Konopnickiej 28. Occupying the reception of the former *Forum Hotel*, this hugely popular café-bar extends out onto the riverbank in summer, offering deckchairs, film shows, food fairs and an indie-retro musical mix. A decent food menu (veggie curry 18zł) and fantastic views of the Wawel add to its list of attributes. Daily 11am–2am.

House of Beer ul. św. Tomasza 35. This roomy and convivial Old Town pub is the ideal place to plough your way through a selection of the increasingly excellent ales turned out by Poland's small breweries. Guest ales on tap (from 7zł/0.5lt). Daily 2pm–2am.

Les Couleurs ul. Estery 10. A smoky and colourful Parisian-style café-bar serving light meals and alcoholic beverages of every description: cocktails around 14zł. Mon–Thurs & Sun 8am–midnight, Fri & Sat 8am–2am.

Mostowa Art Café ul. Mostowa 8. Located on the approach to the Podgórze footbridge, *Art Café* lives up to its name with a pop-art styled interior and contemporary canvases on the walls. Star attraction is the fridge full of craft beers from Poland and beyond. Sun–Thurs noon–10pm, Fri & Sat noon–midnight.

CLUBS

Frantic ul. Szewska 5. With two dancefloors, there's plenty of space here for grooving to a mix of r'n'b and old-school hits. Cocktails from 15zł. Wed–Sat 9pm–4am.

Piec'Art ul. Szewska 12 ⊛piecart.pl. One of the city's most reliable and enduring jazz bars, with live music 2–3 times a week in a sleek and snazzy brick-lined cellar. Entrance on gig nights 15–20zł; draught Tyskie beer 8zł/0.5lt. Daily 2pm–3am.

Piękny Pies ul. Bożego Ciała 9. The big back room of legendary bohemian hangout "Beautiful Dog" is devoted to live gigs and DJ action, with everything from alternative rock to electro to get your limbs shaking. Mon–Thurs & Sun 4pm–3am, Fri & Sat 4pm–5am.

ENTERTAINMENT

Cinema tickets are 12–22zł throughout the city.
Ars ul. św. Jana 6 ⊛ars.pl. Offers a mixture of Hollywood and international art films in an old-style cinema.

Kino Pod Baranami Rynek Główny 27 ⊛kinopodbaranami.pl. Screens a range of Western, Polish and Bollywood titles in an old-fashioned cinema setting.

SHOPPING

Touristy Floriańska and the boutiques in the Rynek contain a few bargain art dealers among the overpriced souvenirs. Kazimierz is filled with reasonably priced galleries and secondhand shops and, on Sun, pl. Nowy becomes a colourful flea market of cheap clothes and jewellery.

Galeria Krakowska next to the train station. An international "mall experience", with all the fashionable global brands that you could wish for, in addition to a large Carrefour supermarket. Mon–Sat 9am–10pm, Sun 10am–9pm.

Massolit Felicjanek 4. You can find a good selection of English used books, including translations of Polish authors, at this café/bookshop, which also serves some of Kraków's best apple pie. Mon–Thurs & Sun 10am–8pm, Fri & Sat 10am–9pm.

DIRECTORY

Consulate US, ul. Stolarska 9 ☎12 424 5100.

Exchange To avoid the large commission charged at the banks, check the *kantor* exchanges that fill the streets around the Rynek for the best rates.

Hospital Gabriel Narutowicz Hospital (Szpital im. Gabriela Narutowicza) north of the Old Town at ul. Prądniczka 35 (☎012 416 2266).

Left luggage The train station has a left-luggage depot (daily 7am–10pm; 5zł/24hr).

Pharmacies Bobilewicz, ul. Grodzka 26 (Mon–Fri 8am–9pm, Sat 9am–6pm, Sun 10am–5pm), and Pod Złotą Głową, Rynek Główny 13 (Mon–Fri 9am–9pm, Sat 9am–4pm).

Post office ul. Westerplatte 20 (Mon–Fri 8am–8.30pm, Sat 8am–3pm).

AUSCHWITZ-BIRKENAU (OŚWIĘCIM)

Lying 70km west of Kraków and within easy day-trip range, the complex of camps known as **AUSCHWITZ-BIRKENAU** (⊛auschwitz.org) has become synonymous with World War II and the Holocaust. The camps lie on the western fringes of **OŚWIĘCIM**, which is in all other respects a perfectly nondescript middle-sized Polish town.

Auschwitz was established by the Germans in 1940 to house Polish political prisoners but swiftly expanded to accommodate Soviet POWs. The Birkenau annexe, built in 1941 to cope with growing numbers, became the site of one of the Nazi regime's most notorious death camps: about 1.3 million people, ninety percent of them Jews, were murdered here. The Germans failed to destroy the camp before they left and over

---

KRAKÓW FESTIVAL CITY

In spring and summer hardly a week goes by in Kraków without at least one cultural **festival** taking place. Many events are held on the Main Market Square, or in outdoor locations elsewhere in the city. Stand-out events include the **Jewish Culture Festival** (June/July; ⊛jewishfestival.pl), with exhibitions, seminars and enjoyable Klezmer concerts in Kazimierz; the **Summer Jazz Festival** (July/Aug; ⊛cracjazz.com), with big names taking to a variety of outdoor stages; and **Kraków Live Festival** (Aug; ⊛livefestival.pl), with three days of international pop-rock (Franz Ferdinand and The Chemical Brothers are among previous headliners) in an open-air location – camping is available. One of the most enjoyable and accessible events is the spectacular annual **Dragon Parade** organized by the Groteska Theatre (early June; ⊛groteska.pl), when people from all over Poland parade their dragons prior to a "Battle of the Dragons" son-et-lumière show beside the Wisła.

25

60,000 prisoners survived – which is why the horrors perpetrated here are so well documented. The two sites, Auschwitz and Birkenau, are 3km apart, but are linked by shuttle bus. Together they are visited by over 1.3 million visitors a year.

Auschwitz

Most visitors start at Auschwitz (daily: Feb 8am–4pm; March & Oct 8am–5pm; April, May & Sept 8am–6pm, June–Aug 8am–7pm; Dec & Jan 8am–2pm; English-language tours on the hour 9.30am–3.30pm; guided tour 40zł; non-guided visits free), which is 3km west of Oświęcim town centre. From April to October participation in guided tours is compulsory between 10am and 3pm, so if you want to visit the Auschwitz site on your own, arrive outside these times. Once beyond the entrance gate (bearing the notorious cast-iron inscription *Arbeit Macht Frei*), the site consists of a series of red-brick barrack blocks, many of which contain a museum display relating to a particular aspect of the camp or a particular nation whose citizens were deported here.

Block 13 contains an account of Europe's Roma and Sinti communities (an estimated 20,000 of whom died here); block 5 contains rooms full of spectacles, prosthetic limbs, pots and pans, all confiscated from inmates of the camp and abandoned here when the Germans retreated. The prison blocks finish by a gas chamber and a pair of ovens where the bodies were incinerated.

Birkenau

The enormous **Birkenau** camp (same hours as Auschwitz; allow 1–2hr to explore the site fully) was designed as a death camp in 1942, when the Nazis developed their policy of exterminating European Jewry. Large gas chambers at the back of the camp were damaged but not destroyed by the fleeing Nazis in 1945. Victims arrived in closed trains, and those who were fit to work (around 25 percent) were immediately separated from those who were driven straight to the gas chambers. The railway line is still there, just as the Nazis abandoned it.

One of the few buildings still standing here is the so-called Sauna, where the newly arrived were undressed, shaved and assigned camp clothes – a matter-of-fact museum display takes you methodically through the process.

ARRIVAL AND DEPARTURE

By bus You can catch one of the regular buses (2–3 hourly; 1hr 45min) to the main Auschwitz site from Kraków's main bus station. There's an hourly shuttle-bus service (April–Oct) to the Birkenau section from the car park at Auschwitz. Taxis are also available; otherwise it's a 3km walk.

THE TATRAS AND ZAKOPANE

Some 80km long, with peaks of up to 2500m, the **Tatras** are the most spectacular part of the mountain range extending along Poland's border with Slovakia. They are as beautiful as any mountain landscape in northern Europe, the ascents leading along boulder-strewn trails beside woods and streams and culminating in breathtaking, windswept peaks. The peaks are topped with snow for most of the year, making it a great area for skiing (from mid-Dec to March). The mountains are a protected national park and harbour rare species such as lynx, golden eagles and brown bear.

The main base for skiing and hiking on the Polish side is the popular resort of **Zakopane**. There are good road and rail links with Kraków, 60km north, as well as several mountain resorts across the border in Slovakia.

WHAT TO SEE AND DO

Skiing here is cheap, with the premier slopes of Kasprowy Wierch just a few minutes out of town, and plenty of places in the town centre to rent equipment. **Hikers** may want to avoid the 9km path to the lovely but busy Morskie Oko Lake in high season, but there's no shortage of other, more secluded, trails. Zakopane's

> ### INTO SLOVAKIA
> The coach company Strama runs 5 daily buses (mid-Oct to mid-June 2 daily) to **Poprad** (2hr; 22zł; ⓦstrama.eu), a Slovakian skiing and hiking centre.

market at the bottom of ul. Krupówki sells a wide range of traditional local goods, including *oscypek* (smoked sheep's cheese) and small woodcarvings. This latter local tradition is intriguingly displayed in the whimsical wooden tombs of the nearby Old Cemetery (Stary Cementarz).

ARRIVAL AND DEPARTURE

By train Zakopane station is on ul. Kosciuszki, a 10min walk east of the pedestrianized main street, ul. Krupówki.
Destinations Kraków (3 daily; 3hr 40min).

By bus The bus station is located next to the train station.
Destinations Kraków (every 20min; 2hr).

INFORMATION

Tourist information Tourist office just west of the stations at ul. Kościuszki 17 (March–June & Sept to mid-Dec Mon–Fri 9am–5pm; July & Aug daily 9am–5pm; ☎ 018 201 2211, ⓦ promocja.zakopane.pl).

Tatra National Park Information Centre near the park entrance at ul. Chałubińskiego 44 (daily: Jan–April & Oct 7am–4pm; May & June 7am–5pm; July & Aug 7am–6pm; Nov & Dec 7am–3pm; ☎ 18 202 3300, ⓦtpn.pl); provides good-quality maps and information on hiking routes.

ACCOMMODATION

Finding a place to stay is rarely a problem in Zakopane as, in addition to the hostels, many homeowners in town offer private rooms.

★**Goodbye Lenin** ul. Chłabówka 44 ☎ 18 200 1330, ⓦzakopane.goodbyelenin.pl. Lying 3.5km out of town, this cosy house in the woods is the perfect place to focus on hiking and skiing. Call ahead for a ride from the bus station. Dorms 35zł, doubles 120zł

Hotel Fian ul. Chałubińskiego 38 ☎ 18 201 5071, ⓦfian .pl. With a sauna and jacuzzi to ease hiking aches, this place also prides itself on the "gastronomic experience" offered by its resident chef. Breakfast included. Doubles 235zł

Stara Polana ul. Nowotarska 59 ☎ 18 206 8902, ⓦstarapolana.pl. A warm wood-panelled interior, satellite TV and friendly service make this hostel excellent value. Dorms 40zł, doubles 120zł

Villa Orla ul. Kościeliska 50 ☎ 18 201 2697, ⓦwillaorla .pl. Traditional partly timbered house with cosy rooms, many with sloping attic ceilings. The buffet breakfast is served up in a sunny room stuffed with vintage clocks. Doubles 160zł

EATING, DRINKING AND NIGHTLIFE

Head to the area around ul. Krupówki where you'll find plenty of lively bars and restaurants.

Bar Mleczny ul. Krupówki 1, entrance from ul. Nowotarska. Pricey for a milk bar, but still the cheapest eats in town with

hearty Polish mains for 9–15zł. Daily 9am–7pm.

★**Café Piano** in a secluded courtyard behind ul. Krupówki 63. Contemporary design meets rustic chic here, with swings instead of bar stools and a garden patio thick with shrubs and ferns. Daily noon–midnight.

Dobra Kasza Nasza ul. Krupówki 48. Wooden pavilion decorated with banquettes and lounge-bar stylings, offering bowls of baked buckwheat (*kasza*) with a variety of savoury accompaniments – ranging from bacon and mushroom to chicken curry. Filling, inexpensive, and actually rather good. Daily noon–11pm.

Owczarnia ul. Galicy 4. Giant grilled steaks, *kielbasa* (sausage) and local trout are the specialities in this lively grill-house. Mains 12–35zł. Daily 10am–midnight.

Western Poland

Tossed for centuries back and forth between the Poles, Germans and Czechs, Poland's southwestern province of Silesia is a fascinating blend of cultures, languages and architectural styles. Its main city, **Wrocław**, is the focus of Poland's new economic dynamism. Vibrant **Poznań** to the north, the heart of the original Polish nation, is one of the country's oldest cities and a key commercial link to Western Europe.

WROCŁAW

WROCŁAW (pronounced "vrots-waf"), the fourth-largest city in Poland, is used to being rebuilt. For centuries it was known as Breslau and inhabited by Germans, but this changed after the war, as thousands of displaced Poles flocked to the ruined city. The various influences are reflected in Wrocław's architecture, with its mammoth Germanic churches, Flemish-style mansions and Baroque palaces. The latest rebuilding came after a catastrophic flood in the early 1990s, which left most of the centre underwater. Fortunately, the reconstruction that followed has rejuvenated the pretty Old Town. Wrocław's term as European Capital of Culture in 2016 gave a significant boost to tourism and the arts, and the city boasts the vigorous air of a place on the rise.

25

WHAT TO SEE AND DO

Wrocław's historical centre is delineated by the former city walls, bordered by a moat and a shady park, and by the River Odra to the north, whose pretty islands are home to a handful of churches.

The Market Square

In the heart of the town is the vast **Market Square** (Rynek) and the thirteenth-century town hall, with its magnificently ornate facades. The hall now houses the applied art collections of the **Town Museum** (Wed–Sat 10am–5pm, Sun 10am–6pm; 20zł). In the northwest corner of the square are two curious Baroque houses known as **Jaś i Małgosia** (Hansel and Gretel), linked by a gateway giving access to **St Elizabeth's**, the finest of Wrocław's churches. Its 90m tower (Mon–Sat 10am–7pm, Sun noon–7pm; 5zł) is the city's most prominent landmark.

Jewish quarter

Southwest of the square lies the former **Jewish quarter**, whose inhabitants were driven from their tenements during the Third Reich. One of the largest synagogues in Poland, the **Synagoga pod Białym Bocianem** (Synagogue Under the White Stork; Mon–Thurs 10am–5pm, Fri 10am–3pm, Sun 11am–4pm; free), lies hidden in a courtyard at ul. Włodkowica 9, and contains an absorbing museum of Jewish life.

The Racławice Panorama and the National Museum

East of the city centre, a rotunda houses the famous **Panorama of the Battle of Racławice** (mid-April to Sept daily 9am–5pm; Oct Tues–Sun 9am–5pm; Nov to mid-April Tues–Sun 9am–4pm; shows every 30min but expect queues; 30zł, including entrance to the National Museum). This painting – 120m long and 15m high – was commissioned in 1894 for the centenary of the Russian army's defeat by Tadeusz Kościuszko's militia at Racławice, a village near Kraków. You can also visit the nearby **National Museum** (Wed–Fri & Sun 10am–5pm, Sat 10am–6pm; closes 1hr earlier Oct–March; 15zł, Sat free), with its colourful

exhibition of twentieth-century Polish installation artists like Jozef Szajna.

University quarter

North of the Market Square is the historic and buzzing **university quarter**, full of bargain eateries and tiny bookshops. At its centre is the huge Collegium Maximum, whose Aula Leopoldina assembly hall, upstairs at pl. Uniwersytecki 1 (Mon, Tues & Thurs 10am–4pm, Fri–Sun 10am–5pm; 12zł), is one of the greatest secular interiors of the Baroque age.

Wyspa Piasek and Ostrów Tumski

Northeast from the Market Hall, the Piaskowy Bridge leads to the attractive island of **Wyspa Piasek** and the fourteenth-century church of St Mary of the Sands, with its majestically vaulted ceiling. Two elegant little bridges connect the island with **Ostrów Tumski**, the city's ecclesiastical heart, home to several Baroque palaces and the vast Cathedral of St John the Baptist.

Centennial Hall and the Afrykarium

Two kilometres east of the centre in Szczytnicki Park (trams #4 and #10) looms the huge dome of the **Centennial Hall** (Hala Stulecia), a celebrated modernist masterpiece dating from 1913. Inside, the **Discovery Centre** (Centrum Poznawce; Mon–Thurs & Sun 9am–6pm, Fri & Sat 9am–7pm; 12zł) contains an audio-visual display devoted to modern architecture.

A short walk south, **Wrocław Zoo** (Mon–Fri 9am–6pm, Sat & Sun 9am–7pm; 40zł) is well worth visiting for the **Afrykarium**, a striking contemporary pavilion whose huge aquaria hold manatees, crocodiles and other denizens of the African continent.

ARRIVAL AND DEPARTURE

By plane Take bus #106 from the airport to Wrocław's (reasonably central) main train station (30min; 3zł). The equivalent taxi ride costs 50–70zł.

By train The main train station, Wrocław Główny, faces the broad boulevard of ul. Piłsudskiego, a 15min walk south of the Market Square.

Destinations Dresden (3 daily; 3hr 30min); Gdańsk (4 daily; 5hr); Kraków (every 2 hours; 3hr 10min); Poznań (hourly; 2hr); Warsaw (5 daily; 3hr 40min).

By bus The main station is just to the south of the train station.

INFORMATION

Tourist information The tourist office at Rynek 14 (daily 9am–7pm; ☎71 344 03111, ⓦwroclaw-info.pl) books accommodation.

ACCOMMODATION

Boogie Hostel ul. Ruska 35 ☎71 342 4472, ⓦboogiehostel.com. Spacious and colourful, with clean, modern rooms and a tendency to attract a party crowd. Dorms **40zł**, doubles **130zł**

Cinnamon ul. Kazimierza Wielkiego 67 ☎71 344 5858, ⓦcinnamonhostel.com. Pleasant, airy rooms and friendly, attentive-to-detail staff make this spice-themed hostel a winner. Board games in the common room help to keep things sociable. Dorms **35zł**, doubles **135zł**

Grampa's Hostel pl. św. Macieja 2/1 ☎71 787 8444, ⓦgrampahostel.com. On the north bank of the Odra, this bright, clean and friendly place has plenty of common-room space. Free wi-fi and breakfast included. Dorms **40zł**, doubles **165zł**

Mleczarnia ul. Włodkowica 5 ☎71 787 7570, ⓦmleczarniahostel.pl. Comfortable bohemian hangout, situated in an old building above a candlelit coffee bar. Retro furnishings and vintage lamps add to the atmosphere. Dorms **45zł**, doubles/apartments **220zł**

Stop Wrocław ul. Sienkiewicza 31 ☎51 911 5075, ⓦstopwroclaw.pl. Just north of the centre across the river, this cute and welcoming guesthouse offers small but comfortable rooms, with access to a kitchen and free tea/coffee. Four-person apartments also available. Doubles **139zł**, apartments **260zł**

EATING

Bazylia ul. Kuźnicza 42. Stylishly minimalist canteen, with food priced by weight (2.69zł/100g) and a wonderful view onto the Collegium. Expect tasty soups, vegetable side dishes, chicken escalopes and lots of salads. Daily 8am–7pm.

Bułka z masłem ul. Włodkowica 8a. Charming little café with a famously leafy garden terrace, serving everything from late breakfasts to gourmet burgers. Draws a crowd on weekdays due to the excellent two-course set lunch (28zł). Mon–Sat 10am–midnight, Sun 11am–midnight.

Mis ul. Kuźnicza 48. Extremely popular and well-known milk bar that provides quick, filling grub for the student crowd. Mains 4zł. Mon–Fri 7am–6pm, Sat 8am–5pm.

Pod II Strusiem ul. Ruska 61. Set in a rejuvenated former lavatory, this place dishes out some tasty pizzas (18–28zł). Particularly good for those who like their pizzas hot – the Ognista ("Fiery One") comes in four varying levels of spiciness; Level Four is definitely a challenge. Mon–Thurs noon–11pm, Fri–Sun noon–midnight.

★**TREAT YOURSELF**
JaDka restaurant ul. Rzeźnicza 24/25, ☎071 343 6461. A meal at this renowned restaurant may not be cheap (though some classics like *pierogi* come in at 27–39zł), but you can be assured of world-class Polish cuisine and excellent service. Daily 1–10pm.

DRINKING AND NIGHTLIFE

Art Café Kalambur ul. Kuźnicza 29a. This ornate Art Nouveau pub, with its period bronze-work and retro vibe, is a hangout for theatre types and hosts occasional live music. 0.5lt beer 7.50zł. Mon–Thurs & Sun noon–2am, Fri & Sat noon–4am.

Barbarka Wyspa Słodowa 6. Consisting of a riverside pontoon and a deckchair-scattered stretch of lawn, thus popular "beach" bar attracts an outdoor café crowd in the daytime and bopping revellers at night. May–Sept Mon–Thurs & Sun 9am–midnight, Fri & Sat 9am–3am.

Bezsennosc ul. Ruska 51. Just 10min away from the Rynek in the bar-packed Pasaż Niepolda courtyard, this graffiti-lined cellar resounds to a fun mix of indie, electronic and reggae tunes. Cocktails 15–20zł. Mon–Wed & Sun 7pm–3am, Thurs–Sat 7pm–5am.

Nagi Kamerdyner ul. św. Mikolaja. Retro-Americana bar that looks like something out of pulp-film noir, serving up cheap drinks and traditional snacks (*pierogi*, white sausage, herring) to an every-night-is-Friday-night crowd. Snacks 8zł, pizzas 18–24zł, vodka 5zł. Mon–Thurs 5pm–4am, Fri & Sat 5pm–7am, Sun 5pm–3am.

POZNAŃ

Thanks to its position on the Berlin–Warsaw rail line, **POZNAŃ** is many visitors' first taste of Poland. It's a city of great **diversity**, encompassing tranquil medieval quarters, a fine main square, dynamic business districts and an arty-bohemian subculture.

WHAT TO SEE AND DO

The sixteenth-century **town hall** that dominates the **Old Town Square** (Stary Rynek) has a striking eastern facade, which frames a frieze of notable Polish monarchs. Inside is the **Poznań Historical Museum** (mid-June to mid-Sept Tues–Thurs 11am–5pm, Fri noon–9pm, Sat & Sun 11am–6pm; mid-Sept to mid-June Tues–Thurs 9am–3pm, Fri noon–9pm, Sat & Sun 11am–6pm; 7zł; Sat free),

25

worth visiting for the Renaissance Great Hall on the first floor. East of the Old Town Square, a bridge crosses to the quiet holy island of **Ostrów Tumski**, dominated by Poland's oldest cathedral, the **Cathedral of St John the Baptist**. Most of the building was reconstructed after the war, and Poland's first two monarchs are buried in the crypt. Just east of the cathedral, the **Porta Posnania** museum at ul. Gdańska 2 (Tues–Fri 9am–6pm, Sat & Sun 10am–7pm; 15zł; w bramapoznania.pl) presents multi-media exhibitions about the history of Poznań in an award-winning contemporary building.

ARRIVAL AND DEPARTURE

By plane Poznań's airport is 7km west of the Old Town and is served by bus #59 (30min; 4.60zł), which runs to the Rondo Kaponiera just north of the train station, and by bus #L to the station itself (4.60zł). The 10min taxi ride from the airport is 50–60zł.

By train The main train station, Poznań Główny, is 2km southwest of the historic quarter; tram #5 runs from the western exit on ul. Glogowska to the city centre.
Destinations Berlin (4 daily; 2hr 50min–3hr 15min); Gdańsk (5 daily; 3hr); Kraków (4 daily; 5–7hr); Toruń (9 daily; 1hr 30min); Warsaw (hourly; 2hr 45min–3hr); Wrocław (hourly; 2hr).

By bus The main bus terminal is a 15min walk south from the Old Town Square, at the intersection of ul. Ratajczaka and ul. Królowej Jadwigi.

INFORMATION

Tourist information Tourist office at Stary Rynek 59/60 (May–Oct Mon–Fri 10am–8pm, Sat & Sun 10am–6pm; Oct–April Mon–Fri 10am–6pm, Sat & Sun 10am–5pm; t 61 852 6156, w cim.poznan.pl).

GETTING AROUND

By public transport Poznań's public transport works on a timed basis; a 15min (3zł) ticket should be adequate for any travel within the centre.

ACCOMMODATION

The city's trade fairs, which take place throughout the year (except July & Aug), can cause hotel prices to double, so always book ahead.

Melange ul. Rybaki 6a t 50 707 0107, w melangehostel .com. In a slightly tatty old building 10min south of the centre, but the rooms are comfortable and nicely decorated, and staff are friendly. Dorms 40zł, doubles 120zł

Melody Hostel Stary Rynek 67 (entrance on ul. Kozia) t 61 851 6060, w melody-hostel.com. Central location, a good choice of either dorms or privates, popular-music-themed decor and a buffet breakfast make this an outstanding choice. Dorms 55zł, doubles 139zł

Mini Hotelik al. Niepodległości 8a t 61 633 1416. This little place not far from the train station may look a bit frumpy, but its rooms are clean, good value and have TVs. Some have shared facilities, others en suite. Doubles 139zł

EATING

Café Ptasie Radio ul. Kościuszki 74. A favourite with the arty elite, this sophisticated and cosy café provides good breakfasts, pasta dishes, salads and tasty desserts. Leave room for *Ptasie*'s celebrated chocolate cake. Mains 19–39zł. Mon–Sat 8am–midnight, Sun 10am–11pm.

Spaghetti Bar Piccolo ul. Rynkowa 1. The buffet here comprises simple but tasty spaghetti dishes that are ready as you enter. Mains from 5.50zł. Mon–Sat 10am–9pm, Sun noon–9pm.

Warung Bali ul. Żydowska 1. Authentic Indonesian food that hasn't been blanded out to suit Central European taste buds, served in a bright interior. Mains from 35zł. Mon–Sat noon–11pm, Sun noon–9pm.

Wynarnia pod czarnym kotem ul. Wolsztynska 1. This welcoming suburban wine bar a 20min walk from the centre draws dedicated diners thanks to its mix of global fusion mains and Mediterranean tapas. Live gigs, open-air film screenings and a great choice of wine provide extra reasons to venture out this far. Mains 20–30zł. Daily 1–11.30pm.

DRINKING AND NIGHTLIFE

Brovaria Stary Rynek 73. This bar in the Old Town Square may be predictably pricey, but the house-brewed *piwo* is some of Poland's finest. 0.5lt mulled honey beer 10zł. Daily 10am–1am.

Cuba Libre ul. Wroclawska 21. A Latin dance club popular with the student crowd, offering the best late-night party in town. 0.5lt beer 8zł. Mon–Wed 9pm–3am, Thurs–Sat 9pm–5am, Sun 9pm–1am.

Dragon ul. Zamkowa 3. Roomy pub with mix-and-match furniture, a buzzing beer garden and a live music venue (anything from free jazz to freak folk) in the basement. Mon–Thurs & Sun 10am–3am, Fri & Sat 10am–5am.

Meskalina Stary Rynek 6. Dive into the Arsenal art gallery on the main square to find this throbbing hipster pub popular with a student and post-university set. There's a menu of soups and bites, and frequent live gigs. Mon–Thurs & Sun 5pm–1am, Fri & Sat 5pm–4am.

Za kulisami ul. Wodna 24. Cosy two-room affair stuffed full of vintage domestic oddments and old books. Attracts a colourful and varied student-to-mad-professor crowd. Draught honey beer 10zł. Mon–Thurs 4pm–1am, Fri & Sat 4pm–3am, Sun 6pm–1am.

STEAM TRAIN, DOURO VALLEY

Portugal

HIGHLIGHTS

❶ A night out in Lisbon Check out the Bairro Alto and dance till dawn. **See p.870**

❷ Queima das Fitas, Coimbra Join in this university town's end-of-term celebrations in May. **See p.879**

❸ Port wine lodges, Porto Numerous lodges offer tours and tastings. **See p.883**

❹ The Douro Rail Route Beautifully scenic line along the Douro river valley. **See p.888**

❺ The Algarve beaches The Ilha de Tavira has some of the best. **See p.894**

HIGHLIGHTS ARE MARKED ON THE MAP ON P.861

ROUGH COSTS

Daily budget Basic €45, occasional treat €65

Drink Bottle of *vinho verde* in shop €3.50

Food Grilled sardines €8

Hostel/budget hotel €20/€45

Travel Train: Lisbon–Faro €22.20; bus: Porto–Lisbon €20

FACT FILE

Population 10.4 million

Language Portuguese

Currency Euro (€)

Capital Lisbon

International phone code ☎351

Time zone GMT

Introduction

Although Portugal is perhaps best known for the "fun in the sun" resorts of the Algarve, there's much more to the Iberian Peninsula's lesser-visited country than beautiful beaches. Portugal is geographically diverse yet small enough to travel around easily, with lively cities, mountain ranges, rural villages and a stunning coastline all within easy reach of each other. Another draw is the relaxed, laidback pace of life, meaning that, even in the biggest metropolises, stress and bustle are remarkably rare. And most importantly for the budget traveller, Portugal is one of the cheapest countries in Western Europe.

Scenically, some of the most interesting parts of the country are in the north: a verdant area home to Portugal's only national park, **Peneda-Gerês**, as well as the sensational gorge and valley of the **Douro**, followed along its course by the spectacular Douro Rail Route. For contemporary Portugal, spend some time in **Lisbon** and **Porto**, the two major cities, both treasure-troves of cultural attractions with big party scenes to boot. And if it's monuments you're after, head to the centre of the country – above all, **Coimbra** and **Évora** – which retain a faded grandeur. The coast is virtually continuous beach, and apart from the **Algarve** and a few pockets around Lisbon and Porto, resorts remain relaxed, often sleepy. The loveliest of all are the wild, isolated beaches of the southern **Alentejo**.

CHRONOLOGY

219 BC The Romans capture the Iberian Peninsula from the Carthaginians, taking the settlement of "Portus Cale" in the process.

711 The Islamic Moors take control of large parts of present-day Portugal.

868 Establishment of the First County of Portugal, within the Kingdom of León.

1095 Crusaders help Portuguese to defeat the Moors.

1139 Afonso I, of the Burgundy dynasty, declares himself king of an independent Portugal.

1386 The Treaty of Windsor, the oldest diplomatic alliance in the world, is signed between England and Portugal, securing mutual military support.

1500s Portugal builds a large empire with colonies across the world including Mozambique, Goa and Brazil.

1580 During a succession crisis, Philip II of Spain invades and crowns himself Philip I of Portugal.

1703 Signing of the Methuen trade treaty with England, following which port wine becomes popular internationally.

1755 An enormous earthquake destroys much of Lisbon.

1822 Brazil declares independence from Portugal.

1916 Portugal joins World War I on the side of the Allies.

1926 Military coup sees Portugal fall under a right-wing dictatorship that would last until 1974.

1939 Portugal remains neutral during World War II.

1974 Government overthrown in a near bloodless coup.

1975 Independence is granted to all Portuguese African colonies.

1976 First free elections are held.

1986 Portugal joins the European Community.

2007 Mass demonstrations against the Portuguese government's economic reforms.

2012 Unemployment exceeds fifteen percent as Portugal struggles through the ongoing European sovereign debt crisis.

2016 An anti-austerity government takes over, tourism booms and the Portuguese football team wins the 2016 Euros in France.

ARRIVAL AND DEPARTURE

Mainland Portugal's three main **airports** are Faro, Lisbon and Porto. Faro and Lisbon in particular are well linked to the rest of Europe by the budget airlines (notably Ryanair and easyJet), with services to and from Faro increasing during the summer rush. **Bus** is the quickest and most convenient method of overland transport from Spain, particularly if you are arriving from the south. Common daily routes include Seville–Faro, Seville–Lisbon and Madrid–Lisbon. **Trains** are a more costly but usually more comfortable option; the Madrid–Lisbon *trenhotel* runs nightly.

26

PORTUGAL

HIGHLIGHTS

1. A night out in Lisbon
2. Queima das Fitas, Coimbra
3. Port wine lodges, Porto
4. The Douro Rail Route
5. The Algarve beaches

26

GETTING AROUND

BY TRAIN

CP (ⓦcp.pt) runs Portugal's **trains**, which are very reasonably priced – particularly in the case of suburban services from Porto and Lisbon. Those designated *Regionais* stop at most stations. *Intercidades* are twice as fast and more expensive. The fastest and most luxurious are the *Rápidos* (known as "Alfa"), which speed between Lisbon, Coimbra and Porto. **InterRail passes** are valid, though you must reserve a seat on Alfa services (payable at the train station; €5). You can check timetables online (select "*Horários*

y preços") or call the information line on ☏808 208 208.

BY BUS

The **bus** network, made up of many regional companies, is more comprehensive and services are often faster, while for long journeys buses can sometimes be slightly cheaper than trains. On a number of major routes (particularly Lisbon–Algarve), express coaches can knock hours off standard multiple-stop bus journeys; Rede Expressos (ⓦrede-expressos.pt) is the largest bus operator. Other key operators include Rodonorte in the north (ⓦrodonorte.pt), Rodotejo in central

Portugal (⊛rodotejo.pt), Rodoviária do Alentejo in the Alentejo (⊛rodalentejo .pt) and EVA (⊛eva-bus.com) and Frota Azul (⊛frotazul-algarve.pt) in the Algarve. For 24hr national bus information call ☎707 22 33 44.

26

BY BIKE

Cycling is popular, with a growing number of facilities to support cyclists. In the north and centre of the country the terrain is hilly, flattening out south of Lisbon. Bikes can be transported on trains for free, as long as there is space. Bus companies' policies vary so enquire before travelling.

ACCOMMODATION

There are more than fifty state-owned **youth hostels** in Portugal (*Pousadas de Juventude*; ⊛pousadasjuventude.pt); most stay open all year and some impose a curfew. All require a valid HI card; for details see ⊛hihostels.com. Alternatively, these hostels in Portugal can provide you with a guest card, which must be stamped every night that you stay (€2 per stamp); once you have five stamps you're a fully paid-up member of HI. A dormitory bed costs €12–17, depending on season and location; double and twin rooms in these hostels cost €30–45. There is also a growing number of **independent hostels**, particularly in Lisbon and Porto; they're a pricier alternative to official youth hostels but tend to be more conveniently located, and the best have hotel-quality facilities, plus free access to wi-fi and a well-stocked kitchen.

In almost any town you should be able to find a single room for around €30 and a double for under €50; cities are slightly more expensive. The main budget stand-bys are *alojamentos particulares* (guesthouses). Hotels tend to be more expensive. Seaside resorts invariably offer cheaper **rooms** (*quartos*) in private houses; tourist offices have lists. At the higher end of the scale are **pousadas** (⊛pousadas.pt), often converted from old monasteries or castles, which charge at least four-star hotel prices. No matter what type of accommodation you select, **breakfast** will usually be included (exceptions are noted in this chapter).

Portugal has more than two hundred **campsites**, most small and attractively located, and all remarkably inexpensive – you'll rarely pay more than €8 a person, plus an additional fee for your tent. You can get a map list from any tourist office, or find details online at ⊛roteiro-campista .pt. Camping rough is banned; beach areas are especially strict about this.

FOOD AND DRINK

Portuguese **food** is cheap and served in large portions. Virtually all cafés dish up a basic meal for less than €10, and for a little more you have the run of most of the country's restaurants. **Snacks** include *tosta mistas* (cheese and ham toasties), *pastéis de bacalhau* (cod fishcakes) and *sandes* (sandwiches). In **restaurants** you can usually have a substantial meal by ordering a *meia dose* (half-portion), or *uma dose* (one portion) between two. Most serve an *ementa turística* (set meal), which can be good value, particularly at lunchtime and in cheaper workers' cafés or *churrasqueiras* (grill restaurants serving meat and fish dishes). It's often worth opting for the *prato do dia* (dish of the day), usually the cheapest dish on the menu.

Meals may begin with unordered appetizers (from bread, butter and olives to more elaborate entrées), which often carry a hefty price tag if eaten – don't be afraid to send these back if you don't want them. Typical **dishes** include *sopa de marisco* (shellfish soup), *caldo verde* (finely shredded kale leaves in broth) and *bacalhau* (dried cod, cooked in myriad ways). *Caldeirada* is a fish stew cooked with onions and tomatoes, *arroz marisco* a similar stew cooked with seafood and rice. *Cabrito assado* (roast kid) is common in the north of the country, while down south you're sure to see *frango piri-piri* (chicken with chilli sauce) on the menu. **Puddings** include *arroz doce* (rice pudding) and *pudím molotoff* (a kind of lightly toasted meringue drenched in caramel sauce). **Cakes** – *bolos* or *pastéis* – are often at their best in *pastelarias* (patisseries), though you'll also find them in cafés and *casas de chá* (tearooms). Among the best are custard tarts (*pastéis de nata*).

PORTUGUESE

	PORTUGUESE	**PRONUNCIATION**
Yes	*Sim*	Sing
No	*Não*	Now
Please	*Por favor*	Por favor
Thank you	*Obrigado* [said by men]/	Obrigado/obrigada
	Obrigada [said by women]	
Hello/Good day	*Olá*	Orla
Goodbye	*Adeus*	Adayoosh
Excuse me	*Desculpe*	Deskulp
Where?	*Onde?*	Ond?
Good	*Bom*	Bom
Bad	*Mau*	Maw
Near	*Perto*	Pertoo
Far	*Longe*	Lonje
Cheap	*Barato*	Baratoo
Expensive	*Caro*	Karoo
Open	*Aberto*	Abertoo
Closed	*Fechado*	Feshardoo
Today	*Hoje*	Oje
Yesterday	*Ontem*	Ontaygn
Tomorrow	*Amanhã*	Amanya
How much is...?	*Quanto é...?*	Kwantoo eh...?
What time is it?	*Que horas são?*	Kay orash sow?
I don't understand	*Não compreendo*	Now comprendoo
Do you speak English?	*Fala Inglés?*	Farla inglayz?
Where is the station?	*Onde é a estação?*	Ond e a estasow?
On the left/right	*A esquerda/direita*	A eeshkerdah/deeraitah
A ticket to...	*Um bilhete para...*	Oom beelyet para...
What time is the train/bus to...?	*A que horas é o comboio/	A kay oras e o convoyo/
	autocarro para...?	autocarro para...?
I would like a room	*Queria um quarto*	Kereea um kwarto
(single/double)	*individual/casal*	individooal/cazal
May I see the room?	*Posso ver o quarto?*	Posso ver o kwarto?
A table for one/two	*Uma mesa para uma*	Uma mehzah para ooma
	pessoa/duas pessoas	pessoa/duash pessoash
I'm a vegetarian	*Sou vegetariano/a*	So vejetarianoh/ah
A bottle of water/wine	*Uma garrafa de água/*	Ooma garrafuh de
	vinho	aigua/vinyo
One	*Um/Uma*	Oom/ooma
Two	*Dois/Duas*	Doysh/dooash
Three	*Três*	Treysh
Four	*Quatro*	Kwatroo
Five	*Cinco*	Sinkoo
Six	*Seis*	Saysh
Seven	*Sete*	Set
Eight	*Oito*	Oytoo
Nine	*Nove*	Nove
Ten	*Dez*	Desh

26

DRINK

Portuguese **wines** (*tinto* for red, *branco* for white) are inexpensive and of high quality. The fortified **port** (*vinho do Porto*; see p.883) and madeira (*vinho da Madeira*) wines are the best known. The light, slightly sparkling **vinhos verdes**, produced in the Minho, are excellent served chilled. **Brandy** comes in two varieties, Macieiera and Constantino,

26

SURFING IN PORTUGAL

Portugal boasts some of Europe's best beaches for surfing. Popular spots include **Peniche** in central Portugal, **Guincho beach** near **Cascais** in Lisbon, the **Alentejo coast** and the west coast of the **Algarve**, north of Sagres. First-timers would do well to try a **surf school** such as Peniche Surf Camp (€550 for a week in high season; ⓦpenichesurfcamp.com) or The Surf Experience in Lagos (€467 for a week in high season; ⓦsurf-experience .com); accommodation is included in courses. For those with a bit more experience, equipment is available for rent in all popular surfing spots (around €60–70 for a week's board rental).

while Lisbon specializes in the cherry brandy *Ginjinha*, which is served at tiny hole-in-the-wall bars throughout the city. The two most common Portuguese **beers** (*cervejas*) are Sagres and Super Bock.

CULTURE AND ETIQUETTE

Portugal is a **Catholic** country, so it's wise to show respect when visiting churches (bare shoulders should be covered and short skirts may be frowned upon), and avoid visiting during services, which take place on Sundays and sometimes on other days at around 9.30am. Learning a few basic phrases in **Portuguese** (see box, p.863) will certainly endear you to locals. Outside the main tourist areas in the north, French is more widely understood than English. In restaurants, it is usual to **tip** five to ten percent if you're satisfied with the service.

Lone women travellers should face no problems, but might attract a bit of curiosity from locals.

SPORTS AND OUTDOOR ACTIVITIES

In Portugal, **football** isn't just a sport: it's a national passion. During all major matches, the streets fall quiet as people flock inside – usually to restaurants and bars – to watch the game. The three biggest and most successful football clubs

are FC Porto, Sporting Lisbon and Benfica. **Surfing** is also popular (see box above), and has become a key part of Portugal's tourist industry. Portugal's **natural parks** (*parques naturais*) and its one **national park**, the Parque Nacional de Peneda-Gerês in the north, provide superb hiking opportunities. More information about the parks can be found at ⓦicnf.pt, while tourist offices near the parks can provide maps and walking routes.

COMMUNICATIONS

Free **wi-fi** is available at nearly every hostel and café, as well as at libraries and via wi-fi hotspots in most town centres. There are no **mobile phone** roaming charges for EU citizens; non-EU citizens should consider buying a local SIM card, such as Lycamobile (ⓦlycamobile.co.uk /en/Portugal). **Post offices** (*correios*) are generally open Monday to Friday 9am to 6pm, Saturday 9am to noon.

EMERGENCIES

Lisbon, Porto and the larger tourist areas are prone to **petty crime**, such as pickpockets. Pilfering from dorms is relatively rare, but it's wise to use the lockers provided or buy a padlock for your luggage. Travel on trains and buses is safe, with thefts a rarity. Portuguese **police** are stationed in most towns, and can be recognized by their dark blue uniforms. Lisbon and Porto have separate **tourist police** to deal with issues affecting visitors.

For minor health complaints go to a **pharmacy** (*farmácia*); pharmacists generally speak good English and can dispense many drugs without a prescription. Normal opening hours are Monday to Friday 9am to 1pm and 3 to 7pm, Saturday 9am to 1pm. A sign at each one will show the nearest 24hr pharmacy. You can get the address of an English-speaking **doctor** from a pharmacy, hotel or consular office.

EMERGENCY NUMBERS

All emergencies ☏ 112.

INFORMATION

You'll find a **tourist office** (*turismo*) in almost every town. Staff can help you find a room (usually with commercial partners), and provide local maps and leaflets.

MONEY AND BANKS

Portugal's currency is the euro (€). **Banks** are open Monday to Friday 8.30am to 3pm; in Lisbon and in the Algarve, **exchange offices** may open in the evening to change money. ATMs are easy to find and credit cards are widely accepted.

OPENING HOURS AND HOLIDAYS

As a general guide, most shops' **opening hours** are Monday to Friday 9am to 12.30/1pm and 2/2.30 to 6/6.30pm, plus Saturday 9am to 12.30/1pm. Larger supermarkets tend to stay open until 8pm, but most shops are closed on Sunday, with some exceptions in the Algarve. Museums, churches and monuments open from around 9/10am to 6pm, with many state institutions free on the first Sunday of the month; almost all close on Mondays and at Easter; smaller

places often close for an hour or more at lunch. Restaurants often close on Sunday evenings. The main **public holidays** are: January 1, February carnival, Good Friday, April 25, May 1, Corpus Christi, June 10, June 13 (Lisbon only), August 15, October 5, November 1, December 1, December 8 and December 25.

26

Lisbon and around

There are few more immediately likeable European capitals than **LISBON** (*Lisboa*). A lively city, it remains in some ways curiously provincial, and rooted as much in the 1920s as the twenty-first century. Wooden trams clank up outrageous gradients, past mosaic pavements, Art Nouveau cafés and the medieval quarter of Alfama, which hangs below the São Jorge castle. The city invested heavily for Expo 98 and the 2004 European Football Championships, reclaiming run-down docks and improving communication links, and today it combines an easy-going pace and manageable scale with a vibrant, cosmopolitan identity.

Lisbon has a huge amount of historic interest. Though the **Great Earthquake** of 1755 (followed by a tsunami and fire) destroyed most of the grandest buildings, several monuments from Portugal's sixteenth-century golden age survived and frantic reconstruction led to the building of many impressive new palaces and churches across the city's seven hills.

WHAT TO SEE AND DO

Many of Lisbon's historical sights, such as the Sé (cathedral) and the Castelo de São Jorge, are located in the centre's eastern portion, best reached by following Rua de Conceição and its continuations as they wind away from the **Baixa**, the city's eighteenth-century core, towards the ancient district of **Alfama**. The city centre can be explored on foot, but a quick hop on a **tram** or **elevador** is a less strenuous way of scaling Lisbon's hills. Public transport is also necessary to reach

26

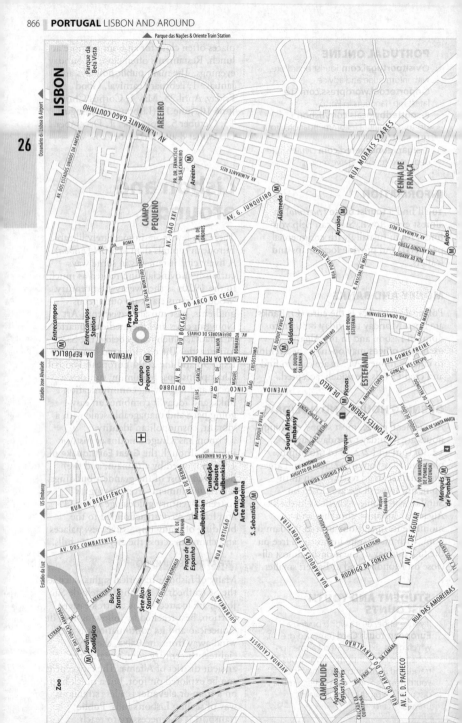

LISBON

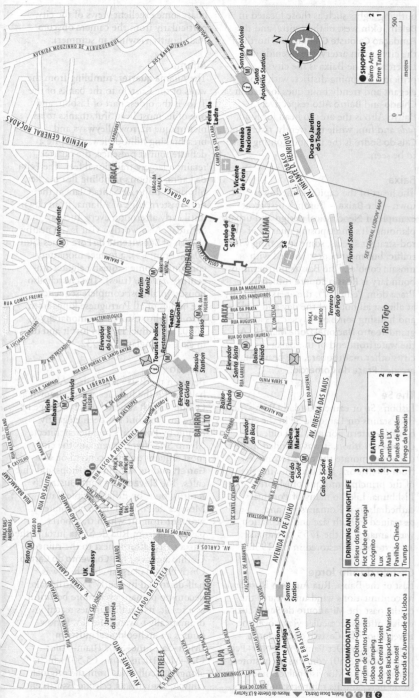

26

● SHOPPING

Bairro Arte 2
Entre Tanto 1

0   metres   500

■ ACCOMMODATION

Camping Obitur-Guincho 2
Jardim de Santos Hostel 3
Lisboa Camping 2
Lisboa Central Hostel 5
Oasis Backpackers' Mansion 4
People Hostel 7
Pousada de Juventude de Lisboa 6

■ DRINKING AND NIGHTLIFE

Coliseu dos Recreios 3
Hot Clube de Portugal 6
Incógnito 5
Lux 8
Main 4
Pavilhão Chinês 7
Trumps 1

● EATING

Bom Jardim 6
Cantina LX 7
Pastéis de Belém 8
Prego da Peixaria 1

26

outlying sights such as those located in **Belém**, 6km west of the centre, and the **Fundação Calouste Gulbenkian**, north of the city's main artery, the Avenida da Liberdade. The Baixa is the city's principal shopping district, with more elegant and trendy boutiques located in **Chiado** and **Bairro Alto** respectively. Bairro Alto is the area to head for food, *fado* and fun, while the trendy, riverfront **Cais do Sodré** is the up-and-coming place to be seen.

Baixa

The heart of the capital is the lower town – the **Baixa** – Europe's first great example of Neoclassical design and urban planning. It's an imposing quarter of rod-straight streets, some streaming with traffic, but most pedestrianized with mosaic cobbles. The Baixa's northernmost boundary is **Rossio Square** (officially Praça dom Pedro IV), the area's hub, busy at almost all hours of the day and night and housing some old-style cafés and the grand **Teatro Nacional Dona Maria II**. At the waterfront end of the Baixa lies the city's other main square, the beautiful arcaded **Praça do Comércio**.

The Sé

Lisbon's **Sé** or cathedral (daily 9am–7pm; free) stands on Largo da Sé in the city centre's eastern portion. The oldest church in Lisbon, it was founded in 1147 to commemorate the city's reconquest from the Moors, and occupies the site of the principal mosque of Moorish Lishbuna. Like so many of Portugal's cathedrals, it is Romanesque and restrained in both size and decoration. It was damaged in the 1755 earthquake, and extensively restored in the 1930s.

Castelo de São Jorge

East of the Baixa, Rua Augusto Rosa and its continuations wind up towards the castle, past the **Miradouro de Santa Luzia**, which offers spectacular views over the River Tejo. The **Castelo de São Jorge** (daily: March–Oct 9am–9pm; Nov–Feb 9am–6pm; €8.50) contains the restored remains of the Moorish palace that once stood here, and its ramparts and towers

boast some excellent views of the city, particularly from the **camera obscura** (half-hourly viewings in summer).

Alfama

The **Alfama quarter**, tumbling from the walls of the Castelo to the banks of the Tejo, is the oldest part of Lisbon, and one of its most beautiful, thanks to its picturesque narrow alleyways and breathtaking hilltop views. Despite a definite tourist presence, the quarter retains a largely traditional feel. The **Feira da Ladra**, Lisbon's rambling flea market, fills the Campo de Santa Clara at the northeastern edge of Alfama, from dawn until early afternoon every Tuesday and Saturday. Also worth a visit is the nearby church of **São Vicente de Fora** (Tues–Sun 10am–6pm; €5), a former monastery containing some exquisite eighteenth-century *azulejos* (tiles). The church also houses, in almost complete sequence, the bodies of all Portuguese kings from João IV, who restored the monarchy in 1640, to Manuel II, who lost it and died in exile in England in 1932.

Chiado

Between the Baixa and Bairro Alto, halfway up the hill, lies an area known as **Chiado**, which suffered much damage in a fire in 1988 but has been elegantly rebuilt by Portugal's premier architect, Álvaro Siza Viera. It remains the city's most affluent quarter, centred on **Rua Garrett** and its fashionable shops and chic cafés. The **Elevador de Santa Justa** (€5 return), built by Eiffel disciple Raul Mésnier de Ponsard, is an elaborate wrought-iron lift which transports passengers from Rua de Santa Justa in the Baixa to a platform next to the ruined Gothic arches of the **Convento do Carmo**. Once Lisbon's largest church, it was half-destroyed by the 1755 earthquake, becoming perhaps even more beautiful as a result, its vaulted arches reaching dramatically towards the sky. It now houses an **archeological museum** (Mon–Sat: June–Sept 10am–7pm; Oct–May 10am–6pm; €3.50) which, alongside sculptures from the original church, contains an eclectic assortment

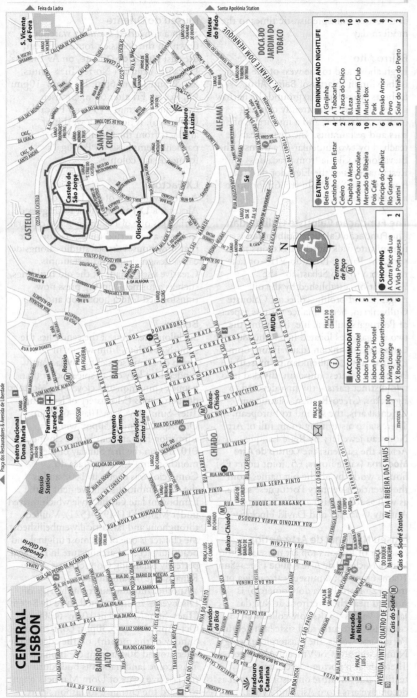

DRINKING AND NIGHTLIFE

A Ginjinha	1
A Tabacaria	6
A Tasca do Chico	3
B.Leza	10
Ministerium Club	9
Music Box	5
Park	4
Pensão Amor	8
Povo	7
Solar do Vinho do Porto	2

EATING

Beira Gare	
Cantinho do Bem Estar	
Celeiro	
Chapitô à Mesa	
Landeau Chocolate	
Mercado da Ribeira	
Pois Café	
Príncipe do Calhariz	
Rio Grande	
Santini	

SHOPPING

A Outra Face da Lua	1
A Vida Portuguesa	2

ACCOMMODATION

Goodnight Hostel	2
Lisbon Lounge	5
Lisbon Poet's Hostel	4
Lisbon Story Guesthouse	1
Living Lounge	3
LX Boutique	6

26

of treasures from prehistoric times to the modern day.

Bairro Alto

High above and to the west of the Baixa is the vibrant quarter of **Bairro Alto**, Lisbon's after-dark playground. Its narrow streets are lined with trendy clothing outlets, *fado* clubs, and a multitude of bars and restaurants. The district can be reached by two funicular-like **trams** – the Elevador da Glória from Praça dos Restauradores or the Elevador da Bica from Rua de São Paulo (€3.60 for up to two trips).

The Fundação Calouste Gulbenkian

The **Fundação Calouste Gulbenkian** is a ten-minute walk north of Lisbon's main park, the Parque Eduardo VII – or take the metro to São Sebastião. The Foundation, established by the oil magnate and prolific collector Calouste Gulbenkian, helps finance various aspects of Portugal's cultural life, including the two art galleries located here. The **Museu Calouste Gulbenkian** (daily 10am–6pm; €5, free Sun; ⑩gulbenkian.pt/museu) is Portugal's greatest museum, divided into two distinct parts – the first devoted to Egyptian, Greco-Roman, Islamic and Oriental arts, the second to European. There's also a stunning room full of Art Nouveau jewellery by René Lalique. Across the gardens, the **Centro de Arte Moderna** (same hours; €5, joint ticket €8) houses works by all the big names from the twentieth-century Portuguese scene, as well as top British artists such as Antony Gormley and David Hockney.

Museu Nacional de Arte Antiga

Another of Lisbon's top art museums, the **Museu Nacional de Arte Antiga** (Tues–Sun 10am–6pm; €6; ⑩museudearteantiga.pt; tram #25 from Praça do Comércio) is situated near the riverfront at Rua das Janelas Verdes 95. Its core collection comprises fifteenth- and sixteenth-century Portuguese works, the masterpiece being Nuno Gonçalves' St Vincent Altarpiece. There are also Portuguese ceramics, textiles and furniture on display, as well as decorative arts from Asia and Africa.

Museu do Oriente

Set in a converted *bacalhau* warehouse down on the docks en route to Belém, the vast **Museu do Oriente**, on Av Brasília, Doca de Alcântara Norte (Tues–Thurs, Sat & Sun 10am–6pm, Fri 10am–10pm; €6, free on Fri after 6pm; ⑩museu dooriente.pt; tram #15 from Praça do Comércio), is home to a wealth of artefacts from the Orient, with a particular emphasis on Portugal's former Asian colonies.

LX Factory

A short walk west of the Doca de Alcântara, **LX Factory** (Rua Rodrigues de Faria 3) is one of Lisbon's coolest cultural spaces – a converted former factory site that now houses artists' studios alongside cafés, design shops and restaurants. Creative use is made of the old buildings, such as a former printing press now transformed into a bookshop and bar.

Belém

Six kilometres west of the centre lies the suburb of **Belém**, from where, in 1497, Vasco da Gama set sail for India. Partly funded by a levy on all spices other than pepper, cinnamon and cloves, the **Mosteiro dos Jerónimos** (Monastery of Jerónimos; Tues–Sun: May–Sept 10am–6.30pm; Oct–April 10am–5.30pm, with last admission half an hour before closing; €10, free on the first Sunday of the month; tram #15 from Praça do Comércio) was begun in 1502 and is the most ambitious achievement in the flamboyant late Gothic style which thrived under Manuel I (1495–1521). Vaulted throughout and fantastically embellished, the cloister is one of the most original and beautiful pieces of architecture in Portugal, perfectly balancing Gothic forms and Renaissance ornamentation.

Another monument from the Age of Discoveries is the turreted **Torre de Belém** (Tues–Sun: May–Sept 10am–6.30pm; Oct–April 10am–5.30pm; €6, free first Sunday of the month), on the edge of the river around 500m from the monastery. This iconic landmark was built during the last five years of Dom Manuel's reign to guard the entrance to Lisbon's port.

Commemorating the era in contemporary style is the vast concrete **Padrão dos Descobrimentos** (Monument to the Discoveries; March–Sept daily 10am–7pm; Oct–Feb Tues–Sun 10am–6pm; last admission 30min before closing; €4), built in 1960 to mark the 500th anniversary of the death of Henry the Navigator, King João I's son, who began Portugal's worldwide explorations; inside is a video exhibition tracing Lisbon's history. A lift takes you to the top for spectacular views.

Step back into the present day at the **Centro Cultural de Belém** (Mon–Fri 8am–8pm, Sat & Sun 10am–6pm; free; ⓦccb.pt), a modern space which hosts a varied programme of concerts and excellent temporary exhibitions of contemporary art and photography. It's also home to the **Colecçao Berardo** (daily 10am–7pm; free), a captivating collection of modern art including works by Andy Warhol, Paula Rego and Picasso.

Parque das Nações and the Oceanarium

Built on reclaimed docklands for Expo '98, the **Parque das Nações** (Park of Nations), 5km east of the centre, has become a popular entertainment park, containing concert venues, theatres, restaurants and a large shopping centre, Centro Vasco da Gama. The park occupies a traffic-free riverside zone with water features and some dazzling modern architecture. The main attraction is the **Oceanário de Lisboa** (daily: May–Sept 10am–8pm, Oct–April 10am–6pm; €14; ⓦoceanario.pt; ⓜOriente), one of Europe's largest oceanariums, an awe-inspiring collection of fish and sea mammals based around a central tank the size of four Olympic swimming pools.

Football stadiums

Lovers of the beautiful game will find Lisbon a paradise, with two top-ranking Portuguese clubs based in the city. Benfica's home is the impressive **Estádio da Luz** (daily 10am–6pm except match days; museum €10, or €15 including stadium tour); ⓦslbenfica.pt; ⓜColegio Militar/Luz), built for Euro 2004.

Sporting's **Estádio Jose Alvalade** was also constructed for the same event, and is equally modern (Mon–Fri 11am–6pm except match days; museum including stadium tour €10; ⓦsporting.pt; ⓜCampo Grande). If you're in town on a match day (season runs Sept–June; see websites for fixtures), head to the stadium a few hours before kick-off to secure a ticket (from €20–50).

ARRIVAL AND DEPARTURE

By plane From Humberto Delgado airport, 7km northeast of the centre, the Aerobus (every 20–30min, 7am–11.20pm; 20min; €3.50 single) runs from outside arrivals to Praça dos Restauradores, Rossio, Praça do Comércio and Cais do Sodré. Metro trains on the red line (see below) run from the airport to Oriente train station and to Alameda metro stop where you can change line for services to Rossio and Baixa-Chiado in the city centre.

By train Trains to and from northern and central Portugal stop at Santa Apolónia Station, a 15–20min walk from Praça do Comércio or a quick hop on the metro (take the blue line from Terreiro do Paço). Trains from the Algarve and Évora terminate at Oriente station, at the end of the red metro line. Local trains from Sintra arrive and depart from Rossio station at the northwestern end of the square.

Destinations from Santa Apolónia Braga (13 daily; 3hr 30min–4hr 30min); Coimbra (20 daily; 2–2hr 45min); Porto (18 daily; 2hr 45min–3hr 10min); Tomar (hourly; 2hr).

Destinations from Oriente Faro (6 daily; 3hr–3hr 30min); Madrid (2 nightly; 10hr–11hr 30min); Tavira (5 daily; 4–5hr).

Destinations from Rossio Sintra (every 20–30min; 40min).

By bus The main Rede Expressos bus station is next to the Jardim Zoológico metro stop.

Destinations Alcobaça (4 daily; 2hr); Coimbra (at least hourly; 2hr 20min); Évora (hourly; 1hr 40min); Faro (6–8 daily; 3hr 45min); Lagos (3–8 daily; 4hr 30min); Madrid (2 daily; 7hr 45min–11hr 30min); Porto (hourly; 3hr 30min–4hr); Seville (2 daily; 7hr–7hr 30min); Tomar (3 daily; 1hr 45min–2hr 30min); Vila Nova de Milfontes (3–4 daily; 3hr 30min).

INFORMATION

Tourist information The main tourist office is the Lisboa Welcome Centre, on the corner of Praça do Comércio and Rua do Arsenal (daily 9am–8pm; ☎210 312 700, ⓦvisitlisboa.com). There are also Ask Me Lisboa kiosks around the city, including one at the airport (daily 7am–midnight) and one at Santa Apolónia station. Staff at these booths can book accommodation, but only with associated partner hotels.

26

GETTING AROUND

By metro Lisbon's metro (6.30am–1am; ⓦ metrolisboa .pt) has four lines: blue (*azul*), green (*verde*), red (*vermelha*) and yellow (*amarela*). Single tickets within the central zone cost €1.40 each, while a 24hr pass allowing unlimited travel costs €6. If you buy a rechargeable Viva Viagem card (€0.50, added to first purchase), however, a single journey only costs €1.25. Note that a Viva Viagem card bought at a metro station cannot be used on train services (you will need to buy another one).

By tram and bus Trams and buses (ⓦ carris.pt) are the most enjoyable way of getting around. When bought on board, tram tickets cost €2.85 and bus tickets €1.80.

By taxi A short taxi journey within the city centre shouldn't cost more than €10–12, but taxis can be hard to find at night – if you're leaving a bar or club book one by phone from Rádio Táxis de Lisboa (☏ 218 119 000) or Teletáxis (☏ 218 111 111).

Discount card Tourist offices sell the Lisboa Card (€18.50/€31.50/€39 for 24/48/72hr; ⓦ askmelisboa.com), which allows free travel on buses, trams, metro services and the train from Rossio to Sintra, as well as free admission to 25 museums and monuments.

ACCOMMODATION

Although prices have risen recently, Lisbon still has plenty of small, cheap guesthouses, many around Rua das Portas de Santo Antão and the Baixa, as well as an excellent selection of funky, well-equipped hostels. Accommodation is easy to find outside Easter and the peak summer months. Addresses below written as 53-3°, for example, describe the street number followed by the floor.

TRAM #28 TO PRAZERES

The picture-book **tram #28** is one of the city's greatest rides, but because it's so popular there are often queues to get on and standing room only. Built in England in the early twentieth century, the trams are all polished wood and chrome and give a bumpy ride up and down Lisbon's steepest streets, at times coming so close to shops that you could almost take a can of sardines off the shelves. From Graça, the tram plunges down through Alfama to the Baixa and up to **Prazeres**, west of the centre. Take care of belongings as pickpockets also enjoy the ride. For a less crowded tram ride, try the equally attractive #25, which heads from the bottom of Elevador da Bica along the waterfront and up through Lapa and Estrela to Prazeres.

HOSTELS

Goodnight Hostel Rua dos Correeiros 113-2° ☏ 213 430 139, ⓦ goodnighthostel.com; ⓜ Rossio; map p.869. Friendly and well-designed hostel in the heart of the Baixa. There's a TV lounge, and a guitar for evening sing-alongs. Dorms €21, doubles €63

★**Jardim de Santos Hostel** Largo Vitorino Damásio 4-2° ☏ 213 974 666, ⓦ jardimdesantoshostel.com; ⓜ Cais do Sodré (trams #25 and #28 also stop nearby); map pp.866–867. Wooden floors and colourful "string art" displays thread their way through this second-floor hostel, with roomy dorms, a relaxed lounge and knowledgeable staff. Dorms €14, doubles €48

Lisboa Central Hostel Rua Rodrigues Sampaio 160 ☏ 309 881 038, ⓦ lisboacentralhostel.com; ⓜ Marquês de Pombal; map pp.866–867. Sturdy bunks, a TV room and a small outdoor terrace make this friendly and well-maintained hostel a good, sociable option. Some private rooms are en suite. Dorms €21, doubles €64

Lisbon Lounge Rua de São Nicolau 41, Baixa ☏ 213 462 061, ⓦ lisbonloungehostel.com; ⓜ Rossio; map p.869. Upmarket hostel near Rossio with spacious, airy dorms and an impressive kitchen where nightly 3-course meals are served for €10. Dorms €22, doubles €32

Lisbon Poet's Hostel Rua Nova da Trindade 2-5° ☏ 213 461 241, ⓦ lisbonpoetshostel.com; ⓜ Baixa-Chiado; map p.869. Arty hostel with a spacious lounge and a range of rooms, the best of which overlook the tram #28 route. Evening meals on request. Dorms €25, doubles €60

Living Lounge Rua do Crucifixo 116-2°, Baixa ☏ 213 461 078, ⓦ lisbonloungehostel.com; ⓜ Baixa-Chiado; map p.869. *Lisbon Lounge*'s conveniently located sister hostel has huge individually designed rooms, bike rental plus free tea and coffee. Dorms €30, doubles €34

Oasis Backpackers' Mansion Rua de Santa Catarina 24, Chiado ☏ 213 478 044, ⓦ oasislisboa.com; tram #28; map pp.866–867. Lively, well-equipped hostel with its own bar, located below the Miradouro de Santa Catarina. Dorms €24, doubles €71

People Hostel Rua dos Jerónimos 16, in Belém ☏ 218 289 567, ⓦ peoplehostel.com; tram #15E from Cais do Sodré; map pp.866–867. Clean but slightly cramped, this brightly painted hostel has a pop-art theme running throughout. Great location near the Mosteiro do Jerónimos. Dorms €12, doubles €30

Pousada de Juventude de Lisboa Rua Andrade Corvo 46 ☏ 213 532 696, ⓦ pousadasjuventude.pt; ⓜ Picoas; map pp.866–867. Well-run hostel with good facilities and en-suite doubles, located near Parque Eduardo VII. Dorms €17, doubles €42

GUESTHOUSES

★**Lisbon Story Guesthouse** Largo de São Domingos 18, Baixa ☏ 218 879 392, ⓦ lisbonstoryguesthouse.com;

★TREAT YOURSELF

LX Boutique Rua do Alecrim 12
ⓜCais do Sodré ❶213 474 394,
ⓦlxboutiquehotel.pt; map p.869. In a
stylishly renovated old townhouse, *LX
Boutique* is a popular small hotel with a
chic restaurant right next to Cais do
Sodré's hippest street. Its themed floors
are named after Portuguese poets and
fado singers, and the smart rooms are
individually decorated, with shutters and
tasteful lighting. Doubles **€110**

ⓜRossio; map p.869. Combining the best of hostel and
hotel, *Lisbon Story* offers eight simple yet stylish private
rooms with a Lisbon theme, a kitchen and a lounge
stocked with travel books. Great breakfast. Doubles **€50**

CAMPSITES

Camping Obitur-Guincho Lugar da Areia, Guincho
❶214 870 450, ⓦorbitur.pt; train from Cais do Sodré to
Cascais, then bus to Guincho; map pp.866–867. A well-
located site 12km out of the city in surfer's paradise
Guincho, with a restaurant, supermarket and sports
facilities. Per tent **€24**
Lisboa Camping Parque Florestal Monsanto ❶217 628
100, ⓦlisboacamping.com; bus #714 from Praça Figueira;
map pp.866–867. Well-equipped campsite in a large park
6km west of the centre, with pool and shops. The entrance
is on Estrada da Circunvalação on the park's west side. Per
person **€7.60**, plus per tent **€7.50**

EATING

Lisbon has some great cafés and restaurants serving large
portions of food at reasonable prices. Lunch is particularly
good value, with bargain dishes of the day and set menus
on offer. Alongside the usual Portuguese restaurants
serving grilled meat and fish, there are lots of seafood
places, plus inexpensive options offering food from former
colonies (including Angola, Goa and Macau).

CAFÉS, CHEAP EATS AND SNACKS

Celeiro Rua 1 de Dezembro 65; ⓜRossio; map p.869. Just
off Rossio in the basement of a health-food supermarket,
this inexpensive self-service place offers tasty vegetarian
spring rolls, quiches, pizza and the like from around €6.
There's also a streetside café offering drinks and snacks.
Mon–Fri 9am–6pm & Sat 9am–5pm.
Landeau Chocolate Rua das Flores 70; ⓜBaixa-Chiado;
map p.869. You might smell this café before you see it. The
dreamy scent of the devilishly good chocolate cake (€4)
wafts into the street, drawing in a steady stream of locals
and tourists. Daily noon–7pm.

Mercado da Ribeira Avenida 24 Julho; ⓜCais do Sodré;
map p.869. Most of Lisbon's main market building is now
given over to a vibrant food hall, with an impressive range
of stalls (most representing top chefs and well-known
outlets in Lisbon) and plenty of benches to sit at. You can
buy everything from hams, cheeses and grilled chickens to
gourmet burgers, seafood, organic salads and chocolates.
Food stalls Sun–Wed 10am–midnight, Thurs–Sat
10am–2am.
Pastéis de Belém Rua de Belém 84–92; tram #15 from
Cais do Sodré or Praça do Comércio; map pp.866–867. This
huge, well-known *pastelaria* could easily have made the
move into tourist-trap territory, but its deliciously flaky
pastéis de nata still go for under €2. Daily: June–Sept
8am–midnight; Oct–May 8am–11pm.
Pois Café Rua São João da Praça 93–95, Baixa; ⓜTerreiro
do Paço; map p.869. Eclectically furnished café with a
relaxed atmosphere and plenty of international books and
papers to peruse. Serves brunch, quiche, sandwiches (from
€6.50) and daily specials, including vegetarian options.
Mon noon–11pm, Tues–Sun 10am–11pm.
Santini Rua do Carmo 9, Chiado; ⓜBaixa-Chiado; map
p.869. Italian-style ice-cream parlour serving more than a
dozen divine home-made flavours. Pay first, then choose
which ones you'll go for. Daily 11am–midnight.

RESTAURANTS

Beira Gare Praça Dom João de Câmara 4;
ⓜRestauradores; map p.869. Well-established restaurant
opposite Rossio station, serving bargain snacks and full
meals from €7. Grab a stool at the counter if there are no
tables. Daily 9am–10pm.
Bom Jardim Trav. De Santo Antão 11–18;
ⓜRestauradores; map pp.866–867. A fairly touristy
restaurant, where chicken is the dish to choose – half a
roast chicken with chips costs around €8. It's so popular
that it's spread over three buildings on either side of a
pedestrianized alley, with some outdoor seats as well.
April–Sept daily noon–11.30pm; Oct–March Mon, Tues &
Fri–Sun noon–11.30pm, Thurs 7–11.30pm.
Cantina LX Rua Rodrigues de Faria 103; tram #15 from
Cais do Sodré or Praça do Comércio; map pp.866–867.
Former factory canteen serving daily specials from
€10. There's a well-shaded seating area around the side.
Mon & Sun noon–3pm, Tues–Sat noon–3pm &
7.30pm–midnight.
Cantinho do Bem Estar Rua do Norte 46, Bairro Alto;
ⓜBaixa-Chiado; map p.869. The staff might be stroppy,
but this tiny place is great value for money – its portions of
Portuguese classics (around €12.50) feed two with ease.
Go early. Tues–Sun noon–2.30pm & 7.15–11.30pm.
Chapitô à Mesa Rua Costa do Castelo 7, Castelo;
ⓜTerreiro do Paço; map p.869. Two-in-one venue with
tapas and barbecued meat served in a buzzing courtyard,

26

and more expensive international dishes on offer in the upstairs restaurant. Both have excellent river views. Mon–Fri noon–midnight, Sat & Sun 7.30pm–midnight.

Prego da Peixaria Rua Escola Politécnica 40; bus #758 from Cais do Sodré; map pp.866–867. Traditional *pregos* are steak sandwiches, but this fashionable restaurant has embraced a whole host of varieties. Choose from the likes of bacalhau, tuna, mushroom or salmon with octopus from around €9–13. Daily noon–10pm.

Príncipe do Calhariz Calçada da Combro 28–30; Ⓜ Baixa-Chiado; map p.869. Busy barbecue joint serving grilled chicken and fillets of fish. Not so hungry? Go for one of the half portions (€6). Mon–Fri & Sun noon–3pm & 7–10.30pm.

★ **Rio Grande** Rua Nova do Carvalho 55; Ⓜ Cais do Sodré; map p.869. On a street full of hip bars, *Rio Grande* is reassuringly traditional, with *azulejos* on the walls beneath an arched ceiling. The spacious restaurant serves good-value Portuguese classics such as pork steaks and an array of fresh fish for under €9. Mon, Tues & Thurs–Sat 12.30pm–3am & 6pm–11pm.

DRINKING, NIGHTLIFE AND ENTERTAINMENT

The densest concentration of bars and clubs is in Bairro Alto and around Rua Nova Carvalho in Cais do Sodré. Lisbon's gay scene centres around Praça do Príncipe Real in the north of Bairro Alto. Clubs don't really get going until at least 2am and tend to stay open till 6am. Admission fees range from €10 to €20 (usually including a drink). What's-on listings can be found in the monthly *Agenda Cultural*, available free at tourist offices, or at Ⓦ lisbon.angloinfo.com.

BARS

A Ginjinha Largo de São Domingos 8, Baixa; Ⓜ Rossio; map p.869. The original *ginjinha* (cherry brandy) bar, this small stand-up place located in lively Largo de São Domingos is a great place to start a night out in Lisbon. Small shot of Ginjinha €1.40. Daily 9am–10pm.

A Tabacaria Rua de São Paulo 75–77; Ⓜ Cais do Sodré; map p.869. In a wonderful old tobacco shop dating from 1885 – with many of the original fittings – this small, friendly bar specializes in cocktails (from around €7), made from gin, vodka, whisky and whatever fruits are in season. Mon–Fri noon–1am, Sat 6pm–2am.

Park Calçada do Combro 58, Bairro Alto; tram #28; map p.869. Reached via a poky entrance inside a car park, this chic rooftop bar comes as quite a surprise. There are potted plants and trees, great cocktails and bar snacks, and a stunning view across the river. At weekends there are often guest DJs and cultural events. Tues–Sat 1pm–2am, Sun 10am–8pm.

Pavilhão Chinês Rua Dom Pedro V 89, Bairro Alto; bus #758 from Cais do Sodré; map pp.866–867. Ideal for a

cocktail, this famous (and pricey) drinking den is decorated with kitsch toys and models. Daily 6pm–2am.

Pensão Amor Rua do Alecrim 19; Ⓜ Cais do Sodré; map p.869. The "Pension of Love" is a former brothel, which has retained its eighteenth-century burlesque fittings for its current incarnation as a trendy bar with risqué photos, frescoes and mirrors: also hosts occasional live concerts. Mon–Wed noon–2am, Thurs–Sat noon–4am.

Povo Rua Nova do Carvalho 32–26; Ⓜ Cais do Sodré; map p.869. Hear *fado* from up-and-coming stars (Tues–Thurs and Sun from 9.30pm) and late-night weekend DJs at this fashionable tavern in the heart of "pink street" (the tarmac is dyed pink). Daily 6pm–4am.

Solar do Vinho do Porto Rua de São Pedro de Alcântara 45, Bairro Alto; bus #758 from Cais do Sodré; map p.869. Over 200 types of port, with ten-year-old tawnies for around €3 a glass. Mon–Fri 11am–midnight, Sat 3pm–midnight.

CLUBS

B.Leza Cais da Ribeira Nova Armazém B; Santos station from Cais do Sodré; map p.869. Boisterous African club, with live music and occasional dance lessons on offer. Wed–Sun 10.30pm–4am.

Incógnito Rua Poiais de São Bento 37, Bairro Alto Ⓦ incognitobar.com; Ⓜ Baixa-Chiado/Cais do Sodré; map pp.866–867. Student-friendly mainstay spinning synth, new wave and indie sounds until the early hours. Wed–Sat 11pm–4am.

Lux Cais da Pedra Santa Apolónia Armázem A, opposite Santa Apolónia station Ⓦ luxfragil.com; Ⓜ Santa Apolónia; map pp.866–867. The city's best-known club, often hosting top DJs and electronic acts, like Fatboy Slim and Hot Chip. See website for events and times.

Main Av 24 de Julho 68, opposite Santos station Ⓦ mainlisbon.pt; Ⓜ Cais do Sodré; map pp.866–867. Swanky place with a minimalist vibe and house tunes, attracting diners and dancers. Thurs–Sat 11.30pm–6am.

Ministerium Club Ala Nascente 72, Praça do Comércio Ⓦ ministerium.pt; Ⓜ Terreiro do Paço; map p.869. Fresh from the US, Ibiza and beyond, big-name DJs come to rock Lisbon's former finance ministry. Sat 11pm–6am, plus occasional events on other nights.

Trumps Rua da Imprensa Nacional 104b, Rato Ⓦ trumps.pt; bus #758 from Cais do Sodré; map pp.866–867. The biggest gay venue in Lisbon, with themed parties in the summertime and a year-round "hetero-friendly" policy. Fri & Sat 11.45pm–6am.

FADO AND LIVE MUSIC

A Tasca do Chico Rua do Diário de Notícias 39; bus #758 from Cais do Sodré; map p.869. Make like the locals and catch some amateur *fado* in this bar during the week. Free entry. Daily 7pm–2am, with performances on Mon & Wed.

26

Coliseu dos Recreios Rua Portas de Santo Antão 96 Ⓦ coliseulisboa.com; Ⓜ Restauradores; map pp.866–867. Portuguese stars fill much of the programme, but this concert hall also attracts international bands. See website for event times.

Hot Clube de Portugal Praça da Alegria 48 Ⓦ hcp.pt; Ⓜ Avenida; map pp.866–867. The longest-running jazz club in Portugal, with live performances five nights a week. Tues–Sat 10pm–2am.

Music Box Rua Nova do Carvalho 24 Ⓦ musicboxlisboa .com; map p.869. Live music venue near Cais do Sodré, with a schedule packed full of DJs and bands playing almost every musical style imaginable. Mon–Sat 11pm–6am.

SHOPPING

A Outra Face da Lua Rua da Assunção 22; Ⓜ Baixa-Chiado; map p.869. Vintage emporium stocking a mishmash of goodies, from clothing to toys. There's also an in-store café. Mon–Sat 10am–8pm, Sun 10am–7pm.

A Vida Portuguesa Rua Anchieta 11; Ⓜ Baixa-Chiado; map p.869. From tiles to sardines, if it's Portuguese, you'll find it here. Many of the old-fashioned brands on sale would have disappeared had this chain store not made them cool again. Mon–Sat 10am–8pm, Sun 11am–8pm.

Bairro Arte LX Factory, on Rua Rodrigues Faria; tram #15 from Cais do Sodré or Praça do Comércio; map pp.866–867.

FADO

Often described as somewhere between the blues and flamenco, the emotional and melodramatic musical genre of **fado** (literally "fate") is as Portuguese as custard tarts and Cristiano Ronaldo. *Fado* has its roots in early nineteenth-century Alfama, where it thrived until the early twentieth century, when it was subject to censorship. Despite the authorities' efforts, the genre continued to develop, and still features in the charts today thanks to a new generation of performers. Lisbon is the best place to hear *fado*, specifically in Bairro Alto, where many restaurants put on performances (from €25 upwards, including dinner), although Coimbra also has its own style (see p.879). To get the most out of a show, first visit the modern **Museu do Fado** at Largo do Chafariz de Dentro 1 (Tues–Sun 10am–6pm; €5), for an excellent audioguide introduction to the history of the genre and its brightest stars, including *grande dame* Amália Rodrigues and younger talent Joana Amendoeira.

One of three *Bairro Arte* shops in Lisbon (the others are in Bairro Alto and Chiado), selling all manner of quirky retro and designer goods. Worth a browse. Daily 9am–midnight.

Entre Tanto Rua Escola Politécnica 42; bus #758 from Cais do Sodré; map pp.866–867. Set in a rambling seventeenth-century building, Entre Tanto is an intriguing jumble of stores and fashionable boutiques selling everything from shoes and hip clothes to perfume and surfboards. There's a lovely terrace café, too, overlooking the Botanical Gardens. Daily noon–8pm.

DIRECTORY

Banks and Exchange Main bank branches in the Baixa. Exchange office at the airport (24hr) and at Santa Apolónia station (daily 8.30am–3pm).

Embassies Australia, Av da Liberdade 200 ☎ 213 101 500; Canada, Av da Liberdade 198–200 ☎ 213 164 600; Ireland, Av da Liberdade 200-4° ☎ 213 308 200; South Africa, Av Luis Bívar 10 ☎ 213 192 200; UK, Rua de São Bernardo 33 ☎ 213 924 000; US, Av das Forças Armadas ☎ 217 273 300.

Hospital The main hospital is Hospital de Santa Maria, Avenida Prof. Egas Moniz ☎ 217 805 000, Ⓜ Jardim Zoológico.

Left luggage Available at Oriente (daily 6.40am–10pm) and Santa Apolónia (daily 6.40am–10pm) stations from €5/7hr.

Pharmacy Throughout the city, including Farmácia Azevedo & Filhos, Rossio 31 (24hr).

Post office Praça dos Restauradores 58 (Mon–Fri 8am–10pm, Sat & Sun 8am–6pm).

Tourist police Palácio Foz, Praça dos Restauradores (☎ 213 421 634).

BEACHES AROUND LISBON

The coast around Lisbon offers ample opportunities to escape from the summer heat of the capital. Half an hour south of the capital, dunes stretch along the **COSTA DA CAPARICA**, a thoroughly Portuguese resort popular with surfers and crammed with restaurants and beach cafés. Solitude is easy enough to find, though, thanks to the **transpraia** (mini-railway) that runs along the 8km of dunes in summer.

Another popular seaside escape is the former fishing village of **CASCAIS**, forty minutes to the west of the city, which boasts three beaches and a campsite. Cascais has a particular appeal to surfers due to its proximity to Guincho beach (see box, p.864), reached by local bus,

26

which has hosted the World Surfing Championships.

ARRIVAL AND DEPARTURE

Costa da Caparica Ferry from Cais do Sodré in Lisbon to Cacilhas (every 15–20min), then the #135 TST bus (every 30min). Buses stop along Avenida Doutor Aresta Branco, close to the main square Praça da Liberdade, and a 3min walk east of the beach.

Cascais Train from Cais do Sodré (every 15–30min; 40min).

SINTRA

The cool, hilltop woodland setting of **SINTRA** once attracted Moorish lords and the Portuguese kings from Lisbon during the summer months; the palaces they constructed remain among Portugal's most spectacular attractions. Sintra can be visited on a day-trip from Lisbon, though there are certainly enough sights to keep you occupied for several days. Combined tickets reduce the price of admission to the sights; enquire at the tourist office for the latest offers.

WHAT TO SEE AND DO

An amalgamation of three villages, Sintra can be confusing, but there are plenty of local buses connecting the sights.

Palácio Nacional

The **Palácio Nacional** (daily: March–Oct 9.30am–7pm; Nov–Feb 9.30am–5.30pm; €10), about fifteen minutes' walk from the train station, is an obvious landmark, with its distinctive conical chimneys. The palace probably existed under the Moors, but takes its present form from the rebuilding commissioned by Dom João I and his successor, Dom Manuel, in the fourteenth and fifteenth centuries. Its style is a fusion of Gothic and the latter king's Manueline additions. The **chapel** and its adjoining chamber are well worth seeing, as is the curious Magpies Room, decorated with hundreds of paintings of the birds with the motto "*Por Bem*" ("For the good") in their beaks.

Quinta da Regaleira

Also within walking distance of the centre is another must-see site, the beautiful

Quinta da Regaleira (daily: Feb, March & Oct 10am–6.30pm; April–Sept 10am–8pm; Nov–Jan 10am–5.30pm; €6, or €10 for guided visits booked in advance on ☎219 106 650). One of Sintra's most elaborate private estates, it lies ten minutes' walk west of the Palácio Nacional on the Seteais–Monserrate road. The house and its fantastic gardens were built at the beginning of the twentieth century by an Italian theatrical set designer for one of the richest industrialists in Portugal. One highlight is the **Initiation Well**, inspired by the initiation practices of the Knights Templar and Freemasons. The vast gardens are full of surprising delights, with chapels, follies and fountains at every turn.

Monserrate

Beyond Quinta da Regaleira, the road leads past a series of beautiful private estates to recently renovated **Monserrate** (daily: March–Oct 9.30am–7pm; Nov–Feb 10am–5pm; €8) – about an hour's walk from the Palácio Nacional – a Moorish-style folly of a palace whose 75-acre **garden**, filled with exotic trees and subtropical shrubs and plants, extends as far as the eye can see.

Moorish castle and Palácio da Pena

Two of Sintra's main sights can be reached on bus #434 (the €5 ticket allows you to hop on and off at each one), starting at the train station. The bus stops outside the Praça da República tourist office before proceeding to the ruined ramparts of the **Castelo dos Mouros** (Moorish castle; daily 9.30am–8pm, last ticket 7pm; €8), from where the views over the town and surrounding countryside are extraordinary. Further on, the bus stops at both entrances to the immense **Pena Park**, at the top of which rears the fabulous **Palácio da Pena** (daily: March–Oct 9.45am–7pm; €14, or park only €7.50; Nov–Feb 10am–6pm; €11, park only €6), a wild, nineteenth-century fantasy of domes, towers and a drawbridge that doesn't draw. The cluttered, kitschy interior has been preserved as left by the royal family on their flight from Portugal in 1910.

ARRIVAL AND INFORMATION

By train Trains run from Lisbon's Rossio station to the centre of Sintra. From here it's a 10min stroll southeast to the main tourist office.

Destinations Lisbon (Rossio) (every 15–30min; 45min).

Tourist information There's one small tourist office at the train station (daily 10am–6pm) and a larger one (daily 9.30am–6pm, until 7pm Aug; **☏** 219 231 157) just off the central Praça da República.

ACCOMMODATION AND EATING

★ Café Saudade Av Doutor Miguel Bombarda 6. On the site of an old cheesecake factory, with beautifully ornate ceilings, this café/gallery near the train station does excellent salads for €7. Daily 8.30am–8pm.

Estrada Velha Rua Consiglieri Pedroso 16. On the road to the Quinta da Regaleira, this good-value café-bar with an old-fashioned but cosy interior serves sandwiches, burgers and other quick bites. Daily 11am–2am.

Moon Hill Hostel Rua Guilherme Gomes Fernandes 17 **☏** 969 831 095, **⊛** moonhillhostel.com. Near Sintra station, this modern hostel has friendly staff, stylish decor and a range of contemporary rooms from en-suite doubles with a view of the castle to tidy dorms with smart wooden bunk beds. Dorms **€20**, doubles **€60**

Central Portugal

Central Portugal embraces the historic regions of the Beiras, Estremadura and Ribatejo that have played crucial roles in each phase of the nation's history – and the monuments are here to prove it. The vast central plains are dominated by **Coimbra**, an ancient university town and Portugal's former capital. South of here lie fertile rolling hills, which boast an extraordinary concentration of vivid architecture and engaging towns such as **Alcobaça** and **Tomar**, both housing famously grand religious monuments. This region also boasts some of Portugal's best surf beaches round the old fishing port of **Peniche**.

PENICHE

Gangs of fishermen still repair their nets at **Peniche** harbourside, which despite a fair amount of development, retains an interesting walled town of narrow streets. This is dominated by a sixteenth-century fortress (Tues–Fri 9am–12.30pm & 2–5.30pm, Sat–Sun 10am–12.30pm & 2–5.30pm; €2), a much-feared jail during the years of Portugal's dictatorship. Still a formidable place of bare yards and high walls, it now houses the municipal museum, while on the top floor you can see the old cells and solitary-confinement pens.

Next to the fortress, boats depart from the marina to the **Ilha da Berlenga** (mid-May to June & early Sept 1 daily; July & Aug 3 daily; €20 return; 45min), a craggy island 10km offshore. It's now a bird reserve with a tiny beach and seventeenth-century fortress.

Either side of town, you'll find long stretches of duned **surf beaches**. The best of these are at **Baleal**, 5km northeast of Peniche, an islet-village joined to the mainland by a narrow causeway, with fine sand beaches either side, and bar-restaurants overlooking the sands at both ends.

ARRIVAL AND INFORMATION

By bus Peniche's bus station lies outside the town walls – it's a 10min walk into the centre, across the Ponte Velha to the main Rua Alexandre Herculano.

Destinations Alcobaça (1–2 daily; 1hr 40min); Baleal (Mon–Fri approx hourly; Sat & Sun 8 daily; 10min); Lisbon (9 daily; 1hr 35min).

Tourist information Turismo at Rua Alexandre Herculano (daily 9am–1pm & 2–7pm; Oct–May closes at 5pm; **☏** 262 789 571, **⊛** cm-peniche.pt).

ACCOMMODATION AND EATING

A Sardinha Rua Vasco da Gama 81–93. The best of the backstreet options, this good-value, family-run place serves a range of fish and seafood, from sardines to clams,

> ### PENICHE SURF-CAMPS
>
> Peniche boasts some of Portugal's best and most consistent **surfing**. Its *turismo* hands out a free guide to the nearby beaches and you can rent gear from any of the local **surf-camps**, including PH Surf School (**⊛** penichehostel.com), and Baleal Surfcamp (**⊛** balealsurfcamp.com), and Peniche Surf Camp, both in Baleal (**⊛** penichesurfcamp.com). Expect to pay from €35 for group lessons, €80 for individual sessions.

26

26

and a superb mixed grilled fish for €12.50 (big enough for two). You can sit outside on the narrow street in summer. Daily 11.30am–4pm & 6.30–10.30pm.

Peniche Hostel Backpackers Rua Arquitecto Paulino Montêz 6–1° ☏ 969 008 689, ⓦ penichehostel.com. A friendly surfers' and backpackers' place in a renovated house just inside the town walls, across from the *turismo*. It's kind of boutiquey, with a kitchen and lounge. They can arrange lessons at their own surf school, and you can also rent boards and bikes. Dorms €20, doubles €50

ALCOBAÇA

The pretty town of **Alcobaça** is dominated by the vast, beautiful **Mosteiro de Santa Maria de Alcobaça** (daily: April–Sept 9am–6pm; Oct–March 9am–5pm; €6, free first Sun of the month). From its foundation in 1147 until its dissolution in 1834, this Cistercian monastery was one of the greatest in the world. Its **church** (free) is one of the largest in Portugal, with a Baroque facade that conceals an interior stripped of most of its later adornments and restored to its original simplicity.

The monastery's most precious treasures are the fourteenth-century **tombs** of Dom Pedro and Dona Inês de Castro, sculpted with incredible detail to illustrate the story of Pedro's love for Inês, the daughter of a Galician nobleman (see box below). The monastery's most impressive room is the **kitchen**, featuring a gigantic conical chimney, and a stream tapped from the river to provide Alcobaça's famously gluttonous monks with a constant supply of fresh fish.

TILL DEATH US DO PART: DOM PEDRO AND DONA INÊS DE CASTRO

Dom Pedro's father, Afonso V, forbade his marriage to **Dona Inês de Castro**, which nevertheless took place in secret. Afonso ordered Inês's murder, and Pedro waited for his succession to the throne before exhuming her corpse and forcing the royal circle to acknowledge her as queen by kissing her decomposing hand. Their tombs have been placed foot to foot so that on Judgement Day the lovers may rise and immediately see one another.

ARRIVAL AND INFORMATION

By bus Alcobaça's bus station is a 5min walk from the monastery in the centre of town, across the bridge.

Destinations Coimbra (1–2 daily; 1hr 25min); Lisbon (4 daily; 2hr); Peniche (1–2 daily; 1hr 40min); Porto (Sept–June 1 daily; 4hr 30min); Tomar (3 daily; 2hr).

Tourist information Tourist office at Rua 16 de Outubro 17, a short walk north of the monastery (daily 9am–1pm & 2–6pm; ☏ 262 582 377).

ACCOMMODATION AND EATING

Corações Unidos Rua Frei António Brandão 39 ☏ 262 582 142. Neat, clean *pensão* with modern bathrooms facing the monastery. The restaurant below serves good-value regional cooking (mains €9). Doubles €40

Real Baça Directly opposite the monastery on Praça 25 de Abril. Relaxed *pastelaria* that serves a good selection of local pastries and cakes (around €1.50), plus ice-cold drinks. Daily 8am–8pm.

Ti Fininho Rua Frei António Brandão 34. Cheap grilled fish and meats, omelettes, and wine by the jug at this simple restaurant a short walk from the monastery. *Bacalhau á casa* €8. Daily 11am–3.30pm & 6–10pm.

TOMAR

Riverside **TOMAR** is famous for its spectacular headquarters of the Portuguese branch of the Knights Templar, which overlooks the town from a wooded hill. It's also an attractive town in its own right – especially during the lively **Festa dos Tabuleiros**, a festival of music and dancing, held once every four years at the beginning of July.

WHAT TO SEE AND DO

Built on a simple grid plan, Tomar's centre preserves its traditional charm, with whitewashed houses lining narrow cobbled streets. West of the central Praça da República is the former Jewish quarter, where at Rua Joaquim Jacinto 73 you'll find an excellently preserved fourteenth-century synagogue, now the **Museu Luso-Hebraicoa Abraham Zacuto** (Wed–Sun: May–Sept 10am–1pm & 3–7pm; Oct–April 10am–1pm & 2–6pm; free), one of the few surviving synagogues in Portugal.

A fifteen-minute walk uphill from the town centre, the **Convento de Cristo** (daily: June–Sept 9am–6.30pm; Oct–May 9am–5.30pm; €6) was founded in 1162 by Gualdim Pais, first Master of the Knights Templar, and became the Order's headquarters. At the heart of the complex, surrounded by serene cloisters, is the **Charola**, the high-ceilinged, sixteen-sided temple from which the knights drew their moral conviction. The beautiful adjoining two-tiered **Principal Cloister** is one of the purest examples of the Renaissance style in Portugal. Next door to the convent, but accessed from a separate entrance off Av Dr Vieira Guimarães, the extensive, partly wooded former convent grounds, the **Mata dos Sete Montes** (daily: May–Sept 8.30am–7.30pm; Oct–April 8.30am–5.30pm; free), makes a lovely place for a picnic.

ARRIVAL AND INFORMATION

By train The train station is on Av dos Combatentes de Grande Guerra, 10min south of the town centre.
Destinations Lisbon (15 daily; 1hr 50min–2hr).
By bus Buses pull in at a lot beside the train station.
Destinations Coimbra (1 daily; 2hr 10min); Lisbon (3 daily; 1hr 45min–2hr 30min); Porto (1 daily; 4hr).
Tourist information Tourist office at the top of Av Dr Cândido Madureira (daily 9am–12.30pm & 2–6pm).

ACCOMMODATION

Parque de Campismo ☎ 249 329 824. ⓦ campingtomar .wordpress.com. Tomar's campsite is a short walk east of Rua Marquês de Pombal. It's a good-sized site with plenty of trees providing shade and a helpful front desk. Per person €4.20, plus per tent €2.65
União Rua Serpa Pinto 94 ☎ 249 323 161. Faded but appealing guesthouse in a nineteenth-century building on the main street. Cheap walk-up rates and a friendly, English-speaking owner. Doubles €45

EATING AND DRINKING

Café Paraiso Rua Serpa Pinto 127. A Tomar institution with marble pillars and tables on the main pedestrianized street, ideal for a drink (espresso 80c) at any time of day. Mon 9am–2pm, Tues–Sat 8am–2am, Sun 8am–8pm.
Jardim Rua Silva Megalhães 54. With a separate entrance on Rua Sacadura Cabral, this huge warren of a place has several dining areas and an appealing garden. Good for large portions of grilled fish or meat from €8. Mon & Wed–Fri 9am–3pm & 6pm–midnight, Sat 6pm–midnight.

COIMBRA

Portugal's capital from 1143 to 1255, **COIMBRA** ranks behind only Lisbon and Porto in historic importance, while its university, founded in 1290, is one of the oldest in the world.

WHAT TO SEE AND DO

For a provincial town Coimbra has significant architectural riches. Its many students create a vivacious atmosphere during term time – especially in May, when they celebrate the end of the academic year with the **Queima das Fitas**, a symbolic tearing or burning of their gowns and faculty ribbons followed by some serious partying. This is when you're most likely to hear the Coimbra *fado*, distinguished from the Lisbon version by its mournful pace and complex lyrics.

The old town

Old Coimbra sits on a hill on the right bank of the River Mondego, with the university crowning its summit. The main buildings of the **Old University** (daily: mid-March to Oct 9am–7.30pm; Nov to mid-March 9.30am–1pm & 2–5.30pm; €7), dating from the sixteenth century, are set around a courtyard (entrance free) dominated by a Baroque clock tower and a statue of João III. The **chapel** is covered with *azulejos* and intricate decoration, but takes second place to the **library**, a Baroque fantasy with *trompe-l'oeil* ceilings. It also has some unusual inhabitants: a colony of bats. Other areas included in the visit are the graduation hall and the academic prison. Halfway down the hill towards the centre stands the solid and simple **Sé Velha** (Old Cathedral; Mon–Sat 10am–5.30pm; €2.50), one of Portugal's most important Romanesque buildings.

Central Coimbra

Restraint and simplicity certainly aren't the chief qualities of the flamboyant **Igreja de Santa Cruz** (Mon–Fri 9am–5pm, Sat 9am–12.30pm & 2–5pm, Sun 4–5.30pm; €2.50), at the bottom of the hill on Praça 8 de Maio. It houses the tombs of Portugal's first kings, Afonso Henriques and Sancho I, and an elaborately carved pulpit.

Across the river is the beautifully restored convent of **Santa Clara a Velha**

26

26

(Tues–Sun: May–Sept 10am–7pm; Oct–April 10am–5pm; €4). Due to the rising tide of the Mondego, its resident nuns moved to higher and higher floors before abandoning the convent for **Santa Clara a Nova** up the hill in 1677. A century ago, the building had all but disappeared beneath the river: the convent visitor centre shows a film (with English subtitles) about its restoration, as well as detailing life in medieval Portugal.

Other areas of interest include the epicentre of the students' social scene, **Praça da República**, a ten-minute walk from Praça 8 de Maio up Rua Olímpio Nicolau Rui Fernandes, and the rambling **Botanic Garden** (daily: April–Sept 9am–8pm; Oct–March 9am–5.30pm; free), which sits in the shadow of the sixteenth-century **aqueduct** to the east of Praça da República. The gardens also have a fine tree-top adventure course, **Sky-Garden**, full of zip wires and ropes (w skygardenadventure.com; €24).

ARRIVAL AND DEPARTURE

By train Intercity trains stop at Coimbra B, 3km north of the city, from where there are frequent connecting services to Coimbra A in the town centre.
Destinations Lisbon (hourly; 2hr–2hr 50min); Porto (hourly; 1hr 20min–2hr).
By bus The bus station is on Av Fernão de Magalhães, a 15min walk from the centre – turn right out of the bus station and head down the main road. Some buses from the north stop on Av Emídio Navarro.
Destinations Alcobaça (1–2 daily; 1hr 25min); Lisbon (at least hourly; 2hr 20min); Porto (roughly hourly; 1hr 30min).

INFORMATION

Tourist information The main tourist office is on Avenida Emídio Navorro near the bridge (Easter–Sept Mon–Fri 9am–8pm, Sat & Sun 9.30am–1pm & 2.30–6pm; Oct–Easter Mon–Fri 9am–6pm; ☎ 239 488 120, w www.turismodocentro.pt).

GETTING AROUND

By bus The local bus network is run by SMTUC (w smtuc.pt) – bus #103 runs from Coimbra A station via the market up to the university, while the #3 runs along the same route to Praça da República. The little electric Linha Azul buses (Mon–Fri, plus Sat mornings in summer) run on a circular route through the otherwise pedestrianized Baixa (lower town). A one-way journey bought on board costs €1.60; 3 tickets bought in advance at a newsstand cost €2.20 or a one-day pass is €3.50.

ACCOMMODATION

Grande Hostel de Coimbra Rua Antero de Quental 196 ☎ 239 108 212, w grandehostelcoimbra.com. Long-established hostel near Praça da República, set in a big old house with a garden, lounge and kitchen providing free tea and coffee. A good place to meet fellow travellers. Dorms €18, doubles €40

Pousada de Juventude Rua Dr. Henrique Seco 14 ☎ 239 829 28, w pousadasjuventude.pt; bus #7 from Av Emídio Navarro. Basic but cheap hostel 10min north of Praça da República. Dorms €12, doubles €30

Serenata Next to Sé Velha at Largo Sé Velha 21–23 ☎ 239 853 130, w serenatahostel.com. Palatial hostel with dorms, twins and doubles, plus a hotel-like living room, games room and sun terrace. Dorms €15, doubles €39

EATING, DRINKING AND NIGHTLIFE

Most of the town's restaurants can be found tucked away in the alleys between Largo da Portagem – the place to head for cafés – and Praça 8 de Maio.

★**Adega Paço do Conde** Rua Paço do Conde 1. Atmospheric, locally renowned *churrasqueira* serving tasty barbecued meat and fish (around €5–12), with a dining room either side of a shady covered terrace. Mon–Sat noon–midnight.

Café Tropical Praça da República. The pick of the República bars, this is a favourite haunt of students, with outdoor tables and cheap drinks. Gets packed out at weekends, both inside and out. Daily 10am–5am.

Fado ao Centro Rua do Quebra Costas 7. A good place to hear Coimbra *fado*, with nightly performances at 6pm (€10 for 50min, including a glass of port). It's only open in the evening for the duration of the performance, though tickets are sold throughout the day.

Quebra Rua de Quebra Costas 45–49. Coimbra's top student music bar. There's a tiny terrace for drinks, and live music and DJ sets later in the evening. Mon–Fri noon–4am, Sat 2pm–4am.

Zé Manel dos Ossos Beco do Forno 12. Not much more than a few tables, this atmospheric little joint serves excellent regional food – around €15 for a decent meal, from soup to coffee. To avoid the queues, arrive at opening time. Mon–Fri noon–3pm & 7.30–10pm, Sun noon–3pm.

Northern Portugal

Porto, the country's second-largest city, is an attractive and convenient centre from which to explore this region. Magnificently located on a rocky cliff astride the River Douro, it is perhaps most famous for the port-producing suburb of **Vila Nova de Gaia**, on the south side of the river. From Porto, the **Douro Valley** runs east, traced by a spectacular rail route, passing the vineyards that supply the port lodges.

North of Porto lies some of Portugal's most beautiful landscapes, a lush wilderness of rolling mountain forests and rugged coastlines (the Costa Verde), with some of the most unspoilt beaches in Europe. A quietly conservative region, its towns have a special charm and beauty, among them the religious centre of **Braga**, and the self-proclaimed birthplace of the nation, **Guimarães**, both of which can be visited by day-trip from Porto, but which also make good bases from which to explore the rest of the region.

PORTO

Capital of the north, **PORTO** (sometimes called "Oporto" in English) is very different from Lisbon – unpretentious and unashamedly commercial, yet extremely welcoming. As the local saying goes: "Coimbra sings; Braga prays; Lisbon shows off; and Porto works." Possessing considerable historical appeal, it also boasts such modern attributes as an efficient metro system, state-of-the-art football stadium and a top concert venue, the Casa da Música.

WHAT TO SEE AND DO

The waterfront Ribeira district is Porto's historic heart, with narrow, winding alleys so picturesque that the area has been declared a UNESCO World Heritage Site. **Boat trips** up the Douro (€10; 50min) depart regularly from Cais da Estiva and, across the river, Cais de Gaia, and are a great way to observe Porto's beauty.

Ribeira

Despite being Porto's most touristy quarter, life in the **Ribeira** continues unaffected by visitors, as a wander through its alleyways will soon reveal. The district is also home to many restaurants and bars, as well as the extraordinary **Igreja de São**

Francisco on Rua Infante Dom Henrique (daily: March–June & Oct 9am–7pm; July–Sept 9am–8pm; Nov–Feb 9am–6pm; €3.50 including museum). Now deconsecrated, its rather plain facade conceals a fabulously opulent, gold-covered interior, refurbished in the eighteenth century. Around the corner on Rua Ferreira Borges is the **Palácio da Bolsa** (Stock Exchange; daily: April–Oct 9am–6.30pm; Nov–March 9am–12.30pm & 2–5.30pm; €8), which ceased trading years ago and now offers informative tours every thirty minutes. The highlight is the ornate *Salão Árabe* (Arab Room), its Moorish style emulating that of the Alhambra palace in Granada, Spain.

Cordoaria to Mercado de Bolhão

The **Museu Nacional Soares dos Reis** at Rua Dom Manuel II (Tues 2–6pm, Wed–Sun 10am–6pm; €5, free Sun 10am–2pm) lies a few minutes' walk west of Aliados, in the Cordoaria area. Portugal's first national museum, it shows an impressive selection of works by home-grown artists and a vast collection of applied and decorative arts. The museum is named after local nineteenth-century sculptor António Soares dos Reis, and displays his *O Desterrado* ("The Exiled"), probably the best-known work in Portugal. A short walk away on Campo Mártires da Pátria, in a former prison, the **Centro Português de Fotografia** (Portuguese Photography Centre; Tues–Fri 10am–12.30pm & 3–6pm, Sat & Sun 3–7pm; free) houses changing photography exhibitions. East of the Photography Centre, the **Torre dos Clérigos**, attached to the Baroque Igreja dos Clérigos on Rua São Filipe Nery (daily: April–Oct 9.30am–1pm & 2–7pm; Nov–March 10am–noon & 2–5pm; €2), offers superb views of the city. Nearby, on Rua das Carmelitas, **Lello & Irmão** bookshop (Mon–Fri 10am–7.30pm, Sat 10am–7pm) is worth a look for its stunning Art Nouveau interior, featuring a fabulously ornate staircase, carved wood panelling and stained glass.

Downhill from here is the city's biggest boulevard, the transport hub of **Avenida**

26

26

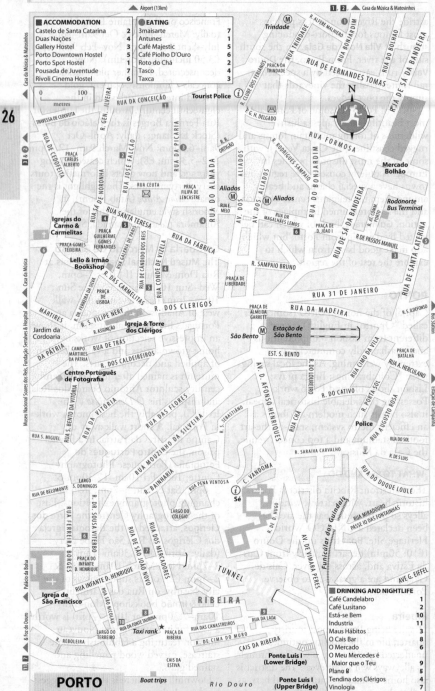

■ ACCOMMODATION
Castelo de Santa Catarina	2
Duas Nações	4
Gallery Hostel	3
Porto Downtown Hostel	5
Porto Spot Hostel	1
Pousada de Juventude	7
Rivoli Cinema Hostel	6

● EATING
3maisarte	7
Antunes	1
Café Majestic	5
Café Piolho D'Ouro	6
Roto do Chá	2
Tasco	4
Taxca	3

■ DRINKING AND NIGHTLIFE
Café Candelabro	1
Café Lusitano	2
Está-se Bem	10
Industria	11
Maus Hábitos	3
O Cais Bar	8
O Mercado	6
O Meu Mercedes é Maior que o Teu	9
Plano B	5
Tendina dos Clérigos	4
Vinologia	7

PORTO

Rio Douro

Boat trips

Ponte Luís I (Lower Bridge)

Ponte Luís I (Upper Bridge)

Cable Car, Tourist Info & Port Lodges ▼ ▼ Vila Nova de Gaia & ⑦

dos Aliados, a short walk east of which is the **Mercado de Bolhão** (Mon–Fri 7am–5pm, Sat 7am–1pm), which sells fresh produce every day except Sunday, while the city's main shopping area is located a little further east around Rua de Santa Catarina.

Casa da Música

The west of the city is home to some of Portugal's most exciting cultural centres, not to mention some daring architecture. Dominating the Avenida da Boavista and accessible by metro, 3km west of the centre, **Casa da Música** (ticket office Mon–Sat 9.30am–7pm, Sun 9.30am–6pm; tours in English daily 11am–4pm; €7.50; ⊕casadamusica.com) is a vast, irregularly shaped and strangely beautiful white concrete building designed by Rem Koolhaas. Concerts are held here most nights, though you can peek inside its impressive interior for free.

Fundação Serralves

Three kilometres west of Casa da Música is another architectural gem and one of Porto's key attractions, the **Fundação Serralves** (April–Sept Tues–Fri 10am–7pm, Sat & Sun 10am–6pm; Oct–March Tues–Fri 10am–6pm, Sat & Sun 10am–5pm; €8.50, park only €4; free Sun 10am–1pm; bus #502 from Bolhão), which comprises the modernist **Museum of Contemporary Art**, hosting an exciting array of temporary exhibitions by Portuguese and international artists, and the Art Deco **Serralves Villa** (which also puts on occasional exhibitions), set in a vast, beautiful park. If the exhibition isn't to your taste, skip it and head straight for the **park**, encompassing everything from formal gardens to wild woods, and even a farm featuring species from northern Portugal.

Foz do Douro

The coastline at **Foz** makes an easy escape from the city, reached via tram #1 (€2.50 one-way) from Rua Nova da Alfândega. The old wooden tram clanks along the coastline to Passeio Alegre, from where you can take a one-hour stroll along the beachside promenade to the curiously

named **Castelo do Queijo** (Cheese Castle) before taking bus #502 back to the centre. For much of the year the Atlantic Ocean is too chilly for all but the hardiest of swimmers, but the beaches fill with sun-worshippers in summer. Foz is also home to a buzzing nightlife scene.

Vila Nova de Gaia

South of the river and essentially a city in its own right, **Vila Nova de Gaia** (usually referred to as Gaia) is dominated by the port trade. From the Ribeira, the names of the various companies, spelled out in neon letters above the terracotta roofs of the wine lodges, leave you in no doubt as to what awaits you. You can walk to Gaia across the **Ponte Dom Luís I**: the most direct route to the lodges is across the Lower Bridge from the Cais da Ribeira, but taking the metro across the top level to the Jardim do Morro stop has the bonus of breathtaking views. Another scenic option is the **Teleférico de Gaia** cable car (daily: April to mid-Sept 10am–8pm; mid-Sept to Oct 10am–7pm, Nov–March 10am–6pm; €5 single, €8 return), which connects Vila Nova de Gaia's waterfront with the top level of the bridge (though doesn't actually cross the river). Most port lodges offer basic **tours** (€5–6) explaining the history of the company and port production and ending with a tasting of one or two ports

> ## PORT
>
> Port wine comes in a variety of types and ages, as you'll discover on an afternoon tour of Vila Nova de Gaia's **port lodges**. The relatively little-known **white ports** are served as an aperitif, and can be dry or sweet; another refreshing option is Croft's "Pink", which was one of the first **rosé** ports on the market. After dinner come either tawny or ruby ports: nutty-tasting **tawnies** are made from a blend of different barrel-aged wines, while deep red **rubies** age in the bottle. Further varieties include Late Bottled Vintage (**LBV**), made from good-quality grapes gathered in a single harvest and aged for five years, and the crème de la crème, **Vintage** port, which uses only the best grapes from a particularly fine harvest.

(more expensive options such as vintage ports are available for an extra fee). If all this sampling whets your appetite, head to *Vinologia* (see p.886) to learn and taste more.

ARRIVAL AND DEPARTURE

By plane From the Francisco Sá Carneiro airport, 13km north of the city, take metro line E (daily 6am–1am; €2.45, including purchase of rechargeable Andante card) to the centre.

By train Most trains from the south stop at the distant Estação de Campanhã; you may need to change here for a connection to the central Estação de São Bento (frequent; 5min). Metro line B will also take you into the centre from Campanhã.

Destinations Braga (every 30min–1hr; 1hr); Coimbra (hourly; 1hr 30min–2hr 30min); Guimarães (hourly; 1hr 20min); Lisbon (hourly; 3hr 20min–4hr).

By bus The main bus terminal (Rede-Expressos) is on Rua Alexandre Herculano, a short walk east of São Bento, while the Rodonorte terminal is at Rua Ateneu Comercial do Porto 19, near Bolhão market.

Destinations Braga (every 30min; 1hr); Coimbra (approx hourly; 1hr 30min); Guimarães (2–3 daily; 1hr 15min); Lisbon (at least hourly; 3hr 30min).

INFORMATION

Tourist information The main tourist office is just north of Av dos Aliados at Rua Clube dos Fenianos 25 (daily: June–Oct 9am–8pm; Nov–May 9am–7pm; ☎ 222 393 472, ⌨ visitporto.travel). There's also a smaller office opposite the Sé at Terreiro da Sé (daily: June–Oct 9am–8pm; Nov–May 9am–7pm; ☎ 222 393 472), and an information kiosk at Avenida Diogo Leite 242 in Vila Nova da Gaia (Mon–Sat 10am–1pm & 2–6pm), which gives out the helpful Caves do Vinho do Porto leaflet, outlining timetables and prices of port lodge tours.

Tourist passes All tourist offices sell the Porto Card, which offers free public transport and free or discounted entry to most of the city's sights (1/2/3-day for €13/€20/€25). The cheaper one-day card (€5) provides the same discounts, excluding public transport.

GETTING AROUND

Tickets The blue rechargeable Andante card covers the metro, tram, the funicular from opposite the Ponte Luis I to Praça da Batalha, and most bus lines. It costs €0.60, added to the price of your first ticket, and is available at the airport, all metro stations and the main tourist office. Once purchased, it can be loaded with one-way journeys or a 24hr pass (€7, valid on all forms of transport). The card must be validated at the start of each trip (or part thereof). When using a "Z2" (zone 2) pass, for example, you can change freely between vehicles within that zone, revalidating the card each time. When you first validate the card, you are given an hour. As long as your final validation of the card falls within that hour, you will be able to continue to your final destination without paying for a new single-trip pass – so long as it is within the same zone. If you revalidate the card after the first hour is up, you will be charged for a new journey.

By metro Porto's sleek, six-line metro system (daily 6am–1am) is cheap and efficient. A single trip in the central zone costs €1.20 with an Andante card.

By bus One-way bus tickets can be purchased on board for €1.85, or €1.20 with an Andante card.

By taxi Taxis are cheap and plentiful (expect to pay around €8 for a ride across town); two useful ranks are located at Praça da Ribeira and the Rotonda da Boa Vista, near Casa da Música.

ACCOMMODATION

Well-located, good-value rooms can be found in the streets to the east and west of Av dos Aliados. There are also some bargain rooms in the slightly run-down area around Praça da Batalha, east of Estação de São Bento. In addition to guesthouses, Porto has some central, well-equipped hostels.

HOSTELS

★ **Gallery Hostel** Rua Miguel Bombarda 222 ☎ 224 964 313, ⌨ gallery-hostel.com; ⓜ Aliados/Trindade. Superb, spacious, hostel-cum-gallery in Porto's emerging artists' quarter. The house, built in 1906 and carefully restored, has its own library, bar and TV room. The helpful family running it offer free tours and trips to local galleries. Dorms **€20**, doubles **€70**

Porto Downtown Hostel Praça Guilherme Gomes Fernandes 66-1° ☎ 220 018 094, ⌨ portodowntown hostel.com; ⓜ Aliados. Friendly, spotlessly clean and central place with different-sized dorms and three double rooms. There's also an inviting lounge and a decent kitchen. Dorms **€29**, doubles **€68**

Porto Spot Hostel Rua Gonçalo Cristovao 12 ☎ 224 085 205, ⌨ spot-oportohostel.com; ⓜ Trindade. A little way out of the city, this smart and sociable hostel has key-card access, clean minimalist rooms and a garden. Dorms **€25**, doubles **€100**

Pousada de Juventude Rua Paulo da Gama 551, Pasteleira ☎ 226 177 257, ⌨ pousadasjuventude.pt; bus #504 from ⓜ Casa da Música, or #207 from São Bento. It's a bit of a way out, but Porto's main hostel has wonderful views of the Douro as it drains into the Atlantic. Dorms **€15**, doubles **€40**, apartment for four **€70**

Rivoli Cinema Hostel Rua Dr Magalhães Lemos 83 ☎ 220 174 634, ⌨ rivolicinemahostel.com; ⓜ Aliados/São Bento. Efficiently run, cinema-themed hostel which offers dorms and spacious twin rooms. There's also a roof terrace. Dorms €25, doubles €58

GUESTHOUSES

Castelo de Santa Catarina Rua de Santa Catarina 1347 ☏ 225 095 599, ⓦ castelosantacatarina.com.pt. A 30min walk from the centre or bus #701/#702/#703 from Mercado do Bolhão, this turreted folly of the most romantic kind makes a superb city retreat. The rooms aren't grand or expensive, but are furnished in period style, while breakfast is eaten in the lush *azulejo*-tiled gardens. Doubles €76

Duas Nações Praça Guilherme Gomes Fernandes 59 ☏ 222 081 616, ⓦ duasnacoes.com.pt; ⓂAliados/São Bento. A deservedly popular option, with bright, decent-sized rooms, most of which are en suite. No breakfast. Dorms €15, doubles €38

EATING

Porto's culinary speciality is the mighty *francesinha* – an acquired taste, it's a gut-busting sandwich of steak, ham and *Linguiça* sausage, covered in a layer of melted cheese and a spicy beer and tomato sauce. Restaurants in the city are good value, particularly the workers' cafés, which usually offer a set menu at lunchtime (but close around 7.30pm and at weekends). Prime areas are Rua do Almada and Rua de São Bento da Vitória. For Italian, Indian and other international cuisines, head to the riverside Cais de Gaia complex in Vila Nova de Gaia.

CAFÉS, CHEAP EATS AND SNACKS

3maisarte Largo Joaquim Magalhães 12, Vila Nova de Gaia. Perfect for a small lunchtime snack, this delightful tiny warehouse is a community organization that sells local arts and crafts, rescues cats and also serves wine and tapas. You'll pay about €7 for a selection of cheeses, meats and a glass of wine. Daily 11am–11pm.

Café Majestic Rua de Santa Catarina 112; ⓂBolhão/Aliados. Voted one of the world's most beautiful cafés, with *belle époque* mirrors and cherubs adorning its walls. Perfect for an elegant (if expensive) snack (sandwiches from €6). Mon–Sat 9.30am–midnight.

Café Piolho D'Ouro Praça de Parada Leitão 45; ⓂSão Bento. Near the university, this diner is popular with students and serves incredibly cheap food throughout the day (mains under €7), before morphing into a packed bar at night. Mon–Sat 7am–4am.

Roto do Chá Rua Miguel Bombarda 457; ⓂAliados. Choose from around 300 different brews at this chilled-out tea shop, a 15min walk from the metro station. There's a tranquil garden at the back and daily lunch specials for €7.50. Mon–Thurs 11am–8pm, Fri–Sat noon–midnight, Sun 1–8pm.

Taxca Rua Da Picaria 26; ⓂAliados. The best place in town for ham or pork sandwiches (their speciality), soups and octopus salad (dishes around €5), all served below hams

hanging above the bar. Mon–Tues noon–10.30pm, Wed–Sat noon–2am.

RESTAURANTS

Antunes Rua do Bonjardim 525; ⓂAliados. Rustic restaurant that famously cooks its daily specials in wood-fired ovens – notably melt-in-the-mouth roast pork, served with roast potatoes. Add a dessert and a carafe of house *rosado*, and you'll eat for €15. Mon–Sat noon–3pm & 7–10pm; closed four weeks in Aug/Sept.

Tasco Rua do Almanda 151A; ⓂAliados. A traditional restaurant serving meat, fish and seafood dishes such as octopus, steak and cod. Expect to pay €16 for steak, side of potatoes and glass of wine or sangria with local dessert. Daily noon–1am.

DRINKING AND NIGHTLIFE

The Ribeira area offers a fairly laidback drinking scene, while Cais de Gaia is good for sophisticated sipping. Livelier late-night bars (open until around 4am at weekends) can be found around Rua Galeria de Paris, near the university. Most of the city's big clubs are in the outlying Matosinhos district or near Foz.

BARS

★**Café Candelabro** Rua da Conceição 3; ⓂAliados. Low-key, cool bar and bookshop with bookcase-lined walls and huge glasses of quality wine for under €2. Also a popular spot for breakfast, with warm croissants. Mon–Fri 10.30am–2am, Sat 2pm–2am, Sun 2.30pm–midnight.

Café Lusitano Rua de José Falcão 137; ⓂAliados. Fun and lively bar with chandeliers dangling from the ceiling, art on the walls and a mixed gay/straight crowd. Wed–Sat 9.30pm–4am.

Está-se Bem Rua da Fonte Taurina 70–72; ⓂSão Bento. A nice little *tasca* where a pre-club crowd hangs out, probably because drinks are cheap and there's no cover charge. Mon–Sat 6pm–4am.

O Cais Bar Rua da Fonte Taurina 2; ⓂSão Bento. Relaxed bar with a clientele as varied as the soundtrack. Serves petiscos snacks, foreign beers and jugs of sangria for €9. Daily 9.30pm–3am.

O Mercado Praça do Infante Dom Henrique; ⓂSão Bento. Skip the indoor restaurant of this renovated market building in favour of the terrace bar, which overlooks Jardim do Infante Dom Henrique, and grab yourself a cool glass of port and tonic. Mon–Thurs & Sun 10.30am–midnight, Sat–Sun 2.30pm–2am.

O Meu Mercedes é Maior que o Teu Rua da Lada 30; ⓂSão Bento/Jardim do Morro. This stalwart of the Ribeira scene not only wins the Porto bar name prize ("My Mercedes is bigger than yours") but is a wonderfully atmospheric stone-walled wine cellar with regular gigs. Wed–Sat 10pm–4am.

26

26

Plano B Rua de Cândido dos Reis 30; ⓜ Jardim do Morro. A popular late-night bar with weekend DJs and a programme of live music and performance art. Tues–Wed 10pm–2am, Thurs 10pm–4am, Fri & Sat 10am–6pm.

★**Vinologia** Rua de São João 28–30; ⓜ São Bento. Innovative bar offering a huge selection of port (from €1.50/glass), with knowledgeable, friendly staff. Even an expert could learn a lot here. Daily 11am–midnight.

CLUBS

Porto's clubs are mostly outside the city centre; catch the #500 to Foz or one of the night buses from Aliados or Casa da Música if you can't afford a taxi.

Indústria Centro Comercial do Foz, Av do Brasil 835–0000; bus #500. A sophisticated dance club out in Foz do Douro, that gets packed in summer and sees Portugal's best DJs play to a cosmopolitan crowd. Thurs–Sat midnight–6am.

Maus Hábitos Rua Passos Manuel 178-4° ⓦ maushabitos.com; ⓜ Bolhão. Cultural space and bar opposite the Coliseu do Porto theatre, hosting live bands, singer-songwriters and pumping DJ sets. Check the website for listings. Also does veggie lunches until 3pm on weekdays. Bar Wed, Thurs & Sun 10am–2am, Fri–Sat 10am–4am.

Tendina dos Clérigos Rua Conde Vizela 80 ☎ 222 011 438, ⓦ tendinhadosclerigos.com; ⓜ Aliados/São Bento. One for rockers – a cave-like bar and club with pool table and dancefloor, that's also a regular venue for up-and-coming bands. Tues–Sat 1–6am.

DIRECTORY

Hospital Centro Hospitalar do Porto at Largo Prof Abel Salazar, near the university (☎ 222 077 500, ⓦ chporto .pt). In an emergency, call ☎ 112.

Left luggage At Trindade metro station (daily 6am–1am; from €1/hr).

Post office The main post office is on Praça General Humberto Delgado, by the town hall; ⓜ Aliados (Mon–Fri 8am–9pm, Sat 9am–6pm).

Tourist police Rua Clube dos Fenianos 11 ☎ 222 833 081 (daily 8am–2am).

BRAGA

BRAGA is Portugal's religious capital – and the scene of spectacular **Easter celebrations** with torchlight processions. But it's not all pomp and ceremony; it's also a lively university town, with a compact and pretty historical centre.

WHAT TO SEE AND DO

Rua Andrade Corvo leads from the train station to the centre, entered via the sixteenth-century **Arco da Porta Nova**.

The City

Just beyond the city gate lies the oldest cathedral in the country, the extraordinary **Sé** (daily: May–Sept 8am–7pm; Oct–April 8am–6.30pm; free), which dates back to 1070 and encompasses Gothic, Renaissance and Baroque styles. The most impressive areas of the Sé, the Gothic chapels – especially the *Capela dos Reis* (Kings' Chapel), built to house the tombs of Henry of Burgundy and his wife Theresa, the cathedral's founders – and the upper choir may only be visited by guided tour (same hours as cathedral; €5 for tour of museum, chapels and sacristy). Nearby on Rua dos Biscaínhos, the **Palácio dos Biscaínhos** (Tues–Sun 9.30am–12.45pm & 2–5.30pm; €2, free on first Sun of the month) is a beautiful seventeenth-century mansion housing a collection of decorative arts, paintings and sculptures. Just behind the palace lies the lovely **Jardim de Santa Bárbara**, an oasis of topiary and rose gardens. Braga's main square, the buzzing, café-lined **Praça da República**, is a short walk northwest of the garden.

Bom Jesus do Monte

Braga's real gem is **Bom Jesus do Monte**, set on a wooded hillside 3km above the city – its glorious ornamental stairway is one of Portugal's most iconic images. A monumental place of pilgrimage, Bom Jesus was created by Braga's archbishop in the early eighteenth century. The #2 bus runs from Braga's Avenida da Liberdade to Bom Jesus (2 hourly; €1.65). Save the ancient wooden funicular (€1.20) for the return journey and ascend the wide, tree-lined staircases to watch Bom Jesus's simple allegory unfold. Each landing holds a small fountain and a chapel containing rather crumbling tableau depictions of the life of Christ, leading up to the Crucifixion scene on the altar of the Neoclassical church which sits atop the staircase. Beyond the church are wooded gardens and a number of hotels and restaurants.

ARRIVAL AND INFORMATION

By train Braga's train station is almost 1km west of the centre, down Rua Andrade Corvo.

Destinations Lisbon (approx hourly; 3hr 30min–4hr 45min); Porto (at least hourly; 55min–1hr 10min).

By bus The bus station, a regional hub, is north of the centre on Av General Norton de Matos.

Destinations Coimbra (4–6 daily; 2hr–2hr 40min); Guimarães (every 30min; 25min); Lisbon (up to 12 daily; 4hr 30min); Porto (every 30min; 1hr); Vila do Gerês (for Parque Nacional da Peneda-Gerês; 5–11 daily; 1hr 30min).

Tourist information Av da Liberdade 1 (Mon–Fri 9am–1pm & 2–6.30pm, Sat 10am–1pm & 2–6pm; ☎ 253 262 550, ⓦ www.cm-braga.pt).

ACCOMMODATION

Albergaria da Sé Rua Dom Gonçalo Pereira 39–51 ☎ 253 214 502. Friendly guesthouse in a great position on a pedestrianized street a stone's throw from the cathedral. The rooms are simple and clean, in a traditional style. **€45**

Pousada de Juventude Rua de Santa Margarida 6 ☎ 253 263 279, ⓦ pousadasjuventude.pt. Fairly basic but good value, with eight- and ten-bed dorms and three en-suite doubles. Dorms **€12**, doubles **€30**

Truthostel Av da Liberdade 738 ☎ 253 609 020, ⓦ truthostel.com. A reboot of an old guesthouse, this is a cheery budget haven with rooms to suit most pockets. The best rooms overlook the flower-filled pedestrianized avenue below. Dorms **€15**, doubles **€35**

EATING AND DRINKING

A Brasileira Largo Barão de São Marinho. Bustling café in the pedestrianized centre with drinks, light meals and sandwiches (from €2) served at pavement tables. Mon–Thurs 7.30am–midnight, Fri–Sat 7.30am–2am.

Livraria Mavy Rua Diogo de Sousa 129–133. The glorious old *Cruz* bookshop, vintage 1888, has been reborn as a hip café-bar. It's a coffee-and-cake place during the day (cheap lunches too) and more of a cocktail and drinks joint at night, with the beautiful interior doubling as a *galeria* for the work of local artists. Daily 9am–2am.

Taperia Palatu Rua Dom Afonso Henriques 35–37. Cool café-bar that serves a range of Spanish-influenced dishes (€8–12), from tapas and *revueltos* (fancy scrambled eggs) to steaks and sharing platters. In spring and summer, the small patio garden comes into its own. Daily noon–2am.

GUIMARÃES

The first capital of Portugal, **GUIMARÃES** remains an atmospheric and beautiful university town. In recent years its prosperity has been helped by the fact that it was named (along with Maribor

in Slovenia) as the 2012 European Capital of Culture. The town's chief attraction is the hilltop **castle** (daily 10am–6pm, free; keep €1.50), whose square keep and seven towers are an enduring symbol of the emergent Portuguese nation. Built by the Countess of Mumadona and extended by Henry of Burgundy, it became the stronghold of his son, Afonso Henriques, Portugal's first independent king. Afonso launched the Reconquest from Guimarães, which was replaced by Coimbra as the capital city in 1143.

Other key sights include the **Paço dos Duques de Bragança** (daily 9am–6pm; €5) near the castle, a fifteenth-century palace which was perfectly restored and used as a presidential residence for Salazar, Portugal's former dictator. In the picturesque medieval centre, the pretty **Praça de Santiago** is a popular spot for an alfresco coffee by day, and comes alive again at night.

Guimarães is overlooked by the **Penha** peak (617m), which you can reach via the **Teleférico de Guimarães** (daily 10am–6.30pm; Aug open til 8pm; €2.30 return), just a five-minute walk from the edge of the old town.

ARRIVAL AND INFORMATION

By train The train station is south of town, connected to the centre by Av D. Afonso Henriques.

Destinations Braga (up to 16 daily; 1hr 20min–2hr); Porto (hourly; 50min–1hr 20min).

By bus Guimarães's bus station is a 15min walk west of town in a vast shopping centre. Follow Av Conde de Margaride to reach the town centre.

Destinations Braga (every 30min; 40min–1hr); Coimbra (3 daily; 2hr–2hr 30min); Lisbon (2 daily; 5hr); Porto (2–3 daily; 1hr–1hr 15min).

Tourist information Tourist office on Alameda de São Damaso 83 (daily 10am–10pm; ☎ 300 402 012, ⓦ guimaraesturismo.com); there's also a branch office at Praça de Santiago 37 (Mon–Fri 9.30am–6.30pm, Sat & Sun 10am–6pm; ☎ 253 421 221).

ACCOMMODATION AND EATING

Pousada de Juventude Largo da Cidade 8 ☎ 253 421 380, ⓦ pousadasjuventude.pt. Stylish, modern hostel with excellent facilities including four-bed apartments: the best-value accommodation in town. Dorms **€13**, doubles **€36**, apartments **€65**

26

Trinas Rua das Trinas 29 ☎253 517 358. Well-run guesthouse in a historic building in the heart of the old town, with clean, comfortable en-suite rooms, free wi-fi and in-room TVs. Doubles €40

EATING AND DRINKING

Casa Amarela Rua do Donães 16–24. A funky townhouse with weekend gigs and DJs upstairs in a smallish contemporary bar that opens onto a roof terrace; good food is served downstairs, from tapas to bacalhau, steak or veggie mains (tapas €4, mains €10–13). Sun–Thurs 10am–midnight, Fri & Sat 10am–2am.

Mumadona Rua Serpa Pinto 260. The cheapest food in town is the set lunch that gets you soup, a choice of main dish, drink and coffee, though it's not much pricier choosing off the menu – generous half-portions start at €5 in this bustling family-run restaurant. Mon–Sat noon–3pm & 7–10pm.

THE DOURO RAIL ROUTE

The Douro Valley, a narrow, winding gorge for the majority of its route, offers some of Portugal's most spectacular scenery. The **Douro Rail Route**, which joins the river about 60km inland (shortly after Livração) and then sticks to it across the country, is one of those journeys that needs no justification other than the trip itself.

Porto is a good place to begin a trip, though there are also regular connections along the line as far as

---

PARQUE NACIONAL DA PENEDA-GERÊS

Encompassing mountains, valleys and moors, Portugal's only national park is heaven for nature lovers, with ample opportunities for hiking, as well as more extreme sports. The main bases for exploration are the spa town of **Vila do Gerês** and **Ponte da Barca**, where the park's Regional Development Association, Adere-PG, is located. It's worth visiting them at Largo da Miséricordia 10 in Ponte da Barca (Mon–Fri 9am–12.30pm & 2.30–6pm; ⓦadere-pg.pt) for information on walking routes and accommodation, including a booking service. Vila do Gerês is easily reached by bus from Braga (5–11 daily; 1hr 30min), as is Ponte da Barca (3–8 daily; 1hr).

Peso da Régua, the depot through which all port wine must pass on its way to Porto. Beyond Régua, there are less frequent connections to **Tua** and **Pocinho**, which marks the end of the line. The trip from Porto to Pocinho takes just over three hours (€13).

Southern Portugal

The huge, sparsely populated plains of the **Alentejo**, southeast of Lisbon, are overwhelmingly agricultural, dominated by vast cork plantations. This impoverished province provides nearly half of the world's cork but only a meagre living for its rural inhabitants. Visitors to the Alentejo often head for **Évora**, the province's dominant and most historic town. But the **Alentejo coast**, the Costa Azul, is a breath of fresh air after the stifling plains of the inland landscape, and offers a low-key alternative to the busy Algarve.

With its long, sandy beaches and picturesque rocky coves, the southern coast of the **Algarve** is the most visited region in the country. West of **Faro**, the region's capital, you'll find the classic postcard images of the Algarve – a series of tiny bays and coves, broken up by rocky outcrops and fantastic grottoes, which reach their most spectacular around the resort of **Lagos**. To the east of Faro lie the less developed sandy offshore islets, **the Ilhas** – which front the coastline for some 40km – and the lower-key towns of **Olhão** and **Tavira**. In summer it's wise to book accommodation in advance, as the Algarve is a popular package-holiday destination.

ÉVORA

ÉVORA, a UNESCO World Heritage Site, is one of southern Portugal's most attractive towns and worth a day's exploration. The Romans and the Moors were in occupation for four centuries apiece, leaving their stamp in the tangle of narrow alleys that rise steeply among the whitewashed houses. Most of the monuments, however, date from the fourteenth to the sixteenth centuries, when, with royal encouragement, the city was one of the leading centres of Portuguese art and architecture.

WHAT TO SEE AND DO

The **Templo Romano** in the central square is the best-preserved Roman temple in Portugal, its remains consisting of a small platform supporting more than a dozen granite columns with a marble entablature. Next to the temple lies the church of the **Convento dos Lóios**. The convent is now a luxury *pousada*, but the church (Tues–Sun 10am–6pm; €7), dedicated to São João Evangelista, contains beautiful *azulejos* and an ossuary under the floor. Nearby, the Romanesque **cathedral** (daily 9am–5pm; Oct–May closed 12.30–2pm; cloisters and cathedral €2.50, with tower €4) was begun in 1186, about twenty years after the reconquest of Évora from the Moors. The most memorable sight in town is the **Capela dos Ossos** (daily 9am–12.30pm & 2.30–5pm; €3) in the church of **São Francisco**, just south of Praça do Giraldo. A gruesome reminder of mortality, the walls and pillars of this chilling chamber are covered with the bones of more than five thousand monks; an inscription over the door reads, *Nós ossos que aqui estamos, Pelos vossos esperamos* – "We bones here are waiting for your bones". Just below the church lies a beautiful, shady park with resident peacocks, a duck pond and a small café.

ARRIVAL AND INFORMATION

By bus Évora's bus station is 1km west of the old town.
Destinations Faro (3 daily; 4hr); Lisbon (approx hourly; 1hr 40min).
By train Trains pull in south of the old town, a 15min walk from the central Praça do Giraldo.
Destinations Lisbon (3–4 daily; 2hr 10min).
Tourist information Tourist office at Praça do Giraldo 73 (daily 9am–7pm; ☏ 266 777 071).

ACCOMMODATION

Évora's tourist appeal pushes accommodation prices above the norm. In addition to the places listed below, there are

also some attractive *turismo rural* properties in the nearby countryside; the tourist office has details.
★ **Hostel Namaste** Largo Doutor Manuel Alves Branco, 12 ☏ 266 743 014, ⓦ hostelnamasteevora.pt. Cool, breezy house in a quiet part of town with a shady courtyard, a sun terrace and big, bright dorms and en-suite doubles. There's a ten percent discount for artists, teachers and students. Dorms **€17**, doubles **€45**
Parque de Campismo Estrada de Alcáçovas ☏ 266 705 190, ⓦ orbitur.pt; bus #41 from Praça do Giraldo. This well-equipped campsite is 2km out of town on the Alcáçovas road. Per tent **€22**
Policarpo Rua Freiria de Baixo 16 ☏ 266 702 424, ⓦ pensaopolicarpo.com. Beautiful, rambling old place full of rustic charm. As well as doubles, there are also rooms sleeping three or four. Doubles **€40**
Pousada de Juventude Rua Miguel Bombarda 40 ☏ 266 706 050, ⓦ pousadasjuventude.pt. In a very grand building, this excellent youth hostel has pristine double rooms and four-bed dorms. There's a pleasant communal lounge and a roof-top terrace with great views. Dorms **€14**, doubles **€42**

EATING AND DRINKING

A Choupana Rua dos Mercadores 16–20. Pick a stool along the wooden bar or a seat in the attached restaurant, where bow-tied waiters serve, and tuck into some tasty tapas, such as the *alheira* (chicken) sausage (€8). Daily noon–1am.
O Combinado Rua de Machede 95a. Near the university, this small, popular local does very good-value dishes such as fish of the day for under €10, and a bargain tourist menu at around €12. Mon & Wed–Fri 9.30am–3pm & 7–10pm, Sat & Sun 11am–10pm.
Páteo Beco do Espinhoso, off Rua 5 de Outubro. This lovely patio café-bar, with tables and chairs beneath shady olive and lemon trees, serves soups and snacks from around €6 and hosts occasional exhibitions. May–Sept daily 11.30am–midnight; March–Oct Mon–Sat 11.30am–8pm, Sun 11.30am–2pm.

★ **TREAT YOURSELF**

The Évora Inn 11 Rua da República ☏ 266 744 500, ⓦ evorainn.com. Tucked away off Praça do Giraldo, this designer guesthouse has smart, individually styled rooms with themes such as pop, travel and revolution. All the double rooms and (slightly pricier) suites come with high-end designer furnishings by the likes of Philippe Starck, and the communal areas boast pieces by Portuguese artists. Doubles **€60**

26

THE ALENTEJO COAST

South of Lisbon, the **Alentejo coast** features towns and beaches as inviting as those of the Algarve. Some of the most attractive are the relaxed resort of **Vila Nova de Milfontes**, and the surfers' haven of **Zambujeira do Mar**. Though exposed to the winds and waves of the Atlantic and with colder waters than the Algarve, the Alentejo coast is fine for summer swimming and far quieter than its neighbouring region. Outside the summer season, the area is blissfully peaceful. **Surfing** is popular along the Alentejo coast, with Milfontes being a good spot for beginners: Surf Milfontes in Vila Nova de Milfontes (❶914 732 652, ⓦsurfmilfontes.com) gives lessons from €40.

Vila Nova de Milfontes

The attractively low-key resort of **VILA NOVA DE MILFONTES** sits on the estuary of the River Mira, whose sandy banks merge into the coastline. This is the most popular as well as one of the most beautiful resorts in the region, its streets lined with houses and hotels painted in the typical Alentejan white and blue. Adding to the charm is a handsome little castle and an ancient port, reputed to have harboured Hannibal and his Carthaginians during a storm.

Zambujeira do Mar

Southwest of Odemira, southern Alentejo's main inland town, is the tiny village of **ZAMBUJEIRA DO MAR**. Here a large cliff provides a dramatic backdrop to the beach, which is prime **surfing** territory. Quieter than Vila Nova de Milfontes, the village livens up in summer, with an annual music festival (ⓦmeosudoeste.pt) attracting international names.

ARRIVAL AND DEPARTURE

By bus Express buses from Lisbon (Rede Expressos; ⓦwww.rede-expressos.pt) take you within easy reach of the whole coastline, stopping at Vila Nova de Milfontes (3hr 30min) and Zambujeira do Mar (3hr 40min).

Destinations from Vila Nova de Milfontes Portimão (1 daily; 2hr 20min); Zambujeira do Mar (2 daily; 25min).

ACCOMMODATION

Accommodation is plentiful in both Vila Nova de Milfontes and Zambujeira do Mar, but it's wise to book ahead during the summer months.

VILA NOVA DE MILFONTES

Camping Milfontes Pousadas Novas, just north of town ❶ 283 996 104, ⓦcampingmilfontes.com. Well-equipped campsite with its own saltwater pool. There are also bungalows and two-person teepees for rent. Per person €4.40, plus per tent €5.40

Casa Amarela Rua Dom Luis Castro e Almeida ❶ 283 996 632, ⓦcasaamarelamilfontes.com. Dorm beds, attractive en-suite rooms and a guest kitchen can be found at this backpackers' favourite. Reductions for longer stays. Dorms €20, doubles €65

ZAMBUJEIRA DO MAR

Camping Zambujeira About 1km east of the cliffs ❶ 283 958 407, ⓦcampingzambujeira.com. Campsite with 2-person apartments, plus its own minimarket and pools. Camping/person €6.25, plus per tent €6, apartments €75

FARO

FARO is the capital of the Algarve, with excellent beaches within easy reach, but as regional capitals go, it's surprisingly laidback. While its suburbs may be modern, Faro retains an attractive historic centre south of the marina.

WHAT TO SEE AND DO

The **Cidade Velha**, or Old Town, is a semi-walled quarter entered through the eighteenth-century town gate, the **Arco da Vila**. Here you'll find the majestic **Sé** (Mon–Fri 10am–6.30pm, last admission 6pm, Sat 10am–1pm, last admission 12.30pm; €3), which offers superb views from its bell tower. The nearby **Museu Municipal** (April–Sept Tues–Fri 10am–7pm, Sat & Sun 11.30am–6pm; Oct–March Tues–Fri 10am–6pm, Sat & Sun 10.30am–5pm; €2) is housed in a sixteenth-century convent on Largo Dom Alfonso III; the most striking exhibit is a third-century Roman mosaic of Neptune and the four winds, unearthed near Faro train station.

Faro's most curious sight is the Baroque **Igreja do Carmo** (Mon–Fri 10am–1pm & 3–6pm, Sat 10am–1pm), near the central post office on Largo do Carmo. A door to the right of the altar leads to a macabre **Capela dos Ossos** (€1.20), its walls decorated with bones disinterred from the adjacent cemetery. The nearby **beach** (Praia de Faro) can be reached by bus from the Avenida da República stop opposite the bus station, or by boat from the harbour. Up to five boats a day also go to the more tranquil **Ilha do Farol**; the tourist information office has timetables or you can check the website of local operator Silnido (ⓦsilnido.com).

ARRIVAL AND DEPARTURE

By plane Taxis from the airport, 6km west of town, to the centre cost €12–14, or take bus #14 or #16 (every 45min, 7am–8pm; 20min; €2.25). To get to the airport, catch the bus from the stop opposite the bus station.

By train The train station is a couple of minutes' walk north beyond the central bus station, up Av da República.

Destinations Lagos (7–9 daily; 1hr 40min); Lisbon (5 daily; 3hr–3hr 30min); Olhão (up to 13 daily; 11min); Tavira (up to 13 daily; 35min).

By bus Buses use the station below the *Hotel Eva*, just north of the marina.

Destinations Évora (3 daily; 4hr); Lagos (6 daily; 2hr 10min); Lisbon (6–8 daily; 3hr 45min); Olhão (1–2 hourly; 20min); Seville, Spain (4 daily; 2–3hr); Tavira (up to 11 daily; 1hr).

INFORMATION

Tourist information The main tourist office is near the harbour at Rua da Misericórdia 8–12 (Mon–Fri 9am–6pm, Sat–Sun 9am–1pm & 2–6pm; ☎289 803 604, ⓦturismodoalgarve.pt); there's also a branch at the airport (daily 8am–11.30pm).

ACCOMMODATION

Adelaide Rua Cruz dos Mestres 7 ☎289 802 383, ⓦadelaideresidencial.net. A short walk north of the old town, this friendly guesthouse has bright, simply styled en-suite rooms with a/c, cable TV and free wi-fi. Welcoming staff. Doubles **€70**

★TREAT YOURSELF

Aeromar Av Nascente 1, Praia de Faro ☎289 817 542, ⓦaeromar.net. With its own restaurant, this simple hotel has decent doubles right opposite the beach at Praia de Faro. A five-minute bus ride from the airport, it makes a great first or last night's stay – or longer if you want to lounge on this long sand-spit beach. Doubles **€70**

★**Casa D'Alagoa** Praça Alexandre Herculano 27 ☎289 813 252, ⓦfarohostel.com. Beautifully restored, 300-year-old house converted into a sociable hostel with its own courtyard, kitchen and roof terrace. Clean dorms, solid wooden bunks with proper mattresses and lots of late-night sangria sessions. Dorms **€35**, doubles **€60**

Pousada de Juventude Rua da Polícia de Segurança Pública 1 ☎289 826 521, ⓦpousadasjuventude.pt. Basic but friendly hostel a 10min walk east of the centre; some rooms are en suite. Dorms **€14**, doubles **€42**

EATING AND DRINKING

A Venda Rua do Compromisso 60. Small local with a living-room like interior, a great place to sample *petiscos* (most €3.50–6) such as salt-cod rissoles and blood sausage. Bench-like seats outside on an attractive cobbled backstreet. Tues–Sat noon–11pm.

Adega Nova Rua Francisco Barreto 24. A good-value restaurant that seats diners on long, shared benches in a barn-like building. It's always crammed with locals, who come for tasty dishes such as grilled pork steaks (€12). Daily noon–11pm.

Columbus Lounge Bar Jardim Manuel Bivar. Close to the harbour, this fashionable bar has outdoor seats beneath the arcades of a former hospital plus a cosy lounge bar inside with a relaxed, friendly atmosphere and tangy mojitos. Daily 11am–1am.

Fim do Mundo Rua Vasco da Gama 53. This narrow restaurant serving good-value fish and grills from around €7 is a lot more cheery than its name (End of the World) suggests. Mon noon–3pm, Wed–Sun noon–midnight.

Poncha's Bar Rua do Rasquinho 26. Popular student bar with an outside terrace serving inexpensive beer, sangria and, of course, *poncha*, a punchy Madeiran cocktail made from honey, lemon and firewater. Mon–Sat 9pm–4am.

LAGOS

The seaside town of **LAGOS** is one of the Algarve's most popular destinations and attracts large numbers of visitors each summer, drawn by its beautiful beaches and lively nightlife. Lagos was also favoured by Henry the Navigator, who used it as a base for African trade.

WHAT TO SEE AND DO

On the waterfront and to the rear of the town are the remains of Lagos's once impregnable fortifications, devastated by the Great Earthquake. One rare and beautiful church which did survive was the **Igreja de Santo António**, on Rua General Alberto Silveira; decorated

26

26

around 1715, its gilt and carved interior is wildly obsessive, every centimetre filled with cherubic youths struggling with animals and fish. The church is part of – and can be visited in tandem with – the adjacent **Museu Municipal** (Tues–Sun 10am–1pm & 2–6pm; €3), housing an eclectic collection of artefacts including Roman busts and deformed animal foetuses. Across the square from here, the arcaded former **Customs House** on Praça do Infante lies on the site of Europe's first slave market, opened in 1444. It now houses a museum tracing the history of the lamentable trade (Mon–Sat 10am–12.30pm & 2–5.30pm; €3).

Lagos's main attraction, however, is its splendid array of beaches, the most secluded of which lie below extravagantly eroded cliff faces south of town. **Praia de Dona Ana** is considered the most picturesque, though its crowds make the smaller coves of **Praia do Pinhão**, down a track just opposite the fire station, and **Praia Camilo**, a little further along, more appealing. Over the river east of Lagos is a splendid sweep of sand – **Meia Praia** – where there's space even at the height of summer. Meia Praia is ideal for **watersports** enthusiasts, as various companies based here offer sailing, sea kayaking and waterskiing lessons. Those who like to keep their feet dry might prefer an excursion to the extraordinary rock formations around **Ponta da Piedade**, a headland that can be viewed by boat (from €15 for an hour, or €20 for longer trips) from the marina. Smaller boats have the advantage of gaining access to some of the smaller grottoes.

ARRIVAL AND INFORMATION

By train The train station is across the river, a 15min walk from the centre across the swing bridge to the marina.
Destinations Faro (7–9 daily; 1hr 40min); Lisbon (5 daily, change at Tunes; 4hr).
By bus The bus station is slightly closer to the town centre, just off the main Av dos Descobrimentos.
Destinations Faro (2–5 daily; 2hr 10min); Lisbon (3–8 daily; 4hr 35min); Seville, Spain (2–4 daily; 4hr 15min).
Tourist information The tourist office is inside the old town hall on Praça Gil Eanes, in the central pedestrianized zone (daily 9am–6pm; ☎282 763 031). Available from hostels, bars and restaurants around town, the *Good Times*

Guide to Lagos (🌐goodtimeslagos.com) includes a map of the local area.

ACCOMMODATION

Algarve Surf Hostel Urb Cerro das Mos Lote 55 🌐algarvesurfschool.com. Villa-style hostel a 15min walk from the centre and set around a swimming pool, with sociable areas for playing pool, drinking and barbecuing. Arranges surf trips to nearby beaches. Dorms **€29**, doubles **€80**

Campismo da Trindade Rossio da Trindade ☎282 763 893. Small, busy campsite close to the sea and just south of the town centre. To reach it, follow the main road 200m beyond the fort. Open all year. Per tent **€10**

Gold Coast Hostel Rua Gil Vicente 48 ☎916 594 225, 🌐goldcoast.lagoshostels.com. Friendly, relaxed hostel with a shared kitchen and a cool outdoor terrace. Not as party-focused as some of the other Lagos hostels. Dorms **€22**, doubles **€58**

Jah Shaka Surf Lodge Estrada da Luz-Burgau, on the outskirts of Luz, about 8km west of Lagos ☎282 764 848, 🌐jahshakasurf.com. Well-equipped villa, with a pool, TV room and volleyball court. The best dorm has sea views and a big en-suite bathroom. The owners can arrange land- and sea-based activities in the area. Call to arrange free pick-up from town or take a taxi (€15). Camping/tent **€35**, dorms **€30**, doubles **€40**

Pousada de Juventude Rua Lançarote de Freitas 50 ☎282 761 970, 🌐pousadasjuventude.pt. Busy, well-equipped hostel in a central location, with both the beach and the main after-dark watering holes within easy reach. Dorms **€17**, doubles **€45**

Rising Cock Hostel Travessa do Forno 14 ☎968 758 785, 🌐risingcock.com. Popular party hostel with a female-only dorm and free crêpes for breakfast. The facilities are a little worn, but this is still the best place for meeting other travellers. Dorms **€30**

EATING, DRINKING AND NIGHTLIFE

Key areas for restaurants and nightlife are the streets around central Praça Gil Eanes, with the cheaper options further back from the water. Avoid the restaurants around the marina, which tend to charge over the odds for very average food.

Adega da Marina Av dos Descobrimentos 35. A great barn of a place with rows of tables serving very good-value food, including huge portions of charcoal-grilled meat and fish; there's occasional live music, too. Most mains under €10. Daily noon–2am.

Bon Vivante Rua 25 Abril 105. This late-night bar/club at the top of the main pedestrianized street has drinking on three floors and a superb roof terrace – a great spot to watch the sun go down. Daily 2pm–4am.

★**Bora Café** Rua Conselheiro Joaquim Machado 17. On both sides of a narrow backstreet, serving decent tapas (around €5 a plate) among the wind chimes and cushioned benches. Mon–Sat 8.30am–8.30pm, Sun 9.30am–8.30pm.

Eddie's Bar Rua 25 de Abril 99. Friendly, intimate bar on the main drag – the loud music, TV football and good-value happy hours attract a lively expat crowd. Daily noon–2am.

Fresco Beco Senhora do Loreto. Good value glass-fronted corner café selling fresh, international dishes with a wide selection of veggie options and a three-course menu that changes daily (€8.50). Mon–Fri 9am–6pm.

The Garden Rua de Lançarote de Freitas 27. The big draw here is a large patio garden, with tables beneath shady trees. There's a bit of everything on the menu, from good cocktails, pasta and burgers (from €7) to more pricy Moroccan-influenced mains such as couscous, tagines and *kefta*. Daily 1pm–1am.

Nahnahbar Travessa do Forno 14. A good spot for dinner or drinks, with home-made burgers (around €9), salads, pasta dishes and cocktails served up by a young, international team. Daily 6–11pm; Oct–March closed Tues.

OLHÃO AND THE ISLANDS

OLHÃO, 8km east of Faro, is the largest fishing port in the Algarve and an excellent base for visiting the local sandbank islands. The narrow streets of the pedestrianized centre, close to the seafront, are pretty yet free of tourist hordes, ensuring the town retains much of its charm.

WHAT TO SEE AND DO

Although Olhão has no sights to speak of, its café-strewn centre is worth a wander, and there's one of the Algarve's best **food markets** in two buildings on the waterfront Avenida 5 de Outubro (Mon–Fri 7am–2pm, Sat 6.30am–3pm). The town's main attraction, however, is its close proximity to, and good connections with, two of the sandbank islands that comprise the **Ria Formosa Natural Park**. The islands of Armona and Culatra boast some superb, spacious beaches, so expansive that they still feel uncrowded even in the height of summer. **Ferries** to the islands run year-round, and depart regularly (up to 9 daily) from the jetty to the left of the municipal gardens. The service to **Armona** (30min; €3.70 return) drops

you off at a long strip of holiday chalets and huts that stretches right across the island on either side of the main path. On the ocean side, the beach disappears into the distance and a short walk will take you to totally deserted stretches of sand. Boats to **Culatra** (30min; €3.70 return) call first at Culatra town, a working fishing village around twenty minutes' walk from a fine ocean-facing beach. The same boat then continues to **Praia do Farol** (1hr; €4.30 return), considered to be one of the most beautiful beaches on the sandbank islands. Heading east, away from the holiday homes, the beach becomes quieter, and eventually leads to the peaceful Praia dos Hangares.

ARRIVAL AND INFORMATION

By train Olhão train station is just east of Av da República, towards the north of town.

Destinations Faro (10–13 daily; 11min); Tavira (10–13 daily; 20min).

By bus The bus station is nearby, to the west of the Avenida.

Destinations Faro (1–2 hourly; 20min); Lisbon (3–4 daily; 4hr).

Tourist information Tourist office at Largo Sebastião Martins Mestre 6a (Mon–Fri 9.30am–1pm & 2–5.30pm; ☎ 289 713 936).

ACCOMMODATION AND EATING

Bela Vista Rua Teófilo Braga 65–67 ☎ 289 702 538. A long-standing favourite, with neat and tidy en-suite rooms with a/c set round an internal courtyard: there's also a roof terrace. No breakfast. Doubles €45

★**Bicuar** Rua Vasco da Gama 5 ☎ 289 714 816, ⊛ pensionbicuar.com. Spotless guesthouse with a kitchen, roof terrace, and pleasant rooms (sleeping up to four) with shower and sink. Minimum two nights' stay in July & Aug. No breakfast. Doubles €55

Camping Olhão Pinheeiros de Marim ☎ 289 700 300. Large, upmarket, well-equipped campsite with a pool, 3km east of town, next to the Quinta da Marim nature reserve. In summer a bus runs from near the municipal garden. Per tent €8.50

Tapas e Lendas Rua Dr Manuel Ariega 18. This attractive tapas bar has seats outside and an upstairs terrace. It serves a good range of drinks and excellent tapas such as goat's cheese with honey in filo pastry, and local sausage, from around €4.50. Mon 6–10pm, Tues–Sat noon–3pm & 6–10pm.

26

26

TAVIRA

TAVIRA is a handsome little town made up of cobbled streets, and split into two pretty halves by the River Gilão. The Romans and Moors who once ruled Tavira left behind monuments that contribute to the town's appeal, though the main tourist attractions, the superb island beaches of the **Ilha de Tavira**, lie offshore. **Boats** to the island depart approximately once an hour from the quayside on Rua do Cais (June–Sept 9am–6.30pm; July–Aug 8am–7pm; Oct 10am–4.30pm, last return 30min after final departure; €2 return), with year-round boats from Quatro Águas (every 15min–1hr; 5min; €1.50 return), 2km east of town. The beach is backed by dunes and stretches west for some 11km. Despite some development – a small chalet settlement, a **campsite**, and a handful of bars and restaurants facing the sea – it's easy to find your own peaceful patch of sand.

Back in central Tavira, the small **Núcleo Islâmico** museum, on Praça da República (Tues–Sat 9am–4.30pm; €2), traces the town's Islamic heritage, with three floors of tiles and utensils from the time the town was under Moorish rule, including an earth-and-stone wall left *in situ*.

Elsewhere, it's worth wandering up to the remains of the **Moorish castle** (Mon–Fri 8am–5pm, Sat & Sun 10am–7pm; free), perched high above the town, with its walls enclosing a pretty garden that affords splendid views. Close to the castle, at Calçada da Galeria 12, a former water tower has been converted into a **camera obscura**, offering views of the town (Feb–June Mon–Fri 10am–5pm; July–Sept Mon–Fri 10am–5pm, Sat 10am–1pm; Oct–Jan Mon–Fri 10am–4pm; €4).

ARRIVAL AND INFORMATION

By train The train station is 1km southeast of the town centre, at the end of Av Doutor Mateus Teixeira de Azevedo. Destinations Faro (around 10–13 daily; 35min); Olhão (10–13 daily; 25min).

By bus Buses pull up at the terminal by the river, a 2min walk from the central square, Praça da República. Destinations Faro (7–11 daily; 1hr); Lisbon (3–4 daily; 4hr 20min).

★ TREAT YOURSELF

Aquasul Rua Dr Augusto Silva Carvalho 11 ☎ 281 325 166. Perfectly cooked international dishes, stonebaked pizzas (from €9.50) and daily specials are the order of the day at friendly *Aquasul*. Seasonal starters include beetroot carpaccio with goat's cheese and rocket followed by mains like confit of duck with red cabbage (€13–15). The setting is pretty and peaceful, with pastel-coloured tables spilling out of the restaurant onto a pedestrianized cobbled street. Tues–Sat 6.30–10.30pm.

Tourist information Praça da República 5 (Mon–Fri 9am–1pm & 2–6pm, with extended hours July & Aug; ☎ 281 322 511, ⓦ cm-tavira.pt).

ACCOMMODATION

Camping Tavira Ilha de Tavira ☎ 281 321 709. Busy campsite with a great location on the Ilha de Tavira; follow the path opposite the ferry dock to reach it. Open Easter–Sept. Per tent **€12**

Lagoas Rua Almirante Cândido dos Reis 24 ☎ 281 328 243, ✉ al.lagoas@hotmail.com. Long-established guesthouse in an old house with small rooms, some of which have en-suite facilities. There are two sun terraces, the highest of which has views across Tavira. Doubles **€55**

Pousada de Juventude Rua Miguel Bombarda 36–38 ☎ 217 326 731 101, ⓦ pousadasjuventude.pt. Pristine hostel with excellent facilities, including a relaxed communal lounge area, simple dorms and attractive private rooms (some of which have en-suite facilities). Dorms **€17**, doubles **€47**

EATING AND DRINKING

Casa Simão Rua Rua João Vaz Corte Real 10. This is where the locals go to fill up on Portuguese steaks and grills from €6–9 – it's a bustling place which gets busy early, but if you can't get a seat, *Os Arcos* next door is a good backup. Mon–Sat 11am–11pm.

Tavira Lounge Rua Gonçalo Velho 16–18. A smart riverside place that acts as a café/ice-cream parlour by day and a restaurant/tapas bar by night. Tapas from around €4. Mon–Thurs & Sun noon–2am, Fri & Sat noon–3am.

Zeca da Bica Rua Almirante Cândido dos Reis 22–24. The setting may be basic, but the food can't be faulted – fresh, tasty portions of Portuguese classics such as grilled sardines from around €8. Mon, Tues & Thurs–Sun noon–3pm & 7–10pm.

SIGHIŞOARA, TRANSYLVANIA

Romania

HIGHLIGHTS

❶ **Bucharest** Stalinist architecture, pretty residential streets, plus fabulous dining and banging nightlife. **See p.901**

❷ **Sighişoara** Beautiful medieval citadel in the heart of Transylvania, with authentic Dracula connections. **See p.910**

❸ **The Carpathians** Stunning mountain scenery under two hours from the capital. See p.910

❹ **Museum of Traditional Folk Civilization, Sibiu** A fascinating open-air museum of Romanian village architecture, set in a scenic landscape. **See p.912**

HIGHLIGHTS ARE MARKED ON THE MAP ON P.897

ROUGH COSTS

Daily budget Basic €25, occasional treat €40

Drink Beer €1.80; bottle of Romanian wine €5

Food *Tochitura moldoveneasca* (Moldavian stew) €2

Hostel/budget hotel €10/€30

Travel Bus: Bucharest–Braşov €10; train: €10

FACT FILE

Population 19 million

Language Romanian

Currency Leu (RON); plural: lei

Capital Bucharest

International phone code ☏40

Time zone GMT +2hr

Introduction

Nowhere in Eastern Europe defies preconceptions quite like Romania. It still suffers from a poor image abroad, but don't be put off – this intriguing country, dotted with picturesque towns and rural communities following traditions little changed since the Middle Ages, is easily accessible and a pleasure to explore.

Romanians trace their ancestry back to the Romans and tend to stress their Latin roots, although they have Balkan traits too. Viewing their future as firmly within the Euro-Atlantic family, they were delighted to join NATO and then, in 2007, the European Union.

The capital, **Bucharest**, is perhaps daunting for the first-time visitor – its savage recent history is only too evident, not least in the form of the Communist-era Centru Civic – but parts of this once-beautiful city have retained their appeal. More attractive by far, and easily accessible on public transport, is **Transylvania**, an ancient region offering some of the most beautiful mountain scenery in Europe as well as a uniquely multi-ethnic character. Its chief cities, such as Braşov, Sibiu and Sighişoara, were built by Saxon (German) colonists, and there are also strong Hungarian and Roma (Gypsy) presences here. In the border region of the **Banat**, also highly multi-ethnic, Timişoara is Romania's most Western-looking city and famed as the birthplace of the 1989 revolution.

CHRONOLOGY

513 BC The Dacian tribe inhabit the area of present-day Romania.

106 AD The Roman Emperor Trajan conquers the Dacian tribe.

271 Following attacks from the Goths, the Romans withdraw from the area.

1000s Hungary conquers and occupies parts of present-day Romania.

1200s Division of Romanian population into different principalities including Wallachia, Moldavia and Transylvania.

1400s Principalities of Moldavia, Transylvania and Wallachia come under attack from the Turkish Ottomans but remain independent.

1448 Vlad "the Impaler" becomes Prince of Wallachia; he is later credited as the inspiration for the character of Dracula.

1700s The Austrian Habsburgs take control of large parts of the Romanian principalities after military successes over the Ottomans.

1862 After battling for independence, Wallachia and Moldavia unite to form Romania. Bucharest is declared the capital.

1878 Romania's claim to independence is formalized by the Treaty of Berlin.

1881 Carol I is named the first King of Romania.

1918 After invasion by the central powers during World War I, Romania is freed and her borders increased.

1939–45 Romania sides with Germany at start of World War II, but changes allegiance to the Allies towards the end. Soviets take large parts of Romanian territory.

1947 Soviet influence remains and the Communist Party comes into power in Romania.

1965 Nicolae Ceauşescu becomes Communist Party leader and adopts a foreign-policy stance independent of the Soviets.

1989 Revolution leads to the overthrow of the Communist regime.

2004 Romania joins NATO.

2007 Romania joins the European Union.

2012 Following almost a decade of strong economic growth, severe recession and austerity measures trigger widespread unrest and the resignation of Prime Minister Emil Boc.

2014 Romanians are permitted to work without restriction throughout the EU.

ARRIVAL AND DEPARTURE

All flights into and out of Bucharest use Otopeni (Henri Coandă) airport, but there are half a dozen regional airports (of which Cluj-Napoca, Iaşi and Timişoara are the most important), served by a growing number of budget airlines such as Wizz Air (ⓦwizzair.com), Blue Air (ⓦblueairweb .com) and easyJet (ⓦeasyjet.com).

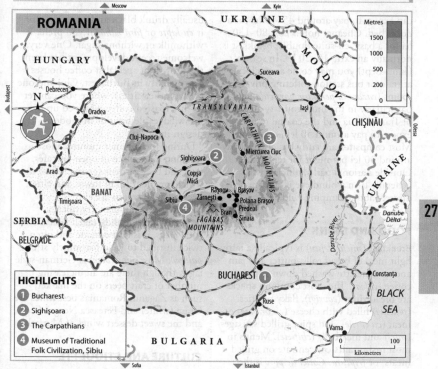

HIGHLIGHTS

1 Bucharest
2 Sighişoara
3 The Carpathians
4 Museum of Traditional Folk Civilization, Sibiu

Travelling to Romania by **train** is fairly simple via Paris, Vienna and Budapest, and there are also through trains from Istanbul, Chişinău and Sofia. This will usually cost more than flying into the country, but works well as part of a larger Europe-wide trip using a pass or point-to-point ticket options (see p.34), including **InterRail** (for European residents) and **Eurail** (for non-European residents).

GETTING AROUND

There are two types of **train**: InterRegio trains are the fastest and only call at major towns, while Regio trains stop everywhere and are generally pretty grubby and crowded. Some overnight trains have **sleeping carriages** (*vagon de dormit*) and **couchettes** (*cuşet*) for a modest surcharge. InterRegio tickets include a seat reservation. You'll also need a seat reservation for **international trains** even if you do not require one before entering Romania, so be sure to book a

seat before departure or face a fine. The best place to **buy tickets** and book seats is at the local Agenţia SNCFR (generally Mon–Fri 7.30am–7.30pm, Sat 8am–noon; ⓦcfrcalatori.ro).

The **bus** (*autobuz*) network is incredibly confusing, and there are often several bus stations in one town, so it's best to check bus times in advance at ⓦautogari.ro. **Minibuses** (*maxitaxi*) are also prevalent on many routes, and are generally faster and more frequent than buses; they do also make some surprisingly long inter-city journeys; expect to pay roughly the same as the Regio train fare.

Taxis are cheap and an attractive alternative to crowded public transport, but be sure to choose a taxi with a clearly marked company name, and check that the meter is working.

ACCOMMODATION

Most cities, and some towns, have a reasonable selection of **hostels**, and you

27

can expect to pay around 45–55 lei for a dorm bed. Cheaper **hotels** cost 80–130 lei for a basic en-suite double; breakfast is normally an extra 15–20 lei. In season (June–Sept) you may come across locals at train or bus stations offering **private rooms** (*cazare la persoane particulare*), particularly in the more touristy areas of Transylvania and the coastal resorts; expect to pay around 50 lei per person. Most **campsites** are fairly basic; you'll pay around 30 lei per night for tent space. Outside national parks, officials will generally turn a blind eye if you are discreet about camping wild.

FOOD AND DRINK

Breakfast (*micul dejun*) is typically a fairly light meal of bread rolls, butter and jam and an omelette washed down with a coffee (*cafea*). The most common **snacks** are bread rings (*covrigi*), flaky pastries (*pateuri*) filled with cheese (*cu brânză*) or meat (*cu carne*), and spicy grilled sausages (*mici*) and meatballs (*chiftele*). Menus in most **restaurants** concentrate on grilled meats, or *friptura*. *Cotlet de porc* is the common pork chop, while *mușchi de vacă* is fillet of beef.

Traditional **Romanian dishes** can be delicious. The best known of these is *sarmale* – pickled cabbage stuffed with rice, meat and herbs, usually served with sour cream – and *tochitură moldovenească*, a pork stew, with cheese, polenta (*mămăligă*) and a fried egg on top. **Vegetarians** could try asking for *cașcaval pane* (hard cheese fried in breadcrumbs), *ghiveci* (mixed fried veg), *ardei umpluții* (stuffed peppers), or vegetables and salads. **Cakes** and **desserts** are sweet and sticky, as throughout the Balkans. Romanians also enjoy pancakes (*clătite*) and pies (*plăcintă*) with various fillings.

DRINK

Most **cafés** (*cafénea* or *cofetărie*) serve the full range of beverages, from coffee (and occasionally tea) to soft drinks and beer, while many also offer cakes, pastries and ice cream. Coffee, whether *cafea naturală* (finely ground and brewed Turkish-style), *filtru* (filtered) or *nes* (instant), is

usually drunk black and sweet; ask for it *cu lapte* or *fără zahăr* if you prefer it with milk or without sugar. One very welcome recent development has been the growth of specialist coffee houses (particularly in Bucharest, Cluj and one or two other cities), where you can get freshly roasted coffee whipped up by knowledgeable baristas in modern design interiors.

During the summer months, most **drinking** takes place in open-air cafés, bars and beer gardens (*gradina de vară*), which are plentiful in towns and cities; beer cellars (*cramas*) are also tremendously popular. Try *țuică*, a powerful plum brandy taken neat; in rural areas, it is home-made and often twice distilled to yield fearsomely strong *palincă*. Most **beer** (*bere*) is German-style lager, though there are an increasing number of craft beers on the market, such as Zăganu. Romania's best **wines** are Grasa (white) and Feteasca Neagră (red), and the sweet dessert wines of Murfatlar.

CULTURE AND ETIQUETTE

Generally speaking, Romanians tend to be very open and friendly people. They will think nothing of striking up a conversation on buses and trains, even if they don't speak much English, and will try their best to communicate through any language barrier.

When speaking to older people, it is respectful to address them using either *Domnul* (Mr) or *Doamnă* (Mrs), while shaking someone's hand is the most common and familiar way of **greeting** – although bear in mind that a Romanian man may well kiss a woman's hand on introduction. The welcoming attitude of the Romanians may mean you are invited to someone's home; it is considered polite to bring a small **gift** with you, which you should also wrap.

Tipping in restaurants is not necessary, although it will be appreciated. **Smoking** is officially banned in any indoor public space, including all restaurants, cafés and bars.

Over the past decade, Romania has made good progress in its attitude

27

ROMANIA ONLINE

Ⓦ**romaniatourism.com** Official tourism site.

Ⓦ**mountainguide.ro** Hiking information and links.

Ⓦ**eco-romania.ro** Association of ecotourism operators.

Ⓦ**inyourpocket.com/romania** Irreverent, up-to-date city guides.

Ⓦ**bucharestlife.net** Regularly updated blog by long-term resident and editor-in-chief of the In Your Pocket guides.

Ⓦ**romania-insider.com** Daily news and features from Romania.

towards gay and lesbian culture; Accept (☎021 2525620, Ⓦaccept-romania.ro) is the best source of up-to-date information on the scene.

SPORTS AND ACTIVITIES

Romania's landscape is dominated by the spectacular Carpathian Mountains. A continuation of the Alps, they encircle Transylvania and provide the country with a rocky backbone perfect for activities ranging from hiking and skiing to caving and mountain biking.

The main mountain ranges, the Bucegi, the Făgăraş, the Apuseni and the Retezat, provide the best-known destinations for **hiking**. There are numerous well-marked trails allowing day-trips or longer expeditions, sleeping in a mountain refuge (*cabana*); these are usually very friendly and sociable places, and make good bases for hiking, caving or climbing. All of the trails are marked on the excellent Hartă Turistica (Ⓦharta -turistica.ro) maps, which can be found in hiking shops and bookshops in most major towns. Some *cabanas* also sell maps. Spring and summer are the best seasons to explore the mountains, and a large number of trails should only be attempted in warmer weather.

Between November and April, Romania offers some of Europe's cheapest **skiing** and **snowboarding** (Ⓦski-in-romania.com), the most popular resorts being Poiana Braşov,

near Braşov, and Sinaia; other resorts include Buşteni and Predeal – on the main road north from Bucharest – Păltiniş near Sibiu, Borşa to the north in Maramureş, and Ceahlău and Durău on the border of Moldavia. Most of the larger resorts all have a number of easy and medium pistes and at least one black run.

COMMUNICATIONS

Post offices (*poşta*) in major cities are open Monday to Friday 7am to 8pm, Saturday 8am to noon; in smaller places they may close an hour or two earlier. You can **phone** from the orange cardphones (though these are increasingly rare) or post offices. Phonecards (10 or 15 lei – get the latter for international calls) are available from post offices and news kiosks. Cheap **SIM cards** are available from Romania's three main mobile network providers (Orange, Telekom and Vodafone). **Wi-fi** is widespread and universally excellent.

EMERGENCIES

Watch out for pickpockets in crowded buses and trams and don't leave bags unattended. EU residents carrying a European Health Insurance Card are entitled to free medical treatment in Romania, but are advised to have travel insurance nonetheless, as state hospitals outside Bucharest and other large towns may not be up to Western standards. Bucharest's central emergency **hospital** is up to Western standards, while Medicover Unirii, at 64–66 Marasesti Blvd (☎021 3353940, Ⓦmedicover.ro), also offers Western-standard care, with English-speaking doctors. **Pharmacies** (*farmacie*) are open Monday to Saturday from 9am until 6pm, though most towns and cities will have one that's open 24 hours.

EMERGENCY NUMBER

In all emergencies call ☎112.

ROMANIAN

	ROMANIAN	PRONUNCIATION
Yes	*Da*	Da
No	*Nu*	Noo
Please	*Vă rog*	Ve rog
Thank you	*Mulţumesc*	Mult-sumesk
Hello/Good day	*Saluu/bunā ziuā*	Saloot/boonā zhewa
Goodbye	*La revedere*	La re-ve-dairy
Excuse me	*Permiteţi-mi*	Per-mi-tets-may
Where?	*Unde?*	Oun-day?
Good	*Bun/bine*	Boon/Bee-ne
Bad	*Rău*	Rau
Near	*Apropiat*	A-prope-reeat
Far	*Departe*	D'par-tay
Cheap	*Ieftin*	Yeftin
Expensive	*Scump*	Scoomp
Open	*Închis*	Un-keez
Closed	*Deschis*	Des-keez
Today	*Azi*	Az
Yesterday	*Ieri*	Ee-airy
Tomorrow	*Mâine*	Mwee-ne
How much is...?	*Cât costa...?*	Cuut costa...?
What time is it?	*Ce ora este?*	Che ora est?
I don't understand	*Nu înţeleg*	Noo unts-eledge
Do you speak English?	*Vorbiţi Englezeste?*	Vor-beetz eng-lay-zeste?
One	*Un, una*	Oon, oona
Two	*Doi, doua*	Doy, doo-a
Three	*Trei*	Tray
Four	*Patru*	Pat-ru
Five	*Cinci*	Chinch
Six	*Şase*	Shass-er
Seven	*Şapte*	Shap-tay
Eight	*Opt*	Opt
Nine	*Nouă*	No-ar
Ten	*Zece*	Zay-chay

INFORMATION

Tourist offices remain few and far between, but can be found in most cities and some of the bigger towns; even then, information is often limited. Opening hours are generally Monday to Friday 9am to 4pm.

MONEY AND BANKS

Romania's currency is the **leu** (plural lei, abbreviation RON), comprising coins of 1, 5, 10 and 50, and notes of 1, 5, 10, 50, 100, 200 and 500 lei. At the time of writing, exchange rates were around €1=4.40 lei, £1=5.60 lei and US$=3.90 lei. Some hotels, rental agencies and other services quote prices in euros. **ATMs**, even

in the smallest towns, are ubiquitous. **Changing money** is best done at banks, which are generally open Monday to Friday between 9am and 4pm, though there are exchange offices (*casa de schimb valuta*) all over the place, some open 24hr; neither banks nor exchange offices charge commission. Never change money on the streets. **Credit cards** are accepted in most hotels, restaurants and shops.

OPENING HOURS AND HOLIDAYS

Shop **opening hours** are Monday to Friday 9am to 6pm, Saturday 9am to 1pm, with many food shops open until 10pm (or even 24hr), including weekends. Museums and castles also open roughly 9am to 6pm, though most are closed on Mondays. Churches are generally open, with no set times. **National holidays** are: January 1 and 2, Easter Monday, May 1, December 1, December 25 and 26.

Bucharest

Arriving in **BUCHAREST** (Bucureşti), most tourists want to leave as quickly as possible; yet to do so would mean missing out on Romania's most vibrant city. The capital does have its fair share of charm and elegance – it just takes a little seeking out. Among the ruptured roads and disintegrating buildings you'll find leafy squares, beautiful, eclectic architecture (albeit often crumbling), and dressed-up young Romanians bringing a touch of glamour to the surroundings. What's more, it's a dynamic city, changing faster than any other in Romania as new office towers sprout up and shops and bars multiply.

Head south of the centre into the Centru Civic and you'll come across myriad unfinished projects from Ceauşescu's reign – seeing the true scale of what a dictatorship can set in motion is something you won't forget, and reason enough to spend a day or two in the capital.

WHAT TO SEE AND DO

The heart of the city lies to the north of the **Dâmboviţa River**, between two north–south avenues; it's a jumble of modern hotels, ancient Orthodox churches and decaying apartment blocks, relieved by the buzzing **historic quarter** and some attractive parks. Beyond lies Ceauşescu's monstrously compelling **Centru Civic**, centred on the extraordinary **Palace of Parliament**. The northern outskirts, dotted with woodlands and lakes, also boast a couple of hugely diverting museums.

Piaţa Revoluţiei

Most inner-city sights are within walking distance of Calea Victoriei, an avenue of

vivid contrasts, with vestiges of *ancien régime* elegance in among the apartment blocks, glass and steel facades, and cake shops. Fulcrum of the avenue is **Piaţa Revoluţiei**, created during the 1930s on Carol II's orders to ensure a field of fire around the Royal Palace.

On the north side of the square is the **Athénée Palace Hotel** (now a Hilton), famous for its role as an "intelligence factory" from the 1930s until the 1980s, with its bugged rooms, tapped phones and informer prostitutes. To its east are the grand **Romanian Atheneum**, the city's main concert hall, and the **University Library**, torched, allegedly by the Securitate, in the confusion of the 1989 revolution, but since rebuilt and reopened.

To the southeast of the square is the former Communist Party HQ, now the **Senate**, where Nicolae Ceauşescu made his last speech from a low balcony on December 21. His speech drowned out by booing, the dictator's disbelief was broadcast to the nation just before the TV screens went blank. He and his wife Elena fled by helicopter from the roof, but were captured and executed on Christmas Day.

The Royal Palace

The **Royal Palace**, on the western side of Piaţa Revoluţiei, now contains the excellent **National Art Museum** (Wed–Sun: May–Sept 11am–7pm; Oct–April 10am–6pm; 15 lei; ⓦmnar.arts.ro), the highlight of which are marvellous collections of medieval and modern Romanian art, the former holding a superb assemblage of icons and fresco fragments, the latter featuring the country's most revered painter, Grigorescu, and the great modern Romanian sculptor Brâncuşi.

The Creţulescu Church and Cişmigiu Park

Standing opposite the Senate, the eighteenth-century **Creţulescu Church** is the city's most celebrated historic building. Badly damaged during the 1989 fighting, but now handsomely restored, it fronts a tangle of streets

27

27

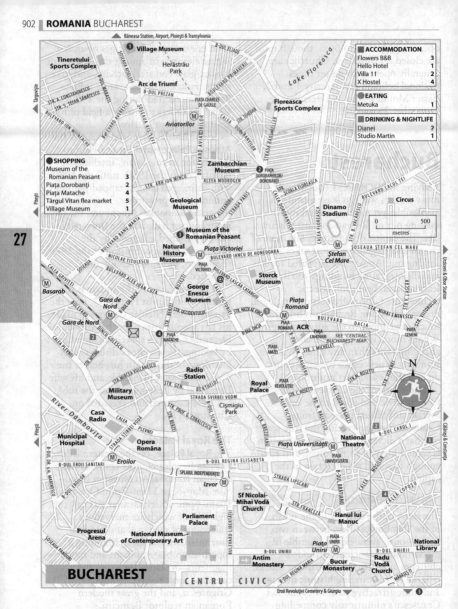

Băneasa Station, Airport, Ploieşti & Transylvania

0 Village Museum

Tineretului
Sports Complex

Herăstrău
Park

Arc de Triumf

B-DUL ELIADE

BULEVARDUL PRIMĂVERII

PIAŢA CHARLES
DE GAULLE

B-DUL PREZAN

Lake Floreasca

Floreasca
Sports Complex

■ ACCOMMODATION
Flowers B&B   3
Hello Hotel   1
Villa 11   2
X Hostel   4

● EATING
Metuka   1

■ DRINKING & NIGHTLIFE
Dianei   2
Studio Martin   1

Aviatorilor

Zambacchian
Museum

2 PIAŢA
DOROBANŢILOR/
DOROBANŢI

● SHOPPING
Museum of the
Romanian Peasant   3
Piaţa Dorobanţi   2
Piaţa Matache   4
Târgul Vitan flea market 5
Village Museum   1

Geological
Museum

Museum of the
Romanian Peasant **3**

Natural
History
Museum

Piaţa Victoriei

BULEVARD IANCU DE HUNEDOARA

PIAŢA
VICTORIEI

George
Enescu
Museum

BULEVARD LASCĂR CATARGIU

Storck
Museum

Dinamo
Stadium

Circus

0   500
metres

Ştefan
Cel Mare

ŞOSEAUA ŞTEFAN CEL MARE

Piaţa
Romană

Basarab

Gara de
Nord

Gara de Nord

PIAŢA
MATACHE

Piaţa
Romană   ACR

BULEVARD   DACIA

PIAŢA
LAHOVARI

SEE "CENTRAL
BUCHAREST" MAP

PIAŢA
GEMENI

Radio
Station

Military
Museum

Casa
Radio

River Dâmboviţa

Municipal
Hospital

Opera
Română

Eroilor

Royal
Palace

Cişmigiu
Park

PIAŢA
REVOLUŢIEI

National
Theatre

PIAŢA
UNIVERSITĂŢII

Piaţa Universităţii

B-DUL REGINA ELISABETA

STRADA LIPSCANI

SPLAIUL INDEPENDENŢEI

Izvor

Sf Nicolai-
Mihai Vodă
Church

B-DUL CAROL I

Hanul lui
Manuc

Parliament
Palace

National Museum
of Contemporary Art

Progresul
Arena

BULEVARD LIBERTĂŢII

PIAŢA
UNIRII

Piaţa
Unirii

Antim
Monastery

Bucur
Monastery

Radu
Vodă
Church

National
Library

BUCHAREST

CENTRU   CIVIC

Eroii Revoluţiei Cemetery & Giurgiu

wending west towards **Cişmigiu Park**, Bucharest's oldest, containing a boating lake, playgrounds, summer terrace cafés and chess players.

The Military Museum

West of Cişmigiu Park, near the Gara de Nord station, the **Military Museum** (Tues–Sun 9am–5pm; 8 lei) has a fine

display on the army's role during the 1989 revolution. Among the most moving exhibits are the personal belongings of both civilians and soldiers, including the blood-splattered uniform worn by the then Minister of Defence, General Vasile Milea, the manner of whose death is not entirely clear (some say that he was executed, others that he committed suicide) following his refusal to carry out orders to shoot civilians.

The historic centre

The regeneration of Bucharest's **historic centre**, known locally as Lipscani after the street of the same name, at the southern end of B-dul Brătianu, is ongoing, but in any case it's now the focal point for the city's best nightlife, with a massive influx of bars, cafés and restaurants. Just southwest of Strada Lipscani stands the diminutive **Stavropoleos Church**; built in the 1720s, it has gorgeous, almost arabesque, patterns decorating its facade, and an elegant columned portico.

The Centru Civic

The infamous **Centru Civic** was Ceaușescu's pet urban project. After an earthquake in 1977 damaged much of the city, Ceaușescu took the opportunity to remodel the entire southern portion of central Bucharest as a monument to Communism. By the early 1980s bulldozers had moved in to clear the way for the Victory of Socialism Boulevard (now Bulevardul Unirii), taking with them thousands of architecturally significant houses, churches and monuments. Now colossal apartment blocks line Bulevardul Unirii, at 4km long and 120m wide slightly larger – intentionally so – than the Champs-Élysées on which it was modelled.

Parliament Palace

Dominating the entire project is the **Parliament Palace** (Palatul Parlamentului) – also known as Casa Nebunului ("Madman's House") – supposedly the second-largest administration building in the world. Started in 1984 – though still not complete by the time of Ceaușescu's death – the building contains 1100 rooms, 4500 chandeliers and a nuclear shelter, and now houses the Romanian Parliament. Guided tours in English (daily 10am–4pm, last tour 3.30pm; 25 lei, plus 30 lei for the use of cameras; ⓦcic.cdep.ro) usually take in about ten

rooms, the most dazzling of which is the magnificent Sala Unirii (Unification Hall); the entrance is to the right of the building as you face it. You must bring your passport to gain entry.

Piața Universității

You're bound to pass through busy **Piața Universității**, overshadowed by the *Hotel Intercontinental* on B-dul Carol I. This is where students pitched their post-revolution City of Peace encampment, which was violently overrun, together with the illusion of true democracy, by the miners called in by President Iliescu to "restore order" in June 1990. The miners returned to Bucharest in 1991, this time in protest against the government rather than to protect it.

Museum of the Romanian Peasant

Stretching north from Piața Victoriei, Șoseaua Kiseleff leads into the more pleasant, leafy suburbs. At no. 3, the **Museum of the Romanian Peasant** (Muzeul Țăranului Român; Tues–Sun 10am–6pm; 8 lei; ⓦmuzeultaranuluiroman.ro) is a must-see, giving an insight into the country's varied rural traditions, with exhibits on everything from costume and textiles to painted glass icons; there are also several superbly reconstructed buildings, including an eighteenth-century windmill and a timber church. In the basement there's a fascinatingly curious exhibition of Communist iconography, while to the rear of the museum there's an excellent souvenir shop and café.

Herăstrău Park and the Village Museum

North of the centre, traffic heading for the airports and Transylvania swings around a familiar-looking Arc de Triumf, commemorating Romania's participation on the side of the Allied victors in World War I. To the right, in **Herăstrău Park** (the city's largest), is the **Village Museum** (Muzeul Satului; daily 9am–5pm; 10 lei; ⓦmuzeul-satului.ro), a fabulous ensemble of wooden houses, churches, windmills and other structures from various regions of the country.

27

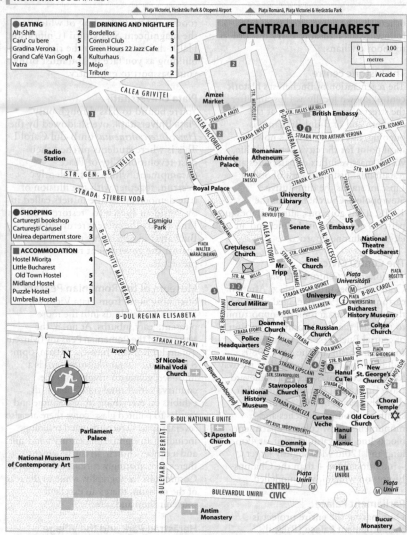

EATING
Alt-Shift ... 2
Caru' cu bere ... 5
Gradina Verona ... 1
Grand Café Van Gogh ... 4
Vatra ... 3

DRINKING AND NIGHTLIFE
Bordellos ... 6
Control Club ... 3
Green Hours 22 Jazz Cafe ... 1
Kulturhaus ... 4
Mojo ... 5
Tribute ... 2

SHOPPING
Cartureşti bookshop ... 1
Cartureşti Carusel ... 2
Unirea department store ... 3

ACCOMMODATION
Hostel Miorita ... 4
Little Bucharest
  Old Town Hostel ... 5
Midland Hostel ... 2
Puzzle Hostel ... 3
Umbrella Hostel ... 1

ARRIVAL AND DEPARTURE

By plane Otopeni (Henri Coandă) airport (☎021 204 1000, ⊚ bucharestairports.ro) is 17km north of the centre. Express bus #783 (24hr; daily every 15–20min, every 40min through the night; 8 lei, return ticket only) departs from under the international arrivals hall and goes to Piaţa Unirii via Piaţa Romană and Piaţa Universităţii. Express bus #780 (daily every 30min; same price) heads directly to the Gara de Nord. Ignore all offers of a taxi within the terminal and book one via one of the touch screens in the main arrivals hall; it costs around 50 lei to the city centre.

By train Virtually all trains terminate at the Gara de Nord, from where it's a 30min walk into the centre, or a short ride on the metro (take line M1 to Piaţa Victoriei then change for line M2 to reach Piaţa Universităţii or Piaţa Unirii).

Destinations Braşov (every 60–90min; 2hr 30min–3hr 45min); Sibiu (3 daily; 5hr 40min); Sighişoara (4 daily; 5hr 15min); Timişoara (5 daily; 9hr).

By bus Bucharest doesn't have a central bus station, but Filaret, on Piaţa Filaret to the south of the city, is where many buses depart from. Otherwise, there are several maxitaxi stations around Gara de Nord. Your best bet is to check ⊚ autogari.ro, which lists daily schedules along with the relevant departure and arrival points.

Destinations Braşov (every 30–45min; 2hr 45min); Sibiu (hourly; 5hr); Sighişoara (8 daily; 5hr 30min); Timişoara (3 daily; 11hr 30min).

INFORMATION AND TOURS

Tourist information The official tourist office is in the Piaţa Universităţii underpass at Universitate metro station (Mon–Fri 9am–6pm, Sat 9am–1pm; ☎ 021 305 5500).

Tour agencies For information you're much better off going to the privately run Mr Tripp at Calea Victoriei 68–70 (Mon–Sat 10am–8pm, Sun 10am–5pm; ☎ 021 211 2266, ⓦ mrtripp.ro), which also runs the city's best tours. In any case, try and get hold of the excellent English-language listings magazine *Bucharest in Your Pocket*.

GETTING AROUND

Public transport Although chaotic and crowded, public transport is very cheap. The most useful lines of the metro system are the M2 (north–south) and M3 (a near-circle). Tickets for two journeys cost 5 lei, and for ten rides cost 20 lei (a daily ticket costs 8 lei). For travel on buses, trams and trolleybuses (which run around 5am–11.30pm; night buses run thereafter), you will need to purchase an Activ Card, which costs 3.70 lei and can be bought from kiosks at major stops. The cards can be charged with credit that is debited every time you swipe them over the orange terminals (1.30 lei for a single journey); a day pass costs 10 lei.

By taxi Fares are cheap, at about 1.70 lei/km; the most reputable companies are Cristaxi (☎ 021 9461), Cobalcescu (☎ 021 9451) or Meridian (☎ 021 9444) – make sure the meter is running.

ACCOMMODATION

Bucharest is jammed with great hostels, most of which offer private rooms as well as dorm beds, and there's also a reasonable choice of affordable hotels, mostly around the Gara de Nord.

HOSTELS

Little Bucharest Old Town Hostel Str Smârdan 15 ☎ 0786 055 287, ⓦ littlebucharest.ro; map p.904. A busy, cheerful hostel in a plum location among the bars, clubs and restaurants of the Old Town, with six-, eight- and twelve-bed dorms, plus comfy doubles. Good-sized kitchen too. Dorms €10, doubles €35

Midland Hostel Str Biserica Amzei 22 ☎ 021 314 5323, ⓦ themidlandhostel.com; map p.904. This modern hostel has a great central location, with three large dorms sleeping four, eight and twelve, and shared bathrooms; breakfast is included. Laundry is extra. Dorms €9

Puzzle Hostel Str Luigi Cazzavillan 44 ☎ 0733 128 887, ⓦ puzzlehostel.ro; map p.904. A 10min walk from Gara de Nord, this place is a mixture of very smart dorms and private

rooms within an attractive old house. Dorms €9, doubles €28

★ **Umbrella Hostel** Str General Christian Tell 21 ☎ 021 212 5051, ⓦ umbrellahostel.com; map p.904. A fine old building with a range of rooms, from doubles to eight-bed dorms, incorporating handcrafted wooden furnishings and coffee tables; the lovely yard is perfect for a sundowner. Dorms €10, doubles €30

Villa 11 Str Institutul Medico-Militar 11 ☎ 0722 495 900, ⓦ vila11.hostel.com; map p.902. Friendly, family-run hostel just a 5min walk from Gara de Nord, with two-, three-, four- and six-bed rooms, some with bathroom. Price includes a pancake breakfast. Laundry and bike rental available. Dorms €11, doubles €26

X Hostel Str Balcesti 9 ☎ 021 367 4912, ⓦ xhostel.com; map p.902. Its party hostel reputation is well deserved, so don't come here in search of a good night's sleep. In its favour are modern facilities and a central location close to Piaţa Unirii metro station. Dorms €11, doubles €45

HOTELS

Flowers B&B Str Plantelor 2 ☎ 021 311 9848, ⓦ flowersbb .ro; map p.902. First-rate and very hospitable bed and breakfast, with elegant en-suite rooms and a lovely summer terrace. Take bus #65 or #85 to B-dul Carol I, from where it's a 5min walk. Breakfast included. Doubles €45

★ **Hello Hotel** Calea Grivitei 43 ☎ 0372 121 800, ⓦ hellohotels.ro; map p.902. A 2min walk from the train station, this large, modern hotel has colourful, good-sized rooms with wall-mounted TVs. Breakfast costs 25 lei. Doubles €38

Hostel Miorita Str Lipscani 12 ☎ 021 312 0361, ⓦ hostel -miorita.ro; map p.904. A hotel rather than a hostel, the comfortable *Miorita* has a great central location, with six spacious en-suite rooms incorporating flat-screen TVs and small fridges. Breakfast included. Doubles €42

EATING

Bucharest's thriving restaurant scene has a wide selection of ethnic cuisines to choose from, as well as traditional Romanian food. Look out for restaurants offering daily set menus; these two- or three-course meals are typically available weekdays between noon and 5pm and cost around 20–25 lei.

Alt-Shift Str Constantin Mille 4 ⓦ altshift.ro; map p.904. Cool, industrial-chic restaurant offering delicious fresh pasta made on the premises (red pesto tagliatelle with prosciutto, 25 lei); the restaurant's long hours make it a perfect spot for post-drinking munchies. Sun–Thurs noon–2am, Fri & Sat noon–6am.

★ **Caru' cu bere** Str Stavropoleos 5 ⓦ carucubere.ro; map p.904. Superb restaurant housed in a spectacular nineteenth-century beer-house replete with carved wooden balconies, stained-glass windows and uniformed waiting staff. The menu features a broad range of

27

Romanian dishes (15–50 lei), and beer is still brewed on the premises. Daily 8am–midnight.

Gradina Verona Str Pictor Arthur Verona 13–15; map p.904. Located to the rear of the Cărtureşti bookshop, this laidback café is one of the city's best and is a great place to relax with a coffee or glass of wine and a good read. Daily 9am–midnight.

Grand Café Van Gogh Str Smârdan 9 @ vangogh.ro; map p.904. Effortlessly cool Old Town café with a smart orange-tinted interior, smooth wooden tables and big bay windows, not to mention a fabulous terrace. Excellent drinks menu as well as breakfasts (10 lei), toasted sandwiches (9 lei) and platters (28 lei). Daily 8.30am–midnight.

Metuka Bul. Lascar Catargiu 7 @ metuka.ro; map p.902. Warm, colourful restaurant offering simple, freshly prepared dishes like chicken with lemon and sour cream (25 lei); helpful, cheery staff to boot. Mon–Sat 11am–9am.

Vatra Str Brezoianu 23 @ vatra.ro; map p.904. Very central, very affordable, with simple but tasty Romanian dishes such as *ciorba* (soup; 10 lei) and *mici* (spicy grilled sausages; 12 lei). Daily noon–midnight.

DRINKING AND NIGHTLIFE

Busy all year round, Bucharest's historic quarter is awash with bars, pubs and clubs, while in summer, the clubs and restaurants around Herăstrău lake are also extremely popular. For more detailed information on the city's nightlife check out the free local listings guide *Sapte Seri* (@ sapteseri.ro) or *Bucharest in Your Pocket* (@ inyourpocket.com/bucharest).

Bordellos Str Şelari 9–11 @ bordello.ros; map p.904. One of the more appealing Old Town hangouts, this vibrant pub has good draught beers, great tapas and big screens for all your sporting kicks. Daily noon–3am.

★ **Control Club** Str Constantin Mille 4 @ control-club.ro; map p.904. Marketed as "the club for people who don't like clubs", this pub transforms into a frenetic venue where anything goes, with live music and local DJs playing out on the fabulous vine-covered terrace. Daily noon–6am.

Dianei Str Dianei 4 @ dianei4.translucid.ro; map p.902. Vaguely hipster joint serving some of the best craft beers and wines in the city, but which is also known for its evenings of music, theatre and comedy; terrific weekend brunches too. Daily 10am–2am.

Green Hours 22 Jazz Cafe Calea Victoriei 120 @ greenhours.ro; map p.904. Cramped cellar-bar with frequent live music and arty theatre shows that attract a lively alternative crowd. In summer, the action moves outdoors to the leafy courtyard. Daily 9am–1am.

Kulturhaus Str Sf. Vineri 4 @ kulturhaus.ro; map p.904. Slightly left-field but massively popular club, with tunes to suit many tastes including folk rock, new wave, punk and indie; there's usually a live band once a week. Thurs–Sat 11pm–6am.

Mojo Str Gabroveni 14 @ mojomusic.ro; map p.904. Cracking Old Town venue offering three floors of fun: the basement "Brit Room" for gigs (by both the resident house band and visiting groups); a ground-floor bar; and a top-floor acoustic room for karaoke, comedy and the like. Daily 1pm–5am.

Studio Martin B-dul Iancu de Hunedoara 61, near Piața Victoriei @ studiomartin.ro; map p.902. For serious clubbers, this place attracts ravers with its international guest DJs (playing techno and house) and gay-friendly atmosphere. Fri & Sat 11pm–5am.

Tribute Calea Victoriei 118 @ tribute.ro; map p.904. Arguably the city's most dynamic live music venue, there's a stellar programme of guest acts, as well as performances by the resident house band. Thurs–Sat 10am–5am.

SHOPPING

Cartureşti bookshop Str Pictor Arthur Verona 13; map p.904. Superb for English-language books (including Romanian history and literature) and all kinds of music; great café out back too. Daily 10am–10pm.

Cartureşti Carusel Str Lipscani 55; map p.904. Stunningly renovated, this is first and foremost a bookshop, but also offers up souvenirs, a gallery and café. Daily 10am–midnight.

Museum of the Romanian Peasant and **Village Museum**; map p.902. These museum shops are by far the best place in the city to find authentic peasant handiwork, including ceramics, textiles and clothing. Tues–Sun 10am–6pm.

Piața Dorobanți and **Piața Matache**; map p.902. The best of the city's daily food markets, the latter great for stocking up on goodies ahead of a long train journey from the nearby Gara de Nord. Both 6am–2pm.

Târgul Vitan flea market Calea Vitan; Dristor I metro; map p.902. The city's largest flea market is chaotic yet fascinating. Sun 8am–4pm.

Unirea department store Piața Unirii 1; map p.904. Built during the communist era, this enormous central shopping centre is a good place to find familiar labels. Daily 10am–10pm.

DIRECTORY

Embassies and consulates Australia, Str Praga 3 @ 021 2062200; Canada, Str Tuberozelor 1–3 @ 021 307 5000; Ireland, Str Buzesti 50–52 @ 021 310 2131; UK, Str J. Michelet 24 @ 021 201 7200; US, B-dul Liviu Librescu 4–5 @ 021 200 3300.

Hospitals Spitalul Clinic de Urgenţa, Calea Floreasca 8 @ 021 599 2300; Medicover Unirii, 64–66 B-dul Marasesti @ 021 310 1599, @ medicover.ro.

Left luggage *Bagaj de mână* (8 lei; 24hr) at the Gara de Nord, on the concourse opposite platforms 4 and 5.

Pharmacies Sensiblu has branches throughout the city,

including 24hr pharmacies at Str B-dul Bălcescu 7 and Radu Beller 6. Helpnet has a 24hr pharmacy at B-dul Ion Mihalache 92.

Police B-dul Lascăr Catargiu 22 ☎ 021 212 5684.

Post office Str M. Millo 10 (Mon–Fri 8am–7pm) and inside the Gara de Nord (Mon–Fri 8am–9.30pm, Sat & Sun 8am–1pm).

Transylvania

From Bucharest, trains carve their way north through the spectacular Carpathian mountain range into the heart of **Transylvania**. Thanks to centuries of migration and colonization, the region's population is a mix of Romanians, Magyars, Germans, Roma and others. The 1920 Trianon Treaty placed the region within the Romanian state, but the character of many towns still reflects those past patterns of settlement, even if only through architecture. With their defensive towers and fortified churches, the most striking of them are the former seats of Saxon power. Indeed, **Sighişoara** (the most picturesque of the lot) could be the Saxons' cenotaph: their houses and churches remain, yet the living culture has evaporated, as it threatens to do in **Braşov** and **Sibiu**.

The Carpathians, meanwhile, offer Europe's cheapest skiing in winter and wonderful hiking during the summer, along with caves, alpine meadows, dense forests sheltering bears, and lowland valleys with quaint villages.

BRAŞOV

With an eye for trade and invasion routes, the medieval Saxons sited their largest settlements near Transylvania's mountain passes. **BRAŞOV**, which they called Kronstadt, grew prosperous as a result, and Saxon dominance lasted until the Communist government brought thousands of Moldavian villagers to work in the new factories. As a result, there are two parts to Braşov: the Gothic and Baroque centre beneath Mount Tâmpa, which looks great, and the surrounding sprawl of flats, which doesn't. The central square, surrounded by restored merchants' houses, is now the heart of a buzzing city with a raft of exciting bars and restaurants.

WHAT TO SEE AND DO

Buses from the station will leave you near the central square, **Piaţa Sfatului**. Leading northeast from the square, the pedestrianized **Strada Republicii** is the hub of Braşov's social and commercial life.

Piaţa Sfatului

Piaţa Sfatului is overshadowed by the Gothic pinnacles of the city's most famous landmark, the **Black Church** (Tues–Sat 10am–7pm, Sun noon–7pm; 6 lei), which stab upwards like a series of daggers. An endearingly monstrous hall-church that took almost a century to complete (1383–1477), it is so-called for its soot-blackened walls, the result of being torched by the Austrian army in 1689. Inside, by contrast, the church is startlingly white, with oriental carpets

27

THE FORTIFIED CHURCHES OF TRANSYLVANIA

Transylvania's Saxon legacy is clearly apparent in the fortified churches erected throughout the region's villages following the migration of the Saxons to Romania, invited by Hungary's King Géza II in 1150. The **Transilvania Card** (50 lei/€11; ⓦ transilvania-card.ro) gives access to fifty Saxon churches across southern Transylvania, which can be obtained from the main churches in Braşov, Sighişoara and Sibiu or from the Foundation for Fortified Churches in Sibiu (Str Gen. Magheru 4; ☎ 0269 221010, ⓦ fortified-churches.org). The Mioritcs Association (Piaţa Muzeului 6, Sighişoara; April–Oct Tues–Sun 10am–6pm; ☎ 0788 115511, ✉ sighisoara@mioritics.ro) is also dedicated to preserving the fortified churches and developing tourism around them. A few (on UNESCO's World Heritage List) attract a lot of tourists, but there are many less well-known ones. Most are accessible with their original gate-key, which is usually kept by one of the elder villagers for safekeeping. Simply ask in the village for the key-holder, who should be able to open up the church and show you around. It is normal to pay them a small amount (about 5 lei) for their trouble.

creating splashes of colour along the walls of the nave. In summer (June & Sept Tues; July & Aug Tues, Thurs & Sat at 6pm), the church's 4000-pipe organ is used for concerts.

The fifteenth-century council house (Casa Sfatului) in the centre of Piaţa Sfatului now houses the **History Museum** (Tues–Sun 10am–6pm; 10 lei), which has a small exhibition dedicated to the Saxon guilds that dominated Braşov in medieval times.

Museum of Urban Civilization

On the south side of the square, the new Museum of Urban Civilization, Piaţa Sfatului 15 (Tues–Sun: May–Sept 10am–6pm; Oct–April 9am–5pm; 7 lei; ⓦmcubrasov.ro), occupies a merchant's house that's typical of the Transylvanian Renaissance style, with beautifully

restored sixteenth- and eighteenth-century murals. Exhibits focusing on the city's trading past include re-creations of shops with painted chests, gingerbread moulds, guns and swords, a home interior and costumes, embroidery and millinery (including rabbit-fur felt).

Mount Tâmpa

A length of fortress wall runs along the foot of **Mount Tâmpa**, behind which a **cable car** (Tues–Sun 9.30am–5.30pm; 10 lei one-way/16 lei return) whisks tourists to the summit. However, the trails up offer a challenging walk (1hr) and some fantastic views.

Museum of the Bârsa Land Fortifications

Of the original seven bastions (towers maintained by the city's trade guilds), the

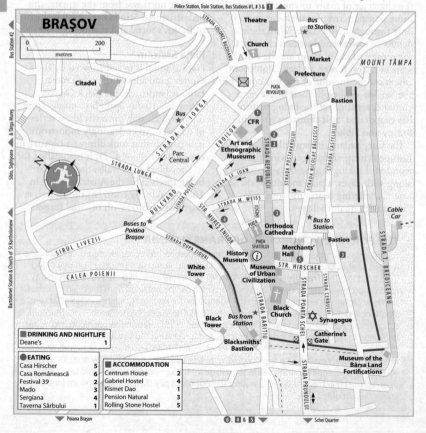

DRINKING AND NIGHTLIFE
Deane's 1

EATING
Casa Hirscher 5
Casa Românească 6
Festival 39 2
Mado 3
Sergiana 4
Taverna Sârbului 1

ACCOMMODATION
Centrum House 2
Gabriel Hostel 4
Kismet Dao 1
Pension Natural 3
Rolling Stone Hostel 5

best preserved is that of the weavers, on Strada Coşbuc. This complex of wooden galleries and bolt holes now contains the **Museum of the Bârsa Land Fortifications** (Tues–Sun 10am–5.30pm; 7 lei). Inside are models and weaponry recalling the bad old days when the region was repeatedly attacked by Tatars, Turks, and by Vlad the Impaler, who left hundreds of captives on sharp stakes to terrorize the townsfolk. The Saxons' widely publicized stories of Vlad's cruelty unwittingly contributed to Transylvania's dark image and eventually caught Bram Stoker's attention as he conceived *Dracula*.

ARRIVAL AND DEPARTURE

By train Braşov's train station is northeast of the old town, 2km from the centre – take bus #4 into town or spend around 8 lei on a taxi.

Destinations Bucharest (hourly; 2hr 45min); Sibiu (6 daily; 2hr 30min); Sighişoara (12 daily; 2hr 15min); Timişoara (1 daily; 10hr).

By bus Buses arrive and depart from either Autogara 1 next to the train station, or Autogari 2, a 5min walk east of the train station opposite the football stadium.

Destinations From Autogari 1: Bucharest (hourly; 3hr 30min); Sibiu (6 daily; 2–3hr); Sighişoara (8 daily; 2hr). From Autogari 2: Bran (Mon–Fri every 30min, Sat & Sun hourly; 45min); Timişoara (2 daily; 9hr 30min); Zărneşti (Mon–Fri hourly, Sat 8 daily, Sun 2 daily; 1hr).

INFORMATION AND TOURS

Tourist office In the History Museum, Piaţa Sfatului 30 (daily 9am–5pm; ☎0268 419 078, ⊚ brasov.ro).

Tours Active Travel at Str Toamnei 2 (☎0268 321515, ⊚ activetravel.ro) is a well-established agency that runs hiking, biking, rafting and skiing trips throughout the region as well as tours of Braşov and day-trips to Bran castle; you can also rent bikes here.

ACCOMMODATION

Centrum House Str. Republicii 58 ☎0727 793 169, ⊚ hostelbrasov.eu. Ridiculously central, this new hostel above a couple of noisy bars (bring earplugs) has a good choice of dorms and private rooms plus a kitchen. Dorms €10, triples €30

Gabriel Hostel Str Vasile Saftu 41a ☎0744 844 223, ⊚ brasovtrips.com. In the historic Schei district (bus #51), this quiet, pleasant place has small dorms with segregated male and female bathrooms and a kitchen. Dorms €10, doubles €14

Kismet Dao Str Neagoe Basarab 8 ☎0268 514 296, ⊚ kismetdao.com. Busy, popular hostel just 5min from the

centre, with decent dorms and private rooms, and a large kitchen. Dorms €10, doubles €27

★**Pension Natural** Str Castelului 58 ☎0744 321273, ⊚ pensiuneanatural.ro. Immaculate little family-run hotel with a tranquil garden beside the city walls. Doubles 220 lei

Rolling Stone Hostel Str Piatra Mare 2a ☎0268 513 965, ⊚ rollingstone.ro. Friendly, sociable hostel with clean, attractive dorms, private rooms and immaculate bathrooms. Pleasant garden terrace with pool and basement bar. Dorms €10, doubles €27

EATING

Casa Hirscher Piaţa Sfatului 12–14 ⊚ casahirscher.ro. This lovely restaurant, in an atmospheric seventeenth-century building, serves quality Romanian and international specialities. Mains 20–50 lei. Daily 9am–midnight.

Casa Românească Piaţa Unirii 15 ⊚ restaurant -casaromaneasca.ro. Friendly and cheap restaurant convenient for the hostels, with a courtyard offering views of the *piaţa*. Traditional Romanian cuisine, and good-sized portions. Mains 15–40 lei. Daily 11am–midnight.

Festival 39 Str Republicii 62 ⊚ festival39.com. This beautiful Art Nouveau bistro is always lively, with particularly good desserts (try the *tort de lămâia* or lemon tartlets), a long cocktail list and live jazz twice a week. Daily 7am–midnight.

Mado Str Republicii 10 ⊚ madobrasov.ro. Popular restaurant with outdoor seating and a spacious interior. The dishes include traditional Romanian and Turkish specialities; you can also try some Romanian wines, such as *vin fiert*, the hearty and spicy hot tipple favoured in rural Transylvania during winter. Home-made cakes too. Mains 15–35 lei. Daily 10am–midnight.

Sergiana Str Mureşenilor 28 ⊚ sergianagrup.ro. Serves wholesome and tasty Transylvanian food in its warren of atmospheric cellars. Mains 15–30 lei. Daily 11am–1am.

Taverna Sârbului Str Republicii 55. Capacious brick-cellar restaurant dishing up gut-busting portions of meat-heavy Romanian and Serbian food. Mains 15–35 lei. Daily noon–midnight.

DRINKING AND NIGHTLIFE

Deane's Str Republicii 19. Perennially popular Irish boozer which puts on some form of entertainment most evenings (music, comedy, karaoke, quizzes). Live sport on TV and a darts room too. Daily 10am–3am.

BRAN

Cosy little **BRAN**, 28km southwest of Braşov, is situated at the foot of the stunning Bucegi Mountains. Despite what you may hear, its **castle** (daily

27

27

9am–6pm, Mon from noon; 35 lei; ⓦbran-castle.com) has only tenuous associations with Dracula, aka Vlad the Impaler, who may have attacked it in 1460. Hyperbole is forgivable, though, as Bran really does look like a vampire count's residence. The castle was built in 1377 by the Saxons of Braşov to safeguard what used to be the main route into Wallachia, and it rises in tiers of towers and ramparts from among the woods, against a glorious mountain background. A warren of stairs, nooks and chambers around a small courtyard, the interior is filled with elaborately carved four-poster beds, throne-like chairs and portraits of grim-faced boyars.

ARRIVAL AND DEPARTURE

Hotels and hostels throughout the country arrange trips to Bran Castle, while Braşov-based Active Travel (see p.909) runs day-trips on Tuesdays, Thursdays and Saturdays.
By bus Buses from Braşov arrive in the centre of town, in view of the castle.

ACCOMMODATION

The Guesthouse Str General Traian Mosoiu 365B ☎0745 179 475, ⓦguesthouse.ro. A comfortable place run by an affable British expat, set in a large garden, with kitchen facilities and immaculate en-suite doubles. Doubles €35
Pension Carina Str Principala 484 ☎0268 238 303, ⓦpensiunea-carina.ro. Sporting some bright colour schemes, this pleasant guesthouse is smart and modern, with a lovely garden. Doubles 80 lei

RÂSNOV AND ZĂRNEŞTI

A more low-key but no less satisfying destination than Bran is nearby **RÂSNOV**, where the hilltop fortress (daily 8am–8pm; 6 lei) and the views are

stunning. North of Bran is **ZĂRNEŞTI**, a charming small town that is the perfect jumping-off point for trips into the Făgăraş Mountains.

ARRIVAL AND DEPARTURE

There's a regular bus service between Braşov and Moeciu de Jos (southwest of Bran) via Râşnov and Bran. Buses and trains run from Braşov to Zărneşti via Râşnov.

ACCOMMODATION

Pensiunea Mosorel 1 Str Dr Senchea 162, Zărneşti ☎0744 368 432, ⓦpensiuneamosorel.ro. Charming family-run guesthouse with large en-suite rooms, delicious home-cooked food, and a pleasant garden with space for tents. Doubles (half-board) 230 lei, camping/person 12 lei
Pensiunea Mosorel 2 Just south of Zărneşti ☎0745 024 471, ⓦpensiuneamosorel.ro. For a near-medieval mountain escape, spend a night here in the picturesque hamlet of Magură, on the flanks of the Piatra Craiului Mountains. Phone ahead and the owners will pick you up from the bus in Zărneşti. Doubles (half-board) 230 lei

SIGHIŞOARA

The citadel of **SIGHIŞOARA**, perched on a hill overlooking the Târnave Mare valley, presents a forbidding silhouette of looming battlements and needle spires; it seems fitting that this was the birthplace of Vlad Ţepeş, the man known to posterity as **Dracula**. Look out for the Medieval Arts and the Inter-ethnic Cultural **festivals** held annually in July and August, when Sighişoara may be overrun by thousands of beer-swillers.

WHAT TO SEE AND DO

The route from the train station to the centre passes the **Romanian Orthodox**

WOLF AND BEAR TRACKING IN THE CARPATHIANS

Romania has the largest **wolf** and **brown bear** populations in Europe. Transylvanian Wolf (☎0744 319 708, ⓦtransylvanianwolf.ro) offers guided walks (around 300 lei for up to 5 people, 65 lei for each extra person) tracking wolves, bears, red deer and lynx under the eagle eye of Dan Marin, an award-winning tracker who works closely with conservation organizations and the new **Piatra Craiului National Park**.

In winter there's the chance to see some spectacular snow-covered landscapes, and take part in sleigh rides and cross-country skiing. Treat yourself and stay in the Marin's spectacular family **guesthouse** (Str I. Metianu 108, Zărneşti; €30 per person), where all meals (breakfast, dinner and packed lunch) are home-cooked and included in the price. Birdwatching and botany tours are also available.

Cathedral, its gleaming white, multi-faceted facade a striking contrast to the dark interior. Across the **Târnave Mare** river, the **citadel** dominates the town from a hill whose slopes support a jumble of ancient houses. Steps lead up from the lower town's main square, **Piaţa Hermann Oberth**, to the main gateway, above which rises the mighty **clock tower**. This was built in the fourteenth century when Sighişoara became a free town controlled by craft guilds – each of which had to finance the construction of a bastion and defend it in wartime.

Sighişoara grew rich on the proceeds of trade with Moldavia and Wallachia, as attested by the regalia and strongboxes in the clock tower's **museum** (May 15–Sept 15 Tues–Fri 9am–6.30pm, Sat & Sun 10am–5.30pm; Sept 16–May 14 Tues–Fri 9am–3.30pm, Sat & Sun 10am–3.30pm; 10 lei; ⓦmuzeusighisoara .ro). The ticket also gives access to the seventeenth-century **torture chamber** and the **Museum of Armaments** next door, with its small and poorly presented "Dracula Exhibition".

In 1431 or thereabouts, the child later known as Dracula was born at Strada Muzeului 6 near the clock tower. At the time, his father – Vlad Dracul – was commander of the mountain passes into Wallachia, but the younger Vlad's privileged childhood ended eight years later, when he and his brother Radu were sent to Anatolia as hostages to the Turks. There Vlad observed the Turks' use of terror, which he would later turn against them, earning the nickname of "The Impaler". Nowadays, Vlad's birthplace is a mediocre tourist restaurant.

ARRIVAL AND INFORMATION

By train Sighişoara's train station is on the northern edge of town, on Str Libertăţii.
Destinations Braşov (6 daily; 2hr 30min); Bucharest (3 daily; 5hr); Sibiu (2 daily; 3hr).
By bus The bus station is close to the train station on the same road. For Sibiu change buses at Mediaş.
Destinations Braşov (9 daily; 2hr); Bucharest (9 daily; 5hr 30min).
Tourist office Opposite the clock tower at Piaţa Muzeului 6 (Tues–Sun 10am–6pm; ☏0788 115 511, ⓦinfosighisoara.ro).

★ TREAT YOURSELF

Casa cu Cerb Str Şcolii 1 ☏0265 774 625, ⓦcasacucerb.ro. This extremely classy hotel occupies a seventeenth-century mansion with an abundance of atmospheric period features. It's a good choice for romantics, with bathtubs big enough for two, while the most expensive rooms have four-poster beds. The restaurant is among the town's best. Doubles **€42**

ACCOMMODATION

Burg Hostel Str Bastionului 4–6 ☏0265 778 489, ⓦburghostel.ro. Central, atmospheric hostel in a seventeenth-century building with clean dorms and doubles. There's a bar in the cellar, internet access and free wi-fi. Breakfast isn't included, but there is a good-value restaurant in the courtyard. Dorms **45 lei**, doubles **100 lei**
Pensiunea Cristina şi Pavel Str Cojocarilor 1 ☏0744 119 211, ⓦpensiuneafaur.ro. The private rooms offered by the Faur family in the citadel are some of the town's best. Guests have use of a kitchen, and bicycle rental is available. Doubles **120 lei**
Pensiunea Gia Str Libertăţii 41 ☏0722 490 003, ⓦhotelgia.ro. A simple hotel that has doubles and triples, and a shared kitchen; no breakfast. Conveniently close to the train station. Doubles **99 lei**
Villa Franka Camping Str Dealu Garii ☏0265 771 046, ⓦsighisoara-tourism.com. Boasting wonderful views from its hilltop position high above the train station, this idyllic tree-shaded campsite (open April to mid–Nov) also has clean wooden bungalows and a good restaurant. Camping/person **€3**, double bungalows **€16**

EATING AND DRINKING

Casa cu Cerb Str Şcolii 1. In the hotel of the same name, this is one of the best restaurants in the citadel, with good breakfasts, light meals and more expensive dinners. There's also a lovely, sunny outdoor seating area. Mains 20–45 lei. Daily 10am–11pm.
Culture Pub In the basement of the *Burg Hostel* (see above), with some live rock/pop music, mainly weekend evenings. Daily till 3am.
International Café Piaţa Cetăţii 8. A cosy café serving delicious and filling sandwiches and cakes (10 lei), and just about the only quiche (12 lei) in Transylvania. Mon–Sat 8am–6pm; June–Aug till 7pm.
Jo Pub Piaţa Hermann Oberth 7. Probably the best of the fairly mass-market *terasas* on the lower town's main square, serving good pizza as well as local dishes such as bean soup in a half-loaf of bread. Daily 11am–midnight.

27

Quattro Amici Str Octavian Goga 12. In the lower town, this enjoyable pizzeria offers fabulous oven-baked pizzas and fresh salads, and there's outdoor seating facing a field. Mains 10–25 lei. Daily 9am–midnight.

SIBIU

The narrow streets and gabled houses of SIBIU's older quarters are the stuff of fairytales. Like Brașov, Sibiu was founded by Germans invited by Hungary's King Géza II to colonize strategic regions of Transylvania in 1143. Its inhabitants dominated trade in Transylvania and Wallachia, but their citadels were no protection against the tide of history which eroded their influence after the eighteenth century. The Saxon community is now mostly gone from Romania, but Sibiu still has stronger and more lucrative links with Germany than any other Transylvanian town, and its stint as European Capital of Culture in 2007 meant its buildings were handsomely refurbished. The city also stages some cracking festivals, not least the International Theatre Festival in late May, with open-air stages across all the main squares.

WHAT TO SEE AND DO

To reach the old town cross the square from the train station and follow Str Gen. Magheru to **Piața Mare**, one of three conjoined squares that form the centre.

Piața Mare

On the western side of Piața Mare stands the handsome eighteenth-century **Brukenthal Palace**, housing the eponymous **museum** (Tues–Sun 10am–6pm; closed Tues mid-Oct to mid-March and 1st Tues of month; European Art 20 lei, Romanian Art 12 lei; ⍟brukenthalmuseum.ro), one of the finest in Romania with an evocative collection of works by Transylvanian and Western painters – look out for Jan van Eyck's *Man in Blue Turban*. The city's **History Museum** (same hours; 20 lei) is nearby in the impressive Old City Hall. On the northern side of Piața Mare, the huge Catholic church stands next to the **Council Tower** (daily 10am–6pm), which offers fine views to the Carpathians.

The cathedral

Just beyond the Council Tower, on Piața Huet, the **Evangelical Cathedral** (May–Oct Mon–Sat 9am–8pm, Sun 11.30am–8pm; Nov–April Mon–Sat 9am–5pm; Sun 11.30am–5pm; 5 lei, tower 5 lei) is a massive Gothic hall-church raised during the fourteenth and fifteenth centuries.

Museum of Traditional Folk Civilization

Set aside most of a day to explore Sibiu's wonderful open-air **Museum of Traditional Folk Civilization** (Muzeul Astra; daily 10am–6pm; 17 lei; ⍟muzeulastra.ro) at Strada Pădurea Dumbrava 16, south of the centre; take bus #13 to the end of the line. Set against a mountain backdrop, the museum offers a fantastic insight into rural life, with authentically furnished wooden houses, churches and mills; there's also a traditional inn serving local food and drink.

ARRIVAL AND INFORMATION

By train Sibiu's train station is on Piața 1 Decembrie 1918, 400m northeast of the main square.

Destinations Brașov (7 daily; 3–4hr); Bucharest (4 daily; 5hr 30min–6hr); Sighișoara (2 daily; 3hr); Timișoara (1 daily; 7hr).

By bus The bus station is adjacent to the train station. For Sighișoara change buses at Mediaș.

Destinations Brașov (13 daily; 2hr 45min); Bucharest (12 daily; 5hr); Timișoara (3 daily; 6–7hr).

Tourist office Sibiu's central tourist office is inside the City Hall at Str Brukenthal 2 (May–Sept Mon–Fri 9am–8pm, Sat & Sun 10am–6pm; Oct–April Mon–Fri 9am–5pm, Sat & Sun 9am–1pm; ☎0269 208913, ⍟turism.sibiu.ro).

ACCOMMODATION

Ela Str Nouă 43 ☎0269 215 197, ⍟ela-hotels.ro. A friendly, family-run hotel, with a pleasant garden, eight spotless en-suite rooms and a guest kitchen. From the train station take Str 9 Mai, turn right onto Str Rebreanu, then first left onto Str Nouă. Breakfast is 15 lei. Doubles **100 lei**

Old Town Hostel Piața Mică 26 ☎0269 216 445, ⍟hostelsibiu.ro. Located above a historic pharmacy in a 450-year-old building, the hostel has three large, airy dorms and also offers en-suite doubles at a different location. Breakfast is not included but there's a kitchen, plus free tea and coffee and internet access. The hostel can also arrange bike rental. Dorms **50 lei**, doubles **150 lei**

27

Pan Geea Hostel Str Avram Iancu 4 ☎0369 801 232, ⓦsibiuhostel.ro. The funkiest hostel in town, with two dorms, one double room, and lockers, kitchen, PC and washing machine; there's also a café-bar downstairs. Dorms **€11**, doubles **€30**

Podul Minciunilor Str Azilului 1 ☎0269 217 259, ⓦela -hotels.ro. A small, central, family-run guesthouse near the Liar's Bridge, with five en-suite doubles and one triple. No breakfast. Doubles **100 lei**

Smart Hostel Pasajul Scarilor 1 ☎0731 147 049, ⓦsmart-hostel.ro. In a fifteenth-century building just below the cathedral, this hostel feels like staying in a friend's stylish modern flat, with comfy sofas and a decent guitar. There are twin and double rooms and six- and eight-person dorms, with reading lights, individual sockets and lots of storage space. There's a good kitchen. and a hearty breakfast is included. Dorms **50 lei**, doubles **130 lei**

EATING AND DRINKING

Crama Sibiu Vechi Str Ilarian 3 ⓦsibiulvechi.ro. Traditional Transylvanian restaurant in the cellar of a fifteenth-century building. This is the best place for something typically Romanian such as *tochitură* (meat stew), *ghiveci* (vegetable stew) or *fasole bătută* (mashed beans), served by staff in national costume. There's also live folk music and cheap wine on tap. Mains 15–40 lei. Daily noon–midnight.

Go In Piața Mică 9 ⓦgoin-sibiu.ro. Popular central restaurant serving great pizzas (10–26 lei) and pasta. Cocktails are good too. Daily 9.30am–midnight.

Imperium Club Str Bălcescu 24. A good old-school music pub with regular live sessions of quality acoustic and rock music. Good beer too. Daily 5pm–2am.

La Turn Piața Mare 1 ⓦlaturnsibiu.ro. Atmospheric spot next to the Council Tower with an impressive range of seafood and Italian dishes. Mains 20–35 lei. Daily 10am–2am.

Pasaj Str Turnului 3a. Sprightly pizzeria with a cool brick interior, also offering a varied selection of salads and pasta, as well as chicken, beef and vegetarian options (and wi-fi). Friendly service but it can be slow. Mains 20–30 lei. Mon–Fri 11am–11pm, Sat & Sun noon–11pm.

The Banat

Once a much larger territory that's now divided between Romania and neighbouring Hungary and Serbia, the featureless plains of the **Banat** were ruled from **Timișoara** until the Turks conquered it in 1552; they governed until 1716,

when they were ousted by the Habsburgs. The region's current frontiers were drawn up during the Versailles conference of 1918–20. Today, Romanian Banat is still home to a diverse population that for centuries has included Slovaks, Bulgarians, Ukrainians and Germans living alongside Serbians, Romanians and Hungarians. Besides the picturesque villages scattered throughout the region, the Banat's main attraction is its capital, Timișoara, with its thriving cultural scene and old town centre packed with historic buildings.

TIMIȘOARA

The engaging city of **TIMIȘOARA**, 250km west of Sibiu near the Serbian border and the rail junction at Arad, is Romania's most West-leaning city, its good location and multilingual inhabitants attracting much foreign investment. The city's fame abroad rests on its crucial role in the overthrow of the Ceaușescu regime. A Calvinist minister, Lászlo Tökes, stood up for the rights of the Hungarian community and, when the police came to evict him on December 16, 1989, his parishioners barred their way. The bloody riots that ensued inspired the people of Bucharest to follow, meaning that Timișoara sees itself as the guardian of the revolution.

WHAT TO SEE AND DO

Approaching from the train station, you'll enter the centre at the attractive pedestrianized **Piața Victoriei**, with fountains and flowerbeds strewn along its length. North of here, trams trundle past the Baroque **Town Hall** on the central Piața Libertății, while two blocks further north is the vast **Piața Unirii**.

Piața Victoriei

The focal point of Piața Victoriei is the huge **Romanian Orthodox Cathedral**, completed in 1946 with a blend of neo-Byzantine and Moldavian architectural elements – this is where most of the protesters were gunned down in 1989. At the opposite end, the unattractive Opera House stands near the castle, which now houses the **Museum of the Banat** (currently closed for long-term renovation), with a broad collection of archeological and historical artefacts.

Piața Unirii

Piața Unirii is dominated by the monumental **Roman Catholic** and **Serbian Orthodox cathedrals**. Built between 1736 and 1773, the former (to the east) is a fine example of Viennese Baroque; the latter is roughly contemporaneous and almost as impressive.

The Museum of the Revolution

The superb **Museum of the Revolution** at Str Oituz 2B (Mon–Fri 8am–4pm, Sat 9am–1pm; 10 lei donation; ⓦmemorialulrevolutiei.ro) soberly documents the remarkable events of December 1989, courtesy of photos, newspaper cuttings and film footage, including the extraordinary moment when the Ceaușescus were informed of their impending execution.

Banat Village Museum

Situated 5km northeast of the centre and accessible by bus (#46), the wonderful **Banat Village Museum** (May–Sept Tues–Sat 10am–6pm, Sun noon–8pm; Oct–April Tues–Fri 9am–4pm, Sat & Sun 10am–5pm; 5 lei; ⓦmuzeulsatuluibanatean.ro) is an outdoor affair featuring a fascinating ensemble of nineteenth-century cottages collected from local villages and reconstructed within the museum's wooded grounds. Architectural styles include German, Slovak, Hungarian, Ukrainian and Romanian.

ARRIVAL AND INFORMATION

By train Timișoara Nord train station is a 15min walk west of the centre along B-dul Republicii.
Destinations Brașov (1 daily; 9hr 30min); Bucharest (4 daily; 9–12hr); Sibiu (1 daily; 6hr 40min).
By bus The main bus station (Autogara Autotim) is just southwest of the train station.
Destinations Brașov (3 daily; 9hr); Bucharest (2 daily; 11hr 30min); Sibiu (4 daily; 6hr 30min).
Tourist information The tourist office (April–Sept Mon–Fri 9am–8pm, Sat 9am–5pm; Oct–March Mon–Fri 9am–6pm, Sat 10am–3pm; ☎0256 437 973,

ⓦtimisoara-info.ro), on the ground floor of the opera building at Str Alba Julia 2, has maps and copies of the free quarterly English-language guide *Timișoara What Where When* as well as the Romanian-language weekly listings guide *Șapte Seri* (ⓦsapteseri.ro).

ACCOMMODATION

Camping International Calea Dorobanților 83, 4km west of town ☎0256 217 086, ⓦcampinginternational.ro. Open all year, this well-kept campsite also has huts sleeping one to four people. Take trolleybus #11 from the train station or centre. Camping/person __30 lei__, double huts __90 lei__

Freeborn Hostel Str Patriarh Miron Cristea 3 (street also known as Asanesti), Apartment 1 ☎0743 438 534, ⓦfreebornhostel.com. Very central hostel with two spacious dorm rooms and a double, each with their own bathroom. There's also a shaded courtyard with barbecue and table tennis. Dorms __€10__, doubles __€30__

Hostel Costel Str Petru Sfetca 1 (street also known as Vidra) ☎0356 262487, ⓦhostel-costel.ro. Lovely hostel with huge dorm rooms in a stylishly refurbished old house, just a short walk northeast from the centre. Dorms __€11__, doubles __€30__

EATING

Baroque Piața Unirii 14. This place lives up to its name, with wrought-iron tables and chairs outside and a decadent array of teas, coffees, milkshakes and hot chocolate (both alcoholic and non-alcoholic). Breakfasts for around 15 lei, hot drinks from 5 lei. Daily 8am–1am.

Cora Pizzaria Str Eugeniu de Savoya 13 ⓦpizzeriacora.ro. First-rate pizzeria in the heart of the city (18–25 lei). Daily 10am–1am.

Harold's Aleea Studenților 17 ⓦharolds.ro. Understated and classy restaurant in a studenty area, with a wide selection of Romanian, Chinese and Mexican dishes, including vegetarian options. Most mains 16–36 lei. Daily 11.30am–midnight.

DRINKING AND NIGHTLIFE

Club 30 Piața Victoriei 7. In the Cinema Timiș, this small basement club plays classic oldies and often puts on live jazz and blues. Daily 6pm–3am.

The Note Pub B-dul Mihai Eminescu 2. A lively pub with a pleasant deck at the rear that does pretty average food (burger and chips, or menu of the day for 20 lei) and hosts live bands and cabaret. Mon–Wed & Sun 8am–midnight, Thurs–Sat 8am–5am.

Piranha Club Str Alecsandri 5. A popular drinking den with a range of cocktails and truly eye-catching surroundings, complete with fish tanks, live lizards and snakes. Open around the clock, it's also a pleasant place for morning coffee.

THE PETER AND PAUL FORTRESS, ST PETERSBURG

Russia

HIGHLIGHTS

❶ **The Kremlin** See the Orlov diamond, stunning churches and the treasures of the Armoury Chamber. **See p.924**

❷ **Ice-skating** Glide along the frozen pedestrian pathways of Moscow's Gorky Park in the depths of winter. **See p.926**

❸ **White Nights** Darkness never falls in St Petersburg and the midsummer partying goes on around the clock. **See p.930**

❹ **The Hermitage** View thousands of priceless treasures at Russia's premier museum. **See p.930**

❺ **Peterhof** Explore Peter the Great's imperial palace and its magnificent gardens in the suburbs of St Petersburg. **See p.938**

HIGHLIGHTS ARE MARKED ON THE MAP ON P.917

ROUGH COSTS

Daily budget Basic €60, occasional treat €75

Drink Beer (*pivo*) €3

Food Pancake (*blini*) €1.50

Hostel/budget hotel €15–25/€45

Travel Train: Moscow–St Petersburg from €25

FACT FILE

Population 143.5 million

Language Russian

Currency Rouble (R)

Capital Moscow

International phone code ☏ 7

Time zone GMT +3hr

Introduction

European Russia stretches from the borders of Belarus and Ukraine to the Ural mountains, over 1000km east of Moscow; even without the rest of the vast Russian Federation, it constitutes by far the largest country in Europe. Formerly a powerful tsarist empire and a Communist superpower, Russia continues to be a source of fascination for travellers. While access is still made relatively difficult by lingering Soviet-style bureaucracy – visas are obligatory and application forms lengthy – independent travel is increasing every year, and visitors are doubly rewarded by the cultural riches of the country and the warmth of the Russian people.

28

Moscow, Russia's bustling capital, combines the frenetic energy of an Eastern city with the cosmopolitan feel of a Western one. With its dense human traffic and show-stopping architecture – from the Kremlin's tsarist palaces and onion domes of St Basil's Cathedral, through the monumental relics of the Communist years to today's massive building projects – the metropolis can feel rather overwhelming. By contrast, with its beautiful canals and graceful buildings, **St Petersburg**, Russia's second city, is nicknamed "the Venice of the north". Founded as a seaport by the eighteenth-century tsar Peter the Great, who wanted the Russian fleet to be the strongest in the world, the city was intended to emulate the best of Western European elegance. Today, its people are more relaxed and friendly than the capital's, and its position in the delta of the River Neva is unparalleled, giving it endless watery vistas. Uneven – and often ostentatious – wealth creation in both cities has made them twin figureheads for Russia's recent high-speed renaissance.

The Russian financial crisis of 2014 has strongly affected the country's economy and financial markets, with the rouble losing half its value within weeks of the onset of the crisis. The plus for travellers is that Russia is, at the time of writing, more affordable than ever. Check the exchange rate (see p.921) before your trip to see if the situation has changed.

CHRONOLOGY

862 AD A Scandinavian warrior, Rurik, founds the state of Rus' (Русь).

989 Grand Duke Vladimir I adopts Orthodox Christianity.

1552 Ivan the Terrible conquers the Tatars and builds the famous domed St Basil's Cathedral in Red Square, Moscow.

1613 Michael Romanov is elected as Tsar of Russia, ushering in 300 years of Romanov rule.

1725 Peter the Great builds the new capital of St Petersburg after defeating Sweden in the Great Northern War.

1751 First recorded reference to "vodka" is made in a decree made by Empress Elizabeth.

1812 Napoleon invades Russia but is defeated.

1869 Tolstoy writes *War and Peace*.

1892 Tchaikovsky composes the famous ballet, *The Nutcracker*.

1905 Revolution leads to the masses gaining both a constitution and a parliament.

1914 Russia enters World War I on behalf of the Allies.

1917 The October Revolution witnesses the Communist Bolsheviks, led by Lenin, overthrowing the monarchy and government.

1924 Joseph Stalin takes control of the Soviet Union.

1941 The Nazis invade Russian territory; after intense fighting and victory at Stalingrad, the Red Army repel the Germans from Russia.

1961 Yuri Gagarin becomes the first human being to travel into space, aboard the *Vostok*.

1962 The Cuban Missile Crisis heightens tensions with the US during the Cold War.

1991 The Soviet Union collapses; many former Soviet countries declare independence. Boris Yeltsin is elected president.

1999 Yeltsin resigns and is replaced by Vladimir Putin.

2007 Russian relations with the US deteriorate over their plans to install anti-missile launchers around Russia's borders.

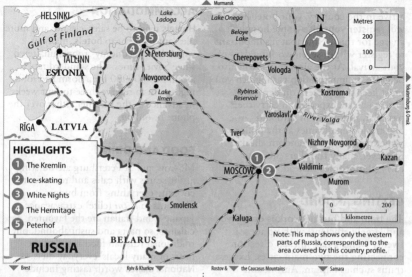

HIGHLIGHTS
1. The Kremlin
2. Ice-skating
3. White Nights
4. The Hermitage
5. Peterhof

RUSSIA

Note: This map shows only the western parts of Russia, corresponding to the area covered by this country profile.

2008 Russia goes to war with Georgia over Georgia's offensive against Southern Ossetia.

2009 President Medvedev announces Russia's rearmament plan, which includes nuclear force.

2011 Russia wins bid to host the football World Cup in 2018.

2012 Putin is sworn in for his second stint as president in May; protests ensue. In August Russia joins the WTO.

2014 Russia takes over Crimea; the US and Europe impose sanctions. In December the Russian rouble begins to drop dramatically, soon losing half its value.

2015 Russia carries out air strikes in Syria.

2016 Russian forces withdraw from Syria. A number of Russian athletes are banned from international competitions for state-sponsored doping.

ARRIVAL AND VISAS

International flights serve Moscow's Sheremetyevo and Domodedovo airports and St Petersburg's Pulkovo Airport. All **airports** are connected with their respective cities by regular and efficient public transport. Besides being the main hub for all domestic **trains**, including the trans-Siberian ones, Moscow is served by trains from Rīga, Tallinn, Warsaw, Berlin and Budapest, while European train routes into St Petersburg include arrivals from Helsinki, Rīga and Vilnius. Train stations in both Moscow and St Petersburg are well connected to the metro; all Moscow's *vokzal* (train

stations) link to a stop on the (brown) circle line. The most convenient way to come to St Petersburg for travellers arriving from the Baltic States may be by **bus**, as they are more frequent than trains. **Ferries** into St Petersburg from Helsinki arrive at the Vasilyevskiy Island ferry terminal.

All tourists travelling to Russia require a **tourist visa**, which entitles visitors to a 30-day stay in the country. To obtain a visa, travellers need to have been "invited" by a hotel or hostel (note that hostels charge a fee for invitation letters). If booking **accommodation** in advance, your hotel or hostel can provide this document for you. Should you wish to find accommodation upon arrival, you can obtain a letter of invitation through a **visa agency** (see box below) for a fee, which states that you will be staying at a randomly selected hotel – there is no obligation to actually do so once in Russia. Once you

EMBASSY AND VISA CONTACTS

ⓦ**russianembassy.net** Russian embassies and consulates.

ⓦ**visitrussia.org.uk** The Russian National Tourist Office provides an efficient visa service.

28

arrive in the country, your hotel/hostel will **register your visa** (some hostels charge for this). Note that it's important to register within seven working days of your arrival. At the airport you will also be given an **immigration card** which you must keep and present on departure. Foreigners are expected to carry their passport, immigration card and registration at all times as the police sometimes carry out random checks. However, many travellers prefer to carry **photocopies** instead.

GETTING AROUND

The **train** and **bus** network is extensive and largely efficient, with up to twenty trains a day in each direction connecting the two main cities. Express trains such as Sapsan, Aurora and Er-200 make the journey in under five hours in the early evening, but cheapest and most atmospheric are the **overnight** services, a quintessentially Russian experience, which take around eight and a half hours. Trains are generally safe, reliable and cheap (one-way from approximately R950 seated only, R1500 in a sleeping compartment). Buy tickets in advance online (⊕rzd.ru), from Leningradskiy station in Moscow or Moskovskiy station in St Petersburg. Regular buses connect the two cities, but the long ten- to twelve-hour journey (around R1400) rarely makes it worthwhile. **City transport** in Moscow and St Petersburg centres on the punctual metro; overground transport includes buses, trams, trolleybuses and minibuses (*marshrútki*). Official taxis can be very expensive, whereas unofficial ones are not necessarily safe – it's best to use a taxi app such as Uber. **Bike** rental in St Petersburg offers a pleasant way to see the city's quieter outer corners, but cycle in Moscow at your peril. As you make your way around the cities, know that the word "ulitsa" (street) is often abbreviated as "ul.", "pereulok" (lane) becomes "per.", "ploshchad" (square) becomes "pl.", and "naberezhnaya" (embankment) becomes "nab."

ACCOMMODATION

Hostels tend to be safer, cleaner and more pleasant than cheap **hotels**, many of which have "economy" rooms unaltered since Soviet times. The standard rate is around R800–900 for a dorm bed for a night; aim to reserve three to four weeks in advance in the summer either over the phone or online.

FOOD AND DRINK

Moscow and St Petersburg are bursting at the seams with cafés and restaurants covering everything from budget blowouts to *elitni* (elite) extravagance. Japanese and Italian are the favoured cuisines, so pasta and sushi abound, but traditional Russian food is still at the heart of many locals' everyday diets. **National dishes** worth tasting include *borshch* (beetroot soup), *shchi* (cabbage soup) and *pirogi* (small pies stuffed with potato, cabbage or a kind of cottage cheese known as *tvorog*). Try these at one of the *stolovaya* (canteen-style) restaurants, such as *Dachniki* in St Petersburg (see p.936). Cheap *blini*, available from the ubiquitous and much-loved *Teremok* fast-food chain, subdivide into *blinchiki*, pancake wraps stuffed with meat or berries, and flat pancakes, served with honey, condensed milk, *smetana* (sour cream) or *krasnaya ikra* (red caviar). In summer, Russians go mad for *morozhenoe* (ice cream).

DRINK

Vodka (*vódka*) is, of course, the national drink, knocked back in one gulp and chased with a bite on black bread or salted cucumber. **Beer** (*pivo*) is essential in summer; try Baltika (rated in strength from 3 to 9), Stariy Melnik or Nevskoe. Be sure to sample the excellent semi-sweet Georgian **wines** too (Khvanchkara was Stalin's favourite). For cheap eating and drinking, stock up at a *produkti* (small grocery shop), or at *rynki* (markets), scattered across both cities, though concentrated in the suburbs. These sell the full range of Russian dairy delights such as *kefir* (sour milk), plus salami, sausages and cheap fresh fruit and vegetables. Traditionally, breakfast is eaten between 7am and 9am and lunch between 1pm and 2pm; evening meals tend to be taken around 8pm.

CULTURE AND ETIQUETTE

Although the Western practice of eating out is now widespread, Russians love to entertain at home; if you're invited over, always bring a small present: men traditionally offer flowers while women bring chocolates. **Tipping** is today the norm at most cafés and restaurants, with five to ten percent given as standard. In **churches**, women should cover their head and shoulders, and men in shorts may be refused entry; you'll also notice that locals avoid turning their back to the iconostasis that screens the altar. Russians are rather superstitious: you'll see people rubbing the noses of the dog statues at the Metro Ploshchad Revolyutsii in Moscow for good luck. Old-fashioned chivalry is alive and well, with men opening doors for women and offering to help with heavy lifting. You'll notice, too, that young people give up their seats to the elderly on public transport: follow their example before being told to.

Russia has a negative attitude towards homosexuality and, in 2013, passed a law banning any so-called "propaganda" supportive of "non-traditional" sexual orientations.

SPORTS AND ACTIVITIES

Spectator sports centre on **football**, with Moscow's biggest teams being Dinamo (Leningradskiy prospekt 36 ☏495 642 7172, ⓦfcdynamo.ru; ⓜDinamo) and Spartak (Otkrytiye Arena, Volokolamskoye shosse 69 ☏495 111 1922, ⓦspartak.com; ⓜSpartak), while Petersburgers support Zenit (Petrovskiy stadium, Petrovskiy Island ☏812 244 8888, ⓦfc-zenit.ru; ⓜSportivnaya).

Skating is as much part of Russian culture as drinking vodka or eating *blinis*. Moscow has plenty of likely spots in winter, including the frozen-over paths at the vast Gorky Park (Krymskiy Val ul. 9 ⓦpark-gorkogo.com; ⓜPark Kultury) or

the smaller, more intimate Hermitage Garden (ul. Karetniy Ryad 3 ⓦmosgorsad.ru; ⓜPushkinskaya). Skates can be rented at both Gorky Park and the Hermitage Garden.

Summer or winter, **swim** in the open-air lidos at Chayka (Turchaninov per. 3/1 ⓦchayka-sport.ru; ⓜPark Kultury), or Luzhniki, currently undergoing refurbishment work and due to reopen in early 2018 (Luzhnetskaya nab. 24; ⓜSportivnaya).

Cycling enthusiasts can see St Petersburg with a **bike tour** (Skatprokat Rent a Bike, Goncharnaya ul. 7 ⓦskatprokat.ru; ⓜPl. Vosstaniya). Alternatively, take a **guided walk** (Peter's Walking Tours, ⓦpeterswalk .com; R1500 for 4–5hr).

COMMUNICATIONS

Most **post offices** are open Monday to Saturday 8am to 7pm, and blue postboxes are affixed to walls across both cities. However, local mail is slow and not particularly reliable, so use DHL for urgent letters. Most hostels offer internet access and wi-fi for free, while virtually all cafés and restaurants also have **wi-fi**. For **international calls** get a pre-paid international phonecard such as the Zebra Telecom card or Evroset card, usable from any phone. Ask at a telecoms kiosk for a *telefonnaya karta*. Non-Russian **mobiles** work on roaming via local providers, but you'll pay a fortune. However, the fact that there is wi-fi virtually everywhere, including on the Moscow metro, means you'll be able to access the net and your phone apps via your smartphone. You could also consider getting a local SIM card (free, you only pay what you top up; bring your passport with you to buy one). Note that when calling a local number from a Russian mobile or landline you need to dial 8 before the number. However, if dialling from an international mobile the 8 is not necessary. Dial the country code +7 followed directly by the number.

EMERGENCIES

Beware of **petty crime**, particularly pickpockets in the metro and in bus and

28

RUSSIAN

	RUSSIAN	PRONUNCIATION
Yes	да	Da
No	нет	Nyet
Please	пожалуйста	Pazháaloosta
Thank you	спасибо	Spaséeba
Hello/Good day	здравствуйте	Zdrávstweetye
Goodbye	до свидания	Da svidáaneya
Excuse me	извините	Izvinéetye
Sorry	простите	Prostitye
Where?	где?	Gdye?
Good/Bad	хороший/плохой	Khoróshee/Plokhóy
Near/Far	близко/далеко	Bléezki/Dalyekó
Cheap/Expensive	дешевый/дорогой	Deshóvy/Daragóy
Open/Closed	открыто/закрыто	Otkryto/Zakryto
Today	сегодня	Sevódnya
Yesterday	вчера	Vcherá
Tomorrow	завтра	Závtra
How much is…?	сколько стоит…?	Skólka stóyit…?
What time is it?	Который час?	Katóree chass?
I don't understand	я не понимаю	Ya ne ponimáyou
Do you speak English?	вы говорите по-английски?	Vwee gavoréetye po angliyski?
Where are the toilets?	где туалет?	Gdye tualyét?
My name is…	меня зовут…	Menyá zavoót…
What is your name?	как вас зовут?	Kak vas zavóot?
I don't speak Russian	я не говорю по-русски	Ya nye gavaryóo pa-róosski
Can I have….	можно…	Mózhna…
Tea	чай	Chay
Beer	пиво	Péeva
Juice	сок	Sok
I am a vegetarian	я вегетарианец	Ya vegetariyánets
The bill, please	счет пожалуйста	Shchyot, pazhálooista
Men's toilet (often seen as M)	мужчины	Moózhshini
Women's toilet (often seen as Ж)	женщины	Zhénshini
Breakfast	завтрак	Závtrak
One	один	Adéen
Two	два	Dva
Three	три	Tree
Four	четыре	Chetéeri
Five	пять	Pyat
Six	шесть	Shest
Seven	семь	Syeem
Eight	восемь	Vósyem
Nine	девять	Déyvyat
Ten	десять	Déysyat

train stations during rush hour. Don't leave valuables in your hotel room. If you are dark-skinned, exercise extra caution, especially at night, as racist attacks are not unknown. Your embassy will be able to advise you on what to do if you get robbed. The **police** (полиция) wear blue-grey uniforms; always make sure you have photocopies of your passport, visa, immigration card and registration on you, as they do stop people at random and often look for an excuse to fine you.

When traversing busy roads, look for an underground crossing (*perekhod*/переход) as many drivers do not honour zebra crossings. High-street pharmacies (*aptéka*) offer many familiar medicines over the counter. Foreigners tend to rely on expensive **private clinics** for treatment, so travel insurance is essential. St Petersburg **water** may still contain the giardia parasite, which can cause severe diarrhoea – metranidazol is the cure and can be bought over the counter. The tap water of both cities contains high levels of heavy metals, so it's best to drink the bottled stuff.

INFORMATION

St Petersburg is well prepared for visitors, with numerous tourist offices dotted around town. The main Tourist Information Office (Sadovaya ul. 14; ⓂNevsky prospekt) has plenty of maps and information in English. At the time of research, **Moscow** did not have an official Tourist Information Office. For up-to-the-minute restaurant and bar listings see the excellent *In Your Pocket* guide (Ⓦinyourpocket.com/russia) which you can pick up at some hotels, as well as at restaurants catering to expats. Hostel and hotel receptions carry leaflets and

maps, and you can get the latest bar, restaurant and entertainment listings and reviews from **English-language papers**. The *Moscow Times* and the more ponderously pro-Kremlin *Moscow News* are well established. Find **maps** in English at bookshops like Dom Knigi (large branch in Moscow at ul. Novy Arbat 8; ⓂArbatskaya).

A useful website with detailed practical advice is Ⓦwaytorussia.net.

MONEY AND BANKS

Russia's currency is the **rouble**, divided into 100 kopeks. There are coins of 1, 5, 10, 20 and 50 kopeks and 1, 2, 5 and 10 roubles, and notes of 50, 100, 500, 1000 and 5000 roubles. Everything is paid for in roubles, although some hostels make a habit of citing prices in either euros or dollars. At the time of writing £1=R98, €1=R79 and US$1=R69. Only **change money** in an official bank or currency exchange. Most **exchange offices** are open Monday to Saturday 10am to 8pm or later, and **ATMs** are plentiful. In general, prices in both cities range from "New Russian" levels down to what the average local salary will cover, making many shops, bars and cafés affordable for the budget-conscious traveller.

OPENING HOURS AND HOLIDAYS

Most **shops** are open Monday to Saturday 10am to 8pm or later; Sunday hours are slightly shorter. **Museums** tend to open 9am to 5pm, with last ticket sales an hour before closing time, and they are invariably shut one day a week, with a day each month put aside for cleaning. **Churches** are accessible from 8am until the end of evening service. **Clubs** stay open until late – many until 6am or later – or don't close at all, morphing into early-morning cafés.

Russian **public holidays** fall on the following dates: January 1 (New Year's Day) and 7 (Christmas), February 23 (Defender of the Fatherland Day), March 8 (Women's Day), May 1 (Labour Day), May 9 (Victory Day), June 12 (Russia Day) and November 4 (Day of Popular Unity).

28

Moscow

Russia's capital, **MOSCOW** (Москва), is a modern, energetic city, but its chaotic spirit is never far beneath the surface: people bribe their way into nightclubs or out of scrapes with the law, supercars tussle for space with barely roadworthy wrecks and, come nightfall, the party mindset is truly no-holds-barred.

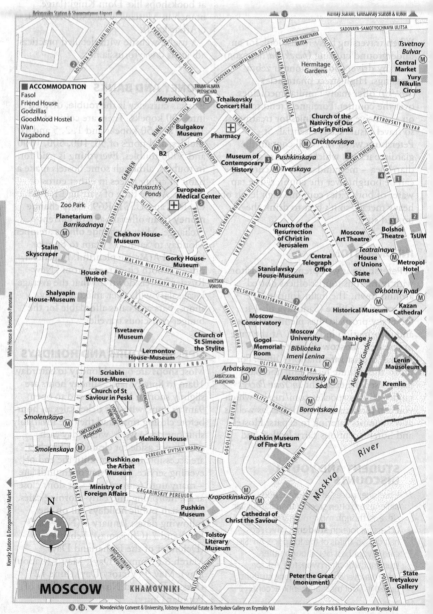

28

ACCOMMODATION

Fasol	5
Friend House	4
Godzillas	1
GoodMood Hostel	6
iVan	2
Vagabond	3

MOSCOW · KHAMOVNIKI

A humble wooden town in the twelfth century, contemporary Moscow is Russia's Manhattan, with brash and opinionated locals, a "whatever, whenever" approach to retail and a startling contrast between its glitzy, cosmopolitan heart, catering to a well-heeled elite, and pockets of extreme poverty. For visitors, the city is, above all, an assault on the senses – spend 24 hours navigating its golden-domed churches, people-crushed subway, designer shops and cliquey nightspots, and you'll need another 24 to recover.

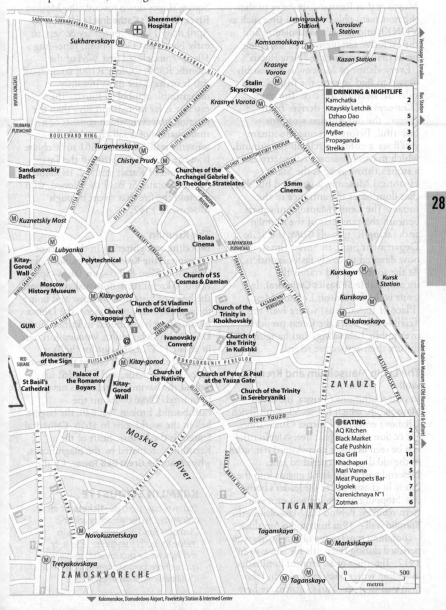

DRINKING & NIGHTLIFE

Kamchatka	2
Kitayskiy Letchik Dzhao Dao	5
Mendeleev	1
MyBar	3
Propaganda	4
Strelka	6

EATING

AQ Kitchen	2
Black Market	9
Café Pushkin	3
Izia Grill	10
Khachapuri	4
Mari Vanna	5
Meat Puppets Bar	1
Ugolek	7
Varenichnaya N°1	8
Zotman	6

28

Kolomenskoe, Domodedovo Airport, Paveletsky Station & Intermed Center

28

Moscow's centre is compact enough to explore on foot, with the general **layout** a series of concentric circles and radial lines emanating from Red Square and the Kremlin. You can map the city's principal sights as strata of its history: the old Muscovy that Russians are eager to show; the now retro-chic Soviet-era sites such as VDNKh and Lenin's Mausoleum; and the exclusive restaurants and shopping malls that mark out the "New Russia".

Every visitor to Moscow is irresistibly drawn to **Red Square**, the historic and spiritual heart of the city. The name (*Krasnaya ploshchad*) derives from *krasniy*, the old Russian word for beautiful. Before entering the square you'll see a golden circle on the ground, which marks Moscow's Kilometre Zero; a stone's throw away is the State Historical Museum, a large red building that dominates the entrance to the square. The Lenin Mausoleum squats beneath the ramparts of the **Kremlin** and, facing it, sprawls **GUM**: the State Department Store in Soviet times, it is now devoted to costly fashion outlets. At the southern end stands the incomparable **St Basil's Cathedral**. In front is the fenced-off Lobnoe Mesto (Place of Executions) where Ivan the Terrible and Peter the Great presided over public beheadings and hangings during their respective reigns.

The Lenin Mausoleum and Kremlin wall

In post-Communist Russia, the **Lenin Mausoleum**, which houses Vladimir Ilyich Ulianov's embalmed corpse (Tues–Thurs, Sat & Sun 10am–1pm; free; ⍟lenin.ru), can be seen as either an awkward reminder of the old days or a cherished relic. Descend past stony-faced guards into the dimly lit chasm where the leader's body lies. Stopping or giggling will earn you stern rebukes. Behind the Mausoleum, the **Kremlin wall** – 19m high and 6.5m thick – contains a **mass grave** of Bolsheviks who perished during the battle for Moscow in 1917. The ashes of an array of luminaries, including writer Maxim Gorky and the first man in space, Yuri Gagarin, are here

too. Beyond lie the graves of a select group of Soviet leaders, each with his own bust; Stalin still gets the most flowers.

St Basil's Cathedral

With its multicoloured onion domes silhouetted against the skyline where Red Square slopes down towards the Moskva River, **St Basil's Cathedral** (early Nov to April daily 11am–5pm; May & Sept to early Nov daily 11am–6pm; June–Aug 10am–7pm; closed first Wed of the month; R350, student R100; ⍟saintbasil .ru) is perhaps the most instantly recognizable symbol of Russia. The exterior is far more impressive than the interior, however, which consists of a stone warren of small chapels and souvenir stalls. Built in 1561 to celebrate Ivan the Terrible's capture of the Tatar stronghold of Kazan in 1552, its name commemorates St Basil the Blessed, who foretold the fire that swept through Moscow in 1547.

The Kremlin

Brooding and glittering in the heart of the capital, the **Kremlin** (Aleksandrovsky Sad; Mon–Wed & Fri–Sun 10am–5pm; R500; ⍟kreml.ru; Ⓜ Borovitskaya) is both the heart of historical Moscow and home to its present-day parliament, the Duma. Its founding is attributed to Prince Yuriy Dolgorukiy, who built a wooden fort here in about 1147. Look out for the **Tsar Cannon**, cast in 1586: one of the largest cannons ever made, and intended to defend the Saviour Gate, it has never been fired. Close by looms the earthbound, broken **Tsar Bell**, the largest bell in the world, cast in 1655. **Cathedral Square** is the historic heart of the Kremlin, dominated by the magnificent, white **Ivan the Great Bell Tower**. Of the

---

KREMLIN ETIQUETTE

You may only purchase **tickets** for set entry times to the Armoury and the Diamond Fund. You will still have to queue for both attractions separately and watch tour groups and people with connections being ushered in before you. It's all part of the experience.

square's four key churches, the most important is the **Cathedral of the Assumption**, with a spacious, light and echoing interior, walls and pillars smothered with icons and frescoes, and temporary exhibitions housed in its belfry. The **Cathedral of the Archangel** houses the tombs of Russia's rulers from Grand Duke Ivan I to Tsar Ivan V, while the golden-domed **Cathedral of the Annunciation** hides some of Russia's finest icons, including works by Theophanes the Greek and Andrey Rublev.

The Armoury Chamber

The unmissable **Armoury Chamber** (ticketed entry at 10am, noon, 2.30pm and 4.30pm; R700), inside the Kremlin, boasts a staggering array of treasures, among them the tsars' coronation robes, jewellery and armour. A separate part of the Armoury Chamber houses the **Diamond Fund** (ticketed entry Mon–Wed & Fri at 20min intervals 10am–1pm and 2–5pm; R500) – a priceless collection of jewels, including the 190-karat Orlov diamond – which belonged to Catherine the Great – and the world's largest sapphire.

The State Central Museum of Contemporary History

The **State Central Museum of Contemporary History** at Tverskaya ul. 21 (Tues, Wed & Fri–Sun 11am–7pm, Thurs noon–9pm; R250; ⓦsovrhistory .ru; ⓜTverskaya) brings the Communist past alive with striking displays of Soviet propaganda posters, photographs and state gifts, although there's a frustrating lack of English translation.

The Pushkin Museum of Fine Arts

Founded in 1898 in honour of the famous Russian poet, the **Pushkin Museum of Fine Arts** at Volkhonka ul. 12 (Tues–Sun 11am–8pm, Thurs & Fri until 9pm; R550, student R300, separate fee for Impressionist wing; ⓦarts-museum .ru; ⓜKropotkinskaya) holds a hefty collection of **European paintings**, from Italian High Renaissance works to Rembrandt, and an outstanding display of Impressionist works.

Cathedral of Christ the Saviour

Built as a symbol of gratitude to divinity for having aided the Russians' defeat of Napoleon in 1812, the **Cathedral of Christ the Saviour** (daily 10am–6pm; ⓦxxc.ru; ⓜKropotkinskaya), opposite the Pushkin Museum of Fine Arts at Volkhonka ul. 15, was demolished in 1931 in favour of a monument to socialism. The project was soon abandoned; years later, under Khrushchev's rule, the site was turned into the world's largest public swimming pool. In 1994 the Cathedral was rebuilt and is now a symbol of Moscow's (and Russia's) post-Communist religious revival.

House-Museums

Admirers of Bulgakov, Chekhov, Gorky, Tolstoy and Stanislavsky will find their former homes preserved as museums. Anton Chekhov lived at Sadovaya-Kudrinskaya ul. 6, in what is now the **Chekhov House-Museum** (Tues–Sun 11am–6pm, Thurs until 8pm; closed last day of the month; R150; ⓜBarrikadnaya), containing humble personal effects, while the **Gorky House-Museum** (Wed–Sun 11am–5.30pm, closed last Thurs of the month; free; ⓜArbatskaya) at Malaya Nikitskaya ul. 6/2 is worth seeing if only for its raspberry-pink Art Nouveau decor. Leo Tolstoy admirers should head to the wonderfully preserved **Tolstoy Memorial Estate** on ul. Lva Tolstogo 21 (Wed, Fri–Sun 10am–6pm, Tues & Thurs

---

★TREAT YOURSELF

Get the city grit out of your skin at Russia's oldest public bathhouse, the exquisitely elaborate **Sandunovskiy baths** (Neglinnaya ul. 14 bldg 3–7 ⓦsanduny.ru; ⓜKuznetskiy Most), founded in 1808. Join Russian businessmen and socialites in the *banya*, a wooden hut heated with a furnace, where you are invited to sweat out impurities, get beaten energetically with birch twigs, and finally plunge into ice-cold water. Men's (2hr sessions from R1600) and women's baths (3hr sessions from R1800) are separate, with the women's section more like a modern spa. Daily 8am–10pm.

28

noon–8pm, closed last Fri of the month; R200; ⓜPark Kultury) where the Tolstoy family lived after moving to Moscow from their country estate in 1881, and where the novelist wrote *War and Peace*. The **Bulgakov Museum**, at Bolshaya Sadovaya ul. 10 (Tues–Sun noon–7pm, Thurs 2–9pm; R150; ⓦbulgakovmuseum.ru; ⓜMayakovskaya), is the flat where the novelist lived from 1921 to 1924, and contains personal effects, photographs and copies of his manuscripts. Thespians should not miss the **Stanislavsky House-Museum** (Wed & Fri noon–7pm, Thurs noon–9pm, Sat & Sun 11am–6pm; R250; ⓜTverskaya) at Leontyevskiy per. 6, where the renowned theatre director and founder of the Moscow Arts Theatre, Constantin Stanislavsky, once lived with his wife and children. Stanislavsky transformed his house into a makeshift theatre, with regular performances taking place in the main hall, while the adjoining dining area served as a make-up studio and held furniture for rehearsals.

Patriarch's Ponds

One of Moscow's most exclusive neighbourhoods, **Patriarch's Ponds** (ⓜTverskaya) is a pleasant spot for a summer stroll or an ice-skate on its frozen waters in the depths of winter – note that there's just one pond, despite the name. The area is also known for being the location of the opening scene of Mikhail Bulgakov's magical realist novel *The Master and Margarita*.

Novodevichiy Convent

A cluster of domes shining above a fortified rampart belongs to the lovely **Novodevichiy Convent** (daily 9am–5pm; R300, student R100; ⓜSportivnaya), founded by Ivan the Terrible in 1524. At its heart stands the white Cathedral of the Virgin of Smolensk. In its **cemetery** lie numerous famous writers, musicians and artists, including Gogol, Chekhov, Stanislavsky, Bulgakov and Shostakovich.

The State Tretyakov Gallery

Founded in 1892 by the financier Pavel Tretyakov, the **State Tretyakov Gallery** at Lavrushinskiy per. 10 (Tues, Wed & Sun 10am–6pm, Thurs, Fri & Sat 10am–9pm; R400, combined ticket with Tretyakov Gallery on Krymskiy Val R700; ⓦtretyakovgallery.ru; ⓜTretyakovskaya) displays an outstanding collection of pre-Revolutionary Russian art. Icons are magnificently displayed, and the exhibition continues through to the late nineteenth century, with the politically charged canvases of the iconic realist Ilya Repin and the Impressionist portraits of Valentin Serov, including *The Girl with Peaches*, one of the gallery's masterpieces.

The Tretyakov Gallery on Krymskiy Val

Opposite the entrance to Gorky Park at Krymskiy Val 10, the **Tretyakov Gallery on Krymskiy Val** (Tues, Wed & Sun 10am–6pm, Thurs, Fri & Sat 10am–9pm; R400, combined ticket with State Tretyakov Gallery R700; ⓦtretyakovgallery.ru; ⓜPark Kultury; Oktyabrskaya) takes a breakneck gallop through twentieth-century Russian art, from the avant-garde of the 1910s and 20s to contemporary artists. Full and illuminating commentary in English is a bonus.

Gorky Park

Gorky Park on ul. Krymskiy Val (ⓜPark Kultury; ⓦpark-gorkogo.com) occupies an area of over 700 acres along the river. In the winter the frozen-over paths become one of the city's largest ice rinks, while in the warmer months you can rent bikes, rollerblades and paddle boats, and take yoga and tango classes. Within the park is the **Garage Museum of Contemporary Art** (ⓦgaragemca.org), which hosts contemporary art projects and design fairs, and there are several cafés and restaurants too.

VDNH

To see Soviet triumphalism at its most prolific, visit the Exhibition of Economic Achievements, or **VDNH**, pronounced "Vee-Dee-En-Kha" (ⓦvdnh.ru; ⓦVDNKh), with its statue upon statue of ordinary workers in heroic poses. Adding to the scene is the permanent exhibition centre, host to everything from fairs and festivals to concerts and congresses, housed in the grandiose Stalinist architecture of the All-Union Agricultural Exhibition of 1939. There's also the People's Friendship Fountain, flanked by Soviet maidens, each symbolizing a Soviet republic. In the 1960s, space exploration became a central theme at VDNH, and a pavilion was created for spacecraft, with a 38m replica of the rocket *Vostok*, in which Yuri Gagarin made the world's first manned flight.

ARRIVAL AND DEPARTURE

By plane Flights from Western Europe arrive either at Sheremetyevo, 30km north of the centre, or Domodedovo, 45km to the south. Aeroexpress trains run between Shremetyevo and Belorusskiy station, connected to ⓜBelorusskaya, on the green and brown lines (every 30min 5am–12.30am; 35min; R470; ⓦaeroexpress.ru). Aeroexpress trains to and from Domodedovo serve Paveletsky station (every 30min 6am–midnight; 46min; R470; ⓦaeroexpress.ru) which is connected to ⓜPaveletskaya; express shuttle buses (every 15min 6am–midnight; 40min; R100) and express taxis (every 15min 6am–midnight; every 40min midnight–6am; 30min; R120) run between Domodedovo and ⓜDomodedovskaya 25km southeast of the centre.

By train All mainline stations are conveniently located by a metro station. Trains from Minsk and Warsaw arrive at Belorusskiy station (Belorusskiy vokzal, Tverskaya Zastava pl. 7; ⓜBelorusskaya) while Rizhsky station (Rizhsky vokzal, Rizhskaya pl. 1; ⓜRizhskaya) serves Latvian destinations such as Rīga. Leningradsky station (Leningradsky vokzal, Komsomolskaya pl. 3; ⓜKomsomolskaya) is the departure point for northern destinations including frequent trains to St Petersburg; Kievsky station (Kievsky vokzal, pl. Kievskogo Vokzala 1; ⓜKievskaya) serves Kiev, Odessa, Budapest and Bucharest. Yaroslavsky station (Yaroslavsky vokzal, Komsomolskaya pl. 5; ⓜKomsomolskaya) is the starting point for trans-Siberian adventures.

Destinations Helsinki (1 daily; 14hr 30min); Rīga (1 daily; 16hr 20min); St Petersburg (standard service: 6–16 daily; 7–9hr; Sapsan express: up to 16 daily; 4hr); Tallinn (1 daily; 15hr); Vilnius (1–2 daily; 14hr 15min); Warsaw (1–3 daily; 18–19hr).

By bus Ecolines buses from Germany and the Baltic States terminate at VDNKh bus station on pl. Charles de Gaulle opposite Hotel Kosmos at ul. Kosmonavtov 2A (ⓜVDNKh). Moscow's main bus station with intercity departures is at Schelkovskoye shosse 75, ⓜShcholkovskaya (☎499 748 8029, ⓦmosoblvokzaly.ru), 16km northeast of the city

centre. Most long-distance foreign destinations require a change at Rīga.

Destinations Rīga (1 daily; 15hr); St Petersburg (21 daily; 10–12hr); Vilnius (2 daily via Rezekne in Latvia; 17hr).

INFORMATION

Tourist office At the time of research Moscow did not have a tourist office. Your best bet is to ask for information at your hostel or get hold of the handy *Moscow In Your Pocket* guide, which can be downloaded from ⓦinyourpocket.com/moscow.

GETTING AROUND

By bus Buses cost R50 per journey; stops are marked with yellow signs.

By metro With its Soviet mosaics, murals and statuary, Moscow's metro (5.30am–1am) is world-famous and is by far the best way to get around, given the city's congested roads. Stations are marked with a large "M" and you can plan your journey on ⓦmetroway.ru. A one-way fare costs R50; you can also buy a card of two (R100) or twenty (R650) journeys (ask at the *kassa* for *dva/dvatsat póezdok*). There are also one-day (R210) and three-day tickets (R400). The metro has free wi-fi.

By minibus *Marshrutki* are cheap (around R35 a journey). They wait to fill up with passengers, then take the route advertised on the side. You can ask to get out at any point. Pay the driver on board.

By tram and trolleybus Moscow's terrible traffic means trolleybuses and trams are often at a standstill, although they can at times be useful to tackle a major road such as the Garden Ring. Stops have blue-and-white signs. Most routes operate from 5am to 1am; fares cost R50 on board; the same tickets are used for buses.

ACCOMMODATION

HOSTELS

★ **Fasol** Arkhangelskiy per. 11/16, bldg.3 ☎499 390 8982, ⓦfasolhotels.ru; ⓜChistye Prudy. Tucked away off a side street in the pleasant neighbourhood of Chistye Prudy, this trendy hostel has stylish interiors. The kitchen

28

28

features wooden stools and a long table that allows for communal dining, while dorm beds have privacy curtains, lockers, reading lights and sockets. Breakfast is R150. Dorms R900, doubles R2900

Friend House Petrovka 17 ☎929 693 0733, ⓦfriend -house.ru; ⓜChekhovskaya. Located off elegant ul. Petrovka a short walk from the Bolshoi Theatre, this pleasant hostel features modern black and white interiors. The comfortable communal area has an open-plan kitchen and black-and-white photos adorning the walls. Rooms are painted in different tones, from pastel hues to vibrant colours, and dorm beds have curtains ensuring a little privacy. Dorms R650, doubles R2300

Godzillas Bolshoi Karetniy 6 ☎495 699 4223, ⓦgodzillashostel.com; ⓜTsvetnoy bulvar/Tverskaya. Relaxed, popular hostel a short walk from the centre. Rooms are pleasantly decorated with quirky wallpaper, minimalist furniture and parquet floors. Helpful staff provide lots of Moscow information. Dorms US$12, doubles US$45

GoodMood Hostel Ul. Maroseyka 9/2 bldg.6 ☎985 962 2635, ⓦgoodmoodhostel.ru. A friendly hostel in the district of Kitay Gorod that is a short walk away from restaurants, bars and major sights. There's a communal area with bare brick walls, sofas and books, and there's a fully equipped kitchen for guests' use. Dorm beds have privacy curtains, reading lamps and power sockets. Private rooms are on the small side. Dorms R1200, doubles R3200

iVan Petrovsky per. 1/30, apt.23 ☎916 407 1178, ⓦivanhostel.com; ⓜChekhovskaya. Clean hostel with bright and airy interiors located just off swanky ul. Petrovka with free morning coffee, all-day tea and single-sex dorms with lockers. Dorms R1200, doubles R3200

Vagabond Tverskaya 19A apt.61 ☎968 404 9404, ⓦvagabondhostel.com. A small and cosy hostel with one spacious mixed dorm featuring large windows overlooking Tverskaya, Moscow's main artery, along with a smaller female-only dorm and a couple of private rooms. Friendly, helpful staff can help book tickets for performances and attractions in town, and there's a fully equipped kitchen for guests' use. Dorms R700, doubles R3000

EATING

Take advantage of the great-value business lunches offered by cafés and restaurants during the week between noon and 4pm.

AQ Kitchen Bolshaya Gruzinskaya 69 ☎499 393 3224, ⓦaq.kitchen; ⓜBelorusskaya. Inventive dishes are served at this bustling restaurant with floor-to-ceiling windows, low-hanging light bulbs and colourful ceiling designs. The menu includes Astrakhan perch with quinoa, broccoli and olive oil sauce (R760) and Moroccan-style chicken with couscous and pear chutney (R590). Daily noon–11pm.

Black Market Ul. Usacheva 2 ☎495 989 0445 ⓦblackmarketcafe.ru; ⓜSportivnaya. Decorated to

resemble a black-market warehouse, this airy café and restaurant with glass-fronted windows serves international cuisine, from modern American dishes to Asian and Italian specialities. Mains R650. Mon–Thurs & Sun 10am–midnight, Fri & Sat 10am–2am.

Izia Grill Ul. Lva Tolstogo 16 ☎495 755 8727, ⓦizia -grill.ru; ⓜPark Kultury. Airy buzzing café and restaurant with open plan kitchen, colourful murals and tree stumps serving as table legs. The food is Middle Eastern (think hummus, falafel and *shawarma*), but there are also juicy burgers (R400) and plenty of grilled meats (R450) to choose from. Mon–Thurs & Sun 8am–midnight, Fri & Sat 24hr.

★**Khachapuri** B. Gnezdnikovskiy 10 ☎985 764 3118, ⓦhacha.ru; ⓜTverskaya. Some of the city's tastiest Georgian grub is served at this cosy and inexpensive café, with live piano recitals laid on in the evenings. The exquisite meat *khinkali* (large dumplings; R80) and the *khachapuri* (bread oozing with melted cheese; R190) are unmissable. Superb-value business lunches (R290–540). Mon–Thurs 10am–11pm, Fri 10am–1am, Sat 11am–1am, Sun 11am–11pm.

★**Mari Vanna** Spiridonevskiy per. 10a ☎495 650 6500, ⓦmarivanna.ru; ⓜTverskaya. Set out like a 1960s Soviet flat, with mock black-and-white TV, floral decor and old-world memorabilia, this expat favourite is a great little place to savour traditional Russian dishes. The exquisite *borshch* soup (R490) is served at the table with a little fanfare, and the home-made meat *pelmeni* (R670) are delicious. Roaming pets add to the welcoming homely atmosphere, as does the doorbell you need to ring upon arrival. Daily 9am–midnight.

Meat Puppets Bar Novoslobodskaya ul. 16/18 ☎495 787 3402, ⓦmeatpuppets.ru; ⓜMendeleevskaya. Passionate carnivores must not miss this restaurant

---

★**TREAT YOURSELF**

Café Pushkin Tverskoy Bulvar 26A ☎495 739 0033, ⓦcafe-pushkin.ru; ⓜTverskaya. You will feel like you've stepped back into the nineteenth century as soon as you cross the threshold of this upmarket restaurant serving historic dishes of the Russian nobility. The Baroque-style interiors of the Library Room feature ceiling-high bookshelves, English chiming wall clocks and a large floor-standing globe. Tuck into an authentic beef stroganoff as you soak in the views of Tverskoy Bulvar, particularly striking on a snowy winter's day. Mains from R800. There's an excellent-value two-course lunch for R620. Open 24hr.

serving top-notch cuts of meat, including glazed pork ribs (R666) and stewed bull tail (R555). There's even bacon cheese cake to finish. Interiors feature chunks of wood jutting out of the wall and papier-mâché lampshades. Mon–Thurs & Sun noon–midnight, Fri & Sat noon–3am.

★**Ugolek** Ul. Bolshaya Nikitskaya 12 ☎ 495 629 0211, ⓦ ugolecafe.ru; ⓜ Okhotny Ryad. At this trendy restaurant with dimly lit interiors, wooden tables and sofas, the creatively presented food (French, Italian and Russian) is cooked on an open charcoal oven, giving the dishes a smoky flavour. Book ahead. Mon–Wed & Sun noon–midnight, Thurs–Sat noon–2am.

Varenichnaya N°1 Arbat 29; ⓜ Arbatskaya. This café-cum-restaurant, decorated with all manner of Soviet knick-knacks, rustles up 80–100kg of exquisite handmade *vareniki* (Ukrainian dumplings; R190) every day. Daily 10am–midnight.

Zotman Ul. Bolshaya Nikitskaya 23/14/9 ☎ 499 426 2603, ⓦ zotman.ru. Shabby-chic place featuring white bare-brick walls serving tasty Neapolitan-style pizzas (R460) in a pleasant buzzing environment. Daily 11am–midnight.

DRINKING AND NIGHTLIFE

Moscow's famous nightlife is marred by the practice of "face control", excluding the not-so-beautiful people from *elitni* clubs. The venues listed here are largely accessible.

Kamchatka Kuznetskiy Most 7 ☎ 495 624 8825, ⓦ novikovgroup.ru/restaurants/kamchatka; ⓜ Kuzneyskiy Most. Lively drinking hole that recalls a Soviet beer house of the 70s and 80s with a self-service system on the ground floor offering cheap local beer (R120) and fried sausages to snack on. Downstairs food is served in a large canteen-style hall, which comes alive in the evenings when DJs spin Russian and Soviet retro classics. Mon–Thurs 10am–11pm, Fri 10am–3am, Sat noon–3am, Sun noon–1am.

Kitayskiy Letchik Dzhao Dao Lubyanskiy proezd 25/12, ⓦ jao-da.ru; ⓜ Kitay-gorod. Descend to this artfully scuffed-up basement labyrinth, which hosts some outstanding alternative bands at weekends (R200–500). Open 24hr.

★**Mendeleev** Ul. Petrovka 20/1 ☎ 495 625 3385; ⓜ Chekhovskaya or Teatralnaya. Walk through the black curtain to the right of the counter of *Lucky Noodles*, a cheap Chinese takeaway joint, and you'll enter the this much sought-after basement bar and speakeasy. Locals and foreigners flock here for the well-prepared cocktails (R500) and trendy atmosphere; it gets packed at the weekends when DJs spin tracks until the early hours. Tues, Wed & Sun 6pm–1am, Thurs 6pm–3am, Fri & Sat 8pm–6am.

MyBar Ul. Kuznetsky Most 3, bldg.2 ☎ 916 583 5279; ⓜ Teatralnaya. Fun, relaxed hangout that makes for a refreshing change from Moscow's glitzy bars, playing a mix of pop and rock classics at the weekends, which attract quite a crowd. There are live gigs on Thursdays, from rock to blues. Beers from R99, long drinks from R199. Daily 6pm–6am.

Propaganda Bolshoy Zlatoustinsky per. 7 ⓦ propaganda moscow.com; ⓜ Kitay-gorod. With this popular club's bare brick walls and bright lights, you might be backstage at a Hollywood film set. Mild face control so it's best to book a table for dinner to ensure entry. Gay nights on Sun. Mon–Fri 11.30am–6am, Sat & Sun noon–6am.

Strelka Bersenevskaya nab. 14 ⓦ strelka.com; ⓜ Kropotkinskaya. An unmissable venue in the summer months, featuring a spacious rooftop terrace overlooking the Moscow River and the Cathedral of Christ the Saviour. Hipsters come here for the tasty food, great cocktails and unobstructed views, which are particularly evocative at sunset. Cocktails R500. Mon–Thurs 9am–midnight, Fri 9am–3am, Sat noon–3am, Sun noon–midnight.

ENTERTAINMENT

Theatre, classical music and ballet all have superb vintages in Russia and won't necessarily break the bank, provided you ask for the cheapest ticket available (*samiy deshoviy bilyet*).

LIVE MUSIC

B2 Bolshaya Sadovaya 8/1 ⓦ b2club.ru; ⓜ Mayakovskaya. With a capacity of 2000 people, *B2* is a staple venue on the live music scene, with a variety of bands playing anything from jazz to ska music. Thurs & Sun R400 after 8pm, Fri & Sat R600 after 8pm, free beforehand. Concert admission from R300. Daily noon–6am.

Tchaikovsky Concert Hall Triumfalnaya pl. 4/31 ⓦ meloman.ru; ⓜ Mayakovskaya. Soak in some classical music at Moscow's premier musical venue. The hall has excellent acoustics and hosts all manner of performances, from soloist acts to symphony orchestras. Tickets start at R100.

THEATRE

Bolshoi Theatre Teatralnaya pl. 1 ⓦ bolshoi.ru; ⓜ Teatralnaya. The sumptuous, recently renovated theatre is home to the world's most famous ballet and regularly stages operas and operettas. Tickets from R2500.

CINEMA

The cinemas listed below screen films in their original language.

35MM Pokrovka 47/24 ⓦ kino35mm.ru; ⓜ Chistye Prudy. Specializes in independent foreign films.

Rolan Cinema Chistoprudny Boulevard 12a ⓦ 5zvezd.ru; ⓜ Chistye Prudy. Art-house films – mainly new classics – and festival screenings.

28

SHOPPING

Dorogomilovsky Market Mozhaisky Val 10; Ⓜ Kievskaya. Plenty of fresh produce on offer, including cheeses, meats, fish and seafood as well as an excellent selection of fruit and veg. Daily 7am–10pm.

Vernissage in Izmailovo Izmailovskoye shosse 73; Ⓜ Partizanskaya. Open-air market with Moscow's best (and cheapest) Soviet paraphernalia and memorabilia including coins, fur hats, *matrioshka* dolls, Soviet posters and postcards. It is open daily but you're best going at weekends 9am–6pm when there are more stalls. In winter make sure you get there before 3pm.

DIRECTORY

Embassies Australia, Podkolokolny per. 10a/2 ☎ 495 956 6070, Ⓜ Kitay-gorod; Canada, Starokonyushenny per. 23 ☎ 495 925 6000, Ⓜ Kropotkinskaya; Ireland, Grokholski per. 5 ☎ 495 937 5911, Ⓜ Prospekt Mira; New Zealand, Prechistenskaya nab. 3 ☎ 495 956 3579, Ⓜ Park Kultury; UK, Smolenskaya nab. 10 ☎ 495 956 7200, Ⓜ Smolenskaya; US, Bolshoi Devyatinskiy per. 8 ☎ 495 728 5000, Ⓜ Barrikadnaya.

Health European Medical Center, Spiridonievskiy per. 5, bldg. 1 ☎ 495 933 6655, ⊛ emcmos.ru, Ⓜ Tverskaya; Intermed Center, Monotchikovsky per. 1/6, bldg. 3 ☎ 495 9375757, ⊛ intac.ru, Ⓜ Paveletskaya. Both have English-speaking doctors and are recognized by international insurance companies.

Pharmacies There are 24hr "36,6" pharmacies at ul. Tverskaya 25/9, Ⓜ Mayakovskaya, and at Leninskiy prospect 12, Ⓜ Oktyabrskaya.

Post offices Tverskaya 7, Ⓜ Tverskaya (Mon–Fri 8am–1pm & 2–8pm, Sat 9am–1pm & 2–6pm). Express postal service: DHL c/o Marriott Tverskaya at ul. 1ya Tverskaya-Yamskaya 11; Ⓜ Mayakovskaya

St Petersburg

ST PETERSBURG (Санкт-Петербург), Petrograd, Leningrad and St Petersburg again – the city's succession of names mirrors Russia's turbulent history. Founded in 1703 by **Peter the Great** as a "window in the West", self-assured, future-focused St Petersburg still retains more of a Western European feel than Moscow more than three hundred years on. A sophisticated capital of the tsarist Empire, the cradle of the Communist Revolution of 1917, and a symbol of Russian stoicism due to the city's heroic endurance of a three-year Nazi siege

during World War II, present-day St Petersburg has eased into modernity without sacrificing any of its old-world magnificence and charm, with shopping malls and nightclubs sitting alongside opulent palaces. The pace of life here is relaxed, and the people are more open and laidback than their Muscovite counterparts. The best **time to visit** is during the midsummer White Nights (mid-June to mid-July), when darkness never falls, and the partying can reach fever pitch. Roughly from May to October (navigation season depends on the weather) bridges across the River Neva are raised from around 1.30am to 5am (each bridge has its own schedule, which changes yearly). It's a beautiful sight, best experienced from a boat.

WHAT TO SEE AND DO

St Petersburg's centre lies on the south bank of the Neva, with the curving River Fontanka marking its southern boundary. The area within the Fontanka is riven by a series of avenues fanning out from the golden spire of the Admiralty on the Neva's south bank. Many of the city's top sights are located on and around **Nevsky prospekt**, the backbone and heart of the city for the last three centuries, stretching from the Alexander Nevsky Monastery to Palace Square. Across the Neva is **Vasilevskiy Island**, home to the Kuntskamera, while over the Birzhevoy Bridge lies the Peter and Paul Fortress. To the east of the centre, beyond the River Fontanka, lies the **Smolniy Institute**, where the Bolsheviks fomented revolution in 1917.

The Winter Palace and Hermitage

Sited on the banks of the River Neva, the 200m-long Baroque **Winter Palace** is the city's largest and most opulent, and was the official residence of the tsars, their court and 1500 servants until the revolution of 1917. Today the building houses one of the world's greatest museums, the **Hermitage** (Tues–Sun 10.30am–6pm, Wed & Fri 10.30am–9pm; R600, free to students, free admission first Thurs of every month; ⊛ hermitagemuseum.org;

Admiralteyskaya), launched as Russia's first public art museum in 1852. It occupies five palaces along with the General Staff Building located on Palace Square, which houses an impressive collection of Impressionist and Post-Impressionist paintings. The elaborately decorated staterooms of the Winter Palace are works of art in their own right, with ceiling frescoes, sumptuous chandeliers and elaborate gild work. The collection embraces over three million treasures and artworks, from ancient Scythian gold and giant malachite urns to Cubist pieces.

Kazan Cathedral

Curving **Kazan Cathedral** (daily 9am–6pm; Nevsky prospekt), built between 1801 and 1811, was modelled on St Peter's in Vatican City and is unique in die-straight St Petersburg. The cathedral was built to house a venerated icon, Our Lady of Kazan, reputed to have appeared miraculously overnight in Kazan in 1579 and later transferred to St Petersburg, where it resided until its disappearance in 1904. In Soviet times the cathedral housed the Museum of Atheism, dedicated to proving that "religion is the opium of the people". Today it teems once more with worshippers.

The Church of the Saviour on the Spilled Blood

The multicoloured, onion-domed **Church of the Saviour on Spilled Blood** at 26 Kanala Griboedova embankment (Mon, Tues & Thurs–Sun 10.30am–6pm, last entry 5.30pm; R250, student R150; cathedral .ru; Nevsky prospekt) was built in 1882 on the very spot where Tsar Alexander II was assassinated by student radicals a year earlier. With a stunning mosaic-covered interior, the church is one of St Petersburg's most striking landmarks, quite unlike the dominant Neoclassical architecture.

The Russian Museum

The Mikhailovsky Palace, worth a visit for its beautifully decorated rooms alone, houses the main part of the **Russian Museum** (4 Inzhenernaya ul.; Mon 10am–8pm, Wed & Fri–Sun 10am–6pm, Thurs 1–9pm; R450,

student R200; rusmuseum.ru; Gostiny dvor). Its collection of Russian art is the world's finest, ranging from fourteenth-century icons to the particularly impressive avant-garde collection from the early twentieth century in the Benois Wing.

The Summer Garden and around

Most popular of all St Petersburg's public gardens is the **Summer Garden** (Mon & Wed–Sun 10am–8pm; rusmuseum.ru; Gostiny dvor) on Kutuzov Embankment. It was commissioned by Peter the Great in 1704 and rebuilt by Catherine the Great in the informal English style that survives today. Also charming are the Mikhailovsky Gardens behind the Russian Museum (May–Sept daily 10am–10pm; Oct–March 10am–8pm; closed April; rusmuseum.ru), and Marsovo Pole (the Field of Mars) on the other side of the River Moyka where a flame burns for the fallen of the Revolution and civil war (1917–21).

The Admiralty and Decembrists' Square

The **Admiralty**, perched at the northwestern end of Nevsky prospect (Admiralteyskaya), was founded in 1704 as a fortified shipyard. It extends 407m along the waterfront from Palace Square to **Decembrists' Square**, named after a group of reformist officers who, in December 1825, marched three thousand soldiers into the square in a doomed attempt to proclaim a constitutional monarchy. Today, Decembrists' Square is dominated by the *Bronze Horseman*, Falconet's 1778 statue of Peter the Great and the city's unofficial symbol.

St Isaac's Cathedral

Looming above Decembrists' Square, **St Isaac's Cathedral** (Mon, Tues & Thurs–Sun 10.30am–6pm; colonnade until 10.30pm May–Oct; R250, student R150, colonnade R150; cathedral.ru; Admiralteyskaya) is one of the glories of St Petersburg's skyline, its gilded dome the third largest in Europe. The opulent interior is equally impressive, decorated with fourteen kinds of marble. Climb the

28

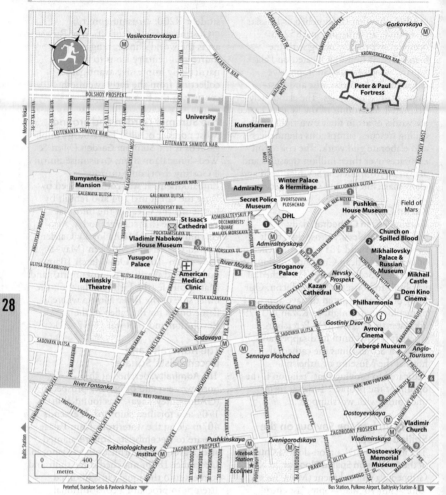

Morskoy Vokzal ◄

◄ Baltic Station

28

Peterhof, Tsarskoe Selo & Pavlovsk Palace ▼

Bus Station, Pulkovo Airport, Baltiyskiy Station & ⑥ ▼

262 steps to the outside colonnade to appreciate the cathedral's height (101.5m) and for an expansive view of the city. From June 1 to August 20 the colonnade is open until 4.30am.

The Peter and Paul Fortress

Across the Neva from the Winter Palace stands the **Peter and Paul Fortress**, built to secure Russia's hold on the Neva delta. The Fortress (daily 6am–8pm; May–Sept until 11pm; free; ⓦspbmuseum.ru; ⓜGorkovskaya) shelters a cathedral as well as rotating exhibitions in the Engineers' and

Commandant's House. Completed in 1733, the Dutch-style Peter and Paul Cathedral (Mon & Thurs–Sun 10am–6pm, Tues 10am–5pm; May–Sept until 7pm; R600, student R350) remained the tallest structure in the city until the 1960s. Sited around the nave are the tombs of **Romanov monarchs** from Peter the Great to Nicholas II, excluding Peter II and Ivan VI. The Nevskaya panorama walk (daily 10am–7.30pm; May–Sept until 9pm; separate ticket required R300), along the rooftops of the fortifications, gives an excellent view of the Winter Palace.

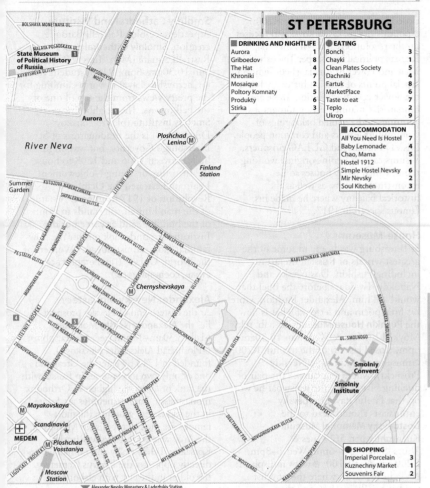

ST PETERSBURG

■ DRINKING AND NIGHTLIFE		● EATING	
Aurora	1	Bonch	3
Griboedov	8	Chayki	1
The Hat	4	Clean Plates Society	5
Khroniki	7	Dachniki	4
Mosaique	2	Fartuk	8
Poltory Komnaty	5	MarketPlace	6
Produkty	6	Taste to eat	7
Stirka	3	Teplo	2
		Ukrop	9

■ ACCOMMODATION	
All You Need Is Hostel	7
Baby Lemonade	4
Chao, Mama	5
Hostel 1912	1
Simple Hostel Nevsky	6
Mir Nevsky	2
Soul Kitchen	3

● SHOPPING	
Imperial Porcelain	3
Kuznechny Market	1
Souvenirs Fair	2

28

Cruiser Aurora

Anchored a short walk along the Neva from the Peter and Paul Fortress is the **Cruiser Aurora** (under renovation at the time of research; ⓦ aurora.org.ru; ⓜ Gorkovskaya), the famous battle ship that fired the opening shot of the revolution of 1917.

Kunstkamera

The **Kunstkamera** at Universitetskaya nab. 3, Vasilevsky Island (Tues–Sun 11am–6pm, closed last Tues of the month; R250; ⓦ kunstkamera.ru; ⓜ Vasileostrovskaya) is Russia's oldest public museum, founded by Peter the Great in 1714 in order to promote scientific research and educate the general public in the sphere of medical research. One of the richest ethnographical museums in the world, the unique collection includes a selection of rather morbid items, from malformed fetuses to infants' hearts, carefully preserved in vinegar or vodka.

State Museum of Political History of Russia

The **State Museum of Political History of Russia** at ul. Kuibysheva 2/4 (Mon, Tues & Fri–Sun 10am–6pm, Wed 10am–8pm, closed last Mon of the month; R200; ⊛polithistory.ru; Ⓜ Gorkovskaya) focuses on the revolutions and wars that shaped Russia's political landscape. The exhibition, Man and Power in Russia, sheds light on crucial points of Russian history, while in the Soviet Epoch exhibition, there are human-size mannequins, photographs, paintings and personal belongings of Communist leaders and common people, NKVD officers and GULAG prisoners. Visitors can see Lenin's original working room, which today houses some reconstructed items, as well as the historical balcony where he made his famous speech in 1917.

House-Museums

St Petersburg was home to some of the greatest writers of Russian literature, including Pushkin, Dostoevsky and Nabokov. Two days before the duel that would kill him, Alexander Pushkin wrote his final poem and letter at what is now the **Pushkin House-Museum**, at nab. reki Moyki 12 (Mon & Wed–Sun 10.30am–6pm, closed last Fri of the month; R200; ⊛museumpushkin.ru; Ⓜ Nevskiy Prospekt), where you can see the pair of duelling pistols and the waistcoat he wore on that fateful day. Dostoevsky enthusiasts should head to the **Dostoevsky Memorial Museum** at Kuznechny per. 5/2 (Tues & Thurs–Sun 11am–6pm, Wed 1–8pm; R200, student R100; ⊛www.md.spb.ru; Ⓜ Vladimirskaya), where the novelist resided briefly in 1846 and then again from 1878 until his death three years later. Here he initially worked on his first story *The Double*, and later on his last novel *The Brothers Karamazov*. The former home of the prose master behind *Lolita* is the **Vladimir Nabokov House-Museum** at Bolshaya Morskaya 47 (Tues–Fri 11am–6pm, Sat & Sun noon–5pm; free entry; ⊛nabokov .museums.spbu.ru; Ⓜ Admiralteyskaya), where the novelist lived until 1917. You can watch a video interview with Nabokov as well as peruse curious memorabilia, including part of the butterfly collection that inspired many of his novels.

Smolniy Cathedral and Institute

A peerless ice-blue Rastrelli Baroque creation, **Smolniy Cathedral** at 3/1 Rastrelli Square (Mon, Tues & Thurs–Sun 10.30am–6pm; R150, student R90; Ⓜ Chernyshevskaya) is worth climbing for the pretty views from the top of one of the bell towers. The neighbouring **Smolniy Institute** (pl. Proletarskoy Diktatury 3) is the headquarters of St Petersburg's Governor, but was originally built between 1806 and 1808 to house the Institute for Young Noblewomen; Lenin orchestrated the October Revolution of 1917 from here. A statue of the man himself still stands in front of the building, and as you enter the Institute's grounds look out for the now familiar Communist slogan: "Workers of the World, Unite!" (Пролетарии всех стран, соединяйтесь!).

Alexander Nevsky Monastery

At the eastern end of Nevsky prospekt lies the **Alexander Nevsky Monastery** (daily 5.30am–11pm; free, ⊛lavra.spb.ru; Ⓜ Ploshchad Aleksandra Nevskogo), founded in 1713 by Peter the Great and one of only two monasteries in Russia with the rank of *lavra*, the highest in Orthodox monasticism. Four **cemeteries** are located in the monastery grounds; the most famous are the Necropolis for Masters of the Arts, where Dostoevsky, Rimsky-Korsakov, Tchaikovsky and Glinka lie, and, directly opposite, the Lazarus Cemetery, the oldest in the city with elaborately decorated tombs. Tickets are required for entry to both (daily 10am–6pm; R150; combined ticket R250). Long trousers and shirts should be worn when entering the monastery and cathedral; women should also use a headscarf.

Rumyantsev Mansion

Along the Neva embankment to the west of the Admiralty, the focal point of the **Rumyantsev Mansion** at Angliyskaya nab. 44 (Mon & Thurs–Sun 11am–6pm, Tues 11am–5pm; R200, student R100; ⊛spbmuseum.ru; Ⓜ Sadovaya) is the exhibition on Leningrad during the Great Patriotic War, which details the horrors of life in a desperate city, besieged by the

Nazis between 1941 and 1944. The most harrowing exhibit is the diary of 11-year-old Tanya Savicheva, who continued going to school as, one by one, her entire family died of starvation.

Yusupov Palace

Purchased by the aristocratic Yusupov family in 1830, the elaborately decorated **Yusupov Palace** at nab. reki Moyki 94 (daily 11am–5pm; R700, including audioguide; ⓦyusupov-palace.ru; ⓜNevsky prospekt) is a unique architectural ensemble of styles from the eighteenth to twentieth centuries, and is one of the few aristocratic mansions in the city where it's possible to gain an insight into the sumptuous lives of the Yusupov family. The palace was the scene of the murder of Grigori Rasputin, a Siberian peasant who was the spiritual mentor and family friend of the Romanovs at the beginning of the twentieth century. The assassination took place in the living quarters of young Prince Felix Yusupov, which today house a historical documentary exhibition that recounts the events of that brutal December evening.

Fabergé Museum

Located in the sumptuous eighteenth-century Shuvalov Palace, the **Fabergé Museum** at nab. reki Fontanki 21 (daily 9.30am–9pm; R450; tours in Russian every 20min, in English daily at 4.10pm; ⓦfabergemuseum.ru; ⓜGostinyy Dvor) houses an impressive collection of Russian jewellery art, including the world's most complete collection of Fabergé masterpieces. On display are nine imperial Easter eggs that were made to the order of Alexander III and Nicholas II, including the very first imperial egg, the Hen Egg, given on Easter Day 1885, and the last imperial egg made during the years of World War I. The collection also includes Russian porcelain, accessories, clocks, icons and Russian and European paintings of the nineteenth and twentieth centuries.

ARRIVAL AND DEPARTURE

By plane International flights arrive at Pulkovo Airport (☎812 337 3822, ⓦpulkovoairport.ru). Express city bus #39Ex (every 25–30min; 20min; R30) and city bus #39

(every 12–20min; 35min; R30) leave from the bus stop in front of the Arrivals Hall and travel to ⓜMoskovskaya, from where it's a 15–20min metro ride to the centre. Minivan K39 travels the same route (every 5min; 15–20min; R40). A taxi to the centre is about R1000.

By train Services from Finland use Finland station (Finlyandskiy vokzal) at pl. Lenina 6 (ⓜPloshchad Lenina) and Ladozhskiy station (ⓜLadozhskaya). Trains from the Baltic States and Eastern Europe terminate at Vitebsk station (Vitebskiy vokzal) on Zagorodny Prospekt (ⓜPushkinskaya). Trains from Moscow draw into Moscow station (Moskovskiy vokzal) on pl. Vosstaniya (ⓜPloshchad Vosstaniya).

Destinations Helsinki (standard service: 1 daily; 6hr 55min; Sapsan express: 4 daily; 3hr 30min); Moscow (standard service: 6–16 daily; 7–9hr; Sapsan express: up to 16 daily; 4hr); Riga (1 daily; 16hr); Vilnius (1 daily; 17hr 10min).

By bus Most buses arrive at the central bus station, nab. Obvodnogo kanala 36, ⓜObvodnyy Kanal. Lux Express services from Riga and Tallinn arrive at Mitrofanyevskoe shosse 2-1 outside Baltic station (Baltiyskiy vokzal; ⓜBaltiyskaya). The Ecolines (ⓦecolines.ru) buses stop outside Vitebsk station (Vitebskiy voksal; ⓜPushkinskaya) at the corner of Vedenskiy kanal and Zagarodniy prospekt. Ecolines ticket office is a short walk away at Podyezdnoy per. 3. A number of shuttle bus companies have services to Helsinki (6–8hr), including Scandinavia (call ☎901 314 56 74 to book, ⓦscandinavia.spb.ru), whose shuttle buses depart from the corner of Ligovsky Prospekt and Nevsky prospekt by *Hotel Oktyabrskaya* (ⓜPloshchad Vosstaniya).

Destinations Helsinki (3 daily; 7hr 30min); Moscow (21 daily; 10–12hr); Riga (9 daily; 11hr); Tallinn (6–9 daily; 7hr).

By ferry St Peter Line (ⓦstpeterline.com) operates ferries to Helsinki (12–13hr), with some ferries travelling on to Stockholm and Tallinn. They dock at the Morskoy vokzal, Morskoy Slavy 1 (ⓜVasilieostrovskaya), at the western end of Vasilevskiy Island (metro or minibus from the centre).

INFORMATION

The main tourist office centre at Sadovaya ul. 14 (Mon–Sat 10am–7pm; ☎812 310 2231, ⓦvisit-petersburg.ru; ⓜNevsky prospekt) has plenty of material in English. There are a number of tourist points around town, including at Isaakievskaya Pl 4/1 (Saint Isaac's Square) and at the Peter and Paul Fortress.

GETTING AROUND

By metro The St Petersburg metro, the deepest in the world, runs from 5.30am to midnight. Small numbers of journeys (R35 a journey) are sold using tokens (*zhetoni*), which you feed into ticket machines. For ten or more rides to be used over a fixed number of days, buy a plastic card.

By bus and trolleybus There are often the best way to navigate a major road like Nevsky prospekt, while overground transport is more useful in the compact city centre than the metro, with its lengthy escalators. Buy tickets from the driver (R30, or use the plastic metro card which is also valid for trams, trolleybuses and buses). Trolleybus #7 goes from Moskovskiy vokzal train station right to the upper end of Nevsky prospekt.

By boat One of the best ways to see the city is by boat (May–Sept) – either a private motorboat from any bridge on Nevsky prospekt (about R3000/hr/boat), or a large tour boat from behind the Hermitage (about R700/person). AngloTourismo (T 921 989 4722, W anglotourismo.com) offer 1hr 30min boat tours in English (R1000, students R850) from the pier at nab. Reki Fontanki 27 (M Gostiny dvor).

On foot AngloTourismo (T 921 989 4722, W anglotourismo.com) offer free 3hr walking tours in English daily at 10.30am that leave by the pier at nab. Reki Fontanki 27.

28

ACCOMMODATION

HOSTELS

All You Need Is Hostel Rubinshteina 6 T 921 950 0574, W youneedhostel.ru; M Mayakovskaya. A colourful hostel with spacious dorms and a communal area full of comfy beanbags, a TV and PlayStation, and all manner of musical instruments to try your hand at. Bike rental is offered. Dorms R650, doubles R2500

Baby Lemonade Inzhenernaya 7 T 812 570 7943, E babylemonadehostel@gmail.com; M Gostiny dvor. This friendly hostel offers rooms inspired by the 1960s, 70s and rock 'n' roll. There's a pleasant open-plan kitchen that is a great spot to mingle. Dorms R650, doubles R3600

★**Chao, Mama** Grazhdanskaya ul. 27/30 T 812 570 0444, W chaomama.ru; M Sadovaya. This stylish hostel offers comfortable, spotless dorms with privacy curtains and lockers, a communal kitchen and a number of modish apartments with kitchenette; apartment guests are given their own key card and enter and exit the block independently. Dorms R1100, apartments R15,000

Hostel 1912 Chapaeva 2A T 921 305 5558, W hostel1912.com; M Gorkovskaya. This itty-bitty place is the city's smallest hostel and one of the few backpacker digs located on the northern side of the Neva River. It only sleeps twelve, which is ideal for those seeking a calm hostel experience. A corridor with bare brick walls and black-and-white photographs of the city leads to the three rooms: a four-bed female only dorm, six-bed dorm and a double room. There's a small kitchen and dining area where guests are encouraged to socialize. Dorms R790, doubles R1990

Mir Nevsky Nevsky prospekt 16 T 911 755 6001, W mirhostel.com; M Admiralteyskaya. Contented travellers here regularly scribble their comments in colourful chalk on the walls of the attractive, parquet-floored communal area. Dorms are clean and spacious and staff even take care of your laundry at no extra cost. Rates include breakfast. Dorms R690, doubles R3000

★**Simple Hostel Nevsky** Nevsky Prospekt 78 T 812 499 4945, W simplehostel.com; M Admiralteyskaya. The exposed brick pipes and bare brick walls give this trendy hostel an industrial-chic feel. The spacious living area with TV is a great spot to mingle with other travellers, while the comfortable dorms have reading lamps and lockers. Dorms R999, doubles R3990

★**Soul Kitchen** Nab. reki Moyki 62/2, apt.9 T 965 816 3480, W soulkitchenhostel.com; M Admiralteyskaya. Cool and funky hostel that boasts a large, modern kitchen and bright, spacious dorms with individual reading lamps, lockers and privacy curtains. Premises are kept spick and span, and staff organize activities ranging from pub crawls to Hermitage trips. Dorms R1400, doubles R5200

EATING

★**Bonch** Bolshaya Morskaya 16 W bonchcoffee.ru; M Admiralteyskaya. A bright and airy café with cushioned seating by large windows that is a great pit stop for brunch (English breakfast R370) or for a slice of home-made cake (R290). Mon–Fri 8.30am–11pm, Sat 10am–11pm, Sun 10am–9pm.

Chayki Nab. Reki Moyki 19 W chaykibar.com; M Admiralteyskaya. A short walk away from the Hermitage, this is a great little place to refuel after a long day of sightseeing. Basement interiors feature chalk-stained walls, small wooden tables, and artworks for sale adorning the walls. The menu includes soups (R200), sandwiches (R330), salads (R330), pasta dishes (R370) and burgers (R390). Mon–Thurs & Sun noon–midnight, Fri & Sat noon–3am.

Clean Plates Society Gorokhovaya ul. 13 W cleanplatescafe.com; M Admiralteyskaya. This popular restaurant serves good-value food in a laidback, modern setting with a hint of faded glamour. In the evenings a DJ livens up the scene. The menu includes steaks (R690), large salads (R390) and burgers (R330). Daily noon–2am.

Dachniki Nevsky prospekt 20; M Admiralteyskaya. Laid out in true Russian *dacha* style with log cabin-style walls, chintzy curtains and Soviet films running back to back on the TV screen. The traditional food is excellent, from borsch (R240) to stroganoff (R390). Daily noon–1am, Fri & Sat until 3am.

Fartuk Ul. Rubinshteina 15/17; M Dostoyevskaya. This welcoming place with bare brick walls and low lighting buzzes at most times of the day. Small wooden tables are tightly packed together, and the handful of books and board games add to the cosy atmosphere. The menu includes pasta dishes (R480) as well as more substantial mains such as beef stroganoff (R560). Mon–Thurs & Sun 10am–midnight, Fri & Sat 10am–3am.

MarketPlace Nevsky pr. 24 ⓦmarket-place.me; ⓜNevsky prospekt. This excellent self-service chain offers affordable tasty food cooked in front of your very eyes. Watch the chefs as they skewer meats and prepare a variety of pastas to order, then take it upstairs to the cosy dining area overlooking Nevsky prospekt. As it's open till early morning, you can even refuel here after a heavy night out. Daily 8am–5.30am.

★**Taste to eat** Nab. Reki Fontanki 82 ⓦtastetoeat .ru; ⓜZvenigorodskaya. This modish restaurant serves delicious new Russian cuisine in a very pleasant setting. Warm interiors feature comfortable leather seating and dim lighting, and dishes are beautifully presented. The menu includes exquisite chicken kiev (R450) and cod with vegetables (R440). Daily 1–11pm, Fri & Sat until midnight.

Teplo Bol. Morskaya 45 ⓦv-teplo.ru; ⓜAdmiralteyskaya. This popular place serves up international cuisine in a warren of cosy partitioned rooms, some with sofas, that will have you lingering longer than you intended. Mains R500. Book ahead. Mon–Thurs & Sun 9am–midnight, Fri 9am–1am, Sat 11am–1am, Sun 1pm–midnight.

Ukrop Marata 23 ⓦcafe-ukrop.ru; ⓜVladimirskaya. Bright and airy veggie café with leafy flowerpots and knick-knacks dotted around. The menu features all manner of vegan and veggie delights, including mushroom soup (R220), beetroot risotto (R320) and buckwheat noodles with vegetables and shiitake (R270). Daily 9am–11pm.

DRINKING AND NIGHTLIFE

Aurora Pirogovskaya nab. 5/2 ☏812 907 1917, ⓦaurora -hall.ru; ⓜPloshchad Lenina. Large concert hall that can accommodate up to 1500 visitors, hosting concerts, festivals and gigs. Check the calendar of events on the website.

Griboedov Voronexhskaya ul. 2A ⓦgriboedovclub.ru; ⓜLigovskiy Prospekt. A labyrinth of underground rooms hosting cultural events and gigs that attracts a friendly laidback crowd. Upstairs, *Griboedov Hill* café hosts concerts as well as exhibitions, DJ sessions and lectures. There's tasty grub here too, so make sure you get there early to nab a table. Mon–Fri noon–6am, Sat & Sun 3pm–6am.

The Hat ul. Belinskogo 9 ⓦhatgroup.ru; ⓜMayakovskaya. Set out like an old New York City bar, this popular drinking hole attracts barflies looking for some live jazz and a few whiskies (there are over 70 types). Jam sessions daily 11pm. Daily 7pm–3am.

Khroniki Nekrasova 26 ⓜChernyshevskaya. Small student hangout that gets particularly packed at the weekends, with drinks scribbled on a blackboard. The simple interior has gilded Soviet chandeliers and

white-washed walls. Neat potent alcohol is the order of the day here, although there are plenty of cocktails (R350) and beers (R200), too. Daily 6pm–2am, Fri & Sat until 5am.

Mosaique Konyushennaya pl. 2; ⓦmosaique-space.com; ⓜNevsky prospekt. A cool techno club that is hugely popular among electronic music connoisseurs, with bunker-like architecture and colourful avant-garde light installations that give the place a unique atmosphere. Fri & Sat 11pm–8am.

Poltory Komnaty ul. Mayakovskogo 34; ⓜCherny shevskaya. Experienced barmen shake up creatively presented cocktails at this small and intimate bar. Drinks are served on slates, trays or wooden boards, often accompanied by nibbles such as olives and pickles. Daily 6pm–3am.

Produkty Nab. reki Fontanki 17; ⓜNevsky prospekt. The retro decor of this little old-school bar includes a jukebox and countless odds and ends brought over from Berlin. It's a great spot to sip a cocktail (R250) as you enjoy some new-wave favourites spun by the DJ. Daily 2pm–2am, Fri & Sat until 6am.

Stirka Kazanskaya ul. 26 ⓦ40gradusov.ru; ⓜSennaya. This small grungy haunt attracts an alternative crowd. When live bands aren't playing you can lounge about on the worn sofas and enjoy the pretty decent sound system. Mon–Thurs & Sun 9am–11pm, Fri & Sat 10am–1am.

ENTERTAINMENT

Theatres tend to close for the summer until mid-Sept. For listings and events pick up the quarterly freebie *Where St Petersburg, In Your Pocket* or the Friday *St Petersburg Times*.

CLASSICAL, OPERA AND BALLET

Mariinskiy Theatre Teatralnaya pl. 1 ☏812 326 4141, ⓦmariinskiy.ru; ⓜSadovaya. Tickets €8–120. Opera and ballet performances at 7pm, matinees at noon.

Philharmonia Mikhaylovskaya ul. 2 ☏812 312 9871, ⓦwww.philharmonia.spb.ru; ⓜNevsky prospekt. Draws international classical musicians as well as Russia's finest. Performances at 7pm. Tickets from R250.

CINEMA

Avrora Nevsky prospekt 60 ⓦavrora.spb.ru; ⓜNevsky prospekt. Screens original-language mainstream films.

Dom Kino Karavannaya 12 ⓦdomkino.spb.ru; ⓜGostiny dvor. Specializes in art-house movies, as well as international cinema weeks.

SHOPPING

Imperial Porcelain Pr. Obukhovsky Oborony 151 ⓜLomonosovskaya; ⓦipm.ru. Originally established in 1744, this was the first porcelain manufactory in Russia to produce wares for the ruling family. There are various

28

branches in town, although this factory outlet offers porcelain at discounted prices. Items are expensive but the quality is high. Daily 10am–8pm.

Kuznechny market Kuznechniy per. 3; Ⓜ Vladimirskaya. With its mouthwatering displays of sweets and cakes, salted cucumbers, sausages, plaited cheese rinds and caviar, this is the place to come for Russian speciality foods. Daily 8am–8pm.

Souvenirs Fair Nab. kanala Griboedova 2, opposite the Church of the Saviour on the Spilled Blood; Ⓜ Nevsky prospekt. Nearly 200 stalls open all year round with plenty of souvenirs from paintings to handicrafts. Daily 9am–10pm.

DIRECTORY

Consulates Australia, Petrovsky pr. 14 ☎ 812 325 7334, Ⓜ Sportivnaya; UK, pl. Proletarskoy Diktatury 5 ☎ 812 320 3200, Ⓜ Chernyshevskaya; US, Furshtatskaya ul. 15 ☎ 812 331 2600, Ⓜ Chernyshevskaya.

Health American Medical Clinic, nab. reki Moyki 78 ☎ 812 740 2090, Ⓦ amclinic.com, Ⓜ Admiralteyskaya; MEDEM International Clinic, ul. Marata 6 ☎ 812 336 3333, Ⓦ medem.ru, Ⓜ Mayakovskaya.

Pharmacy Petropharm, Nevsky prospekt 22 (24hr).

Post offices Main office at Pochtamtskaya ul. 9 (open 24hr; Ⓜ Nevsky prospekt). Express letter post: DHL (Nevsky prospekt 10; Mon–Fri 9am–9pm, Sat & Sun 10am–4pm; Ⓦ dhl.ru; Ⓜ Admiralteyskaya).

DAY-TRIPS FROM ST PETERSBURG

The imperial palaces of **Peterhof** and **Tsarskoe Selo**, half an hour to an hour outside the city, are both splendid day-trips. Although entering the palaces is increasingly expensive, you can slip away from the crowds into the surrounding parks. As you leave St Petersburg on the bus, look out for the awe-inspiring war monument to Leningrad's World War II sacrifice, and Lenin "hailing a taxi" near Finland station.

Peterhof

Most visitors with time for just one day-trip opt for **Peterhof** (Grand Palace Tues–Fri & Sun 10.30am–7pm, Sat 10.30am–9pm, closed last Tues of month; R600, student R300; park daily 9am–8pm, fountains from 11am; R700, student R250), 29km west of St Petersburg, known as the "Russian Versailles" and famed for its marvellous

fountains and impressive cascades. Though originally built between 1709 and 1724 for Peter the Great, each of the subsequent rulers made their mark here. Travel by hydrofoil between May and September (every 15min to 1hr, depending on weather conditions; first hydrofoil at 10am; R750 each way or R1300 return; 30–40min) from outside the Winter Palace or take minibus #224, #300 or #424 from Ⓜ Avtovo, or #103 or #420 from Ⓜ Leninsky prospekt.

Tsarskoe Selo and Pavlovsk Palace

The small town of **Tsarskoe Selo** (also known as Pushkin, after the "Russian Shakespeare" who was educated at the neighbouring Lyceum school), 30km south of St Petersburg, centres on the **Catherine Palace** (palace: May & Sept Mon & Wed–Sun noon–7pm; June–Aug Mon & Wed–Sun noon–8pm; Oct–April Mon & Wed–Sun 10am–6pm; Oct–April closed last Mon of the month; R580, students R290; grounds: May–July daily 7am–11pm; Aug daily 7am–10pm; rest of the year daily 7am–9pm; R120, student R60; Ⓦ tsar.ru). The ostentatious blue-and-white Baroque structure built by Catherine the Great is surrounded by a richly landscaped park. Scottish architect Charles Cameron's elegant Neoclassical gallery stretches high above it. To get to Pushkin, take minibus #342 or #545 from Ⓜ Moskovskaya or bus #186 from Ⓜ Kupchino; alternatively, take a train to Tsarkoe Selo from Vitebsky or Kapuchino stations, then bus #371 or #382.

From Tsarskoe Selo buses #286 and #370 take you 5km further south to the more intimate **Pavlovsk Palace** (May–Sept Palace daily 10am–6pm, closed first Mon of the month, Park daily 6am–midnight; Oct–April Palace Mon–Thurs, Sat & Sun 10am–6pm, closed first Mon of the month, Park daily 6am–9pm; Oct–April free admission to the park on weekdays, palace R500, student R250; park R150, student R80; Ⓦ pavlovskmuseum.ru), its magnificent Neoclassical interior set amid luxurious 1500-acre grounds.

CITY HALL, SUBOTICA

Serbia

HIGHLIGHTS

❶ Belgrade Explore the nightlife and café culture of Serbia's hectic, hedonistic capital city. **See p.944**

❷ Novi Sad Admire the view from Petrovaradin, the hilltop fortress that hosts the EXIT Festival every summer. **See p.951**

❸ Subotica Enjoy the city's unspoilt feel and fantastical Secessionist architecture. **See p.953**

❹ Studenica Monastery The finest of Serbia's fresco-laden, medieval monastic churches. See p.954

HIGHLIGHTS ARE MARKED ON THE MAP ON P.941

ROUGH COSTS

Daily budget Basic €25, occasional treat €40

Drink Beer (0.5l) €1

Food *Pljeskavica* (hamburger) €1–2

Hostel/budget hotel €12/€35

Travel Bus: Belgrade–Novi Sad €6; train: Belgrade–Niš €7

FACT FILE

Population 7.5 million (excluding Kosovo)

Language Serbian

Currency Dinar (din)

Capital Belgrade

International phone code ☏ 381

Time zone GMT +1hr

29

Introduction

Serbia is a buzzy and boisterous country, compact enough for visitors to sample both Belgrade's urban hedonism and the gentler pace of the smaller towns or national parks within a few days – and it's one of Europe's most affordable destinations to boot. Grittier than its blue-eyed neighbour Croatia, it is nevertheless an integral part of any backpacker's Balkan tour: at the heart of the region, it gives easy access to the cluster of cultures and histories crammed into this small corner of Europe.

Serbia's young, European-minded population brings a bubbling energy to its bars, cafés and clubs, producing an adrenaline-charged nightlife unmatched anywhere else in the Balkans. The general determination to have a good time confounds the expectations of many a traveller, arriving with memories of the 1990s, when Serbia's name was not often off war reporters' lips. Today, it's just as likely to attract headlines for the annual EXIT festival in Novi Sad, or the exploits of tennis superstar, Novak Djoković.

Serbia's capital, **Belgrade**, is a sociable, hectic city that energizes and exhausts by turns. Northwest of the city on the iron-flat Vojvodina Plain sits lovely **Novi Sad**, window to the **Fruška Gora** hills, while further north – a stone's throw from the border with Hungary – enchanting **Subotica** is sprinkled with early twentieth-century Secessionist architecture. Deep in the mountainous tract of land to the south of Belgrade are three key struts of Serbia's religio-cultural heritage – Žiča, Studenica and Sopoćani **monasteries**. East of here, **Niš** is a pleasant small city to pause in en route to or from Bulgaria or Macedonia.

CHRONOLOGY

168 BC The Romans defeat the Illyrian tribe and establish their rule of the area of present-day Serbia.

630 AD Serbs settle in the region.

1166 Stefan Nemanja, leader of the Serbs, declares independence from Byzantine rule.

1219 The Serbian Orthodox Church is established.

1389 The Ottomans defeat the Serbs in the Battle of Kosovo, ushering in four centuries of direct rule.

1804 National hero Karađorđe ("Black George") begins the First Serbian Uprising against the Ottomans.

1913 The Ottomans lose their remaining authority in Serbia during the Balkan wars.

1918 Following World War I the Kingdom of Serbs, Croats and Slovenes is formed.

1929 The Kingdom is renamed Yugoslavia.

1945 Following World War II, Serbia is absorbed into Socialist Yugoslavia.

1989 Slobodan Milošević, a Serbian communist, becomes President of Serbia.

1992 The wars of the disintegration of Yugoslavia begin. Fighting ends three years later.

1993 The International Criminal Tribunal for the former Yugoslavia is set up in The Hague to try those accused of war crimes.

1998 Serbia launches a violent campaign against the ethnic Albanian community in Kosovo, costing thousands of lives.

1999 NATO's "Operation Merciful Angel" – a ten-week war from the air to end Milošević's ethnic cleansing campaign – drives Yugoslav National Army forces out of Kosovo.

2000 Mass protests lead to the resignation of Milošević.

2003 Serbian prime minister, Zoran Đinđić, is assassinated in Belgrade.

2006 Milošević dies in prison, awaiting trial at the International Criminal Tribunal for the former Yugoslavia on charges of genocide.

2006 Montenegro peacefully gains independence from Serbia.

2008 Kosovo declares independence from Serbia after nine years under UN administration. Serbia does not recognize Kosovo as an independent state.

2011 Ratko Mladić arrested and transferred to the War Crimes Tribunal in The Hague.

2014 EU accession talks begin.

2016 Radovan Karadžić found guilty of genocide and war crimes at the War Crimes Tribunal in The Hague.

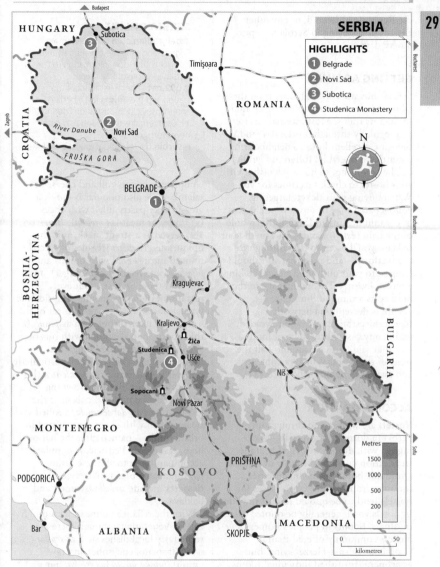

ARRIVAL AND DEPARTURE

Flight operators from the UK include Wizz Air (ⓦwizzair.com) and Air Serbia (ⓦairserbia.com). Cuts to services mean that Serbia's **rail** connections with neighbouring countries are now fairly limited: from Belgrade there are currently three daily services to Budapest in Hungary, two to Skopje in Macedonia, two to Zagreb in Croatia (both of which continue to Ljubljana in Slovenia), two to Sofia in Bulgaria (via Niš), and two to Podgorica (and Bar on the coast) in Montenegro – this last trip is one of Europe's most scenic. There are currently no services to Romania or Bosnia. No visas are needed for nationals of the US, Canada, Australia, New Zealand, the UK,

29

the Republic of Ireland, or any other EU country staying in Serbia for up to ninety days.

GETTING AROUND

Serbia's **bus** network (Ⓦbas.rs) is on the whole efficient and reliable – much more so than its trains. Most internal services run regularly throughout the day, and there are excellent links to neighbouring countries. Timetables (often in Cyrillic) can be confusing, so it's well worth asking your hostel to check bus times for you. When buying your ticket, targeting younger staff may improve your chances of communicating in English. Keep hold of the coin (*žeton*) handed back with your ticket – you'll use it to pass through to the platform – and note that you should hang onto your outbound ticket if taking a return journey. Putting luggage in the hold costs around 40din.

Serbia's decrepit **rail** network (Ⓦzeleznicesrbije.com) is best avoided, and in any case, likely to be of limited use; that said, fares are around half the price of the buses. Where possible, try and avoid the *putnički* (slow) services.

ACCOMMODATION

Hostels are widespread throughout Serbia (a dorm bed costs €10–15 a night), with dozens in Belgrade alone. In addition you'll find freshly decorated, affordable **hotels** in the major cities (doubles from around €40). Prices for hostels tend to be quoted in euros, while in hotels you'll generally be quoted prices in dinars. **Rooms** in people's homes (*sobe*) are less commonly offered than in Croatia or Bosnia-Herzegovina, but **apartmani** (furnished individual rooms or suites) are available, with doubles starting at around €40.

FOOD AND DRINK

In common with other Balkan countries, Serbian **cuisine** is overwhelmingly dominated by meat, and many dishes manifest Turkish or Austro-Hungarian influences. **Breakfast** (*doručak*) typically

SERBIA ONLINE
Ⓦ**belgradian.com** Comprehensive English-language site covering everything from local transport information to the fast-changing nightlife scene.
Ⓦ**b92.net** Venerable broadcasting station and the driving force behind anti-Milošević demonstrations during the 1990s; it remains the country's most newsworthy site.
Ⓦ**serbia.travel** Official tourist board site.

comprises a coffee, roll and cheese or salami, while also popular is *burek*, a greasy, flaky pastry filled with cheese (*sa sirom*) or meat (*sa mesom*). *Burek* is also served as a **street snack**, as is the ubiquitous *ćevapčići* (rissoles of spiced minced meat served with onion) and *pljeskavica* (oversized hamburger). You will find these on just about every **restaurant** (*restoran*) menu, alongside the typical starter, *čorba* (a thick meat or fish soup), and **main dishes** such as *pasulj* (a thick bean soup flavoured with bits of bacon or sausage), the Hungarian-influenced, paprika-red *gulaš*, particularly popular in Vojvodina, and *kolenica* (leg of suckling pig). But the crowning triumph of the national cuisine is the gut-busting *karađorđe šnicla*, a rolled veal steak stuffed with cheese and coated in breadcrumbs – named after the national hero, Karađorđe Petrović. A popular accompaniment to all these dishes is *pogača*, a large bread cake. Typical **desserts** include *strudla* (strudel) and baklava.

With the reliance on meat, it's a tough call for **vegetarians**, though there are some tasty local dishes such as *srpska salata* (tomato, cucumber and raw onion), *šopska salata* (as *srpska*, but topped with grated *kashkaval* white cheese) and *burek*.

DRINK

You will not want for **coffee** (*kafa*) in Serbia, but sadly the traditional Turkish kind (thick, black, with grounds in) is now mainly just consumed in homes. Balkan **beer** (*pivo*) brands like Lav, Jelen and Montenegrin Nikšićko are very palatable – the first two are lager-like beers, the last one is available in both light and dark varieties. Craft beers are starting to make their mark; look out for Kabinet, which you'll find mostly in the capital. On the whole, **wine** tends to be disproportionately pricey on restaurant menus, but Montenegrin Vranac and Macedonian Tikveš are more affordable. Everyone should sample *slijvovica* – plum *rakija* – but pace yourself to avoid waking up with a shocked head and raw throat.

CULTURE AND ETIQUETTE

Even though tourists are quite a rarity in some parts, part of the charm of travel in Serbia is a sense of "live and let live" – you are unlikely to be quizzed intrusively or pestered to buy wares. Serbian culture as a whole is far from conservative – a fact you'll quickly grasp from the fashion choices youngsters make. You should cover arms and legs in Orthodox churches, however. Although **smoking** is not permitted in most indoor public spaces, it is one of the few European countries where it is still allowed in cafés, restaurants and bars, which can make dining out quite an unpleasant experience, if you are not a smoker that is. **Tipping** in restaurants is not essential, but in the nicer places you should leave ten percent.

SPORTS AND ACTIVITIES

Serbia's countryside is beautiful, varied and never more than a short bus ride away. In the summer, **hike** or walk in the Fruška Gora National Park

---

SERBIAN

Serbia uses the **Cyrillic alphabet** as well as the Latin one. Many street signs (see box, p.946) and bus and train timetables are in Cyrillic only, so it's worth being able to decode at least the first few letters of a word. Serbian, like Bosnian, is very closely related to Croatian (see p.158), and all three languages will be understood in all three countries.

EMERGENCY NUMBERS

Police ☎92; Ambulance ☎94; Fire ☎93; Road assistance ☎987.

(⊚npfruskagora.co.rs); in winter hit the **ski** slopes with Balkan daredevils at Kopaonik National Park (⊚eng.infokop .net). The locals love their **football**, and a derby between Belgrade's Red Star (⊚crvenazvezdafk.com) and FK Partizan (⊚partizan.rs) is invariably fiery, and frequently violent (outside the ground). For something more sedate, head to Novi Sad's FK Vojvodina (⊚fkvojvodina.com). Basketball, too, is a major spectator sport, with Red Star (⊚kkcrvenazvezda.rs) and Partizan (⊚kkpartizan.rs) the dominant forces.

COMMUNICATIONS

Wi-fi is available in most cafés and bars, while you may find it available in some public spaces in the cities. Most hostels and hotels offer it as standard. **Internet cafés** are now rare, but where you do find one, expect to pay around 100din per hour. **Public phones** use Halo cards, sold with 300din and 600din credit at post offices, kiosks and tobacconists. Most **post offices** (*pošta*) are open Monday to Friday 8am to 7pm. **Stamps** (*markice*) can also be bought at newsstands.

EMERGENCIES

The **crime** rate, even in Belgrade, is low by European standards, though the usual precautions apply; be particularly wary of pickpockets on the city buses.

Pharmacies (*apoteka*) tend to follow shop hours of around Monday to Friday 8am to 8pm and Saturday 8am to 3pm.

INFORMATION

All the towns covered in this chapter have a **tourist information office** (*turističke informacije*), stocking good-quality materials in English. Another good source of information is *In Your Pocket* (⊚inyourpocket.com), which currently

29

publishes online guides to Belgrade, Novi Sad and Niš.

MONEY AND BANKS

The currency is the **dinar** (usually abbreviated to din), comprising coins of 1, 2, 5, 10 and 20din (and also 50 para coins – 100 para equals 1din), and notes of 10, 20, 50, 100, 200, 1000 and 5000din. At the time of writing, exchange rates were €1 = 120din, £1 = 150din and US$1 = 100din. **Exchange offices** (*menjačnica*) are everywhere, while **ATMs** are widely available in towns. Credit/debit cards are accepted in most hotels, restaurants and shops. Note that accommodation prices are normally quoted in euros, but you pay in dinars.

OPENING HOURS AND HOLIDAYS

Most **shops** open Monday to Friday 8am to 7/8pm (sometimes with a break for lunch), plus Saturday 8am to 2pm, and sometimes later in Belgrade. Most **museums** are open Tuesday to Sunday 9/10am to 5/6pm. Shops and banks close on **public holidays**: January 1, 2 and 7, February 15, and May 1 and 2. The Orthodox Church celebrates Easter between one and five weeks later than the other churches.

Belgrade

BELGRADE (Београд; Beograd) is a vigorous, high-energy city, especially in spring and summer, when all ages throng the streets at all hours. With a seemingly endless supply of bars and clubs, the city's pulsing nightlife is one of the unexpected high points on any European itinerary.

The city sits at a strategic point on the junction of the Danube and Sava rivers, something that has proved a source of weakness as well as strength over the ages: Belgrade has been captured as many as sixty times by Celts, Romans, Huns, Avars and more. The onslaught continued right through the twentieth century, when the city suffered heavy shelling

during World War II and in 1999 withstood 78 days of NATO airstrikes.

Visually, the mingling and merging of architectural styles can be off-putting, particularly when a row of beautiful older frontages is interrupted by a postwar interloper. Yet this mishmash also makes the city what it is: alongside all the Yugoslav experimentation, the grand nineteenth-century buildings and Art Nouveau facades bear eloquent witness to the days of Ottoman and Austro-Hungarian rule.

WHAT TO SEE AND DO

The city's most attention-grabbing attraction is the **Kalemegdan Fortress**, while just outside the park's boundary is the **Old City**, whose dense lattice of streets conceals Belgrade's most interesting sights. South of here is Belgrade's central square, **Trg Republike**, and the old bohemian quarter of **Skadarlija**, centred on charming, cobbled Skadarska, though it's little more than the venue for several tourist-trap restaurants. Beyond here lie several more sights worth seeing, including the Church of St Sava, one of the world's largest Orthodox churches, and the very worthwhile **Nikola Tesla Museum**. For a spot of rest and recuperation, head west across the Sava to the verdant suburb of **Zemun**, in New Belgrade, or further south towards the island of **Ada Ciganlija**, Belgrade's own miniature beach resort.

Kalemegdan Fortress

Splendidly sited on an exposed nub of land overlooking the confluence of the Sava and Danube rivers, **Kalemegdan Park** is dominated by the **fortress** (ⓦbeogradskatvrdjava.co.rs) of the same name. The whole complex is a paean to Serbian heroism, topped with the proud Victory Monument of 1912. Originally built by the Celts in the third century BC, before expansion by the Romans, the fortress has survived successive invasions; most of what remains is the result of a short-lived Austrian occupation in the early eighteenth century. The best of the attractions is the **Military Museum** (Tues–Sun 10am–5pm; 150din), where a

29

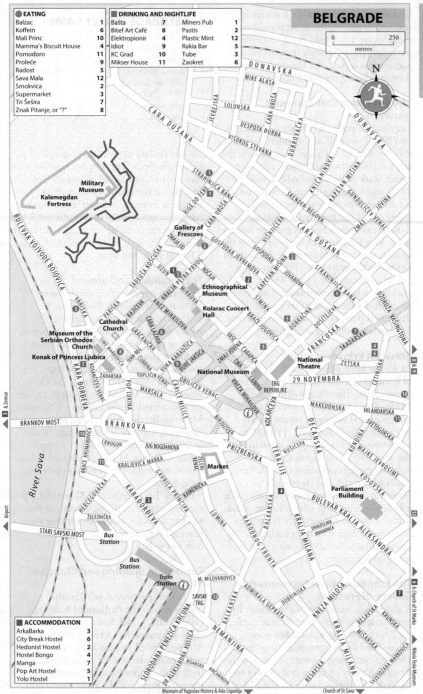

◀ &Zemun

◀ &Zemun

▶ 8 & 9

◀ Airport

▶ 12

▶ 6 & Church of St Marko

▶ Nikola Tesla Museum

EATING

Balzac	1
Koffein	6
Mali Princ	10
Mamma's Biscuit House	4
Pomodoro	11
Proleće	9
Radost	5
Sava Mala	12
Smokvica	2
Supermarket	3
Tri Šešira	7
Znak Pitanje, or "?"	8

DRINKING AND NIGHTLIFE

Bašta	7	Miners Pub	1
Bitef Art Café	8	Pastis	2
Elektropionir	4	Plastic Mint	12
Idiot	9	Rakia Bar	5
KC Grad	10	Tube	3
Mikser House	11	Zaokret	6

BELGRADE

0 _____ 250
metres

N

ACCOMMODATION

ArkaBarka	3
City Break Hostel	6
Hedonist Hostel	2
Hostel Bongo	4
Manga	7
Pop Art Hostel	5
Yolo Hostel	1

Museum of Yugoslav History & Ada Ciganlija ▼   Church of St Sava ▼

29

history thick with conflict is divertingly presented; among the most prestigious exhibits are Tito's field dress and other personal effects, though its most prized acquisition is part of a US stealth bomber downed during the 1999 conflict.

The Orthodox Cathedral and museum

Leaving the park and crossing Pariska, you'll find yourself in the oldest part of the city. On Kneza Sime Markovića is the city's main **Cathedral Church**, a modest, rather stark Neoclassical edifice built in 1840 and featuring a fine Baroque tower; it's also the resting place for several members of the mighty Obrenović dynasty, as well as Serbia's greatest literary hero, Vuk Karadžić. Directly opposite the church stands the **Museum of the Serbian Orthodox Church** (Mon–Fri 8am–4pm, Sat 9am–noon, Sun 11am–1pm; 100din), where a small collection of bejewelled Bibles and other gorgeously decorated paraphernalia is housed in the headquarters of the Patriarchate.

Konak of Princess Ljubica

At Kneza Sime Markovića 8, the **Konak of Princess Ljubica** (Tues, Wed & Fri 10am–5pm, Thurs noon–8pm, Sat 11am–5pm, Sun 10am–2pm; 100din; ⓦ mgb.org.rs) was built on the orders of Prince Miloš Obrenović in 1831 to accommodate his family. Eventually the abode of a nineteenth-century noblewoman, it underlines the Balkans' position as a cultural crossroads: a Napoléon III–themed room sits alongside a Turkish-style room with a Koran stand. It seems nineteenth-century Belgraders loved socializing too: there's a big semicircular sofa for chatting guests in nearly every room.

The Ethnographical Museum and Gallery of Frescoes

A short walk northeast of the Konak lie two intriguing museums. At Studentski trg 13, the **Ethnographical Museum** (Tues–Sat 10am–5pm, Sun 9am–2pm; 150din; ⓦ etnografskimuzej.rs) is a lively people's history of crafts and clothes in the Balkans. Beyond here, at Cara Uroša

20, the **Gallery of Frescoes** (Tues, Wed & Fri 10am–5pm, Thurs & Sat noon–8pm, Sun 10am–2pm; 200din) houses replicas of 1200 of the country's most fêted medieval frescoes – a must if you don't have the opportunity to visit the originals at the monasteries of southern Serbia and Kosovo. The style is fresh and colourful – lots of puce and blue.

Trg Republike and around

The main street leading south from Kalemegdan is Kneza Mihailova, a pedestrianized *korzo* (promenade) with narrow, pretty fronts concealing an array of fancy shops. It becomes more commercialized and hulkish at its southern end as it approaches **Trg Republike** (Republic Square), the city's main square. An irregularly shaped space, it's dominated by the imperious National Museum (having been closed for years, hopes are high for its reopening, finally, in 2017), in front of which is a grand statue of Prince Mihailo on horseback – this is the traditional meeting place for Belgraders.

East of Trg Republike is **Skadarlija**, the former bohemian district; south of the square, the wide swathe of **Terazije** slices through the commercial and business hub of the city.

Parliament Building and Church of St Marko

A left turn partway down Terazije brings you to the **Parliament Building** (Skupština), which has seen its fair share of drama. In October 2000, after Milošević tried to claw back the presidential election he'd lost, hundreds of demonstrators forced their way into the parliament building and threw fake ballot papers out of the windows as the building blazed inside. It remains the scene for political protests, such as those that followed Kosovo's declaration of independence in 2008.

More aesthetically pleasing is the **Church of St Marko** just up the road, a grandiose, five-domed neo-Byzantine structure modelled on the revered monastery of Gračanica in Kosovo. It holds the tomb of the Serbian Emperor, Tsar Dušan, protected by muscled stone guards.

Church of St Sava

A twenty-minute walk south of Trg Republike is the magnificent gilded dome of the **Church of St Sava**, on Svetosavski trg in the Vračar district. Built on the spot where the Turks supposedly burnt the bones of the founder of the Serbian Orthodox Church in 1594, it is a perfect example of the way religious and national identities fuse here. Standing some 70m high, it also stakes a fair claim to be one of the largest Orthodox churches in the world, with a cavernous interior that has been under stop-start construction for over a hundred years. There is literally nothing, decorative or otherwise, inside, but it is worth a peek for its gob-smacking size.

Nikola Tesla Museum

A short walk north of the Church of St Sava, at Krunska 51, is the engaging **Nikola Tesla Museum** (Tues–Sun 10am–6pm; 150din; Ⓦtesla-museum .org), which celebrates the pioneering work of the eponymous nineteenth-century inventor and engineer. Tesla (1856–1943) is credited with inventing the AC current, while other notable achievements include the development of wireless communications and remote control technologies. Alongside papers, tools and personal effects, the museum contains the urn with his ashes. Demonstrations of his experiments are held on the hour.

The Museum of Yugoslav History

Well worth the trip is the **Museum of Yugoslav History** (Tues–Sun 10am–6pm;

400din; Ⓦmij.rs; bus #40 or #41 from Kneza Miloša), located around 1.5km south of the centre on Botićeva 6. The museum comprises three components, the centrepiece of which is the **House of Flowers**, designed in 1975 as Tito's winter garden and now housing the former president's tomb, as well as that of his wife, Jovanka, who died in 2013. The rooms either side hold a selection of Tito's personal effects, most notably a silver writing set presented to him by John F. Kennedy in 1961, and hundreds of batons used in the annual "relay of youth" which took place on May 25 each year to celebrate Tito's birthday. The adjoining **Old Museum** holds a wealth of exhibits pertaining to the former Yugoslavia's convoluted history, but inevitably the focus is on Tito himself, notably a bewildering array of gifts presented to him by foreign dignitaries. The **May 25 Museum**, meanwhile, has temporary exhibitions, which are invariably concerned with the former Yugoslavia.

Ada Ciganlija and Ada Bridge

In the summer months Belgraders flock to **Ada Ciganlija** (literally, "gypsy island"), a stretch of wooded park along the bank of the Sava just south of the centre. The island's sandy beaches have earned it the local nickname "Belgrade's seaside", and city-dwellers enjoy its giant water slides, waterskiing and naturist area; there's even bungee-jumping. Skirting the easternmost tip of the island is the gleaming **Ada Bridge**, a seven-span superstructure over 950m long, and rising to a height of some 200m, which makes it the largest single pylon suspension bridge in the world – the views of it from the island are stunning. To get to Ada Ciganlija, take bus #53 or #56 from Zeleni Venac.

Zemun

If you're after peace and quiet, head across the Sava River to New Belgrade and the west bank suburb of **Zemun**, a jumble of low-slung houses and narrow winding streets centred around the hilly waterside district of Gardoš, which holds

29

the Baroque **Nikolajevska Church**, the city's oldest Orthodox church. To get here, take bus #15 from Zeleni Venac, or bus #83 from outside the train station, and alight on Glavna, the main street.

ARRIVAL AND DEPARTURE

By plane Belgrade's Nikola Tesla airport (☎ 11 209 4000, ⊛ beg.aero) is 18km northwest of the city in Surčin, and connected to the centre by bus #72 (5.15am–midnight, Mon–Fri every 30min, Sat & Sun hourly; 150din), which departs from in front of the departures hall (one level above arrivals) and terminates at the Zeleni Venac market. If you wish to travel to the centre by taxi, avoid the sharks in the arrivals hall and instead head to the Taxi Info sign, where you can order a taxi for 1800din (€18).

By train The main train station (*železnička stanica*) is on Savski trg, a 15min walk southwest of the centre.

Destinations Budapest (3 daily; 8hr); Ljubljana (2 daily; 10hr); Niš (6 daily; 4hr 30min–5hr 30min); Novi Sad (every 1–2hr; 1hr 30min–1hr 50min); Skopje (2 daily; 9hr 30min); Subotica (5 daily; 3hr 50min); Zagreb (2 daily; 7hr 30min).

By bus The main bus station (*autobuska stanica*) is adjacent to the train station on Železnička. Note that bus arrivals stop by the park across the road from the station itself.

Destinations Kraljevo (every 1hr–1hr 30min; 2hr); Niš (every 1hr–1hr 30min; 3hr); Novi Pazar (every 1hr–1hr 30min; 3hr); Novi Sad (every 30–45min; 1hr 20min); Sarajevo (7 daily; 7–8hr); Subotica (every 45min–1hr; 3hr 30min); Zagreb (6 daily; 5–6hr).

INFORMATION

Tourist information The main information centre is at Knez Mihailova 5 (daily 9am–7pm; ☎ 11 263 5622, ⊛ tob .rs/en), with other branches at the train station (Mon–Sat 7am–1.30pm) and at the airport arrivals hall (daily 9am–9.30pm). Free city walking tours are offered daily at 11am & 4pm, departing from Trg Republike.

GETTING AROUND

By bus, trolleybus and tram There's an extensive network of buses, trolleybuses and trams throughout the city; the cheapest way to travel is to buy a BusPlus pass (40din), which you load with credit (72din per journey); these can be bought from a kiosk or newsstand; alternatively, pay once you get on (150din), though you will need the exact change – either way, make sure you validate the ticket in the machine on board. It's actually easier to purchase either a one-day (290din), three-day (740din) or five-day ticket (1100din); these prices include the BusPlus pass. Night buses depart from Trg Republike, operating between midnight and 4am (150din payable on the bus; daily tickets are not valid for night buses).

By taxi Give short shrift to the baying mob at the bus station and under no circumstances take a taxi from outside the train station; instead, grab one from the street or at any small rank; better still, call one of the following reliable firms: Beogradski Taxi (☎ 11 9801), Pink Taxi (☎ 11 9803) and Beotaxi (☎ 11 970). It is 200din from the outset, after which it's around 65din/km.

ACCOMMODATION

Belgrade is awash with hostels, though many are of dubious quality – unless listed here, avoid those opposite the stations. The vast majority of hostels are located in apartment blocks, and usually on the top floor too, so be prepared to climb a lot of steps. None of the below offers breakfast, but they do have facilities to make your own, and you are likely to be offered a shot of *rakija* upon arrival.

ArkaBarka Bulevar Nikole Tesle bb ☎ 64 925 3507, ⊛ arkabarka.net. This floating hostel is a cool concept exactly executed, with snug cabin-like rooms, on-board entertainment (playlists on the laptop), and drinks on deck (the small balcony edging the raft). To reach it, head towards the river through Ušće Park. Dorms €15, doubles €40

City Break Hostel Beogradska 41 ☎ 62 636442, ⊛ citybreakhostel.rs. Quiet, low-key hostel near Tašmajdan Park, with a welcoming atmosphere and a range of dorms, including one double. Trams #2, #3 or #7. Dorms €10, doubles €24

★**Hedonist Hostel** Simina 7 ☎ 11 328 4798, ⊛ hedonisthostelbelgrade.com. Occupying an old town house, this fantastic hostel is a superb antidote to the ubiquitous apartment-style places that proliferate – bare brick walls and low, wooden-beam ceilings lend it considerable charm. There's also a games room with PlayStation, and the owners lay on regular barbecues in the pretty garden, which is where they also show films and sporting events on a big screen. Bike rental too (€5). Dorms €14, doubles €50

★**Hostel Bongo** Terazije 36 ☎ 11 268 5515, ⊛ hostelbongo.com. Impeccably clean, chirpily run hostel on the ground floor of an apartment block offering five- and six-bed dorms plus a couple of doubles, all bursting with colour. Excellent kitchen-cum-lounge featuring a superb breakfast bar. Dorms €11, doubles €34

Manga Resavska 7 ☎ 11 324 3877, ⊛ mangahostel.com. Opened by enthusiastic couchsurfers, *Manga* occupies a small chalet, with a range of colourfully decorated dorms, plus one single room and an apartment. There's also a cosy exposed-brick cellar, which doubles up as a kitchen/ lounge. Dorms €11, doubles €36

Pop Art Hostel Karađorđeva 69 ☎ 11 218 5908, ⊛ poparthostel.com. As funky as its name suggests, this colourful place offers four superbly conceived rooms (sleeping two, four, six and eight), themed on artists

Warhol and Basquiat, The Doors' frontman Jim Morrison, and cartoonist Stan Drake. Dorms €12, doubles €30

Yolo Hostel Uzun Mirkova 6 ❶ 64 200 8817, ⓦyolostel.rs. In a super location, the classy *Yolo* offers three brightly coloured, parquet-floored rooms (two four-bed dorms and one six-bed dorm) all with shared shower facilities. Dorms €11, doubles €35

EATING

Belgrade's restaurant scene has improved markedly in recent years and you'll now find an increasing number of ethnic restaurants alongside those serving traditional Serbian food, all at easy-to-the-pocket prices. If you fancy a spot of open-air (though entirely unexceptional) dining, complete with live music and a bit of tourist tack, then head to one of the traditional tavernas lining Skadarska.

CAFÉS

Koffein Uskočka 8. Decent coffee used to be hard to come by in Belgrade, but no longer, thanks in part to this buzzy, artisan coffeehouse, which roasts its own beans on site; every type of caffeine fix you could wish for. Daily 8am–11pm.

Mali Princ Palmotićeva 27. In the shadow of a giant linden tree, this refined little coffeehouse makes for a relaxing stop, with a range of coffees and some delectable cakes and chocolates. Mon–Sat 8am–11pm, Sun 10am–11pm.

Mamma's Biscuit House Strahinjića Bana 72a. By day this cool, curiously named café satisfies those seeking great coffee and cake; by night it services a more boisterous drinking crowd. Daily 8am–midnight.

Supermarket Uzun Mirkova 8. If Belgrade hasn't already sharpened your sense of the surreal, check out this "concept store", a café-cum-fashion shop with a futuristic aesthetic. Sip a freshly squeezed juice, lick an ice cream or down a craft beer. Mon–Sat 10am–10pm, Sun noon–8pm.

RESTAURANTS

Balzac Strahinjića Bana 13. A good spot for alfresco dining, this sparky little place hits a wide range of price points, from chicken risotto (560din) to salmon fillet (1100din). It also offers a cracking-value two-course menu of the day (noon–5pm) for 600din. Mon–Sat 10am–midnight.

Pomodoro Hilandarska 32. This fairly simple-looking place knocks up some of the city's best pizzas (700din) from its wood-burning stove, in addition to some terrific pasta dishes and cooked breakfasts (330din). Mon–Sat 9am–midnight, Sun noon–midnight.

Proleće Vuka Karadžića 11. There's no fuss or fanfare at this very ordinary-looking restaurant, just a steady flow of locals tucking into honest Serbian grub such as *sarma* (cabbage leaves stuffed with ground pork and rice) with

sauerkraut (510din), white beans with roast pork (530din) and *šopska salata* (350din; cheese, tomato and cucumber salad). Daily 9am–11pm.

★**Radost** Pariska 3. In this city of meat-eaters, it's both surprising and refreshing to find this top-notch veggie restaurant; paprika tofu and pickles, and shiitake quesadilla (740din) are typical dishes, and super-friendly staff to boot. Tues–Sat 2–11pm, Sun 1–9pm.

Sava Mala Savski trg 7. This restaurant's location, opposite the stations, couldn't be any less distinguished, but don't let that put you off. Perfect for a pre- or post-journey fill-up, the menu offers the standard Serbian grills (600din) plus dishes like *prebanac* (Serbian beans) and the mighty *karađorđe šnicla* (stuffed veal steak). Daily 7am–11pm.

Smokvica Kralja Petra 73. Named after the fig tree that shades its slightly wonky stone-and-brick terrace, the "little fig" is a terrific place to tuck into a scrumptious *smokvica* burger (550din) or tandoori roll (460din); also available are some fabulous cooked breakfasts (320din). Daily 9am–midnight.

Tri Šešira Skadarska 29. Skadarlija's oldest restaurant, *The Three Hats* is a great place to be introduced to the robust charms of Serbian dining – the mixed grill (900din) includes no fewer than six types of meat. It's all rather hammed up for the tourists, but great fun if you can bear that. Daily 11am–midnight.

Znak Pitanja, or **"?"** Kralja Petra 6. Run through with atmosphere and history, and furnished with low wooden tables and stools, the city's oldest inn is the best place to get your chops round a gut-busting *pljeskavica* with *kajmak* (500din). Daily 8am–midnight.

DRINKING AND NIGHTLIFE

Not for nothing is Belgrade regarded as one of Europe's foremost party towns. There are a staggering number of places to drink and dance, though the scene moves frequently and it's hard to keep up. The current cool spots are Savamala, an area just west of the stations near the waterfront, and beyond here the Beton Hala Complex. Better still is Cetinjska ulica, specifically a cluster of alternative bars that have set up within several abandoned buildings of the old Belgrade Brewery. In summer, it's all aboard the *splavovi* – floating bars and clubs – to dance the night away. Most are concentrated on the banks of the Danube behind the *Hotel Jugoslavija* – a conspicuous block on the main road towards Zemun – and along the Sava around the Brankov Bridge; two of the most popular are *Freestyler* and *Blaywatch*. Most clubs don't get going until at least 11pm and usually stay open until around 4am.

BARS

Miners Pub Rīga od Fere 16. As the name suggests, this subterranean, brick-vaulted den resembles a mining pit,

29

and jolly good fun it is too; best of all, though, they have the finest selection of craft beers – many on tap – in the city. Daily 2pm–midnight.

Pastis Strahinjića Bana 52b. This French-style bistro bar is one of the street's more down-to-earth venues, with a constant stream of drinkers packed cheek-by-jowl inside, or, in warmer weather, huddled round wooden barrels outside. Daily 8am–12.30am, Fri & Sat till 1.30am.

Rakia Bar Dobračina 5. How could you come to Belgrade and not sample a glass or two of the country's finest? This place has in excess of one hundred varieties – your only problem will be deciding which ones to try, and how many. Daily 9am–midnight.

Zaokret Cetinjska 15. One of several alternative-minded bars to have recently moved in to the old brewery premises, the groovy, retro-designed *Zaokret* offers craft beers, DJ evenings and live music, and a cracking vibe. Daily 9am–1am, Fri & Sat til 4am.

CLUBS AND LIVE MUSIC

★ **Bašta** Mala Stepenice 1A ⓦ jazzbasta.com. Just one of the many venues down by the popular Beton Hala Complex near Brankov Bridge, *Bašta* (meaning "The Garden") is a stupendously ace jazz café-cum-club, with live music (jazz, blues, soul, bossa nova) most nights of the week. One not to miss. Mon–Thurs 5pm–1am, Fri–Sat noon–2am.

Bitef Art Café Skver Mire Trailović 1 ⓦ bitefartcafe.rs. Ever-popular café offering a regular and energetic programme of live funk, soul and jazz – as well as an eclectic mix of cultural events – in a converted Evangelical church.

Elektropionir Cetinjska 15. One of the new gang of bars and clubs occupying the grounds of the old Belgrade Brewery, this rocking place has a regular programme of concerts (mainly dance and rock), but is also a good place to chill during the day.

Idiot Dalmatinska 13, 1km southeast of Džordža Vašingtona, off Ruzveltova. Students and artists swarm into this small basement club by the Botanic Gardens. The terrace, too, is a great spot in warmer weather.

KC Grad Braće Krsmanović 4 ⓦ gradbeograd.eu. Occupying a former harbourside warehouse, *KC* is one of the most diverse establishments down in the Savamala district, staging an innovative programme of events, including concerts (jazz every Wednesday), film, poetry and debates, among other things. Mon–Sat 7am–2am.

Mikser House Karadordeva 18 ⓦ house.mikser.rs. This fabulous place in Savamala is a real hub of design and creativity, variously staging concerts, theatre, cabaret, dance and mini-festivals. Mon–Thurs & Sun noon–8pm, Fri–Sat noon–2am.

Plastic Mint Takovska 34. Although not quite the mega-popular venue of yore, this split-level two-in-one club (consisting of *Plastic* and *Mint*) still pumps out some of the best house music in Belgrade; often visited by international DJs and pop stars. Thurs–Sat.

Tube Simina 21. This super-cool underground warren is the city's top dog for all strands of electronica, attracting some of Europe's leading DJs; the defining feature of its superbly conceived interior is a narrow, 25m-long dance-floor. Thurs–Sat.

ENTERTAINMENT

Tickets for concerts and events are on sale at the Bilet Servis ticket agency, inside the Kulturni Centar at Trg Republike 5 (Mon–Fri 9am–8pm, Sat 10am–8pm).

Kolarac Concert Hall Studentski trg 5 ⓦ kolarac.rs. Hosts many of the concerts of the Beogradska Filharmonija. Tickets 200–500din; box office Mon–Fri 10am–8.30pm, Sat 10am–2pm.

National Theatre Francuska 3 ⓦ narodnopozoriste .co.rs. Tickets to opera, ballet and plays are a bargain, ranging from 200–1200din. Box office 11am–3pm & 5pm till performance.

SHOPPING

Kalenić Pijaca Maksima Gorkog bb. Belgrade's biggest open-air food market, a 20min walk southeast of Trg Republike in the Vračar district (just east of the Church of St Sava). You can stock up on edible souvenirs or essentials for hostel cooking: smallholders sell fresh fruit and veg, breads, honey and national delicacies like *kajmak* (clotted cream) and *ajvar* (pepper and aubergine purée). Daily 6am–7pm.

Ušće Shopping Centre Bulevar Mihajla Pupina 4. Across the river in New Belgrade, the city's premier shopping complex harbours some 150 shops, as well as a host of entertainment facilities. Daily 10am–10pm.

DIRECTORY

Embassies and consulates Australia, Vladimira Popovića 38–40 ☎ 11 330 3400; Canada, Kneza Miloša 75 ☎ 11 306 3000; Ireland, Kosančićev venac 2/1 ☎ 11 218 3581; UK, Resavska 46 ☎ 11 306 0900; US, Kneza Aleksandra Karadjordjevica 92 ☎ 11 706 4000.

Exchange There are "Menjačnica" signs everywhere.

Hospital Emergency Centre, Pasterova 2 ☎ 11 361 8444 (24hr).

Left luggage (пртљаг – *prtlag*). At bus and train stations (150din/24hr).

Pharmacies Prvi Maj, Kralja Milana 9 ☎ 11 324 1349; Sveti Sava, Nemanjina 2 ☎ 11 264 3170. Both 24hr.

Police Savski trg 2 ☎ 11 264 5764.

Post office Zmaj Jovina 17 (Mon–Sat 8am–7pm) and inside bus station (Mon–Fri 8am–9pm, Sat 8am–2pm).

Northern Serbia

North of Belgrade, stretching up towards the Hungarian border and spanning the southern part of the fertile Pannonian Plain, is **Vojvodina**, one of Serbia's most ethnically eclectic regions, with a large Hungarian minority. The region's capital, **Novi Sad**, is a charming spot that's a feasible day-trip from the capital or a handy springboard north to **Subotica** and Hungary. It's also an ideal base for forays into **Fruška Gora**, the gently undulating hills to the south peppered with medieval Orthodox monasteries.

NOVI SAD AND AROUND

Situated on the main road and rail routes towards Budapest some 75km northwest of Belgrade, **NOVI SAD** (Нови Сад) has long charmed visitors with its comely buildings – remnants of Austro-Hungarian rule. Today it's an emphatically young town – especially in the summer, when thousands of international revellers swarm to Petrovaradin Fortress for the four-day EXIT festival.

WHAT TO SEE AND DO

The hub of the city is **Trg Slobode** (Freedom Square), a spacious plaza bounded on either side by the neo-Gothic **Catholic Church of the Virgin Mary** and the neo-Renaissance town hall. Running east from here is bustling Zmaj Jovina, which, together with the adjoining bar-filled alleyway Laze Telečkog and wide, pedestrianized Dunavska, forms the town's central nexus of streets for eating, drinking and socializing. At the bottom end of Dunavska, occupying no. 35, the enlightening **Museum of Vojvodina** (Tues–Fri 9am–7pm, Sat & Sun 10am–6pm; 150din; w muzejvojvodine.org.rs) explores the region's many nationalities, including its significant Hungarian, Romanian and Slovak minorities; the prize exhibit, however, is a gold-plated Roman parade helmet.

Sun-lovers should head for the **Štrand** (May–Sept; 100din), a sandy beach on the Danube's north bank, opposite the fortress, which has bars, cafés and a "school's out" vibe.

The south bank and Petrovaradin Fortress

Novi Sad developed in tandem with the huge **Petrovaradin Fortress** (open access) on the Danube's south bank. The fortress rises picturesquely from rolls of green hillside, its delicate lemon-yellow buildings set inside sturdy fortifications. It took its present shape in the eighteenth century when the Austrians tried to create an invincible barrier against the Turks. Unfortunately its defences quickly became outdated, and the authorities decided to imprison independent-minded troublemakers here instead – including Karađorđe and, a century later, a young Tito. The fortress **museum** (Tues–Sun 10am–6pm; 150din) relays the history of

---

MONASTERIES AROUND NOVI SAD

Shadowing the city to the south are the low rolling hills of the **Fruška Gora**, once an island in the now evaporated Pannonian Sea. These days, its orchards and vineyards comprise a national park carved up by a web of simple hiking trails. The hills – known among devotees as the Holy Mountain – also house sixteen monasteries (there were once 35). About 15km south of Novi Sad, just off the main road before the village of Irig, is **Novo Hopovo**, where a Byzantine church is housed within a picturesque monastery. Not far off are two more sixteenth-century monastic churches: elegant white **Krušedol**, and **Vrdnik-Ravanica**, which has Tsar Lazar's collarbone on display.

Accessing the monasteries is nigh on impossible without a car; expect to pay around €30–35 for a day's rental with a firm such as Europcar (Bulevar Jaše Tomića 1; ☎21 443 188, w europcar.rs). Alternatively, contact the tourist office in Sremski Karlovci (see p.952), who can, with some warning, organize group sightseeing tours of the main monasteries (around 1200din) or arrange for a driver (around 2000din for 3hr).

29

both the fortress and the town, though is more interesting for its wealth of eighteenth- and nineteenth-century applied art. As you approach from town, look out for the **plaque** on the right of the bridge commemorating Oleg Nasov, who was killed during the NATO bombing – Novi Sad was one of the cities hardest hit in the spring of 1999, losing all its bridges.

Beyond the fortress, climb the steps to the right of the church; you'll arrive just under the **clock tower**. From this vantage point, the functional twentieth-century architecture of Novi Sad itself looks less alluring than the fortress does from the opposite bank, but the views of the surrounding countryside are magnificent.

Sremski Karlovci

On the eastern fringes of the Fruška Gora National Park, the enchanting small town of **Sremski Karlovci** (Сремски Карловци) makes for a great little trip out of Novi Sad. Its main square, Branka Radičevića, with the Orthodox and Catholic churches side by side and the Four Lions fountain, is highly picturesque, but Sremski Karlovci's status as a national treasure comes courtesy of its speciality wine, **Bermet**, made exclusively here since 1770. Drunk with desserts or as an aperitif, Bermet was popular in the Austro-Hungarian court and served on board the *Titanic*'s maiden voyage. The tourist information office on the main square can point you to the delightful **wine cellar** owned by the Živanović family (Mitropolita Stratimirovića 86b; daily 10am–7pm; ⓦ muzejzivanovic.com), where you can buy your own supplies – swing open the side-gate to enter their orchard; there's also a quaint beekeeping museum. Alternatively, relax with a glass or two on the outdoor decking of the hotel of the same name on the main square.

Sremski Karlovci is a ten-minute taxi ride from Novi Sad (around 500din); catch a cab from the rank on Ilije Ognjanovića.

ARRIVAL AND DEPARTURE

By train Novi Sad's train station is just under 1km north of the centre on Bulevar Jaše Tomića. To reach the centre, take

---

THE EXIT FESTIVAL

For four days at the beginning of July the grounds of Petrovaradin Fortress are overrun by **EXIT Festival** revellers (ⓦ exitfest.org). Now established as one of the premier music events in Europe, EXIT attracts some of the very biggest names in pop, techno and hip-hop. Buy tickets and camping passes via the website. You can rent rooms in Novi Sad for the duration: check ⓦ exittrip.org, which helps with booking accommodation and transport.

---

bus #4 (70din) from in front of it; walking takes about 30min – head straight down Bulevar Oslobođenja and turn left into Jevrejska at the market. A taxi into the centre should cost no more than 200din.

Destinations Belgrade (every 2hr; 2hr); Budapest (2 daily; 6hr); Subotica (10 daily; 2hr).

By bus The bus station is adjacent to the train station.

Destinations Belgrade (every 30–45min; 1hr 20min); Sarajevo (2 daily; 8hr); Subotica (every 30min–1hr; 1hr 30min).

INFORMATION

Tourist information Mihaila Pupina 9 (daily 8am–6pm) and Jevrejska 10 (daily 9am–5pm; ☎ 21 421 811, ⓦ novisad.travel). There's free wi-fi in Trg Slobode.

ACCOMMODATION

All of Novi Sad's accommodation gets booked up well in advance of the EXIT Festival, and just about all of them double their prices for this period.

Hostel 021 Pavla Papa 6 ☎ 63 573 073. Located on a small side street across from the National Theatre, the clean and welcoming *021* has four- to six-bed dorms, a triple and a double with TV, plus a spacious communal area and a small kitchen. Breakfast not included. Dorms **€10**, double **€30**

Hostel Downtown Njegoševa 2 ☎ 21 524 818, ⓦ hostelnovisad.com. A quiet, unassuming hostel just a few paces along from the main square, with a range of dorm sizes (some with bathrooms), kitchen and laundry facility. Breakfast not included. Dorms **€12**, doubles **€40**

Hostel & Caffe Bar Rookies Jevrejska 13 ☎ 21 662 1889, ⓦ hostelrookies.com. Super-friendly, super-clean hostel in the heart of the city with three- and five-bed dorms as well as doubles. The downstairs café/bar offers a terrific range of food and beverages. Dorms **€10**, doubles **€26**

Sova Hostel Ilije Ognjanovića 26 ☎ 21 527 556, ⓦ hostelsova.com. Located just off the main square, the "owl" is an appealing apartment hostel offering hip four- to ten-bed rooms, a cosy communal space, and kitchen. Breakfast not included. Dorms €10, doubles €30

★ **Varad Inn Hostel** Štrosmajerova 16 ☏ 21 431 400, ⊛ varadinn.com. Brilliantly located at the foot of the fortress, this early eighteenth-century building has been converted into a sparkling hostel featuring beautifully designed en-suite rooms, all with a/c. Wonderful café and garden too. Breakfast not included. Dorms €10, doubles €30

EATING AND DRINKING

Astal Saren Mite Ružića 4. The aroma of grilled meat will have you sniffing out this homely little Serbian diner, located up a tiny side street off Laze Telečkog; big, caloric plates of grilled sausages, *čevapi* (a type of kebab) and *pljeskavica*, served with roast or fried potatoes and pickled salad (450din). Daily 9am–11pm.

Café Nublu Žarka Zrenjanina 12. Welcoming, gay-friendly café/bar located at the back of the city's best bookshop; the bare-bricked interior is replete with dimly lit lanterns, quirky clocks and lots of mismatched furniture, while the colourfully graffitied garden terrace completes the look. Daily 9am–11pm.

Foody Modena 1–3. Committed cost-cutters will warm to this bright, functional canteen, with soups, sandwiches, *pljeskavica* (150din) and much more. Sit down or takeaway. Mon–Sat 7.30am–11pm, Sun 9.30am–11pm.

Kuća Mala Laze Telečkog 4. A refreshing antidote to the string of brasher venues along this street, the "little house", with its cosy decor and checked tablecloths, is great for a hot sandwich (250din), pizza (650din) or a cracking cooked breakfast. Daily 9am–11pm, Fri & Sat till 1am.

Moritz Eis Laze Telečkog 2. This modern, snappy-looking *gelateria* serves the best ice cream in the city, bar none; chestnut, pear, and banana and cinnamon are just three of the simple but sensational varieties on offer. Daily 11am–11pm.

Pivnica Gusan Zmaj Jovina 4. Narrow brick-vaulted cellar restaurant doling out juicy mixed grills and kebabs (690din); alternatively, just stop by for a beer at the long wooden bar or outside on the buzzy terrace. It's through a passageway by the Diesel shop sign. Daily 8am–midnight.

★ TREAT YOURSELF

Zak Šafarikova 6 ☏ 021 447 545. Novi Sad's finest restaurant, with exquisitely thought-out dishes such as deer fillet with red cabbage and juniper sauce (1200din), and chocolate leaves with white mousse and morello cherries. Fine wines and impeccable service round things off beautifully. Mon–Fri 8am–11pm, Sat 10am–1am, Sun 11am–11pm.

SUBOTICA

Some 175km north of Belgrade, Vojvodina's second city, **SUBOTICA** (Суботица; Hungarian: Szabadka), is a wonderful counterpoint to the capital, its Secessionist buildings, green spaces, wide pavements and burghers riding around on old-fashioned bicycles all contributing to its unspoilt, wholesome air. Just a stone's throw from Hungary, Subotica feels tangibly more like its northern neighbour. Historically, the ties are close: Subotica reached its apotheosis in the years of the Austro-Hungarian Empire, when it was granted the status of a Royal Free Town.

WHAT TO SEE AND DO

The heart of the town is grassy **Trg Republike**, fronted by a hulking city hall built in 1912; its gingerbread-like windows and colourfully patterned roof are almost too gaudy to look at in full sunlight. In front stands a brilliant blue fountain. Adjoining Trg Republike is Trg Slobode, behind which runs the Korzo, a busy pedestrianized street featuring the fairytale **Piraeus Bank** building, with its door and windows straight out of a medieval castle, created by architects Dezsó Jakab and Marcell Komor at the start of the twentieth century.

Further out, northwest of the city centre is another Jakab/Komor collaboration: the dignified but now deserted 1902 **synagogue**, where a moving plaque remembers the "4000 Jewish citizens with whom we lived and built Subotica".

Likovni Susret Contemporary Art Gallery

Occupying the wildly colourful 1904 mansion of architect Ferenc Raichle on Rajhlov Park Square is the **Likovni Susret Contemporary Art Gallery** (Mon–Fri 8am–7pm, Sat 9am–1pm; 100din), exhibiting work by local artists. The real draw, however, is the attention-seeking interior decor, from the cutesy hearts at the entranceway to the bulbous alcoves upstairs.

29

Cathedral of St Theresa

A five-minute walk west of the centre, on Harambašićeva, the **Catholic Cathedral of St Theresa** is a curiously moving place; in the surrounding square, the scattered statues are a poignant mix of classical piety (the two hands clasped in prayer) and postwar brutalism (the enormous monument to the "victims of fascism" who died during World War II).

ARRIVAL AND DEPARTURE

By train The train station dominates one side of Rajhlov Park, a 5min walk from the centre.
Destinations Belgrade (6 daily; 3hr 30min–5hr); Budapest (2 daily; 2hr 30min); Novi Sad (10 daily; 2hr).
By bus The bus station is on Senćanski Put, a 15min walk from the centre on the road to Novi Sad.
Destinations Belgrade (hourly; 3hr 30min); Novi Sad (hourly; 1hr 30min); Szeged, Hungary (every 2hr; 1hr 30min).

INFORMATION

Tourist information Trg Slobode 1, to the rear of the City Hall (Mon–Fri 8am–6pm, Sat 9am–1pm; ☎ 24 670 350, ⓦ visitsubotica.rs). There are plenty of brochures and maps on both the town and Lake Palić.

ACCOMMODATION

Hotel Patria Đure Đakovića bb ☎ 24 554 500, ⓦ hotelpatria.rs. Between the bus station and the centre, this budget four-star hotel proves you get more bang for your buck outside Belgrade. Breakfast included. Doubles €60
Incognito Huga Badalića 3, left off Maksima Gorkog ☎ 62 666 674, ⓦ hostel-subotica.com. This large hostel is a 5min walk from the central square, with basic but clean rooms, all with TV and wi-fi. Breakfast not included. Dorms €10, doubles €24

EATING AND DRINKING

Boss Matije Korvina 7–8. Just behind the Likovni Susret mansion, this atrium pizzeria and bar is where people come to be seen; the adjoining statue-strewn courtyard is a fabulous place to sup a beer. Pizza 500din, pasta 580din. Daily 7am–midnight.
Stara Picerija Matije Korvina 5. Opposite *Boss*, on a cute cobbled alleyway, this place excels at pizza (450din), hot sandwiches and much more besides; attractive interior and cheerful feel-good classics on the stereo. Mon–Thurs & Sun 9am–midnight, Fri & Sat till 1am.

Southern Serbia

South of Belgrade, the softly rolling hillsides studded with low red-roofed houses are the setting for three of the country's most precious medieval monasteries: **Žiča, Studenica** and **Sopoćani**. Elsewhere, the south's main city, **Niš**, conveniently straddles major road and rail routes to Bulgaria and Macedonia, and is an attractive small town with some fascinating sights.

ŽIČA, STUDENICA AND SOPOĆANI

In the hilly stretch south from the town of Kraljevo – itself some 170km south of Belgrade – to Novi Pazar lie some of Serbia's most impressive **monasteries**. Just 4km southeast of Kraljevo, **Žiča** was a thirteenth-century creation of St Sava – Serbia's patron saint and the first archbishop of the independent Serbian Church – with a vivid red exterior that evokes the red Serbs use to paint eggs at Easter.

The first and greatest of the Serbian monasteries, however, is **Studenica**, set against the wild, roaming slopes some 12km (and accessible by bus) from the village of Ušče. It was established in 1190 by Stefan Nemanja, founder of the Nemanjić dynasty, whose marble tomb lies in the Church of the Virgin Mary. Studenica's **superb frescoes** were the

> ### VISITING THE MONASTERIES
>
> While Žiča is easily accessible by bus from Kraljevo (every 30–45min; 50min), you'll need a car if you want to see more than one monastery in a day. In Niš try Inter Rent-A-Car (P.C. Ambasador Lok 23; ☎ 18 528 852, ⓦ rentacarnis.rs); prices start at around €35 per day. If you have more time, you could try public buses: on the Kraljevo–Novi Pazar route, you can get off at Ušče, from where there are 2–3 daily buses to Studenica. Monasteries are generally open from 8am to 6pm, and are free to enter.

work of an innovative but still anonymous Greek painter who created *trompe-l'oeil* images to resemble mosaics.

Around 16km from Novi Pazar is the **Sopoćani** monastery, a thirteenth-century construction that once stretched across a whole complex, but of which only the Holy Trinity Church remains. *The Assumption of Virgin Mary* is the most famous of its unusually large Byzantine frescoes; the bright colours and expressive faces are said to prefigure the Italian Renaissance.

NIŠ

The pleasant university town of **NIŠ** (Ниш), 235km southeast of Belgrade, is a useful stopover point between Belgrade and Sofia or Skopje. Its inhabitants have a definite small-town pride, as well they might: this is the birthplace of Constantine, the Roman emperor responsible for the conversion of the whole empire to Christianity. Its collection of intriguing – if macabre – sights is a gritty reminder of the darker sides to Serbia's history, but the focus in the cafés and bars crammed with students is all on having a good time.

WHAT TO SEE AND DO

The city's centrepiece is its main square, **Trg Kralja Milana**, which sits across the Niöava River from **Niš Fortress**.

The fortress

A Roman fortress once stood here – a circle of Roman tombstones remains inside – but the current fortifications date from the beginning of the eighteenth century. Enter from the main Istanbul Gate facing the bridge; inside, the town authorities have put real effort into making this a place residents can enjoy, with the beautiful **mosque of Bali Bey** converted into an exhibition space, and the row of cafés in the shadow of the fortress's inner wall a cool spot to unwind. Each August the whole fortress is given over to the Nisville jazz festival (www.nisville.com).

The first of the city's rather grim sights is to your right as you leave the fortress:

look out for the miniature blue-domed **memorial chapel** perched on the lawn, which commemorates the local people killed in the NATO bombings.

Ćele Kula

East of the centre on Brače Taskovича, **Ćele Kula** (The Skull Tower; Tues–Sun 9am–8pm; 150din; take any bus towards Niška Banja) makes for gruesome sightseeing. It dates from 1809, when Stevan Sinđelić, commander of a nationalist uprising, found his men surrounded by the Turkish army on nearby Čegar Hill and took drastic action against his adversaries, firing into his gunpowder supplies and blowing up most of the Turks and all the Serbs around him. Following the battle, to deter future rebellion the ruling Pasha ordered that the heads of the Serbian soldiers killed in the battle be stuffed and mounted on the tower; 952 went into creating this macabre totem pole, though today only 58 remain.

Crveni Krst

The derelict **Crveni Krst** (Red Cross; Tues–Sun 9am–6pm; 150din) World War II concentration camp, a ten-minute walk down busy Bulevar 12 Februar from the bus station, is powerfully evocative: the hand-painted German signs for the washroom, messroom and kitchen make it all seem very recent. The barbed-wire fences and watchtowers, so familiar from camps in Poland and Germany, are a reminder that the displacement and genocide of millions was a truly pan-European operation.

ARRIVAL AND DEPARTURE

By train The train station is 2km west of town on Dimitrija Tucovića. Buses #1, #5 and #6 all run to the centre.
Destinations Belgrade (6 daily; 4hr 30min–6hr); Skopje (2 daily; 4hr 45min); Sofia (2 daily; 5hr).
By bus The bus station is a 5min walk from town, west of the fortress on Bulevar Februar 12.
Destinations Belgrade (every 30–45min; 3hr); Kraljevo (6 daily; 3hr); Skopje (6 daily; 4–5hr); Sofia (2 daily; 2hr 30min).

INFORMATION

Tourist information Voždova Karađorđa 7 (Mon–Fri 9am–8pm, Sat 10am–3pm; ☎ 18 521 321, www.visitnis.com), and inside the fortress (Mon–Fri 9am–8pm, Sat 9am–4.30pm, Sun 10am–3pm; ⓣ 18 250 222).

ACCOMMODATION

Aurora Hostel Petra Vucinic 18 ⓣ 18 214 462, ⓦ aurorahostel.rs. Occupying what was once the Turkish consulate, this tidy little hostel has three- and eight-bed dorms, all with a/c and their own bathrooms. A well-equipped kitchen and neat terrace round things off nicely. Breakfast not included. Dorms **€10**

Downtown Hostel Kej Kola Srpskih Sestara 3/2 ⓣ 18 526 756, ⓔ office@downtownhostel.rs. Occupying a renovated apartment just metres from the riverfront, this place is enthusiastically run and features an eight-bed dorm and several doubles (all with a/c), plus kitchen and lounge. Dorms **€12**, doubles **€30**

EATING AND DRINKING

Cobbled Kazandžijsko Sokače (Tinker's Alley), just south of Trg Kralja Milana, is the town's social hub, thronging with café-bars.

Crazy Horse Davidova 8. An Irish pub, but it's pretty much the liveliest place in town right now; good beer and chat, sport on the telly, and loads of great live music. Daily 8am–2am, Fri & Sat till 4am.

Hamam Tvrđava bb. Named after the Turkish baths it's housed in (just inside the fortress entrance), this is the place to try some grilled lamb or oven-baked fish (400–500din), frequent evenings of live music enliven proceedings. Daily 10am–midnight.

Mamma Nade Tomić 10. Quirkily designed pizzeria with a terrific wood-fired oven; serious carnivores should have a stab at the house pizza, which comes topped with five types of meat (500din). Mon–Sat 10am–midnight, Sun noon–11pm.

Sinđelić Nikole Pašića 36. Named after the kamikaze general behind the Tower of Skulls episode, *Sinđelić* excels at simple, hearty Serbian food; try the gourmet *pljeskavica*, stuffed with pork and spices (500din). Located near the Kalča shopping mall. Daily 8am–1am.

SPIŠ CASTLE

Slovakia

HIGHLIGHTS

❶ **Bratislava** Try out the chic coffeehouses and cool underground bars. **See p.963**

❷ **Banská Štiavnica** Climb a volcano or swim in a mine. **See p.968**

❸ **High Tatras** Admire the majesty of Slovakia's highest peaks. **See p.970**

❹ **Levoča** Explore the crumbling backstreets of this beautiful walled town. **See p.973**

❺ **Spiš Castle** Step into the Middle Ages at this atmospheric pile. **See p.973**

❻ **Košice** Enjoy this laidback and youthful eastern city. **See p.974**

HIGHLIGHTS ARE MARKED ON THE MAP ON P.959

ROUGH COSTS

Daily budget Basic €35, occasional treat €45

Drink Beer €1.70

Food Gnocchi with bacon €4

Hostel/budget hotel €15/€30

Travel Bratislava–Košice (train): 5hr–6hr, €19

FACT FILE

Population 5.4 million

Language Slovak

Currency Euro (€)

Capital Bratislava

International phone code ☎421

Time zone GMT +1hr

Introduction

Hungarians and Turks came to Slovakia for its natural resources, and so does today's tourist. A broad band of sprawling mountains means lots of good skiing and snowboarding, while Karst areas are for caving, and the rambling hilly midlands are a hiker's paradise.

30

One of Europe's most low-key capitals, **Bratislava** is a warren of cobbled streets, low arches and tiny squares. It's small enough to explore in a day, but big enough to hold your interest for a long weekend. In Central Slovakia, you'll find lovely **Banská Štiavnica**, a UNESCO-protected medieval mining town in a lunar landscape of dead volcanoes. East and north are the **High Tatras**, as decent a mountain range as any in Central and Eastern Europe. They've long been the site of enthusiastic skiing, hiking and sonnet-writing. Heading east towards Ukraine is the wild, rocky **Spiš** region, home to the mammoth medieval **Spiš Castle** and the twelfth-century walled town of **Levoča**. Continuing south, almost to the Hungarian border, you'll find Slovakia's second city, lively **Košice**.

Sharing borders with Poland, the Czech Republic, Austria, Hungary and Ukraine, Slovakia is landlocked, with high mountains in the north, low mountains in the centre, hills to the west, and the Danube basin to the south. The population is fairly diverse, with over half a million ethnic **Hungarians**, hundreds of thousands of **Roma** (Gypsies), and several thousand **Rusyns** in the east.

CHRONOLOGY

450 BC Celts inhabit present-day Slovakia.
623 AD Samo becomes King of the Slavs after defeating the Avarians near Bratislava.
828 First Christian church consecrated in Slovakia.
863 First Slavic alphabet written in Greater Moravia by saints Cyril and Methodius.
895 The Magyars (Hungarians) gradually begin to conquer and occupy the territory.
1241 Mongol invasion of Slovakia results in heavy losses.

1526 Hungary loses Buda to the Turks; the Habsburgs move their capital to Bratislava.
1800s Growth in Slovak nationalism.
1895 Czechs and Slovaks form a strategy of mutual cooperation against dual monarchy Austria-Hungary.
1918 The independent republic of Czechoslovakia is established on the defeat of Austria-Hungary in World War I.
1939 Germany takes Sudetenland in Czechoslovakia, before occupying the rest of the country.
1945 Slovak National Uprising against German occupation is successful, but thousands of Slovakian Jews have already been sent to the camps.
1948 The Communist Party comes to power in Czechoslovakia.
1989 The Velvet Revolution heralds the end of Communism in Czechoslovakia.
1993 Czechoslovakia splits peacefully into two states.
2004 Slovakia joins NATO and the EU.
2009 The euro replaces the Slovak crown as the national currency.
2016 In national elections the ultra-right-wing ĽSNS enters parliament for the first time.

ARRIVAL AND DEPARTURE

Slovakia's main international airport is M.R. Štefánika, often referred to as **Bratislava Airport** (☎02 3303 3353, ⊛bts.aero), 9km northeast of central Bratislava. There are also international airports in **Košice**, operating flights to and from Prague, Vienna, London and Dublin, and in Poprad, operating mainly business flights to and from various European cities. Another option is to fly into Vienna; the two capitals are only 60km apart, flights to Vienna are sometimes cheaper, and Slovaklines (hourly; 1hr) and MeinFernbus/FlixBus (hourly; 1hr) both run shuttle-bus connections for €5–15 one-way. For a more romantic arrival, there's the Vienna–Bratislava hydrofoil (see p.965).

Slovakia has good **rail connections** with Austria, Hungary, Poland and the Czech Republic. Most international trains terminate at Bratislava, but trains from Budapest, Kraków and Prague also run to Košice, and there's a direct service between Prague and Poprad.

Eurolines buses connect European cities to Bratislava (ⓦeurolines.sk), while **Student Agency's** (ⓦstudentagency.cz) domestic and international coaches are cheap and comfortable.

GETTING AROUND

BY TRAIN

Train journeys are slow but scenic. Slovak Railways (Železnice Slovenskej Republiky or ŽSR; ☎18188, ⓦslovakrail .sk) runs fast *rýchlik* trains that stop at major towns; *osobný* (local) trains stop everywhere. You can buy **tickets** (*lístok*) for domestic journeys at the station (*stanica*) before or on the day of departure. Supplements are payable on all EuroCity (EC) trains, and occasionally for InterCity (IC) and Express (Ex) trains of Slovak Railway trains. ŽSR runs reasonably priced sleepers and couchettes. Book in advance no later than six hours before departure.

InterRail passes are valid; **Eurail** passes require supplements.

BY BUS

Buses (*autobus*) cover a far more extensive network. The former state bus company is Slovenská Autobusová Doprava or SAD though there are now myriad other companies operating services such as Slovaklines (ⓦslovaklines.sk). Buy your **ticket** from the driver or book in advance from the station if you're travelling at the weekend or early in the morning on one of the main routes. Bus (and train) timetables are available online at ⓦcp.atlas.sk.

BY BICYCLE

Although much of Slovakia is mountainous and not ideal for **cyclists**, the countryside around Bratislava has well-maintained bike paths that stretch into Austria and Hungary. More demanding rides can take you into the Little Carpathians. Most trains allow bikes.

ACCOMMODATION

New B&Bs are opening all the time, and hostel provision has been increasing for years. There's no network of **hostels** in

30

Slovakia, though a few are affiliated to HI (⊕hihostels.com). Bratislava has plenty of good private hostels, and in the High Tatras you can find chalet-style **boarding houses** (*chata*) in the mountains, with basic dorm beds from around €10 per bed. There are plenty of **campsites** in Slovakia, which usually rent out basic wooden huts (*chata*), fun if you share with friends.

In summer the cheapest accommodation is sometimes **university halls**; ask at the local tourist office for details. **Private rooms** are also cheap, and can be organized through the local tourist office as well. If you're a student, get hold of an ISIC (International Student Identity Card), as you'll need it to get student rates. Check websites for online booking discounts. Smaller places are often understaffed so pre-book and give an estimated arrival time, or you might find yourself locked out.

FOOD AND DRINK

Slovak **cuisine** is an edifice resting on three mighty columns: the potato, the pig and the cabbage. Because of their many neighbours, you'll find strong hints of Polish, Ukrainian and especially Hungarian fare, too. Main courses are usually a combination of meat with potatoes (*zemiaky*), or dumplings. Slovak dumplings (*halušky*) are small and smooth, like gnocchi. Meat is usually breaded and fried, or cooked in a sauce. The main meal of the day is lunch, which starts with **soup** (*polievka*) – perhaps garlic (*cesnaková*) or sauerkraut (*kapustnica*). You can often find game meats, like boar, rabbit and venison, on menus, as well as pork, beef, chicken, duck and goose.

A classic mid-morning **snack** is *párok*, a hot frankfurter. A Slovak delicacy is *jaternica*, made from pig's blood and rice. *Bryndza*, sheep's cheese made in the region since the Middle Ages, is light, salty and delicious. *Bryndzové halušky*, the national dish, is dumplings served with *bryndza* and bacon. Another favourite is *pirohy*; unleavened boiled dumplings stuffed with cheese, a little like ravioli. Hungarian goulash is popular, and so is *langoše* – deep-fried dough topped with crushed garlic, cheese, ketchup or sour cream.

Some popular **desserts** are strudel (apple or curd cheese), *palacinky* (crêpes filled with chocolate, fruit or jam, and usually cream) and *lievance*, which look like Scotch or American pancakes, and are served with hot fruit. An unusual Slovak speciality is sweet noodles (*rezance*), with poppy seeds and butter or curd cheese and sugar.

Outside the major cities, restaurant **closing time** is usually 9 or 10pm, while pubs often have cheap lunchtime deals from 11.30am to 1.30pm.

DRINK

The Romans brought **wine** to Slovakia. Vineyards in the southeast produce good whites, the most distinctive being Tokaj, a sweet dessert wine. For a few weeks in September you can get fresh *burčák*, a fruity, bubbly semi-fermented white with which Slovaks and Czechs toast the harvest. *Slivovica*, made with plums, and *borovička,* made with juniper berries, are popular spirits, but Slovaks will gladly make alcohol from any fruit. The national soft drinks are Kofola, an aniseedy Coca-Cola substitute, and Vinea, made with red or white grapes. The best-known bottled **beer** is Zlatý Bažant (Golden Pheasant). You'll find a pub (*krčma*) in every town, as well as a wine bar (*vináreň*), which will usually have later closing hours and often doubles as a nightclub. The legal drinking age is 18 and you may be asked for ID in shops, pubs or clubs. **Coffee** is traditionally served strong and black, though coffeehouses now serve cappuccino, latte and the like. Teahouses (*čajovňa*) are popular, especially with young people, and stock dozens of types of **tea**.

CULTURE AND ETIQUETTE

Learning a few Slovak words helps break down Slovak reserve, even just "hello", "goodbye" and "thank you" (see box, p.962). If you've been travelling eastwards, your Czech will do fine, as all Slovaks understand Czech.

When **tipping**, Slovaks usually round up to the nearest euro or two. When you are introduced to strangers, shake hands, and don't use first names when addressing older people. Casual greetings like *ahoj* are only for close friends. Wish fellow diners a good meal (*dobrú chut*) before starting, and make a toast (*na zdravie*) before drinking. If you are invited to a Slovak home you must take off your shoes at the door, even when told not to (they're just being polite), and if you're invited to eat, bring wine or chocolates.

SPORTS AND ACTIVITIES

Slovaks love football and **ice hockey**, which you can see live on screens in bars across the Republic. You can go to ice hockey games in stadiums from September to April (ⓦhcslovan.sk, in Bratislava); tickets cost between €13 and €50 and can be bought from the arena on match days. There's plenty of **hiking**, **skiing**, **snowboarding** and **rafting** in the High Tatras (ⓦtatry.sk) and caving in the Slovak Karst in east Slovakia (ⓦssj.sk). Walking is a popular national pastime, particularly in the plentiful woodlands on Saturday afternoons.

COMMUNICATIONS

Most **post offices** (*pošta*) open Monday to Friday 8am to 5pm. You can buy stamps (*známky*) from tobacconists (*trafika*) and street kiosks, and it's also worth asking in

SLOVAKIA ONLINE

ⓦ**slovakia.org** Political, historical, cultural and economic information.
ⓦ**slovakia.travel** Tourist information in a variety of languages with travel tips and event information.
ⓦ**spectator.sme.sk** English-language weekly with news and listings.
ⓦ**slovak-republic.org** Upcoming events and attractions as well as other travel information.

EMERGENCY NUMBERS

General emergency ☎112.

anywhere that sells postcards. Cheap local calls can be made from any phone, but for international calls it's best to buy a **phonecard** (*telefónna karta*) from a tobacconist or post office.

EMERGENCIES

Violent crime is fairly rare and pickpocketing or petty theft is the biggest danger. You should carry a photocopy of your passport with you, as ID is (in theory at least) required by law. Small ailments can be dealt with by the **pharmacist** (*lekáreň*); for bigger problems go to the nearest **hospital** (*nemocnica*).

INFORMATION

Most towns have some kind of **tourist office** (*informačné centrum*), usually with English-speaking staff. In summer they're generally open Monday to Friday 9am to 6pm, Saturday and Sunday 9am to 2pm; in winter they tend to close an hour earlier and all day Sunday. **Maps** are available from tourist offices, bookshops and some hotels. The Slovak for town plan is *plán mesta*.

MONEY AND BANKS

The euro became Slovakia's currency in 2009. **Credit** and **debit cards** are accepted in upmarket hotels and restaurants and some shops, and there are plenty of **ATMs** in larger towns. **Exchange offices** (*zmenáreň*) can be found in big hotels, travel agencies and department stores, but it's usually better value to change your money in a bank.

STUDENT DISCOUNTS

To get a student discount (which is often as much as fifty percent) you'll need an ISIC, as most places won't accept your university ID card.

30

SLOVAK

	SLOVAK	PRONUNCIATION
Yes	Áno	Uh-no
No	Nie	Nyeh
Please	Prosím	Pro-seem
Thank you	Ďakujem	Dya-koo-yem vam
Hello/Good day	Dobrý deň/Ahoj	Doh-rie den[y]/a-hoy
Goodbye	Dovidenia	Do-vid-en-ya
Excuse me	Prepáčte	Pre-patch-teh
Where	Kde	Gde
Good	Dobrý	Dob-rie
Bad	Zlý	Zlee
Near	Blízko	Bli-sko
Far	Ďaleko	D[y]a-lek-o
Cheap	Lacný	Lats-nie
Expensive	Drahý	Dra-hie
Open	Otvorený	Ot-vor-eh-nie
Closed	Zatvorený	Zat-vor-eh-nie
Today	Dnes	Dnes
Yesterday	Včera	Ftch-er-a
Tomorrow	Zajtra	Zuyt-ra
How much is…?	Koľko stojí…?	Kol-ko stat[y]…?
What time is it?	Koľko je hodín?	Kol-ko ye hod-in?
I don't understand	Nerozumiem	Ne-ro-zoom-yem
Do you speak English?	Hovoríte po anglicky?	Hov-or-i-te po ang-lits-ky?
Entrance	Vchod	FHod
Exit	Výstup	VeeStoop
Ticket	Lístok	Leestok
Hotel	Hotel	Hotel
Toilet	Záchod	ZaHod
Square	Námestie	Nahmestee
Station	Stanica	Stani-tza
Do you have a…?	Máte…?	Ma-te…?
Single room	Jednoposteľovú izbu	Yed-no-pos-tye-lyo-voo iz-bu
One	Jeden	Yed-en
Two	Dva	Dva
Three	Tri	Tri
Four	Štyri	Shtir-i
Five	Päť	Pyat[y]
Six	Šesť	Shest[y]
Seven	Sedem	Sed-em
Eight	Osem	Oss-em
Nine	Deväť	Dev-yat[y]
Ten	Desať	Dess-at[y]

OPENING HOURS AND HOLIDAYS

Opening hours for local shops are in the region of 9am to 6pm on weekdays and 9am to noon Saturdays, with supermarkets staying open later and sometimes on Sundays. Smaller rural shops close for an hour at lunchtime. Opening hours for **sights** and **attractions** are usually Tuesday to Sunday 9am to 5pm, though low season hours are often restricted to weekends and holidays. Most **castles** are closed in winter. When visiting a sight, ask for English (*anglický*) text. Admission rarely costs more than €4. **Public holidays** include January 1, January 6, Good Friday, Easter Monday, May 1, May 8, July 5, August 29, September 1, September 15, November 1, November 17, December 24, 25 and 26.

Bratislava

Straddling the Danube in the southwest corner of Slovakia, **BRATISLAVA** is one of Europe's quieter capitals, its meandering streets and tiny but grand buildings attracting far fewer tourists than Vienna or Prague. In fact, with its slightly small-town atmosphere, on a hot afternoon a flock of sheep wouldn't look out of place grazing on Františkánske Square. The Old Town showcases the skill of Slovak town planners, who crammed a city's worth of palaces, shops, cafés, pubs, restaurants, museums and churches into a few blocks.

The area has been settled since the Neolithic era (about 500 BC), making it centuries older than Prague or Budapest. It has always been an international city – Romans, Hungarians, Germans, Austrians, Turks, Czechs, Jews and Roma have all left their mark. The locals are less visitor-weary and cynical than the natives of most capitals, characterized by a friendly reserve.

WHAT TO SEE AND DO

The **Old Town** (Staré Mesto) lies on the north bank of the Danube, 1km south of the train station, east of the stout **castle** and southwest of the shops and housing blocks of **New Town** (Nové Mesto). A pedestrian zone stretches between Hodžovo námestie in the north down to the river in the south. South of the city is Hungary and west is Austria. Bratislava is the only capital city that borders two independent countries.

Old Town

You can enter the Old Town via the only surviving medieval gateway, **Michalská brána a veža** (St Michael's Gate and Tower; Tues–Fri 10am–5pm, Sat & Sun 11am–6pm; €4.30), which contains a military museum and a tower with a view. Michalská and Ventúrska, two halves of one street, are lined with stately **Baroque palaces**, the university library and dozens of places to eat. At number 10 is **Mozart House**, where the six-year-old Mozart performed for the Palffy clan,

while the former Hungarian parliament stands at Michalská 1.

A little northeast are the adjoining squares of the **Old Town** – Hlavné námestie and Františkánske námestie. Hlavné, dotted with street cafés, hosts the Christmas and Easter markets, and a few stalls most weeks. On Františkánske, you'll find the Rococo **Mirbach Palace** (Františkánske nám. 11; Tues–Sun 11am–6pm; €3.50, students €2), home of the City Gallery's Baroque collection.

Primate's Palace

Neoclassical **Primate's Palace** (Primaciálne nám 1; Tues–Sun 10am–5pm; €3.50) contains the Hall of Mirrors, where Napoleon and Austrian Emperor Franz I signed the Peace of Pressburg (as Bratislava was then called) in 1805. In 1903 city authorities restored the palace, and discovered six seventeenth-century English tapestries concealed behind the plaster, which are now the palace's other main attraction.

Cathedral of St Martin

On the edge of the Old Town is the fine Gothic Cathedral of St Martin. This was the **coronation church** for the kings and queens of Hungary between 1563 and 1830, and houses the remains of the seventh-century saint Joan the Merciful.

> ### ACTIVE BRATISLAVA
>
> **Cycling** and **rollerblading** along the Danube, towards Austria (upstream) or Hungary (downstream), are popular activities: for information on bike rental see p.966. The Small Carpathian mountains surrounding Bratislava are beautiful and make for a good day's **cycling** or **walking**; see ⓦ bratislava sightseeing.com for suggested routes and guided tours.
>
> Action Park offers a number of activities including zorbing, kiting, bungee trampoline and a shooting gallery (zorbing €6, archery €9/1hr; ⓦ actionpark.sk).

30

30

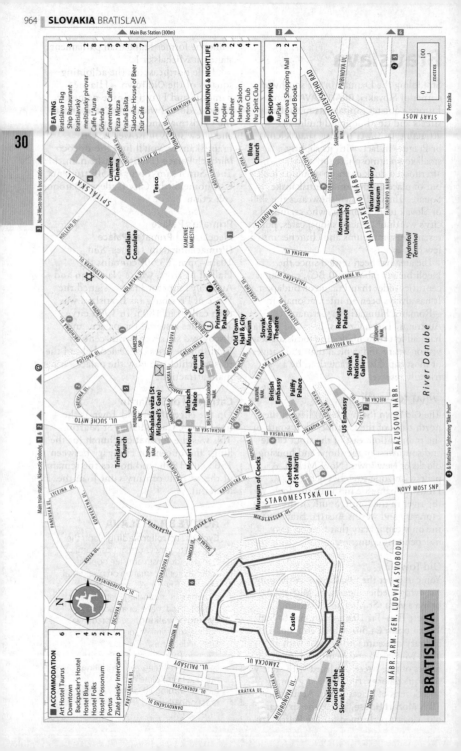

BRATISLAVA

Main Bus Station (300m)

■ ACCOMMODATION
Art Hostel Taurus	6
Downtown	1
Backpacker's Hostel	4
Hostel Blues	5
Hostel Folks	2
Hostel Possonium	7
Portus	7
Zlaté piesky Intercamp	3

● EATING
Bratislava Flag	3
Ship Restaurant	2
Bratislavský	8
mestiansky pivovar	8
Caffe L'Aura	5
Govinda	1
Greentree Caffe	9
Pizza Mizza	4
Prašná Bašta	6
Sladovňa-House of Beer	6
Štúr Café	7

● DRINKING & NIGHTLIFE
Al Faro	5
Dopler	3
Dubliner	2
Harley Saloon	6
Norton Club	4
Nu Spirit Club	1

● SHOPPING
AuPark	3
Eurovea Shopping Mall	2
Oxford Books	1

River Danube

Nový most

A whimsical moment in Slovak communist functionalism, **Nový most** (New Bridge) was formerly called Most SNP, and is now nicknamed the UFO bridge, due to the tower rising from one end that resembles a flying saucer speared by a twig. You can ascend the tower by elevator and dine at the restaurant, which looks like the *Starship Enterprise* (daily 10am–11pm), or gaze at Bratislava from the viewing deck – locals say it's the best view of the city, because it's one of the few places you can't see the Nový most.

The castle and museums

Bratislava's **castle** (*hrad*; Tues–Sun: April–Oct 10am–6pm; Nov–March 9am–5pm; ⓦbratislavskyhrad.eu) sits on a strategic hill between the Alps and Carpathians, first fortified in 3500 BC. On a clear day you can see Slovakia, Austria and Hungary. The current castle, a boxy four-towered rectangle, is a 1950s reconstruction of Emperor Sigismund's fifteenth-century fortification, which burnt down in 1811: it now houses the **Slovak Historical Museum** (Historické Múzeum Tues–Sun 9am–6pm; €7; ⓦsnm.sk). Winding down the castle hill is what's left of the former Jewish quarter (Židovská), which contains the **Museum of Clocks** on Židovská 1 (Tues–Fri 10am–5pm, Sat & Sun 11am–6pm; €2.30, students €1.50; ⓦmuzeum .bratislava.sk).

Slovak National Gallery

There are two entrances to the **Slovak National Gallery** (Tues, Wed & Fri–Sun 10am–6pm; Thurs noon–8pm; free; ⓦsng.sk): the entrance on the embankment leads to the main building, a

converted barracks housing the principal collection, while the entrance on Štúrovo námestie leads to the **Esterházy Palace** wing, used for temporary exhibitions, mostly contemporary art.

The Blue Church

A short walk east from the Old Town is the Church of St Elizabeth (Kostol svätej Alžbety) or **Blue Church**, Bezručova 2 (Modrý kostolík, ⓦmodrykostol.fara .sk), which rises out of the suburbs like an Art Nouveau wedding cake. Built in the early twentieth century, the church is in the Hungarian Secessionist style, playfully combined with oriental, Romanesque and classical features. It's consecrated to a medieval princess and saint, a native of Bratislava, who risked her rank by giving alms to the poor; she stars in some mosaics inside.

The Artificial Beach

Every year from mid-June to August, hundreds of tonnes of sand are dropped on the banks of the Danube to give locals a taste of the beach. **Tyršovo nábrežie**, on the south bank facing the Old Town, is friendly, hot and crowded. Entry, hammocks, deckchairs, parasols and sports equipment are free, and there are cocktail bars, live music, table football, volleyball and snack bars.

ARRIVAL AND DEPARTURE

By plane From Bratislava Airport (ⓣ02 3303 3353, ⓦbts.aero), take bus #61 to the main train station, and from there walk or catch the tram into the centre. You can also take a taxi (see p.966).

By train Main station, Bratislava-Hlavná stanica, is within walking distance – 1km north – of the centre, or you can take bus #93. Some trains, particularly those heading for west Slovakia, pass through Bratislava Nové Mesto station, 4km northeast of the centre, which is linked to town by tram #6.

30

DAY-TRIP TO AUSTRIA

From Bratislava it takes 1hr 30min to get to Vienna by **hydrofoil**. Add that to higher prices in Austria and there's an argument for making Vienna a day-trip rather than an overnight affair. You can catch the hydrofoil from Rázusovo Nábrežie Embankment (up to 3 daily; €20–35 one-way, depending on the day and time; reservations required; ⓦtwincityliner.com). For a less scenic but cheaper trip you can get a Slovaklines bus from the main bus station (1hr 20min; from €5; ⓦslovaklines.sk). Trains also make the run with two services an hour leaving from either the main station or Petržalka station.

30

Destinations Brno (9 daily; 1hr 25min); Košice (approx hourly; 6hr); Poprad (9 daily; 4hr 40min–5hr); Prague (to Praha-Hlavní nádraží; 7 daily; 4–5hr); Vienna (2 hourly; 1hr).

By bus The main bus station is Bratislava autobusová stanica, on Mlynské nivy, just over 1km east of the centre. Trolleybus #210 connects it to the main train station, while #206 goes to the centre.

Destinations Bánska Štiavnica (2 direct buses daily, or change in Žarnovica; 3hr 20min); Brno (at least hourly; 1hr 30min–2hr 30min); Poprad (3 direct daily; 5–6hr); Prague (Florenc station; at least hourly; 4hr 15min–4hr 45min); Vienna (at least hourly; 1hr 20min).

INFORMATION

Tourist office Klobučnícka 2 (Daily: April–Oct 9am–7pm; Nov–March 9am–6pm; ☎ 02 216 186, ⓦ bratislava.sk): it can book centrally located private rooms. There's also a branch at the airport with varying hours, usually opening 8.30–9.30am and closing 6.30–7.30pm, sometimes later depending on flights.

Discount card The Bratislava City Card is available from both the centre and airport tourist offices: it lasts for up to three days, costs up to €16, and gets you discounts to city attractions, a one-hour walking tour, and free transport, including night buses.

GETTING AROUND

Walking is the only way to see the pedestrianized Old Town, but it's less than five minutes end to end so you're unlikely to get tired.

By tram, bus and trolleybus Buses are slower than trams and trolleybuses. Public transport runs from 4.30am until approximately 11pm. Night buses run roughly every hour; let the driver know where you're going, as the stops are by request only.

Tickets Buy your ticket before you board and validate it in one of the orange machines inside. Inspectors target routes going to the airport and bus and train terminals; fines are €50. Buy one-way tickets from machines at the tram terminus and newsagents: €0.70/15min; €0.90/up to 30min. A day-pass costs €4.50 and a three-day pass €8; you can buy these from shops at both the main bus and train stations (ⓦ imhd.sk). In theory you also need a half-fare ticket for bulky luggage, though few bother with this.

By bike Although there are currently no designated bike paths in Bratislava, ⓦ bratislava.info/trips/bike has plenty of information on cycling in the country. Bikes can be rented from Bratislava Sightseeing (☎ 0944 103 432, ⓦ bratislavasightseeing.com; €6/hr, €15/day), who also run bike tours leaving from the *UFO* restaurant car park, at Viedenská cesta.

By taxi Taxis are equipped with a meter, but even so it's normal to bargain the price before your journey. It's best to order in advance rather than hailing one on the street; try Radio Taxi (☎ 02 16303) or Personal Express (☎ 0903 588 070, ⓦ personalexpress.sk), which takes bookings by email.

ACCOMMODATION

Art Hostel Taurus Zámocká 24–26 ☎ 02 2072 2401, ⓦ hostel-taurus.com. Gleaming white, central hostel with only eight rooms. There's a dining area, sofas dotted around and a stage and musical instruments in case you want to jam. All rooms have a private bathroom and locker. Breakfast included. Dorms €16, doubles €50

Downtown Backpacker's Hostel Panenská 31 ☎ 0905 259 714, ⓦ backpackers.sk. Arty, colourful HI-affiliated hostel on the edge of the Old Town with 24hr reception, a restaurant-bar, common room with a tuneless old piano, books and games. There's also a kitchen and laundry room. Dorms €18, doubles €53

★ **Hostel Blues** Špitálska 2 ☎ 0905 204 020, ⓦ hostelblues.sk. Great concrete slab of a building which unexpectedly contains a warm, inviting hostel. The space given over to socializing (bar/reception with live weekly concerts, living room and a big kitchen) makes for a friendly atmosphere, and the staff are helpful and well informed. Rooms and dorms (female or mixed) are clean and towels are provided. Dorms €17.50, doubles €62.50

Hostel Folks Obchodná 2 ☎ 0903 725 252. Right in the thick of the downtown action, this crisply maintained if slightly bland hostel offers IKEA-furnished dorms and private rooms as well as a kitchen. Dorms €15, doubles €42

Hostel Possonium Šancová 20 ☎ 02 2072 0007, ⓦ possonium.sk. Great little hostel a 3min walk from the station, which means a 5min tram ride to the Old Town. There's a popular horror-themed bar (inspired by the film *Hostel*) and a garden where guests chat and barbecue in the summer. Some of the dorms are pretty small, but all have intriguing wall decor. Dorms €19, doubles €55

Portus Paulínyho 10 ☎ 0911 978 026, ⓦ portus.sk. Well-located *pension* close to the river. Large dull rooms, but gleaming bathrooms and friendly staff. Doubles €60

Zlaté piesky Intercamp ☎ 02 4425 7373, ⓦ intercamp .sk. Lakeside campsite 8km northeast of the city centre. Lifeguard services and a beach, as well as two restaurants on site and chalets (sleeping three) to rent. Take tram #4 from town to the end stop, Zlaté Piesky. May to mid-Oct. Camping/person €3.50, chalets €31

EATING

CAFÉS

Caffe L'Aura Rudnayovo nám 4. Packed with creaking chairs, antique pitchers and cracked oil paintings, this unruly café-bar is a good place to wait out a rainstorm. In better weather sit on the terrace overlooking the cathedral. Sun–Thurs 10am–midnight, Fri 10am–1am, Sat noon–1am, Sun 11am-10pm.

Greentree Caffe Ventúrska 20. Part of a likeable Italian-owned local chain. There are five dotted around town, but this is possibly the best of the lot, housed in an atmospheric vaulted cellar. Mon–Thurs 8am–8.30pm, Fri 8am–9pm, Sat 9am–9pm.

Štúr Café Štúrova 8 ⓦ sturcafe.sk. Elegant but laidback café modelled on the glamorous coffeehouses of interwar Austria-Hungary. Freshly baked cakes, hearty sandwiches, and famous spiced home-made lemonade. There's a second branch on Panská. Mon–Fri 8am–midnight, Sat & Sun 9am–midnight.

RESTAURANTS

★**Bratislava Flag Ship Restaurant** Nám SNP 8 ⓦ bratislavskarestauracia.sk. Cavernous, echoing restaurant with decor that's half Charles Dickens half Las Vegas. The food is very decent and inexpensive, the atmosphere is warm and there's a terrace on the square. Mains €4.50–16. Mon–Sat 10am–midnight, Sun noon–midnight.

Bratislavský meštiansky pivovar Drevená 8 ⓦ mestianskypivovar.sk. Old-style pub that brews its own beer and serves meaty Slovak staples. It can be hard to get a table on a Friday night but you could always try the other branch at Dunajská 21. Mains €6–19. Mon–Thurs & Sat 11am–midnight, Fri 11am–1am, Sun 11am–11pm.

Góvinda Obchodná 30 ⓦ govinda.sk. Good, inexpensive Indian vegetarian buffet on a busy shopping street: a plate of tasty veggie Indian food costs roughly €3.50. Mon–Fri 10.30am–5.30pm.

Pizza Mizza Tobrucká 5 ⓦ pizzamizza.sk. Reckoned to be the smartest pizza joint in Bratislava (though that's not saying much), *Pizza Mizza* is a decent place for a cheap, filling meal (pizza €3.50–14). They have branches dotted all over town, and also do home delivery via the website. Mon–Fri 10am–11pm, Sat & Sun 11am–11pm.

Prašná Bašta Zámočnícka 11 ⓦ prasnabasta.sk. Tucked in a quiet courtyard off Michalská gate, *Prašná Bašta* is an elegant, low-key restaurant loved by locals. The delicious food combines Slovak and international flavours, there's a handsome vaulted interior, summer terrace and live jazz and classical music. Mains €7–19. Daily 11am–11pm.

Sladovňa: House of Beer Ventúrska 5. Decent local cuisine and good beer, outdoor seating (street or courtyard) in summer, and an atmospheric beer cellar in winter. Mains €7–16. Mon–Wed 11am–1am, Thurs–Sat 11am–2am, Sun 11am–11pm.

DRINKING AND NIGHTLIFE

Al Faro Eurovea Shopping Mall, Pribinova 8/A ⓦ alfaro.sk. Strange to say, one of the nicest places for a cold drink on a hot evening is the mall: Eurovea, a 15min walk from Old Town, has a row of bars, cafés and restaurants along the riverbank, while *Al Faro* has a summer terrace on a pier over the river furnished with sofas and parasols. Daily 11am–midnight.

Dopler Prievozská 18. Bratislava's biggest and most raucous nightclub is a taxi ride from the centre, popular with students and high schoolers. Mon–Sat 9pm–5am.

Dubliner Sedlárska 6 ⓦ irish-pub.sk. Busy Irish pub providing sports games and live music at the weekends. Located on a street of bars, so if this one doesn't work you have plenty of nearby options. Daily 9am–3am.

Harley Saloon Rebarborová 1/a ⓦ harley.sk. Big place, heaving at weekends, with a retro 1980s and 1990s playlist. It's on the edge of town so you'll need to take a trolley bus or taxi. Mon–Thurs 10am–midnight, Fri 10am–6am, Sat 11am–6am, Sun 11am–midnight.

Norton Club Panská 29. British motorcycle-theme bar, though you are unlikely to meet any bikers as it's on a pedestrian street. Sun–Thurs 1pm–midnight, Fri–Sat 1pm–2am.

30

FESTIVALS

Bratislava hosts a raft of excellent festivals, especially for music-lovers. Here are a few of the best:

Cultural Summer ⓦ bkis.sk. Performance festival from June to September which floods Bratislava with theatre, opera, visual arts and dance.

Coronation Celebration ⓦ bratislava-info.sk. Once a year history-lovers don their codpieces and stockings to celebrate the coronation of a certain ruler: check website for current date and king.

Jazz Days ⓦ www.bjd.sk. Brief but exuberant jazz festival which has been held every year since 1975. Typically held in October.

Bratislava Music Festival ⓦ bhsfestival.sk. Classical music heavyweight organized by the Slovak Philharmonic every autumn, holding about 25 chamber and symphonic concerts each year.

Nu Spirit Club Pasáž Luxor, Štúrova 3 ⓦ nuspirit.sk. Nudisco, drum'n'bass, funk, hip-hop, house and disco, DJ nights, stand-up comedy, live concerts and jam sessions. The owners also run a good bar on Medená St (same name). Mon–Fri 10am–3am, Sat 5pm–3am, Sun 5pm–1am.

ENTERTAINMENT

The tourist office stocks *Kam do mesta*, a monthly listings magazine (free; ⓦ kamdomesta.sk), while the weekly English-language *Slovak Spectator*, available from kiosks and hotels, has news and listings. There are open-air classical music concerts in summer in courtyards and squares across the city, such as outside the Jesuit church by Michalská. Ask at the tourist office for details, or check ⓦ bkis.sk.

Slovak National Theatre ⓦ snd.sk. You can watch theatre performances at the impressive modern New Slovak National Theatre (Pribinova 17) and the Historic Slovak National Theatre (Hviezdoslavovo nám). Tickets can be bought at either building one hour before the show (€8–30). Some of the less well-known performances in the studio cost as little as €3.

Reduta Palace On the corner of nám Štúra and Medená. This is home to the Slovak Philharmonic Orchestra (ⓦ filharmonia.sk).

Lumière Cinema Špitálska 4 ⓦ www.aic.sk /kinolumiere. Arthouse joint in the city centre showing old and new Slovak, European and world films.

Cinema City In the Eurovea Shopping Mall, Pribinova 8 ⓦ cinemacity.sk. Cinema showing new releases.

SHOPPING

Michalská and Ventúrska streets in the Old Town are good for souvenir shopping – good bets are ceramics and wooden items.

AuPark Einsteinova 18 ⓦ aupark.sk. Large 240-shop mall with a Cinema City and food court. Mon–Fri 10am–9pm, Sat & Sun 9am–9pm.

Eurovea Shopping Mall Pribinova 8 ⓦ eurovea.com. A 15min walk from the Old Town, Eurovea contains mainstream, big-name chain shops, plus riverside bars and restaurants (see p.967) and a multiplex cinema (see p.968). Daily 10am–9pm.

Oxford Books Laurinská 9 ⓣ 02 5262 2029, ⓦ oxfordbookshop.sk. Good browsing and a wide selection of English-language books. Mon–Fri 10am–7pm, Sat 10am–5pm.

DIRECTORY

Embassies and consulates UK, Panská 16 ⓣ 02 5998 2020; US, Hviezdoslavovo nám 5 ⓣ 2 5443 0861.

Hospital Poliklinika Ružinov, Ružinovská 10 (trams #8, #9, #14 and #50; ⓣ 02 4827 9111, ⓦ ruzinovskapoliklinika.sk).

Internet There's free wi-fi access in certain parts of town, including Primaciálne nám, Hlavné nám and Františkánske nám. Most cafés and bars also offer free wi-fi.

Left luggage Main train station (daily 6.30am–11pm).

Pharmacies Lekáreň Pod Manderlom, nám SNP 20 (ⓣ 02 5443 2952). Lekáreň Pokrok, Račianske Mýto 1 (24hr; ⓣ 02 4445 5291, ⓦ lekarenpokrok.sk).

Police Foreign police and passport services, Hrobáková 44 (ⓣ 0961 036 855).

Post office Slovenská pošta, nám SNP 35 (Mon–Fri 7am–8pm, Sat 7am–6pm, Sun 9am–2pm).

Central Slovakia

If you're partial to an undulating hill or a winding mossy way, **Central Slovakia** is your kind of place. Quiet and agrarian, it's the heart of Slovakia; the cradle of Romantic Nationalism in the nineteenth century and the seat of the Slovak National Uprising in 1944. The way of life is slow, as are the trains, but what it lacks in zip it repays in beauty.

BANSKÁ ŠTIAVNICA

Lying in a great caldera created by the collapse of a long-since extinct volcano, **BANSKÁ ŠTIAVNICA** is Slovakia's oldest mining town. In the third century the Huns discovered precious metal here, and by the Middle Ages it was the largest source of gold and silver in the Hungarian Empire. During the Ottoman Wars the town sprouted fortifications, watchtowers and a castle to repel marauding Turks. As the metal reserves dwindled the inhabitants migrated, leaving the town with a slightly frozen-in-time feel.

WHAT TO SEE AND DO

Main square **Námestie sv Trojice** is dominated by the Holy Trinity column, a red marble monolith marking the end of the plague in 1711. Southeast is Radničné Námestie, the Gothic Church of St Catherine and the Town Hall (Radnica), the latter with a clock that marks hours with its big hand and minutes with its little hand – according to an unusually credible local legend it was the work of a drunk clockmaker. Continuing southeast, you'll come to the minimalist **New Castle** (Nový Zámok) and **Church of Our Lady of the Snows**.

The Old Castle

To the west of the main square is the **Old Castle** (Starý zámok; May–Sept daily 9am–5pm; Oct–April Wed–Sat 8am–4pm; €4), not a castle at all but a fortified Romanesque church used as a storage facility for municipal wealth. It's part of the Slovak Mining Museum, and exhibits Baroque sculptures, archeological remains and medieval blacksmithery. You can also discover what life was like in a medieval jail.

Klopačka

Up A. Sládkoviča street is the **Clapping Tower** (Klopačka), home to a giant clapping contraption built for waking up miners. Today it claps for the amusement or irritation of tourists, and contains a teahouse (see p.970).

Museums

Štiavnica is a museum-rich town. First up is the **Jozef Kollár Gallery** on Námestie sv Trojice, which exhibits everything from medieval madonnas to twentieth-century watercolours. A few doors down is the **Mineral Museum**, which houses exhibits on the technical development of mining, while **New Castle**, at Novozámocká 22, contains a little museum about the Ottoman Wars in Slovakia. All of these museums are run by the **Slovak Mining Museum** (wmuzeumbs.sk) and have the same opening hours and prices (May–Sept Tues–Sat 9am–5pm; Oct–April Mon–Fri 8am–4pm; €2).

At the **Open Air Mining Museum**, J.K. Hella 12 (April–June & Sept–Oct Tues–Sun 9am–5pm; July & Aug Mon noon–5pm, Tues–Sun 9am–6pm; tours hourly; €5), 1.5km from town, you can take a trip down the old mines, while 3km from town, the **Museum of St Anton**, 72 Svätý Anton (Tues–Sat 9am–3pm; sometimes opens earlier and closes later in high season; wmsa.sk; €5–8, depending on how much of the museum you wish to see) is the kind of

tapestry-heavy, trophy-stuffed manse that helps to while away a rainy morning.

Around Banská Štiavnica

The hills around Štiavnica are perfect for strolling, berry-picking and idling. Centuries of mining with gunpowder left the hills scarred with pits, which in time became lakes. On a hot day you can hike, swim, picnic, and be back by teatime. The most interesting walk is up to **Calvary** (Kalvária, 1km northeast of Old Town), a cluster of red and white Baroque chapels and churches perched on an inactive volcano, each one representing a stage in Christ's journey to the Cross. Hiking maps are available at the tourist office and hotels.

ARRIVAL AND DEPARTURE

By train The train station is a 2km walk through the suburbs from the old town. There's no direct train-only service to Bratislava.

By bus The bus stop is 100m closer to town than the train station, and is next to the big Billa supermarket at Križovatka, a steep climb up to the centre.

Destinations Bratislava (hourly indirect connections, change in Žarnovica or Žiar nad Hronom; 3hr 20min–3hr 50min); Nitra (approx hourly indirect services with a change in Žarnovica or Žiar nad Hronom; 2hr 15min–2hr 40min).

INFORMATION

Tourist office Nám sv Trojice 3 (daily: May–June & Sept 9am–5pm; Oct–April 8am–4pm; July & Aug 9am–6pm; ☏ 046 949 653, wbanskastiavnica.sk, wbanskastiavnica.org).

SPA TREATMENT

Do you have backache after lugging that backpack across Europe? Then hop on a bus at Križovatka and whizz over to **Sklené Teplice Spa**, Ul. A. Pécha 2 (wkupele-skleneteplice.sk), where you can jump into w springs and take cold showers alternately – an ordeal that leaves you exhausted to the point of relaxation. The spring is 42°C, with high levels of magnesium and calcium, and the spa claims it heals visitors with muscle and muscular-skeletal conditions. There's also a pool, saunas and massage.

30

GETTING AROUND

Public transport You can walk from one side of the Old Town to the other in 10min. Cheap shuttle buses run through town; you can stop them anywhere by waving, and the fare is €0.50. Taxis are useful if you want to get out into the country but operators rarely speak English, so ask your hotel or hostel to order and agree the fee for you. Firms include Ju-Ma taxi (☎09 1010 0300) and T Taxi (☎09 10 525 999).

ACCOMMODATION

Archanjel Radničné nám 10b ☎0915 365 371, ⦿archanjel.com. Smart rooms in an old townhouse above a local bar, with a shared kitchenette. The rooms are far from perfect but quite good value for an en-suite room. Doubles **€35**

Hostel Skautský dom A. Pécha 2 ☎0905 382 885, ⦿hostel.stiavnica.sk. Štiavnica's cheapest; a rambling, echoey hostel and tiny campsite below the castle. Camping/person **€7**, dorms **€8**, doubles **€24**

Penzion Kachelman Kammerhofská 18 ☎045 692 2319, ⦿kachelman.sk. Large and pristine hotel located halfway between the bus station and the town centre. There's a restaurant, pizzeria, sauna and jacuzzi on site. Doubles **€45**

★**Penzion Nostalgia** Višňovského 3 ☎0905 360 307, ⦿penzion-nostalgia.sk. One of Slovakia's finest B&Bs, *Nostalgia* is a seventeenth-century townhouse with a wood-burning stove, oak beams and crisp linen sheets. It's right in the centre of town, with views of the Old Town synagogue. Breakfast €4.50. Doubles **€40**, apartments **€60**

EATING AND DRINKING

Art Café Akademická 2. Bustling café, bar, exhibition space and sometime-cinema. It stocks a good range of local wines. Follow the staircase behind their terrace for views of the town. Sun–Thurs 10am–11pm, Fri & Sat 10am–2am.

Čajovňa Klopačka A. Sládkoviča 7 ⦿klopacka.com. Teahouse of the red cushion, smoky incense variety popular with Slovak students. There are 150 types of tea and water pipes. Mon–Thurs 11am–11pm, Fri & Sat 10am–midnight, Sun 10am–11pm.

★**TREAT YOURSELF**

4 Sochy Kammerhofská 16, ⦿4sochy.sk. If you fancy a splurge, this café-restaurant, stylishly furnished with antiques, serves a higher class of cuisine than rural Slovakia normally offers. Mains €10–23. Tues–Thurs 11.30am–8pm, Fri & Sat noon–9pm, Sun noon–8pm.

★**Kaviareň Divná pani** Andreja Kmeťa 8 ⦿divnapani .sk. Decorated like a flamboyant Roman library, this oddly named café-bar (the name translates as "strange woman") offers beer on tap, liquors, coffee and cakes, columns, statues and old books. The closing times are often later than advertised on busy nights. Mon–Thurs 7.15am–10pm, Fri 7.15am–midnight, Sat 8.30am–midnight, Sun 9am–10pm.

Pivovar ERB Novozámocká 2 ⦿pivovarerb.sk. Shiny tourist-orientated microbrewery and restaurant with specialities including smoked pork knuckles and sausages in vinegar brine. Mains €8–22. Sun–Thurs 11am–10pm, Fri & Sat 11am–midnight.

★**Terasa u Blaškov** Jazero Počúvadlo ⦿terasaublaskov .sk. If you're in town on a balmy Friday or Saturday evening, take a long hike to *Terasa u Blažkov* (7km from Štiavnica). It's a traditional rustic night out with a whole pig roasted on a spit, fresh bread, salad and a folk band. Dinner is €5–8 and the taxi home around €7 extra. It starts at 5pm, and if you arrive early you can swim in the adjoining lake. June–Sept daily 10am–11pm.

Tulsi Radničné nám 13 ⦿tulsi.sk. The risottos, sushi and salads at this tea house and restaurant provide a break from *halušky* and a sporting chance for vegetarians. Mains €4–9: daily menu €4. Mon–Wed 11am–9pm, Thurs & Fri 11am–10pm, Sat noon–10pm, Sun noon–9pm.

THE TATRAS

Defining the border with Poland, the **HIGH TATRAS** (Vysoké Tatry) are Slovakia's pride and joy and a popular lure for tourists too. The highest peak, pyramid-shaped Gerlach, is the tallest mountain in northern and eastern Central Europe at 2655m high. The beauty and splendour of the mountains made them a magnet for Romantic and Nationalistic types in the eighteenth century, and in 1844 a student in Bratislava composed a song beginning with the words "There is lightning over the Tatras" – today the national anthem. The peaks and their foothills are awash with rare flora and fauna, and if you're lucky you might glimpse a lynx, wild boar, brown bear or Tatra chamois (goat-antelope).

Poprad is an excellent transport hub, directly linked with Bratislava, Prague, Budapest and Kraków; however, there's not much happening to keep you there. From Poprad you can catch a train or bus to the **Smokovec** resorts (divided into two adjoining halves, Nový (new) and Starý (old), bustling ski resort **Tatranská Lomnica**, or spindly **Ždiar**, one endless street of painted wooden cabins. Wherever you stay you'll want to move between the villages; if you're using public transport you'll have to plan ahead a little because the trains and buses are erratically timed.

ARRIVAL AND DEPARTURE

By train The main-line train station for the Tatras is Poprad-Tatry in Poprad. From there tiny red electrical trains (TEŽ; hourly; 25min to Starý Smokovec; €1.50) trundle across the mountains, linking Poprad with Smokovec and Tatranská Lomnica.

Destinations (from Poprad) Bratislava (9 daily; 4hr 40min–5hr); Košice (hourly; 1hr 15min–1hr 50min).

By bus Buses also move between the cities listed above, but the train is usually quicker and more convenient. Ždiar isn't on the train line so you'll have to get the bus, which leaves Poprad roughly hourly and takes an hour.

Destinations (from Poprad) Bratislava (4 daily; 6hr); Levoča (hourly; 30min–1hr); Prešov (6 daily; 1hr 30min–2hr).

By plane There is a small airport on the western outskirts of Poprad, Poprad-Tatry (ⓦwww.airport-poprad.sk), which runs infrequent flights to and from a number of European destinations, including Luton in the UK.

INFORMATION

Tourist office In Poprad: at the western end of námestie sv Egidia in the Dom Kultúry building (Sept–May Mon–Fri 9am–5pm, Sat 9am–noon; June–Aug Mon–Fri 8am–8pm, Sat 9am–1pm, Sun 2–5pm; ☎052 436 1192, ⓦpoprad.sk). In Starý Smokovec: in the Mountain Rescue Service building (daily 8am–8pm; ☎052 442 3440, ⓦtatry.sk). In Tatranská Lomnica: on the main street opposite Penzión Encián (Mon–Fri 8am–6pm; ☎052 446 8119, ⓦtatry.sk).

ACTIVITIES

AquaCity Športová 1, Poprad ⓦaquacity.sk. AquaCity has outdoor thermal pools (30–38°C) and a 50m pool,

tobogganing, a beauty centre, massage, slides, restaurants, bars and a club. Perfect for a break after a few days' skiing. €15–24 for a 3hr package. Mon 11am–10pm, Tues–Sun 8am–10pm.

Belianska Cave The north slope of Kobylí Hill, near to Tatranská Kotlina (☎052 446 7375, ⓦwww.ssj.sk). A 70min tour of Belianska Cave, which was discovered by gold prospectors in the 1700s, leads you past subterranean waterfalls, stalagmites and the Musíc Hall – so-called because of the melodious sound of water drops on the still pool. It's below freezing even in summer, so dress warmly. The nearest bus stop is Tatranská Kotlina. Tour hourly 9am–4pm; times fluctuate, so check beforehand; €8, students €7.

Climbing Inexperienced mountaineers should go with a certified guide, available at the Association of Mountain Guides (Spolok horských vodcov). Their services are expensive, starting at €175/hike (Vila Alica, Starý Smokovec; ☎0905 428 170, ⓦtatraguide.sk).

Bikes, scooters and tubing Tatry Motion rental, Starý Smokovec (☎0911 410 945, ⓦvt.sk) and Tatranská Lomnica (☎0903 112 200, ✉info@vt.sk). Scooter €7.50/ride, bike €12/day, tubing (at Hrebienok) €4–5 rides. There's also a bike park (ⓦvt.sk) at Hrebienok (accessible by funicular from Starý Smokovec) with easy and difficult routes; bikes €35/day (9am–6pm dependent on weather).

Rafting at Červený Kláštor Pieniny sport centrum, Červený Kláštor 37, Pieniny National Park (☎0907 477 412, ⓦrafting-pieniny.sk). It's a little over two hours by bus to the Dunajec River in Pieniny National Park, on the Slovak–Polish border, but worth the trip. You can rent a kayak, canoe or mountain bike or take a rafting trip with a guide. May–Sept only; equipment rental 9am–6pm. Bus Poprad–Červený Kláštor, with a change in Spišská St.Ves (7 daily; 1hr 50min).

Skiing and snowboarding The season is Dec–March. Tatranská Lomnica is an ideal place to ski and snowboard, with heated chairlifts and cable cars, long runs, routes for all abilities, good black runs plus off piste. Bachledova Dolina is a great, affordable option – a day-pass is €25.30, ski rental is €12, and the restaurants on the slopes are cheap too. There's a 2km run, beginners' slopes in the

30

MOUNTAIN SAFETY

On average, twenty people a year die in the High Tatras – these are serious mountains not to be underestimated. Keep safe by hiking with two or more people and making sure someone knows where you are going. Wear layers, a waterproof and windproof coat, and hiking boots. Always take plenty of water and some food. Buy a whistle – the emergency signal is 6 blasts. Weather conditions change fast, so check the prognosis before you leave; the Mountain Rescue Service in Starý Smokovec will give you a forecast. If you get in trouble, call Mountain Rescue (☎18300) right away. Don't think of them as an easy fall-back, though; they charge a large fee for call-outs.

30

ON YER HIKE

If you're not a hiker, there are plenty of shorter routes to leave the heel unblistered. Ask for maps or recommendations at any of the tourist offices.

Štrbské pleso–Popradské pleso A scenic stroll between two lakes that takes less than two hours. On the way you'll pass the Symbolic Cemetery, a memorial garden to those who died in the Tatras.

Biela voda–Chata pri Zelenom plese Takes a little under three hours, and it ends on a high, with beautiful mountain panoramas around the chalet.

Kriváň peak When you've got your mountain legs, hike up this high, hook-nosed peak (2495m – a hike for summer only), beloved of Slovak Romantic poets. It's one of the highest mountains in the Tatras and the walk takes a full day. You can start from Štrbské pleso and follow the red trail towards Podbanské. Peruse our safety tips (see box, p.971) before starting out.

villages (Strednica and Strachan), and blue, red and black routes at Bachledova. Štrbské Pleso hosts national and international skiing events and it's a beautiful place, but it's pricey and the skiing is pretty similar to Lomnica: see ⓦ skibachledova.sk/en/skiing.

Tatrabob Tatranská Lomnica 29 ☎ 0944 503 069, ⓦ tatrabob.sk. Pint-sized mountainside roller coaster plus archery. €3/ride.

ACCOMMODATION

In high season (ski season and high summer) prices often double. All prices listed are for high season. The tourist offices in any of the resorts can help you arrange accommodation.

★**Ginger Monkey Hostel** Ždiar 294 ☎ 052 449 8084, ⓦ gingermonkey.eu. Many the eye of a hardened backpacker mists over at the mention of *Ginger Monkey*, a wooden-cabin hostel on the edge of Ždiar. There are chickens in the garden, books in the kitchen, mountains outside the window and a yellow dog for company. From Poprad, the bus stop is the fourth in Ždiar – keep an eye out for the sign that says "Petrol Station 500m" and alight at the next stop. Eggy breakfast included. Dorms €14, doubles €34

Hotel Café Razy Námestie sv. Egídia 58, Poprad ☎ 052 776 4101, ⓦ hotelcaferazy.sk. New hotel on Poprad's main square offering large and comfortable two-floor rooms. Friendly staff and a decent breakfast (€5). Located above a restaurant so may be a bit noisy. Doubles €44

Penzion Aqualand Štefánikova 893, Poprad ☎ 0903 412 482. This *pension*, a 10min walk from the bus and train stations, is neat and friendly. Plus, guests get a discount at the nearby waterpark. Doubles €40

Penzion Mon Ami Nový Smokovec 31 ☎ 0911 786 518, ⓦ monami.sk. Clean, comfortable B&B in a delightful, traditional wood-framed guesthouse on the high street in Smokovec, with views over the mountains. All rooms are en-suite doubles. €54

Penzión Slalom Tatranská Lomnica 94 ☎ 052 446 7216, ⓦ slalom.sk. Friendly little B&B close to both bus and train

stations. Nearly all rooms have a balcony. Breakfast is an extra €7. Doubles €41

Penzión Ždiar Ždiar 460 ☎ 052 449 8138, ⓦ penzionzdiar.sk. Large, friendly wooden guesthouse with equestrian equipment and painted plates on the walls. Rooms for 1–5 people; en-suite rooms cost €14 per person. Dorms €9

MOUNTAIN CABINS

For an authentic mountain experience, hike to one of the wooden huts (*chata*) in the hills. Sleeping is often in dorms, and most huts offer dinner and breakfast.

Bilíkova Chata ☎ 052 442 2439, ⓦ bilikovachata.sk. Hotel-like hut, with wood-panelled dorms, single and double rooms for a cosy lie down after a long hike. Breakfast €5. Dorms €29, doubles €58

Zbojnícka ☎ 0903 638 000, ⓦ zbojnickachata.sk. All oak beams and open fires, with one dorm sleeping 16. Breakfast is €6 extra. Dorm €26

EATING AND DRINKING

Cukráreň Tatra Starý Smokovec 66. Follow the warm scent of vanilla to this delightful *cukráreň* (café-bakery), which serves great cakes, ice cream, chocolate and real coffee. Daily 9am–8pm.

Hotel Atrium Bowling Bar Nový Smokovec 42. An amusing evening out in a village low on nightlife. Mon–Thurs 1–11pm, Fri & Sat 9am–1am, Sun 9am–11pm.

Humno Tatranská Lomnica 14640. Swish alpine chalet that's a bar, café, pub, and on Fridays and Saturdays a nightclub (the best in the mountains). There's an open fire, leather sofas, a snow plough coming out the wall (the DJ booth) and a cadillac that once belonged to Madonna. Sun–Thurs 11am–midnight, Fri & Sat 11am–4am.

Rustika Ždiar 334. Wood shack that on the inside looks more like a junk shop than a pizzeria. Specializes in inexpensive pizzas and salads plus there's beer on tap. Pizza €5, monster pizza (50cm) €12. Daily 3–10pm.

Sabato Sobotské nám 6, Poprad ⓦsabato.sk. Medieval-style restaurants combine large slabs of meat and ludicrously dressed waiters, and this is a good example of the genre. Mains €8–21. Daily noon–11pm.

Tatratom Ždiar 288. Traditional pub serving excellent, old-timey meals. The garlic soup is hot and piquant, and the fruit dumplings are a dream. Mains €4–9. Daily 9am–7pm.

U Friga Nový Smokovec 44 ⓦpizzeriaufriga.com. Pizza, pasta, salads and *halušky* in comfy environs. Mains €4.50–6.50. Mon–Sat 5–10pm.

Vila Park Tatranská Lomnica. With a sunny summer terrace overlooking the village green, 3min from the train station, this restaurant serves up decent modern Slovak food. Mains from €6. Daily noon–10pm.

East Slovakia

Slovakia's folksy **east** (východoslovenský kraj) could be said to have one foot firmly in the past. Protected from the west by the Tatras, traditional dialects and customs thrive, and the land is bleaker and grander than the west. The area stretches northeast up the Poprad Valley to the Polish border, while east along the River Hornád towards Prešov is the **Spiš** region, for centuries a semi-autonomous province in the Hungarian kingdom.

LEVOČA

What inspired the great Hungarian writer Kálmán Mikszáth to make **LEVOČA** the star of his 1910 revenge saga *The Black Town* is a mystery. The medieval town is as neat and respectable as a privet hedge, and if there are any passions seething they're well buried. The town's main attraction is the wonderful religious art at the Church of St James, but it's also a good base for visiting **Spiš** castle (see box below), and a gateway to beautiful Slovak Paradise National Park.

WHAT TO SEE AND DO

Levoča is a grid-plan town. The main streets run from **Námestie Majstra Pavla** (the main square) to the city walls, becoming darker and a touch shabbier as they go. Churches, hotels and museums congregate in the main square, with the cheaper *pensions*, hostels and pubs scattered near the town walls. From the north side of **Námestie Majstra Pavla** you can see the graceful white church at Mariánska hora (Mary's Mountain), a Catholic pilgrimage site.

Church of St James

The splendid **Church of St James** (Chrám sv Jakuba; Tues–Sat 8.30am–4pm) soars above the north side of the main square. It houses a magnificent 5.5m-high wooden altarpiece containing the *Last Supper*, and a baby-faced Madonna, both the work of sixteenth-century master-carver Pavol of Levoča. The church can only be visited with a guide, and tours (€2) are conducted on the hour. The ticket office is opposite the main entrance. A small and uninspiring **museum** (daily 9am–5pm; €3.50), dedicated to Master Pavol, stands opposite the church and exhibits replicas of the art in the church.

Town Hall and Lutheran Church

Between St James and the squat, Neoclassical **Lutheran church** (Evanjelický kostol) is a wrought-iron contraption called the **Cage of Shame** (*klietka hanby*), built in a flourish of sixteenth-century misogyny: women caught on the streets after dark were imprisoned here overnight in their

> ## SPIŠ CASTLE
>
> An endless mass of ramshackle bone-white walls, roads and broken towers, **Spiš Castle** (Spišský hrad; daily: April & Oct 9am–4pm; Nov 10am–3pm; May–Sept 9am–6pm, last entry 5pm; €6, students €4; ⓦspisskyhrad.com) is a monumental twelfth-century fortress built over a much older castle. It's a bleak, dreamlike place, so isolated that the only sounds are birds and crickets. Inside are exhibits giving a clear picture of medieval life (short and dirty), audioguides and a tower to climb. You can catch a bus from Levoča to Spišské Podhradie (2 hourly; 30min) and then it's about an hour's walk to the castle.

30

30

petticoats, heads shorn, as an example to other females. Inside the third building on the square, the old **Town Hall**, you'll find the **Spiš Museum** (daily 9am–5pm; €3.50; ⓦspisskemuzeum.com), which exhibits paintings and icons.

ARRIVAL AND INFORMATION

By bus The bus station is 1km southeast of Levoča old town. If you're coming from the east, alight one stop earlier at the Košice gate.

Destinations Poprad (hourly; 30min–1hr); Košice (2 direct daily; 2hr, or change in Prešov).

By train Levoča is not on the train line, but you can get a taxi or catch a bus to Spišská Nová Ves (2 hourly; 20min), and from there catch the direct train to Bratislava (8 daily; 4–5hr), which also stops at Poprad.

Tourist office Nám Majstra Pavla 58 (daily 9am–noon & 12.30–5pm; ☎053 451 3763, ⓦik.levoca.eu).

ACCOMMODATION

Autocamp Levoča Levočská Dolina ☎053 451 2705, ⓦautocamplevoca.sk. Campsite with wooden bungalows and a *pension* 5km northwest of town: there's bike rental, a café, sauna and whirlpool. Camping/person **€3.50** plus per pitch **€1.80**, bungalows/person **€7.50**, doubles **€38**

Barbakan Košická 15 ☎053 451 4310, ⓦbarbakan.sk. The kind of solid, old-fashioned hotel that smells of floor wax and pink soap. Breakfast €5. **€46**

Oáza Nová 65 ☎053 451 4511, ⓦoaza.weblib.sk. Well-scrubbed, no-frills accommodation in a family-run boarding house a few minutes' walk from the main square. You can get a private room or share, but it's popular with contract workers. Dorms **€10**

EATING

Arkáda Nám Majstra Pavla 26 ⓦarkada.sk. Vaulted, dramatically uplit stone cellar tavern stashed beneath one of the bigger hotels. Draught beer, local wine and Slovak staples. Mains €5–14. Daily 7am–10pm.

Kupecká bašta Kukučínová 2 ⓦkupeckabasta.sk. Housed in a defensive tower in the old town walls, this has a tastefully renovated interior, a roaring fire in winter, and some nice folksy and antique touches. The food is a mixed bag of Slovak staples and imaginative European dishes. Mains €6–12.50. Mon–Thurs 9am–10pm, Fri & Sat 9am–11pm; May–Oct also Sun 9am–10pm.

Peko Spiš Košicka ulica. The town's best bakery selling bread and pastries – perfect for self-caterers seeking breakfast. Mon–Fri 6am–6pm, Sat 6am–noon.

Planéta Nám Majstra Pavla 38a ⓦplanetalevoca.sk. Every sleepy provincial town needs a *Planéta*; a café at 4pm, a restaurant at 7pm and a bar at 10pm. The menu is

simple (pizza, salads, pasta) but fresh. Lunch menu €4.50, dinner menu €5. Mon–Fri 8am–11pm, Sat & Sun 9am–10pm.

Restaurácia Slovenka Nám Majstra Pavla 62 ⓦrestauraciaslovenka.sk. Quite traditional restaurant serving cheap and filling Slovak fare on oddly shaped wooden platters. The service here is good. Mains €1.50 11. Daily 10am 10pm.

Restaurácia U Leva Nám Majstra Pavla 24 ⓦuleva.sk. The nicest mid-range restaurant in Levoča, combining Mediterranean (carpaccio, *insalata caprese*) and Slavic dishes (duck breast with cherry sauce, chicken liver with wild mushrooms), and doing both well. Mains €4.20–11.90. Daily 10am–10pm.

KOŠICE

KOŠICE was once a vital commercial crossroads for the Hungarian Empire, and today its pleasing centre forms a kilometre-long promenade, lined with historical buildings, churches, cafés and restaurants. Warm days see residents emerging in packs to enjoy the sun and listen to the musical fountain located in the park next to the State Theatre. A lively university town, Košice was European Capital of Culture in 2013, and makes for a pleasant stop-off for a couple of days.

WHAT TO SEE AND DO

Košice's action is pretty much centred on its main street, **Hlavná**, which is lined with parks interspersed with some historical sites. Wandering the side streets provides some interesting sightseeing; this is also where you'll find various places to stay.

St Elizabeth's Cathedral

The symbol of the city's patron, **St Elizabeth's Cathedral** (Dóm svätej Alžbety; Mon 1–5pm, Tues–Fri 9am–5pm, Sat 9am–1pm; cathedral only €1.50, cathedral, tower and St Michael's Chapel €5) is Slovakia's largest place of worship. It houses an intriguing rare Gothic double spiral staircase, and a sundial dating from 1477. The cast-iron altar, reportedly the only one in Europe, is said to have been crafted from weapons used in World War I. For a view of the town and out to the hills, climb the 60m-high northern **tower**.

WARHOL'S ROOTS

Pop artist **Andy Warhol** has Slovak roots; his parents emigrated to the US in the early 1900s. Born Andrej Varhola Jr, the artist has been commemorated in the town of Medzilaborce (120km north of Košice) with the Andy Warhol Museum of Modern Art, which displays his works of art and artefacts from his childhood and life. There are a couple of direct buses a day from Košice, but to reach the town by train you have to change in Hummené. Otherwise, arrange a tour at Košice's tourist office, which includes a visit to Warhol's parents' village.

St Michael's Chapel

The small, charming **St Michael's Chapel** (Kaplnka Sv. Michala; Mon–Fri 9.15am–6pm, Sat 9.15am–noon; €1.50) sits next to St Elizabeth's and was originally surrounded by the city's cemetery, which has now been turned into an attractive park.

Lower Gate

Reconstruction of Hlavná street in the mid-1990s uncovered the original gateway to the city and parts of the original fortifications. **Lower Gate** (Dolná brána; mid-May to mid-Sept Tues–Sun 10am–6pm; €0.90) has been turned into an underground museum of sorts in which you can see these ancient constructions.

Vojtech Löffler Museum

Famed local sculptor Vojtech Löffler donated a significant body of work to the city, leading Košice to open the **Vojtech Löffler Museum**, Alžbetina 20 (Tues–Sat 10am–6pm, Sun 1–5pm; €2 ⓦ lofflermuzeum.sk), dedicated to him and his work. In addition to his sculptures and painted portraits of local personalities, the museum also hosts temporary exhibitions by contemporary artists.

ARRIVAL AND INFORMATION

By plane Košice's airport (ⓦ www.airportkosice.sk) is 6km south of the city and offers regular flights to Bratislava, Prague and Vienna.

By train The train station is a 10min walk from the city centre; head through the park and down Mlynská. There's a left luggage desk in the train station.
Destinations Bratislava (approx hourly; 6hr); Budapest (1 daily; 3hr 30min); Poprad (hourly; 1hr 15min–1hr 50min); Prague (1 night train, 10hr; 2 daily, 7hr 30min–8hr 30min).
By bus The bus station is next to the train station. Check ⓦ eurobus.sk for international connections.
Destinations Budapest (1 daily; 3hr 30min); Levoča (2 direct daily; 2hr, or change in Prešov); Prešov (hourly; 35–55min).
Tourist office Hlavná 59, in the Old Town Hall (Mon–Fri 10am–6pm, Sat 10am–3pm; ☏ 055 625 8888, ⓦ visitkosice.eu).

ACCOMMODATION

Košice Hostel Jesenského 20 ☏ 0907 933 462, ⓦ kosicehostel.sk. In a handy location near the train station, this bare-bones place offers very basic but spotlessly clean dorm rooms, doubles and triples with cheap, colourful furniture and minuscule TVs. Dorms **€11**, doubles **€26**
Rokoko Gorkého 9 ☏ 055 796 6800, ⓦ rokoko.sk. *Rokoko* has clean, good-sized doubles and is about a 5min walk from the main square. Breakfast is included. Doubles **€60**
Villa Regia Dominikánske námestie 3 ☏ 055 625 6510, ⓦ villaregia.sk. Located in the shadow of the Dominican Church, this hotel offers contemporary rooms in warm colours. Their restaurant is one of the best in town, serving up delicious marinated ribs and traditional Slovak mushroom soup. Breakfast is included. Doubles **€69**

EATING AND DRINKING

Aida Hlavná 44. Confectionery overload in this most famous of Košice's sweet shops, where you can bag a slice of fresh cake for under a euro. Summer sees a massive queue for the ice cream. Daily 8am–9pm.

FESTIVALS AND EVENTS

Some of the city's festival highlights include Košice City Day (the first week in May), followed by the City Festival at the end of the month, both offering a variety of medieval entertainment including crafts, historic parades, battling knights and other such merriment. There's a birthday party for Andy Warhol at the beginning of August (see box above) and the Košice Wine Festival in mid-September. Europe's oldest marathon, the Košice Peace Marathon, is run on the first Sunday in October.

30

30

Bageteria Hlavná 102. Chain sandwich shop selling fresh and affordable sandwiches (from around €20, with fillings ranging from ham and cheese to Indian and Balkan. Mon–Thurs 7am–9pm, Fri 7am–11pm, Sat & Sun 9am–11pm.

Diesel Pub Hlavná 92 ⓦ irishpubkosice.com. The ubiquitous Irish pub; Košice's is large, with a great back garden, and offers regular disco nights. Decent food with Guinness, Kilkenny and Cashel's Cider on draught. Mon–Wed 11am–midnight, Thurs & Fri 11am–2.30am, Sat 4pm–2.30am, Sun 4–11pm.

Med Malina Hlavná 81 ⓦ www.medmalina.sk. For a taste of Central European slow food, eaten in a room reminiscent of Granny's, head to *Med Malina* on the main square. Try the traditional Polish soup, *žurek*, or splurge on roast duck with potato pancakes. Mains €4–14. Mon–Sat 11am–11pm, Sun 11am–10pm.

Pivovar Golem Dominikánske námestie 15 ⓦ pivovargolem.sk. The only place in Košice still brewing beer – and it's light to say the least. However, they make up for it with generous portions of heavy Slovak pub food served up in two large rooms, one with more of a dining feel, the other all pub with views to the brewing vats. Mains €4.60–7.50. Daily 10am–10pm.

SOČA VALLEY

Slovenia

HIGHLIGHTS

❶ **Old Town, Ljubljana** Wonderful architecture, a hilltop castle and atmospheric riverside bars. See p.983

❷ **Škocjan Caves** Magnificent underground canyon. See p.989

❸ **Piran** Historic coastal town with gorgeous Venetian Gothic architecture. See p.990

❹ **Lake Bohinj** The pearl of Slovenia's alpine lakes. See p.992

❺ **Soča Valley** Stunningly scenic location for hiking, rafting and skiing. See p.993

❻ **Ptuj** Slovenia's oldest, most endearing settlement. See p.996

HIGHLIGHTS ARE MARKED ON THE MAP ON P.979

ROUGH COSTS

Daily budget Basic €45, occasional treat €65

Drink *Pivo* (beer) €2.50 for half a litre

Food Pizza €5–7

Hostel/budget hotel €18/€60

Travel Train: Ljubljana–Maribor €9; bus: Ljubljana–Bled €7

FACT FILE

Population 2 million

Language Slovene

Currency Euro (€)

Capital Ljubljana

International phone code ☎ 386

Time zone GMT +1hr

Introduction

Stable, prosperous and welcoming, Slovenia is a charming and comfortable place to travel, with architecturally grand, cultured cities, and lush pine-forested countryside, perfect for hiking and biking in summer and skiing in winter. The country managed to avoid much of the strife that plagued other nations during the messy disintegration of the Yugoslav Republic, and has integrated quickly with Western Europe, joining the eurozone at the start of 2007. Administered by German-speaking Habsburg overlords until 1918, Slovenes absorbed the culture of their rulers while managing to retain a strong sense of ethnic identity through their Slavic language.

31

Slovenia's sophisticated capital, **Ljubljana**, is a delight, pleasantly compact and cluttered with fabulous Baroque and Habsburg buildings. A short ride away, the Julian Alps provide stunning mountain scenery, most accessible at the majestic twin lakes of **Bled** and **Bohinj**, while the **Soča Valley**, skirting the country's western border, is even more memorable. Further south are spectacular caves, notably at **Postojna** and **Škocjan**, while the short stretch of Slovenian coast is punctuated by two starkly different towns: historic **Piran** and party-oriented **Portorož**. In the eastern wine-making regions, **Ptuj** is Slovenia's oldest and best-preserved town, while the country's second city, **Maribor**, is a worthwhile stopover point on the way to Austria.

CHRONOLOGY

181 BC The Romans conquer the area of present-day Slovenia.

550 AD Slavs begin to inhabit the area.

600s The first Slovenian state, the Duchy of Carantania, is established.

745 The Frankish Empire takes over Carantania, and converts the Slavs to Christianity.

1267 Coastal Istria officially becomes the territory of the Venetian Republic. It remains under Venetian rule until 1797.

1335 The Habsburgs take control of Slovenian regions through marriage.

1550 The first book is published in the Slovenian language.

1867 Slovenia is brought under the direct control of Austria.

Late 1800s Growth of Slovenian nationalism.

1918 Following the collapse of the Austro-Hungarian Empire after World War I, Slovenia is incorporated into the Kingdom of the Serbs, Croats and Slovenes.

1929 The Kingdom is renamed Yugoslavia.

1945 After being occupied by the Germans during World War II, a liberation force led by Slovenian General Tito incorporates Slovenia into the Republic of Socialist Yugoslavia.

1950s The industrialization of Slovenia leads to rapid economic development.

1980 General Tito dies; disintegration of Yugoslavia begins.

1990 Slovenians vote for independence in a referendum.

1991 Slovenia declares its independence from Socialist Yugoslavia, leading to a ten-day war with the Yugoslav army. The Slovenians win.

2003 The oldest wooden wheel in the world, thought to be 5000 years old, is discovered in Slovenia.

2004 Slovenia joins NATO as well as the EU.

2007 Slovenia is the first former Communist state to adopt the European single currency.

2012 Maribor is the European Capital of Culture.

2016 Ljubljana is the European Green Capital.

ARRIVAL AND DEPARTURE

Flight operators from the UK include easyJet (ⓦeasyjet.com), flying from London Stansted; Wizz Air (ⓦwizzair .com), flying from Luton; and the Slovenian national carrier, Adria (ⓦadria .si), flying from London Gatwick. By **train**, there are services from Ljubljana to Belgrade, Budapest, Vienna and Zagreb, though there are currently no direct services to Italy. By **bus**, you can travel from Ljubljana to Belgrade, Budapest, Sarajevo and Zagreb. Access to the

Slovene coast is also straightforward: buses arrive daily from Trieste (Italy) and Pula (Croatia), and between May and September you can travel by **catamaran** between Venice and Piran.

GETTING AROUND

Slovene Railways (Slovenske železnice; ⓦslo-zeleznice.si) is smooth and efficient. **Trains** (*vlaki*) are divided into slow (LP), and Intercity (IC) express trains, as well as the fast Inter City Slovenia trains (ICS) between Ljubljana and Maribor, some of which continue to Koper in the summer. Seat reservations (*rezervacije*; €3.60) are obligatory for all services marked on a timetable with a boxed R (effectively, all ICS trains and some international services). Most timetables have English notes; "departures" is *odhodi*, "arrivals" is *prihodi*. Eurail and InterRail passes are valid.

The **bus** network consists of an array of local companies offering a comprehensive and reliable service, with buses reaching a far wider range of destinations than trains, though services are significantly reduced on Sundays. Towns such as Ljubljana, Maribor and Koper have big bus stations, where you can buy your tickets in advance – elsewhere, simply pay the driver or conductor. You'll be charged extra for cumbersome items of baggage.

Slovenia is a superb destination for **cycling**, with quiet roads, fabulous

CAR RENTAL

Slovenia's quiet roads and inspiring scenery make the country a driver's dream. If you can stretch your budget to a few days of **car rental**, you will afford yourself unlimited access to rural and mountainous regions such as the Soča Valley, which can prove challenging to reach using public transport. There are branches of most major car rental companies at Ljubljana airport; typical costs are €35 per day, €120 per week.

31

scenery and a well-established network of adventurous Alpine trails for mountain bikers. The lakes, the Soča Valley and the eastern wine roads are all pleasant places to explore on two wheels, and many hotels and hostels rent bikes for free or a small charge. The website ⓦmtb.si is a useful resource for mountain bikers.

ACCOMMODATION

Accommodation is universally clean and good quality. Slovenia has a decent spread of **hostels**, many of which are highly original in their conception. In addition, you'll find basic student dorms (*dijaški dom*) that significantly boost capacity during the summer. Hostels are not especially cheap; expect to pay about €18–22 per person per night in high season; student dorms are around €10. **Campsites** are numerous and generally have very good facilities, often including sporting equipment, restaurants and shops; two people travelling with a tent can expect to pay €20–30, and the majority of campsites are open from April or May to September. Camping rough without permission is punishable by a fine.

In the capital, double rooms at a two-star **hotel** start around €60. Family-run *pensions* and tourist farms in rural areas, especially the mountains, offer many of the same facilities as hotels but usually at a lower price. **Private rooms** (*zasebne sobe*) are available throughout Slovenia, with bookings often made by the local tourist office or travel agents like Kompas. Rooms are pretty good value at about €35–50 for a double, although stays of three nights or less are usually subject to a surcharge in peak season. Self-catering **apartments** (*apartmaji*) are also plentiful in the mountains and on the coast.

FOOD AND DRINK

Slovene **cuisine** draws on Austrian, Italian and Balkan influences. There's a native tradition, too, based on age-old peasant recipes, which you may encounter at tourist farms across the country, but

traditional Slovene dishes are becoming harder to find on restaurant menus increasingly dominated by Italian pizzas and pasta. For breakfast and snacks, *okrepčevalnice* (snack bars) and street kiosks dole out *burek*, a flaky pastry filled with cheese (*sirov burek*) or meat (*burek z mesom*). Sausages come in various forms, most commonly *kranjska klobasa* (big spicy sausages). Menus in a restaurant (*restavracija*) or inn (*gostilna*) will usually include roast meats (*pečenka*) and schnitzels (*zrezek*). Goulash (*golaž*) is also common. Two traditional dishes are *žlikrofi*, ravioli filled with potato, onion and bacon; and *žganci*, once the staple diet of rural Slovenes, a buckwheat or maize porridge often served with sauerkraut. Few local dishes are suitable for **vegetarians**, though international restaurants usually offer a choice of dishes without meat. On the coast you'll find plenty of fresh fish (*riba*), mussels (*žkoljke*) and squid (*kalamari*). Typical **desserts** include strudel filled with apple or rhubarb; *štruklji*, dumplings with fruit filling; and *prekmurska gibanica*, a delicious local cheesecake.

DRINK

Daytime **drinking** takes place in small café-bars, or in a *kavarna*, where a range of cakes, pastries and ice cream is usually on offer. **Coffee** (*kava*) is generally served with milk (*kava z mlekom*), or strong and black, as is tea (*čaj*), unless specified otherwise. Slovene beer (*pivo*) is refreshingly crisp and is dominated by two brands: Laško, from the town of the same name, and Union, from Ljubljana, though, more excitingly, there is an increasing number of craft breweries on the scene; two to look out

SLOVENIA ONLINE

ⓦ**www.burger.si** Superb interactive maps and panoramic photos.

ⓦ**inyourpocket.com/slovenia** Up-to-date and irreverent online listings from the ever reliable *In Your Pocket* series.

ⓦ**slovenia.info** Official tourist board site.

ⓦ**visitljubljana.com** Detailed information on sights and events in the capital.

for are Humanfish and Pelican. Most breweries also produce *temno pivo* ("dark beer"), a Guinness-like stout. Although still somewhat under the radar, Slovenian **wine** (*vino*) is superb; *črno* is red, *belo* is white. Even if you can't make it to any of the country's beautiful wine-growing regions, you'll find them in several of Ljubljana's excellent wine bars, while any restaurant worth its salt will have a decent selection. Favourite aperitifs include *slivovka* (plum brandy), the fiery *sadjevec*, a brandy made from various fruits, and the gin-like *brinovec*.

CULTURE AND ETIQUETTE

Slovenes are welcoming people who speak a very high level of English and are only too willing to help tourists. The predominant religion is Catholicism, and respectful attire (no sleeveless tops or above-the-knee skirts) should be worn inside churches and around religious sites. Although **tipping** is not obligatory, it is polite to round the bill up to a convenient figure in restaurants and when taking a taxi. **Smoking** is banned in all indoor public spaces, including cafés, bars and restaurants.

SPORTS AND OUTDOOR ACTIVITIES

There are few more active nations in Europe than Slovenia – the national sport is skiing, with several prestigious competitions held throughout the country each year. The most popular **spectator sports** are basketball, handball and football.

The country's dramatic and varied landscape – particularly in the Julian Alps (see p.993) – provides superb opportunities for a host of outdoor pursuits, most obviously **hiking**, **climbing** and **cycling** in summer, and **skiing** in winter. Moreover, the country's mountains, forests, lakes and rivers provide ample opportunity for adventure-seekers, with **rafting**, **canyoning** and **paragliding** among the most popular activities. Local tourist offices have comprehensive relevant information.

EMERGENCY NUMBERS
Police ☎ 113; Ambulance & Fire ☎ 112.

COMMUNICATIONS

Wi-fi is widely available, offered free in most hostels and hotels and in many public spaces; most tourist information offices will have a PC for use. Most **post offices** (*pošta*) are open Monday to Friday 8am to 6/7pm and Saturday 8am to noon. Stamps (*znamke*) can also be bought at newsstands.

Public **phones** use cards (*telekartice*; €4.25 or €14.85), available from post offices, kiosks and tobacconists. Make long-distance and international calls at a post office, where you're assigned to a cabin. Better still, buy a **SIM card** from one of the main Slovenian mobile operators, which are Telekom Slovenije, Si.mobil and Telemach; these typically cost around €6, and include some starting credit.

EMERGENCIES

The **police** (*policija*) are generally easy-going and likely to speak a decent level of English. **Pharmacies** (*lekarna*) are typically open Monday to Friday from 7am to 7/8pm, Saturday 7am to 1pm, and a rota system covers night-time opening; details are in the window of each pharmacy.

INFORMATION

Just about every town and resort has a well-stocked and helpful **tourist information office**, which can usually arrange accommodation too. Most offices stock an excellent range of maps,

---

STUDENT AND YOUTH DISCOUNTS
Even if you already have the European Youth Card (see p.44), consider purchasing the affiliated SŽ-EURO<26 (€18; from most train stations) to get an additional 30 percent off train fares within Slovenia, and 25 percent off international rail travel.

31

SLOVENE

	SLOVENE	PRONUNCIATION
Yes	*Ja*	Ya
No	*Ne*	Ne
Please	*Prosim*	Proseem
Thank you	*Hvala*	Huala
Hello/Good day	*Živijo/dober dan*	Zheeveeyon/donburr dnan
Goodbye	*Nasvidenje*	Nasveedehnye
Excuse me	*Dovolite mi, prosim*	Dovoleeteh mee, proseem
Where?	*Kje?*	Kye?
Good	*Dobro*	Dobro
Bad	*Slabo*	Slabo
Near	*Blizu*	Bleezoo
Far	*Daleč*	Daalech
Cheap	*Poceni*	Potzenee
Expensive	*Drago*	Drago
Open	*Odprto*	Odpurto
Closed	*Zaprto*	Zapurto
Today	*Danes*	Danes
Yesterday	*Včeraj*	Ucheray
Tomorrow	*Jutri*	Yutree
How much is…?	*Koliko stane…?*	Koleeko stahne…?
What time is it?	*Koliko je ura?*	Koleeko ye oora?
I don't understand	*Ne razumem*	Ne razoomem
Do you speak English?	*Ali govorite angleško?*	Alee govoreete angleshko?
One	*Ena*	Ena
Two	*Dve*	Dve
Three	*Tri*	Tree
Four	*Štiri*	Shteeree
Five	*Pet*	Pet
Six	*Šest*	Shest
Seven	*Sedem*	Sedem
Eight	*Osem*	Osem
Nine	*Devet*	Devet
Ten	*Deset*	Deset

including a variety of hiking and cycling maps. Look out, too, for the superb (and free) *In Your Pocket* guides, which are also available online (ⓦinyourpocket .com/slovenia).

MONEY AND BANKS

Slovenia's currency is the **euro** (€). **Banks** (*banka*) generally open Monday to Friday 9am to noon and 1 to 5pm, Saturday 8.30am to 11am/noon. You can also change money in tourist offices, post offices, travel agencies and exchange bureaux (*menjalnica*). **Credit cards** are accepted in most hotels, restaurants and shops, while **ATMs** are widespread.

OPENING HOURS AND HOLIDAYS

Most **shops** open Monday to Friday 8am to 7pm and Saturday 8am to 1pm, with a few also open on Sunday mornings. Museum times vary, but many close on Mondays. All shops and banks are closed on the following **public holidays**: January 1 and 2, February 8, Easter Monday, April 27, May 1 and 2, June 25, August 15, October 31, November 1, December 25 and 26.

Ljubljana

Prosperous and elegant, the Slovene capital **LJUBLJANA** gracefully fans out from its castle-topped hill, the old centre marooned in the shapeless modernity that stretches out across the plain. The city's museums, galleries and architecture are only part of the picture; above all, Ljubljana is a place to meet people and enjoy the nightlife.

WHAT TO SEE AND DO

An eminently walkable city, most of Ljubljana's sights are located in or around the gorgeous **Old Town**, spread directly below the castle on the right bank of the River Ljubljanica, and the **nineteenth-century quarter** situated to the west, where the principal museums and galleries are. Beyond here, **Tivoli Park** is the city's engaging green heart.

The Old Town

The hub around which everything in the **Old Town** revolves is **Prešernov trg**, so named after Slovenia's national poet, France Preseren (1800–49), whose statue graces the centre of this bustling square. Close by, the seventeenth-century Baroque **Church of the Annunciation** (daily 10am–6pm) blushes a sandy red; it's worth a look inside for Francesco Robba's marble high altar, richly adorned with spiral columns and plastic figurines. Robba, an Italian architect and sculptor, was brought in to remodel the city in its eighteenth-century heyday. His best piece, a beautifully sculpted **fountain** that symbolizes the meeting of the rivers Sava, Krka and Ljubljanica, lies across the river, in front of the town hall on Mestni trg – this, though, is a copy; the original sits in the National Gallery (see p.984). To get there, cross the elegant **Tromostovje** (Triple Bridge), the city's most iconic sight and one of many innovative creations by celebrated Ljubljana-born architect Jože Plečnik (1872–1957); the city is run through with his classically inspired designs, most of which were incorporated between the two world wars.

St Nicholas' Cathedral and the market

A little east of Mestni trg, on Ciril-Metodov trg, **St Nicholas' Cathedral** (daily 6am–noon & 3–6pm) is the most sumptuous and overblown of Ljubljana's Baroque statements. Completed in 1706

and decorated with fabulous frescoes painted by Quaglio, this is the best preserved of the city's ecclesiastical buildings. Along the riverside, you can't miss Plečnik's bustling **colonnaded market** (closed Sun), while just beyond is the striking Art Nouveau **Dragon Bridge**, each corner plinth guarded by a copper dragon – the city's symbol.

The castle

Opposite the market, Študentovska ulica winds up the thickly wooded hillside to the **castle** (daily: June–Sept 9am–11pm; April, May & Oct 9am–9pm; Nov–March 10am–8pm), which is also reachable via the **funicular railway** (€4 return). Originally constructed in the twelfth century, its present appearance dates from the sixteenth century, following an earthquake in 1511. The castle grounds comprise four principal attractions (daily: June–Sept 9am–9pm; April, May & Oct 9am–8pm; Nov–March 10am–6pm; €7.50, €10 including funicular): the **Virtual Castle**, an enlightening twelve-minute projection chronicling the city's development; the exhibition of **Slovenian History**, with particularly fascinating coverage of the Ten-Day War; the wonderfully engaging **Museum of Puppetry**, which documents one of Slovenia's most-cherished art forms; and lastly, the **clock tower**, which affords superlative views of the Old Town below and the magnificent Kamniške Alps to the north.

Metelkova

The alternative face of Ljubljana, **Metelkova**, situated a five-minute walk east of both the bus and train stations, is one of the city's most colourful quarters. The former barracks complex of the Yugoslav People's Army, its graffitied streets now accommodate a cosmopolitan array of independent societies, underground clubs, bars and galleries (see p.987), alongside a couple of more mainstream cultural attractions. Foremost among these is the marvellous **Ethnographic Museum** (Tues–Sun 10am–6pm; €4.50; www.etno-muzej .si), housing a voluminous collection of

31

31

anthropological artefacts from all over the world; close by at Maistrova 3, the **Museum of Contemporary Art** (Tues–Sun 10am–6pm; €5; ⓦmg-lj.si) exhibits modern art from the 1960s onwards.

Kongresni trg and around

Framed by some architectural gems, such as the early eighteenth-century **Ursuline Church**, the buttermilk-coloured Slovene Philharmonic Hall and the neo-Renaissance University building – not to mention a stack of cafés and bars – the grassy expanse of **Kongresni trg** is one of the city's most atmospheric spots. Heading south from Kongresni trg, you can't miss the chequered pink, green and grey brickwork of the **National and University Library**, arguably Plečnik's greatest work. Just behind here, the fine **City Museum** (Tues–Sun 10am–6pm; €4; ⓦwww.mgml.si) is devoted to the lives and times of the city's inhabitants (*ljubljancani*), though do keep an eye out for the usually excellent temporary exhibitions held here. Virtually next door is the seventeenth-century monastery complex of **Križanke**, originally the seat of a thirteenth-century order of Teutonic Knights, now an atmospheric concert venue. In the centre of Trg Francoske revolucije, opposite, the **Illyrian Monument** was erected in 1929 in belated recognition of Napoleon's short-lived attempt to create a fiefdom of the same name centred on Ljubljana.

Museums west of Slovenska

The town's leafy cultural quarter boasts several impressive museums and galleries. The best of these is the **National Gallery** at Prešernova 24 (Tues–Sun 10am–6pm, Thurs until 8pm; €7; ⓦng-slo.si), which is rich in local medieval Gothic work, although most visitors gravitate towards the halls devoted to the Slovene Impressionists, and in particular the outstanding paintings by Ivan Grohar and Rihard Jakopič. Diagonally across from here the **Museum of Modern Art** at Tomšičeva 14 (Tues–Sun 10am–6pm; €5; ⓦmg-lj.si)

effectively takes over from where the National Gallery stops, showcasing more experimental work from the mid-twentieth century onwards. Lastly, the **National Museum** (daily 10am–6pm, Thurs till 8pm; €4; ⓦnms.si), at Prešernova 20, has an outstanding collection of archeological finds from all over the Slovene territory, though the most intriguing are those retrieved from the Ljubljanica River; the building also houses the **Natural History Museum** (same hours and ticket), whose star exhibit is the only complete mammoth skeleton found in Europe.

Tivoli Park

Beyond the galleries lies elegant **Tivoli Park**, an expanse of lawns and tree-lined walkways leading to dense woodland. It's a lovely retreat from the busy city centre. A Baroque villa at the edge of the park contains the **National Museum of Contemporary History** (Tues–Sun 10am–6pm; €3.50; ⓦwww.muzej-nz.si), with interactive displays and carefully presented artefacts creating an evocative journey through Slovenia's conflict-riddled twentieth-century history, including some fascinating objects from the Ten-Day War in 1991, including the tail of a Yugoslav National Army Gazelle helicopter shot down on nearby Rožnik Hill.

ARRIVAL AND DEPARTURE

By plane Ljubljana's Jože Pučnik airport (☏ 04 206 1000, ⓦlju-airport.si) is in Brnik, 25km north of the city, and connected by bus (Mon–Fri hourly, Sat & Sun every 2hr; 50min; €4.10), or the quicker shuttle bus (€9). Taxis should cost around €35–40.

By train The train station (*železniška postaja*) is on Trg Osvobodilne fronte, a 10min walk north of the centre.

Destinations Divača (hourly; 1hr 30min); Koper (3 daily; 2hr 30min); Maribor (hourly; 1hr 45min–2hr 30min); Postojna (hourly; 1hr); Ptuj (2 daily; 2hr 30min).

By bus The station (*Avtobusna postaja*) is beside the train station.

Destinations Bled (hourly; 1hr 20min); Bohinj (hourly; 2hr); Bovec (4 daily; 3hr 30min–4hr 15min); Divača (7 daily; 1hr 30min); Kobarid (3 daily; 3–5hr); Koper (10 daily; 2hr); Maribor (4 daily; 2hr 30min–3hr); Piran (6 daily; 2hr 45min); Portorož (5 daily; 2hr 30min); Postojna (hourly; 1hr).

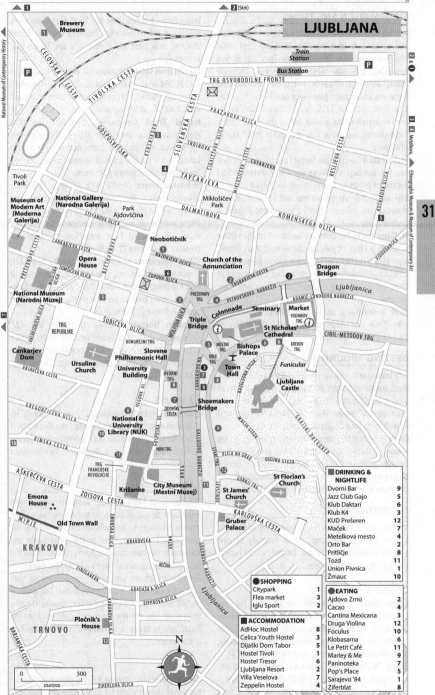

LJUBLJANA

National Museum of Contemporary History

2 & 1

3 4 Metelkova, Ethnographic Museum & Museum of Contemporary Art

31

1 (5km)

Brewery Museum

Train Station

Bus Station

P

P

TRG OSVOBODILNE FRONTE

CELOVŠKA CESTA

TIVOLSKA CESTA

GOSPOSVETSKA

KERSNIKOV

SLOVENSKA CESTA

TRDINOVA

CIGALETOVA ULICA

MIKLOŠIČEVA CESTA

CUFARJEVA

RESLJEVA CESTA

KOTNIKOVA ULICA

PRAŽAKOVA ULICA

TAVČARJEVA

Tivoli Park

Museum of Modern Art (Moderna Galerija)

National Gallery (Narodna Galerija)

Park Ajdovščina

Miklošičev Park

KOMENSKEGA ULICA

VIDOVDANSKA

STEFANOVA ULICA

DALMATINOVA

Neobotičnik

CANKARJEVA CESTA

TOMSIČEVA ULICA

BEETHOVNOVA

Opera House

NAZORJEVA ULICA

ČOPOVA ULICA

Church of the Annunciation

TRUBARJEVA CESTA

Dragon Bridge

Ljubljanica

PREŠERNOVA ULICA

MIKLOŠIČEVA ULICA

National Museum (Narodni Muzej)

PREŠERNOV TRG

PETKOVŠKOVO NABREŽJE

ADAMIČ-LUNDROVO NABREŽJE

ŠUBIČEVA ULICA

Colonnade

Seminary

Market

VODNIKOV TRG

Triple Bridge

St Nicholas' Cathedral

KREKOV TRG

CIRIL-METODOV TRG

VALVASORJEVA ULICA

TRG REPUBLIKE

KONGRESNI TRG

Slovene Philharmonic Hall

MESTNI TRG

Bishops Palace

Cankarjev Dom

Ursuline Church

University Building

DVORNI TRG

RIBJI TRG

Town Hall

Funicular

ERJAVČEVA CESTA

VEGOVA UL.

CANKARJEVO NAB.

ŽIDOVSKI STEZA

Shoemakers Bridge

Ljubljana Castle

RAZTEGOVA STEZA

MAČJA STEZA

GRADAŠKA CESTA

GREGORČIČEVA ULICA

National & University Library (NUK)

GOSPOSKA UL.

NOVI TRG

BREG

GALLUSOVO NABREŽJE

STARI TRG

ULICA NA GRAD

OSOJNA STEZA

RIMSKA CESTA

AŠKERČEVA CESTA

TRG FRANCOSKE REVOLUCIJE

ZOISOVA CESTA

Križanke

City Museum (Mestni Muzej)

LEVSTIKOV TRG

GORNJI TRG

St Florian's Church

Emona House

Old Town Wall

EMONSKA ULICA

KRAKOVSKA

VRTNA

St James' Church

Gruber Palace

KARLOVŠKA CESTA

MIRJE

KRAKOVO

FINŽGARJEVA

REČNA

SHOPPING
Citypark   1
Flea market   3
Iglu Sport   2

BARJANSKA CESTA

GRADAŠKA ULICA

EIPPROVA ULICA

Ljubljanica

GRUDNOVO NABREŽJE

ACCOMMODATION
AdHoc Hostel   8
Celica Youth Hostel   3
Dijaški Dom Tabor   5
Hostel Tivoli   1
Hostel Tresor   6
Ljubljana Resort   2
Villa Veselova   7
Zeppelin Hostel   4

Plečnik's House

TRNOVO

KARUNOVA CESTA

ZIHERLOVA ULICA

N

0   300
metres

DRINKING & NIGHTLIFE
Dvorni Bar   9
Jazz Club Gajo   5
Klub Daktari   6
Klub K4   3
KUD Prešeren   12
Maček   7
Metelkova mesto   4
Orto Bar   2
Pritličje   8
Tozd   11
Union Pivnica   1
Žmauc   10

EATING
Ajdovo Zrno   2
Cacao   4
Cantina Mexicana   3
Druga Violina   12
Foculus   10
Klobasarna   6
Le Petit Café   11
Marley & Me   9
Paninoteka   7
Pop's Place   5
Sarajevo '84   1
Ziferblat   8

31

INFORMATION AND TOURS

Tourist information The Slovenian Tourist Information Centre (STIC) is at Krekov trg 10 (June–Sept daily 8am–9pm; Oct–May Mon–Fri 8am–7pm, Sat & Sun 9am–5pm; ☎01 306 4576), with the main Ljubljana Tourist Information Office (TIC) next to the Triple Bridge on Stritarjeva ulica (daily: June–Sept 8am–9pm; Oct–May 8am–7pm, ☎01 306 1215, ✆ visitljubljana.com), there's another branch in the arrivals hall at the airport (daily 10am–10pm). You can pick up *Ljubljana in Your Pocket* at all of these.

Tourist card The Ljubljana Tourist Card, Urbana (€25/one day; €30/two days; €35/three days), is available from all the tourist offices and covers travel on Ljubljana's buses, free bike rental, one guided tour and entrance to most museums and galleries; there's a ten percent discount if you buy online.

Walking tours The Ljubljana Tourist Information Office organizes a range of pleasant 2hr walking tours (April–Sept; €10) of the Old Town, as well as special interest tours. CurioCity (✆ curiocity.si) offer more offbeat walking tours (from €25), including Express Your Selfie and Lazy Sundays.

Boat tours Barka Ljubljanica (✆ barka-ljubljanica.si) offer 45min river cruises, which depart from Novi trg on the hour (11am–9pm; €8).

GETTING AROUND

City transport Ljubljana's buses are cheap and frequent; there are no cash fares on buses, so you must buy an Urbana public transport card (€2), available at tourist information offices, news kiosks and post offices, and top it up with credit for your journeys, which cost €1.20.

Bikes Bikes can be rented from various central docking stations including the Central Market and Tivoli Park through Ljubljana's "Bicike" scheme (register at ✆ bicikelj .si; free up to 1hr, €1/2hr, €2/3hr). The Slovenian Tourist Information Centre also rent bikes (€2/2hr, €8/day).

ACCOMMODATION

Ljubljana has a terrific stock of hostels, in addition to student dorms (*dijaški dom*), which generally become available in late June/early July. Decently priced budget hotels are few and far between.

HOSTELS

AdHoc Hostel Cankarjevo Nabrežje 27 ☎051 268 288, ✆ adhoc-hostel.com. Super location in the heart of the Old Town for this sprawling, yet surprisingly quiet, hostel, with graffitied walls and large communal spaces. No breakfast, but there are kitchens for use. Dorms €20, doubles €54
Celica Youth Hostel Metelkova 8 ☎01 230 9700, ✆ hostelcelica.com. Brilliantly original hostel in a former military prison at the centre of artistic Metelkova, with

bright dorms and two/three-bed "cells", each designed by a different architect or artist. Breakfast included. Expect concerts, exhibitions and parties here too. Dorms €22, doubles €60
Dijaški Dom Tabor Vidovdanska 7, entrance at Kotnikova 4 ☎01 234 8840, ✆ hostel.ddt.si. Busy, central student hostel, with decent, very cheap beds on offer in July and August only. Breakfast included. Dorms €11, doubles €38
Hostel Tivoli Lepodvorska 2 ☎059 160 974, ✆ hosteltivoli.com. Sweet little place a short walk from the stations, with just two dorms, each with three-high bunks, and a double; all with shared shower facilities. Breakfast included. Dorms €21, double €60
★Hostel Tresor Čopova ulica 38 ☎01 200 9060, ✆ hostel-tresor.si. This former bank building has been utilized to great effect: the spacious dorms are wonderfully bright and the old vaults now function as the breakfast room and games/chill-out area. Superb atrium too. Breakfast €3. Dorms €12, doubles €36
Villa Veselova Veselova 14 ☎059 926 721, ✆ vilaveselovahostel.com. Charming hostel in a historic villa bordering peaceful Tivoli Park, with large, colour-themed dorms and one en-suite private room. Breakfast included. Dorms €22, double €60
Zeppelin Hostel Slovenska 47 ☎059 191 427, ✆ zeppelinhostel.com. Sociable, centrally located option with four-, six-, and ten-bed dorms as well as doubles with or without bathroom. Breakfast included. Dorms €22, doubles €64

CAMPING

Ljubljana Resort Dunajska 270 ☎01 589 0130, ✆ ljubljanaresort.si. Superbly equipped site 4km north of the centre in Ježica; also has chalets sleeping four, a water park, restaurant, bar and shop. Bus #6 or #8 from Slovenska cesta. Per person €13.70

EATING

The streets of Ljubljana's Old Town are packed with restaurants to suit all budgets, and during the warmer months it's lovely to dine alfresco on the banks of the Ljubljanica. For snacks, head to the many kiosks and stands near the stations selling *burek*, *pljeskavica* and the local *gorenjska* sausages. There's a lively food market on Vodnikov trg (closed Sun) where you can pick up tasty seasonal produce, while the nearby Market Colonnade is packed with little food shops selling breads, cheeses, sandwiches and the like. Every Friday on neighbouring Pogačarjev trg, the open-air kitchen is great for street food at bargain prices.

CAFÉS

Cacao Petkovškovo Nabrežje 3. This stylish riverside café-bar serves the city's best ice cream; take your pick from delicious flavours like pistachio, melon and forest strawberry (€1.50 per scoop), or just kick back with a refreshing fruit juice or coffee. Daily 8am–midnight.

Le Petit Café Trg Francoske revolucije 4. This cosy, long-standing Parisian-style café, in a lovely spot by Križanke, is perfect for a big mug of *bela kava* (white coffee) during the day or a glass of wine later on. Daily 7.30am–1am.

Paninoteka Jurčičev trg 3. Cracking riverside setting by the Shoemaker's Bridge for this cool sandwich bar serving a range of piping-hot panini, ciabattas and wraps. Takeaway too. Daily 9am–11pm.

★ **Ziferblat** Vegova 8. The concept is quite simple: the longer you stay, the more you pay (€0.50/min, €3/hr); and for that, all your drinks (sadly, none of the alcoholic variety) are free, as is use of the considerable space/facilities, including a hammock. Daily 9am–10pm.

RESTAURANTS

Ajdovo Zrno Trubarjeva 7. Excellent veggie canteen in a pleasant courtyard, with a self-service salad bar, soups, sandwiches and tortillas (€3–4), plus daily specials like cannelloni and risotto. Mon–Fri 8am–5pm.

Cantina Mexicana Knafljev prehod. On a lively alleyway between Slovenska cesta and Wolfova ulica, this brash, colourfully painted restaurant serves decent Mexican fajitas and tortillas (€8–12), as well as cocktails. Mon, Tues & Sun 10am–1am, Wed & Thurs until 2am, Fri & Sat until 3am.

Druga Violina Stari trg 21. Occupying an enviable Old Town spot, this delightful restaurant – part of a project to help people with disabilities assimilate into mainstream society – specializes in simple Slovenian classics like *jota* and *štruklji* (€5). Daily 8am–midnight.

Foculus Gregorčičeva 3. Strong contender for the city's best pizzeria, this wonderfully decorated place offers an enormous menu of pizzas (including dessert pizzas) and salads, from around €6. Daily 11am–midnight.

Klobasarna Ciril-Metodov trg 15. There's one item on the menu: sausage. But what a sausage it is; the mighty *kranjska klobasa* comes sliced and is served with a roll and huge dollops of mustard and horseradish (€5.90). Mon–Sat 10am–11pm, Sun 10am–3pm.

Marley & Me Stari trg 9. An enticing possibility in this busy little Old Town street, with well-prepared Mediterranean classics such as tagliatelle with shrimp (€11). Daily 11am–11pm.

Pop's Place Cankarjevo Nabrežje 3. You'll do well to grab a table in this tiny restaurant, but it's well worth the wait for the juiciest burgers and ribs this side of the Atlantic, possibly (€8–10); there's a terrific selection of craft beers to boot. Daily noon–1am.

★ **Sarajevo '84** Nazorjeva ulica 12. Decked out with sporting paraphernalia in homage to Sarajevo's staging of the winter Olympics, this fun Bosnian restaurant serves, among other things, the classic Balkan grilled meats, *čevapčiči* and *pljeskavica* (€7). Mon–Wed 11am–midnight, Thurs & Fri 11am–1am, Sat noon–2am.

DRINKING AND NIGHTLIFE

Despite its diminutive size, Ljubljana has an impressively varied and energetic choice of bars and clubs, and a leisurely stroll along the banks of the Ljubljanica will yield a locale every 20m or so. Similarly, you'll find plenty of places along Mestni trg and Stari trg, and around Kongresni trg. The city has always maintained a strong independent spirit, manifest in numerous progressive venues offering a wide programme of alternative events. *Ljubljana In Your Pocket* is your best bet for the most up-to-date listings.

BARS

★ **Dvorni Bar** Dvorni trg 2. If you don't get to Slovenia's beautiful wine-growing regions, fear not; this classy bar has offerings from all over the country, be it the straw-coloured Rebula from Goriška Brda or the ruby-red Teran from the Karst (€3–4/glass). Mon–Sat 8am–1am, Sun 9am–1am.

Klub Daktari Krekov trg 7. The decor really makes this convivial place special, with restored antique furniture, corner piano and shelves packed with books. Live music, cabaret and jam sessions. Mon–Sat 8am–1am, Sun 9am–midnight.

Maček Krojaška 5. This lively, bohemian café-bar is arguably the most popular of the riverside watering holes, its large terrace perfect for people-watching with a glass of wine. Mon–Sat 9am–12.30am, Sun 9am–11pm.

Tozd Galusovo Nabrežje 27. Located down by the quieter, southern stretch of the river, this is a great spot to cool off with a beer at sundown; the hip brick and enamel interior is plastered with all manner of random objects. Daily 8.30am–midnight.

Union Pivnica Celovška 22. Prepare for a rollicking good time at this cavernous, industrial-styled bar inside the brewery of the same name, selling a delicious range of draught and bottled beers alongside juicy beer sausages to soak it all up. Mon–Sat 11am–1am.

Žmauc Rimska 21. The graffiti-daubed exterior of this happy, hippy dive gives some indication of what to expect; the small buzzy terrace is packed throughout the day. Mon–Fri 7.30am–1am, Sat 10am–1am, Sun 6pm–1am.

CLUBS AND LIVE MUSIC

Jazz Club Gajo Beethovnova 8 ⓦ jazzclubgajo.com. Suitably atmospheric venue for the genre, with quality live offerings and jam sessions every Mon at 9pm.

Klub K4 Kersnikova ⓦ klubk4.org. Legendary stalwart of Ljubljana's alternative scene with a terrific rota of music: mainly electronic, but also rock, jazz and folk, plus regular gay and lesbian nights.

31

31

LJUBLJANA FESTIVALS

There's a wonderful roster of annual festivals in the capital.

Druga Godba Ⓦdrugagodba.si. Brilliant three-day annual world music festival at the end of May featuring concerts at atmospheric venues throughout the city.

International Summer Festival
Ⓦljubljanafestival.si. Long-running programme of internationally renowned orchestral artists, with concerts at various venues between July and mid-Sept.

Ljubljana Jazz Festival Ⓦljubljanajazz.si. Ljubljana's four-day jazz festival at the beginning of July is up there with the best in Europe; better still, most concerts take place at the wonderful Križanke open-air theatre.

KUD Prešeren Karunova 14 Ⓦwww.kud.si. Superb gig venue and cultural centre in Trnovo that also hosts regular literary events, workshops and art exhibitions. Also stages the excellent *Trnfest* festival in Aug.

★**Metelkova mesto** Metelkova cesta Ⓦmetelkova mesto.org. The city's counter-cultural hub, with a left-field cluster of clubs, bars and galleries; one of the most banging venues here is *Gala Hala*, with several live performances a week during the summer.

Orto Bar Grablovičeva 1 Ⓦorto-bar.com. Energetic club east of the train station; also one of the city's principal rock venues, with typically one or two gigs a week.

Pritličje Mestni trg 5 Ⓦpritlicje.si. Vibrant cultural centre (and comic store) that also functions as a café/bar and live music venue; expect all kinds of fun happenings on a daily basis.

ENTERTAINMENT AND EVENTS

Ljubljana has a busy calendar of dance, music and theatre at its purpose-built venues.

Cankarjev Dom Prešernova 10 ☎01 241 7100, Ⓦcd-cc .si. The city's cultural headquarters, hosting major orchestral and theatrical events, art exhibitions, and folk and jazz concerts.

National Opera and Ballet Theatre Župančičeva 1 ☎01 241 1740, Ⓦopera.si. An impressive nineteenth-century Neoclassical theatre staging ballet and opera.

SHOPPING

Citypark Šmartinska 152 Ⓦcitypark.si. Slovenia's largest shopping centre, out on the northeastern fringes of the capital, with more than a hundred stores. Buses #2, #7, #12 and #27. Mon–Fri 9am–9pm, Sat 8am–9pm. Sun 9am–3pm.

Flea market Wonderful antiques market along the right bank of the Ljubljanica where, among other things, you can pick up Tito-era memorabilia. Sun 8am–2pm.

Iglu Sport Petkovškovo 31 Ⓦiglusport.si. Stocks camping and outdoor gear; useful for trips to the lakes or mountains. Mon–Fri 9am–2pm & 3–7pm, Sat 9am–1pm.

DIRECTORY

Embassies and consulates Australia, Železna cesta 14 ☎01 234 8675; Canada, Linhartova cesta 49A ☎01 252 4444; Ireland, Palaca Kapitelj, Poljanski nasip 6 ☎01 300 8970; UK, Trg Republike 3 ☎01 200 3910; US, Prešernova 31 ☎01 200 5500.

Exchange At the train station and at post offices.

Hospital Zaloška Cesta 2 ☎01 522 5050, Ⓦkclj.si.

Left luggage Lockers at the train station (€2–3/24hr depending on locker size).

Pharmacy Centralna Lekarna on Prešernov trg (Mon–Fri 7.30am–7.30pm, Sat 8am–3pm; ☎01 230 6100); 24hr pharmacy at Prisojne 7 ☎01 230 6230.

Post office Slovenska cesta 32 (Mon–Fri 8am–7pm, Sat 8am–noon).

Southwest Slovenia

Not to be missed while you're in Ljubljana is a visit to either the **Postojna** or **Škocjan caves** – both spectacular, and both easily manageable either as a day-trip from the capital or en route south to the coast. A trip easily combined with Postojna is to **Predjama Castle**, a sombre fortress craftily embedded into the karst landscape. On the small stretch of Adriatic coastline are a number of charismatic towns, heavily influenced by a legacy of Venetian rule. Of these, **Piran** is by far the most rewarding, its fishing-village charm and gorgeous architecture contrasting starkly with the brash modernity of neighbouring **Portorož**.

POSTOJNA

Hourly trains run the 65km route from Ljubljana to **POSTOJNA**, though the walk to the caves is much shorter from the bus stop. Once in the town, signs direct you to the **caves** (daily: Jan–March, Nov & Dec 10am–3pm; April & Oct

10am–4pm; May, June & Sept 9am–5pm; July & Aug 9am–6pm; tours every 1–2hr; 90min; €24, combined ticket with Predjama Castle €31.90; ⓦpostojnska-jama.eu); inside, a train whizzes you through spectacular preliminary systems for 3.5km before the guided 1.5km walking tour starts. The vast and fantastic jungles of rock formations are breathtaking and there's also an opportunity to catch a rare glimpse of the cave-dwelling "human fish", a blind amphibian that can live for up to 100 years, before the climactic finale of the 40m-high "concert hall". Bring a jacket and appropriate footwear; the air inside the caves is decidedly chilly. To avoid the considerable crowds, visit first thing in the morning or late afternoon.

Once done there, pop along to the brilliantly designed **EXPO Postojna Cave Karst** exhibition (same times as caves; €8.90), which guides visitors through the history of the caves and the local karst region, covering its geology, archeology and biology, including in-depth coverage of the many fascinating cave-dwelling animals that lurk within.

PREDJAMA CASTLE

Nine kilometres northwest of the caves, but not served by public transport, is the precariously sited **Predjama Castle** (daily: Jan–March, Nov & Dec 10am–4pm; April & Oct 10am–5pm; May, June & Sept 9am–6pm; July & Aug 9am–7pm; €11.90; combined ticket with the caves €31.90). Built into and around an elevated cave entrance in the midst of the dramatic karst landscape, this sixteenth-century fortress is a striking sight and affords excellent views of the surrounding countryside. Its damp, sparsely filled interior is less rewarding, though it is fun exploring the many passageways, galleries and alcoves, and you can see weaponry and artefacts dating back to its heyday as the castle of the legendary knight Erazem Lueger. For those with a ticket for both the castle and caves, there is a free shuttle bus operating in July and August; otherwise, the easiest way to get here is to rent bikes from the *Hotel Sport* at Kolodvorska 1 in Postojna (€15/day).

ŠKOCJAN CAVES

Much less visited, but even more dramatic than Postojna, the **Škocjan Caves** are a stunning system of echoing chambers, secret passages and collapsed valleys carved out by the Reka River, which begins its journey some 50km south near the Croatian border. Daily **tours** (June–Sept hourly, 10am–5pm; Oct–May 2–3 daily, 10am–3pm; €16; ⓦpark-skocjanske-jame.si) take you through several stalactite-infested chambers and halls, before you reach the breathtaking **Murmuring Cave**, reputedly the world's largest subterranean canyon; here you get to cross the remarkable, vertiginous 45m-high **Cerkvenik Bridge**, under which the Reka flows. To get here, follow the 3km footpath from Divača train station (see map at the station).

PORTOROŽ

Easily reached by bus from the train terminus in Koper, **PORTOROŽ** ("Port of Roses") sprawls at the beginning of a long, tapering peninsula that projects like a lizard's tail north into the Adriatic. Popular since the end of the nineteenth century for its mild climate and the health-inducing properties of its salty mud baths, today the resort's big draw is high-rise hotels, glitzy casinos and buzzing nightlife. The main "beach" is just a continuation of the concrete promenade, and though there's nothing by way of culture here, the town's vibrant bars and clubs are unrivalled on this stretch of the coast.

ARRIVAL AND INFORMATION

By bus The small, principal bus terminal is on the main coastal strip, Obala, though buses stop all along here. Destinations Ljubljana (5 daily; 2hr 30min).
Tourist office Just down from the bus terminal at Obala 16 (daily: July & Aug 9am–10pm; Sept–June 9am–5pm; ☎05 674 2220, ⓦportoroz.si).

31

ACCOMMODATION

Private rooms (double €30–50) can be booked through Maona, at Obala 14b (☎05 674 0363, ⓦmaona.si), or Turist Biro at Obala 57 (☎05 674 1055, ⓦturistbiro-ag.si).

Hostel Panorama Šentjane 25 ☎031 678 767, ⓦhostelportoroz.si. Large hostel with a range of dorms and apartments located high up in the hills halfway between Portorož and Piran, with fine views of the Istrian coast. There's no public transport up to here, so expect a stiff 30min walk. Breakfast included. Dorms **€23**, doubles **€48**

EATING AND DRINKING

Take your pick from any number of beachside bars and clubs, many of which stay open until dawn.

Alaya Obala 22. Sprawling, tropically themed, open-air beach bar just south of the main beach and watersports centre, which also stages live music and regular party nights. Mon–Sat 9am–3am.

Cacao Obala 14. Near the tourist office, this laidback bar sports a cool, loungey interior and deck terrace facing the beach; but best of all, it serves the finest ice cream anywhere along the coast. Mon–Thurs & Sun 8am–10pm, Fri & Sat 8am–midnight.

PIRAN

PIRAN, at the tip of the peninsula, 4km from Portorož, couldn't be more different. Its web of arched alleys, tightly packed ranks of houses and little Italianate squares is delightful. The centre, 200m around the harbour from the bus station, is **Tartinijev trg**, a striking, marble-surfaced square fringed by Venetian palaces and an imposing Austrian town hall. The square is named after Giuseppe Tartini, an eighteenth-century Italian violinist and composer who was born in a cream villa up a small flight of stairs on the square's east side; now a **commemorative house** (June–Aug daily 9am–noon & 6–9pm; Sept–May Tues–Sun 11am–noon & 5–6pm; €2), it features scores, diaries and letters as well as his death mask. From the square's eastern edge, follow Rozmanova ulica all the way up to the commanding Baroque **Church of St George**, crowning a spectacular spot on the far side of Piran's peninsula. Climb the monumental belfry (€1) for superlative views of the Adriatic.

ARRIVAL AND INFORMATION

By bus Buses pull up on Cankarjevo nabrežje, a 5min seafront walk from the main square, Tartinijev trg.

Destinations Ljubljana (7 daily; 2hr 45min); Portorož/Koper (every 15–20min; 10/45min); Trieste (Mon–Sat 1 daily; 1hr 30min).

Tourist information Tartinijev trg 2 (daily: July & Aug 9am–10pm; Sept–June 9am–5pm; ☎05 673 4440, ⓦportoroz.si).

ACCOMMODATION

Private rooms (double €30–50) can be booked through Maona, at Cankarjevo nabrežje 7 (☎05 674 0363, ⓦmaona.si), between the bus station and the square.

Fiesa Camping Fiesa 57b ☎05 674 6230. Decent site 1km east of Piran (follow the path from the Church of St George). Open May–Sept. Per person **€11.50**

Hostel Piran Vodopivčeva 9 ☎031 627 647, ⓦhostelpiran.com. Smart little hostel with a range of doubles, triples and quads, either with shared or private bathrooms. Kitchen for use too. Dorms **€25**, doubles **€50**

Val Hostel Gregorčičeva 38a ☎05 673 2555, ⓦhostel-val.com. Friendly and well run, with a comfortable guesthouse feel; one-, two- and three-bedded rooms, laundry facilities and a good restaurant. Breakfast included. Doubles **€60**

EATING AND DRINKING

Čakola Partizanska ulica 2. Charming corner café much frequented by locals enjoying a morning coffee and croissant or, a little later in the day, a glass or two of the excellent local wine. Daily 8am–midnight.

Da Noi Prešernovo nabrežje 4. Popular, cellar-like bar, with a cool, breezy seafront terrace too. Mon–Thurs & Sun 8am–1am, Fri & Sat till 3am.

Pirat Zupančiceva 24. A pleasant antidote to the town's touristy restaurants, with no-frills seafood served in copper bowls and a good-value daily tourist menu for €10. Daily 10am–11pm.

Pri Mari Dantejeva ulica 17. Just beyond the bus station, this warm, trattoria-style place offers some terrific dishes like spicy squid pasta, and fillet of tuna on a bed of rocket salad (€12). Tues–Sat 2–4pm & 6–10pm, Sun 2–6pm.

Northwest Slovenia

Within easy reach of Ljubljana are the stunning mountain lakes of **Bled** and **Bohinj**. The magnificent **Soča Valley**, on the western side of the Julian Alps, is much less touristed, while the small towns of **Kobarid** and **Bovec** are excellent bases for hiking and adventure sports.

BLED

Perhaps the most visited place outside of the capital, the lake resort of **BLED** has all the right ingredients for a memorable visit – a placid mirror lake with a romantic island, a medieval cliff-top castle and a backdrop of snowcapped mountains. In summer, the lake is the setting for a whole host of watersports – including major rowing contests – and in winter the surface becomes a giant fairytale skating rink.

WHAT TO SEE AND DO

The best way to appreciate the lake is to walk around it: a leisurely stroll should take no more than two hours. Otherwise, a constant relay of stretched gondolas leaves from below the *Park Hotel*, by the *Pension Mlino* and by *Vila Prešeren*, ferrying tourists back and forth to Bled's picturesque **island** (€14 return). With an early start, and by renting your own rowing boat (€10–15/ hr) from the Castle Boat House or *Pension Pletna*, you can beat them to it. Crowning the island, the Baroque **Church of Sv Marika Božja** (€6) is the last in a line of churches on a spot that's long held religious significance: under the present building lie remains of a pre-Roman temple.

From the north shore a couple of paths wind steeply uphill to **Bled Castle** (daily: April to mid-June & mid-Sept to Oct 8am–8pm; mid-June to mid-Sept 8am–9pm; Nov–March 8am–6pm; €10), originally an eleventh-century fortification whose present appearance dates from the seventeenth; its museum contains a well-presented collection of local artefacts relating to the settlement of Bled, including many fascinating items retrieved from the lake, while the lovely courtyard has magnificent views across the lake and towards the Alps. In the shade of the castle rock lies a clean, well-equipped **bathing area** with changing rooms (June to late Sept).

Vintgar Gorge

The main attraction in the outlying hills is the **Vintgar Gorge** (late April–Oct daily 8am–7pm; €4), 4km north of town, an impressive defile accessed via a series of wooden walkways and bridges suspended from the rock face. To get here, take the daily tourist bus (June–Sept 10am; July & Aug additional bus at 9am; return at 12.30pm; €2.30) to the village of Zasip, climb to the hilltop chapel of **Sv Katarina** and pick up a path through the forest to the gorge entrance.

ARRIVAL AND DEPARTURE

By train Trains from Ljubljana stop at Bled-Lesce, 4km southeast of Bled, from where there are regular buses (€1.50) to the lake. Trains on the Jesenice–Nova Gorica branch call at Bled Jezero, a 5min walk from the northwest corner of Bled.

Destinations Ljubljana (every 1–2hr; 40min–1hr); Bohinjska Bistrica (7 daily; 20min); Most na Soči for the Soča Valley (7 daily; 55min).

By bus The station is a 5min walk northeast of the lake on Grajska cesta.

Destinations Ljubljana (hourly; 1hr 15min); Ribčev Laz for Lake Bohinj (hourly; 40min).

INFORMATION

Tourist office Cesta svobode 10, opposite the *Park Hotel* (mid-April to June, Sept & Oct Mon–Sat 8am–7pm, Sun 10am–4pm; July & Aug Mon–Sat 8am–9pm, Sun 9am–5pm; Nov to mid-April Mon–Fri 8am–6pm, Sat & Sun 9am–4pm; ☏ 04 574 1122, w www.bled.si). Bikes can be rented from here (and elsewhere in town), costing €6/3hr, €10/day.

Triglav National Park Information Centre Ljubljanska cesta 27 (daily: mid-April to mid-Oct 8am–6pm; rest of year 8am–4pm; ☏ 04 578 0205, w tnp.si); superb visitor centre where you can get all the information you need on visiting the national park; there's also an exhibition on the park's flora, fauna and architecture, a café and souvenir shop.

31

ACCOMMODATION

Private rooms are available through Kompas in the shopping centre at Ljubljanska 4 (☎04 572 7501, ⓦ kompas-bled.si).

★**Camping Bled** Kidričeva 10 ☎04 575 2000, ⓦ sava -hotels-resorts.com. Beautifully located amid the pines at the western end of the lake, this family-friendly campsite has first rate facilities. For glampers, there are superb wooden huts with double beds and hot tubs; the breakfast basket (€9) is fab. Easter–Oct. Camping/person **€13.80**, huts **€61**

Pension Bledec Grajska 17 ☎04 574 5250, ⓦ bledec.si. This high-quality hostel's comfortable dorms and doubles feature traditional furniture and each has its own bathroom. No kitchen but a good restaurant. Breakfast €5. Dorms **€22**, doubles **€56**

Travellers Haven Riklijeva cesta 1 ☎05 904 4226, ⓦ travellers-haven.si. Close to *Pension Bledec*, with tastefully furnished dorms, a kitchen and common area, and free bike rental and laundry facilities. Breakfast not included but there's a supermarket opposite. Dorms **€19**, doubles **€48**

EATING AND DRINKING

The best places for eating are in the hillside area between Bled's bus station and castle, though many of the lake's waterfront *pensions* offer decent food too. The ugly concrete shopping centre on Ljubljanska is home to some strangely popular bars.

Chilli Cesta svobode 9. Popular bar and restaurant with a pleasant terrace and an appropriately spicy menu of Mexican and Mediterranean dishes from around €8. Daily 11am–1am.

Gostilna Pri Planincu Grajska 8. Opposite the bus station, this historic pub and restaurant has been serving up hearty Slovene home cooking since 1903; the mixed grill (€12.50) is worth chomping into after a hard day's hike. Daily 9am–midnight.

Šmon Grajska 3. "The Bear" café has been going even longer (since 1880) and is the best place to try the ubiquitous Bled *Kremna Rezina* (cream cake; €2.50) alongside a steaming mug of *bela kava* (white coffee). Daily 7.30am–9pm.

LAKE BOHINJ

From Bled hourly buses make the 25km trip through the verdant, mist-laden Sava Bohinjka Valley to **Lake Bohinj**. In appearance and character Lake Bohinj is utterly different from Bled: the lake crooks a narrow finger under the wild mountains, evergreen woods slope gently down to the water, and in the relative absence of visitors, a lazy stillness hangs over all.

Ribčev Laz

RIBČEV LAZ (referred to as Jezero on bus timetables), at the eastern end of the lake, is where most facilities are based. **Walking trails** lead round both sides of the lake (the 12km circumference can be walked in around four hours), or north on to the eastern shoulders of the Triglav range. One route leads north from the enchanting village of Stara Fužina into the Voje valley, passing through the dramatic **Mostnica Gorge** (€2.50), a local beauty spot.

Ukanc, Mount Vogel and the Valley of the Seven Lakes

About 5km from Ribčev Laz at the western end of the lake is the hamlet of **UKANC** (sometimes referred to as Zlatorog), where a **cable car** (daily 7am–7pm, every 30min; closed Nov; €14 return) whizzes you vertiginously up to the summit of **Mount Vogel** (1535m) in no time – if the Alps look dramatic from the lakeside, from Vogel's summit they're breathtaking; at the top, you can grab a bite to eat at the excellent, and cheap, restaurant. Ukanc is also the starting point for a one-hour walk north to the photogenic **Savica Waterfalls** (daily weather permitting 8am–8pm; €3). From here, the serious hiking can commence, either as a day-trip to the **Valley of the Seven Lakes** – an area strewn with eerie boulders and hardy firs – or as an expedition to scale Mount Triglav itself.

ARRIVAL AND DEPARTURE

By train Trains on the Jesenice–Nova Gorica line call at Bohinjska Bistrica, some 6km from the lake back in the direction of Bled. From here two morning shuttle buses run back towards Bled.

Destinations From Bohinjska Bistrica: Bled Jezero (7 daily; 20min); Most na Soči for the Soča Valley (6–8 daily; 40min).

By bus Buses stop outside the *Hotel Jezero* in Ribčev Laz, terminating in Ukanc on the lake's southwestern corner.

Destinations Bled (hourly; 40min); Bohinjska Bistrica (hourly; 15min); Ljubljana (hourly; 1hr 45min).

INFORMATION

Tourist office Ribčev Laz 48, just up from the main bus stop next to the Mercator supermarket (July & Aug Mon–Sat 8am–8pm, Sun 8am–6pm; Sept–June

Mon–Sat 8am–6pm, Sun 9am–3pm; ☎04 574 6010, ⓦbohinj-info.com). There's free public wi-fi in the immediate vicinity of Ribčev Laz.

ACCOMMODATION

The tourist office offers a plentiful choice of private rooms and apartments around Ribčev Laz and in the idyllic villages of Stara Fužina and Studor, 1km and 3km north respectively. **Hostel Pod Voglom** Ribčev Laz ☎04 572 3461, ⓦhostel-podvoglom.com. Rather old-fashioned, but very social, hostel occupying a prime lakeshore spot some 2km along the road to Ukanc; the mix of differently sized rooms come with both private and shared bathroom facilities. Breakfast included. Dorms €18, doubles €44

★**Rustic House 13** Srednja Vas ☎03 146 6707, ⓦstudor13.si. Exceptional hostel in a tastefully renovated historic house 3km from the lake, with immaculate singles, doubles, triples and quads, and a well-equipped self-catering kitchen. Free pick-up from Bohinj. Breakfast included. Dorms €27, doubles €60

Zlatorog Ukanc 2 ☎04 572 3482. Extremely basic but splendidly located campsite on the lake's western tip; conveniently located for trips up the mountains. May–Sept. Per person €9

EATING AND DRINKING

Gostišče Erlah Ukanc 67. Good-value fish dishes such as fresh trout (€7), direct from their own farm, and grilled salmon feature on the menu at this friendly inn at the western end of the lake. Daily noon–9pm.

Pizzerija Ema Srednja Vas 73. The fabulous mountain views from the terrace and *Ema's* extensive menu of affordable, tasty pizzas and pasta dishes more than justify the 4km hike from the lake to the pretty village of Srednja Vas. Daily 9.30am–11pm.

THE SOČA VALLEY

On the other, less touristy, side of the mountains from Bohinj, the brilliantly turquoise **River Soča** streaks through the western spur of the Julian Alps, running parallel with the Italian border. During World War I, the Soča marked the front line between the Italian and Austro-Hungarian armies; now memorial chapels and abandoned fortifications nestle incongruously amid awesome Alpine scenery. The valley is a major centre for activity-based tourism, with the river providing first-class **rafting** and **kayaking** conditions throughout the spring and summer, and the mountain slopes perfect for **skiing** and **snowboarding** in winter.

The main tourist centres are **Kobarid** and **Bovec**, both small towns boasting a range of fabulous walking possibilities. The GZS 1:50,000 Zgornje Posočje **map** covers trails in the region.

Kobarid

It was at the little Alpine town of **KOBARID** that German and Austrian troops finally broke through Italian lines in 1917, almost knocking Italy out of World War I in the process. The 29 months of fighting in the region are relayed in the excellent **Kobarid Museum**, Gregorčičeva 10 (daily: April–Sept 9am–6pm; Oct–March 10am–5pm; €6), via a twenty-minute multimedia presentation and a series of sobering photographs, maps and mementoes. It's also the starting point for the superb **Kobarid Historical Trail** (3–5hr), a steep 5km loop where remote woodland paths are punctuated by forgotten wartime landmarks. From the town's main square you climb up to a striking three-tiered **Italian War Memorial**, opened by Benito Mussolini in 1938, before hiking further into the hills to see surviving military fortifications. At the trail's farthest point from town bubbles the **Kozjak waterfall** (40min walk), less impressive for its height than for the cavern-like space that it has carved out of the surrounding rock. Maps of the trail are available from the museum and tourist office.

ARRIVAL AND INFORMATION

By bus Buses stop on the small main square, Trg Svobode. Destinations Bovec (3–5 daily; 20min); Ljubljana (2 daily; 3hr 30min).

Tourist office Trg Svobode 16 (July & Aug daily 9am–8pm; April–June & Sept Mon–Fri 9am–1pm & 2–7pm, Sat & Sun 9am–1pm & 4–7pm; Oct–March Mon–Fri 9am–1pm & 2–4pm, Sat 10am–2pm; ☎05 380 0490, ⓦlto-sotocje.si). Adjoining the museum, the excellent Walk of Peace centre provides a wealth of information on the valley's World War I sights and organizes guided walks.

ACCOMMODATION

Camp Koren Drežniške Ravne 33 ☎05 389 1311, ⓦkamp-koren.si. 500m out of town near the end of the historical walk trail, this superbly well-equipped site also has six log cabins sleeping up to six. Camping/person €13, chalets €65

31

ADVENTURE SPORTS

In **Kobarid** the main adventure sports company is X-Point, at Trg Svobode 6 (☎05 388 5308, ⓦxpoint.si); they organize rafting (€40), kayaking (€45) and canyoning (€50), among other activities guaranteed to raise your heart rate. Popular outfits in **Bovec** include Soča Rafting (☎05 389 6200, ⓦsocarafting.si), opposite the tourist office at Trg Golobarskih 14, and Avantura (☎41 718 317, ⓦavantura.org), further down the same street, who specialize in tandem paragliding (€145). They all offer similar prices for activities.

Hostel X-Point Trg Svobode 6 ☎05 388 5308, ⓦxpoint .si. Clean, modern hostel run by the adventure sports company; two- and three-bed rooms, shared bathrooms and self-catering kitchen. Dorms €16, doubles €40

EATING AND DRINKING

Pri Vitku Pri Malnih 41. Small, welcoming place in a residential street a 10min walk south of town (follow signs), offering pizza, pasta and grilled meat dishes (€6). Daily noon–midnight.

Topli Val Trg Svobode 1. If you can afford to spend just a little more, then head to this classy restaurant inside the *Hotel Hvala*; on offer is a marvellous fish and seafood menu featuring the likes of trout, crayfish and mussels (€15). Daily noon–10pm.

Bovec

Twenty five kilometres up the valley from Kobarid, the village of **BOVEC** straggles between imperious mountain ridges. Thanks to its status as a winter ski resort, it has a greater range of accommodation options and sporting agencies than Kobarid, so enjoys a more vibrant atmosphere. The quickest route into the mountains from here is provided by the **gondola** that departs on the hour 1km south of the village (June–Sept 8am–4pm; €13 return), which ascends to the pasture-cloaked Mount Kanin over to the west.

ARRIVAL AND INFORMATION

By bus Buses terminate outside the *Letni Vrt* restaurant on the main square, Trg Golobarskih žrtev.
Destinations Kobarid (3–5 daily; 20min).
Tourist office Trg Golobarskih žrtev 8 (daily 9am–6pm; ☎05 384 1919, ⓦbovec.si).

ACCOMMODATION

Adrenaline Check Eco Place Podklopca 4 ☎041 383 662, ⓦadrenaline-check.com. Some 12km from Bovec, Europe's first sustainable outdoor hostel offers riverside camping (with tents for rent too) and fully equipped lean-tos. Free pick-ups. Camping/person €13, rented tents €18, lean-to €25

Hostel Soča Rocks Mala Vas 120 ☎041 317 777, ⓦhostelsocarocks.com. Rocks by name, rocks by nature, this cracking hostel – featuring colourful six-bed dorms and doubles, along with lots of activities on offer – certainly lives up to its name. Dorms €15, doubles €40

Eastern Slovenia

The lush landscapes to the east of Ljubljana – where many of the country's most reputable vineyards are concentrated – are generally less explored by travellers. However, as host to Slovenia's second city, **Maribor**, and oldest settlement, **Ptuj**, which lie on the main routes to Austria and Hungary respectively, the region can reward the passing visitor with its rich historical heritage, traditional culture and fine wine.

MARIBOR

Located 122km northeast of Ljubljana, **MARIBOR** is perched snugly on the Drava River between hillside vineyards and the Pohorje mountain range. Though it has been beset by war and occupation, the old town's beautiful architecture preserves myriad historical and cultural influences, and the nightlife is second only to Ljubljana.

WHAT TO SEE AND DO

Maribor's main attractions are condensed in a pedestrianized centre, beginning on Trg Svobode. Here Maribor Castle houses the **regional museum** (Tues–Sat 10am–6pm; €3), which presents particularly fine ethnological and cultural history sections. Across the square is the labyrinth of underground catacombs that make up the **Vinag Wine Cellar**, where you can stop by to sample some of the region's acclaimed vintages (tours Mon–Thurs

11am & 2pm, Fri–Sun 11am, 2pm & 4pm; €5 for three wines). On the western fringe of the pedestrianized zone sits the photogenic **Slomškov trg**, a serene, leafy opening surrounded by a few landmarks, including the university building and the elegant **Slovene National Theatre**. Opposite the university, and mimicking its distinct yellow colour, is the sixteenth-century Gothic **Cathedral Church** (daily 10am–6pm), with a bell tower (€2) that offers fantastic views to the edges of the city and beyond. South of Slomškov is Maribor's most charming square, **Glavni trg**, which epitomizes the hotchpotch architectural styles of the city. Its centrepiece is the Baroque **Plague Memorial**, erected after the deadly disease wiped out a third of the town's population in the seventeenth century.

Lent

Between Glavni and the Drava River, the streets become narrow and uneven, as you enter the oldest part of town, **Lent**, which hosts myriad open-air events during the Lent festival in late June each year, comprising two entertaining weeks of street theatre, dance performances and jazz, rock and classical concerts. It is here that the world's oldest productive vine, a protected national monument, grows majestically outside the **Old Vine House** (daily: May–Sept 10am–8pm; Oct–April 10am–6pm; free). Inside, a small exhibition complements the range of top-quality, reasonably priced local vintages, some of which you can taste (€4 for three samples).

Pohorje

Just a short bus ride (#6 to vzpenjača; €1.10) or cycle southwest from the centre is the sprawling **Pohorje** mountain range. Take the hourly cable car (daily 8am–8pm; €6 return) up the slope, where – depending on the season – you can hike, mountain bike, horseride and ski, or simply sit and admire the glorious views of Maribor and the countryside surrounding it. The website ⓦ mariborskopohorje.si has detailed information on activities in the area.

ARRIVAL AND DEPARTURE

By train Partizanska cesta 50. Turn left out of the exit and the road curves directly into the town centre. Left luggage lockers €2–3/24hr.

Destinations Ljubljana (every 1–2hr; 1hr 50min–2hr 30min); Graz, Austria (2 daily; 1hr); Ptuj (8 daily; 45min–1hr); Vienna, Austria (2 daily; 3hr 40min).

By bus Mlinska ulica 1 (just off Partizanska cesta).

Destinations Ljubljana (4 daily; 3hr); Ptuj (every 30–45min; 40min).

INFORMATION

Tourist office Partizanska cesta 6a, next to the Franciscan church (April–Oct Mon–Fri 9am–7pm, Sat & Sun 9am–5pm; Nov–March Mon–Fri 9am–7pm, Sat 10am–5pm; ☎ 02 234 6611, ⓦ maribor-pohorje.si). They rent out bikes (€5/3hr, €10/day) and provide helpful cycling maps to explore the vineyards. There is free wi-fi in public spaces throughout the city.

ACCOMMODATION

The tourist office can book private accommodation (from €20/person).

Hostel Pekarna Ob železnici 16 ☎ 059 180 880, ⓦ mkc -hostelpekarna.si. Part of Maribor's foremost alternative cultural centre, this sparky hostel in Tabor (on the south side of the Drava) offers four-bed dorms as well as studio rooms and apartments. Breakfast included and free bike rental. Dorms €̶2̶1̶, doubles €̶5̶4̶

Tavas Hostel Vetrinjska ulica 5 ☎ 040 894 492. Small, very basic, but very clean hostel smack-bang in the centre of the city, with a ten-bed dorm and one apartment (sleeping two or three), shared bathroom facilities and kitchen for use. Dorms €̶1̶7̶

EATING AND DRINKING

★ **Bistro Arty** Slovenska ulica 20. Easy to spot by virtue of the row of colourful potted plants lining the windowsill, this delightful, veggie-oriented café serves the likes of dandelion soup and garlic pie €5. Mon–Fri 7am–6pm, Sat 7am–3pm.

Gril Ranca Dravska 10. Down in the riverside Lent district, this is fast food Serbian style, with *čevapčiči* and *pljeskavica* grilled meats (€6) comprising pretty much the entire menu. Cheap, filling and very tasty. Mon–Sat 11am–11pm.

KGB Vojašniški trg 5 ⓦ klub-kgb.si. The most popular joint in Maribor, this lively underground cellar bar attracts all ages, with an eclectic programme of regular live music. Mon–Sat 7pm–2am.

Satchmo Jazz Klub Strossmayerjeva ulica 6 ⓦ satchmo .si. Hosts high-calibre jazz and rock sessions, but also ideal for a mellow drinking session. Tues–Thurs 7pm–3am, Fri & Sat 7pm–5am.

31

31

Takos Mesarski prehod 3. Tucked away on a cobbled alley, this cheap-and-cheerful Mexican also serves cocktails, becoming a club at weekends. Mon, Wed & Thurs 11am–10pm, Tues, Fri & Sat 11am–3am.

PTUJ

PTUJ is arguably Slovenia's most attractive town, rising up from the Drava valley in a flutter of red roofs, and topped by a charming castle. The streets themselves are the main attraction, with scaled-down mansions standing shoulder to shoulder on scaled-down boulevards, and medieval fantasies crumbling next to Baroque extravagances.

WHAT TO SEE AND DO

Ptuj's main street is **Prešernova ulica**, an atmospheric thoroughfare which snakes along the base of the castle-topped hill. At its eastern end is **Slovenski Trg**, home to a fine-looking sixteenth-century bell tower (though now just a souvenir shop) and the **Church of St George**, dating from the twelfth century, with an interior distinguished by some spectacular frescoes. At either end of Prešernova, cobbled paths wind up to the **castle** – featuring an agglomeration of architectural styles from the fourteenth to the eighteenth centuries – which now houses the carefully presented collections of the **Ptuj Regional Museum** (daily: May to mid-Oct 9am–6pm; mid-Oct to April 9am–5pm; €5). There's much to take in, including Baroque tapestries, a Turqueries collection (paintings with Turkish motifs), and a marvellous assemblage of musical instruments, but the real highlight is the colourful display of *kurenti* masks, which appear each February as part of the Kurent carnival, one of the country's most celebrated events.

ARRIVAL AND DEPARTURE

By train The station is on Osojnikova cesta, a 5min walk northeast of town.

Destinations Ljubljana (2 daily; 2hr 25min); Maribor (8 daily; 1hr).
By bus The station is 200m from the train station.
Destinations Maribor (every 45min–1hr; 45min).

INFORMATION

Tourist information Slovenski trg 5 (daily: May–Sept 9am–8pm; Oct–April 9am–6pm; ☎ 02 779 6011, ⓦ ptuj .info). The Centre for Free Time Activities, just across from the bus station in the modern buildings at Osojnikova 9 (Mon–Fri 9am–6pm; ☎ 02 780 5540, ⓦ cid.si), is also super helpful.

ACCOMMODATION

Hostel Sonce Zagrebška cesta 10 ☎ 031 361 982, ⓦ hostel-sonce.com. Very neat and very bright family-run hostel a 5min walk from the centre, across the river; all rooms (from singles up to five-bed dorms) are en suite and come with TV and a/c. Breakfast €3. Dorms **€25**
★ **Musikafe** Vrazov trg 1 ☎ 02 787 8860, ⓦ muzikafe.si. Seven beautifully conceived rooms brimming with colour and creativity in this warm and welcoming B&B. Breakfast included. Doubles **€52**
Terme Ptuj Pot v Toplice ☎ 02 749 4100, ⓦ sava-hotels -resorts.com. Across the river, 2km west of town, this pleasant resort-style campsite also has enormous wine barrels that have been ingeniously converted into pod-like accommodation; guests can also use the on-site Thermal Park pools and saunas. Camping/person **€14.30**, wine-barrel glamping **€66**

EATING AND DRINKING

Gostilna PP Novi trg 2. Cheap and very cheerful canteen-style joint knocking up fast and filling daily specials, though it's best known for its local chicken dishes (€4–5). Mon–Fri 7am–6pm, Sat 7am–4pm.
★ **Musikafe** Vrazov trg 1. Wonderful hangout that combines an inviting stone terrace with a richly painted, retro furnished interior where you can chill out to an eclectic playlist. Superb live music in both the garden (summer) and cellar (winter). Daily 8am–11pm, Fri & Sat till midnight.
Ribič Dravska ulica 9. The exceptional seafood at this riverside restaurant with a lovely terrace overlooking the Drava justifies the slightly higher price tag, which is typically around €12–15 a dish. Tues–Thurs & Sun 10am–10pm, Fri & Sat 10am–11pm.

MUSEO GUGGENHEIM, BILBAO

Spain

HIGHLIGHTS

❶ **Madrid** World-class museums and legendary nightlife. **See p.1003**

❷ **Alhambra, Granada** Evocative Moorish palace atop this charming Andalucian city. **See p.1037**

❸ **Barcelona** Perhaps Europe's most alluring city. **See p.1053**

❹ **San Sebastián** Stunning beaches and mouth-watering cuisine. **See p.1072**

❺ **Museo Guggenheim, Bilbao** The building is as big an attraction as the art it houses. **See p.1074**

❻ **Santiago de Compostela** The end point of Europe's most famous pilgrim trail. **See p.1079**

HIGHLIGHTS ARE MARKED ON THE MAP ON P.999

ROUGH COSTS

Daily budget Basic €65; occasional treat €85

Drink €1.70–2.50 per *caña* (small beer)

Food *Menú del día* €10–12

Hostel/budget hotel €16–35/€35–80

Travel Madrid–Barcelona: bus €32–43; train €60–125

FACT FILE

Population 47.3 million

Languages Spanish, Catalan, Basque, Galician, Aranese

Currency Euro (€)

Capital Madrid

International phone code ☏ 34

Time zone GMT +1hr

Introduction

Spain has so much more to offer than the clichés of bullfights, crowded beaches, paella and flamenco. You don't have to travel for very long to discover ancient castles, world-class museums, idyllic whitewashed villages, isolated coves and beaches, and a wealth of art and architecture. The separate kingdoms that made up the original Spanish nation are still very evident today, encompassing a medley of languages, cultures and traditions.

Of the regions, vibrant **Catalunya** in the northeast is fiercely independent of spirit; the fishing region of **Galicia** in the northwest a seafood lover's dream; the **Basque country** a remarkable contrast between post-industrial depression and world-class architecture and food; and **Castilla y León** and the **south** still, somehow, quintessentially "Spanish". There are definite highlights: the three great cities of **Barcelona**, **Madrid** and **Seville**; the Moorish monuments of **Andalucía** in the south and the Christian ones of **Castilla y León** in the west; beach life on the island of **Ibiza**, the **Costa del Sol** or on the more deserted Costa de la Luz near **Cádiz**; some of the best trekking in Europe in the **Pyrenees**, and winter sports in **Andorra**.

Spain can be visited all year round, though Madrid, Extremadura and parts of Andalucía get unbearably hot in summer. Depending on what you're after, you can party at local festivals, engage in all manner of outdoor pursuits, sample the regional specialities, take in the varied architecture that traces Spain's multicultural heritage and enjoy some of Europe's best nightlife. The country recently suffered crippling financial woes, and although the economy is picking up, youth unemployment remains high. However, this has done little to dampen the nation's spirits: town centres remain buzzing with life, and Spain's enthusiasm for sport remains as strong as ever.

CHRONOLOGY

1000 BC Phoenicians colonize the Iberian Peninsula, establishing the cities of Cádiz and Málaga.
400s BC Carthaginians exert power over large parts of present-day Spain.
200s BC The Romans capture "Hispania" during the Punic Wars and rule it for over 500 years.
711 AD The Islamic Moors conquer Spain, and Moorish culture flourishes.
1085 With the capture of Toledo, Spanish Christians begin to diminish the influence of the Moors in Spain.
1480 The Spanish Inquisition persecutes non-Christians, leading to mass conversions and expulsion of Jews.
1492 Christopher Columbus discovers lands in the Americas for the Spanish Crown.
1605 The world's first "novel", *Don Quixote* by Cervantes, is published.
1714 The British capture Gibraltar.
1800s Spanish colonies in the Americas gain their independence.
1931 Surrealist artist Salvador Dalí completes arguably his most famous painting, *The Persistence of Memory*.
1936 The Spanish Civil War breaks out as Nationalist forces led by General Franco defeat Republican forces.
1939 Spain remains neutral at the outbreak of World War II.
1975 Franco dies and is replaced by King Juan Carlos.
1977 First free elections are held in almost four decades.
2004 Bombs detonated on busy Madrid trains leave 191 people dead. An Islamic group takes responsibility.
2007 The government's struggle with Basque separatists, ETA, continues as the group end their ceasefire.
2008 Spain's construction boom brought to an end by international financial meltdown, and unemployment soars from 6 percent to 20 percent.
2010 Spain wins the FIFA World Cup.
2013 Spain's unemployment rate climbs to record high, with 55 percent of under-30s out of work.
2014 King Juan Carlos abdicates in favour of his son, Felipe VI.

ARRIVAL AND DEPARTURE

The quickest – and cheapest – way to get to Spain is on one of the budget-airline **flights** (Vueling, easyJet, Ryanair and Norwegian Air). All major airlines serve Barcelona and Madrid. Other major

HIGHLIGHTS

1. Madrid
2. Alhambra, Granada
3. Barcelona
4. San Sebastián
5. Museo Guggenheim, Bilbao
6. Santiago de Compostela

32

airports include Alicante, Málaga, Valencia, Seville and Mallorca. **Trains** from France serve San Sebastián (from Biarritz), Barcelona (from Toulouse and Perpignan) and Girona (from Perpignan), while trains from Portugal run from Lisbon to Madrid via Cáceres and from Porto to Santiago de Compostela. Regular **ferries** from Morocco serve the ports of Algeciras, Gibraltar and Tarifa.

GETTING AROUND

Spain's public transport is budget traveller-friendly. While the high-speed trains are often more comfortable than buses for longer journeys, they are significantly more expensive.

BY TRAIN

RENFE (⊛renfe.es) operates three types of train: *cercanías* (local commuter trains); *media distancia* (intercity trains); and *larga distancia* (long-distance) trains, which include the high-speed *AVE* (routes connect Madrid with Alicante,

Barcelona, Córdoba, Málaga and Seville) and *Euromed* (Valencia–Barcelona) trains, and the somewhat slower *Talgo* (Valencia–Alicante and Murcia) and *Alvia* (Madrid–Bilbao). To avoid queuing, buy tickets online from the RENFE website and print the ticket out at the station. Return fares (*ida y vuelta*) often get a ten to twenty percent discount, as do advance online bookings. **InterRail** and **Eurail** passes are valid on all RENFE trains and also on *Euromed*; supplements are charged on the fastest trains. Book well in advance, especially at weekends and holidays. The InterRail Spain Pass is only worth it if you're planning on a lot of train travel within a short space of time.

BY BUS

Alsa (⊛alsa.es) is the biggest **bus** company, covering most of the country. There are regular services between major cities, and many smaller villages are accessible only by bus. In some cases it is faster to take the bus than a regional train. Frequency is reduced on Sundays

ON YOUR BIKE

Though few large Spanish cities have cycle lanes, Spain is becoming more bicycle friendly, with **public bicycle** systems introduced in cities such as Barcelona, Madrid, Seville, Valencia, Mérida and Zaragoza; dozens of pick-up/drop-off points are scattered around the streets.

and holidays. For long-distance buses, you can buy your ticket in advance online, which is often cheaper.

BY BOAT

Regular ferries and hydrofoils connect mainland Spain to the Balearic Islands and Tangier, Ceuta and Melilla. Acciona Trasmediterránea (⊛trasmediterranea.es) is the main national ferry company; you can book seats or sleeping berths for its fast, modern passenger ferries. The Balearic Islands are served by Baleària (⊛balearia.com) and Iscomar (⊛www.iscomar.com) ferries.

ACCOMMODATION

Book accommodation well in advance if planning on staying during a festival. Prices in popular areas drop considerably in low season.

HOTELS AND HOSTELS

There are several types of budget accommodation available. **Pensiones** (P) are simple guesthouses without breakfast, most rooms sharing a bathroom. Slightly more expensive are **hostales** (H) – budget hotels – offering single and double rooms, mostly en suite. Madrid, Barcelona and other big cities have a large network of centrally located independent **hostels** with a full range of facilities, such as guest kitchens and tour booking. Beds are generally €20–35. HI-affiliated **youth hostels** (*albergues juveniles*; ⊛reaj.com) can be inconveniently located and are sometimes block-reserved by school groups. At €17–27 per person (more without an HI card), they offer basic accommodation in dorms, usually including breakfast. These options generally offer free wi-fi.

CASAS RURALES, CAMPING AND REFUGIOS

Nationwide, **agroturismo** (⊛agroturismo rural.com) and **casa rural** programmes offer cheap accommodation in rural areas. A room in a private house costs around €40 for a double, and €25 for a single. Tourist offices have full lists. There are hundreds of **campsites** throughout Spain, charging around €6 per person plus the same for a tent; see ⊛vaya camping.net. In popular mountain areas, particularly on the Camino de Santiago pilgrim trail, you'll find *refugios* (mountain shelters) offering dorm-style accommodation on a first-come, first-served basis (€10–15 per night). Some have a cooking area and/or serve hot meals; bring your own bedding and cooking equipment.

FOOD AND DRINK

Bars and cafés are best for **breakfast**, which can consist of *churros con chocolate* (tubular deep-fried doughnuts dipped in thick drinking chocolate), *tostadas* (toast), or *tortilla* (omelette). **Coffee** and **pastries** are on offer at the many excellent *pastelerías* and *confiterías*, while *bocadillos* (sandwiches) are available everywhere. *Tabernas, tascas, bodegas, cervecerías* and bars all serve **tapas** or *pintxos*: tiny sandwiches, mini portions of meat, *tortilla* or fried potatoes with *alioli* for €1.50–4.50 a plate; the most elaborate tapas are found in the Basque country. Their big brothers, **raciones** (€8–16), make a meal in themselves. Most restaurants offer a weekday lunchtime two- or three-course meal, *menú del día* (€10–13), or *platos combinados* (€7–10), a single dish such as meat with fries and a side of salad, drink included. **Fish** and **seafood** are excellent, particularly regional specialities such as Galician fish stew (*zarzuela*), grilled octopus and *gambas a la plancha* (grilled prawns). Spain's most famous dish is the rice-based paella, which can be made with seafood, meat and vegetables. There's also *fideuá* (similar to paella but made with vermicelli instead of rice), especially popular in Valencia and Alicante. Andalucía's staples include *gazpacho* and *salmorejo* – cold summer soups – with Granada and Almería adding North African food to the mix. Inland Spain is famous for its *carnes asados* (roasted meats), hearty stews and delicious **cured meats** – particularly *jamón iberico de bellota* – a highly prized dry-cured ham. Big cities cater best to **vegetarians**, while gourmets should make a beeline for the Basque country and Catalunya – the two regions responsible for some of the most adventurous cuisine in the world. San Sebastián in particular is known for its proliferation of bars serving imaginative tapas.

DRINK

Wine (*vino*) – *tinto* (red), *blanco* (white) or *rosado* (rosé) – is generally good quality. The best reds are Rioja and Ribera, while Catalunya and Galicia produce the best whites (Penedès or Peralada and Albariño respectively); Catalunya is also home to *cava* – a sparkling white wine that's champagne in everything but name. Vino de Jerez, Andalucían **sherry**, is served chilled and available in *fino/manzanilla* (dry), *amontillado* (medium) or *oloroso/dulce* (sweet) varieties. *Cerveza*, lager-type **beer**, includes Mahou, San Miguel, Cruzcampo, Alhambra and Estrella. In bars, you usually order a *caña* (small glass) of beer with your tapas. *Tinto de verano* (red wine spritzer) is a popular summer drink. **Sangría**, a red wine-and-fruit punch, and **sidra**, a dry cider most typical in Asturia and the Basque Country, are well worth sampling. **Coffee** is invariably espresso, unless you specify *cortado* (with a drop of milk), *con leche* (a more generous amount) or *americano* (weaker black coffee). **Tea** is drunk black, though you can order it *con la leche aparte*, and most eating establishments offer *infusiones* (herbal teas).

CULTURE AND ETIQUETTE

Lunch is usually eaten between 2 and 4pm and dinner from 8.30pm. In the largest Spanish cities, a lot of shops, tourist offices and restaurants stay open all day, whereas smaller towns and especially villages are dead between 2 and 5pm. **Tipping** is not the norm; ten percent in restaurants is considered generous. When paying by credit/debit card in shops, you may need photo ID.

SPORTS AND ACTIVITIES

The beaches on the south coast are the best for **swimming**, while the north coast (and Spain's southernmost tip) are ideal for watersports such as **windsurfing** and **surfing**: Playa de Zurriola in San Sebastián is a popular choice, as is Santander's Sardinero beach. Tarifa, at the southernmost tip of Spain, is a year-round paradise for kitesurfers and windsurfers. The Mediterranean waters of Costa Brava and Costa del Sol, as well as the Balearic Islands, offer numerous good scuba-diving and snorkelling spots. Whitewater junkies can head to Catalunya's Noguera Pallaresa River or Cantabria's Carasa River for kayaking and rafting. There are great paragliding destinations along the Mediterranean coast and in Aragón. The Aragonese Pyrenees, Picos de Europa and the Sierra Nevada, in Andalucía, are excellent in winter for **skiing** and equally good for **hiking** in summer. The **Camino de Santiago** (see box, p.1079) makes a superb long-distance hike or bike ride. Spain has numerous scenic and challenging cycling options throughout the country, including *bici todo terreno* (off-road tracks for mountain bikes).

SPECTATOR SPORTS

A match at Real Madrid's Estadio Santiago Bernabéu is a must for any **football** fan (☏913 984 300, ⊛realmadrid.es), as is a game at the Camp Nou, FC Barcelona's 100,000-seater stadium (☏902 189 900, ⊛fcbarcelona.com). For something quite different, try the electrifying spectacle of **bull running** (or *encierros*), the most famous of which take place every July in Pamplona during the Fiesta de San Fermín (see box, p.1071). While **bullfighting** remains a subject of great passion in Madrid and Andalucía (particularly in Seville, Málaga and Ronda), its popularity is waning with

32

32

EMERGENCY NUMBERS

For the police, ambulance services or fire brigade, call ☎112.

the younger generation, and it has been outlawed in Catalunya since 2012.

COMMUNICATIONS

Post offices (*correos*) are open Monday to Friday 8.30am to 8.30pm (with a siesta break in smaller towns), Saturday 9am to 1pm. In larger cities, there are also lots of discount call centres (*locutorios*). Alternatively, buying a prepaid SIM card is inexpensive. The international access code is ☎00, the Spain country code is ☎34 and local area codes are incorporated into the phone numbers. Free **wi-fi** is common, so internet cafés are now rare.

EMERGENCIES

Violent crime is rare, but watch out for pickpockets and scam artists. Be particularly vigilant around market areas, on public transport and during fiestas. Report robberies to the **Policía Nacionál**; you can report your loss by phone (☎902 102112) or online under *Denuncias* at ⓦpolicia.es. For minor **health** complaints, go to a pharmacy (*farmacia*). In more serious cases, head to *Urgencias* at the nearest **hospital**, or get the address of an English-speaking doctor from the *farmacia* or tourist office.

INFORMATION

The **Spanish National Tourist Office** (*Oficina de Turismo*) has a branch in

STUDENT AND YOUTH DISCOUNTS

Most museums and attractions offer a student or under-26 discount, which can give a significant reduction or even free entry. To make the most of these, buy an **ISIC** (International Student) or **IYTC** (International Youth) card. For more information see ⓦisiccard.com. Many museums also have free entry on Sundays.

SPAIN ONLINE

ⓦ**spain.info** Comprehensive website of the Spanish tourist board.
ⓦ**guiadelocio.com** Nationwide restaurant and entertainment listings, updated weekly (in Spanish only).
ⓦ**tourspain.org** Useful site for visitors, with city guides and accommodation listings.

virtually every major town, giving away city maps and brochures. There are also provincial or regional *Turismos*, which stock information on the entire province.

MONEY AND BANKS

Spain's **currency** is the euro (€). **Banks** have branches in all but the smallest towns, open Monday to Friday 8.30am to 2pm; some are also open Saturday 9am to 1pm. In tourist areas, you'll also find **casas de cambio**, with more convenient hours, but worse exchange rates. **ATMs** (*cajeros automáticos*) are widespread, and all major credit cards are accepted in most shops, restaurants and hotels.

OPENING HOURS AND HOLIDAYS

Shops **open** Monday to Saturday 9am to 8pm; in Madrid and Barcelona some open for a shorter time on Sunday. Smaller towns and cities take a **siesta** between 2 and 5pm. Tapas bars are typically open from lunchtime until late, while restaurants are typically open 1–4pm and 8–11pm or 1–11pm, with many closed on Sunday evenings and on Mondays. In nightclubs, things only really get going after midnight. Shops and banks are closed on the following national public holidays (plus local ones): January 1 and 6, Maundy Thursday and Good Friday, May 1, August 15, October 12, November 1, December 6, 8, 24 and 25.

FESTIVALS

Each town and city celebrates its own annual **fiesta** in honour of its patron saint. Don't miss: the decadent **Carnaval** in Cádiz (Feb/March); Valencia's **Las**

SPANISH

	SPANISH	PRONUNCIATION
Yes	*Sí*	See
No	*No*	Noh
Please	*Por favor*	Por fahvor
Thank you	*Gracias*	Grath-yass
Hello/Good day	*Hola*	Ola
Goodbye	*Adiós*	Ad-yoss
Excuse me	*Con permiso*	Con pairmeeso
Sorry (strong)	*Lo siento*	Loh see-en-toh
Sorry (mild)	*Perdón*	Pear-don
Where?	*¿Donde?*	¿Donday?
Good	*Bueno*	Bwaynoh
Bad	*Malo*	Maloh
Near	*Próximo*	Prox-eemo
Far	*Lejos*	Layhoss
Cheap	*Barato*	Bar-ahto
Expensive	*Caro*	Cahro
Open	*Abierto*	Ahb-yairto
Closed	*Cerrado*	Thairrado
Today	*Hoy*	Oy
Yesterday	*Ayer*	A-yair
Tomorrow	*Mañana*	Man-yana
Toilet	*Aseo/baño*	Ahseyoh/ bahnio
I don't eat meat	*No como carne*	Noh cohmoh carnay
The bill	*La cuenta*	Lah kwentah
How much is…?	*¿Cuánto cuesta…?*	¿Kwanto kwesta…?
What time is it?	*¿Tiene la hora?*	¿Tee-eynay-la ora?
Do you speak English?	*¿Habla inglés?*	¿Ahblah eenglays?
Where is…?	*¿Dónde está…?*	¿Don-des-ta…?
I don't understand	*No entiendo*	Noh ent-yendo
I would like…	*Quisiera…*	Ki-si-yeah-ra…
One	*Un/Uno*	Oon/Oon-oh
Two	*Dos*	Doss
Three	*Tres*	Tress
Four	*Cuatro*	Kwatro
Five	*Cinco*	Theenko
Six	*Seis*	Say-eess
Seven	*Siete*	See-ettay
Eight	*Ocho*	Oh-cho
Nine	*Nueve*	Nwa-vay
Ten	*Diez*	Dee-yeth

32

Fallas (March 15–19) – processions, fireworks and carousing around the clock; **Semana Santa** (week leading up to Easter Sunday) in Seville, Málaga and Córdoba – spectacular processions, feasting and fireworks, followed by Seville's **Feria de Abril** (late April); Pamplona's **San Fermín** festival (second week of July) – the famous running of the bulls; or **La Tomatina** in Buñol, near Valencia (second to last or last Wed in Aug) – messy fun with tomatoes.

Madrid

When Philip II moved the seat of government to **MADRID** in 1561 his aim was to create a symbol of Spanish unification and centralization. Given its lack of natural advantages, such as a sea port, and extreme temperatures in winter and summer, it was only the determination of successive rulers to promote a strong central capital that ensured its success.

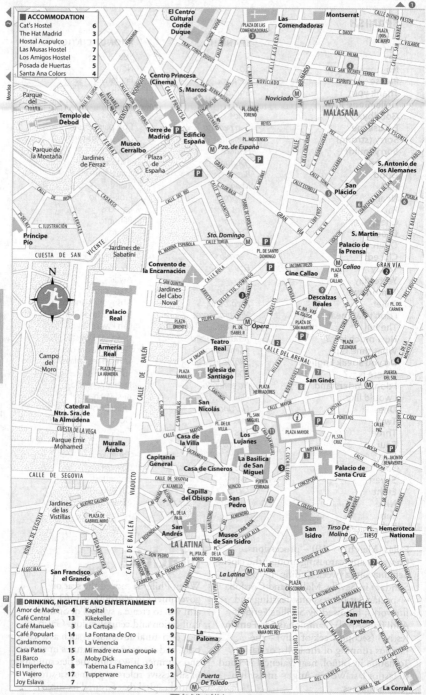

ACCOMMODATION

Cat's Hostel	6
The Hat Madrid	3
Hostal Acapulco	1
Las Musas Hostel	7
Los Amigos Hostel	2
Posada de Huertas	5
Santa Ana Colors	4

32

DRINKING, NIGHTLIFE AND ENTERTAINMENT

Amor de Madre	4	Kapital	19
Café Central	13	Kikekeller	6
Café Manuela	3	La Cartuja	10
Café Popular	9	La Fontana de Oro	14
Cardamomo	11	La Venencia	12
Casa Patas	15	Mi madre era una groupie	16
El Barco	5	Moby Dick	1
El Imperfecto	8	Taberna La Flamenca 3.0	18
El Viajero	17	Tupperware	2
Joy Eslava	7		

Estadio Vicente Calderón

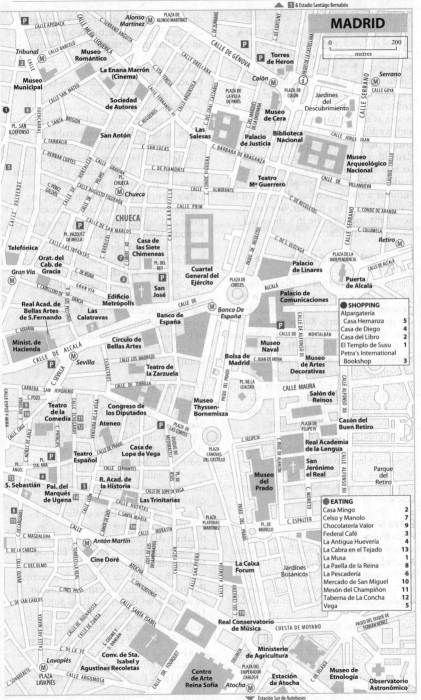

MADRID

0   200
metres

& Estadio Santiágo Bernabéu

Alonso Martínez
PLAZA DE ALONSO MARTÍNEZ
Tribunal
Museo Romántico
La Enana Marrón (Cinema)
Museo Municipal
Sociedad de Autores
San Antón
Torres de Heron
Colón
PLAZA DE LA VILLA DE PARÍS
Museo de Cera
Jardines del Descubrimiento
Serrano
Las Salesas
Palacio de Justicia
Biblioteca Nacional
Museo Arqueológico Nacional
Chueca
CHUECA
Teatro Mª Guerrero
Telefónica
Casa de las Siete Chimeneas
Orat. del Cab. de Gracia
Gran Vía
Palacio de Linares
Retiro
Edificio Metrópolis
San José
Cuartel General del Ejército
Puerta de Alcalá
Real Acad. de Bellas Artes de S.Fernando
Las Calatravas
Banco de España
Palacio de Comunicaciones
Minist. de Hacienda
Sevilla
Círculo de Bellas Artes
Banco De España
Museo Naval
Museo de Artes Decorativas
Teatro de la Zarzuela
Bolsa de Madrid
Salón de Reinos
Teatro de la Comedia
Congreso de los Diputados
Ateneo
Museo Thyssen-Bornemisza
Casón del Buen Retiro
Teatro Español
Casa de Lope de Vega
R. Acad. de la Historia
Real Academia de la Lengua
San Jerónimo el Real
Parque del Retiro
S. Sebastián
Pal. del Marqués de Ugena
Las Trinitarias
Museo del Prado
Antón Martín
Cine Doré
La Caixa Forum
Jardines Botánicos
Real Conservatorio de Música
Lavapiés
Conv. de Sta. Isabel y Agustinas Recoletas
Ministerio de Agricultura
Museo de Etnología
Centro de Arte Reina Sofía
Estación de Atocha
Observatorio Astronómico
Atocha

Estación Sur de Autobuses

32

● **SHOPPING**
Alpargatería	
Casa Hernanza	5
Casa de Diego	4
Casa del Libro	2
El Templo de Susu	1
Petra's International Bookshop	3

● **EATING**
Casa Mingo	2
Celso y Manolo	7
Chocolatería Valor	9
Federal Café	3
La Antigua Huevería	4
La Cabra en el Tejado	13
La Musa	1
La Paella de la Reina	8
La Pescadería	6
Mercado de San Miguel	10
Mesón del Champiñón	11
Taberna de La Concha	12
Vega	5

WHAT TO SEE AND DO

Today, Madrid's streets are a beguiling mix of old and new, with narrow, atmospheric alleys and wide, open boulevards. It is also home to some of Spain's best art, from the Museo del Prado's world-renowned classical collection, to the impressive modern works at the Reina Sofía. Galleries and sights aside, much of Madrid's charm comes from immersing yourself in the daily life of the city and tapping into its frenetic energy: hanging out in the traditional cafés and *chocolaterías* or the summer *terrazas*, packing the lanes of the Sunday Rastro flea market, or playing very hard and very late in a thousand bars, clubs and discos.

Puerta del Sol and the Plaza de Cíbeles

Central **Puerta del Sol** is officially the centre of the nation: a stone slab in the pavement outside the main building on the south side marks **Kilómetro Zero**, from where six of Spain's *Rutas Nacionales* (National Routes) begin. The city's emblem, a statue of a bear pawing a *madroño* bush, lies on the northeast side. To the west, c/Arenal heads directly towards the Teatro Real and Palacio Real, but there's more of interest along **c/Mayor**, one of Madrid's oldest thoroughfares, which runs southwest through the heart of the medieval city. Down c/Alcalá to the east, the Cibeles fountain is the unofficial bathing spot for Real Madrid fans, who congregate here to celebrate their team's victories.

Plaza Mayor

Plaza Mayor is one of the most important architectural and historical landmarks in Madrid and the centrepiece of Madrileño life for centuries. In this beautiful seventeenth-century square, *autos-da-fé* (trials of faith) and executions were held by the Inquisition, kings were crowned, demonstrations, festivals and bullfights staged. These events were watched by up to 50,000 spectators and by royalty from the frescoed **Real Casa de la Panadería** (Royal Bakery). Today, the plaza is a pleasant but expensive place to have a

drink. In summer, it's an outdoor theatre and music stage; in autumn, a book fair, and a Christmas market in mid-December.

Palacio Real

Palacio Real, or Royal Palace, on C de Bailén (daily 10am–8pm; €11; ⓜpatrimonionacional.es; ⓂÓpera), built after the earlier Muslim Alcázar burned down in 1734, was the principal royal residence until Alfonso XIII went into exile in 1931, but is now used only on state occasions. The building, which claims more rooms than any other European palace, features a **library** with one of the biggest collections of books, manuscripts, maps and musical scores in the world; an **armoury** with an unrivalled and often bizarre collection of weapons dating back to the fifteenth century, including armour for war horses and children; and an original **pharmacy** – a curious mixture of alchemist's den and early laboratory. Take your time to contemplate the extraordinary opulence of the place: acres of Flemish and Spanish tapestries, endless Rococo decoration, bejewelled clocks and pompous portraits of the monarchs.

The Gran Vía

Central Plaza de España, home to the statues of Cervantes, Don Quixote and Sancho Panza, joins **Gran Vía**, once the capital's major thoroughfare, which effectively divides the old city to the south from the newer parts. Permanently crowded with shoppers and sightseers, the street is appropriately named, with quirky Art Nouveau and Art Deco facades fronting its banks, offices and apartments, and huge posters on the theatres. At the beginning of the street, by the magnificent cylindrical **Edificio Metropolis**, it joins with c/Alcalá on the approach to Plaza de Cibeles. Just across the junction is the majestic old **Círculo de Bellas Artes** (museum Tues–Sun 10am–3pm; €4, free Wed; ⓦcirculo bellasartes.com; ⓂSevilla), a cultural centre for up-and-coming artists which also boasts a roof terrace bar with the best views of Madrid (Azotea; Mon–Thurs 9am–11pm, Fri 9am–2am, Sat & Sun 11am–2am; €4).

MADRID FOR FREE

You can see most of Madrid's top sights for free, as long as you time your visits carefully. Get there before the free opening times, or you'll have to contend with crowds. Free entry is as follows: **Museo Nacional Centro de Arte Reina Sofía** (Mon, Wed–Sat 7–9pm, Sun 1.30–7pm; always free to university students); **Museo del Prado** (Mon–Sat 6–8pm, Sun & hols 5–8pm; always free to under-25 EU students); **Museo Thyssen-Bornemisza** (Mon noon–4pm); **Palacio Real** (Mon–Thurs last 2hr of opening for EU citizens). Many other sights also offer reduced rates for students or people under 26. You can also take a free city tour (donations welcome; ⓦnewmadrid-tours.com), which departs several times daily from the Plaza Mayor.

Museo del Prado

Madrid's **Museo del Prado**, on Paseo del Prado (Mon–Sat 10am–8pm, Sun 10am–7pm; €14/27.20 combined ticket with Museo Thyssen-Bornemisza and Centro de Arte Reina Sofía; ⓦmuseodelprado.es; ⓜAtocha), has been one of Europe's key art galleries ever since it opened in 1819. It holds a collection of over 8600 paintings, including the world's finest collections of Goya, Velázquez, Rubens and Bosch. The central downstairs gallery houses the **early Spanish collection**, and a dazzling array of portraits and religious paintings by El Greco, among them his mystic and hallucinatory *Crucifixion* and *Adoration of the Shepherds*. Beyond this are the Prado's **Italian** treasures: superb Titian portraits of Charles V and Philip II, as well as works by Tintoretto, Bassano, Caravaggio and Veronese. Upstairs are Goya's unmissable *Pinturas negras* (*Black Paintings*), so called due to their dark hues and the distorted appearance of their subjects, hinting at the artist's unsettled state of mind. The outstanding presence among Spanish painters is Velázquez – among the collection are intimate portraits of the family of Felipe IV, most famously his masterpiece *Las Meninas*.

Museo Thyssen-Bornemisza

The **Museo Thyssen-Bornemisza** (Mon noon–4pm, Tues–Sun 10am–7pm; €12; ⓦmuseothyssen.org; ⓜBanco de España) occupies the grand Palacio de Villahermosa, diagonally opposite the Prado. Acquired by the state in 1993, this was perhaps the world's greatest private art collection, belonging to the late Baron Thyssen-Bornemisza. There are important works from every major period and movement: from Duccio and Holbein, through El Greco and Caravaggio, to Schiele and Rothko; from a strong showing of nineteenth-century Americans to some very early and very late Van Goghs; and side-by-side hangings of parallel Cubist studies by Picasso, Braque and Mondrian.

Museo Nacional Centro de Arte Reina Sofía

As well as the collection of twentieth-century art, the **Museo Nacional Centro de Arte Reina Sofía**, at c/Santa Isabel 52 (Mon & Wed–Sat 10am–9pm, Sun 10am–7pm; €8; ⓦmuseoreinasofia.es; ⓜAtocha), features a cinema, excellent art and design bookshops, a print, music and photographic library and edgy temporary exhibitions. However, it is **Picasso's Guernica** – his signature Cubism piece – that most visitors come to see, and rightly so. Superbly displayed along with its preliminary studies, this icon of twentieth-century Spanish art and politics – a response to the Fascist bombing of the Basque town of Guernica in the Spanish Civil War – carries a shock that defies all familiarity. Other halls are devoted to **Dalí** and Surrealism, early twentieth-century Spanish artists

32

STAYING COOL

With Madrid often unbearably hot In summer, sometimes there's only one thing for it – taking refuge in one of the city's open-air **swimming pools**. Usually open from June to August, the largest of them is in Casa de Campo (daily 11am–8.30pm; €6; ⓜLago). Search for *"piscinas aire libre"* at ⓦmadrid.es for others, or ask at the tourist office.

including **Miró** and post-World War II figurative art, mapping the beginning of abstraction through to Pop and avant-garde.

The Rastro

The **Rastro flea market** (Sun 8am–3pm) is as much a part of Madrid's weekend ritual as a Mass or a *paseo*. The stalls sprawl south from ⓜ La Latina to the Ronda de Toledo, selling everything from flamenco records to imitation designer gear to old photos of Madrid. Expect a great atmosphere, but you'll have to search hard for bargains among the junk. Keep a tight grip on your possessions. Afterwards, while away the afternoon in the bars and *terrazas* around Puerta de Moros.

Parque del Buen Retiro and Parque del Oeste

The most central and most popular of Madrid's parks is the **Parque del Buen Retiro** (daily: May–Sept 6am–midnight; until 11pm rest of the year; ⓜ Retiro or Ibiza) behind the Prado, a stunning mix of formal gardens and wilder spaces. You can row a boat, picnic, check out a travelling art exhibition at the beautiful **Palacio de Velázquez** and the nearby **Palacio de Cristal** and, above all, promenade like half of Madrid. You can also visit the "Hill of the Absents" – a mound constructed in memory of those who died in the Madrid bombing of 2004. Although charming by day, Retiro is best avoided at night. The **Parque del Oeste** on the city's western edge (ⓜ Ventura Rodríguez) boasts a genuine Egyptian temple – Templo de Debod, donated to Spain by Egyptian president Nasser in 1968 as a gesture of thanks to Spanish archeologists who saved it from the rising waters of Lake Nasser.

Estadio de Santiago Bernabéu

Even non-football fans may enjoy a tour of Real Madrid's Bernabéu stadium (non-match days Mon–Sat 10am–7pm, Sun 10.30am–6.30pm; match days closes 5hr before kickoff; €19; ⓦ realmadrid .com; ⓜ Santiago Bernabéu) in northern Madrid. With multimedia exhibitions charting the club's rich history, and visits to the trophy room, players' dugout and away team's dressing room, there's enough here to keep you entertained for a few hours. A café and restaurant overlooking the pitch serve reasonably priced meals. In summer, there's also an outdoor nightclub in the stadium, *La Terraza del Bernabéu* (€10 entry including a drink; drinks €12 thereafter).

ARRIVAL AND DEPARTURE

By plane Barajas airport (ⓦ www.aena.es), 15km northeast of the centre, is served by all major airlines from Europe, North and Latin America. To reach the city, metro line #8 runs to ⓜ Nuevos Ministerios (daily 6am–2am; 12min; €4.50). The fast, reliable 24hr Exprés Aeropuerto bus leaves terminals 1, 2 and 4 (every 15–35min; €5), stopping at c/O'Donnell, Plaza de Cibeles and Atocha (the last stop only between 6am and 11.30pm). AeroCITY minibuses (24hr; ☏ 917 477 570, ⓦ aerocity.com) drop passengers off door-to-door from €8–25.

By train In the north of the city, Estación de Chamartín is used by trains for the north and west of Spain. The more central Estación de Atocha serves the south and east of Spain.

Destinations from Chamartín Bilbao (4 daily; 5hr–6hr 30min); El Escorial (hourly; 55min); León (12 daily; 2hr 15min–4hr 30min); Salamanca (12 daily; 1hr 35min–3hr 5min); Santander (7 daily; 4hr 10min–7hr); Segovia (1–2 hourly; 30min–2hr 5min).

Destinations from Atocha Barcelona (25 daily; 2hr 30min–3hr 10min); Cáceres (4 daily; 3hr 40min–4hr 10min); Cádiz (10 daily; 3hr 55min–5hr 30min); Córdoba (1–2 hourly; 1hr 40min–2hr); Granada (2 daily; 4hr); Lisbon (1 daily; 10hr 30min); Málaga (12 daily; 2hr 20min–2hr 50min); Mérida (3 daily; 4hr 40min–5hr 10min); Pamplona (7 daily; 3hr–4hr 10min); Paris (5 daily; 10hr–12hr 30min, change in Barcelona); San Sebastián (6 daily; 5hr 20min–7hr 30min); Santiago de Compostela (3 daily; 5hr–5hr 30min); Seville (22 daily; 2hr 30min); Toledo (13 daily; 30min); Valencia (15 daily; 1hr 40min–3hr 40min).

By bus Terminals are scattered throughout the city, but the two main stations are the Estación del Sur (ⓜ Méndez Alvaro) on c/Méndez Alvaro, south of Estación de Atocha, for destinations south, east and west of Madrid, and the Intercambiador de Avenida de América (ⓜ Avenida de América) for destinations in the north.

Destinations Alicante (5–8 daily; 5hr–6hr 30min); Almería (2 daily; 10hr 30min); Barcelona (20 daily; 7hr 30min–8hr); Bilbao (13 daily; 4hr 10min–4hr 45min); Cáceres (7 daily; 4hr–4hr 30min); Cádiz (13 daily; 12hr 45min–16hr 30min); El Escorial (hourly; 1hr); Granada (14 daily; 4hr 30min–5hr); León (10 daily; 3hr 30min–4hr 15min); Málaga (4–8 daily; 6hr); Mérida (3 daily; 4hr 15min–5hr); Pamplona (8 daily; 5hr–6hr 30min); Salamanca (22 daily; 2hr 30min–3hr); San Sebastián (9 daily; 6hr); Santander (8 daily; 5hr 45min); Santiago de Compostela (5 daily; 8–9hr); Segovia (10 daily; 1hr 30min); Seville (8 daily; 6hr); Toledo (every 30min 6.30am–10pm; 1hr–1hr 30min); Valencia (13 daily; 3hr 15 min–4hr 15min).

INFORMATION

Tourist information Centro de Turismo de Madrid is at Plaza Mayor 27 (daily 9.30am–9.30pm; ☎ 914 544 410, ⓦ www.esmadrid.com; Ⓜ Sol). Branches at Plaza de Colón (Ⓜ Colón) and Terminal 4 at the airport (both daily 9.30am–8.30pm). Events listings are detailed in free English-language monthly *In Madrid* (ⓦ inmadrid.com) and Spanish *Guía del Ocio* (ⓦ guiadelocio.com).

GETTING AROUND

By bus Buses (ⓦ emtmadrid.es) operate from 6.30am to midnight; there are also 26 night buses known as *búhos* (owls) which run from Plaza de Cibeles (midnight–6am; every 15min). Single fare €1.50.
By metro The metro (ⓦ www.metromadrid.es) runs 6am–2am. Fares are €1.50–2 within central zone A, or €12.20 for a ten-journey ticket that is also valid on buses.
By taxi Taxi ranks are located throughout the city centre. Fares start from €2.40 7am–9pm during the week; higher fares in the evening and at weekends. Charges per km are €1.05–1.20; supplementary charges apply for journeys to and from train and bus stations. There's a €30 flat fare to and from the airport.

ACCOMMODATION

The best budget accommodation is in the area surrounding Plaza Santa Ana. Other good areas include Gran Vía and along c/Fuencarral towards Chueca and Malasaña.

HOSTELS

Cat's Hostel c/Cañizares 6 ☎ 913 692 807, ⓦ catshostel .com; Ⓜ Antón Martín. Party hostel located in a converted eighteenth-century palace with beautiful central patio. Rooms are a bit cramped but there's a lively cellar bar, nightly tapas bar crawls, and free wi-fi. Dorms €30, doubles €80
The Hat Madrid c/Imperial 9 ☎ 917 728 572. *The Hat* has a sustainable focus, small, stylish dorms and a top location, but the real draw is its rooftop bar with spectacular city views. Dorms €20, doubles €60
Las Musas Hostel c/Jesus y María 12, 3rd floor ☎ 915 394 984, ⓦ lasmusashostel.com; Ⓜ Tirso de Molina. This stylish hostel is a favourite with international backpackers who congregate in its large kitchen/lounge or on its roof terrace before hitting the many nearby bars. Dorms €16, doubles €65

Los Amigos Hostel c/Arenal 26 4 Izq ☎ 915 592 472, ⓦ losamigoshostel.com; Ⓜ Ópera. Popular, friendly hostel with bright a/c dorms, lockers and kitchen. Bike rental available. Dorms €21, doubles €60
Posada de Huertas c/de las Huertas 21 ☎ 914 295 526, ⓦ posadadehuertas.com; Ⓜ Antón Martín. Spacious, secure and colourful dorms with lockers. Helpful staff, nightly tapas bar tours, free breakfast, wi-fi and kitchen facilities are just some of the perks at this hostel in the heart of Madrid's nightlife. Dorms €20

HOTELS

Hostal Acapulco c/de la Salud 13, 4th floor ☎ 915 311 945, ⓦ hostalacapulco.com; Ⓜ Gran Vía. You're guaranteed not to go loco here: the spotless, sunny rooms with marble floors and balconies overlook cute little Plaza del Carmen. Doubles €65
Santa Ana Colors c/de las Huertas 14, 2nd floor ☎ 914 296 935, ⓦ santaanacolors.com; Ⓜ Antón Martín. Modern, budget hotel that's as brightly coloured as the name suggests. Each minimalist, comfortable room comes with flat-screen TV and free wi-fi, and the location is hard to beat. Doubles €50

EATING

Madrid has an incredible variety of restaurants, and it's easy to dine out on a tight budget. Most tapas bars are known for a particular speciality – Madrileños will have a drink and a tapa in one bar before moving on to another. Most places serve food 1–4pm and 8–11.30pm, unless otherwise stated.

CAFÉS AND TAPAS BARS

One of the best areas to enjoy tapas is La Latina, with myriad bars clustered along its little streets.
Chocolatería Valor Postigo de San Martín; Ⓜ Callao. One of the best spots in town for *chocolate con churros*, with an incredible array of dipping chocolate for the doughnuts.
La Cabra en el Tejado c/Santa Ana 29; Ⓜ La Latina. Relaxed café-bar serving cheap drinks (€1 beer or vermouth) and decent tapas. Try the €6 mezze plate for a bargain feed.
Mercado de San Miguel Plaza de San Miguel; Ⓜ Sol. Transformed into a gleaming modern venue with numerous food counters and perpetually busy tables, one of Madrid's oldest markets is now a top spot for tapas (from €1), drinks and people-watching.
Mesón del Champiñon c/Cava de San Miguel 1; Ⓜ Sol. Tuck into a plate of the house speciality (mushrooms with or without chorizo) washed down with a glass of wine. Mushrooms €6.
★**Taberna de La Concha** c/de la Cava Baja 7; Ⓜ La Latina. Friendly tapas bar with downstairs seating and an

32

array of tapas (some gluten-free). Try the baked red peppers with cheese and béchamel (€6). Kitchen 1pm–midnight.

RESTAURANTS

Casa Mingo Paseo de la Florida 34; ⓜPríncipe Pío. Asturian cider house with a cheap, no-nonsense menu. If the roast chicken doesn't grab you, go for the *chorizo a la sidra* (C0).

Celso y Manolo c/Libertad 1; ⓜChueca. Stylish but surprisingly good-value restaurant offering a huge range of traditional *raciones* with a creative twist. Try the cod and green pepper omelette (€8).

Federal Café Pl. de las Comendadoras 9; ⓜNoviciado. If meaty tapas and fried foods are all too much, try this Australian-inspired oasis for tasty brunch options such as scrambled eggs with avocado and halloumi. Great quality coffee. Mon–Sat 9am–midnight, Sun 9am–5.30pm.

La Antigua Huevería c/San Vicente Ferrer 28; ⓜTribunal. "The old egg shop" is a cosy little restaurant/ bar serving great pizzas (from €10) and, appropriately, *huevos rotos* – eggs lightly scrambled over potato, onion and sometimes ham or sausage.

La Musa c/Manuela Malasaña 18 ⓦgrupolamusa.com; ⓜBilbao. Always heaving with a young clientele, and serving a deliciously different menu – try the fried green tomatoes with goat's cheese (€6.50). There's another branch on Pl. de la Paja.

La Paella de la Reina c/de la Reina 39; ⓜGran Vía. This is where Madrileños head to sate their rice cravings. Like any good *arrocería*, this place only cooks paella for two people or more, so take a friend. The *arroz negro* (€18/ person) is delicious.

★**La Pescadería** c/Ballesta 32 ⓦlamuccacompany.com; ⓜTribunal. Trendy restaurant with a buzzing atmosphere, strong service and great quality tapas and mains – all at a reasonable price. Try the cod fritters (€7.50).

Vega c/Luna 9; ⓜCallao. Vegan bar and restaurant, more hipster than hippy. The €12 *menú del día* features quinoa salads, stuffed aubergines and more. In the evening, take your pick of Vega's *raciones* washed down with craft beer.

DRINKING AND NIGHTLIFE

Clubs open from midnight until well beyond dawn; the best areas are hipster Malasaña, gay-friendly Chueca and multicultural Lavapiés/Antón Martín.

BARS

Amor de Madre c/San Joaquín 14; ⓜTribunal. A skateboarder's paradise in terms of decor, "mother's love" is a laidback, friendly bar right in the heart of Malasaña.

Café Manuela c/San Vicente Ferrer 29; ⓜTribunal. Splashes of marble and gilt trims give this place a certain old-fashioned grandeur, but the vibe's relaxed. Enjoy a milkshake or cocktail over a board game.

El Imperfecto Pl. de Matute 2; ⓜSol. Far from being imperfect, this is an excellent cocktail bar with an intriguingly decorated interior. There's occasional live music.

El Viajero Pl. de la Cebada 11; ⓜLa Latina. Ideal spot for a beer on a warm night, when you can gaze out at the city's comings and goings from the open-air rooftop terrace.

Kikekeller c/Corredera Baja de San Pablo 17; ⓜCallao No, it's not a design shop, but a trendy bar where the furniture's for sale and the waiters wear leather skirts. Perfect people-watching territory.

★**La Venencia** c/Echegaray 7; ⓜSevilla or Sol. Old-school sherry bar where nothing seems to have changed for years (except perhaps the quantity of dust on the bottles behind the bar). Sherry from €1.70 a glass.

CLUBS

Joy Eslava c/Arenal 11; ⓜSol. Former theatre converted into a glamorous nightclub, popular with an international crowd. Thursday is student night. Entry from €15 including drink.

Kapital c/Atocha 125; ⓜAtocha. Popular megaclub with seven levels and a roof terrace featuring different dancefloors – everything from hip-hop to salsa to r'n'b. All this fun doesn't come cheap – and you need to dress up – but the €20 admission includes a drink. Fri & Sat midnight–6am.

La Cartuja c/de la Cruz 10 ⓜSol. Fun, unpretentious place popular with a young crowd, playing mostly chart music. Entry €8 with drink. Wed–Sat 10pm–6am.

Mi madre era una groupie c/Santa Polonia 5; ⓜAntón Martín. One for the less-than-hardcore clubbers, this little place has a friendly atmosphere and a playlist that features Britpop and classic hits. Free entry. Thurs–Sat until 3.30am.

Tupperware Corredera Alta de San Pablo 26; ⓜTribunal. This little club is fun through-and-through, from its über-kitsch decor to its eclectic playlist – soul, indie and Sixties and Seventies classics, enjoyed by a 30-something crowd. Free entry. Daily 9pm–3am.

ROOFTOP BARS

During summer, Madrid's nightlife takes to the sky: rooftop bars are the places to see and be seen. The **Azotea del Círculo de Bellas Artes** (c/Alcalá 42) may charge a €4 entrance fee, but it boasts the best views of Madrid and drinks are reasonably priced compared to other roof terraces. The bars at **Gymage** (c/de la Luna 2) and **Palacio de Cibeles** (Plaza de Cibeles) are also worth checking out.

ENTERTAINMENT

Big rock concerts are usually held at Palacio Vistalegre, Utebo 1 (🚇 Oporto). Flamenco is at its best in the summer, especially during the Suma Flamenca, a fortnight of special concerts in June (🌐 esmadrid.com/agenda/sumaflamenca).

LIVE MUSIC

Café Central Pl. del Ángel 10 🌐 cafecentralmadrid.com; 🚇 Sol. Attracting big international musicians, this is one of the best places in the world to hear live jazz. Open from noon for drinks, with music nightly from 9–11pm; arrive early to secure weekend tickets (€12–17).

Café Populart c/de las Huertas 11 🚇 Sol. Well-established venue with nightly jazz performances. Free admission.

El Barco c/del Barco 34 🌐 barcobar.com; 🚇 Tribunal. Popular bar/club in Malasaña with a varied programme of gigs, from flamenco to rock. Nightly from 10pm.

La Fontana de Oro c/Victoria 3 🚇 Sol. Popular with a young crowd, this bar offers regular free concerts, specializing in rock.

Moby Dick Avda de Brasil 5 🌐 mobydickclub.com; 🚇 Santiago Bernabéu. Popular nautical-themed venue attracting live rock bands, both local and international.

FLAMENCO

Cardamomo c/Echegaray 15 🌐 cardamomo.es; 🚇 Sevilla. Atmospheric bar with nightly *tablaos* (performances). Pricey (from €25 including drink), but the shows are some of the city's most recommended. Three shows daily from 6pm.

Casa Patas c/Cañizares 10 🌐 casapatas.com; 🚇 Antón Martín. Classic flamenco club with bar and restaurant, and incredible shows. Best nights Thurs & Fri from 8.30pm; can get rather crowded. Entrance €38 including drink. Check website for performance times.

Taberna La Flamenca 3.0 Ronda de Segovia 28; 🚇 Puerta de Toledo. This popular bar offers a budget flamenco alternative, with occasional shows in an intimate atmosphere. Check their Facebook page for details.

CINEMA

Cine Doré c/Santa Isabel 3; 🚇 Antón Martín. Offers a bargain (€2.50) programme of classic films, a pleasant bar and, in summer, an outdoor *cine-terraza*; home to the national film library.

Cines Princesa c/de la Princesa 3; 🚇 Plaza de España. Films shown in their original language – from English-language Hollywood blockbusters to international art films.

La Enana Marrón Travesía de San Mateo 8 🌐 laenanamarron.org; 🚇 Alonzo Martínez. Artsy and independent Spanish-language films and alternative theatre.

BULLFIGHTING

Plaza de Toros Monumental de las Ventas c/de Alcalá 237; 🚇 Ventas. Hosts regular bullfights during summer, especially during the May/June San Isidro festivities; ticket prices start from around €3 for standing *sol* (sun) tickets, with *sombra* (shade) tickets from €5. Tickets for all but the biggest events are available at the box office (☎ 913 562 200, 🌐 las-ventas.com). To find out about the history of bullfighting with none of the gore, visit the museum (Mon–Fri 9.30am–2.30pm; free).

SHOPPING

The main shopping streets are Gran Vía (where you'll find chain stores) and c/Fuencarral (for Spanish and international brands and designers, plus some independent shops). If you're looking for quirky clothing or jewellery, try the boutiques and vintage stores of Chueca and Malasaña. The area from Plaza Mayor to Puerta de Toledo is filled with shops selling everything from religious icons to embroidered shawls – great for browsing and picking up the odd authentic souvenir, but often quite expensive.

Alpargatería Casa Hernanza c/de Toledo 18; 🚇 Ópera. This purveyor of traditional rope-soled sandals and shoes has been in business since 1840.

Casa de Diego Puerta del Sol 12; 🚇 Sol. The place to go for handcrafted *abanicos* (fans). Prices for more basic models start at under €10.

Casa del Libro Gran Vía 29; 🚇 Gran Vía. A huge bookshop with a large selection in English.

El Templo de Susu c/del Espíritu Santo 1; 🚇 Tribunal. One of Malasaña's best-stocked vintage emporiums.

Petra's International Bookshop c/de Compomanes 13; 🚇 Ópera. Lets you swap your old books for other secondhand ones.

DIRECTORY

Embassies Australia, Torre Espacio, Paseo de la Castellana 259d, 24th floor ☎ 913 536 600; Canada, Torre Espacio, Paseo de la Castellana 259d ☎ 913 828 400; Ireland, Paseo de la Castellana 46, 4th floor ☎ 914 364 093; New Zealand, c/de Pinar 7 ☎ 915 230 226; UK, Torre Espacio, Paseo de la Castellana 259d ☎ 917 146 300; US, c/Serrano 75 ☎ 915 872 200.

Hospitals Anglo-American Medical Unit (Unidad Médica) at c/del Conde de Aranda 1 (☎ 914 351 823, 🌐 unidadmedica.com; 🚇 Retiro) has Spanish- and English-speaking staff. Hospital General Gregorio Marañón at c/del Doctor Esquerdo 46 (☎ 915 868 000; 🚇 Sáinz de Baranda) is the main public hospital.

Left luggage Estación de Atocha has lockers (daily 5.30am–11.50pm), as does Estación de Chamartín (daily 7am–11pm). There is a *consigna* (left luggage) at the Estación Sur de Autobuses (6.30am–11.30pm). There are also 24hr *consignas* at the airport (terminals 1, 3 and 4).

32

Pharmacies Farmacia Mayor at c/Mayor 13 (☏913 664 616) and Farmacia Velázquez at c/Velázquez 70 (☏915 756 028) are both open 24hr.

Post office Paseo del Prado 1, Pl. de Cibeles (ⓜBanco de España).

Day-trips from Madrid

Surrounding the capital are some of Spain's most fascinating towns and cities, all an easy day-trip from Madrid.

EL ESCORIAL

Fifty kilometres northwest of Madrid, nestled in the foothills of the Sierra de Guadarrama, are **SAN LORENZO DEL ESCORIAL** and the monastery of **El Escorial** (Tues–Sun: April–Sept 10am–8pm; Oct–March 10am–6pm; €10, free Wed pm for EU citizens). The city grew around this enormous, severe-looking building, which resembles a fortress rather than a palace. Start at the monastery's west gateway, which leads into the **Patio de los Reyes** and the impressive Basilica. Move on to the **Salas Capitulares**, outside and around to the left, to see works by El Greco, Velázquez and Ribera. Nearby, the staircase next to the Sacristía leads down to the **Panteón de los Reyes**, the final resting place of virtually all Spanish monarchs since Charles V, where they lie in gilded tombs. You'll pass the **Pudería**, where corpses are left to rot for twenty years, and the eerie **Panteón de los Infantes**, with its tiny marble coffins. The spartan Habsburg apartments inside the **Palace** itself, inhabited by Philip II, house the chair that supported his gouty leg and the deathbed from which he looked down into the church.

ARRIVAL AND INFORMATION

By train From both of Madrid's train stations, C8 *cercanías* run to El Escorial (hourly; 1hr; €3.40). Take a connecting local bus up to the town centre (€1.20); otherwise it's a 20min walk uphill.

By bus Bus #661 runs between Moncloa and the bus station in El Escorial (Mon–Fri every 15min Sat & Sun hourly; 50min; €3.60). From here, it's a 10min walk to the monastery.

Tourist office c/Grimaldi 2 (Mon–Sat 10am–2pm & 3.30–6pm, Sun 10am–2pm; ☏918 905 313, ⓦsanlorenzoturismo.org).

SEGOVIA

Located 87km northwest of Madrid, **SEGOVIA** has a remarkable number of architectural achievements for a small city. Known to locals as the "stone ship", from a bird's-eye view the city resembles a boat, with its three most celebrated attractions at the stern, bow and mast: the Alcázar, Aqueduct and cathedral, respectively.

The Aqueduct

The **Aqueduct**, a magnificent structure that looms over the Plaza del Azoguejo, stretches over 800m and towers 30m high. As if these dimensions weren't impressive enough, the entire structure stands up without a drop of mortar. No one knows exactly when it was built, but it was probably around the end of the first century AD under the Emperor Trajan.

The cathedral

Dominating the Plaza Mayor in the heart of the old city, the impressive **cathedral** (daily 9.30am–6.30pm; €3) takes the Gothic style to its extreme, with pinnacles and flying buttresses tacked on at every conceivable point.

The Alcázar

Beside the cathedral, c/Daoiz leads on to a small park in front of the **Alcázar** (daily 10am–7pm; €5.50, free for EU citizens Tues 2–6pm; tower access €2 extra). This extraordinary castle with narrow towers and turrets, rebuilt in 1862 after the original was destroyed by fire, is said to have inspired Walt Disney's design for Sleeping Beauty's castle. Inside, you can admire the splendid Sala de Reyes, the three-dimensional frieze depicting all the monarchs of Asturias, Castilla and León, the peculiar "pine cones" decorating the ceiling in the Sala de Las Piñas, and the unsurpassed view of the city and the

32

snow-tipped mountains behind it from the summit of the Torre de Juan II. It's worth investing in an audioguide (€3), as information inside is scarce.

Vera Cruz

The most impressive of Segovia's churches is **Vera Cruz** (Tues 4–7pm, Wed–Sun 10.30am–1.30pm & 4–7pm; €2), a remarkable twelve-sided building in the valley facing the Alcázar, erected by the Knights Templar in the early thirteenth century.

ARRIVAL AND INFORMATION

By train The fast AVE train (up to 17 daily; 28min; from €12) from Madrid Chamartín stops at Segovia-Guiomar station, 6km from town: take bus #11 to the Aqueduct (every 15min; €1).

By bus Frequent buses (every 45min; 1hr 30min; €8) run from Madrid's Moncloa bus station (Ⓜ Moncloa). The entrance to the old city is a 10min walk up Avda de Fernández Ladreda.

Tourist office Plaza del Azoguejo 1 (daily 10am–7pm, Sat until 8pm; ☎ 921 466 720, ⓦ turismodesegovia.com); guided city tours available (€13.80/person).

ACCOMMODATION AND EATING

Hostal Juan Bravo c/de Juan Bravo 12 ☎ 921 463 413, ⓦ hostaljuanbravo.blogspot.com.es. Superbly located, friendly *hostal*, its spotless rooms brightened up with cheerful art prints. Request one of the back rooms for the awesome views of the Sierra de Guadarrama. Doubles **€45**, with shared bathroom **€35**

La Judería c/Judería Vieja 5. Great for vegetarians, this restaurant offers fresh Indian cuisine, with a few Spanish dishes thrown in for good measure. The €9 lunch deal will fill you up for an afternoon's sightseeing. Daily 1–3.30pm & 8–11pm.

Maribel c/Padre Claret 16. A local favourite which specializes in Segovia's delicacy of *cochinillo asado* (suckling pig), although the roast lamb is also excellent. Prices are moderate too – around the €12 mark for generous portions. Mon lunch only, closed Tues, otherwise 1–4pm & 8–11pm.

TOLEDO

Capital of medieval Spain until 1560, UNESCO World Heritage Site **TOLEDO** is the spiritual heart of Catholic Spain and a city redolent of past glories. Famous for having been home to the "three cultures" over the years, Toledo

retains a captivating selection of Christian, Jewish and Muslim monuments. Set against a bleak landscape, Toledo's haphazard maze of cobbled streets rests on a rocky mound isolated on three sides by a looping gorge of the Río Tajo. The imposing military fortress of the Alcázar dominates the view. To see the city at its finest, lose yourself in the backstreets or stay the night; by 6pm, the tour buses have all gone home.

The Catedral

The **Catedral** is at the heart of the city (Mon–Sat 10am–6.30pm, Sun 2–6.30pm; €8 including audioguide). This Gothic construction took almost three centuries to complete (1227–1493) and is bursting with treasures. The sacristy and museums are home to the most opulent paintings, most notably by Zurbarán, Velázquez and El Greco. Behind the Capilla Mayor's huge altarpiece is the Baroque *Transparente*, with marble cherubs and clouds, especially magnificent when the sun reaches through the strategically placed opening in the roof above.

The Judería

On c/Samuel Levi in the **Judería**, the old Jewish Quarter, the beautifully restored **Sinagoga del Tránsito**, built along Moorish lines by Samuel Levi in 1366 and housing the **Sephardic Museum** (March–Oct Tues–Sat 9.30am–7.30pm; Nov–Feb Tues–Sat 9.30am–6pm; all year Sun 10am–3pm; €3, free Sat from 2pm), maps Jewish culture and tradition in Spain, exhibits including ceremonial artefacts and costumes. A short walk away at c/Reyes Católicos 17 is the

32

THE TOLEDO MONUMENTAL

The **Toledo Monumental** tourist bracelet (€9) allows you access to the Sinagoga Santa María la Blanca, Mezquita Cristo de la Luz, San Juan de los Reyes Monastery, Iglesia del Salvador, Iglesia de las Jesuitas, Real Colegio de las Doncellas Nobles and El Greco's painting, *The Burial of the Count of Orgaz*.

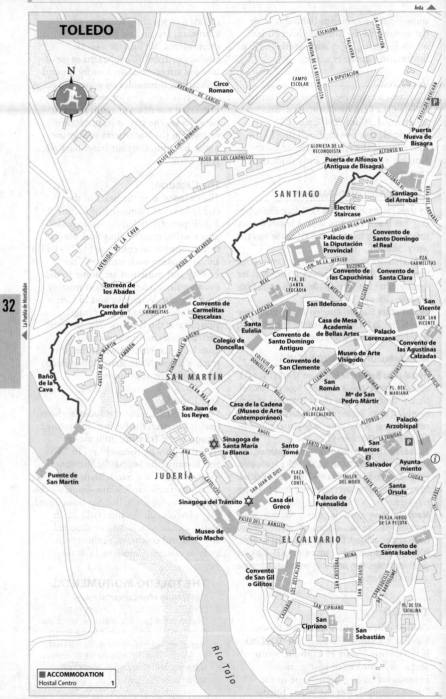

TOLEDO

Ávila

32

La Puebla de Montalbán

ACCOMMODATION
Hostal Centro 1

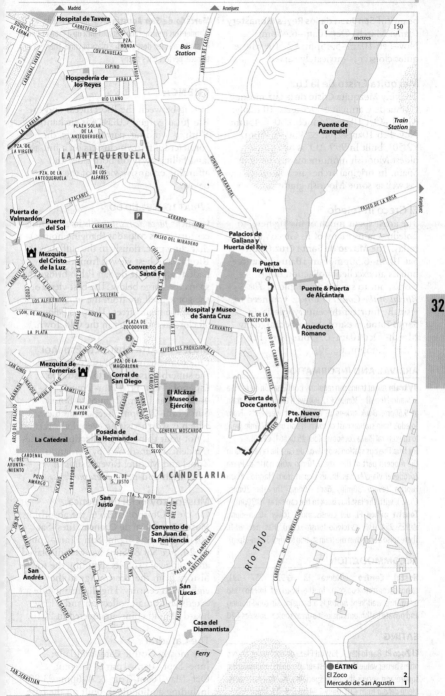

Madrid ▲   Aranjuez ▲

Hospital de Tavera

DUQUES DE LERMA

CARRETEROS

HONDA

LOS

AVENIDA DE CASTILLA

PZA. HONDA

COVACHUELAS

TRINITARIOS

ESPINO

Bus Station

Hospedería de los Reyes

PERALA

RÍO LLANO

LA CARRERA

PLAZA SOLAR DE LA ANTEQUERUELA

Puente de Azarquiel

Train Station

PZA. DE LA VIRGEN

LA ANTEQUERUELA

PZA. DE LA ANTEQUERUELA

PZA. DE LOS ALFARES

RONDA DEL GRANADAL

AZACANES

PASEO DE LA ROSA

Aranjuez ▶

Puerta de Valmardón

Puerta del Sol

CARRETAS

GERARDO LOBO

PASEO DEL MIRADERO

P

Palacios de Galiana y Huerta del Rey

Mezquita del Cristo de la Luz

CARMELITAS CRISTO DE LA LUZ

CODO

NÚÑEZ DE ARCE

LOS ALFILERITOS

CIÓN. DE MENORES

LA PLATA

Convento de Santa Fe

CUESTA DE ARMAS

LA SILLERÍA

NUEVA

CABEZAS

PLAZA DE ZOCODOVER

SANTA FE

Hospital y Museo de Santa Cruz

CERVANTES

PL. DE LA CONCEPCIÓN

Puerta Rey Wamba

Puente & Puerta de Alcántara

Acueducto Romano

Mezquita de Tornerías

COMERCIO SIERPE

SAN GINÉS

GRANADA SINAGOGA

HOMBRE DE PALO

Corral de San Diego

PZA. DE LA MAGDALENA

CUESTA DE CARLOS V

ALFÉRECES PROVISIONALES

PASEO DEL CARMEN

CERVANTES

DE JUANELO

PLAZA MAYOR

JUAN LABRADOR

HORNO DE LOS BIZCOCHOS

El Alcázar y Museo de Ejército

GENERAL MOSCARDÓ

Puerta de Doce Cantos

Pte. Nuevo de Alcántara

TAJO

La Catedral

ARCO DEL PALACIO

CARDENAL

PL. DEL AYUNTA-MIENTO

POZO AMARGO

SIXTO RAMÓN PARRO

Posada de la Hermandad

CISNEROS

SAN PEDRO

VICARIO

BARCO

PL. DEL SECO

PL. DE S. JUSTO

CTA. S. JUSTO

LA CANDELARIA

RÍO TAJO

C.IÓN DE JESÚS

AVE. MARÍA

POZO

CAPEDA

San Justo

San Andrés

PABLO

SAN

BJDA. DEL BARCO

AMARGO

PLEGADERO

Convento de San Juan de la Penitencia

CUESTA DEL CAN

PASEO DE LA CAMPEARÍA

CABESTREROS

CARRETERA DE CIRCUNVALACIÓN

San Lucas

PASEO

Casa del Diamantista

Ferry

SAN SEBASTIÁN

0 — 150
metres

32

●**EATING**
El Zoco | **2**
Mercado de San Agustín | **1**

beautiful **San Juan de los Reyes Monastery** (daily: March–Oct 10am–6.45pm; Nov–Feb 10am–5.45pm; €2.50), whose quiet cloister is intricately carved.

Mezquita Cristo de la Luz

The tiny **Mezquita Cristo de la Luz** mosque, Cuesta de Carmelitas Descalzos 10 (daily: March–Oct 10am–2pm & 3.30–6.45pm; Nov–Feb 10am–2pm & 3.30–5.45pm; €2.50), built in 999 AD, is one of the oldest Moorish monuments surviving in Spain. Its original arches are still intact (as well as some Moorish graffiti).

El Greco in Toledo

The artist spent much of his life here, so Toledo retains many of El Greco's works today. The **Museo de Santa Cruz** (Mon–Sat 10am–6.30pm, Sun 10am–2pm; free) houses an excellent collection of his works, but to see his masterpiece, *The Burial of the Count of Orgaz*, you need to visit the fourteenth-century **Iglesia de Santo Tomé**, west of the cathedral (daily March–Oct 10am–6.45pm; Nov–Feb 10am–5.45pm; €2.50).

ARRIVAL AND INFORMATION

By train Avant trains run regularly from Estación de Atocha in Madrid (hourly; 30min; €12.90), with the last return train at 9.50pm. Book tickets in advance at weekends. From Toledo's train station east of town, it's an uphill 20min walk to the central Plaza Zocódover (bus #5 or #61; €1.50).

By bus The bus station is on Avda de Castilla la Mancha in the modern part of the city, a 10min walk north of Plaza Zocódover via c/Armas. Buses depart from Madrid's Plaza Elíptica (every 30min, 6am–10pm; 1hr–1hr 30min; €5.42), with the last bus back to the capital at 10.30pm.

Tourist office Pl. del Consistorio 1 (daily 10am–6pm; 📞 925 254 030, 🌐 toledo-turismo.com). Has free wi-fi. There's also a branch at the train station (daily 9.30am–3pm).

ACCOMMODATION

Hostal Centro c/Nueva 13 📞 925 257 091, 🌐 hostalcentrotoledo.com. In the heart of Toledo's old town, this well-kept *hostal* is a bargain. Air-conditioning and private bathrooms make it a great choice. Doubles €40

EATING

El Zoco Pl. Barrio Rey 7. Just off Plaza de Zocódover, *El Zoco* offers better value than the restaurants on its neighbouring square and serves the local speciality, *perdiz* (partridge). *Menú del día* from €10. Daily 1–4pm & 8–11.30pm.

Mercado de San Agustín c/Cuesta del Aguila 1 & 3. Wander this gourmet market and pick up a tapa or two at its stalls, washed down with a glass of wine. There's also a terrace, perfect if it's sunny.

CUENCA

Sitting between the Río Huécar and the Río Júcar gorges, **CUENCA** is enchanting. With its winding, narrow streets, the compact Old Town clusters on a hill, the land falling away on both sides and affording expansive views of the valleys below.

WHAT TO SEE AND DO

Cuenca's *pièce de résistance* is its sixteenth-century **casas colgadas** (hanging houses) that cling precariously to the cliff above Río Huécar, best viewed from the pedestrian Puente de San Pablo bridge that spans the gorge below. The best views of the gorge itself are from the *mirador* at the top of the main street. The sites below are all close to each other in the Old Town.

Museo de Arte Abstracto Español

One of the hanging houses contains the superb **Museo de Arte Abstracto Español** (Tues–Fri 11am–2pm & 4–6pm, Sat 11am–2pm & 4–8pm, Sun 11am–2.30pm; free; 🌐 march.es), which is worth visiting even if abstract art is not your thing. The collection includes the delicate *Jardín Seco* by Fernando Zóbel and Manuel Rivera's sinister wire-mesh-and-paint *Metamorfosis*.

Museo Provincial de Cuenca

On c/del Obispo Valero 6, the absorbing **Museo Provincial de Cuenca** (Tues–Sat 10am–2pm & 4–7pm, Sun 11am–2pm; €1.20, free Sat & Sun) has well-displayed archeological exhibits spanning the town's history from the Bronze Age to the eighteenth century. Highlights include an extensive Roman collection and a large hoard of gold coins, uncovered in 2010.

The Catedral

The mostly Gothic **Catedral** (daily: June–Sept 10am–1pm & 4–7pm; Oct–May 10am–1pm & 4–6pm; €3.80 including audioguide), built on the base of a former mosque, dominates the main square and features some splendid stained-glass windows.

ARRIVAL AND INFORMATION

By train Slow trains for Madrid use the station on central c/Mariano Catalina, a block from the bus station. High-speed trains arrive at the AVE station 3km outside of Cuenca; the #12 bus connects it to the town's bus station (every 30min, less frequent in winter; €1.20), from where you can catch bus #1 to the Old Town.
Destinations Madrid (6 daily; 1hr 10min–3hr 30min); Valencia (6 daily; 1hr 15min–4hr).
By bus The bus station is on c/Fermín Caballero, a 10min walk from Cuenca's Old Town.
Destinations Madrid (8 daily; 2hr 10min–2hr 30min); Toledo (1 daily; 2hr–3hr 20min).
Tourist office c/Alfonso VIII 2 (Mon–Sat 10am–2pm & 5–7pm, Sun 9am–2.30pm; shorter hours in winter; ☎ 969 176 100, ⓦ turismo.cuenca.es). Pick up the free booklet *Paseos por Cuenca*, which details walks starting from the Old Town.

ACCOMMODATION, EATING AND DRINKING

Bar Clásicos c/Severo Catalina 5. Little bar serving good-value lunch menus (€10). Arrive early to grab a table on the terrace overlooking the Río Júcar. Daily 1–4pm & 8–11.30pm.
La Bodeguita de Basilio c/Fray Luís de León 3. One of the town's best watering holes, this place is ideal for those on a budget – each drink (around €3) comes with a sizeable free tapa. Daily 1–4pm & 8–11.30pm.
Posada de San Julián c/de las Torres 1 ☎ 969 211 704, ⓦ posadasanjulian.es. At the foot of the hill leading up into the Old Town, this comfortable place has simple rooms with their own toilets (but shared showers), wi-fi access and a popular restaurant on the ground floor. Doubles €42

Extremadura

The harsh environment of **Extremadura**, west of Madrid, is known as the "cradle of the conquistadors". Remote before and forgotten since, the area enjoyed a brief golden age when the conquerors of the Americas returned with their gold to live in a flourish of splendour. **Cáceres** preserves an entire town built with conquistador wealth, the streets crowded with the ornate mansions of returning empire-builders. An even more ancient past is tangible in the wonders of **Mérida**,

the most completely preserved Roman city in Spain. The province attracts fewer tourists in June and July, as temperatures get unbearably hot.

CÁCERES

Old **CÁCERES** was built largely on the plunders of the New World and is home to the University of Extremadura. The Ciudad Monumental – a maze of tiny, winding streets, lined with immaculate historical buildings – is enclosed by medieval stone walls, with storks nesting on every rooftop. Beautiful Cáceres may appear staid, but there's a lively restaurant and bar scene, with locals getting the party started after lunch every Saturday.

WHAT TO SEE AND DO

Almost every building in the **Plaza Mayor** is magnificent, featuring ancient walls pierced by the low **Arco de la Estrella**, the **Torre del Horno**, one of the best-preserved Moorish mud-brick structures in Spain, and the **Torre del Bujaco** – whose foundations date back to Roman times and which you can climb for a great view of the city (daily 10am–2pm & 5.30–8.30pm; €2.50). Enter the UNESCO World Heritage-listed Ciudad Monumental via the old city gate, the **Arco de la Estrella**. For a great view of the walled city, climb the tower at the **Concatedral de Santa María** (Mon–Sat 10.30am–1.30pm & 5.30–7.30pm; €2). North of here, you'll find the **judería** (former Jewish quarter) – narrow lanes of whitewashed houses with window boxes of bright flowers. Another sight worth seeking out is the **Museo de Cáceres** (Tues–Sat 9am–3.30pm & 5–8.30pm, Sun 10.15am–3.30pm; €1.20, EU citizens free), on the Plaza de las Veletas, which has jewellery, statuary, national costume and fine arts sections and whose highlight is the *aljibe* (cistern) of the original Moorish Alcázar, with rooms of wonderful horseshoe arches.

ARRIVAL AND DEPARTURE

By train The station is 3km out of town. Bus #L1 runs every 15min to central Plaza de San Juan, near the Plaza Mayor.

32

Destinations Madrid (4 daily; 3hr 40min–4hr 10min); Mérida (5 daily; 1hr).

By bus The station faces the train station across the Carretera Sevilla.

Destinations Madrid (7 daily; 3hr 40min–5hr); Salamanca (4 daily; 3hr 30min); Seville (8 daily; 4hr).

INFORMATION

Tourist office c/Tiendas 3 (daily 10am–2pm & 5.30–8.30pm; ⓣ 927 111 222, ⓦ turismo.ayto-caceres.es).

ACCOMMODATION

Albergue Las Veletas c/Margallo 36 ⓣ 927 211 210, ⓦ alberguelasveletas.es. Bright, spacious dorms and rooms with modern furnishings and a/c. Friendly staff make it popular with groups of young Spaniards. Breakfast for €3.50. Dorms **€21**, doubles **€50**

Hostal Goya Plaza Mayor 11 ⓣ 927 247 482. Simple, old-fashioned en-suite rooms with a/c. In a prime location: you pay €10 extra for a view of Plaza Mayor. Doubles **€48**

EATING AND DRINKING

32

If you're in Cáceres over the weekend, be sure to check out the lively day-to-night scene around Calle Pizarro.

Bouquet Pl. de Publio Hurtado 1. A stone's throw from the Plaza Mayor, *Bouquet* offers top tapas and salads in the more informal *tapería*, or full meals in the restaurant. Try the tuna and strawberry salad.

★ **La Cacharrería** c/Orellana 1. Make sure to arrive early at this justifiably popular tapas bar, where the modern decor and tapas contrast with its Ciudad Monumental location. Good selection of local wines. Pork cheeks with coriander €4.50. Daily 1.30–4pm & 8.30pm–midnight.

Mastropiero c/Fuente Nueva 4. Two venues in one: the upstairs gastrobar serves tapas and main meals with an international influence (around €6 per dish), while the downstairs bar is a staple on the Cáceres nightlife scene. The garden terrace is a popular spot on summer nights. Daily 7pm–2.30am.

Restaurante Tapería Ibérico Pl. San Juan 12. Extremadura's local cuisine is meat-heavy, and there's no better place for a feast than this traditional restaurant serving local specialities. Try the excellent hams and cheeses. *Menú del día* €12.50. Daily 1–4pm & 8–11.30pm.

MÉRIDA

MÉRIDA, 70km south of Cáceres, contains one of Europe's most remarkable concentrations of Roman monuments, including two impressive aqueducts and a theatre which still stages performances.

WHAT TO SEE AND DO

The beautiful **Teatro Romano** and **Anfiteatro** were gifts to the city from Marcus Agrippa in around 15 BC. The stage is in a particularly good state of repair, and in July and August it's the scene for a season of classical plays (ⓦ festivaldemerida.es; tickets from €12). In its day, up to fifteen thousand people would gather in the adjacent amphitheatre to watch gladiatorial combats and wild animal fights. By the theatre's entrance is the superb **Museo Nacional de Arte Romano** (April–Sept Tues–Sat 9.30am–8pm, Sun 10am–3pm; Oct–March Tues–Sat 9.30am–6.30pm, Sun 10am–3pm; €3, free Sat pm, Sun and for EU students), with an impressive collection including portrait statues of Augustus, Tiberius and Drusus, plus some glorious mosaics, coins and other Roman artefacts. Further south, behind the Plaza de Toros, is the **Casa de Mitreo** – the remains of a Roman villa with an impressive mosaic. To the east of town you'll find the outline of the **Circo Romano**, which accommodated up to 30,000 people during chariot races. Also worth seeing is the magnificent **Puente Romano**, the pedestrian Roman bridge across the Río Guadiana on the city's west side – sixty arches long, and defended by an enormous Moorish **Alcazaba fortress**, built in 835 AD.

An **Entrada Conjunta** gives access to all six archeological sites (check at tourist office for latest timetables, which are changeable; combined ticket €15).

ARRIVAL AND DEPARTURE

By train The station is a 10min walk along c/Mártir Santa Eulalia from the town centre.

Destinations Cáceres (4 daily; 1hr); Madrid (4 daily; 4hr 30min–5hr 30min).

By bus Mérida's bus station is on Avda de la Libertad, a 15min walk across the Lusitania bridge or a short bus ride (bus #4 or #6) to the city centre.

Destinations Madrid (3 daily; 4hr 15min–5hr); Salamanca (5 daily; 4hr 10min–5hr); Seville (5 daily; 2hr 15min–2hr 45min).

INFORMATION

Tourist office c/Santa Eulalia 62 (daily 9am–8pm; ⓣ 924 380 191, ⓦ turismomerida.org).

ACCOMMODATION

El Flor de Al-Andalus Avda Extremadura 6 ☎ 924 313 356, ⓦ laflordeal-andalus.es. Guesthouse with rooms decorated in Moorish style and scrupulously clean private bathrooms. Close to the train station and main attractions. Doubles **€52**

Hostal Emeritae c/Sagasta 40 ☎ 924 303 183, ⓦ hostalemeritae.com. The pick of the budget options in the centre, this recently refurbished spot is more like a boutique hotel. Modern bathrooms and a patio with outdoor seating. Doubles **€70**

EATING AND DRINKING

Fusiona Gastrobar c/José Ramón Melinda 15. Take a perch on one of the stools or grab a terrace table, and tuck into some good-value tapas that branch out from Mérida's meaty mainstays. Strong on vegetarian and gluten-free options. Tues–Sun 12.30pm–midnight.

Nico Jiménez c/José Ramón Melinda 24. Sample local cooking and *embutidos* (cured meats) in this friendly, informal bar-cum-shop: you can even take some produce home with you. Daily 1–4pm & 8–11pm.

Pizzeria Gallileo c/John Lennon 28. Choose from over thirty pizzas and calzones, with prices as low as €4. Make sure to visit the basement for an exclusive glimpse of the Roman ruins. Tues–Sun 1–4pm & 8pm–midnight.

Castilla y León

The foundations of modern Spain were laid in the kingdom of **Castilla y León**, west and north of Madrid. A land of frontier fortresses – the *castillos* from which it takes its name – it became the most powerful and centralizing force of the Reconquest. The monarchs of this triumphant and expansionist age were enthusiastic patrons of the arts, endowing their cities with superlative monuments above which, quite literally, tower the great Gothic cathedrals of **Salamanca** and **León**.

SALAMANCA

SALAMANCA is home to arguably the oldest and what was once the most prestigious university in Europe. It's a compact city, home to many golden sandstone monuments and an attractive arcaded Plaza Mayor. As if that weren't enough, Salamanca's student population ensures an active nightlife during term time.

WHAT TO SEE AND DO

For a postcard-worthy view of Salamanca, cross the city's oldest surviving monument, the much-restored, 400m-long **Puente Romano** (Roman Bridge) at the southern end of the Old Town. Then start your exploration proper at the grand **Plaza Mayor**, its centre enclosed by a four-storey Baroque building decorated with iron balconies and medallion portraits, the restrained elegance of the designs heightened by the changing position of the sun. Be sure to wander Salamanca's streets by night, when the glorious architecture is subtly lit by street lights; the pedestrianized Calle de la Compañía has the best views.

Casa de las Conchas and the Universidad

The celebrated fifteenth-century **Casa de las Conchas** at c/Compañía 2 (Mon–Fri 9am–9pm, Sat 9am–2pm & 4–7pm, Sun 10am–2pm & 4–7pm; free), or House of Shells, is so called because its facades are decorated with rows of carved scallop shells, symbol of the pilgrimage to Santiago de Compostela. It now houses a library. From here, c/Libreros leads to the **Patio de las Escuelas Menores** and the Renaissance entrance to the **Universidad** (April–Oct 15 Mon–Sat 10am–7pm, until 8pm rest of year, Sun 10am–2pm; €10). The ultimate achievement of Plateresque art, a Spanish style characterized by ornate decoration, this reflects the tremendous reputation of Salamanca in the early sixteenth century, when it was Europe's greatest university with the most important astronomy department in the world, consulted by Columbus before he set off on his sea voyage. Spotting the legendary "*rana de suerte*" (lucky frog) on its intricately sculpted facade allegedly brings you a year of good luck (spoiler: look closely at the skulls on the right column). The university's highlight is its incredible **library**, with its carved wooden ceiling and a collection of around 2800 manuscripts, a contrast to the rather plain lecture theatres also open to visitors.

32

32

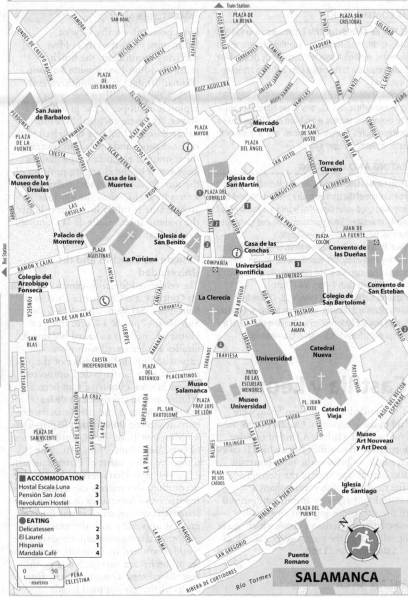

The cathedrals

Sumptuous and intricate, the late Gothic **Catedral Nueva** (daily: April–Sept 10am–8pm; Oct–March 10am–6pm; €4.75) was begun in 1512, and acted as a buttress for the Catedral Vieja, which was in danger of collapsing. Entry to the

Catedral Vieja (same hours and ticket) is inside the Catedral Nueva. Tiny by comparison and a stylistic hotch-potch of Romanesque and Gothic, its most striking feature is the fifteenth-century Renaissance altarpiece, its 54 tablets depicting the life of Christ. As you look at the Catedral Nueva from the Plaza de Anaya, try to spot the ice-cream cone and the astronaut, carved into the Puerta de Ramos during the last restoration. Inside the cathedral, you will find yourself dwarfed by its monolithic proportions. Entry to the cathedral complex also includes the **Ieronimus exhibition** (same hours), a visit to which affords views of both the old and new cathedrals and excellent views over Old Salamanca, plus history and art exhibitions hidden in a maze of little rooms.

The convents

The **Convento de San Esteban** (daily 10am–2pm & 4–8pm; €3.50) is a short walk down c/Tostado from the Plaza de Anaya. Its Gothic-Renaissance cloisters may be magnificent, but they're rivalled by those at the **Convento de las Dueñas** (Mon–Sat 10.30am–12.45pm & 4.30–5.30pm; €2). Built on an irregular pentagonal plan, its upper-storey capitals are wildly carved with writhing demons and human skulls.

ARRIVAL AND DEPARTURE

By train The main Salamanca station is 15min walk northeast of the centre. Bus #11 runs to the historical centre. The Salamanca–Alamedilla stop is more central; a 10min walk to Plaza Mayor down Gran Vía.
Destinations Barcelona (1 daily; 8hr 30min); Bilbao (3 daily; 4hr 55min–6hr 18min); Madrid (10 daily; 1hr 35min–3hr 45min); San Sebastián (3 daily; 5hr 20min–6hr 20min).
By bus The station is a 10min walk northwest from the centre on Avda de Filiberto Villalobos. Bus #4 runs along the Old Town perimeter.
Destinations Cáceres (8 daily; 3hr–3hr 30min); León via Zamora (1–2 daily; 3hr 15min); Madrid (15 daily; 2hr 30min); Mérida (6 daily; 4hr 30min); Santiago de Compostela (1 daily; 7hr); Seville (6 daily; 7hr 30min).

INFORMATION

Tourist office Pl. Mayor 32 (April till mid-Oct Mon–Fri 9am–2pm & 4.30–8pm, Sat 10am–8pm, Sun 10am–2pm; mid-Oct till March Mon–Fri 9am–2pm & 4–6.30pm, Sat 10am–6.30pm, Sun 10am–2pm); ☎923 218 342, ⓦsalamanca.es).

ACCOMMODATION

Accommodation is hard to find during fiesta time – the first week of September.

★**Hostal Escala Luna** c/Mélendez 13 ☎923 218 749, ⓦhostalescalalunasalamanca.com. Just metres from the Plaza Mayor, this friendly guesthouse is clean, comfortable and a/c. Prices drop sharply out of season, especially mid-week. Doubles €60
Pensión San José c/Jesús 24 ☎923 265 461, ⓦpensionsanjose.com. Spotless, airy singles, doubles and triples, some en suite, located right near the cathedrals on a quiet street. Doubles €40
Revolutum Hostel c/Sánchez Barbero 7 ☎923 217 656, ⓦrevolutumhostel.com. Central, chic boutique hostel with brightly decorated en-suite rooms and dorms, a trendy common lounge with egg-like seats and outdoor chill-out terrace. The friendly staff are happy to mix you a cocktail at the bustling on-site bar. Dorms €24, doubles €55

EATING AND DRINKING

For cheap tapas and drinks, try student-friendly street c/Van Dyck.
Delicatessen c/Mélendez 25. Chic, modern tapas bar and restaurant serving salads, pasta, meat and fish dishes. Arrive early to bag a table in the pretty winter garden. Daily 10am–2am.
El Laurel c/San Pablo 49. Smart, well-priced vegetarian restaurant with a wide variety of dishes served in huge portions, including pumpkin and courgette risotto (€8.75). Tues–Sat 1.30–5pm & 9pm–12.30am, lunch only on Sun.
Hispania 20 Pl. del Corillo 20. Skip the more formal restaurant and try some tapas in the bar. To keep the menu interesting, the chef takes inspiration from all the different regions of Spain. €3 per tap. Daily 9am–11.30pm.
★**Mandala Café** c/de Serranos 9–11. With an emphasis on fresh ingredients, this bright spot gets busy due to its superb three-course *menú* (€10.50 mid-week, €12.50 Friday night and weekends), which includes dishes like *arroz negro*, and a number of vegetarian choices – try the stuffed aubergine. Daily 1–4pm & 8–11.30pm.

LEÓN

The old town of **LEÓN** is steeped in history: in 914 AD, as the Reconquest edged its way south from Asturias, the city became the Christian capital, and along with its territories it grew so rapidly that by 1035 the county of Castile had matured into a fully fledged kingdom. For the next two centuries, Castilla y León jointly spearheaded the war against the Moors, but by the thirteenth century Castilla's power had eclipsed that of even her mother territory.

32

WHAT TO SEE AND DO

Historic sights aside – most notably the monumental Catedral – León has an attractive and enjoyable centre. Its Barrio Húmedo is where to head for a lively spot of tapas bar-hopping.

The Catedral

León's enormous Gothic **Catedral** (May–Sept Mon–Fri 9.30am–1.30pm & 4–8pm, Sat 9.30am–noon & 2–6pm, Sun 9.30–11am & 2–8pm; Oct–April Mon–Sat 9.30am–1.30pm & 4–7pm, Sun 9.30am–2pm; €6, including audioguide) dominates the Old Town. Dating back to the city's final years of greatness, it is perhaps the most beautiful of Spanish Gothic cathedrals. The kaleidoscopic stained-glass windows, covering an amazing 1800 square metres, are one of the most magical and harmonious spectacles in Spain, best appreciated from the inside. The audioguide provides an informative tour.

Real Basílica de San Isidoro

The city's other great attraction is the **Real Basílica de San Isidoro** (daily 7.30am–11pm; free), a few minutes' walk west from the Catedral. It was commissioned by Ferdinand I, who united the two kingdoms in 1037, as a shrine for the bones of San Isidoro, and royal mausoleum. Its **Panteón Real** (July–Sept Mon–Thurs 10am–2pm & 4–7pm, Fri & Sat until 8pm, Sun 10am–3pm; Oct–April Mon–Sat 10am–2pm & 4–7pm, Sun 10am–2pm; €5), a pair of twelfth-century, crypt-like chambers, features some of the most imaginative and impressive paintings of Romanesque art, as well as a mummified finger of San Isidoro. It once contained the bones of eleven kings and twelve queens, but now lies empty, the French troops having destroyed the graves during the Napoleonic wars.

Convento de San Marcos

The opulent **Convento de San Marcos**, on the Plaza de San Marcos west of the city's old pedestrianized quarter, was built in 1168 for the Knights of Santiago, one of several chivalric orders founded in the twelfth century to lead the Reconquest. It served as a resting point for weary pilgrims on their way to Santiago de Compostela, and is now part of a sumptuous *Parador* hotel, though non-guests can peek inside at the beautiful cloisters. The church's sacristy houses the small **Museo de León** (July–Sept Tues–Sat 10am–2pm & 5–8pm; Oct–June Tues–Sat 10am–2pm & 4–7pm, Sun 10am–2pm; €0.60), containing some beautiful statuary and portraits of the Knights of Santiago.

Museo de Arte Contemporaneo (MUSAC)

A short walk north of the Convento de San Marcos is the award-winning **Museo de Arte Contemporaneo** (Tues–Fri 11am–2pm & 5–8pm, Sat & Sun 11am–3pm & 5–9pm; €3, free Sun pm; ⓦ musac.es), its exterior covered with 37 shades of glass, known for its excellent, thought-provoking temporary exhibitions by contemporary artists, which include Spanish and international photography, sculpture and video installations.

ARRIVAL AND DEPARTURE

By train The train station is at the end of Avda de Palencia across the bridge from the city centre. The *casco antiguo* (old city) is a 10min walk along Avda de Ordoño II.

Destinations Barcelona (3 daily; 8hr–8hr 40min); Bilbao (1 daily; 4hr 50min); Madrid (15 daily; 2hr 10min–5hr); San Sebastián (1 daily; 5hr); Santiago de Compostela (1 daily; 5hr 40min).

By bus The bus station is near the train station on Paseo Ingeniero Saenz de Miera.

Destinations Cáceres (3 daily; 6hr 15min); Madrid (10 daily; 3hr 30min–4hr); Santander (7 daily; 5hr–5hr 40min); Seville (3 daily; 10hr 30min); Zaragoza (3 daily; 6hr 15min–9hr 15min).

> ★ **TREAT YOURSELF**
>
> **Real Colegiata de San Isidoro** Pl. de Santo Martino 5 ☎ 987 875 088, ⓦ hotelrealcolegiata.es. Rest your weary bones in the super-comfortable beds at this hotel, stunningly located in the Colegiata section of the Real Basílica de San Isidoro church complex (see above). Set around a beautiful cloister, it's a surprisingly affordable oasis of luxury if you book out-of-season deals. Doubles **€75**

INFORMATION

Tourist office Pl. San Marcelo 1 (daily 9am–8pm; ☎987 878 327, ⓦturismoleon.org). Offers cheap bike rental (from €4 per half day).

ACCOMMODATION

Alda Centro León Hostel c/La Torre 3, 1º ☎987 225 594, ⓦaldacentroleon.es. Basic budget rooms with private bathrooms. The friendly owner offers laundry service and a shared kitchen. Doubles €30

Hostal San Martín Pl. Torres de Omaña 1, 2º ☎987 815 187, ⓦsanmartinhostales.es. Plain, bright rooms (some en suite) and a warm welcome near Barrio Húmedo. Doubles €43, shared bathroom €30

EATING AND DRINKING

Free tapas is the name of the game in the Barrio Húmedo around Plaza San Martín.

Bar Altar c/Platerías 2. Lively, friendly tapas bar a few metres from the Plaza Mayor with a range of free tapas plus cheap *montaditos* (small sandwiches). Daily 1–11.30pm.

El Llar Plaza San Martín 9. Stalwart Leonese bar with dark wood interior and terracotta walls. The *patatas alioli* (potatoes with garlic mayonnaise) – free with every drink – are brilliant. Daily 1–4pm & 7.30pm–1am.

El Rincón del Gaucho c/Azabachería 1. Barrio Húmedo classic, specializing in *sopa de ajo* (garlic soup), although the other tapas are great too (free with a drink, or €2.50–3 a dish). Daily 1–4pm & 8–11.30pm.

Parilla Louzao c/Juan Madrazo 4. Smart but moderately priced restaurant serving local meat dishes in large portions. Try the pork chops (€25 to share). Daily 1–4pm & 8–11.30pm.

Andalucía

The southern region of **Andalucía**, the sun-kissed, passionate home of **flamenco** and **bullfighting**, is all tradition and fierce pride. Evidence of the **Moors**' sophistication remains visible to this day in **Córdoba**, **Seville**, and, particularly, in **Granada's Alhambra**. Extending to either side of **Málaga** is the **Costa del Sol**, Europe's most developed resort area, but you can find unspoiled beaches even there, and along the **Costa de la Luz**, on the way to **Cádiz**, one of Spain's oldest cities. Andalucía is also where Europe stops and Africa begins: from **Tarifa**, a kite-surfer's paradise on Europe's most southerly tip, that great continent appears almost close enough to touch.

SEVILLE (SEVILLA)

SEVILLE (Sevilla) is the great city of the Spanish south, one of the earliest Moorish conquests (in 712 AD) and, as part of the Caliphate of Córdoba, the second city of al-Andalus. Under the Almohad dynasty, Seville became the capital of the last real Moorish empire in Spain from 1170 until 1212 before being conquered by Fernando III in 1248. Its monopoly on trade with the New World meant the city grew in wealth and influence; centuries on, it remains one of the most prosperous and beautiful of Spain's cities. Illustrious history aside, it is Seville's vitality that remains the great attraction, expressed on a grand scale at the city's two great festivals: **Semana Santa**, the week before Easter, and the **Feria de Abril**, a week at the end of April. While thoroughly modern, the soul of the city lies in its latticework of narrow streets, patios and plazas, where minarets jostle for space among cupolas and orange trees, and in its atmospheric flamenco bars.

WHAT TO SEE AND DO

Seville's three architectural gems – the Alcázar, Catedral and La Giralda – occupy the southern corner of the maze-like Barrio Santa Cruz.

La Giralda and the Catedral

Topped with four copper spheres, the 90m-tall **La Giralda** (Puerta de San Cristóbal; Mon 11am–3.30pm, Tues–Sat 11am–5pm, Sun 2.30–6pm; €9; ⓦcatedraldesevilla.es), erected by the Almohads between 1184 and 1198, still dominates the skyline today, and you can ascend the former minaret for a view of the city. The Giralda was so venerated by the Moors that they wanted to destroy it before the Christian conquest of the city. Instead, in 1402 it became the bell tower of the **Catedral**, the world's largest Gothic church, and the world's largest cathedral by volume. Its centre is dominated by a vast Gothic *retablo* composed of 45 carved scenes from the life of Christ, making up the largest altarpiece in the world. The cathedral is also the final resting place of Christopher Columbus. On your way

32

Hospital (7km) & Airport (10km)

SEVILLE (SEVILLA)

0   250
metres

Estación FF.CC.
Santa Justa

Jardines
del Valle

Convento
Sta. Paula

S. M. del
Socorro

PLAZA
JERÓNIMO
DE CÓRDOBA

Jardín de
Capuchinos

San
Hermenegildo

Convento
Sta. Isabel

Sta. Catalina

Convento de
Capuchinos

S. Marcos

PLAZA PONCE
DE LEÓN

PL. DE LOS
TERCEROS

Iglesia de
Sta. Marina

PL.SAN
MARCOS

S. Pedro

Palacio de
las Dueñas

City
Walls

Metropol
Parasol

Hospital de
la Sangre

Iglesia de
San Luis

PLAZA DE LA
ENCARNACIÓN

Arco
de la
Macarena

San Gil

LA MACARENA

Universidad
Antigua

Basílica de
la Macarena

Omnium
Sanctorum

C E N T R O

Alameda de Hércules

S. Lorenzo y
Jesús del
Gran Poder

PLAZA DE
GAVIDIA

Convento de
Sta. Clara

PZA. DE
S. LORENZO

S. Vicente

Monasterio de
S. Clemente

Río Guadalquivir

Parque
Jardín del
Guadalquivir

Telecabina

La Cartuja &
Centro Andaluz de
Arte Contemporáneo

■ DRINKING, NIGHTLIFE
AND ENTERTAINMENT

Bar Garlochí	4
Casa Anselma	6
Fun Club	5
La Carbonería	1
La Casa del Flamenco	2
Pura Vida Terraza	3

● EATING

Catalina	1
Eslava	5
Heladería la Fiorentina	4
Il Vesuvio	3
Mercado Lonja del Barranco	6
Vinería San Telmo	2

■ ACCOMMODATION

Feetup Samay Hostel	1
Oasis	3
Pensión Nuevo Suizo	4
TOC	2
Triana Backpackers	5

32

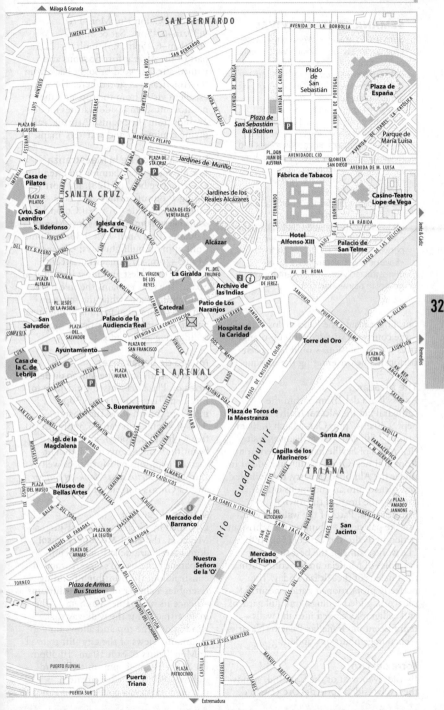

SAN BERNARDO

AVENIDA DE LA BORBOLLA

JIMENEZ ARANDA

SAN BERNARDO

AVENIDA DE MÁLAGA

AVENIDA DE CARLOS V

Prado
de
San
Sebastián

A AVENIDA DE PORTUGAL

Plaza de
España

DEMETRIO DE LOS RIOS

LUIS MONTOTO

CONTRERAS

AIDA DE CÁDIZ

Plaza de
San Sebastián
Bus Station

A AVENIDA DE ISABEL LA CATÓLICA

Parque de
María Luisa

PLAZA DE
S. AGUSTÍN

MENÉNDEZ PELAYO

Jardines de Murillo

PL. DON
JUAN DE
AUSTRIA

AVENIDADEL CID

GLORIETA
SAN DIEGO

AVENIDA DE M. LUISA

IMPERIAL S. ESTEBAN

PLAZA DE STA. CRUZ

STA. Mª. LA BLANCA

MARISCAL

Fábrica de Tabacos

Casa de
Pilatos

SANTA CRUZ

CONDE DE IBARRA

LEVIES

Jardines de los
Reales Alcázares

S. FERNANDO

Casino-Teatro
Lope de Vega

PLAZA DE
PILATOS

XIMENEZ DE ENCISO

PLAZA DE LOS
VENERABLES

LA RÁBIDA

Cvto. San
Leandro

S. JOSE

AGUA

Hotel
Alfonso XIII

S. Ildefonso

Iglesia de
Sta. Cruz

MATEOS GAGO

Alcázar

PEDRO DE LA FRONTERA

Palacio de
San Telme

VÍRGENES

C. AIRE

DEL REY D. PEDRO

BOTEROS

ABADES

PL. DEL
TRIUNFO

PLAZA
ALFALFA

LUCHANA

ARGOTE DE MOLINA

PL. VÍRGEN
DE LOS
REYES

La Giralda

PASEO DE LAS DELICIAS

PL. JESÚS
DE LA PASIÓN

FRANCOS

ALEMANES

Catedral

Archivo de
las Indias

PUERTA
DE JEREZ

AV. DE ROMA

San
Salvador

PLAZA
DEL
SALVADOR

Palacio de la
Audiencia Real

AVENIDA DE LA CONSTITUCIÓN

Patio de Los
Naranjos

SANJURJO

PUENTE DE SAN TELMO

JUAN S. ELCANO

COMPAÑIA

CUNA

Ayuntamiento

VIÑUESA

TOMÁS IBARRA

SANTANDER

Hospital de
la Caridad

PLAZA DE
CUBA

ASUNCIÓN

Casa de
la C. de
Lebrija

SIERPES

TETUÁN

PLAZA DE
SAN FRANCISCO

DOS DE MAYO

Torre del Oro

AV. REP.
ARGENTINA

VELÁZQUEZ

PLAZA
NUEVA

EL ARENAL

JOAQUIN

SALADO

RIOJA

MÉNDEZ NÚÑEZ

MORATÍN

SANTAS PATRONAS

CASTELAR

ADRIANO

ANTONIA DÍAZ

PASEO DE CRISTÓBAL COLÓN

RABIDA

S. Buenaventura

GALERA

Plaza de Toros de
la Maestranza

Santa Ana

ARDILLA

Igl. de la
Magdalena

SAN PABLO

ZARAGOZA

Capilla de los
Marineros

BETIS

PUREZA

TRIANA

FARMACÉUTICO
E. M. HERRERA

SAN ELOY

O'DONNELL

GRAVINA

CANALEJAS

ALMANSA

REYES CATÓLICOS

BETIS

RODRIGO DE TRIANA

EVANGELISTA

PLAZA
AMADEO
JANNONE

Museo de
Bellas Artes

BAILEN

P. DEL TORO

ALBUERA

P. DE ISABEL II (TRIANA)

PL. DEL
ALTOZANO

SAN JACINTO

PAGÉS DEL CORRO

San
Jacinto

ALFONSO XII

PLAZA
DEL MUSEO

PLAZA
DE PARADAS

TRASTAMARA

Mercado del
Barranco

Río Guadalquivir

SAN JORGE

MARQUÉS DE PARADAS

C. DE ARJONA

PLAZA
DE LA LEGIÓN

Mercado
de Triana

PAGÉS DEL CORRO

TORNEO

PLAZA DE
ARMAS

AV. DEL CRISTO DE LA EXPIRACIÓN

Nuestra
Señora
de la 'O'

ALFARERÍA

Plaza de Armas
Bus Station

PUENTE DEL CACHORRO

ALFARERÍA

CASTILLA

PUERTO FLUVIAL

CLARA DE JESÚS MONTERO

MANUEL ARELLANO

Puerta
Triana

PLAZA
PATROCINIO

CASTILLA

TEJARES

PUERTA SUR

32

Jerez & Cádiz

Remedios

SEMANA SANTA SURVIVAL

Semana Santa (Holy Week) is the most exciting time to be in Seville, with its eerie processions of hooded faithful from different *hermandades* (brotherhoods). To navigate your way around during this frenetic time, here are some tips:

Do your sightseeing in the mornings, since most processions take place in the afternoons and evenings.

• Find out the day's procession routes and make sure you know how to get back to your accommodation.

• Stock up on water and snacks, as many central shops will be closed.

• To get past a procession, shuffle along the side, NOT down the middle.

• Don't sit on the wooden chairs along the procession routes; people will have paid between €70 and €800 for each seat.

• Splurge on a balcony space for an unobstructed view – locals rent theirs out; expect to pay around €60.

out, linger inside the Patio de los Naranjas – the courtyard studded with 66 orange trees where ablutions would have been performed before entering the mosque.

The Alcázar

Across Plaza del Triunfo from the cathedral lies the **Alcázar** (daily: April–Sept 9.30am–7pm; Oct–March 9.30am–5pm; €9.50; ⦿ alcazarsevilla.org), a site that rulers of Seville have occupied from Roman times. Often rebuilt and added to, under the Almohad dynasty, the complex was turned into an enormous citadel, forming the heart of the town's fortifications. Parts of the walls survive, but the palace was rebuilt in the Christian period by Pedro the Cruel (1350–69). His works, some of the best surviving examples of Mudéjar architecture, form the nucleus of the Alcázar today. The perfectly proportioned patios, beautiful tile work, gilded ceilings, tranquil gardens and calligraphy carved into the walls – reminiscent of Granada's Palacios Nazaríes – encourage hours of wandering.

Torre del Oro

By the river, west of the Catedral, stands the twelve-sided **Torre del Oro** (Paseo de Cristóbal Colón s/n; Mon–Fri 9.30am–6.45pm, Sat & Sun 10.30am–6.45pm; €3), built in 1220 as part of the Alcázar fortifications and named after the gold brought back from the Americas was stored here. There are excellent views from the top, and the nautical museum inside features models of ships from the Spanish Armada, early diving equipment and seafarers' maps.

Plaza de Toros de la Maestranza

Even if you're not planning on attending a *corrida* (see box, p.1028), it's worth taking a tour of Seville's venerable **bullring** (Paseo de Cristóbal Colón 12; tours every 20min, daily: Nov–March 9.30am–7pm; April–Oct 9.30am–9pm, until 3pm on bullfight days; €7, free Mon 3–7pm; ⦿ realmaestranza.com) – one of the oldest and most beautiful in Spain. The tour explains the role of the bullfighting team, while the museum features costumes of famous bullfighters and *corrida*-related artworks by Goya, a bullfighting aficionado.

Museo de Bellas Artes

There's superb art at the **Museo de Bellas Artes** on Plaza del Museo (mid-June to mid-Sept Tues–Sun 9am–3.30pm; mid-Sept to mid-June Tues–Sat 9am–8.30pm, Sun 9am–3.30pm; €1.50, free with EU passport), housed in a beautiful former convent. Highlights include paintings by Murillo, as well as Zurbarán's *Carthusian Monks at Supper* and El Greco's portrait of his son.

Metropol Parasol

Designed by German architect Jürgen Mayer H, the 2011 **Metropol Parasol** dominates Plaza de la Encarnación. Apparently the world's largest wooden construction, the 30m-high building resembles a cluster of giant mushrooms – hence its nickname "Las Setas". The main attraction is the walkway that winds along the top and allows for panoramic views of the city (lift to level 2; Mon–Thurs & Sun 10am–10.30pm, Fri & Sat 10am–11pm; mirador and walkway €3). In the basement, a museum displays a collection of Roman ruins, which were discovered during construction (Tues–Sat 10am–7.30pm, Sun 10am–1.30pm; €2.10).

Triana

Across the river lies **Triana**, a *barrio* that was once home to Seville's gypsy community. At its northern edge is **La Cartuja** (Avda Américo Vespucio 2; Tues–Sat 11am–9pm, Sun 10am–3.30pm; €1.80 includes entry to CAAC, free Tues–Fri 7–9pm & Sat; ⓦwww.caac.es), a fourteenth-century former Carthusian monastery, where Columbus allegedly planned his early voyages – home to the **Centro Andaluz de Arte Contemporáneo**, which hosts edgy painting, sculpture and photography exhibitions.

ARRIVAL AND DEPARTURE

By plane Los Amarillos (ⓦlosamarillos.es) shuttle bus runs every 20–30min from Seville's domestic and international Aeropuerto San Pablo to Plaza de Armas and stops at the Estación de Santa Justa en route (4.30am–midnight; 30min; €4 one-way). Taxis cost around €22–25.

By train Estación Santa Justa is northeast of the centre, on Avda Kansas City; bus #C1 (€1.40) connects it to the centre and to the San Sebastián bus station.

Destinations Almería (4 daily; 6hr); Barcelona (8 daily; 5hr–11hr 30min); Cádiz (15 daily; 1hr 30min); Córdoba (every 30min 6.50am–9.35pm; 40min–1hr 20min); Granada (4 daily; 3hr); Madrid (17 daily; 2hr 30min–6hr 40min); Málaga (15 daily; 2hr–2hr 30min); Valencia (4 daily; 4hr–7hr 30min).

By bus The main bus station is at Plaza de Armas, but buses for destinations within Andalucía (plus Barcelona, Alicante and Valencia) leave from the more central terminal at Plaza de San Sebastián. Buses #C4 and #C21 connect the two.

Destinations Almería (3 daily; 5hr 30min–9hr); Cáceres (7 daily; 3hr–4hr 10min); Cádiz (10 daily; 1hr 45min–2hr); Córdoba (7 daily; 1hr 45min–2hr 15min); Granada (9 daily; 3hr–4hr 30min); Madrid (8 daily; 6hr 10min–6hr 30min); Málaga (6 daily; 2hr 30min–4hr); Mérida (10–13 daily; 3hr); Ronda (5 daily; 2hr 30min); Tarifa (4 daily; 2hr 55min–3hr 15min).

INFORMATION

Tourist office Pl. del Triunfo (Mon–Fri 9am–7.30pm, Sat & Sun 9.30am–7.30pm; ⓣ954 210 005, ⓦturismosevilla.org).

ACCOMMODATION

The most attractive area to stay is Barrio Santa Cruz, near the Catedral. During Easter Week and the Feria de Abril, prices double (prices below are regular high season) – book several months in advance.

Feetup Samay Hostel Avda Menendez Pelayo 13 ⓣ955 100 160, ⓦfeetuphostels.com. Top budget choice in a modern, marble-floored building with light, spacious and secure en-suite dorms, and a large roof terrace. Dorms €14, doubles €65

Oasis c/Compañia 1 ⓣ955 228 287, ⓦoasisbackpackershostels.com. Fantastic backpacker favourite, with helpful staff and clean dorms on several floors festooned with greenery. Rooftop pool and nightly tapas bar crawls. Dorms €19

Pensión Nuevo Suizo c/Azofaifo 7 ⓣ954 229 147, ⓦnuevosuizo.com. Creaky, wooden house that's in the heart of the action, particularly during Semana Santa. Friendly staff and free tea and coffee; some rooms share bathrooms. Doubles €36

TOC Miguel Mañara 18 ⓣ954 501 244, ⓦtochostels.com. Über-cool, design hostel moments from the Catedral and Alcázar. The vibe here is more hotel than hostel: spacious, modern rooms, a stylish bar and even a boutique-style indoor cinema. Book in advance online for discounts. Dorms €21, doubles €94

Triana Backpackers c/Rodrigo de Triana 69 ⓣ954 459 960, ⓦtrianabackpackers.com. Friendly and sociable place in Triana, whose staff organize lots of events. Clean dorms inside the attractively tiled building have a/c – a godsend in summer. Dorms €15, twin €38

EATING

There are numerous choices in the Barrio Santa Cruz, around Plaza Nueva and Triana. Seville is one of the great bastions of the tapa – the city claims to be its birthplace – so you'll be spoilt for choice here.

Catalina Paseo Catalina de Ribera 4 ⓣ954 412 412. Vegetarians are welcome at this restaurant with an outdoor terrace; the sumptuous aubergines with grilled goat's cheese is one of the house specials. Mains €9–14. Daily 9am–1am.

★**Eslava** c/Eslava 3 ⓦespacioeslava.com. Prepare to wait – this award-winning tapas bar gets busy. The inventive dishes, such as brie pastry cigars with cuttlefish and algae, are surprisingly good value (from €2.90). Tues–Sat 12.30pm–12.30am, Sun 12.30–4.30pm.

★**Heladería la Fiorentina** c/Zaragoza 16 ⓣ954 221 550. For over twenty years, Joaquín Lira's innovative ice creams have been capturing the flavours of Seville. Try the *crema de flor de azahar*, which evokes the smell of orange blossoms in springtime, or the *dulce de palmera*, which is inspired by a traditional Semana Santa sweet. March–Dec daily 1pm–1am.

Il Vesuvio c/Sierpes 54. At this authentic Italian restaurant, choose from a short menu of home-made pasta and fish or steak mains, then finish off with a

32

better-than-average tiramisu. Mains from €9. Daily 1–4.30pm & 7.30–11pm.

Mercado Lonja del Barranco c/Arjona s/n ⓦmercadolonjadelbarranco.com. Housed in a renovated glass and wrought-iron, nineteenth-century building is Seville's foodie must-visit destination. Choose from twenty stalls (prices start around €2.99) ranging from cheese specialists and gourmet croquettes to pulled-pork burgers and wine bars. Mon–Thurs & Sun 10am–midnight, Fri & Sat 10am–2am.

Vinería San Telmo Paseo Catalina de Ribera 4 ☎954 410 600. This tapas bar with alfresco terrace has a wonderful signature dish – the *rascocielo* or "skyscraper" of smoked salmon, grilled aubergine, goat's cheese and tomatoes. Tapas from €3.50. Daily 4.30–8pm.

DRINKING, NIGHTLIFE AND ENTERTAINMENT

The Plaza Alfalfa area, north of the Catedral, is particularly lively at night. Also popular with tourists and Seville's gay population is c/Betis in Triana.

BARS

Bar Garlochí c/Boteros 26. Weird and wonderful bar that's popular with *Sevillanos*. There's a mock-Semana Santa theme and a sacrilegious house special – the Sangre de Cristo cocktail. Daily 9pm–late.

Fun Club Alameda de Hércules 86. A music club where live bands play a mix of funk, jazz and Latino. Entry €5–7 on live music nights. Thurs–Sat 11.30pm–7am.

Pura Vida Terraza Hotel Fontecruz Sevilla Seises, c/Segovias ☎667 71 74 44. Kick back with a cocktail (€9) at this sun-trap rooftop bar. There's a chilled, beachy vibe and up-close views of the cathedral and Giralda. April–Sept daily 3–10pm, Oct–March Tues & Thurs–Sun 3–10pm.

FLAMENCO

Flamenco is staged across the city. A good place to head is c/Rodrigo de Triana, home to a handful of flamenco academies.

BULLFIGHTING

The season starts on Easter Sunday, reaches a peak around Feria de Abril, and continues until the end of September; most *corridas* are held on Sunday evenings. Love it or hate it, Seville's **bullring** is probably the best in Spain, with only bullfighters who have "made it", such as El Cid and El Juli, fighting on its sands. Tickets from the Plaza de Toros de la Maestranza, Paseo de Colón 12 (☎902 5223 506), start at €7–38 for a *sol* (sun-exposed) seat, and can cost up to €68 for *sombra* (shade).

Casa Anselma c/Pagés de Corro 49. Thick with cigarette smoke and packed with local flamenco aficionados, all waiting for a spontaneous performance to break out. There's no sign, so look for the yellow building whose facade is decorated with a mosaic; it's on the corner of c/Antillano Campos in Triana. Mon–Sat midnight–late.

La Carbonería c/Levíes 18. Tapas bar in an old coal merchant's building, with free flamenco performances at 11pm and midnight most nights.

La Casa del Flamenco c/Ximénez de Enciso 28 ☎954 500 595, ⓦlacasadelflamencosevilla.com. Fantastic daily performances at this intimate cultural centre (eighty or more spaces) at 7/8.30pm. Book tickets in advance (€18).

DIRECTORY

Hospital Hospital Universitario Virgen Macarena, Avda Dr Fedriani 3 (☎950 080 000), has English-speaking doctors. For emergencies, call ☎061.

Left luggage There are lockers at the train and bus stations.

Post office Avda de la Constitución 32.

CÁDIZ

CÁDIZ is among the oldest settlements in Spain, founded in around 1100 BC by the Phoenicians, and has long been one of the country's principal ports. In the eighteenth century it enjoyed a virtual monopoly on the Spanish–American gold and silver trade. It's also the spiritual home of flamenco, and has a tremendous atmosphere – slightly seedy, somewhat in decline, but still full of mystique. Cádiz's big party is its annual **Carnaval**, complete with costumed revelry, normally held in February and early March.

WHAT TO SEE AND DO

Built on a peninsular island, with grand open squares, winding alleys and high, turreted houses, Cádiz is fascinating to wander around.

Torre Tavira

For 360-degree views of the city, climb the **Torre Tavira** at Marqués del Real Tesoro 10 (daily: May–Sept 10am–8pm; Oct–April 10am–6pm; €6; ⓦtorretavira.com), the tallest of the city's 126 lookout towers – a legacy of the pirate age. The price includes tours showcasing the *camera obscura* – a device that uses mirrors to zoom in on any part of the city and project an image onto a surface inside the tower.

Catedral Nueva and Torre de Poniente

The huge, white, sea-facing **Catedral Nueva** (Pl. de la Catedral s/n; Jan–March, Nov & Dec Mon–Sat 10am–7pm, Sun 11am–7pm; April–June, Sept & Oct Mon–Sat 10am–8pm, Sun 11am–8pm; July & Aug Mon–Sat 10am–9pm, Sun 11am–9pm; €5, free Sun 11am–1.30pm; ⍵ catedraldecadiz.com) is a blend of High Baroque and Neoclassical styles as a result of it taking 116 years to build, decorated entirely in stone. Climb the adjacent **Torre de Reloj** (same hours and ticket) for splendid views of the city.

Museo de Cádiz

The well-lit interior at the **Museo de Cádiz** on Plaza de Mina (Jan to mid-June & mid-Sept to Dec Tues–Sat 9am–8.30pm, Sun 9am–3.30pm; mid-June to mid-Sept Tues–Sun 9am–3.30pm; €1.50, free for EU citizens) showcases the Phoenician marble sarcophagi, Roman statuary and other archeological treasures. Upstairs are masterpieces by Zurbarán and Murillo – including the last altarpiece he painted before a fatal fall from the scaffolding.

Coastal walk and beaches

A 4.5km **coastal walk** runs along the outside of the Old Town, taking in two beautiful parks – the Alameda Apodaca, running along the Bay of Cádiz, and the large, sculpted Parque Genovés, home to numerous exotic plants. Cádiz also has two main **beaches**: the often-crowded little crescent Playa de la Caleta at its western end, complete with Castillo San Sebastian (daily 9.30am–5pm; free), and Playa de la Victoria's wide stretch of white sand (take bus #2 south along Avda del Puerto).

ARRIVAL AND DEPARTURE

By train The station is at the southeastern end of the Old Town, a 5min walk from Plaza de San Juan de Dios.
Destinations Córdoba (13–20 daily; 2hr 25min–3hr 30min); Madrid (9–15 daily; 4hr 20min–5hr 10min); Seville (11–15 daily; 1hr 30min–1hr 50min).
By bus The bus station is opposite the train station.

Destinations Almería (1 daily at 3pm; 7hr 45min); Córdoba (4 daily; 3hr 30min–4hr); Granada (4 daily; 5hr 15–5hr 45min); Málaga (4 daily; 3hr 45min–4hr 45min); Ronda (2 daily; 3hr 20min); Seville (9 daily; 1hr 45min–2hr); Tarifa (6 daily; 1hr 30min–1hr 45min).

INFORMATION

Tourist office Paseo de Canalejas (June–Sept Mon–Fri 9am–7pm, Sat & Sun 9am–5pm; Oct–May Mon–Fri 8.30am–6.30pm, Sat & Sun 9am–5pm; ☎ 956 241 001, ⍵ cadiz.es).

ACCOMMODATION

Cadiz Inn Backpackers c/Botica 2 ☎ 956 262 309, ⍵ cadizbackpackers.es. A super-central hostel, with helpful staff and a sunny roof terrace. Dorms **€20**, doubles **€50**
Casa Caracol c/Suárez de Salazar 4 ☎ 956 261 166, ⍵ casacaracolcadiz.com. This backpacker favourite has laidback staff, dorms and doubles (most en suite), and a plethora of activities on offer, from rooftop parties to day-trips. Dorms **€21**, doubles **€45**
Pensión España c/Marqués de Cádiz 9 ☎ 956 285 500, ⍵ pensionespana.com. This friendly, central guesthouse offers clean singles, doubles and triples, most with shared bathrooms. Doubles **€40**

EATING

Cádiz is the birthplace of takeaway fried fish so make sure to try one of the *friedurías* (fried-fish shops). For drinks and seafood, head to c/Virgen de la Palma in the Barrio de la Viña, just east of Playa de la Caleta, or to Plaza de Las Flores.
El Aljibe c/Plocia 25 ☎ 956 266 656. Trendy, stone-walled, wooden-beamed bar serving some of Cádiz's most inventive tapas, from spinach and shrimp lasagne to baby squid in ink. Tapas €2.20–4. Daily 9.30am–1am.
Freiduría Las Flores Pl. de las Flores. A Cádiz institution, this *freiduría* serves up large, cheap portions of fish. Try the excellent *tortilla de camarónes* (shrimp patty). Tapas €1.20–2.40. Daily 9am–4pm & 7pm–midnight.
★**La Candela** c/Feduchy 3 ☎ 956 221 822. Small, popular place that's been decorated with quirky touches. Tapas dishes range from classics to more unusual offerings like pork *bao* topped with a fried egg. There are also sharing plates and mains (from €8). Daily 1.30–4pm & 8.30–11.30pm.

TARIFA

If there's one thing that defines tiny **TARIFA**, it is the powerful prevailing wind, which has made the southernmost point in mainland Europe one of the world's most popular kitesurfing and windsurfing destinations. The place charms with its laidback atmosphere and maze of narrow streets, plus Africa lies on the horizon, and is easily accessible, via the ferries that run to Tangier in Morocco (see box below).

(see box below).

WHAT TO SEE AND DO

There are two principal things to keep you occupied: enjoying the waves and the wind and searching for whales.

Kitesurfing and windsurfing

The 10km white, sandy **beaches**, **Playa de los Lances** and **Ensenada de Valdevaqueros**, are the places for watersports. You can book a course or rent equipment from a number of outfitters in town, such as Bull Sails & Kites (c/Braille 22; ☎956 68 04 59, ⓦbullschool.com), which run kiteboarding, surfing and stand-up paddle-boarding courses (group courses start at €20/person/hr), and rent out equipment.

32

Whale-watching

The Strait of Gibraltar is an excellent place for spotting killer whales, pilot whales, sperm whales and dolphins. Several operators run daily two-hour **whale-watching boat trips**, including Firmm, c/Pedro Cortés 4 (April–Oct; €30; tours include a 30min talk on marine mammals; ☎956 627 008, ⓦfirmm.org), who are dedicated to the research and conservation of the local

population of marine mammals, and Whalewatch Tarifa at Avda de la Constitución 6 (from €33; ☎956 627 013, ⓦwhalewatchtarifa.net), a non-profit conservation association.

ARRIVAL AND DEPARTURE

By bus Comes (☎956 681 038, ⓦtgcomes.es) buses arrive at the station at Batalla del Salado s/n (near the petrol station). The centre is a 10min walk south.
Destinations Algeciras (8–12 daily; 30min); Cádiz (5 daily; 1hr 45min); Málaga (3 daily; 2hr 45min); Seville (4 daily; 3hr).
By boat FRS at Avda Andalucía 16 (☎956 681 830, ⓦfrs.es) runs fast ferries and tours to Morocco (see box below).

INFORMATION

Tourist office Paseo de la Alameda s/n (Mon–Fri 10am–1.30pm & 4–6pm, Sat & Sun 10am–1.30pm; ☎956 680 993, ⓦaytotarifa.com).

ACCOMMODATION

From July to mid-Sept, book accommodation well in advance.
Camping Paloma 11km northwest of town ☎956 684 203, ⓦcampingpaloma.com. Situated 500m from Playa de Valdevaqueros, this shady campsite has a full range of facilities, including on-site restaurant, supermarket and swimming pool. There are also forty bungalows (sleeping two to six people; minimum two nights). Powered pitches cost extra. Check website for discounts during low season. Camping/person **€6.48** plus per tent **€4.86**, bungalow for two **€54**

MOROCCO-BOUND

The main reason to visit the gritty, busy post of **Algeciras** is to take a ferry to **Tangier** in Morocco, or the Spanish enclave of **Ceuta**. FRS ferries (ⓦfrs.es) are the fastest and most frequent (depending on the weather): buy tickets directly from their office at the port. However, Tarifa (see above) is a more salubrious departure point for Tangier, with FRS selling straightforward ferry tickets (one-/two-day trip €60/89; ☎956 681 830), as well as guided one-day tours and customized two- or three-day trips to Tangier, Tetouan, Asilah or Chefchaouen. Bring your passport.

FERRIES TO MOROCCO

From Algeciras Ceuta (5–6 daily; 1hr; €32 one-way, €64 return); Tangier (7 daily; 1hr 45min; €30 one-way, €40.80 return).
From Tarifa Tangier (4–8 daily; 35min; €37 one-way, €66 return).

ONWARD TRAVEL FROM ALGECIRAS

If arriving in Algeciras, you can travel on to other Spanish cities from the bus station on c/San Bernardo

and the adjacent train station.
By train Córdoba (4 daily; 3hr 10min–4hr 30min); Granada (3 daily; 4hr 15min–4hr 40min); Madrid (3 daily; 5hr 30min); Ronda (5 daily; 1hr 25min–1hr 50min).
By bus Granada (4 daily; 3hr 30min–5hr 45min); La Línea de la Concepción (every 30min; 45min); Málaga (18 daily; 1hr 45min–4hr 40min); Tarifa (6 daily; 30min).

GIBRALTAR

Backed by the enormous Rock, visible from many kilometres away, and long coveted for its strategic position at the entrance to the Mediterranean, the British territory of **Gibraltar**, at the southern tip of Spain, has been the source of tension between the two countries for nearly three hundred years since it was ceded to **Britain** under the Treaty of Utrecht.

Now a somewhat clichéd slice of Britain, Gibraltar comes complete with red postboxes, Marks & Spencer, chippies and, of course, the pound.

Relations between the UK and Spain can be strained over Gibraltar, with Spain enforcing tough, time-consuming border checks. **Buses** run from several Spanish destinations to La Línea. To get to Gibraltar, walk across the border and follow Winston Churchill Ave into town (10min).

Hostal Africa c/María Antonia Toledo 12 ☎ 956 680 220, ⓦ hostalafrica.com. Popular with kitesurfers, this central guesthouse has attractive marble-floored rooms and a partially covered roof terrace for lounging. Cheaper rooms share bathrooms. Doubles €50

Melting Pot Hostel c/Turriano Gracil 5 ☎ 956 682 906, ⓦ meltingpothostels.com. Backpacker and kitesurfer haven with fully equipped kitchen and a cosy lounge/bar. En-suite dorms are somewhat cramped, but the ambience is great. Dorms €26, doubles €60

EATING

★ **Café 10** c/Ntra. Sra. de la Luz 10 ☎ 671 23 79 41. Petite and beachy, *Café 10* is stylishly decked out with stone floors and whitewashed wood panelling. A popular breakfast haunt, the all-day menu features toasties (€4.50), crêpes (€6), fresh juices and home-made cakes. Daily 9–2am.

Chilimosa c/Peso 6. Compact vegetarian restaurant/takeaway serving up healthy food with an eastern twist. The changing menu includes a range of main dishes (€3–8) and the *plato degustación* (€9.80) which features falafel, hummus and salad. Don't miss the cheesecake. Daily 12.30–3.30pm & 7–11pm.

Lola c/Guzmán el Bueno 5. In the evenings, tables spill out of this friendly tapas bar onto the street. The highlights on the menu include the garlic prawns and *el revuelto de abuela* (fancy scrambled eggs). Tapas from €1.50; *raciones* €4–17. Daily 1–4pm & 7.30pm–midnight.

★ **No. 6 Cocina Sencilla** C/Colón 6 ☎ 671 23 79 41. The owner of *Café 10*'s latest venture boasts a cool interior that blends exposed brick, a stone archway and pendant lights. Try the sweet potato *patatas bravas* with wasabi aioli

(€3.50); if your budget can stretch to it, the *ración* of impossibly tender pan-seared octopus with soy mayonnaise for €13 is worth every penny. Mon & Wed–Fri 7.30pm–12.30am, Sat & Sun 1–4pm & 7.30pm–12.30am.

RONDA

Built on an isolated ridge of the sierra, and ringed by mountains, the spectacular *pueblo blanco* of **RONDA**, a large cluster of attractive whitewashed houses, was made famous in Hemingway's *For Whom The Bell Tolls*. The town is split in two by a gaping river **gorge** with a sheer drop, spanned by an incredible eighteenth-century arched bridge from which hundreds of people were thrown to their deaths during the Spanish Civil War.

WHAT TO SEE AND DO

Most sights of interest lie in the tiny old quarter on the eastern side of the gorge.

Plaza de Toros y Museo Taurino

In the modern El Mercadillo quarter, the Plaza de Toros, Spain's oldest **bullring**, is where three generations of the Romero family shaped the rules of bullfighting during the eighteenth and nineteenth centuries (daily: March & Oct 10am–7pm; April–Sept 10am–8pm; Nov–Feb 10am–6pm; €7). The on-site **Museo Taurino** showcases *corrida* memorabilia, including numerous *trajes de luz* – the colourful costumes of the *matadores*.

Old Quarter sights

The principal gate of the town, through which the Christian conquerors passed, stands beside the **Alcázar**, destroyed by the French in 1809. Sights in the Old Quarter include the well-preserved thirteenth- and fourteenth-century **Baños Árabes** (c/San Miguel s/n; Mon–Fri 10am–7pm, Sat & Sun 10am–3pm; Oct–March Mon–Fri closes 6pm; €3, free Tues from 3pm), with their distinctive horseshoe arches, reachable via a flight of steps and a path along a section of the old city wall. The **Palacio de Mondragón** (Mon–Fri 10am–7pm, Sat & Sun 10am–3pm; €3, Tues free from 3pm for EU citizens), located on its namesake plaza, was probably once the palace of

32

the Moorish kings and is now home to exhibitions on the history of the area. On nearby Plaza Duquesa de Parcent stands the **Iglesia de Santa María la Mayor** (daily: April–Sept 10am–8pm; Oct & March 10am–7pm; Nov–Feb 10am–6pm; €4.50), built on the site of Ronda's main mosque. The whimsical **Museo Lara** at c/de Armiñán 29 (daily: June–Oct 11am–8pm; Nov–May 11am–7pm; €4; w museolara.org) houses an ever-expanding private collection of antique objects, ranging from eighteenth- and nineteenth-century weaponry to early cameras and horse carriages. A macabre exhibit on witchcraft and the Inquisition is (fittingly) located in the cellar.

Local walks

The Old Quarter's **Jardínes de Forestier** ascend the gorge in a series of stepped terraces, offering superb views of the river and the remarkable stairway of the **Casa del Rey Moro**, an early eighteenth-century mansion on the north side of the gorge. For a classic shot of the Puente Nuevo that spans the gorge, head to the Jardines de Cuenca. There are also some fantastic day hikes around Ronda, ranging from 2.5km to 9.1km, outlined in a booklet available at the tourist office (€5).

ARRIVAL AND DEPARTURE

By train The train station is at Avda de la Victoria 31, off Avda Andalucía, a 15min walk from the Old Quarter.
Destinations Algeciras (5 daily; 1hr 30min–1hr 50min); Córdoba (4 daily; 1hr 45min–2hr); Granada (3 daily; 2hr 30min–3hr); Madrid (3 daily; 4hr); Málaga (3 daily; 2hr–2hr 20min).
By bus The bus station is near Plaza Redondo.
Destinations Cádiz (2 daily; 3hr 15min–3hr 30min); Málaga (7 daily; 3hr 30min); Seville (6 daily; 1hr 45min).

INFORMATION

Tourist office Opposite the entrance to the bullring at Pl. de Toros (April–Sept Mon–Fri 10am–7pm; Oct–March Mon–Fri 10am–6pm; all year Sat 10am–5pm, Sun 10am–2.30pm; t 952 187 119, w turismoderonda.es).

ACCOMMODATION

Prices rise in April and May, when you should book in advance.
Hotel Morales c/Sevilla 51 t 952 871 538, w hotelmorales.es. Friendly, central cheapie with warm staff and spotless en-suite rooms. Doubles €35

Hotel San Francisco c/María Cabrera 18 t 952 873 299, w hotelsanfrancisco-ronda.com. Elegant budget option, with Moorish archways in the dining room and cosy rooms equipped with a/c. Check website for discounts. Doubles €44

EATING AND DRINKING

Bodega San Francisco c/Ruedo Alameda 32, just outside the Carlos V gate t 952 878 162, w bodegasanfrancisco.com. Old-school tapas bar, with hams hanging from the ceiling, serving fantastic *tortilla de camarones* (prawn omelette), mini-*pinchos* (grilled meat on sticks) and other favourites. Tapas from €1. Mon–Wed & Fri–Sun 11am–midnight.
La Vita E Bella c/Nueva 5. Cheerful Italian-run joint with a big selection of pizzas (from €6.50), delicious home-made pasta dishes and a range of fish and meat mains. April–Oct daily noon–4pm & 7.30pm–midnight; Nov–March Mon noon–4pm, Wed–Sun noon–4pm & 7.30pm–midnight.
★ **Tragatapas** c/Nueva 4 t 952 877 209. Ronda's most imaginative tapas, such as pork cheeks au gratin on ciabbata and fried pig's ear with a spicy sauce. Also serves sharing plates (from €8) and fusion mains such as curried duck. Tapas from €1.85; mains €10.50–22. Tues–Sat 1–4pm & 8–11pm, Sun 1–4pm.

MÁLAGA

MÁLAGA is the second city of the south after Seville, one of the oldest in Spain, and also the gateway to the rest of the Costa del Sol, the richest resort area in the Mediterranean.

WHAT TO SEE AND DO

The charming historic centre may be unchanged – as are the clusters of high-rises that surround it – but much of Málaga has undergone a transformation. The once-drab port has been revamped into the sleek Muelle Uno, and the city that was home to Picasso is rapidly fulfilling its mission to become a Spanish cultural hub (see box opposite).

The Picasso museums

Málaga's most famous native son, born here in 1881, is honoured in the immensely popular **Museo Picasso Málaga**, c/San Agustín 8 (daily: March–June, Sept & Oct 10am–7pm; July & Aug 10am–8pm; Nov–Feb 10am–6pm; €8, free last 2hr on Sun;

MÁLAGA'S CHANGING ART SCENE

The millions of euros that have been pumped into Málaga's **art scene** are unveiling themselves in an impressive array of sights. Stealing the show is the pop-up **Pompidou** (El Cuba, Muelle Uno; mid-June to mid-Sept Mon & Wed–Sun 11am–10pm; mid-Sept to mid-June Mon & Wed–Sun 9.30am–8pm; permanent exhibition €7, temporary €4, combined €9; ⓦ centrepompidou-malaga.eu), in a striking building topped with a multi-coloured glass cube. On loan for five years, the collection houses works from big names such as Frida Kahlo and Pablo Picasso. Another foreign foray, the **State Russia Museum Collection** is calling an old tobacco factory home for ten years (Edificio de Tabaclera, Avda Sor Teresa Prat 15; mid-June to mid-Sept Tues–Sun 11am–10pm, mid-Sept to mid-June Tues–Sun 9.30–8pm; permanent exhibition €6, temporary €4, combined €8; ⓦ coleccionmuseoruso.es). Meanwhile, the up-and-coming **SOHO** district is becoming an open-air **street-art** canvas – grab a free street art map from Maus (ⓦ mausmalaga.com), or join a tour by CAC (3 daily on Mon; free).

ⓦ museopicassomalaga.org), which displays an intimate collection spanning Picasso's career; temporary exhibitions feature his contemporaries. Serious fans shouldn't miss the **Casa Natal de Picasso**, Plaza de la Merced 15 (April–Oct daily 9.30am–8pm; Nov–March Mon & Wed–Sun 9.30am–8pm; €3; ⓦ www .fundacionpicasso.es), where the artist was born, with choice works of his displayed upstairs.

Catedral

Founded in 1528, Málaga's **Catedral** on Calle Molina Lario (Mon–Fri 10am–6pm, Sat 10am–5pm; €5) towers above the Old Town. It features a melange of architectural styles, having taken 260 years to complete: its interior is Renaissance and Baroque while the northern entrance is Gothic. Since it features one tower when the original plans included two, it is affectionately known as La Manquita (one-armed woman).

Alcazaba and Castillo de Gibralfaro

Just east of the Old Town rises Mount Gibralfaro where the Moorish citadels of the 1057 **Alcazaba** and **Castillo de Gibralfaro** (both daily: April–Oct 9am–8pm; Nov–March 9am–6pm; lift shut on Mon; each €2.20, free Sun from 2pm, joint ticket €3.55), built in the eighth century by Abd ar-Rahman I and rebuilt in the fourteenth and fifteenth, tower above the ruins of a Roman theatre. The viewpoint on the way to the castle offers spectacular city views.

Centro de Arte Contemporáneo (CAC)

Housed inside a converted 1930s wholesale market on Calle Alemana, this cutting-edge **contemporary art museum** (Tues–Sun: mid-June to Sept 10am–2pm & 5–9pm; Oct to mid-June 10am–8pm; free; ⓦ cacmalaga.org) features exhibits of twentieth- and twenty-first-century installations, painting and sculpture by international artists.

Beaches

Sunbathers favour the white-sand Playa de la Malagueta, ten minutes' walk from the Old Town. The old fishing villages of El Palo and Pedregalejo, 4km east of the centre, boast grey-sand **beaches** and a promenade lined with some of the best **fish and seafood restaurants** in the province; catch bus #11 along Paseo del Parque.

ARRIVAL AND DEPARTURE

There's luggage storage at the bus and train stations.

By plane Málaga's Pablo Picasso Airport (ⓣ 952 048 484, ⓦ aena.es) is linked to the train station by electric train (every 20min 5.20am–11.30pm; €1.80); continue another stop to Málaga Centro: Alameda for the city centre. The airport bus (#A) goes to the city centre, via the main bus station (every 20–30min; 6.25am–11.30pm; €3).

By train The station is a 20min walk southwest of the centre at Explanada de la Estación, s/n. Buses #1, #3, #5, #10 and #16 run to the city centre.

Destinations Barcelona (4–7 daily; 5hr 35min–11hr 20min); Córdoba (19 daily; 1hr); Madrid (13–16 daily; 2hr 25min–3hr 45min); Seville (11 daily; 1hr 50min–2hr 50min); Valencia (3 daily; 4hr 10min–7hr 30min).

By bus The bus station (ⓣ 952 350 061) is roughly opposite the train station, on the Paseo de los Tilos. Buses #4 and #11 run to the Alameda Principal.

32

Destinations Almería (7 daily; 3hr–5hr 15min); Córdoba (4 daily; 2hr 30min–4hr); Granada (18 daily; 1hr 30min–2hr); Madrid (8 daily; 6hr–7hr 20min); Ronda (11 daily; 2hr 45min); Seville (6 daily; 2hr–3hr 15min).

INFORMATION

Tourist office Pl. de la Marina 11 (daily: April–Sept 9am 8pm; Oct March 9am 6pm; ☎951 926 020, ⓦ malagaturismo.com).

ACCOMMODATION

Casa Babylon c/Pedro de Quejana 3 ☎952 267 228, ⓦ casababylonhostel.com. Colourful, sociable and full of character, this is the place to meet fellow travellers, though don't expect much sleep if your room is near the common room. The location – in Málaga's historical centre – is hard to beat. Dorms €17, doubles €40

La Casa Mata c/Molinillo del Aceite 8 ☎951 252 776. On the edge of the Old Town, this quiet secure hostel features bright private rooms (doubles, twins and triples), a well-stocked kitchen and friendly management. The singles are tiny. Call ahead if arriving after 8pm. Doubles €44

★**Lights Out** c/Torregorda 3 ☎951 25 35 25, ⓦ lightsouthostel.com. New hostel set up by people who know what travellers want: plenty of bathrooms, powerful showers, friendly staff, well-designed dorms (beds have sockets and reading lights), and great communal areas – including a sociable beanbag-strewn roof terrace. Dorms €19, doubles €90

EATING AND DRINKING

Málaga specialities – *fritura malagueña* (battered and fried fish and squid) and *espeto* (sardines grilled on bamboo spears) are served at seaside restaurants along the El Palo and Pedregalejo beaches.

El Rincón del Cervecero C/Casas de Campos 5b ☎952 226 426. In artsy SOHO, this beer shop and bar is helping drive Málaga's craft beer movement. There are 250 beers on offer, tasting sessions and homebrew workshops. The owners also make their own brews for Semana Santa and the Feria. Mon–Wed 7pm–midnight, Thurs–Sat noon–4pm & 7pm–12.30am.

★**El Tapeo de Cervantes** c/Cárcer 8 ⓦ eltapeode cervantes.com. In this atmospheric bar you'll be sitting cheek by jowl with other diners, hungrily awaiting tapas such as Ibérico pork with pumpkin and pineapple relish and lamb stew with couscous. Get there early, as the place gets packed. Tapas from €2.50. Tues–Sat 1–3.30pm & 7.30–11.30pm, Sun 7.30–11.30pm.

★**Mamuchis** Casa de Campos 27 ☎951 994 517. Eating here is like being welcomed into someone's home; owners Marcel and Leiticia have decorated the place with

mementos from their travels and the menu of healthy sharing plates (from €5) mirrors this, featuring dim sum and Greek-style courgette burgers. Tues 2–8pm, Wed–Sat 2–11pm, Sun 2–4pm.

Recyclo Bike Café Marqués de Villafiel 4 ⓦ recyclobike .com. With bikes hanging from the ceiling, this laidback joint serves toasties and burgers (from €5), and has plenty of vegetarian options. Combine breakfast with renting wheels from their bike shop next door (Mon–Fri 10–2pm & 5–8.30pm, Sat 10–2pm) before cycling off to Málaga's quieter beaches. Daily 9am–midnight.

CÓRDOBA

CÓRDOBA was once the largest city of Roman Spain, then for three centuries the heart of the great medieval caliphate of the Moors, before becoming the second-largest headquarters of the Inquisition. It's an engaging, compact and atmospheric city that is easily explored on foot.

WHAT TO SEE AND DO

Córdoba's main attraction is **La Mezquita** – the grandest and most beautiful mosque ever constructed by the Moors in Spain. This stands right in the centre of the city, surrounded by the labyrinth of old Jewish and Moorish quarters.

La Mezquita

Córdoba's domination of Moorish Spain began thirty years after the conquest, in 756 AD, when the city was placed under **Abd ar-Rahman I**, who established control over all but the north of Spain. He began the building of the Great Mosque – in Spanish, **La Mezquita** (March–Oct Mon–Sat 10am–7pm; Nov–Feb Mon–Sat 10am–6pm; all year Sun 8.30–11.30am & 3–6pm; €8, free Mon–Sat 8.30–9.30am) – which is approached through the **Patio de los Naranjos**, a classic Islamic court preserving both its orange trees and fountains for ritual purification before prayer. Inside, nearly a thousand twin-layered red and white archways combine to mesmerizing effect, the harmony culminating only at the foot of the beautiful **mihrab** (prayer niche), decorated with gold mosaic cubes – a gift from Nicephoras II Phocas, the Christian emperor of Byzantium. In the centre of

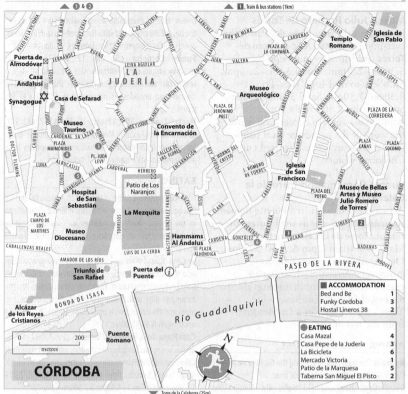

Iglesia de
San Pablo

Templo
Romano

Puerta de
Almodóvar ⊠

Casa
Andalusí

LA
JUDERÍA

Museo
Arqueológico

PLAZA DE LA
CORREDERA

Synagogue ✡

Casa de Sefarad

Museo
Taurino ❹

PLAZA DE
JERÓNIMO
PÁEZ

Convento de
la Encarnación

PLAZA DE LA
CORREDERA

Plaza
Maimónides ❹

PL. JUDA
LEVÍ

PLAZA
CAÑAS

PLAZA
SOCOMO

Hospital
de San
Sebastián ❺

Patio de Los
Naranjos ⊠

Iglesia
de San
Francisco

Museo de Bellas
Artes y Museo
Julio Romero
de Torres

PLAZA
CAMPO DE
LOS
MÁRTIRES

La Mezquita

Museo
Diocesano

Hammams
Al Ándalus ❻

PLAZA DE
POTRO

LINEROS ❷

Triunfo de
San Rafael

Puerta del ⓘ
Puente

PASEO DE LA RIVERA

32

■ ACCOMMODATION	
Bed and Be	1
Funky Cordoba	3
Hostal Lineros 38	2

Alcázar
de los Reyes
Cristianos

RONDA DE ISASA

Río Guadalquivir

● EATING	
Casa Mazal	4
Casa Pepe de la Judería	3
La Bicicleta	6
Mercado Victoria	1
Patio de la Marquesa	5
Taberna San Miguel El Pisto	2

0　　　　200
metres

Puente
Romano

N

CÓRDOBA

▼ Torre de la Calahorra (25m)

one of the world's most beautiful mosques, you'll find the incongruous presence of a Renaissance cathedral, built in 1523, though it's the mihrab that commands most of the attention.

La Judería and around

North of La Mezquita lies **La Judería**, Córdoba's old Jewish quarter, a network of narrow, atmospheric lanes and small plazas. At c/Judíos 20 is a tiny fourteenth-century **synagogue** with fine stuccowork (Jan to mid-June & mid-Sept to Dec Tues–Sat 9am–8.30pm, Sun 9am–3.30pm; mid-June to mid-Sept Tues–Sun 9am–3.30pm; €0.30, free for EU citizens), one of only three in Spain that survived the Jewish expulsion of 1492. Nearby, on the corner of c/Judíos and c/Averroes, the beautiful fourteenth-century **Casa de Sefarad** (Mon–Fri 10am–6pm, Sat & Sun 11am–7pm, closed one week in Nov & two weeks in Jan; €4; ⓦcasadesefarad.es)

explores the Sephardic-Judaic tradition. Its collections include weavings with gold thread and ceremonial objects; upstairs, exhibits are devoted to the contribution of Sephardic Jews to Islamic Córdoba and their persecution by the Inquisition. Some evenings there are live shows, from flamenco to theatre, in the candle-lit courtyard.

Alcázar de los Reyes Cristianos

Near La Mezquita is the thirteenth-century **Castle of the Christian Monarchs** (Pl. Campo Santo de los Mártires s/n; Tues–Fri 8.30am–8.45pm, Sat 8.30am–4.30pm, Sun 8.30am–2.30pm; €4.50, free Tues–Fri 8.30–9.30am), originally home to Alfonso X and then the headquarters of the Inquisition between 1490 and 1821. Highlights include the beautiful sculpted gardens, a third-century Roman sarcophagus and the view from one of the Alcázar's towers.

Museo Julio Romero de Torres

Located on the tiny Plaza del Potro, the ever-popular **Museo Julio Romero de Torres** (mid-June to mid-Sept Tues–Sat 8.30am–2.30pm, Sun 9.30am–2.30pm; mid-Sept to mid-June Tues–Fri 8.30am–7.30pm, Sat 9.30am–4.30pm, Sun 9.30am–2.30pm, €4.50, ⓦmuseojulioromero.cordoba.es) features the work of the namesake local painter, whose signature works depicted curvy Córdoban women.

Puente Romano and Torre de la Calahorra

Across the pedestrianized **Puente Romano** (Roman Bridge) stands the fourteenth-century **Torre de la Calahorra** (daily: May–Sept 10am–2pm & 4.30–8.30pm; Oct–April 10am–6pm; €4.50; ⓦtorrecalahorra.com), housing an entertaining museum that brings the history of Islamic Córdoba to life. There's a great view of a La Mezquita from the top of the tower.

ARRIVAL AND DEPARTURE

By train The train station is along the Glorieta de las Tres Culturas, 1km northwest of the old town.

Destinations Barcelona (13 daily; 4hr 30min–10hr 10min); Cádiz (14–22 daily; 2hr 20min–4hr); Granada (6 daily; 2hr–2hr 40min); Madrid (25–30 daily; 1hr 45min–5hr 30min); Málaga (15 daily; 1hr); Seville (35 daily; 45min–2hr 20min).

By bus The bus station is behind the train station. Bus #3 (€1.50) runs down c/San Fernández, just east of the Judería.

Destinations Granada (8 daily; 2hr 40min–4hr); Madrid (7 daily; 4hr 45min); Málaga (4 daily; 2hr 25min–3hr); Seville (7 daily; 1hr 45min–2hr).

INFORMATION

Tourist office Pl. de Triunfo s/n (Mon–Fri 9am–7.30pm, Sat & Sun 9.30am–3pm; ☎902 201 774, ⓦwww.turismodecordoba.org).

ACCOMMODATION

The intensely hot summers drive tourists away from Córdoba; come in April and May for a more pleasant stay but expect a spike in accommodation prices.

★**Bed and Be** c/Cruz Conde 22 ☎661 420 733, ⓦbedandbe.com. Stylish yet welcoming place, with light rooms, high ceilings, whitewashed shutters and quirky touches. There's a sunny terrace, bikes to rent, and friendly owner, José, is passionate about making sure guests see the best of the city – and with the clued-up staff and social events you're guaranteed that. Dorms **€15**, doubles **€38**

Funky Cordoba c/Lucano 12 ☎957 473 234, ⓦfunkycordoba.com. Central hostel with helpful staff, a roof terrace and guest kitchen. However, the place could be cleaner and breakfast is not included. Dorms **€11.50**, doubles **€30**

Hostal Lineros 38 c/Lineros 36–38 ☎957 482 517, ⓦhostallineros38.com. Moorish-style guesthouse that's more hotel than hostel, with luxurious four-poster beds and hammam-style bathrooms. Doubles **€48**

EATING

Córdoba's cuisine is some of the best in Andalucía, and it's fast becoming one of the most exciting foodie destinations in the region. Don't miss dishes such as *salmorejo* (a thicker, more savoury gazpacho) and *ajoblanco* (cold garlic and almond soup).

★**Casa Mazal** c/Tomas Conde 3. A tiny passageway leads into the flower-adorned, cobbled courtyard of Córdoba's only Sephardic restaurant. Their vegetarian dishes (try the aubergine pâté with home-made bread) are the best in town and their couscous is perfection. Mains €8–18. Daily noon–4pm & 8–11.30pm.

Casa Pepe de la Judería c/Romero 1 ☎957 200 744. Prop up the bar at this Córdoban institution, and don't miss their *salmorejo* and *berenjenas con miel* (aubergines with honey). Tapas from €3; mains from €9. Mon–Fri 1–4pm & 7.30–11.30pm, Sat & Sun 1–4.30pm & 7.30pm–midnight.

★**La Bicicleta** c/Cardenal Gonzalez 1. Behind a windowsill laden with fresh fruit hides a warren of rooms with exposed brickwork and pendant lights. Try the home-made cake of the day (€4.25) and freshly squeezed juices (€2.95). If you turn up on a bike they'll give you a discount on your food and drink. Mon–Fri 10am–1am, Sat & Sun noon–1am.

Mercado Victoria Paseo de la Victoria ⓦmercadovictoria.com. Billed as Andalucía's first gourmet market, thirty stalls fill this restored nineteenth-century pavilion. There's everything from *jamón ibérico* and Spanish cheeses, to international dishes and a handful of bars. Mon–Wed & Sun 10am–midnight, Thurs 10am–1am, Fri & Sat 10am–2am.

Patio de la Marquesa c/Manriquez 4. This traditional house in the Judería has been transformed into one of Córdoba's newest culinary ventures. Within the interconnected patios is a gastro-market offering Andalucían classics, international cuisine and a terrace-bar. Mon–Fri noon–4.30pm & 7.30–11pm, Sat & Sun noon–12.30pm, bar open till 3am.

Taberna San Miguel El Pisto Pl. San Miguel 1 ⓦcasaelpisto.com. Over a hundred years old, this place serves excellent Montilla wine, accompanied by regional tapas, such as *salmorejo*. Tapas from €2.40, mains from €8.50. Mon–Sat noon–4pm & 7.30pm–midnight.

GRANADA

If you see only one town in Spain, it should be **GRANADA**, with its wonderful backdrop of the **Sierra Nevada** mountains, and Spain's most visited monument, the **Alhambra**. Granada was established as an independent kingdom in 1238 by **Ibn Ahmar**, a prince of the Arab Nasrid tribe. The Moors of Granada maintained their autonomy for two and a half centuries, but by 1490 only the city itself remained in Muslim hands. On January 2, 1492, Granada fell to the army of Ferdinand and Isabella following a seven-month siege, and the Christian Reconquest of Spain was complete, followed by the expulsion of Jews from Spain and the persecution of its Muslim population. Today Granada is a vibrant city, combining modern infrastructure with astounding Moorish architecture.

WHAT TO SEE AND DO

The main attraction is the **Alhambra**, the stunning Moorish palace complex perched on a hill overlooking the city. However, Granada's centre has some fine architecture of its own, including the **cathedral** and the **Capilla Real**. On an adjacent hill to the Alhambra lies the **Albaicín** – a maze of cobbled medieval streets and houses with Moorish touches. In fact, Granada retains much of its North African legacy, from *teterías* offering shisha and mint tea, to its hammams and Arabic doorways.

The Alhambra: the Alcazaba and the Palacios Nazaríes

The standard approach to the **Alhambra** is along the Cuesta de Gomérez that climbs uphill from Plaza Nueva, either on foot or by taking the #C3 bus from Plaza Isabel la Catolica (every 7–8min; 7am–11pm; €1.20). The earliest, most ruined part of the fortress is the **Alcazaba**, furthest from the main entrance. It was this building's distinctive hue that gave the complex its name – "al-Hambra" means "red" in Arabic. At the summit is the **Torre de la Vela**; from the tower and ramparts there's a fine view of the whitewashed houses on the hillside opposite.

32

The buildings in the **Palacios Nazaríes** – undoubtedly the Alhambra's gem – show a brilliant use of light and space with ornamental stucco decoration, in rhythmic repetitions of supreme beauty. Elegant Arabic inscriptions from the Koran cover the palace walls. Look closely, and you'll see the remains of ancient paint behind the calligraphy. The sultans used the **Palacio del Mexuar**, the first series of rooms, for business and judicial purposes. In the **Serallo**, beyond, they received distinguished guests: here is the royal throne room, known as the **Hall of the Ambassadors**, the largest room in the palace. The last section, the **Harem**, formed their private living quarters. These are the palace's most beautiful rooms, and include the **Patio de los Leones** with its elegant, fluted columns and the restored lions around the fountain, which have become the archetypal images of Granada. Come back to the Palacios Nazaríes at night to see the serene reflection in the pool of the Patio delos Arrayanes and the buildings subtly lit up.

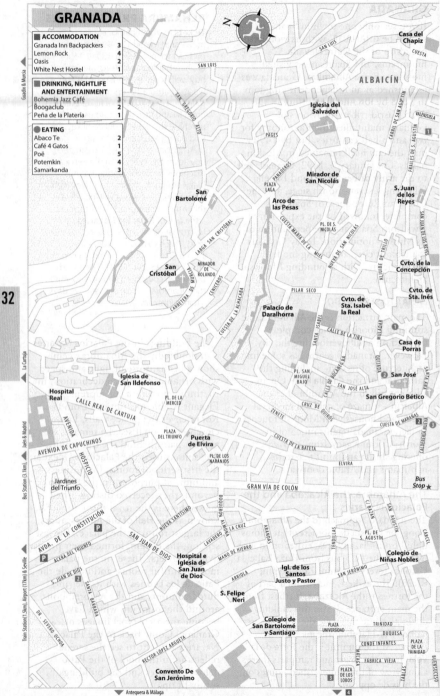

GRANADA

■ ACCOMMODATION
Granada Inn Backpackers	3
Lemon Rock	4
Oasis	2
White Nest Hostel	1

■ DRINKING, NIGHTLIFE AND ENTERTAINMENT
Bohemia Jazz Café	3
Boogaclub	2
Peña de la Platería	1

● EATING
Abaco Te	2
Café 4 Gatos	1
Poë	5
Potemkin	4
Samarkanda	3

32

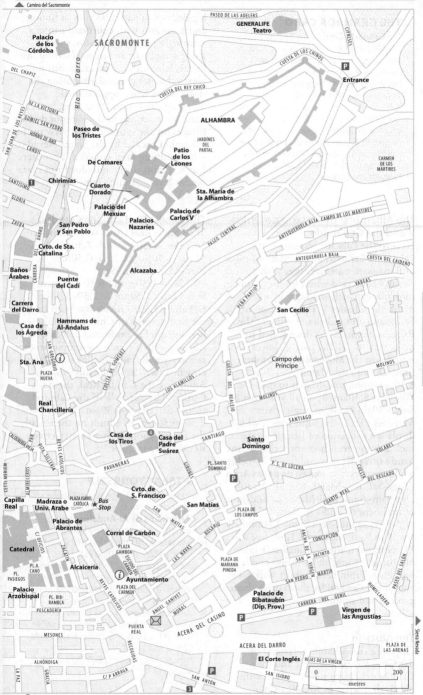

PASEO DE LAS ADELFAS

GENERALIFE
Teatro

CUESTA DE LOS CHINOS

Palacio
de los
Córdoba

SACROMONTE

CIPRESES

P

Entrance

DEL CHAPIZ

CUESTA DEL REY CHICO

RÍO Darro

ALHAMBRA

CARMEN
DE LOS
MÁRTIRES

DE LA VICTORIA

GUMIEL SAN PEDRO

SAN PEDRO

Paseo de
los Tristes

JARDÍNES
DEL
PARTAL

HORNO DE ORO

CANDIL

Patio
de los
Leones

De Comares

SANTISIMO 1

Chirimías

GLORIA

Cuarto
Dorado

Sta. María de
la Alhambra

ZAFRA

Palacio del
Mexuar

Palacio de
Carlos V

San Pedro
y San Pablo

Palacios
Nazaríes

CAMPO DE LOS MÁRTIRES

ANTEQUERUELA ALTA

Cvto. de Sta.
Catalina

PASEO CENTRAL

Baños
Árabes

Alcazaba

ANTEQUERUELA BAJA

CUESTA DEL CAIDERO

Puente
del Cadí

PEÑA PARTIDA

VARGAS

Carrera
del Darro

San Cecilio

BELÉN

Casa de
los Ágreda

Hammams de
Al-Andalus

MOLINOS

Sta. Ana

Campo del
Príncipe

PLAZA
NUEVA

LOS ALAMILLOS

MOLINOS

Real
Chancillería

SANTIAGO

Casa de
los Tiros

Casa del
Padre
Suárez

SANTIAGO

Santo
Domingo

SOLARES

P. S. DE LUCENA

PAVANERAS

PL. SANTO
DOMINGO

P

CUARTO REAL

DEL PESCADO

Cvto. de
S. Francisco

Capilla
Real

Madraza o
Univ. Árabe

PLAZA ISABEL
CATÓLICA

Bus
Stop

San Matías

PLAZA
DE
LOS CAMPOS

Palacio de
Abrantes

Corral de Carbón

CONCEPCIÓN

Catedral

PLAZA
GAMBOA

LAS NAVAS

PLAZA DE
MARIANA
PINEDA

SAN PEDRO

MARTIR

Alcaicería

Ayuntamiento

PLAZA DEL
CARMEN

Palacio
Arzobispal

PL. BIB-
RAMBLA

PESCADERÍA

ANGEL GANIVET

Palacio de
Bibataubín
(Dip. Prov.)

CARRERA DEL GENIL

P

Virgen de
las Angustias

MESONES

PUERTA
REAL

ACERA DEL CASINO

PLAZA DE
LAS ARENAS

ALHÓNDIGA

ACERA DEL DARRO

GRACIA

El Corte Inglés

REJAS DE LA VIRGEN

0   200
metres

SAN ISIDRO

5 (100m)

32

Sierra Nevada

32

THE GRANADA CARD

The **Granada Card** (3-day €33.50; 5-day, €37.50) provides entry to the city's major sites, which works out cheaper than paying for each sight separately. It also lets you jump lengthy queues and includes a handful of free bus trips. Purchase it in advance at ⓦ en.granadatur .com and collect it from the tourist information office. The card includes the Alhambra, but you must still book a time slot in advance for the Palacios Nazaríes – this can be done when buying your Granada Card online.

The Alhambra: the Palacio de Carlos V and the Generalife

Next to the Palacios Nazaríes is the **Palacio de Carlos V**, an ostentatious piece of Renaissance architecture, with a circular courtyard where bullfights once took place, which was built by its namesake Charles V, the grandson of Ferdinand and Isabella. A wing of the Palacios Nazaríes was demolished to make way for it. The palace's lower floor is home to the **Museo de la Alhambra** (mid-Oct to mid-March Wed–Sat 8.30am–6pm; mid-March to mid-Oct Wed–Sat 8.30am–8pm; all year Tues & Sun 8.30am–2.30pm; night visits May–Sept Fri 9–11.30pm; free), which displays a collection of Islamic artefacts, such as a fourteenth-century chessboard, handwritten Korans and fine tile work, while upstairs, the **Museo de Bellas Artes** (Tues–Sat: Jan–March & mid-Oct to Dec 9am–6pm; mid-March to mid-June & mid-Sept to mid-Oct 9am–7.30pm; mid-June to mid-Sept 9am–3.30pm; all year Sun 9am–3.30pm; €1.50, free for EU citizens) features a small collection of Hispano-Moorish paintings and sculpture. From here, a short walk takes you to the **Generalife**, the cypress-shaded gardens and summer palace of the sultans.

The Albaicín

Opposite the Alhambra, framed by the Gran Vía on the west and the Carrera del Darro to the south, is the old Arab quarter of the **Albaicín**, a higgledy-piggledy collection of houses and mansions with courtyard gardens seemingly piled on top of one another along steep, narrow streets. Getting lost in this labyrinth is a pleasure, but mind your valuables particularly during the siesta hours when opportunistic mugging can occur. From here, you can wind your way up to the **Mirador de San Nicolás** for the quintessential view of the Alhambra backed by the Sierra Nevada – it's stunning (and crowded) at sunset. Bus #31 runs to the mirador from Plaza Nueva (every 10min, 7am–11pm; €1.20).

The Capilla Real and the Catedral

The **Capilla Real** (April–Oct Mon–Sat 10.15am–1.30pm & 4–7.30pm, Sun 11am–1.30pm & 2.30–6.30pm; Nov–March Mon–Sat 10.15am–1.30pm & 3.30–6.30pm, Sun 11am–1.30pm & 2.30–5.30pm; €4) along Calle Oficios was built in the first decades of Christian rule as a mausoleum for Ferdinand and Isabella. Although their tombs are simple, in the sacristy you'll find Isabella's sceptre and crown, as well as Ferdinand's sword. Adjoining the Capilla Real, the stark Gothic-Baroque bulk of the **Catedral** (Mon–Sat 10am–6.30pm, Sun 2.30–6.30pm; €5), built on the site of the former mosque, has an attractive Renaissance interior.

★ TREAT YOURSELF

Immerse yourself (literally) in Andalucía's Moorish culture by visiting one of the **Hammams de Al-Andalus** (book in advance; ⓦ hammamalandalus.com). Granada boasts the oldest Arabic bath in Spain (c/Santa Ana 16; ☏ 958 229 978), but there are others in Córdoba (c/Corregidor Luis de la Cerda 51; ☏ 957 484 746) and Málaga (Pl. de los Mártires 5; ☏ 952 215 018). Inside, you alternate in semi-darkness between hot and cold pools and then you can relax over some sweet tea. For the bath only prices are: Granada €28; Córdoba €24; Málaga €30; with a massage it is: Granada €40; Córdoba €36; Málaga €43.

ARRIVAL AND DEPARTURE

By plane The airport lies 17km west of the centre; Autocares J González buses run to Gran Vía de Colón (7 daily; 40min; €3; ⓦ autocaresjosegonzalez.com). Taxis cost €25–30.

By train The station is 1.5km west of the centre on Avda de Andaluces, off Avda de Constitución, connected to the centre by the LAC and SN1 bus lines.

Destinations Almería (4 daily; 2hr 30min); Barcelona (2 daily; 7hr 40min); Córdoba (7 daily; 2hr 30min–3hr); Madrid (5 daily; 4hr–4hr 15min); Ronda (3 daily; 2hr 30min–3hr); Seville (4 daily; 3hr 10min–3hr 20min); Valencia (1 daily on Fri, Sat & Sun; 5hr 40min–6hr).

By bus The station is in the northwest of the city on Carretera de Jaén; bus SN1 runs to Gran Vía de Colón (every 7min; 15min).

Destinations Almería (7 daily; 2hr 15min–4hr 25min); Cádiz (4 daily; 5hr–5hr 30min); Córdoba (8 daily; 2hr 45min–4hr 10min); Madrid (20 daily; 4hr 30min–5hr); Málaga (17 daily; 1hr 30min–2hr); Seville (7 daily; 3hr–4hr 30min).

INFORMATION

Tourist office In the Ayuntamiento, Pl. del Carmen s/n (Mon–Fri 9am–9pm, Sat 10am–8pm; ☎902 405 045, ⓦ granadatur.com); regional office, Santa Ana 4 (Mon–Fri 9am–7.30pm, Sat & Sun 9.30am–3pm; ☎958 575 202, ⓦ andalucia.org).

ACCOMMODATION

★**Granada Inn Backpackers** c/Padre Alcover 10 ☎958 285 284, ⓦ granadabackpackers.es. Stay in a backpacker apartment (four-bed €82, eight-bed €127) at this renovated historical building, where you share the kitchen, terrace and lounge with other travellers, or else opt for a regular dorm or room. Beds are firm, rooms are spotless, showers are powerful and staff are fantastic. Breakfast is €3.50. Dorms €14, doubles €40

Lemon Rock c/Montbalbán 6 ☎958 096 975, ⓦ lemonrockhostel.com. Achingly cool design-hostel, that feels more like a hotel. The stunningly restored building boasts wooden beams, glimpses of exposed brick, and a huge wall of caged lightbulbs. Doubles and dorms are light and spotless but the hub here is the bar/restaurant that hosts live music events from acoustic sessions to jazz. Dorms €16, doubles €71

Oasis Placeta Correo Viejo 3 ☎958 215 848, ⓦ oasisgranada.com. Firm backpacker favourite, this sociable hostel has spotless en-suite dorms arranged around a central courtyard. There's a roof terrace and young staff lay on tapas bar crawls. Dorms €18

White Nest Hostel c/Santísimo 4 ☎958 994 714, ⓦ nesthostelsgranada.com. This friendly place distinguishes itself not just by its psychedelic colour scheme, but the helpfulness of its staff, rooftop terrace with great views of the Alhambra and multiple free daily tours on offer. Dorms €13, doubles €45

EATING

Granada is renowned for being one of the few places left in Spain where many bars still offer free tapas with your drink: pick up the *Granada de tapas* booklet from the tourist office. For a taste of the city's Moorish legacy, sip on sweet mint tea in one of the shisha-hazed *teterías* on Calderería Nueva and Calderería Vieja.

Abaco Te Alamo del Marqués 5 ⓦ abacote.com. Perched high in Albaicín, a steep climb from Plaza San Gregorio, this place serves a selection of teas (from €2.50), juices (from €3) and sweet treats. There's a cushion-strewn sloping attic and a sought-after balcony with a view of the Alhambra towering above a sea of rooftops. April–Sept Mon–Fri 3–10pm, Sat & Sun 3–11pm; Oct–March Mon–Fri 4–10pm, Sat & Sun 4–11pm.

★**Café 4 Gatos** Placeta Cruz Verde 6 ☎680 460 363. Tiny café with a clutch of tables on the cobbled street where you can catch a peep of the Alhambra. There's a fantastic all-day breakfast – don't miss the toast topped with smoked salmon, cream cheese, tomatoes and capers (€3.50) or the carrot cake. Mon & Tues 8.30am–6pm, Wed–Fri 8.30am–midnight, Sat 9am–midnight, Sun 9am–midnight.

Poë c/Paz ⓦ barpoe.com. This intimate British–Angolan tapas bar has been a popular gathering spot for locals and visitors alike for years. One of the few places in a spice-shy country where you can find truly fiery tapas, such as the spicy chicken livers or the piri-piri pork stew. Tapas €1.40. Tues–Sun 8pm–12.30am, bar open later.

Potemkin Placeta Hospicio Viejo 3 ☎630 718 569. Compact and bustling tapas bar with tables spilling out onto the quiet square. On Wednesdays and Saturdays they mix it up with popular sushi nights – either opt for single portions (€1.20) or take advantage of their sushi and bottle of wine deal (€20). Daily 8am–1am.

Samarkanda c/Calderería Vieja 3 ☎958 210 004. Vegetarians rejoice, for the vegetable couscous (€8) at this Lebanese spot is very good, as is the *labneh* (yogurt) with flatbread. There are also meaty options such as lamb tagine (€12.75), and a cluster of outdoor tables. Mon, Tues & Thurs–Sun 1–4pm & 7.30–11.30pm.

DRINKING, NIGHTLIFE AND ENTERTAINMENT

Granada would be a rather sedate city if it weren't for the lively student population that crowds the city's discobars – join the action around the university areas near Gran Capitán and c/San Juan de Dios. The monthly *Guía de Granada* lists the top entertainment venues and tapas bars.

32

Bohemia Jazz Café Pl. de los Lobos 11. Quirky bar with live jazz music, crammed full of an array of oddities: a piano that doubles as a table, a hairdresser's chair, an old juke box, typewriters, and shelves lined with messages in bottles. Thurs–Sun 3pm–2am, Fri & Sat 3pm–3am.

Boogaclub c/Santa Barbara 3 ⓦ boogaclub.com. Reggae, funk, house and soul are the order of the day at this popular club; international DJs are regular guests. Tues–Thurs midnight–7am, Fri–Sun 11pm–7am.

Peña de la Platería Placeta de Toqueros 7 ☎ 958 210 605. Tucked away in the Albaicín, this serious flamenco club claims to be the oldest in Spain. Performances take place on Thursdays at 10.30pm and cost €10; Saturday nights only are members only.

ALMERÍA

Founded by the Phoenicians, and having risen to prominence as the main port of Moorish Córdoba, **ALMERÍA** is an attractive, prosperous port city sandwiched between the Mediterranean and looming, barren mountains.

32

THE GOOD, THE BAD AND THE CORNY

In the 1960s and the 1970s, the rocky desert landscape north of Almería was used as the setting for such Hollywood classics as *Lawrence of Arabia* and later for the likes of *Indiana Jones and the Last Crusade*, as well as around 150 "spaghetti westerns"; Clint Eastwood's career was launched here in *A Fistful of Dollars*. You can visit the Wild West sets to watch a bank hold-up and shoot-out (shows daily noon & 5pm) at **Oasys Mini Hollywood** (daily: June & Sept 10am–7.30pm; July & Aug 10am–9pm; Oct–May 10am–6pm; €22.50; ☎ 902 533 532, ⓦ oasysparquetematico.com), where the ticket also includes entry to the adjoining Reserva Zoológica. Nearby **Fort Bravo** (daily: April–Sept 9am–8pm, Oct–March 9am–6pm; €19.40; ⓦ fortbravo.es) offers similar attractions. Both sites are around 25km north of Almería, off the Tabernas turn-off from the A92. You'll need your own car to get there, which you can rent from any major car company at Almería airport.

WHAT TO SEE AND DO

The town is dominated by the **Alcazaba**, but also take a look at Almería's **cathedral** (Mon–Sat 10am–7pm, Sun 1.30–7pm; €5), built in 1524, and fortified to withstand the frequent pirate raids from North Africa and Turkey in the sixteenth century. Behind it, on c/Pintor Díaz Molina 9, the **Centro Andaluz de la Fotografía** (daily 11am–2pm & 5.30–9.30pm; free; ⓦ www.centroandaluz delafotografia.es) houses excellent temporary photography exhibitions by international names.

Alcazaba

The grand, crumbling, tenth-century **Alcazaba** (Tues–Sat: April to mid-June 9am–8.30pm; mid-June to mid-Sept 9am–3.30pm & 7–10pm; mid-Sept to March 9am–6.30pm; all year Sun 9am–3.30pm; free) was built into the hillside by the Córdoba Caliph Abd-ar Rahman III and subsequently altered by the Christian monarchs. During its heyday, the fortress complex held up to 20,000 people and was said to rival Granada's Alhambra with the beauty of its palaces and sculpted gardens. Little remains, but it's worth visiting if only for the fabulous coastal views.

ARRIVAL AND DEPARTURE

By plane To reach Almería airport, 10km east of the city, catch the #L22 bus from outside the bus/train station.

By train Trains pull in at the Estación Intermodal on Carretera La Ronda, a 10min walk from the city centre. No luggage storage.

Destinations Barcelona (1 daily; 13hr 30min–14hr 30min); Granada (4 daily; 2hr 30min); Madrid (2 daily; 6hr 30min–7hr 15min); Seville (4 daily; 5hr 30min–5hr 45min); Valencia (1 daily; 8hr 30min– 9hr 30min).

By bus Buses use the same Estación Intermodal as trains.

Destinations Barcelona (3 daily; 12hr–14hr 30min); Granada (8 daily; 2hr–4hr 45min); Madrid (5 daily; 6hr 30min–7hr); Málaga (7 daily; 2hr 30min–5hr 30min); Seville (3 daily; 5hr 30min–8hr 30min); Valencia (4 daily; 6hr 30–8hr 30min).

INFORMATION

Tourist office c/Parque Nicolás Salmerón s/n at Martínez Campos (Mon–Fri 9am–7.30pm, Sat, Sun & holidays 9.30am–3pm; ☎ 950 175 220, ⓦ andalucia.org).

EL CABO DE GATA

Only 15km east of Almería lies **Cabo de Gata**, a **national park** comprising dramatic cliffs, desolate scrubland, fishing villages and some of the most unspoiled beaches in the south. You can explore the park on a bike, enjoy incredible views of the coast from Torre Vigia Vela Blanca (an eighteenth-century watchtower), camp at the seaside villages and enjoy the pristine beauty of Playa de los Genoveses – the cape's prettiest beach. The only village you can reach by bus from Almería is **San José** (2–3 daily with Autocares Bernardo; ⓦautocaresbernardo.com), where you'll also find the greatest variety of accommodation and the National Park **information office** (Avda de San José 27; Mon–Sat 10am–2pm & 5.30–8.30pm, Sun 10am–2pm; ⓦcabodegata-nijar.com).

ACCOMMODATION

Hotel La Perla Pl. del Carmen 7 ☎950 238 877, ⓦhotellaperla.es. Multistorey budget hotel with compact, spotless en-suite rooms and pleasant staff. Little character, but it's hard to beat the central location. Wi-fi is temperamental. Doubles €50

Hotel Sevilla c/de Granada 25 ☎950 230 009, ⓦhotelsevillaalmeria.net. Spick-and-span a/c rooms with thimble-sized but modern bathrooms at this centrally located hotel. Breakfast not included. Doubles €43

EATING

★**Casa Puga** c/Jovellanos 7. Packed and lively, this place feels the real deal: hams hang from the ceiling, walls feature traditional tiles, and your bill is chalked down in front of you onto the marble bar. Tapas, such as *boquerones en vinagre* (fresh anchovies in vinegar), cost from €1.50. Mon–Sat noon–4pm & 8pm–midnight.

★**Joseba Añorga Taberna** Pl. de la Constitución 4 ☎950 268 623. Basque mini-masterpieces are the order of the day at this *donostia*. Choose from the likes of cod *croquettas* or grilled foie gras with apple sauce, and wash them down with a glass of Txacolí. *Pintxos* from €3; mains €8–20. Tues–Sat 7am–midnight, Sun 8.30am–5pm.

Tetería Almedina c/Aurora Paz 2. This local legend is tucked into a maze of streets just 5min walk from the Alcazaba. A cosy Moorish restaurant that really delivers with its tagines, couscous and anything with aubergine. Try the superb *rghifa* pancakes, and don't miss the home-made mint lemonade. On Saturday evenings, from 10pm, they stage Spanish dance performances and North African music concerts. *Pinchitos* from €2, mains €10–20. Tues–Sun 11.30am–11pm.

Valencia and Alicante

Much of the coast around **Valencia** and further south on the **Costa Blanca** has been insensitively overdeveloped, suffering from mass package tourism and its associated ills. The main cities, however – vibrant **Valencia** and relaxed **Alicante** – are appealing and worth a stop for anyone travelling along the east coast.

VALENCIA

VALENCIA has worked hard to shed its provincial reputation and has emerged as an exciting, cosmopolitan city to rival Madrid and Barcelona. The City of Arts and Sciences complex is the best example of this, but Valencia's exuberance is also evident in its diverse nightlife. The city also takes pride in its museums, easily accessible beach and, of course, its main festival: the world-famous **Las Fallas**. Also in the region are international music festival **Benicassim** and the riotous **Tomatina**, held in Buñol.

WHAT TO SEE AND DO

A few blocks north of the train station, the adjoining squares of **Plaza de la Reina** and **Plaza de la Virgen** are Valencia's heartbeat, with many of its principal sights nearby. Pedestrianized Plaza de la Virgen is a perfect spot to while away an hour with a drink and a cathedral view. The most interesting area for wandering is the maze-like **Barrio del Carmen**, with its arty, bohemian atmosphere. Stretching north of the Mercado Central up to the river bed of the Río Turia, it's full of historic buildings being renovated. Valencia's beach, **Playa de la Malvarrosa**, is easily accessible (bus #1 from Torres Serranos and metro line #5 to Maritim-Serrería).

The town centre

Plaza de la Reina is home to the impressive thirteenth-century **Catedral** (Oct–April Mon–Sat 10am–5.30pm, Sun 2–5.30pm; May–Sept Mon–Sat 10am–6.30pm, Sun

32

VALENCIA

■ ACCOMMODATION	
Center Valencia	1
Hôme Youth Hostel	2
Pensión Paris	4
Red Nest Hostel	3

■ DRINKING AND NIGHTLIFE	
Café Negrito	1
Calcutta	2
Radio City	3

● EATING	
The Good Whale	4
La Lluna	2
La Pepica	3
La Pitusa	1

32

2–6.30pm; €4.50), whose bell tower, the **Miguelete** (daily 10am–7.30pm; €2), gives stunning city views. Southwest of the cathedral lies the enormous **Mercado Central**, a modernist iron and glass structure housing over one thousand stalls selling local fruit, vegetables and seafood until 2pm (closed Sun). Opposite is the city's former silk exchange, **La Lonja** (entrance at c/de la Lonja 2; mid-March to mid-Oct Tues–Sat 10am–7pm, Sun 10am–3pm; mid-Oct to mid-March Tues–Sat 10am–6pm, Mon & Sun 10am–3pm; €2, free Sun), a stunning Gothic building whose main hall features intricately crafted spiral columns and a vaulted ceiling.

The museums

Contemporary art lovers will find **IVAM**, the modern art museum at c/Guillém de Castro 118 (Tues–Sun 10am–7pm; €2, free Sun; ⓦivam.es), a treat, with its permanent sculpture collection plus two floors of changing exhibitions of work by Spanish and international artists. If you prefer your art a little older, make time for the **Museo de Bellas Artes** (c/San Pío 5; Mon 11am–5pm, Tues–Sun 10am–7pm; free), which has a vast display of works by painters including Goya, Velázquez and local boy Joaquín Sorolla. The highlight of the city's museums, however, is the **Ciudad de las Artes y las Ciencias** (City of Arts and Sciences; see website for times of individual sights; €36.90 for 3-day ticket to all sights; ☎902 100 031, ⓦcac.es). Sitting at the end of the Jardines del Turia, a 7km-long landscaped park that was built in the old river bed of the Río Turia, this breathtaking collection of futuristic concrete, steel and glass architecture comprises five buildings, four of which were designed by locally born superstar architect Santiago Calatrava. The complex includes the **Hemisfèric**, an eyeball-shaped IMAX **cinema** (€8.80), a vast **science museum** (€8), a huge **aquarium** with beluga whales, sharks and turtles (€28.50), and a dramatic pistachio nut-shaped **arts centre**. The complex itself is free to enter, and well worth a visit to check out the architecture if you can't afford museum entry. Take bus #19 from Plaza del Ayuntamiento, or #35 from Avenida Marqués de Sotelo.

ARRIVAL AND DEPARTURE

By plane Valencia airport is 8km west of the centre, and is accessible by metro (lines #3 and #5; 25min; 5.30am–11.30pm; €3.90).

By train Trains to and from Alicante and Murcia use the central Estació del Nord on c/Xàtiva (Ⓜ Xàtiva). Trains between Madrid and Barcelona use the Estació Joaquim Sorolla, 500m further south.

Destinations Alicante (10 daily; 1hr 35min–2hr 15min); Barcelona (15 daily; 3hr–5hr 20min); Granada (1 daily; 7hr 40min); Madrid (16 daily; 1hr 40min–3hr 40min).

By bus The station is northwest of the centre, on the far bank of the Río Turia river bed (Ⓜ Turia); bus #8 (or a 30min walk) to Pl. del Ayuntamiento.

Destinations Alicante (20 daily; 2hr 30min–5hr); Barcelona (10 daily; 4hr–5hr 45min); Madrid (13 daily; 4hr); Seville (3 daily; 9hr 45min–11hr 40min).

By ferry Bus #19 connects the Balearic Ferry Terminal with Pl. del Ayuntamiento.

Destinations Ibiza (6 weekly; 6hr 30min); Mahon (1 weekly; 15hr); Palma (6 weekly; 8hr).

INFORMATION

Tourist office The office at c/Paz (c/Pau) 48 covers both Valencia city and the surrounding region. (Mon–Sat 9am–7pm, Sun 10am–2pm; ☎ 963 986 422, Ⓦ turisvalencia.es). Hands out the free listings guides *Hello Valencia* and *24-7 Valencia* (Ⓦ 247valencia.com).

Discount cards The Valencia Tourist Card (€15/20/25 for 1/2/3 days, or €10 for 7 days without transport) gives you unlimited travel on buses and metro and discounts in some museums, shops and restaurants. Available at tourist offices or at Ⓦ valenciatouristcard.com.

GETTING AROUND

By bus and metro Most of Valencia's key sights are walkable from the town centre, but the public transport system is efficient and easy to use. Bus and metro

journeys in the central zone cost €1.50, while the metro costs €3.90 to the airport. The metro runs 5.30am–midnight.

ACCOMMODATION

Although prices given here are for high season, many hostels put prices up further for Las Fallas.

Center Valencia c/Samaniego 18 ☎ 963 914 915, Ⓦ center-valencia.com; Ⓜ Xàtiva. Clean, basic dorms with good facilities, roof terrace, laundry service and breakfast. Dorms €12

★ **Hôme Youth Hostel** c/La Lonja 4 ☎ 963 916 229, Ⓦ homehostelsvalencia.com; Ⓜ Xàtiva. One of two *Hôme* hostels in the city. Well-designed, comfortable accommodation with kitchen and TV room, in a great central location. Dorms €23, doubles €67

Pensión Paris c/Salvá 12 ☎ 963 526 766, Ⓦ pensionparis .com; Ⓜ Colón. Rooms are basic, but prices are low and the location is central. Doubles €34

Red Nest Hostel c/Paz (c/Pau) 36 ☎ 963 427 168, Ⓦ rednesthostel.com; Ⓜ Colón. Bright, fun decor and lots of communal space, with pool table and table football. Dorms €16, doubles €65

EATING

There are plenty of decent options near the Mercado Central and in the Barrio del Carmen, but avoid touristy places too near the plazas de la Reina and de la Virgen. Most restaurants serve food daily 1–4pm and 8–11.30pm; exceptions cited below.

The Good Whale c/Salamanca 46. Trendy tapas spot in the Ensanche district serving up tasty modern treats with

32

international influences, like gyozas and fish and chips with *chimichurri* mayonnaise. Daily noon–12.30am.

La Lluna c/San Ramón 23. Filling vegetarian grub plus organic beers and wines in a homely atmosphere. The bargain €8.20 weekday lunch menu features treats such as a spinach and squash "cake". Closed Sun.

★**La Pepica** Paseo Neptuno 6. A few mouthfuls of *La Pepica's* paella will show you why this beachside restaurant is renowned for serving up the best rice dishes in the city. The three-course *menu degustación* (€28.50, min two people) makes the experience more affordable. Sun 1–4pm only.

La Pitusa c/del Pare d'Orfens 4. *La Pitusa* draws on the Valencian community's reputation as the "garden of Spain" to serve up market-fresh produce in a modern setting. The €8.95 weekday lunch menu is a good deal.

DRINKING AND NIGHTLIFE

The action in Valencia is quite widely dispersed, but the city centre's best nightlife is in the Barrio del Carmen (c/Caballeros, c/Quart and c/Alta). Ruzafa is a chilled, hipster-friendly alternative nightlife area. The best gay bars and clubs are around c/Quart. Clubs open around midnight, but don't get going until 2am.

Café Negrito Pl. Negrito. Set in a lively square, this café-bar is the perfect spot to kick off your night in Valencia.

Calcutta c/del Rellotge Vell 4. Dance the night away to pop, house and r'n'b in this restored palace in the Barrio del Carmen. Fri & Sat until 7am.

Radio City c/Santa Teresa 19 ⓦ radiocityvalencia.com. Iconic space with a varied programme of exhibitions, films, dance and music performances. Free entry most nights. Tuesday is flamenco night (€15, book via the website).

DIRECTORY

Banks Main branches of most banks are around Pl. del Ayuntamiento or along c/Xàtiva near the train station.

Hospital Hospital General, Avda Tres Cruces 2; ☎ 961 972 000; ⓜ Nou d'Octubre.

Left luggage Lockers available at both train stations (daily 7am–10pm; €2.40–4.50/24hr) and the bus station (24/7; €3–4/24hr). You'll need the exact change.

Pharmacies C/San Vicente Martir 107 (☎ 963 411 729). 24hr.

Police Gran Vía de Ramón y Cajal 40 (☎ 963 539 539).

Post office Pl. del Ayuntamiento 24.

ALICANTE

ALICANTE is a thoroughly Spanish city, despite its proximity to a strip of package-holiday resorts. With good beaches nearby, lively nightlife and plenty of cheap hotels, it's worth a short stopover.

WHAT TO SEE AND DO

Wide esplanades give the town an elegant air, and around the Plaza de Luceros and along the seafront *paseo* you can relax beneath palm trees at terrace cafés. Try to time your visit to coincide with the **Hogueras fiesta** of processions, fire and fireworks, which culminates in an orgy of burning on the night of June 23/24. The cliff-top fortress of **Castillo de Santa Bárbara** (daily: April–Sept 10am–10pm; Oct–March 10am–8pm; €2.70 for the lift, last ascent is at 7.20pm, last descent 7.40pm) is Alicante's main sight, with pleasant park areas and a tremendous view from the top. Access to the lift is from beach-side Avenida de Jovellanos via a tunnel. Also worth a visit is the **Museum of Contemporary Art** (Tues–Sat 10am–8pm, Sun 10am–2pm; free) on Plaza de Santa María, a light, airy space with a permanent collection of twentieth-century (mostly Spanish) art, including works by Miró and Picasso, plus temporary exhibitions. **Playa Postiguet** is the city beach, but it gets crowded in summer: try the beaches at **Playa San Juan**, ten minutes from the town, on the half-hourly #L4 tram.

ARRIVAL AND DEPARTURE

By plane The airport is 12km south of town. The #L6 airport bus (every 20min 6am–11.10pm; €3.85) stops near the train station and at Pl. Luceros.

By train The main train station is on Avda Salamanca, a 15min walk from the town centre.

Destinations Barcelona (8 daily; 4hr 45min–5hr 35min); Madrid (12 daily; 2hr 12min–5hr 14min); Valencia (12 daily; 1hr 30min–2hr 11min).

By bus Local and long-distance services arrive at the bus station on c/Portugal, a 15min walk from the town centre.

Destinations Barcelona (8 daily; 7hr 45min–9hr 15min); Granada (5 daily; 5hr–6hr 40min); Madrid (9 daily; 4hr 15min–6hr 15min); Málaga (7 daily; 5hr–6hr 50min); Valencia (22 daily; 2hr 30min–5hr 20min).

INFORMATION

Tourist office Avda Rambla Méndez Nuñez 23 (Mon–Fri 9am–6pm, Sat & Sun 10am–2pm; ☎ 965 200 000, ⓦ alicanteturismo.com). There are other offices inside the train and bus stations, and at the airport.

★ **TREAT YOURSELF**

El Portal c/Bilbao 2 ☎ 965 143 269, ⓦ elportaltaberna.com. Gourmet tapas and *raciones* served at the bar or in the chic restaurant. The menu features lots of local produce, including rice dishes and a salad made with Raf tomatoes (€7.50), plus creative options such as baked scallops with cauliflower, almonds and truffles (€8.90). Booking recommended. Daily 1pm–1.30am.

ACCOMMODATION

Outside July and August, finding accommodation should be easy, with most budget options concentrated at the lower end of the Old Town, especially on c/San Fernando, c/Jorge Juan and c/Castaño.

Albergue Juvenil La Florida Avda de Orihuela 59 ☎ 965 918 250, ⓦ www.gvajove.es. Fairly institutional HI hostel (card obligatory), with café and laundry facilities. From October to June many spaces are reserved for students, so booking ahead is essential. Dorms (under-25s) **€12.50**, over-25s **€16.70**, full-board **€21.50/25.50**

Camping Costa Blanca c/Convento 143, El Campello ☎ 965 630 670, ⓦ campingcostablanca.com. In a small town, Campello, 10km to the north of Alicante, and close to the beach. Accessible by L1 or L3 tram, or bus #21. Also has bungalows sleeping 4–6 people. Camping/person **€6**, plus per tent **€6**, bungalows **€86**

★ **Hostal Les Monges Palace** c/San Agustín 4 ☎ 965 215 046, ⓦ lesmonges.es. Elegant, stylishly decorated rooms, with excellent facilities for the price. Great central location. Doubles **€60**

Pensión San Nicolás c/San Nicolás 14 ☎ 965 217 039, ⓦ alicantesanicolas.com. Comfortable rooms (some en suite) with little extras such as kettles and bathrobes, plus a fridge for visitor use. Close to the nightlife, so can be noisy at weekends. Doubles **€45**

EATING AND DRINKING

Known locally as El Barrio, the concentration of streets stretching north from the main Rambla to the castle contains over a hundred bars and is without a doubt the best place for eating and drinking. Another key area for summer nightlife is c/Castaños. For eating, it can be hard to find budget options now that Alicante's gastronomic scene is booming; avoid touristy places on the Esplanade.

★ **Alioli** c/Miguel Soler 12. Relaxed, friendly wine and tapas bar serving local and national wines by the glass, plus a selection of cold tapas including meats and cheeses. Tapas around €4, wine from €2.20. Mon–Fri noon–4pm & 8pm–midnight, Sat & Sun 8pm–midnight.

Desdén c/Labradores 22, El Barrio. Lively, late-opening bar playing dance, jazz and funk music. Several similar options on the same street. Daily until late.

★ **El Cisne de Oro** c/César Elguezábal 23. Popular tapas bar full of locals sampling delicious Alicante specialities, such as *pulpo* and *pastel de tortilla* from €4. Daily 1–4pm & 8–11pm.

DIRECTORY

Consulate UK, Edificio Espacio, Rambla Méndez Nuñez 28–32 ☎ 965 140 528.
Post office Plaza Gabriel Miró 7.

The Balearic islands

The largest **Balearic islands** – Ibiza, Mallorca and Menorca – each maintain a character that is distinct from the mainland and from each other. **Ibiza** is synonymous with all-night summer clubbing, though it also boasts some lovely beaches and traditional villages. While **Mallorca**, the largest of the Balearics, attracts mass tourism with brash resorts crammed along the Bay of Palma, away from these there are soaring pine-forested mountains, traditional villages, lively fishing ports, incredible cycling terrain, beautiful coves and the Balearics' one real city, **Palma**. The furthest island from the mainland, **Menorca**, is more tranquil than its sisters, its topography less dramatic. Along with an abundance of unspoilt coves lapped by waters turquoise enough to rival the Caribbean, Menorca is also famous for the prehistoric monuments that dot the island. Prices on all the Balearic islands are considerably above the mainland, and from mid-June to mid-September budget **rooms** are in short supply, so book in advance.

GETTING TO THE ISLANDS

Ferries from mainland Spain and inter-island connections are relatively expensive considering the distances involved, and budget **flights** from the Spanish mainland with Ryanair and

32

Vueling mean it can be cheaper, as well as quicker, to fly; in summer there are plenty of international flights to all three islands. The three main ferry companies are **Trasmediterranea** (ⓦ trasmediterranea.es), **Balearia** (ⓦ balearia.com) and **Iscomar** (ⓦ www .iscomar.com): they operate from Barcelona, Valencia and Dénia (just south of Valencia) on the mainland and have connections to and between Ibiza, Palma, Port d'Alcúdia, Maó and Ciutadella on the islands. Ferry timetables and prices vary hugely, and some services, particularly the fast boats, only run in summer. For the latest fares and schedules, see ⓦ directferries.co.uk, a useful one-stop shop (in English) for all routes and services.

IBIZA

32

IBIZA (Eivissa in Catalan) is an island of excess, internationally heralded as one of the world's top clubbing destinations. Each summer the world's best DJs play at its venues, attracting scores of holidaymakers looking to party 24/7. Yet it also has a quieter side, particularly in the north, with beautiful beaches and a bohemian vibe, a legacy from the 1960s when the island was a hippy hang-out. Out of season, the sun keeps shining but the crowds depart, leaving behind a relaxing island oasis.

WHAT TO SEE AND DO

IBIZA TOWN is arguably the most attractive place on the island. Set around a dazzling natural harbour, it's one of the Mediterranean's most cosmopolitan small capitals. The mighty city walls enclose the ancient quarter of **Dalt Vila**, with its labyrinthine alleyways, attractive Gothic cathedral, and the excellent **Museu d'Art Contemporani** (Ronda de Narcís Puget; Tues–Fri 10am–2pm & 6–9pm, Sat & Sun 10am–2pm; free). Below Dalt Vila, the port area is a maze of streets lined with bustling bars and expensive boutiques, with a small, lively produce market just opposite the fortress entrance. The island's second town, **SANT ANTONI**

(accessible by bus #3 from Ibiza Town; every 30min 7.30am–midnight, when the Discobus takes over), is handy for club access but rather charmless. To make the most of this compact island and to explore its isolated coves and traditional villages, it's well worth renting a car.

ARRIVAL AND DEPARTURE

By plane The airport is 7km southwest of Ibiza Town. Regular bus #10 (daily 6.15am–12.20am; €3.50) connects it to the port area via the city centre.

By boat The terminal on Passeig des Moll serves ferries to and from the mainland and Mallorca; boats from Formentera use the dock on Avda Santa Eularia.

By bus Ibiza is well connected by bus. For timetables see ⓦ ibizabus.com.

INFORMATION

Tourist office The main office is on Plaça de la Catedral (Mon–Sat 10am–2pm & 6–9pm, Sun 10am–2pm; ☏ 971 399 232, ⓦ eivissa.es), but there's a smaller branch with longer opening hours at Passeig Vara de Rey 1 (Mon–Sat 9am–8pm, Sun 9am–2pm). Both provide information on the entire island, including cycle routes.

ACCOMMODATION

★ **Apartamentos Llobet** c/Alejandro Llobet 6-8 ☏ 971 304 124, ⓦ apartamentosllobet.com. This recently refurbished apart-hotel on the beachfront at Figueretas (10min walk from Ibiza Town) boasts friendly staff, big breakfast buffets, apartments with spacious terraces and a swimming pool. Prices drop significantly out of season. Four-bed apartment **€190**

DETOUR TO FORMENTERA

Just 20km south of Ibiza Town, the fourth-largest Balearic island, **Formentera**, lures day-trippers from Ibiza with its stunning beaches and clear turquoise waters (Ses Illetes, Llevant and Migjorn are top choices), and alternating landscapes of rugged cliffs and fields. Formentera is small enough to be explored end to end by bike in a day: numerous kiosks at the harbour rent bicycles from €8 per day. Plentiful mid-range restaurants focus on seafood and rice dishes (most open May–Oct). Companies including Baleària–Trasmapi (ⓦ balearia.com) run at least ten times daily during peak season; the cheapest option is Aquabus (ⓦ aquabusferryboats .com; one-way from €9.50).

BEST OF THE BEACHES

Of Ibiza's many beaches, particular gems include the following: **Cala Llenya**, 2km northeast of Santa Eulària, with calm azure waters against a backdrop of pine trees; tiny, sheltered **Cala Mastella**, covered in bark-like Poseidonia seagrass; **Cala Boix** with its deep, turquoise water and a steep descent; golden-sand Platges de Comte on the western tip of the island; and the long white crescent behind a pine grove that is **Platja de Ses Salines**, south of the airport, past the salt marsh, accessible by bus #11 (hourly 9.30am–7.30pm).

Camping Cala Nova Platja Cala Nova ☎ 971 331 774, ⓦ campingcalanova.com. Located 20km north of Ibiza Town – but only 50m from the Cala Nova beach. Good watersports base; bungalows available. Buses run from nearby Santa Eulària to Ibiza Town every 20min. Per tent **€8.90**, plus per person **€8.90**

Hostal Giramundo c/Ramón Muntaner ☎ 971 307 640, ⓦ hostalgiramundoibiza.com. Brightly coloured backpacker joint with themed rooms, tiny bathrooms and an in-house bar-café, just a block from Figueretas beach and a 10min walk from the centre of Ibiza City. Dorms **€35**, doubles **€70**

Hostal La Bartola c/Catalunya 4. Comfortable, well-decorated hostel in a central location. No kitchen. Dorms **€45**, doubles **€60**

Hostal Las Nieves c/Juan de Austria 18 ☎ 971 190 319 ⓦ hostalibiza.com. Clean and friendly *hostal* several blocks away from the Old Town. Doubles without bathroom **€80**, with bathroom **€100**

Hostal Rosalía c/Rosalía 5, Sant Antoni ☎ 971 340 709, ⓦ hostalrosalia.com. Refurbished budget hotel with a small pool, popular with clubbers who like to stay a short walk away from *Es Paradis*. Prices drop steeply outside Aug. Doubles **€95**

EATING AND DRINKING

Opening hours are daily 1–4pm & 8–11pm unless otherwise stated.

★**Can Terra** Avda d'Ignasi Wallis 14. If you're on a budget, fill up on the flavoursome *pintxos* topping the bar. If you're looking for a full meal at a reasonable price, take a seat on the garden terrace. It's a popular spot, so go early. Tapas from €2.50.

Comidas Bar San Juan c/Guillem de Montgrí 8. Long-standing family-run restaurant-bar, with good-quality fish dishes. Arrive early to avoid queuing and expect to share tables. Mains from €8. Closed Sun.

Guillemis Gastro Bar c/Enmig 15. Great choice close to the harbour, with innovative tapas and *raciones*. Top-notch cooking for a decent price – sharing dishes from €6. Daily 11am–3am.

Madagascar Café Pl. del Parque 4. Set on a buzzing square, *Madagascar* dishes up wallet-friendly sandwiches, salads and pizzas (from €6.50), plus a long list of drinks.

Tapas Restaurant & Lounge Bar Cami des Reguero 4, Sant Antoni. Yes, it attracts a large tourist contingent, but their *patatas bravas* and prawns with chorizo stand out, and the Sunday roasts tempt homesick Brits. Tapas from €4.50, mains from €12.

CLUBS

Ibiza's world-famous temples to hedonism draw hundreds of thousands of revellers during the party season (June–Sept), with entertainment provided by world-class DJs. The action tends to take place 1–6am, with each megaclub specializing in a different theme, be it foam parties, fancy dress or even striptease. Entry fees can be anything from €35 upwards, not including drinks (from €10 each); look out for touts selling discounted tickets around the port bars each night, and club promoters handing out free invites on the beaches. Ibiza also has one of the best gay scenes in Europe, with a lot of the action centred in the port and another cluster of bars on c/de la Virgen; many mainstream clubs hold a weekly gay night. The Discobus (check ⓦ discobus.es for timetables; €3 one-way) links these clubs with the centre of town. Alternatively, head to Platja d'en Bossa to party day and night at the famous beach bar *Bora Bora* (free entry; ⓦ boraboraibiza.net). If you're looking for some more chilled daytime action, try low-key beach clubs such as *Jockey Club* at Ses Salines.

Amnesia Ibiza Town–Sant Antoni road, km6 ⓦ amnesia .es. Busy mega-club which plays host to top DJs including Calvin Harris. There's a choice of two rooms, so there's no chance of getting bored. Check out Cream on Thursday if you like your superstar House DJs. June–late Sept.

Anfora c/San Carlos 7, Dalt Vila ⓦ discoanfora.com. Ibiza's only dedicated gay club. Late May–Oct.

Es Paradis c/Salvador Espriu 2, Sant Antoni ⓦ esparadis .com. Arguably Ibiza's most beautiful superclub, with its

32

glass pyramid, roofless dancefloor, and pounding sound system. Extremely popular for its water parties (Tues & Fri), when the dancefloor is flooded, and Glow, its Sunday night Neon Paint Party. Late May–late Sept.

Pacha Avda 8 d'Agost ⓦ pacha.com. Think: mirror balls, large dancefloor with a capacity of over three thousand; a variety of music, including Spanish pop, soul and funk, but predominantly techno and house; DJs such as David Guetta; and a chillout terrace. Open year-round.

Privilege Ibiza Town–Sant Antoni road, km7 ⓦ privilegeibiza.com. The biggest club in the world has a capacity of 10,000 and superstar DJs doing their thing from a cabin suspended above the pool. Check out sunrise at the Vista Club. Late May–early Oct.

Ushuaia Platja d'en Bossa 10 ⓦ ushuaiabeachhotel.com. A Platja d'en Bossa hotel swimming pool sounds a cheap choice for an open-air club venue, but *Ushuaia* is pure glam. With lavish surroundings and spectacular special effects, famous DJs such as Avicii and Axwell Ingrosso are almost the supporting acts.

MALLORCA

32

MALLORCA has a split identity. There are sections of its coast where the concrete curtain of high-rise hotels is continuous, but these areas are easy to avoid. Elsewhere the island is as appealing as it gets in the Mediterranean, particularly in the northwest where several stunning coves and pretty villages are framed by the dramatic backdrop of the rugged Tramuntana mountains. The northwest and northeast coasts also hold great appeal for serious cyclists, with steep switchback bends extending down to the Sa Calobra cove and running all the way to Cap de Formentor, Mallorca's northernmost tip.

Palma

Much to the surprise of many visitors, **PALMA** is an attractive, historic and cosmopolitan city filled with atmospheric narrow streets, stylish boutiques and lively bars and restaurants. The main

---

★ **TREAT YOURSELF**

Wind down from a busy day's sightseeing on the terrace bar at **Es Baluard**. From this excellent vantage point, you can watch the sun set over Palma's harbour, gin & tonic in hand, as a DJ spins chill-out tunes. Drinks from €4. Daily until midnight.

---

focal point is the vast Gothic **cathedral** (Mon–Fri 10am–6.15pm, Sat 10am–2.15pm; €7) at c/del Palau Reial 9, which was built in recognition of the Christian Reconquest of Mallorca, and later worked on by Gaudí. Make sure to pick up the free audio/video guide for the lowdown on the stunning interior. Next door is the imposing **Palau de l'Almudaina** (Tues–Sun 10am–8pm; €7), an Islamic fort turned royal residence; you can visit the spartan chambers and royal apartments. More interesting is the private art collection at *casa-palacio* **Palau March** (Mon–Fri 10am–6.30pm, Sat 10am–2.15pm; €4.50), which includes sculptures by Rodin and Barbara Hepworth. Above the harbour, the old city bastion is now a contemporary art gallery **Es Baluard**, Porta de Santa Catalina 10 (Tues–Sun 10am–8pm; €6, €4 temporary exhibitions, free Tues; ⓦ esbaluard.org), housing a permanent collection of twentieth-century art (including a substantial Miró section) and excellent temporary exhibitions.

ARRIVAL AND INFORMATION

By plane Palma airport, 8km east of the city, is served by bus #1 (every 15min; €3) with various stops in the city and port area.

By boat The large ferry port is 3.5km west of the city centre, connected to Palma by bus #1.

Tourist office Pl. de la Reina 2 (Mon–Fri 9am–8pm, Sat 9am–2pm; ☎ 971 173 990, ⓦ infomallorca.net).

Car rental Palma airport has plenty of options, or try Europcar along the seafront in Palma (Avda Ingeniero Gabriel Roca 19 ☎ 902 105 055).

Bike rental From €6 per day from Lock and Go at Plaça de Espanya bus and train station.

ACCOMMODATION

Central Palma Pl. de José María Quadrado 2 ☎ 971 101 215, ⓦ centralpalma.com. Official youth hostel in a quiet square in the heart of Palma. Well equipped, with laundry facilities and bike rental. Dorms **€27**

Hostal Apuntadores c/Apuntadores 8 ☎ 971 713 491, ⓦ apuntadoreshostal.com. Centrally located multistorey cheapie with simple, a/c rooms, friendly English-speaking staff and a roof terrace offering great views of the city. Doubles **€60**

Pura Vida Hostel c/San Sebastiá 2 1 ☎ 635 027 871. Backpacker hostel a stone's throw from Palau March. Shared bathrooms and kitchen access. Dorms **€35**, doubles **€75**

EATING AND DRINKING

The best places to search for a bite to eat are the largely pedestrianized La Lonja area and the newly hip Santa Catalina neighbourhood a short walk west of the centre. Opening hours are daily 1–4pm & 8–11pm unless otherwise stated.

Bar El Día c/Apuntadores 18. Simple tapas bar, overflowing with locals, that specializes in large portions of *patatas alioli*, garlicky *gambas al ajillo*, *pimentos padrón* and more. Tapas from €4. Closed Mon.

Celler Pagès Off c/Apuntadores at c/Felip Bauza 2. Small, unpretentious restaurant serving traditional Mallorcan food – try the stuffed marrows with home-made mayonnaise. Good-value lunch menu at €14. Closed Sun.

La Golondrina c/Sant Magi 60. Popular vegan bar and restaurant in Santa Catalina. The menu has international influences and includes soups, snacks, sharing dishes and full meals (around €16 per head for a full meal, sharing dishes average €10). Often features live music in the evening.

La Rosa Vermutería c/de la Rosa 5. Slick space serving up traditional tapas with a modern slant, washed down with drink-of-the-moment vermouth. Fill up on the cod and green pepper omelette (€9). Mon 7.30pm–midnight, Tues–Sun noon–4pm & 7.30pm–midnight.

Sóller and around

Set beneath the dramatic Tramuntana mountains, where the air is scented by orange and lemon groves, the beautiful

---

> ### PALMA–SÓLLER TRAIN RIDE
>
> The **train ride from Palma to Sóller** (4–7 daily; €16 one-way, €30 return including tram; ⓦ trendesoller.com) makes a great day-trip out of the city. The narrow-gauge railway was built in 1912 to carry fruit to Palma. Today, the wooden carriages rattle along the outskirts of the capital before a cross-country climb up mountain passes and through tunnels, passing almond and lemon groves, tiny towns and craggy peaks topping a thousand metres. In Sóller, you can then hop on the antique 1913 tram that rumbles down to Port de Sóller (1–2 hourly; €6 one-way), where you'll find a pretty bay with a sandy beach and restaurants at the water's edge.

town of **SÓLLER** is dominated by the Baroque Església de San Bartolomé, whose modernist facade was designed by Gaudí disciple Joan Rubió. Don't miss the superb local ice cream at the Sa Fabrica de Gelats (ⓦ gelatsoller.com) on the Plaça de Mercat: try a scoop flavoured with local oranges. The best way to get here is by train (see box above). From Sóller it's only 2km to the picturesque village of **Biniaraix**, and another 2km to **Fornalutx**. The winding Ma-10 hugs the coast, heading southwest, passing through the mountain village of **Deià**, the former home of Robert Graves, before arriving in **Valdemossa**, famous for its monastery where Chopin and George Sand stayed in 1838–39.

Eastern Mallorca

While many beaches along Mallorca's east coast have been ruined by mass tourism, the beaches north of Cala Ratjada are still relatively unspoiled, with white sand and clear waters. Inland you'll find the quiet town of **Artà**, dominated by a fourteenth-century hilltop fortress, from which you get a fantastic view of the surrounding countryside, while south along the coast, near the town of Porto Cristo, are the island's most spectacular caves – Coves del Drac (ⓦ cuevasdeldrach.com for tour times; €15), known for their vast size, strange rock formations and subterranean lake.

> ### CYCLING MALLORCA
>
> The rugged terrain, pine forests and winding roads along Mallorca's northwestern coast make for some challenging cycling, and lycra-clad enthusiasts tackle in it droves. Don't miss the scenic ride to Cap de Formentor – the **lighthouse** at the island's northernmost tip. When you climb to the first viewpoint, past the Port de Pollença, a minor road winds its way uphill to your right. If you reach the top, there are fantastic views of the island from the perilous watchtower. Heading south along the Ma-10, it's well worth stopping in Pollença for the Calvari – a 365-stone-step climb to the hilltop chapel. Further southwest, the most picturesque of Mallorca's turquoise-water coves, Sa Calobra, is reached by a series of steep hairpin bends. Bikes are available at rental outlets in Palma and in Alcúdia on the north coast; they can be transported in the luggage section of buses.

32

ARRIVAL AND DEPARTURE

By bus Frequent buses from Palma run to Artà and Cala Ratjada, but to get to the caves and some of the more isolated beaches you need your own transport.

MENORCA

In 1993 **MENORCA** was declared a biosphere reserve, and as such the island has largely avoided the rampant development seen elsewhere in the Balearics. Instead, idyllic coves, tranquil bays and rolling countryside, dotted with prehistoric sights, take their place. It's possible to get to some of the beaches with local transport from the main towns of **Maó** or **Ciutadella**, but you'll need your own wheels if you want to discover the more isolated beauty spots. Cycling is a great option as the roads are flat and quiet.

Maó

As most visitors stay in resorts along the coast, the Menorca capital of **MAÓ** is relatively free from tourists and so retains a low-key feel, its lovely old streets lined with Georgian houses remaining from Menorca's period of British rule. Maó has the second-largest natural harbour in the world: take a boat trip from **Moll de Llevant** for great vistas. In town, explore the **Mercat des Claustre del Carme**

MENORCA'S PREHISTORIC SITES

Unlike its neighbours, Menorca is dotted with stone constructions dating as far back as 2000 BC. There are three types of edifices: *taulas*, unique to Menorca, are horseshoe-shaped constructions with T-shaped pillars at the centre; *talayots* are stone mounds that served as ancient watchtowers; *navetas* are constructions that resemble upturned boats and possibly served as tombs or places of gathering. The most impressive include **Naveta des Tudons** (Mon & Tues 9am–2pm, Wed–Sun 9am–7.30pm; €2), a large, intact stone burial chamber near the 40km mark along the Ciutadella–Maó road, and **Torre d'en Galmés** (Tues–Sun 10am–2pm; €3), where you can check out the three hilltop *talayots* and underground chambers. Outside set hours and peak season the sites can be visited free of charge.

(Mon–Sat 7.30am–8.30pm, Sun 8.30am–2pm), a church cloister elegantly converted into a market. Local buses provide access to nearby attractions, such as the lunar landscape of the **Cap de Favaritx**, the whitewashed seaside town of **Fornells** – home of Menorca's signature dish, *caldereta de langosta*, slow-cooked lobster stew – or the beach resorts in the southeast, such as **Cala en Porter**.

ARRIVAL AND DEPARTURE

By plane Menorca's international airport is 5km southwest of Maó. Bus #10 (€2.65) every 30min from 6am to midnight to Maó's central bus station.
By bus TMSA runs hourly buses to Ciutadella via various towns including Alaior (1hr; €4.50), plus five express buses taking a direct route (Mon–Fri; 45min; €5.10). Five daily Autos Fornells buses run to Fornells (30min).
By boat Ferries from Palma and Barcelona arrive at Maó harbour, a short walk from the town centre.

INFORMATION

Tourist office Plaça S'Esplanada (Mon–Fri 9am–1.30pm & 5–7.30pm, Sat 9am–2pm; ☎ 971 355 952, ⊛ menorca.es).
Bike rental Autos Mahon Rent, Moll de Levant 35–36 ⊛ autosmahonrent.com. Rents bicycles (€12/24hr), scooters and cars.

ACCOMMODATION

Hostal Jume c/Concepción 6 ☎ 971 363 266, ⊛ hostaljume.com. Cheap central choice with a/c rooms and a warm welcome. Doubles **€57**
Hostal La Isla c/Santa Caterina 4 ☎ 971 366 492, ⊛ hostal-laisla.com. Centrally located, friendly guesthouse with simple, comfortable rooms. Doubles **€63**

EATING AND DRINKING

The best places for eating and drinking are down by the port, where the bars and restaurants are open mainly in July and August, and around Plaça Bastió, an appealing square with lots of tapas options.
★ **Bar à Vins** Pl. de la Conquesta 5. Trendy wine bar and restaurant with hip decor designed by a Menorcan tattoo artist. Offers high-quality seasonal cooking encompassing meat, fish and vegetable dishes, with lunch menus from €8. Closed Sun.
Sa Bodega Pl. de la Constitució. Cosy spot to sample Menorcan cheese and other cold cuts washed down with local wine or vermouth.
Ses Forquilles Rovellada de Dalt 20. Gourmet dishes such as suckling pig, tuna *tataki* and chorizo lollipops served in a low-key setting. Creative tapas also available in the upstairs bar. Tapas from €3, mains from €12. Closed Sun.

32

Ciutadella and around

Well-preserved **CIUTADELLA** has a lovely old quarter and harbour, and is Menorca's prettiest town. Wandering around the narrow, cobbled streets and quiet plazas, lined with colourful houses and seventeenth-century churches, is a real pleasure. Nearby are some of the most beautiful and secluded virgin beaches in the Mediterranean, such as **Cala Turqueta** (10km) and **Macarella** (13km) – both have soft white sand and turquoise waters and are about a twenty-minute drive from Ciutadella (also easily reachable by bike) through countryside and pine forest. There are no facilities at Turqueta, so bring a picnic. A short walk from Macarella over the white stone gorge takes you to the even prettier bay of **Macarelleta**.

ARRIVAL AND DEPARTURE

By bus TMSA buses serve Maó (hourly; 45min–1hr; ⓦ tmsa.es) and arrive and depart from Plaça de la Pau, a few minutes' walk from the centre of town. Buses to the beaches are operated by Torres and leave from Plaça des Pins.

By boat Ferries from Alcúdia in Mallorca arrive at the ferry port about 4km south of the centre, which is best reached by taxi.

Bike and motorbike rental Velos Joan, c/Vila Juaneda 23 (ⓣ 971 381 576, ⓦ velosjoan.com).

INFORMATION

Tourist office Pl. Catedral 5 (Mon–Sat 9am–3pm & 5–9pm; ⓣ 971 484 155, ⓦ menorca.es).

ACCOMMODATION

Hostal Ciutadella c/Sant Eloi 10 ⓣ 971 383 462, ⓦ hostalciutadella.com. In a quiet area of the Old Town, this simply furnished *hostal* features typical Menorcan window-shutters. Rooms are simple and immaculately clean, staff are friendly and breakfast is served in the downstairs restaurant. Doubles **€70**

Hostal Oasis c/Sant Isidre 33 ⓣ 630 018 008, ⓦ hostaloasismenorca.es. Comfortable, spacious rooms in an Old Town house with pretty garden, where breakfast is served in summer. Doubles **€66**

EATING AND DRINKING

The lively produce market (Plaça Llibertat; Mon–Sat mornings) is a good place to pick up provisions or enjoy a coffee. For nightlife, hit the port, where bars and clubs (in high season) stay open until 6am.

El Imperi Pl. d'es Born 5. A Ciutadella classic with a smart old-school interior and black-aproned waiters. The prices don't match the setting: delicious *sobrasada* and honey sandwiches cost from €1.60 and the wine's a steal at €2 a glass.

★ **La Cayena** c/Alaoir 40. Internationally inspired restaurant with a boho-chic interior. The wide-ranging menu features Thai, Indonesian and Mexican meals plus home-made desserts. Pad Thai €12.50. Dinner only, closed Sun.

Restaurante Vegetariano Fang I Aram c/Gabriel Marti I Bella 11. A short walk from the centre, this airy café-restaurant serves daily three- or four-course lunch menus of meat-free home cooking. Lunch menu from €10.90. Mon–Sat 10am–noon & 1–3.30pm, plus Sat 8–11.30pm.

Catalunya

With its own language, culture and, to a degree, government, **Catalunya** (Catalonia in English) has a unique identity. **Barcelona**, the capital, is very much the main event – one of the most vibrant and exciting cities in Europe. Inland, the monastery of **Montserrat**, Catalunya's premier sight, is perched on one of the most unusual rock formations in Spain and makes for a great day-trip from Barcelona. To the north, the rugged **Costa Brava** is shaking off its unfortunate touristy image and boasts the best beaches in the region, along with some appropriately wacky and wonderful homages to Surrealist artist Salvador Dalí. Just south of Barcelona, the beach town of **Sitges** draws visitors with its beaches and a raucous Gay Pride event in June.

BARCELONA

Cool and hip as they come, **BARCELONA** is Catalunya's cosmopolitan and self-confident modern capital. A thriving port, and the most prosperous commercial centre in the Iberian peninsula, its sophistication and cultural dynamism are way ahead of the rest of Spain – the city seems far more in tune with Milan and Paris than with Madrid or Lisbon. Barcelona also evolved a quirky and very individual identity of its own, most perfectly expressed in the eccentric Art Nouveau architecture of **Antoni Gaudí** and his contemporaries, but

32

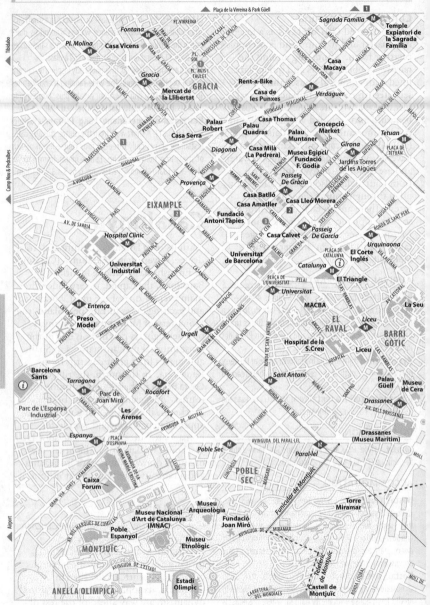

also evident in the huge diversity of the city's cultural events.

WHAT TO SEE AND DO

Though it boasts outstanding **Gothic** and **Art Nouveau** buildings, and some great

museums – most notably those dedicated to Picasso, Miró and Catalan art – Barcelona's main appeal lies in getting lost in the narrow side streets of the **Barri Gòtic** (Gothic Quarter), rising, eating and drinking late, hitting the beach or lazing in the parks, and

ACCOMMODATION	
Equity Point Centric	2
Sant Jordi Sagrada Familia	1

● EATING	
Can Tosca	1
La Cava	2
Lateral	3

■ DRINKING AND NIGHTLIFE	
La Fira	2
Luz de Gas	1

generally soaking up the atmosphere. As in any large city, beware of pickpockets.

La Rambla
One of the most popular avenues in Europe, **La Rambla** teems with sightseers,

tourist bars, postcard stalls and human statues. As it bisects the city, La Rambla remains a useful point of reference, so it's worth strolling down to orient yourself before getting lost in the more interesting maze of side streets in the Barri Gòtic to

CATALAN (CATALÀ)

	CATALAN	PRONUNCIATION
Yes	*Sí*	See
No	*No*	Noh
Please	*Si us plau*	See-uus-plow
Thank you	*Graciès*	Gra-see-ess
Hello	*Hola*	Oh-la
Goodbye	*Adéu*	A-day-uu
Excuse me	*Perdoni*	Perdoni
Where?	*On?*	On?
Good	*Bon/Bona*	Bon/Bonna
Bad	*Mal*	Mal
Near	*A prop*	A prop
Far	*Lluny*	Yoon
Cheap	*Barat*	Barat
Expensive	*Car*	Carr
Open	*Obert*	Oo-berrt
Closed	*Tancat*	Tun-cat
Today	*Avui*	A-boo-ee
Yesterday	*Ahir*	A-hear
Tomorrow	*Demà*	Du-maa
How much?	*Quant val?*	Kwant val?
What time is it?	*Quina hora és?*	Kina ora es?
I don't understand	*No ho entenc*	No oo antenk
Do you speak English?	*Parles anglès?*	Par-les ang-lays?
One	*Un/Una*	Oon/Oona
Two	*Dos/Dues*	Doss/Doo-guz
Three	*Tres*	Trays
Four	*Quatre*	Kwa-tra
Five	*Cinc*	Sing
Six	*Sis*	Seess
Seven	*Set*	Set
Eight	*Vuit*	Bweet
Nine	*Nou*	No
Ten	*Deu*	Dayoo

the east or El Raval to the west. If you are walking down La Rambla towards the sea, just off to your right is the highly photogenic **La Boqueria**, the city's main food market (Mon–Sat 8am–8.30pm; wboqueria.info), a splendid gallery of sights and smells that's frequented by locals and tourists alike. By the namesake metro station stands the **Liceu**, Barcelona's celebrated opera house (guided tours Mon–Fri at 9.30am & 10.30am; €16; several "express visits" daily, check website for times; €6; 934 859 914, wliceu barcelona.cat). Further south, just off La Rambla and into the Barri Gòtic, is the elegant nineteenth-century **Plaça Reial**, crowded with hundreds of alfresco diners and drinkers. Across La Rambla and just

into El Raval, **Palau Güell** (daily: April–Oct 10am–8pm; Nov–March 10am–5.30pm; €12; wpalauguell.cat) at c/Nou de la Rambla 3–5 is a must for any Gaudí fan: the interiors showcase some of his best work and are simply breathtaking. At the harbour end of La Rambla, Columbus stands perilously perched atop a tall, grandiose column, the **Mirador de Colom** (daily 8.30am–8.30pm; €4). Take the lift to his head for a bird's-eye view of the city.

El Raval

The once-notorious red-light district of **El Raval** lies on the west side of La Rambla. With its two universities and numerous bars, clubs and arts centres, Raval is now one of the most diverse areas of the city. For a taste of the area's regeneration, walk up the **Rambla de Raval** – a boulevard with pavement cafés and bars – on your way to the **Museu d'Art Contemporani de Barcelona** or **MACBA** (Mon & Wed–Fri 11am–7.30pm, Sat 10am–9pm, Sun 10am–3pm; €10, valid for one month; ⓦmacba.cat), an arresting white-walled and glass edifice, which houses a permanent collection of Spanish and Catalan art from the 1950s onwards, as well as thought-provoking temporary exhibitions by international and national artists. Next door is the **Centre de Cultura Contemporània de Barcelona** or **CCCB** (Tues–Sun 11am–8pm; €6 one exhibition, €8 two exhibitions; ⓦcccb.org). Firmly at the cutting edge of contemporary culture, this creative space hosts film cycles, exhibitions, installations and more, including Sónar (see box, p.1062).

Barri Gòtic

The **Barri Gòtic** dates principally from the fourteenth and fifteenth centuries, when Catalunya reached the height of its commercial prosperity. The quarter is centred on **Plaça de Sant Jaume**, just behind which lies Barcelona's **cathedral**, **La Seu** (daily 8am–12.45pm & 5.15–8pm; €6 1–5.30pm, free other times; ⓦcatedralbcn.org), one of Spain's great Gothic buildings. Barcelona's finest Roman remains were uncovered nearby, beneath the beautiful **Plaça del Rei**, and now form part of the wonderful **Museu d'Història de Barcelona** (Tues–Sat 10am–7pm, Sun 10am–8pm; €7, free Sun from 3pm, all day first Sun of the month; ⓦmuseuhistoria.bcn.cat), which takes you into the nitty-gritty of the city's development, all the way from its Roman fish sauce-making factory to the present day. You'll also be able to see the interiors of the Plaça del Rei's finest buildings – including the famous **Saló del Tinell**, on whose steps Ferdinand and Isabella stood to receive Columbus on his triumphant return from his famous voyage of 1492. Along c/de Marlet, in the centre of El Call, Barcelona's medieval Jewish quarter, you'll come across the tiny **Sinagoga**

Major (Mon–Fri 10.30am–6.30pm, Sat & Sun 10.30am–2.30pm; €2.50), one of the oldest synagogues in Europe and all that remains of Spain's largest Jewish community.

La Ribera and Parc de la Ciutadella

Heading east from Barri Gòtic, you cross Vía Laietana into **La Ribera** and reach the **Carrer de Montcada**, crowded with beautifully restored old buildings. One of these houses the **Museu Picasso** (Tues–Sun 10am–7pm, Thurs till 9.30pm; €11, free Sun from 3pm, all day first Sun of the month; ⓦbcn.cat/museupicasso), one of the world's most important collections of Picasso's work. Continue down the street and at its end you'll find yourself opposite the stunning basilica of **Santa Maria del Mar** (daily 9am–1.30pm & 4.30–8.30pm; free, but €6 Mon–Sat 1–5pm & Sun 2–5pm), built on what was the seashore in the fourteenth century. The elongated square leading from the church to the old Mercat del Born is the **Passeig del Born**, heart of the trendy **El Born** neighbourhood, a pleasant area for wandering. A few minutes' walk from here is the green and peaceful **Parc de la Ciutadella**, whose attractions include the meeting place of the Catalan parliament, a lake and Gaudí's monumental fountain.

Port Vell, Barceloneta and Port Olímpic

The attractive **Port Vell** area, centred on the Maremàgnum complex, features an upmarket shopping mall, an aquarium with an 80m-long shark tunnel, and a multitude of expensive restaurants. The other side of the port, past the marina, the **Barceloneta** district, in contrast, is one of the few remaining *barris* harbouring genuine local Catalan life. Here, you'll find popular and not terribly clean **beaches**, the city's most famous **seafood** restaurants and the excellent **Museu d'Història de Catalunya** (Tues–Sat 10am–7pm, Wed till 8pm, Sun 10am–2.30pm; €4.50; ⓦmhcat.net), a stampede through 2000 years of Catalan history, including the Muslim occupation of Barcelona and the Civil War. A **cable car**, the **Teleférico de Barcelona** (daily:

32

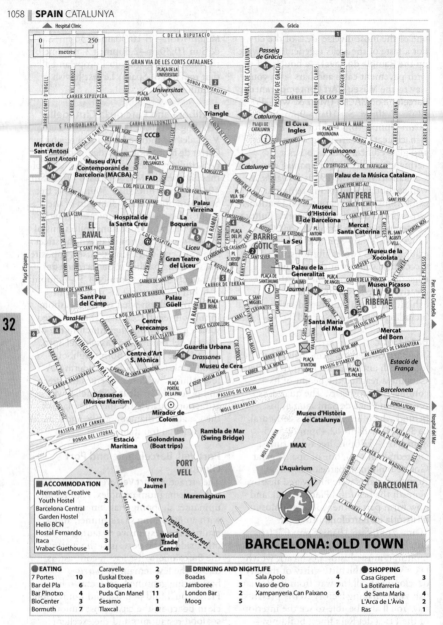

BARCELONA: OLD TOWN

ACCOMMODATION	
Alternative Creative Youth Hostel	2
Barcelona Central Garden Hostel	1
Hello BCN	6
Hostal Fernando	5
Itaca	3
Vrabac Guethouse	4

EATING			
7 Portes	10	Caravelle	2
Bar del Pla	6	Euskal Etxea	9
Bar Pinotxo	4	La Boqueria	5
BioCenter	3	Puda Can Manel	11
Bormuth	7	Sesamo	1
		Tlaxcal	8

DRINKING AND NIGHTLIFE			
Boadas	1	Sala Apolo	4
Jamboree	3	Vaso de Oro	7
London Bar	2	Xampanyeria Can Paixano	6
Moog	5		

SHOPPING		
Casa Gispert	3	
La Botifarreria de Santa Maria	4	
L'Arca de L'Àvia	2	
Ras	1	

March to early June & mid-Sept to late Oct 10.30am–7pm, early June to mid-Sept 10.30am–8pm; late Oct to Feb 11am–5.30pm; €11 one-way, €16 return) makes its high, perilous-seeming journey from the tip of Barceloneta to Montjuïc hill (see p.1059). Walk 1km north along the beach promenade and you'll find **Port Olímpic** with its myriad bars and restaurants. At night, the tables are stacked up, dancefloors emerge and the area hosts one of the city's liveliest (and brashest) bar and club scenes.

Sagrada Família

Barcelona offers – above all through the work of **Antoni Gaudí** (1852–1926) – some of the most fantastic and exciting modern architecture anywhere in the world. Without doubt his most famous creation is the incomplete **Basílica de Sagrada Família** (daily: April–Sept 9am–8pm; Oct–March 9am–6pm; €15 basic, including towers €29; Ⓦsagradafamilia.cat), in the northeastern sector of the Eixample district. Construction is ongoing, with the projected completion date being the hundredth anniversary of Gaudí's death, and it's fascinating to watch Gaudí's last-known plans being slowly realized. The size alone is startling, with eight spires rising to over 100m. If you choose the "top views" ticket, be sure to take the lift, or climb up one of the towers, and you can enjoy a dizzy view down over the whole complex and clamber still further round the walls and into the towers.

L'Eixample

Barcelona's Eixample (the street-grid zone) abounds with wonderful modernista (Art Nouveau) buildings. The top two are Gaudí's **Pedrera** at Passeig de Gràcia 92 (daily: 9am–8.30pm & 9–11pm; €20.50 including audioguide; Ⓦlapedrera.com), its quirky roof terrace providing a spectacular view of the city's skyline, and, nearby, his **Casa Batlló** at Passeig de Gràcia 43 (daily 9am–8pm; €20.35/16.30; Ⓦcasabatllo.cat), a wonderfully surreal residential building; check out the front window in the form of a dragon's mouth. Inside, you'll find no straight lines – just curves, twists and undulations. Casa Batlló shares a block with two other great Art Nouveau buildings, the Casa Amatller at no. 41 and the Casa Lléo Morera at no. 35.

Barcelona's other Art Nouveau masterpiece is the 1908 **Palau de la Música Catalana** concert hall in c/Sant Pere Més Alt (daily 10am–3.30pm; July & August until 6pm; tours every 30min; €18, with limited places, so buy in advance online; Ⓦpalaumusica.org), where the multicoloured columns of the facade are just a taster of the wonders within, in particular the amazing stained-glass roof.

Gràcia and Park Güell

The residential neighbourhood of **Gràcia**, north of the centre, has a bohemian, village-like feel, and is a good place for an authentic night out. Popular with arty student types, the bars are best stumbled upon by chance – try your luck around the Plaça de la Virreina.

In the eastern part of Gràcia, **Park Güell** (daily: winter 8.30am–6pm; summer 8am–9.30pm; €8; Ⓦparkguell.cat) is Gaudí's most ambitious project after the Sagrada Família. This almost hallucinatory experience consists of a hillside park featuring, among other creations, giant decorative lizards and a vast Hall of Columns, containing a small **museum** (daily 10am–6pm) with some of the furniture Gaudí designed. To get here, take the metro to Vallcarca or Lesseps (15min walk from either) or bus #24 from Plaça de Catalunya to the eastern side gate.

Montjuïc

The green hill of **Montjuïc**, with its winding paths and botanical gardens, provides a refuge from the bustle of the city, while at the same time featuring a couple of great museums and a superbly sited castle. You can approach it from **Plaça d'Espanya** and walk from there up the imposing Avenida de la Reina María

32

DAY-TRIP: MONTSERRAT

The bulbous mountains of **Montserrat**, 60km northwest of Barcelona, make for an interesting day-trip out of the city. As well as some short hikes (1–3hr) through the national park's unusual rock formations, the main attraction is the Benedictine monastery, with its well-preserved sixteenth-century basilica housing a twelfth-century image of La Moroneta, patron saint of Catalunya. To get here, take the R5 train from Plaça Espanya (every hour at 36min past; 1hr 5min) to Montserrat Aeri (for the cable car), or to Monistrol de Montserrat (for the rack railway to the town).

Cristina, past the **Font Màgica**, a large fountain that comes alive with lights to the tune of "Barcelona" by Freddie Mercury and Montserrat Caballé in the evenings. To start with the castle, take the **Funicular de Montjuïc** (daily: Mon–Fri from 7.30am, Sat & Sun from 9am; summer till 10pm; winter till 8pm; every 10min; fare included in metro tickets), from Paral.lel metro station to the start of the **Telefèric de Montjuïc** (daily: March–May & Oct 10am–7pm; June–Sept 10am–9pm; Nov–Feb 10am–6pm; €8 one-way, €12 return), which in turn leads to the **Castell de Montjuïc** (daily: April–Sept 9am–8pm; Oct–March 9am–6pm; €5, free Sun from 3pm), an eighteenth-century fortress that offers magnificent city views and often hosts concerts in summer.

MNAC, the Poble Espanyol and the Fundació Joan Miró

The Palau Nacional, set at the back of Montjuïc, is the grand peach-coloured home to one of Spain's great art museums, the **Museu Nacional d'Art de Catalunya** or **MNAC** (May–Sept Tues–Sat 10am–8pm, Sun 10am–3pm; Oct–April Tues–Sat 10am–6pm, Sun 10am–3pm; €12, free Sat from 3pm & first Sun of month; ⊕mnac.es). Its enormous bounty includes a Romanesque collection that is the best of its kind in the world and a substantial number of Gothic, Baroque and Renaissance works, as well as a large modern art section and changing temporary exhibits. Nearby is the **Fundació Joan Miró** (Tues, Wed & Fri: Nov–March 10am–7pm; April–Oct 10am–8pm; all year Thurs 10am–9.30pm, Sat 10am–8pm, Sun 10am–2.30pm; €12; ⊕bcn.fjmiro.es), devoted to the largest collection of works by one of the greatest Catalan artists, with Miró's drawings, bold abstract paintings, sculpture and textile creations on display in an appealing, light-filled building. Downhill and to the west of MNAC is the **Poble Espanyol** or "Spanish Village" (Mon 9am–8pm, Tues–Thurs & Sun 9am–midnight, Fri 9am–3am, Sat 9am–4am; €12; ⊕poble-espanyol.com), consisting of replicas of famous or characteristic buildings from all over Spain, and with a lively bar scene at night.

ARRIVAL AND DEPARTURE

By plane The main Aeroport del Prat is 12km southwest of the city centre and is linked by train (daily 5.45am–11.30pm, every 30min; €3.50) to Barcelona Sants, and Pg. de Gràcia in the city centre, both served by ⓜL3 to Liceu or Pl. de Catalunya. The Aerobús (6am–1am, every 5–10min from Terminal 1, every 10–20min from Terminal 2; €5.90; ⓦaerobusbcn.es) runs to Pl. d'Espanya and Pl. de Catalunya. Some Ryanair flights land at Girona airport (see p.1065).

By train Barcelona Sants (ⓜSants) is the city's main train station, for national and some international arrivals – many national buses also stop here.

Destinations Girona (1–2 hourly; 38min–1hr 30min); Madrid (1–2 hourly; 2hr 30min–7hr); Tarragona (2–4 hourly; 31min–54min); Valencia (15 daily; 3–5hr); Zaragoza (1–2 hourly; 1hr 30min–4hr 45min).

By bus The main bus terminal for international and long-distance services is the Estació del Nord (ⓦbarcelonanord .com; ⓜArc de Triomf).

Destinations Alicante (9 daily; 7hr 30min–9hr 45min); Madrid (17 daily; 7hr 20min–7hr 50min); Valencia (9 daily; 4hr–5hr 30min); Zaragoza (15 daily; 3hr 30min).

By ferry Balearics ferries dock at the Estació Marítima (ⓜDrassanes). Acciona Trasmediterranea (ⓦtrasmedi terranea.es) and Balearia (ⓦbalearia.com) are the main ferry companies with regular services from Barcelona to Palma de Mallorca, Maó on Menorca and Ibiza Town. Grandi Navi Veloci ferries (ⓦwww.gnv.it) run three or more luxury ferries to Genoa, Italy (19hr), and Tangier, while Grimaldi Ferries (ⓦwww.grimaldi-lines.com) run to Civitavecchia not far from Rome, Livorno in Tuscany and Porto Torres in Sardinia.

INFORMATION

Tourist office Pl. de Catalunya 17 (daily 8.30am–8.30pm; ☎932 853 834, ⓦbarcelonaturisme.com; ⓜCatalunya).

GETTING AROUND

By metro and bus The easiest way of getting around is by metro (Mon–Thurs & Sun 5am–midnight, Fri till 2am, Sat all night). Numerous bus routes (roughly 6am–10.30pm; ⓦtmb.cat) pass through Plaça de Catalunya; every bus stop displays route maps. Yellow night buses run between 11pm and 3/5am every 30–45min; all pass through Plaça de Catalunya. Pick up a free transport map at TMB customer service centres at Barcelona Sants, and at Universitat, Diagonal, La Sagrera and Sagrada Familia metro stations.

Tickets Ticket prices for bus and metro are as follows: zone 1 single (covers all major sights) €2.15; a ten-ride *targeta* "T-10" €9.95 which is valid for the train to El Prat airport; 1/2/3/5-day Hola BCN! Pass €14/20.50/26.50/32.

Discount cards The Barcelona Card, available from any tourist office (3/4/5 days €45/55/60, 10 percent discount online), covers all city transport including to/from airport, plus between 15 and 50 percent discounts at many museums and some tours, shops and restaurants. Worthwhile only if you're planning on huge amounts of sightseeing in a short period. The Articket (€30, available at the tourist office and participating museums; ⓦarticketbcn.org) covers entry to six of the city's main art galleries: it's worth getting if you plan on visiting at least four of them. Student ticket prices in museums and galleries are often only available to those who are both a student and under 25.

Bicycles Many hostels rent out bikes, or try Rent-a-Bike, c/Perill 29 (€11/day; ☏672 367 145, ⓦrentabikebarcelona .com).

Taxis The black-and-yellow taxis charge a minimum of €2.05, plus €0.93/km Mon–Fri 8am–8pm, €1.18 at other times: a cross-town journey costs around €8–12.

ACCOMMODATION

Accommodation in Barcelona is among the most expensive in Spain, and you're strongly advised to book ahead, particularly at busy times such as Sónar (see box, p.1062) and September's Festes de la Mercè, when the city celebrates its patron saint with a riot of *castellers* (human castles), *correfocs* (fire runs) and other revelry. Most of the cheapest accommodation is in the side streets off and around La Rambla and in El Raval.

★**Alternative Creative Youth Hostel** Ronda de la Universitat 17 ☏635 669 021, ⓦalternative-barcelona .com; ⓜCatalunya; map p.1058. Great location, friendly atmosphere that encourages communal dinners (without this being a party hostel), wonderfully helpful staff and fast wi-fi. Dorms €30

Barcelona Central Garden Hostel c/Roger de Llúria 41 ☏935 006 999, ⓦbarcelonacentralgarden.com; ⓜCatalunya; map p.1058. Near the main attractions, with lovely patio, common area with book exchsange, and sparsely decorated but comfortable rooms. Quiet time after midnight guarantees a good night's sleep. Dorms €28, doubles €80

Equity Point Centric Passeig de Gràcia 33, Eixample ☏932 156 538, ⓦequity-point.com; ⓜPasseig de Gràcia; map pp.1054–1055. Stunning mansion conversion in a prime location right near La Rambla and Plaça Catalunya with comfy beds, great terrace bar and decent guest kitchen. Breakfast included. Dorms €30

Hello BCN c/Lafont 8–10, Poble Sec ☏934 428 392, ⓦhellobcnhostel.com; ⓜParal.lel; map p.1058. Secure, well-located hostel popular with a young crowd. Crowded dorms but an excellent common room with great atmosphere; also has sun terrace, kitchen, laundry service and a bar. Dorms €28, doubles €100

Hostal Fernando c/Ferran 31, Barri Gòtic ☏933 017 993, ⓦwww.hfernando.com; ⓜLiceu; map p.1058. Refurbished stone-walled *hostal* offering spacious, sparkling rooms, plus top-floor dorm accommodation and a tapas bar downstairs. Breakfast included. Dorms €29.50, doubles €85

Itaca c/Ripoll 21 ☏933 019 751, ⓦitacahostel.com; ⓜJaume I; map p.1058. Friendly, stylish little hostel in the heart of Barri Gòtic, with spacious mixed dorms (and one women-only dorm), plus plenty of communal spaces, helpful staff and a small kitchen. Dorms €34, twins €70

Sant Jordi Sagrada Familia c/Freser 5 ☏934 460 517, ⓦsantjordihostels.com; ⓜSant Pau/Dos de Maig; map pp.1054–1055. Not far from its namesake attraction, this super-clean, skateboard-themed hostel scores high points for the sociable vibe, huge guest kitchen and group nights out. Great place to meet people. Dorms €20

Vrabac Guethouse c/Portaferrissa 14 ☏663 494 029, ⓦvrabacguesthouse.wordpress.com; ⓜLiceu; map p.1058. Lovely small guesthouse in Barri Gòtic, its individually decorated rooms arranged around a peaceful central courtyard. Good breakfast is included and the owner is very helpful. Doubles €85

EATING

Barcelona is a fairly expensive place to eat out. The best bet for a cheap meal is a weekday lunchtime *menú del día* that many places offer, with three courses with wine and bread for as little as €12. There are many excellent tapas bars in the Old Town; avoid the overpriced ones on La Rambla. Opening hours are daily 1–4pm & 8–11pm unless otherwise stated.

7 Portes Passeig d'Isabel II 14; ⓜBarceloneta; map p.1058. Expect white linen, smart-looking career waiters and expertly cooked large portions of paella, *arroz negro* (rice in sepia ink) and *fideuá*. One of the few *arrocerías* where you can order a paella for one. Mains around €15.

★**Bar del Pla** c/Montcada 2; ⓜJaume I; map p.1058. Top tapas bar close to the Picasso Museum. Petite and perennially packed, it serves tasty takes on classics such as *patatas bravas* and more inventive daily specials made with market-fresh produce. Mon–Thurs noon–11pm, Fri & Sat noon–midnight.

Bar Pinotxo La Boquería; ⓜLiceu; map p.1058. Perpetually busy with locals, this tapas bar at the back of La Boquería dishes up such delights as caramel pork belly or seared squid. Tapas from €4. Sept–July Mon–Sat 6am–5pm.

BioCenter c/Pintor Fortuny 25 ⓦrestaurantebiocenter .es; ⓜCatalunya; map p.1058. One of the best-value vegetarian lunchtime menus in town – €10.45 weekdays, €12.45 weekends. If you're eating à la carte, try the lentil burger or "bravissimo" potato selection with a choice of sauces.

Bormuth Pl. Comercial 1; ⓜJaume I; map p.1058. Trendy tapas bar in El Born that serves modern versions of Spanish classics. Start your night right with a

32

vermouth, the trendiest drink in Barcelona and *Bormuth's* speciality. Mon–Wed & Sun 12.30pm–1.30am, Fri & Sat 12.30pm–2.30am.

Can Tosca c/del Torrent de l'Olla 77; ⓦFontana; map pp.1054–1055. Unassuming neighbourhood bar that serves a mean breakfast (try the *butifarra* sausage sandwich), home-style lunches – and unexpectedly morphs into a popular spot for a gin & tonic on weekend nights. Mon–Thurs 8am–8pm, Fri & Sat 8am–3am.

★**Caravelle** c/Pintor Fortuny 31; ⓦCatalunya; map p.1058. Airy café restaurant close to La Rambla serving top brunch options such as baked eggs with chorizo and corn fritters with avocado. Also serves lunch and dinner. Good for vegetarians. Brunch or main dishes average €8. Mon 9.30am–5.30pm, Tues–Fri 9.30am–1am, Sat 10am–1am, Sun 10am–5.30pm.

Euskal Etxea Placeta de Montcada 1 ⓦeuskaletxeataberna.com; ⓦJaume I; map p.1058. Basque *taberna* specializing in a great range of mouthwatering *pintxos* (tapas) from €2 each.

★**La Boquería** La Rambla; ⓦLiceu; map p.1058. Barcelona's most famous produce market, heaving with locals and tourists. Shop here for fruit, veg, chorizo, jamón, cheese, bread, cake and fresh fruit juices, and head for the tapas stalls at the back for lunch or snacks. Mon–Sat 8am–8.30pm.

La Cava c/Corsega 339; ⓦDiagonal; map pp.1054–1055. At the Gràcia end of expensive l'Eixample, this hip bar-restaurant serves a range of vermouths (and cocktails incorporating the popular tipple), plus a changing menu of tempting tapas and *raciones*. Mon–Fri 7pm–midnight, Sat 4pm–midnight.

Lateral c/Consell de Cent 329; ⓦPasseig de Gracia; map pp.1054–1055. Sleek, minimalist decor and a menu bursting with fresh, modern tapas choices. Try the salmon and avocado tartare or the vegetable tempura. Service is quick and efficient, and you can eat well for around €12.

MUSIC FESTIVALS

If electronica is your thing, make sure you're in town for **Sónar** (ⓦsonar.es), an internationally respected multimedia art and progressive music festival, held every June in Barcelona. Day tickets bought online cost €54, night tickets €72, while a pass for the entire festival will set you back €195.

If you're more into indie and rock, check out **Primavera Sound** (ⓦprimavera sound.com), a three-day festival held at the end of May/beginning of June. Day tickets €80, three-day tickets from €125.

Puda Can Manel Pg. Joan de Borbó 60 ⓦcanmanel.es; ⓦBarceloneta; map p.1058. *Bodega* with large wooden barrels, specializing in grilled meats and Catalan favourites such as *calçots* (grilled spring onions). Good-value €16 *menú del día*, best washed down with a jug of their cava sangría. Closed Mon & Sun eve.

Sesamo c/Sant Antoni Abat 52; ⓦSant Antoni; map p.1058. Cheerful, friendly vegetarian restaurant in El Raval. Three-course lunches are a steal at €10 and there are fresh juices and pastries if you prefer a snack. Closed Wed & Sun eve.

Tlaxcal c/Comerç 27 ⓦtlaxcal.com; ⓦJaume I; map p.1058. Hugely popular Mexican joint with thirteen types of tacos and fantastic home-made salsas. Weekday lunchtimes are a bargain, with fresh guacamole, a portion of tacos and dessert for €10.50. Closed Mon.

DRINKING AND NIGHTLIFE

Barcelona's nightlife is some of Europe's best, though it's not cheap. High-end bars and clubs are concentrated mainly in the Eixample, especially around c/Ganduxer, Avda Diagonal and Vía Augusta. Laidback and alternative places can be found in the streets of El Raval and El Born, while the waterfront Port Olímpic area is a more mainstream summer-night playground, where the big, brash clubs are. Music bars close at 3am, the clubs at 4 or 5am, though later at weekends. For listings, pick up a copy of *Butaxaca*, a free weekly guide available in most bars and clubs (ⓦbutxaca.com), or buy the weekly *Guía del Ocio* from any newsstand (ⓦguiadelociobcn.com). The thriving gay scene (ⓦgaybarcelona.net) is centred around the so-called Gaixample, a few square blocks northwest of the main university.

BARS

Boadas c/Tallers 1, El Raval; ⓦCatalunya; map p.1058. Old-school cocktail bar just off La Rambla once frequented by Hemingway. Mixologists create their signature daiquiris and pour over thirty types of gin. Mon–Thurs noon–2am, Fri & Sat noon–3am.

La Fira c/Provença 171; ⓦProvença; map pp.1054–1055. Barcelona at its quirkiest: fairground rides and circus paraphernalia adorn this long-standing theme bar. Tues–Sat from 11pm till late.

London Bar c/Nou de la Rambla 34–36; ⓦLiceu; map p.1058. Here you can prop up the bar that Picasso and Miró once graced, or check out the live acts on the small stage at the back.

Vaso de Oro c/Balboa 6; ⓦBarceloneta; map p.1058. A tiny but lively bar, packed with locals and serving a good selection of artisan beer.

Xampanyeria Can Paixano c/Reina Cristina 7; ⓦBarceloneta; map p.1058. The place to sip champagne while snacking on tiny sandwiches. Very popular (read: very, very crowded). Mon–Sat 9am–10.30pm, Sun to 1pm.

CLUBS

Jamboree Pl. Reial 17; Ⓦ masimas.com/jamboree; Ⓜ Liceu; map p.1058. Cavernous basement club with an international crowd dancing to hip-hop, funk and r'n'b (cover charge around €15). The top DJs take to the decks at 12.30am, but there are live jazz performances at 8 and 10pm. Daily until 5.30am.

Luz de Gas c/Muntaner 246; Ⓜ Diagonal. Stylish club with a glamorous retro feel. Popular with a young crowd, and often hosts top Catalan and international DJs.

Moog c/Arc del Teatre 3 Ⓦ masimas.com/moog; Ⓜ Drassanes; map p.1058. If you're into your electronica, *Moog* is the place to go for regular appearances from big-name UK and Euro DJs. Despite the large, industrial setting, the atmosphere is relaxed and both gay- and straight-friendly. Cover charge €15. Daily midnight–5am.

Sala Apolo c/Nou de la Rambla 113 Ⓦ sala-apolo.com; Ⓜ Paral.lel; map p.1058. Live gigs from international acts and burgeoning stars from the worlds of alternative electronica, rock and techno. "Nasty Mondays" are very popular. Daily 10pm–5am.

SHOPPING

The big names of the fashion industry occupy the Passeig de Gràcia and the waterside shopping centre Maremagnum. The crooked passages of La Ribera and El Born are home to dozens of little boutiques, while in El Raval, trendy vintage shops lie along the Carrer de la Riera Baixa. There are also a number of excellent speciality food retailers in the city, and chocolate shops are scattered throughout the Ciutat Vella.

Casa Gispert c/Sombrerers 23 Ⓦ casagispert.com; Ⓜ Barceloneta or Jaume I; map p.1058. Freshly roasted nuts, dried fruits, speciality chocolates and *turrons* (marzipan and nougat bars), with sweet teeth catered to since 1851.

La Botifarreria de Santa María c/Santa María 4; Ⓜ Barceloneta or Jaume I; map p.1058. Sells fabulous speciality hams, cheeses and their famous *botifarras* (Catalan sausages).

L'Arca de L'Àvia c/Banys Nous 20; Ⓜ Liceu; map p.1058. An incredible collection of vintage clothing – so much so that these guys have supplied the set of *Titanic* and other films.

Ras c/Doctor del Dou 10; Ⓜ Universitat; map p.1058. Beautiful bookshop and gallery selling books on art and architecture, as well as photography.

DIRECTORY

Consulates Canada, Pl. de Catalunya 9 1st floor, 2a ☎ 932 703 614; Ireland, Gran Vía Carles III 94 ☎ 934 915 021; UK, Avda Diagonal 477, 13th floor, Eixample ☎ 933 666 200; US, Pg. Reina Elisenda de Montcada 23, Sàrria ☎ 932 802 227.

Exchange Most banks are located in Pl. de Catalunya and Pg. de Gràcia. ATMs and money exchange available at the airport, Barcelona Sants, the Pl. Catalunya tourist office, and at *casas de cambio* throughout the centre.

Hospitals 24hr accident and emergency centres at the following: Hospital Clínic, c/Villaroel 170 ☎ 932 275 400, Ⓜ Hospital Clínic; Hospital dos de Maig, c/Dos de Maig 301, Ⓜ Sant Pau–Dos de Maig.

Left luggage Lockers at Sants station (daily 5.30am–11pm) and at Locker (Estruc 36, Barri Gòtic, Ⓜ Catalunya; daily: summer 8.30am–10pm; winter 9am–9pm).

Pharmacies At least one *farmacía* in each neighbourhood is open nights and weekends. Try Farmàcia Clapés (La Rambla 98, Ⓜ Liceu).

Police Guàrdia Urbana (City Police), La Rambla 43 ☎ 092, Ⓜ Liceu; open 24hr.

Post office Pl. Antoni López, Barri Gòtic, Ⓜ Jaume I (Mon–Fri 8.30am–8.30pm, Sat 8.30am–2pm).

THE COSTA BRAVA

Stretching for 145km from the French border to the town of Blanes, the **Costa Brava** (Rugged Coast) boasts wooded coves, high cliffs, popular beaches and deep blue water. The more rugged northern part, dominated by the spectacular **Cap de Creus** headland and park, and the whitewashed fishing town of **Cadaqués**, is the most attractive yet least crowded, with a natural appeal all its own. Inland is **Girona**, the beautiful medieval capital of the region, and **Figueres**, Dalí's birthplace and home to his outrageous **museum. Buses** in the region are almost all operated by SARFA (☎ 902 302 025, Ⓦ sarfa.com), with an office in every town. To visit the smaller and more picturesque coves, a car or bike is useful, or walk the fabulous Camí de Ronda necklace of footpaths running along the coastline.

Figueres

The northernmost parts of the Costa Brava are reached via **FIGUERES**, a provincial Catalan town with a lively *rambla*. The town's major highlight is one of Spain's most visited museums, the surrealist creation that is the **Teatre-Museu Dalí** (March–May & Oct Tues–Sun 9.30am–6pm; June daily 9.30am–6pm; July–Sept daily 9am–8pm; Nov–Feb Tues–Sun 10.30am–6pm; €14; Ⓦ salvador-dali.org). Born in Figueres, Dalí died here in the tower and the

32

museum showcases some of his most eccentric work. The extraordinary pink facade, topped with enormous eggs and suits of armour balancing baguettes on their heads, sets the tone for the exhibitions inside, which include collages, sculptures and mechanical contraptions requiring audience participation, and the ticket price includes entry to the Dalí Jewels exhibition – 39 precious creations based on the artist's designs. Between late July and late August, the whole experience gets even more surreal during cava-fuelled night visits (daily 10pm–1am; €15).

ARRIVAL AND DEPARTURE

By train AVE trains from Barcelona, Girona and Madrid arrive at Figueres Vilafant just outside the centre; take the shuttle bus. Local trains use the central station; from here (about 600m), simply follow the "Museu Dalí" signs to reach the centre.

Destinations Barcelona (hourly; 55min); Girona (hourly; 30–40min); Madrid (12 daily; 3hr 40min–4hr 44min).

By bus The bus station is around 200m away from the main train station, towards the city centre. SARFA buses run to Cadaqués (4–8 daily; 1hr).

INFORMATION

Tourist office Pl. de l'Escorxador 2 (July–Sept Mon–Sat 9am–7pm, Sun 10am–2pm; Oct–June Mon–Fri 10am–2pm; ☏ 972 503 155, ⓦ visitfigueres.cat).

ACCOMMODATION AND EATING

It's easy to go to Figueres as a day-trip from either Barcelona or coastal destinations, but it might be worth staying overnight to beat the bussed-in crowds. The restaurants around Museu Dalí tend to be sub-par and overpriced.

Creperie Bretonne c/Cap de Creus 6. The decor draws on the absurdist theme, and the wide range of sweet and savoury stuffed crêpes and salads (set lunch menu from €9) is equally enticing. Daily 1–4pm & 8–11pm.

Hostal Sanmar c/Rec Arnau 31 ☏ 972 509 813, ⓦ hostalsanmar.com. Budget choice 400m from the Museu Dalí. Worn furnishings, but clean and perfectly acceptable for an overnight stay. Doubles €60

Cadaqués

The picture-postcard fishing village of **CADAQUÉS**, an hour by SARFA bus (4–8 daily; 1hr) from Figueres, with whitewashed houses, tiny beaches and narrow cobbled streets straddling a hill

topped by an imposing church, was Salvador Dalí's home from 1930 to 1982, and attracted an arty crowd during its heyday. The tiny fishing village of Portlligat, 1.25km walk from Cadaqués, features the **Casa-Museu Dalí** (by advance booking only; daily mid-Feb to mid-June, Nov & Dec 10.30am–6pm; mid-June to Oct 9.30am–9pm; closed Tues mid-Feb to mid-March & Nov; €11; ☏ 972 251 015, ⓦ salvador-dali.org), a labyrinthine ramble of a house decorated according to the whims of Dalí and his beloved wife. Bizarre ornaments catch your eye in every room and a visit to the artist's intimate quarters offers an enthralling (and surprising) glimpse into his private life.

INFORMATION

Tourist office c/del Cotxe 1 (summer Mon–Sat 9am–9pm, Sun 10am–1pm & 5–8pm; winter Mon–Thurs 9am–1pm & 3–6pm, Fri & Sat Mon–Thurs 9am–1pm & 3–7pm; ☏ 972 258 315).

ACCOMMODATION

Camping Cadaqués Ctra Port-Lligat 17 ☏ 972 258 126, ⓦ campingcadaques.com. Campsite in an attractive location with a large pool; very basic facilities. Open mid-March to Sept. Per person €8.70, plus per family tent €11.50

Hostal Vehí Carrer de l'Església 5 ☏ 972 258 470, ⓦ hostalvehi.com. Friendly budget option near the church, with wonderfully clean a/c rooms with en-suite bathrooms. Doubles €65

EATING AND DRINKING

For a drink or a meal, the seafront is the liveliest. Look out for *suquet* – the town's signature fish and potato stew.

Pilar c/de la Miranda 4. Some of Cadaqués's best paella and other rice dishes, as well as grilled fish and seafood. Mains €16–20. Daily 1–4pm & 8–11pm, closed Sun eve.

Girona

GIRONA, 37km south of Figueres and 100km from Barcelona, is one of Spain's loveliest unsung cities – especially in May during the nine-day Temps de Flors flower festival. Alleyways wind through the compact old town, the **Barri Vell**, to the atmospheric streets of **El Call** – the beautifully preserved medieval Jewish quarter – at its core. The star attraction here is the **Museu d'Història dels Jueus de Girona** (July & Aug Mon–Sat 10am–8pm, Sun 10am–2pm; Sept–June

Tues–Sat 10am–6pm, Sun & Mon
10am–2pm; €4) at Carrer de la Força 8,
an excellent museum that tells the story
of Catalunya's second most important
Jewish community, from daily rituals to
contributions to medieval medicine and
relentless persecution by the Inquisition.
Girona was fought over every century
since the Romans first set foot here, and
is dominated by its towering **cathedral**
(daily: April–Oct 10am–6.30pm;
Nov–March 10am–5.30pm; €7 including
audioguide) nearby. The town's eclectic
past is tangible in its **medieval walls**,
which you can walk on for a great view of
the city from above.

Girona is also popular with hikers and
cyclists who use the city as a base for the
many great routes in the area, details of
which are available at the tourist office.

ARRIVAL AND DEPARTURE

By plane The airport (@ barcelona-girona-airport.com),
11km out of town, served by Ryanair flights from the UK, is
connected to Girona's bus/train station by regular Sagalés
(@ sagales.com) buses (30min).
By train The station is off the Barcelona Crta, a 10min
walk southwest from the centre.
Destinations Barcelona (2–4 hourly; 40min–1hr 20min);
Figueres (hourly; 30–40min); Madrid (10 daily; 4hr–10hr
20min).
By bus The station is next to the train station.
Destinations Barcelona (3–5 daily; 1hr 20min); Cadaqués
(2–3 daily; 1hr 45min).

INFORMATION

Tourist office c/Joan Maragall 2 (Mon–Fri 8am–8pm,
Sat 8am–2pm & 4–8pm, Sun 9am–2pm; ☎ 872 975 975,
@ girona.cat).

ACCOMMODATION

Girona can easily be visited as a day-trip from Barcelona
but staying overnight allows you to soak in the atmosphere
after crowds of day-trippers leave.
Pensió Margarit c/Ultònia 1 ☎ 972 201 066,
@ hotelmargarit.com. Between the train station and the
Old Town, this budget hotel offers comfortable rooms,
though light sleepers beware: walls are thin and the sound
really carries. Doubles €57
Room in Girona c/Santa Clara 9, third floor ☎ 972 426
480, @ roomingirona.com. In a perfect location close to
the river, this backpacker hostel is fairly basic, but offers
free wi-fi, a laundry service and bike rental. Dorms €20,
twins (shared bathroom) €45, private bathroom €55

EATING AND DRINKING

For evening drinking it's best to head into the Barri Vell or
the area around Pl. Independència, where you'll find most
of the bars and clubs.
Draps c/de la Cort Reial 2 Traditional restaurant in an
arcaded riverside square, serving Catalan classics such as
esquixada (salt cod salad). The €14 lunch menu will fill you
up for an afternoon's sightseeing. Daily 12.45–4pm &
8–11pm.
El Vermutet Can Gombau c/Bonaventura, Carreras i
Peralta 7. Lively bar specializing in popular Catalan
aperitif vermouth. Go before dinner to soak up the
atmosphere. Wed–Sat noon–3pm & 6.30–11pm, Sun
noon–3pm.
Rocambolesc c/de Santa Clara 50. You may not be able to
afford (or secure a table at) the world's top restaurant *El
Celler de Can Roca*, but you can sample one of the Roca
brothers' imaginative ice creams here. Flavours change,
but include seasonal options like caramelized apple and
lavender From €3.50. Mon–Thurs & Sun 11am–11pm, Fri
& Sat 11am–midnight.

32

Andorra

A tiny country nestled in the Pyrenees,
Andorra is one of the oldest nations in
Europe. Set up by Charlemagne in the
eighth century as a buffer between
France and the Islamic Moors, it
became an independent, democratic
principality in 1993. It's the only
country in the world with Catalan as its
official language, although Spanish and
French are also widely spoken, as is
basic English.

Duty-free shopping, winter sports and
summer hiking are the main attractions
of this picturesque alpine nation: the
capital, **Andorra la Vella**, offers the
widest range of accommodation and
cuisine, while next-door **Escaldes-
Engordany** lays claim to the biggest
thermal spa in Europe. To the northwest
is the popular ski resort of **Pal-Arinsal**,
while the hills around **Ordino** boast
challenging trails and splendid valley
views. East of Ordino, a road weaves
through appealing mountainscapes to
Canillo, home to a captivating
Romanesque chapel, and near the
French border are sleepy **Soldeu** and
the busy ski slopes of **Grandvalira**.

ARRIVAL AND INFORMATION

Andorra doesn't have an airport, but regular **buses** link the tiny nation to the nearest international ones three to four hours' drive away in Barcelona (225km) and Toulouse (180km). Alsina Graells (☎902 335 533, ⓦmovelia.es) has eight daily services from Barcelona (€28, 3hr 15min–4hr 20min), as does Nadal Autocars (from €29.50; Andorra ☎805 151, ⓦautocarsnadal.com), while Novatel (☎803 789, ⓦandorrabybus.com) does airport transfers from both Barcelona (7 daily; €33) and Toulouse (3 daily; €36). Alsa also offers a coach service (8 daily) from Barcelona Nord to Andorra's central bus station, via Lleida.

Alternatively, you can travel by **train** from Zaragoza or Barcelona Sants to Lleida and then take a Montmantell minibus (5 daily; €23; ☎973 982 949 or Andorra ☎807 444, ⓦwww.montmantell .com) from in front of the train station to Andorra la Vella.

The international phone code for Andorra is ☎376 and the currency is the euro.

ENTRY REQUIREMENTS

Passports are generally required to cross the Andorran border. You'll be asked to show your passport when buying a bus ticket.

GETTING AROUND

Its small size makes Andorra easy to get around – most places can be visited as day-trips from Andorra la Vella, with efficient public bus links to most towns and villages.

ACCOMMODATION

Good **budget hotels** are scarce in the capital. Prices peak in high season – July to August (when reservations are a must) and December to March – expect to pay

EMERGENCY NUMBERS

Police ☎110; Ambulance and Fire ☎118; Medical ☎116; Mountain Rescue ☎112.

at least €50 for a double room in most places. There are many well-equipped **campsites** throughout Andorra, and in summer you can stay for free in one of the 26 state-run **refugis** – simple mountain cabins; information is available at tourist offices. Camping in the wild is illegal except around *refugis*.

ANDORRA LA VELLA

The name of the national capital **ANDORRA LA VELLA** is a bit of a misnomer: "Old Andorra" is for the most part a spread-out collection of ski lodges, touristy restaurants, bars and ageing storefronts that cater to duty-free shoppers and skiers. However, with a backdrop of towering mountains, its setting has an undeniable appeal.

WHAT TO SEE AND DO

The capital is bisected by the Avinguda del Príncep Benlloch, which further east becomes the shop-filled Avinguda de Meritxell and then, on towards neighbouring Escaldes-Engordany, Avinguda de Carlemany. Towards the western end of town, **Barri Antic** is the capital's old quarter, with pleasant cobbled streets and quiet *plaças*; at its centre is the **Casa de la Vall**, one of the oldest – and smallest – parliaments in Europe.

ARRIVAL AND DEPARTURE

By bus Most international buses (see p.1066) use the Central d'Autobusos, just southeast of the small Parc Central, 5min south of the city centre. Buses to Lleida, run by Montmantell (ⓦmontmantell.com), leave from Caldea Spa but can also make stops in the centre on request.

★ TREAT YOURSELF

The **Caldea Spa** (opening hours vary, check website; €35 for 3hr, €30 for 2hr evening session; ☎800 999, ⓦcaldea.com; bus #L3 from Avda Meritxell), 1km east of Casa de la Vall, in Escaldes-Engordany, is the largest health centre on the continent, pumping in water from the nearby thermal springs. Rich in sodium, silica and sulphur, the water here is reputed to have healing effects for skin and respiratory ailments.

32

▼ Bus Station

ANDORRA LA VELLA (BARRI ANTIC)

32

Domestic buses run along Avda Meritxell and connect the capital to all the main towns and villages. Check ⊛www.transportpublic.ad for schedules.

Destinations Barcelona (15 daily; 3–4hr); Lleida for Zaragoza and Madrid (4–6 daily; 2hr 30min); Toulouse (2 daily; 3hr 15min).

INFORMATION

Tourist office Pl. de la Rotonda (Mon–Fri 9am–8pm, Sat 9am–9pm, Sun 9am–2pm; ☎750 100, ⊛visitandorra.com).

ACCOMMODATION

★**Hostel Barri Antic** c/de la Vall 20 ☎845 969, ⊛hostalbarriantic.com. Right in the heart of the old town, this biker bar-cum-guesthouse is the most welcoming establishment in town. Brightly coloured rooms and kitchen available for use. With Jägermeister on tap in the bar, you won't fail to have fun here. Doubles €44, quadruple €80

Hotel Sant Jordi Avda Príncep Benlloch 45 ☎876 201, ⊛hotelsantjordi-andorra.com. Ordinary rooms with a good view of the old town. There's a pleasant restaurant downstairs where you can have breakfast (included), which offers more under its "continental" description than most budget accommodation. Doubles €35

Pensió La Rosa c/Antic Carrer Major 18 ☎821 810. One of the cheapest *pensions* in the country, and the location is unbeatable. Be sure to call before you arrive, as the bell-for-entry system isn't terribly effective. Doubles €32

EATING

Cisco de Sans c/Anna Maria Janer 4. Romantic tapas restaurant with an excellent selection of local cheeses (€7 for a plate) and cured meats (€2.50/100g). Mon–Wed 7pm–1am, Thurs–Sat 7pm–3am.

★**La Adelita** Plaça Príncep Benlloch 4. Colourful *taqueria* named after a revolutionary Mexican folk song. The menu offers a selection of tacos, including the super-tender tacos *carnitas* (€7.90 for four), home-made guacamole and tortilla chips (€6.95) and, of course, shots of Don Julio tequila. Daily 1–4pm & 7.30–11pm.

L'Escenari de Pizzes Avda Dr Mitjavila 19. Unassuming place near the Pont du Paris with the best pizzas in Andorra (€9–15). Only a handful of tables, so either arrive early or book. Cards not accepted. Mon–Sat 1–4pm & 8–11pm, Sun 1–4pm.

DRINKING

La Birreria c/de la Vall 3. Every inch of wall here is lined with bottled beers. It's big on community spirit, with an everyone-welcome house ethos. Mon–Wed 4.30–11pm, Thurs 4.30pm–1am, Fri & Sat 4.30pm–2am.

DIRECTORY

Hospital Hospital Nostra Senyora de Meritxell, next to Caldea Spa (☎871 000).

Pharmacy Les Tres Creus, c/Canals 5 (daily 9.30am–8pm; ☎820 212, ⊛farmacialestrescreus.com).

Post offices Spanish PO at c/Joan Maragall 10 (Mon–Fri 8.30am–2.30pm, Sat 9.30am–1pm); French PO at c/Pere d'Urg 1 (Mon–Fri 8.30am–1.30pm, Sat 9am–noon).

LA MASSANA

A twenty-minute bus ride away through a verdant valley from Andorra la Vella (bus #L5 or #L6 from Avda Princep Benlioch, every 15min 7am–9pm, €1.80), **LA MASSANA** is a good base for hiking or skiing. Get information at the helpful tourist office (Avda Sant Antoni 1, Pl. les Fontetes; Mon–Sat 9am–1pm & 3–7pm, Sun same hours when the ski station is open; ☎835 693, ⓦlamassana .ad), and pick up the *Trails of Andorra* booklet which covers all the walks in detail (€5).

ACCOMMODATION AND EATING

Alberg Borda Jovell Avda Del Jovell, Sispony ☎836 520. Turn up the mountain at La Massana's Museu Casa Rull and you'll arrive at this chalet hostel. Good Spanish and a willingness to mingle helps. Dorms €25

★ **Mon Bohemi** Cami Ral, Complex Tabola ☎837 076. Cultural café and book exchange in an old parking lot. The home-made pizzas are delicious (slice for €2.10), as are the burgers (€6). Wed–Mon 2pm–2am.

PAL AND ARINSAL

At the western end of La Massana commune lies **PAL** (bus #M2 from La Massana; 4 daily), one of the best-preserved villages in Andorra, hugging the slopes that veer up to Pal-Arinsal, part of the popular Vallnord ski complex (ⓦvallnord.com). Pal is also a great base for summertime activities – ask at the tourist office in La Massana for details. Head back down to La Massana to take the road up to **ARINSAL**, 2km northwest (bus #L5 from Avda Princep Benlloch in Andorra la Vella via La Massana, every 30min), which is much bigger than Pal – it is also a great base for summer treks and known for its lively **nightlife**.

ACCOMMODATION AND EATING

Fugazzeta Ctra de Arinsal. Laidback café where boarders chill with a beer (Estrella €1.50) and a slice (pizzas €7–9). Marinated beef empanadas offer themselves up on the bar for €1.90. Daily 7.30am–11.45pm.

Surf Next to the cable-car station, Arinsal. An Argentine steakhouse (*parilla* meats from €11.50) until 11.30pm, when it becomes a raucous bar for the après-skiers. Mon–Wed & Sun 12.30–11.30pm, Thurs–Sat 12.30pm–5am.

Xixerella Park Ctra de Pal – Erts ☎718 613, ⓦxixerellapark.com. A scenic campsite on the road between La Massana and Pal with a swimming pool and riverside pitch and putt. Per person €6.60, per tent €6.60

The Pyrenees

The area around the Spanish Pyrenees is little visited; most tourists who come here travel straight through, but in so doing they miss out on some of the most wonderful scenery in Spain, and some of the country's most attractive trekking, with several beautiful **national parks** as a focus for exploration. To the south lies Aragón, and most especially its capital, **Zaragoza**, with its fine architecture and stately pace of life. One place that attracts tourists is **Pamplona**, the capital of **Navarra** and famous for its bull-running fiesta, but a great place to visit at any time of the year.

ZARAGOZA

ZARAGOZA is the capital of Aragón, and easily its largest and liveliest city, with over half the province's one million inhabitants and the majority of its industry. There are some excellent bars and restaurants tucked in among its remarkable monuments, and it's also a handy transport centre, with good connections into the Pyrenees and east towards Barcelona.

WHAT TO SEE AND DO

Many places of interest are clustered around the Plaza del Pilar, near the Río Ebro. Other beautiful medieval monuments are a short walk away. Try and be in town for the October **Fiestas del Pilar**, a lively festival in honour of the town's patron saint.

Aljafería

The city's only surviving legacy from Moorish times, the **Aljafería** (April–Oct daily 10am–2pm & 4.30–8pm;

Nov–March Mon–Sat 10am–2pm & 4.30–6.30pm, Sun 10am–2pm, sometimes closed Thurs & Fri am for parliamentary meetings, check with tourist office; €3, free on Sun; ⓦcortesaragon.es), was built in the eleventh century by the independent dynasty of Beni Kasim. After Zaragoza was reconquered in 1118, the palace was Christianized and used by the *reconquista* kings of Aragón. From the original design, the foremost relic is a tiny and beautiful mosque adjacent to the second courtyard, the intricately decorated **Patio de Santa Isabel**. From here, the **Grand Staircase** (added in 1492) leads to a succession of rooms remarkable chiefly for their carved ceilings.

Basílica de Nuestra Señora del Pilar

The most imposing of the city's churches, majestically fronting the Río Ebro, is the **Basílica de Nuestra Señora del Pilar** (daily: summer 6.45am–8.30pm; winter 6.45am–8.30pm). It takes its name from the column that the Virgin is said to have brought from Jerusalem during her lifetime to found the first Marian chapel in Christendom. Topped by a diminutive image of the Virgin, the pillar forms the centrepiece of the Holy Chapel and is the focal point for pilgrims, who line up to kiss an exposed section encased in a silver sheath. Visitors can climb the **tower** (daily 10am–2pm & 4–6pm; €3) for excellent city views.

San Salvador

In terms of beauty, the interior of the Basílica de Nuestra Señora del Pilar can't compare with the nearby Gothic-Mudéjar cathedral, **San Salvador**, or **La Seo** (Mon–Fri 10am–2pm & 4–6.30pm, Sat 10am–12.30pm & 4–6.30pm; €4), at the far end of the pigeon-thronged Plaza del Pilar.

Roman remains

The city has brought to light its Roman past through several underground excavations: there's the **Forum** and **River Port** (close to La Seo), as well as the **Roman Baths** and the **amphitheatre** on c/San Jorge (all Tues–Sat 10am–1.30pm

& 5–8.30pm, Sun 10am–2pm; €4, free first Sun of the month, combined ticket €7). Following the semicircle of c/Coso and c/Cesar Augusto, the **Roman walls** are steadily being excavated; the best place to view them is at c/Echegaray at the junction with c/Coso, where remains of towers and ramparts can be seen.

ARRIVAL AND DEPARTURE

Zaragoza's modern Delicias station serves all train and bus destinations. It's on Avda Navarra, about a 30min walk from the centre and connected by bus #51 to Paseo de Pamplona, at the southern end of Avda de la Independencia (every 11–12min, 8am–midnight). Some regional trains also call at the more central Goya station.

By train Barcelona (at least 1 hourly; 1hr 30min–2hr 50min); Bilbao (2 daily; 4hr 30min); Madrid (17 daily; 1hr 20min–4hr 10min); Pamplona (2 daily; 1hr 45min–2hr 15min).

By bus Barcelona (13 daily; 3hr 30min–4hr 15min); Madrid (18 daily; 3hr 30min–4hr); Pamplona (10 daily; 1hr 50min–3hr).

INFORMATION

Tourist office Pl. del Pilar (daily 10am–8pm; ☎ 976 201 200, ⓦzaragozaturismo.es); also at Torreón de la Zuda (Mon–Sat 10am–2pm & 4.30–8pm, Sun 10am–2pm), and in Delicias train station and airport (daily 10am–8pm).

Discount card The Zaragoza Card (24hr €20/48hr €23; ⓦzaragozacard.com) includes entrance to the majority of the city's museums and monuments and offers discount on transport, restaurants and hotels.

ACCOMMODATION

Albergue Zaragoza Hostel c/de los Predicadores 70 ☎ 976 282 043, ⓦbehostels.com/zaragoza. Five-hundred-year-old building with a rock bar in its cellar. Not the best facilities but a perfect location for discovering the city. Dorms **€16**

Hostal Navarra c/de San Vicente de Paúl 30 ☎ 976 291 684, ⓦhostalnavrra.net. Just 200m from Plaza España, this hostel has an unbeatable location. Comfy sofas in the lounge area – perfect for enjoying the view. Doubles **€30**

Hotel Sauce c/Espoz y Mina 33 ☎ 976 205 050, ⓦhotelsauce.com. Worth a stay for the name alone, *Hotel Sauce* has a prime location around the corner from Pl. del Pilar, comfortable, en-suite rooms and friendly staff. The on-site café serves great home-made cakes. Doubles **€49**

Pensión Iglesias c/Verónica 14-2° ☎ 976 293 161, ⓦpensioniglesias.com. In a great location with some rooms overlooking the Roman amphitheatre. Doubles have basins and a shower but separate toilets. Doubles **€32**

32

32

EATING AND DRINKING

El Tubo, the name given to the streets around c/Estébanes and c/Libertad, is the best place for bar-hopping and tapas, while the bars around the church of Santa María de Magdalena have a more bohemian, alternative vibe. Zaragoza's main fresh-food market, Mercado Central, is on c/Caesar Agosto (Mon–Sat 9am–2pm & 5–8pm). Most places open 1–4pm and 8–11.30pm.

Bar La Viña c/del Arzobispo Apaolaza. Aromas of herbs and spices emanate from this popular tavern. A few *cervezas* in, friends share kebabs (€2.50) and battered aubergine fries (€2).

★ **Birosta** c/de la Universidad 3, Barrio de la Magdalena. Healthy, vegetarian *pinxtos*, with daily specials that include mushroom pâté with caramelized onions and home-made falafel with a citrus sauce (€1.20). The shop indoors sells alternative veggie and vegan products.

Café Botanico Santiago 5. Garden store meets café at this hip arcade venue. Choose from a drool-inducing selection of cakes, made and replenished in store throughout the day. Try the coconut and mascarpone or house favourite, chocolate and orange (€2 per slice).

Café at Museo Teatro c/San Jorge 12. To see half the museum without paying an entrance fee, opt for the coffee and tortilla combo (€2.50, before 1pm) and enjoy it on the terrace, in the grounds of the old amphitheatre.

Taberna Doña Casta c/Estébanes 6. This popular bar elevates the humble *croqueta* to an art form, with delicious specialities (€2.40 each) including *arroz negro*. Ever-popular *jamón* is paired with walnut for a tasty twist.

PARQUE NACIONAL DE ORDESA

For summertime walking, there's no better destination than the **Parque Nacional de Ordesa** (ⓦordesa.net), focused on a vast, trough-like valley flanked by imposingly striated limestone palisades. From Zaragoza's Intercambiador de Actur you'll need to take a bus to **Sabiñánigo** (up to 10 daily; 2hr) and from there catch a bus to **Torla** (1–2 daily; 55min), the best base for the park. Note that bus services between Torla and Sabiñánigo are very limited, so plan your journey well – see ⓦalosa.es for details. At Torla, a regular shuttle bus (every 30min from 6am) takes you to and from the park, but trekkers should opt instead for the lovely trail (1hr 30min) on the far side of the river, well marked as the GR15.2. Further **treks** can be as gentle or as strenuous as you like, the most popular outing being an all-day trip

to the **Circo de Soaso** waterfalls. For detailed information on the park, contact either Torla's tourist office (July–Sept Thurs–Tues 9.30am–1.30pm & 5–9pm; ☎974 486 378) or the park's **Centro de Visitantes**, which is also in Torla (daily 9am–2pm & 4.15–7pm; ☎974 486 472),

ACCOMMODATION AND EATING

Reserve well in advance for accommodation in July and August; the three most scenic campsites, *San Antón* (☎974 486 063), *Camping Ordesa* (☎974 117 721) and *Camping La Gorga* (☎974 502 357), strung out between 1km and 3km north, often fill up. Make sure to bring a sleeping bag along to the *refugios*.

Refugio L'Atalaya c/A'Ruata ☎974 486 022. Torla's real refuge. A cosy restaurant downstairs offers a fireplace, head-tilting art and some of the nicest tapas in town (€7–9). Open all year. Dorms €15

PAMPLONA

PAMPLONA (Iruña in Basque) has been the capital of the old kingdom of Navarra since the ninth century, and long before that was a powerful fortress town defending the northern approaches to Spain. Even now it has something of the appearance of a garrison city, with its hefty walls and elaborate pentagonal citadel. The fast-flowing River Arga runs through it, providing many appealing bankside picnic spots.

WHAT TO SEE AND DO

Though most visitors flood the city during the Fiestas de San Fermín (see box opposite), the compact and lively streets of the Old Town have plenty to look at. Highlights include the elaborately restored Gothic **cathedral** with its magnificent cloister, the **Museo Diocesano** (summer Mon–Sat 10.30am–6pm; winter Mon–Sat 10.30am–4pm; €5; ⓦcatedraldepamplona.com), and the colossal **city walls** and **citadel**. Don't miss the excellent **Museo de Navarra** (Tues–Sat 9.30am–2pm & 5–7pm, Sun 11am–2pm; €2, free Sat pm & Sun; ⓦwww .cfnavarra.es/cultura/museo); besides the wealth of archeological treasures, from Paleolithic tools to vast Roman mosaics and an intricately carved eleventh-century chest from Islamic Spain, there's a superb art collection – from medieval and Renaissance ecclesiastical works to Navarrese art from the nineteenth and twentieth centuries. The city also has a wealth of parks, including the beautiful, if surreal, **Parque La Taconera**, home to herds of deer, peacocks and other unusual bird species.

ARRIVAL AND DEPARTURE

By train 800m from the old part of town; bus #9 runs every 15min to the end of Paseo de Sarasate, a short walk from the central Pl. del Castillo – there is a RENFE ticket office at c/Estella 8.

Destinations Barcelona (7 daily; 3hr 15min–4hr 15min); Madrid (7 daily; 3hr 15min–3hr 30min); San Sebastián (4 daily; 1hr 40min); Zaragoza (6 daily; 2hr).

By bus c/Yanguas Miranda in front of the citadel.

Destinations San Sebastián (11–15 daily; 1–2hr); Zaragoza (9–12 daily; 1hr 50min–3hr); Barcelona (2–3 daily; 6hr); Madrid (10–11 daily; 5hr–5hr 45min).

INFORMATION

Tourist office Avda Roncesvalles 4 (Mon–Sat 10am–2pm & 3–7pm, Sun 10am–2pm; ☎848 420 420, ⓦturismo.navarra.es), opposite the monument to the running of the bulls.

ACCOMMODATION

Rooms are in short supply during summer, and at fiesta time you've virtually no chance of a place without booking

months in advance. Most places quadruple their prices during San Fermín, so you're better off staying nearby (San Sebastián is a viable option) and travelling to Pamplona to enjoy the night-long festivities and early morning running of the bulls. Many end up sleeping rough; remember that there is safety in numbers – head for one of the many parks such as Vuelta del Castillo or Media Luna and bring a sleeping bag. Prices below are high season, outside of fiesta time.

★ **Hostel Hemingway** c/Amaya 26-1º ☎948 983 884, ⓦhostelhemingway.com. The only proper hostel in town, with cool decor, large guest kitchen and staff who go out of their way to help. Dorms **€17**

Hotel Horno de Aralar c/San Nicolás 12 ☎948 221 116, ⓦasador-aralar.com. Sea-blue rooms with basic amenities. Close to Plaza Castillo. Popular *asado* (barbecue) restaurant below. Doubles **€40**

Pensión Arriazu c/Comedias 14 ☎948 210 202, ⓦhostalarriazu.com. Fourteen prim, pastel-shaded rooms at this former theatre in a location that couldn't get more central. Doubles **€64**

EATING AND DRINKING

The Mercado de Santo Domingo is the town's main produce market (Mon–Sat 8am–2pm). The highest concentration of restaurants and bars is along c/San Nicolás and c/Estafeta in the Casco Antiguo.

La Granja c/de Estafeta 71. One of the few restaurants in the city to stay open through siesta time. Their menu of the day, with highlights such as skirt steak and seafood paella, is an absolute bargain for €10.90. Thurs & Sat open till 3am.

32

SAN FERMÍN: THE RUNNING OF THE BULLS

From midday on July 6 until midnight on July 14, Pamplona embraces the riotous nonstop celebration of the **Fiestas de San Fermín**. The focus is the **encierro**, or the running of the bulls – which has evolved from a way of herding cattle to the market to a nail-bitingly exciting spectacle. The *mozos* (runners) are a mix of daring locals and outsiders, mostly male (women were originally forbidden from participating, but still do) and fuelled by alcohol and bravado. The course – from the Plaza Santo Domingo to the bullring – is 825m long. At 8am two rockets are fired to signify the release of the six bulls from their corral and the participants start running. Once you're in, you're in till the end; if you lose your nerve halfway through the run and try to scramble up the wall alongside the course, you'll be pushed back in. Particularly dangerous parts are where c/Mercaderes meets c/Estafeta and the slope down from c/Estafeta to the bullring. Every year there are gorings, particularly when a bull becomes separated from the rest of the herd. The spectacle is over in minutes; to watch the *encierro* it's essential to arrive early and to stake out a spot along the route. If you can't afford a spot on a balcony, buy a ticket for the bullring to watch the end of the proceedings, when bullocks with padded horns are let loose on the crowd inside the bullring. The bulls that participate in the *encierro* are then killed in the afternoon bullfights. If you watch the actual running, you won't be able to get into the bullring, so go on two separate mornings to see both. At midnight on July 14, there's a mournful candlelit procession, the **Pobre De Mi**, to wind up the festivities. See ⓦsanfermin.com for more details. There's also a PETA-organized anti-bullfighting event, the **Running of the Nudes** (ⓦrunningofthenudes.com), held two days before the first bull run; participants mostly wear a red scarf and plastic horns, but little else.

La Servicial Vinícola Navarro Villoslada 11. Locals sipping regional wine among maps of Navarra: this is the real Pamplona. A generous *menú del día* for €10 or a variety of *bocadillos* – tortilla, flank steak, cheese (€4) – are on offer.
Sarasate c/San Nicolás 19. A great vegetarian restaurant that serves the likes of ratatouille and spinach and feta strudel. Daily set menu €11. Daily 1–5pm, Fri & Sat also 8.30pm–1am.

The north coast

Spain's **north coast** veers wildly from the typical conception of the country, with a rocky, indented coastline full of cove beaches and fjord-like *rías*. It's an immensely beautiful region – mountainous, green and thickly forested, with frequent rains often shrouding the countryside in a fine mist. In the east, butting against France, is the **País Vasco** (**Euskadi**, or **Basque Country**), with a strongly independent character. Note that the Basque language, Euskera, bears no relation to Spanish, or any other known language (we've given the alternative Basque names where popularly used) – it's perhaps the most obvious sign of Spain's strongest separatist movement. **San Sebastián** is the big seaside attraction, with superb beaches and some of the most imaginative food in Spain. There are any number of lesser-known, equally attractive coastal villages from the border with France all the way to **Bilbao** – home to the iconic Guggenheim – and beyond. To the west lies pastoral **Cantabria**, centred on the port of **Santander**, with more good beaches and superb trekking in the mountains of the **Picos de Europa**. In the far west, green and lush **Galicia** is Spain's main fishing region; unsurprisingly, its population goes crazy for all manner of seafood. This province also treasures its independence, and Gallego, which has much in common with Portuguese, is still spoken by around 85 percent of the population. For travellers, the obvious highlights are the world-class city of **Santiago de Compostela**, the greatest goal for pilgrims in medieval Europe, and the strenuous, 800km **Camino de Santiago**, one of Europe's finest hikes.

SAN SEBASTIÁN

The undisputed queen of Basque resorts, **SAN SEBASTIÁN** (Donostia), European Capital of Culture in 2016, frequently entices even the most time-strapped travellers to stay longer. With excellent beaches and a gastronomic scene whose Michelin-star count is rivalled only by Paris, it's unsurprising that San Sebastián is so infectious. The town's *kilometre zero* rule means that markets and restaurants pledge to serve local ingredients, where possible, so food is always at its freshest and money filters back into the community. San Sebastián has always been a fashionable place to escape the heat of the southern summers. Its **festivals** include an International Jazz Festival (late July; ⊛heinekenjazzaldia .com) that attracts top performers to play in different locations around town, the **Semana Grande** (Big Week) in mid-August, featuring music, races and an international fireworks contest, and the **San Sebastián Film Festival** in mid-September.

WHAT TO SEE AND DO

San Sebastián is beautifully situated around the deep, still bay of **La Concha**. The **Parte Vieja** (old quarter) sits on the eastern promontory, while newer development has spread inland along the banks of the River Urumea and around the edge of the bay to the foot of **Monte Igeldo**.

Parte Vieja

The **Parte Vieja**'s cramped and noisy streets are where crowds congregate in the evenings to wander among the small bars or sample the shellfish from the traders down by the fishing harbour. Here, too, are the town's chief sights: the gaudy Baroque facade of the church of **Santa María** and the more elegant and restrained, sixteenth-century **San Vicente**. The centre of the Old Town is the Plaza de la Constitución, known locally as "La Consti"; the numbers on the balconies of the buildings around the square date back to the days when it was used as a bullring. Behind La Consti, winding footpaths crisscross up to the top of **Monte Urgull**.

32

From the mammoth figure of Christ on its summit, there are great views out to sea and back across the bay to town.

Monte Igeldo

For wonderful views of the curving bay, the city and the mountains beyond, head to the top of **Monte Igeldo**: take bus #16 or walk around the coastline to its base, from where a **funicular** (spring & June Mon–Fri 11am–8pm, Sat & Sun 10am–9pm; July & Aug Mon–Fri 10am–9pm, Sat & Sun 10am–10pm; rest of the year Tues, Thurs & Fri 11am–6pm, Sat & Sun 11am–7pm; €1.75 single, €3.15 return; ⓦwww.monteigueldo.es) will carry you to the summit.

City beaches

La Concha beach is the most central and most celebrated, a wide crescent of yellow sand stretching round the inlet from the town. Out in La Concha bay is a small island, **Isla de Santa Clara**, which makes a good spot for picnics; glass-bottom boats (*servicio visión submarina*) leave from the Paseo Mollaberria (June–Sept 10am–8pm; every 60–90min; €6; ⓦmotorasdelaisla.com).

Ondarreta, considered the best beach in San Sebastián for swimming, lies beyond the rocky outcrop that supports the **Palacio Miramar**, west of La Concha. Far less crowded, and popular with surfers, **Playa de Zurriola** and the adjacent **Playa de Gros** have breakwaters to shield them from dangerous currents, with the latter particularly good for beginners; Pukas

---

TABAKALERA

Renovation work began on San Sebastián's old tobacco factory in 2011, with an exquisite redesign by Jon and Naiara Montero. **Tabakalera** (Plaza de las Cigarreras 1; Mon–Thurs 8am–10pm, Fri 8am–11pm, Sat 10am–11pm, Sun 10am–10pm; ⓦtabakalera.eu) is now a centre for contemporary culture, with an art-house cinema and space for temporary exhibitions, which hosts the city's annual film festival in September. Take the lift to the top floor; the city view is incredible.

(Avda Zurriola 24; Mon–Fri 10am–2pm & 4–8pm, Sat 8.30am–2pm & 4–8pm, Sun 8.30am–2pm; ☎943 320 068, ⓦpukasurf.com) offers surf lessons, wetsuit and board rental. Weekend surf courses cost €64; board rental is €11 for an hour or €26 for a day.

ARRIVAL AND DEPARTURE

By train The RENFE train station (Estación del Norte) is across the Río Urumea on Paseo de Francia, a 10–15min walk to the historical centre. The EuskoTren from Bilbao's Atxuri station in the Ibaiondo district will take you to San Sebastián's Amara in central Easo Plaza (every 30min; 2hr 30min; €6.30).

Destinations Barcelona (2 daily; 6hr); Madrid (6 daily; 5hr 30min–7hr 40min); Pamplona (2 daily; 1hr 40min); Salamanca (7 daily; 6hr 15min–8hr); Zaragoza (2 daily; 3hr 40min).

By bus National buses arrive at Paseo Frederico Garcia, close to the train station.

Destinations Bilbao (13–25 daily; 1hr 20min); Madrid (12 daily; 5hr–6hr 45min); Pamplona (10–15 daily; 1–2hr).

INFORMATION

Tourist office Alameda del Boulevard 8 (Mon–Thurs 9.30am–1.30pm & 3.30–7pm, Fri & Sat 10am–7pm, Sun 10am–2pm; ☎943 481 166, ⓦsansebastianturismo .com). Runs good local walking tours (tickets from €10; book at ⓦsansebastianreservas.com).

ACCOMMODATION

During busy July and August prices are inflated. High season extends to September when the film festival takes place.

★**A Room in the City** Easo Kalea 20 ☎943 429 589, ⓦaroominthecity.eu. The trendiest hostel on the coast, with touches of character everywhere you look. A 5min walk to La Concha Beach, and 10min to the old town. The staff all speak perfect English, and are generous with their time and knowledge. Dorms €25

Downtown River Hostel San Martin Kalea 2 ☎943 56 34 66, ⓦdowntownriverhostel.es Modern, no-frills hostel with a party vibe. Close to train/bus stations. Dorms €27

Green Nest Hostel Uba Aterpetxea Uba Bidea 43 ☎943 457 117, ⓦnesthostelsansebastian.com; EuskoTren to Intxaurrondo or #33 bus from Avda de la Libertad to Otxoki Pasealekua. Central digs booked up, or can't pay the extortionate last-minute prices? *Green Nest*, set in a beautiful wooded area 4km out of the city, might be your answer. Private bathroom for each dormitory. Dorms €25

Pensión Larrea c/Narrica Kalea 21-1º ☎943 422 694, ⓦpensionlarrea.com. Run by a super-helpful *señora*, this *hospedaje* offers sparkling mid-sized rooms with polished wooden floors, tiny balconies, soundproof windows, and powerful, spacious showers in the shared bathrooms. Minimum stay two nights in high season. Doubles **€60**

Surfing Etxea Zabaleta 32 ☎ 943 265 832, ⓦ surfingetxea.com. Community comes first at this surf house – a perfect place to chill after hitting the waves. Dorms are well equipped with comfy bedding and personal reading lamps. Surfboards and wetsuits available for rent. Dorms **€37**

EATING AND DRINKING

Food in the Basque country is considered some of the best in Spain and it's easy to see why in San Sebastián. The Parte Vieja is crammed with bars serving gourmet *pintxos* (bite-sized tapas), washed down with Basque country cider or Txacolí (young white wine). Opening hours are daily 1–4pm & 8–11pm unless otherwise stated.

Atari Gastroteka c/Mayor 18. An array of imaginative *pintxos*, both cold (try the *jamón*, goat's cheese and onion marmalade, €3) and hot (the *revuelto de bacalao*, €2.50, is superb). Also table service for an à la carte menu with *raciones* from €8 each and a curious *helado queso* (cheese ice cream) for €3.50. Daily till 2/3am.

Belgrado Avda de Navarra 2. Café-cum-deli-cum-shop, *Belgrado* is the pinnacle of San Sebastián's cool. It can't get much better than biting into their Fritilla Burger (€6), while looking over Playa de Gros's swell.

★ **Borda Berri** c/Fermín Cabetón 12. Traditional Basque *pintxos* made fresh to order. Eat elbow-to-elbow with locals enjoying the rich food and wine. The best of the menu is the melt-in-your-mouth calf's cheek (€3.20) cooked in red wine, and the *risotto con queso de Idiazabal* (local cheese risotto) for €2.70.

Giroki Enbeltran Kalea 4. Nautical-feeling place with friendly barmen. For a tender *milanesa*, try the Carolina Sandwich (€4.90) with *Giroki's* house sauce. Huge *platos combinados* from €7.50. Fri & Sat till 1am; closed Wed eve.

Juantxo Enbeltran Kalea 6. Come to this old-town tavern for a hearty brunch. Flavoursome tortillas (plain for €3.15, with chorizo for €3.70) come by themselves or in *bocadillos*.

NIGHTLIFE

Dabadaba Mundaitz Kalea 8 ⓦ dabadabass.com. Converted warehouse with live indie/rock bands, followed by DJs spinning vinyl on the weekends. Check website for listings. Mon–Thurs 9am–1pm & 5–11pm, Fri 9am–1pm & 5pm–4am, Sat 5pm–4am, Sun 5–11pm.

Gu De Alderdi Eder Parkea 1 ⓦ gusansebastian.com. Twenty-four-hour bar/club with entry deals before 11pm. Architecturally impressive, with panoramic views over La Concha. Splash out on the Willy Wonka cocktail (€10), made with white chocolate liqueur. Closed Sun.

BILBAO

Although traditionally a gritty industrial city, **BILBAO** (Bilbo) has been given a makeover In the last couple of decades and is now a must for any lover of art or architecture. A state-of-the-art metro, designed by Norman Foster, links the city's widely spread attractions: the monumental titanium-and-glass Museo Guggenheim by Frank Gehry – along with Jeff Koons' puppy sculpture in flowers – is the city's highlight, while the airport and one of the many dramatic river bridges are Calatrava-designed, and the compact Casco Viejo (Old Town) is a beguiling maze of medieval streets. The city's vibrant, friendly atmosphere, elegant green spaces and some of the best *pintxo* bars in Euskadi combine to make Bilbao an appealing destination. From the first Saturday after August 15, the whole city goes totally wild during the annual bullfighting extravaganza, **La Semana Grande**, with scores of open-air bars, live music and impromptu dancing.

WHAT TO SEE AND DO

The **Casco Viejo**, the old quarter on the east bank of the river, is focused on the beautiful **Teatro Arriaga**, the elegantly arcaded **Plaza Nueva** and the fourteenth-century Gothic **Catedral de Santiago** (Mon–Fri entry at 11am, 1pm & 7.30pm; Sat & Sun after mass at 1pm).

Museo Guggenheim

A good route leads from the Casco Viejo down the river past the Campo Volantín footbridge and the Puente Zubizuri to the sensual, gleaming titanium curves of the **Museo Guggenheim** (daily July & Aug 10am–8pm; Sept–June Tues–Sun 10am–8pm; €13, €16 joint pass with the Museo de Bellas; ⓦ guggenheim-bilbao .es), described as "the greatest building of our time" by architect Philip Johnson. Replacing an industrial wasteland, the Guggenheim, with its promontories, soaring columns, and wonderful use of light inside its vast atrium, is at least as interesting as the treasures it houses. The permanent collection, which includes works by Kandinsky, Klee, Mondrian, Picasso, Chagall and Warhol, to name a few, is housed in traditional galleries, while the superb temporary exhibitions and individual artists' collections are displayed in the huge sculpted spaces nearer the river. There are free guided tours in English every day at 12.30pm (arrive 30min before).

Museo de Bellas Artes

A five-minute walk from the Guggenheim, on the edge of the Parque de Doña Casilda de Hurriza, is the **Museo de Bellas Artes** (Mon & Wed–Sun 10am–8pm; €7, free on Wed & also for under-25s Sun 2–8pm; ⍵museobilbao .com), which focuses on three main specialisms: classical art, such as works by Goya, Murillo, Zurbarán and El Greco; more recent art by the likes of Gauguin; and Basque art, such as sculpture by Quintín de Torre. There are also some fine temporary exhibitions.

ARRIVAL AND DEPARTURE

By plane From the airport (☎902 404 704, ⍵aena.es), 12km north of town, the Bizkaibus #A3247 runs to Pl. Moyúa in the centre (daily 5.20am–10pm; every 20min; 30min; €1.80).

By train The FEVE and RENFE train stations are located at Abando, just over the river from the Casco Viejo.

Destinations Madrid (6 daily; 4hr 45min); Pamplona (Mon–Sat 9 daily, Sun every 3–4hr; 2hr 30min); Santander (FEVE; 3 daily; 3hr).

By bus Buses arrive at Termibús in San Mamés, connected to the train station by *cercanías* trains to the Casco Viejo by metro.

Destinations Barcelona (4 daily; 8hr–8hr 25min); Madrid (15 daily; 4–5hr); San Sebastián (13–26 daily; 1hr 10min–2hr); Santander (29 daily; 1hr 15min–1hr 45min).

INFORMATION

Tourist office Pl. Circular 1 (daily 9am–9pm; ☎944 795 760, ⍵bilbao.net), with another useful branch in the Guggenheim (daily 10am–7pm), and at the airport.

GETTING AROUND

Standard metro rates are €1.45 for a single journey in the central zone, €4.50 for a day-pass; single tickets on the *cercanías* trains cost €1.60, while EuskoTren tram-line

tickets are €1.50 for a single, €4.50 for a day-pass (validate your ticket in the platform's machine before boarding). If you're going to be using the metro a lot, it's worth purchasing a Barik card (€3), saving you an average of €0.80 per journey. Buses (€1.25 single) run alongside trams, connecting every part of the city.

ACCOMMODATION

In summer and at weekends, booking ahead is advisable.

★**Bilbao Akelarre Hostel** c/Morgan 4-6º ☎944 057 713, ⍵bilbaoakelarrehostel.com. See a different side to the city in this character-packed hostel, which is run by three friends. The black, white and red walls are covered with illustrations and quirky observations, and the bunks are comfy. Closest metro is Duesto. Dorms **€17.50**

Hotel Bilbi c/Miribima 8 ☎94 415 2811 ⍵www .hotelbilbi.com. Well-organized hotel close to Merkuata La Ribera. All rooms have a/c; ones on the top floor boast impressive views over the city. Doubles **€57**

Ganbara Hostel c/Prim 13 ☎944 053 930, ⍵ganbarahostel.com. A couple of minutes' walk from the Casco Viejo, this is a favourite with backpackers and pilgrims alike. Dark bedrooms are alleviated by an open, friendly communal area. Could do with more bathrooms. Dorms **€19**

Pil Pil Hostel Av Sabino Arana 14 ☎944 345 544, ⍵pilpilhostel.com. Bright decor, spacious twelve-person dorms with lockers and a backyard patio for socializing. Close to the bus station. Dorms **€19**, doubles **€56**

EATING AND DRINKING

The highest concentration of *pintxo* bars is around Plaza Nueva in Casco Viejo. Opening hours are daily 1–4pm & 8–11pm unless otherwise stated.

Charly Pl. Nueva 8 ⍵barcharly.com. Amid the stiff competition of Plaza Nueva, you could miss little *Charly*, tucked in its corner. Though you pay for the setting, the *pintxos* (€1.95 each) are fresh and delicious, with regional speciality *balacao* (cod) being the standout.

Kubrick Villarías Kalea 2. Bilbao's personality comes to the fore in this riverside café. Intriguing posters and display pieces invite you into Stanley Kubrick's mad world. Fresh tapas from €4–7 and the café latte is perfection (€2). Closed Mon.

Melia Y Fez Hurribide Kalea. Low-key tavern where *moronus de cordero* (skewered pork, €2.40) sizzle on the grill in front of you. Fancy something else? Four different types of tortilla are displayed on the bar.

Muga Muga Taberna c/María Muñoz 8. This colourful bar offers a menu dedicated to all things veggie. Try the imaginative tofu shitake burger or the falafel teriyaki with chilli sauce (€7), accompanied by a selection of craft ales. Casco Viejo metro is just opposite.

32

★**Ria Oja** Txakur Kalea 4. Bright, informal place, serving up the best in Basque cuisine. Choose your *plato tipico* from a dozen pans stretched across the bar. Be brave and try the squid served in a sauce of its own ink (€9). Closed Mon.

DIRECTORY

Hospital Santa Marina, Ctra Santa Marina 41 ☎ 944 006 900.
Post office Vda De Espalza (Mon–Fri 8.30am–8.30pm, Sat 9.30am–1pm).

SANTANDER

Long a favourite summer resort of Madrileños, the port of **SANTANDER** has an elegant feel, meaning hotels and restaurants tend to be at the upper end of the price scale. Though severely damaged by a fire in 1941 that left the town with few historical buildings of interest, the setting is such that time can easily be whiled away wandering the promenade – stretching 3km along the spectacular Bahía de Santander – and scoping out some of the city's excellent beaches.

32

WHAT TO SEE AND DO

While the city's main draw is its wealth of white-sand beaches, there are also a couple of entertaining museums. All attractions are easily reachable either on foot or by catching city buses along the coastal road.

Museo de Arte Moderno y Contemporáneo

The three floors at the excellent **Museo de Arte Moderno y Contemporáneo** (c/de Rubio 6; Tues–Sat 10am–1.30pm & 5.30–9pm, Sun 11am–1.30pm; free) feature twentieth-century paintings, sculpture, photography and installations, with an emphasis on artists from Santander and wider Cantabria.

Museo Marítime del Cantábrico

Located along the waterfront c/de San Martín de Bajamar, the well-presented **Museo Marítimo del Cantábrico** (Tues–Sun: May–Sept 10am–7.30pm; Oct–April Sun 10am–6pm; €8) thoroughly immerses you in Cantabria's long relationship with the sea. On the ground

floor, enormous whale skeletons overlook the entrance to a shark-infested **aquarium**. The other two floors focus on Cantabria's nautical history, with models of boats and nets and displays on life at sea.

The beaches

Heading east of the town centre along the **Bahía de Santander** you reach the **beaches** in the following order: Playa de Los Peligros, Playa de Magdalena, Playa de Bikinis, Playa del Camello, Playa de la Concha and Playa El Sardinero. The first three beaches are sheltered by cliffs, with calm waters, while the 1.25km stretch of white sand that is Playa El Sardinero faces the ocean, its waves attracting surfers in autumn and winter. Playa de Bikinis nestles along the south side of the Península de Magdalena, a wooded headland featuring the **Palacio Real de Magdalena**, the summer residence of the royal family until 1930. Playa El Sardinero is divided in two by the **Jardínes de Piquío**, an attractive palm-studded park with benches overlooking the beach from above. From the north end of the beach, a beautiful cliff-side trail skirts the headland, leading to **El faro de Cabo Mayor** lighthouse. Buses #1, #4, #7 and #15 run to the beaches along the waterfront from the centre; #4 also leaves from the bus station (€1.30). If you find these too crowded, make for surf-haven **Playa del Somo** (buses take just over 30min from the bus terminal) or **Playa del Puntal**, just before Somo; jump on a *lancha* taxi-ferry (May–Sept every 30min; boats run until 8pm, €4 return; ⏱losreginas.com) from Los Reginas, on the waterfront by the Palacete del Embarcadero.

ARRIVAL AND DEPARTURE

By plane The airport is 5km from town, served by Vueling and Iberia flights to main Spanish cities and Ryanair flights from major European destinations. Buses run to Santander bus station (daily: every 30min, 6.30am–10.30pm).
By train The RENFE and regional FEVE train stations are centrally located near the waterfront at Plaza de las Estaciones.
Destinations Madrid (3 daily; 4hr 30min); Bilbao (3 daily; 3hr); Oviedo (2 daily; 5hr).

By bus The station is over the road from the train stations. Destinations Bilbao (22–26 daily; 1hr 30min); Oviedo (7–10 daily; 2hr 15min–3hr 15min); Madrid (7 daily; 5–6hr); Santiago de Compostela (2 daily; 7hr 15min–9hr 45min).

INFORMATION

Tourist office Municipal: Jardines de Pereda (mid-June to mid-Sept Mon–Sat 9am–7pm, Sun 10am–2pm; mid-Sept to mid-June daily 9am–9pm; ☎942 203 000, ⓦsantander.es). Regional: Mercado del Este, c/de Hernán Cortés 4 (daily 9am–9pm; ☎901 111 112, ⓦturismodecantabria.com).

ACCOMMODATION

Some places shut down outside the peak summer season of mid-June to mid-September.

Hostal San Fernando c/San Fernando 16 ☎942 371 984, ⓦhostalsanfernando.es. Rooms, though clad in dark wood and lace, are decent value for money. Centrally located, 10min walk from the bus and train stations. Doubles **€50**

Hostel Santander Paseo Pereda 15 ☎942 223 986. Three-tiered bunks in light, spacious rooms, and a common room that is more than comfortable. The balcony overlooks the city's busy promenade. Dorms **€24**

Pensión Plaza c/Cadiz 13 ☎942 212 967, ⓦpension -plaza.com. Impersonal hotel close to the bus station and sea front. Large, comfortable beds and 24hr reception. Triple rooms available. Doubles **€60**

Surf to Live Hostel c/Cayuso 33, Somo ☎639 232 230, ⓦsurftolive.com. The first of its kind along the coast, this well-kept guesthouse appeals to surfers in search of respite and inspiration. It's just a walk away from gorgeous Playa Somo so wetsuits and boards are – naturally, dude – available for rent. Dorms **€15**

EATING AND DRINKING

The richest pickings are found along c/Daoíz y Velarde and c/Hernán Cortés. Opening hours are daily 1–4pm & 8–11pm unless otherwise stated.

Bodega Fuente De c/de la Peña Herbosa 5. Unpretentious tavern, which serves some of the best regional dishes. Stews to share change daily; their *cocido montañés* (Cantabrian fava bean stew, €8) is the most flavoursome. Closed Sun.

Cerveceria 100 Montaditos Calderón de la Barca 19. This busy, cheap beer house is a perfect place to line your stomach for a long night. Mini sandwiches are on the menu – fillings from tortilla to goat's cheese with pesto. Everything is €1 on Wednesday and Sunday. Fri & Sat until 1am.

La Casa del Indiano c/Hernán Cortés 4. A 360-degree bar in buzzing Mercado Este where locals sip sangria and pick from a choice of *pintxos* (€4 each, 3 for 2) or share hearty *raciones* (the *patatas indianas*, €3.20, are worth a try). All tapas are €1 on Thursday afternoons. Closed Sun eve.

La Rana Verde Daíz y Velarde 30. Descend a few steps and you're in the world of "the green frog". Illuminated cabinets display hundreds of frog-themed ornaments; the menu is simpler. The owner's wife will flip you an honest burger for €3 (€3.50 with cheese). Variety comes in the form of a *patatas* platter.

Restaurante Olleros c/Enseñanza 6. Situated just beyond the cathedral, *Olleros* serves the best croquettes in town. Order them *de casareras* and receive a lightly battered variety (9 for €8). Complimentary *pintxo* while you wait.

PARQUE NACIONAL PICOS DE EUROPA

The **Picos de Europa** (ⓦpicosdeeuropa .com) offers some of the finest hiking, canoeing and mountain activities in Spain. The densely forested national park boasts two glacial lakes, a series of peaks over 2400m high, wildlife including otters and bears, and a jaw-dropping funicular. Choose which of the three sides you enter the park from carefully as there are no through-roads between León's Caín and Cantabria's Fuenté De (via Potes), and between Fuenté De and Covadonga in Asturias. The mountain weather is notoriously capricious, so bring warm and waterproof gear whatever the time of year.

ARRIVAL AND INFORMATION

By bus From Oviedo, ALSA buses run to Cangas de Onís, a major gateway to the park (12 daily; 1hr 30min); there are at least five buses daily from Cangas de Onís to Covadonga, a village on the park's northwestern edge. From Santander's main bus terminal to the park's southeastern hub Potes (2 daily; 2hr–2hr 30min).

By car From Santander, about 80km to the east, the park is reached by passing through San Vicente de la Barquera, Unquera and Cares; alternative access is from Oviedo in the south.

Tourist office Cangas de Onís has a tourist office (Nov–June Mon–Sat 10am–2pm & 4–7pm, Sun 10am–2pm; July–Sept 9am–8pm; closed Oct; ☎985 848 614, ⓦcangasdeonis.com/turismo). Potes' tourist office is on Pl. de la Independencia (daily: June–Sept 10am–2pm & 4–8pm; Sept–June 10am–2pm & 4–6pm; ☎942 738 126).

32

ACCOMMODATION

Albergue Cangas de Onis ☎669 350 843, ⓦalberguecangasdeonis.com. A converted village school, this is the only conventional hostel in the national park, 2km north of Covadonga. Join a mountain activity group or rent some gear – canoes, kayaks, harnesses – and go it alone. Fully equipped kitchen. Dorms **€20**

Albergue El Portalón ☎942 736 018, ⓦalbergue elportalon.com. Old stone building in the quaint village of La Vega, which sits along the River Quivies (accessible from Potes by bus). Dormitories are set around a romantic courtyard. Dorms **€22**

★**Camping La Isla** Carretera Potes Fuente De ☎942 730 896, ⓦcampinglaislapicosdeeuropa.com. Campsite and bungalows in a riverside setting, 1km walk along the road to Potes from Fuenté De. Large outdoor swimming pool and bar (in summer). Camping/person **€5**, plus per tent **€4**, double bungalows **€55**

OVIEDO

The capital of the ancient principality of Asturias under King Alfonso II, thriving **OVIEDO** is best known for its *sidrerías* (cider bars), whose waiters artfully sling the smoky-tasting local brew (more like scrumpy than commercial cider) from above head height into glasses held at waist level to give it some fizz. The *sidrerías* are concentrated in the attractive Old Town, a warren of beautiful squares and narrow streets.

WHAT TO SEE AND DO

Though a sizeable place, Oviedo is easy to navigate on foot as most attractions are found in and around the compact old quarter. Look out for the profusion of street sculptures strewn across the city, which include a statue of Woody Allen (who expressed a fondness for Oviedo) on c/Milicias Nacionales and an enormous bottom on c/Pelayo.

Catedral de San Salvador and the Cámara Santa

Oviedo has a couple of unusual ninth-century churches, dating from a time when Asturias was an independent kingdom, and the only part of Spain under Christian rule. One of these churches, the **Cámara Santa**, now forms part of the city's otherwise Gothic **Cathedral** (Mon–Sat 10am–2pm & 4–8pm; entry to Cámara Santa €5, €7 including Diocesan Museum and cloister). The treasures here include a jewel-studded gold cross donated by Alfonso II, and the Santo Sudario, a bloodstained cloth said to have been wrapped round Christ's head (displayed just three times a year).

Iglesia de San Julián de los Prados

The ninth-century **Iglesia de San Julián de los Prados** (Mon–Sat 10am–noon; €2, free first Mon of the month) is a treasure of the pre-Romanesque era. With colourful frescoes, and a "secret chamber" in the walls, it's worth the ten-minute walk northeast to c/Segal, next to the Oviedo–Gijón highway.

Museo de Bellas Artes

The **Museo de Bellas Artes** at c/Santa Ana 1 (Tues–Fri 10.30am–2pm & 4.30–8.30pm, Sat 11.30am–2pm & 5–8pm, Sun 11.30am–2.30pm; free; ⓦmuseobbaa.com) is a labyrinth of discovery. Within a complex design, linking four different buildings, works by some of Spain's most important painters since the fourteenth century are shown. The Palacio de Velarde section presents El Greco's portraits of the twelve Apostles, a couple of Goyas and the Romantic era at large. Picasso's *Mosquetero con Espada y Amorcillo* and Dalí's impressive *Metamorfosis de Ángeles en Mariposa* are displayed in the museum's modern wing. Be sure to acquire a map from reception.

ARRIVAL AND DEPARTURE

By train RENFE and FEVE trains both leave from the train station on Avda de Santander, a 10min walk northwest of the old quarter.

Destinations León (4 daily; 2–3hr); Madrid (5 daily; 4hr 15min–6hr 30min); Santander (FEVE; 2 daily; 5hr); Zaragoza (5 daily; 8hr).

By bus Avda de Pepe Cosmen, 200m north of the train stations.

Destinations Bilbao (9–10 daily; 3hr 35min–4hr 50min); Madrid (18–21 daily; 5hr 15min–6hr); Santander (8–12 daily; 2hr 15min–3hr 50min); Santiago de Compostela (8–10 daily; 4hr 45min–7hr).

32

INFORMATION

Tourist office Municipal: Pl. de la Constitución 4 (daily 9.30am–7pm; ⓣ 985 086 060, ⓦ turismo.ayto-oviedo.es), with booths at c/Marquéz de Santa Cruz 1 (daily: summer 9am–8pm; rest of the year 10.30am–6pm). Regional: Pl. de la Constitución 4 (daily 9.30am–7pm; ⓦ asturias.es).

ACCOMMODATION

Hostal Fidalgo c/Jovellanos 5 ⓣ 985 213 287, ⓦ hostalfidalgo.es. Little English is spoken here, but the owners will make you feel comfortable. Rooms are spacious and all come with a private bathroom. Ask for a room with a view of the plaza. Doubles €35

Hotel Rural La Balconada Lugar Faro de Arriba 33 ⓣ 985 793 792, ⓦ hotellabalconada.com. Antique-laden rooms and a delightful rural setting. Complimentary breakfast is served in the conservatory, which overlooks the entire city and out to the Picos de Europa. Doubles €45

Santa Clara Hotel c/de Santa Clara 1 ⓣ 985 087 070, ⓦ hotel-santaclara.es. Large, clean rooms with wl-fl. Good location – same side of the Campo de San Francisco as Woody Allen's statue. Breakfast on offer in the bar downstairs. Doubles €40

EATING AND DRINKING

There are several shops dotted around the Old Town where you can buy Asturian specialities like cider, cheese and meats. Camilo de Blas (c/de Jovellanos 7; Mon–Sat 9am–9pm; ⓦ camilodeblas.com) has been selling the traditional *carboyones* (€2.80) – almond pastries – since 1914. Loli Arrieta (c/Suárez de la Riva 2; Mon–Sat 9.30am–3pm & 3.15–8pm, Sun 9.30am–2.30pm; ⓦ www.loliarrieta.com) is the best bet for local wines and cured meats.

Cerveceria La Sureña Pl. Tres Colores. Well-priced *raciones* (croquettes for €6, glass of beer for €1) in Oviedo's prettiest plaza. Patio tables catch the sun in the afternoon. Daily 1.30–4pm & 8–11pm.

La Mal Quierda c/Indalecia Pieto 6. Unfussy *sidrería* off the main drag. Large plates to share from €8. Bottle of house *sidra* (€2.50) poured for you traditionally, but over buckets in the corner. Daily 11am–1.30am.

Tierra Astur c/de Gascona 1. Asturia's favourite home-food chain, *Tierra Astur*'s seriously extensive menu has a plate to suit all. If you can forgive the impersonal service, their *fabada* (traditional Asturian stew, €10) is worth a try. Mon–Fri 8.30am–1.30am, Sat 8.30am–2.30am, Sun 10am–1am.

SANTIAGO DE COMPOSTELA

SANTIAGO DE COMPOSTELA, built in warm golden granite, is one of the most beautiful of all Spanish cities and deservedly declared a national monument. The **pilgrimage to Santiago** (see box below) captured the imagination of medieval Christian Europe on an unprecedented scale, peaking at half a million pilgrims each year during the eleventh and twelfth centuries. The route continues to be well trodden by the faithful, as well as hikers and cyclists who enjoy the challenge, ensuring that the medieval streets of Galicia's regional capital are filled with a lively buzz.

32

WHAT TO SEE AND DO

With many pedestrianized areas, picturesque plazas and a wealth of beautiful architecture, Santiago is ideal to discover on foot. Most sights are clustered near each other in the compact historic **Old Town**. The large **Parque de Alameda** separates the old centre from

THE CAMINO DE SANTIAGO

The most famous Christian pilgrimage in the world, the **Camino de Santiago** – or Way of St James – traces a route through France and Spain to Santiago de Compostela (Saint James of the Field of Stars), the supposed burial place of St James the Apostle and the third-holiest site in Christendom after Jerusalem and Rome. There are 39 routes across the Iberian Peninsula, but the majority of pilgrims take the so-called Camino Francés into Galicia. Pilgrims identify themselves by attaching a large scallop shell to their backpack, and many carry a *credenciál*, or "pilgrim passport", available from tourist offices and *refugios*, that permits overnight stay in some mountain refuges. Accommodation along the way consists mostly of pilgrim *albergues*, where you can sleep in a basic dorm for around €10. Along the way, pilgrims collect stamps in order to receive a Compostela (certificate of completion) from the Church authorities. To be eligible, you must walk at least 100km or cycle 200km of the 800km-long route. Aside from those motivated by faith, people are drawn by the physical challenge and the stunning countryside; while half the pilgrims come from Spain, the rest make up a very international crowd. For more details, see ⓦ xacobeo.es.

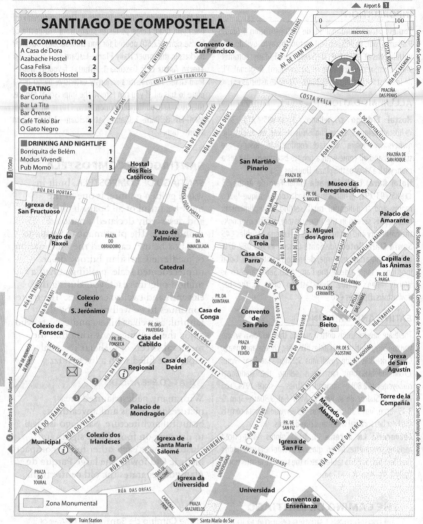

SANTIAGO DE COMPOSTELA

ACCOMMODATION
A Casa de Dora	1
Azabache Hostel	4
Casa Felisa	2
Roots & Boots Hostel	3

EATING
Bar Coruña	1
Bar La Tita	5
Bar Örense	3
Café Tokio Bar	4
O Gato Negro	2

DRINKING AND NIGHTLIFE
Borriquita de Belém	1
Modus Vivendi	2
Pub Momo	3

the modern new town, which boasts many bars and cafés.

Catedral de Santiago

All roads lead to the **cathedral** (daily 7am–8.30pm, visits allowed outside Mass), on Praza do Obradoiro. The fantastic granite pyramid adorned with statues of the saint was built in the mid-eighteenth century by an obscure Santiago-born architect, Fernando Casas y Novoa. Just inside this facade is the building's original west front: the

stupendous **Pórtico de Gloria**. So many millions have pressed their fingers into the roots of its sacred Tree of Jesse that five deep holes have been worn into the solid marble. Behind, the **High Altar** symbolizes the spiritual climax of the pilgrimage. Visitors climb steps behind the altar to the *Most Sacred Image of Santiago*, kiss his bejewelled cape, place their hands on the silver scallop shell on the back of his throne and receive a Latin certificate called a Compostela – a procedure that's seven centuries old. The elaborate pulley system in front of the altar is for moving the immense incense burner – **El Botafumeiro** – which, operated by eight priests, is swung in a vast ceiling-to-ceiling arc across the transept. This takes place only during certain festival services (check with the tourist office). Visiting the **cathedral museum** (daily: April–Oct 9am–8pm; Nov–March 10am–8pm; €6) is worthwhile, as is a tour of the cathedral roof (€12), which offers stupendous views of the Old Town.

The convents and monasteries

The enormous Benedictine **San Martín Pinario monastery** stands close to the cathedral, the vast altarpiece in its church depicting its patron riding alongside St James. Nearby is the **Convento de San Francisco**, reputedly founded by the saint himself during his pilgrimage to Santiago. In the north of the city are Baroque **Convento de Santa Clara**, with a unique curving facade, and, a little southwards, **Convento de Santo Domingo de Bonaval**. This last is perhaps the most interesting of the buildings, featuring a magnificent seventeenth-century triple stairway.

The museums

Museo do Pobo Galego at Rúa San Domingos de Bonaval is a fascinating glimpse into Galician culture (Tues–Sat 10am–2pm & 4–7.30pm, Sun 11am–2pm; €3, Sun free; ⓦmuseodopobo.gal), from the region's fishing history to traditional crafts. Just next door is the **Centro Galego de Arte Contemporánea** (Tues–Sun 11am–8pm; free; ⓦcgac .xunta.gal), which hosts temporary exhibitions by international artists.

ARRIVAL AND DEPARTURE

By plane Lavacolla airport, 11km northeast of town (☎981 547 500, ⓦaena.es), is linked to the bus and train stations by Freire buses (every 30min; €3 one-way, €5 return).
By train The train station is a 15min walk south of the Old Town along Rúa do Horreo.
Destinations Bilbao (2 daily; 10–16hr); León (2 daily; 4hr 30min–5hr 20min); Madrid (6 daily; 5hr–5hr 45min).
By bus The bus station is on Praza de Camillo Díaz Baliño, a 20min walk northeast of the centre; bus #5 (€1) runs

every 16–30min to Pr. Galicia at the old city's southern edge.
Destinations Bilbao (3 daily; 9hr 45min–11hr 30min); Lisbon (1 daily; 9hr 45min); Madrid (8–9 daily; 8hr–9hr 45min); Oviedo (4 daily; 4hr 30min–6hr 45min); Porto (1–2 daily; 4hr 15min); Santander (5 daily; 8–10hr).

INFORMATION AND GETTING AROUND

Tourist office The helpful Turismo de Santiago office is at Rúa do Vilar 63 (Easter & June–Sept daily 9am–9pm; rest of year Mon–Fri 9am–7pm, Sat & Sun 9am–2pm & 4–7pm; ☎981 555 129, ⓦsantiagoturismo.com). The Turismo de Galicia office is at Rúa do Vilar 32 (Mon–Fri 8am–8pm, Sat 11am–2pm & 5–7pm, Sun 11am–2pm; ☎981 584 081, ⓦturgalicia.es) and has info on the Camino de Santiago and the rest of the province.
Local buses All local destinations are €1 one-way.

ACCOMMODATION

★**A Casa de Dora** Rúa Granxa do Castiñeiriño 42 ☎609 082 072, ⓦwww.acasadedora.com. Quiet and clean hostel, 25min walk (or a short bus ride) out of town. Friendly owner Manuel will help you (in English or Spanish). Dorms are spotless; huge, automatic blinds mean they're bright in the day and extremely easy to sleep in at night. Dorms €20
Azabache Hostel Rúa da Acibechería 15 ☎981 071 254, ⓦazabache-santiago.com. Large and airy hostel. Doesn't offer much in the way of character, but it's cheap, well located and has a fully fitted kitchen. Dorms €16
Casa Felisa Rúa da Porta da Pena 5 ☎981 582 602, ⓦcasafelisa.es. *Pension* with compact, bright rooms (some with monastery views), squeaky-clean shared bathrooms and an attractive outdoor restaurant. A friendly retriever will be at the door to welcome you. Doubles €40
Roots & Boots Hostel Rúa do Cruceiro do Gaio 7 ☎699 631 594, ⓦrootsandboots.es. Large hostel adjacent to the Parque Alameda, with attractive garden and view of the cathedral. Can get noisy at night, so bring earplugs if you're an early riser. Dorms €15

EATING

There are plenty of restaurants in the historic centre, particularly Rúa do Franco and Rúa da Raíña. Saunter just off the main streets, however, and you'll find the cheaper tapas bars. Galicia is famous for its seafood – the province's signature dishes are *polvo da feira* (boiled, spicy octopus) and the famous *tarta de Santiago* (almond cake). You can purchase fresh produce at the Mercado de Abastos along Pl. de Abastos (Mon–Sat 7am–6pm). Opening hours are daily noon–4pm & 8–11pm unless otherwise stated.
Bar Coruña Rúa de Raíña 17. The seafood aroma hits you as soon as you enter this friendly watering hole. Mussels in

32

the *salsa de la casa* (€5.50) are a must. Menu of the day for €8. Closed Sun.

Bar La Tita Rúa Nova 46. This popular bar-restaurant offers a free slice of tortilla with every drink. Huge tapas (€6) and salads (€3.50–6), so come hungry. Mon–Sat 8am–midnight.

Bar Orense Rúa de Raiña 25. Make sure to order the speciality sandwich (€2) – a *bocadillo* with Galician cheese and anchovies – at this locals' spot. Wine served in traditional bowls (€1) straight from the barrel. Closed Sun.

Café Tokio Bar Avda Figueroa 6 & 7. Strong coffee (€1–2), complimentary *churros*, and the best view of Parque Alameda. Come early to get a seat out on the terrace.

★ **O Gato Negro** Rúa de Raiña s/n. What this bare-boned tavern lacks in atmosphere, it makes up for in flavour. Copy the locals and order the velvety *pulpo*, served on a platter in a garlic sauce; a half portion (€7) is enough for one. Closed Sun eve & Mon.

DRINKING AND NIGHTLIFE

Borriquita de Belem Rúa de San Paio de Antealtares 22. Busy, compact bar with live rock music and jam sessions every Wed, Thurs & Sat. Closed Sun.

Modus Vivendi 1 Praza de Feixóo. Sip a generous whisky (€5) and admire the trinkets in display cabinets at the oldest bar in the city, while a jazz/funk soundtrack places. Daily till 4.30am.

Pub Momo Virxe de Cerca 23. Around since the 1980s, this indoor/outdoor bar has bags of character, and is known for its retro music, beers (€2) and cocktails (from €3). Daily till 4/4.30am.

DIRECTORY

Pharmacy Rúa de Vilar 54 (Mon–Fri 9.30am–2pm & 4.30–8.30pm, Sat 9.30am–2pm).

Post office Rúa do Franco 4 (Mon–Fri 8.30am–8.30pm, Sat 9.30am–1pm).

OLD TOWN (GAMLA STAN), STOCKHOLM

Sweden

HIGHLIGHTS

❶ **Stockholm** Perhaps the most beautiful setting of any European capital. **See p.1089**

❷ **Gothenburg** Hop on a tram and explore Sweden's second city. **See p.1098**

❸ **Malmö** Fun-sized city with its own sandy beaches. **See p.1103**

❹ **Gotland** Join the summer exodus to Sweden's party island. **See p.1106**

❺ **Inlandsbanan** Whistle past endless forests en route to Lapland. **See p.1108**

❻ **Icehotel** A chilly treat worth breaking the budget for. **See p.1111**

HIGHLIGHTS ARE MARKED ON THE MAP ON P.1085

ROUGH COSTS

Daily budget Basic €60, occasional treat €80

Drink *Spendrups* draught beer (40cl) €5

Food *Korv med bröd* (Swedish hotdog) €2.50

Hostel/budget hotel Dorm bed €22/hotel room €75

Travel Train: Stockholm–Gothenburg €40; bus: Stockholm–Gothenburg €38

FACT FILE

Population 9.8 million

Language Swedish

Currency Swedish krona (kr)

Capital Stockholm

International phone code ☎46

Time zone GMT +1hr

33

Introduction

Sweden combines stylish, sophisticated cities with a vast wilderness of dense forests and crystal-clear mountain lakes. Quality of life is high, almost everyone speaks fluent English, and even a short visit here leaves you with the impression that the Swedes have somehow got things "right". While the country is not entirely populated by blonde, blue-eyed sauna-loving eco-warriors, you'll find plenty to reinforce the stereotype.

As with the rest of Scandinavia, Sweden can prove a challenge for the budget traveller. However, it's still considerably cheaper than Norway. If you stick to hostels, eat out only at lunch and resist the temptation to buy a round of drinks, you can still manage to explore beyond a flying visit.

First on the list for almost any traveller is **Stockholm**. One of Europe's most beautiful capital cities, it's a bundle of islands hosting a picture-postcard old town, fine museums (some free) and the country's most active nightlife. Although Stockholm laps up most of the international attention, Sweden's other main cities – **Gothenburg** and **Malmö** – are both eminently likeable, and well worth exploring for a couple of days each. The university towns of **Lund** and **Uppsala** make excellent day-trips from Malmö and Stockholm respectively.

In summer, Sweden's interior beckons with the opening of the 1300km **Inlandsbanan** rail line running along the spine of the country past pine forests and shimmering lakes as far as the **Arctic Circle**. Summer is also the time to join the rush to **Gotland**, Sweden's Baltic island escape. If you're in Sweden between December and mid-April, you shouldn't miss the chance to splurge on a night at the *Icehotel* near **Kiruna**, in the country's far north.

CHRONOLOGY

98 AD Tacitus refers to a Scandinavian tribe known as the "Suiones".

800s The Swedish Vikings become a powerful force in Europe over the following few centuries.

1255 City of Stockholm founded.

1397 The Kalmar Union unites Sweden with Denmark and Norway through a marriage arrangement.

1520 Hundreds of nobles are killed by Danish forces during the "Stockholm Bloodbath". A counter-attack is led by Swede Gustav Vasa.

1523 Gustav is crowned King Gustav I and leads the Protestant Reformation of Sweden.

1536 Sweden leaves the Kalmar Union, asserting independence.

1628 The *Vasa* battleship sinks outside Stockholm – a national embarrassment now turned into a money-spinning tourist attraction.

1721 Sweden is defeated by a coalition led by Russia in the Great Northern War, ending the success of the Swedish Empire.

1814 Sweden invades and conquers Norway.

1901 First Nobel Prize ceremony held, as part of the will of Swedish inventor Alfred Nobel.

1905 Sweden peacefully concedes Norwegian independence.

1914 Sweden remains neutral during World War I.

1939 Sweden declares neutrality during World War II.

1943 The first IKEA store is opened by founder Ingvar Kamprad.

1974 ABBA top the charts after winning the Eurovision Song Contest with "Waterloo".

1986 Prime Minister Olof Palme is assassinated in Stockholm; the crime is still unresolved.

1995 Sweden joins the EU after a closely fought referendum.

2003 Swedish voters reject the adoption of the euro.

2006 After twelve years of rule, the Social Democrats lose an election to the centre-right Alliance for Sweden.

2010 A four-day celebration ends with Crown Princess Victoria marrying a "commoner" at Stockholm Cathedral.

2014 The far-right Sweden Democrats party (Sverigedemokraterna) wins 49 seats in the general election.

2016 Sweden is granted a non-permanent seat on the UN Security Council.

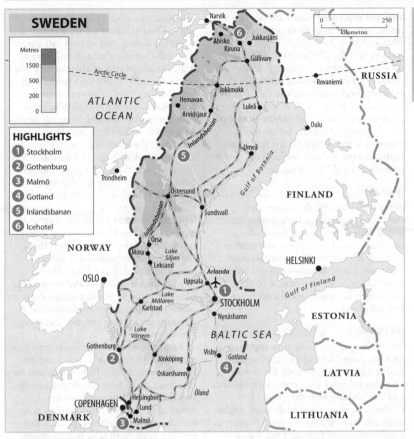

SWEDEN

Metres

1500
500
200
0

HIGHLIGHTS

1 Stockholm
2 Gothenburg
3 Malmö
4 Gotland
5 Inlandsbanan
6 Icehotel

Narvik
Jukkasjärri
Abisko
Kiruna
Gällivare
Arctic Circle
Rovaniemi
RUSSIA
Jokkmokk
Hemavan
Luleå
Arvidsjaur
Oulu
**ATLANTIC
OCEAN**
Umeå
Inlandsbanan
Trondheim
Gulf of Bothnia
Östersund
FINLAND
Sundsvall
Inlandsbanan
Orsa
NORWAY
Mora
Lake
Siljan
Leksand
HELSINKI
Arlanda
Uppsala
OSLO
Lake
Mälaren
Karlstad
STOCKHOLM
Nynäshamn
Gulf of Finland
ESTONIA
Lake
Vänern
BALTIC SEA
Gothenburg
Jönköping
Visby Gotland
Oskarshamn
Öland
LATVIA
COPENHAGEN
Helsingborg
Lund
DENMARK
Malmö
LITHUANIA

0   250
kilometres

ARRIVAL AND DEPARTURE

Most travellers arrive and depart from one of Stockholm's three international **airports**. The largest and most convenient, Arlanda, is served by the big international carriers like Finnair and SAS, plus a few budget airlines like easyJet and Norwegian. Ryanair uses Skavsta and Västerås airports, both around 100km from Stockholm; the budget airline also flies in and out of Gothenburg, a three- to four-hour train ride from Stockholm.

International **trains** and **buses** from Norway and Denmark stop at Stockholm, Malmö and Gothenburg. In the north, Kiruna is usually the first stop in Sweden for visitors arriving from northern Norway.

International **ferry routes** include: Stockholm–Tallinn (Estonia), Helsinki

and Turku (Finland); Helsingborg–Helsingør (Denmark); Gothenburg–Kiel (Germany) and Frederikshavn (Denmark).

GETTING AROUND

BY TRAIN

The most comfortable way to explore Sweden is by train. The extensive **state-run rail network**, SJ (wsj.se), runs as far north as Abisko, 250km inside the Arctic Circle. There are also other companies in charge of regional routes, most of which are visible on the SJ website. The scenic **Inlandsbanan** line (winlandsbanan.se), which travels through central and northern Sweden, is privately run and only operates from late June to August (see box, p.1108).

33

InterRail and **Eurail** passes are valid on all trains, but you must book a place in advance (from 35–375kr) for overnight services and the 200km/hr X2000 trains, which run between the south's major cities. Heavily **discounted tickets** (for example Stockholm–Malmö for 195kr) are available if you book ninety days in advance, and cheap **last-minute tickets** go on sale exactly 24 hours before trains depart (see the SJ website for full details). Reduced rates are also available for passengers aged 25 and under.

BY BUS

Buses are considerably cheaper than trains and, although a little slower, are worth considering if you don't have an InterRail/Eurail pass. Buses also tend to be more reliable during snowy weather. The main national companies are Swebus (Ⓦswebus.se) and Nettbuss.se (Ⓦnettbuss .se), which both offer good rates when booked ahead.

BY PLANE

The main operators of **internal flights** are SAS (Ⓦsas.se), Norwegian (Ⓦnorwegian .no) and BRA (Ⓦflygbra.se). Gotlandsflyg (Ⓦgotlandsflyg.se) also connects Stockholm and Gothenburg with the island of Gotland. Be wary, though: domestic flights often cost more than a trip from Sweden to a different part of Europe. Even if you book ahead with SAS, for example, a one-way flight from Stockholm to Kiruna will set you back around 1000kr.

BY BOAT

Ferries can help you make the most of Sweden's long coastline and the mass of disparate islands that speckle the cold blue water. Information on accessing the islands of Stockholm's archipelago and Gotland is given later in the chapter (see p.1097 & p.1107).

ACCOMMODATION

Sweden has an excellent network of well-maintained **hostels** (*vandrarhem*) mostly operated by STF (Ⓦsvenskaturist foreningen.se). They are found all over the country, often in incongruous

surroundings, such as former prisons or ships. Double rooms are usually available as well as dorms, and virtually all hostels have self-catering kitchens and serve a buffet breakfast. Prices are relatively low (generally 200–350kr for a hostel bed), but you may have to pay extra for sheets and breakfast (usually 70–100kr extra each), so it can be worth bringing your own sheets and seeking out cheaper breakfasts elsewhere. Free wi-fi is almost always included. Non-STF members have to pay an additional charge of around 50kr per night. There are also many non-STF hostels, run by SVIF (Ⓦsvif.se) or private companies.

Hotels and **B&Bs** can be good value, especially in Stockholm and the bigger towns during the summer when they slash their rates; breakfast is almost always included in the price. The tourist-office websites of the major cities often advertise weekend package deals including hotel accommodation and a discount card giving free city transport and entry to sights.

Practically every village has at least one **campsite**, generally of a high standard. Pitching a tent costs 180–320kr, and for that price up to four people can usually stay the night. This varies, however, reflected in the differing camping price formats throughout the chapter. Most sites are open from June to September, some year-round. Many sites also have cabins, usually with kitchen equipment but not sheets, for around 600–800kr for a two-bedded affair. For a list of campsites, and how to get the Camping Key Europe (150kr), which you need to pitch a tent in some campsites, see Ⓦcamping.se. Swedish law permits free, wild camping for one night at a time, but there are strict rules about what you can and cannot do. For helpful pointers in English, visit the Naturvårdsverket website (Ⓦswedishepa.se).

FOOD AND DRINK

Thanks in part to IKEA, Swedish meatballs (*köttbullar*) are familiar across the world. However, there is rather more to the national cuisine than this. **Seafood** is particularly good, with marinated salmon (*gravlax*) and herring (*strömming*), the latter pickled, smoked and even fermented, being served everywhere; you'll often find them offered as part of a classic **smörgåsbord** buffet with potato salad, rye bread, cheeses and fruit. Other specialities include reindeer and elk (both surprisingly tasty), crayfish (especially on the west coast) and sweet cloudberries (delicious with ice cream).

Breakfast (*frukost*) is invariably a help-yourself buffet of juice, cereals, bread, boiled eggs, jams, salami and coffee or tea. For **snacks**, a *gatukök* (simple takeaway) or *korvkiosk* (hot-dog stand) will serve hot dogs, burgers, chips and the like for around 50kr. Coffee shops are predominantly where Swedes come to *fika* (chat over coffee and cake), but usually they also serve a good range of *smörgåsar* – open sandwiches piled high with toppings (40–80kr) – and freshly made salads.

Lunch (*lunch*; usually served around noon) is, from a budget traveller's perspective, the best time to eat out, with most places offering a **set meal** (*dagens rätt*) of a main dish with bread, salad and coffee at 80–130kr. Otherwise meals in restaurants, especially at **dinner** (*middag*), can be expensive: around 250–400kr for two courses, plus drinks. Much cheaper are kebab shops, pizzerias and simple Thai restaurants.

DRINK

Sweden remains one of the most expensive places in Europe to **drink alcohol**. In a simple bar or pub you'll pay around 40kr for a 40cl glass of one of the main national brands, *Spendrups* or *Falcon*. Order a Guinness or an imported lager, and the price will rise to around 70–80kr. In clubs, it's normal for a cocktail (or even just a shot with a mixer) to cost upwards of 120kr.

No surprise, then, that many Swedes load up on shop-bought alcohol before hitting the town. The only places licensed to sell drinks with an alcohol content above 3.5 percent are the government-run **Systembolaget** shops, where alcohol costs around a third of what you'll pay in a bar

SWEDEN ONLINE

33

Ⓦ**cityguide.se** Up-to-date events listings in the main Swedish cities.
Ⓦ**thelocal.se** English-language news, views, listings and blogs on life in Sweden.
Ⓦ**routesnorth.com** Money-saving tips for travelling in Sweden.

(you need to be at least 20 years old to buy alcohol at Systembolaget, as opposed to 18 in bars). There are at least one or two branches in even the smallest towns, but opening hours are deliberately restrictive, with most shops closing in the early evening. All outlets are closed on Sundays.

CULTURE AND ETIQUETTE

Swedes are a mix of apparent contradictions: fiercely patriotic yet globally minded, confident yet self-deprecating, orderly yet creative. Throughout the country you'll find the small ritual of *fika* – a verb that means something like "to have a coffee and a bun and a chat with a friend or two" – is a common pastime, along with singalongs and complaining about winter. **Traditional festivities** like Midsummer's Day and Easter inspire enormous enthusiasm, and on holidays young and old alike head for the countryside to celebrate. The vast majority of Swedes speak some **English** and most speak it with disarming fluency, so Anglophone travellers will have no problem striking up conversations.

SPORTS AND OUTDOOR ACTIVITIES

Football is Sweden's national sport, with a club or two in most of the main cities. Naturally enough, **winter sports** are where the Swedes excel on the world stage, and skiing, snowboarding and ice hockey are all very popular. The best ski resorts are in Åre, Kittelfjäll, Riksgränsen and Ramundberget. In summer, everyone flocks to Sweden's exquisite, unpolluted lakes and to Stockholm's archipelago for **swimming**, **kayaking** and **sailing**. Sweden is a fantastic place for

33

SWEDISH

	SWEDISH	PRONUNCIATION
Yes	Ja	Ya
No	Nej	Nay
Please	Varsågod	Vaa-show-go
Thank you	Tack	Tak
Hello/Good day	Hej	Hay
Goodbye	Hejdå	Hay-dor
Excuse me	Ursäkta	Urh-shekta
Where?	Var?	Vaar?
Good	Bra	Braa
Bad	Dålig	Doo-ah-lig
Near	Nära	Nehra
Far	Avlägsen	Arv-lessen
Cheap	Billig	Billi
Expensive	Dyr	Deyur
Open	Öppen	Upp-en
Closed	Stängd	Stengd
Today	I dag	Ee daa
Yesterday	I går	Ee gor
Tomorrow	I morgon	Ee morron
How much is…?	Vad kostar det…?	Vaa kostar day…?
What time is it?	Hur mycket är klockan?	Hoor mucker er clockan?
I don't understand	Jag förstår inte	Yaa fur-stor int-eh
Do you speak English?	Talar du engelska?	Taalar doo eng-ul-ska?
One	Ett	Ett
Two	Två	Tvo
Three	Tre	Tree-a
Four	Fyra	Feera
Five	Fem	Fem
Six	Sex	Sex
Seven	Sju	Shoo
Eight	Åtta	Otta
Nine	Nio	Nee-o
Ten	Tio	Tee-o

hiking, with some of Europe's most unspoilt wildernesses to explore. The most trekked path is the 500km Kungsleden (King's Trail; see p.1112).

COMMUNICATIONS

The Swedish **postal service** scrapped normal post offices in 2001. Instead, you can send and receive mail and buy stamps at supermarkets, newsagents and tobacconists (look for the blue postal sign). **Free wi-fi** is widely available in cafés, bars and restaurants across the country, and you can usually get a decent mobile internet connection, even in the remotest parts of the north. **Mobile phone** coverage is excellent across most

of the country and calls and data are affordable. Pay-as-you-go SIM cards are available at newsagents and supermarkets across the country.

EMERGENCIES

The **police** are generally courteous and fluent in English. Medical treatment is free for anyone with a European Health Insurance Card (EHIC), although a small administration fee may be charged (around 300kr for a consultation with a doctor). **Pharmacies** operate normal shop opening hours with a rota system for late opening. Stockholm has a 24-hour pharmacy (see p.1097).

STUDENT AND YOUTH DISCOUNTS

The main cities all have **tourist cards** or passes, which offer either free or discounted entry to museums, free or discounted use of local transport (often including ferries), and sometimes other goodies, such as discounts in cafés and restaurants. An **ISIC card** can halve the price of museums, and give discounts on accommodation, shops, restaurants and transport (for example, up to 22 percent off Swebus journeys, and up to 30 percent off train journeys with SJ). Many of the state-run museums are free; others offer substantial student discounts.

INFORMATION

Almost all towns have a **tourist office**, giving out good-quality maps and timetables; they are also usually able to book accommodation and rent out bikes. Information on regional tourist offices can be found at ⓦvisitsweden.com. If you want a detailed map to use when you go hiking, try ⓦkartbutiken.se (Swedish only), which stocks a wide range.

MONEY AND BANKS

Sweden's currency is the **krona** (abbreviated to kr; plural: kronor). There are coins of 1kr, 2kr, 5kr and 10kr, and notes of 20kr, 50kr, 100kr, 200kr, 500kr and 1000kr. At the time of writing €1 was worth 9.4kr, US$1 was 8.48kr, and £1 was 11.42kr. **Banks** are generally open Monday to Friday 9.30am to 3pm, but most have later opening hours (until around 6pm) at least one day per week.

CASHLESS SWEDEN

Sweden is well on its way to becoming one of the world's first **cashless societies**. By 2012, just three per cent of all of the country's transactions involved notes and coins. Despite the locals' preference for paying with plastic, most bars, shops, restaurants and supermarkets do (for the time being at least) still accept cash. On many buses and trams, however, that option no longer exists – so make sure you buy your ticket from the station in advance.

Outside these hours you can **change money** at airports and ferry terminals, as well as at Forex offices, which usually offer good rates (minimum 50kr commission). **ATMs** are plentiful.

OPENING HOURS AND HOLIDAYS

Generally, **shops** open Monday to Friday 9am to 6pm, and on Saturday from 9am to 1/4pm. Most larger stores stay open until 8/10pm, and the majority are also open until 8/10pm on Sundays. Banks, offices and shops close on **public holidays** (Jan 1, Jan 6, Good Fri, Easter Sun & Mon, May 1, Ascension, Whit Sun & Mon, June 20 & 21, Nov 1, Dec 24–26 & 31). They may also close early the preceding day.

Stockholm

With the air of a grand European capital yet on a small, Scandinavian scale, **STOCKHOLM** is a vibrant and instantly likeable city. Built across fourteen islands, water and green space dominate the landscape, but there are still plenty of distinctly urban attractions to fill your days, from elegant museums and royal palaces to achingly cool bars and clubs.

WHAT TO SEE AND DO

Taking a **boat tour** is the classic way to see Stockholm. After checking into your accommodation, head straight to Strömkajen, the harbour fronting the *Grand Hotel*, where operators sell tickets for sightseeing trips (see p.1094). Once you have a fix on the city's layout you can cover most ground on foot or take the T-bana **metro** for cross-city trips.

The key **sights** are Gamla Stan (the Old Town), Vasa Museum, Moderna Museet (modern art museum), the Fotografiska photography museum and Sodermalm's SoFo neighbourhood. Aside from these it's best, in summer at least, to stroll around the parks and gardens (especially Djurgården) or take a trip to the Stockholm Archipelago. In winter, the city's ice rinks and cosy coffee houses come into their own.

33

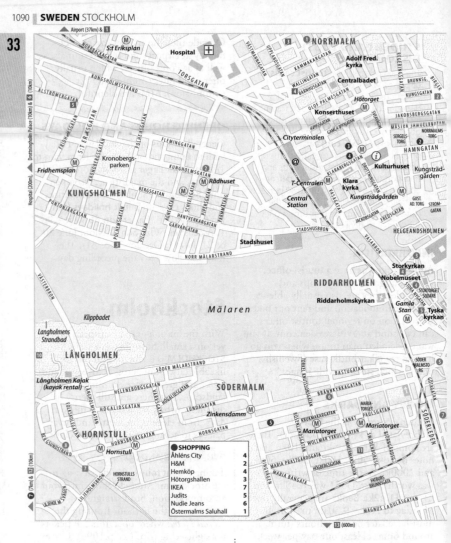

Central Station and the Stadshuset

The first impression of Stockholm for most people is the vast and sometimes confusing **Central Station**, the city's main transport hub. Cityterminalen, the bus station, is just across the road and the ⓜ Centralen metro station is underneath. A short walk west across the Stadshusbron bridge to Kungsholmen is one of the city's most recognizable buildings: the **Stadshuset** (City Hall) at Hantverkargatan 1 (daily guided tours only, in English hourly 10am–3pm; April–Oct 100kr; Jan–March &

Nov–Dec 70kr; ⓜ Centralen), which hosts the annual Nobel Prize banquet. Climbing the hall's 106m-high **tower** (daily: May & Sept 9am–3.50pm; June–Aug 9am–5.10pm; 50kr), which is topped by three golden crowns, is worth the effort for unrivalled views of the city.

Gamla Stan

One of the best-preserved medieval towns in Europe, **Gamla Stan** is packed with sights to explore. However, the real joy is in simply strolling around, particularly in the evening after the tourists depart and

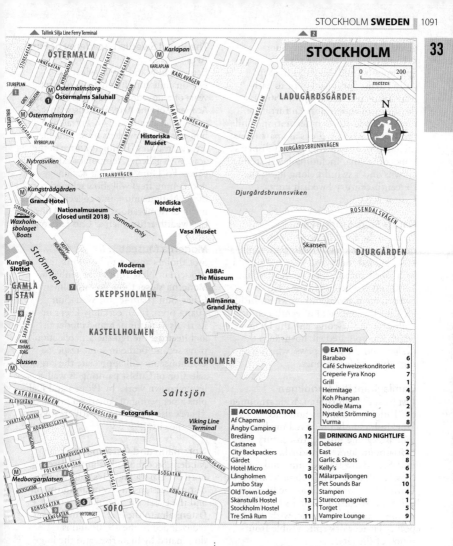

STOCKHOLM

● EATING	
Barabao	6
Café Schweizerkonditoriet	3
Creperie Fyra Knop	7
Grill	1
Hermitage	4
Koh Phangan	9
Noodle Mama	2
Nystekt Strömming	5
Vurma	8

■ ACCOMMODATION	
Af Chapman	7
Ängby Camping	6
Bredäng	12
Castanea	8
City Backpackers	4
Gärdet	2
Hotel Micro	3
Långholmen	10
Jumbo Stay	1
Old Town Lodge	9
Skanstulls Hostel	13
Stockholm Hostel	5
Tre Små Rum	11

■ DRINKING AND NIGHTLIFE	
Debaser	7
East	2
Garlic & Shots	8
Kelly's	6
Mälarpaviljongen	3
Pet Sounds Bar	10
Stampen	4
Sturecompagniet	1
Torget	5
Vampire Lounge	9

the lamp-lit streets become more intimate.

Stortorget, the main square, is surrounded by beautiful terracotta and saffron-coloured eighteenth-century buildings – look out for no. 7 where you'll see a cannonball lodged into the wall, supposedly fired during the Stockholm Bloodbath of 1520. Art shops, restaurants and bars line the surrounding narrow streets. The informative **Nobelmuseet** at Stortorget 2 (June–Aug daily 9am–8pm; Sept–May Tues 11am–8pm, Wed–Sun 11am–5pm;

100kr; ⓦnobelmuseum.se) showcases the work of Nobel Prize winners since 1901.

Gamla Stan: Kungliga Slottet
The monumental **Kungliga Slottet** (Royal Palace; ⓜGamla Stan) is a beautiful Renaissance successor to Stockholm's original castle. The Swedish Royals don't actually live here, having relocated to the Drottningholm Palace 10km west of the city, but no one seems to have told the royal guards who put on a display of pomp, pageantry and shouting at the daily changing of the

33

guard (Mon–Sat 12.15pm, Sun 1.15pm). Inside are the royal **apartments** (mid-May to mid-Sept daily 10am–5pm; mid-Sept to early May Tues–Sun noon–4pm; 150kr), a dazzling collection of regal furniture, tapestries and Rococo decoration, while the **Treasury** (same times as apartments; included in apartments ticket) displays ranks of regalia, including jewel-studded crowns and a sword belonging to the sixteenth-century Swedish king Gustav Vasa.

Gamla Stan: Storkyrkan

Close to the royal palace, Stockholm's cathedral, **Storkyrkan** (daily 9am–4pm; 40kr, guided tours cost 40kr and should be booked ahead), was consecrated in 1306 and is where the monarchs of Sweden are married and crowned. Inside, look for the animated fifteenth-century sculpture of St George and the Dragon, which incorporated elk horns into the design, and the royal pews, which look more like golden thrones.

Gamla Stan: Riddarholmen

Just west of Gamla Stan, Riddarholmen or "Knights' Island" is home to Stockholm's only preserved medieval monastery, the thirteenth-century **Riddarholmskyrkan** (mid-May to mid-Sept daily 10am–5pm, mid-Sept–Nov Sat & Sun 10am–4pm; 50kr). Until 1950 it was used as the burial place for Swedish monarchs but today its role is purely aesthetic, with its pointy latticework spire visible from much of the city.

STOCKHOLM BY KAYAK

Seeing Stockholm by boat is one thing, but getting right down to water level on a **kayak** gives you a terrific sense of freedom – you can stop off just about anywhere – plus a unique view of the city. The best place to rent kayaks is **Långholmen Kajak** at Alstaviksvägen 3 on the island of Långholmen (daily: mid-May–June & late Aug 11am–9pm; July to mid-Aug 10am–9pm; early Sept 11am–6pm; 200kr/2hr; ⓦlangholmenkajak.se).

The Royal Swedish Academy of Fine Arts

Between now and 2018, when the Nationalmuseum finally reopens after years of renovations, **The Royal Swedish Academy of Fine Arts**, at Fredsgatan 12 (ⓦkonstakademien.se; ⓜCentralen), will house some of Sweden's most valuable artistic treasures. Taking up three of the academy's galleries, temporary exhibitions (Tues–Fri 11am–5pm, Sat & Sun noon–4pm; free) will show selected parts of the Nationalmuseum's collection, which includes Rembrandts, Renoirs and pieces by Swedish artists such as Carl Larsson.

Moderna Museet

Stockholm's answer to London's Tate Modern or New York's Guggenheim, **Moderna Museet**, on Skeppsholmen (Tues–Sun 10am–8pm, Wed–Sun 10am–6pm; free), certainly keeps up with its rivals in terms of grand modernist architecture, though the art collection plays second fiddle in some respects. Connoisseurs will appreciate the large selection of Cubist painting as well as lesser-known works by Picasso and Dalí, plus a peppering of American pop art. There's also a restaurant with great views over the city.

Norrmalm and Östermalm

Modern Stockholm lies immediately north of Gamla Stan. It's split into two distinct sections: the central **Norrmalm** and the classier residential streets of **Östermalm** to the east. Norrmalm was redeveloped in the 1970s and is dominated by high-rises and the huge public-square-cum-roundabout, Sergels Torg. Taking up most of the east side of the square is the **Kulturhuset** (Mon–Fri 9am–7pm; Sat & Sun 11am–5pm; free; ⓦkulturhusetstadsteatern.se), which puts on plays and dance productions.

Östermalm, east of Norrmalm, is the address of choice for wealthy Stockholmers. It also hosts the city's most exclusive nightlife – particularly on and around Stureplan, where you'll find legions of designer-clad revellers queuing round the block for ultra-expensive nightclubs. The main attractions during the day are the **Östermalms Saluhall** food market (see p.1096) and **Historiska Muséet** (June–Aug daily 11am–6pm; Sept Mon, Tues & Thurs–Sun 11am–6pm, Wed 11am–8pm; Oct–May Tues–Fri noon–6pm, Sat & Sun 11am–6pm; free; ⓦhistoriska.se; ⓜKarlaplan). Highlights here include a Stone Age household and a mass of Viking weapons, boats and, most interestingly, gold – over 52kg of the stuff.

Södermalm and Långholmen
Stockholm's hippest island is **Södermalm**, just south of Gamla Stan. Head south from the traffic hub of Slussen along Götgatan, past Medborgarplatsen, to arrive at the central district of **SoFo** (South of Folkungagatan), which bristles with cool bars, clubs and boutiques. To the west of central Södermalm, **Hornstull** is SoFo's quieter cousin, with a cluster of bars and restaurants along Hornsgatan and around Bergsundstrand. It's a short walk north from here to the peaceful island of **Långholmen**, whose leafy woodlands and small sandy beach are perfect for summertime picnics.

Fotografiska
Behind the brick facade of a former customs building that hugs Södermalm's north coast is **Fotografiska** (Sun–Wed 9am–11pm, Thurs–Sat 9am–1am; 120kr; ⓦfotografiska.eu), Stockholm's contemporary photography centre. Here, 2,500 square metres of exhibition space is given over to inspirational pictures by local and international snappers. On Thursdays, Fridays and Saturdays, when the museum is open late, there's usually live music in the upstairs bistro.

Djurgården and its museums
A former royal hunting ground, **Djurgården** is the nearest large expanse of park to the city centre and home to several interesting museums. You could walk to the park from Central Station, but it's quite a hike: it's quicker to take a bus, tram or ferry instead. Bus #67 makes the journey from Karlaplan, while tram #7 runs from Sergels Torg, via Nybroplan. Ferries leave year-round from Slussen, dropping off at the Allmänna Gränd jetty.

On the west shore of Djurgården, **Vasa Museet** (daily: June–Aug 8.30am–6pm; Sept–May 10am–5pm, Wed open till 8pm; 130kr; ⓦvasamuseet.se) is one of the country's top tourist attractions, displaying a famous Swedish design disaster: the top-heavy *Vasa* warship, which sank in Stockholm harbour just twenty minutes into its maiden voyage in 1628. Preserved in mud, the ship was raised in 1961 and painstakingly restored. It really is an incredible sight close up and the museum does an excellent job of evoking the atmosphere of the time. The palatial **Nordiska Museet** (daily 10am–5pm, Oct–May Wed open till 8pm; 100kr, Oct–May free on Wed evenings; ⓦnordiskamuseet.se), nearby, showcases Swedish cultural history in an accessible fashion, with a particularly interesting section on the Sami – the indigenous people of Sweden's northern reaches.

Further south on the western shore of Djurgården, at Djurgårdsvägen 68, is Stockholm's blockbuster attraction, **ABBA: The Museum** (May–Aug daily 10am–8pm; Sept–April Mon, Tues & Fri–Sun 10am–6pm, Weds & Thurs 10am–8pm; 195kr, payment by card only; ⓦabbathemuseum.com), which uses interactive exhibits to tell the story of Sweden's most successful band.

ARRIVAL AND DEPARTURE

By plane The main airport is Arlanda, 37km north of the city. A high-speed rail line connects it with Central Station (every 5–10min; 20min; 280kr one-way, 540kr return; half-price with ISIC card, free with InterRail/Eurail; under 25s also get a discount; ⓦarlandaexpress.com). Alternatively, buses (45min; 99kr one-way, 198kr return; ⓦflygbussarna.se) run frequently into the city, arriving at Cityterminalen. Skavsta and Västerås airports, each around 100km from the capital, are also well connected by bus (1hr 20min; 139kr one-way, 238kr return; discount for under 25s; ⓦflygbussarna.se).

By train Trains arrive and depart from Central Station, a busy terminal on Vasagatan in Norrmalm. All branches of the Tunnelbana, Stockholm's metro, meet at ⓜCentralen, the station directly below Central Station.

Destinations Copenhagen (up to 5 daily; 5hr); Gothenburg (at least hourly; 3hr by X2000, 5hr by Intercity); Jönköping (1 daily; 3hr 15min); Kiruna (1 nightly; 18hr); Lund (at least hourly; 4hr 15min); Malmö (at least hourly; 4hr 30min); Nynäshamn (every 30min; 1hr); Oslo (1 daily;

33

6hr); Östersund (3–4 daily; 5–9hr); Umeå (up to 4 daily; 7–9hr); Uppsala (several hourly; 40min).

By bus Cityterminalen, adjacent to Central Station, handles almost all bus services, both domestic and international.

Destinations Gothenburg (up to 15 daily; 6–7hr); Jönköping (up to 16 daily; 4–5hr); Lund (2 daily; 8hr); Malmö (2 daily, 8hr 10min), Nynäshamn (4 daily; 1hr); Oslo (3 daily; 8hr); Östersund (2 weekly; 7hr 30min); Umeå (4 daily; 9hr); Uppsala (up to 13 daily; 1hr 20min).

By ferry Viking Line (ⓦ vikingline.se) ferries serving Helsinki and Åland arrive and depart from Stadsgårdskajen in Södermalm, towards the south of the city. The terminal is a 30min walk from Central Station, or 15min from ⓜ Slussen. The main terminals for Tallink Silja Line (ⓦ tallinksilja.com) ferries – Frihamnen and Värtahamnen – are in the northeastern reaches of the city, both around a 15min walk from ⓜ Gärdet station. Polferries (ⓦ polferries.se) from Gdansk and Gotland ferries (ⓦ destinationgotland.se) from Visby dock at Nynäshamn, 58km south of the city centre.

Destinations from Stadsgårdskajen Helsinki (Helsingfors; 1 daily; 16hr); Mariehamn (3 daily; 6hr 25min).

Destinations from Värtahamnen Helsinki (Helsingfors; 1 daily; 17hr); Tallinn (1 daily; 15hr).

Destinations from Frihamnen Rīga (1 daily; 17hr).

Destinations from Nynäshamn Gdansk (at least 6 monthly; 19hr); Visby (up to 5 daily; 3hr 15min).

GETTING AROUND

Tickets Buses, trams and trains (both T-bana/ underground and local) are operated by Storstockholms Lokaltrafik (SL; ⓦ sl.se). In zone A, it costs 36kr (20kr for under-20s) for up to 75min of travel on trams, T-bana services and buses – buy tickets from the automatic machines. If you're going to travel around the city a lot, it's worth buying the SL Access card (20kr from SL ticket offices) and loading it with a 24/72hr pass (115kr/230kr).

By metro The clean, efficient Tunnelbana (T-bana; Mon– Thurs & Sun 5am–roughly 1am, Fri & Sat 24hr) has three lines (red, green and blue), and is worth considering once you've tired of walking.

By bus There are four main "blue bus" lines that run across the city centre, numbered #1 to #4; numerous other lines serve suburban destinations. Buy tickets before you board.

By tram Trams run between Sergels Torg in Norrmalm and Waldermarsudde, on the southern tip of Djurgården.

By ferry Frequent ferries link Slussen with Djurgården, travelling via Skeppsholmen. Individual tickets cost 36kr.

By taxi Taxis are expensive (the meter starts at 45kr) and are only really a good option if you are in a group. Due to the risk of overcharging, it's best to stick with one of the main companies; try Taxi Stockholm (ⓣ 08 15 0000, ⓦ taxistockholm.se).

By bike The Stockholm City Bikes scheme (April–Oct only; ⓦ citybikes.se) offers a quick, affordable way to rent cycles from around 100 locations across the city. Buy the city bike card at any tourist office or an inner-city hostel/hotel (165kr/3 days) and then swipe it at the bike stand to unlock a cycle (max hire time 3hr).

INFORMATION AND TOURS

Tourist information The helpful main tourist office is at Sergels Torg 5 in Norrmalm, right next to Kulturhuset (see p.1092) (May to mid-Sept Mon–Fri 9am–7pm, Sat 9am–4pm, Sun 10am–4pm; mid-Sept to April Mon–Fri 9am–6pm, Sat 9am–4pm, Sun 10am–4pm; ⓣ 08 508 28 508, ⓦ visitsweden.com). There's also an office inside Terminal 5 at Arlanda Airport.

Boat tours Strömma (ⓦ stromma.se) runs a hop-on, hop-off boat tour (late April to early Sept; 180kr/24hr) stopping at the Vasa Museum, Skeppsholmen (Moderna Museet) and Gamla Stan. Buy tickets online or at the main office at Nybroplan. Winter sightseeing tours also available.

ACCOMMODATION

HOSTELS

★ **Af Chapman** Flaggmansvägen 8, Skeppsholmen ⓣ 08 463 22 66, ⓦ stfchapman.com. A Stockholm landmark, *Af Chapman* is a tall sailing ship converted into probably the world's most elegant hostel. If you can't get a bed on board (from 375kr) there are cheaper rooms on dry land in the hostel building, which houses the reception and a breakfast room plus a decent café. Dorms **395kr**, doubles **850kr**

Castanea Kindstugatan 1, Gamla Stan ⓣ 08 22 35 51, ⓦ castaneahostel.com. The Old Town location of this quiet, second-floor hostel (just a few min from the Royal Palace) takes some beating. Inside are clean, bright dorms. Dorms **280kr**, doubles **750kr**

★ **City Backpackers** Upplandsgatan 2a, Norrmalm ⓣ 08 20 69 20, ⓦ citybackpackers.org. Fun, sociable hostel with everything from private en-suite rooms to 12-bed dorms. Free pasta, wi-fi and, this being Sweden, sauna. Dorms **300kr**, doubles **840kr**

Gärdet Sandhamnsgatan 59a, Östermalm ⓣ 08 463 22 99, ⓦ stfturist.se/gardet; ⓜ Gärdet and 10min walk, or blue bus #1 from Cityterminalen to Östhammarsgatan and 50m walk. There are 53 modern rooms at this hotel/hostel on the edge of a quiet park, northeast of the centre. It's a pleasant 2km walk from here to Djurgården and the Vasa Museum. Doubles **895kr**

Långholmen Långholmsmuren 20, Långholmen ⓣ 08 720 85 00, ⓦ langholmen.com; ⓜ Hornstull, turn left and follow the signs. Located within an old prison on leafy Långholmen island. Spend the night in a converted cell: there are single-sex dorms with shared facilities, plus en-suite doubles and pricier hotel rooms. Dorms **285kr**, doubles **640kr**

33

Skanstulls Hostel Ringvägen 135, Södermalm ☎ 08 643 02 04, ⓦ skanstulls.se. Bright modern hostel within easy walking distance of SoFo's bars and restaurants. The decor is funky and fresh, and there's a good mix of dorms and private rooms. Dorms 235kr doubles 590kr

Stockholm Hostel Alströmergatan 15, Kungsholmen ☎ 07 156 55 25, ⓦ stockholmhostel.se; a few mins' walk from ⓂFridhemsplan. It's not in the best location and you have to book an entire room, but this bright, clean hostel is still a sociable option, with a huge, spotless kitchen and bathrooms in every room. Doubles 720kr

HOTELS AND PENSIONS

Hotel Micro Tegnérlunden 8, Norrmalm ☎ 08 545 455 69, ⓦ hotelmicro.se. Bargain prices for central Stockholm. The rooms are windowless but pleasant enough and there are clean men's and women's bathrooms along each corridor. Online discounts. Doubles 595kr

Old Town Lodge Baggensgatan 25, Gamla Stan ☎ 08 20 44 55, ⓦ oldtownlodge.se. This cosy little place in the heart of the Old Town dates back to the 1600s. As a result its 19 rooms are a little small, but they feel modern inside and are most certainly comfortable. Note, though, that the cheapest rooms are windowless. Doubles 557kr

Tre Små Rum Högbergsgatan 81, Södermalm ☎ 08 641 23 71, ⓦ tresmarum.se; ⓂMariatorget. The name means "three small rooms" but there are now seven at this good-value hotel in the heart of Södermalm. A delicious buffet breakfast is served in the lovely kitchen area and there are bikes to rent for 85kr/day. Doubles 795kr

CAMPSITES

Ängby Camping Blackebergsvägen 25 ☎ 08 37 04 20, ⓦ angbycamping.se; Ⓜ Ängbyplan, then a 5–10min walk. Basic campsite 10km west of the city on Lake Mälaren, close to the beach. Open all year, but phone ahead to book Sept to April. Per tent 150kr

Bredäng Stora Sällskapets Väg ☎ 08 97 70 71, ⓦ bredangcamping.se; Ⓜ Bredäng, then a 10min walk.

★ TREAT YOURSELF

Jumbo Stay Jumbovägen 4, Arlanda Airport ☎ 08 593 60 400, ⓦ jumbostay .com. Flying visit? Consider treating yourself to a night at a working hotel and hostel built into the shell of an old Boeing 747. Up front in the flight deck, with two adjustable beds and a flat-screen TV, the Cockpit Suite (1850kr per person) is the reserve of first-class travellers. Thankfully there's cheaper accommodation further back in the fuselage, where cattle class used to be. Dorms 450kr, doubles 1200kr

---

Decent spot with hostel and restaurant on site, 10km southwest of the centre by Lake Mälaren. Open all year though only the campsite's cabins are open between mid-Oct and mid-April. Camping/tent 135kr, dorms 240kr, doubles 600kr

EATING

CAFÉS, CHEAP EATS AND SNACKS

Barabao Hornsgatan 66; Ⓜ Mariatorget. Decorated with hanging plants, this small, Asian-inspired restaurant serves beautifully soft steamed buns loaded with everything from pork belly to slow-cooked beef with green apple chutney (around 100kr). Mon–Thurs 11.30am–2pm & 5–9pm, Fri 11.30am–2pm & 5–11pm, Sat 1–4pm & 6–11pm, Sun 5–9pm.

Café Schweizerkonditoriet Västerlånggatan 9, Gamla Stan; Ⓜ Gamla Stan. The most homely and welcoming café in a very touristy (and expensive) part of the Old Town. Coffee is served in great big cereal bowls, and you can get tasty pies with salad for less than 100kr. Daily 7am–7pm, occasionally longer at weekends.

Hermitage Stora Nygatan 11, Gamla Stan; Ⓜ Gamla Stan. Cheery, Old Town canteen serving vegetarian food from around the world. On weekdays the lunch buffet (11am–3pm) costs 120kr. Mon–Fri 11am–8pm, Sat & Sun noon–8pm.

Noodle Mama Kungsholmsgatan 22; Ⓜ Rådhuset. Steaming bowls of soba noodles with fragrant meat and vegetables (from 89kr) are served at this *kawaii* Japanese kitchen in Kungsholmen. Mon–Fri 11am–8pm, Sat & Sun noon–7pm.

Nystekt Strömming Södermalmstorg, just outside the T-bana stop; Ⓜ Slussen. This tiny but well-known takeaway cart serves fried herring with mash or Swedish crispbread (*knäckebröd*) for less than 80kr. It's always busy, and rumour has it that the food works wonders for a hangover. Daily 10am–9pm.

Vurma Bergsunds strand 31; Ⓜ Hornstull. Kitsch and cosy café just back from the waterfront in Hornstull. The *Vurma* brand has become something of a Stockholm institution, with three branches now open across the city. Good option for breakfast (from 50kr). Daily 9am–7pm.

RESTAURANTS

Creperie Fyra Knop Svartensgatan 4, Södermalm; Ⓜ Medborgarplatsen/Slussen. Good-value crêpes (from 50kr) are served in this dark, evocative restaurant, which is fashionably tatty and often packed. Daily 5–11pm.

★ Grill Drottninggatan 89, Norrmalm; Ⓜ Rådmansgatan. It's the lavish boudoir-style decor (with velvety sofas and mannequins standing in the windows) that first lures passing shoppers into *Grill*. But the daily lunch buffet (120kr), with tasty dishes like seafood paella on offer, also happens to be great value. Mon–Thurs Fri 11am–1.30pm

33

& 5pm–1am, Fri 11am–2pm & 5pm–1am, Sat 4pm–1am, Sun 3pm–midnight.

Koh Phangan Skånegatan 57, Södermalm ☎ 08 642 50 40; ⓜ Medborgarplatsen. Very popular Thai restaurant-bar with an interior resembling a tropical forest. The food (mains around 150kr) struggles to match the decor, but it's competently put together. Booking recommended. Mon–Fri 11am–midnight, Sat & Sun noon–1am.

DRINKING AND NIGHTLIFE

BARS AND PUBS

East Stureplan 13, Östermalmstorg; ⓜ Östermalmstorg. Lively Japanese bar-restaurant with a heated outdoor area. Always packed at weekends, when DJs play late into the night. Mon–Sat 11.30am–3am, Sun 5pm–3am.

Garlic & Shots Folkungagatan 84; ⓜ Medborgarplatsen. Garlic is offered with just about everything at this American-style bar – including the draught beer. For something a little sweeter, check out the excellent list of long and short drinks. Daily 5pm–1am.

★ **Kelly's** Folkungagatan 49, Södermalm; ⓜ Medborgarplatsen. Big, brash and student-friendly rock bar right near Medborgarplatsen, serving what must be some of the city's cheapest beer. If you don't have a coat to hang up (20kr) it's free to get in, too. Min age 23. Daily 4pm–3am.

Pet Sounds Bar Skånegatan 80, Södermalm; ⓜ Medborgarplatsen. One of the most popular places in SoFo for a drink, run by the eponymous record store a few doors down; the basement bar hosts live music and DJs on Fri and Sat. Tues 5pm–midnight, Wed–Sat 4pm–1am, Sun 4pm–midnight.

Vampire Lounge Östgötagatan 41, Södermalm; ⓜ Medborgarplatsen. Subterranean cocktail bar – comfy red sofas, bare stone walls and hip clientele. Kick-start your evening with a Vampire Martini cocktail, or go for a cheap beer. Min age 20/21. Wed–Fri 5pm–1am, Sat 7pm–1am.

CLUBS AND LIVE MUSIC

Debaser Hornstulls Strand 9 ⓦ debaser.se; ⓜ Hornstull. Big-name DJs and live bands top the bill at this venue near the waterfront in Hornstull – expect anything from house to hip-hop. There's also an American-style bar and a Mexican restaurant. Minimum age 20 on Fri and Sat. See website for event times.

Stampen Stora Nygatan 5, Gamla Stan ⓦ stampen.se; ⓜ Gamla Stan. Two floors of jazz, swing and blues, right in the heart of the Old Town. Live music almost every night. Tues–Fri 5pm–1am, Sat 2pm–1am.

Sturecompagniet Sturegatan 4 ⓦ sturecompagniet.se; ⓜ Östermalmstorg. This Stockholm staple boasts a terrific light-show with house and techno sounds blaring long into the night. Dress to impress and start queuing early. Over-23s only. Thurs–Sat 10pm–5am.

GAY STOCKHOLM

Mälarpaviljongen Norr Mälarstrand 64, ⓦ malarpaviljongen.se; ⓜ Rådhuset. Open-air bar-restaurant down by the water with great views of Gamla Stan. It attracts a mixed gay/straight crowd and puts on events during the annual Stockholm Pride. April–Sept daily 11am–1am.

Torget Mälartorget 13 ⓦ torgetbaren.com; ⓜ Gamla Stan. This elegant place is Stockholm's main gay bar, good for a drink at any time, and always busy. The modern Swedish food here is justifiably popular, so always reserve ahead if you want to eat. Daily 5pm–1am.

SHOPPING

FASHION AND LIFESTYLE

Åhléns City Klarabergsgatan 50, near the T-bana stop; ⓜ Centralen. Sweden's biggest department store is the place to stock up on Björn Borg undies and skinny Acne jeans. Mon–Fri 10am–9pm, Sat 10am–7pm, Sun 11am–7pm.

H&M Hamngatan 37 ⓜ Hötorget. The main Stockholm branch of one of Sweden's biggest retail success stories; wall-to-wall with cut-price fashion. Mon–Fri 10am–8pm, Sat 10am–6pm, Sun 11am–6pm.

IKEA Modulvägen 1, Skärholmen (7km southwest of Stockholm). If you're dying to see the world's largest IKEA then hop on one of the free shuttle buses leaving from Vasagatan 18 (Mon–Fri approx hourly 10am–7pm). Daily 10am–8pm.

Judits Hornsgatan 75 ⓦ judits.se; ⓜ Zinkensdamm. Fantastic secondhand clothes emporium selling shoes and accessories at affordable prices. Mon–Fri 11am–6pm, Sat 11am–4pm.

Nudie Jeans Skånegatan 75 ⓦ nudiejeans.com; ⓜ Medborgarplatsen. Organic khakis and jeans draw style-conscious Stockholmers to this concept store on Skånegatan. Mon–Fri 11am–6.30pm, Sat 11am–5pm, Sun noon–4pm.

FOOD AND MARKETS

Hemköp Directly below Åhléns City, Mäster Samuels gatan 57. Super-central supermarket with an excellent deli counter and an in-house bakery. Mon–Fri 7am–11pm.

Hötorgshallen Hötorget ⓦ hotorgshallen.se; ⓜ Hötorget. A truly international market, selling everything from oolong tea and Gruyère cheese to fresh Finnish bread. There's a branch of Systembolaget here, too (closes at 3pm on Sat). Mon–Thurs 10am–6pm, Fri 10am–7pm, Sat 10am–4pm.

Östermalms Saluhall Östermalmstorg; ⓜ Östermalmstorg. Neo-Gothic food hall, built in 1888, with wine bars and restaurants surrounding the stalls. It's closed for refurbishment until 2018, so a temporary food hall is open next door. Mon–Fri 9.30am–7pm, Sat 9.30am–6pm.

DIRECTORY

Embassies Australia, Klarabergsviadukten 63, 8th floor ☎ 08 613 29 00; Canada, Klarabergsgatan 23, 6th floor ☎ 08 453 30 00; Ireland, Hovslagargatan 5 ☎ 08 54 50 40 40; UK, Skarpögatan 6–8 ☎ 08 671 30 00; US, Dag Hammarskjöldsväg 31 ☎ 08 783 53 00.

Hospital St Görans Sjukhus, St Göransplan 1 ☎ 08 587 010 00, ⊛ stgoran.se/english (24hr).

Left luggage Lockers in Central Station and Cityterminalen (70/90kr per 24hr, depending on size).

Pharmacy Apoteket C.W. Scheele, Klarabergsgatan 64 ☎ 07 714 504 50 (24hr).

Post office You can send packages from the information desks in branches of Hemköp and Ica, with a branch of the latter on Kungsholmstorg, just north of Strömkajen (daily 8am–11pm).

Around Stockholm

One of the key excursions from Stockholm is to the royal palace of Drottningholm, on the shores of Lake Mälaren, west of the capital. In summer the pine-clad islands of Stockholm's **archipelago** make an enticing escape from the city, while history buffs should head to the elegant town of **Uppsala**, a short train ride away.

DROTTNINGHOLM PALACE

Just 10km west of Stockholm, **Drottningholm Palace** (April & Oct Fri–Sun 11am–3.30pm; May–Sept daily 10am–4.30pm; Nov–March Sat & Sun noon–3.30pm; 120kr; ⊛ kungahuset.se) is a Versailles-like monument to excess dating from the mid-seventeenth century. The Swedish royal family made it their permanent residence in 1981, and, while you're unlikely to spot any of them, you are free to wander through sections of the palace on guided tours and visit the manicured gardens.

ARRIVAL AND DEPARTURE

By boat The most fun way to get here is on one of the majestic old steam ships which leave from the quay near Stadshusbron five times a day (mid-April to Oct; 205kr return; ⊛ stromma.se).

By metro and bus You can also reach it on the less regal combination of T-bana to Brommaplan followed by the #177 bus.

THE STOCKHOLM ARCHIPELAGO

For 80km east of the capital stretches the **Stockholm archipelago** (Stockholms Skärgård), made up of 30,000 islands, most of which are little more than lumps of rock rising up from the sea. In summer, the area bristles with tourists, day-trippers, sailing boats and locals making use of their summer homes.

ARRIVAL AND DEPARTURE

By boat Boats to some of the islands leave from Strömkajen in Stockholm and are run by Waxholmsbolaget (☎ 08 614 64 50, ⊛ waxholmsbolaget.se; from 60kr one-way).

Vaxholm and Kyrkogårdsön

Just an hour's scenic boat ride from Stockholm and also connected by road, **Vaxholm** is the most easily accessible of the archipelago islands, which means it can be swamped with visitors in summer. However, it's still a charming spot, only 3.2km long and with an elegant harbour on its eastern edge, where you'll find restaurants, cafés and shops.

An hour's ferry ride north of Vaxholm is the cute little island of **Kyrkogårdsön**, which locals rave about. Siaröfortet is the name of the island's small naval fort, built during World War I. The fort has been turned into a museum but the real attraction is the island's indented coastline – perfect for kayaking and swimming.

ARRIVAL AND INFORMATION

By ferry Blidösundsbolaget ferries do day-trips from Strömkajen to Kyrkogårdsön (May to mid-Aug; 180kr return; ⊛ blidosundsbolaget.se; get off at Siaröfortet).

Tourist information Vaxholm's tourist office is on Rådhustorget, a short walk north of the harbour (hours vary but it's always manned daily between 11am–2pm; ☎ 08 541 314 80).

ACCOMMODATION

Bogesunds Slottsvandrarhem South across the bridge at Per Brahes Väg 1, Vaxholm ☎ 08 541 750 60, ⊛ bogesundsslottsvandrarhem.se; bus #681 from Söderhamnsplan (near the harbour) until you reach

33

Bogesunds Gård. Though accommodation is expensive on the island itself, this peaceful hostel is a good choice. Doubles <u>510kr</u>

STF youth hostel By the beach, Kyrkogårdsön ☏ 08 243 090, ⓦ svenskaturistforeningen.se. If you want to stay on Kyrkogårdsön, this is a lovely hostel with a wood-fired sauna. Open mid-May to mid-Oct only. Dorms <u>250kr</u>, doubles <u>500kr</u>

UPPSALA

Forty minutes' train ride north of Stockholm, the pretty university town of **UPPSALA** makes an excellent day-trip. Just north of the restaurant- and bar-lined River Fyris, which bisects the town, you'll find the vast Gothic **Domkyrkan** (daily 8am–6pm), Scandinavia's largest cathedral. Poke around and you'll see the tombs of Reformation rebel monarch Gustav Vasa and his son Johan III, as well as local hero Carl Linnaeus, the famous botanist.

Also worth seeking out are the remarkable royal burial mounds at **Gamla (Old) Uppsala**. Thought to have been created by the Svea tribe some 1500 years ago, they were once the site of gruesome human sacrifices – with unfortunate victims strung up from a tree. The place where this took place is marked by the **Gamla Uppsala Kyrka**, St Eriks torg 7 (daily 9am–6pm), a church built when the Swedish kings first took baptism in the new faith. The worthwhile **Gamla Uppsala Museum**, Disavägen (April, May & Sept daily 10am–4pm; June–Aug daily 11am–5pm; Oct–March Mon, Wed, Sat & Sun noon–4pm; 80kr), fills you in on all the background.

ARRIVAL AND INFORMATION

By train Trains pull in at Uppsala Centralstation, a couple of blocks northeast of the river.
Destinations Stockholm (at least 3 per hour; 40min); Leksand/Mora (2–3 daily; 2hr 30min–3hr 10min); Östersund (around 4 daily; 4hr 20min–6hr 30min).
By bus Swebus and Nettbuss services to Stockholm are frequent, departing from Stationsgatan.
Destinations Stockholm (at least hourly; 1hr).
Tourist information Signs show the way to the cathedral and tourist office at Kungsgatan 59 (Mon–Fri 10am–6pm, Sat 10am–3pm; ☏ 018 727 48 00, ⓦ destinationuppsala.se).

ACCOMMODATION AND EATING

Max Stora Torget 6–8 (the main square). Part of a nationwide chain, this fast-food joint has a few veggie options on the menu, and also give details of each burger's carbon footprint. Most meals 60–80kr. Mon, Tues & Sun 10am–midnight, Wed & Thurs 10am–3am, Fri & Sat 10am–5am, Sun 10am–midnight.

Uppsala City Hostel St Persgatan 16, northwest of the station off Kungsgatan ☏ 018 10 00 08, ⓦ uppsalacity hostel.se. Conveniently located hostel with good-value dorms and rooms in satisfyingly simple Swedish style. Dorms <u>220kr</u>, doubles <u>560kr</u>

Southern Sweden

Southern Sweden is dominated by endless expanses of farmland, and its coastline is famous for its superb beaches. Local dialects are strong and cause much mirth among metropolitan Stockholmers. Yet to portray the area as a rural backwater would do it a disservice. Here you'll find the gritty port city of **Gothenburg**, which buzzes with student life. South of here, **Malmö** is Sweden's culturally diverse gateway to the rest of Europe, while **Lund**, a medieval cathedral and university town, is an essential day-trip. Lying 90km off the southern coast in the Baltic Sea is the attractive and historically important island of **Gotland**, whose beaches and bars are awash with visitors over the summer.

GOTHENBURG

Sweden's second city, **GOTHENBURG** (Göteborg, pronounced *Yuh-teh-borr*) is Scandinavia's largest seaport and home to some of Sweden's biggest brands, including Volvo and Ericsson. Beyond the industrial gloom of its shipyards you'll find an attractive, unpretentious city with broad avenues, leafy parks and several outstanding museums and galleries. With students making up an eighth of the population it's also a fun, youthful city with plenty of quirky bars, nightclubs and coffee shops – not to mention some of Sweden's best restaurants.

33

GOTHENBURG

■ ACCOMMODATION
Eklanda B&B	5
Kärralund Camping Liseberg	3
Kvibergs Vandrarhem & Stugby	1
Slottsskogens Vandrarhem	4
Stigbergsliden	2

■ DRINKING AND NIGHTLIFE
Henriksberg	4
Pustevik	2
Rock Baren	3
Yaki-da	1

● EATING
Bönor & Bagels	9
Café Santo Domingo	7
Feskekôrka	3
Gourmet Korv	8
Hagabions	6
Holy Moly	4
Moon Thai Kitchen	1
Strömmingsluckan	5
Yammy Kitchen	5

Airport (25km)

Central Station

Nils Ericson Terminalen

Nils Ericson Terminalen

Maritiman

Opera House

Lilla Bommen Harbour

Docks

Göta River

HISINGEN

Stenpiren

Gamla Ullevi Stadium

Scandinavium

Liseberg Amusement Park

Universeum

Museum of World Culture

Näckrosdammen

Göteborgs Konstmuseum

Konserthuset

VASASTAN

Trädgårds-föreningen

Röhsska Museet

University Main Building

University Library

Nordstan Shopping Centre

Radhus

Göteborgs Stadsmuseum

Antikhallarna

Cathedral

Paddan Boat Tours

Kungsparken

Vasaparken

HAGA

LINNÉ

Skansparken

Slottsskogen Park

Stena Line Terminal

Naturhistoriska Museum

metres
0 — 300

N

33

WHAT TO SEE AND DO

Exploring Gothenburg by tram is one of the great pleasures of the city, but almost all its sights can be covered on foot. Most visitors head straight towards the main shopping street, Avenyn, which leads uphill towards the Konstmuseum, though from here it's only a short stroll to Liseberg, Scandinavia's biggest theme park, and the Universeum science centre. If you have time, dedicate a lazy afternoon to Slottsskogen, the city's most attractive swathe of green space, or head out to explore the rocky islands of the Southern Archipelago.

Maritiman and the Opera House

A short walk north from the station, at **Maritiman** (April Sat & Sun 11am–4pm; May & Sept daily 11am–5pm; June–Aug daily 10am–6pm; 120kr; ⓦmaritiman.se) you can clamber aboard a destroyer and descend into a submarine moored at the quayside. It's worth coming here just to look at the dockyards beyond, which frame the ship-shaped **Gothenburg Opera House** (ⓦen.opera.se).

Avenyn and the Röhsska Museet

Running southeast from the central area around the Nordstan shopping centre, Kungsportsavenyn is Gothenburg's showiest thoroughfare. Known simply as **Avenyn** (the Avenue), this wide strip was once flanked by private houses fronted by gardens and is now lined with some of the city's most popular – and overpriced – restaurants and bars. About halfway down, the excellent **Röhsska Museet** at Vasagatan 37–39 (Wed noon–8pm; Thurs & Fri noon–5pm, Sat & Sun 11am–5pm; 40kr, free for under 25s;

FIVE MUSEUMS FOR THE PRICE OF ONE

Pay the 40kr admission fee at any of the five museums listed here and you'll receive a **pass** that lets you visit the Röhsska Museet, Konstmuseum, Naturhistoriska Museum and two other city museums (Sjöfartsmuseet Akvariet and Göteborgs Stadsmuseum) as many times as you like over a twelve-month period.

ⓦrohsska.se) traces the history of design from 1850 to the present day, and also hosts regular fashion shows by young designers from Gothenburg University.

Göteborgs Konstmuseum

At the far southern end of Avenyn is Gothenburg's museum of art, the **Konstmuseum** (Tues & Thurs 11am–6pm, Wed 11am–8pm, Fri–Sun 11am–5pm; 40kr, free for under-25s) housing a unique collection of Nordic masterpieces. Among the highlights are paintings by Edvard Munch, P.S. Krøyer and Carl Larsson, but there are also works by Picasso, Van Gogh and Rembrandt. The square outside the museum, **Götaplatsen**, is home to a city icon – Carl Milles' 7m-high bronze statue of Poseidon in all his naked glory.

Liseberg Amusement Park

Liseberg, five minutes' walk southeast of Götaplatsen, is a gorgeous inner-city amusement park (late April to early Oct, and then again at Christmas; opening times vary; the Allt-i-ett, or all-in-one, pass costing 440kr gives access to the park and unlimited rides all day; ⓦliseberg.com), with restaurants, bars and adrenaline-pumping rides set among acres of landscaped gardens. It's the biggest theme park in Scandinavia, and Balder, the rickety wooden roller coaster, is one of the best of its kind in the world. Atmosfear, a needle-like tower rising 116m into the sky, is Europe's tallest free-fall ride.

Universeum and the Museum of World Culture

Nearby, **Universeum** (daily: mid-June to mid-Aug 10am–8pm; mid-Aug to mid-June 10am–6pm; ⓦuniverseum.se; 180–245kr, depending on the season) is a fun if expensive science discovery centre – it's worth getting a Gothenburg City Card (see opposite) just to visit this place. The main attraction is a huge, climate-controlled tropical forest but there's also a large seawater aquarium with its own shark tunnel, plus a section full of deadly reptiles.

Adjacent to Universeum, the **Museum of World Culture** (Tues, Thurs & Fri noon–5pm, Wed noon–8pm, Sat & Sun

11am–5pm; free, but extra to access certain galleries; ⓦvarldskulturmuseerna .se) runs exhibitions on global issues such as HIV/Aids, human trafficking and fair trade as well as more upbeat topics such as Bollywood and hip-hop. There are also regular screenings of English and foreign-language films.

Haga and Linnégatan

The old working-class district of **Haga**, a few minutes' walk west of Avenyn, is now a picturesque area of cobbled streets lined with cafés, clothing boutiques and antique shops. Tree-lined **Linnégatan**, further west still, is a prettier and more refined version of Avenyn, with relaxed bars and restaurants leading almost all the way to Slottsskogen.

Slottsskogen Park and Naturhistoriska Museum

Slottsskogen (tram #1, #2 or #6 to Linnéplatsen) is the city's largest park, a lovely expanse of woodland, lakes and wide paths perfect for joggers and cyclists. Several vantage points offer sweeping views over the city, and there's also a small zoo area with penguins and a seal pond. The nearby **Naturhistoriska Museum** (Tues–Sun 11am–5pm; 40kr; under-25s free; ⓦgnm .se) houses the world's only stuffed blue whale. It was once possible to go inside the huge marine mammal, but since a couple of visitors were caught in a compromising embrace in its mouth, the whale has been kept as a purely visual exhibit.

Southern Archipelago

Saltholmen (the southernmost stop on tram #11) is the jumping-off point for trips to Gothenburg's craggy **Southern Archipelago**. Ferries run from here to inhabited islands like Vargö, Bränö and Styrsö, which make great spots for swimming and sunbathing in the summertime. Tram tickets are valid for ferry journeys, too.

ARRIVAL AND DEPARTURE

By plane The city's commercial airport, Gothenburg Landvetter, is 25km east of the city; buses (every 20min; 30min; 105kr; 95kr if booked online; ⓦflygbussarna.se) connect to the Nils Ericson terminal next to Central Station.

By train Trains arrive and depart from Central Station on Drottningtorget, just north of the centre; an underground walkway leads into Nordstan, the city's central shopping mall.

Destinations Copenhagen (hourly; 3hr 50min); Helsingborg (hourly; 2hr); Lund (hourly; 3hr); Malmö (hourly; 3hr 10min); Oslo (3 daily; 4hr); Stockholm (at least hourly; 3hr by X2000, 5hr by Intercity).

By bus Buses from all destinations use the Nils Ericson bus terminal, which adjoins Central Station. For onward travel to regional destinations like Copenhagen and Oslo, served by Swebus (ⓦswebus.se) and Nettbuss (ⓦnettbuss.se), book ahead online.

Destinations Copenhagen (up to 7 daily; 4hr 30min–5hr); Helsingborg (up to 18 daily; 2hr 40min); Lund (up to 15 daily; 3hr–3hr 30min); Malmö (up to 20 daily; 3hr 30min–4hr); Oslo (up to 21 daily; 3hr 30min–4hr); Stockholm (up to 15 daily; 6–7hr).

By boat Stena Line ferries from Frederikshavn in Denmark and Kiel in Germany dock within a 20min walk of the centre. Trams #3, #9 and #11 run from nearby Masthuggstorget to the centre.

Destinations Frederikshavn (at least 4 daily; 2hr–3hr 30min); Kiel (1 daily; 14hr 30min).

INFORMATION AND TOURS

Tourist information Gothenburg has two helpful and well-informed tourist offices: a main office at Kungsportsplatsen 2 (June–Aug daily 9.30am–6/8pm; Sept–May Mon–Sat 9.30am–2/5pm; ☎031 368 4200, ⓦgoteborg.com) and a glass kiosk in the middle of the Nordstan shopping mall (Mon–Fri 10am–8pm, Sat & Sun 10am–6pm). Both offices sell the Gothenburg City Card (375/525/675kr for 24/48/72hr), giving unlimited bus and tram travel, free or half-price museum and attraction entry, free Paddan boat tours and a fifty percent discount on a day-trip to Frederikshavn in Denmark.

Boat tours Open-topped Paddan boats (ⓦstromma.se) take tourists on 50min tours (April–Oct; 170kr or free at certain times with Gothenburg City Card) along the city's canals. Boats depart from Kungsportsplatsen.

GETTING AROUND

By tram There are 13 colour-coded tram routes operated by Västtrafik – pick up a map from any hotel or tourist office, or use the English-language journey planner at ⓦvasttrafik.se. Tickets (28kr or free with Gothenburg City Card) can usually be bought from the on-board vending machines. A more reliable option is the Västtrafikkort, which can be purchased at any branch of Pressbyrån. You pay a 50kr deposit for the card, and can then top it up with 100, 200 or 500kr at a time. Touch the card against the on-board scanner when you start each journey and you'll pay slightly less than the usual per-journey fee.

33

By bike Cycle paths criss-cross the city. You can rent bikes (200kr/day) from Cykelkungen at Chalmersgatan 19 (ⓦ cykelkungen.se) or buy a three-day pass for the city's bike rental scheme, Styr & Ställ (25kr, plus a 140kr deposit; ⓦ goteborgbikes.se). The first 30min of every journey is free.

ACCOMMODATION

Gothenburg can be an affordable place to treat yourself to a proper hotel room, thanks to the Gothenburg Package (from 775kr/person), run by the city's tourist board. This deal gets you a double room in a central hotel, with breakfast and a free Gothenburg City Card worth 375kr – book ahead at ⓦ goteborg.com.

★**Eklanda B&B** Eklandagatan 3 ☎031 18 79 94, ⓦ eklandabochb.com. High up in an attractive townhouse near Universeum and Liseberg (no sign outside), this privately run B&B has two immaculate doubles that share a bathroom and a relaxed lounge area. Buffet breakfast included. Booking essential. Doubles 695kr

Kärralund Camping Liseberg Olbergsgatan ⓦ liseberg.se; from Brunnsparken in the city centre, take tram #5 to Welandergatan (direction Torp). Busy campsite 4km from the centre aimed mostly at families visiting the Liseberg amusement park. There is also a youth hostel on site (dorms only, sleeping up to four people, and you must book the whole room). Camping/tent (sleeping 4) 295kr, dorms 995kr

Kvibergs Vandrarhem & Stugby Lilla Regementsvägen 35 ☎031 43 50 55, ⓦ vandrarhem.com; tram #7 or #11 towards Kviberg. A 10min ride from the centre, this peaceful place offers a range of decent accommodation, from dorms (though you have to rent the entire room) to private rooms. There are also self-contained, five-person wooden cabins with kitchens. Doubles 560kr, cabins 1050kr

★**Slottsskogens Vandrarhem** Vegagatan 21 ☎031 42 65 20, ⓦ sov.nu; tram #1, #2 or #6 to Olivedalsgatan. This huge hostel is in a great location near Slottsskogen park, 2min walk from Linnégatan. There's a sauna, free wi-fi and a chill-out area, and dorms come with lockers built into the bunks. Dorms 195kr, doubles 500kr

Stigbergsliden Stigbergsliden 10 ☎031 24 16 20, ⓦ hostel-gothenburg.com; tram #3, #9 or #11 from the city centre to Stigbergstorget. Comfortable hostel in a charming, nineteenth-century sailor's mission, close to the Stena Line ferry terminal and the bars of Andra Långgatan. Check-in closed noon–4pm. Dorms 245kr, doubles 600kr

EATING

CAFÉS, CHEAP EATS AND SNACKS

Bönor & Bagels Linnégatan 48. Cracking little café on one of the city's most attractive streets. Grab a latte, some soup and a bagel (around 70kr), then sit outside and watch the trams roll by. Mon–Fri 8am–6pm, Sat & Sun 9am–6pm.

Café Santo Domingo Andra Långgatan 4a. With stacks of old LPs for sale and Dominican coffee steaming away on the counter, this roomy record store attracts a mixed crowd of music lovers. There's cheap vegetarian soup each weekday lunchtime. Live bands every Fri. Mon–Fri 9.30am–6.30pm, Sat 10am–4pm.

Feskekörka Rosenlundsvägen by the waterfront. Built in 1874, this lively church-like building (its name literally means fish church) is where locals come to stock up on locally caught crayfish or natter over a takeaway shellfish salad from Kerstins Delikatesser (89kr). Tues–Fri 10am–6pm, Sat 10am–3pm.

Gourmet Korv Södra Larmgatan 6. Choose from 50 different kinds of hotdog sausage – including one flavoured with cognac and juniper berries – at this tiny yet central kiosk. The sausage of the day, served with potato salad and a drink, costs 79kr. A second branch in Nordstan has longer hours. Mon–Fri 10am–6pm, Sat 11am–4pm.

Hagabions Linnégatan 21. Eat vegetarian food or drink a creamy glass of Stigbergets IPA (brewed in Gothenburg) at this film-themed café inside an arthouse cinema showing pictures from around the globe. Daily 5pm–1am.

Strömmingsluckan In the car park near Magasinsgatan 17. Insanely popular takeaway van serving a truly Swedish take on fast food: fried herring with mashed potatoes and lingonberries (65kr). Mon–Fri 11am–3pm, Sat noon–4pm.

RESTAURANTS

Holy Moly Andra Långgatan 31. Tiny, softly lit Mexican place that attracts a young and chatty crowd. There's often live music and the cheap finger food is a nice accompaniment to the cold beer. Mon–Thurs & Sun 4pm–1am, Sat & Sun 4pm–2am.

★**Moon Thai Kitchen** Kristinelundsgatan 9. Still the best Thai restaurant in town, with twinkling fairy lights strewn across its interior, and surprisingly authentic curries (from 139kr) grouped according to spiciness and cost. Mon–Thurs 4–11pm, Fri 11am–1am, Sat noon–1am, Sun noon–11pm.

Yammy Kitchen Andra Långgatan 5. For sizzling soups and beef stews, look no further than this Korean-run place, whose huge menu also includes sushi boxes (from 72kr). Veggie and vegan options are available, too. Mon–Thurs 3–10pm, Fri 3–11pm, Sat noon–11pm, Sun 2–10pm.

DRINKING AND NIGHTLIFE

For cheap beer and good times, Andra Långgattan ("second long street") is a safe bet – it's one of the few places you can buy a beer for under 50kr and there are plenty of cheap-ish restaurants, though things are starting to get gentrified.

Henriksberg Stigbergsliden 7. A fun place to meet Swedish students, with cheap beer (from 46kr) and pub games like pool and shuffleboard helping to keep things consistently lively. Upstairs is a terrace with views over the harbour, and at weekends bands play in the venue downstairs. Sun–Wed 5pm–1am, Thurs–Sat 5pm–2am.

Pustervik Järntorgsgatan 14. Live bands and/or DJs play almost nightly at this former theatre, which draws in a good mix of local talent and international acts. Try to visit on Mon (free entry) when you can take part in the venue's surreal ping-pong competition. Mon–Thurs 11am–2am, Fri 11am–3am, Sat & Sun 5pm–3am.

Rock Baren Kristinelundsgatan 14. Two floors of noisy rock 'n' roll action, just steps from the swanky clubs of Avenyn. Head in between 5–10pm for the daily happy hour, when a draught beer costs just 32kr. Minimum age 20. Sun–Thurs 5pm–2am, Fri & Sat 5pm–3am.

Yaki-da Storgatan 47. Homely sofas, framed portraits and old-fashioned lampshades decorate the themed rooms of this sprawling club, just off Avenyn. The well-mixed Negronis (135kr) are easier on the tongue than they are on the wallet. Minimum age 23; entry around 150kr. Wed, Fri & Sat 8pm–3am.

MALMÖ

Linked to Denmark by the impressive Öresund Bridge, **MALMÖ** is Sweden's most cosmopolitan city. More than a hundred languages are spoken on its streets and you'll find Turkish and Thai food as popular as meatballs and herring. In fact, Malmö didn't even become Swedish until 1658, having been Denmark's second city for generations. Today it's Sweden's third-largest town, an attractive mix of chocolate-box medieval squares and striking modern architecture, most notably the Turning Torso skyscraper, Scandinavia's tallest building.

WHAT TO SEE AND DO

Mostly flat and home to an extensive cycle network, Malmö is the perfect place to rent a bike and explore at leisure. Most of the sights are squeezed into the compact medieval centre, although the **beaches** and modern **docklands** to the north make a tempting excursion. South of the old centre is the bohemian district of **Möllevångstorget**, where you'll find many of the best places to eat and drink.

Stortorget

The city's main square, **Stortorget** is as impressive today as it must have been when it was first laid out in the sixteenth century. It's flanked on one side by the imposing **Rådhus** (town hall), built in 1546 and covered with statuary and spiky accoutrements. To its rear stands the fine Gothic **St Petri Kyrka** (daily 10am–6pm), while to the south runs **Södergatan**, Malmö's main pedestrianized shopping street.

Lilla Torg

A late sixteenth-century spin-off from Stortorget, **Lilla Torg** is everyone's favourite part of the city. Edged by cafés and restaurants, it's usually pretty crowded at night, with drinkers kept warm under patio heaters and bars handing out free blankets. On the south side of the square, through an archway, is the **Form/Design Center** (Tues–Sat 11am–5pm, Sun noon–4pm; free; ⓦformdesigncenter.com), which showcases cutting-edge Swedish furniture, textiles and lighting. There's also a café stocked with magazines and journals on design trends.

Malmöhus Slott

Handsome **Malmöhus Slott** is a low, heavily fortified castle defended by a deep moat and two circular keeps. Taking its current form in the mid-sixteenth century, when Danish king Christian III wanted to assert his power over the region, the castle was later used as a prison. Now it houses **Malmö Museer** (daily 10am–5pm; 40kr; ⓦmalmo.se /museer), a disparate but fascinating collection of exhibitions on everything from geology to photography – and an aquarium, too. Small lakes and an old windmill dot the three leafy parks that surround the castle grounds.

The Turning Torso and Öresund Bridge

A good twenty-minute walk or five-minute cycle ride north of the station is Malmö's most iconic sight, the 190m-high **Turning Torso** skyscraper. A towering helix of glass and steel, the structure was completed in 2005 and remains Scandinavia's tallest building. You can't go up in the tower, but the area immediately

33

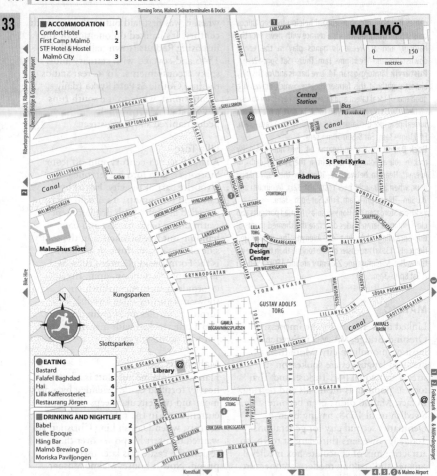

■ ACCOMMODATION
Comfort Hotel	1
First Camp Malmö	2
STF Hotel & Hostel	
Malmö City	3

MALMÖ

0   150
metres

● EATING
Bastard	1
Falafel Baghdad	5
Hai	4
Lilla Kafferosteriet	3
Restaurang Jörgen	2

■ DRINKING AND NIGHTLIFE
Babel	2
Belle Epoque	4
Häng Bar	3
Malmö Brewing Co	5
Moriska Paviljongen	1

around it is still worth a wander. On a wall just to the west is an electronic eye (made from LEDs by Swedish artist Annika Svenbro), which seems to change its appearance throughout the day. Heading coastward takes you to a viewpoint of the **Öresund Bridge**: this 17km engineering marvel links the city with Copenhagen (a journey of just 35min by train) and is the iconic centrepiece of the Scandi noir thriller series *The Bridge*.

The beach
Ribersborgsstranden, or "Ribban", as city residents call it, is Malmö's artificial sandy beach, created in the 1920s. A long access path, busy in summer with rollerbladers

and cyclists, leads down to the sections of beach, each indicated by a jetty. Just offshore is **Ribersborgs Kallbadhus** (May–Aug Mon, Tues, Thurs & Fri 9am–8pm, Wed 9am–9pm, Sat & Sun 9am–6pm; Sept–April Mon, Tues, Thurs & Fri 10am–7pm, Wed 10am–8pm, Sat & Sun 9am–6pm; 65kr; ⓦ ribersborgskal lbadhus.se), where locals come to take a naked dip in the icy sea then warm up in one of the five oven-like saunas.

Möllevångstorget
Known as **Möllan**, this giant cobbled square towards the south of the city was once the heart of working-class Malmö. By day it hosts a busy market selling

everything from cassava to Arabic sweets, while by night it becomes the alternative hangout of choice for the city's student population.

ARRIVAL AND DEPARTURE

By plane Copenhagen/Kastrup Airport is just 20min by train from Malmö's Central Station; trains leave round the clock and cost 111kr. Malmö's own airport, Sturup, is used mostly by Swedish airlines flying to domestic destinations and the odd Wizz Air service to Poland or Hungary. It's 30km southeast of the city; buses run once or twice per hour (40min; one-way journey costs 115kr, or 105kr if booked online; W flygbussarna.se).

By train All trains terminate at Central Station, including the local Pågatåg services that run from Helsingborg and Lund (rail passes are valid). Trains bound for Copenhagen, on the other side of the Öresund Bridge, also depart from here.

Destinations Copenhagen (every 20min; airport 20min, city 35min); Gothenburg (hourly; 3hr 10min); Helsingborg (roughly every 20min; 40–50min); Lund (every 10min; 10–15min); Stockholm (hourly; 4hr 30min).

By bus The main bus terminal, served by local buses and long-distance Swebus and Nettbuss services, is just east of Central Station on Centralplan. Occasionally, long-distance buses drop off and pick up at Norra Vallgatan, 200m south of the train station.

Destinations Copenhagen (up to 9 daily; airport 45min, city 1hr); Gothenburg (up to 20 daily; 3hr 30min–4hr); Lund (up to 16 daily; 25min); Helsingborg (up to 18 daily; 50min–1hr 15min); Stockholm (4 weekly; 8hr 25min); Oslo (up to 13 daily; 7hr 30min–8hr).

INFORMATION

Tourist information The main tourist office is across from the train station at Skeppsbron 2 (Mon–Fri 9am–5pm, Sat & Sun 10am–2pm; ☎040 34 12 00, W malmotown.com).

GETTING AROUND

By bus City buses are run by Skånetrafiken (W skanetrafiken.se), whose desk inside the glass part of the train station (Mon–Fri 6.30am–8pm, Sat 9am–6pm, Sun 10am–6pm) sells a 24hr pass that allows unlimited travel on inner-city bus routes (65kr).

By bike Bike rental available from Fridhems Cykelaffär, Tessins Väg 13, about two blocks along Tessins Väg west from the castle (150kr for the first day, then 100kr/day thereafter).

ACCOMMODATION

Comfort Hotel Carlsgatan 10c ☎040 33 04 40, W choice .se. Bright, comfortable rooms just a 2min walk from

Central Station. Room rates include free organic breakfast, wi-fi and access to the on-site gym. Book ahead for the best deal. Doubles ~~699kr~~

First Camp Malmö Strandgatan 101 ☎040 15 51 65, W firstcamp.se; bus #4 from Central Station. Huge beachside campsite with views of the Öresund Bridge. Per person ~~20kr~~, plus per tent ~~200kr~~

STF Hotel & Hostel Malmö City Rönngatan 1 ☎040 611 62 20; bus #8 from the train station to Davidshall. Simple, clean and very popular STF hostel 1km south of the centre in a great location for nightlife and shops. Dorms ~~320kr~~, doubles ~~925kr~~

EATING

Bastard Mäster Johansgatan 11. There aren't many animal parts the tattooed chefs at *Bastard* won't cook. Its adventurous menu includes dishes like blood sausage with apple and pine nuts, and a grilled rabbit for two (375 kr). Tues–Thurs 5pm–midnight, Fri & Sat 5pm–2am.

Falafel Baghdad Annelundsgatan 59. Malmö is famous for its falafel and this simple place near Rosengård, where local hero Zlatan Ibrahimović grew up, is one of the originals. Daily 10am–11pm.

Hai Davidshallstorg 5. Malmö's best sushi and sashimi is served in this buzzing restaurant on elegant Davidshallstorg. There's a new lunch menu (95kr) every weekday. Mon–Thurs 11.30am–10pm, Fri 11.30am–11pm, Sat noon–11pm, Sun 2–9pm.

Lilla Kafferosteriet Baltzarsgatan 24. Caffeine-hungry Swedes flock to this mustard-coloured café, which specializes in coffee made from newly roasted beans. The breakfast buffet (8–11am on weekdays; 95kr) is a great way to kick-start the day. Mon–Fri 8am–6pm, Sat 10am–5pm, Sun 11am–5pm.

Restaurang Jörgen Inside the Frans Suell och Jörgen Kocks Gymnasium (high school) at Kungsgatan 44. Lunch at this restaurant, run by trainee students, includes a hot main, salad and a dessert. At 65kr, it's unbeatable value. Mon–Thurs 11.30am–12.45pm, Fri 11.30am–12.15pm during term time.

DRINKING AND NIGHTLIFE

★**Babel** Spångatan 38 W babelmalmo.se. This old red-brick church spends most of its time shaking to the sounds of local bands, but it also hosts club nights, comedy shows and documentary screenings. Entry usually 80–140kr. Hours vary with each event; see website.

Belle Epoque Södra Skolgatan 43 W belle-epoque.se. Eating here is expensive (mains around 200kr) so come later on in the evening, when DJs play to a young crowd of cocktail-sipping party people. Wed–Sat 6pm–1am.

Häng Bar Kristianstadsgatan 7b. With a covered seating area out front and a menu that features cheap nibbles like chicken wings (50kr), this is a decent spot for slurping a

33

beer (from 48kr), listening to music and people-watching. There are occasional comedy shows, too. Daily 4pm–1am. **Malmö Brewing Co** Bergsgatan 33. Sup pale ales, pilsners and porters at the city's best microbrewery. The pub is open late, and on Friday evenings you can take a tour of the brewery itself. Mon–Thurs 4pm–midnight, Fri 4pm–3am, Sat noon–3pm.

Moriska Paviljongen Norra Parkgatan 2 ⓦmoriskapaviljongen.se. This quirky Moorish-style pavilion in a park puts on various club nights throughout the year, covering everything from afrobeat to rock. It's best to buy tickets in advance if you can. See website for specific event times.

LUND

Just a short hop inland from Malmö, the pretty university town of **LUND** makes for a pleasant afternoon wander. It's often voted one of the best places to live in Sweden, and with its quaint cobbled streets, relaxed pace of life and mix of well-heeled residents and students from across the world, it's easy to see why. The high student population may account for the huge number of bikes you'll see across the city.

The main sight in town is the impressive, twin-towered **cathedral** (Mon–Fri 8am–6pm, Sat 9.30am–5pm, Sun 9.30am–6pm), one of Scandinavia's finest medieval buildings. Inside is a quirky attraction: a fifteenth-century astronomical clock from which two mechanical knights pop out and clash swords as the clock strikes (Mon–Sat noon & 3pm, Sun 1pm & 3pm). Surrounding the cathedral are several grand nineteenth-century buildings belonging to the university. Also nearby is the entrance to the vast **Kulturen** open-air museum (May–Aug daily 10am–5pm; 120kr; Sept–April Tues–Sun noon–4pm; 90kr; ⓦkulturen.com), a village in itself – full of perfectly preserved cottages and permanent exhibitions covering everything from Viking weapons to modernist design. Student discounts offered.

ARRIVAL AND INFORMATION

By train The train station is towards the west of town, an easy walk from the centre.

Destinations Gothenburg (hourly; 3hr); Helsingborg (every 10min; 30–40min); Malmö (every 5–10min; 10min); Stockholm (hourly; 4hr 20min).

By bus Frequent buses arrive and depart from the train station.

Destinations Gothenburg (5–6 daily; 3hr 25min); Copenhagen (1–2 daily; 1hr 35min).

Tourist information The tourist office is just off Stortorget at Botulfsgatan 1a (June–Aug Mon–Fri 10am–6pm, Sat 11am–3pm, Sun 11am–3pm; Sept–May Mon–Fri 10am–6pm, Sat 10am–3pm; ☎046 35 50 40, ⓦvisitlund.se).

GETTING AROUND

By bike To rent a bike, head to Fridhems Cyckelaffär at Bredgatan 32, a 10min walk from the train station (150kr for first day, 100kr/day thereafter).

ACCOMMODATION AND EATING

Since Lund's famous train hostel closed down, there's been a serious shortage of affordable rooms (nearby Malmö is a much better bet for budget travellers).

CheckInn Hantverksgatan 6 ☎072 329 08 00, ⓦcheckinn.se. If you get stuck in Lund, this hotel-style B&B in a couple of pretty houses (with single and double rooms) is one of the cheaper spots. Doubles discounted by 100kr Fri & Sat. Doubles **995kr**

Saluhallen Mårtenstorget 1. This indoor market has all the ingredients you need to put together a cheap picnic. Inside, *Gröna Deli* sells tasty salads with smoked salmon (69kr). Most shops Mon–Fri 10am–6pm, Sat 10am–4pm.

Winstrup Hostel Winstrupsgatan 3 ☎072 329 08 00, ⓦwinstruphostel.se. The only proper hostel in Lund is run by the same folks as *CheckInn* (above). It's clean, modern and comfortable, with bright dorms and a roomy kitchen. Prices are high, though. A breakfast buffet is available in the mornings for 95kr per person. Dorms **595kr**

GOTLAND

Sweden's largest island, **GOTLAND** is packed with historical intrigue, lined with great beaches, and, in summer at least, full of partying students. The star attraction is the beautifully preserved medieval town of **Visby**, though the rest of the island is also well worth exploring, especially by bike or car.

WHAT TO SEE AND DO

Once the Baltic's main trading centre, **VISBY** is a heavily fortified and beautifully preserved medieval town, full of crumbling churches and cute half-timbered houses. The best approach is to simply get lost in its warren of cobbled alleyways, using the thirteenth-century walls circling the town as a reference point. After a while you'll find your way to the main open space, **Stora Torget**, where bars and restaurants cater to a happy crowd of holidaying Swedes.

Visby's museums

Established in the late nineteenth century, **Gotlands Fornsal** (daily 10am–6pm; 120kr, under 20s free; ⓦgotlandsmuseum.se) has exhibitions about everything from Viking rune stones and gold to the macabre discovery of shallow graves that held the bones of townsfolk executed in the Middle Ages.

Behind the museum is Visby's art gallery or **Konstmuseum** (daily 10am–6pm; 80kr, or 160kr with entry to Gotlands Fornsal), mostly focused on paintings by islanders and Swedes from further afield.

Visby cathedral and church ruins

Visby's graceful **cathedral**, St Maria (daily 9am–5pm), is a short walk west of Stora Torget. Its three towers, two octagonal and one square, can be seen for kilometres around. Of the town's ruined churches, the most impressive and photogenic are **St Hans** on St Hansgatan and **St Katarina** on the eastern side of Stora Torget.

The rest of the island

Tofta Strand, 20km south of Visby (take bus #10 or rent a car; see below), is one of the island's most picturesque sandy beaches. It's packed out in summertime, especially during week 29 (otherwise known as Stockholm Week; most Swedes can tell you off the top of their head which week of the year we are in) when rich kids from the capital invade the island, sending prices sky-high. To avoid the crowds it's often worth checking out the beaches on the eastern side of the island instead. Buses run across the island but services are infrequent, so renting a car makes things easier. With your own wheels you can also take a trip up to **Fårö**, Gotland's tiny sister island (the ferry is free, with frequent crossings during summer), where you'll find the beach resort of Sudersand, and the mysterious-looking sea stacks known as Langhammars, on the wind-battered

north coast. Halfway to the ferry port on Gotland, the caves at **Lummelunda**, a 14km drive north of Visby (daily: May to mid-July & mid-Aug to Sept 10am–1/5pm, mid-July to mid-Aug 9am–6pm; 140kr), make for an interesting stop. Take bus #1 from Visby if using public transport.

ARRIVAL AND INFORMATION

By plane Several airlines, including BRA (ⓦflygbra.se), SAS (ⓦsas.se) and Norwegian (ⓦnorwegian.com), fly to Gotland, with year-round services running from Stockholm and Gothenburg. Book ahead and it's possible to fly Stockholm–Visby one-way for around 400kr, even in high season. The airport is 4km north of Visby. An infrequent bus service runs into the centre of town in summer (June–Aug; 60kr; see ⓦflygbussarna.se for times). Otherwise, a taxi costs around 150kr.

By ferry Visby is accessible by ferry from the mainland ports of Nynäshamn, a 1hr train ride south of Stockholm, and Oskarshamn, in Sweden's southeast. Both crossings are run by Destination Gotland (☏0771 22 33 00, ⓦdestinationgotland.se), arriving at the harbour, a 10–15min walk west of Visby. One-way tickets start at 258kr for adults and 206kr for under-25s. If you have an InterRail pass you're eligible for a discount, but you'll need to call ahead to get it.

Destinations Nynäshamn (for Stockholm; up to 5 daily; 3hr 15min); Oskarshamn (for southern Sweden; up to 3 daily, 3hr).

Tourist information Donners Plats 1, near the ferry terminal (daily 9am–6pm; ☏0498 20 17 00, ⓦgotland .com).

GETTING AROUND

By bus Visby's main bus terminal is beyond the town wall to the east, on Kung Magnus Väg. Tickets for single trips start at 25kr.

By car Car rental at Mickes Biluthyrning, down by the ferry terminal (☏0498 26 62 62, ⓦmickesbiluthyrning.se; summer 350kr/day, otherwise 300kr/day). Good selection of old VWs and the like at bargain prices.

By bike Bike rental from Gotlands Cykeluthyrning, Skeppsbron 2, near to the tourist office (June–Aug daily 9am–6pm; May & Sept daily limited hours; from 80kr/day; ☏0498 21 41 33, ⓦgotlandscykeluthyrning.com).

ACCOMMODATION

Accommodation prices skyrocket in summer, putting all but the cheapest hostels out of the reach of budget travellers. However, some of Gotland's mid-range hotels cut their rates by as much as fifty per cent at colder times of the year, making a winter break more affordable.

33

STF Hostel Lärbro/Grannen Around 1km north of Lärbro, in the north of the island ☏ 0498 22 50 33, ⓦ svenskaturistforeningen.se. In a peaceful wooded area 35km from Visby, this no-frills hostel has small rooms, a sauna and a sociable TV area. Doubles 490kr

Visby Fängelse Skeppsbron 1 ☏ 0498 20 60 50, ⓦ visbyfangelse.se. Striking youth hostel in a converted prison near the waterfront, with beds in "cells" that sleep between 2 and 6 guests. Book ahead in summer. Dorms 450kr, doubles 750kr

Visby Logi St Hansgatan 31/Hästgatan 14 ☏ 070 752 20 55, ⓦ visbylogi.se. Two beautiful historic homes in the heart of Visby converted into double and single rooms (shared bathroom). No breakfast but kitchen facilities available. Doubles 650kr

Visby Strandby 4km northeast of Visby ☏ 049 821 21 57. Holiday houses and a pleasant campsite just beside Snäckviken beach, about 4km from the town centre. Discount on camping prices for under-25s. Camping/person 195kr, cabins 700kr

EATING, DRINKING AND NIGHTLIFE

Black Sheep Arms St Hansgatan 51. English-style bar serving up pub grub (fish and chips 169kr) and a wide selection of beers; a favourite with locals and tourists alike. Sun–Thurs noon–midnight, Fri & Sat 5pm–1am.

Gutekällaren Lilla Torggränd 3 ⓦ gutekallaren.com. With bars inside and out, this club complex is heaving with bronzed, dressed-up twenty-somethings all summer, when it attracts Sweden's top DJ talent. Entry sometimes free before 11pm. June–Aug daily 9pm–3am.

★ **Munkkällaren** Stora Torget 1 ⓦ munkkallaren.se. Visby nightlife stalwart with live bands and a big party vibe later in the evening, particularly on Thurs and Fri. The restaurant serves up decent grub, and much of the large beer selection is reduced during happy hour (4–6pm Fri). Daily 4pm–3am.

Score Hamnplan 5. This American-style sports bar by the water is best visited on a Friday night, when dishes on the special after-work menu (pizza, ribs and onion rings) cost 99kr. Fri 4pm–late, Sat noon–late.

Surfers Södra Kyrkogatan 1 ⓦ surfersvisby.se. An unusual concept for medieval Visby: sweet and peppery Szechuan food served tapas style, with each dish costing 85kr (there's a discount for takeaway orders). Good cocktail list too. Daily 5pm–late.

Central Sweden

The rural Sweden of most visitors' imaginations begins in the central areas of the interior: vast tracts of forest,

THE INLANDSBANAN

Among the most enthralling of Europe's train journeys, the **Inlandsbanan** (Inland Railway) cuts a route through 1300km of Sweden's best-looking scenery. The quaint, toy-like line links central Sweden with Gällivare in the north, a two-day trip if attempted without a break. The full railway (☏ 0771 53 53 53, ⓦ inlandsbanan .com) is open from June to the end of August only.

Tickets Fares are calculated per kilometre – for example, Mora to Östersund costs 596kr, Östersund to Gällivare is 1378kr; reserving a seat costs 50kr per journey.

Discounts and rail cards InterRail and Eurail pass holders travel for free apart from the optional seat reservation fee. Students receive a 25 percent discount. The Inlandsbanan Card (1995kr) offers unlimited travel on the line for fourteen days.

peaceful lakes and log cabins. Deep-blue **Lake Siljan**, at the heart of the province of Dalarna, is a major draw, particularly in midsummer when it's a focus of festivities celebrating the long days and warm weather. From here one of Europe's classic rail journeys, the **Inlandsbanan**, begins its slow route north to the Arctic Circle via the towns of Orsa and Östersund.

LAKE SILJAN

Lake Siljan (ⓦ siljan.se) holds a special, misty-eyed place in the Swedish heart. Thousands head here in summer to stay at its iconic red lakeside cabins, paddle lazily in canoes and kayaks and hike deep into the surrounding countryside. If you happen to be here around Midsummer's Eve (*midsommarafton*), head to the town of **Leksand** at the south end of the lake, which holds a huge festival with maypole dances and longboat races.

Mora, at the north end of Siljan, has more facilities and is the starting point for the Inlandsbanan rail route (see box above). Right near the *STF Mora* hostel is the finish line for Vasaloppet – the gruelling 90km-long cross-country ski race held annually on the first Sunday in March. The small **Vasaloppet museum** here (July & Aug daily 10am–5pm; Sept–June Mon–Wed & Fri 8am–noon & 1pm–4.30pm; Thurs 8am–noon & 1pm–3pm; free; ⓦvasaloppet.se) tells the story of the event's ninety-five-year history.

ARRIVAL AND INFORMATION

By train From Stockholm, direct trains (at least 3 daily; roughly 4hr) make the scenic journey to Mora. There's also a direct service from Gothenburg (1 daily; 6hr 30min).

Tourist information The tourist office (Mon–Fri 10am–5pm, Sat 10am–2pm; ☎0250 59 20 20) across from Morastrand station at Köpmannagatan 3a gives out information on activities around the lake.

ACCOMMODATION

STF Mora 600m northeast of the tourist office at Fredsgatan 6 ☎0250 381 96. Rustic but welcoming hostel in a pleasant location by the Vasaloppet finish line. Sauna on site. Dorms 250kr, doubles 600kr

ORSA

The Inlandsbanan, having begun in Mora, makes its first stop at **ORSA**, fifteen minutes up the line, where the nearby **Orsa Björnpark** (daily 10am–3/6pm; 270kr; ⓦorsabjornpark.se; bus #342 to Grönklitt) provides the best chance to see the brown bears that roam over swathes of central Sweden. In winter, there's some great skiing, snowshoeing and walking to be done here.

ACCOMMODATION

Grönklitts Vandrarhem ☎0250 462 00, ⓦorsagronklitt.se. The Orsa Björnpark's on-site hostel has nice clean two- and four-bedded rooms in a building at the foot of one of the slopes. Twins 310kr

ÖSTERSUND

ÖSTERSUND, halfway point on the Inlandsbanan, is a very provincial but welcoming town on the shores of **Lake Storsjön**. It's most famous for the Loch Ness-style monster, the Storsjöodjur, said to inhabit the lake. More prosaically the town is also a major inland rail junction: as well as the Inlandsbanan, routes head east to Stockholm and west to Trondheim in Norway.

WHAT TO SEE AND DO

Apart from monster-spotting (there are eight official "observation points" along the lakeshore), the main thing to do is visit **Jamtli** (daily 11am–5pm; Sept–May closed Mon; free), a family-friendly, partly open-air **museum**, fifteen minutes' walk north from the centre along Rådhusgatan. The key exhibits are the ninth-century **Överhogdal tapestries**, whose simple hand-woven patterns of horses, dogs and other beasts date from the Viking Age.

From near Östersund's **harbour** you can take the bridge over the lake to **Frösön** island, site of the original Viking settlement here. In the colder months, when the lake freezes and is turned into an enormous winter park, it's possible to skate or walk from one side to the other.

ARRIVAL AND DEPARTURE

By plane Daily SAS flights from Stockholm land at Åre Östersund Airport on Frösön, a 15min bus ride from the city centre. Bus journeys are scheduled to match flight times. See ⓦnettbuss.se for exact times.

By train It's a 5min walk north into the centre from Östersund Centralstation.

Destinations Gällivare, for trains to Kiruna (1 daily; 14hr); Mora (1 daily, summer only; 6hr); Orsa (1 daily, summer only; 5hr 45min); Stockholm (2 daily; 5–6hr); Uppsala (2 daily; 4hr 15min–6hr).

By bus The main bus station is on Gustavs III Torg, off Rådhusgatan.

Destinations Kiruna, via Gällivare (1 daily; 12hr 45min); Mora (1–2 daily; 5hr 15min); Orsa (1–2 daily; 4hr 45min); Stockholm (1 daily; 8hr).

INFORMATION

Tourist information The tourist office is at Rådhusgatan 44 (Sept–May Mon–Fri 9am–5pm; June–Aug Mon–Fri 9am–5pm, Sat & Sun 10am–3pm; ☎063 701 17 00, ⓦvisitostersund.se).

ACCOMMODATION

Frösö Camping ☎077 110 12 00, ⓦfroso .nordiccamping.se; bus #3 from the centre. This is the most picturesque of Östersund's campsites, with views over Storsjön lake and several easy walking trails in the surrounding area. Open mid-May to mid-Sept. Per tent 245kr

Jamtli Hostel ☎063 150 300, ⓦjamtli.com. Quaint, appealing hostel in the grounds of the Jamtli open-air museum, with bright, clean dorms. Booking ahead is essential. Dorms 270kr

33

A FOODIE TOUR OF ÖSTERSUND

Östersund is no culinary capital, but there's plenty of good **local food** to wrap your taste buds around – from elk and wild mushrooms to tangy Jämtland cheese. One of the best ways to find out what the locals eat is to visit some of the quirky food shops dotted around town. The local tourist office (see p.1109) can provide you with all the info you need for a self-guided food tour. Although some of the restaurants are pricey, there are boutiques selling good-value, locally produced food – much of it organic.

Östersund Ledkrysset Biblioteksgatan 25 ☎ 063 10 33 10, ⊛ ostersundledkrysset.se. The most modern and sociable of the city's hostels, with immaculate dorms and private rooms housed in an attractive former fire station near the centre. Dorms 220kr, doubles 600kr

EATING AND DRINKING

Captain Cook Hamngatan 9. Australian-themed drinking haunt with decent food to boot. Try the Aussie burger, served with beetroot and a sourdough bun (169kr). Mon–Thurs 4–11pm, Fri 4pm–2am, Sat 1pm–2am.

Wedemarks Konditori Prästgatan 27. Popular bakery with a cosy downstairs lunch bar that serves up such treats as the delicious prawn-topped open sandwiches (85kr). Mon–Fri 8am–6pm, Sat 10am–5pm, Sun 11am–4pm.

Northern Sweden

Northern Sweden – Swedish Lapland – is the wildest, strangest part of the country. The region is famous for the Northern Lights and midnight sun as well as the Sámi people – reindeer herders who were once the sole inhabitants here. The Sámi are still visible, especially in the small town of **Jokkmokk**, which almost straddles the Arctic Circle. A couple of hundred kilometres further north, **Kiruna** is the access point for the celebrated **Icehotel**, a once-in-a-lifetime stay if you're feeling flush.

ARRIVAL AND DEPARTURE

By plane and train The most atmospheric way to reach the far north of the country is the Inlandsbanan rail line (see box, p.1108), although you can also get here via

regular rail services from Stockholm and by air to Kiruna. Flights also run to the east-coast city of Luleå, which has a direct train to Kiruna and Abisko.

THE ARCTIC CIRCLE AND JOKKMOKK

After brief stops at Arvidsjaur and Moskosel, the Inlandsbanan finally crosses the **Arctic Circle** at a point 7km south of Jokkmokk. Painted white rocks indicate this latitudinal milestone, making it an essential photo stop; killjoys will point out that the real Arctic Circle (66°33') has shifted a further kilometre north owing to changes in the earth's orbit, but no one seems to care.

JOKKMOKK itself is a welcome oasis after hours on a tiny train. The town is a renowned handicraft centre, with a Sámi educational college keeping the language and culture alive, and a lively winter market. The **Ájtte Museum** (mid-June to mid-Aug daily 9am–6pm; mid-Aug to mid-June Tues–Fri 10am–4pm, Sat 10am–4pm; 80kr) on Kyrkogatan takes a respectful look at Sámi culture. The permanent exhibitions house vivid Sámi costumes and a fascinating section on how the industrial age has affected the region and its people. Jokkmokk's **Great Winter Market** (first Thurs, Fri & Sat of Feb; ⊛ jokkmokksmarknad.se) is the best and busiest time to visit; you'll need to book accommodation a good six months in advance.

INFORMATION

Tourist information The tourist office is at Stortorget 4 (Mon–Fri 8.30am–noon & 1–4pm, with longer hours in summer; ☎ 0971 222 50, ⊛ destinationjokkmokk.se).

ACCOMMODATION

Arctic Camp Jokkmokk ☎ 0971 12370, ⊛ arcticcampjokkmokk.se. If you're washed out from the long journey to get here, try this campsite which also has family-friendly, 2-bed cabins plus heated swimming pools in a lakeside location 3.5km east of Jokkmokk. Camping/tent 185kr, cabins 440kr

Jokkmokk Hostel Åsgatan 20 ☎ 070 366 46 45, ⊛ stfturist.se. A good alternative to camping, this grand 1920s house has modern rooms plus some single-sex dorms. There's a small reading room upstairs, and handy kitchen facilities. Dorms 300kr, doubles 700kr

KIRUNA

With its nearby airport, rail connections to Norway and proximity to the *Icehotel* (see box below), **Kiruna**, 145km north of the Arctic Circle, has become the unlikely tourist hub for Swedish Lapland. The city is dominated by its iron ore mine, the world's largest, and became a focus during World War II, when the supply of iron was fought over by the Germans and Allies. Be sure to take plenty of photos of Kiruna as you walk around: the vast mine is continuing to expand, threatening the city's vital infrastructure, and many of today's landmarks have already been scheduled for demolition. Between now and 2035, 2500 homes plus shops, schools and many of Kiruna's best-known buildings – including the huge town hall – will be knocked down and rebuilt 3km to the east.

To see why the city has to move, you can take a tour of the **mine** (in English at 11am and 3pm daily during summer; book ahead at the tourist office; 345kr; student discounts available), run by mining company LKAB. Descending more than 500m below the surface, you'll learn about the mine's history and the techniques used for extracting iron ore.

★ TREAT YOURSELF

Icehotel 17km west of Kiruna in the small village of Jukkasjärvi ⓦ icehotel .com; bus #501 from Kiruna, get off at Jukkasjärvi. If you've made it this far north, a visit to Sweden's world-famous *Icehotel* is a tempting prospect. Although the hotel operates year-round, the obvious time to come is Dec–April when the fairytale-like ice structure is in place; a visitor pass (325kr) allows you a look inside the rooms. If you can stump up the cash, you could consider spending a night in its igloo-like conditions; temperatures hover around -5°C to -8°C, although you'll be toasty warm, wrapped up tight in an army sleeping bag and lying on reindeer skins. A cheaper alternative is a night in the hotel's regular, heated chalets. Doubles **4060kr**, chalets **2060kr**

ARRIVAL AND DEPARTURE

By plane Kiruna's airport is 10km southwest of the city. An airport bus (110kr) is on hand for the 20-minute journey; otherwise take a shared taxi (350kr/car).

By train Kiruna's original train station is now closed because of the ongoing project to move the city. Train services now call at a temporary station, 1.5km north of the city. Free shuttles meet the trains and take you into the centre.

Destinations Abisko Turiststation (4 daily; 1hr 30min); Luleå (up to 7 daily; 3hr 30min–5hr); Narvik (4 daily; 3hr); Stockholm (1 daily; 18hr).

By bus The bus station is at the top of Skolgatan, just across the road from the old city hall.

Destinations Luleå (1–2 daily; 5hr 10min); Gällivare (2–3 daily; 1hr 30min–1hr 50min); Jukkasjärvi (for the *Icehotel*; at least 2 daily; 30min–1hr).

INFORMATION AND TOURS

Tourist information Inside Folkets Hus, on the main square at Lars Janssonsgatan 17 (Mon–Fri 8.30am–5pm, Sat 8.30am–11.15am & noon–3pm; ☎ 0980 188 80, ⓦ kirunalapland.se).

Tours If you want to get out into the countryside but don't fancy doing it alone, contact Kiruna Guidetur (☎ 098 08 11 10, ⓦ kirunaguidetur.com), which arranges elk safaris, snowmobile excursions (including a trip from Kiruna to the *Icehotel*) and dogsled rides.

ACCOMMODATION

Camp Ripan Campingvägen 5 ☎ 098 063 000, ⓦ ripan.se/en. Family-oriented hotel with an on-site restaurant, spa and swimming pool. You can also camp here and – light pollution permitting – may be able to see the Northern Lights. Camping/tent **225kr**, doubles **1115kr**

Kiruna Vandrarhem Bergmästaregatan 7 ☎ 098 017 000, ⓦ kirunahostel.com. Sociable hostel a 5min walk from the bus station, with TV, sauna and kitchen facilities. Breakfast is available in the attached restaurant. Dorms **265kr**, doubles **945kr**

Yellow House Hantverkaregatan 25 ☎ 0980 137 50, ⓦ yellowhouse.nu. A cosy independent hostel that spreads across two yellow houses. It's a little dated but it's cosy and warm enough to be welcoming on a winter's day. Advance booking recommended in summer. Dorms **170kr**, twins **440kr**

EATING AND DRINKING

Bishops Arms Föreningsgatan 6. English-style pub selling burgers (169kr) and overpriced beer. Options are limited in Kiruna, and this place acts as one of the town's few social hubs. Sun & Mon 4–11pm, Tues–Thurs 4pm–midnight, Fri 4pm–1am, Sat noon–1am.

33

Landströms Kök & Bar Föreningsgatan 11. More expensive than the *Bishops Arms* pub, with most mains 200–270kr, but the menu includes specialities such as reindeer and Arctic char. Mon, Tues & Thurs 6–11pm, Wed 6pm–12.30am, Fri & Sat 6pm–1am.

Thai Kitchen Vänortsgatan 8. A friendly little Thai place near the tourist office, where you can enjoy a yellow curry with king prawns for 00kr. This food is perfect when you're frozen to the bone. Mon–Fri 11am–9pm, Sat noon–8pm.

ABISKO AND THE KUNGSLEDEN TRAIL

Sweden's premier trek, **Kungsleden** (the King's Trail) winds through 500km of wilderness from Abisko, 98km west of Kiruna, south to Hemavan. Mountain huts are spaced every 10–20km along the route to allow for a day's walk between them. The northern section of the trail between Abisko and Kebnekaise (86km) is the most popular and well worth tackling if you have around a week to spare.

Abisko, just an hour and twenty minutes by train from Kiruna on the Narvik line, is considered one of the world's best places for watching the Northern Lights. For more information on each section of the trail, visit ⓦstfturist.se.

ACCOMMODATION

Abisko Turiststation ⓦabisko.nu. This incredibly popular hostel/hotel is the starting point for the King's Trail (see above), and the slopes surrounding the outpost are popular with skiers and snowboarders alike. Dorms 425kr, doubles 1690kr

Switzerland

HIGHLIGHTS

❶ **Lausanne** Lively and extremely hilly town in a beautiful setting on Lake Geneva. **See p.1121**

❷ **Luzern** Covered wooden bridges, lake cruises and mountain views. **See p.1125**

❸ **Zürich** Trendy bars, cutting-edge clubs and a beautiful medieval Old Town. **See p.1128**

❹ **Jungfrau Region** Jaw-dropping Alpine scenery plus unlimited hiking and adventure sports. **See p.1132**

❺ **The Matterhorn** Iconic mountain, with a glacier delivering year-round skiing and snowboarding. **See p.1135**

HIGHLIGHTS ARE MARKED ON THE MAP ON P.1115

ROUGH COSTS

Daily budget Basic €60, occasional treat €90

Drink Beer €5

Food Fondue €22

Hostel/budget hotel €40/€100

Travel Train: Geneva–Zürich €30; bus: St Moritz–Lugano €74

FACT FILE

Population 8.3 million

Languages German, French, Italian, Romansch

Currency Swiss Franc (Fr.)

Capital Bern

International phone code ☏41

Time zone GMT +1hr

Introduction

All the stereotypes are true – cheese, chocolate, clocks, snowcapped mountains – but Switzerland also displays a winning blend of rural and urban, historic and modern. The major cities are cosmopolitan and vibrant, transport links are excellent, and the scenery takes your breath away. The country is diverse and multilingual, and almost all Swiss speak some English along with at least one of the country's four official languages.

34

In the French-speaking west, chic **Geneva** and sophisticated **Lausanne**, both on the shores of Lake Geneva, are at the heart of Suisse-Romande. Of the German-speaking cities, **Zürich** has diverse sightseeing and Switzerland's most LGBT-friendly scene, as well as easy access to the tiny principality of **Liechtenstein**. **Basel** and the capital, **Bern**, are quieter, each with an attractive historic core, while genteel **Luzern** has an appealing setting among lakes and mountains. The picturesque **Bernese Oberland** is the most visited Alpine area, although the loftiest Alps lie further south, where the **Matterhorn** towers above **Zermatt**. South of the Alps, Italian-speaking **Ticino** seems a world apart, particularly the palm-fringed lakeside towns of **Lugano** and **Locarno**.

CHRONOLOGY

800–58 BC A Celtic tribe, the Helvetians, inhabit what is now Switzerland.
58 BC Julius Caesar conquers the Helvetians.
1291 AD Three valleys unite against Habsburg rule, forming the basis of the Swiss Confederation.
1388 The Swiss Confederation defeats the Habsburgs.
1648 The Holy Roman Empire recognizes Swiss independence.
1719 Liechtenstein becomes an independent principality of the Holy Roman Empire.
1803 The Swiss start to produce chocolate.
1803–15 After a series of wars between France and other European powers, Napoleon is defeated and Switzerland's current borders are established.
1864 Red Cross founded in Geneva.
1880–81 Johanna Spyri writes *Heidi*.
1914 Switzerland remains neutral during World War I.
1920 The League of Nations headquarters are based in Geneva.
1921 Liechtenstein adopts Swiss currency.

1939–45 Swiss neutrality during World War II is tainted by the acceptance of Nazi plunder by Swiss banks.
1971 Swiss women are among the last in Europe to gain the vote.
1993 Liechtenstein elects Europe's youngest leader, Mario Frick, at the tender age of 28.
1998 Swiss banks agree to pay US$1.25 billion in compensation to Holocaust survivors and families.
2013 Swiss tennis number one, Roger Federer, is the most successful male player in the history of the game, having won seventeen Grand Slam titles.
2016 The new Gotthard Base Tunnel opens – the world's longest and deepest traffic tunnel and the first flat, low-level route through the Alps.

ARRIVAL AND DEPARTURE

Switzerland's main **airports** are at Geneva (wgva.ch), Zürich (wzurich-airport.com) and Basel (weuroairport.com), and to a lesser extent Bern (wflughafenbern.ch). Travelling to Switzerland from the continent, it's most likely you'll arrive by **train**. Services run from Paris to Geneva, Lausanne, Basel, Bern and Zürich. Geneva is also reached by trains from Lyon, southern France and Barcelona. Travelling via Strasbourg, or southwestern Germany, you'll probably arrive at Basel. Zürich is the main hub for trains from Bavaria, Austria, Italy and Eastern Europe. The most scenic way to arrive is by **ferry**, crossing Lake Maggiore from Italy, Lake Geneva from France or Lake Constance from Germany.

GETTING AROUND

Public transport is comprehensive. **Train** travel is comfortable, hassle-free and scenic, with many mountain routes attractions in their own right. The national

HIGHLIGHTS
1. Lausanne
2. Luzern
3. Zürich
4. Jungfrau Region
5. The Matterhorn

34

network, run by SBB-CFF-FFS, is seamlessly integrated with many routes, especially Alpine lines, operated by local companies. **Buses** take over where the rails run out – generally yellow postbuses, departing from train station forecourts. InterRail, Eurail and the Swiss Travel Pass (specified in the text as "IR", "ER" and "SP" respectively) give free travel on SBB and most minor lines. Bargain Supersaver train tickets are available up to two weeks in advance at ⓦrail.ch. The Swiss Pass also gives a fifty percent discount on most lake ferries, mountain railways, cable cars and postbuses (although some Alpine routes require a supplement), as well as free entrance to 490 museums and exhibitions across the country. There are also **regional passes** such as the Tell Pass in central Switzerland (ⓦtell-pass.ch), the Berner Oberland Regional Pass (ⓦregionalpass -berneroberland.ch) or the Léman-Alpes Regional Pass (ⓦgoldenpass.ch), giving some days of free travel and others at half-price. Most lake **ferries** run from April to October, and may duplicate routes covered more cheaply and quickly by rail.

ACCOMMODATION

Accommodation, although expensive, is invariably excellent. Tourist offices can often book rooms for free; some have boards detailing local hotels on the street or at railway stations, complete with courtesy phone. When you check in, ask for a **guest card**, giving free local transport and other discounts. **Hostels** (*Jugendherberge*; *Auberge de Jeunesse*; *Albergo/Ostello per la Gioventù*) offer great value for money (book ahead June–Sept). Part of the global HI hostels (ⓦhihostels .com) group, Swiss Youth Hostels (ⓦyouthhostels.ch; designated SH in this guide) has 52 properties around the country, with double and family rooms as well as dorms, plus dedicated "wellness" hostels, while Swiss Hostels (ⓦswiss hostels.com) has some lively, centrally located properties. Dorm beds typically cost around Fr.40, with reductions for members of the above groups. **Campsites** are clean and well equipped, charging Fr.6–13 per person plus Fr.7–13 per tent. Many require an international camping carnet. Camping outside official sites is illegal. **Hotels** are first-rate, but will stretch your budget; shared-bath doubles start around Fr.90 (average Fr.120), en suites around Fr.140.

FOOD AND DRINK

Eating out in Switzerland can punch a hole in your wallet. Burgers, pizza slices, kebabs and falafel are universal **snack** standbys, as

34

are *Bratwürst* sausages. Dairy products find their way into most dishes: cheese **fondue** – a pot of wine-laced molten cheese into which you dip cubes of bread – is the national dish. Another speciality is **raclette** – piquant molten cheese scraped over potatoes and pickles. A Swiss-German staple is **rösti**, grated potatoes topped with cheese, chopped ham or a fried egg. Almost everywhere offers vegetarian alternatives. **Cafés** and **restaurants** usually serve meals at set times (noon–2pm & 6–10pm), with only snacks available in between. To get the best value, make **lunch** your main meal, and opt for the dish of the day (*Tagesmenu, Tagestelle, plat/assiette du jour, piatto del giorno*) – substantial nosh for around Fr.20 or less. The same meal in the evening, or choosing à la carte anytime, can cost double. Major department stores, and some Coop or Migros supermarkets, have excellent-value self-service restaurants: a small/large plate costs about Fr.9/15, with as much fresh salad or hot food as you can pile onto it. There are supermarkets in most large stations, which open late seven days a week. Cafés are open from breakfast till midnight or 1am and often sell alcohol; **bars** and **pubs** tend to open from late afternoon into the evening only. **Beers** are invariably excellent, at Fr.5–8 for a glass (*e'Schtange, une pression, una birra*). Even the simplest places have **wine**, most affordably as *Offene Wein, vin ouvert, vino aperto* – a handful of house reds and whites chalked up on a board (small glass Fr.5–7).

ADVENTURE SPORTS IN SWITZERLAND

With its mountains, glaciers, deep gorges and fast-flowing rivers, Switzerland is made for **adventure sports**. In winter it's home to some of the world's best **ski and snowboard** resorts, while in summer countless outfits offer activities such as **kayaking** (Fr.80/half-day), **river-rafting** (Fr.100/half-day), **bungee-jumping** (from Fr.130), **zorbing** (Fr.125), **zip lining** (Fr.40), **hang-gliding** (Fr.200), **paragliding** (Fr.170) and **skydiving** (Fr.410). You can book most of these activities in various locations across the country through Swiss Raft (ⓦswissraft.ch).

CULTURE AND ETIQUETTE

It's not customary to **tip**; if you're impressed by the service, round up your bill to the nearest franc.

SPORTS AND ACTIVITIES

Spectacular scenery and an excellent transport infrastructure combine to make Switzerland one of Europe's top destinations for skiing, hiking and climbing. For **skiers and snowboarders**, the choice is overwhelming: Verbier is renowned for its challenging off-piste skiing, while scenic Zermatt is suitable for all abilities. The picturesque resorts of the Jungfrau region – Grindelwald, Mürren and Wengen – are better suited for intermediates. Lift passes cost Fr.60–75 a day, from Fr.330 for six days. Glaciers at Saas Fee and Zermatt enable summer skiing. The Swiss love **hiking** – with over 60,000km of marked trails, most boasting stunning Alpine vistas, it's easy to see why. The Jungfrau and Matterhorn regions are particularly popular. Hiking trails are clearly signed in yellow; red signs mark the nationwide **cycling** network. Bikes (and trailers, e-bikes etc) can be rented from main stations (from Fr.27 half-day, Fr.35 day), and in summer the largest cities have free bike schemes (such as Züri rollt and Genèveroule). Ask at tourist offices or consult ⓦmyswitzerland.com for routes and tips.

COMMUNICATIONS

Main **post offices** open Monday to Friday 7.30am to 6pm, Saturday 8 to 11am. Most **public phones** take credit cards, some take Swiss Francs and euros. Phonecards (*taxcards*) are available from post offices and news kiosks and Swisscom shops. EU roaming regulations don't apply in Switzerland, so **mobile phone** costs are high – buying a prepaid Swisscom SIM card (from Swisscom shops, post offices and kiosks) is good value. **Wi-fi** (known as WLAN) is widespread, available free at most cafés, hotels and hostels.

SWITZERLAND AND LIECHTENSTEIN ONLINE

Ⓦ **myswitzerland.com** Tourist office site – vast, detailed and authoritative.

Ⓦ **postbus.ch** and Ⓦ **sbb.ch** Details of the postbus and rail networks, including Alpine routes.

Ⓦ **swissinfo.ch** News database in English, with good links.

Ⓦ **tourismus.li** The Liechtenstein tourist board.

EMERGENCIES

EU nationals with a valid European Health Insurance Card (EHIC) can claim state healthcare free or at reduced cost. Alternatively, pay **hospital** (*Spital, hôpital, ospedale*) bills up-front then claim the money back from your insurance provider. Every district has at least one 24-hour **pharmacy** (*Apotheke, pharmacie, farmacia*), the details of which are provided outside each local pharmacy.

INFORMATION

Tourist offices (*Verkehrsverein* or *Tourismus; Office du Tourisme; Ente Turistico*) distribute maps, accommodation and transport information, and are typically located near train stations. Staff usually speak English. Offices in smaller towns often close over lunch.

MONEY AND BANKS

Both Switzerland and Liechtenstein use the **Swiss franc** (CHF or Fr.), divided into 100 Rappen (Rp), centimes or centisimi (c). There are coins of 5c, 10c, 20c, 50c, Fr.1, Fr.2 and Fr.5, and notes of Fr.10, Fr.20, Fr.50, Fr.100, Fr.200 and Fr.1000. It's easiest to **change money** in train stations. **Banks** usually open Monday to Friday 8.30am to 4.30pm; some in cities and resorts also open Saturday 9am to 4pm. **Post offices** give a similar exchange

EMERGENCY NUMBERS

Police ☏ 117; Fire ☏ 118; Ambulance ☏ 144.

STUDENT AND YOUTH DISCOUNTS

With an **ISIC** card, you can take advantage of **student discounts** (up to fifty percent) at almost all **museums** and galleries. Although there is no student discount on cable-car tickets, in winter many resorts offer a youth discount on **lift passes**.

rate to banks, and **ATMs** are everywhere. Many shops and services, especially in tourist hubs, accept euros. At the time of writing, €1 was roughly equal to Fr.1.10, US$1 to Fr.0.97 and £1 to Fr.1.30.

OPENING HOURS AND HOLIDAYS

Shop hours are Monday to Friday 9am to 7pm, Saturday 8.30am to 4pm, sometimes with a lunch break and earlier closing in smaller towns. Many **museums** and attractions close on Monday. Almost everything is closed on **public holidays**: January 1, Good Friday and Easter Monday, Ascension Day, Whit Monday, December 25 and 26. In Switzerland, shops and banks close for all or part of the national holiday (Aug 1) and on a range of local holidays. Liechtenstein keeps May 1 as a public holiday, and August 15 as the national holiday.

Lake Geneva

French-speaking Switzerland, or Suisse Romande, occupies the western third of the country, comprising the shores of **Lake Geneva** (Lac Léman) and the hills and lakes to the north. **Geneva**, at the southwestern tip of Europe's largest Alpine lake, was once a haven for freethinkers from across Europe; now it's a city of diplomats and big business, but you'll see its more relaxed side by the lakeside on a warm day. Visible from the city is **Mont Blanc**, Western Europe's highest mountain (4807m). Halfway around the lake, **Lausanne** is a cultured, energetic town full of young people, with breathtaking views across the water to the French Alps. Further east is the stunning medieval **Château de Chillon**, which transfixed Byron and the Romantic poets. On a sunny day, the train ride around the northern shore is memorably scenic, though the excellent boat trip (ER & SP free, IR 50 percent; ⓦcgn.ch) brings home the full grandeur of the setting.

34

GENEVA

The struggle of **GENEVA** (Genève) for independence is inextricably linked with Puritanism. By 1602, when it won independence from Savoy, the city's religious zeal had painted it as the "Protestant Rome". Geneva joined the Swiss Confederation in 1815, with a reputation for being somewhat dull that it still struggles to shake off. Today, there is plenty for budget travellers, with its attractive lake, beautiful Old Town and many galleries.

WHAT TO SEE AND DO

The **Rive Gauche**, on the south bank, is a grid of waterfront streets comprising the main shopping and business districts, with the Old Town, Switzerland's largest, above them. Further south is **Carouge**, characterized by picturesque Italianate architecture and artisans' shops. Behind the grand hotels lining the northern waterfront, **Rive Droite**, is the main station and the cosmopolitan (and in places sleazy) **Les Pâquis** district, full of cheap ethnic eateries. Further north are the dozens of international bodies headquartered in Geneva, including the UN.

Rive Gauche and the Old Town

The roaring 140m-high plume of Geneva's trademark **Jet d'Eau** erupts on the Rive Gauche, beyond the ornamental flowerbeds of the Jardin Anglais. South of Rive Gauche is the main thoroughfare of the **Old Town**, the steep, cobbled Grande Rue. Here, among jewellery shops and galleries, you'll find the seventeenth-century **Hôtel de Ville** and arcaded armoury. A block away, the predominantly Gothic **Cathédrale St-Pierre** (June–Sept Mon–Fri 9.30am–6.30pm, Sat 9.30am–5pm, Sun noon–6.30pm; Oct–May Mon–Sat

10am–5.30pm, Sun noon–5.30pm) has an eighteenth-century Neoclassical facade, and is where Calvin preached from 1536–64 – climb the cathedral's 157 steps for sweeping city and lake views. Behind the cathedral, in the eighteenth-century Maison Mallet, the **Musée Internationale de la Réforme** (Tues–Sun 10am–5pm; Fr.13; ⓦmusee-reforme.ch) documents Geneva's contribution to the Reformation. Just beyond is the hub of the Old Town, **Place du Bourg-de-Four**, a picturesque split-level square ringed by cafés. Alleys wind down from here to a lovely terrace, the Promenade de la Treille, with the world's longest wooden bench (126m). Beneath this, in the university park, the **Wall of the Reformation** (1909–17) has statues of the leading reformist preachers.

The Musée d'Art et d'Histoire

Just east of the Old Town, the sizeable **Musée d'Art et d'Histoire**, Rue Charles-Galland 2 (Tues–Sun 11am–6pm; permanent collection free, temporary exhibitions Fr.5; ⓦmah-geneve.ch), houses impressive collections of archeology, armour and weaponry, and fine arts.

Quartier des Bains

In a former industrial area west of the Old Town on Rue des Bains, the **Quartier des Bains** (ⓦquartierdesbains.ch) is home to nine galleries and five cultural institutions dedicated to contemporary art. The highlights of the district include **MAMCO** (Tues–Fri noon–6pm, Sat & Sun 11am–6pm; Fr.8, students Fr.6; free first Sun of month and first Wed from 6–9pm; ⓦmamco.ch), which hosts thought-provoking exhibitions by emerging international artists, and the **Centre d'Art Contemporain de Genève** (Tues–Sun 11am–6pm; Fr.5; ⓦcentre .ch), which has shown works by the likes of Olaf Breuning, Gilbert & George and KLAT in its time.

Palais des Nations, Musée International de la Croix-Rouge and the Jardin Botaniques

About 1km north of the station stands the imposing UN complex (tram #15 to Nations). One-hour tours of the **Palais**

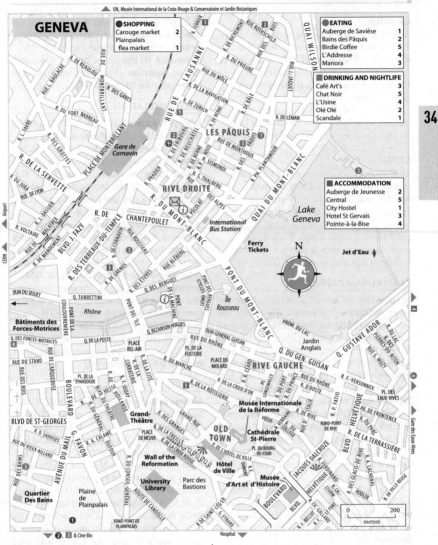

GENEVA

● **SHOPPING**
Carouge market 2
Plainpalais
flea market 1

● **EATING**
Auberge de Savièse 1
Bains des Pâquis 2
Birdie Coffee 5
L'Addresse 3
Manora 3

■ **DRINKING AND NIGHTLIFE**
Café Art's 3
Chat Noir 5
L'Usine 4
Olé Olé 2
Scandale 1

■ **ACCOMMODATION**
Auberge de Jeunesse 2
Central 5
City Hostel 1
Hotel St Gervais 3
Pointe-à-la-Bise 4

34

des Nations (April–Aug Mon–Sat 10.30am, noon, 2.30pm & 4pm; Sept–March Mon–Fri 10.30am, noon, 2.30pm & 4pm; Fr.12; passport required; ⓦunog.ch) start in the new wing (entry 14 Av de la Paix) and continue to the original Palais des Nations, built from 1929–38 to house the League of Nations. The highlight is the Council Chamber, with allegorical ceiling murals by José-Maria Sert. Just beyond the UN, the thought-provoking **Musée International**

de la Croix-Rouge (Tues–Sun 10am–5pm, April–Oct until 6pm; Fr.15, students Fr.7; ⓦredcrossmuseum.ch; bus #8 to Appia) explains the Red Cross's work and its response to humanitarian crises. Between the lake and the UN, the **Conservatoire et Jardin Botaniques** (daily April to late Oct 8am–7pm; late Oct to March 9.30am–5pm; free; ⓦcjb-geneve .ch) boasts 70 acres of gardens and one of the world's largest collections of preserved plants.

34

Carouge

Ten minutes south of the centre by tram #12 or #15, **Carouge** was built by the king of Sardinia in the 1750s as a separate town for Catholics and Jews. Its low Italianate houses and leafy streets now house fashion designers and small galleries, and the area's reputation as an outpost of tolerance and hedonism lives on in its numerous cafés and music bars.

CERN

Twenty minutes northwest of Cornavin station (tram #13), CERN Globe of Science and Innovation (Mon–Sat 10am–5pm; free; ⓦcern.ch/expoglobe) houses the Universe of Particles exhibition, a surprisingly fascinating exploration of particle physics. Reserve online in advance and bring ID.

ARRIVAL AND DEPARTURE

By plane Trains and buses (#5/10) run regularly from the airport, 4km northwest, into central Geneva. Get a free public transport ticket (valid for 80min) from the machines in the baggage reclaim hall.

By train The central station, Cornavin, lies at the head of Rue du Mont-Blanc. Trains from Paris, Lyon and southern France arrive in a separate French section of the station; local French trains from Annecy/Chamonix terminate at Gare des Eaux-Vives, east of town (tram #12/16/17 into the centre).

Destinations Basel (2 hourly; 2hr 55min); Bern (every 30min; 1hr 50min); Lausanne (7 hourly; 50min); Lyon (8 daily; 1hr 55min); Marseille (daily; 3hr 45min); Milan (3 daily; 4hr); Paris (8 daily; 3hr 15min); Zürich (every 30min; 2hr 50min).

By bus The international bus station (Gare Routière) is on Place Dorcière in the centre.

Destinations Chamonix (2 daily; 2hr 5min); Grenoble (5 daily; 2hr 15min); Paris (3 weekly (overnight); 8hr 10min).

By ferry Boats dock along the Quai du Mont-Blanc.

Destinations Lausanne (April–Oct 1–2 daily; 3hr 15min–4hr 50min).

INFORMATION

Tourist information Tourist offices at Rue du Mont-Blanc 18 (Mon 10am–6pm, Tues–Sat 9am–6pm, Sun 10am–4pm; ⓣ022 909 7000, ⓦgeneve.com) and at the airport (daily 8am–10pm).

GETTING AROUND

By public transport When you check in to any Geneva hotel, hostel or campsite, pick up a Geneva Transport Card for free transport across the city, including the lake *mouette* ferries. Alternatively, you can buy a Geneva Pass (Fr.26/37/45

for 24/36/72 hours) for free public transport, plus free and/or discounted access to museums, attractions and activities.

By bike The Genèveroule scheme (mid-April to mid-Oct; ⓦgeneveroule.ch) provides free bikes for 4 hours from Place de Montbrillant 17 (daily 8am–9pm), and other locations across the city (daily 9am–7pm).

ACCOMMODATION

Auberge de Jeunesse (HI) Rue Rothschild 30 ⓣ022 732 6260, ⓦyouthhostel.ch & ⓦyh-geneva.ch. A big, bustling and well-maintained 360-bed hostel. It has no kitchens but breakfast is included. Dorms **Fr.36**, doubles **Fr.100**

Central Rue de la Rôtisserie 2 ⓣ022 818 8100, ⓦhotelcentral.ch. This small, contemporary hotel just south of the Old Town has quiet, good-value, top-floor rooms, all of which have their own balconies. Doubles **Fr.115**

★**City Hostel** (SH) Rue Ferrier 2 ⓣ022 901 1500, ⓦcityhostel.ch. A friendly 100-bed backpacker place near the station. No meals are provided, but there's a kitchen on each corridor. Dorms **Fr.32**, doubles **Fr.89**

Hotel St Gervais Rue des Corps-Saints 20 ⓣ022 732 4572, ⓦstgervais-geneva.ch. Modest, atmospheric hotel just a 2min walk from the lake and Cornavin station. Its budget rooms come with a shared shower. Doubles **Fr.115**

Pointe-à-la-Bise ⓣ022 752 1296, ⓦcampingtcs.ch; bus #E or #G. Lakeside site in Vésanaz, some 7km northeast of the city, located by a nature reserve. Open March–Oct. Per person **Fr.12**, plus per tent **Fr.22**

EATING

Auberge de Savièse Rue des Pâquis 20 ⓣ022 732 8330. This friendly restaurant specializes in fondue (Fr.23–28) and raclette (Fr.6.50 for one portion, Fr.35 for all-you-can-eat), as well as lasagne and vegetarian dishes for Fr.23. Great for groups; book for weekends. Daily 10.30am–11pm.

Bains des Pâquis Quai du Mont-Blanc 30. This popular café-bar at the lakefront swimming area (Fr.2 entry) is a great spot to soak up some sun. Breakfast until 11.30am, then *plat du jour* (Fr.15). Mon–Sat 10am–9pm, Sun 9am–9pm.

Birdie Coffee Rue des Bains 40 ⓦbirdiecoffee.com. Quirky café where the masterful baristas serve some of Geneva's best coffee. They also dish up home-baked pastries (Fr.4), generous sandwiches (Fr.12) and vast salads (Fr.14). Mon–Fri 8am–2.30pm, Sat & Sun 10am–2.30pm.

L'Addresse Rue du 31 Décembre 32 ⓦladress.ch. Smart, urban loft in a former artists' workshop with a rooftop terrace. Serves Mediterranean cuisine, such as luxurious croque-monsieur (Fr.17) and gnocchi (Fr.15). Tues–Fri noon–2pm & 7.30–10pm, Sat noon–3pm & 7.30–10pm.

Manora Rue Cornavin 6. Deli counters on the ground floor of this department store sell good takeaway *foccacine* (Fr.4), pizza slices (Fr.4.80) and curries (Fr.6). There's also a self-service restaurant with roof terrace, serving salads, pizza and dishes of the day from Fr.11. Mon–Wed

8.30am–7pm, Thurs 8.30am–9pm, Fri 8.30am–7.30pm, Sat 8am–6pm.

DRINKING AND NIGHTLIFE

Café Art's Rue des Pâquis 17 ⓦcafe-arts.ch. Café-bar with a Parisian-style terrace and relaxed bohemian feel serving panini (Fr.12), omelettes (Fr.13), beer (Fr.8 for half a litre) and cocktails (Fr.15). Mon–Thurs 11am–2am, Fri 11am–4am, Sat 8am–4am, Sun 8am–2am.

Chat Noir Rue Vautier 13, Carouge ⓦchatnoir.ch. Bar and cellar venue with DJs, live music that could include anything from world to techno, and tasty tapas. Mon–Thurs 6pm–4am, Fri & Sat 5pm–5am.

L'Usine Place des Volontaires 4 ⓦusine.ch. Converted factory hosting diverse arts and music events, including club nights (hip-hop, breakbeat, electronica) by Zoo (ⓦlezoo.ch), while *leREZ* puts on gigs here. See website for times and details of gigs.

★ **Olé Olé** Rue de Fribourg 11. Lively tapas bar with great cocktails (Fr.15), wine (Fr.5 a glass) and beer (Fr.8 a bottle), as well as tapas (Fr.8) plus salads and burgers (Fr.12). Mon–Fri 11am–2am, Sat 5pm–2am.

Scandale Rue de Lausanne 24 ⓦlescandale.ch. Retro bar with comfy armchairs and DJs several nights a week. It also serves food; dish of the day Fr.18 and drinks from Fr.6. Mon & Sat 5pm–2am, Tues–Fri 11am–2am.

ENTERTAINMENT

In July and August, films are screened on the lakeside Quai Gustave-Ador (ⓦorangecinema.ch), and from mid-July to mid-August mainstream Hollywood films are screened open-air by the lakeside at Port-Noir (ⓦcinedulac.ch).

Cinéma Bio Rue St-Joseph 47, on the Place du Marché, Carouge ⓦcinema-bio.ch. A charming arthouse cinema with two screens, dating from 1912. Films cost Fr.16.50, students Fr.13.

Alhambra Rue de la Rôtisserie 10 ⓦalhambra-geneve.ch. Historical building housing a contemporary concert hall with bohemian café. Performances typically cost Fr.20–40.

SHOPPING AND MARKETS

Carouge market Carouge in general is a good choice for affordable and whimsical shopping; it's crammed with cute boutiques and hosts a colourful market. Wed & Sat 8am–1.30pm.

Plainpalais flea market Head for this flea market near the Old Town, where you can pick up anything from old records and retro kitchenware to gemstones. Wed & Sat 6am–6pm.

DIRECTORY

Consulates Australia, Chemin des Fins 2 ☎022 799 9100; Canada, Av. de l'Ariana 5 ☎022 919 9200; New Zealand, Chemin des Fins 2 ☎022 929 0350; US, Rue Versonnex 7 ☎022 840 5160. Embassies are in Bern.

Exchange At the train station by the ticket office (Mon–Fri 7am–8pm, Sat 7am–7pm, Sun 9am–1.30pm & 2.30–5.50pm).

Hospital Hôpitaux Universitaires, Rue Gabrielle-Perret-Gentil 2 ☎022 372 8120.

Left luggage At the train station (Mon–Fri 8.30am–6.45pm, Sat 9am–1pm & 2–6.30pm); also 24hr lockers (Fr.7–8).

Post office Rue du Mont-Blanc 18 (Mon–Fri 7.30am–6pm, Sat 9am–4pm).

Pharmacy Amavita, in the train station (Mon–Sat 7am–11pm, Sun 10am–11pm).

LAUSANNE

LAUSANNE is attractive and vibrant, set on a succession of south-facing terraces above Lake Geneva, with the Old Town at the top, the train station and commercial districts in the middle, and the former fishing village of **Ouchy**, now prime territory for waterfront café-lounging and strolling, at the bottom. Switzerland's biggest university makes this a lively, fun city. For chilled-out bars, head for the trendy Flon district.

WHAT TO SEE AND DO

To reach the central **Place St-François** from the train station, walk up the steep **rue du Petit-Chêne**, or take the metro to **Flon**; from the metro platforms, lifts raise you to the level of the giant Grand Pont, between **Place Bel-Air** on the left and Place St-François on the right. From here, rue St-François drops down into a valley and up again to the cobbled **Place de la Palud**, an ancient, fountained square flanked by the Renaissance town hall.

The Cathedral and around

From Place de la Palud the medieval Escaliers du Marché lead up to the **Cathedral** (daily 9am–7pm, winter closes 5.30pm; ⓜBessières), a fine Romanesque-Gothic jumble. Opposite is the **MUDAC Musée de Design et d'Arts Appliqués Contemporains** (July & Aug daily 11am–6pm; Sept–June Tues–Sun 11am–6pm; Fr.10, students Fr.5; ⓦmudac .ch), displaying contemporary glass and temporary exhibitions upstairs. Just across the road from the cathedral, with its main entrance on Place de la Riponne, the

34

34

Musée Cantonale des Beaux Arts, in a neo-Renaissance palace (Tues–Thurs 11am–6pm, Fri–Sun 11am–5pm; Fr.10, students Fr.5; ⓦmcba.ch), houses collections of fine arts from around the world, as well as smaller museums dedicated to history and zoology.

Lausanne suffered many medieval fires, and is the last city in Europe to keep alive the tradition of the **nightwatch**: every night, on the hour (10pm–2am), a sonorous-voiced civil servant calls from the cathedral tower "C'est le guet; il a sonné l'heure" ("This is the nightwatch; the hour has struck").

Collection de l'Art Brut

Ten minutes' walk west of Palud on Avenue Vinet (or bus #2, #3 or #21 to Beaulieu), the fascinating **Collection de l'Art Brut**, 11 av des Bergières (Tues–Sun 11am–6pm; July & Aug also Mon; Fr.10, students Fr.5, free first Sat of month; ⓦartbrut.ch), is devoted to utterly absorbing "outsider art".

Ouchy, The Olympic Museum and Musée de l'Elysée

Ouchy's waterfront hosts regular free music events in summer, and people come down here for a spot of café sunbathing or rollerblading. In a fine lakefront park just to the east, **The Olympic Museum** (Tues–Sun: May to mid-Oct 9am–6pm; mid-Oct to April 10am–6pm; Fr.15, students Fr.10; ⓦolympic.org/museum) features high-tech displays on the history of the Games. Above it in the same park, the **Musée de l'Elysée** (Tues–Sun 11am–6pm; Fr.8, students Fr.4, first Sat of month free entry and guided tours; ⓦelysee.ch) is an excellent photography museum.

ARRIVAL AND DEPARTURE

By train From the train station, metro line 2 runs down to Ouchy by the lake and up to Flon, Riponne and Bessières, for the cathedral area.

Destinations Basel (3 hourly; 2hr 15min); Bern (every 30min; 1hr 10min); Geneva (6 hourly; 35min); Milan (4 daily; 3hr 20min); Paris (5 daily; 3hr 40min); Zermatt (hourly, change at Visp; 3hr); Zürich (every 30min; 2hr 10min).

By ferry The ferry port is on Quai Jean-Pascal Delamulaz – head out of Ouchy metro station to the lake and it's just to the left/east. Note that ferries run mid-April to mid-Dec only.

Destinations Chillon (up to 4 daily; 1hr 30min–2hr 45min); Geneva (up to 18 daily; 3hr 15min–5hr); Montreux (up to 9 daily; 1hr 30min–2hr 15min); Vevey (up to 5 daily; 1hr–2hr 50min). Check times before you travel at ⓦcgn.ch.

INFORMATION

Tourist information Lausanne has three tourist offices (☎021 613 7392, ⓦlausanne-tourisme.ch): one in the train station (daily 9am–7pm); one facing Ouchy metro station (daily: May–Sept 9am–7pm; Oct–April 9am–6pm); and one in the Cathedral (Mon–Sat 9.30am–6.30pm, Sun 1–5.30pm; Oct–March closes 1–2pm).

ACCOMMODATION

Camping de Vidy ☎021 622 5000, ⓦcamping lausannevidy.ch; bus #1/2/6 west to Maladière and 5min walk (past the ruins of Roman Lousana). Large lakeside campsite with a supermarket and restaurant (April–Sept). Open all year. Per person **Fr.9**, plus per tent **Fr.16**

Jeunotel (HI) Chemin du Bois-de-Vaux 36 ☎021 626 0222, ⓦyouthhostel.ch/lausanne. Huge HI hostel beside the *Vidy* campsite with four-bed dorms and double rooms, plus cheap meals on request (Fr.17.50). Dorms **Fr.40**, doubles **Fr.98**

★**Lausanne Guest House** (SH) Chemin des Epinettes 4 ☎021 601 8000, ⓦlausanne-guesthouse.ch. Fabulous, friendly hostel with lake views, a kitchen, garden, plus four-bed dorms and double rooms. Dorms **Fr.40**, doubles **Fr.98**

Pension Bienvenue Rue du Simplon 2 ☎021 616 2986, ⓦwww.pension-bienvenue.ch. Respectable women-only guesthouse behind the station. It's very clean and friendly, with shared WCs and showers, wi-fi, kitchen and a good breakfast. Long stays available. Doubles **Fr.140**

EATING

Café des Artisans Rue Centrale 16. A lively bistro that is popular with students. It serves up simple food from wraps (Fr.8) and pasta (Fr.12) to steak & fries (Fr.24). Mon–Fri 8am–midnight, Sat 10am–midnight.

Café Romand Place St-François 2. The go-to spot for Lausanne's literati since 1951, this bustling, heart-warming place has cosy alcoves for beer, coffee and hearty Swiss fare. Dish of the day Fr.19. Mon–Sat 7am–midnight.

Holy Cow Rue Cheneau-de-Beurg 17, ⓦholycow.ch. A hip burger and craft beer joint that first launched here in Lausanne and has subsequently become one of Switzerland's most popular chains. Burgers Fr.10, beers Fr.6.90. Mon & Tues 11am–10pm, Wed–Sat 11am–11pm.

Laxmi Escaliers du Marché 5, ⓦlaxmi.ch. Authentic North Indian food, with plenty of vegetarian choices (mains around Fr.18). The all-you-can-eat lunch buffet (Mon–Thurs; Fr.19.80) is popular; takeaways are available. Mon–Sat 11.30am–2pm & 6.30–11pm, Sun 6.30–11pm.

Le Barbare Escaliers du Marché 27. Among the Old Town's rooftops, this atmospheric café makes Lausanne's

LAUSANNE FESTIVALS

The **Lausanne Estivale** (ⓦlausanne.ch), founded in 1986, runs from June to September with countless concerts, theatre productions, performances and impromptu events across the city. The big party is the free **Festival de la Cité** in early July (ⓦfestivalcite.ch), featuring music, dance and drama on open-air stages in the Old Town.

MONTREUX JAZZ FESTIVAL

The sleepy lakeside town of Montreux livens up during its star-studded **Montreux Jazz Festival** (ⓦmontreuxjazz .com), held in the first half of July. Since 1966, it's attracted the likes of Miles Davis and Ray Charles, but "jazz" is now something of a misnomer; today's festival features big-name acts from most music genres. Check online for tickets (Fr.60–240 for specific shows, Fr.1,420 for a Festival Pass), or just join the street parties and free entertainment around the lake.

best hot chocolate as well as pizzas and croque-monsieurs. There's a sun-trap terrace for summer and cosy interiors for winter. Mon–Sat 8.30am–midnight.

DRINKING AND NIGHTLIFE

Bleu Lézard Rue Jenni Enning 10 ⓦbleu-lezard.ch. Fashionable, lively café-bar with regular live music sets downstairs and excellent, seasonal, veggie-friendly food (including Sun brunch). Mon–Thurs 7am–1am, Fri 7am–2am, Sat 8am–2am, Sun 8am–1am.

Brasserie du Château Place du Tunnel 1 ⓦbiereduchateau.ch. Bar with tasty home-brewed beers, pub grub and funky music (DJs Thurs–Sat). Mon–Thurs 11am–1am, Fri & Sat 11am–2am, Sun 4pm–1am.

D! Club Place Centrale, Flon ⓦdclub.ch. Popular club in a former theatre with live acts plus DJs spinning electro and house. Thurs is student night. Thurs–Sat 11pm–5am.

MAD (Moulin à Danse) Rue de Genève 23, Flon ⓦmad .ch. At the hub of trendy Flon, this boisterous club boasts four dancefloors with cutting-edge DJs, plus a theatre, art galleries and alternative-style café. Daily 11pm–5am.

The Great Escape Rue de la Madeleine 18 ⓦthe-great .ch. A trendy, informal pub with a great terrace that is popular with locals. Mon–Thurs 11.30am–1am, Fri 11.30am–2am, Sat 10am–2am, Sun noon–1am.

DIRECTORY

Exchange At the train station (Mon–Wed & Fri 8am–6.30pm, Thurs 8am–8.30pm, Sat 8am–6pm, Sun 9am–1.20pm & 2.40–6pm).

Left luggage At the train station (Mon–Fri 8.30am–6.45pm, Sat & Sun 9am–1pm & 2–6.30pm).

CHÂTEAU DE CHILLON AND CHAPLIN'S WORLD

The highlight of a journey around Lake Geneva is the spectacular thirteenth-century **Château de Chillon** (daily: April–Sept 9am–7pm; March & Oct 9.30am–6pm; Nov–Feb 10am–5pm; Fr.12.50, students Fr.10.50; ⓦchillon.ch),

one of Europe's best-preserved medieval castles. Jutting into the lake and framed by craggy mountains, the whimsical castle was inspiration for Byron's poem *The Prisoner of Chillon*. To get here, take the hourly train to Veytaux-Chillon, the ferry (dating from 1904) from Lausanne or Montreux (4 daily; Fr.32, students Fr.10) or bus #1 east from Montreux station (every 10min).

Chillon is also home to **Chaplin's World**, Route de Fenil 2 (daily 10am–6pm; Fr.23, students Fr.21; ⓦchaplinsworld.com; bus #212 from Vevey), set in a 10-acre lakeside park. The famous film star's former house, it's now a museum dedicated to Chaplin, exhibiting his personal belongings and his studio, where you can watch a documentary about silent film.

The Swiss heartland

The Mittelland – between Lake Geneva and Zürich, flanked by the Jura range to the north and the high Alps to the south – is a region of lakes, gentle hills and some higher peaks. There's a wealth of cultural and historical interest in the cities of **Basel**, **Luzern** and the federal capital, **Bern**. Wherever you are, the mountains are never more than a couple of hours away by train.

BASEL

Sitting astride the Rhine where Switzerland, France and Germany touch,

BASEL (Bâle in French) is neither as picturesque as Bern or Luzern, nor as vibrant as Zürich. Yet it's a wealthy city, with a charming Old Town, excellent museums and galleries and some striking contemporary architecture. It also hosts the three-day Fasnacht **carnival** in February or March (@fasnacht.ch), beginning at 4am the Monday after Mardi Gras.

34

<hr>

WHAT TO SEE AND DO

The River Rhine curves through the city, with most attractions found in affluent **Grossbasel** (Greater Basel) on the south bank, including the historic Old Town (some 1km north of the station), which is centred on **Barfüsserplatz**. Across the river on the north bank, **Kleinbasel** (Little Basel) is the city's historical working-class quarter. The rivalry between the two districts is displayed by a replica statue of the Lällekeenig (Tongue King) near Mittlere Brücke: the original was built in 1640 on the Grossbasel bank, sticking his tongue out at Kleinbasel.

Historisches Museum and the Münster

The city's pre-eminence in the fifteenth and sixteenth centuries is demonstrated in the **Barfüsserkirche**, home since 1894 to the **Historisches Museum** (Tues–Sun 10am–5pm; Fr.15; free first Sun of month; @hmb.ch); don't miss the sumptuous medieval tapestries hidden behind protective blinds. On a terrace between the river and the Historisches Museum, the **Münster** (summer Mon–Fri 10am–5pm, Sat 10am–4pm, Sun 11.30am–5pm; winter Mon–Sat 11am–4pm, Sun 11.30am–4pm) contains the tomb of Renaissance humanist Erasmus.

Kunstmuseum and Museum für Gegenwartskunst

Just east of the Old Town at St Alban-Graben 16, Basel's **Kunstmuseum** (Tues–Sun 10am–6pm; Fr.15; free first Sun of month; @kunstmuseumbasel.ch) has a dazzling array of twentieth-century art, plus an outstanding medieval section, including the world's largest collection of paintings by Holbein. The riverside **Museum für Gegenwartskunst**, St Alban-Rheinweg 60 (Museum of

Contemporary Art; Tues–Sun 11am–5pm; Fr.12), displays installations by Frank Stella and Joseph Beuys.

Museum Jean Tinguely

On the north bank of the Rhine at Paul Sacher-Anlage 2, the **Museum Jean Tinguely** (Tues–Sun 11am–6pm; Fr.18, students Fr.10; @tinguely.ch), designed by Ticino architect Mario Botta, is dedicated to one of Switzerland's best-loved artists. Tinguely used scrap metal, plastic and everyday junk to create vast, grotesque and comical Monty Pythonesque machines that judder into life with the touch of a button.

Fondation Beyeler

Northeast of the Rhine, at Baselstrasse 101, the **Fondation Beyeler** (Mon, Tues & Thurs–Sun 10am–6pm, Wed 10am–8pm; Fr.25; @fondationbeyeler.ch) displays impressive artworks by the likes of Rodin, Cézanne, Mark Rothko and Paul Klee. Belonging to former art dealers Ernst and Hildy Beyeler, the collection is housed in a striking Renzo Piano building.

ARRIVAL AND DEPARTURE

By train Basel has two train stations serving three countries. The main Basel SBB is in Switzerland, but has a notionally French section entitled Bâle SNCF at its west end which handles trains from Paris and Strasbourg. Trams #8 and #11 shuttle to Barfüsserplatz. Some trains from Germany terminate at the notionally German Badischer Bahnhof (Basel Bad. for short), on the north side of the river, from where tram #6 runs to Barfüsserplatz.

Destinations Frankfurt (10 daily; 2hr 50min); Geneva (3 hourly; 2hr 40min); Interlaken (2 hourly; 2hr); Lausanne (2 hourly; 2hr 15min); Lugano (2 hourly; 3hr 55min); Luzern (4 hourly; 1hr 30min); Paris (6 daily; 3hr); Strasbourg (hourly; 1hr 20min); Zürich (5 hourly; 1hr).

INFORMATION

Tourist information Tourist offices at Steinenberg 14 (Mon–Fri 9am–6.30pm, Sat 9am–5pm, Sun 10am–3pm; ☎061 268 6868, @basel.com) and in the main train station (Mon–Fri 8.30am–6pm, Sat 9am–5pm, Sun 9am–3pm). Either office can provide a full list of Basel's museums and galleries. If you stay overnight you're entitled to a Mobility Ticket, giving free city transport; ask for it when you check in.

Basel Card This card (Fr.20/27/35 for 24/48/72hr) gives half-price museum entry, free city tours and discounts at restaurants, bars and clubs.

ACCOMMODATION

Basel Backpack (SH) Dornacherstr. 192 ☎ 061 333 0037, ⓦ baselbackpack.com; tram #15 or #16 to Tell Platz. Good hostel in a funky renovated factory/arts complex behind the station. Colour-coded dorms or numbered guesthouse rooms, bar, kitchen and industrial-style bathrooms. Dorms **Fr.32**, doubles **Fr.99**

Jugendherberge St Alban (HI) St Alban-Kirchrain 10 ☎ 061 272 0572, ⓦ youthhostel.ch. A former silk factory that has been refurbished by celebrated Swiss architects Buchner & Bründler, this hostel is in the central yet semi-secret St-Alban-Tal. Dorms **Fr.41**, doubles **Fr.132**

EATING

Consum Rheingasse 19 ⓦ consumbasel.ch. Excellent, popular wine bar in Kleinbasel that specializes in salamis and cheese, with lunch sandwiches around Fr.9 and sharing platters at Fr.15. Mon–Sat 11am till late, Sun 5pm till late.

Parterre Klybeckstr. 1. Lively Kleinbasel hangout with several outlets, this being the original. The menu is creative and vegetarian-friendly; mains Fr.19–35. Mon–Wed 10am–11pm, Thurs–Sat 9am–midnight, Sun 11am–11pm.

Zum Roten Engel Andreasplatz 15. This busy café serves up coffees and pastries on a pedestrianized cobbled square. There's a good Sunday brunch (11am–4pm) for Fr.19. Mon–Sat 9am–midnight, Sun 11am–10pm.

DRINKING AND NIGHTLIFE

Atlantis Klosterberg 13 ⓦ atlan-tis.ch. A Basel institution ('tis to locals) this restaurant and lounge-bar hosts jam-packed club nights at weekends. Minimum age women 18, men 20 – bring ID. Entry Fr.15. Club Fri & Sat 11pm–4am; restaurant Tues–Thurs 11.30am–2pm & 5pm–midnight, Fri 11.30am–2pm & 5–11pm, Sat 6–11pm.

Bird's Eye Kohlenberg 20 ⓦ birdseye.ch. Basel's main jazz venue, with live music by local and international musicians. Also hosts jazz workshops for adults and kids, some in English. Entry Fr.8–24. June–Aug Wed–Sat 8–11.30pm; Sept–May Tues–Sat 8–11.30pm.

Die Kuppel Binningerstrasse 14 ⓦ kuppel.ch. Popular local hangout near Basel Zoo. Expect everything from local to global bands, live DJs, reggae and funk to hip-hop. Thurs–Sat 10am–late.

Sud Burgweg 7 ⓦ sud.ch. Industrial-style Kleinbasel club in a converted brewery, which plays diverse music till the

small hours. There's also a small theatre and café on site. Thurs 9pm–1am, Fri & Sat 9pm–4.30am, Sun 10am–4pm.

LUZERN (LUCERNE)

An hour south of Basel, beautiful **LUZERN** offers captivating mountain views, lake cruises and a picturesque medieval quarter.

34

WHAT TO SEE AND DO

To the right of the train station, you're greeted by the striking KKL concert hall; busy Pilatusstrasse is to the left, where, 100m further along, you'll find the **Sammlung Rosengart gallery** (daily: April–Oct 10am–6pm; Nov–March 11am–5pm; Fr.18, students Fr.10), with its superb collection of twentieth-century art, notably by Picasso and Klee. The alleyways of the Old Town span both riverbanks, linked by two covered wooden bridges. The fourteenth-century **Kapellbrücke** was rebuilt after a fire in 1993; some of the seventeenth-century paintings fixed to its roof beams have been replaced by facsimiles. Northeast of the Old Town is **Löwenplatz**, dominated by the **Bourbaki Panorama** (daily: April–Oct 9am–6pm; Nov–March 10am–5pm; Fr.12; SP free), a 110m by 10m circular mural, depicting the flight of General Bourbaki's 87,000-strong army into Switzerland during the Franco-Prussian War. Just off the square is the **Löwendenkmal**, a dying lion hewn out of a cliff-face to commemorate seven hundred Swiss mercenaries killed by French revolutionaries in 1792.

Sonnenberg Bunker

Built beneath central Luzern during the Cold War, the seven-storey **Sonneberg Bunker** could accommodate 20,000 people, complete with a hospital, radio station and prison. Two-hour English-speaking tours of the bunker start from outside the Jesuitenkirche (Jesuit church), at Bahnhofstrasse 11a, at 11am on the last Sunday of the month (advance booking essential; Fr.30; ☎ 079 797 0917, ⓦ unterirdisch-ueberleben.ch).

Lake Luzern

Switzerland's most beautiful and dramatic by far, **Lake Luzern** has thickly wooded slopes rising sheer from the water. Don't leave town without taking a **boat trip** (every 30min; Fr.11–45, hop-on/hop-off day ticket Fr.24, ER & SP free, IR 50 percent discount; ⓦlakelucerne.ch).

ARRIVAL AND INFORMATION

By train The station sits at the south end of the Seebrücke, facing the docks for boats on Lake Luzern.

Destinations Basel (2 hourly; 1hr); Bern (hourly; 1hr 30min); Interlaken (hourly; 2hr 20min); Lausanne (hourly; 2hr 30min); Zürich (3 hourly; 50min).

Tourist information Tourist office at Zentralstr. 5 (May–Oct Mon–Fri 8.30am–7pm, Sat 9am–7pm, Sun 9am–5pm; Nov–March Mon–Fri 8.30am–5.30pm, Sat 9am–5pm, Sun 9am–1pm; ☎041 227 1717, ⓦluzern .org), on the west side of the railway station.

GETTING AROUND

By public transport Everything in the centre is easily reached on foot. If you book accommodation through Luzern Tourism (ⓦluzern.com) you'll receive a Visitor Card which gives free travel within the city.

By bike Bikes can be rented at the Velostation on the east side of the station (daily 7/8am–7pm), the HI hostel or *Backpackers Lucerne*.

ACCOMMODATION

Backpackers Lucerne (SH) Alpenquai 42 ☎041 360 0420, ⓦbackpackerslucerne.ch. A friendly place, with kitchen and bike rental but no breakfast, a 10min walk east from the station along the lake. Dorms **Fr.33**, doubles **Fr.78**

HI Jugendherberge Am Rotsee, Sedelstrasse 12 ☎041 420 8800, ⓦyouthhostel.ch/luzern; bus #18. A friendly modern hostel not far from the centre (the bus takes a roundabout route from the Bahnhof to Jugendherberge); it's a bit of a maze but has lots of pleasant common areas. Dorms **Fr.32**, doubles **Fr.95**

Lido Lidostr. 19 ☎041 370 2146, ⓦcamping -international.ch. A shady lakeside site that is open all year. Also with bunk-bed dorms (holding up to 8). Camping/person **Fr.10**, plus per tent **Fr.10**, dorms **Fr.34**

EATING AND DRINKING

Bourbaki Löwenplatz 11. As well as an arthouse cinema, this place encompasses a bistro-bar serving panini and salads from Fr.8.50. Tables spill out onto the Löwenplatz in summer. Sun–Thurs 9am–11.30pm, Fri & Sat 9am–12.30am.

LUZ Bahnhofplatz. A lovely café on the lake by the station, serving good-value food, such as *würst* (sausage), baked potatoes, ciabattas and salads (all from Fr.10). Also available to take away for picnics. Daily 7.30am–12.30am.

Mill'Feuille Mühlenplatz 6. A real locals' favourite, this buzzing café stays open all day with breakfast served until

6pm. Dishes include bagels and focaccia (Fr.8), mains at dinner (from Fr.24) and bar snacks (Fr.8). Mon–Sat 7.30am–late, Sun 9am–late.

Roadhouse Pilatusstr. 1. A lively pub, facing the west side of the station, that hosts jam sessions, live gigs and themed parties most weekends. Mon–Thurs 7am–5am, Fri 7am–5am, Sat 9am–close, Sun 9am–4am.

World Café In the KKL building, Europaplatz 1. This place has changing specials with a global twist from Fr.18, as well as real coffee and a wine bar. Daily 8.30am–9pm.

ENGELBERG

Under fifty minutes from Luzern by train is the picturesque Alpine resort of **ENGELBERG**, from where a revolving cable car (Fr.89 return; ER, IR & SP fifty percent reduction) serves the snowbound summit of Mount Titlis (3239m), the highest point in Central Switzerland (ⓦtitlis.ch). Countless outlets here rent out skis, mountain bikes, scooters and DevilBikes.

BERN

Shoehorned onto a steep-sided peninsula in a crook of the River Aare, **BERN** is one of Switzerland's most captivating cities. Its quiet cobbled lanes, lined with arcaded sandstone buildings, have changed little in five hundred years. It's sometimes hard to remember that this petite town of just 140,000 people is the nation's capital.

WHAT TO SEE AND DO

The heart of Bern's compact old town is **Spitalgasse**. Heading east from the Bahnhofplatz, this becomes **Marktgasse**, Kramgasse and then Gerechtigkeitsgasse, before crossing the river to the **Bärengraben** (bear pits). The main museums are on Helvetiaplatz, on the south bank of the river, across the Kirchenfeldbrücke.

The Old Town and Münster

Marktgasse, lined with attractive seventeenth- and eighteenth-century buildings and arcaded boutiques, leads you past various landmarks, including the Zytglogge, a medieval city gate converted to a clock tower in the sixteenth century. To the left, on Kornhausplatz, the notorious **Kindlifresserbrunnen** fountain depicts an ogre devouring a baby. Münstergasse, one block south, brings you to the fifteenth-century Gothic **Münster** (Mon–Sat 10am–5pm, Sun 11.30am–5pm), with a magnificently gilded high-relief *Last Judgement* above the main entrance. Climb its 444-stepped tower (closes 30min earlier; Fr.5), Switzerland's tallest, for terrific views. Nearby Munsterplattform hosts a craft market on the first Saturday of the month from March to November.

The Bärengraben

At the eastern end of the centre, the Nydeggbrücke crosses the river to the **Bärengraben**, Bern's famed bear pits, which held generations of bears from the early sixteenth century to 2009. Sloping down to the river, the spacious new **Bear Park** (daily 9.30am–5pm; ⓦbaerenpark -bern.ch) houses rather more content bears. Legend has it that the town's founder, Berchtold V of Zähringen, named Bern after killing one of the beasts during a hunt.

The Kunstmuseum

Bern's **Kunstmuseum**, near the station at Hodlerstrasse 8 (Tues 10am–9pm, Wed–Sun 10am–5pm; Fr.7; ⓦkunst museumbern.ch), is one of the country's best art galleries, especially strong on twentieth-century art, notably Matisse, Kandinsky, Braque, Picasso and Hodler.

The Bernisches Historisches Museum

South of the river, the **Bernisches Historisches Museum**, on Helvetiaplatz (Tues–Sun 10am–5pm; Fr.13, students Fr.8; ⓦbhm.ch), details the city's history. It's also home to the **Einstein Museum** (Fr.18 for both museums, students Fr.13), which documents the physicist's family life and chequered early career.

Zentrum Paul Klee

East of the centre at Ostring, the **Zentrum Paul Klee** (Tues–Sun 10am–5pm; Fr.20; ⓦzpk.org; bus #12) houses the world's largest collection of works by the artist, who spent much of his life in Bern. The triple-arched building was designed by star Italian architect Renzo Piano.

ARRIVAL AND INFORMATION

By train The train station is on Bahnhofplatz, to the west of the Old Town.

Destinations Basel (every 30min; 1hr); Geneva (every 30min; 2hr); Interlaken (every 30min; 1hr); Lausanne (3 hourly; 1hr 15min); Luzern (hourly; 1hr); Milan (4 daily; 3hr 30min); Paris (hourly; 4hr 30min); Zermatt (2 hourly, change at Visp; 2hr 15min); Zürich (every 30min; 1hr).

Tourist information In the train station (Mon–Sat 9am–7pm, Sun 10am–6pm; ☎031 328 1212, ⓦbern.com).

GETTING AROUND

Bern's Old Town is compact and can easily be covered on foot.

By bus Bus #12 runs from the train station through the Old Town to the Bärengraben and then to the Zentrum Paul Klee.

By bike Bike rental available all year at the Velostation in the train station (daily 8/10am–7pm; first 4hr free, Fr.1/ hour thereafter; ⓦbernrollt.ch): you need photo ID and Fr.20 deposit and must return bikes the same day. Also May–Oct at Hirschengraben and Zeughausgasse.

ACCOMMODATION

Camping Eichholz Strandweg 49 ☎031 961 2602, ⓦcampingeichholz.ch; tram #9 from south of Bahnhofplatz to Wabern. Good-value riverside campsite with kitchen and restaurant. Open April–Sept. Per person **Fr.12**, plus per tent **Fr.8**

HI Hostel Weihergasse 4 ☎031 326 1111, ⓦyouthhostel .ch/bern. Good hostel in a quiet riverside site just below the Bundeshaus, with a large terrace for alfresco dining and chilling. Breakfast included. Dorms **Fr.35**, doubles **Fr.93**

Hotel National Hirschengraben 24 ☎031 552 1515, ⓦnationalbern.ch. Grand, family-run hotel with the original 1908 lift, plus an on-site theatre and club (Fri & Sat 7pm–3.30am). Budget doubles feature a private shower & WC across the corridor. Doubles **Fr.120**

Landhaus (SH) Altenbergstr. 4 ☎031 331 4166, ⓦalbertfrida.ch. Excellent hostel in an old house near the Bärengraben. Full of character, with wonky wooden stairs leading to a modern extension and lively downstairs bar (live jazz on Thurs). Dorms have neat 2-bed cubicles. Breakfast included with doubles only. Dorms **Fr.38**, doubles **Fr.120**

EATING AND DRINKING

For picnic supplies and takeaways, try the supermarket at the train station, or visit the produce market on Bärenplatz.

Altes Tramdepot Grosser Muristalden 6. Microbrewery with views across the river to the Old Town, serving Swiss dishes such as rösti (Fr.19.50) and *Flammkuchen* (Fr.18.50). Summer Mon–Fri 11am–12.30am, Sat & Sun 10am–12.30am; winter daily 10am–12.30am.

Anker Kornhausplatz 16. Cheery place for local beer and a selection of twenty different rösti dishes (Fr.19.50). Also serves fondue (Fr.26.50) and Schnitzel (Fr.24.50). Mon–Fri

8am–midnight, Sat 9am–midnight, Sun 9.30am–6pm.

★ **Le Lötschberg** Zeughausgasse 16. Relaxed, trendy wine bar and deli serving a range of cheese platters, veggie dishes (Fr.17–35) and salads (Fr.11–18). Mon–Thurs 10am–midnight, Fri & Sat 9am–midnight, Sun 11am–11pm.

Tibits Bahnhofplatz & Gurtengasse 3. Excellent vegetarian self-service restaurants, dishing up a great selection of salads and hot dishes. Pay by weight. Mon–Wed 6.30am–11.30pm, Thurs–Sat 6.30am–midnight, Sun 8am–11pm.

34

NIGHTLIFE

Bern hosts the huge open-air rock concert, Gurtenfestival (ⓦ gurtenfestival.ch), each July.

Dampfzentrale Marzilistr. 47 ⓦ dampfzentrale.ch. Lively arts centre offering live music, dance and clubs (Sat), plus food and drink. Mon–Fri 11am–11.30pm, Sat 2pm–12.30am, Sun 10am–11pm; Oct–March closed Sun & Mon.

Reitschule Neubrückstr. 8 ⓦ reitschule.ch. This cultural and political arts squat is at the heart of Bern's alternative clubbing scene: it also hosts theatre, films and flea markets. See website for events and times.

DIRECTORY

Embassies Canada, Kirchenfeldstr. 88 ☎ 031 357 3200; Ireland, Kirchenfeldstr. 68 ☎ 031 352 1442; UK, Thunstr. 50 ☎ 031 359 7700; US, Sulgeneckstr. 19 ☎ 031 357 7011.

Hospital Inselspital, Freiburgstr. 8 (☎ 031 632 2111).

Internet Weblane, Kramgasse 47 (basement; daily 9am–11pm; Fr.4/30min).

Left luggage In the station (Mon–Sat 8am–7pm, Sun 10am–7pm; lockers 5.45am–1am; left luggage Fr.7/10, lockers Fr.6/9).

Pharmacy Bahnhof Apotheke, in the station (daily 6.30am–10pm).

Post office Post Parc, behind the station; also at Kramgasse 1.

ZÜRICH

Astride a river and turned towards a crystal-clear lake and distant snowy peaks, beautiful **ZÜRICH** is Switzerland's most vibrant and engaging city. Two of the city's twelve districts demand the most attention: the old town of Niederdorf, complete with cobbled alleyways and medieval buildings clustered on the eastern shores of the River Limmat; and the post-industrial district of Züri-West, a gritty, arty area, packed with quirky shops, restaurants and bars.

WHAT TO SEE AND DO

Zürich's west bank is the main commercial district, with the prestigious shopping street **Bahnhofstrasse** running south from the station to the lake. This is where Zürchers stroll and shop in department stores and boutiques, which become increasingly expensive towards the lake.

Across the River Limmat from the station, the narrow lanes of medieval **Niederdorf** stretch south. Its waterfront is lined with fine Baroque *Zunfthäuser* (guildhalls), whose arcaded lower storeys, fronting the quayside, now house chic restaurants. One block in is **Niederdorfstrasse**, whose touristy shops can be avoided by browsing around its cobbled side alleys and courtyards.

Cabaret Voltaire

The birthplace of the Dada art movement, **Cabaret Voltaire** at Speigelgasse 1, just south of Hirschenplatz (Tues–Sun 12.30–6.30pm; Fr.5; ⓦ cabaretvoltaire .ch), hosts controversial art exhibitions and cabaret performances: it also has a café and bar.

The Grossmünster

Just south of Niederdorfstrasse is Zürich's **Grossmünster** (Great Minster; daily: March to Oct 10am–6pm; Nov–Feb 10am–5pm), where Huldrych Zwingli, father of Swiss Protestantism, started preaching the Reformation in 1519. Look out for the vivid choir windows (1933) by Augusto Giacometti.

The Kunsthaus

Switzerland's best gallery, the **Kunsthaus**, Heimplatz 1 (Tues, Fri–Sun 10am–6pm, Wed & Thurs 10am–8pm; Fr.15, students Fr.10; ⓦ kunsthaus.ch), is uphill from the Grossmünster. It's wide-ranging collection includes Gothic paintings, Venetian and Flemish masters, some stunning international twentieth-century art, plus works by some of Switzerland's greatest Swiss artists such as Fuseli and Klee.

Schweizerisches Landesmuseum

Immediately north of the main train station at Museumstr. 2, the eclectic **Schweizerisches Landesmuseum** (Federal History Museum; Tues, Wed & Fri–Sun 10am–5pm, Thurs 10am–7pm; Fr.10; ⓦ nationalmuseum.ch) gives a definitive

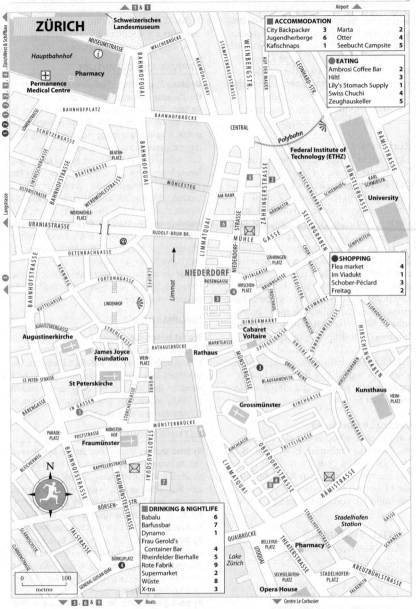

ZÜRICH

Schweizerisches
Landesmuseum

Hauptbahnhof

Pharmacy

**Permanence
Medical Centre**

34

Federal Institute of
Technology (ETHZ)

University

NIEDERDORF

Cabaret
Voltaire

Augustinerkirche

**James Joyce
Foundation**

St Peterskirche

Rathaus

Grossmünster

Kunsthaus

Fraumünster

Stadelhofen
Station

Pharmacy

*Lake
Zürich*

Opera House

N

0   100
metres

---

account of Switzerland's historical and
cultural development.

Lindenhof and St Peterskirche

The area between Bahnhofstrasse and the
river is **Lindenhof**, site of a Roman fort

that gives fine views over the river.
Nearby, at Augustinergasse 9, is the
James Joyce Foundation (Mon–Fri
10am–5pm; free) – Joyce wrote *Ulysses* in
Zürich (1915–19), and the foundation
can direct you to his various hangouts

and grave. Steps away is St Peterskirche (Mon–Fri 8am–6pm, Sat 10am–4pm, Sun 11am–5pm), with its vast sixteenth-century clock faces – Europe's largest. Immediately south rises the slender-spired Gothic **Fraumünster**, Münsterhof 2 (Mon–Sat 10am–4/6pm, Sun 11.30am–6pm), with its spectacular stained glass by Marc Chagall.

Züri-West

Dominated by the 126m-high Prime Tower, the alternative district of **Züri-West** (eight minutes by train from the Hauptbahnhof to Zürich Hardbrücke) is home to **Frau Gerold's Garten**, Geroldstrasse 23 (shops Mon–Fri 11am–7pm, Sat 11am–6pm; restaurants Mon–Sat 11am–midnight, Sun noon–10pm; ⊛fraugerold.ch), a community-run food market, beer garden and collection of hip bars and shops amid shipping containers and flowerbeds made from reclaimed railway sleepers. From here, follow Viaduktstrasse west for the hip food and shopping complex **Im Viadukt** (see p.1132), or head north for **Schiffbau** (⊛schauspielhaus.ch), a former ship-building factory that now houses three theatre stages, a jazz club, swanky restaurant and bar.

Centre Le Corbusier

On the eastern shores of Lake Zürich, the **Centre Le Corbusier**, Höschgasse 8 (July–Sept Wed–Sun noon–6pm; Fr.12; ⊛centrelecorbusier; tram #2 & #4 from the Hauptbahnhof), is the Swiss architect's last building, commissioned in 1960 by

WILD SWIMMING

Lake and river swimming is a Zürich obsession. Favourite bathing spots include Seebad Enge for lake swimming with mountain views; the 250m-long beach at Strandbad Mythenquai; and the women-only Frauenbad am Stadthausquai. These beaches all have a summer *Bädi-Bar*, with food and live music. Unterer Letten combines river swimming, beach volleyball, a lively bar & restaurant and Filmfluss open-air cinema (July).

Heidi Weber. The colourful pavilion contains a collection of Corbusier's drawings, paintings and books.

ARRIVAL AND DEPARTURE

By plane Zürich's airport (Flughafen), 11km northeast of the city centre, is served by frequent trains.

By train Zürich's giant Hauptbahnhof (HB) is served by trains from all over Europe. Extending three storeys below ground, it includes a shopping mall, supermarket, some decent places to eat and a Wednesday food market.

Destinations Basel (5 hourly; 1hr); Bern (4 hourly; 1hr); Geneva (every 30min; 2hr 45min); Innsbruck (every 2hr; 3hr 30min); Interlaken (every 30min; 1hr 55min); Lausanne (4 hourly; 2hr 10min); Lugano (2 hourly; 2hr 40min); Luzern (3 hourly; 50min); Milan (hourly; 4hr); Munich (6 daily; 4hr 15min); Paris (6 daily; 4hr); Sargans (2 hourly; 1hr); Schaffhausen (2 hourly; 40min); St Moritz (change at Chur; hourly; 3hr 20min); Stuttgart (every 2hr; 3hr); Vienna (4 daily; 7hr 30min).

By bus The bus station is located 50m north of the train station, on Sihlquai, with departures to and from the Balkans/Central Europe.

INFORMATION

Tourist information Tourist office on the train station concourse (May–Oct Mon–Sat 8am–8.30pm, Sun 8.30am–6.30pm; Nov–April Mon–Sat 8.30am–7pm, Sun 9am–6pm; ☎044 215 4000, ⊛zuerich.com) can book rooms for free, and sells the 24/48-hour ZürichCARD (Fr.24/48), allowing free public transport and free or discounted entry to museums and attractions.

GETTING AROUND

By tram and bus Although most sites can be covered on foot, the tram and bus system (⊛zvv.ch) is easy to use, with all tickets valid on trams, buses, "S-Bahn" city trains and some boats. Tickets are available from machines at any stop: either the green button (24hr; Fr.8.60); blue button (1hr; Fr.4.30); or yellow button (short one-way hop; Fr.2.80). You'll need a multi-zone ticket to get to or from the airport.

By bike Free bikes (Fr.20 deposit and ID required) are available year-round at the Velostation Nord and Sud, on either side of the Hauptbahnhof (daily 8am–9.30pm), and elsewhere in the city (May–Oct Mon–Fri 9am–9.30pm, Sat & Sun 9am–9.30pm).

By boat Zürichsee and Limmat River ferries leave from Bürkliplatz (⊛zsg.ch); the shortest trips (up to 90min) are covered by public transport tickets.

ACCOMMODATION

City Backpacker (SH) Niederdorfstr. 5 (Rosenhof) ☎044 251 9015, ⊛city-backpacker.ch. Good atmosphere and central location as well as a kitchen, laundry and free wi-fi, though rather cramped when full. No check-in after 10pm. Dorms **Fr.37**, doubles **Fr.118**

Jugendherberge (HI) Mutschellenstr. 114 ☎043 399 7800, ⓦ youthhostel.ch/zuerich; tram #7 to Morgental or train to Wollishofen, then a 5min walk. Rather institutional hostel, out in a southwestern suburb. Breakfast included. Dorms **Fr.40**, doubles **Fr.106**

Kafischnaps Kornhausstr. 57 ☎043 538 8116 ⓦ kafischnaps.ch. Five funky rooms with a shared bathroom above a hipster coffee bar in an old butcher's shop between the Wipkingen and Unterstrass districts. Breakfast included. Doubles **Fr.108**

Marta Zähringerstr. 36 ☎044 251 4550, ⓦ martahaus.ch. Female-owned and run budget hotel in the Old Town, with a café and laundry as well as rooms for up to four friends. Breakfast included. Doubles **Fr.125**

Otter Oberdorfstr. 7 ☎044 251 2207, ⓦ hotelotter.ch. Quirky and friendly with vibrantly decorated rooms, shared bathrooms, good breakfasts and a lively bar. Balcony rooms have Old Town views and the top-floor apartment sleeps four. Doubles **Fr.150**, apartment **Fr.240**

Seebucht Campsite Seestr. 559 ☎044 482 1612; bus #161 or #165 from Bürkliplatz to Stadtgrenze. Well-serviced site on the lakeside, 2km south of the centre. Open May–Sept. Per person **Fr.9**, plus per tent **Fr.12**

EATING

The Niederdorf district is home to dozens of eating options, among them sausage, noodle and French-fry stands, plus beer halls serving daily specials for about Fr.13.

Ambrosi Coffee Bar Viaduktstr. 37. Lively, all-day place under the Im Viadukt railway arches. Does a generous breakfast buffet and serves authentic pasta (Fr.15), pizza (Fr.13.50) and focaccia (Fr.12.50). Mon–Thurs 8am–midnight, Fri 8am–2am, Sat 10am–2am, Sun 10am–10pm.

Hiltl Sihlstr. 28 Long-established vegetarian restaurant, with budget takeaway prices. Daily specials Fr.16.50. Mutates into a trendy cocktail bar with DJs at weekends. Restaurant Mon–Sat 6am–midnight, Sun 8am–midnight; bar Thurs–Sun 11pm–4am.

Lily's Stomach Supply Langstr. 197 & Sihlfeldstr. 58. Bustling pan-Asian noodle-bar serving huge stir-fries from Fr.15 (Fr.10 takeaway, until 10pm). Mon–Thurs 11am–midnight, Fri & Sat 11am–1am, Sun noon–12.30am.

Swiss Chuchi Rosengasse 10. Enjoy huge portions of fondue or raclette for Fr.26.50, while taking advantage of the fantastic people-watching opportunities in summer when tables spill out onto the Hirschenplatz. Daily 11.30am–11.15pm.

Zeughauskeller Banhofstr. 28a. In a fifteenth-century arsenal, this traditional establishment dishes up Swiss classics such as *Züri Geschnetzeltes* (veal in a cream sauce) and *Bürgermeister Schwert* (veal wrapped around a sword blade). Daily specials from Fr.21.50. Daily 11.30am–11pm.

DRINKING AND NIGHTLIFE

Zürich boasts lively music venues and clubs plus a thriving LGBT scene. The hip quarter around Langstrasse, west of the centre, is full of DJ bars, while the best clubs hide in the former industrial quarter of Züri-West. The annual Pride parade (ⓦ zurichpridefestival.ch) takes place in June, with the techno street dancing Saturday Street Parade (ⓦ street-parade.com) in mid-Aug. The *ZüriTipp* (ⓦ zueritipp.ch) listings magazine is available at the tourist office.

BARS

Babalu Schmidgasse 6 ⓦ babalubar.ch. Trendy little DJ-bar in the Old Town with Brazilian cocktails and house music. Mon–Tues 5pm–midnight, Wed & Thurs 5pm–1am, Fri & Sat 5pm–2am.

Barfussbar Stadthausquai ⓦ 12 barfussbar.ch. Set in an original Art Nouveau swimming baths, this venue takes its name (barefoot bar) literally – visitors leave their shoes at the door for barefoot chilling and dancing. Wed, Thurs & Sun 8pm–midnight.

Frau Gerold's Container Bar Geroldstr. 23 ⓦ fraugerold.ch. Set in a quirky beer garden in Züri-West (see opposite), this lively bar has been constructed from shipping containers. Mon–Sat 11am–midnight, Sun noon–8pm.

Rheinfelder Bierhalle Niederdorfstr. 76. Founded In 1870 and still the best of the beerhalls, filled with locals and serving cheap, filling daily specials, such as the aptly named Jumbo Jumbo Cordon Blue (Fr.28). Daily 9am–midnight.

Wüste In *Hotel Otter*, Oberdorfstr. 7. Mellow, relaxed cellar bar located near the Grossmünster and attracting a young bohemian crowd. Live music on Thurs–Sat nights. Mon–Thurs 4pm–midnight, Fri & Sat 4pm–2am.

X-tra Limmatstr. 118 ⓦ x-tra.ch. Stylish bar-restaurant, with popular upstairs lounges and club hosting DJs and a range of gigs, from folk to electro. Wed 10pm–2.30am, Thurs 9pm–2.30am, Fri & Sat 10pm–4am.

CLUBS

Dynamo Wasserwerkstr. 21 ⓦ dynamo.ch. City-run youth centre that hosts music courses, theatre groups and alternative, punkish bands. There's also a restaurant. Gig nights start around 7 or 8pm, though the club doesn't fill up till later.

Rote Fabrik Seestr. 395 ⓦ rotefabrik.ch. Alternative bands, big-name DJs, art studios, a cheap and funky restaurant and a great riverside bar, all in a former factory complex. Tues–Sun 11am–midnight.

Supermarket Geroldstr. 17 ⓦ supermarket.li. Popular gay-friendly club in the Züri-West district, that attracts international DJs playing techno, electronica and house till the early hours. Minimum age 21. Thurs–Sat 8pm–late.

34

34

SHOPPING

Kirchgasse and Niederdorfstrasse have a high concentration of secondhand bookshops, antiques shops and galleries.

Flea market Bürkliplatz ⓦflohmarktbuerkliplatz.ch. Since 1971, this has been the place to look for jewellery, antiques and other secondhand treasures. May–Oct Sat 8am–4pm.

Im Viadukt Viaduktstrasse. Beneath the railway arches of Züri-West ⓦ im-viadukt.ch. Food market hall plus collection of cafés, delis and hip fashion, design and interiors shops. Mon–Thurs 10am–8pm, Fri & Sat 8am–8pm.

Schober-Péclard Napfgasse 4 ⓦpeclard-zurich.ch. Good option for over-the-top chocolates and cakes, from either the jewel-like shop or the upstairs café. Mon–Wed 8am–7pm, Thurs–Sat 8am–11pm, Sun 9am–7pm.

Freitag Geroldstr.17 ⓦfreitag.ch. The Freitag brothers recycle colourful truck tarpaulins into waterproof accessories in their shop, a pile of shipping containers by Frau Gerold's garden. Mon–Fri 11am–7.30pm, Sat 10am–6pm.

DIRECTORY

Banks and exchange At the station (daily 6.30am–9.30pm) or UBS, Bahnhofstr. 45 & 72 (Mon–Fri 8.15am–4.30pm).

Consulates Ireland, Claridenstr. 25 ☎044 289 2515; UK, Hegibachstr. 47 ☎044 383 6560; US, Dufourstr. 101 ☎043 499 2960. Embassies are in Bern.

Hospital Permanence Medical Centre, Bahnhofplatz 15 ☎044 215 4444 (reception daily 7am–10pm).

Left luggage North side of the station (daily 7.30am–7.45pm).

Pharmacy Bellevue, Theaterstr. 14 ☎044 266 6222; and Bahnhof Apotheke, Bahnhofplatz 15 ☎044 225 4242 (both 24hr).

Post office Sihlpost, Kasernenstr. 95, beside the station (Mon–Fri 6.30am–10.30pm, Sat 6.30am–8pm, Sun 10am–10.30pm).

THE RHINE FALLS

It's a great half-day trip from Zürich north to Europe's largest waterfalls, the Rhine Falls (ⓦrhinefalls.com), 3km west of **SCHAFFHAUSEN**. They are magnificent, not so much for their height (just 23m) as for their impressive breadth (150m) and sheer drama, with spray rising in a cloud of rainbows above the forested banks and the turreted castle, **Schloss Laufen** (now an HI hostel), on the south bank. In summer, the best views are from the daredevil boats, which leave from Schloss Laufen (Fr.6–19; ⓦmaendli.ch) and scurry about in the spray.

Take a train to Schaffhausen then bus #1 to Neuhausen Zentrum, or a local train to either Laufen am Rheinfall (below the castle; April–Oct) or Neuhausen; you can also walk (30min) from Schaffhausen to the bridge above the falls.

The Swiss Alps

South of Bern and Luzern, and east of Lake Geneva, lies the grand Alpine heart of Switzerland, a massively impressive region of classic Swiss scenery – high peaks, sheer valleys and turquoise lakes – that makes for great summer hiking and world-class winter sports. The Bernese Oberland, centred on the **Jungfrau Region**, is the most accessible and touristed area, but beyond this first great wall of peaks is another even more daunting range on the Italian border in which the **Matterhorn** is the star attraction.

THE JUNGFRAU REGION

The spectacular **Jungfrau Region** is named after a grand triple-peaked ridge – the Eiger, Mönch and Jungfrau – which crests 4000m. Switzerland's most popular mountain railway, the **Jungfrau Railway**, dating from 1912, trundles south from **Interlaken** before coiling up across mountain pastures, and tunnelling through the Eiger to emerge at the **Jungfraujoch** (3454m), a dramatic col beneath the Jungfrau summit and Europe's highest railway station. It's a scenic journey, but pricey and very slow, journey (2hr 20min from Interlaken, with two changes to progressively smaller trains) – try to pick a clear day, for the spectacular panoramic views from the Sphinx Terrace (3571m) to Germany's Black Forest in one direction, and across gleaming mountains to the Italian Alps in the other. If you can, splash out Fr.14.40 extra to upgrade to First Class, for plush cabins with glass ceilings.

The cable-car ride up the **Schilthorn** (2970m) offers an equally scenic ride with impressive views, and it's quicker and cheaper. A return trip from Interlaken takes six hours to the Jungfraujoch, or four hours to the Schilthorn (both allowing an hour at the summit).

The most beautiful countryside is the **Lauterbrunnen valley**, overlooked by the village of **Mürren**, an excellent base for winter skiing and summer hiking, as is **Grindelwald**, in the next valley east. The region's transport hub is bustling Interlaken, a handy, if less tranquil, base.

ARRIVAL AND DEPARTURE

By train There are two routes up the Jungfrau from Interlaken, changing trains at either Lauterbrunnen or Grindelwald (most people go up one way and down the other). The routes meet at the spectacularly sited station of Kleine Scheidegg, where you change for the final pull to the Jungfraujoch. The adult return-trip fare from Interlaken to the Jungfraujoch is a budget-crunching Fr.204.40 (IR no discount; ER 25 percent discount; SP free to Grindelwald and Lauterbrunnen, then half-price to Kleine Scheidegg and 25 percent off to the top). Discounted "Good Morning" tickets, valid May–October for travel on the first or second trains of the day (at 6.35am & 7.05am from Interlaken Ost) cost Fr.145 from Interlaken, and Fr.135 from Lauterbrunnen or Grindelwald.

By cable car The Schilthorn cable car, compared to the Jungfraujoch ride, is a bargain. From Stechelberg to the top is Fr.102 return, from Mürren Fr.80 (IR no discount; ER

25 percent discount; SP free to Mürren, then 50 percent). Going up between 7.40am and 9.10am or after 3.40pm knocks the fare down to Fr.82 (Fr.64 from Mürren).

INTERLAKEN

INTERLAKEN is centred on its long main street, Höheweg, which is lined with cafés and hotels, and has a train station at each end, although the best way to arrive is by boat. The town lies on a neck of land between two of Switzerland's loveliest lakes, and it exists primarily to amuse trippers on their way to the mountains. Coming from Luzern, you could get out at Brienz and do the last stretch to Interlaken Ost by boat (ER & SP free, IR 50 percent). Likewise, from the Bern/Zürich direction, you could take a boat from Thun to Interlaken West.

ARRIVAL AND INFORMATION

By train Interlaken West station serves the town centre; from here Bahnhofstr. leads east, becoming the main street, Höheweg, with Interlaken Ost station, the main interchange, at its far end.

Destinations Bern (every 30min; 55min); Grindelwald (every 30min; 45min); Jungfraujoch (change at Grindelwald or Lauterbrunnen, then Kleine Scheidegg;

34

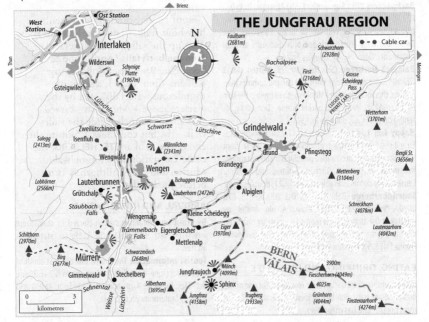

THE JUNGFRAU REGION

34

EXTREME INTERLAKEN

Interlaken is a hub for **extreme sports**, with paragliders spiralling above and landing right in the town centre: Skywings (☎ 033 266 8228, ⓦ skywings.ch) will take you **paragliding** for Fr.170. Agencies such as Alpin Raft, Hauptstr. 7, Matten (☎ 033 823 4100, ⓦ alpinraft.com), can arrange everything from **rafting** or **canyoning** (both Fr.119) to **ice climbing** (Fr.180), and can be booked direct or through hostels.

every 30min; 2hr 30min); Lauterbrunnen (every 30min; 25min); Luzern (hourly; 2hr); Zürich (change at Bern; every 30min; 2hr).

Tourist information Tourist office beneath the town's tallest building at Höheweg 37 (May–Sept Mon–Fri 8am–6pm, Sat 8am–4pm; July & Aug Mon–Fri 8am–7pm, Sat 8am–7pm, Sun 10am–7pm; Oct–April Mon–Fri 8am–noon & 1.30–6pm, Sat 9am–2pm; ☎ 033 826 5300, ⓦ interlaken.ch).

ACCOMMODATION

Accommodation fills up quickly in the high seasons, so advance booking is advised. Interlaken Adventure (ⓦ interlaken-adventure.com) can book accommodation and excursions.

Backpackers Villa Sonnenhof (SH) Alpenstr. 16 ☎ 033 822 1643, ⓦ villa.ch. Excellent hostel with rooms sleeping two to seven, some with south-facing balconies; free swimming pool access included plus discounts at local restaurants. Dorms **Fr.47**, doubles **Fr.74**

Balmer's Herberge (SH) Hauptstr. 23, Matten ☎ 033 822 1961, ⓦ balmers.com. With a DJ bar and summer beer garden, this sociable hostel 10min south of town is the hub of Interlaken's lively backpacker scene. Dorms **Fr.34**, tented dorms **Fr.25**, doubles **Fr.95**

Happy Inn Lodge Rosenstrasse 17 ⓦ happy-inn.com. Cosy hostel in the heart of town (a 5min walk from Interlaken West station) with a popular bar and restaurant, live music in summer, kitchen facilities and parking. Female-only dorms available. Dorms **Fr.21**, doubles **Fr.62**

Jugendherberge Bahnhofplatz Ost (HI) ☎ 033 826 1090, ⓦ youthhostel.ch/interlaken. A big hostel by Interlaken Ost station, with rooms for up to six, many en suite and some with balcony, plus billiards and good food. Dorms **Fr.35.50**, doubles **Fr.125**

EATING, DRINKING AND NIGHTLIFE

In the evenings most backpackers congregate at one of the busier hostel bars: *Balmer's Herberge* (see above) is the most popular and has cheap beer.

Club Caverne Hauptstr. 36, Matten ⓦ caverne.ch. Located in the *Funny Farm* hostel, this place attracts party-goers till the small hours with its pumping house music and maverick staff. Daily 10.30pm–2am.

Migros Rugenparkstrasse 1. Opposite Interlaken West station, a reliable supermarket for cheap, self-service staples. There's also an inexpensive, yet consistently good, restaurant serving excellent rotisserie chicken (Fr12.50). Mon–Thurs 8am–7pm, Fri 8am–9pm, Sat 8am–5pm.

My Little Thai Hauptstrasse 19 ⓦ mylittlethai.ch. Small, authentically Thai restaurant, adorned with photos of the Thai royal family. Owner Eddie makes juicy spring rolls, excellent Pad Thai and rich curries. Takeaway available. Wed–Sun 11am–2pm & 5–10pm.

PizPaz Centralstr. Located just off Bahnhofstrasse, this large and lively place dishes up big portions of affordable Italian favourites: pizza and pasta cost from Fr.15 (20 percent discount for takeaway). Daily 10am–11pm.

LAUTERBRUNNEN

It's hard to overstate the impact of the **Lauterbrunnen valley**. An immense U-shaped cleft with bluffs on either side rising 1000m sheer, doused by some 72 waterfalls, it is utterly spectacular. The **Staubbach falls** – Switzerland's highest at nearly 300m – tumble just beyond the village of **LAUTERBRUNNEN** at the valley entrance.

From Lauterbrunnen, it's a scenic half-hour walk, or an hourly postbus, 3km up the valley to the spectacular **Trümmelbach falls** (April–June & Sept–Nov 9am–5pm; July & Aug 8.30am–6pm; Fr.11), a series of thunderous waterfalls – fed by the glaciers above – which have carved corkscrew channels inside the valley walls. The bus continues 1.5km to the end of the road at **STECHELBERG**; the **cable-car** station for Gimmelwald, Mürren and the Schilthorn is 1km before the hamlet.

ARRIVAL AND INFORMATION

By train Lauterbrunnen station (served by trains from Interlaken Ost) is opposite the cable-car station for Mürren.

Tourist information The tourist office is just south of the station (June–Sept daily 8.30am–noon & 2–6.30pm; Oct–May Tues–Sat 9am–noon & 1.30–5pm; ☎ 033 856 8568, ⓦ lauterbrunnen.ch).

ACCOMMODATION

Camping Jungfrau 033 856 2010, camping
-jungfrau.ch. Great views and facilities, including a decent
restaurant serving Swiss dishes, pizza and pasta, plus a
minimarket. Also has family chalets (minimum week-long
rental). Camping/person **Fr.13**, plus per tent **Fr.13**,
chalets **Fr.1140**

SH Valley Hostel 033 855 2008, valleyhostel.ch. A
cosy place with 7 dorms (4–8 bunk beds in each), most
with balcony, and just one double, plus kitchen, laundry
and drying facilities. Dorms **Fr.30**, double **Fr.43**

MÜRREN AND UP TO THE SCHILTHORN

The cable car sets out north of
Stechelberg, passing through the hamlet
of **GIMMELWALD** before continuing to
the car-free village of **MÜRREN**. It's
worth the journey for the views alone:
the valley floor is 800m down, and a
panorama of snowy peaks fills the sky.
Mürren is also accessible from
Lauterbrunnen, by taking a cable car
to **Grütschalp** then a spectacular little
cliff-edge train from there (one-way
Fr.11/return Fr.22; IR no discount;
ER 25 percent discount; SP free). It's
easy to do a loop by cable car and train.
A cable car continues from Mürren on a
scenic (20min) ride to the 2970m peak
of the **Schilthorn** (schilthorn.ch),
where you can admire jaw-dropping
panoramas while sipping cocktails in
the revolving *Piz Gloria* restaurant,
famed as Blofeld's hideout in the Bond
film *On Her Majesty's Secret Service*.
Next to the restaurant, you can venture
onto the **Skyline Walk**, a reinforced glass
platform suspended some 3000m above
the ground.

HIKING IN THE JUNGFRAU REGION

Hiking some sections of the Jungfrau
Region is perfectly feasible in summer,
and can save a great deal on train tickets.
Excellent transport networks and
vista-rich footpaths linking all stations
mean that with a hiking map – such
as the *Wanderkarte Wengen-Mürren-
Lauterbrunnental* (1:40,000) – you can
see and do a great deal in a day.

ACCOMMODATION

Mountain Hostel 033 855 1704, mountainhostel
.com. A chalet hostel in Gimmelwald with a scenic terrace
where you can enjoy beer, pizza and great views. Closed
early April & Nov. Breakfast included. Dorms **Fr.45**

GRINDELWALD

34

Valley-floor trains from Interlaken Ost run
to the popular resort of **GRINDELWALD**,
nestling under the craggy trio of the
Wetterhorn, Mettenberg and Eiger.
Numerous trails around **Pfingstegg** and
especially **First** – both reached by gondolas
from Grindelwald – offer excellent hiking.

INFORMATION

Tourist information 200m east of the station (Mon–Fri
8am–6pm, Sat & Sun 9am–6pm; April, May, Oct & Nov
closed Sat & Sun; 033 854 1212, grindelwald.ch).

ACCOMMODATION

Camping Gletscherdorf 033 853 1429,
gletscherdorf.ch. A quiet site by a stream to the east of
the village, with electric hook-ups and a basic food kiosk.
Open May to late Oct & Nov–April on request. Per person
Fr.8.50, plus per tent **Fr.10**

HI Jugendherberge Geissstutzstr. 12 033 853 1009,
youthhostel.ch/grindelwald. In a quiet lane above the
village, this is an excellent hostel in a huge chalet with
restaurant and massive mountain-view terrace. Closed
mid-April to mid-May & mid-Oct to early Dec. Dorms
Fr.35.70, doubles **Fr.124.40**

Mountain Hostel (SH) 033 854 3838,
mountainhostel.ch. A lively, well-run hostel on the
valley floor by Grindelwald-Grund station (served by trains
from Grindelwald to Kleine Scheidegg). Some of the
contemporary 2-, 4- and 6-bedded rooms have views of
the Eiger. Dorms **Fr.35**, doubles **Fr.98**

ZERMATT AND THE MATTERHORN

One of Europe's highest peaks, the iconic,
shark's-tooth **Matterhorn** (4478m) is
Switzerland's best-known mountain, and
one of the last to be climbed – it was
finally conquered by Edward Whymper
in 1865. Over 500 alpinists are estimated
to have died on the Matterhorn since
then, including Whymper on his descent,
making it one of the world's most
notorious mountains. Sticking up from
an otherwise uncrowded horizon above
ZERMATT, it stands alone, its pointy

34

shape so distinctive that the Swiss chocolate Toblerone was modelled on it.

WHAT TO SEE AND DO

Zermatt's main street buzzes year-round with climbers, skiers, tour groups, backpackers and fur-clad socialites, while its **Old Town** boasts ancient timber chalets. It's car-free, with electric buses and taxis ferrying people between the train station at the town's northern end and the cable-car terminus 1km south. You can find out about Zermatt's rich history at the **Zermatlantis Matterhorn Museum** on Kirchplatz (daily: July–Sept 11am–6pm; Oct–June 3–6pm; Fr.10; SP free).

Zermatt's many **cable cars and trains** bring you to trailheads and spectacular views: opposite the station, Gornergrat-Bahn trains (ER 25 percent discount, SP 50 percent; cheaper after 1.40pm) afford spectacular Matterhorn views (sit on the right) as they climb to the **Gornergrat**, where there's a panorama of 29 peaks over 4000m high, including Switzerland's highest, the **Dufourspitze** (4634m).

The Furi-Schwarzsee gondola climbs from the southern end of Zermatt to **Schwarzsee** (2583m), the start of a two-hour zigzag hike to the *Hörnli Hut* (3260m) on the flank of the Matterhorn. Lifts continue up to the **Matterhorn Glacier**, where 21km of ski runs and a half-pipe are open all summer (day pass Fr.84; SP 50 percent).

ARRIVAL AND INFORMATION

By train The only access to Zermatt is on the spectacular narrow-gauge MGB train line (ER no discount, IR 50 percent, SP free; ⊚ mgbahn.ch); change at Visp from main-line trains. The most celebrated way to arrive is on the *Glacier Express*, a day-long journey from St Moritz by panoramic train (reserve at any train station; ER 25 percent discount, IR Youth Pass 50 percent, SP free; ⊚ glacierexpress.ch).
Destinations Brig (2 hourly; 1hr 20min); St Moritz (1–4 daily; 6hr 30min–7hr 30min); Visp (2 hourly; 1hr 10min).
Tourist information Tourist office outside the station (mid-June to Sept daily 8.30am–6pm; Oct to mid-June Mon–Sat 8.30am–noon & 1.30–6pm, Sun 9.30am–noon & 4–6pm; ⊚ zermatt.ch).
Snow and Alpine Centre Bahnhofstr. 58 (⊕ 027 966 2460, ⊚ alpincenter-zermatt.ch), includes the mountaineering centre (mid-June to Sept daily 9am–noon & 3–7pm), for booking climbing guides, fixed-rope courses

and ice-climbing, and the Ski & Snowboard School (Nov–May daily 8am–noon & 3–7pm).

ACCOMMODATION

Hotel Tannenhof Englischer Viertel 3 ⊕ 027 967 3188, ⊚ rhone-web.ch/tannenhof. A good-value hotel that is particuarly popular with climbers. It has cosy doubles, with or without private bathroom, and a generous buffet breakfast included. Doubles **Fr.90**
Matterhorn Campsite Bahnhofstr. ⊕ 027 967 3921, ⊚ campingzermatt.ipeak.ch. Not accessible to cars, this basic tents-only grassy campsite is a 2min walk from the station and has a bus stop for access to the cable cars. Open June–Sept. Per person **Fr.11**
Zermatt Youth Hostel Staldenweg. 5, Winkelmatten (HI) ⊕ 027 967 2320, ⊚ youthhostel.ch/zermatt. Excellent hostel above town in a sustainably constructed building. Good 3-course dinners (Fr.17.50) are served up and breakfast is included. Dorms **Fr.36**, doubles **Fr.131**

EATING AND DRINKING

Brown Cow Bahnhofstr. 41. A popular pub, serving soups, hot dogs and burgers (Fr.10–14.50). It's also home to the *Broken Bar* disco. Bar daily 9am–2am; food till 11pm, disco daily 11pm–3.30am.
Gee's Bar & Brasserie Bahnhofstr. 70 ⊚ zermattgees .com. One of Zermatt's most popular venues where you can eat tacos (Fr.9), salads (Fr.19.50) and soups (Fr.11.50), washed down by cocktails: there's also live music most nights. Daily 11am–2am.
The Bubble Kirchstrasse 38 ⊚ zermattbubble.com. Run by a young local team, *Bubble* serves excellent burgers (Fr.24) and ribs (Fr.36). It sister restaurant, *North Wall*, Steinmattstrasse 71, is good for pizzas (Fr.22) and nachos (Fr.18). Both daily 6–10pm.

Ticino

Italian-speaking **Ticino** (Tessin in German and French) occupies the balmy, lake-laced southern foothills of the Alps. A little pocket of Italy in Switzerland, its culture, food, architecture and attitude owe more to Milan than Zürich, although Switzerland has controlled the area for more than 500 years. The region's main attractions are the lakeside resorts of **Locarno** and **Lugano**, where mountain scenery meets subtropical flora. The best way to enjoy these chic towns is to join the locals promenading with ice creams.

In 2016, the world's deepest and longest train tunnel, the **Gotthard Base Tunnel** (57km long), opened, enabling train passengers to hurtle through the Gotthard massif at 250km per hour.

LOCARNO

A branch line heads west from Bellinzona (whose three superb castles are on UNESCO's World Heritage list) to **LOCARNO**, a charming town on **Lake Maggiore** with piazzas overhung by subtropical shrubbery. Overrun with glamorous visitors from Milan and Zürich on summer weekends and during the Locarno Film Festival (early August; ⓦpardolive.ch), the town exudes well-heeled, sun-drenched cool.

WHAT TO SEE AND DO

The **Piazza Grande**, where well-groomed locals parade on summer nights, is near the lake, with the Renaissance Old Town rising gently behind. The fifteenth-century church of **Madonna del Sasso** (daily 7am–6.30pm) is an impressive ochre vision high on a crag. It's a glorious walk up, or take the funicular (Fr.7.20 return) from just west of the station to Orselina, Ticino's greatest photo-op, looking down on the church and lake.

From here a cable car climbs steeply to **Cardada** amid fragrant pine woods with walking routes; a spectacular chairlift whisks you further up to **Cimetta**, where the restaurant terrace offers memorable views.

A short bus ride east of Locarno in Valle Verzasca, you can re-enact the opening of the James Bond film *Goldeneye* by bungee-jumping 220m off the **Verzasca Dam** (April–Oct daily; Fr.255, students Fr.195; ☏091 780 7800, ⓦtrekking.ch).

ARRIVAL AND INFORMATION

By train Station 150m northeast of Piazza Grande.
Destinations Basel (hourly; 4hr); Bellinzona/Giubiasco (for Lugano; 3 hourly; 20min); Domodossola (for Brig and southwestern Switzerland; 7–11 daily; 1hr 58min); Luzern (hourly; 3hr); Zürich (hourly; 3hr). Journey times may reduce once trains run regularly via the Gotthard Base Tunnel.
By boat The landing stage is between the train station and Piazza Grande; boats (late March to mid-Sept; ⓦnavigazionelaghi.it) sail to nearby Swiss and Italian resorts.

Destinations Ascona (hourly; 20–30min); Stresa (for Milan; 2 daily; 2hr 20min–3hr 30min).
Tourist information In the Casino opposite the landing stage (Mon–Fri 9am–6pm; March–Oct also Sat 10am–6pm, Sun 10am–1.30pm & 2.30–5pm; ☏0848 091 091, ⓦascona-locarno.com).

ACCOMMODATION

Delta campsite Via Respini 7 ☏091 751 6081, ⓦcampingdelta.com. Expensive but well-equipped campsite 20min walk south by the lake (just past the lido). Open March–Oct. Per tent **Fr.34**, caravans **Fr.69**
HI hostel "Palagiovani" Via Varenna 18 ☏091 756 1500, ⓦyouthhostel.ch/locarno; bus #1/#2/#7 from opposite the station to Cinque Vie. A friendly hostel, just 10min walk from the centre. Dorms **Fr.41.50**, doubles **Fr.122**

EATING AND DRINKING

Appunto Piazza Grande 2. Great snack bar on Piazza Grande serving sandwiches, pizza slices and salads (Fr.6–9). Service can be slow, which gives more time for people-watching. Mon–Sat 8am–6.30pm.
Bar Lungolago Via Bramantino 1. Lively bar and restaurant on the promenade that is ideal for leisurely lunches and evening drinks. It serves up pizzas (Fr.14.30), pasta (Fr.15) and ice cream. Thurs–Tues 7am–1am.

LUGANO

With its lush promenades and piazzas, chic **LUGANO** is Ticino's most alluring city. The tree-lined lakefront promenade **Lungolago** wraps around Lake Lugano, while **Piazza della Riforma**, packed with cafés, marks the heart of the city. Through the maze of steep lanes northwest of Riforma, Via Cattedrale dog-legs up to the **Cattedrale San Lorenzo**, with its fine Renaissance facade, interior frescoes and spectacular views. Also from Riforma, the narrow, boutique-lined Via Nassa heads southwest to the medieval church of **Santa Maria degli Angioli**, home to a wall-sized fresco of the Crucifixion. Further south on Piazza Luini, the **Lugano Arte e Cultura (LAC)** (Tues, Wed & Sun 10.30am–6pm, Thurs–Sat 10.30am–8pm; Fr.15, students Fr.10; ⓦluganolac.ch) includes in its permanent collection works by Ticinese artists as well as big names such as Degas, Pissarro and Renoir. Some 20 minutes further south from the district of Paradiso, a funicular rises 600m to **San Salvatore**, a rugged sugarloaf pinnacle offering fine views of the lake.

34

34

ARRIVAL, INFORMATION AND TOURS

By train Lugano's train station overlooks the town from the west, linked to the centre by a short funicular (SP free) or by steps down to Via Cattedrale.

Destinations Luzern (3 hourly; 2hr 30min); Milan (hourly; 1hr); Zürich (hourly; 2hr 40min).

By bus Postbuses bookable at the train station.

Destinations St Moritz (mid-June to mid-Oct daily, mid-Oct to mid-June 3 weekly; 4hr).

Tourist information On Palazzo Civico, off Riforma (Mon–Fri 9am–7pm, Sat 9am–6pm, Sun 10am–5pm; ☎058 8666609, ⱳ luganotourism.ch).

Tours Boat tours around the lake (April–Oct; Fr.5.45–26, SP free; ⱳ lakelugano.ch) depart from directly opposite the tourist office.

ACCOMMODATION AND EATING

HI Hostel Via Cantonale 13, Savosa ☎091 966 2728, ⱳ youthhostel.ch/lugano; bus #5 to Crocifisso from 200m north of the train station. Excellent, quiet hostel with a large garden and swimming pool. Dorms **Fr.37**, doubles **Fr.96**

Hotel Pestalozzi Piazza Indipendenza ☎091 921 4646, ⱳ pestalozzi-lugano.ch. Some 150m from the lake, with clean, white, recently refurbished rooms, and a great (alcohol-free) restaurant with friendly staff. Doubles **Fr.110**

La Tinèra Via dei Gorini, behind Piazza della Riforma. Classic locals' restaurant hidden in a basement, serving great pasta and tasty Ticinese chicken stews (Fr.19) and *zabaglione* to finish. Mon–Sat 11.30am–3pm & 5.30–11pm.

Pasta e Pesto Via Cattedrale 16. Buzzing little place with a small terrace, spitting distance from the cathedral: it serves up mountains of tasty pasta (Fr.9.80–12). Mon & Tues 9.30am–7pm, Wed–Sat 9.30am–9.30pm.

TCS Camping Lugano La Piodella Via alle Foce 4 ☎091 994 7788, ⱳ campingtcs.ch. Attractive lakeside campsite with restaurant in Muzzano, 3km west by FLP train from the platform opposite the main station. Per tent **Fr.25**

Liechtenstein

Barely larger than Manhattan, **Liechtenstein** is the world's sixth-smallest country – and one of the richest. Tucked between Switzerland and Austria, amid dramatic mountain ranges whose peaks are topped with turreted castles, Liechtenstein is a constitutional monarchy, ruled by His Serene Highness Prince Hans Adam II. You can see the whole country on a day-trip from Zürich, two hours away by train. Swiss francs are

legal tender, but the phone system is separate (country code ☎423).

VADUZ

Liechtenstein's capital is the tiny, photogenic **VADUZ**, crowned with the Prince's sixteenth-century castle. The hub of its modern, rather soulless centre is the main bus stop, between the highway, Äulestrasse, and the more appealing pedestrianized Städtle. On either side of the bus stop are the **Kunstmuseum** (Tues–Sun 10am–5pm, Thurs till 8pm; Fr.15, students Fr.10), displaying temporary art exhibitions from the Prince's private collection, and the **Landesmuseum** (Tues–Sun 10am–5pm, Wed till 8pm; Fr.10, students Fr.7), with excellent coverage of local history. Stroll northeast to the appealing district of **Mitteldorf**, where medieval houses overlook the Prince's vineyards.

ARRIVAL AND INFORMATION

By bus From Sargans train station on the Zürich–Chur line, bus #1 shuttles over the Rhine to Vaduz. Buses stop on Vaduz's main street, by the post office. They serve all of Liechtenstein, as well as Sargans in Switzerland, and Feldkirch in Austria, from where trains serve Bregenz, Innsbruck and Vienna.

Destinations Feldkirch (Austria; every 30min; 30min); Sargans (Switzerland; every 30min; 25min).

Tourist information Städtle 39 (May–Oct daily 9am–6pm; Nov–April daily 9am–5pm; ☎239 6363, ⱳ tourismus.li).

ACCOMMODATION

HI Hostel Schaan-Vaduz Under Rüttigass 6 ☎232 5022. Quiet rural location, looking out over fields and mountains, 5min from Mühleholz bus stop and 2km north of Vaduz. Open March–Oct. Dorms **Fr.34.50**, doubles **Fr.92**

Mittagsspitze campsite ☎392 3677, ⱳ camping triesen.li. Tranquil rural campsite with swimming pool, some 5km south of Vaduz, near the Säga bus stop. Per person **Fr.9**, plus per tent **Fr.6**

EATING AND DRINKING

Burg Brasserie Städtle 15 ⱳ adler.li. Brasserie serving sandwiches, burgers and a salad buffet from Fr.12.60, with the smarter *Cesare* Italian restaurant upstairs. Brasserie Mon–Fri 8.30am–midnight, Sat & Sun 9.30am–midnight.

New Castle Aeulestrasse 22 ⱳ new-castle.li. A comfortable restaurant serving hearty local fare, such as fillet steaks (Fr.34), breaded Schnitzels (Fr.28.50) and generous, good-value daily specials from Fr.18.50. Mon–Sat 9am–midnight.

THE COVERED BAZAAR, ISTANBUL

Turkey

HIGHLIGHTS

❶ Istanbul A sensory overload with historical sights, fantastic nightlife and delicious cuisine. See p.1146

❷ Ephesus One of the world's best-preserved ancient cities. See p.1162

❸ Kaş A great base for swimming, ancient sites and adventure sports. See p.1167

❹ Olympos Explore well-preserved seaside ruins and spend the night in a treehouse in a tranquil valley. See p.1167

❺ Cappadocia A lunar landscape, complete with rock-cut churches and underground cities. See p.1173

HIGHLIGHTS ARE MARKED ON THE MAP ON P.1141

ROUGH COSTS

Daily budget Basic €30, occasional treat €45

Drink *Rakı* €4.50, beer (*Efes*) €4

Food Kebab with side order €5–6

Hostel/budget hotel €12 (dorm)/€55

Travel Bus: Istanbul–Ankara €19

FACT FILE

Population 77.6 million

Area 783,562 sq km

Language Turkish

Currency Turkish lira (₺ or TL)

Capital Ankara

International phone code ☎90

Time zone GMT +2hr

Introduction

Turkey has multiple identities. Poised between East and West, it's a place where mosques coexist with churches, and Roman ruins crumble alongside ancient Hittite sites. The country is politically secular, though the majority of the population is Muslim, and it's an immensely rewarding place to travel, not least because of the people, whose reputation for friendliness and hospitality is richly deserved.

Much of the country's delights are inexpensive pleasures. Whether it's indulging in tasty *gözleme* (stuffed flatbreads) or dancing in backstreet bars, there are plenty of activities to consume your time but not your budget.

Most visitors begin their trip in **Istanbul**, a heady mixture of European shopping districts, Byzantine and Ottoman architecture and Anatolian cultural influences. South from here small country towns are interspersed by swathes of olive groves and several ancient sites, notably **Ephesus**. Beyond the functional city of **İzmir**, the **Aegean coast** is dotted with tourist resorts, including hedonistic party towns such as **Bodrum** and **Marmaris**. The aptly named Turquoise Coast is home to resorts such as **Fethiye** and **Kaş**, famous for their fabulous water- and adventure-sports facilities. Inland is spectacular

Cappadocia, with its well-known rock churches, subterranean cities and landscape studded with cave dwellings. Further north, **Ankara**, Turkey's capital, is a planned city whose contrived Western feel gives some indication of the priorities of the modern Turkish Republic. Further south, **Konya** is the birthplace of the Mevlevi (whirling dervish) sufi sect.

CHRONOLOGY

1250 BC According to Homer's *Iliad* Troy is cleverly taken by the Greeks who sneak into the city in a wooden horse.

334 BC Alexander the Great marches through Anatolia, present-day Turkey.

129 BC Romans conquer Anatolia.

54 AD St Paul brings Christianity to Anatolia.

330 Emperor Constantine founds Constantinople, calling it the new Rome and establishing the Byzantine Empire.

1288 The Islamic Ottoman Empire starts to expand across present-day Turkey.

A DIFFICULT NEIGHBOURHOOD

The unravelling of Turkey's southeastern neighbours, first **Iraq** (from 2003) then **Syria** (from 2011), has had inevitable consequences on a nation strategically located between Europe and the Middle East. By early 2016 Turkey was home to up to three million Syrian refugees, an enormous strain on the economy, as well as a bone of contention with Europe, to where many moved on. ISIS (Islamic State), spawned from the chaos of a decaying Iraq and developing strength in the vacuum of war-torn Syria, launched several suicide bomb attacks within Turkey in 2015 and 2016, targeting both Ankara and Istanbul. Following the breakdown of "peace talks" between the Turkish government and the outlawed Kurdish Workers Party (PKK), the situation in Turkey was further complicated by renewed fighting between the state security forces and PKK militants. An extremist offshoot of the PKK launched two suicide bomb attacks in Ankara in 2016. Although fewer than a total of twenty foreigners were killed in the ISIS and PKK-splinter group blasts, the repercussions on Turkey's tourism industry were severe; an attempted coup in summer 2016 further complicated the situation. Despite the troubles, Turkey remains a relatively safe place to visit, but make sure that you check your home country's **foreign travel advice** before travelling – for the UK this is ⓦ gov.uk/foreign-travel -advice/turkey.

35

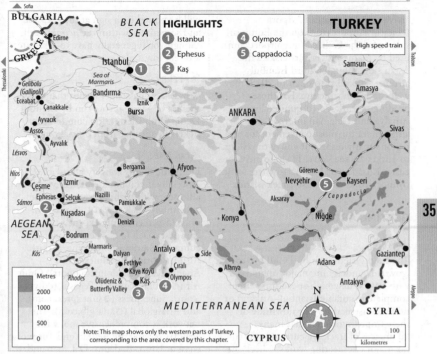

1526 The Ottomans defeat the Habsburgs, taking large areas of Europe.

1832 Following more than ten years of heavy fighting, the Greeks gain independence from Ottoman Turkey.

1918 The Ottomans, having aligned with Germany in World War I, are defeated by the Allies.

1923 After its War of Independence, Turkey is declared a republic led by President Mustafa Kemal Atatürk.

1928 The Turkish constitution declares Turkey to be a secular state.

1938 Atatürk dies on November 10.

1945 Turkey remains neutral during World War II.

1960 A military coup results in the dismissal of the ruling Democrat Party and the hanging of its leaders.

1980 Once more the army overthrows government. Governance is given back to civilians a couple of years later.

1993 Tansu Çiller becomes Turkey's first female prime minister.

2005 Talks about Turkish accession to the EU are held.

2007 Tens of thousands of secularists protest in Ankara against Islamist Prime Minister Erdoğan's proposed run for president.

2010 Istanbul becomes a European Capital of Culture. Nine Turkish citizens aboard a Gaza-bound relief ship are killed by Israeli commandos.

2011 Ten thousand Syrian refugees travel over the border into Turkey. PM Erdoğan criticizes his former ally Assad.

2013 Protests against plans to develop Istanbul's Gezi Park turn into a summer of demonstrations and discontent across the country. The heavy-handed response by the government and police is condemned at home and abroad.

2015 The Islamist AKP (Justice and Development Party) win a record fourth term in office. Turkey finds itself home to around 2.5m Syrian refugees.

2016 Suicide bomb blasts in Istanbul and Ankara kill over seventy people; in July sections of the army try, and fail, to overthrow Erdoğan in a coup.

ARRIVAL AND DEPARTURE

Tourist **visas** are required for individuals from most countries, and cost between US$20 and US$60. You must apply in advance and online for an electronic visa (e-visa) from ⓦevisa.gov.tr. Visas issued for most nationalities allow for multiple entry and are valid for 90 days in 180.

The most common point of **arrival** is Istanbul, with **overland travellers** arriving at the bus station some distance from the centre. **International flights** to Istanbul arrive at either Atatürk Airport (waturkairport.com) on the European side or Sabiha Gökçen (wsgairport.com), used by many budget carriers, on the Asian side, though a third Istanbul airport, scheduled to open in 2018, may well change this picture. For those heading to Turkey's Turquoise Coast, Antalya and Dalaman international airports are the most convenient for the region's many resorts. If you're travelling to Turkey **by sea** you're likely to arrive at either Kuşadası or Marmaris where ferries connect Turkey with the Greek islands.

<h2>35</h2>

GETTING AROUND

BY TRAIN

The **train** system, run by TCDD (wtcdd .gov.tr) is undergoing major upgrades, with several new high-speed lines either completed (notably Istanbul–Ankara) or under construction. The downside of these improvements is that many kilometres of track are currently closed for major engineering works. Check the TCDD website or, more reliably, wseat61.com, for the latest news on routes. Reserve in advance for sleeper cabins on overnight services; seat reservations are usually only necessary at weekends or on national holidays. An ISIC card gets a twenty percent discount. InterRail passes are valid; Eurail aren't.

BY BUS

The **long-distance bus** network is extensive, reliable and affordable. Most destinations are served by several competing firms, which all have ticket booths at the bus station (*otogar* or terminal) from which they operate, as well as an office in the town centre. Book ahead if you're travelling in high season or on a public holiday. **Fares** vary only slightly between companies: expect to pay about ₺15 per 100km. Bus companies usually provide a free shuttle bus between the *otogar* and town centre. For short hops you're most likely to use a **dolmuş** (shared taxi), a **car** or **minibus** that follows a set route, picking up and dropping off along the way. Sometimes the destination will be posted on a sign at the kerbside, and sometimes within the *dolmuş* itself, though you'll generally have to ask. Fares are very low.

BY FERRY

Vehicle and passenger **ferries** that cross the Sea of Marmara are run by Istanbul Deniz Otobüsleri (wido.com.tr). Buy tickets in advance from official outlets.

BY PLANE

Domestic flights are very affordable, especially if you book reasonably well in advance, with flights between Istanbul and Antalya as low as ₺100 one-way, only 25 percent more expensive than the cheapest coach fare. There are many competing airlines, including Turkish Airlines (wturkishairlines.com), Anadolujet (wanadolujet.com.tr), Onur Air (wonurair.com.tr), Pegasus (wflypgs .com), Sunexpress (wsunexpress.com) and Atlasglobal (watlasglb.com). The network is comprehensive too, with airports serving the Aegean and Turquoise coast at İzmir, Bodrum, Dalaman and Antalya, while Cappadocia has airports at Kayseri and Nevşehir.

ACCOMMODATION

Finding **accommodation** is generally no problem, except in high season in Istanbul, at the busier coastal resorts and in the larger towns. Basic ungraded **hotels** or **pansiyons** (*pensions*) offer fairly spartan rooms, with or without bathroom, for €40–70. There's also a well-established network of **backpacker hotels** that generally cost €10–20 for a dorm bed, €50–70 for a private double room (€10–20 less if there's no bathroom). You'll also find triple and quad rooms offered at attractive rates at most hotels. Many resort-based places close in winter, so it's wise to call ahead. Almost everywhere offers wi-fi and a/c in each room, and, unless otherwise indicated, includes a Turkish buffet breakfast in the price. **Campsites** are common only on the coast and in national parks and cost around €8–13 per person.

FOOD AND DRINK

At its finest, Turkish food is one of the world's great cuisines, and prices are on the whole affordable. **Breakfast** (*kahvaltı*) served at hotels and *pansiyons* is usually a buffet, offering bread with butter, cheese, cucumber, tomatoes, olives, jam, honey, and tea or coffee. Many workers start the morning with *poça*, pastries filled with meat, cheese or potato that are sold at bakeries, *büfes* (stall/café) or at street carts. Others make do with a simple *simit* (sesame-seed bread ring). Snack vendors hawk *lahmacun*, small "pizzas" with meat-based toppings, and, in coastal cities, *midye dolma* (stuffed mussels). A more substantial option is *pide*, or Turkish pizza – flatbread with various toppings.

Meat dishes in **restaurants** include several variations on the kebab (*kebap*). Fish and seafood are good, if usually pricey. **Meze** – an extensive array of cold appetizers – comes in all shapes and sizes, the most common being *dolma* (peppers or vine leaves stuffed with rice), *patlıcan salata* (aubergine in tomato sauce) and *acılı ezme* (a mixture of tomato paste, onion, chilli and parsley). Many restaurants are alcohol-free.

For **dessert**, there's every imaginable concoction at a *pastane* (sweet shop): best are the honey-soaked baklava, and a variety of milk puddings, most commonly *sütlaç*. Other sweets include *aşure* (Noah's pudding), a sort of rosewater jelly laced with pulses, raisins and nuts; and *lokum* or Turkish delight.

Restaurant **opening hours** vary widely, but in general they are open all day; some open as early as 7am, others open for lunch at around 11am and close between 11pm and 1am. In smaller cities, such as Bursa and Edirne, many tend to shut by around 9pm. Bars are generally open 11am or noon–2am. Clubs are usually open after 11pm until 5/6am.

DRINK

Tea (*çay*) is the national drink, with sugar on the side but no milk. **Turkish coffee** (*kahve*) is strong, bitter and served in tiny cups. Nescafé pretty much holds a

NARGILES

Smoking has been banned in public places, including restaurants, shopping centres and public transport, for many years. However, the country remains very much enamoured with tobacco and the prohibition has not been as effective here as in some other countries. A variety of bars exist specializing in **nargile** (waterpipe) smoking. *Nargiles* use special flavoured tobacco with varieties ranging from chocolate to strawberry. Government plans to ban outdoor as well as indoor smoking may well affect the future of Turkey's nargile café culture.

35

monopoly on instant coffee, but fresh filter coffee and even international favourites like flat whites and lattes are popular in trendier cafés. **Fruit juices** (*meyva suyu*) can be excellent but are usually sweetened. You'll also come across **ayran**, watered-down salted yoghurt, which makes a refreshing drink. The main locally brewed brands of **beer** (*bira*) are Efes Pilsen and Tuborg. The national aperitif is anis-flavoured *rakı* – a strong spirit consisting of 45 percent alcohol. It's usually topped up with water and enjoyed with meze. There are plenty of decent Turkish-produced wines, though, like all alcoholic beverages, they are surprisingly expensive because of high taxes.

CULTURE AND ETIQUETTE

Turkey's unspoken codes of conduct can catch the first-time visitor off guard. Away from the main cities you should **dress modestly** and avoid shorts and revealing attire – this is particularly important the further east you travel. If you are a female traveller, it is essential to take a headscarf or shawl if you plan on **visiting a mosque**. These are generally open during daylight hours, except for prayer time (around half an hour following the call to prayer). Both sexes should remember to remove their shoes.

In almost every sphere of social interaction, **tea drinking** plays an important role. You'll notice shop

HAGGLING

Shopping in Turkey requires more than just money. In bazaars, market stalls and independent shops, you should try **haggling** – the original price quoted can be three times the price of the item's actual value. Avoid displaying too much enthusiasm over your desired item, and if the price quoted sounds expensive, either make to walk away or inform the shopkeeper that you would like to shop around for a better deal – this might result in a better offer.

salesmen commonly invite you to peruse their goods over tea.

Although interaction between Turkish men and women is quite formal, single **female travellers** may experience harassment and should take care, particularly in the evenings. Note also that, while many young Turkish women visit bars and clubs, few of them go out unaccompanied at night, and you should observe this rule away from tourist areas.

SPORTS AND ACTIVITIES

Undoubtedly Turkey's most popular sport is **football**, with Istanbul's "big three", Galatasaray, Beşiktaş and Fenerbahçe, being the nation's favourite teams. To find out about games and buy tickets, visit ⊕biletix.com.

Most tour operators in the established resorts have information about both summer and winter **adventure sports**. **Scuba diving** is popular, and Kaş in particular offers some of the best in the Med. Other picturesque spots along the coast have skies full of **paragliders**, while **hikers** will find all manner of great trails, not least the Lycian Way from Fethiye to Antalya.

COMMUNICATIONS

Most **post offices** (PTT) open Monday to Saturday 9am to 5pm, with main branches open till 7/8pm and also on Sunday. Use the *yurtdışı* (overseas) slot on postboxes. **Phone calls** can be made from Turk Telecom booths and the PTT. Post offices and kiosks sell phonecards (30, 60 and 100 units) and also have metered phones. Some payphones accept credit cards. Numerous private phone shops (*Kontürlü telefon*) offer metered calls at dubious, unofficial rates. For longer stays it might be worthwhile purchasing a local SIM card from one of the three major operators – Turkcell, Avea or Vodafone. There are **internet** cafés in most towns, but almost every hotel and hostel has free **wi-fi** and often a computer for use by residents. Many bars, cafés, restaurants – and even the long-distance buses – also have free wi-fi.

EMERGENCIES

Street **crime** is uncommon and theft is rare; however, lone women should pay attention and be very wary of going out alone after dark. **Police** wear dark blue uniforms with baseball caps, with their division – *trafik*, *narkotik*, etc – clearly marked. There's a tourist police centre at Yerebatan Cad 6 (☎0212 527 4503) in Sultanahmet with some English-speaking officers. In rural areas, you'll find the camouflage-clad Jandarma, a division of the regular army. For minor **health** complaints, head for the nearest pharmacy (*eczane*). Night-duty pharmacists are known as *nöbetçi*; the current rota is posted in every pharmacy's front window. For more serious ailments, go to a hospital (*klinik*) – either public or the much higher-quality and cleaner private (*Özel Hastane*).

INFORMATION

Most towns of any size have a **tourist office** (Turizm Danışma Bürosu), generally open Monday to Friday 8.30am to 12.30pm and 1.30 to 5.30pm. Staff usually speak English, and should be able to help you with accommodation, and you'll generally find a good range of brochures and maps.

EMERGENCY NUMBERS

Police ☎ 155; Ambulance ☎ 112; Fire ☎ 110.

TURKISH

	TURKISH	PRONUNCIATION
Yes	*Evet*	Evet
No	*Hayır/yok*	Hi-uhr/yok
Please	*Lütfen*	Lewtfen
Thank you	*Teşekkürler/mersi/sağol*	Teshekkewrler/sa-ol
Hello/Good day	*Merhaba*	Merhabuh
Goodbye	*Hoşçakalın*	Hosh-cha kaluhn
Excuse me	*Pardon*	Pardon
Where?	*Nerede?*	Neredeh?
Good	*İyi*	Eeyee
Bad	*Kötü*	Kurtew
Near	*Yakın*	Yakuhn
Far	*Uzak*	Oozak
Cheap	*Ucuz*	Oojooz
Expensive	*Pahalı*	Pahaluh
Open	*Açık*	Achuhk
Closed	*Kapalı*	Kapaluh
Today	*Bugün*	Boogewn
Yesterday	*Dün*	Dewn
Tomorrow	*Yarın*	Yaruhn
How much is?	*Ne kadar…?*	Ne kadar…?
What time is it?	*Saatınız var mı?*	Saatiniz var muh?
I don't understand	*Anlamıyorum*	Anlamuh-yoroom
Do you speak English?	*İngilizce biliyor musunuz?*	Eengeeleezjeh beeleeyor moosoonooz?
Sorry	*Özür dilerim*	Erzer delereem
Do you have?	*…var mı?*	Öva mur?
I would like	*…istiyorum*	Öe-stee-yo-rum
What is your name?	*Adınız ne?*	A-denurz nay?
I'd like the bill	*Hesabı Istiyorum*	Hes-ab ee-stee-yo-rum
One	*Bir*	Bir
Two	*İki*	Iki
Three	*Üç*	Ewch
Four	*Dört*	Durt
Five	*Beş*	Besh
Six	*Altı*	Altuh
Seven	*Yedi*	Yedi
Eight	*Sekiz*	Sekiz
Nine	*Dokuz*	Dokuz
Ten	*On*	On

MONEY AND BANKS

Currency is the **Turkish lira** (₺ or TL), divided into 100 kuruş. There are coins of 1, 5, 10, 25, 50 kuruş and ₺1, and notes of ₺1, 5, 10, 20, 50, 100 and 200. The symbol ₺, introduced in 2012, is phasing out the old system, where the price was suffixed by the letters TL, as in 10TL, but plenty of places still use the acronym. Exchange rates for foreign currency are always better inside Turkey; at the time of writing they were approximately £1 = ₺4.1, €1 = ₺3.2,

US$1 = ₺2.9. Many *pensions* and hotels, particularly in the popular destinations, often quote prices in **euros**, and you can usually pay in either euros or Turkish lira.

Banks open Monday to Friday 8.30am to noon and 1.30pm to 5pm; some, notably Garanti Bankası, are open at lunchtimes and on Saturday. Some of the **exchange booths** run by banks in coastal resorts, airports and ferry docks charge a small commission. Private exchange offices have competitive rates and no commission. Almost all banks have

TURKEY ONLINE

Ⓦ **goturkeytourism.com** Turkey's official tourism portal.

Ⓦ **hurriyetdailynews.com** The best source of Turkish (and international) news in English.

Ⓦ **timeoutistanbul.com/en** A reliable listings site for the latest exhibitions, gigs and films.

Ⓦ **turkeytravelplanner.com** Turkey expert's personal guide to the country.

ATMs. **Post offices** in sizeable towns also sometimes change cash and cheques.

OPENING HOURS AND HOLIDAYS

Shops are generally open Monday to Saturday 9am to 7/8pm, and possibly Sunday, depending on the owner. There are two **religious holidays**. **Kurban Bayramı** (the Feast of the Sacrifice) falls on August 31 to September 4 in 2017, August 24 to 28 in 2018 and August 10 to 14 in 2019. **Şeker Bayramı** (Sugar Holiday) marks the end of the Muslim fasting month of Ramadan. If either falls midweek, the government may choose to extend the holiday period to as much as nine days. Many shops and restaurants close as their owners return to their home towns for the holiday. Banks and public offices are also closed on the **secular holidays**: January 1, April 23, May 19, August 30, October 28 and 29.

Istanbul

Arriving in **ISTANBUL** can result in sensory overload: backstreets teem with traders pushing handcarts, the smell of grilled food from roadside vendors lingers in the air and the call to prayer rings out from tall minarets. Yet this is merely one aspect of modern Istanbul. With the bustling bars, cafés, boutiques and art galleries in Beyoğlu, a distinctly European influence also pervades.

Istanbul is the only city in the world to have played capital to consecutive Christian and Islamic empires, and retains features of both. Named **Byzantium** after the Greek colonist Byzas, the city was an important trading centre. In the fourth century it was renamed **Constantinople** when Constantine chose it as the new capital of the Roman Empire. The city later became an independent empire, adopting the Greek language and Christianity as its religion. In 1453 the city was captured by the Ottoman Turk **Mehmet the Conqueror**. By the nineteenth century, the glory days of the Ottoman empire were over. After the War of Independence (1919–23), the territorial boundaries of modern-day Turkey were set and Istanbul lost its status as the **capital** to Ankara under the country's leader, **Mustafa Kemal Atatürk**. The city remains the country's economic and cultural heart, though, with a population of over 15 million.

WHAT TO SEE AND DO

The city is divided in two by the **Bosphorus**, a stretch of water that runs between the Black Sea and the Sea of Marmara, dividing Europe from Asia. At right angles to it, the inlet of the **Golden Horn** cuts the European side in two. Most visitors stay on the European side of the Bosphorus, basing themselves either in the old city, centred on the historic **Sultanahmet** district, or in the arty, Europeanized district of **Beyoğlu**, north of the Golden Horn. Sandwiched between the two is **Eminönü** and the old Levantine area of Galata, now **Karaköy**, home to one of the city's most famous landmarks, the Galata Tower. **Taksim Square** is a convenient base, and comes into its own at night as a centre of cultural and culinary activity.

Haghia Sophia

The former Byzantine cathedral of **Haghia Sophia** or **Aya Sofya** in Turkish (daily April–Oct 9am–7pm, last entry 6pm; Nov–March 9am–5pm; ₺30; Ⓦ ayasofya muzesi.gov.tr), readily visible thanks to its massive domed structure, is perhaps the single most compelling sight in the city. Commissioned in the sixth century by the Emperor Justinian, it was converted to a mosque in 1453, after which the minarets were added; it's been a museum since 1934. For centuries this was the largest enclosed space in the world, and the interior – filled with shafts of light from the high windows around the dome – is still profoundly impressive. There are a few features left over from its time as a mosque – a mihrab (niche indicating the direction of Mecca), a mimber (pulpit) and the enormous wooden plaques which bear sacred names of God, the Prophet Mohammed and the first four Caliphs. There are also remains of abstract and figurative mosaics.

Topkapı Palace

Immediately north of Aya Sofya, **Topkapı Palace** (daily except Tues: April–Oct 9am–7pm, last entry 6pm; Nov–March 9am–5pm; ₺30; ⓦtopkapisarayi.gov.tr) is Istanbul's second unmissable sight. Built between 1459 and 1465, the palace was the centre of the Ottoman Empire for nearly four centuries. The ticket office is in the first courtyard, followed by the beautifully restored Divan, containing the Imperial Council Hall in the second courtyard. Around the corner is the Harem, well worth the additional ₺15 (tickets sold outside Harem entrance). The only men once allowed in here were eunuchs and the imperial guardsmen, who were only employed at certain hours and even then blinkered. Back in the main body of the palace, in the third courtyard, the throne room was where the sultan awaited the outcome of sessions of the Divan.

The Blue Mosque

With its six minarets, the **Blue Mosque** or **Sultanahmet Camii** (Mon–Thurs, Sat & Sun 9am–1hr before dusk prayer call, Fri

9am–noon prayers; free; remove your shoes before entering) is instantly recognizable; inside, its four "elephant foot" pillars obscure parts of the building and dwarf the dome they support. It's the 20,000-odd blue tiles inside that lend the mosque its name. Outside the precinct wall is the **Tomb of Sultan Ahmet** (daily 9am–4pm), where the sultan is buried along with his wife and three of his sons.

The Museum of Turkish and Islamic Art

Located in the former palace of İbrahim Paşa, the **Museum of Turkish and Islamic Art** (daily April–Oct 9am–7pm; Nov–March 9am–5pm; ₺20) houses one of the best-exhibited collections of Islamic artefacts in the world. Ibrahim Paşa's magnificent audience hall is devoted to a collection of Turkish carpets, while on the ground floor, in rooms off the central courtyard, is an exhibition of the folk art of the Yörük tribes of Anatolia.

TROUBLED TIMES

Istanbul, and Taksim Square in particular, was the scene of several demonstrations and clashes throughout 2013. A small protest against plans to redevelop Taksim Square's Gezi Park (one of the few areas of green space left in the city) flared into a much larger expression of dissatisfaction with the government that elicited a heavy-handed response and unrest across the country.

Much worse followed when, in January 2016, an Islamic State (ISIS) suicide bomber killed twelve tourists in the historic Sultanahmet district. Another suicide bomb attack resulted in five foreign nationals losing their lives on busy İstiklal Caddesi in March 2016.

35

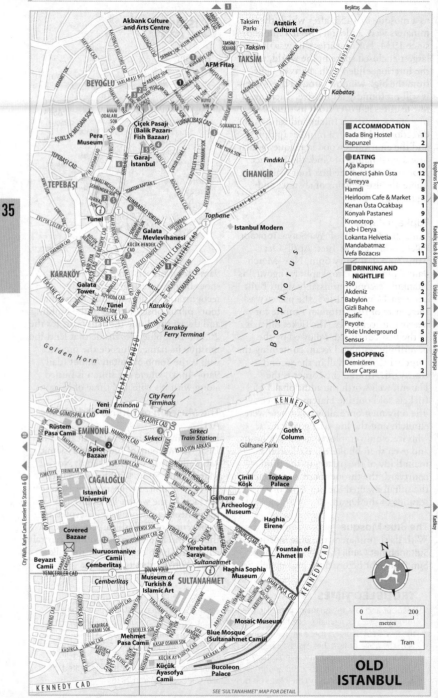

Beşiktaş

Akbank Culture
and Arts Centre

Taksim
Parkı

Atatürk
Cultural Centre

TAKSİM

Taksim

AFM Fitaş

BEYOĞLU

Kabataş

Çiçek Pasajı
(Balık Pazarı–
Fish Bazaar)

Pera
Museum

Garaj-
İstanbul

Fındıklı

CİHANGİR

TEPEBAŞI

Tünel

Tophane

İstanbul Modern

Galata
Mevlevihanesi

Bosphorus

KARAKÖY

Galata
Tower

Tünel

Karaköy

Karaköy
Ferry Terminal

Golden Horn

City Ferry
Terminals

Yeni
Cami

Eminönü

KENNEDY CAD

Rüstem
Paşa Camii

EMİNÖNÜ

Sirkeci

Sirkeci
Train Station

Goth's
Column

Spice
Bazaar

Gülhane Parkı

CAĞALOĞLU

Çinili
Köşk

Topkapı
Palace

Istanbul
University

Gülhane
Archeology
Museum

Haghia
Eirene

Covered
Bazaar

Yerebatan
Sarayı

Fountain of
Ahmet III

Beyazıt
Camii

Nuruosmaniye
Camii
Çemberlitaş

Sultanahmet

Haghia Sophia
Museum

Çemberlitaş

Museum of
Turkish &
Islamic Art

SULTANAHMET

Hippodrome

Mosaic Museum

Mehmet
Paşa Camii

Blue Mosque
(Sultanahmet Camii)

Küçük
Ayasofya
Camii

Bucoleon
Palace

KENNEDY CAD

SEE 'SULTANAHMET' MAP FOR DETAIL

**OLD
ISTANBUL**

- Bosphorus Tour
- Kadıköy, Hasır & Kanga
- Üsküdar
- Harem & Haydarpaşa
- Kadıköy

City Walls, Kariye Camii, Esenler Bus Station &

■ **ACCOMMODATION**
| Bada Bing Hostel | 1 |
| Rapunzel | 2 |

● **EATING**
Ağa Kapısı	10
Dönerci Şahin Usta	12
Fürreyya	7
Hamdi	8
Heirloom Cafe & Market	3
Kenan Usta Ocakbaşı	1
Konyalı Pastanesi	9
Kronotrop	4
Leb-i Derya	6
Lokanta Helvetia	5
Mandabatmaz	2
Vefa Bozacısı	11

■ **DRINKING AND
NIGHTLIFE**
360	6
Akdeniz	2
Babylon	1
Gizli Bahçe	3
Pasific	7
Peyote	4
Pixie Underground	5
Sensus	8

● **SHOPPING**
| Demirören | 1 |
| Mısır Çarşısı | 2 |

N

0   200
metres

Tram

The Archeology Museum and around

Just west of Topkapı, **Gülhane Parkı**, once the palace gardens, houses the **Archeology Museum complex** (Tues–Sun: April–Oct 9am–6pm; Nov–March 9am–4pm). The three museums are covered by one ticket (₺15). In the **Archeology Museum** is a superb collection of sarcophagi, sculptures and other remains of past civilizations. The adjacent **Çinili Köşk** is the oldest secular building in Istanbul, now a Museum of Ceramics housing a select collection of İznık ware and Selçuk tiles. Nearby, the **Museum of the Ancient Orient** contains a small but dazzling collection of Anatolian, Egyptian and Mesopotamian artefacts.

The Covered Bazaar

Off the main street of Divan Yolu Caddesi lies the district of Beyazıt, centred on the Kapalı Çarşı or **Covered Bazaar** (Mon–Sat 9am–7pm; Beyazıt T1 tram stop), a huge web of passageways housing more than four thousand shops, each with chatty, persuasive salesmen. Give yourself an hour or so to negotiate its network of alleyways and to soak up the bustling atmosphere. There are carpet shops everywhere catering for all budgets, shops selling leather goods, gold jewellery, slippers, ceramics and mass-produced souvenirs. If you do decide to buy something, don't forget to haggle (see box, p.1144).

Kadiköy

On the Asian (or Anatolian) side of the city, **Kadiköy** makes a great day-trip or base for a few days. It's a fun residential district and relatively free of tourists; many locals live here and commute to work on the European side. Ferries between the Asian and European sides are cheap and frequent, take twenty minutes and operate from around 6am to 11.30pm.

Karaköy and Beyoğlu

Across the Galata Bridge from Eminönü is **Karaköy** (formerly Galata) and **Beyoğlu**. Karaköy was previously the capital's "European" quarter, and has been home to Jewish, Greek and Armenian minorities. Today you'll find boutiques, crafts shops and small art

> ### HIT THE HAMMAM
>
> No trip to Turkey is complete without a trip to a traditional Turkish bath. One of the city's finest historical public baths is **Çemberlitaş Hammam** at VezirHan Cad 8, Çemberlitaş. At the entrance you'll be given a *peştamal* (cotton towel) to wrap yourself in, and a scrubbing mitt; ladies will also be given disposable underwear. Men and women bathe in separate areas. Once you've changed and put any personal items in a locker you'll be led into the *sıcaklık*, a hot room with a heated marble platform on which you lie down and relax for fifteen minutes or so until you start to sweat. If you've opted for a soap scrub, your attendant will spend fifteen minutes washing, scrubbing and rinsing you, removing grime and dead skin cells. Otherwise you wash yourself. Afterwards, take a dip in the hot tub or relax in the cool lounge afterwards with a cup of tea or fresh fruit juice. Allow at least an hour for the entire process. Basic entry ₺60; entrance plus soap scrub by an attendant ₺95.

galleries, and it's where locals and clued-up overseas visitors meet in international coffee shops, world-class restaurants and lively clubs; this is the place to come for a night out without the tourist hordes you get in Sultanahmet. The **Galata Tower** (daily 9am–8pm; €6.50 or ₺ equivalent), built in 1348, is the area's most obvious landmark; its viewing galleries, café and ridiculously expensive restaurant offer the best panoramas of the city, with queues to match. **Istanbul Modern** by the Bosphorus (Tues–Sun 10am–6pm; ₺17; ⊛istanbulmodern.org) is worth a visit too. With a focus on modern art from contemporary Turkish artists as well as international talent, this is Turkey's answer to the Tate Modern in London.

Up towards İstiklal Caddesi, Beyoğlu's main shopping boulevard, an unassuming doorway leads to the courtyard of the **Galata Mevlevihanesi** (daily 9.30am–5pm, closed Wed; ₺10), a former monastery and ceremonial hall of the Whirling Dervishes, a sect founded in the thirteenth century. Staged dervish

35

ceremonies take place here (April–Sept most Sun at 5pm; Oct–March twice monthly; tickets around ₺50).

The **Pera Museum** (Tues–Sat 10am–7pm; Sun noon–6pm; ₺10; Ⓦperamuseum.org) on Meşrutiyet Cad 65, housed in a beautiful nineteenth-century building, displays changing exhibitions of contemporary art, historical oil paintings of old Istanbul, ceramic tiles and a collection of historical weights and measures. İstiklal Caddesi ends at **Taksim Square**, a busy tourist and transport hub, home to Gezi Park and scene of numerous demonstrations over the years (see box, p.1147).

ARRIVAL AND DEPARTURE

By plane Istanbul's Atatürk airport is 24km west of the city. The cheapest option to get to Sultanahmet is to take the M1 metro from the airport to Zeytinburnu, then change onto the T1 tram. For Beyoğlu/Taksim take the M1 metro to Yenikapı, then the M2 metro to Şişhane or Taksim. Either journey requires the purchase of two travel *jetons*, costing ₺4 each. A taxi will cost around ₺50 to Sultanahmet or ₺60 to Taksim; make sure they use the meter. The Havataş bus (4am–1am every 30min; 40–60min; ₺11) is a reliable option; the bus terminates at Taksim, but get off at Aksaray and take the T1 tram for Sultanahmet.

Istanbul's Sabiha Gökçen airport is 35km southeast of central Istanbul. Shuttle buses (every 30min; 4am–1am; 1hr 30min; ₺14) terminate at Taksim. A taxi from Sabiha Gökçen airport to Sultanahmet will cost around ₺90.

By train Istanbul's historic European-side station, Sirkeci, has been closed to all bar local metro trains. At the time of writing, due to line upgrading in Thrace, train travellers were being bussed into Istanbul from the Turkish-Bulgarian border. When line works are completed (2018), trains from Europe will terminate at a western suburb of Istanbul, where they'll connect with the city's metro system. Haydarpaşa station, the terminal for trains from Asia on the east bank of the Bosphorus, was also closed at the time of writing for the construction of high-speed rail lines and the Marmaray Rail Transport Project, due for completion in 2018. Trains on the high-speed line to Ankara depart from the Asian-side Istanbul suburb of Pendik, but may well depart from Haydarpaşa once all works are completed. Check their site (Ⓦtcdd.gov.tr) and Ⓦseat61.com for the latest developments.

Destinations Ankara (5 daily via Eskisehir; 4hr 15min); Konya (2 daily; 4hr 30min); London (5 days); Sofia, Bulgaria (1 daily; 13hr).

By bus From Istanbul's bus station (*otogar*) at Esenler, 15km northwest, the better bus companies run courtesy minibuses to various points in the city, although if you're heading for Sultanahmet it's often quicker to take the M1 metro (₺43). Some buses also stop at the Harem bus station on the Asian side, from where there are regular *dolmuşes* to Haydarpaşa station. Taxis to Sultanahmet cost approximately ₺40 from the main *otogar*. Watch out for drivers who offer their services near to the departure area. These are usually unlicensed and do not operate a meter.

Destinations Ankara (hourly; 6hr); Antalya (4 daily; 12hr); Athens, Greece (2 weekly; 22hr); Bodrum (8 daily; 12hr); Bursa (hourly; 4hr); Çanakkale (hourly; 6hr); Edirne (hourly; 3hr); Göreme (5 daily; 12hr); İzmir (hourly; 10hr); Konya (7 daily; 11hr); Kuşadası (5 daily; 9hr); Marmaris (4 daily; 13hr); Nevşehir (3 daily; 12hr); Sofia, Bulgaria (12hr).

By ferry Sea bus, car and passenger services from Yalova and Bandirma arrive at the Yenikapı terminal, just south of Aksaray.

INFORMATION

Tourist office The most central office is in Sultanahmet, near the Hippodrome on Divan Yolu Cad (daily 9am–5pm; Ⓣ0212 518 8754). Staff aren't particularly helpful but will hand out free city guides. Smaller branches are at the airport (24hr) and Sirkeci station.

GETTING AROUND

Istanbul boasts an impressive choice of transport, from ferries and trams to metros and an underground funicular. The city's eleven million commuters mean public transport is often crowded.

Tickets It's worth getting hold of an İstanbulkart, a pre-paid smartcard purchased from kiosks near busy transport hubs. It costs a refundable ₺6 for the card; top it up with as much credit as you're likely to need. The İstanbulkart can be used on buses, the metro, trams and ferries. Journeys work out around 40 percent less than using the alternative, travel *jetons*, small plastic tokens that cost ₺4 per journey and are available from booths or vending machines near many transport stops.

By bus Istanbul's buses are either run by the municipality, and are marked by an "IETT" logo, or one of several private companies. The main bus stops boast large route maps and lists of services. Most services run from early in the morning (around 6.30am) to late at night (11.30pm).

By tram The European side has two tram lines. The T1 runs from Kabataş through Sultanahmet to outlying suburbs. The other "toy" tram runs along İstiklal Cad from Beyoğlu to Taksim using an antique tram.

By metro The two most useful lines for visitors are the M1 metro, linking Atatürk Airport with Yenikapı, in the old city, and the M2 metro which runs across the Golden Horn from the old city to Beyoğlu and Taksim. The Marmaray metro links the old city with the Asian side of Istanbul.

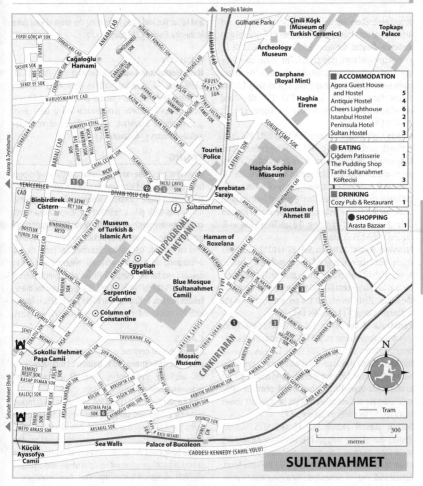

Gülhane Parkı

Çinili Köşk
(Museum of
Turkish Ceramics)

Topkapı
Palace

Archeology
Museum

Darphane
(Royal Mint)

Haghia
Eirene

Çağaloğlu
Hamamı

Tourist
Police

Haghia Sophia
Museum

ACCOMMODATION
Agora Guest House and Hostel	5
Antique Hostel	4
Cheers Lighthouse	6
Istanbul Hostel	2
Peninsula Hotel	1
Sultan Hostel	3

Yerebatan
Sarayı

Sultanahmet

Fountain of
Ahmet III

EATING
Çiğdem Patisserie	1
The Pudding Shop	2
Tarihi Sultanahmet Köftecisi	3

Binbirdirek
Cistern

Museum of Turkish &
Islamic Art

Hamam of
Roxelana

DRINKING
Cozy Pub & Restaurant	1

SHOPPING
Arasta Bazaar	1

35

HIPPODROME
(AT MEYDANI)

Egyptian
Obelisk

Blue Mosque
(Sultanahmet
Camii)

Serpentine
Column

Column of
Constantine

Sokollu Mehmet
Paşa Camii

Mosaic
Museum

CANKURTARAN

N

Tram

0   300
metres

SULTANAHMET

Küçük
Ayasofya
Camii

Sea Walls   Palace of Bucoleon

CADDESI KENNEDY (SAHIL YOLU)

Dolmuş *Dolmuşes* have their point of departure and destination displayed somewhere about the windscreen or painted on the bonnet. Several depart the streets around Taksim Square to various points in the city.

By boat Regular ferries run between Eminönü and Karaköy on the European side, and Üsküdar, Kadiköy and Haydarpaşa in Asia; buy your *jeton* (₺4 one-way) from the dockside kiosks. Ferries depart every 15–20min from around 6am to 9pm; crossings take 20min. Sightseeing Bosphorus cruise boats leave from the Boğaz İskelesi terminal near the Galata Bridge and stop for a long lunch break at Anadolu Kavağı, a distant village up the Bosphorus on the straits' Asian side. The cruise takes approximately 7hr return and costs ₺25. For more information on ferries, see ⊛ sehirhatlari.com.tr.

ACCOMMODATION

There are numerous small hotels and *pansiyons* in Sultanahmet, particularly around Yerebatan Cad and the backstreets between the Blue Mosque and the sea. Taksim is a great base, and is handy for nightlife and boutique shopping and bustling cafés. From Eminönü and Aksaray, many buses pass through either Karaköy or Taksim, or both. Kadiköy on the Asian side offers a less touristy option.

SULTANAHMET

Agora Guest House and Hostel Amiral Tafdil Sok 6 ☎ 0212 458 5547, ⊛ agoraguesthouse.com; map p.1151. Blurring the lines between hotel and guesthouse, this excellent budget choice is right in the heart of the old city. The tastefully furnished communal breakfast/lounge area has a massive flat-screen TV, a cool terrace and a great

atmosphere. There are ten well-appointed doubles, and dorms range from four to ten beds. Dorms €17, doubles €80
Antique Hostel Kutlugün Sok 51 ☎0212 638 1637, ⓦantiquehostel.com; map p.1151. The rooms are a little stuffy but good-looking nonetheless. The sea-view terrace is perched atop the city like an eyrie, with an island bar and decent food available (mains ₺12–15). Wi-fi and breakfast included. All rooms have a/c. Dorms €11.50, doubles €39
Cheers Lighthouse Çayıroğlu Sok 18 ☎0212 458 2324, ⓦcheershostel.com; map p.1151. This cosy eighteen-bed, five-room hostel spread over three floors offers a wide range of accommodation for visitors who appreciate the communal hostel vibe yet want plenty of privacy, with both suite rooms and dorms. On the ground floor is a great lobby, bar and terrace restaurant with views over the now defunct suburban railway line to the sea. There's free wi-fi, tea and coffee too. Dorms €18
Istanbul Hostel Kutlugün Sok 35 ☎0212 516 9380, ⓦistanbulhostel.net; map p.1151. Friendly long-running hostel, with 68 beds plus a terrace and bar. The basement dorm is justifiably popular and they have log fires during the winter. Hostel guests get ten percent discount in the restaurant. Dorms €11, doubles €45
Peninsula Hotel Adliye Sok 6 ☎0212 458 6850, ⓦhotelpeninsula.com; map p.1151. Comfortable budget accommodation on a quiet side street, the eleven simply furnished rooms (laminate floors and plain pastel walls) nonetheless boast a/c, central heating and double glazing as well as flat-screen TVs. Rooms and bathrooms are on the small side, but at these prices that's to be expected; there's also a roof terrace with great views. €45
Sultan Hostel Akbıyık Cad 17 ☎0212 516 9260, ⓦsultanhostel.com; map p.1151. The bar-restaurant is a social focal point on Istanbul's main hostel street, with music blaring and dorm beds empty until the early hours. Abrupt staff and not somewhere for a good night's sleep, but a lively spot. Fine views from the terrace and top-floor twenty-bed dorm. Dorms €12, doubles €46

BEYOĞLU

Bada Bing Hostel Serçe Sok 6, Karaköy ☎0212 249 4111, ⓦbadabinghostel.com; map p.1148. In the hip former docklands of Karaköy, this cool place has a/c dorm rooms ranging from four- to ten-bed, with an eight-bed, female-only option. There are stylishly decorated private rooms as well, plus a massive lounge area and roof-top terrace complete with bean-bags and cool beers for sipping. Dorms €12, doubles €50
★**Rapunzel** Bereketzade Camii Sok 3 ☎0212 292 5034, ⓦrapunzelistanbul.com; map p.1148. Hard to find, but worth the effort. Housed in a more original building than many others, it features nineteenth-century stone walls and all manner of decorative curiosities. Staff are young

and full of tips and ideas for making the most of your time in the city. Dorms €20, doubles €70

KADIKÖY

Hush Hostel and Lounge Rasimpaşa Mah, Rıhtım Cad, İskele Sok 46, Kadiköy ☎0216 450 4363, ⓦhushhostelistanbul.com. This spacious and clean hostel has a well-equipped kitchen, roof terrace and a large back garden. Buffet breakfast, wi-fi and use of computer included. Dorms €14, doubles €31

EATING

Istanbul offers all the range of food and drink you'd expect from a major world city, and provides a number of top spots to sample Turkish delights. From high-end restaurants with prices to match to super-cheap street carts, there are plenty of ways to fill up. Fresh orange and pomegranate juice are worth picking up from street stalls; corn on the cob, less so. Sultanahmet has some decent restaurants, although the principal concentrations are in Beyoğlu and Taksim. The Balık Pazarı, particularly, behind the Çiçek Pasajı (off İstiklal Cad), is a great area for meze, kebabs and fish. In Kadiköy you'll find plenty of bars (many with live music) and restaurants but relatively few tourists.

CAFÉS

Istanbul has undergone a coffee renaissance in recent years, and while strong, thick, traditional Turkish coffee is still available everywhere, international brews are increasingly sold at new coffee shops.
Ağa Kapısı Nazir Izzet Efendi Sok 11; map p.1148. Tucked away on a dead-end street just below the Süleymaniye Camii the *Ağa Kapısı* boasts the picture window beyond compare, giving a stunning panoramic view down over the Galata Bridge and the Bosphorus beyond. Try the *gözleme* (a kind of paratha stuffed with goat's cheese) and a glass of tea (₺2), traditional Turkish style. Daily 8am–midnight.
Çiğdem Patisserie Divan Yolu Cad 62; map p.1151. One of many patisseries in the area but among the best, with forty years of experience serving delectable baklava (₺8 per portion). Daily 8am–11pm.
★**Heirloom Café & Market** Adile Naşit Sok 6; map p.1148. Hard to find (their only sign looks like a homeless person's piece of cardboard) but worth seeking out. A quiet spot set in the garden of a 115-year-old building offering "pour over" coffee (₺7) made from Italian espresso machines, as well as pastries, panini and salads (₺10–18). Daily 8.30am–8.30pm.
Konyalı Pastanesi Ankara Cad, by the tram stop near Sirkeci train station, Eminönü; map p.1148. This place goes back to 1897 and they have their Turkish coffee down to a T. Couple it with the rich sesame *çörek*. Mon–Sat 7am–8pm.
Kronotrop Yeniçarşı Cad 5; map p.1148. There's no room to sit down in this popular spot, but their take-out flat

white (₺8) and Americano (₺7) coffees are from freshly roasted single origin beans and are sublime. Mon–Sat 8.30am–8pm, Sun 11am–7pm.

Mandabatmaz Olivia Geçidi off İstiklal Cad; map p.1148. This tiny Turkish coffee joint, opened in 1967, is more of an institution than a café. Pull up a stool in the cramped interior or on the street outside and, for ₺4, enjoy one of the best Turkish coffees in Istanbul – thick, velvety and like chocolate – the result of its custom roasted coffee beans.

Vefa Bozacısı Katip Çelebi Cad 104/1 ☎ 0212 519 4922, ⓦ vefa.com.tr; map p.1148. Worth a look just to see the interior: old tiled floor, dark-wood shelves, ornate Victorian-style mirrors and bottles of vinegar with label designs unchanged for decades The *boza* (₺3), a cloudy, viscous drink made by fermenting millet with sugar and water, is delicious. Daily 7am–midnight.

RESTAURANTS

SULTANAHMET

Dönerci Şahin Usta Nuruosmaniye Kılıçlar Sok 7; map p.1148. Proper authentic kebabs (₺12) served from an establishment the size of an en-suite bathroom. Justifiably popular with locals working in the bazaar and sold out and closed up by mid-afternoon. Mon–Sat 10am–3pm.

The Pudding Shop (Lale Restaurant) Divan Yolu Cad 6; map p.1151. Dating back to 1957, this Sultanahmet hotspot became the essential meeting place for hippies making the trek to India in the 1960s. It's still popular, offering canteen-style dining (vegetarian bean dishes for ₺11; *köfte* at ₺15) and its famous desserts. Daily 7am–11pm.

Tarihi Sultanahmet Köftecisi Divan Yolu Cad; map p.1151. An Istanbul institution popular with celebrities (many of whose mugs beam down from the wall). You'll probably have to queue, especially at lunchtime, but the *köfte* (₺16) – six meaty fingers of lamb with a flash of pink inside, accompanied by a white bean salad, chillies and chilli sauce – are sufficient recompense. Daily 11am–11pm.

BEYOĞLU AND EMİNÖNÜ

Fürreyya Serdar-ı Ekrem Sok 2B, Galata ☎ 0212 252 4853 ⓦ furreyyagalata.com; map p.1148. A little gem of a fish restaurant near the Galata Tower, *Fürreya* serves up perfectly cooked seafood with a few modern touches, at very reasonable prices. The fish wrap, prawn casserole and fishcakes with basil sauce all come highly recommended. Mains from ₺12. Daily noon–11pm.

Hamdi Tahmis Cad Kalçin Sok 17 ☎ 0212 528 0390; map p.1148. Third-floor restaurant next to the spice bazaar. Fresh meze and kebabs are all served to a high standard. Highly popular and touristy but the views of the Golden Horn are irresistible. Reservations advised. Mains from ₺24. Daily 11am–midnight.

★ **Kenan Usta Ocakbaşı** Kurabiye Sok 18; map p.1148. Master grillsman Kenan has been perfecting his art for

GET YOUR FRESH FISH HERE

Fresh fish and seafood are delicious in Istanbul. At either end of **Galata Bridge** you can buy freshly grilled fish sandwiches (₺6) from fishermen with mobile carts or fresh off a bobbing boat. At the Karaköy end walk past the fish market, settle down at the plastic chairs and tables and order a whole grilled fish, chips and salad for around ₺15. Times vary, but food is generally served until 10pm daily.

four decades, and a visit to his basement charcoal grill to watch him in action is a must. Locals gather around the huge fire pit as he cooks meat to perfection before sending it out with a red onion and parsley garnish, lightly toasted *lavaş* (tortilla-style bread) and a variety of fresh meze. Meat mains from ₺20. Daily 10am–2pm.

Leb-i Derya Kumbaracı Yokuşu 57 6, Tünel; map p.1148. This is one of the best bar-restaurants from which to see the city from up high. The food and the cocktails are as good as the view, though prices are not budget. Expect to part with at least ₺70 per head. The street is steep and narrow, leading off from the main drag, İstiklal Cad. Mon–Thurs & Sun 11am–2am, Fri & Sat 11am–3am.

Lokanta Helvetia General Yazgan Sok 8/a; map p.1148. It may be small but the buffet-style lunches and dinners make this one of Beyoğlu's best bargains (it's ₺15 a plate). Mon–Sat 8am–10pm.

DRINKING AND NIGHTLIFE

Many backpackers gather in the bars on Akbıyık Cad in Sultanahmet, but Karaköy, Galata and Beyoğlu are much livelier and frequented by arty and alternative locals as well as visitors. In Kadıköy go to Kadife Sok, aka "bar street", for the liveliest places.

BARS

★ **360** Mısır Apartmanı 32 309, Istiklal Cad, Tünel ⓦ 360istanbul.com; map p.1148. Actually a restaurant, bar and club, as its name suggests this pricey place has panoramic views best appreciated at night. At weekends the place rocks till the small hours, but it's really all about the view. Mon–Thurs noon–2am, Fri noon–4pm & 6pm–4am, Sat 6pm–4am, Sun 6pm–2.30am.

Akdeniz Nevizade Sok 25, Beyoğlu; map p.1148. Rambling, multistorey student bar, with rock music and cheap drinks. Some of the artwork is a bit dodgy but it's a great spot to chill out with friends – or on your own – with an Efes or two. Daily until late.

Cozy Pub & Restaurant Divan Yolu Cad 66; map p.1151. A dark wood-panelled bar on a corner perfect for people-watching that's been serving locals and tourists alike since

1846. Order some Turkish or international food (₺18–30) or just a beer (₺12) and observe the human traffic flowing by. Daily 10am–2am.

Gizli Bahçe Nevizade Sok 27, Beyoğlu; map p.1148. Cutting-edge dance music in a dilapidated Ottoman townhouse bar. Probably looks like a squat in daylight. This is hipster Istanbul, with languidly cool staff. Daily noon–2am.

Karga Kadife Sok 16, Kadıköy. A hip yet friendly bar spread across several floors and furnished with lots of dark chunky wood tables. DJs and live music. Daily 11am–2am.

Pasific Sofyalı Sok ☎0212 292 7642; map p.1148. Small, friendly bar with a good selection of rock music and well-priced beer (₺10 for draught). It's a struggle to find a seat on the alleyway tables in summer, though the *Kino Garden* next door, jointly with *Pasific*, has a garden out back. Daily 10am–2am.

Sensus Büyükhendek Cad 5, Galata ☎0212 245 5657, ⓦ sensuswine.com; map p.1148. Just a stone's throw from the Galata Tower, this basement "wine and cheese boutique" has character and dozens of local Turkish wines (from ₺10 a glass) and tasty cheese platters. Daily 10am–11pm.

CLUBS

★Babylon Tarihi Bomonti Bira Fabrikası, Birahane Sok 1, Bomonti, Şişli ⓦ babylon.com.tr; map p.1148. This state-of-the-art venue, housed in a converted historic brewery, attracts the most exciting, alternative Turkish and international acts. Tues–Thurs 9.30pm–2am, Fri & Sat 10pm–3am.

Peyote Sahne Sok 24, Beyoğlu ⓦ peyote.com.tr; map p.1148. Run by people in bands (generally a good sign), this live music club boasts several floors and a much-needed roof terrace for cooling after. Beers are around ₺10 and entry charges start from ₺14. Daily 10pm–4am.

Pixie Underground Toşbaşağa Sok 12; map p.1148. This small venue is musically one of the most cutting-edge clubs in Beyoğlu. Istanbul's only bass music club, the emphasis is on dubstep, drum'n'bass and jungle. Beers are a respectable price, entry often free. Daily 2pm–4am.

ENTERTAINMENT

For listings pick up monthly *Time Out Istanbul* from newsstands, bookshops, hotels and hostels.

AFM Fitaş İstiklal Cad 24–26. A popular ten-screen cinema near Taksim Square, with a pub upstairs. Open daily; Wed is discount day.

Akbank Culture and Arts Centre (Akbanksanat) İstiklal Cad 8, Beyoğlu. A multipurpose centre boasting café, dance studio, music room, library and theatre. The centre hosts film festivals and the annual Akbank Jazz Festival. Tues–Sun 10.30am–7.30pm.

Garajistanbul Kaymakan Reşit Bey Sok 11, Beyoğlu. A hip performing arts venue in a converted car park, offering cutting-edge films, art projects and workshops. Opening hours vary depending on the programme.

SHOPPING

Istanbul is famous for its bazaars, where you can pick up pretty much anything, from mass-produced trinkets and souvenirs to hand-woven carpets. Shops lining İstiklâl Cad are the place to head for clothes (you'll find European and American brands here) and the network of narrow streets in Beyoğlu is home to numerous boutiques, secondhand and vintage shops, as well as owner-maker artist studios where you can buy one-off craft items for affordable prices.

BAZAARS

Arasta Bazaar Mimar Mehmet Ağa Cad 14, Sultanahmet; map p.1151. Good for handmade crafts and carpets. Daily from 10am.

Mısır Çarşısı (Spice Bazaar) Çiçek Pazarı Sok, 5min southwest of Eminönü tram stop; map p.1148. Everything from spices to jewellery, natural apple tea and aphrodisiacs including chewy sweet-like blocks of Viagra. Daily 8am–7.30pm.

SHOPS

Demirören İstiklal Cad, Beyoğlu ⓦ www .demirorenistiklal.com; map p.1148. Opened to great fanfare in 2011 by Real Madrid and Portugal legend Cristiano Ronaldo, this conveniently located mall includes a Virgin Megastore, Mothercare and Gap among many other shops, as well as a cinema. Daily 10am–10pm.

DIRECTORY

Consulates Australia, Askerocağı Cad 15, Elmadağ, Şişli 34367 ☎0212 243 1333; New Zealand, İnönü Cad No 48/3, Taksim 80090 ☎0212 244 0272; UK, Meşrutiyet Caddesi 34, Beyoğlu ☎0212 334 6400; US, Kaplıcalar Mevkii Sok 2, İstinye 34460 ☎0212 335 9000.

Hospitals American Hospital, Güzelbahçe Sok 20, Nişantaşı ☎0212 444 3777; International Hospital, İstanbul Cad 82, Yeşilköy ☎0212 468 4444.

Internet Wi-fi is available at almost every café or hostel, so the number of dedicated internet cafés has declined massively and what's left are largely for gaming.

Left luggage Facilities are available at both of the city's airports, Atatürk (₺20 for a suitcase) and Sabiha Gökçen (comparable prices). Open 24hr daily.

Police Tourist Police, Yerebatan Cad, Sultanahmet ☎0212 527 4503.

Post office The central office is on Büyük Postane Caddesi (☎0212 526 1200).

The Sea of Marmara

Despite their proximity to Istanbul, the shores and hinterland of the Sea of Marmara are usually neglected by foreign travellers – but there are good reasons to explore the region: not least **Bursa**, the first Ottoman capital and home to some superb Islamic buildings. Many visitors also stop off at the extensive World War I battlefields and cemeteries of the **Gelibolu** peninsula (Gallipoli), using either the port of **Eceabat** as a base, or, more commonly, **Çanakkale**. The border town of **Edirne**, meanwhile, is a charming spot to break a journey into Europe.

BURSA

Draped along the leafy lower slopes of Uludağ, a mountain that towers more than 2000m above, **BURSA** – first capital of the Ottoman Empire and the burial place of several sultans – is a charming city in which to spend a few days. Gathered here are some of the finest early Ottoman monuments in Turkey, in a tidy and appealing city centre.

WHAT TO SEE AND DO

Flanked by busy Atatürk Caddesi, compact **Koza Parkı**, with its fountains, benches and cafés, is the heart of Bursa. On the far side looms the fourteenth-century **Ulu Cami**, whose interior is dominated by a huge *şadırvan* pool for ritual ablutions. A little way north is Bursa's covered market, the **Bedesten**, given over to the sale of jewellery and precious metals, and the **Koza Hanı**, flanking the park, still entirely occupied by silk and brocade merchants.

Yeşil Cami, Yeşil Türbe and the Art Museum

Across the river to the east, the **Yeşil Cami** (daily 8am–8.30pm) is easily the most spectacular of Bursa's imperial mosques. The nearby hexagonal **Yeşil Türbe** (daily 8am–noon & 1–7pm) contains the sarcophagus of Çelebi Mehmet I and

assorted offspring. Just north of Yeşil Türbe is the small **Museum of Turkish and Islamic Art** (daily: April–Oct 9am–7pm; Nov–March 9am–5pm; ₺5), with Çanakkale ceramics, glass items and clothing. The peaceful courtyard is a nice place to chill out.

The Hisar and around

West of the centre, the **Hisar** ("citadel") district was Bursa's original nucleus. Narrow lanes wind up past dilapidated Ottoman houses, while walkways clinging to the rock face offer fabulous views. The best-preserved dwellings are a little way west in medieval **Muradiye**, where the Muradiye Külliyesi mosque and *medrese* complex was begun in 1424. This is the last imperial foundation in Bursa, although it's most famous for its tombs, set in lovingly tended gardens.

ARRIVAL AND INFORMATION

By bus The bus station is 5km north on the main road to İstanbul, from where bus #38 (every 15min) runs to Koza Parkı.
Destinations Çanakkale (hourly; 4hr); Istanbul (hourly; 4hr); İznik (hourly; 2hr).
Tourist office Corner of Koza Parkı (Mon–Fri 8am–noon & 1–5pm, Sat 9am–12.30pm & 1.30–6pm; ☎ 0224 220 1848).

ACCOMMODATION

Hotel Çeşmeli Gümüşçeken Cad 6 ☎ 0224 224 1511. A Female-run place with a handy location that makes up for its somewhat quaint aesthetic. Centrally located with an excellent self-service breakfast. Doubles ₺140
Hotel Güneş İnebey Cad 75 ☎ 0224 222 1404. Cheap, clean and friendly. Extremely basic but full of character. Prices are cheaper if you can forgo a bath for the night. Breakfast is ₺9 extra. Doubles ₺70
Kitap Evi Kavaklıdere Cad, Burçüstü Sok 21 ☎ 0224 225 4160, ⓦ kitapevi.com.tr. This one-time bookshop has been

THE EVIL EYE

Take a short stroll around any Turkish town and it won't be long until you spot one of the ubiquitous **evil eye** symbols. This circular blue and white emblem with a dot in the middle is a good luck charm designed to ward off evil spirits. As well as being proudly displayed in homes and businesses, the symbol is also printed on pendants, bracelets and brooches.

35

turned into a swish boutique hotel. The place to come if you need pampering – one room boasts a private hammam. Doubles €95, suite with private hammam €185

EATING AND DRINKING

Everything closes pretty early in Bursa with the exception of popular baklava cafés. Sakarya Cad is a pretty cobbled street of fish and seafood restaurants that fill with post-work locals after dark. Mains around ₺18.

Çiçek Izgara Belediye Cad 15. An elegant restaurant with a slightly inflated price to match. However, the food is reliable and the main Ottoman-inspired dishes, including *köfte* and *sütlü tel kadayıfı*, are worth a try. Mains ₺12–18. Mon–Sat 10am–midnight.

Kebapçı İskender Ünlü Cad 7 ⓦ iskender.com.tr. A local institution. Queues form early at lunch and the restaurant closes early, but it's a great choice for trying Bursa's speciality, the *İskender kebap* – lamb with tomato sauce, yoghurt and hot butter poured from a saucepan at the table (₺23). Daily 11am–6.30pm.

Üç Köfte İvaz Paşa Çarşısı 3. Cheap and cheerful *köfte* specialists just north of the main bazaar offering delicious meatballs with tasty trimmings. Mains ₺10–15. Mon–Sat 11am–3pm.

ÇANAKKALE

ÇANAKKALE is a progressive, modern city celebrated for its setting on the Dardanelles and as a popular base for visiting Gelibolu (Gallipoli) and Troy. There's a big university here, and the 15,000-odd students, together with Aussie and Kiwi backpackers visiting Gallipoli, make for a busy nightlife scene. You'll find no shortage of bars, clubs and budget places to eat, and English-speaking voices drift across the seafront nightly. Almost everything of interest – park, **Naval Museum** (Tues, Wed & Fri–Sun 9am–noon & 1.30–5pm; ₺6.5) and **Archeological Museum** (daily: April–Oct 8am–7pm; Nov–March 8am–5pm; ₺5) – is within walking distance of the ferry docks, close to the start of the main Demircioğlu Caddesi. Stroll past the Trojan horse on the seafront promenade near the ferry terminal; you might recognize the wooden structure from the 2004 film *Troy*.

ARRIVAL AND INFORMATION

By bus The bus station is on the coastal highway, Atatürk Cad, a 15min walk from the waterfront; if you're arriving

from Istanbul, get off at the ferry terminal in the centre of the city rather than at the bus station.
Destinations Istanbul (hourly; 6hr 30min); İzmir (11 daily; 5hr 30min); Selçuk (8 daily; 7hr).

By ferry Ferries run hourly between Çanakkale and Eceabat and take 25min. Tickets can be bought at the ferry terminal for ₺3.50.

Tourist office Beside the ferry docks (daily 8.30am–5.30/7pm depending on season; ☎ 0286 217 1187).

ACCOMMODATION

Except for a crowded couple of weeks during the Çanakkale/Troy Festival (mid-Aug), or on ANZAC Day (April 25), when the town is inundated with Antipodeans, you'll have little trouble finding budget accommodation.

Anzac House Hostel Cumhuriyet Meydanı 61 ☎ 0286 213 2550, ⓦ anzachouse.com. A pretty basic hostel offering well-kept rooms over several floors. Bathrooms are shared and there's no lift. Breakfast is ₺6 extra. Dorms ₺30, single ₺45, double ₺80

★ **Grand Anzac Hotel** Kemal Yeri Sokak ⓦ anzachotel.com. One of several Anzac hotels run by the same owners (try the *Comfort Anzac*, *Anzac* or *Kervansarary* – below – if this one is full). A big and buzzy popular spot in the centre of the city, with a large indoor/outdoor breakfast area. Singles €30, doubles €40

Kervansaray Hotel Fetvane Sok No. 13 ☎ 0286 217 7777, ⓦ otelkervansaray.com. The former home of an Ottoman judge: you'll find big plush rooms, a pretty garden and a quality buffet breakfast waiting in the morning. Be sure to get a room in the main, old building, as the annexe at the back of the garden has far less character. Singles €45, doubles €58

Yellow Rose Kemal Paşa Mah ☎ 0286 217 3343, ⓦ yellowrose.4mg.com. A good-value hostel with a homely feel that lets you economize further by using the kitchen. Breakfast can be taken near the table-tennis tables in the attractive garden. Dorms €15, doubles €35

EATING AND DRINKING

The seafront is jammed with restaurants and some of the best bars are tucked away in the streets just behind. Be sure to seek out the *peynir helvası* – the city's famous cheese dessert – it's much tastier than it sounds.

Caféka Cumhuriyet Meydanı 28. For a break from traditional Turkish cuisine try trendy *Caféka*, with salad bowls, pasta dishes and chicken fajitas just some of the Mediterranean-style cuisine on offer. Good lattes and other coffees too. Mains ₺14–30. Daily noon–11pm.

★ **Cevahir** Fetvane Sok 15/a. Small, family-run corner café serving tasty home-style Turkish food. Buffet-style food served on small, medium and large plates (₺8–10); salad and bread included. Dishes might include aubergine and chicken, sweet grated carrot with yogurt, or bean salad. Daily until early evening.

Sardunya Fetvane Sok 11. One of several *ev yemekleri* (home-style cooking) places, this local favourite offers filling stews and salads at bargain prices (mains from ₺12). Daily noon–10pm.

Seaside Eski Balıkhane Sok 3. One of the better seafront restaurants, offering fresh fish for around ₺30 per head, live entertainment and a relaxed atmosphere. Daily until around 11pm.

THE GELİBOLU (GALLIPOLI) PENINSULA

Though endowed with splendid scenery and beaches, the slender **Gelibolu** (Gallipoli) peninsula, which forms the northwest side of the Dardanelles, is known chiefly for its grim military history. In April 1915 it was the site of Winston Churchill's plan to land Allied troops, many of them **Australian** and **New Zealand** units, with a view to putting Turkey out of the war. Huge strategic mistakes, as well as a fierce opposition headed by the gifted officer Mustafa Kemal (later known as Atatürk), led to the dismal failure of the operation, incurring massive casualties. This was the first time Australians and New Zealanders had seen action under their own commanders, and the date of the first landings, April 25, is celebrated as **ANZAC Day**.

WHAT TO SEE AND DO

The World War I battlefields and Allied cemeteries are by turns moving and numbing in the sheer multiplicity of graves, memorials and obelisks. The first stop on most tours is the **Çanakkale Destanı Tanıtım Merkezi** (Çanakkale Epic Presentation Centre; daily 8.30am–6pm; ₺10), with

several audio-visual and interactive exhibits as well as eleven galleries over four floors packed with fascinating war-time artefacts. Beyond the centre are the **Beach, Shrapnel Valley** and **Shell Green** cemeteries, followed by **Anzac Cove** and **Arıburnu**, site of the ill-fated ANZAC landing. Most tourists then bear right for **Büyük Anafartalar** village and **Çonkbayırı hill**, where there's a massive New Zealand memorial and a Turkish memorial detailing Atatürk's words and deeds. Working your way back down towards the orientation centre, you pass **The Nek, Walker's Ridge** and **Quinn's Post**, where the trenches of the opposing forces lay within a few metres of each other: the modern road corresponds to no-man's-land.

ARRIVAL AND DEPARTURE

By bus Buses from Istanbul to Çannakale stop at Eceabat. Destinations Istanbul (hourly; 5hr).

By ferry Ferries run hourly between Çanakkale and Eceabat and take 25min.

ACCOMMODATION

Crowded House Hostel İskele Hüseyin Avni Sok 4, Eceabat ☏ 0286 814 1565, ⓦ crowdedhousegallipoli.com. A 30min ferry ride from Çanakkale in Eceabat, this hostel offers 26 rooms all with private bathroom, and an outdoor restaurant and bar serving barbecued meat and fish. It also has its own travel agency (see box below). Doubles €30̶

TJ's Cumhuriyet Cad 5, Eceabat ☏ 0286 814 3121, ⓦ tjshotel.com. Also in Eceabat, this hostel-cum-hotel offers both dorm beds and cheerful double rooms complete with LCD TVs and a/c. Like *Crowded House*, it has an in-house travel agency (see box below). Dorms €30̶, doubles €70̶

EDİRNE

Bordering both Greece and Bulgaria, the small sleepy town of **EDİRNE** boasts an impressive number of elegant

35

BATTLEFIELD TOURS

Various companies offer **battlefield tours**. The reliable Hassle Free Tours (Cumhuriyet Meydan 61, Çanakkale; ☏ 0286 213 5969, ⓦ anzachouse.com) put on a seven-hour tour of the major sites, including a boat-trip of the landing beaches and lunch, for €40. Over in Eceabat, *TJ's Hostel* (☏ 0286 814 3121, ⓦ anzacgallipolitours.com) offer a similar tour for slightly less money, as does the *Crowded House Hostel*'s travel agency (see above). Both have very good reputations and have been doing these tours for many, many years. For those short of time there are gruelling day-trips to the battlefields from Istanbul with Hassle Free, who have a branch on Akbıyık Cad 10, Sultanahmet (☏ 0212 458 5500), for around €99. *TJ's* and *Crowded House* also offer similar day tours from Istanbul.

monuments. It springs to life for the week-long oil-wrestling festival of Kırkpınar (end of June) but is a relaxing alternative to Istanbul (some 230km southeast) at any time of year.

WHAT TO SEE AND DO

You can see the sights on foot in a day. The best starting point is the **Eski Cami** (open to visitors during daylight hours aside from prayer times; free) bang in the centre, the oldest mosque in town, begun in 1403. Just across the way, the **Bedesten** was Edirne's first covered market and was restored in the 1980s. The beautiful **Üç Şerefeli Camii** (also open to visitors outside prayer times; free) dates from 1447 and has four idiosyncratic minarets, the tallest of which has three galleries for the muezzin. A little way east of here is the masterly **Selimiye Camii** (daily; free), designed by Minar Sinan. Its four slender minarets, among the tallest in the world, also have three balconies; the interior is most impressive, its dome planned to surpass that of Istanbul's Haghia Sophia (Aya Sofya). The main **Archeological Museum** (Tues–Sun 9am–5pm; ₺5), just northeast of the mosque, contains an assortment of Greco-Roman fragments and some Neolithic finds. A stroll south in the direction of Karaağaç, crossing the iconic Mecidiye bridge over the River Meriç, is also a pleasant way to spend a morning.

ARRIVAL AND INFORMATION

By train The train station is 5km southeast of the centre. *Dolmuşes* run into town from here (₺2). However, owing to the upgrade of the line in Thrace all services from Istanbul were suspended at the time of writing.
By bus The bus station is 8km southeast of the centre. When you arrive, walk through the terminal to the car park on the other side – here you'll find *dolmuşes* that go to the centre of town (₺2). Get off either near the main shopping area or at the Eski Cami mosque.
Destinations Ankara (10pm & 11am; 10hr); Çanakkale (4 daily; 4hr 30min); Istanbul (every 30min; 3hr); İzmir (4 daily; 10hr); Plovdiv, Bulgaria (3hr).
Tourist office Hürriyet Meydanı 17 (daily 8.30am–5.30pm; ☎0284 213 9208).

ACCOMMODATION

Efe Hotel Maarif Cad 13 Kaleiçi ☎0284 213 6166, ⓦefehotel.com. Stylish boutique hotel with impressive rooms, all manner of quirky knick-knacks strewn about, and an outdoor bar. Breakfast included. Doubles ₺175
Hotel Aksaray Alipaşa Ortakapı Cad ☎0284 212 6035. A small *pension* with a friendly English-speaking welcome, but the rooms are slightly scruffy and it feels a bit like an elderly relative's home. No breakfast. Doubles ₺85
Taşhan Hotel Çavuşbey Mahallesi Ağaçpazarı Cad 4 ☎0284 225 1413. Housed in a 500-year-old building in the centre of town, this place has been thoughtfully renovated, with cool brick walls and wooden floors a major feature. Breakfast served in a quiet courtyard. Doubles €60

EATING AND DRINKING

Hanedan Karaağaç Mah. İki Köprü Arası Cad 2. A well-situated riverside spot offering meze from ₺6 and a variety of kebabs (₺14–22). Daily until late evening.
Melek Anne Kayseri Mantısı Maarif Cad 18. Friendly, all female home-cooking joint specializing in Turkish-style ravioli (*mantı*) and other traditional favourites. Nice garden and free wi-fi add to the appeal. Daily 8am–9pm.
Niyazi Usta Alipaşa Ortakapı Cad 9. A renowned *ciğerci* (liver purveyor) in a town specializing in them, where the fried slices (₺14) are piled high and served with *cacık* (cucumber and yoghurt, ₺5). Proper fast food, served with lots of onion and salad. Closes at 9.30pm.
Pena Cafe Pub Alipaşa Ortakapı Cad 6. Sash windows usher cool breezes into this café-bar made up of small rooms with wooden floorboards and panelling. A youthful atmosphere in a middle-aged-feeling town. Daily 9am–1pm.

CROSSING TO BULGARIA

Edirne (see above) is a popular base for travellers crossing the border into **Bulgaria**. Regular buses leave from Edirne to Plovdiv and tickets cost ₺35–50 for the 4hr journey. If visiting Edirne for the day, bring your passport along even if you don't intend to cross the border. Officials at the bus station may ask to see it to make sure you haven't entered Turkey illegally.

The Aegean coast

The **Aegean coast** is one of Turkey's most enticing destinations, home to some of the best of its antiquities and the most appealing resorts. The city of **İzmir** serves as a base for day-trips to nearby sights and beaches. Visitors continuing south will be spoilt for sightseeing choices as the territory is rich in Classical, Hellenistic and Roman ruins, notably **Ephesus** and the remains inland at **Hierapolis** – sitting atop the famous pools and mineral formations of **Pamukkale**. The coast itself is better down south, too, and although the larger resorts, including **Kuşadası**, have been marred by the developers, **Bodrum** still has a certain charm despite the growing number of hedonistic holidaymakers.

İZMİR

İZMİR – ancient Smyrna – was mostly burned down in the Greco-Turkish war of 1919–22, and was largely built from scratch afterwards. Nowadays it's Turkey's third-largest city, a booming, cosmopolitan and relentlessly modern place that's home to around four million people. Orientation can be confusing in places, but most points of interest lie near each other, and walking is the most enjoyable way of exploring, especially along the waterfront.

WHAT TO SEE AND DO

İzmir doesn't have a single centre, although the district of **Konak**, where you'll find a busy park, the city bus terminal and **Konak Pier** on the waterfront, is where visitors spend most time. Head north and you'll reach the **Kültur Parkı**, a large park with regular outdoor entertainment, particularly in the summer. Continue in the same direction and you'll soon reach the district of **Alsançak** – the hub of evening entertainment with alfresco bars and restaurants and, on the seafront, the **Atatürk Museum** (Tues–Sun 8.30am–5.30pm) on Atatürk Caddesi. This beautiful nineteenth-century seafront house is where Atatürk stayed when he visited the city in the 1930s. If you fancy a walk, head south along the waterfront for about twenty minutes to the city's free elevator, **Asansör**, which has wonderful views over the city and Gulf of İzmir.

Archeological Museum and Ethnography Museum

Southwest of the Konak Camii is İzmir's **Archeological Museum** (Tues–Sun:

April–Oct 8am–9pm; Nov–March 8am–5pm; ₺10). The collection consists of finds from all over İzmir province, including some stunning marble statues and sarcophagi. Next door in an old Turkish house is the charming **Ethnography Museum** (Tues–Sun 8am–5.30pm; free) where you can learn about the local tradition of camel wrestling and see examples of Anatolian crafts such as clog-making, lacemaking and the ubiquitous "evil eye" beads.

Kemeraltı Bazaar

Immediately east of Konak is **Kemeraltı**, İzmir's bazaar. The main drag, Anafartalar Caddesi, is lined with clothing, jewellery and shoe shops; Fevzipaşa Bulvarı and the alleys just south are strong on leather garments. A pleasant, relaxed alternative to the bazaar is the street market at the northernmost end of Sevgi Yolu, where you can browse jewellery, scarves, leather bracelets and lots of books, including English ones. When you've finished shopping, enjoy a Turkish coffee (₺5) at one of the many street cafés.

Kadifekale

A symbol of İzmir's historic past, the castle ruins of **Kadifekale** (always open; free), about 3km from Konak, provide great views of İzmir's metropolitan expanse. To get to the castle, take a red-and-white city bus #33 from Konak and get off shortly after you see the national flag flying from the top of the hill. Buses back to Konak are from the bus shelter at the corner of the road approaching the castle.

ARRIVAL AND DEPARTURE

By plane İzmir's Adnan Menderes airport is approximately 15km outside of the city. A taxi from the airport to Çankaya is about ₺50. A cheaper alternative is to catch the Havaş shuttle bus (30min; ₺10). The Havaş service to the airport runs hourly 3.30am–11.30pm every day from the northern end of Gaziosmanpaşa Bul.

By train Intercity trains to Denizli pull in at Basmane station, 1km from the seafront at the eastern end of Fevzipaşa Bul. Longer distance trains depart from Alsancak, north of the city centre.

35

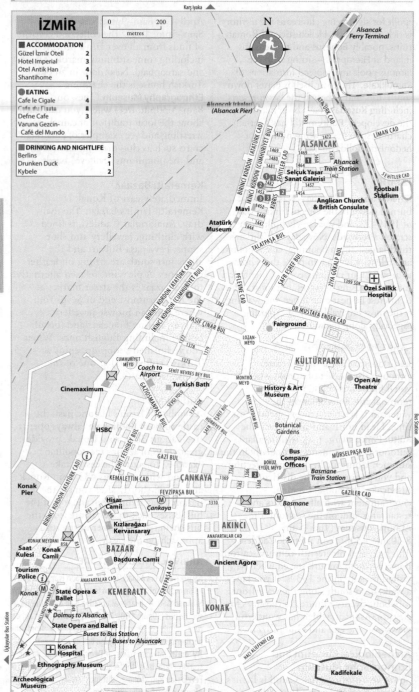

İZMİR

0 _____ 200
metres

ACCOMMODATION

Güzel İzmir Oteli	2
Hotel Imperial	3
Otel Antik Han	4
Shantihome	1

EATING

Cafe le Cigale	4
Cafe du Flauta	2
Defne Cafe	3
Varuna Gezcin-Café del Mundo	1

DRINKING AND NIGHTLIFE

Berlins	3
Drunken Duck	1
Kybele	2

35

Karş iyaka

N

Alsancak
Ferry Terminal

Alsancak İskelesi
(Alsancak Pier)

ALSANCAK

Selçuk Yaşar
Sanat Galerisi

Alsancak
Train Station

Football
Stadium

Anglican Church
& British Consulate

Mavi

Atatürk
Museum

Özel Saılkk
Hospital

Fairground

KÜLTÜRPARKI

Open Air
Theatre

Cinemaximum

Coach to
Airport

Turkish Bath

History & Art
Museum

Bus
Station

Konak
Pier

HSBC

Botanical
Gardens

Bus
Company
Offices

Basmane
Train Station

Konak
Pier

Hisar
Camii

Çankaya

ÇANKAYA

Basmane

Kızlarağazı
Kervansaray

AKINCI

Saat
Kulesi

Konak
Camii

BAZAAR

Başdurak Camii

Ancient Agora

Tourism
Police

State Opera &
Ballet

KEMERALTI

KONAK

Dolmuş to Alsancak

State Opera and Ballet
Buses to Bus Station
Buses to Alsancak

Konak
Hospital

Kadifekale

Ethnography Museum

Archeological
Museum

Destinations From Alsancak: Ankara (1 daily; 13hr); Istanbul via ferry from Bandirma (1 daily; 14hr). From Basmane: Denizli (6 daily; 5–6hr); Selçuk (8 daily; 1hr 15min).

By bus The main bus station for onward journeys is 8km east of the centre; on arrival you can jump on one of the bus companies' free shuttles or grab a taxi from around ₺40. Buses to and from Çeşme depart from the Uçkuyular bus station 10km west of the centre.

Destinations Ankara (every 30min; 8hr); Bodrum (hourly; 3hr); Bursa (hourly; 5hr); Çanakkale (10 daily; 5hr); Fethiye (15 daily; 7hr); Istanbul (hourly; 9hr); Konya (1 daily; 8hr); Kuşadası (every 30min; 1hr 30min); Marmaris (hourly; 4hr); Selçuk (every 20min; 1hr).

INFORMATION

Tourist office 1344 Sok 2. Housed in a grand building near the seafront just off Atatürk Cad near the junction with Gazi Bul (daily 8.30am–5.30pm; ☎0232 483 5117). Helpful English-speaking staff.

GETTING AROUND

By bus To use city buses you need to buy a Kent Kart (₺6), widely available from kiosks and shops across the city. To get to Alsancak from Konak (₺2.25) take the #169, #554 or #8, all from the same bus stop on the opposite side of the road from Atatürk Kültür Merkezi (Atatürk Culktural Centre) on Mithatpaşa Cad.

By metro The handy metro system (6am–midnight; tickets ₺2.25 or use the Kent Kart) links Basmane station (the metro is located at the bottom of the escalators behind the station), Çankaya and Konak. Ticket office 7am–9.30pm.

ACCOMMODATION

Although İzmir is one of Turkey's major cities, its tourism industry is only just developing. Consequently, good-quality budget hotels are hard to come by, especially now that İzmir is a major congregating point for Syrian and other refugees en-route to Europe.

Güzel İzmir Oteli 1368 Sok 8 ☎0232 483 5069, ⊕guzelizmirhotel.com. A bright and airy central spot boasting a fitness centre (just a handful of machines dumped in a basement). Includes breakfast and wi-fi. Doubles ₺120

Hotel Imperial 1296 Sok 54 ☎0232 425 2051. A museum piece from the 1970s on a street littered with budget hotels. The rooms are mournful but well looked after, and some have half-decent views. Doubles ₺80

Otel Antik Han Anafartalar Cad 626 ☎0232 489 27 50, ⊕otelantikhan.com. Friendly, with a pretty courtyard where you can enjoy breakfast. Close to the ancient agora. Parking available. Doubles ₺135

Shantihome 1464 Sok 15 ☎0546 235 0805, ⊕shantihome.org. İzmir's only hostel is a bright,

traveller-friendly place with curtained-off bunks and a fully equipped kitchen. There are even bicycles for rent. Dorms ₺30

EATING

Head to Sok numbers 1482, 1453 and 1452 in Alsancak for a night out. 1482 and 1453 have a certain grunginess about them, while narrow 1452 is a little smarter, though still young. Many of the bars change ownership and concept frequently, so exploring these streets can yield unexpected results.

Café La Cigale Fransız Kültür Merkezi, Cumhuriyet Bul 152 ☎0232 421 4780. Tucked away in the pleasant gardens of the French Cultural Institute, this place is worth a splurge, with delicious French and pasta dishes for around ₺20. Daily 8.30am–10.30pm.

Cafe du Fiesta Sok 1482. A wood-panelled café housed in a 150-year-old Greek mansion, packed out with teenagers, students and musicians knocking back good coffee and burgers (₺8). Daily 9am–11.30pm.

Defne Café 1452 Sok. Cosy little place on a cute side street where Efes is ₺10 and a steak sandwich is just ₺15. Daily lunch & dinner.

★Varuna Gezcin-Café Del Mundo 1482 Sok. A busy bar and restaurant full of students taking advantage of happy hour (until 9pm) and chowing down on international cuisine and downing a wide (for Turkey) array of international beers. Good for cocktails too. Licence plates all over the walls and booming rock music add to the atmosphere. Meal and a drink around ₺35. Daily until late.

DRINKING AND NIGHTLIFE

Opening hours vary, but most clubs and bars stay open until midnight and beyond.

Berlins Alsancak Sok 1453. Jugs of mojitos and a thumping reggae and r'n'b soundtrack are the order of the day here, though many nights are given over to retro Turkish pop.

Drunken Duck 1482 Sok 15. A small but friendly bar with live music and mildly inebriated locals.

Kybele 1453 Sok 28. Live music club specializing in alt-rock and jazz with a tiny stage and super-speedy bar staff. Entrance price varies depending on who's playing (generally ₺18–35).

ENTERTAINMENT

Atatürk Kültür Merlezi Mithat Paşa Cad 92. Home to the city's own symphony orchestra, with most concerts taking place Fri & Sat eve.

Cinemaximum Atatürk Cad 19. Cinema with recent Hollywood releases. Student discount available.

State Opera and Ballet Milli Kütüphane Cad, Konak ☎0232 484 3692. A diverse programme of concerts ranging from classical to jazz and pop.

35

35

KUŞADASI

KUŞADASI is one of Turkey's most bloated resorts, yet the old town has its charms. Ferry services link it with the Greek island of Sámos, and the resort is a port of call for Aegean cruise ships, though this business was hit in 2016 by bombings elsewhere in Turkey, which caused several companies to temporarily suspend stops in Turkish ports.

WHAT TO SEE AND DO

Liman Caddesi runs from the ferry port up to Atatürk Bulvarı, the main harbour esplanade, from which pedestrianized Barbaros Hayrettin Bulvarı ascends the hill. To the left of here, the **Kale** district, huddled inside the town walls, is the oldest and most appealing part of town, with a mosque and some fine traditional houses. Kuşadası's most famous beach, **Kadınlar Denizi**, 3km southwest of town, is a popular strand, often overcrowded in summer. The best beach in the area is **Pamucak**, at the mouth of the Kücük Menderes River, 15km north, an exposed 4km stretch of sand that is comparatively less developed; in season it's served by regular *dolmuşes* from both Kuşadası and Selçuk.

ARRIVAL AND INFORMATION

By bus The combined *dolmuş* and long-distance bus station is about 2km out, past the end of Kahramanlar Caddesi on the ring road to Söke, while the *dolmuş* stop is closer to the centre on Adnan Menderes Bulvarı.

FERRIES TO GREECE

Between April and October one ferry daily departs Kuşadası at 9am to the Greek island of **Sámos** (€35 one-way, €40 day return, €55 open return; 1hr 15min). Between the beginning of July and mid-October an additional ferry departs **Kuşadası** on Tuesday, Thursday and Sunday at 5pm. Meander on Kıbrıs Cad (right by the ferry port ☏0256 614 3859, ⓦmeandertravel.com) runs up to two boats daily in summer. From Sámos, a popular follow-on destination is the party island **Íos** (see p.530). Tickets from Sámos to Íos can be bought from ITSA or By Ship travel agents located near the pier.

Tourist office Right by the ferry port (Mon–Fri 8am–5pm; summer also Sat & Sun; ☏0256 614 1103).

ACCOMMODATION AND EATING

Avlu Cephane Sok 15/a. Serves a wide range of kebabs, stews, steamed vegetables and meze in an outdoor courtyard (meze from ₺7, kebabs from ₺15). Daily 8am–midnight.

Sezgin Hotel and Guesthouse Aslanlar Cad 68 ☏0256 614 4225, ⓦsezginhotel.com. A great-value spot boasting a lovely garden and swimming pool. Doubles **€29**

SELÇUK

Once a small farming village, **SELÇUK** was catapulted into the tourism limelight by its proximity to the ruins of **Ephesus**, once the wealthy capital of Roman Asia and now a UNESCO World Heritage Site. Pleasant Pamucak beach (see above) is easily accessible by *dolmuş* or bike (9km).

WHAT TO SEE AND DO

The sights and attractions in Selçuk itself can easily be seen in a day. **Ayasoluk** hill (daily: April–Oct 8am–7pm; Nov–March 8am–5pm; ₺10) to the northwest of the centre is the traditional burial place of St John the Evangelist, who died here around 100 AD; it boasts the remains of a basilica built by Justinian that was one of the largest Byzantine churches in existence. Just behind the tourist office, the **Efes Archeological Museum** (daily 8.30am–6pm; ₺10) has galleries of finds from Ephesus, while beyond the museum, 600m along the road towards Ephesus, are the scanty remains of the **Artemision** or sanctuary of Artemis.

Ephesus

Ephesus (Efes in Turkish; daily: April–Oct 8am–7pm; Nov–March 8am–5pm; ₺30), 3km southwest of Selçuk, is one of the largest and best-preserved ancient cities around the Mediterranean. Situated close to a temple devoted to the goddess Artemis, its location by a fine harbour was the source of its wealth, which resulted in an array of fine buildings.

In the centre of the site is the **Arcadian Way**, which was once lined with hundreds of shops and illuminated at night. The nearby theatre has been partly restored to allow its use for open-air concerts; climb to the top for views of the surrounding countryside. About halfway along Marble Street is a footprint, a female head and a heart etched into the rock – an alleged signpost for a brothel. Across the intersection looms the elegant **Library of Celsus**, erected by the consul Gaius Julius Aquila between 110 and 135 AD. Just uphill, a Byzantine fountain looks across the Street of the Curetes to the **public latrines**, a favourite photo opportunity with visitors.

ARRIVAL AND DEPARTURE

By train The train station lies a little east of the aqueduct.
Destinations Denizli (7 daily; 3hr); İzmir (8 daily; 1hr 15min).
By bus and dolmuş The bus and *dolmuş* terminal is a few minutes' walk south from the centre of town. Ephesus is a quick taxi ride or 40min walk away.
Destinations by bus Bodrum (3–4 direct daily; 3hr); Marmaris (1 direct daily; 4hr).
Destinations by dolmuş Kuşadası (frequent until 8–9pm; 30min); Pamucak beach (hourly; 30min); Şirince (every 30min until 7pm).

INFORMATION

Tourist office Opposite the bus terminal. Efficient rather than helpful, and no use for hotel or restaurant recommendations (daily 8.30am–noon & 1–5.30pm; winter Sat & Sun only; ☎0232 892 6945).

ACCOMMODATION

ANZ Guesthouse 1064 Sok 12 ☎0232 892 6050, ⓦ anzephesusguesthouse.com. Popular backpacker choice with bicycles for rent. Free breakfast buffet on roof terrace. Check a few rooms as some are better than others. Dorms €10, doubles €30
★ **Barım** 1045 Sok 34 ☎0232 892 6923, ⓦ barimpension .com. In an atmospheric old house complete with a charming garden, this is one of the best value options in town, with traditionally decorated rooms with exposed stone walls. ₺80
Boomerang Guest House 1047 Sok 10 ☎0232 892 4879, ⓦ ephesusboomerangguesthouse.com. A centrally located and spotlessly clean establishment comprising a number of private rooms and a decent twelve-bed dorm. There's a roof terrace and residents get ten percent discount in the restaurant. Dorms €10, doubles €40
★ **Homeros Pansiyon** Atatürk Mah Asmalı/1048 Sok 17 ☎0232 892 3995, ⓦ homerospension.com. This

SURVIVING EPHESUS

Ephesus is Turkey's most popular tourist site and often swarming with visitors, mostly from the cruise ships which drop off in Kuşadası. Be sure to visit early in the morning to avoid the worst of the crowds and blistering heat (you can easily walk to the site, but most accommodation offers free drop-offs from Selçuk). If you're tempted to hire a guide, do so at the tourist office in Selçuk rather than the sharks touting their services at the site itself (audioguides are available but there are few information boards). Remember to bring a hat and water (there's next to no shade).

35

super-friendly family-run *pension* is one of the best places to stay in the area. The bedrooms (some with a balcony, all with a/c) are cosy and are richly decorated with colourful carpets, blankets and knick-knacks. The roof terrace has fabulous views of the town. Free pick-up from the bus or train station and bikes available. Doubles €40
Nişanyan House Şirince village ☎0232 898 3208, ⓦ nisanyan.com. A peaceful boutique hotel high on the hillside, with a private hammam and spectacular views. Rooms are individually decorated and the traditional Turkish breakfast is made on site by the talented kitchen staff. Doubles ₺350

EATING AND DRINKING

Café Carpouza Argenta Cad 6. This popular café, set in a huge garden, is run by the municipality so prices for the coffees and beer are reasonable. A meatball sandwich will fill you up for around ₺8. Daily 9am–midnight.
★ **Mehmet and Alibaba Kebab House** 1047 Sok 4/a ☎0232 892 3872. By far the most popular restaurant in town. While the food is decent enough (ranging from kebabs at ₺15 to generous plates of mixed veg meze for ₺12), the affable owners are a real draw too. Apple tea, orange tea and regular tea are free to diners. It's licensed too. Daily 9am–11.30pm.
Old House 1005 Sok 1/a ☎0232 892 9357. Carefully prepared mains including grills, seafood and Turkish standards for ₺10–25, served up in a shady little garden courtyard. Alcohol served. Daily 8am–midnight.
Selçuk Köftecisi Şahabettin Dede Cad ☎0232 892 6696. Easily overlooked because of its basic, rather bland appearance, but with forty years' experience behind it this place is all about the food. Smoky bread cooked in a wood oven, known as Şirince bread, accompanies mains. Soups ₺5–6, meaty mains around ₺15. Daily 6am–10pm.

PAMUKKALE: THE "COTTON CASTLE"

The rock formations of **PAMUKKALE** (literally "Cotton Castle"), 190km east of Selçuk, are well worth a detour, a series of white terraces saturated with dissolved calcium bicarbonate, bubbling up from the feet of the Çal Dağı mountains beyond. The spring emerges in what was once the ancient city of **Hierapolis**, the ruins of which would merit a stop even if they weren't coupled with the natural phenomenon. One ticket gives entry to the travertine terraces and the archeological zone of Hierapolis behind (daily; April–Oct 8am–9pm; Nov–March 8am–5pm; ₺25). Tucked in among the ruins is **Pamukkale Thermal Baths**, home to the sacred pool of the ancients (daily April–Oct 8am–9pm; Nov–March 8am–5pm; ₺32), open for bathing in the 35°C mineral water.

Buses from İzmir, Selçuk, Antalya and Bodrum (and many other places in Turkey) run to Denizli, 20km from Pammukale. Some bus companies have a free minibus running onto Pamukkale village, but there is also a good *dolmuş* service. Pamukkale village is a very pleasant **place to stay**, with plenty of good-value *pensions* and hotels. There are day-trips to Pamukkale from several coastal resorts, but they are rather gruelling.

35

BODRUM

In the eyes of its devotees, **BODRUM** – ancient Halicarnassos – with its whitewashed houses and subtropical gardens, is an attractive Turkish resort, a quality outfit in comparison to its upstart Aegean rivals. It's much favoured by yachting types, well-off urban Turks and party animals. However, in 2015 it became an exit point to Greece (the island of Kos is just 7km offshore) for Syrian refugees. The photograph of a drowned Syrian Kurdish child, 3-year-old Alan Kurdi, which touched millions of hearts around the world, was taken on a Bodrum beach in September 2015.

WHAT TO SEE AND DO

The town's centrepiece is the **Castle of St Peter** (Tues–Sun: April–Oct 8.30am–6.30pm; Nov–March 8.30am–4.30pm; ₺25), built by the Knights of St John over a Selçuk fortress between 1437 and 1522. Inside, the various towers house a **Museum of Underwater Archeology**, which comprises several different display halls. These include the Glass Wreck Hall, complete with a 33m-long Byzantine ship dating to 1025, the Uluburun Wreck Hall containing nautical remains from three ancient wrecks, and the Carian Princess Hall, with a sarcophagus enclosing the skeleton of a noblewoman who died in the fourth century BC.

Immediately north of the castle lies the bazaar, from where you can stroll up to Türkkuyusu Caddesi to see what's left of the **Mausoleum** (Tues–Sun: April–Oct 8am–7pm; Nov–March 8am–5pm; ₺10), the burial place of Mausolus, ruler of Halicarnassos from 376–353 BC and the origin of the word mausoleum.

ARRIVAL AND DEPARTURE

By bus The bus station is 500m up Cevat Şakır Cad, which divides the town roughly in two.

Destinations Fethiye (7 daily; 5hr); Istanbul (hourly; 12hr); İzmir (hourly; 3hr, 30min); Kuşadası (3 daily; 3hr); Marmaris (hourly; 3hr 15min); Selçuk (hourly; 3hr).

By ferry Ferries dock at the jetty west of the castle. Bodrum Ferryboat Association (☎0252 316 0882, ⌨ bodrumferryboat.com) runs ferries to Kos and Datça, while Bodrum Express Lines (☎0252 316 1087, ⌨ bodrumexpresslines.com) handles hydrofoils to Kos, Rhodes and domestic services to Marmaris.

Destinations Datça (two daily; 90min); Kos (April–Oct 2 daily; 1hr); Rhodes (July & Aug daily; 2hr).

INFORMATION

Tourist office Barış Square 48, close to the jetty (Mon–Fri 8am–noon, 1–5.30pm; summer daily 8.30am–5.30pm; ☎0252 316 1091). Friendly staff will help you book accommodation and boat trips.

ACCOMMODATION

Bodrum Backpackers Atatürk Cad 37/b ☎0252 313 2762, ⌨ bodrumbackpackers.net. Lively backpackers' hostel – not the place to go if you want some beauty sleep. During the summer, when all the beds are full, you can sleep on the terrace for ₺30. Breakfast and wi-fi included. Dorms/singles ₺60, doubles ₺120

Hotel Güleç Üçkuyular Cad 22 📞0252 316 5222, ⓦhotelgulec.com. Pretty standard accommodation considering the price, but nice and secluded from the chaos. It's on a quiet street a short walk from the beach and bars. Breakfast included. Singles ₺120, doubles ₺160

Mars Otel Turgut Reis Cad, İmbat Çıkmazi 29 📞0252 316 6559, ⓦmarsotel.com. Clean, friendly and decent value, especially outside the peak July to August months when prices are around 40 percent less than those quoted here. Quiet central location. Small swimming pool, and bikes for rent. Breakfast included. Singles ₺120, doubles ₺200

Myndos Pansiyon 1017 Sok 11 📞0252 313 4422, ⓦmyndospansiyon.com. Pleasant *pension* with a conveniently central – but quiet – location. Plain walls, kilim-bedecked floors and petals on the bed on arrival and after each bed make-up make this a reasonably cheap option in overpriced Bodrum. ₺210

EATING AND DRINKING

Bodrum is packed with places hugging the shoreline, and offers numerous opportunities to dine in the dark on the sand. Many places are complacent and pricey, but there are a few gems to be found if you dig a little.

Le Man Kültür Cumhuriyet Cad 161 📞0252 316 5316, ⓦlmk.com.tr. Theme chain based on the popular Turkish satirical comic of the same name, it's a great place for well-priced burgers, pizza and pasta dishes (from ₺12) and beer, and attracts affluent young Turks down from Istanbul, İzmir and Ankara for their holidays. Daily 8am–2am.

Ox Wine and Burger Bar Cumhuriyet Cad 175. A decent burger joint with a spectacular wine list, so a good choice if you're starting to tire of Efes and kebabs. Not too pricey considering the location. Gourmet burger, chips saltier than the Dead Sea and beer around ₺35. Daily noon–midnight.

★**Piknik** Atatürk Cad 65 📞0252 313 7049. One of the best-value places in town, so many of your fellow diners here will be locals. Try the spicy Adana kebab for ₺16. They also do a full range of *pide*. Open 24hr.

NIGHTLIFE

Hadigari 1025 Sok 2. A Bodrum stalwart that still pulls in 2000-odd punters on summer nights. Find it at the marina near Bodrum Castle and dance till daybreak under the stars. Open until 5am at weekends.

Halikarnas At the far end of the bar strip this renowned nightclub has an entry price to match its reputation (expect to pay around ₺75 to get in and bring a stuffed wallet if you want to drink). However, the place is enormous, the atmosphere electric, and varied themed shows will keep you on your feet until dawn. Daily 10pm–late.

The Mediterranean coast

The first stretch of Turkey's Mediterranean coast, dominated by the Akdağ and Bey mountain ranges and known as the "**Turquoise Coast**", is its most popular, famed for its pine-studded shore, minor ruins and beautiful scenery. In the west, **Fethiye** is a perfect base for visits to **Ölüdeniz**, **Kaya Köyü** and **Butterfly Valley**. The scenery becomes increasingly spectacular as you head towards the site of **Olympos**, and **Kaş**, which offers great scuba diving, before reaching the port and major city of **Antalya**.

35

FETHİYE

FETHİYE is well situated for access to some of the region's ancient sites, many of which date from the time when this area was the independent kingdom of Lycia. The best **beaches**, around **Ölüdeniz lagoon**, are now too crowded for comfort, but Fethiye remains a charming market town and has been able to spread to accommodate increased tourist traffic.

WHAT TO SEE AND DO

Fethiye itself occupies the site of the Lycian city of Telmessos, little of which remains other than the impressive ancient theatre, and a number of Lycian rock tombs on the hillside. You can also visit the remains of the medieval fortress behind the harbour area of town. In the centre of town the tiny **museum** (Tues–Sun: June–Sept 8am–7pm; Oct–May 8am–5pm; ₺5) has some fascinating exhibits from local sites and a good ethnographic section. There are numerous boats on the harbour offering **island-hopping trips** (see p.1166).

Kaya Köyü

One of the most dramatic sights in the area is the ghost village of **Kaya Köyü** (daily 8am–5pm; ₺5), 7km out of town, served by *dolmuşes* departing from a stop by the Yeni Cami (New Mosque). The village, once known as Levissi, was abandoned in 1923, when its Anatolian-Greek population was relocated, and all you see now is a hillside covered with more than two thousand ruined cottages and a couple of churches.

Ölüdeniz lagoon

The warm waters of **Ölüdeniz lagoon** make for pleasant swimming although the crowds can reach saturation level in high season – in which case the nearby beaches of Belceğiz and Kıdrak are better bets. Ölüdeniz is about two hours on foot from Kaya Köyü or a thirty-minute *dolmuş* ride from Fethiye.

ARRIVAL AND DEPARTURE

By bus Fethiye's bus station is 2km east of the centre.
Destinations Istanbul (5 daily; 12hr); Kaş (hourly; 4hr); Marmaris (hourly; 3hr).
By dolmuş *Dolmuşes* leave from near the Yeni Cami (New Mosque), which is beyond the town hall and the PTT on Atatürk Cad.
Destinations Kaya Köyü (30min; hourly); Ölüdeniz (hourly; 30min).

INFORMATION, TOURS AND ACTIVITIES

Tourist office Close to the theatre, near the harbour at Fevzi Kakmak Cad 9/d (summer Mon–Fri 8am–8pm & Sat 10am–5pm; winter Mon–Fri 8am–noon & 1–5pm; ☏0252 612 1527).
Tours Daily boat tours generally cost around ₺50, lasting from 10.30am to 6.30pm. Tickets can be bought through your accommodation.

> ### BUTTERFLY VALLEY
>
> Popularized in the 1980s by hippies, **Butterfly Valley** (Kelebek Vadisi) is a peaceful spot worth a detour. Boasting a deserted beach, a handful of shady restaurants, a waterfall and not much else, it's reached by boat from Ölüdeniz (3 return trips daily), and usually open from March to October. As the name would suggest, it's home to a colony of butterflies, including the Jersey Tiger, although they can be pretty elusive.
> You can get a feel for the place in a day, but if you want to linger longer basic accommodation is on offer – in tents (₺34) or bungalows (₺64); prices include a buffet breakfast and dinner. Book via ⓦyenikelebeklervadisi.org/en.

Scuba diving Divers Delight (ⓦdiversdelight.com) runs several diving courses as well as try-a-dive day-trips (₺100) and snorkelling for non-divers (₺45).

ACCOMMODATION

Duygu Pension Karagözler Ordu Cad 54 ☏0252 614 3563, ⓦwww.duygupension.com. Eleven rooms, some with amazing views of the bay, kept in great condition. Swimming pool and free bus station pick-up. Family-run and friendly. Doubles ₺100
★ **Ferah Pension (Monica's Place)** Karagözler Orta Yol 23 ☏0252 614 2816, ⓦferahpension.com. This *pansiyon* has lovely sea views from the upstairs rooms. Despite being part of a chain, it's pleasantly personal and well run. Free transfers from the bus station. Excellent food. Dorms ₺40, doubles ₺120
Villa Daffodil Fevzi Çakmak Cad 115, İkinci Karagözler ☏0252 614 9595, ⓦvilladaffodil.com. Bright yellow, mock-Ottoman structure in one of the quieter shoreline corners, with a pool, on-site restaurant, hammam and landscaped grounds, as well as fair-sized, pine- and white-tile rooms. ₺180
Yıldırım Guesthouse Fevzi Çakmak Cad 53 ☏0252 614 4627, ⓦyildirimguesthouse.com. Backpackers' favourite run by the friendly Ömer. Plain but tidy carpeted rooms include three dorm rooms, one male, one female and one mixed. Generous breakfast and you can make free tea or coffee all day. Dorms ₺35, doubles ₺100

EATING AND DRINKING

Car Cemetery Bar Hamam Sok 33. Look out for the car bonnet protruding incongruously from the wall along Fethiye's liveliest street. This is a hip spot where shots and tasty cocktails are the order of the day (or night). Tues–Sat 6pm–4am.
The Duck Pond Eski Cami Sok 41. Bag a table next to the pond in welcome shade, sip on a beer (₺10) and nibble on a plate of the best mixed meze in town or treat yourself to a Turkish casserole. Mains from ₺18. Daily till late.
Meğri Lokantası Çarşı Cad. This *lokanta*, a humbler version of *Meğri Restaurant* round the corner, has a nice setting by the duck pond and delivers good traditional Turkish grub. Mains ₺18–25. Daily 9.30am–1am.
Mercan Balık Restaurant Hal ve Balık Pazarı, Zabıta Bürosu Yanı. One of numerous restaurants surrounding the little fish market, which will cook the fish you buy and give you salad and bread into the bargain. The fish market can get popular with tourists so arrive early. Open daily.
★ **Öztoklu** Meyve Pazarı (fruit market). Buy fresh fish from the adjacent fish market and have it cooked for a mere ₺8, which includes salad, bread or garlic bread and a special sauce. Drinks are only slightly overpriced. Daily noon–midnight.

KAŞ

KAŞ sprang to prominence after about 1850, when it established itself as a Greek fishing and timber port. It is beautifully located, nestled in a small curving bay below rocky cliffs. But what was once a sleepy fishing village is fast becoming an **adventure-sports centre** for backpackers, with nightlife to match.

WHAT TO SEE AND DO

In ancient times Kaş was the site of **Antiphellos**, and a few remains of the Lycian city are scattered around town. Five hundred metres west of town lies an almost complete **Hellenistic theatre**, behind which is a unique Doric tomb named Kesme Mezar, again almost completely intact. Kaş is also well situated for the nearby ruins of Kekova and Patara. On Fridays there is a big market behind the bus station.

ARRIVAL AND INFORMATION

By bus and dolmuş All buses and *dolmuşes* arrive at the small bus station just north of the town at the top of Elmalı Cad.
Destinations Antalya (18 daily; 7hr); Bodrum (3 daily; 6hr); Fethiye (10 daily; 2hr).
Tourist office In the town square at Cumhuriyet Meydanı 5 (May–Oct Mon–Fri 8.30am–7pm, Sat & Sun 10am–7pm; Nov–April Mon–Fri 9am–5pm; ☎0242 836 1238).

ACTIVITIES

Kaş is a handy base for paragliding and mountain biking, and offers some of the best scuba diving in Turkey. Many of the *pensions* listed can organize these activities, or try one of the numerous operators in town, such as Bougainville (☎0242 836 3737, ☻bougainville-turkey.com).

ACCOMMODATION

Most *pensions* are located in the streets close to the bus station, particularly around Recep Bilgin Cad and immediately beyond.
Ateş Pension Yeni Cami Sok 3 ☎0242 836 1393, ☻atespension.com. Meals can be eaten up on the pleasant rooftop terrace, where a barbecue with up to fifteen meze will set you back ₺35. Check the rooms before agreeing – prices are negotiable on the less appealing ones. You can use the pool at the *Hideaway Hotel* across the road. Dorms ₺50, doubles ₺150
★ **Hideaway** Eski Kilise Arkası 7 ☎0242 836 1887, ☻hotelhideaway.com. Situated at the fringes of the village, so terrace views are spectacular. The roof bar

serves alcoholic drinks and proper coffee. A cut above the rest in town and run by an engaging Turkish-Belgian couple. Doubles €55
Hilal Pension Süleyman Yıldırım Cad ☎0242 836 1207, ☻hilalpension.com. The really attentive owner here can help with all manner of excursions and activities. The rooms are decent and you can often feast on reasonably priced fish from the barbecue in the evening. A convivial spot. Doubles €35
Kaş Otel Hastane Cad 20 ☎0242 836 1271, ☻myhotelkas.com. Spartan but superbly located, right on the seafront with its own sun loungers and a ladder into the sea. Try to get a balconied room near the water; the ones behind have no views to speak of. ₺120

EATING AND DRINKING

Bahçe Uzun Çarşı ☎0242 836 2370. The broadest range of cold and hot meze in town, served in the garden (*bahçe* in Turkish). Nearby, their seafood annexe *Bahçe Balık* serves meze and mains including swordfish fillet (₺30). Daily 10am–midnight.
Bar Celona Uzunçarşı Gürsoy Sok 2/a. This lively place, set on a busy people-watching corner, attracts a good mix of locals, expats and holiday-makers. Owner Haldun is an engaging host, the beers are well priced and the cocktails delicious. Daily until late.
Kaş'ım Öztürk Sok 15. Chicken stew, *pide* pizzas and good old kebabs are all cooked to delicious perfection. Perpetually popular. Daily 9am–11pm.
★ **Şaraphane** Hastane Cad, Yeni Cami Sok 3 ☎0242 836 2715. On a quiet side street leading to the Yeni Cami, this mellow wine bar is the perfect place to share a tasty cheeseboard (₺20) and bottle of locally produced Likya Vineyard wine (a bargain ₺30). They also do decent mains from ₺20. Daily 10am–midnight.
Sultan Garden Hükümet Cad. Set in an atmospheric spot up the hill across the harbour and offering excellent meze, this family business has played host to several weddings. Daily until late.

OLYMPOS

The Lycian site of **OLYMPOS**, 50km before Antalya, is located on a beautiful sandy bay and the banks of a largely dry river. It's an idyllic location with a small village that is now firmly on the backpacker circuit. You can while away several hours rambling among the overgrown **ruins** (daily: April–Oct 8am–7pm; Nov–March 9am–5.30pm; ₺5, including access to the beach) before chilling out on the sand. The ruins include some recently excavated tombs,

35

the walls of a Byzantine church and a theatre, though most seats are long gone. On the north side of the river are more striking ruins, including a well-preserved marble temple entrance. Beyond is a Byzantine bathhouse, with mosaic floors, and a Byzantine canal that would have carried water to the heart of the city.

Çıralı and the Chimaera

A 1.5km walk along the pebbly beach from Olympos is the quieter holiday village of **ÇIRALI**. About an hour's well-marked stroll above the village's citrus groves flickers the dramatic **Chimaera** (open 24hr; ₺6), a series of eternal flames issuing from cracks in the bare rock, and particularly beautiful at night (take a torch for the walk there and back); many hostels in Olympos organize trips here for a small fee. The Chimaera fires have been burning since antiquity, and inspired the Lycians to worship the god Hephaestos (or Vulcan to the Romans).

ARRIVAL AND INFORMATION

By bus Catch any Kaş–Antalya bus to the minibus stop on the main highway, 11km up from the shore; in season a minibus departs every 15min from the main road to Olympos. In winter minibuses run but there are fewer of them so be prepared to take a taxi from the main road to Olympos village. There are also one or two minibuses a day from Antalya to Çıralı in season.

Money Note that there are no banks or ATMs in Olympos or Çıralı, so make sure you have enough cash before arriving. Many of the *pensions* can accept card payment for accommodation. There's no tourist office but hotels can help with tours and travel plans.

ACCOMMODATION

Most places in Olympos offer a choice of dorm beds or private bungalow; Çıralı is largely *pensions*.

Barış Pansiyon Just behind the beach near the restaurants, Çıralı ☎ 0242 825 7080. A choice of spartan, older en-suite rooms, a new wing of part-balconied upper-floor units (₺20 extra) and three wooden chalets, plus ample parking. Doubles ₺110, chalets ₺150

Bayram's Olympos ☎ 0242 892 1243, ⍟ bayrams.com. Accommodation ranges from bungalow shacks to tree-houses. Excellent facilities include laundry service and internet access. Prices include breakfast and dinner. Dorms ₺50, Treehouse doubles ₺100, bungalow ₺150

★ **Kadir's** Olympos ☎ 0242 892 1250, ⍟ kadirstree houses.com. With 338 dorm and bungalow beds mostly set in treehouses, plus space for campers, a volleyball court, the eclectic *Hangar Bar* for cocktails and the lively *Bull Bar* alfresco nightclub (from midnight till very late), it's no surprise this is the backpacker hangout of choice. No TVs in the rooms. Dorms ₺40, treehouses ₺45, bungalows ₺65

Orange ☎ 0242 892 1317, ⍟ olymposorangepension .com. Professionally run and offering better-quality cabins than others. Good wholesome grub too, including a decent vegetarian buffet. Prices can be bargained down a little. Dorms ₺30, bungalows ₺140

Şaban Olympos ☎ 0242 892 1265, ⍟ sabanpansion.com. Tranquil, treehouse-style *pension* set among pomegranate and lemon trees, with low-slung hammocks in shady spots, excellent home-made Turkish food offered as part of the room rate and a friendly, relaxed atmosphere. English and German spoken. Dorms ₺35, treehouses ₺60, bungalows ₺80

EATING AND DRINKING

Most hotels provide evening meals, but there are plenty of shady restaurants with locals preparing stuffed *gözleme*.

Cactus Café Olympos village. Chilled-out place playing reggae, set amid a pretty orange grove. Basic fare such as omelettes, salads, sandwiches and pasta dishes (from ₺8). Beer ₺9. Open daily.

Çıralı Gözleme Çıralı village between the Orange Market and Olympos Rent A Car, close to the *Orange Motel*. The most succulent specimens of *gözleme* hereabouts. Open daily.

Eski Yeni Olympos village ☎ 0242 892 1342. This dedicated live music venue draws some surprisingly well-known Turkish bands to its stage, with an emphasis on World Music old and new. Daily noon–2am.

Zakkum Olympos village. Another great spot to fill up on cheap *gözleme*. Choose from meat, cheese, potato or spinach – or all of the above – for less than ₺10. Open daily.

ACTIVE OLYMPOS

Olympos, with its beautiful scenery, calm warm sea and plenty of sunshine, is perfect for the outdoor life. *Kadir's* (below) offer a whole host of activities, including scuba diving, trekking on Turkey's first marked long-distance trail, the Lycian Way (⍟ culterouresinturkey.com), sea kayaking, rock-climbing and mountain-biking. Prices start from €25. If you're heading to Fethiye, you can opt for the three-night *gület* boat trip with V-Go (☎ 0252 612 2113, ⍟ boatcruiseturkey .com; from €199/person), which stops en route at archeological sites, small villages and Butterfly Valley (see box, p.1166).

ANTALYA

ANTALYA is backed by spectacular mountains, has two long swimming beaches either end of the city and, despite the grim appearance of its concrete sprawl, is an agreeable place. The main area of interest for visitors is confined to the relatively small walled old quarter, though the nearby mountain-set ancient city of **Termessos** is a major draw.

WHAT TO SEE AND DO

Antalya is dominated by the **Yivli Minare** or "Fluted Minaret", erected in the thirteenth century. Downhill from here is the old **harbour**, recently restored and site of the evening promenade. North is the **bazaar**, while south, beyond the Saat Kalesi (clock tower), lies Kaleiçi or the **old town**, with every house now a carpet shop, café or *pension*. On the far side, on Atatürk Caddesi, the triple-arched **Hadrian's Gate** recalls a visit by the emperor in 130 AD; Hesapçı Sokak leads south past the Kesik Minare to the cliff-edge and pretty **Karaalioğlu Park** and its tea gardens.

Antalya Archeological Museum

The one thing you shouldn't miss is the **Antalya Archeological Museum** (Tues–Sun: April–Oct 9am–7pm; Nov–March 8am–5pm; ₺20), one of the top five archeological collections in the country, with some superb statues from the nearby ancient city of Perge and many other artefacts; it's on the western edge of town at the far end of Kenan Evren Bulvarı, easily reachable by a period tram that departs from the clock tower in Kaleiçi.

Termessos

The spectacular remains of **Termessos** (daily: April–Oct 8am–7pm; Nov–March 8am–5pm; ₺5), a small but superbly situated ancient city that even Alexander the Great failed to capture, is set 1000m above sea level in a beautiful national park 30km northwest of Antalya. A dramatically situated cliff-edge theatre is the centrepiece of this gorgeously overgrown site, but the rock-cut tombs run it a close second.

ARRIVAL AND INFORMATION

By plane The airport is 12km northeast; Havaş buses into town (₺10) depart from the domestic terminal, 5min walk from the international terminal. A taxi into the centre costs around ₺40. There are city buses but they require a travel smart card not available at the airport.

By bus Antalya's main bus station is 7km north of town. From the bus station take bus #93 to Hadrian's Gate (Üçkapılar) then walk into the old town, or take the Antray tram (you may have to purchase an Antray travel card from the terminal to do this).

Destinations Fethiye, by inland route (6 daily; 4hr); İzmir (6 daily; 9hr 30min); Kaş (6 daily; 5hr); Konya (6 daily; 5hr 30min); Olympos (every 30min; 2hr).

Tourist office A 15min walk west from the clock tower on Cumhuriyet Cad (daily 8am–6/7pm; ☎ 0242 241 1747).

GETTING AROUND

By tram A period tram runs along Atatürk Cad, ending its route at the museum. Tickets (₺1.75) can be bought on board.

ACCOMMODATION

Most budget accommodation is in the area sandwiched between Hadrian's Gate and the back of the bazaar.

Atelya Art Hotel Civelek Sok 21 ☎0242 2481 6416, ☻ atelyahotel.com. One of the old quarter's longest-established hotels fashioned from a superb Ottoman-era house, with several annexes of equal charm and vintage. Doubles **€50**

Özmen Pension Zeytin Çıkmazı 5 ☎0242 241 6505, ☻ ozmenpension.com. Friendly place well located on the western edge of the old walled city. Spotless rooms and a pleasant terrace, all overseen by engaging hosts Deniz and Aziz. Doubles **€35**

Sabah Pansiyon Hesapçı Sok 60/a ☎0242 247 5345, ☻ sabahpansiyon.com. Backpacker-friendly place with decent rooms and a sleepy courtyard. Price includes breakfast. Dorms **€25**, doubles **€50**

White Garden Kaleiçi Kılıçaslan Hesapçı Geçidi 9 ☎0242 241 9115, ☻ whitegardenpansion.com. Charming Ottoman restoration with fifteen immaculate rooms with large en suites. The owners also run the nearby *Secret Palace Hotel* and *Hadrians*, two equally pretty establishments with shady gardens, charging comparable prices. Doubles ₺140

EATING AND DRINKING

Antalya's restaurants and bars are generally open from the morning until late evening.

★**Castle Bar & Restaurant** Hıdırlık Kulesi Sok 48 ☎0242 248 6594. Perhaps the best-located of the old quarter's bar-cum-restaurants, right on the cliff-edge in the shadow of a Roman watchtower. Spectacular views across the bay, freezing beers (₺12) and a Turkish-international mix menu (mains from ₺16). Daily 8am–1pm.

Parlak Restaurant Kazım Özalp Cad Zincirlihan 7. It might not look too appealing from the outside but this popular spot is worth a visit. Try the slow-roasted chicken or lovely fresh meze. Mains ₺18–35. Daily 9am–11pm.

Salman Patisserie Fevzi Çakmak Cad. Uluç Apt 7. ☏ 0242 316 7738. Treat yourself to a sumptuous breakfast buffet or baklava and a top-notch cappuccino. Daily 7am–10pm.

Seraser Karanlık Sok 18 ☏ 0242 247 6015. A cut above the budget joints in town, serving well-presented fresh fish and other Turkish delights. Good for a special night out with fish mains from ₺22. Daily 11am–midnight.

★ **Sim Restaurant** Kaledibi Sok 7. Tucked away from the crowds, but well worth seeking out. A charming husband-and-wife-run place; tables are either upstairs in a small dining room decorated with antiques or outdoors on the quiet street beneath shady vines. Mains from ₺25. Daily 11am–1pm.

Central Turkey

Sandwiched between the Black Sea and the Mediterranean, Central Turkey, or **Anatolia**, comprises several interesting spots. **Ankara** grew as a result of immigration from the Anatolian villages to become the metropolis it is now. Southeast of here is the bizarre landscape of **Cappadocia**, where water and wind have created fantastic forms from the soft tufa rock, including forests of cones, table mountains and canyon-like valleys. Further south still, **Konya** is best known as the birthplace of the mystical Mevlevi sufi order and makes a convenient place to stop over between Cappadocia and the coast.

ANKARA

Modern **ANKARA** is really two cities, a double identity that is due to the breakneck pace at which it has developed since being declared capital of the Turkish Republic in 1923. Until then Ankara – known as Angora – had been a small provincial city, famous chiefly for the production of soft goat's wool. This city still exists, in and around the old citadel

that was the site of the original settlement. The other Ankara is the modern metropolis that has grown up around a carefully planned attempt to create a seat of government worthy of a modern, Western-looking state. Often overlooked, it merits a detour of a couple of days, especially if you're travelling from Istanbul to Cappadocia.

WHAT TO SEE AND DO

The city is bisected north–south by **Atatürk Bulvarı**, and everything you need is within easy reach of this broad and busy street. At the northern end, **Ulus Meydanı**, a large square and an important traffic intersection marked by a huge equestrian Atatürk statue, is the best jumping-off point for the old part of the city – a village of narrow cobbled streets and ramshackle wooden houses centring on the **Hisar**, Ankara's old fortress and citadel. To the south, the modern shopping district of **Kızılay** sees Turkish students congregate on its streets. At night, the area is awash with entertainment, bars and restaurants, as are the neighbouring districts of **Kavaklıdere** and **Çankaya**.

The Museum of Anatolian Civilizations

Located in Ulus, at the end of Kadife Sokak, is the **Museum of Anatolian Civilizations** (daily: April–Oct 8.30am–6.45pm; Nov–March 8.30am–5.15pm; ₺15), which boasts an incomparable collection of archeological objects housed in a restored Ottoman *bedesten*, or covered market. Hittite carving and relief work form the most compelling section of the museum, mostly taken from Carchemish, near the present Syrian border. There are also Neolithic finds from Çatal Höyük, the site of one of Anatolia's oldest settlements and widely regarded as the world's first "city".

Hisar

A steep walk up Hisarpark Cad brings you to the **Hisar**, a small citadel amid the old city walls. Most of what can be seen today dates from Byzantine times, with substantial Selçuk and Ottoman

35

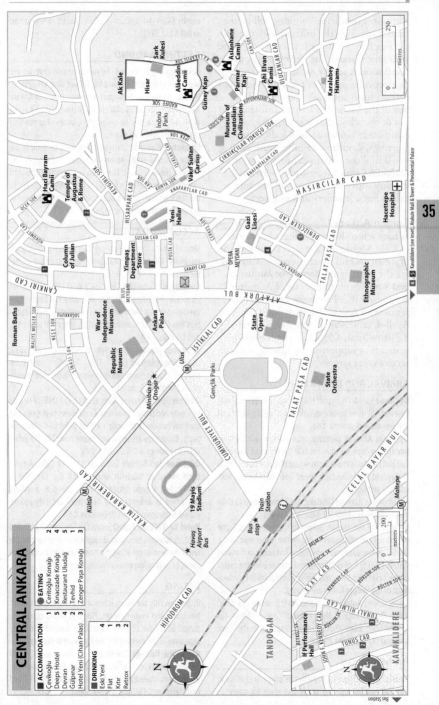

CENTRAL ANKARA

ACCOMMODATION
Çevikoğlu	1
Deeps Hostel	5
Devran	4
Gülpınar	2
Hotel Yeni (Cihan Palas)	3

DRINKING
Eski Yeni	4
Flat	1
Kitir	3
Retrox	2

EATING
Ceritoğlu Konağı	2
Kınacızade Konağı	4
Restaurant Uludağ	5
Tevhid	1
Zenger Paşa Konağı	3

35

Kavaklıdere (see inset), Atakule Mall & Tower & Presidential Palace

Bus Station

additions. Inside the confines, follow the steps leading up the hill and look out for the flag flying in the distance as you wend your way through the narrow lanes, and you'll soon reach **Ak Kale**, a castle ruin that provides a perfect perch for viewing Ankara from above. A walk around the rest of the Hisar will let you amble in and out of the alleys that intersect the ramshackle houses as local kids shout greetings. Continue to head south and you'll find the twelfth-century mosque, **Alâeddin Camii**, along with a series of touristy souvenir stalls selling handmade carpet bags, jewellery and crockery.

Roman Ankara

What's left of Roman Ankara lies north of Ulus Meydanı. First stop is the **Column of Julian** on Hükümet Meydanı. Close by are the ruins of the **Temple of Augustus and Rome**, built in honour of Augustus around 20 BC. Northeast of here are the remains of Ankara's **Roman baths** (daily: April–Oct 8.30am–7pm; Nov–March 8.30am–5pm; ₺5). Only the foundation stones that supported the heating and service areas remain.

ARRIVAL AND DEPARTURE

By plane Esenboğa airport is 28km north of town. Havaş buses (₺10) meet incoming Turkish Airlines flights; a taxi will set you back around ₺80.

By train Ankara's pleasant train station, with a new terminal for high-speed trains, is at the corner of Talat Paşa Cad and Cumhuriyet Bul, from where frequent buses run to Kızılay and Ulus. The high-speed line links Ankara with Istanbul and Konya.

Destinations Istanbul (10 daily; 4hr 20min); İzmir (1 daily overnight; 13hr); Konya (7 daily; 1hr 45min).

By bus The bus station is 5km to the southwest. Some companies run minibuses to the centre, otherwise take a *dolmuş* or the easy and convenient Ankaray rapid transit system (₺3) to Kızılay (10min) and change onto the metro (same ticket) for Ulus (red line towards Batıkent), where most of the budget hotels are located.

Destinations Antalya (12 daily; 7hr); Bodrum (10 daily; 12hr); Bursa (hourly; 6hr); Istanbul (every 30min; 4hr 45min–6hr); İzmir (hourly; 8hr); Konya (hourly; 3hr); Nevşehir (12 daily; 4hr 30min).

INFORMATION

Tourist office There's a small but helpful tourist office in the train station offering maps and ideas for day-trips

nearby (Mon–Fri 8.30am–5.30pm, closed at weekends; ☎0312 231 5572).

GETTING AROUND

Tickets for city buses and the metro system cost ₺3 per journey – or buy a travel card for ₺5 and save ₺1 per trip.

By bus As well as displaying numbers, buses in Ankara also display the names of their destinations, so it's easy to work out which one to catch. Most buses stop running between midnight and 1am.

By metro/Ankaray The metro runs from Batıkent in the northwest and splits at Kızılay where it becomes the Ankaray (light railway). The Ankaray heads to either Aşti (where the bus station is based) or Dikimevi in the east. In the summer, the metro stops running at midnight and in the winter it terminates at 11pm.

ACCOMMODATION

Most of the cheaper hotels are in the streets east of Atatürk Bul in the Ulus district. Standards are pretty basic across the board.

Çevikoğlu Çankırı Cad, Orta Sok 2 ☎0312 310 4535. Set on a quiet backstreet, this budget choice has better than average decor in the rooms and is extremely well kept – plus there's a decent buffet breakfast to set you up for the day. Doubles ₺80

★ **Deeps Hostel** Atac Sok 2 ☎0312 213 6338, ⌨deepshostelankara.com. This friendly hostel is spotlessly clean, with wood laminate floors and cheery decor. Dorms ₺27, doubles ₺85

Devran Opera Meydanı, Ulus ☎0312 311 0485. Friendly welcome and professional feel. Great views of the city and stadium but could do with a lick of paint and plaster in parts. Bathrooms are clean and rooms have TVs. Breakfast costs an additional ₺8. Doubles ₺80

Gülpınar Hacı Bayram Cad 6 ☎0312 311 5998. A basic hotel aimed at transient workers and the like, this is nonetheless a good option as it's as cheap as anything you'll find in Ankara. Small but clean and tidy rooms, shared bathrooms. No wi-fi. Doubles ₺55

Hotel Yeni (Cihan Palas) Sanayı Cad 5/b, Ulus ☎0312 310 4720, ⌨hotelyeni.com. A good couple of notches up from the rest of the town's more affordable hotels. Quiet and respectable and open to haggling on room prices. Doubles ₺280

EATING

Ulus, especially the Hisar, is home to a number of decent lunchtime and evening spots. *Pide* and kebab places are dotted about the city. For something smarter and more expensive in the evening try the Kavaklıdere district.

Ceritoğlu Konağı Kalekapısı Sok, Hisar ☎0312 324 3622. A quirky café offering *gözleme* for a mere ₺6, yoghurt-smothered *mantı* (Turkish ravioli) for ₺12 and breakfasts for ₺15. Daily 8am–7.30pm.

Kınacızade Konağı Kalekapısı Sok 28, Hisar. Guns, waistcoats, records, tankards and hookahs are just some of the random objects hanging from the walls in this intriguing spot. Especially good for its monumental, all-inclusive breakfast spread (₺60 for two). Daily 8am–1am.

Restaurant Uludağ Denizciler Cad 54, Ulus. It doesn't look like much from the outside but it has been going since 1956 and still offers some of the best kebabs and other grills in Ankara. Decent selection of desserts, too. Closes around 9pm.

Tevhid Anafartlar Cad 10 ☎0312 310 4851. This unassuming place is well known for its succulent *İskender kebap* (₺18), though its other kebabs and grilled meats are just as tasty. Vegetarians or the impecunious can go for the tasty *pide* (₺8 and up). Daily 7am–10pm.

Zenger Paşa Konağı Doyran Sok 13, Hisar. Just climbing up to the restaurant is a treat. Atmospheric location for a splurge, with hearty fixed menu evening meals starting from ₺70, which includes a couple of alcoholic drinks. Mon–Sat 10am–midnight.

DRINKING AND NIGHTLIFE

★ **Eski Yeni** İnkılap Sok 6, Kızılay. A lively spot on a busy bar street entertaining enthusiastic drinkers with live music inside and a large courtyard outside. Daily until late.

Flat Tunus Cad 54, Kavaklıdere ☎0312 466 6311. Marking its territory by flames and Balearic tunes, this spot serves top cocktails to a hip, young crowd while a shot bar on the pavement aims to entice more in. A sign reads "Music, drinks, people", which has it about right. Daily 2.30pm–1am.

Kıtır Tunalı Hilmi Cad 114 24, Kavaklıdere. A sprawling treat, full of locals packed into wooden booths and perusing beer-stein-shaped menus to a thumping rock and pop soundtrack. Snacks such as hotdogs and *kokoreç* (spiced stuffed lamb's intestines) are popular – best washed down with a large Efes beer (₺12) or two. Daily 11am–midnight.

Retrox Tunus Cad 53, Kavaklıdere ☎0312 465 0053. A dark and convivial spot, where the lights are low and the conversation kept to a murmur. Brick walls and black-and-white photography add to the ambience. Burgers, pasta dishes and the like keep the patrons' hunger at bay. Daily noon–2am.

ENTERTAINMENT

Anadolu Gösteri Kongre Merkezi Türkocağı Cad Balgat. Large performance hall for theatre or music concerts. See ⊕biletix.com for tickets.

If Performance Hall Tunus Cad 14/a, Kavaklıdere ☎0312 418 9506, ⊕ifperformance.com. Bands perform nightly – a stalwart of the Ankara music scene.

State Opera Atatürk Bul ☎0312 324 2210, ⊕dobgm .gov.tr. Classic operas and occasional piano recitals and classical concerts. Tickets (₺30 and up) from the Dost bookshop in Kızılay or the venue.

DIRECTORY

Embassies Australia, Nenehatun Cad 83, Gaziosmanpaşa ☎0312 459 9500; Canada, Cinnah Cad 58, Çankaya ☎0312 409 2700; New Zealand, Iran Cad 13 4, Kavaklıdere ☎0312 467 9054; UK, Şehit Ersan Cad 46/a, Çankaya ☎0312 455 3344; US, Atatürk Bul 110, Kavaklıdere ☎0312 455 5555.

Hammam Karacabey Hamamı, Talat Paşa Bul 101 (daily 10am–10pm; from ₺25).

Hospital Hacettepe University Medical Faculty, west of Hasırcılar Sok, Sıhhıye ☎0312 305 500.

Internet Chatlak Net Café Fevzi Çakmak Sok 22-B Kızlay.

Left luggage The train station has lockers you can use 24 hours.

Post office Merkez Postahane, on Atatürk Bul, Ulus.

CAPPADOCIA

A land created by the complex interaction of natural and human forces over vast spans of time, **CAPPADOCIA**, around 150km southeast of Ankara, is a superlative visual experience. Its weird formations of soft, dusty rock have been adapted into caves and even underground cities over centuries by many cultures. A short flight from Istanbul, Cappadocia is an essential destination thanks to the wide selection of competitively priced accommodation, restaurants and activities on offer. Many backpackers choose to stay in the touristy spot of **Göreme**, but alternatives include sleepier **Uçhisar** or **Ürgüp**, a small town where many of the old abandoned cave dwellings have been renovated into guesthouses and private homes. Less appealing is the working city of **Nevşehir**, which acts as a transport hub for the region.

WHAT TO SEE AND DO

A relatively easy 1km walk from Göreme village, the **Göreme Open-Air Museum** (daily: April–Oct 8am–7pm; Nov–March 8am–5pm; ₺20) is the site of more than thirty cave churches, mainly dating from the ninth century to the end of the eleventh century and a treasure-trove of detailed frescoes in dark recesses – many of which have been defaced in distant centuries.

Outdoor pursuits include walking in the valleys, in particular **Ihlara Valley**; allow two to four hours per walk and don't miss a stop at one of the rustic farmer-run teashops en route. Note that there are no detailed maps of the area and waymark signs tend to be arrows painted on rocks. The best routes are Pigeon Valley between Göreme and Uçhisar, and the Red Valley from Ortahisar to the village of Çavuşin. The open-air museum at **Zelve** (daily: April–Oct 8am–7pm; Nov–March 8am–5pm; ₺10), meanwhile, was occupied for some 4000 years until as recently as the 1920s, and was the site of a monastery from the ninth to the thirteenth centuries.

Derinkuyu and Kayamaklı

Among the most extraordinary phenomena of the Cappadocia region are the remains of a number of underground settlements, some of them large enough to have accommodated up to 30,000 people. The cities are thought to date back to Hittite times, though the complexes were later enlarged by Christian communities. Most thoroughly excavated is **Derinkuyu** (daily: April–Oct 8am–7pm; Nov–March 8am–5pm; ₺20), 29km from Nevşehir and accessible by *dolmuş*. The city is well lit, and the original ventilation system still functions remarkably well, though some of the passages are small and cramped. The excavated area consists of eight floors and includes stables, wine presses and a dining hall or schoolroom with two long, rock-cut tables, plus a cruciform church and dungeon.

Some 10km north of Derinkuyu is **Kaymaklı** (daily: April–Oct 8am–7pm; Nov–March 8am–5pm; ₺20), where only five of its underground levels have been excavated to date.

ARRIVAL AND DEPARTURE

By plane The region is served by two main airports, Kayseri Erkilet Airport about 1hr from Göreme, and Nevşehir, which is much closer and more convenient. Taxis and shuttles run from the latter, but your hotel may arrange transport.
Destinations from Kayseri Istanbul (6 daily; 90min).
Destinations from Nevşehir Istanbul (2 daily; 90min).
By bus Direct services arrive at the Göreme bus station, located in front of Müze Cad, in the centre of town. However, some firms will drop you off in Nevşehir, from where you'll have to continue by local bus or *dolmuş*. The

dolmuş runs between Nevşehir and Ürgüp, calling at Göreme, several times an hour from 7am to 11pm. You shouldn't have to wait long for a ride. When buying your bus ticket, be sure to check the end destination.
Destinations from Nevşehir Ankara (7 daily; 5hr); Konya (6 daily; 3hr).

INFORMATION, TOURS AND ACTIVITIES

Numerous travel agencies offer tours of the region, which take in the best of Cappadocia's panoramic points, underground cities, monasteries and other attractions.
Tourist office By Göreme bus station (daily 5am–8pm); it offers accommodation lists and maps but not much in the way of help.
Middle Earth Travel Göreme ☎0384 271 2559, ⌨ middleearthtravel.com. From €60/person for hikes in the Ihlara valley; from €190 for two-day climbs up Erciyes Dağı or Hasan Dağı; from €590 for a one-week trek, including accommodation and meals.
Argeus Travel ⌨ argeus.com.tr. Specialize in cycling and hiking trips (between $435 and $755 for a three-night hiking tour including accommodation, depending on group size), while bicycles, mopeds and jeeps can be rented from a number of spots in Göreme.
Kapadokya Balloons ☎0384 271 2442, ⌨ kapadokyaballoons.com. The original balloon operator offers standard flights (1hr) beginning at dawn and costing €175/person, including transfers, insurance and champagne breakfast.

GETTING AROUND

By dolmuş *Dolmuşes* operate regularly between Cappadocia's villages, departing Göreme for example every 15min from 7am to around 10.30pm.

ACCOMMODATION

Cave hotels are the most popular form of accommodation in Cappadocia, but there are alternatives – often with great views – for those not keen on a night underground. Some hostels/hotels can be tricky to find, though most are walkable from bus stations. If you're staying in another village, ask your accommodation, as many will arrange a free transfer from the bus station.

GÖREME

Kookaburra Konak Sok 10 ☎0384 271 2549, ⌨ kookaburramotel.com. Well-established and well-run hostel that ticks all the right boxes – quiet location, clean rooms, friendly owner (İhsan) and lovely roof terrace. Dorms €10, doubles €40
Köse Pension Ragıp Üner Cad, Göreme ☎0384 271 2294, ⌨ kosepension.com. Large, homely *pension* near the bus station with swimming pool, shady outdoor and rooftop areas to relax in. The mattress-strewn dorm is in a

large wooden hall on the roof. Free wi-fi. Breakfast and evening meal, served daily, are extra. Dorms ₺20, doubles ₺120

Rock Valley Pension Isali Mah, İceri Dere Sok, Göreme ☎ 0384 271 2153. Attractive mix of same- and mixed-sex dorms and private rooms. Big pool with the valley looming up all around. A pleasant, low-key option. Breakfast included. Dorms ₺22, doubles ₺90

UÇHİSAR

★**Kale Konak** Kale Sok 9, Uçhisar ☎ 0384 219 2828, ⓦ kalekonak.com. A wonderfully cosy and labyrinthine hotel at the foot of Uçhisar Castle. All fifteen rooms are spectacular and the affable owner keeps large tour groups away. A private session in the marble hammam (free) is the ultimate indulgence. A top place to blow the budget for a night or two. Doubles €140

ÜRGÜP

★**Esbelli Evi** Esbelli Sok 8, Ürgüp ☎ 0384 341 3395, ⓦ esbelli.com. Magnificent views and sumptuous boutique rooms in caves with private terraces and secluded courtyard gardens at one of Cappadocia's finest – and oldest – hotels. Laptops with Skype in each room. Well worth stretching your budget for. Includes breakfast. Doubles €135

EATING AND DRINKING

In Göreme, several restaurants and bars are on Müze Cad, behind the bus station. Most places in the region are open every day until quite late in the evening during high season.

GÖREME

Dibek Hakkı Paşa Meydanı, Göreme ☎ 0384 271 2209. It won't take long for someone to tell you about this place's *testi kebap* (₺42) but it takes the restaurant a long time to cook it – you need to order it when you make your reservation. The building is nearly 500 years old. Daily 8am–late.

Fatboys Belediye Cad ☎ 0536 936 3652. Emphasizing the clientele's international origins rather than its Central Anatolian location, this is the place to come to relax with a local or imported beer and eat pizza, burgers or hummus. Board games and big-screen sports add to the backpacker vibe. Daily 9am–late.

Top Deck Efendi Sok 15 ☎ 0384 271 2474. Run by a welcoming Turkish-South African couple, this atmospheric cave-set restaurant offers great meze (from ₺9) and tasty mains from ₺22. There are plenty of vegetarian options, and hearty desserts are dished up with a scoop of ice cream. Reservations essential. Mon–Thurs, Sat & Sun 6–10pm.

ÜRGÜP

★**Ziggy's** Yunak Mah, Tevfik Fikret Cad 24, Ürgüp ☎ 0384 341 7107. Delicious meze, superb mains (including a

spectacular liver dish), an outdoor terrace and charming owners make this an essential, if pricier, stop. Booking essential. Around ₺60 per head including local wine. Daily noon–11pm.

KONYA

Roughly midway between Antalya and Nevşehir, **KONYA** is an unremarkable city but an essential place of pilgrimage for the Muslim world – the home of Celaleddin Rumi or the Mevlâna ("Our Master"), the mystic who founded the Mevlevi or **Whirling Dervish** sect, making it a centre of Sufic mystical practice and teaching.

The Mevlâna Museum

The **Mevlâna Museum** (daily: April–Oct 9am–6.30pm; Nov–March 9am–4.40pm; free) is housed in the first lodge (*tekke*) of the Mevlevi dervish sect, at the eastern end of Mevlâna Bulvarı, recognizable by its distinctive fluted turquoise dome. Inside are the tombs of the Mevlâna, his father and other notables. The original *semahane* (ceremonial hall) exhibits some of the musical instruments of the first dervishes, the original illuminated poetical work of the Mevlâna, and a 500-year-old silk carpet from Selçuk Persia (supposedly the finest ever woven). In the adjoining room, a casket containing hairs from the beard of the Prophet Mohammed is displayed alongside illuminated medieval Korans and other sacred texts.

Karatay Tile Museum

Built by Emir Celaleddin Karatay in the thirteenth century, the interior of the **Karatay Tile Museum** (Alâeddin Bulvarı; daily: April–Oct 9am–6.40pm; Nov–March 9am–4.40pm; ₺5) is as fascinating as the ceramics on show, with a beautifully decorated domed central ceiling and ornamental green tiles.

ARRIVAL AND DEPARTURE

By plane Konya's airport is 18km from the city. Havaş shuttle buses take 30min to the centre (₺10); a taxi will cost around ₺50. (₺40 by taxi). Head to the Turkish Airlines office at Feritpaşa Cad 10/b in the city for the return journey.

35

By train The train station is 2km out of the centre at the far end of İstasyon Cad, connected to the centre by regular *dolmuş*.

Destinations Ankara (7 daily; 1hr 45min); Istanbul (2 daily; 4hr 35min); İzmir (1 daily; 11hr 30min).

By bus The bus station is 10km out of town, from where the *otogar dolmuş* and tramway connects with the town centre. Follow the tramway signs and purchase a pass at the small ticket booth.

Destinations Ankara (hourly; 3hr); Antalya (8 daily; 5hr); Istanbul (every 40min; 10hr); Nevşehir (10 daily; 3hr 30min).

INFORMATION

Tourist office Azize Mahallesi, Aslanlı Kışla Cad 5. By the Mevlâna Museum and very helpful (daily 8am–5pm; ☎ 0032 353 4021, ext 147).

GETTING AROUND

By tram The city has one main tram line running from Alâeddin in the centre to the outskirts via the Otogar. Buy tickets from booths by the stops.

ACCOMMODATION

Deluxe Otel Ayanbey Sok 22 ☎ 0332 351 1546, ⓦ konyadeluxeotel.com. All 25 rooms are en suite with a/c, minibar and flat-screen TV at this hotel, with a business-style feel but impressive for the money. Little English but welcoming nonetheless. Doubles ₺90

Hich Hotel Aziziye Mah Celal Sok 6 ☎ 0332 353 4424, ⓦ hichhotel.com. Located in an impressive historic

---

WHIRLING DERVISH CEREMONY

This meditational ceremony, where worshippers spin around to draw closer to God, is held at the Mevlâna Cultural Centre near the museum. The ceremony is free and takes place every Saturday night. No need for a ticket; just turn up (8pm winter; 9pm summer). You'll find plenty of background reading on ⓦ mevlana.net.

---

building opposite the Mevlâna Museum, this small boutique-style hotel offers a different experience to standard Konya hotels. Wrought-iron furniture gives a traditional feel; espresso machines and iPhone docks a touch of modernity. Doubles €80

Rumi Hotel Durakfakih Sok 5 ☎ 0332 353 1121, ⓦ rumihotel.com. A comfortable and very centrally located hotel opposite the Mevlâna Museum, with spectacular views from the rooftop breakfast terrace. Large rooms and decent bathrooms. Doubles ₺150

★ **Ulusan** Off Alâeddin Cad on side road behind the PTT ☎ 0332 351 5004, ⓔ ulusanhotel@hotmail.com. A family-run place helmed by an eccentric and amiable host with great English. Stuffed toys and knick-knacks throughout. Shared bathrooms but decent rooms and a home-away-from-home feel. Doubles ₺90

EATING AND DRINKING

Konya has a handful of half-decent restaurants but no reputable bars or pubs to speak of. Locals prefer to hang out around a *nargile*, and few women venture out at night alone. The area around Alâeddin Parkı is where younger people congregate, although there's not a lot to do there either.

Ali Baba Firin Kebab Şeref Şirin Sok ☎ 0532 581 560. A Konya speciality is lamb slow-cooked in a wood-fired oven. This is the place to try it, served up with tender, warm *pide* bread and sliced onions. Prices, based on grams, start from ₺12. Mon–Sat 10am–5pm.

Mevlevi Sofrası Nazimbey Cad 1/a. Smart, spacious terrace with sweeping views of the museum garden. If you're hungry after a museum visit, try the *adana kebap* (₺14) or a tasty meat and vegetable casserole known as *güveç* (₺18). Daily 8am–11pm.

Osmanlı Çarşısı Ince Minare Sokak. A classic *nargile* and coffee place with Ottoman-style rooms spread over several floors. It is behind the İnce Minare Medresesi on an atmospheric street flooded with green lights. Daily until late.

Somatçı Akçeşme Mahallesi Mengüç Cad 36. A converted Ottoman house on a quiet and atmospheric cobbled street serving traditional food to a mostly local clientele. Photos on the wall are testament to the many happy punters since it opened. Mains from ₺20. Daily 8am–10pm.

PECHERSKA LAVRA, KYIV

Ukraine

HIGHLIGHTS

❶ Chornobyl Museum, Kyiv Learn about the world's worst nuclear accident and the heroism of those who cleared it up. **See p.1184**

❷ Pecherska Lavra, Kyiv Experience Orthodox-Christian spirituality first-hand at this centuries-old religious site. **See p.1185**

❸ Odesa Soak up the sun then party all night at Arkadia beach. **See p.1187**

❹ L'viv Old Town Lose yourself in the café-filled alleys and courtyards of this Central European jewel. **See p.1189**

HIGHLIGHTS ARE MARKED ON THE MAP ON P.1179

ROUGH COSTS

Daily budget Basic €40, occasional treat €60

Drink *horilka* (vodka; 50ml shot) €1

Food Ukrainian *borshch* €0.80

Hostel/budget hotel €8/€30

Travel Train: Kyiv–Odesa €10; bus €18

FACT FILE

Population 45.5 million

Languages Ukrainian, Russian

Currency Hryvnia (Hr/UAH)

Capital Kyiv

International phone code ☏ 380

Time zone GMT +3hr

Introduction

The second-largest country in Europe, Ukraine has not always had clearly defined frontiers and has spent large tracts of its history under foreign rule. However, it has long had a clear sense of national identity, which has been strengthened by the 2014 Euromaidan revolution and the ensuing political tension between Ukraine and Russia. National pride coexists with a mixture of cultural influences: Ukrainians living in Kyiv, Odesa and the east may well speak the Russian language at home and on the streets, while those living in L'viv and the west speak Ukrainian in all social situations – and are enormously proud of the fact.

Despite being a country of large distances and time-consuming travel, Ukraine is not as far away as you might think, and its three key cities are well worth fitting in to a wider European trip. Ukraine's fast-paced capital **Kyiv** offers a fascinating insight into a country in the throes of transformation, with chic boutiques and slick bars sprouting up along broad, cobbled boulevards. Glittering church domes and steeples show off the city's medieval glories. One of Europe's great maritime cities, **Odesa** exudes a sense of Tsarist-Empire grandeur, while its bars and beaches provide a vibrant hedonistic edge. In total contrast is the western city of **L'viv**, a Central European city that looks like an estranged cousin of Vienna or Prague, and has the cultural attractions and café life to match. Situated within easy travelling distance of Central European cities, L'viv is the one Ukrainian city that you should squeeze into your itinerary.

CHRONOLOGY

Tenth century AD A strong Slav state known as "Rus" emerges, centred on Kyiv.

988 Prince Vladimir of Kyiv accepts Christianity.

1240 Kyiv is sacked by the Tatars.

1362 After the Battle of the Blue Waters, much of Ukraine is absorbed into the Grand Duchy of Lithuania.

1569 The Union of Lublin creates the Polish-Lithuanian Commonwealth, with most of Ukraine falling under direct Polish rule.

1648 Cossack leader Bohdan Khmelnitskyi leads an uprising against the Commonwealth.

1654 Khmelnitskyi swears allegiance to Tsarist Russia, bringing central and eastern Ukraine into the orbit of Moscow. Western Ukraine remains in Polish, then Habsburg, hands.

1709 An anti-Russian revolt under Ivan Mazepa is defeated.

1780s Russia drives the Ottoman Turks from southern Ukraine and the Crimea.

1794 Russian Empress Catherine the Great founds the Black Sea port of Odesa.

1917–21 The Russian Revolution sparks failed attempts to re-create an independent Ukrainian state. Central and Eastern Ukraine are absorbed into the Soviet Union, while Western Ukraine becomes part of Poland.

1932–33 Stalinist collectivization policies lead to the Holodomor or Great Famine, resulting in anything between 2.5 and 7.5 million deaths.

1941 Nazi Germany invades Ukraine, meeting fierce resistance in Kyiv and Odesa.

1945 International borders are redrawn: Western Ukraine is absorbed into the Ukrainian Soviet Republic.

1986 A fire at the Chornobyl power plant leads to the world's worst nuclear accident.

1991 The USSR is dissolved and Ukraine becomes an independent state.

2004 Viktor Yanukovych wins a presidential election regarded by many as fraudulent. Popular protests spark the so-called Orange Revolution. A re-vote is won by pro-Western Viktor Yushchenko.

2009 The Orange Revolution runs out of steam: Viktor Yanukovych is re-elected president.

November 2013 President Yanukovych's failure to sign a long-awaited association agreement with the EU sparks the protest movement known as Euromaidan.

February 2014 Yanukovych signs a compromise agreement with EU mediators and then flees to Russia, leaving a power vacuum filled by parliament.

March 2014 Moscow exploits Ukraine's weakness by staging a takeover of Crimea and stoking rebellion in Ukraine's Russian-speaking east.

February 2015 Ukraine and Russia sign the so-called Minsk II ceasefire agreement, although tension in the east remains.

UKRAINE

Warsaw
0   100
kilometres

BELARUS

Minsk   Moscow

RUSSIA

Kovel
Chornobyl
Kyivske
Reservoir   **1**   KYIV

Kraków

Lutsk   Rivne

Kharkiv

POLAND

L'viv   **4**   Zhytomyr   Kremenchutske
Reservoir   Poltava

Ternopil   Khmel'nyts'kyi   Cherkasy   **2**

Luhansk

SLOVAKIA

Ivano-
Frankivs'k   Kamianets-
Podil's'kyi   Vinnytsya   Kremenchuk

Kirovohrad   Dnipropetrovsk   Donetsk

Budapest

Chernivtsi   Kryvy Rih

HUNGARY

ROMANIA   Kakhovske
Reservoir   RUSSIA

HIGHLIGHTS

Metres

1500

900

300

0

1 Chornobyl Museum, Kyiv
2 Pecherska Lavra, Kyiv
3 Odesa
4 L'viv Old Town

Mykolayiv   Kherson

Odesa   **3**

Sea of
Azov

N

BLACK SEA   Simferopol

Sevastopol   Yalta

Bucharest

ARRIVAL AND DEPARTURE

The main hub for arrivals **by air** is Kyiv Borispil, which is served by major European and transatlantic airlines. The smaller Kyiv Zhulyany is used by the budget carrier Wizz Air, while the airports at Odesa and L'viv receive a limited number of flights from other European cities. Kyiv Central Railway Station (sometimes marked on timetables as Kyiv Pasazhirs'kyi) is the main international **train station**, served by overnight trains from Budapest, Kraków and Warsaw. The western Ukrainian city of L'viv is the easiest to reach from Central Europe, served by trains from Budapest, Moscow, Warsaw and Kraków, as well as **buses** from Kraków, Warsaw and Prague.

GETTING AROUND

Ukraine's principal cities are a long distance apart and travelling between them usually takes a whole day or night. Trains and buses are frequently booked solid days in advance so it is wise to plan ahead. **Public transport** in Ukraine's cities is cheap, with flat fares rarely exceeding 5Hr. Many urban transport routes are operated by privately owned **minibuses** known as *marshrutki*. They are speedier than regular buses and trams, but can be overcrowded.

BY TRAIN

Train is the cheapest way to travel, though only one or two daytime trains run each way on the Kyiv–L'viv and Kyiv–Odesa routes; all other services are overnight. The cheapest tickets are for *platskart* or third class, a cramped open carriage in which the (hard) seats are turned into bunks at night. The next step up is *kupe*, a second-class compartment with four bunks, while *luks* are private one- or two-person sleeping compartments that are three times more expensive. Whichever class you travel in, your carriage will be controlled by an attendant (*provodnitsa*) who serves tea but also prevents you from wandering around from carriage to carriage. Dining cars are rare, so bring your own food and drink. **Train stations** (*vokzal*) are confusing places with little in the way of Latin-script labelling and a proliferation of counters selling different types of ticket. Counters selling tickets for today are marked "*Dobovoho prodazhu*"; those for advance bookings are marked "*Poperednyoho prodazhu*". International tickets are bought from counters marked "*Mizhnarodnoho spolucheniya*".

BY BUS

Intercity bus services are slightly quicker than trains and usually run during daylight hours, although tickets are more expensive. Companies such as Avtolyuks

36

(ⓦautolux.ua) and Gunsel (ⓦgnslines.ua) run services between Kyiv and Odesa and have booking offices at the main bus stations (*avtovoksal*) in each city. Kyiv–L'viv services are operated by a range of smaller private companies. Several operators provide "VIP" or "Експресс" services that are quicker and slightly more expensive than the regular buses; tickets sell out fast and should be booked well in advance.

ACCOMMODATION

Backpacker **hostels** are common in the main cities. They're often rough-and-ready affairs in converted apartments, although most offer a mixture of multi-bed dorms (€7–10 per bed/190–270Hr) and private doubles, with a kitchen and/or common room to lounge around in and socialize.

Hotels are the most unpredictable category of accommodation, with informal B&Bs, Soviet-era concrete blocks and modern business-oriented establishments all charging similar prices for hugely varying levels of comfort. In Kyiv it is easy to find a habitable double room for less than €50/1300Hr; prices are cheaper still in Odesa and L'viv.

Local agencies rent out **private rooms** and apartments to tourists in Odesa, where a small self-catering apartment can be cheaper than a double room in a hotel.

FOOD AND DRINK

Ukrainian cities are well supplied with restaurants (*restoran*) and cafés, while pubs frequently have a full menu of food. Cheap and convenient are the self-service **canteens** (*stolova*), which serve local food and help-yourself salads at hard-to-resist prices.

Ukraine is one of the original homelands of **borshch**, the pinky-hued beetroot soup. Ukrainian *borshch* often includes cabbage, along with bits of pork or other meat. A summer alternative to *borshch* is *okroshka*, a cold soup consisting of sour milk, cucumber, bits of ham and boiled egg. Other staples include *varenyky*, ravioli-like parcels of dough with potato,

cottage cheese or minced-meat fillings; *sirniki*, cylindrical little cheese cakes with a sweet-and-savoury taste; and a whole range of pancakes (*mlintsi*) stuffed with a variety of ingredients. Pork, beef and chicken figure prominently among the main courses; fish (particularly anchovy and mackerel) is common on the Black Sea coast. Buckwheat (*hrechka*) is a staple side order, while bread with *salo* (pork fat) is a traditional snack. Central Asian dishes once popular across the Soviet Union and still ubiquitous in Ukraine include *shashlik* (shish-kebab) and *cheburek* (a deep-fried meat pasty).

DRINK

Horilka (vodka) is very much the national drink. It usually comes in classic, clear form, although flavoured varieties are also available – *medova s pertsem* (honey vodka with hot red pepper) is the one you must try at least once. The standard measure for spirits is 5cl (almost a double by Western standards), so consume in moderation. Ukrainian **beer** (*pivo*) is on the whole excellent, with Obolon, Slavutich, L'vivske and Chernihivske among the main mass-market brewers. Most produce a regular lager-type brew (*svitle*) alongside a dark porter (*tamne*) and a "white" unfiltered beer (*bile*). In addition, an increasing number of brewpubs serve up their own-brand ales, and a good number of small-scale breweries (notably Stare Misto in Western Ukraine) are producing a cracking range of tasty beers.

There is a handful of domestic red and white **wines** from the Crimea, although most bars and restaurants in Kyiv and L'viv tend to serve European, Australian and American imports.

Hookah pipes (*kalyan*) with flavoured tobaccos are very popular among young adults and are a regular feature of Ukrainian bars.

CULTURE AND ETIQUETTE

The majority of Ukrainians are Orthodox Christians. In churches and monasteries, women should cover their heads and shoulders (there may well be stalls outside selling cheap scarves and shawls for precisely this purpose), while men should don long trousers. **Tipping** is not required if you are just having a drink in a café, but ten percent is common in restaurants.

SPORTS AND OUTDOOR ACTIVITIES

Football is the most popular spectator sport, with Shakhtar Donetsk (UEFA Cup winners in 2009) and Dinamo Kyiv enjoying mass support. Karpaty L'viv have had their moments, playing in the group stages of the Europa League in 2010.

Ukraine's main **hiking** area is in the smooth green hills of the Carpathian range, with the 2061m Mount Hoverla (Ukraine's highest) the main target. The trailheads are a good three to four hours' drive southeast

of L'viv so you will need to plan a two- to three-day trip to make the most of it.

COMMUNICATIONS

Post offices (*poshta*) in major cities are open Monday to Saturday 9am to 9pm, Sunday 10am to 5pm. Increasingly rare, public phones on the street can only be used for local calls and take phonecards (purchased at the post office). Long-distance and international calls are best made from a **telephone office** (usually attached to the main post office), where you pay a deposit before being assigned a cabin to make your call. Cheap **international calls** are also available at many of the internet cafés spread throughout city centres. **Mobile phone**

UKRAINIAN

	UKRAINIAN	PRONUNCIATION
Yes	*Так*	Tak
No	*Ні*	Nyi
Please	*Будь ласка*	Bood-la-ska
Thank you	*Дякую*	Dya-koo-yoo
Hello/Good day	*Доброго дня*	Do-bro-ho dnya
Goodbye	*До побачення*	Do po-ba-che-nya
Excuse me/sorry	*Вибачте*	Vee-bach-teh
Today	*Сьогодні*	Syo-hod-nyi
Yesterday	*Вчора*	Fcho-ra
Tomorrow	*Завтра*	Zaf-tra
I don't understand	*Я не розумію*	Ya ne roz-um-i-yoo
How much?	*Скільки?*	Skil-ki?
Do you speak English?	*Ви розмовляєте англійською мовою?*	Vi roz-mov-lya-ee-tee an-hlee-sko-yoo mo-vo-yoo?
Where is the..?	*Де?*	Deh?
Hotel	*Готель*	Hotel
Bus	*Автобус*	Af-to-boos
Plane	*Літак*	Li-tak
Train	*Поїзд*	Po-yizd
I would like a…	*Я хочу*	Ya ho-chu
Open	*Відчинено*	Vid-chi-ne-no
Closed	*Зачинено*	Za-chi-ne-no
One	*Один*	O-din
Two	*Два*	Dva
Three	*Три*	Tri
Four	*Чотири*	Cho-ti-ri
Five	*П'ять*	Pyat
Six	*Шість*	Shist
Seven	*Сім*	Sim
Eight	*Вісім*	Vi-sim
Nine	*Дев'ять*	Dev-yat
Ten	*Десять*	Des-yat

roaming charges are slightly more expensive in Ukraine than elsewhere in Europe; if you are likely to use your mobile phone a lot then consider buying a prepaid local SIM card. If you are travelling with a laptop, **wi-fi** is free in many hostels, hotels and city-centre cafés.

EMERGENCIES

Ukraine is a relatively safe country to travel in, although tourists are frequently the target of pickpockets and petty thieves. Ukrainian **police** occasionally carry out spot checks on foreigners, so always carry your passport with you. They rarely speak English.

High-street **pharmacies** (*apteka*) sell familiar medicines over the counter. Each city has a 24hr pharmacy in the centre. Staff in Ukrainian public **hospitals** are unlikely to speak English and you are advised to seek private treatment in the event of illness or injury – so make sure you are insured before you travel.

INFORMATION

L'viv is the only Ukrainian city that has a **tourist information office** and Latin-alphabet signage in the streets. In Kyiv and Odesa, hostel staff and private tourist agencies are the most likely sources of information.

MONEY AND BANKS

Currency is the **hryvnia** (Hr/UAH), divided into 100 kopinky. Coins come in 1, 2, 5, 10, 25 and 50 kopinky denominations; and notes in 1, 2, 5, 10, 20, 50, 100 and 200 hryvnias. At the time of writing, £1 = 32Hr, €1 = 27.50Hr, US$1 = 24.50Hr. **Banks** (Mon–Fri 9am–6pm, Sat 9am–noon) and exchange offices (*obmin valyut*) offer similar exchange rates. **Credit and debit cards** are accepted in larger hotels and city-centre shops, but will be refused elsewhere. ATMs are fairly widespread.

> ### EMERGENCY NUMBERS
> Fire ☎ 101; Police ☎ 102; Ambulance ☎ 103.

OPENING HOURS AND HOLIDAYS

An increasing number of shops in Ukrainian cities are open 10am to 6pm daily, although some have restricted hours on Saturdays and are closed on Sundays. Most museums and historic sights are closed one day a week, and one day at the end of the month for cleaning. **Public holidays** are January 1, January 7, January 8, March 8, Easter Sunday & Monday, May 1, May 9, Pentecost (50 days after Easter), June 28 and August 24.

Kyiv

Sprawling, energetic but never overwhelming, **KYIV** (Київ) combines the stately aura of a great historical city with the raw vigour of a rapidly changing society. Golden-domed churches recall the city's role as the birthplace of Christian Rus – the medieval Slav civilization that subsequently gave rise to both the Ukrainian and Russian nations. Designer-label boutiques, flashy bars and top-of-the-range jeeps offer a jarringly contemporary contrast. With attractions aplenty and a fast-developing nightlife scene, it's a city that is easy to enjoy. It also remains an easy-to-explore capital despite its scale: walking distances between the main sights are not too taxing, and the city's metro system provides quick and cheap transport from one neighbourhood to the next.

WHAT TO SEE AND DO

At the heart of the city is **Khreschatyk**, a broad, tree-lined boulevard that leads to **Maidan nezalezhnosti**, the square that gave its name to the Euromaidan revolution of 2014. A brace of historic churches occupies the high ground above, while downhill to the northeast is Podil, an area of serene Neoclassical buildings bordered by residential streets. Linking the two is **Andriivs'kyi uzviz** ("St Andrew's Descent"), the winding cobbled street that best captures the atmosphere of nineteenth-century Kyiv. A short southbound hop on the metro is **Kyivo-Pecherska Lavra**, a rambling

36

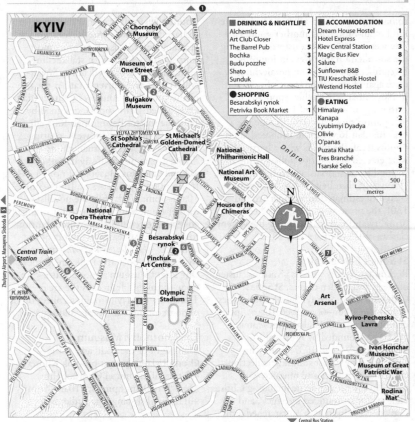

KYIV

■ DRINKING & NIGHTLIFE
Alchemist	7
Art Club Closer	1
The Barrel Pub	5
Bochka	3
Budu pozzhe	6
Shato	2
Sunduk	4

● SHOPPING
| Besarabskyi rynok | 2 |
| Petrivka Book Market | 1 |

■ ACCOMMODATION
Dream House Hostel	1
Hotel Express	6
Kiev Central Station	3
Magic Bus Kiev	8
Salute	7
Sunflower B&B	2
TIU Kreschatik Hostel	4
Westend Hostel	5

●EATING
Himalaya	7
Kanapa	2
Lyubimyi Dyadya	6
Olivie	4
O'panas	5
Puzata Khata	1
Tres Branché	3
Tsarske Selo	8

36

monastery complex famous for its icon-rich churches and candlelit catacombs. Bordering the monastery complex to the south, a swathe of riverside park is dominated by **Rodina Mat'**, the imperious statue that symbolizes Soviet Ukraine's struggles against Nazi Germany during the "Great Patriotic War" of 1941–45.

Khreschatyk and around
Lined by shops and cafés, Khreschatyk is the place where many Kyivans come to sip coffee during the day and stroll on summer evenings. At its southwestern end, the boutiques of the Metrograd underground shopping centre provide a contemporary contrast to the pre-World War I Besarabs'kyi Rynok, the indoor market hall that fills daily with fresh produce.

Opposite the Rynok on the corner of Velyka Vasylkivs'ka and Baseina, the **Pinchuk Art Centre** (Tues–Sun noon–9pm; free; ⓦpinchukartcentre.org) displays contemporary art on four storeys, with major international names featuring heavily in the programme. The top-floor café is decked out in minimalist all-white style and comes with roofline views of downtown Kyiv.

Maidan nezalezhnosti
A horseshoe-shaped square at the eastern end of Khreschatyk, Maidan nezalezhnosti or "Independence Square" has long served as the symbolic heart of the city. During the Soviet period it hosted a statue of Lenin, removed by pro-independence protesters in 1991 and replaced in 2001 with a gilded **statue of Berehynia**, the pre-Christian spirit adopted by

36

romantically inclined Ukrainians as some kind of all-protecting mother-goddess. The scene of mass demonstrations during the so-called Orange Revolution of December 2004, Maidan nezalezhnosti once again became the focus of protest in November 2014, when spontaneous gatherings in support of European integration snowballed to become the Euromaidan Revolution. Billboard-sized photos recall the places where barricades were erected against riot police, while shrine-like memorials remember the "Heavenly Hundred" (Nebesna sotnya; currently estimated to number around 130), the protesters killed by police brutality and sniper fire during the violent clashes of February 19–21, 2015.

St Sofia's Cathedral

Beckoning visitors with its vivacious cluster of green and golden domes, **St Sofia's Cathedral** at Volodymyrs'ka 24 (Mon, Tues & Fri–Sun 10am–6pm, Wed 10am–5pm; complex 3Hr, cathedral and museums 50Hr) was founded by Prince of Rus Yaroslav the Wise in 1037. Inside the church is Kyiv's most stunning collection of medieval frescoes and mosaics, with scenes in the central dome including Christ Pantocrator surrounded by angels, and a resplendent Virgin with outstretched arms.

St Michael's Golden-Domed Cathedral

Standing opposite St Sofia's at the far end of a long square, **St Michael's** (daily 8am–7pm) was demolished by the Soviets in the 1930s and faithfully reconstructed six decades later. A medieval church given a thorough Baroque makeover in the eighteenth century, it was the first church in Kyiv to sport gilded domes, a practice later picked up by most of the other churches in the city. The church interior contains fragments of original twelfth-century mosaics and frescoes, taken to St Petersburg in 1937 and returned to Kyiv in 2008.

Andriivs'kyi uzviz

Still paved with its original cobblestones and lined with nineteenth-century houses, the steep and winding

Andriivs'kyi uzviz is one of the few streets to have preserved its pre-Revolutionary appearance. It is also Kyiv at its most tourist-laden, lined with stalls selling Ukrainian embroidered shirts, Soviet-era collectables and souvenir tat. At the top of the street is St Andrew's Church (daily except Wed 10am–6pm), designed by Baroque master Bartolomeo Rastrelli, its slender dome-topped towers spearing skywards like a gargantuan clump of divine asparagus. Halfway down, the **Mikhail Bulgakov Museum** at no. 13 (Mon noon–5pm, Tues & Thurs–Sun 10am–5pm; 60Hr) fills the novelist's former home with a theatrically arranged collection of exhibits, drawing attention to the more fantastical elements of the author of *The Master and Margarita*'s work. At the bottom of the street, the **One Street Museum** at no. 2 (Tues–Sun noon–6pm; 50Hr) recalls the area's Tsarist-era heyday through a collection of period costumes and sepia photographs.

The Chornobyl Museum

Main sight of the Podil area is the **Chornobyl Museum** at proulok Khoreviy 1 (Natsional'niy muzei Chornobyliu; Mon–Fri 10am–6pm, Sat 10am–5pm; 40Hr; English-language audioguide

---

CHORNOBYL TOURS

Tours of the 30km exclusion zone around the **Chornobyl reactor** are offered by a growing number of local tour agencies. It's a long (and relatively expensive) day-trip but is definitely worthwhile – a uniquely numbing memorial to government stupidity and the selfless sacrifice of those who cleared up afterwards. **Tours** pass near the reactor before visiting the ghost town of Pripyat alongside other eerily deserted sites within the exclusion zone. Despite the high levels of radiation within the zone, one day's exposure is thought to be too insignificant to have an adverse effect on a visitor's health. Prices range from US$130–500 per person depending on how many individuals sign up for the tour. Tours are advertised by almost all hostels and hotels in Kyiv; otherwise contact one of the agencies in town (see p.1186).

80Hr; ⓦchornobylmuseum.kiev.ua), an informative and frequently moving account of the events of April 1986 – when an explosion at Chornobyl nuclear power station, 100km north of Kyiv, released a radioactive plume of smoke that travelled over much of Central Europe. The 50,000-strong city of Pripyat was evacuated, and a 30km exclusion zone established – it still exists today. The museum is mostly labelled in Ukrainian, although the photographs and newsreels on display tell the story eloquently enough. It's certainly an affecting tribute to the emergency crews who risked their lives in the aftermath of the disaster.

Kyivo-Pecherska Lavra

Few sights in Kyiv pack the historical and spiritual punch of **Pecherska Lavra**, the "Cave Hermitage" founded on a bluff overlooking the River Dnipro in the eleventh century. Located 1.5km southeast of Khreschatyk, just beyond the Arsenal'na metro station, this sprawling complex of churches, monastery buildings and museums is regarded as the birthplace of Ukrainian and Russian Orthodoxy, and is swarming with pilgrims all year round.

The Lavra is divided into two parts, the **Upper Lavra** to the northwest and the Lower Lavra to the southeast. The Upper Lavra centres on the **Cathedral of the Dormition** and its accompanying bell tower, a five-storey Baroque beauty topped by a gilded dome. Also inside the Upper Lavra compound is the worthwhile **Museum of Ukrainian Folk Art** (Mon & Wed–Sun 10am–6pm; 20Hr), containing the phantasmagorical paintings of self-taught village artist Mariya Pryimachenko.

Highlight of the **Lower Lavra** is the system of caves used by medieval monks as burial vaults, the dry subterranean air helping to mummify many of the bodies laid to rest there. Entrance to the largest group of catacombs, the **Near Caves**, is inside the **Church of the Raising of the Cross** (daily 9am–6pm). Among the coffins stored in niches are the Lavra's founder, Anthony of Athos, eleventh-century folk hero Ilya Muromets, and twelfth-century chronicler Nestor.

The Ivan Honchar Museum

Right outside the Lower Lavra's boundary wall, the **Ivan Honchar Museum**, Ivana Mazepy 29 (Tues–Sun 10am–6pm; 30Hr), is an attractively arranged ethnographical collection rich in ceramics, costumes and musical instruments.

Rodina Mat'

Rising imperiously from the riverbank to the south of Pecherska Lavra, the 68m-high sword-wielding statue of **Rodina Mat'** ("Homeland Mother") was raised in 1981 in memory of Kyiv's suffering in World War II. Constructed from plates of steel bolted together, she looks like a cross between a classical goddess and a gargantuan robot. The statue's cone-shaped pedestal holds a **Museum of the Great Patriotic War** (as World War II was known in the Soviet Union; daily 10am–6pm; 20Hr), recalling Kyiv's two-year occupation by the Germans. An observation deck (50Hr extra) at the top of the pedestal provides a sweeping panorama of the Kyiv riverside. An open-air section of the museum (5Hr extra) is packed with post-World War II Soviet hardware, MIG jets and rocket launchers included.

Mamayeva sloboda

If there is one historical community associated with Ukraine it's the Cossacks – and it's only fitting that they have their own theme park in the shape of **Mamayeva sloboda** (daily 10am–6pm, 50Hr; ⓦmamajeva-sloboda.ua). Situated 7km west of the centre on vul. Dontsya (trolleybus #27 from ⓜShulyavs'ka), it's basically a re-creation of a typical seventeenth-century Cossack settlement, complete with thatched dwellings and a timber-built church. Displays of folk crafts, horseriding and swordsmanship are held at weekends, and traditional dishes washed down with vodka are available in the *Shynok* restaurant (open till 11pm).

ARRIVAL AND DEPARTURE

By plane Most international flights arrive at Boryspil, 29km southeast of the city, which has three main terminals (B, D and F). The terminals are within a 5–10min walk of each other, and there is also a shuttle bus connecting them all. Sky Bus buses from the stops in front of terminals B and F run to the

36

Central Railway Station (every 15min, 6am–8pm, then every 45–60min till 6am the following morning; 50min; 60Hr). Some budget flights arrive at Zhulyani airport, which is 8km west of the centre (bus #9 runs to the central train station).

By train International trains terminate at the Central Railway Station (Tsentralniy vokzal) on the western fringes of the centre. Leave the main exit and turn left to find the Voksal'na metro station: downtown Khreschatyk is only two stops from here.

Destinations Budapest (1 daily; 25hr); Kraków (change at L'viv and Przemysl; 1 daily; 14hr); L'viv (7 daily; 5hr–9hr 20min); Moscow (3 daily; 10–13hr); Odesa (4 daily; 8hr 30min–11hr); Warsaw (1 daily; 18hr).

By bus Many inter-city buses use an informal cluster of stops, known colloquially as "Bus Station Kiev", in front of the Central Railway Station. Otherwise the city's Central Bus Station (Tsentralnyi avtovoksal) is at pl. Moskovska, 4km southwest of the centre. Demiivs'ka metro station is a 5min walk west of the bus station; otherwise taxis will take you into town for 80–100Hr.

Destinations from Bus Station Kiev: L'viv (4 daily; 8hr); Odesa (2 daily; 6hr).

From Central Bus Station: L'viv (3 daily; 8hr); Odesa (10 daily; 5hr 30min–7hr 30min); Warsaw (4 weekly; 16hr).

TOURS

Tours Free Tours (☎066 851 855, ⌨freetours.kiev.ua) offers a daily choice of two 3hr walking tours of the city sights. Solo East, Prorezna 10 (☎044 279 3505, ⌨tourkiev .com) and Tour2Kiev (☎044 451 6171, ⌨tour2kiev.com) both run Chornobyl trips.

GETTING AROUND

By bus and trolleybus One-way tickets cost 1.50Hr and should be bought from newspaper kiosks before boarding. **By metro** Kyiv has three metro lines (red, blue and green). All of them intersect at central Khreschatyk. One-way fares cost 2Hr; buy a plastic token from the *kassa* and push it into the slot at the entrance barriers. You can travel with a compact rucksack on the metro but not large items of luggage.

By minibus Yellow-coloured *marshrutki* operate on many routes. Pay the driver (2–3Hr; the price will be displayed on the side of the bus).

ACCOMMODATION

HOSTELS

Dream House Hostel Andriivskyi uzviz 2-D ☎044 580 2169, ⌨dream-hostels.com; ⓜKontraktova. Large hostel in a courtyard just off Kyiv's most characterful pedestrianized street. Common areas are chic and spacious, dorms and private rooms neat and modern. Breakfast is included. Dorms 190Hr, doubles 650Hr

Kiev Central Station Hoholivs'ka 25, apt 11 ☎093 758 7468, ⌨kievcentralstation.hostel.com; ⓜUniversytet. In a

nicely kept apartment with parquet floors and cheerful colours, this is the most convenient hostel for early-morning getaways, with the central train station a 15–20min walk away. The usual mix of doubles and dorms, plus kitchen-diner chill-out zone. Dorms 200Hr, doubles 700Hr

Magic Bus Kiev Saksahans'koho 31 ☎097 336 0303, ⌨magicbushostels.com; ⓜL. Tolstoho. Ideally located between the train station and centre, *Magic Bus* looks like a quirky hippy flat but is neat and well run into the bargain. Cosy common area with a piano provides the requisite community spirit. Dorms 130Hr, doubles 450Hr

TIU Kreschatik Hostel Khreshchatyk 8b, apt 11 ☎066 932 3676, ⌨tiu-kreschatik.com; ⓜMaidan Nezalezhnosti. Small, intimate and friendly place with only one dorm and one private room. Good kitchen and a decent-sized lounge help generate a family atmosphere. Dorms 230Hr, doubles 560Hr

HOTELS

Hotel Express Shevchenka 38/40 ☎044 234 2113, ⌨expresskiev.com.ua; ⓜUniversytet. This ungainly tower block is a perfectly situated 10min walk from the train station and has frumpy but acceptably clean en-suite rooms with TV and tiny balcony. The top-floor breakfast room (complete with tropical fish) is a major plus. Doubles 1200Hr

Salute Ivana Mazepy 11-B ☎044 494 1420, ⌨salute.kiev .ua; ⓜArsenal'na. Something of an 1980s design classic or Soviet-era eyesore depending on your point of view, this sci-fi concrete cylinder contains modest but comfortable en-suite rooms – many with superb views. Doubles 1300Hr

Sunflower B&B Kostel'na 9–41 ☎044 279 3846, ⌨sunflowerhotel.kiev.ua; ⓜMaydan Nezalezhnosti. Superbly central but discreetly tucked away in a courtyard, this intimate B&B offers bright rooms, warm colours and friendly customer service. Doubles 1500Hr

Westend Hostel Kiev Zahidna 12 ☎066 365 9009, ⌨westend.com.ua; ⓜShulyavs'ka. Despite being called a hostel, this is a cosy and welcoming guesthouse in a block of flats, with functional doubles and a communal kitchen/ lounge for hanging out. No breakfast but there are cafés nearby. Doubles 400Hr

EATING

Himalaya Chervonoarmiys'ka 80; ⓜOlimpiys'ka. Decked out in warm colours and a tasteful collection of Eastern objets d'art, this well-established Indian restaurant serves authentic food with plenty of spice – and a good range of vegetarian options. Mains from 150Hr. Daily 11.30am–11.30pm.

Kanapa Andriivs'kyi uziv 19a ☎044 425 4548; ⓜZoloti vorota. In an old wooden house with an atmospheric courtyard, this semi-formal restaurant is a great place to try traditional Ukrainian dishes cooked the haute-cuisine way. The borscht with nettles (89Hr) is superb – or splash out on the stewed Carpathian goat (210Hr). Daily 10am–midnight.

★**Lyubimyi Dyadya** Pankovska 20; ☎044 289 1885; Ⓜ Vokzal'na. A culinary experiment, the "Favourite Uncle" mixes Ukrainian and Middle Eastern cuisine with real aplomb. A cosy, mildly arty feel brings in a relaxed bohemian crowd. Main courses 250Hr. Daily 8am–11pm.

Olivie Khmel'nyts'koho 16; Ⓜ Teatral'na. A self-service canteen with a long line of dishes laid out on hotplates, this is a good place to sample local favourites such as *kievski kotlet* (chicken kiev), *vareniki* (ravioli-like dumplings stuffed with savoury fillings), and more. Main courses 25–80Hr. Daily 8am–11pm.

O'panas Tereschenkivs'ka 10; Ⓜ Teatral'na. This restaurant in Taras Shevchenko park has plenty of garden seating and an interior that looks like a giant-sized peasant's hut. The menu is Ukrainian-international, ranging from *vareniki* with cabbage (58Hr) to rib-eye steak (300Hr). Daily 8am–midnight.

Puzata Khata Kontraktova 2/1; Ⓜ Kontraktova. Cafeteria on three floors overlooking Kontraktova pl, where staff dressed in folksy costumes serve a broad range of Ukrainian dishes. A convenient place to grab a bite in Podil, with *borshch* from 10Hr. Daily 8am–11pm.

Tres Branché Lysenka 4; ☎044 278 6125; Ⓜ Zoloti vorota. Cosy, French-themed café-restaurant that's perfect for a quick coffee and croissant or a classic French-Mediterranean main. The wine list is full of temptations. Mains 200–300Hr. Daily 8am–11pm.

Tsarske Selo Ivana Mazepy 42/1; Ⓜ Arsenal'na. Ukrainian food, waiting staff dressed in traditionally embroidered blouses, and an interior strong on wooden benches and wall-mounted textiles – try the veal roulade with spinach (320Hr). Daily 8am–1am.

DRINKING AND NIGHTLIFE

Alchemist Shota Rustaveli 12; Ⓜ Teatral'na. Suave dark-brown interior, a well-stocked bar and frequent weekend gigs/DJs ensure a steady stream of night creatures to this chic but welcoming early-hours bar. The cocktails are well worth a flutter. Daily noon–5am.

Art Club Closer Nizhnryutkovs'ka 31 Ⓦ facebook.com /closerkiev; Ⓜ Tarasa Shevchenka. Former factory space hosting all kinds of cultural activity, from indie rock to free jazz, film projections and stomp-til-dawn DJ events. Admission 100–150Hr. Daily 4pm–8am.

Barrel Pub Khmelnyts'koho 3; Ⓜ Teatral'na. Popular microbrewery pub serving their own brew on tap alongside plenty of other Ukrainian beers. There's also an extensive menu of main meals and snacks. Set in a courtyard with a colonnaded terrace decorated with hanging baskets, it's a relaxing spot for a beer. Another branch of the same business, *Bochka*, in the courtyard behind Khreshchatyk 21, has a more raucous beer-hall feel. Both 24hr.

★**Budu pozzhe** Kurtyi spusk 6/2; Ⓜ Tolstoho. This artfully distressed bare-brick place is more mellow than some of the other central bars, offering wines by the glass and excellent

cocktails to a twenty- to thirty-something chattering crowd. Mon–Thurs & Sun 10am–2am, Fri & Sat 10am–3am.

Shato Khreschatyk 24; Ⓜ Khreschatyk. Pricier than most but still enjoyable, this roomy brewpub is one of the few spots along Khreschatyk that has a street-side terrace. Excellent own-brand beer, and traditional snacks such as sausages and pigs' ears. 24hr.

Sunduk Mykhailivs'ka 16; Ⓜ Universytet. A laidback and cosy pub on a quiet but central street, serving up its own-brew lager beer (25Hr/0.5Lt) as well as more mainstream names. The food menu ranges from pizza to ribs, and there's a pleasant outdoor terrace under the trees. Daily 11am–11pm.

SHOPPING

Besarabskyi rynok Ⓜ L. Tolstoho. A pungent collection of fresh fruit, vegetables, fish and flowers in a nineteenth-century covered market hall. Tins of caviar 400Hr. Daily 8am–6pm.

Petrivka Book Market Ⓜ Petrivka oskovsky. A warren of stalls selling new and secondhand books, maps, stationery and computer software. Daily 9am–5pm.

DIRECTORY

Embassies Canada, Kostelna 13a ☎ 044 590 3100, Ⓦ kyiv.gc.ca; Ireland, Kreshchatyk 32B ☎44 279 3200, Ⓦ irishconsulate.kiev.ua; UK, Desyatynna 9 ☎44 490 3660, Ⓦ www.gov.uk/government/world/ukraine; US, Sikorskoho 4 ☎44 521 5000, Ⓦ ukraine.usembassy.gov.

Hospital American Medical Center, Berdychivs'ka 1 (☎044 490 7600; Ⓜ Luk'yanivs'ka).

Left Luggage At the central train station: luggage lockers in the basement – buy a token from the cashier (24hr; 30Hr/item). Also at the bus station (6am–10.30pm; 20Hr/item).

Pharmacy 03 Apteka Shevchenka 58 (24hr).

Post office Khreschatyk 22 (Mon–Sat 8am–9pm, Sun 9am–7pm).

Odesa

Founded by Russian Empress Catherine the Great in 1794, **ODESA** (Одеса) is both busy port and beach resort, exuding a seductive blend of commercial swagger and riviera-town style. Well-preserved nineteenth-century buildings provide a sense of historical grandeur, while the bars of Deribasivs'ka and nightclubs at the nearby beaches ensure that you're never too far away from a party. It's a town popular with tourists all over the Russian-speaking world, and a holiday atmosphere reigns for much of the spring and summer.

36

36

WHAT TO SEE AND DO

With a grid of predominantly nineteenth-century streets, Odesa is a welcoming and easily stroll-able city. The pedestrianized, café-lined strip of Deribasivs'ka is the centre's main focal point, with a deliciously pink-and-cream Art Nouveau shopping arcade at its western end providing an irresistible architectural flourish. From Deribasivs'ka, Yekaterynyns'ka curves down towards the Potemkin Stairs and the port area, passing stately rows of Neoclassical buildings on the way. Odesa's sandy beaches spread for several kilometres along the southeastern side of the city; the most famous of them is Arkadia, a twenty-minute tram ride from the centre.

The Potemkin Stairs

Completed in 1841, the 192-step sweep of the Potemkin Stairs was immortalized in Sergei Eisenstein's 1925 film *Battleship Potemkin* – in which Tsarist troops march remorselessly down the steps firing on demonstrators, famously upsetting a baby's pram on the way. It remains one of the most iconic locations in the whole of Ukraine, and it's here that every visitor to Odesa comes to be photographed.

The tree-lined Prymors'ka promenade runs either side of the top of the steps. At the eastern end of the promenade a statue of Alexander Pushkin (resident here 1823–24) stands in front of **Odesa City Hall**, a Neoclassical building boasting a Corinthian columned portico.

Beaches

Stretching east of town is a string of sandy beaches, each backed by a clutch of cafés and restaurants. They are linked by Trasazdoroviya ("The Path of Health"), a tree-shaded path that runs along the coast from central Odesa – pick it up from the Monument to the Unknown Sailor in Shevchenko Park. Nearest to the centre is **Lanzheron**, packed with city folk on summer weekends. One kilometre further on is **Otrada**, famous for the rudimentary cable car (each car resembling a metal bucket) that links the beach to bul. Frantsuzsky, the main street that runs along the high ground above.

Best known of the beaches is **Arkadia**, 5km from the centre (near the terminus of tram #5 if you don't fancy the walk), and main focus of the city's party life. It's a small but undoubtedly beautiful crescent of sand, much of which is administered by beach-side cafés renting out sun loungers and parasols (150–200Hr for the day). On the edges are "free" stretches of beach where you can lay your towel – although they are crowded at weekends.

Odesa catacombs

Stay at one of Odesa's backpacker hostels and you'll inevitably be offered the chance to go on a tour of Odesa's so-called **catacombs**, the honeycomb of tunnels carved by nineteenth-century limestone miners and used by anti-Nazi partisans during World War II. Led by local speleologists, the tours are unofficial, at-your-own-risk affairs that pay scant regard to health-and-safety regulations – you may get a pair of overalls but you're unlikely to be issued a hard hat. The tours usually focus on the catacombs near Nerubays'ke, 10km north of Odesa, and frequently include a visit to the **Partizanska Slava** memorial complex, where a few short stretches of tunnel have been opened as an official museum. Expect to pay from 650Hr per person for the guided tour and taxi transfer.

ARRIVAL AND DEPARTURE

By plane Odesa airport is 12km south of the centre. *Marshrutka* #117 runs from here to the central Yekaterins'ka.
By train Odesa train station is 2km south of the main downtown area. Bus #220 runs from here to Hrets'ka, a stone's throw from the main Deribasivs'ka.
Destinations Kyiv (4 daily; 8hr 30min–11hr); L'viv (1 daily; 12hr).
By bus Odesa's central bus station is 4km west of the centre at Kolontayivs'koi 58. Tram #5 runs from here to the train station.
Destinations Kyiv (12 daily; 5hr 30min–7hr 30min).

GETTING AROUND

By bus, trolleybus and tram Tickets (1.50Hr) are bought from conductors on board.

ACCOMMODATION

Outside the train station, landladies hawk rooms (*kvartiri*) for 300–400Hr per night – have a map handy to check locations before accepting any offers.

Babushka Grand Mala Arnauts'ka 60 ☎630 705 535, ⓦbabushkagrand.com. Close to the train station, *Babushka* offers a taste of Odesa's faded glories, with nineteenth-century chandeliers and ceiling mouldings presiding over a snug collection of dorm beds and private rooms. It's good for mellow socializing and the staff have excellent local knowledge. Dorms 230Hr, doubles 700Hr

Deribas Deribasivs'ka 27 ☎048 795 2874, ⓦhotel -deribas.com. Hidden in an alleyway linking Deribasivs'ka with pl. Hrets'ka, and somewhat tricky to find, this apartment-hotel offers pristine modern doubles and 3- to 4-person studios in a superbly central spot. Breakfast available for 70Hr. Doubles 1100Hr

Dream Hostel Odessa Soborna 12, apt 7 ☎067 696 2932, ⓦdream-hostels.com. Bunk bed dorms, a couple of private doubles and a small kitchen in a converted nineteenth-century flat that's big on atmosphere. Excellent location just off the main pedestrianized strip. Dorms 140Hr, doubles 450Hr

EATING

Bazilik Deribasivs'ka 1. Cute café with arty-rustic interior and a terrace shaded by tassled awnings, serving good teas and coffees and an extensive menu of Mediterranean-influenced food. Salads (120Hr), pastas (140Hr). Daily 9am–midnight.

Bernardazzi Bunina 15 ☎048 785 5585. The best place in Odessa for a slap-up meal (which, by western European standards, is still quite affordable). Located in the Philharmonic Orchestra building, *Bernardazzi* serves French-Mediterranean fare in old-school starched-napkin surroundings. Try the roast sea bream or sea bass (250Hr), or duck breast with apricots (290Hr). Daily 11am–11pm.

Pizza Olio Gavanna 7 and Bunina 35. Justifiably popular Mediterranean-themed place serving speedy and reliable thin-crust pizzas plus a range of pasta dishes, with mains in the 95–125Hr bracket. Daily 9am–11pm.

Robin Bobin Soborna 2. Occupying a comfy timber porch facing a leafy park, *Robin Bobin* offers traditional Ukrainian dishes and also plenty of salt- and freshwater fish. Try the pan-fried fillets of pike-perch (*sudak*) for 160Hr. Daily 10am–11pm.

Zelen Kanatna 85. Smart café-restaurant near the railway station serving vegetarian food with a range of global culinary influences. They also make refreshing smoothies and ice creams. Mains 95–150Hr. Daily 10am–10pm.

DRINKING AND NIGHTLIFE

Fanconi Katerynyns'ka 15. Swish café-bar whose street-facing terrace is hugely popular with the mid-evening cocktail-sipping crowd. The menu takes in sushi, cakes, ice cream and other fancy food. 24hr.

Ibiza Arkadia ⓦibiza.ua. Popular beach club with a dancefloor right by the sea and bizarre white pods that serve as "VIP" boxes; it hosts a busy programme of DJs and Ukrainian pop stars throughout the summer. May–Sept 10pm–5am.

Itaka Arkadia ⓦitaka-club.com.ua. With palm trees, swimming pools and fluted columns reminiscent of a classical Greek temple, this is an enjoyably kitsch beach club attracting international DJs and party-hungry locals. May–Sept 9pm–5am.

Pivnoy sad Havanna 6. Brew pub with a big subterranean dining hall and a terrace facing the lush city gardens. With a couple of own-brand lagers and porters there's plenty of ale to sample, plus a food menu of soups, grilled sausages and other pub grub. Daily 11am–midnight.

Vyhod/Exit Bunina 24. It's worth exploring the streets south of the Deribasivs'ka strip to uncover this gem of a bar. The semi-submerged space hosts gigs, DJs and poetry evenings, drawing a dedicated but far from cliquey clientele. Daily 8pm–3am.

ENTERTAINMENT

National Opera Chaikovs'koho 1 ☎048 703 4040, ⓦopera .odessa.ua. Nothing sums up Odesa's *belle époque* more than the grandeur of its opera house, built in 1883. It hosts top-quality performances of classic opera and ballet, and tickets are comparatively cheap. No shorts, T-shirts or trainers.

SHOPPING

Novy rynok Torhova. Not the biggest of Odesa's markets but certainly the handiest central place to stock up on picnic provisions, with smoked Black Sea mackerel, fresh cheese and other scrumptious local produce. Daily 7am–6pm.

Pl. Soborna This centrally located square fills up daily with stalls selling crafts and souvenirs in spring and summer. Daily 9am–9pm.

Starokonny rynok Starokonny pereulok; tram #5 to Kosvenna. A neighbourhood market near the bus station that hosts a huge flea market on Sun, with vendors selling wares on the pavements of several surrounding streets. Old clothes, crockery, kids' toys, Soviet-period junk and more. Sun 7am–3pm.

L'viv

Home to a burgeoning café scene and an ever-growing stock of backpacker hostels, forward-looking **L'VIV** (Львів) represents Ukraine at its most tourist-friendly. For centuries subject to Polish then Habsburg overlords, L'viv still looks and feels like a slice of Central Europe, its welter of Catholic, Orthodox and Armenian churches attesting to a multicultural past. Historically the centre of the Ukrainian national movement, L'viv remains an avowedly Ukrainian-speaking city. With

36

uneven cobbled streets, creaky-floored art galleries and trams screeching their way around tracks that were laid generations ago, the city has the look of a well-preserved nineteenth-century survivor. A night spent exploring the city's addictively eccentric bars will soon dispel any ideas that this is just a museum piece.

WHAT TO SEE AND DO

A fistful of churches and palaces lies within a pedestrian-friendly **Old Town**, its neat grid of streets arranged around the spacious Rynok (Market Square). An irregular circle of broad boulevards and park-like greenery separates the Old Town from the nineteenth-century suburbs beyond. A short hike up **Visokyi Zamok** hill, just north of the Old Town, provides an expansive panorama of central L'viv and is a good way to get your bearings.

The Rynok

Surrounded by stately mansions and a warren of courtyards, the Rynok is the centre of L'viv's social life, abuzz with outdoor cafés in the summer. At its centre is the Neoclassical **Town Hall** or Ratusha, its castellated **tower** (daily: May–Sept 9am–6pm; Oct–April 10am–5pm; 25Hr) a nineteenth-century copy of an earlier medieval version. Most eye-catching of the buildings on the Rynok's eastern side is the **Black House** at no. 4, with statues of saints protruding from its grime-encrusted sixteenth-century facade. Next door at no. 6 is the **Kornyakt Palace**, famous for its arcaded Renaissance courtyard (nowadays a daytime café).

Around the Old Town

Just off the southwestern corner of the Rynok, the fourteenth-century **Latin Cathedral** (the city's main Catholic church) contains a show-stopping sequence of Baroque altarpieces. Have your camera at the ready for the adjacent **Boim Chapel**, at Katedral'na 1 (Tues–Sun 10am–5pm; 30Hr), encrusted both inside and out with an animated collection of seventeenth-century statuettes. Although built on the model of medieval Armenian churches, the **Armenian Cathedral**, a block north of the square on Virmens'ka, contains a delicious

collection of Art Nouveau frescoes by Józef Mehoffer and Jan Henryk Rosen.

Arguably the finest of L'viv's churches, the **Bernardine Cathedral** on pl. Soborna boasts a Dutch-Renaissance facade and bulbous belfry, its profile recognizable from countless tourist brochures.

Fragments of L'viv's fortifications still survive along Pidval'na, where the sixteenth-century **Arsenal** at no. 5 (Mon, Tues & Thurs–Sun 10am–5.30pm; 20Hr) contains a display of helmets, breastplates, pikes and early firearms.

Prospekt Svobody

Running along L'viv's Old Town to the west is **Prospekt Svobody** ("Freedom Avenue"), a broad two-lane street with a strip of fountain-splashed park running up the middle. Presiding haughtily over the scene is L'viv Opera House, dating from 1900 and topped with a trio of winged statues symbolizing the arts. Diagonally opposite at Svobody 20, the **National Museum** (Tues–Sun 10am–6pm; 30Hr) holds an impressive collection of Ukrainian Orthodox icons.

The Brewery Museum

Two kilometres northwest of the centre at bul. Kleparivs'ka 18, L'viv's brewery was a highly respected brand throughout the Habsburg and Soviet eras, and continues to churn out well-regarded local-recipe brews. Right beside the brewery gate is the **Brewery Museum** (admissions Mon & Wed–Sun at 10.30am, noon, 1.30pm, 3pm, 4.30pm & 5.30pm; museum 15Hr, museum and beer tasting 30Hr), a small but entertaining display that tells the history of beer brewing from its origins in the ancient Middle East to the present day.

Occupying the huge barrel-vaulted cellars underneath the museum, the **Robert Doms House of Beer** (daily noon–midnight) is named after the Swiss entrepreneur who owned the brewery in the mid-nineteenth century, and serves up draught L'vivs'ke by the litre.

Lychakivs'ke Cemetery

Entered from Mechnikova 3km southeast of the centre, **Lychakivs'ke Cemetery** (daily 10am–6pm; 10Hr; tram #7 or #8 to

Pekars'ka) is one of Central Europe's classical burial grounds, park-like in its landscaped beauty and brimming with over two centuries' worth of funerary monuments. Originally laid out in 1786, it is now a museum reserve: indeed, the sheer profusion of ornate family chapels, sculpted angels and statues of the deceased gives the place the appearance of an outdoor art gallery. The southeastern corner of the cemetery is dominated by the **Cemetery of the Eagles**, a memorial built by the interwar Polish state to commemorate the (mostly very young) volunteers who beat off pro-independence Ukrainian forces in the winter of 1918/1919. Right next to it is a towering, pillar-top statue of the **Archangel Michael**, honouring the Ukrainians who fell in the same conflict.

Folk Architecture Museum

Spread over a forested hillside to the north of Lichakivs'ke Cemetery at Chernecha Hora 1, the **Folk Architecture Museum** (daily 10am–6pm; 20Hr; tram #2, #7 or #8 to Mechnikova then walk uphill) consists of a collection of timber-built houses and barns from all over Western Ukraine that provide the ideal introduction to the region's much-cherished rural traditions. The most spectacular buildings are the fairytale Carpathian churches, their belfries raised in pagoda-like tiers.

ARRIVAL AND DEPARTURE

By plane L'viv airport is 6km southwest of the city centre. Trolleybus #9 (40min; 2Hr) and *marshrutka* #95 (35min; 3Hr) run into town; otherwise a taxi costs 150–200Hr.

By train The train station is 2km west of the centre at the top of Chernivets'ka. ATMs are in the arrivals hall, and the "lux" waiting room (5Hr/hr) offers free wi-fi. Trams #1 & #9 run to the centre. Taxis cost 50–100Hr depending on how gullible you look. International tickets are sold from a counter upstairs in the "Hall of Enhanced Comfort". Reservations for international trains frequently sell out a few days in advance, so don't bank on leaving town this way.

Destinations Budapest (1 daily; 13hr); Kraków (1 daily: 8hr); Odesa (1 daily; 12hr).

By bus The main bus station is at bul. Striys'ka 109, 6km southeast of the centre. Trolleybus #4 runs to Shota Rustaveli, a 10min walk south of the main square. A taxi will set you back 100–150Hr. *Marshrutki* minibuses from Medyka-Shehyni (the Polish–Ukraine border) arrive at the train station.

Destinations Prague (5 weekly; 17hr); Riga (4 weekly; 16hr).

INFORMATION

Tourist information The tourist office in the town hall, Rynok 1 (May–Sept: Mon–Fri 10am–8pm, Sat & Sun 10am–6pm; Oct–April: Mon–Fri 10am–6pm, Sat & Sun 10am–4pm; ☎ 032 254 6079, ⊕ touristinfo.lviv.ua), has free town maps and can advise on accommodation.

Maps Knigarnya E, pr. Svobodi 7 (Mon–Fri 9am–9pm, Sat 10am–3pm), is the place to stock up on maps.

GETTING AROUND

By tram, bus and trolleybus Almost everything in central L'viv is walkable but you will need to use the city's mixture of trams, buses and trolleybuses to get to train and bus stations as well as outlying attractions such as Lychakivs'ke Cemetery and the Folk Architecture Museum. Buy single-journey tickets (2Hr) from kiosks or from the driver.

ACCOMMODATION

Art Hostel Rynok 3 apt. 4 ☎ 6730 88 066, ⊕ arthostel .lviv.ua. Located up several flights of magnificently creaky stairs, this hostel looks directly out onto the main square, with a multi-bed dorm, a private double and a small kitchen. Breakfast available for an extra few hryvnia. Dorms 120Hr, double 320Hr

Gar'is Hostel Kopernika 16 ☎ 098 877 3993, ⊕ garishostel .com. Newish, clean and smoothly run hostel just outside the Old Town, with a good mixture of dorms, doubles and quads. The attic doubles are particularly cute. No breakfast, but there is a kitchen. Dorms 155Hr, doubles 450Hr

George Hotel Mitskievycha 1 ☎ 032 232 6236, ⊕ georgehotel.com.ua. A charming Habsburg-era hotel that has retained many of its interior features, the *George* offers high ceilings, sturdy furnishings and parquet floors at decidedly old-school prices: ensuite doubles cost 1300Hr. Doubles 580Hr

Leotel Lukyanovychka 3 ☎ 032 238 2190, ⊕ leotel.lviv .ua. This slightly old-fashioned but smart mid-range hotel is an affordable budget choice, offering plush en-suite comforts a short hop away from the Old Town. Doubles 800Hr

Old City Hostel Beryndy 3 ☎ 032 294 9644, ⊕ oldcityhostel .lviv.ua. This new hostel in a nineteenth-century apartment block with plush furnishings and parquet flooring will suit those who like their accommodation squeaky clean. There's a fully equipped kitchen. Dorms 140Hr, doubles 450Hr

EATING

Amadeus Katedral'na pl. 7. For quality pan-European cuisine in a picturesque city-centre square, you can't do much better than *Amadeus*. The food ranges from humble *varenyky* (stuffed pastry parcels) to fancy Adriatic seafood with plenty of pork-chop fare in between; expect to fork out 150–230Hr for mains. Daily 11am–11pm.

Kumpel Vynnychenka 7. Microbrewery and restaurant whose huge copper vats form an attractive centrepiece to

36

36

the dining room. Steaks, stews, sausages and schnitzels are the main items on the menu. Wash it down with *Kumpel*'s own-brand *svitle* (a pale, refreshing lager) or *burshtinove* (a more rounded brown-coloured ale). Mains 140–180Hr. Daily 11am–midnight.

L'vivs'ka maysternya shokoladu Serbs'ka 3. Strong coffee, velvety drinking chocolate and in-house ice creams at this enjoyable re creation of a nineteenth-century coffee house. The delectable range of own-brand, handmade chocolates makes repeat visits pretty near essential. Daily 10am–8pm.

Livyi bereh prospekt Svobody 28. Beneath the opera house, this bare-brick cellar restaurant is decked out with musical memorabilia and hosts an eclectic range of live music at weekends. The inexpensive menu is mostly Ukrainian, with *varenyky* dumplings at 65Hr. Daily 11am–2am.

Myasa ta spravedlivost Bernardine Monastery courtyard (access from Halyts'ka pl). An open-sided barn with medieval torture masks hanging from the beams, "Meat and Justice" serves up sausage, chicken, steak and other grilled fare, with staff dressed in serving-wench garb and food arriving on wooden platters. Theatrical it may be, but the young locals love it. Mains 70–200Hr. Daily 11am–midnight.

Puzata Khata Sichovykh Striltsiv 12. City-centre branch of the trusty self-service canteen chain, especially strong on *varenyky*, *mlintsi* and other Ukrainian staples. Frequently packed with Polish tour groups, who know a good culinary bargain when they see one. Fill up your plate for under 60Hr. Daily 8am–11pm.

Stargorod pl. Mytna. A huge pub-restaurant with a vaguely Czech theme, serving excellent own-brewed beer (half litre/30Hr) accompanied by meat-heavy dishes such as sausage (90Hr) and roast duck (175Hr). The roomy interior incorporates a re-creation of L'viv main square, and the beer garden is truly vast. 24hr.

DRINKING AND NIGHTLIFE

BARS

Bilya Diani Rynok. With chairs and tables scattered around the statue of Diana in the Rynok's southwestern corner, this outdoor café serves up thirst-quenching, own-brand light and dark ales (25Hr/0.5Lt) as well as a range of nibbles – the *sudzhuk* (spicy beef sausage) platter goes down a treat. May–Sept daily 9am–11pm.

Dim lehend Staroevreys'ka 48. The five-storey "House of Legends" begins with a souvenir shop on the ground floor and a sequence of wackily decorated drinking rooms above, culminating in a dizzying roof terrace. Fills nightly with young L'vivians enjoying draught beers and a menu of snacks. Daily 11am–2am.

★**Dzyha** Virmens'ka 35. Cult art centre comprising a gallery, a café-pub (*Pid Klepsydroyu*) with a varied food menu, and an upstairs performance space (*Kvartyra 35*)

that hosts folk and jazz concerts as well as being a cool place to drink. Daily 11am–midnight.

Gasova Lyampa Virmens'ka 20. Head down the steps and then up a spiral staircase to reach this characterful bar occupying four cramped storeys of a tall and narrow house. Draught beers and meaty snacks are served up in rooms decorated with pictures of gas lamps and oil derricks: a statue of Ignacy Lukasiewicz, oil pioneer and inventor of the kerosene lamp, sits outside. Daily 11am–2am.

Kabinet Vynnychenka 12. Literary café with book-filled shelves and a programme of cultural events, *Kabinet*'s collection of armchairs and sofas makes it an ideal venue for a relaxing evening drink. Also serves a menu of inexpensive eats. Daily 10am–11pm.

Masoch Serbs'ka 7. Author of *Venus in Furs* Leopold von Sacher-Masoch was born in L'viv in 1836, and this café-bar serves as some kind of kinky tribute. The decor (lacy fabrics, whips) is charming rather than over the top, and cocktails (from 85Hr) have corny names like *Burning Desire*. Your bill is delivered in a high-heeled shoe. Daily 4pm–4am.

Music Lab Bratyv Rohatintsyv 27. DJ bar decked out with vinyl records and other bits of musical memorabilia, serving shots and cocktails to a style-conscious crowd. Daily 24hr.

CLUBS

Metro Zelena 14 ⓦmetroclub.com.ua. Big city-centre club with a dancefloor policy ranging from commercial Euro-pop to cutting-edge trance and techno. Good social mix of local youngsters and international students. Cover 40–70Hr. Daily 9pm–6am.

Picasso bul. Zelena 88 ⓦpicasso.lviv.ua. Seventeen years old and still going strong, *Picasso* is the place to catch incoming DJs and live jazz and rock acts. Open as a café during the daytime. Cover 50–200Hr depending on event. Café noon–8pm; gigs and club nights 8/10pm–4am.

SHOPPING

Krakivsky rynok ul. Bazarna. Covered market selling fruit, veg and dairy products, bordered by a lively strip of outdoor clothes stalls. Daily 8am–3pm.

Souvenir market cnr Teatral'na and Lesi Ukrainky. Open-air stalls selling embroidered tablecloths and blouses, near-antique collectables and kitschy souvenir trash by the bag-load. Daily 9am–6pm.

DIRECTORY

Hospital Emergency dept, Mykolaychuka 9 (☎032 252 7590).

Left luggage At the train station (24hr with breaks at 11am–noon & 2–3am; 10Hr/item).

Pharmacy Apteka, cnr Brativ Rohatyntsiv & Halyts'ka (24hr).

Post office Slovats'koho 1 (Mon–Fri 9am–7pm, Sat 10am–4pm, Sun 10am–3pm).

Small print and index

1194 Small print

1197 Our writers

1198 Index

1207 Map symbols

Rough Guide credits

Editors: Alice Park, Amanda Tomlin, Neil McQuillian
Layout: Jessica Subramanian
Cartography: Rajesh Mishra, Rajesh Chhibber
Picture editor: Aude Vauconsant
Proofreader: Jan McCann
Managing editor: Monica Woods
Assistant editor: Divya Grace Mathew

Production: Jimmy Lao
Cover photo research: Sarah Stewart-Richardson
Editorial assistant: Aimee White
Senior DTP coordinator: Dan May
Programme manager: Gareth Lowe
Publishing director: Georgina Dee

Publishing information

This fifth edition published March 2017 by
Rough Guides Ltd,
80 Strand, London WC2R 0RL
11, Community Centre, Panchsheel Park,
New Delhi 110017, India
Distributed by Penguin Random House
Penguin Books Ltd, 80 Strand, London WC2R 0RL
Penguin Group (USA), 345 Hudson Street, NY 10014, USA
Penguin Group (Australia), 250 Camberwell Road,
Camberwell, Victoria 3124, Australia
Penguin Group (NZ), 67 Apollo Drive, Mairangi Bay,
Auckland 1310, New Zealand
Penguin Group (South Africa), Block D, Rosebank Office
Park, 181 Jan Smuts Avenue, Parktown North, Gauteng,
South Africa 2193
Rough Guides is represented in Canada by DK Canada, 320
Front Street West, Suite 1400, Toronto, Ontario M5V 3B6
Printed in Singapore
© Rough Guides, 2017
Maps © Rough Guides

A catalogue record for this book is available from the
British Library
ISBN: 978-0-24127-033-2
The publishers and authors have done their best to
ensure the accuracy and currency of all the information
in **The Rough Guide to Europe on a Budget**, however,
they can accept no responsibility for any loss, injury, or
inconvenience sustained by any traveller as a result of
information or advice contained in the guide.
1 3 5 7 9 8 6 4 2

MIX
Paper from
responsible sources
FSC www.fsc.org   FSC™ C018179

Help us update

We've gone to a lot of effort to ensure that the
fifth edition of **The Rough Guide to Europe on a
Budget** is accurate and up-to-date. However, things
change – places get "discovered", opening hours are
notoriously fickle, restaurants and rooms raise prices
or lower standards. If you feel we've got it wrong or
left something out, we'd like to know, and if you can

remember the address, the price, the hours, the phone
number, so much the better.

Please send your comments with the subject line
"Rough Guide Europe on a Budget Update" to mail
@uk.roughguides.com. We'll credit all contributions and
send a copy of the next edition (or any other Rough Guide
if you prefer) for the very best emails.

Acknowledgements

Kiki Deere wishes to thank all the kind people who helped with the update of this book, in particular ENIT in London, Chiara Crovella and Erika Carpaneto at Turismo Torino.

Lottie Gross extends a huge thanks to Dritan Xhengo at Past & Present for his indispensable advice and support on the ground; cheers to the team at Drive Albania & Balkan Secrets, and props to Catherine and Alfred in Valbona for their seriously hard work.

Eva Hibbs would like to thank Steffi from Hondarribia for being so generous with her time and knowledge.

Gabriella Le Breton would like to thank Sara Roloff and Harry White of Switzerland Tourism who were instrumental in setting up her whirlwind trip.

Anna Kaminski says a big thank you to Georgia Platman and Genie Khmelnitski in London, Linda in Liverpool, Graham Shultz in Manchester, Pete in Oxford, Christian Geib in Glasgow, Brendon Griffin in Edinburgh, Nicolas in Orkney, and Cristian Pizarro and Peter Selman in Fort William.

Norm Longley would like to thank Monica and Alice at Rough Guides, Tine Murn in Ljubljana, Nika Pirnar in Ljubljana, Zorica Jovanov and Ivana Vucelic in Belgrade, and Christian, Luka, Anna and Patrick.

John Malathronas would like to thank George Tziachris, Tina Kyriakis (Athens), Papadias Valsamakis (Athens), Alexia Petonis (Mykonos), Clive Birch (Iráklion), Katerina Manoff (Olympia), Kim Mach, Paul Jansen, Frank James (Crete)

and Carola Scupham (Crete) for all their help with research in Greece; Törőcsik Gábor (Eger), Bankó Péter (Balaton), Nemes Nikoletta (Pécs), Szűcs-Balás Vera (Szentendre), Pirosné Blénessy Erika Emma (Kecskemet) and Nora Erdei (Debrecen) for their assistance in Hungary.

Olivia Rawes extends thanks to everyone who made travelling in Andalucía so enjoyable, especially José at Bed and Be in Córdoba, Rosa Pavón in Seville, and Daniel Galán in Granada. At Rough Guides, thanks to Monica Woods, Neil McQuillan, and my editor Alice Park. Finally a special thanks to my family for their constant support, Kaz for making even the longest drives entertaining, and to Jack for joining me on this adventure and keeping me laughing – and well-fed – throughout the whole trip.

Jeroen van Marle would like to thank Neil McQuillian and Mandy Tomlin at Rough Guides, Tim Burford, Daphne Damiaans and Germany's enthusiastic tourist office staff, especially Sonja Bukvicki in Stuttgart, Anja Dietrich in Weimar, Karola Gärtner and Ingrid Jourdant-Kammerer in Nuremberg, Fabian Hoersch in Bonn and Holger Mohring in Freiburg. As always, a special shukran to Soulafa.

Luke Waterson offers a thank you to all the wonderful people working in Finnish and Danish tourism who helped me with this update: particularly Kirsi Eskola, Alana Fogarty, Olga Henriksson, Heli Jokela, Kathrine Lind Gustavussen, Marjatta Sarre, Salla Tauriainen and Henrik Thierlein.

Readers' updates

Thanks to all the readers who have taken the time to write in with comments and suggestions (and apologies if we've inadvertently omitted or misspelt anyone's name):

Jonathan Allum, Edward Aves, Daniel Bamford, Nancy Barker, Katie Bennett, Rob Benzies, Alex Berry, Helen Booth, Stephen Hardwick, Manon Hekel, Stuart Hicks, Vivien Hilson, Begoña Larive Iragüen, Janet Jardine, Trina King, Samuel Knoblauch, Micha Lazarus, Kate Lock, Graham Lockwood, George MacBride, Patrick Martin, Andrea Mays, Rachel Mills, Geoffrey Morris, Hollie Panther, Martin Peters, Sarah Potter, Timothy Shepherd, Steve Simpson, Jane Speedie, Jeremy Stanford, Alan Stones, Martin Thomas, A. Turnbull, Michael de Weymarn.

A ROUGH GUIDE TO ROUGH GUIDES

Published in 1982, the first Rough Guide – to Greece – was a student scheme that became a publishing phenomenon. Mark Ellingham, a recent graduate in English from Bristol University, had been travelling in Greece the previous summer and couldn't find the right guidebook. With a small group of friends he wrote his own guide, combining a contemporary, journalistic style with a thoroughly practical approach to travellers' needs.

The immediate success of the book spawned a series that rapidly covered dozens of destinations. And, in addition to impecunious backpackers, Rough Guides soon acquired a much broader readership that relished the guides' wit and inquisitiveness as much as their enthusiastic, critical approach and value-for-money ethos. These days, Rough Guides include recommendations from budget to luxury and cover more than 120 destinations around the globe, from Amsterdam to Zanzibar, all regularly updated by our team of roaming writers.

Browse all our latest guides, read inspirational features and book your trip at **roughguides.com**.

Photo credits

All photos © Rough Guides, except the following:
Key: a-above; b-below/bottom; c-centre; l-left; r-right; t-top)

OUR WRITERS

Jonathan Bousfield
Croatia, Estonia, Latvia,
Lithuania, Poland, Ukraine

Tim Burford
Romania

Kiki Deere
Italy, Russia

Marc Di Duca
Czech Republic,
Slovakia

Darragh Geraghty
Ireland

Emma Gibbs
France

Lottie Gross
Albania

Matthew Hancock
Portugal

Eva Hibbs
Spain

Daniel Jacobs
Morocco

Anna Kaminski
Great Britain

Gabriella Le Breton
Switzerland

Phil Lee
Norway

Norm Longley
Bosnia, Romania,
Serbia, Slovenia

John Malathronas
Greece, Hungary

Olivia Rawes
Spain

Terry Richardson
Turkey

Emma Thomson
Belgium &
Luxembourg,
The Netherlands

Kate Turner
Spain

Jeroen van Marle
Germany

Steve Vickers
Sweden

Neville Walker
Austria

Luke Waterson
Denmark, Finland

Matt Willis
Bulgaria, Macedonia,
Montenegro

Index

Maps are marked in grey

A

Å 826
Aachen 391
Aalborg...................... 233–235
Aarhus ....see Århus
Abbaye de Fontevraud..........302
Aberystwyth....................476
Abisko.......................... 1112
Abri de Cap Blanc..............313
accommodation 36
Acrocorinth....................511
Aegean Coast (Turkey)
...........................1158–1165
Agnóndas.......................536
Agrigento 676
Airbnb...........................37
Aix-en-Provence...............328
Ajaccio 346
ALBANIA 47–60
Albania 49
Alcobaça.........................878
Alentejo coast..................890
Ålesund 821
Algarve, the 890–894
Algeciras 1030
Alghero..........................680
Alhambra, Granada............1037
Alicante 1046
Almería 1042
Alps (France) 343–345
Alps (Germany) 409–411
Alps (Switzerland) ...1132–1136
Alsace........................ 305–307
Alta..............................829
Amalfi..........................666
Ambleside......................465
Amboise.........................302
Amsterdam 779–788
Amsterdam.................. 780–781
   accommodation.............................785
   arrival...784
   coffeeshops..................................787
   drinking and nightlife 787
   eating..786
   entertainment................................788
   gay Amsterdam...............................788
   shopping.......................................788
   sights.................................... 779–784
   tourist information 785
   tours..785
   transport.......................................785
Anacapri.........................666
Ancona 658
Åndalsnes.......................822
Andalucía 1023–1043

Andorra 1065–1068
Andorra la Vella 1066
Andorra la Vella 1067
Angla.............................250
Anglesey 478
Ankara 1170–1173
Ankara 1171
Antalya 1169
Antibes 335
Antwerp...................... 100–103
Antwerp...................... 101
Apollonía 526
Aran Islands 593
Arctic Circle (Sweden)...........1110
Ardennes 108
Areópolis 515
Argostóli 539
Arhéa Kórinthos 511
Århus 230–233
Århus 231
Arinsal 1068
Arles.............................324
Armona 893
Arnhem 799
Artà 1051
Assisi.............................657
Athens 502–510
Athens 504–505
   accommodation...........................507
   arrival......................................506
   crime..507
   drinking and nightlife 509
   eating.......................................508
   entertainment.........................508, 509
   ports..506
   shopping...................................509
   sights..................................502–506
   tourist information 507
   transport...................................507
ATMs..............................43
Auschwitz-Birkenau...................853
AUSTRIA..........................61–86
Austria............................ 63
Austvågøy.......................825
Aviemore 491
Avignon 326–328
Avignon 327
Ayía Efimía 539
Áyios Górdhis 538
Áyios Nikólaos 515, 542, 548

B

B&Bs 36
Bacharach........................393

Bachkovo Monastery 145
Badacsony........................560
Baden-Württemberg... 398–405
Bakken 224
Balaton, Lake....................559
Bâle .... see Basel
Baleal............................877
Balearic islands 1047–1053
Balestrand 820
Banat, the........................913
banks.............................. 43
Banská štiavnica 968–970
Bansko 140
Bar 736
Barcelona 1053–1063
Barcelona 1054–1055
Barcelona Old Town........ 1058
   accommodation........................... 1061
   arrival...................................... 1060
   drinking and nightlife 1062
   eating...................................... 1061
   shopping................................... 1063
   sights................................1054–1060
   tourist information 1060
   transport.................................. 1060
Barèges..........................316
Bari..............................667
Basel 1123–1125
Basque Country 1072–1076
Bastia............................345
Bath 443–445
Battle of the Oranges..............620
Bavaria 405–414
Bay of Kotor 732–734
Bayeux 297
Bayonne 315
Beacon Way, The 476
Beatles, The.....................462
Beaune 304
Beethoven, Ludwig van..........390
Belfast 596–600
Belfast 597
BELGIUM..........................87–112
Belgium and Luxembourg... 89
Belgium's languages 92
Belgrade 944–950
Belgrade 945
Belianska Cave....................971
Ben Nevis........................491
Benicassim 1045
Berat 57
Berchtesgaden 410
Bergen 816–820
Bergen 817
Berlenga, Ilha de................877
Berlin............................ 358–370

Berlin, Central 360–361
Berlin: Kreuzberg &
  Friedrichshain 364
Berlin: Mitte & Prenzlauerberg
  362
  accommodation 366
  arrival...365
  drinking and nightlife 368
  eating 367
  entertainment...............................369
  excursions......................................369
  gay Berlin......................................368
  sights.....................................358–365
  tourist information.......................366
  transport..366
Bern 1126–1128
Biarritz 314
Bihać 123
Bilbao 1074–1076
Birkenau 854
Bitola 724
Black Forest, the 400–402
Black Mountains 475
Black Sea coast (Bulgaria)
  148–152
Black Valley 588
Blagaj 126
Blasket Islands 590
Bled..991
Blue Grotto 666
Bodensee (Germany) 404
Bodø...824
Bodrum 1164
Bohemia 197–203
Bohinj, Lake 992
Bol 172
Bologna 640–642
Bolshoi Ballet, Moscow 929
Bonifacio.................................349
Bonn..390
Bordeaux 309–312
Bordeaux 310
Bosnia 122
BOSNIA-HERZEGOVINA
  113–126
Bosnia-Herzegovina 115
Boulogne 295
Bovec 994
Bowness..................................465
Brač 172
Braga 886
Brajčino 724
Bran 909
Brașov 907–909
Brașov 908
Bratislava 963–968
Bratislava 964
Brecon (town) 475
Brecon Beacons.....................475
Bremen....................................385
Brighton 439–441
Brighton 440

Brindisi..................................667
Bristol........................... 445–447
Brittany 297–299
Brno.............................. 203–205
Brno 204
Bruges........................ 106–108
Bruges 107
Brugge.........................see Bruges
Brussels....................... 93–100
Brussels 94–95
Bruxelles.............see Brussels
Bucharest 901–907
Bucharest 902
Bucharest, Central 904
București..............see Bucharest
Budapest 551–558
Budapest 553
  accommodation......................556
  arrival......................................555
  baths..555
  drinking and nightlife..........557
  eating 556
  entertainment......................557
  excursions.............................558
  sights...............................551–555
  tourist information.............556
  tours..556
  transport................................556
budget airlines 29
budget tips 40
Budva 734–736
Budva 735
bulbfields (The Netherlands)
 790
BULGARIA.................... 127–152
Bulgaria 129
bullfighting..........................1001
bulls, running of the (Pamplona)
 1071
bunkers in Albania.................54
burčák......................................203
Burgas....................................150
Burgundy 303–305
Burren, The.............................590
Bursa 1155
bus and train times........ 32–33
Busabout 35
buses 30, 35
Butrint.......................................60
Butterfly Valley 1166

C

Cabo de Gata, El...................1043
Cáceres 1017
Cadaqués 1064
Cádiz 1028
Caernarfon 478
Cagliari 678
Calais.......................................295

Calvi.......................................348
Camargue..............................326
Cambridge 454–457
Cambridge......................... 456
Camino de Santiago.............1079
camping 37
Çanakkale 1156
Canal du Midi.........................320
cannabis..................................777
Cannes....................................334
Canterbury............................438
Caparica, Costa de................875
Cape Kolka.............................696
Cape Soùnio 510
Cappadocia..............1173–1175
Capri......................................666
Carcassonne 319
Cardiff 473–475
Carpathian Mountains..........910
Carrick-a-Rede 601
Casablanca................... 763–766
Casablanca 764–765
Cascais....................................875
Cashel, Rock of 584
Castilla y León 1019–1023
Catalunya 1053–1065
cell phones...............................44
CERN 1120
Český Budějovice..................198
Český Krumlov.......................199
Cetinje 738
Ceuta 752
Chamonix...............................344
changing money 43
Chaplin's World.....................1123
Chefchaouen..........................752
Chenonceau, château de.......301
Chepstow 475
Chernobyl..............................1184
Chester....................................464
Chia...679
Chillon, Château de 1123
Chinon 301
Chornobyl..............................1184
Cinque Terre...........................629
Ciutadella 1053
Çıralı......................................1168
Cliffs of Moher 590
clothing size conversions.........45
coffeeshops (The Netherlands)
  .... 777, 787
Cognac....................................308
Coimbra 879
Cologne 386–390
Cologne 387
Combarelles, Grotte des 313
Como, Lake 626
Constance, Lake....................404
contraceptives 42
Conwy.....................................478

Copenhagen 213–224
Copenhagen 214–215
  accommodation 219
  arrival 218
  drinking and nightlife 222
  eating 220–222
  entertainment 222
  excursions 224
  gay Copenhagen 223
  shopping 223
  sights 215–218
  tourist information 218
  tours 219
  transport 219
Córdoba 1034–1036
Córdoba 1035
Corfu 537–539
Cork 585–587
Cork 586–587
Corsica 345–350
Corte 348
Costa Brava 1063–1065
Costa da Caparica 875
costs 40
Côte d'Azur 334–338
Côte Vermeille 322
couchsurfing 37
County Clare 590
Craignure 493
credit cards 43
Crete 540–544
Crete 540–541
Crickhowell 475
crime 40
CROATIA 153–182
Croatia 155
Cuenca 1016
Culatra 893
Curonian Spit 713
customs 41
Cyclades islands 525–532
CZECH REPUBLIC 183–206
Czech Republic 185

D

D-Day beaches 298
Dachau concentration camp
  409
Dalí, Salvador 1063, 1064
Dalmatian Coast (Croatia)
  167–182
Dartmoor 447
De Koog 798
debit cards 43
Debrecen 567
Deià 1051
Delft 793
Delos 526
Delphi 517

Den Burg 798
Den Haag 790–793
Den Haag 791
DENMARK 207–236
Denmark 209
Derinkuyu 1174
Derry-Londonderry 601
dervishes, whirling 1176
Derwent Water 466
Dhiakoftó–Kalávryta Railway
  510
Dijon 303
Dingle 589
Dingle Peninsula 590
disabilities, travellers with 45
doctors 42
Dodecanese islands 532–535
Donegal Town 595
Doolin 590
Douro valley 888
Dover 437
Dracula, Count 909, 910, 911
Dresden 370–374
Dresden 371
Drottningholm Palace 1097
drugs 41
Drumnadrochit 492
Duart Castle 493
Dublin 575–582
Dublin 576
Dubrovnik 178–182
Dubrovnik 178
Durham 469
Durmitor National Park 740

E

Eagle's Nest 410
Eden Project 449
Edinburgh 479–485
Edinburgh 480
Edirne 1157
Eger 564
EHIC 42
Eisenach 378
El Escorial 1012
electricity 41
Elgol 494
Elterwater 466
email 43
emergencies 42
Engelberg 1126
ENGLAND 421–472
Ephesus 1162
Epidaurus 512
Ercolano 664
Ermoúpolis 525
Essaouira 771

ESTONIA 237–254
Estonia 239
Etna, Mount 674, 675
euro, the 43
Eurolines 30, 35
Europe Park 402
European Health Insurance Card
  (EHIC) 42
European Youth Card 44
Euskadi 1072–1078
evil eye 1155
Évora 888
EXIT Festival 952
Extremadura 1017–1019

F

Fabergé Museum, St Petersburg
  935
fado 875
Faliráki 534
Faro 890
Faroe Islands 236
ferries 30, 35
Fès .... see Fez
festivals 37
Fethiye 1165
Fez (Fès) 755–760
Fez, Fès el Bali 756
Fez, Ville Nouvelle 758
Figueres 1063
FINLAND 255–274
Finland 257
Finnmark 828
Fionnphort 493
Fíra 531
Firenze .... see Florence
Fishguard 476
Fiskárdho 539
fjords (Norway) 816–822
Flakstadøya 826
Flåm 819
flights 29, 30, 31
Florence 644–650
Florence 646–647
Fnideq 752
Font de Gaume, Grotte de 313
Formentera 1048
Fort Bravo 1043
Fort William 491
Foz do Douro 883
FRANCE 275–350
France 277
Frankfurt 394–397
Frankfurt 396
Freiburg im Breisgau ... 400–402
Fruška Gora 951
Funen 227–229
Füssen 409

G

Galičica National Park 726
Gallipoli 1157
Galway 591–593
Galway 592
Gap of Dunloe 588
Garden Festival 169
Gateshead 470
Gavarnie 316
gay travellers 42
Gdańsk 843–846
Gdańsk 844
Geirangerfjord 821
Geliboli peninsula 1157
Geneva 1118–1121
Geneva 1119
Genoa 626–628
Genova ....see Genoa
Gent .... see Ghent
Gentse Feesten 105
GERMANY 351–414
Germany 353
Ghent 103–106
Ghent 104
Giant's Causeway 600
Gibraltar 1031
Gimmelwald 1135
Girona 1064
Giverny 294
Gjirokastra 58
Glasgow 485–489
Glasgow 486
Glastonbury Festival 447
Glen Coe 491
Glenbrittle 494
Glencolmcille 595
Glendalough 582
Golfe de Porto 347
Göreme 1173
Górtys 541
Gothenburg 1098–1103
Gothenburg 1099
Gotland 1106–1108
Gotthard Base Tunnel 1137
Gouda 796
GR20 349
Granada 1037–1042
Granada 1038–1039
Graz 75–77
Graz 75
GREAT BRITAIN 415–494
Great Britain 417
Great Plain (Hungary)
....565–568
GREECE 495–544
Greece 497
Grenen 235
Grenoble 343
Grindelwald 1135

Guaja National Park 695
guesthouses 36
Guimarães 887

H

Haarlem 789
Hadrian's Wall 472
Hague, The 790–793
Hague, The 791
Halkidhikí 523
Hallstatt 82
Hamburg 379–383
Hamburg 380
Haniá 543
Hannover 384
health 42
Heidelberg 398–400
Heidelberg 399
Helsingør 224–226
Helsinki 261–267
Helsinki 262
Herceg Novi 732
Herculaneum 664
Hermitage Museum,
  St Petersburg 931
Hersónissos 542
Herzegovina 123–126
Hierapolis 1164
Hill of Crosses 711
Hillerød 224
Hoge Veluwe National Park ...799
Hohenschwangau Castle 409
Holyhead 476
Honningsvåg 829
Hóra (Mýkonos) 526
Hóra (Pátmos) 534
hospitals 42
hostels 36
hotels 36
Humlebæk 224
HUNGARY 545–568
Hungary 547
Hungerburg plateau 85
Hvar 173

I

Ía 531
Ibiza 1048–1050
Icehotel (Sweden) 1111
Ihlara Valley 1173
Inari 274
Inisheer 594
Inishmaan 594
Inishmore 593
Inlandsbanan, the 1108

Innsbruck 83–86
Innsbruck 84
insurance 42, 43
Interlaken 1133
International Youth Travel Card
 44
internet 43
InterRail passes 34
Inverness 492
Ioánnina 519
Iona, Isle of 493
Ionian islands 537–539
Íos 530
Iráklion 540
IRELAND 569–602
Ireland 571
Ireland, Northern 596–602
ISIC 44
Istanbul 1146–1154
Istanbul City 1147
Istanbul, Old 1148
Istanbul: Sultanahmet 1151
  accommodation 1151
  arrival 1150
  drinking and nightlife 1153
  eating 1152
  entertainment 1154
  shopping 1154
  sights 1146–1150
  tourist information 1150
  transport 1150
Istria 164–167
ITALY 603–680
Italy 605
itineraries 22–27
Ivrea 620
İzmir 1159–1161
İzmir 1160

J

Jajce 122
Jarve 250
Jokkmokk 1110
Jostedalsbreen 820
Jotunheimen National Park ...814
Jungfrau Region 1132–1135
Jungfrau Region 1133
Jūrmala 693
Jutland 229–236

K

Kaali 250
Kafka, Franz 192
Kalambáka 518
Kamáres 526
Kamári 532

Kaprun............................83
Kardhamýli....................515
Karlovy Vary..................201
Kaş...............................1167
Kassándhra....................523
Kastráki........................518
Kástro...........................526
Kaunas...................708–712
Kaunas........................709
Kávos............................538
Kaymaklı......................1174
Kecskemét....................565
Kefalloniá.....................539
Kérkyra....................see Corfu
Keswick........................466
Keszthely......................560
Keukenhof....................790
Kiev.........................see Kyiv
Kilkenny.......................583
Killarney.......................588
Kilronan........................593
Kinhu...........................252
Kiruna..........................1111
Klaipėda.......................712
Knockreer Estate...........588
Knossós........................541
Kobarid........................993
København...see Copenhagen
Köln..........................see Cologne
Komiža.........................175
Konstanz.......................404
Konya...........................1175
Koprivshtitsa.................145
Korčula....................176–178
Kórinthos......................510
Košice.....................974–976
Kotor.....................732–734
Kotor..........................733
Koukounariés................535
Kraków...................848–853
Kraków.......................849
Kravice Waterfalls.........126
Kremlin, the..................924
Kruja.............................56
Krušedol........................951
Ksamil...........................60
Kungsledden Trail..........1112
Kuopio.........................271
Kuressaare....................250
Kuşadası.......................1162
Kutná Hora...................197
Kyiv.......................1182–1187
Kyiv..........................1183
Kyrkogårdsön................1097

L

L'viv......................1189–1192
La Massana....................1068

La Roche-en-Ardenne.............109
La Rochelle...........................307
Lacanau................................310
Lagos..........................891–893
Lahemaa National Park.........249
Lahinch................................590
Lake Bohinj..........................992
Lake Constance......see Bodensee
Lake District (England)
...........................464–467
Lake District, Southern Lakes
....465
Lake Geneva............1117–1123
Lake Luzern.........................1125
Lake Maggiore.....................1137
Lake Matka...........................723
Lake Ohrid............................725
Lake Region (Finland)
...........................269–272
Lake Siljan..........................1108
Lake Skadar..........................739
Land's End............................449
Langdale..............................466
languages
   Albanian..............................51
   Arabic (Moroccan).............747
   Bosnian..............................118
   Bulgarian............................132
   Catalan.............................1056
   Croatian.............................158
   Czech................................187
   Danish...............................213
   Dutch................................778
   Estonian.............................240
   Finnish...............................260
   French................................280
   German..............................357
   Greek.................................500
   Hungarian..........................550
   Irish..................................574
   Italian................................609
   Latvian...............................684
   Letzebuergesch....................92
   Lithuanian..........................701
   Macedonian........................719
   Montenegrin.......................730
   Norwegian..........................806
   Polish................................836
   Portuguese.........................863
   Romanian...........................900
   Russian..............................920
   Serbian..............................943
   Slovak...............................962
   Slovene..............................982
   Spanish.............................1003
   Swedish............................1088
   Turkish..............................1145
   Ukrainian...........................1181
   Welsh................................473
Lapland (Finland).........272–274
Lapland (Sweden)....1110–1112
Las Fallas...........................1045
Lascaux...............................313
LATVIA.......................681–696
Latvia.........................683

Lausanne..................1121–1123
Lauterbrunnen.....................1134
Le Corbusier.........................330
Le Puy-en-Velay....................339
Lecce...................................669
left luggage............................43
Leiden.................................789
Leipzig.......................375–377
León.................................1021
Les Calanques......................332
Les Eyzies............................313
lesbian travellers....................42
Levoča.................................973
LGBT travellers.......................42
Liechtenstein.......................1138
Lille....................................295
Líndhos...............................534
Linz......................................73
Lisboa.....................see Lisbon
Lisbon........................865–875
Lisbon........................866–867
Lisbon, Central...................869
   accommodation..................872
   arrival...............................871
   beaches.............................875
   drinking and nightlife..........874
   eating...............................873
   entertainment....................874
   fado..................................875
   shopping...........................875
   sights........................865–871
   tourist information..............871
   transport...........................872
Lisse...................................790
LITHUANIA................697–714
Lithuania....................699
Litóhoro..............................525
Liverpool..................461–464
Ljubljana...................982–988
Ljubljana....................985
Llanberis.............................477
Locarno..............................1137
Loch Ness............................492
Lofoten Islands.....................825
Loire Valley................299–303
London.......................421–437
London.......................422–423
London: West End............425
   accommodation..................432
   arrival...............................429
   drinking and nightlife..........434–436
   eating...............................433
   entertainment....................436
   gay London........................436
   shopping...........................437
   sights.........................421–429
   tourist information..............430
   transport...........................430
Londonderry.........................601
Lorraine.....................305–307
Lourdes...............................316
Lübeck................................383
Lucerne..............................1125
Lugano................................1137

Lumbarda 177
Lund 1106
LUXEMBOURG 110–112
Luxembourg City 110–112
Luxembourg City 11
Luzern 1125
Lydford 447
Lyon 339–343
Lyon 340

M

Maastricht 799
MACEDONIA 715–726
Macedonia 717
Mackintosh, Charles Rennie....487
MADRID 1003–1012
Madrid 1004–1005
  accommodation 1009
  arrival 1008
  drinking and nightlife 1010
  eating 1009
  entertainment 1011
  excursions 1012–1017
  shopping 1011
  sights 1006–1008
  tourist information 1009
  transport 1009
Magerøya 828
Maggiore, Lake 1137
mail 43
Mainz 391
Málaga 1032–1034
Malbork 846
Mália 542
Mallorca 1050–1052
Malmö 1103–1106
Malmö 1104
Malovište 724
Manchester 457–460
Manchester 459
Manganári 530
Máni peninsula 515
Mantova .... see Mantua
Maó 1052
maps 43
Marathoníssi 514
Maribor 994–996
Marina Piccola 666
Marmara, Sea of 1155
Marrakesh 767–771
Marrakesh 768
Marseille 329–334
Marseille 331
Matera 668
Matka, Lake 723
Matterhorn 1135
Mavrovo 724
Mavrovo National Park 723
Međugorje 126

Meissen 375
Meknes 753–755
Meknes 754
Melk 73
Menorca 1052
Mérida 1018
Metéora 518
midges 493
Midnight Sun (Norway) 827
Milan 622–626
Milan 624–625
Minack Theatre 448
Mini Hollywood 1042
Minotaur 541
mobile phones 44
Monaco 338
Monemvasiá 514
money 40, 43
Mont Blanc 344
Mont St-Michel 299
Monte Carlo 338
MONTENEGRO 727–740
Montenegro 729
Montpellier 320
Montreux Jazz Festival 1123
Montserrat 1059
Moravia 203–206
Moreška, the 176
MOROCCO 741–772
Morocco 743
Moscow 922–930
Moscow 922–923
  accommodation 927
  arrival 927
  drinking and nightlife 929
  eating 928
  entertainment 929
  shopping 930
  sights 924–927
  tourist information 927
  transport 927
Mosel, River 394
Moskenes 826
Moskenesøya 826
Moskva .... see Moscow
Mostar 123–125
Mount Athos 523
Mount Dajti 56
Mount Etna 674, 675
Mount Olympus (Greece) 524, 525
Mount Snowden 477, 478
Mount Toukbal 769
Mount Vogel, Slovenia 992
Mourne Mountains 600
Mozart, Wolfgang Amadeus.... 79
Muckross Estate 588
Mull, Isle of 493
München .... see Munich
Munich 405–409
Munich 406
Mürren 1135

Mycenae 511
Mykínes 511
Mýkonos 526–528
Mýkonos Town 527
Mylopótas 530
Mystra 513

N

Náfplio 512
Namur 108
Nancy 305
Nantes 299
Náoussa 528
Naples 659–663
Naples, Bay of 663–665
Naples: Centro Storico 660
Napoli .... see Naples
nargiles 1143
Náxos 529
Nesebar 150
NETHERLANDS, THE 773–800
Netherlands, The 775
Neuschwanstein Castle 409
Newcastle-upon-Tyne 470–472
Newgrange 582
Newquay 450
newspapers 44
Nice 335–338
Nice 336
Nida 714
Nîmes 323
Niš 955
Nora 679
Nordkapp 830
Nordpark 86
Normandy 297–299
Northern Lights (Norway) 827
NORWAY 801–830
Norway 803
Novi Sad 951–954
Novo Hopovo 951
Nuremberg 412
Nuremberg 412
Nürnberg .... see Nuremberg

O

Odense 227–229
Odense 227
Odessa 1187–1189
Ohrid 725
Okehampton 447
Oktoberfest 409
Old Man of Storr 494

Old Sarum 442
Olhão 893
Olomouc 205
Ölüdeniz lagoon 1166
Olympia (Greece)......................516
Olympos (Turkey) 1167
Olympus, Mount (Greece).....524, 525
Open'er Festival 816
Oporto ....see Porto
Ordesa, Parque Nacional de 1070
Orléans 303
Orsa 1109
Ortygia......................................675
Oslo 807–813
Oslo 808–809
Östersund................................1109
Oświęcim 854
Oudeschild................................798
Oulu 273
Oviedo 1078
Oxford 450–453
Oxford 451

P

Padova .... see Padua
Padua 631–633
País Vasco 1072–1076
Pal 1068
Palanga 712
Palermo 670–673
Palermo, Central 672
Palio, Siena...............................653
Palma 1050
Pamplona 1070
Pamukkale................................1164
Parikiá 528
Paris.............................. 281–294
Paris 282–283
Paris, Central 286–287
  accommodation 289
  arrival.....................................288
  drinking and nightlife 292
  eating 290–292
  entertainment.............................293
  excursions....................................294
  gay Paris 293
  shopping....................................294
  sights 281–288
  tourist information........................289
  transport 289
Parma......................................642
Pärnu 251
Páros..528
Parque Nacional de Ordesa 1070
Pátmos.......................................534
Pátra 516

Pavlovsk Palace 938
Peak District.............................460
Pécs 562–564
Pélekas.....................................538
Pelister National Park 724
Peloponnese, the......... 510–517
Pembrokeshire 476
Peneda-Gerês, Parque Nacional du..................................888
Peniche....................................877
pensions 36
Penzance..................................448
Périgueux 312
Paríssa.....................................532
Perpignan 322
Perugia 655–657
Peso da Régua 888
Peterhof, the............................938
Phaestos...................................541
phones 44
Piatra Craiului National Park..910
Picasso, Pablo 1032, 1033
Picos de Europa..................... 1077
Pilsen...........................see Plzeň
Piran 990
Pisa...650
Plakiás......................................543
Plitvice Lakes...........................162
Plovdiv 142–145
Plovdiv 143
plugs 41
Plzeň 200
Počitelj.....................................126
Podgorica.................................738
Pohorje 994
POLAND........................ 831–858
Poland 833
police 41
Pompeii 664
Pont du Gard............................323
Ponte de Barca 888
Poprad 970
port..883
Porto (Portugal) 881–886
Porto (Portugal) 882
Porto (Corsica) 347
Portorož 989
Portree.....................................494
Portstewart..............................601
PORTUGAL 859–894
Portugal 861
Porvoo 267
post.. 43
Postojna...................................988
Potsdam....................................369
Potter, Beatrix 466
Poznań......................................857
Prague 188–197
Prague 190–191
  accommodation 194
  arrival.....................................193

drinking and nightlife...................195
  eating 194
  entertainment.............................196
  shopping....................................197
  sights 189–193
  tourist information........................193
  transport 193
Praha..........................see Prague
Predjama Castle 989
Priekestolen.............................816
Primavera Sound 1062
Provence....................... 323–338
Ptuj..996
Pula (Croatia)...........................165
Pula (Italy) 679
Pulpit Rock...............................816
punting 452
Pyrenees (France) 316
Pyrenees (Spain) 1068–1072

R

Rabat............................ 760–763
Rabat 761
rail passes.............................34, 35
Randstad, The.............. 788–798
Rapallo.....................................629
Râşnov 910
Ravello 668
Ravenna....................................643
Regensburg...............................411
Reims 296
Réthymnon...............................542
Rhine Falls 1132
Rhine Gorge..............................392
Rhodes 532–534
Rhodes Town 533
Ria Formosa..............................893
RibčevLaz 992
Rīga 686–693
Riga 687
Rīga, Old 688
Rila Monastery.........................140
Ring of Kerry............................589
Riviera di Levante 628
Rock of Cashel 584
ROMANIA 895–914
Romania 897
Romantic Road.........................405
Rome 610–619
Rome, Central............... 612–613
  accommodation 616
  arrival.....................................615
  drinking and nightlife 618
  eating 617
  entertainment.............................619
  festivals....................................619
  shopping....................................619
  sights 610–615
  tourist information........................616

tours.................................616
transport.............................616
Ronda..............................1031
Roskilde..............................226
Rothenburg ob der Tauber....413
Rotterdam.................794–797
Rotterdam..........................795
Rouen.................................297
Rovaniemi............................273
Rovinj.................................166
Royal Shakespeare Company
  (RSC)................................454
Rundāle Palace.......................694
Ruskin, John..........................466
RUSSIA.........................915–938
Russia.............................917

S

Saaremaa.............................250
Saariselkä.............................274
Sachsenhausen concentration
  camp.................................370
Sächsische Schweiz..................374
safety..................................40
St Andrews.............................490
St David's..............................476
St Ives.................................449
St-Malo.................................298
St Michael's Mount 448
St Petersburg..............930–938
St Petersburg...........932–933
  accommodation......................936
  arrival..............................935
  drinking and nightlife.................937
  eating...............................936
  entertainment.......................937
  excursions..........................938
  shopping............................937
  sights.........................930–935
  tourist information..................935
  transport............................935
St Wolfgang.............................81
Saintes-Marie-de-la-Mer........326
Salamanca................1019–1021
Salamanca..........................1020
Salaspils...............................694
Salisbury...............................442
Salzburg.......................77–81
Salzburg.............................78
Samarian Gorge.......................543
Sámi...................................539
Sámi, the..............................830
San Fermín, Fiestas de.........1071
San Gimignano.......................654
San Lorenzo del Escorial......1012
San Sebastián..........1072–1074
Sant Antoni.........................1048
Santa Margherita Ligure........628
Santander...........................1076

Santiago de Compostela
.................................1079–1082
Santiago de Compostela
....1080
Santoríni..............................531
Sarajevo.................118–122
Sarajevo: Baščaršija..........119
Saranda.................................59
Sardinia.....................677–680
Saumur.................................302
Savonlinna.............................270
Schaffhausen........................1132
Schauinsland..........................401
Schiltorn.............................1135
Schwangau.............................409
SCOTLAND 479–494
Scottish Highlands..................491
Sea of Marmara......................1155
Segovia..............................1012
Selçuk................................1162
SERBIA.......................939–956
Serbia.............................941
Seville.....................1023–1028
Seville 1024–1025
sexual harassment.....................46
Shakespeare, William..............453
shoe size conversions 45
Sibiu..................................912
Sicily 670–677
Siena 651–654
Siena 652
Sífnos..................................526
Sighişoara 910–912
Sigulda................................694
Siljan, Lake 1108
Sintra.................................876
Siófok.................................559
Siracusa...............................675
Sithonía...............................523
Sitía..................................542
Skadar, Lake..........................739
Skagen.................................235
Skála..................................534
Skiathos...............................535
Škocjan Caves.........................989
Skópelos...............................536
Skopje 720–723
Skopje.............................721
Skye, Isle of........................494
Skýros.................................536
Slea Head..............................590
Slieve League.........................595
Sligo..................................594
Slitere National Park..............696
SLOVAKIA 957–976
Slovakia.............................959
SLOVENIA 977–996
Slovenia.............................979
Smokovec..............................970
Snowdonia..............................477
Soča valley............................993

Sofia 133–139
Sofia.............................134
Sognefjord............................820
Sóller................................1051
Sónar.................................1062
Sopoćani..............................954
Sopot..................................846
Sopron.................................561
Sorrento...............................665
Sound of Music, The................79
Sozopol................................151
SPAIN..........................997–1082
Spain.............................999
Spárti.................................513
Spiš Castle............................973
Split 169–172
Spoleto................................657
Sporades islands.........535–537
Sremski Karlovci......................952
Staffa, Isle of.......................493
Stamsund...............................825
Stari Bar..............................736
Stavanger..............................814
Stáyira................................523
Stechelberg..........................1134
Stirling...............................489
Stockholm 1089–1097
Stockholm..............1090–1091
Stockholm archipelago........1097
Stonehenge.............................443
Stoúpa.................................515
Strasbourg.............................305
Strasbourg. 306
Stratford-upon-Avon...............453
Studenica..............................954
student discounts 44
study..................................38
Stuttgart......................402–404
Subotica...............................953
Supetar................................172
surfing (Portugal) 864, 877
Sveti Jovan Bigorski................724
Sveti Stefan...........................737
Svolvær................................825
SWEDEN...................1083–1112
Sweden............................1085
SWITZERLAND.........1113–1138
Switzerland........................1115
Sýros..................................525
Szeged.................................566
Szentendre.............................558
Sziget Festival.......................557

T

Tallinn 241–249
Tallinn 243
Tampere................................269

Tangier.....................748–752
Tangier.....................750–751
Taormina...........................673
Tara Canyon.....................740
Tarifa 1029–1031
Tartu 252–254
Tartu 253
Tatra mountains (Poland)......854
Tatra mountains (Slovakia)
.................................970–973
Tatranská Lomnica...................971
Tavira...............................894
telephones..........................44
Tetouan............................752
Texel................................798
Theseus.............................541
Thessaloníki................520–523
Thessaloníki..................521
Thíra...............................531
Thy.................................233
Ticino........................1136–1138
time zones...........................45
time zones..........................46
Timişoara..........................913
Tintern Abbey.....................475
Tirana........................52–56
Tirana............................53
Tirol.......................see Tyrol
Tisno...............................169
Tobermory.........................493
Toledo 1013–1116
Toledo 1014–1015
Tomar...............................878
Tomatina, La......................1045
Torino....................see Turin
Toruń..............................847
Toukbal, Mount...................769
Toulouse 317–320
Toulouse 318
tourist information.................45
Tours..............................300
trains 30, 31
train and bus times........32–33
Trakai..............................707
Transylvania.................907–913
travel agents.......................31
travellers with disabilities........45
Travnik............................122
Trebinje...........................126
Trier...............................393
Trollstigen Highway..............822
Tromsø.............................827
Trondheim.................822–824
Tsarkoe Selo......................938
Turaida Castle.....................694
Turin..............................620
TURKEY 1139–1176
Turkey.........................1141
Turku 267–269
Tuscany 644–655

U

Uig.................................494
Ukanc..............................992
UKRAINE 1177–1192
Ukraine 1179
Ulcinj..............................737
Umbria 655–659
Umbria Jazz Festival.............656
Uppsala...........................1098
Urbino.............................658
Utrecht............................797

V

Vaduz.............................1138
Valbona.............................57
Valdemossa......................1051
Valencia...................1043–1046
Valencia.......................1044
Van Gogh, Vincent...............325
Varna...............................148
Vathý.............................526
Vatican............................615
Vátos..............................538
Vaxholm...........................1097
Veliko Tarnovo...................146
Venezia...................see Venice
VENICE 633–640
Venice 634
Venice, Central 636–637
accommodation..............639
arrival..............................638
drinking and nightlife............640
eating..............................639
entertainment...................640
festivals..........................640
sights..........................633–638
tourist information..............638
transport.........................638
Ventspils..........................695
Vergina............................524
Vermilion Coast..................322
Verona.............................630
Versailles..........................294
Vestvågøy.........................825
Vesuvius...........................664
Vevčani............................726
Vézère Valley 313
Vialattea...........................620
Vienna.......................65–73
Vienna.......................66–67
Vila do Gerês......................888
Vila Nova de Gaia................883
Vila Nova de Milfontes..........890
Villandry, château de 301
Vilnius 702–707
Vilnius.........................703
Vintgar Gorge....................991
Virpazar...........................739

Vis.................................175
visas................................41
Visby..............................1106
Vlad the Impaler.....909, 910, 911
vodka..............................842
Vrdnik-Ravanica..................951

W

WALES 472–478
Warhol, Andy.....................975
Warsaw 837–843
Warsaw 838
Wartburg Castle..................378
water................................42
Weimar.............................377
Werfen..............................81
whale-watching, Spain.........1030
wheelchair access 46
whirling dervishes................1176
wi-fi.................................43
Wicklow............................582
Wien ....see Vienna
Wild Atlantic Way, The 588
Wimdu..............................37
Windermere........................465
women travellers...................46
Wordworth, William..............466
work.................................38
Wrocław 855–857

Y

Yíthio..............................514
York 467–469
York..........................468
youth discounts 44
youth hostels 36

Z

Žabljak.............................740
Zadar..............................167
Zagreb 159–164
Zagreb 160
Zakopane..........................854
Zambujeira do Mar...............890
Zappa, Frank......................705
Zaragoza.................1068–1070
Zărneşti...........................910
Zdiar...............................971
Zealand......................224–227
Zell am Zee 83
Zermatt...........................1135
Žiča...............................954
Zürich.....................1128–1132
Zürich.........................1129

Map symbols

The symbols below are used on maps throughout the book

— — - -	International boundary	♠	Place of interest	Ⓣ	Tram stop
▬▬ ■ ■	State/province boundary	∴	Ruins	🅿	Parking
	Motorway	♙	Monastery	▲	Mountain peak
	Road	♙	Mosque	⌃⌃⌃	Mountain range
	Pedestrianized road	♜	Castle	⌢⌢⌢	Rocks
	Steps	♜	Stately home	/|\	Hill
- - - -	Path	♙	Monument	⌣	Bridge
	Railway	✿	Ferris wheel	⌂	Cave
⊦⊦⊦⊦⊦	Funicular	⚚	Lighthouse	⩍	Campsite
●-- ●	Cable car	⚘	Viewpoint		Church
— —	Ferry route	⚘	Waterfall		Building
▬▬▬	Wall	✡	Synagogue		Pedestrianized area
✕✈	Airport	⚲	Swimming pool		Market
★	Transport stop	⊙	Statue		Stadium
⛴	Boat	♟	Museum		Park/national park
🚂	Train	⊤	Fountain/gardens		Beach
🚌	Bus	⊠	Gate		Marsh
@	Internet café/access	⊖	London Underground		Glacier
✉	Post office	Ⓢ	S-bahn		Christian cemetery
ⓘ	Tourist office	Ⓜ	Metro		Jewish cemetery
⚐	Windmill	Ⓤ	U-bahn		Muslim cemetery
⊞	Hospital				

Listings key

- ■ Accommodation
- ● Eating
- ■ Drinking/nightlife
- ● Shopping

Long bus journey?
Phone run out of juice?

👉 **TEST YOUR KNOWLEDGE** WITH OUR ROUGH GUIDES TRAVEL QUIZ

1 Denim, the pencil, the stethoscope and the hot-air balloon were all invented in which country?

a. Italy
b. France
c. Germany
d. Switzerland

2 What is the currency of Vietnam?

a. Dong
b. Yuan
c. Baht
d. Kip

3 In which city would you find the Majorelle Garden?

a. Marseille
b. Marrakesh
c. Tunis
d. Malaga

4 What is the busiest airport in the world?

a. London Heathrow
b. Tokyo International
c. Chicago O'Hare
d. Hartsfield-Jackson Atlanta International

5 Which of these countries does not have the equator running through it?

a. Brazil
b. Tanzania
c. Indonesia
d. Colombia

6 Which country has the most UNESCO World Heritage Sites?

a. Mexico
b. France
c. Italy
d. India

7 What is the principal religion of Japan?

a. Confucianism
b. Buddhism
c. Jainism
d. Shinto

8 Every July in Sonkajärvi, central Finland, contestants gather for the World Championships of which sport?

a. Zorbing
b. Wife-carrying
c. Chess-boxing
d. Extreme ironing

9 What colour are post boxes in Germany?

a. Red
b. Green
c. Blue
d. Yellow

10 For three days each April during Songkran festival in Thailand, people take to the streets to throw what at each other?

a. Water
b. Oranges
c. Tomatoes
d. Underwear

1:b / 2:a / 3:b / 4:d / 5:b / 6:c / 7:d / 8:b / 9:d / 10:a